WOMEN IN WORLD HISTORY

A Biographical Encyclopedia

WOMEN IN WORLD HISTORY

A Biographical Encyclopedia

VOLUME
16
Vict-X

Anne Commire, Editor
Deborah Klezmer, Associate Editor

YORKIN PUBLICATIONS

GALE GROUP

THOMSON LEARNING

Detroit • New York • San Diego • San Francisco
Boston • New Haven, Conn. • Waterville, Maine
London • Munich

Yorkin Publications

Anne Commire, *Editor*
Deborah Klezmer, *Associate Editor*
Barbara Morgan, *Assistant Editor*

Eileen O'Pasek, Gail Schermer, Patricia Coombs, James Fox,
Catherine Cappelli, Karen Rikkers, *Editorial Assistants*
Karen Walker, *Assistant for Genealogical Charts*

Special acknowledgment is due to Peg Yorkin who made this project possible.

Thanks also to Karin and John Haag, Bob Schermer, and to
the Gale Group staff, in particular Dedria Bryfonski, Linda Hubbard, John Schmittroth, Cynthia Baldwin,
Tracey Rowens, Randy Bassett, Christine O'Bryan, Rebecca Parks, and especially Sharon Malinowski.

The Gale Group

Sharon Malinowski, *Senior Editor*
Rebecca Parks, *Editor*
Laura Brandau, *Assistant Editor*
Linda S. Hubbard, *Managing Editor*

Margaret A. Chamberlain, *Permissions Specialist*
Mary K. Grimes, *Image Cataloger*

Mary Beth Trimper, *Production Director*
Evi Seoud, *Assistant Production Manager*

Cynthia Baldwin, *Product Design Manager*
Tracey Rowens, *Cover and Page Designer*
Michael Logusz, *Graphic Artist*

Barbara Yarrow, *Graphic Services Manager*
Randy Bassett, *Image Database Supervisor*
Dan Newell, *Imaging Specialist*
Christine O'Bryan, *Graphics Desktop Publisher*
Dan Bono and Ryan Cartmill, *Technical Support*

Library of Congress Catalog Card Number 99-24692
A CIP record is available from the British Library

ISBN 0-7876-4075-1
Printed in the United States of America.

Library of Congress Cataloging-in-Publication Data

Women in world history : a biographical encyclopedia / Anne Commire, editor, Deborah Klezmer, associate editor.
   p. cm.
  Includes bibliographical references and index.
  ISBN 0-7876-3736-X (set) — ISBN 0-7876-6436-7 (v.13). —
  ISBN 0-7876-4073-5 (v. 14) — ISBN 0-7876-4074-3 (v.15) — ISBN 0-7876-4075-1 (v.16) — ISBN 0-7876-4076-X (v.17)
   1. Women—History Encyclopedias.2. Women—Biography Encyclopedias.
  I. Commire, Anne. II. Klezmer, Deborah.
   HQ1115.W6 1999
   920.72'03—DC21

99-24692

10 9 8 7 6 5 4 3 2 1

Vict

Victoire, Duchesse de Nemours
(1822–1857).

See Victoria of Saxe-Coburg.

Victoire, Madame (1733–1799)

French princess. Born Victoire Louise Marie Thérèse at Versailles, France, in 1733; died on June 8, 1799; daughter of Louis XV (1710–1774), king of France (r. 1715–1774), and *Marie Leczinska (1703–1768); sister of Adelaide (1732–1800) and *Louise Marie (1737–1787), as well as Louis le dauphin (father of Louis XVI).

Youngest and jolliest of King Louis XVI's aunts, the pious Victoire blindly obeyed her elder sister *Adelaide (1732–1800). When her father King Louis XV came down with small-pox, however, she was the one with the courage to nurse him, staying with him until he died.

Victor, Frances (1826–1902)

American novelist and historian. Name variations: Frances Fuller; Frances Auretta Fuller Victor; (pseudonym) Florence Fane. Born Frances Fuller on May 23, 1826, in Rome, New York; died on November 14, 1902, in Portland, Oregon; daughter of Adonijah Fuller and Lucy A. (Williams) Fuller; sister of Metta Victor (1831–1885); educated at a female seminary in Wooster, Ohio; married Jackson Barritt, in 1853 (divorced March 1862); married Henry Clay

Victor (a naval engineer), in May 1862 (died 1875); no children.

Moved to New York with younger sister Metta (1848); wrote poetry and fiction in New York (late 1840s); moved west with first husband (1853); left husband and moved back to New York; wrote for "Dime Novels" series (1862); moved west with second husband (1864); wrote historical works on Western subjects (1870s–90s).

Selected works: Anizetta, the Guajira: or the Creole of Cuba *(1848);* Poems of Sentiment and Imagination *(with Metta Victor, 1851);* East and West; or, The Beauty of Willard's Mill *(1862);* The Land Claim: A Tale of the Upper Missouri *(1862);* The River of the West *(1870);* All Over Oregon and Washington *(1872, rev. ed. published as* Atlantis Arisen, *1890);* The New Penelope *(stories, 1877);* The History of Oregon *(2 vols., 1886–88);* The History of Washington, Idaho, and Montana *(1890);* The History of Nevada, Colorado, and Wyoming *(1890);* The Early Indian Wars of Oregon *(1894);* Poems *(1900).*

The older sister of **Metta Victor*, the prolific writer of dime novels, Frances Victor also followed a literary path, writing fiction and poetry before turning to history in her later years. She was born in Rome, New York, in 1826, and her family moved first to Erie, Pennsylvania, and then to Wooster, Ohio, where the two sisters attended an all-female school. They began to write, sending their stories and poems first to local publications and then farther afield. Frances' adventure romance *Anizetta, the Guajira: or the Creole of Cuba* was published in Boston in 1848, the same year the sisters moved to New York City. In 1851, they jointly wrote and had published *Poems of Sentiment and Imagination.*

After the death of her father in 1850, Victor moved back to the Midwest to rejoin her family. Living in Michigan near Detroit, she married a man named Jackson Barritt, who took her west to a new homestead in Nebraska. Apparently not cut out for pioneer life, she left her husband and went back to New York to rejoin her sister, who had married Orville James Victor, editor of a new series of cheap adventure stories called "dime novels."

Metta contributed prolifically to the catalogue of dime novels brought out by the publishing house of Beadle and Adams, and Frances also wrote several dime novels, drawing on her Nebraska experiences in *East and West; or, The Beauty of Willard's Mill* and *The Land Claim: A Tale of the Upper Missouri*, both published in 1862. That year, she married Orville Victor's brother Henry Clay Victor, a naval engineer with whom she moved west again, this time to the Pacific Coast. She took up residence in San Francisco, contributing to several periodicals there, sometimes under the pseudonym Florence Fane, and accompanied her husband to Oregon late in 1864.

Finding herself once again in pioneer country, Victor turned to a different genre of writing and became a serious historian, one of the few active at that time in the Pacific Northwest. She chronicled the life of a mountain man, *The River of the West* (1870), and wrote a travelers' guide, *All Over Oregon and Washington* (1872), as well as a temperance tract, *The Women's War with Whisky* (1884). She continued writing after her husband's death in a shipwreck in 1875, publishing poems, stories, newspaper columns, and more historical writing. Victor supported herself by working on Hubert Howe Bancroft's monumental *History of the Pacific States*, a 28-volume opus completed in 1890. Though Bancroft put his name to the entire project, four volumes (*The History of Oregon* [2 vols., 1886–88], *The History of Washington, Idaho, and Montana* [1890], and *The History of the Nevada, Colorado, and Wyoming* [1890]) and parts of three others were actually written by Victor. On commission from the Oregon legislature, she also wrote *The Early Indian Wars of Oregon* (1894). Her works of Western history are still considered fundamental to further study of these regions.

After again spending some time in New York, Victor passed the last years of her life in Salem and Portland, Oregon. She published her last book, *Poems*, in 1900, and died in Portland two years later.

SOURCES:

James, Edward T., ed. *Notable American Women, 1607–1950*. Cambridge, MA: The Belknap Press of Harvard University, 1971.

McHenry, Robert, ed. *Famous American Women*. NY: Dover, 1980.

James M. Manheim,
freelance writer,
Ann Arbor, Michigan

Victor, Metta (1831–1885)

American writer. Name variations: Metta Victoria Fuller Victor. Born Metta Victoria Fuller on March 2, 1831, in Erie, Pennsylvania; died of cancer on June 26, 1885, in Ho-Ho-Kus, New Jersey; daughter of Adonijah Fuller and Lucy A. (Williams) Fuller; sister of Frances Victor (1826–1902); graduated from an all-female school in Wooster, Ohio; married Orville J. Victor (an editor), in July 1856; children: Lillian (b. 1857); Alice (b. 1859); Bertha (b. 1860); Winthrop (b. 1861); Lucy (b. 1863); Guy (b. 1865); Metta (b. 1866); twins Vivia and Florence (b. 1872).

Moved with sister Frances to New York City (1848); with husband, edited Cosmopolitan Art Journal *(late 1850s); edited* Home *(from 1860); wrote over 100 dime novels and other works of fiction (1860–85).*

Selected writings: The Senator's Son, or, The Maine Law: A Last Refuge *(1851);* Mormon Wives *(or* Lives of the Female Mormons, *1856);* Miss Slimmens' Window *(1859);* Alice Wilde, The Raftsman's Daughter *(1860);* The Backwoods Bride *(1860);* Maum Guinea, and Her Plantation "Children" *(1862);* Too True: A Story of To-Day *(1868);* The Blunders of a Bashful Man *(1875);* A Bad Boy's Diary *(1880);* A Naughty Girl's Diary *(1884).*

Even in her own day her name was hardly known, for she wrote anonymously or under a pseudonym, yet Metta Victor must be ranked as one of the founding figures of American popular culture. She was a prolific creator of dime novels, the action-packed mass entertainment phenomenon of the mid-to-late 19th century, and the readership of her more than 100 works included not only ordinary Americans but also one as renowned as President Abraham Lincoln. She was born Metta Victoria Fuller in 1831 in Erie, Pennsylvania, where she spent some of her childhood before moving to Wooster, Ohio. She and her older sister *Frances Victor received formal schooling at an all-female institution in Wooster, and began to write. They sent stories to hometown newspapers, and Victor's first novel, a fanciful recreation of life in Mayan times called *The Last Days of Tul*, was published when she was 15. Emboldened by the acceptance for publication of one of their writings by a New York magazine called the *Home Journal*, the sisters moved to New York City in 1848, when Metta was only 17.

In New York, they made contacts in the literary world, particularly editor Rufus Wilmot Griswold, and published a volume entitled *Poems of Sentiment and Imagination* in 1851. That same year, Metta finished a pro-temperance novel, *The Senator's Son, or, The Maine Law: A Last Refuge*. It was published both in the United States and in England, appearing in a number of editions, and launched her literary career in earnest. By 1856, she had published at least two more full-length works, one of which was a condemnation of the lives of women in the polygamy-practicing Mormon Church. Her professional and personal lives converged fortuitously in July 1856, when she married an editor named Orville J. Victor.

The couple jointly edited the *Cosmopolitan Art Journal*, published first in Sandusky, Ohio, where they lived before moving to New York City in 1858. Her first child had been born in 1857, and she would have eight more by 1872, but Victor nonetheless became the editor of the monthly magazine *Home*, published by the house of Beadle and Adams, in 1859. She also speedily contributed a popular *Dime Cook-Book* to their catalogue. Her husband worked closely with the same publisher, and in 1860 he turned the art journal over to his wife so that he could devote full time to a new venture in mass-production publishing, the Beadle and Adams "Dime Novels."

"Dime Novels" took off, eventually becoming ubiquitous, and Metta Victor immediately tried her hand at them. By the end of 1860, she had written and published both *Alice Wilde, The Raftsman's Daughter* and *The Backwoods Bride*. She would go on to write nearly 100 more novels in the form; 1862's *Maum Guinea, and Her Plantation "Children"* (Dime Novel No. 33) was widely popular and played a role in the antislavery movement at the height of the Civil War. President Lincoln praised the book, although, like her other dime novels, its title page did not bear its author's name.

Victor became well established as a writer, and later in life was able to earn handsome prices for her work. She sometimes worked outside the dime novel genre, as with *Miss Slimmens' Window* (1859), a collection of short satires, and *The Blunders of a Bashful Man* (1875), and continued to contribute to the numerous periodicals of the day. Attuned to the tastes of the times, after the Civil War she abandoned the reform novels that no longer appealed to a war-weary public and turned instead to gentle humor and light domestic satire. One of her last books, *A Naughty Girl's Diary*, was published in 1884, only a year before her death from cancer at age 54, in Ho-Ho-Kus, New Jersey.

SOURCES:

James, Edward T., ed. *Notable American Women, 1607–1950*. Cambridge, MA: The Belknap Press of Harvard University, 1971.
McHenry, Robert, ed. *Famous American Women*. NY: Dover, 1980.

James M. Manheim,
freelance writer,
Ann Arbor, Michigan

Victor, Wilma (1919–1987)

Native American educator. Name variations: Wilma L. Victor. Born in Idabel, Oklahoma, on November 5, 1919; died in Idabel on November 15, 1987; attended University of Kansas; Milwaukee State Teachers College (now University of Wisconsin-Milwaukee), B.A.; University of Oklahoma, M.A. in education.

Wilma Victor devoted her career to the creation of new institutions that reflected the needs of Native American students and prepared them to meet the wider world. Born in 1919 in Idabel, Oklahoma, where the Choctaw tribe had been allocated territory after traveling the dreadful Trail of Tears in the 1830s, Victor was a full-blooded Choctaw. Imbued as a child with an understanding of the value of education, she aspired to attend college, a rare goal for a young woman of Native American descent before World War II. A friend who worked for the Federal Bureau of Indian Affairs (BIA) arranged for her to receive a two-year scholarship to the University of Kansas. While there, she caught the attention of the BIA's education director, Willard Beatty, who persuaded her to enter a teaching career and procured for her another scholarship, this one at Milwaukee State Teachers College (now the University of Wisconsin at Milwaukee). Victor's student teaching assignment took her to Shiprock, New Mexico, on the land of the Navajo tribe. The Navajos, who inhabit their ancestral homeland, have succeeded in maintaining many of their cultural traditions, and Victor began to think about the ways in which Native American culture could be integrated with modern educational methods.

After a stint in the Women's Army Corps during World War II (serving mostly in Kentucky), Victor took a BIA teaching post at the new Intermountain School in Utah, again on Navajo land. She spent 13 years there, and then moved to Santa Fe, where she assisted in the establishment of the Institute of American Indian Arts. She played a key role in developing the curriculum of this institution, which focused on Native artistic traditions, and she came to believe strongly in the capacity of Native Americans to create their own solutions to the social problems that faced them. In the 1960s, she returned to the Intermountain School, this time as its supervisor. She received a Federal Women's Award in 1967, was a keynote speaker at the first National Indian Workshop for Indian Affairs, and was named one of "seven women of the 70s" by the state of Utah. In 1970, she received the Indian Achievement Award. The height of her career came in 1971, when she was named special assistant to Rogers C.B. Morton, secretary of the interior under President Richard Nixon, a post that made her the highest ranking Native American woman in government at the time.

SOURCES:

Gridley, Marion E. *American Indian Women*. NY: Hawthorn Books, 1974.

James M. Manheim,
freelance writer,
Ann Arbor, Michigan

Victoria (d. around 253 CE)

Italian martyr and saint. Executed in or about 253 CE; daughter of noble Tivoli parents; sister of Anatolia; never married; no children.

Born into one of the noblest families of Tivoli, Victoria and her sister **Anatolia** were renowned for their beauty. Raised as Christians, the sisters had been promised in marriage by their parents to two of the region's most eligible and noble—and pagan—bachelors. Victoria, betrothed to Eugenius, eagerly anticipated her wedding, while Anatolia, pledged to Titus Aurelius, bitterly opposed the match her parents had made for her and looked for any excuse she could find to postpone the wedding. Titus Aurelius beseeched Eugenius to urge Victoria to convince her sister to proceed with plans for her marriage. Citing holy scripture, Victoria reminded Anatolia that God looked favorably upon the state of marriage, inasmuch as most of the church's patriarchs and prophets had themselves married in days gone by. Had not God smiled upon them and their descendants, Victoria asked. Anatolia responded to her sister with such a persuasive argument in favor of chastity that Victoria, once so eager to join Eugenius in wedlock, was convinced to break off her engagement. She also sold off her jewelry and donated the proceeds to the benefit of Tivoli's less fortunate citizens.

Frustrated and angry, Eugenius and Titus Aurelius sought relief from the emperor, who agreed to allow the two to carry their intended brides off to the men's country homes in the hope that there they might persuade them to renounce their faith and marry. Alternating between gentle persuasion and violent coercion, the men tried every tactic they could conceive to convince the sisters that marriage was the proper course, but neither sister showed any sign of yielding.

Finally, Titus Aurelius killed Anatolia in a fit of anger. Eugenius, however, was convinced that in time, Victoria would come around to his point of view with regard to marriage, and continued to alternate between sweetness and violence in his persuasive efforts. For a time, he allowed her only a single piece of bread each day. Years went by, but Victoria showed no sign of turning from her faith and her determination to resist marriage. In fact, so strong was her faith that she managed to convert many of those who spent time near her, including the man set to guard her.

Finally, Eugenius grew frustrated beyond control, especially when she refused to sacrifice to his gods, and prevailed upon Julian, prefect of the Capitol in Rome and count of the temples, to supply him with the services of Liliarcus, the state executioner. At the direction of Eugenius, Liliarcus stabbed Victoria through the chest with a single thrust of his sword. Legend has it that in the wake of the execution, Liliarcus developed leprosy and died six days later. Victoria was later canonized. It is generally agreed that she was a historical figure, although the exact story of her life and death that has come down to us is probably a myth. Her feast day is December 23.

SOURCES:

Englebert, Omer. *The Lives of the Saints*. London: Thames and Hudson, 1951.

Don Amerman,
freelance writer,
Saylorsburg, Pennsylvania

Victoria (1819–1901)

Queen of England from 1837 to 1901 who restored the damaged prestige of the British monarchy and presided over the most confident years of British imperial and industrial dominance. Queen of Great Britain (r. 1837–1901), empress of India (r. 1876–1901). Born Alexandrina Victoria on May 24, 1819, in Kensington Palace, London, England; died on January 22, 1901, at Osborne House, Isle of Wight, England; buried at Windsor, Berkshire, England; daughter of Edward Guelph, duke of Kent (son of King George III) and Victoria of Coburg; married Prince Albert of Saxe-Coburg, on February 10, 1840 (died 1861); children: Victoria Adelaide (1840–1901); Albert Edward (1841–1910, future Edward VII, king of England, r. 1901–1910, who married Alexandra of Denmark); Alice Maud Mary (1843–1878, mother of Alexandra Feodorovna of Russia); Alfred (1844–1900, who married Marie Alexandrovna [1853–1920]); Helena (1846–1923); Louise (1848–1939); Arthur (1850–1942); Leopold Albert (1853–1884, duke of Albany, and father of Princess Alice of Athlone [1883–1981]); Beatrice (1857–1944).

Descendants: H.M. Queen Elizabeth II and the House of Mountbatten-Windsor; Wilhelm II of Hohenzollern, last German emperor; kings Carl XVI Gustaf of Sweden and Juan Carlos I of Spain, and Queen Margrethe II of Denmark; the former kings of Greece, Rumania, and Yugoslavia; the head of the former Russian imperial house of Romanov.

Death of William IV; Victoria succeeded to throne (1837); coronation (June 28, 1838); Sir Robert Peel became prime minister (1841); Irish Potato Famine (1845–49); repeal of the Corn Laws (1846); Lord John Russell became prime minister (1847); continental revolutions throughout Europe; in Britain, the Chartist Movement (1848); Great Exhibition (1851); Crimean War (1853–56); Lord Palmerston became prime minister (1855); Indian Mutiny threatened British control of subcontinent (1857); death of Prince Albert (1861); Second Reform Act passed (1867); Gladstone became prime minister (1868); Franco-Prussian War (1870–71); Disraeli became prime minister (1874); Disraeli made Victoria the empress of India (1877); Third Reform Act enfranchised farm laborers (1884); Lord Salisbury became prime minister (1886); Victoria celebrated her Diamond Jubilee (1897); South African War (1899–1902); Victoria died at age 81, having reigned 63 years (1901).

Queen *Charlotte of Mecklenburg-Strelitz and King George III had 15 children but most of them were idle, debt-ridden, and licentious. As George deteriorated into insanity, he had no legitimate grandchildren and so the throne had no secure line of succession. Princess Victoria was born just before George III died, and the rapid extinction of her three elderly and childless uncles would give her the throne at age 18. She ruled Britain and its expanding empire for the next 64 years, restored the sagging prestige of the monarchy, worked tirelessly, and came to impart a moral and aesthetic style to an entire age and way of life.

She was the daughter of George III's fourth son Edward, duke of Kent. The duke and the king both died in the year 1820, so Victoria was brought up, often lonely, by her mother *Victoria of Coburg, a German princess still trying to adjust to life in Britain. At her mother's instigation, Victoria learned the Western European languages and was fluent throughout her life in French, German, and Italian. She was also tutored in history, geography, natural history, music, dancing, and drawing, the regimen being supervised by a talented cleric, George Davys, whom she later rewarded with appointment as bishop of Peterborough.

As she was growing up two of her uncles occupied the throne, first George IV, then William IV. Both of them died childless and in consequence Victoria inherited the kingdom in 1837, when she was 18. She wrote in her diary on learning the news: "Since it has pleased Providence to place me in this station, I shall do my utmost to fulfil my duty towards my country; I am very young and perhaps in many, though not in all things, inexperienced, but I am sure, that very few have more real good will and more real desire to do what is fit and right than I have." "Victoria was a woman of peerless common sense; her common sense, which is a rare gift at any time, amounted to genius," writes E.F. Benson. "[C]ommon sense poured out from her, grey and strong, like the waters of the Amazon."

Victoria at once faced a conflict with her mother whose close advisor Sir John Conroy aimed to become a power behind the new queen. Victoria disliked and mistrusted Conroy and made it quite clear that she would not be governed by him—she even broke off all conversation with her mother over the issue, until she got her own way and had Conroy dismissed. She also resolved to see her ministers alone, beginning at once to break out of the close chaperonage which her mother had exercised until then. As queen, she was for the first time able to sleep in her own room rather than sharing one with her mother. She confirmed Prime Minister Lord Melbourne in his office on her first day as a monarch, and enjoyed his tutelage through the early years of her reign. He was a friendly and gifted politician, impressed by the young queen's abilities, and worked harmoniously with her until he was ousted by a defeat in the House of Commons. She was now supposed to invite the leading Tory member of Parliament, Sir Robert Peel, to form a government, but balked when Peel asked her to introduce more Tories at court. Peel withdrew, Melbourne was temporarily restored, and the queen's early popularity suffered a dent, for she seemed to be politicking improperly—the event was nicknamed "the Bedchamber Crisis."

Her marriage to Prince Albert of Saxe-Coburg in 1840 restored much of her credibility. He was her cousin; they had met and enjoyed each other's company previously, and now she decided that she would like to marry him. As queen she, rather than he, proposed the match and was gladly accepted. Victoria idolized Albert, and they were inseparable for the duration of their marriage. Its early days were fraught with tension, however, because Albert did not take kindly to being his wife's subordinate, as she, the queen, insisted. After the birth of their first child, Princess *Victoria Adelaide, he finally won her consent to take care of some state affairs. Impressed by Albert's judgment, the queen soon came to rely on it, and he felt his wounded pride suitably soothed by his newly important role.

Victoria was crowned at age 18.

Alice Maud Mary.
See Alexandra Feodorovna (1872–1918) for sidebar.
❧➤

The couple had nine children, the first being born less than a year after the marriage, and the last in 1857: Victoria Adelaide (1840–1901); Albert Edward (1841–1910, future Edward VII, king of England, who married ***Alexandra of Denmark**); ❧ **Alice Maud Mary** (1843–1878, mother of ***Alexandra Feodorovna** of Russia); Alfred (1844–1900, who married ***Marie Alexandrovna** [1853–1920]), ❧➤ **Helena** (1846–1923); ***Louise** (1848–1939); Arthur (1850–1942); Leopold Albert (1853–1884, duke of Albany, and father of Princess ***Alice of Athlone**

She ruled for
64 years.

❧►
See sidebars
on the
following page

[1883–1981]), and ❧ **Beatrice** (1857–1944). Victoria found pregnancy vexing and difficult, and was glad to avail herself of chloroform to ease the pain of her last two deliveries—her decision set off a vogue for the new anaesthetic throughout Europe.

The royal family lived a vigorous life in the 1840s, dancing, riding, and traveling in the royal yacht on visits to France, Germany, Scotland, and Ireland. They showed a keen interest in the technological innovations of the era which were then making Britain the world's predominant in-

❧ Helena (1846–1923)

Duchess of Schleswig-Holstein-Sonderburg-Augustenberg. Name variations: Helena of Saxe-Coburg; Princess Christian of Schleswig-Holstein. Born Helena Augusta Victoria on May 25, 1846, in Buckingham Palace, London, England; died on June 9, 1923, in London, England; third daughter of Queen *Victoria (1819–1901) and Prince Albert Saxe-Coburg; sister of King Edward VII of England; married Christian of Schleswig-Holstein-Sonderburg-Augustenberg, on July 5, 1866; children: Christian; Albert, duke of Schleswig-Holstein-Sonderburg-Augustenberg; Helena Victoria (1870–1948); Marie-Louise (1872–1956); Harold.

❧ Beatrice (1857–1944)

Princess of England. Name variations: Beatrice of Battenberg; Princess of Battenberg; Princess Henry of Battenberg; Beatrice Saxe-Coburg; Beatrice of Saxe-Coburg. Born Beatrice Mary Victoria Feodora (or Feodore) on April 14, 1857, at Buckingham Palace, London, England; died on October 26, 1944, in Balcombe, West Sussex, England; fifth and youngest daughter of Queen Victoria (1819–1901) and Prince Albert Saxe-Coburg; sister of King Edward VII of England; married Prince Henry Maurice of Battenberg, on July 23, 1885 (died 1896); children: Alexander Mountbatten, marquess of Carisbrooke (1886–1960); Victoria Eugenie of Battenberg (1887–1969, who married Alphonso XIII, king of Spain, and was known as Queen *Ena); Leopold Mountbatten; Maurice Mountbatten.

Of all Queen *Victoria's children, the last born Beatrice was the closest to her; she was the queen's constant companion for 40 years. When Prince Albert died, Victoria had written of Beatrice in her usual third person: "The Queen can only pray that this flower of the flock may never leave her, but be the prop, comfort and companion of her widowed mother to old age." The only daughter left at home, Beatrice had a lonely childhood, consoling herself with her music and animals. She was called "Baby" well into her adulthood.

On March 2, 1882, while returning to Windsor by carriage with her mother, Beatrice caught sight of a man in the crowd as he raised a gun and took aim at the carriage. The shot missed and the would-be assassin, Roderick MacLean, was thrown to the ground by the throng. Victoria was awestruck by Beatrice's composure; from then on, she depended on her daughter even more. Beatrice became confidante, secretary, factotum, and nurse—

until the day that she fell in love with a Prussian, Prince Henry of Battenberg. Her mother was so angry that for six months she would only communicate with Beatrice by notes shoved across the breakfast table.

Finally, the queen relented; but only if the couple would live in the royal household after their marriage. Henry agreed, giving up his commission in the Prussian army. They were married in 1885 in a small church at Whippingham on the Isle of Wight, the first time a monarch's daughter was married in an English parish church. The queen allowed a two-day honeymoon. Fortunately, Victoria grew fond of her son-in-law, as did the British. He was made governor of the Isle of Wight.

The couple had four children and for the next ten years shared a happy marriage while undertaking many ceremonial engagements throughout England. But Henry grew weary. When trouble broke out in West Africa, Henry, backed by Beatrice, received permission to join the British Expeditionary Force being sent to quell the angry Ashanti. Far from home, he died after contracting malaria in 1896. After a month spent away from the castle while in mourning in France, the longest she had been away from her mother, Beatrice returned to her mother's side and remained there. She also took on her husband's duties as governor of the Isle of Wight.

Following her mother's death in 1901, Princess Beatrice spent the next 30 years editing her mother's letters and journals (Victoria had scrupulously kept a diary from age 13 until her death). Beatrice recopied them into a series of blue notebooks, striking out anything that might put her mother in a bad light, sometimes rewriting total passages. She then burned the originals, to the shock and horror of historians of British history. The 111 volumes of edited journals reside in the Royal Archives at Windsor.

During World War I, Beatrice had to leave the Isle of Wight. She moved into Kensington Palace and spent most of the war setting up the Princess Henry of Battenberg hospital for Officers in Hill Street, London. At war's end, George V stripped the German names from royal titles and adopted the surname Windsor, and Beatrice's sons became Mountbattens rather than Battenbergs. Beatrice, like her mother, went on with her duties even when nearly blind with cataracts by 1935. She spent the last years of her life at Brantbridge Park, Balcombe, dying there on October 26, 1944, and was buried at Windsor Castle. She was the last of Queen Victoria's children to die. Her body now resides next to her husband's at Whippingham.

SUGGESTED READING:

Packard, Jerrold M. *Victoria's Daughters*. St. Martin's, 1998.

dustrial power: they experimented with rail travel and replaced the old royal yacht with a new steam-powered one. They patronized the new craft of photography and were one of the first families in the world to have their lives extensively documented by photograph—Victoria herself eventually had more than a hundred family photograph albums. When Albert designed a new house for them at Osborne on the Isle of White, it was in large part prefabricated, and built in record time. Albert was also an accomplished musician, played the organ and wrote music which was sometimes performed at official functions. He and Victoria were enthusiastic supporters of the Great Exhibition of 1851 which demonstrated the technical progress of the era in a spectacular glass building, the Crystal Palace. They opened the exhibition and returned to admire it several times that summer.

Melbourne's fall at the election of 1841 had led to the appointment of Peel as prime minister. Despite the embarrassing memory of the Bedchamber Crisis, Victoria and he soon developed a mutual respect, and, from then on, throughout the rest of her reign, she always managed to work effectively with her ministers, even those she did not particularly like. The only one to rival Melbourne in her later affections was the Tory premier Benjamin Disraeli, who was an artful flatterer and consummate politician; by contrast, she always found William Gladstone, Disraeli's great Liberal rival, rigid and unyielding, and Lord Palmerston (who had once made improper advances to one of her ladies-in-waiting) an untrustworthy profligate. Disraeli observed: "Gladstone treats the Queen like a public department; I treat her like a woman." He recognized her broad streak of obstinacy and bent as far as possible to accommodate it. He also saw that she grasped political issues in personal terms, and learned how to present them to her in that form.

Disraeli particularly delighted Victoria by making her empress of India in 1877 after a reorganization of British administration on the subcontinent. India as the "jewel in the crown" became a catchphrase of the imperial era, and Victoria always gloried in imperial adventures—she found Gladstone's "Little England" policy incomprehensible and unfairly blamed him for the death of General Charles Gordon, an imperial legend, at the Siege of Khartoum, in 1885. Disraeli managed to insinuate that all the triumphs of his foreign policy (acquisition of the Suez Canal, for example) were her own work, with him merely crossing the t's and dotting the i's. Victoria reciprocated Disraeli's chivalrous gestures by violating her own court protocol and allowing him to sit in her presence. When he died in 1882, she went to his estate and placed her personal tribute on his grave.

Disraeli's ascendancy still lay in the future during the 1850s when Victoria and Albert ruled confidently side by side, through the crises of the Crimean War, the Indian Mutiny, and the onset of the American Civil War. The Crimean War (1854–56) saw Britain allied with France, her traditional enemy, against Russia. Victoria and Albert visited Paris during the war, on a sumptuous state visit to Emperor Napoleon III and Empress *Eugénie, with Victoria herself noting the incongruity of fraternizing with the nation which had been Britain's deadliest enemy in her grandfather's era. After the French Revolution of 1870, Napoleon III and Empress Eugénie fled to England as exiles. Their only son later died in Africa after volunteering to serve in a British regiment in the Zulu Wars.

Victoria and Albert witnessed the maturing of their large family, and Victoria gave birth for the last time in 1857, while already planning marriages with suitable non-Catholic European royalty for her older children. The oldest son and heir, "Bertie," prince of Wales (the future Edward VII), was a source of perpetual annoyance to Victoria—he learned his lessons more slowly than his sisters as a boy and then discovered sex at about the age of 20, soon developing a taste for promiscuity. His parents, sternly puritanical in sexual affairs, were furious; throughout the following decades, Victoria's disapproval of her heir's conduct was a recurrent theme in British public life. Another son, Prince Leopold, was a hemophiliac, and Victoria's daughters, without suffering it, carried this disability, which spread through most of Europe's monarchies in the wake of Victoria's matrimonial alliances. After marrying her elder children to all possible European candidates, Victoria permitted one of the younger daughters, Princess Louise, to marry a commoner, the Marquess of Lorne, in 1869. She planned to prevent her youngest child, Princess Beatrice, from marrying at all and consented to her match with Prince Henry of Battenberg only if the couple agreed to remain with her as permanent companions. There was a furious stand-off for half a year, with mother and daughter communicating only by curt notes, but in the end the couple agreed, married in 1885, then settled in with the queen for the rest of her long life.

After 21 years of marriage, Prince Albert caught typhoid in 1861. Victoria was not alarmed at first, because she had survived it in childhood, but he soon sank and died. The death of Albert came to her as a shattering blow, and, though she lived on for another 40 years, she never subsequently cast off her mourning clothes (and mourning was required of all at court right into the 1890s, even among those born after Albert's demise). At first, Victoria was so distracted with grief that she refused to see even her ministers, though her strong sense of duty soon reasserted itself. More long-lasting was her decision to withdraw from public life. As years passed and she still remained entirely out of the public eye, her reputation began to decline. Death of loved ones at any stage of life was still common in mid-19th-century Britain, and, though a period of mourning was seemly, it should not, Britons agreed, go on indefinitely. Members of Parliament with republican sympathies declared that the government should not grant the queen her large annual income if she refused to reciprocate by fulfilling her official duties—for many years she declined even to preside at the official opening of Parliament. In an age of rapid political transformations (the unifications of Italy and Germany, the Franco-Prussian War, the Paris Commune), it seemed possible to her advisors that Victoria might erode the authority of the monarchy to the point that it too would collapse, though, in actuality, it never faced a dangerously strong political challenge.

Rumors circulated in London—and reached all the way to the Russian court in St. Petersburg—that the queen had gone mad, unhinged by grief. For the rest of her life, she acted in many ways as though Albert were still with her, ordering hot shaving water to be carried to his room every morning, for example. Lord Clarendon saw the queen in 1862 and could not help noticing that she repeatedly referred to the "Prince's opinions and acts as if he was in the next room." Clarendon "found it difficult not to think so for everything was set out on his table, the blotting book open with a pen upon it, his watch going, fresh flowers in the glass, etc." Victoria's elaborate grieving for her lamented husband yielded some public benefits. The Albert Hall, the Victoria and Albert Museum, the Museum of Natural History, and the Albert Memorial, now central fixtures of British cultural life, were all projects initiated by the queen in her eagerness to pay him tribute.

During her years of retirement from public life, Victoria spent long periods at her Scottish castle, Balmoral, attended by a loyal servant named John Brown who soon became a favorite, gaining easier access to the queen than even her own children. Court gossip alleged that he had become her lover, even that they had married se-

cretly, and Victoria's children became resentful of his influence over their mother. His ascendancy increased in 1872 when an Irish republican pointed a pistol at the queen (one of seven assassination attempts she survived during her long reign). Brown jumped from the carriage they were riding in and pinned the assassin to the ground until help arrived. When Brown died in 1883, Victoria even tried to write a eulogistic biography of him until her ministers managed to discourage the project (they were already dismayed by her decision to publish long sections of her diaries almost verbatim). Later still, she became deeply attached to another servant, an Indian Muslim named Abdul Karim whom she nicknamed "the Munshi," or teacher, because he gave her lessons in Hindustani. He became an advisor to her on Indian affairs, and she stubbornly took his side in every dispute relating to his conduct. Most of her children and courtiers, sharing the typical racism of the era, were enraged by his presence and his influence, but powerless to prevent it in the face of the queen's unbending dedication to him. The Munshi himself became increasingly self-important and arbitrary, stole jewels from the queen, and used her favor to avenge himself on his personal enemies. In the end, her trusted doctor, Sir James Reid, warned her that the gentlemen of her household would resign en masse if the Munshi were not dismissed, and that he himself might even be forced to declare her insane if she insisted on sticking by her favorite. Even then, she defied her advisors, weathered the storm, and encouraged the Munshi to stay by her side, where he could still be found at the time of her death.

The long succession of anguished scenes over the Munshi showed that the queen, always bossy and obstinate, was becoming more tyrannical with age. When Gladstone died in 1898, she showed none of the affectionate gratitude to his memory that she had accorded Disraeli. Her son and heir the prince of Wales had often supported Gladstone and now provoked his mother by acting as a pallbearer at the funeral. "The Queen was so incensed that she telegraphed to enquire what advice he had sought and what precedent he had followed. The Prince's reply was unusually curt. He had sought no advice and knew of no precedent. There was but one Gladstone."

Whatever the rumblings of discontent behind the scenes in public, the queen's reputation, long in eclipse, revived in the last years of her 64-year reign as she emerged from her self-imposed seclusion. Many of her subjects enjoyed the revelations in her published diaries, and she herself seems to have had an instinctively middle-class taste which made her easily able to appreciate the hopes and fears of what had become the most important and influential section of the British public. On the other hand, she never showed much awareness of the widespread suffering of her poorest subjects—she would mention in her diary the signs of poverty and suffering she had seen on her travels, but never threw her energy into the cause of social and industrial reform.

In 1897, her Diamond Jubilee celebrations featured all the pomp and circumstance of the empire. As historian Theo Aronson notes:

> Queen Victoria's Diamond jubilee confirmed her position as the most celebrated, most instantly recognizable person in the world. In that small, dignified figure seemed concentrated all the glory, all the power, all the wonder of majesty. She was by now an almost mythical creature: the Doyenne of Sovereigns, the Great White Queen, the Shah-in-Shah-Padshah, the Grandmamma of Europe, Victoria Regina et Imperatrix, a monarch who ruled over the greatest empire that the world had ever known.

She died four years later after presiding over the turn of the century, when the ugly Boer War was already showing new problems in store for the empire. Her reign had been an immense success in terms of restoring the dignity of the monarchy, and the fact that her name was attached to the age, and to an entire way of life, "Victorian," suggests the breadth and durability of her influence.

SOURCES:

Aronson, Theo. *Heart of a Queen: Queen Victoria's Romantic Attachments*. London: John Murray, 1991.

Ashdown, Dulcie. *Victoria and the Coburgs*. London: Robert Hale, 1981.

Benson, E.F. *As We Were: A Victorian Peepshow*. London: Blue Ribbon, 1934.

Longford, Elizabeth. *Victoria R.I.* London: Pan Books, 1976.

Mullen, Richard and James Munson. *Victoria: Portrait of a Queen*. London: BBC Books, 1987.

St. Aubyn, Giles. *Queen Victoria: A Portrait*. London: Sinclair-Stevenson, 1991.

RELATED MEDIA:

Mrs. Brown (105 min. film), starring **Judi Dench** and Billy Connolly, directed by John Madden, Miramax, 1997.

Victoria Regina (play) by Laurence Housman, starred **Helen Hayes*, 1935.

Victoria

"Victoria Regina" (television presentation), on NBC's "Hallmark Hall of Fame," starred *Julie Harris, 1961.

Victoria the Great (118 min. film), starring *Anna Neagle and Anton Walbrook, directed by Herbert Wilcox, 1937.

Patrick Allitt,
Professor of History,
Emory University, Atlanta, Georgia

Victoria (1866–1929)

*Prussian princess. Name variations: Victoria Hohenzollern. Born Frederica Amelia Wilhelmina Victoria on April 12, 1866, in Potsdam, Brandenburg, Germany; died on November 13, 1929, in Bonn, Germany; daughter of *Victoria Adelaide (1840–1901) and Frederick III (1831–1888), emperor of Germany (r. 1888); sister of Wilhelm II, emperor of Germany (r. 1888–1918); married Adolph of Schaumburg-Lippe, on November 19, 1890; married Alexander Anatolievitch Zoubkoff, on November 19, 1927.*

Victoria (1868–1935).

See Alexandra of Denmark for sidebar.

Victoria (1977—)

*Swedish crown princess and duchess of Västergötland. Name variations: Victoria Bernadotte. Born Victoria Ingrid Alice Désirée on July 14, 1977, in Stockholm, Sweden; daughter of Carl XVI Gustavus, king of Sweden, and *Silvia Sommerlath (1943—); studied French at a French university in 1996; studied political science at Uppsala University.*

Swedish crown princess Victoria, who grew up romping with her sister *Madeleine (b. 1982) and brother Carl Philip at Drottningholm, a 17th-century palace outside Stockholm, was long known for her fun-loving ways and talent for school and sports. When she turned 18, her birthday photos showed a smiling, round-faced teenager in good health. But a weekly women's magazine, *Svensk Dam Tidning*, noted that the heir to the throne looked as if she had "eaten too many hamburgers." The editors were jubilant two years later when a sleeker version of Victoria began to emerge and featured her on their cover nine times, once in a bikini.

On November 29, 1997, a week after Victoria wore an evening gown that revealed her skeletal shoulders, the director of the Information and Press Department of the royal court confirmed public suspicions: "The crown princess is suffering from an eating disorder. She is receiving therapeutic help."

Victoria Adelaide (1840–1901)

Princess royal of Great Britain and German empress. Name variations: Vicky; Victoria; Victoria Adelaide Mary Louise; Empress Frederick. Born Victoria Adelaide Mary Louise on November 21, 1840, in Buckingham Palace, London, England; died of cancer on August 5, 1901, in Friedrichshof, Germany; eldest child of Queen Victoria (1819–1901) and Prince Albert Saxe-Coburg; sister of King Edward VII of England; educated by a French governess and her father; married Friedrich Wilhelm also known as Frederick III (1831–1888), emperor of Germany (r. 1888), on January 25, 1858; children: Wilhelm (William) II (1859–1941), emperor of Germany; Charlotte of Saxe-Meiningen (1860–1919); Henry of Prussia (1862–1929); Sigismund (1864–1866); Victoria (1866–1929); Waldemar (1868–1879); Sophie of Prussia (1870–1932, who married Constantine I, king of the Hellenes); Margaret Beatrice (1872–1954).

Advocate of constitutional government; active in philanthropic and educational endeavors; founded Berlin Industrial Art Museum and the Victoria House and Nursing School (1881); founded Victoria Lyceum, the first institution in Germany dedicated to women's higher education.

Victoria Adelaide, eldest child of Queen *Victoria and her husband Prince Albert, was born in Buckingham Palace on November 21, 1840. Known within the family as Vicky, the young princess was doted on by her parents and enjoyed an idyllic childhood in the royal family's numerous comfortable homes. Particular attention was paid to her education. A gifted and responsive child, she could speak English, French, and German with some fluency by the age of three.

In 1851, at age 11, she met her future husband, Prince Friedrich Wilhelm (Frederick III), when he visited London with his father, Prince Wilhelm (I), to attend the Great Exhibition. Prince Albert, an ardent advocate of German unification who saw Prussia as the potential vanguard of a nationalist movement, began discussing an English-Prussian marriage as early as 1853. After receiving the reluctant blessing of Prince Wilhelm's brother, Frederick William IV, king of Prussia, the couple were engaged when Vicky was just 15. The engagement was not publicly announced until April 1856, on the conclusion of the Crimean War by the Treaty of Paris, but the news was received coolly in both countries.

Prior to her marriage, Vicky's education was pursued with her future position in mind. Prince Albert devoted an hour a day to her personal instruction, debating political and social questions with her and fostering in her his own liberal sympathies. At his suggestion, she translated into English Johann Gustav Droysen's "Karl August und die Deutsche Politik," a plea for a liberal national policy in Germany.

Married in London on January 25, 1858, the 17-year-old princess met with a warm welcome in Prussia but soon found her new life there difficult. Not only were the living conditions in Prussian palaces far more primitive than in their English counterparts, but the Prussian court was more narrow in matters of religion, politics, and etiquette. Her outspoken views on the benefits of constitutional government were unwelcome, and she chafed under the strict surveillance of her mother-in-law *Augusta of Saxe-Weimar. In the Neue Palais in Berlin's Unter den Linden, Vicky gave birth to her first child, the future emperor Wilhelm II, in January 1859. Seven other children were to follow within the next 13 years: *Charlotte of Saxe-Meiningen (1860–1919); Henry of Prussia (1862–1929); Sigismund (1864–1866); *Victoria (1866–1929); Waldemar (1868–1879); *Sophie of Prussia (1870–1932, who married Constantine I, king of the Hellenes); and *Margaret Beatrice (1872–1954). Still tutored by her father, to whom she sent weekly political reports and historical essays, Vicky enjoyed a strong influence over her husband, which made her increasingly unpopular in court circles.

Vicky and Frederick became crown princess and crown prince of Prussia in January 1861, when King Wilhelm I succeeded his brother, inaugurating a year of traumatic change in Vicky's life. Her beloved father died suddenly that December and delicate health prevented her from attending the funeral. In March 1862, Wilhelm I dismissed his liberal cabinet and asked Otto von Bismarck and the conservative Junker Party to help him rule Prussia. Bismarck was to become a lifelong opponent of Vicky and Frederick, who despised his rejection of constitutional principles. The couple withdrew from court entirely, leaving Berlin in October 1862.

After Frederick made an open protest against Bismarck's absolutist government in a speech in Dantzig in 1863, the prince was forced to retire from all political activity. By 1864, the whole of their retinue had been replaced by Bismarck's followers, and Vicky was singled out for attack by the conservative press. Queen Victoria was dissuaded with some difficulty from active intervention on her daughter's behalf. Bismarck excluded the crown prince completely from the business of state.

Vicky found herself constantly in opposition to Bismarck over issues like the Schleswig-Holstein succession and the 1866 Austro-Prussian conflict, during which, despite their personal opposition to the war, Frederick commanded an army unit and Vicky organized hospitals. She became the focus of anti-English opinion during the Franco-Prussian war of 1870–71, despite indefatigable philanthropic efforts recruiting nurses and organizing hospitals for wounded Germans.

Her interests extended beyond politics to education, art and literature, and Vicky cultivated a broad social circle. A keen artist, she was elected a member of the Berlin Academy in 1860 and was instrumental in the founding of the Berlin Industrial Art Museum, which opened in 1881. Following her exhaustive 1872 report on hospital organization, the Victoria House and Nursing School was established in Berlin in 1881, informed by *Florence Nightingale's reforms in England.

Victoria Adelaide

Vicky's liberal beliefs and hospital experience developed into a concern for the social conditions of the working classes, and she founded a society for the promotion of health in the home in 1875, as well as hospitals, workhouses, schools, and libraries. She espoused the cause of education for women, founding the Victoria Lyceum, the first German institution dedicated to women's higher education. Her activity on behalf of women's education brought real social change throughout Germany, where she founded over 40 educational or philanthropic institutions.

As the old emperor's health declined and Frederick's accession at last seemed possible, the crown prince fell ill with a disease of the throat. By the time the old emperor died in March 1888, it was clear that the new emperor was dying as well. No longer able to speak, he relied on Vicky to help pursue his political program. Bismarck, jealous of her influence, initiated a press campaign against the proposed match of her second daughter, helping to create a family quarrel by enlisting Crown Prince Wilhelm's support. Just three months after his accession, Frederick died, leaving Victoria isolated and estranged from both Bismarck and her eldest son, Bismarck's protégé, now Emperor Wilhelm II. After Bismarck's fall from grace in 1890, Victoria's relationship with her son improved, although he tormented her with anti-English sentiments. Most of her widowhood was spent in Cronberg, where she built Friedrichshof, her country seat, making frequent visits home to England. She attended Queen Victoria's Diamond Jubilee procession in 1897 but was diagnosed with cancer following a fall from a horse soon after. Outliving her mother by only six months, Vicky died at Friedrichshof on August 5, 1901, and was buried beside her husband in the Friedenskirche at Potsdam.

SOURCES AND SUGGESTED READING:

Bennett, Daphne. *Vicky: Princess Royal of England and German Empress.* NY: St. Martin's Press, 1971.

Packard, Jerrold M. *Victoria's Daughters.* NY: St. Martin's Press, 1998.

Pakula, Hannah. *An Uncommon Woman: Empress Frederick, Daughter of Queen Victoria, Wife of the Crown Prince of Prussia, Mother of Kaiser Wilhelm.* NY: Simon & Schuster, 1995.

Paula Morris, D.Phil.,
Brooklyn, New York

Victoria Adelaide of Schleswig-Holstein (1885–1970)

Duchess of Albany. Name variations: Victoria Adelheid, princess von Schleswig-Holstein. Born Victoria Adelaide of Schleswig-Holstein-Saxe-Coburg-Glucks- *burg on December 31, 1885, in Grunholz, Holstein, Germany; died on October 3, 1970, in Coburg, Bavaria, Germany; daughter of Frederick Ferdinand (1855–1934), duke of Schleswig-Holstein-Glucksburg (r. 1855–1934) and *Caroline Matilda of Schleswig-Holstein (1860–1932); married Charles Edward Saxe-Coburg, 2nd duke of Albany, on October 11, 1905; children: John Leopold (b. 1906), prince of Saxe-Coburg; *Sybilla of Saxe-Coburg-Gotha (1908–1972); Hubertus Frederick (b. 1909, a pilot in the Luftwaffe); Caroline Matilda Schnirring (1912–1983, who married Max Otto Schnirring, a captain in the Luftwaffe), duchess of Saxony; Frederick (b. 1918).*

Victoria Alexandra Alice Mary (1897–1965).
See Mary.

Victoria Eugenia (1887–1969).
See Ena.

Victoria Eugenie of Battenberg (1887–1969).
See Ena.

Victoria Frederica of Schleswig-Holstein (1860–1932).
See Caroline Matilda of Schleswig-Holstein.

Victoria Louise (1892–1980)

Duchess of Brunswick-Lüneburg. Born Victoria Louise Adelaide Matilda Charlotte on September 13, 1892, at Marble Palace, Potsdam, Brandenburg, Germany; died on December 11, 1980, in Hanover, Lower Saxony, Germany; daughter of *Augusta of Schleswig-Holstein (1858–1921) and Wilhelm II (1859–1941), emperor of Germany (r. 1888–1918); married Ernest Augustus of Cumberland (1887–1953), duke of Brunswick-Luneburg (r. 1923–1953), on May 24, 1913; children: Ernest Augustus (1914–1987); George (b. 1915); *Fredericka (1917–1981, queen of Greece); Christian (1919–1981); Welf-Henry (b. 1923); Monika of Solms-Laubach (b. 1929).

Victoria Louise Sophia Augusta Amelia Helena (1870–1948).
See Helena Victoria.

Victoria Mary Louisa (1786–1861).
See Victoria of Coburg.

Victoria Mary of Teck (1867–1953).
See Mary of Teck.

Victoria Melita of Saxe-Coburg
(1876–1936)

Grand duchess of Hesse-Darmstadt. Name variations: Victoria of Saxe-Coburg; Grand Duchess Kiril or Cyril; (nickname) Ducky; known as Marie Feodorovna following her second marriage. Born in Malta on November 25, 1876; died of a stroke in Amorbach, Germany, on March 2, 1936; daughter of Alfred Saxe-Coburg, duke of Edinburgh, and *Marie Alexandrovna (1853–1920); sister of *Alexandra Saxe-Coburg (1878–1942), *Beatrice of Saxe-Coburg (1884–1966), duchess of Galliera, and *Marie of Rumania (1875–1938); married Ernest Louis, grand duke of Hesse-Darmstadt, on April 19, 1894 (divorced 1901); married Cyril Vladimirovitch (grand duke and grandson of Alexander II of Russia), on October 8, 1905; children: (first marriage) Elizabeth of Hesse-Darmstadt (1895–1903) and one son (1900–1900); (second marriage) *Marie of Russia (1907–1951); *Kira of Russia (1909–1967); Vladimir Cyrillovitch (1917–1992).

SUGGESTED READING:

Sullivan, Michael John. *A Fatal Passion: The Story of Victoria Melita, the Uncrowned Last Empress of Russia.* NY: Random House, 1997.

Victoria of Baden (1862–1930)

Queen of Sweden. Born Sophia Mary Victoria on August 7, 1862, in Karlsruhe, Baden-Wurttemberg, Germany; died on April 4, 1930, in Rome, Italy; buried in Stockholm, Sweden; daughter of Frederick I, grand duke of Baden, and *Louise of Baden (daughter of William or Wilhelm I, emperor of Germany, and *Augusta of Saxe-Weimar); married Gustav or Gustavus V (1858–1950), king of Sweden (r. 1907–1950), on September 20, 1881; children: Gustavus VI Adolphus (1882–1973), king of Sweden (r. 1950–1973); William Bernadotte, prince of Sweden (b. 1884, who married *Marie Pavlovna of Russia); Eric Gustaf Louis, duke of Vestmanland (1889–1918).

Victoria of Battenberg (1887–1969).
　　See Ena.

Victoria of Coburg (1786–1861)

Duchess of Kent. Name variations: Victoria of Leiningen; Victoria of Saxe-Coburg; Victoria Mary Louisa von Saxe-Coburg. Born Victoria Mary Louisa of Saxe-Coburg-Saalfeld on August 17, 1786, in Coburg, Bavaria, Germany; died on March 16, 1861, in Windsor, Berkshire, England; interred at Frogmore, Windsor; daughter of Francis, duke of Saxe-Coburg-Saalfeld,

and *Augusta of Reuss-Ebersdorf (1757–1831); sister of Leopold I, king of the Belgians; married Emich, 2nd prince of Leiningen, on December 21, 1803; married Edward Guelph also known as Edward Augustus, duke of Kent, on July 11, 1818, at Kew Palace, Surrey; children: (first marriage) Charles, 3rd prince of Leinigen, and *Feodore of Leiningen (1807–1872); (second marriage) Queen *Victoria (1819–1901).

SUGGESTED READING:

Packard, Jerrold M. *Victoria's Daughters.* St. Martin's, 1998.

Victoria of Baden

Victoria of Hesse-Darmstadt (1863–1950)

Princess of Hesse-Darmstadt. Name variations: Princess Victoria, marchioness of Milford Haven. Born Victoria Alberta Elizabeth Matilda Mary on April 5, 1863, in Windsor Castle, Berkshire, England; died on September 24, 1950, in Kensington Palace, London, England; daughter of Grand Duke Louis IV of Hesse-Darmstadt and Princess *Alice Maud Mary (daughter of Queen *Victoria); married Louis of Battenberg, 1st marquess of Milford Haven, on April 30, 1884; children: *Alice of Battenberg (1885–1967); *Louise Mountbatten (1889–1965, who married Gustavus VI Adolphus); George, 2nd marquess of Milford Haven (1892–1938); Lord Louis Mountbatten (1900–1979, who married *Edwina Ashley Mountbatten).

Victoria of Mecklenburg-Strelitz
(1878–1948)

Prussian aristocrat. Born Victoria Marie Augusta Louise Antoinette Caroline Leopoldine on May 8, 1878; died on October 14, 1948, in Obercassel; daughter of Adolphus Frederick V, grand duke of Mecklenburg-Strelitz, and Elizabeth of Anhalt-Dessau; married George Jametel, on June 22, 1899 (divorced 1908); married Julius of Lippe, in August 1914; children: (first marriage) two; (second marriage) two.

Victoria of Saxe-Coburg (1822–1857)

Duchess of Nemours. Name variations: Victoria of Saxe-Coburg-Gotha. Born on February 14, 1822;

died on November 10, 1857; daughter of Ferdinand Saxe-Coburg (b. 1785) and *Antoinette Kohary (1797–1862); sister of Ferdinand Saxe-Coburg (1816–1885, who married *Maria II da Gloria, queen of Portugal); cousin of Queen *Victoria (1819–1901); married Louis (1814–1896, son of Louis Philippe I, king of France), duke of Nemours, on April 27, 1840; children: Gaston (b. 1842), count of Eu; Ferdinand (b. 1844), duke of Alençon; Margaret d'Orleans (1846–1893, who married Ladislaus Czartoryski); Blanka d'Orleans (1857–1932).

Victoria of Saxe-Coburg (1876–1936).

See Victoria Melita of Saxe-Coburg.

Vidal, Mary Theresa
(1815–1869 or 1873)

British-born Australian writer. Born in 1815 in Devon, England; died in 1869 or 1873; married a minister; children.

A relative of the 18th-century British portraitist Joshua Reynolds, Mary Theresa Vidal was one of the first women to write fiction in Australia. Born in Devon, England, in 1815, she moved with her minister husband in 1840 to Australia, a wild, pioneer land once primarily a penal colony set up to relieve the overcrowding of British jails. While in Australia, Vidal wrote *Tales for the Bush*, a collection of moralistic short stories that warned servants and other working folk against drink and dereliction. *Tales for the Bush* was published in Sydney in 1845; despite the book's title, the stories' subject matter had little to do with Australia. That same year, Vidal returned to England. Once home, she did create two works set in Australia, a story called "The Cabramatta Store" (1850) and the novel *Bengala: Or, Some Time Ago* (1860). These touch mostly on domestic concerns, but also include depictions of colonial and pioneer life. "The Cabramatta Store" uses the drought, fires, and flood of the harsh Australian environment as a backdrop. In addition, Vidal published eight other works of fiction. The date of her death has been variously given as 1869 and 1873.

SOURCES:

Buck, Claire, ed. *The Bloomsbury Guide to Women's Literature.* NY: Prentice Hall, 1992.

Wilde, William H., Joy Hooton, and Barry Andrews. *The Oxford Companion to Australian Literature.* Melbourne, Australia: Oxford University Press, 1985.

James M. Manheim,
freelance writer,
Ann Arbor, Michigan

Vidar, Jorunn (1918—)

Icelandic composer, pianist and teacher often featured on Icelandic radio and television. Born in Reykjavik, Iceland, on December 7, 1918; studied music first with her mother and Pall Isolfsson; later enrolled at the Reykjavik College of Music, studying with Arni Kristjansson and graduating in 1936; studied at the Berlin Hochschule für Musik, 1936–38; continued musical education at the Juilliard School in New York, 1943–45; studied piano in Vienna with Viola Tern, 1959–60.

The volcanic North Atlantic island of Iceland boasts perhaps the highest literacy rate in the world (99.9%), and with a population of only 200,000 may well be the smallest nation to have a language and literature that is over 1,000 years old. Icelanders are also immensely proud of the fact that their Parliament (*Althing,* or general assembly), which first met in the year 930 CE, makes them the oldest continuous practitioners of democracy in the world. Women have made great strides in Iceland in the 20th century, including *Vigdís Finnbogadóttir's election to the office of president. In culture, Icelandic women too have been able to successfully assert themselves. One of the pioneer women in Icelandic music was the multitalented Jorunn Vidar who left a deep impression on Icelandic culture. Her compositions were able to combine traditional Icelandic melodies with the subtleties of the prevailing international style. Some of her best-known works include the ballet *Fire* (1951), *Five Meditations on Icelandic Themes* for piano (1965), and a Suite for Violin and Piano to commemorate the 1,100-year-old settlement of Iceland (1973).

John Haag,
Athens, Georgia

Viebig, Clara (1860–1952)

German novelist and short-story writer. Name variations: Clara Viebig Cohn. Born in 1860 in Trier, Germany; died in 1952 in Berlin, Germany; educated in Düsseldorf and at the Berlin High School of Music; married Fritz Theodor Cohn (a publisher).

Selected writings: Kinder der Eifel *(Children of the Eifel, 1897);* Das Weiberdorf *(Village of Women, 1900);* Das tägliche Brot *(1900, published in English as* Our Daily Bread, *1909);* Die Wacht am Rhein *(The Watch on the Rhine, 1902);* Das schlafende Heer *(1904, published in English as* The Sleeping Army, *1929);* Einer Mutter Sohn *(1907, published in English as* The Son of His Mother, *1913);* Das Kreuz im Venn *(The Cross in Venn, 1908);* Die vor den Toren *(Those*

Outside the Gates, 1910); Töchter der Hekuba *(1917, published in English as* Daughters of Hecuba, *1922)*; Insel der Hoffnung *(1933)*; Der Vielgeliebte und die Vielgehasste *(1936).*

Born in 1860 in the Eifel region of Germany, Clara Viebig used the area of her birth for the settings of her early novels, an area that had been featured very rarely in earlier German literature. It was Viebig who familiarized German readers with the region's bleak highlands of volcanic origin, forbidding swamplands, and vast pinelands. The novelist showed an uncanny talent for blending her characters and the landscape of Eifel, a technique that perhaps can best be seen in the story "Am Totenmaar" from her 1897 collection of short stories *Kinder der Eifel.* In that tale the austere physical setting of the Eifel countryside perfectly reflects the moral rigor of an aging shepherd, and the loneliness of his abandoned child.

Viebig's early work also clearly reflects the influence of *Gabriele Reuter*'s landmark 1895 novel *Aus guter Familie* (From a Good Family), the story of a sensitive young woman of the upper middle class whose conservative, prudish education and social training doom her to a life of sadness. Viebig, however, went much further than Reuter in her examination of life's erotic side, a subject treated with a humorous touch in *Das Weiberdorf* (Village of Women), published in 1900.

In 1904's *Das schlafende Heer* (*The Sleeping Army*), Viebig considers how the seemingly servile demeanor of Polish peasants conceals feelings of patriotism and a seething hatred for the Germans who occupy their homeland. In *Das Kreuz im Venn* (The Cross in Venn), published in 1908, she similarly paints a somewhat contemptuous portrait of the masses, who in the book often act in concert with little thought about the nature or the consequences of their actions. In this particular work the novelist explores the actions and reactions of religious pilgrims to the shrine at Echternach in the Eifel region.

Of all Viebig's novels, *Die Wacht am Rhein* (The Watch on the Rhine, 1902) received the greatest international acceptance and acclaim. Set in Düsseldorf, where she had lived for a time during her childhood, the novel (not to be confused with *Lillian Hellman*'s later play) details some of the diversity of the German peoples in a three-generation study of a Rhineland family into which a Prussian has married.

After marrying successful publisher Fritz Theodor Cohn, Viebig spent much of her adult life in Berlin. The city also became the setting for several of her later novels, most of which focused on social interaction among the classes of German society. In 1900's *Das tägliche Brot* (*Our Daily Bread*), she offers an extremely sympathetic portrait of the day-to-day life of a woman toiling as a servant in the homes of the lower middle class. Viebig showed a particular facility for portraying characters motivated by the most basic of human needs and emotions. This is particularly evident in two of her later novels, *Einer Mutter Sohn* (*The Son of His Mother*, 1907) and *Töchter der Hekuba* (*Daughters of Hecuba*, 1917). Another of her later works, *Die vor den Toren* (Those Outside the Gates, 1910), explores the difficulties faced by people affected by Berlin's urban expansion. At the turn of the century, Viebig was one of Germany's most read novelists, and many of her works were translated into English. She died in Berlin in 1952.

SOURCES:

Buck, Claire, ed. *The Bloomsbury Guide to Women's Literature.* NY: Prentice Hall, 1992.

Columbia Dictionary of Modern European Literature. 2nd ed. NY: Columbia University Press, 1980.

Don Amerman,
freelance writer,
Saylorsburg, Pennsylvania

Vieira da Silva, Maria Elena

(1908—)

Portuguese-born French painter. Name variations: Maria Helena. Born on June 13, 1908, in Lisbon, Portugal; only child of Marcos Vieira da Silva (an economist) and Maria (Graca) Vieira da Silva; educated in Lisbon; studied in Paris, learning sculpture with Bourdelle and Despiau, engraving with Hayter, and painting with Friesz and Léger; married Arpad Szénes (a painter), on February 22, 1930.

Selected works: Forest of Errors *(1941);* The City *(1948);* Morning Mist *(1952);* Iron Bridges *(1953);* Theatre *(1953);* Nocturnal Space *(1954);* Overhead Railway *(1955).*

Portuguese-born painter Maria Elena Vieira da Silva was born in 1908 and grew up in her native Lisbon, the only child of economist Marco Vieira da Silva and **Maria Graca Vieira da Silva**; one of her relatives was the founder of *O Seculo*. She traveled extensively with her family, and her mother, aunt, and uncle all encouraged her toward a career in painting, leaving her in Paris at the age of 19 to study sculpture with Bourdelle and Despiau, engraving with Hayter, and painting with Friesz and Léger.

In Paris, Vieira da Silva married Hungarian painter Arpad Szénes in 1930 and held the first of her several one-woman shows in 1933. Her reputation was established early in her career by a semi-abstract style notable for its soft colors, gentle light, and often poetic moods. Vieira da Silva believed that a painting should "have its heart, its nervous system, its bones, and its circulation. In its movements it should be like a person and have the tempo of a person's movements."

Vieira da Silva spent World War II in Brazil, living from 1939 to 1947 in Rio de Janeiro, but she spent the vast majority of her adult life in France, ultimately becoming a French citizen. While in Rio, she continued to paint, creating murals for the University of Agriculture, until her return to Paris in 1947.

During the 1940s and 1950s, Vieira da Silva exhibited at the Venice and Sao Paolo Biennales, as well as in London, Paris, and New York City. After her 1956 American show, the *New York Herald Tribune* described her as "one of the most interesting talents to develop in Europe since the end of the war." Vieira da Silva's work is highly collectible and hangs in major museums and galleries around the world. A typical Vieira da Silva work, *Overhead Railway* (1955), can be seen in the Nordsheim-Westfälen Kunstsammlung in Düsseldorf.

SOURCES:
Current Biography. NY. H.W. Wilson, 1958.

Paula Morris, D.Phil.,
Brooklyn, New York

Vieregg, Elizabeth Helene

*Queen of Denmark and Norway. Second wife of Frederick IV (1671–1730), king of Denmark and Norway (r. 1699–1730); no children. Frederick IV had two other wives: *Louise of Mecklenburg-Gustrow and *Anne Sophie Reventlow.*

Viertel, Salka (1889–1978)

*Central European actress and writer, now known chiefly for her screenplays for Greta Garbo, who hosted a brilliant salon in Hollywood and provided aid to European refugees in the years before and during World War II. Born Salomea Sara Steuerman or Steuermann in 1889 in Sambor, Galicia (part of the Austro-Hungarian Empire); died on October 20, 1978, in Klosters, Switzerland; daughter of a prominent Jewish attorney and town mayor and a mother who chose marriage over a career as a singer; married Berthold Viertel (a director), on April 30, 1918 (later separated, died 1953); children: John Viertel; Peter Viertel (b. 1920, a writer who married *Deborah Kerr); Thomas Viertel.*

After the sudden death of her fiancé, went to Vienna at age 16 to study theater (1905); landed a position with the Deutsches Theater led by Max Reinhardt; with husband, founded acting ensemble Die Truppe in Berlin; driven by rising anti-Semitism, left Germany with her husband and children for Hollywood (1928); became a screenwriter, chiefly for Greta Garbo, writing the scripts for Queen Christina and Anna Karenina, among others; established a salon at her Mabery Road house where the most famous actors and intellectuals from Europe and America gathered; left the U.S. for Switzerland after the House Un-American Activities Committee implied she was a Communist (1953); wrote autobiography The Kindness of Strangers (1969).

On a cold Christmas Eve in 1953, two women in their 60s, a gentile and a Jew, sat sharing an improvised supper and enjoying the flickering candles on a tiny Christmas tree. Friends for many years, both had lived for a long time in the United States, their adopted country where they had built new lives. Now, with friends and families scattered, they sat in the candlelight sharing memories, then raised glasses of vodka in toast to each other. Salka Viertel sat with the legendary film star *Greta Garbo, welcoming Christmas with a hearty Scandinavian "Skol!"

Viertel was born Salomea Sara Steuermann in 1889 and grew up in a house called Wychylowa in Sambor, Galicia, a region of the Austro-Hungarian Empire situated between the city of Warsaw and the Ukraine. Her father, a prominent attorney, was the first Jew to be elected the town's mayor. Her mother had studied singing before deciding to marry rather than pursue a musical career. Salomea, called Salka, was the eldest of four children, followed by **Ruzia**, Edward, and Zygmunt. The Steuermanns lived on a grand scale: their large home, filled with servants, was surrounded by fields and orchards, and the children were educated by governesses. Salka's brother Edward was a gifted pianist, while she herself loved to perform onstage.

Sambor was a garrison town and a tolerant, multicultural place, where troops of many nationalities serving the empire were stationed. Salka's family was Jewish, but many of their friends and neighbors were gentile. Galicia had been a part of Poland until 1773, when that portion of the country came under the Austro-Hungarian rule of the Habsburgs, who had controlled their empire for hundreds of years, well before the rise of the modern nation-state. Within its bounds, loyalty was not to one's ethnic group but to the emperor. At the same time, it was considered natural to speak several languages and to be at ease with different cultures. Salka, who grew up speaking Polish at home and also learning Russian, Ukrainian, French, and German, would live her whole life with her homeland's tolerance, respecting others no matter what their ethnicity.

At age 16, she was engaged to Stanislav Eisenstein, a partner in her father's law firm, but he died unexpectedly during surgery. Heartbroken, Salka fled to Vienna, where she took consolation in diction and acting lessons. She became determined to pursue a career in the theater, even though acting was not considered an especially respectable career. She managed to rid her fluent German of the Polish accent she had picked up at home, and famous German director Max Reinhardt accepted her as a player at his Deutsches Theater in Berlin. Roles in other German cities, as well as in Austria and Switzerland, followed. She was joined in Berlin by Edward, who came there to study music with composer Arnold Schoenberg, and the siblings soon knew many people who were to have a lasting impact on modern music, including Alban Berg, Anton von Webern, and Hanns Eisler.

The Steuermann family was vacationing together in the beautiful High Tatra Mountains, in what is now Poland, in June 1914, when Archduke Franz Ferdinand, heir to the throne of the Austro-Hungarian Empire, was assassinated with his wife *Sophie Chotek in the Balkan city of Sarajevo. While Austria-Hungary and its ally Germany were determined to avenge the deaths, the governments of Great Britain and France vehemently opposed the use of military force against the Balkans. After weeks of tension, war was declared. The Steuermanns fled to Vienna, where they stayed for several months before returning to Sambor. There they found that their home had been looted by troops; only the walls and roof remained. The family settled in nevertheless, and Salka and her sister Ruzia volunteered at the local hospital, where they witnessed the enormous casualties of the world's first modern war.

After a time, Salka returned to acting in Vienna. There she met a young lieutenant in uniform, stage director Berthold Viertel, who was separated from his wife. The two were married on April 30, 1918, shortly after his divorce. It was the year of the influenza pandemic which killed millions, and the newly married Salka

nearly died of the disease. That November, the war finally came to an end. In 1919, she gave birth to the first of three sons, John Jacob, followed in quick succession by Peter and Thomas.

Life was precarious in postwar Europe. The collapse of the Austro-Hungarian Empire had given rise to such countries as Czechoslovakia, Poland, Hungary, and Yugoslavia. Russia's revolution of 1917 had also brought the Russian Empire to an end, and a flood of refugees was pouring into the West from Lenin's Soviet Union. The financial reparations demanded of Austria and Germany by the victorious Allied nations brought enormous economic hardship to people already left impoverished by war. Inflation wiped out families' lifetime savings; a loaf of bread could cost millions of marks. Under the onslaught of inflation, immigration, and reparations, the stability of Germany and Austria-Hungary disappeared. Those struggling to end sovereign rule and establish democratic institutions had to do as best they could in almost impossible circumstances.

Salka
Viertel

The harsh environment seemed nevertheless to unleash creative forces. In Berlin and Vienna especially, concert halls, theaters, and cafés flourished, and the Viertels enjoyed many new opportunities. While Berthold got work directing new plays in Vienna and Berlin and films in London, Salka performed in Germany's leading theaters, appearing in classic German plays as well as contemporary European dramas. Together, they founded an ensemble of actors called Die Truppe. Among their new friends were the artist Oscar Kokoschka, the playwright Bertolt Brecht, and the actor Oscar Homolka.

The cultural ferment in Berlin attracted worldwide attention, especially in America, where the burgeoning film industry began luring foreign actors, directors, and artists to Hollywood with promises of enormous sums of money. Within a few years, as Adolf Hitler's small group of thugs expanded in size and gained in respectability, it would be politics rather than money that caused German artists and intellectuals to flee the Nazi party's increasing influence in daily life for the more tolerant atmosphere of California.

By 1928, Berthold Viertel's growing reputation as a film director led to a contract offer in California. Undaunted by the prospect of learning a new language in a new land, he signed a three-year contract with Fox, and the family departed for America on February 22. The Viertels at first found California to be a strange land, but many Germans had preceded them, and Salka soon learned to drive. Exploring the area around Los Angeles, she fell in love with Santa Monica, which was then considered hopelessly rural, and rented a house at 165 Mabery Road. Berthold's ample salary allowed the couple to employ a staff to care for the children and maintain their house and grounds, and Salka made a policy of employing people in serious need of the money, including African-Americans who were subject to work discrimination and European refugees fleeing anti-Semitism. All who worked there were made to feel part of the family.

Viertel, approaching her mid-30s, adjusted to the fact that her theatrical career was virtually non-existent. She set about learning yet another language, English, and meeting the many interesting people who lived or visited in Hollywood. Salka was an excellent cook, and people gravitated to Mabery Road; her list of new acquaintances soon included Albert Einstein, the brothers Heinrich and Thomas Mann, André Malraux, Sergei Eisenstein, Upton Sinclair, Aldous Huxley, Charlie Chaplin and the actress Greta Garbo.

In 1928, Garbo was at the peak of her success. Her home was not far away from the Viertels', and the two women became fast friends, often taking early morning walks together on the beach. Berthold recognized more than anyone how much his wife had given up in leaving Germany, and when Greta urged her to try screenwriting, he concurred. Salka had a bit part in Garbo's *Anna Christie*, and during filming she came across a biography of Queen *Christina of Sweden. After hearing her describe the queen's remarkable life, Garbo asked Salka to write a screenplay about it. Despite Viertel's recent acquaintance with English, she soon finished the script for what would become *Queen Christina* (1933), which many consider Garbo's finest film. When Garbo signed a new contract with Metro, she introduced Viertel to the dynamic young director Irving Thalberg, who hired her as a screenwriter at $1,000 a week (an enormous sum at the time, but typical for Hollywood). Viertel had a new career. Over the next two decades, she worked on many films, although, with screenplays for such films as *Anna Karenina* (1935) and *Conquest* (1937), she remained best known as "Garbo's writer."

Berthold and Salka Viertel both had other love interests, but their bond would remain strong. Tiring of Hollywood, the restless Berthold eventually accepted a job in New York, then went on to London and Paris. He and Salka wrote, called, and sent telegrams constantly. He was back in Berlin working on a film project on January 30, 1933, shortly after Hitler's ascent to power, when his salary was cut because he was Jewish. Jews were meanwhile increasingly being attacked on the city's streets, and Berthold left Berlin in April. Salka Viertel's career was by this time going strong. *Queen Christina* was in production, directed by Rouben Mamoulian, and its star came to stay at Mabery Road during the shooting. While there, Garbo was continually harassed by the press, as usual.

Berthold's descriptions of anti-Semitic incidents had convinced Viertel that she had to get members of her family to America. Her brother Edward came first, followed by her sister, while *Queen Christina* became one of the last American films shown in the Third Reich before the Nazi government banned them because of the many Jews associated with Hollywood. In the summer of 1939, Viertel went to Europe to do research for a potential Garbo film on *Marie Curie and to procure visas for her mother and her younger brother Zygmunt, who were still in Poland. Paperwork by then made it almost impossible for Jews wishing to emigrate to leave

Europe, and procuring visas for the U.S. was especially difficult. Salka left for the States on September 1, 1939, the day the German army invaded Poland, unable to bring her family with her.

Back in America, Viertel remained generous in providing companionship, work and material resources to newly arrived refugees. Whether sending money to the great Soviet director Sergei Eisenstein or providing living quarters for an African-American friend whose wife was white, she demonstrated a generosity of spirit that later would cost her dearly.

Following the Japanese bombing of Pearl Harbor on December 7, 1941, that brought the U.S. into World War II, Viertel's sons joined the military. Before that year was out, her mother escaped Poland via the Soviet Union and Japan, and arrived finally in California. Zygmunt's fate would not be known until the end of the war, when it was learned that he had perished in the Holocaust.

Viertel was deeply upset by the U.S. government's internment of Californians of Japanese descent. Her home on Mabery Road meanwhile became a haven for German and Central European refugees, who told her of friends, husbands, wives, children, and parents fallen victim to the Nazis. "As the years went by, my life ceased to be solely my own," she wrote. "It became like the estuary of a big river into which other streams flowed." Over the years some of the greatest artists of the 20th century gathered in her living room, bringing to Hollywood a quality of cultural and intellectual life not known before or since.

By the end of World War II, the Viertels had been living separate lives for many years. Berthold's career as a director never truly flourished after he left Germany, and for a long time Salka was his sole support, even after she encouraged him to remarry. She endured difficulties in those years as well; her elderly mother died, she learned of Zygmunt's death, and her sons returned from the war and married. Garbo stopped making movies, and her screenwriting work dried up.

Additionally, her many kindnesses began to be held against her, as the House Un-American Activities Committee (HUAC) started subpoenaing people who had helped leftists or Communists during the war. While those in Hollywood less courageous than she found it prudent to distance themselves from former friends, Viertel remained proud of her assistance to those in need, no matter their political beliefs.

But the movie industry began blacklisting individuals who were thought to be Communists, leftists, or "fellow travelers," and with less and less work available, she was forced to accept the support of friends.

Berthold died in 1953, by which time "red-hunting" was in full bloom, with a congressman from California, Richard Nixon, and a senator from Wisconsin, Joseph McCarthy, establishing national reputations by ferreting out so-called subversives. Viertel decided it was time to leave the United States for Europe. (Chaplin and Brecht were among those who had already left.) Shortly afterward, at age 64, she started yet another life, this time in Switzerland. Settling near a group of friends from Hollywood who had taken up residence in Klosters, she wrote her autobiography, *The Kindness of Strangers*, which was published in 1969. Salka Viertel died at the age of 89, on October 20, 1978, after a two-year struggle with cancer. She was buried in Klosters, in the small cemetery of the Protestant church, in sight of the Swiss mountain peaks.

SOURCES:

Clurman, Harold. "Salka's Incorrigible Heart," in *The Nation*. May 5, 1969, p. 580.

Cook, Bruce. "Salka Viertel, Sundays in Mabery Road," in *Affairs of the Mind: The Salon in Europe and America from the 18th to the 20th Century*. Ed. by Peter Quennell. Washington, DC: New Republic Books, 1980.

Heilbut, Anthony. *Exiled in Paradise: German Refugee Artists and Intellectuals in America, from the 1930s to the Present*. Boston, MA: Beacon Press, 1983.

Houseman, John. *Front and Center*. NY: Simon and Schuster, 1979.

I.M. "Salka Viertel," in *The Times* [London]. November 4, 1978, p. 16.

"Salka Viertel," in *Variety*. November 1, 1978.

Viertel, Peter. *Dangerous Friends*. NY: Doubleday, 1992.

Viertel, Salka. *The Kindness of Strangers*. NY: Holt, Rinehart, and Winston, 1969.

John Haag,
Associate Professor,
University of Georgia, Athens, Georgia

Vigée-Le Brun, Elisabeth

(1755–1842)

Celebrated French painter during the late 18th and early 19th centuries who is best known for her portraits of Marie Antoinette and other members of the French court and aristocracy prior to the French Revolution. Name variations: Elisabeth Vigee; Elisabeth Vigee LeBrun; Mme Le Brun, le Brun, or Lebrun. Born Marie Anne Élisabeth Louise Vigée on April 16, 1755, in Paris, France; died in 1842 in Paris; daughter of Louis Vigée and Jeanne (Maissin) Vigée; had little formal education; attended convent school until age

11, then self-taught; married Jean Baptiste Pierre Le Brun, in 1776; children: **Jeanne Lucie Louise Le Brun Nigris** *(1780–1819).*

Left convent school (1767); death of father (1768); elected to the Royal Academy of Painting (1783); fled France during French Revolution and traveled throughout Europe (1789–1801); elected to the Academy and Institute of Bologna (1789); elected to the St. Petersburg Academy (1795); traveled to London (1802–05); returned to Paris (1805).

Selected works: Over 660 portraits and other paintings, some of the most famous of which are Madame Vigée-Le Brun and Her Daughter, Mother Love, The Girl With the Muff, Venus Tying the Wings of Love, *several self-portraits, portraits of Marie Antoinette and the Royal Family, and portraits of members of the French and European aristocracy during the late 18th and early 19th centuries.*

Publications: Memoirs of Mme. Elisabeth Louise Vigée-Le Brun *(c. 1834).*

Elisabeth Louise Vigée was born on April 16, 1755, in Paris. Her father Louis Vigée was a pastel and oil painter who produced landscapes and portraits. Her mother **Jeanne Maissin Vigée** was a beautiful, austere woman known for her piety. Elisabeth was sent to a convent to study at the age of six, where she remained until she was eleven. She later recalled developing a fascination with drawing from these early years. She had been "born with a passion to paint."

Vigée-Le Brun remembered her father very fondly as a jovial and warm man. During her frequent visits home from the convent school, he allowed her to use the paints and crayons in his studio. When she was seven or eight, she showed him a sketch she had made of a man with a beard, at which he exclaimed, "You will be a painter, my child, if ever there was one." As a painter, Louis was considered adequate but not outstanding. Vigée-Le Brun admitted in her *Memoirs* that many prominent members of society came to have their portraits painted by him "on account of his delightful conversation."

In 1767, 11-year-old Elisabeth left the convent for good and joyfully returned home to her family. She began to study oil painting with Davesne, a friend of her father's. But her happiness was shattered the following year with the passing of her father, who suffered an exceptionally painful death, even by 18th-century standards. He swallowed a fish bone, which lodged in his stomach, and was made to undergo numerous exploratory surgeries to try to remove it. The wounds became infected, and he died on May 9,

1768. She recalled that her mother "wept day and night." Vigée-Le Brun was so devastated that she found it impossible to paint for many months. She eventually returned to her easel as the only way of "assuaging my sorrow and reclaiming me from my sad thoughts."

By the time Elisabeth turned 14, she was gaining some notoriety in Paris for her work. She was introduced to the painter Joseph Vernet, who advised her, "don't follow any system or school." Instead, he encouraged her to study the great Italian and Flemish masters and to paint from nature, which he called "the first of all masters." Vigée-Le Brun and her mother visited the art galleries frequently, and gained admission to the best private art collections in Paris as well. Especially entranced by the works of Rubens, Rembrandt, Raphael, and Van Dyck, Elisabeth pored over their works excitedly, for hours at a time, in order to gain a better understanding of their representation of light and delicate flesh tones.

Because her father had left little money behind when he died, Jeanne soon felt obliged to marry again, in order to provide for the maintenance of the household and the college expenses for her brother. She married a rich jeweler, Le Sèvre, who turned out to be a horrible miser. Although Elisabeth turned over all the money she received for painting portraits, which by that time comprised a considerable sum, Le Sèvre refused to give them even a minimal allowance for necessities. To Elisabeth's horror, he also took all of her late father's clothing, which he wore without bothering to have them altered to fit his own frame. Joseph Vernet urged Vigée-Le Brun to give her stepfather a set amount of money for room and board and keep the remainder of the profits from her own work, but she refused, in fear of further impoverishing her mother.

During this period, Vigée-Le Brun became increasingly in demand as a portrait painter, which gave her an entrance into Parisian high society. She was invited by *Louise Marie of Bourbon, duchess of Chartres, to paint her picture, soon after which she was besieged by requests from other fashionable members of the aristocracy. Vigée-Le Brun's services were also enthusiastically sought by several male admirers, who hoped to use the excuse of a sitting to woo her with their charms. Elisabeth was completely engrossed in her art, and so she recalled that "as soon as I realized they wished to make eyes at me, I painted them with their gaze averted; which prevents the sitter from looking at the painter. At the least movement of their pupils in my direc-

Self-Portrait in a
Straw Hat, *by
Elisabeth Vigée-
Le Brun.*

tion, I would say: 'I'm doing the eyes.' That would annoy them a little, as you can imagine."

Vigée-Le Brun's *Memoirs* depict the vibrant and sophisticated Parisian society that existed before the French Revolution. Walking in the many public parks was a popular pastime among women, and frequent dinners and suppers, often lasting for many hours, were given by those who were part of the upper-class social circle. Social engagements at the time were not limited to the hereditary aristocracy; many of the participants were musicians, poets, actors, and artists. Vigée-Le Brun's great talent, beauty and pleasant manner secured opportunities that few of her contemporaries could boast.

In 1776, her stepfather retired from business and the family went to live at a house owned by Jean Baptiste Pierre Le Brun, a painter and picture dealer who readily loaned her pictures from his collection to copy. Six months after their arrival, he asked Elisabeth to marry him. She was torn: "I was twenty years old and leading a life free from any anxiety as to my future, for I was earning a good deal of money and felt no desire whatever to get married." She was persuaded to accept Le Brun's proposal by her mother, who argued that the wealthy Le Brun would be a "profitable match" for her daughter. Elisabeth grudgingly agreed to the marriage, only to be told by her new husband that the wedding would have to be kept secret, because he had previously agreed to marry the daughter of a Dutch dealer with whom he did business, and wanted to conclude his business with him before his marriage to Elisabeth became public.

If the victims of that execrable time had not had the noble pride to die courageously, the Terror would have been ended much sooner. Men of undeveloped intelligence have too little imagination to be moved by an inward suffering, and the people's pity is much more easily excited than its admiration.

—Elisabeth Vigée-Le Brun

Within days of the marriage, Elisabeth began to regret her decision. Several friends, under the impression that the wedding had not yet taken place, came to her to warn her not to marry Le Brun, who already had a reputation for gambling. When the marriage was finally announced, Elisabeth threw herself back into her painting and tried to make the best of the situation. Pierre turned out to be an obliging man, with a "mixture of gentleness and vivacity" which made him popular in society, but he eventually squandered his own fortune, as well as his wife's commissions from painting, by "his unbridled passion for women of bad morals, joined to his fondness for gambling." Pierre spent the money from Elisabeth's portraits without apology. Although she would earn over 1 million francs by the outbreak of the Revolution in 1789, she would flee France that same year with less than 20 francs.

The only happiness that Vigée-Le Brun received from her marriage was the birth of her daughter, Jeanne Lucie Louise, in 1780. Elisabeth had not allowed her pregnancy to interfere with her profession, and even in the throes of labor pains, she continued her work on *Venus Tying the Wings of Love*. Vigée-Le Brun doted on her daughter, who became the subject of many of her paintings, including the famous portraits of the two of them which still hang in the Louvre.

By the late 1770s, Vigée-Le Brun was painting for an increasingly select clientele. In 1776, she painted Monsieur (later Louis XVIII), king Louis XVI's brother, who regaled her endlessly with light chatter and off-key (and somewhat off-color) singing. When he asked her "How do you think I sing, Madame Le Brun?," she cleverly replied, "Like a Prince, Monseigneur!" Eventually, Vigée-Le Brun painted every member of the royal family except for the youngest brother, the count of Artois (later Charles X). Her favorite model among the royal family was the queen, *Marie Antoinette, whom she first painted in 1779. Elisabeth described Marie Antoinette's complexion as "brilliant" and "transparent." She also admired the queen's carriage, recalling that "she walked better than any other woman in France, holding her head well up with a majesty that stamped her as sovereign in the midst of all her Court, without, however, detracting in any way from what was kind and gentle in her aspect." Although awed by the queen at first, Vigée-Le Brun soon became impressed with her kindness, remarking, "I do not believe Queen Marie-Antoinette ever failed to say something pleasant to those who had the honor of approaching her, while the kindness she always showed to me is one of my sweetest memories."

In 1783, Vigée-Le Brun was proposed by Joseph Vernet to become a member of the Royal Academy. Her acceptance was opposed by the chief painter to the king, who questioned the reception of women into the society (although one woman, *Anne Vallayer-Coster, had already been accepted). Elisabeth was eventually admitted to the Royal Academy, possibly in part because of the influence of Marie Antoinette.

Although she painted through most of the daylight hours, Vigée-Le Brun often attended sumptuous dinners, and even entertained in her own small apartment a dazzling assortment of "grand ladies, grand gentlemen, outstanding men of letters and art . . . where the crowd was often so big that the marshals of France sat on the floor for want of a seat." Her soirees boasted "the best music in Paris," and later she recalled, "In the days when I gave my concerts, one had both taste

Madame Vigée-
Le Brun and
Her Daughter,
*by Elisabeth
Vigée-Le Brun.*

and leisure for amusement." She served simple suppers of "a fowl, a fish, a plate of vegetables and a salad," at about ten o'clock, after which the guests would play charades, perform music, read poetry, act out plays, or engage in other intellectual pursuits until midnight. When she attended the suppers of others, she much preferred musical evenings to balls, "never having any fondness for dancing." Theaters, concert halls, and galleries were the frequent meeting places of Parisian society, punctuated by retreats to sumptuously furnished country homes.

Pre-revolutionary France was not without its darker side, however. As far back as the 1760s, Elisabeth's father had returned home one night from a dinner of "Intellectuals," including Denis Diderot, Claude Helvétius, and Jean d'Alembert, to note grimly, "all that I've just heard, my dear friend, makes me think that the world will soon be upside down." By the 1780s, it was impossible for Vigée-Le Brun to ignore that unrest and dissatisfaction were manifesting themselves among the French lower class. In 1788, she traveled into the countryside to Romainville, to spend a few days at the home of some friends, and recalled: "On our way we noticed that the peasants no longer doffed their hats to us. On the contrary, they looked at us insolently, while some even threatened us with their sticks." After one of her supper parties, which she had spent 15 francs in arranging, rumor inflated the cost of the party to 20,000 francs. When she painted a portrait of the finance minister, Calonne, for which she received 4,000 francs, rumor had it that she had been given a sum sufficient to ruin the royal treasury.

In June 1789, while Vigée-Le Brun was staying at the royal residence at Marly with a friend who was in service to Marie Antoinette, she witnessed an incident which convinced her that destructive events were on the horizon. When the women saw a drunken trespasser enter the courtyard, they sent a manservant out after him. The manservant returned with some papers that had fallen out of the man's pocket which read, "Down with the Royal Family! Down with the nobles! Down with the priests!" and contained "a lot of dreadful predictions, written in a way that made one's hair stand on end." They sent for the military guards to take him away and question him. The manservant quietly followed the guards outside after they arrived, and saw them join arms with the man as soon as they were out of sight, singing and making merry. The incident struck fear in Vigée-Le Brun's heart: "What were we coming to, my God! when the public authority made common cause with the guilty?" Elisabeth showed the papers to the queen, who insisted, "These things are impossible. I will never believe they are planning such atrocities."

When the French Revolution did begin in 1789, Vigée-Le Brun quickly decided to make plans to take her daughter and leave the country: "Society seemed to be breaking up altogether, honest folk being without any protection whatever, for the Garde Nationale was so oddly made up that it revealed a mixture as weird as it was frightful." She became thin and pale, and found it impossible to eat or to paint: "My imagination was darkened and wilted by so many horrors, and ceased to find satisfaction in my art." She left several portraits unfinished; "For me there was no longer any question of success and fortune. The only question was how to save one's head." The final straw for Elisabeth was when a dirty group of national guardsmen forced their way into her drawing-room and forbade her to leave. When they left, two other national guardsmen, who were her neighbors, came to her house and urged to her leave immediately, by public stage rather than her private carriage. In the midst of the torrent of emigration taking place at the time, it took two weeks for her to get a place on a coach. She finally left Paris on October 5, the same day that the king and queen were forced to leave Versailles for Paris by bread rioters.

During the harrowing trip to the French border, Vigée-Le Brun sat across from a filthy man who bragged of having stolen several watches and of hanging people from lampposts. On the seat next to her was a Jacobin, who addressed crowds of curious onlookers at every stop with assurances that the king and queen had been forced into Paris, and now would be made to accept a Constitution. Elisabeth had taken the added precaution of wearing a working woman's dress and a kerchief over part of her face, to avoid being recognized on the trip, as she had recently exhibited one of her portraits of herself with her daughter in her arms. Vigée-Le Brun was terrified that she would be recognized when the Jacobin began talking about the exhibition and even praised her portrait. She endeavored to keep her face averted, and "thanks to that and my costume," she later recalled, "I came through with nothing worse than a little fear."

During the years that the Terror raged in France, Vigée-Le Brun and her daughter traveled from city to city, beginning in Italy, and settling for a time in Naples, Rome, Berlin, Vienna, and St. Petersburg. Wherever she went, she was a welcome guest, even in Bologna, where a city ordinance forbade French travelers to remain overnight. An exception was made for Vigée-Le Brun, and she was even made a member of their Academy and Institute in November 1789. As she traveled, she made her living by painting. Her dissolute husband, back in France, spent everything she had left behind, and even wrote her repeatedly asking for more, which she sent. She never lacked for eager clients, as her fame had spread far beyond her native land. Her brother, who had also remained behind, sent her frequent letters detailing the horrors of the Terror, including, in 1793, the executions of Louis XVI and Marie Antoinette. Another of her old friends, *Madame du Barry, was also condemned to death by the Revolutionary Tribunal, and, unlike most of the victims, cried out to the crowd in terror and begged for mercy as she was being taken to the scaffold. Moved by her incessant pleas, the crowd quieted and the executioner disposed of her quickly. Elisabeth later surmised: "If the victims of that execrable time had not had the noble pride to die courageously, the Terror would have been ended much sooner. Men of undeveloped intelligence have too little imagination to be moved by an inward suffering, and the people's pity is much more easily excited than its admiration."

In April 1795, Vigée-Le Brun left Austria for Russia. In the later years of Empress *Catherine II the Great, St. Petersburg had a great reputation as a mecca for artists. Elisabeth, who was introduced to Catherine by the French ambassador, described the empress as small and very stout, "but she still had a fine face." Catherine welcomed her warmly to St. Petersburg, and agreed to sit for a portrait. Unfortunately, a few days before the sitting was to have taken place, Catherine became ill and soon died. Vigée-Le Brun watched the funeral from her window and was amazed by its splendor. She was dazzled by the gold-armor-clad guardsman (who dropped dead of fatigue after the ceremony) and by the ladies enveloped in long trains and black veils, who walked through the snow in the long procession.

Vigée-Le Brun was elected as a member of the St. Petersburg Academy, much to her delight. She described the costume worn by the women members as "a riding-habit, a little violet vest, a yellow petticoat, and a black-feathered hat." During her stay, she attracted some of the wealthiest clients in Russia. Her enjoyment of the artistic circle in St. Petersburg was blighted, however, when her daughter Jeanne, who had grown into a young woman during their travels, fell in love with a penniless Russian named Nigris. Although Elisabeth refused to give her blessing to what she considered an ill-fated match, Jeanne eventually obtained permission from her father in Paris, and Vigée-Le Brun was powerless to prevent the marriage. The wedding and the dowry swallowed up all the money she had been able to save in Russia, and soured relations between her and her daughter for the rest of their lives.

In 1801, after the Terror had abated and France had become more stable, Vigée-Le Brun's name was struck off the list of émigrés, and it became safe for her to go back to her native land. She returned home, after 12 years' absence, in the autumn of 1801, where she was warmly greeted by her brother, her husband, who had redecorated her apartments for her arrival, and those who remained of her friends. She was relieved to be home, but distressed by the vestiges of revolution which she saw around her: "Liberty, Fraternity and Death" was still visible on every wall, and the colorful and extravagant fashions of the pre-revolutionary days had been cast aside in favor of "black coats and black hair." At the first public play which she attended, she was recognized and applauded by the crowd, which warmed her immensely. She was invited to lunch with *Josephine and Napoleon Bonaparte, while he was serving as First Consul. She renewed old friendships and made new ones, but she found it impossible to shake the feeling of depression and loss that came upon her with every reminder of the Revolution she saw in Paris.

In April 1802, during a lull in the fighting between France and England, she resolved to leave Paris again and settle in London for a time. As she did not speak a word of English, she found the transition difficult. She also found the persistent fog oppressive, and the somber dinner parties of the English aristocracy bored her. Vigée-Le Brun studied the portraits of Joshua Reynolds (who had died a decade previously) and struck up friendships with several of the French émigrés residing in England, however, and remained there for three years.

She returned to Paris in 1805 to see her daughter, who was visiting without her husband. As Elisabeth had predicted, the marriage had proved disastrous, but even Jeanne's recognition of that fact did not completely heal the old wounds; their relationship was never the same. Aside from a trip to Switzerland in 1808–09 and one to Bordeaux in 1820, Vigée-Le Brun remained in France, and she even purchased a little country house at Louveciennes, a village on the Seine, where she spent eight months out of every year. Her husband Pierre died in 1813, followed by her daughter in 1819 and her brother in 1820.

Vigée-Le Brun continued to paint, writing to a friend at the age of 68 that "painting is always for me a distraction that will only end when I die." She continued painting well into her 80s and still held social events frequented by the beautiful women and distinguished men of Paris, "to whom she never wearied in talking of Marie Antoinette." In her later years, she was cared for by her niece, Eugénie Le Brun, whom she came to regard as a daughter. Elisabeth Vigée-Le Brun died in Paris, at age 88, in 1842, and was buried in the 13th-century church there.

During her lifetime, Elisabeth painted some 660 portraits, only a few of which hang in public galleries. Her most famous works are those depicting herself and her small daughter. They reveal an incredible richness of detail as well as a depth of feeling which foreshadowed the Romantic period. Vigée-Le Brun used her incredible talents and personal charm to make acquaintances among the most famous figures in Europe during the late 18th century. Through her portraits and her memoirs, she has left us with an unparalleled personal account of those turbulent times.

SOURCES:

Brooks, Geraldine. *Dames and Daughters of the French Court.* NY: Thomas Y. Crowell, 1904.

Dobson, Austin. *Old Kensington Palace and Other Papers.* London: Oxford University Press, 1926.

Kirkland, Winifred, and Frances Kirkland. *Girls Who Became Artists.* NY: Harper and Brothers, 1934.

Tallentyre, S.G. *The Women of the Salons and Other French Portraits.* NY: Longmans, Green, 1901.

Vigée-Le Brun, Elisabeth Louise. *The Memoirs of Mme. Elisabeth Louise Vigée-Le Brun, 1755–1789.* NY: George H. Doran, 1927.

SUGGESTED READING:

Sheriff, Mary D. *The Exceptional Woman: Elizabeth Vigée-Lebrun and the Cultural Politics of Art.* Chicago, IL: University of Chicago Press, 1996.

Kimberly Estep Spangler,
Vice Chair of Religion and Humanities
and Assistant Professor of History,
Friends University, Wichita, Kansas

Vigilantia (c. 485–?)

*Byzantine royal. Born around 485; daughter of swineherds; sister of Emperor Justinian I (482–565); children: Justin II, emperor of Byzantium and Rome (r. 518–527, who married *Sophia [c. 525–after 600]).*

Vigri, Caterina dei (1413–1463).

See Catherine of Bologna.

Vijaya Lakshmi Pandit (1900–1990).

See Pandit, Vijaya Lakshmi.

Vike-Freiberga, Vaira (1937—)

President of Latvia. Name variations: Vaira Vîke-Freiberga; Vaira Vike-Freibergs. Born in Riga, Latvia, on December 1, 1937; daughter of Karlis and Annemarie (Rankis) Vike; University of Toronto, B.A., 1958, M.A., 1960; McGill University, Ph.D., 1965; married Imants F. Freibergs, on July 16, 1960; children: Karl Robert; Indra Karoline.

Clinical psychologist, Toronto Psychiatric Hospital (1960–61); assistant professor, department of psychology, University of Montreal (1965–72); associate professor (1972–77), became professor (1977); director of Latvian Youth Ethnic Heritage Seminars Divrei-izdivi (1979); president, Social Science Federation of Canada (1980); chair of NATO special program panel on human factors (1980).

Sworn in as president of Latvia on July 8, 1999, Vaira Vike-Freiberga became the first democratically elected woman president in Eastern Europe. She was born in Riga, Latvia, in 1937, and as a child fled with her family to escape the advancing Red Army, hiding in ditches and enduring the rigors of a refugee camp, where her infant sister died in the winter of 1945. Following the war, the family lived in Casablanca, then emigrated to Canada.

Vike-Freiberga earned her undergraduate and master's degrees from the University of Toronto, then received her Ph.D. in clinical psychology from McGill University in 1965. In the interim, she married and had two children. She was employed at Toronto Psychiatric Hospital and later as a professor at the University of Montreal. Though she became a Canadian citizen, Vike-Freiberga never forgot her beleaguered homeland. She became an expert in Latvian folklore and culture, and lobbied Western governments not to recognize the annexation of the Baltics by the Soviet Union. When the captive nations regained independence in 1991, many émigrés declared their mission complete. Before the decade was out, however, Vike-Freiberga found herself the symbol of renewed hope for her country. Elected on January 17, 1999, following five failed rounds, she took office in Latvia just as the nation was eager for change.

As pointed out in *The Economist* (August 1999), the new president had several strikes against her. Although fluent in five languages, she spoke no Russian, the mother tongue of a third of the country; she had no political base, having been elected by Parliament as a deadlock-breaking outsider; and she had little day-to-day power, although she did have the authority to call for a referendum in which voters could either vote out the president or Parliament.

Vike-Freiberga is possessed of great charm, intelligence, and popularity, however, which may indeed be enough to overcome any of her weaknesses. Coming to her job as an outsider, she also owed no political favors, another plus. Naming admission to the European Union (EU) and NATO as her first priorities, the new president immediately went to work. One of her earliest promises was her intention to learn Russian herself. "I thought it would be fun," she said, "a challenge to those who have spent 50 years not learning Latvian." Another immediate consideration was the EU's concerns that laws on citizenship and language, established after 1991, discriminate against Russians in Latvia. Addressing the issue early on, Vike-Freiberga rejected a particularly harsh new language law passed in Parliament which demanded that private commercial transactions should be in Latvian. Parliament seemed likely to agree to her softening amendment, which bodes well for her attempt to establish her country on a more even playing field.

SOURCES:
"Vaira Vike-Freiberga, a Canadian-European," in *The Economist*. August 21, 1999.

Viktoria.
Variant of Victoria.

Vilbushevich, Manya (1878–1961).
See Shochat, Manya.

Vilhelmina or Vilhelmine.
Variant of Wilhelmina or Wilhelmine.

Villard, Fanny Garrison
(1844–1928)

American philanthropist, suffragist, and activist. Name variations: Helen Frances Garrison. Born Helen Frances Garrison on December 16, 1844, in Boston, Massachusetts; died on July 5, 1928, in Dobbs Ferry, New York; daughter of William Lloyd Garrison (the abolitionist) and Helen Eliza (Benson) Garrison; educated at the Winthrop school in Boston; married Henry Villard (a newspaper publisher and businessman), on January 3, 1866 (died 1900); children: Helen Villard; Oswald Garrison Villard; Harold Garrison Villard; Henry Hilgard Villard.

Cofounded the National Association for the Advancement of Colored People (1909); founded the Women's Peace Party with Jane Addams (1915); founded the Women's Peace Society (1919); participated in the founding of Barnard and Radcliffe colleges; published William Lloyd Garrison and Non-Resistance *(1924).*

Fanny Garrison Villard, the fourth of seven children and only daughter of famous abolitionist William Lloyd Garrison and **Helen Benson Garrison**, was born in Boston in 1844 at the height of her father's anti-slavery crusade. She grew up both inspired by her father's activism and aware of its perils, although the latter never prevented her from having the courage of her convictions. Villard's lifelong respect for her fa-

ther's work inspired her to write *William Lloyd Garrison and Non-Resistance*, which was published in 1924, only four years before her death at the age of 83.

Villard was educated at Boston's Winthrop school and then taught the piano to help support the family until her marriage to German immigrant Henry Villard in 1866. Henry's early career as a newspaper correspondent was transformed into the politically influential role of publisher of the New York *Evening Post* and the *Nation* after substantial financial success in the 1870s, when he became president of the Northern Pacific Railroad and co-founder of the Edison General Electric Company.

The first decade of the Villards' marriage was spent traveling for business extensively in the United States and Europe, and rearing four children: **Helen Villard**, Oswald Garrison Villard, Harold Garrison Villard, and Henry Hilgard Villard (who died at seven). In 1876 the family settled in New York City.

Her husband's business success gave Fanny Villard the leisure and wealth she needed to pursue a life of activism and philanthropy, and his purchase of the two journals in 1881 meant that she was in frequent contact with national political leaders. In 1878, she took up her first charity, the Diet Kitchen Association, serving as president from 1898 to 1922 and becoming a dedicated consumer activist for nutritional education and milk stations.

The 1880s and 1890s saw Villard spending increasingly large amounts of time and money on charity work. Particularly concerned with the educational opportunities for blacks and women, she took an active role in the founding of both Barnard and Radcliffe colleges, the American College for Women in Constantinople, and numerous schools for black students in New York and the South, including Hampton Institute in Virginia. Sharing her father's beliefs in freedom and nonviolence, Villard was a co-founder of the National Association for the Advancement of Colored People (NAACP) in 1909.

Although her active involvement in charitable and educational institutions continued into the 20th century, Villard's interests shifted to the political realm after her husband's death in 1900 and her son Oswald's rise to prominence as the outspoken, liberal editor of the New York *Evening Post*. Her decades of experience in charity work and exposure to social agencies resulted in a new perspective on the causes of urban poverty, and she began looking beyond work with individuals in order to effect a more profound social change.

In 1906, she became a member of the suffrage movement, joining three New York suffrage clubs and serving as president of one, the William Lloyd Garrison Equal Suffrage Club. A tireless speaker at debates, public meetings, suffrage street parades, and legislative hearings, Villard expounded on her belief that suffrage held great promise for both the "welfare and moral uplift" of the American people.

The second great cause of Villard's life was the peace movement. In 1915, she was a co-founder of the Women's Peace Party, under the presidency of *Jane Addams, giving the cause of nonviolence her total attention after the success of the New York suffrage referendum in 1917. Opposed to United States involvement in World War I, Villard led peace parades, lobbied political figures—including the president—and spoke at conventions and public forums. Her vehement pacifism resulted in her leaving the executive board of the party in 1917, after the United States entered the war, and devoting her time and money to refugee relief and aid for conscientious objectors. In 1919, she founded her own Women's Peace Society in New York on a platform of total disarmament and nonresistance.

An extremely attractive and warm-hearted woman, Villard was considered by contemporaries to be indefatigable rather than fanatical. Her son once described her as "certain of the triumph of every cause to which she gave her devotion." Her idealism was put to the test in the last decades of her life, but she remained both resolutely unreligious and politically active into the 1920s. Villard died of heart disease at the family estate in Dobbs Ferry, New York, at age 83, and was buried in the nearby Sleepy Hollow Cemetery.

SOURCES:

James, Edward T., ed. *Notable American Women, 1607–1950.* Cambridge, MA: The Belknap Press of Harvard University, 1971.

Weatherford, Doris. *American Women's History.* NY: Prentice Hall, 1994.

Paula Morris, D.Phil.,
Brooklyn, New York

Villedieu, Catherine des Jardins, Mme de (c. 1640–1683)

French novelist and playwright. Name variations: Madame de Villedieu; Marie Catherine Desjardins or Marie-Catherine Desjardins; Marie-Catherine Boesset; Marie-Catherine de Chaste. Born Marie-Catherine Hortense Desjardins or des Jardins around 1640, probably in Alençon, France; died in 1683 in Paris; daughter of Guillaume Desjardins and Catherine (Ferrand) Desjardins; associated with Antoine de Boesset de Villedieu; married Claude-Nicolas de Chaste, in 1677; children: Louis de Chaste (b. 1678).

The celebrated writer known to contemporaries as Madame de Villedieu was born around 1640 into a poor family of Alençon, France, where she lived until 1655. In that year, she fell in love with her cousin. They planned to marry but her father opposed the match, filing a lawsuit to break off the engagement. Villedieu's mother **Catherine Ferrand** subsequently left her husband and moved with her two children to Paris, where she became a maid in the household of **Madame de Montbazon**. It was in this household that Ferrand's daughter, the young Catherine, was educated, an unusual privilege for a girl of her class, and discovered a talent for composing poetry. In 1658, she met a lieutenant in the regiment of Picardy, Antoine de Boesset, sire of Villedieu, and they fell in love. The next year marked the beginning of her literary career at age 18, with the publication of a sonnet, "Jouissance," in a Parisian journal, followed by the publication of several essays and more poetry. In 1661, she published to critical success *Alcidamie*, an unfinished romance. Her increasing popularity led to the publication of a collection of poetry in 1662, along with two plays, both tragedies. A prolific writer, Villedieu completed her second novel in 1663. Its success led to an invitation to meet King Louis XIV at Versailles.

In 1664, Catherine solemnized her relationship with Antoine de Boesset with a formal engagement, just as he was leaving France with his regiment. On his return in 1667, however, de Boesset disavowed his promise of marriage and married another before following the army to Flanders. Catherine continued to consider his promises binding, and insisted that she still be referred to as Madame de Villedieu, the title she had taken for herself in 1664.

Her third play, *Le Favori* (The Favorite), completed in 1664, brought her the friendship and support of the well-known playwright Moliére, who staged the drama to great success at the Palais Royal in 1665. It was the first by a female playwright to be honored by a command performance by the king, who had it staged at Versailles. The play also brought its author the patronage of *Marie d'Orleans, duchess of Nemours, who would remain a good friend and patron of Madame de Villedieu for many years.

Following her final break with de Boesset in 1667, Villedieu left France for the Netherlands.

Despite her literary success, she faced financial difficulties at home, and hoped to win a property lawsuit she had pending in the Netherlands. While staying in Belgium, she was shocked to learn that de Boesset had sold her personal letters to him, and despite her efforts she was unable to prevent their publication. In August 1667, she learned that de Boesset had died in battle, at the same time that she lost her lawsuit and learned of the death of her father. Heartbroken and impoverished, Villedieu stayed with the duchess of Nemours for almost a year, returning to Paris in 1668.

There she began the most important phase of her literary career, permanently adopting Madame de Villedieu as her public name. Her first major novel, *Cléonice*, was published in 1669, earning her a place among France's most popular writers. Whether prose or poetry, Villedieu's works were always concerned with issues of love, romance, and gallantry, using strong and outspoken female protagonists, often based on historical figures and events, to portray the desires and emotions of women. Modern critics now credit her with creating a new kind of French novel, the "nouvelle galante" (gallant novel), which broke away from the predominant genre of heroic adventure novels set in exotic lands.

Although her works were widely read and translated, Madame de Villedieu chose to retire to a convent in 1672, at the height of her popularity. Monastic life soon proved too constricting for her, however, and in 1673 she returned to Paris and took up her writing again. The year 1675 saw the publication of the last of her works to appear during her life, *Les desordres de l'amour* (*The Disorders of Love*). In 1676, she was granted a royal pension by Louis XIV in recognition of her literary contributions to her country. The next year she married formally, about age 35, to 55-year-old Claude-Nicolas de Chaste, sire of Chalon. It seems to have been a marriage of convenience, Villedieu still seeking financial security and the stability of permanent home life. They had one son, Louis, born in 1678.

About two years later de Chaste died, leaving Villedieu again with pressing financial needs. Louis XIV granted her son a modest pension in addition to her personal pension, but she was still unable to make ends meet and retired to her family's farm in Clinchemore. There she died in 1683, about age 43. The Parisian bookseller who had published her private letters to de Boesset collected her manuscripts and published some of her unfinished works in 1685. Villedieu's works continued to be printed and sold widely throughout the 18th century and into the 19th century. In recent years many of her writings, including some of her letters to other prominent French literary figures, are again becoming available.

SOURCES:

Klein, Nancy D., ed. *Selected writings of Madame de Villedieu*. NY: P. Lang, 1995.

Wilson, Katharina M. *Encyclopedia of Continental Women Writers*. NY: Garland, 1991.

Laura York, M.A. in History,
University of California,
Riverside, California

Villegas, Micaela (1748–1819)

Actress and singer who as "La Perricholi" was the mistress of Peruvian viceroy Manuel de Amat, and became to later generations the most famous Peruvian woman of her age and the subject of plays, operas, and novels. Name variations: La Périchole, La Perricholi, or La Pirricholi; (nickname) Miquita. Born in Lima, Peru, on September 28, 1748; died on May 16, 1819, in Lima; daughter of José Villegas and Teresa Hurtado de Mendoza; married Vicente Fermín Echarri y Gorózabal, on August 4, 1795; children: (with Manuel de Amat) Manuel (b. 1769); and a daughter (name unknown).

Became comic actress (c. 1763); met Viceroy Manuel de Amat (1766); banned from the stage by Amat (1773); reconciled with Amat and returned to stage (1775); withdrew from public life when Amat was replaced as viceroy and returned to Spain (1776); with Vicente Echarri y Gorózabal, became theatrical entrepreneur (1780s).

The most celebrated Peruvian woman of her age, Micaela Villegas lived a life that was filled with controversy and, following her death, clouded by legend. Popular opinion held for many years that she was born in the town of Huánuco, high in the Andes to the east of Lima. Others argued that Lima, the City of the Kings, was her birthplace. Some claimed she was born in 1739, others in 1748. The date of her death varied from 1812 to 1819. To many Peruvians, the historical facts of her life were less important than the legends which had sprung up to make Micaela Villegas into a national icon.

Nonetheless, the discovery of a parish document recording her birth and baptism established that Micaela was born in Lima on September 28, 1748. She was the first child of José Villegas, a native of Arequipa in southern Peru, and **Teresa Hurtado de Mendoza**, who could trace her genealogy back through many generations to one of the colony's early viceroys. Micaela's parents later had five other children: José Félix (b. 1750), **María Josefa** (b. 1752), José Antonio (b. 1755), José Humberto (b. 1760), and **María Lugarda** (b. 1761). That Micaela became an actress and singer probably indicates that her family was lower class, of modest means. That she was not baptized until December 1, over two months after her birth, may reflect her family's modest circumstances and perhaps her parents' lack of religious fervor. The great Lima earthquake of 1746, which devastated large parts of the capital and the nearby port of Callao, must have made her early years difficult.

As a child, Micaela showed a vivacity and extroversion ideal for the stage. "Miquita," as she was known, loved to perform for family and friends. Her memory for songs was precocious, and she learned to play the guitar and harp, with which she accompanied herself. She also performed popular dances. In 1761, her parents reportedly took her to the Coliseo de Comedias, Lima's popular theater. Though the 1746 earthquake had destroyed it, the city's love for theater was so great that within less than two years the Coliseo had been rebuilt and was staging Hispanic and Peruvian plays. Villegas left the Coliseo enthralled with the performance of Bartolomé Massa, a famous actor, and with the applause and finery. Although the costumes were roughly sewn, they must have seemed luxurious to the young girl.

> One can ask everything of men when one has rendered them ridiculous.
>
> —Ventura García Calderón

At home, Miquita spent hours practicing her singing and dancing, her mind filled with dreams of starring on the stage of the Coliseo herself. With her parents' permission, she began to give public performances at age 15, and she quickly attracted the attention of impresarios from the Coliseo. Massa, who was also the theater's director, opened a career to her. She became his mistress, although her ability as a comic actress and her skill as a dancer and singer were more important to her success. With her fiery personality and natural talent, she soon rose from the chorus to more important roles. By age 20, she had become one of the capital's favorite actresses, especially famed for her zest and her songs between acts. The male audience received her with great enthusiasm and on more than one occasion carried her in triumph from the theater.

Meanwhile, the other chief actor in Villegas' story had taken the stage. He was Manuel de Amat, a Catalan who arrived in Lima in 1761 to rule as viceroy. A soldier by temperament, the 57-year-old bachelor soon developed Lima's love for the theater. The Coliseo had a sumptuously decorated box reserved for the viceroy, and Amat began to use it. He became a fixture at the spectacles, and in 1771 promulgated a special set of ordinances to regulate the Coliseo. Although the theater was subject to censorship, the viceroy proved remarkably tolerant. Mild indulgence seemed the order of the day.

Enamored as he was of the theater, it was perhaps inevitable that Amat became enamored also of its actresses. At some point, perhaps in 1766, he took notice of Villegas and became completely infatuated: "She was better than beautiful, she was charming. Small and on the plump side, she was pretty." Her pale brown skin, long black hair, tiny feet and hands, and beauty mark above the upper lip exuded a liveliness that entranced the elderly ruler. From then on, Amat's attendance at the Coliseo was constant. As a viceroy, he had a reputation for harshness, but watching Villegas he shouted, applauded, beat time with his cane, and generally behaved outlandishly.

Rumor reported that Amat eventually invited her to the palace, insisting she keep the visit secret. But such was his enthusiasm that he trumpeted his liaison with the actress. Popular attention focused more intensely on her. In a hierarchical society dominated by patronage and personal connections, ambitious Peruvians found it wise to flatter the viceroy: what better way than to show their public approval of the young actress. Of course, the social elite faced a dilemma: the Lima aristocracy despised Villegas as a social inferior, but could not publicly challenge Amat's liaison. Due to her relationship with the viceroy, people approached Micaela hoping to obtain favors from Amat.

Playing her part shrewdly, the young actress became a primary beneficiary of the viceroy's largesse. One of her biographers noted, "Micaela thought only of applause, and even more of doubloons." He provided Villegas with a sumptuous house, complete with stage and vast gardens. According to rumor, an underground passage linked it to the gardens of the viceregal palace. She loved jewels, and he covered her with them. On the weekends, the two stayed at Miraflores outside Lima at the estate of Amat's nephew. When they traveled there, protocol prevented anyone from riding beside the viceroy in his carriage, and consequently Villegas followed behind on horseback in public view. "She dressed like a man, or else wore a long sky-blue skirt embroidered with gold fringes and a toque of feathers." Tongues wagged, both admiring and censorious.

In 1769, Villegas gave birth to a son, whom she called Manuel de Amat, after his father. She dressed him in finery, and the couple's sycophants fawned over the young boy. The Spaniard did not officially recognize the child as his son, but Villegas hoped he would. In the meantime, she continued to star at the Coliseo, refusing to give up the stage. The theater was for Villegas "a form of expression and liberation, to show off her charms, to win admirers, to keep herself 'in shape' for elegance and love." Amat loved her both as a woman and an actress. He often attended "rehearsals and gave the actors advice." The viceroy even mediated disputes within the company. Villegas was the first lady of the Peruvian stage, although the aristocrats never would have considered her a real lady.

Then, in 1773, her hot temper caused a conflagration on the stage of the Coliseo. Perhaps she had spent too little time rehearsing, given the demands of her semi-public private life. Perhaps Massa, the director and chief actor, resented the fact that the public often attended to see the viceroy's mistress rather than the plays. On stage with Massa, a distracted Villegas stumbled over her part. Massa told her to put more spirit into the role and in a loud whisper said that Inesilla could do better. Inesilla, or **Inés Mayorga**, was her great rival, and Villegas flew into a rage. With the light cane already in her hand, she slashed the actor's cheek. The curtain fell, interrupting the play, while the audience called for her arrest. (According to some reports, the crisis occurred during a rehearsal of *Fuego del Dios en el querer bien*, by Calderón de la Barca; other versions hold that it was during a public performance of the play.) At any rate, scandalized by her behavior, Amat angrily broke off their relationship.

Villegas was not worried, because Amat had always reconciled with her after other tantrums. This time, however, the old man was adamant. He prohibited her from acting, allegedly declaring: "She'll never return to the

Anna Magnani portrayed Villegas in Jean Renoir's Le Carrosse d'or.

theater, and if she makes me angry, I'll make her go out on the stage on her knees and ask the public's pardon and after that an executioner will kick her out forever." For over a year, the viceroy refused to see her.

Some also claim that it was during this crisis that he first referred to her as *la Perricholi*, the term by which Villegas became most famous. According to that version of her story, the word represented the Catalan Amat's angry attempt to pronounce *perra chola* (half-breed bitch). Another version holds that the word derived from the Catalan *petritxol*, a term of gallantry meaning "my joy" or "my delight." In this case, Amat shouted the term to Villegas while she was on stage, and the public soon used it to refer to her also. Perhaps neither is correct. Peruvian historian Guillermo Lohmann Villena discovered the existence of persons with the surname Perricholi living in Lima around 1750. Thus, neither the origin nor the precise meaning of the term is clear. Nonetheless, it is certain that Micaela Villegas became *la Perricholi* to the Hispanic world.

Stubborn as they might be, the two succumbed to a reconciliation by September 1775. Villegas prevailed upon Amat to let her return to the stage. Her first appearance was on November 4, with the viceroy shouting encouragement from his box. He also insisted that Massa ask her pardon and raise her monthly salary from 100 to 150 pesos. "Wilder than ever, with burning eyes and a smile of triumph on her lips, she reconquered her public, who acclaimed her like a long-lost queen." Inesilla, who had replaced Villegas as the star of the Coliseo, found herself arbitrarily banished to Chile.

In 1775 and 1776, la Perricholi was at the height of her influence. She dressed little Manuel in silk with a wide, red ribbon, imitating the Order of St. Januarius of which his father was a member. Some talked of her as though she were the viceroy's wife; rumor held that Amat had proposed marriage. One night she feigned thirst until Amat, clad in his nightshirt, went out into the street and fetched her water from the fountain. La Perricholi split her time between the stage and a Peruvian imitation of Versailles.

One of Villegas' greatest triumphs occurred in mid-1776, when Lima celebrated the feast day of Portiuncula. It was customary for the viceroy in his coach to head a procession to the Alameda. Villegas had pleaded with Amat for permission to ride with him. When he refused, she asked him to provide her with a coach of her own. Amat knew that only the high aristocracy enjoyed such a privilege, but he succumbed to her entreaties. Perhaps this was his way of humiliating the elite who had resisted his rule. As her blue and gold coach made its way through the streets, to the scandal of the aristocrats, it met two candle bearers and a priest going to administer the last rites to a dying parishioner. Remorse, or grand theater, overwhelmed Villegas. She descended from the coach, asked the priest to get in, and tearfully followed on foot in her ball gown as he went about his sacred duty. In a further dramatic gesture, she donated the carriage to the parish.

Amat turned over power to his successor in July 1776, and the aged lover left for Spain a few months later. Recriminations and lawsuits proliferated against the former viceroy. These included a theatrical lampoon, *El drama de los palanganas*, which accused Amat and Villegas of all sorts of corruption and debauchery. Perhaps la Perricholi had hoped Amat would take her with him, or send for her; perhaps not. He did neither but, in 1779, married a young woman whom his nephew had jilted. Amat died on February 14, 1782, without recognizing his paternity of Villegas' son.

Meanwhile, in Lima, she withdrew from public life, benefiting from property left her by Amat. Eventually she teamed with Vicente Fermín Echarri y Gorózabal to manage the Coliseo de Comedias, with Villegas providing most of the capital. As entrepreneurs, they prospered and wielded enough influence in 1788 to prevent competitors from building a new, rival theater. On August 4, 1795, she married Echarri and seemed delighted when people called her Echarri's *señora*. Echarri died in 1807.

In her final years, la Perricholi showed determination to make a way for herself into respectable middle-class society. She sent her son Manuel to Europe for polishing. He returned embittered after finding that being the illegitimate son of a viceroy conferred no advantages in Spain. When Manuel tried to marry a beautiful seamstress, his mother had him jailed for several months until he agreed to what she considered a more suitable union. Villegas reportedly passed her final years dressed in a nun's habit. She stipulated in her will that her heirs give her a simple funeral and use the money saved to give alms to the poor. When she died on May 16, 1819, her estate amounted to more than 60,000 pesos. She also left a number of books, evidence of her literacy.

After her death, Villegas became symbolically even more important. From humble origins, she had conquered the affections of a viceroy. She had challenged the prejudices of the

Peruvian aristocracy, and her later popularity perhaps reflects the people's admiration of her social defiance. Idolized in popular legend, Villegas became the subject of Jacques Offenbach's opera *La Périchole*, and the romantic drama by M. Théaulon, *La Périchole*. She also figured prominently in Thornton Wilder's *The Bridge of San Luis Rey*.

SOURCES:

Descola, Jean. *Daily Life in Colonial Peru 1710–1820*. London: George Allen and Unwin, 1968.

Flores y Caamaño, Alfredo. *Un virrey y su favorita*. Lima, 1955.

García Calderón, Ventura. *La Périchole*. Paris: Gallimard, 1940.

Lohmann Villena, Guillermo. *El arte dramático en Lima durante el Virreinato*. Madrid: Estades, 1945.

Saénz-Rico Urbina, Alfredo. *El Virrey Amat: precisiones sobre la vida y la obra de don Manuel de Amat y de Junyent*. 2 vols. Barcelona: Museo de Historia de la Ciudad, 1967.

Sánchez, Luis Alberto. *La Perricholi*. Lima: Universidad Nacional Mayor de San Marcos, 1963.

SUGGESTED READING:

León y León D., Gustavo. *La Perricholi: apuntes histórico-genealógicos de Micaela Villegas*. Lima: CONCYTEC, 1990.

Ruiz Cano y Saenz Galiano, Francisco Antonio, marquis of Soto Florido. *Un tríptico del Perú virreinal; el Virrey Amat, el marqués de Soto Florido y la Perricholi: el drama de dos palaganas y su circunstancia*. Edition and preliminary study by Guillermo Lohmann Villena. Chapel Hill, NC: University of North Carolina Press, 1976.

Kendall W. Brown,
Professor of History,
Brigham Young University,
Provo, Utah

Villems, Sigbrit (fl. 1507–1523).

See Willums, Sigbrit.

Villena, Isabel de (1430–1490)

Spanish abbess and author. Born in 1430; died in 1490 in Valencia, Spain; illegitimate daughter of Enric de Villena (a nobleman and writer); educated at the court of Alphonso V (1396–1458), king of Aragon (r. 1416–1458); never married; no children.

Abbess of Trinity Convent in Valencia (1463–90); author of Vita Christi *(1497).*

Isabel de Villena was born in 1430, the illegitimate daughter of Spanish noble Enric de Villena. Like her father, she became a writer, although she was to surpass him in both fame and influence. Villena entered Trinity Convent in Valencia at the age of 15, after an education at the court of Alphonso V (known as the Magnanimous). In 1463, Villena was elected abbess of Trinity Convent for life and became an increasingly important voice in Valencian society, particularly after the accession of the "Catholic kings," *Isabella I of Castile and Ferdinand II of Aragon. The work for which Villena is best known, *Vita Christi*, was published posthumously in 1497.

Paula Morris, D.Phil.,
Brooklyn, New York

Villeneuve, Gabrielle-Suzanne de (c. 1695–1755)

French novelist. Name variations: Mme de Villeneuve; Gabrielle-Suzanne Barbot Gallon de Villeneuve. Born around 1695; died in 1755; widowed around 1730.

Selected writings: (novels) Le Phénix conjugal *(The Phoenix of Marriage, 1733),* La Jeune américane *(The Young American, 1740–41),* Le Beau-frère supposé *(The Presumed Brother-in-Law, 1752),* La Jardinière de Vincennes *(The Gardener of Vincennes, 1753),* Le Juge prévenu *(The Biased Judge, 1754),* Anecdotes de la cour d'Alphonse XI *(Anecdotes from the Court of Alphonso XI, 1757),* Mlles de Marsanges *(1757),* Le temps et la patience *(Time and Patience, 1768); (play)* Les belles solitaires *(Lonely Beauties, 1745); (stories)* Les Contes de cette année *(This Year's Tales, 1744),* Contes de Mme de Villeneuve *(The Tales of Madame de Villeneuve, 1765).*

Little is known of Gabrielle-Suzanne de Villeneuve's early life. Her career as a writer did not begin until she was widowed and left with an insufficiently small income. Living in Paris, Villeneuve supported herself by writing, producing over 12 volumes during the latter half of her life. She is credited with writing the fairy tale *Beauty and the Beast* (*La Belle et la bête*, in vol. XXVI of *Cabinet des fées*). Both 1733's *Le Phénix conjugal* (The Phoenix of Marriage) and 1753's *La Jardinière de Vincennes* (The Gardener of Vincennes), the latter considered her best work, focus on the position of women in society, portraying lower-class women as empathetic, admirable heroines.

Paula Morris, D.Phil.,
Brooklyn, New York

Villers, Mme (fl. late 18th c.)

French artist. Active in the late 18th and early 19th centuries.

Madame Villers is an enigmatic figure in the history of French art, with little known about her background. Scant and confusing information has been found in the Paris Salon catalogs of 1799, 1801, and 1802, all years when a Mme Villers exhibited a handful of paintings. It is believed that her maiden name was either Lemoine or Nisa, and that she studied with an artist named either Giraudet (an unknown figure), Girardet (one of a large family of Swiss artists), or possibly Anne Louis Girodet-Trioson (1767–1824). Work exhibited by Villers in those three Salons included the accomplished if conventional *A Baby in its Cradle* (exhibited in 1802) and the charming *Portrait of Mme Soustras*, which was possibly also exhibited in 1802 under the title *A Study of a Woman from Nature*. Its subject, possibly a dancer, is depicted bending over to lace up her slipper, a popular pose with artists of Villers' day (most notably Goya in *Bien tirada está*), as was the painting's landscape setting, which is suggestive of Girodet-Trioson's *Portrait of J.B. Belley* (1797).

SOURCES:

Harris, Anne Sutherland, and Linda Nochlin. *Women Artists, 1550–1950*. Los Angeles, CA: Los Angeles Country Museum of Art, 1976.

Paula Morris, D.Phil.,
Brooklyn, New York

Villiers, Anne (d. 1688)

*Countess of Portland. Died on November 30, 1688; daughter of Sir Edward Villiers and Lady *Frances Villiers (c. 1636–1677); sister of *Elizabeth Villiers (c. 1657–1733); married Hans William Bentinck, earl of Portland, on February 1, 1678; children: **Mary Bentinck** (1679–1726, who married Algernon Capell, 2nd/22nd earl of Essex, and Hon. Sir Conyers D'Arcy); **William Bentinck** (b. 1681); **Henry Bentinck** (b. 1682), 1st duke of Portland; **Anne Margaretta Bentinck** (1683–1763, who married Arend de Wassenaer-Duvenvoirde, Baron de Wassenaer); **Frances Wilhemina Bentinck** (1684–1712, who married William Byron, 4th Baron Byron); **Eleanor Bentinck** (b. 1687), a nun; **Isabella Bentinck** (1688–1728, who married Evelyn Pierrepont, duke of Kingston-on-Hull).*

Villiers, Barbara (d. 1708)

*Viscountess FitzHardinge. Died on September 19, 1708; interred on September 23, 1708, at Westminster Abbey, London; daughter of Sir Edward Villiers and Lady *Frances Villiers (c. 1636–1677); married John Berkeley, 4th Viscount FitzHardinge.*

Villiers, Barbara (c. 1641–1709)

Countess of Castlemaine and duchess of Cleveland who was the powerful and influential mistress of Charles II of England for over ten years. Name variations: Barbara Palmer; Lady Castlemaine; Countess of Southampton; Baroness Nonsuch. Born autumn 1641 (some sources cite 1640 or 1642) at Westminster, England; died at Chiswick on October 9, 1709; only daughter of William Villiers, 2nd Viscount Grandison, and Mary (Bayning) Villiers; educated in impoverished circumstances; married Roger Palmer, in 1659; became mistress of King Charles II, in 1660; had affair with John Churchill, duke of Marlborough; married Robert (Beau) Feilding or Fielding (d. 1712), on November 25, 1705, a union which was declared void on May 24, 1707, as Feilding had a wife, Mary Wadsworth, still living; children: (with Charles II) Anne Palmer (b. 1661); Charles, duke of Southampton (1662–1730); Henry, 1st duke of Grafton (1663–1690); Charlotte Fitzroy (1664–1717); George, duke of Northumberland (1665–1716); (with John Churchill) Barbara Palmer (b. 1672).

Moved to London in early teens; married Roger Palmer (1659); became mistress of Charles II (1660); created countess of Castlemaine (1662) and appointed lady-in-waiting to queen; converted to Catholicism (1663); given large pension and created duchess of Cleveland (1669); had affair with John Churchill (1672); removed from queen's household due to Test Act (1672); moved to Paris (1677); remained at court during reign of William and Mary; married Robert Feilding (November 1705) after death of first husband; bigamy trial of Feilding (1706); marriage declared null (1707); fell ill (July 1709) and died from dropsy (October 1709).

Barbara Villiers was born into a family that was known for its loyalty to the crown. The Villiers family rose to power, wealth, and prominence during the reign of James I, whose favorite, George Villiers, duke of Buckingham, secured influential places at court for his brothers and sisters. During the ill-fated reign of Charles I, Barbara's father William Villiers, 2nd viscount Grandison, fought on the royalist side while his daughter, in turn, became the powerful and prominent mistress of Charles II. The grandeur of her life, however, was not foreshadowed at the outset.

In 1641, the year of Barbara's birth, England was on the brink of civil war. The nobility in Scotland had already challenged the king's authority, and the English Parliament was engaged in a battle of wills with Charles I over his arbitrary use of the royal prerogative. One year later, Britain was at war. Throughout most of the civil war, Barbara was sheltered from much of the ongoing political turmoil and lived with her moth-

er **Mary Bayning** in the countryside. Her father, however, immediately took up the king's standard and raised an army. A year later, in July 1643, he died from a gunshot wound sustained in battle. Barbara and her mother were left to fend for themselves.

Little is known about the early years of Villiers' life. She was forced to live in reduced circumstances and was brought up by relatives in the countryside until her early teens. From an early age, however, observers noted her beauty and charm. Later portraits confirm that she had auburn hair, a voluptuous figure, and dark blue eyes. In 1656, 15-year-old Barbara joined her mother in London, who had been living there for some years with her second husband. Here, Barbara caught the eye of several young gentlemen including Philip Stanhope, 2nd earl of Chesterfield, whose reputation as a "rake" and seducer of young women was well known. Consequently, Villiers' family soon became worried that her friendship with him would lead to something more serious. Although some historians argue that she had an affair with Chesterfield, there is little reliable evidence to support their claims. Nevertheless, her reputation as one of the most beautiful and enchanting women in London was growing, and her fortunes were about to be altered forever when the political situation changed.

In 1659 and after ten years of republican rule under Oliver Cromwell, the political tide turned back towards monarchical government. One year later, Charles II returned to govern the kingdom he had been forced to leave a decade ago. Those men who had remained loyal to the Royalist cause were eager to regain the power and prestige they had lost during the Cromwellian regime. One of these Royalists was 24-year-old Roger Palmer who had recently been captivated by, and won the hand of, Barbara Villiers. They were married on April 14, 1659. One year later, in the spring of 1660, Palmer and his 19-year-old wife were sent to Brussels to assist with preparations for Charles II's return. Here, their lives were changed forever. Although no one knows exactly what happened when the king and Barbara Palmer met, that encounter signaled the beginning of an intense, passionate, and long-lasting relationship.

Tall, dark, athletic and intelligent, Charles II was instantly captivated by the vivacious and very beautiful Mrs. Palmer, and they became lovers sometime in May 1660. The king's obvious infatuation with her was confirmed when, upon his return to England, he spent his first night with Barbara at the palace of Whitehall. From this point on, Villiers was seen with the king at formal and public events and was quickly acknowledged as his mistress. After the birth of a daughter ✥ **Anne Palmer**, Villiers' first child with the king, Roger Palmer was created baron of Limerick and earl of Castlemaine in December 1661 as consolation. Although he acknowledged this child as his own, Palmer knew that his marriage was one in name only, and he retreated from court to concentrate on his career as a member of Parliament.

Life at the Restoration court was a welcome change from previous years of puritanical restraint. Vibrant, colorful and gay, the new court was both intellectually and sensually stimulating. Although Charles left many of the political matters in the hands of his capable chancellor, Edward Hyde, earl of Clarendon, he did not abandon his kingly duties. A primary concern, of course, was to find the king a suitable wife. Royal marriages were based on political rather than emotional concerns, and by 1662 it had been decided that the king would marry the Portuguese princess, *Catherine of Braganza. A new wife did not mean that Charles would give up Lady Castlemaine, however, and when Catherine arrived in England on May 13, 1662, the king did not go out to greet her but spent the evening with Villiers instead.

Charles, Barbara's second child with the king, was born in June 1662. Once again, however, Roger Palmer acknowledged the child as his own and, having recently converted to Catholicism, had him baptized according to Roman Catholic rites. This action gave Villiers the pretext she needed to leave her husband officially, and, from this point on, they rarely saw one another. Charles II, on the other hand, was endeavoring to keep Barbara even closer to him by arranging her appointment as lady-in-waiting to Queen Catherine. Although homesick and isolated, Catherine of Braganza had fallen in love with her husband and refused his request to have the royal mistress in her presence. Charles retaliated by sending the majority of Catherine's Portuguese servants back home. The king's resolve in this matter, and his loyalty to Villiers, was unshakable. When he learned that Chancellor Clarendon was in favor of blocking Barbara's appointment, he is recorded as having said: "I am resolved to go through with this matter, let what will come on it. Whosoever I find to be my Lady Castlemaine's enemy in this matter, I do promise, upon my word, to be his enemy as

---

✥➤ **Palmer, Anne** (1661–1722)

Countess of Sussex. Name variations: Lady Dacre; Anne Lennard. Born in February 1661; died in 1722; daughter of Barbara Villiers (c. 1641–1709) and probably Charles II, king of England; married Thomas Lennard, Lord Dacre, in 1674, who was created earl of Sussex in 1684 (died 1715).

King Charles II was probably the father of *Barbara Villiers' first child, Anne, though, at the time, the paternity was also attributed to one of Barbara's earliest reputed lovers, Philip Stanhope, 2nd earl of Chesterfield (1633–1713).

---

long as I live." By August, two distinct factions had formed, one which supported the queen, the other Lady Castlemaine. Nevertheless, the opposition underestimated both Villiers' intelligence and her influence with the king. Two months after the issue arose, Barbara was given official lodgings at Whitehall and a position in the queen's household. Her rooms soon became the center of opposition against Clarendon.

By 1663, rumors were circulating that not only was Lady Castlemaine supplanted in the king's affections by a new mistress but that she had taken a new lover herself. It is difficult to prove whether or not these rumors were true, and Barbara's birth of a third child (Henry) with the king in September and the lavish gifts he presented to her at Christmas suggests that they were false. Her conversion to Catholicism in December 1663 may have been an attempt to consolidate her position in the king's circle because many of his closest friends were secret Catholics. Regardless of her motivations, she maintained both her faith and her status as the official mistress of the king and, with him, gave birth to another child, &▶ **Charlotte Fitzroy** (1664–1717).

In 1665, when the plague was raging in London, Villiers traveled with the royal court to Salisbury and Oxford. Despite public criticism, her position at court remained strong. Her influence was recognized by the French king, Louis XIV, who ordered his ambassador to coax as many state secrets from Lady Castlemaine as possible. Unfortunately, the ambassador's attempts in this regard were never rewarded.

In December 1665, Barbara gave birth to George, her fifth and last child with the king. Charles II was preoccupied with foreign affairs, most notably a naval war with the Dutch. The Anglo-Dutch war continued for two years and signaled the end of Villiers' chief political rival, the earl of Clarendon, who took the blame for this unpopular war. While it is difficult to determine whether or not she played an active role in securing the chancellor's downfall, she was, nevertheless, pleased when he was finally removed from office in 1667. Charles II, however, was in no hurry to appoint a successor and remained without a chief minister for several years after Clarendon's fall.

Villiers' position remained secure even when she learned that the king's attentions had now turned to actresses. Realizing that she would have to share her royal lover with other women, Lady Castlemaine continued to hold a powerful sway over the king. Public criticism against her position, however, continued. In April 1668, an anonymous pamphlet entitled "The Poor Whores' Petition" circulated throughout London. Addressed to Lady Castlemaine, it asked for her protection since she was "one of us." A few days later, an anonymous "answer" to the petition was written. As a means of publicly acknowledging his regard for her, and in an obvious, if futile, attempt to sway public opinion, Charles gave Villiers an annual pension of £4,700 as well as a large house across from St. James's Palace. She lived there for two years with her three youngest children during which time the king visited her every day.

> *H*er achievement had been impressive, for at a time when women had few opportunities for advancement she had succeeded in winning herself a fortune, a title, and independence by the age of thirty.
>
> —Ronald Hutton

In 1670, Barbara was created Baroness Nonsuch, countess of Southampton, and duchess of Cleveland. She continued to receive various pensions, jewels and properties from the king. In addition to these royal gifts, Villiers, who was an astute businesswoman, accepted bribes from foreign diplomats as well as English courtiers. She continued to rely on her own beauty, charms, and influence to secure both money and property for her children. In this regard, she was wise to collect what revenues she could, as the situation for Catholics in England was becoming increasingly tense. Much of this was due to the king's foreign policy.

In 1670, Charles signed the Treaty of Dover with France. Under the terms of this agreement, France and England united to make war against the Dutch. While this clause of the treaty was publicized, some other, more serious and secret promises were also made. In return for a promise to convert to Catholicism, Charles was to receive £166,000 as well as additional financial subsidies from Louis XIV over the next eight years. Shortly before war was declared on Holland two years later, Charles issued a Declaration of Indul-

---

&▶ **Fitzroy, Charlotte** (1664–1717)
Countess of Lichfield. Name variations: Charlotte Lee. Born in 1664; died in 1717 (some sources cite 1718); illegitimate daughter of Charles II, king of England, and *Barbara Villiers (c. 1641–1709); married Edward Henry Lee, earl of Lichfield, in 1677 (died 1716).

gence which suspended penal laws against Catholics and non-conformists. The English House of Commons, which was anti-Catholic and anti-French, was outraged by the king's action and refused to grant money for the Dutch war until the king withdrew the Declaration. Parliament then passed the Test Act which prohibited anyone who was not a member of the Church of England from holding public office. Consequently, all Catholic officials, including the king's brother, James, duke of York (later James II), were driven from office. Barbara, duchess of Cleveland, also lost her position in the queen's household as a result of this legislation.

Although he continued to lavish gifts and pensions upon her, it was becoming increasingly clear that Barbara's influence over the king was dwindling, particularly as a succession of women had supplanted her as royal mistress. (Charles had a legion of mistresses throughout his reign, including Lady **Elizabeth Byron, Marguerite Carteret, ◄ Elizabeth Killigrew, *Nell Gwynn, ◄ Moll Davies, *Hortense Mancini, ◄ Catherine Pegge, *Louise de Kéroüalle, *Frances Stuart,** and ***Lucy Walter**.) The duchess, however, was never one to lie low. She, in her turn, had a series of liaisons with several men, including John Churchill (afterwards duke of Marlborough) with whom she had a daughter ◄ **Barbara Palmer** in 1672. She also made concerted and successful efforts to secure wealthy and influential marriages for all of her children.

When many of these family matters had been settled, Villiers moved to Paris in 1677. Her motivations for doing so are unclear. Some historians suggest that she left England to escape from her creditors while others argue that she preferred to have her daughter brought up in a Catholic convent. Whatever the reasons, the duchess remained in Paris for several years, during which time she had an affair with the

English ambassador, Ralph Montague. She returned to England for several short visits, primarily to collect the rents from her various properties. She was present in England, however, just shortly before the death of Charles II in February 1685. It is not known how she reacted to the news of his death, but she must have grieved for the man who had changed her life so substantially.

Although she had little influence at court after the death of Charles II, Villiers continued to fare well under the successive reigns of James II and William III. She was allowed to remain at court, although the income she was to receive from her various pensions was not always paid regularly. In addition, she began to gamble heavily and by the mid-1690s she was £10,000 in debt. Fortunately, William III finally came to her aid and in 1699 not only paid off her debts but granted her a regular, if small, pension, for the rest of her life.

By the turn of the century, however, her personal life had taken a turn for the worse. In July 1705, she became a widow when her husband Roger Palmer died. Four months later, she married Robert Feilding. Unfortunately, Villiers' choice of a second husband was unwise. One year after their marriage, Feilding was arrested for threatening and maltreating his wife and, more seriously, it was soon discovered that he had married another woman just two weeks before his marriage to Villiers. Feilding went on trial for bigamy, and on May 23, 1707, sentence was passed declaring her second marriage null and void. From this point on, Villiers' health deteriorated, and in July 1709 she fell ill with dropsy. Three months later, she died on October 9, 1709, at the age of 68.

SOURCES:

Andrews, Allen. *The Royal Whore: Barbara Villiers, Countess of Castlemaine*. Philadelphia, PA: Chilton, 1970.

Gilmour, Margaret. *The Great Lady: A Biography of Barbara Villiers, Mistress of Charles II*. NY: Alfred Knopf, 1941.

Hamilton, Elizabeth. *The Illustrious Lady: A Biography of Barbara Villiers, Countess of Castlemaine and Duchess of Cleveland*. London: Hamish Hamilton, 1980.

SUGGESTED READING:

Hutton, Ronald. *Charles the Second: King of England, Scotland and Ireland*. Oxford: Clarendon Press, 1989.

Margaret McIntyre,
Instructor in Women's History,
Trent University, Peterborough, Ontario, Canada

Villiers, Elizabeth (c. 1657–1733)

Countess of Orkney. Name variations: Elizabeth Hamilton, Countess of Orkney; Mrs. Villiers. Born

---

❧► **Killigrew, Elizabeth.** *See Gwynn, Nell for sidebar.*

❧► **Davies, Moll.** *See Gwynn, Nell for sidebar.*

❧► **Pegge, Catherine.** *See Gwynn, Nell for sidebar.*

❧► **Palmer, Barbara** (1672–1737)

Daughter of Barbara Villiers. Born in 1672; died in 1737; daughter of Barbara Villiers (c. 1641–1709) and possibly John Churchill, duke of Marlborough; children: (with James Douglas) Charles Hamilton.

The reputed daughter of John Churchill, duke of Marlborough, and *Barbara Villiers, Barbara Palmer entered a nunnery in France. Later, with James Douglas (1658–1712), afterwards 4th duke of Hamilton, she had an illegitimate son, Charles Hamilton (d. 1754).

---

around 1657; died in London on April 19, 1733; daughter of Colonel Sir Edward Villiers of Richmond and Frances (Howard) Villiers (c. 1633–1677); sister of *Anne Villiers (d. 1688); married cousin, Lord George Hamilton (5th son of the 3rd duke of Hamilton), 1st earl of Orkney (r. 1696–1737), on November 25, 1695; children: Anne Hamilton (b. 1694), countess of Orkney; Henrietta Hamilton.

Born around 1657, Elizabeth Villiers was the daughter of Sir Edward Villiers and Lady *Frances Villiers, who, as governess to the princesses *Mary (II) and *Anne, secured a place for her children in Mary's household. Elizabeth's brother Edward Villiers (1656–1711), afterwards created 1st earl of Jersey, became master of the horse, while Elizabeth and her sister Anne were among the maids of honor who accompanied Mary to The Hague on her marriage to William III, prince of Orange (future William III of England).

Elizabeth became William III's acknowledged mistress in 1680. It is said that she tried to ward off his advances by encouraging the attentions of a Captain Wauchoop, a Scottish mercenary working for the Dutch. William summarily dismissed Wauchoop. "Elizabeth was no great beauty," writes Charles Carlton in *Royal Mistresses*. "She was ungainly, had a passable figure, and a long white neck." But when she grew older, she had "intelligence and wit enough" to keep Jonathan Swift "up all night laughing," and as a young woman she had the bearing to fascinate William of Orange.

After his accession to the English crown, William conferred on Elizabeth a large share of the confiscated Irish estates of King James II. This grant was revoked by Parliament, however, in 1699. Queen Mary, who was always painfully aware of her husband's relationship with Elizabeth, wrote a letter to William, to be opened after her death, begging him to break with his mistress for the sake of his soul. Following Mary's death in 1694, a grieving William heeded his wife's wishes and separated from Villiers. He was never again seen with her in public. In November 1695, Elizabeth married her cousin, Lord George Hamilton, fifth son of the 3rd duke of Hamilton. Early the next year, William granted her husband the titles of earl of Orkney, viscount of Kirkwall, and Baron Dechmont. The marriage proved to be a happy one. Elizabeth Villiers died in London on April 19, 1733.

SOURCES:
Carlton, Charles. *Royal Mistresses*. London: Routledge, 1990.

Villiers, Frances (c. 1633–1677)

Duchess of Richmond. Name variations: Lady Frances Howard. Born around 1633 (one source cites c. 1636); died on November 27, 1677; interred at Westminster Abbey, London; daughter of Theophilus Howard (1584–1640), 2nd earl of Suffolk (r. 1626–1640), and *Elizabeth Hume (c. 1599–1633); married Colonel Sir Edward Villiers of Richmond; children: Edward Villiers (1656–1711), 1st earl of Jersey; Henry Villiers; *Elizabeth Villiers (c. 1657–1733); Katherine Villiers (who married Colonel William Villiers and Louis James Le Vasseur, marquess de Purissar); *Barbara Villiers (d. 1708); *Anne Villiers (d. 1688, who married Hans William Bentinck, earl of Portland); Henrietta Villiers (d. 1719, who married John Campbell, 2nd earl of Breadalbane); Mary Villiers (d. 1753, who married William O'Brien, 3rd earl Inchiquin).

Villiers, Margaret Elizabeth Child- (1849–1945)

English philanthropist. Name variations: Margaret Elizabeth Leigh, countess of Jersey. Born Margaret Elizabeth Leigh on October 29, 1849, in Stoneleigh Abbey, England; died on May 22, 1945; daughter of William Henry Leigh (b. 1824), 2nd Baron Leigh, and Caroline Amelia (Grosvenor) Leigh; married Victor Albert George Child-Villiers (1845–1915), 7th earl of Jersey (r. 1859–1915), on September 19, 1872; children: George Henry Robert Child-Villiers (b. 1873), 8th earl of Jersey; Margaret (1874–1874); Margaret Child-Villiers (b. 1875, who married Walter FitzUryan Rhys, 7th baron Dynevor); Beatrice Child-Villiers (b. 1880); Arthur George Child-Villiers (b. 1883).

Was the founder and president of Victoria League (1901–27); awarded DBE (1927).

Born in England a decade after Queen *Victoria's accession, Margaret Villiers, countess of Jersey, was to live through the reigns of five different monarchs. The daughter of the second Baron Leigh, Villiers married a peer in 1872, the 7th earl of Jersey. Known for much of her life as a society hostess, entertaining widely at both Middleton Park, Bicester, and Osterley Park, Isleworth, Villiers took an active interest in children's welfare. She was also one of the founders and president of the Victoria League, an organization that promoted international relations between countries in the British Empire (now the Commonwealth). Villiers worked on the League's behalf from 1901 to 1927, when she was named Dame Commander of the British Empire (DBE) in recognition of her services to the community.

Paula Morris, D.Phil.,
Brooklyn, New York

Villiers, Susan

*Countess of Denbigh. Daughter of Sir George Villiers and Mary Beaumont, countess of Buckingham; married William Fielding, 1st earl of Denbigh (r. 1622–1643), around 1607; children: Basil Fielding, 2nd earl of Denbigh; George Fielding, 1st earl of Desmond; *Mary Hamilton (1613–1638); Anne Fielding (d. 1636, who married Baptist Noel, 3rd viscount Campden); Elizabeth Fielding, countess of Guildford (who married Lewis Boyle, viscount Kynalmeaky).*

Villoms, Sigbrit (fl. 1507–1523).

See Willums, Sigbrit.

Vilmorin, Louise de (1902–1969)

French novelist and poet. Born in 1902 in Verrières-le-Buisson, France; died in 1969; married second husband, Count Paul Palffy, late 1930s.

Selected writings: (novels) Sainte-Unefois *(Saint Onetime, 1934),* La Fin des Villavides *(The Last of the Villavides, 1938),* Le Lit à colonnes *(The Tapestry Bed, 1941),* Le Retour d'Erica *(Erica's Return, 1948),* Julietta *(1951),* Madame de . . . *(1951),* La Lettre dans un taxi *(Letter in a Taxi, 1958); (poetry)* Fiançailles pour rire *(Betrothal in Jest, 1939),* L'Alphabet des aveux *(Alphabet of Avowals, 1954).*

Louise de Vilmorin was born in Verrières-le-Buisson in 1902 and published her first, largely autobiographical novel, *Sainte-Unefois* (Saint Onetime), at age 32. By the end of the 1930s, Vilmorin had had one unsuccessful marriage, embarked on a second—with Count Paul Palffy—and published her first poetry collection, *Fiançailles pour rire* (Betrothal in Jest, 1939). Although she was to publish more poetry later in life, Vilmorin received most acclaim for her novels. A number of her fictional works were made into films, including *Le Lit à colonnes* (The Tapestry Bed, 1941), *Julietta* (1951), and *Madame de . . .* (1951).

Vilmorin's elegant, ironic style, combined with her elaborate (and sometimes fantastic) plots, sophisticated settings, and characters drawn from high society, made many of her novels great popular successes, including *La Fin des Villavides* (The Last of the Villavides, 1938), *La*

Lettre dans un taxi (Letter in a Taxi, 1958), and *Le Retour d'Erica* (Erica's Return, 1948). She was awarded the Grand Prix Littèraire de Monaco in 1955, and died in 1969.

SOURCES:
Columbia Dictionary of Modern European Literature. 2nd ed. NY: Columbia University Press, 1980.

Paula Morris, D.Phil.,
Brooklyn, New York

Vince, Marion Lloyd (1906–1969)

American fencer. Born in Brooklyn, New York, on April 16, 1906; died on November 2, 1969; married.

Won national championship (1928 and 1931); member of the Helms Hall of Fame.

Marion Lloyd Vince was born in Brooklyn in 1906 but did not begin fencing until 1925. She quickly proved her abilities, winning the national championship in 1928 and 1931. In the 1932 Olympics, she was the first U.S. woman to attain the fencing finals. Her husband, who was also a fencer, directed the Salle Vince team which won ten national team championships. Marion Lloyd Vince, a key member of those winning teams, was named to fencing's Helms Hall of Fame, and the under-19 national championship trophy awarded by the Amateur Fencing League of America was named for her.

SOURCES:
Markel, Robert, Nancy Brooks, and Susan Markel. *For the Record: Women in Sports.* NY: World Almanac, 1985.

Karin Loewen Haag,
Athens, Georgia

Vincent, Mrs. James R. (1818–1887).

See Vincent, Mary Ann.

Vincent, Mary Ann (1818–1887)

British-born American actress who was noted for her roles in comedies, particularly She Stoops to Conquer *and* The Rivals. *Name variations: Mrs. J.R. Vincent; Mrs. James R. Vincent. Born Mary Ann Farlow on September 18, 1818, in Portsmouth, England; died on September 4, 1887, in Boston, Massachusetts; daughter of John Farlow (a naval worker); married James R. Vincent (an actor), in 1835 (died 1850); married John Wilson (an expressman), on December 16, 1854 (deserted 1866, later divorced); no children.*

The actress who came to fame under the name Mrs. J.R. Vincent was born Mary Ann Farlow, probably in Portsmouth, England, in

1818. Both her mother and her father, John Farlow, who worked for the navy, were dead by the time she was four years old, so she was raised in Portsmouth by her grandmother and aunt.

An untrained novice, Vincent made her stage debut on April 25, 1835, in Cowes, the principal town on the Isle of Wight, playing the role of the chambermaid Lucy in George Colman's *The Review, or the Wags of Windsor*. Still only 16, she married fellow actor James R. Vincent and the couple worked together as traveling players in England, Ireland, and Scotland. Mrs. Vincent, as she was now known, showed great aptitude and versatility, even playing the part of the Nurse in *Romeo and Juliet* before she was 19 years old.

In October 1846, the Vincents sailed from Liverpool—where they had spent two seasons at the Theater Royal—to Boston, engaged as players by William Pelby's National Theater. Their first American performance, on November 11, 1846, was in John B. Buckstone's *Popping the Question*, and Mary Vincent remained a member of the company until 1852. Her personal life during the 1850s and 1860s was extremely difficult and unhappy. James committed suicide on June 11, 1850, and her second husband, an expressman named John Wilson who was 11 years her junior, left her in 1866 after 12 turbulent years of marriage.

Her standing in Boston's theatrical world, however, was to prove both happy and enduring. When the old National Theater burned down in April, 1852, Vincent moved to the Boston Museum theater, beginning a long association with that beloved institution which would last until her death. The only break in her tenure took place during the 1861–62 season, following a disagreement with the manager. That season she appeared at the Howard Athenaeum in Boston, with **Lucille Western**'s company in Baltimore, and in Washington, where President Abraham Lincoln was said to have been an admirer of her acting.

An intelligent, natural performer, Vincent enjoyed a popular and long-lived career at the Boston Museum that was founded on a wide repertoire, from Shakespeare to classical comedy to melodrama. She was an accomplished comedian, particularly in character and old-woman roles. On April 25, 1885, Mary Vincent performed two of her most famous roles—Mrs. Hardcastlein *She Stoops to Conquer* and Mrs. Malaprop in *The Rivals*—on the same day, when the Boston Museum celebrated her 50th anniversary on the stage with gala performances of both those plays.

Called "the dear old lady," Vincent was well known in Boston both for her acting and for her charitable works. She supplemented her income by letting rooms and renting out costumes and properties for amateur theatricals like Harvard's Hasty Pudding Club, but her generosity to individuals, charities, and animals in particular meant she was always impoverished. The actor E.A. Sothern, whom she had befriended as a young thespian, created a Christmas fund of $100, replenishing the fund whenever Vincent needed to draw on it for one of her causes.

On August 31, 1887, Mary Vincent appeared on stage for the last time, taking ill after a performance of *The Dominie's Daughter*. She died at home of an apoplectic stroke on September 4. The funeral was held at St. Paul's Episcopal Church, where she had been a dedicated member. After her death, money for the Vincent Memorial Hospital (dedicated 1891) was raised in her honor, with the help of Bishop Phillips Brooks of Trinity Church, and the Vincent Club was formed to raise funds for the hospital's support. She was buried in Mount Auburn Cemetery, Cambridge.

SOURCES:

James, Edward T., ed. *Notable American Women, 1607–1950*. Cambridge, MA: The Belknap Press of Harvard University, 1971.

Paula Morris, D.Phil.,
Brooklyn, New York

Vincent, Mother (1819–1892)

Irish-born Australian nun and educator. Name variations: Sister Mary Vincent; Ellen Whitty. Born Ellen Whitty on March 3, 1819, near Oilgate, County Wexford, Ireland; died on March 9, 1892, in Brisbane, Australia; daughter of William Whitty (a farmer) and Johanna (Murphy) Whitty; trained as a teacher.

Born one of six children in the farming family of William and **Johanna Murphy Whitty** in Ireland in 1819, Ellen Whitty trained as a teacher before joining a religious order of the Sisters of Mercy at the age of 19. *Catherine McAuley—one of the founders of an order begun in 1831 with the aims of both education and social work—became both friend and mentor to the young novitiate, known after 1840 as Sister Mary Vincent.

Outgoing and intelligent, she became novice mistress and bursar before her election in 1849 as Reverend Mother. Preoccupied with social work resulting from the great Irish famine of the 1840s, Mother Vincent prepared a number of her order to travel with emigrants in 1854 and was also involved in sending sisters to nurse the wounded during the Crimean War, an initiative backed by her brother, Father Robert Whitty, who was vicar-general to Cardinal Wiseman in Westminster. After the war ended, Mother Vincent continued the social work of her order by creating homes for neglected children and unmarried mothers.

In 1860, Mother Vincent was invited by Bishop James Quinn to become one of the first women religious in the newly formed diocese of Queensland, Australia. She arrived in Brisbane with five sisters in May 1861, despite a reluctance within her community to see her leave Ireland, which was overcome only by the direct command of Archbishop Cullen.

Mother Vincent had always found it easy to make and keep friends, but she was faced with several problems when she arrived in Queensland. She discovered that Australia tended towards centralized, secular school education, and, even worse, she found Bishop Quinn autocratic. Forced to accept his wish to choose teachers and texts, Mother Vincent found his interference in convent matters unbearable. The conflict between them resulted in her demotion in 1865. But in 1870, having sent her home to Ireland to recruit nuns, Quinn appointed her assistant to the Queensland head of the Order, an office she held for the rest of her life.

Their relationship remained problematic. Her desire to start a health-care center for Aborigines was vetoed by Bishop Quinn. However, by the time of her death in 1892, she had created 26 Mercy schools in Queensland, with 222 sisters and 7,000 pupils, as well as a Mercy Training College for teachers. She started All Hallow's, the state's first Catholic secondary school. Mother Vincent also introduced the types of social work she had pioneered in Dublin and encouraged regular home visitation, emphasizing the link between the different forms of social service. Despite the difficulties of her missionary work in Australia, in both education and social work, Mother Vincent left an important and lasting legacy.

SOURCES:
Radi, Heather, ed. *200 Australian Women: A Redress Anthology.* NSW, Australia: Women's Redress Press, 1988.

Paula Morris, D.Phil.,
Brooklyn, New York

Vining, Elizabeth Gray (1902–1999)

American tutor to the crown prince of Japan and author of many books for children and adults. Name variations: Elizabeth Janet Gray. Born on October 6, 1902, in Philadelphia, Pennsylvania; died on November 27, 1999, in Kennett Square, Pennsylvania; *daughter of John Gordon Gray (a businessman) and Anne Moore (Iszard) Gray; educated at Germantown Friends School; Bryn Mawr College, A.B., 1923; Drexel Institute School of Library Science, B.S., 1926; married Morgan Vining, on January 31, 1929 (died).*

Writing career began at age 17 when she contributed story to Young Churchman *(1919); wrote several books under name Elizabeth Janet Gray; won Newbery Medal for* Adam of the Road *(1943); was recipient of* Herald Tribune *Spring Festival award for book* Sandy *(1945); tutored Crown Prince Akihito of Japan (1946–50); wrote bestselling book,* Windows for the Crown Prince *(1952), about her experiences in Japan.*

Selected writings—all under Elizabeth Janet Gray unless otherwise noted: Meredith's Ann *(1929);* Tilly-Tod *(1929);* Meggy MacIntosh *(1930);* Tangle Garden *(1932);* Jane Hope *(1933);* Beppy Marlowe of Charles Town *(1936);* Young Walter Scott *(1938);* Penn *(1938);* Contributions of the Quakers *(1939);* The Fair Adventure *(1940);* Anthology with Comments *(1942);* Adam of the Road *(1942);* Sandy *(1945); (under Elizabeth Gray Vining)* Windows for the Crown Prince *(1952);* The World in Tune *(1954);* The Virginia Exiles *(1955);* Friend of Life: The Biography of Rufus M. Jones *(1958);* The Cheerful Heart *(1959);* Return to Japan *(1960);* I Will Adventure *(1962);* Take Heed of Loving Me *(1963);* Flora: A Biography *(1966);* I, Roberta *(1967); (under Elizabeth Gray Vining)* Quiet Pilgrimage *(autobiography, 1970); (under Elizabeth Gray Vining)* The Taken Girl *(1972); (under Elizabeth Gray Vining)* Being Seventy: The Measure of a Year *(1978).*

Born into an old Philadelphia Quaker family on October 6, 1902, Elizabeth Gray Vining received her early schooling at Germantown Friends School and graduated from Bryn Mawr College in 1923. She was the daughter of **Anne Izard Gray** and John Gordon Gray, a businessman who made surveying instruments used by Admiral Robert Peary at the North Pole and in the building of the Trans-Siberian railroad. Following her college graduation, Vining taught school and had several stories published in Sunday school magazines. In 1926, she obtained a degree in library science from Drexel University in Philadelphia, and went on to teach at the University of North Carolina at Chapel Hill, where she met Morgan Vining, the associate director of the university's extension division, whom she married on January 31, 1929. Her husband died in an automobile accident a few years later.

After writing several books under the name Elizabeth Janet Gray, she was named the recipient of the prestigious Newbery Medal for her children's book *Adam of the Road* (1943). She also won the *Herald Tribune* Spring Festival award for her book *Sandy* in 1945. In 1946, through her work with the American Friends Service Committee, Vining was suggested as a possible English tutor for Crown Prince Akihito of Japan. Her first reaction to the idea was one of disbelief and hesitancy, but in the end she decided to take the position if she were asked, though she would not lift a finger to get it. With the approval of the emperor of Japan, Vining was selected to tutor Akihito, and in 1946 she arrived at the imperial court intent on making some "small contribution to the cause of peace among nations." She also hoped that she might help improve the lowly position of women in Japan, not knowing that, abetted by *Beate Sirota, Japanese women had already been given the right to vote shortly before her arrival there. Her duties in Japan soon included teaching English to other members of the royal family as well as lecturing to various groups.

Vining's experiences in Japan led her to write two books, the bestselling *Windows for the Crown Prince* (1952) and *Return to Japan* (1960). In *Windows for the Crown Prince*, she gives a clear picture of the dedicated attempts of many Americans in Japan who, after World War II, attempted to build a new and democratic country. She also details the bewilderment the Japanese often experienced while trying to learn American democratic principles. Descriptions of Japanese customs, traditions and holidays are included, as well as detailed notes on school life, the royal family and the imperial court, the crown prince's first meeting with General Douglas MacArthur, and the Japanese reaction to the outbreak of war in Korea in 1950. Tutoring the crown prince from 1946 to 1950, Vining forged a strong friendship with him, one that was retained throughout her lifetime.

Vining wrote more than 60 books for children and adults, including biographies, contemporary fiction, historical novels and an autobiography. Her last, also autobiographical in nature, was *Being Seventy: The Measure of a Year* (1978), a daily journal of the changes, thoughts and wisdom Vining encountered during her 70th year. A return visit to Japan and reminiscences of her days teaching the crown prince are included.

Vining served as the vice-president of trustees of Bryn Mawr from 1951 to 1971 and held memberships in the Authors League and PEN (New York). She was awarded 14 honorary degrees, was the recipient of the *Constance

Elizabeth Gray Vining

Lindsay Skinner Award and the American Women's Eminent Achievement Award, and named Distinguished Daughter of Pennsylvania. The Japanese government presented her with the Third Order of the Sacred Crown, an award with eight possible degrees of merit. When it was explained to her that the first and second degrees of merit were reserved for princesses, she was asked whether she would mind the third. Vining replied, "*Mottai nai*" (It's too good).

Elizabeth Vining died on November 27, 1999, at Kendal-at-Longwoods, a retirement community in Kennett Square, Pennsylvania, at the age of 97.

SOURCES:

Commire, Anne, ed. "Elizabeth Janet Gray," in *Something about the Author*. Vol. 6. Detroit, MI: Gale Research, 1974.

"Elizabeth Vining," in *The Economist*. December 11, 1999.

Obituary in *The Day* [New London, CT]. December 1, 1999.

Jo Anne Meginnes,
freelance writer,
Brookfield, Vermont

Vinson-Owen, Maribel (1911–1961).

See Owen, Marible Vinson.

Vintimille, Pauline Félicité, Marquise de (1712–1741).

See Pompadour, Jeanne-Antoinette for sidebar.

Violante.

Variant of Violet, Yolanda or Yolande.

Violante of Bavaria (d. 1731).

See Medici, Violante Beatrice.

Violante of Hungary (1215–1251).

See Iolande of Hungary.

Violante of Montferrat (fl. 1300).

See Irene of Montferrat.

Violante Visconti (c. 1353–1386).

See Visconti, Violet.

Violette, La (1724–1822).

See Veigel, Eva-Maria.

Violetti, Eva Maria (1724–1822).

See Veigel, Eva-Maria.

Violet Visconti of Milan (c. 1353–1386).

See Visconti, Violet.

Vionnet, Madeleine (1876–1975)

French fashion designer. Born in 1876 in Chileurs aux Boix, near Paris, France; died in 1975; daughter of a plumber and a café owner.

Worked in ateliers of Kate Reilly, Callot Soeurs, and Jacques Doucet; began own fashion house (1912); pioneered bias-cut clothing; awarded Chevalier of the Legion of Honor (1929).

Born in 1876 in Chileurs aux Boix, near Paris, to a plumber and a café proprietor, Madeleine Vionnet was apprenticed to a dressmaker at the age of 14. She moved to London in 1896 in order to work for the dressmaker **Kate Reilly**. On her return to Paris around 1900, she worked for Callot Soeurs and then, after 1907, for Jacques Doucet. Vionnet opened her own fashion house in 1912, although she was forced to close it during World War I. She reopened in 1918, but had to shut down business permanently in 1940 after the German invasion of Paris.

From 1919 on, Vionnet was a dominant influence in women's fashion. That year she designed the first of her tubular dresses which slipped over the head, developing the revolutionary bias-cut dresses that were to become her trademark. Vionnet, who claimed to be responsible for models discarding their corsets, pioneered the use of flowing fabrics like crepe and silk and popularized "handkerchief point" skirts. One of her unusual practices was eschewing sketches in favor of draping designs on specially made quarter-sized wooden mannequins, after which full-sized patterns were made. Vionnet's customers, who included many rich and prominent personalities, admired her subtle color sense as well as her flair for cut; she preferred a pale palette and was fond of geometric designs that worked with the three-dimensional figure of the owner.

Vionnet's progressive attitudes were not confined to fashion. As an employer, she provided social services and facilities for her staff, such as clinics and gymnasiums. She was appointed Chevalier of the Legion of Honor in 1929.

Paula Morris, D.Phil.,
Brooklyn, New York

Vipsania Agrippina (?–20 CE)

*Roman matron. Died in 20 CE; daughter of Marcus Vipsanius Agrippa and his first wife *Pomponia; half-sister of *Agrippina the Elder; married (future emperor) Tiberius (divorced 11 BCE); married Asinius Gallus; children: (first marriage) Drusus the Younger.*

In the year 14 CE, Caesar Augustus forced Tiberius to divorce Vipsania Agrippina, the mother of his child, and marry the emperor's own recently widowed daughter *Julia (39 BCE–14 CE). In love with Vipsania, Tiberius was very unhappy with his marriage to Julia, who had a scandalous reputation. Wrote Suetonius: "One day, [Tiberius] accidently caught sight of Vipsania and followed her with tears in his eyes and intense unhappiness written on his face." Henceforth, safeguards were taken to ensure that he would never see her again.

Virdimura of Sicily (fl. 1376)

Jewish physician of Sicily. Flourished in 1376 in Sicily; married Pasquale of Catania (a doctor).

Virdimura was a Jewish woman who worked as a physician in Sicily. Her husband and tutor was another doctor, Pasquale of Catania, a university-trained surgeon who taught his highly intelligent wife the art of surgery and herbal medicine. At the time, most women were forbidden to practice medicine, although in Italy the rules were more lax than in other regions. Virdimura, eager to build a lawful practice and win recognition for her healing abilities, petitioned the court for the right to treat patients as a professional.

As part of the hearing process, she brought in patients who attested to her great knowledge and skill, as well as other physicians who verified her learning and supported her petition. Virdimura also had to take several exams to determine the extent of her knowledge, which she passed easily. Thus in 1376, she was fortunate enough to have the Sicilian royal court grant her a license to practice medicine throughout the state. She chose not to work among the wealthy nobles who could afford to pay her well, but instead healed the poor of Sicily, often for free or for a very reduced fee.

SOURCES:
Echols, Anne, and Marty Williams. *An Annotated Index of Medieval Women.* NY: Markus Wiener, 1992.

Laura York, M.A. in History,
University of California,
Riverside, California

Virgilia.

See Volumnia in joint entry under Veturia and Volumnia.

Virgin Mary (20 BCE–40 CE).

See Mary the Virgin.

Virgin Queen, The (1533–1603).

See Elizabeth I.

Visconti, Agnes (c. 1365–1391)

*Italian noblewoman. Name variations: Agnese; Agnesina; Agnes Gonzaga. Born around 1365 in Milan; beheaded in February 1391 in Mantua (some sources cite 1395); daughter of Bernabo Visconti, lord of Milan (r. 1354–1385), and Beatrice della Scala (1340–1384); sister of Catherine Visconti (c. 1360–1404) and *Virida Visconti (c. 1354–1414); married Francesco Gonzaga (1366–1407), 4th captain general of Mantua (r. 1382–1407) and lord of Mantua (r. 1388–1407), in 1381; children: daughter Alda Visconti (b. 1391).*

Agnes Visconti was born into the ruling family of Milan, one of 15 children of Bernabo Visconti and *Beatrice della Scala. In 1381, her parents arranged a marriage for her with Francesco Gonzaga, heir to Ludovico, ruler of the city-state of Mantua and a powerful player in Italian politics. Agnes' dowry of 50,000 gold florins demonstrates her family's wealth, as well as their desire to secure a political alliance with the Gonzaga. The wedding, symbolic of a new friendship between Milan and Mantua, was celebrated in August in Milan. Both Agnes and her new husband were about 15 years old. Ten years later, their only child, Alda, was born.

In the late 1380s, Agnes was caught up in the Visconti family's political struggles. In 1385, her father Bernabo was overthrown by her cousin Gian Galeazzo Visconti. Francesco Gonzaga quickly forgot about his alliance with Bernabo, who soon died in prison, and sought an alliance with Gian Galeazzo instead. Agnes despised Gian Galeazzo for deposing her father and causing his death, and deeply resented Francesco's alliance with her hated cousin. After Francesco became lord of Mantua in 1388, he made several treaties with Gian Galeazzo, helping him maintain control of Milan against Agnes' dispossessed brothers. Agnes' resentment of her husband's ally and her open rejoicing at his defeats put Francesco in an awkward diplomatic position. Her hostility also led her to break off relations with Gian Galeazzo's wife, her sister *Catherine Visconti, who seems to have supported his actions as a wife was expected to do.

Agnes' refusal to put the Gonzagas' interests before her own, coupled with her failure to bear sons to secure the succession, led her into a precarious position at the Mantuan court. It is perhaps unsurprising that by 1390 scandals involving Agnes were spreading there. It was rumored that she was plotting with her brothers against Gian Galeazzo and his allies. Late in 1390, Gian Galeazzo himself contributed to these rumors. He told Francesco that he had evidence that Agnes was conspiring to kill her husband. Apparently inclined to believe the story, Francesco had Agnes, along with several of her retinue, arrested and confined to her apartments in January 1391. She was charged not with conspiracy, however, but with adultery. A young courtier, Vicenzo da Scandiano, was arrested and under torture confessed to an affair with Agnes. Given the hostile political climate of the Gonzaga court towards Agnes and Gian Galeazzo's role in her arrest, however, Agnes' guilt is at the very least questionable.

In February, Agnes and Vicenzo were found guilty of adultery and sentenced to death. Agnes was beheaded on February 7, while her supposed lover was strangled in prison. Francesco Gonzaga's real motivations and involvement in Agnes' downfall are difficult to ascertain. There is little evidence that he had any affection for his wife during their marriage, and he had responded quickly to Gian Galeazzo's accusations against Agnes. Further, he married Margherita Malatesta (*Margherita Gonzaga) within a few months of Agnes' execution. Yet some witnesses reported that he was overcome with grief after the execution and locked himself in his room for days. He did turn against Gian Galeazzo Visconti soon after, suggesting that he now believed Gian Galeazzo had used him in a plot against Agnes. In 1397, Francesco sent an army to attack Milan, giving as his reason the unavenged death of Agnes. Whether this was an honest motivation or simply a pretext for war remains unclear.

SOURCES:

de Mesquita, D.M. Bueno. *Giangaleazzo Visconti, Duke of Milan.* Cambridge: Cambridge University Press, 1941.

Muir, Dorothy. *A History of Milan Under the Visconti.* London: Methuen, 1924.

> **Laura York**, M.A. in History,
> University of California,
> Riverside, California

Visconti, Beatrice (d. 1334).

See Este, Beatrice d'.

Visconti, Bianca Maria (1423–1470)

Duchess of Milan. Name variations: Bianca Maria Sforza; Blanca Maria. Born in 1423 in Milan, Italy; died in 1470 (some sources cite 1468) in Milan; daughter of Duke Filippo Maria Visconti (r. 1402–1447) and his mistress Agnes del Maino; married Francesco Sforza (1401–1466), 4th duke of Milan (r. 1450–1466), in 1441; grandmother of *Caterina Sforza (c. 1462–1509); children: Galeazzo Maria Sforza (1444–1476), 5th duke of Milan (r. 1466–1476); Ascanio (1445–1505, a cardinal); *Ippolita (1446–1484, who married Alphonso II, king of Naples); Sforza Maria (1449–1479), duke of Bari; Lodovico il Moro Sforza (1451–1508, who married *Beatrice d'Este [1427–1497]); Ottaviano. Francesco had two illegitimate children: Sforza "Secondo" (1433–1501), count of Borgonovo, and Tristano (d. 1477, who married *Beatrice d'Este da Correggio [1427–1497]).

Bianca Maria Visconti

Bianca Maria Visconti was the only child of the duke of Milan, Filippo Maria Visconti, and his mistress **Agnes del Maino**. When she was about nine years old, Filippo betrothed her to his ally, the Italian noble Francesco Sforza, whom she married in 1441. Bianca had six children with Francesco. On Duke Filippo's death in 1447, he named Alphonso II of Aragon, king of Naples, as his heir to Milan; Bianca and Francesco, who believed that Bianca should succeed as Filippo's only child, went to war with Alphonso for the right of succession. The battle eventually involved many other Italian city-states which had a vested interest in who controlled the powerful and prosperous Milanese duchy. Three years later, Francesco and Bianca emerged victorious, and co-ruled Milan until Francesco's death in 1466. Bianca then continued to rule with her eldest son, Galeazzo Maria, before retiring; she was also responsible for the upbringing of *Caterina Sforza, Galeazzo's illegitimate daughter, who would become a powerful force in Italian politics. Bianca Maria Visconti was known for her generous patronage of artists and charitable contributions to religious establishments. She was adored by the people as a champion of the oppressed, and was also known as a peacemaker. She died in 1470 at age 46.

SOURCES:

Echols, Anne, and Marty Williams. *An Annotated Index of Medieval Women.* NY: Markus Wiener, 1992.

Jackson, Guida. *Women Who Ruled.* Santa Barbara, CA: ABC-Clio, 1985.

> **Laura York**, M.A. in History,
> University of California,
> Riverside, California

Visconti, Caterina (c. 1360–1404).

See Visconti, Catherine.

Visconti, Catherine (c. 1360–1404)

*Duchess and regent of Milan. Name variations: Caterina Visconti; Caterina di Bernabo Visconti. Born around 1360 in Milan; died in October 1404 in Monza, Italy; daughter of Barnabas, Barnabo or Bernabo Visconti, lord of Milan (r. 1354–1385), and Beatrice della Scala (1340–1384); sister of *Virida Visconti (c. 1354–1414) and *Agnes Visconti (c. 1365–1391); married her cousin Giangaleazzo or Gian Galeazzo Visconti, later 1st duke of Milan (r. 1396–1402), in November 1380; children: Gian Maria Visconti (1388 or 1389–1412), duke of Milan (r. 1402–1412); Filippo Maria Visconti (1392–1447), duke of Milan (r. 1402–1447). Gian Galeazzo was first married to Isabelle of France (1349–1372), daughter of John II, king of France, and *Bona of Bohemia. He also had many illegitimate children, including son Gabriele Maria Visconti with Agnese Mantegazza and possibly two other sons with a woman named Lusotta.*

Catherine Visconti was the third daughter born to Bernabo Visconti and *Beatrice della Scala, rulers of Lombardy in northern Italy. She grew up in a large household in the fortress of Milan, being a middle child of 15. Like those of most of her siblings, Catherine's marriage was arranged when she was a child by her parents for their political benefit. In Catherine's case, the husband chosen for her was Gian Galeazzo Visconti, count of Pavia, her first cousin and her father's political rival. He was 30 years old and already a widower when his marriage to 20-year-old Catherine was celebrated in November 1380. It was well known that Gian Galeazzo coveted Bernabo's position as lord of Milan; Bernabo in turn wanted to add Gian Galeazzo's lands to his own. He coerced Gian Galeazzo into the marriage alliance, seeking to use his daughter Catherine as a sort of spy on Gian Galeazzo's movements. But as it turned out, Catherine was much more of an asset to her husband than to her father.

Far from resenting the wife imposed on him by his uncle, Gian Galeazzo came to trust her judgment and loyalty, and to appreciate Catherine's intelligence and political skills. Nor did his marriage prevent Gian Galeazzo from continuing to plot means of overthrowing his father-in-law, now with Catherine's assistance. She was a consistent aid to him in his constant attempts to conquer neighboring Italian city-states. Unlike many aristocratic women, Catherine advised her husband on policy issues and was given some authority in his administration, responsible for appointing state officials. She also fulfilled the responsibilities more common to aristocratic women, presiding over the court of Pavia and patronizing artists and writers.

In 1384, Catherine's mother Beatrice died. As her mother's heir, Catherine had a legitimate claim to rule the city of Verona. After a protracted struggle, the Veronese finally accepted Catherine as their rightful ruler, adding to the couple's growing power. The next year Gian Galeazzo finally realized his long-held dream of overthrowing Bernabo Visconti. He captured the elderly ruler and declared himself lord of Milan and ruler of Lombardy. The Milanese accepted Gian Galeazzo's rule with little resistance; Catherine's father died in prison a few months later.

Catherine had her first child, Giovanni Maria, in 1388. Her second son, Filippo Maria, was born four years later. Catherine also acted as a foster mother for her numerous young brothers and sisters, whom she had brought to Pavia after her mother's death. Gian Galeazzo was remarkably different in his personal life than most Italian aristocrats. He was close to his children (he had four with his first wife *Isabelle of France [1349–1372]) and preferred to remain with his wife and family in Pavia rather than accompany his troops into battle. In fact, he and Catherine lived so secluded a life but experienced such an increase in political power that it was commonly believed he practiced black magic in secret. This suspicion was only heightened in 1395 when the Holy Roman emperor created Milan as a duchy and named Gian Galeazzo the first duke of Milan.

In 1402, Gian Galeazzo died after a brief illness. He had named Catherine to be regent for their ten-year-old son Giovanni Maria, who became the second duke of Milan. Catherine and her advisors attempted to keep the news of Gian Galeazzo's death a secret, fearing that Milan's many enemies would attack the city-state when they found out its lord was only a young boy. This is, in fact, exactly what happened. Catherine and her sons spent most of the next two years besieged in their fortress in Milan, attempting to fight off one invading army after another. Their short-lived success is attributed to conflicts between Milan's enemies, each of whom wanted to conquer Milan for himself.

As regent, Catherine negotiated with various noble families, seeking assistance, but in the end she could not build enough alliances to save the Milanese state for her son; Milan simply had too many enemies. In 1404, Giovanni Maria turned against his mother and took the reins of government himself. Only 16 years old, he was an incompetent and inexperienced leader, and hastened Milan's fall. Catherine fled Milan but her son had her captured and imprisoned at Monza to prevent her from exercising her influence. She died at Monza only a few months later, in November 1404. It was commonly believed that she had been murdered on her son's orders. Fearing a popular reaction against him, Giovanni had the castellan of Monza executed on charges of murdering the duchess. This satisfied few of the Milanese, who remembered the reign of Gian Galeazzo and Catherine as a time of prosperity, pride, and peace for Lombardy.

SOURCES:
de Mesquita, D.M. Bueno. *Giangaleazzo Visconti, Duke of Milan.* Cambridge: Cambridge University Press, 1941.
Muir, Dorothy. *A History of Milan Under the Visconti.* London: Methuen, 1924.

Laura York, M.A. in History,
University of California,
Riverside, California

Visconti, Elizabeth (d. 1432)

*Duchess of Bavaria. Name variations: Elisabetta Visconti. Died in 1432; daughter of Bernabo Visconti, lord of Milan (r. 1354–1385), and *Beatrice della Scala (1340–1384); married Ernst or Ernest (1373–1438), duke of Bavaria (r. 1397–1438); children: Albert III the Pious (b. 1401, sometimes referred to as Albert II), duke of Bavaria (r. 1438–1460).*

Visconti, Regina (1340–1384).

See della Scala, Beatrice.

Visconti, Thaddaea (d. 1381)

*Duchess of Bavaria. Name variations: Taddea; Thaddia. Died on September 28, 1381; daughter of Bernabo Visconti, lord of Milan (r. 1354–1385), and *Beatrice della Scala (1340–1384); married Stephen III the Magnificent, duke of Bavaria (r. 1375–1413), on October 13, 1364; children: *Isabeau of Bavaria (1371–1435); Louis VII the Bearded (1365–1447), duke of Bavaria (r. 1413–1443, deposed). Stephen III married Elizabeth of Cleves (daughter of Adolf III, count of Cleves) on January 16, 1401.*

Visconti, Valentina (1366–1408)

*Duchess of Orléans. Name variations: Valentina of Milan; Valentine Visconti; Valentine of Milan. Born in 1366 in Milan; died in 1408 in France; daughter of John Galeas Visconti also known as Gian Galeazzo Visconti, lord of Milan (r. 1378–1402), duke of Milan (r. 1396–1402), and Isabelle of France (1349–1372); married Louis (1372–1407), duke of Orléans, in 1388 (died 1407); children: Charles (1391–1465), duke of Orléans; Jean or John (b. 1404), count of Angoulême; Philippe, count of Vertus; *Marguerite of Orleans (d. 1466).*

Valentina Visconti was born in 1366 in Milan, the daughter of Princess *Isabelle of France and the Milanese duke Gian Galeazzo Visconti. Raised in the best tradition of the Italian nobility, she was highly literate, and read and spoke Latin, French, and German fluently. She collected books and manuscripts throughout her life, and was in addition an accomplished harpist. In 1388, she married Louis, duke of Orléans (brother of French king Charles VI), by proxy. She could not move to France to join him, however, until two years later, when her father had finally gathered the 500,000 gold francs that served as her dowry.

Once in France, Valentina developed a great rivalry with the French queen *Isabeau of Bavaria (1371–1435); Valentina's station as the wife of the popular and powerful Louis, who often acted as regent of the country, put her in an influential position almost similar to Isabeau's. Moreover, Valentina was a popular duchess, respected as a kind and beautiful woman, while Isabeau made enemies all her life and was perhaps France's most despised queen. They vied to create the most opulent court and to have the most beautiful, richest wardrobes—superficial rivalries, to be sure, but ones which disguised the political rivalries each faced in the other. These conflicts intensified when Duke Louis began an affair with Queen Isabeau, and when subsequently the insane King Charles VI showed Valentina so much kindness that rumors of an affair between them were widely believed.

Queen Isabeau fueled most of the rumors against Valentina herself, and even accused her of witchcraft. Louis did little to protect his wife, but had her moved away from Paris, ostensibly for her own safety. Louis was assassinated in 1407, and for the next year, until she herself died, Valentina Visconti tried to re-establish herself in Paris with some success, based on her previous good reputation and popularity.

SOURCES:
*Tuchman, Barbara. *A Distant Mirror: The Calamitous Fourteenth Century.* NY: Ballantine, 1978.

Laura York, M.A. in History,
University of California,
Riverside, California

Visconti, Violante (c. 1353–1386).

See Visconti, Violet.

Visconti, Violet (c. 1353–1386)

Duchess of Clarence. Name variations: Violante. Born around 1353; died in November 1386 (some sources cite 1404); daughter of Galeazzo II, lord of Milan (r. 1354–1378), and *Blanche of Savoy (c. 1337–?); became second wife of Lionel of Antwerp (1338–1368), duke of Clarence, on May 28, 1368 (died); married Marquis of Montferrat (died); married Louis also known as Ludovico Visconti (son of Bernabo Visconti), in 1380. Lionel of Antwerp's first wife was *Elizabeth de Burgh (c. 1332–1363).

Visconti, Virida (c. 1354–1414)

Archduchess of Austria. Name variations: Verde Visconti; Virda Visconti; Viridis Visconti. Born around 1354 (some sources cite 1350 and 1351) in Milan, Italy; died in 1414 in Sittich, Karnten; daughter of Bernabo Visconti, lord of Milan (r. 1354–1385), and Beatrice della Scala (1340–1384); sister of *Catherine Visconti (c. 1360–1404), and *Agnes Visconti; married Leopold of Habsburg also known as Leopold III (1351–1386), archduke of Austria, Styria, and Carniola, co-emperor of Austria (r. 1365–1379), on February 23, 1365; children: Friedrich IV (b. 1368); William (b. 1369, who married *Joanna II of Naples); Margarethe (1370–c. 1400), margravine of Moravia; Leopold IV (1371–1411); Archduke Ernst or Ernest the Iron (1377–1424, who married *Cimburca of Masovia); Elisabeth (b. 1378); Katharine (b. 1380); Friedrich or Frederick IV (1382–1439), duke of Austria-Tyrol.

Born around 1354 into the ruling family of Milan, Virida Visconti was one of seven children of Bernabo Visconti and ***Beatrice della Scala**. She became duchess of Austria on her marriage about age 14 to the Austrian prince Leopold von Habsburg (later Leopold III), also 14. He was duke and co-ruler of Austria with his brothers until 1379, when he gave up his claim to Austria proper and became duke of Styria and Tyrol. The couple made their court at Bruck-am-der-Mur, in the province of Steiermark, Austria. Duchess Virida had seven children between 1368 and 1380. After Leopold's death in 1386 while fighting the Swiss army at the battle of Sempach, her children became the wards of Leopold's brother Albert III. Virida, still young, retired from court but remained in Austria the rest of her long life. She outlived all but two of her children, dying at age 63, and was buried at Sittich, Karnten, Austria.

SOURCES:

Muir, Dorothy. *A History of Milan under the Visconti.* London: Methuen, 1924.

Wheatcroft, Andrew. *The Habsburgs: Embodying Empire.* NY: Viking, 1995.

Laura York, M.A. in History,
University of California,
Riverside, California

Viseu, duchess of.

See Beatrice of Beja (1430–1506).

Vishnevskaya, Galina (1926—)

Russian soprano who, with her husband, lost her Soviet citizenship for supporting dissidents. Name variations: Vishnevskaiia. Born Galina Pavlovna Vishnevskaya in Leningrad (now St. Petersburg), USSR, on October 25, 1926; married Mstislav Rostropovich (the cellist and conductor), in 1955.

Galina Vishnevskaya's career was divided between the United States and the former Soviet Union, although not by choice. Trained in Leningrad (St. Petersburg) by **Vera Garina**, Vishnevskaya joined the Bolshoi Theater's operatic

*Galina
Vishnevskaya*

staff in Moscow in 1952. Three years later, she married Mstislav Rostropovich, the cellist and conductor, with whom she frequently appeared in concert. In 1961, Vishnevskaya appeared with the Metropolitan Opera in New York. Despite the fact that she and her husband were stars in the USSR, both had repeated political clashes with the Communist government. When they took Aleksander Solzhenitsyn, the dissident writer, into their home, it was a bold challenge to the Soviet regime. In 1974, they decided to emigrate to the West, settling in Washington, D.C., where Rostropovich was appointed musical director of the National Symphony Orchestra in 1977. The couple were stripped of their citizenship in 1978. Vishnevskaya published her biography, *Galina: A Russian Story*, in 1984. In 1990, her citizenship was restored. Vishnevskaya's voice was warm and her style passionate. One of the high points of her career was her performance of Benjamin Britten's moving *War Requiem* with Peter Pears and Dietrich Fischer-Dieskau, conducted by the composer. When released on record, this was considered by many critics to be one of the great recordings of the century.

SOURCES:
Sadie, Stanley, ed. *New Grove Dictionary of Music and Musicians*. 20 vols. NY: Macmillan, 1980.

John Haag,
Athens, Georgia

Vitti, Monica (1931—)

Italian actress and director. Born Maria Luisa Ceciarelli on November 3, 1931, in Rome, Italy; trained at National Academy of Dramatic Art, graduated 1953.

Selected filmography: Ridere, Ridere, Ridere *(Laugh, Laugh, Laugh, 1955);* L'avventura *(The Adventure, 1960);* La Notte *(The Night, 1961);* L'eclisse *(The Eclipse, 1962);* Chateau en Suede *(Nutty, Naughty Chateau, 1963);* Il deserto rosso *(Red Desert, 1964);* Modesty Blaise *(1966);* La ragazza con la pistola *(The Girl with the Pistol, 1969);* Dramma dela gelosia *(The Pizza Triangle, 1970);* La pacifista *(The Pacifist, 1971);* A mezzanotte va la ronda del piacere *(Guilty Pleasures, 1975);* An Almost Perfect Affair *(1979); (and author)* The Flirt *(1983); (and author)* Francesca e mia *(1986); (and director and co-author)* Scandalo Segreto *(Secret Scandal, 1989);* Wind over the City *(1996).*

Monica Vitti is the stage name of Maria Luisa Ceciarelli, an actress born in Rome in 1931. Vitti appeared in a number of amateur plays from the age of 15 and went on to study at the National Academy of Dramatic Art, graduating in 1953. After her stage debut that same year in Machiavelli's *La mandragora*, Vitti made her name in both classical roles and in comedy and revue. In 1955, after she began appearing on television, she was awarded the Noce d'oro as the most promising actress in Rome. Vitti joined director Michelangelo Antonioni's theater group in the mid-1950s and appeared as Sally Bowles in his 1957 version of *I am a Camera.*

Vitti's reputation results chiefly from the numerous films she made in a movie career that began in 1955 with Edoarto Anton's *Ridere, Ridere, Ridere* (Laugh, Laugh, Laugh). Described as the perfect Antonioni heroine because of her ability to be intense, cool, and expressive, she is particularly known for her leading roles in his films *L'avventura* (1960), *La Notte* (The Night, 1961, with Marcello Mastroianni and *Jeanne Moreau), *L'eclisse* (The Eclipse, 1962, with Alain Delon), and *Il deserto rosso* (Red Desert, 1964). She worked mainly in Italy, where she became extremely famous, known for both her blonde beauty and for her comedy performances. She also appeared in Roger Vadim's *Chateau en Suede* (Nutty, Naughty Chateau) in 1963, Joseph Losey's *Modesty Blaise* with Dirk Bogarde in 1966, and Miklós Janscó's *La pacifista* in 1971. Vitti continued appearing in films throughout the 1970s and 1980s, writing the scripts for *Flirt* in 1983 and *Francesca e mia* in 1986; she also directed and co-wrote her own film, *Scandalo Segreto* (Secret Scandal), in 1989.

Paula Morris, D.Phil.,
Brooklyn, New York

Vittoria della Rovere (d. 1694).

See Medici, Vittoria de.

Vivanti, Annie (1868–1942)

Italian poet and novelist. Born in 1868 in London, England; died in 1942 in Turin, Italy; daughter of an Italian father and Anna Lindau (a German writer); trained as a teacher of singing and languages; mentored by Italian poet Giosuè Carducci; married John Chartres (a lawyer), in 1908; children: one daughter.

Selected writings: (poetry) Lirica *(Lyric, 1890);* Marion, artista da caffè concerto *(Marion, Café Entertainer, 1891);* The Devourers *(1910); (play)* L'invasore *(The Invader, 1917);* Zingaresca *(Gypsy Love, 1918);* Naja Tripudians *(1921); (short stories)* Perdonate Eglantina! *(Forgive, Eglantina!, 1926); (travel)* Terra di Cleopatra *(Cleopatra's Land, 1925).*

Annie Vivanti was born in 1868 in London to an Italian father and a German mother, the writer **Anna Lindau**. While her first ambition was to become an actress, she trained as a teacher of singing and languages, although she did not pursue a teaching career. Instead she followed in her mother's footsteps by becoming a writer.

In 1908, Vivanti married Irish lawyer and patriot John Chartres, and they spent some time in the United States, his adopted home. Prior to her marriage, Vivanti had lived in Italy, where she had become intimate with Giosuè Carducci (1835–1907), the dean of Italian poets. Carducci sponsored both her first book of poetry, *Lirica* (Lyric, 1890) and her novel *Marion, artista da caffè concerto* (Marion, Café Entertainer, 1891); her own influence can be detected in his late poetry. Despite Carducci's endorsement, critical response to both of these early works was dismissive.

In 1910, she published a novel in English, *The Devourers* (issued in Italian in 1911 as *I divoratori*), then followed it with over 20 books, including novels, short stories, plays, and travelogues. Like her first novel, many of Vivanti's longer works of fiction were largely autobiographical and preoccupied with the dilemmas facing the woman artist; *The Devourers*, for example, explored the way children can destroy the lives of their mothers.

Despite this prolific output, Vivanti's reputation had declined by the Second World War. The last few years of her life were spent entirely alone, after her daughter's death in an aerial bombardment early in the war. Vivanti died in Turin in 1942.

SOURCES:
Buck, Claire, ed. *The Bloomsbury Guide to Women's Literature.* NY: Prentice Hall, 1992.
Columbia Dictionary of Modern European Literature. 2nd ed. NY: Columbia University Press, 1980.

Paula Morris, D.Phil.,
Brooklyn, New York

Vivian.

See Bibiana (d. 363).

Vivien, Renée (1877–1909).

See Barney, Natalie Clifford for sidebar.

Vivonne de Savelli, Catherine de
(1588–1665).

See Salonnières for sidebar on Marquise de Rambouillet.

Vjera.

Variant of Vera.

Vlachos, Helen (1911–1995)

Greek publisher and legislator. Name variations: Eleni Vlachos. Born on December 18, 1911, in Athens, Greece; died on October 14, 1995, in Athens; daughter of George Vlachou (a newspaper publisher); educated abroad; married Costas Loundras.

Began career as reporter (1935); published newspapers, including influential daily Kathimerini (1951–87); closed her three newspapers after military takeover (1967); escaped to London while under house arrest (1967); published autobiography The House Arrest (1970); returned to Greece and elected to Parliament (1974).

Helen Vlachos was born Eleni Vlachou in Athens in 1911, the daughter of newspaper owner George Vlachou. After receiving her education abroad, Vlachos returned to Athens to work for her father, first as a bookkeeper and, from 1935, as a reporter. During her journalistic career, she covered everything from Greek earthquakes to Mussolini in Libya and events in the Far East. From her father, who ran the respected daily paper *Kathimerini*, Vlachos learned the power and effects of political opposition through

Helen Vlachos

the pages of a newspaper; he was jailed by more than one Greek government, and one of his newspapers was taken over by the Nazis in 1941 after he refused them cooperation.

In the late 1940s, Vlachos began writing a witty political column in *Kathimerini*, in which she regularly criticized the government. Her popularity and fame as a journalist increased, and in 1951 she assumed control of *Kathimerini*, as well as *Messimvrini*, another daily newspaper, and the weekly picture magazine *Eikones*. In a dramatic move that garnered international attention, Vlachos closed all three publications in 1967 when a group of army colonels seized power, instituting censorship and mandating pro-government daily reports. The military dictators had expected her support because of Vlachos' outspoken anti-Communism, but she refused to serve as a conduit for the regime's propaganda. Vlachos not only closed her high-circulation dailies but told an Italian newspaper, "They can't tell me how to run newspapers any more than I can tell them how to run their tanks." She was placed under house arrest and charged with "insulting authorities."

During her arrest, despite the very real threat of imprisonment, Vlachos made light of the situation in her typically witty and irreverent manner, asking prison officials to note that her favorite dish was meatballs. Later in 1967, she made a daring escape to London, with her hair dyed black and carrying a fake passport. During the escape, Vlachos hid in a cramped bordello while her husband Costas Loundras walked around their Athens apartment in high-heeled shoes, fooling the guards stationed below into thinking that she was still at home.

In London, Vlachos led the public campaign against the junta and published a book about her career and escape, *The House Arrest* (1970). She returned home after the junta fell in 1974, reopened her newspapers, and was elected to Parliament as a member of the conservative New Democracy Party. Vlachos remained the publisher of *Kathimerini* until 1987, when she sold her media holdings. A legend in Greek journalism, she died in Athens in 1995, age 85.

SOURCES:

Steinhauer, Jennifer. "Helen Vlachos," in *The New York Times News Service*. October 16, 1995.
Time. October 30, 1995.

Paula Morris, D.Phil.,
Brooklyn, New York

Vladimir, grand duchess (1854–1920).

See Maria of Mecklenburg-Schwerin.

Vlasek, June (b. 1915).

See Lang, June.

Voegtlin, Marie (1845–1916).

See Vögtlin, Marie.

Vogel, Dorothy (1935—)

American art collector. Born Dorothy Hoffman on May 14, 1935, in Elmira, New York; studied at University of Buffalo, 1953–55; Syracuse University, B.A., 1957; University of Denver, M.A. in library studies, 1958; married Herbert Vogel (a postal worker), in 1962.

Dorothy Vogel was born in 1935 and raised in Elmira, New York, the daughter of a stationery store owner. She began her studies at the University of Buffalo in 1953, graduating from Syracuse University with a B.A. in English literature and library studies in 1957. After completing an M.A. at the University of Denver the following year, she moved to New York City to work at the Brooklyn Public Library.

In 1962, she married postal clerk Herb Vogel, a New York City native who had cultivated his love for art at New York University, where he took classes in painting and art history, and at the Cedar Tavern, an artists' hangout in Greenwich Village. Herb introduced Dorothy to the world of art, encouraging her to take a drawing class and going with her to museums and galleries. "We learned about art by studying everything that was going on," she said. "We read catalogs. We went to lectures and all the shows and, significantly, the studios of artists." Although they were by no means wealthy, the young enthusiasts began making shy appearances, and occasional purchases, at New York galleries. In 1965 they made their first important art purchase, buying one of the earliest works that Sol LeWitt—a founding member of the minimal school—ever sold. Using Dorothy's salary as a librarian for their modest living expenses, the couple reserved Herb's earnings for art. A life of art collecting had begun.

Rather than buying fashionable Pop art or the bold Abstract Expressionism of artists like Jackson Pollock and Willem de Kooning, the Vogels concentrated on minimalism and conceptualism, eventually amassing a collection of more than 2,000 paintings, drawings, and sculptures, all housed in their one-bedroom apartment in New York. Their home was famous for being full of pets and art, with little room for furniture. "A joke went round that I kept art in the oven," said Vogel, who relied on her librarian's training to keep track of all the pieces stored in crates and closets.

Never members of high society, museum boards, or patrons' circles, the Vogels bought pieces as they could afford them and came to be highly respected by artists for not viewing art as a commodity. Sol LeWitt once characterized them as "idealistic and supportive" and "a breath of fresh air" in an art world increasingly compromised by greed and pretension. They collected a large number of works by LeWitt and Richard Tuttle; more than 200 artists are represented in their collection.

By the 1980s the Vogels were known and respected in the art world, and their collection was much in demand for exhibitions. Quiet and unassuming amid the wealthy and fashionable of the art world—now eager for their opinions—the couple continued to spend their Saturdays visiting galleries by subway, sometimes seeing as many as 25 shows in one day. In 1992 Dorothy and Herb Vogel bequeathed their collection to the National Gallery of Art in Washington, D.C.—a museum they first visited 30 years earlier on their honeymoon—which they chose because it has never sold a painting.

SOURCES:

Ash, Lee, ed. *Biographical Directory of Librarians.* Chicago, IL: American Library Association, 1970.

Gardner, Paul. "An extraordinary gift of art from ordinary people," in *Smithsonian.* October 1992.

Paula Morris, D.Phil., Brooklyn, New York

Vogelstein, Julie (1883–1971).

See Braun-Vogelstein, Julie.

Vögtlin, Marie (1845–1916)

Swiss medical pioneer, the first woman in Switzerland to earn a medical degree, who established a successful career as a gynecologist and served as director of the pediatric division of Zurich's Swiss Nurses' School. Name variations: Marie Heim-Vögtlin; Marie Vogtlin or Marie Voegtlin. Born in Bözen, Canton Aargau, Switzerland, on October 7, 1845; died in Zurich on November 7, 1916; daughter of a minister; married Albert Heim (1849–1937, a geologist), in 1876; children: daughter Helene; son Arnold; (foster daughter) Hanneli.

Marie Vögtlin played a key role in pioneering women's educational and professional rights. In the late 1860s and early 1870s, Vögtlin and six other female medical students—❧▶ **Nadezh**-

da **Suslova** and **Maria Bokova** (Russian), **Louisa Atkins** and **Elizabeth Morgan** (English), Eliza Walker (Scottish), and *Susan Dimock (American)—completed their studies at the University of Zurich with distinction. By impressing the all-male faculty with their abilities, the women were able to influence a world that had hitherto regarded women's potential to benefit from higher education, particularly medical education, with skepticism if not outright hostility.

Although a handful of American women, including *Elizabeth Blackwell, had been able to receive medical degrees in the 1840s and 1850s, the institutions from which they graduated did not compare favorably to European universities of the day. It was in Switzerland, specifically in Zurich, that medical coeducation on a world-class level would be realized for the first time. Starting in the late 1860s, women began to study medicine side-by-side with men. After the graduation of that small band of pioneers in the early 1870s, dozens and soon hundreds of new enrollments of women followed. Ultimately, Zurich's medical school would be able to boast of the largest number of female medical students anywhere in the world before 1914. Along with Paris, which soon followed the Swiss example, the universities of Switzerland (Bern, Geneva, Lausanne and Zurich) led the world for half a century in their openness to women seeking higher educational opportunities.

Founded in 1833, the Zurich's Hochschule (it would be officially granted the title Universität Zurich in 1912) was by the 1860s an important component of a thriving bourgeois city increasingly aware of its importance as a center of expanding commerce and liberal innovation, features that made Zurich a haven for political refugees and radical émigrés. In 1864, a Russian woman, **Maria Knjaznina**, successfully applied for permission to attend lectures at the university's medical school. The following spring, another Russian woman, Nadezhda Suslova, was allowed to attend lectures. By December 1867, when Suslova successfully defended her thesis before the medical faculty, it was becoming clear that change was in the air. At the conclusion of Suslova's impressive defense of her original research, surgeon Edmund Rose, who along with the other examining professors had questioned the candidate sharply, simply noted: "Soon we are coming to the end of slavery for women, and soon we will have the practical emancipation of women in every country and with it the right to work." Suslova was the first modern woman to be the recipient of a medical degree from a recognized university of high academic standards.

Suslova, Nadezhda. See Liubatovich, Olga for sidebar.

Two members of the group who would go down in history as the Zurich Seven arrived in Zurich in the fall of 1868. Susan Dimock, a native of North Carolina, and Marie Vögtlin, a minister's daughter from a conservative farming town in canton Aargau, quickly became close friends. Vögtlin had grown up in a family that valued books and education. Engaged at age 17 to Friedrich Erismann (who would later marry Nadezhda Suslova), Marie was encouraged by him to pursue her intellectual and political interests. She became an avid reader, devouring books by such leading liberal thinkers of the day as John Stuart Mill and Giuseppe Mazzini. Vögtlin's enthusiasm for Mazzini's gospel of human progress became even more intense after she met the venerable idealist while he was visiting Zurich.

Following the end of her engagement to Erismann, Vögtlin determined to become a physician. Her father initially agreed to her plans, but he retreated in the face of opposition both from family and community after they became known nationally. For a time, much of Swiss public life was centered on debating whether or not Marie Vögtlin should be permitted to study medicine "like those Russian women." Eventually, however, Vögtlin's father consented and became a strong supporter of her aspirations. A beacon of liberalism in a nation that was in many aspects still profoundly conservative, the University of Zurich admitted Vögtlin in autumn 1868. Marie wrote to a friend, "I want to break new pathways, will I succeed? The responsibility I have taken on myself is great. I feel that I stand here in the name of my entire sex and if I do poorly I can become a curse to my sex."

Like all the others in the pioneering group, Vögtlin did not "do poorly," being instead a dedicated and excellent student of all facets of medical theory and practice. As did Dimock, whom she called her "faithful companion," Vögtlin found Zurich's professors and the rest of the medical students to be supportive. In a letter, she described the school's rector as being "like an angel to me; the professors . . . are all extremely friendly; concerning the students all one hears is how decently they treat the women." With their morale high and their success clearly in sight, Dimock and Vögtlin excelled in their studies. Confiding to a friend, Vögtlin noted: "Miss Dimock and I are probably the best in the entire anatomy class." Dimock successfully completed her studies in 1871, and for the two friends parting was a painful experience. Marie described it as being comparable to dying, "for we will probably never see each other again."

Four years later, Dimock, by then a successful physician in Boston, would look forward to a European study tour and a reunion with Vögtlin and other friends from her years in Zurich. Tragically, she died in May 1875, when the steamship *Schiller* sank near the coast of England with the loss of nearly all on board.

Vögtlin was the last of the band of seven to finish her doctorate. Unlike the others, she had had no previous training in medicine before her enrollment, and thus after completion of her course work in 1872 took additional courses in Germany. At the University of Leipzig (where she was the only woman among 3,200 students), she found the other students to be "repulsive" in their loud and insulting behavior toward her. She completed her studies at Dresden, writing a thesis under the supervision of noted gynecologist Franz von Winckel. Back in Zurich, on July 11, 1874, Vögtlin passed her doctoral examination in the same room where all but one—Elizabeth Morgan—had preceded her. By this time, the "Zurich experiment" in women's medical education was seen as a clear success. Never again would a serious question be raised about the admission of women to medical schools, although restrictions on the medical education of women (except in France) would continue for the rest of the 19th century. As late as 1907, neither Germany, Great Britain, Russia, nor the United States had opened their medical schools to women as widely and with as much liberality as had Switzerland. By that time, more than a thousand women were studying medicine in Swiss universities, a number greater than in the rest of Europe combined and equal to the total enrollment of women in the 150 medical schools of all kinds, including women's schools, in the United States.

Two years after receiving her medical degree, Vögtlin married Albert Heim, a geologist four years younger than she. Both shared interests in the wonders of nature and the promise of modern science. Both also had social consciences, showing concern over the class divisions and injustices that were threatening the stability of European society. Vögtlin opened her medical practice in gynecology and quickly became well known throughout Zurich. Putting into practice a "Socialism of the Good Deed" (*Sozialismus der helfenden Tat*), Vögtlin offered her medical services to indigent as well as affluent patients. To avoid shaming her poor patients, she charged them a nominal fee, so they would not regard themselves as "mere charity cases."

In her long, active career, Vögtlin received full support from her husband, whose work as a geologist also flourished over the next decades. The busy couple often spent pleasant hours together at home, where they worked at a large desk in a study they shared. Vögtlin was able to combine the roles of successful physician and mother, giving birth to a son Arnold when she was 37 and a daughter Helene when she was 40. Besides raising their own children, she and her husband added a third child to the family, a foster daughter named Hanneli.

Starting in 1896, in association with two other Swiss women physicians, *Anna Heer and **Ida Schneider**, Vögtlin worked on a plan to build a professional nursing school in Zurich. Overcoming many professional and financial obstacles, the Swiss Nurses' School (Schweizerischen Pflegerinnenschule) opened its doors in 1901. With Heer as its chief physician, the school could boast of a dedicated staff of highly trained and experienced women professionals, including Vögtlin as head of its pediatric division. For over a decade, she worked to maintain and even raise the school's standards, which quickly gave it a sterling reputation beyond Switzerland. Advancing years finally took their toll on Vögtlin, and in the winter of 1913–14 her health broke down. By the end of 1913, when it became clear that she was suffering from a serious case of tuberculosis, she had no choice but to retire from the Swiss Nurses' School and end her practice as a gynecologist. Almost as painful for Vögtlin as accepting the termination of a long and successful career in medicine was her realization that because of World War I Europe was involved in a savage bloodbath lacking in moral significance. Disgusted by the attitudes of both the French and German sides in the conflict, she concluded in a letter, "one cannot sympathize with any nation." Mourned not only by women physicians whose cause she had pioneered so many decades earlier, but also by countless individuals whose lives had been enriched as a result of her practical idealism, Marie Vögtlin died in Zurich on November 7, 1916.

SOURCES:

Albert Heim, 1849–1937: Professor für Geologie an ETH und Universität Zürich: Katalog zur Gedenkausstellung 1987. Zurich: ETH-Bibliothek, 1988.

Blake, Catriona. *The Charge of the Parasols: Women's Entry to the Medical Profession.* London: Women's Press, 1990.

Bonner, Thomas Neville. "Rendezvous in Zurich: Seven Who Made a Revolution in Women's Medical Education, 1864–1874," in *Journal of the History of Medicine and Allied Sciences.* Vol. 44, no. 1. January 1989, pp. 7–27.

———. *To the Ends of the Earth: Women's Search for Education in Medicine.* Cambridge, MA: Harvard University Press, 1992.

Brockmann-Jerosch, Marie Charlotte, Arnold Heim, and Helene Heim. *Albert Heim: Leben und Forschung.* Basel: Wepf, 1952.

Craig, Gordon Alexander. *The Triumph of Liberalism: Zurich in the Golden Age, 1830–1869.* NY: Scribner, 1988.

Heim-Vögtlin, Marie. *Die Aufgabe der Mutter in der Erziehung der Jugend zur Sittlichkeit. Vortrag, gehalten an der Jahresversammlung des Zürcher Frauenbundes zur Hebung der Sittlichkeit am 19. V. 1904.* 4th ed. Zurich: Zürcher & Furrer, 1907.

———. *Die Pflege des Kindes im ersten Lebensjahr: Zehn Briefe an eine junge Freundin, im Auftrag des schweizerischen gemeinnützigen Frauenvereins verfasst.* 3rd rev. ed. Leipzig: R. Gerhard, 1907.

Hildebrandt, Irma. *Die Frauenzimmer kommen: 16 Zürcher Portraits.* 2nd rev. ed. Munich: Eugen Diederichs, 1997.

Holmes, Madelyn. "'Go to Switzerland, Young Woman, If You Want to Study Medicine,'" in *Women's Studies International Forum.* Vol. 7, no. 4, 1984, pp. 243–245.

Lovejoy, Esther Pohl. *Women Doctors of the World.* NY: Macmillan, 1957.

"Marie Heim-Vögtlin, Ärztin," in *Neue Zürcher Zeitung.* November 17, 1916.

Marks, Geoffrey, and William K. Beatty. *Women in White.* NY: Scribner, 1972.

Siebel, Johanna. *Das Leben von Frau Dr. Marie Heim-Vögtlin, der ersten Schweizer Ärztin, 1845–1916.* Zurich: Rascher, 1919.

Marie Vögtlin

Staatsarchiv Zürich. Collection "Frauenstudium 1864–1879."

Vögtlin, Marie. *Über den Zustand der Genitalien im Wochenbett.* Leipzig: S. Hirzel, 1874.

Woodtli, Susanna. *Gleichberechtigung: Der Kampf um die politischen Rechte der Frau in der Schweiz.* 2nd rev. ed. Frauenfeld: Verlag Huber, 1983.

John Haag,
Associate Professor of History,
University of Georgia, Athens, Georgia

Voigt-Diederichs, Helene

(1875–1961)

German novelist and short-story writer. Born in 1875 in Schleswig-Holstein, Germany; died in 1961; educated at home; married Eugen Diederichs (a publisher), in 1898 (separated 1911).

Selected writings: (poetry) Unterstrom *(Undercurrent, 1901): (novels)* Regine Vosgerau *(1901),* Dreiviertel Stund vor Tag *(Three-Quarters of an Hour Before Daybreak, 1905),* Auf Marienhoff: das Leben einer deutschen Mutter *(Marienhoff, the Life of a German Mother, 1925),* Ring um Roderich *(A Ring about Roderich, 1929),* Der Verlöbnis *(The Engagement, 1942),* Waage des Lebens *(The Scale of Life, 1952); (story collections)* Kinderland *(The Land of Children, 1907),* Mann und Frau *(Husband and Wife, 1921),* Der grüne Papagei *(The Green Parrot, 1934),* Der Zaubertrank *(The Enchanted Drink, 1948),* Die Bernsteinkette *(The Amber Necklace, 1951); (travel books)* Wandertage in England *(Wandering in England, 1912),* Gast in Siebenbürgen *(Visitor in Siebenbürgen, 1936).*

Helene Voigt-Diederichs was born in 1875 in Marienhoff, a family estate in Schleswig-Holstein, and lived and studied there with private tutors until she was 14. After several years of travel throughout Europe, she married Leipzig publisher Eugen Diederichs in 1898. The couple moved to Jena, where they lived until separating in 1911. Voigt-Diederichs then moved to Brunswick, returning to live in Jena only in 1931.

Voigt-Diederichs' writing career began during her marriage. She published her only volume of poetry, *Unterstrom* (Undercurrents), and the novel *Regine Vosgerau* in 1901, beginning a writing life that was to span 50 years. With a literary style described as typically North German and marked by a cool, somber restraint, Voigt-Diederichs' work centered on the life of rural communities and the problems of marriage; many of her books were based on her own experiences, like *Regine Vosgerau* and *Dreiviertel Stund vor Tag* (Three-Quarters of an Hour Before Daybreak, 1905). In her 1925 book *Auf Marienhoff: das Leben einer deutschen Mutter* (Marienhoff, the Life of a German Mother), she described her mother's life, and also explored marital conflicts in the stories in *Mann und Frau* (Husband and Wife, 1921) and in the novel *Ring um Roderich* (A Ring about Roderich, 1929). Voigt-Diederichs is also known for her stories about children, such as *Kinderland* (The Land of Children, 1907) and *Der grüne Papagei* (The Green Parrot, 1934), and for her travel books *Wandertage in England* (Wandering in England, 1912) and *Gast in Siebenbürgen* (Visitor in Siebenbürgen, 1936). She died in 1961.

SOURCES:

Columbia Dictionary of Modern European Literature. 2nd ed. NY: Columbia University Press, 1980.

Paula Morris, D.Phil.,
Brooklyn, New York

Voilquin, Suzanne (1801–1877)

French feminist, midwife, and writer. Born in 1801 in France; died in 1877 in France; married and divorced.

Trained as midwife; practiced in France, Egypt, and Russia; was editor of Tribune des femmes *(Women's Tribune, 1832–34); was a member of the Saint-Simonian movement; published Claire Démar's* Ma loi d'avenir *(My Law for the Future, 1834); wrote autobiography* Souvenirs d'une fille du peuple *(Memories of a Daughter of the People, 1866).*

Suzanne Voilquin was born in France in 1801 and rose to prominence as a working-class feminist and active member of the Saint-Simonian movement. From 1832 to 1834, she was editor of the feminist journal *Tribune des femmes* (Women's Tribune), in which she gave a public account of the breakdown of her marriage. At the end of her tenure at the *Tribune*, despite their differences in views on morality, Voilquin published a radical work by **Claire Démar** called *Ma loi d'avenir* (My Law for the Future) in 1834.

Joining an expedition to Egypt, Voilquin trained as a midwife, a profession that enabled her to gain access to and help women in Egyptian harems. On her return to France, she resumed her activism, this time on behalf of her fellow midwives, campaigning for better pay and conditions. She also worked for a time as a midwife in Russia, where she is credited with introducing homeopathic medical practices. In 1866, Voilquin wrote her autobiography, *Souvenirs d'une fille du peuple* (Memories of a Daughter of the People), which is notable for its frank account of her sexual experiences. She died in France in 1877.

SOURCES:
Buck, Claire, ed. *The Bloomsbury Guide to Women's Literature*. NY: Prentice Hall, 1992.

Paula Morris, D.Phil.,
Brooklyn, New York

Voisin, La.

See French "Witches" for Catherine Deshayes.

Voisins, countess of.

See Taglioni, Maria (1804–1844).

Volchetskaya, Yelena (1943—)

Soviet gymnast. Born in the Soviet Union in December 1943.

Yelena Volchetskaya won an all-around team gold medal in gymnastics at the Tokyo Olympics in 1964.

Volhard, Christiane (b. 1942).

See Nüsslein-Volhard, Christiane.

Volkonskaya, Maria (1805–1863)

Russian aristocrat who joined her husband in Siberian exile and became known as the Princess of Siberia for her leadership and charitable work among the exiled families. Name variations: Maria Raveskaya, Princess of Siberia; Maria Volkonsky. Pronunciation: Vole-kun-SKY-ya. Born Maria Raveskaya on December 25, 1805, on her family's estate in the Ukraine; died on August 10, 1863, in St. Petersburg, after a long illness; daughter of Nikolai Nikolaevich Ravesky (a military officer in the campaign against Napoleon) and Sophia Konstantinova Raveskaya (a descendant of the celebrated 18th-century poet and scientist M.V. Lomonosov); education typical of the Russian aristocracy; married Prince Sergei Volkonsky, on January 12, 1825; children: Nicholas (b. January 2, 1826, died young); son Misha and daughter Elena.

Became friends during adolescence with celebrated poet Alexander Pushkin; married Prince Sergei Volkonsky (1825); Volkonsky implicated in revolt against the tsar (December 14, 1825); followed Volkonsky into exile, leaving son behind (1827); husband's imprisonment ended after ten years but exile continued, in a large house staffed with servants, in Irkurtsk; returned from exile to St. Petersburg, where Decembrists were fêted for their courage and liberal ideals (1856).

A horse-drawn sledge raced across the white Siberian landscape, a tiny speck on a barren snowfilled plain. The young woman inside, in her early 20s, was leaving behind the glittering palaces and comfort of family and friends she had always known. Now thousands of miles from home and her infant son, she raced toward prison and exile. She had committed no crime. Everyone, including Tsar Nicholas I, had implored her not to go. But the young Princess Maria Volkonskaya was determined to be with her husband, and for that she would become known as the Princess of Siberia, the savior of the Decembrists.

Born on December 25, 1805, Maria Raveskaya was the third daughter and fifth child of Nikolia Nikolaevich Ravesky, a military officer soon to become a well-known hero in the campaign against Napoleon's attempt to conquer Russia. Maria's mother **Sophia Konstantinova Raveskaya** was a descendant of the celebrated 18th-century poet and scientist M.V. Lomonosov, and lavished most of her attention on her two sons. Maria was quite different from her sisters and brothers. She was a musical child, with dark eyes and hair, a great spirit, and an almost exotic air. She was her father's favorite, and returned the adoration of the tall, commanding general.

Like most members of the Russian upper classes, Maria grew up speaking French and learning English and German. She knew far less Russian, which was considered the language of servants. Her family spent their summers at Boltshka, the family estate in the Ukraine, and passed their winters in the sun-drenched Crimea, enjoying its lush fruits and soft breezes. Maria enjoyed the seasonal rounds of dancing, horseback riding, shooting parties, and picking wild mushrooms. When she was 14, the great Russian poet Alexander Pushkin was a guest of her family, while temporarily exiled to the countryside for his liberal thinking. Pushkin wrote several poems to the young girl, and they maintained a lifelong friendship.

Maria grew up accepting the pattern of Russian society without question. In her eyes, it was natural that most people were serfs tied to the land while a few ruled over them. Some members of the nobility believed this feudal social order was destructive, and that Russia was a backward and oppressive country, badly in need of reform. The relatively recent American and French revolutions led some of the nobility to dream of a freer, more inclusive society which granted all its members liberty and equality. One of these was Prince Sergei Volkonsky, a well-read and sophisticated young noble, who belonged to an ancient and noble family (his mother was first lady of the bedchamber to the dowager empress, *Sophia Dorothea of Wurttemberg). An officer in the army, he had traveled widely in Europe, made friends in England and France, and witnessed the more open behavior of people in Western Europe compared to autocratic Russia. Acquainted with the writings of French philosophers and American revolutionaries who advocated a more liberal form of government, Volkonsky idealized the United States and hoped he would someday have the opportunity to visit the new country.

*M*y parents were convinced that they had assured me the most brilliant future, but I felt strangely uneasy, as if through my wedding veil I had been able to discern the dark fate that awaited us.

—Maria Volkonskaya

When Maria met Prince Volkonsky, she was still in her teens. A graceful girl with enormous dark eyes, she was visiting his sister-in-law, Princess **Zenaida Volkonskaya**, in Odessa. When the two married, on January 12, 1825, in Kiev, the groom was 35 and the bride had just turned 20. The Volkonskys moved in elevated social circles, and Prince Volkonsky was considered a great catch.

Maria went to live at the family palace of her husband in St. Petersburg, a cold, dark place for someone accustomed to spending the winter in the warmth of the Crimean sun. In their first year of marriage, military duties kept Sergei from her for all but three months. When she saw him, he often seemed preoccupied. A day never passed, however, that she did not receive a note, a present, or some piece of jewelry from him.

When Maria became pregnant, she returned to her parents' home in Odessa to flourish in the warmth of her family circle. On a night early in December 1825, her husband arrived unexpectedly and began to burn some of his papers. Then a terrible argument erupted between her father and her husband. The general accused the prince of "sheer stupidity and selfishness" and of ruining the future of his daughter and grandchild. The following morning, Sergei left.

The general had come to realize that his son-in-law was in mortal danger. In fact, since before his marriage, Volkonsky had been involved in a plot to overthrow the tsar. Liberal ideas widely discussed in the army had led him to join a group led by Pavel Ivanovich Pestel and Nikita Muraviev, who were conspiring to replace Russia's system of serfdom and autocracy with more open institutions. On November 27, 1825, Tsar Alexander I had unexpectedly died, and for almost three weeks the country remained in a state of suspension, not knowing whether the ruler would be succeeded by his brother Constantine or by Nicholas, his son. Constantine had no wish for the throne, hoping to avoid the fate of his own father, who had been assassinated, and by December 12 it was clear that Nicholas would be tsar. The conspirators, thinking the new tsar was weak, chose this time to strike, wanting to rescue their leader Pestel, who had already been arrested for conspiracy, and also expecting all of Russia to answer their call for revolution by rising up and demanding reform.

Unfortunately, on December 14, 1825, only a few thousand joined the cause of the revolutionaries. Nicholas, furious at the treachery among men he had known as friends, called on loyal troops. Many in the opposition were massacred, and the remaining leaders of the uprising were rounded up and imprisoned in the Peter and Paul Fortress. In a towering rage, Nicholas interviewed every member of the nobility who had betrayed him and personally decided their fate. Five ringleaders, including Pestel, were executed by hanging. Volkonsky and others were ordered into exile in Siberia.

On January 2, 1826, while Volkonsky was being held in Peter and Paul Fortress, Maria Volkonskaya gave birth to a son named Nicholas, after a long labor without the aid of a midwife. Childbed fever kept her in bed for two months, but she finally recovered and managed with great difficulty to visit her husband in prison. Shortly afterward, Volkonsky departed with other prisoners for Siberia.

Few in the nobility, including the prince's own mother, showed the slightest remorse about the fate of the revolutionaries, known by then as the Decembrists. Maria's father, grief stricken over having arranged this disastrous marriage for his favorite child, made his position clear: she was not yet 21, it would be relatively easy for her to obtain an annulment and begin her life anew; she should forget Volkonsky.

Maria instead began to petition the tsar for permission to join her husband in exile. When the embittered Nicholas finally acquiesced, he made his conditions harsh. Maria must leave her son behind with the Volkonskys; even if her husband should die in exile, she could never return to European Russia; all future children born to their marriage would be serfs, not nobles. She could own no valuables and hire no domestics. The Princess Maria Volkonskaya would henceforth have the status of the wife of a state criminal.

Maria
Volkonskaya

Thus began the sledge-drawn journey to Nerchinsk, where Maria arrived with her maid Masha, who followed her into exile, and with provisions that even included a piano. Prepared as she was for the intense cold of Siberia, she soon found her new way of life a great shock, as she witnessed for the first time how most Russians lived, and the harshness of the rule of the tsar toward the common people.

At Nerchinsk, she met Princess **Katherine Trubetskaya,** the first wife among the Decembrist exiles to have departed for Siberia, only a week behind the prisoner convoy that had left in July 1826. On her initial visit to the prison,

Maria found her husband looking thin and pale, in rags and leg irons. All the men suffered from being forced to do hard labor every day in the freezing mines. Soon Maria managed to sneak into the mines, bringing the Decembrists letters from home and their first glimmer of hope.

More wives of the banished men, drawn from various ranks of society, eventually joined their husbands. Princess Trubetskaya was a plain woman who gave the appearance of being from earthy peasant stock, but her charm had made her a beloved figure in Russian upper-class society. She was a member of the Laval family, known for great social entertaining and the outstanding art collection in the family palace (which today houses the central archives of the former Soviet Union). The princess had met Sergei Petrovich Trubetskoy in Paris and much of her existence revolved around her husband. Countess **Alexandrina Grigorevna Muravieva** left two sons and a daughter to join her husband in exile, and fared poorly under the harsh conditions. She lost a premature infant, and then her husband became ill. She died in 1832, followed by her husband in 1835. She was buried in the tiny cemetery adjacent to the local church, where her crypt was well tended and a flame was kept lit. Years later, survivors who returned found the flame still burning.

Two of the Decembrists' wives were French. In the years following the French Revolution in 1789, a number of French royalists and members of the nobility had made their way to Russia and taken jobs as governesses, seamstresses, or other service positions among the Russian upper classes. **Pauline Geueble Annenkova** was from Nancy, and was representing a French fashion firm in Russia when she met Ivan A. Annenkov, a wealthy young lieutenant. She was musically gifted, a talented seamstress and cook, and in love with the Russian lieutenant at the time of his arrest. A few months later, she gave birth to his daughter, and joined her lover in Siberia in March 1828. Though they were allowed to marry, Annenkova's lack of social standing increased the hardships of her exile. Eventually she was recognized as a valued member of the colony. **Camilla Petrovna Ledantu** was one of three daughters of a governess who had married a prominent landlord, V. Gigorovich. Camilla fell in love with Vasili Petrovich Ivashev, a young man of noble birth who had been groomed for a military career, but her lower social status would have prevented their marriage under ordinary conditions. After Pauline Geueble was permitted to marry Ivan Annenkov, Camilla petitioned Tsar Nicholas I for permission to marry Ivashev, who was not even aware of the depth of her affection at the time. The permission was granted, and the couple was married in 1831; their first child died. In 1839, Camilla died when she was eight months pregnant and in serious need of medical attention.

Mme **E.P. Naryshkina**, Mme **Yental'tseva**, **Anna Rozan**, and **Sashenka Davydova** were other women in the Decembrists' circle, as well as Masha, the maid of Volkonskaya. At times, the women shared a common household, and Volkonskaya gradually emerged as their leader. She wrote constantly to relatives and friends demanding funds and needed items, such as warm clothes, sometimes sending 30 letters a day. Over 100 men were imprisoned and some had less than others. Maria took charge of the received funds, which were pooled so that every prisoner had the right to a portion of the money for extra food, tobacco, clothes, and other necessities. Over time, the colony thus grew, ironically, into a community of people living the ideals for which they had sacrificed their freedom. At the same time, Volkonskaya never forgot her aristocratic upbringing, and along with her female companions always dressed in her finest. To most Siberians, these wives of state criminals looked like ladies of the court.

In 1830, the small colony moved from a prison at Chita to another specially constructed facility at Petrovsky zavod, a suburb of Nerchinsk. Although the conditions left much to be desired, the Decembrists and their wives were fortunate in their commandant at the new site. General Stanislav Romanovich Lepardsky was fair minded and believed in treating those in his charge decently. With the help of Volkonskaya's organizational efforts, life for the prisoners and their families was gradually transformed. Warmer clothes and better food became available; books, newspapers, rugs, and other signs of civilization began to reach the prison, and the men were even allowed to spend time outside the prison walls. Summer gardens were planted, discussion groups were allowed to meet, and performances of string quartets were organized. At Petrovsky zavod, the women were allowed to occupy a string of huts which they called Ladies Street (*Damskaya ulitsa*), a name which endures to this day, where the men could spend time with their wives and growing families. Eventually, the community had more than 20 children, and with their advent came schooling. Prisoners or their wives commonly spent several hours a day tutoring the children, and because the Decembrists were generally highly educated men, the children became knowledgeable on a variety of topics and often spoke flawless French. Often there were gatherings at tea time, holiday celebrations, or walks when the weather was fine.

In Siberia, Volkonskaya received news of the death of her first son, and she lost another infant in exile. In 1832, she gave birth to another son Misha, who eventually had a sister **Elena Volkonskaya**. The Volkonskys' marriage was not without difficulties, however. Sergei adjusted to Siberia less well than did Volkonskaya, who found freedom in the life far from St. Petersburg, learned to enjoy the country, and became adept at the language of the local Buritan tribe. For awhile, she fell in love with a close friend of her husband, Alessandro Poggio, but the three managed to maintain a lifelong devotion to each other without destroying the marriage.

After ten years of imprisonment, the men were released and allowed to live in Siberian towns. The breakup of the small colony severed important relationships and required new adjustments. In the fall of 1844, Maria bought a large house in Irkurtsk which she staffed with 25 servants, and took up her habit of good works in the town, improving the orphanage and the local hospital. In Irkurtsk, she became known as the Princess of Siberia, and the governor and townspeople felt honored, by this time, to associate with the Volkonskys.

After the death of Tsar Nicholas I in February 1855, his son came to power as Alexander II. Over three decades, the story of the men who had risked everything for liberty and the women who had joined them in exile had become a powerful example to younger Russians, and even the new tsar was an admirer of the Decembrists. He issued a pardon allowing their return to European Russia in 1856. After 28 years, Trubetskaya and others were dead, and some of the Decembrists who remained now thought of Siberia as home. But the Volkonskys returned to Moscow and St. Petersburg, where they were widely fêted as heroes. Sergei, now a distinguished silver-haired gentleman, doted on his wife and blossomed in the drawing-room society he had enjoyed in his youth. Maria felt the loss of her parents, long dead, but was able to see her son and daughter returned to their place in society and was able to make successful marriages for them. The Volkonskys enjoyed several happy years together before her death on August 10, 1863. After that, Sergei went into decline. He retired to Voronky to "place my life beside her, who saved it for me," and died in 1865.

SOURCES:

Crankshaw, Edward. *The Shadow of the Winter Palace. Russia's Drift to Revolution 1825–1917.* NY: Viking, 1976.

Mazour, Anatole G. *The First Russian Revolution, 1825: The Decembrist Movement, Its Origins, Development and Significance.* Berkeley, CA: University of California Press, 1937.

——. *Women in Exile: Wives of the Decembrists.* Tallahassee, FL: The Diplomatic Press, 1975.

Raeff, Marc. *The Decembrist Movement.* Englewood Cliffs, NJ: Prentice Hall, 1966.

Sutherland, Christine. *The Princess of Siberia: The Story of Maria Volkonsky and the Decembrist Exiles.* NY: Farrar, Straus, Giroux, 1984.

Venturi, Franco. *Roots of Revolution. A History of the Populist and Socialist Movements in Nineteenth Century Russia.* NY: Grosset & Dunlap, 1960.

Karin Loewen Haag,
freelance writer,
Athens, Georgia

Volkonsky, Maria (1805–1863).

See Volkonskaya, Maria.

Volkova, Vera (1904–1975)

Russian ballet dancer and master teacher who trained the finest dancers of the day in the Vaganova technique of which she was the leading exponent in the West. Name variations: Mrs. Hugh Finch Williams. Born Vera Volkova on June 7, 1904, in St. Petersburg, Russia; died in Copenhagen, Denmark, on May 5, 1975; daughter of a Russian military officer; married Hugh Finch Williams (a British architect), in 1936.

Awards: granted the title Knight of Dannebrog by the Danish government (1956); received the Carlsberg Memorial Legacy (1974).

Entered the Russian Choreographic School (1920); joined the State Theater for Opera and Ballet (1925–29); toured the Soviet Far East (1928); made second tour, including China and Japan (1929); defected while on a tour of the Far East (1929); settled in Shanghai, China (1929); moved to Hong Kong (1932); moved to London (1937); danced with the International Ballet (1941); founded a school in London (1943); taught at the Sadler's Wells Ballet (1943–50); was advisor to the Teatro La Scala, Milan (1950); was a guest teacher at the Royal Danish Ballet, Copenhagen (1951), then artistic director (1952) and permanent instructor in dance (1952–75); toured the U.S. with the Royal Danish Ballet; was guest instructor with the Joffrey Ballet (1958); was guest instructor with the Harkness Ballet (summers 1964, 1965); created a Knight of Dannebrog (1956).

Vera Volkova was born into the aristocracy of imperial Russia and was raised in St. Petersburg in a wealthy home overlooking the River Neva. Her father was a career officer in an elite hussar regiment; her mother was a lady of taste and refinement, who encouraged her three children in their respective careers. Her elder sister became a painter and her brother a doctor. The exact date of Volkova's birth was long uncertain as she was skittish about her age, but it now appears certain that it was on June 7, 1904. After an initial education under the care of French governesses, Vera and her elder sister were sent to the Smolny Institute, the elite boarding school founded by *Catherine II the Great as a private girls' academy reserved solely for daughters of the nobility. There, Volkova was educated in the French language and in the deportment thought necessary to a young woman who would soon be traveling in the highest circles of tsarist society. The school was under imperial patronage and manners suited to the imperial court were rigorously taught and enforced.

With the outbreak of World War I, the sheltered and genteel life of Vera Volkova began to crumble. Her father left for the front and never returned, having fallen in combat in 1917. As the revolution approached and the situation deteriorated in Petrograd, as St. Petersburg had been renamed at the beginning of the war, Volkova's mother sent her and her older sister, together with a French governess, to Odessa, far—it was thought—from the increasing food shortages and other difficulties in the capital. At first, all went well, and the girls continued their education even after the fall of the tsar, but in 1918, as the Russian Civil War drew nearer to Odessa, their governess fled to a French warship which was evacuating all French citizens from the beleaguered port, leaving the Volkova sisters with only enough money to return to Petrograd. The two girls secured a train but were unable to get further than Moscow where they were stranded and forced to support themselves by helping other refugee mothers with their children in exchange for food. Eventually they did succeed in returning to Petrograd, where they found their mother living in a single room of their mansion which under Soviet rule had now been divided among working-class families. These were years of privation that lasted until well into the 1920s. During this period, Volkova's health was undermined to the extent that her constitution was permanently weakened. She suffered several serious illnesses later in her life.

As the widow of a tsarist officer, Madame Volkova was in a difficult social situation vis à vis the new regime, but fortunately the Lenin government had decided to allow the ballet to continue despite its elitist associations, and apart from the Marinsky school, it also allowed other ballet schools to emerge. As a result, in 1920 Vera was able to secure ballet training at the new Russian Choreographic School founded and directed by the influential ballet critic Akim Volynsky (1863–1926) with the distinguished dancers ◀❧ **Maria Romanova** and *Agrippina Vaganova** (1879–1951) as his instructors. Romanova was an excellent teacher whose daughter, *Galina Ulanova**, went on to become the first great soviet *prima ballerina assaluta*. Though now in her late teens, an advanced age at which to begin ballet training, Volkova advanced rapidly to a great extent. Not having had prior ballet training, she had less to unlearn than some of the other dancers from the Maryinsky who had been trained in the earlier tradition of imperial Russia.

Here at Volynsky's school, where Volkova studied for five years, new techniques were taught, especially by Vaganova, and in years to come Volkova would be the first to bring the knowledge of these to the world of Western ballet.

Agrippina Vaganova, who was later to attain near mythic status as the founder of the Soviet ballet, had retired as a dancer in 1916, after long years of dissatisfaction with the teaching of ballet in imperial Russia. Before the revolution, three traditions had existed in Russian dance: the French school with its soft, gentle and artificial manner of performance which made it difficult to develop virtuosity, the Italian school which emphasized strength and endurance at the expense of lyricism and harmony, and the Russian school with its rich emotional and spiritual content. Vaganova's goal and her life's work was to consolidate the three traditions into one coordinated system that would nurture the best element in each. Since anything new and supposedly revolutionary was warmly welcomed in the years immediately following the revolution, Vaganova received strong support from the Soviet government, and it was under her tutelage that there emerged the first generation of Soviet dancers, including Galina Ulanova (1910–1980), *Olga Lepeshinskaya** (1916—) and *Natalya Dudinskaya** (1912—). This was important because the coming of the revolution had seen the departure of most of the great dancers of the previous era, including such luminaries as *Matilda Kshesinskaia** (1872–1971), *Anna Pavlova** (1881–1931), *Tamara Karsavina** (1885–1978), and Vaslav Nijinsky (1890–1950).

In 1925, Volkova was able to secure a position with the State Theater for Opera and Ballet (GATOB), formerly the Maryinsky and later the Kirov Theater and Ballet, where she performed until 1929. At first, she had little opportunity to dance in public, and as the daughter of the old upper class her chances for a career in the increasingly radical and despotic Soviet Union were highly uncertain. In 1928, however, the authorities thought it a good idea to send small companies of selected dancers to perform in the Soviet Far East and other remote places where dancers were unlikely to defect, and Volkova was chosen as part of a group sent to Harbin in Manchuria, a town then under Soviet rule. Although several dancers took the opportunity to flee the company while there, Volkova chose to return to her family in Leningrad, as Petrograd had been renamed in 1924.

Life in Leningrad was difficult, however, and even though Vera was able to continue per-

❧▶
Romanova, Maria. *See Ulanova, Galina for sidebar.*

forming with GATOB until 1929, it became increasingly clear that the Soviets were thwarting the careers of the children of the old expropriated classes. Volkova's mother encouraged her to seek a career abroad. Since no one was allowed to leave Russia without special permission, when an opportunity arose for a second tour to the Far East Madame Volkova urged her daughter to join the group and this time to defect to Shanghai, which had become a focal point for many Russian refugees who had fled the new regime. At first, Vera was unable to secure the necessary permits to travel but by a piece of sheer good fortune the official to whom she made her final application remembered having served under her father during the war and he approved her journey.

This second Soviet tour (1929) took Volkova to China and Japan and then back to Russia. Once in Vladivostok, she managed to defect without difficulty and, making her way to China, soon found herself in the cosmopolitan world that was Shanghai between the two world wars. Initially, she supported herself as an acrobatic dancer along with other former dancers and students of the Russian ballet who survived by performing in the many nightclubs and theaters of the bustling city. In time, however, she was dancing with Georgi Goncharov, another expatriate Russian dancer who had formed a company and a school in Shanghai. As a "White Russian" (an émigré from the Soviet Union), Volkova soon became accepted in the European society of the teeming city. Among her newfound friends, she counted the Hookham family, whose daughter Margaret was taking ballet lessons with Goncharov and who appeared to Vera to be extremely talented. It was Volkova who encouraged the family to take their daughter to England and secure more formal training for her. The girl, as *Margot Fonteyn, would become the first great English ballet dancer and one of the greatest dancers of the mid-20th century and a devoted pupil and friend to Volkova for decades afterward.

It was at a party in Shanghai that Volkova met a young English architect, Hugh Finch Williams, and soon the two were in love. Williams planned to marry Vera but was forced to return to Hong Kong where his firm was engaged in the construction of the first high-rise building—the Hong Kong-Shanghai Bank. The attempts of Williams to bring Volkova to join him in Hong Kong failed at first because before she could obtain the necessary papers to enter the British Crown colony she was required to have secured employment there. Eventually,

however, Williams hit upon a scheme whereby he would establish a school in Hong Kong announcing children's ballet lessons soon to be available from the Russian dancer Vera Volkova. A location was chosen, a studio fitted up, and with this as security Vera received a Nansen passport of the kind devised by the Norwegian humanitarian Fridtjof Nansen for displaced persons without proper papers after World War I.

Once in Hong Kong, Volkova became seriously ill for several weeks and after her recovery moved into the Helena May Institute, an English hostel for single women, where she began the study of the English language. As soon as she had acquired sufficient English, a language that she never fully mastered, she was able at last to open her school in 1932. The venture proved a great success and, as the teacher of children of the more prominent members of the English community in the colony, Volkova was soon drawn into their tumultuous social life.

In 1936, Williams returned to England. Having obtained a promotion that enabled him to support a wife, he sent for Vera, and they were married in 1937. After studying briefly with *Olga Preobrazhenska in Paris, Volkova settled in Britain with her husband where eventually she became a naturalized British subject. In 1941, she joined the newly formed International Ballet Company of **Mona Inglesby** but then abandoning her career for a time, she settled down to a domestic life in the elegant Maida Vale district of London. With the coming of the war, Williams joined the army and was posted to India for the duration during which Volkova, with time on her hands, became a fire watcher during the German bombing of London known as the Blitz. Since this wartime role did not fully occupy her hours, she began giving lessons again. In 1943, she opened a school in Basil Street, Knightsbridge, which as her reputation as an excellent and innovative teacher spread was transferred to larger quarters at West Street in the fashionable West End, where most of the better dance schools were located and where Goncharov himself had opened a studio. Here the rising young Margot Fonteyn began taking lessons with her and in time most of the Sadler's Wells Company were taking afternoon classes as well. *Ninette de Valois, director of the Sadler's Wells Ballet, having heard of her work from Fonteyn, attended Volkova's classes as an onlooker and was sufficiently impressed to invite her to come regularly to teach at Sadler's Wells, which she did from 1943 to 1950.

Advancing the system of Vaganova, Volkova adapted it for the training of individual dancers, and the innovations in ballet technique learned from Vaganova drew many dancers to her studio, including not only her former pupil Margot Fonteyn but also Robert Helpmann (1909–1986) and *Moira Shearer (1926—), both of whom would become ornaments of the English ballet world by the middle of the century. "British dancers were a challenge for they were beautifully trained," said Volkova in 1959. "But their legs were more developed than their upper bodies. And so I had to find just the right approach to add harmony of arms and shoulders, and to release them a bit emotionally. Frankly, I don't think that Cecchetti technique is especially good for British dancers. It is too precise and confining. It was more suited to the Russian dancers of the Diaghilev era because they needed to be toned down. The British dancers need the reverse."

> Dance historians are preoccupied with the past. I care about the future.
>
> —Vera Volkova

Once the war was over, dancers came from all over to study under Volkova and for a time it was assumed that she would be invited to serve as a teacher with the newly forming Royal Ballet. Ninette de Valois offered her the position of resident ballet teacher with the company on the condition that she close her school on West Street. This, however, Vera refused to do, whereupon not only was the offer withdrawn but de Valois' dancers were forbidden to attend classes with Volkova. As a result, her school began to falter. In later years, both sides came to realize that a major mistake had been made. The future Royal Ballet had been deprived of the benefits of a great teacher, and Volkova had lost a great opportunity to continue her career in her adopted homeland. Instead, she began to look elsewhere to pursue her art. Meanwhile her husband had returned from the war and, taking advantage of his wife's success, gave up architecture and began to pursue painting which had always been his first love. His choice of a new career was not only successful but gave him the freedom to follow his wife wherever her work might take her. Their marriage was a happy one, and Williams and Volkova remained together until her death.

In 1950, she was invited to serve as an advisor to La Scala in Milan where the famed opera company was undertaking a reorganization of its corps de ballet. Volkova did the best that she could but was startled to find the Italian dancers lacking in the discipline and seriousness in which she had been trained in Russia and that she had found in her English pupils. The following year, however, she received an invitation from Harald Lander (1905–1971), director of the Royal Danish Ballet, to come to Copenhagen as a guest teacher for two months. Vera readily accepted, but upon her arrival found that Lander had been dismissed, and Niels Bjørn Larsen (1913–1992) had been pressured into taking his place, thus projecting Volkova into a political thicket in which she had no interest but soon became entangled. Larsen welcomed her, however, and when the two months were completed invited her to remain as artistic director of the company. It was soon clear to Volkova that the Royal Danish Ballet and its school were deeply entrenched in the Bournonville ballet tradition that was far from what was becoming the norm in the Western world, and that a great deal of hard work would be necessary to bring the company up to the standards of the mid-20th century.

August Bournonville (1805–1879), dancer, choreographer and teacher, was the artistic director of the Royal Danish Ballet from 1830 to 1877 and was responsible for its having become a company of international stature. Rejecting the romantic tradition sweeping European ballet in the 19th century, with its emphasis on anguish and melancholy, he chose to emphasize the positive so that ballet would ennoble its audience. Rejecting too the increasing emphasis on the ballerina that in many cases had led to the male dancers becoming mere *porteurs*, he continued the Danish tradition of stressing the importance of masculine roles. Volkova had no problem with the importance of the male dancer, and she felt that the Vaganova system complemented that of Bournonville rather than competing with it, which was important because the Danes were dearly attached to what was considered to be the national tradition. What she tried to do at the Royal Danish Ballet was to update its technique using her understanding and development of the Vaganova system and to try to develop a cadre of first-class female dancers to complement the males. Senior members of the company predictably found it difficult to adapt to the new style, but younger members took to it rapidly and Henning Kronstam (1934—), Flemming Flindt (1936—) and **Kirsten Simone** (1934—) were the first dancers who succeeded in mastering the Vaganova technique as interpreted by Volkova. One of her pupils, the Anglo-Danish Stanley Williams (1925–1997), proved to be more interested in choreography than in dancing, and when he went to America he took the Vaganova technique with him, introducing it to the ballet world of New York.

As artistic director at the Royal Danish Ballet, Volkova, while welcoming the production of new choreographic creations, insisted on the continued production of the great classics of ballet—*Swan Lake, Giselle, Les Sylphides,* etc.—because she knew that it was by the standards of these masterpieces that the quality of a ballet company and of its individual dancers must be judged. During her tenure, she was able to draw some of the greatest talents of Western ballet to Copenhagen for teaching visits of varying lengths. Balanchine came from New York to stage *Apollo* and Frederick Ashton came from London to create his *Romeo and Juliet* especially for the company.

Ultimately the strains of the political aspects of being a foreigner directing a national ballet led Volkova to resign as artistic director, but she continued to teach in Copenhagen, contenting herself with the knowledge that teaching was by far the most important aspect of the development of a ballet company and of great individual dancers. Extremely conscientious, Volkova watched almost every performance of the Royal Ballet and used what she saw to govern her teachings in class the following day. The years spent in Copenhagen proved to be the most important of her career. It was she who took the good but still relatively provincial Danish ballet and turned it into one of the great companies of the Western world, and who through its internationally renowned and respected dancers spread the influence of her version of the Vaganova system throughout the world of Western classical dance. As a result, the reputation of the Royal Danish Ballet grew with every passing year. The company was enormously acclaimed during its American tours, and every summer was the centerpiece of the summer ballet festival in Copenhagen. Dancers came from all over to study under Volkova, not only young newcomers but also defectors from Russia and luminaries such as Margot Fonteyn. In 1961, Volkova was approached in Copenhagen by the young Rudolf Nureyev (1938–1993), who, recently defected from the Kirov Ballet and knowing little English, took his first lessons in the West from her and who remained her friend for the rest of her life. Later Mikhail Baryshnikov (1946—), another famous Soviet defector, studied with her as well. In 1956, her paramount role in the transformation of the Royal Danish Ballet into a company of international stature was recognized by the Danish government which awarded her the title Knight of the Order of Dannebrog.

But though the years in Copenhagen may have been the summit of her career, Volkova did not spend all of her time there. From 1958 to 1970, she taught regularly at Kurt Jooss' Folkwang Schule in Essen, Germany, and in the summers of 1964 and 1965 she was a guest teacher for the Harkness Ballet at its headquarters in Rhode Island. In her later years, Volkova became interested in the work of a certain Dr. Thomasen of Aarhus, Denmark, a famous orthopedic surgeon who had taken a great interest in the injuries to limbs and joints brought about by the demands of ballet dancing. The human body was not designed to be dropped to the floor from great heights, and it was notorious that many great dancers had been forced to terminate rewarding careers because their knees had given way. Working with Thomasen, Volkova developed a series of exercises designed to renew the joints after surgical operations and in this way extended the careers of several of her dancers as well as enabling others to return to their work when previously they would have been unable to do so.

In Denmark, Vera Volkova had a profound influence on such dancers as Erik Bruhn, **Lis Jeppsen**, Henning Kronstram, Adam Lüder, Peter Martins, Peter Schaufuss, and Kirsten Simone, while Frank Andersen preserved her influence in Copenhagen, where for many years he directed the Royal Danish Ballet. Frederick Ashton, Michael Somes, Peter Schaufuss, and **Merle Park** brought some of her technique to London, Erik Bruhn to Canada, the American-born John Neumeier to the Hamburg Ballet, and the Hynds to Munich.

Vera Volkova was a small, lovely woman with dark hair, large brown eyes, and a warm expression. Her actual performing career was extremely brief, and she is best known in ballet history for her qualities as a master teacher with an uncanny eye for the detection of genius in a budding dance student. As a teacher of ballet, she saw herself as a link in the chain from the early teachings of Vaganova in Petrograd to the development of such Western companies as Sadler's Wells and the Royal Danish Ballet. Devoted to her students, she was a mentor, counselor, and guide, as well as a stern taskmaster to those unwilling to apply themselves with the intensity demanded of the ballet dancer's art. Curiously, though she spent 23 years in Denmark, she seems never to have even attempted to learn Danish and conducted all of her classes as well as her other affairs in a colorful and somewhat broken English. Her students held her in great devotion, however, and when she died in 1975 her funeral at Holmans Church was attended by a large number of dancers who came great distances to pay her their last respects.

SOURCES:
Boscawen, Penelope. "Remembering Vera Volkova," in *Dancing Times* (London). October 1985.
Hering, Doris. "America Meets Vera Volkova," in *Dance Magazine*. September 1959.
Kragh-Jaconsen, Svend. "Interview with Vera Volkova," in *Ballet Review*. Vol. 5, no. 4. 1975–1976.
Music Collection, Free Library of Philadelphia.
The New York Times (obituary). May 7, 1975.
Zoete, Beryl de. "Vera Volkova," in *Ballet*. January–February 1951.

SUGGESTED READING:
Clarke, Mary. *The Sadler's Wells Ballet*. London, 1955.

Robert H. Hewsen,
Professor of History,
Rowan University,
Glassboro, New Jersey

Voloshenko, P.S. (1853–1935).
See Ivanovskaia, Praskovia.

Volumnia.
See joint entry under Veturia and Volumnia.

von Arnim, Bettina (1785–1859).
See Arnim, Bettine von.

von Arnim, Elizabeth (1866–1941).
See Arnim, Elizabeth von.

von Arnstein, Baroness (1758–1818).
See Arnstein, Fanny von.

von Bacheracht, Therese (1804–1852).
See Bacheracht, Therese von.

von Bingen, Hildegard (1098–1179).
See Hildegard of Bingen.

von Ehrenweisen, Baroness Hilla Rebay (1890–1967).
See Rebay, Hilla.

Von Ertmann, Dorothea (1781–1849)
German-Austrian pianist. Born in Offenbach am Main, Germany, on May 3, 1781; died in Vienna, Austria, on March 16, 1849; studied with Beethoven who was her great admirer.

Although she was born in Offenbach am Main, Germany, in 1781, Von Ertmann moved to Vienna and quickly established herself as a famous performer and member of that city's cultivated social elite. Von Ertmann's playing was a constant delight to Beethoven. She studied with him briefly in 1803 and often performed his new compositions in concerts and recitals. His great Sonata No. 28 in A major, Op. 101, is dedicated to her.

John Haag,
Athens, Georgia

von Hahn-Hahn, Ida (1805–1880).
See Hahn-Hahn, Ida, countess von.

von Harbou, Thea (1888–1954)
German screenwriter, novelist, director and actress who is best known for her novel and screenplay Metropolis. *Born on December 27, 1888, in Tauperlitz bei Hof, Bavaria; died in West Berlin on July 1, 1954; daughter of Theodor von Harbou and Clotilde (d'Alinge) von Harbou; married Rudolf Klein-Rogge, in 1914; married Fritz Lang (a director), around 1918 (divorced 1934).*

Thea von Harbou was born into a financially unstable aristocratic family in 1888, the same year emotionally unstable Wilhelm II became kaiser of Germany. Her father worked as a chief forester, and young Thea grew up surrounded by woods and meadows. After finishing her secondary education at a girls' academy in Dresden, the stagestruck young Thea embarked on an acting career in 1906 in Düsseldorf, but despite considerable exertions on her part she did not achieve any significant success over the next few years. Convinced that she had a talent for writing, von Harbou began to send manuscripts to publishers, and by 1910 one of her novels, *Die nach uns kommen* (The Next Generation), had appeared in print, earning both good reviews and healthy sales.

From 1910 to 1952, von Harbou published two dozen novels, many of which became bestsellers. A strongly conservative and nationalistic bias is detectable in virtually all these works: *Der Krieg und die Frauen* (War and Women, 1913); *Deutsche Frauen* (German Women, 1914); *Der unsterbliche Acker* (Immortal Soil, 1915); *Der junge Wacht am Rhein* (The Young Watch on the Rhine, 1915), and *Die deutsche Frau im Weltkrieg* (The German Woman in the World War, 1916). The fierce nationalism and racism found in von Harbou's wartime writings, while hardly a unique point of view, was presented in popular and entertaining formats which made her a well-known personality on the extreme right of the political spectrum in the last years of imperial Germany. Her nationalistic fervor became if anything even more uncompromising in the books and articles she published after the collapse of the monarchy in November 1918. In these works, Germany was invariably depicted as the innocent victim in a world of evil foes. As they turned the pages of her books, von Harbou's readers learned again and again of a Fatherland that had been wronged by its implacable traditional geopolitical and philosophical adversaries, France and Great Britain. Many of her books appeared under the Scherl Verlag imprint, a publishing firm that was part of the media empire of Alfred Hugenberg, a politically ambitious industrialist who despised the democratic republic that had emerged in 1918. Starting in the late 1920s, Hugenberg provided substantial subsidies to Adolf Hitler's violently anti-democratic Nazi Party.

Married in 1914 to actor Rudolf Klein-Rogge, Thea divorced him soon after the war to marry Fritz Lang, a rising filmmaker. She was fascinated by the relatively new film medium. Endowed with a gift for understanding what mass audiences desired, von Harbou began writing screenplays for Lang. Beginning with his 1920 film *Das wandernde Bild* (*Wandering Image*), she wrote all Lang's motion pictures—works of cinematic art that are now regarded as landmarks in the history of film and are studied in classrooms around the globe. Of the ten screenplays she wrote between 1920 and 1933, the best known are *Dr. Mabuse, der Spieler* (*Dr. Mabuse, the Gambler*, 1922), *Die Nibelungen* (1922–24), *Metropolis* (1927), *M* (1931), and *Das Testament des Dr. Mabuse* (*The Testament of Dr. Mabuse*). By the mid-1920s, Thea von Harbou was acknowledged to be the leading writer of the German cinema, equal in talent to Carl Mayer.

In her most successful screenplay, *Metropolis*, a technically impressive science-fiction film which Lang shot in 1927, von Harbou gave voice to the deeply felt fears of mechanization and urban life that embodied a significant aspect of conservative intellectuals' cultural criticism of Weimar Germany. Skyscrapers in the film appear as tall, dark forms that make city streets little more than suffocatingly narrow canyons. The workers in *Metropolis* have completely lost all freedoms and human dignity, having been enticed and seduced by a robot that brings not social stability but profound dissatisfaction. Set in the year 2000, Metropolis is a cautionary tale of a city that has become totally polarized, with a hedonistic elite that seeks its pleasures above ground, their way of life made possible by the exploitation of a subterranean proletariat that has been ground down to a dehumanized state. The film remains visually impressive, in part because of the 35,000 extras used in its many crowd scenes. In production for 17 months, it cost what was then the vast sum of over 2 million reichsmarks, and presented such starkly memorable images as a Tower of Babel sequence in which a thousand men and women appear with their heads shaved.

Portrayed by von Harbou as essentially dull witted, the workers of Metropolis appear visually as drones laboring in their underground industrial complex. A ray of hope appears in the figure of Young Fredersen, scion of the master of the city, who is moved by the virginally pure woman Maria. She kindles in him a growing social conscience concerning the miseries of the workers. After a massive uprising of the workers is halted by Maria, who convinces them that their grievances will be addressed by a mediator who will unify and redeem the entire community, she is kidnapped by Young Fredersen's father. An evil scientist clones Maria into a malevolent robot who now spreads a spirit of rebellion among the easily misled workers. Mindlessly they turn to mob violence, going on a Luddite rampage and destroying the city's machines. A massive flood apparently drowns the city's children, enraging the grief-stricken masses who burn Maria's robot version as a witch. At the end, Young Fredersen and the real Maria are able to effect a heroic rescue of the children, thus destroying the scientist's power as well as ending class hatred that had threatened to destroy the city. This goal of social reconciliation is achieved when Young Fredersen's father, having experienced a moral awakening, joins with the liberated workers to become their leader as the wisely paternalistic "glorious father" they had always yearned for.

Although *Metropolis* was a smash hit both in Germany and abroad, its story line was harshly criticized from the start by liberal and leftist intellectuals. Although some writers merely dismissed her work as little more than forgettable, trashy entertainment, others detected more ominous ideas and ideals lurking in von Harbou's screenplay. The critic Axel Eggebrecht condemned the film for extolling social mysticism and denying "the unshakable logic of the class struggle." Both the novel *Metropolis* and the Fritz Lang film version of it have been the subject of criticism which has discerned conservative, reactionary and even proto-fascist tendencies in the story line. *Metropolis'* depiction of the workers as brainless slaves who become destructive at a whim has been compared to neo-conservative ideals of the period that called for a return to a social order based on hierarchies which would bring the uncontrolled masses back in line.

Adolf Hitler regarded *Metropolis* as a splendid motion picture, emphasizing as it did a community's triumph over class divisions through the appearance of a messianic leader. It is more than likely that Hitler identified himself with the film's hero Young Fredersen, comparing the goals of his own Nazi movement to the pseudo-liberation achieved by the workers when they willingly bowed to accept Fredersen senior's rule. The industrialist's authoritarian benevolence paralleled Nazi ideology, which promised to banish class antagonisms in an organic *Gemeinschaft*. Where the film appeared to most of its viewers to contain a criticism of the dangers of enslavement posed by humanity's growing dependence on technology, Hitler apparently could see only a celebration of a people's embrace of subordination to authority and hierarchy.

After *Metropolis*, von Harbou continued to write popular novels and screenplays. Her successful 1928 novel *Frau im Mond* (The Girl in the Moon) was transformed by Lang the following year into a popular film. Her screenplay for the 1931 film *M*, starring Peter Lorre as the child murderer brought to justice by the underworld, remains a classic of the Weimar cinema. In 1922 and again in 1933, Lang filmed von Harbou screenplays about the character Dr. Mabuse, a pathological criminal. In the 1933 version, *Das Testament des Dr. Mabuse* (*The Testament of Dr. Mabuse*), words closely resembling those of Hitler are put in madman Dr. Mabuse's mouth, and the film has been described as an anti-Nazi allegory. Most likely this is not the case, given the fact that von Harbou had joined the Nazi Party in 1932 as a sign of her enthusiastic support of all that Hitler stood for. That same year, von Harbou and her husband separated, at least in part because of irreconcilable political as well as personal reasons; their divorce became final in 1934.

In early 1933, soon after the Nazis came to power, propaganda minister Joseph Goebbels asked Lang to remain in Germany, promising that he could continue to make films and indeed could expect to become head of the entire German film industry. Given the fact that Lang's mother was Jewish, this was a remarkable concession on the part of the Nazis. Goebbels also confided to Lang that after he had viewed *Metropolis*, Hitler made an announcement regarding Lang's role in the coming Third Reich: "That's the man to make National Socialist films." Lang left Germany the same evening. Von Harbou, on the other hand, remained and went on to have a successful career in the Third Reich, continuing to write screenplays as well as trying her hand as a director on two occasions (with only moderate success). In 1933, she was elected chair of the Association of German Sound Film Authors, a body that signaled its Nazification by purging itself of Jews and anti-fascists. She eagerly worked as a script doctor for propaganda films and provided scripts for several films directed by the notorious Veit Harlan.

By the end of the war, in 1945, Thea had become notorious as a last-ditch Nazi, particularly because of her screenplay for *Kolberg*, a historical epic that appealed to the German people to fight to the bitter end, pending a military miracle that might still change the course of the war. Declared a Nazi by German courts, she was banned from working in films for several years, but by the late 1940s was once more active in the industry, writing dubbing scripts for Deutsche London Film. Von Harbou's last screenplay was for the 1953 film *Dein Herz ist meine Heimat* (Your Heart is My Home). Critical opinion then and now has concluded that this, her final work, was no better than mediocre. Thea von Harbou died in West Berlin on July 1, 1954.

SOURCES:

Bruns, Karin. *Kinomythen 1920–1945: Die Filmentwürfe der Thea von Harbou*. Stuttgart: Metzler, 1995.

Dixon, Wheeler Winston. "von Harbou, Thea," in Amy L. Unterburger, ed., *Women Filmmakers and Their Films*. Detroit, MI: St. James Press, 1998, pp. 439–441.

*Eisner, Lotte H. *Fritz Lang*. London: Secker & Warburg, 1976.

Frame, Lynne-Marie Hoskins. "Forming and Reforming the New Woman in Weimar Germany." Ph.D. dissertation, University of California, Berkeley, 1997.

Gill, Anton. *A Dance Between Flames: Berlin Between the Wars*. NY: Carroll & Graf, 1993.

Grafe, Frieda, Enno Patalas, and Hans Helmut Prinzler. *Fritz Lang*. Munich: Carl Hanser, 1976.

Harbou, Thea von. *M: A Film by Fritz Lang*. Trans. by Nicholas Garnham. NY: Simon and Schuster, 1968.

Huyssen, Andreas. "The Vamp and the Machine: Technology and Sexuality in Fritz Lang's *Metropolis*," in *New German Critique*. No. 24–25. Fall–Winter 1981–1982, pp. 221–237.

Kaplan, E. Ann. *Fritz Lang: A Guide to References and Resources*. Boston, MA: G.K. Hall, 1981.

Keiner, Reinhold. *Thea von Harbou und der deutsche Film bis 1933*. Hildesheim: G. Olms, 1984.

Kracauer, Siegfried. *From Caligari to Hitler: A Psychological History of the German Film*. Princeton, NJ: Princeton University Press, 1947.

Kreimeier, Klaus. *The Ufa Story: A History of Germany's Greatest Film Company 1918–1945*. Translated by Robert and Rita Kimber. NY: Hill and Wang, 1996.

Lang, Fritz. *Metropolis*. NY: Simon & Schuster, 1973.

Rutsky, R.L. "The Mediation of Technology and Gender: *Metropolis*, Nazism, Modernism," in *New German Critique*. No. 60. Fall 1993, pp. 3–32.

Schulte-Sasse, Linda. *Entertaining the Third Reich: Illusions of Wholeness in Nazi Cinema*. Durham, NC: Duke University Press, 1996.

Zimnik, Nina. "The Formation of Feminine Fascist Subjectivity: Thea von Harbou and *Leni Riefenstahl*." Ph.D. dissertation, State University of New York at Buffalo, 1997.

John Haag,
Associate Professor of History,
University of Georgia,
Athens, Georgia

von Heygendorf, Frau (1777–1848).
See Jagemann, Karoline.

von Hillern, Wilhelmine (1836–1916).
See Birch-Pfeiffer, Charlotte for sidebar.

von Kärnten, Margarete (1318–1369).
See Margaret Maultasch.

von Krüdener, Baroness (1764–1824).
See Krüdener, Julie de.

von La Roche, Sophie (1730–1807).
See La Roche, Sophie von.

von Meck, Nadezhda (1831–1894)

Wealthy Russian patron of music who supported one of her country's greatest composers during a critical period in his career, maintaining years of correspondence that provide valuable insights into the daily life and creative mind of Peter Ilyich Tchaikovsky. Name variations: Naddezhda, Nadeja, or Nadejda von Meck; Madame von Meck. Born Nadezhda Philaretovna Frolovskaya (also seen as Frolowskaya) in Znamenskoye, near Smolensk, Russia, on February 10, 1831; died on January 13, 1894, in Wiesbaden, Germany; father was an avid amateur violist; married Karl Fyodorovich von Meck (an engineer), in 1847; children: 18, of whom 11 survived.

Married at 16, encouraged her husband to leave the work he despised as a bureaucrat to strike out as a railroad entrepreneur; widowed, after her husband had garnered an enormous fortune, by his sudden death at age 46; turned to music, commissioning pieces from the young composer Peter Ilyich Tchaikovsky, who entreated his patron for a subsidy that would allow him to devote himself entirely to composing; began an intense 14-year correspondence with Tchaikovsky (1876); ended the relationship suddenly for reasons unknown (1890); death of Tchaikovsky followed by hers, only two months later (1894).

Patronage has long been central to art. The Greek Acropolis, the Sistine Chapel, and the operas of Mozart are all works created as a result of support from individuals or governments. One of the most famous examples of private patronage in history was that provided by the wealthy Nadezhda von Meck to the Russian composer Peter Ilyich Tchaikovsky, to whom she gave extraordinary moral and financial support for 14 years while he was establishing his reputation. The great legacy of Nadezhda von Meck includes not only the beautiful music of one of the world's best-known composers, but the lengthy correspondence that documents the unique friendship of this patron and artist and opens a window onto the creative workings of Tchaikovsky's mind.

Nadezhda Frolovskaya was born on February 10, 1831, near the Russian city of Smolensk, west of Moscow. Her youth was typical of an upper-class girl growing up in imperial Russia at that time, except for the intensity of her love for music and skill at the piano, cultivated by her father, who was a keen amateur violinist. Just before her 17th birthday, Nadezhda married Karl Fyodorovich von Meck, a 28-year-old engineer employed as a bureaucrat by the Moscow-Warsaw railway. Nadezhda soon gave birth to the first of 18 children, 11 of whom survived.

Karl's earnings were modest, and in the first years of marriage, life for the couple was hard. "I had to be wet-nurse, nanny, servant, tutor, and seamstress to all my children, and my husband's valet, book-keeper, secretary and aide," wrote von Meck. Such duties were unusual in the life of an upper-class woman. Nadezhda urged him to strike out on a new career. "In the civil service," she later wrote, "a man must forget he has a reason, will, human dignity—he is just a puppet, an automaton. I was unable to stand it, and begged my husband to resign. . . . When he did, we found ourselves in such straits that all we had was some twenty kopecks per day."

But the period of hardship was to pay off. During the 1860s, railways were being built throughout imperial Russia. At Nadezhda's urging, Karl found a financial backer and became a builder of railways. He quickly amassed a huge fortune, and the couple began to enjoy a life of luxury, moving between their sumptuous townhouses and large estates. The business acumen and foresight von Meck showed in encouraging her husband into entrepreneurship was rarely to fail her.

A beautiful, passionate woman, Nadezhda grew restless in her marriage and became involved with her husband's young secretary, Aleksandr Iolshin. While Karl remained unaware of the affair, their older children knew that their youngest sister, **Liudmila**, known as "Milochka," had a different father. When Milochka was four years old, one of the children revealed Nadezhda's transgression to Karl, and family legend has it that in response he suffered the fatal heart attack that killed him at age 46.

Left a wealthy widow, Nadezhda von Meck was nevertheless unprepared for her husband's untimely death. She became a recluse, and except for doting on her children, showed little interest in anything except music. She already employed a cellist to accompany her at playing the piano, and she soon hired a violinist, Iosif Kotek, to live with the family. Music was a commonplace and relatively inexpensive form of home entertainment for the wealthy. It was not unusual, in this preelectronic era, for Russians to hire musicians and composers to provide occasional music in their households. Kotek, a former pupil of Tchaikovsky, adored his teacher's music. It was he who suggested that von Meck commission Tchaikovsky to compose pieces especially written for piano and violin. Tchaikovsky agreed, and in late 1876 he and von Meck began to correspond.

You are the only person in the world from whom I am not ashamed to ask for money. In the first place, you are very kind and generous; secondly, you are wealthy. I should like to place all my debts in the hands of a single magnanimous creditor by whom I should be freed from the clutches of moneylenders.

—Peter Ilyich Tchaikovsky to Nadezhda von Meck

Peter Ilyich Tchaikovsky had been born into a family that had served Russia's tsars for several generations, mostly as army officers. His uncle and namesake had fought against Napoleon's troops when they invaded Russia in 1812. His father Ilya, a mining engineer of prominence in the mining town of Votkinsk, had many serfs and a hundred cossacks at his disposal. As an important civil servant, the elder Tchaikovsky could provide for his large family, and he married three times, losing his first two wives to illness and death. Tchaikovsky's mother **Alexandra** gave birth to six children, adding to the two by the first marriage. Tchaikovsky was 14 when his mother died, and he mourned her passing all his life. His father's third wife had no children, but Peter maintained lifelong attachments to all his siblings.

Tchaikovsky showed an early interest in music and began to study the piano at a young age. When his father retired and moved the family to St. Petersburg, Tchaikovsky obtained a law degree and a position at the Ministry of Justice. He was handsome and charming and created a brilliant social life on the fringe of high society, but he was dissatisfied with the practice of law. When he resigned from the ministry to devote himself entirely to music, he imposed an economic hardship on a family fortune that had never been large. At first he earned money giving piano lessons and accompanying singers. At age 26, he became a professor of harmony at the Moscow Conservatoire, where he composed his first three symphonies, his first Piano Concerto, three operas, the tone poem *Romeo and Juliet*, and the ballet *Swan Lake*. He was on the brink of fame but still struggling economically when Iosif Kotek contacted him about writing music for Nadezhda von Meck.

Peter Ilyich Tchaikovsky was high strung and intense, a complex person whose moods lapsed at times into depression. He has been described as "over-sensitive, over-shy, weak of will and overwhelmingly, frighteningly strong of emotion," and it was not unusual for him to avoid concert halls where his music was being performed, or to shun his family and friends. Seeming at times to flee human society, he could also be attractive and charming, and was greatly loved by those who knew him. The composer Rimsky-Korsakov described Tchaikovsky as "sympathetic and pleasing to talk to, one who knew how to be simple of manner and always speak with evident sincerity and heartiness. A man of the world in the best sense of the word, always animating the company he was in." The loss of his mother, inborn emotional complexity, and creative genius explain much about the character of Tchaikovsky, but his homosexuality also accounts for some aspects of his personality. Living in morbid fear of discovery, he eventually went so far as to marry to disguise his sexual persuasion.

In late 1876, the 36-year-old Tchaikovsky was delighted to obtain a commission from the 45-year-old widow, but he remained in dire financial straits nonetheless. It was Nikolai Rubinstein, virtuoso pianist and Tchaikovsky's superior at the Moscow Conservatory, who suggested to the young composer that he apply to his new mentor for a loan. After von Meck wrote that she would like to know the composer better, their relationship blossomed through a correspondence which grew voluminously into hundreds of letters written over a 14-year period.

From the outset, however, it was a basic tenet of this remarkable friendship that von Meck and Tchaikovsky would never meet. Still a recluse at this stage, von Meck may have feared repeating the physical relationship which might have resulted in her widowhood. In any case, she wrote to the composer, "the more fascinated I am by you, the more I fear acquaintance." Tchaikovsky, shy as he was, and fearful his homosexuality might be discovered, was more than happy to honor her request. Although the two lived near each other at times, and occasionally saw each other at a distance, they met only twice, and then by accident.

Von Meck quickly assumed a central role in Tchaikovsky's emotional and professional life. In 1877, the year after their correspondence began, the composer wrote that he had decided to marry **Antonina Ivanovna Milyukova**, who was a virtual stranger to him. He perhaps hoped that Milyukova would look after his needs, but the marriage proved from the outset to be a disaster. Writing to von Meck, Tchaikovsky never describes his problems with a physical union but dwells on the incompatibility existing between bride and groom. Von Meck, who wrote of her great reservations about the marriage, also offered him what epistolary support she could during the months when the relationship was dissolving. By the end of the first year, the intensity of both correspondents had made the composer and his patron emotionally dependent on one another. But when Madame von Meck suggested that they should assume the intimate form of address with one another, Tchaikovsky declined to do so.

Nevertheless, the relationship assumed a more intimate dynamic. After von Meck asked for photographs not only of Tchaikovsky but other members of his family, large numbers of pictures were exchanged. Their letters were also filled with comments about political events, gossip, family events, and personal observations. The two were compatible as conservative Russians devoted to the tsar and the Orthodox Church during a period when the imperial system was under attack from radicals. Music, of course, was also an important topic. Von Meck did not like Mozart's music, for example, while Tchaikovsky adored it. He endeavored to change her musical taste, and wrote about his works in progress, explaining sections as they were composed. A great deal of what is known about his composition of *Eugene Onegin* and the Fourth Symphony comes from their correspondence, and his Fourth Symphony was dedicated to von Meck, his "beloved friend."

Von Meck's support began as occasional subsidies, and gradually increased until she was sending Tchaikovsky a generous monthly stipend amounting to more money in two months than he had made teaching at the Moscow Conservatory in a year. When he eventually decided to resign his post to devote himself to composing full time, the decision met with von Meck's full support. Her generous patronage allowed not only new creative freedom but a chance for the composer to travel abroad. She also made her estates, including the magnificent Brailov, available for him to visit often for relaxation.

Tchaikovsky was never a prudent money manager, and it was not unusual for him to give away large amounts of the money von Meck bestowed upon him. When his funds were low, she sent more or doubled his monthly allowance. This extraordinary generosity and moral support continued until the composer was professionally well established and financially secure.

How and why the end of this unique relationship came about is not clear. At the time, she wrote to him that financial catastrophe meant her subsidies must be discontinued, and although it is true that her family suffered a temporary setback, railroads were soon booming again. Other members of von Meck's family wrote to the composer that her health had deteriorated, making it impossible for her to continue writing, and Tchaikovsky probably feared that she had been put off by learning of his homosexuality. This may even have been true, because stories about his liaisons circulated continuously. More probably, however, von Meck's many living children resented their mother's financial output, especial-

Nadezhda von Meck

ly after his compositions had begun to earn him a great deal of money. Whatever the reason, Tchaikovsky bitterly resented the end of this friendship, and it is said that her name was on his lips when he died of typhoid three years later, at age 53. Von Meck died two months later.

Tchaikovsky, in a sense, was the wealthy patron's dream. Without her support of him, Nadezhda von Meck would have been just another wealthy Russian widow. With it, he produced some of his greatest compositions, including such major works as the *Sleeping Beauty* ballet, his Fifth and Sixth symphonies, *Hamlet*, and *Eugene Onegin*. Von Meck, in turn, was the artist's dream—a non-judgmental figure, and a haven, perhaps even the mother that he always missed. Tchaikovsky wrote her, "I have never in my life encountered another soul as kindred and close to me as yours, responding so sensitively to my every thought, my every heartbreak." And for posterity, there is not only the music but the mind of the musician, revealed through his moods, his attitudes, and his intimate views on his own compositions throughout the hundreds of letters he wrote to his patron.

SOURCES:

Bennigsen, Olga. "A Bizarre Friendship: Tchaikovsky and Mme von Meck," in *The Musical Quarterly*. Vol. 22, no. 4. October 1936, pp. 420–429.

———. "More Tchaikovsky von Meck Correspondence," in *The Musical Quarterly*. Vol. XXIV, no. 2. April 1938, pp. 129–146.

Bowen, Catherine Drinker and Barbara von Meck. *"Beloved Friend": The Story of Tchaikowsky and Nadejda von Meck*. NY: Random House, 1937.

Brown, David. *Tchaikovsky: A Biographical and Critical Study*. Vol. I. NY: W.W. Norton, 1981.

———. *Tchaikovsky: The Crisis Years 1874–1878*. Vol. II. NY: W.W. Norton, 1983.

———. *Tchaikovsky: The Final Years 1885–1893*. Vol. IV. NY: W.W. Norton, 1993.

———. *Tchaikovsky: The Years of Wandering 1878–1885*. Vol. III. NY: W.W. Norton, 1986.

Craft, Robert. "Love in a Cold Climate," in *The New York Review of Books*. Vol. 40, no. 19. November 18, 1993, pp. 37–41.

Garden, Edward, and Nigel Gotteri, eds. *"To my best friend": Correspondence between Tchaikovsky and Nadezhda von Meck 1876–1878*. Trans. by Galina von Meck. Oxford: Clarendon Press, 1993.

Griffiths, Paul. "Perfect Partners: The romantic dialogue of a melancholy composer and a passionate lady," in *The Times* [London] *Literary Supplement*. No. 4705. June 4, 1993, p. 18.

Tchaikovsky, Piotr Ilyich. *Letters to his Family: An Autobiography*. Trans. by Galina von Meck. NY: Stein and Day, 1981.

Volkoff, Vladimir. *Tchaikovsky. A Self-Portrait*. London: Robert Hale, 1975.

John Haag,
Associate Professor,
University of Georgia,
Athens, Georgia

Von Mises, Hilda (1893–1973).

See Geiringer, Hilda.

Von Nagy, Käthe (1909–1973)

German film actress. Name variations: Kathe von Nagy. Born on April 4, 1909, in Szabadka, Hungary; died in 1973; daughter of a bank director; attended school in St. Christiania (Frohsdorf); married Constantin J. David (a film director); married Jacques Fattini, around 1935.

Worked briefly at Hungarian newspaper Pester Hirlop; *began career as a film actress (1927); appeared in German, French, and Italian films of both silent and early sound eras; associated with Nazi-era German cinema, particularly comedies.*

Selected filmography: Männer vor der Ehe *(Men Before Marriage, 1927);* Republik der Backfische *(Teenager's Republic, 1928);* Rotaie *(Rails, 1929);* Der Andere *(The Other One, 1930);* Ronny *(1931);* Der Sieger *(The Victor, 1932);* Ich bei Tag, Du bei Nacht *(I by Day, You by Night, 1932);* Flüchtlinge *(Refugees, 1933);* Prinzessin Turandot *(1934);* Liebe, Tod und Teufel *(Love, Death and the Devil, 1934);* La Route impériale *(The Imperial Road, 1935);* Unser kleine Frau *(Our Little Wife, 1938).*

Käthe Von Nagy was born on April 4, 1909, in Szabadka, Hungary, a town that was to be annexed to Yugoslavia after World War I, and was the daughter of a prosperous bank director who worked and owned considerable property in the village of Paličs. Von Nagy's quiet, bourgeois upbringing included studying French and German with nuns in St. Christiania (Frohsdorf), languages that were to prove invaluable in her later career. At the age of 15, she ran away to Budapest in order to fulfil her ambition of becoming a writer of short stories, although the police soon found her at the elegant Hotel Ragusa, where she had registered under a false name. In order to keep her occupied, her father offered her a job working in his office, overseeing all German correspondence, but Von Nagy's taste of big-city life had made her eager for more. Her literary ambitions forgotten, she persuaded her father to send her to Berlin to become an actress.

Von Nagy spent a fruitless year in Berlin trying to attract the attention of one of the numerous film companies there. Her dark complexion, pitch-black eyes, and willowy figure were striking but not fashionable, and she eventually admitted defeat, returning to Budapest to work answering correspondence for the newspaper *Pester*

Hirlop. But in 1927 she won a supporting role in a Deulig company production called *Männer vor der Ehe* (Men Before Marriage), chosen by the Corsican director Constantin J. David, who directed a number of her films and eventually became her husband. Under David's tutelage, Von Nagy transformed herself from a girlish amateur into a shrewd, hard-working professional actress. Her breakthrough role was in 1928's *Republik der Backfische* (Teenager's Republic), in which her appealing, insouciant performance as a girl leading a band of young women to found a new state brought her public recognition.

Von Nagy's first real dramatic role came in Mario Camerini's classic Italian film *Rotaie* (Rails, 1929), to which a musical soundtrack was later added. Von Nagy and Maurizio D'Ancora, an actor who was to become better known as a member of the Gucci family fashion dynasty, played a poor couple who, finding a wallet stuffed with bills, live the high life for a while before choosing to return to their jobs in a factory. Her first sound film, *Der Andere* (The Other One, 1930), was based on the phenomenon of the split personality, enabling Von Nagy—playing the girlfriend of a public minister with a double life—to reveal new depths as a performer.

Like many actors of the era, Von Nagy found the adjustment to sound films difficult (technicians had to remind her not to fidget with her pearl necklace, as the sound was distracting). But she soon became an accomplished comic actress, often typecast in the role of a minx, in a constant stream of frothy, escapist films, many of which were made in both German and French versions. Among the most successful were *Der Sieger* (The Victor, 1932), also starring Hans Albers in his usual role of bon vivant, as well as *Ronny* (1931), *Ich bei Tag, Du bei Nacht* (I by Day, You by Night, 1932), and *Prinzessin Turandot* (1934), all featuring film operetta star Willy Fritsch. *Prinzessin Turandot* was written by *Thea von Harbou (1888–1954), one of the most prolific and creative of Germany's female screenwriters, who chose to remain in Germany with the Nazis rather than emigrate to the United States with her husband, director Fritz Lang, whom she divorced in 1934.

Von Nagy also acted in some serious films during this period, demonstrating considerable gifts in both *La Route impériale* (The Imperial Road, 1935) and *Flüchtlinge* (Refugees, 1933), again with Albers. *Flüchtlinge* was considered by propaganda minister Joseph Goebbels to be a prime example of the "new film" which would reflect Nazi ideals of the "national revolution."

Hans Albers' name was not mentioned at the ceremony when *Flüchtlinge* won an award for best film, because he had just married the Jewish actress **Hansi Burg** in Switzerland.

By the mid-1930s, Von Nagy was living in Paris with her second husband Jacques Fattini, although she continued to make films in Germany and Italy (the 1938 premiere of *Unser kleine Frau*, made at Cinecittà, was held in Naples on board the American cruiser *Milwaukee*). Unlike many Teutonic actresses of the period, Von Nagy was best suited to flirtatious, saucy, and sometimes provocative roles in light comedies or exotic tales like *Liebe, Tod und Teufel* (Love, Death and the Devil, 1934). She became one of the most popular stars of Nazi-era cinema in Germany, despite the fact that she had neither an Aryan heritage nor appearance. Von Nagy died in 1973.

SOURCES:
Romani, Cinzia. *Tainted Goddesses: Film Stars of the Third Reich*. NY: Sarpedon, 1992.

Paula Morris, D.Phil.,
Brooklyn, New York

von Nissen, Constanze (1762–1842).

See Mozart, Constanze.

Vonnoh, Bessie Potter (1872–1955)

American sculptor. Name variations: Bessie Potter. Born Bessie Onahotema Potter in 1872 in St. Louis, Missouri; died in 1955; studied at the Art Institute of Chicago under Lorado Taft, in a studio that included sculptors Janet Scudder and Julia Bracken Wendt; married Robert W. Vonnoh (an artist), in 1899.

Traveled to Paris (1895); best known for small genre subjects like The Young Mother *(1896); moved to New York City (1899); held one-woman show at Brooklyn Museum (1913); work of the 1920s and 1930s includes the* Burnette Fountain *in Central Park and a fountain for the Roosevelt Bird Sanctuary in Oyster Bay, Long Island; portrait commissions include Major General S. Crawford* for the Smith Memorial, Philadelphia, *and James S. Sherman* for the U.S. Capitol.

Bessie Potter Vonnoh was born Bessie Potter in St. Louis, Missouri, in 1872, and studied at the Art Institute of Chicago with Lorado Taft, whose studio yielded a generation of women sculptors, including *Janet Scudder and *Julia Bracken Wendt. Known as one of Taft's "White Rabbits," the young Bessie was hired to assist with his sculptures for the 1893 Columbian Exposition in Chicago, where she found artistic inspiration in the elegant bronze figurines by

Else von Richthofen

Prince Paul Troubetskoy that were exhibited in the Italian section of the fair. In Taft's opinion, this exposure was crucial to Vonnoh's development, although her attempts to emulate Troubetskoy's style meant some critics found her early work derivative. Taft encouraged her throughout this formative period, later describing her as "another eager spirit out of the West whose little bronzes are welcome the world over."

After a 1895 trip to Paris, where she may have been influenced by the simple, domestic subjects chosen by painters Auguste Renoir and *Mary Cassatt, Vonnoh became famous for her small genre subjects, which were characterized by a spontaneous feel, including her most popular works, *The Young Mother* (1896), *Girl Dancing* (1897), *Enthroned* (1902), *A Modern Madonna* (1905), and *Beatrice* (1906). A copy of *The Young Mother* is on display in New York City in the Metropolitan Museum of Art.

In 1899, Bessie married well-known painter Robert Vonnoh and moved to New York City to continue her work, staging a one-woman show at the Brooklyn Museum in 1913. Like Cassatt, Vonnoh concentrated on the details of serene middle-class domesticity in her work, though in the 1920s and 1930s she turned her focus to larger pieces, including the *Burnette Fountain* in Central Park and a fountain for the Roosevelt Bird Sanctuary in Oyster Bay, Long Island. Her major portrait commissions were of Major General S. Crawford for the Smith Memorial in Philadelphia and James S. Sherman for the U.S. Capitol. Vonnoh was awarded a bronze medal at Paris in 1900, and a gold medal at St. Louis in 1904; she was elected an associate of the National Academy of Design in 1906 and a member in 1921. She died in 1955, at the age of 83.

SOURCES:

Bailey, Brooke. *The Remarkable Lives of 100 Women Artists.* Holbrook, MA: Bob Adams, 1994.

Rubinstein, Charlotte Streifer. *American Women Artists.* Boston, MA: G.K. Hall, 1982.

Paula Morris, D.Phil., Brooklyn, New York

von Reibnitz, Marie-Christine (b. 1945).

See Michael of Kent.

von Richthofen, Else (1874–?)

German intellectual and social activist, sister of Frieda Lawrence, who was the first woman appointed by the state to monitor the rights of women factory workers. Born in the French city of Metz, in Lorraine, in 1874; eldest of three daughters of Friedrich von Richthofen (a civil engineer) and Anna (Marquier) von Richthofen; sister of Frieda Lawrence (1879–1956) and Johanna "Nusch" von Richthofen; attended boarding school in Freiburg; Heidelberg University, Ph.D., 1901; married Edgar Jaffe, in 1902 (died 1921); children: (with Edgar Jaffe) three; (with Otto Gross) one son.

The eldest and brainiest of the three von Richthofen sisters, Else was a beauty as well—tall and blonde, with elegant, fine features. She aspired early to an intellectual life, becoming a schoolteacher at 17 in order to pay for her advanced studies. As a young woman, she was a student and disciple of sociologist Max Weber and also attended lectures by sociologist Georg Simmel and economists Adolph Wagner and Gustav Schmoller in Berlin. She received her doctorate degree in economics from the University of Heidelberg in 1901, where she was one of only a handful of matriculating female students at the time. Her doctoral thesis, which examined the changes in attitude since 1869 of the authoritarian political parties in Germany toward worker-protection legislation, was suggested by Weber, and he was also instrumental in her pioneering appointment as a factory inspector. The first woman appointed to such a post, Else was mandated to monitor factory conditions and to protect the rights of women workers. As a social activist, she won the respect and admiration of the country's feminists (among them *Gertrud Baümer, *Helene Lange, and *Alice Salomon), and as a scholar, she was a respected member of the intellectual community.

Many of Else's feminist friends and admirers were surprised and disappointed when, in 1902, she gave up her career to marry Edgar Jaffe, a wealthy but rather dull teacher of political economy. It seemed that she did not love him, and in a letter to a woman friend she later described their relationship as "*freundschuftlich*," a kind of friendship. As early as 1905, Else had an affair with Freudian psychologist and free-love advocate Otto Gross, who was also involved with her sister *Frieda Lawrence at the time. Else had a son with Gross in 1907, which caused a rift between the sisters that lasted several years. In 1910, Max Weber declared his love for Else, and though it was evident that she loved him, she could not betray his wife *Marianne Weber, who also exercised great influence over her life. Spurning Max, Else formed an alliance with his unmarried brother Alfred Weber (also a sociologist), with whom she traveled to Italy twice a year, assisting him in his study of culture. Despite her relationships with other men, Else remained married to Jaffe, giving birth to their third and last child in 1909.

After the deaths of Max Weber (1920) and her husband (1921), Else eventually went to live with Alfred Weber, becoming his reader, translator, and traveling companion until his death in 1958, at the age of 90. She spent the last years of her life in a Heidelberg nursing home, not wishing to become a burden to her family.

Aside from their brief estrangement around 1907, Else remained close to her sister Frieda, supporting her both emotionally and financially throughout Frieda's tumultuous relationship with D.H. Lawrence. Like all the von Richthofens, Else occasionally turns up in a Lawrence story: as Mary Lindley, for example, in "Daughters of the Vicar" ("a long slim thing with a fine profile and a proud, pure look of submission to a higher fate"), which also explores the Jaffe marriage. In "The Sisters," Lawrence examined the complex relationship between Frieda and Else.

SOURCES:
Green, Martin. *The von Richthofen Sisters: The Triumphant and the Tragic Modes of Love*. NY: Basic, 1974.

von Richthofen, Frieda (1879–1956).
See Lawrence, Frieda.

von Saltza, Chris (b. 1944).
See Fraser, Dawn for sidebar.

von Schlegel, Dorothea (1764–1839).
See Mendelssohn, Dorothea.

von Stade, Richardis (d. 1152).
See Stade, Richardis von.

von Steinbach, Sabina (fl. 13th c.).
See Steinbach, Sabina von.

von Strauss und Torney, Lulu (1873–1956).
See Strauss und Torney, Lulu von.

von Suttner, Bertha (1843–1914).
See Suttner, Bertha von.

Von Trapp, Maria (1905–1987)

Mother of the world-famous Trapp Family Singers, whose flight from Nazi-occupied Austria in 1938 inspired the musical play and motion picture **The Sound of Music**. *Name variations: Baroness Maria Von Trapp. Born Maria Augusta Kutschera on January 26, 1905, on a speeding train en route to Vienna, Austria; died on March 28, 1987, at Copley Hospital, Morrisville, Vermont; daughter of Karl Kutschera and Augusta (Rainer) Kutschera; educated in Austrian primary and secondary schools; graduated from the State Teachers College for Progressive Education, Vienna; married Baron Georg Ritter Von Trapp (1880–1947), on November 26, 1927; children: Rosmarie (b. 1929); Eleonore (b. 1931); Johannes (b. 1939); stepchildren: Rupert (1911–1992); Agathe (b. 1913); Maria (b. 1914); Werner (b. 1915); Hedwig (1917–1972); Johanna (1919–1994); Martina (1921–1951).*

Awards: Merenti (Papal Decoration, 1948); Golden Book Award of Catholic Writers Guild for The Story of the Trapp Family Singers (1950); Catholic Mother of the Year (1956); Austrian Honorary Cross for Science and Art (1967); numerous honorary degrees, civic honors and citations.

Worldwide concert tours with the Trapp Family Singers (1935–56); emigrated with family from Salzburg, Austria, to U.S. (1938); organized and directed Trapp Family Music Camp, Stowe, Vermont (1944–56); organized Trapp Family Austrian Relief,

Inc. (1947); recorded with family for RCA Victor, Concert Hall Society and Decca recording companies (1938–59); lectured and appeared on radio and television (1938–84); managed Trapp Family Lodge, Stowe, Vermont (1948–69).

Selected writings: The Story of the Trapp Family Singers *(1949);* Yesterday, Today and Forever *(1952);* Around the Year with the Trapp Family *(1955);* A Family on Wheels *(1959);* Maria: My Own Story *(1972);* When the King was Carpenter *(1976); and numerous magazine articles.*

For Maria Von Trapp, the 1965 Academy Award-winning film *The Sound of Music* forever captured a portion of her early life and immortalized her as a modern heroine. Starring **Julie Andrews** as Maria, the movie depicted the tale of a young Austrian nun who left her Salzburg convent to serve as governess to the seven motherless children of Baron Georg Von Trapp. The romantic courtship of Maria and Georg, their marriage and escape from Nazi Austria in 1938, summarized a segment of the Trapp saga.

The true story of Von Trapp's life far outshines the movie version in drama, excitement, and fame. Her life was rooted in belief in following God's will for herself and her family. This religious conviction led her through Nazi oppression, loss of home, life as a refugee, and life as a world-famous musician. "You have inside of you a very fine voice which you train yourself to listen to. When that moment of great importance comes which can significantly change your life, it will tell you the right decision for you to make," Von Trapp explained.

Nothing in Von Trapp's early life suggested her future role as a devoutly religious matriarch of a large family. Her childhood was a lonely one, full of insecurity and disdain for her Catholic faith. As the only child of Karl and **Augusta Kutschera**, she was orphaned by age nine. In the Vienna home of her guardian, an agnostic, Von Trapp constantly heard the Catholic Church described in derisive terms. After World War I, Austria dismissed its emperor, and the new regime secularized the country. "All the Bible stories I had loved in my early childhood were now branded as silly old legends," Von Trapp recalled. "[S]uddenly God was out of my life."

Von Trapp entered Vienna's State Teachers College for Progressive Education, a school known for innovative teacher training. There she spent four years during the early 1920s. In her final year, she claimed she was given "a special mercy of God" and rediscovered her Catholic faith. While on a class trip high in the Austrian Alps, Von Trapp committed her life to God and decided to enter a convent. Nonnberg, the Benedictine convent in Salzburg, accepted her as a candidate to the novitiate.

Von Trapp's earthy, active manner and liberal ideas of education were often at odds with the cloistered nuns and the school they operated. Though she was frequently corrected by her superiors, she remembered her two years at Nonnberg as momentous in her religious life and the development of her character. "The marvelous Benedictines of Nonnberg worked first to make a girl out of a boy, and then to make a nun out of that," she said.

In 1926, Von Trapp was sent by Nonnberg to fill a temporary need for a governess at the home of Baron Georg Von Trapp. His first wife **Agathe Whitehead** had died in 1922, leaving seven children. Captain Von Trapp was known throughout Austria as a World War I naval hero. His work with primitive submarine warfare produced daring feats. When Austria was stripped of its seacoast after World War I, the much-decorated captain retired to a villa in the Salzburg suburb of Aigen.

When the 21-year-old governess reported to the Trapp villa, she was met with seven children, ranging from five to fifteen in age: Rupert, **Agathe**, **Maria**, Werner, **Hedwig**, **Johanna**, and **Martina**. The lonely children fell under the spell of the athletic, outgoing, musical Maria, who joined them in games and noticed their musical abilities. Soon she started introducing them to group singing of folk songs and madrigals. Though Von Trapp expected to return to convent life, the captain proposed. With the blessing of Nonnberg, the two were married on November 26, 1927. Maria was 22; her husband 47.

Singing and hiking became the predominant hobbies of the Trapp family. They made frequent excursions into the Austrian Alps and to the Adriatic Sea. Von Trapp joined her seven stepchildren in singing, and the eight voices blended in unique harmony. They particularly enjoyed singing church music for religious devotions.

Maria Von Trapp added two children to the family: **Rosmarie** and **Eleonore**. World events disrupted their life when the captain's fortune was wiped out by the Depression. The Trapps economized by taking over duties on their estate and opening the house to paying guests, mostly students and priests. In 1935, Father Franz Wasner arrived at the Trapp home to celebrate Mass. Wasner (1905–1992) was an eminent musician, an organist and instructor of Gregorian chant at

Maria
Von Trapp

Seminarium Majus in Salzburg. When he learned of the Trapp family's interest in choral singing, he offered to coach them.

Under Wasner's guidance, the Trapps mastered music of the 14th, 15th and 16th centuries.

"We sang for the joy of singing," Von Trapp recalled. All of their music was learned from memory and despite their talent for group singing, the early efforts were limited to church services. "When you sing, you pray twice," she remarked. In addition to harmonizing, the Trapps learned ancient instruments: recorders, viola da gamba and spinet, but most of their singing was a capella.

In 1936, opera diva *Lotte Lehmann overheard the Trapps singing in their garden. Urging them to become professional, she persuaded them to enter a Salzburg competition for group singing. The family was so well received that radio performances and a command performance for the chancellor of Austria followed.

> *The most important thing in life is to find out the Will of God and then go and do it.*
>
> —Maria Von Trapp

Von Trapp clearly thrived on the growing fame of the family choir, despite her husband's initial discomfort at the notion of his children singing in public for money. When the group appeared at the Salzburg Festival in 1937, they were offered contracts to tour throughout Europe and America. A December 1937 tour took them to Italy, Belgium, Holland, and England.

As hobby evolved into profession, the Trapps were shaken by Austria's annexation by Nazi Germany in March 1938. The Trapps hated the Nazi philosophy, and found it increasingly difficult to hide their sentiments. They refused an invitation to sing for Hitler, would not fly a Nazi flag at their home, and the captain turned down an offer to command German submarines. Son Rupert Von Trapp, a newly graduated doctor, rejected a Nazi offer to serve at a hospital. The Trapps understood that to preserve their faith and ideals they must flee their homeland.

Nine members of the Trapp family, along with their musical conductor Franz Wasner, left home for a vacation to Italy during the summer of 1938. Their ultimate destination was America and freedom, using a singing contract offered by a New York concert manager as their means of escape. In October 1938, the family arrived in New York and began their first tour as the Trapp Family Choir.

The Trapp experiences in America constitute a typical refugee-immigrant tale. They struggled with the language and new customs. "We were pitiful ill-fits," Von Trapp remembered. Their combined capital when they arrived was four dollars. Fees from their concerts supported them during the first months, but Von Trapp was expecting a child, and the tour came to an end in December 1938. The family settled in Germantown, Pennsylvania, where the tenth and last child, Johannes, was born in January 1939.

When their visitor visas expired, the Trapps returned to Europe to tour Scandinavia during the summer of 1939. Fortunately, they were readmitted to the United States in October 1939. Eventually, they found excellent management from the Columbia Concerts Agency in New York. With a varied and less formal repertoire, the Trapp Family Singers became a popular attraction. Their friendly, sincere manner, colorful Austrian costumes and folk pageantry, combined with exquisite musicianship, made them one of the concert world's most sought-after attractions.

Von Trapp served as on-stage hostess, introducing the family and the selections they performed. Her communication skills added to the aura the Trapp Family Singers projected to audiences. A 1942 concert reviewer in Bangor, Maine, commented on the singers' charm and Von Trapp's role:

> Baroness Von Trapp, exceedingly charming, acted as the spokesperson. Her rare loveliness and restraint, as she introduced the numbers, was a high point. . . . The Trapp family always sing without accompaniment and their infallible pitch is a marvel. . . . [It] brought an ovation from [the] audience. Music of the highest order was heard when this talented family presented a program ranging from church music to the lovely songs of the Austrian Tyrol.

The Trapp Family Singers became one of America's most heavily booked attractions. For 17 consecutive seasons (1938–55), they toured in 49 of the States and in Canada. Each season brought a new repertoire. Father Wasner required constant rehearsals and strict discipline. His musical research produced music that was sometimes performed for the first time in America. The group sang in dozens of languages, as they incorporated folk music from many lands in their programs. Christmas concerts added to their renown as they reenacted customs and music familiar from their Austrian home. With proceeds from their singing, the Trapps bought a farm in the Green Mountains near Stowe, Vermont, in 1941. Between tours, they worked to farm the land and build a house. The farm became known as "*Cor Unum*," meaning "One heart, one soul."

During World War II, Rupert and Werner Von Trapp served in the American army. Rupert then resumed his medical career and no longer performed, while Werner rejoined the singers and grew interested in farming. The Trapp Family Singers eventually included the three youngest children: Rosmarie, Eleonore, and Johannes.

The Trapps became so well known as a symbol of family togetherness that they were often asked for advice on successful family life. In

1944, they opened the Trapp Family Music Camp near their home in Stowe, to serve as a summer retreat for music-making and an example of group living and customs. The camp operated for 12 successful seasons.

In 1947, Georg Von Trapp died at 67 and was buried near the family home. Through his family's concertizing, he had not sung on stage, but he accompanied them on tours and assisted in their work. Before his death, he helped form the Trapp Family Austrian Relief, a charity founded to assist the needy in postwar Austria. The Trapps were credited with shipping over 275,000 pounds of supplies to their homeland. After the captain's death, the singing group was reorganized almost annually. Rosmarie no long wished to sing and four of the others married between 1947–49. Meshing individual lives with the demands of the singing career was taxing, and non-related singers sometimes filled gaps left by family members.

As leader of the group, Von Trapp was anxious to continue the Trapp Family Singers, whose demand persisted unabated. In 1950, they toured South America and Europe. In 1952, their travels included the Hawaiian Islands. In 1955, the group concertized for six months in Australia and New Zealand. "For twenty blissful years we had traveled the world together, bringing music to the people," Von Trapp reflected. But in 1956, the group retired from the stage. Despite their adventures and the experiences of exotic travels, the family members had made many personal sacrifices to achieve a log of 2,000 concerts for millions of listeners in over 30 countries.

Von Trapp noted that "in the adventure of faith there is no such thing as a closed door." Three of the Trapp children served as missionaries in New Guinea, while their mother and Father Wasner toured the mission fields of the South Pacific for the Catholic Church. With the family home in Stowe increasingly vacant, it was turned into the Trapp Family Lodge, a year-round resort. Von Trapp continued to live there, but was often absent. She forged a career for herself on the stage alone—as a much sought-after lecturer.

During the 1960s and 1970s, Von Trapp took her message of faith to audiences across America. She related the story of her family and stressed that "if God's Will had turned out so well in the case of the Trapp Family, it can also work for you." She emphasized "the art of loving" and the need for compassion and charity in everyday life. With the proceeds from her appearances, Von Trapp helped support missions and carried on quiet charity work for the remainder of her life.

When *The Sound of Music* debuted on the Broadway stage in 1959, a new measure of fame surrounded the Trapp Family. With *Mary Martin in Maria's role and Rodgers and Hammerstein's music, the play became a Broadway legend. It was a money-maker for everyone but the original family. Soon after her book *The Story of the Trapp Family Singers* was published, Von Trapp sold rights to the story for $9,000. Despite huge profits earned by the play and the movie, she never received more than a tiny fraction of one percent of the profits. This money was divided among the family and Father Wasner, who returned to Europe. "It's simply not so that we are rolling in millions," Von Trapp stated in 1980. "People write that *Sound of Music* strengthened their trust in God. That is enough for me."

Crowds came to the Trapp Family Lodge to catch a glimpse of "the real Maria from *The Sound of Music*." Von Trapp operated a gift

From the movie The Sound of Music, *starring* Julie Andrews.

shop on the property, where she mingled with visitors, visiting each table in the lodge dining room. She oversaw the lodge operation until her son Johannes became manager in 1969.

The Von Trapp children were occasional visitors at the lodge, but none ever resumed a musical career. Rupert became a New England doctor, with six children. Werner operated a Vermont dairy farm, with help from his six offspring. Agathe participated in operating a Maryland kindergarten. Maria served 30 years as a missionary in New Guinea. Hedwig assisted at the lodge and taught until her death. Johanna raised seven children in Austria. Martina died with her first baby. Rosmarie studied nursing and retained an interest in music. Eleonore raised seven daughters. Johannes graduated from Yale Forestry School; his two children were raised on the Trapp Family Lodge property.

In 1980, the Trapps lost their home for the second time when a flash-fire sent guests fleeing the wooden lodge. Von Trapp escaped unharmed but saw her home leveled by flames. "I lost just plain everything," she said. The Trapps were encouraged by former guests and friends to rebuild their lodge, and a new version was opened in 1983. At a celebration of the reopening, the family gathered in one of their rare reunions. Once again they sang and reminisced over their lives. "My life," Maria Von Trapp remarked, "has been like a story, a very, very beautiful story." Her experience included both tragedy and success, fame and public adulation. Most significant to Von Trapp was the concept that God had guided her through all her experiences.

Von Trapp spent her last years living quietly in Stowe. When she died at the age of 82 in 1987, she left behind her the image of a determined woman, true to her convictions, and the image of the heroine of one of the most popular films ever made.

SOURCES:

Anderson, William. "America's Trapp Family," in *American History Illustrated.* December 1986, p. 36.
Von Trapp, Maria Augusta. *Maria: My Own Story.* Carol Stream, IL: Creation House, 1972.
———. *The Story of the Trapp Family Singers.* Philadelphia, PA: J.B. Lippincott, 1949.
Von Trapp Family members. Interviews with the author, 1980, 1984, 1993.

SUGGESTED READING:

Hirsch, Julia Antopol. *The Sound of Music: The Making of America's Favorite Movie.* Contemporary Books, 1993.

RELATED MEDIA:

The Sound of Music, starring Julie Andrews and Christopher Plummer, produced by Twentieth Century-Fox, 1965.

Trapp Family Singers. "The Best of the Trapp Family Singers" (2-cassette set), MCA Corporation, 1991.
Trapp Family Singers. "Everywhere Christmas" CD, Trapp Family Lodge, Stowe, VT, 1993.

William Anderson,
author of numerous books and magazine articles,
including *The World of the Trapp Family*

von Wedemeyer, Maria (c. 1924–1977).

See Wedemeyer, Maria von.

von Westphalen, Jenny (1814–1881).

See Marx, Jenny von Westphalen.

von Wiegand, Charmion
(1899–1993)

American abstract painter and collage artist. Born in 1899 in Chicago, Illinois; died in 1993; studied at Barnard College; married second husband Joseph Freeman (a magazine editor), in 1932.

Grew up in San Francisco; began painting (1926); writer for art magazines; met friend and mentor Piet Mondrian (1941); learned to paint Chinese characters and developed abstract collage style (1940s); organized Kurt Schwitter's exhibition of collages (1948); inspired by theosophy and Tibetan Buddhism.

Charmion von Wiegand was born in 1899 into a prosperous, middle-class family in Chicago and spent her childhood in San Francisco. That city—in particular the vibrant life of Chinatown—was one of her strong early influences, along with her father's theosophist religion, which incorporated elements of Buddhism.

Trying to meet her family's expectations, von Wiegand attended the prestigious women's college Barnard in New York and made a socially acceptable marriage. By the time she reached her late 20s, she was a very unhappy society wife living in Darien, Connecticut. Von Wiegand sought the help of a psychoanalyst, and in 1926 began to paint. She divorced her husband and, declining his financial help, began working as a journalist, painting only in her spare time. In 1932, von Wiegand married again, to magazine editor Joseph Freeman, and became a writer for art magazines.

Through her journalistic research, von Wiegand became increasingly interested in abstract art. In 1941, she interviewed the Dutch artist Piet Mondrian and found that her background in theosophy fit with his philosophy of order and harmony in art. He became both a good friend and artistic mentor, encouraging her to explore non-objective painting. The 1940s was a period of great experimentation for von Wiegand, leading her to an informal collage style that incorporated both paper and cloth, and juxtaposed symbols and solids. In 1948, she was one of the organizers of Kurt Schwitter's exhibition of collages.

Some of von Wiegand's collages incorporated Chinese characters painted in ink, and in the late 1940s, inspired by its religious symbolism, she began studying Tibetan Buddhist art. This combination of Buddhist and abstract art became the defining characteristic of von Wiegand's work. She expanded her knowledge with trips to India in the 1970s, and continued studying, writing, and producing collages well into her 80s. She died in 1993, at the age of 94.

SOURCES:

Bailey, Brooke. *The Remarkable Lives of 100 Women Artists.* Holbrook, MA: Bob Adams, 1994.

Paula Morris, D.Phil.,
Brooklyn, New York

Vorlova, Slavka (1894–1973)

Czech composer, conductor, pianist, singer and teacher. Name variations: Miroslava; (pseudonym) Mira Kord. Born in Nachod, Czechoslovakia, on March 15, 1894; died in Prague on August 24, 1973.

Was the first woman in Czechoslovakia to receive a music degree in composition (1948); composed over 100 works, including over 20 symphonic works and three operas; also composed jazz and modern music.

Slavka Vorlova lost her voice while studying singing under **Rosa Papier** at Vienna's Music Academy, so she studied composition under Vitezslav Novak and piano under Vaclav Stephan in Prague. Following her marriage in 1919, she established musical evenings which became quite well known. At the end of World War II, she decided to study composition at the Prague Conservatory and in 1948 became the first woman to receive a degree in composition in Czechoslovakia. Vorlova was a prolific composer who wrote over 100 works which cover a wide range of styles. *Rozmarynka* is a folk opera set in a 19th-century Czech village. Although folk music greatly influenced her, she also made unusual use of instruments. Aleatorics, dodecaphony and serial techniques played an increasing role in her music after 1960. Using the name Mira Kord, Vorlova composed many jazz works and songs.

SOURCES:

Cohen, Aaron I. *International Encyclopedia of Women Composers.* 2 vols. NY: Books & Music (USA), 1987.

Sadie, Stanley, ed. *New Grove Dictionary of Music and Musicians.* 20 vols. NY: Macmillan, 1980.

John Haag,
Athens, Georgia

Vorontsova, Ekaterina (1744–1810).

See Dashkova, Ekaterina.

Vorse, Mary Heaton (1874–1966)

American labor journalist. Born in New York City on October 9, 1874; died in Provincetown, Massachusetts, on June 14, 1966; only child of Hiram Heaton and Ellen (Blackman) Heaton; privately educated, including art school in Paris (1893) and New York City (1896–98); married Albert White Vorse, in 1898 (died 1910); married Joe O'Brien, in 1912; children: (first marriage) Heaton Vorse (b. 1901) and Ellen Vorse (b. 1907); (second marriage) Joel O'Brien (1914).

Writings: hundreds of articles and short stories, two plays, and sixteen books, including Men and Steel *(1920),* Strike! *(1930), and* Time and Town *(1942).*

When Mary Heaton Vorse was in her 80s, she wrote: "You must understand that when I was young, Life said to me, 'Here are two ways—a world running to mighty cities, full of

*Mary
Heaton
Vorse*

Boyce, Neith.
See Glaspell,
Susan for
sidebar.

**Eastman,
Crystal.** See
Balch, Emily
Greene for
sidebar.

the spectacle of bloody adventure, and here is home and children. Which will you take, the adventurous life or a quiet life?' 'I will take *both*.' I said." Her decision to live a full life as a journalist, traveling the world, and have a family for which, by virtue of being twice widowed, she was the sole provider, was not always easy. Her relationships with her children, especially her daughter **Ellen Vorse**, were frequently strained. Money was often in short supply, and Vorse was not above turning out short stories she called "lollipops" to make some easy cash. Nonetheless, in old age, her children rallied round her, and her career as a labor journalist had no rival. In an age when women rarely tried to combine family responsibilities with a career, Mary Heaton Vorse did indeed do both.

She was born in New York City in 1874, the only child of Hiram and **Ellen Blackman Heaton**. Her mother had been a wealthy widow with five teenagers when she met and married Hiram Heaton. Mary Heaton Vorse's childhood was a comfortable one, with homes in New York City and Amherst, Massachusetts, and yearly trips to Europe. Somewhat of a rebel and very much wanting to be a "New Woman," Vorse convinced her parents to send her to Paris for a year of art school. Even though her mother accompanied her, Vorse saw this as her first break from familial restraints. In 1896, she took more art classes in New York and, with her parents in Amherst most of the time, secretly married Albert White Vorse. A second ceremony with their families in attendance took place six months later. Albert, a sailor, explorer and writer, earned almost enough to provide his family a comfortable lifestyle, including trips to Europe and a summer home in Provincetown, Massachusetts.

Mary Heaton Vorse had given up painting for writing by 1903, turning out short stories for extra income while her husband worked on a book. Their marriage, initially so passionate, grew strained due to Alfred's unfaithfulness, and by the time he died in 1910, the two had drifted apart. Vorse's mother died the same day, and the two deaths and the financial pressure of caring for her children pushed Mary Heaton Vorse not to a breakdown but to a new career—that of labor journalist.

Her coverage of the 1912 Lawrence, Massachusetts, "Bread and Roses" textile strike established Vorse as more than a labor journalist; she was a sympathetic, even at times participatory reporter. During the Lawrence strike, Vorse met Industrial Workers of the World (IWW) leader *Elizabeth Gurley Flynn who was to become a

lifelong friend. It was also in Lawrence that Vorse met her second husband, the radical journalist Joe O'Brien. Although their marriage was to be brief, the two spent magical summers in Vorse's Provincetown house, surrounded by their radical and literary friends, such as Hutchins Hapgood and ◄ **Neith Boyce**, Max Eastman, John Reed, and *Susan Glaspell. To amuse themselves one summer night, the group put on a play on Vorse's dock and the Provincetown Players were born. Winters were spent in New York, where Vorse worked as an editor for the radical journal the *Masses*. In 1912, she and several other like-minded women, including Elizabeth Gurley Flynn, ◄ **Crystal Eastman** and **Henrietta Rodman**, formed the Heterodoxy Club. In 1914, Vorse and O'Brien's son Joel was born; a year later, Joe O'Brien was dead, a victim of stomach cancer. Once again, Vorse was left a widow, now with three children to support.

For the next 40 years, she would travel from one strike to the next, reporting the horrible conditions of labor which drove workers to strike, and the police brutality they frequently faced on the picket line. From the Mesabi Range copper miners' strike in 1916 to the massive steel strike of 1919, from the textile workers' strike in Gastonia, North Carolina, in 1926 to the Flint, Michigan, auto workers' sitdown strike of 1937, Vorse passionately recorded in articles, books, and even novels the efforts of workers to achieve dignity in the face of oppression. At the same time, her personal life continued to be difficult. There never seemed to be enough time to be a good mother and a good writer. A two-year affair with the political cartoonist and Communist Robert Minor ended in 1922 with Vorse suffering a miscarriage and Minor leaving her for another, younger woman. After her miscarriage, the 47-year-old Vorse was prescribed morphine to which she became addicted for a few years. Once again, however, she found within herself the strength to go on—for the sake of her children and for the sake of her career.

Mary Heaton Vorse remained active until the end. In the 1950s, still a friend of labor but not necessarily of the big unions which represented workers, she wrote an article exposing corruption within the longshoremen's union. Always short of cash, Vorse gratefully accepted money from supporters, only to give most of it away, beginning in the 1950s, to various Southern civil-rights groups, and later in the 1960s, to Cesar Chavez, leader of the Chicano farmworkers' movement. Now almost 90, Vorse carried out her activism closer to her beloved Provincetown home. In the early 1960s, she was part of the effort to establish a national park on Cape

Cod, and she fought the dumping of nuclear waste. When the local Episcopalian minister spoke out against the Vietnam War and displeased much of his congregation, Vorse in turn spoke out on his behalf.

In 1962, the United Auto Workers (UAW) presented Vorse with their first Social Justice Award. UAW president Walter Reuther and his brother Victor had heard that their friend, the great labor journalist, was in need of money, and the award was designed as a cover for the "honorarium" which went with it. However, four years later, when Mary Heaton Vorse died at the age of 92, Walter Reuther released a statement to the press which summarized why Vorse was worthy of a social justice award. "She was one of the great labor writers of all time," he said. "She wrote with deep compassion of the human need for working class people. . . . Mary Heaton Vorse was part of the UAW." In reality, Vorse was part of a much larger community, that of workers everywhere. She earned her place through her writing, which resonated with a passion for simple justice.

SOURCES:

Garrison, Dee. *Mary Heaton Vorse: The Life of an American Insurgent*. Philadelphia, PA: Temple University Press, 1989.

COLLECTIONS:

Mary Heaton Vorse Papers, Archives of Labor History and Urban Affairs, Wayne State University, Detroit, Michigan.

Kathleen Banks Nutter,
Manuscripts Processor at the
Sophia Smith Collection, Smith College,
Northampton, Massachusetts

Voynich, Ethel (1864–1960)

Irish-born British writer and translator. Born Ethel Lilian Boole in 1864 in Cork, Ireland; died in 1960 in New York City; daughter of George Boole (a mathematician) and Mary Everest Boole (a feminist philosopher); educated in Irish schools and in Berlin; married Wilfrid Michael Voynich (1865–1930), in 1891.

Worked for periodical Free Russia *in London; drew on husband's political experiences for the first and best known of her novels,* The Gadfly *(1897), made into a film in Soviet Union (1955); moved to United States (1916).*

Selected writings: (novels) The Gadfly *(1897),* Jack Raymond *(1901),* Olive Latham *(1904),* An Interrupted Friendship *(1910),* Put Off Thy Shoes *(1945); (translations)* Stories from Garshin *(1893),* The Humour of Russia *(1895),* Chopin's letters *(1931).*

Ethel Voynich was born Ethel Lilian Boole in 1864 in Cork, Ireland. Daughter of eminent mathematician George Boole and feminist philosopher **Mary Everest Boole**, Ethel Boole was educated in Irish schools and later in Berlin, also traveling as a young woman to Russia.

In 1891, she married Wilfrid Michael Voynich, a young Polish exile who in 1890 had escaped to England from exile in Siberia, where he had been sent in 1885 because of his involvement in the anti-tsarist Polish nationalist movement. In England, he had anglicized his name from Habdank-Woynicz after becoming a naturalized British subject. Ethel Voynich worked for a time in London for the periodical *Free Russia*.

Voynich's first novel, *The Gadfly* (1897), drew heavily on her husband's political experience and idealistic revolutionary zeal, with which she sympathized. A vehemently anti-clerical novel, *The Gadfly* is set in pre-1848 Italy and features both a revolutionary young Englishwoman and the "gadfly" hero of the title. A popular success, the book went through eight impressions in four years, selling in vast quantities in translation in Eastern Europe and the Soviet Union, where it was made into a film in 1955 (with a score by Dmitri Shostakovich).

Voynich's reputation as a writer is largely based on *The Gadfly*, but she published other novels featuring revolutionary heroes, such as *Jack Raymond* (1901), the story of a rebel and a Polish patriot's widow; *Olive Latham* (1904), about an English nurse and a Russian revolutionary; and *An Interrupted Friendship* (1910), which continues the story of *The Gadfly*. None of her later novels are considered the equal of her first, and are chiefly characterized by an obsession with violence and physical suffering.

In addition to novels, Voynich published two translations of Russian stories, *Stories from Garshin* (1893) and *The Humour of Russia* (1895), and a translation of Chopin's letters (1931). In 1916, Voynich and her husband moved to the United States, where she continued writing, publishing her last novel, *Put Off Thy Shoes*, in 1945. She died in 1960 in New York.

Ethel Voynich

SOURCES:

Drabble, Margaret, ed. *The Oxford Companion to English Literature.* 5th ed. Oxford: Oxford University Press, 1985.

Shattock, Joanne. *The Oxford Guide to British Women Writers.* Oxford: Oxford University Press, 1993.

Paula Morris, D.Phil.,
Brooklyn, New York

Vreeland, Diana (1903–1989)

Parisian-born fashion icon, style setter, and innovative editor of Vogue *and* Harper's Bazaar, *who created the annual extravagant fashion exhibitions at the Metropolitan Museum of Art as consultant to its Costume Institute. Born Diana Dalziel in Paris on July 29, 1903; died at Lenox Hill Hospital in New York City on August 22, 1989, of a heart attack; daughter of Frederick Y. Dalziel (a Scottish stockbroker) and Emily Key (Hoffman) Dalziel (an American socialite); had apparently little formal education, aside from the Brearley School in New York City for a few months, and ballet classes with Russian choreographer Michel Fokine; married T. Reed Vreeland (a banker), in 1924 (died 1966); children: Thomas R. Vreeland, Jr. (who became an architect in California); Frederick Vreeland (who entered the diplomatic service and served as American ambassador to Morocco); grandchildren: Alexander Vreeland (U.S. director of marketing for Giorgio Armani).*

Awards: various, including Council of American Fashion Designers Salute for her work at the Metropolitan Museum; chevalier of the French National Order of Merit; and honors from the Rhode Island School of Design and the Italian fashion industry.

As World War I approached, family left Paris for New York (1914); made her debut (1922); following marriage in New York City, lived in Albany where husband was a banker trainee (1924–28); moved to Europe; briefly ran an exclusive lingerie shop in London; returned to U.S. (1936); began writing a column for Harper's Bazaar, *"Why Don't You" (1937); was fashion editor of* Harper's *(1937–62); moved to* Vogue *as fashion editor (1962), became editor-in-chief (1963); dismissed from* Vogue *(1971); took four-month hiatus and traveled to Europe; became consultant to the Costume Institute of the Metropolitan Museum of Art (1972), producing a range of costume exhibitions for 14 years.*

Selected writings: Allure *(Doubleday, 1980); (memoirs)* D.V. *(Alfred A. Knopf, 1984).*

"I want this place to look like a garden, but a garden in hell," said Diana Vreeland, when she invited her friend and decorator Billy Baldwin to transform her Park Avenue apartment. She wanted it red, her favorite color: "It makes all other colors beautiful." Notes art historian Mario Praz, if "the surroundings become a museum of the soul," then Vreeland's apartment was her own theatrical backdrop; it remained unchanged for more than 30 years. An invitation to dinner at her home, where she served simple American food along with her anecdotes and distinctive ideas, was prized. Although Vreeland's relatively small apartment on Park Avenue could accommodate only about eight for dinner, the illusion was luxurious. Her guests were a range of famous faces, from entertainment superstar Mick Jagger to *Jacqueline Kennedy. Candles and incense were always burning, while her numerous bibelots personalized the room: photos of friends, schools of brass fish, a Zuolaga scene of Easter Sunday in Seville which was a gift from her husband, porcelain leopards, horn snuffboxes from Scotland, seascapes of shells, needlepoint pillows she made herself, a plaster cast of her mother, her favorite portrait by William Acton, and more. Her material things, though not of great monetary value, had style and personal significance. "She wanted it to seem as though hers was a home of leisure—the flowers, pillows, scents, objects—but in fact, everything was obsessively organized," noted her friend and colleague Katell le Bourhis.

Her scarlet office at the Metropolitan Museum of Art's Costume Institute during her years there as a special consultant reflected the same kind of underlying discipline. After her death, a staff memorandum was featured in a 1993 show commemorating Vreeland. Among the list of what her red oilcloth-covered table must "ALWAYS HAVE" were "green or brown pencils in pencil holders," including "Thuro Black editorial pencils—these are hard to get" and a carton of Lucky Strikes. There was a diagram detailing exactly how her 1:30 PM lunch table should be set, with assigned places for her yellow raisins, cigarettes and lighter, bottle of scotch, and black coffee.

Vreeland, whose life bridged more than 80 years of cultural change, was a visionary, famous for her aphorisms, discourse, and mode of dress. She became an icon in the world of fashion who transcended her position as a fashion editor to influence more than half a century of attitude and style. She also propelled fashion into the forefront of culture through her popular fashion extravaganzas at the Metropolitan Museum of Art's Costume Institute. When she died in 1989, *Newsweek* called her, "The seismograph of chic . . . [whose] most famous creation turned out to be herself."

Vreeland's critics alluded to *Gertrude Stein's "Very interesting, if true" to characterize her memoirs, *D.V.* In the book, she wrote that her parents, who met in Paris, were part of the transition between the formal Edwardian era and the modern world. Her Scottish father Frederick Y. Dalziel was a "continental Englishman"—a stockbroker who never made money. Even so, the family lived well in Paris where Diana was born in 1903.

Her childhood harbored some family problems, which Vreeland characteristically did not dwell on. The Dalziels, who lived for pleasure, displayed little emotion. Her mother **Emily Key Hoffman** was a beautiful American socialite who had numerous lovers. Diana, who emulated Emily's sense of drama, loved dancing, especially the tango, and "adored" dressing and making up to go out. As a young woman, Vreeland covered her upper body with stark white theatrical makeup, reveling in the contrast of makeup and scarlet nails against the background of her escort's black dinner jacket. Later in life, her makeup routine would include those trademark scarlet nails and lipstick, scarlet streaks of rouge on her cheeks, forehead and earlobes. She enjoyed asking her companions, "Is it Kabuki enough?" (Japanese Kabuki theater was among her loves.) "Performance is all I cared about as a child," she said, "and it's all I care about now. I don't go to see a great play, I go to see a great *interpreter.*"

According to her memoirs, Vreeland's education consisted of observation; she had very little formal schooling. Most days, she and her sister would go to the Bois de Boulogne to play; Wednesdays, she went to the Louvre with her grandmother's secretary. In the Paris of her childhood, the women of the demimonde, the beautiful actresses and mistresses of royalty and the rich, were the great personalities. Seeing their clothes in the park stimulated her lifelong passion for fashion.

Her other passion was horses. In 1914, the Dalziels moved to New York to escape World War I. When there was an outbreak of infantile paralysis in the East, she and her sister were sent to Cody, Wyoming, where Vreeland claimed she learned to ride from Buffalo Bill Cody. In New York, her formal education consisted of several months at the exclusive Brearley School for Girls. She also studied ballet with Russian masters, including choreographer Michel Fokine, and developed a discipline which would later serve her well.

Two years after making her debut in 1922, she met T. Reed Vreeland, a handsome Yale graduate, while on vacation in Saratoga, New York. Diana admired his glamour and professed she only felt comfortable about her looks after she married. Days before the ceremony in 1924, a scandal involving her mother and a lover appeared in the newspaper, and on the wedding day the guests did not arrive because her mother had forgotten to mail the invitations. The newlyweds moved to Albany, where Reed had a job as a bank trainee, and their first child Thomas was born. The family then moved to Europe when Reed was hired by a bank in London, and Diana gave birth to her second son Frederick.

For Vreeland, who educated herself by reading, books were a major influence; the family read aloud together and eventually amassed several thousand volumes. While in London, she ran a custom lingerie business where she first met Wallis Warfield Simpson, the future *Duchess of Windsor, as a customer. Like Diana's father, her husband was not a successful capitalist. Though he and Diana never spoke of business, they managed to live luxuriously and travel to offbeat places in a Bugatti, accompanied by a housemaid and a chauffeur. "When I lived in London," she told *New York Magazine*, "if you were sufficiently well-born and well known, you could mount bills *forever.*" The Vreelands were a popular couple in the social whirl of London and Paris. Appearing everywhere as a fashionable young woman, Diana was handed complimentary couture clothing—a *prix jeune fille*—from the top designers before the war.

As a lover of haute couture, after their return to New York in 1936, Vreeland missed Europe, which was to be always a more comfortable environment for her. Notes fashion publicist **Eleanor Lambert**, "In Europe, the great style setters were never beauties. Diana knew that she fit into that tradition." One night in New York, **Carmel Snow**, the *Harper's Bazaar* editor who made *Harper's* the most innovative fashion magazine of its time, noticed Vreeland dancing at the St. Regis, wearing a white lace *Coco Chanel dress with a bolero jacket and red roses in her hair. Her flair caught Snow's eye, and she was invited to write a column for the magazine despite her protest that she lacked experience. Vreeland needed the income, and Snow needed a new editor who traveled in international society. In summer 1936, Vreeland's "Why Don't You" column debuted in *Harper's Bazaar*, providing fantasy in the midst of hard economic times. Vreeland remembered it as frivolous, but the column was widely read. "Why don't you wash your blond child's hair in dead champagne to keep it gold, as they do in France?" she'd ask.

Vreeland was flattered when humorist S.J. Perelman parodied the column in *The New Yorker*.

The following year, she was promoted to fashion editor, a position that required an amalgam of talents—film director, propmaster, seamstress, and beautician. On a visit to the museum of Pompeii, she observed the figures of a woman and her slave making love preserved in volcanic ash. Vreeland copied the slave's footwear: a strap between the toes, thin layers of leather for a sole, and a strap around the ankle attached to the heel. Voilà: the thonged sandal.

Of course, you understand, I'm looking for the most farfetched perfection.

—Diana Vreeland

From the magazine's art director Alexey Brodovitch, she learned to develop a photo spread of contrasting scale by opposing two pictures. Vreeland incorporated the uncommon images of photographers like Man Ray and Richard Avedon, and she developed a long working relationship with *Louise Dahl-Wolfe, who photographed American fashion outdoors. When the war cut off fashion news from Paris, American designers were inspired by Vreeland's imagination. But when Snow retired in 1958, she alerted the publisher, the Hearst organization, that Vreeland did not have the discipline and judgment to be editor-in-chief. Snow's niece, **Nancy White**, was named her successor, and Vreeland stayed on for four more years. During her 28-year career at *Harper's Bazaar*, she earned less than $20,000 annually. In 1962, when *Vogue* courted her with money and, wrote Vreeland, "an endless expense account and Europe whenever I want to go," she became *Vogue*'s fashion editor.

Addressed by her staff as Mrs. Vreeland (her friends called her Dee-Ann), she proceeded to remake *Vogue* in her own image, which meant shaking up the status quo and creating friction with some of the staff. "In many ways, she acted like a brilliant theatrical producer," recalled Alexander Liberman, editorial director of Condé Nast publications. "She visualized *Vogue* as theater." When editor **Jessica Daves** retired angrily, Vreeland's name replaced hers as editor-in-chief on the January 1963 *Vogue* masthead. Vreeland's style was an intrinsic part of her persona. "What she presented was not who she was," wrote Avedon. "Diana lived for imagination ruled by discipline." At *Vogue*, she wore a simple "uniform" of black sweater, beige skirt, and comfortable, ankle-strap low-heel sandals. She loved aristocratic luxury of earlier periods, and she also embraced the avant-garde. After years

of wearing her hair in a snood, she opted for a jet-black helmeted mane. Maintenance in all things was key: an early enthusiast for physical fitness, she was sleekly groomed and fashionably thin; her many bags and shoes were religiously maintained with daily polishing and waxing by her maid. Described by Cecil Beaton as an "authoritative crane . . . [who] walked like a ballet dancer," Vreeland was noted by her collaborator on *Allure*, Christopher Hemphill, for a voice which "almost allows one to *see* the italics she speaks in[;] her choice of words is even more arresting than her delivery. She naturally introduces foreign words into conversation" and "gives the impression of inventing her own syntax as she goes along." For example, she broke down corduroy into its original components—*cord du roi*. Vreeland became famous for her observations—like "Peanut butter is the greatest invention since Christianity," or "Pink is the navy blue of India."

With a credo of "Give them what they never knew they wanted," Vreeland sent her photographers and models to locations around the world for the exotic images that transformed fashion journalism. To describe her vision of the magazine's essence to **Kate Lloyd**, her assistant features editor, Vreeland used the phrase "*Vogue* is the myth of the next reality." Though in her 60s when she came to the magazine (her colleagues thought of her as years younger), she understood the times—the 1960s youth culture, rock 'n' roll, John F. Kennedy's presidency, and the Vietnam War. In a world of material affluence, she not only reported on the latest fashion news but also influenced it. Vreeland coined the word "youthquake" and welcomed miniskirts and bikinis, "the biggest thing since the atom bomb." Young people were creating their own styles, in dress and behavior, and Vreeland's enthusiasm for this youth movement was reflected in the pages of *Vogue*. For Vreeland, Mick Jagger was "the creature of the '60s," while the pouty French actress **Brigitte Bardot** represented the '50s: "Her lips made Mick Jagger's lips *possible*," she wrote in *Allure*. She found the perfect model for the bikini, the German countess **Veruschka**. When Veruschka wanted her name mentioned in *Vogue*, Vreeland agreed, launching the cult of celebrity-models. She discovered *Twiggy, used women of color, and moved beyond conventional beauty by using women with strong features.

During her tenure, she highlighted the work of photographers such as Avedon, Beaton, Irving Penn, and **Deborah Turbeville**. Avedon worked with her at *Harper's Bazaar* and *Vogue* for over

40 years, and paid her high tribute: "Vreeland invented the fashion photographer." Photographers, who learned not to take what she said literally and to understand her idiosyncratic code, gave her the imaginative pictures she wanted. The paparazzi style—the snapshot that caught the unintended and revealed personality—fascinated Vreeland. "Laying out a beautiful picture in a beautiful way is a bloody bore. I think you've got to blow it right across the page and on the side, crop it, cut it in half, combine it with something else . . . *do* something with it." A perfectionist, she worked closely with photographers, supervising reshoots until she was satisfied. Unprecedented composite photos were used to create the perfect whole: legs, arms, torsos were mixed and matched. Artifice for dramatic effect was a hallmark of her style.

While Vreeland's years at *Vogue* were that of an unmistakable innovator, Liberman notes that she was an uncontrollable force at the magazine, and the planning required to run the publication was not there. As the 1970s ushered in feminism and a new austerity in light of economic recession, her extremes—editorial and finan-

Diana
Vreeland

cial—were seen to be getting out of hand. Vreeland had alienated many Seventh Avenue designers by featuring fashions that were not practical or available in stores. They felt that *Vogue* needed redirection, and in 1971 Vreeland was dismissed. Associate editor **Grace Mirabella** became editor-in-chief of the publication.

Characteristically, Vreeland forged ahead with stoicism. After her husband's death of cancer in 1966, she had continued her lavish lifestyle and now needed to work. Her friend, Metropolitan Museum curator Thomas Rousseau, suggested to the museum director, Thomas Hoving, that Vreeland become a special consultant to the Met's Costume Institute; her salary would be contributed by a number of friends. Although that financial arrangement did not materialize, Vreeland signed on in 1972 and more than proved her worth in revitalizing the institute, a primarily scholarly wing of the museum, giving it high visibility. Her annual exhibits, beginning in 1973, attracted hundreds of thousands of new visitors to the Metropolitan and made it a focal point for the Beautiful People, the monied upper class who were her friends, bringing in new patrons and thousands of dollars in donations. Her involvement was timely: Vreeland's spectaculars supported a new trend in the museum world—commercialization and expansion to keep them viable, including glittering fund-raising events, blockbuster exhibits, and retail shops. For 14 years, she would conceive a range of annual costume spectaculars which strengthened her position as stylemaker extraordinaire.

Although Vreeland knew what would sell to the public and patrons, not everyone was happy with her performance. Her selective historical view was solely from the standpoint of style and fashion, which concerned some museum officials; her outrageous bills, accumulated during scouting trips for costumes around the world, did not endear her to the financial powers at the museum; and she angered some of the curatorial staff when she called on her socially prominent and designer friends to critique an exhibit prior to opening.

During the 1980s—the "Me Decade" with its newly rich elite seeking status through cultural affiliation and a Reagan presidency that garnered criticism for its sense of aristocracy and fantasy—some critical voices were raised about corporate sponsorship of Vreeland's exhibitions and their content. Luxury, opulence, and glamour—an emphasis on surface over substance—were a constant, no matter what the period or subject. Richard Martin and Harold Koda, curators of her own 1993 tribute at the Costume Institute, offered another interpretation in the ex-

hibition catalogue. Unlike the traditional museological approach of a curator, Vreeland worked more like the editor she was, interpreting costume, creating elements of mystery and magic, and employing a nonchronological, subjective late-20th-century view of history.

From the start, Vreeland's exhibitions reflected her experience with fashion photography. In her first show, which featured the work of haute couture designer Cristobal Balenciaga, she animated the mannequins—a figure in a flamenco dress appeared to be dancing—and she used lighting like a studio photographer, employing shadows to form a path through the gallery. Some subsequent shows would include period posters and paintings, providing background to enhance the costumes. Borrowing works from some curators to satisfy this styling, however, conflicted with their more academic approach.

Many of Vreeland's exhibitions generated criticism for various reasons, from their suitability to their historical accuracy, but this did not stop her from attracting great numbers of museumgoers. Among her spectaculars were "Romantic and Glamorous Hollywood Design" (1974), for which the inclusion of **Barbra Streisand**'s costume for the then-unreleased film *Funny Girl* raised questions; "The Glory of the Russian Costume" (1976), with a catalogue written by Vreeland's friend, Jacqueline Kennedy (both women were instrumental in negotiating with the government of the Soviet Union to lend costumes and accoutrements; asked by government functionaries her opinion of the Soviet Union, Vreeland lauded Russian cheekbones and the simplicity of Russian dress); and "The Manchu Dragon: Costumes of China, the Ch'ing Dynasty," which drew criticism from historian **Deborah Silverman** who claimed that the exhibit projected a fantasy of wealth, power and leisure within a fashion-show environment, without regard for historical accuracy or context.

"The Eighteenth Century Woman" (1981) focused on women's luxurious dress, but ignored contemporary social criticism of such extravagance in France before the Revolution and failed to explain the meaning of the revolutionary dress code of *sans-culottes*, the common man's trousers versus the aristocrat's knee breeches. "The Belle Epoque" (1982), for all its beauty and influence on designers and perfume manufacturers, was a misnomer; it was not a French golden age, but a *fin de siècle*, a period of decline and political and social upheaval to end the century. The focus was on women who had intrigued Vreeland from childhood—demi-mondaines, actresses, and mistresses who derived their own power from powerful men. Vreeland featured women's cycling outfits as sportswear, but gave no indication that this was controversial clothing that symbolized the new freedom and mobility of women.

Glamorous fund-raising events launched each exhibit and the crowds continued to pour in, but the critics were vigilant. Silverman noted that particular themes were apparent in Vreeland's period exhibits: elites about to collapse, and the power of women derived from their appearance and seduction rather than their intelligence.

Vreeland's "Twenty-five Years of Yves Saint Laurent" (1983) was the first museum tribute to a living designer, and her most obviously commercial exhibit, "Man and the Horse" (1984), celebrated her lifelong equestrian passion. The latter provided its sponsor, Ralph Lauren, with a unique advertising and marketing opportunity for his $350,000 grant. The generous grant enabled Lauren's name and logo to appear on everything from the Costume Institute's benefit invitations to the exhibit gallery walls. Lauren's designs, criticized as lacking in originality, would be elevated by association with the museum. Admiring the "integrity of man and the beautiful beast," Vreeland used the precision and chic related to horsemanship as components in her exhibit. In acknowledgment of her childhood adventure out West, she included Buffalo Bill Cody's jacket.

By 1983, Vreeland's eyesight had grown weaker and she was becoming frail. During preparation time for "Royal India," which was scheduled to open in December 1985, she communicated mostly by phone and came to work infrequently. Even in a wheelchair, she wore shoes that grabbed attention, black slippers with large 18th-century rosettes. Vreeland told Veruschka that she didn't need to see anything; she could visualize the show down to its minute details. Veruschka was so fascinated by Vreeland's descriptions that she forgot that Vreeland was nearly blind. In 1985, the Council of American Fashion Designers lauded Vreeland for her contribution to fashion as art and bringing it to such a vast public. She died of cancer four years later, on April 22, 1989, at Lenox Hill Hospital in New York City.

Vreeland was a hard-to-identify, charismatic, obsessive visionary. Critics questioned her artifice, choice of surface over substance, and successful elevation of fashion as art, tempered by subjectivity instead of historical context. In the catalogue for "Diana Vreeland: Immoderate Style" (1993), the Metropolitan Costume Institute's own tribute to Vreeland, she has the last word on style: "The energy of imagination, deliberation, and invention, which falls into a natural rhythm totally one's own, maintained by innate discipline and a keen sense of pleasure. These are the ingredients of style."

SOURCES:

Avedon, Richard. "In Memorium; Diana Vreeland," in *Vanity Fair.* January 1990, p. 158.

Baldwin, Billy, with Michael Gardine. *Billy Baldwin: An Autobiography.* Boston, MA: Little, Brown, 1985, pp. 244–245.

Beaton, Cecil. *The Glass of Fashion.* Garden City, NY: Doubleday, 1954, pp. 359–361.

Collins, Amy Fine. "The Cult of Diana," in *Vanity Fair.* November 1992, pp. 177–190.

Curtis, Charlotte. "Sort of an Empress-of-Fashion Thing," in *The New York Times.* June 17, 1984, p. 13.

Darnton, Nina. "Museums of Modern Garb," in *Newsweek.* February 27, 1989, p. 78.

Kanfer, Stefan. "Madame de Style," in *The New Republic.* July 30, 1984, pp. 37–40.

Koenig, Rhoda. "The Voice of the Peacock," in *New York Magazine.* June 4, 1984, pp. 75–76.

Kornbluth, Jesse. "The Empress of Clothes," in *New York Magazine.* November 29, 1982, pp. 30–36.

Langway, Lynn, with Lisa Whitman. "High Priestess of 'Allure,'" in *Newsweek.* September 22, 1980, pp. 51–52.

Martin, Richard, and Harold Koda. *Diana Vreeland: Immoderate Style.* NY: Metropolitan Museum of Art, 1993.

McGuigan, Cathleen. "The Divine Madame V," in *Newsweek.* September 4, 1989, p. 62.

Morris, Bernadine. "Celebrating the Flair that was Vreeland," in *The New York Times.* December 7, 1993, p. B14.

———. "Diana Vreeland, Editor, Dies; Voice of Fashion for Decades," in *The New York Times.* August 23, 1989, p. 5.

Mullarkey, Maureen. "Fake It! Fake It!," in *The Nation.* November 1, 1986, pp. 437–440.

Storr, Robert. "Unmaking History at the Costume Institute," in *Art in America.* February 1987, pp. 15–23.

Talley, André Leon. "Bridled Passion," in *Vogue.* December 1984, pp. 358–405.

———. "Lady in Red," in *House & Garden.* May 1989 p. 216.

Vogel, Carol. "Vreeland's Touches," in *The New York Times.* April 1, 1990, pp. 61–63.

Vreeland, Diana. *D.V.* NY: Alfred A. Knopf, 1984.

———, and Christopher Hemphill. *Allure.* Garden City, NY: Doubleday, 1980.

RELATED MEDIA:

Allure (27 min. sound recording), adapted from the book by Diana Vreeland and Christopher Hemphill, produced and recorded by Matthew Nast under a grant from the National Endowment for the Arts; first performed January 1982.

Funny Face (color film, 103 min.), starring *Audrey Hepburn, Fred Astaire, and *Kay Thompson; directed by Stanley Donen, 1957 (Astaire's role is based on photographer Richard Avedon, who is credited as visual consultant; as a magazine editor, Kay Thompson ["Think pink"] satirizes Vreeland).

Blowup (color film, 111 min.), starring **Vanessa Redgrave**, David Hemmings, Sarah Miles, Veruschka; music by Herbie Hancock; directed by Michelangelo Antonioni, 1966.

Laurie Norris,
freelance writer,
New York, New York

Vronsky, Vitya (1909—)

Russian pianist. Name variations: Viktoria. Born in Evpatoria, Russian Crimea, on August 22, 1909; married Victor Babin (1908–1972, a pianist), in 1933.

Vitya Vronsky was born in Evpatoria, Russian Crimea, in 1909, and began her studies at the Kiev Conservatory. After she and her family fled Russia, she studied in Berlin with Artur Schnabel and Egon Petri; additional studies were undertaken in Paris with Alfred Cortot. Vronsky began her concert career in 1930. After she married Victor Babin in 1933, they established a highly successful duo-piano team. They emigrated to the United States in 1937, where their joint career blossomed. The Babin-Vronsky duo made many recordings over the decades.

John Haag,
Athens, Georgia

Barbara F. Vucanovich

Vucanovich, Barbara F. (1921—)

American politician. Born Barbara Farrell on June 22, 1921, in Camp Dix, New Jersey; educated at Miss Quinn's School, Albany, New York; graduated from Albany Academy for Girls, 1938; attended Manhattan College of the Sacred Heart, New York, 1938–39.

Was a delegate to the Nevada State Republican conventions (1952–80); served as district staff assistant for U.S. Senator Paul Laxalt (1974–82); was a delegate to the Republican National conventions (1976 and 1980); elected as Republican to the 98th through 104th Congresses (1983–97).

Born Barbara Farrell in Camp Dix, New Jersey, in 1921, Barbara F. Vucanovich grew up in Albany and was educated at both Miss Quinn's School and the Albany Academy for Girls, from which she graduated in 1938. After two years at the Manhattan College of the Sacred Heart in New York, she moved to Nevada in 1949. In the 1960s, Vucanovich was a businesswoman, the owner of a travel agency and an Evelyn Woods Reading Dynamics School.

7But her political interests—she became a delegate to the Nevada State Republican Convention in 1952—eventually spelled a change of career. For 20 years Vucanovich worked for U.S. Senator Paul Laxalt, first as a local organizer and later as his North Nevada representative, holding the position of district staff assistant. This long-term commitment to the Republican Party and her experience in party politics helped secure her the Republican nomination for the newly created Second District seat in 1982. Vucanovich, a Reno resident, was elected to the 98th Congress, taking her seat in 1983, and represented the district encompassing most of the land area of Nevada for six subsequent Congresses.

As a member of the House of Representatives, Vucanovich focused on a number of issues of concern to her constituency, including federal wilderness and national park policy, public land use, and nuclear waste disposal. She served on the Committee on Interior and Insular Affairs (where she was ranking Republican on the Subcommittee on General Oversight and Investigation) and the Committee on House Administration (where she was ranking Republican on the Subcommittee on Accounts). Vucanovich was also a member of the Select Committee on Children, Youth, and Families. In the latter half of her Congressional career she served on the Committee on Appropriations, chairing the Subcommittee on Military Construction during her final term. After 14 years in the House of Representatives, Vucanovich did not seek reelection to the 105th Congress.

SOURCES:
Women in Congress, 1917–1990. Washington, DC: U.S. Government Printing Office, 1991.

Paula Morris, D.Phil.,
Brooklyn, New York

Vukotich, Milena (1847–1923).

See Milena.

Vuldetrade (fl. 550)

Queen of Metz (Austrasia). Name variations: Vuldetrada. Flourished around 550; daughter of Wacho, king of the Lombards; married Thibaud also known as Theodovald or Theudebald (d. 555), king of Metz (Austrasia, r. 548–555); seventh wife of Chlothar, Clothaire, Clotar or Lothair I (497–561), king of Soissons and the Franks.

Vultrogotha (fl. 558)

Queen of Paris. Name variations: Ultrogotte. Flourished around 558; married Childebert (d. 558), king of Paris (r. 511–558), around 558.

Vyroubova, Nina (1921—)

Russian-born French ballerina. Born in 1921 in Gourzouv, USSR; educated at the Lycée Jules Perry, Paris; studied ballet with Vera Trefilova, Olga Preobrazhenska, Victor Gsovsky, Boris Kniaseff, Lubov Egorova, Serge Lifar, Nicholas Zverev, and Yves Brieux.

Appeared in Irene Lidova's Soirées de la Danse *(1944); had first major success in* La Sylphide, Les Ballets des Champs Élysées *(1946); was première danseuse étoile of Paris Opéra (1949–56); ballerina with Grand Ballet du Marquis de Cuevas (1957–61); won Prix Pavlova of the Institut Chorégraphique de Paris (1957); was guest ballerina with Ballet Russe de Monte Carlo (1961–62), and ballet of the Colón Theater, Buenos Aires (1964).*

Nina Vyroubova was born in 1921 in Gourzouv in the Crimea and began studying dance as a child with her mother, a ballet teacher. She continued her education at the Lycée Jules Perry in Paris, and her teachers included *Vera Trefilova, *Olga Preobrazhenska, Victor Gsovsky, Boris Kniaseff, *Lyubov Egorova, Serge Lifar, Nicholas Zverev, and Yves Brieux. Vyroubova first began attracting attention in the mid-1940s, appearing in *Soirées de la Danse*, organized by **Irene Lidova**, in 1944 (dancing with Roland Petit in *Giselle* and *Nightingale and the Rose*) and creating the principal role in Petit's *Les Forains* in 1945.

Her first major success came in 1946, when she danced the title role of *La Sylphide*, recreated by Victor Gsovsky from Filippo Taglioni's original ballet of 1832 for Les Ballets des Champs Élysées. In 1949, Vyroubova became the première danseuse étoile of the Paris Opéra, one of the few dancers trained outside the company to attain such a position.

She continued at the Paris Opéra until 1956, her repertoire including the classic ballets as well as *Blanche Neige*, *Firebird* (the Lifar version), and *Les Noces Fantastiques*. From 1957 to 1961, Vyroubova was ballerina with the Grand Ballet du Marquis de Cuevas, dancing *Giselle*, *Swan Lake*, and *L'Amour et son Destin*, among others. In 1957, her performance in *Giselle* won the Prix Pavlova of the Institut Chorégraphique de Paris.

She was one of the Auroras in the Marquis de Cuevas' final production, *The Sleeping Beauty*. After his death, she appeared as guest ballerina with a number of companies, including the Ballet Russe de Monte Carlo (for their United States tour of 1961–62) and the ballet of the Colón Theater in Buenos Aires, Argentina (1964). She then returned to France to continue dancing and teaching.

Paula Morris, D.Phil.,
Brooklyn, New York

W

Waddell, Helen (1889–1965)

Irish scholar of medieval literature and poet. Born Helen Jane Waddell in Tokyo, Japan, on May 31, 1889; died in London, England, on March 5, 1965; youngest child of Hugh Waddell and Jane Martin Waddell; educated at Victoria School for Girls, Queen's University, Belfast, and at Somerville College, Oxford; never married; no children.

Awards: A.C. Benson Foundation Medal, Royal Society of Literature (1928); fellowship of Royal Society of Literature (1928); member of the Royal Irish Academy (1932); Hon. D.Litt, University of Durham (1932), Columbia University, New York (1935), University of St. Andrew's (1936).

Selected writings: The Wandering Scholars *(Constable, 1927);* Medieval Latin Lyrics *(Constable, 1929);* Abelard *(Constable, 1933);* The Desert Fathers *(Constable, 1936);* Poetry in the Dark Ages *(Constable, 1948).*

Helen Waddell was born in Tokyo in 1889 to a Presbyterian missionary family. Her mother died when she was two, and her father subsequently married his cousin **Martha Waddell**, with whom Helen had a difficult relationship. She was educated at the Victoria School for Girls in Belfast, one of the best secondary schools in Ireland. Headmistress *****Margaret Byers** was so impressed with Helen's abilities that she offered to educate the girl for nothing, but Helen won enough scholarships and prizes to see her through. In 1908, Waddell went to Queen's University, Belfast, from which she graduated in 1911 with a first class B.A. in English language and literature. The following year, she was awarded a master's degree for research on Milton.

The visiting professor in English at Queen's was George Saintsbury, from Edinburgh University, whom Waddell admired greatly; he in turn respected her gifts as a scholar. They would remain in close contact until Saintsbury's death. She also developed a close friendship with the Reverend George Taylor and his wife, who were Presbyterian missionaries, and they wrote each other weekly letters until his death in 1920. These friendships helped her through a stifling and unhappy home life. Her studies at Queen's were often curtailed by her obligation to look after her stepmother, an invalid who disapproved of novels and thought that plays were the devil's work. In 1915, Waddell's brother George, a Presbyterian minister, died suddenly, and his passing deeply affected Helen. She became even closer to her sister **Margaret** at Kilmacrew in County Down, and Margaret's children were the initial audience for the Bible stories which Helen contributed to the Presbyterian magazine *Daybreak*.

Waddell decided to forego further postgraduate study in order to look after her invalid stepmother. In a letter to her sister in 1935, she wrote candidly: "I didn't actually hate mother but I had a deep festering grudge against all the ways she had thwarted me, the things she had taken from me, and never a word of thanks. . . . I knew that if only I had mastered that grudge inwardly as well as outwardly, those years would have been far richer." When her stepmother finally died in February 1919, Waddell suffered a nervous reaction after "the long years," as she termed them. In November 1920, she arrived at Somerville College in Oxford to study for a doctorate. Her academic career soon prospered, and the following year she was appointed to a lectureship under the Cassell Trust Fund.

However, Waddell never settled in Oxford, though she made many friends there. She found the all-female atmosphere suffocating, and she disliked the constrictions of academic work. "I am horribly afraid that artists and journalists are more my sort than academic people," she told George Saintsbury. Waddell moved to London to find freelance work and earned money by marking school and university exams. "I've never felt so alive," she wrote. "I feel as if those two years in Oxford were a bad dream." She refused offers from a number of the women's colleges to return to Oxford. However, she did accept the Susette Taylor Travelling Scholarship from Lady **Margaret Hall** which enabled her to go to Paris to do research for what became *The Wandering Scholars*. When Waddell returned to London in 1925, she started writing that book, and became friends with Otto Kyllmann of Constable, the company that would publish nearly all her work.

The Wandering Scholars was released in 1927 to considerable acclaim. Waddell followed this in 1929 with *Medieval Latin Lyrics*. In 1931, she published *A Book of Medieval Latin* for schools which went into 10 editions over the next 30 years. She enjoyed literary and artistic life in London, and her literary friends included W.B. Yeats, Æ (George Russell), Stephen Gwynn, *Virginia Woolf, Enid Starkie, Gustav Holst, and Paul Henry. Waddell maintained her links with Ireland and with Irish friends and regularly visited her sister's home at Kilmacrew, "the kindest house I know and the most human" she once said. It was Æ who urged her to write about the French medieval theologian Peter Abelard. (*See Heloise.*) She immersed herself in the study of Abelard's theology but progress on the book was slow: "I felt for so long that once *Abelard* was written the thing for which I was born would be done." When *Abelard* was published in 1933, it went through three editions in six months and was translated into nine languages.

Shortly after the publication of *Abelard*, Waddell bought a large house at Primrose Hill in London which was to prove something of a burden to her in later years. In 1935, a play she had written in the early 1930s, *The Abbé Prévost*, was produced in London but was not a success. She never attempted another drama, although she often considered adapting *Abelard* for the stage. Waddell then returned to medieval scholarship, and in April 1936 her book *The Desert Fathers* was published to much praise; her introduction was hailed as a piece of superlative prose.

Waddell stayed in London throughout the war. She became the assistant to F.A. Voigt, editor of the journal *Nineteenth Century* which was published by Constable. This caused her considerable frustration because of the time it took away from her writing, although she did publish a number of poems. The noise and disruption caused by air raids also caused increasing strain, which was not helped by the placement of anti-aircraft guns near her house. She kept open house for various nieces and nephews who were passing through London, but was devastated when two of her sister's sons died in accidents in 1941 and 1942. In the last months of the war, her house suffered considerable damage in two air raids, and by the end of the war she was near to physical and mental exhaustion.

Waddell rallied after the armistice. Her Ker lecture at the University of Glasgow in 1947 on "Latin Poetry in the Dark Ages" was a great success, and she developed a warm friendship with the poet Siegfried Sassoon. But her health began to deteriorate once more, and she told Sassoon, "I have been like something lost in a fog for most of the year." Kyllmann encouraged her to write, but she never completed her book on John of Salisbury, one of Abelard's students. Waddell, who realized that her mental faculties were failing, consulted specialists about her worsening memory losses but nothing could be done. She was nursed in her last years by her housekeeper and friend, Mrs. Luff. When Waddell died in March 1965, she was buried in the churchyard near Kilmacrew. Sassoon once praised her "unique quality of integrity and illuminativeness. . . . The eclipse of her magnificent intelligence was a disaster to me."

SOURCES:

Blackett, Monica. *The Mark of the Maker: A Portrait of Helen Waddell*. London: Constable, 1973.

Dictionary of National Biography 1961–1970. Edited by E.T. Williams & C.S. Nicholls. Oxford: Oxford University Press, 1981.

Deirdre McMahon,
lecturer in history at Mary Immaculate College,
University of Limerick, Limerick, Ireland

Waddingham, Dorothea

(1899–1936)

English murderer. Name variations: Dorothea Leech; Nurse Waddingham. Born Dorothea Nancy Waddingham in 1899 in England; hanged on April 16, 1936, in Nottingham, England; married Thomas Willoughby Leech (died before 1935); lover of Ronald Joseph Sullivan.

It is not certain that the woman known as Nurse Waddingham had any nursing training at all before she opened her own private nursing home on Devon Drive in Nottingham, England, in 1935. By this time, her husband Thomas Willoughby Leech was dead, and she had resumed use of her maiden name. Despite her haggard, even ghoulish appearance, Dorothea Waddingham had a powerful hold over her lover, Ronald Joseph Sullivan, a World War I hero who performed all the heavy chores in the nursing home and demonstrated almost servile devotion to Waddingham.

After receiving accreditation from the County Nursing Association, Waddingham admitted her first patients: the 89-year old Mrs. Baguley, who suffered from senility, and her daughter **Ada Baguley**, 50, who had creeping paralysis. Shortly after arriving in Nurse Waddingham's home, Ada changed her will, leaving her entire estate of around £2,000 to Waddingham and Sullivan. On May 12, 1935, Mrs. Baguley died; the cause of death was listed as old age. However, when Ada died on September 12—supposedly of a cerebral hemorrhage brought on by eating too many chocolates—suspicions were raised by the haste with which Waddingham wanted the body cremated. Dr. Cyril Banks, the medical officer asked to approve the cremation, ordered an autopsy on Ada's corpse, despite the fact that Waddingham produced a letter dated August 29, 1935, purportedly written by Ada, in which she stated her desire to be cremated. The letter was later declared a forgery.

The autopsy of Ada Baguley—along with the subsequent autopsy on her mother's body—revealed that both women had been given excessive amounts of morphine. Both Waddingham and Sullivan were arrested, although only Waddingham was charged with murder. At her trial, which began on February 4, 1936, a calm Waddingham contended that Dr. H. Manfield, the doctor who signed both of the Baguleys' death certificates, had directed her to give the patients morphine. Manfield's testimony to the contrary ("I never prescribed them. I never gave them") undermined her story. Waddingham also admitted to feeding Ada Baguley a large, heavy meal the night before the patient's death, belying her claim that Ada was already suffering from severe abdominal pains that required morphine. The prevailing opinion, summed up by the judge, was that no nurse with common sense would have served such a dinner to a suffering patient. Waddingham was found guilty of both counts of murder, and although the jury recommended that mercy be shown, she was hanged on April 16, 1936.

SOURCES:
Nash, Jay Robert. *Look for the Woman*. NY: M. Evans, 1981.

Paula Morris, D.Phil.,
Brooklyn, New York

Waddington, Marianna Bacinetti-Florenzi (1802–1870).

See Bacinetti-Florenzi, Marianna.

Waddles, Charleszetta (1912–2001)

African-American religious leader and humanitarian.
Name variations: Reverend Mother Charleszetta Waddles; Mother Waddles; Charleszetta Lena Campbell. Born Charleszetta Lena Campbell on October 7, 1912, in St. Louis, Missouri; died July 12, 2001, in Detroit, Michigan; daughter of Henry Campbell and Ella (Brown) Campbell; educated only until age 12; married three times, first to Clifford Walker (died around 1922); last husband was Payton Waddles (died 1980); children: ten.

Moved to Detroit (1940s); opened a "thirty-five cent restaurant" in Detroit (1950); opened her own church, the Perpetual Help Mission (1950s); was ordained a Pentecostal minister; established ten nonprofit urban missions, including two in Africa; wrote several books, including two cookbooks; received more than 300 awards and honors; was the subject of PBS documentary Ya Done Good *(1989).*

Charleszetta Campbell, known as Mother Waddles, was born in 1912 in St. Louis, Missouri, the oldest of Henry Campbell and **Ella Brown Campbell**'s seven children and one of three to survive beyond childhood. Her family sank into poverty during her early years, and she was forced to leave school at 12, after her father's death, to help support the family. Waddles' experience of watching her father "stand on corners, for hours at a time," demoralized and socially ostracized because of his unemployment, made a lasting impression that was to inform her life's work with the poor and underprivileged.

Married and a mother by the age of 14, Waddles was "treated like a little toy" by her first husband, Clifford Walker, who was 19 when they married and "not what he said he was." Widowed before she turned 20, Waddles married again the following year, this time to a man twice her age who moved the family to Detroit. She eventually left him, returning to St. Louis with her seven children to help care for her ailing mother. After her mother's death and another unhappy relationship with a man in St. Louis, Charleszetta returned to Detroit. She eventually married for the third time, to Payton Waddles, while she and her children—numbering nine at this point—were living on welfare in Detroit. Raising money for a church function, she met Payton when he stopped by to sample her barbecue. "I've never been back on welfare," she said after his death in 1980, "and I'm still living off the love that he gave me."

In 1950, Waddles opened a "thirty-five cent restaurant," where all the meals cost just 35 cents, and she did all the cooking and laundry. Many restaurant patrons paid more than the asking price for their food in order to help subsidize the venture—sometimes as much as $3 for a cup of coffee. Every customer, regardless of how much they paid, was offered the same food choices and same quality of service.

At age 36, before meeting her third husband, Waddles had a vision that told her to "create a church that had a social conscience, that would feed the hungry, clothe the naked, and take folks in from outdoors." In the mid-1950s, she opened her own church, the Perpetual Help Mission, founded on the principles of charity and humanitarianism. Ordained as a Pentecostal minister, Waddles focused her considerable energy, creativity and drive on the plight of the needy, eventually establishing ten non-profit urban missions, including two in Africa, assisting thousands of people with job training, health care, food distribution, budgeting and emergency aid. To help raise money for the work of the missions, Mother Waddles wrote several books, with subjects including philosophy and self-esteem; her two cookbooks sold more than 85,000 copies.

Believing that dignity did not have to be a casualty of poverty, Mother Waddles dedicated her life to feeding, guiding, educating and empowering her constituency of urban poor, with particular concern for the black community. Her work has been recognized with more than 300 awards and honors, and she was the subject of a 1989 PBS documentary called *Ya Done Good*. Recovering from a recent heart attack, Mother Waddles died on July 12, 2001, in her Detroit apartment.

SOURCES:
Obituary, *The Detroit Free Press,* July 20, 2001.
Obituary, *The Detroit News,* July 13, 2001.
Smith, Jessie Carney, ed. *Notable Black American Women.* Detroit, MI: Gale Research, 1992.

Paula Morris, D.Phil.,
Brooklyn, New York

Waddy, Harriet (1904–1999)

One of the highest-ranking African-American officers in World War II. Name variations: Harriet West; Harriet West Waddy. Born Harriet West on June 4, 1904; died on February 21, 1999, in Las Vegas, Nevada.

Harriet Waddy, born Harriet West, stepped into the limelight in April 1943, when she made a radio broadcast on behalf of the Army to urge black women to join the armed forces. First Officer West—as Waddy was then known—told black Americans that joining a segregated military that did "not represent an ideal of democracy" should not be considered "a retreat from our fight," but rather "our contribution to its realization."

Waddy was to become one of the highest-ranking black officers in the Women's Army Corps (WAC) during World War II and its wartime adviser on racial issues. Created in 1942 as the Women's Army Auxiliary Corps, the WAC attracted 6,500 black women into the service. Unfortunately, the military's policy of segregation forced many of these enlistees into service as uniformed domestic servants, assigned to cleaning officers' clubs. Waddy lobbied to change this state of affairs after she was promoted to major and named an aide to the WAC director, Colonel *Oveta Culp Hobby.

Waddy's experiences during the war included traveling to the South to hear the grievances of black WACs, and fighting racially insulting Army decrees; she recommended, for example, that official memoranda not differentiate between "white and colored personnel." Major West and Major **Charity Adams**, who commanded the only unit of black WACs sent overseas in World War II, were the only two black women to attain the rank of major in the wartime WAC. In old age, Charity Adams Earley recalled Harriet Waddy as a "charming" woman who was "well-disciplined, as we were all trained to be." Waddy died in Las Vegas in 1999, at the age of 94.

SOURCES:
Obituary. *The Day* [New London, CT]. March 8, 1999.

Paula Morris, D.Phil.,
Brooklyn, New York

Wade, Virginia (1945—)

Wimbledon tennis champion, known for her aggressive play and ability to recover from mistakes, who brought a sense of high drama to the court and was tremendously popular with fans. Born Sarah Virginia Wade on July 10, 1945, in Bournemouth, England; daughter of an Anglican cleric.

Learned to play tennis in South Africa, where her family moved when she was a child; first qualified for Wimbledon (1962); finally won the Wimbledon singles championship (1977); by the time she retired from professional play (1987), was third in world rankings for number of titles won, including singles titles at Wimbledon and the U.S. and Australian opens; inducted into the International Tennis Hall of Fame (1989).

Little disturbed the quiet neighborhood of Durban, South Africa, around the Anglican Church of St. Paul's. It was, in those pre-apartheid days, solidly British, its rows of neatly kept houses and fastidiously trimmed lawns comfortably settled in suburban tranquility.

*V*OLUME *S*IXTEEN   **97**

There was only one slight annoyance to break the spell—the nearly constant *thwack* of tennis ball against racquet, followed by the inevitable *plock* of the ball hitting the pristine white paint of the Wade home, the two-stroke sequence monotonously repeating itself for hours on end. "Tennis was an obsession," Virginia Wade once said of her childhood passion, so much so that her father complained about the black marks spattered over the white facade of the house and forced Virginia to practice against the more secluded garage.

She had always been an energetic child, following in the footsteps of her older siblings—two brothers and a sister—who all excelled at athletic pursuits and who carried their enthusiasms with them to South Africa from Bournemouth, England, where Virginia had been born on July 10, 1945. She was barely a year old when her father, an Anglican cleric, accepted a position in a parish in Cape Town, South Africa, just after the end of World War II. Four years later, he was appointed the archdeacon of St. Paul's in Durban. "I was so energetic I don't know how Daddy kept me quiet long enough to concentrate on his sermons," Wade said. But that was before she discovered a long-forgotten tennis racquet hidden away in the junk closet she had been assigned to clean one day when she was nine years old. "I loved the quick and visible results when the ball and racquet connected," she said, "and I was tantalised by the idea that there was something very exact about it."

It was not unusual for a young white girl of comfortable means growing up in South Africa in the 1950s to take up tennis, a popular leisure time activity for the middle and upper classes and one that could be pursued year round thanks to the country's mild climate. All the Wade children played tennis at one time or another, but only Virginia became obsessed with the game because, she later claimed, "I cared more about it than the others did." Wade was soon playing in local junior tournaments and advanced to open tournament play, but presently found herself bored with the level of competition she was facing. Her frustration became apparent when what few players she could find at her level complained she was slamming the ball too often and without reason. Virginia admitted her play was becoming tinged with anger. "I was angry with myself at my mistakes," she said of a growing reputation for emotional volatility. "It was an unfortunate signature to be stuck with." Her future in tennis seemed doomed when her father announced in 1956 that the family would be moving back to England, where she knew the lack of a well-developed training system like South Africa's would mean fewer chances to find qualified teachers and more challenging opponents. But it was the elder Wade's opinion that racial divisions were worsening in South Africa to such an extent that his friendly relations with several black clerics might place his family in danger. Incredibly, he picked out a house in the one place in England where Virginia might feel most comfortable. "I had always thought Wimbledon was the name of the place where tennis was played," she once recalled, not realizing it was also a suburb of London.

Her first months in Britain were not encouraging. "Winter was hideous," Wade later remembered of the family's arrival in Southampton on a dreary February day, a stark contrast to the semitropical warmth of South Africa. "My clothes were not remotely thick enough. The dream was over." But at least there was tennis at some of the local courts, and just down the road from her new home was Wimbledon itself, where Virginia would wait in line for hours for standing-room tickets to watch all her favorite players. Then, too, there was the Queen's Club, where much to her surprise Virginia found an active junior training program under the tutelage of an Australian coach named George Worthington. By 1962, Wade had qualified for an inter-school tournament to be played at Wimbledon itself, the first time she stepped onto that hallowed ground as a player rather than as a spectator. Even better, her team won the tournament thanks to Virginia's energetic, if still unfocused, play. By the end of that year, she had been seeded No. 1 in the British Junior ranks and was being called Britain's most promising junior player.

But it was now that the temper for which she had become known in South Africa came back to haunt her. During a juniors match she played against an equally peppery opponent, the audience watched in shocked fascination as the two young women hurled insults at each other and threw racquets to the ground in alternating fits of pique. "It's a wonder we didn't blacken each other's eyes," Wade said of the match that would lead to her later characterization in the press as the "Wild Woman" of tennis. The fact that her game actually got worse when she tried to control her temper did not help matters. "Getting mad made me feel guilty, and suppressing myself scuttled my involvement in the match," she said. It would be a personality trait that would taint her entire career. Only *Billie Jean King seemed to get through to Wade some years later by suggesting, "You never have time on the court to waste getting mad."

Opposite page

*V*irginia

*W*ade

New challenges awaited when Virginia entered Sussex University, which had no strong tradition of team sports and which made it even harder for Wade to keep up her practice schedule. She spent hours on slow, stuffy trains shuttling between Sussex and London for practice at the Queen's Club and played badly when she was picked for Britain's Wightman Cup team in 1964—the first of what would be a record-breaking 21 consecutive years of Wightman Cup play. Court wags thought she was a powerful player, hitting the ball hard and racing to make difficult returns that would elude more timid players; but, they said, she had no control over the ball. Only Worthington remained convinced that "Ginny," as she was now universally called, had the makings of a world champion. "One day she'll prove I'm right," he confided to friends. Worthington's confidence was sorely tested in the next three years, as Virginia struggled to keep to her studies and advance in the rankings at the same time, at one point taking final exams in a room hired for her next to Wimbledon. So it was with some relief that Virginia finally took her degree in mathematics in 1966, looking back on three years of Wimbledon and Wightman Cup play with little to her credit. "Foolishly, I thought Wimbledon's galvanizing effect would be all I'd ever need to win," she said of those difficult years. "Success at Wimbledon requires virtually a twelve-month preparation. Somehow I thought that providence would see that it all just happened."

She stubbornly continued to hold that view even after being freed from her studies, devoting nearly all her time to tennis, setting as her goal the U.S. Open and departing for America on her 21st birthday to begin play on the U.S. tennis circuit to qualify. Among her colleagues on the U.S. Tennis Association roster were a young *Chris Evert, *Evonne Goolagong and *Martina Navratilova; and signing up for the fledgling Virginia Slims circuit, she faced players like Billie Jean King, *Rosie Casals, and *Margaret Smith Court. There were a few victories, mostly in doubles play, but Wade returned to England at the end of the season with a lackluster singles record, no further toward her goal. There followed another round of international touring. Although her record improved only slightly, Wade felt her game was getting better. "My best tennis was better than it had been," she once recalled; but added, "My worst was still bad." The low point for her was a Caribbean tour, playing a grueling schedule in sweltering heat from Jamaica to Venezuela to Colombia and losing to a string of much lower seeded opponents. Return-

ing to England at the end of the tour, she played her way to the quarterfinals at Wimbledon, which she considered some consolation after her first full year of non-stop tennis. But her patchwork record was attracting attention in the press, which used words like "tempestuous," "explosive" and "glowering" to describe her.

In 1968, Wade decided to join the ranks of many of her peers and turn pro, although she had mixed feelings about the decision. "I was adamant that I shouldn't be a puppet of the professional promoter," she said. "If the money was there, that was fine. If not, I wasn't going to go out of my way to procure it." Her ambivalence became evident when she won her first Open tournament in her hometown of Bournemouth. She refused to accept the £800 in prize money, the amount, she said, being too much less than that awarded to the winner of the men's tournament. Despite the predictable press attention her announcement attracted, Wade felt that her 1968 win at Bournemouth justified another try at Wimbledon.

I always felt I could get better. That's the whole incentive.

—Virginia Wade

The accepted entry points for Wimbledon at the time were the Wightman Cup and the Davis Cup, both played on Wimbledon courts and both important tests for the bigger matches that lay ahead at the prestigious site. Wade had unsuccessfully competed on four Wightman Cup teams, but this time she rocketed to both the singles and doubles titles against the American team. Virginia faced the American **Nancy Richey** in the singles championships, a replay of a match between them two years before which Wade had lost in the third set. But this time, victory was hers; and this time, the press concentrated more on the game she had played than on her by now famous temper. "This was a performance as controlled, as disciplined, as intelligent as had ever been produced by this unpredictable player," one journalist wrote of the match with Richey.

Now, Wimbledon lay ahead, barely a week after the Wightman Cup victory. But as Wade began play in her first match, on courts sodden with four days of rain, her winning streak quickly dissipated, and she was easily defeated by a Swedish player she had faced with success in past years. "It was an embarrassing nightmare," Wade said later. "This was the year my target was to reach the semifinals at least, and I was beaten in the first round." She had serious doubts about pressing on with her plans to trav-

el to Forest Hills for the U.S. Open, but the chance to leave the constant sniping and gossip about her public play and private life in England proved irresistible. Seeded sixth for the tournament, Virginia managed to win her early matches, handily defeating the formidable Rosie Casals and **Judy Tegart** to arrive at the semifinals. Much to the surprise of the crowd, her victories had come without the expected displays of irritation and outright bad temper. "Only once had I winced at a bad bounce," Wade later boasted, "and then thought 'Shut up and get on with it.'" She maintained her newfound concentration and cool during her semifinal play against **Ann Jones**, an important rival for best player in Britain; and in 43 unruffled minutes, Wade played her way to a 7–5, 6–1 win to enter finals play against Billie Jean King. It was the most important final in which she had played so far in her career. This time, it took only 42 minutes to send King down to defeat at 6–4, 6–2 and capture her first U.S. Open title. Wade was the first British woman to do so since 1930.

She returned to England as the toast of the sporting press, and the win at Forest Hills supplied her with more than just a title. The novel experience of playing an important match without losing her concentration to bad temper proved that her approach of past years—"wanting victory without the slogging," as Wade put it—had worked against her. "This is when you discover that instinct alone cannot sustain you," she said. "Improvisation isn't sufficient. You need mental technique. Being good isn't good enough. You have to know why and how." Wade worked on that technique for the next two years of nearly constant play, often without the professional guidance of the kind of coaching found in the United States. She played to the semifinals at Forest Hills in 1970, losing to Rosie Casals; became the Italian women's champion in 1971; and was confident of another victory at the U.S. Open that year when she slipped during play at a small tournament in New Jersey and badly sprained her ankle, putting her out of competition for the rest of the year. But in 1972, she fought back to capture the singles title at the Australian Open and could tell reporters: "I can honestly say that I am enjoying every moment on court."

By 1975, after winning the U.S. Open, the Australian Open, and capturing the Italian title, Wade was telling friends that she had no doubt she would win Wimbledon; and it seemed her prediction was accurate when, at the last tournament leading up to that year's Wimbledon play, she defeated both Martina Navratilova and Billie Jean

King to take the tournament title. At Wimbledon itself, she played superbly to the semifinals to face Australia's Evonne Goolagong in what was generally conceded to be the best match of the entire tournament due to the precise control displayed by both women. But the victory went to Goolagong, who defeated Wade by just two points. In a display of her new self-confidence, however, Virginia decided to learn from the defeat instead of giving in to despair. "I wasn't going to be defeated twice in one day," she said. "What I had to do was correct my technical weaknesses and leave the press and public to sort out their image of me in whatever way they liked."

Over the next year, she practiced relentlessly and learned, as she later explained, to recreate at will the mental focus on the court that would produce her best play, able to react to conditions fluidly. She compared it to an actor learning lines. "The first thing he has to do is get the words out of the way," she said. "On stage, his concentration is no longer on stringing them together or picking up his cues. Now he is free to create and spontaneously react to what is happening on stage. It's the creative process you take out on the court with you." Admitting for the first time that she couldn't win Wimbledon without professional guidance, she sought help from Jerry Teeguarden, who had coached Margaret Smith Court to world championship status. Teeguarden set to work on Wade's serve—called by the press "the best serve in women's tennis" but, as Teeguarden pointed out, one that took too much energy from the rest of her game.

By the time the 1977 Wimbledon matches came around, Wade felt the goal was in reach as she defeated her old opponent and good friend Rosie Casals in the quarterfinals. Even when it became apparent that she would be facing Chris Evert in the semifinals, her confidence never wavered. Evert was at the time considered the world's best tennis player and virtually unbeatable. "I knew I could beat her," Wade later wrote. "I wanted to." She felt "fully rehearsed" for the match everyone was sure Evert would win. But it was Virginia who triumphed, battling back after losing the middle of three sets to advance to the finals. She faced **Betty Stove**, whom Wade had often played in past years and whom she had often defeated; and her training and newfound concentration carried the day as she quickly defeated Stove 4–6, 6–3, 6–1 to capture Wimbledon at last after 17 years of trying. To add even more significance to the victory, Queen *Elizabeth II presented Wade with the prized Wimbledon trophy, it being the centennial year for the tourna-

ment, as the crowd broke into a joyful rendition of "For She's a Jolly Good Fellow."

Wade's subsequent career could never surpass the personal triumph represented by her 1977 Wimbledon victory, although she returned to Wimbledon's Centre Court in the two subsequent years, during which she again faced Evert in semifinals play but this time lost to the American superstar. In succeeding years, she advanced only as far as the quarterfinals, in 1979 and in 1983. By the time of her retirement in 1987, she was 63rd in the international rankings; but she had played at Wimbledon for a record 28 years, had remained in the top-ten rankings for 13 straight years, from 1967 to 1980, and had placed second during 1968. In 1989, Wade was inducted into the International Tennis Hall of Fame.

But it was Wimbledon in 1977 that would always remain the crowning achievement of her career and her voyage of self-discovery. "One has the right, which need never be surrendered, to graduate, to ascend," Virginia Wade wrote during that remarkable year. "To use every possible source of inspiration to confront the issues that separate you from what you want, is the spiritual inheritance of each of us."

SOURCES:
Wade, Virginia, with Mary Lou Mellace. *Courting Triumph*. London: Hodder & Stoughton, 1978.

Norman Powers,
writer-producer, Chelsea Lane Productions,
New York, New York

Wagner, Cosima (1837–1930)

Daughter of one great musician and wife of another who was instrumental in helping found Bayreuth, the festival featuring her husband's operas, and ensuring its survival as an annual event of worldwide fame.

Born Cosima Liszt in Bellagio, on Lake Como, on December 24, 1837; died in Bayreuth, Germany, on April 1, 1930; illegitimate daughter of Franz Liszt (the pianist and composer) and Countess Marie d'Agoult (who wrote under the pseudonym Daniel Stern); educated in Paris; married Hans von Bülow (the conductor), on August 18, 1857 (divorced 1870); married Richard Wagner (the composer), on August 25, 1870; children: (first marriage) daughters Blandine von Bülow and Daniela von Bülow (Wagner); (conceived with Wagner during first marriage) Isolde Wagner and Eva Wagner; (with Wagner before second marriage) Siegfried Wagner.

Every year opera lovers from around the world gather in the small German town of Bayreuth for the only festival dedicated exclusively to the works of a single composer, Richard

Wagner. For well over a century, this small town has been transformed annually by the arrival of some of the world's best conductors, prima donnas, set decorators, and costume designers, converging to stage productions for audiences willing to pay premium prices to hear Wagner's most famous works, and especially to watch the sagas of Teutonic gods unfold, transporting the audience in a wash of beautiful music from Bayreuth to the Nordic halls of Valhalla. Although the festival was conceived because of Richard Wagner's genius, its survival and prosperity are due largely to his wife Cosima, who made the performances there both artistically viable and financially profitable. Although Cosima Wagner was not a musician, her influence on the music world has been incalculable, and it was under her leadership particularly that the Bayreuth Festival grew from a German event into one of international stature.

What love has done for me, I shall never be able to repay.

—Cosima Wagner

From the time of her birth, the life of Cosima Liszt defied social convention. She was born in Bellagio on Lake Como on December 24, 1837, the illegitimate daughter of Countess ❧ **Marie d'Agoult**, who wrote under the pseudonym of Daniel Stern and was often compared with *George Sand, and the famous composer and pianist Franz Liszt. Cosima was one of three children born to the couple, and grew up largely in Paris, although she often went to her father's residence in Weimar. She also spent time with her paternal grandmother and under the care of various governesses. From birth, she was at the center of European cultural life, acquainted with the most famous musicians, artists, and writers of the period. Her life was one of extremes, in which her parents were lionized but she was illegitimate. She was by nature a quiet and orderly person, and yet her bohemian origins would always play a central role in her long and productive life.

After receiving an excellent education in Paris, Cosima married Hans von Bülow, the conductor and pianist, on August 18, 1857, a few months before her 20th birthday. The couple had two daughters, **Blandine von Bülow** and **Daniela von Bülow (Wagner)**. Among her husband's associates was the composer Richard Wagner, notorious throughout Europe as a ladies' man as well as a musical and political revolutionary. When Cosima was still a child, Richard had been caught up in the Revolution of 1848 that swept across the Continent, further shaking the already weakened foundations of the old medieval Europe.

A typical Romantic, Richard Wagner was a strange combination of revolutionary and conservative, pushing for a new and different future while desiring a return to the past. He had come to Paris to find backers to produce his operas and did not always have great success. Except for meeting Cosima, Richard's memories of Paris would not be happy ones.

When Richard entered Cosima's life, he was 51 and separated from ❧ **Minna Wagner**, his wife of 29 years. Cosima was 26. While he was known for his many liaisons, and she was a young wife and mother, it was not surprising that he should be especially taken by Cosima, whom he described as "young and exceptionally gifted, the very image of Liszt, but intellectually his superior." In 1864, thanks to subsidies paid by King Ludwig II of Bavaria, Richard and Hans von Bülow were working on a musical collaboration when the attraction between the composer and the conductor's wife blossomed into an affair. Cosima regarded her marriage as empty and loveless, and was so drawn to Richard, whom both she and her husband regarded as a genius, that all risks seemed worthwhile. When she became pregnant with Richard's child, Von Bülow was aware of the situation but did not intervene. All three feared that if King Ludwig learned of their domestic triangle, he would withdraw his support. When Cosima's daughter was born, she was named **Isolde (Wagner)**, and the triangle continued.

By November 1868, Cosima had given birth to a second child, **Eva (Wagner)**, with Richard. The composer's first marriage had produced no children, and he delighted in his daughters. In 1868, Cosima left von Bülow, and in 1870 she married Richard Wagner, almost a year after their son, Siegfried, was born.

A month after she officially left von Bülow, Cosima began to keep a diary. What emerges from these writings is a complex justification of the life she had chosen with her lover. As an illegitimate child who had become a faithless wife, Cosima always saw her personal life as less than ideal, and it was partly in order to justify her life with Richard to their children that she began to write down the events of daily life and to document her husband's creative activity. While Richard's personal life had also been less than perfect, Cosima believed that his music symbolized the triumph of German ideals, and all that was pure and good in the German people. Regarding him as a genius whose philosophy would not only revolutionize music but change the world, the adoring young woman 25 years his junior was ready to support him completely.

For Cosima and Richard, their relationship was larger than life; there is no doubt of their passionate love for each other. In her first entry in the diary, Cosima wrote that their alliance was "not sought after or brought about myself: Fate laid it on me." Certainly she brought a soothing element to the life of this tempestuous genius. Alternately depressed and exhilarated, Richard was overwhelmed by haunting fantasies and dreams. He loved and hated passionately, and was prone to spending enormous sums of borrowed money on extravagant purchases. Quietly and efficiently, Cosima organized their daily life, listened to her husband's scores, took walks with the children, and invited in friends for intimate gatherings in the evening. While flaunting social convention, she remained selflessly devoted to him, believing that no sacrifice was too great for genius. But life with Richard was never easy.

On June 21, 1868, *Die Meistersinger* premiered in Munich to a triumphant reception, ensuring the further support of King Ludwig. Richard's operas were increasingly performed, but the composer sought even greater outlets for his music. His dream now was to bring together Europe's finest singers, musicians, and set designers to produce his entire cycle of four operas, *Das Rheingold*, *Die Walküre*, *Siegfried*, and *Götterdämmerung*, known collectively as *The Ring of the Nibelungen*. It would be an unprecedented event in the history of music.

The Wagners had conceived the idea of a yearly festival of his works, and gained the generous support of King Ludwig and other patrons, by 1872, when the foundation stone for the theater was laid in the town of Bayreuth, in Germany's Upper Franconia. In 1874, the Wagners had moved to their new home in Bayreuth, called Wahnfried. Two years later, the first *Ring* cycle was produced, and received largely positive reviews, but production costs were enormous. As a financial venture, it was not a great success, but as an artistic event, these productions proved a musical and cultural turning point in European history. Richard Wagner's powerful music, combined with exquisite staging, was like nothing

---

Agoult, Marie d' (1805–1876)

French author and salonnière. Name variations: Marie de Flavigny, comtesse d'Agoult; (pseudonym) Daniel Stern. Born Marie Catherine Sophie de Flavigny in Frankfurt am Main, Germany, on December 31, 1805; died in Paris, France, on March 5, 1876; married the Comte d'Agoult, in 1827, but left him and formed a liaison with the Hungarian composer Franz Liszt; children: (with Liszt) three daughters, including *Cosima Wagner (1837–1930).

Marie d'Agoult wrote the semi-autobiographic romance *Nélida* (1845), *Lettres Républicaines* (1848), *Histoire de la Révolution de 1848* (1851), *Mes Souvenirs, 1806–33* (1877), *Florence et Turin* and *Dante et Goethe*. Her *Esquisses Morales et Politiques* (1849) is considered her best work.

Wagner, Minna (c. 1800–1866)

German actress. Born Minna Planer around 1800; died in Dresden, Germany, in February 1866; married Richard Wagner (the composer), on November 22, 1836; children: an illegitimate daughter; (with Wagner) no children.

A beautiful and gifted young actress, Minna Planer met Richard Wagner in 1834 while he was chorusmaster and assistant conductor with the Bethmann Company in Magdeburg and she was a young and sought-after actress in the company. She was almost four years older than Wagner and at age 16 had had an illegitimate daughter whom she passed off as her sister. They were married two years later. Theirs was a tumultuous relationship. At the time, Richard's finances were in a terrible state; Minna had to sell a bracelet to redeem his *Das Liebesverbot* from the copyist. A year later, she returned to her parents' home in Dresden, and Richard sold their wedding presents to pursue her. She eventually rejoined him, and they continued to flee borders and creditors for the next couple of years. Richard borrowed from relatives, pawned all of his and Minna's possessions, then sold the pawn tickets.

By 1840, Richard Wagner was in debtors' prison in France, and the by-now-faithful Minna wrote desperate letters to friends who eventually bailed him out. Their lives changed in 1842 with the successful production of Wagner's *Rienzi* in Dresden. Seven years later, infatuated with **Mathilde Wesendonk**, Richard wrote Minna that he could not continue his life with her. But the marriage limped along for three or four more years, Minna ill with heart disease, until he turned his attention to *Cosima Liszt (Wagner). As Minna lay dying in Dresden, the now-affluent Wagner did not visit while he was in the city. She wrote a friend: "Every three months I get a crumb from Richard's abundance." She died in February 1866.

ever seen before. The success of Bayreuth would consume Cosima and Richard for the rest of their lives, and his operas would gain an enduring place in opera repertory.

There was a dark side, however, to this musical legacy. Believing that Germany had depended for too long on French and Italian cultural influence, Richard had always wanted the German people to return to their history and roots to create their own literature, music, and art. In 1870, Otto von Bismarck had succeeded in unifying Germany politically, and the flowering of Richard Wagner's music coincided with a new sense of nationalistic pride, especially since the stories of the *Ring* cycle were based on Teutonic myth. Reinforced along with these themes was the attitude shared by many Germans that their culture should be "purified" of all foreign influences—Jewish as well as French and Italian. Taking this stance, Richard became increasingly anti-Semitic, as did Cosima along with him.

Cosima concurred, in fact, in all of her husband's opinions. Raised in Paris, with French as her native language, she rarely spoke it once she learned German, because Richard felt that France was culturally inferior. In her diary, she faithfully recorded many nights of conversation in which the couple discussed German racial purity and Richard voiced prejudices against Jews that were shared by many in their culture. In his opinion, Jewry embodied materialistic capitalism, which he saw as a threat to the new German nation. Despite this prejudice, the Wagners had many close Jewish friends, including Jacques Fromental Halévy, the operatic composer, Karl Tausig, the celebrated pianist, and Joseph Rubenstein, who belonged to the family's most intimate circle.

Richard's hatred of Jews as a race but love of individuals as friends was shared by Cosima, whose relationships were very like her husband's. Hermann Levi, the first conductor of *Parsifal*, was Jewish and close to both the composer and his wife; Levi's friendship with Cosima continued after her husband's death. Of his Jewishness, Levi wrote to Cosima, "I should begin by thanking you for bearing with me, for being able to stand me; for I can hardly stand myself." Cosima did not find such racial self-hatred strange, but took it for granted. The Wagners were cultural rather than biological anti-Semites, believing that if Jews adopted German Christian culture, it would be best for them and for Germany. Although this was a less virulent form of anti-Semitism than the biological racism that later would be espoused by the Nazis, it

paved the way for what ultimately followed, and Cosima and Richard and many like them share some responsibility for the virulent racial hatred which ultimately snuffed out millions of lives.

As Richard aged, his health declined, and he became more opinionated. He slept poorly, was tormented by erysipelas and indigestion, and told his children, "You see what a man looks like who is writing his last opera." His fits of anger became worse, and he suffered from heart spasms. Through it all, Cosima smoothed the waters, inviting friends to join them for musical evenings or reading Shakespeare with her husband. As a couple, they were happy and enjoyed their children. Richard remained devoted to Cosima, and believed that without her he never would have written *Die Meistersinger*, the *Ring* cycle or *Parsifal*. He composed songs for her and once, on her birthday, she awoke to the strains of a 45-piece orchestra that had been hired by her husband to surprise her with his exquisite new serenade for their son, the "Siegfried Idyll." When Richard was particularly difficult, Cosima's response was "what can a poor woman do but suffer in love and passion." Despite her devotion, however, Cosima always felt guilty about leaving Hans von Bülow, and suffered because of her separation from the two daughters of that marriage, with whom she was eventually reunited.

Richard Wagner died in 1883, of a heart attack in Venice. Because so much of her life had been devoted to him, friends worried about what would happen to Cosima. Countless times they had heard her say, "Yesterday and today, I put my whole being into a prayer: to die together with Richard." In fact, reality proved quite different. Cosima survived her husband for 47 years, living to age 92, and it was during this period that she blossomed most fully into her own person.

The music world soon learned that Cosima was gifted at more than matters of her family and household. By 1886, she had complete and unchallenged control of the Bayreuth Festival. She proved a much better business manager than Richard had been, and under her guidance the festival became extremely profitable. She also began to shape productions, deciding on musicians, staging, and interpretation in her own way, according to what she felt her husband would have approved or disapproved. Dressed in widow's black, she became a myth in her own right, as "the absent god's semi-divine representative."

In 1906, increasing blindness caused her to turn the directorship of the festival over to her son, Siegfried. Almost 70 by then, and increasingly frail, she remained a strong cultural presence in Bayreuth, and in opera houses around the world where her husband's works were performed. Her imprint was so great that today it is impossible to separate her contributions from his work.

Cosima Wagner's devotion to her husband was combined with intelligence and determination, and her importance in the music world is unquestioned. Bayreuth would never have become the important musical center it remains without her leadership after Richard Wagner's death, and once on her own she made substantial contributions to the staging of some of the world's most beautiful music.

SOURCES:

Connelly, Kenneth. "Wagner: His Wife, his Life, his Art," in *Yale Review*. Vol. 68, no. 4. June 1979, pp. 581–589.

Fest, Joachim. "Richard Wagner. A Sketch Drawn from Cosima's Diaries," in *Encounter*. Vol. 53, no. 3. September 1979, pp. 7–17.

Field, Geoffrey G. *Evangelist of Race: The Germanic Vision of Houston Stewart Chamberlain*. NY: Columbia University Press, 1981.

"Frau Wagner," in *The Times* [London]. April 2, 1930, p. 19.

Gutman, Robert W. "Notes from Valhalla," in *New York Review of Books*. Vol. 25, no. 17. November 9, 1978, pp. 20, 22–23.

Millington, Barry. *Wagner*. Princeton, NJ: Princeton University Press, 1992.

Skelton, Geoffrey. *Richard and Cosima Wagner: Biography of a Marriage*. Boston, MA: Houghton Mifflin, 1982.

Sojoloff, Alice. *Cosima Wagner, Extraordinary Daughter of Franz Liszt*. NY: Dodd, Mead, 1969.

Steinberg, Michael. "The Genius Day-to-Day," in *The New York Times Book Review*. January 25, 1981, pp. 8–10.

Wagner, Cosima. *Cosima Wagner's Diaries*. 2 vols. Martin Gregor-Dellin and Dietrich Mack, eds. NY: Helen and Kurt Wolff Book, 1978, 1980.

Werner, Eric. "Jews around Richard and Cosima Wagner," in *Musical Quarterly*. Vol. 17, no. 2, 1985, pp. 172–199.

Westernhagen, Curt von. *Wagner: A Biography*. 2 vols. Cambridge: Cambridge University Press, 1978.

John Haag,
Associate Professor, University of Georgia,
Athens, Georgia

Wägner, Elin (1882–1949)

Swedish writer and activist who espoused pacifism and women's emancipation. Name variations: Elin Wagner. Born Elin Matilda Elisabeth Wägner in 1882 in Lund, Sweden; died in 1949; educated at a girls' school; married John Landquist (a critic), in 1910 (divorced 1922).

Selected writings: Från det jordiska muséet (From our Earthly Museum, 1907); Pennskaftet (The Penholder, 1910); Släkten Jernploogs framgång (The Success of the Family Ironplough, 1916); Åsa-Hanna (1918); Väckarkloka (Alarm Clock, 1941); and a biography of Selma Lagerlöf.

Elin Wägner was born in Lund, Sweden, in 1882. Her mother died when she was three, and her father, a headmaster, shared the responsibility of raising her with her grandparents in Småland, where she spent some of her childhood. She attended a girls' school for seven years and later became a journalist, drawing on her journalistic skills when she began writing books.

A radical thinker who supported the causes of pacifism, women's emancipation and environmental preservation, Wägner wrote most of her novels as parts of a public debate. Her first book *Från det jordiska muséet* (From our Earthly Museum) was published in 1907, followed by *Pennskaftet* (The Penholder) in 1910, a work that was groundbreaking in its erotic insights and views on women's suffrage. That year she married critic John Landquist; they divorced in 1922.

During World War I, Wägner published her pacifist novel *Släkten Jernploogs framgång* (The Success of the Family Ironplough, 1916) and also the work considered her best, *Åsa-Hanna* (1918), the story of a strong woman in immoral surroundings, set at the end of the 19th century. Wägner continued to write novels and endorse causes throughout her life, even writing a feminist "new age" book—*Väckarkloka* (Alarm Clock, 1941)—40 years before the concept of New Age gained popularity. For her biography of *Selma Lagerlöf, Wägner was awarded a seat in the Swedish Academy in 1944. She died in 1949.

SOURCES:

Buck, Claire, ed. *The Bloomsbury Guide to Women's Literature*. NY: Prentice Hall, 1992.

Paula Morris, D.Phil.,
Brooklyn, New York

Wagner, Friedelind (1918–1991)

German author and lecturer, granddaughter of Richard Wagner, who broke with her family's tradition of nationalism and racism and fled Nazi Germany while maintaining her influential link with Wagnerian scholarship. Born in Bayreuth, Germany, on March 29, 1918; died in Herdecke, Germany, on May 8, 1991; daughter of Siegfried Wagner and Winifred (Williams) Wagner; granddaughter of Richard Wagner and Cosima Wagner (1837–1930);

had brothers Wieland, Wolfgang and sister Verena; never married.

From the day of her birth in 1918, Friedelind Wagner had little choice but to cope with the legacy—and burden—of being a descendant of one of the greatest musical geniuses of all time, Richard Wagner. The fact that the Wagner legacy was not only a musical one but also represented a cultural and political agenda, one that emphasized a German mission that was hostile to Jews and other alien influences, represented another challenge. A final issue facing Friedelind as she grew up was her mother *Winifred Wagner's uncritical support of Adolf Hitler and the Nazi ideology. That she was able to survive and even prevail over these challenges is a testimonial to her strength of character.

Friedelind Wagner was born in Bayreuth, Bavaria, on March 29, 1918. Her name, Friedelind, was derived from the female heroine in her father's opera *Der Schmied von Marienburg* (The Smith of Marienburg), the composition he was working on at the time she was born. From birth, her family legacy was an extraordinary one. Her father Siegfried Wagner was the only son of Richard Wagner and *Cosima Wagner, whose father had been another of the musical giants of the 19th century, Franz Liszt. Friedelind's mother Winifred was born in England in 1897, but at age ten she had been adopted by a German musician, Karl Klindworth, whose wife was a cousin of Richard Wagner.

Friedelind grew up in Bayreuth, home of annual Wagner Festivals since 1876, in a bustling environment that included her sister **Verena Wagner** and brothers Wieland and Wolfgang. The Wagner household included not only four children but three maids, a gardener, a cook, a nanny named **Emma Baer**, a music teacher, Fräulein **Anna Mann**, and two servants for the elderly lady always looming in the background—Siegfried's widowed mother Cosima. Friedelind and her siblings were instructed never to mention Richard Wagner in their grandmother's presence, but this did not prevent them from playing with items The Master had left in his study when he died in 1883 and which had lain untouched there ever since. Friedelind adored her father Siegfried, who not only ran the Wagner Festivals but was a conductor and composer of operas in his own right. He allowed her to attend rehearsals, and was always patient with her, never acting as if his precocious daughter were in the way. As a child, Friedelind was known in family circles as *Mausi* (little mouse) or *Die*

Maus (the mouse), an affectionate nickname she was to retain throughout her life within a growing clan of Wagner nieces and nephews.

The Wagner Festivals attracted music lovers from all over the world, but for some Richard Wagner embodied not only great music and musical drama but a message of cultural and political redemption as well. Among Wagner's less attractive traits was his ability to hate. For much of his life, Richard disseminated a political message as well as an artistic one, the most unattractive element of which was his hatred of what he was convinced were destructive Jewish influences in modern civilization. In his essay *Das Judentum in der Musik* (Judaism in Music) and elsewhere, Richard Wagner attacked Jews as the enemies of all that was profound and authentic in culture. After his death in 1883, Cosima kept her husband's "ideals" alive, and her son-in-law, English-born Houston Stewart Chamberlain, wrote influential books that fleshed out Wagnerian anti-Semitism along more modern racist lines. Cosima would remain loyal to these doctrines until her death in 1930. Even more important, Cosima's daughter-in-law Winifred, who married Siegfried in 1915, became an uncritical believer in such extreme views. In the early 1920s, she was attracted to Adolf Hitler's fledgling Nazi Party (Nationalsozialistische Deutsche Arbeiterpartei, or NSDAP), becoming one of its pioneer members.

Siegfried Wagner, on the other hand, never shared his wife's ultra-Teutonic racist beliefs. As early as 1921, when an influential Viennese critic and anti-Semite advocated that as director of Bayreuth Siegfried should prohibit Jews from performing at or even attending the festival, Siegfried refused. In an eloquent letter of response, Siegfried repudiated the anti-Semitic argument, emphasizing Bayreuth's freedom from racial bias and formulating its aim as being that of "a true work of peace." Until his sudden death in 1930, many Jewish singers such as Friedrich Schorr were invited to perform on the Bayreuth stage.

After Siegfried Wagner's death, the situation at Bayreuth rapidly changed. Friedelind, only 12 at the time, was devastated by the loss, and her sole consolation was the beginning that year of a lifelong friendship with the great conductor Arturo Toscanini, about whom she would later write, "It was as if in the hour of my father's death, heaven sent me another." The aged Cosima Wagner died that same year, and Winifred Wagner found herself thrust into a leadership role in both the family and the Festival. Winifred became ever more intoxicated with the Nazi movement, which was now aspiring to power in Germany, and enjoyed a close relationship with Hitler (unfounded rumors circulated about their imminent marriage). What was certain was that in the early 1930s Hitler was indeed a frequent visitor in the Wagner household, and with Winifred's encouragement he assumed the role of a surrogate father for the Wagner children. After Hitler came to power in 1933, Friedelind would sometimes lunch with the Führer. On these occasions, the bright and intellectually independent teenager sometimes offered her criticisms of Nazi policies, which not surprisingly would enrage Hitler.

By the time she was in her late teens, Friedelind Wagner's personality was fully formed. Years later, she characterized herself in a few words: "I was always stubborn and independent." Like others in her family, she was not only intelligent and artistically inclined but strong-willed as well. Her antipathy toward the Nazis had increased over the years, and she differed with her mother not only over Nazi ideals and policies in general, but in particular over the blatant propaganda uses Hitler and his regime had made of the Wagner Festivals. She was particularly upset when, during the Festivals, the Wagner family villa, Wahnfried, and its grounds were filled with ominous-appearing SS troops and Hitler's personal bodyguard, the Leibstandarte Adolf Hitler. Friedelind not only disagreed with her mother over Nazism, but found Hitler abhorrent, noting: "I had only to listen to Hitler rant and rave to be disgusted and horrified."

On the eve of World War II, Friedelind decided to leave Germany and a family environment in which she could no longer live. Fortunately, she had a place to escape to, Lucerne, Switzerland, where she was given refuge by her two aged aunts who resided at the Triebschen villa that had long since entered into Wagnerian lore as the site of the first performance in 1870 of Richard Wagner's tender serenade for his infant son, the "Siegfried Idyll." In the summer of 1939, only weeks before the outbreak of the bloodiest war in history, Friedelind and her aunts found themselves among a few invited guests for a unique performance of the "Siegfried Idyll" conducted by Arturo Toscanini. Uncertain about whether she could continue to stay in Switzerland, Friedelind was assured of safety when Toscanini arranged with the mayor of Lucerne that she could remain in the country. Some months later, with Europe already engulfed in war, Friedelind was visited by her mother Winifred. Winifred told her daughter

that her anti-Nazi views, which were being reported in the European press, were a cause of regret not only to her but to the Führer, particularly because they came from the lips of a descendant of Richard Wagner. Winifred made it clear to Friedelind that henceforth she would have to be silent, or return to Bayreuth. Failing that, she was informed, "If these measures fail, the order will be given. You will be exterminated at the first opportunity."

Sensing that the warnings her mother had personally delivered to her were serious, Friedelind took advantage of an offer from Arthur Beverly Baxter, a British journalist and member of Parliament, to get her admitted to Great Britain on an emergency basis. However, after arriving in London in the spring of 1940, Friedelind was frustrated in her plans to continue her war against the Nazis by making BBC broadcasts to Germany when she was interned with thousands of other anti-Nazis, many of them Jewish refugees, on the Isle of Man. Concerned about the possibility that some of the émigrés might be Nazi spies, a panicky Winston Churchill had decided simply to intern all of them, indicating on a memo that officials should "collar the lot." Released after three months, Friedelind

Friedelind
Wagner

found herself in a London now under relentless aerial attack by Hitler's Luftwaffe. Once again her friend Toscanini came to her rescue, pressuring British officials to let her go to Argentina, which she did in March 1941. Toscanini also was able to use his influence to get a United States entry visa for Friedelind, who arrived in New York from South America at the end of 1941.

Once in America, Friedelind made many friends in the music world, including Jewish artists who had fled the Nazi regime she detested. She deepened her friendship with the Toscanini family, not only with her surrogate father Arturo, but with the conductor's daughter **Wally Toscanini** as well. To support herself, Friedelind wrote articles in the musical press, spoke out in the media against Nazi Germany, worked on a book that would be published at the end of the war under the title *Heritage of Fire*, and, when funds were scarce, made ends meet by giving lectures, working as a secretary, and even by waitressing for a time. In 1946, Friedelind was able to fulfill a dream by producing a version of Richard Wagner's *Tristan und Isolde*.

In 1951, the Wagner Festivals resumed under the direction of Friedelind's brother Wieland. Wieland, a gifted man of the theater, modernized the staging of Wagnerian music dramas, transforming them from stuffy Victorian relics to modern and powerful works of musical art. In 1953, having been invited to Bayreuth by Wieland, Friedelind made the difficult decision to return to what had once been her home. To the citizens of Bayreuth, as well as to her mother Winifred, who would live in Bayreuth until her death in 1980, Friedelind Wagner would remain controversial. For some, she was a brave woman who had defied not only her family but an evil regime as well. To others, however, she was little more than a traitor who had abandoned her country in wartime to side with its enemies.

Friedelind ignored the gossip and intrigues, plunging eagerly into a new career as a lecturer and organizer of master classes at Bayreuth, which were first given in 1959. With her knowledge of music and opera, she was able to attract advanced musicians from throughout the world for ten weeks of intensive study. Under her tutelage, Friedelind's pupils immersed themselves not only in Wagner, but in the whole art of opera. In an interview at the end of her life, she described the philosophy that underlay her master classes as "a complete program of training" designed to present all facets of "Richard Wagner's ideal of total theater," which included conducting, stage design, direction, acoustics, and

lighting—the end result being that, having mastered these areas, the graduate would be more confident in organizing "every aspect of a theater from the inside out." Friedelind was given a rare opportunity to put her own ideas into theatrical practice when she produced *Lohengrin* at Bielefeld in 1966.

Over the years that she gave her master classes, from 1959 through 1966, Friedelind Wagner's manic energies and magnetism enabled her to win over countless visitors to Bayreuth, including such celebrities as *Agatha Christie, who visited and became a good friend. Although she had lived there only briefly at the start of World War II, Friedelind reserved a special place in her heart for England. Among her ambitions was one of establishing a permanent experimental theater where she could try out her own and other artists' innovative ideas. The nearest she would ever come to fulfilling this dream was at Norton Priory on Teesside in the north of England, where she resided for some years at Stockton-on-Tees. In the late 1960s and early 1970s, she was a regular visitor to the Wagner performances given by the English National Opera at the London Coliseum. On these occasions, she gave many talks on her grandfather's musical achievements, charming all with a manner that was both outgoing and warm. American music lovers also were given the opportunity to benefit from her decades of musical experience when in her later years she taught at the Southlands summer school in Cleveland, Ohio. Friedelind's last opportunity to produce a musical work occurred in 1975, when she organized a concert performance of her father's opera *Der Friedensengel* (The Angel of Peace).

Once more sensing that Bayreuth was not a congenial place in which to live, in 1984 Friedelind Wagner again decided to "emigrate" from Germany, choosing as her final home a house in Lucerne with a fine view of Triebschen. On her last visit to Bayreuth, in April 1990, she accompanied her good friend Leonard Bernstein. Only months before his death, and doubtless with mixed feelings about Richard Wagner, the great Jewish-American musician had decided to visit the anti-Semitic Richard Wagner's *Festspielhaus* in the company of the composer's granddaughter ("the landlord was absent," he said). After that last visit to her former home, Friedelind Wagner died a little over a year later, in the Ruhr city of Herdecke, on May 8, 1991.

SOURCES:

Barkas, Janet. "Frau Wagner," in *Opera News*. Vol. 37, no. 1. July 1972, pp. 20–21.

"The Case of Wagner's Granddaughter," in *The Times* [London]. December 4, 1940, p. 9.

Donner, Wolf. "Winifred, Wahnfried, Wagner: A Silence is Broken in Bayreuth," in *Encounter*. Vol. 45, no. 6. December 1975, pp. 32–37.

"Friedelind Wagner," in Deborah Andrews, ed., *The Annual Obituary 1991*. Detroit, MI: St. James Press, 1992, pp. 310–311.

"Friedelind Wagner," in *The Times* [London]. May 13, 1991, p. 16.

"Good Old Adolf," in *Time*. Vol. 106, no. 7. August 18, 1975, p. 33.

Harford, Robert. "Friedelind Wagner," in *The Independent* [London]. May 17, 1991, p. 20.

Kiesel, Markus. "So wie er—Friedelind Wagner (1918–1991)," in *Musica*. Vol. 45, no. 4. July–August 1991, pp. 268–269.

Lipman, Samuel. "Wagner's Holy Family," in *Commentary*. Vol. 66, no. 5. November 1978, pp. 68–73.

Sachs, Harvey. *Toscanini*. Philadelphia, PA: J.B. Lippincott, 1978.

Schostack, Renate. *Hinter Wahnfrieds Mauern: Gertrud Wagner, ein Leben*. 2nd rev. ed. Hamburg: Hoffmann und Campe, 1998.

Skelton, Goeffrey. *Wieland Wagner: The Positive Sceptic*. London: Victor Gollancz, 1971.

Spotts, Frederic. "Winnie and the Big Bad Wolf," in *The Sunday Times* [London]. July 27, 1997.

Sutcliffe, Tom. "No Love Lost for Uncle Adolf," in *The Guardian* [London]. May 10, 1991.

Teichman, Jennifer S. "A Triumvirate of Women in the Third Reich: *Leni Riefenstahl, *Gertrud Scholtz-Klink, and Winifred Wagner," M.A. thesis, Central Missouri State University, 1999.

Thomson, J.M. "Masterclass Mania," in *The Guardian* [London]. May 28, 1991.

Thomson, John Mansfield. "The Path to Bayreuth: Friedelind Wagner's 1962 Masterclass and the Influence of Walter Felsenstein (1901–1973)," in *Liber amicorum John Steele: A Musicological Tribute*. Stuyvesant, NY: Pendragon, 1997, pp. 453–470.

Wagner, Friedelind. "Memories of Wahnfried," in *Opera News*. Vol. 6, no. 13, January 12, 1942, pp. 6–8, 13.

———, and Page Cooper. *Heritage of Fire: The Story of Richard Wagner's Granddaughter*. 3rd ed. NY: Harper & Brothers, 1945.

———, and Paul Hess. "Siegfried Wagner: A Daughter Remembers Her Father," in *The Opera Quarterly*. Vol. 7, no. 1. Spring 1990, pp. 43–51.

Wagner, Gottfried. *Twilight of the Wagners: The Unveiling of a Family's Legacy*. Trans. by Della Couling. NY: St. Martin's Press, 1999.

———. *The Wagner Legacy*. London: Sanctuary, 2000.

Wagner, Nike. *The Wagners: The Drama of a Musical Dynasty*. Trans. by Ewald Osers and Michael Downes. Princeton, NJ: Princeton University Press, 2001.

Wagner, Wolf Siegfried. *The Wagner Family Albums: Bayreuth 1876–1976*. London: Thames & Hudson, 1976.

Wagner, Wolfgang. *Acts: An Autobiography of Wolfgang Wagner*. Trans. by John Brownjohn. London: Weidenfeld & Nicolson, 1995.

"Wagnerian Issue," in *Time*. Vol. 36, no. 25. December 16, 1940, pp. 40, 42.

RELATED MEDIA:

"Family of the Ring: Siegfried. Introduction by Friedelind Wagner" (3 VHS videos), Princeton, NJ: Films for the Humanities, 1981.

"The Making of the Ring: A Documentary" (video, includes interviews with Friedelind Wagner, Wolfgang Wagner and others involved in Patrice Chéreau's centenary Bayreuth productions, 1976–80, of Richard Wagner's "Der Ring der Nibelungen"), Philips Video Classics, 1987.

Syberberg, Hans-Jürgen. *Winifred Wagner and the History of Wahnfried House, 1914–1975* (348 min. documentary film in 6 episodes), Syberberg-Filmproduktion, co-produced with Bayerischer Rundfunk and ORF Wien-Österreichischer Rundfunk, 1975.

Wagner, Friedelind. "Wagner's Ring" (video), Princeton, NJ: Films for the Humanities, 1982.

John Haag,
Associate Professor of History,
University of Georgia, Athens, Georgia

Wagner, Johanna (1826–1894)

German soprano who created the role of Elisabeth in Tannhäuser. *Name variations: Johanna Jachmann-Wagner. Born on October 13, 1826, in Lohnde, Germany; died on October 16, 1894, in Würzburg, Germany; adopted daughter of tenor and producer Albert Wagner (1799–1874), composer Richard Wagner's brother; niece of *Cosima Wagner (1837–1930); married Alfred Jachmann.*

Johanna Wagner was born in Lohnde, Germany, in 1826. The adopted daughter of Albert Wagner, a tenor and opera producer who was also the brother of composer Richard Wagner, Johanna began her own opera career in 1844. With a voice described by Richard as "incomparably beautiful," she also possessed a charming stage personality. Johanna performed in major opera houses in cities throughout Europe, including Hamburg, Berlin and London. Her roles included Tancredi, *Lucrezia Borgia, Fidès and Ortrud, and she created the role of Elisabeth in *Tannhäuser*. Richard Wagner had hopes that she would become the "representative" of his music—and his first Brünnhilde—but was eventually disillusioned, calling his niece vain and self-seeking. Johanna Wagner, who married Alfred Jachmann, died in Würzburg, Germany, in 1894.

Paula Morris, D.Phil.,
Brooklyn, New York

Wagner, Minna (c. 1800–1866).

See Wagner, Cosima for sidebar.

Wagner, Winifred (1897–1980)

British-born Nazi supporter and close friend of Adolf Hitler who was a key figure in the Bayreuth Festival in the 1930s and 1940s. Born Winifred Williams in England in 1897; died in 1980; married Siegfried

Wagner (the son of composer Richard Wagner); children: Wolfgang Wagner (director of Bayreuth Festival); *Friedelind Wagner (1918–1991).

Born Winifred Williams in 1897 in England, Winifred Wagner was around ten when she was adopted by a German musician, Karl Klindworth, whose wife was a cousin of the composer Richard Wagner. Winifred married Siegfried Wagner, son of Richard and *Cosima Wagner. In marrying into the Wagner operatic dynasty, Winifred was to become a key figure in the Bayreuth Festival and the controversy that has dogged it since World War II. Virulently anti-Semitic, Winifred Wagner was an outspoken admirer of Adolf Hitler, to whom she sent the manuscript paper on which he wrote his manifesto, *Mein Kampf*, while in prison for a failed 1923 coup.

Wagner never met her famous father-in-law; he died in 1883, before either she or Hitler were born. However, the composer's infamous anti-Semitic writings exercised a powerful influence over the Nazi leader. Winifred Wagner ran the Bayreuth Festival in the 1930s and played a key role in forging its alliance with Hitler, an association that has haunted both the Wagner family and the festival ever since. Under Winifred's directorship, Hitler helped fund the Bayreuth Festival and was allowed to play a role in artistic decisions. Although she later sought to play down her Nazi sympathies, insisting she paid only the minimum monthly party dues, Winifred courted controversy after the war by inviting widows of top Nazis to Bayreuth. According to her grandson Gottfried Wagner, she referred to Hitler as "USA"—which stood for "*unser seliger Adolf*" (our blessed Adolf)—and dismissed the Holocaust as "lies and insults."

After her death in 1980, Winifred Wagner's support for Hitler remained an incendiary issue for Wagner scholars and family members alike. In 1999, a Bayreuth exhibition marking her 100th birthday was canceled, possibly for fear of controversy. Winifred's son Wolfgang Wagner, estranged from his son Gottfried since the 1999 publication of Gottfried's *Twilight of the Wagners*—a family history extremely critical of Winifred Wagner—announced that more research was needed to determine "the historical truth" about his mother.

SOURCES:
"Composer Wagner's heirs feuding over family's Nazi legacy," in *The Day* [New London, CT]. July 28, 1997.

Wagner, Gottfried. *Twilight of the Wagners: The Unveiling of a Family's Legacy.* Picador, 1999.

SUGGESTED READING:
Braun, Julius. "Winifred Wagner and Pater Laurent Hora," in *Richard Wagner-Jahrbuch*. Graz: Österreichische Richard-Wagner-Gesellschaft, 1988, pp. 209–216.

Scholz, Dieter David. *Richard Wagner Antisemitismus.* Würzburg: Könighausen & Neumann, 1993.

Spotts, Frederic. *Bayreuth: A History of the Wagner Festival.* New Haven, CT: Yale University Press, 1994.

"Winifred Wagner, Opera Figure," in *The New York Times Biographical Service*. March 1980, p. 467.

Wistrich, Robert S. *Who's Who in Nazi Germany.* NY: Macmillan, 1982.

RELATED MEDIA:
Syberberg, Hans-Jürgen. "Winifred Wagner and the History of Haus Wahnfried, 1914–1975" (6 videos), Syberberg-Filmproduktion, Bayerischer Rundfunk, Österreichischer Rundfunk, 1975–85).

Paula Morris, D.Phil.,
Brooklyn, New York

Waite, Catherine (1829–1913).

See Bradwell, Myra for sidebar.

Waitz, Grete (1953—)

Norwegian marathon runner who played a central role in changing the image of women's long-distance running. Born Grete Andersen on October 1, 1953, in Oslo, Norway; daughter of Reidun and John Andersen; married Jack Waitz, in 1975.

At 16, won the Norwegian Junior title in the 400 and 800 meters; set a European Junior record in the 1,500 meters with a time of 4 min. 17 secs. (1971); competed in her first Olympics (1972) but failed to medal; set a record in the 3,000 meters (1975); won the inaugural World Cup in 3,000 meters (1977), placed fifth in the 1,500 meters in the European championships, and won five world cross-country titles in Norway; finished first in the New York marathon (1978), taking two minutes off the world record; won 9 out of 13 New York marathons (1978–91); took five minutes off her 1978 record, becoming the first woman to run a marathon in under two and a half hours (1979); won the London Marathon and the first World Track and Field championship marathon in Helsinki (1983); was an Olympic silver medalist in Los Angeles (1984); selected Sportswoman of the Year by Women's Sports *magazine; voted the best female distance runner of the past 25 years by* Runner's World *(1991); formed the Grete Waitz Foundation to helped teenage female runners get started.*

Grete Waitz was born Grete Andersen in 1953 in Oslo, Norway, the daughter of John and **Reidun Andersen**. In her youth, she played handball and participated in gymnastics and track. At age 12, when she found an old pair of spikes lying about, she started running back and forth behind the apartment house where she lived with her parents and two older brothers. Waitz already knew she could run fast. In the cops and robbers games she played with other children, no one wanted to be the cop who had to chase robber Grete. Not even the boys could catch her.

Young Grete quickly realized she needed a more substantial training program than running on the lawn could provide, so she joined the Vidar Sports Club of which she is still a member. Waitz ran with the older boys of the club who consented to take her along on their six-mile workouts, during which she sustained their 6.30-mile pace with difficulty but determination. She was soon identified as a long-distance runner.

At 16, Waitz became the Norwegian Junior champion in the 400 and 800 meters; later that year, she made her first national senior team, which meant an invitation to compete in Canada. Her success convinced her parents that she was serious about the pursuit of running. They bought her an athletic bag and a pair of running shoes. More important, they agreed to let her discontinue the piano lessons which she had resented throughout her childhood.

At 17, she experienced the highs and lows indigenous to the career of anyone who stands out in the crowd. She had set Norwegian records in the 800 and 1,500 meters and thereby raised everyone's expectations for her performance in the upcoming European championships in Helsinki. Unprepared for the psychological demands of an international race, she ran poorly and afterwards retired to the bathroom where she cried for two hours before emerging with a internal promise to "show them" in the Rome championships in 1974.

But the death of her boyfriend in 1972 almost put an end to Grete's career; she lost her desire to run, to eat, to live. Only the steady efforts of her brothers and their friends in the Vidar club, among them Jack Waitz, whom she would marry in 1975, got her back on the track. She did not place in the Munich Olympics that summer, but the Games brought back her desire to participate and to compete once again. Her mind made up, she began a winning streak in Norway which was to last 12 years.

Winning a bronze medal in the 1,500 meters in the 1974 European championships in Rome earned her the Athlete of the Year title in Norway; the following year, she was ranked No. 1 in the world for the 1,500 and 3,000 meters. The Montreal Olympics of 1976, however, proved a disappointment. Waitz made it to the semifinals—a race sensational enough to make *The Guinness Book of World Records*—but missed the finals by two tenths of a second. The disappointment of her nation weighed so heavily on her she decided to run in future without the support of the Norwegian Federation scholarship, responsible only to herself. In the 1978 European championships in Prague, she took "only the bronze" and a Norwegian paper ran a headline "Sorry Norway" above a picture of her pointing thumbs down.

At this point, Waitz considered retiring from running. For years, she had kept up a grueling training schedule, at one time running as much as 125 miles a week. She was tired, disappointed, and ready to hang up her Adidas. Then her husband talked her into running a marathon. "I never really wanted to run the marathon," she said.

When Waitz lined up for the New York City Marathon in 1978, she was an insecure schoolteacher from Norway. "My longest run, even in training had been only 12 miles. But my husband urged me to try, just to see how I would do." The world record she set that day was as much a surprise to her as it was to the watching crowd. It opened up a new realm of invitations to travel and compete, astonishing to someone who had always set her goals for winning and improving rather than racing against a clock and a record. Her four marathon world records brought her glory, success and financial security as well as a career in health and fitness after retirement from running.

From 1978 to 1991, Waitz won 9 out of 13 New York marathons. In 1979, she shaved five minutes off her 1978 record, becoming the first woman to run a marathon in under two and a half hours. She won the London Marathon and the first World Track and Field championship marathon in Helsinki in 1983. In the first Olympic marathon in Los Angeles in 1984, Grete was dealing with back spasms and finished second to *Joan Benoit Samuelson**. In 1991, Waitz was voted the best female distance runner of the past 25 years by *Runner's World*.

In addition to earning prize money, Waitz has made product endorsements and run clinics, carefully selected activities which have proved lucrative enough to let her buy a house on a hill overlooking the Oslo Fjord. The Grete Waitz Foundation supports girls in track and field, and the Grete Waitz Run for Women offers encouragement to all women runners. Charities such as

Save the Children and the Cystic Fibrosis Foundation have also benefited from Grete Waitz's success.

SOURCES:

Condon, Robert J. *Great Women Athletes of the 20th Century.* Jefferson, NC: McFarland, 1991.

Waitz, Grete, and Gloria Averbuch. *World Class.* NY: Warner, 1986.

Woolum, Janet. *Outstanding Women Athletes.* Phoenix, AZ: Oryx, 1992.

Inga Wiehl,
a native of Denmark, teaches
at Yakima Valley Community College, Yakima, Washington

Waizero (1876–1930).

See Zauditu.

Waka Yamada (1879–1956).

See Yamada Waka.

Wake, Margaret of Liddell
(c. 1299–1349).

See Margaret Wake of Liddell.

Wakefield, Priscilla (1751–1832)

English writer of children's books. Born Priscilla Bell on January 31, 1751, in Tottenham, England; died on September 12, 1832, in Ipswich, England; daughter of Daniel Bell of Stamford, Middlesex, and Catherine Barclay (both Quakers); aunt of prison reformer Elizabeth Fry; grandmother of politician Edward Gibbon Wakefield and colonist William Hayward Wakefield; married Edward Wakefield (a merchant), in 1771 (died 1826); children: one daughter; two sons (who became well-known economists).

Selected writings: Leisure Hours; or Entertaining Dialogues *(1794–96);* An Introduction to Botany in a Series of Familiar Letters *(1796);* Juvenile Anecdotes founded on Facts *(2 vols., 1795–98);* Reflections on the Present Condition of the Female Sex, with Suggestions for its Improvement *(1798);* The Juvenile Travelers *(1801);* A Family Tour through the British Empire *(1804).*

Born Priscilla Bell in Tottenham, England, in 1751, Priscilla Wakefield was the daughter of Daniel Bell of Stamford, Middlesex, and **Catherine Barclay,** the granddaughter of a noted Quaker apologist. Wakefield herself was a member of the Society of Friends throughout her life, although she did not conform to its codes on either dress or amusements. In 1771, she married Edward Wakefield, a London merchant, with whom she had two sons and a daughter. Throughout the 1770s and 1780s, she was engaged in philanthropic activities, creating a charity for lying-in women in

Tottenham and promoting "frugality banks," savings banks for women and children, the first of their kind in Great Britain. She started writing only when the family's fortunes began to decline in the 1790s. Her books were chiefly instructive works for children, and she specialized in natural history and travelogues. Several became extremely popular and continued to be reprinted even after her death, including *An Introduction to Botany in a Series of Familiar Letters* (1796), *Juvenile Anecdotes founded on Facts* (2 vols., 1795–98), and *The Juvenile Travelers* (1801), the story of an imaginary tour of Europe, in its 19th edition by 1850.

Other works included *Leisure Hours; or Entertaining Dialogues* (1794–96) and *A Family Tour through the British Empire* (1804). Her one work for adults, *Reflections on the Present Condition of the Female Sex, with Suggestions for its Improvement* (1798), advocated greater educational and vocational opportunities for women, including science, teaching, shop work, portrait painting and farming. Wakefield was the aunt of prison reformer *Elizabeth Fry and grandmother of the Radical politician Edward Gibbon Wakefield and the colonist William Hayward Wakefield, who founded the city of Wellington, New Zealand. She died in Ipswich, England, in 1832.

SOURCES:

Concise Dictionary of National Biography. Oxford: Oxford University Press, 1992.

Kunitz, Stanley J., and Howard Haycraft, eds. *British Authors of the Nineteenth Century.* NY: H.W. Wilson, 1936.

Shattock, Joanne. *The Oxford Guide to British Women Writers.* Oxford: Oxford University Press, 1993.

Paula Morris, D.Phil.,
Brooklyn, New York

Wakeling, Gwen (1901–1982)

American movie costume designer. Born on March 3, 1901, in Detroit, Michigan; died in June 1982 in Los Angeles, California.

Worked for Cecil B. De Mille at Pathé and Paramount; was head costume designer at Fox (1933–42); worked on over 120 films for a number of studios (1927–65); also designed for television, stage plays and light opera companies; nominated for Academy Award for Samson and Delilah *(1950).*

Gwen Wakeling was born in Detroit, Michigan, in 1901. She began work at Pathé and Paramount as a costume designer when she was discovered by Cecil B. De Mille. Her first film was his 1927 movie *King of Kings.* In 1933, she became head costume designer at Fox, and between 1927 and 1965 she worked on over 120 films, mostly in the early 1930s and 1940s. Wakeling was the costume designer for numerous *Shirley Temple (Black) films, including *The Littlest Rebel, Poor Little Rich Girl, Dimples, Heidi, Rebecca of Sunnybrook Farm, Little Miss Broadway, Just Around the Corner, The Little Princess,* and *Young People.* She also designed costumes for John Ford's 1939 Oscar-winning version of *The Grapes of Wrath,* starring Henry Fonda. In 1950, she was nominated for an Academy Award for De Mille's 1949 picture *Samson and Delilah.*

In addition to her movie work for Columbia, United Artists, Republic, RKO and Warner Bros., Wakeling also designed costumes for stage plays, productions at the Los Angeles Civic Light Opera Association and for NBC-TV.

Paula Morris, D.Phil.,
Brooklyn, New York

Walberga (c. 710–777).

See Walpurgis.

Walburg, Walburga, or Walburge (c. 710–777).

See Walpurgis.

Walcott, Mary.

See Witchcraft Trials in Salem Village.

Walcott, Mary Morris (1860–1940)

American artist and naturalist. Born Mary Morris Vaux on July 31, 1860, in Philadelphia, Pennsylvania; died of a heart attack on August 22, 1940, in St. Andrews, New Brunswick, Canada; daughter of George Vaux and Sarah Humphreys (Morris) Vaux; graduated from the Friends Select School of Philadelphia, 1879; married Charles Doolittle Walcott (secretary of the Smithsonian Institution), on June 30, 1914 (died 1927).

Became first woman to climb Mount Stephen (1900); moved to Washington, D.C., upon marriage (1914); published her wildflower paintings in North American Wild Flowers *(1925); joined the Society of Woman Geographers (1926) and was elected national president of the Society (1933); appointed by President Calvin Coolidge to her deceased brother's seat on the Board of Indian Commissioners (1927); contributed paintings to* Illustrations of North American Pitcher Plants *(1935).*

Mary Morris Walcott was the eldest of three children raised in a prominent Pennsylvania Quaker family who spent many of their summers in the mountains of the Canadian west. Her

Gwen
Wakeling

brother, George Vaux, Jr., became a well-respected Philadelphia attorney and later was appointed by President Theodore Roosevelt to the U.S. Board of Indian Commissioners, a post Walcott herself would assume following George's death. After her mother **Sarah Humphreys Vaux** died in 1879, Walcott was left to manage both the household and the family dairy farm.

Walcott developed gradually into an amateur naturalist and painter. Over the summers in the Canadian Rockies, she became interested in glaciers through her uncle, an amateur mineralogist. After 1887, she began spending almost every summer in western Canada and became an avid mountaineer. Walcott had displayed artistic talent since childhood and often painted landscapes. After a botanist in British Columbia asked her to paint a rare alpine flower, she began focusing her painting on wildflowers, and always took her watercolors along on her mountain treks. In Philadelphia, her family was active in the Academy of Natural Sciences.

In 1900, at age 40, the independent Walcott became the first woman to scale Mt. Stephen in British Columbia. In 1913, at 53, she met the man she would marry—64-year-old Charles D. Walcott, a geologist and paleontologist who was secretary of the Smithsonian Institution in Washington, D.C. The Walcotts continued to spend summers in western Canada and led a busy public and social life in Washington. Mary Walcott assisted Charles on various projects while continuing her painting, and in 1925 the Smithsonian published a five-volume limited edition collection of 400 of her wildflower watercolors. The successful publication was praised for its quality of bookmaking and color printing, and prompted some to call her the "Audubon" of American wildflowers.

Walcott joined the Society of Woman Geographers the following year and later served two terms as its elected president. She was appointed to fill her brother's seat on the Board of Indian Commissioners after his death in 1927, was reappointed by President Herbert Hoover, and served there until 1932. She was active throughout her life in the Society of Friends, and was a major force behind the building of the Florida Avenue Friends Meeting House in Washington, D.C. At 75, she contributed 15 paintings to another Smithsonian botanical publication, and it is reported that she spent her 77th birthday riding 20 miles in the mountains.

Mary Walcott died at age 80 in New Brunswick, Canada. Her estate was added to the scientific support fund her late husband Charles had created, and as she had contributed much to the public awareness of botanical research, the income from her published works went to establish the Mary Walcott Fund for Publications in Botany. In British Columbia, Canada, a mountain reaching to 10,881 feet fittingly carries the maiden name of the tall, graceful, and strong-willed woman who loved the mountains and the flowers that covered them in summer.

SOURCES:

James, Edward T., ed. *Notable American Women, 1607–1950.* Cambridge, MA: The Belknap Press of Harvard University, 1971.

McHenry, Robert, ed. *Famous American Women.* NY: Dover, 1980.

Jacquie Maurice, freelance writer, Calgary, Alberta, Canada

Wald, Florence (1917—)

American dean of Yale School of Nursing who played a key role in launching the hospice movement in the United States in the early 1970s. Name variations: Florence S. Wald. Born Florence Schorske in New York City on April 19, 1917; daughter of Theodore Alexander Schorske and Gertrude (Goldschimdt) Schorske; graduated from Mt. Holyoke College, 1938; Yale University, M.A. in nursing, 1941; married Henry J. Wald; children: Joel David Wald; Shari Johanna Wald.

Established the first hospice in the United States, the Connecticut Hospice, in Branford (1974); numerous honors include being inducted into the National Women's Hall of Fame (1998).

Modern medical technology prides itself on its many strategies of keeping death at bay, but while the ability to prolong life is often welcome, there are times the situation of the terminally ill patient is stripped of its human dimension to become little more than a series of technical decisions in which the individual and family are excluded from active participation. In recent decades, the profound issues raised by dying and death have been restored to the center of medical care as a result of the hospice movement. The modern movement was founded by Dr. *Cicely Saunders, who established St. Christopher's Hospice in London in 1967. In the United States, it was primarily because of the efforts of Florence Wald that the hospice movement became a significant part of the spectrum of health care for the terminally ill.

Born in New York City in 1917, Florence Wald graduated from Mt. Holyoke College in 1938, going on to Yale University, where she was awarded a master's degree in nursing in 1941. For a year after leaving Yale, in 1941–42, she worked as a staff nurse at the Children's Hospital in Boston. She then moved to Manhattan, where she was employed for a year with the Henry Street Visiting Nurse Service. This was followed over the next 15 years by various positions in the New York area, including a period when Wald worked as a research assistant in the cornea research laboratory of the New York City Eye Bank. She also served briefly in the final stages of World War II in the nursing branch of the Women's Army Corps, leaving the service with the rank of second lieutenant.

By 1957, Florence Wald's varied experiences led to her being appointed to the faculty of the Yale University School of Nursing as director of that institution's mental health and psychiatric nursing program. Within a year of starting her work at Yale, Wald was appointed acting dean of the nursing school. The next year, 1959, the appointment became a permanent one, and she would remain dean until 1967.

In 1963, Wald's career and life were transformed when she met a remarkable woman. While touring the United States to inform medical professionals of her successes with the hospice concept, Cicely Saunders stopped for several days at the Yale University Medical Center. Saunders made "an indelible impression" on Wald and most of the other faculty and students with whom she came in contact. Saunders' approach to patients suffering from terminal cancer, which was broadly based on her many years' experiences as a nurse, almoner and physician, emphasized aggressive measures to ease the pain of the illness. Once this was achieved, Saunders argued persuasively, patients and families could get on with the business of attending to precious relationships in the closing chapters of life.

From the outset, Saunders' "vision of patient and family in the foreground and medical treatment in the background and her conviction that listening was an essential act" took hold of Florence Wald. She saw the great value of these ideas for patients with terminal illnesses and their families and determined to transplant them to the United States. But she was also a realist, and because of her experiences as a dean of one of the leading nursing schools in the United States harbored few illusions as to how difficult it would be to change the thinking of a deeply conservative medical profession, as well as to revamp curriculums, develop new services, and change long-accepted practices. In her favor was the *zeitgeist* of the 1960s, which was a time of profound changes and challenges to old ideas and institutions. Massive protests against the Vietnam war, the search for happiness through radical experimentation in lifestyles, and attacks on orthodoxies of all stripes characterized the entire decade. In the medical profession, intellectual and institutional ferment began seriously to challenge a health-care hierarchy in which male physicians had long reigned as virtual demigods. The women's movement inspired new ideas and attitudes among nurses. All of these changes made it easier for Wald to organize the solid foundations of a coalition that would eventually bring about the successful implementation of the hospice concept in the United States.

By 1966, Wald was able to organize 30 medical professionals at Yale in a workshop with activities that included a visit by Cicely Saunders. Some of the individuals who came from beyond the Yale campus included *Elisabeth Kübler-Ross, who was then teaching at the University of Chicago, and Colin Murray Parkes of the University of London. By 1969, Wald had been able to secure Saunders as the mentor of what was now a permanent group determined to create the first hospice in the United States. After a month's internship spent working directly with Saunders at St. Christopher's Hospice in London, Wald returned to Yale to continue her planning activities with her interdisciplinary team, whose core members included Dr. Morris Wessel and Dr. Ira Goldenberg and, as director of religious ministry, Reverend Edward Dobihal. Other key members of Wald's group included nurse **Katherine L. Klaus** and Catholic priests Don McNeil and Robert Canney, as well as Lutheran pastor Fred Auman.

For several years, from 1969 through 1971, the team led by Wald gathered data and compared ideas in order to have a solid foundation on which to transform their dream of America's first hospice from an abstraction to a reality. As they began to plan a hospice that would serve the greater New Haven area, volunteers clamored to help with the fund raising, publicity, office chores, and, eventually, inpatient care. "The surge and interest were unstoppable," said Wald. Her husband Henry J. Wald, a health-facility planner, also became involved in the project, and in 1974, having been incorporated as an independent, not-for-profit institution, the Connecticut Hospice in Branford began providing home care. In 1980, the Connecticut Hospice added an inpatient facility.

Wald's work as a medical pioneer has earned her many honors, including induction into the National Women's Hall of Fame in 1998. Still active in her 70s and 80s, she spent countless hours as an advocate of the creation of hospice units in America's too-numerous prisons. In a 1999 interview, she argued persuasively for hospice care for the terminally ill, describing it as "the end piece of how to care for patients from birth on. It is a patient-family-based approach to health care that belongs in the community with natural childbirth, school-based health care, mental health care, and adult care." In a remarkable career rich in achievements, Florence Wald played a crucial role in "taking what was essentially a hidden scene, death, an unknown, and making it a reality. We are showing people that there are meaningful ways to cope with this very difficult situation."

SOURCES:

Blau, Eleanor. "Ministry to the Dying, a Heartfelt Turn in Theology," in *The New York Times*. December 30, 1972, pp. 23, 26.

Brockman, Elin Schoen, and Dianne Hales. "Women Who Make a Difference," in *Family Circle*. Vol. 103, no. 8. June 5, 1990, pp. 15–17.

Corless, Inge B., and Zelda Foster, eds. *The Hospice Heritage: Celebrating our Future*. NY: Haworth Press, 1999 (*The Hospice Journal*, Vol. 14, no. 3–4).

Fellman, Bruce. "Dimensions of Dying," in *Yale Alumni Magazine*. Vol. 58, no. 1. October 1994, pp. 54–57.

"Florence Wald Inducted into the Connecticut Women's Hall of Fame," in *Connecticut Nursing News*. Vol. 72, no. 2. June–August 1999, p. 2.

Friedrich, M.J. "Hospice Care in the United States: A Conversation With Florence Wald," in *JAMA: The Journal of the American Medical Association.* Vol. 281, no. 18. May 12, 1999, pp. 1683–1685.

Siebold, Cathy. *The Hospice Movement: Easing Death's Pains.* Toronto: Maxwell Macmillan Canada, 1992.

Wald, Florence S. "The Emergence of Hospice Care in the United States," in Howard M. Spiro, *et al.,* eds., *Facing Death: Where Culture, Religion, and Medicine Meet.* New Haven, CT: Yale University Press, 1996, pp. 81–89.

———. "A Nursing Perspective on Patient Care," in Lillian G. Kutscher, *et al.,* eds., *Hospice U.S.A.* NY: Columbia University Press, 1983, pp. 139–143.

RELATED MEDIA:

Flattery, Kevin. "The Hospice Movement in America" (video), Kansas City, MO: University of Missouri-Kansas City, School of Medicine-Hospice Care of Mid-America, 1984.

John Haag,
Associate Professor of History,
University of Georgia, Athens, Georgia

Wald, Lillian D. (1867–1940)

American public health nurse, social reformer, settlement house leader, and feminist who worked to improve the health and welfare of women and children. Born Lillian D. Wald (the initial does not stand for anything) on March 10, 1867, in Cincinnati, Ohio; died on September 1, 1940, in Westport, Connecticut, after a long illness brought on by a cerebral hemorrhage; daughter of Max D. Wald (an optical goods dealer) and Minnie (Schwartz) Wald; attended various private schools, including Miss Martha Cruttenden's English and French Boarding and Day School for Young Ladies and Little Girls in Rochester, New York, until the age of 16; granted nursing diploma, New York Hospital Training School for Nurses, 1891; attended Woman's Medical College of New York, 1892–93; never married; no children.

Founded the Henry Street Settlement and organized the Henry Street Visiting Nurse Service (1893); founded the National Child Labor Committee (1904); helped establish a department of nursing and health at Teachers College (Columbia University, 1910); elected first president of the National Organization for Public Health Nursing (1912); helped establish the Children's Bureau (1912); awarded gold medal of the National Institute of Social Sciences (1912); headed Committee on Home Nursing, Council of National Defense (1917–19); founded League of Free Nations Association (1919); retired as head of Henry Street Settlement (1933); was co-chair, Good Neighbor League (1936); awarded the New York City Distinguished Service Award (1937).

Selected works: The House on Henry Street *(Henry Holt, 1915);* Windows on Henry Street *(Little, Brown, 1934).*

In 1893, a young medical student named Lillian D. Wald was teaching a course in hygiene and home nursing to a group of immigrant women from the Lower East Side of Manhattan. One day, a child came to Wald's classroom and asked her to look in on her sick mother, who was a student in Wald's class. Wald, who had completed nurses' training before entering medical school, agreed to look in on the patient. On the way to the child's home, she encountered a street environment she described in her autobiography, *The House on Henry Street*:

> Over broken asphalt, over dirty mattresses and heaps of refuse we went. The tall houses reeked with rubbish. . . . I will not attempt to describe the place, the filth, the smell, or the sanitary conditions, which were too foul for words. . . . There were two rooms and a family of seven not only lived here but shared their quarters with boarders.

In the late 19th century, such conditions were in fact not unusual for impoverished areas of New York City and other large cities, but for Wald, like many middle-class women of her time, such a degree of poverty and misery was beyond her ken. Arriving at the flat, she did her best to tidy up the meager surroundings and make her student comfortable, and when she was finished, "that poor woman kissed my hands." Recalling that the moment left her "ashamed of being part of a society that permitted such conditions to exist," Wald wrote, "that morning's experience was my baptism of fire. That day I left the laboratory and the [medical] college. What I had seen had shown me where my path lay."

Wald herself came from a background far removed from the squalor of Manhattan's Lower East Side. Born in 1867 in Cincinnati, Ohio, she was the second daughter and third of four children of Max D. Wald and **Minnie Schwartz Wald.** Both the Wald and Schwartz families were descended from a long line of rabbis, merchants, and professional men from Poland and Germany, and there was even a legendary ancestor said to have been the king of Poland for a day. Like many immigrants, the Walds and the Schwartzes had come to America hoping to find greater economic opportunity and political and social freedom than were available in their own countries, and their hopes were soon fulfilled. Max Wald prospered as a dealer in optical goods, and was able to provide his four children—Alfred, **Julia,** Lillian, and Gus—with a carefree and luxurious childhood. Lillian described herself as a "spoiled child" who was seldom punished, and who was showered with expensive gifts and treated to luxurious excursions by her parents and her indulgent paternal grandfather, Goodman Schwartz. The Walds and the Schwartzes were also avid connoisseurs of fine literature, music, and art. Lillian recalled her mother Minnie as a woman who was both "beautiful and loved beauty" in her surroundings, and taught all of her children to appreciate "good works, good books, and good talk."

Max Wald's business eventually took the family from Cincinnati to Dayton and finally to Rochester, New York, which Lillian regarded as her hometown long after she had moved on to her life's work in Manhattan. In Rochester, the Walds joined a prominent German-Jewish community that enjoyed a lavish social life and tended to be conservative in its politics and attitudes toward social reform. Like other rapidly growing industrial cities of the time, Rochester had its share of working-class families who suffered from the deleterious effects of low wages, long working hours, poor nutrition, and a bad living environment, but there is no indication that Lillian was aware of their plight. Her parents appear to have been equally unconcerned with the situation of the poor. Although they occasionally performed private acts of charity, they were not involved in social causes of any kind, and devoted most of their time to ensuring their place among Rochester's elite professional class.

Like most young women of her social standing, Wald was not expected to earn wages outside the home or to be educated in preparation for a professional career. Instead, she was sent to private "finishing" schools that would give her the skills and manners expected for marriage, in particular Miss **Martha Cruttenden**'s English and French Boarding and Day School for Young Ladies and Little Girls. Although the school aimed to "make scholarly women and womanly scholars," and included standard college preparatory courses, such as languages, trigonometry, astronomy, physics, and chemistry, it did not actually intend to prepare students for either college or career. Instead, Miss Cruttenden hoped to transform the students into "elegant young ladies" suitable for marriage to equally well-mannered young gentlemen.

Although Lillian appreciated the social advantages of the school, she gradually became dissatisfied with the quality of education offered there. At age 16, when Lillian decided to apply to Vassar College in Poughkeepsie, New York, her parents, who held somewhat stereotypical ideas about women's education, were surprised but allowed her to proceed with the application. After the president of Vassar decided that Lillian

was too young to enter the college then, and suggested that she reapply in a few years, Wald reluctantly returned to her studies at Miss Cruttenden's, and entered into the stylish social life of Rochester with the intention of finding a wealthy husband.

Although Lillian enjoyed wearing pretty clothes and attracting male attention, she quickly grew bored with the social whirl of Rochester, and began to search for something more interesting to do with her life. Her options were limited, as young women of her background did not work for wages or leave their childhood homes before marriage; she could have gone to Vassar or some other women's college eventually, but her initial rejection seems to have quelled that ambition. When her father helped her obtain a respectable clerical job that she could perform at home, she found the opportunity uninspiring. In 1889, while visiting her pregnant older sister Julia, she began to find her direction. During the visit, Julia became ill and needed the care of a trained nurse; the woman assigned to her was a graduate of the Bellevue nursing school, then one of the best programs in the country. She was the first member of the nursing profession whom Wald had ever met, and the experience, according to Lillian, was "the opening of a window on a new world." On her application to nursing school, Wald expressed her reasons for wanting to enter:

> My life hitherto has been—I presume—a type of modern American young womanhood, days devoted to society, study, and housekeeping duties. . . . This does not satisfy me now, I feel the need of serious, definite work. A need perhaps more apparent since the desire to become a professional nurse has had birth. I choose this profession because I feel a natural aptitude for it and because it has . . . appeared to me womanly, congenial work, work that I love and which I think I could do well.

When Wald entered the New York Hospital Training School in 1889, her family did not entirely approve. Nursing was regarded by many as little more than specialized domestic service, and an unsuitable occupation for well-bred ladies. Seeing that her heart was set on this career, however, and being the indulgent parents that they were, the Walds had grudgingly allowed Lillian to attend. After graduating in 1891, she took a nursing job at the Juvenile Asylum, an orphanage in New York City. She found the institutional treatment of children to be appalling, and left the position after only a year.

In 1892, Wald decided to supplement her nursing training and enrolled in the Woman's

Medical College in New York, an institution she described as "one of those schools founded in protest against the exclusive attitude adopted by the men's colleges." A year later, she agreed to organize home nursing classes at a school for immigrant women on the Lower East Side, and there underwent the experience that changed her life. After her firsthand look at living conditions of the urban poor, Wald decided to leave medical school to do something to help.

Wald's reform activities were strongly influenced by the work of the settlement house movement then under way, in which young, college-educated women and men lived among the urban poor to teach them job skills, money-saving strategies, cooking and cleaning methods, and other ways of improving their daily lives. Educated women found settlement work especially attractive, for it provided one of the few alternatives to marriage and motherhood at the time.

A major source of Wald's inspiration was the College Settlement Association, founded in 1887 by seven Smith College graduates who were dismayed by the lack of professional opportunities available to college-educated women, and sought to help the poor while providing themselves with independent, meaningful careers. In 1889, the Association set up the College Settlement at 95 Rivington Street in Manhattan, which Wald visited several times during her early forays into the Lower East Side. Together with **Mary Brewster**, a friend from nurses' training school, Wald decided in 1893 to create a "Nurses' Settlement," which would provide inhabitants of a poor neighborhood with nursing care and teach them the rudiments of healthy living.

During the first few years, Wald and Brewster worked out of makeshift quarters in the College Settlement and a tenement building on Jefferson Street. Eventually the generous contributions of Jacob H. Schiff, a wealthy New York banker, allowed Wald and Brewster to acquire a permanent home at 265 Henry Street. The two nurses were soon joined by nine other residents, many of whom were also trained nurses. By 1913, Wald had a thriving Visiting Nurses' Service consisting of 92 nurses who made more than 200,000 visits per year from the Henry Street headquarters and branch settlements in upper Manhattan and the Bronx. The service provided low-cost home health care for invalids, first aid stations, convalescent facilities, and follow-up care for patients recently released from the hospital.

Wald's nursing activities soon moved beyond Henry Street as she became involved in a nationwide movement to reform American nursing. For centuries, nursing had been a lowly occupation that was usually performed by women in charitable religious orders, or by untrained women in hospitals, many of whom were former prostitutes and/or recently recovered patients. Nurses typically had no control over their work environment, and were entirely subservient to physicians and hospital administrators, almost all of whom were men. Consequently, nurses were viewed by most people as little more than housemaids, and in need of little if any training.

By the late 19th century, however, nurses and their supporters were dissatisfied with the lowly status of their work. To many of these women, their situation was a microcosm of women's subordinate status in American society in general, and they identified the uplifting of nursing with the aims of the larger feminist movement then under way to grant women full equality with men. In her memoirs, Wald recalled that she and many of her colleagues regarded nursing as "a gauge and an inseparable part" of the "eternal woman movement." One of their major goals, therefore, was to free nursing from the domination of male physicians and hospital administrators, and give nurses themselves full control over educational standards, licensing, and the nature of their work. Wald's visiting nursing service at Henry Street was a particularly important advance in this area, for the visiting nurse worked independently of the controlling influence of physicians.

The Henry Street model of nursing care spread rapidly beyond New York City as similar programs were set up across the country and around the world, culminating in the birth of a new profession that Wald called public health nursing. Central to Wald's concept of public health nursing was the idea that the nurse should do more than simply care for sick patients, by working to prevent illness before it starts through improvement of the clients' environment and their education in the principles of a healthy lifestyle.

In addition to the Henry Street Visiting Nurse program, Wald helped to create a number of institutions that extended the concepts of public health nursing beyond the settlement movement. In 1902, she convinced the New York City Board of Health to establish the first public-school nursing program in the United States. In 1909, Wald persuaded the Metropolitan Life Insurance to adopt a public health program for industrial workers to prevent these clients from succumbing to premature death or disability.

Lillian D. Wald

Three years later, with the help of the American Red Cross, she set up a Town and Country Nursing Service, which gave individuals in rural and suburban areas access to visiting nurse services. That same year, Wald was recognized for her pioneering efforts in this new profession, and was named the first president of the National Organization of Public Health Nursing.

Wald's accomplishments in the area of social reform were equally impressive, and a logical extension of her activities in public health. Although Henry Street had begun as a nursing settlement, Wald soon realized that her clients needed more than good nursing care; in order to remain healthy, they also needed good jobs, decent wages, safe housing, and clean physical surroundings. Through a variety of civic campaigns, Wald became involved in providing the poor with improved housing, sanitary drinking water and bathroom facilities, and parks and playgrounds for their children. She was also an avid supporter of the organized labor movement, offering rooms at Henry Street for labor union meetings, and became a major ally of the Women's Trade Union League.

Wald was especially concerned with abolishing child labor, which she saw as not only causing ill health among the young, but also reducing the wages of working women who competed with children for jobs. Wald was a lifelong member of the New York Child Labor Committee and the National Child Labor Committee, both of which pushed for legislation to outlaw child labor. Her work in this area convinced her of the need for a federal governmental agency to protect the health and welfare of the nation's children. She first recommended such a national agency to President Theodore Roosevelt in 1905, bitterly noting that there was a bureau to investigate the state of the nation's crops and livestock but none to preserve the well-being of American children. In 1912, her campaign resulted in the creation of the federal Children's Bureau, with fellow children's rights leader *Julia Lathrop as the agency's first chief.

Throughout the 1910s and 1920s, Wald's political activism broadened. In 1909, she was a key figure in the establishment of the National Association for the Advancement of Colored People (NAACP). In 1914, she and other settlement leaders protested the "hideous wrong" as World War I got under way when they founded the American Union against Militarism with Wald as its first president. After the U.S. became a combatant in the war, Wald served as head of the committee on home nursing of the Council of National Defense, and enlisted her Henry Street nurses to care for wartime victims of contagious diseases. Her service was especially valuable during the influenza pandemic of 1918, when she served as the chair of the Nurses' Emergency Council. When the war ended, she continued her pacifism and concern for civilian victims of war by founding the League of Free Nations Association as successor to her anti-militarist union.

Wald's main passion during this time, however, was the battle for woman's suffrage. From 1909 to 1917, she served as honorary vice chair of the New York State Woman Suffrage Party, which succeeded in winning the vote for New York women in 1917. Upon hearing the news that women had finally received the right to vote, Wald wrote to her friend and fellow settlement leader *Jane Addams, "We are nearly bursting over our citizenship. . . . I had no idea that I could thrill over the right to vote."

With the suffrage victory in hand, Wald and her associates at Henry Street worked hard to educate women in the socially responsible use of their new political power. One major accomplishment often attributed to the women's vote was the passage in 1921 of the Sheppard-Towner Maternity Bill, which offered federal matching funds for maternal and infant health care. Wald and other reform leaders were faced with a conservative political climate during the 1920s, however, and were disappointed to discover that many women did not share their liberal views. The Sheppard-Towner Bill was overturned in the late 1920s, and Wald and her associates found it increasingly difficult to drum up popular support for other reform causes.

By the mid-1920s, Wald was approaching age 60, and deteriorating health forced her to cut back on many activities, both at Henry Street and in national politics. In 1933, a debilitating heart attack and stroke forced her to resign from Henry Street altogether, and she retired to her country home in Westport, Connecticut. Even in retirement, she maintained her enthusiasm for political causes and was a major ally of Franklin Delano Roosevelt and the New Deal.

Despite her frail condition, she served as chair of the Good Neighbor League in 1936, and helped persuade independent voters to join the Democratic Party. She also continued to back nurses' struggle for professional autonomy. When the visiting nurses at Henry Street balked at her successor, who was not a trained nurse, Wald supported their decision to secede from the settlement house, saying that the "nurses must speak for themselves" if they were to have full control of their profession. Wald even found the energy to pen *Windows on Henry Street* (1934), a sequel to her much-acclaimed autobiography, *The House on Henry Street* (1915).

On March 10, 1937, Lillian Wald made one of her few trips outside Westport to attend a celebration in New York in honor of her 70th birthday. Thousands of well wishers attended joint ceremonies at Henry Street and in Westport, and Wald received hundreds of gifts, cards, and letters from around the world congratulating her on her lifetime accomplishments. Her highest acclaim came from New York City Mayor Fiorello La Guardia, who awarded her the city's Distinguished Service Award.

Later that year, Wald suffered another heart attack and stroke, which confined her to Westport for the remainder of her life. She died in September 1940, and her ashes were buried in her family's plot in Rochester. In November of that year, 2,500 people attended a memorial service in her honor held at Carnegie Hall in New York City. President Roosevelt sent a telegram praising her for her "discernment and vision, a heart overflowing with compassion . . . [and] indefatigable industry. She did her great work without thought of self. The Henry Street Settlement with its superb record in bringing light to dark places and joy to the hearts that had known only sorrow is her true monument."

SOURCES:

Coss, Clare, ed. *Lillian D. Wald: Progressive Activist.* NY: Feminist Press, 1989.

Daniels, Doris Groshen. *Always a Sister: The Feminism of Lillian D. Wald.* NY: Feminist Press, 1989.

Duffus, Robert L. *Lillian Wald: Neighbor and Crusader.* NY: Macmillan, 1938.

Rogow, Sally M. *Lillian Wald: The Nurse in Blue.* Philadelphia, PA: Jewish Publication Society of America, 1966.

Wald, Lillian. *The House on Henry Street.* NY: Henry Holt, 1915.

———. *Windows on Henry Street.* Boston, MA: Little, Brown, 1934.

SUGGESTED READING:

Davis, Allen. *Spearheads for Reform.* NY: Oxford University Press, 1967.

Melosh, Barbara. *"The Physicians' Hand": Work Culture and Conflict in American Nursing.* Philadelphia, PA: Temple University Press, 1982.

Muncy, Robyn L. *Creating a Female Dominion in American Reform, 1890–1930.* NY: Oxford University Press, 1991.

Reverby, Susan M. *Ordered to Care: The Dilemma of American Nursing, 1850–1945.* NY: Cambridge University Press, 1987.

COLLECTIONS:

Lillian D. Wald Papers, Rare Book and Manuscript Library, Columbia University; Lillian D. Wald Papers, Manuscript and Archives Division, New York Public Library; Archives of the Visiting Nurse Service of New York (all New York City).

RELATED COLLECTIONS:

Jane Addams Papers, Peace Collection, Swarthmore College.

*Florence Kelley Papers, Rare Book and Manuscript Library, Columbia University.

*M. Adelaide Nutting Papers, Nursing Archives in Special Collections, Milbank Memorial Library of Teachers College, Columbia University.

Heather Munro Prescott,
Associate Professor of History,
Central Connecticut State University, New Britain, Connecticut

Wald, Patricia McGowan (1928—)

American judge who was one of the first two women trustees of the Ford Foundation. Born on September 16, 1928, in Torrington, Connecticut; daughter of Joseph F. McGowan and Margaret (O'Keefe) McGowan; Connecticut College for Women in New London, B.A., 1948; Yale Law School, LL.B., 1951; married Robert L. Wald, on June 22, 1952; children: Sarah; Douglas; Johanna; Frederica; Thomas.

Admitted to D.C. bar (1952); served as clerk for U.S. Circuit Court of Appeals judge (1951–52); associate at firm of Arnold, Fortas & Porter, Washington (1952–53); was a member of the D.C. Crime Commission (1964–65); worked at Department of Justice (1967); worked at Neighborhood Legal Service, D.C. (1968–70); was co-director, Ford Foundation Project Drug Abuse (1970), Center for Law and Social Policy (1971–72), and Mental Health Law Project (1972); was assistant attorney general for legislative affairs, Department of Justice (1977–79); became judge, U.S. Court of Appeals for D.C. (1979), became chief judge (1986).

Born in 1928, Patricia McGowan Wald earned her undergraduate degree at the Connecticut College for Women in New London in 1948, before moving on to law school at Yale University in New Haven. After graduation in 1951, her career path led her to the Ford Foundation to join **Dorothy Nepper-Marshall** as the first two women trustees of the foundation in 1971. The following year, she joined the Mental Health Law Project, which served as a springboard to her appointment as assistant U.S. attorney general for legislative affairs from 1977 to 1979. Thereafter, she served the justice system as a judge in the Washington, D.C., circuit of the United States Court of Appeals, becoming chief judge in 1986.

SOURCES:

Read, Phyllis J., and Bernard L. Witlieb. *The Book of Women's Firsts.* NY: Random House, 1992.

Jacquie Maurice,
freelance writer,
Calgary, Alberta, Canada

Waldeck and Pyrmont, duchess of.

See Helen of Nassau (1831–1888).

Waldegrave, Frances (1821–1879)

English countess and society leader. Name variations: Countess Waldegrave. Born Frances Elizabeth Anne Braham in 1821; died in 1879; daughter of well-known singer John Braham; married John Waldegrave, in 1839; married Lord George Edward, 7th earl Waldegrave, in 1840 (died 1846); married George Granville Harcourt, in 1847 (died 1861); married Chichester (later Lord) Fortescue, in 1863.

Frances Waldegrave was born in 1821 into English society as the daughter of famed Jewish singer John Braham. Following her third marriage, the witty and radiant Frances, Countess Waldegrave, established herself as a London society leader, and is also known for her restoration of Strawberry Hill. In addition to throwing frequent "galas" in her Carlton Gardens home, she was skilled at politics and often hosted more serious gatherings of the influential Whigs and Liberals of her day.

Jacquie Maurice,
freelance writer,
Calgary, Alberta, Canada

Waldegrave, Maria, dowager countess of.

See Walpole, Maria (1736–1807).

Waldetrude (c. 628–688).

See Wandru.

Waldmann, Maria (1842–1920)

Austrian opera singer. Born in 1842 in Vienna, Austria; died on November 6, 1920; studied with Passy-Cornet in Vienna, and with Lamperti in Milan; married and retired in 1878.

Considered by Giuseppe Verdi, who gave her away at her wedding, to be the ideal mezzo-soprano, Maria Waldmann debuted her "velvety tone" in St. Petersburg in 1865. Throughout the 1870s, she sang in Milan, Paris, Moscow, Vienna, Trieste, and Cairo. Highlights of her short career include singing Amneris in the first Italian *Aïda*, and creating the alto part in Verdi's *Requiem*.

Jacquie Maurice,
freelance writer,
Calgary, Alberta, Canada

Waldo, Ruth Fanshaw (1885–1975)

American advertising executive. Born on December 8, 1885, in Scotland, Connecticut; died on August 30, 1975, in Bridgeport, Connecticut; daughter of Gerald Waldo and Mary (Thomas) Waldo; graduated from Adelphi College, 1909; Columbia University, A.M., 1910; never married.

Worked for the J. Walter Thompson Company advertising agency (1915–60); appointed first female vice president of the Thompson Company (1944).

Born in 1885 and raised on an eastern Connecticut farm, Ruth Waldo was the eldest of three children. After studying languages at Adelphi College and attending Columbia University until 1910, she spent four years in New York City as a social worker before deciding to find a career that would allow her more room to advance. In 1915, she became an apprentice copywriter at the New York office of the J. Walter Thompson Company, an advertising agency; the job was offered to her by an acquaintance whose husband was just taking ownership of the company.

Between 1915 and 1930, Waldo's chosen field boomed as it became commonplace for large companies to spend millions on brand-name advertising, and her career skyrocketed as well. Her creativity and knack for writing concise, attention-getting copy that appealed to women as mothers, housewives, and individuals earned her an impressive reputation. After spending some years working in the agency's Chicago and London offices, in 1930 Waldo returned to New York and began supervising all of the Thompson Company's women's copy. A "high-intensity" person, Waldo promoted the practice at the New York offices of female copywriters wearing hats to avoid being mistaken for secretaries.

Waldo's ability to develop superior advertising campaigns allowed her control over creative issues most of the time, while she left the business of agency-client relations to the all-male account executives. She was, however, very intelligent and well aware of how the economics of a depression, a war, and then television impacted her profession. Through the 1930s and 1940s, slogans that she and her colleagues dreamed up became household phrases, and in 1944 the driven and intense Waldo was appointed the first female vice-president of the company.

One of the industry's most prominent women at the time, Ruth Waldo called getting along well with people—especially difficult people—her "hobby," and took pride in the women she had trained who had followed her into a vice-presidency at the company. Consumed by her interest in her work and never having married, in 1960 she retired after 45 years at the J. Walter Thompson Company. She died 15 years later, at age 89. Her trust fund money went to Adelphi University and the American Friends Service Committee, and her 18th-century homestead was left to the public.

SOURCES:

Sicherman, Barbara, and Carol Hurd Green, eds. *Notable American Women: The Modern Period.* Cambridge, MA: The Belknap Press of Harvard University, 1980.

Jacquie Maurice,
freelance writer,
Calgary, Alberta, Canada

Waldrada (fl. 9th c.)

Queen of Lorraine. Flourished around the 9th century; briefly second wife of Lothair also known as Lothar II (b. 826–869), king of Lorraine, also known as Lotharingia (r. 855–869), after 855; children: Hugh (b. around 855). (See Tetberga.)

Walenska, Maria (1786–1817).

See Walewska, Marie.

Walentynowicz, Anna (1929—)

Polish worker and labor leader at the Lenin Shipyard in Gdansk, whose firing in August 1980 triggered a massive strike movement leading directly to the birth of Solidarity. Name variations: (nickname) "Mala" (the little one). Born Anna Lubczyk in 1929 in Wolyn (Volhynia) province, Poland (now Ukraine); orphaned at the age of ten and ended her formal education in the fourth grade; married Kazimierz Walentynowicz (a locksmith), in 1964 (died 1973); children: son, Janusz.

Fired as a worker at the Lenin Shipyard in Gdansk (August 1980), triggering a massive strike movement that led directly to the birth of the Solidarity union and set in motion a process that by the end of the decade would bring about the end of Communist rule in Poland; despite the crucial role played in the Solidarity movement by Walentynowicz and countless other women, they quickly found themselves marginalized once its male leadership achieved recognition as a legitimate political force; both before and after her retirement (1991), was highly critical of many of her former Solidarity colleagues, particularly Lech Walesa.

The people of Poland have a long tradition of resistance and rebellion dating back to the late 18th century, when their nation lost its independence and was partitioned between its Austrian, Prussian and Russian neighbors. Bloody but failed national uprisings in 1830–31 and again in 1863–64 helped to forge a tradition of massive resistance to the hated foreign occupiers, in both of these instances tsarist Russia. In all of these uprisings, as well as during the difficult decades of national occupation and humiliation that marked Polish history until the restoration of independence in 1918, women played important roles, even participating in armed resistance, as personified in the life and martyr's death of the hero of the 1830–31 revolt, *Emilja Plater. Polish women were active in the anti-German resistance during World War II, and fought alongside men both in the Warsaw Ghetto and the general Warsaw uprisings of 1943 and 1944.

After World War II, the situation of women in Poland became more complex, depending on their place in society and their political views. In theory, the Communist government that took control of the country in the years after 1945 brought about their full economic and social emancipation. In practice, the social egalitarianism proclaimed in Marxist-Leninist ideology was often not achieved. Women were not incorporated into the inner policymaking circles of the ruling Polish United Workers' Party (PZPR), and in the workplace, they suffered from significant discriminations, including being rarely offered higher-paying jobs and facing many more obstacles to being promoted than did male workers. Although women constituted one-half of postwar Poland's labor force, they would earn on average only about two-thirds the salary of men.

It was into this complex and frustrating world that a woman of courage, Anna Walentynowicz, appeared to play a role that would change the course of Polish and indeed world history. Anna Lubczyk was born into rural poverty in 1929 in the province of Wolyn (Volhynia). Orphaned at age ten, she was adopted by a farm family who withdrew her from school when she was in fourth grade so that she could work. After the difficult years of World War II, she moved to the Gdansk (formerly Danzig) region, where she worked for awhile as a farmhand. In November 1950, Anna found employment as a welder in Gdansk's Lenin Shipyard, working in a brigade named after the Polish-born revolutionary *Rosa Luxemburg. During this time she became an unmarried mother, giving birth to her only child, a son named Janusz, whom she placed in child care so that she could keep working. Almost from the start of her career, Walentynowicz was aware of the injustices and inequities of her workplace. In 1953, she voiced her complaints that the Lenin Shipyard's women workers were not receiving the same prize money as work incentives that male workers got. As a result of her defiant attitude, she was arrested and interrogated for eight hours, before being released with a warning.

As a young woman from an impoverished background and with only a limited formal education, Walentynowicz was willing to rally behind the government of "People's Poland," which had the unenviable task of rebuilding a shattered nation out of the devastation and rubble of a war that had cost at least six million lives. In 1951, she joined the Polish Youth Union, one of the mass organizations the Communist state relied on to rally popular support for its policies, and traveled to East Berlin to attend a world youth congress. During these years, Anna was "in awe" of the PZPR that ruled Poland, believing she was not worthy of joining it because "only the best and brightest belonged to it, and that excluded me."

Throughout the 1950s and early 1960s, Walentynowicz toiled at the Lenin Shipyard as a model worker who believed in the slogans prominently displayed all around her on huge red banners, including ones exhorting workers to "Care For Your Fellow Worker." During those years, she hoped that such slogans based on the idea of individuals willingly sacrificing themselves for the common good would "become reality, not just propaganda." At production meetings, she spoke out in favor of the current Five Year Plan, even demanding more work. At the same time, she also spoke out in favor of just distribution of bonuses, insisting that these go to workers who had in fact been more productive, rather than to those who were deemed loyal and ideologically correct. Amid the hard work and occasional turbulence of her job, Anna also found some stability in her private life during this period when in 1964 she married Kazimierz Walentynowicz, a locksmith who worked at the shipyard (he would die in 1973).

In 1965, health problems compelled Anna Walentynowicz to give up her job as a welder at the Lenin Shipyard, becoming instead a crane operator. Respected for her honesty and outspokenness, she gained a reputation throughout the shipyard for activism on behalf of her fellow workers. As a member of her division's workers' council, as well as of the division commission (which she chaired for a time), Walentynowicz instinctively uncovered shady dealings and outright corruption by management. On one occasion, she discovered that a fund designated for sick leaves and emergency drug prescriptions was being diverted by a corrupt official, who used it to purchase lottery tickets for himself. She was particularly outraged when she learned that this same official had transferred a pregnant woman worker from the production line to his office so that she could spend full time filling out the lottery tickets. On another occasion, after publicly criticizing the local PZPR leader for his ineptitude, Walentynowicz was interrogated by SB (security police) officials who accused her of listening to Radio Free Europe and being a Jehovah's Witness. By 1968, Walentynowicz had gained such a reputation as a "troublemaker," who could neither be intimidated nor bribed into keeping quiet, that she was fired from her job.

During the decades that saw Walentynowicz gain a reputation for integrity and devotion to her work, Poland went through many crises. In 1956, worker uprisings created massive pressure and brought into power a reform-minded government that made significant concessions on both the cultural and economic fronts, but by the late 1960s stagnation and repression had set in once again. In 1968, intellectuals and students demanded democratic reforms, but their cause was weakened when workers did not join them. By December 1970, worsening economic conditions had triggered massive worker demonstrations on the Baltic coast, including in Gdansk. Many workers were killed by the organs of state repression, and most of Poland was plunged into a state of chaos. Not surprisingly, in Gdansk Walentynowicz played a significant role in December 1970, as one of the leaders of a strike that succeeded in shutting down the Lenin Shipyard. In late January 1971, she was a member of the strikers' presidium that met with new PZPR First Secretary Edward Gierek, negotiations that were able to gain solid concessions for Gdansk's shipyard workers. In December 1971, Walentynowicz helped organize the activities that (illegally) commemorated the first anniversary of the bloody events that had taken place in Gdansk and other Baltic cities a year earlier.

By the late 1970s, the reforms initiated by Gierek had largely failed to create economic prosperity or social peace, and once more a new spirit of defiance began to assert itself among Polish workers and intellectuals. In 1970, there had been little cooperation between striking workers and angry intellectuals, a fact that served to benefit the regime as it strove to regain its power in the aftermath of the turmoil. In the mid-1970s, as Gierek's star as a reformer rapidly lost its luster, workers and intellectuals finally began to work together to find effective means to create a united front that could stand up to the regime. In June 1976, Polish workers once again launched massive protests against declining living standards and other social ills. Unlike earlier crises, however, on this occasion workers and intellectuals were able to bridge the gaps that divided them. In September 1976, intellectuals created the Komitet Obrony Robotników (Workers' Defense Committee, or KOR), which was successful in establishing contacts between the intelligentsia and workers, and over the next years developed an extensive network of collaborators and sympathizers throughout Poland.

It was at a KOR session held in Walentynowicz's modest living room in the late 1970s that she first met a militant young worker named Lech Walesa. Born into a poor peasant family as she had been, Walesa had been an electrician at the Lenin Shipyard in December 1970, serving at the time as a member of the strike committee. Fired from his shipyard job in 1976 for speaking out against the Gierek regime, he became a member of the Free Trade Unions (Wolne Zwiazki Zawodowe, or WZZ), and although he was branded a troublemaker from this point forward, and would lose several more jobs, Walesa persisted. From her first encounter with Walesa, Walentynowicz recognized his leadership qualities, but also sensed that since both she and he possessed strong personalities, "I felt that we wouldn't see eye to eye." By December 1978, Walentynowicz too found herself in trouble with the state. Arrested by the security police, she was threatened by them, but while she was in custody they tried to recruit her to work for them by offering "a better job, better apartment, [and] travel abroad." Walentynowicz refused the offer, telling her captors she did not "care about my life because it isn't worth much," and to cease their threats "because I no longer care." Thereupon, the police released her.

In September 1977, the KOR organization had progressed to the point that it was able to print and effectively distribute an illegal biweekly newspaper, *Robotnik* (The Worker). On the Baltic coast, which included Gdansk, activist workers such as Walentynowicz and Walesa distributed *Robotnik*, eventually even publishing a local edition for that region. Issue No. 35 of *Robotnik*, dated December 1, 1979, is crucial in the history of Poland because it published a document entitled the Charter of Workers' Rights that is regarded as a major step toward the Solidarity movement that emerged less than a year later. Signed by 107 intellectuals and workers, including Walentynowicz and Walesa, the Charter dealt with issues of interest to workers, including a minimum living wage, work safety and health concerns, Saturday and Sunday holidays for miners, a 40-hour work week, and promotions being decided only on the basis of merit rather than the individual's beliefs and opinions. By the end of 1979, a frightened regime was resorting to threats and outright violence to crush worker dissent. Lech Walesa and others were arrested and interrogated. The state usually stopped short of killing dissidents, but one militant worker's mutilated body was found in a river. Among those who were physically mistreated during this period was activist **Maryla Plonska**, who was dragged into a police car by her hair, followed by two days of incarceration.

On December 16, 1979, increasingly angry workers at the Lenin Shipyard reacted to the detention of some of their colleagues with a short warning strike. On December 31, 80 workers at the shipyard began another strike to demand that the management abandon its plan to punish Anna Walentynowicz, whose WZZ activities had grown in recent months, by transferring her to a different department. In April 1980, Walentynowicz was detained and kept under arrest for

two days. On this occasion, she was kicked in the legs, her injuries being serious enough for her to receive a five days' excuse from work from a physician. When she mentioned to a militia member violations of the constitution (described by her as "a splendid document [that] is not observed"), "the officer just laughed." That same spring, she was finally transferred to a new division within the shipyard and put in "quarantine" by the management who barred her from using the canteen. Finding that her defiant attitudes had not changed, on August 9, 1980, the management fired Walentynowicz from her job as a crane operator at the Lenin Shipyard.

Within days after Walentynowicz's dismissal, the workers of the shipyard rose to her defense, and on August 14 they went on strike to protest her firing as well as to press for a number of reforms. Known to many of them simply as "Mala" (the little one), the diminutive crane operator with the fiery temperament was greatly respected as a "woman of iron," unafraid of those with power who exercised that power unjustly. A crowd of a thousand shipyard workers angrily countered the shipyard's PZPR secretary, who attempted to justify Walentynowicz's firing for "disciplinary reasons" by reminding him

Anna Walentynowicz kneeling next to Lech Walesa at a mass during the Gdansk strike.

that she had worked there for three decades, earning three service medals for her labor. On the first day of the strike, Lech Walesa, who had been out of work since his latest firing in January 1980, climbed over the fence and quickly began to play a leading role in the rapidly escalating crisis. Although the immensely popular Walentynowicz was asked by a number of workers to lead the strike committee, she turned it down, noting, "We have equality of the sexes and all that, but the leader has got to be a man." An alarmed government quickly made a number of concessions to the strikers, including the reinstatement of both Walentynowicz and Walesa to their jobs, and a monument to the victims of the 1970 uprising. Some days later, while negotiations between the strikers and the government were proceeding, an exhausted Lech Walesa, now the recognized leader of the strike, suggested that since a number of important concessions had been made to the workers, the time had come to end the strike. Walentynowicz and other militants were shocked and disappointed by this, given the fact that the government had not given in on the issue of release of political prisoners. Thereupon Walentynowicz made a dramatic speech in which she insisted that the jailed activists would not be abandoned. The strike continued. In all, there had been 21 demands made by the strikers, and on August 31, 1980, the government acceded to all of these, including the release of jailed political prisoners. Significantly, neither Walentynowicz nor any other woman was delegated to place her signature on the historic Gdansk accords. Neither were any women present for the signing of the equally significant Szczecin accords.

Anna Walentynowicz's independent stance and indeed defiance of Lech Walesa would cost her dearly in the next years. Almost from the start, their relationship had been tense, not surprising in view of the fact that her extreme frankness sometimes directly challenged Walesa's leadership of what had now become a mass movement—Solidarity (*Solidarnosc*). By the end of September 1980, an astonishing ten million Polish men and women had joined Solidarity, virtually stripping the state-backed national labor union, the Central Council of Trade Unions (Centralna Rada Zwiazków Zawodowych, or CRZZ), of its membership and legitimacy. From this point on, women would participate less and less in the actual strikes, acting more as "stay-behind" forces at home, giving support to the movement through "their men." By January 1981, when Walentynowicz and Walesa were invited to the Vatican to meet with fellow Pole

Pope John Paul II, their always wary relationship had deteriorated badly, and they bickered even in front of the pontiff over who would be first in line to receive his autograph.

In April 1981, still unwilling to kowtow to Walesa, Walentynowicz found herself ousted from the influential Interfactory Founding Committee. Her accelerating erosion of power and influence was echoed by a rapid erosion of women's influence within the Solidarity organization. In 16 out of 41 areas in the elections of July 1981, not a single woman, not even Walentynowicz, was chosen as a delegate to the first National Solidarity Congress. The exclusions continued on the National Commissions of the new union: only 1 woman and 18 men on the Conciliatory Commission, 3 women and 18 men on the Auditing Commission, and 1 woman to 82 men on the National Commission. In total, only 63 women were elected to other Solidarity panels, a mere 7% of all delegates. Reflecting the views of the devout Roman Catholic Lech Walesa and the majority of male Poles, from 1981 on Solidarity projected a conservative position on women's issues, not only by ignoring inequities based on sex, but also by pressing for social policies that would allow women to devote more time to family and child rearing. Within Polish Communist circles after 1980, women's role in public life was also drastically diminished. In 1981, the Ninth Extraordinary Congress of the PZPR dropped the existing quota system for women's representation, the result being that the number of women elected was half that of previous years.

In December 1981, the Polish government cracked down on Solidarity, banning the organization and declaring a state of martial law. Along with Walesa and other leaders, Walentynowicz would be arrested and interned. When tanks broke through the Lenin Shipyard gates that December, she had to be restrained by her friends from standing in their way. When first arrested, Walentynowicz went on a hunger strike to protest prison conditions. Upon her release, she defied a ban by smuggling herself into the shipyard, working there illegally for a day. Perplexed officials sent her to a facility for psychiatric evaluation, but after six weeks they could not agree on a diagnosis and transferred her to prison, where upon arrival she was greeted warmly by prison workers with flowers and kisses. On this occasion, she declared, "We struggle with our hearts, not with violence. Solidarity is a volcano that cannot be capped." After being banned, Solidarity refused to die, simply going underground instead. The organization was kept alive largely through the efforts of innumerable women who, being regarded by the regime as "invisible," were able to undertake activities vital to the organization's continued existence. After the end of the Communist regime in 1989, these women would often be marginalized and their heroism largely forgotten. The record of their contributions has been restored to historical memory in **Shana Penn**'s pioneering article "The National Secret," published in the *Journal of Women's History* in 1994.

At her March 1983 trial for her 1981 actions, Walentynowicz pleaded not guilty to charges of attempting to requisition a water cannon from a local fire brigade to enable strikers to repulse security forces (these exploits of hers would later be featured in Andrzej Wajda's film *Man of Iron*). Walentynowicz was found guilty of having incited a sitdown strike following the proclamation of martial law, but the three-judge court gave her a suspended sentence in view of the delicate state of her health and her reputation as "an excellent worker." She could have been sentenced to a maximum of ten years of imprisonment, but the judges displayed considerable political prudence, acknowledging her value as a symbol of defiance and deciding she might well be less dangerous to the system out of prison than behind bars.

Throughout the 1980s, as the Warsaw regime tried to weaken the illegal Solidarity movement, Walentynowicz continued to agitate on its behalf. With her lectures in church halls throughout Poland, she organized church hunger strikes to protest the government's arrest of young men who had renounced their military service obligations. This initiative resulted in the unleashing of moral energies that led to the conscripts' Freedom and Peace Movement. Increasingly disillusioned by Walesa's leadership of Solidarity, she openly accused him of having cynically and selfishly betrayed the movement's original ideals, and by the mid-1980s Walentynowicz began to agitate for the establishment of a new political party. Because she displayed a lack of political shrewdness or indeed any ability to make compromises, however, the idea died on the vine. In 1987, seeking a respite from life in a nation in permanent crisis, she spent six months in the United States, where among the honors she received was the naming of a housing project in Buffalo, New York, after her.

Anna Walentynowicz remained as critical as ever of those in power when a Solidarity movement led by Lech Walesa came to share power in 1989 with General Wojciech Jaruzelski, who had imposed martial law in 1981. She accused Walesa and his circle of an act of betrayal, becoming even more embittered when Gdansk's shipyard closed as a result of Poland's shock-therapy transition to capitalism in the early 1990s. Walentynowicz retired in 1991 in Gdansk on a modest pension of 1,000 zlotys ($229) a month. When Walesa was elected president of Poland in December 1990, she was not impressed. One night he called to offer her a ministerial post, but her response was blunt indeed: "I said, 'You are disgusting—an illiterate president offering a high position to an illiterate person. What would it mean for the country?.'" Walesa would later deny having made the telephone call. In 1995, as the now highly unpopular Walesa fought a losing political battle for the presidency, Walentynowicz herself ran for a seat in the Sejm (Parliament). After receiving only a handful of votes—1,300 in total—she continued her feud with her former ally from the Lenin Shipyard, accusing him in an article of various reprehensible actions ranging from embezzlement to spying. Even as she entered old age, Walentynowicz gave up little of her stubbornly combative spirit, retaining the formidable personality befitting a true "woman of iron."

SOURCES:

Ascherson, Neal. *The Struggles for Poland.* NY: Random House, 1987.

Atkinson, Jane. "The Woman Behind Solidarity: The Story of Anna Walentynowicz," in *Ms.* Vol. 12, no. 8. February 1984, pp. 96–98.

The Birth of Solidarity: The Gdansk Negotiations, 1980. Trans. and introduced by A. Kemp-Welch. NY: St. Martin's Press, 1983.

Ekiert, Grzegorz. "Rebellious Poles: Political Crises and Popular Protest Under State Socialism, 1945–89," in *EEPS: East European Politics and Societies.* Vol. 11, no. 2. Spring 1997, pp. 299–338.

Held, Joseph. *Dictionary of East European History Since 1945.* Westport, CT: Greenwood Press, 1994.

Jastrun, Tomasz. *Zycie Anny Walentynowicz.* Warsaw: Niezalezna Oficyna Wydawnicza, 1985.

Kenney, Padraic. "The Gender of Resistance in Communist Poland," in *The American Historical Review.* Vol. 104, no. 2. April 1999, pp. 399–425.

Korbonski, Andrzej. "Dissent in Poland, 1956–76," in Jane Leftwich Curry, ed., *Dissent in Eastern Europe.* NY: Praeger, 1983, pp. 25–47.

Kubik, Jan. *The Power of Symbols Against the Symbols of Power: The Rise of Solidarity and the Fall of State Socialism in Poland.* University Park, PA: The Pennsylvania State University Press, 1994.

Laba, Roman. *The Roots of Solidarity: A Political Sociology of Poland's Working-Class Democratization.* Princeton, NJ: Princeton University Press, 1991.

Lee, Hongsub. "Transition to Democracy in Poland," in *East European Quarterly.* Vol. 35, no. 1. March 2001, pp. 87–107.

Lipski, Jan Józef. *KOR: A History of the Workers' Defense Committee in Poland, 1976–1981.* Trans. by

Olga Amsterdamska and Gene M. Moore. Berkeley, CA: University of California Press, 1985.

Long, Kristi S. *We All Fought for Freedom: Women in Poland's Solidarity Movement.* Boulder, CO: Westview Press, 1996.

Malinowska, Ewa. "Socio-Political Changes in Poland and the Problem of Sex Discrimination," in *Women's Studies International Forum.* Vol. 18, no. 1. January–February 1995, pp. 35–43.

Masterman, Sue, and Anton Koene. "The Two Baltic Miracle Makers," in *Maclean's.* Vol. 93, no. 37. September 15, 1980, p. 35.

Miller, Stefania Szlek. "Solidarity Trade Union, Gender Issues, and Child Care In Poland," in *Canadian Slavonic Papers.* Vol. 30, no. 4. December 1988, pp. 417–437.

Ost, David. *Solidarity and the Politics of Anti-Politics: Opposition and Reform in Poland Since 1968.* Philadelphia, PA: Temple University Press, 1990.

Penn, Shana. "The National Secret," in *Journal of Women's History.* Vol. 5, no. 3. Winter 1994, pp. 55–69.

Reading, Anna. *Polish Women, Solidarity and Feminism.* London: Macmillan, 1992.

Sanford, George and Adriana Gozdecka-Sanford. *Historical Dictionary of Poland.* Metuchen, NJ: Scarecrow Press, 1994.

Siemienska, Renata. "Women and Social Movements in Poland," in *Women & Politics.* Vol. 6, no. 4. Winter 1986, pp. 5–35.

"Solidarity Aide Is Put On Trial," in *The New York Times.* March 10, 1983, p. A3.

"Suspended Sentence for Solidarity Aide," in *The Washington Post.* March 31, 1983, p. A30.

"Walentynowicz, Anna, neé Lubczyk," in Juliusz Stroynowski, ed., *Who's Who in the Socialist Countries of Europe.* 3 vols. Munich: K.G. Saur, 1989, vol. 3, p. 1280.

Walentynowicz, Anna, and Anna Baszanowska. *Cien Przyszlosci.* Gdansk: Wydawnictwo Albatros, 1993.

Wavell, Stuart. "Poland's Woman of Iron: Solidarity Activist Anna Walentynowicz," in *The Guardian* [London]. June 18, 1986.

Williamson, Elizabeth. "Little Solidarity Left Between Two Polish Union Heroes," in *The Wall Street Journal.* September 1, 2000, p. A9.

"Worker Who Spawned Solidarity Is Arrested," in *The New York Times.* June 18, 1986, p. A5.

RELATED MEDIA:

Man of Iron (Polish film), directed by Andrzej Wajda.

John Haag,
Associate Professor of History,
University of Georgia, Athens, Georgia

Wales, Nym (1907–1997).

See Snow, Helen Foster.

Wales, princess of.

See Eleanor of Montfort (1252–1282).
See Joan of Kent (1328–1385).
See Anne of Warwick (1456–1485).
See Caroline of Ansbach (1683–1737).
See Augusta of Saxe-Gotha (1719–1772).
See Caroline of Brunswick (1768–1821).
See Caroline of Brunswick for sidebar on Charlotte Augusta (1796–1817).
See Alexandra of Denmark (1844–1925).
See Mary of Teck (1867–1953).
See Diana (1961–1997).

Wales, queen of.

See Edith (fl. 1063).
See Angharad (d. 1162).

Walewska, Marie (1786–1817)

Polish noblewoman who became the mistress of Napoleon Bonaparte in order to promote the restoration of independence to her country. Name variations: Maria Walenska; Maria Walevska; Countess Valeska. Pronunciation: Va-LEV-skah. Born Marie Laczynska in the Polish town of Brodno near her family's estate of Kiernozia outside Warsaw on December 7, 1786; died in Paris, France, on December 11, 1817, of kidney disease complicated by a recent pregnancy; daughter of Matthew Laczynski and Eva (Zaborowska) Laczynska (members of the Polish nobility); educated by private tutors, and at the Convent of Our Lady of the Assumption in Warsaw, 1800–1803; married Anastase Colonna Walewski (a Polish noble, landowner, and former chamberlain to King Stanislaus Poniatowski of Poland), probably on June 17, 1804 (divorced 1812); married General Philippe Antoine Ornano (cousin to Napoleon), on September 7, 1815; children: (first marriage) Anthony Basil Rudolph; (second marriage) Rodolphe Auguste; (with Napoleon) Alexander Florian Joseph Colonna Walewski.

Death of her father in battle of Maciejowice against the Russians (1794); left family estate for schooling in Warsaw (1800); while French army occupied Warsaw, met Lieutenant Charles de Flahaut and worked in French military hospitals (1806); became Napoleon's mistress, visited him at Finckenstein castle, and creation of Grand Duchy of Warsaw (1807); visited Paris (1808); fled from Warsaw to Thorn during Austrian invasion of Poland and joined Napoleon in Vienna and Paris (1809); after Napoleon married Archduchess Marie-Louise of Austria, moved permanently to Paris (1810); presented at French imperial court (1811); when Napoleon invaded Russia, returned to Warsaw (1812); returned to Paris (1813); visited Napoleon on Elba (1814); had two final meetings with Napoleon (1815).

Countess Marie Walewska stands in the midst of two momentous developments in European history at the start of the 19th century. Her native Poland had recently been removed from the map as an independent country, and patriotic Poles like Marie were searching for a way to restore the once powerful Polish state. Secondly, the European scene was dominated as never before by a single man: the French dictator, Napoleon Bonaparte. As Napoleon's mistress starting in the eventful year of 1807, Marie shared his intimate life; she also apparently had an opportunity to make him personally receptive to the hopes of the Polish people.

Poland was the only major European country of the 18th century to be partitioned among its neighbors and to vanish as a sovereign state. Once the second largest country in Eastern Europe (after Russia) and the greatest power in the region, Poland had fallen into a political abyss. Its powerful nobility not only elected the country's monarch, the nobility increasingly reduced the monarch and the entire central government to impotence.

Meanwhile, the growing strength of Poland's ambitious and expanding neighbors—imperial Russia, the Austrian Empire, and the kingdom of Prussia—created a deadly danger to Polish independence. Each of the three possessed a relatively efficient centralized government and powerful military forces. In the course of the 18th-century rivalry among the three, Poland loomed large as a prize ripe for the taking. In the end, they compromised some of their differences by dividing Poland among themselves. Thus, starting in the 1770s, her three potent neighbors carved up Poland. There were three separate partitions: in 1772, 1793, and 1795. After the last one, Poland, although not the Polish people and their hopes, had ceased to exist.

By the time the third partition of Poland had taken place, Napoleon Bonaparte was a rising young general in the French army. Over the next decade, he took power as military dictator, and in 1804 he crowned himself as the French emperor. The following year, he launched a spectacular series of wars. Striking eastward, he began to defeat the very countries that had partitioned Poland: Austria and Russia were his victims at the battle of Austerlitz in 1805, Prussia was humiliated by the French the following year at the battle of Jena.

Napoleon claimed to be the heir of the French Revolution, and he offered the oppressed peoples of Europe relief from the evils of the old regime. Thus, by the time French armies began to penetrate Polish territory after Jena, Napoleon had become the center of hope for Polish patriots. Polish soldiers had fought as volunteers in the French army ever since the 1790s,

and Polish leaders like Prince Joseph Poniatowski, the nephew of the last king, half hoped, half expected that Napoleon would be the godfather of a restored, independent Poland.

In his personal life, Napoleon had long been known for his relentless pursuit of attractive young women. His marriage to *Josephine Beauharnais in 1796 was soon shaken, first by her infidelity, then by his. By the time he reached Poland in early 1807 and made the acquaintance of the beautiful young Countess Walewska, Napoleon was accustomed to having his way with most women who caught his eye.

The woman who stands as one of the greatest loves of Napoleon's life was the daughter of an aristocratic Polish family. The Laczynski family could trace their noble lineage back at least three centuries, but their wealth had been severely diminished by Poland's difficulties with its neighbors. Much of the family land was lost when Prussia shared in the 1772 partition. Thus, at the time of Marie's birth in 1786, Poland was already shrinking. Her country's last efforts to fend off her greedy neighbors made the young girl an orphan. In 1794, when she was only eight, her father died in the battle of Maciejowice fighting with a ragtag volunteer force defend-

*Marie
Walewska*

ing Warsaw against the Russian army. She was raised by her mother on their diminished estate. The family fortunes went into further decline, since **Eva Laczynska** was unable to manage the remaining family lands successfully.

The young girl was educated by private tutors until just before she became 14. Then she left Kiernozia to complete her schooling at the Convent of Our Lady of the Assumption in Warsaw. Marie's biographer **Christine Sutherland** finds the roots of the young countess' patriotism in both her early years at Kiernozia and these teenage years in her nation's cultural center. At the family estate, her most important teacher was a young Frenchman named Nicholas Chopin, who would later father the great Polish composer of the 19th century. Nicholas had become a fervent Polish patriot after arriving in his adopted country, and he had fought in the same force of civilian volunteers as Marie's father. In addition to the patriotic lessons he taught her, Marie heard her new school friends in Warsaw speak glowingly about the restoration of Polish independence. By then, Napoleon had a prominent place on the European scene, and many of Marie's aristocratic schoolmates looked to him as Poland's savior.

Yet her sacrifice for Poland was to prove all in vain, so it was as well that she came to be genuinely attached to Bonaparte.

—**Correlli Barnett**

The young countess was a strikingly beautiful woman, with blonde hair, a milk-white complexion, and lovely, blue eyes. Her first love was the son of a Russian general. But in the end, she married a wealthy and elderly Polish noble from a nearby estate. There is some doubt about the date of the wedding, which may have occurred in 1803 but most likely took place in 1804. There is none about the disparity in their ages. She was at most only 18, while Anastase Walewski was in his late 60s. The marriage took place at the insistence of her mother, and Sutherland describes their wedding as one joining "the melancholy little bride, bereft of feeling, and the old gentleman, beaming with self-satisfaction."

The unlikely couple took up residence in the Polish countryside, and married life seemed to point Marie toward an uneventful, somber existence. Anastase Walewski had been an important figure in the Polish court before the country's independence was extinguished, but now he chose to spend much of his time in his rural retreat. The most important event in the early years of their marriage was the birth of a son in

June 1805. Then, the world of European power politics intervened.

As Napoleon's conquests extended into Eastern Europe in the winter of 1806, Marie's life became intertwined with that of the French leader. Following the French victory over the Prussian army at Jena in October 1806, advance parties of French troops entered western Poland and occupied Warsaw. Napoleon soon followed.

Even before Napoleon's arrival Marie had an important contact with the French. The first troops to reach her husband's estate included the glamorous young officer Lieutenant Charles de Flahaut, illegitimate son of Count Talleyrand. A number of historians believe that Flahaut informed Talleyrand, then the French foreign minister and a proponent of a restored Poland, of the attractive young Polish aristocrat. These authorities suggest that Talleyrand saw to it that Napoleon met Marie. Thus, the emperor's sexual energies could be put in the service of Polish independence. In any case, along with other Polish noblewomen, Marie went to Warsaw to work in military hospitals in support of the French army. Her husband, now in his 70s and in poor health, openly expressed his jealousy as she moved into such activities that put her in contact with attractive young men.

Historians differ on how Napoleon and Marie first met. Some contend Marie first contacted her future lover in the small town of Bronia as he made his way toward Warsaw in January 1807. Marie and a single companion supposedly accosted the leader of Napoleon's escort and successfully pleaded to meet the great man. Thus, the first encounter took no more than a moment, but the lovely young Polish noblewoman made a lasting impression.

Whether or not this initial meeting occurred, it is certain Napoleon met the striking Marie at the grand ball welcoming him to Warsaw on January 7, 1807. The attention he paid her there was obvious to Polish leaders who were also present. When Napoleon sent the young beauty two admiring notes and received no answer, he became even more fascinated by her. The French dictator was not accustomed to having his romantic initiatives ignored in this fashion.

From the early stages of their relationship, Polish politics entered upon the scene. The leaders of Napoleon's personal entourage contacted Prince Poniatowski, the leader of Poland's nationalist movement, to ask his help in getting Marie to receive the attentions of the French dictator. Polish leaders like Poniatowski were well aware that Napoleon's friendship, backed by French arms, offered the best hope for a resurrected and independent Poland. Marie's brother Benedict, who had served for years in the French army, added his voice to those urging her to accept Napoleon's overtures. In the end, Marie relented. As R.F. Delderfield has noted, "Had she been less of a patriot it is extremely doubtful whether she could have been persuaded to yield to the enormous pressures put upon her by her fellow countrymen." Despite her conservative family background and devotion to her Roman Catholic religious beliefs, Marie agreed to see the French emperor. In short order, she became his mistress.

The political situation into which Marie now entered was a complex one. Napoleon could see the advantage of sponsoring a revived Polish kingdom with its population linked by ties of gratitude to France. On the other hand, promoting Polish independence meant a severe strain on France's relationship to the Austrian and Russian empires. In the end, Napoleon refused to bend his political policies or to stray far from his pursuit of gain even for Marie. But the French dictator used the promise of his friendship for Poland in wooing Marie. He noted in one letter to her that "your country will be even dearer to me if you have compassion on my heart." Nonetheless, the two lovers soon went beyond a mere physical relationship to a tie of genuine affection. They had a rare chance for an extended time together in the first months of 1807 as Napoleon resumed his war against the Russians. Following a bloody stalemate at the battle of Eylau on February 8, Napoleon retired to his headquarters at the castle of Finckenstein in East Prussia. Marie joined him there in April while he planned the next stage in the campaign.

She now frankly accepted her role as Napoleon's mistress, and they spent approximately two months together at Finckenstein. In his memoirs written years later on St. Helena, Napoleon recalled how his feelings for Marie changed during this interlude. She ceased to be merely a target of his sexual desires and stimulated his deepest feelings of love and devotion. In June, Napoleon's forces triumphed over the Russians at the battle of Friedland. In the ensuing settlement Napoleon reached with Russia's Tsar Alexander I, Russia kept most of its Polish lands. Napoleon was willing only to carve out a small Polish state; this newly formed Grand Duchy of Warsaw now emerged as a French satellite. These actions were a clear indication that Napoleon would not bend his ambitions to satisfy the desire of Poland's patriots. Marie's role as an emissary for her nation had failed.

When the French leader returned to Paris, Marie followed six months later in the spring of 1808. But her visit was brief. After his arrival home, Napoleon renewed his continuous quest for other sexual partners. He also immersed himself in maintaining control over the European continent. France's invasion of Spain was going badly, and he had to leave to deal personally with the crisis. With her lover gone, Marie felt no reason to remain and returned to Poland. For the next year and a half, her only contact with Napoleon came through letters.

The second major interlude they had together came in 1809. The Austrian Empire, Napoleon's most stubborn opponent among the powers of Europe, went to war against France once again in April of that year. Napoleon had a difficult campaign in dealing with his old antagonist. Austrian troops even penetrated Poland, forcing Marie and other pro-French aristocrats to flee from Warsaw. The decisive French victory over the Austrians came only in July 1809 at the battle of Wagram. Marie then joined the victori-

Polish stamp issued in 1970 in honor of Marie Walewska.

MARIA WALEWSKA
mal. Jacquotot Marie-Victoire

2,50 ZŁ POLSKA

ous French leader at the Schönbrunn Palace outside Vienna. Their stay at Schönbrunn was the longest time the two had together. By September, Marie found that she was pregnant. She returned to Poland to have their child in May 1810, a boy whom she named Alexander.

By then, Napoleon's personal and political lives had led him to turn away from her. In order to gain a sense of respectability for his rule and to have a suitable and legitimate heir, the French dictator first divorced Josephine, his wife of 14 years' standing, then sought a second wife from the ranks of European royalty. He was unable to get the younger sister of Tsar Alexander I as his bride, and he then turned to the Habsburg rulers of Austria. In March 1810, he married the Habsburg princess *Marie Louise of Austria (1791–1847), and, almost exactly one year later, she gave him a legitimate son. Ironically, Marie Walewska's pregnancy probably helped to convince him that Josephine's childlessness was not his fault. Thus, his Polish lover inadvertently pushed him into his divorce and remarriage.

Nonetheless, Napoleon made it clear that he wished Marie nearby. In late 1810, at his request, she settled in Paris with her young son. Napoleon provided her with a lavish residence in the city as well as a country retreat. It is uncertain whether he saw her and their child frequently, but Marie herself was presented at the imperial court in 1811.

Napoleon's reign over Europe faced its most dramatic crisis in 1812. His invasion of Russia brought disaster. The vast international army that he led into Russia was almost totally destroyed. It had been the foundation stone of his power, and now much of Europe rose up against him. Before leaving for Russia, Napoleon had made financial provisions to secure the future of Marie and Alexander. Shortly after his departure for the fateful campaign, Marie herself returned to Poland. Following her arrival home, she obtained a divorce from her husband on the grounds that she had been coerced in marrying the aged Polish nobleman.

Faced with calamity in Russia, Napoleon deserted the remnants of his defeated army. On his way back to France in December 1812, the French leader passed within a short distance of Marie's home. He considered visiting her, but he was quickly persuaded not to by his aides. They reminded him of the pressing danger to his political fortunes.

In 1813, as Marie watched from her home in Paris with her two children at her side, the disasters mounted up. Napoleon hurled newly raised armies into Central Europe but was defeated by a coalition of his enemies at the battle of Leipzig in October. Marie's health deteriorated as a result of the strain she experienced watching Napoleon's fortunes collapse. In the spring of the following year, France itself was invaded and Paris was occupied. Faced with exile, Napoleon attempted suicide. When Marie tried to see him at Fontainebleau in the aftermath of his attempt to end his life, she was unable to gain entrance to his room. The French leader left for Elba in April 1814. His new home, the political realm which he now ruled, was just a tiny island off the Italian coast.

At Elba, Marie and Napoleon had their last encounter. In September 1814, five months after the beginning of his exile, Napoleon greeted his Polish mistress and his four-year-old son, Alexander. Historians attribute a variety of motives to Marie's effort to meet him. One view holds that she wanted to remain with him as his mistress. A second possibility is that she had come to secure her financial future. As Delderfield notes, Walewska was no longer the romantic and patriotic young woman Napoleon remembered. Napoleon's financial arrangements to care for Marie and Alexander had not been carried out. Thus, "she had come to Elba to discuss money." A third possibility is that she used her financial needs as an excuse to see him and to plead her case to remain with him.

The meeting took place in an uncomfortable environment. Napoleon was trying desperately to get his Austrian wife and his legitimate son to join him on Elba. Thus, he made every effort to prevent news of Walewska's visit from becoming public. And he made sure it was a brief one. The two had a bittersweet family reunion, the one occasion when Napoleon was able to get to know the love child he and Marie had produced. After a stay of less than two days, mother and child were gone.

The lovers had their final meetings in 1815. Napoleon slipped away from his island prison in March of that year, landed in southern France, and marched triumphantly to Paris to retake power. His brief interlude of political success was shattered at the battle of Waterloo in June 1815. And in these dramatic and sad moments, Marie met the French leader two more times. The two saw each other just before Napoleon left for the Waterloo campaign, and he saw her and Alexander several days after his climatic defeat. At the second meeting, they spoke in private for an hour and had a final embrace. In the film *Conquest*, the plot presents Marie and Napoleon meeting at the port of Rochefort. He is about to board the British navy vessel that will take him to his final place of exile, the island of St. Helena in the remote reaches of the South Atlantic. She urges him to escape and offers to help. He gallantly refuses. The scene is emotionally stirring. And it is pure fiction.

The glamorous Polish noblewoman, still beautiful almost a decade after she had attracted Napoleon's eye, had a brief and tragic second marriage. Her first husband, the elderly count, died in January 1815. After Napoleon began his exile in the South Atlantic, Marie fell in love with General Philippe Ornano, a distinguished officer in the Napoleonic army whom she had known for several years. Ironically, he was also Napoleon's cousin. Their marriage produced Marie's third child, a son she named Rodolphe. By this time, however, she was in very fragile health. The strain of the pregnancy weakened her even further, and she died in Paris on December 11, 1817, scarcely two years after her wedding. According to her wishes, she was buried in Poland but her heart was removed and placed in a cemetery in France.

Marie Walewska's love affair with Napoleon failed to bring the political aims that the patriotic countess had sought. Poland remained divided and under foreign control until the aftermath of World War I. But the child produced by their relationship went on to a distinguished career. Alexander Walewski fought in Poland's rebellion of 1830 against Russian rule, became an officer in the French Foreign Legion, and rose to become French foreign minister under his cousin, Emperor Napoleon III. He died in 1868.

Marie's love affair illuminates important features of Napoleon's personality. Accounts of their moments together, whether at Finckenstein, Vienna, or, briefly, at Elba, show a Napoleon capable of great tenderness. For many of Napoleon's biographers, Marie and Josephine were the only women he ever loved. At the same time, his tie to her reflected his practical, even ruthless nature. The Poland she loved, and whose fortunes had first placed her in Napoleon's arms, found no help from her powerful friend.

SOURCES:

Barnett, Correlli. *Bonaparte*. London: George Allen & Unwin, 1978.

Cronin, Vincent. *Napoleon: An Intimate Biography*. NY: William Morrow, 1972.

Delderfield, R.F. *Napoleon in Love*. NY: Simon and Schuster, 1959.

Sutherland, Christine. *Marie Walewska: Napoleon's Great Love*. Paris: Vendome, 1979.

SUGGESTED READING:

Bernard, J.F. *Talleyrand: A Biography*. NY: Putnam, 1973.

Bierman, John. *Napoleon III and his Carnival Empire*. NY: St. Martin's Press, 1988.

Normington, Susan. *Napoleon's Children*. Dover, NH: Alan Sutton, 1993.

Stacton, David. *The Bonapartes*. NY: Simon and Schuster, 1966.

RELATED MEDIA:

Conquest (112 min. film), starring Charles Boyer and *Greta Garbo, directed by Clarence Brown, Metro-Goldwyn-Mayer, 1937.

Neil M. Heyman,
Professor of History,
San Diego State University, San Diego, California

Walford, Lucy (1845–1915)

Scottish novelist. Born Lucy Colquhoun on April 17, 1845, in Portobello, near Edinburgh, Scotland; died on May 11, 1915; daughter of John Colquhoun and Frances Sara (Fuller-Maitland) Colquhoun; educated at home by governesses; married Alfred Saunders Walford, in 1869 (died 1907); children: two sons and five daughters.

Selected writings: Mr. Smith: A Part of his Life *(1874);* Pauline *(1877);* Troublesome Daughters *(1880);* The Baby's Grandmother *(1884);* Cousins *(1885);* The History of a Week *(1886);* A Mere Child *(1888);* A Stiff-Necked Generation *(1889);* The Havoc of a Smile *(1890);* The Mischief of Monica *(1892);* A Pinch of Bubble *(1895);* Sir Patrick the Puddock *(1899);* A Dream's Fulfillment *(1902);* The Enlightenment of Olivia *(1907); (autobiography)* Recollections of a Scottish Novelist *(1910);* David and Jonathan on the Riviera *(1914).*

Lucy Walford was born in 1845 in Portobello, near Edinburgh, Scotland, and raised in a well-connected family. Her father John Colquhoun was an author, and her aunt was the novelist *Catherine Sinclair. By the time she was seven, Walford was already an avid reader, and she later professed that her first exposure to *Jane Austen's work in 1868 influenced her immeasurably. After her marriage to Alfred Saunders Walford, she wrote secretly, contributing stories to *Blackwood's Magazine* and working on her first book, *Mr. Smith: A Part of his Life*. Her family voiced disapproval when the book was published in 1874, but it was a great success and earned her an audience with Queen *Victoria. Walford went on to write 45 books and was particularly adept at light-hearted domestic comedy, as seen in her books *Pauline* (1877), *The Baby's Grandmother* (1884), *Cousins* (1885), *The History of a Week* (1886), *A Mere Child* (1888), *A

Stiff-Necked Generation (1889), *The Havoc of a Smile* (1890), *The Mischief of Monica* (1892) and *Sir Patrick the Puddock* (1899). She also contributed to several London magazines, and worked as London correspondent for the New York *Critic* from 1889 to 1893. She produced two nonfiction works in 1910 and 1912 before publishing her last novel in 1914 at the age of 70, the year before her death.

SOURCES:

Buck, Claire, ed. *The Bloomsbury Guide to Women's Literature.* NY: Prentice Hall, 1992.

Shattock, Joanne. *The Oxford Guide to British Women Writers.* Oxford: Oxford University Press, 1993.

Jacquie Maurice,
freelance writer,
Calgary, Alberta, Canada

Walkenshaw, Clementina (c. 1726–1802).

See Walkinshaw, Clementina.

Walker, A'Lelia (1885–1931).

See Women of the Harlem Renaissance.

Walker, Cath (1920–1993).

See Walker, Kath.

Walker, Madame C.J. (1867–1919)

African-American entrepreneur who, as a laundress and daughter of former slaves, invented hair-care products for black women which she turned into a multimillion-dollar business. Name variations: Sarah Walker; Sarah Breedlove McWilliams Walker; Sarah Breedlove McWilliams. Born Sarah Breedlove on December 23, 1867, on a cotton plantation in Delta, Louisiana; died at the mansion she built in Irvington, New York, on May 25, 1919; third child of Owen Breedlove and Minerva Breedlove (field hands and former slaves); married Moses (Jeff) McWilliams (a laborer), in 1881 (died 1887); married John Davis, around 1890 (divorced around 1903); married Charles J. Walker (a journalist), on January 4, 1906 (divorced 1912); children: (first marriage) Lelia McWilliams, later A'Lelia Walker (b. June 6, 1885).

Orphaned at seven during a yellow fever epidemic; moved to Vicksburg with her sister when she was ten (1877); at 14, married Moses McWilliams (1881), who died in an accident (1887); with infant daughter, moved to St. Louis where she supported herself as a laundress and attended night school; developed a formula to straighten hair, targeted to black female customers (1905); traveled the country to promote her product and established offices in various cities, a correspondence school, Lelia College, in Pittsburgh to train her representatives, and a factory in Indianapolis; amassed a personal fortune, contributing to various black causes, from education to social protest.

Sarah Breedlove took care to wear immaculate, freshly starched clothing to advertise her skills as a laundrywoman. Thus attired, she sat in the audience of the National Association of Colored Women at the St. Louis World's Fair of 1904 listening to *Margaret Murray Washington, the wife of the black educator Booker T. Washington. Washington's elegance and calm authority amazed Sarah, who had been orphaned at seven, widowed at twenty. Years of labor over a washtub enabled her to send her daughter to college. Still she was as much at the mercy of the elements as a farmer—submerging her hands and arms into hot soapy water whether the day was scorching or the temperatures freezing, left powerless on days when rain or snow made it impossible to hang clothes outside.

The difficulties of her life and the rigors of her work took a toll on her body. Her hair was split and her scalp was balding in patches and the sight of Margaret Washington dressed in silk and lace with her hair pulled serenely from her brows inspired Sarah to try to make more of her looks. In the weeks that followed, she tried beauty products that supposedly promoted hair growth. Soon, in her spare time, she was selling them door-to-door. Then, confident she could improve upon the products she represented, she was experimenting with her own formulas. At 37, Sarah Breedlove, the daughter of slaves, set her feet on the path that would make her Madame C.J. Walker, one of the greatest capitalists in America.

In later years, she would synopsize her story by making it a myth: "As I bent over the washboard and looked at my arms buried in the soapsuds, I said to myself, 'What are you going to do when you grow old and your back gets stiff?'" God, she said, answered her prayers. "One night I had a dream, and in that dream a big black man appeared to me and told me what to mix up for my hair. Some of the remedy was grown in Africa, but I sent for it, mixed it, put it on my scalp, and in a few weeks my hair was coming in faster than it had ever fallen out." In time, through enterprise and inventiveness, money was coming in too.

Sarah Breedlove was born in 1867 on the Louisiana plantation where her parents, former slaves, worked in fields owned by the family that once owned them. After her parents died in a yellow fever epidemic when Sarah was seven,

Madame
C.J.
Walker

she and her brother and sister were unable to work the land, and so they eventually moved across the river to Vicksburg, Mississippi. When Sarah's sister **Lovenia** married in 1879, Sarah lived briefly with the couple, but at 14 she married laborer Moses McWilliams to escape her domineering brother-in-law. McWilliams died in an accident when Sarah was 20, leaving her with her two-year-old daughter Lelia, later ◄❧ **A'Lelia Walker**, to support. Walker traveled to St. Louis where she heard a laundress like herself could make higher wages.

With a black population of 35,000, St. Louis had one of the largest African-American communities in the nation and was a mecca for migrants from the South. It supported more than 100 black-owned businesses and three newspapers. With its advantageous position on the Mississippi, it boasted the nation's largest brewery, its key drug manufacturer, and largest tobacco factory. Doing the hard labor of laundering clothes at home, which then meant boiling vats of hot water and immersing hands and arms in strong detergents, starching and pressing shirts and dresses with heavy irons heated on coal stoves, enabled Sarah to stay home with her growing child. Walker's great-granddaughter **A'Lelia Perry Bundles** offered a picture of the future millionaire at this time, writing in her book: "When she delivered her laundry, she walked with dignity, a basket of neatly folded clothes balanced atop her head."

Sarah joined the St. Paul African Methodist Episcopal Church, founded by blacks, which before the Civil War had defied anti-literacy laws and taught blacks to read and write. The women of the church helped her, and she responded by assisting impoverished members of the community in the Mite Missionary Society, where for the first time she came in contact with cultured, successful black women. By the time Walker attended the 1904 St. Louis World's Fair, the coverage of Margaret Washington's speech there was the first time a black woman was treated positively in the city's press.

While the image of her sisters rose in her eye, Sarah's sense of her own appearance suffered. She dressed cleanly and crisply to promote her services as a laundress, but she was conscious of her broken hair and balding temples. Poor nutrition, a hard life, and harsh treatments advertised in black publications undoubtedly undermined her appearance. The late 19th century was a time of conformity and the idealization of the wasp-waisted Gibson Girl with long upswept hair, which few women of any race could achieve. While black women wanted their own identity, hairstyles inspired by Africa were unheard of. Gripped by the idea of the financial and psychological profits to be made from helping black women improve their appearance, Walker supplemented her income by working as a sales agent for *Annie M. Turnbo Malone's Poro Company, which sold patented hair mixtures door-to-door. Disappointed in the products she sold, Walker experimented to improve them. Sometime between 1900 and 1905, she developed her own hair grower whose secret ingredient was probably sulphur. She found that her ointment, applied with heated steel combs which had just been developed, straightened hair safely and effectively. Her system encompassed a shampoo, a pomade "hair grower," vigorous brushing, and heated combs that softened curls and promoted a luscious sheen.

Using contacts and skills she honed working for the Poro Company, Walker began to sell door-to-door in St. Louis. Though confident of success, she wanted to avoid direct competition with Annie Malone. With her daughter A'Lelia enrolled at Knoxville College, a black institution in Tennessee, and $1.50 in savings, Walker moved to Denver where her late brother had died, leaving four daughters. Having lived on the steamy Mississippi River all her life, she was astonished by the majesty of Colorado's mountains and its dry bracing air. She found a job as a cook, probably at the home of E.L. Scholtz, a druggist. Conceivably, he provided technical advice on ingredients as she continued to develop her formulae and test them on her nieces. When results satisfied her, she named her three improved products Wonderful Hair Grower (which contained medication for the scalp), Glossine, and Vegetable Shampoo. She left her full-time job and took in laundry two days a week, and the rest of the time sold door-to-door by offering free demonstrations. She used her profits to buy raw materials and advertising, much of it mail order. Her own before and after photographs were convincing sales tools. Unlike other manufacturers who used light-skinned women as models, she put a picture of herself, a "typical" black woman, but one with long flowing hair, on her labels.

C.J. Walker, a newspaperman from St. Louis, had been corresponding with her and offering advice. When he came to visit her in Denver, the two married on January 4, 1906. Soon he helped her expand her mail-order business and added "C.J. Walker's Blood and Rheumatic Remedy." To evoke the glamour of France and to avoid homier sobriquets like "Aunt Sarah," Sarah began calling herself Madame Walker.

❧▶
Walker, A'Lelia.
See Women of
the Harlem
Renaissance.

Against the advice of her husband and other counselors, she embarked on an 18-month sales trip to nine states, including New York, speaking in churches, Masonic and public halls and demonstrating her products. According to A'Lelia Bundles, this trip increased her sales to $35 a week, more than double the earnings of the average white American male. On the road, she trained sales agents who earned a share of the company's profits and quickly increased company sales tenfold. In 1908, she established the headquarters of the Madame C.J. Walker Manufacturing Company in Pittsburgh, to operate the mail-order business more efficiently. She and her daughter A'Lelia opened a training center for Walker agents there and called it Lelia College. "Hair culturists," as her graduates were known, were able to earn in one week what they would have earned in a month as housekeepers, laundresses, or teachers. These agents making in-home sales accounted for the bulk of the business. Their mission was not just to sell but to educate customers in "cleanliness and loveliness."

Walker stressed that hygiene and personal appearance were cornerstones of self-respect. In 1919, *The Crisis*, the magazine of the National Association for the Advancement of Colored People, said that in her lifetime Madame Walker "revolutionized the personal habits and appearance of millions of human beings." She formed the Mme. C.J. Walker Culturists Union of America, with dues of 25 cents a month, which entitled their beneficiaries to a $50 payment at their death. The unions engaged in charitable and educational work as well as business matters. She gave cash prizes to the "Walker Clubs" that did the most philanthropic work in their communities.

In 1910, the Walkers moved to Indianapolis where Sarah established a manufacturing plant. The city served eight railway systems, and had a large black community to provide employees. At that time, it was the center of the country's automobile industry and used the Indianapolis Speedway to test cars. Within the year, the company had 950 agents across the country and a monthly corporate income of $1,000.

One of her few and favorite relaxations was the movies. A fan of Charlie Chaplin and the epics of Cecil B. De Mille, Walker went to the local Isis Theater one afternoon, slid her dime across the counter to buy a ticket, and was told that since she was "colored," she would have to pay 25 cents. Enraged, she told her attorney to sue. The matter was settled out of court, but when she built The Walker Building to house her factory and offices, she included an elegant theater specifically for black people. Over time, she and her husband had mounting disagreements over control of the company. In 1912, they divorced. She retained his name and he remained a Walker agent. A'Lelia, now known as A'Lelia Walker Robinson, had also divorced, but she adopted a poor 13-year-old girl named **Mae Bryant**, whose intelligence and beauty made her a natural Walker model.

In 1913, Sarah and A'Lelia expanded their operations to New York City. Between 1913 and 1915, they purchased two houses at 108–119 West 136th Street, which they remodeled to include a façade of Indiana limestone. The lower floors housed a beauty parlor and school while the two women lived on the upper floors, where they established a social center, a meeting place for accomplished individuals of both races. In the 1920s, A'Lelia became a leading hostess of the Harlem Renaissance, inviting to her home such intellectuals and entertainers as W.E.B. Du Bois, Countee Cullen, Langston Hughes, *Alberta Hunter, *Rebecca West, Osbert Sitwell, Carl Van Vechten, and European royalty. Walker left management of the overall business to Freeman B. Ransom, a lawyer, although she wrote him letters almost daily, instructing him on operations, and also sending mounting bills to pay.

> *It is given to few persons to transform a people in a generation. Yet this was done by the late Madame C.J. Walker.*
>
> —**W.E.B. Du Bois**

Walker became a speaker not only for her products, but for her race and gender. In July 1912, at the National Association of Colored Women, she met *Mary McLeod Bethune, a 37-year-old educator who was attempting to expand education for blacks in Florida. Walker led a fund-raising effort on her behalf. She also worked to end lynching and during World War I joined a delegation that met with President Woodrow Wilson to protest segregation policies in the War Department. In late 1918, she considered going to the Versailles Peace Conference to promote the rights of blacks. The government disapproved of this action and blocked her request for a passport. Her products were known in Europe, however. When the uninhibited dancing and vivid personality of *Josephine Baker seized the French imagination, her use of the Walker System was publicized. A French company quickly marketed similar products under the name "Baker-Fix."

Walker numbered among her friends Booker T. Washington, Mary McLeod Bethune, and

*Mary Morris Talbert, but her relations with competitors became increasingly rancorous. Black businessmen were reluctant to acknowledge her achievement or that of her rivals Annie Malone, with her Poro System and Poro College, and Madame ◄❀ Sarah Spencer Washington, with her Apex products. At a 1912 convention of the National Negro Business League, Booker T. Washington did not include Walker on the podium, but she became the talk of the convention when she made an unscheduled speech from the floor. "Surely you are not going to shut the door in my face," she shouted to Washington, who had ignored her for three days. "I have been trying to tell you what I am doing. I am a woman who came from the cotton fields of the South. I was promoted from there to the washtub. Then I was promoted to the cook kitchen. And from there I promoted myself into the business of manufacturing hair goods and preparations. I know how to grow hair as well as I know how to grow cotton. I have built my own factory on my own ground." She then outlined the steps by which she turned a $1.50 investment into a $117,000 business in eight years. The next year, Washington made her a featured speaker.

The physical demands that Walker placed on herself undermined her health, and she suffered from hypertension. She went for rest cures at Hot Springs, Arkansas, in 1916 and at Battle Creek Sanitarium in Michigan in 1917. Otherwise, she did not relax her pace or put herself in the hands of physicians. In April 1919, she became gravely ill in St. Louis and returned to New York. Fearing she was at the end of her life, she summoned Freeman Ransom and gave him a list of black organizations and institutions she wished to help. Bedridden a few weeks later, she said, "I want to live to help my race," and then fell into a coma from which she never emerged. She died of chronic interstitial nephritis at Villa Lewaro, her country home, on May 25, 1919, at the age of 51.

In 1922, her estate was valued at $509,864. She owned a city block in Indianapolis and various other lots, property in Los Angeles, Chicago, Savannah, St. Louis, as well as in Idlewild, Michigan, and Gary, Indiana. Her personal holdings included various properties in New York City, besides her Harlem houses, and a manor in Irvington-on-Hudson, which was situated near the estates of John D. Rockefeller and Jay Gould. Enrico Caruso had persuaded her to name it Villa Lewaro, based on the initials of her daughter's name (LWR). It included a piano and Victrola covered in gold leaf and other luxuries that bolstered her image as a woman of wealth, but drained on her finances needlessly.

Sales of her products reached a peak of $595,000 in 1920, then slowly declined. In 1933, in the depths of the Depression, they were $48,000. The company endured, however, and continued to provide work and service to black people until it was purchased by an Indianapolis businessman in 1985.

SOURCES:

Bundles, A'Lelia Perry. *Madame C.J. Walker.* NY: Chelsea House, 1991.

——. *On Her Own Ground: The Life and Times of Madam C.J. Walker.* Scribner, 2001.

Gates, Henry Louis, Jr. "Madam's Crusade," in *Time 100* special.

Sicherman, Barbara, and Carol Hurd Green, eds. *Notable American Women: The Modern Period.* Cambridge, MA: The Belknap Press of Harvard University, 1980.

SUGGESTED READING:

Lewis, David Levering. *When Harlem was in Vogue.* NY: Alfred A. Knopf, 1981.

McKay, Claude. *Harlem: Negro Metropolis.* NY: E.P. Dutton, 1940.

Sterling, Dorothy, ed. *We Are Your Sisters: Black Women in the Nineteenth Century.* NY: W.W. Norton, 1984.

COLLECTIONS:

Indiana Historical Society, Indianapolis, Indiana.

Kathleen Brady,
author of *Lucille: The Life of Lucille Ball* (Hyperion) and
Ida Tarbell: Portrait of A Muckraker (University of Pittsburgh Press)

❀► **Washington, Sarah Spencer** (1889–?)

African-American entrepreneur. Name variations: Sara Washington. Born in Berkley, Virginia, on June 6, 1889; death date unknown; daughter of Joshua and Ellen (Douglass) Phillips; educated at the Lincoln Preparatory School in Philadelphia, Pennsylvania, and the Norfolk Mission College, Norfolk, Virginia; studied beauty culture in York, Pennsylvania, and advanced chemistry at Columbia University.

Starting out as a dressmaker, Sarah Spencer Washington turned to the field of beauty culture in 1913, founding a small hairdressing shop in Atlantic City, New Jersey. Like *Madame C.J. Walker and *Annie Turnbo Malone before her, Washington began a house-to-house campaign to sell her wares. By 1919, she was the sole owner of Apex Hair and News Company, conducting classes and setting up supply stations throughout New York and New Jersey. By 1939, her regular staff had grown to 215, with 35,000 agents throughout the United States. Washington was also generous with her money, giving often to the black community.

Walker, Edyth (1867–1950)

American opera singer and teacher. Born Minnie Edith Walker on March 27, 1867, in Hopewell, New York; died on February 19, 1950, in New York City;

daughter of Marquis de Lafayette Walker and Mary (Purdy) Walker; graduated from the Rome Free Academy in Rome, New York, 1884; studied with Anna Aglaia Orgeni at the Dresden Conservatory, Germany; never married.

Taught school in Rome, New York, for several years after graduation; made opera debut in Berlin (1894); was lead mezzo-soprano at Vienna's Imperial Opera (1898–1903); debuted at Metropolitan Opera in New York City as Amneris in Aïda (1903); left the Metropolitan (1906); debuted at Covent Garden, London (1908); joined Munich Opera (1912–17); retired from the opera (1918); taught at the American Conservatory in Fontainebleau (1933–36).

Born in 1867, the youngest of six children in an upstate New York family, Edyth Walker showed an early talent for music; she was singing solo at her local church by age 14. Her family did little to encourage her ability, but thanks to a gift of $1,000 from a local doctor who had heard her sing, in 1889 Walker was able to travel to Germany to study under **Anna Aglaia Orgeni**, an acclaimed Hungarian coloratura soprano. To pay her way in Germany while studying there, Walker taught singing and English, and confidently asked a rich New Yorker who was then traveling in Vienna for financial backing. William K. Vanderbilt reportedly sent her $1,000 with only the request that he hear her sing when she had made a name for herself.

A year after her opera debut in Berlin as Fidés in *Le Prophète*, Walker went on to the Vienna Opera, where her performance of the lead role in *Der Evangelimann* in 1896 so dazzled the Austrian emperor Franz Joseph that he made her a Kammersängerin, the highest honor given in Austria and Germany to an opera singer. She debuted at New York's Metropolitan Opera in 1903 to favorable reviews and spent three years there before leaving to return to Europe. Although she later signed a contract with the Chicago Opera, its cancellation upon the outbreak of World War I permanently ended her American performance career.

In Europe, the vibrant and talented Walker spent several years with the Berlin and Hamburg operas and later sang at London's Covent Garden, taking the lead in the English premiere of *Elektra*. After appearing with the Munich Opera for about five years, she retired and moved to Holland for a few years. She then taught in Paris for awhile, before returning once more to New York City to teach there, counting among her pupils *Blanche Thebom and Irene Dalis. She

died at age 82 and left her estate to the Christian Science Church, of which she was a member. An accomplished cellist as well as opera singer, Edyth Walker inspired her students and was one of the first Americans to gain success in German opera.

SOURCES:
James, Edward T., ed. *Notable American Women, 1607–1950.* Cambridge, MA: The Belknap Press of Harvard University, 1971.

Jacquie Maurice,
freelance writer,
Calgary, Alberta, Canada

Walker, Kath (1920–1993)

First Australian Aborigine to publish a book of poems. Name variations: Cath Walker; (Aboriginal name) Oodgeroo Noonuccal. Born on November 3, 1920, on Minjerriba (North Stradbroke Island), Queensland, Australia; died in 1993; educated to primary school level; children: two sons.

Received Jesse Litchfield Award (1967) and the Mary Gilmore Medal (1977); established an Aboriginal educational and cultural center on Stradbroke Island; lectured and tutored at several institutions including the University of the South Pacific.

Selected writings: We Are Going *(1964);* The Dawn Is at Hand *(1966);* My People *(1970); (compilation of Aboriginal legends)* Stradbroke Dreamtime *(1972);* Father Sky and Mother Earth *(1981);* Little Fella: Poems by Kath Walker *(1987);* Kath Walker in China *(1988);* The Rainbow Serpent: O.N. and Kabul Oodgeroo Noonuccal *(1990);* My People: Oodgeroo *(1990);* Shoemaker *(1994).*

Born in 1920 and brought up in the traditional Aborigine manner on an island off the southern coast of Queensland, Kath Walker was initiated into the European world via a primary school education. Although she was proficient in both cultures, her primary identity was as an Aboriginal, and from an early age she was active in civil liberties groups (including the Communist Party of Australia). Walker was especially active in support of the referendum of 1967, which delivered to Aborigines the suffrage that, in those states where it had existed, had been eradicated under the Australian Constitution in 1901, and also in the politics of land rights and conservation. She also served on a variety of arts and social services boards, including the Federal Council for the Advancement of Aborigines and Torres Strait Islanders and the Aboriginal Advancement League, to press for the civil rights of her people. She established a school, Moongalba, for the advancement of her people, and en-

Lucy
Walker
(1836–1916)

joyed a significant national and international reputation as an assertive and charismatic artist and black activist. As the first poet of her race to be published in English, she became an inspiration to a younger generation of writers. Though she was named a Member of the Order of the British Empire (MBE) in 1970, she so strongly identified with her people that she rejected the honor in 1988 in protest of England's bicentennial celebrations of European settlement, one she described as "200 years of humiliation and brutality to the Aboriginal people." That year she officially changed her name to the Aboriginal Oodgeroo Noonuccal.

Walker became the first Aborigine to publish a book of poems with the appearance of *We Are Going* in 1964. In a 1960s Australia that was comparatively wealthy and complacent but fearful of Communism, Walker's satiric and polemical verse brought on shock. She wrote plainly and bluntly about her people's economic mistreatment in such poems as "Aboriginal Charter of Rights," which was notable for its firm and seemingly confident assertion of rights that at the time did not constitutionally exist. Walker implicitly attacked the practice of Christianity in Australia and charged government and

welfare with bureaucratic paternalism and with relegating her people to a permanent underclass. To white Australia at the time, it was seditious, and certainly dangerously socialist in tone. It was easy for the formalist aesthetes of the academic establishment of the day to denigrate her poetry as propagandist and regressive in its craft, because the influence of an older bush balladry was clearly evident in it. This manifesto, and other poems in the same vein, made a plea for human and Christian rights to be extended to Aborigines, and pointed to a long list of discriminatory practices. At times, her poetry works more obliquely, as in her much-anthologized "We Are Going," which nostalgically contrasts a demoralized present with an implied presettlement golden age when the tribes are represented as having been in harmony and identity with every feature of their environment. In poems like "No More Boomerang," she is laconically satiric about the "advances" of white civilization, which are contrasted unfavorably with traditional values. Many poems lament the passing forever of a lifestyle that she perceived to be in the best interests ecologically of the land she loved and of all Australians.

Walker's controversial poetry sometimes had critics among her own people. Mudrooroo, the leading black-identified intellectual of his generation, viewed her less as a poet than as a polemicist (he invented the term "poetemics" for her work), and pointed out that the genres she used are those internalized as a result of her white education. However, he noted that her use of simple meters and diction are part of her enduring appeal to both her own people and to a more numerous readership of white readers. Other critics, informed by postcolonial theory, debated whether the critical frameworks of the mainstream are appropriately applied to her work, and cited features of the verse entailing the use of Aboriginal forms of rhetoric that are not visible to white readers. Some pointed to the performance dimension of her art and its roots in mythic ritual and political oratory.

Although she was committed to exposing the dispossession of Aboriginal society by the white "invaders," Walker avoided the role of victim and worked actively and resistantly to build Aboriginal pride, identity, and solidarity. An important aspect of her educational program was her commitment to writing down stories of her almost traditional growing up at Minjerriba, and recovering and illustrating—in a delicate and accomplished traditional manner—the myths and stories of her own people and place for a younger generation of both black and white readers.

Walker was awarded honorary doctorates by Griffith and Macquarie universities and the Queensland University of Technology. In 1967 she won the *Jessie Litchfield Award for Literature, and in 1977 the Fellowship of Australian Writers Patricia Weickhardt Award and the *Mary Gilmore Award. Her work has the rare distinction in Australia of being continually reprinted and of having struck a note of optimistic hope for a self-respecting Aboriginality that remains potent decades later. She died of cancer in 1993, at age 72.

SOURCES:

Buck, Claire, ed. *The Bloomsbury Guide to Women's Literature.* NY: Prentice Hall, 1992.

Encyclopedia of World Literature. Vol. 3: L–R. Detroit, MI: St. James Press, 1999.

"Oodgeroo Noonuccal," in *The New York Times Biographical Service.* September 1993.

Jacquie Maurice,
freelance writer,
Calgary, Alberta, Canada

Walker, Lelia (1885–1931).

See A'Lelia Walker in Women of the Harlem Renaissance.

Walker, Lucy (1836–1916)

English mountaineer. Born in 1836; died in 1916; daughter of Francis Walker (a mountaineer); sister of Horace Walker (a mountaineer); lived in Liverpool.

Made first woman's ascent of the Matterhorn (1871); served as president of the Ladies' Alpine Club (1913–15), which was founded in 1907.

In her childhood, Lucy Walker went on many Alpine expeditions with her mountaineer father. In 1859, at age 23, having shown an interest in climbing the Altels in the Bernese Oberland, Walker was introduced by her father to the guide Melchior Anderegg; this was the beginning of a climbing partnership that lasted many years and 90 climbs. For all these climbs, Lucy wore a white print dress.

Invariably with Anderegg, sometimes with her family, Walker climbed Finsteraarhorn and the Monte Rosa (Dufourspitze) in 1862, the second highest peak in Europe. In 1864, she climbed the Eiger, Rimpfischorn, and Balmhorn. The following years saw the ascent of the Jungfrau, the Weisshorn, Dom des Mischabels, and the Mönch. In 1870, she ascended the Aiguille Verte. While she was on the mountain, her material needs, and those of the group, were looked after by her mother in the base camp below. The following year, Lucy Walker made her greatest climb—the Matterhorn.

Many had died on the Matterhorn (14,690 ft.), a pyramid that sits on the Swiss-Italian border. In 1865, four climbers had fallen to their deaths. Another was killed in 1868. Thus, when Walker attempted the Matterhorn, the world took note. On July 20, 1871, Lucy, her father, Fred Gardiner, Anderegg, and four other guides climbed the Matterhorn by the Hörnli route. It was the 19th ascent of the mountain and the first by a woman. For all her earlier climbs, her ascents to this point had been little known. Britain's *Punch* did its best to make the world catch up:

> A lady has clomb to the Matterhorn's summit,
> Which almost like a monument points to the sky.
> Steep not very much less than the string of a
>   plummet
> Suspended, which nothing can scale but a fly.
>
> This lady has likewise ascended the Weisshorn,
> And, what's a great deal more, descended it too,
> Feet foremost; which, seeing it might be named
>   Icehorn,
> So slippery 'tis, no small thing to do.

From 1858 to 1879, Lucy Walker missed only two climbing seasons—the first, when her father died in 1872.

Walker, Lucy (1903–1987).

See Sanders, Dorothy Lucie.

Walker, Maggie Lena (1867–1934)

African-American, first female bank president in the United States, who was a champion of racial and women's equality. Born Maggie Lena on July 15, 1867, in Richmond, Virginia; died of diabetes gangrene on December 15, 1934; daughter of ex-slave Elizabeth Draper, later Elizabeth Draper Mitchell, and (likely) Irish-American abolitionist Eccles Cuthbert; attended public grammar and primary schools; graduated from Armstrong Normal and High School, 1883; awarded honorary M.S., Virginia Union University, 1925; married Armstead Walker, on September 14, 1886; children: Russell Eccles Talmage Walker (b. 1890); Armstead Mitchell Walker (1893–1893); Melvin DeWitt Walker (b. 1897).

Mother married William Mitchell (May 27, 1868); half-brother Johnnie Mitchell born (1870); stepfather died (February 1876); joined mutual aid society, Independent Order of Saint Luke (1881); taught school (1883–86); named executive secretary treasurer of St. Luke's (1899–1934); founded St. Luke Herald (1902); became president of Saint Luke Penny Savings Bank of Richmond (1903); founded department store, Saint Luke Emporium (1905); suffered debilitating fall that injured legs (1907); son, Russell, killed Armstead Walker by accident (1915); ran unsuccessfully for Virginia state superintendent of public instruction on Lily-Black Republican Party ticket (1921); became chair of the board, Consolidated Bank and Trust Company (1930).

As the 19th century drew to a close, the Independent Order of Saint Luke (IOSL) stood on the verge of collapse. The mutual aid society, which included 57 chapters in a number of African-American communities, had only $31.61 in its treasury and $400 in unpaid bills. The IOSL then turned to a leading activist in the organization, Maggie Lena Walker of Richmond, Virginia, who agreed to become its new executive secretary-treasurer. Under the direction of this remarkable woman, it grew into one of the most successful mutual benefit societies in the country. By 1925, the number of local chapters rose to 1,500, membership climbed from 3,400 to 50,000, and its assets stood at $400,000. And Walker, the individual most responsible for this success, had emerged as one of Richmond's most respected and powerful women.142

Maggie Walker was born in Richmond on July 15, 1867, the first child of Elizabeth Draper, a former slave who worked as a cook in the home of *Elizabeth Van Lew. According to family legend to which Walker herself subscribed, her natural father was the abolitionist Eccles Cuthbert, but there is little evidence to either support or refute this. In any event, "Lizzie" Draper, as she was generally known, married William Mitchell shortly after Maggie's birth, and he came to assume the role of the male head of the family. The Van Lew house would have provided a relatively good environment for an African-American child to grow up in, because the wealthy, unmarried mistress of the home had been an opponent of slavery and a Northern sympathizer. But William Mitchell got a job as the head waiter at the exclusive St. Charles Hotel in central Richmond. He moved his family to a two-story clapboard house in College Alley between Broad and Marshall streets when Maggie was still very young. In 1870, **Elizabeth Draper Mitchell** had a second child, Johnnie.

Until the mid-1870s, the Mitchells lived quite comfortably compared to most black families of the period. William continued to work at the St. Charles Hotel while his wife supplemented this income by taking in laundry. Then, in February 1876, William failed to return home from work one night. After a five-day search, his body was found in the James River. The coroner listed death by suicide, but it is likely he was robbed and murdered. Deprived of the majority of their income, the family faced a crisis that threatened to render them paupers. But Lizzie refused to give up their house and independence without a fight. She started taking in as much laundry as she could, and young Maggie, only nine, worked alongside her mother many hours a day. As Walker put it years later, "I was not born with a silver spoon in my mouth; but instead, with a clothes basket almost upon my head."

Elizabeth Mitchell and her daughter began their laundering work early every morning. They would build a fire, sort the clothes, and draw and then heat the water. Washing was a tiring, arduous task that involved scrubbing the clothing by hand on washboards and finishing the job by wringing out the cleaned articles. Walker would help roll the clothes in preparation for ironing. She and her younger brother would also be responsible for picking up and delivering the loads of laundry which they toted in wicker baskets. The hard work paid off, though, as the Mitchells maintained a successful operation serving white clients for many years.

Lizzie also dedicated herself to ensuring that her children received a decent education, though such opportunities for Richmond's black youth were extremely limited at the time. Maggie attended a segregated public grammar and primary school, then the Armstrong Normal and High School. She graduated at the top of her class in 1883. There was a great deal of controversy associated with the commencement ceremony that year, as Maggie and her nine classmates demanded that they be honored at the same function as white students. Each year, white graduates of public schools held their exercises in the Richmond Theater, while black students received their diplomas in a church. Arguing that the parents of all children were taxpayers and thus deserved equal treatment, Maggie's class asked principal **Elizabeth Knowles** to help them bring about the integration of the ceremony in the theater. Knowles was sympathetic to the desires of her African-American students and managed to work out a compromise. School officials and the faculty agreed to hold a single commencement, but insisted that whites and blacks sit in separate locations, with the latter restricted to the balcony. The African-American students balked at this compromise, however, and elected to get their diplomas in the Normal School auditorium. In effect, they conducted what was probably the first student-directed strike against a public school system on the part of American blacks.

Upon graduation at the age of 16, Walker went to work as a schoolteacher in her old

Maggie
Lena
Walker

grammar school. She taught for the next three years, starting at $35 a month, and attended night courses in accounting and sales. She also did some work for the Woman's Union, an insurance company she helped create. Deeply religious, Maggie belonged to the Old First Baptist Church. She attended Thursday night "Sunday school" meetings and later taught Sunday school classes. The church represented the center of her social life, and it was here she met Armstead Walker, a young building contractor, whom she married on September 14, 1886. As was customary, she quit working outside the home and began to devote herself to domestic duties. The Walkers had two sons who survived infancy. Russell Eccles Talmage was born in 1890 and Melvin DeWitt in 1897. A third child, Armstead Mitchell, died in the year of his birth, 1893.

When she was 14, Maggie had joined a local chapter of the Independent Order of Saint Luke. Begun by ◀ **Mary Ann Prout** in Baltimore, Maryland, in 1867, this self-help society was founded primarily as a women's sickness and death mutual benefit association. When Maggie became a member, it contained chapters in Virginia and New York as well as Maryland, and admitted men. Walker devoted much of her free time to St. Luke's Good Idea Council No. 16, ultimately becoming its chief, and she attended a number of IOSL conventions beginning in 1883. Her influence quickly spread beyond the local level, and by the mid-1890s she was a recognized leader of the group. In 1895, she organized the juvenile branch of the order, which was directed by female members at the chapter level, and became Grand Matron of the Juvenile Department.

In 1899, the IOSL held its 32nd annual meeting in Hinton, West Virginia. The organization was in crisis with membership declining and funds dwindling. Its secretary-treasurer, William M.T. Forrester, had served this role since 1869. But more interested in his job as head of the Odd

Fellows, and certain the organization was dying, he refused to accept reappointment. Some members would not give up hope for the society, though, and Maggie Walker's name was placed into nomination as new St. Luke's executive secretary. Strong willed and optimistic, she accepted this honor and won election to the post.

The appointment of Walker proved to be the turning point of the IOSL. It was obvious from the beginning that the new leader was a brilliant businesswoman and charismatic organizer. She was forceful, but possessed a kind, modest manner and great skill as an orator. Most important, people trusted and liked her. She traveled extensively to existing chapters throughout the eastern United States, and personally founded new ones. She spoke about the evils of segregation and the many hardships that African-Americans faced. But her message was always one of hope. She advocated self-help and economic independence from whites, promoted race pride, and called for women's rights. Within a year, St. Luke's membership doubled.

At the 1901 annual meeting, Maggie Walker proposed the creation of a newspaper and a savings bank. On March 29, 1902, the *St. Luke Herald* began publication, and the paper was far more than a fraternal newsletter. The *Herald* announced it was "against mob law, against 'Jim Crow' cars, against the curtailment of Public

---

❧▶ Prout, Mary Ann (1801–1884)

African-American school founder and educator. Name variations: Aunt Mary Prout. Born, possibly in Baltimore, Maryland, on February 14, 1801 (some sources cite born in 1800, while another source maintains that she was born a slave in South River, Maryland); died in Baltimore in 1884; daughter of mixed-African parentage.

Although there is confusion concerning the date and circumstances of her birth, it is likely that Mary Ann Prout was born free in Baltimore, Maryland, where she was converted at age 12 and became a devoted member of Bethel African Methodist Episcopal Church. "During the early days of Bethel, when it was poor and in debt, Prout was constantly devising ways and means of relieving it," recalled Bishop James Anderson Handy. She remained devoted to the church for her entire life, serving as a member of the church association known as the Daughters of Conference at Bethel AME, and singing in the choir.

It is not known where Prout received her education, but around 1830, she founded a day school in Baltimore,

where she taught for over 30 years. After the school closed in 1867, she continued to pursue humanitarian work, becoming one of the two black trustees of the Gregory Aged Women's Home, also in Baltimore. She additionally served as the president of the association in charge of the home, the National Reform Educational Association.

Also in 1867, Prout founded a secret order which evolved into the Independent Order of St. Luke, a black organization which provided financial aid to the sick and funds for burial of the dead. The Order eventually split in two, one section taking up headquarters in Richmond, under the leadership of *Maggie Lena Walker, who frequently paid homage to Prout as its founder. Under Walker, the Order flourished and in 25 years had grown from 57 local chapters to 1,500, and had accrued assets of nearly $400,000. It also spawned several other institutions that benefited blacks, including a newspaper, a savings bank, and a short-lived department store. Mary Ann Prout died in Baltimore in 1884.

SOURCES:

Smith, Jessie Carney, ed. *Notable Black American Women.* Detroit, MI: Gale Research, 1992.

School privileges and against the enactment and enforcement of laws which place a premium upon white literacy and treat black illiteracy as a crime." While Walker was the weekly newspaper's guiding force, **Lillian Payne** served as managing editor. The periodical included a children's page devoted to publishing poems and short pieces written by young people, and contained advice from Right Worthy Grand Matron Walker.

Maggie Walker also convinced her St. Luke colleagues: "We need a savings bank, chartered, officered, and run by the men and women of this order." To prepare for directing this enterprise, Walker spent many hours in the Merchants' National Bank of Richmond as an observer. The new institution was then chartered in 1903 as the Saint Luke Penny Savings Bank of Richmond. The IOSL purchased 200 shares of stock in the bank, three quarters of which were made available solely to organization members. Maggie Walker assumed the duties of bank president, the first woman to hold this position in the United States. She would earn a salary of $25 a week, an amount which hardly compensated her for the exhaustive efforts on her part to make the project work. She became the project's principal promoter who called on each individual at Saint Luke "to open an account, if for even so small amount as a dollar" and to purchase "at least one share of stock which costs $10.00 and can be paid for upon monthly installments of one dollar per month."

The bank's first day proved to be a success. The *Richmond News Leader* reported: "The main office has been crowded all day with colored people representing all stations of Afro-American society"; 280 people made deposits totalling over $8,000, and $1,247 worth of stock was sold. African-American leaders from throughout the mid-Atlantic states made the trip to Richmond for the opening to deposit money. But it was the common folk of Richmond, and particularly women, who became the backbone of the institution. Many of the first customers were laundresses, including Maggie's own mother.

The Saint Luke Penny Savings Bank grew slowly but consistently in subsequent years. Once success seemed assured, it moved its offices from St. James Street to 112 East Broad Street in 1905, purchasing the structure for $13,500. Deposits rose from about $21,000 to over $85,000 between 1904 and 1910. Then changes in Virginia's banking and insurance laws placed the enterprise at risk. As regulation became more extensive, two rival black-run financial institutions closed down. Secret orders were also prohibited from banking, so the Penny Savings Bank had to be separated from the IOSL. Walker navigated the treacherous waters of banking reform, and helped reorganize the institution as the Saint Luke's Bank and Trust Company, a separate entity from the parent organization. It continued to flourish for many years.

Soon after Maggie Walker saw two of her ideas achieve fruition—the newspaper and the bank—she set out to create a department store. In 1905, 22 women from the Order of St. Luke collectively founded the Saint Luke Emporium. The goal was to provide goods at lower prices for the African-American community. The three-story establishment stood on East Broad Street in central Richmond and employed 15 women as sales clerks. But the enterprise faced stiff resistance from the white business community from the start. The white Retail Dealers' Association pressured wholesale merchants not to sell to the Emporium. Fearful that black merchants would "get a few dollars which would otherwise go to the white merchant," the Retailer's Association threatened to boycott the wholesalers. White competitors also made new efforts to appeal to black customers, and many chose not to abandon the older, white-run stores in favor of the new Emporium.

As the department store began to lose money, Maggie Walker appealed to the African-American community to support the store. At a mass meeting in 1906, she asked:

> Hasn't it crept into your minds that we are being more and more oppressed each day that we live? Hasn't it yet come to you, that we are being oppressed by the passage of laws which not only have for their object the degradation of Negro manhood and Negro womanhood, but also the destruction of all kinds of Negro businesses? There is a lion terrorizing us, preying upon us, and upon every business effort which we put forth. The name of this insatiable lion is prejudice.

Walker went on to associate that discrimination with the "the white press, the white pulpit, the white business associations," and the state legislature, and warned that the "only way to kill the Lion is to stop feeding it." In the long run, however, pleas like this too often fell upon deaf ears. Many blacks continued to frequent the older, white-owned stores. Seven years after the Emporium opened, it closed its doors for good in January 1912.

The failure of the Saint Luke Emporium represented the most significant disappointment of Maggie Walker's public career. Throughout her many years of leadership in Saint Lukes, the bank, and her community, she weathered most ordeals with an unyielding positive outlook. But the same cannot be said of her personal life. In 1905, her family moved into a new home at 110½ East Leigh Street. A nice two-story brick row house when they took possession of it, the Walkers expanded it over the next few years until it included twenty-two rooms, including eight bedrooms. Her entire extended family lived there, including her sons, and ultimately, their wives and children. It was on the porch of this house that Maggie experienced a bad fall in 1907 that injured her knees. In subsequent years, she suffered from severe leg pain, and her ultimate reliance on a wheelchair by the late 1920s may have been related to this accident.

A worse tragedy struck the Walkers on that same porch in 1915 when oldest son Russell shot and killed his father there. Russell was arrested before the coroner's inquest, which ultimately determined the death to be accidental. But rumors continued to swirl around Richmond that the son had murdered his father. An investigation led to a murder charge. The body was exhumed for further examination, and the family agonized for five months waiting for the trial to open. Finally, on November 12, the case went before a jury, and witnesses provided a day of testimony about the affair. Walker faced examination for three hours, and Russell testified on his own behalf. He claimed that he had mistaken his father for a prowler who had been reported in the neighborhood. The testimony was concluded by 10:00 PM that night, but the court adjourned until Monday. As Maggie described the delay in learning the verdict:

> My son was carried to jail to spend that time. I hated awfully to see him go. He said, "Mama, it is my papa; I don't mind going." He stayed in jail Saturday night, Sunday, and on Monday morning at 10:00 a.m. we were all back in the court to get the final verdict. . . . When the jurors returned, a death-like silence filled the court room. The verdict was "Not Guilty."

Even after the acquittal, this ordeal was not over. Maggie Walker's rivals in the Order of St. Luke tried to wrest power from her under the pretext of saving the organization from the taint of scandal. Walker's long-time friend, Wendell P. Dabney, who later wrote a biography of her, believed the murder charge had actually been instigated by "a certain group of our colored men [who] secured the services of [a lawyer] to assist the prosecuting attorney." Though Russell was found innocent, they called for Maggie's resignation at the next annual meeting. But the strong-willed matron of the order would not back

down, and after a passionate speech announcing her intent to continue, "an ovation, the like of which Richmond had never seen," greeted her determination.

It proved fortunate for the IOSL in general and the bank that she won this battle, for both continued to flourish. By 1920, the bank had financed black ownership of 645 houses in Richmond. During the next decade, it continued to experience growth until it became the strongest black-run financial institution in the city. In 1929 and 1930, it merged with two other African-American banks, the Second Street Savings Bank and the Commercial Bank and Trust Company, to form the Consolidated Bank and Trust Company. Maggie Walker was named chair of the board of directors at the time of the merger, a position she held for the rest of her life.

Though her duties as a businesswoman commanded a great deal of her time, Maggie Walker also emerged as a prominent community activist, as well as a leader of a number of national reform organizations. She founded the Richmond Council of Colored Women (CCW) in 1912 and served as its president for over two decades. This organization raised funds for various causes, including the Piedmont Tuberculosis Sanitorium for Negroes at Burkeville, a visiting nurse program, and the Virginia Industrial School for Colored Girls. Walker served on the board of the latter institution, which was created by *Janie Porter Barrett's Virginia Federation of Colored Women's Clubs, to which Maggie belonged. The CWW also purchased a house on Clay Street as a community center. Among other purposes, this building provided an office for the National Association for the Advancement of Colored People (NAACP). Walker had co-founded the local branch of the NAACP and later served on the national board. She was also one of the organizers of Virginia's Negro Organization Society, which was created to unite every African-American organization in the state into a force to promote black education and similar goals.

Maggie Walker, moreover, served as a board member of the National Urban League, the Virginia Interracial Committee, and Colored Women's Clubs, while belonging to a host of other reform and community service groups. In 1921, she ran unsuccessfully for state superintendent of public instruction on the Lily-Black Republican Party ticket, and served as the treasurer of the National League of Republican Colored Women.

Throughout her long career as an activist, Maggie Walker never missed an opportunity to promote racial equality and justice. She believed that African-Americans, working collectively, could undermine the barriers imposed by white intolerance and oppression. As she argued in an address in 1909, blacks could not rely on anyone else to help them, other than God. But even His "help is something that comes only when we are doing, striving and making the best effort of which our brains and hands are capable. We can do; we will do; we are going to do now." The commitment to "race uplift," moreover, was something women must play a leadership role in. She called on black women to "band themselves together, . . . put their mites together, put their hands and their brains together and make work and business for themselves." She believed that women should seek gainful employment, and that this work would strengthen the family, not weaken it as was widely argued at the time. A woman who uses "her powers, ability, health and strength" in the workplace will help a marriage succeed. "What stronger combination could ever God make," she asked, "than the partnership of a businessman and a businesswoman?"

Maggie Walker's own marriage had been just such a union before Armstead's tragic death in 1915. They had lived according to Maggie's creed that "the woman and man are equal in power and should by consultation and agreement mutually decide as to the conduct of the home and the government of the children." Then Walker carried on as the sole head of the household, an extended family that included her mother, children, grandchildren, the informally "adopted" **Polly Anderson Payne** (and eventually Polly's husband), and sometimes others. Walker loved to be surrounded by family and friends, and she revelled in the fact that the house was a center of civic activism in Richmond. Maggie's granddaughter recalled that "there were always guests seated at the large dining room table" who might be members of Richmond's African-American political and business elite or prominent black leaders such as W.E.B. Du Bois and Langston Hughes.

In her later years, Maggie Walker was the recipient of many awards and honors. In 1924, a "testimonial of life" celebration was held for her in the city auditorium, sponsored by the Order of St. Luke and people of Richmond. Virginia Union University awarded her an honorary master of science degree in 1925. She received an honorable mention in the 1927 Harmon Award for Distinguished Achievement in the business category. These acknowledgements, however, were hardly evidence that Walker was drifting into retirement. Though difficulty in walking

had led her to seek treatment at spas, use braces, and ultimately, rely on a wheelchair and chauffeured automobile (she had her Packard altered to accommodate the chair), her work slowed down very little after her 60th birthday.

In the fall of 1934, some African-American organizations decided to designate October as Maggie Walker Month in recognition "of her outstanding achievements as Christian mother, fraternalist, banker, philanthropist, and minister of international good will," as the *Richmond News Leader* noted. By that point, the Independent Order of Saint Luke had chapters in 14 states and a record of $3 million in paid claims. The Consolidated Bank and Trust Company had met the challenges associated with the darkest days of the Great Depression, and stood poised to offer its services for many decades to come. Maggie had seen her beloved mother pass away in 1922, a loss followed all too quickly by the death of son Russell the next year. But the remaining members of her family enjoyed relative prosperity; in fact, all but Russell's widow, **Hattie Walker**, and her daughter, **Maggie Laura Walker**, had moved away from the Leigh Street mansion to their own houses.

The celebration of Maggie Walker Month would prove to be the last honor the great activist and businesswoman would receive during her lifetime. On December 15 of that year, she died of diabetes gangrene, and was buried on December 19 in Evergreen cemetery. The service at the First American Baptist Church proved to be among the largest in city history. The day before the funeral, the *Richmond News Leader* eulogized the beloved grandmother:

> Mrs. Maggie Walker was the greatest of all Negro leaders of Richmond. She probably was the most distinguished Negress ever born in Richmond and, in solid achievement, one of three or four ablest women her race ever produced in America.

Of course, a more fitting tribute to this champion of racial justice and gender equality would be to omit the references to the color of her skin and her sex and to simply appreciate the amazing accomplishments and decency of this great American.

Today, in Richmond, a street, theater, and high school bear the name of Maggie Walker. Her home, at 110½ East Leigh Street, has been designated the Maggie L. Walker National Historic Site. The house has been restored, complete with many original furnishings, to its appearance at the time of her death. The museum's existence ensures that people of many generations to come will be familiar not only with the name of Maggie Walker, but leave inspired by the story of how the daughter of an ex-slave laundress achieved wealth and fame through hard work, intelligence, and kindness.

SOURCES:

Brown, Elsa Barkley Brown. "Womanist Consciousness: Maggie Lena Walker and the Independent Order of Saint Luke," in *Signs: Journal of Women in Culture and Society*. Vol. 14. Spring 1989, pp. 610–633.

Dabney, Wendell P. *Maggie L. Walker: Her Life and Deeds*. Cincinnati, OH: Dabney Publishing, 1927.

Simmons, Charles Willis. "Maggie Lena Walker and the Consolidated Bank and Trust Company," in *Negro History Bulletin*. Vol. 38. February–March, 1975, pp. 345–349.

SUGGESTED READING:

Bird, Caroline. *Enterprising Women: The Innovators*. NY: W.W. Norton, 1976.

Daniel, Sadie Iola. *Women Builders*. Washington, DC: Associated, 1931.

COLLECTIONS:

Maggie Lena Walker Papers, Maggie L. Walker National Historic Site, Richmond, Virginia.

John M. Craig,
Professor of History,
Slippery Rock University, Slippery Rock, Pennsylvania,
author of *Lucia Ames Mead and the American Peace Movement*
and numerous articles on activist American women

Walker, Margaret (1915–1998)

African-American writer whose poetry and prose, especially her novel Jubilee, *have become a recognized part of the African-American literary canon. Born Margaret Abigail Walker on July 7, 1915, in Birmingham, Alabama; died on November 30, 1998, in Chicago, Illinois; daughter of the Reverend Sigismund Walker (a minister in the United Methodist Church) and Marion Dozier Walker (a music teacher); graduated from high school in New Orleans; granted a bachelor's degree from Northwestern University, 1932; University of Iowa, M.A., 1940, Ph.D., 1965; married Firnist James Alexander, on June 13, 1943 (died); children: Marion Elizabeth Alexander (b. 1944); Firnist James Alexander, Jr. (b. 1946); Sigismund Walker Alexander (b. 1949); Margaret Elvira Alexander (b. 1954).*

Awards: first Black poet chosen for Yale University's Series of Younger Poets (1941); named to Honor Roll of Race Relations (1942); given Rosenthal fellowship (1944), Ford fellowship (1954), Houghton Mifflin Literary fellowship (1966), and Fulbright fellowship (1971); awarded National Endowment for the Humanities (1972); Doctor of Literature, Northwestern University (1974); Doctor of Letters, Rust College (1974); Doctor of Fine Arts, Denison University (1974).

Selected writings: For My People *(1942);* Jubilee *(1966);* Ballad of the Free *(1966);* Prophets for a New Day *(1970);* How I Wrote Jubilee *(1972);* October Journey *(1973); (with Nikki Giovanni)* A Poetic Equation: Conversations between Nikki Giovanni and Margaret Walker *(1974);* This Is My Century *(1989);* Richard Wright: Daemonic Genius *(1985);* How I Wrote Jubilee *(1990); also contributed to numerous anthologies.*

In a 1993 interview with **Maryemma Graham**, Margaret Walker identified the focus of her literary contributions as springing from her interest in a historical point of view, a view that reflected and encouraged the development of African-Americans approaching the 21st century. Some of Walker's first memories were those of a segregated world, the Jim Crow South. She remembered riding on segregated streetcars, attending a segregated one-room schoolhouse, watching movies in a segregated theater, and her father being chased home by an angry policeman who "resented" her father's possession of a fountain pen.

Margaret Walker was born on July 7, 1915, in Birmingham, Alabama. Her father Sigismund C. Walker was born in Jamaica Buff Bay, Jamaica, British West Indies. He came to the United States for ministerial study, graduating from Cammon Theological Seminary in Atlanta. Extremely well educated, he spoke five languages and read three more. Margaret Walker described him as a man who loved and lived in the world of books. While a theology student in Atlanta, Sigismund Walker met and married a college-educated music teacher, **Marion Dozier (Walker)**. The couple moved from Atlanta to Birmingham, where Margaret's father pastored a Methodist church and where she and three younger siblings were born.

Margaret Walker was an intelligent, precocious child, reading by the age of four, completing elementary school by age eleven, high school by age fourteen, and college at nineteen. Walker's parents instilled their religious beliefs, somewhat stern moralistic code, and unequivocal sense of duty into each of their children. They expected their children to be achievers, to strive for excellence, and to excel academically. The family moved often during Walker's early childhood as her father accepted various posts within the United Methodist Church. When Walker was ten, the family relocated to New Orleans where her parents accepted professorial positions at New Orleans University. Walker attended Gilbert Academy in New Orleans and then the university where her parents taught. After hearing Langston Hughes read his poetry at New Orleans University, Walker approached the well-known poet with her own poetry. He read her work, then encouraged her to continue writing and encouraged her parents to get her out of the South. Walker and Hughes remained friends for the next 35 years, until Hughes' death.

Walker left the South while still a teenager to attend Northwestern University in Evanston, Illinois. She was 19 years old and still a student when W.E.B. Du Bois published her first poem, "Daydreaming," in *The Crisis*, the journal of the NAACP. Her creative writing teacher, E.B. Hungerford, also arranged for her to be admitted to the Northwestern chapter of the Poetry Society of America. During her senior year at Northwestern, Walker worked as a volunteer on a recreation project sponsored by the Works Progress Administration (WPA). She was given a group of "delinquent" girls—shoplifters and prostitutes—to befriend, in hopes that her influence would have a beneficial effect. After completing her degree in English at Northwestern in 1935, Walker was employed with the WPA Writers' Project in Chicago. She wrote her first novel during these years, "Goose Island," a portrait of the Italian-black neighborhood surrounding Division Street, in which she had worked as a student. Although the novel was never published, Walker's characters and images reappear later in her poetry.

While employed by the WPA, Walker met a number of well-known writers, including Arna Bontemps, *Gwendolyn Brooks, and Richard Wright. She worked closely with Wright during her tenure with the Writers' Project, helping him research and edit his novel *Native Son*, and receiving help from him in the revision and rewriting of her poetry. She soon learned that Wright, who had no formal education, was paid $125 dollars per month, while Walker received only $85. Though Wright explained that he had a mother, aunt, and brother to support as head of a family, while Walker had only a sister, Walker remembered the $40 disparity in pay as an example of gender discrimination. Walker's political consciousness grew during her years in Chicago, and, influenced by Wright, she read a number of socialist and Marxist works. Unlike Wright, however, she did not join the Communist Party, but she did advocate unionization and socialist political cooperation between African-Americans and whites.

Walker's work with the WPA ended in 1939, as did her friendship with Wright, a breach that was never healed. She claimed later that mutual "friends" told him that she was critical of some of his decisions, so he snubbed her and broke off the friendship. She eventually

wrote to him, and he to her, but the connection was not reestablished. Walker left Chicago in 1939 to begin graduate studies at the University of Iowa, working toward a master's degree in writing. Since she had little money, she labored to finish her second degree in one year. She completed her master's in 1940, writing a volume of poems as her thesis. This collection was published in 1942 under the title *For My People*, the first book of poetry by a black woman to be issued since 🔖➤ Georgia Douglas Johnson's *The Heart of a Woman and Other Poems* (1918). The poems in Walker's book honor ordinary African-Americans, those who have faced and overcome terrible obstacles in a race-conscious, often racist, society. She calls on African-Americans to reclaim their power to make a better world for themselves and others.

Walker began her teaching career in January 1941 with a position at Livingstone College in Salisbury, North Carolina. Since she had a master's degree but no teaching experience, she was paid only $130 per month. She won the Yale Award for Younger Poets during the summer of 1941 for *For My People*, the first African-American to win that competitive award, and the volume was subsequently published as part of the

Margaret Walker

◀❧
Johnson, Georgia Douglas. See *Women of the Harlem Renaissance.*

Yale Series. The award brought her a degree of recognition and several job offers. Before she had a chance to choose a suitable position, however, her parents accepted a post for her at West Virginia State College. Unfortunately, she found the living arrangements there untenable, moving five times in one semester. She finally found herself living in a dormitory on campus, a living situation that had been denied her when she arrived. After one year at West Virginia State College, Walker accepted a contract from the National Concert Artists Corporation Lecture Bureau to lecture and read poetry, a contract that was to last for five years, from 1943 to 1948. She returned to Livingstone College as professor of English for one year, 1945–46, while under contract with National Artists. In September 1949, Walker began teaching at Jackson State College in Mississippi, where she remained for 26 years, until 1979.

Margaret Walker . . . [w]as a Black woman who sought and achieved her identity in a white, male world that allowed some few Black men access, tolerating no women, let alone Black ones.

—Maryemma Graham

On June 13, 1943, Margaret Abigail Walker married Firnist James Alexander, a disabled veteran. They would have four children: **Marion Elizabeth Alexander**, Firnist James Alexander, Jr., Sigismund Walker Alexander, and **Margaret Elvira Alexander**. When Walker accepted the teaching position at Jackson State, she had three children, the youngest being only nine weeks old. Her husband was ill, thus Walker was the primary breadwinner for the family. Margaret Walker did not write extensively about her family, though she dedicated one of her books to her husband, whom she describes as her "lover, sweetheart, best boy-friend, and . . . ever-loving husband for more than thirty years." She also wrote an essay, "How I Told My Child about Race," in which she narrates the heartbreak of honestly responding to her oldest child's questions, telling her about racism in the United States. The essay was published in 1951, while the Alexander family was living in Mississippi, long before separate public facilities and overt, hostile segregation were ended in the South.

Although Walker was classified as the equivalent of a Ph.D. at Jackson State because she was a poet, in reality her salary did not reflect such a classification. In fact, for the first 11 years of her tenure at Jackson State, her salary remained well under $6,000 per year. As her children grew older, Walker determined to raise her salary in order to provide the money for their college educations. She decided to return to graduate school. In the summer of 1961, she borrowed money to enroll in summer school at the University of Iowa, taking her two youngest children with her. While there, she inquired about the doctorate degree and about using the Civil War novel (later to become *Jubilee*) she had started, based on her great-grandmother's life, as her dissertation. She returned to Jackson State for one more year, bargaining with the administration for partial salary and study leave; for the next two years, she would receive half her salary from Jackson State College, borrowing upon her salary for a third year. Thus, in the fall of 1962, with her mother caring for her younger children, Margaret Walker returned to graduate school at the University of Iowa as a candidate for a Ph.D. By then, her older children were in college; one of them would graduate a week before her mother. The writing of *Jubilee*, with Paul Engle as her advisor, was the focus of her study at the University of Iowa. *Jubilee* is Walker's only published novel. Although the book initially received mixed reviews, it won the Houghton Mifflin Literary Fellowship Award, and is currently an integral part of the African-American canon.

According to Walker, the dissertation she wrote at the University of Iowa was a story she had literally been writing for 30 years. In "How I Wrote *Jubilee*," Walker says she had been conceiving the story of her great-grandmother, based on family stories her grandmother told her as a child, from her early adolescence. Walker began historical research for the work while she was working on her master's degree at Iowa. Her poetry, however, became her thesis, and she discontinued her research for several years. In 1944, she was awarded a Rosenwald fellowship to continue her research on the topic, and by 1948, she had written a rough outline of the book. She had titles for the chapters, most of which were taken directly from her grandmother's words. She gathered material from slave narratives, history books, Civil War newspapers, as well as the Georgia and National Archives. *Jubilee*, as a historical novel, spans the era from slavery through Reconstruction. Walker's heroine Vyry emerges from the bonds of slavery as a strong, capable human whose children are the center of her life. Critics argued that Vyry's lack of bitterness and her forgiving spirit were not realistic, but Walker countered that Vyry's forbearance was a faithful rendering of her great-grandmother and reflected the oral history passed to her from her grandmother. *Jubilee*, undoubtedly Walker's most successful literary effort, has sold millions of copies, has been translated into six languages, and has been produced as an opera. The book remains in print.

In addition to her novel *Jubilee*, Walker published a second volume of poems in 1966, *Ballad of the Free*. Two years later, she became director of Jackson State University's Institute for the Study of the History, Life, and Culture of Black People. In 1970, Walker published another volume of poetry, *Prophets for a New Day*. This collection identifies civil-rights leaders with Biblical prophets, and like *Jubilee*, reflects the deep religious convictions of the author. Although she decries the racism and corruption of the era, she also offers the reader hope for a new day, a day of redemption brought by leaders such as Malcolm X and Martin Luther King, Jr. She also celebrates the historical leaders, both black and white, who sacrificed their lives to political commitment. In 1973, Walker published her third collection of poetry, *October Journey*. Although this volume lacks the cohesiveness of her first two collections, it demonstrates her commitment to celebrating the wide variety of black voices, from an epitaph for her father to pieces about Paul Laurence Dunbar and *Harriet Tubman. She also collaborated with poet **Nikki Giovanni** to produce a book entitled *A Poetic Equation: Conversations between Nikki Giovanni and Margaret Walker* in 1974. In her conversation with Giovanni, Walker discusses her deep spirituality, reveals her role as a healer, and shows her commitment to humanity in general.

In 1977, Walker brought suit against Alex Haley, author of *Roots*, alleging that he had copied part of his plotting from her novel *Jubilee*. Although the suit was dismissed, she maintained that Haley plagiarized parts of her work. In 1979, Walker retired from Jackson State University, intending to devote herself to her writing and to public speaking. Unfortunately, she found herself embroiled in the court battle against Haley. She also faced publication delays, a rather lengthy illness, and the death of her husband. These events did not prove permanent obstacles to her career, however. In the late 1980s, she produced two major works. In 1988, she published the critical biography, *Richard Wright: Daemonic Genius*. Critics consider the work ambitious but uneven, with a rather weak, poorly synthesized ending. Walker also drew upon her earlier relationship with Wright, revealing her resentment of his rejection of her. The year following her book on Wright, Walker published *This Is My Century: New and Collected Poems*. Her poems celebrate the 20th century and the progress of the modern and post-modern eras. In the volume, Walker contrasts her youthful visions of life with those of her later years. She affirms her belief in shared humanity, a humanity that provides dignity for all. In 1990, Walker published *How I Wrote Jubilee and Other Essays on Life and Literature*. The essays, in part autobiographical, describe the devastating effect of racism on Walker as a child, the discrimination and harassment she faced as a black woman in academia, and the process and production of her masterpiece, *Jubilee*. In addition, she included essays and poems dedicated to exploring the work of African-American literary leaders as well as the African-American literary tradition itself.

In the early 1990s, Walker was writing a sequel to *Jubilee* called "Minna and Jim" and another novel titled "Mother Broyer." She was also working on her autobiography and editing an anthology of African-American literature. At the time of her death in Chicago in 1998, Houghton Mifflin was preparing to launch a new trade paper edition of *Jubilee*.

SOURCES:

Baechler, Lea, and A. Walton Litz, eds. *African American Writers*. NY: Scribner, 1991, pp. 1219–1220.

Davis, Arthur P. *From the Dark Tower: Afro-American Writers 1900 to 1960*. Washington, DC: Howard University Press, 1974.

Draper, James P. *Black Literature Criticism*. Detroit, MI: Gale Research, 1992.

Evans, Mari, ed. *Black Women Writers, 1950–1980: A Critical Evaluation*. NY: Doubleday, 1984.

Giovanni, Nikki, and Margaret Walker. *A Poetic Equation: Conversations Between Nikki Giovanni and Margaret Walker*. Washington, DC: Howard University Press, 1974.

Graham, Maryemma. "The Fusion of Ideas: An Interview with Margaret Walker Alexander," in *African American Review*. Summer 1993.

May, Hal, and James G. Lesniak, eds. *Contemporary Authors*. Vol. 26. New Revision Series. Detroit, MI: Gale Research, 1989.

Metzger, Linda, ed. *Black Writers: A Selection of Sketches from Contemporary Authors*. Detroit, MI: Gale Research, 1989.

Salem, Dorothy C., ed. *African American Women: A Biographical Dictionary*. NY: Garland, 1993.

Tate, Claudia, ed. *Black Women Writers at Work*. NY: Continuum, 1983.

Walker, Margaret. *How I Wrote Jubilee and Other Essays on Life and Literature*. Ed. by Maryemma Graham. NY: The Feminist Press, 1990.

Yvonne Johnson,
Associate Professor of History,
Central Missouri State University, Warrensburg, Missouri

Walker, Mary Edwards (1832–1919)

Surgeon awarded the Congressional Medal of Honor for her service during the Civil War, who asserted the rights of women in the medical profession, became an active supporter of suffrage and broader divorce rights for women, and challenged the impractical and unhealthy nature of women's dress. Born on November 26, 1832, in Oswego, New York; died in Oswego on February 21, 1919; daughter of Alvah Walker (a carpenter-farmer) and Vesta (Whitcomb) Walker; received a common school education in Oswego until 1850, then attended Falley Seminary in Fulton, New York, for two terms; obtained medical degree from Syracuse Medical College, 1855, and second medical degree from Hygeia Therapeutic College (New York), 1862; married Dr. Albert Miller, in 1855 (divorced 1869); no children.

Taught in Minetto, New York (1852); began medical practice in Columbus, Ohio (1855); moved practice to Rome, New York (1855); wrote letters to Dr. Lydia Sayer Hasbrouck's publication Sybil *that helped to launch a crusade for dress reform (1857); elected a vice-president of National Dress Reform Association (1860 and 1863); became volunteer assistant to Union Army surgeon at Patent Office Hospital in Washington, D.C. (1861); assigned to tent hospital near Fredericksburg (1862); assigned as surgeon to the 52nd Ohio Infantry regiment in Tennessee (1863); captured by Confederates (April 10, 1864); released after four months in prisoner exchange from Castle Thunder, in Richmond (August 1864); commissioned as acting assistant surgeon (October 1864); awarded Congressional Medal of Honor (1866); elected president of National Dress Reform Association (1866); made lecture tour of England (1866); helped organize Women's Suffrage Association for Ohio (1869); published* Hit, *about divorce (1871); published* Unmasked, or the Science of Immorality, *about infidelity in men (1878); was a candidate for Congress (1890); was a candidate for U.S. Senate (1891); was a delegate to Democratic National Convention (1892); published "Crowning Constitutional Argument," on women's franchise (1907).*

In late 1863, the 52nd Ohio Infantry regiment of the Union Army was located southeast of Chattanooga, Tennessee, when Mary Edwards Walker arrived there as a volunteer surgeon, dispatched by General George H. Thomas, Union commander of the Cumberland, to replace the regiment's doctor who had recently died. Those to whom her services were offered were outraged. According to Walker's biographer Charles McCool Snyder, the director of the medical staff under General Thomas' command, a Dr. Perin, considered the idea of a female surgeon a "medical monstrosity," and called for a review by an army medical board of Walker's qualifications. The board itself doubted "whether she has pursued the study of medicine" and concluded that her medical knowledge in areas other than obstetrics was "not much greater than most housewives." According to the regimental historian, Reverend Nixon B. Stewart, the men of the 52nd Ohio not only worried about the new doctor's skills, but suspected that her frequent excursions from camp to care for local residents nearby might be a cover for her activities as a spy.

At the end of the war, Dr. Mary Walker paid a visit to the regiment, suggesting that strong personal attachments had developed despite the men's initial resistance. During her tour of duty, according Snyder, the regiment was in "good health," allowing Walker the opportunity to care for residents of the area, and even help young men hiding out in nearby swamps to avoid Confederate impressment. In January 1866, her unique service to her country was acknowledged when she was awarded the Congressional Medal of Honor, presented to her by President Andrew Johnson.

Her choice of careers was not the only way Mary Edwards Walker defied the conventions of her day. At a time when corsets and hoopskirts were meant to define a woman's attractiveness and gentility, she spurned such dress as uncomfortable, impractical, and such a hindrance to free movement as to limit women's labor potential.

The strength of Mary Walker's belief in the fulfillment of women's potential is not surprising in light of her childhood. She was born on November 26, 1832, three months after her family moved to a 33-acre farm near Oswego, New York, on Lake Ontario. Her parents were Alvah Walker, a native of Greenwich, Massachusetts, and a carpenter by trade, and **Vesta Whitcomb Walker**, who had given birth to four older daughters—**Vesta**, **Aurora**, **Luna**, and **Cynthia**. In 1822, soon after their marriage, the couple had set out for Kentucky, but a stop at Vesta's uncle's homestead in Owasco, New York, had persuaded them that the Erie Canal being built nearby offered much work for a young carpenter, so they had settled first in Syracuse. Ten years later, Oswego was also booming, as the Oswego Canal connected it with the Erie Canal. On his land, Alvah built the town's first schoolhouse, where his daughters, and his son, Alvah, Jr., born in 1833, were educated.

In this family of mostly daughters, girls supplied the farm labor. The elder Alvah did not expect his daughters to wear restrictive clothing like

Opposite page
ℳary
ℰdwards
𝒲alker

corsets in their work, and he intended for all of his children to be educated for professional careers. Vesta became licensed to teach in the county, and after Mary showed an interest in her father's medical books, acquired when he had contracted measles, she was encouraged to pursue medicine.

In the 1840s, upstate New York was fertile intellectual ground for a progressive-minded young woman. In 1848, when Mary Walker was 16, the first Women's Rights Convention met at nearby Seneca Falls. The Walkers were evangelicals and believers in the Abolitionist movement who attended Methodist and Baptist services held by revivalist evangelical preachers roaming throughout the area. During the winters of 1850–51, Mary was educated at Falley Seminary in nearby Fulton, previously attended by her sisters Luna and Aurora; beginning in 1852, she taught at Minetto, New York, and saved money for her medical studies.

Despite social restrictions, the 1850s gave some benefits to women wanting to enter the medical profession. As the U.S. frontier expanded westward, doctors were in high demand, causing the opening of many medical schools. As competition for students increased among these schools, some became willing to accept women, and Mary Walker was admitted to Syracuse Medical College in December 1853. In June 1855, after courses in anatomy and physiology, surgery, medical pathology, obstetrics, diseases of women and children, therapeutics and pharmacy, chemistry, and medical jurisprudence, she received her medical degree, the only woman in her class.

That same year, Dr. Walker moved to Columbus, Ohio, the hometown of her father's sister, to open her first medical practice. According to Snyder, people there were reluctant to visit a female doctor, but Walker had another reason to leave, when she received a marriage proposal from Dr. Albert Miller of Rome, New York. The marriage took place that year, and the couple set up a common practice in Rome, where Mary demonstrated her independence by declining to use the surname Miller.

Four years later, after her husband proved unfaithful, the couple separated, and Walker moved into smaller rooms for her living quarters and office. Information on her financial status at the time is sketchy, but though competition was stiff, she offered a viable medical alternative to the people of Rome, and appears to have enjoyed some success. The *Rome Sentinel* commented on one of her ads, "Those . . . who prefer the skill of a female physician . . . have now an excellent opportunity to make their choice."

In 1857, Walker began to contribute to *Sybil*, the publication of Dr. *Lydia Sayer Hasbrouck of Middletown, New York. Hasbrouck had participated in the Bloomerite movement in the late 1840s, named after *Amelia Jenks Bloomer, which encouraged women to wear breeches, or pants. Now Walker began to address the issue of conventional women's dress as a barrier to their good health and successful labor. She herself wore a tunic or dress coat, gathered at the waist, which extended slightly below the knees, over pants and a high-collared undergarment. Walker championed this style over the long skirts or dresses worn with hoops and corsets, which could restrict circulation to the legs, place too much weight on the shoulders, and also pick up and carry dirt. Worn in public, especially on trains and carriages, according to Walker's claims, the space-consuming styles also added to the difficulties of transportation, encumbering women and annoying men.

Women cannot be deprived of God-given rights, or of Republican rights, without men being sufferers as well as women.

—Mary Edwards Walker

In 1857, Walker's published views earned her a place on the program of the second Reform-Dress Association Convention, in Syracuse. That December, she lectured on reform dress in Black River, New York, near Watertown, and in 1860 she was one of nine vice-presidents elected at the National Dress Reform Association Convention in Waterloo, New York.

During the summer of 1860, Walker was in Delhi, Iowa, the hometown of a family friend, hoping to secure a divorce under that state's more lenient laws. The following summer, she returned to Rome without her divorce, probably because of her concerns due to the outbreak of the Civil War. Shortly after the Battle of Bull Run in July 1861, the war's first large-scale battle, Walker arrived in Washington, D.C., to volunteer her medical services. Her first assignment was to the hospital established in the U.S. Patent Office, where she became a de facto assistant to Dr. J.N. Green. Despite recommendations made by Green, she was never commissioned by Surgeon General Clement Finley. Her authority in the hospital eventually became comparable to Green's, however, and her volunteer status gave her the freedom to come and go as she pleased. At one point, she personally accompanied a critically wounded soldier to his home in Rhode Island. Also in 1861, Walker helped to organize the Women's Relief Association, designed to provide lodging for the wives, mothers, and children of soldiers with nowhere to go in Washington. When necessary, she opened her own home to these women. In 1862, posted to Forest Hall Prison in Georgetown, she decided her services were not crucial and returned to New York to attain a second medical degree, from Hygeia Therapeutic College.

By November 1862, Walker was back in Washington. During the last weeks of 1862 and early in 1863, following the Battle of Fredericksburg, she was treating the wounded at a nearby tent hospital, where she made at least an attempt to reform medical military treatment, cautioning stretcher bearers not to carry the wounded downslope with the head lower than the feet. She also believed many amputations were unnecessary, and encouraged several wounded soldiers at the Patent Office Hospital to refuse the surgery. According to Snyder, her volunteer status and aversion to the procedure suggest that she did not actually perform amputations during the war.

Two anecdotes about Walker during her service at the Patent Office Hospital demonstrate her independence of mind about proper female roles. When *Dorothea Dix, head of the nursing corps for the Union army, paid a visit, Dix declared her disapproval of the presence of the "young and good-looking" doctor. Dix wanted to minimize the possibility of impropriety by hiring only older, plain women for hospital work, a position which Walker found absurd. At another time, Walker took a walk outside the hospital to get a breath of fresh air on a warm evening. When a man asked where she was going, she pulled out a revolver, aimed at him, and then fired into the air. Years later, she recalled that she was never again accosted by a man after that.

During her service with the 52nd Ohio Infantry Regiment, Walker once held troop inspection for Colonel McCook, the regimental commanding officer, on a morning when he was called away. On one of her journeys to care for people in the countryside, she was captured by a Confederate sentry, and spent the next four months as a prisoner of war at Castle Thunder, near Richmond, Virginia. In captivity, her complaints about the lack of grain and vegetables in the prisoners' diet led the Confederates to add wheat bread and cabbage to the Union rations at Castle Thunder. On August 12, 1864, she was released in a prisoner exchange for a Confederate surgeon with the rank of major.

Walker continued her appeal for a commission throughout her service in Tennessee. Her request for placement—in a female wing of a hospital or anywhere the army might need her—was carried all the way to President Abraham Lincoln, and refused. In September 1864, she was granted $432.36 for her services since March 11 of that year, although she had been in Castle Thunder most of the time. On October 5, she finally became the only female surgeon commissioned in the army, with the title of acting assistant surgeon and a monthly salary of $100.

After her release from Castle Thunder, Walker served for about six months at the Women's Prison Hospital in Louisville, where she was quickly disillusioned by the ingratitude and disloyal talk of the prisoners and the unwillingness of other officers to impose discipline. She next administered an orphan asylum in Clarksville, Tennessee, until her discharge on June 15, 1865.

The Congressional Medal of Honor awarded her in 1866 made Walker no less controversial. That year in a New York City milliner's shop, she was surrounded by a crowd because of her unorthodox dress. For her protection, the shopkeeper called the police, but when she defiantly refused to identify herself to the arriving officer, he arrested her. Walker later took action against the officer, gaining a hearing before the police commissioner; he agreed that she had every right to wear her preferred outfit, and assured her that she would no longer be bothered by police officers. In the 1870s, boys in Washington harassed her by asking her for chewing tobacco, but she did not back down. In fact, her attire grew even less conventional, as she began to don coats and shirts with ties.

Following the war, Walker worked to get relief bills for war nurses through Congress, but the bills died in committee. Efforts to gain a pension for herself were especially frustrating. An eye injury sustained during the war had resulted in partial muscular atrophy, for which she received $8.50 per month. Walker, believing the optical problem to be temporary, claimed to have refused an earlier offer of $25 per month, but the disability continued to interfere with her medical work. Beginning in 1872, she asked for either a $24 monthly stipend or a $10,000 lump sum. Reportedly, her unorthodox wardrobe was one reason why the 1872 petition to Congress was rejected; finally, in 1890, she was granted $20 per month, including the earlier $8.50 pension.

Walker earned most of her money by going on the lecture circuit immediately after the war. In 1866–67, she toured Great Britain for six months, lecturing on her own experiences, dress reform, and women's rights, and arguing that women should certainly enjoy voting rights in a country with a queen (*Victoria) on the throne. In November 1866 and February 1867, she lectured at St. James's Hall in London, and received favorable reviews despite cat-calls and police intervention for order.

Back in the United States, Walker resumed her crusade for dress reform and women's suffrage, lecturing and writing for publications. In 1868, she gave a speech before the Universal Franchise Association in Washington and testified with *Belva Lockwood before the Judiciary Committee of the District of Columbia House of Delegates (then the district's legislative body), which was considering a bill to allow women in the district to vote; the bill did not pass.

In 1866, Walker had been elected president of the National Dress Reform Association. In 1869, she and her long-time friend Dr. Lydia Hasbrouck addressed the Mutual Dress Reform and Equal Rights Association in Washington. That September, she joined *Susan B. Anthony and *Lucy Stone in Cincinnati to organize the Women's Suffrage Association for Ohio; in August, she had also participated as a D.C. delegate in the National Working Men's Convention in Philadelphia. As well, she served on the Central Women's Suffrage Bureau, coordinating activities for suffrage.

In 1869, Walker was finally granted a divorce by the State of New York. Two years later, in 1871, she published her views on divorce in the book *Hit*. Her concern was for more equitable divorce laws so that women and children would not be trapped in unhappy homes. Tied to this point, she realized, was the need for women to vote: "[U]ntil women have a voice in making [marriage laws], they must of necessity be imperfect, as are all laws, where . . . woman has had no voice in their making." She used the language of republicanism in her discussion of marriage, believing that it should be a "contract" between "equal" partners: "No young lady, when she is being courted . . . for a moment supposes that *her* lover *can* . . . ever wish her to be his slave."

In 1878, her second book, *Unmasked, or The Science of Immorality*, discussed the issue of unfaithful men, and blamed men's toleration of their own sexual improprieties on their childhood education, suggesting that the experience of her marriage was still a painful memory.

After the failure of the D.C. women's voting rights bill, Walker and Lockwood decided to create a legal challenge by joining with five other women in bringing petitions before the D.C. election board, requesting that they be registered to vote. Here also, Walker employed a republican argument, telling the board, "You imprison women for crimes you have forbidden women to legislate upon." The request was refused.

In 1872, after Walker was again rebuffed when she tried to vote in Oswego, a subsequent strategy left her separated from the mainstream suffrage movement. When Susan B. Anthony was indicted and fined for illegally voting in Rochester, most of the leadership, including Anthony, Lockwood, and *Anna Howard Shaw, decided to push for a constitutional amendment for suffrage rights. Walker believed that since the Constitution was addressed to "We the People," without mention of gender, and allowed the several states to determine eligible voters for Congress, such an amendment was unnecessary. In her view, what was needed were state acts declaring all restrictions on women's voting rights null and void; then women could be electors for the House of Representatives. She also favored a declaratory act to give women the same voting rights protection given to male blacks under the 15th Amendment.

These were the beliefs summarized in Walker's "Crowning Constitutional Argument," published in pamphlet form in 1907, and previously supported by U.S. Senator Charles Sumner of Massachusetts and Chief Justice Salmon P. Chase in the 1870s. In 1912 and 1914, Walker made her argument before the House Judiciary Committee, and before the New York State Constitutional Convention's Suffrage Committee in 1915. Feelings on the issue ran so deep that Mary called the suffrage movement's leadership "desirous of graft" when they raised funds for trips to Washington that would have been rendered unnecessary if her argument had been carried out.

Assertive and unrelenting in her political activism, Walker became alienated from the Republican Party after President Ulysses S. Grant failed to support temperance reform, continued to use tobacco, and was accused of nepotism. In 1890, she declared herself a candidate for Congress in Oswego, and in 1891 she campaigned for a U.S. Senate seat. The following year, she paid her own way to the Democratic National Convention.

After her father's death in 1880, Walker inherited the Bunker Hill Farm, where she lived during the last decades of her life, traveling often between Washington and Oswego. According to Snyder, she was sometimes overbearing toward farm tenants, and she quarreled with her brother Alvah when he took in their mother, though their father's will had named Walker to care for her. When Walker refused to allow Alvah use of her stables in compensation, he was angered. Walker remained more attached to her sister Aurora, who cared for her affairs when Walker was away until Aurora's death in May 1900. After that time, Mary planned to use the farm as a colony for young single women wanting to learn farming and domestic tasks before marriage. In April 1917, during World War I, she even wrote to Kaiser Wilhelm II, offering her land as the site of a German-American peace conference, but neither of these plans was ever realized.

In 1917, Mary Edwards Walker was 85 years old when she fell on the Capitol steps in Washington. She never completely recovered and died two years later, on February 21, 1919, while staying at the home of a neighbor in Oswego. That year saw the ratification of the 19th Amendment which she had opposed. But she had also lived to see the advent of the automobile and changes in women's dress. Mary Edwards Walker was inducted into the Women's Hall of Fame at Seneca Falls, New York, in the autumn of 2000.

SOURCES:

Snyder, Charles McCool. *Dr. Mary Walker: The Little Lady in Pants.* NY: Vantage Press, 1962.

U.S. 63rd Congress, 2nd Session. House Committee on the Judiciary Hearings on Women's Suffrage, Serial 11, Part 1, March 3, 1914. Washington: Government Printing Office, 1914.

Walker, Mary Edwards. *A Woman's Thoughts about Love and Marriage* (alternative title of *Hit*). NY: James Miller, 1871.

COLLECTIONS:

Walker papers located at Syracuse University and at the Oswego (New York) County Historical Society.

Wes Borucki, doctoral candidate, Department of History, the University of Alabama, Tuscaloosa, Alabama

Walker, Nancy (1922–1992)

American actress, comedian, and director. Born Anna Myrtle Swoyer on May 10, 1922, in Philadelphia, Pennsylvania; died of lung cancer on March 25, 1992, in Studio City, California; daughter of comedian Dewey Swoyer (stage name Dewey Barto) and Myrtle (Lawler) Swoyer; attended Bentley School and the Professional Children's School, New York, 1930–40; married Gar Moore (divorced); married David Craig (a dancer and vocal coach); children: Miranda Craig.

Made stage debut on Broadway (1941), as Blind Date in Best Foot Forward; *continued on Broadway (1941–60); appeared in several films (1943–76); made*

television guest appearances (late 1950s); appeared in various television series (1970–92); directed several television series episodes (mid-1970s); received Emmy nominations for work on "McMillan and Wife" (1973, 1974, 1975), and "Rhoda" (1975); known as the Bounty paper towel spokeswoman; appeared in her last role on the television sitcom "True Colors" (1991–92).

Television series: "Family Affair" (1970); "McMillan and Wife" (1971–76); "The Mary Tyler Moore Show" (1970s); "Rhoda" (1973–78); "The Nancy Walker Show" (1976); "Blansky's Beauties" (1976); "True Colors" (1991–92).

Born Anna Myrtle Swoyer in Philadelphia in 1922, the child of a dancer and a vaudeville acrobat, Nancy Walker traveled the vaudeville circuit with her parents. She made her first public show-stopping appearance in 1923, at ten months old, when she crawled on stage. By age ten, she decided to be a performer; by the time she was a teenager, her father's agent was helping her book minor singing engagements. A mix-up at the audition for the 1941 Broadway musical comedy *Best Foot Forward* permanently changed her name. After Anna Swoyer was mistakenly introduced as the established singer **Helen Walker** to producer George Abbott, the last name stuck when his appreciation for the diminutive redhead's plucky singing style led him to create a lead role for her.

Now known as Nancy Walker, she had a brassy, confident stage presence and talent for comedy that earned her much critical praise and soon had her career humming. After *Best Foot Forward* closed, Walker signed with Metro-Goldwyn-Mayer and moved to Hollywood, where she appeared in a series of musical-comedy films. She missed the pace of Broadway, however, and spent the next several years commuting between Hollywood and New York. In 1956, she made her directorial debut with *UTBU* on Broadway. In 1957, after the musical comedy *Copper and Brass* made a disappointing run, despite Walker's good reviews, she moved back to California to try television work. She made a few guest appearances on such programs as "The Ed Sullivan Show."

Walker soon became a well-known fixture on American television. In the early 1970s, her interpretation of the brash, candid Ida Morgenstern on "The Mary Tyler Moore Show" was so well liked that her character earned a starring role in the series "Rhoda." Walker was nominated for an Emmy award three times for her portrayal of the

housekeeper Mildred on the series "McMillan and Wife." She directed several episodes of "The Mary Tyler Moore Show," "Rhoda," and "Alice," and appeared in several films during the 1970s as well.

Nancy Walker

Walker was also readily recognized as the waitress Rosie in the Bounty paper towel commercials. Many film and television actors found commercial appearances beneath them, but Walker did not. "One minute's work done well is just as important as one hour," she said. Although she was adept at playing outspoken, audacious characters, offstage Walker was a more subdued, thoughtful, and observant person who wasn't quite sure why she was so successful at comedy. "I have this effect on people," she said, "so when I walk onstage, they start laughing."

SOURCES:
Annual Obituary 1992. Detroit, MI: St. James Press, 1993.
Herbert, Ian, ed. *Who's Who in the Theatre.* 16th ed. London: Pittman, 1977.

Jacquie Maurice,
freelance writer,
Calgary, Alberta, Canada

Walker, Nellie (1891–1964).

See Larsen, Nella.

Walker, Sarah Breedlove (1867–1919).

See Walker, Madame C.J.

Walkinshaw, Clementina

(c. 1726–1802)

Countess of Alberstroff. Name variations: Clementina Walkenshaw. Born around 1726; died in 1802; mistress of Prince Charles Edward Stuart (d. 1788), known as Bonnie Prince Charlie, the Young Pretender; children: Charlotte (b. 1753), countess of Albany.

Clementina Walkinshaw was the mistress of Prince Charles Edward Stuart (d. 1788), also known as Bonnie Prince Charlie, the Young Pretender, and was alleged to have been a Hanoverian spy.

Wallace, Lila Acheson (1889–1984)

Canadian-born philanthropist who was the co-founder and publisher of Reader's Digest *magazine.*
Born Lila Bell Acheson on December 25, 1889, in Virden, Manitoba, Canada; died in May 1984 in Mount Kisco, New York; daughter of T. Davis Acheson and Mary E. (Huston) Acheson; graduated from University of Oregon in Eugene, 1917; married DeWitt Wallace (a publisher), on October 15, 1921.

Became a director of the New York Central Railroad (1954); received, with husband DeWitt, the distinguished service award from the Theodore Roosevelt Association (1954), and the distinguished service to journalism award from Syracuse University (1955); received Medal of Freedom from President Richard Nixon (1972).

Lila
Acheson
Wallace

Born in 1889 in Canada, a middle child in a family of five, Lila Bell Acheson moved with her family to the United States and lived in several states while growing up. As a girl, she learned to enjoy hunting and horseback riding from her fa-

ther T. Davis Acheson, a Presbyterian minister. She studied English at college in Nashville, Tennessee, and at the University of Oregon, in Eugene, completing her four-year degree in less than three years. After graduation in 1917, she returned to Washington state where she taught high school for two years and managed a Young Women's Christian Association (YWCA) summer home on an island in Puget Sound. During and after World War I, Acheson continued doing social service work for the YWCA, the Interchurch World Movement, and the U.S. Labor Department.

After the war, the "dainty" Lila moved to New York City. In 1921, she married a longtime friend from Minnesota, DeWitt Wallace, who had himself just moved to New York to start up a new magazine called *Reader's Digest*. Founding the magazine on borrowed funds, on their wedding day the couple mailed out hundreds of advertisements from their Greenwich Village apartment. When they returned from their honeymoon, they found some 1,500 subscription checks awaiting them. They published the first issue of their innovative magazine in February 1922. Working from a modest basement office, the Wallaces created the unique format of *Reader's Digest* by going to the library and selecting and copying articles from other magazines for reprint. Reprint permission was easy enough to obtain, and the magazine's popularity mushroomed. By 1929, *Reader's Digest* was grossing over $600,000, and the Wallaces could afford to pay for reprint rights.

The magazine began publishing some of its own articles in 1933, and by offering some of these articles to other magazines for free publication, the Wallaces expanded their own supply pool. *Reader's Digest* did so well, even during the Great Depression, that in the mid-1930s the couple began making plans to construct a $1.5 million four-story suburban plant. Lila was in charge of the design of the building and applied her exceptional talent for art and architecture to the task. The result was "one of the industrial showplaces of the nation," noted the Los Angeles *Times*, and sightseers from all over the globe enjoyed tours of the buildings and grounds. In 1938, the magazine went international when the first British edition was published; Spanish and Portuguese editions followed, and by 1956 it was being published in 11 languages.

Until 1955, *Reader's Digest* accepted no advertising for the domestic edition, and even then the Wallaces insisted it be limited. They would not accept ads for certain products such as liquor.

The Wallaces suffered criticisms that their editorial policies were "reactionary" and the magazine's content was "intellectually mediocre." However, an ever-growing circulation, which in 1955 nearly equaled that of the next two most widely distributed magazines combined, made the Wallaces very wealthy. Lila Wallace became the only woman member of the board of directors of a major railroad in 1954. They won several joint awards and became known as philanthropists, contributing to many causes.

The Wallaces together built a global publishing empire from an idea which was ridiculed by others in the industry. They adhered to an editorial ethic which emphasized selecting from a wide variety of subjects and presenting stories of achievement, decency, and simple virtues in an uncomplicated way. Their business practices were equally principled. The Lila and DeWitt Wallace Foundation donated generously to many arts organizations and to media such as National Public Radio and educational television.

SOURCES:

Canning, Peter. *American Dreamers: The Wallaces and Reader's Digest: An Insider's Story.* NY: Simon and Schuster, 1996.
Current Biography 1956. NY: H.W. Wilson, 1956.

Jacquie Maurice,
freelance writer,
Calgary, Alberta, Canada

Wallace, Lucille (1898–1977)

American pianist whose career centered around the proper historical and musical interpretation of piano music. Born in Chicago, Illinois, on February 22, 1898; died in London, England, on March 21, 1977; married Clifford Curzon (the pianist), in 1931.

Lucille Wallace was born in Chicago in 1898 and educated at the Bush Conservatory there before continuing her education at Vassar College. In 1923, she enrolled at the University of Vienna to study music history with Guido Adler and social history with Alfons Dopsch. In 1924, she went to Paris to study with *Nadia Boulanger. Having by this time developed a strong interest in playing the harpsichord, Wallace took lessons in Paris from *Wanda Landowska. She also studied piano with Artur Schnable in Berlin. A musical scholar as well as a performing artist, throughout her active career Wallace grappled with the most difficult problems of proper interpretation and historical accuracy. In 1931, she married the brilliant British pianist Clifford Curzon. In the early 1950s, she gave up her performing career in order to devote

her full time and energy to raising the two orphaned sons of the singer *Maria Cebotari.

SOURCES:

"Lucille Wallace," in *The Times* [London]. March 23, 1977, p. 18.
Salter, Lionel. "Wallace, Lucille," in *New Grove Dictionary of Music and Musicians.* Vol. 20. London: Macmillan, 1980, p. 175.

John Haag,
Athens, Georgia

Wallace, Sippie (1898–1986)

African-American blues singer and pianist. Name variations: Beulah Belle Wallace. Born Beulah Belle Thomas on November 1, 1898, in Houston, Texas; died in November 1986 in Alameda, California; daughter of George Thomas and Fanny Thomas; coached in music by older brother George Thomas, Jr.; married Frank Seals (divorced); married Matthew Wallace.

Began singing in church choir as a pre-teen; released "Jack O' Diamond Blues" (1926); recording career ended (1929); toured Europe on folk-blues festival circuit (1966); sang at Lincoln Center in New York City (1977).

Sippie Wallace was born Beulah Belle Thomas in 1898, the fourth of thirteen children in a religious Houston, Texas, family. Her musical abilities were recognized early on when she sang and played piano in her family's Baptist church. Wallace was never educated much past elementary school, but her older brother George Thomas, Jr., and her older sister **Lillie Thomas** encouraged her talent and taught her how to write songs and sing. When she was 15, George moved to New Orleans to begin his musical career, and the attractive young Sippie followed him. They settled in the Storyville district where George's friends included the up-and-coming entertainer Louis Armstrong.

By the time she was 20, Sippie had endured a short and miserable marriage in New Orleans to Frank Seals, and her parents had passed away. Wallace returned to Houston to live with her brothers and sisters, but had not lost her desire to perform. She joined the tent shows in Houston on the Theatre Owner's Booking Association (TOBA) circuit, serving as an assistant and maid to the snakedancer Madame Dante and hoping for a break. Her talent soon earned "The Texas Nightingale" a place singing with small bands as she traveled around Texas. While she was still in her early 20s, her brother George, by then a successful composer, sent for her to join him in Chicago. She moved there with her young teenage brother Hersal Thomas, a piano prodigy, and her niece **Hociel Thomas**, who also wanted to be a blues singer.

Boosted by George's influence and position in the recording industry, the three talented Thomas siblings soon made a name for themselves. Sippie's dynamic recordings of "Shorty George" and "Up the Country Blues" outshone even George's 1922 hit "Muscle Shoals Blues." Her first recording reportedly sold 100,000 copies, a testament to the popularity of her singing style, which was a mix of Southwestern rolling honky-tonk and Chicago shouting moan. Sippie also wrote her own blues songs, drawing on personal experiences. Her "Jack O' Diamond"—the recording which featured Louis Armstrong—was born out of financial troubles caused by her second husband, the handsome gambler Matthew Wallace. Sippie Wallace's recording and stage career soon had her both headlining in traveling TOBA shows and working in studios. In the mid-1920s, she and her husband Matt, with Hociel and Hersal, who had made records themselves, moved to Detroit.

Sippie
Wallace

Then at the peak of her career, Wallace suffered a cluster of personal tragedies. In 1925, her mother Lillie died, in June 1926 Hersal succumbed to food poisoning, and in 1928 George was fatally struck down by a Chicago streetcar. The brilliant Thomas trio collaboration was over, and Wallace stopped recording the blues. In 1929, she signed a contract with Victor Records and put out a few strong recordings, including "Mighty Tight Woman." However, the Great Depression, shifts in musical tastes, and the lack of her brother's guidance all worked against her, and by 1932 she had faded into anonymity. Over the next 30 years or so, she focused her efforts on her family and worked in her church as a nurse and part of the choir.

Wallace made two recordings, in 1945 and 1959, which proved she had not lost her gift for the blues, and in the late 1960s she was convinced by a friend to take advantage of the folk-blues revival that was then taking hold. Wallace toured Europe in 1966 and performed to enthusiastic young audiences. In the early 1970s, younger artists such as **Bonnie Raitt** helped promote interest in the singing style of Wallace and others like her. In 1977, at age 80, Sippie Wallace sang her powerful brand of blues at New York's Lincoln Center. Even age and arthritis could not stop her from singing in Germany only six months before her death in 1986.

SOURCES:

Bailey, Brooke. *The Remarkable Lives of 100 Women Artists.* Holbrook, MA: Bob Adams, 1994.
Smith, Jessie Carney, ed. *Notable Black American Women.* Detroit, MI: Gale Research, 1992.

Jacquie Maurice,
freelance writer,
Calgary, Alberta, Canada

Wallace, Zerelda G. (1817–1901)

American temperance and suffrage leader. Born Zerelda Gray Sanders on August 6, 1817, in Millersburg, Kentucky; died of a bronchial ailment on March 19, 1901, in Cataract, Indiana; daughter of John H. Sanders and Polly C. (Gray) Sanders; attended boarding school, 1828–30; married David Wallace (lieutenant governor of Indiana), on December 26, 1836 (died 1859); children: Mary Wallace; Agnes Wallace Steiner (who married John H. Steiner); David Wallace, Jr.; three who died in childhood; and three stepchildren, including the writer General Lew Wallace.

Organized the Indiana state Women's Christian Temperance Union (WCTU, 1874); served as Indiana WCTU president (1877, 1879–83); helped organize the Indianapolis Equal Suffrage Society and became first president (1878); headed Franchise (suffrage) Department of the national WCTU (1883–88).

Born the daughter of a successful physician in Kentucky in 1817, Zerelda G. Wallace ended her formal education after two years of boarding school, but she was well read and enjoyed intellectual and religious conversations with her father. After moving to Indiana, she married the state's widowed lieutenant governor, David Wallace, when she was 19. As her husband moved on to become governor and then a U.S. congressional representative, young Zerelda Wallace took on increasing social duties and soon became a distinguished citizen of Indianapolis. David Wallace died in 1859, and over the next 14 years Zerelda Wallace had little interest in civic causes or a public career.

In 1873, however, the extremely religious Wallace became caught up in the temperance movement. The following year she attended a Cleveland convention of the Women's Christian Temperance Union (WCTU) and, being a well-known and respected citizen, she was installed on two influential committees. Upon her return to Indianapolis, she established the Indiana branch of the WCTU, of which she would serve twice as president. In 1875, she turned her attention to suffrage when she found that the signatures of 10,000 women on a temperance memorial meant little to the Indiana legislature. She was convinced that prohibition would never become law unless women were allowed to vote, and was instrumental in the passage that same year of a national WCTU resolution supporting the female vote on prohibition issues.

Interestingly, Wallace was not very concerned with suffrage itself, but instead viewed it as "the most potent means for all moral and social reforms." With that viewpoint, in 1878 she established the Indianapolis Equal Suffrage Society along with *May Wright Sewall. Previously affiliated with a suffrage society formed by *Lucy Stone's American Woman Suffrage Association, in 1887 Wallace nevertheless founded a group loyal to *Susan B. Anthony's National Woman Suffrage Association, and served as its vice-president at large for three years. During most of the 1880s, she served as head of the national WCTU's Franchise Department and lobbied for prohibition and suffrage in Indiana and other state legislatures.

Wallace became well known in the 1880s for her popular, effective, and inspirational, if lengthy, suffrage and temperance lectures. She spoke with purpose, and her average, sturdy looks were said to reflect the strength of her convictions. Four years after her last major speaking engagement in Washington in 1888, she suffered a major illness but still continued to lecture periodically. Alert but weakening after 1898, she spent her last years in the home of her daughter **Agnes Wallace Steiner**. Zerelda Wallace was also the inspiration for the character of Ben-Hur's mother in the 1880 novel *Ben-Hur*, which was written by her stepson General Lew Wallace.

SOURCES:
James, Edward T., ed. *Notable American Women, 1607–1950*. Cambridge, MA: The Belknap Press of Harvard University, 1971.

Jacquie Maurice,
freelance writer,
Calgary, Alberta, Canada

Wallada (fl. 11th c.)

Spanish poet. Name variations: Walladah bint al-Mustakfi. Flourished in the 11th century in Cordova.

Wallada, a poet of Spain, came from a ruling Arabic family, the daughter of the caliph of Cordova. She led a rather leisured life and spent most of her years in intellectual pursuits. Wallada gathered around her poets, artists, and scholars from across Arabic Spain, patronizing their works and composing her own verse. Apparently she never married, instead taking lovers as she wished, including Ibn Zaidun, one of early medieval Spain's greatest poets. Able to live fairly independent of male control, she reportedly even refused to wear the traditional veil of her culture. Numerous poems attributed to Wallada have survived; all are part of poetic "conversations" she held with Ibn Zaidun.

SOURCES:
Cosman, Carol, ed. *The Penguin Book of Women Poets*. NY: Penguin, 1978.

Laura York,
Riverside, California

Walladah bint al-Mustakfi (fl. 11th c.).
See Wallada.

Waller, Judith Cary (1889–1973)

American broadcasting executive. Born on February 19, 1889, in Oak Park, Illinois; died of a heart attack on October 28, 1973, in Evanston, Illinois; daughter of John Duke Waller and Katherine (Short) Waller; graduated from Oak Park High School, 1908.

Became manager of radio station WGU, later WMAQ (1922); produced first radio broadcast of a college football game (1924); brought the "Amos 'n'

Andy" show to WMAQ (1928); became vice-president and general manager of WMAQ (1929); became educational director of the National Broadcasting Company's (NBC) Central Division (1931); wrote Radio, The Fifth Estate *(1946); retired from NBC (1957).*

Judith Waller was born in 1889 in Oak Park, Illinois, the eldest of four daughters. After a wealthy aunt subsidized her trip to Europe upon her high school graduation, Waller returned and enrolled in a business college. She then worked for various firms, including the J. Walter Thompson advertising agency, for several years. On her European tour, she had met the business manager for the *Chicago Daily News*, and in 1922 he offered her a job managing the Chicago radio station the newspaper had just acquired, WGU. Though she was unsure of her ability to handle the unfamiliar job, Waller accepted and soon demonstrated her talents for programming at the prominent station, which later became WMAQ.

She created a classical music format for WMAQ, with her first program spotlighting a visiting opera star with piano and violin backup. Working with a staff of only two—herself and an engineer—Waller canvassed local music schools and the like for performers, wrote press releases to publicize the show, and announced and produced the programs herself. She produced the first play-by-play radio broadcast of a college football game in 1924, and the following year persuaded the owner of the Chicago Cubs to allow WMAQ to broadcast the team's home games. Waller also masterminded innovative political programming, brought about the first radio broadcast of the Chicago Symphony Orchestra, and was instrumental in the exceptional popularity of the "Amos 'n' Andy" show on radio, and later, television.

Waller was most well known for the program "University of Chicago Round Table." Begun in 1931 on WMAQ and later picked up by NBC, it "set the standard for intellectual excellence in broadcasting" and embodied Waller's high expectations for the educational potential of radio and television. She had already developed educational programming, creating the first successful television show for pre-schoolers, "Ding Dong School." The stalwart, pioneering Waller was a renowned leader in her industry; she helped form the National Association of Broadcasters (NAB), participated in all four national radio conferences of the 1920s, and threw herself into the deliberations over advertising in broadcasting.

Rather than envisioning the radio business from the conventional perspective, as a private, for-profit enterprise, Waller believed that radio ought to serve the public interest. She worked vigorously to promote collaborations between radio and education. In 1931, she left WMAQ to serve as an educational director at NBC, and later became public service director there. She served on the board of the University Association for Professional Radio Education, on the NAB's Educational Standards Committee, and on the Federal Radio Education Committee. She worked with Northwestern University to establish a summer broadcasting school there in 1942, and became co-director of the resulting NBC-Northwestern University Summer Radio Institute. Her 1946 textbook, *Radio, the Fifth Estate*, was used extensively in broadcasting courses.

Judith Waller, who was said to have a "tough, original, critical mind," achieved a widely respected, distinguished rank at a time when American radio industry leaders were primarily male. She continued her work after her retirement from NBC in 1957, lecturing at Northwestern University and leading television workshops at Purdue University. Waller died of a heart attack in 1973.

SOURCES:
Sicherman, Barbara, and Carol Hurd Green, eds. *Notable American Women: The Modern Period*. Cambridge, MA: The Belknap Press of Harvard University, 1980.

Jacquie Maurice,
freelance writer,
Calgary, Alberta, Canada

Wallmann, Margarethe
(1901–1992)

German-born dancer, choreographer, and teacher, a leading exponent of expressionist dance in pre-Hitler Germany, who later became the first woman to achieve international acclaim as an opera director. Name variations: Margarita Wallmann; Margaret Wallmann; Margarete Wallmann; Margherita Wallmann. Born, probably in Berlin, on July 22, 1901 (some sources cite in 1904 in Vienna); died in Monte Carlo, Monaco, on May 2, 1992.

Margarethe Wallmann enjoyed an extraordinary career, one extending over more than six decades in both Europe and the New World, in which she achieved fame as a dancer, teacher, director of a dance company, choreographer, ballet director, and last but certainly not least, as the first woman in history to be an opera director. She was born most likely in Berlin in 1901, and studied ballet there under **Eugenia Eduardowa** and *****Olga Preobrazhenska**, and later in Munich with Heinrich Kröll and **Anna Ornelli**, as well as for a time in Paris. As a dance student in Munich, she was, she wrote, "a little dancer who was besotted with music." In 1923, Wallmann moved to Dresden to study modern dance with *Mary Wigman. For a time, she was a member of Wigman's touring company, whose members also included such future dance stars as *Hanya Holm and *Gret Palucca. In 1927, Wallmann founded a dance school at which she taught the new style pioneered by Wigman, and the next year traveled to the United States to introduce the Wigman approach there.

By 1929, Wallmann had founded her own dance company, the Tänzer-Kollektiv (Dancers' Collective). It was in Munich in 1930 that she performed with her dance ensemble a "movement drama" entitled *Orpheus Dyonisos*, to the music of Christoph Willibald von Gluck, with the American dancer Ted Shawn, who proclaimed her to be "Germany's newest genius." Wallmann's choreography for *Orpheus Dyonisos* won her the first prize at the International Dance Congress of 1930. In the summer of 1931, the Wallmann troupe were guest performers at Austria's Salzburg Festival. There, as exponents of contemporary expressionist dance (*Ausdruckstanz*), she and her dancers staged the premiere of *Das jüngste Gericht* (The Last Judgment) to music by Georg Friedrich Händel, deemed a success by both audiences and critics. In 1932, Wallmann was placed in charge of the choreography for the Salzburg staging of Carl Maria von Weber's *Oberon*. Thanks to these artistic triumphs, Wallmann would be a regular guest at the Salzburg Festival until 1937, serving that prestigious institution as its chief choreographer. In 1933, she also made her debut in Salzburg as an opera producer with Gluck's *Orpheus and Eurydice*. That same year at Salzburg she choreographed Max Reinhardt's acclaimed version of Goethe's *Faust*.

In 1932, Wallmann closed her dance school in Berlin, after an accident ended her active career as an expressionist dancer. Being both Jewish and a champion of artistic modernism, she fled Germany in 1933 when the Nazis came to power. Fortunately, the successes she had already achieved in Austria allowed her to continue her career there, but her relocation coincided with her turning away from Wigman's ideas on modern dance. From this point on, Wallmann would direct her energies to making the best uses of more traditional ballet-oriented dance styles. The opportunity to do this soon arose, for in 1934 she was appointed the "ballet mistress" of Vienna's world-renowned Staatsoper (State Opera), with additional duties as director of the

Margarethe Wallmann, with Willy Franz, 1934.

State Opera's ballet school. The indefatigable perfectionist Wallmann quickly earned the admiration and respect of many of her colleagues, including Staatsoper director Dr. Erwin Kerber.

During her years in Vienna, which were marked by growing political tensions (on at least one occasion, Nazis released stink bombs during a Staatsoper performance to protest appearances by Jewish singers), Wallmann began to display her extraordinary versatility as an artist. While working full time at the State Opera, as well as at the Salzburg Festival every summer, she also began to take foreign assignments, including work at Prague's New German Theater and Milan's fabled La Scala Opera House. Her La Scala achievements in the 1930s included choreographing operas by Boïto, Gluck, and Verdi, and ballets by the contemporary Italian composer Ottorino Respighi (*The Birds* and *Ancient Airs and Dances*). Wallmann's growing fame even brought her to Hollywood, where among other projects she choreographed the *Greta Garbo film *Anna Karenina* (1935). Back in Vienna, she produced a number of works reflecting Austria's desperate attempt to forge a national cultural identity distinct from that of (Nazi) Germany, including such artistically conservative ballets (or ballet-pantomimes) as *Weihnachtsmärchen* (Christmas Fairy Tale, 1933), **Fanny Elssler* (1934), *Österreichische Bauernhochzeit* (Austrian Peasant Wedding, 1934), and *Der liebe Augustin* (1936).

One of Wallmann's last triumphs was her choreography for Bizet's *Carmen*, staged at Vienna's Staatsoper in December 1937, with Bruno Walter conducting. In March 1938, time ran out for Austrian independence. Jewish artists like Wallmann and Walter now fled Nazi terror. Fortunately for Wallmann, she enjoyed a worldwide reputation for excellence in both theater and dance, and by the end of that year she was in Buenos Aires, having been offered a contract by Argentina's famed Teatro Colón, where she directed the opera house's ballet. Her much-acclaimed work in Buenos Aires over the next decade included choreographing Lothar Wallerstein's productions of Beethoven's *Fidelio*, and Wagner's *Tannhäuser* and *Die Meistersinger von Nürnberg*. Among Wallmann's most noted dance sequences done at the Teatro Colón were her productions of Richard Strauss' *Don Juan* and *Die Josephslegende*. In 1947, she also ventured into opera direction with her version at the Teatro Colón of a contemporary work, Arthur Honegger's *Jeanne d'Arc au bucher*, which earned her the highest critical praise from both audiences and critics that year. She encored the Honegger work in 1948.

After returning to Europe in 1948, Wallmann concentrated her career energies on opera direction. For the next four decades, she would be involved in an extraordinary number of opera productions. She was not only the first woman in the world to work as an opera director, but would virtually monopolize this position until the 1960s. By 1949, she was active in Italy, where she would direct an astonishing number of operas—14 by Verdi alone, including such rarities as his early *La Battaglia di Legnano* and *Luisa Miller*—many of these at La Scala. As late as 1982, Wallmann would direct a Verdi opera (*Un ballo di maschera*), in this instance not in Italy, but in France at Avignon's municipal theater. While directing operas across the entire range of the lyric repertory, including **Maria Callas* in *Norma* and *La Gioconda*, Wallmann enjoyed specializing in modern works, including operas by contemporary composers such as Richard Strauss, Igor Stravinsky, Manuel de Falla, Darius Milhaud, Mario Castelnuovo-Tedesco, Krzysztof Penderecki, and Francis Poulenc.

Wallmann's artistic relationship with the French composer Francis Poulenc would turn out to be a particularly fruitful one, for in 1957 she directed the world premiere of his great opera *Dialogues des Carmélites* at the Paris Opera as well as at La Scala. In her memoirs, Wallmann wrote with pride of her work with Poulenc who had become a sort of "big brother." Over a friendship lasting decades, she gave him valuable advice, including a way to end the first act of *Dialogues des Carmélites*. "Francis looked at me in amazement. 'It's wonderful, it's amazing!,' and he lifted me in his arms and carried me round the room like a whirlwind."

Wallmann's style, described by Alan Blyth as "representational, flamboyant and luxurious, requiring elaborate scenery," was budget-busting and had largely gone out of fashion by the mid-1970s. In her heyday, however, she was incomparable and worked successfully with some of the operatic world's most eminent designers, including Nicola Benois and Salvador Dali. Besides working at such opera houses as Vienna's Staatsoper (where she directed imposing and long-lived productions of *Don Carlos* and *Turandot* under Herbert von Karajan's baton), Buenos Aires' Teatro Colón, and London's Covent Garden, Wallmann also directed operas in the United States at New York's Metropolitan Opera (Ponchielli's *La Gioconda* in 1966–67, and Donizetti's *Lucia di Lammermoor* from 1964 through 1976), and at Chicago's Lyric Opera (Bizet's *Carmen* in 1959–60). Even the Iron Curtain did not stand in her way, for in 1964 she found a way to direct *Lucia di Lammermoor*, as well as Puccini's *Turandot*, at Moscow's Bolshoi Theater. Wallmann continued to direct well into her 80s. In 1983, she helmed her first *Zauberflöte* (Mozart's Magic Flute) at the Teatro Colón. In 1987, she presented Richard Strauss' *Der Rosenkavalier* at the Grand Theater of Monte Carlo, which received praise from the critic of the journal *Opera*, who noted simply that Wallmann, "an old friend of Richard Strauss," had presented this classic opera in "an authentic way... [and] ... with so little indulgence on [her] part that the Faninal escapes caricature and even Ochs retains a trace of dignity." In 1988, Wallmann directed one final opera in her long and remarkable career, Puccini's *Madama Butterfly*, also at Monte Carlo's Grand Theater. It was in Monte Carlo that she died on May 2, 1992.

SOURCES:

Amort, Andrea. "Die Geschichte des Balletts der Wiener Staatsoper, 1918–1942," Ph.D. dissertation, University of Vienna, 1981.

———. "Wallmann, Margarete," in Selma Jeanne Cohen et al., eds., *International Encyclopedia of Dance.* 6 vols. NY and Oxford: Oxford University Press, 1998, Vol. 6, pp. 357–358.

———. "Wallmann, Margarethe," in Taryn Benbow-Pfalzgraf and Glynis Benbow-Niemier, eds., *International Dictionary of Modern Dance.* Trans. by Zoran Minderovic. Detroit, MI: St. James Press, 1998, pp. 808–809.

Blyth, Alan. "Wallmann, Margarita," in Stanley Sadie and Christine Bashford, eds., *The New Grove Dictionary of Opera.* Vol. 4. London: Macmillan, 1992, p. 1096.

Caamaño, Roberto. *La Historia del Teatro Colón, 1908–1968.* 3 vols. Buenos Aires: Editorial Cinetea, 1969.

Chiavarone, Luigi M. "La Wallmann e Visconti: Regia lirica al Teatro alla Scala (1953–1962)," Ph.D. dissertation, Università del Sacro Cuore, Milano, 1992.

Craine, Debra, and Judith Mackrell. *The Oxford Dictionary of Dance.* Oxford, UK: Oxford University Press, 2000.

Douer, Alisa, and Ursula Seeber, eds. *Wie weit ist Wien? Lateinamerika als Exil für österreichische Schriftsteller und Künstler.* Vienna: Picus, 1995.

Fabian, Imre. "'Es ist das beste Theater der Welt': Gespräch mit der Regisseurin Margherita Wallmann über das Teatro Colón," in *Opernwelt.* Vol. 20, no. 5, May 1979, p. 43.

"In Memoriam," in *NZ: Neue Zeitschrift für Musik.* Vol. 153, no. 7–8, July–August 1992, p. 96.

Larner, Gerald. "Monaco: Wallmann and 'Rosenkavalier,'" in *Opera.* Vol. 38, no. 7. July 1987, p. 807.

"Margarete Wallmann: Zum Tode der Choreographin und Regisseurin," in *Tanzdrama.* No. 19, 1992, pp. 8–11.

Mayer, Tony. "Orange: A New Broom," in *Opera.* Vol. 33, no. 11. November 1982, pp. 1132–1133.

"Obituaries: Margarethe Wallmann," in *Dance Magazine.* Vol. 66, no. 11. November 1992, p. 36.

"Obituary: Margarita Wallmann," in *Opera.* Vol. 43, no. 9. September 1992, p. 1043.

Rode-Breymann, Susanne. *Die Wiener Staatsoper in den Zwischenkriegsjahren.* Tutzing: Hans Schneider, 1994.

Seebohm, Andrea, ed. *The Vienna Opera.* NY: Rizzoli, 1987.

Shawn, Ted. "Germany's Newest Genius," in *Dance Magazine.* August 1930.

Veroli, Patrizia. "La regia d'opera in Italia: il caso di Margherita Wallmann," in *Nuova Rivista Musicale Italiana.* Vol. 32, no. 1–4. January–December 1998, pp. 351–369.

Wallmann, Margarita. *Les balcons du ciel.* Paris: Editions Robert Laffont, 1976.

"Wallmann, Margarethe," in Frithjof Trapp, *et al.*, *Handbuch des deutschsprachigen Exiltheaters 1933–1945.* Vol. 2: *Biographisches Lexikon der Theaterkünstler.* Munich: K.G. Saur, 1999, Part 2, pp. 983–984.

COLLECTIONS:

Walter Toscanini Collection of Research Materials in Dance, New York Public Library Research Collection.

John Haag,
Associate Professor of History,
University of Georgia, Athens, Georgia

Waln, Nora (1895–1964)

American journalist and author. Born on June 4, 1895, in Grampian, Pennsylvania; died on September 27, 1964; daughter of Thomas Lincoln Waln and Lilla (Quest) Waln; educated at Swarthmore College in Swarthmore, Pennsylvania; married George Edward Osland-Hill (in British government service), in 1922; children: one daughter.

Published House of Exile *(1933), based on her experience of living with a Chinese family for two years; on eve of World War II, published a perceptive book on Nazi Germany,* The Approaching Storm: One Woman's Story of Germany, 1934–1938 *(released in the United States under title* Reaching for the Stars, *1939).*

Nora Waln was born in 1895 in Philadelphia to a sea-faring Quaker family which had actively participated in trade with China in the 1800s. As a girl, she studied early family records and found that the Walns had "hereditary traditions" of friendship and trade with a Chinese family in Hopei Province. Waln discovered that this aristocratic family, the Lins, still lived in their ancestral family homestead, called "The House of Exile." The notion of this family connection stayed with Waln as she grew up. She attended college until the United States entered World War I, when she left to edit a Washington, D.C., newspaper page about women and the war. She later worked in New York as a publicity director for the Near East Relief Committee.

In 1920, Waln sailed for China. After a day's trip from Peking (Beijing), she located the Lin family compound on the Grand Canal. The first foreigner ever to set foot in the home in the entire 650 years of its existence, she was welcomed as a "daughter of affection" and shared the family's daily lives for the next two years. She kept detailed notes on the experience. On a boat during a visit home, the trim, blonde Waln met George Osland-Hill, who was working in Peking for the British foreign service. They married in Shanghai in 1922 and later had one daughter. Waln was forced to relocate to England and Japan during troubled political times in China, but was finally able to return to the Lin home. She had composed a book, *House of Exile*, from the notes she made during her first stay with the family, and after critiquing it they finally allowed her to publish it. The book was a bestseller in 1933.

After George Osland-Hill's resignation from his government post, Waln accompanied him to Dresden, Germany, in 1934. The popular *House of Exile* had been widely translated, and the couple was welcomed by German admirers, including some Nazi elite. Adolf Hitler himself had purchased 35 copies of the book. Over the following four years, Waln began another book about her perceptions of Nazism and the emergence of National Socialism in Germany. Her sentiments were not complimentary, and in 1938, when German security officers seized part of the manuscript she had sent to London publishers, Waln and her husband were deported with only a 24-hour notice. Before leaving, Waln had attempted to mail three copies of the manuscript to London from three different postal stations within Germany. None of them ever made it, however, and Waln had to rewrite the book from memory and the notes she had managed to keep.

The Approaching Storm: One Woman's Story of Germany, 1934–1938 (titled *Reaching for the Stars* in the United States), was published in 1939 to wide approval. The book was full of admiration for the German people, but some criticized Waln's Quaker mildness in not condemning the Nazi government harshly enough. Before her death in 1964, Waln wrote magazine articles and reported on the Nuremberg trials, the Korean War, and postwar Japan.

Jacquie Maurice,
freelance writer,
Calgary, Alberta, Canada

Walpole, Maria (1736–1807)

Countess of Waldegrave and duchess of Gloucester. Name variations: Maria, Lady Waldegrave; Maria, Dowager Countess of Waldegrave; Maria of Waldegrave; Maria Gloucester. Born Maria Walpole on July 10, 1736 (some sources cite 1735), at St. James's Palace, Westminster, London, England; died on August 22, 1807, at Oxford Lodge, Brompton, Middlesex, England; buried at St. George's Chapel, Windsor, Berkshire, England; illegitimate daughter of Sir Edward Walpole (elder brother of Horace Walpole) and **Dorothy Clement** *(a milliner's apprentice); married James, 2nd earl of Waldegrave, on May 15, 1759 (died 1763); married William Henry Hanover (1743–1805), 1st duke of Gloucester and Edinburgh (brother of George III, king of England), on September 6, 1766; children: (first marriage) Anne Horatio Waldegrave (1759–1801, who married Lord Hugh Seymour); Elizabeth Laura, countess of Waldegrave (1760–1816, who married George, 4th earl of Waldegrave); Charlotte Maria Waldegrave (1761–1808, who married George Henry, duke of Grafton); (second marriage) Sophia Matilda (1773–1844); Caroline Augusta Mary (1774–1775); William Frederick (1776–1834), duke of Edinburgh and Gloucester. William Henry Hanover*

also had a daughter with Lady **Almeria Carpenter**: *Louisa Maria (1762–1835, who married Godfrey Bosville, 3rd baron of Slate).*

Maria Walpole was one of five children born to Edward Walpole (son of the great British minister Robert Walpole) and his mistress **Dorothy Clement**, a shopgirl. When her mother died in 1739, Maria and her siblings were moved to their father's estate near Egham, where they were brought up like other aristocratic children despite their illegitimate birth. As a child, Maria became very attached to her uncle, the celebrated diarist Horace Walpole, who claimed her as his favorite niece because of her intelligence, ambition, and beauty.

In 1759, Horace Walpole arranged a marriage for Maria with his friend, James, earl Waldegrave. Waldegrave was twice her age, wealthy, and a respected politician in Parliament. He held numerous important posts in the British government, including Lord of the Treasury and tutor to the prince of Wales. Maria's surviving correspondence and her uncle's memoirs show that she consented to the arrangement readily; it was a better marriage than she could have hoped for, given her illegitimacy. They were married on May 15, 1759; a week later, Maria was presented at court to the king, George II.

Maria had three daughters with Waldegrave: **Anne Horatio Waldegrave** (1759–1801, who married Lord Hugh Seymour); **Elizabeth Laura**, countess of Waldegrave (1760–1816, who married George, 4th earl of Waldegrave); and **Charlotte Maria Waldegrave** (1761–1808, who married George Henry, duke of Grafton). They became a close couple over the course of their marriage despite their age difference. Maria and the earl worked together on the earl's memoirs; much of the original manuscript is in her handwriting. Then, in 1763, her husband contracted smallpox and, despite Maria's dedicated nursing, died some weeks later. He made his 26-year-old wife the executor of his will, which provided well for her family's support. Maria was also left in control of the earl's copious correspondence, memoirs, and other papers, many of which were eventually published and provide insight into the daily politics of 18th-century England.

The young, wealthy widow found herself the target of numerous aristocratic suitors. Maria surprised London society by refusing all offers of marriage, until it was learned that she was spending much of her time in the company of King George III's younger brother, William

Henry, eight years her junior and duke of Gloucester. Her family became deeply concerned for her reputation. The duke, next in line to the throne, could not possibly marry her, it was thought, because of her illegitimate birth; the king would never approve of William's marriage to a commoner. But Maria refused to heed her family's warnings to break it off, and was seen constantly in public with the duke for several years. She even traveled across Europe with him in 1771, and took quarters at his palace of Hampton Court. The king, fearful that William Henry would indeed marry Lady Waldegrave, issued the Royal Marriage Act of 1772, stipulating that no member of the royal family could marry without the consent of the crown. William Henry had promised his brother he would never marry Maria Walpole; he even censured his other brother, Henry, duke of Cumberland, for marrying *Ann Horton. Royalty did not marry subjects.

But in 1772 Maria finally confessed to her father that she had indeed already married the duke, in a private ceremony in 1766. She explained that she had not told anyone because she feared for her honor, that of her late husband, and that of her own family. Sir Edward revealed Maria's secret to others, and soon their marriage was open knowledge across English society. On September 13, 1772, King George received a letter from William Henry: "I am grieved much at finding myself obliged to acquaint Your Majesty with a thing which must be so disagreeable to you, but I think the world being so much acquainted with my marriage, whilst Your Majesty is still supposed to be ignorant of it, is neither decent nor right." The letter was well timed; Maria Walpole was pregnant.

The duke of Gloucester's furtive nuptials hurt the king deeply. The brothers, who had been confidants, now became estranged for years. "He must be displeased," wrote Maria Walpole to a friend, "but his behaviour has been such upon the occasion that we have all the reason in the world to be grateful to him." Pariahs among the royalty, the two dukes and their wives were taken up by the royal opposition. Wrote Lady **Louisa Stuart**: "Never were princesses so reverenced and Royal Highnessed by patriots."

Despite her letter, Maria Walpole had nothing but antipathy for the king and his queen *Charlotte of Mecklenburg-Strelitz. Lady **Elizabeth Luttrell** called her a female roué, who governed her family with a high hand "and led the way in ridiculing the King and Queen. . . . A mighty scope for satire was afforded by the Queen's wide mouth and occasionally imperfect English, as well as by the King's trick of saying What! what!"

The king, outraged by his brother's behavior, said he could never forgive him, and forbade them, and anyone who associated with them, from coming to court. He could not undo the marriage, however, and permitted it to be legally validated by Parliament before the birth of Maria and William's first child, *Sophia Matilda, in May 1773. A second daughter Caroline Augusta Mary followed in June 1774, but died the following year.

Banned from court, the duke and duchess established a small court of their own at Gloucester House in London, although few nobles visited out of fear of the king's anger. The couple was deeply in debt; Maria's inheritance from Waldegrave provided mostly for his children, now living with their great-uncle Horace Walpole. The duke's requests for an increased allowance from the king were rejected. Despite these hardships, Maria and William Henry traveled in Italy and France from 1775 to 1777, hoping to improve the duke's always frail health. In Rome, Maria gave birth to her last child and only son, William.

The ducal couple returned to England in 1777 when they believed the duke to be dying. He recovered, and by 1784 they were back in Italy again for another three-year stay. Except for their children, they believed there was little in England for them; banned from court, despised and avoided by the aristocracy, alienated from much of their families, they had little reason to remain there.

By 1787, however, Maria's 20-year relationship with William Henry was deteriorating. They had grown apart, and the duke had begun an open affair with one of Maria's ladies-in-waiting. On their return to England, the duke wrote to the king that Maria could remain in his house only if she agreed to limit her visits with their children. Clearly he was attempting to reconcile with George III by distancing himself from the marriage which had proven to be so disadvantageous. But Maria did remain at Gloucester House, refusing to reveal to the outside world the collapse of the marriage for which she had risked her own and her family's honor.

A loving mother, she was compelled to agree to the duke's demands in order to continue to see Sophia and little William. Maria maintained close relationships with all five of her surviving children, corresponding with them frequently even during her years abroad. Her married daughters from her first marriage—known as "the three Ladies Waldegrave"—visited their mother often after 1787, co-hosting her many parties. She also kept up a lively and frank correspondence with her uncle Horace Walpole, who served as a friend and advisor until his death in 1797.

The duke and duchess seem to have reconciled somewhat after 1787; they were on friendly terms, but they were never again as close as they had been. In 1805, the duke of Gloucester died at age 62. His 70-year-old widow moved to Gloucester Lodge, a new house in Brompton, with her youngest daughter. She divided her days between her many charities and her children and grandchildren. Maria also turned to religion in her last years, developing a close friendship with the renowned religious writer *Hannah More. In August 1807, Maria Walpole suddenly became ill and died a few days later at age 72. She was buried after an elaborate funeral in the same tomb in Windsor Castle as the duke of Gloucester.

SOURCES:

Biddulph, Violet. *The Three Ladies Waldegrave and Their Mother*. London: Peter Davies, 1938.

Clark, J.C.D., ed. *The Memoirs and Speeches of James, 2nd Earl Waldegrave, 1742–1763*. Cambridge: Cambridge University Press, 1988.

Laura York, M.A. in History, University of California, Riverside, California

Walpura or Walpurga (c. 710–777).

See Walpurgis.

Walpurgis (c. 710–777)

English saint and missionary. Name variations: Walberga; Walburg; Walburga; Walburge; Walpura; Walpurga. Born around 710; died in 777 (some sources cite 779) at the monastery of Heidenheim (also seen as Heidenham), Germany; sister of St. Willibald and St. Winibald; never married; no children.

Christians of early England revered Walpurgis as a saint. She was the daughter of a petty noble of Wessex; when he died, Walpurgis entered the convent of Wimborne. After several years, the abbess of Wimborne was approached by the missionary St. Boniface, who asked her to send some of her nuns with him to Germany to help convert the Germanic tribes. The intelligent, well-educated, and deeply pious Walpurgis was chosen to accompany Boniface, as were *Lioba and a number of other nuns. Walpurgis spent two years traveling among the German people; then she was made abbess over the nuns at the foundation of Heidenheim, a double monastery established several years earlier by Walpurgis' own brothers, Saint Willibald and Saint Winibald.

On Winibald's death, Walpurgis was given responsibility for the monks as well, putting her in a position of considerable power. She managed the house and its adjacent lands with competence, all the while developing a reputation for having a special relationship with God. Walpurgis was believed to be able to effect miracles of healing, and was widely sought out by the ill for this power. After her death and subsequent canonization, miraculous powers were also attributed to her relics; the nuns at Heidenheim sent them, upon request, to churches across Germany, Belgium, and other countries, for Saint Walpurgis' reputation had spread across Western Europe.

Though Engelbert's *Lives of the Saints* lists her feast days as February 25 and May 1, Walpurgis Night is commonly celebrated on April 30, the eve of May Day. During Walpurgis Night, witches were supposed to ride on broomsticks to the ancient places of sacrifice in order to revel with Satan. One of the best known of witch hills was the highest point of the Harz, the Brocken, in Germany, the scene of the witches' Sabbath in Goethe's *Faust*.

SOURCES:

Dunbar, Agnes. *Dictionary of Saintly Women, vol. I*. London: G. Bell and Sons, 1904.

Laura York, M.A. in History, University of California, Riverside, California

Walpurgis, Maria Antonia (1724–1780).

See Maria Antonia of Austria.

Walsh, Adela Pankhurst (1885–1961).

See Pankhurst, Adela.

Walsh, Stella (1911–1980)

Polish-American track-and-field star, the first woman to run the 100-yard dash in under 11 seconds, who set numerous world records in 30 years of competition, was posthumously accused of being a man, and later was cleared of this accusation by an Olympic Committee. Name variations: Stanislava Walaciewicz; Stanislawa Walasiewicz-Olson; (nickname) the Polish Flyer. Born Stanislawa Walasiewicz on April 3, 1911, in Rypin, Poland; murdered on December 4, 1980, in Cleveland, Ohio; married briefly to Harry Olson; no children.

Collected 1,100 trophies in track and field over a 30-year career; astounded the track-and-field world by running the 50-yard dash in 6.1 seconds in Madison Square Garden (1930); ran 100 yards in 10.8 sec-

onds (1930), the first time a woman clocked under 11 seconds; competed for Poland in the Olympics, winning a gold medal in the 100 meters with a world-record time of 11.9 seconds (1932); won a silver medal for Poland in the Olympics in the 100 meters with a time of 11.7 seconds (1936); broke the AAU women's national record for 70 yards with a time of 8.2 seconds (1935); became an American citizen (1947); organized track, field and other women's sports and recreation programs for the Cleveland recreation program (1970s); also edited the sports section of a Polish newspaper in Cleveland.

In the 1930s, Stella Walsh was known as a "wonder woman" in the sports world, the first woman to run the 100-yard dash in under 11 seconds. Like *Sonja Henie and *Babe Didrikson Zaharias, Walsh was a household name. For 23 years, from 1930 until 1953, she won over 1,000 medals in major track-and-field events; her competitive career, astonishingly, lasted a full 30 years. She is little known today, however, and her name is associated more often with events that happened after her death than with the heights of athletic achievement, a circumstance that would no doubt deeply sadden her.

Stanislawa Walasiewicz was born in Rypin, Poland, on April 3, 1911, and emigrated with her family to Cleveland, Ohio, while she was still a baby. When she was a schoolgirl, her teachers suggested she change her name to Stella Walsh, to make it easier for Americans to pronounce. Walsh would retain an allegiance to both her adopted country and the land of her birth throughout her life, and she would compete for both. Although she spent most of her life in the United States, she traveled frequently to Poland, retaining close ties to her family there. Her Polish was fluent, and in later years she wrote and edited a sports column for a Polish newspaper in Cleveland. "I was born in Poland as Stella Walasiewicz," she once said, "and came to this country in the arms of my mother at the age of ten months. Almost since then, I have been running—in streets, playgrounds, and high school gymnasiums. I like competition. I must have inherited it from my mother and my maternal grandfather." (When he was 70, her grandfather challenged the young girl to a dash around the family barn, and Stella had to push hard to beat him.) Stella's mother encouraged her daughter's athletic skills, and her training was intense. In 1930, she commented:

> My stride had to be built up step by step. I began with a simple exercise—which I still do about ten times a day for four minutes

at a time—merely raising my knee straight up until it almost hits my chin, and then snapping the lower part of the leg up and out as far as I can. It's extremely simple, but it works. It develops the hip muscles, loosens them, and helps develop that long, high stride.

In the early years of the 20th century, track and field was not considered an appropriate area of athletic competition for women. When the first 800-meter race for women was held at the 1928 Amsterdam Olympics, **Lina Radke** won in world-record time (2:16.8), but *The New York Times*, convinced that the decision to permit women to compete in such events was idiotic, reported: "At the finish six of the runners were completely exhausted and fell headlong to the ground" while "eleven wretched women" were strewn about the cinder track. This was the mindset that greeted the 19-year-old Walsh when she burst onto the American track-and-field scene that same year, competing in the (otherwise) all-male Melrose Games at New York's Madison Square Garden. The 16,000 spectators

Stella Walsh (left), with Canadian Hilde Strike and American Wilhelmina Von Bremen, 1932.

were stunned and thrilled when the young woman from Cleveland ran the 50-yard dash in 6.1 seconds, breaking a world record. Stella Walsh was named outstanding performer of the Melrose Games. Soon known as "the Polish Flyer," she would be a bright star in the sports world for years to come.

Walsh also threw the discus, a sport which brought her headlines three years later. During the discus throw at a 1931 track-and-field meet in New Jersey, members of the crowd—some 15,000 strong—pressed closer and closer to the contestants. As Walsh prepared to make her throw, the discus slipped from her hand and struck an onlooker who had gotten too close. Knocked unconscious, he was taken by ambulance to a nearby hospital while the park commissioner threatened to arrest her immediately. Cooler heads prevailed, and Walsh was permitted to defend her title in the 220-yard dash. She won the event before being taken into custody ("Stella Walsh, Star Sprinter, Is Arrested in Jersey City as Platter Fells a Man," trumpeted a headline on the sports page of *The New York Times*). The matter was swiftly dropped.

In 1932, on her 21st birthday, Walsh applied for citizenship, and Americans looked forward to her competing as an American in that year's Los Angeles Olympics. Then economics came into play. Participation in Olympic competition hinged on an athlete's conformance to a very strict definition of "amateur" status—athletes who attempted to support themselves through sports-related jobs were not allowed to compete—and the Great Depression was in full swing. Walsh had been supporting herself by working as a filing clerk for the New York Central Railroad, but her department was suddenly shut down and she was out of a job. Although the city of Cleveland offered her work in its Municipal Recreation Department, she had to decline; such a job would have meant she was a "professional sportswoman" and ineligible for the Games. The strictures of this rule made life extremely difficult for athletes like Walsh who came from poor families. Thus, when she appeared in federal court to take her oath of allegiance on July 9, 1932, the last step in becoming an American citizen, she sadly refused. Her trainer, Dan Griffin, pleaded with her, but could not change her mind. On July 12, she announced that she had accepted a job with the Polish Consulate in New York, as a Polish citizen, and would compete for that country in the Olympics.

In the 1932 Games, America's loss was Poland's gain. Walsh captured the 100-meter race with a time of 11.9 seconds. In taking the gold medal, she beat Canadian **Hilde Strike** and American **Wilhelmina Von Bremen**. She also finished 6th in the discus throw with 100'3". After her triumph at the Games, Walsh competed throughout Europe while studying at the Physical Culture Institute in Warsaw. Despite her decision to run for Poland, Americans continued to regard Walsh as one of their own, referring to her as "the girl from Cleveland." She made the headlines again early in January 1934: "Stella Walsh Injures Foot; Athletic Career Imperiled," announced *The New York Times*. The newspaper reported that Walsh had "dislocated or broken a joint in her foot" while skiing in the Carpathian Mountains. Two weeks later, accounts were more optimistic: she had "twisted her ankle" but was "entirely recovered." Just before leaving Poland to sail to New York, she was received by Poland's President Ignacy Moscicki, a sign that Poles, like Americans, continued to regard her as their own.

That year, Walsh clocked a world record of 7.2 seconds in the 60-yard dash at the Polish Falcon Athletic Club Games in Brooklyn, New York. By now there was a new American track star competing against the Polish Flyer—*Helen Stephens, a high school sensation from Missouri. The rivalry between Walsh and Stephens remained a hot topic on sports pages throughout the nation. At the 1935 AAU indoor meet, Stephens beat Walsh in the 50-yard dash, a blow to Walsh who held women's world records in the 60-, 80-, and 100-meter dashes and was considered a "near champion" in hurling the discus. The year brought other problems as well: the old specter of losing her amateur status loomed once more. The AAU suspended Walsh from competition for 30 days because she had played with an amateur girls' basketball team in Buffalo, New York, on January 27, 1935. The women's game had preceded a professional contest, and the AAU forbade any amateur to "participate on the same program with professionals." This narrow interpretation of the rule angered Walsh who told reporters, "I didn't know there was such a rule. I didn't know my amateur standing was in danger. If I wanted to turn professional, I could have done it long ago—and made plenty of money." Since the rule had been adopted only the month before, Walsh was let off "lightly."

The rivalry between Walsh and Stephens continued as the 1936 Olympics loomed. On May 4, 1935, Walsh broke the women's national AAU record for the 70-yard distance with a time of 8.2 seconds, clipping two-tenths of a second off the old mark. That same day, Stephens ran the 50-meter dash in 5.9 seconds, bettering the listed women's world record. Since the race had been held without starting blocks, a common practice at the time, the record was not recognized, but the feat demonstrated that Stephens was hot on Walsh's heels. The press was hoping for a rematch at the AAU outdoor meet the following month, but Walsh refused to compete, claiming she was "concentrating on her studies at Notre Dame Academy." Stephens ran the 100 meters in 11.8 seconds, besting Walsh's previous record of 11.9 in St. Louis on June 1. At the Northeastern Ohio AAU meet one week later, Walsh also ran the 100 meters in 11.8 and ran the 220-yard race in 0:24.3 seconds, bettering the accepted women's world record. Americans followed the competition between the two women runners with great interest. Walsh was scheduled to compete again for Poland in the upcoming Olympics, and Stephens would be running for America; there was much speculation on the potential outcome.

The 1936 Berlin Olympics, held in Nazi Germany, were controversial for many reasons. Some felt the Nazis were using the event for propaganda purposes. Many others felt that Adolf Hitler had brought order and economic prosperity to Germany, and regarded charges of anti-Semitism as attempts to tarnish these accomplishments. There were several skirmishes over participation in the Games by Jewish athletes. Although the American Olympic Committee did protest when *Helene Mayer, the German fencing star, was not allowed to enter the Games because she was half Jewish, the Nazis' eventual decision to allow her to participate was generally held as proof that they were not serious racists. Walsh would have none of this whitewashing. Conditions for Jews in Germany, she told reporters, were "very bad indeed." She witnessed racism firsthand when a Jewish woman on the national Polish team was insulted. Unlike others, Walsh did not duck the controversy: "I hate to see politics mixed with sport," she said. "Like every other athlete, I'd hate to have anything prevent the Olympic Games. I hope things can be straightened out. Yes there are anti-Jewish signs up. The Jews have to compete against themselves in their own clubs. The press smooths things over now." But at a time when the world press minimized the actions committed by the Nazis, Walsh was in the minority in her determination to speak out against the Third Reich.

In Berlin, Walsh was forced to concentrate on her chief rival, Helen Stephens. Although the star of the Polish team ran her fastest time in the 100 meters, clocking in at 11.7, Stephens took

the gold medal with a time of 11.5; Walsh had to be content with the silver. After the Games, she continued to compete in Europe until World War II forced her return to the United States. Although she was in her 30s, she gave no thought to retiring and, during the 1940s, dominated AAU competition.

> The Athletic Congress unanimously passed a resolution saying accusations that Walsh was a man are inaccurate.
>
> —*Atlanta Journal and Constitution*, December 7, 1991

In 1947, Walsh finally became an American citizen. When Poland became a Communist country, she refused to represent its government as an athlete. In 1953, at age 42, she entered the western regional meet of the Women's National AAU pentathlon. Although she was considered well past her prime, she won the five-event competition with a record-breaking performance. At age 44, Walsh petitioned the Olympic Committee to allow her to compete as an American in the 1956 Olympics. Told she was ineligible because she previously had competed for Poland, she threatened to retire unless she were permitted to try out. But she failed to qualify for the team in 1956, and again in 1960 when she was almost 50. "Every year I think of retiring," the perennial contender explained, "but I get out on the track with the youngsters and want to run myself." Like her grandfather who could sprint around the barn at age 70, Walsh retained her athletic abilities as she grew older. When she finally retired, she had accumulated 1,100 trophies in her 30-year career and captured 25 outdoor AAU titles in the 100-yard dash, 220-yard dash, and the long dash.

Athletic competition was never easy for Walsh, and the economic aspects of remaining an amateur athlete were especially difficult. She was forced to support herself at non-sports-related jobs for most of her life. For many years, she eked out a living by writing for a Polish newspaper in Cleveland. In the 1970s, Mayor George Voinovich recognized Walsh as a "Cleveland institution" and decided it was time for the city to pay for her many talents. She was placed in charge of organizing track and field and other women's sports for the Cleveland recreation program, a position that finally gave her financial independence after many years of near poverty.

Stella Walsh had all but disappeared from the country's media when her untimely death received coverage nationwide. On the night of December 4, 1980, she had gone shopping at a local discount store to buy ribbons for a welcoming ceremony for the Polish Olympic women's basketball team, scheduled to play at Kent State University the following week. The store was robbed at gunpoint while she was there, and Walsh was caught in the crossfire. Found lying next to her car, she was rushed to St. Alexis Hospital with a bullet wound to her abdomen. She died during surgery, at the age of 69. Lauded in Cleveland for her many accomplishments, Walsh was buried with honors. Unfortunately, her death caused far more controversy than she had ever known in life.

During her career, Walsh was sometimes accused of being a man. She was not alone, as many female athletes with muscles, slim hips, or a physical shape that was not considered "feminine" faced the same allegation. Such accusations were routine during a period when women were thought incapable of competing successfully in athletics, and continue to surface on occasion up to this day. As a matter of fact, however, the one imposter known to have competed in the Games, a man named Hermann Ratjen who called himself Dora while representing Nazi Germany in the high jump during the same 1936 Games that Walsh competed in, did not win a medal.

The coroner's report filed after Walsh's autopsy fed the old rumors about her, for Cuyahoga County coroner Samuel R. Gerber revealed that Walsh had had underdeveloped, non-functioning male sex organs. She had been born with what the medical world terms an "intersex state," and a genetic makeup of one X and one Y chromosome. While women as a general rule have two X chromosomes and men have one X and one Y chromosome, on occasion (less infrequently than might be thought) babies are born with some other combination of chromosomes. This genetic condition, known as "mosaicism," affects the sexual organs and the body's development to varying degrees; in some cases it may be apparent immediately or by puberty, while in others it is detectable only by genetic testing or surgery. In Walsh's case, apparently, her male genitalia were so underdeveloped that her parents, who always considered her female, the man to whom she was briefly married, and she herself never realized her condition.

In 1991, 11 years after Walsh's death, The Athletic Congress (TAC), which is the governing body of U.S. track and field, addressed the question of her gender. **Roxanne Atkins Andersen**, a Canadian who had been an Olympic hurdler in the 1936 Games, felt that Walsh had been a man

and should be stripped of her titles and Olympic medals. "She ran like a man," said Andersen. "She was muscled all over, very slim and trim in the hips." The key issue was whether Walsh's condition gave her an advantage as an athlete because she produced male hormones such as testosterone which increases muscle mass. Dr. **Mona Shangold**, a sports gynecology expert, maintained that Walsh's condition gave her no unfair advantage. Walsh's old rival Helen Stephens said, "I don't think she was a man. . . . I don't think she had any advantage. Let bygones be bygones. Let the woman rest." Walsh's ex-husband Harry Olson also defended her, noting that he had never noticed her condition when they were intimate (though they had always turned out the lights). He continued, "People in Cleveland seem torn between loving her and destroying her. All of this vicious energy should have been organized toward finding her murderer." Many in Cleveland stuck up for Walsh. One of them noted, "She trained children until her dying day. You can just imagine what her medals meant to her. She was so honored, she worked hard for it." In the end, Walsh's accomplishments stood this trial by fire. Andersen withdrew her motion to strip the athlete of her medals, and The Athletic Congress unanimously passed a resolution declaring that the accusations about Walsh were inaccurate.

Stella Walsh faced many obstacles during her life, including economic hardship, immigrant status, sex discrimination, and ageism, but she never stopped fighting. When a stray bullet ended her life prematurely, she was subjected to further indignity for a condition over which she had no control and may have had no knowledge. As is so often the case, the public was all too willing to dismiss her achievements. In more than one contemporary history, she is written off as a male imposter. In *Olympics Factbook* it states blandly, "Walsh's story came to a tragic end—and her record was amended—when she was caught in the middle of a holdup; the post-shooting autopsy revealed that Stella Walsh was a man." The highly respected *Women's Sports* by Allen Guttmann also continues to perpetuate the all-black, all-white approach. Discussing an international competition held in France, Guttmann wrote: "The brightest star of the individual events was Poland's Stanislava Walaciewicz, subsequently known in the United States as Stella Walsh. She won three gold medals for races over 60, 100, and 200 meters. (Decades later, alas, an autopsy revealed that Stella Walsh was a man.)" Reputation muddied, laurels tarnished, she is slowly being dropped from sports compilations, as if she were an embarrassment better left unheralded. (In the meantime, her story is frequently cited in the growing field of gender studies.) This is grossly unfair, because Stella Walsh was one of the 20th century's most talented women runners. A phenomenal athlete who set numerous world records, she deserves a permanent place in the starting lineup of the history of sports.

SOURCES:

"A.A.U. Suspends Miss Walsh for 30 Days for Appearing on Same Program With Pros," in *The New York Times.* February 16, 1935, p. 17.

"Cinder Path Sisters," in *Newsweek.* Vol. 16, no. 3. July 15, 1940, pp. 45–46.

"Discus Hits Onlooker; Woman Athlete Held. Stella Walsh, Star Sprinter, Is Arrested in Jersey City as Platter Fells Man," in *The New York Times.* July 26, 1931, p. 25.

Guttmann, Allen. *Women's Sports.* NY: Columbia University Press, 1991.

Hornbuckle, Adam R. Porter. "Walsh, Stella 'The Polish Flyer,'" in *Biographical Dictionary of American Sports: Outdoor Sports.* Edited by David L. Porter. NY: Greenwood Press, 1988.

"Intersex States," in *The Merck Manual of Diagnosis and Therapy.* 15th ed. Rahway, NJ: Merck, 1987.

McMillen, Larry. "A Question of Gender," in *New Orleans Times-Picayune.* December 5, 1991.

———. "Stella Walsh to Maintain Sprint Marks," in *New Orleans Times-Picayune.* December 7, 1991.

"Missouri Girl Ties World Dash Mark," in *The New York Times.* June 2, 1935, section V, p. 4.

"Miss Walsh Breaks U.S. 70-Yard Mark," in *The New York Times.* May 5, 1935, section V, p. 4.

"Miss Walsh Clips Mark," in *The New York Times.* June 10, 1935, p. 24.

"Miss Walsh Denies Reports of 'Run-Out'; Track Star Will Sail for Poland Today," in *The New York Times.* June 19, 1935, p. 26.

"Miss Walsh, Given Job in Polish Consulate, To Represent Native Land in the Olympics," in *The New York Times.* July 13, 1932, p. 21.

"Miss Walsh Refuses Citizenship Papers; Remains Ineligible for U.S. Olympic Team," in *The New York Times.* July 9, 1932, p. 14.

"Miss Walsh Ties Marks," in *The New York Times.* July 28, 1936, p. 12.

"Moscicki Sees Stella Walsh," in *The New York Times.* October 19, 1933, p. 21.

Olympics Factbook. Detroit, MI: Visible Ink Press, 1992, p. 528.

"Poland Honors Miss Walsh," in *The New York Times.* June 23, 1934, p. 7.

"Report Says Stella Walsh Had Male Sex Organs," in *The New York Times.* January 23, 1981, p. 18.

Rosen, Karen. "Gender of '32 Gold Medalist To Be Debated," in *Atlanta Constitution.* December 5, 1991.

———. "TAC Finds No Evidence That Female Winner Was A Man," in *Atlanta Journal Constitution.* December 7, 1991.

"Stella Walsh Again Training; Recovered From Ankle Injury," in *The New York Times.* February 10, 1933, p. 20.

"Stella Walsh Injures Foot; Athletic Career Imperiled," in *The New York Times.* January 22, 1933, p. 5.

"Stella Walsh Is Freed on Charge," in *The New York Times.* October 11, 1944, p. 22.

"Stella Walsh Slain. Olympic Track Star," in *The New York Times Biographical Service.* December 1980, pp. 1825–1826.

"Takes Citizenship Step. Miss Walsh, Sprint Star, Applies for Papers on 21st Birthday," in *The New York Times.* April 8, 1932, p. 29.

"Track Star Asks Ruling," in *The New York Times.* October 15, 1955, p. 11.

"2 Charged in Ohio Murder," in *The New York Times.* May 28, 1983, section I, p. 6.

Von Stein, Josef W. "Breaking Records is Stella's Favorite Indoor Sport," in *The American Magazine.* Vol. 110, no. 4. October 1930, pp. 71–72.

"Walasiewicz-Olson, Stanislawa," in *Wielka Encyklopedia Powszechna.* Warsaw: Panstwowe Wydawnictwo Naukowe, 1969.

"Woman Athlete Here Fears Anti-Semitism. Stella Walsh, Polish Champion, Tells of German Insult to Jewish Girl at Meet," in *The New York Times.* October 23, 1935, p. 9.

Karin Loewen Haag,
freelance writer,
Athens, Georgia

Walsingham, Frances (d. 1631)

Countess of Essex. Name variations: Frances Devereux. Interred on February 17, 1631, at Tonbridge Church; daughter of Francis Walsingham and **Ursula St. Barbe**; *married Sir Philip Sidney; married Robert Devereux, 2nd earl of Essex, in 1590; married Richard de Burgh, 4th earl of Clanricarde, before April 8, 1603; children: (first marriage) Elizabeth Sidney; (second marriage)* ***Frances Devereux** (d. 1674);* **Robert Devereux** *(b. 1591), 3rd/20th earl of essex;* **Dorothy Devereux** *(d. 1636, who married Henry Shirley, Bt. 2nd); (third marriage)* **Honora de Burgh**.

Walter, Cornelia Wells (1813–1898)

American journalist. Born on June 7, 1813, in Boston, Massachusetts; died on January 31, 1898, in Boston; daughter of Lynde Walter and Ann (Minshull) Walter; married William Bordman Richards (an iron and steel dealer), on September 22, 1847 (died 1877); children: Annie (died at age three); Elise Bordman (b. 1848); twins (b. 1853) Walter (died at six months) and William Reuben; and possibly one other child.

A woman known for her warmth and beauty, Cornelia Walter entered the field of journalism when she took over her older brother Lynde Minshull Walter's position as editor at the *Boston Transcript* after his death in 1842. The quality of her work and her sharp mind earned her the admiration of her peers. A crisp writing style characterized Walter's columns about

Boston social and literary life. She spoke boldly through her pen in opposition to female suffrage, unorthodox religious theories, the Mexican War, and the annexation of Texas, and in support of higher education for women. She also traded snide barbs with author Edgar Allan Poe. Upon her marriage in 1847, however, she retired as editor and devoted herself to domestic duties, thereafter contributing occasionally to the *Transcript*. That same year, Walter published a history of Cambridge's famous cemetery, *Mount Auburn Illustrated*. She died at age 84 in 1898.

SOURCES:

Sicherman, Barbara, and Carol Hurd Green, eds. *Notable American Women: The Modern Period*. Cambridge, MA: The Belknap Press of Harvard University, 1980.

Jacquie Maurice,
freelance writer,
Calgary, Alberta, Canada

Walter, Judith (1845–1917).

See Gautier, Judith.

Walter, Lucy (c. 1630–1658)

Welsh mistress of Charles II. Name variations: Mrs. Barlow or Lucy Barlow; incorrectly Lucy Walters and Lucy Waters. Born around 1630 in Paris, France; died in 1658 in Paris; daughter of Richard Walter of Haverfordwest; mistress of Colonel Robert Sidney, in 1644; mistress of Charles II (1630–1685), king of England (r. 1661–1685), from 1648 to 1650; mistress of Henry Bennet, in 1650; children: (with Charles II) James Crofts Scott, duke of Monmouth (April 9, 1649–1685); possibly Mary Crofts (b. May 6, 1651, who married William Sarsfield).

Lucy Walter, also known as Mrs. Barlow and sometimes incorrectly as Lucy Walters or Lucy Waters, had gone to The Hague in 1644 and been a colonel's mistress there before becoming the famed mistress of England's King Charles II between 1648 and 1650. In 1649, she gave birth to Charles' illegitimate son, James. James later became the duke of Monmouth and led the unsuccessful Monmouth Rebellion in 1685, after Charles' brother James (II) had been made king. After 1650, Walter became a mistress to a succession of other men. In 1656, she was in Cologne when Charles' friends bribed her to return to England, where she was arrested as a spy and sent back to Holland. She died in Paris two years later. Between 1673 and 1680, it was widely rumored that Charles II had legally married Walter before a cleric and a witness, an allegation he denied with three declarations issued in 1678.

*Elizabeth Goudge wrote a historical novel about Walter, *The Child from the Sea* (1970).

Jacquie Maurice,
freelance writer,
Calgary, Alberta, Canada

Walter-Martin, Steffi

East German Olympic luge champion. Name variations: Steffi Martin.

East Germany's Steffi Walter-Martin had already won a gold medal in the dangerous sport of luge at the 1984 Sarajevo Winter Olympics when she took the 1987 season off to have a child. To the dismay of competitors who hoped she might retire, the defending world champion went immediately back into vigorous training and qualified for the 1988 Winter Olympics in Calgary. There Walter-Martin again took the gold with a time of 3:03.973 while two of her teammates took second and third, maintaining the East Germany domination that had begun with the sport's inception in 1964.

Jacquie Maurice,
freelance writer,
Calgary, Alberta, Canada

Walters, Barbara (1929—)

Award-winning television journalist, particularly known for her celebrity interviews and news specials, who was the first woman to co-host a major network news program. Born on September 25, 1929, in Boston, Massachusetts; daughter of Lou Walters (a show-business entrepreneur) and Dena (Seletsky) Walters; educated in private schools in Florida and New York before graduating from Sarah Lawrence College in 1951 with a degree in English; married Bob Katz (a businessman), in 1955 (divorced 1958); married Lee Gruber (a producer), in 1963 (divorced 1976); married Merv Adelman (a movie studio executive), in 1986 (divorced 1992); children: one adopted daughter, Jacqueline Gruber.

Had first job in broadcasting with WNBC in New York City writing press releases; hired as a writer for "Today" (1961) and eventually given on-screen reporting segments on topics the network deemed of interest to women; improved journalistic fortunes when she became part of the press corps traveling to Egypt with Jacqueline Kennedy (1962); became co-host for "Today" (1974); became the industry's first news anchor to earn a salary of $1 million when she moved to ABC to co-anchor its evening newscast (1976); in the years since, has interviewed everyone from Fidel Castro to Ronald Reagan, co-hosted ABC's long-running *news magazine show "20/20" as well as a string of Barbara Walters Specials and "The View," and has been presented with seven Emmy awards for her work.*

Barbara Walters has always considered the worst moment in her long career of talking to the world's famous and infamous to be her 1977 interview with *Katharine Hepburn, when she asked the now-legendary question, "If you were a tree, what kind of tree would you be?" (Undaunted, Hepburn promptly replied that she would like to be an oak.) But it was typical of Walters that she was more than willing to share the moment with millions of viewers in a 1996 television special looking back over more than 30 years of questioning major world figures and covering the world's most important events. Her formula for a successful interview has remained unchanged. "I want to know what *everyone* wants to know," she says.

Walters had been used to being around famous people even before she was old enough to frame a question. Her father Lou Walters was a show-business entrepreneur successful enough to afford the 18-room house in Newton, Massachusetts, in which Barbara, the second of his two daughters, was born on September 25, 1929. Lou had married **Dena Seletsky (Walters)** in 1920 just as he opened his first booking agency. The couple's first daughter, **Jacqueline Walters**, had been diagnosed with moderate mental retardation shortly after her birth in 1926, but the Walters Booking Agency's prosperous early years assured good care for Jacqueline and a comfortable home for Barbara. Even the stock market crash of 1929 couldn't keep Lou Walters down, for he soon parlayed a job managing a Boston restaurant into enough investment capital to open the first of his legendary Latin Quarter nightclubs. Stars from Maurice Chevalier to Jimmy Durante dandled young Barbara on their knees during visits to the Walters' new home in affluent Brookline, Massachusetts. Admitting years later that her father's business embarrassed her when she entered Lawrence Elementary School, Barbara kept to herself and conscientiously did her homework backstage at the Latin Quarter at night. Still, she later credited Lou Walters with her success. "He was sensitive, amusing, utterly cultivated, charming, never without a book," she said shortly after her father's death in 1977. "If I have any writing ability, I get it from him."

The mercurial fortunes of her father's business interests only added to Barbara's early sense of isolation. After he moved his family to Palm Island, Florida, to open a second Latin Quarter in 1940, she spent several years in what was then a rural suburb of Miami with few other children, driven to a private school by a chauffeur each morning; two years later, she was living in New York City, where Lou Walters opened a third Latin Quarter, and attending an exclusive girls' school. By the time she was ready for tenth grade, Walters was whisked back to Miami as her father planned the expansion of that city's Latin Quarter, only to return to New York in a matter of months when her father's gambling debts and mismanaged finances forced the closing of the Boston and Florida clubs. Still, there was enough money to enroll Barbara in Manhattan's prestigious Birch Walthen School for Girls, where her academic performance was to such a high standard that she was accepted on graduation to Sarah Lawrence College, then a revolutionary experiment in education in which exceptionally gifted students designed their own curricula and study plans under the guidance of a faculty adviser. Although Walters studied theater during her years at Sarah Lawrence and appeared without much success in a school production of Sean O'Casey's *Juno and the Paycock*, her talents seemed more suited to the printed page. She served as the drama critic for her school's newspaper, attracting attention for perceptive reviews of both Broadway and Off-Broadway productions. There was a lively social life at Sarah Lawrence, too, Walters emerging from her shell to host parties at her parents' New York apartment and theater evenings with friends. But it wasn't the theater or a newspaper that provided her first paying job on her graduation in 1951 with a degree in English. It was the relatively new medium of television.

Walters had the good fortune to enter the business just as America was beginning its love affair with TV, the bulky boxes inhabiting a corner of the living room in 90% of American homes by 1950. There were no women holding important positions in the industry at the time, and Walters' first job was a modest one writing press releases for NBC's New York affiliate. It would not be until 1964 that *Marlene Sanders would become the first woman to host a nightly news program, and even then only for one appearance when the regular, male anchor had fallen ill. Despite the unfavorable atmosphere, Walters was offered the chance to produce a daily children's show for WNBC less than two years after joining the staff. "Ask the Camera" was a live, 15-minute program that was canceled after a year, but the experience paid off in 1955 when CBS hired Walters for the staff of its new "Morning Show," planned as a competitor to

NBC's more established "Today." Although she had been hired as a researcher and talent coordinator, Walters made her network debut during a fashion segment she produced for the program, filling in for a model who failed to appear. "She always knew she wanted to be in front of the camera," one of her co-workers later said, and the "Morning Show"'s producers seemed to agree with Walters once they saw her on-screen. Further on-camera assignments dealing with "women's issues" followed. "I never minded doing the so-called female things—the fashion shows, cooking spots, whatever," Walters told a magazine reporter many years later. "But at the same time, it bothered me that I wasn't allowed to participate in a Washington interview." The same year she began work for the "Morning Show" on CBS, Walters married businessman Bob Katz after a short engagement.

Unfortunately, both the job and the marriage were short-lived. Ratings for the "Morning Show" never posed a serious challenge to its competitors, and the show was canceled in 1958, the same year that Walters' divorce from Katz was finalized. Her long days at the network, starting as early as four o'clock in the morning and lasting into the evening, left little time to build a stable marriage. Adding to the turmoil of that year was Lou Walters' bankruptcy after the failure of a new club he had opened in New York, followed by charges of tax evasion filed against him by the IRS. The government eventually confiscated the Walters' sumptuous Florida and New York homes. "I not only had to support myself, but my parents and my sister," Walters recalled in 1982. "I knew I'd have to work all my life so I'd never feel financial pressure." But her initial efforts to find another job in television were unsuccessful, and she was forced to take a job at $60 a week at a public relations firm representing clients to television and film producers. Walters would later characterize the years from 1958 to 1961 as the low point of her fortunes, but a reputation at the firm for probing, incisive interviews with potential clients led the producers of NBC's "Today" to accept her proposal for a 13-week trial period.

By 1961, "Today" was entering its ninth year as America's most popular morning television program, and the training ground for journalists such as John Chancellor, Frank Blair, **Jane Pauley** and Walters' eventual co-host for "20/20," Hugh Downs. Barbara's skill as a writer and her on-air presence proved NBC's gamble well worthwhile. Within a year, she was given her first major assignment as part of the press corps traveling to Egypt in 1962 with then-first lady *Jacqueline Kennedy. Walters followed the tour with a well-received article for *Good Housekeeping* on Jackie Kennedy's sister **Lee Radziwell** and interviewed Jackie's official biographer, **Joan Braden**, on "Today." There quickly followed two developments that firmly established the name Barbara Walters in the public mind. The first was John Chancellor's replacement in 1962 as host on "Today" by Hugh Downs. Downs became Walters' staunchest ally in the internal politics of the show and soon convinced the show's producers to try Barbara out as a "'Today' girl," the attractive young lady who delivered weather reports and engaged in occasional banter with the host. The second development came on the day assigned for Walters' trial run for the job, November 22, 1963, when President John Kennedy was assassinated in Dallas, Texas. As the "Today" staff scrambled to cover the tragedy, Walters found herself thrust into the spotlight, staying on the air and on-camera for five consecutive hours fielding reports from journalists in Dallas and in Washington and interviewing without preparation government officials and other important figures. Her cool professionalism in the midst of the country's grief and anger assured her future. By 1964, Walters was no longer a "'Today' girl" but a full-fledged reporter on America's most popular daytime network news show.

Her expertise in the art of the intimate interview quickly drew comparisons to Edward R. Murrow's esteemed "Person to Person" interviews of the late 1950s. Walters merely claimed that she asked her subjects the kinds of things everyone wanted to know, rather than engaging in a show of intellectual gamesmanship; and while she conversed easily with some of the world's most famous people, from Hollywood stars to international jetsetters, her choice of subject material also included stories on anti-Semitic housing practices in Michigan, conditions in a women's prison in Maryland, and the life of a cloistered nun. Most famously, she enrolled in Hugh Hefner's Playboy Bunny training program and reported on the working conditions in Hefner's vast empire of Playboy clubs. She fearlessly descended into a dark Welsh coal mine when the two male reporters traveling with her refused, and so completely won the trust of Dean Rusk, Lyndon Johnson's secretary of state during that administration's tortured Vietnam War experience, that the time he devoted to her interview was broadcast in a three-part series. "If any NBC vice-president gives you a hard time, show them this letter and tell them to leave you alone," Rusk wrote to her.

Opposite page
ℬarbara
𝒲alters

Not everyone shared Rusk's enthusiasm, for there were frequent complaints from within the network and from reporters for other networks—most of them male—of Walters' ruthless pursuit of a story and the demands she placed on the assistants and technicians who worked with her. The trust placed in her by the notoriously press-hostile Richard Nixon, and her inclusion as one of only three reporters allowed to travel with him during Nixon's ground-breaking visit to China in 1972, only increased the animosity of some of her peers. Walters never apologized for her determination to get her story or denied that she demanded only the best from her co-workers; and there were an equal number of stories about her motherly treatment of the growing retinue that traveled with her—of the best doctors sought to treat crew members who fell ill on the road, of the small gifts given in appreciation of hard work, of the praise for a job well done passed on to network executives.

The 1960s brought changes in Walters' personal life, too. In 1961, she had met through mutual friends theater producer Lee Gruber. She and Gruber married two years later and, after three attempts to have a child ended in miscarriages, adopted a baby girl they named after Barbara's sister Jacqueline in 1968. "I wanted a child very, very badly," Walters told *McCall's* a year after the adoption. "You have to want a child very badly if you're in this business. Jacqueline has been the home. She is what makes it a home." But Walters made it plain that she had no intention of sacrificing her career to child-rearing. She resumed her normal schedule at the network soon after the adoption, relying on nannies and cooks for support while she once again made the nation sit up and take notice with her frank discussion of birth control on an NBC special in 1969, "From Here to the Seventies," and by publishing the bestselling book *How to Talk to Practically Anybody about Practically Anything* in 1970. The following year, Walters added to her "Today" schedule by taking over hosting duties on "For Women Only," a morning chat show on the network's New York affiliate, WNBC-TV, taping a week's worth of shows in one night before a live audience while reporting to work on "Today" before dawn each morning. Walters pointedly renamed the show "Not For Women Only" and expanded its content to include discussions of such then-controversial issues as marijuana use and the growing feminist movement. The show's ratings tripled within six months as *The New York Times* called it "one of the most improved and provocative shows in the entire early morning

schedule." Walters stayed with "Not For Women Only" for four years, then left the show for the biggest promotion of her career to date.

It was well known that Walters' relations with "Today"'s host Frank McGee were as icy as her relationship with Hugh Downs had been warm. McGee's resentment of Walters' skills made itself apparent whenever the two of them conducted an interview together on the show. Walters was allowed to ask a question only after McGee had asked the first three, and McGee flatly refused to allow her access to any interviews with political figures. Barbara retaliated by threatening to leave the show unless the network agreed to a contract clause that gave her the co-host slot should McGee leave the show. Given her popularity and ratings, NBC had no choice; and when McGee died of bone cancer in 1974, the network dutifully made Walters the first female co-host of a major network news program in television history. She was joined by Jim Hartz, with whom she established a cordial relationship both on and off camera, while NBC made sure to point out to an audience in the throes of a vocal feminist movement that "Today" was the only show on television with a female co-host. Walters' ascendancy was confirmed a year after she assumed her new role when she was awarded her first Emmy as Outstanding Host in a Talk, Service or Variety Series, was named Broadcaster of the Year by the International Radio and Television Society, and was included among *Time*'s 100 most influential Americans of 1975.

> *You're a marvelous girl, but stay out of television.*
>
> —ABC producer Don Hewitt to Barbara Walters, 1957

Walters' heightened celebrity did not come without a price. Her ten-year marriage to Lee Gruber came to an end when the couple separated in 1973 and formally divorced five years later; and the network's high expectations for her were dashed when, despite her popularity, "Today"'s ratings began a precipitous slide during 1975. Although she and Hartz worked well together, there seemed little personal dynamism between them on-camera and audiences found the pair rather boring. Further troubles ensued when Walters convinced the network to produce a lavish afternoon special for the soap opera audience called "Barbara Walters Visits the Royal Lovers," an outgrowth of a "Today" segment she had done on the marriage of Britain's Princess *Anne. Although it was the first of

what would become a distinguished line of "Barbara Walters Specials," the show was a ratings and review disaster. Given all these factors, NBC balked at Walters' conditions for her contract renewal in 1976, which included a substantial salary increase and complete autonomy from network control over the content and topics of her stories. While the contract dispute was the talk of the industry, no one was prepared for what happened next.

ABC's "Evening News" was, at the time, running a distant third in the ratings behind its two older competitors—so distant that ABC executives made the bold decision to make Barbara Walters not only the industry's first woman to co-anchor a nightly newscast but the first network on-camera professional, male or female, to be paid an annual salary of $1 million. Walters' decision to accept ABC's offer to join Harry Reasoner for such an unprecedented amount of money on its nightly newscast stunned the broadcasting industry. Walters received her own office staff, wardrobe and makeup artists, as well as first-class tickets and luxury accommodations while traveling. For her part, Barbara would not only co-anchor the evening news with Reasoner five nights a week, but would appear on a dozen programs of ABC's weekly current-events series "Issues and Answers" and host four "Barbara Walters Specials" each year. Even more shocking to the industry's old guard was the fact that Walters' huge salary would be split between the network's news and entertainment divisions, an uncomfortable blurring of the line between the two. CBS' Walter Cronkite complained of a "sickening sensation that we are all going under, that all of our efforts to hold television news aloof from show business have failed." Even the solid support given to her by *The New York Times* began to slip when the newspaper published a feature article titled "Is Barbara Walters Worth a Million?" Barbara was further stung by Harry Reasoner's disapproval of the network's decision to hire her, a decision Reasoner regarded as nothing more than "a stunt" to boost ratings and which he worried would reduce the quality of the "hard news" content at the expense of Walters' emphasis on human interest stories. Others complained of reverse sexism, pointing out that Reasoner was paid a fifth of the salary given to Walters (although ABC raised the amount to $500,000 when Barbara was hired). As if to taunt her even further, NBC's comedy show "Saturday Night Live" regularly began to feature *Gilda Radner's "Baba Wawa," lampooning Barbara's trademark Boston accent and lisp. Walters' supporters amid the furor ranged from John Wayne ("Don't let the bastards get you down," he wrote to her) to then-President Gerald Ford's economic adviser Allen Greenspan, to the millions of fans who wrote to her offering encouragement.

Walters debuted on the "ABC Evening News" on October 4, 1976, and at first it seemed as if the network's gamble had paid off; ratings after the first week rose by an impressive 2%. But after two months, they had fallen back to their pre-Walters levels and ABC once again found its evening newscast in third place, as it struggled to smooth the increasingly tense relations between its new star and Harry Reasoner. The dislike grew so strong that the two refused to sit near each other during public appearances and sat so far apart on the "Evening News" set that the network was obliged to use separate cameras to cover them individually and never showed them together in the same frame. "Harry Reasoner . . . seems as comfortable on camera with Barbara Walters as a governor under indictment," *New Republic* reported, while Walters herself later described her time on the "Evening News" as "the worst period in my professional life." Even her first ABC Special in 1976 drew professional ridicule for her questions to successful presidential candidate Jimmy Carter (especially Walters' curiosity about the Carters' sleeping arrangements and whether they would take one bed or two from their Georgia home to the White House) and her melodramatic conclusion to the interview as she pleaded with Carter to "be wise with us . . . be good to us" as president. In a trend that has marked the rest of her career, the program was criticized by her journalistic peers while at the same time scoring high ratings with her audience.

There were moments, however, when Walters' news instincts seemed to triumph over her interest in her subjects' love lives and domestic arrangements. Interviewing Fidel Castro while the two of them bumped through the Cuban countryside in a Jeep, Walters suddenly interrupted her questions about his marriages and his cigar-smoking to ask pointed questions about the Cuban military's presence in strife-torn Angola; and her hard-edged questions to Egypt's president Anwar Sadat earlier that same year later led to Sadat's acceptance of Walters' invitation to be jointly interviewed with Israeli Prime Minister Menachem Begin during Sadat's historic visit to Jerusalem in 1977. But even Barbara's high-profile interviews couldn't save ABC's evening news program from the animosity between her and Reasoner, forcing the network to hire a new production team headed by Roone Arledge in January 1978. Arledge's tactic of giving Walters more out-of-studio assignments to keep her away from Reasoner failed to solve the problem, which Reasoner himself solved by resigning later that same year to go to work for CBS. Arledge took advantage of the break to re-style the program as "World News Tonight," with three male co-anchors in New York, Chicago and Washington (Peter Jennings, the New York co-anchor, would later assume solo duties in 1983), while Walters was assigned to a "Special Coverage Desk" in New York. Although it was seen as a demotion by some, Walters claimed the change suited her perfectly. "From the day I was hired, I asked them not to put me on the air *just* to read," she said, and it was true that her new position left her more time for the personal interviews that were her strong point.

Walters was sufficiently comfortable with the new arrangement to renew her contract with ABC in 1981, expanding her presence on the air with more "Barbara Walters Specials" and by co-hosting the network's successful news magazine show, "20/20," with her old friend Hugh Downs. The two comfortably shared the camera on "20/20" until Downs' retirement in 2000. "If Hugh had not fought for my opportunity to appear regularly on 'Today,' I would not have happened in this business," she once said. With Downs' support, Walters chose to emphasize on "20/20" the stories of ordinary people in extraordinary circumstances, saving her celebrity interviews for her specials. Among her subjects on "20/20" have been **Jean Harris,** imprisoned for shooting to death her lover; tennis great Arthur Ashe, who publicly acknowledged to Walters his infection with AIDS in an interview in the mid-1980s; and Dr. Jack Kevorkian, whose advocacy and public practice of assisted suicide made him one of the most controversial figures of late-20th-century America.

Walters was herself embroiled in controversy over her unwitting involvement in the Iran-Contra scandal of 1986, in which the Reagan Administration was suspected of trading arms destined for anti-government rebels in Nicaragua for the release of American hostages held by Iranian revolutionaries. Walters had interviewed the two major figures in the story, Saudi Arabian business executive Adnan Khashoggi and an Iranian arms dealer named Manuchar Ghorbanifar. After her interview with Ghorbanifar, Walters rashly agreed to deliver to the White House what Ghorbanifar claimed were highly secret documents detailing payments made to Iranian arms suppliers. She later claimed she had made the decision in the belief that it might help free American hostages held in Teheran, but the news industry and the American public saw it differently. Walters was severely criticized for her personal involvement in what was supposed to be an unbiased news report and for abandoning her journalistic principles to act as a carrier of secret information for the government. ABC admitted she had "violated a literal interpretation of news policy" but refused to take disciplinary action against her. Indeed, it agreed to her contract renewal demands later that same year.

As "20/20"'s ratings climbed to make it one of network television's most popular programs, Walters turned more attention on her personal life. She had met film producer Merv Adelman in 1984 on a blind date arranged by friends; in May 1986, the two were married in a private ceremony in California with her daughter Jacqueline serving as maid of honor. Although neither of them was willing to give up their careers, with Barbara spending most of her time on the East Coast and Adelman remaining in Los Angeles, the marriage managed to survive for four years before the couple announced an amicable separation in 1990 and a divorce in 1992.

Walters' celebrity interviews continue to earn ABC some of its highest ratings of any time period, but Barbara herself began to grow tired of them and stipulated in a contract renewal of the early 1990s that she do fewer of them. Most of the stars, she complained, were only interested in promoting their latest book or movie; it was tremendously difficult to elicit anything of interest from them. "What I hate is the preparation of the questions," she has said. "People say 'Oh, isn't if fun?' It *isn't* fun! [The challenge is to] get them to say something interesting." But her talks with public figures have provided television with some of its most riveting and touching moments. One of her most moving interviews was in September 1995, when Walters talked to actor Christopher Reeve, left paralyzed in a wheelchair from spinal cord injuries after a riding accident, and his wife **Dana**. "She gave us room to express [the despair I once felt] and also to talk about how much joy, hopefulness, laughter and love remain in our life," Reeve later said. The interview raised public awareness and support for research into spinal cord injuries and so touched the nation that Walters was given the prestigious Peabody Award for journalistic excellence for the interview. Her sensitive questioning of former Olympic diving champion Greg Louganis followed in 1996, after Louganis had admitted knowing he was HIV-positive during his gold-medal performance at the 1992 Olympic games. Louganis' discussion of his ho-

mosexuality and his struggles with AIDS under Walters' gentle questioning won the appreciation of the Gay and Lesbian Alliance against Defamation, which awarded her its first Excellence in Media Award. Equally impressive was Walters' interview with Los Angeles attorney **Marcia Clark**, who had been one of the lead prosecutors in California's murder case against O.J. Simpson. Barbara used the interview to explore sexual discrimination in the courtroom and made her audience see Clark's admission to a rehabilitation clinic after the trial was over as a symptom of that discrimination.

By the end of the century, Barbara Walters had become the highest-paid and longest-employed woman in broadcasting, had won seven Emmy Awards, and had become the first woman inducted into the American Academy of Television Arts and Sciences' Hall of Fame. "She is an institution now," ABC's Mike Wallace said of her late in 1999, but Walters has no intention of assuming such an exalted status by retiring from the job that has made her world famous. "With the grace of God and a good lighting director," Walters said in 1996, at the age of 67, "I look forward to doing it for a long time."

SOURCES:
Oppenheimer, Jerry. *Barbara Walters: An Unauthorized Biography*. NY: St. Martin's Press, 1990.
Remstein, Henna. *Barbara Walters*. Philadelphia, PA: Chelsea House, 1999.

Norman Powers,
writer-producer, Chelsea Lane Productions,
New York, New York

Walters, Lucy (c. 1630–1658).

See Walter, Lucy.

Wambaugh, Sarah (1882–1955)

American author, lecturer, and consultant on international affairs. Born on March 6, 1882, in Cincinnati, Ohio; died on November 12, 1955; daughter of Eugene Wambaugh and Anna S. (Hemphill) Wambaugh; graduated from Radcliffe College in Cambridge, Massachusetts, 1902, master's degree, 1917; began graduate study at the London University School of Economics, 1920.

Assistant in history and government at Radcliffe College (1902–06); member of the League of Nations secretariat (1920–21); studied in Europe (1922–c. 1924); worked in Washington, D.C., and Lima, Peru (mid-1920s); awarded the Gold Decoration of the City of Arequipa (1926); became professor of the French-language Academy of International Law in the Netherlands (1927); appointed to help draft regula-

tions for the Saar Plebiscite (1934); lectured at the Institute for Advanced International Studies in Geneva (1935); received honorary doctorate in social sciences from the University of Geneva (1935), LL.D degrees from Ohio State University and Western Reserve University, and an L.H.D. from Tufts University (1935); received Knight's Cross, 1st Class, of the Austrian Order of Merit (1935); received LL.D from Columbia University (1936); named an Officer of the Peruvian Order of the Sun (1937); received LL.D from Russell Sage College (1938); received the Heraldic Order of Christopher Columbus of the Dominican Republic (1940); was technical adviser to 600 Americans designated to observe Greek elections (1946).

Selected works: Monograph on Plebiscites *(1920);* La pratique des plébiscites internationaux *(1928);* Plebiscites Since the World War *(1933);* The Saar Plebiscite *(1940).*

Sarah Wambaugh was born in 1882 in Cincinnati, Ohio. At age ten, she moved to the intensely academic environment of Cambridge, Massachusetts, when her father Eugene Wambaugh, a specialist in constitutional and international law, was appointed to the faculty at Harvard Law School. After graduating from Radcliffe College in 1902 and later working as an assistant there, she earned her master's degree in international law and political science in 1917.

Following World War I, some plebiscites (a direct vote by an entire people on an important issue) were held in disputed border territories. Looking for authoritative books on the subject, Wambaugh could find only one thin, turn-of-the-century French volume, written by a citizen of Alsace. So in 1920, while doing graduate work in London, Wambaugh published a comprehensive study on the topic, *Monograph on Plebiscites,* for the Carnegie Endowment for International Peace. It became the standard text on the subject of plebiscites and was widely used in foreign offices as well as at the U.S. Department of State.

That same year, Wambaugh took an opportunity to substitute temporarily for an American member of the League of Nations, and relocated with the League from London to Geneva. There she found working with people from all over the world extremely engaging, writing in an article, "Greek, Serb, Dane, Briton, Spaniard, so they were. . . . [I]n a few weeks they had become to me just so many interesting, courteous, and friendly men and women, working unselfconsciously together for a common purpose for a common cause." After teaching for a semester at Wellesley College, in 1922 Wambaugh again left

the United States and traveled across Europe studying postwar plebiscites. In 1924, the ardent student of politics returned to her favorite place to study and work: the League of Nations in Geneva. There she served as an expert advisor on the Saar Basin and the Free City of Danzig (now Gdansk).

In 1925–26, Wambaugh served again as an expert advisor, this time to the Peruvian government on the Tacna-Arica plebiscite, and she divided her time between Lima, Peru, and Washington, D.C. Following this position, in 1927 she became a professor at an academy in the Netherlands capital and wrote several texts between then and the early 1930s. In 1935, she helped draft the regulations for the Saar Plebiscite, a vote held to decide the difficult question of whether that productive industrial area would belong to Germany or France.

During her lifetime, Wambaugh was honored many times over by organizations, universities and governments worldwide. The citation which accompanied the University of Geneva's honorary doctorate bestowed upon her in 1935 described her as "the brilliant historian [and] . . . one of the great artisans of peace . . . who represents the greatest technical competence in this field." Sarah Wambaugh died in 1955.

SOURCES:
Current Biography 1946. NY: H.W. Wilson, 1946.
Current Biography 1956. NY: H.W. Wilson, 1956.

Jacquie Maurice,
freelance writer,
Calgary, Alberta, Canada

Wanda of Poland (fl. 730)

Queen of Poland. Flourished in 730 in Poland; daughter of Krak, king of Poland.

Since no authenticated information is available for the period before the Kingdom of the Piasts was founded in Poland around 962, few facts remain of Wanda of Poland's life. She inherited the kingdom of Poland as the only surviving child of the powerful King Krak, who founded Krakow (Cracow). Queen Wanda spent her long and successful reign strengthening Poland's military forces, even leading battles herself at times. Poland was under an almost constant barrage of invasions from all its neighbors, particularly from the German forces of King Ridger. Wanda was a strong, intelligent, and politically acute monarch, and she successfully repelled most of her enemies.

Laura York, M.A. in History,
University of California,
Riverside, California

Wandru (c. 628–688)

Belgian saint. Name variations: Waldetrude; Waldetrudis; Waldetrud; Waudru. Born around 628 in Cousolre, Belgium; died on April 9, 688, in Mons, Belgium; daughter of (Saint) Walbert, count of Hainault, and (Saint) Bertilia; sister of Aldegund (c. 680–684); married Madelgaire (the future St. Vincent Madelgar); children: (all saints) Landry or Landric; Dentlin or Dentilinus; Madelberte; Aldetrude.

A Benedictine abbess, Wandru is the patron saint of the city of Mons, Belgium. She was born around 628 into the ruling family of Hainault to exceptionally devout parents, Count Walbert and his wife **Bertilia**, both of whom were later canonized. Wandru had one sister, *****Aldegund**, also made a saint, who founded the abbey of Maubeuge and served as its abbess. Perhaps surprisingly, given her upbringing, Wandru did not choose a cloistered life but married instead. Her husband was a minor noble called Madelgar; the two were well suited to one another and raised four children, all of whom chose religious lives and were canonized. In their later years, however, Madelgar and Wandru wanted to devote their lives to prayer and service. Wandru encouraged her husband to found a monastery at Haumont and supported his retirement into the abbey. Two years later, Wandru herself decided to withdraw from the world. She considered joining her sister Aldegund at the convent of Maubeuge, but felt that life there would not give her the solitude she sought. However, both of her daughters **Aldetrude** and *****Madelberte** each eventually served as abbess of their aunt's abbey of Maubeuge.

Wandru chose instead to retire to a small religious establishment which became known as Châteaulieu, or Castrilocus, in Monte. There she spent her time in prayer, becoming famous for her miracles of healing. Her piety attracted settlers to Châteaulieu, which led to the founding of a Benedictine monastery where Wandru served as abbess until her death in 688. Eventually the town of Mons grew up around Wandru's small abbey. Saint Wandru's relics are still kept in Mons, where they are carried through the town once a year in honor of the town's patron saint.

SOURCES:
The New Catholic Encyclopedia. Washington, DC: Catholic University of America, 1967.

Thurston, Herbert, and Donald Attwater, eds. *Butler's Lives of the Saints.* Vol. II. London: Burns & Oates, 1956.

Laura York, M.A. in History, University of California, Riverside, California

Warburg, Agnes (1872–1953)

English pictorialist photographer. Born in 1872 in London, England; died in 1953 in Surrey, England; daughter of Frederick Warburg and Emma Warburg; educated at home by governesses.

Exhibited at the Photographic Salon of the Linked Ring (1900); continued showing with Linked Ring for nine more years; helped found the Halyon Women's Club and exhibited there (1914); exhibited at the London Salon of the British Photographic Society and the Royal Photographic Society (1916); was a founding member of the Royal Photographic Society's Pictorial Group (1920); helped found the Royal Photographic Society's Colour Group (1927); left London during World War II.

Born in London in 1872, Agnes Warburg first took up photography around 1880, following in her older brother John's footsteps. Agnes was an early experimenter with the autochrome and Raydex color photographic processes, and was one of the foremost pictorialists of the early 20th century. As snapshot photography became more and more accessible to the new middle-class, the pictorialist movement sought to bring art back into photography through complex composition and intricate printing methods.

Warburg, like other pictorialists, preferred to portray nature as more dignified for having been controlled and tamed by the human hand. Her photographs emphasize not only the beauty of the natural world, but the beauty of natural things as cultivated and ordered by man. Warburg photographed everywhere she went, from Britain to Sweden, France, and Spain and later to Africa and Yugoslavia in the 1930s. She eventually settled in a fittingly domesticated landscape in Surrey, England, and died there in 1953.

SOURCES:
Williams, Val. *The Other Observers.* London, England: Virago, 1986.

Jacquie Maurice, freelance writer, Calgary, Alberta, Canada

Ward, Barbara (1914–1981)

British economist, intellectual journalist, and advocate of Third World development who was an influential figure in academia and politics throughout the mid-20th century. Name variations: Barbara Ward (1914–50, and thereafter in publications); Barbara Jackson (1950–73); Dame Barbara Ward (1974–76); Baroness Jackson of Lodsworth (1976–81). Born Barbara Ward on May 23, 1914, in York, England; died at home in Sussex, southern England, shortly after her 67th birthday, on May 31, 1981; daughter of Walter Ward and Teresa Mary (Burge) Ward; attended Catholic schools, England; the Lycee Molière and Sorbonne, Paris; and Somerville College, Oxford University; married Sir Robert Gillman Jackson, in 1950 (separated 1973); children: one son, Robert (b. 1956).

Worked as foreign editor of The Economist *(1939–50); served as governor of the British Broadcasting Corporation (BBC, 1946–50); was Harvard Professor of International Development (1958–67); was economic advisor to President Lyndon Johnson (1964–67), and Schweitzer Professor of International Economic Development, Columbia University (1968–73); served as president of International Institute for Environment and Development (1973–81).*

Selected writings: The International Share-Out *(1938);* Hitler's Route to Baghdad *(1939);* Turkey *(1941);* The West at Bay *(1948);* Policy for the West *(1951);* Faith and Freedom *(1954);* The Interplay of East and West *(1957);* Five Ideas that Change the World *(1959);* India and the West *(1961);* The Rich Nations and the Poor Nations *(1962);* Spaceship Earth *(1966);* Nationalism and Ideology *(1966);* The Lopsided World *(1968);* The Widening Gap *(1971);* Only One Earth *(with Rene Dubos, 1972);* The Home of Man *(1976). Contributor to many others.*

Barbara Ward was an outstanding intellectual journalist on political and economic affairs who became influential in British and American liberal circles. A fluent stylist with what she called "a fatal facility for words," she assimilated vast quantities of difficult information quickly and was able to summarize and explain it lucidly and persuasively. These gifts, coupled with an unflagging capacity for hard work, made her an influential figure in journalism, academia, and political life throughout the middle decades of the 20th century. Rarely ahead of her time, she embodied the wisdom of the moment raised to its highest power. Fiercely anti-fascist in the 1930s, anti-Communist in the late 1940s, anti-colonialist in the 1950s, a "global villager" in the 1960s, and an environmentalist in the 1970s, she lent her powerful pen and persuasive rhetoric to each of these causes in turn. She was, besides, a consistent advocate of the rights of the individual, the needs of poor nations, and the sovereignty of the Roman Catholic Church.

Ward grew up in East Anglia, mainly in the seaside and port town of Felixstowe, daughter of a provincial lawyer. Her mother was a devout Roman Catholic and sent her to convent schools, but her father was a Quaker, and pointed out to her the class injustices of English society. Ward surprised her school friends by defending the British trade unions when they launched the General Strike of 1926 in support of coal miners facing pay cuts. After two years of "finishing" education in Paris and Germany, during which she became fluent in both French and German, she went to Somerville College, Oxford, one of the elite women's colleges, where her initial plan to become an operatic soprano gave way to the study of politics and economics. She gained a first class honors degree in 1935 and won a three-year postgraduate award to study economic and political conditions in Central Europe. There she witnessed at firsthand the Fascist transformation of Austria and Italy and studied the dilemma of the Austrian Roman Catholic Church. She lectured on politics and economics in Cambridge University's extension program between 1936 and 1939.

Ward's first book, *The International Share-Out* (1938), criticized the economic injustices of British imperialism. She was an enthusiastic

Barbara Ward

member of the Labour Party and her lucid, persuasive writing on Labour and colonial issues led to an invitation from editor Geoffrey Crowther to write for *The Economist*, Britain's leading left-wing journal on political and economic affairs. She became a member of *The Economist*'s permanent staff in 1939 and was its foreign editor throughout the Second World War and the late 1940s, a period which one writer described as the journal's "twentieth century zenith of dignity and influence." She also gave radio talks on the BBC during the war, becoming part of the "Brains Trust" (a cluster of professional broadcasting geniuses), and lectured in America, Sweden, and on British army bases, becoming one of the distinctive broadcasting voices of the war and a national celebrity before the age of 30. Ward served on the BBC's board of governors between 1946 and 1950, and was a governor of the Old Vic Theater and the Sadler's Wells opera company in London.

She was a devout Roman Catholic and tried to energize her Church towards more radical social reform. On good terms with the English Catholic primate, Cardinal Hinsley, Ward belonged to the Sword of the Spirit Movement, a Catholic activist group during the 1940s, and contributed to *A Christian Basis for the Post-War World* (1941). In the 1960s, in the pontificate of Paul VI, she was to become an advisor to the papacy and a member of the Pontifical Commission for Studies of Justice and Peace, making her one of the first women to enter the ancient male preserve of the papal curia.

Like many members of the Labour Party, Ward was a democratic Socialist, fervently opposed to the undemocratic character of Soviet Communism. Catholicism intensified her anti-Communist fervor. Her 1951 book *Policy for the West* blamed the Soviet leaders for throwing away the chance for peace in 1945. "Those who mold Russian policy," she wrote, "have been trained in an atmosphere precisely calculated to produce in them a deadly mixture of arrogance and suspicion" and a "profound scorn for all who do not accept the absolute and eternal truths of Marxist doctrine." At the same time, she recognized that theoretical Marxism "has the magnificent sweep of a great epic," making it all the more a temptation to be resisted. Ward was herself strongly attracted to wide-ranging intellectual systems, praising in particular those of Arnold Toynbee and her fellow Catholic Christopher Dawson.

In the Cold War era, she urged a resolute anti-Communist foreign policy, based on the economic strength of a broad free-trade area in Western Europe, and she praised the statesman-like generosity of President Harry Truman for his support of the Marshall Plan in rebuilding a shattered Europe at the end of the war. It was the kind of selfless international scheme she most favored, and in later works she often referred back to the Marshall Plan as a model for bold international incentives led by the wealthy nations of the West. In her 1954 book *Faith and Freedom*, Ward argued that the Christian West's tradition of individual dignity and spiritual freedom ought to attract Third World peoples emerging from colonialism but that, as a sign of good faith, these benefits must be accompanied by economic aid and effective mechanisms for redistributing the world's wealth. Central to Ward's thinking about economics was the fact that the world no longer lived with scarcity. "I often wonder whether this fact has really reached the profounder levels of our imagination, or whether we do not still live in an imagined age of scarcity, still reacting as though the difficulty of securing enough materials to accomplish even basic needs ought to dominate public thinking." Too often, by the mid-20th century, the advanced nations suffered from *over*-production so that redistribution abroad could be commensurate with self-interest.

Faith and Freedom, her most philosophical book, also demonstrated how acutely Ward could read—and share—the mood of a generation. It coincided with the Western vogue of existentialism in the early 1950s, arguing that humanity is condemned to freedom and that the challenge of life is to accept freedom, and use it wisely. Combining it with her religious faith in a manner strongly reminiscent of the Protestant theologian Paul Tillich, she ended her plea for the world with an assertion that the existence of a good God could still be demonstrated: "The firmest proofs of religion are rooted in the nature of reality—in the necessities of reason, in the underivative character of such concepts as truth and goodness." And she did not hesitate to assert the superiority of Christianity over the other world religions because it most fully recognized the centrality of time, change, and history. "It is . . . the unique character of Christianity, among all the world religions, to have grasped not only the infinitude of the Creator but also the dynamism of His creation. For all its evil and suffering and sin, the world is rescued from the last horror—the horror of meaninglessness."

Ward was married in 1950 to Robert Gillman Jackson, an Australian civil servant and later assistant secretary of the United Nations.

With him, she moved first to Australia and then in 1953 to Ghana, where he worked as an economic advisor to the post-colonial government of Kwame Nkrumah, as it planned and built the Volta Dam. Although Ghana remained her home base for the next 15 years, she was often away, teaching on economic development at Harvard every winter semester between 1957 and 1968, touring other newly independent British colonies including India and Pakistan, and giving lectures throughout the English-speaking world. Her experience of de-colonization and her visits to these lands forced on her, in the most vivid way, the terrible disparities between the rich and poor nations, and she became convinced that world political stability depended on transforming this unequal relationship. She argued persuasively that, so long as the developing nations were primarily exporters of raw materials, they would be at a permanent disadvantage beside the exporters of manufactured goods. Asia, she noted in a 1960 lecture, "became primarily an exporter of raw materials and an importer of manufactures" in the colonial era. "This is the least profitable of commercial relationships; yet Western trade policy is still in some measure designed to hinder rapid industrialization in the emergent lands." Her lecture series were regularly published and caught the attention of important figures. Lyndon Johnson said of her book *The Rich Nations and the Poor Nations* (1962), "I read it like I do the Bible," and he frequently invited her to the White House for unofficial advice on economic affairs between 1963 and 1967. But unlike President Johnson, Ward had no experience of actual government or administration. Her writings—confident, decisive, sweeping, and theoretical—never addressed the practical complications involved in changing the direction of the entire world's economic conduct. And at crucial points her deep learning and analysis shaded off into utopian pleas for moral, political, and economic transformations.

Ward, like many liberal intellectuals during the 1960s, became convinced that technology had led to an acceleration of history itself, that the world was becoming a "global village," and that the application of good will and technical expertise could solve its residual problems, ushering in an age of peace and plenty. Her lectures at Carleton University, Ottowa, reprinted as *Nationalism and Ideology* (1966), were devoted to this theme, and to lamenting the continuing grip of nationalist ideas, even among groups like the Americans who ought to know better. She was correspondingly dismayed to see her friend President Johnson becoming ever more heavily involved in the Vietnam War, which seemed to give the lie to these optimistic ideas.

A few years later, Ward became one of the first liberal intellectuals to pay systematic attention to environmental deterioration, another of the drawbacks of advanced industrial societies, and as she came to understand it better, she abandoned the boundless technological optimism which had colored her speeches and writings in the early 1960s. She argued now against the relentless urbanization of America, and the imbalance created in poor countries like Ghana by the rapid growth of cities and depopulation of the countryside.

> *The* great paradox of this century is that we have reached an extreme pitch of national feeling all around the world just at the moment when, from every rational point of view, we have to find ways of progressing beyond nationalism. This point needs great emphasis because, in this field, our reason and our emotion probably do not work in the same direction.
>
> **—Barbara Ward**

Environmentalists in the 1960s believed that overpopulation was one source of the crisis. Most favored birth-control programs for the Third World and were strong supporters of reducing population growth rates. That view made the Catholic Church, which banned artificial contraception, seem like an obstacle to progress. Ward was one of many liberal Catholics who hoped that the Vatican would change its teaching on the birth-control question, as it seemed ready to do in 1966, after the upheavals of the Second Vatican Council. At a Catholic congress of the laity, she wrote a petition advocating such a change. But when Paul VI issued his encyclical letter *Humanae Vitae* (1968), upholding the old prohibition, she swallowed her doubts and defended the pope's decision. Redistribution of wealth was more important than population restraint, she argued, formulating the point at a Vatican press conference where she declared: "If a man asks you for bread and you give him a pill he'll spit in your eye!"

In 1967, Ward was named Albert Schweitzer Professor of International Economic Development at Columbia University. The university's economics department challenged her appointment on the grounds that she was a talented economic journalist rather than an original scholar, but the administration overruled it and installed her. Her prestige and influence enabled her to summon world leaders to conferences there, emphasizing the theme of wealth inequalities between the first and third worlds.

Ward's concern for environmental affairs intensified in the 1970s. With Rene Dubos, she co-wrote *Only One Earth*, a preparatory study for a United Nations' environmental conference in Stockholm in 1973. It summarized the environmental issues then coming under political scrutiny and, as usual for Ward, argued that fuller knowledge and more intensive study, coupled to vigorous co-operative political action, were essential. "The first step to devising a strategy for planet Earth" she wrote in her chapter on "strategies for survival," "is for the nations to accept a *collective* responsibility for discovering more—much more—about the natural system and how it is affected by man's activities and vice versa." And in the chapter on population, Ward pointed out that rising living standards rather than government support for birth-control plans had led to shrinking family size and population stability in the advanced nations—a point which enabled her to reconcile her environmental concerns with her orthodox Catholicism.

That same year, 1973, Ward resigned from her Columbia chair to accept the presidency of the International Institute for Environment and Development in London. She spent the later years of her life back in England but continued to travel widely, working for more generous aid to the developing world and becoming engrossed in the anti-nuclear movement. Her last work was a pamphlet commissioned by Catholic bishops on the duties of the rich, both individuals and nations, and she ended with words which could summarize the mission of her adult life: "Could it be the vocation of this generation to give the planet the institutions of unity and cooperation that can express this mystery [of Christ's incarnation]? Is the need not all the greater since, just as we have discovered the fragilities of our natural systems, we have invented, in nuclear weapons, a possible means of destroying ourselves and them together?" Barbara Ward died shortly after her 67th birthday, at home in Sussex, southern England in 1981.

SOURCES:

"Barbara Ward," in *Current Biography 1977*. NY: H.W. Wilson, 1977, pp. 424–427.

"Outstanding Contribution to Economic Thought," in *The Times* (London). June 1, 1981, p. 16.

Nowell, Robert. "Barbara Ward's Last Cry for World Justice," in *The Times* (London). July 27, 1981, p. 12.

Ward, Barbara. *Faith and Freedom*. NY: Norton, 1954.

———. *Five Ideas that Change the World*. NY: Norton, 1959.

———. *The Legacy of Imperialism*. Chatham College, 1960.

———. *Nationalism and Ideology*. NY: Norton, 1966.

———. *Policy for the West*. London: George Allen and Unwin, 1951.

———. *The Spirit of '76: Why Not Now?* Williamsburg: Colonial Williamsburg Press, 1963.

———, and Rene Dubos. *Only One Earth: the Care and Maintenance of a Small Planet*. NY: Norton, 1973.

Patrick Allitt,
Professor of History, Emory University,
Atlanta, Georgia

Ward, Catharine Barnes

(1851–1913)

American photographer, writer and lecturer. Name variations: Catharine Barnes. Born Catharine Weed Barnes in Albany, New York, on January 10, 1851; died in 1913 in Hadlow, England; granddaughter of Thurlow Weed; attended Albany Female Academy and the Friends School of Providence, Rhode Island; attended Vassar College, 1869–1871; married Henry Snowden Ward, in 1893 (died 1911).

Catharine Barnes Ward was born in 1851 in Albany, New York, the granddaughter of Thurlow Weed, a journalist and New York politician. During the 1860s, she attended Albany Female Academy and the Friends School of Providence, Rhode Island. From 1869 to 1871, she studied at Vassar College and in 1872 toured Russia with her parents.

Returning to America, Ward traveled the United States and in 1877 began caring for her sick mother. She took up photography in 1886 at her mother's suggestion and, in 1888, received a photographic diploma in Boston. Upon her mother's death, she kept house for her father and built an attic studio to pursue her work as a photographer. In 1890, Ward became the associate editor of *American Amateur Photographer*. She quickly built a reputation as an advocate for female photographers, as well as a noted writer and lecturer in photography.

As a member of both the Society of Amateur Photographers of New York and the Photographic Society of London, Catharine worked to establish ties between the two countries' photographic communities. She demonstrated this connection in her own marriage to Henry Snowden Ward, the 28-year-old Brit who founded and edited *Practical Photographer*, in 1893. Together they founded several photography magazines. In 1896, she published and illustrated *Shakespeare's Town and Times*. She followed this with a series of other illustrated works, including books on Dickens, the Canterbury pilgrimages, and Exmoor, the land of Lorna Doone. Ward returned to the United States with her husband, where they toured the country, working to raise funds for the Dickens centenary. After Henry Ward died in New York in 1911, Ward returned to England, where she died in 1913.

SOURCES:
Rosenblum, Naomi. *A History of Women Photographers.* NY: Abbeville, 1994.

Judith C. Reveal,
freelance writer,
Greensboro, Maryland

Ward, Clara Mae (1924–1973)

African-American singer whose career with the Ward Trio and the Clara Ward Singers popularized gospel music in the mainstream music industry. Born on April 21, 1924, in Philadelphia, Pennsylvania; died on January 16, 1973, in Los Angeles, California; daughter of George Ward and Gertrude May (Murphy) Ward.

Clara Mae Ward was born in Philadelphia in 1924, the second daughter of George Ward and **Gertrude Murphy Ward**. The family had moved from South Carolina in search of a better life, but during the Great Depression, Gertrude supported her family by serving wealthy white families as a domestic. Following a revelation in a dream, Gertrude began singing gospel music in 1931, and performed in churches throughout the Philadelphia area. In 1934, she added her daughters Clara and **Willa Ward** to the act to create the Ward Trio. Clara Ward had been singing since the age of five and had started piano a few years after. Considered a gifted musician, she was especially regarded for her singing talent.

In 1943, while performing with the Ward Trio at the National Baptist Convention in Philadelphia, Clara was officially introduced to the national gospel circuit. The Ward Trio experienced phenomenal success at the Philadelphia Convention, and they began to tour extensively. Although a popular group, they received little money for their efforts. This situation improved in 1949 when the Ward Trio added **Marion Ward** and **Henrietta Waddy** to the group. It was also during this time that they met their lifelong friend, preacher and songwriter W. Herbert Brewster.

Although she was just 5'3" and weighed only 103 pounds, Clara Ward's small stature belied her powerful performances. She possessed enormous energy, and her skillful artistic direction enthralled those who saw her perform. Ward assumed control of the group and gave them a more sophisticated image through strik-

ing gowns and new, mature hair-styles. As a result, the Ward Singers were ranked among the most successful female gospel groups of the 1950s. As their popularity grew during that decade, they also established a lifelong relationship with the Reverend C.L. Franklin. His daughter **Aretha Franklin** was profoundly influenced by her exposure to Clara Ward. (It was at the funeral of her aunt that the 12-year-old Franklin, transfixed by Ward's exuberant singing, decided to become a singer herself.)

Clara Ward was considered an emotional singer who produced a long list of bestselling gospel records, including "Surely, God Is Able," "How I Got Over," "Come in the Room" and "The Day Is Past and Gone." Ward's popularity filled auditoriums and churches wherever she performed. Her affinity for writing and performing new music led to the establishment of Ward's House of Music, a successful publishing company. The business published not only music, but booklets and song collections, including many of the over 500 songs written by Ward herself.

From 1943 to 1957, the Ward Singers traveled more than a million miles throughout the gospel circuit. In 1955, they performed at the Apollo Theater in Harlem, but "The Big Gospel Cavalcade of 1957" took them to a different city each night of the week but Saturday. Their success with the Cavalcade tour earned them an invitation to perform at the 1957 Newport Jazz Festival on an all-gospel matinee program.

The Ward Singers grew from performing free concerts to receiving $5,000 for single performances. Although 1958 brought unrest within the group due to personnel changes and a shift in artistic direction, "Mother" Gertrude Ward was able to draw the group back together, and they continued their upward climb. In 1959, they went on an immensely successful Scandinavian tour. And with Clara Ward's 1961 decision to perform at the Village Vanguard in New York City, the group began to expand their following. Ward's Vanguard audiences were captivated by what they saw and heard, and engagements at other clubs—such as the Elegant, Birdland, and the Blue Angel—soon followed. A 2-week engagement at the New Frontier Hotel in Las Vegas in 1961 turned into a highly publicized and profitable 40-week gig. Repeated the following year, it was the longest consecutive booking at the time for any performer in Las Vegas history.

The name of the group changed from the Ward Singers to the Clara Ward Specials and finally to the Clara Ward Singers. In 1962, the Clara Ward Singers first appeared in Disneyland.

After that performance, they became a regular attraction. Their rigorous travel schedule included worldwide performances as far away as Vietnam and the Far East. They appeared with Jack Benny at the Ziegfeld Theater in New York City, and myriad television hosts, including Ed Sullivan, Mike Douglas, Danny Thomas, Steve Allen, and Tennessee Ernie Ford, sought them as guest performers. Continuing to break barriers, the Clara Ward Singers performed at the Philadelphia Academy of Music in 1967—the first gospel group do so. They also recorded with other groups, such as the Isley Brothers. As well, Ward's career took her to Broadway as musical director and co-star with Lou Gossett, Jr., of Langston Hughes' *God's Trombones.*

Ward's progression from traditional gospel to pop-gospel had taken nearly 20 years. Despite her musical transition from "Precious Lord" to "Zippety-Dooh-Dah," she never lost her spiritual center or her concern that her early supporters would misunderstand her motives. Although she permitted no serving of alcohol during her performances, her appearances in nightclubs remained a point of contention between her and her good friend of many years, *Mahalia Jackson.

While performing in a Florida hotel, Ward suffered a stroke, which left her temporarily unable to sing. Yet her drive to perform was so strong that she took on the role of accompanist for the group. Five weeks after her first stroke, Ward suffered a second stroke and died on January 16, 1973, in Los Angeles. Her mother Gertrude organized two funerals. The first, a "service of triumph," took place in Philadelphia on January 23, 1973, at the old Metropolitan Opera House. Aretha Franklin sang "The Day Is Past and Gone," one of Clara Ward's greatest hymns. The second service was held at the Shrine Auditorium in Los Angeles. More than 4,000 mourners appeared and the performance included former Ward Singers Marion Williams singing "Surely, God Is Able," and Gertrude Ward singing "When the Storms of Life Are Raging." Clara Ward was buried in the Freedom Mausoleum at Forest Lawn in Glendale, California.

SOURCES:

Smith, Jessie Carney, ed. *Notable Black American Women.* Detroit, MI: Gale Research, 1992.

Judith C. Reveal,
freelance writer,
Greensboro, Maryland

Ward, Elizabeth Stuart Phelps

(1844–1911)

American author and social reformer. Name variations: Mary Gray Phelps; Lily. Born Mary Gray Phelps on August 31, 1844, in Boston, Massachusetts; died on January 28, 1911, in Newton, Massachusetts, of myocardial degeneration; daughter of Austin Phelps (a minister) and Elizabeth Wooster Stuart Phelps (1815–1852, a writer); attended Abbott Academy and Mrs. Edwards' School; married Herbert D. Ward (a writer), in October 1888; no children.

Selected writings: Ellen's Idol *(1864);* Up Hill; or, Life in the Factory *(1865);* Mercy Gliddon's Work *(1865);* Tiny *(1866);* Gypsy Breynton *(1866);* Gypsy's Cousin Joy *(1866);* Gypsy's Sowing and Reaping *(1866);* Tiny's Sunday Nights *(1866);* Gypsy's Year at the Golden Crescent *(1867);* I Don't Know How *(1868);* The Gates Ajar *(1868);* Men, Women, and Ghosts *(1869);* The Trotty Book *(1870);* Hedged In *(1870);* The Silent Partner *(1871);* What to Wear? *(1873);* Trotty's Wedding Tour and Story Book *(1873);* Poetic Studies *(1875);* The Story of Avis *(1877);* My Cousin and I *(1879, published as* An Old Maid's Paradise, *1885);* Sealed Orders *(1879);* Friends: A Duet *(1881);* Doctor Day *(1882);* Beyond the Gates *(1883);* Songs of the Silent World and Other Poems *(1884);* Burglars in Paradise *(1886);* The Madonna of the Tubs *(1886);* The Gates Between *(1887);* Jack, the Fisherman *(1887);* The Struggle for Immortality *(1889);* The Master of the Magicians *(with Herbert Dickinson Ward, 1890);* Come Forth *(with H.D. Ward, 1890);* Fourteen to One *(1891);* Austin Phelps: A Memoir *(1891);* A Lost Hero *(with H.D. Ward, 1891);* Donald Marcy *(1893);* A Singular Life *(1895);* Chapters from a Life *(1896);* The Story of Jesus Christ: An Interpretation *(1897);* Loveliness: A Story *(1899);* The Successors of Mary the First *(1901);* Within the Gates *(1901);* Avery *(1902);* Confessions of a Wife *(as Mary Adams, 1902);* Trixy *(1904);* The Man in the Case *(1906);* Walled In: A Novel *(1907);* Though Life Us Do Part *(1908);* The Whole Family: A Novel by Twelve Others *(with others, 1908);* Jonathan and David *(1909);* The Oath of Allegiance and Other Stories *(1910);* Comrades *(1911).*

Elizabeth Phelps Ward was the eldest child and only daughter of the Reverend Austin Phelps and his first wife **Elizabeth Stuart Phelps,** a noted writer. She was baptized Mary Gray Phelps and nicknamed "Lily" by the family; however, after her mother's death from a lengthy illness when Elizabeth was only eight, she chose to be known thereafter by her mother's name. She grew up in Andover, Massachusetts, where her father, a Congregational minister and professor of sacred rhetoric at the local seminary (and later the president of Andover Theological Seminary), carefully guided her education. According to **Mary Bortnyk Rigsby**, as a child, Elizabeth considered herself a tomboy and displayed "willful disregard for proper behavior." Although life in Andover was pervaded by rigid Calvinistic doctrine that relegated women to the domestic realm, Elizabeth was encouraged to pursue academic studies. She attended Abbott Academy, a private girls' school, and Mrs. Edwards' School for Young Ladies, an institution that offered a curriculum similar to men's colleges except for Greek and trigonometry. She also received a religious education, which taught her to value hard work and eschew worldliness.

Influenced by her mother's love of writing, the young Elizabeth wrote several short stories for Sunday school readers during her early years, none of which survive. At age 16, she encountered *Elizabeth Barrett Browning's blank verse novel *Aurora Leigh*, about a young woman artist, and later attributed her own literary aspirations to it. Concurring with Browning's assertion that poets should represent the age in which they live, and should not allow imagery to compromise that vision, Elizabeth Stuart Phelps Ward helped to usher in the genre of literary realism in the 19th century.

Ward's opportunities to write were significantly hindered when her father became an invalid in 1861 and she was compelled to devote her time to the household duties she disdained. She still managed to write, often in unheated, out-of-the-way rooms of the house, while wrapped in her mother's old fur cape. After losing a close friend in the Battle of Antietam during the Civil War, Ward turned the event into the story "A Sacrifice Consumed," which was subsequently accepted for publication in the January 1864 issue of *Harper's New Monthly*. Earning $25 and her father's approval, Elizabeth felt encouraged to continue.

Ward penned two series of Sunday-school books ("Tiny" and "Gypsy"), which she considered necessary to support herself. Rigsby suggests, however, that although these volumes are "conventional and undistinguished" when considered with her other books for young girls, they "indicate her emerging interest in critiquing social expectations of how women lived their lives." A pivotal point in Ward's intellectual development had occurred in 1860 with the disastrous fire at Andover's Pemberton Mill in which 88 young women died. Elizabeth researched the event thoroughly and, in 1866, wrote a fictional account of the fire, which was published in the March 1868 issue of *The Atlantic Monthly*, earning praise from such literary figures as John Greenleaf Whittier and Thomas Wentworth Higginson.

The year 1868 also brought Ward's most significant success with the publication of *The Gates Ajar*, which became a literary and cultural phenomenon. The novel posits her own view of heaven as a paradise comprising all the best aspects of life on Earth. Largely a series of conversations between the two main characters—Mary Cabot and her aunt Mrs. Forceythe—as they deal with the recent deaths of loved ones, the book tapped into the religious current of the time, which rejected the harsh Calvinistic doctrine of predestination in favor of a more merciful God who admitted the truly repentant into heaven regardless of their transgressions. Not only was the novel an immediate bestseller, its popularity endured for almost 30 years. Rigsby notes that by 1897, the book had sold more than 81,000 copies in the United States and more than 100,000 copies in England, in addition to translations into French, German, Dutch, and Italian. It also inspired a wide range of products that were marketed bearing its name, everything from patent medicines to Gates Ajar floral arrangements and musical compositions for funerals. "The success of the novel in the United States," writes Rigsby, "can be attributed to the emotional needs of a readership suffering from the pain of Civil War, but this explanation cannot be so easily applied to international sales." She adds that other critics have suggested that the novel comforted the "spiritual disquiet" that had resulted from an increasingly scientific perspective of the human condition. In the midst of the religious controversy that ensued, Ward was accused of heresy by the church, but for most readers who wrote to her, the book had been a comfort.

The success of *The Gates Ajar* secured Ward's writing career and enabled her to rebuild the summer house, used by her mother as a study, into a studio. For the next 20 years, observes Rigsby, Ward "honed her understanding of American patriarchal culture, writing in support of women's political rights, educational and occupational opportunities, dress reform health concerns, and financial independence." Although

Elizabeth Stuart Phelps Ward

her books were widely read, none repeated the triumph of *The Gates Ajar*. Most of her novels concerned simple New England girls going about their daily lives. Her second novel, *Hedged In* (1870), defended fallen women, relating the story of factory girls in a mill town near Andover. She published a series of articles in *The Independent* magazine in which she advocated for dress reform and suffrage and expressed her scorn at the confinement placed on women by domesticity. She also expressed these views in her fiction, patterning the idealized heroine of her 1877 novel *The Story of Avis* after her own mother, who had struggled to combine her writing with married life. Rigsby points out that "*The Story of Avis* was the first American novel, to focus exclusively on the subject of a failed marriage." Ward, who had professed a desire never to marry for most of her life, revisited that theme in *Doctor Zay* (1882). Despite her stated desire to remain single, in 1888, Elizabeth married Herbert Dickinson Ward, a writer 17 years her junior, who was the son of her longtime friend and frequent publisher William H. Ward, managing editor of *The Independent*. Except for the early years, their marriage was not happy; the couple spent much of their time apart and had no children. However, they did collaborate on three unsuccessful Biblical romances: *The Master of the Magicians* (1890), *Come Forth* (1890), and *A Lost Hero* (1891). Ward continued her own writing after her marriage, producing, among other works, a biography of her father, *Austin Phelps: A Memoir* (1891), and her autobiography, *Chapters from a Life* (1896).

In later life, Ward suffered from chronic insomnia and was an invalid for many years preceding her death from myocardial degeneration, which occurred at her home in Newton, Massachusetts, on January 28, 1911. Her ashes were buried in Newton Cemetery. During her career, she produced more than 150 short stories and 20 adult novels, in addition to poetry, plays, essays, and children's books. And although her literary stature diminished after the 19th century, contemporary studies in American culture are revisiting her work. As Jean Ferguson Carr writes: "She is gradually being rediscovered . . . [and] valued for her ardent investigations, in fiction and prose of the unarticulated lives of the industrial poor, of the elderly, and of women."

SOURCES:

Carr, Jean Ferguson. "Elizabeth Stuart Phelps," in *Dictionary of Literary Biography*, Vol. 74: *American Short-Story Writers Before 1880*. Detroit, MI: The Gale Group, 1988, pp. 288–296.

James, Edward T., ed. *Notable American Women, 1607–1950*. Cambridge, MA: The Belknap Press of Harvard University, 1971.

McHenry, Robert, ed. *Famous American Women*. NY: Dover, 1980.

Rigsby, Mary Bortnyk (assisted by Heidi L.M. Jacobs and Jennifer Putzi). "Elizabeth Stuart Phelps," in *Dictionary of Literary Biography*, Vol. 221: *American Women Prose Writers, 1870–1920*. Detroit, MI: The Gale Group, 2000, pp. 294–304.

Judith C. Reveal,
freelance writer,
Greensboro, Maryland

Ward, Geneviève (1838–1922)

American actress and opera singer who was the first actress to be named a Dame Commander of the British Empire (1921). Name variations: Genevieve Ward; Lucy Geneviève Teresa Ward; Ginevra Guerrabella; Dame Geneviève Ward. Born Lucy Geneviève Teresa Ward on March 27, 1838 (one source cites 1837), in New York City; died on August 18, 1922; daughter of Samuel Ward (a planter and businessman) and Lucy Lee (or Leigh) Ward; studied with San Giovanni, Lamperti, and Fanny Persiani; married Count Constantin de Guerbel, on November 10, 1856.

Geneviève Ward was born Lucy Geneviève Teresa Ward in New York City, the daughter of **Lucy Ward** and Colonel Samuel Ward and the granddaughter of Gideon Lee, former mayor of New York. In the course of her education in Europe, Ward sang for composer Gioacchino Rossini, who urged her to study with an opera director in Florence, Italy. In addition to developing her voice under such teachers as San Giovanni and Lamperti, Ward became involved with a Russian count she met there, Constantin de Guerbel. They were married in a civil ceremony in 1856 at the American consulate in Nice, France, but the groom failed to appear for the church ceremony in Paris which would have made their marriage legal in Russia. Her outraged parents tracked him down in Warsaw, where government intervention forced him to proceed with the church wedding. It was essentially meaningless, however, as Geneviève never saw her husband again after the Ward family returned to Italy.

Ward continued to train her with various instructors, including diva **Fanny Persiani**, and made her opera debut in the title role of Donizetti's **Lucrezia Borgia* at La Scala in Milan in 1857. Singing under the stage name Ginevra Guerrabella, she toured throughout Europe for the following five years in such roles as Elvira in *Don Giovanni*, Maid Marian in *Robin Hood*, and Elvira in *I Puritani*, which was her first performance of an Italian opera in London.

She also returned to the United States in 1862 to play Violetta in *La Traviata* at the Academy of Music in New York.

During the winter of this same year, Ward contracted diphtheria while touring Cuba, and, although she recovered, the disease destroyed her singing voice. She taught singing for several years, but so missed performing that she decided to pursue a career as a stage actress. Within ten years, she had established a second successful career. Performing under her real name, in 1873 Ward traveled to England and made her first dramatic stage appearance as Lady Macbeth at Manchester's Theatre Royal to rave reviews. Her careful study of the craft resulted in a highly successful acting career in that country as well. In 1875, she appeared in two plays written expressly for her: Lewis Wingfield's *Despite the World* and William G. Willis' *Sappho*. She experienced one of her greatest early successes with the dual role of Blanche de Valois and Unarita in *The Prayer in the Storm*, a performance she repeated 162 times. Her repertoire and popularity continued to grow with such roles as Julia in *The Hunchback*, Portia in *The Merchant of Venice*, the Countess Almaviva in *The School for Intrigue*, Rebecca in *Ivanhoe*, Margaret Elmore in *Love's Sacrifice*, and Emilia in *Othello*, the last of which, according to *American National Biography*, caused her to be hailed as the "best Emilia of our generation." Although she received many offers to act on the Continent (and did, in fact, play Lady Macbeth in Paris to strong reviews in 1877), Ward preferred the English stage, where she spent the majority of her acting career, returning to America only for brief engagements.

Ward expanded her international reputation after obtaining the rights to Herman Merivale's *Forget-Me-Not*, which opened in London in 1879. Her performance as Stephanie de Mohrivart in the play was a huge success and made her famous in the United States, Canada, India, South Africa, and Australia. She spent the next 13 years on a world tour before settling down with Henry Irving's Lyceum company in 1893.

At the beginning of the 20th century, Ward devoted her skill and energy to teaching young actors, although she continued to appear on stage sporadically until 1922, when she gave a final performance at St. James's Theater in London as Queen Margaret in Shakespeare's *Richard III*. In 1921, she became the first actress to be conferred the order of a Dame Commander of the British Empire for her accomplishments as a tragic actress. The honor, which is usually announced on New Year's Day, was so unique that it was issued in the form of a personal greeting from Windsor Castle on the morning of Ward's 83rd birthday. The selection was controversial since it was the first to be given to an actress, and George V had chosen an American to receive it. Many British subjects felt the honor should have gone to *Ellen Terry, an adored English actress of the day. On August 18, 1922, Geneviève Ward died, at the age of 85.

SOURCES:

Garraty, John A., and Mark C. Carnes, eds. *American National Biography*. NY: Oxford University Press, 1999.
Johns, Eric. *Dames of the Theatre*. New Rochelle, NY: Arlington House, 1974.
Who Was Who in the Theatre: 1912–1976. Detroit, MI: Gale Research, 1978.

Judith C. Reveal,
freelance writer,
Greensboro, Maryland

Ward, Hortense (1872–1944)

American lawyer and reformer. Born Hortense Sparks on July 20, 1872, near Simpsonville, Texas; died on December 5, 1944; daughter of Frederick Sparks (a cattleman, surname originally Funks) and Louisa Marie (La Bauve) Sparks; married Albert Malsch (a tinner), in 1891 (divorced 1906); married William Henry Ward (a lawyer), in 1909; children: (first marriage) Mary Louise, Marguerite, and Hortense.

Was the first woman to pass the bar examination in Texas (August 1910); fought for a married women's property rights law, which was known as the Hortense Ward law upon its passage (1913); was the first Texas woman admitted to practice before the U.S. Supreme Court (February 1915); also gained women the right to vote in political primaries in Texas (1918).

Hortense Ward was born near Simpsonville, Texas, in 1872. Her father Frederick Sparks was a German-born deputy hide inspector and cattle raiser; her mother **Louisa Marie La Bauve** was descended from an old French family in Louisiana. Hortense lived her entire life in Texas, attending public schools in Edna and graduating from Nazareth Academy in Victoria in 1890.

Ward's brief teaching career ended with her marriage to Albert Malsch on January 4, 1891. The couple had three daughters, but separated when Hortense moved to Houston to take a position with the Wolf Cigar Company in the summer of 1903. Although her husband and children joined her that fall, Ward's ambition surpassed that of her husband, and they divorced in 1906. Now a stenographer and notary, Hortense shared office space with the legal firm of Hogg, Gill & Jones, which sparked her interest in law as a career. For two years, she studied by correspondence course while also working as a court reporter. In 1909, she married lawyer William Henry Ward, who helped her to complete her law studies. She became the first woman in Texas to pass the bar examination and was admitted to the Texas bar in Galveston on August 30, 1910.

Ward and her husband soon established the firm of Ward & Ward, active in civil cases. Though her husband was a trial lawyer, Hortense never appeared in court, confining herself to briefings and consultations. She chose to use her understanding of law to benefit women by advocating on several fronts as a lobbyist. Her 1912 letter to a local Houston newspaper concerning married women's property law drew the interest of the *Delineator* magazine, which provided national publicity for her cause and printed and distributed her pamphlet "Property Rights of Married Women in Texas." In 1913, after considerable effort and lobbying by Ward on the issue, the Hortense Ward law granting married Texas women property rights was passed. That same year her efforts on behalf of worker's compensation and the establishment of a 54-hour work week for employed women also became law. A proponent of prohibition, Ward also supported the establishment of a division for women in the state's labor department and a court for domestic issues. She also lobbied for the right of married women to serve as officers of corporations. During World War I, she became president of the Harris County Equal Suffrage Association. Ward was behind another major advancement for women when the women's primary law gave Texas women the right to vote in party primaries in 1918.

In February 1915, Ward was admitted to practice before the Supreme Court of the United States; she is considered to be the first Texas woman to achieve this feat. Although she mounted an unsuccessful bid for the Democratic nomination to a judgeship in 1920, she used her political savvy to oppose Texas governor James Ferguson following his derogatory remarks about higher education for women. Her opposition to Ferguson, however, did not extend to his wife *Miriam A. Ferguson's run for the governorship in 1924 on an anti-Ku Klux Klan platform. Ward's aversion to the Klan also took her to Maine in support of an anti-Klan candidate there. A strong Democratic campaigner, she championed Oscar Underwood's bid for the Democratic nomination for president in 1924 and Al Smith's similar attempt in 1928.

In 1925, Ward was named chief justice to a temporary Texas supreme court arranged specifically for the case of *Johnson v. Darr*. The case involved a fraternal order to which all the justices belonged, thus requiring their disqualification. The governor appointed Ward and two other women to hear the case. During that same year Ward served as acting judge of the city of Houston's corporation court. Upon the death of her husband and because of her own arthritic condition, Ward closed her law office in 1939 and thereafter limited her practice to consulting for selected friends and former clients. She died on December 5, 1944, and was buried in Hollywood Cemetery.

SOURCES:
James, Edward T., ed. *Notable American Women, 1607–1950*. Cambridge, MA: The Belknap Press of Harvard University, 1971.
McHenry, Robert, ed. *Famous American Women*. NY: Dover, 1980.

Judith C. Reveal,
freelance writer,
Greensboro, Maryland

Ward, Mrs. Humphry (1851–1920)

Prolific English novelist, critic, journalist, memoirist, settlement house organizer, and opponent of women's suffrage who was the author of Robert Elsmere *(1888), one of the most famous religious novels of the 19th century. Name variations: Mary Augusta Arnold (1851–1871); Mary Augusta Ward (1871–1920); Mrs. Humphry Ward (in all publications). Born Mary Augusta Arnold in Hobart Town, Tasmania, on June 11, 1851; died in London, England, on March 24, 1920; eldest of eight children of Thomas Arnold (second son of Dr. Thomas Arnold, headmaster at Rugby) and Julia (Sorrell or Sorell) Arnold (1826–1888); sister of *Julia Arnold Huxley (1862–1908); married Thomas Humphry Ward, in 1872; children: Dorothy Ward (b. 1874); Arnold (b. 1876); Janet Ward (b. 1879).*

Selected writings: (translation) Journal Intime of Henri Frederic Amiel *(1885);* Robert Elsmere *(1888);* Helbeck of Bannisdale *(1898);* The Testing of Diana Mallory *(1908);* Daphne *(1909);* Delia Blanchflower *(1914);* England's Effort *(1916);* A Writer's Recollections *(1918, 2 vols.) and many others—40 books in all.*

In her heyday, 1890–1910, Mrs. Humphry Ward was one of the most influential novelists in the English-speaking world. She published 25 novels and 15 other books of social and literary criticism, played a prominent role in the settlement house movement, was an active society hostess, and a leader in the campaign against women's suffrage. Tolstoy declared her the greatest English novelist of her day; William Dean

Howells, the dean of American letters, ranked her fiction as almost the equal of George Eliot's (*Mary Anne Evans) and most other Edwardian critics agreed that she stood in the honorable line of women novelists from *Jane Austen through the *Brontës, *Elizabeth Gaskell, and Eliot. By the end of the 20th century, however, while these others remained honored figures, central to the canon of English literature, Mrs. Ward was forgotten. Even her best novel, *Robert Elsmere* (1888), was regarded by most critics more as an illuminating historical document than as a work of literature in its own right.

Mary Ward came from a distinguished family. Her grandfather was the famous Dr. Thomas Arnold, a pioneer of English educational reform and headmaster of Rugby School; one of her uncles was Matthew Arnold, the leading Victorian essayist, and the family was connected to Britain's political and intellectual elite. Her father Thomas Arnold was also a successful scholar as a young man but an impractical dreamer. After graduating from Oxford, he emigrated to New Zealand where he tried to clear wild land and create a homestead farm. The physical labor was too much for him, however, and he accepted, instead, the job of educational advisor to the governor of Australia and Tasmania, where Mary herself was born in 1851.

When she was an infant her father fell under the spell of John Henry Newman's writings. Newman, a prominent Anglican minister and Oxford don, had horrified many of his contemporaries ten years before by converting to Roman Catholicism, after concluding that it represented the genuine line of theological descent from St. Peter to the present. In 1856, when Mary was five, her father converted to Catholicism, in Hobart, Tasmania. Her mother **Julia Sorrell Arnold**, a devout Protestant, was furious and threw a brick through the window of the Catholic church in which the ceremony was taking place. This conversion caused him to lose his job—public education in British colonies was a strictly Anglican preserve, and the family migrated back to Britain. Her father found a job working with Newman himself, first in Dublin, then as a teacher at Newman's Birmingham oratory school for Catholic boys. Mary lived partly at home, torn in affection between her parents but always loyal to the Church of England, and partly at an Anglican boarding school near Bristol. In 1869 at the age of 18, she published her first story, having already drafted numerous (never published) novels as a teenager.

After nine years as a Catholic, meanwhile, Thomas Arnold had reverted to Anglicanism and won a job as an Oxford don—he was an expert in Early English. But after another decade, just when he was about to be appointed to the coveted Rawlinson Professorship of Anglo-Saxon, he became a Catholic for a second time, and lost his chance. The family's fortunes fell on hard times again and Julia Arnold, enraged for a second time, separated from him, with the result that young Mary experienced one of the jarring religious controversies of the century in the midst of her own family life. (Her parents were never reconciled, and her mother died of cancer in 1888.) This fraught religious situation of her childhood provided material for several of Mary's later novels, particularly *Helbeck of Bannisdale.*

Growing up in Oxford, Mary proved to be exceptionally gifted intellectually but was denied the chance of formal higher education because Oxford was then an all-male university. In the 1870s, she contributed to the foundation of Somerville Hall (later the College at which *Dorothy Sayers and *Margaret Thatcher studied), the first women's educational institution there. At the age of 20, in 1872, she married T. Humphry Ward, a fellow of Brasenose College, Oxford, and from then on always took her husband's name. At that time, Oxford fellows had been forbidden to marry, and Humphry still needed to get permission from the university's proctors and surrender his fellowship, becoming a tutor instead. The couple continued to live in Oxford for another decade, where she gave birth to their two daughters and one son, but then they moved to London where he switched to a successful career as art critic for Britain's most influential newspaper, the London *Times.* Both spouses contributed regularly to the leading journals, with whose editors they were on friendly terms, including the *Manchester Guardian, Pall Mall Gazette, Nineteenth Century,* and *Macmillan's Magazine.* Mary, despite her lack of formal higher education, was invited to write a book on Spanish history for an Oxford series, and contributed dozens of learned articles to the *Dictionary of Christian Biography.*

Her first book, *Millie and Ollie,* a light-hearted story for children, appeared in 1881 when she was 30. Her second, *Miss Bretherton* (1884), much more serious, was a study of the theatrical and intellectual development of an actress in the form of a novel, and was filled with learned discussion of aesthetic theory. She began it after going with Henry James, one of her many literary friends, to see the performance of a famous American actress, *Mary Anderson.* She followed it the next year with a translation from French of Henri Frederic Amiel's *Intimate*

Journal, the self-exploration of a Swiss agnostic who found himself unable to believe in literal revealed Christianity in light of modern Biblical criticism and the scientific revolution. This book, along with her own experiences and her studies in ancient and modern philosophy, notably the works of Hegel, all contributed to her next and greatest book, *Robert Elsmere*. It was one of the dozens of religious theme novels published in 19th-century Britain. Newman himself had written a fictional transfiguration of his own conversion in *Loss and Gain* (1848), and it is clearly a forerunner of Ward's book, with each character representing a distinct set of religious ideas, and the drama of the book arising out of these theological views in conflict.

She is an aristocrat—not a vulgar aristocrat but an intellectual aristocrat, one whose ideal is of a small governing class of exquisite souls who would behave nicely to the poor, make just laws for them, and generally keep them in their proper station with a firm but gentle hand.

—Alfred George Gardiner

Published in 1888, *Robert Elsmere* was an explosive bestseller and remained in print almost without interruption for the next century. It describes sympathetically the plight of an Anglican cleric who loses his faith after studying modern science and Biblical criticism. He tries to create a new form of religion, the New Brotherhood, which takes Jesus as an inspiring human example instead of a supernatural figure. Elsmere's intellectual voyage paralleled Ward's own. Her studies in ancient history had introduced her to the idea that Biblical literature should be scrutinized with the same dispassionate care as all other ancient texts, and that much of it could be shown to derive from a primitive and magical world-view, which was no longer convincing to sophisticated minds in the progressive 19th century. In the same way Mrs. Ward puts into Elsmere's struggles the scientific revolution brought about by Lyell's geology and Darwin's biology, which showed the Earth to be far older than mankind, and the Genesis story of the Garden of Eden to be no more than a myth or allegory.

The novel's dramatic tension comes from the fact that Elsmere's wife Catherine, despite her deep love for him, is unconvinced by his arguments and clings to the severe evangelical Protestant faith she had learned as a girl from her father. A respectful but argumentative 23-page review by William Gladstone, the former Liberal prime minister, in the prestigious *Nineteenth Century*, gave the novel a crucial boost. Sales reached 30,000 in Britain in the first year, and four or five times as many copies (mostly pirated editions) sold in America. The book, widely discussed (pro and con) in the newspapers and learned journals, went through dozens of editions over the next decade, first in English, then in numerous translations. In *The Case of Richard Meynell* (1911), Ward reintroduced Catherine Elsmere and her daughter, 26 years on, to a second trial between traditional and modern Christianity, and in this sequel, as in the original, showed every character preoccupied with religious issues. As critic William Peterson notes, however, "she had not taken sufficiently into account the growing secularization of the contemporary world, the decline of all institutional forms of Christianity . . . and the widespread indifference to theological questions" by the second decade of the 20th century.

From *Robert Elsmere* onwards, Ward never ceased from regular publication of fiction, half of it straight romance, the other half organized around issues and causes in contemporary life. She also wrote literary criticism, including introductions to a new edition of the works of the Brontë sisters (whose influence is evident in much of her own work). Immensely hard working despite a growing number of ailments (rheumatism, gallstones, nervous exhaustion), she gathered around herself a growing entourage of helpers. **Lizzie Smith**, her maid, served her from 1880 until Ward's death in 1920, and Ward's daughter **Dorothy Ward** also devoted most of her young adult life to her mother's many causes. In 1893, Ward helped establish a social settlement house, the Passmore Edwards Settlement, in the poor East End of London, which was later renamed Mary Ward House in honor of her. The idea of settlement-house pioneers was to introduce the example of healthy middle-class living into the slums in the hope that they could uplift the poor and reform their vicious habits. Passmore Edwards specialized in giving poor children a place to play safely while their parents were at work, and in giving care to disabled children, for whom there was then no public education available. It remained a lifelong interest, for which she lobbied hard among her numerous political acquaintances.

Mrs. Ward's second outstanding novel was *Helbeck of Bannisdale* (1898), a story of Catholic conversion and the social and personal stress it caused in 19th-century England. Its central figure, Laura Fountain, is a young liberal

Protestant who falls in love with Alan Helbeck, the head of an old Catholic family from the north of England. Her relatives have the common anti-Catholic prejudices of the day, but she defies them and plans to convert to Catholicism and marry him. Eventually, however, she finds the Catholic Church dogmatic, inflexible, and intolerant of individuality. Unable to deny either her love for Alan Helbeck or her Protestant liberty, she commits suicide by drowning. Helbeck becomes a Jesuit priest. The novel, didactic but ingenious, makes a careful case for the Catholic religion in its first half, but builds up an anti-Catholic momentum as the possibility of the marriage increases. Ward was drawing from her own family history, and partially rewrote the book for the sake of her father's approval before publishing it. She had never been tempted to convert herself, despite her love for her father, but remained throughout her life a "progressive" Broad Church Anglican, taking the view that the Church of England should accommodate itself to a wide variety of intellectual and theological positions.

Among her friends were Gladstone, Henry James, Walter Pater (her next-door neighbor in Oxford), the mathematics don Charles Dodgson (better known as Lewis Carroll, author of *Alice in Wonderland*), Leslie Stephen (***Virginia Woolf**'s father), and many others prominent in British political and intellectual life. With her family, she visited the United States and Canada in 1908, finding the British colony more to her liking than the independent republic to its south. Her novel *Canadian Born*, published in 1910, drew on her visit to famous Canadian landmarks. Her fame had preceded her to America, however, and President Theodore Roosevelt invited her to dinner at the White House, where they became friends. They corresponded regularly after that, he visited her in England in 1910, and in 1916 her "open" letters to Roosevelt were published in the American press, explaining Britain's role in the First World War and urging the United States to join in the conflict against Germany. Her novel *Daphne* (1909) was an attack on the relative laxity of American divorce laws, which offended her sense that marriage was a sacrament, not merely a social arrangement.

Among the more dramatic social movements of the early 1900s was the campaign for women's suffrage. Mrs. Ward was horrified by suffragism and became one its most outspoken opponents. She was not, in her own eyes, against the advancement of women—indeed, she was an active exponent of higher education for women at the universities. But she believed that political rights for women would be more likely to hinder than help. Her first foray into the anti-suffrage cause was an 1889 article in *Nineteenth Century* entitled "An Appeal Against Female Suffrage." She argued that men and women were different by nature, that they had complementary roles to play in the world, that their differences ought not to be diminished, and that votes for women would undermine the moral foundations of family life. She also believed that women were too ignorant, even though her own life belied the claim. "It is of course true," she admitted in one newspaper arti-cle, "that many men in a democracy are politically ignorant. True; it is the great risk of democracy. But men are not *necessarily* ignorant." Her novels *The Testing of Diana Mallory* (1908) and *Daphne* (1909) introduced the issue of women's suffrage and depicted it in a harshly negative light.

In 1908, alarmed to find the idea of women's suffrage becoming more respectable in society, Ward became a founding member and the first president of the Women's National Anti-Suffrage League. Meanwhile the pro-suffrage forces, led by ***Emmeline Pankhurst** and her daughters ***Christabel** and ***Sylvia**, were organizing marches, arson attacks, shop-window smashing campaigns, and other forms of political direct action. They hoped to force the Liberal government to grant women's suffrage, though it actually retaliated by imprisoning Emmeline Pankhurst and her colleagues and force-feeding them when they went on hunger strike. Ward denounced them in dozens of speeches around Britain and wove her arguments into an anti-suffrage novel, *Delia Blanchflower* (1914), in which Gertrude Marvell, the suffragist leader (modeled on Mrs. Pankhurst), is burned to death in one of her own arson attacks.

Although she suffered from a wide variety of ailments as she aged, Ward continued her writing and publishing career at an exhausting pace. Her son Arnold, a brilliant scholar at Oxford but, like her father, an impractical man, was briefly a member of Parliament (1910–11) and later worked as a foreign correspondent for the London *Times*, but gambled recklessly and accumulated immense debts, which she tried valiantly to pay off. Humphry, her husband, suffered increasingly from amnesia and spent the last 15 years of his life largely as an invalid. She wrote three exuberantly patriotic books about the First World War while it was in progress, *England's Effort, Towards the Goal*, and *Fields of Victory*. The most famous poetry and fiction about the First World War, such as Remarque's *All Quiet on the Western Front* and Hemingway's *A Farewell to Arms*, are written from the point of view of disillusionment at the futility of the struggle. Mrs. Ward's books, by contrast, are full of vigor and propaganda pep: she took seriously the idea that it was a war for civilization and against German barbarism. Knowing personally the leading members of the government, she was able to visit munitions factories, the British fleet, and even the trench lines in northeastern France and Belgium. In effect she was, by these travels, becoming the first female war correspondent in British history. She also used the war as setting for three more novels, *Missing, The War and*

Elizabeth, and *Cousin Philip*, which followed the conventions of her earlier romances and intensified them with the danger of war and the heroic self-sacrifice of the men.

Despite her opposition to women's suffrage, Ward was impressed on visiting factories where women were now doing industrial work previously confined to men, and doing it well for the sake of the war effort, and she recognized that the war was causing a social revolution in gender relations that was not entirely bad. When, at the end of the war, British women were finally given the vote and other political rights, she benefited in an unexpected way, by being one among the first seven women to be appointed magistrates. By then, however, she was too sick to take up her duties. Suffering nervous disorders and bouts of temporary paralysis and rheumatism since the 1890s, worsened by eczema, and often necessitating morphine, she was ultimately diagnosed with a heart condition and died in March 1920. The 1920s vogue for D.H. Lawrence and James Joyce and the other daring modernists meant that her reputation, already (as she knew) in decline, faded rapidly. A revival of scholarly interest in the 1970s and 1980s has restored to historians and literary critics an awareness of Mrs. Humphry Ward and an appreciation for her novels, but it has not restored her to the pre-eminence she enjoyed in her lifetime.

SOURCES AND SUGGESTED READING:

Bindslev, Anne M. *Mrs. Humphry Ward: A Study in Late Victorian Feminine Consciousness.* Stockholm: Almqvist and Wiksell, 1985.

Colby, Vineta. *The Singular Anomaly: Women Novelists of the Nineteenth Century.* NY: New York University Press, 1970.

Jones, Enid Huws. *Mrs. Humphry Ward.* London: Heinemann, 1973.

Smith, Esther M.G. *Mrs. Humphry Ward.* Boston, MA: Twayne, 1980.

Sutherland, John. *Mrs. Humphry Ward: Eminent Victorian and Preeminent Edwardian.* Oxford, England: Clarendon Press, 1990.

Thesing, William B. and Stephen Pulsford. *Mrs. Humphry Ward: A Bibliography.* St. Lucia: University of Queensland, Australia, 1987.

COLLECTIONS:

Humphry Ward Manuscript Collection: Honnold Library, Claremont College, California; Pusey House, Oxford, UK; Mary Ward Center, Tavistock Place, London, UK.

Patrick Allitt,
Professor of History, Emory University,
Atlanta, Georgia

Ward, Ida Caroline (1880–1949)

British phonetician and West African language scholar. Born on October 4, 1880, in Bradford, Yorkshire, England; died on October 10, 1949, in Guildford, England; daughter of Samson Ward (a wool merchant) and Hannah (Tempest) Ward; educated in Bradford and at the Darlington Training College; Durham University, B.Litt., 1902; London University, Ph.D., 1933; never married.

Born in 1880 in Yorkshire, England, Ida Caroline Ward was the eighth child of Samson and **Hannah Ward,** and received her early education in her hometown of Bradford. After attending the Darlington Training College, she went on to graduate from Durham University with a bachelor's degree in 1902.

Ward taught secondary school for 16 years before entering the phonetics department of London's University College in 1919 and becoming an expert in the major European languages. Her interest in African languages grew into a specialty and in 1932, after joining the staff of what later became London University's School of Oriental and African Studies, she earned a doctorate from that institution on the strength of her scholarly research, published as *Phonetic and Tonal Structure of Efik.* Her study focused scientifically on the tonal importance of African language, a subject she pursued further with the groundbreaking *Introduction to the Ibo Language,* published in 1936. A year later, Ward was appointed head of the university's new department of African languages and cultures. From its humble beginnings, Ward established the department as an internationally recognized center for research on Africa, which was consulted by numerous missionary, educational and governmental bodies. Although Ward engaged herself in instructing English colonial officers to the African cultures they were to govern, she also taught Africans how to study their own language to perpetuate the scholarly study in African universities. She was instrumental in the development of the International African Institute's *Handbook of African Languages,* and her other scholarly works, *Practical Phonetics for Students of African Languages* (1933) and *Introduction to the Yoruba Language* (posthumously published in 1952), were no less important to the field.

England officially recognized Ward's numerous contributions to language study by making her a Commander of the British Empire in 1948, the same year she officially resigned her chair at the university and began a tour of American learning institutions. Ward lived with her widowed sister and passed away in Guildford, England, on October 10, 1949.

SOURCES:

The Dictionary of National Biography, 1941–1950. Edited by L.G. Wickham Legg and E.T. Williams. Oxford: Oxford University Press, 1959.

Judith C. Reveal,
freelance writer,
Greensboro, Maryland

Ward, Irene (1895–1980)

English politician. Name variations: Irene Mary Berwick Ward; Baroness Ward. Born in England in 1895; died in 1980; daughter of architect A.J. Berwick Ward; educated at Newcastle Church High School.

Was a member of Parliament (1931–45, 1950–74), which made her the longest serving woman member at the time; made a Dame of the British Empire (1951), and a Companion of Honor (1973); created a baroness (1974), and served in the House of Lords (1974–80).

Born in England in 1895, Irene Ward lost her father to tuberculosis when she was a young child; one of her most potent memories was of the financial struggles that her widowed mother then endured. Although she avoided the term "feminist," Ward was a lifelong advocate for disadvantaged women like her mother and, throughout her political career, stretched the boundaries for women's rights. Following her education at Newcastle Church High School, Ward worked as secretary to an industrialist, and also began her career in English politics as a volunteer with the Conservative Party.

Before she turned 30, Ward had made her first run for a seat in Parliament. Undeterred by her losses in that election and the one that followed five years later, she finally won election in the Wallsend campaign of 1931. A member of the government's delegation to the League of Nations during the 1930s, she retained her seat until 1945 when a Labour landslide ejected numerous Conservative incumbents like Ward. Her first term in office was marked by a concern for women's rights at home and in India as well. World War II gave Ward further opportunities to promote women's causes as chair of the Woman Power Committee, a group that influenced the most effective utilization of women during the labor shortage. Ward was an able advocate in pressuring the government to improve wages and working conditions for women; she was particularly outraged by the government's compensation package for injured individuals, which gave more to men than women.

Ward won re-election to Parliament in 1950, representing Tynemouth. Maintaining a firm hold on this seat, she served for 24 years in this position, becoming the longest-serving female Parliament member at the time. She continued to champion equal pay and was no respecter of parties when it came to calling the government to account on broken promises made to women during the crisis of the war. Ward achieved some of her economic objectives when the government guaranteed equal wages to teachers and civil servants in 1954. She then turned her focus to the needs of fixed-income households, particularly the plight of widows with young children. She also threw her support behind the unsuccessful Deserted Wives Bill, which would have averted homelessness among abandoned English women by transferring ownership of the family dwelling to the wife upon a husband's desertion.

Upon her retirement in 1974, Ward switched from the House of Commons to the House of Lords with her ascendancy to the title Baroness Ward of North Tyneside. Although fully supportive of the Sex Discrimination Bill of 1975, she demonstrated conservative political leanings in other areas. For example, she argued against liberalizing divorce and abortion laws, and defended the use of flogging for serious crimes. However, she by no means toed the party line when it came to her insistence on rights for women. She fought for greater representation in politics, the trade union movement, industry, civil service and other public bodies. Her commitment to women's rights kept the discrimination issue alive in England throughout the duration of her long career in politics.

SOURCES:

Banks, Olive. *The Biographical Dictionary of British Feminists, Vol. Two: A Supplement, 1900–1945.* NY: New York University Press, 1990.

Uglow, Jennifer S., comp. and ed. *The International Dictionary of Women's Biography.* NY: Continuum, 1985.

Judith C. Reveal,
freelance writer,
Greensboro, Maryland

Ward, Mary (1586–1645)

English nun and founder of the Institute of the Blessed Virgin Mary, a model for modern Catholic women's institutes. Born on February 2, 1586 (some sources cite January 23, 1585), in Yorkshire, England; died on January 20, 1645, in Hewarth, Yorkshire, England; daughter of Marmaduke Ward and Ursula (Wright) Ward.

Born in England in 1586 to prosperous parents, Mary Ward grew up in the Catholic faith that would become the focus of her life's work. Since Catholic religious orders were forbidden in Britain after Anglicanism became the state church, she entered a Poor Clares convent in the Netherlands in 1606 at the age of 20. Unable to submit to a cloistered existence, she left the convent to establish a new order based upon that of the Jesuits, which augmented a contemplative life with good works. Calling it the Institute of the Blessed Virgin Mary (IBVM), she and her followers established a new community for Englishwomen near Gravelines in northern France in 1607, and dedicated themselves to the founding of free schools for women. Her efforts opposed church restrictions regarding women religious, which forbade nuns from leaving the convent for any reason. It also differed in that it functioned without a choir, religious habits, or diocesan supervision.

In 1624, Pope Urban VIII rejected the plan Ward had submitted to him and effectively suppressed the society, closing the IBVM in Rome. Nevertheless, interest continued to grow, and, because the sisters were not easily identified by their dress, they were able to assist parishioners without drawing attention from the government. Although Ward experienced tremendous persecution during this time, the IBVM was able to extend its activities throughout France, Germany, Holland, Italy, Austria, and England. Resistant to the institute on the basis of its lack of enclosure, a papal bull dissolved the IBVM, and Ward was imprisoned for heresy in 1631. In 1637, she returned to England, and in 1639 the pope granted her permission to form a modified order there. She continued her work in Catholic education and moved to Yorkshire in the 1640s, dying in 1645. She was buried in Osbaldwick churchyard near York.

The rule of the institute she had founded was approved in 1703 by Pope Clement XI. In 1877, Pope Pius IX fully restored it as the Institute of Mary, and modern Catholic women's institutes use it as a model. Officially recognized by the Catholic Church in 1909 as the founder of the IBVM, Ward was also acknowledged in 1951 by Pope Pius XII for her religious work in England during the 17th century.

SOURCES:

Bell, Maureen, George Parfitt, and Simon Shepherd. *A Biographical Dictionary of English Women Writers, 1580–1720*. Boston, MA: G.K. Hall, 1990.

The Cambridge Biographical Encyclopedia. Edited by David Crystal. Cambridge: Cambridge University Press, 1998.

The Concise Dictionary of National Biography. Oxford: Oxford University Press, 1992.

Delaney, John J., and James Edward Tobin. *Dictionary of Catholic Biography*. Garden City, NY: Doubleday, 1961.

McClory, Robert. "Catholic dissent: When wrong turns out to be right," in *U.S. Catholic*. May 1999.

The New Catholic Encyclopedia. Catholic University Press, 1967.

Uglow, Jennifer S., comp. and ed. *The International Dictionary of Women's Biography*. 2nd ed. NY: Continuum, 1985.

Judith C. Reveal,
freelance writer,
Greensboro, Maryland

Ward, Mary (1827–1869)

Irish author, artist, naturalist, astronomer and microscopist. Name variations: Mary King. Born in 1827 in Ferbane, Ireland; died in 1869; married Henry Ward, later 5th Viscount Bangor.

Born in Ireland in 1827, Mary Ward built on her private education to become a noted astronomer and scientist. Her skill with microscopes and telescopes produced two significant works: *Sketches with the Microscope* and *Telescope Teachings* (1859). The former enjoyed such success that it was reprinted eight times between 1858 and 1888 under the title *The World of Wonders as Revealed by the Microscope*. The revision of the book appeared as *Microscope Teachings*. Her equally accomplished *Telescope Teachings* sprang from her experience with what was then the world's largest telescope, located on the grounds of Birr Castle. Ward's numerous publications benefited from her skill as an illustrator, a talent she employed in works by other writers such as Sir David Brewster's *Life of Newton*. The fame of her books extended to the 1862 International Exhibition at the Crystal Palace at which two of them were on display. Seven years later, Ward perished in a steam carriage accident.

SOURCES:

Newman, Kate, comp. *Dictionary of Ulster Biography*. Belfast: Institute of Irish Studies, Queen's University, 1993.

Judith C. Reveal,
freelance writer,
Greensboro, Maryland

Ward, Mary Augusta (1851–1920).

See Ward, Mrs. Humphry.

Ward, Nancy (1738–1822).

See Nanye'hi.

Ward, Winifred Louise (1884–1975)

American children's theater specialist. Born on October 29, 1884, in Eldora, Iowa; died following a stroke on August 16, 1975, in Evanston, Illinois; daughter of George Ward (a lawyer and city official) and Frances

Allena (Dimmick) Ward; graduated from Cumnock School of Oratory in Evanston, Illinois, 1905; University of Chicago, Ph.B. in English, 1918; never married.

Winifred Louise Ward was born in 1884 in Eldora, Iowa, the third of four children and the youngest daughter of George Ward and **Frances Dimmick Ward**. Her father served as mayor and school board member as well as county attorney. Her mother devoted her energies to raising the family and participating in civic activities whenever possible. Fond of her father's dramatic readings and her mother's cultivated tastes in music, Ward entered the Cumnock School of Oratory in Evanston, Illinois, after completing her public school education in Eldora in 1902. She finished the diploma course in oratory in 1905 and directed plays for two years. She then returned to Cumnock to complete postgraduate studies in oratory. Ward moved to Adrian, Michigan, where she taught in the public schools for eight years before entering the University of Chicago in 1916, where she earned a Ph.B. in English.

Upon completing her graduate work in 1918, Ward joined the faculty of the Cumnock School, which became the Northwestern University School of Speech in 1920. With assistance and support from the dean, Ward strengthened the speech education curriculum at the school during her first decade there. Extending study to 12 courses, she also negotiated with the Evanston public school system to field-test her theories regarding story dramatization with children. This partnership with the Evanston schools led to her appointment as the supervisor of dramatics. In 1925, with the sponsorship of Northwestern University, she co-founded the Children's Theater of Evanston, which provided a venue for students to develop their technical skills and their proficiency in acting, directing, and producing. The theater, which Ward directed until 1950, was a joint project between the university and the community. According to *Notable American Women*, the theater was unique in that it utilized college students for all adult roles and children from the public schools for all juvenile parts.

In 1930, Ward produced her first book, *Creative Dramatics*, which advocated a child-centered approach to instruction. She carefully distinguished between drama "with" children and drama "for" children. Drama "with" children focused on the process of creating, while drama "for" children focused on the end product. Her second book, *Theatre for Children* (1939), expanded upon these ideas. Her third book, *Playmaking With Children*, completed in 1947, was aimed at young people interested in the dramatic arts, not the trained specialist. Considered one of the most comprehensive manuals available for inexperienced creative dramatics leaders, it became a standard text in its field. In 1952, Ward published her last book, *Stories to Dramatize*, a compilation of stories suitable for dramatization with children. It, too, is considered a standard text in its field.

Ward was an active participant in numerous professional organizations, including the American Educational Theater Association, which requested her to chair a committee on children's theater in 1936. It was through her work in this capacity that she founded the influential Children's Theater Conference at Northwestern University in 1944. For more than 50 years, Ward lived with her closest friend and colleague at Northwestern, **Hazel Easton**. In 1975, Ward died of a stroke in Evanston.

SOURCES:

Sicherman, Barbara, and Carol Hurd Green, eds. *Notable American Women: The Modern Period*. Cambridge, MA: The Belknap Press of Harvard University, 1980.

Judith C. Reveal,
freelance writer,
Greensboro, Maryland

Wardlaw, Elizabeth (1677–1727)

Scottish poet. Name variations: Elizabeth Halket. Born in April 1677; died in 1727; daughter of Janet (Murray) Halket and Sir Charles Halket; married Sir Henry Wardlaw, on June 13, 1696.

Lady Elizabeth Wardlaw was born Elizabeth Halket in April 1677 in Fife, the daughter of **Janet Murray Halket** and Sir Charles Halket of Pitfarraine. In 1696, she married Sir Henry Wardlaw of Pitcruivie. Lady Wardlaw is best remembered as the supposed author of the ballad "Hardyknute," which she claimed to have discovered as a fragment in a vault in Dunfermline. It was published in 1719 as an example of an ancient Scottish epic, and in 1724 Allan Ramsay published it in *The Ever Green*. The authenticity of the ballad was called into question in 1765 when it appeared in *Reliques of Ancient English Poetry* by Bishop Thomas Percy, and the controversy gave rise to false speculation that Lady Wardlaw might also have reworked the ballad "Sir Patrick Spens."

Judith C. Reveal,
freelance writer,
Greensboro, Maryland

Warfield, Wallis (1895–1986).

See Windsor, Wallis Warfield, duchess of.

Waring, Anna Letitia (1823–1910)

British hymnwriter. Name variations: Anna Laetitia Waring. Born on April 19, 1823, in Plas-y-Velin, Neath, Glamorganshire; died on May 10, 1910; daughter of Elijah Waring and Deborah Waring; never married.

Anna Letitia Waring was born in 1823 in Plas-y-Velin, Neath, Glamorganshire, the second daughter of Elijah and **Deborah Waring**, both active members of the Society of Friends. She began writing hymns at an early age and followed in the footsteps of her uncle, Samuel Miller Waring, a hymnwriter who left the Society of Friends to join the Church of England. Like her uncle, Waring also left the Society to join the Church of England. She learned to read Hebrew and studied the Psalms on a daily basis, as well as the Hebrew poetry of the Old Testament.

In 1846, at age 23, Waring wrote "Father, I know that all my life," one of her most popular works. Her hymns were widely embraced and her volume *Hymns and Meditations*, written in 1850 and containing 18 hymns, was reprinted through many editions in both the 19th and 20th centuries. As she continued to produce hymns, she added them to successive editions, until the 1863 publication contained 38 songs. Waring was a prolific religious writer, whose works included *Additional Hymns* (1858) and *Days of Remembrance* (1886). She never married and continued writing hymns until her death in 1910.

Judith C. Reveal,
freelance writer,
Greensboro, Maryland

Waring, Laura Wheeler (1887–1948)

African-American artist and educator. Born in 1887 in Hartford, Connecticut; died on February 3, 1948; daughter of Robert Foster Wheeler (a minister) and Mary (Freeman) Wheeler; attended the Pennsylvania Academy of Fine Arts; attended the Académie de la Grande Chaumière in Paris; married Walter E. Waring.

Laura Wheeler Waring was born in Hartford, Connecticut, in 1887, into a progressive and prominent African-American family. Her father Robert Foster Wheeler graduated from Howard University's theology school and served as minister of the Talcott Street Congregational Church. Waring was a bright student and a gifted artist. Her early education in Hartford included Arsenal Grade School and the Hartford High School. Her artistic talents then drew her to Philadelphia where she enrolled in the Pennsylvania Academy of Fine Arts in September 1906. Displaying originality and mastery in her technique, Waring was awarded the Cresson Travel Scholarship in 1914, which enabled her to journey to many Western European countries to further her studies. Her early works reflect the scenes she witnessed during her first trips to such capitals as London, Dublin, Paris, and Rome. With the onset of World War I, she returned to America and completed her studies in Philadelphia.

Waring became director of the art and music departments at Cheyney State Teachers College, remaining there for three decades and influencing hundreds of students. During this tenure, she produced many of her best-known portraits, including those of Leslie Pickney Hill, president emeritus of Cheyney, and numerous trustees and faculty. Although well known for her portraits, Waring also produced excellent landscapes of Chester and Delaware County, Pennsylvania. According to *Notable Black American Women*, she developed a style in these works that combined impressionism and academicism. In 1924, Waring again traveled to Paris, where she enrolled in the Académie de la Grande Chaumière. Here, she was influenced by the French masters Boutet de Monvel and Eugène Delécluse. She also visited Italy and North Africa.

Still Life with Heather, by Laura Wheeler Waring.

Waring began to enjoy increased recognition, and in 1926 she was the official in charge of the Negro Art section at the Sesquicentennial Exposition in Philadelphia. In 1927, she performed a similar function at the Texas Centennial Exposition. That same year, she won a gold medal in the annual Harmon Foundation Salon. Waring was also invited to exhibit in well-known galleries, such as the Pennsylvania Academy of Fine Arts, the Philadelphia Museum of Art, the Carlen Galleries, the National Collection of Arts, the Corcoran Gallery, the Art Institute of Chicago, the Brooklyn Museum, and Howard University. She made a third and final trip abroad, where she held a one-woman show at the Galerie du Luxembourg in Paris.

Known primarily as a portrait painter, Waring was praised for her use of color, her vivid imagination, and a steady strength of line. Her work is especially significant for having preserved the images of many distinguished African-Americans who were instrumental in securing freedom in America, in particular such great personalities as W.E.B. Du Bois, John Haynes Holmes, *Marian Anderson, and ❧ Jessie Redmon Fauset. In 1946, two years before her death, Waring began a series of religious paintings depicting her understanding of the Negro spiritual, including *Jacob's Ladder*, *The Coming of the Lord*, and *Heaven, Heaven*.

SOURCES:

Rubinstein, Charlotte Streifer. *American Women Artists.* NY: Avon, 1982.

Smith, Jessie Carney, ed. *Notable Black American Women.* Detroit, MI: Gale Research, 1992.

Judith C. Reveal,
freelance writer,
Greensboro, Maryland

❧▶
Fauset, Jessie Redmon. See Women of the Harlem Renaissance.

Warner, Anna Bartlett (1827–1915).

See joint entry under Warner, Susan Bogert and Anna Bartlett Warner.

Warner, Susan Bogert and Anna Bartlett Warner

Warner, Susan Bogert (1819–1885). Writer who was the first American to sell over a million copies of a book. Name variations: (pseudonym) Elizabeth Wetherell. Born Susan Bogert Warner on July 11, 1819, in New York City; died on March 17, 1885, in Highland Falls, New York; daughter of Henry Whiting Warner and Anna (Bartlett) Warner; sister of Anna Bartlett Warner (1827–1915); educated privately.

Selected writings: The Wide, Wide World (1852); Queechy (1852); American Female Patriotism: A Prize Essay (1852); The Law and the Testimony (1853); The Hills of Shatemuc (1856); The Old Helmet (1863); Melbourne House (1864); Walks from Eden (1865); The House of Israel (1866); Daisy (1869); Daisy in the Field (1869); The Broken Walls of Jerusalem and the Rebuilding of Them (1870); "What She Could" (1870); The House in Town (1870); Opportunities (1871); Lessons on the Standard Bearers of the Old Testament (1872); Trading (1872); The Little Camp on Eagle Hill (1873); Sceptres and Crowns (1874); Willow Brook (1874); Bread and Oranges (1875); The Flag of Truce (1875); The Rapids of Niagara (1876); Pine Needles (1877); Diana (1877); The Kingdom of Judah (1878); My Desire (1879); The End of a Coil (1880); The Letter of Credit (1881); Nobody (1882); Stephen, M.D. (1883); A Red Wallflower (1884); Daisy Plains (1885).

Warner, Anna Bartlett (1827–1915). American author who was the first to publish a do-it-yourself gardening book. Name variations: (pseudonym) Amy Lothrop. Born Anna Bartlett Warner on August 31, 1827, in New York City; died on January 15, 1915, in Highland Falls, New York; daughter of Henry Whiting Warner and Anna (Bartlett) Warner; sister of Susan Bogert Warner (1819–1885); educated privately.

Selected writings: Carl Krinken: His Christmas Stocking (1853); Say and Seal (1860); Dollars and Cents (1852); Gardening by Myself (1872); Wych Hazel (1876); The Gold of Chickaree (1876); Susan Warner (1909).

Susan Bogert Warner and Anna Bartlett Warner were born eight years apart in New York City to prosperous lawyer Henry Whiting Warner and Anna Bartlett Warner. Their mother died when the girls were still young, and they were raised by an aunt. Susan, the only one of the Warners' first four children to survive, was of a nervous temperament and remarkably different from her more boisterous younger sister. Both girls received a private education in music and Italian from tutors while their father oversaw their studies in history, literature, and the classics. In 1836, Henry Warner purchased Constitution Island on the Hudson River near West Point, and moved his family to this remote location. He had envisioned the former Revolutionary outpost—complete with the ruins of an old fort—as a summer retreat, but the economic panic of 1837 forced the family to give up their expensive quarters in the city and live on the island full-time. The family's financial straits had a profound impact on the Warner girls. Now responsible for their own cooking, cleaning, and gardening, they also assumed such tasks as chopping firewood and rowing to the mainland for supplies and mail. Susan felt the loss of the family's position in society more keenly than did Anna, since she had been on the cusp of her society debut, but the hardship drew the sisters together despite their differing temperaments.

Economic necessity also propelled the sisters into writing careers. According to **Ruth K. MacDonald**, all of the novels by the Warner sisters "deal with the genteel society the two had known during their family's prosperous period and with the evangelical Protestantism which they both professed." Writing under the pseudonym Elizabeth Wetherell, Susan Warner published her first book, *The Wide, Wide World* (1852), which featured a character not unlike a female Huck Finn. Numerous publishers refused her manuscript before it was accepted and published by Putnam. The novel, like her other works, has religious overtones and a rural setting. Phenomenally popular, in part because of favorable theological reviews, it outsold Charles Dickens' *David Copperfield* in England, making Susan the first American to sell more than a million copies of a book, and was read into the 20th century. Shedding her pen name, she followed this success with two more novels, *Queechy* (1852) and *The Law and the Testimony* (1853), which both experienced moderate success. In 1856, Susan Warner published *The Hills of the Shatemuc*, which sold 10,000 copies on the day of its release. A prolific writer, she published at least one book each year from 1856 until her death in 1885.

Anna Warner's first book, *Dollars and Cents*, was also published in 1852. A mildly humorous story about a once-prosperous family who experienced financial hardship and had to move to the country, it was a moderate parallel to her own family's circumstances. She also developed a popular educational card game called "Robinson Crusoe's Farm," which was sold for many years through the George P. Putnam store. Anna Warner went on to publish some 25 books, including children's fiction, religious subjects, and gardening. She took great pleasure in gardening and in 1872 published *Gardening by Myself*, which deals with the planning, preparation and attention to her own garden. Extremely popular, this book was reprinted 50 years after its first publication. Anna's religious works included verse and the words to several hymns, her best-known efforts being "Jesus Loves Me, This I Know," and "Jesus Bids Us Shine." Although Susan was the more popular and successful of the two authors, Anna's writing displays greater versatility and a lighter touch. Her last book, published in 1909, was a biography of Susan.

Economic necessity forced Susan to sell her rights to *The Wide, Wide World*, and due to a lack of copyright protection, she did not receive payment when it was published abroad. Although the sisters never became rich from their writings, they were able to support themselves. Religion was a very important part of their lives and, in addition to their writing, they conducted Bible classes for West Point cadets, which included serious reading and discussion sessions followed by tea and gingerbread. In the winter, the classes were held at the academy; during warmer months, they were held on the island and provided time and opportunity for the cadets to explore the area.

Although Susan and Anna were not particularly close as children, given the difference in their ages, their isolated existence on Constitution Island and their interests in reading and writing eventually drew them together. In addition to their individual efforts, the sisters collaborated on several children's books. According to MacDonald, critical interest in their work has not revealed a lasting influence upon children's literature; however, as successful authors in the 19th century, they inspired the domestic fiction of other women writers.

Susan Warner died in Highland Falls, New York, in 1885. Anna remained on the island for the next 30 years. During this time, she was offered considerable sums of money for Constitution Island but steadfastly refused to sell. The sisters had wanted the island to become part of West Point, but bills to acquire it repeatedly failed to pass Congress. It was eventually purchased by *Margaret Olivia Sage, who presented it to the government in 1908 in her name and that of Anna Warner. Anna died in 1915 and is buried with her sister in the government cemetery at West Point, where their graves overlook Constitution Island.

SOURCES:

Edgerly, Lois Stiles, ed. *Give Her This Day*. Gardiner, ME: Tilbury House, 1990.

James, Edward T., ed. *Notable American Women, 1607–1950*. Cambridge, MA: The Belknap Press of Harvard University, 1971.

MacDonald, Ruth K. "Susan Bogert Warner," in *Dictionary of Literary Biography*, Vol. 42: *American Writers for Children Before 1900*. Detroit, MI: Gale Group, 1985, pp. 362–367.

Read, Phyllis J., and Bernard L. Witlieb. *The Book of Women's Firsts*. NY: Random House, 1992.

Stern, Madeline B., and Leona Rostenberg. "Susan Bogert Warner," in *Dictionary of Literary Biography*, Vol. 3: *Antebellum Writers in New York and the South*. Detroit, MI: Gale Group, 1979, pp. 348–349.

Weatherford, Doris. *American Women's History*. NY: Prentice Hall, 1994.

Judith C. Reveal,
freelance writer,
Greensboro, Maryland

Warner, Sylvia Ashton (1908–1984).

See Ashton-Warner, Sylvia.

Warner, Sylvia Townsend

(1893–1978)

British author who, over a period of 50 years, won critical acclaim and a large readership in England and the U.S. for her novels, poetry, short stories, and biography of writer T.H. White. Born Sylvia Townsend Warner at Harrow, Middlesex, England, on December 6, 1893; died at home in Maiden Newton, Dorset, on May 1, 1978; only child of George Townsend Warner (an assistant master at the famed Harrow School for Boys) and Eleanor Mary (Nora) Hudleston (who was raised in Madras where her father was an officer in the Indian army); educated at home by parents and by Harrow's distinguished musicologist, Dr. Percy Buck, who all marvelled at her erudition, phenomenal memory, and musicality; lived with Valentine Ackland for 30 years.

During World War I, interrupted her budding career as a composer to work as a shell machinist in a munitions factory; served as one of four editors of the ten-volume Tudor Church Music *(1917–29); published first volume of poetry,* The Espalier *(1925); found fame and a comfortable income with first novel,* Lolly Willowes *(1926); published two other novels,* Mr. Fortune's Maggot *and* The True Heart, *which added to her reputation as one of England's leading writers (1927–29); formed a relationship with the poet Valentine Ackland that lasted until the latter's death in 1969 (1930); frustrated by the continuing economic depression and England's appeasement of Hitler, joined the Communist Party along with Ackland (1935); after the outbreak of the Spanish Civil War, spent three weeks in Barcelona, Spain, working with a Red Cross Unit aiding the anti-fascist Spanish Republic (1936); along with Ackland, attended as a British delegate the Second Congress of the International Association of Writers for the Defense of Culture held in Madrid (1937); with Ackland, left for U.S. (mid-1939) to attend the Third Congress of American Writers, cutting short visit after World War II began; published two novels,* Summer Will Show *(1936) and* After the Death of Don Juan *(1939), which reflect her political commitment to Marxism and deep admiration for the Spanish people's fight against Fascism; involved in war work in Dorset until Germany's surrender in May 1945; her novel about 14th-century nuns,* The Corner That Held Them, *revived interest in her work (1947), as did her last novel,* The Flint Anchor *(1954); for the remainder of her life, wrote some poetry and many short stories*

published in both England and U.S.; her biography of T.H. White was universally praised (1967); grieved by the death of her companion Valentine (1969); edited two volumes of Ackland's poems (early 1970s); published her last collection of short stories, Kingdoms of Elfin, *to wide acclaim (1977); died at the home shared with Ackland for 30 years, Frome Vauchurch, in Maiden Newton, Dorset (1978).*

Selected writings: in addition to the seven novels mentioned above, Sylvia Townsend Warner published eight volumes of verse and thirteen volumes of stories, many of which first appeared in The New Yorker. *Her* T.H. White: A Biography *(1967) was published in Great Britain and the United States, as was most of her fiction and poetry. Her earlier translation of Marcel Proust's* Contre Saint-Beuve *appeared in 1958.*

In the early hours of December 6, 1893, one of Great Britain's most original writers, Sylvia Townsend Warner, was born to George Townsend Warner and **Nora Hudleston Warner** at Harrow-on-the-Hill in Middlesex. George Townsend Warner had been a brilliant student at Cambridge, and following in the footsteps of his father and grandfather, who had been masters at Newton College and Harrow School, respectively, was an assistant master at Harrow School at the time of his daughter's birth. Sylvia's mother Nora had grown up in Madras, India, and years later Warner recalled that her mother's "recollections of her childhood in India were so vivid to her that they became inseparably part of my own childhood, like the arabesques of a wallpaper showing through a coating of distemper."

Warner was a highly intelligent but solitary child who at age six was removed from a local kindergarten for disruptive behavior. She was educated at home by her mother, with whom she studied the Bible, geography, history, French, Shakespeare, and Dickens. Later they studied the Russian novelists Tolstoy, Dostoevsky, and Turgenev together. Her father, judged one of the best teachers of his time, gave her intensive classes in history during the school holidays. At a young age, Sylvia felt like an outsider, and was very much aware that she was an only child and a female child who, at Harrow, was living in a world totally dedicated to the education of boys. It did not help that her mother's love diminished when it was clear, by adolescence, that Warner was not beautiful. However, her father doted on her and encouraged her to study with Harrow's distinguished musicologist, Dr. Percy Buck (knighted in 1936). At age 16, Sylvia was studying piano and organ, as well as composition and the history and theory of music, rising every morning at seven to practice the piano.

In 1914, Warner had planned to study composition abroad with Arnold Schoenberg, but the outbreak of World War I made that impossible. She continued to compose on her own, and developed a strong interest in 15th- and 16th-century music. In 1915, she interrupted her musical studies to work as a shell machinist in a Vickers munitions factory. She found the work monotonous and difficult, noting that "the noise eats [the workers] like a secret poison."

In late September 1916, Warner suffered a devastating blow when her father died suddenly. Buck, Sylvia's teacher and mentor, was aware that Nora Warner had little use for an uncongenial and unmarried daughter. Through Buck's influence, Warner was appointed one of the four editors of a monumental project to gather, record, and publish Tudor church music. The project was funded by the American Carnegie Trust and lasted for ten years; the last of the ten volumes of *Tudor Church Music* appeared in 1929. Warner's salary of £3 a week made it possible for her to live on her own in London.

Sylvia
Townsend
Warner

While still engaged as an editor of the project, Warner began to write poetry. In 1925, an influential friend, Charles Prentice of Chatto & Windus (which was to publish all of Warner's work in England), persuaded the firm to publish her first volume of verse, *The Espalier*. The discriminating novelist and critic *Virginia Woolf recorded in her diary that she had met Chatto & Windus' "new poetess" and had liked Warner's traditional yet original poems well enough to spend two shillings and sixpence for a copy of *The Espalier*.

The following year Chatto & Windus published Warner's first novel, *Lolly Willowes*, to wide acclaim on both sides of the Atlantic. Some 90 reviews of the work, all of them favorable, appeared in 1926 and 1927. The novel, still in print, concerns a spinster who finds liberation from a life of dependency by becoming a witch. Warner was inspired to write the novel after reading **Elizabeth Murray**'s *The Witch Cult in Western Europe* (1921), a study that gave a new respectability to witchcraft. Murray, an Egyptologist whom Warner was delighted to meet after the novel's appearance, argued that witchcraft was a pagan religion that had deep and wide roots in Western Europe and was never totally displaced by Christianity. After reading *Lolly Willowes*, Virginia Woolf invited the author to lunch and asked Sylvia how it was that she knew so much about witchcraft. Warner answered, matter of factly but with tongue in cheek, "because I am one."

I think musical considerations—form, modulation, tempi and so on—have always been an influence in my work.

—Sylvia Townsend Warner

When *Lolly Willowes* was chosen as the first offering by the Book-of-the-Month Club in the United States, Warner discovered, to her astonishment, that she could earn a living from something that gave her great pleasure: her writing. As a matter of fact, except for some lean years during the Depression and the immediate post-World War II era, she enjoyed a comfortable income from her writing for the remainder of her life. Warner had always been generous to friends in need, even when she earned only £3 a week, and when she died in 1978 she left legacies to all her surviving friends, young and old.

Inspired by the written account of a spinster missionary's experiences in Polynesia, Warner wrote her second novel, *Mr. Fortune's Maggot*, at breakneck speed, publishing it in 1927. The novel was a daring work for its time, as her missionary,

Mr. Fortune (a *most* unfortunate man), is clearly homosexual. After a year's effort, Mr. Fortune converts only one native (with whom he has fallen in love), and loses his own faith after his male convert, Lueli, relapses into paganism. Warner later wrote that by age seven she was as agnostic as a cat, and her novel clearly reflects her antipathy towards both Anglicanism and imperialism.

By 1929, on the eve of the Great Depression, Warner herself was feeling depressed and lonely, despite her continued success as a writer. (The publication, in 1929, of her third novel, *The True Heart*, a retelling of the Cupid and Psyche myth set in Victorian England, had added to her fame.) Her interests in art, architecture, music, history, drama, and literature continued unabated, and Warner could count on many loyal and interesting friends in London and in Dorset, in southern England. But alas, something vital was missing: "this thing called love." She had recently ended a long and very discreet affair with her mentor, Percy Buck, and when she became attracted to a graduate of Harrow, the sculptor Steven Tomlin, her pride was deeply wounded when he made it clear that he found her physically unappealing.

In 1927, Warner was introduced by a close friend and fellow writer, Theodore Powys, to a tall, beautiful and unpublished poet by the name of **Valentine Ackland**. At first, Warner was uninterested in Ackland, but in time they became friends. In 1930, Ackland's landlord abruptly terminated her lease on a cottage in the village of West Chaldon, Dorset, after Valentine had invited Sylvia to use the cottage whenever the latter wished to escape the heat and noise of London. Feeling remorseful, Warner rented a cottage not far from the village and offered to share it with Ackland. One night in October 1930, Sylvia heard Valentine's plaintive voice through the partition that separated their bedrooms. When she heard Ackland cry out that she felt utterly unloved, Sylvia, who probably felt the same way, took Valentine in her arms.

In modern-day vernacular, the two women became domestic partners, and every January 12th, the day they took their own vows, they celebrated their wedding anniversary. In their diaries and letters, they always referred to their nearly 40-year relationship as a marriage, and after Ackland's death in November 1969, Warner described herself as a widow. Their love was, in Shakespeare's words, "an ever-fixéd mark that looks on tempests and is never shaken." They did indeed look on tempests in their long relationship, and, in 1939, Warner was badly shaken when Ackland fell in love with **Elizabeth Wade White**, an American poet and biographer of *Anne Bradstreet. Despite Ackland's infidelity, Warner adhered to her promise always to stand by her. Ackland, who had the habit of twisting herself in knots, consumed by guilt and worry, finally terminated her on again-off again relationship with White by the early 1950s. Ackland had always known that she could not live without Warner.

Sharon B. Watstein points out in her essay on Warner in *Gay and Lesbian Literature* (1994) that "Warner and Ackland neither hid nor emphasized their lesbianism or their relationship." The only time they celebrated their love for each other in print seems to have been in a collection of poems, *Whether a Dove or Seagull*, which Warner's American publisher, Viking Press, published in 1933. Half of the 110 poems, none of which was signed and only a few of which were titled, were written by Warner and the other half by Ackland. In a note to the reader, they explained that the book was "a protest against the frame of mind, too common, which judges the poem by the poet, rather than the poet by the poem."

The very year *Whether a Dove or Seagull* was published Hitler came to power in Germany. Alarmed and outraged by the deepening economic depression and Great Britain's mealy-mouthed response to Hitler, both Warner and Ackland became political activists. By 1935, when it was clear that only the Soviet Union was taking a stand against a rearmed and threatening Nazi Germany, both Warner and Ackland joined the British Communist Party, an obligation they kept until after World War II ended. Warner's political commitment to Marxism is reflected in her fourth novel, *Summer Will Show*, published

Ackland, Valentine (1906–1969)

British author. Born Mary Kathleen McCrory Ackland in 1906 in London, England; died of breast cancer on November 9, 1969, in Dorset, England; sister of Joan Ackland, eight years older; married Richard Turpin; lived with Sylvia Townsend Warner for 30 years; no children. Selected works: (with Sylvia Townsend Warner) Whether a Dove or Seagull (1934); Country Conditions (1936); The Nature of the Moment (1973); Further Poems (1978); For Sylvia, An Honest Account (1985).

Mary Kathleen Ackland's strict Anglo-Catholic upbringing in London and Norfolk brought her into conflict when, at convent school, she had an intimate encounter with a female school friend. Upon discovering this, her father distanced her from the family. Still in her late teens, Ackland moved to London, becoming an unusual figure in 1920s society and good friends with poet, publisher, and activist *Nancy Cunard. Taking the androgynous name "Valentine," Ackland began to write and publish poetry seriously. She also began her first serious involvement with a woman, Tory speaker **Bo Foster**. The two maintained their affair even after Ackland married Richard Turpin. The union was a sham, and husband and wife never consummated their marriage. Instead, Ackland became pregnant by another man and miscarried, to her great disappointment, when she slipped down a bank at Chaldon. Her marriage to Turpin was annulled.

At the turn of the decade, Ackland ended her relationship with Foster and began a long live-in relationship with novelist *Sylvia Townsend Warner. Their dedication to one another was apparent in their writing. When apart, Ackland and Warner wrote letters to one another twice a day. In their poetry, the two wrote separately but published together, without individual attribution. They also expressed strong political and social opinions through their poetry, essays and stories, which appeared in such publications as *The New Statesman* and *Women Today*. In 1935, reacting against the growing trend toward Fascism in Europe, Ackland and Warner joined the Communist Party of Great Britain and briefly served in an ambulance unit during the Spanish Civil War. No political party encompassed their beliefs, however, and they shortly grew disinterested in Communism as well.

A longterm drinking problem and an affair with **Elizabeth Wade White** temporarily separated Ackland from Warner. Ultimately, Ackland reaffirmed her Catholicism and reunited with Warner, with whom she lived in Dorset. Ackland continued to write and publish, mostly nonfiction, until her death from metastasized breast cancer in 1969. Two volumes of her poetry were published posthumously, as well as *To Sylvia*, written for Warner, which was Ackland's account of her vices, guilt, and views of their relationship. Much of her unpublished work is held at the Dorset County Museum.

SOURCES:

Maxwell, William, ed. *Letters: Sylvia Townsend Warner*. NY: Viking Press, 1982.

Mulford, Wendy. *This Narrow Place: Sylvia Townsend Warner and Valentine Ackland: Life, Letters and Politics, 1930–1951*. London: Pandora Press, 1988.

Crista Martin,
Boston, Massachusetts

in 1936 and set in France during the Revolution of 1848. While the critics found the novel interesting, it did not sell as well as her earlier work. However, 1936 also marked the year that *The New Yorker* first published a short story by Warner. During the next 40 years, *The New Yorker* published an additional 143 of her stories, which attest to both her fine narrative skills and her considerable popularity among American readers. The income from *The New Yorker* helped Sylvia and Valentine through some hard times in the late 1930s and after.

Shortly after the publication of *Summer Will Show* and in November 1936, Warner and Ackland journeyed to Spain for three weeks to show their support for the beleaguered Spanish Republic, returning again the next summer. In July 1936, the Spanish Civil War had erupted, a conflict that pitted the left-wing Republic against a conservative-fascist coalition led by General Francisco Franco and aided by Hitler and Mussolini. Warner, like many other writers and intellectuals of her time, never forgot her vivid impressions of a people in arms against Fascism. Shortly after Franco's triumph in April 1939, her fifth novel, *After the Death of Don Juan*, appeared. Set in rural Spain, the novel concerns the defeat, by heartless and greedy landowners, of peasants seeking land, liberty, and justice. Warner's homage to Spain did not sell well at the time, but it was republished in the 1990s.

When World War II broke out in September 1939, Warner and Ackland were in the United States attending a Writers' Congress. They were urged to remain in America, but, loyal to their embattled country, they returned to Great Britain and were both involved in war work until the conflict in Europe ended in May 1945. After the war was over and in 1947, Warner published her sixth novel, *The Corner That Held Them*. Set in a 14th-century English convent where the nuns are distracted by financial woes, the novel drew from Warner's wartime experience of working exclusively with other women. The novel was better received than her political novels of the 1930s, as was her seventh and last novel, *The Flint Anchor*, published in 1954. The latter concerned a tyrannical and hypocritical *pater familias* living in an English east coast fishing port. Anthony West, writing in *The New Yorker* on October 9, 1954, thought *The Flint Anchor* "beautifully written . . . and psychologically profound about family relationships."

After 1954, Warner ceased writing novels for the remaining 24 years of her life, and instead concentrated on poetry and short stories.

In addition, after the sudden death of T.H. White in early 1964, Warner was persuaded to write a biography of the author of *The Once and Future King* and other Arthurian legends that inspired *Camelot*, the wildly popular musical. *T.H. White: A Biography* was a critical and popular success, and its publication in 1967 led to a lasting revival of interest in Warner's novels and other writings. But Ackland's death of breast cancer at the age of 63 in November 1969 plunged Warner into remorseful despair. Unlike Warner, Ackland never enjoyed literary success and is largely remembered not as a poet, but as the lifelong companion of Sylvia Warner.

In time, Warner recovered from her grief and loneliness, made new friends, and returned to her writing. In the early 1970s, she had two volumes of Ackland's poems privately printed. In 1977, a year before her own death in her 84th year, Warner's last volume of stories, *Kingdoms of Elfin*, appeared. In 1973, she had written friends that she was writing in a new vein, and in some ways the stories are a departure from her previous work, as they concern elves rather than human beings. On the other hand, *Kingdoms of Elfin* marked a return to a fantastic world that Warner created in her first novel, *Lolly Willowes*, where Satan and witches and warlocks were as unremarkable as ordinary persons. The work won instant and universal acclaim from critics and the reading public, just as *Lolly Willowes* had done over 50 years before. One critic, William Jay Smith, wrote in 1977 that *Kingdoms of Elfin* "has all the freshness, wit, originality of perception and clarity of insight that have won for her rhythmical prose so many admirers over so long a time."

On May 1, 1978, Sylvia Townsend Warner died and her ashes were interred beside those of Ackland, under the epitaph that Ackland had chosen nine years before: *Omnis non moritur* (Death is not the end). Death was certainly not the end for Warner, and since her passing her diaries and letters and other unpublished writings have appeared. In addition, many of her novels, poems and stories have been reprinted, while in the late 1980s **Claire Harman** and **Wendy Mulford** each published an excellent biography of Warner. Sardonic to the end, Warner hoped that she had annoyed a great number of persons during her lifetime. No doubt she did, but Sylvia Townsend Warner has also delighted millions of readers for years. Her wit, humor, irony, compassion and marvelous imagery will no doubt enchant readers for many generations to come.

SOURCES:

Harman, Claire. *Sylvia Townsend Warner: A Biography*. London: Chatto & Windus, 1989.

———, ed. *The Diaries of Sylvia Townsend Warner*. London: Chatto & Windus, 1994.

Maxwell, William, ed. *Sylvia Townsend Warner: Letters*. NY: The Viking Press, 1982.

Mulford, Wendy. *This Narrow Place: Sylvia Townsend Warner and Valentine Ackland: Life, Letters and Politics, 1930–1951*. London: Pandora Press, 1988.

Warner, Sylvia Townsend. *Lolly Willowes, or The Loving Huntsman*. Chicago, IL: Academy Chicago, 1979.

———. *Summer Will Show*. London: Chatto & Windus, 1936.

SUGGESTED READING:

Harman, Claire, ed. *Collected Poems*. NY: Viking, 1983.

Steinman, Michael, ed. *The Element of Lavishness: Letters of Sylvia Townsend Warner and William Maxwell, 1938–1978*. Counterpoint, 2001.

Warner, Sylvia Townsend. *Selected Stories*. NY: The Viking Press, 1988.

Anna Macías,
Professor Emerita of History,
Ohio Wesleyan University, Delaware, Ohio

Warren, Althea (1886–1958)

American librarian. Born Althea Hester Warren on December 18, 1886, in Waukegan, Illinois; died on December 20, 1958; daughter of Lansing Warren and Emma Newhall (Blodgett) Warren; University of Chicago, Ph.B., 1908; University of Wisconsin Library School, B.S.L.S., 1911.

Served as the president of the California Library Association (1921–22); as city librarian, successfully maneuvered the Los Angeles Public Library through difficult eras of budget cuts; assumed the directorship of the Victory Book Campaign, collecting five million books for military personnel during World War II; served as president of the American Library Association (1943–44).

After earning a Ph.B. from the University of Chicago and a library science degree from the University of Wisconsin Library School, Althea Warren became branch librarian for the Chicago Public Library in 1911, serving a poor immigrant community on the city's northwest side. She left that position in 1912 to work as a librarian for Sears, Roebuck and Company before joining her widowed mother **Emma Blodgett Warren** in San Diego and accepting a position at the San Diego Public Library in 1915. Within one year, she had assumed the duties of head librarian there. Her ten-year administration of the library had as its defining characteristic her strong belief in a democratic workplace. The San Diego staff was involved with all facets of the library throughout its dramatic reorganization. Recognizing her capabilities, her colleagues elected her president of the California Library Association in 1921.

While on a leave of absence from the San Diego Public Library to care for her ailing mother, Warren accepted an offer to become the assistant city librarian for the Los Angeles Public Library. She once again demonstrated her talent for handling major changes when she assumed the responsibility of moving the library's collection from a rented building to the new facility. She also launched a careful study of book turnover and set in motion a proposal for salary increases that made Los Angeles librarians some of the highest paid in the country. By 1933, she was named city librarian. Warren took charge of the library system during the difficult Depression era, when universal belt-tightening resulted in severe budget cuts. She minimized the impact of shorter hours, personnel cuts, and reduced services through successful juggling of her small resources and masterful public relations work. She guided the Los Angeles Public Library through a similar financial crisis during World War II, combating book and personnel shortages by extending the hours and initiating special war programs. At the same time, she took on the daunting task of organizing a national campaign to collect millions of books for military personnel at the request of the American Library Association president, Charles H. Brown. As director of the Victory Book Campaign, Warren helped the campaign reach its goal of five million books within four months. In 1943, she was elected to the presidency of the American Library Association, the first Californian so honored. In her year's service in this post, she actively lobbied for federal grant money for American libraries, while also working to enact changes within the association itself.

Warren's retirement from the city librarian position in 1947 did not end her work with public libraries. She moved into the academic arena as an instructor at the Library School of the University of Southern California, which led to invitations to teach at the University of Michigan and the University of Wisconsin. Her teaching career ended where it began, at the University of Southern California, in 1957. She died a year later.

SOURCES:
Current Biography 1942. NY: H.W. Wilson, 1942.
Dictionary of American Library Biography. Edited by Bohdan S. Wynar. Littleton, CO: Libraries Unlimited, 1978.

Judith C. Reveal,
freelance writer,
Greensboro, Maryland

Warren, Eleanor Clark (1913–1996).

See Clark, Eleanor.

Warren, Elinor Remick

(1900–1991)

American composer and pianist whose works were widely acclaimed throughout her nearly 50-year career. Born Elinor Remick Warren in Los Angeles, California, on February 3, 1900; died on April 27, 1991; only child of Maude Remick Warren (a non-professional pianist) and James Garfield Warren (a businessman); studied piano with Kathryn Cocke at the Westlake School for Girls; after attending Mills College, studied in New York with Frank LaForge, Ernesto Beruman, and Clarence Dickenson; studied with Nadia Boulanger in Paris in 1959; married Raymond Huntsberger (a physician), in 1925 (divorced 1929); married Z. Wayne Griffin (a producer in radio, film, and television), on December 12, 1936 (died 1981); children: (first marriage) James (b. 1928); (second marriage) Wayne (b. 1938); Elayne (b. 1940).

Had choral symphony The Legend of King Arthur *broadcast over the Mutual Network (1940); premiered* Suite for Orchestra *(1955) and* The Crystal Lake *(1958) with Los Angeles Symphony; named* Woman of the Year in Music *by* The Los Angeles Times *as well as by the National Federation of Music Clubs; in addition to choral works, composed numerous works for orchestra.*

Music was the central theme in the life of composer Elinor Remick Warren from the moment of her birth on February 23, 1900. Both her parents were musical: her mother Maude played the piano and her father James, a businessman, had a tenor voice of professional caliber. Elinor displayed her own musical talent at the age of 13 months, astonishing her parents by humming part of a lullaby, "Rock-a-bye Baby," perfectly. By age three, she was picking out short pieces on the piano which her mother copied into notebooks. (Years later, pianist Harold Bauer examined the notebooks and declared the compositions to be in perfect form.)

At age five, Warren began piano lessons with **Kathryn Cocke**, a young New England Conservatory graduate who applied the principles of kindergarten teaching to music. Under Cocke's sensitive tutelage, Warren progressed rapidly, learning harmony and theory along with her piano studies, and composing pieces which she could now write down herself. As a student at the Westlake School for Girls in Los Angeles, she excelled in academics and also developed a talent for acting and writing. While still a schoolgirl, Warren wrote "A Song of June," which she was urged to send to the New York

publisher Schirmer. They accepted the song and sent her a contract.

As a teen, Warren studied theory and harmony with composer **Gertrude Ross** for several years. Following her graduation from Westlake, she stayed home for a year, working on advanced composition with Ross and continuing piano lessons with **Olga Steeb**. In 1919, she attended Mills College in Oakland and studied singing, "which was funny because I can't sing," she said later. After a year, her voice coach realized her talent for composition and urged her to go East to study.

After convincing her reluctant parents to let her live in New York, Warren began studying accompaniment and the art song with Frank LaForge, and orchestration and counterpoint with Dr. Clarence Dickinson. She continued to write and publish songs at a steady pace, and by 1922 her choral works began to appear in print. At LaForge's suggestion, she also started touring as an accompanist for opera star **Florence Easton**, with whom she formed a lifelong friendship. Warren also performed periodically with Lawrence Tibbett and Richard Crooks, occasionally appeared as a soloist with symphony orchestras, and made piano recordings for the Okeh label.

During the five or so years she was in New York, Warren returned to Los Angeles each summer. In the course of one of these visits, she began dating a childhood friend, Raymond Huntsberger, now a physician. In 1925, they married, but the union had problems from the beginning and ended four years later, shortly after the birth of a son, James. After her divorce, Warren left her son with her parents and continued to tour as an accompanist. She also embarked on an intensive study of orchestration and wrote her first orchestral work, *The Harp Weaver*, set to a narrative poem by *Edna St. Vincent Millay. The work, large in scope, received its premiere at New York's Carnegie Hall in 1936, conducted by *Antonia Brico. That same year, Warren married Wayne Griffin, a promising tenor who because of ill health had given up a career as a singer to work as a producer in radio, film, and television. Over the next six years, the couple established a happy, supportive relationship and moved several times to accommodate a growing family that included son Wayne Griffin, Jr., and daughter **Elayne Griffin**.

Warren's second major composition for orchestra, *The Legend of King Arthur*, had been brewing in her mind since her days at the Westlake School when she read Alfred, Lord Tennyson's *Idylls of the King*. "I was so thrilled with that part of it called 'The Passing of Arthur,'"

she recalled. "It just took hold of me, and, though it was beyond me then, I knew that one day, I would set it to music." The work had its world premiere in 1940, conducted by Britain's Albert Coates, who was in the United States for a series of appearances with the Los Angeles Philharmonic. "There is not a measure that does not fit cannily into the musical flux, which surges and glistens with radiant orchestral color, and flows in luminous tonal strands through massed choral forces," wrote a critic for the *Los Angeles Daily News*.

The premiere performance was also broadcast to a nationwide radio audience, giving Warren her first national exposure. The press picked up on her unusual story, running articles and pictures of the young mother feeding her two-year-old son with one hand while correcting a score with the other. When asked about combining motherhood and career, Warren always maintained that her family came first. Her husband provided her with unending encouragement and saw to it that the children respected their mother's working schedule. ("Only if you break a leg may you interrupt your mother when she's composing," he jokingly admonished them.) Warren, who was characterized as a private and introspective woman, had no difficulty surrendering to the isolation of the creative process. "Don't plan on going out to lunch," she once wrote. "You will rarely see even the friends dear to your heart. No phone calls, either, to break the concentration. How can one listen to the inner voice except in aloneness?"

Throughout the 1940s and 1950s, Warren composed some of her most important works, among them *The Sleeping Beauty*, *The Crystal Lake*, *Along the Western Shore*, *Singing Earth*, *Transcontinental*, *Suite for Orchestra*, and *Abram in Egypt*. In 1959, once again encouraged by her husband, she studied briefly in Paris with *Nadia Boulanger, with whom she formed a close friendship.

In 1963, Warren received the commission to compose *Requiem*, a project that occupied her for three years and one she called "engrossing and monumental." The work had its world premiere at the *Dorothy Chandler Pavilion of the Los Angeles Music Center on April 2, 1966. Critics were overwhelming in their praise of the piece. Patterson Greene of the *Los Angeles Herald-Examiner* called it "a devout, quietly intense work . . . a dignified, meditative and distinguished contribution to choral literature."

Commissions continued to occupy Warren, whose advancing age failed to slow her down. She produced several additional major works throughout the 1970s, including *Symphony in One Movement* and *Good Morning, America!*, for chorus, narrator and orchestra. In 1980, with her husband, she selected 12 of her 60 songs for a new collection, *Selected Songs by Elinor Remick Warren*, published by Carl Fischer. The publisher's copies reached Warren just months after her husband's death from cancer in 1981. Devastated by the loss, Warren was sustained by continuing to compose and play the piano. At age 86, she appeared as the accompanist on a compact disc of her songs produced by Cambria Records, marking the beginning of a comprehensive CD survey of her music. Warren continued to work almost up until the time of her death from pancreatic cancer in April 1991.

In summing up Warren's extraordinary career, **Christine Ammer** notes that Elinor never set herself apart from the mainstream as a "woman" composer, but frequently expressed her view that "there was no gender in music." Another biographer, **Virginia Bortin**, points out that unlike many of her contemporaries, the composer never compromised her musical ideals to achieve popularity. "Warren possessed a passionate romantic soul and was deeply moved by nature, beauty and the sublime," she writes. "Her music reflects her inner being and seems at times to come from a secluded, distant place."

SOURCES:

Blivins, Pamela J. "Elinor Remick Warren: Requiem for a Composer," in *The *Maud Powell Signature: Woman in Music*. Vol. 1, no. 1. Summer 1995.

Bortin, Virginia. *Elinor Remick Warren: A Bio-Bibliography*. Westport, CT: Greenwood Press, 1993.

Cohen, Aaron I. *International Encyclopedia of Women Composers*. 2 vols. NY: Books & Music (USA), 1987.

Barbara Morgan,
Melrose, Massachusetts

Warren, Lavinia (1841–1919)

American performer who turned her genetically endowed dwarfism to her advantage through the showmanship of P.T. Barnum. Name variations: Mrs. Tom Thumb; Mrs. Charles Sherwood Stratton; Mercy Lavinia Stratton. Born Mercy Lavinia Warren Bump or Bumpus on October 31, 1841, on a farm in Middleboro, Massachusetts; died of chronic interstitial nephritis on November 25, 1919, in Middleboro; daughter of James S. Bump and Huldah (Warren) Bump; married Charles Sherwood Stratton (also known as General Tom Thumb), on January 10, 1863; married Count Primo Magri, in 1885; children: none, though one was reported.

There are two general types of genetic dwarfism, one involving a body that usually develops normally, but with truncated limbs; Lavinia Warren belonged to the other type, accurately described by the showman P.T. Barnum, who found her to be "a perfectly developed woman in miniature." She was born Mercy Lavinia Warren Bump or Bumpus in 1841 in Middleboro, Massachusetts, the daughter of parents who were six feet tall. Though Lavinia appeared normal at birth, her growth stopped when she reached age ten. She had eight sisters and brothers, all of whom were of normal height except for her younger sister **Minnie (Newell)**, who was also a dwarf.

Growing up, Lavinia did what other New England girls did. She went to school, learned to cook and sew, and did fancywork; with her predilection for music, poetry, and the fine arts, she studied to be a teacher and taught third grade in Middleboro. By age 20, she was 32 inches tall and weighed 29 pounds. Lavinia also had the wanderlust.

Capitalizing on a mid-19th-century trend, she set out touring on a Mississippi showboat. At that time, Phineas T. Barnum had made the exhibition of little people fashionable as one of the great attractions of his "living museum." His biggest publicity buildup had been for General Tom Thumb, three feet tall, whose real name was Charles Sherwood Stratton. In both England and America, lines had formed for a glimpse of him; England's Queen *Victoria met with him three times. Originally hired at three dollars a week, Stratton had become Barnum's partner, then toured independently. In 1862, when Lavinia Warren joined Barnum's American museum, General Tom Thumb was very rich and had been happily retired from exhibiting since the previous year.

When Barnum signed Warren to a long-term contract, she was 21 and Tom Thumb was 24. Their romance was a press agent's dream. According to **Helen Woodward**, Lavinia Warren was the "Victorian ideal of the doll-woman." At the height of her fame, a *New York Times* reporter found her "intelligent, pleasant, modest . . . very lively in conversation . . . speaks with all confidence and even wit." There was even the real-life drama of a romantic triangle.

Tom Thumb's rival was another Barnum dwarf named George Washington Morrison McNutt, known as Commodore Nutt, the son of a New Hampshire farmer. The suitors came to much-publicized blows, but Lavinia Warren had eyes only for Charles Sherwood Stratton. When the wedding plans were announced, the two agreed to go on display for one last time, and with the curious clamoring for a looksee, the museum raked in $3,000 a day.

The wedding took place at Manhattan's Grace Church on February 10, 1863. Included among the 2,000 invited guests were Mrs. Cornelius Vanderbilt (*Sophia Johnson Vanderbilt), whose husband was also a commodore, and General Ambrose Burnside, who lent his name to side whiskers. Outside the church, crowds were cordoned off, and when the tiny couple strolled down the aisle, along with Minnie as bridesmaid,

an "audible giggle ran through the church," reported *The New York Times*. In the midst of the Civil War, the New York *World* tossed battlefield headlines off the front page to banner "Much Ado about Very Little," and the couple honeymooned in Washington, D.C., where they met Abraham and *Mary Todd Lincoln. Ten months later, it was ballyhooed that Warren had given birth to a three-pound baby girl who was said to have died shortly after her first birthday. But according to Barnum biographer Irving Wallace, there was no real daughter, only "Barnum's brainchild, invented for publicity."

In 1869, accompanied by Warren's sister Minnie and Commodore Nutt, the couple set off on a world tour that lasted three years and covered 56,000 miles. The foursome traveled to Australia, India, and Japan; they met Pope Pius IX, Napoleon III, and Victor Emmanuel. (When Minnie was nearly 30, she would marry an English skater who was slightly taller than a dwarf, known as General Grant, Jr.; Minnie later died in childbirth.)

Before their marriage, Charles "Tom Thumb" Stratton had made it clear that his wife would never work. The two were happily married for more than 20 years, but the general was extrava-

Lavinia Warren

gant, spending his fortune on sailing sloops and pedigreed horses. By the time of his death, of apoplexy (probably a stroke), on July 15, 1883, at age 45, all that was left for his widow were a few pieces of property and $16,000. Two years later, Warren married a young Italian dwarf, Count Primo Magri, a piccolo player and pugilist who stood 3'9". Unfortunately for Magri, he became known as "Mrs. Tom Thumb's husband."

According to Wallace, Warren's last years were "a nightmare of one night stands." To earn a living, she and her new husband toured the country with a dwarf opera company, appeared in vaudeville and at world's fairs, made four movie comedies, and wintered in the sideshow at Coney Island. When she and Magri finally retired, in Marion, Ohio, she joined the Eastern Star and the Daughters of the American Revolution (DAR), and became a dedicated Christian Scientist. Their miniature home was a tourist attraction.

When Lavinia Warren died in 1919, at age 78, she was buried at the Mountain Grove Cemetery in Bridgeport, Connecticut, next to her beloved Tom Thumb, who had been laid to rest under a 40-ft. column of Italian marble, topped by his lifesize statue in granite. Next to him, the plain headstone over Warren's child-size grave reads simply, "His wife."

SOURCES:

Wallace, Irving. *The Fabulous Showman: The Life and Times of P.T. Barnum.* NY: Knopf, 1959.

Woodward, Helen Beal. *The Bold Women.* NY: Farrar, Straus, 1953.

Warren, Mary.

See Witchcraft Trials in Salem Village.

Warren, Mercy Otis (1728–1814)

Articulate and eloquent poet, playwright, political thinker, and traditional Puritan homemaker who demonstrated convincingly that gender was no barrier to intellectual equality. Born Mercy Otis on September 25, 1728, in Barnstable, Massachusetts; died on October 19, 1814, at home in Plymouth, Massachusetts; daughter of Mary Allyne Otis (1702–1767) and Colonel James Otis, Sr. (1702–1778); educated with her older brothers by a private tutor; married James Warren, Sr. (1726–1808), on November 14, 1754; children: James, Jr. (October 18, 1757–1821); Winslow (March 24, 1760–1791); Charles (April 14, 1762–1785); Henry (March 21, 1764–1828); George (September 20, 1766–1800).

Attended brother James, Jr.'s graduation from Harvard (1743); married and took up residence in her husband's family home on the Eel River near Plymouth (November 14, 1754); purchased the Winslow House in Plymouth (1757); published The Adulateur, a Tragedy *(1772); published* The Defeat, a Play *(1773); purchased the Thomas Hutchinson country estate in Milton (1781); son Charles died (1785); sold Milton estate and returned to Plymouth town home and farm (1788); published* Observations on the New Constitution, and on the Federal Conventions *(1788); published* Poems, Dramatic and Miscellaneous *(1790); son Winslow killed fighting Indians (1791); son George died (1800); published* History of the Rise, Progress and Termination of the American Revolution, interspersed with Biographical and Moral Observations *(1805); corresponded with John Adams regarding her unfavorable depiction of Adams in her* History *(1807).*

Mercy Otis Warren combined the role of traditional wife and mother with that of the foremost female intellectual of her day to become an effective speaker for American independence and the principles of liberty, equality, and democracy. With a caustic pen and a ready wit, this Plymouth housewife demonstrated a talent, a vitality, and a determination which commanded attention in the male-dominated society of the American revolutionary era and early national period.

As the third child (oldest daughter) of the thirteen born to **Mary Allyne Otis** and Colonel James Otis, Sr., Mercy's ancestral roots went deep into the inhospitable soil of colonial Massachusetts. She was born into and grew up in a Puritan family of enviable influence and prominence. From her mother, Mercy inherited a respectability which came naturally from being descended from one of the signers of the famous Mayflower Compact. As the signer and a founder of the Plymouth colony, her great-grandfather Edward Dotey was a progenitor of a family which practiced assiduously the Puritan values of learning, hard work, public service, and steady habits.

It was from her father, however, that Mercy inherited what would constitute near-aristocratic status in 18th-century New England. The Otises were part of the Great Puritan Migration of the 1630s, arriving in 1631 and settling in Hingham. They soon acquired substantial landholdings and a reputation for integrity and public service. In 1683, Warren's grandfather Otis moved south to the Cape Cod village of Barnstable where he soon became prominent as a merchant and politician. As a farmer, merchant, lawyer, judge, militia officer, and local politician,

Warren's father was able to give to his growing progeny a competence and a respectability which provided her with opportunities denied most girls in Puritan New England. Although not formally schooled, Colonel Otis saw to it that his sons (and interestingly also his oldest daughter Mercy) were provided with the best education then available.

Like most Puritan children, Warren learned to read at an early age. It was likely that it was her mother who taught the eager Mercy to read, so she would be appropriately prepared to assume the role of housewife and mother. The education of most girls stopped at this point, but Mercy was allowed, even encouraged by her father, to continue. In the company of her two older brothers, James and Joseph, Warren came under the educational influence of her uncle Russell. As a Yale-trained cleric, the Reverend Jonathan Russell was well schooled in literature, history, theology, and the classics. For several years, Warren was exposed to a rigorous program of reading and disputation. She found that she could keep up with her precocious brothers, both of whom were being prepared to enter Harvard College. She read primarily Greek and Roman literature in translation, history, and literature. Her writings as an adult reflected especially this early and substantial acquaintance with history and the classics. She especially loved to read history. Purportedly Walter Raleigh's *History of the World* was her favorite, and it was probably at this early age that she conceived of the idea of writing history. Unlike most girls of the age, Warren also learned not only the basics but also the intricacies of composition. In fact, she practiced her writing constantly and soon became highly skilled in presenting complex concepts and ideas. At first, her writing was somewhat stilted and convoluted, but with diligence she soon acquired the ease of written expression which characterized her adult works.

It was during the time of her tutelage with Uncle Russell that Mercy became particularly close to her brother Jemmy (James Otis, Jr.), who became her dearest friend and intellectual companion. With the help and encouragement of her mercurial brother, Warren came to the realization that she was the intellectual equal of men. Although her opportunities for education and a career outside of the home were greatly restricted, she participated vicariously in the political and literary world of 18th-century Massachusetts first through her brother Jemmy and later through her husband James Warren and her friend John Adams. What she learned was that gender was no barrier to intellectual equality.

Jemmy's graduation from Harvard in 1743 provided the first opportunity for the 14-year-old Mercy to see the world outside Barnstable. The Harvard commencement was one of the highlights of the year, and the entire Otis clan traveled to Cambridge for the graduation and accompanying festivities. It is likely that at this time, the young, impressionable Mercy first met her brother's college-mate James Warren. Two years behind Mercy's brother at the college, James came from a prominent Plymouth family. This early acquaintance would, after a number of years, develop into a romance which led to marriage in November 1754.

As James Warren's wife, Mercy joined a family equally as prominent as her own. The Warrens, like the Otises, were descended from the first Pilgrim settlers and had, by the mid-18th century, achieved the status as one of the first families of Plymouth. In the hierarchical and patriarchal society of colonial Massachusetts, Mercy Otis Warren, both before and after marriage, lived a life of relative ease, comfort, and affluence. Throughout her life, there were always servants to do most of the menial jobs, allowing her time—denied most—to read, reflect, and write. However, in the male-dominated world of Puritan Massachusetts, Warren readily accepted the traditional view of a secondary role for women. As she wrote in a poem in 1779:

> Critics may censure, but if candour frowns
> I'll quit the pen, and keep within the bounds
> The narrow bounds, prescribed to female life
> The gentle mistress, and the prudent wife.

As a young wife, Warren would be a homemaker first and then a writer and political thinker. She would always be "the gentle mistress, and the prudent wife."

With her marriage, Mercy moved into the Warren family home and into the highest political and social circles of Plymouth. With the death of James' father in 1757, her husband inherited the Eel River farm ("Clifford"). Also in 1757, the young bridegroom purchased a Plymouth town house. Except for a brief hiatus in the 1780s, Mercy and James would spend their lives in the Plymouth town house and nearby farm.

At regular intervals between 1757 and 1766, Warren gave birth to five boys. Providentially all of her sons grew to maturity, though three of them predeceased her. James, Jr. was born in 1757, followed by Winslow in 1759, Charles in 1762, Henry in 1764, and George in 1766. Although she loved all of her sons and was in fact a caring and compassionate mother to all, Winslow seems to have been a favorite. Her letters to her second son revealed an especially strong mother-son bond. Ironically, it was Winslow who gave his mother the greatest grief. Although intelligent and personable, Winslow possessed an unpuritan fondness for the hedonist life. He refused to attend Harvard and instead jumped from one career to another with no success. In his early 30s, he did obtain a commission in the U.S. Army and soon afterwards was killed in General Arthur St. Clair's infamous defeat at the hands of Indians in 1791. Of the other sons, the oldest James, Jr., although he outlived his mother, sustained a wound which made necessary having one of his legs amputated while serving in the navy during the Revolutionary War; the third son Charles contracted tuberculosis and died in 1785 at the age of 23; and the youngest George contracted an unknown but fatal disease and died in 1800 at the age of 34. Only the fourth son Henry was to marry and give Mercy the grandchildren she so dearly loved.

Critics may censure, but if candour frowns,

I'll quit the pen, and keep within the bounds,

The narrow bounds, prescribed to female life,

The gentle mistress, and the prudent wife.

—Mercy Otis Warren, *On Primitive Simplicity*

The 1760s and 1770s were exciting times for the Warrens. Raising five boys was a full-time job for the mother. Partly because her husband was frequently away serving on various revolutionary committees or in the legislature, Mercy assumed, somewhat begrudgingly, the arduous and time-consuming task of managing the Plymouth town house and Eel River farm. In addition, it was Mercy who supervised the early education of all of the five sons. As a result of her diligence and persistence, all of her boys learned their three "Rs" and more at an early age. It was during these busy years that Warren began to write seriously. The extant poems from this period show a writer who is slowly but surely learning her craft. In addition to poetry, Warren also wrote numerous letters in which she honed her writing skills while commenting intelligently on the complex social and political issues of the day.

During the 1760s, Mercy became involved, at first vicariously but later more directly, in the anti-English furor which eventually led to American independence. Although both the Otises and the Warrens had long been active politically, it was for Mercy her brother Jemmy's involvement in the Writs of Assistance controversy that constituted her inauguration into the morass of Massachusetts politics. James Otis, Jr.'s famous speech before the Superior Court of Massachusetts in which he challenged the validity of the writs was, according to the always biased sister, "the foundation of a revolution." John Adams later claimed: "Then and there the child Independence was born." Because of his brilliant defense of colonial rights, Jemmy quickly became, along with Samuel Adams, John Hancock, John Adams, and James Warren, a leader of the country or opposition party. The court or English party was headed by Thomas Hutchinson and the Oliver family. Because of numerous prior political snubs and deliberate slights, some dating back to the 1740s, and because the Hutchinson-Oliver clan was the chief defender and indeed the major benefactor of English policies, the Otis-Warren family became the implacable foe of Thomas Hutchinson and his political cronies.

Much of the planning and discussions of the country party leaders took place in the Warren house. Thus it was that Mercy met and got to know well many of the prominent radical leaders. She in fact became involved in the discussions and planning which led eventually to "the shot heard around the world" at Lexington and Concord. Warren shared the radical political views of her mercurial brother Jemmy and her more staid husband James. Particularly after Jemmy's increasingly frequent bouts with insanity rendered him unable to continue as an opposition leader, Mercy became the family's voice of opposition. She took pen in hand to oppose Britain's continuing attacks on American liberty.

Warren's first published play was an attack on the Hutchinson-Oliver family. *The Adulateur, a Tragedy* appeared in two installments in the *Massachusetts Spy* in the spring of 1772. The play, probably written to be read and not performed on stage, was an ill-disguised satire on the current political situation in Massachusetts. The targets of the cleverly written spoof were Governor Thomas Hutchinson and Lieutenant Governor Andrew Oliver. The heroes were, not surprisingly, James Otis, Jr., James Warren, and John Adams. Although the play was published anonymously, it was soon widely known that James Warren's Plymouth housewife was the author of this widely distributed propaganda tract. In *The Adulateur*, Mercy warned of all the evil intentions of the Hutchinson-Oliver clan. The governor and his "fawning courtiers" would, she wrote, stop at nothing to subvert the people's liberties.

Warren followed her first published success with the anonymous publication of *The Defeat*, *a Play* in the summer of 1773. Although not as well crafted as her first endeavor, this play continued the attack on the now-discredited governor and his fawning minions. By 1775, Mercy Otis Warren had become the leading "penwoman" of the entire revolutionary movement.

During the period of the American War for Independence, Warren met, and corresponded, with many of the radical leaders. It was at this time that she met John Adams and his wife Abigail. Mercy became *Abigail Adams' female mentor. Although she was 16 years younger and less formally educated than the Plymouth housewife, Abigail's letters to Mercy showed a sophistication and intellectual maturity which delighted the house-bound Mrs. Warren. Also of great interest was Mercy's long-time correspondence with English historian *Catharine Macaulay. As the author of the celebrated *History of England from the Accession of James I to that of the Brunswick Line*, Macaulay became the female intellectual role model for Mercy. It was Catharine Macaulay indirectly (by example) and John Adams directly (by constant badgering) who encouraged Mercy to undertake the writing of the history of the American Revolution. During the conflict, Warren started collecting manuscripts, letters, and pamphlets in preparation for the publication of what would become her magnum opus.

With the advent of peace in 1783, the 55-year-old Warren continued her interest in writing and politics. For most of the 1780s, James and Mercy lived in Milton having purchased, in 1781, the elegant Thomas Hutchinson mansion. Hutchinson of course was living in brooding exile in England. The irony of James Warren purchasing Hutchinson's mansion was not lost on Mercy. Although much closer to Boston, "Tremont" (as the Warrens called their new acquisition) proved to be too expensive to maintain. After seven years of financial struggle, the Warrens sold their "dream house" and returned to live more simply and thriftily in their Plymouth townhouse and nearby Eel River farm.

During the 1780s, Mercy viewed with increased alarm the growing nationalistic movement which would eventually lead to the 1787 Constitutional Convention. In fact, when the proposed constitution was first made public in the fall of 1787, Warren quickly became one of its most severe and articulate critics. Like most anti-federalists, Mercy felt that the Constitution of 1787 represented a betrayal of the American Revolution. Specifically, she objected to the national government being given the power to tax, the power to regulate trade and commerce, and the

Mercy Otis Warren

power to enforce its acts. Both Warren and her husband rushed to publish anti-federalist tracts. Posing as "A Republican Federalist," James issued a series of seven tracts in which he claimed the proposed constitution was illegitimate because the founding fathers had exceeded their instructions in drafting an entirely new organic law.

Warren's opposition appeared as *Observations on the New Constitution, and on the Federal Conventions*. In this widely distributed tract, Mercy reiterated several of the standard anti-federalist arguments such as the lack of a bill of rights, the possibility of a standing army during peacetime, and the enhancement of national power at the expense of the states. She then went on to claim that the new constitution was a "many-headed monster; of such motley mixture, that its enemies cannot trace a feature of Democratick or Republican extract." With the 1788 publication of this strident attack on the proposed constitution, both Warren and her husband completed the political estrangement, started earlier over Shay's Rebellion, with most of their conservative Plymouth neighbors and with most of the federalist-leaning political leaders in Massachusetts. James essentially retired from active politics and public service after several electoral defeats, while Mercy finished writing her majestic history of the American Revolution.

In 1790, Warren published *Poems, Dramatic and Miscellaneous*. In this, her first book-length publication, she included numerous poems, several political tracts written during the Revolution, and two of her more recently written plays. Unlike her earlier dramas, women played leading roles in *The Ladies of Castile* (written in 1784) and *The Sack of Rome* (1785). This volume reflected Warren's growing maturity as a writer and her emergence as a leading advocate of women's rights. By making the lead characters women, Warren seemed to be saying that women are indeed the equal of men if given equal opportunities for education and public service. Her first book brought the public acclaim which had eluded her earlier for her anonymously written plays and political tracts. She was now recognized as the leading female playwright and political commentator and perhaps more important as the foremost female intellectual and literary figure of her day and age.

At the urging of her husband and John Adams, Warren finally submitted for publication her long-awaited history of the Revolution. *The History of the Rise, Progress and Termination of the American Revolution, interspersed with Biographical and Moral Observations* was a tour de force consisting of 1,298 pages (31 chapters) in three volumes. Published in 1805, it was the anti-federalist, Jeffersonian answer to John Marshall's ponderous, federalist-oriented five volumes on the *Life of George Washington*. Of particular merit are Warren's biographical sketches of the leading figures, both male and female, of the revolutionary era. From personal acquaintance and diligent research, Warren produced a historical tome which still commands attention. Significantly, her magnum opus was the first major published historical work written by an American woman. Thus Mercy Otis Warren was the first published woman historian in the United States; a fact for which she was proud and well aware. *The History* has become her most enduring published legacy.

The History also became the cause of an unseemly political estrangement with her longtime friend and political mentor John Adams. In a series of ten caustically written letters, the former president attacked Warren's scholarship and her audacity in even undertaking a historical project of such magnitude and scope. What the overly sensitive Adams wrote was "History is not the Province of the Ladies." What he meant was Mercy had unjustly, in his view, criticized him for his alleged "monarchical" leanings, his polit-

ical conservatism, and his "Pride of talent and much ambition." Her attempts to answer Adams rationally and logically only spurred him on to renewed vindictiveness. The alienation caused by this one-sided missive verbal assault was never fully healed. Although the Warren-Adams correspondence was resumed after some four years, it never reached the cordiality and intimacy of former times.

The few years left to James and Mercy together were lived in virtual political isolation. Warren was largely consoled, however, by the frequent visits of her nine grandchildren (all belonging to son Henry and his wife **Polly Winslow Warren**) and by the return home of her oldest son James. After the publication of *The History*, Warren wrote but little. Instead, she assumed the role of matriarch of the Warren family.

In November 1808, Mercy lost "the first friend of her heart." In 54 years of marriage, James had always been her confidant, compassionate husband, political compatriot, and gentle literary critic. As she wrote to her oldest son, "Your father is the philosopher and the Christian:—he is the best husband, the best father—the best friend." In 1772, she had written to her then husband of 18 years: "All my Earthly Happiness depend[s] on the continuance of [your] Life." With the death of her 82-year-old husband, the 80-year-old Mercy knew her years were numbered.

Warren had never enjoyed robust health. Frequently she was bedridden for weeks on end with a variety of physical illnesses or periods of severe depression. As early as 1775, her eyes began to give her trouble, forcing her to refrain from reading and writing for long periods. Her final illness came suddenly. Early in the morning of October 19, 1814, Warren died of now unknown causes at the age of 86.

Mercy Otis Warren's enduring legacy is that she overcame the rigid social and political strictures of her day to become the first published woman historian and a respected political thinker and writer. She was able to combine the traditional role of wife and mother with that of a published writer of great merit, influence, and ability. Her life and manifold accomplishments are proof that a woman, although living under a handicap in the patriarchal society in which she was born, could achieve literary and intellectual gender equality.

SOURCES:

Anthony, Katharine. *First Lady of the Revolution: The Life of Mercy Otis Warren*. Port Washington, NY: Kennikat Press, 1958.

Brown, Alice. *Mercy Warren*. NY: Scribner, 1896.

Smith, William Raymond. *History as Argument: Three Patriot Historians of the American Revolution.* The Hague: Mouton, 1966.

Zagarri, Rosemarie. *A Woman's Dilemma: Mercy Otis Warren and the American Revolution.* Wheeling, IL: Harland Davidson, 1995.

SUGGESTED READING:

Hoffman, Ronald, and Peter J. Albert, eds. *Women in the Age of the American Revolution.* Charlottesville, VA: University Press of Virginia, 1989.

Kerber, Linda K. *Women of the Republic: Intellect and Ideology in Revolutionary America.* NY: W.W. Norton, 1980.

Norton, Mary Beth. *Liberty's Daughters: The Revolutionary Experience of American Women, 1750–1800.* Boston, MA: Little, Brown, 1980.

Waters, John J., Jr. *The Otis Family in Provincial and Revolutionary Massachusetts.* Chapel Hill, NC: University of North Carolina Press, 1968.

COLLECTIONS:

Mercy Warren Letter Book and Mercy Warren Papers, The Massachusetts Historical Society, Boston.

Joseph C. Morton,
Professor of History, Northeastern Illinois University,
Chicago, Illinois

Warren and Surrey, countess of.

See Isabel of Vermandois (d. before 1147).

See Marshall, Maud (d. 1248).

See Isabella of Angoulême for sidebar on Alice le Brun (d. 1255).

See Joan de Vere (fl. 1280s).

Warrenne, Adelicia de (d. 1178).

See Adelicia de Warrenne.

Warrenne, countess of.

See Isabella of Angoulême for sidebar on Alice le Brun (d. 1255).

Warrenne, Eleanor de (c. 1250–?).

See Eleanor de Warrenne.

Warrenne, Isabel de.

See Isabel de Warrenne (c. 1137–1203).

See Isabel de Warrenne (b. 1253).

See Isabel de Warrenne (d. 1282).

Warrenne and Surrey, countess of.

See Isabel of Vermandois (d. before 1147).

See Marshall, Maud (d. 1248).

See Isabella of Angoulême for sidebar on Alice le Brun (d. 1255).

See Joan de Vere (fl. 1280s).

Warwick, countess of.

See Mortimer, Catherine (c. 1313–1369).

See Despenser, Isabel (1400–1439).

See Neville, Cecily (1415–1495).

See Beauchamp, Anne (1426–1492).

See Rich, Mary (1625–1678).

See Greville, Frances Evelyn (1861–1938).

Warwick, Daisy (1861–1938).

See Greville, Frances Evelyn.

Warwick, Dionne (1940—)

Popular African-American vocalist who collaborated with Burt Bacharach and Hal David to produce 30 hit singles. Name variations: Dionne Warwicke. Born Marie Dionne Warrick on December 12, 1940, in East Orange, New Jersey; daughter of Mancel (some sources cite Marcel) Warrick (a chef and gospel music promoter) and Lee Warrick (manager of a gospel group); earned a master's degree in music from the Hartt College of Music at the University of Hartford, 1976; married Bill Elliot (a drummer and actor), in September 1967 (divorced 1975); children: David, Damion.

Selected discography: Presenting Dionne Warwick *(1964);* Anyone Who Had a Heart *(1964);* Make Way for Dionne Warwick *(1964);* The Sensitive Sound of Dionne Warwick *(1965);* Here I Am *(1965);* Dionne Warwick in Paris *(1965);* Here Where There Is Love *(1967);* On Stage and in the Movies *(1967);* Windows of the World *(1967);* The Magic of Believing *(1967);* Valley of the Dolls and Others *(1968);* Soulful *(1969);* Greatest Motion Picture Hits *(1969);* Dionne Warwick's Golden Hits, Volume 1 *(1969);* Dionne Warwick's Golden Hits, Volume 2 *(1970);* I'll Never Fall in Love Again *(1970);* Very Dionne *(1971);* Promises, Promises *(1971);* From Within, Volume 1 *(1972);* Dionne *(1973);* Just Being Myself *(1973);* Then Came You *(1975);* Track of the Cat *(1975);* Love at First Sight *(1977);* Dionne *(1979);* No Night So Long *(1980);* Hot! Live and Otherwise *(1981);* Heartbreaker *(1983);* Dionne and Friends *(1986);* Anthology, 1962–1971 *(1986);* Masterpieces *(1986);* Reservations for Two *(1987);* Dionne Warwick Sings Cole Porter *(1990);* Hidden Gems: The Best of Dionne Warwick *(1992);* Friends Can Be Lovers *(1993);* Aquarela do Brasil *(1994);* From the Vaults *(1995);* Dionne Sings Dionne *(1998).*

Five-time Grammy winner Dionne Warwick was born Marie Dionne Warrick in East Orange, New Jersey, in 1940. Her parents, devout Methodists, were both in the music business: her father Mancel Warrick was the director of gospel music promotion for Chess Records while also working as a chef and butcher, and her mother **Lee Warrick** managed the Drinkard Singers, a popular gospel group. The family included Warwick's younger sister and brother, Dee Dee Warrick and Mancel Warrick, Jr.

During the mid-1950s, Warwick, her sister, and two cousins formed a group called The Gospelaires and performed primarily as a back-up group for other singers. Anticipating a career as a music teacher in the public schools, Warwick accepted a scholarship to study piano, music, and voice at the University of Hartford's Hartt College of Music. However, in 1960, during a summer vacation from college, Warwick rejoined The Gospelaires as back-up accompaniment to The Drifters on their recording of "Mexican Divorce." Burt Bacharach, the composer of the song, was directing the session. Captivated by Warwick's voice, he and his lyricist Hal David asked her to cut a demonstration recording of one of their other compositions, and Warwick soon signed a contract with Scepter Records, a small rhythm-and-blues label. For her first Scepter release in 1962, Warwick sang more Bacharach-David material, and the "B" side, "Don't Make Me Over," immediately soared to the #21 position on the Billboard chart.

Throughout the 1960s, the Warwick-Bacharach-David collaboration produced 30 hit singles and nearly 20 bestselling albums. Some of the more famous titles include "Anyone Who Had a Heart" and "Walk on By" (both 1964), "Message to Michael" (1966), "I Say a Little Prayer for You" (1968), and "This Girl's in Love with You" (1969). Other hits included "Trains and Boats and Planes," "Alfie," "You'll Never Get to Heaven," and "Make It Easy on Yourself." Warwick won the Grammy Award for Contemporary Pop Vocal twice during this period—for "Do You Know the Way to San Jose?" (1968) and "I'll Never Fall in Love Again" (1970). Although numerous other performers made hits of Bacharach-David material, it was the duo's work with Warwick that best exemplified their distinctive style. According to Notable Black American Women, Warwick was "one of the few singers who could do justice to Bacharach's unusual, rhythmically challenging, and difficult compositions."

Warwick appealed to a wide audience, much like Nat King Cole had a decade earlier. Her immense talent and popularity led to a command performance for Queen *Elizabeth II in 1968—the first black female performer to be so honored. However, when the Bacharach and David partnership disintegrated in 1972, it left Warwick facing a breach of contract suit from Warner Bros. since she would be unable to cut a new album of their material. She successfully sued Bacharach and David, settling out of court.

In 1974, Warwick collaborated with The Spinners on the single "Then Came You,"

which went to the top of the Billboard chart. However, for much of the 1970s, Warwick's career waned. Her personal life also reached a low point when her 1967 marriage to musician and actor Bill Elliott began to founder. On the advice of an astrologer and numerologist, Warwick added an "e" to the end of her last name, which had been misspelled on her first record, in the hope of improving her fortunes. The extra letter did not help. She and Elliott were divorced in 1975, and two years later Warwick's father died unexpectedly and her mother suffered a stroke. However, Warwick maintains a strong belief in the power of numerology and astrology. In the 1990s, she became a spokeswoman for the Psychic Friends Network.

Warwick's career revived in 1979 when Arista Records president Clive Davis, who would also be instrumental in the career of Warwick's cousin **Whitney Houston**, signed Warwick to a contract. He also arranged for Barry Manilow to produce her first Arista album, Dionne. Warwick was initially concerned that Manilow might give the album the "disco" sound that Warwick had deliberately avoided; however, their collaboration was spectacularly successful. Some of their hits include "I'll Never Love This Way Again" and "Deja Vu," Warwick's initial platinum record. Both songs earned Grammy Awards for Warwick, making her the first female artist to win in both the Pop Female Vocal and the Rhythm and Blues Female Vocal categories.

In June 1980, Warwick began hosting the television show "Solid Gold," which featured a countdown of the week's top hits and guest appearances by popular recording artists. She was fired the following spring, ostensibly because the producers thought a younger host would attract a younger audience; however, rumors circulated that Warwick was temperamental and difficult. Although Warwick acknowledged being a perfectionist, she believed that racism and sexism resulted in her abrupt departure from the show. The controversy did not affect Warwick's popularity, however, as she proved when the title song from her 1982 album Heartbreaker rose to the top ten on the Billboard chart. During the 1980s and 1990s, she co-hosted and helped originate "The Soul Train Music Awards" program and hosted her own television program, "Dionne and Friends."

Warwick is known for her humanitarian work, devoting much of her time to charitable activities. In 1984, she joined 45 other top performers to produce the hit single "We Are the World," the proceeds of which benefited Africa's

Dionne Warwick

hunger-relief program. Warwick also brought together Stevie Wonder, **Gladys Knight**, and Elton John to join her on the recording "That's What Friends Are For," written by Bacharach, with whom Warwick had reconciled. In January 1986, the song soared to #1 on the *Billboard* chart and raised an estimated $2 million for AIDS research. Warwick, who hosted countless fund-raising benefits for AIDS research, also became involved in boosting awareness of other health issues, including Sudden Infant Death Syndrome (SIDS) and sickle-cell anemia. To focus attention on blood diseases generally, she founded the group Blood Revolves Around Victorious Optimism (BRAVO) in the mid-1980s. On behalf of her work on these health issues, she was U.S. Ambassador for Health during this decade.

Still touring and recording regularly, in 1992 she released the album *Friends Can Be Lovers*, which featured the song "Sunny Weather Lover," Warwick's first Bacharach-David material in 20 years. Another notable album is *Aquarela do Brasil* (Watercolors of Brazil), a collection of Brazilian music released in 1994. Warwick first visited Brazil in the early 1960s and was so enthralled by the South American country that she made her home there and studied Portuguese. As the 20th century came to a close, Warwick celebrated her decades-long career with the album *Dionne Sings Dionne* (1998), comprising her classic hits and lesser-known "gems." More recently, she has created Carr-Todd-Warwick Productions, Inc., a production company that focuses on film and television projects.

SOURCES:

Phelps, Shirelle, ed. *Contemporary Black Biography, Vol. 18*. Detroit, MI: Gale Research, 1996.

Smith, Jessie Carney, ed. *Notable Black American Women*. Detroit, MI: Gale Research, 1992.

Judith C. Reveal,
freelance writer,
Greensboro, Maryland

Washburn, Margaret Floy

(1871–1939)

American experimental psychologist, one of the premier women in the field in the early 20th century, who was the second woman selected to the National Academy of Sciences. Born Margaret Floy Washburn on July 25, 1871, in Harlem, New York; died of a cerebral hemorrhage on October 29, 1939, in Poughkeepsie, New York; daughter of Francis Washburn (a businessman and Episcopal cleric) and Elizabeth (Floy) Davis Washburn; attended Ulster Academy, Kingston, New York; Vassar College, A.B., 1891; Cornell University, Ph.D., 1894; Wittenberg College, honorary D.Sc., 1927; never married; no children.

Was professor of psychology, philosophy and ethics at Wells College (1894–1900); was a warden at Sage College and instructor of social psychology and animal psychology at Cornell University (1900–02); headed the psychology department at the University of Cincinnati (1902–03); was associate professor (1904–08) and then professor of psychology (1908–37) at Vassar College, where she established (1912) and served as first head of the psychology depart-

ment; Washburn Commemorative Volume of the American Journal of Psychology issued (1927); became the second woman elected to National Academy of Sciences (1931).

Selected writings: "Some Apparatus for Cutaneous Stimulation," in American Journal of Psychology *(vol. 6, 1894, pp. 422–426);* "Über den Einfluss der Gesichtassociationen auf die Raumwahrnehmungen der Haut," in Philosophische Studien *(vol. 2, 1895, pp. 190–225); (trans. with E.B. Titchener and J.H. Gulliver)* Wilhelm Wundt's Ethical Systems *(1897);* "The Psychology of Deductive Logic," in Mind *(vol. 7, 1898, pp. 523–530);* "The Genetic Function of Movement and Organic Sensations for Social Consciousness," in American Journal of Psychology *(vol. 14, 1903, pp. 73–78);* The Animal Mind: A Text-Book of Comparative Psychology *(1908);* "The Physiological Basis of Rational Processes," in Psychological Bulletin *(vol. 6, 1909, pp. 369–378);* "The Function of Incipient Motor Processes," in Psychological Review *(vol. 21, 1914, pp. 376–390);* Movement and Mental Imagery: Outlines of a Motor Theory of the Complexer Mental Processes *(1916);* "The Social Psychology of Man and the Lower Animals," in Studies in Psychology: Titchener Commemorative Volume *(Wilson, 1917);* "Some Thoughts on the Last Quarter Century in Psychology," in Philosophical Review *(vol. 26, 1917, pp. 46–55);* "Introspection as an Objective Method," in Psychological Review *(vol. 29, 1922, pp. 89–112);* "A Questionary Study of Certain National Differences in Emotional Traits," in Journal of Comparative Psychology *(vol. 3, 1923, pp. 413–430);* "Emotion and Thought: A Motor Theory of Their Relations," in M.L. Reymert, Feelings and Emotions: The Wittenberg Symposium *(Worcester, MA: Clark University Press, 1928, pp. 104–115);* "Autobiography: Some Recollections," in C. Murchison, A History of Psychology in Autobiography *(Worcester, MA: Clark University Press, 1932, vol. 2, pp. 333–358); (with C. Wright)* "The Comparative Efficiency of Intensity, Perspective, and the Stereoscopic Factor in Producing the Perception of Depth," in American Journal of Psychology *(vol. 51, 1938, pp. 151–155); (with Richard Albert and Edward Brooks)* The Diary of Michael Floy Jr. Bowery Village 1833–1837 *(New Haven, CT: Yale University Press, 1941).*

Margaret Floy Washburn, considered one of the most prominent women psychologists in America, devoted her lifelong work to the understanding of human and animal emotions. One of the few women to earn a Ph.D. in the nascent field of psychology in the 19th century, she was so influential that she became the second woman ever elected to the National Academy of Sciences. Her intellectual awakening came early, she recalled, when on her fifth birthday she was walking along the path of her family's large garden and suddenly realized that "thinking about myself was agreeable." This epiphany would lead to increased self-awareness and later to her professional training as an experimental psychologist.

Born on July 25, 1871, at her family's home in Harlem, New York, she was the only child of Francis and **Elizabeth Floy Davis Washburn**. Her father, a businessman, was intellectual and temperamental, noted Washburn, while her mother was well balanced, strong, and kind. Both were educated, and the family was wealthy from the fortune Elizabeth Washburn had inherited. The Harlem of Margaret's happy childhood was one of mansions; the Washburns' frame house at 125th Street, surrounded by several acres of land, had been built by her great-grandfather Michael Floy, a prominent florist and nurseryman who had emigrated from Devonshire, England. A woman physician was among the conglomeration of Europeans and professionals from whom she was descended. Washburn was a humorous and perceptive child who enjoyed reading books at an early age. Her parents encouraged her academic pursuits, and without siblings for company, she had plenty of quiet time to read and think. She also wrote stories, although she did not think she had talent as a writer. Formal schooling was not so pleasant. In 1878, when her father became an Episcopal cleric for Hudson Valley parishes, the family moved upstate to Walden, where, Washburn claimed, "I learned very little." She attended the Ulster Academy in Kingston, New York, from 1883 to 1887, considering the school dull and examinations "below contempt."

After graduating from high school, 16-year-old Margaret decided to attend Vassar College, where her aunt had been a member of the first graduating class. Her mother's inheritance meant that she had ample funds to pay for her undergraduate and graduate education. During her freshman year, she became intrigued by chemistry and French. She then explored classes in biology and philosophy. "At the end of my senior year I had two dominant intellectual interests, science and philosophy," she wrote. "They seemed to be combined in what I heard of the wonderful new science of experimental psychology." In college, Margaret also developed a love of poetry, embraced ideas regarding freedom of religion, and grew to dislike sanctimonious people. To respect her family, she publicly attended Episcopal services, but privately considered herself to be agnostic. She graduated Phi Beta Kappa with an A.B. degree in 1891.

Washburn focused on the emerging field of experimental psychology. Aware of James McKeen Cattell, an American leader of experimental psychology who had studied with Wilhelm Wundt at the University of Leipzig in Germany and established a psychological laboratory at Columbia University, she "determined to be his pupil," because he had come "from the fountain-head, the Leipzig laboratory." Most graduate schools of the era did not admit women, and administrators refused to allow Washburn to become a full-time graduate student when she applied to study at Columbia. She persisted, trying to convince Cattell to let her attend his classes as a "hearer" even if she were unable to enroll at the school formally. Columbia's trustees debated for an entire semester before agreeing to permit her to audit Cattell's lectures. He welcomed her and treated her as an equal, expecting her to do the same work as male students in addition to independent study and reading. "While I was thus being initiated into Cattell's objective version of the Leipzig doctrine," Washburn recalled, "the influence of William James' *Principles* was strong." She also noted, "I feel an affectionate gratitude to [Cattell], as my first teacher, which in these later years I have courage to express; in earlier times I stood too much in awe of him."

Both Cattell and Washburn realized the gender limitations at Columbia, and he recommended her to Edward Bradford Titchener, who had established a psychological laboratory at Cornell University, a school which both permitted women to enroll as regular graduate students and offered scholarships. Titchener "did not quite know what to do with me," she wrote. Having recently received training at Oxford and at Leipzig with Wundt, he was in his first year at Cornell, and Washburn was his only graduate student. They were also about the same age, which helped her feel more comfortable with him and less in awe. A second student, Walter B. Pillsbury, arrived the following year, and the trio worked closely together. Margaret "was a brilliant conversationalist," said Pillsbury. "Her keen sense of humor was fully developed at this time." Titchener was attempting to establish psychology on a scientific basis, and he discussed with his two students the introspective experimental psychology Wundt had taught him. According to Pillsbury, Titchener had not yet worked out the theories of structuralism for which he later would become well known.

"When the more rigid system developed, Miss Washburn showed a lack of sympathy with the more extreme tenets," said Pillsbury.

During her three years at Cornell, Washburn studied philosophy as well as psychology. Her dissertation research analyzed the skin's perception of distances and directions, revealing the influence of visual imagery on tactile judgments. Of her final doctoral oral examination, said Washburn, "the occasion was a pleasant one." She was honored when Wundt published her dissertation in his German journal. Receiving her Ph.D. in 1894, Washburn became the experimentalists' first eminent student. She would remain in contact with these men as well as several Cornell philosophers throughout her career.

A young woman when she completed her Ph.D., Washburn had no immediate career plans and briefly considered marrying a philosophy professor. Rejecting this idea, she instead set out to pursue experimental psychology full time. In 1894, she joined the American Psychology Association, becoming one of its first women members. For six years, she taught psychology, philosophy, and ethics at nearby Wells College, visiting the library, laboratories, and seminars at Cornell weekly for intellectual stimulation. As well, she collaborated with Titchener and *Julia Henrietta Gulliver in translating Wundt's three-volume *Ethical Systems* from the German, and also indexed the revised text. Providing English-language philosophy students with access to this germinal treatise for the first time, the translation was considered excellent and faithful to the original work. Washburn lectured at Cornell on social psychology, and began work on animal psychology while teaching a course on the subject there in 1901. Motivated by her own "almost morbidly intense love of animals," especially cats, and interest in their behavior, she began investigating whether animals have any conscious experiences. In the same years, from 1900 to 1902, she also served as warden of a women's dormitory at Sage College. Women scientists often were expected to perform such supervisory tasks in addition to their academic work, but Washburn intensely disliked her warden role, which involved monitoring female students' behavior and social functions and took valuable time away from research. Eager to quit, late in 1902 she accepted a year's position in charge of psychology at the University of Cincinnati.

Washburn believed that women's education should be the same as men's education, and so when she was approached by Vassar College about a faculty position she had to be convinced to teach at a women's college rather than at a co-educational institute. Nonetheless, in 1904, she returned to Vassar as an associate professor of philosophy. Four years later she became Vassar's first professor of psychology, and, after establishing a department of psychology there in 1912, its first department head. She also taught psychology at Columbia University's summer school. She was considered a good teacher and administrator, and her Vassar department became a premiere psychological center. Washburn pioneered lectures in social psychology, and according to **Elizabeth M. Hincks**, "Her lectures were brilliant, exact, clear, with such a wealth of references and citing of original sources as almost to overwhelm a student as yet unable to appreciate the breadth of the scholarship and the painstaking labor involved in the construction of a single lecture," while Edwin G. Boring, a Harvard psychology professor who disliked most women in the profession, noted that "Her clear, incisive mind made her classroom lectures effective and popular." Vassar president Henry Noble MacCracken praised her because "she loved and stimulated her pupils." Many students enrolled at Vassar solely to obtain their undergraduate training under Washburn; though somewhat fearful of her demanding, scholarly demeanor, they found her stimulating and fair.

A prolific writer of over 200 articles and book reviews, Washburn was known as a thorough scholar, and was considered by colleague Herbert S. Langfeld as an "ideal experimenter" who "never acknowledged defeat." Her exuberance attracted supporters within both the Vassar and the psychological communities. "A woman of great personal charm," said Langfeld, "she also possessed in high degree the desire and ability to collaborate on terms of perfect equality with all colleagues, male and female, young and old." To familiarize her psychology majors with experimental research, she collaborated with them on psychological problems; she outlined a problem and method of research, and the assigned student conducted the experiment and tallied results. Washburn then wrote the article, and, unlike many of her colleagues, gave the student credit. In this manner she wrote 70 articles with joint authors in the well-known series *Studies From the Psychological Laboratory of Vassar College*. This successful collaboration resulted in many substantial professional contributions while also enabling Washburn to continue productive research despite a busy teaching schedule. By encouraging undergraduates to pursue meaningful research, she inspired many students to choose careers in psychology and to seek graduate training. She did not, however, develop a graduate program at Vassar, because she believed that coeducational schools provided a better environment for advanced study. She emphasized that students needed to interact with and be criticized by authorities and peers, most of whom were, at the time, male and at major universities. As well, Vassar lacked sufficient funds to subscribe to the professional psychological journals necessary for advanced training. She wrote, "I wouldn't have a graduate student under any circumstances," supporting instead a Vassar graduate fellowship for alumnae to use at other institutions. Without graduate students, however, she had few disciples to extend her experimental work, and her students' names are usually connected with those of their graduate school professors rather than Washburn herself.

Most of the projects on which Washburn collaborated with her laboratory students were explorations of topics related to her major research emphases, such as spatial perception, memory and emotions, differences between individuals, aesthetic preferences of colors and sounds of speech, and the color vision of animals. (In the summer of 1905, she had worked with Madison Bentley on observing the color vision of trout.) In her laboratory, Washburn pioneered the field of exploring emotional and temperamental traits, using methods to distinguish such personality characteristics as optimism and pessimism.

Her most important scientific publication, however, dealt with animal psychology. She had begun collecting scattered publications about animal behavior in 1901, with the intention of centralizing them in an accessible format. Washburn wanted to learn as much as she could not only about animals' external behavior but also about their conscious experiences, such as senses, space perception, memory, and problem solution. She realized that she would be unable to demonstrate conscious experiences in animals logically, but thought she needed to show that they existed, for example the manner in which animals reacted to changes in light. In *The Animal Mind: A Text-Book of Comparative Psychology*, first published in 1908, Washburn compiled and analyzed experimental work and literature on animal behavior. A pioneering treatise, the book helped to develop the field of animal psychology. In it she argued against her opponents, the behaviorists, who claimed that animals exhibited only behavior, not conscious experiences, and used human experiences as examples to test hypotheses in animal behavior. Washburn believed that consciousness and behavior were two different types of phenomena, but endorsed that psychologists should compromise and not exclude phenomena such as feeling or smelling odors from scientific research. Washburn would emphasize that the purpose of her book was "to organize the literature on the patterns of animal consciousness and to argue that they are both open to and worth investigation." Comparative psychological experimentation was in its formative stages, and her work to show evidence of animals' minds through sensory discrimination, reactions, perceptions, and subsequent modification of conscious processes filled a need for research methodology. Three revised editions appeared between 1917 and 1936, introducing new facts as advances in comparative psychology were made, further insights on conscious processes were revealed, and psychological schools of interpretation such as behaviorism were replaced by more subjective analyses like the configurational school. *The Animal Mind* was translated into Japanese, and in its various editions became a classic taught in courses throughout the world. It is still considered among the greatest psychological treatises, posing future research questions for scholars.

Washburn's next scientific achievement was the publication, in honor of the 50th anniversary of Vassar College, of her motor theory of consciousness in *Movement and Mental Imagery: Outlines of a Motor Theory of the Complexer Mental Processes* (1916). Similar to *The Animal Mind* in theory, her second book posited that mental functions, including all thoughts and perceptions, create some type of motor reaction, and that motor phenomena play an essential role in psychology. While stating, "No topic dealt with in the book is treated in anything like an exhaustive manner" because "I have not aimed at a thorough presentation of the literature of my subject, but simply at an outline development of my own views," Washburn allied psychology with physical sciences by suggesting that all perceived or imagined emotions arouse some bodily movement or muscle action. She noted that just as humans can revive their sensory impressions of how absent objects look, sound, or feel, they could reenact motor responses of approaching, manipulating, or avoiding different objects. Recalling her previous behavioral studies, she remarked, "the only sense in which we can explain conscious processes is by studying the laws governing these underlying motor phenomena," although she admitted, "The movements of a living being are of all forms of movements the most complicated and difficult to study." She connected mental and physical movement into a scientific aspect of psychology, and insisted that psychology must not focus solely on behavior but include movement as well as consciousness. Like her mentors Wundt and Titchener, Washburn believed that mind and matter—the conscious processes and behavior—were two different events, and that humans and animals reacted to perceptions by moving in some way, no matter how small. By examining the neglected motor processes of slight muscular contractions and consciousness, she transformed traditional psychology thought. *Movement and Mental Imagery*, while technical, was written to permit individuals lacking in psychological expertise to understand her ideas.

Despite her expertise and pioneering work, Washburn, like other female professionals, was excluded from the World War I Army Psychological Testing Program. This omission prevented Washburn and her female peers from securing important scientific and professional contacts that served male psychologists well in the postwar era, while also denying the army her valuable input. After the war, she worked with music professor George S. Dickinson on exploring "the emotional effects of instrumental music," winning the Edison Company prize of $500 in 1921. That same year, in a mark of respect from her peers, she became the second woman elected president of the American Psychological Association. In her presidential address, she argued her belief in a dualism of physical and mental processes. Washburn considered herself an experimentalist, not a theorist, and frequently emphasized that "The results of experimental work, if it is successful at all, bring more lasting satisfaction than the development of theories." Although she never established a psychological school of thought, she formed neutral ground between introspectionists, who studied only consciousness, and behaviorists.

Despite the fact that he was Washburn's mentor, Titchener refused to allow her or any other professional female psychologist to join his Society of Experimental Psychologists, an informal round table where men discussed research in progress. Hiding her anger at being excluded from Titchener's club and the professional benefits of networking with eminent colleagues, she never protested publicly. Washburn, who was considered conservative and noncontroversial when compared to vocal psychologist *Christine Ladd-Franklin, realized her omission had little to do with her ability but much to do with male psychologists' irrational fears that standards would be lowered if women were admitted to their society. She nonetheless continued receiving laurels from her peers, and in 1927 was elected

vice-president of the American Association for the Advancement of Science. That year she received an honorary D.Sc. from Wittenberg College, and a special issue of the *American Journal of Psychology*, entitled the "Washburn Commemorative Volume," celebrated her career. She also was starred as a distinguished psychologist in the first edition of *American Men of Science*. In 1929, Washburn's closest friend, Karl Dallenbach, with whom she edited a psychology journal, succeeded Titchener at Cornell and, despite the astonishment of male members, welcomed her into the Society of Experimental Psychologists. (Two years later, Washburn arranged for the group to meet at Vassar.)

In 1931, Washburn received the signal honor of becoming the second woman to be elected to the National Academy of Sciences (the first was anatomist *Florence Sabin in 1925). Because women scientists received only minor professional encouragement, few women ever attained this status. Selection relied on having the male panel first recognize a scientist's merit and then support her or him despite peer resistance. Although ten to twenty men were elected to the academy every year, Washburn and Sabin would remain the only women so honored until 1944, when *Barbara McClintock was chosen.

Washburn actively edited numerous journals, serving as one of four coeditors of the *American Journal of Psychology* and initiating *Psychological Abstracts*. She also contributed editorial advice to the *Psychological Bulletin*, *Psychology Review*, *Journal of Comparative Psychology*, and *Journal of American Behavior*. Although Vassar was well endowed, Washburn had scant access to research funds and, with a full teaching load, little time for research. After being denied either teaching assistance or a reduced courseload, she resigned her editorial duties, telling her editor-in-chief, "I doubt if anyone else on the board is teaching eighteen hours a week, as I am. I simply must cut down my work somewhere." She nonetheless accepted committee responsibilities to survey the academic status of psychology and its teachers, and was active in the New York Academy of Science and chaired psychology sections in the National Research Council and represented the United States at international psychology conventions.

Washburn's personality won her many friends. Boring described her thus: "In manner Miss Washburn was direct and frank, but her criticism was blunted sometimes by a gracious diplomacy, sometimes by a friendly humor. She was reserved but not shy, with a few devoted friends, a host of admirers, and some others who feared her a little." Said MacCracken: "The key to her personality was a unique attitude, in which were combined a detached objective devotion to experimental science and a passionate joy of living." He noted her love of literary, musical, and artistic efforts; she enjoyed oil painting, singing, dancing, piano playing, and amateur acting. She also collected 17th- to 19th-century manuscripts on English political history and had a scholarly interest in classical literature. According to Robert S. Woodworth, "She had a keen sense of humor and a cheerful and even buoyant disposition, though she was not blind to human frailties." Often aloof and private, enjoying quiet time to herself as she had when she was a child, Washburn believed that she was "never less alone than when alone." Throughout her life she shared a close relationship with her parents, who lived only 16 miles from Vassar, and her mother moved in with her after her father's death. A tactful, deliberate, and logical woman, she often served as a mediator on campus and in the psychological community. Washburn was not known as a feminist, and although she supported equal educational opportunities for women she criticized suffrage groups for what she believed were inconsistent methods of seeking the vote. Privately, she protested separate gender spheres, but publicly she did not demonstrate. One rare exception of sorts to this standard occurred in 1934, when she ate in the men-only dining hall during a meeting at the Harvard Faculty Club. This rupture of the rules upset Boring, whom she tried to soothe by saying that, far from being fueled by any feminist motives, she had mistakenly believed that women were allowed in the dining hall on that singular occasion.

As Washburn's career wound down, her scientific writing tailed off, and she began to write the obituaries of her mentors and colleagues. She also began editing and annotating the diary of her grand uncle Michael Floy, Jr. (Vassar later would publish her unfinished transcription posthumously, in honor of the college's 75th anniversary.) After 25 years at Vassar, her students gave her a purse containing $15,407.04 for her personal enjoyment, which she in turn gave to the college, endowing the Margaret Floy Washburn Fund for Promising Students in Psychology. She retired in 1937. Her hand-picked successor **Josephine Gleason** did not have sufficient publications to her credit to be chosen chair of the psychology department, and a heated controversy ensued while the college tried to find a woman chair. Ultimately, a man named Lyle Lanier was selected as chair, demonstrating the profession's

continued resistance to naming women to top psychological positions. Still, her influence in the field remained strong. Her professional legacy, according to colleagues, has endured: "she is best known for her dualistic psychophysiological view of the animal mind, and for her strongly argued view that all thought can be traced to bodily movement." A 1968 study by an international group of psychologists rated Washburn as one of the most prominent women in her field.

After having enjoyed good health most of her life, Washburn suffered a series of strokes and a cerebral hemorrhage the same year she retired. Her health deteriorated, and she lived in a nursing home at Poughkeepsie, New York, until her death on the afternoon of October 29, 1939. Her last intelligible words were: "I love every living thing." A memorial service was held in her honor at Vassar, to which she had willed her estate, and her ashes were buried in the Washburn family plot in a rural cemetery near White Plains, New York.

SOURCES:

Dallenbach, Karl M. "Margaret Floy Washburn, 1871–1939," in *The American Journal of Psychology*. Vol. 53. January 1940, pp. 1–5.

Goodman, Elizabeth S. "Margaret F. Washburn (1871–1939): First Woman Ph.D. in Psychology," in *Psychology of Women Quarterly*. Vol. 5. Fall 1980, pp. 69–80.

Hincks, Elizabeth M. "Tribute of a Former Pupil," in *Vassar Alumnae Magazine*. Vol. 25. January 1940, p. 6.

Pillsbury, Walter B. "Margaret Floy Washburn (1871–1939)," in *The Psychological Review*. Vol. 47. March 1940, pp. 99–109.

Washburn Commemorative Volume. *American Journal of Psychology*, 1927.

Woodworth, Robert S. "Biographical Memoir of Margaret Floy Washburn, 1871–1939," in *Biographical Memoirs of the National Academy of Sciences*. Vol. 25. Washington, DC: National Academy of Sciences, 1949, pp. 275–295.

SUGGESTED READING:

Boring, Edward G. *A History of Experimental Psychology*. NY: Century, 1929.

Mull, Helen K. "A Bibliography of the Writings of Margaret Floy Washburn: 1894–1927," in *American Journal of Psychology*. Vol. 39, 1927, pp. 428–436.

Kambouropoulous, Polyxenie. "A Bibliography of the Writings of Margaret Floy Washburn: 1928–1939," in *American Journal of Psychology*. Vol. 53. January 1940, pp. 19–20.

Rossiter, Margaret W. *Women Scientists in America: Struggles and Strategies to 1940*. Baltimore, MD: Johns Hopkins University Press, 1982.

COLLECTIONS:

The Christine Ladd-Franklin Papers (includes correspondence with Washburn) are held in Special Collections, Butler Library, Columbia University, New York City.

The Edward Bradford Titchener Papers and Karl Dallenbach Papers are located at the Cornell University

Archives and Regional History Office, Ithaca, New York.

The Edwin G. Boring Papers (includes correspondence with Washburn) are held in the Harvard University Archives, Cambridge, Massachusetts.

The James McKeen Cattell Papers are held by the Library of Congress, Manuscript Division, Washington, D.C.

Washburn's biographical file is located in Deceased Members Records, National Academy of Sciences-National Research Council Archives, Washington, D.C.; faculty files and the Christine Ladd-Franklin Diaries are located at the Vassar College Archives, Poughkeepsie, New York; course notes are available in various collections of former pupils at the Archives of the History of American Psychology, University of Akron, Akron, Ohio; correspondence, manuscripts, lecture notes, photographs, and memorabilia are located in the Robert M. Yerkes Papers, Yale University, New Haven, Connecticut.

Elizabeth D. Schafer, Ph.D.,
freelance writer in history of technology
and science, Loachapoka, Alabama

Wa Shi (1498–1560)

Zhuang warrior, noted general, and shrewd political figure in southern China in the latter years of the Ming Dynasty, who became the most famous woman in the history of the Zhuang ethnic minority. Pronunciation: Wah Shrrr, rhymes with Hah Brrr. Born Wa Shi (which means flower in her native Tai dialect but often erroneously thought by the Chinese to mean flower-tile), in 1498; daughter of Cen Zhang (a great feudal lord of the Zhuang minority people of the Sino-Vietnamese frontier region of southern China); married the Zhuang lord Cen Meng; children: a son, Cen Bangzuo.

Trained in the art of combat and known for her strength, was briefly married to the most powerful and wealthy of the Zhuang lords; returned with her son to her father's court; after the death of her former husband at her father's hands, created shrewd alignments that allowed the Zhuang people to live in peace with the Chinese, gaining great influence for her family and protection for her people; chosen as the general to lead an army against Japanese pirates plaguing the Chinese coast, achieved military success (1557).

In the southern province of China that adjoins Vietnam, the people of the ethnic minority known as the Zhuang have long been accorded an unusual degree of autonomy, largely because of the political and military role they have played in maintaining the Chinese border. A millennium ago, the Zhuang shamaness *A Nong fought for the identity of her people against the Chinese and lost. Five hundred years later, the famous Zhuang warrior Wa Shi helped to guar-

antee the survival of her people by serving the Chinese Empire with distinction. A shrewd politician, as well as skilled in the traditional martial arts, she ably led her family through continuous internecine quarrels while avoiding direct Chinese control, becoming the most famous woman in the history of the Zhuang and one of the very few women ever to hold the rank of general in the Chinese imperial armies.

The Chinese had begun their expansion into Zhuang regions as far back as the 3rd century BCE, and had been resisted by them for many centuries. By the time Wa Shi was born in 1498, the numbers of the Chinese were beginning to exceed those of the Zhuang, who were becoming a minority in their own lands.

Wa Shi's father Cen Zhang was a powerful lord of the Cen clan, a dominant clan of the Zhuang by the year 1500. Her mother's clan was the Wa, also an important local family. Like all Zhuang women then, and most Chinese women today, Wa Shi kept her maiden name after her marriage. Clan members traced their descent through common male ancestors. In earlier periods, before the Chinese impact, the Zhuang had traced their descent bilaterally, through both male and female lines.

As the head of his clan, Cen Zhang controlled a large territory by virtue of his leadership of many warriors. The region of the Zhuang was mountainous terrain, where communication was difficult and the topography impeded political or cultural unity. In terms of providing its inhabitants with a living, it was also poor, and mercenary service in the armies of the Chinese (and Vietnamese) had long been an attractive alternative to the back-breaking labor of mountain farming.

The forbidding lands were also spectacularly beautiful, however, with sharply drawn limestone crags called karsts that jut up suddenly from verdant valleys. The forested highlands are inhabited by tropical parrots, finches, and delicate deer, and in Wa Shi's lifetime by wolves, tigers, wild elephants, and bears. Typhoons from the South China Sea bring violent winds and heavy rains to the region, and when conditions are right, fog lingers in the valleys and wreaths the mountain peaks. It was this atmosphere that served as the primary inspiration for traditional Chinese landscape painting, and for an active girl like Wa Shi it must have seemed a lovely, if sometimes dangerous, playground.

Although the Chinese migration had changed Zhuang society significantly by the time of Wa

Shi's birth, the two cultures remained quite different, particularly in terms of the roles of women. Zhuang women were independent, accustomed to hard physical labor, and accorded social equality to match their responsibilities. Women often maintained their own households, and it was not uncommon for a husband to move in with his bride's family rather than establish a male-dominated household. The Chinese appear to have viewed Zhuang women as wild and somewhat fearsome, and even to have credited them with supernatural powers, while also finding them alluring.

Many Zhuang women trained as warriors. The Cen clan of Wa Shi's father had a long military tradition, and was one of the few which kept a military handbook for the training of its men, along with an elaborate code of behavior for warriors on campaign. As the daughter of a lord, Wa Shi might have been kept safe from war because of her status. On the other hand, it also gave her exposure to the best possible training in the military arts, and she proved to be a talented, aggressive student. She became particularly adept at fighting with a long straight sword in each hand, a style of combat that required great coordination and dexterity. She also became expert with the long spear and was noted for her physical strength.

By the time Wa Shi was growing up, the Ming rulers of the Chinese Empire, in power since the mid-14th century, had been forced to recognize a degree of autonomy among the Zhuang people rather than continually face fierce Zhuang soldiers in prolonged and costly wars. Instead, they had attempted to co-opt Zhuang lords by recognizing their local power through the grant of Chinese titles, and by requiring them to pay taxes to the Chinese court. They also made a continuous effort to restrict the autonomy they had allowed, however, and during Wa Shi's youth, they moved to do away with the hereditary status and incorporate the region as another imperial province. Wa Shi must have heard many heated arguments among the men and women of her family about how to deal with the Chinese. Without the hereditary titles they had been granted, the Zhuang lords would be reduced to the status of local landholders with no special rights or privileges. As well, incorporation of the region would have meant an end to the cultural identity of the Zhuang people as a whole. Compared to this relatively small group, China was a huge multiethnic empire, which had successfully absorbed a great diversity of peoples in the past, melding them into the Chinese people.

It was during this period that Wa Shi married a noted Zhuang lord, Cen Meng, becoming one of his four wives. A violent, ambitious man, Cen Meng also proved shrewd in resisting the Chinese while continually expanding his domains at the expense of weaker Zhuang lords. When it served his purposes, he lent his armies to Chinese campaigns against other regional minorities, like the Yao and Miao. Because he was useful to them, and also a formidable local lord, the Chinese rulers chose to ignore his rapacious appetite for power.

Zhuang lords lived in elaborate palaces built in the Chinese style, guarded by eunuch gatekeepers and waited upon by numerous servants. Cen Meng was immensely wealthy, and Wa Shi must have possessed an abundance of the gold and silver ornaments by which the Zhuang displayed their wealth. At the time of her marriage, Wa Shi seems to have been regarded as Cen Meng's primary wife, and there is evidence that the couple initially loved each other deeply. Wa Shi subsequently gave birth to a son, Cen Bangzuo. Before many years had passed, however, the couple grew apart. Cen Meng expelled Wa Shi from his household, and she returned to her father's holdings with her young son.

> [She] fought with two swords and knew how to defeat the pirates.
>
> **—Chinese poem**

In 1524, Cen Meng came to an open break with the Chinese. After three years of successful resistance, he was attacked by a massive Chinese army before he could prepare adequate defenses. In the hope of raising additional troops, he fled to the territory of Cen Zhang. But Cen Zhang was enraged that Cen Meng had put Wa Shi aside, thereby depriving the father-in-law's family of any rights to Cen Meng's vast holdings. The failing war also endangered the powers of all the Zhuang lords, and while holding a feast for his former son-in-law, Cen Zhang had him poisoned. At the time of his death in 1527 Cen Meng was the most powerful Zhuang lord since King Nong Zhigao, during the Song era, when A Nong lived.

Ordinarily, Wa Shi's divorce from Cen Meng should have signaled the end of her personal power, since she no longer had direct rights to her former husband's holdings. But in the very unsettled period following Cen Meng's death, while the Chinese were attempting to consolidate direct control over his holdings, there were unusual opportunities for the daring Wa Shi, who maneuvered skillfully among the quarreling Zhuang lords.

In a clever compromise that brought her the support of other Zhuang clans, Wa Shi first came to terms with Cen Meng's other wives, by putting forward as Cen Meng's heir one of the sons of the primary wife, rather than her own son. Then, however, she ensured her continued control over the boy and the estates of Cen Meng by raising the designated heir as her own child. When another son of Cen Meng, Bangxiang, grew to adulthood, he waged a war against Wa Shi's influence. After Wa Shi succeeded in capturing Bangxiang's household, she strangled him with her own hands, and other claimants for power suddenly became less ambitious.

Wa Shi, now in her maturity, became the dominant lord of the Zhuang heartland. For several decades, she was noted for her benevolent but disciplined rule. Because she could field tens of thousands of professional warriors, the Chinese took care not to antagonize her. Again showing her genius for necessary compromise, she made her peace with the Chinese, indicating that she recognized the inevitability of their rule. In turn, the Chinese took care to preserve the essential elements of power among the Zhuang lords, allowing important titles to remain hereditary.

In the years Wa Shi was consolidating her power in the south, China faced a crisis on its eastern coast. The end of a long period of feudal warfare in Japan had demobilized thousands of professional Japanese warriors, many of whom took to sea rather than settle down, and became pirates. In 1522, recognizing that eastern China was weakly defended, they had begun making daring raids along the coast, sometimes following the rivers hundreds of miles inland. Some of these raids were made up of as many as 20,000 brigands aboard hundreds of vessels. The raiders, known derisively to the Chinese as *Wako* (dwarf pirates), brought the coastal economy to a halt. Peaceful Chinese peasants and fishermen fled the vulnerable coastal lowlands, leaving large areas depopulated.

The Ming court, now grown weak and corrupt, was entering upon its last century of rule. The Chinese sent ever-larger armies against the Japanese, who proved too fierce and too mobile, while the Chinese court was hindered by clique politics. Court ministers were using the military coffers to amass personal fortunes, and armies were often sent out ill-equipped and poorly trained. If the ponderous Chinese military forces succeeded in making contact, the Japanese simply melted away in small groups and regained their ships off-shore.

Finally, a Chinese general who had fought against Cen Meng thought of the Zhuang. The Chinese court offered Wa Shi a general's commission to form an expedition to face the pirates. In 1557, at age 59, Wa Shi set out for the coast at the head of an army of 6,000 hand-picked Zhuang infantry, known to the awe-struck Chinese as *Langbing* (Wolf Soldiers). Along the way, her headquarters was guarded by a band of 40 female warriors. The trip took months and rations ran low, but the hardy troops foraged and found food where other armies might have starved.

Arriving at the coast, Wa Shi led her troops in an initial skirmish in which she herself fought hand-to-hand, wielding a heavy cutlass-like Dao sword against the armored pirates. The Zhuang were victorious, and Wa Shi later led a column of Zhuang in a lightning-fast attack on the main body of the pirates, dealing them their first serious defeat.

But despite Wa Shi's ability and the skill of her soldiers, the Ming court proved too corrupt to sustain the fight. A quarrel among the cliques resulted in the execution of the Chinese general who had recruited Wa Shi, and the Chinese force became so weakened and demoralized that Wa Shi sought permission to return home. For the next 20 years, the pirates remained a periodic problem.

Wa Shi lived another year before her death, in 1560. A local religious cult grew up around her, and the temple built to her spirit was maintained well into the 20th century. Descendants of the Cen line continued to serve the Chinese nation with great distinction, usually as generals and political figures. Even now, the Cen name is famous in the Guangxi Zhuang Autonomous Region, where China and Vietnam meet. The indigenous inhabitants of this frontier region, known in China today as the Zhuang, and in Vietnam as the Nung, are one of the world's largest ethnic groups without a state structure of their own, numbering more than 15 million people. Many other Zhuang have made noted contributions to Chinese history, as poets, artists, politicians, warriors, and generals. But the most famous of all Zhuang women remains the formidable Wa Shi.

SOURCES:

Barlow, Jeffrey G. "The Zhuang Minority in the Ming Era," in *Ming Studies*. No. 28. Fall 1989.

Dreyer, June Teufel. *China's Forty Millions*. Cambridge, MA: Harvard University Press, 1976.

Eberhard, Wolfram. *China's Minorities, Yesterday and Today*. Belmont, CA: Wadsworth, 1982.

SUGGESTED READING:

Barlow, Jeffrey G. "The Zhuang Peoples of the Sino-Vietnamese Frontier in the Song Period," in *Journal of*

Southeast Asian Studies. Vol. XVII, no. 2. September 1987.

Hucker, Charles O., ed. *Chinese Government in Ming Times: Seven Studies*. NY: Columbia University Press, 1969.

Jeffrey G. Barlow,
Professor in the Department of Social Studies at
Pacific University, Forest Grove, Oregon

Washington, Dinah (1924–1963)

African-American blues and pop singer whose successful career, enhanced by her crossover into the white musical world, was cut short by her early death. Name variations: Ruth Jones. Born Ruth Lee Jones in Tuscaloosa, Alabama, on August 8(?), 1924; died in Detroit on December 14, 1963, from an apparently unintentional overdose of sleeping pills; daughter of Ollie Jones and Alice Jones; married John Young, in 1941 (divorced within a year); married George Jenkins (a drummer), in 1946 (divorced July 1947); married Robert Grayson, in 1947 (divorced within a year); married a saxophonist (divorced); married a cabdriver, in 1959 (divorced 1960); married an actor (divorced); married Dick Lane (a quarterback for the Detroit Lions), in July 1963; children: (first marriage) George Jenkins, Jr. (b. 1947); (second marriage) Robert Grayson, Jr. (b. August 1948).

Moved with her mother to Chicago at the start of the Great Depression; began playing the piano and singing in church choirs as a young girl; after winning a singing contest, began singing in local clubs, the owner of one of which gave her the stage name by which she would be known (1939); began touring with the Lionel Hampton Band as a blues singer (1942); became such a popular rhythm and blues artist (mid-1940s) that she left Hampton's band and put together her own act; known for the intense emotionalism of her interpretations, crossed over to the pop charts (1959) with her recording of "What a Diff'rence a Day Makes" and reached a mainstream audience.

It seemed like the usual crowd filling the dim, smoky upstairs lounge of the Sherman Hotel on Chicago's South Side as the blues singer everyone knew as Ruth Jones began her first set of the evening. But there was one difference that night in 1942, for among the shadowy silhouettes huddled around the tables or leaning on the bar was Lionel Hampton, a former percussionist with Benny Goodman. Hampton now had his own big band and was looking for a female vocalist. "After listening to a few bars, I knew she was the girl I was looking for," he later said of his first exposure to the singer he would make famous to audiences across the country as Dinah Washington.

It was the break that had eluded Ruth's mother **Alice Jones** since she had moved with her daughter and son, Harold, to Chicago from Tuscaloosa, Alabama, in 1929. Ruth had been born five years earlier, although the exact birth date in August has never been pinned down, birth certificates not being routinely issued for the children of poor blacks in the Depression-era South. The date most often given is August 8, 1924. Abandoned by her husband Ollie Jones not long after Ruth was born, Alice decided to follow the great African-American migration north to Chicago to look for work. The only thing her daughter would remember about Alabama was the loneliness of those early years.

At first, conditions didn't seem much better in Chicago. "They were living in the projects, and there were rats and roaches, and they didn't have food or enough clothes to wear," a family friend once recalled. Most of Chicago's African-Americans in those days were crowded into the city's South Side, traveling to the wealthier white sections of town to work as domestics or on street crews. Others opened bars and "juke joints," where the hardships of daily life could be shared through that most native of American music forms, the blues, carried north from the fields and slums of the South. Alice Jones, however, would have none of it, finding her solace at St. Luke's Baptist Church, where she played piano for the choir and saw to it that young Ruth learned how to play, too. To her delight, Ruth also showed a great talent for singing, so much so that she became a celebrity on the church circuit for her ability to put over a rousing gospel song and bring a congregation to its feet. Soon, little Ruth Jones had come to the attention of **Sallie Martin**, Chicago's undisputed gospel star of the 1930s, who had formed a famous touring gospel choir and organized an annual Gospel Singers Convention. Ruth, Sallie told Alice, not only had a powerful voice but perfect diction and would be a great addition to the Sallie Martin Colored Ladies Quartet, a smaller group of Martin's more talented singers.

Ruth was soon touring with the Quartet, but it became evident that her interests lay elsewhere than gospel music. Her idol, she admitted, was *Billie Holiday, whom she admired not only for her blues treatment of popular tunes but also for the fact that Holiday seemed to be making money as a singer whereas she, Ruth, was making very little indeed. Martin quickly noticed, too, that as Ruth entered her teens and her figure blossomed, it was the money that men could offer that was proving a real danger. "She could really sing," Martin later said, "but, shoot, she'd catch the eye of some man and she'd be out of the church before the minister finished the doxology." Neither Martin nor Ruth's mother knew that Ruth had been singing blues in clubs and juke joints one or two nights a week, using a different name each time, after winning a talent contest at the Regal Theater and coming to the attention of club owners. When Ruth's secret was finally discovered, it was too late. She left Sallie Martin's gospel singing behind and, at 17, married a man named John Young, who said he could find her work as a singer. "He talked my language and said he would help me get into show business," Dinah recalled. "I was seventeen and absolutely dumb about the ways of the world."

When you get inside of a tune, the soul in you should come out.

—Dinah Washington

Even though the marriage lasted less than a year, Young did manage to find her work, first as the opening act at a new lounge in the Sherman Hotel called the Down Beat room, where Fats Waller was the headliner. Jobs at other clubs followed, although club managers didn't pay her a regular salary, and the only money Ruth made was from tips from customers. It was no different at the even more prestigious Garrick Stage Lounge's upstairs club, but a big bonus for Ruth was that Billie Holiday was booked downstairs in the first floor lounge. In between her own sets, Ruth would be sure to watch Holiday's act and soon began to mimic her idol in her own performances, swaying her body slightly and softly snapping her fingers as she sang. Soon, customers were nearly as numerous upstairs as they were below, for Ruth's emotional range during a song—from a soft-spoken tenderness to a high-pitched intensity drawn from her gospel-singing days—made any number she tackled distinctly her own. Impressed by her growing audience, the Garrick's owner paid Ruth her first real salary, $50 a week; and, by the time Lionel Hampton came to see her, had come up with the name Dinah Washington which, he said, "rolls off people's tongues like rich liquor."

Hampton had been touring with his band for five years by the time he hired Washington, whose blues style proved to be the perfect complement to his penchant for big band rhythms. From Dinah's perspective, Hampton's band gave her what Chick Webb's band had given *Ella Fitzgerald ten years earlier—a much wider audi-

ence, and a home. While Hampton refined Washington's repertoire and stage presence, his wife **Gladys Hampton** took Dinah's wardrobe and deportment as her own responsibility. By the time Washington opened with Hampton at New York's Apollo Theater in December 1943, standing ovations for her performance had become routine. The influential jazz composer and critic Leonard Feather was as impressed as everyone else when he first heard Dinah sing at the Apollo, but he thought the pop standards Hampton had given Washington to sing were too restrictive. Feather suggested to Hampton that Dinah and some of the players from the band record a few blues numbers he'd written for a small, private label. "I thought she'd make a wonderful blues singer," he said. "She had a very biting quality to her voice, and unique timbre. She didn't sound like *Bessie Smith, but it was in the same tradition, just a generation later—a more sophisticated sound."

Hampton was so agreeable to Feather's suggestion that he and five musicians from the band backed Washington up at Feather's recording session, even though Hampton's contract with Decca prohibited him or any members of his band from playing on anybody else's label. When Dinah's treatment of Feather's "Evil Gal Blues" was released, listing the Lionel Hampton Sextet as the backup, Decca successfully sued to halt distribution of the single; but the release got enough airplay on the radio to put Dinah's name on the black music charts and considerably increase her influence with the band; so much so that Decca finally relented and allowed Washington to legally record another Feather number, "Blowtop Blues," released in 1945. Dinah's star power had risen sufficiently by now, so much so that when Hampton demanded rights to the song so his band could perform it without her, Dinah refused and left the band in 1946 to form a solo act, when she was just 21. Hampton, she complained, would only let her sing big band tunes when it was the blues that was making her money.

Signing with an independent record label, Apollo Records, Washington churned out 12 blues singles, made her first tour of the West Coast, and married a drummer, George Jenkins, all within the first seven months of her new solo career. Soon pregnant, Dinah returned to Chicago to give birth to George Jenkins, Jr., early in 1947. Jenkins *pére* was not in attendance at the birth. The marriage disintegrated and ended in divorce in July 1947. Washington returned to touring, but not before marrying for a third time, taking as her new husband Robert Grayson who, as the son of the pastor at St. Luke's in Chicago, she had

Dinah Washington

known as a girl. The birth of Robert Grayson, Jr., followed in August 1948. Dinah, accompanied by a girlhood friend to look after the children, went back to touring and recording after the birth of her second child. Once again, her marriage ended within a year even as her prestige as an important new blues and jazz singer increased with recordings featuring innovative instrumentalists like Max Roach and Charles Mingus.

By mid-century, with white audiences discovering the blues and *Billboard* changing the name of its "Race Records" chart to "Rhythm and Blues," Washington's audience grew even larger when she signed with mainstream Mercury Records. "Baby Get Lost," released in 1949, went to No. 1 on the new R&B lists; and when Dinah began inserting more pop-oriented tunes into her repertoire, even *Variety* sat up and took notice. "Uninhibited as a rule, the buxom Miss Washington is considerably toned down in chirping the sedate *Without A Song*," *Variety* said of Washington's appearance at the Apollo in 1949. Dinah was now earning over $100,000 a year and could afford to take a suite of rooms at a hotel near the Apollo during her appearance. She was, in fact, approaching full diva status, with expensive wardrobe, volatile temper and lavish habits to match. "If she didn't like you, she would cuss you out in a minute," said a close friend. Among those Dinah chose to disparage were the three husbands she had gone through since divorcing Robert Grayson, as well as *Ebony* magazine, which was careless enough to call her "plump, good-natured Dinah." She had developed a fondness for good brandy, expensive automobiles and luxury gifts for those who pleased her, running up such bills that she was forced to tour and record nearly constantly to pay for it all. It must have brought some relief when Mercury offered her a $20,000 advance for a new five-year contract. With her work schedule now even heavier, Washington turned to prescription drugs to keep her awake during show times and put her to sleep at night. "A lot of people thought she was on street stuff," one friend pointed out, "but it was all prescription, all legit." Legal or not, Dinah's drug usage took its toll on her personal life. Her fifth husband walked out one night when Dinah smashed his saxophone against a brick wall during an argument about that night's performance.

By the late 1950s, with rock 'n' roll beginning to encroach on rhythm-and-blues territory ("It'll die out," Dinah predicted), Mercury decided to move Dinah's repertory even further toward pop standards. Dinah's first purely pop album, *Look to the Rainbow*, was released in 1956. Backed by a full, lush string section, she crooned her way through songs like "Smoke Gets in Your Eyes" and "More Than You Know." Radio stations were at first resistant to playing anything from the album. "At that time, if you brought a record by a black artist to a pop disk jockey, you were dead," recalled Washington's Mercury producer Bobby Shad. "They would refuse to play them. I remember bringing up records, and I would refuse to tell them who the singer was. I'd say, just listen to the record."

"Look to the Rainbow" was not a success, but white audiences slowly began to pick up on Dinah's talent for taking a song everyone had heard before and making it sound new. "Getting inside a tune is so important," Washington said, "and when you do, there's a feeling that comes out. It should flow out of you. That's what I want and try to do." Her second pop album, *Land of Hi-Fi*, sold somewhat better than its predecessor; but it wasn't until Mercury put its first black producer in charge of Washington's next recording, "What a Diff'rence a Day Makes," that Dinah won full acceptance from white listeners. The song had been brought to her by composer Arnold Shaw, who had originally called it "What a Difference a Day Made." Dinah's insistence on changing the title and lyric to the present tense was a perfect example of "getting inside a tune." Shaw personally promoted the record on its release in the spring of 1959. By June, it had crossed over from the R&B listings to the pop charts, where it rose to No. 9. Arguably Dinah's most famous recording, "What a Diff'rence" won her a Grammy award that year as best R&B artist.

Mercury was sufficiently encouraged to send Washington on her first European tour in the fall of 1959, to Stockholm and London. Assured of her reputation as "queen of the jukebox," Dinah caused a stir in the British capital when she told her audience that "there's one heaven, one earth, and one queen—and your Elizabeth is an imposter." Aboard ship between the two cities, Dinah married a cabdriver she had met on the way to the New York ship terminal (she had flown him to Europe for the occasion). It lasted no longer than her other marriages, ending in divorce in 1960.

On her return to the United States, the toll taken by 20 years of nearly constant touring began to become apparent. Her reliance on brandy during her rare off hours was now supplemented by sips of champagne during long recording sessions, so many of them in between takes that she often had to be led from the studio. Added to the diet pills she used to control her weight were weekly injections of mercury which, Washington claimed, "drew water from the body." Even the most innocuous comment about her weight would send her into a rage, Dinah once pulling a revolver on a dressmaker who thought one of her dresses should be let out. Even more telling, Washington began missing gigs. "A lot of times she just didn't feel up to performing," said a friend of those days in the early 1960s. "She was taking those pills, and her voice began to come and go, and she couldn't hit the notes like she wanted to. And if somebody said something to her, then she'd get nasty." Friends hoped that Washington's purchase of a failed Chicago nightclub, which she renamed Dinahland, would give more focus to her life. But her venture into club management, and marriage to an actor she had met while touring, both ended within a year. Hopes rose again when, in July 1963, Dinah married Dick Lane, a quarterback for the Detroit Lions who seemed devoted to her and to as normal a home life as could be arranged by two stars of the sports and music worlds. Plans had been made for a family Christmas in Detroit with Lane's children from a previous marriage when word came of Dinah's death from an overdose of sleeping pills. She had died at home while Lane was in Chicago picking up the children for the trip back to Detroit. The death was ruled accidental, and Lane theorized that Washington had simply forgotten how many of the pills she had taken in her search for desperately needed sleep. She was just 39 at her death.

At Dinah Washington's funeral in Chicago, Lane spoke of her ability to reach people of all backgrounds through her music. "It was unbelievable how she could take kings and bring them under her spell," he said, "and she could take the tramp out there in the street and the prostitute and do the same thing." It was Washington's great talent to find her own soul in her music and teach her audiences that it was their soul, too.

SOURCES:

Haskins, Jim. *Queen of the Blues: The Story of Dinah Washington*. NY: Morrow, 1987.
Sadie, Stanley, ed. *The New Grove Dictionary of Music and Musicians*. 2nd ed. NY: Macmillan, 2001.
Slonimsky, Nicholas, ed. *Baker's Biographical Dictionary of Musicians*. 8th ed. NY: Schirmer, 1992.

Norman Powers,
writer-producer, Chelsea Lane Productions,
New York, New York

Washington, Fredi (1903–1994)

African-American actress and founder of the Negro Actors Guild of America. Name variations: Edith Warren. Born Fredricka Carolyn Washington on December 23, 1903, in Savannah, Georgia; died on June 28, 1994, in Stamford, Connecticut; graduated from Julia Richmond High School in New York; attended Egri School of Dramatic Writing and the Christophe School of Languages; married trombonist Lawrence Brown (divorced); married dentist Anthony H. Bell (died).

Selected theater: Shuffle Along *(1921);* Black Boy *(1926);* Sweet Chariot *(1930);* Singin' the Blues *(1931);* Run, Little Chillun *(1933);* Mamba's Daugh-ters *(1939);* Lysistrata *(1946);* A Long Way from Home *(1948);* How Long Til Summer *(1949).*

Selected filmography: Hot Chocolates *(1929);* Great Day *(1929);* Black and Tan Fantasy *(1929);* The Emperor Jones *(1933);* The Old Man of the Mountain *(1933);* Mills Blue Rhythm Band *(1933);* Imitation of Life *(1934);* Drums of the Jungle *(1935);* Quanga *(1936);* One Mile from Heaven *(1937).*

Actress Fredi Washington, who was typecast in mainstream films as the "tragic mulatto" during her early career, worked to improve dramatic roles for black actors through the Negro Actors Guild of America, which she founded. She was born in 1903 in Savannah, Georgia, to a black mother and a white father. She picked up the nickname "Fredi" from her mother who died when the girl was only 11 years old. As the eldest daughter, Washington assumed responsibility for running the household until her father's remarriage, after which she and her sister **Isabell (Powell)** entered Saint Elizabeth's Convent in Cornwell Heights, Pennsylvania. Eventually Washington moved to New York to live with her grandmother and an aunt. She graduated from ***Julia Richmond** High School and completed further studies at two professional schools, Egri School of Dramatic Writing and the Christophe School of Languages.

Washington began her stage career at age 16 as a chorus member of the Happy Honeysuckles. While working as a bookkeeper at W.C. Handy's Black Swan Records in the early 1920s, she learned of a dance audition for the black musical *Shuffle Along*. Although she had no formal dance training, Washington landed a spot in the chorus with the assistance of black choreographer **Elida Webb**, earning $35 a week.

During a stint at Manhattan's Club Alabam, producer Lee Shubert recommended that she audition for the Broadway play *Black Boy* (1926), based on the life of prizefighter Jack Johnson and starring Paul Robeson. Under the stage name Edith Warren, she landed the part of a fair-skinned black girl who passes for white but in the end identifies with the black community. The play opened to mixed reviews, but Washington earned critical notice and the play drew theatergoers curious to see if she were as white as reputed by the media. The play established an unfortunate precedent in that Washington became typecast as the "tragic mulatto"—a fair-skinned black woman who decides to pass for white. After taking a break from acting to tour Europe as a dancer at the end of the decade, she returned to America and starred in

Fredi Washington

several films, including *Hot Chocolates* and *Great Day* (both 1929).

The film *Black and Tan Fantasy* (1929) was primarily a vehicle for Duke Ellington and his orchestra, but it also established Washington as a dancer in the eyes of American movie audiences. She also appeared in *Sweet Chariot* (1930), a musical play based on Marcus Garvey's Universal Negro Improvement Association. In 1931, Washington and her sister Isabell starred in *Singin' the Blues*, a melodramatic depiction of Harlem night life. Two years later, she won a starring role in Hall Johnson's folk drama *Run, Little Chillun.*

During the 1930s, Washington was regarded as one of the most prominent black dramatic actresses of the day, creating strong roles in such movies as 1933's *The Emperor Jones* in which she played a Harlem prostitute opposite Robeson, the protagonist who rises from a Pullman car porter to emperor of an island of blacks. Her appearance in this movie disquieted the Will Hays Office—the movie industry's censoring agency—which insisted that she reshoot her scenes in dark makeup so that audiences would not perceive the light-skinned Washington as a white woman making love to a black man.

Washington went on to experience success in other films, such as *The Old Man of the Mountain* and *Mills Blue Rhythm Band* (both 1933), but it was the movie *Imitation of Life* (1934), based on the novel by *Fannie Hurst and co-starring *Claudette Colbert and *Louise Beavers, that would provide her greatest success as well as her greatest failure. In the role, she passes as a white woman, rejecting her black mother (Beavers) and then experiencing intense remorse upon her mother's death. Although the film met with mixed critical reviews, it was a success at the box office. According to *Notable Black American Women*, the film "served to deepen society's ambivalence toward her as a person and as an actress." And although Washington was praised for her performance, she realized that serious dramatic roles outside the stereotypically tragic mulatto evaded her. In 1935, she played a half-breed in *Drums of the Jungle.* Two years later, she played a woman who rears a white foundling and later becomes her governess and maid in *One Mile From Heaven.* In the late 1930s Washington returned to the Broadway stage when she appeared opposite *Ethel Waters in *Mamba's Daughters.* On stage, Washington felt she did not experience the same typecasting as in film.

Sensing that typecast roles had been her undoing, Washington became more politically oriented and founded the Negro Actors Guild of America, serving as its first executive secretary from 1937 to 1938. The guild's mission was to improve roles for black actors and also to eliminate racially biased material from plays and shows. Washington also became the theater editor and columnist for *The People's Voice*, a weekly newspaper published by Adam Clayton Powell, Jr.

Behind the scenes during the 1940s and 1950s, Washington worked as a casting consultant for such films as *Carmen Jones* (1943), *Porgy and Bess* (1943), and *Cry, the Beloved Country* (1952). She continued to perform on stage in *A Long Way From Home* (1948) and *How Long Til Summer* (1949), and appeared on "The Goldbergs," a weekly television drama that starred *Gertrude Berg.

A civil-rights activist, Washington was an active participant in the Joint Actors Equity Theater League Committee on Hotel Accommodations and, through the NAACP, worked for more black participation in the arts. She died on June 28, 1994, in Stamford, Connecticut, at the age of 90.

SOURCES:

Obituary, in *The Day* [New London, CT]. June 30, 1994.
Obituary, in *Time.* July 11, 1994, p. 15.
Smith, Jessie Carney, ed. *Notable Black American Women.* Detroit, MI: Gale Research, 1992.

Judith C. Reveal,
freelance writer,
Greensboro, Maryland

Washington, Josephine (1861–1949)

African-American writer. Born Josephine Turpin on July 31, 1861, in Goochland County, Virginia; died in 1949; daughter of Augustus A. Turpin and Maria V. Turpin; educated in Richmond's public elementary and high schools; attended Richmond Institute (later Richmond Theological Seminary); graduated from Howard University, 1886; married Samuel H.H. Washington (a physician), in 1888.

Born in Virginia in 1861, Josephine Turpin Washington was taught by a family employee to read at an early age and attended public schools in Richmond. She studied at Richmond Institute, which later became the Richmond Theological Seminary, before entering Howard University, where she spent her summer vacations working as a copyist in the office of Frederick Douglass, the black abolitionist who was then recorder of deeds in the District of Columbia. After her marriage to physician Samuel Washington, the couple moved to Birmingham, Alabama.

Washington's literary career began in 1877 when the *Virginia Star*, the state's only black publication, published her article "A Talk about Church Fairs," in which she protested the selling of wine at social functions designed to benefit the church. Most of her writings, however, focused on racial problems and women's issues. She believed that men and women were equal and advocated for improving women's lives through education. In an essay entitled "Impressions of a Southern Federation," published in *Colored American Magazine*, Washington dealt with the problems of both race and gender. The article detailed the topics addressed at the State Federation of Colored Women's Clubs held in Mobile, Alabama, in 1904. However, in addition to describing the city, the attire worn by the attendants, and the various activities sponsored by the clubs, she also discussed black womanhood, motherhood, morality, and character and spoke of the establishment of a reformatory for youths convicted of minor offenses. A deeply religious woman, Washington expressed her convictions through prose and poetry. She is also credited with playing a significant role in the development of Selma University in Alabama, founded in 1878 to train ministers and teachers. Little is known about Washington's later life.

SOURCES:

Smith, Jessie Carney, ed. *Notable Black American Women.* Detroit, MI: Gale Research, 1992.

Judith C. Reveal,
freelance writer,
Greensboro, Maryland

Washington, Margaret Murray

(c. 1861–1925)

African-American educator and lecturer who, while married to Booker T. Washington, played a significant role in the administration of Tuskegee Institute. Born Margaret James Murray on March 9, around 1861 (though her tombstone is inscribed 1865); died on June 4, 1925; buried on the campus of Tuskegee Institute; daughter of Lucy Murray (a washerwoman) and an unknown white father born in Ireland; became third wife of Booker T. Washington (1856–1915, founder of Tuskegee Normal and Industrial Institute and one of the great African-American leaders), on October 12, 1892; stepchildren: (one daughter) Portia Marshall Washington; (two sons) Booker Taliaferro Washington, Jr., and Ernest Davidson Washington.

Although Margaret Murray Washington was probably born in 1861, her birth year is listed as 1865 on her gravestone. The editor of the *Booker T. Washington Papers*, Louis R. Harlan, suggests that she may have altered her age upon entering Fisk Preparatory School in 1881. Her mother **Lucy Murray** was a washerwoman, and there is no written trace of her white father, an Irish immigrant, other than a published statement that he died when she was seven.

It took Margaret eight years to complete Fisk University's preparatory school and college. During that time, she was associate editor of the

student newspaper and served as president of a literary society. She also formed an enduring friendship with fellow student W.E.B. Du Bois. In 1889, after earning her degree, she began teaching at Tuskegee Institute. A year later, she assumed the position of lady principal at a salary of $500 a year, plus board. She first met her future husband, head of Tuskegee Institute Booker T. Washington, at a dinner of graduating seniors just prior to the June 1889 Fisk commencement, about a month after the death of his second wife *Olivia Davidson Washington (his first wife **Fanny Norton Smith Washington** had died on May 4, 1884). The course of the affection that developed between Margaret and Booker is not easily discernable from surviving documents. However, by late 1891 he had proposed.

Margaret's poor relationship with Booker's family initially influenced her to reject his proposal. She quarreled with Booker's favorite brother James Washington and could not tolerate James' wife. Although she enjoyed a good association with Washington's two sons from his previous marriage, she and his eldest child, **Portia Washington**, were hostile toward each other for years. Nevertheless, on October 12, 1892, Booker and Margaret were married in Tuskegee. Scholars have had difficulty assessing the Washingtons' marriage since few published letters between them exist. Although Booker T. Washington had yet to deliver his speech at the Atlanta Exposition of 1895, an event that would propel him into national celebrity, he was away from home as much as six months of the year speaking and fund-raising and had little time for his family. Margaret often joined him and, in 1899, accompanied him on a European trip. Some historians judge their marriage as one of practicality and convenience in which Margaret provided the stability of a home life for her busy husband. However, Margaret was clearly working hard to achieve their common goals, and no visible disunity between them can be documented.

Margaret was an able assistant in fund-raising, as well. According to *Notable Black American Women*, it was Andrew Carnegie's admiration for her, plus the fact that she was a Fisk graduate, that enabled her husband to persuade Carnegie to withdraw the stipulation that his $25,000 gift to Tuskegee be matched. Moreover, evidence suggests that in the early years Margaret advised her husband on his speeches and frequently spoke on the same program. While Booker T. Washington was addressing civic leaders and clergy during the day and community meetings at night, Margaret would be speaking with local women during the afternoons.

Wishing to exercise financial independence, Margaret continued working at Tuskegee following her marriage, serving in several capacities. In 1900, she was the director of the department of domestic science, which included laundering, cooking, dressmaking, and sewing. She was also involved in the development of Dorothy Hall, which housed the girls' industries. She served on the executive committee, which ran Tuskegee during Booker T. Washington's absences. And eventually she became dean of women, continuing her service to the institution after her husband's death in 1915. Her marriage also meant that she was responsible for the tasks traditionally assigned to a president's wife—receiving and entertaining the numerous distinguished visitors drawn by Tuskegee's favorable reputation. She was also active in the school's woman's club, which focused on temperance work in its meetings twice a month. Margaret supported the institution's tradition of reaching out to African-American farmers by performing plantation work at a settlement eight miles away. She also devoted her Saturdays to the mothers' meeting in Tuskegee, which by 1904 had grown to an attendance of nearly 300 women.

Through her position and commitment to social reform, Margaret dedicated substantial energy to the women's club movement. In July 1895, she attended a meeting in Boston that resulted in the formation of the National Federation of Afro-American Women, and became its vice-president. When she assumed the presidency a year later, the number of affiliated clubs had more than doubled. About a year after that, the group merged with the Colored Women's League to become the National Association of Colored Women; Margaret served as secretary of the executive board, becoming president in 1914.

From 1919 until her death in 1925, Washington presided over the Alabama Association of Women's Clubs. During her tenure as president, plans for the Rescue Home for Girls in Mt. Meigs were completed. She also influenced the approach of black club women to the Commission on Interracial Cooperation (CIC), a primarily white organization founded in 1918. As well, she was involved in an attempt to bring black and white club women together for a common program of action in 1920. That same year, Washington was instrumental in founding the International Council of Women of the Darker Races, which promoted the appreciation of the history and achievements of people of color worldwide. However, in 1925, before the group could become firmly established, Margaret Murray Washington died.

SOURCES:

Smith, Jessie Carney, ed. *Notable Black American Women.* Detroit, MI: Gale Research, 1992.

Judith C. Reveal,
freelance writer,
Greensboro, Maryland

Washington, Martha (1731–1802)

First first lady of the United States who, despite the loss of all four of her children, maintained a simple dignity as one of Washington's warmest hostesses.

Born Martha Dandridge on June 2, 1731, at Chestnut Grove plantation, on the Pamunkey River in New Kent County, Virginia; died at Mount Vernon Plantation, Fairfax County, Virginia, on May 22, 1802; daughter of John Dandridge (a planter) and Frances (Jones) Dandridge; taught by tutors and parents at home; married Daniel Parke Custis (died 1757), on May 15, 1750 (some sources cite 1749); married George Washington, on January 6, 1759 (died 1799); children (first marriage) Daniel Parke Custis II (b. 1751, died in infancy); Frances Parke Custis (b. 1753, died in infancy); Martha "Patsy" Parke Custis (1754–1773); John "Jacky" or "Jackie" Parke Custis (1755–1781).

Inherited one-third of large estate (dower right) upon first husband's death (1757); courted by George Washington (spring 1758); married to Washington (January 1759); became mistress of Mount Vernon plantation; spent winters at Washington's headquarters during the Revolutionary War; lived at the nation's capitals during Washington's presidency (1789–97), New York (1789–90), and Philadelphia (1789–97); was responsible for management of Mount Vernon and the other plantations of George Washington after his death (1799–1802).

Martha Washington's simple dignity, devotion to her husband and family, and acceptance of public duty exemplified the virtues extolled by Americans during the era of the founding of a new nation. Giving much attention to domestic concerns, she was always the supportive wife and discreet in social functions so as not to say or do anything that might be of embarrassment to her husband.

Martha Dandridge was the eldest of eight children of Colonel John Dandridge and **Frances Jones Dandridge**. Although the Dandridges did not rank among the first tier of Virginia gentry, Martha could boast a distinguished lineage. Her great-grandfather, Reverend Rowland Jones, immigrated from England, and became the first rector of Bruton Parish Church, and her grandfather Orlando Jones served in the Virginia House of Burgesses. In 1715, John Dandridge, Martha's father, came to Virginia at age 15, and by 1730 owned 500 acres on the south bank of the Pamunkey River, where he built Chesnut Grove, a two-story frame house, with chimneys at each end and a hip roof. John Dandridge and Frances Jones were married on July 22, 1730. John evidently had a basic education, for he was clerk of the New Kent County Court for 25 years and also vestryman for St. Peter's Church. Martha's mother Frances must have received some learning, since her father possessed one of the largest libraries in the colony. Learning from her parents and probably also from itinerant tutors, Martha acquired the rudiments of reading and writing and useful knowledge of household management, cooking, and needlework. She learned how to play the spinet, and in later years instructed family members how to play it. Like all young ladies of the time brought up in proper society, she mastered dancing—the minuets, quadrilles, and country dances.

Despite her family being of moderate means, Martha had opportunity to mingle in the company of Virginia's elite. With light brown hair and hazel eyes, though a bit on the plump side, she was considered a very attractive young woman. Important genteel families lived in her neighborhood, and her own home was only 30 miles from the colonial capital at Williamsburg. The Dandridges hobnobbed with the best of families. Thus, Martha could expect to attract attention from any of a number of prospective suitors. At age 15, she met Daniel Parke Custis. Daniel was the son of Colonel John Custis, one of the wealthiest men in the colony and a member of the governor's council. A romance developed between Martha and Daniel, who was still a bachelor and old enough to be her father. Colonel Custis disapproved of marriage between the two, because the Dandridge estate was too small. Daniel, a dutiful son and not wishing to lose an inheritance, bent to the wishes of his father. But, after skillful diplomacy by friends who momentarily caught the old colonel in the right mood, consent to the marriage was finally obtained. Eighteen-year-old Martha Dandridge married Daniel Parke Custis, age 38. When John Custis died on November 22, 1749, either before or shortly after the wedding, Daniel inherited the bulk of the estate, which included five plantations (17,000 acres), the White House (the family homestead), and also Six Chimney House in Williamsburg.

Martha and Daniel had seven blissful years, during which four children were born. Daniel Parke Custis II (b. 1751) and Frances Parke

Custis (b. 1753) died in infancy. **Martha "Patsy" Parke Custis** was born in 1754, and John "Jacky" Parke Custis the next year. When Daniel Parke Custis died of a heart attack on July 8, 1757, age 45 and nine months, he died intestate, which meant under Virginia law that Martha inherited outright one-third of the estate, and, as sole executrix, acted in trust for the administration of the rest of the estate until the two surviving children reached their majority. Martha, at age 26, was probably the richest widow in Virginia.

In spring 1758, while visiting the neighboring plantation of Richard Chamberlayne, Martha met George Washington, who was on his way to Williamsburg to consult a doctor for dysentery and other ailments he had contracted while serving in the military campaign against the French along the Pennsylvania frontier. A wealthy planter, Colonel Washington had already achieved a most respected reputation as commander of Virginia's armed forces, and recently had been elected burgess for the Virginia Assembly. Washington soon returned to the theater of war, but after victory over the French in November 1758, he resigned his commission and returned to Virginia. On January 6, 1759, Martha and George were married at the Custis homestead. After the wedding, the couple resided at the Six Chimney House in Williamsburg while Washington attended the legislative session. Thereafter, they lived at Washington's Potomac River plantation, Mount Vernon, which Washington was leasing from **Ann Fairfax Washington**, the widow of his half-brother Lawrence Washington, and which became his sole possession upon her death in 1761. According to the law of the time, Washington now also controlled all of Martha's property under her dower rights, and eventually, upon the death of Martha's two other children, the whole of the Daniel Parke Custis estate. Besides Mount Vernon, Washington owned several other plantations. On June 12, 1759, he wrote the English firm of Capel & Osgood Hanbury: "I must now desire that you will please to address all your Letters which relate to the Affairs of the Deceas'd Colo. Custis to me."

Martha kept busy at Mount Vernon, managing the household and supervising domestic production. She often had 16 spinning wheels constantly in motion. Especially, she attended to the curing of meat in the smokehouse. Lund Washington, after a visit to Mount Vernon, wrote George Washington in January 1776 that "Mrs. Washington's charitable disposition increases in the proportion as her meat house." Martha was

$\mathcal{M}$artha
$\mathcal{W}$ashington

deeply religious. She maintained close contact with women friends and relatives. Mount Vernon became known for its hospitality, with visitors staying over almost every day. Martha also looked after the welfare of some 200 slaves.

Family tragedy struck frequently. Within four years, Martha had lost her first husband, two children, and a younger sister; by 1775, five brothers had also died; in 1785, she lost her mother and last brother. The deaths of her last two children in early life would bring unremitting sorrow. George Washington adored the children, Patsy and Jacky, and, though trying hard to be an exacting parent, George, like Martha, was indulgent. It has been said that if George and Martha Washington ever had children on their own (which they did not), George would have been somewhat a failure as a parent. Yet the two Custis children were turning out well, though Jacky was lazy and easy-going, knowing full well that he was to be, and was briefly, one of the wealthiest men in Virginia. Patsy was an amiable and loving child. As a teenager, she was regarded as a beauty, often referred to as the "dark lady" because of her brunette complexion. At age 17, Patsy died suddenly during one of her epileptic seizures, on June 17, 1773. George Washington wrote: "This sudden, and unexpected blow . . .

has almost reduced my poor Wife to the lowest ebb of Misery."

Washington looked after Jacky's education, putting him in a school conducted by the Reverend Jonathan Boucher in Annapolis, Maryland. Sent to King's College in New York, Jacky was back home after three months. In February 1774, he married ❧ **Eleanor "Nellie" Calvert** of Mount Airy, Maryland. The newlyweds made their home upriver from Mount Vernon at Abingdon and had four children. Jacky would be an aide to his father at the battle of Yorktown. Contracting "camp (typhoid) fever," he would die on November 6, 1781, at age 26. The two youngest of his four children, ❧ **Eleanor "Nelly" Parke Custis** (age two) and George Washington Parke Custis (age six months), would be raised by George and Martha Washington at Mount Vernon.

The Revolutionary War brought long separations between Martha and George Washington. Only twice, between 1775 to 1783, did George visit Mount Vernon. Martha, however, regularly visited George at the army's winter encampment. From December 11, 1775, to April 20, 1776, she and her son Jacky stayed with George at the Cambridge, Massachusetts, headquarters. The trip was considered somewhat a necessity since it was feared that the royal governor of Virginia would descend upon Mount Vernon with loyalist troops. Such an attempt was made in July 1776, but was repelled by Virginia militia. Martha endured the severe winters at Morristown, Valley Forge, Middlebrook, New Windsor, and Newburgh. She acted as the official host at headquarters, and together with wives of other generals helped to create a society atmosphere, in which there was much dancing. General and Lady Washington (a title that she bore for the rest of her life) had dinner guests daily from the officer corps. Martha once said that she timed her visits to the army between the closing guns of one campaign and the beginning of another. When the war ended, George submitted a bill of £1,064 to Congress for the "lawful" expenses incurred during Martha's sojourns in camp. During the war, she dressed only in clothes spun and woven by servants at Mount Vernon.

Back home after the war, the Washingtons entertained a stream of guests, even strangers.

❧▶ **Custis, Eleanor "Nellie" Calvert** (fl. 1775)

Daughter-in-law of Martha Washington. Name variations: Mrs. John Parke Custis; Nellie Custis. Born Eleanor Calvert in Mt. Airy, Maryland; flourished around 1775; married John "Jacky" Parke Custis, in February 1774; children: (first marriage) Martha Parke Custis (who married Thomas Peter); *Eleanor "Nelly" Parke Custis (1779–1852); George Washington Parke Custis (b. 1781), and one other; (second marriage) 16 children.

Eleanor Calvert Custis married John "Jacky" Parke Custis in February 1774; they had four children. Following the death of her husband, Eleanor kept two of her children, her older daughters; the other two were sent to live with her in-laws, George and ***Martha Washington**. Eleanor would later remarry and give birth to 16 more children.

❧▶ **Custis, Eleanor "Nelly" Parke** (1779–1852)

Granddaughter of George and Martha Washington who was raised by her grandparents at Mount Vernon. Name variations: Eleanor Custis Lewis; Nelly Custis. Born Eleanor Parke Custis in 1779; died in obscurity on her son's farm in the Shenandoah Valley in March 1852; daughter of John Parke Custis and Eleanor Calvert Custis; granddaughter of George and Martha Washington; married Lawrence Lewis, on February 22, 1799 (died 1839); children: Francis Parke Lewis; Agnes Lewis; Angela Lewis (d. 1839); Lorenzo Lewis; and four others.

Like her grandmother ***Martha Washington**, Nelly Custis knew sorrow; during her lifetime, she sat bedside for most of the deaths of seven of her eight children. Nelly grew up in the heady atmosphere of the capital, while her step-grandfather George Washington was president of the United States, and leaned heavily on her grandparents. In 1804, on the death of her grandmother, and having already lost two of her children, Nelly wrote to her friend **Elizabeth Beale Bordley**: "I look back with sorrow, & to the future without hope. It appears to be a dream long passed away, so heavily has time passed to me." In later years, she suffered many illnesses and watched as her husband's poor management ate into their money. Following the death of her husband and daughter in the same year (1839), Nelly went to live with her son Lorenzo on an isolated estate in the Shenandoah Valley. She died there in 1852, having despaired for many years.

SUGGESTED READING:
American Heritage. February 1977, pp. 80–85.

George confided in his diary of June 30, 1785: "Dined with only Mrs. Washington which I believe is the first instance of it since retirement from public life." Retirement at Mount Vernon proved only temporary. Martha had thought that at the end of the war, as she later wrote *Mercy Otis Warren, no "circumstances" could possibly "have happened which would call the General into public life again. I had anticipated, that from this moment we should have been left to grow old in solitude and tranquility togather [sic]." George traveled alone to his presidential inauguration in New York City; Martha followed several weeks later with her two grandchildren, being greeted by dignitaries and military honors along the way, culminating with the firing of 13 cannon in New York City. At the nation's capitals, first New York City and then Philadelphia, Martha endured stoically the restraints of being the president's wife. She complained to her niece, **Fanny Bassett Washington**, in October 1789:

> I live a very dull life hear and know nothing that passes in the town—I Never goe to any publick place, indeed I think I am more like a state prisoner than anything else, there is certain bounds set for me which I must not depart from—and as I can not doe as I like I am obstinate and stay at home a great deal.

Yet Martha made friendships with other women, and occasionally visited them. "We live upon terms of much Friendship & visit each other often," wrote *Abigail Adams, wife of the vice-president. "Mrs. Washington is a most friendly, good Lady, always pleasent and easy." Although always interested in fashion, Martha kept her appearance unpretentious. An Englishman wrote in 1794: "Mrs. Washington struck me as being older than the president. She was extremely simple in dress, and wore her gray hair turned up under a very plain cap." The head covering became a trademark for Martha, who thought it made her look taller and slimmer, but which in reality had the opposite effect. Becoming a little more plump as she aged, Martha also developed a "portly double chin."

While President Washington held an official reception each Tuesday, known as a "levee," for men only, Lady Washington hosted every Friday evening a reception, which she called a "drawing room." This function was an open house, without special invitation, for women and men of prominent political or social connections. Martha remained seated while receiving guests. Tea, coffee, and cakes were served as refreshments. President Washington mingled with the guests.

After the Washingtons came home to stay in 1797, Martha delighted in the domestic life, free from the public limelight. She wrote **Lucy Knox**, wife of Washington's secretary of war, that "I am again fairly settled down to the plesant duties of an old fashioned Virginia house-keeper, steady as a clock, busy as a bee, and as cheerful as a cricket."

> She reminded me of the Roman matrons of whom I had read so much, and I thought that she well deserved to be the companion and friend of the greatest man of the age.
>
> —Peter Stephen Du Ponceau

When George Washington died on December 14, 1799, Martha supposedly said: "Tis well, I have no more trials to pass through, I shall soon follow." By Virginia law, Martha received one-third of the estate, and, according to Washington's will, the "use and benefit" of the entire estate during her lifetime. According to custom, Martha closed off her and George's bedroom, and made her chamber in a small room on the third floor of Mount Vernon. George Washington also decreed that all of his personal slaves would be freed upon Martha's death. Martha, however, did not wait. She granted 123 slaves their freedom on January 1, 1801. Those slaves not freed had been inherited by Martha from her first husband and were partly owned by the children of that marriage.

During her last years, Martha Washington had the company of her two grandchildren and George's nephew Lawrence Lewis. Lawrence and Eleanor Parke Custis were married at Mount Vernon on George Washington's last birthday, February 22, 1799. After George died, Lewis stayed on to manage the estate's farms. Martha continued to receive visitors.

Martha Washington died of a prolonged "severe fever" and was entombed next to her husband at the family vault at Mount Vernon. She left her portions of the estate to the two grandchildren and the nephews and nieces. By George's will, Mount Vernon passed to Bushrod Washington (appointed a Supreme Court justice in 1798), son of George's younger brother, John Augustine Washington, who had predeceased George.

Martha Washington gained admiration from all who knew her. Not born to aristocracy, she attained the height of social status. Still she maintained throughout her life a simple dignity and a plain style in appearance and in her relations with people. Her foremost concern was the welfare of her family. Although not particularly keen of wit, she charmed everyone by the warmth of her personality. As one obituary fittingly said: "The silence of respectful grief is our best eulogy."

SOURCES:

Freeman, Douglas S. *Washington: A Biography.* 7 vols. NY: Scribner, 1949–57.

Thane, Elswyth. *Washington's Lady.* NY: Dodd, Mead, 1960.

Wharton, Anne H. *Martha Washington.* NY: Scribner, 1897 (reprint ed., 1967).

SUGGESTED READING:

Desmond, Alice C. *Martha Washington: Our First Lady.* NY: Dodd, Mead, 1942.

Wilson, Dorothy C. *Lady Washington.* Garden City, NY: Doubleday, 1984.

COLLECTIONS:

Fields, Joseph E., ed. *"Worthy Partner": The Papers of Martha Washington.* Westport, CT: Greenwood Press, 1994.

Jackson, Donald, *et al.*, eds. *The Diaries of George Washington.* 6 vols. Charlottesville, VA: University Press of Virginia, 1976–79.

Harry M. Ward,
Professor of History, University of Richmond, Richmond, Virginia, and author of *American Revolution/ Nationhood Achieved, 1763–1788*, St. Martin's Press, 1994

Washington, Olivia Davidson

(1854–1889)

African-American educator who founded Tuskegee Institute with her husband Booker T. Washington. Name variations: Olivia America Davidson. Born Olivia America Davidson on June 11, 1854, in Mercer County, Virginia; died on May 9, 1889, in Boston, Massachusetts; daughter of Elias Davidson (a free laborer and former slave) and Eliza (Webb) Davidson; attended Hampton Institute, 1878–79; graduated from the State Normal School in Framingham, Massachusetts, on June 29, 1881; married Booker T. Washington (1856–1915, one of the great African-American leaders), on August 11, 1886; children: Booker T. Washington, Jr. (b. 1887); Ernest Washington (b. 1889); stepdaughter Portia Washington.

Olivia Davidson Washington, founder of Tuskegee Institute with her husband Booker T. Washington, was born free on June 11, 1854, in Mercer County, Virginia. Her father Elias, who was listed as a slave in the 1846 will of his owner, Joseph Davidson, appears in the 1850 census as a free laborer. Records suggest that her mother **Eliza Webb** was the daughter of a "free colored" woman. When Virginia became too dangerous for free blacks, the Davidsons migrated to southern Ohio, settling in Ironton. There were ten children in the Davidson family and since it is known that the older ones attended school in Ironton, it is believed that Olivia,

who turned six in 1860, began her schooling there as well. Olivia is thought to have attended high school in Gallipolis, Ohio, where she was living with her sister **Mary Davidson (Elliott)** and her sister's doctor husband, Noah Elliott. **Margaret Davidson**, another sister, was a teacher, and Olivia accompanied her to Memphis, Tennessee, to teach among the freedmen in the South. Historians believe that Olivia eventually moved there to be near Margaret and their brother Joseph, who was residing with Margaret at the time. Soon after Olivia's arrival, Margaret died and, shortly after that, Joseph was murdered by the Ku Klux Klan. Devastated, Olivia returned to Ohio to teach school; she was barely 16 years of age. Whether through financial need or devotion alone, though, Olivia began to teach in Mississippi and Arkansas during her summer vacations.

In 1874, she accepted a position as a sixth-grade teacher at the Clay Street School in Memphis. The opening of this new school was marked by controversy over integrated staffs at black schools; blacks demanded that their schools be staffed only by black teachers and administrators. Despite the conflict and perpetually inadequate funding, Olivia gained experience in newer teaching methods and changes in curricula. Exhausted from a heavy workload, however, and still grieving the loss of her sister and brother, she returned to Ohio for a summer of relaxation in 1878. That fall, she received a scholarship from *Lucy Webb Hayes, wife of President Rutherford B. Hayes, to enroll in the senior class program at Hampton Institute. The ambitious program included the study of reading, English literature, algebra, bookkeeping, history, political economy, elements of agriculture, civil government, grammar, chemistry, and the Bible. At her graduation the following May, she delivered an essay on "Decision of Character." The postgraduate speaker was Booker T. Washington and, together, they formed a partnership to found an institute of higher learning for the black population that would become Tuskegee Institute in Alabama.

At the age of 25, Olivia received support for two years of study at the State Normal School in Framingham, Massachusetts. During her stay there, she learned advanced teaching techniques and made several important friendships. Upon graduating with honors in 1881, Olivia became ill and returned to Hampton Institute to recuperate and to provide schooling for Native Americans during the summer. Although poor health prevented her from joining Booker T. Washington for the opening of Tuskegee Institute on July 4, she arrived there in late August and devoted all her energy to the school's success. Since the state provided little in the way of financial support, fund-raising was an ongoing and vital aspect of the school's survival. Land acquisition and the construction of buildings accounted for a large portion of Tuskegee's budget; however, salaries also needed to be paid and impoverished students needed assistance. Olivia was instrumental in organizing local fund-raising efforts and traveling to the North whenever necessary, utilizing contacts she had made while a student at Framingham. She also brought to her role at Tuskegee the vast experience she had gained as a teacher. In the position of lady principal, she oversaw the female students in all aspects of their on-campus lives—dormitory living, industrial work, and class work. As the equal partner of Booker T. Washington in the administration of the school, her influence was felt everywhere; he credited her above everyone else with Tuskegee Institute's success.

Olivia's strenuous schedule, however, taxed her fragile strength, and she again fell ill in late 1883. During the course of her long convalescence, Booker T. Washington's first wife **Fanny Norton Smith Washington** passed away, and in 1886 he and Olivia were married. According to *Notable Black American Women*, their relationship appears to have been warm and loving, despite her consistently poor health. She also established a good relationship with his daughter from his first marriage, **Portia Washington**. Their first son, Booker, Jr., was born in 1887, and despite concern over her health for a number of months, their second son Ernest Davidson was born early the next year. Two days after his birth, their home caught fire, and Olivia, who was having increasing problems with her throat, was taken out into the early morning chill and never recovered from the exposure. Seeking medical treatment first in Montgomery and then in Boston, she died of tuberculosis of the larynx on May 9, 1889, at Massachusetts General Hospital.

SOURCES:

Smith, Jessie Carney, ed. *Notable Black American Women*. Detroit, MI: Gale Research, 1992.

Judith C. Reveal,
freelance writer,
Greensboro, Maryland

Washington, Ora (1899–1971)

African-American tennis and basketball player. Born on January 16, 1899, in Philadelphia, Pennsylvania; died in May 1971 in Philadelphia, Pennsylvania.

Played in segregated tennis and basketball leagues (1920s and 1930s); was undefeated singles champion of the all-black American Tennis Association (ATA, 1929–35); played with the Philadelphia Tribune and the Germantown Hornets basketball teams.

Born in Philadelphia in 1899, Ora Washington originally took up tennis as a way of deflecting the grief she felt after her sister's death. At the time she began playing, segregation in America prevented her from competing with whites, but she became a dominant force in the all-black leagues in which she played. In 1924, she won her first national championship at Baltimore's Druid Hill Park, defeating **Dorothy Radcliffe**. From 1929 until 1935, Washington remained undefeated as the singles champion of the all-black American Tennis Association (ATA), returning as champion again in 1937, and went nearly undefeated in the African-American National Tennis Organization. She was also part of the doubles championship team for seven consecutive years. Considered an unorthodox player in her presentation, Washington preferred to play without first warming up, grasped the racket halfway up the handle, and rarely took a full swing. Washington retired from the ATA twice. After her first retirement, she was goaded back into the game by a challenge from singles champion **Flora Lomax** of Detroit; although she lost that game, she won a special match to regain the title. Her dominance of the game, however, intimidated younger hopefuls, so she retired for a second time to encourage the players who represented the future of the sport.

While making a huge impact on the world of tennis, Washington also put her mark on women's basketball. She played as star center on the *Philadelphia Tribune* women's squad for 18 years and was the team's top scorer for a time. She also played for the Germantown Hornets and served as team captain from 1929 to 1930. While with the *Philadelphia Tribune*, she toured the country with her teammates, who presented clinics and offered demonstrations of their skill to any and all challengers. The team only lost six games in nine years of touring while traveling thousands of miles throughout the country.

Washington's heyday came years before any African-American could expect to see financial success in a sporting venture. She worked in domestic service during the time she played tennis and basketball and by 1961 owned an apartment building. During her career, she received more than 200 trophies. Washington was also well known for her generous work with young people at community tennis courts in her hometown, where she frequently conducted free training sessions. She died in 1971.

SOURCES:

Johnson, Anne Janette. *Great Women in Sports*. Detroit, MI: Visible Ink Press, 1998.

Judith C. Reveal,
freelance writer,
Greensboro, Maryland

Washington, Sarah Spencer (b. 1889).

See Walker, Madame C.J. for sidebar.

Wasilewska, Wanda (1905–1964)

Polish-born Russian politician and writer. Name variations: *Vanda L'vovna Vasilievskaia; Wanda Wassilewska.* Born on January 21, 1905, in Cracow (Kraków), Poland; died on July 29, 1964, in Kiev, Ukraine; daughter of Leon Wasilewski (a politician); graduated from the University at Kraków, 1927; married a university student and revolutionary (died);

Polish stamp issued in 1983 in honor of Wanda Wasilewska.

married Marion Bogatko (a mason); married Ukrainian-born Alexander Korneichuk (a playwright and politician); children: one daughter, Eva.

Aligned herself with the Soviet Union during a border dispute with Poland in the early 1940s; was head of the Soviet-backed Union of Polish Patriots and deputy chair of the Polish Committee of National Liberation which later became the provisional government of Poland after its liberation from the Nazis.

Selected writings: The Image of the Day *(1934);* Motherland *(1935);* Earth in Bondage *(1938);* Flames in the Marshes *(1939);* The Rainbow *(1942).*

Wanda Wasilewska was born in 1905 to revolutionary parents in Kraków, Poland. Her father Leon Wasilewski, a member of the Polish Socialist Party, helped create the Polish-Soviet border through his drafting of the Treaty of Riga of 1921. Her parents' political activities often usurped their time with their daughter, whose earliest playmates were children of the workers of Kraków. Wasilewska's early exposure to the poor laborers nourished in her a deep abhorrence for those who exploited the poor. Because of her parents' increasing involvement with the Polish nationalist movement, with the onset of World War I Wasilewska was sent to live with her grandmother in the country, where her affiliation with the downtrodden intensified.

As a student at the university in Kraków, Wasilewska specialized in philology and associated with the working classes. Her strong political convictions led to her participation in an unsuccessful revolutionary uprising in 1923, and cemented her relationship with her first husband, a fellow student and revolutionary who later died. Wasilewska graduated from the university in 1927 and became a high school teacher. However, her leftist political leanings as a member of the Polish Socialist Party and her association with the illegal Polish Communist Party forced her to change jobs frequently. She combined her profession with her ideology by joining a Polish teachers' union and organizing a teachers' strike in the 1930s.

Wasilewska's childhood interest in poetry gradually evolved into prose writing as an expression of her sympathy for the working class. The 1930s saw her publication of major novels with proletarian themes: *The Image of the Day* (1934), *Motherland* (1935), *Earth in Bondage* (1938), and the trilogy *Flames in the Marshes* (1939). The first was banned in Poland immediately after publication, but the other three found an audience in the Soviet Union through several different language translations. All of the novels depict the suffering of the working classes in contrast to the luxuries enjoyed by others at their expense. Wasilewska's 1942 novel *The Rainbow* was the only one to reach an American audience through an English translation. The first edition of *The Rainbow* sold 400,000 copies in two days. Considered propagandistic by many, the novel won the Soviet Union's Stalin Prize of 100,000 rubles as the most outstanding work of 1943 in the field of belles-lettres.

After losing her job as editor of the Warsaw children's magazine *Płomyk* in 1937, because of her Communist associations, Wasilewska began work with *Nowe Widnokregi* (New Horizons), a radical Polish publication. Two years later, when Nazi Germany annexed Poland to start the aggression of World War II, she left her native country for Soviet Russia. Although she became a Soviet citizen, she maintained strong ties to her Polish origins, developing the Russian-sponsored Union of Polish Patriots, an organization composed of Polish leftists living in Russia, around 1943. That year, Wasilewska also took on the role of editor to the Polish-language newspaper *Volna Polska* (Free Poland) and correspondent to the Red Army. She helped establish a Polish division of the Red Army and was made an honorary colonel for her efforts. In addition, she became a deputy to the Supreme Soviet of the Soviet Union during this time.

Despite her dual identity as a Pole and a Soviet citizen, Wasilewska made her allegiance very clear during the Russo-Polish border dispute in 1943. The conflict between Russia and the Polish government, which had been set up in exile in London during Germany's occupation of Poland, came about over Poland's refusal to give up the territory it had acquired after World War I. As the dispute became more heated, both sides leveled accusations of the other's misdeeds, which culminated in the Polish government's investigation into allegations that Russians had murdered 10,000 Polish officers near Smolensk in 1940. The Polish government's lending of credence to this Nazi-generated charge caused the Soviet government to break off relations with the Polish government-in-exile. Wasilewska applauded the decision, believing that Poland could survive only through democratic activity by citizens within its borders, not by émigrés.

By the beginning of 1944, Russia clearly indicated that the removal of anti-Soviet elements from the Polish Cabinet was a necessary move before Russo-Polish relations could be reestablished. Wasilewska's Union of Polish Patriots seemed poised to become the Polish governing body officially recognized by the Soviet Union when the announcement went out that the Union of Polish Patriots had formed a National Council within Poland. Comprising representatives from Poland's leftist political groups, this council claimed to have majority support within occupied Poland. The international community worried that the Soviet-backed council could succeed in erecting a Communist government in Poland, and their fears appeared to be confirmed by reports that Wasilewska had met with Soviet ruler Joseph Stalin in May 1944 to apprize him of the situation in Poland.

As the Red Army began liberating Poland from the retreating Nazis, many Poles considered it an exchange of one oppressor for another. The Soviets continued to ignore the Polish government-in-exile, and the newly formed Polish Committee of National Liberation—with Wasilewska acting as one of two deputy chairs—took control of the liberated territory by the authority of the Soviet Union. In addition to performing civil functions, the committee took command of both the underground Polish army and the Polish division of the Red Army. Renamed the Lublin Committee after the area in which it was headquartered, it announced its status as the provisional government of Poland at the end of 1944. Wasilewska's name had disappeared from the list of members by this time, possibly because she may have offended Stalin by protesting his presentation of the Order of Suvorov to a Polish general. (The great Russian general Alexander Suvorov had taken Warsaw in 1794, killing over 32,000 Poles the process.)

By this time, Wasilewska was married to her third husband, Alexander Korneichuk, a Ukrainian-born playwright, novelist and politician. Korneichuk, also a recipient of the Stalin Prize, was formerly vice-commissar of Foreign Affairs in Russia and became foreign minister of the new Ukrainian Republic in 1944. Wasilewska had one daughter, Eva, from a previous marriage.

SOURCES:
Current Biography, 1944. NY: H.W. Wilson, 1944.
Current Biography, 1964. NY: H.W. Wilson, 1964.

Judith C. Reveal,
freelance writer,
Greensboro, Maryland

Waterbury, Lucy McGill (1861–1949).

See Peabody, Lucy.

Waters, Ethel (1896–1977)

Oscar-nominated African-American singer and actress, enormously popular on both stage and screen, who brought black art into the white world and was a towering presence in American entertainment for decades. Born Ethel Perry on October 31, 1896, in Chester, Pennsylvania; died on September 1, 1977, in Chatsworth, California; illegitimate daughter of Louise Anderson who had been raped at knifepoint at age 12 by John Waters; had one stepsister, Genevieve Howard; married Merritt "Buddy" Punsley, in 1913 (divorced 1915); married Clyde Matthews, around 1930 (divorced around 1933); married Edward Mallory (dates unknown); no children.

Received a minimal education before going to work as a cleaning woman and laundress at age eight; at 17, began appearing in traveling vaudeville shows and in nightclubs, performing and popularizing blues songs which have since become standards of the genre; starred on Broadway in a number of successful musicals and dramatic plays (starting 1927); generally credited with being the first African-American woman to receive star billing in legitimate theater and, later, on screen; though nominated for an Academy Award for her role in the film Pinky *(1949), is best remembered for her performance in both the stage and screen versions of Carson McCullers'* The Member of the Wedding; *published two autobiographies before her death (1977).*

Filmography: On with the Show *(1929);* Gift of Gab *(1934);* Tales of Manhattan *(1942);* Cairo *(1942);* Cabin in the Sky *(1943);* Stage Door Canteen *(1943);* Pinky *(1949);* The Member of the Wedding *(1952);* The Heart Is a Rebel *(1956);* The Sound and the Fury *(1959).*

The dressing room at New York's Empire Theater may have seemed empty to the stage manager who called out the five-minute warning one night in 1939, but for the actress to whom he delivered his message, the room was crowded with the memories of some of the great ladies of the stage who had heard the same message in that room over the years—*Katharine Cornell, *Ethel Barrymore, *Helen Hayes. Now, Ethel Waters, whom African-American audiences had known for years as a singer and bawdy comedian, was about to step in front of an elegant, mostly white Broadway audience for her debut as the leading lady of a dramatic play, *Mamba's Daughters*. "I could have looked back over my shoulder and blown a kiss to all my yesterdays in show business," Waters remembered many years later. "That was *the* night of my professional life." The audience must have agreed, for at the end of the evening Waters received 17 curtain calls.

There was a time when Ethel Waters would have laughed at the idea of making a living in

show business, despite the fact that she had been entertaining audiences on the black vaudeville circuits of the early 20th century as "Sweet Mama Stringbean." During those years, show business had merely been an escape from the poverty and conflicts of a troubled childhood in and around Philadelphia. Waters was the illegitimate daughter of **Louise Anderson**, who had been raped at knifepoint at the age of 12 by a man named John Waters, a "mixed colored" with both white and black grandparents. Louise gave birth to her daughter on October 31, 1896, in Chester, Pennsylvania, and soon left the child in the care of her own mother, **Sally Anderson**. Sally instilled in Ethel a deep mistrust of white people or anyone "bright-skinned," as John Waters had been. Even the name "Waters" was banned from Sally's household, so Ethel spent most of her early years as Ethel Perry, taking the last name of a man her grandmother said was one of her early suitors. Ethel always considered Sally as her mother, even referring to her as "Mom" while Louise was "Momweeze." Louise, who later married and had a second child with her husband, made only occasional visits to see her first child and would maintain a strained relationship with Ethel until both were well along in years. In addition to a wariness toward whites, Sally Anderson gave her granddaughter a second lifelong preoccupation, one that would eventually cancel out the first—a deeply felt spiritual yearning that stemmed from Sally's devout Roman Catholicism, the "rock and the light" of Ethel Waters' life.

Although Ethel maintained a deep respect for "Mom" throughout her life, most of her childhood was spent on the streets of Chester and, later, Philadelphia, where she often stayed with an aunt while Sally Anderson was "living in" with white employers. "I never was a child," she once said. "I never was coddled, or liked, or understood by my family. I never felt I belonged." The few warm memories Waters had of her childhood revolved around singing, a talent shared by her numerous aunts, uncles, and cousins, all of whom harmonized and sang unaccompanied. Waters loved the stories the songs told and was thrilled at her first public appearance, at age five, in a children's program staged by a small church in Philadelphia. She appeared as "Baby Star," reciting poetry and singing a simple melody her aunt had taught her.

Of more direct influence, however, was the street life of Philadelphia's red-light district, not far from her aunt's home. During a year spent in the ward known as the "Bloody 8th" when she was six, Ethel ran errands for local brothels and

kept a lookout for police while the prostitutes did business, claiming later it was these very activities that kept her away from drugs or alcohol. "Whatever moral qualities I have," she once observed, "come, I'm afraid, from all the sordidness and evil I observed firsthand as a child. By the time I was seven, I knew all about sex and life in the raw." At eight, Ethel was put to work for a white woman doing household chores, but she soon returned to the streets, leading grandmother Sally to place her in a Catholic school in Philadelphia when Ethel was nine. Many years later, Waters remembered the love with which she was treated by the nuns and the kindness shown to her by the parish priest who, rather than reveal anger or shock at Ethel's first confession of her sins, merely told her not to swear anymore and to pray. Not long after, at a children's revival meeting, Ethel remembered, "Love flooded my heart and I knew I had found God and that now and for always I would have an ally, a friend close by to strengthen me and cheer me on."

Ethel's newfound faith was sorely tested as she matured. Living conditions remained as stark and unsanitary as ever, and years later Waters would recall her childhood dream of sleeping alone in a bed free of lice and fleas. Her relatives drank to excess and bickered constantly, so much so that Waters once pleaded with the nuns at school to put her in an orphanage, only giving up her request when grandmother Sally finally took her home to Chester to live. Then came trouble with men.

I was scared to work for white people. I didn't know very much about them, and what I knew I didn't like.

—Ethel Waters

Tall and lithe by the time she was just 11 years old, Waters found herself fending off the unwanted attentions of older men. Her grandmother felt compelled to accompany her granddaughter to the dance halls where Ethel had already begun winning singing and dancing contests and was being given free admission in exchange for dance lessons for the clientele. But even Sally failed to protect Ethel from the wooing of a 23-year-old man named Merritt Punsley, whom Ethel married when she was 13 years old, in 1909. Punsley was intensely jealous of his new young bride and strove to keep her away from her friends and her dancing, often by using his fists to impose his will. After a year, the two separated, and were divorced in 1911.

Waters' next chance to escape the poverty and turmoil of her family didn't come until six years later, when she attended a Halloween dance in Philadelphia. By now, she later recalled, "I had developed into a really agile shimmy shaker. I sure knew how to roll and quiver, and my hips would become whirling dervishes." The crowd at the party called her back for three encores before she was approached by two song-and-dance men from the vaudeville circuit named Braxton and Nugent, who offered her a paid job singing and dancing at the Lincoln Theater in Baltimore for ten dollars a week. It was as "Sweet Mama Stringbean" that Waters introduced W.C.

Handy's "St. Louis Blues," the song that would become her trademark during these vaudeville years; she sang it in a way that was new to audiences used to the powerfully emotional styles of blues queens like *Ma Rainey and *Bessie Smith. "They loved them and all the other shouters," Waters said. "I could always riff and jam and growl, but I never had that loud approach." Instead, Waters sang the number in a soft, clear, bell-like voice, full of understated pain and suffering at the loss of her man. The approach worked to such effect that the stage was littered with coins and bills when she finished, a phenomenon repeated each night Waters played at the Lincoln, sometimes doing her first show at nine in the morning and continuing well into the night.

With word spreading about the new singer from Philadelphia, Waters joined up with two sisters, **Maggie** and **Jo Hill**, to form an act with which she toured the black vaudeville circuit, playing theaters like the old Monogram in Chicago, as well as smaller venues in Lima, Ohio, Charleston, South Carolina, and Savannah, Georgia. Within six months, advance publicity for "The Hill Sisters" had given way to banners proclaiming, COMING! SWEET MAMA STRINGBEAN IN PERSON, SINGING ST. LOUIS BLUES!

But Waters' experiences away from the stage only seemed to prove Sally Anderson's warnings about whites. Ethel labored under a double burden, being known as a "Yankee nigger," and would often tell the story of the car crash in which she was involved in Birmingham, Alabama. She and four other performers from her current show went on a joyride at the invitation of a chauffeur who had commandeered his boss' car for the evening. Waters' right leg was severely injured in the crash and one of the other passengers was pinned under the car, but the two white men who were the first to happen on the scene refused to help until Ethel pleaded with them; and Waters claimed that the emergency room doctor, also white, told her, "This is what all you niggers should get when you wreck white people's cars." On the road, the troupe was often forced to stay in brothels, there being no hotels open to them; and Ethel would never forget the family in Macon, Georgia, with whom she was staying who learned their only son had been lynched by a white mob for talking back to a white man. The boy's body was thrown into the lobby of Waters' theater as a warning to "uppity" blacks. Ethel, however, merely considered bigoted whites as "odd and feeble-minded," and preferred to remember the many whites who were kind and helpful to her during her time touring the vaudeville circuit. She reserved her most venomous anger for her own people, so-called "society Negroes" who patronized or openly scorned less socially mobile African-Americans, including herself. "We have lived through so much together," Waters once said, "that I'll never understand how some of us who have one way or another been able to lift ourselves a little above the mass of colored people can be so insanely brutal as to try to knock the hell out of our own blood brothers and sisters."

Despite her professional success during her tour, Waters never considered it more than a stroke of luck that would come to an end sooner or later, as it did by 1920. Back in Philadelphia, she moved in with her relatives and went to work in a restaurant, sure that "some sense of order and good meals at regular times of the day," as she verbalized her dreams, would come by one day finding a job as a lady's maid to a wealthy white woman. But show business beckoned again when the white owner of a Philadelphia saloon, Barney Gordon, offered her a singing job at $15 a week. Gordon, who catered to a mostly black clientele and who had been told about Ethel by some of them, was the first white man from whom Waters accepted employment and money. Soon after she began work at the saloon, another offer came for a week's work at Harlem's Lincoln Theater. Waters found herself plunged into the excitement and opportunity offered by what was then the center of black entertainment and culture. She introduced new numbers into her act, including more pop-oriented material like "A Pretty Girl Is Like a Melody" and "Rose of Washington Square," along with her old standby, "St. Louis Blues." By the time she had finished the Lincoln Theater dates and gone to work at a nightclub called Edmond's Cellar, on 132nd Street, New York's café society, black and white, traveled uptown to hear her. During the summers of the early 1920s, Waters appeared in Atlantic City, New Jersey, then a hotbed of jazz and blues, where she sang for the first time to a mostly white audience at Rafe's Paradise. Even *Sophie Tucker, that "red hot Mama" of the jazz era, came out to hear her. Waters relished telling the story of being asked up to Tucker's hotel room, where she was paid to sing so Sophie could study Ethel's phrasing and movements.

The heyday of blues and jazz brought Waters her first recording contract with W.C. Handy's Black Swan Records. Ethel received $100 for each recording, a considerable sum in those days. Black Swan's A&R man at the time was Fletcher Henderson, who soon left the company to form the swing band that would gain nationwide fame during the 1930s. Henderson persuaded Waters to go out on tour with him for six months as the "girl singer" for his Jazz Masters. The increased exposure brought Ethel an audition for the African-American musical, *The Chocoate Dandies*, in 1924. The producers of the show thought she wasn't aristocratic enough which, as it turned out, was fortunate. The show was a disaster and closed after two performances. Waters did manage to land a job with a touring African-American revue called *Hello 1919!*, which played to mostly white audiences in the Midwest and convinced her that her future lay not with vaudeville or as a nightclub singer, but with legitimate musical theater. Her hopes were confirmed by her many offers from white producers to appear in major productions, but all were shows in which she would be the only black performer, and Waters turned them down. "The very idea of appearing on Broadway in a cast of ofays made me cringe in my boots," she said.

It was a song-and-dance man whom Waters knew from her Harlem club days, appropriately named Earl Dancer, who persuaded Ethel to bring her talents to a wider audience. "If you only let the white people hear you sing," he prophetically told her, "they'd love you for the rest of your life." Although Waters was skeptical, Dancer convinced her to work up an act with him in which she sang the same blues numbers she'd done for black audiences, but modified with a certain amount of extemporaneous talking to emphasize the story each number told. Opening at the Kedzie Theater in Chicago, one of the premier theaters on the mainstream vaudeville circuit, Waters was convinced at the end of their act that it had been a failure. Unlike black audiences, who yelled, screamed, and stomped their feet in approval, this white audience merely applauded politely. She was packing her bags for New York when the theater management appeared in her dressing room and offered Waters and Dancer $350 a week—a sum that would be raised to $500 per week by the time their contract ended. Returning to New York, Waters and Earl Dancer played all the big vaudeville houses, in which Ethel once again introduced non-blues numbers into her act—including "My Man," then being sung to great acclaim by *Fanny Brice in the Ziegfeld Follies, and a number Waters sang entirely in Yiddish. But it was back in Chicago that Ethel Waters finally came to the attention of a national audience, with her performance in 1924's *Plantation Revue*. Ashton Stevens, an influential, nationally syndicated theater critic, praised her talents so much that Ethel's future on the stage was assured.

By the mid-1920s, Waters had become the toast of New York's theater world, appearing in her first Broadway musical, *Africana*, which was produced by Earl Dancer, as well as appearing at the city's most chic night spots and receiving top billing for a charity show at the venerable Palace Theater with such headliners as Will Rogers and Katharine Cornell. Now feeling more comfortable in the company of whites, Waters was the guest of honor at elegant Park Avenue dinner parties given by writer and social liberal Carl Van Vechten, where she hobnobbed with such theater luminaries as Noel Coward, Cole Porter, and Eugene O'Neill. Toward the end of the decade, she was earning more than $1,200 a week, recording with Tommy Dorsey and Benny Goodman, and appearing in her first film, the 1929 Warner Bros. musical *On with the Show*, in which she sang two numbers, "Am I Blue?" and "Birmingham Bertha." "Dressed to the nines," critic Donald Bogle later wrote of the film, "her energy and attitude ('don't mess with this chile,' is what she seems to be telling us) were wholly new to the American cinema." Early the next year, Waters married her second husband, Clyde Matthews, a Cleveland businessman who accompanied her on an eight-month European tour during which she played Paris, London, and Cannes. By now, Ethel could be amused at the white society matrons on the transatlantic voyage who avoided being anywhere near "Mrs. C.E. Matthews" until discovering she was the famous Ethel Waters, after which they besieged her with requests for autographs and invitations to tea.

Although the Depression had gripped the United States by the time Waters returned, her popularity was such that she was hardly affected. Almost immediately after arriving in New York, she took to the road again with a tour of the musical revue *Rhapsody in Black*, which played Washington and Chicago as well as Broadway; then appeared at Harlem's legendary Cotton Club, where she introduced Harold Arlen's "Stormy Weather"—a song Waters felt might have been written especially for her, since her marriage to Matthews had begun to fall apart. The two would become legally separated the next year, with a formal divorce following shortly thereafter. "I was telling things I couldn't frame in words," she said of the song's lyrics. "I was singing . . . the story of the wrongs and outrages done to me by people I had loved and trusted." In the Cotton Club audience one night was Irving Berlin, who approached her with an offer to appear in a new musical he had written called *As Thousands Cheer*. Although most of the show was an airy, thinly plotted musical revue, Berlin had written a poignant song called "Supper Time" for the show's second act—one of three numbers he gave to Waters. "Supper Time" is sung by a black woman who has just learned of her husband's lynching and is faced with the task of telling her children why their father will not be sharing the evening meal. Waters, remembering the family in Georgia whose son had been similarly killed, fought a last-minute attempt to drop the number from the show and brought the theater to complete silence on opening night. Audiences were astounded at her versatility, for her other numbers in the show—the infectious "Heat Wave" ("She started the heat wave by making her seat wave," wrote one wag) and the nostalgic "Harlem on My Mind"—were equally effective. "Ethel Waters had frankness, vitality, and grinning good humor that gave audiences complete confidence in anything she did," *The New York Times'* Brooks Atkinson told his readers. By the time *As Thousands Cheer* closed, Waters was the highest paid female performer then on Broadway, earning $1,000 a week. Atkinson was equally enthusiastic about Waters' work in her next revue, 1935's *At Home Abroad*, which was directed by Vincente Minnelli and co-starred comedian *Bea Lillie. Waters was "a gleaming tower of regality," Atkinson wrote, "who knows how to make a song stand on tiptoe."

The reception given to "Supper Time," which Waters always felt she acted rather than sang, encouraged her to begin seeking dramatic roles in legitimate theater. It was a bold decision on her part, for at the time there were no leading African-American actresses, the only roles available to black women being minor parts as maids or other menials. It was a tribute to Waters' talent that several roles in major productions had been offered to her even before *As Thousands Cheer*, but none of them appealed to her. "Those plays never seemed quite true to life to me," she once pointed out. "The characters in them had either been created by white men or by Negro writers who had stopped thinking colored." But the exception proved to be DuBose Heyward, a Southern writer who had come to national attention with his novel *Porgy* (on which the Gershwins' *Porgy and Bess* was based) and who had adapted his second novel, *Mamba's Daughters*, with his wife *Dorothy Heyward, for the stage. The work had an overpowering attraction for Waters, who saw her grandmother Sally in the Heywards' matriarch, Mamba, and her own mother, Louise, in Hagar, the character the Heywards wanted her to play. "All my life," she said,

"I'd burned to tell the story of my mother's despair and long defeat, of Momweeze being hurt so by a world that then paid her no mind." Although few backers wanted to take on a dramatic play with an all-black cast and a leading actress with no dramatic experience, the Heywards eventually did raise the money when director Guthrie McClintic (Katharine Cornell's husband) agreed to helm the production. *Mamba's Daughters* opened in January 1939, co-starring **Alberta Hunter* and Canada Lee, to nearly unanimous praise. "In the playing of Ethel Waters," one reviewer wrote, "Hagar becomes magnificently like a force of nature." "Ethel Waters establishes herself as one of the finest actresses, black or white," wrote another. The one holdout was Brooks Atkinson, who cared neither for Ethel's performance nor the play itself, prompting a full-page ad in the *Times* taken out by **Tallulah Bankhead*, Oscar Hammerstein, **Judith Anderson*, and Ethel's old friend Carl Van Vechten, praising her performance and placing her in the top echelon of dramatic performers. More important, Waters had become the first black actress to appear in a leading role in a major dramatic production on Broadway.

The next year, she scored another triumph with her performance as Petunia in Vernon Duke's musical *Cabin in the Sky*, and this time Atkinson was back in her camp. "Ethel Waters . . . made playgoers very happy indeed with the gleam and gusto with which she sang 'Taking a Chance on Love,'" he enthused. But for most of the war years, Waters was in Hollywood, where she appeared in the film version of *Cabin in the Sky*, as well as 1942's *Cairo* and 1943's *Stage Door Canteen*. Now approaching 50, Waters had permanently shed the raunchy, earthy image of her Sweet Mama Stringbean days and had assumed the dignified air of a black matriarch. "In her hands," Bogle points out, "the mammy stereotype had been transformed into the black earth mother figure."

The time in Hollywood, however, proved a detriment to her career, largely because of a disastrous relationship with a much younger man whom Waters claimed was a "protégé." She ac-

Ethel Waters with Julie Harris and Brandon DeWilde in Carson McCullers' Member of the Wedding.

cused him in public of robbing her of some $10,000 in cash and $35,000 in jewelry while staying in her home. The negative publicity, generated when Waters filed formal charges and testified at the trial which sent the young man to prison, turned many former supporters against her. The incident was the beginning of a decline in her fortunes during the mid-1940s, professionally and personally. Movie roles dwindled, there were no offers from Broadway, and the Internal Revenue Service filed charges against her for back taxes it claimed Ethel owed on her income during the 1930s. Waters admitted she had been careless with her money ("Where I come from," she pointed out, "people don't get close enough to money to have a working acquaintance with it") and agreed to give back a sizeable portion of her earnings to the government. The first signs of the diabetes with which she would later be diagnosed began to plague her, and her weight increased dramatically in cruel contrast to the lissome Waters of 20 years before. Even worse, Ethel felt the religious faith which had sustained her for so long slipping away. "I knew I had hate in my heart," she said, "and that wasn't fair to God." By the end of World War II, Waters had moved back to Harlem and was living in a rooming house, trying to ignore the entertainment press' opinion that her career was over.

Fortunately, not everyone thought so. Offers to sing in small nightclubs outside New York sustained her, and Waters might have found some comfort after a show in Philadelphia in 1948 when her mother Louise appeared in her dressing room. The two had been estranged for many years, but now Louise hugged her daughter and told her, "You're pretty, Ethel, and you're a good daughter. [God] will bring you back." As if proving Louise right, Waters was cast the next year in the film role for which she would be nominated for an Oscar, the part of Aunt Dicey in 1949's *Pinky*, a then-controversial film about a light-skinned black girl who tries to pass for white. Ethel played the benevolent grandmother to *Jeanne Crain's Pinky, and opposite *Ethel Barrymore's portrayal of the crusty Miss Em. Both Ethels were nominated for Best Supporting Actress that year. As she had in *Mamba's Daughters* and her rendition of "Supper Time," Waters drew upon her own experiences to create her performance, in this instance recalling her grandmother, Sally Anderson. "As a dramatic actress, all I've ever done is remember," she once said. "I try to express the suffering or the joy I've known in my own lifetime; or the sorrow and happiness I've sensed in others."

The role for which Ethel Waters will always be remembered materialized the following year, although she originally turned down the part of the gospel-singing cook Berenice Sadie Brown in *Carson McCullers' *The Member of the Wedding*. As McCullers wrote her, Ethel felt, Berenice was a bitter woman "with no God in her"; and she objected to the original form of what would become the most famous scene in the play, in which Berenice sings to her two young, white charges, the roughneck girl Frankie and the sensitive boy John Henry. Waters later claimed that McCullers had Berenice singing a Russian lullaby to the children, and in a meeting with McCullers after her initial rejection of the role, Ethel told the author, "I never heard of a colored woman . . . who had ever sung a Russian ditty to a child!" When McCullers asked what Berenice *would* sing, Ethel closed her eyes and softly began the African-American spiritual she had learned as a young girl back in Philadelphia, "His Eye Is on the Sparrow," which concluded with:

> For Jesus is my portion,
> My constant friend is He,
> For His eye is on the sparrow,
> And I know He watches me.

Waters tactfully offered to delete the line containing "Jesus" in case it might offend some theatergoers, but by then, she later remembered, McCullers had crossed the room, buried her face in Waters' lap, and was crying; she later agreed to let Ethel adapt the role to her own liking. Directed by Harold Clurman, *The Member of the Wedding* opened on January 5, 1950, at the Empire Theater (where Waters had had her dramatic debut in *Mamba's Daughters* nearly 30 years before), with *Julie Harris as Frankie and Brandon DeWilde as John Henry. The critical and popular reaction to the play was nearly universal praise, and Ethel brought Berenice to national audiences by touring with the show after it closed in New York and recreating her performance with the Broadway cast in Columbia's 1952 screen version of the play, directed by Fred Zinnemann, for which Julie Harris was nominated for an Oscar as Best Actress.

From then on, Waters never lost her place as one of the entertainment world's best-loved performers. Throughout the 1950s and 1960s, she kept busy with film work, starred in the television series "Beulah" (succeeded by *Hattie McDaniel and then *Louise Beavers) and on "GE Theater," and toured with her own one-woman show, *An Evening with Ethel Waters*, during 1957. Also during this period, Waters met and married her third husband, Edward Mallory. Health problems continued to plague her, however, and when her weight rose to well over 300 pounds, she was warned that the strain on her heart might be fatal. Put on a strict diet, she slimmed down to 160 within two years. But best of all, she rediscovered her religious strength after meeting evangelist Billy Graham in New York in the late 1950s. Throughout the '60s and into the early '70s, Waters frequently appeared with the Billy Graham Crusade, speaking of her spiritual journey and never neglecting to sing "His Eye Is on the Sparrow." She always referred to Graham as "my precious child," and dedicated her second autobiography to him. *To Me It's Wonderful* was Ethel's way of reconciling herself to her own faults. She admitted lying about her age in her first book, in which she claimed to have been born four years later than she actually was, although she wrote that it began as an innocent attempt to help friends who needed her to join a group insurance plan which required all its members to have been born no earlier than 1900. More important, she finally laid to rest her troubled relationship with whites. "I hadn't always loved white people," she wrote. "I'll be candid, I did *not* love them! [But] if you stop to think about it, we're all colored. I'm one color and you may be another. And when I say there's no difference under the skin, I mean mainly that we're all sinners in need of a Savior. That same Savior who loves us all alike."

With her health in decline, Waters retired from show business and the Graham Crusade in the mid-1970s. On September 1, 1977, she died at her home in Chatsworth, California, of heart and liver failure, ending a 60-year career by rediscovering the spiritual peace that had sustained her as a child. "I was born naked and hungry, and [God] fed me and clothed me and made me strong enough to make my way on my own," she once said. "There is no greater destiny, I think."

SOURCES:

Atkinson, Brooks. *Broadway*. NY: Macmillan, 1970.

Bogle, Donald. *Blacks in American Film and Television*. NY: Garland, 1988.

Waters, Ethel, with Charles Samuels. *His Eye Is on the Sparrow*. NY: Doubleday, 1951.

Waters, Ethel, with *Eugenia Price and Joyce Blackburn. *To Me It's Wonderful*. NY: Harper and Row, 1972.

Norman Powers,
writer-producer, Chelsea Lane Productions,
New York, New York

Waters, Lucy (c. 1630–1658).

See Walter, Lucy.

Watkins, Frances Ellen (1825–1911).

See Harper, Frances E.W.

Watkins, Margaret (1884–1969)

Scottish photographer. Name variations: Meta Gladys Watkins. Born in 1884 in Hamilton, Canada; died in 1969 in Glasgow, Scotland.

Margaret Watkins was born Meta Gladys Watkins in 1884 in Hamilton, Canada, to Scottish parents, and became interested in photography in 1900. She studied her craft with Clarence White in New York City from 1914 to 1916, at which time he invited her to join the staff of his school. In 1916, Watkins became a professional photographer, associated with the studio on Jane Street in Greenwich Village. From 1916 until 1930, she produced still lifes, portraits, landscapes and nudes and exhibited throughout the United States and abroad. Her work influenced many young photographers including Anton Bruehl, *Laura Gilpin, Paul Outerbridge, Ralph Steiner and *Doris Ulmann. Watkins joined the Pictorial Photographers of America and in 1920 edited the organization's journal. During the 1920s, she worked for J. Walter Thompson, a New York ad agency, where she did advertising photography for Macy's department store.

In 1928, Watkins traveled throughout Europe and the Soviet Union, and in 1930 she produced documentary photos in both Moscow and Leningrad. She traveled to Glasgow, Scotland, in 1931, where she lingered to care for four elderly aunts, remaining with them until the last one died in 1939. With the onset of World War II, she found herself stranded in Scotland where she subsequently lived for the next 30 years. Watkins led a quiet, reclusive life and died there in 1969. Her neighbor and executor, Joseph Mulholland, discovered over 200 photographs after her death.

SOURCES:

Rosenblum, Naomi. *A History of Women Photographers*. NY: Abbeville, 1994.

Judith C. Reveal,
freelance writer,
Greensboro, Maryland

Watson, Edith (1861–1943)

American photographer. Born in 1861 in New England; died in 1943, probably in Canada; companion of writer Victoria Hayward.

Edith Watson created portraits, landscapes and social documentation as a photographer in the late 19th and early 20th centuries. From the mid-1890s until 1930, she traveled extensively through Canada, photographing Canadians at work. She was especially well known for her work on the Quebecoises in 1910 and the Doukhobors in 1919. Her photographs of Mennonites in the prairies and clam diggers and fishermen in Cape Breton are among her most popular. Watson's work was widely published in magazines. In 1911. she entered into a relationship with writer **Victoria Hayward** which continued until her death from a ruptured ulcer in 1943.

SOURCES:

Rosenblum, Naomi. *A History of Women Photographers.* NY: Abbeville, 1994.

Judith C. Reveal,
freelance writer,
Greensboro, Maryland

Watson, Ella (1861–1889).

See Watson, Ellen.

Watson, Ellen (1861–1889)

American homesteader accused of cattle rustling who became the first woman lynched in Wyoming Territory, in a hanging carried out by a group of ranchers for their self-interests. Name variations: Ella Watson; Ellen Liddy Pickell; "Cattle Kate"; also mistakenly known as Kate Champion and Kate Maxwell (see below). Born Ellen Liddy Watson on July 2, 1861, in Arran Township, Ontario, Canada; died on July 20, 1889, in Sweetwater Valley of Wyoming Territory, by hanging; daughter of Thomas Lewis (a farmer) and Frances (Close) Watson; learned to read and write at homestead school; married William A. Pickell, on November 24, 1879 (divorced 1886); married James Averell or Averill, on May 17, 1886; no children.

Moved with family to farm near Lebanon, Kansas (1877); after leaving first marriage, worked as cook and domestic employee in Nebraska and Wyoming until filing a homestead claim in Sweetwater Valley, Wyoming; accused, with Averell, of cattle rustling by cattle ranchers who seized and lynched them (1889); newspapers owned by cattle interests charged her with being a prostitute and accepting stolen cattle as payment.

On July 20, 1889, a bright Saturday afternoon in the Sweetwater Valley of Wyoming Territory, a small group of men pulled Ellen Watson and Jim Averell from their separate homes, accused the couple of rustling cattle, and took them to a secluded area nearby where they hanged them. A day and a half later, the bodies were taken down and buried on Averell's homestead. Ellen Watson was the first woman to be hanged in Wyoming, and only the third in the

frontier history of America's West; the other two had committed murder.

These are the bare facts at the heart of an incident that still causes animated debate among area residents and historians alike. In the frontier code of law, rustling was not a capital offense and hanging a woman was not acceptable under any but the most appalling circumstances. Subsequent newspaper and personal accounts of the incident demonstrate considerable differences about the events leading up to the lynching, and cast doubt on the traditional characterizations of the primary participants. One point of dispute revolves around whether the legendary "Cattle Kate" ran a "hog ranch," or bordello, to supplement the income of the store and saloon run by her lover and husband, Jim Averell. If a cowhand had no cash, this frontier madame was alleged to accept cattle stolen from the boss rancher's herd or mavericks captured before the spring roundup.

Ellen Watson was a tall woman for her time, probably 5'8" or so; the few photos of her show her to be a large, attractive, capable-looking young woman. The first description published after the lynching portrayed her as "the equal of any man on the range. Of robust physique she was a daredevil in the saddle, handy with a six-shooter and adept with the lariat and branding iron. . . . [T]hat she was a holy terror all agreed." Descriptions by friends and family members, however, suggest a very different person, and cast doubt on the motives of the perpetrators, and the truth of the early reports that became the legend of "Cattle Kate."

Ellen Liddy Watson was born on July 2, 1861, in Arran Township, Ontario, Canada. Her father Thomas Lewis Watson had immigrated to Ohio from Scotland with his family in 1837, then run away to Canada where he met and married **Frances Close**. Of Ellen's nine siblings, seven were born in Canada and three in America, after the family's move to Kansas in 1877. Thomas filed a homestead claim there and developed a small farm where the children worked hard and learned to read and write at an elementary school nearby. The siblings reportedly had thick Scottish accents, and Ellen was said to have had a brogue throughout her life.

About 1878, Ellen was sent to Smith Center, Kansas, to work as cook and housekeeper for a local banker. She would keep in touch with her family, however, until shortly before her death. In Smith Center, she caught the attention of a young homesteader, William A. Pickell, and married him in 1879, at age 18. Pickell was alco-

Ellen
Watson

holic, and it was common knowledge that he beat Ellen when drinking. Within two years, she went back to her family and obtained a job as cook and domestic worker on a neighboring farm, while Pickell tried to convince her to return to him.

In 1883, Ellen moved to Red Cloud, Nebraska, just over the state border, to get away from Pickell's continued attention. She took a job in the Royal Hotel and filed for divorce the following year, after establishing legal residency, on grounds of extreme cruelty and infidelity. The divorce would not be finalized until March 1886, when she was living in Wyoming, and then only on Pickell's grounds of desertion. After filing her divorce request, Ellen reverted to using her family name, Watson, shortly before leaving Red Cloud for Denver City, Colorado, where her brother lived. Before the end of 1884, she moved north to Cheyenne, Wyoming, where the cattle industry economy was booming, and took another job as a cook and servant at Rawlins House in Cheyenne, where she worked from 1884 to 1886.

During this time, an incident occurred that later created a confusion of identities affecting Ellen Watson's story. In Fetterman, Wyoming, a prostitute named **Ella Wilson** was involved in a widely reported shooting incident in a saloon. The similarity in names later caused some people to claim that Watson had a history of prostitution. But it is extremely unlikely that Watson was involved in the episode, which occurred during the period she was en route from Nebraska through Colorado to Cheyenne, since she was new to the area and reports of the shooting indicate that Wilson was well established. Watson was a common name and easily confused with Wilson. "Ella," the family's nickname for Watson, was a popular name of that era, but the name "Ellen," which Watson always used for her signature, was not. Ellen Watson was literate, though Ella Wilson was not, a fact shown by official documents signed by Wilson with an X as her mark.

> This notorious and significant historical tragedy must now be viewed in a fresh, new light, and from an altogether different perspective.
> —George W. Hufsmith

Physical descriptions of the two women are also quite different. Watson was tall and Celtic in appearance, weighed about 160 pounds, and was 23 years old at the time. Wilson was described as fair and frail, a "half-breed," and 40 years old. Family members of Watson in Ohio received letters written from various places along her travel route, but none from Fetterman, and, following the lynching, no one interviewed in Fetterman acknowledged knowing an Ellen Watson. In practical terms, Fetterman was a defunct military town, not on any main route, and a woman planning to go into business as a prostitute would have little reason to go there instead of the booming city of Cheyenne.

In February 1886, Watson met James Averell when he made a trip into Cheyenne to file for a second homestead. Averell was a widower who operated a combination store and saloon, known as a road ranch, on his first homestead, and was also postmaster and justice of the peace in the sparsely populated Sweetwater Valley.

Despite claims after their deaths that Watson and Averell were not married, official documents show that a marriage license was granted to them on May 17, 1886, in Lander, Wyoming, a few months after Watson's divorce became final. Watson and Averell probably kept the marriage secret for the same reason that many other homesteaders did: Watson planned to make a homestead filing in the Sweetwater Valley town of Rawlins, the logical place for the marriage, and it was not legal for people of the same family to file individual claims. Probably as a further disguise, Watson used a different surname, Andrews, although she continued to use her actual first and middle names, Ellen Liddy, and gave her correct age and address. In so sparsely populated an area, the likelihood of another "Ellen Liddy" of her age and address is almost nil. Marriage licenses of the time were in three parts—the application, the license and the certificate—and the first two parts made the marriage legal. Many people did not go through with the ceremony to complete the third part, and this appears to be what Watson and Averell did.

When Ellen Watson filed for a homestead adjoining Averell's, close to Horse Creek, the location of their properties probably had more to do with precipitating subsequent events than any other single factor in their story. The problem was that both homesteads lay in an area desired for grazing by the local cattle baron Albert Bothwell.

Before homesteaders moved into Wyoming Territory, herds of cattle were grazed over the entire range, with two roundups per year to sort out the animals before they were driven to market. The new cattle of that year, as yet unbranded, were called mavericks, and were rounded up each spring with the branded animals, then divided up among the ranchers according to the relative size of their herds. With the arrival of the homesteaders and small ranchers, this division became increasingly inequitable, because larger owners still got most of the mavericks while the small owners were prevented even from keeping the mavericks they could identify as born to animals in their herds. When the homesteaders began putting up fences to keep their animals separate and designate their property claims, the cattle barons began bringing their power and money to bear to institute laws through the Territorial Legislature for the protection of their herds. In the resulting conflict, some ranchers attempted to intimidate and run off the homesteaders, or at least prevent them from proving up their claims, while homesteaders found that they could file for water rights which allowed them to divert out of the range cattle's reach rivers and streams that were formerly free-running. This period of conflict lasted from 1875 to 1900, and became known as the range wars.

Informal testimony from the homesteading neighbors and regular customers of Ellen Watson and Jim Averell suggest that they were good neighbors, unassuming and hardworking. Watson went at least once to stay for several days with a sick neighbor, and Averell's customers said he was well liked, even by most of the cowmen in the area. Watson and Averell may have taken in a young boy, Gene Crowder, from a family whose widowed father was a drunkard. Crowder worked and lived at Watson's homestead. Watson may have worked both her own place and Averell's during the day, returning to her own small home at night, in order to meet residency requirements.

But the homestead improvements that Watson and Averell undertook, including putting up fencing and digging irrigation ditches, were guaranteed to arouse the ire of other ranchers and particularly Bothwell, who was reputed to have a volatile personality. Later testimony asserted that Bothwell and others had attempted on several occasions to intimidate Watson, Averell and other homesteaders. In 1887, a rancher friend of Bothwell's filed a claim against Watson, but she won the case in court. Then, in February 1889, Averell wrote a letter to the *Casper Weekly Mail* protesting the illegal practices of the large cattlemen in the Sweetwater Valley. Averell was a Democrat who had received several state and federal appointments in the territory, among ranchers who were generally Republican. He was also vocal in his support of homesteaders and small ranchers who favored a proposal that was controversial at the time, to split Carbon County into two smaller counties.

In the spring of 1889, Watson purchased some cattle. Witnesses and records indicate that they were legally purchased, although it is possible that some rustled calves were included in the small herd. Cattle rustling was always a serious

Isabelle Huppert (with Kris Kristofferson) portrayed Ellen Watson in Michael Cimino's Heaven's Gate.

issue among ranchers. Rustling took many forms, but the most common practice, collecting unbranded calves before the spring roundup, had been made illegal by the Maverick Law of 1884. The law, especially after modifications in 1886, had handed the advantage to large ranch owners over the homesteaders by making all unbranded cattle that got loose the property of the Wyoming Cattle Growers Association, even if the original owner could identify the animals. The usual drastic market fluctuations had meanwhile been intensified in 1886–87 by extreme weather conditions, and the advent of the homesteaders had changed ranching forever. Unemployed ranch hands wandered the territory, looking for any means of livelihood; while working cowboys and owners of smaller ranches rustled to make extra money or to increase their own herds.

Watson's cattle were not newly marked with her brand until early in the summer of 1889, probably because she had bought them between February 15 and the beginning of spring roundup, when branding was illegal. Her purchase would have taken place shortly before many of the cows gave birth, or when they were still weakened by the conditions of the winter, and branding would have imposed an extra hardship on the animals, risking the loss of some cows or calves. The lasting question, once the accusation of rustling was made against Watson, is whether the charge was due to a conspiracy, or was simply a mistake. Witnesses aware of the conflict between Watson and Bothwell reported that Bothwell tried on several occasions to buy Watson out or to give her money to prove up her claim early. He therefore had opportunities to see her herd and to know that it was legally hers, and if he truly believed otherwise, he could have brought legal action against her long before July.

On Saturday, July 20, Watson had left her homestead to visit an Indian encampment nearby, to purchase beadwork. A group of six men, including ranchers and their hands, arrived on her property and began running her cattle out of the fenced pasture. When Watson returned, they accused her of rustling and pulled her into a wagon, despite her request to change her dress and pleas to be taken to Rawlins, where she could show proof of purchase. The group then rode to Averell's road ranch and took him.

According to the version given by the ranchers and their supporters, they had found the couple sitting in Averell's house, drinking and smoking, with guns lying about the room. Eyewitness testimony given in legal proceedings, including statements by Gene Crowder and John DeCorey, declared the ranchers' story untrue. According to Crowder and DeCorey, they rounded up the cattle, patched the fence, and headed for Averell's. Finding Averell gone, they alerted his nephew, Ralph Cole, and a friend, Frank Buchanan. Buchanan rode off in search of the ranchers, hid behind some rocks at the lynching site and fired at the group, hitting one man, but he was outnumbered and ran out of ammunition. Helpless, he crouched and watched the lynching of Watson and Averell.

Some who were witnesses to the abduction but not to the lynching indicate some degree of conspiracy. The editor of the *Sweetwater Chief* newspaper and his assistant apparently had been alerted to the ranchers' plans when they stood atop their building in the newly established town of Bothwell and watched the procession depart from Averell's place. On climbing down, they told some cowboys that "Averell and Watson were hung," without actually seeing the lynching and before reports of it reached town.

It may be that the original plan was to only frighten Watson and Averell, then escalated in the heat of the moment. According to witnesses, when Averell and Watson realized their captors were going to carry out their threats, Averell began to beg for mercy and Watson fought against her abductors. They were placed on a low rock, unbound, and the ropes around their necks were thrown over the tree branch. When their feet were pushed off the rock, there was not enough height to break their necks and bring immediate death, and they strangled slowly while struggling to free themselves.

While Buchanan fled for his life from the scene, one of the perpetrators rode into Rawlins to tell the news and have it telegraphed to Cheyenne. The next day, the first newspaper account appeared in the *Cheyenne Daily Leader*. Written by Edward Towse, it characterized Averell as "always feared because he was a murderous coward" and Watson as "a virago who had been living with him as his wife for some months." In the form that was fed to Towse, the story may have been an attempt to justify lynching a woman; at any rate, his article contains the seed upon which the legend of "Cattle Kate" was built. Towse continued these characterizations in succeeding articles that were picked up by newspapers around the country, repeating the images of Watson and Averell as hard-living, drunken rustlers, and the ranchers as victims driven to extremes by thieving trickery.

In Sweetwater Valley, an inquest was instated the next evening prior to the burial of the couple at Averell's homestead. Eyewitnesses identified the abductors as six cowboys and ranchers, including Bothwell, and all were arrested within days but allowed to post bail for each other and return home. In the next several months, all who had been witnesses disappeared or died under mysterious circumstances. While a second inquest did not dislodge the findings of the first, it was revised to state that the lynching was done by "persons unknown." In August, Watson's father arrived to find out what happened, and he stayed for some time. But upon his return to Kansas, the continued reports about his daughter's character caused him to forbid mention of her.

In October, when a grand jury was impaneled, Frank Buchanan, the only witness for the prosecution left alive, disappeared. Whether he was murdered, bribed, or fled was never discovered, although numerous theories and suggestions of evidence were advanced by contemporaries and in later research.

Soon after the lynching, all but two of the accused, ostracized and feared by their neighbors, left the Sweetwater area. Albert Bothwell, alleged to be the instigator of the entire scheme, took over the land and buildings developed by Watson and Averell, and continued to squabble over land issues with other residents and the federal government into the next century. When he died many years later in California, it was said among some of the Sweetwater Valley oldtimers that he died "utterly insane."

No information ever gave credence to the view that Ellen Watson had been a prostitute. The charge began with Towse's stories in the *Daily Leader*, which seemed deliberately to confuse Watson with ❧▶ **Kate Maxwell**, who operated a gambling hall, saloon, dance hall and brothel in Bessemer, Wyoming, some ten miles south of Casper and a day's ride northeast of the Sweetwater post office where Jim Averell was postmaster.

The men of the Wyoming Cattle Growers Association were thus successful, not only at killing Watson but at branding her with an unwarranted reputation lasting down through the years. As late as 1981, a book by Jay Robert Nash, with the interesting title *Look for the Woman*, carried this portrayal:

> Not too bright, Ella Watson had been a bar shill and prostitute until moving to Rawlins, Wyoming, where she met cattle rustler Jim Averill who set her up with her very own whorehouse. The bordello was really a front. Into the large pens behind the property, Averill and Ella herded hundreds of cows they had stolen from neighboring ranches, selling the

---

❧▶ **Maxwell, Kate** (fl. 1886)

American frontier woman. Name variations: "Cattle Kate." Flourished around 1886; married a man named Maxwell.

Kate Maxwell, a seriocomic singer from Chicago, was brought to Wyoming about 1886 by a cattleman named Maxwell, and apparently married him after she arrived. Kate Maxwell operated a gambling hall, saloon, dance hall and brothel in Bessemer, Wyoming, some ten miles south of Casper and a day's ride northeast of the Sweetwater post office where Jim Averell was postmaster and had his homestead next to *Ellen Watson's.

Maxwell was referred to in the press as "Cattle Kate" long before the lynching of Ellen Watson and Jim Averell. Perhaps the first to make such reference was the *Bessemer Journal*. Some of the print reports state that she did associate with rustlers, shoot a man, rob a gambler, and operate various businesses in Bessemer. Prostitution was not illegal in the frontier West; rather it was tolerated as a business that would develop, regardless of laws, in a territory where there were few women. It was not, however, an acceptable job for a decent woman.

In his newspaper articles after the Watson-Averell lynching, Edward Towse seemed deliberately to confuse Watson with Kate Maxwell. He identified Maxwell and Watson as the same person, giving them the same background. Towse said Maxwell imported race horses and jockeys who raced against Native Americans, as well as bulldogs to fight coyotes and wolves. According to Towse, Maxwell was said to have poisoned her husband, and allowed the ranch to become a center for thieves. Eventually, she was robbed of horses and jewels, her cattle scattered, the foreman and others left. Then, Towse said, she joined Averell at his road house.

Reporter W.R. Hunt, working for the *Chicago Inter Ocean* at the time of the lynching, wrote in a personal notebook about his 1890 trip to the Sweetwater Valley to interview residents and witnesses. The journal was discovered in the Kansas City attic of a woman whose sister was said to be a friend of Hunt's. He wrote, on April 12, 1890, during an investigative trip to Casper, that "Kate Maxwell was another woman altogether, . . . [who s]old her services to the Army stationed [at Bessemer City]," and that she was at that time "[s]till alive."

beef for quick and heavy profits. Ella was soon known in the area as "Cattle Kate."

In 1980, the movie *Heaven's Gate*, loosely based on the homesteader conflict known as the Johnson County wars, added a further level of confusion to the actual identity of the murdered homesteader, depicting Ella Watson as a "notorious brothel keeper" in love with both Jim Averill and Nate Champion. In reality, there was a Nate Champion, reputed variously to be a cattle rustler and a defender of the rights of the homesteaders and small ranchers. Champion was indeed hanged by the men of the Wyoming Cattle Growers Association, but in 1892, three years after the death of Ellen Watson.

More reliably, contemporary interviews of Sweetwater residents, and later ones recording what descendants related of their family histories, indicate that the legend of "Cattle Kate" is at least partly a fabrication that served cattle-ranching interests. At best, the life of Ellen Watson deserves to be reclaimed as that of a hardworking and courageous homesteader like many who lived and died in the Wyoming Territory.

SOURCES:

Clay, John. *My Life on the Range*. Introduction by Donald R. Ornduff. Norman, OK: University of Oklahoma Press, 1962.

Hufsmith, George W. *The Wyoming Lynching of Cattle Kate, 1889*. Glendo, WY: High Plains Press, 1993.

Nash, Jay Robert. *Look for the Woman*. NY: M. Evans, 1981.

Ray, Grace Ernestine. *Wily Women of the West*. San Antonio, TX: Naylor, 1972.

SUGGESTED READING:

Horan, James D., and Paul Sann. *Pictorial History of the Wild West*. NY: Crown, 1954.

Lamar, Howard R., ed. *The Reader's Encyclopedia of the American West*. NY: Thomas Y. Crowell, 1977.

McLoughlin, Denis. *Wild and Woolly: An Encyclopedia of the Old West*. Garden City, NY: Doubleday, 1975.

Myres, Sandra L. *Westering Women and the Frontier Experience: 1800–1915*. Albuquerque, NM: University of New Mexico Press, 1982.

COLLECTIONS:

Newspaper reports, legal documents and photographs concerning this incident and the range wars are collected in the Wyoming State Archives and Historical Department in Cheyenne, Wyoming, and in the Historical Research Division, Coe Library, University of Wyoming, Laramie. Private collection of correspondence and papers about Ellen Watson is held by George W. Hufsmith of Jackson, Wyoming.

Margaret L. Meggs,
independent scholar on women's and disability issues and on feminism and religion, Havre, Montana

Watson, Janet Vida (1923–1985)

English geologist. Born on September 1, 1923, in Hampstead, London, England; died on March 29, 1985, in Ashtead, England; daughter of David Meredith Seares Watson (a paleontologist) and Katherine Margarite Watson; graduated from Reading University, 1943; Imperial College in London, Ph.D., 1949; married John Sutton (a geologist), in 1949; children: two daughters (both died at birth).

Studied some of the world's most ancient rocks; wrote two foundation texts in the study of geology, Introduction to Geology *(1962) and* Beginning Geology *(1966); served as first woman president of the Geological Society of London (1982–84).*

Janet Vida Watson was born in 1923 into an intellectually stimulating English household. Her father David Meredith Seares Watson was both a vertebrate paleontologist and a professor of zoology and comparative anatomy at the University of London, while her mother **Katherine Margarite Watson** had engaged in embryological research prior to their marriage. Janet excelled in her studies at Reading University, from which she graduated with first-class honors in biology and geology in 1943.

After graduation, Watson worked as a researcher on chicken growth and diet, but boredom led her first to teaching at a girls' school and then to the field of geology by the end of World War II. She attended London's Imperial College, where H.H. Read convinced her to undertake a study of the Lewisian gneisses, the oldest rocks of the British Isles. The unique nature of the rocks required that Watson and fellow researcher John Sutton create a new technique in geological research, for which they were commended by the Geological Society of London in 1951. Watson and Sutton were married in 1949 and continued their professional partnership throughout their lives. Having already earned her Ph.D., Watson received a senior studentship in 1951 that enabled her to continue studying the Lewisian while also embarking on a study of ancient rocks in Tanzania.

Watson's groundbreaking work in geology earned her a position as Read's assistant in 1952. Her fascination with the geological problems of these ancient rocks often combined with her interests in Scotland, mineralization, heat flow through the Earth's crust, and geochemistry, and her expertise produced two foundation texts in the field of geology: *Introduction to Geology* (1962) and *Beginning Geology* (1966). She wrote the former with Read 12 years before she became a professor herself, joining her husband who became chair of the geology department at Imperial College in 1958.

Watson was co-recipient with her husband of the Bigsby medal and the Lyell medal from the Geological Society of London, and in 1982 was elected the society's first female president. Soon thereafter, she became vice-president and council member of the Royal Society. In 1983, her analytical skills led to an important study in which she reversed the accepted hypothesis for uranium deposits in Italy, and she presented numerous papers to professional societies on her findings. She died two years later, after a painful illness.

SOURCES:

The Concise Dictionary of National Biography. Oxford: Oxford University Press, 1992.

The Dictionary of National Biography, 1981–1985. Edited by Lord Blake and C.S. Nicholls. Oxford: Oxford University Press, 1990.

Judith C. Reveal,
freelance writer,
Greensboro, Maryland

Watson, Lillian (b. 1950).

See Watson, Pokey.

Watson, Maud (b. 1864)

English tennis champion. Born Maud Edith Eleanor Watson in Harrow, Middlesex, England, in 1864; daughter of a rector in Berkswell, England; sister of Lillian Watson.

In 1884, Maud Watson became the first woman champion at Wimbledon, when she and 13 other women vied for the trophy. Wearing a corset and an ankle-length dress, Maud beat her older sister **Lillian Watson** in a tough final, 6–8, 6–3, 6–3. She repeated her win in 1885, triumphing over *****Blanche Bingley** (**Hillward**), 6–1, 7–5. In 1886, Bingley handily beat Watson, 6–3, 6–3. A Wimbledon face-off between two sisters would not be repeated until the year 2000, when **Venus Williams** beat her little sister **Serena Williams** in the semifinals on centre court.

Watson, Pokey (1950—)

American Olympic swimmer. Name variations: Lillian Watson. Born Lillian Debra Watson in Mineola, Long Island, New York, on July 11, 1950; married Allen Richardson (an all-American swimmer), in 1971; children: three.

Born Lillian Watson in 1950 in Long Island, New York, Pokey Watson entered her first Olympic competition at age 14 in 1964. As a member of the 4x100-meter freestyle relay swim team (which included *****Sharon Souder, *****Donna

de Varona**, and **Kathleen Ellis**), Watson won the gold medal in world-record time. She followed up this victory with consecutive U.S. national titles, first in the outdoor freestyle 100-meter event and then in the 200-meter event. During those years, Watson also played on the national women's water polo championship team at the Santa Clara Swim Club.

Watson built on third and fourth place finishes in the 100-meter and 200-meter events at the 1967 Pan American Games in preparation for the 1968 Olympics in Mexico City, Mexico. Becoming bored with freestyle swimming, she switched to the backstroke on a whim the summer before the Olympics and pulled off a first-place finish in the Olympic 200-meter backstroke the year it became open to women. She was the first woman to accomplish this feat, with a time of 2:24.8 seconds.

SOURCES:

Read, Phyllis J., and Bernard L. Witlieb. *The Book of Women's Firsts.* NY: Random House, 1992.

Judith C. Reveal,
freelance writer,
Greensboro, Maryland

Wattles, Santha Rama Rau (b. 1923).

See Rama Rau, Santha.

Wattleton, Faye (1943—)

President of the Planned Parenthood Federation of America (PPFA) from 1978 to 1992. Name variations: Alyce Faye Wattleton. Born Alyce Faye Wattleton on July 8, 1943, in St. Louis, Missouri; daughter of George Edward Wattleton (a factory worker) and Ozie (Garrett) Wattleton (a seamstress and preacher); graduated from Ohio State University Nursing School, 1964; Columbia University, New York, M.S., 1967; married Franklin Gordon, in 1973 (divorced 1981); children: daughter Felicia Gordon (b. 1975).

Faye Wattleton was the first African-American, the first woman since founder *****Margaret Sanger**, and the youngest individual to serve as president of the Planned Parenthood Federation of America (PPFA). For 14 tumultuous years as the leader of an organization that advocates women's reproductive freedom, Wattleton was embroiled in a national controversy over legalized abortion, especially during the administrations of Ronald Reagan and George Bush. With unflagging clarity of vision and eloquence, Wattleton articulated the tenets and goals of the PPFA's pro-choice platform in a professional and nonthreatening manner. Carefully discerning between "pro-choice" and "pro-abortion" throughout her tenure, she kept the focus upon the essential rights of women to make choices about their own bodies without the intrusion of government or the courts.

An only child, Faye Wattleton was born on July 8, 1943, in St. Louis, Missouri, the daughter of George Wattleton, a factory worker, and **Ozie Wattleton**, a seamstress and itinerant fundamentalist preacher. Ozie was one of Faye Wattleton's role models, along with Martin Luther King, Jr., and John F. Kennedy. Although the family was poor, they lived their politics, stressing the importance of helping those who were less fortunate than they. Missionary work was an important part of their lives.

Wattleton entered Ohio State University Nursing School at age 16 and earned a bachelor's degree in 1964, becoming the first person in her family to do so. After graduation, she found a position as a maternity nursing instructor at the Miami Valley Hospital School of Nursing in Dayton, Ohio. There, she was exposed to the aftermath of illegal abortions, the memory of which would later inspire her to ensure the availability of legal abortions. In 1966, Wattleton

Faye Wattleton

moved to New York to study at Columbia University on a full scholarship; a year later, she received an M.S. in maternal and infant health care, with certification as a nurse-midwife. While a student at Columbia, she interned at Harlem Hospital, where the importance of access to safe abortion became even more apparent to her.

Returning to Dayton in 1967, Wattleton worked as a consultant and assistant director of Public Health Nursing Services for the city. Asked to join the local Planned Parenthood board, Wattleton became its executive director less than two years later. Under her leadership, the number of clients tripled, and the budget increased from less than $400,000 to just under $1 million. In 1973, she married Franklin Gordon, a social worker raised in Roxbury, Massachusetts. Two years later, she became a mother as well as the chair of the national executive director's council of PPFA. She was appointed to the presidency in 1978, which surprised many who thought she lacked the experience to assume such a highly visible, highly paid position in the largest voluntary health agency in America. As it turned out, however, Wattleton was an ideal choice as a speaker for Planned Parenthood. According to *Contemporary Black Biography*, "She effectively bridged the gap between the organization's mostly white, middle- and upper-class membership and the mostly poor women being served in the clinics. Her race helped her to challenge complaints that Planned Parenthood was helping to promote genocide by providing birth control to black women." Wattleton argued that the greater threat was black women bearing numerous children against their will.

Wattleton soon began to change the direction of Planned Parenthood, which until then had been recognized primarily for its 850 clinics in 46 states, serving some 3 million each year with everything from infertility counseling and birth control to prenatal care. Wattleton thought Planned Parenthood should also assume a strong advocacy role for women's rights and reproductive freedom, especially at a time when conservative opposition to the Supreme Court's *Roe* v. *Wade* decision by political groups such as the Moral Majority and the Right to Life movement was strengthened by the support of Republican administrations. Although abortion continued to be protected under the law, conservative groups succeeded in getting the Hyde Amendment passed in 1977, which severely restricted federal funding for the controversial procedure. And by 1989, the Supreme Court's *Webster* decision enabled states even greater power to restrict abortion.

Diffusing the political battle to several fronts, the Reagan administration fought to repeal the U.S. family planning program, Title I of the Public Health Service Act. President Reagan also attempted to enact a requirement that federally funded clinics receive parental consent before distributing contraceptive devices to minors. Wattleton, however, argued that parental notification would merely lead to an increase in teen pregnancies. The administration also proposed a rule to prevent abortion counseling by federally funded family-planning agencies. Meanwhile, conservative opposition to Planned Parenthood began to express itself in more extreme and sinister ways through the burning and bombing of clinics in Minnesota, Virginia, Nebraska, Vermont, and Ohio. Wattleton herself had been targeted by hate mail and death threats, necessitating the hiring of bodyguards.

As family planning services and their funding were threatened, Wattleton worked even harder to bring PPFA into public view, making numerous guest appearances on radio and television talk shows to rally support. Although the organization lost a few corporate sponsors as it heightened its political visibility, private donations increased dramatically. Under Wattleton, the organization's budget tripled. Film personalities and Hollywood executives demonstrated their support publicly, and the organization participated in massive rallies in the nation's capital and elsewhere. On each occasion, Wattleton stood at the forefront delineating Planned Parenthood's goals and arguing that PPFA was working to level the playing field in terms of access to health care between the rich and the poor, since the poor were especially vulnerable to reductions in federal funding.

Equal access was not the only issue raised concerning reproductive choice and freedom. Wattleton attempted to locate the reproductive issue in a wider context of federal neglect. In her view, the Reagan-Bush administration tried to dismantle programs designed to confront not only the issue of inadequate health care but also homelessness and poor education. Thus, sex education and information about contraceptives became crucial elements of PPFA's platform. While using the media to promote those issues, Wattleton also co-authored the book *How to Talk to Your Child About Sex*, which sold more than 30,000 copies. In her view, children needed to be taught about sexuality before they became adolescents. She attributed the increase of teen pregnancies to children's contradictory exposure to sex.

Wattleton's professional prestige continued to soar as she accumulated honors and awards, including the 1986 American Humanist Award and the Jefferson Award for the Greatest Public Service Performed by a Private Citizen in 1992. She also became a member of numerous organizations, among them the National Academy of the Sciences' Institute of Medicine's Study Committee on the Role of State and Local Public Health Departments, the advisory committee of the Women's Leadership Conference on National Security, and the President's Advisory Council on the Peace Corps.

Amidst dissension in PPFA's ranks regarding its public role in reproductive rights battles, however, Wattleton resigned from her post in 1992. The following year, she was inducted into the National Women's Hall of Fame. In 1995, she established a women's policy think tank, the Center for Gender Equality, to promote a national dialogue on the economic, political, and educational aspects of women's lives in addition to health and reproductive rights.

SOURCES:

Encyclopedia of World Biography. 2nd ed. Detroit, MI: Gale Research, 1998.

Mabunda, L. Mpho, ed. *Contemporary Black Biography*. Vol. 9. Detroit, MI: Gale Research, 1995.

Smith, Jessie Carney, ed. *Notable Black American Women*. Detroit, MI: Gale Research, 1992.

Judith C. Reveal,
freelance writer,
Greensboro, Maryland

Watts, Helen (1927—)

Welsh contralto, known chiefly for oratorio and opera roles, who was also an interpreter of lieder and 20th-century songs. Born on December 7, 1927, in Milford Haven, southwest Wales; studied under Caroline Hatchard and Frederick Jackson at the Royal Academy of Music in London.

Welsh contralto Helen Watts received her vocal training as a student at the Royal Academy of Music in London, studying under noted teachers **Caroline Hatchard** and Frederick Jackson. She got her start in the choruses of the Glyndebourne Festival and the BBC, making her first solo appearance in 1953. Her 1955 performance of Bach arias under the baton of Sir Malcolm Sargent at the London Promenade Concerts was the springboard to a successful concert career on European and North American circuits.

In addition to her concert performances, Watts embarked on an opera career in 1958 as Didymus in *Theodora* with the Handel Opera Society. She was a regular performer with the society for the next six years, and then debuted at the Salzburg Festival as the First Maid in *Elektra*. Other notable performances included her Lucretia during a tour of Russia with the English Opera Group, her initial appearance at Covent Garden in London as the first Norn in *Götterdammerung* in 1965, her American debut in *A Mass of Life* in 1966, and her Mistress Quickly at the Welsh National Opera in 1969. With the last company, she enjoyed a long run as a leading member until her retirement in 1983. In 1978, she was made a Commander of the Order of the British Empire.

Judith C. Reveal,
freelance writer,
Greensboro, Maryland

Wauneka, Annie Dodge

(1910–1997)

Navajo public health activist and tribal leader who was the first woman elected to the Navajo Tribal Council and the first Native American to win the U.S. Presidential Medal of Freedom. Name variations: Anne Wauneka. Name variations: known to the Navajo nation as "Our Legendary Mother." Born on April 10, 1910, near Sawmill, Arizona; died of Alzheimer's disease on November 10, 1997, in Flagstaff, Arizona; daughter of Henry Chee Dodge (a rancher and politician) and K'eehabah (also seen as Kee'hanabah); University of Arizona, B.S. in public health; married George Wauneka, in October 1929; children: Georgia Anne Wauneka; Henry Wauneka; Irma Wauneka; Franklin Wauneka; Lorencita Wauneka; Sallie Wauneka; and two who died young.

Annie Dodge Wauneka was born in a Navajo hogan near Sawmill, Arizona, in 1910. Her father Henry Chee Dodge was a Navajo rancher and politician; her mother **K'eehabah** was one of Dodge's three wives. Traditional Navajo society was matrilineal and permitted polygamy. Since wives were usually related to one another, children born to them were considered full siblings. At one year of age, Annie was taken from her mother and brought to live with her father, together with her half-siblings. Dodge, who was fluent in English, had been an interpreter for the government. He was also a tribal council leader and the owner of a large ranch with all the modern conveniences, including servants. However, he encouraged humility in his children by assigning them chores, such as sheep herding.

Annie and her siblings received their early education at a white school. At age eight, she attended the government school at Fort Defiance, and then went to the government school at Albu-

querque where she learned English. When she returned home, Wauneka developed a close bond with her father and frequently accompanied him on trips around the reservation, assisting him with translations. Through her travels, she witnessed a high level of illness and poverty and understood the ideals and goals her father had for the tribe. She also became aware of the importance of education in the resolution of these problems.

Annie broke with tribal tradition when she chose her own husband rather than wait for the family to arrange her marriage. In October 1929, she married George Wauneka, a schoolmate from Albuquerque; the couple would have eight children, two of whom died young. Although she devoted most of her time to her family, she continued to travel with her father around the reservation, and after his death she dedicated herself to perpetuating his work. In 1951, Wauneka became the first woman elected to the Navajo Tribal Council. She was re-elected again in 1955 and 1959. Her concerns about tribal health also led to her appointment as chair of the health committee.

Wauneka assumed her role with enthusiasm, focusing first on tuberculosis, the reservation's most pernicious problem. She realized that conventional Western European medicine might be the solution but that she needed to bridge the gap between cultures first. She approached traditional families with the idea of changing their food preparation techniques and sanitizing their cooking and eating areas as a way of improving the health of their families. She also tried to convince medicine men, whom the Navajo respected and trusted, to try conventional medicine, so that they might convince others. Wauneka returned to college in the mid-1950s, earning a B.S. in public health from the University of Arizona. She studied for three months in the hospitals and laboratories of the U.S. Public Health Service. She also wrote a Navajo dictionary to help her people understand the illnesses they faced, and the cures and treatments that were available to them. In addition to her studies on tuberculosis, Wauneka brought understanding to other health areas, including improved gynecological, obstetric, and pediatric care. She advocated regular eye and ear exams, and fought alcohol abuse.

During the next decade, Wauneka enlarged her sphere of influence by serving on the New Mexico Committee on Aging and becoming a member of advisory boards of the U.S. Surgeon General and the U.S. Public Health Service. In 1958, she won the Josephine Hughes Award and the Woman of Achievement Award from the Ari-

zona Press Women's Association. She was named Outstanding Worker in Public Health of the Arizona Public Health Association in 1959 and was honored with the Indian Achievement Award of the Indian Council Fire of Chicago that year as well—an award her father had won in 1945. In 1960, Wauneka hosted her own daily radio show on KGAK in Gallup, New Mexico. Broadcasting in Navajo, she provided general interest items along with important health issues. She was also active in the Head Start program and participated as a leader in the Girl Scouts.

On December 6, 1963, President Lyndon B. Johnson awarded the Presidential Medal of Freedom to Wauneka for her contributions to healthcare services. She received an honorary doctorate in public health from the University of Arizona in 1976, and in 1984 the Navajo council honored her as the legendary mother of the Navajo people. She still served as an advisor to the Navajo Tribal Council into her 80s. On May 9, 1996, her alma mater, the University of Arizona, awarded her a second honorary doctorate. Wauneka died of Alzheimer's disease on November 10, 1997, at Flagstaff Medical Center. "She made us proud to be Navajo," said her grandson, Navajo tribal president Albert Hale. In the autumn of 2000, Annie Dodge Wauneka was inducted into the Women's Hall of Fame at Seneca Falls, New York.

SOURCES:

Bataille, Gretchen M., ed. *Native American Women.* NY: Garland, 1993.

Encyclopedia of World Biography. Detroit, MI: Gale Research, 1999.

Gridley, Marion E. *American Indian Women.* NY: Hawthorn, 1974.

"Obituary," in *The Day* [New London, CT]. November 16, 1997.

Rooney, Terrie M., ed. *Contemporary Heroes and Heroines.* Detroit, MI: Gale Research.

SUGGESTED READING:

Niethammer, Carolyn. *I'll Go and Do More: Annie Dodge Wauneka, Navajo Leader and Activist.* Lincoln, NE: University of Nebraska Press, 2001.

Judith C. Reveal,
freelance writer,
Greensboro, Maryland

Way, Amanda M. (1828–1914)

American preacher and social reformer. Born on July 10, 1828, in Winchester, Indiana; died on February 24, 1914; daughter of Matthew Way and Hannah (Martin) Way; attended Randolph Seminary in Winchester; never married.

Worked on behalf of women's rights and for temperance in Indiana and Kansas; was the first woman to be elected Grand Worthy Chief Templar of the Independent Order of Good Templars; served as first president of the Women's Christian Temperance Union in Kansas.

Born in 1828, Amanda M. Way was the second of eight children of Matthew and **Hannah Martin Way**, both Quakers. She was educated in public schools and at Randolph Seminary in Winchester, Indiana. A brief teaching career ended when she opened a millinery and dressmaking shop to help support her widowed mother and a sister's orphaned children.

In 1851, Way attended an anti-slavery meeting in Greensboro, Indiana, where she proposed a resolution calling for a state women's rights convention. As a result, the Indiana Woman's Rights Society was formed and, during her nine years of service, Way became vice-president and later president. In addition to her administrative duties, she assisted **Sarah Underhill** in editing the *Woman's Tribune*, an Indianapolis newspaper; she also contributed to the temperance movement, organizing the Woman's Temperance Army in Winchester in 1854. Way lectured and organized for the temperance-oriented Independent Order of Good Templars and was the first woman to be elected Grand Worthy Chief Templar.

With the onset of the Civil War, Way's reform activities ceased when she followed four of her brothers who had joined the Union Army to become a nurse, serving both in hospitals and on the battlefield. Following the war, she resumed her work for women's rights by initiating another call for a state-wide convention in 1869. The subsequent reorganization of the prewar women's movement resulted in the creation of the Indiana Woman Suffrage Association. In January 1871, Way read a memorial from the state society to the state legislature, asking for an amendment to the Indiana Constitution granting women the right to vote. That same year, she became a licensed preacher of the Methodist Episcopal Church, to which she had converted from Quakerism several years before. In 1872, her ministry took her to Kansas where she continued to lecture on temperance and the women's movement. After the General Conference of the Methodist Episcopal Church discontinued licensing women preachers in 1880, she returned to her Quaker faith and served as a minister for the remainder of her life.

Way founded the Women's Christian Temperance Union in Kansas and served as its first president. She served as a delegate to a Chicago convention of the National Woman Suffrage Association in 1880 and would address the convention again in 1905 as one of the few survivors from the pre-Civil War suffrage movement. Around that time, Way left Kansas for the West and, after a short stay in Idaho, made her home in California. She settled in Whittier, where she died in 1914.

SOURCES:

James, Edward T., ed. *Notable American Women, 1607–1950.* Cambridge, MA: The Belknap Press of Harvard University, 1971.

Judith C. Reveal,
freelance writer,
Greensboro, Maryland

Weatherspoon, Teresa (1965—)

African-American basketball player. Name variations: Spoon; T-Spoon. Born on December 8, 1965, in Pineland, Texas; daughter of James Weatherspoon and Rowena Weatherspoon; graduated from Louisiana Tech University with a degree in physical education, 1988.

Was a member of three gold-medal basketball teams in international competition (1986–87); led her college basketball team, the Lady Techsters, to an NCAA championship (1988); won a gold medal with the women's Olympic basketball team (1988), and a bronze medal (1992); joined the New York Liberty team in the first year of the Women's National Basketball Association (1997); named the WNBA Defensive Player of the Year (1997).

Teresa Weatherspoon, nicknamed "Spoon" by her family and friends and "T-Spoon" by her fans, was born in 1965 in Pineland, Texas, the youngest of six children, and raised in a sports environment. Her father James Weatherspoon, who played minor league baseball for the Minnesota Twins, holds the record for the most grand-slam home runs in a single game. Her mother **Rowena Weatherspoon** encouraged her early interest in sports and urged her to play on the boys' teams with her brothers. Teresa therefore played Little League baseball, rather than softball with the other girls, as a child. During her high school years, she excelled both on the basketball court and in the classroom, graduating as valedictorian. By the time she began attending Louisiana Tech University, she had proven herself to be a star in the making.

Weatherspoon led the Lady Techsters to the NCAA finals twice and to a national championship in 1988. Both in 1987 and in 1988, she was named a Kodak All-American and a Wade Trophy winner. Her senior year brought a host of prestigious honors, including the Broderick Cup and being named Louisiana State Player of the Year. The NCAA listed her on its Women's Basketball Team of the Decade, and she was chosen as the 1988 NCAA tournament's most valuable player. By the time Weatherspoon graduated with a physical education degree in 1988, she was the university's career leader in steals and assists. Her level of play was such that she landed spots on the U.S. national teams in the 1986 FIBA World championships, the 1986 Goodwill Games, and the World University Games. Weatherspoon brought home gold medals in all three international competitions. She also competed in her first Olympic games in 1988 when the American team brought home the gold.

Following graduation, Weatherspoon could continue her career in basketball only by going abroad, as there was no professional basketball league for women in the United States. She played professionally in Italy for eight years and in Russia for two before returning to America to compete with the U.S. Olympic team, taking a bronze medal at the 1992 games. On January 22, 1997, however, Weatherspoon signed with the newly formed Women's National Basketball Association (WNBA) and was assigned to the New York Liberty. That first season she posted impressive numbers and earned the honor of being the league's Defensive Player of the Year, in addition to leading the league in steals. She repeated that feat in 1998, while also being among the leaders in assists. Weatherspoon enjoyed a successful 1999 season as well when she led the Liberty to the WNBA final rounds, sinking a half-court shot that won the game against the Houston Comets and keeping the Liberty in the

Teresa Weatherspoon

competition. Although her team eventually lost that championship, Weatherspoon vowed to play until her team succeeded in winning a championship. An All-Star starter in 1999 and 2000, Weatherspoon has an aggressive style of play that makes her a league favorite. For the thousands of girls and young women for whom she's a role model, she co-wrote a motivational book, *Basketball for Girls*, in which she encourages them to be aggressive in achieving their goals.

SOURCES:

Leland, John. "Up in the Air," in *Newsweek*. September 1, 1997, pp. 57–62.

Page, James A. *Black Olympian Medalists*. Libraries Unlimited, 1991.

Judith C. Reveal,
freelance writer,
Greensboro, Maryland

Weaver, Harriet Shaw (1876–1961)

English publisher who championed the publication of James Joyce's Ulysses *in 1922. Born Harriet Shaw Weaver in 1876 in Frodsham, Cheshire, England; died in 1961 in Saffron Walden, near Cambridge; daughter of Frederick Poynton Weaver.*

Harriet Shaw Weaver was born in Victorian England in 1876, the sixth of eight children, and raised according to the tenets of the Church of England. Until the age of 18, she was taught by a series of governesses, and supplemented her education by attending lectures and traveling. Weaver volunteered to work for **Dora Marsden**'s new venture, the magazine *The Freewoman*, which Marsden had founded in 1911. Financial troubles caused the magazine to fold, although Weaver revived it as *The New Freewoman*, and again as *The Egoist*, assuming editorship of the last incarnation in 1914. Marsden eventually handed full control to Weaver, although the two women remained in contact.

Weaver's interest in avant-garde novelists quickly drew her to the work of Irish writer James Joyce. She began serializing Joyce's *A Portrait of the Artist as a Young Man* until 1915, when Joyce determined to publish it in hardcover. After three publishers in London rejected the manuscript, Weaver proposed to reorganize *The Egoist* into a book press in order to publish the work herself. However, this plan was thwarted by England's strict obscenity laws, which held printers accountable for setting in type any "morally questionable" material. Undeterred, Weaver took the manuscript to B.W. Huebsch in the United States, and guaranteed its distribution in England. When he published it at the end of 1916, Weaver became the figurehead publisher early the next year.

Joyce received advances for the serial rights—£50 on publication and £25 more from Weaver—but Weaver ended up financing the author in much larger amounts, despite his frequent bouts of drunkenness and his infamous ability to deplete formidable amounts of money with impressive speed. According to W.G. Rogers, Weaver's commitment to Joyce is difficult to explain, given the fact that she did not even meet the man until 1922. However, she was known to have a keen sympathy for those who were injured or ill, and Joyce, who had an uncanny instinct for finding people who would sacrifice their finances to his art, seemed to exploit this tenderness by providing Weaver with an ongoing account of the details of his seriously deteriorating eyesight.

By 1918, Joyce had progressed well with his novel *Ulysses* and had a pressing need for a publisher. Its frank sexual content compelled Huebsch to require certain cuts in the manuscript, but Joyce refused to be censored. In 1919, Weaver attempted to interest Leonard and *Virginia Woolf of the Hogarth Press in the manuscript, but without success. Fearing for Joyce's state of mind in the midst of the delay, Weaver mailed him £200 as an advance on the publication, which still had no immediate future.

A breakthrough finally occurred when Weaver and *Sylvia Beach, owner of Paris' Shakespeare and Company book shop, approached Maurice Darantière, a printer in Dijon, France. Joyce was now kept busy, working 17 hours a day to prepare copy for the printer. After the first edition appeared in Paris in 1922, Weaver began to coordinate the proposed English edition with Darantière. The publication history in itself was constantly eventful: serialization in *Margaret Carolyn Anderson's *Little Review* was stopped by court action in America; copies were burned on the docks in England; and a pirated serialization was protested by many of the world's intellectuals. It was not until a 1933 court decision declared that it was not obscene that *Ulysses* was published in the United States.

Throughout the duration of the project, Joyce was careful not to offend his benefactor, as Weaver was his source of ready financial security. Prior to meeting him in July 1922, she had already given him £8,500 and a house in the country. A year after they met, she provided another gift of £12,000. Although reports of Joyce's profligate ways disturbed her, she is reported to have promised him additional sums which she expected to inherit. His demands on her were endless, as he required her to do his press notices, write his thank-you notes to various people, process checks and tend to the needs of his increasingly mentally ill daughter **Lucia Joyce**. As the interest from the endowment fund she had given him rapidly depleted and he began to burrow into the principal, Weaver timidly suggested that he leave the nest egg untouched. For a short time he did, but as he returned to this trough, he made it clear to Weaver and her solicitors that he did not care for their interference. Notes Rogers, it was perhaps to her advantage that some distance separated her from Joyce.

Joyce died during World War II, and his wife *****Nora Joyce** died in 1951. They left behind a sorely troubled daughter Lucia, who required constant attention. Weaver took on the burden of her care as Joyce's literary executor. The British courts appointed Weaver receiver for Lucia, and she also managed Joyce's vast estate. As old age descended upon her, Weaver eventually relinquished many of her responsibilities as well as original manuscripts from Joyce to the British Society of Authors. The one responsibility she would not give up was the care of Lucia, for whom she faithfully provided a home and nursing attendants. She eventually placed Lucia at St. Andrew's in the care of a godchild.

During the 1930s, Weaver's support for the British Labour Party grew into an interest in Communism. She ultimately joined the Communist Party, working at routine tasks in one of their neighborhood offices. Rogers suggests that Weaver's devotion to Joyce extended to a concern for the general welfare of society, and can best be expressed through Karl Marx's dictum, "From each according to his abilities, to each according to his needs." During the blitz in World War II, she withdrew to Oxford to live with a friend. Her final move occurred when she went to live in the home of her brother's widow in Saffron Walden not far from Cambridge. She died there in 1961.

SOURCES:
Rogers, W.G. *Ladies Bountiful.* NY: Harcourt, Brace & World, 1968.

Judith C. Reveal,
freelance writer,
Greensboro, Maryland

Weavers, The.

See Gilbert, Ronnie (b. 1926).

Webb, Beatrice (1858–1943)

Social researcher and reformer who became a member of the Fabian Society and, with her husband Sidney Webb, helped instigate many of the welfare and educational reforms adopted in Great Britain in the early part of the 20th century. Name variations: Bee or Bo Potter. Born Beatrice Potter on January 22, 1858, in Standish House, her family's home in Gloucestershire, England; died on April 30, 1943, of kidney disease at her home in Passfield Corner, England; daughter of Richard Potter (a wealthy businessman) and Lawrencina or Laurencina (Heyworth) Potter; educated by governesses, with one year spent at Stirling House, a finishing school in Bournemouth, England, at age 17; married Sidney James Webb, on July 23, 1892; no children.

Lived at various homes her family had in England; traveled to North America with her father and to Europe with various family members; enjoyed the social season in London; assumed the management of her father's houses upon her mother's death (1882); began charitable work (1882); decided to become a social investigator; studied the conditions of the dock workers, the "sweated trades," the co-operative movement, and the development of trade unions; became a socialist; devoted her life to social investigation, writing, and reform programs; established, with Sidney Webb, the London School of Economics and Political Science (1895); served on the Royal Commission on the Poor Law (1905–09) and later on various other governmental commissions; kept a diary throughout most of her life.

Selected writings: The Co-operative Movement in Great Britain *(1891); (Fabian tracts)* Women and the Factory Acts *(1896) and* The Abolition of the Poor Law *(1918);* Men's and Women's Wages: Should They be Equal? *(1919);* My Apprenticeship *(1926); (edited and published posthumously)* Our Partnership *(1948); many other works jointly authored with Sidney Webb.*

Victorian England expected upper-class women to conform to certain roles—wife, mother, household manager, society hostess—which required no extensive education or any great intellectual development. Women were assigned positions of subordination and generally were thought to be inferior intellectually to men. Although born into an upper-middle-class family, Beatrice Webb did not conform to her society's expectations, nor did she accept any pre-imposed limitations upon her intellectual development.

Beatrice Webb's parents came from wealthy backgrounds—from the classes risen to wealth during the heyday of industrialization. Her father's fortune came from the timber industry and from railroads; he served as the director of railroads in Great Britain and in Canada. Her maternal grandfather Lawrence Heyworth made his fortune in the textile industry. The Potters lived mostly at Standish House in Gloucestershire, where Beatrice Potter was born on January 22, 1858, but throughout her childhood the family moved frequently from one of their elegant houses to another, depending upon the season. Moving as they did was evidently unsettling to young Beatrice, as she confided to her diary that her childhood was a lonely, unhappy one. Given the fact that she was the eighth of nine daughters (a boy, who lived only four years, was born between Webb and her youngest sister), it seems strange that she would feel lonely. However, her mother, sorrowing over the loss of her only son, did not exhibit any affection for Beatrice and then lavished her attention upon the last daughter, **Rosalind Potter**, when she was born a few months after the son died. **Laurencina Potter**, herself considered something of an intellectual, actually judged Beatrice to be mentally inferior to her other children. Richard Potter's love for all his daughters compensated greatly for his wife's indifference. All the Potter girls received their education from governesses in a schoolroom provided at home, and the only time Webb was sent away to a "finishing" school was to Stirling House in Bournemouth, when she was 17. Although Beatrice had a very limited formal education, her father allowed his daughters to read and study whatever interested them, and Beatrice read the classics, history, economic theory, and philosophy. In addition, the Potter household frequently entertained prominent guests—scientists, clerics, entrepreneurs, government officials, philosophers, all friends of Richard Potter—and the young daughters conversed, discussed and even argued with some of the finest minds of the era. The philosopher Herbert Spencer, a longtime friend of the family, became one of Webb's intellectual mentors. From him and his writings, she learned the importance of the scientific method in making inquiries and coming to conclusions.

At age 18, Beatrice Potter made her debut into society and enjoyed the social scene for the next six years, until her mother's death in 1882 thrust upon her, as the older of the two unmarried daughters still at home, the management of her father's household. Not only did Potter rely upon Webb to handle his domestic concerns, but he also depended upon her assistance with his business affairs, which she managed so competently that he even considered making her officially a business associate.

Since these familial duties did not occupy all her time, in 1883 Webb began a short associa-

tion with the Charity Organization Society (COS) in London as a "visitor" to the slums in Soho. Voluntary work with such an organization was considered appropriate for unmarried women from the upper classes. The COS' role was to make sure that only the "deserving poor" received help. In November 1883, Beatrice, disguised as a "Miss Jones" from Wales, visited a town, Bacup in Lancashire, from which her maternal ancestors had come. She was impressed by the spirit of community she found there. In 1885, Webb became a manager and rent-collector for Katharine Buildings, a group of dwellings for the working class located near St. Katharine Dock in London. This experience provided her with insight into the ordinary lives of the working class. However, her activities were curtailed by her father's stroke in November 1885, since his care fell primarily upon her shoulders. Her older sisters soon realized that she needed relief from the constant attendance upon their father, and they arranged for her to have four months each year to carry on her own endeavors.

In early 1886, Webb began to interview dock workers in London as part of Charles Booth's research to determine the numbers and conditions of the poor in that city. Booth, a wealthy shipowner who was married to Beatrice's cousin, did not believe the accusations of the Social Democratic Federation, a Marxist group, that one-fourth of the city's population lived in poverty. (The results of his investigations proved that in reality one-third were at the poverty level.) In talking with the dock workers, Webb perfected her interviewing techniques, which she had begun to develop at Katharine Buildings. She also became more concerned about the causes of poverty.

When she began her charity work and her social investigations, Webb was still very much influenced by Herbert Spencer, whose philosophy stressed individualism and laissez-faire. After witnessing the lives of the poor, Beatrice came to see this system of thought as self-centered and rapacious. She began to search for a replacement, for a "creed" in which she could believe. She had, while a teenager, begun to doubt Christianity, although throughout her life she had a mystical longing and found solace and comfort in visiting churches and in praying. During these years, Webb also sought a "craft" which she could pursue as her life's work.

The importance of having a craft seemed vital to Beatrice, since she had come to the conclusion that she would not marry. Beautiful and intelligent, Webb had had suitors, but she did not

Beatrice Webb

reciprocate their feelings. The one great romantic attraction she did develop, at age 25, was for Joseph Chamberlain, then age 47. Chamberlain, a member of Parliament, had been a popular mayor of Birmingham and would later serve as colonial secretary. He had been widowed twice and was seeking a new mate. From 1883 to 1887, the two visited and corresponded with each other. However, as Beatrice related in her diary, she came to realize that his domineering personality would stifle her intellectual growth. After 1887, she put aside any consideration of marrying him and dedicated herself to the craft she had decided suited her best—that of a social investigator.

During these years, Webb had also investigated the "sweated" industry (clothing manufacturing), working briefly, and ineptly, at making trousers. By 1888, she had gained some renown for her research-related articles, which appeared in a few newspapers and journals. Based on that recognition, she was called to testify before a House of Lords committee investigating the "sweated" industries. Her research methods, attention to details, and presentation of her findings were gaining recognition. She felt confident in her work.

Beatrice then decided to study the co-operative movement in Great Britain, which led to the publication of *The History of Co-operation in Great Britain* in 1891. Her studies of the working class, her research of the co-operative movement, her interviews of dock workers during their strikes, her interest in trade unionism—all had convinced her that the prevailing laissez-faire capitalism was based upon individual greed and that community-oriented consciences had to be developed. The underlying causes of poverty had to be eliminated. Her search for a creed gradually led her to socialism and to Sidney James Webb.

In 1890, while collecting data for her book on co-operatives, Beatrice sought advice from Sidney Webb, a member of the socialist group the Fabian Society. From their first meeting, it seems, Sidney fell in love with Beatrice, and over the next two years tried to convince her to marry him. She was not romantically attracted to him, but she recognized his intellectual ability and literary talent. Finally, after the death of her father in January 1892, the two were married the following July 23. Many of her friends warned she had made an unwise choice, because the homely Sidney did not have the wealth nor social standing the Potters enjoyed. Nevertheless, Beatrice realized that she needed companionship and that marriage to Sidney would allow her to continue her social research. Soon she came to love her husband as much as he loved her, and the marriage turned into a partnership, or "the firm of Webb," as Beatrice referred to their union, which produced a prodigious amount of research, books, articles, reports, and speeches dealing with trade unions, local government, the poor laws, prisons, and many other topics. Biographers of each of the Webbs have stated that it is almost impossible to separate their work and assign specific credit to one or the other.

Two years after their marriage, the Webbs published their widely acclaimed *History of Trade Unionism*. Planned initially by Beatrice and based upon voluminous research and travel, this work proved how well their minds complemented each other. Another early and important result of the partnership was the founding of the London School of Economics and Political Science. Using a legacy left by a deceased Fabian member, the Webbs initiated the school in 1895. Beatrice not only helped conceive the plans for the school, but she also raised most of the additional revenue needed for its establishment. Sidney, by then a member of the London County Council and chair of its Technical Education Board, was also successful by 1898 in changing the University of London into a teaching institution instead of an examining and degree-granting body. The London School of Economics soon became one of the colleges of the University of London.

Whereas Sidney was generally in the public's view because of his elections to the London County Council, Beatrice was content to engage in the tedious research for their many subsequent volumes, especially for those on local government and on the poor laws. However, from 1905 to 1909, she, too, shared the public limelight. Appointed to the Royal Commission on the Poor Law in December 1905, Beatrice welcomed this opportunity for public service, especially as she believed the current Poor Law, which had undergone no major changes since 1834, was drastically in need of revision. Belief in Social Darwinism prevailed among the ruling classes in Britain at that time, and many people believed that the poor themselves were to blame for their conditions. Beatrice disagreed: unemployment and other situations beyond their control accounted for the vast number of poor people. She firmly believed that the government had a responsibility to provide what she called a "national minimum" of living standards—in employment, in education, in health benefits—for all citizens. Soon after the 20 commissioners assembled, Beatrice realized that the evidence to be presented by key witnesses and the data to be accumulated were controlled by the majority of members, who favored retaining the old principles behind the Poor Law. She did her best to present materials from her own research, to direct the Commission to the conclusion that it was better and, in the long run, cheaper to prevent unemployment and disease than to deal with them after the fact. Her diary entry of July 17, 1906, expresses this:

> In listening to the evidence brought by the C.O.S. members in favour of restricting medical relief to the technically destitute, it suddenly flashed across my mind that what

we had to do was to adopt the exactly contrary attitude, and make medical inspection and medical treatment compulsory on all sick persons—to treat illness, in fact, as a public nuisance to be suppressed in the interests of the community.

Although Beatrice badgered the majority of commissioners to change their views, she was unsuccessful. Thereupon, in 1909, she decided to submit a Minority Report expressing her conclusions. Sidney, the better of the two at writing, quickly drafted the document, and three other commissioners joined Beatrice in signing and presenting it. This report, the basis for welfare measures adopted in the future, gained for Beatrice an honorary doctorate in 1909 from the University of Manchester. (Later the University of Edinburgh and the University of Munich also conferred honorary degrees upon her.)

To gain support for the Minority Report, the Webbs formed the National Committee for the Prevention of Destitution in 1909. However, their attempts to convince leading Liberals and Conservatives to accept the report failed. Instead, the National Insurance Act, passed in 1911, effectively ended the hopes for Beatrice's remedies. The Insurance Act provided relief for the unemployed and the aged, and medical care for the destitute, but it did not address underlying causes of poverty.

After the grueling and unsuccessful campaign on behalf of the Minority Report, the Webbs went abroad on a world tour from 1911 to 1912. Beatrice, whose health was always frail, was exhausted by her intense work on the Commission. In 1898, they had previously traveled in Canada, the United States, New Zealand, and Australia. This trip took them to the Far East—to Japan, China, India. (Beatrice's inheritance provided the bulk of their livelihood and allowed for such travels, which were basically the only luxury they allowed themselves. However, she firmly believed that those with uncarned income had an obligation to serve the community.) Her diary entries during her journeys reveal a disquieting amount of elitism and chauvinism toward other cultures, which seems out of character for one so concerned about the poor of her own country.

Upon their return in 1913, the Webbs founded a weekly journal, *The New Statesman*. The controversy generated by the Minority Report made them realize that their socialistic programs needed wider publicity. Too many in Britain still feared socialism as a revolutionary movement. The Webbs, as members of the Fabian Society, believed not in violent upheaval, but, as they phrased it, "in the inevitability of gradu-

alness," i.e., in a gradual evolution toward a socialistic society. The new journal, although independent, was intended to explain evolutionary socialism more thoroughly to the general public.

During World War I, both Webbs served on governmental committees. In 1916, Beatrice was appointed to the Statutory Pensions Committee, and in 1917 she served on a few subcommittees of the Reconstruction Committee. In the summer of 1918, she was on the War Cabinet Committee on Women in Industry, which studied the amount of wages paid to women doing jobs formerly held exclusively by men. This committee reported that promises of pay equity had not been fulfilled, but the war ended shortly thereafter, and nothing was done about the report.

> The die was cast, the craft was chosen. Through the pressure of circumstances and the inspiration of the time-spirit, I had decided to become an investigator of social institutions.
>
> —Beatrice Webb

In 1918, women over the age of 30 received the right to vote in Great Britain. Beatrice had originally opposed woman suffrage on the grounds that women had no obligation in the political arena. However, gradually she came to realize that the government was increasingly involved in the private lives and welfare of the people and that women needed the vote to help direct public policy. The year 1918 was also an important milestone in the reformation of the Labour Party. A new constitution, written by Sidney, allowed for individual party membership rather than group affiliation, and the party's policy was definitely socialistic. Previously the Webbs had not wholeheartedly supported the Labour Party, for they had directed their efforts at permeation of their socialist goals into the two major parties. Failing at that, they realized the need to work through the Labour Party. In 1921, Beatrice formed the Half-Circle Club in the Labour Party to educate women about party policies and to familiarize them with political procedures so they could become informed voters. She chose the name for the club because it admitted only women. When Sidney was elected to the House of Commons as a Labour candidate in 1922, Beatrice also worked with the women of his constituency, Seaham, meeting with them occasionally, and regularly sending them newsletters about issues before Parliament.

In early 1924, the Labour Party formed the government for the first time, and Sidney became a Cabinet member, heading the Board of Trade. The Webbs had recently purchased a country house, Passfield Corner, and Beatrice, for reasons of health, began to spend more time there away from London, which had been their residence since their marriage. Although she realized Sidney had responsibilities to his office and his constituents which kept him in London, she resented the time they were apart. The first Labour government lasted less than a year, but Sidney was returned to Commons from Seaham until 1929, when he did not seek reelection.

During these years, while continuing her research and writing, Webb decided to publish her autobiography. Based on her diary and published in 1926, the volume covered her life to 1892. She titled it *My Apprenticeship*, since those were the years when she acquired the interests and skills for her life's work, the years which prepared her for the partnership with Sidney. Reviewers of *My Apprenticeship* praised Webb's candid evaluation of her life and the fact that she never sought to retaliate against her and Sidney's detractors. In the late 1930s, Beatrice began a second volume of her autobiography and worked on it until shortly before her death. Also based on her diary entries and entitled *Our Partnership*, the book was edited by her friend *Margaret Cole and her niece Barbara Drake and published in 1948.

In June 1929, the Labour Party, forming the government for the second time, wanted Sidney to serve in the Cabinet again. Since he had not sought reelection to Commons in 1929, he was given a peerage and a seat in the House of Lords as Lord Passfield so he could become colonial secretary. He held this post until Labour lost its majority in 1931. Beatrice, however, refused to be recognized as Lady Passfield and tried to avoid ceremonies at which protocol demanded that she be addressed by that title. In 1931, Beatrice was made a Fellow in the prestigious British Academy, the lone woman member.

When the Labour Party's second government failed to solve the economic depression of the early 1930s, Beatrice became very depressed about ever achieving their ideal socialistic society. It was then that the Communist experiment underway in the Union of Soviet Socialist Republics (USSR) began to attract the Webbs' attention. They traveled to Russia in 1932 and were eagerly welcomed and escorted around the country. They returned to England believing they had witnessed the utopia of their dreams, discounting the fact that they had been shown only what the Soviet leaders wanted them to see.

They could not believe the reports of police-state tactics they heard from others. They saw the Communist Party officials as dedicated, selfless public servants working for the good of all the Soviet people. In 1935, the Webbs published *Soviet Communism: A New Civilization?*, praising the Soviet system. (They omitted the question mark in the second edition.) Their detractors have subsequently used this to condemn them as undemocratic. However, others have preferred to assess their enchantment with the USSR as the last hope of two aging socialists to see their dreams accomplished. Their earlier works, especially *A Constitution for the Socialist Commonwealth of Great Britain*, published in 1920, clearly indicate that they believed in democracy and envisioned a government which represented all segments of society.

Beatrice, whose health had been failing for some time, died of kidney disease at Passfield Corner on April 30, 1943, at age 85. Her body was cremated, and her ashes were buried on their property. However, at Sidney's death in 1947, her ashes, along with his, were placed in Westminster Abbey—the only married couple to be interred there.

Although Beatrice did not live to see most of their plans for reform implemented, the Webbs' research and writing prepared the way for many of the welfare programs adopted by the Labour Party when it formed the government after World War II. Beatrice, true to her creed and her craft, had dedicated herself to social research, which she hoped would lead to improvement in the lives of all citizens.

SOURCES:

Cole, Margaret I. *Beatrice Webb*. London: Longmans, Green, 1945.

Muggeridge, Kitty, and Ruth Adam. *Beatrice Webb: A Life, 1858–1943*. London: Secker & Warburg, 1967.

Radice, Lisanne. *Beatrice and Sidney Webb: Fabian Socialists*. NY: St. Martin's Press, 1984.

Webb, Beatrice. *My Apprenticeship*. London: Longmans, Green, 1926.

———. *Our Partnership*. Ed. by Barbara Drake and Margaret I. Cole. London: Longmans, Green, 1948.

SUGGESTED READING:

Caine, Barbara. *Destined to be Wives: The Sisters of Beatrice Webb*. London: Oxford University Press, 1987 (explores the lives of Beatrice and her eight sisters).

MacKenzie, Norman, and Jeanne MacKenzie. *The Fabians*. NY: Simon and Schuster, 1977.

Seymour-Jones, Carole. *Beatrice Webb: A Life*. Ivan R. Dee, 1992.

COLLECTIONS:

Beatrice Webb's diary, correspondence, and related materials are deposited in the British Library of Political and Economic Science, along with those of Sidney's, as the Passfield Papers.

Patricia A. Ashman,
Professor of History, Central Missouri
State University, Warrensburg, Missouri

Webb, Catherine (1859–1947)

English cooperative leader. Born in 1859; died in 1947.

Catherine Webb became a force in the women's cooperative movement in England towards the end of the 19th century, through her establishment of the Battersea branch of the Women's Cooperative Guild in London in 1886. Her book *Woman with a Basket* (1927) detailed the history of the guild, and she also contributed to its visibility through lectures. She inherited her interest in the cooperative movement from her coppersmith father who was also director of the Cooperative Wholesale Society. Webb's progressive outlook could be traced to her mother whose wide-ranging interests included astronomy and polar exploration, which was then a matter of considerable public fascination.

In addition to her efforts on behalf of the Battersea guild, Webb became a member of the Cooperative Union's Central Board and contributed to a better understanding of the cooperative movement in general with her editing of what became its standard text, *Industrial Co-operation*, in 1904. Her later years brought an increasing interest in adult education, and she served as governor of Morley College in south London prior to her death in 1947.

Judith C. Reveal,
freelance writer,
Greensboro, Maryland

Webb, Electra Havemeyer

(1888–1960)

Collector of American folk art whose founding of the Shelburne Museum contributed to the popularization of "Americana" as fine art. Born on August 16, 1888, in Babylon, Long Island, New York; died on November 19, 1960; daughter of Henry O. Havemeyer (a sugar refiner) and Louisine (Waldron) Elder Havemeyer (1855–1929, an art collector); attended Miss Spence's School in New York City; married J(ames) Watson Webb, in 1910; children: five.

Born on Long Island, New York, in 1888, Electra Havemeyer Webb enjoyed a privileged upbringing as the daughter of Henry O. Havemeyer, the president and a founder of the American Sugar Refining Company, and ❧▶ **Louisine Have-**meyer, a well-known art collector. The Havemeyers made sure that their daughter acquired the skills expected of young society women, supplementing her education at Miss Spence's School in New York City with a private study of fine art. Electra began collecting American folk art at the age of 18 when she purchased a cigar-store Indian. Her fascination with "Americana" baffled her parents and many others, who considered such items outside the realm of art. At the time of Louisine's death in 1929, Electra inherited her mother's collection of Chinese bronzes and Tanagra figurines and such grand masters as Degas, Corot, and Manet. Although she had developed a keen appreciation for this art, she was happiest collecting the works of anonymous artisans. She treasured everyday objects that were simple and unpretentious, anticipating a trend that would take another 20 years to develop.

Electra's marriage in 1910 to J. Watson Webb, the great-grandson of *Sophia Johnson Vanderbilt and railroad tycoon Cornelius Vanderbilt I, brought her into extraordinary wealth. J. Watson Webb built on the family money by founding the Webb and Lynch insurance company in 1933. Among the many properties owned by the Webbs was a magnificent estate in Shelburne, Vermont, which boasted the largest hackney breeding stud farm and the first private golf course in the country. The Webbs and their five children lived in a 110-room house, while the horses resided in a barn as big as Madison Square Garden.

After her marriage, Electra Webb continued to pursue her collections, and the idea of creating a museum occurred to her shortly after her mother's death. Her early collections of dolls grew to include those made of Bisque, china, papier mâché, wax, wood shells, rubber, rawhide, rag, and celluloid. Unable to resist such collectibles, she expanded her collection to include their accouterments such as clothing, houses and carriages. Her keen enthusiasm for collecting in quantity soon progressed into other categories, until she eventually acquired more than 125,000 objects, among them quilts, rugs, furniture, pewter, glass, ceramics, toys, carriages, sleighs, tools, folk art, clothes, and decoys. After her husband saved a small, brick Vermont-type house on his father's property from being destroyed, it became the nucleus of their summer home in Vermont and was expanded to include numerous wings to accommodate her collections. In 1947 she began to establish an outdoor museum at this house on Shelburne Farms.

By this time both of her in-laws had died, and the family gathered to determine what to do

Havemeyer, Louisine. See Cassatt, Mary for sidebar.
❧

with the grand collections of carriages. The Webbs secured eight acres of land on Route 7, south of the village of Shelburne, and constructed an appropriate building for a public display. By the time of its completion, Webb had collected additional carriages as well as fire equipment, wagons, sleighs, and coaches. She also began acquiring architecture, including a red-brick schoolhouse from 1830, a small barn, and the Stagecoach Inn, built in 1783. When she learned of the planned destruction of a double-lane covered bridge in Vermont, she purchased the structure, had it disassembled and moved it to the museum grounds where she created a large lily pond to accommodate it. She also acquired a lighthouse, a stone jail, a wooden meeting house, and stores, in addition to boats and trains.

Webb, who had accompanied her own father duck shooting and on trips to the West when she was young, loved the outdoors and especially enjoyed hunting for game animals. Between 1931 and 1941, the Webbs had traveled to Alaska and the Canadian Northwest seven times, with Electra usually the only woman in the party. It was during these trips that she began collecting specimens of large and small game, and many of her trophies continue to hold official records for size and quality. Although Webb could have settled into a luxurious routine of international travel and hunting excursions with her husband, she was active throughout both world wars. She drove an ambulance during World War I, and was rewarded for her efforts with a promotion to assistant director of the Motor Corps of the Red Cross. She became more involved with blood-drive recruitment during World War II as assistant director of the Red Cross' Blood Bank and was the first Vermont donor to give 16 pints of blood during the course of the war.

The Shelburne Museum, opened to the public in 1952, is neither a reconstruction nor a restoration but a collection of everything Americana. By 1953, Webb had saved the S.S. *Ticonderoga*, a steamboat 220' long and three decks high. Although it had been used for several years as a tourist attraction in Burlington, Vermont, the costs associated with it made it impossible to maintain, so Webb made the inevitable decision to move the *Ticonderoga* to the museum. The Shelburne Museum, which occupies more than 40 acres of land and comprises nearly as many buildings, preserves an extraordinary record of America's heritage. In 1956, in recognition of the discernment and affection with which the collections were assembled and displayed, Webb received an honorary degree of Master of Arts from Yale University, one of only five women ever so honored at that time. She died in 1960.

SOURCES:

Garraty, John A., and Mark C. Carnes, eds. *American National Biography*. NY: Oxford University Press, 1999.

*Saarinen, Aline B. *The Proud Possessors*. NY: Random House, 1958, pp. 287–306.

Judith C. Reveal,
freelance writer,
Greensboro, Maryland

Electra Havemeyer Webb

Webb, Jane (1807–1858).

See Loudon, Jane Webb.

Webb, Mary (1881–1927)

English novelist and poet whose work became widely celebrated only after her early death. Born Gladys Mary Meredith on March 25, 1881, in Leighton, Shropshire, England; died in St. Leonards, Sussex, on October 8, 1927; daughter of George Edward Meredith (a schoolmaster) and Sarah Alice (Scott) Meredith;

educated at home and at a boarding school in Southport, Lancashire, 1893–95; married Henry Bertram Law Webb, in 1912; no children.

At age one, moved with parents to The Grange, a small country house near Much Wenlock, Shropshire; between 12 and 21, lived at Stanton-on-Hine Heath, six miles from Shrewsbury, followed by ten years in Meole Brace, one mile from Shrewsbury; after marriage, lived for two years in Weston-super-Mare, Somerset, before returning to Shropshire, to live in Pontesbury, where she was a market gardener, and Lyth Hill; in the last few years of her life, divided her time between Hampstead, London, and Shropshire; her writing career developed from about 1916 and continued until her death.

Selected writings: The Golden Arrow *(Constable, 1916);* The Spring of Joy *(J.M. Dent, 1917);* Gone to Earth *(Constable, 1917);* The House in Dormer Forest *(Hutchinson, 1920);* Seven for a Secret *(Hutchinson, 1922);* Precious Bane *(Cape, 1924). Her collected works were published in 1928, by Cape in London and Dutton in New York, and included the unfinished* Armour Wherein He Trusted.

On January 14, 1927, Stanley Baldwin, the British prime minister, wrote from his official residence at 10 Downing Street to Mary Webb:

> I hope you will not think it an impertinence on my part if I tell you with what delight I have read *Precious Bane*. My people lived in Shropshire for centuries before they migrated to Worcestershire, and I spent my earliest years in Bewdley, which is on the border. In your book I seem to hear again the speech and turns of phrase which surrounded me in the nursery. I think it is really a first-class piece of work and I have not enjoyed a book so much for years. It was given to me by one of my secretaries and I read it at Christmas within sight of the Clee Hills, at home. Thank you a thousand times for it.

This spontaneous praise—the two had never met or exchanged correspondence—would have delighted any author, particularly one as little read and uncelebrated as Mary Webb. Yet, although Baldwin's acclaim was to bring her name before a wide public, it came too late for her to benefit personally. Still only in her mid-40s, Mary Webb was mortally ill, and within nine months would be laid to rest in the earth of her native Shropshire.

The county of Shropshire lies in the west of England and runs along the border with Wales. Those parts of it known as the borderlands are mostly rural, with some deep, wooded valleys and craggy hills that impart a unique atmosphere. A hundred or so years ago, both local

customs and a distinctive dialect survived in forms little changed in centuries. In her early years, Mary Webb absorbed the characteristics of the place and people and immortalized them in her novels, essays and poems. Her father George Meredith was a man of education, a graduate of Cambridge University who tutored young men preparing for civil service and similar examinations. He had, however, deep roots in the area; both his father and grandfather had been vicar of Leighton Parish Church (where Mary was christened), and he delighted in roaming about the countryside and collecting the anecdotes and proverbs of the local people. Her mother **Sarah Scott Meredith** was the daughter of an Edinburgh doctor who claimed to be of the clan of Sir Walter Scott, the author of *Rob Roy, Ivanhoe*, and many other novels. For seven years, Mary was the Merediths' only child, and then between 1888 and 1894 three brothers and two sisters were born. In keeping with the common attitude towards girls, George Meredith seems not to have educated his daughter very systematically. He taught her to read and write, and at age 12 she went, for two lonely years, to a school of modest educational standards in Southport. Fortunately, she was a quick learner who devoured books avidly. A novel that had a particular influence in stimulating her sense of social justice was *Uncle Tom's Cabin* by *Harriet Beecher Stowe. Her father did, however, kindle her imagination during their walks together about the countryside, and many of his stories were retold when she began to write.

Although not wealthy, the large Meredith family lived comfortably, in a manner similar to that of the local gentry. To accommodate his pupils, George Meredith rented a large house, and was able to keep servants and ride to hounds. Mary's only serious difference with her father was over the question of hunting, which she regarded as cruel and unnecessary. In her teens, as part of her system of personal morality, she decided to become a vegetarian. By this time she had been brought home from the school in Southport after her mother suffered a riding accident. Sarah Meredith, probably due to a psychiatric disorder, then withdrew to her bedroom where she remained for the greater part of five years. Mary helped to take charge of the household and, later aided by a governess, the upbringing of her brothers and sisters. As befitted the Merediths' social standing, Mary was expected to undertake charitable work among less fortunate neighbors, such as visiting the sick and reading the Bible to a blind man. On these occasions, she absorbed more of the local speech and was able to make a close study of the type of village characters who were later represented in her fiction.

When Webb was about 20, her mother resumed her place in the household. Very soon after, Mary's health began to fail. She became depressed and withdrawn, to such an extent that a psychosomatic illness has been suggested as the cause. However, her symptoms may have been due to the onset of a thyroid condition known as Graves' disease or thyrotoxicosis. This illness, which medical science was not then able to cure, led to intense headaches, giddiness, delusions and irrational actions in those who suffered from it. The patient's neck became swollen and the eyes appeared to bulge in their sockets. Although Mary had periods of respite, so sensitive was she about her appearance that she became reclusive. Her illness led her to behave eccentrically at times, and she always dressed in high-necked clothes in an attempt to conceal her distended throat. As an outlet for her emotions, and with the encouragement of the family's governess, she began to write sketches and poems, though seldom allowing even family members to read them. On her better days, she continued to ramble about the countryside and visit the local cottagers. She remained, too, a voracious reader, of poetry, Shakespeare, natural history and folklore. Several modern writers—Thomas Hardy, Rudyard Kipling, and Richard Jeffries among them—also gave her pleasure.

Those who knew Mary began to regard her with sympathy, as a gentle and kindly person who seemed doomed to the short, unfulfilled life of the invalid. There was much surprise, therefore, when her engagement was announced to the son of a local doctor. On July 12, 1912, she married Henry Webb, a Cambridge graduate and a schoolmaster (like her father, who had died in 1909), and six years younger than Mary. Her intelligence and loving disposition, it seems, mattered more to him than her handicaps. Instead of her sisters, she arranged for her bridesmaid to be the three-year-old daughter of the gardener and invited as her guests all the old people from the local almshouse at which she had been a regular visitor. In the early years of the marriage, Henry Webb indulged his wife's unusual fancies. He resigned from his post at a school in Somerset so that they could move back to Shropshire and for a time made a precarious living from market gardening. The Webbs would carry their flowers and fruit to Shrewsbury market, where Mary enjoyed the conversation of customers and other stallholders.

With Henry's encouragement, Mary began to offer her writings to magazines and was able to get accepted a few nature studies, sketches of the pleasure to be found among the plants and sounds of the countryside. In the spring of 1915, during three weeks of intense creativity, she wrote a lengthy novel, *The Golden Arrow*. Critics agree that the character of John Arden was based on George Meredith and that Deborah, his daughter, was Mary Webb's representation of herself. A melodrama of Shropshire village life, taking its title from a local legend concerning a search for a golden arrow, it was published in 1916, when some reviewers compared it to the work of Thomas Hardy. It enjoyed sufficient success for another publisher to bring out a collection of her nature studies in 1917. Relatively little income came from Mary Webb's writings, and much of what she did receive was spontaneously given to those who seemed in need. Childless herself, she had a deep fondness for children and made a point of giving presents at Christmas and on birthdays to those in the village.

By the beginning of 1917, she had completed her second novel, *Gone to Earth*, the tragic story of Hazel Woodus, a wild, shy girl, the daughter of a Welsh Gypsy (Rom) and a half-mad beekeeper. Torn between two men, Hazel dies, along with her unborn child, in a vain attempt to save her pet fox from the hunt. Written at the height of the Great War, the novel has been seen as an allegory. It is true that, even in a remote part of the country, Mary Webb was deeply aware of the war. Although her husband, who had poor eyesight, was exempt from military service, her three brothers were in the army. In *Gone to Earth* there is a conflict between good and evil which symbolizes the war as Mary Webb saw it, but much of its appeal was in the strength and intensely poetic nature of the prose. Few made a direct link between the huntsmen—described as "fiery-faced and fiery-coated, with eyes frenzied by excitement, and open, cavernous mouths, they were like devils emerging from hell"—and the ferocities of the war. Indeed, the novelist John Buchan, in his introduction to a later edition of the book, wrote that "in the dark days of 1917" he read *Gone to Earth* as a relief from the world at the time. As well as human frailties, the beauty of nature was constantly present in Mary Webb's work. It was in this respect that Buchan made a point, shared by others who have studied her novels, that she "is curiously insensitive to the cruelties of nature"; to her, evil arises from man and his works, while nature is a benign and pure force. Although she regarded herself as a member of the Church of England, there was a mystical, pantheistic element in her beliefs.

Henry Webb, never a successful or fulfilled market gardener, was able to obtain after a few years another teaching post, in Shrewsbury. The Webbs moved from their smallholding at Pontesbury to temporary accommodation, until a small bungalow was built for them on Lyth Hill. Their new home, with its extensive views of unspoiled countryside, brought Mary an interlude of greater happiness. Her illness was less debilitating, while the modest success of her books brought her better financial terms for a new novel, *The House in Dormer Forest*. This attracted an American publisher, George H. Doran, who also undertook to pay for her next book. Though it was not large, she did have a circle of discriminating readers, along with the approval of those critics who warmed to her vivid prose and a treatment of natural beauty that contrasted with the imperfections of humankind. Just as, in *Gone to Earth*, it is the fate of Hazel Woodus to die, in *The House in Dormer Forest*, the symbolic ending is the burning down of Dormer Old House and the death of the character who started the fire.

By the time her fourth novel, *Seven for a Secret*, appeared in 1922, the Webbs had set up home in Hampstead, north London. In late 1920, Mary's health had worsened, in part due, her doctor suggested, to the solitary nature of a life which led her to brood about herself and her symptoms. There is some evidence too that Henry Webb was finding it too great a strain to adjust to his wife's style of life. She was indifferent to housekeeping and, as her illness became more acute, reproached him with her jealous suspicions. (Possibly not all these were unfounded: two years after her death, Henry Webb married **Kathleen Wilson**, who had been one of his students.) London, it seemed, would provide both with a greater social life, especially as Mary had a number of literary contacts made through her novels and short stories. For a time, she did move in circles frequented by other writers, though she also retreated regularly to the cottage on Lyth Hill. *Seven for a Secret* has been compared to *Emily Brontë*'s *Wuthering Heights* for the sense of profound emotion that pervades it, though most would find the over-melodramatic plot inferior in concept and execution. The theme is one common to all Mary Webb's novels, the conflict between a love that is sacred and one that is profane. The main female character, Gillian Lovekin, is infatuated by Ralph Elmer, an inn landlord who symbolizes profane love, and allows herself to be seduced by him. She then learns that he is married to Rwth, a dumb Gypsy, used by him as a drudge. Once Elmer is

unmasked, Gillian marries a poetical shepherd, Robert Rideout. Mary Webb dedicated the book to Thomas Hardy.

Seven for a Secret has been criticized for an over-reliance on coincidence in the plot, a tendency to use stock characters of a type that appeared in her earlier novels, and a labored prose style. It is notable, therefore, that in her next book, *Precious Bane*, Mary Webb recovered her artistic power to the extent of producing what is usually regarded as her finest piece of work. This success in part arises from the technical skill involved in writing a novel in the first person. It is an approach that requires the character who tells the story not only to be plausibly present in every scene (or have reason to be informed about what has occurred) but also to convey the thoughts and motivations of all the other characters. In *Precious Bane*, the narrator is Prudence Sarn, the daughter of a Shropshire farmer in the early 19th century. Some reviewers did doubt that a girl of these origins would have the command of language that the narrative shows,

Mary Webb

but admirers of the novel have been unaffected by such a criticism. Moreover, the way in which dialect words, popular beliefs and historical details are deployed makes the narrator's account seem plausible. A theme of the story is the evil that results from the love of money (as hinted in the title which is taken from a line in Milton's *Paradise Lost*: "Let none admire/ That riches grow in Hell; that soyle may best/ Deserve the precious bane"). Gideon Sarn sacrifices his life through greed, but his sister Prudence is finally rewarded for her unselfish love when she becomes the wife of the good weaver Kester Woodseaves. Prudence has been mistreated because of her harelip, which the superstitious peasants regard as a sign of evil, and this has been interpreted as a fictional representation by Mary Webb of her swollen neck.

Much of the noble work of Mary Webb might be called the prose poems of a Shropshire Lass.

—G.K. Chesterton

Other characters too have been identified as having their origins in their creator's own life, the minor figures drawn from Mary's village acquaintances and the more virtuous main ones from her family circle. The wicked, however, have been criticized as rather stock figures, melodramatically based on the villains of popular fiction. Moreover, even those who praised her gift for description found her characters insufficiently convincing. **Grace Chapman**, for example, in reviewing the collected works of Mary Webb in 1931, noted "an exquisite feeling for Nature in all its manifestations" but went on to write: "The good remain irritatingly righteous, the bad monotonously wicked; while the comic are at all costs facetious, and the faithful persevere in unswerving devotion." The satirical pen of *Stella Gibbons in her novel *Cold Comfort Farm* (1932) was another response to Mary Webb's rural types. Gibbons had in mind several writers on rustic themes, including *Sheila Kaye-Smith, but Mary Webb was the principal target of her parody.

Precious Bane brought new admirers, and it remains, despite adverse criticism, the best regarded of her novels. In 1925, it was awarded a literary prize, the Femina Vie Heureuse, though the citation that accompanied it—the award was for an imaginative work by an author who had not gained sufficient recognition—served to emphasize Mary Webb's lack of literary standing. Some fellow authors sought to enhance her reputation; *Rebecca West, for example, had been among the first to praise *Gone to Earth*. Another admirer, the publisher Hamish Hamilton, passed a copy of *Precious Bane* to a civil servant who worked with the prime minister. As a result, Baldwin in January 1927 sent the aforementioned letter. But although Mary replied to it gratefully, she did not seek from him any public endorsement. In the last months of her life, she wrote short stories and reviews and, rather fitfully, worked on a historical romance, *Armour Wherein He Trusted*, the manuscript of which she almost destroyed in a mood of despair. As well as Graves' disease, which was gradually destroying her system, Mary Webb was suffering from pernicious anaemia, also beyond the power of doctors to cure. It was agreed that a visit to Miss Lory, her old governess, at St. Leonards on the Sussex coast, might be of benefit, but on her arrival she had to be taken to a nursing home. A few days later, on October 8, 1927, Mary Webb died. Her body was returned for burial to Shrewsbury in Shropshire.

Her death was little noticed. On April 25, 1928, Stanley Baldwin spoke at the annual dinner of the Royal Literary Fund, referred to Mary Webb as a novelist of genius and expressed surprise at her neglect. The report of his speech led to a level of interest in her books that had not existed before. The publishing firm of Jonathan Cape quickly organized a collected edition of seven volumes, each prefaced by a well-known literary figure, except for *Precious Bane* which was introduced by Baldwin. In the 1930s, her books sold well; Cape issued them in cheaper editions and some were translated into various European languages. Quiet Shropshire villages were invaded by tourists, intent on discovering what one guidebook termed "the haunts of Mary Webb." In 1950, *Jennifer Jones starred as Hazel Woodus in a film version of *Gone to Earth* (released in the United States as *The Wild Heart*). Since then, Mary Webb's books have been regularly reprinted, and collections of her poems have been issued. Some critics have suggested that she is a greater poet than novelist, and others that her romances reveal a feminist perspective. Academic opinion, however, remains more doubtful about the claims made on behalf of her work. Although she has received scholarly attention, it has been on a minor scale, and, as in her lifetime, those who find genius in the work of Mary Webb fail to persuade the majority.

SOURCES:

Barale, Michèle Aina. *Daughters and Lovers: The Life and Writings of Mary Webb*. Middletown: CT: Wesleyan University Press, 1986.

Chapman, Grace. "Mary Webb," in *London Mercury*. Vol. 23, no. 136. February 1931, pp. 364–369.

Coles, Gladys Mary. *The Flower of Light: A Biography of Mary Webb*. London: Duckworth, 1978.

McNeil, W.K. "The Function of Legend, Belief and Custom in *Precious Bane*," in *Folklore*. Vol. 82, no. 2. Summer 1971, pp. 132–146.

Moult, Thomas. *Mary Webb: Her Life and Work*. London: Cape, 1932.

Pitfield, Robert Lucas. "The Shropshire Lass and her Goitre: Some Account of Mary Meredith Webb and her Works," in *Annals of Medical Science*. Vol. 4, no. 4. July 1942, pp. 284–293.

Wrenn, Dorothy P.H. *Goodbye to Morning: A Biographical Study of Mary Webb*. Shrewsbury: Wilding & Son, 1964.

SUGGESTED READING:

Cavaliero, Glen. *The Rural Tradition in the English Novel 1900–1939*. London: Macmillan, 1977.

Cockburn, Claud. *Bestseller: The Books that Everyone Read 1900–1939*. London: Sidgwick & Jackson, 1972.

RELATED MEDIA:

The Wild Heart (82 min. film), starring Jennifer Jones, Emeric Pressburger, Cyril Cusack and *Sybil Thorndike, released in 1950.

D.E. Martin,
Lecturer in History,
University of Sheffield, Sheffield, England

Webb, Stella (1902–1989).

See Gibbons, Stella.

Weber, Aloysia (c. 1761–1839).

See Lange, Aloysia.

Weber, Constanze (1762–1842).

See Mozart, Constanze.

Weber, Helene (1881–1962)

Pioneering German social worker who was also a leading political figure in Germany's Catholic Center Party during the 1920s and in its successor, the Christian Democratic Party, after World War II. Pronunciation: Hell-EEN VEHB-err. Born on March 17, 1881, in Elberfeld, Germany; died in a hospital in Bonn, Germany, on July 25, 1962; second of six children of Wilhelm Weber (a schoolteacher) and Agnes Christiane (van Gent) Weber; attended grade school and women's school in Elberfeld; had teacher-education training in Aachen and Elberfeld; studied history, French, philosophy, and sociology at universities in Bonn, Germany, and Grenoble, France.

Passed the qualifying examination to become a schoolteacher (1900); taught at schools in Aachen and Elberfeld (1900–05); studied at the universities of Bonn and Grenoble (1905–10); taught at women's secondary schools in Bochum (1909); became principal of the Kaiserina Augusta School in Cologne (1911); assumed the leadership of the new social welfare school of the German Catholic Women's Federation (1916); became editor of the Federation journal (1917); was elected to the constitution-writing convention for the Weimar Republic (1919); was appointed to ministerial rank in the Prussian Ministry for Social Welfare (1919); was a member of the Prussian Landtag (1922–24); traveled to the United States as a representative of the German Catholic Women's Federation (1923); served as a deputy in the Reichstag (1924–33); received an honorary doctorate from the University of Münster (1930); released from her ministerial position by the new Nazi government of Germany on the grounds of "political unreliability" (June 1933); moved to her sister's home in Marburg after her home in Berlin was destroyed by bombing (1945); served as a member of the Landtag of the German state of North Rhine-Westphalia (1946); served as a member of the German Bundestag in West Germany (1949–62); served as president of the women's branch of the Christian Democratic Party (1949–58); became president of the women's committee of the Bundestag (1957); attended the World Eucharistic Congress in Rio de Janiero (1955); received the West German government's highest civilian award, the Grosse Bundeverdienstyrenz (1957).

Helene Weber's interests combined two areas not often found together: politics and social work. Although she was active in a German political party which for a long time opposed the right to vote for women, Weber played a role in convincing party leaders eventually to accept suffrage for women. But she insisted that the emancipation of women also meant that women should assume more responsibilities, and she split her own career between political service and efforts to expand and professionalize social work in Germany. Her path was unusual enough that fellow Germans coined a new term—"social politics"—to describe her work.

Born in Elberfeld, Germany, in 1881, the daughter of a schoolteacher, Weber originally trained for elementary school teaching. After instructing at that level for five years at Aachen and Elberfeld, she took advantage of new opportunities for women to study in universities by taking courses in history, French, philosophy, and sociology at the universities of Bonn, Germany, and Grenoble, France. She then worked as a school administrator. In 1911, she was appointed principal of the Kaiserina Augusta school in Cologne. In 1916, she was named the head of the first social welfare school of the German Catholic Women's Federation, first in Cologne and then in Aachen, where she had a heavy influence in shaping a curriculum that included theology, medicine, economics, and the basics of law. She later served as president of the Federation.

World War I altered the course of her life and career. During the war, the German government urged women to be part of "citizen service." Weber responded by immersing herself in social work, helping found a series of organizations and activities to aid the families of soldiers who were at the front. Born in the heavily industrialized Rhineland area of Germany, she was well aware of working conditions in German factories. She worried especially about women who assumed dangerous homefront jobs during the war, particularly in factories (she was especially concerned for munitions workers), as well as women who worked on farms and in hospitals.

A devout Catholic, Weber came to see social work as a religious imperative. Speaking in the Reichstag building in Berlin in 1916, she told a general meeting of the German Catholic Women's Federation that young women, in particular, should be motivated by "a Christian impulse" to join in social work.

This woman has a better sense of politics in her little finger than most people have in their entire hand.

—Konrad Adenauer

The collapse of the imperial German government at the end of the war, and the flight to Holland of the German emperor, opened the way for the establishment of a democracy in Germany. Weber, although active in the leadership circles of the Catholic Center Party since 1903, found herself at odds with the leadership of the party, which had traditionally opposed women's suffrage. Elected in 1919 to the body which wrote a new constitution for Germany, in effect creating the Weimar Republic, Weber proved to be an influential political figure. Of the more than 420 delegates, 36 were women. Weber was one of the six women representing the Catholic Center Party. When it became apparent that the new constitution would grant the right to vote to women aged 21 and older, conservative commentators in Germany noted the extent to the which Catholic women, including Weber, had influenced their party to accept women's suffrage.

Appointed to a ministerial position in the newly created Prussian Ministry of Social Welfare in 1920 (changed in 1932 to the Prussian Ministry for Science, Art, and Education), Weber also served in the Landtag, the lower legislative house of Prussia, during the 1920s. She frequently proved to be an independent figure politically. She was in the minority of Center Party leaders opposing the German signing of the Treaty of Versailles, which ended World War I, because she believed that it was unnecessarily harsh on Germany.

Weber's ideas on social work were also iconoclastic. She pledged that her goals within the Prussian Ministry of Social Welfare were to find "new ways to achieve the renewal" of German women and create "helpful guidance" for German youth. During the decade of the 1920s, she continued to argue that the goals of the German women's movement had to comprise not only emancipation but also social concern. Equality, she said, "is not the same thing as making everyone act alike or be alike. Equality recognizes the differences between the sexes, as well as the intrinsic worth of both sexes." She added that social work should help women workers without ignoring women who had "stayed at home." "We are," she insisted, "beyond the first period of securing legal rights for women. Now we are in the second period, when we expect that promises made will be fulfilled."

Weber's political work brought her into contact with social workers in other countries. When she visited *Jane Addams' Hull House settlement in Chicago in 1923 as part of a Federation delegation to the United States, she noted the "wide influence" of Addams' social work ideas in Germany. She was instrumental in the merger, in 1925, of 20 schools of social work, in Europe and the United States, into the Union Catholique Internationale de Service Social (UCISS). In recognition of her efforts to promote social work and provide women's leadership in politics, the University of Munster awarded her an honorary doctorate of politics in 1930.

In March 1933, Weber was one of the prominent Center Party members who opposed the Enabling Act. This law, which much of the Center Party leadership was tricked into approving, eventually allowed Adolf Hitler to assume dictatorial powers in Germany. In the aftermath, she realized, "My tenure in the ministry was no longer possible for political reasons." She was "summarily dismissed" from the Prussian Ministry on June 3, 1933, and was given 24 hours to remove her belongings from her office. She chose to regard her firing as a "liberation from work"—a kind of "blessing," because her work in the ministry could no longer be in accord with "Christian principles to help youth and provide a social education for them."

But she later observed, "I did not go into hiding" from the summer of 1933 through the end of World War II. For awhile, she remained in Berlin and immersed herself in the "social, cultural, and religious work" of the German

Catholic Women's Federation. Her colleague Josef Schmitt declared that by the mid-1930s, "people of resistance to the Nazi regime" were gathering in her home for frequent meetings.

The social work organizations that she headed were never banned by the government, although the Nazi regime attempted to limit participation by legal threats and the searches of some social workers' homes. Weber tried to stay in touch with Catholic social workers by frequent tours throughout the country, concentrating on the German cities. She reported discovering that the racial discrimination laws of the Nazi regime, plus the pressure for sterilization of some ill or handicapped children, caused great anxiety in some social workers. When Catholic social workers were forced by the Nazi government into German "work fronts," her influence as "supervisor" and "teacher" of those social workers who were associated with the Federation was greatly diminished.

When, in 1939, the journal of the Federation was banned by the Nazi government, Weber contributed a poem to its last issue which read:

> All that we bear
> Will be suffered in private
> Only in Silence will the great Love be fulfilled
> All that we have
> Will be lost in death
> Only in death is the great Love to be understood.

Remaining in Berlin during World War II, Weber worried about a brother, who was in a Russian prison camp and would, in fact, die in the camp at the end of the war. When her home in Berlin was destroyed by bombing in 1945, she moved in with a sister in Marburg.

At the end of the war, she once again entered the political arena. During the years 1946–48, she was a member of the citizens advisory council to the British occupation forces in West Germany, which had the goals of normalizing life in Germany and laying a basis for a non-Nazi government. During 1946, she served as a member of the Landtag, or parliamentary body, of the German state of North Rhine-Westphalia. During the 1950s, Weber was a German delegate to what eventually became the European Community.

Weber was a member of the group which wrote the constitution for the Federal Republic of Germany, the government of non-Communist West Germany during the Cold War years. She assumed a prominent role as party secretary when the Christian Democratic Party was founded after World War II as a successor to the Center Party. It became the dominant party in West Germany during the 1950s and 1960s. During the years 1949 through 1962, Weber sat in the Bundestag, the popularly elected lower house of West Germany's Parliament, as part of the Christian Democratic government of Chancellor Konrad Adenauer. She served as chair of the women's committee of the Bundestag and president of the women's branch of the Christian Democratic Party.

Weber continued her social work. At the end of World War II, speaking to a Düsseldorf meeting of social workers, she tied the fate of Germany with the peace of Europe and "Christian responsibility." She became president of the Maternity Care Service. She helped revive the Union Catholique Internationale de Service Social and served on the organization's steering committee from 1950 to 1958. In 1950, she was a representative of the UCISS to a Eucharistic Congress in Brazil.

Upon her death in 1962, one of Germany's leading politicians said, "Those of us who have worked closely with Helene Weber know that our country will miss not only her intelligence and iron will in politics, but also her maternal way of doing political business." After her death, her contributions to German life were

Postal stamp issued by the Federal Republic of Germany in honor of Helene Weber.

recognized in two different ways. A school was named after her in Berlin—the Helene Weber Academy—and she was one of several women honored in a special series of German postage stamps, issued in 1969, under the motif of "50 years of Women's Suffrage."

SOURCES:

Hellwig, Renate, ed. *Die Christdemokratinnen: Unterwegs zur Partnerschaft.* Stuttgart and Herford: Seewald, 1984.

Prégardier, Elisabeth, and Anne Mohr. *Helene Weber (1881–1962): Ernte eines Lebens: Weg einer Politikerin.* Annweiler-Essen: Ploeger, 1991.

———. *Politik als Aufgabe: Engagement christlicher Frauen in der Weimarer Republik.* Annweiler-Essen: Ploeger, 1990.

SUGGESTED READING:

Evans, Richard J. *The Feminist Movement in Germany, 1894–1933.* Beverly Hills, CA: SAGE, 1976.

Kall, Alfred. *Katholische Frauenbewegung im Deutschland: Eine Untersuchung zur Gründung katholisches Frauenvereine im 19. Jahrhundert.* Paderborn: Schöningh, 1983.

Zeender, John. *The German Center Party.* Philadelphia, PA: American Philosophical Society, 1976.

Niles Holt,
Professor of History,
Illinois State University, Normal, Illinois

Weber, Helene Marie (b. 1824).

See Bloomer, Amelia for sidebar.

Weber, Jeanne (1875–1910)

Infamous murderer responsible for the strangling deaths of 8 children in France (1905–08), who may have killed as many as 20. Name variations: Ogre de la Goutte d'Or; Madame Moulinet; Marie Lemoine. Born in 1875 in northern France; died in 1910 in Mareville, France; married, in 1893.

Jeanne Weber holds the dubious honor of being one of the most heinous murderers in French history. She managed to elude conviction for a series of child killings between 1905 and 1908, despite convincing evidence that the children in her charge had been strangled. Local doctors who misdiagnosed the cause of the deaths, and misguided sympathizers who won her release from prison not once, but twice, allowed her killing spree to continue until she was finally caught in the act and declared insane in 1908.

Jeanne Weber was born in northern France in 1875, and made her way to Paris at age 14. In 1893, she married an alcoholic, and the couple had three children, two of whom died. Weber, her husband, and her remaining child lived in a tenement area known as Passage Goutte d'Or.

Weber's first known murders occurred in March 1905, and began with children in her own extended family. While babysitting her sister-in-law's two toddlers on March 2, 1905, she choked the youngest, a murder interrupted by the mother's premature return. Not suspecting that Weber was to blame for her daughter's choking fit, the mother left the child in Weber's care after she started breathing normally again, only to find her dead when she returned three hours later. Despite the black-and-blue marks on the baby's neck, Weber was so completely clear of suspicion that the mother asked her to babysit the remaining child a little over a week later. That child, too, died in Weber's care, but the cause of her death was ruled as convulsions.

Two weeks after the second death, Weber struck again when she babysat her brother's seven-month-old daughter. As with the first murder, the baby was initially saved when her grandmother, who lived below the family flat, twice came to investigate the child's cries and found the infant choking. The young girl's breathing returned to normal, and the grandmother did not suspect that Weber was to blame for the strange red marks on the child's neck. Weber returned the next day to offer her babysitting services, and her brother and his wife left their daughter in her care. The child was dead before they returned home, a victim of diphtheria according to the doctor who examined the body. Three days later, Weber's own remaining son died of what the doctors determined to be the same illness, although the red marks on his throat could not be explained.

No one suspected that Weber's sudden interest in her large extended family had a murderous motive, so when she invited two more sisters-in-law to dinner on April 5, one of them brought her ten-year-old son. At Weber's suggestion, the two women left the boy with Weber while they ran errands. This time, however, when the mother returned early and found the boy unconscious with suspicious marks on his neck, she accused Weber of attempting to strangle him, setting off a frenzy of public outrage against the suspected child-killer. Weber's presumed guilt in the public mind attracted a prominent defense lawyer, Henri Robert, to her cause.

In the course of the nine-day trial, the prosecution drew a convincing picture of a mass murderer as they detailed the number of children who died in Weber's care, including all three of Weber's own offspring, the three children of her sisters-in-law, plus two other children. Yet Robert proved brilliant in Weber's defense, relying solely on the convincing testimony of Dr. Leon Henry Thoinot, a leading forensic scientist of the day, that the children had died of natural causes. Robert's emotional speech at the close of the trial also made a tremendous impact on the jury. The mob outside the courthouse suddenly converted to Weber's side in jubilant celebration when she was declared not guilty of the charges on February 7, 1906. The woman who had become known as the "Ogre de la Goutte d'Or" was free to kill again. Thoinot collaborated with his mentor, Dr. Paul Camille Hippolyte Brouardel, and published a medical report on the affair that essentially credited them for their unerring medical decisions.

Although Weber had won her freedom, life after the trial proved to be difficult. Her husband deserted her shortly after her acquittal, neighbors who believed her guilty hounded her, and she was generally shunned. After complaining about being persecuted, she disappeared for 15 months, only to resurface in the French province of Indre, where she took a position as housekeeper and mistress under the assumed name "Madame Moulinet" sometime in 1907. On April 17 of that year, she strangled the nine-year-old son of her employer. Unlike the other physicians who had examined Weber's victims, the attending doctor became immediately suspicious of the discoloration on the boy's neck, as well as the odd behavior of "Moulinet," who had scrubbed and dressed the boy in his best clothes after he died. He took the matter to the local police, but the police-appointed doctor ruled that the boy's death had stemmed from convulsions. However, the older sister of the dead boy discovered newspaper clippings from Weber's first trial—some of which had photos proving that Madame Moulinet and Weber were the same person—among Weber's personal belongings, and took them as evidence of her guilt to the police. A doctor performing a second autopsy on the dead boy reached the conclusion that the boy had indeed been strangled, possibly by a handkerchief wrapped around his neck.

Weber's arrest on May 4, 1907, incited another public outcry, as the public had not forgotten the trial less than a year before. Still believing her innocent, Henri Robert took up Weber's cause again for the second trial and attacked the local authorities as inept and backward in their investigation. Dr. Thoinot made another appearance as an expert medical witness and declared, after examining the boy's badly decomposed body, that the child had died of typhoid fever.

Once again the defense team of Robert and Thoinot proved potent in the courtroom as Weber won her release in December of that year.

Robert hailed the trial as a victory of forensic science over public emotion before the distinguished Paris Society of Forensic Medicine on January 13, 1908. Robert's and Thoinot's influence was such that the president of the Society for the Protection of Children provided Weber with a job in his Children's Home in Orgeville to offset the injustice of her "persecution." Now known as "Marie Lemoine," Weber was caught choking a sick child only a few days after starting work. The president quietly fired her. Too embarrassed by his lapse in judgment, he did not report her to the authorities.

Weber returned to Paris and was arrested as a vagrant. After declaring to local police that she was the woman behind the child-killings in the Goutte d'Or (although she later denied it), she was sent to a mental asylum where she was declared sane. After this, Weber rapidly spiraled downward, becoming the mistress of one man, turning to full-scale prostitution, and finally running away with a railway worker named Emile Bouchery. On May 8, 1908, they took a room at an inn run by the Poirot family and Weber helped Madame Poirot around the inn with chores. Complaining that her "husband" beat her, Weber asked Madame Poirot if Poirot's ten-year-old son could sleep in her bed as an assurance against future violence. However, the household was awakened in the night by the sound of a struggle coming from Weber's bedroom, and a guest, **Madame Curlet**, arrived to find Weber in a frenzied state, straddling the boy and strangling him with a handkerchief. He was to be her last victim.

Any doubt regarding Weber's guilt vanished, and a final trial found her to be insane on October 25, 1908. Her conviction and placement in a mental hospital in Mareville inspired waves of indignation throughout France, although one of her chief defenders—Thoinot—never assumed responsibility for twice setting her free to kill again. Doctors made periodic visits to her cell at the mental hospital to study her as she experienced fits of frenzy and sexual fantasy, which they suspected might have been the driving force behind the murders. Although Weber murdered 8 children for certain, she may have been responsible for as many as 20 deaths. In 1910, Weber was discovered dead in her cell. One account reports that she was found with her own hands gripped around her throat, nails piercing the skin in a death lock.

SOURCES:

Nash, Jay Robert. *Look for the Woman*. NY: M. Evans, 1981.

Judith C. Reveal,
freelance writer,
Greensboro, Maryland

Weber, Louise (1869–1929).

See Goulue, La.

Weber, Lois (1881–1939)

American film director, one of the most important and prolific in the era of silent films, who brought to the screen her concerns for humanity and social justice. Name variations: Mrs. Phillips Smalley. Born Florence Lois Weber on June 13, 1881, in Allegheny City, Pennsylvania; died on November 13, 1939, in Los Angeles, California; second daughter of George Weber (an upholsterer and decorator) and Mary Matilda (Snaman) Weber; married Phillips Smalley, in May 1905 (divorced 1922); married Captain Harry Gantz; no children.

Toured as a concert pianist at age 17; after giving up music, joined the Church Army Workers as a missionary worker in the slums of Pittsburgh; joined a theatrical touring company, where she met Phillips Smalley; began work as writer, actor, and director for Gaumont film company (c. 1907); working with Smalley as a team, moved from Gaumont to Reliance Studio, then to Rex Company (1909); with Smalley, was put in charge of Rex, by then under control of Universal Studios, where she became important as a director (1912); elected mayor of Universal City; moved to Bosworth Company (1914); returned to Universal (1915); established own studio with financial help from Universal (1917); signed contract with Paramount to direct five films (1920); Paramount deal withdrawn (1921); divorced Smalley (1922); suffered nervous collapse, but returned briefly to directing (1926); worked as script doctor and directed screen tests at Universal (early 1930s); directed last film, her only sound film (1934).

Selected filmography as director: (also writer and actress) The Jew's Christmas (1913); (also writer and actress) False Colors (1914); (also writer) Hypocrites (1914); (also writer) It's No Laughing Matter (1914); (also writer and actress) The Leper's Coat (1914); Like Most Wives (1914); (also actress) The Merchant of Venice (1914); (also writer) The Dumb Girl of Portici (1915); (also actress) The Scandal (1915); (also actress) Sunshine Molly (1915); Discontent (1916); The French Downstairs (1916); (also writer and actress) Hop, the Devil's Brew (1916); John Needham's Double (1916); (also actress) The People vs. John Doe (1916); (also writer and actress) Saving the Family Name (1916); Shoes (1916); Where Are My Children (1916); Even As You and I (1917); (also actress) The Hand that Rocks the Cradle (1917); For Husbands Only (1917); The Man Who Dared God (1917); The

Mysterious Mrs. M (1917); The Price of a Good Time (1917); There's No Place Like Home (1917); Borrowed Clothes (1918); The Doctor and the Woman (1918); Forbidden (1919); Home (1919); Mary Regan (1919); (also writer) Midnight Romance (1919); Scandal Managers (1919); When a Girl Loves (1919); (also writer) The Blot (1921); To Please One Woman (1921); (also writer) Too Wise Wives (1921); (also writer) What Do Men Want? (1921); (also writer) What's Worth While? (1921); A Chapter in Her Life (1923); (also writer) The Marriage Clause (1926); Angel of Broadway (1927); (also writer) Sensation Seekers (1927); (also writer) White Heat (1934).

Since early silent films seldom included screen credits, it is not easy to determine who was writer, director, or cinematographer on many of the industry's earliest works. In the first references to the work of Lois Weber in the trade papers, she was generally credited along with her husband Phillips Smalley for the films they produced together as Smalley Productions, so it is not clear to what extent Smalley contributed to the creative process. What is certain, however, is that Weber's reputation as both writer and director soon surpassed that of her husband. The little else that is known about Weber's early years indicates that she was a person of outstanding gifts combined with a personal fragility that would remain in evidence throughout her career.

Few facts are available about Weber's youth, except that she was born in 1881, in Allegheny City, Pennsylvania, the daughter of George and **Mary Matilda Weber**, was educated in Pittsburgh, and was touring as a concert pianist by the age of 17. According to a profile written by **Bertha H. Smith** for *Sunset* magazine in 1914, Weber's musical career ended during a concert in South Carolina, when a piano key came off in her hand, leaving her confidence so shattered that she could no longer play.

When Weber returned home to Pittsburgh, the idealism that was to be a mark of her film work prompted her to join the Church Army Workers, a missionary group that sang hymns on street corners and helped the poor in the city's industrial slums. In 1905, after an uncle suggested that the stage might be a better platform for her interest in reforming audiences, she joined the Vance and Sullivan stock company in a touring production of the melodrama *Why Girls Leave Home*. Phillips Smalley was the company manager, and the two married that year in Chicago. As an actress, Weber garnered favorable reviews, but the couple disliked the long separations that touring imposed, and she soon settled in New York to establish a home.

The early 1900s were formative years in the film industry. Filmmakers were experimenting with improving their story-telling techniques through the use of close-ups, changes in the position of the camera, and the editing of scenes. Short narrative films found audiences through vaudeville exhibitors, who set up film projectors in stores to show programs of several short films, and people flocked into these nickelodeons. As the demand for films grew, the newborn industry welcomed talented people who could write scripts, direct films and play leading roles. As it turned out, Lois Weber could do all three. By about 1907, she had become interested in film and joined the Gaumont film company.

Before long, Phillips Smalley joined Weber at Gaumont; from Gaumont, the couple moved to Reliance Studio, then in 1909 to Rex Company, which had been established by Edwin S. Porter, one of the most important innovators in silent film. In 1912, Porter left, and Rex Compa-

ny became part of Universal, where Weber and Smalley took charge of productions still being made under the Rex name.

Together with Smalley, Weber assembled a company of actors and produced two two-reelers a month. The scripts were written by Weber, while the couple co-directed and also played leading roles. Four of these early works were *His Brand* (1913), *The Jew's Christmas* (1913), *The Leper's Coat* (1914), and *The Career of Waterloo Peterson* (1914). The last of these was a light comedy about studio life; the other three all carried clear moral messages: the brand that a cowboy inflicts on his wife appears on his newborn son; racial prejudice can be overcome by the love of parents; and fear of disease can produce its symptoms.

As the film industry began to establish its permanent home in California, Weber and Smalley joined the westward migration of talented people in the field. Weber's popularity with the staff at Universal led to her election as mayor of Universal City. Then in her early 30s, Weber had also built a reputation for dealing in a forthright way

Lois Weber

with bold subject matter. As she told Smith, "I can preach to my heart's content, and with the opportunity to write the play, act the leading role, and direct the entire production, if my message fails to reach someone I can blame only myself."

In the autumn of 1914, Weber and Smalley left Universal to join the Bosworth Company, a production company formed by actor Hobart Bosworth. There, Weber completed several longer, four- and five-reel films, which were released through Paramount. Three, entitled *False Colors* (1914), *It's No Laughing Matter* (1914), and *Sunshine Molly* (1915), were melodramas dealing with family life. Reviewers for *Variety* praised *False Colors* as "a powerful melodrama"; labeled *It's No Laughing Matter* "a winner" with a farmer character never before seen "in such a natural way on the screen"; and noted that Weber "made quite a big story out of a simple romance, with very good results" in *Sunshine Molly*.

In 1914, Weber also made *The Hypocrites* for Bosworth. The story of the film involves a young minister who unveils a statue of The Naked Truth, causing a crowd to stone him and destroy the statue. The statue is transformed into a naked young woman who wanders about holding up a mirror that reflects the hypocrisy in human nature, in business, in politics and in society. In filming the young woman, Weber appears to have used a double-exposure technique that the reviewer for *Variety* described as creating "the essence of sweetness in purity." But the same reviewer, anticipating that the story would provoke controversy, commented: "[I]t would not be surprising, after seeing this film, that the maker should decide to present it as a special picture show." The film did create a sensation with audiences in New York, and was met elsewhere with outright hostility; in Ohio, it was banned by the board of censors, and the mayor of Boston demanded that clothes be hand-painted on the nude woman, frame by frame. Two years after its release, when *The Hypocrites* was booked into the Strand Theater in New York, the critic for *The New York Times* wrote, "There is nothing objectionable about the picture, which is indeed superior to the majority that have followed in the two years since it was made. It is at least intelligent."

In April 1915, Weber returned to Universal, where she directed *Jewel* that year (she would later remake it in 1923 under the title *A Chapter in Her Life*). In both versions, the heroine brings happiness to others with the aid of principles very close to those of Christian Science, although the film contained no direct reference to the religious sect.

When Universal decided to make a film featuring the world-famous ballerina *Anna Pavlova and the Ballets Russes dance company, Weber was chosen to direct. *The Dumb Girl of Portici* was Pavlova's first and only dramatic film, made in 1915 and based on the opera *Masaniello*. Critics and audiences were disappointed with Pavlova's acting debut, and reviews were mixed. The *New York Dramatic Mirror* reviewer found it a "good spectacle," but a "great disappointment in so far that it gave the star so little opportunity to dance."

With *Where Are My Children* and *The People vs. John Doe* (both 1916), Weber returned to scripts that carried a strong message. Anticipating controversy over the subject matter of *Where Are My Children*, she used opening titles that took what seems a surprisingly modern approach, suggesting that the film might not be suitable for children, unless they attended with parents, in which case it might do them an immeasurable amount of good. As the film opens, a district attorney is following the trial of a young doctor accused of distributing literature advocating birth control. Although the doctor argues that the conditions he finds in the slums have convinced him of the need for worldwide enlightenment about birth control, he is convicted. The wife of the district attorney, along with many of her socially active women friends, is childless, and after her brother seduces the housekeeper's daughter, the wife recommends the girl to her own doctor, who performs an abortion that leads to death of the girl and this doctor's conviction. As the doctor is led away, he warns the district attorney to look in his own home, and when the district attorney checks the physician's account book, he is horrified to discover that abortions are the reason that his wife and many of her friends are childless. The story is framed by special effects depicting the floating souls of unborn children at the opening of the film and ghostly images of children superimposed around the husband in the closing scenes while he wonders, "where are my children."

For audiences, the film carried equally strong dual arguments, for birth control and against abortion. Universal was concerned about the reaction of censor boards and scheduled an exclusive showing at the Globe Theater in New York, resulting in record attendance and excellent critical reviews. The National Board of Review, which had rejected the film as unsuitable for mixed audiences, reconsidered, and the film was approved for adult audiences. Though the controversy continued, the film was banned only in Pennsylvania, and *Where Are My Children* reportedly earned the studio some $3 million.

The People vs. John Doe, which the critic for *The New York Times* called "a terrific indictment of a system that permits a man to be convicted and sentenced to death on purely circumstantial evidence," was based largely on an actual criminal case. When it opened in New York, Mischa Applebaum, founder of the Humanitarian Cult, addressed the audience after the film to "supplement with words the moral of the picture." According to the *Times* critic, it "seems not to be a drama acted before the camera, but a transcript of life itself," and for those interested in film art, this film "offers an absorbing study."

Through such works, Weber became one of the most important directors at Universal, with her films listed as Weber Productions and a salary of $5,000 a week. By the summer of 1917, she had decided to organize her own company, Lois Weber Productions, and with financial help from Universal, she bought an estate, with acres of grounds that could be used for outdoor locations and buildings for studio space (which she leased while fulfilling the remainder of her Universal contract).

In 1917–19, Weber directed six more films for Universal, all featuring actress *Mildred Harris. Critics found these lighter films—*The Price of a Good Time, For Husbands Only, The Doctor and the Woman, Borrowed Clothes, Home,* and *Forbidden*—entertaining but not great, though they had compliments for Weber. "Miss Weber has a facility for . . . the presentation of the natural things of life—which after all, is true art," wrote *Variety* in a review for *Borrowed Clothes*. "Her little touches of detail do more for her pictures than possibly anything else."

In 1920, Weber signed a contract with Paramount to produce five films. The terms called for payment of $50,000 per film plus half the profits. In October 1919, she had begun her first independent production, *To Please One Woman*, starring a young, unknown actress, *Claire Windsor, for release in 1921. But audience tastes were changing. Interest in the reform movements that characterized the early years of the century was waning, and filmgoers now preferred mostly to be entertained. The moralistic messages of Weber's earlier films had lost their appeal. Studios, under increasing pressure from censors, were also inclined to avoid controversy in choosing scripts.

To Please One Woman was not well received by reviewers or the public. *Variety* thought it "failed to make much of an impression either for merit in direction or distinction in story value," and Weber's next two films, *What's Worth While* and *Too Wise Wives* (both 1921), met with no more enthusiasm. Paramount then dropped its distribution contract, and the last two of her five films, *The Blot* and *What Do Men Want*, were distributed that year by a small independent company.

Things were also not going well in Weber's private life. In 1922, she and Smalley divorced, and film historian Anthony Slide refers to reports of a suicide attempt. Others refer to a nervous collapse. According to Slide, after her marriage to Captain Harry Gantz, Weber felt able to return to making movies. Back at Universal, she directed two more silent features, *The Marriage Clause* (1926) and *Sensation Seekers* (1927). Reviewers for both *Variety* and *The New York Times* lamented the weak story lines while praising Weber's skill as a director, but it was now increasingly difficult for her to find work.

> *L*ois was often mistakenly taken to be a Christian fundamentalist, but she was more of a libertarian, opposing censorship and the death penalty and championing birth control. . . . [I]f there was a single maxim that underlay each film it was that selfishness and egocentricity erode the individual and the community.
>
> —Cari Beauchamp

Out of friendship, an executive at Universal offered her work doctoring scripts and directing screen tests of young starlets. Then Cecil B. De Mille asked her to direct what was to be her last silent film, *The Angel of Broadway* (1927). Weber undoubtedly drew on her early missionary experiences in filming this story of a nightclub entertainer who begins by studying a Salvation Army girl to create a parody for her act and ends up converted to the cause.

Weber's final film was a talkie, *White Heat* (1934), financed by Seven Seas, a small independent company. The reviewer for *The New York Times* found it "a humorless account of the amorous difficulties of a young sugar planter" that compensated for its technical inferiority with "the reality and beauty of its Hawaiian setting." That same year, Weber advocated the use of film as a classroom teaching tool, but she failed to find takers for her ideas and scripts.

Reports of Weber's final years are sketchy. Over the years, she had acquired real-estate holdings and at one time reportedly managed an apartment building in Los Angeles. According to Slide, mismanagement of her assets left her almost penniless at the time of her death of a gastric hemorrhage at Good Samaritan Hospital in Los Angeles, on November 13, 1939, at age 57 (she had suffered from a gastric ulcer for many years). Her funeral expenses were paid by *Frances Marion, a screenwriter to whom Weber had given her first film job.

Lois Weber was a prolific director. By her own reckoning, she made over 400 films. Over the years, however, many have disappeared, and because of sketchy early records, others are difficult to authenticate. Today, about 50 films have been positively identified as directed by Weber. Prints of some of these are available in archives in the United States and Great Britain.

During the silent-film era, Weber was highly respected within the film industry for her talent and skill. "I would trust Miss Weber with any sum of money that she needed to make any picture that she wanted to make," said studio executive Carl Laemmle, when Weber was the peak of her career. "She knows the motion picture business as few people do and can drive herself as hard as anyone I have ever known."

SOURCES:

Beauchamp, Cari. *Without Lying Down: Frances Marion and the Powerful Women of Early Hollywood.* NY: Scribner, 1997.

Brownlow, Kevin. *Behind the Mask of Innocence.* NY: Alfred A. Knopf, 1990.

Koszarski, Richard. *History of the American Cinema.* NY: Scribner, 1990.

———. "The Years Have Not Been Kind to Lois Weber," in *Village Voice.* November 10, 1975, pp. 140–141.

Nash, Jay Robert, and Stanley Ralph Ross. *The Motion Picture Guide.* Chicago, IL: Cinebooks, 1987.

The New York Times Film Reviews. NY: The New York Times and Arno Press, 1970.

Parish, James Robert, and Michael R. Pitts. *Film Directors: A Guide to Their American Films.* Metuchen, NJ: Scarecrow, 1974.

Slide, Anthony. *Early Women Directors.* NY: A.S. Barnes, 1977.

Smith, Bertha H. "A Perpetual Leading Lady," in *Sunset.* March 1914, pp. 634–636.

Variety Film Reviews. NY: Garland Press, 1983.

SUGGESTED READING:

Acker, Ally. *Reel Women: Pioneers of the Cinema.* NY: Continuum, 1991.

Kay, Karyn, and Gerald Perry, eds. *Women and the Cinema.* NY: Dutton, 1977.

Lucy A. Liggett,
Professor of Telecommunications and Film,
Eastern Michigan University, Ypsilanti, Michigan

Webster, Alice (1876–1916).

See Webster, Jean.

Webster, Augusta (1837–1894)

English poet, dramatist, and essayist. Name variations: Julia Augusta Davies; (pseudonym) Cecil Home. Born Julia Augusta Davies on January 30, 1837, in Poole, Dorset, England; died on September 5, 1894, in Kew, London, England; daughter of George Davies (vice-admiral in the British navy) and Julia Augusta (Hume) Davies; studied at the Cambridge School of Art; married Thomas Webster (a lawyer), in 1863; children: one daughter.

Selected writings: Blanche Lisle and Other Poems *(1860);* Lesley's Guardians *(1864);* Dramatic Studies *(1866);* A Woman Sold and Other Poems *(1867);* Portraits *(1870);* A Housewife's Opinions *(1878);* A Book of Rhyme *(1881);* In a Day *(play, 1882);* The Sentence *(play, 1887);* Mother and Daughter *(1895).*

Augusta Webster was born Julia Augusta Davies in Poole, Dorset, England, in 1837, the daughter of **Julia Hume Davies** and naval officer George Davies. She grew up in several areas of England, including a stint on board a ship docked in Chichester Harbor. In addition to attending the Cambridge School of Art, Webster studied French in Paris and Geneva. She expanded her language studies to include Italian, Spanish, and Greek, the last of which she taught her younger brother.

Webster began her career as an author in 1860, with *Blanche Lisle and Other Poems*, which she published under the masculine pseudonym "Cecil Home." Three years later she married Thomas Webster, a law lecturer at Trinity College in Cambridge with whom she would have one daughter, and began publishing under her married name of Augusta Webster. The poem *Lilian Gray* and her only novel, *Lesley's Guardians*, both published in 1864, were followed by *Dramatic Studies* (1866), a collection of dramatic monologues. These eight monologues, including three spoken exclusively by women, drew heavily from poets Robert Browning and *Elizabeth Barrett Browning and marked Webster's first important contribution to poetry. That same year, she issued a well-received translation from the Greek of *Prometheus Bound*; a translation of *Medea* would meet with equal success in 1868. (Her maternal grandfather, Joseph Hume, had earlier translated Dante.) Webster's 1867 collection *A Woman Sold and Other Poems* showed more diversity in her poetic forms as well as the influence of Alfred, Lord Tennyson. She returned exclusively to the monologue form in *Portraits* (1870), which highlighted her feminism through an exploration of the predicaments faced by women in the mid-1800s, particularly regarding marriage and the dilemma of the single woman. *Vita Sackville-West would later praise "A Castaway," the monologue of a prostitute, and another monologue drew comparisons with the work of Dante Gabriel Rossetti. *Portraits* proved so successful that it went into a second edition before the year ended.

In 1870, Webster also moved with her family from Cambridge to London, where her husband practiced as a lawyer. Despite the success with which her poems had met, she wrote less poetry after the move, although in 1881 she did introduce to English audiences the *risputti* or *stornelli*, an Italian stanza poem, in *A Book of Rhyme* (1881). Instead, she focused on plays and essays, and also devoted her energy to the campaign for better education for women. As part of this effort, she was twice elected to the London School Board, serving from 1879 to 1882. Among her plays were *The Auspicious Day* (1872) and *Disguises* (1879), neither of which received performances, and *In a Day*, written in 1882 and produced with her daughter in the starring role in 1890. *Christina Rossetti and her brother William Michael Rossetti were among those who thought highly of Webster's *The Sentence* (1887), a three-act tragedy detailing the life of Caligula; the latter poet called it "one of the masterpieces of European drama."

A firm supporter of women's suffrage, Webster wrote a series of essays on the issue which were published in the *Examiner* and reprinted by the Women's Suffrage Union in 1878. The *Examiner* also published her series of essays on married women, published in book form as *A Housewife's Opinions* (1878). Webster was unable to complete her last work, a sonnet sequence, before her death on September 5, 1894. It was published posthumously as *Mother and Child* the following year.

SOURCES:

Buck, Claire, ed. *The Bloomsbury Guide to Women's Literature*. NY: Prentice Hall, 1992.

The Concise Dictionary of National Biography. Oxford: Oxford University Press, 1992.

Kunitz, Stanley J., and Howard Haycraft, eds. *British Authors of the Nineteenth Century*. NY: H.W. Wilson, 1936.

Shattock, Joanne. *The Oxford Guide to British Women Writers*. Oxford: Oxford University Press, 1993.

Ann M. Schwalboski, M.A., M.F.A., University of Wisconsin-Baraboo/Sauk County, Wisconsin

Webster, Jean (1876–1916)

American writer whose best-known work was Daddy-Long-Legs. *Born Alice Jane Chandler Webster on July 24, 1876, in Fredonia, New York; died after giving birth to her only child on June 11, 1916, in New York; daughter of Charles Webster (a publisher) and Annie (Moffett) Webster; graduated from the Lady Jane Grey School in Binghamton, New York; Vassar College, B.A., 1901; married Glenn Ford McKinney (a lawyer), in 1915; children: Jean Webster McKinney (b. 1916).*

Selected works: When Patty Went to College (1903); The Wheat Princess (1905); Jerry, Junior (1907); The Four Pools Mystery (1908); Much Ado About Peter (1909); Just Patty (1911); Daddy-Long-Legs (1912); Dear Enemy (1914).

Born in New York State in 1876, Jean Webster was the daughter of **Annie Moffett Webster**, a niece of Mark Twain (Samuel Clemens), and Charles Webster, who published Twain's *Huckleberry Finn* and the memoirs of Ulysses S. Grant. Although she was christened Alice Jane, she began calling herself Jean while boarding at the Lady *Jane Grey School in upstate New York. After boarding school, Webster attended Vassar

Jean Webster

College, where she published short stories in the *Vassar Miscellany* and wrote a weekly column for the *Poughkeepsie Sunday Courier* to earn extra money. She also started an enduring friendship with fellow classmate **Adelaide Crapsey**, later a well-known poet. It is thought that Crapsey provided the inspiration for the stories Webster began writing about a college student named Patty, some of which were serialized while she was still at Vassar. After graduating with a bachelor's degree in English and economics in 1901, Webster continued freelance writing and traveled throughout Europe. *When Patty Went to College*, a collection of the Patty stories, was published in 1903. Her European travels became the basis for her next two books: *The Wheat Princess* (1905), which told of her winter stay in an Italian convent, and *Jerry, Junior* (1907).

Returning to the U.S., Webster settled in New York City's Greenwich Village and focused her attention on improving the deplorable conditions of orphanages. Her love of children sparked Webster to write what would become her most-loved book, *Daddy-Long-Legs* (1912), the story of a young woman raised in an orphanage who gets the opportunity to go to college with the sponsorship of an unknown, wealthy bachelor. *Daddy-Long-Legs* was first serialized in the popular women's magazine *Ladies' Home Journal*, and became a bestseller upon its publication in book form. Two years later, Webster adapted *Daddy-Long-Legs* into a play that provided *Ruth Chatterton with her first smash role during its long run on Broadway. *Daddy-Long-Legs* later was filmed several times, first in 1919 with *Mary Pickford; again in 1931; as *Curly Top* with *Shirley Temple (Black) in 1935; and as a musical (minus the hyphens in the title) with Fred Astaire, **Leslie Caron**, and *Thelma Ritter in 1955. The popularity of Webster's book also led to a New York State Charities Aid Association movement to establish groups in colleges that would each pay for the education of one orphaned child.

A diligent worker, Webster mercilessly edited and rewrote her books to create intelligent, direct, and witty stories for all ages. Her last book *Dear Enemy* (1914), a sequel to *Daddy-Long-Legs*, also became a bestseller. In 1915, Webster married Glenn Ford McKinney, a lawyer, with whom she lived in New York City and the Berkshire Hills in Massachusetts. She gave birth to her only child, **Jean Webster McKinney**, the following year, and died a few hours later.

SOURCES:

Edgerly, Lois Stiles, ed. *Give Her This Day*. Gardiner, ME: Tilbury House, 1990.

James, Edward T., ed. *Notable American Women, 1607–1950*. Cambridge, MA: The Belknap Press of Harvard University, 1971.

Kunitz, Stanley J., and Howard Haycraft, eds. *Twentieth Century Authors*. NY: H.W. Wilson, 1942.

McHenry, Robert, ed. *Famous American Women*. NY: Dover, 1980.

Ann M. Schwalboski, M.A., M.F.A.,
University of Wisconsin-Baraboo/Sauk County

Webster, Kate (1849–1879)

Irish murderer. Born in 1849 in Killane, County Wexford, Ireland; hanged on July 29, 1879, in London, England; never married; children: one son.

Kate Webster, born in 1849 in Ireland, was first a thief, then a murderer. She began her life of crime as a child, when her bold, recurrent stealing brought not only many arrests but also many lectures from the local priest. Webster escaped further arrests and lectures by using money she had stolen to sail to Liverpool, England. Not possessed of the swiftest of pickpocketing techniques, however, she soon was caught there and convicted. After serving a four-year sentence, she left her criminal record behind once again and moved to London.

There, Webster became a maid, but also supported herself through prostitution. She soon turned to lodging-house robbery. Renting a different room every few days, she would steal anything she could carry to the local pawnbroker. She was also frequently arrested, racking up over 30 counts of larceny on one occasion. Throughout the mid-1870s, she spent many days in jail, including an 18-month sentence in Wandsworth prison.

By January 1879, now an unmarried mother, Webster had moved to the Richmond area of London. Through the charity of a local woman named **Mrs. Crease**, she found work as a maid for the wealthy and reclusive Mrs. **Julia Martha Thomas**. Webster left her son (to whom she was apparently quite attached) with Mrs. Crease while she lived with and worked for Thomas. After an initial period during which she seemed to be a model maid, working hard to complete her chores each day, Webster began working less and playing more at the local pub, the Hole-in-the-Wall. Her employer disapproved of this kind of behavior, and fired her only one month after she had been hired.

Webster responded to news of her dismissal by waiting for Thomas to return from church, where she had gone immediately after telling Webster to leave, and then attacking her with an axe. Striking her on the head with the side of the axe, Webster next pushed Thomas down a staircase before delivering a fatal blow to the head. To dispose of the evidence, she dragged Thomas' body into the kitchen, stripped it, cut it up, and threw it into a copper pot she already had boiling. Unable to tolerate the horrific stench, she then went drinking at the Hole-in-the-Wall pub for awhile before returning to the house to finish the job. She packed what was left of Thomas in a box and scrubbed the entire house, including the copper pot. The following day she burned Thomas' bones in the fireplace. Webster's greed was such that she sold her victim's gold bridgework (with several false teeth still attached), and she reportedly attempted to sell some of the boiled-down remains as cooking fat.

Having thrown Thomas' head into the river (it was never found), Webster enlisted the help of Robert Porter, a young man who had been pub-hopping with her, to help her carry the box of Thomas' remains to the Richmond Bridge. She sent him on his way after explaining that a friend would be picking up the box, and then dumped it in the Thames. She was so certain she had committed the perfect crime that she told new acquaintances she had inherited (from "a dear aunt") Thomas' house, and began negotiating the sale of the dead woman's furniture.

The following day, however, the box she had dumped floated to the surface of the river, and fishermen who opened it made the gruesome discovery of the unidentifiable remains. Although this evidence in itself did not point to Webster as the murderer—indeed, no one had even noticed that Thomas was missing—a neighbor called the police when she saw Thomas' furniture being taken away without the supervision of either Thomas or her maid. Police arrived at the house to investigate the matter, and Webster fled. Her flight confirmed guilt, and she erred further by attempting to hide out in her home town of Killane, Ireland, where authorities, now convinced that Thomas had been murdered, easily tracked her down on March 28, 1879. She was still wearing Thomas' dress and rings.

Webster did not go quietly to her fate. When returned to London and faced with John Church, the man who had tried to purchase Thomas' furniture and had agreed to identify her for police, she pointed at him and shouted dramatically, "Here's your murderer!" He was arrested, much to his shock, but then quickly released after proving his whereabouts on the day of Thomas' murder. Webster then tried to shift the blame to the father of her pub-hopping friend Robert Porter, but this, too, was proved to be a lie. The circumstances of her crime—particularly her grisly methods of disposing of the body—had horrified all England, and her trial, begun on July 2, 1879, was widely covered in the papers. Webster was routinely described during the trial as "savage, barbaric, callous, fiendish," and on July 9 she was found guilty. After the death sentence was pronounced, she claimed that a man who had been her lover (she offered no name) had committed the crime. The court did not believe her. She then "pled her belly" (the executions of pregnant women were postponed until after they gave birth), but an examination proved that she was not pregnant. Webster continued making wild accusations up until the night before her execution, when she finally admitted to a prison chaplain and the warden that she had indeed killed Thomas. She nonetheless appeared unremorseful, and the following day, July 29, 1879, showered obscenities on observers at Wandsworth prison as she was escorted to the hangman's noose.

SOURCES:
Nash, Jay Robert. *Look for the Woman.* NY: M. Evans, 1981.

Ann M. Schwalboski, M.A., M.F.A., University of Wisconson-Baraboo/Sauk County

Webster, Margaret (1905–1972)

American actress and director who devoted her career to bringing theater, particularly Shakespeare, to the greater public. Name variations: Peggy Webster. Born on March 15, 1905, in New York City; died on November 13, 1972, in London, England; only child of Benjamin Webster III (an actor) and Mary Louisa (Whitty) Webster, known as May Whitty (1865–1948); graduated from Queen Anne's School, Caversham, England, in 1923; attended Etlinger Dramatic School, London, England; never married; no children.

Once called "America's foremost Shakespearean director," Margaret Webster was to the theater born. The only child of renowned actors Benjamin Webster III and Dame *May Whitty, Margaret spent her early childhood living variously in New York and London, frequently in the care of relatives while her parents toured. She made her own theatrical debut at the age of eight, performing the prologue to the *York Nativity Play*, directed by *Ellen Terry. "My parents objected to a stage career with the usual insincerity of theatrical parents," Webster once said, adding that her mother frequently let her watch from the wings while she performed and sometimes allowed her to "walk on" in a mob scene. It was also her mother who read Shakespeare to her from the age of three.

In 1924, after completing a private school education, Webster enrolled in the Etlinger Dramatic School. She made her professional debut that same year in the chorus of a London production of Euripides' *The Trojan Women*. She spent the next years honing her craft as the member of various stock companies, including the Macadona Players, the Oxford Players, and Ben Greet's Shakespeare Company. With the latter group, Webster toured England playing in outdoor Shakespeare productions in a variety of conditions. "You had to learn to play Lady Macbeth up and down on a fire escape," she wrote in *Shakespeare Without Tears*, "and convince an audience of irreverent children that you were really sleepwalking at the same time."

In 1929, she joined the Old Vic, playing second leads during her first season, but returning three years later as Lady Macbeth during the 1932–33 season. Between 1934–36, Webster

Margaret Webster

acted in 14 plays, among them *Queen of Scots*, *Viceroy Sarah*, *Parnell*, and *Girl Unknown*, which she also adapted from a play by Ferenc Molnar. During this time, Webster had her first directorial experience, staging an outdoor pageant-production of *Henry VIII*, under the auspices of the Women's Institute, throughout the county of Kent. "The principal parts were played by the same actors throughout, but each of the different crowd scenes was allocated to a separate village or locality," she explained in her family memoir *The Same Only Different*. "The Baptism Scene at the end was to bring together the entire cast of more than eight hundred people."

In 1935 and 1936, while pursuing her acting career, Webster also directed nine productions, most of them new tryout plays, with the exception of a revival of Ibsen's *Lady from the Sea*. In 1937, she was invited by Maurice Evans to direct his New York production of *Richard II*, the first Broadway presentation of the play since 1878, and Webster's first experience with New York actors. "I soon discovered certain fundamental differences between American and English actors, especially when confronting Shakespeare," she wrote. "The Americans worked harder, were more concentrated and more direct. They were also more self-conscious. The English actor would toss a Shakespearean part lightly over his left shoulder, as something all in the day's work; but the American treated it as something very special and rather awesome."

Winning unanimous critical acclaim for her direction (the play ran an unprecedented 171 performances), Webster continued to work with Evans on productions of *Hamlet* (1938), *Henry IV, Part I* (1939), *Twelfth Night* (1940), and *Macbeth* (1941). In 1939, she also staged abbreviated versions of four of Shakespeare's comedies for the Globe Theater at the New York World's Fair. Amid her directing duties, Webster also made her American acting debut on March 28, 1938, playing Masha in a Theatre Guild production of Anton Chekhov's *The Seagull*, which starred Alfred Lunt and *Lynn Fontanne. Critic Brooks Atkinson praised her as "the only member of the cast who plays with perception of the evanescent life that is hovering under and around the written skeleton of the drama."

In 1942, Webster created a stir when she cast black actor Paul Robeson as the Moor in a production of *Othello*, which also starred *Uta Hagen and José Ferrer. Although it was predicted that the production would fail because of the casting, it ran for a record 295 performances. Webster chanced a second bit of daring casting in a subsequent production of *The Tempest* (1945), choosing the ballerina *Vera Zorina as Ariel and the black ex-boxer Canada Lee as Caliban. It too was a box-office smash, establishing Webster, in the words of George Jean Nathan, as "the best director of the plays of Shakespeare that we have."

Webster's projects were by no means limited to Shakespeare. She also directed Euripides' *The Trojan Women* (1941), Tennessee Williams' *Battle of Angels* (1941), Chekhov's *The Cherry Orchard* (1942), and Thomas Job's *Thérèse* (1945), adapted from the Emile Zola novel *Thérèse Raquin*. (Webster's mother Dame May Whitty had roles in both *The Trojan Women* and *Thérèse*.)

In 1945, Webster joined with *Eva Le Gallienne and *Cheryl Crawford to found the American Repertory Theater, which they hoped would serve to keep the dramatic classics of the past in production along with new plays of merit. The venture lasted only a single season, after which Webster used the equipment from the failed company to begin a new initiative. Wanting to bring the theater to those who had previously had little or no experience with live production, she formed the Margaret Webster Shakespeare Company, a troupe that toured the United States and Canada, performing in schools, colleges, and public halls. The company toured for two years, covering over 36 states and three Canadian provinces. Webster thought the company was her greatest contribution to the American theater.

In 1950, Webster directed a production of Verdi's *Don Carlos* at New York's Metropolitan Opera, becoming the first woman ever to direct for the Met. It was such a success that she continued to direct opera throughout the 1950s, putting her creative stamp on productions of *Aïda* (1951) and *Simon Boccanegra* (1960), both at the Met, as well as *Troilus and Cressida* (1955), *Macbetto* (1957), *The Taming of the Shrew* and *The Silent Woman* (both 1958) for the New York City Opera.

Webster's career suffered a severe blow in 1951, when José Ferrer, under pressure, named her before the House Committee on Un-American Activities. Although she was eventually cleared of all charges labeling her a Communist sympathizer, she was blacklisted and had difficulty finding work in the United States. She returned to England, directing at Stratford-upon-Avon and at the Old Vic. She regained her former status in the United States in 1961, when the State Department invited her to travel to South Africa as a member of its American Specialists Program. During the tour, she lectured, performed concert readings of Shakespeare, and directed a production of Eugene O'Neill's *A Touch of the Poet*. Her later work during the 1960s included a series of visiting lecturer positions at various American universities where she taught, directed, and performed her one-woman shows on Shakespeare and George Bernard Shaw.

Webster, who never married, eventually retired to Martha's Vineyard, Massachusetts, where she wrote a family memoir, *The Same Only Different* (1969), and her autobiography, *Don't Put Your Daughter on the Stage* (1972). Her death, in London in 1972, not only ended a brilliant career but brought an end to a 150-year-old English theatrical dynasty.

SOURCES:

Current Biography 1950. NY: H.W. Wilson, 1950.

Garraty, John A., and Mark C. Carnes, eds. *American National Biography.* Vol. 22. NY and Oxford. Oxford University Press, 1999.

Sicherman, Barbara, and Carol Hurd Green, eds. *Notable American Women: The Modern Period.* Cambridge, MA: The Belknap Press of Harvard University, 1980.

Webster, Margaret. *The Same Only Different.* NY: Alfred A. Knopf, 1969.

Wilmeth, Don B., and Tice L. Miller, eds. *Cambridge Guide to American Theater.* NY: Oxford University Press, 1993.

Barbara Morgan,
Melrose, Massachusetts

Webster, Mary Louise "May"
(1865–1948).

See Whitty, May.

Webster, Peggy (1905–1972).

See Webster, Margaret.

Weddington, Sarah R. (1945—)

American lawyer and politician who argued Roe v. Wade *before the Supreme Court. Born Sarah Ragle on February 5, 1945, in Abilene, Texas; daughter of Herbert Doyle Ragle (a Methodist minister) and Lena Catherine (Morrison) Ragle; McMurry College, B.S., 1965; University of Texas Law School, J.D., 1967; married Ron Weddington (divorced 1974).*

Argued the case of Roe v. Wade *before the Supreme Court (1971, 1972); elected to the Texas House of Representatives (1972); advised President Jimmy Carter on issues affecting women (1978–80); returned to private practice and became a popular college lecturer.*

Sarah R. Weddington was born on February 5, 1945, in Abilene, Texas, the daughter of a Methodist minister who had an itinerant ministry in central Texas. An excellent student, she entered McMurry College at age 16, majoring in speech and education. However, she decided against a teaching career and after graduating from college in 1965 entered the University of Texas Law School. She and her classmate **Linda Coffee** were among the five women who earned degrees from the law school in 1967.

Though Weddington graduated in the top 25% of her class, discrimination against women in the field of law made it difficult for her to find work in Texas. While Coffee turned to bankruptcy law, Weddington worked on the American Bar Association's project to standardize legal ethics. Her career took a definite turn, however, after her husband Ron Weddington, still in school, introduced her to some graduate students who worked on *The Rag*, an underground feminist paper in Austin. These women were also involved with birth-control counseling, which included informing women with unwanted pregnancies which illegal abortion clinics in Mexico were reasonably safe. They consulted Weddington on whether they would be criminally liable for providing such information, which led to the question of a method for challenging the Texas statute (all but unchanged since 1854) banning abortion except in cases where the mother's life was in danger. As she would later explain in her book *A Question of Choice*, the issue interested Weddington partially because, while still in law school, she herself had obtained an illegal abortion in Mexico, going under the anesthetic while wondering whether she would live or die.

Sarah R. Weddington

Although she was still only in her early 20s, with legal experience largely limited to simple divorces and wills, Weddington began compiling arguments, based on the right to privacy guaranteed in the Constitution, against the statute banning abortion. She teamed up with former classmate Coffee to find a woman for whom they could file a class-action suit challenging Texas' abortion laws. In 1969, they found her, an out-of-luck, unemployed and pregnant former carnival barker named **Norma McCorvey**, who in court papers

was called "Jane Roe" to protect her privacy. At age 25, Weddington filed suit against the abortion statute in a federal court in Dallas.

Known as *Roe v. Wade*, the case became one of the most controversial in American history. Neither Weddington nor Coffee had ever tried a case in court before, but they won their class-action suit against the State of Texas. An appeal by the Texas attorney general led the case to the Supreme Court, which agreed to hear it. In mid-1970, Weddington began devoting all her energies to preparing for the case, quitting her job and enlisting law professors and others to hear her potential arguments. (McCorvey, meanwhile, still legally barred from obtaining an abortion, had given birth to a girl whom she put up for adoption. In later years, she worked in an abortion clinic before a religious conversion led her to switch sides on the debate and become a prized opponent of abortion rights.) The first hearing was held before the Supreme Court on December 13, 1971. In her opening argument, Weddington said, "I think it's without question that pregnancy to a woman can completely disrupt her life. It disrupts her body, it disrupts her education, it disrupts her employment, and it often disrupts her entire family life. And we feel that, because of the impact on the woman, this certainly, insofar as there are any rights which are fundamental, is a matter which is of such fundamental and basic concern to the woman involved that she should be allowed to make the choice as to whether to continue or to terminate her pregnancy." The State of Texas, in turn, argued that a fetus was a person, and therefore entitled to protection under the Constitution. A second hearing was held before the nine-member court on October 11, 1972. On January 21, 1973, the court ruled, in a 7–2 decision, that the state cannot prohibit a woman in consultation with her doctor from getting an abortion in the first trimester of pregnancy. The majority opinion, written by Justice Harry Blackmun, found that women's "right of personal privacy" included the right to an early abortion, and state statutes criminalizing such procedures were a violation of the due process clause in the 14th Amendment. (William Rehnquist, then a new member of the court, wrote the dissenting opinion.) The ruling also allowed greater state regulation of abortion in the second trimester and strong regulations in the final trimester.

Meanwhile, in 1972, Weddington had been elected to the Texas state legislature. During her first term, she co-sponsored a health care act that established life-saving procedures for kidney patients and also championed and passed

House Bill 920, which made it illegal to deny credit or loans on the basis of gender. Weddington continued fighting for women's rights in her second term by co-sponsoring, with **Kay Bailey Hutchison**, House Bill 284, which made a woman's past sexual experiences inadmissible as evidence in rape cases. Expanding her focus, in her third term she fought for the establishment of state job agencies, funded school art programs through a city tax on hotel and motel stays and also sponsored a bill to create the Commission on the Status of Women.

In 1977, Weddington left Texas to become general counsel for the U.S. Department of Agriculture in Washington, D.C. As general counsel, she was actively involved in policy-making and also supervised a staff of 350 employees. In September 1978, President Jimmy Carter named Weddington his special assistant for women's issues, arousing protest from anti-abortion groups. As the president's special assistant, Weddington fought hard to make sure that Carter remained committed to passing the Equal Rights Amendment, and worked to rebuild the National Advisory Committee on Women after *Bella Abzug's abrupt departure over policy differences with Carter. In 1980, after Carter lost his bid for reelection and the ERA was not passed, Weddington returned to Texas.

There she established a private law practice, and began teaching pre-law courses at the University of Texas at Austin. Weddington has been the recipient of numerous awards, including the Woman of the Year Award of the Texas Women's Political Caucus and the *Susan B. Anthony Award from the National Organization for Women (both 1973), the **Elizabeth Boyer** Award from the Equity Action League (1978, 1992), the *Margaret Sanger Award from the Planned Parenthood Federation of America (1980), and the Lecturer of the Year Award from the National Association for Campus Activities (1990). This last award was a result of her frequent lectures on college campuses, where she is an accomplished and popular speaker. In 1992, Weddington wrote *A Question of Choice*, both a history of *Roe* v. *Wade* and a reflection on the years since her victory in the case. She commented a year later, "It was a fantastic experience. . . . It is also something that, if anybody had said to me then, you will still be talking about this in twenty years, I would never have believed it. . . . I thought, that's done, now we can move on to other issues. And the current-day situation certainly says just how wrong I was about that."

SOURCES:

Christian Science Monitor. September 26, 1996.

Crawford, Ann Fears, and Crystal Sasse Ragsdale. *Women in Texas.* Austin, TX: State House Press, 1992.

Irons, Peter, and Stephanie Guitton, eds. *May It Please the Court.* NY: The New Press, 1993.

Publishers Weekly. September 13, 1993, p. 10.

The Village Voice. January 27, 1998.

Ann M. Schwalboski, M.A., M.F.A.,
University of Wisconsin-Baraboo/Sauk County

Wedemeyer, Maria von

(c. 1924–1977)

German-born mathematician who was the fiancée of Dietrich Bonhoeffer. Name variations: Maria von Wedemeyer-Weller. Born in Germany around 1924; died of cancer on November 16, 1977, in Boston, Massachusetts; studied math at the University of Göttingen in Germany; Bryn Mawr, M.A., 1950; married Paul Schniewind, in 1949 (divorced c. 1955); married Barton Weller, in 1959 (divorced 1965); children: (first marriage) Christopher; Paul; (stepdaughter) Sue M. Ryan.

Born around 1924, the daughter of German aristocrats, Maria von Wedemeyer was in her early teens when she first met German pastor Dietrich Bonhoeffer, while attending confirmation classes he was giving. By the time they met again during World War II, Wedemeyer's father and brother had died fighting on the Russian front, and Bonhoeffer was a confirmed opponent of the Third Reich, forbidden by the Nazis from speaking in public and secretly using his job in German military intelligence to help the resistance. A struggle was being fought within the German Evangelical Church, and Bonhoeffer was a strong supporter of the "Confessing Church," the small faction that confessed to being led only by Jesus Christ, not by Adolf Hitler. By 1943, despite the difference in their ages—he was 17 years her senior—Wedemeyer and Bonhoeffer were engaged. That April, he was arrested for his role in a plot to assassinate Hitler. They never met alone again, although Wedemeyer was able to visit him under the supervision of guards during his almost two years in Berlin's Tegel Prison. They also corresponded regularly (despite prison censorship), in letters that vividly document both their love and Bonhoeffer's philosophies. Towards the end of the war, Bonhoeffer was transported to first one and then another concentration camp. He was hanged along with other prisoners at Flossenburg on April 9, 1945, less than a month before Germany's surrender.

Wedemeyer attended the University of Göttingen, studying math, and in 1948 immigrated to the United States, where she kept her correspondence with Bonhoeffer in a bank vault. The insight into Bonhoeffer's character that the letters might provide made them of key interest to scholars, but when Wedemeyer donated them to Harvard University in 1967, it was under orders that they were not to be published for another 25 years without her permission. She published limited portions of the letters in an article in the Union Theological Seminary's journal that year.

In the United States, Wedemeyer, whose two marriages and divorces left her the single mother of three children, built on her studies of mathematics to create a successful career at Honeywell, Inc., in Boston. Her work as an engineer in the field of minicomputers, particularly in her development of what was known as emulation capability, placed her firmly at the forefront of the computer age. She died of cancer in Boston in 1977, at age 53. In 1994, her correspondence with Bonhoeffer was published as *Love Letters from Cell 92*.

SOURCES:

Bonhoeffer, Dietrich. *Love Letters from Cell 92: The Correspondence between Dietrich Bonhoeffer and Maria von Wedemeyer, 1943–45*. Trans. by John Brownjohn. Ed. by Ruth-Alice von Bismarck and Ulrich Kabitz. Nashville, TN: Abingdon Press, 1994.

Contemporary Authors, Vol. 148. Detroit, MI: Gale Research, 1996.

The New York Times Biographical Service. November 1977, p. 1574.

Publishers Weekly. February 13, 1995, p. 58.

SUGGESTED READING:

Clements, Keith W. *A Patriotism for Today: Love of Country in Dialogue with the Witness of Dietrich Bonhoeffer*. London: Collins Flame, 1986.

Ann M. Schwalboski, M.A., M.F.A.,
University of Wisconsin-Baraboo/Sauk County, Wisconsin

Wedgwood, C.V. (1910–1997)

British historian, specialist in 17th-century Europe, who was one of the great prose stylists of her profession. Born Cicely Veronica Wedgwood on July 20, 1910, in Stocksfield, Northumberland, England; died on March 9, 1997, in London; daughter of Sir Ralph Wedgwood (chief general manager of a British railroad) and Iris Veronica (Pawson) Wedgwood (an author of books on history and topography); educated privately and at a school in Kensington; studied at Bonn University in Germany and at the Sorbonne in Paris, France, 1927–28; Lady Margaret Hall, Oxford, B.A., 1931.

Selected writings: Strafford, 1593–1641 *(1935);* The Thirty Years War *(1938);* Oliver Cromwell *(1939);* William the Silent *(1944);* Velvet Studies: Essays on Historical and Other Subjects *(1946);* Seven-teenth-Century English Literature *(1950);* The Great Rebellion: The King's Peace, 1637–1641 *(vol. 1, 1955);* The Great Rebellion: The King's War, 1641–1647 *(vol. 2, 1958);* Truth and Opinion: Historical Essays *(1960);* Poetry and Politics Under the Stuarts *(1960);* A Coffin for King Charles: The Trial and Execution of Charles I *(1964);* The World of Rubens *(1967);* Milton and His World *(1969);* Oliver Cromwell and the Elizabethan Inheritance *(1970);* The Political Career of Peter Paul Rubens *(1975);* The Spoils of Time: A World History from the Dawn of Civilization through the Early Renaissance *(1985).*

C.V. Wedgwood, one of England's premier historians, spent her first years in Yorkshire, before her family moved to London. Through her father Sir Ralph Wedgwood, who would serve as chair of British Railways during World War II, she was a descendant of the great 18th-century Staffordshire potter Josiah Wedgwood, while her mother **Iris Pawson Wedgwood** wrote books about history and topography. Cicely Veronica Wedgwood's first history lesson at the age of six opened up a world of possibilities for the young girl. The early inspirations for her writing career included John Habberton's *Helen's Babies*, the *Odyssey*, *Pilgrim's Progress*, and L.T. Meade's *Beyond the Blue Mountains*. She also delighted in *Prometheus Unbound*, ***Anna Sewall**'s *Black Beauty*, and Ernest Thompson Seton's *The Biography of a Grizzly*. At the age of nine, she wrote her first play and then three novels which she eventually discarded. She turned to nonfiction when she was 12 (at the suggestion of her father, who thought she was writing too much poetry), and wrote a history of England which she also threw away. Around that time she learned the importance of primary sources: "One day at school our teacher read us letters to illustrate a lesson, and a fragment of a diary. The immense revelation dazzled me."

Wedgwood continued her education in 1927–28, traveling to study at Bonn University in Germany and then at the Sorbonne in Paris, France. Returning to England, she received a scholarship to Lady Margaret Hall in Oxford, where she earned a "first" in modern history and a bachelor's degree in 1931. She then began working for the Commission on the History of Parliament, assigned to the Civil War and Commonwealth period.

Wedgwood focused most of her attention on the 17th century because she believed it to be the most predominantly significant period in British history. Her first book, *Strafford, 1593–1641* (1935), was a biography of Thomas Wentworth,

1st earl of Strafford and advisor to Charles I, who urged the king to protect his own skin by assenting to Wentworth's execution for treason. (Charles did so, and was himself executed eight years later.) Publisher Jonathan Cape thought "Cicely Veronica" too feminine a name for a war historian, so her name instead appeared on this and subsequent books as C.V. Wedgwood. She next wrote *The Thirty Years War* (1938), which became the definitive work on that complicated subject. Wedgwood researched the book in five languages (learning Dutch to do so) and visited almost all of the places involved in the conflict. She also wrote *Oliver Cromwell* (1939) for the "Great Lives" series of biographies of prominent historical figures, publishing another work on Cromwell in 1970 as *Oliver Cromwell and the Elizabethan Inheritance*. All of her works received fine reviews from the British weekly papers. In a critique of her 1946 collection *Velvet Studies: Essays on Historical and Other Subjects*, the *Times Literary Supplement* noted: "The fine quality of Miss Wedgwood's own production derives from the fact that, writing for a wide public, she presents to them, in the best sense of an abused word, the results of research. Ranging herself, with some bravado, among the 'popularisers,' she is able to claim attention precisely because she is a scholar."

In an essay for *New Writing and Daylight* (Autumn 1944), Wedgwood summed up her thoughts on historians and the need for books about history: "Certainly it is important that good history should be read by more people; the solution is not for *more* books from a *few* historians but for *more* good historians." She believed that "historians should always draw morals," understanding the power to shape opinion inherent in the telling of history. Her particular approach to writing historical accounts included reading every contemporary document she could find regarding the period. When writing about a battle, she outlined the tactics for every hour of the engagement and then traveled to the battle site to visualize how it must have felt to experience it firsthand.

Wedgwood received the University of Edinburgh's prestigious James Tait Black Memorial Prize for *William the Silent* (1944), which has since been translated into at least six different languages. She recaptured the events of the years preceding the Civil War in England in *The Great Rebellion: The King's Peace, 1637–1641* (1955), and those of the war itself in a second volume, *The King's War, 1641–1647* (1958). The *Saturday Review* (September 24, 1955) said of the first volume: "The excitement and color of this narrative are never achieved at the cost of the least violence to scholarly accuracy. Instead, its special fascination results . . . from long soaking in the documents of an exciting and colorful time." Wedgwood went on from *The Great Rebellion* to give the conclusion of the story in *A Coffin for King Charles: The Trial and Execution of Charles I* (1964).

In addition to her historical work, Wedgwood also published several studies of poetry and literature in their historical context, including *Seventeenth Century English Literature* (1950), *Poetry and Politics Under the Stuarts* (1960), *The World of Rubens* (1967), *Milton and His World* (1969), and *The Political Career of Peter Paul Rubens* (1975), and translated several volumes from the German. Literary editor of the journal *Time and Tide* from 1944 to 1950, she also frequently lectured and spoke on the British Broadcasting Corporation, for she was a well-known figure thanks to the popularity of her books. Wedgwood was a fellow of the Royal Historical Society, the British Academy, and the Royal Society of Literature of the United Kingdom, as well as a member of the Royal Commission on Historical Manuscripts (1952–78) and the Institute of Advanced Studies at Princeton University (1953–68). She also served as presi-

C. V. Wedgwood

dent of the English Association (1955–56) and of the Society of Authors (1972–77). Named a Commander of the British Empire in 1956, she was elevated to the rank of Dame in 1968, and the following year became one of the 24 members of the Order of Merit.

Wedgwood's last book, the culmination of years of research, was a volume of world history, *The Spoils of Time: A World History from the Dawn of Civilization through the Early Renaissance* (1985), published when she was 75. After her death in 1997, an obituary in *The Economist* noted, "She had a novelist's talent for entering into the character of the giants of history," echoing a 1965 assessment in *Horizon* magazine: "Wedgwood is that rare treasure, an impeccably accurate historian who, at the same time, has a novelist's feeling for character and plot, and writes about history as the rousing good story it is."

SOURCES:
Current Biography 1957. NY: H.W. Wilson, 1957.
Encyclopedia of World Biography. 2nd ed. Detroit, MI: Gale Research, 1998.
Horizon. Summer 1964, vol. VI, no. 3.

SUGGESTED READING:
"C.V. Wedgwood, 86; Found Vivid Tales in History," in *The New York Times.* March 11, 1997, p. C24.
"Dame Veronica Wedgwood," in *The Times* [London]. March 11, 1997, p. 23.

Susan J. Walton,
freelance writer,
Berea, Ohio

Weed, Ella (1853–1894)

American educator who played a leading role in the development of Barnard College. Born on January 27, 1853, in Newburgh, New York; died on January 10, 1894, in New York City; first of four children of Jonathan Noyes Weed (a banker) and Elizabeth Merritt (Goodsell) Weed; attended Miss Mackay's School in Newburgh; graduated from Vassar College, 1873; never married; no children.

Taught in Springfield, Ohio (1875–82); taught at Miss Mackay's School (1882); became head of the day school at Anne Brown School in New York City (1884); recruited by Annie Nathan Meyer to assist with founding of Barnard College (1888); named chair of the academic committee of the newly founded Barnard College (1889); set the standard for the college, both in curriculum and in entrance standards, while overseeing the college's early development (1889–94).

Born in 1853 in Newburgh, New York, Ella Weed was the eldest child of Jonathan Noyes Weed, a banker, and **Elizabeth Goodsell Weed**. Both parents were well known in the communi-

ty, where her father's family had lived for generations. After receiving her early education at Miss Mackay's School in her hometown, Weed attended Vassar College. She was a talented writer, and before graduating with honors in 1873 helped the school's publication, *Vassar Miscellany*, achieve a high reputation among college periodicals of the time.

Two years after graduating, Weed began teaching at a girls' school in Springfield, Ohio, where her duties centered on helping to prepare students who wished to attend Vassar. At her family's request, in 1882 she returned to Newburgh and a less demanding job teaching at Miss Mackay's School. In 1884, having recovered her strength, Weed obtained the position of head of the day school at the stylish Anne Brown School in New York City. The strong reputation she earned there caught the attention of *Annie Nathan Meyer, a wealthy New Yorker who briefly had attended Columbia University's Collegiate Course, the all-male school's version of higher education for women. The Collegiate Course required women to study on their own, without the benefit of lectures that were open only to men, despite the fact that both female and male students were expected to meet the same standards and pass the same examinations. The injustice of this situation brought about a movement, led by Meyer, to replace the Collegiate Course with a women's annex. Weed's experience at the Anne Brown School had brought her into the acquaintance of many socially prominent people, and in 1888 Meyer sought her assistance in selecting 50 important individuals to sign a petition, to be presented to Columbia's trustees, advocating the establishment of a women's annex to the university. The petition proved successful, and the following year saw the founding of Barnard College for women, complete with lectures provided by Columbia faculty. While the college was distinct both physically and financially from the men's university, its students received a comparable education and their degrees were granted by Columbia University.

Weed continued in her job at the Anne Brown School while also serving as a member of the first board of trustees and chair of the academic committee for Barnard College. In the latter position, she was responsible for all of the academic duties of a college dean, with minimal supervision from Arthur Brooks, chair of the board of trustees. Among her responsibilities were overseeing the college's first location at 343 Madison Avenue and negotiating with Columbia's faculty. She was also active in public relations and fund raising for the college.

While Meyer was a strong presence at the college (and would remain a trustee for five decades), Weed's involvement was vital in helping to establish Barnard as one of the foremost women's colleges. She did not approve of the educational standards of many colleges for women, which like finishing schools emphasized those skills necessary for a wife and a woman of society, and Barnard's policies reflected her conviction that women could gain full intellectual status only by having access to an education equal to that offered to men. She also imposed strict standards upon Barnard's entrance requirements. Despite the limited availability of preparatory Greek instruction for women, Weed insisted on Greek as an entrance requirement since it was a requirement for Columbia University. In addition, she was adamant with regard to insisting on breadth of learning as opposed to specialization and refused special students in all areas but the sciences. In the school's early years, she also refused transfer students so that the measure of the college would be based on students who received their entire education at Barnard. She further guaranteed high standards by requiring Columbia's supervision of all instruction at Barnard.

Weed was described as good humored and possessed of a winning personality, and her personal style contributed highly to her success. She often exhibited such faith in students who were deemed unlikely to succeed that she inspired them with an enthusiasm for learning. Considering women's education to be her personal cause, she largely put her own literary talents and ambitions aside, although she did write a satirical novel, *A Foolish Virgin* (1883), about a Vassar graduate who denies her own good sense and education in an effort to meet society's low standards for female behavior. *Pearls Strung by Ella Weed* (1898), published posthumously, contains selections from some of her favorite authors. Weed's career, however, was cut short when she was just 40. She died in 1894 in New York City, of "nervous prostration" which may have been caused by overwork, and was buried in her hometown of Newburgh.

SOURCES:

James, Edward T., ed. *Notable American Women, 1607–1950*. Cambridge, MA: The Belknap Press of Harvard University, 1971.

Susan J. Walton,
freelance writer,
Berea, Ohio

Weed, Ethel (1906–1975)

American military officer who promoted Japanese women's rights during the U.S. occupation of Japan after World War II. Name variations: Ethel Berenice Weed. Born on May 11, 1906, in Syracuse, New York; died of cancer on June 6, 1975, in Newton, Connecticut; oldest of three daughters and one son of Grover Cleveland Weed (an engineer) and Berenice (Benjamin) Weed; attended grade school in Syracuse, New York, and Lakewood High School in Lakewood, Ohio; Western Reserve University, A.B. in English, 1929.

The daughter of an engineer who encouraged his children to emulate his own love of adventure, Ethel Weed was born in 1906 and moved with her family in 1919 from her hometown of Syracuse, New York, to Cleveland, Ohio. There she became the first member of her family to achieve a college degree, with her graduation in 1929 from Western Reserve University (now Case Western Reserve University). She followed this accomplishment with an eight-year stint as a reporter for the *Cleveland Plain Dealer*. After a brief time of travel in Europe, she worked as assistant executive secretary of public relations for the Women's City Club in Cleveland. This position proved to be a springboard to her own public relations business, begun in 1941, which she conducted largely on behalf of women's groups and other civic organizations.

In 1943, during World War II, Weed made a career change after a client who was a recruiter for the Women's Army Corps (WAC) convinced her to sign up with the military. Basic training and time spent at the Officers' Candidate School in Fort Oglethorpe, Georgia, resulted in her receiving a commission as a second lieutenant in August 1944. She began as a recruiter, but her interest in travel to the Far East led her to apply for a special course in Japanese studies at Northwestern University. Accepted in the course, she became one of only 20 women officers chosen for an assignment in Japan at the end of World War II.

Japan's surrender in 1945 signaled the beginning of the occupation of that country by American forces, and Weed went on the first American convoy to Yokohama in order to assist with the demilitarization and democratization of Japan. That October, she took on the title of Women's Information Officer in the Civil Information and Education Section, with responsibility for drafting policies and developing "programs for the dissemination of information pertinent to the reorientation and democratization of Japanese women in [the] political, economic and social fields." Weed put her recruiting skills to work by surrounding herself with Japanese advisors who could counsel her in this daunting task, the majority of whom had been active in working for suffrage and other women's rights issues in the years before the war.

Weed focused on promoting women's suffrage in preparation for the first postwar election, to be held on April 10, 1946. American authorities were counting on the desire for peace of Japanese women to influence what sort of leadership would be elected, but women had been granted the right to vote only in January, and the press predicted that a mere 10% of those newly enfranchised would go to the polls. Using her extensive public relations skills, Weed launched a campaign that utilized press conferences, radio shows, motion pictures, and other techniques to motivate women to vote. Remarkably, 67% of women voters turned out, electing an astonishing 39 women to seats in Parliament.

Weed also focused vast efforts toward the development of women's organizations that were based on a democratic foundation. Her prior experience with Cleveland women's clubs was invaluable as she assisted with the organization (or reorganization) of groups such as the Women's Democratic Club, the Japanese Association of University Women, the Housewives' Federation, and the Japanese League of Women Voters. All across Japan, women's groups utilized a pamphlet Weed wrote on how to use democratic principles in running their organizations.

In 1946, a number of legal reforms enacted by the Occupation in order to better the status of women in Japan required a revision of the Civil Code. Weed assisted legal experts as they factored in the changes which gave Japanese women the freedom to choose a husband and provided equality with regard to property, divorce, and inheritance. As she had done with the suffrage issue, Weed campaigned across the country in support of these reforms. That same year, her extraordinary efforts were recognized when she was awarded an Army Commendation Ribbon on September 23. In 1947, she resigned from the WAC as a first lieutenant but continued crusading for her various causes as a civilian, playing an important role in the forming of a Women's and Minors' Bureau of the new Japanese Ministry of Labor. She staying with this task until the end of the Occupation in 1952, to guarantee that funds were not compromised by the government. Out of her many accomplishments during this time of upheaval, perhaps the most enduring was her instruction of women's groups on how to use their new rights.

After returning to the United States in 1952, Weed began doctoral studies of East Asia at Columbia University, although she never completed her degree. In 1954, she opened a bookstore that specialized in Asian works, the East and West Shop, with her cousin **Thelma Ziemer**, moving it from New York City to Newton, Connecticut, in 1969. She maintained contact with many of her Japanese friends and in 1971 made a return trip to Japan, where she was honored by both government and civic leaders. She died of cancer four years later, on June 6, 1975, in Newton.

SOURCES:
Sicherman, Barbara, and Carol Hurd Green, eds. *Notable American Women: The Modern Period.* Cambridge, MA: The Belknap Press of Harvard University, 1980.

Susan J. Walton,
freelance writer,
Berea, Ohio

Weekley, Frieda (1879–1956).

See Lawrence, Frieda.

Weeks, Helen C. (1839–1918).

See Campbell, Helen Stuart.

Wehner-Loebinger, Lotte (b. 1905).

See Loebinger, Lotte.

Wehselau, Mariechen (b. 1906).

See Ederle, Gertrude for sidebar.

Weigel, Helene (1900–1971)

Legendary Austrian-born stage actress and theater director who was married to the dramatist Bertolt Brecht. Pronunciation: WHY-gl (g as in go). Name variations: Helen Weigel-Brecht. Born in Vienna on May 12, 1900; died in East Berlin in what was then the GDR in 1971; came from a well-off Jewish family, her father was manager of a textile factory and her mother the owner of a toy store; attended Volksschule in Vienna, 1907–15; attended a Lyzeum (high school) for girls, 1915–18; took acting lessons, 1918; married Bertolt Brecht, in 1929; children: Stefan Sebastian Brecht (b. 1924); Mari Barbara Brecht (b. 1930).

Auditioned with the famous Viennese director Arthur Rundt and made small stage appearances in Vienna (1918–19); acted in Frankfurt, Germany, where she received her first major role as Marie in Georg Büchner's Woyzeck *(1919–23); was on stage at various theaters in Berlin (1922–28), where she met Bertolt Brecht (1923); acted at the Staatstheater Berlin (1928–29); married Brecht (1929); emigrated from Germany (1933), first to Prague, then Vienna, Switzerland, and Denmark; traveled to Moscow (1933); emigrated to Sweden (1939), and to Finland (1940); emigrated to U.S. via the Soviet Union (1941); settled with Brecht and their children in California; returned to Switzerland (1947) and settled in the Com-*

munist-controlled East sector of Berlin (1948); co-founded the Berlin Ensemble with Brecht (1949); was a director of the Berlin Ensemble and lead actress in numerous plays (1949–71).

Major roles: Marie in Georg Büchner's Woyzeck *(Frankfurt, 1921–23); Klara in Friedrich Hebbel's* Maria Magdalena *(Berlin, 1925); Grete in Ernst Toller's* Der deutsche Hinkemann *(Berlin, 1927); the Widow Bebick in Brecht's* Man equals Man *(Berlin, 1927); title role in Maxim Gorky's* The Mother *(Berlin, 1932 and 1951); Therese Carrar in Brecht's* Die Gewehre der Frau Carrar *(The Guns of Mrs. Carrar, Paris, 1937, and Copenhagen, 1938); title role in* Antigone *(Chur, Switzerland, 1948); title role in Brecht's* Mother Courage *(Berlin Ensemble, 1949); Natella in Brecht's* The Caucasian Chalk Circle *(Berlin Ensemble, 1954); with the Berlin Ensemble in London as* Mother Courage *(1956) and as Natella at the Old Vic (1965); Mrs. Luckerniddle in Brecht's* St. Joan of the Stockyards *(1968).*

"What one needs is an actress," the struggling, young dramatist Bertolt Brecht told a friend in Berlin on a late summer evening in 1923. Looking out the window, Brecht's friend remarked that the light had just gone on in Helene Weigel's apartment across the square, "I'll call her up and tell her you're coming." Brecht left immediately, and Weigel invited him in. Later that evening, when it became clear that Brecht wanted to spend the night, Weigel fixed a bed for him on the sofa. In the middle of the night, Brecht knocked on Weigel's bedroom door complaining that he was cold. She gave him another blanket.

Upon Brecht's return to Munich shortly thereafter—though he was still married, had a steady girlfriend, and several lovers—he began pursuing Weigel; he wrote letters, invited her to visit him in Munich, and for a trip to Paris and Italy. Despite his claim that he needed "an actress," Brecht did not work with her until years later. According to Weigel, he at first thought very little of her as an actress. She was to develop, however, into the quintessential Brechtian actress, illustrating to perfection Brecht's theory of the drama. On stage, she captivated the audience with her charismatic personality, and her gestures and expressions—at once simple and complex—not only captured a wide range of emotions, but also inspired intellectual skirmishes over the actions of characters she portrayed on stage. A fan once complimented Weigel on her performance by musing that she had not been acting the part of a lower-class mother, but

she had become that mother. "No," Weigel answered, "I played her, and it must have been her that you liked, not me." One critic remarked that Weigel accomplished more than just making her audience see and listen. She performed not one art, but many. For instance, Weigel taught her audience that generosity and wisdom are forms of art which could and must be learned.

Helene Weigel was born on May 12, 1900, to a wealthy, assimilated Jewish family in Vienna. Her father managed a textile factory, and her mother owned and operated a toy story. Weigel was brought up in one of the most exciting cities of Europe. At the time, Vienna was the home of Freud and psychoanalysis, of writers such as Arthur Schnitzler and Hugo von Hofmannsthal, painters such as Gustav Klimt, Egon Schiele, and Oskar Kokoschka; well known for its intellectual caféhouse culture, Vienna was the city of the waltz, the theater, and the opera. Vienna's *haute bourgeoisie*, which included a numerous and prosperous Jewish element, was known for its mixture of aristocratic sentimentalism, liberalism, and decadence. However, with the Austro-Hungarian Empire coming toward its end, Vienna was also the site of social and political disintegration, and thus a fertile ground for the development of disparate ideological trends, including nationalism, anti-Semitism, zionism, and socialism.

Having two working parents, Weigel and her sister were raised with the help of servants. As was common in upper-class, Jewish circles, Weigel was sent to a girl's *Lyzeum*. The school's director, *Eugenie "Genia" Schwarzwald*, was a suffragist who believed that given the opportunity girls could achieve as much as boys. To prove her point, Schwarzwald invited professionally successful women to the school. The visits of the popular actress **Lia Rosen** and the famous Danish writer *Karin Michaëlis* deeply impressed Weigel and influenced her decision to break out of her sheltered existence and pursue her dream. Against the wishes of her parents, who saw acting as a morally dubious and unstable profession, Weigel decided to conquer the world on stage. With the Austro-Hungarian Empire near its collapse, Weigel left school during the last year of World War I and filched money from her father's pants pockets to pay for her first acting lessons.

In December 1917, Weigel auditioned for the famous Viennese theater director Arthur Rundt. Michaëlis, who was a strong supporter of Weigel, went along for the audition and described later that she had heard in Weigel's voice "the tones of a pipe organ, the rattle of death, the cries of women giving birth, and the joy of love's ecstasy." Throughout her career, Weigel's voice received much attention. It was hailed by some reviewers as "tone hard as steel," or "marked by deep sensitivity of feeling," while others called her the noisiest actress of Berlin, whose horrible screams should be silenced as soon as possible.

In 1918, Weigel made minor stage appearances in Vienna, and in 1919, she moved to Frankfurt, Germany, to join the New Theater, where she played her first major role and reaped her first success as Marie in Georg Büchner's *Woyzeck*. The Frankfurt newspaper called her a "true talent," and others noted that her acting was carried by her excellent mimics and a "hard tone of voice with discerning eccentricity." While in Frankfurt, she also played the prostitute Anna in Hans Johst's *The King*, the old woman in Georg Kaiser's expressionist play *Gas II*, Pauline Piperkarcka in Gerhart Hauptmann's naturalist play *The Rats*, and Meroe in Heinrich von Kleist's *Penthesilea*. Most reviewers noted the vitality Weigel brought to her roles—one reviewer compared her to an erupting volcano—but also thought that her extraordinary talent was in need of discipline and control.

[Helene Weigel was] one of the greatest dramatic geniuses ever born.

—Arthur Rundt

In 1922, Weigel moved to Berlin, where she worked under the direction of Leopold Jessner at the Staatstheater Berlin. Under Jessner, she played many different roles between 1922 and 1929—minor roles in Shakespeare's *Macbeth*, Goethe's *Faust, Part I*, and in comedies by Molière; major, challenging roles as Salome in Hebbel's *Herodes and Mariamne* and the servant girl in Sophocles' *Oedipus*. From 1923 to 1928, she was engaged by several theaters in Berlin, among them the Schauspielertheater, Deutsche Theater, Renaissancetheater, Centraltheater, Junge Bühne, Lessing-Theater, Volksbühne, and the Theater am Schiffbauerdamm. Weigel's first role in a play by Brecht was not on stage but in an adaptation of the play *Man equals Man* for radio in March 1927. She spoke the role of Leokadja Bebick and received positive reviews from critics, although the radio version of the play was generally not well received. In December 1927, she played the same role on stage at the Volksbühne Berlin. Brecht, one critic noted, merely produced words, but coming from Weigel's mouth, these words became so convincing that the audience could not help but believe them.

It came as a great shock to many when Brecht and Weigel married in 1929. Brecht had come to settle in Berlin in 1924. Weigel had given

him her own apartment and had found herself another one nearby. At Weigel's apartment, Brecht came and went as he pleased. He had various lovers, was still married, and had a daughter **Hanne** with his wife **Marianne Zoff** as well as a son from a previous relationship who was later raised by Austrian relatives of Weigel. Brecht's and Weigel's son Stefan had been born in 1924. By 1928, Brecht was divorced and had led several lovers to believe that they would be the next Mrs. Brecht, among them the actress *Carola Neher (1900–1942), the playwright *Marieluise Fleisser (1901–1974), and Brecht's co-writer Elisabeth Hauptmann (c. 1900–1962), who, as has been revealed recently, wrote many songs, parts, and poems attributed to Brecht without ever receiving credit or adequate compensation for her work. Both Fleisser and Hauptmann attempted suicide when they heard about Brecht's marriage to Weigel, but both survived.

According to Fleisser, Brecht made it absolutely plain to Weigel "that both he and his work could not get along without other women." Except for occasional crises, Weigel seemed to accept Brecht's promiscuous lifestyle quietly. In the 1940s, while working at the Berlin Ensemble, she pulled aside a young man who showed a romantic interest in one of the actresses working with Brecht, explaining that her husband got upset and distracted when someone pursued one of his love interests. She then politely asked him to leave.

Weigel's and Brecht's daughter Mari Barbara was born in 1930. Between 1928 and 1933, Weigel performed in various Brecht plays: she continued playing the Widow Bebick in *Man equals Man* under the direction of Brecht; she was an agitator in *The Measures Taken* and Pelagea Wlassowa in *The Mother*, a role for which she was praised as the "greatest proletarian actress." It is said that Brecht's turn toward Communism and Marxism and the increasing politicization of his work was due to Weigel's influence. Weigel had been a Communist since her days in Vienna, where she had come in contact with socialist and leftist ideals. She joined the Communist Party in 1929.

After Hitler's rise to power, Weigel, Brecht, and their children left Germany in February 1933, traveling to Prague and Vienna before settling for a short time in Carona, Switzerland. In June, they moved to Denmark and lived at first at Michaëlis' estate in Thuro and then bought their own house in Svendborg. Weigel could not work in Denmark; she did not speak Danish and lived in a village without a theater. Dissatisfied

with her forced retirement from the stage and eager to help in the anti-Nazi efforts, she traveled to Moscow that autumn. There, she fell ill and had to cancel her planned appearances on Soviet radio. Sick and without money, Weigel asked Brecht in a letter to come to Moscow. He declined, and Weigel had to borrow money to make her way back to Denmark. In October 1937, Weigel played Therese Carrar in Brecht's *The Guns of Mrs. Carrar* at a guest engagement in Paris. In 1938, she played two parts in the Paris opening of Brecht's *99%*.

By 1939, Hitler's Third Reich was expanding rapidly, and the Brecht-Weigel family no longer felt safe in Denmark. In April, they moved to Stockholm, Sweden, where they applied for American immigration visas, and then went on to Helsinki, Finland. Their visas for the U.S. finally arrived in May 1941, and they left Helsinki for the Soviet Union. The family bought tickets for the last five places on the Swedish freighter *Annie Johnson*, sailing from Vladivostok for San Pedro, California. On the night of June 21–22, the German army attacked the Soviet Union, and the *Annie Johnson* was to be the last passenger ship to leave for America for years to come.

The Brecht-Weigel family settled in Santa Monica, California, where Brecht became involved with Hollywood and the movie business. Weigel devoted her time to raising her children and providing her husband with a comfortable home. She could not establish herself in Hollywood, where successful actresses had to be young and beautiful. Weigel lacked conventional beauty, spoke English with a heavy German accent, and was in her 40s. However, she did play a role in the film version of *Anna Seghers' The Seventh Cross*, which also featured Spencer Tracy and *Jessica Tandy.

In November 1947, Brecht and Weigel left California and moved to Switzerland. In Chur, she played Antigone in Brecht's version of Sophocles' play. Some reviewers criticized Brecht's choice for the part, maintaining that Weigel's age should have precluded her from playing the youthful Antigone. While in Switzerland, Weigel and Brecht began to assemble a team and concentrated on finding the right stage for the many works that Brecht and his faithful workers had completed in exile. In 1948, the Soviet authorities extended an invitation to Brecht and Weigel. They were offered financing for the production of Brecht's *Mother Courage* in the Soviet-controlled East sector of Berlin. With Weigel in the title role, the play was a huge success. Deeply moved, the audience sat silently, then stood up and applauded to exhaustion. A Soviet critic saw the play's final scene as a "terrifying symbol of the tragic fate of an entire people." Overnight, Weigel became a legend, now commonly identified as Mother Courage.

In February 1949, when Weigel was given several offices at the Soviet-German cultural club in Berlin, she set out to establish a theater company under her direction, with Brecht serving as head artistic advisor. In April, the ruling Socialist Unity Party approved the creation of a theatrical ensemble under the management of Helene Weigel. The ensemble was the culmination of Brecht's efforts to establish the "epic theater." In contrast to the traditional, Aristotelian theater, the epic theater depicts events not as fate, but as historically constituted processes. Instead of empathy and pity for the fate of a hero, Brecht wanted to raise critical awareness about the conditions prompting a character's actions. The epic theater calls for a new type of actor and actress and a new type of audience. The style of acting is subdued, oscillating from highly affected stylization to naturalistic gestures. The fragmentation of the drama's plot is enhanced by the interspersion of songs and declarations. The emphasis of Brecht's plays lies not upon *what* happens, but upon *how* it happens. The audience is expected to view the play with critical distance, examining and judging the characters for their actions rather than identifying with their suffering.

Weigel became the model actress of the epic theater. She illustrated Brecht's *Verfremdungseffekt*, the alienation effect, by seeming to stand beside the character without identifying with it. However, in her perfection of the epic principles, Weigel unwillingly undermined them. She was so successful in her roles that she mesmerized the audience, thus putting into question its critical distance. In the fall of 1949, the Berlin Ensemble made its debut with Brecht's *Mr. Puntila and his Man Matti* in the newly formed German Democratic Republic. In 1951, Weigel once again played the part of Pelagea Wlassowa in *The Mother*; in 1952, she reprised the role of Teresa Carrar, and, in 1954, Natella in *The Caucasian Chalk Circle*.

After Brecht's death in 1956, Weigel continued her work with the Ensemble, taking *Mother Courage* to London in 1956 and *The Caucasian Chalk Circle* in 1964. She became Brecht's sole heir and guardian of the posthumous papers. Before she died in Berlin in 1971, Weigel received numerous medals and titles from the government of the GDR. Unfortunately, Weigel was not a writer; she did not keep a diary and did not write many letters. Her papers are housed in the former GDR, and to this day little is known in the West about her life. With the opening of the Wall, more researchers will gain access to information housed in East Berlin Archives, and it is to be expected that Weigel's career and life will be more fully explored in the future.

SOURCES:

Fuegi, John. *Brecht and Company: Sex, Politics, and the Making of the Modern Drama*. NY: Grove Press, 1994.

Hayman, Ronald. *Brecht. A Biography*. NY: Oxford University Press, 1983.

Hecht, Walter, and Siegfried Unseld, ed. *Helene Weigel zu Ehren*. Frankfurt: Suhrkamp, 1970.

Schorske, Carl E. *Fin-De-Siècle Vienna*. NY: Random House, 1980.

Karin Bauer,
Assistant Professor of German Studies,
McGill University, Montreal

Weigl, Vally (1889–1982)

Austrian-born American composer, music therapist, and lecturer. Name variations: Valery Weigl. Born Valery Pick in Vienna on September 11, 1889 (some sources cite 1894 or 1899); died in New York on December 25, 1982; daughter of Josef Pick (a prominent attorney); sister of Käthe Leichter (1895–1942), Austrian Social Democratic leader who was murdered at Ravensbrück; married the composer Karl Weigl (1881–1949).

Vally Weigl studied in Vienna under Richard Robert, Guido Adler, and Karl Weigl whom she later married. She and her composer husband came to the United States in 1938, as refugees from the Nazi occupation of their native Austria. Weigl's sister *Käthe Leichter was unable to escape from Nazi-occupied Vienna, and as a Social Democratic activist soon found herself in a Nazi concentration camp, where she was killed in 1942. Weigl's first jobs in New York were teaching positions at the Institute for Avocational Music and the American Theater Wing (1947–58). A lifelong interest in music therapy motivated her to obtain a master of arts degree in that field in 1955 from Columbia University. She became the chief music therapist at New York Medical College and taught at Roosevelt Cerebral Palsy School. She also wrote music therapy programs for UNESCO. Because of her wide experience in the field of music therapy, Weigl was much sought after as a lecturer. Despite her often hectic schedule, she continued composing and was able to find some leisure time for her musical agenda as a fellow of the McDowell Colony where she was twice composer-in-residence. A committed peace activist, Weigl served as a co-founder of the Friends' Arts for World Unity Committee, and her *Peace Is a Shelter* for Chorus, Soloist and Piano (1970) was composed during the Vietnam War. Weigl composed well over 100 vocal pieces, a number of which have been recorded. Besides her own musical efforts, she was tireless in promoting her late husband's compositions.

John Haag,
Athens, Georgia

Wei Kuo fu-jen (1262–1319).

See Guan Daosheng.

Weil, Simone (1909–1943)

French Jewish intellectual, writer, teacher, political activist, and Christian mystic who was "the saint of outsiders." Name variations: (pseudonym) Émile Novis. Pronunciation: See-mon VALE. Born Simone Adolphine Weil on February 3, 1909, in Paris, France; died in Ashford, Kent, England, on August 24, 1943; daughter of Bernard Weil (a physician) and Salomea (Selma) Reinherz Weil; received baccalauréat degree, Lycée Duruy, Paris, 1925; studied philosophy, Lycée Henry IV, Paris, 1925–28; École Normale Supérieure, 1928–31 (passed agrégation, 1931); never married; no children.

Taught at girls' lycée in Le Puy (1931–32); taught in Auxerre (1932–33); taught in Roanne (1933–34); met Leon Trotsky (1933); worked in factories (1934–35); taught in Bourges (1935–36); was active in Spanish Civil War (1936); visited Italy and Assisi (1937); held teaching post in Saint-Quentin, a suburb of Paris (1937–38); took sick leave (1938); lived in Switzerland (spring 1939); returned to Paris (September 1939); family fled Paris (June 1940); stayed in Vichy (June–September 1940); settled in Marseille; fled to Morocco (May 14, 1942); sailed to New York (June 7, 1942); left for England (November 10, 1942); worked for Free French forces, London; hospitalized with tuberculosis (mid-April 1943).

Simone Weil carried two burdens throughout her life—by birth, not by choice, Simone was a female and a Jew. From an early age, she repudiated and minimized her gender and rejected her Jewishness. An idealist in an age of the horrors of two world wars, economic depression, genocide, and forced exile, she sympathized with the working classes and sought solace in Catholicism while deprecating the organized Church. An unsuccessful teacher, a vagabond, an outsider, she stressed the need for roots, for "rootedness," stability and regularity in one's life. Weil never achieved what she valued for others; her life is a life of a mind cultivated and nurtured at the expense of physical and material well-being.

Weil was born in 1909 in her parents' apartment in Paris, the second child of free-thinking bourgeois French Jews who had few ties to the established Jewish community in Paris. Her father's highly orthodox family came from Alsace, her mother was born in Russia. Intelligent and cultured, the Weils provided mental stimulation for their brilliant son André (born in 1906) and for Simone; books were plentiful, but no toys were allowed. During World War I (1914–18), Dr. Weil was called up for medical service. The close-knit family followed him to the various towns where he was stationed. Simone realized early on that her brother was exceptionally gifted (he became a mathematician), and she developed a keen sense of intellectual inferiority. However, she excelled in Latin and Greek, learned English from listening to André's tutor, and German from her parents' conversations. Weil's fragile health as a child and fear of contamination may have been responsible for her increasing aversion to physical contact with others. Moreover, she often could not bear to eat knowing that other children around the world were starving. One biographer remarked that she could not let her body enjoy or be enjoyed by others, thereby making herself "untouchable." Physical deprivation—lack of close, warm friendships and of simple comforts—characterized her entire life from childhood on.

It is necessary to uproot oneself. To cut down the tree and make of it a cross, and then carry it every day.

—Simone Weil

From the age of ten, Weil's education prepared her to enter the world of the French intellectual elite. She attended the most prestigious preparatory schools in Paris where she scored at or near the top of her classes. Simone's mother encouraged her to reject "girlish charms" and cultivate forthrightness to the point of bluntness. Further, Weil adopted a modified style of men's clothing. Her scorn for bourgeois standards for feminine behavior offended many of her fellow students, as did her abrasive intellectualizing and patent moralizing. Simone envied her brother whom she regarded as brighter than she—and "he was he." As Thomas R. Niven points out: "It is as though for her, to be recognized as female was tantamount to being reduced, to being only female."

In June 1925, Weil passed the baccaulauréat and in October entered the top class of the Lycée Henry IV to prepare for entry into the highly selective École Normale Supérieure. She studied philosophy with the famous Alain who influenced her attitude towards religion, art, the working class, and government. Her interest in politics led to involvement with French workers, and trade union movements, and her attraction to Catholicism produced some of her most lyrical and profound writings. At the Sorbonne, Weil ranked at the top of her class (*Simone de Beauvoir ranked second), and in 1928, Weil was the only woman admitted to the Normale that prepared students for an academic career. Her study of Descartes convinced her that work gave life

meaning and value. She believed in action, in doing: ideas must be acted upon. At the Normale, she was called the "red virgin" because of her militant left-wing sympathies and her pacifism. She collected money to aid the unemployed and campaigned for disarmament. She never joined the French Communist Party, but she agreed with its goals of improving the lot of the worker. Weil confided to her friend and biographer **Simone Pétrement**, "What I can't put up with is that people compromise." While a student at the Lycée Henry IV, she had stated that she would choose a career "to do something for the good of humanity." In 1931, she passed her exams, qualifying her to teach in lycées and universities.

Weil was now forced to enter the adult world of work, a system, according to her, that dehumanized the worker, making them into a mere tool of production. Did she regard teaching as a form of servitude, a means of fulfilling her need to serve humanity? In her work "The Iliad, or a poem of the force" (1940–41), she laments the impersonal "force" that transforms man into a "thing," an empty shell, a corpse. This view may explain in part her lack of success as an educator; as a teacher, she was reduced to serving the students, their parents, and numerous school officials. Weil saw herself as a mere cog, a "thing," in the huge national education system. But Simone knew she was at least a "thinking thing." The 17th-century French Christian apologist (and mathematical genius) Blaise Pascal wrote: "Man is only a reed, the weakest found in nature; but he is a thinking reed." Simone Weil exemplified this notion. Assigned to a girls' lycée in the remote town of Le Puy, she taught philosophy, Greek, Latin, and art history with a marked indifference to preparing her students for their national exams. Instead, she devoted her energies to lecturing to miners at the Workers' College in the industrial town of Saint-Étienne, a three-hour train ride from Le Puy. She organized meetings to encourage unity among workers' unions, Socialist and Communist; only through uniting union leadership would workers achieve their revolutionary goals, she believed. And for revolution to succeed, the workers needed to acquire the power of understanding and using language, a power held by their leaders, by industrialists, and politicians. Weil had embraced Marx's notion that revolution would "restore the unity of intellectual and manual labor." In 1934, she wrote her "Reflections on the causes of liberty and of social oppression" (published posthumously) which included analyses of Marxism and political oppression, a theory of a free society, and a critical look at society and its failures. When she participated in a miners' demonstration and wrote articles for *L'Effort*, school officials suggested she transfer to another school.

In 1932, Weil had traveled to Berlin where she witnessed the growing fascist movement and met Leon Trotsky's son. After Hitler was appointed chancellor in 1933, she provided aid for German refugees, often sheltering them in her parents' home in Paris. Leon Trotsky himself visited her in December 1933. Having been reassigned, teaching at lycées in Auxerre and Roanne, Weil decided to take a leave of absence and work in a factory; her experiences are related in her "Reflections" where she criticizes modern industry "in which human labor has been debased to drudgery." Moreover, female workers, she noted, were victims of sexist attitudes, paid less than men, and served as objects of obscene remarks. Despite living and working with factory employees, she remained apart; as one biographer observed, Simone Weil placed herself *with* the workers, the Communists, and later the Catholics, but she was never one of them. Indeed, Simone was a loner, an outsider who lived a spartan life, eschewing physical comforts, often denying her body nourishment and her soul a tranquil existence. She struggled to improve the lot of humankind, to right the wrongs that afflicted them; Weil was near to becoming "a lonely moral scourge," Robert Coles observed, "whose magnificent capacity to dream of what ought to be was imprisoned by pessimism about what can be."

Weil abandoned factory work in August 1935 and traveled with her parents to the Iberian coasts. In a small Portuguese fishing village, she had the first "of three contacts with Christianity that have really counted," as she expressed it. She observed the celebration of a festival honoring the village's patron saint and listened to the women singing plaintive ancient hymns. Suddenly she was struck with "the conviction . . . that Christianity is preeminently the religion of slaves, that slaves cannot help belonging to it, and I among others." But Weil was not a slave, she was an intellectual bourgeois Jew and would never belong to Christianity any more than she belonged to the workers, a political party, or her fellow teachers.

During the academic year 1935–36, Weil taught at Bourges, but continued to work for unity among leftist labor unions and for factory reform, dedicating herself to rescuing manual labor from its "degradation." In June 1936, the Spanish Civil War broke out, and Simone joined up with a motley assemblage of non-Spanish

anti-fascist volunteers at the front. After only a few days, she stepped into a pot of boiling oil and was returned to France by her protective parents who had followed her to Spain. Infection in her leg prevented her from teaching in 1936–37. Suffering from severe headaches and anemia, she went to Italy in the spring of 1937, where she observed fascism in action and experienced her second encounter with Christianity. She visited a chapel in the mountains near Assisi and heard the story of a woman in the 15th century who had disguised herself as a man to gain admittance to the chapel; her identity was discovered only 20 years later when she was beatified. Weil realized that she and this pious woman shared a common burden, that of being female. In the Chapel of Santa Maria degli Angele, as she wrote to her friend, the Dominican priest Father Joseph-Marie Perrin, five years later, "something stronger than I forced me for the first time in my life to get down on my knees."

Weil resumed teaching in October 1937, in a lycée in Saint-Quentin, near Paris, but debili-

Simone
Weil

tating headaches compelled her to take a leave of absence. She never taught again. However, she was able to write—her true vocation—and she contributed numerous articles to journals. During Holy Week (the week before Easter) in 1938, Simone and her mother attended services in a Benedictine abbey near Les Mans to hear Gregorian chant. Here "Christ himself descended and possessed me," she wrote; it was a mystical experience that revealed to her "the possibility of loving the divine love through affliction," and which she kept secret for three years. Relieved of teaching duties, Weil eagerly studied Greek and Roman historiography, the Torah, the Egyptian Book of the Dead, and the Bible. Christianity had a strong appeal to Simone Weil, but she felt it had been contaminated and distorted by Judaism and the ancient Romans. She sought to purge it of these contaminants, thus her study of ancient texts.

After a decade of excruciating headaches, Weil reluctantly consulted a brain surgeon, fearing she had a tumor. Her friend Pétrement claims she contemplated suicide at this time. Not yet 30 years old, she had had to abandon teaching and return to her parents' home. She cherished independence, of body and mind, but found herself dependent and ill. A biographer has suggested that her headaches, which began just when she completed her education, were possibly due to her rejection of having to enter the "adult world of work," a world of responsibility and commitment. Indeed, Weil may have suffered from realizing the "dream of what ought to be" could never be achieved. In a world threatened by dictators—Hitler, Stalin, Mussolini, and Franco—and where depression crushed the worker while concentration camps crushed human bodies and souls, Weil's dream must have been sorely battered "by pessimism about what can be."

When Simone contracted pleurisy in the spring 1939, her parents took her to Switzerland and the south of France. They returned to Paris, filled with apprehension, in September 1939. War had broken out again. Weil needed to be useful and involved in the war effort. She drew up a proposal to create a nurses' corps to tend the wounded and began taking first-aid classes. Six months later, the family had to flee Paris; on June 14, 1940, the Germans occupied Paris, which had been declared an open city to save it from being destroyed. Leaving behind all their possessions, the Weils arrived safely in Vichy where they stayed until mid-September. They had decided to remain in France, despite the risk of becoming victims of German anti-Semitic policies, rather than join André in England. Sur-

prisingly, Weil felt no hatred for the German invaders, but her pacifism was severely tested when French resistance rapidly disintegrated and an armistice was signed. Simone and her family had been uprooted, as so many Jews had throughout history. The words rootlessness, uprootedness, and affliction appear frequently in her writings. She was aware of her own lack of ties, for she was neither Jew nor Christian, and her involvement in teaching and workers' causes had not bound her to any group.

"No aspect of the life of Simone Weil is more problematic—and sad—than her attitudes toward her Jewish background," according to Robert Coles. This is strikingly illustrated in a letter she wrote in August 1940 to the minister of education of the Vichy government (the French government in the unoccupied zone of France), requesting a teaching assignment. "What is a Jew?" she asked. "I do not know the definition of the word 'Jew.' . . . The subject was not included in my education. . . . I myself, who profess no religion and never have, have certainly inherited nothing from the Jewish religion. . . . The Hebraic tradition is alien to me." But anti-Jewish legislation placed severe restrictions on French Jews, and Simone was not allowed to teach. Coles is especially critical of her rejection of her heritage and concludes that "her Jewishness became a cross. . . . [The Jews] deserved better from her. It is sad that Simone Weil did not bring her intelligent, caring comprehension to her own people, her Lord's people."

The family moved on to Marseille and lived there until they left France in May 1942, following rumors that the Germans intended to occupy all of France. Weil began to study Babylonian and Sanskrit, wrote and revised poems and essays, began writing a play, and translated Greek works. She published articles in the journal *Cahiers du Sud*, using the name Émile Novis; this was in open violation of laws forbidding publication of works by Jews. Weil had also refused to comply with a June 1941 law requiring all Jews in the unoccupied zone to register and be identified: she preferred "to go to prison rather than to a ghetto." Obstinate and defiant, she engaged in illegal activities, collecting and distributing food, clothing, and ration coupons (even her parents' coupons) to Vietnamese soldiers and civilian workers interned by the Germans near Marseille, and she courted imprisonment by providing false identity cards for refugees, including Jews. She never joined the French resistance, but she was arrested for handing out anti-Vichy literature and was arraigned in court. When the judge threatened her with prison, she showed no fear and he "dismissed her as a lunatic."

Prevented from teaching, Weil tried to get work on a local farm. Physical labor, she believed, kept one in touch with reality. Through her friend Father Perrin, she was hired by Gustave Thibon. Thibon was closely associated with the French political extreme right wing and was a friend of Marshal Philippe Pétain, head of the Vichy government. But Simone must have believed in him for when she left France she entrusted him with her personal notebooks and some of her writings. She found farm work exhausting but, she wrote, "I regard physical work as a purification . . . on the order of suffering and humiliation . . . [with] instants of profound, nourishing joy." Moreover, "hard physical work was essential for an intellectual, lest the mind become all too taken with itself."

The threat of German takeover of the unoccupied zone and news of the deportation of Jews from Paris forced the Weils to leave France. Since they refused to go without Simone, she accompanied her parents to Morocco on May 14, 1942. After a short internment in a refugee camp in Casablanca, the family sailed for New York. During the four months she lived there, Weil did research on folklore at the New York Public Library and wrote two essays on the French heretical sect, the Cathars. In a long letter to Father Perrin, she reiterated her reasons for not joining the Catholic Church despite her personal commitment to Christianity. A collection of her letters to Perrin, *Attente de Dieu*, was published in 1950; it was then translated and published as *Waiting for God* in 1951.

Feeling she had deserted France, Weil decided to go to London and work in some capacity for the Free French organization there. She left New York on November 10, 1942. In London, she worked as a staff member, reviewing proposals for the regeneration of a liberated France. Her own vision of establishing a just society in a free France is contained in her *L'Enracinement* (*The Need for Roots*, 1943). Here Weil considers what every individual needs: beauty in the world, order ("a certain rhythm and regularity"), obedience, responsibility, and rootedness. And finally for the soul, "The need for truth is more sacred than any other need." Her utopian dreams reflected fear and uncertainty of the future in a time of terrible upheaval. Her concern and hopes for the working class are considered in one of her last essays, "Uprootedness in the Towns." Each worker would have a house and "a bit of garden," but they must also be allowed

"a sense of how they and their particular work fitted into life's overall scheme—in other words, to restore their roots."

In mid-April 1943, Weil contracted tuberculosis. Her desire to be of service to a free France would never be realized. She died of heart failure, aggravated by self-imposed malnutrition, at Grosvenor Sanatorium in Ashford, Kent. Curiously, the young unbaptized Jewish-Christian mystic was buried in the Roman Catholic section of the local cemetery. Simone Weil, whom André Gide called "the saint of outsiders," died in exile, rootless, with no family, religion, or country to anchor her in this world.

SOURCES:

Coles, Robert. *Simone Weil: A Modern Pilgrimage*. Reading, MA: Addison-Wesley, 1987.

McLellan, David. *Simone Weil: Utopian Pessimist*. Baringstoke, England: Macmillan, 1989.

Nevin, Thomas R. *Simone Weil: Portrait of a Self-exiled Jew*. Chapel Hill, NC: University of North Carolina, 1991.

SUGGESTED READING:

Dunaway, John M. *Simone Weil*. Boston, MA: Twayne, 1984.

Fiori, Gabriella. *Simone Weil: An Intellectual Biography*. Athens, GA: University of Georgia Press, 1989.

Little, Pat. *Simone Weil: Waiting on Truth*. Oxford: Berg, 1988.

McFarland, Dorothy Tuck. *Simone Weil*. NY: F. Ungar, 1983.

Pétrement, Simone. *Simone Weil: A Life*. Trans. by Raymond Rosenthal. NY: Schocken, 1988.

White, George Abbott, ed. *Simone Weil: Interpretations of a Life*. Amherst, MA: University of Massachusetts Press, 1981.

Winch, Peter. *Simone Weil: "The Just Balance."* Cambridge: Cambridge University Press, 1989.

COLLECTIONS:

Simone Weil's papers are located in the Manuscript Division of the Bibliothèque Nationale de France, Paris; microfilmed copies of the papers are available in the United States at the Historical Studies and Social Science Library of the Institute for Advanced Study, Princeton University.

Jeanne A. Ojala,
Professor Emerita, Department of History,
University of Utah, Salt Lake City, Utah

Weinbrecht, Donna (1965—)

American freestyle skier. Born in Hoboken, New Jersey, on April 23, 1965; daughter of James Weinbrecht and Caroline Weinbrecht.

Placed 2nd at World championships (1989, 1997); placed 1st (1991), placed 5th (1995); won a gold medal in the moguls in the Albertville Winter Olympics (1992); came in 7th in the moguls at Lillehammer Winter Olympics (1994); won the U.S. championships (1994, 1996), and placed 2nd (1997).

The first great champion in the sport of freestyle skiing, Donna Weinbrecht was also the first Olympic gold medalist in the sport, skiing in a snowstorm at Albertville in 1992 to the accompaniment of "Rock 'n' Roll High School" by the Ramones; nine months later, she suffered a knee injury. With 11 seasons on the tour, Weinbrecht had won 45 World Cup races, more World Cups than any skier in history. Her last two Olympics were disappointing, however; she came in 7th in the moguls at Lillehammer in 1994 (**Stine Lise Hattestad** of Norway took the gold, U.S.'s **Elizabeth McIntyre** the silver) and 4th in Nagano in 1998.

Weinstein, Hannah (1911–1984)

American film producer and political activist. Born Hannah Dorner on June 23, 1911, in New York City; died of a heart attack on March 9, 1984, in New York; daughter of Israel Dorner and Celia (Kaufman) Dorner; New York University, B.A., 1927; married Peter Weinstein (a journalist), in 1938 (divorced 1955); children: daughters Dina Weinstein; Lisa Weinstein (a producer); Paula Weinstein (a producer).

Early in her career, worked for the New York Herald Tribune; *was a political speechwriter for Fiorello H. La Guardia; left the United States after being blacklisted (1950); co-founded Third World Cinema (1972); produced the films* Claudine *(1974),* Greased Lightning *(1977), and* Stir Crazy *(1980).*

Born in 1911, Hannah Weinstein was a native of New York who studied journalism at New York University. While still a teenager, she started her career at the foreign desk of the *New York Herald Tribune*, leaving this job in 1937, after ten years, to work as a speechwriter for New York Mayor Fiorello H. La Guardia. Weinstein remained active on several political fronts after her speechwriting days ended; she organized various artists and scientists on behalf of President Franklin D. Roosevelt, and later worked for the presidential campaigns of Henry Wallace and Eugene McCarthy.

Weinstein's unwavering commitment to her liberal political beliefs did not fall in line with the conservative McCarthy-era "Red Scare," and in 1950, by then a divorced single mother, she moved with her three young daughters to London. There she became interested in filmmaking, producing her first feature, *Fait-Divers à Paris*, in 1952. In partnership with a British television station, she started a production company to create made-for-TV movies and hired

writers blacklisted in the United States, including Ring Lardner, Jr., and Adrian Scott, to work under cover of pseudonyms. Over a ten-year period the company made 435 television films and series, including the highly popular "Robin Hood" series, which ran for five years and was syndicated in the United States.

In 1962, Weinstein returned to the United States. She was strongly opposed to the Vietnam War, and in 1970 organized a rally at Madison Square Garden to raise funds for antiwar candidates for the Senate. The previous year, a meeting with an African-American who was qualified as a cinematographer but unemployable because he could not gain union membership had led her to begin researching racial discrimination in film production. She discovered that there were only 10 black and 3 Puerto Rican members in a technical union with a membership of over 6,000, and, in line with her daughter **Paula Weinstein**'s description of her as "an activist, a doer, not a talker," Hannah became a co-founder of Third World Cinema. The company, whose other founders included James Earl Jones, Ossie Davis and *Diana Sands, was established in 1971 to make films about minorities with minority actors and technicians. Third World Cinema was unique in Hollywood both for its intent and because 40% of its stock was owned by the Harlem-East Harlem Community Association. As executive vice-president, Weinstein furthered her goal of increasing minority presence in filmmaking by acquiring funds for a film-training academy for minorities. She also focused some of her efforts on assisting minorities in finding employment in the film industry, hiring 28 minority crew members for Third World Cinema's first feature film, *Claudine* (1974), starring James Earl Jones and **Diahann Carroll**. Although it was praised as "outstanding" by the trade paper *Variety*, the movie did not do well at the box office. More successful was Weinstein's next film with Third World Cinema, 1977's *Greased Lightning*, which featured a young Richard Pryor in his first starring role. The comedy about a black stock-car racer won audiences over, setting the stage for Weinstein's next movie with Pryor, the hugely popular prison comedy *Stir Crazy* in 1980. Both films, noted critic Dale Pollock of the *Los Angeles Times*, "stood out as intelligent, well-crafted films in an era of violent and sexist black exploitation movies."

Her efforts netted Weinstein significant honors, including the Women in Film Life Achievement Award in 1982 and the Liberty Hill Upton Sinclair Award in 1984. Sadly, she died of a heart attack shortly before the ceremony for the latter award. When it was presented posthumously, a letter from her friend *Lillian Hellman was read aloud by **Jane Fonda**, in which Hellman wrote that Weinstein was "the only person in the world Joe McCarthy was frightened of." Said Fonda, "Hannah taught me something very important: You can be successful and still be true to your values." In addition to the movies she produced and the institutions she founded, Weinstein left a significant legacy to film through her daughters Paula and **Lisa Weinstein**, both of whom followed her into the industry. The first woman vice president at Warner Bros. (in 1975), Paula Weinstein later produced *A Dry White Season* (1989), a film notable for its strong political content.

SOURCES:

Acker, Ally. *Reel Women: Pioneers of the Cinema 1896 to the Present*. NY: Continuum, 1991.

Levy, Margot, ed. *The Annual Obituary 1984*. Chicago, IL: St. James Press, 1984.

SUGGESTED READING:

Ceplair, Larry, and Steven Englund. *The Inquisition in Hollywood: Politics in the Film Community 1930–1960*. Garden City, NY: Anchor Press-Doubleday, 1980.

"Hannah Weinstein, Film and television producer," in *The Times* [London]. March 16, 1984, p. 16.

"Hannah Weinstein, Producer And Political Activist, Is Dead," in *The New York Times Biographical Service*. March, 1984, p. 423.

Susan J. Walton,
freelance writer,
Berea, Ohio

Weir, Irene (1862–1944)

American artist and art educator. Born on January 15, 1862, in St. Louis, Missouri; died of cardiovascular disease on March 22, 1944, in Yorktown Heights, New York; daughter of Walter Weir (a teacher) and Annie Field (Andrews) Weir; enrolled at the Yale School of Fine Arts (1881–82) and was awarded a B.F.A. degree in 1906; received a diploma from the École des Beaux Arts Américaine in Fontainbleau in 1923; never married; no children.

Taught drawing in grammar and high schools in New Haven, Connecticut (1887–90); served as director of the Slater Museum School of Art in Norwich, Connecticut; was teacher and then director of art instruction for Brookline, Massachusetts, public schools; published The Greek Painters' Art *(1905); published* Outlines of Courses in Design, Representation and Color for High School Classes *(with Elizabeth Stone, 1910); taught in the fine arts department of the Ethical Culture School; founded (1917) and served as director of the School of Design and Liberal Arts (1917–29).*

Born on January 15, 1862, in St. Louis, Missouri, Irene Weir continued a 100-year family tradition of devotion to the fine arts through her career as an artist and teacher. She followed in the footsteps of such notable family members as her grandfather Robert Walter Weir (1803–1889), who was both a painter and an instructor at the U.S. Military Academy at West Point for 42 years, and her uncles John Ferguson Weir (1841–1926), a painter who served as director of the School of Fine Arts at Yale University for over four decades, and Julian Alden Weir (1852–1919), a leader in the New York art world. Irene Weir credited her family's ability to combine hard work with a love of beauty for their success in art. She studied art privately under her uncle Julian before enrolling at John Ferguson Weir's School of Fine Arts at Yale in 1881.

After spending a year at Yale, Weir, like many 19th-century American artists, chose to go abroad to further her artistic development, making two trips to Europe to study at galleries in France, Italy, Spain, Holland, and England. Upon her return to the U.S., she embarked on what would be a lengthy and distinguished teaching career, beginning with instruction in drawing at the grammar and high schools of New Haven, Connecticut, from 1887 to 1890. This led to her appointment as director of the Slater Museum School of Art in Norwich, Connecticut, for three years. After a two-month stint at the newly established Denison House settlement in Boston, Massachusetts, she became a teacher and then the director of art instruction in the Brookline, Massachusetts, public school system. During this time, Weir wrote and published *The Greek Painters' Art* (1905) and *Outlines of Courses in Design, Representation and Color for High School Classes* (1910), the latter co-authored with **Elizabeth Stone**.

In 1910, Weir left Brookline for New York City and a job teaching in the fine arts department of the prestigious Ethical Culture School. Seven years later, she founded the School of Design and Liberal Arts, which offered courses in crafts, interior decorating, art education, fashion illustration and commercial design in addition to the more traditional subjects of drawing and painting. Her tenure as director of the school from 1917 to 1929 was interrupted by a trip to France in 1923, during which she earned a diploma from the École des Beaux Arts Américaine.

Weir's own best-known works were posters from the 1890s, flower and landscape paintings, portraits (including one of ***Marie Curie** which now hangs at Memorial Hospital in New York

City), and powerful murals painted during the 1920s. Among these latter works are *Mother and Babe with Jesus*, painted at a prison in New York City, and *Child of Bethlehem*, done for the Washington Cathedral. Like most of her mature works, these were strongly informed by her Episcopal beliefs. Weir exhibited at a number of galleries in New York City and London as well as at the Brooklyn Museum and the Corcoran Gallery in Washington, D.C.

An active member of the art world, Weir served as director of the Art Alliance of America and the Salons of America for several terms. She was also a contributing member of many artists' organizations, such as the Independent Artists of America, the National Society of Etchers, the Founders Group of the Museum of Fine Arts in Houston, Texas, and the London Lyceum Club. Besides teaching, she lectured at museums and at various colleges and universities including Princeton and Vassar.

Weir retired as director of the School of Design and Liberal Arts in 1929, although she remained active and occasionally gave lectures into her late 70s. She died from cardiovascular disease at a nursing home in Yorktown Heights, New York, in 1944, at age 82.

SOURCES:

James, Edward T., ed. *Notable American Women, 1607–1950.* Cambridge, MA: The Belknap Press of Harvard University, 1971.

Susan J. Walton,
freelance writer,
Berea, Ohio

Weis, Jessica McCullough

(1901–1963)

U.S. congressional representative (January 3, 1959–January 3, 1963). Name variations: Judy Weis; Mrs. Charles W. Weis, Jr. Born on July 8, 1901, in Chicago, Illinois; died on May 1, 1963, in Rochester, New York; daughter of Charles H. McCullough, Jr. (president of Lackawanna Steel Company) and Jessie (Martin) McCullough; educated in schools in Buffalo, New York, and graduated in 1916 from Miss Wright's School in Bryn Mawr, Pennsylvania; attended Madame Rieffel's French School in New York City, 1916–17; married Charles William Weis, Jr. (a stockbroker and businessman), on September 24, 1921 (died 1958); children: Charles McCullough Weis; Jessica Weis Warren; Joan Weis Jameson.

Served as vice-chair of the Citizens' Republican Finance Committee (1935); organized motor caravans for Republican presidential nominee Alfred M. Landon (1936); was vice-chair of the Monroe County Re-

publican Committee (1937–52); appointed to the New York State Republican Committee's executive committee (1938); was vice-president of the National Federation of Republican Women's Clubs (1938); elected president of the National Federation of Republican Women's Clubs, and served as delegate-at-large to the Republican National Convention (1940); seconded the nomination of Thomas E. Dewey for president and was associate campaign manager (1948); received appointment to the national advisory board of the Federal Civil Defense Administration (1954); elected to the House of Representatives for New York's 38th District (1958, 1960); coordinated the Republican congressional campaign in New York State (1960).

Jessica McCullough Weis, called "Judy" by her friends, was active in the Republican Party on local, state, and national levels. Born in Chicago, Illinois, in 1901, she moved with her family to Buffalo, New York, while still a young girl, and was educated both in Buffalo and at Miss Wright's School in Bryn Mawr, Pennsylvania. After graduating from Miss Wright's in 1916, she spent a year at Madame Rieffel's French School in New York City. When she was 20, she married Charles William Weis, Jr., a stockbroker who was also chair of a lithograph company, and moved with him to Rochester, New York.

Weis had three children over the next years, but despite the demands of family life made time to become involved in civic activities. In 1923, she founded the Chatterbox Club, a primarily social group that also organized charitable activities. Twelve years later, during the Depression year of 1935, she became vice-president of the Rochester Junior League. Weis also entered politics for the first time that year when she accepted an appointment from Monroe County Republican leader Thomas E. Broderick to be vice-chair of the Citizens' Republican Finance Committee. Her organization of Republican presidential nominee Alfred M. Landon's local motorcades the following year earned her promotion to vice-chair of the Monroe County Republican Committee in 1937.

Weis entered into state politics in 1938, when she was appointed to the New York State Republican Committee's executive committee. That same year, she was named vice-president of the National Federation of Republican Women's Clubs, and in 1940 became the federation's second president as well as a delegate-at-large to the Republican National Convention. She became a fixture at the convention through the 1940s and 1950s as four-time vice-chair of the New York delegation, and beginning in 1943 was a 20-year member of the Republican National Committee. During World War II, she chaired the Rochester Canteen and volunteered with the Red Cross Blood Bank. In 1948, Weis seconded the nomination of Thomas E. Dewey for president and became an associate campaign manager for the Dewey-Warren ticket, the first woman ever to achieve that level within a presidential campaign. While she planned both men's and women's campaign activities, she paid particular attention to gaining the support of women voters by keeping them informed of the Republican Party's plans for appointing women to important government positions. Although Dewey lost that year, in 1954 Weis was appointed to the national advisory board of the Federal Civil Defense Administration by President Dwight D. Eisenhower. That same year she was named an advisor to the United States delegate to the Inter-American Commission of Women. She also headed the committee that reorganized the 1956 Republican National Convention, held in San Francisco.

When Kenneth B. Keating, congressional representative for New York's 38th district, was nominated as the Republican candidate for the U.S. Senate in August 1958, Weis decided to make a bid for his seat in the U.S. House of Representatives. The 38th District covered both rural farmland in Wayne County and the eastern, industrial half of Monroe County, and Weis campaigned at every store, factory and shopping center in the areas, winning a 26,000-vote majority over Democrat Alphonse L. Cassetti. As a member of the 86th Congress, she was assigned to the Committee on Government Operations and the Committee on the District of Columbia. In the following Congress, she left the former to become a member of the Committee on Science and Astronautics. Weis' political philosophy tended toward Eisenhower's ideas of economy in government and a balanced budget. She consistently voted against spending measures on such issues as veterans' housing, airport construction, and water pollution control, and backed changes for the farm program, extension of the military draft, authorization of $180,500,000 for the National Aeronautics and Space Administration, extension of the Renegotiations Act of 1951, the Landrum-Griffin labor bill and statehood for Hawaii. She also supported a proposed Equal Rights Amendment to the Constitution, which eventually failed to achieve ratification.

On behalf of her constituency, Weis went before the Senate Committee on Labor and Public Welfare to seek the continuation of special exemptions for the fruit growers in her district.

Jessica McCullough Weis

She sent out newsletters to her constituents regarding major issues and made regular appearances on a Rochester television and radio program, on which she interviewed political personalities. In 1960, Weis coordinated the Republican congressional campaign in New York State while seeking re-election to her seat in the House. She declined to run for a third term in June 1962 due to health considerations, and died less than a year later, on May 1, 1963.

SOURCES:

Current Biography 1959. NY: H.W. Wilson, 1959.
Current Biography 1963. NY: H.W. Wilson, 1963.
Office of the Historian. *Women in Congress, 1917–1990.* Commission on the Bicentenary of the U.S. House of Representatives, 1991.

Susan J. Walton,
freelance writer,
Berea, Ohio

Weishoff, Paula (1962—)

American volleyball champion who was inducted into the U.S. Volleyball Hall of Fame. Born on May 1,

1962, in Torrance, California; attended the University of Southern California, 1978–79; married Karl Hanold.

Played in the U.S. Junior Olympics (1980); won a gold medal at the NORCECA championships (1981, 1983); won a bronze medal at the World championships (1982); won a silver medal at the Pan American Games (1983); won a team silver medal at the Los Angeles Olympics (1984); played professionally in Italy, Brazil, and Japan (1984–97); won a bronze medal at the Goodwill Games (1986); won a silver medal at the NORCECA championships (1991); won a team bronze medal at the Olympics and at the FIVB Super Four (1992); played professional beach volleyball (1993); won a gold medal at the World Grand Prix (1995); was a member of the Olympic volleyball team (1996); inducted into the U.S. Volleyball Hall of Fame (1998).

Paula Weishoff became known for her incredible ability as a middle blocker in both amateur and professional volleyball. She earned numerous "Most Valuable Player" honors as a member of the U.S. national team and while playing for various teams in the Italian and Japanese professional leagues. A native of Torrance, California, she originally turned to volleyball in an effort to ease the self-consciousness caused by her height, which had reached six feet by the time she was in the eighth grade. (She later grew another inch.) Weishoff began playing volleyball during her freshman year at West Torrance High School, where she would also letter in soccer, track, and softball. In 1978, during her senior year, she helped her volleyball team in reaching the semifinals of the Southern Section playoffs. She was also named volleyball player of the year in the Southern Section 3-A Division. A popular college recruiting target, she finally decided to attend the University of Southern California (USC). In her freshman year, she led the USC Trojans to a 46–4 season and the national championship. She was also honored as the Association of Intercollegiate Athletics Women's Player of the Year. Her coach at USC, Chuck Erbe, described Weishoff as "an intimidating player and a physically imposing athlete. Her power made her a feared player . . . She could do it all."

Later admitting to the *Los Angeles Times* that the main reason she had chosen to attend USC had been to train for the Olympics, Weishoff left college in 1979, after only a year, to join the U.S. national team. In the 1980 U.S. Junior Olympics, she earned All-American and Most Valuable Player citations, and played a vital role on the bronze medal-winning American team at the 1982 World championships. In the 1984 Olympic Games in Los Angeles, California, Weishoff helped Team USA win a silver medal and was honored as the U.S.' Most Valuable Player.

Because there was no women's professional volleyball league in America, Weishoff joined the women's professional league in Italy. She spent the next seven years living there, winning honors while playing for Cassana Dadda (1984–85), Civc Civ Modena (1985–88), and Reggio Emilia (1988–91). Weishoff rejoined the U.S. national team for the 1992 Olympics thanks to a change in the rules, which allowed her to play even though she no longer had amateur status. In the 1992 Olympic Games in Barcelona, Spain, she managed 96 kills and 9 blocks with Team USA to take the bronze medal. She also earned an Outstanding Player of the 1992 Olympics citation.

Returning to professional volleyball in Italy, Weishoff rejoined Civc Civ Modena for the 1992–93 season, and also played beach volleyball in 1993. She spent 1994 playing in Brazil before moving to Japan, where from 1995 to 1997 she played for the Daiei team, winning the pro league title and MVP honors in her first year there. Taking time off in 1996, Weishoff again joined Team USA for the 1996 Olympics. Terry Liskevych, coach for the U.S. volleyball team, called Weishoff one of the "mainstays" of the team and a "big factor" in the team's success. Nonetheless, the U.S. did not win a medal in the 1996 Games in Atlanta, Georgia. After finishing her Japanese contract the following year, Weishoff returned to USC to take a coaching position with her former team. In 1998, she was inducted into the U.S. Volleyball Hall of Fame.

SOURCES:

Johnson, Anne Janette. *Great Women in Sports*. Detroit, MI: Visible Ink, 1998.

Susan J. Walton,
freelance writer,
Berea, Ohio

Weiss, Alta (1889–1964)

American baseball player and physician who pitched for two male semipro teams. Born on February 9, 1889, in Ragersville, Ohio; died on February 12, 1964, in Ragersville; second of three daughters of George Weiss (a physician) and Lucinda Weiss; graduated from Ragersville High School, 1908; attended Wooster Academy, 1908–10; graduated as a Doctor of Medicine from Starling College of Medicine (now Ohio State University Medical College), in Columbus, Ohio, in 1914; married John E. Hisrich (a gas station owner), in 1927 (separated around 1938); no children.

The second of three daughters of a Ragersville, Ohio, physician, baseball player

Opposite page

𝒜lta

𝒲eiss

Alta Weiss began pitching at the age of two, "hurling corncobs at the family cat with wrist-snap and follow-through," writes **Barbara Gregorich**. Growing up, Weiss loved all outdoor sports and with her father's encouragement became an excellent shot with a rifle and shotgun. When she began getting serious about baseball, her father established a two-year high school so that she could play on its baseball team. He also built Weiss Ball Park, where she played with the town team. It would have been inconceivable for a young woman of Weiss' breeding to join any of the sexually integrated barnstorming teams that were beginning to spring up. Thus, if it had not been for her father, she might not have had a chance to pursue the sport.

In August 1907, while the Weisses were vacationing in Vermilion, Ohio, Alta became involved in a pick-up game with a group of local young men who were awed by the speed of her pitches. When the mayor of the town saw Weiss play, he suggested to the manager of the semipro Vermilion Independents that she might make an excellent addition to his team. The manager was reluctant to sign a woman, so the mayor arranged a game between two local teams and enlisted Weiss to pitch for one of them. After she struck out her 15th batter, the manager changed his mind and asked her to join the Independents.

On September 2, 1907, sporting a billowing, long blue skirt, Weiss played her first semipro game, pitching five innings and giving up four hits and one run. She played first base for the remainder of the game, which the Independents won 4–3. During the rest of the 1907 season, she pitched seven more games, each one attracting more and more fans to see the "Girl Wonder." In a 9–3 victory over the Sandusky Shamrocks, Weiss, it was reported, "allowed but seven hits, struck out five men, gave one base on balls, stole a base, scored a run and accepted her only fielding chance." At Cleveland's major league stadium, where the Independents played the Vacha All-Stars of Cleveland, Weiss received $100 for her appearance, an impressive sum for a semipro player of either gender. "She's in there with chimes and bells," wrote a reporter for the *Cleveland Press*. "She struck out the first batter. The next man drove a sizzling liner at her. She made a catch that increased the cheers threefold. It was a beauty that would do credit to any pitcher. Then she fanned the next batter, retiring the side."

Weiss ended her season with the Independents with a 5–3 record. During the off-season, her father built a heated gymnasium on his property, so she could throw practice pitches and lift

weights throughout the winter. Early in 1908, he went so far as to purchase a semipro team for her, the Weiss All-Stars. When they took the field for their first game, Weiss had given up her long skirt for a pair of bloomers "made so wide that the fullness gives a skirtlike effect," she explained, assuring all that her modesty was still intact. While the other players wore white uniforms, however, Weiss was dressed in maroon to stand out.

During the 1908–09 season, the All-Stars toured Ohio and Kentucky, playing for record crowds. Weiss, the star attraction, pitched five innings of each game, then retired to cover first base. During her second season, however, sportswriters began to note Weiss' shortcomings as well as her strengths. The *Messenger-Graphic* reported that she did a good job in the field, but when hitting, "she pushes the bat toward the ball, ungracefully and without force." Gregorich suggests that Weiss may have been ahead of her time, "a natural for the designated-hitter American League, in which pitchers do not bat at all."

Weiss' baseball career was curtailed all too soon. In the fall of 1908, she entered Wooster Academy and two years later began medical training at Starling College of Medicine in Columbus. She continued to make appearances on the mound up until 1910, after which she concentrated on her studies. She received her Doctor of Medicine in 1914, the only woman in her class. However, she apparently did not intend to devote her entire career to medicine. The *Columbus Citizen* announced that following graduation she would spend the summer practicing with her father, then planned to attend Harvard to train as a physical education teacher.

Weiss did return to Ragersville to work with her father, but never made it to Harvard. In 1915, she worked briefly as the resident physician at the girls' reformatory in Delaware, but found it such an ordeal that she had to quit after two months. During World War I, she took over the practice of an enlisted doctor in Sugarcreek, Ohio. "It was a rough experience," she recalled. "Scores of people were dying from the flu, and the roads were so bad in those days that the only way we could get around was by horse and buggy." She called the 1918–19 influenza pandemic one of the most distressing experiences of her life. "I don't think I ever had great enthusiasm for the profession after that."

In 1925, Weiss opened her own practice in Norwalk, Ohio, and two years later married John Hisrich, a Hagersville service station owner. (They would separate around 1936.) When her father died, Weiss took over his prac-

tice in Ragersville, where she lived for the remainder of her life. After her retirement, she frequently spent evenings sitting on her front porch, reading the paper and watching the local children play ball in the street. She gave one of them, a girl by the name of **Lois Youngen**, a baseball that she claimed was signed by Babe Ruth. "I don't know if it really was Ruth's signature or not," Youngen said, "but Alta signed the other side of it. It's her signature, I know, because I witnessed it." Youngen, who kept the baseball, went on to become a catcher for the Fort Wayne Daisies of the All-American Girls Baseball League. Alta Weiss died in 1964.

SOURCES:

Gregorich, Barbara. *Women at Play: The Story of Women in Baseball.* NY: Harcourt Brace, 1993.

———. "You Can't Play in Skirts: Alta Weiss, Baseball Player," in *Timeline.* July–August 1994.

Barbara Morgan,
Melrose, Massachusetts

Weiss, Louise (1893–1983)

French international journalist, writer, film producer, and feminist who was an advocate of realpolitik, peace, and European unity. Pronunciation: loo-EEZ VICE. *Born in Arras (Pas-de-Calais) on January 25, 1893; died in Paris, France, on May 26, 1983, and cremated at Père-Lachaise Cemetery; daughter of Paul-Louis Weiss; her mother's maiden name was Javal; educated at the Lycée Molière, Lady Margaret Hall (Oxford), and the Collège Sévigné, and earned an agrégé in literature; married José Imbert, around 1934 (divorced around 1937); no children.*

Passed the agrégation *examination and founded a small hospital for wounded soldiers (1914); was editor at* Europe Nouvelle *(1918–19); was editor-in-chief of* Europe Nouvelle *(1920–34); went to Russia to observe the Revolution (1921); founded the École de Paix (1930–36); founded La Femme Nouvelle, which promoted women's suffrage (1934–38); was secretary-general of the Refugee Committee (1938–40); went to the United States to obtain pharmaceuticals for France (1940); was editor of the Resistance gazette* La Nouvelle République *(1942–44); undertook a series of travels to Asia, the Mideast, North America, and Africa, resulting in books and documentary films (1946–65); won the Literature Prize of the Académie Française (1947); was secretary-general of the Institut de Polémologie (1964–70); failed election to the Académie Française (1974); elected to the European Parliament (1979–83).*

Selected writings: Délivrance: roman *(A. Michel, 1936);* Souvenirs d'une enfance républicaine *(Denoël, 1937);* La Marseillaise *(Gallimard, 1945);* L'Or, le camion et la croix: un voyage du Mexique en Alaska *(Julliard, 1949)*; Sabine Legrand: roman *(Julliard, 1951)*; La Syrie *(Del Duca, 1953)*; Le Cachemire *(Hachette, 1955)*; Images de l'Empire Soleil *(Oeuvres Libres, 1959)*; Le Voyage enchanté *(Fayard, 1960)*; Souen: le singe pélérin *(Oeuvres Libres, 1962)*; Mémoires d'une européenne *(6 vols., A. Michel, 1968–80)*; Lettre à un embryon *(Julliard, 1973)*; Deniéres voluptés: roman *(A. Michel, 1979)*.

Journalism: her principal collaboration was at Europe Nouvelle *(1918–34); also contributed articles to numerous other journals,* Le Radical *(1915–17?)*; La Revue de Paris *(1915)*, L'Information *(1919)*, Le Petit Parisien *(1921–22)*, La Nouvelle République *(1942–44)*, Le Fer rouge *(1957)*, L'Aurore, Parisien-Libéré, France-Illustration, Guerres et paix, *and* Paris-Match.

Selected documentary films: Une station-service en mer Rouge; Allah aux Comores; Caravaniers de la lune; Le Christ aux sources du Nil; Moi et le lion; Pirates et parfums; Face au volcan, face au cyclone; Ivoire et bois ébène; Une reine, un général, un président; Duel avec le soleil; Survivre; Des chameaux, des poignards, de la boue; O pauvre Virginie; Pitié pour les tortures; Rien avant le pôle Sud; Allah au Cachemire; Catrunjaha; Sainte Colline de la Victoire morale; Aux frontières de l'au-delà ou l'Himalaya trône des dieux.

One of the most eminent journalists of her time, Louise Weiss would have dearly loved to pursue a career in politics, where she probably would have reached the highest levels. But she was 51 years old before French women at last received the vote (1944). She lived a life of great accomplishment yet shadowed by painful might-have-beens planted by a happenstance: the timing of her birth.

She was born in Arras (Pas-de-Calais), in Picardy near the Belgian border, in 1893, the second of five children (two girls, three boys). Her family was well situated financially. Her father Paul-Louis Weiss was the son of a Protestant notary in Strasbourg who, when Paul was three, had emigrated after the Franco-Prussian War (1870–71) because Alsace-Lorraine had come under German rule. Paul was a mining engineer in the coalfields of the northeast and eventually the director of the entire French coal industry during much of World War I (1914–18). Louise's mother was Jewish, a Javal (originally Jacob) related to southern Alsatian bankers and boasting ancestral ties to Jewish families scattered over most of Germany (Baden, Brandenburg, Bavaria) and Austria, as well as cousins in Belgium and England. She was a daughter of a fa-

mous ophthalmologist, Louis-Émile Javal, and granddaughter of a feisty grande dame, **Théodora von Lindenberg** (1821–1911), daughter of a court banker. Louise later wrote that as a child she had acquired "a view of history of rare amplitude" from this great-grandmother who had been born the year Napoleon died.

As a daughter of families from the classic border region of Alsace and related to people all over the Continent, Louise Weiss took a lifelong interest in European cooperation: "My European mark was all but inevitable." She was also, however, a French patriot who recalled bicycle jaunts with her father to visit his conquered Alsatian homeland.

In 1899, the family moved to a fine residence in the west end of Paris. Louise had her first brush with politics there, for the Dreyfus Affair (1894–1906) was at its apogee. Not surprisingly, her family was Dreyfusard; at the Exposition of 1900, her mother even spat in the face of a general who had persecuted the Jewish captain. Her mother—anticlerical, rationalistic, liberal, strong willed, strict, and moralistic—helped Weiss to become spiritually independent. Her grandfather Javal, "a born teacher," a friend of Émile Zola, and like his father a one-term deputy for Yonne in Parliament, also exerted a powerful influence on her. Her mother insisted, over her father's objections, that she attend a girls' preparatory school, the Lycée Molière, in Auteuil. Such schools for girls had existed only since 1880, and to attend one was to make a statement regarding republicanism and the intellectual advancement of women. Louise's father, thoroughly old-fashioned, felt she should think only of preparing to marry. Louise entered the lycée in 1906. In 1907, she spent three months in England to improve her English and then returned to Molière, where she graduated in 1910 decked with honors. An excursion to Syria and Palestine followed. To placate her father, however, she then spent three months at the high-toned Household School of the Grand Duchess of Baden, in Germany, where she learned domestic skills. Weiss hated it and left a month early, but once home she made such an ostentatious display of her new culinary arts that her father ceased his carping.

Two teachers at Molière had especially strong influence on her intellectually and morally. **Marguerite Scott**, from England, was the soul of charity and political idealism—peace, feminism, socialism. **Marie Dugard** "incarnated moral reason." She championed high culture, "a Cartesian in her statements but as much removed from Pascal as from Voltaire." Louise later wrote that Dugard "changed everything" about her life and destiny. When Weiss did not dare at first to continue her education beyond the lycée, Dugard gave her free weekly tutorials. It was Dugard who most inspired her with a love of learning.

But what to do now? She had not taken the *baccalauréat* examination and so was ineligible for the Sorbonne or the Sèvres Normal School. But she could, possibly, study at the Collège Sévigné to prepare for the daunting *agrégation*, which qualifies one to teach in the lycées. Both her mother and (ironically) Dugard saw her future as that of a cultivated wife. For her part, Louise thought that all professions should be open to women. Her mother gave way and supported the Sévigné option, but Dugard held firm, saying that bright though she was she still had little chance of passing and should pursue cultural self-improvement. In a wrenching scene, Weiss broke with Dugard and declared her independence. The choice between work and domesticity was hard for her for decades: she never quite gave up hope that Prince Charming would appear.

For a few months in 1911 Weiss prepared in modern languages at Lady Margaret Hall, Oxford, before settling into a grinding regimen of lectures at Sévigné, eight hours at the Bibliothèque Nationale, and then night study at home. She sat for the *agrégation* in July 1914 and was one of 11 who passed. Her father did not ask how she had done. When she finally got up the nerve to tell him, he turned to her mother and exclaimed, "Do you hear? Your daughter would do better to marry," and then added, "I would have preferred your son graduating first from the Polytéchnique." That was all.

Would she now become a State teacher somewhere? An examiner had taken offense at the rose-decorated straw hat she had boldly worn. The placement officer at the Ministry of Education warned her against such *incartades*. Knowing instantly she could never stomach working in a bureaucracy, she resigned on the spot, walked out, and skipped down the street, bursting with joy. She never lacked the courage to part with persons or situations "incompatible with my nature."

A fortnight later, while she was with her family on their annual vacation in Brittany, the Great War exploded. Weiss later spoke for her generation when she wrote, "The war of 1914 has marked me profoundly. From its massacres I emerged in full youth and revolt into a world in ruins where men of my age had almost all been killed." She choked down a dislike of nursing and started a small hospital at Saint-Quay-Portrieux (Côtes-du-Nord) tending lightly wounded convalescents. After these men were transferred south, she opened a clinic for civilians (until November 26) and, inspired by Romaine Rolland's pacifist appeal from Switzerland, helped care for German POWs housed in an abandoned barracks—not a popular charity.

Back in Paris by the winter of 1914–15, she became—through her father, ironically—a journalist. He had complained about the government's economic incompetence to his friend Senator Justin Perchot, owner of *Le Radical*, a small but influential daily. When Perchot suggested he write articles, he indignantly declined, but Louise seized the chance and volunteered to write anonymously (as "Louise Lefranc") under his inspiration. Her father's well soon ran dry, but she got his permission to continue with subjects of her own choosing and under her own name. She also wrote in the *Revue de Paris*, in February and March 1915, on POWs and French people deported to Germany. Weiss had begun (but never finished) a doctoral thesis on political poetry in the 16th century, but journalism had "hooked" her. She began to take up the cause of independence for the subject nationalities of Central and Eastern Europe and of an international organization to prevent war, the germ of the League of Nations. These themes, which consumed her for the next 20 years, took shape under the impress of her first love affair.

Milan Stefanik, a lieutenant in the French army, had emigrated from Slovakia (Austria-Hungary) just before the war, established political connections as a technologist promoting long-distance radio communication, and by late 1915, when she met him, was working for General Ferdinand Foch to arouse fellow Slovak and Czech soldiers to strike for independence. Though she was entranced by this adventurous genius, she asserted it was not a physical attraction. Their love, she writes, was "a total spiritual communion in a climate of inhuman asceticism." Looking back on it, she concluded that "for the balance and orientation of my young life, no sentimental adventure could have been more harmful." The separation of the moral from the physical in this affair "accentuated the masculine character of the mind with which nature had endowed me and barred me several times from the path of happiness for which I had been raised." In any event, through Stefanik she became closely acquainted with the leaders of the future Czechoslovakia, Thomas Masaryk (1850–1937) and Eduard Benes (1884–1948), and was instrumental in bringing their cause to the attention of the world, especially in the pages of a new publication, *Europe Nouvelle* (New Europe).

This journal resulted from a chance meeting with a financial writer and promoter bearing the Dickensian name of Hyacinthe Philouze. He had money from a bequest, and she suggested creating a weekly review of diplomacy and international economics. Philouze took up the idea and, needing someone with brains and willing to work for a pittance, made her general secretary. The first issue appeared on January 12, 1918, providentially only four days after President Woodrow Wilson's "Fourteen Points" address. It drew instant attention. Its standpoint was basically Wilsonian yet focused not only on idealistic ends but also technical means. Weiss' particular interest lay in the spread of democracy and in freedom for the subject nationalities of Austria-Hungary. In her memoirs, she credits Philouze with teaching her how to write articles rapidly and to exact lengths, dictate directions, and make her way into the most influential circles where news is made.

The end of the war in November 1918 and the Paris Peace Conference of 1919 supplied ample grist for *Europe Nouvelle*'s columns. Meanwhile, Stefanik was working his way toward the top of the nascent Czechoslovak Republic. He served in the Czech Legion in Russia, was decorated and named the republic's minister of war. Angling to replace Benes and become the real power behind Masaryk, he wanted to arrive in Czechoslovakia by air, a sensational act. In a lacerating scene, he told Louise that because he could never be her master or teach her anything, he could not marry her; rather, he had found a very young Italian marquese who fit the bill. He left for Rome on May 4, 1919, and died when his plane crashed near Prague. Weiss read about it in the papers.

She attended the signing of the Versailles Treaty, which she feared carried the seeds of another war, and then in August resigned from *Europe Nouvelle*, having quarreled with Philouze over the review's direction. Later that month, she set off on a four-month professional trip—the first of many during her life—to Prague (visiting Masaryk), Budapest, Warsaw, Vienna, Lvov, etc., while sending bi-weekly articles to *L'Information*.

Back home in 1920 and jobless, dependent on her parents for money, she was astounded when Philouze begged her to return. She drove a hard bargain: editor-in-chief with administrative oversight, and her father as chair of the board of

French stamp issued in honor of Louise Weiss, May 15, 1993.

directors. Trips to London and again to Eastern Europe followed, but she especially wanted to go to Russia. Weiss got her wish when Élie-Joseph Bois, editor of the mass-circulation daily *Le Petit Parisien*, paid her way in return for articles. From September 14, 1921, into November, she interviewed numerous Russian leaders, while incidentally aiding 125 governesses stranded by the Revolution to return to France. Among her subjects she counted Maxim Gorki (writer), Kamenev (Moscow soviet), Lunacharsky (education), Radek (*Pravda*), Chicherin (foreign affairs), Joseph Stalin (nationalities—she learned little), and Leon Trotsky—but not Lenin. Trotsky asked her if she wanted "an interview or a political argument" after she challenged his resentment of criticism, but he let her return several times; his idealism and honesty so appealed to her that later (1946) she visited his widow *Natalia Trotsky in Mexico.

Her visit to Russia proved more important to her than the notoriety she reaped from her articles. As did many idealists of the time, she found the Revolution inspiring in its aims, its leaders unforgettable, and the people marvelously courageous amidst their suffering. But she was profoundly disturbed by evidence of what would soon be called totalitarianism. She drew the lesson that either men are made for principles and then persuaded or forced to conform to them; or that principles are made for men in order to develop, protect, and comfort them—"to help them to die in bed." She opted, permanently, for the latter, quoting Aristide Briand (1862–1932), whom she came to know and admire immensely, that "the art of politics is to conciliate the desirable with the possible."

The grandmother of Europe.
—Chancellor Helmut Schmidt

Until she resigned in January 1934, *Europe Nouvelle* was a remarkable production. (After she left, it would quickly fade.) It was advanced for its time by paying attention not just to politics but also to economic, commercial, and financial questions. It became required reading for the international elite of politics, diplomacy, and business, who also contributed articles (even Benito Mussolini did). Its own staff housed a raft of men (and a few women) who were or became writers of note or came to occupy the highest positions in diplomacy and public administration. She developed an incomparable network of sources and acquaintances and worked nonstop, writing (including pieces for other journals to raise money), interviewing, soliciting funds, attending virtually every international conference and League of Nations annual session in a decade crammed with them, and even, in October–December 1926, undertaking a lecture tour in the United States sponsored by the Foreign Policy Association. In 1925, her friend Premier Édouard Herriot admitted her, at age 32, to the Legion of Honor.

Astonishingly, only with the decoration did her father at last reconcile himself to having a daughter more brilliant than his sons. Until then, she had lived under her parents' roof or, after she had fled, in an apartment, closely watched, even spied upon, for fear she, unmarried, might soil the family's name by some social or sexual indiscretion. She vastly admired her father's intelligence and ability but seemed unable to stop his and her mother's attempts to control her. Why she submitted for so long is a question she seemed unable to answer fully even in six volumes of memoirs.

She also became more independent financially, although sustaining a review was never easy. She had, somewhat out of character, speculated very successfully in German marks in the early 1920s. One result was that she learned much about capitalism's power to unleash individual effort, and in her memoirs she criticized socialism for distributing money to political supporters and "imbeciles and ne'er-do-wells," and French governments for decades of confiscating, devaluating, and nationalizing; by destroying individual sheep, as she put it, they had created a big flock harder to master than a single animal.

By 1930, it was clear that prospects for peace were fading. In 1931, Weiss organized at the Trocadero a large rally (1,095 delegates from 395 associations worldwide) to support an upcoming disarmament conference, but such efforts were taking on an air of futility. She also founded (November 1930) the École de Paix (School of Peace), a private foundation under a component of the Académie de Paris, which sought to develop a "science of Peace." It held weekly public meetings from November to May at the Sorbonne featuring speakers and panel discussions by important people from all over Europe. Resembling both a forum and a think tank, this rather original entity survived until 1936, when participants from the Eastern dictatorships finally made reasoned discussion impossible. By that time, Weiss had been out of *Europe Nouvelle* for two years.

Her disillusionment with the League of Nations, the great hope of her generation, had become profound. It deeply marked the rest of her life. She could no longer stomach "the general lie" infecting this "greatest abortion in history." *Europe Nouvelle* had preached that "idealism gains nothing from feeding on illusions": one must get the facts right and be realistic. She was a pacifist yet no advocate of "peace at any price." Peace with Germany was her dearest wish, but it had to be founded on material security (including reparations for war damage) and enforceable guarantees. Instead, the United States had long ago walked away, Britain was more suspicious of French "imperialism" than of Germany, and France was physically and psychologically bled out. The League had refused to face facts; the diplomats and the secretariat had covered up the real state of affairs, deceiving themselves and the League's supporters. In 1931, well before he came to power (1933), she was warning, "You can't traffic with Hitler." Few were listening yet. In short, her labors had reached a dead end: international law was being trashed, the League was a farce, war was surely coming, and France, lacking the leadership and will to respond, would surely lose it.

The defeat staring her in the face was also, to her, personal. Had this battle been worth the sacrifice of marriage and children? In the eyes of others, she believed, she was "an abnormal woman, that is, a monster of intelligence and authority," while inside, despite all appearances, "I only wanted to be cherished and mastered." Sentiments such as these go far to explain her marriage (c. 1934) soon after she left *Europe Nouvelle*. José Imbert was a talented architect and musician of humble origins who never won much acclaim. The marriage lasted only a few months, a victim, she asserted (again), of her independent spirit. She devoted less than a page to it in her memoirs. Ironically, she noted, marriage and especially the divorce (c. 1937) brought her a civil status which helped her and "opened romantic opportunities that . . . I would not have encountered as a spinster." Rumors, in fact, linked her with several prominent men.

Gone from *Europe Nouvelle*, Weiss found to her chagrin that no journal wanted her in a senior position. At that moment, her political ideals a shambles and while apparently experiencing a deep anxiety about her own womanhood, writes Michael Bess, she was approached by **Marcelle Kraemer-Bach**, who invited her to meet *Cécile Brunschvicg about becoming involved in the UFSF (the French Union for Women's Suffrage). In her memoirs, Weiss says she was first struck forcibly by the suffrage issue when interviewing Idaho's Senator William Borah back in 1926; they were interrupted by a delegation of female constituents to whom Borah was most deferential. It struck her that nothing like that would happen in France, where politicians began speeches with "Ladies and Citizens." In France, she was a prominent, well-connected political journalist, yet voteless.

She quickly warmed to the task. The vote would advance the cause of peace and open the doors for women to all professions. She met Brunschvicg but told her the UFSF was too timid and too linked to a political party (the centrist Radical-Socialists). She decided to form her own organization, La Femme Nouvelle (The New Woman), politically independent, devoted solely to winning the vote, and using methods made famous by England's "suffragettes"—news-making demonstrations and stunts: "Feminism must be dragged out of the salons, where it dilly-dallies uselessly, and the orthodox leagues, where it is becoming petrified." So saying, she launched into "one of the most thankless campaigns of my life, even more exhausting than my apostolate for the League of Nations."

La Femme Nouvelle began with a flourish. It opened an office on the Champs-Élysées on October 6, 1934, its window displaying a large world map with a bold legend, "English women vote, American women vote, Chinese women vote," and so on, ending with "French women do not vote." On October 17, Weiss flew with three female aviators to a large rally in Marseille. In October and November, the political parties were lobbied, and in December a rally at the Paris City Hall during a convention won endorsements from a host of mayors—a coup. There was even a helpful scandal: Weiss was sitting on some steps, knees drawn up, engrossed in a report while waiting to be admitted to the premier's office, when a photographer from the reactionary *Action Française* slipped a camera under her dress and snapped a picture. It was circulated on thousands of postcards, but Weiss, rather than sue, simply quipped, "As you now know, gentlemen, I don't wear *culottes*," thus turning the laughter to her side.

La Femme Nouvelle reached its peak in 1935–36 and then faded until its demise in 1939. In its heyday, it drew much press and newsreel attention and made women's suffrage a lively issue. In 1935, it succeeded in defeating one Senator Duplantier, who had made a grossly insulting speech against women's suffrage to his guffawing colleagues. Weiss "ran" in Montmartre for the Paris Municipal Council, while votes (some 19,000) favoring the suffrage were collected in hatboxes outside the polls (May 5). When the police moved in, they were doused with rose-scented talcum powder, to general hilarity. On May 12, some 45 women chained themselves in pairs at the Bastille column, where they burned hostile newspapers and scattered tracts.

The year 1936 was charged with drama. Accompanied by massive strikes, a left-wing coalition, the Popular Front, came to power under Socialist premier Léon Blum (1872–1950). La Femme Nouvelle militants worked hard to shove Blum and Parliament toward the suffrage. On the final election day, May 3, they launched balloons carrying tracts toward the president's box at the French soccer Cup Final. The hatboxes reappeared and collected 15,000 votes, while Weiss "ran" for Parliament in the Latin Quarter. When the Chamber of Deputies convened on June 1, militants in the visitors' gallery help up placards, and at the Senate on June 2 they tossed darned socks from the gallery to shame a senator who had said mockingly that women wouldn't darn socks anymore if they got the vote. On June 28, they delayed the start of the Grand Prix de Longchamp horserace, to the fury of the crowd, by filing out on the track. They held a rally later that day, mounted a shivaree on July 3 outside the home of a hostile senator, Henri Merlin, and the next day chained themselves together to block the rue Royale. (A policeman, perhaps tongue-in-cheek, told his superior he couldn't arrest Weiss because "she gets her clothes at Molyneux.")

Blum, maneuvering, put three women (*Iréne Joliot-Curie, *Suzanne Lacore, and Brunschvicg) in his Cabinet, but on condition that they not raise the suffrage issue because it would only complicate the current domestic and foreign crises and split the Left, which had always feared women, many under Roman Catholic influence, would support the Right. In her memoirs, Weiss asserts that Blum invited her, but she had rejected the condition. That he ever made her an offer seems quite doubtful. They disliked each other, anyhow; Blum referred to her in private as "la belle grosse Louise." For her part, she had nothing but scorn for the female under-secretaries of state, especially Brunschvicg, as her memoirs amply testify.

The Chamber approved a suffrage bill on July 30, but the shivaree and a brutal jeering of a Brunschvicg speech caused the Senate group favoring the bill to denounce such tactics as "disorderly" and "tasteless." The Senate thus found another excuse to bury it. La Femme Nouvelle now lost support rapidly. Weiss continued to lobby and spoke in the provinces, notably at a large rally at Lille on October 27, 1937. The Senate passed a bill to remove the civil disabilities of married women, which became law on February 20, 1938. Not unjustly, Weiss claimed some credit for it. With her failure in 1938 to persuade the government to create a non-combat women's component in the army, she left the movement to concentrate on international affairs once again.

Weiss' excursion into feminist politics proved disappointing, although she rightly noted it was important that, when Charles de Gaulle simply gave women the vote in 1944, they could hold up their heads for having helped in their own liberation and not merely received a favor from above. It remains true, however, that she turned off the bulk of the conservative mass of women, while most feminist leaders viewed her as an egotistic latecomer, too obviously dismissive of others' efforts. Many, too, raised legitimate doubts as to the wisdom of engaging in provocative acts in the midst of the Depression, when violence or its threat could endanger the regime itself. Nevertheless, in her memoirs she took pride in having had a part in winning the suffrage: "The worldwide accession of women to a civil status identical with that of men is without doubt the most important collective phenomenon of the first half of this century."

As noted, Weiss early on believed another war was coming. She attended Masaryk's funeral (September 1937) and warned Benes not to count on France. The sellout of Czechoslovakia at Munich (September 1938) surprised her not at all. From mid-1938, she worked tirelessly to cope with the oncoming catastrophe. Until its end in June 1940 because of the German invasion, she was secretary-general of the officially sanctioned Refugee Committee, which tried to find housing and jobs for thousands of Jews flooding in from the east. She played a key role in getting permission for the *Saint-Louis*, crammed with Jewish refugees, to disembark at Antwerp (1939) after many countries (including the United States) had refused to accept them. In gratitude, the (Jewish-American) Joint Distribution Fund financed the Mimi-Pinson Canteen she had started in Montmartre which served the mothers, wives, and daughters of soldiers.

She also founded (February 7, 1938) the Union of French Women Decorated with the Legion of Honor, which sought to strengthen the country through non-partisan efforts to improve civil rights and to lobby on questions of general interest, notably public morals and health. The Union founded the Propaganda Center for the Grandeur of the Country, which focused on persuading elite civil service women to support strengthening the family (including raising birth rates) and proclaiming the "civilizing mission" of French womanhood.

Beyond these causes, Weiss worked to educate the public about air raids and passive resistance to invaders, and hence was accused of warmongering. She also tried to persuade the government and the army to institute Women's National Service, whose thousands of enrollees would release men for frontline duty. "Women are patriotic, but timid," so organize them. Weiss took her case to President Lebrun himself, but she battered in vain against a wall of indifference, red tape, bureaucratic bumbling, and political fears. Premier Daladier told her army service for women would ignite demands for the vote, which he opposed. Not until the Germans were advancing on Paris did the government send out a call, but so many women volunteered that the authorities sank under the flood just before the surrender.

In her memoirs, Weiss paints a detailed, devastating picture of France in those tragic years, reserving particular contempt for the wishy-washy Radical-Socialists and above all the Socialists and Blum, whose irresponsible policy of "support without participation" left governments exposed to every wind. Their refusal to face realities—she found they just didn't grasp what Reinhard Heydrich and Heinrich Himmler really were—and their smothering of all bad news to spare the public's nerves paved the road to the debacle.

In 1939, she fell in love—an "*amour délicieux*"—the great love of her life. He was a large landowner in Brie (southeast of Paris), a 40ish decorated veteran whose unfaithful wife had declined into insanity, leading him to cancel his intent to divorce her. The "Chevalier de Magloire"—she would not reveal his name—was called back to service in 1939. They shared passionate trysts during his leaves until the May 1940 invasion. A principled, courageous man, he insisted on frontline service and was killed on June 9 defending the Seine bridge at Andeleys (Eure). She endured six agonizing weeks before she learned he had met the fate she intuitively knew would be his.

As the Germans approached Paris, Weiss went to Bordeaux, where she declined an invitation by Jean Monnet, the future father of the Common Market, to escape to England. After the capitulation, she went to Vichy (capital of the unoccupied zone), where she petitioned Marshal Pétain to let her go to the United States to get medicines for France. On the eve of her journey, she learned of the chevalier's death, but she resolved to return because she had promised to do so and because, she says, her "whole culture and disposition" disposed her toward sharing and relieving France's suffering. She felt obliged, too, not to abandon the women she had led in the suffrage fight.

At her own expense, she left Vichy on July 14 by air and arrived in New York on July 29 from Lisbon. Until December, she shuttled between there and Washington, pleading with all the important people she could collar, including *Eleanor Roosevelt. It was a hard sell: France, especially Vichy, was out of favor because of the defeat. Many feared supplies of any kind would only end up in Nazi hands. The quarrels among French émigrés helped not at all. Weiss walked on eggs. The British finally gave her permission to bring, in person, 200 kilos of medicines through the blockade. She returned by ship to Lisbon and drove to Vichy with her precious cargo. She believed she had established the principle of allowing aid into unoccupied France; only two food ships, however, later went to

Marseille. Weiss proposed a second trip, but when the Vichy authorities asked her to spy, she refused. Banished to the occupied zone, she returned to Paris in February 1941.

She lay low, for she knew she was on the Gestapo's lists. Conning a French official, she obtained a document saying she was pure Aryan. She slipped back to Vichy once to deliver a report to the American ambassador on morale in the occupied zone and to leave some articles for *The New York Times*, which it published anonymously. At the end of 1941, the Germans seized her library (6,000 volumes), a Golden Book of pictures, epitaphs, and commentaries by her friends—a gallery ranging from Raoul Dufy to Thoman Mann, Paul Valéry, *Colette, Hjalmar Schacht, Chaim Weizman, and on and on—and at both her home and the chevalier's they took all her notes and letters from the 1920s and 1930s. She did succeed, however, in saving the papers of the Comte de Saint-Simon (1760–1825), the utopian socialist who had planned for a united Europe. Devastated by her losses, she went to the German police to complain. They promptly turned her over to a high SS officer for interrogation. Terrified, recognizing her naïveté, she yet managed to put on a show of indignant injured innocence to deny she had any Jewish ancestry. Convinced against his will, he let her go. In August 1943, she would play another such scene to persuade a vacillating French prefect to release her arrested brother André.

In 1942, she came into contact with the Resistance in the form of a Masonic network, Patriam Recuperare, containing many important future politicians, and became editor-in-chief of its gazette, *La Nouvelle République*. Until March 1943, when arrests ended the connection, she sent considerable information to London; she also traveled clandestinely all over France, including trips to the Ardennes to develop information on German exploitation of French farm workers which was used later at the Nuremberg Trials. As the Liberation neared, her life became increasingly imperiled. A tip led her to avoid arrest by moving several times. When the Germans retreated at last, she returned to her Paris home to find that officers, who had made it into a casino, had stripped it of its valuable paintings, furniture, documents, and mementos. Her anguish only deepened when *La Nouvelle République* was sold out from under her by its owner. She had hoped to see it become a major newspaper.

Weiss' experiences in the fight for the League of Nations and the suffrage and in the terrible collapse and occupation during the war left her feeling she had been a fool. Her memoirs reflect this bitterness. What is universal in humans is not a thirst for justice, she concluded, but a will to dominate others. Force and will, not the spirit of compromise, shape history. In her chastened state, she vowed to discover new bases for world peace by studying human behavior.

At war's end, Weiss was aged 52, but her career was only half over. In an astonishing display of will and vitality, she would remain active until two months before her death in 1983 at age 90. She began by making her only try at politics (in May 1945) when she joined the Radical-Socialist Party and lost to the Communists in a bid for the municipal council of Magny-les-Hameaux (Seine-et-Oise), where her family owned property. Thereafter, she moved to the Gaullist Right but devoted herself to writing and traveling.

Weiss wrote a long series of articles and books, including novels (the last in 1979). Most analyzed parts of Asia, the Mideast, Africa, and North America she had visited. Six stout volumes of memoirs (published 1968–80) took her 11 years to write. If this were not enough, she lectured widely (often sponsored by the Alliance Française) and, mainly with Pathé-Cinéma and sometimes with government support, produced some 37 documentary films derived from her excursions from 1946 to 1965. These travels arose from her thirst to understand, "if possible, dominate intellectually," the accelerated change of her times. She could not do it from books alone; she had to see for herself. Her writing and films especially investigated human aggression, religion, politics, and the evils ravaging the world. "I have searched for lightening, the lightening of the human spirit," she wrote. "Too often, I have found darkness, bestiality, fetishism, greed." The work was arduous. Her long-time photographer, Georges Bourdalon, recalled her at 71 riding in a jeep for 12 hours in a blazing heat on the fringe of the Sahara to reach a colonial outpost, and then sitting up half the night "fiercely" arguing politics with the locals.

Her writing earned her the Literature Prize of the Académie Française in 1947 for her novel *La Marseillaise* (1945), and she later won other literary prizes. But in 1974, when she posed her own name (a highly irregular act) for election to the Académie—partly to point up the fact that it had never elected a women—she was rebuffed. She had hoped her memoirs in particular might win her the coveted seat. She also failed in a bid for a Nobel Prize which she persuaded influential friends to make on her behalf. In 1976, she

was, however, promoted to Grand Officer of the Legion of Honor and made a delegate to UNESCO; later she received the Robert Schuman Gold Medal for service to European peace and unity. And from 1976 to 1979, she was chosen by Jacques Chirac, president of the Gaullist Party (RPR), to lecture all over Western Europe on European unity.

From 1964 to 1970, she served as secretary-general of the Institut de Polémologie, devoted to the study of the nature of war, and assisted its founder, Gaston Bouthoul, as editor of *Guerres et paix*, funded by the French Ministry of Defense. Bouthoul was probably the "savant" with whom she had a happy 25-year liaison until, with tears, she broke off because he refused to recognize her contributions to "our common creations"; her whole nature and past, she wrote, forbade such an "abdication." She then founded (1970) the Institute of the Sciences of Peace (Strasbourg), devoted to European unity, peace, and the amelioration of human relations; and in 1971, to support it, she set up the Fondation Louise Weiss, which annually awards a prize to a person or institution advancing these causes. Recipients have included Helmut Schmidt, *Simone Veil, Jacques Delors, and Anwar Sadat.

Weiss was something of an anomaly: a peace advocate but on the political Right, defending imperialism and waxing nearly apocalyptic when describing the menace to the West posed by the Soviet Union and China. *Storm over the West* was the title she chose, aptly, for the last volume of her memoirs, which cover the years 1945 to around 1975, when the Cold War and the ending of the Western empires held center stage. (Not that her opinion on the colonies was unique; until the latter 1950s it was shared by a majority in France.) She could write, for example: "The defeat of the Americans in Indochina has shaken the world more than it was once shaken by the fall of Byzantium." Or in *Le Fer rouge* (The Red Iron), a short-lived (seven months) review she founded in 1957 to oppose the retreat from North Africa: "Our present decomposition will take us through a period of indescribable agony, toward a final collapse in favor of an Asiatic Europe which will wipe us off the face of the map." The collapse of the Soviet Union only six years after her death would have astonished her perhaps even more than it did virtually every expert of the day.

Until the mid-1970s, her leading themes were that 1) Europe was being ground between the new world empires of the Soviet Union and the United States and turned into "dishonest and beggarly vassals"; 2) that the Soviet Union and China are powerful and growing more so ("All China needs is time.") while the democracies, including the bumptious, directionless United States, are decaying amidst "laziness, corruption, and abundance"; and 3) that Western civilization, clearly the leading one, threw away, through sheer fecklessness and a misplaced sense of guilt, its opportunity to finish the great work of raising the Third World to its standards of science and material well-being. She was an assimilationist and as such critical of the failure of the French, for example, to grant Westernized, educated natives the same positions as whites.

These views testify to the profound impact on her of the catastrophic failure of the democracies in the 1920s and 1930s and of the overwhelming defeat of France in 1940. The United Nations ("the Machine"), like its sorry predecessor, had become little more than a "club of dictators" from the Communist bloc and the Third World who hypocritically ignore blatant violations of human rights. Would she witness a repetition of all that wretched failure only on an even larger scale? The question haunted the last half of her life.

Her answer was that Europe contained its own—and the world's—best hope. It must recognize its cultural unity and assert its independence. It must summon from its glorious past the courage to face the harsh realities of international life, where force is the last argument and weakness is punished with slavery and death. It must tame the self-indulgence which is rotting its very core. Especially through the 1970s until her death, she preached this gospel with renewed fervor. She was a French patriot to the marrow, believing each country has a right to its own political identity. But she proudly proclaimed, as she had since the 1920s, that she was also a European. Franco-German reconciliation lay especially close to her heart. (She named one of her cats "Bismarck.")

The end of her long life brought a wonderful reward. In 1979, the European Parliament, the principal advisory body to the European Community, was elected by popular vote for the first time. (Previously, members were chosen by national parliaments.) Jacques Chirac placed her fifth on the combined list of the RPR and the group "Defense of French Interests in Europe" (of which she was a member), thus all but guaranteeing her election. When the new Parliament convened at Strasbourg, a place of special meaning to her, she was by virtue of age (86) the temporary president and delivered an inspiring address. She told of her joy, "the greatest joy a human being can experience in the evening of life: the joy of a youthful vocation miraculously come to fruition." She evoked a crowd of historical heroes from every part of Europe and, with her usual verve, challenged her listeners to forge a real European unity. Why not a European constitution, university, academy, museum, and symphony orchestra, and even sport teams? "The [European Economic] Community institutions have produced European sugar beets, butter, cheese, wines, calves, and even pigs. They have not produced Europeans." Full of years and honors, Weiss died in a Paris hospital on May 26, 1983. On June 1, a service was held at the Protestant church on the rue Cortembert and she was cremated at Pére-Lachaise Cemetery.

Few women experienced so intensely so much of the 20th century as did Louise Weiss. Chancellor Helmut Schmidt once dubbed her "the grandmother of Europe." (She didn't like the title, saying it sounded too much like "granny.") Few if any of her contemporaries were her equal in promoting a vision of European unity extending beyond economic integration. She was a lifelong peace advocate, but after the early 1920s she was no dewy-eyed idealist. Writes Bess:

> Weiss clearly understood two fundamental facts of globalism. First, she came squarely to grips with the awesome diversity of the world's cultures, confronting head-on the problem of maintaining order in the pullulating mosaic of human wills. And second, she observed the empirical fact that power in the present world all too often took the shape of domination of some people by others. . . . Hers was the voice of tough-minded, world-weary experience.

Her protean personality shines through her lively, detailed, and opinionated memoirs, a matchless description of persons and events of her time which, nevertheless, must be approached with caution. Nothing, least of all her role, loses in the telling. She was often pessimistic and bitter about the world, frustrated as she was in love and ambition. Her temperament was authoritarian and in tone often sarcastic and cynical. Humble she was not. In truth, her ability, intelligence, and energy left her with little to be humble about. She was witty and loved humor. She possessed an ample endowment of blonde, blue-eyed charm, and used it; and she liked to be courted in turn. Except for those who were her equal in intelligence and success, she did not prefer the company of women. Yet she was a staunch, lifelong feminist. She hated the patronizing of women. When someone mentioned the new Cabinet post of Secretary of State for the Feminine Condition, she drawled, "Why not a Secretary of State for the Canine Condition?" Moreover, in contrast to much of her public image, she loved children, animals, flowers, and decorating her home. Louise Weiss was, in short, one of the more striking individuals of her time. The French have a word for persons of her stamp: *formidable*.

SOURCES:

Bard, Christine. *Les Filles de Marianne: Histoire des féminismes 1914–1940*. Paris: Fayard, 1995.

Bess, Michael. *Realism, Utopia, and the Mushroom Cloud: Four Activist Intellectuals and Their Strategies for Peace, 1945–1989: Louise Weiss (France), Leo Szilard (USA), E.P. Thompson (England), Danilo Dolci (Italy)*. Chicago, IL: University of Chicago Press, 1993.

Carrère d'Encausse, Hélène, *et al*. *Louise Weiss*. Lausanne: Fondation Jean Monnet pour l'Europe, Centre de récherches européennes, 1989.

Conte, Arthur. *Grandes françaises du XXe siècle*. Paris: Plon, 1995. Ch. 1.

Hause, Steven, and Anne Kinney. *Women's Suffrage and Social Politics in the French Third Republic*. Princeton, NJ: Princeton University Press, 1984.

Klejman, Laurence, and Florence Rochefort. *L'Égalité en marche: Le Féminisme sous la Troisième République*. Paris: Presses de la Fondation nationale des sciences politiques/Éditions des Femmes, 1989.

"Louise Weiss: 'la grand-mère de l'Europe,'" in *Historiens et Géographes*. No. 340, 1993, pp. 37–40.

Montbrial, Thierry de. "L'Idéalisme et la réalisme de Louise Weiss [et l'idée d'Europe en 1918]," in *Revue des Deux Mondes*. No. 1, 1992, pp. 87–94.

Nugent, Neill. *The Government and Politics of the European Community*. Durham, NC: Duke University Press, 1989.

Palmer, Michael. *The European Parliament: What It Is, What It Does, How It Works*. Oxford: Pergamon Press, 1981.

Rabaut, Jean. *Histoire des féminismes français*. Paris: Éditions Stock, 1978.

Reynolds, Sian. "Women and the Popular Front in France: The Case of the Three Women Ministers," in *French History* (England). Vol. 8, 1994, pp. 196–224.

Scott, Joan Wallach. *Only Paradoxes to Offer: French Feminists and the Rights of Man*. Cambridge, MA: Harvard University Press, 1996.

Smith, Paul. *Feminism and the Third Republic*. Oxford: Clarendon Press, 1996.

Vallance, Elizabeth, and Elizabeth Davies. *Women of Europe: Women MEPs and Equality Policy*. Cambridge: Cambridge University Press, 1986.

Weiss, Louise. *Mémoires d'une européenne*. 6 vols. Paris: Albin Michel, definitive editions, 1971–1980. I. *Une petite fille du siècle, 1893–1919*; II. *Combats pour l'Europe, 1919–1934*; III. *Combats pour les femmes, 1934–39*; IV. *Le Sacrifice du Chevalier, 3 septembre 1939–juin 1940*; V. *La Resurrection du Chevalier, juin 1940–aôut 1944*; VI. *Tempête sur l'Occident (1945–1975)*.

———. *Souvenirs d'une enfance républicaine*. Paris: Éditions Denöel, 1937 (*Une petite fille du siècle* is a revision of this).

———. *Speeches by Mrs. Louise Weiss, Oldest Member, and Mrs. Simone Veil, President, Strasbourg, 17 and 18 July 1979*. Strasbourg: European Parliament, 1979.

Zand, Nicole. "Européenne et féministe" (obituary), in *Le Monde*. May 28, 1983.

SUGGESTED READING:

Betts, Raymond. *Tricoleur: The French Overseas Empire*. NY: Gordon & Cremonesi, 1978.

Fine, Michele. "A Passion for Action: The Political Crusades of Louise Weiss, 1915–1938." Ph.D. dissertation, UCLA, 1997.

Girardet, Raoul. *L'Idée coloniale en France de 1871 à 1962*. Paris: La Table Ronde, 1972.

Hoffmann, Stanley. *Decline or Renewal? France since the 1930s*. NY: Viking, 1974.

Monnet, Jean. *Memoirs*. Trans. by Richard Mayne. London: Collins, 1978.

Naguères, Henri, *et al*. *Histoire de la résistance en France, de 1940 à 1945*. 5 vols. Paris: Robert Lafont, 1981.

Schmidt, Hans A. *The Path to European Union*. Westport, CT: Greenwood Press, 1981.

Sorum, Paul C. *Intellectuals and Decolonization in France*. Chapel Hill, NC: University of North Carolina Press, 1977.

Talbot, France. "L'Engagement politique d'une femme entre les deux guerres: Louise Weiss." Ottawa: Bibliothèque du Canada, 1983. M.A. thesis, Laval University.

Thornton, A.P. *The Imperial Idea and Its Enemies*. NY: St. Martin's Press, 1985.

Weber, Eugen. *The Hollow Years: France in the 1930s*. NY: W.W. Norton, 1994.

COLLECTIONS:

Weiss' private papers are in the Bibliothèque Nationale, Nouvelles Acquisitions Français, Legs 1977, Côtes 17794–17862, and Legs 1983, Don 84–06. The Bibliothèque du Parlement Européen (Luxemburg) and the Bibliothèque *Marguerite Durand (Paris) contain newspaper clippings on her career. Original prints of her films are housed in the Archives du Film, Bois d'Arcy (Seine-et-Oise).

The Bibliothèque universitaire de Strasbourg and the City of Arras (Pas-de-Calais) received her books; the City of Saverne (Bas-Rhin), her residual heir, houses her memorabilia and art works at the Palais Rohan; the Musée de l'Homme (Paris) contains musical documents from her travels. There exists a European Association of the Friends of the Fondation Louise Weiss.

David S. Newhall,
Pottinger Distinguished Professor of History Emeritus,
Centre College, and author of *Clemenceau: A Life at War* (1991)

Weizmann, Vera (1881–1966)

First first lady of Israel. Name variations: Vera Chatzmann. Born on November 27, 1881, in Rostov, Russia; died on September 24, 1966, in Israel; educated at Marinskaya Imperial Gymnasium and the Rostov Conservatoire of Music; studied medicine at the University of Geneva; married Chaim Weizmann (1874–1952, first president of the state of Israel), in 1906; children: Benjamin (b. 1907) and Michael (1916–1942).

Served as medical officer in Manchester, England (1913–16); founded WIZO (Women's International Zionist Organization, 1920); was joint chair, with Rebecca D. Sieff, of WIZO's world executive committee (1920–40); served as president of Youth Aliyah (1940s); was a Red Cross worker in London during World War II; was involved in Israeli Red Cross and Youth Aliyah (1950s); wrote memoir The Impossible Takes Longer *(published 1967).*

Born in Rostov-on-Don in Cossack Territory in 1881, Vera Chatzmann enjoyed an atypical upbringing for a Jewish girl in tsarist Russia. Her father, recruited into the tsar's army in his youth, enjoyed certain privileges as a result, including the right to live outside the Pale of Settlement, the Jewish enclave created by *Catherine II the Great. The Chatzmanns settled in Rostov, where Vera's father became a wholesale clothes dealer. His seven children enjoyed a comfortable and privileged upbringing as part of the guild merchant class. Learning neither Hebrew nor Yiddish, she and her four sisters received no religious education, growing up with little understanding of Jewish tradition or history, but Vera developed a strong sense of personal pride and dignity that later in her life would be interpreted as an innate snobbishness.

After beginning her school life at a French-speaking kindergarten, Vera studied at the Marinskaya Imperial Gymnasium and then the Rostov Conservatoire of Music. At 14, however, she chose a medical career. As no Russian university offered places for women, she moved to Geneva at the age of 18 to study medicine.

Geneva at that time was a hotbed of political and intellectual activity, where both V.I. Lenin and Leon Trotsky were living in exile. There, in 1900, in Geneva's Jewish Club, Vera met Chaim Weizmann. A talented scientist and ardent exponent of cultural Zionism, Weizmann had been a participant in Zionist congresses since 1898. Vera saw in Chaim a man who "seemed to carry all the burdens of the Jewish world" on his shoulders. Despite their differences in age, background and convictions, they formed a passionate attachment. Chaim ended an engagement to another medical student, **Sophia Getsova**, and embarked on a turbulent, intense five-year courtship with the coolly attractive Vera.

Under Chaim's tutelage, Vera began what she later called her "conversion" to Judaism and Zionist ideology. Although she planned to return to Russia after her graduation, Chaim persuaded her to consider Britain as their home. He had first visited Britain during the Ugandan Crisis in order to galvanize Zionist opposition to the plan to create a Jewish homeland in Africa, helping to ensure the proposal's defeat at the Zionist Congress in 1905. Believing Britain to be the only European country prepared to support the Zionist cause, Chaim moved to England in 1904, where he became a lecturer in biochemistry at the University of Manchester. The couple married in Zopot on August 23, 1906, shortly after Vera's graduation in May.

Vera's early years in England were not happy. An accomplished linguist and musician with little knowledge of housekeeping, and unable to practice medicine in England until 1913, Vera Weizmann found life in Manchester difficult, "both physically and spiritually." The couple's first son, Benjamin, was born in 1907. In 1912, Vera sat British medical exams and the following year was appointed medical officer at the Manchester clinic for expectant mothers. When she began her studies in 1911, there had been only one other practicing woman doctor in the city. Vera spent three years working in the Manchester slums, focusing on improving the diet and health care of babies and their mothers.

As Chaim Weizmann's political influence grew, a move to London became inevitable. During the First World War, her husband emerged as leader of the Zionist movement. He was instrumental in obtaining the British government's support for a Jewish national home in Palestine—beginning with the historic Balfour Declaration of 1917—and his increasing prominence in public life necessitated a change in Vera's focus from a medical career to that of political wife after their move from Manchester in 1916.

Weizmann visited Palestine for the first time in 1919, a trip she later described as "the beginning of my own journey back to my own people." This first visit was a dispiriting experience. Appalled by the primitive conditions and harsh climate, Vera returned to London and took action: in 1920, she enlisted the help of other women in the English Zionist Federation to form the Women's International Zionist Organization (WIZO). At the first meeting of Zionist women's groups from around Europe, Weizmann gave a paper on infant and pre-natal care; one of WIZO's first projects was setting up a home for infants and a domestic science school in Tel Aviv.

Throughout the 1920s, the Weizmanns traveled the world raising money for the Zionist cause, while Vera sponsored the creation of

WIZO groups from Canada to South Africa. With Albert Einstein, they traveled to America, where Einstein was speaking on the future of the Hebrew University in Palestine, which Chaim Weizmann had helped to found in 1918. From 1920 to 1940, Vera served as joint chair, with **Rebecca D. Sieff**, of WIZO's world executive committee, eventually leaving to become president of the children's organization Youth Aliyah.

The Weizmanns maintained a strong but emotionally fraught bond throughout their marriage. Chaim, widely suspected of serial infidelity, formed a number of passionate infatuations and intense friendships with other women, many of whom he was attempting to convert—as he had done with Vera—to the Zionist cause. It has been suggested that the couple separated, at Vera's demand, in July 1925, after which she spent nearly a year living in European resorts with their younger son Michael. She made no mention of this, or any other disruption to their marriage, in her memoir *The Impossible Takes Longer*, published posthumously in 1967.

Their lifestyle was lavish, with the fashionable, elegant Vera presiding over both their household and their political salon, which attracted many diplomats and important guests, including Lord Balfour and T.E. Lawrence. Inspired by the homes of prominent families like the Rothschilds and Astors, Vera created a gracious and calm home for the husband she described as "brilliant but naïve"; he, in turn, attributed his comfort "to her forethought, her devotion and her savoire faire." The reserve of Vera's youth became increasingly perceived as an aloof elitism; even her friends accused her of social climbing, and she disapproved of the Yiddish-speaking friends Chaim invited home.

Family life for the Weizmanns was anything but serene beneath the surface: they had troubled relationships with their two sons, who had been chiefly brought up by nurses and other household staff before being sent away to school. Both Benjamin, whose rage at his parents' neglect was often directed towards his mother, and Michael, the favorite (killed in action in 1942), rejected their father's Zionism, alienated from their parents both politically and personally.

After Chaim was unceremoniously dismissed from his presidency of the World Zionist Organization at the 17th Zionist Congress in 1931, Vera felt bitter and betrayed by their former friends. In 1933, they returned to Palestine, where Chaim planned to build a chemistry and biology research laboratory. The Weizmanns were now financially independent, Chaim having sold his patented acetone process in the United States. Dividing their time between London and the Palestinian village of Rehovot, Vera found life in the Jewish homeland at odds with her "busy, energetic, public and social existence" in Britain. She threw her energies into supervising the design and building of a mansion (known locally as "the White House") befitting her husband's status as head of the Jewish Agency for Palestine. Completed in 1937, the house—with its striking contemporary design and numerous illustrious guests—was the source of much pride for Vera, who later called it "part of the living history of Israel."

During World War II, Vera Weizmann served as a doctor in a Red Cross shelter in the London slums. Grief stricken after her son Michael's death, she busied herself packing food parcels for prisoners of war in Germany. After the war, the Weizmanns returned to Palestine to lay the foundation stone of the Weizmann Institute of Science. As civil unrest and violence increased in Palestine, they traveled to America to lobby President Harry Truman for a Jewish state, and for Chaim to testify in front of a UN Special Committee. With the UN's vote for the partition of Palestine and the eventual proclamation of the State of Israel in 1948, Vera and her ailing but still influential husband experienced "the most hectic period of our lives."

In February 1949, the first elected Parliament of Israel elevated Chaim Weizmann from the presidency of the Provisional State Council to the title of president of the State of Israel. But his role was chiefly symbolic, to Vera's intense frustration. In poor health, her husband was just a figurehead, "the Prisoner of Rehovot," as she called him.

After Chaim's death in 1952, Vera struggled to find a role for herself. She became president of the Israeli Red Cross, and once again became involved with Youth Aliyah. She traveled to the U.S. to visit Truman and met President Juan Perón of Argentina during a trip to South America in 1954, where she spoke on behalf of Israel's bond drive and the Weizmann Institute. Before her death in 1966, Vera Weizmann made a visit to her Russian homeland for the first time in 40 years.

SOURCES:

Rose, Norman. *Chaim Weizmann: A Biography*. London: Weidenfeld & Nicolson, 1986.

Weizmann, Chaim. *Trial and Error: The Autobiography of Chaim Weizmann*. NY: Harper Bros., 1949.

Weizmann, Vera. *The Impossible Takes Longer*, 1967.

Paula Morris, D.Phil.,
Brooklyn, New York

Welch, Joan Kemp (b. 1906).

See Kemp-Welch, Joan.

Weld, Angelina Grimké (1805–1879).

See Grimké, Angelina E.

Weld, Theresa (1893–1978).

See Blanchard, Theresa Weld.

Weld, Tuesday (1943—)

American actress, notorious in the 1960s for her free-wheeling lifestyle, who was dubbed "the archetypal nymphet" by Time *magazine. Born Susan Ker Weld on August 27, 1943, in New York City; daughter of Lathrop Motley Weld and Aileen (Ker) Weld; attended Hollywood Professional School; married Claude Harz (a writer), in 1965 (divorced 1971); married Dudley Moore (an actor), in 1975 (divorced 1980); married Pinchas Zuckerman (a violinist), in 1985; children: (first marriage) Natasha Harz; (second marriage) Patrick Moore.*

Selected filmography: Rock, Rock, Rock *(1956);* The Wrong Man *(1956);* Rally 'Round the Flag, Boys! *(1958);* The Five Pennies *(1959);* Sex Kittens Go to College *(1960);* High Time *(1960);* Because They're Young *(1960);* The Private Lives of Adam and Eve *(1961);* Bachelor Flat *(1961);* Wild in the Country *(1961);* Return to Peyton Place *(1961);* Soldier in the Rain *(1963);* The Cincinnati Kid *(1965);* I'll Take Sweden *(1965);* Lord Love a Duck *(1966);* Pretty Poison *(1968);* I Walk the Line *(1970);* A Safe Place *(1971);* Play It As It Lays *(1972);* Looking for Mr. Goodbar *(1977);* Who'll Stop the Rain *(1978);* Serial *(1980);* Thief *(1981);* Author! Author! *(1982);* Once Upon a Time in America *(1984);* Heartbreak Hotel *(1988);* Falling Down *(1993);* Feeling Minnesota *(1996).*

Tuesday Weld, who would become Hollywood's premiere "sex kitten" in the 1960s before earning respect as an actress of genuine ability, was born in a Salvation Army Hospital in New York City on August 27, 1943. Her mother **Aileen Ker Weld** was the fourth wife of Lathrop Motley Weld, a former investment broker and playboy who was the black sheep of his rich and socially distinguished family. His death of a heart ailment when Tuesday was only three marked the beginning of her career in the spotlight, as her mother pressed the little girl into modeling in order to support the family, which included an older brother and sister. They barely survived in a $20-a-month apartment without hot water in a Manhattan slum, but Aileen Weld refused to accept her in-laws' offer to raise and educate the children because the deal hinged on her never seeing them again.

The burden of keeping the family together fell largely on little Tuesday (then called Susan), as her childhood became a steady round of auditions for modeling jobs. Under the pressure of show-business life, she quickly cracked, later claiming to have had her first nervous breakdown at the age of nine. The family's move to Ft. Lauderdale, Florida, gave Weld the rare opportunity to attend public school on a regular basis, as her schedule in New York had allowed only her nominal enrollment in several city schools. She was still far from having a normal childhood, however, as she developed a drinking problem at age ten.

Increased financial need caused Weld and her mother to return to New York after only two years in Florida, where Aileen left her other children in the care of friends. While still modeling, Weld began acting and dance lessons, and quickly accumulated a number of television roles on such shows as "Playhouse 90," "Kraft Theater," "Alcoa Theater," and "Climax." Her acting success did little to assuage the pain she felt, however, and at age 12 she made the first of several suicide attempts, by ingesting a potentially lethal combination of alcohol, sleeping pills, and aspirin. She emerged from the resultant coma as wild as ever, routinely skipping school to get drunk in Greenwich Village.

Weld's break into films occurred at age 13, in 1956's low-budget *Rock, Rock, Rock*. Her part, described by a critic in *Time* magazine as "the archetypal nymphet, ***Shirley Temple [Black]** with a leer," was to be the first of many such roles she would play in her acting career, and the image for which she became best known. Unable to gain admittance to New York's Actors Studio because of her age, Weld went with her mother to Hollywood and in 1958 landed the role of the sexy young babysitter in the Paul Newman-***Joanne Woodward** vehicle *Rally 'Round the Flag, Boys!*, her first feature film. The following year she legally changed her first name to Tuesday, a childhood nickname, and played the crippled daughter of Danny Kaye in *The Five Pennies* (1959). This led to a featured role in the popular television series "The Many Loves of Dobie Gillis," as Thalia Menninger, one of the title character's girlfriends. Weld moved out of her mother's house at age 16, but, compelled by California's strict child labor laws to remain in school until she was 18, attended the Hollywood Professional School when she was not working. Her stint on

Tuesday
Weld

"Dobie Gillis" proved short, for in 1960 she was dropped because a sponsor thought her teenage sex appeal inappropriate for a family show.

Undaunted by this setback, Weld found that her image was in demand on the big screen and during the early 1960s starred in a series of movies (most of them forgettable, some truly awful) that exploited this quality. Among these were *Because They're Young* (1960), with Dick Clark as a high-school teacher; *High Time* (1960), starring Bing Crosby as a college student;

Sex Kittens Go to College (1960), which featured **Mamie Van Doren** as an ex-stripper turned college science professor; *The Private Lives of Adam and Eve* (1961), with Van Doren, Mickey Rooney—as the devil—and Mel Torme; *Return to Peyton Place* (1961), based on the novel by *Grace Metalious; and *Wild in the Country* (1961), written by Clifford Odets and starring Elvis Presley. In each, Weld played the part of a mindless teeny-bopper, troubled teenager, or luscious nymph, commanding $35,000 per film. Hailed as the successor to *Marilyn Monroe (whose career was then in its final tailspin), Weld attracted a torrent of media attention for her off-screen scandals, which included affairs with some of Hollywood's biggest names, among them Frank Sinatra, Raymond Burr, Albert Finney, John Ireland, George Hamilton, Elvis Presley, and John Barrymore, Jr. Weld flaunted her sex life and further scandalized the press by making no secret of her fondness for liquor and showing up for interviews barefoot. Such behavior would seem almost commonplace by the end of the decade, but in the conservative early 1960s she was vilified by gossip columnists for adding to the moral decay of Hollywood.

Because of the poor quality of the movies she appeared in, Weld's film career had attracted almost no critical attention, but in the years following she began to earn a reputation as an actress of surprising range. Her sensitive portrayal of Jackie Gleason's dim-witted girlfriend in *Soldier in the Rain* (1963) caused **Judith Crist** to hail her as "a lovely blonde who portrays a teen-age submoron to perfection." Playing another backwards girlfriend—this time opposite Steve McQueen—in *The Cincinnati Kid* (1965), Weld again turned critics' heads despite the minor nature of the role. She possessed a knack for elevating even the most typecast roles, such as her shallow high-school beauty whose every wish is granted in *Lord Love a Duck* (1966), causing one reviewer to remark, "Weld is not only sexy but eloquent in what she doesn't say with words." She was rewarded with first runner-up honors in the Best Actress of the Year category from the New York Film Critics Circle Award on the basis of her work in *Pretty Poison*, with Anthony Perkins, in 1968. Weld was runner-up to no one when she won Best Actress honors at the Venice Film Festival in 1972 for her portrayal of a troubled former model-actress in the screen adaptation of **Joan Didion**'s novel *Play It As It Lays*.

Despite her talent, box-office success eluded Weld. In the 1960s, she passed on plum roles in such major films as *Lolita* (in which **Sue Lyon** starred), *Bonnie and Clyde* (**Faye Dunaway** took the role of *Bonnie Parker), *Bob & Carol & Ted & Alice*, *Cactus Flower* (for which **Goldie Hawn** later won an Oscar), and the crowd-pleaser *True Grit*. However, she had a significant cult following by the mid-to-late years of the decade, with Tuesday Weld film festivals springing up in Manhattan and other locations. The cult status of her celebrity allowed Weld to break out of her early Hollywood image to obtain more diverse roles, particularly in television movies which became her primary vehicles from the mid-1970s onward. During this time she was known more for her troubled marriage to actor Dudley Moore, whom she married in 1975 after the break-up of her first marriage in 1971, than for her acting. The 1980s saw even less of Weld, and in the 1990s, despite the respect that now greets her name, she acted in only two major films, *Falling Down* (1993) and *Feeling Minnesota* (1996), in which she played a mother.

SOURCES:

Edgar, Kathleen J., ed. *Contemporary Theatre, Film and Television*. Vol. 18. Detroit, MI: Gale Research, 1998.

Katz, Ephraim. *The Film Encyclopedia*. 3rd ed. NY: HarperCollins, 1998.

Moritz, Charles, ed. *Current Biography Yearbook 1974*. NY: H.W. Wilson, 1974.

Susan J. Walton,
freelance writer,
Berea, Ohio

Welitsch, Ljuba (1913–1996)

Bulgarian soprano. Pronunciation: lyoo-ba VEY-lish. Born Ljuba Velickova or Welitschkova on July 10, 1913, in Borissovo, Bulgaria, a small town on the Black Sea; died in Vienna in September 1996; daughter of a farmer; studied with Gyogy Zlatov in Sofia and with Lierhammer in Vienna.

Sang at Hamburg (1941–43), the Vienna Volksoper (1940–44), and Munich (1943–46); gave a special performance of Richard Strauss' Salome with the composer conducting (1944); joined the Vienna Staatsoper (1946); debuted at Covent Garden (1947), Glyndebourne (1948), and New York's Metropolitan Opera (1949).

Ljuba Welitsch's name is especially associated with the role of Salome as she performed it under Richard Strauss' direction in 1944, and in a notorious production by Peter Brook with decor by Salvador Dali. At the time, *Salome* was regarded as a somewhat scandalous work. World War II interrupted Welitsch's career, confining her to the Continent. In 1949, she debuted at New York's Metropolitan Opera, but her subsequent international career was relatively short lived. By 1955, Welitsch's voice was in decline,

Ljuba
Welitsch

poetry at an early age. Her books include *Early Poems* (1913), *Pride* (1923), *Lost Lane* (1925), *Genesis: An Impression* (1926), *Matrix* (1928), *Deserted House* (1930), *Jupiter and the Nun* (1932), *Sir George Goldie, Founder of Nigeria* (1934), *Poems of Ten Years, 1924–1934* (1934), *Selections from the Poems of Dorothy Wellesley*, with an introduction by William Butler Yeats (1936), *Lost Planet* (1942), *The Poets* (1943), *Desert Wells* (1946), *Rhymes for Middle Years* (1954), and *Early Light: The Collected Poems* (1955). She published her autobiography, *Far Have I Travelled*, in 1952.

Wellington, duchess of.

See Wellesley, Dorothy (1889–1956).

Wells, Alice (1927–1987)

American photographer. Name variations: Alisa Wells. Born in 1927 in Erie, Pennsylvania; died in 1987 in Galisteo, New Mexico; attended Pennsylvania State University in University Park, Pennsylvania; married Kenneth Carl Meyers (divorced 1959); married Richard Witteman, in 1974 (separated 1980); married Roman Attenberger; children: (first marriage) three.

Born in Erie, Pennsylvania, in 1927, Alice Wells became known for her experimental work with montage and assorted photographic processing techniques. After marrying Kenneth Carl Meyers, Wells moved to Rochester, New York, where her husband held a position with Eastman Kodak. In 1952, Wells began working for Kodak as well, in a secretarial position. She took up photography in 1959, the same year she divorced Meyers. In 1961, she attended an Ansel Adams photography workshop in Yosemite National Park, California, followed by a year's worth of study with Nathan Lyons at his home in Rochester, New York. In 1962, Wells resigned her position at Kodak and became Lyons' secretary at George Eastman House (now the International Museum of Photography at George Eastman House) also located in Rochester.

Wells began creating photographs of abstract forms in nature using large-format cameras. In 1964, she had a solo exhibition of those works at Eastman House. She switched to hand-held 35-mm cameras in 1965 and used highly populated urban areas as her subject. Wells experimented with multiple exposures in camera and negative sandwiches in the darkroom. She also worked with solarization, toning, and hand coloring. In 1969, Lyons created the Visual Studies Workshop

which some ascribed to overuse. In her prime, her voice had apparently limitless resources. "Welitsch sang on her nerves," noted Philip Hope-Wallace, "clear stream of tone like [*Elisabeth] Rethberg, a diamond top C like the evening star." She made few recordings but those which survive confirm a theatrical voice.

John Haag,
Athens, Georgia

Wellesley, Dorothy (1889–1956)

English poet. Name variations: Duchess of Wellington. Born Dorothy Violet Ashton in White Waltham, Berkshire, England, on July 20, 1889; died in Withyham, Sussex, England, on July 11, 1956; daughter of Robert Ashton and Lucy Cecilia Dunn Gardner Ashton; tutored at home by foreign governesses; married Lord Gerald Wellesley, 7th duke of Wellington; children: one daughter, one son.

Considered somewhat of a rebel from her upperclass upbringing, Dorothy Wellesley wrote (originally called the Photographic Studies Workshop) in Rochester, where Wells was his assistant until 1972 when she moved to New Mexico. While there, Wells changed her first name to "Alisa" which she spelled in various ways. In 1974, she married Richard Witteman who shared her interest in Zen Buddhism. The couple separated in 1980, and Wells' third marriage to Roman Attenberger lasted until her death in 1987.

SOURCES:

Rosenblum, Naomi. *A History of Women Photographers.* NY: Abbeville, 1994.

Susan J. Walton,
freelance writer,
Berea, Ohio

Wells, Alice Stebbins (1873–1957)

First woman police officer in the United States. Born in 1873 in Kansas; died in 1957; attended public schools in Kansas; attended Hartford Theological Seminary in Connecticut.

Sworn in with full powers of arrest in Los Angeles, California (September 12, 1910); lectured throughout the U.S. on the benefits of women police officers (1910s); retired (1940).

Alice Stebbins Wells' religious background influenced her career path, which led her to become the first woman police officer in the United States and possibly in the world. Born in 1873 and raised in Kansas, she moved to Brooklyn, New York, after high school. She then became an assistant to a local Congregational minister and took up religious studies of her own at the Hartford Theological Seminary in Connecticut. After two years of study, Wells launched her own ministry, traveling across the country and giving lectures on Christian topics. She even earned her own pastorates in Maine and Oklahoma—the first woman to do so in those states—before settling in California.

At this point, Wells combined her Christian principles with an interest in prison reform. She decided that she could be most effective as an actual police officer, and applied for a job on the Los Angeles police force. Although there were no women officers in the city, Wells appealed to prominent citizens for support, and the city responded to the 100 signatures she collected by agreeing to let her join the force.

On September 12, 1910, Alice Stebbins Wells was sworn in as the first woman police officer with full powers of arrest in Los Angeles, California, and in the United States as a whole. She carried no weapon, but otherwise had the same authority to make arrests as did male officers. The novelty of a woman police officer forced Wells into proving to the public that she was, indeed, an officer. She had the most difficulty with streetcar conductors who often accused her of using what they supposed to be her husband's badge to get free rides. To solve the problem, the department issued her a badge that read "Police Woman's Badge No. 1," in large clear letters, and Wells designed a "feminine" yet official-looking uniform to wear. Her initial duties were to facilitate the "suppression of unwholesome billboard displays" and enforce laws regarding "dance halls, skating rinks, penny arcades, picture shows" and other public recreational establishments.

By 1914, there were four more women serving as police officers in Los Angeles. When the police department issued a policy that male police officers could not question young women, policewomen were assigned the task. (It was thought that a policewoman's sympathy and intuition would help gain the confidence of those being questioned.) Women police officers also worked on cases involving abandoned women. With her status as the first female officer in America, Wells worked toward educating other police departments across the country about the significant role of women in law enforcement. In 1914, she spoke on the subject to the Consumers' League in New York City and to the New York State legislature. Shortly thereafter, a bill was passed without opposition allowing ten women to be placed on the New York City police force. By 1916, the year Wells established the International Association of Policewomen, 17 U.S. cities had women police officers. She continued to contribute to the expansion of women in law enforcement by founding the first police training program for women, at the University of California in Los Angeles. Wells retired from the Los Angeles police department on November 1, 1940.

SOURCES:

Axelrod, Alan, and Charles Phillips. *Cops, Crooks, and Criminologists.* NY: Facts on File, 1996.

Felton, Bruce, and Mark Fowler. *Felton & Fowler's Famous Americans You Never Knew Existed.* NY: Stein & Day, 1979.

Griffin, Lynne, and Kelly McCann. *The Book of Women: 300 Notable Women History Passed By.* Holbrook, MA: Bob Adams, 1992.

Read, Phyllis J., and Bernard L. Witlieb. *The Book of Women's Firsts.* NY: Random House, 1992.

Susan J. Walton,
freelance writer,
Berea, Ohio

Wells, Carolyn (1862–1942)

Prolific American author and editor. Born on June 18, 1862 (some sources cite 1869), in Rahway, New

Jersey; died on March 26, 1942, in New York City; daughter of William Edmund Wells (a real estate and insurance salesman) and Anna Potter (Woodruff) Wells; educated in Rahway public schools and the Sauveur School of Languages in Amherst, Massachusetts; married Hadwin Houghton (of the Boston publishing family), in 1918 (died 1919); no children.

Selected writings: At the Sign of the Sphinx (charades, 1899); The Jingle Book (1899); Idle Idylls (verse, 1900); Folly in Fairyland (1901); Abeniki Caldwell (novel, 1902); A Phenomenal Fauna (1902); Folly in the Forest (1902); The Gordon Elopement (novel, with Harry Persons Taber, 1904); Folly for the Wise (verse, 1904); The Matrimonial Bureau (with Taber, 1905); Rubáiyát of a Motor Car (verse, 1906); The Emily Emmins Papers (1907); The Happy Chaps (1908); The Rubáiyát of Bridge (verse, 1909); The Seven Ages of Childhood (verse, 1909); The Lover's Baedeker and Guide to Arcady (1912); The Eternal Feminine (1913); Girls and Gayety (1913); The Technique of the Mystery Story (1913); The Re-Echo Club (1913); Maid of Athens (play, 1914); Baubles (1917); Ptomaine Street: A Tale of Warble Petticoat (1921); A Concise Bibliography of the Works of Walt Whitman with Alfred Goldsmith (1922); The Rest of My Life (autobiography, 1937).

Carolyn Wells

Wrote the "Fleming Stone," "Alan Ford," "Pennington Wise," and "Kenneth Carlisle" crime novel series. Other crime novels: The Disappearance of Kimball Webb ("Rowland Wright" mystery, 1920); More Lives Than One ("Lorimer Lane" mystery, 1923); The Fourteenth Key ("Lorimer Lane" mystery, 1924); The Moss Mystery (1924); Face Cards (1925); The Vanity Case (1926); The Sixth Commandment (1927); Deep-Lake Mystery (1928).

Selected writing for children: The Story of Betty (1899); The Merry-Go-Round (1901); Mother Goose's Menagerie (1901); Patty Fairfield (1901); The Pete and Polly Stories (1902); Eight Girls and a Dog (1902); Patty at Home (1904); In the Reign of Queen Dick (1904); The Staying Guests (1904); The Dorrance Domain (1905); Dorrance Doings (1906); Fluffy Ruffles (1907); Marjorie's Vacation (1907); Patty in Paris (1907); Patty's Summer Days (1908); Dick and Dolly (1909); Marjorie's New Friend (1909); Patty's Pleasure (1909); Dick and Dolly's Adventures (1910); Marjorie in Command (1910); Marjorie's Maytime (1911); Patty's Motor Car (1911); Marjorie at Seacote (1912); Patty's Social Season (1913); Two Little Women (1915); Patty's Romance (1915); Patty's Fortune (1916); Two Little Women and Treasure House (1916); Two Little Women on a Holiday (1917); Doris of Dobbs Ferry (1917); Patty Blossom (1917); Patty-Bride (1918); Patty and Azalea (1919); A Christmas Alphabet: From a Poem (1919).

Carolyn Wells was born in Rahway, New Jersey, in 1862, into the middle-class household of William and **Anna Wells**. A clever, precocious child, she mastered the alphabet at 18 months and reading by the age of three. An attack of scarlet fever at age six, however, left her deaf.

Although she graduated from high school as valedictorian of her class, Wells thought school a waste, and college an even greater waste. She attended the Sauveur School of Languages in Amherst for three summers, studying Shakespeare under the esteemed scholar William J. Rolfe, and delighted in private, informal studies on a variety of subjects, including medieval history, botany, astronomy, German, and French. She also worked for the Rahway Library Association, which gave her limitless access to the library's collection as well as the power to order whatever books and magazines she desired. According to Carlin T. Kindilien, "The flow of books that Carolyn Wells first let loose in 1895 is more than anything else the product of a bright and good-humored librarian."

She wrote her first book, *At the Sign of the Sphinx*, at the encouragement of Rolfe, who knew of her fondness for puzzles. Described as a book of charades, it marked the beginning of a prolific writing career for Wells, who quickly set a pace of publishing three or four volumes a year. All in all, she produced about 180 works of humor, mystery, and children's books in her career. Various magazines published her humorous pieces throughout the 1890s, including *Chap Book, Lark, Philistine, Tatler, Yellow Book, Bookman, Youth Companion*, and *Life*. She became so well known for her parodies and facility with limericks that publishers sought to incorporate her name into titles of humor books, such as *The Carolyn Wells Year Book of Old Favorites and New Fancies for 1909*. Wells herself edited numerous comedic works, produced her own notable collections, and crafted side-splitting parodies that made use of the works of other writers. Both *The Rubáiyát of a Motor Car* (1906) and *The Rubáiyát of Bridge* (1909) were comic models of Edward Fitzgerald's highly popular *Rubáiyát of Omar Khayyám* as the basis for her humorous observations on Americans' love affairs with cars and cards, while Sinclair Lewis' *Main Street* met its comic match in Wells' *Ptomaine Street: A Tale of Warble Petticoat* in 1921.

Of Wells' works, roughly half are from the mystery genre, which earned her the informal title "Dean of American Mystery Writers." Her main character, Fleming Stone, first appeared in 1909 and thereafter became the subject of 60 of Wells' mysteries. Other detectives created by Wells to solve her drawing-room crimes included Kenneth Carlisle, Alan Ford, Lorimer Lane, and Pennington Wise. Some critics found her mystery work formulaic to the point of parodying fellow mystery writers Edgar Allan Poe, *Anna Katharine Green, and Arthur Conan Doyle, but Wells was considered enough of an expert to publish *Technique of the Mystery Story* in 1913.

Wells also made her mark in the genre of children's literature. As with her parodies, she sometimes drew from established literature to create her imaginative stories. Lewis Carroll's combination of humor and fantasy served as a model for Wells' *Folly in Fairyland* (1901) and *Folly in the Forest* (1902), and Rudyard Kipling inspired the title for *The Jingle Book* (1899). Following the trend of children's publishing, Wells produced several popular series for girls such as her "Patty," "Marjorie," and "Two Little Women" narratives around the same time that Edward Stratemeyer's "Tom Swift" and "The Bobbsey Twins" series were achieving fame.

Wells often traveled to England and cultivated a wide circle of literary friends on both sides of the Atlantic. She was also known for her rare book collections of writers such as Walt Whitman, Emerson, Longfellow and Poe. At age 55, Wells married Hadwin Houghton, related to the Boston publishing family, on April 2, 1918. Houghton, who was the superintendent of a varnish manufacturing company, died in 1919. Upon his death, Wells moved to New York City, living in a hotel overlooking Central Park until her death on March 26, 1942. She had suffered from arteriosclerosis and died in a New York hospital after breaking her leg and wrist in a fall. She was buried in the Rahway Cemetery in New Jersey.

SOURCES:

Dresner, Zita Zatkin. "Carolyn Wells," in *Dictionary of Literary Biography*, Vol. 11: *American Humorists, 1800–1950*. Detroit, MI: Gale Research, 1982, pp. 556–560.

Garraty, John A., and Mark C. Carnes, eds. *American National Biography*. NY: Oxford University Press, 1999.

Kindilien, Carlin T. "Carolyn Wells," in *Notable American Women, 1607–1950*. Ed. by Edward T. James. Cambridge, MA: The Belknap Press of Harvard University, 1971.

Kunitz, Stanley J., and Howard Haycraft, eds. *Twentieth Century Authors*. NY: H.W. Wilson, 1942.

McHenry, Robert, ed. *Famous American Women*. NY: Dover, 1980.

Amy Cooper, M.A., M.S.I.,
Ann Arbor, Michigan

Wells, Catherine (d. 1927).

See Richardson, Dorothy for sidebar.

Wells, Charlotte Fowler
(1814–1901)

American phrenologist and publisher. Born Charlotte Fowler on August 14, 1814, in Cohocton, New York; died in West Orange, New Jersey, age 86, on June 4, 1901; daughter of Horace Fowler and Martha (Howe) Fowler; attended local schools and Franklin Academy in Prattsburg, New York; married Samuel Robert Wells, in 1844 (died 1875).

Charlotte Fowler Wells was born in 1814 in Cohocton, New York, into a farming family of eight children. Her formal education consisted of attendance at the district school near her home and six months at the Franklin Academy in Prattsburg, New York. The Wells household was a stimulating environment for Charlotte, however, and her education was supplemented by her family and by self-instruction. She began a career in teaching before she was 20 years old.

Wells became interested in the Austrian "science" of phrenology in the early 1830s. This discipline taught that there were physiological determinants of character, and that character could be determined by the physical characteristics of the cranium. Her brothers Orson Squire Fowler and Lorenzo Niles Fowler adapted the practice for American audiences and helped found and popularize "practical phrenology," which sought to reform personalities and apply phrenology to all aspects of life. They established a phrenological center (including a museum, publishing house, and lecture-booking office) in New York City in 1835, which Wells joined in 1837.

Charlotte was an integral part of the center; she taught the first regular class in phrenology in America, gave readings and helped to manage all aspects of the family's publishing activities. She believed in Spiritualism, which promoted faith based on science and the promise of social reform, and was a vocal supporter for the equal rights of women. She also hosted meetings for the New York Medical College for Women and was a member of its board of trustees from its founding in 1863 until her death.

In 1844, Charlotte married Samuel Robert Wells, a recent convert to phrenology who had joined the family business. In 1855, she and her husband bought Charlotte's brothers' interests in the center, becoming full owners of the business. The Wellses continued to write, publish, and teach, and were instrumental in founding the American Institute of Phrenology. After her husband's death in 1875, Charlotte was the sole proprietor and president of the Fowlers and Wells Company. Into her 80s, Wells continued to teach the public about phrenology, writing a series of articles for the *Phrenological Journal* on the pioneers of the movement. In 1896, she lost sight in one eye after a fall, but still managed to continue lecturing. Charlotte Wells died on June 4, 1901, in West Orange, New Jersey.

SOURCES:

Edgerly, Lois Stiles, ed. and comp. *Give Her This Day.* Gardiner, ME: Tilbury House, 1990.

James, Edward T., ed. *Notable American Women, 1607–1950.* Cambridge, MA: The Belknap Press of Harvard University, 1971.

Read, Phyllis J., and Bernard L. Witlieb. *The Book of Women's Firsts.* NY: Random House, 1992.

Amy Cooper, M.A., M.S.I.,
Ann Arbor, Michigan

Wells, Emmeline B. (1828–1921)

American leader of Mormon women and suffragist.
Name variations: E.W.; Blanche Beechwood; Aunt Em. Born Emmeline Blanche Woodward on February 29, 1828, in Petersham, Massachusetts; died of heart failure on April 25, 1921, in Salt Lake City, Utah; daughter of David Woodward and Deiadama (Hare) Woodward; educated in local grammar schools and the select school for girls in New Salem; married James Harvey Harris, in 1843 (deserted, 1844); married Newel K. Whitney (a Mormon bishop), in 1845 (died 1850); married Daniel Hanmer Wells, in 1852 (died 1891); children: (first marriage) Eugene Henri Harris (died in infancy, 1844); (second marriage) Isabel Modelena (b. 1848), Melvina Caroline (b. 1850); (third marriage) Emmeline (b. 1853), Elizabeth Ann (b. 1859), and Louisa Martha (b. 1862).

Emmeline B. Wells was born in 1828 in Petersham, Massachusetts, one of nine children of David and **Deiadama Woodward**. She was four when her father died. Her mother converted from Congregationalist to the Mormon faith in 1842, and Emmeline followed with baptism into the Mormon Church on March 1, 1842. Her education at the local grammar school and at a school for girls in New Salem resulted in Wells receiving her teaching certificate in 1843. That same year, she began teaching in a country school in Orange, Massachusetts, and married James Harvey Harris, the son of the presiding elder of the local Mormon church. In 1844, Emmeline traveled with her husband to the Mormon city of Nauvoo, Illinois, where she met the Prophet Joseph Smith. James' parents left the church and, in November 1844, he deserted his wife just after the death of their month-old son Eugene. In 1845, Emmeline became the plural wife of the presiding bishop of the Mormon Church, Newel K. Whitney, and in February of the following year she and her family joined the exodus of Mormons from Nauvoo and moved to Salt Lake City. In 1852, two years after the death of Bishop Whitney, Emmeline became the seventh wife of Daniel Hanmer Wells, a high officer in the Mormon Church.

Wells began to devote her time to the work of the church, journalism, and women's suffrage after the birth of her last child in 1862. Becoming a member of the Relief Society, the largest Mormon women's organization, she began contributing to its publication, the *Woman's Exponent*, in 1873. She rose through the ranks of the *Exponent* during the 1870s until she became full editor in 1877. Her lengthy tenure in this position, which lasted until the paper was superseded by the *Relief Society Magazine* in 1914, added to her already sizeable sphere of influence. In her articles, written under the names "Aunt Em," "E.W." or "Blanche Beechwood," she sought to present a balanced representation

Emmeline
B. Wells

of Mormonism and to promote the rights of women. She used the *Exponent* to argue the case for women's suffrage when Congress sought to repeal voting rights for women in the Utah Territory in the 1880s. Brigham Young had influenced the territory's legislature into granting women the right to vote as early as 1870 as a way of counteracting the growing non-Mormon influence, which consisted largely of single men. Wells even traveled to Washington, D.C., as a lobbyist for the cause in 1885.

Although Congress successfully repealed women's suffrage in the territory in 1887, Wells was recognized as a suffragist on a national level as vice-president of the Utah chapter of the National Women Suffrage Association. She was a personal friend of prominent women's rights advocates *Susan B. Anthony and *Elizabeth Cady Stanton, and joined Emily Sophia Richards in founding the Woman Suffrage Association of Utah in 1889 to demand the return of their right to vote. The group's lobbying at Utah's constitutional convention in 1895 achieved its aim when a woman suffrage clause became part of the state's constitution in 1896. A long-time attendee at women's conventions, in 1899 Wells was a delegate to the International Council of Women in London.

Known for her devotion to hard work, Wells managed to find time in the midst of the suffrage campaign to expand her role in the Relief Society. In 1876, Brigham Young made her the president of the Relief Society's Central Grain Committee, which oversaw the storage of grain against famine. She became general secretary of the Relief Society in 1892, and was its president in 1910. Influential outside the church as well as within it, Wells was a member of the Pacific Coast Women's Press Association, founded the Utah Women's Press Club in 1891, and was a charter member of the state's society of the Daughters of the American Revolution. Brigham Young University awarded Wells an honorary degree in 1912, and she was held in high esteem as a valuable public figure until her death in 1921. In 1928, a marble bust of Emmeline B. Wells was placed in the rotunda of Utah's state capitol.

Wells' principal works include editorials and columns as the editor of the *Woman's Exponent* (1877–1914). She edited *Charities and Philanthropies: Woman's Work in Utah* (1893), as a contribution to the Chicago World's Fair. She also published a book of poetry, *Musings and Memories* (1896), and wrote the words for the Mormon song "Our Mountain Home So Dear."

SOURCES:

James, Edward T., ed. *Notable American Women, 1607–1950.* Cambridge, MA: The Belknap Press of Harvard University, 1971.

McHenry, Robert, ed. *Famous American Women.* NY: Dover, 1980.

Amy Cooper, M.A., M.S.I.,
Ann Arbor, Michigan

Wells, Ida B. (1862–1931).

See Wells-Barnett, Ida.

Wells, Kate Gannett (1838–1911)

American reformer and anti-suffragist. Name variations: Catherine Boott Gannett. Born on April 6, 1838, in London, England; died of acute gastritis on December 13, 1911; third daughter of American parents Ezra Stiles Gannett (a minister) and Anna (Tilden) Gannett; married Samuel Wells, on June 11, 1863; children: Stiles Gannett, Samuel, and Louisa Appleton.

Kate Gannett Wells was born in 1838 in London, England, the first of three children and only daughter of Ezra and **Anna Tilden Gannett**, both Americans. She was christened Catherine Boott Gannett, after a Dr. Boott who was then caring for Ezra as he recovered from a nervous breakdown. The colleague and successor of Reverend William Ellery Channing at the (Unitarian) Federal Street Church in Boston and the grandson of President Ezra Stiles of Yale College, Ezra Gannett was a descendant of **Mary Chilton**, one of the first English immigrants to the New World. Anna Gannett died when Kate was eight, so the young girl's childhood was shaped by her father and his austere, orderly life which focused on public service. Kate married Samuel Wells, a prominent Boston lawyer, on June 11, 1863, and this union provided the affluent leisure that allowed her to pursue her own career of public service from the 1870s until her death in 1911.

Kate Gannett Wells' choice of social causes reflected her belief that women should concern themselves only with specifically feminine issues, such as education, health, family, and moral matters. Early in her service career, she was a member of the Massachusetts Moral Education Association, which sought to combat prostitution through better education and increased charity work by Bostonian women. Better education was very much at the forefront of Wells' efforts as a member of the Woman's Education Association of Boston during the 1870s. In 1875, she was elected to the Boston School Committee for one term, and was appointed to three eight-year terms on the Massachusetts State Board of Education beginning in 1888. Wells was active in several other women's organizations, including the New England Women's Club, which she served as secretary in 1882, and the Association for the Advancement of Women. In the 1890s, she led the Massachusetts Emergency and Hygiene Association in the promotion of better health practices in working-class families.

For all her work with women and various social causes, Wells adamantly opposed women's suffrage, going so far as to declare herself a remonstrant against the woman suffrage petition presented annually to the Massachusetts legislature. As a leader in the anti-suffrage movement, Wells argued that the addition of uneducated women to the voting rolls would foster confusion and unnecessary legislation, although she acknowledged that the future presence of educated women in the political process would be beneficial. Kate Gannett Wells died at age 74 in her home in the Back Bay area of Boston on December 13, 1911, and was buried in Mount Auburn Cemetery in Cambridge.

SOURCES:

James, Edward T., ed. *Notable American Women, 1607–1950.* Cambridge, MA: The Belknap Press of Harvard University, 1971.

Amy Cooper, M.A., M.S.I.,
Ann Arbor, Michigan

Wells, Kitty (1919—)

American singer, the first female vocalist to have a number one country music song on the national record charts, whose lengthy and influential career earned her the title of "the Queen of Country Music."
Born Ellen Muriel Deason on August 30, 1919, in Nashville, Tennessee; daughter of Charles Carey Deason (a brakeman) and Myrtle (Street) Deason; graduated from Lipscomb School in South Nashville; attended ninth grade at Howard High School; married Johnny Wright (a musician), on October 30, 1937; children: Ruby Jean, Johnnie Robert III, Carol Sue.

Sang for the first time over the radio (1936); moved to Greensboro, North Carolina, the first of a number of relocations (1941); adopted Kitty Wells as her stage name; moved to Knoxville with family and sang on station WNOX; moved to Raleigh, North Carolina, and performed on station WPTF; appeared on the initial performance of "The Louisiana Hayride" over station KWKH, Shreveport, Louisiana (April 3, 1948); made her first RCA recordings (1949); father died (May 3, 1951); moved to Nashville; recorded "It Wasn't God Who Made Honky Tonk Angels" (May 1952); first duet with Red Foley (1953), with Roy Acuff (1955), with Webb Pierce (1956), and Roy Drusky (1960); mother died (September 18, 1967); premiered "The Kitty Wells-Johnny Wright Family Show" (1969); made her first appearance in Britain at Wembley Festival (1974); elected to the Country Music Hall of Fame (1976); received Academy of Country Music's Pioneer Award (1986); received National Academy of Recording Arts and Sciences' Lifetime Achievement Grammy Award (1991); named a TNN-Music City News Living Legend (1993); elected to Grammy Awards Hall of Fame (1997); went on last concert tour (April 2000).

In explaining the success of her signature song "It Wasn't God Who Made Honky Tonk Angels," recorded in 1952, Kitty Wells once said that it was the right song at the right time. The years of World War II had seen women working in vast numbers in previously male-dominated industries, adjusting themselves to living independently of husbands or fathers, and generally experiencing a higher level of social and personal autonomy while thousands of American men fought against totalitarian regimes overseas. When the war was won and the world again made safe for democracy, the men came home, returning to the jobs that women had filled and expecting social roles and mores to have remained the same. Wells' song was an "answer" and in a certain sense a protest against a hit country-music song of the day, "The Wild Side of Life," which implicitly condoned men's questionable conduct while looking unfavorably on the behavior of a woman (a "honky tonk angel" or one who, heaven forbid, frequented honky-tonks just like men did) who has jilted the male singer. "It Wasn't God Who Made Honky Tonk Angels" reflected many women's understanding of the double standard and sexual inequality that remained in America. It immediately became the nation's most popular country-music song, and even made a respectable showing on the pop charts. An instant star (with years of work already behind her), Wells became the first woman to rise to the top of country music, and there she would stay, in influence if not in sales, as country-music styles changed radically over the decades.

The "Queen of Country Music" was not reared in a palace. She was born Ellen Muriel Deason on August 30, 1919, in Nashville, Tennessee, the daughter of **Myrtle Deason** and Charles Deason, a Tennessee Central brakeman. While her father and mother were unable to give her wealth, Wells inherited a legacy of love, a sincere religious faith, and a passion for country music. She recalled that after a day's work her father would often pick up his guitar and lead a "family sing" at their home on Wharf Avenue. "My mother loved to sing hymns," said Wells. "While I was growing up, we would go to church and to prayer meetings" where Myrtle Deason would "sing her heart out." She also took her young daughter to the Grand Ole Opry. At the time, Wells had no thought of ever being on stage. "To me the performers on stage seemed larger than life. I thought that I'd be like my mother; that is, grow up, get married and raise a family—and not have a career." She spent her childhood and adolescent years like hundreds of other Tennessee girls, faithfully attending Sunday school and learning from her mother how to cook and sew.

At about the age of 14, Wells "really started getting serious about the guitar" and shortly thereafter began playing at prayer meetings and church socials. It was the era of the Great Depression, and her parents' financial resources were limited. She helped supplement the family income by ironing, cleaning, and babysitting outside her home. Wells attended the Lipscomb School in South Nashville, graduated from the eighth grade, and enrolled in high school. She began the ninth grade at Howard High School and then dropped out of school, never to return. Although she dated boys from the family's Nazarene Church, Wells' idea of a good time "was singing and playing" guitar with her best friend **Josephine Allison** or her cousin **Bessie Choate**. Her father, she wrote, "was so pleased that I had learned to play, and could follow myself on the different songs I was singing, that one day he brought his guitar to me." Rather pensively she added, "I never did hear him play anymore after that."

Wells met her future husband Johnny Wright when his sister Bessie, who lived next door to the Deasons, invited her brother to hear Kitty Wells—or Muriel Deason as she was then called—sing. Wright began to visit his sister more often. Around that time, Wells started singing with her cousin Bessie Choate at local dances, billing themselves as the Deason Sisters. In 1936, radio station WSIX in Nashville initiated a Saturday afternoon amateur hour called "The Old Country Store," and the Deason Sisters decided to participate. When they sang "Jealous-Hearted Me," which included the line "it takes the man I love to satisfy my soul," the station judged it too risqué and cut them off the air. However, the Deason Sisters had enough fan support to persuade the station to grant them a regular slot on an early morning show where they sang such standards as "The Crawdad Song" and "There's A Big Eye Watching You." After dating for two years, Wells and Wright were married on Halloween Eve, 1937.

Wells' sister-in-law, **Louise Wright**, then joined Wells and Choate to form a trio, billed as Johnny Wright and the Harmony Girls. Though they performed each morning on WSIX, both Johnny and Kitty kept their regular jobs. Neither earned enough as performers to support a family that on October 27, 1939, increased to three with the birth of their first child, **Ruby Jean Wright** (who would later team up as a singer with ◄❧ **Anita Carter** and **Rita Robbins**). In early 1941, the family moved to Greensboro, North Carolina, where Johnny's band The Happy Roving Cowboys performed on station WBIG. The band's popularity annoyed Charlie Monroe, a WBIG musician who felt Wright was encroaching on his territory. Monroe's clout meant that the Wrights were soon packing their bags and heading for Charleston, West Virginia, where they performed on WCHS, a 50,000-watt station. Despite the fact that the Wright family temporarily had to share a room with Louise and her husband, Wells remained upbeat. At times, Kitty and Louise performed together as the Wright Sisters.

On March 30, 1942, the Wrights welcomed a fourth member to their family when Johnnie

❧►
Carter, Anita.
See Carter,
Maybelle for
sidebar.

Robert Wright III was born at Charleston's St. Francis Hospital. Shortly thereafter, the family moved to Knoxville, Tennessee, where The Tennessee Hillbillies, as Johnny Wright's band was now called, had been invited to perform on WNOX's popular "Mid-Day Merry-Go-Round." At the end of 1942, with the U.S. now fully engaged in World War II, The Tennessee Hillbillies broke up; the family returned to Nashville where Johnny began working for the Dupont Chemical Company. Both Johnny and Kitty, however, missed the stage. When a fellow named "Smiling" Eddie Hill encouraged Johnny to revive the band, Wright agreed to do so, and the family returned to Knoxville and station WNOX. At the suggestion of Lowell Blanchard, WNOX's station manager, Wright urged his wife to become Kitty Wells, after his favorite boyhood ballad, "Sweet Kitty Wells." Wells "started to draw more mail than any other person on the show," said Eddie Ferguson, one member of the band. "She had that little tremor to her voice, and I think that's what sold her."

Wells gave birth to her third child, Carol Sue Wright, on July 8, 1945, the year the family moved to Raleigh, North Carolina, where Wright created the popular "Carolina Barn Dance" on WPTF. One of the performers on this station was Chet Atkins, a new friend and guitarist *par excellence.* For a time Wells seemed content to give all of her time to rearing her children. On April 3, 1948, however, she joined the premiere broadcast of "The Louisiana Hayride" on KWKH in Shreveport, Louisiana. This program, aired on a powerful 50,000-watt station, hoped to rival the "National Barn Dance" on Chicago's WLS, the "Original Jamboree" on WWV out of Wheeling, West Virginia, and the Grand Ole Opry which aired over Nashville's WSM. "The Louisiana Hayride" helped launch the careers of several well-known performers, including Hank Williams, Jim Reeves, and Elvis Presley.

Christmas 1951 saw the Wright family back in Nashville. About that time, country singer Hank Thompson was recording a song titled "The Wild Side of Life" which by May 10, 1952, was the nation's most popular country tune. The song had been written by William Warren in response to his ex-wife's refusal to grant a reconciliation. Though Wells liked the song, she believed that there were two sides to every story and that Thompson's hit presented only the man's side. Songwriter J.D. Miller also believed it was one-sided and "cried" for an answer. The rather accusatory "I didn't know God made honky tonk angels," one line in Thompson's song, provided the title for the song that would make Wells famous. In the prelude to "It Wasn't God Who Made Honky Tonk Angels," she sings of listening to "The Wild Side" on the jukebox and having it evoke "mem'ries when I was a trusting wife." The song continues:

> It wasn't God who made honky tonk angels
> As you said in the words of your song
> Too many times married men think they're still
>   single
> That has caused many a good girl to go wrong.

Nashville music promoter Troy L. Martin, together with Decca Records' Paul Cohen, thought the song might sell.

An instant smash hit, it became the nation's most popular country-music song within three months, and remained so for six weeks. Eventually it would sell over a million records. Kitty Wells had become the first female country music vocalist to climb to the top of the charts, and "It Wasn't God Who Made Honky Tonk Angels" became the first important recording by a woman in country music since *Patsy Montana's 1936 rendition of "I Want to Be a Cowboy's Sweetheart." Saluting Wells, Hank Thompson said, "I think that was the starting point that opened the door for all the very fine girl vocalists we have in country music today."

Wells' second hit, "I'm Paying for That Back Street Affair," was also an answer song, in this case to Webb Pierce's "Back Street Affair." Her "Hey, Joe" was in response to Carl Smith's best-selling tune of the same name. "I'll Always Be Your Fraulein," in 1957, was a reply to Bobby Helm's number-one hit "Fraulein." Her listeners seemed eager to hear Wells present a woman's point of view on a lifestyle that heretofore had seemed to glorify men and denigrate women. By the end of the 1950s, 35 of Wells' songs had become Top 20 choices, with 24 making the Top 10. She continued to experience success in later years, with 11 more tunes becoming Top 10 favorites. She also encountered opposition because of her sex. For example, she was tardily invited to appear on the Grand Ole Opry because, it was said, she "lacked exuberance in performance." Roy Acuff, who came to be called the King of Country Music, took her part, as did Ernest Tubb, the Texas Troubadour. With the support of these and other musicians as well as her own sustained popularity, she eventually made it to the stage of the Grand Ole Opry.

Wells' immense popularity can be attributed to various factors. She teamed up with certain male performers who also were well liked and well known: Roy Acuff, Red Foley (with whom she sang the number-one hit "One by One" in 1954), Webb Pierce, and Roy Drusky. She also recorded several duets with her husband, who was perhaps her biggest booster and forever on the lookout for songs that fit her style. But Wells had much to do with her own success. Sarah Colley Cannon—better known as *Minnie Pearl, a long-time favorite on the Grand Ole Opry—attributed Wells' success to "her soft-spoken, unassuming ways. It was that wholesome image that people loved in Miss Kitty." Pearl declared that there "was a sort of instant communication with an audience" when Wells sang "It Wasn't God Who Made Honky Tonk Angels." "It was as though a spell was cast over the crowd. I was simply amazed at the way she electrified them. I had seen it once before, when Hank Williams sang his 'Lovesick Blues' at the Opry."

Charles Lamb, the one-time publisher of *Music Reporter*, noted, "I think what made Kitty such a big female favorite with country fans was her distinctive sound, vocally and musically." Lamb explained, "Kitty's vocals weren't the lush, sophisticated kind of singing like **Crystal Gayle** today. It was simplicity itself, songs from the heart, bolstered by lots of feelings." He believed that the way Wells projected songs made one feel "she was telling you a true story.

Kitty Wells

The songs were like plays which acted out the woman's dilemma with great emotion and intensity." Her producer Owen Bradley believed that Wells' strength was "a very unique style that's very easily identifiable," similar to that of popular male performers like Tubb, Pierce, and Foley. He described her songs as "sagas" about "misunderstood or mistreated wives." Today her music is described as "traditional." Said Bradley, "I would say it has to be traditional because Wells started all that. She was the first gal to really start it all."

Wells' achievements have been recognized in various ways. In 1976, she became the first living solo female vocalist to be inducted into the Country Music Hall of Fame. "That's probably the highlight of my whole career," said Wells. (One congratulatory note, which read, "Congratulations on being nominated and entered into the Country Music Hall of Fame. One of your devoted fans," came from Ringo Starr.) On April 14, 1986, at the awards telecast of the Academy of Country Music, Wells was named winner of the Pioneer Award. Presenter Crystal Gayle hailed Wells by noting that she had been the top female country singer for 14 years "and no one has ever done that either before or since." On December 17, 1988, the Nashville *Tennessean* reported that a portion of Old Hickory Boulevard was being renamed Kitty Wells Boulevard. In addition, on February 20, 1991, the National Academy of Recording Arts and Sciences bestowed on Wells a NARAS Lifetime Achievement Award. She was in distinguished company that evening; similar citations were also granted to Bob Dylan, John Lennon, and *Marian Anderson. Female singers including *Patsy Cline, Hazel Dickens, Dolly Parton, *Loretta Lynn, Emmylou Harris, Skeeter Davis, *Tammy Wynette and Norma Jean have sung her praises (and her songs) while acknowledging their debts to Wells, who continues to be recognized as the Queen of Country Music.

Even though Wells' "churchy, four-square-singing," as *Newsweek* once characterized it, is not as popular as it was in the 1950s and early 1960s, Wells retains a loyal following. She made personal appearances throughout the world for decades, often with her husband, and as late as 1979 had two hit records. In 1969, she and her husband had begun hosting a syndicated television program, "The Kitty Wells-Johnny Wright Family Show," featuring different members of the Wright family, which ran for several years. Wells made appearances at the Grand Ole Opry and toured through the last years of the 20th century, performing before live audiences across the country. She made her last tour at the age of 80, in the early months of 2000, and has continued to perform live on rare occasions since then, always to enthusiastic audiences who wait to hear her sing songs they love, including "It Wasn't God Who Made Honky Tonk Angels."

SOURCES:

Brown, Charles T. *Music U.S.A.: America's Country and Western Tradition.* Englewood Cliffs, NJ: Prentice-Hall, 1986.

"Country's First Queen," in *Newsweek.* August 12, 1985, p. 60.

Dellar, Fred, Roy Thompson, and Douglas B. Green, eds. *The Illustrated Encyclopedia of Country Music.* NY: Harmony, 1977.

Hitchcock, H. Wiley, and Stanley Sadie, eds. *The New Grove Dictionary of American Music.* Vol. 4. London: Macmillan, 1986.

Larkin, Colin, ed. *The Guinness Encyclopedia of Popular Music.* Vol. 6. NY: Stockton, 1995.

Malone, Bill C. *Country Music, U.S.A.* Austin, TX: University of Texas Press, 1985.

Trott, Walt. *The Honky Tonk Angels.* Nashville, TN: Nova, 1993.

SUGGESTED READING:

Grattan, Virginia L. *American Women Songwriters: A Biographical Dictionary.* Westport, CT: Greenwood Press, 1993.

Marschall, Rick, ed. *The Encyclopedia of Country and Western Music.* Reading, PA: Exeter Books, 1985.

Pendle, Karin, ed. *Women and Music: A History.* Bloomington, IN: Indiana University Press, 1991.

Robert Bolt,
Professor of History, Emeritus,
Calvin College, Grand Rapids, Michigan

Wells, Marguerite Milton

(1872–1959)

Third president of the National League of Women Voters who sought to educate women on the issues and their political rights. Born on February 10, 1872, in Milwaukee, Wisconsin; died of pneumonia in Minneapolis, Minnesota, on August 12, 1959; daughter of Edward Payson Wells (a banker, railroad entrepreneur, and politician) and Nellie (Johnson) Wells; attended Miss Hardy's school in Eau Claire, Wisconsin; graduated from Smith College, 1895; never married.

Became involved with the suffrage movement in its final stages as a member of the Minnesota Woman Suffrage Association (1917); joined the newly formed National League of Women Voters after ratification of the 19th Amendment (1920); became president of the League (1934).

Marguerite Milton Wells was born in Milwaukee, Wisconsin, in 1872. Her parents Edward and **Nellie Wells** moved to Jamestown, a settlement on the edge of Dakota Territory, where Wells spent her childhood. Her father's interests in banking and railroads made him one of the primary figures in the development of the Territory, and Marguerite had the opportunity to watch the territorial government form as an example of democracy in action. The experience gave her an unshakable confidence in the democratic process that would inform much of her philosophy in regards to women's suffrage.

Wells took her teaching examinations at the age of 15 and taught a summer session in a one-room Dakota school before attending Miss Hardy's school in Eau Claire, Wisconsin. In 1891, Wells entered Smith College, thus beginning a longstanding association with the school that would include her graduation in 1895 and her ascension to a trustee post in 1915. The years following her graduation were a combination of European travel, two years of teaching in New Jersey, and volunteer work in Minneapolis, Minnesota, where her family had settled. However, Wells suddenly dropped all responsibilities on various boards in order to devote herself wholeheartedly to the Minnesota Woman Suffrage Association in 1917, even though she had never previously been involved with activist work.

Wells joined the suffrage cause in the final stages of the movement; working closely with **Clara Ueland,** she helped organize the campaign for the ratification of the 19th Amendment in Minnesota. Once the association achieved its goal, Wells switched her focus to the education of the newly enfranchised female voter as part of the new National League of Women Voters in 1920. She served as president of the Minnesota League for ten years, was a member of the national board, and finally succeeded *Belle Sherwin as the third national president of the League in 1934.

Wells' vision for the League was to fashion it into an unbiased and informed voice of the public on various political issues. She believed the League needed to educate voters beyond its own membership rolls, and her philosophy became the background for the League's theory of government. In 1938, Wells wrote *A Portrait of the League of Women Voters at the Age of Eighteen*, promoting action over study. In 1944, Wells' letters to state League presidents were collected and published as *Leadership in a Democracy, Marguerite Milton Wells*, which further highlighted her vision of community representation in government. Wells helped to rework the League's structure to more directly link the national office with local members, promoting these issues until her retirement from the presi-

dency in 1944. She died of pneumonia in 1959 at her sister's home in Minneapolis.

SOURCES:

Sicherman, Barbara, and Carol Hurd Green, eds. *Notable American Women: The Modern Period.* Cambridge, MA: The Belknap Press of Harvard University, 1980.

Amy Cooper, M.A., M.S.I.,
Ann Arbor, Michigan

Wells, Mary (b. 1928).

See Lawrence, Mary Wells.

Wells, Mary (1943–1992)

African-American singer, known as the Queen of Motown, who was the first woman to become a major R&B star on the Motown label. Born Mary Esther Wells on May 13, 1943, in Detroit, Michigan; died of throat cancer in Los Angeles on July 26, 1992; married Herman Griffin, in 1960 (divorced 1962); married Cecil Womack, in 1966 (divorced 1977); children: (second marriage) four, including Stacey Womack.

After graduation from high school, applied for an audition at Berry Gordy's Motown studios, using a song she had written herself at age 15; became the Motown label's first established star with a series of successful releases, including "My Guy" (early 1960s), but her career declined when she left Motown and signed with another label (1964); though she was acknowledged by later Motown artists as an inspiration for their own careers, her personal life was marred by financial difficulties which worsened after she was diagnosed with throat cancer (late 1980s); musical stars of all types contributed to a fund for her welfare as a tribute to her influence.

Singles: "'Bye 'Bye Baby" (1961); "You Beat Me to the Punch" (1962); "Two Lovers" (1963); "My Guy" (1964); "Set My Soul on Fire" (1968); "Dear Lover" (1968); "Dig the Way I Feel" (1970); "Give a Man the World" (1970); "Gigolo" (1982).

On a warm summer evening in 1992, scores of candles flickered to life outside a modest building in a predominantly African-American section of Detroit. The edifice was the original home of Motown Records, and the candlelight vigil was in honor of the woman who had once been known as "Mother Motown." Even so, Mary Wells had died nearly penniless only a few days before in Los Angeles, her last days made more bearable by contributions from a musical family that had been born because of her artistry.

Mary Esther Wells had actually wanted to be a scientist. Born on May 13, 1943, in a poor section of Detroit, Wells spent the first years of her childhood bedridden with spinal meningitis and, later, tuberculosis. When she finally recovered, she dreamed of finding a cure for both diseases when she grew up; but the dreams of a young African-American girl soon had to give way to the realities of life for America's urban blacks. "In Detroit," Wells once said, "there were three big careers for a black girl. Babies, the factories, or daywork." By the time she was 12, her father had died, her two brothers had left home, and Mary was helping her mother scrub the floors of wealthier families afternoons after school and on weekends. Any thoughts of a scientific career had long ago been given up. "We were just two women alone, helpin' each other out," Wells recalled. "Now, church helped. [Mama] always stood better when she come out of there on Sunday, and I was singing there since I was a baby."

The term is oldie but goodie, right?

—Mary Wells

Wells had begun singing in public in the early 1950s, when Detroit was just becoming the center of growing national interest in gospel music and its more commercial relative, rhythm and blues. She sang at first in her church choir and at school events, later at local dances, and began writing songs in her mid-teens, all in the R&B style. During her senior year at Northwestern High School, Mary began to notice the activity at a house not far from her own, over the front of which hung a banner which read "Hitsville U.S.A." It was a record company, everyone said, and the rumor was that an audition could be arranged just by walking in the door.

Less than a year after graduating, Wells boldly sauntered into the studio and asked to sing a number she had written two years earlier for her favorite R&B singer, Jackie Wilson, called "'Bye 'Bye Baby." Wilson was managed by Berry and **Raynoma Gordy**, the couple waiting for her in the studio, and they were as impressed with her performance as with the song itself. Berry Gordy persuaded a stunned Mary to record the song herself, guiding her through 22 takes. It would be the first release for his new label, Motown.

Gordy, an ex-boxer who only a few years before had been working on the assembly line at Ford Motors, had begun his career much like Wells, writing songs in his spare time until persuading Jackie Wilson to record one of them, the 1957 hit "Reet Petite." Realizing that the real money lay in managing and producing, Gordy formed the Five Stars with a group of friends

and wrote songs for them which he produced himself, working out of his apartment. Adding other artists to his new company, he and Raynoma soon formed Rayber Records and, by 1959, had made a deal with United Artists to distribute their R&B material under a new label, Tamla. Moving into larger quarters—the "Hitsville U.S.A." which Wells had noticed—Berry and Raynoma created still other labels for other music genres besides R&B: soul, gospel, rock, and even country music. In 1961, Gordy sensed that a new audience was waiting for a more pop-oriented R&B sound and decided to create yet one more label that would take advantage of it. In a nod to the "Motor Town" that had given him so much success, he called the label "Motown" and had a hunch that Mary Wells, with a rich, fluid voice that one critic would later compare to "burnt honey," would be the right artist for his new venture.

"'Bye 'Bye Baby" wasn't the crossover blockbuster Gordy had been looking for, but it did make #45 on the pop charts as well as the top ten on the R&B charts, encouraging him to put Mary in the hands of a new, young producer who had just joined the company, Smokey Robinson. Although Smokey and his group, The Miracles, would make a name for themselves some years in the future, Robinson was content to produce and co-write a string of hits with Mary Wells during her time at Motown, like 1962's "You Beat Me to the Punch," which made #1 on the R&B charts and, as Gordy had been hoping, made a respectable showing on the pop charts; the million-selling "Two Lovers"; and, in 1964, Mary's biggest hit, "My Guy," written by Robinson. It shot to #1 on *Billboard*'s pop charts in May of that year. Not only had Wells delivered Berry Gordy's first pop hit, she was the first Motown artist to appear on "American Bandstand," a tremendous promotional boost for Gordy's company, and the first of "Gordy's girls" to lend an air of sophistication and maturity to his efforts by appearing on tour in elegant gowns and elbow-length gloves, a style that would be followed by the likes of **Diana Ross** and *The Supremes**, and a host of Motown female groups. "Mary was the established star," says ex-Supreme **Mary Wilson**, one of Mary Wells' closest friends. "She was a hometown girl made good. And she was the first female there in a man's world, so she really gave us initiative."

Despite these successes, the early years of Wells' stardom were bittersweet. "We were . . . just a bunch of kids that cared about each other, just havin' fun," Wells once remembered. "It's something like what I've heard people describe

Mary
Wells
(1943–1992)

about their college years, I guess. Those were *our* years of higher education." In the first flush of success, Wells had married one of Motown's backup singers, Herman Griffin, when she was only 17. By the time they were divorced two years later in 1962, Mary had had two abortions which she later claimed Griffin had forced upon her so she could keep working. On tour, Wells had her first encounters with the racism from which she had been shielded in her African-American milieu in Detroit, although the stage lights were so blinding that she didn't at first notice that she was usually playing to a white orchestra section and a black balcony. But an incident in New Orleans made things all too plain, when Wells walked into City Hall on a sweltering day and stopped to drink from a water fountain. "All these people started *lookin'* at me," she said. "And me, so much a fool, I say to myself, 'Oh, they know who I am, I'm Mary Wells.' Then I look up and see the sign. WHITES ONLY. Me in my little Motown star bubble. All of a sudden everything kind of crushes."

In 1964, Wells became the first Motown artist to play to an audience outside the United States, traveling to Britain when "My Guy" reached the top ten on that country's charts. She toured with the Beatles, who had heard her sing during their first U.S. tour and had been immediately smitten. "John Lennon was funny, but always gentle to me, always respectful," Wells remembered. "I have a *hard* time with the fact that some fool murdered the man."

The year 1964 held another surprise for Berry Gordy and the Motown "family," for in that year, Wells announced that she was leaving. Some said that Herman Griffin had convinced her to accept an offer from 20th Century-Fox, an offer that included not only a $500,000, four-year recording contract, but the possibility of an acting career in films. Others claimed that Wells had used Fox's offer as a bluff to force Berry Gordy to pay her royalties she said had not been forthcoming. (She was to be the first of half a dozen of "Gordy's girls" to make such accusations.) If so, Gordy called her bluff, and Wells left Motown despite the fact that her contract was still in effect. In the lawsuit which Motown filed against her, Mary pointed out that Motown could not enforce an agreement she had signed when still a minor; in the end, the case was settled out of court when Fox merely bought out the disputed contract. **Esther Gordy Edwards**, Berry's sister and a vice-president of Motown at the time, remains convinced that Wells was probably encouraged by others to leave. "We hated to lose her," Edwards has said. "I think she would have been a super superstar if she had stayed with Motown because of the nurturing, and the organization she had here was conducive to a great career."

Once settled in Los Angeles, Wells discovered how important Motown had been to her. With no Smokey Robinson to produce her songs and a weak concert booking office, 20th Century-Fox marked the beginning of a sharp decline in her fortunes. Fox's record producers often forced her to do 30 or more takes of a song, her voice turning hoarse from the strain; and the flurry of movie offers she had been expecting failed to materialize. (She did appear in a small role in one long-forgotten film, 1967's *Catalina Caper*.) After barely a year at Fox, Wells moved to the Atco label, a division of Atlantic Records, only to find that Atco was busy promoting **Aretha Franklin** and would have no time for her until the next year. Three of her songs for Atco reached the charts, including "Set My Soul on Fire" and "Dear Lover," but all remained near the bottom of the lists. Impatient and still searching for another Motown, Mary left Atco in 1969 and moved to Jubilee records, for which she recorded "Dig the Way I Feel" and "Give a Man the World" in 1970. Both failed to sell, and her luck at her next two labels, Reprise and Epic, did not improve.

In 1966, some stability seemed to come into Wells' life with her marriage to Cecil Womack, a singer with a group called The Valentinos and the brother of R&B star Bobby Womack. The couple had four children, the last born after they had divorced in 1977 and Wells had begun a relationship with Cecil's brother, Curtis. "I think the majority of entertainers should never get married," Wells said after her divorce from Cecil. "People expect too much. They're expecting you to wake up like a movie star in the morning, to have a hit record out every day. You are a symbol, a dream, a myth . . . [and] you have to think about living up to it." But Curtis, and especially the children, seemed proud and even a little surprised at Mary's talents as they sometimes traveled with her on tour. "[The kids] see their mama getting people wild and happy," Cecil once told a reporter. "And before you know it, one of them will be saying to me, *Whoa*, look at Mama get *down*!"

Wells' tour schedule during the 1980s must have seemed a far cry from that of 20 years before. Gone were the appearances on top-rated TV shows, interviews with fan magazines, and trips to Europe. Now, after fading into obscurity during the 1970s, she was forced to accept appearances at oldies events in anything from converted beer halls to football stadiums. Admitting she was at first hurt by "this goldie oldie thing," she learned to put it in perspective. "It can't hurt me," she said. "I like to come home, take care of the kids, wash the clothes, clean the house myself . . . and then go back out there and work. I can do both. Mother taught me independence, and I tell you, I need it more than a man or a career."

What Wells didn't say was that she *had* to keep working. Never careful about her business arrangements and lacking a knowledgeable business manager, she had seen her income from touring and royalties on her recordings dwindle steadily since leaving Motown. With four children to raise, she had little choice but to accept whatever appearances were offered. She recorded new versions of her old hits for the Allegiance label, but she had no records on the charts after 1982's "Gigolo." There was briefly cause for hope during the mid-1980s when negotiations were opened to return to Motown after she appeared on a TV special, "Motown 25," in 1983, but the deal fell apart.

By the late 1980s, even her concert appearances were becoming more difficult as her voice began to grow weaker. *Martha Reeves of Martha and the Vandellas remembers that during what would be Mary's last tour in 1989, the singer who had charmed the nation with "My Guy" and "Two Lovers" could barely whisper the lyrics. Forced off the concert circuit, Wells, who had always been a heavy smoker, was told in 1990 that the polyps which had formed on her larynx were malignant.

The course of treatment she underwent was not only painful, but expensive, and whatever money Mary had was quickly used up. When she was threatened with eviction from her home in Los Angeles, her plight came to the attention of The Rhythm and Blues Foundation in Washington, D.C., set up to help R&B artists in difficult financial straits. The Foundation immediately launched a fund drive, and Wells might have taken comfort in the fact that her "family" had not forgotten her, after all. Berry Gordy, who had built Motown into a $60 million business, contributed funds to secure Wells' housing; Diana Ross gave $15,000, and similar amounts poured in from such diverse musical entertainers as Bruce Springsteen, The Temptations, and Phil Collins. The Foundation raised a total of $125,000. "It speaks a lot to the power of her music that we got contributions from all over the world," said the Foundation's executive director, **Suzan Jenkins**, "from people who couldn't even speak English."

Despite the course of radiation therapy and a tracheotomy, doctors found that Wells' cancer had spread to her lungs. But, said her daughter **Stacey Womack**, "She never complained. She only cried because she couldn't do what she liked to do, which was sing." On July 26, 1992, Mary Wells died.

"She was loved," Esther Gordy Edwards told reporters at the candlelight vigil in Mary's honor organized by Smokey Robinson and Martha Reeves. "Everybody loved everybody, and once a part of that Motown family in the 'sixties, you remained part of it forever." But Mary Wells was part of a much larger family, made up of the fans who never forgot her when it seemed everyone else had. One of them, a middle-aged white man born in the bleak New York City suburbs, stood outside her dressing-room door in a smoky New York nightclub in the early 1980s, clutching a yellowed record album he had carefully preserved since first hearing Mary Wells as a young boy. "White kids get their own blues in a two-family dump in Flushing," he told a reporter. "Mary saved me. I love her."

SOURCES:

Garcia, Guy. "Death of a Soul Survivor," in *People Weekly*. Vol. 38, no. 6. August 10, 1992.

Hirshey, Gerry. *Nowhere To Run: The Story of Soul Music*. NY: Times Books, 1984.

Larkin, Colin, ed. *The Guinness Encyclopedia of Popular Music*. 2nd ed. NY: Stockton Press, 1995.

"Motown Star Mary Wells Dead At 49," in *Billboard*. Vol. 104, no. 32. August 8, 1992.

Singleton, Raynoma Gordy, with Bryan Brown and Mim Eichler. *Berry, Me, And Motown*. Chicago, IL: Contemporary Books, 1990.

Stambler, Ed Irwin, ed. *The Encyclopedia of Pop, Rock, And Soul*. Rev. ed. NY: St. Martin's Press, 1989.

Tee, Ralph. *Soul Music: Who's Who*. Rocklin, CA: Prima, 1992.

Norman Powers,
writer-producer, Chelsea Lane Productions,
New York, New York

Wells, Melissa Foelsch (1932—)

American ambassador. Born Meliza Foelsch in Tallinn, Estonia, on November 18, 1932; daughter of Kuno Georg Foelsch (a physicist) and Miliza (Korjus) Foelsch (a singer); became naturalized U.S. citizen, 1941; attended a Catholic women's college; Georgetown University's School of Foreign Service, B.S., 1956; married Alfred Washburn Wells (an officer in the Foreign Service), in 1960; children: Christopher, Gregory.

Served as ambassador to Guinea-Bissau and Cape Verde (1976–77); served as ambassador to Mozambique (1987–90); served as ambassador to Zaire, now the Republic of Congo (1991–93); became ambassador to Estonia (1998); took several positions with the United Nations, including under-secretary general of administration and management; was the first woman foreign service officer to have a child while at her post.

Melissa Foelsch Wells was born in Estonia in 1932, the daughter of physicist Kuno Georg Foelsch and professional singer **Miliza Korjus**. Her parents moved to Hollywood to appear in

MGM films when Melissa was four, and the young girl seemed poised to follow them into show business when she became a show girl and a synchronized swimmer after attending a Catholic women's college. However, when the traveling aquacade troupe with which she performed broke up, her life took a significantly different direction. She enrolled at Georgetown University's School of Foreign Service in Washington, D.C., graduating *cum laude* in 1956. By 1960, she had passed the Foreign Service exam, and had married Alfred Washburn Wells, a fellow officer.

Against precedent, Wells was not asked to resign when she married, or when she and her husband separated one year later. In 1961, she transferred to Trinidad with the couple's child, while her husband went to London. From Trinidad, Wells went to Paris in 1964 and eventually reconciled with her husband in London. She was the first woman officer to have a child while at a post, proving that childbearing did not interfere with embassy work. However, she still had battles to fight as a wife, mother, and For-

eign Service officer, after discovering that women officers were not given family allowances. She took the case to the ambassador and won.

Wells transferred to Brazil in 1975 as a commercial counselor and, after learning Portuguese, was selected the first U.S. ambassador to Guinea-Bissau and Cape Verde in 1976. She became a delegate to the UN Economic and Social Council from 1977 to 1979, before traveling to Uganda for the United Nations. She served in the UN for seven years both in Uganda and Geneva.

Beginning in 1987, Wells served as ambassador to Mozambique, remaining in that post until 1991. There, she convinced the U.S. government to fund Lhanguene, a home for youth who were rendered helpless by the long-time conflict between warring political factions. Wells next became ambassador to another African nation when she went to Zaire (now Republic of Congo) in 1991. This two-year post ended when she took the position of under-secretary general for administration and management with the UN in New York City. In 1998, she was appointed U.S. ambassador to her native Estonia.

SOURCES:

Morin, Ann Miller. *Her Excellency: An Oral History of American Women Ambassadors.* NY: Twayne, 1995, pp. 211–227.

Amy Cooper, M.A., M.S.I.,
Ann Arbor, Michigan

Melissa Foelsch Wells

Wells-Barnett, Ida (1862–1931)

*African-American writer, editor, and organizer, best known for her crusade against lynching. Name variations: Ida B. Barnett; Ida B. Wells; Ida Wells Barnett. Born Ida Bell Wells on July 16, 1862, in Holly Springs, Mississippi; died of uremia in Chicago, Illinois, on March 25, 1931; daughter of Elizabeth Warrenton Wells (a slave, then domestic servant) and James Wells (a slave, then carpenter); attended Rust College intermittently; married Ferdinand Lee Barnett (an attorney, Republican politician, and editor), on June 27, 1895; children: Charles Aked (b. 1896); Herman K. (b. 1897); Ida B. Wells (b. 1901); **Alfreda M. Duster** (b. 1904).*

Taught in Holly Springs and Memphis areas (1878–91); was a weekly columnist for American Baptist *(1886); was part owner and editor,* Memphis Free Speech and Headlight *(1889–92); contributed to various African-American newspapers; served as secretary, National Colored Press Association (1891–93); was a founder of the Southern Afro-American Press Association (1893); organized the Ida B. Wells Club, Chicago (1893); was owner and editor,* Conservator *(Chicago, 1895–97); was a founder of the National*

Association of Colored Women (1896); served as editor for Women's Era *(1896); was a founder of the National Afro-American Council (1898) and secretary (1898–99); headed the Anti-Lynching Bureau (1899–1903); was a national organizer (1900–03); was a founder of the Frederick Douglass Center, Chicago (1904); was a participant at the National Negro Conference (1909) and member of the Committee of Forty; was a founder of the Negro Fellowship League, Chicago (1910); was an early participant of the National Association for the Advancement of Colored People (1909–14); served as president, Chicago bureau, National Equal Rights League (1914); was on the publicity committee, National League of Republican Colored Women (1924); was a national organizer, Illinois Colored Women of Colored Voters Division, Republican National Committee (1928).*

Selected writings: Southern Horrors: Lynch Law in All Its Phases *(New York Age Print, 1892, reprint, Arno, 1969);* A Red Record: Tabulated Statistics and Alleged Causes of Lynching in the United States, 1892–1893–1894 *(Donohue & Henneberry, 1895, reprint, Arno, 1969); (with Frederick Douglass, Garland Penn, and F.L. Barnett)* The Reason Why the Colored American is not in the World Columbian Exposition *(Ida B. Wells, 1893, reprint, University of Illinois Press, 1993);* Lynch Law in Georgia *(Chicago Colored Citizens, 1899);* Mob Rule in New Orleans *(1900, reprint, Arno, 1969);* The Arkansas Race Riot *(Hume Job Print, 1920);* The East St. Louis Massacre: The Greatest Outrage of the Century *(Negro Fellowship Forum, 1917); (Alfreda M. Duster, ed.)* Crusade for Justice: The Autobiography of Ida B. Wells *(University of Chicago Press, 1970); (Trudier Harris, comp.)* Selected Works of Ida B. Wells-Barnett *(Oxford University Press, 1991); (Miriam DeCosta-Willis, ed.)* The Memphis Diary of Ida B. Wells *(Beacon Press, 1995).*

On March 9, 1892, in the city of Memphis, Tennessee, three black males were lynched. Three years earlier, these same men had organized the People's Grocery Company, which was located in a thickly populated suburb on the corner of Walker Avenue and Mississippi Boulevard. Thomas Moss was company president. Calvin McDowell clerked in the store. Will Stuart owned stock in the firm. The new enterprise quickly cut into the profits of the sole competitor, a white merchant named W.H. Barnett, who owned a store across the street and who had enjoyed a monopoly in this racially mixed neighborhood.

Exactly a week before the lynching, some black and white boys fought over a game of marbles. The father of one of the whites whipped one

of the black victors. The black fathers gathered near the home of the offender, at which point whites called the police. This tension led to a violent incident at the People's store between black clerk McDowell and white competitor Barnett, with the specific circumstances of the conflict in dispute. A criminal court judge arrested McDowell, who posted bail and was released.

Three days later, on March 5, nine armed whites, dressed in civilian clothes, entered the People's store and arrested two blacks who had called for dynamiting "white trash." These armed whites were confronted by black armed guards, who fired on them, wounding three deputies in a brief shoot-out. The remaining deputies gathered additional troops, then arrested McDowell and Stuart. The white press magnified the incident, calling it "a bloody riot." Soon the People's store was looted. White deputies, some of them mere boys, broke into over 100 black homes, arresting some 30 black "co-conspirators," including Moss. Within hours, rumors of a black revolt had spread throughout the entire county. A black militia was disarmed.

Four days after the shoot-out, around 3 PM, a group of whites entered the jail and carried Moss, McDonald, and Stuart about a mile north of Memphis. There all three were shot; in addition, McDonald's eyes were gouged out. A grand jury met for two weeks on the matter but failed to indict anyone. No one connected with the lynching was ever arrested.

A 29-year-old African-American woman, who was in Natchez during the entire episode, wrote an editorial in a newspaper, the *Memphis Free Speech*, which she partially owned. She had been an extremely close friend of Moss and his widow, serving as godmother to their daughter. Wrote Ida Wells-Barnett:

> The city of Memphis has demonstrated that neither character nor standing avails the Negro if he dares to protect himself against the white man or becomes his rival. There is nothing we can do about the lynching now, as we are out-numbered and without arms. . . . There is therefore only one thing left we can do; save our money and leave a town that will neither protect our lives and property, nor give us a fair trial in the courts, but takes us out and murders us in cold blood when accused by white persons.

Before the Memphis affair, Wells-Barnett believed that the rape of white women was the prime motive in lynching. As she later recalled:

> Like many another person who had read of lynching in the South, I had accepted the idea meant to be conveyed—that although

lynching was irregular and contrary to law and order, unreasoning anger over the terrible crime of rape led to the lynching; that perhaps the brute deserved to die anyhow and the mob was justified in taking his life.

Now her eyes were opened "to what lynching really was. An excuse to get rid of Negroes who were acquiring wealth and property and thus keep the race terrorized and 'keep the nigger down.'" Sixty-one hundred blacks disposed of their property, leaving the city of Memphis. Leading pastors took entire congregations with them as they headed for Oklahoma Territory. Whites soon shut *Free Speech* down. The world of Ida Wells-Barnett had been permanently shaken.

She was born Ida Bell Wells in 1862 in the northern Mississippi hill town of Holly Springs, of slave parents, the oldest in a family of four boys and four girls. Her mother **Elizabeth ("Lizzie") Warrenton** was the child of a black mother and an Indian father. One of ten children born to slaves in Virginia, she had been beaten frequently by various masters. Moreover, she and two sisters were sold apart, separated from their mother. Her last owner, whom she served as a cook, was a Holly Springs carpenter named Bolling, who proved to be a kind master. Elizabeth's husband James Wells, the acknowledged son of his master, was apprenticed to Bolling to learn the carpentering trade. James could hire himself out while living in the town of Holly Springs. After Ida's parents became free, her mother continued to work as a cook and her father as a carpenter.

I felt that one had better die fighting against injustice than to die like a dog or a rat in a trap.

—Ida Wells-Barnett

Ida's upbringing was strict. On Sunday, only the Bible could be read. When she went to school, her semiliterate mother attended class as well. Wells-Barnett was educated at Holly Springs' Shaw University (informally called Rust College until 1890). Sponsored by northern Methodists, the school educated newly emancipated blacks, providing instruction at levels ranging from elementary instruction to teaching training. She left Shaw temporarily in 1878, when, that September, her parents and an infant brother died in a devastating epidemic of yellow fever that swept the Mississippi Valley. Suddenly, at age 16, Ida had to care for five siblings, the oldest a sister paralyzed below the waist. She later recalled, "After being a happy, light-hearted schoolgirl I suddenly found myself at the head of a family."

Claiming to be 18, Wells-Barnett let down her skirts and put up her hair, so as to make herself look older. The tactic worked, for she secured a position teaching in a one-room school at Holly Springs. Her salary: $25 a month. She taught for three years in neighboring areas and six months in a school in Cleveland County, Arkansas. She continued her studies at Rust between teaching terms. In 1881, at the instigation of aunt **Fannie Wells**, she moved to Memphis, Tennessee, which was 40 miles from Holly Springs. She first served in the nearby town of Woodstock, then after 1884 in Memphis' black schools, where monthly salaries came to $60. At that time almost half of Memphis was black.

Wells-Barnett hated teaching, being troubled by overcrowded classrooms, unruly students, and slim chances for advancement. Yet she felt trapped, finding menial labor the only other option. Besides, being a teacher catapulted her into Memphis' black elite. She became particularly active in literary and dramatic circles and found what she called "a breath of life" in the Memphis Lyceum, editing its newspaper, the *Evening Star*.

Always a devout Christian, Wells-Barnett was active in several Memphis congregations, among them Episcopal, African Methodist, and the Disciples of Christ. To Ida, God was the defender of the persecuted as well as the one who forgave her admittedly strong temper. At the same time, she was frequently scornful of African-American clergy, whom she found corrupt and ignorant.

Wells-Barnett found herself engaged in the struggle for civil rights somewhat inadvertently. In 1883, while traveling from Memphis to Woodstock on the Chesapeake, Ohio & Southwestern Railroad, she purchased a first-class ticket and sat in the "ladies' car." Upon being told to move to the second-class "smoking car," where all African-Americans were expected to sit, she refused to leave. When the conductor grabbed her arm, she bit the back of his hand. As she was being forcibly removed, the white passengers applauded. Filing suit against the railroad, in November 1884 she won her case in circuit court, being awarded $500 in damages. Blacks throughout the nation celebrated the verdict. In April 1887, however, the Tennessee Supreme Court reversed the decision, fining her $200 for court costs. She confided to her diary:

I felt so disappointed, because I had hoped such great things from the suit for my people generally. . . . O God is there no redress, no peace, no justice in this land for us? Thou has always fought the battles of the weak and oppressed. Come to my aid at this moment & teach me what to do, for I am sore-

ly, bitterly disappointed. Show us the way, even as Thou led the children of Israel out of bondage into the promised land.

Wells-Barnett's accounts of the case in a local black newspaper launched her journalism career, though she remained a teacher until 1891.

Then the Memphis school board fired her, doing so because she criticized the substandard, faulty buildings available to black children. At first she wrote gratis for the Memphis *Living Way*, a journal run by two black Baptist ministers. Using the pen name "Iola," she advocated education, self-help, and social reform. By 1884, the African-American *New York Globe* (later the *Freeman* and the *Age*), edited by T. Thomas Fortune, had picked up her articles. Soon she was contributing to a host of African-American journals, including *A.M.E. Church Review*, *Indianapolis World*, *Kansas City Dispatch*, and *Conservator* of Chicago. She became a protégé of the powerful minister William J. Simmons, president of both the National Baptist Convention and a theological school in Louisville and editor of the Black Press Association. In October 1886, Simmons hired Wells-Barnett to write the weekly women's column for his *American Baptist*, putting her on regular salary for the first time. Within a year, she became so popular that a black journalist called her the "Princess of the Press." In 1889, Wells-Barnett invested her savings to buy one-third interest in the *Memphis Free Speech and Headlight*, a paper she edited as well. (She shortened its name to *Free Speech*.) Within a year, she had raised its circulation from 1,500 to 4,000. By 1892, she became half-owner.

Wells-Barnett was soon involved in wider African-American circles. In 1891, she began a two-year term as secretary of the National Colored Press Association. That year she helped form the Southern Afro-American Press Association, an ephemeral body founded by discontented Southern and Western editors in protest against Eastern attempts to dominate black journalism. She also assisted in organizing the National Afro-American League, a body established to fight lynch law and integrate public accommodations.

In 1885, a newspaper described Wells-Barnett as "about four and a half feet high, tolerably well proportioned, and of ready address." Wrote editor Fortune, "She is rather girlish looking in physique, with sharp regular features, penetrating eyes, firm set lips and a sweet voice." However, many black leaders, both male and female, felt ambivalent towards her, finding her writings too militant, her personality too confrontational. Former U.S. Senator Blanche K. Bruce, for example, called her arrogant and egotistical. "Ida B. Wells," he wrote in 1894, "has become so spoiled by the Afro-American press that she has delegated to herself the care and keeping of the entire colored population of the United States."

In 1892, after the Memphis lynching, a frightened Wells-Barnett left Memphis for good. It would be over 20 years before she returned to the South. She became a weekly contributor to Fortune's *New York Age*, which had become the leading black paper in the nation. In June 1892,

the paper published her lengthy attack on lynching, which was reprinted in pamphlet form as *Southern Horrors: Lynch Law in All Its Phases*. Three years later, another work, *A Red Record*, updated her findings. It listed all the lynchings of the past two years, organized by accusations against its victims. The nation's foremost abolitionist, Frederick Douglass, wrote the preface. The *St. Paul Appeal* commented:

> We cannot see what the "good" citizens of Memphis gained by suppressing the *Free Speech*. They stopped the papers of a few hundred [sic] subscribers and drove Miss Ida B. Wells to New York, and now she is telling the story to hundreds of thousands of readers.

In her writings on lynching, Wells-Barnett stressed several themes. She challenged the notion that lynching was perpetuated by poor whites, declaring that leading businessmen led the mobs. Lynchings averaged over twice a week precisely because African-Americans were resisting degradation. Whites, she said, were saying to themselves, "Kill the leaders and it will cow the Negro who dares to shoot a white man, even in self-defense."

In two-thirds of the cases, Wells-Barnett observed, the much-touted accusation of rape was not even charged. Even if one were accused of such a crime, guilt was often doubtful. As part of her argument, she stressed the appeal black males held for white females. She wrote, "There are many white women in the South who would marry colored men if such an act would not place them beyond the pale of society and within the clutches of the law." Similarly she noted many incidents where white males raped black females with impunity. She wrote, "Virtue knows no color line, and the chivalry which depends upon complexion of skin and texture of hair can command no honest respect." She questioned the "manliness" of such a practice, stressing that lynching involved savage acts of uncontrolled fury. Indeed, in the face of such barbarism, African-Americans acted with remarkable restraint.

Wells-Barnett called for black self-defense, claiming that armed resistance had prevented several lynchings. "A Winfield rifle should have a place of honor in every black home," she asserted. "The more the Afro-American yields and cringes and begs, the more he is insulted, outraged and lynched." She herself had bought a pistol as soon as Thomas Moss was murdered.

Soon Wells-Barnett was on the lecture circuit, appearing practically everywhere but the South. By the 1890s, among African-Americans, only Frederick Douglass received more attention. Douglass wrote Wells-Barnett, telling her that her protests against lynching were unequaled. He personally was particularly grateful to her as well, for many African-American women had snubbed his second wife, **Helen Pitts Douglass**, who was white. In fact, when Douglass died in 1895, one could well argue that Wells-Barnett was his logical heir apparent. She had the edge on the other two contenders, then being far more famous than the budding scholar W.E.B. Du Bois and more ideologically compatible with Douglass than Booker T. Washington. There was, however, one major drawback: Wells-Barnett was a woman.

At first, however, she had supported Washington's accommodationist strategy. Washington, finding himself totally dependent upon the white establishment, was insisting that a segregated society could protect blacks while generating their economic self-reliance. In 1890, Wells-Barnett sent him a letter of support. In 1894, she declared that his "quiet, earnest work is a shining light in the Black Belt of Alabama, where it is so needed." In 1899, she spoke at a pro-Washington meeting in Boston and "the Wizard of Tuskegee" soon returned the compliment in New York.

In October 1892, the Ida B. Wells Testimonial Reception Committee, composed of African-American women in the greater New York area, raised about $400 for her anti-lynching crusade. It was reportedly the largest gathering of black club women yet assembled. While visiting Philadelphia, Wells-Barnett met **Catherine Impey**, an English Quaker dedicated to temperance and antipoverty efforts. Impey published the journal *Anti-Caste*, "devoted to the Interest of the Coloured Races." In April 1893, at the request of Impey and Scottish author **Isabelle Mayo** (whose pen name was Edward Garrett), Wells-Barnett left the U.S. to tour the British Isles for several weeks. In her attempt to mobilize sentiment abroad, she was undoubtedly aware of the crucial role played by British cotton purchases in the economy of the American South. Following her first lecture in Mayo's Aberdeen home, the women organized the Society for the Recognition of the Brotherhood of Mankind.

In 1894, Wells-Barnett returned to Britain for six weeks. During her stay she was a correspondent for the *Chicago Inter-Ocean*, a widely circulating daily paper. In both trips she met with major opinion leaders, including the archbishop of York and the duke of Argyle. She helped launch the London Anti-Lynching Committee, the first anti-lynching organization in the world.

During her second trip, she attacked *Frances Willard, American president of the Women's Christian Temperance Union, who was also touring that nation. Willard had accused "the colored race" of drunkenness ("The grogshop is its center of power"). She also appeared to condone lynching: "The safety of women, of children, of the home is menaced in a thousand localities at this moment, so men dare not go beyond the sight of their own roof-tree." (Willard did back down by explicitly condemning lynching, but the two women sniped at each other for years.) Similarly Wells-Barnett assailed evangelist Dwight L. Moody, who acquiesced in segregated revivals in the South.

By now she was firmly ensconced as a Chicago resident. Little wonder that in 1893 Ida joined Frederick Douglass, author Garland Penn, and Chicago attorney Ferdinand L. Barnett to produce a pamphlet denouncing the Chicago World's Fair. Its title: *The Reason Why the Colored American is not in the World Columbian Exposition*. The fair had omitted the black contribution to the United States and failed to note the nation's prevailing racism, hoping to mollify criticism by holding a segregated "Colored Jubilee Day." In the pamphlet, the authors argued that without the contributions of African-Americans over the centuries, there could never have been such an exposition. Some 20,000 copies were distributed to foreign visitors.

On June 27, 1895, Ida Wells was married in Chicago to the widower Ferdinand Lee Barnett. The wedding was widely covered in the nation's press. The son of a slave, Barnett was born about 1856. Raised in Nashville, he graduated from the law department of Northwestern University. He was a successful attorney and owned the Chicago *Conservator*, the city's first black paper. Advising Republican presidents in black appointments, in 1896 and 1900 he headed the Western office of the Republican Negro Bureau. From 1896 to 1911, he was assistant state's attorney. Ida joined her last name to his, becoming Ida Wells-Barnett. She bought the *Conservator* from Ferdinand, editing it from 1895 to 1897.

The couple had four children. Motherhood slowed down Wells-Barnett's public activities but certainly did not stifle them. In 1896, at a meeting held in Washington, D.C., she helped organize the National Association of Colored Women (NACW), serving on the editorial staff of its journal *Women's Era*. Almost immediately, however, she withdrew from the group, for she clashed with NACW president ***Mary Church Terrell**. In part, the tension was created by professional rivalries and personality conflicts. In part, it was rooted in Wells-Barnett's criticism of Terrell's support of Booker T. Washington's conciliatory policies.

In 1898, Wells-Barnett assisted in the formation of the National Afro-American Council (NAAC), a group organized in Rochester, New York, to confront deteriorating race relations. She was the only woman to hold office, serving as secretary until 1899, when she began heading its Anti-Lynching Bureau. She became national organizer in 1900, but finding that all the new officers supported Booker Washington, she left the group within three years.

Wells-Barnett remained highly attuned to violence against African-Americans. In November 1898, a race riot in Wilmington, North Carolina, resulted in the death of 11 blacks. In addressing the matter, Wells-Barnett accused President William McKinley of apathy, in the process challenging Booker T. Washington's assumption that blacks could rise in American society by economic means alone. When that year a black postmaster and his infant were lynched in Lake City, South Carolina, Wells-Barnett was part of a protest delegation that called upon the president. She again attacked Booker Washington when he appeared too slow in protesting the lynching of a Georgia black who was burned alive. The victim, who killed a white man, had supposedly acted in self-defense. Wells-Barnett wrote another pamphlet, *Lynch Law in Georgia* (1899), to publicize the injustice. After the death of a Louisiana black, who had violently resisted what he considered unlawful arrest, she published *Mob Rule in New Orleans* (1900).

By now Wells-Barnett was a major opponent of the "Tuskegee machine." In April 1903, in an article for *World Today* entitled "Booker T. Washington and His Critics," Wells-Barnett found the entire system of vocational education, centering on the "wizard's" Tuskegee Institute, most destructive. "It is," she wrote, "the South's old slavery practice in a new dress."

Speaking at the National Negro Conference called in New York in 1909, Wells-Barnett demanded federal anti-lynching legislation and a government investigating agency. After initially being ignored, she was appointed to the executive committee of the convention's Committee of Forty, which soon established the National Association for the Advancement of Colored People (NAACP). As with other such groups, she withdrew within several years. In this case, she found the body too moderate in tone and too dominated by whites. *Mary White Ovington,

the white chair of the NAACP executive committee, later responded in turn: Wells-Barnett "was a great fighter, but we knew she had to play a lone hand. And if you have too many players of lone hands in your organization, you soon have no game."

In 1919, Wells-Barnett and NAACP assistant secretary Walter White did cooperate in investigating a four-day riot in Elaine, Arkansas, an event that left five whites and many more blacks dead. African-American sharecroppers, forced to sell their cotton below market prices, had attempted to unionize. When whites fired on their organizing meeting, the blacks fought back. Though 12 blacks initially received death sentences, all were soon released. Out of the turmoil came another Wells-Barnett pamphlet, *The Arkansas Race Riot* (1920).

Despite such national activity, Wells-Barnett increasingly centered her activity on Chicago. In 1893, she organized a black woman's organization, which adopted the name the Ida B. Wells Club. Projects included a kindergarten for black children. In 1902, she successfully integrated black women into the League of Cook County Clubs. In 1904, she helped form the city's Frederick Douglass Center, whose projects included a kindergarten, sewing classes, a men's forum, classes in sociology and English, a summer school for black children, and athletic clubs for boys and girls. From 1906 to 1911, she fostered the Pekin Theater, which launched the careers of numerous black entertainers. In 1910, Wells-Barnett set up the Negro Fellowship League, a settlement house for black men just arrived from the South. It maintained a social center, reading rooms, a dormitory, and an employment bureau. During its ten-year life span, she was its president, also editing its *Fellowship Herald* from 1911 to 1914. From 1913 to 1916, she was the first black adult probation officer for the Chicago municipal court. At one time, 200 probationers were under her charge.

Wider encompassing activities also drew her support. In 1913, Wells-Barnett led a successful campaign to block a bill that would have segregated public transportation in Illinois. Both that year and in 1915, she fought congressional proposals to outlaw interracial marriage in the District of Columbia. In 1913, Wells-Barnett and William Monroe Trotter, the militant editor of the *Boston Guardian*, visited Woodrow Wilson, presenting the president with a petition of 20,000 signatures protesting the newly initiated segregation of the Treasury and Post Office departments. A year later, she became president of the Chicago bureau of the National Equal Rights League (NERL), an organization founded by Trotter, who was an impassioned enemy of Booker Washington and his "Tuskegee machine."

Riots in Wells-Barnett's home state in 1917 led to another publication, *The East St. Louis Massacre, The Greatest Outrage of the Century.* Seeking legal aid for the victims, she personally visited the stricken city where 100 African-Americans had been killed. In July 1919, she wrote the *Chicago Tribune*, warning that Chicago faced a similar explosion. On July 27, the predicted outbreak occurred, leaving 23 blacks and 15 whites dead. The Chicago NERL met daily during the riot, serving as liaison with the city government. Wells-Barnett, however, resigned, opposing the group's call to have state attorney general Edward J. Brundage investigate the crisis. (She felt Brundage had been derelict in handling the East St. Louis matter.)

Wells-Barnett was always a strong suffragist. In 1913, she headed the Alpha Suffrage Club, Illinois' first such organization for black women. When, on March 3, 1913, a national parade was held in Washington, D.C., she defied the color line by slipping into the Illinois delegation at the last minute. In June 1916, she led her club members in a famous Chicago parade. Five thousand suffragists marched to the Republican National Convention in a pouring rain, there to seek a suffrage plank in the party platform.

Once the United States entered World War I, the government's Military Intelligence Division found Wells-Barnett disloyal. Why, federal agents asked, did she keep harping on domestic grievances—lynching and segregation being foremost—when the country was at war? Far from being intimidated, she went so far as to defend some 13 African-American soldiers sentenced to death after a race riot in Houston. The Third Battalion of the 24th Infantry, a black unit, had been stationed just outside the city. Experiencing insults because of their race, 100 soldiers marched on the city. In the wake of the insurrection, 20 lay dead, of whom 16 were white and 4 black. In other ways, Wells-Barnett did support the war effort, selling Liberty Bonds and organizing Christmas kits for soldiers.

After the war, both Wells-Barnett and her husband supported Marcus Garvey's United Negro Improvement Association (UNIA), a mass movement led by a Jamaican immigrant and centering on black nationalism and "Back to Africa." (She later wrote that Garvey was too "drunk with power" to be an effective leader.) Both the UNIA and Trotter's National Colored Congress for World Democracy chose Wells-Barnett as a delegate to the Paris Peace Conference of 1919. The federal government, still finding her subversive, would not grant her a passport.

In her last decade, Wells-Barnett was relatively inactive. Now in her 60s, she taught an adult Sunday school class in Chicago's Metropolitan Community Church. She also led such local groups as the Women's Forum and the Third Ward Women's Political Club. In 1922, she lobbied unsuccessfully for the Dyer anti-lynching bill. Two years later, she ran unsuccessfully for the presidency of the NACW president, being defeated by educator *Mary McLeod Bethune. She had equal misfortune with the National League of Republican Colored Women, simply gaining a place on its publicity committee that year. In 1928, she was slightly more successful, being appointed national organizer of Illinois Colored Women, a branch of the Colored Voters Division of the Republican National Committee. Two years later, she failed in a three-way race for the state senate. In 1928, she began her autobiography, a spirited volume in which she refought old feuds. On March 25, 1931, Ida Wells-Barnett died in Chicago of uremic poisoning.

In summarizing her career, editor and critic Walter Goodman finds Wells-Barnett "a sophisticated fighter whose prose was as tough as her intellect." Few important events occurred in the struggle for black rights without her participation. Her uncompromising attitude and prickly personality, however, often prevented effective leadership. Even her leading biographer, **Linda O. McMurry**, finds her unable to work with most people, for "her temper led her tongue to alienate even those who were ideologically compatible." This quality led to her eventual failure to get the credit she deserved, both in her lifetime and long afterwards.

Biographer McMurry finds Wells-Barnett continually forced to choose between competing ideals: "support of black 'manhood' and the need for strong black women; race unity and the belief in the oneness of humanity; political realities and personal integrity; racial uplift and class identity; tolerance and high moral standards; integration and black autonomy; nurturing her family and crusading for justice." Despite a contentious personality, few balanced such rival loyalties so well.

SOURCES:
Duster, Alfreda M., ed. *Crusade for Justice: The Autobiography of Ida B. Wells.* Chicago, IL: University of Chicago Press, 1970.
McMurry, Linda O. *To Keep the Waters Troubled: The Life of Ida B. Wells.* NY: Oxford University Press, 1998.

Thompson, Mildred I. *Ida B. Wells-Barnett: An Exploratory Study of an American Black Woman, 1893–1930*. Brooklyn, NY: Carlson, 1990.

SUGGESTED READING:

Bederman, Gail. "'Civilization,' the Decline of Middle-Class Manliness, and Ida B. Wells' Antilynching Campaign (1891–1894)," in *Radical History Review*. Vol. 52. Winter 1992, pp. 5–30.

DeCosta-Willis, Miriam, ed. *The Memphis Diary of Ida B. Wells*. Boston, MA: Beacon Press, 1995.

Harris, Trudier, comp. *Selected Works of Ida B. Wells-Barnett*. NY: Oxford University Press, 1991.

McMurry, Linda O. "Ida Wells-Barnett and the African-American Anti-Lynching Campaign," in Randall M. Miller and Paul A. Cimbla, eds., *American Reform and Reformers*, 1996.

Schechter, Patrica Ann. "'To Tell the Truth Freely': Ida B. Wells and the Politics of Race, Gender, and Reform in America, 1880–1913." Ph.D. dissertation, Princeton University, 1993.

Townes, Emilie Maurren. "The Social and Moral Perspectives of Ida B. Wells-Barnett as Resources for a Contemporary Afro-American Christian Social Ethic." Ph.D. dissertation, Northwestern University, 1989.

COLLECTIONS:

Ida B. Wells Papers, University of Chicago.

RELATED MEDIA:

Ida B. Wells: A Passion for Justice (documentary film), read by *Toni Morrison, written by William Greaves, produced by William Greaves and Louise Archambault, narrated by Al Freeman, Jr., New York, aired on "American Experience," 1989.

Justus D. Doenecke,
Professor of History, New College of the
University of South Florida, Sarasota, Florida

Welsh, Jane Baillie (1801–1866).

See Carlyle, Jane Welsh.

Welsh, Lilian (1858–1938)

American physician and educator who promoted women's hygiene and public health through the Evening Dispensary for Working Women and Girls and the Woman's College of Baltimore (later Goucher College).

Born in Columbia, Pennsylvania, on March 6, 1858; died in Columbia of encephalitis lethargica on February 23, 1938; daughter of Thomas Welsh (a merchant and later general in the army) and Annie Eunice (Young) Welsh; graduated from Columbia High School, 1873; graduated from the State Normal School of Millersville, Pennsylvania, 1875; graduated from the Woman's Medical College of Pennsylvania, 1889; attended the University of Zurich, 1889–90; never married.

Lilian Welsh was born in Columbia, Pennsylvania, in 1858, the fourth daughter of **Annie Young Welsh** and Thomas Welsh, a military man who first served in the Mexican War and then, after a stint as a merchant, rejoined the army during the Civil War. He rose to the rank of brigadier general and died of an illness contracted during the siege of Vicksburg. Lilian Welsh attended both Columbia High School and the State Normal School in Millersville, Pennsylvania, returning to her alma maters to teach after graduation in 1875. She had been principal of Columbia High School for five years when she tendered her resignation in 1886 to enter the Woman's Medical College of Pennsylvania. She earned her medical degree in 1889, but hoped to become a physiological chemistry teacher and pursued further studies in Zurich in expectation of this career move. However, a teaching position never opened up, which prompted her to become a physician at the State Hospital for the Insane in Norristown, Pennsylvania, in 1890.

Two years later, Welsh made another career change when she teamed up with Dr. *Mary Sherwood, a friend from Zurich, to set up a private practice in Baltimore. The two women shared an interest in preventive medicine and the health of expectant mothers and babies, which became the focus of their professional lives. Although both women were qualified physicians, prejudice against women doctors prevented their practice from flourishing. Undaunted, Welsh took her fight to the Woman's College of Baltimore (later known as Goucher College) when she was appointed physician to the students and professor of physiology and hygiene in 1894. She taught personal and public health matters and promoted physical exercise for women during a time when women were considered far too delicate for either. She became a fixture at the school, noted for both her outspoken manner of teaching and her commitment to proper hygiene for girls.

Around the same time, Welsh and Sherwood took control of the Evening Dispensary for Working Women and Girls, recently founded by physicians *Kate Campbell Hurd-Mead and Alice Hall. This privately held charitable organization provided women physicians the opportunity to practice medicine, and emphasized women's health in the general public. The dispensary was a leader in obstetric care, concerned with both pre-natal and post-natal care for mother and child. Among other innovations, the clinic dispensed pure milk to babies, employed the first visiting nurse in the city, and formed a social service department.

Welsh became secretary of the newly formed Baltimore Association for the Promotion of the University Education of Women in 1897, seeking to secure admission of women into graduate departments within the Johns Hopkins University. She was a member of the National American Woman Suffrage Association, and marched in many street parades supporting the cause. She was also a charter member of Baltimore women's organizations such as the Arundell Club and the Arundell Good Government Club. She returned to her family home in Columbia, Pennsylvania, in 1935, after the death of her long-time companion Mary Sherwood, and died there three years later.

SOURCES:

Edgerly, Lois Stiles, ed. and comp. *Give Her This Day.* Gardiner, ME: Tilbury House, 1990.

James, Edward T., ed. *Notable American Women, 1607–1950.* Cambridge, MA: The Belknap Press of Harvard University, 1971.

Amy Cooper, M.A., M.S.I.,
Ann Arbor, Michigan

Welty, Eudora (1909–2001)

American writer, considered one of the greatest literary figures of the 20th century, whose short stories, novels, and essays evoke the vibrant culture of her native Mississippi. Born Eudora Alice Welty on April 13, 1909, in Jackson, Mississippi; died of pneumonia, age 92, at Baptist Medical Center in Jackson on July 23, 2001; daughter of Christian Webb Welty and Mary Chestina (Andrews) Welty; attended two years at Mississippi State College for Women, 1925–27; University of Wisconsin, B.A. in English literature, 1929; studied advertising at Columbia University School of Business, 1930–31; never married; no children.

Honors and awards: four-time winner of the O. Henry Award (second prize 1941, first prize 1942, 1943, 1968); twice awarded Guggenheim fellowships (1942, 1949); elected to the National Institute of Arts and Letters (1952); William Dean Howells Medal of the American Academy of Arts and Letters for The Ponder Heart *(1954); honorary LL.D. degrees from University of Wisconsin (1954) and Smith College (1956); honorary lecturer at Cambridge University (1955) and Smith College (1956); honorary consultant to the Library of Congress (1958–61); elected to the American Academy of Arts and Letters (1971); Gold Medal for Fiction of the National Institute of Arts and Letters (1972); Pulitzer Prize for Fiction for* The Optimist's Daughter *(1973); National Medal of Literature and Medal of Freedom (1981); National Medal of Arts (1986); Chevalier de l'Ordre des Arts et Lettres in France (1987); inducted into the Women's Hall of Fame at Seneca Falls, New York (autumn 2000).*

Born and raised in Jackson, Mississippi; lived in New York City (1930–31); returned to Mississippi upon the death of her father (1931); served as publici- *ty agent for the Works Project Administration (1933–36); published first short stories (1936); published many short stories and novels (1940s–1950s), while traveling throughout U.S. and Europe; won Pulitzer Prize (1973); gave William E. Massey lectures at Harvard University (1983); resided throughout life in Jackson, Mississippi.*

Selected writings: (short stories) A Curtain of Green *(Doubleday, 1941); (novel)* The Robber Bridegroom *(1942); (short stories)* The Wide Net and Other Stories *(1943); (short stories)* Delta Wedding *(1946); (short stories)* The Golden Apples *(1949); Selected* Stories *and* The Ponder Heart *(1954); Three Papers on Fiction* (1962); (juvenile) The Shoe Bird *(1964); (novel)* Losing Battles *(1970); (short novel)* The Optimist's Daughter *(1972); (nonfiction)* The Eye of the Story *(1978); The Collected Stories of Eudora Welty (1980); One Writer's Beginnings (1984).*

Eudora Welty was praised throughout her literary career for giving voice to the distinctive culture of the American South. Her life was spent primarily in the heart of the South, in Jackson, Mississippi, and her keen observations of the peculiarities of Southern life allowed her to capture in writing the rural Southern attitudes, family structures, relations between races, and speech patterns which are now disappearing in the wake of the growing urbanization and dedication to mass media of the late 20th and early 21st centuries. Throughout her career, Welty's works enjoyed wide appeal that has continued after her death, not only with Southern audiences, but with Northern, Western, and European audiences as well.

Welty's upbringing most certainly contributed to her later choice of vocation. She was born on April 13, 1909, in Jackson, Mississippi, the daughter of a former schoolteacher, **Chestina Welty**, and a gentle and nurturing bookkeeper, Christian Webb Welty. Eudora recalled that both her parents "were from families without much money. They were educated, as it turned out, through their own efforts." The Weltys had an affectionate marriage, and the household was harmonious and scholarly. The loss of their first child, a son, before Eudora's birth made them fiercely protective of Eudora and her two younger brothers, Edward (born 1912) and Walter (born 1915). Chestina Welty was a voracious reader all of her life, and she encouraged her children to cultivate the same passion. Christian and Chestina were sufficiently well-off to provide their children with many books and toys; Eudora recalled she had little interest in the dolls that she received but was thrilled to receive a ten-volume set of children's books entitled *Our Wonder World* when she was nine years old. While confined to bed as a child because of a "fast-beating heart," she recalled, "[i]t did give me a glorious opportunity to do what I loved to do: Read. 'Cause I lay on the bed with books all around me. . . . So that really was a feeling of being perfectly free to read to my heart's content. Or look out the window to my heart's content." Like all well-brought-up Southern girls of her day, Welty also learned to play the piano and to paint; she especially enjoyed working with watercolors.

Welty's upbringing was surprisingly progressive for that time. She was encouraged to excel in her studies, and she was a frequent visitor to the city library, only blocks away from her home. She came into contact with many strong women who no doubt encouraged her to seek her own path. The librarian, Mrs. Calloway, she remembered as a fearsome personage: "Like a dragon she sat at her desk, facing the front door, and refused entrance to any girl whose skirt could be seen through. She allowed patrons to take out only two books at a time and refused to accept them back until at least a day later." The president of Welty's elementary school, **Lorena Duling**, likewise inspired fear and admiration, not only among her students, but with community leaders as well. When she needed something, Miss Duling "telephoned the mayor, or the chief of police, or the president of the power company, or the head doctor at the hospital, or the judge in charge of a case, or whoever, and calling them by their first names, told them what to do."

> *A* sheltered life can be a daring life as well. For all serious daring starts from within.
>
> —Eudora Welty

When Welty completed her elementary and secondary education in 1925, she longed to leave Jackson and experience the wider world. Her parents encouraged her to attend college but were fearful to send her so far away from home, as she was only 16. Eudora relented, and for two years she attended Mississippi State College for Women, 150 miles away in Columbus, Mississippi. Two years later, she persuaded her parents to allow her to transfer to the University of Wisconsin, where she studied English literature and graduated with a bachelor of arts degree in 1929. After graduation, Welty traveled to New York City, where she studied advertising at the Columbia University School of Business from 1930 to 1931. She blissfully remembered the time she spent in the big city, where she attended plays and concerts and the ballet, and spent every Sunday at the Metropolitan Museum of Art.

Welty's exploration of the wider world was suddenly cut short in 1931. The Great Depression had struck the nation, and Eudora received word that her father had fallen ill with leukemia. She immediately returned to Jackson, where her mother was willing to go to any lengths to save her husband. Eudora recalls her mother lying on a cot by her father's, in a desperate attempt to save his life with a blood transfusion. A tube was passed from Chestina's arm to her husband's, but the transfusion was not successful. Welty had a vivid recollection of her father's death: "All at once his face turned dusky red all over. The doctor made a disparaging sound with his lips, the kind a woman knitting makes when she drops a stitch. What the doctor meant by it was that my father had died." By the time of his death at the age of 52, Christian Welty had worked his way up in the Lamar Life Insurance Company in Jackson from bookkeeper to president of the company. His death was a horrible blow for the family and the community.

The death of her father placed a burden upon Welty to help support her two brothers, who were still in school. The most obvious possibility open to a young, unmarried woman with an education was to become a teacher. Eudora had no interest in pursuing this profession, lacking, as she stated, "the instructing turn of mind, the selflessness, the patience." Instead she worked odd jobs in writing and advertising for various newspapers and Jackson radio station WJDX, until in 1933 she was hired as a publicity agent for the Works Progress Administration (WPA). From 1933 to 1936, she traveled to all of Mississippi's towns and rural areas to chronicle successful projects completed through the WPA. She interviewed local officials and wrote newspaper reports. She remembered this experience as "the real germ of my wanting to become a real writer, a true writer. It caused me to attempt it. It made me see, for the first time, what life was really like in this state. It was a revelation." In the process she took over 1,200 photographs of the people she met. Her budding interest in photography would later have a great impact on her literary style: "I learned that every feeling waits upon its gesture, and I had to be prepared to recognize this moment when I saw it. These were things a story writer needed to know."

During her time with the WPA, Welty began writing short stories about the people and culture of Mississippi. From the beginning, her work emphasized "hearing" the dialogue between characters. As she later noted, "I love dialogue, and when I read or write something, I can hear it." In 1936, she submitted two of her stories, "Death of a Travelling Salesman" and "Magic" to *Manuscript*, a small literary magazine. Both were accepted for publication. The editor wrote back to Welty, describing "Death of a Travelling Salesman," "one of the best stories we have ever read." Emboldened by her success, Welty began sending her stories to more prestigious literary journals; some won national prizes. Three days after the appearance of her stories in *Manuscript*, a New York publisher wrote to request that she send some of her material to be considered for publication, but when she submitted a collection of short stories he sent them back with the admonition, "It is quite impossible to publish a volume of stories by a relatively unknown author under the present conditions of the book market." Her stories, he insisted, "show an acute but somewhat unfocussed sensibility. They are charming but vague. Sometimes the architecture of the stories is at war with the content. . . . Often you have no

story to tell at all, but rather a state of mood to convey." He suggested that she write a novel.

Welty's first attempt as a novelist was less than successful. *The Cheated*, which she submitted to Houghton Mifflin in 1938, was rejected as too vague: "You have apprehended rather than thought out the situations and characters, with the result that much of the story has the quality of a dream or fantasy," was the editor's critique. Although she continued to publish her short stories in such prestigious magazines as *Harper's Bazaar* and *Atlantic Monthly*, she floundered in search of a publishing career. In 1940, she secured an agent, Diarmuid Russell, and finally in 1941, her first collection of stories was published by Doubleday as *A Curtain of Green*. The following year, her first novel, *The Robber Bridegroom*, was published, and her writing career was firmly established.

Prizes and travel opportunities quickly followed. In 1942, she placed first in the distinguished O. Henry Short Story award, and placed first again the following year, the first writer ever

Eudora Welty

to do so. She received a Guggenheim fellowship in 1942, and two years later the American Academy of Arts and Letters awarded her $1,000. Welty spent the summer of 1944 in New York City as a staff writer for *The New York Times Book Review*. Her publications continued to appear regularly. In 1943, she published a collection called *The Wide Net and Other Stories*. In 1946, she published *Delta Wedding*; although it received mixed reviews, it soon became a bestseller. Her collection of stories published in 1949 as *The Golden Apples* all centered around the fictional town of Morgana, Mississippi. That year, another Guggenheim fellowship allowed her to go to Britain and Europe for extended travel. While in Ireland, she stayed at Bowen's Court with *Elizabeth Bowen, who described Welty as "very unwriterish and *bien élevée*. A Southern girl from the state of Mississippi; quiet, self-contained, easy, outwardly old-fashioned, very funny indeed when she starts talking. No one would pick her out on sight as 'an interesting woman.' Actually I think she's a genius rather than an interesting woman, which I am glad of as I prefer the former."

The 1950s were also a very busy and productive time for Welty. She won the O. Henry prize once more in 1951, and was elected to the National Institute of Arts and Letters the following year. In 1954, she published *Selected Stories* and *The Ponder Heart*, which received the 1955 William Dean Howells Medal of the Academy of Arts and Letters. She was also selected to give a lecture on "Place in Fiction" that year at Cambridge University. In 1956, a theatrical version of *The Ponder Heart* opened on Broadway, where it was "modestly successful."

Welty's travels slowed somewhat in the 1960s, as her mother's declining health kept her closer to home. She continued to write prodigiously, however. In 1962, she published *Three Papers on Fiction*, and in 1964 she issued her first children's book, *The Shoe Bird*. She spent ten years working on a novel, which she published in 1970 as *Losing Battles*. Both her mother and her brother Edward died in 1966. As a means of dealing with her grief, Welty wrote another short novel, *The Optimist's Daughter*, which she dedicated to her mother when it was published in 1972. It won the Pulitzer Prize for Fiction in 1973.

In 1978, Welty published her first collection of nonfiction, entitled *The Eye of the Story*. In 1980, *The Collected Stories of Eudora Welty* was released. Three years later, she was invited to deliver the William E. Massey lectures at Harvard University. These were published in 1984 as *One Writer's Beginnings*, which became another bestseller. Throughout the 1980s and 1990s, Welty continued to produce stories and essays, to lead conferences and give lectures. She received medals from both Presidents Jimmy Carter and Ronald Reagan, and in 1987 was made a Chevalier de l'Ordre des Arts et Lettres by the French government.

Throughout her life, Welty remained an intensely private person. In an interview, she remarked, "Your private life should be kept private. My own, I don't think would particularly interest anybody, for that matter. But I'd guard it; I feel strongly about that. They'd have a hard time trying to find something about me. I think I'd better burn everything up. It's best to burn letters, but at least I've never kept diaries or journals." Because of her position as a role model for Southern women, Eudora Welty was sometimes pressured to give her views on the modern feminist movement. But she never viewed her upbringing in the intensely conservative South as a roadblock to her literary potential. Welty believed that a piece of literature should be divorced from the writer's gender, race, or background. An author's work, she always maintained, must stand alone. Despite her own celebrity, she never lost her sense of perspective. She was as candid about her early failures as she was about her own successes. In recalling her early work, she remembered having "all the weaknesses of the headlong. I never rewrote, I just wrote. The plots in those stories are weak because I didn't know enough to worry about plots."

Welty's characters provide the focus of all her works. She described a literary character as "a taproot that goes clear down. . . . [W]hat you want is an essence, a dramatic entity, the human being to be shown as unlike any other human being. That's what human beings are, and you've got to show them that way." It was her ability to portray Southerners as fully developed human beings that enabled her to highlight their peculiarities without reducing them to caricatures. As the years passed, she was increasingly cited as one of the century's greatest American writers. In 1999, the Library of America published a two-volume set of Welty's collected works, the first time a living author had been so honored. Her 90th birthday later that year saw the publication of a spate of books and journal articles about her writing and celebrations hosted by fellow writers, friends, and devoted fans. In autumn 2000, she was inducted into the Women's Hall of Fame in Seneca Falls, New York. Welty died on July 23, 2001, leaving behind a wealth of literature invaluable to readers of all cultures. "My wish, my continuing passion," she once wrote, "would be not to point the finger in judgment but to part a curtain, that invisible shadow that falls between people, the veil of indifference to each other's presence, each other's wonder, each other's human plight."

SOURCES:

The Boston Sunday Globe. September 20, 1998, p. N2.

Evans, Elizabeth. *Eudora Welty.* NY: Frederick Ungar, 1981.

Firing Line, "The Southern Imagination," William F. Buckley, Jr. interviewing Eudora Welty and Walker Percy. Columbia, SC: SECA, 1972.

Isaacs, Neil. *Eudora Welty.* Austin, TX: Steck-Vaughn, 1969.

Magill, Frank N., ed. *Great Women Writers: The Lives and Works of 135 of the World's Most Important Women Writers, from Antiquity to the Present.* NY: Henry Holt, 1994.

Newsweek. August 6, 2001, p. 60.

Obituary in *The Boston Globe.* July 24, 2001, pp. A1, A9.

Obituary in *The Day* [New London, CT]. July 24, 2001, p. A3.

Obituary in *The New York Times.* July 24, 2001, pp. A1, B8.

Powell, Dannye Romine. *Parting the Curtains: Interviews with Southern Writers.* Winston-Salem, NC: John F. Blair, 1994.

Preston, Charlotte Ann. "Eudora Welty's Still and Silent Lives." Master's thesis, Kansas State University, Manhattan, Kansas, 1976.

Westling, Louise. *Eudora Welty.* Totowa, NJ: Barnes & Noble, 1989.

SUGGESTED READING:

McHaney, Pearl Amelia, comp. *Eudora Welty: Writers' Reflections Upon First Reading Welty.* Hill Street Press, 1999.

Waldron, Ann. *Eudora.* NY: Doubleday, 1999 (unauthorized biography).

Kimberly Estep Spangler,
Assistant Professor of History and Chair, Division
of Religion and Humanities, Friends University, Wichita, Kansas

Wencheng (c. 620–680)

Chinese princess of the Tang Dynasty who married the first king of Tibet and founded the Jokhang Temple in Lhasa, making her instrumental in establishing Buddhism as the national religion of Tibet. Name variations: WenCheng. Pronunciation: WHEN-chin. Born Wencheng into the family of Emperor Tang Taizong; adopted and raised by his Empress Zhangsun; given the title of princess and provided with a classical Confucian education; enjoyed the educational advantages of Chang-An, then one of the most cosmopolitan capitals of the world; married Songzan Ganbu (or, according to the Tibetan alphabet, Srongbtdan Sgam-po), king of Tibet.

In 607 CE, Songzan Ganbu had unified the mountainous country of Tibet and made Lhasa its capital. Eager to attract the more advanced technology of China to his new country, and desiring to elevate Tibet's standard of living, culture and art, in 634 he approached the court of the Chinese emperor Tang Taizong, asking to be granted a bride of the Han Chinese people.

The request was not unusual for the Tang emperor's court. His dynastic predecessors had often made peace or strengthened military alliances through marriages between princesses and the chiefs of outlying minority tribes to the north and west, helping to secure the state's political safety. Equally important, in areas bordering China, such alliances made trade safer along the legendary Silk Road, the caravan route for sending and receiving goods overland all the way to the Mediterranean. For the leaders of lands around China, political friendship was one advantage gained through diplomatically arranged marriages, but so was the level of culture that could be passed into the vast areas on the periphery of China, where a cultivated Chinese woman could bring religion, writing, silk growing and other forms of agriculture to the less developed kingdoms that were still in transition from their past as loosely organized nomadic tribes.

At the sophisticated Tang court, however, Tibet seemed so remote as to be barely worth notice, and the upstart king at first found his request refused. Frustrated and insulted, Songzan Ganbu responded by declaring war against the Tang, and was defeated. But in 640, when the ambitious ruler from the high country repeated his request, sending his prime minister Ge'erdongzan to the emperor's capital Chang-An, he was better received. One reason, no doubt, was the 5,000 liang (about 9,000 ounces) of gold included as a gift in the prime minister's retinue. At any rate, Emperor Taizong presented the king of Tibet with the lovely, cultured Princess Wencheng as a bride. The marriage alliance marked the beginning of a political link that became the basis for all future claims by China to attachment, and eventually control, of Tibet.

Princess Wencheng was a daughter of a member of the family of Emperor Tang Taizong. She had been adopted and raised by his Empress **Zhangsun** in their luxurious court, given the title of princess, and provided with a classical Confucian education. Living at the beginning of the Golden Age of the Tang dynasty, she enjoyed the educational advantages of Chang-An, then one of the most cosmopolitan capitals of the world. Once the marriage was arranged, she also knew the importance of her role in Tang politics, representing the new bond of friendship between the two countries. As compensation for leaving the sophisticated court behind, Emperor Taizong lavished the princess with a large personal dowry of silk clothes, fine furniture, expensive jewelry, and many books that would find their way into Tibetan libraries, as well as the many gifts she was to share with her new people, such as farming implements, seed-grains, technical manuals and musical instruments. By such gifts, the Tibetan portion of the border of Taizong's empire was to be made secure, and newly formed Tibet was to be bordered by a friendly ally and free to expand its own culture.

Conducted to Tibet by a large convoy of retainers and her escort Li Daocheng, Wencheng reached the Qinzang plateau, where she was met by a party of Tibetans who greeted her with gifts of horses, cattle, yaks and boats. She and her retinue were offered food and drink, then a song was sung to her in welcome:

> Don't be afraid of crossing the prairie
> A hundred horses are waiting for you.
> Don't be afraid to climb over the snow
> A hundred docile yaks are waiting for you.
> Don't be afraid to ford the deep river
> A hundred horse head boats are waiting for you.

It had taken the princess' party one month to travel from Chang-An to Lhasa. Songzan Ganbu met her near Lake Zalin and rode with her into the capital, where she was met with another musical greeting. The king respected her cultivated tastes and dressed in the rich silk clothes she had brought him. They were married in Lhasa, and their nuptial chamber was in the grand Potala palace, built by Songzan Ganbu on the sacred mountain of Putuo Hill. *Potala* means Buddha's Mountain, and the enormous structure placed high on the side of the mountain, facing south, overlooked the entire city of Lhasa. A part of the original palace still remains today. The oldest remaining section is the Guanyin temple in the portion known as the Red Palace, where Princess Wencheng began her life with her new husband. The main section of the surviving Potala is actually a combination of two palaces built during the 17th century by the 5th Dalai Lama. The Red Palace, completed in 1693, and the White Palace built from 1645 to 1653, were added onto the remaining structures of the Potala of Princess Wencheng's time, part of which was destroyed in the 8th century by lightning.

Also brought to Tibet by Princess Wencheng was a gilded bronze statue of the Sakyamuni Buddha. Under her supervision, the Jokhang Temple was built to house this sacred object. The temple, called the *Dazhousi* in Chinese and the *Jokhang* in Tibetan, is considered one of Tibet's holiest places, located in the oldest part of the city. Its great hall and first two stories are the original structure; above the entrance are two enormous copper *dagobas*, covered with gold leaf, and a gilded prayer wheel placed between them is held by two gilded statues of goats. Inside, the Sakyamuni Buddha was set on a gold throne embraced by two pillars of solid silver. Nearby are statues of Wencheng and Songzan Ganbu, as well as of **Princess Tritson**, his Nepalese wife, representing another political alliance through marriage. In addition to Princess Wencheng and Princess Tritson, Songzan Ganbu also had three Tibetan wives, whose children founded Tibet's Tubo dynasty. All lived together in the grand Potala palace, later the home of the Dalai Lamas, filled with thousands of rooms that eventually housed thousands of monks.

While Buddhism was known in Tibet before the arrival of Princess Wencheng, it was her faith and the construction of her Jokhang temple that helped to spread the Buddhist faith, and laid the foundations for the emergence of the Dalai Lamas and the rule of Tibet as a theocracy. It is appropriate, perhaps, that the statue brought by Wencheng was of the historical Buddha who always appears crosslegged on a lotus flower, as in meditation. Before Wencheng's arrival the common local religion was Bon, a faith filled with demons and magic.

To this day, a painting remains showing the arrival of Princess Wencheng in Lhasa. Tradition says that she and her husband knelt before the Jokhang temple after its completion and planted saplings of willow trees she had also brought from Chang-An. The old willow tree trunk which remains in front of the temple-monastery is said to be one of those trees.

From China, Princess Wencheng had also brought artisans to introduce the arts of papermaking, textile weaving and new techniques in metallurgy and architectural design. Also introduced were the principles of grinding wheat, making pottery, constructing field tools, brewing wine, and making ink stock. The Tibetans mastered Han techniques of agriculture, and adopted the Chinese system of planting. Many gave up their animal-skin tents, reminders of their nomadic days, and constructed Chinese-style houses. The upper class eventually adopted silk clothes and cultivated the art of embroidery.

Princess Wencheng introduced the lunar calendar into Tibet, along with seed grains and planting cycles based on the calendar that improved agriculture. The band of musicians she had brought enlivened music at court and changed Tibetan music by introducing stringed instruments. Some of the original instruments she brought as gifts can be seen each year on February 13, according to the Tibetan calendar, and have been well preserved for more than a thousand years.

Songzan Ganbu, eager for every form of improvement, also sent an emissary named Sambhota to India to learn a system of writing, and Sambhota created the Tibetan alphabet, based on the Sanskrit writing of Kashmir. This new system of Tibetan writing was adopted within 20 years, and was widely used to write laws, records and Buddhist scriptures. The new written language stimulated trade and economic exchange with China, and Tibet prospered. At the death of Emperor Taizong, Songzan Ganbu sent 15 different types of elaborate Tibetan jewelry as sacrificial offerings in his honor, and when the next Tang emperor ascended the throne, the king declared his military loyalty in a petition, along with an offering of extravagant gifts. In return, he was made magistrate of Xihai. In 650, at the death of Songzan Ganbu, the Tang emperor sent an emissary to attend the funeral and pay his respects to Princess Wencheng, verifying the good relations between two countries.

During the lifetime of Wencheng, Tibet adopted a postal system similar to the one in China, utilizing riders with mail satchels who rode horses in 100-mile relays akin to the later American pony express, improving communication between Lhasa and Chang-An. After the death of Wencheng, political alliances through marriage were continued when the Tang princess **Jin Cheng** married Tibet's King Chidai Zhudan. In 821 CE, the Tibetan king Chirao Bajin and Tang emperor Tang Muzong commemorated the long interlinking of blood lines with the erection of several stelas bearing the names of the common relatives of the allied nations, along with the inscription: "Cooperate Peacefully as One Family."

Princess Wencheng lived in Tibet for 40 years. Her life is commemorated every year on two dates of the Tibetan calendar: April 15, the day of her arrival in the country, and October 15, her birthday. Plays performed on these occasions retell her story. The goodwill ambassador who married out of diplomacy became much more than an envoy. She instructed Tibet in the Buddhist faith, and irreversibly influenced the fortunes of its people. Before her death, funerals for women of her position were thought to be so unimportant that they were not even recorded. Hers was to be an exception. When

Wencheng died on May 7, 680, the Tibetans held a great funeral in her honor. Her death date is still commemorated by people who recite her good deeds, wearing paper hats and carrying bamboo poles.

By the 10th century, Buddhism had begun to assume political as well as spiritual leadership in Tibet. Monasteries were fortified, their estates grew in wealth and influence, and the Buddhist lamas began to assert authority over the faithful. In 1572, the first Dalai Lama was proclaimed. The title was conferred by the Mongols, whose chief at the time was Altan Khan; *Dalai* means "ocean" and *Lama* means "man of profound wisdom," ascribing a deep knowledge to the bearer of the title. The Dalai Lama, in turn, appointed the Panchen Lama who ruled from Xigaze, 227 miles from Lhasa.

In 1913, the 13th Dalai Lama proclaimed Tibet independent from China, but when the Communists came to power in China in 1949, they reasserted control over Tibet; in 1965, they established Tibet as an "autonomous region" known as Xizang Zizhiqu. During China's Cultural Revolution, many temples and monasteries in Tibet were destroyed, but the Jokhang Temple founded by Princess Wencheng still remains, a symbol of her power and her faith. She is commemorated in legends, plays and songs not only in Tibet but in China as well.

SOURCES:

The author is grateful for consultation with Professor Zhu-lei, chair of the history department, Wuhan University, 1988–89, and Gerard Massacrier, professor of French, Wuhan University, 1988–89.

Booz, Elisabeth B. *Tibet*. Lincolnwood, IL: Passport Books, 1986.

Bo Yang. *Genealogical Tables of Chinese Emperors, Empresses, Princes, and Princesses*. China: Friendship Publishing, 1986.

Ji Zhong. "Princess Wencheng—A Chinese Dance Drama," in *Women of China*. April 1980, pp. 20–21.

"Princess WenCheng," in *The Dictionary of Famous Women of Hua Shia* (China). Trans. from Chinese by Lucia P. Ellis. Beijing: Hua Shia Publishing House, 1988.

Sui Xiaohuan. "A Friendship Carrier who Promoted a Friendship Between Han Chinese and Tibetans," in *Famous Women of Ancient Times and Today*. Ed. by Chinese Woman Magazine (orally trans. from Chinese by Fang Hong). Hebei People's Publishing House, 1986.

Wan Shengnan. *Princess Wencheng*. Zhong Hua Books Bureau.

Xin Anting, Chinese Historical Figures. Gansu People's Publishing House, 1983.

Barbara Bennett Peterson, Ph.D.,
Professor of History, University of Hawaii,
and editor of *Notable Women of Hawaii*
(Honolulu, HI: University of Hawaii Press, 1984)

Wendt, Julia Bracken (1871–1942)

One of the leading women sculptors of the American West. Born Julia Bracken in Apple River, Illinois, on June 10, 1871; died in Los Angeles, California, in 1942; daughter of Andrew Bracken and Mary Bracken; attended the Art Institute of Chicago, 1887, and studied with Lorado Taft, 1887–92; married William Wendt (b. 1865, an artist), on June 26, 1906.

Major works: Illinois Welcoming the Nations *(1893) and* The Three Graces: History, Science and Art *(1914).*

Julia Bracken Wendt was born into a large Irish Catholic family in 1871 in Apple River, Illinois, and moved with her parents to Galena in 1876. Her career began at 17, when she started work as one of Lorado Taft's female assistants, a group known as the "White Rabbits" which included other noted female sculptors *Bessie Potter Vonnoh and *Janet Scudder. Wendt worked with Taft for six years, making a name for herself as an independent artist in Chicago. In 1893, she was commissioned for a sculpture at the Illinois Pavilion at the Chicago World's Fair. She produced *Illinois Welcoming the Nations*, which was placed in the state capitol in Springfield.

Julia left Chicago in 1906 after her marriage to famous California painter William Wendt. They moved to Los Angeles and then to an art colony in Laguna Beach where they built a studio. Julia Wendt's sculptures in bronze, wood, and marble made her one of the more famous figures in the California art community, particularly her series of relief portraits of famous men of the century such as Tolstoy, Emerson, Lincoln, and William Morris. In 1911, she was commissioned to create one of her best-known pieces, an allegory sculpture for the rotunda of the Los Angeles County Museum called *The Three Graces: History, Science and Art*. Completed in 1914, the 11'-tall sculpture depicts three women in bronze holding aloft a globe illumined by electric light. It was the centerpiece of the rotunda for years until it was completely hidden by another exhibit in the 1950s. However, it was returned to a central place in the museum in the 1980s. Among the many honors Wendt received was a gold medal for sculpture at the 1915 San Diego Exposition. She also taught at the Otis Art Institute from 1918 to 1925. One of the most important Los Angeles sculptors of her day, Wendt died in 1942.

SOURCES:

Bailey, Brooke. *The Remarkable Lives of 100 Women Artists.* Holbrook, MA: Bob Adams, 1994.

Rubinstein, Charlotte Streifer. *American Women Artists.* NY: Avon, 1982.

Amy Cooper, M.A., M.S.I.,
Ann Arbor, Michigan

Wenham, Jane (d. 1730)

Last woman convicted of witchcraft in England. Name variations: Witch of Walkern. Died in 1730.

Jane Wenham, who lived in Walkern, Hertfordshire, was the last woman tried for and convicted of witchcraft in England. In 1713, she was tried and found guilty by jury, but the jury's decision to condemn Wenham to death was contrary to the judge's leading. In fact, in response to one of the charges brought against her, the judge declared that there was no law against flying. Wenham was pardoned and her case was debated in legal pamphlets of the day. She died in 1730.

Amy Cooper, MA, MSI,
Ann Arbor, Michigan

Wentworth, Baroness (1837–1917).

See Lovelace, Ada Byron, countess of, for sidebar on Anne Blunt.

Wentworth, Cecile de (c. 1853–1933)

American portrait painter. Name variations: Mme C.-E. Wentworth; Mme C.E. Wentworth; Cecile Smith de Wentworth. Born Cecilia Smith in New York City about 1853; died in Nice, France, on August 28, 1933; educated in convent schools; studied painting in Paris with Alexandre Cabanel and Edouard Detaille; married Josiah Winslow Wentworth, around 1887 (died 1931).

Appeared in the exhibition catalogue of the Paris Salon (1889); won bronze medal for portrait of Pope Leo XIII at the Exposition Universelle in Paris (1900); received title of Grand Commander of the Order of the Holy Sepulcher and the papal title of Marchesa from the pope; awarded title of Chevalier of the Legion of Honor (1901).

Cecile de Wentworth was born Cecilia Smith into a large Roman Catholic family in New York City around 1853. Educated in convent schools, she journeyed to Paris in 1886 to study painting in the studios of the academic painter Alexandre Cabanel and his compatriot Edouard Detaille. Although Wentworth never surrendered her American citizenship, France became her adopted homeland and the place where she achieved her greatest fame as a portrait painter.

Within a few years of her arrival in France, Cecile married Josiah Winslow Wentworth and also appeared in her first exhibit at the Paris Salon under her married name. For the next 30 years, she showed her works at the salon and maintained a studio on the Champs Élysées. Her ability to produce lively, natural expressions in her portraits made her a coveted portraitist whose roster of clients eventually included American presidents Theodore Roosevelt and William Howard Taft, England's Queen *Alexandra of Denmark (commissioned by the king of Spain), and General John J. Pershing, whose portrait hung in the Versailles Museum. Her most famous portrait was of Pope Leo XIII, displayed in the Vatican Museum in Rome, which won her a bronze medal at the Exposition Universelle in Paris in 1900. The pope showed his gratitude by decorating her with the title of Grand Commander of the Order of the Holy Sepulchre, and conferring on her the papal title of Marchesa.

Wentworth achieved other significant honors in her lifetime; France made her a chevalier of the Legion of Honor in 1901, and she was one of the few women artists to have works purchased by the Luxembourg Museum. Her art found homes in several other prestigious museums, including the Musée d'Orsay in Paris, the Metropolitan Museum of Art in New York City, and the Corcoran Gallery in Washington, D.C. But the death of her husband in 1931 virtually bankrupted Wentworth despite her fame, and she was forced to move from her Paris home to cheaper quarters in Nice. She died two years later in the municipal hospital there; the American embassy in Paris helped cover her funeral expenses.

SOURCES:

McHenry, Robert, ed. *Famous American Women.* NY: Dover, 1980.

Rubinstein, Charlotte Streifer. *American Women Artists.* NY: Avon, 1982.

Malinda Mayer,
writer and editor,
Falmouth, Massachusetts

Wentworth, Henrietta Maria

(c. 1657–1686)

British baroness, mistress and supporter of James Scott, duke of Monmouth. Name variations: Baroness Wentworth. Born around 1657; died on April 23, 1686; only child of Sir Thomas Wentworth (1613–1665), Baron Wentworth, and Lady Philadelphia Wentworth (d. 1696, daughter of Ferdinando Carey); mistress of James Crofts Scott (1649–1685), duke of Monmouth (son of Charles II and Lucy Walter, executed 1685).

Inherited the estate of her grandfather the earl of Cleveland and succeeded to the barony of Wentworth (1667); spent several years discharging his debts and establishing her rights; met James Scott, duke of Monmouth, while performing in a masque at court (1674); lived with him on her estate (1680); followed him to exile in Holland (1684); dissuaded him from entering imperialist service against the Turks and supplied funds for him to lead a failed rebellion against King James II (1685); returned to England (1685).

Henrietta Maria, Baroness Wentworth, influenced the course of English history through her liaison with James Crofts Scott, duke of Monmouth, who harbored an ambition to be king of England. Raised on her family estate of Toddington in Bedfordshire, Baroness Wentworth inherited her title and estates from her grandfather in 1667 while she was still a child. Her heritage included considerable debts and a host of creditors' suits that were settled for her by her mother Lady **Philadelphia Wentworth** and her guardian, leaving a still-considerable fortune at her disposal. In due course, she became involved in the social life of the royal court, and in December 1674, when she was about 17, she appeared with other ladies of the court in a masque written by John Crowne entitled *Calisto, or the Chaste Nymph,* performing the role of "Jupiter, in love with Calisto." It was on this occasion that her cousin, Baron John Lovelace, introduced her to the duke of Monmouth who was "one of the men that danced."

The duke, the illegitimate son of King Charles II and *Lucy Walter, had grown up in Paris where his mother settled after being banished for claiming to be the king's wife. In 1662, he returned to England, by all accounts a strikingly handsome and charming man, where he was installed in his natural father's court as a favorite. At the time he met Wentworth, the engaging duke was both married, by arrangement, to the wealthy *Anne Scott, countess of Buccleuch, and in liaison with **Eleanor Needham**, daughter of Sir Robert Needham, with whom he had had several children. Not at all deterred by these encumbrances, he followed Wentworth to her home in Toddington when she and her mother abruptly withdrew from court in 1680, and seems to have succeeded in frustrating a proposed marriage between Wentworth and the earl of Thanet. He lived with her in Toddington for several years, as a plan of the house attests, with rooms set aside for him adjacent to Wentworth's.

Monmouth's position at court at this time was tenuous. He had done well commanding troops as captain of the king's guard in several conflicts and in 1678 had been appointed captain general of all the king's forces in England. Ten years earlier, James (II), duke of York, heir to the throne, had converted to Catholicism and the succession to the throne had become a burning issue, with anti-papal hysteria aroused by rumors of a Catholic plot to seize power. Anthony Ashley Cooper, earl of Shaftsbury, leader of the anti-Catholic Whig Party in Parliament, championed Monmouth for succession. King Charles blocked all attempts to exclude James, and banished Monmouth from the country in 1679. Monmouth defied his father, built up a following and, in 1682 and 1683, was involved in a failed Whig conspiracy against Charles and James known as the Rye House Plot. He fled to Toddington, Wentworth's home, when the plot was discovered, and although he was pardoned, he was again banished from court. He took refuge in the Netherlands where Wentworth followed him. She was received at The Hague by Prince William of Orange as Monmouth's mistress.

Wentworth was one of Monmouth's chief financial supporters. In 1684, she briefly returned to England, probably to raise money for him, and he visited her when he secretly came into England in an attempt to gather followers. Back in Holland, William encouraged Monmouth to join the imperial forces in Hungary in a war against the Turks, but Wentworth wanted him to be king, and to that end placed all her resources, including her rents, her diamonds, and her credit, at his disposal. In 1685, after the death of Charles and the accession of James, Monmouth landed in Lyme Regis, Dorset, with 82 followers in an attempt to start a rebellion among the gentry and be declared king. However, he was unable to rally enough forces and was defeated and captured. On his arrest, a volume was found in his possession containing verses about the bowers of Toddington. On the scaffold several days later, Monmouth maintained that his connection with Lady Wentworth was blameless in the eyes of God, that she had reclaimed him from a licentious life, and that he remained faithful to her, claiming her to be "a lady of virtue and honour, a very virtuous and godly woman." One of his last acts before he was beheaded was to request one of the attendants to convey a memorial to her.

Wentworth remained in Holland until the end of the year, when she returned to England.

She died in April of the following year, and her mother raised an elaborate monument to her. Another memorial left behind, touching in its affectionate simplicity, was her name, which could be traced for many years, carved by Monmouth on a stately oak next to the mansion at Toddington.

Malinda Mayer,
writer and editor,
Falmouth, Massachusetts

Wentworth, Margaret (d. 1550)

English aristocrat. Name variations: Margaret Seymour; Marjory Wentworth. Died in 1550; daughter of Henry Wentworth; descendant of Edward III; married Sir John Seymour (a courtier), before 1500; children: John Seymour (d. 1510); Edward Seymour (who married ***Anne Stanhope**); *John Seymour (d. 1520); Thomas Seymour (c. 1506–1549, who married* ***Catherine Parr**); ***Jane Seymour** *(c. 1509–1537, who married Henry VIII); Henry Seymour; Anthony Seymour (d. 1520);* **Elizabeth Seymour** *(d. 1563);* **Marjory Seymour** *(d. 1520);* **Dorothy Seymour**.

Wenzel, Hanni (1951—)

Champion skier from Liechtenstein. Born on December 14, 1956, in Germany; grew up in Liechtenstein.

Won 32 World Cup titles, including giant slalom (1974, 1980), overall (1978, 1980), slalom (1978), combined (tied with Annemarie Proell-Moser in 1979, 1980, 1983); won four Olympic medals: bronze in slalom (1976), silver in downhill, gold in slalom, gold in giant slalom (1980).

Although she was born in 1951 in Germany, Hanni Wenzel and her brother Andreas grew up in Liechtenstein, one of Europe's smallest countries. Wenzel won the World slalom championship at St. Moritz in 1974. Two years later, she won a bronze medal in slalom at the Innsbruck Olympics. In 1978, she won the World championship. At the 1980 Lake Placid Winter Olympics, Wenzel and her brother won four medals for their tiny nation: Andreas won a silver in the men's giant slalom, while Hanni won gold medals in the giant slalom and slalom, and a silver in the downhill behind ***Annemarie Proell-Moser**. Wenzel went on to make 1980 her best year, winning the slalom, giant slalom, and combined in the World championships. Injury kept her off the slopes in 1982, but she was second to ***Tamara McKinney** in the 1983 World championships. She was not allowed to compete in the 1984 Olympics because she had signed a commercial contract, and guidelines about amateur status were much stricter then than they are currently. **Erika Hess** of Switzerland nudged Wenzel out of a 1984 World Cup overall title. At the end of that year, she retired with 32 World Cup titles.

SOURCES:

Markel, Robert, Nancy Brooks, and Susan Markel. *For the Record: Women in Sports.* NY: World Almanac, 1985.

Woolum, Janet. *Outstanding Women Athletes.* Phoenix, AZ: The Oryx Press, 1992.

Karin Loewen Haag,
Athens, Georgia

Werbezirk, Gisela (1875–1956)

Austrian actress and cabaret performer. Name variations: Giselle Werbesik. Born in Pressburg (Poszonyi), Hungary (now Bratislava, Slovakia), on April 8, 1875; died in Hollywood, California, on April 16, 1956; married Hans Piffl; children: son, Heinrich.

A Viennese superstar of stage and screen for several decades before 1938, Gisela Werbezirk was an unattractive woman with an extraordinary stage presence and inborn sense of dramatic timing. Born in 1875 into a Jewish family in Bratislava (then called Pressburg or Pozsonyi), she moved to nearby Vienna to try her luck on the stage. Werbezirk quickly became a star, with her mastery of the nuances of language earning her praise from the writer Oskar Maurus Fontana who proclaimed: "Werbezirk belongs to Vienna. She needs the climate of this city, its glory and sufferings, its people and its language."

Werbezirk's reputation in Vienna was based on her ability to play the roles of ordinary women whose lives, often tragic and poverty stricken, tested them to the utmost, but who nevertheless found the strength to survive and indeed prevail. For decades, the Viennese public loved her and looked forward to both new roles and those she had made her own. With the looming threat to Vienna from Hitler's Germany, Werbezirk emigrated to the United States in 1938, changing her stage name to Giselle Werbesik. She acted in a number of Hollywood films, including *****Anna Seghers**' *The Seventh Cross.*

SOURCES:

Ahrensfeldt, Fritz. "Die Werbezirk," in *Neue Freie Presse* [Vienna]. July 12, 1925.

Dachs, Robert, Walter Öhlinger and Adelbert Schusser, eds. *Sag beim Abschied . . . Wiener Publikumslieblinge in Bold & Ton. 158. Aussetellung des Historischen Museums der Stadt Wien in Zusammenarbeit mit dem Jüdischen Museum der Stadt Wien, 23. Jänner bis 22. März 1992.* Vienna: Eigenverlag der Museen der Stadt Wien, 1992.

"Gisela Werbezirk. Von akademischem Maler Robert Fuchs," in *Neue Freie Presse* [Vienna]. September 24, 1937.

Horak, Jan-Christopher. "The Other Germany in Zinnemann's *The Seventh Cross* (1944)," in Eric Rentschler, ed. *German Film & Literature.* NY: Methuen, 1986, pp. 117–131.

"Jewish Club of 1933: Cyclus der Künstlerabende," in *Aufbau* [New York]. Vol. 8, no. 2. January 9, 1942, p. 15.

Salten, Felix. "Die Frau Werbezirk," in *Neue Freie Presse* [Vienna]. July 1, 1923.

Torberg, Friedrich. "Die Werbezirk ist tot," in *Neuer Kurier* [Vienna]. April 23, 1956, p. 5.

"Werbezirk, Gisela," in Frithjof Trapp, *et al.,* eds., *Handbuch des deutschsprachigen Exiltheaters 1933–1945,* Vol. 2: *Biographisches Lexikon der Theaterkünstler.* Munich: K.G. Saur, 1999, Part 2, pp. 1012–1013.

Wicclair, Walter. *Von Kreuzburg bis Hollywood.* Berlin: Henschelverlag, 1975.

John Haag,
Associate Professor of History,
University of Georgia, Athens, Georgia

Gisela Werbezirk

Werburga (d. 700?)

Saint and abbess of Sheppey and Ely. Name variations: Werburga of Ely; Werburh. Died around 700; daughter of Wulfhere, king of Mercia (r. 657–675), and *Ermenilda (d. about 700, who was also abbess of Sheppey and Ely).

Werfel, Alma (1879–1964).

See Mahler, Alma.

Werlein, Elizabeth Thomas
(1883–1946)

American socialite who was largely responsible for the preservation of the French Quarter in New Orleans, Louisiana. Born Elizabeth Thomas in Bay City, Michigan, on January 28, 1883; died at her home in New Orleans, Louisiana, on April 24, 1946; elder of two children and only daughter of Henry Thomas (a dynamite manufacturer) and his first wife, Marie Louise Felton Smith; attended public schools in Bay City, Liggett School in Detroit, the Detroit Conservatory of Music, and Miss White's School in Paris, France; married Philip Werlein III (a music publisher and instrument dealer), on August 4, 1908 (died February 1917); children: Betty, Lorraine, Evelyn, and Philip.

Considered a professional singing career; was one of the first women to fly in a plane; taught sewing classes for underprivileged girls; was on the board of New Orleans Philharmonic Society; engaged in war work during World War I; founded and directed the New Orleans Red Cross canteen (1919); became the first president of Louisiana League of Women Voters (1920); assisted Motion Picture Producers and Distributors Association in forestalling legislative censorship (1924–30); supported cultural organizations in New Orleans' French Quarter; sparked interest in restoration of French Quarter mansions (1920s); organized and became first president of Vieux Carré Property Owners Association (1930); instrumental in preservation of Vieux Carré; made honorary member of American Institute of Architects (1942).

Elizabeth Werlein was born in 1883 and raised in Michigan, the daughter of a dynamite manufacturer and his first wife. She attended public schools in her hometown of Bay City as well as the Liggett School in Detroit. Voice lessons at the latter institution and at the Detroit Conservatory of Music made her a promising candidate for a singing career, so she traveled to Paris in 1903 for further training at Miss White's School.

Although two of her teachers were Antonio Baldelli and noted Wagnerian tenor Jean de Reszke, Elizabeth was far too active socially to apply herself to a serious study of voice. The beautiful socialite hunted big game in Africa and made the acquaintance of distinguished European royalty such as Empress *Eugénie, widow of Napoleon III, Emperor Franz Joseph in Vienna, and the family of her fiancé, a Russian prince, in St. Petersburg. After the engagement was broken off, Elizabeth became a member of fashionable society in England, applying her singing skills in a private concert in the Wagnerian role of Brünnhilde and becoming engaged to a new beau, Viscount Charles Yorke Royston. She shared an enthusiasm for ballooning with her new love, and traveled to Belgium in a balloon in 1908, wearing an outfit designed especially for the occasion by Worth of Paris. She was also one of the first women to ride as a passenger in an airplane.

Elizabeth's short visit to America in 1908 became permanent when she met music publisher Philip Werlein III at a party in Louisiana. The pair quickly fell in love and married that year in Elizabeth's hometown of Bay City, but they settled in the city in which Philip was highly active in community and political affairs: New Orleans. In spite of the high-flying nature of her single life, after her marriage Elizabeth Werlein quickly settled down to become fully involved in the civic and social life of New Orleans. She opened and maintained sewing classes for underprivileged girls at Kingsley House, the settlement house managed by **Eleanor McMain**, and applied her own music background to her duties as secretary-treasurer and board member of the New Orleans Philharmonic Society. As such, she was host to many famed artists in the music world, most notably *Nellie Melba** who recovered from a stage accident at the Werlein home.

The death of her husband in the influenza pandemic of 1917 did not slow down Werlein's energetic community work, although she was also raising their four children. Her efforts during World War I included leadership of the Woman's Committee of the New Orleans Liberty Loan drives, the Woman's Division of the Council of National Defense for New Orleans, and the "Landing Fields in Louisiana" Committee. After the war, she threw herself into a variety of volunteer organizations such as the New Orleans Red Cross canteen, which she founded in 1919, and the state League of Women Voters, being elected as its first president in 1920. She later became president of both the Orleans Club and the Quarante Club, and also lent her assistance in the restoration of the paintings at the Louisiana State Museum. In the midst of all her volunteer work, Werlein had one paid position as the public relations director for a chain of movie theaters from 1924 to 1930. As such, she was responsible for the promotion of the Motion Picture Producers and Distributors Association's efforts at self-censorship as a way of forestalling any legislated censorship of the industry.

Werlein expended considerable energy on these projects, but the cause that was most important to her was the preservation of the Vieux Carré, otherwise known as the old French Quarter of New Orleans. As a resident of the district, she vigorously supported its cultural organizations, such as Le Petit Salon, Le Petit Théâtre du Vieux Carré, and Le Quartier Club, and had even published a booklet of photographs, *The Wrought Iron Railings of Le Vieux Carré*, in 1910. Her discovery that some of the railings had been removed even before the book was published indicated to Werlein the necessity of preserving the Quarter's charm. She was particularly sensitive to the decay of the old French and Spanish buildings, and in the 1920s she inspired other business and civic leaders to begin restoring some of the mansions.

Werlein experienced early setbacks in her crusade to preserve the Quarter, particularly as the end of Prohibition brought a flood of nightclubs, bars, and brothels to the area. Rather than give up hope, she fought back by founding the Vieux Carré Property Owners Association to campaign for the enactment and enforcement of zoning laws and strict building codes. The association initially had little public support, but Werlein expertly deflected criticism and gradually won over both the public and government officials. It was largely due to her efforts that the French Quarter came to be recognized as a valuable asset to the national heritage, and her influence was such that any changes to the Vieux Carré had to meet with her approval or be challenged in a court of law. In 1942, the American Institute of Architects made her an honorary member in recognition of her preservation efforts.

Werlein died of cancer in 1946 and was buried in New Orleans. At her death, the *New Orleans Times-Picayune* wrote: "The vigor of her leadership and the breadth of her logic were indispensable in the movement to retain the distinctive architectural character of the Vieux Carré."

SOURCES:

James, Edward T., ed. *Notable American Women, 1607–1950*. Cambridge, MA: The Belknap Press of Harvard University, 1971.

Malinda Mayer,
writer and editor,
Falmouth, Massachusetts

Werner, Ilse (1918—)

German actress who personified the ideal "Aryan girl" in Third Reich propaganda films during World War II. Born on July 11, 1918, in Batavia (later Jakarta), Java, Indonesia; daughter of O.E.G. Still (a Dutch exporter) and Lilly Werner (a German national); attended school in Frankfurt am Main, Germany, from age ten; studied with Max Reinhardt at Vienna's Theater-Akademie, 1936 and 1937; married John de Forest (an American journalist), in 1948 (divorced 1953); married Josef Niessen (an orchestra conductor), in 1954 (divorced).

Made stage debut in Max Dauthendey's Glück *(1937); invited to Berlin; achieved popularity with film* Wunschkonzert *(1940); published memoirs (1941); moved to California with husband (1948); returned to Germany (1953); had hit song with "Baciare" throughout Europe (1960); starred in television series "Eine Frau mit Pfiff" (1967); appeared as Anna in German version of* The King and I *(1970); toured Germany and Switzerland in play directed by Marie Becker (1973); worked on television as moderator and host (1970s); published second volume of memoirs (1981).*

Ilse Werner was born in 1918 in Java, Indonesia, the daughter of a Dutch exporter and his German wife. She returned to her mother's hometown of Frankfurt am Main in Germany at age ten and attended a local school prior to enrolling in Max Reinhardt's Theater-Akademie in Vienna. Her two years of study there concluded with her stage debut in *Glück* (Happiness) with the Josefstädter Bühne in Vienna in 1937. Although she was less than 20 years old, her performance so impressed Nazi officials that she was immediately called to Berlin to personify the ideal Aryan German girl in propaganda films. She made *Die unruhigen Mädchen* (The Restless Girls) in 1938, but it was *Wunschkonzert* (Request Concert), released in 1940, that brought her fame as the faithful German heroine. Werner portrayed a woman who is waiting for the return of a childhood friend and her true love from the war, both of whom are in love with her; the film was intended to encourage German women with loved ones fighting in the war.

The following year Werner starred in *Die schwedische Nachtigall* (The Swedish Nightingale), loosely based on the life of *Jenny Lind. This time her two suitors are writer Hans Christian Andersen and a count, both of whom she rejects in order to pursue her singing career, thereby demonstrating the supremacy of the eternal qualities of art over the temporal nature of love. Werner had the chance to show off her considerable whistling and singing talents in the 1942 movie *Wir machen Musik* (We Make Music), and the following year she starred in *Münchhausen* (The Adventures of Baron Münchhausen), which proved highly popular. Werner balanced her film career with appearances in theater, cabaret, and radio, in addition to her bestselling recordings of modern German songs.

After the war, Werner's marriage to an American journalist in 1948 took her to California, although she continued making German films, such as *Die gestörte Hochzeitsnacht* (The Troubled Wedding Night), in her homeland. Werner's permanent return to Germany following her divorce in 1953 also brought a change in the direction of her career, as she turned to the emerging medium of television. She frequently appeared as a celebrity guest on a variety of German programs and showcased her whistling abilities as the star of her own show "Eine Frau mit Pfiff" (A Woman with a Whistle) in 1967. She also continued to record music, with her song "Baciare" (To Kiss) making its mark on Europe in 1960. Her second husband Josef Niessen was the conductor of the dance orchestra of the Bayerische Rundfunk, the Bavarian Radio network.

Throughout the 1970s, Werner worked as a moderator and hosted a Cologne-based talk show in 1982. As the 1980s came to a close, she appeared in two television series, "Rivalen der Rennbahn" (Rivals of the Racetrack) and "Forstinspektor Buchholz." Her television appearances became more infrequent as the century came to a close, with roles in "Die Hallo-Sisters" in 1991 and "Alles wegen Robert De Niro" in 1996.

In 1970, Werner returned to the stage in the realization of her long-held dream to act in a Broadway musical when she portrayed *Anna Leonowens in the German version of *The King and I*. Three years later, she went on tour in Germany and Switzerland in a play directed by **Marie Becker**. Werner published her memoirs 40 years apart; the first volume, *Ich über mich* (I on Myself), appeared in 1941; the second, *So wird's nie wieder sein* (It Will Never Again be the Same), was published in 1981.

SOURCES:
Romani, Cinzia. *Tainted Goddesses: Female Film Stars of the Third Reich*. NY: Sarpedon, 1992.

Malinda Mayer,
writer and editor,
Falmouth, Massachusetts

Werner, Ruth (1907–2000).

See Kuczinski, Ruth.

Wertmüller, Lina (1928—)

Award-winning Italian filmmaker and writer whose stylish and often controversial films made her one of the first women directors to achieve international acclaim. Name variations: Lina Wertmuller; (pseudonyms) Nathan Wich, George H. Brown. Pronunciation: VERT-mew-ler. Born Arcangela Felice Assunta Wertmüller von Elgg Español von Brauchich on August 14, 1928, in Rome, Italy; daughter of Frederico Wertmüller (a lawyer) and Maria (Santamaria) Wertmüller; attended 15 private Catholic schools; received teacher's certification, Academy of Theater, Rome, 1951; married Enrico Job (an art director), in 1968; no children.

Awards: Silver Sail at the Locarno Film Festival, Switzerland, for The Lizards *(1963); Nino Manfredi received the Silver Ribbon Award for acting in Italy for Wertmüller's* Let's Talk About Men *(1965); Best Director Award at the Cannes Film Festival for* The Seduction of Mimi *(1972); Giancarlo Giannini received the Best Actor Award at Cannes for Wertmüller's* Love and Anarchy *(1973);* Seven Beauties *received four American Academy Award nominations: Best Foreign Film, Giancarlo Giannini for Best Actor, and Wertmüller for Best Director and Best Screenplay (1976).*

Did various work in the theater: produced contemporary plays, toured with a puppet company, wrote plays and scripts for television, acted, designed sets, and worked as a stage manager and publicist (1951–62); worked as assistant director for Federico Fellini for film 8½ (1962); wrote, directed and produced for the cinema, theater, television and radio.

Films—directed: The Lizards *(1963);* "Gian Burrasca's Diary" *(TV, 1965);* Let's Talk About Men *(1965);* "Rita the Mosquito" *(TV, 1966);* "Don't Sting the Mosquito" *(TV, 1967);* *Belle Starr *(1968);* The Seduction of Mimi *(1972);* Love and Anarchy *(1973);* All Screwed Up *(1974);* Seven Beauties *(1975);* Swept Away . . . by An Unusual Destiny in the Blue Sea of August *(1975);* The End of the World in Our Usual Bed in a Night Full of Rain *(1977);* Blood Feud *(Revenge, 1978);* "E Una Domenica Sera Di Novembre" *(TV, 1981);* A Joke of Destiny, Lying in Wait Around the Corner Like a Robber *(1983);* A Jealous Man *(1984);* Complicated Intrigue of Back Alleys and Crimes *(1985);* A Summer Night *(1986);* To Save Nine *(1989);* Saturday, Sunday and Monday *(1990);* Ciao Professore *(1992).*

Scriptwriter: Violent City *(1970);* Brother Sun, Sister Moon *(directed by Franco Zeffirelli, 1972); and for most films she directed.*

Plays: Love and Magic in Mama's Kitchen; Two and Two are No Longer Four *(produced in 1968, directed by Franco Zeffirelli).*

Writings: The Screenplays of Lina Wertmüller; Avrei Voluto Uno Zio Esibizionista *(autobiography).*

${\mathscr{L}}$ina
${\mathscr{W}}$ertmüller

In the family of the Italian moviemaker with the Germanic name, tradition has it that Lina Wertmüller's great-great-grandfather left his native Zurich, Switzerland, for Naples after killing a man in a duel over a woman. True or not, it is a good tale to explain the lineage of a spectacu-

lar storyteller, who also claims to have inherited the same ancestor's fiery temperament. Wertmüller was born Arcangela Felice Assunta Wertmüller von Elgg Español von Brauchich in Rome, on August 14, 1928, while Italy was under the fascist rule of Benito Mussolini. While the dictator known as Il Duce had brought some economic improvements to his floundering country, he headed a repressive government that allowed its people only one political party, and in the 1930s negotiated a pact with Hitler's Germany which drew his country into World War II against the European allies.

Lina's father Frederico Wertmüller, a lawyer, was considered something of a dictator within his own family. He ruled over the household and his wife **Maria Santamaria Wertmüller** with an iron hand. While Frederico's political sympathies were to some extent on the side of Il Duce, the family also had many friends who were against the Mussolini regime, and the Wertmüllers themselves sheltered a family of Jews from the Holocaust, when all European Jews were at risk of being sent to concentration camps. Lina, who grew up with one older brother Enrico (who would serve later as the publicist for her films), remembers her childhood as filled with arguments, especially between herself and her father. Maria Wertmüller, after being submissive for most of her life, would finally rebel against Frederico and divorce him, ending a marriage of 50 years.

𝒲hat I hope to express in my films is my great faith in the possibility of man becoming human.

—Lina Wertmüller

As a girl, Lina's rebelliousness extended to her strict Catholic schools. In fact, her fascination with Hollywood began as she snuck out of school to see movies at the Regina Cinema; she would eventually be expelled from 15 schools. After World War II, she enrolled in law school to please her father, who wanted her to be a lawyer like himself. At the same time, she and her friend **Flora Carabella** (**Mastroianni**) began studying at the Academy of Theater, and it was soon evident that law had lost and drama school won out. She graduated from the Academy of Theater in 1951 and spent the next ten years working in theater and television. For awhile, she and friends had an experimental theater group which eventually failed, partly because they charged no admission for performances. Wertmüller then toured Europe with the puppet troupe of **Maria Signorelli**, alarming audiences with stories by Franz Kafka instead of the usual fairy tales.

In 1961, through her friend Carabella who had married the Italian movie actor Marcello Mastroianni, Wertmüller met the illustrious director Federico Fellini; he hired her as an assistant director on his groundbreaking film *8½*. Not long after its completion, Wertmüller was able, with the support of Fellini and help from some of his crew, to get backing to direct a script she had written called *The Lizards*. Released in 1963, the film centered around life in a small Italian town and three young boys whose chief interests are girls and being in the sun. Shown at the Locarno Film Festival in Switzerland that year, the movie won a Silver Sail Award.

Wertmüller next directed a 1965 television musical, "Gian Burrasca's Diary," for which she also wrote the script. Her second film, *Let's Talk About Men*, about the ways men treat women, garnered a Silver Ribbon, the Italian equivalent of the Academy Award for its male lead, Nino Manfredi. By 1966, Wertmüller's work was well regarded, but she could not get financial backing for another film, so she returned to television to make "Rita the Mosquito" under the name George H. Brown. This was the first time she directed the actor Giancarlo Giannini, whose name was to become virtually synonymous with her films. In 1967, when Wertmüller directed "Don't Sting the Mosquito," the sequel to "Rita," its crew included Franco Fraticelli as film editor and Enrico Job as art director. The following year, Wertmüller married Job, and both he and Fraticelli have worked on Wertmüller's productions ever since. It is Giancarlo Giannini, however, whom Job credits with the blossoming of Wertmüller's career. Giannini recommended her play *Two and Two are No Longer Four* to Franco Zeffirelli, who directed the work with Giannini as the star and Job as designer.

In 1971, Wertmüller was able to direct her new film script, *The Seduction of Mimi*. Again starring Giannini, the comedy concerns a man who goes from youthful idealism to resigned conformism. For her work, Wertmüller was named Best Director at the Cannes Film Festival in 1972. The following year, Giannini received the Best Actor award at Cannes for his role in *Love and Anarchy*, Wertmüller's deeply moving work about a young man who tries to assassinate Mussolini. The film earned its director wide acclaim, and won her the respect of critics like Peter Biskind, who wrote that Wertmüller's films "reveal a mature and major talent." Paul Zimmerman wrote in *Newsweek* that *Love and Anarchy* established "Wertmüller as the most exciting woman director on the international scene."

In 1975, *Swept Away . . . by an Unusual Destiny in the Blue Sea of August*, was another smash hit. Released in the U.S. simply as *Swept Away*, the movie is about a rich society woman on a yacht who dominates an ordinary seafarer during a cruise. When the two become stranded on a small island, their roles are reversed. The man maintains power and control as long as the woman is dependent on him for survival, but when they are returned to civilization, the romance ends as they revert to their previous lives.

By 1975, Wertmüller had achieved both popular and critical success, although not without controversy. Objections arose over a number of her scenes, including the physical abuse inflicted on the woman in *Swept Away*, and the treatment of an extremely heavy-set woman as grotesque in *The Seduction of Mimi*. To capitalize on the publicity, a 1973 Wertmüller production, *All Screwed Up*, was released in the U.S. to mixed reviews, while the film world awaited her much-touted new film, *Seven Beauties*. About an Italian man being held in a German concentration camp who will do anything to survive, including seduce the woman who is in charge, *Seven Beauties* opened in 1975 to critical raves and a firestorm of accusations about its insensitivity. Critic John Simon called the work "an upward leap in seven-league boots that propels her into the highest regions of cinematic art, into the company of the major directors," but *Pauline Kael found it to be "a grotesque vaudeville show."

At the pinnacle of her popular success, Wertmüller was awarded a contract with Warner Bros. to make four films. Going for the long titles she likes, the director made *The End of the World in Our Usual Bed in a Night Full of Rain*, about the marital relationship between an Italian journalist, again played by Giannini, and an American photographer, played by **Candice Bergen**. The film was handsome but talky and not well received; soon afterward the contract was canceled.

When Wertmüller directs, she immerses herself totally in the production. While cast and crew are on the set, they must forget their outside lives. The total dedication makes the atmosphere electric with energy and tension. Wearing her signature white-frame glasses, her red-brown hair styled short, and laden with necklaces, bracelets, and rings, Lina Wertmüller has always demonstrated her own individual style. Her husband Enrico oversees the production design on all her films, in charge of the visual elements, while the two confer on every other aspect of the business end. Job has worked as an artist, producing paintings, sculpture, photography, poetry, and performance art, as well as a stage and set designer. Wertmüller is small in stature, and Job is over six feet tall; she is energetic and he more contained. Together they provide a good balance for each other. They live with Lina's mother in a "penthouse apartment jumbled with ill-assorted artifacts in Rome."

In the late 1970s, Wertmüller continued to write and direct, but failed to draw the attention she had with her earlier works. While most of her stories have been provocative combinations of comedy and tragedy that managed to touch effectively on society, politics, materialism, and sex, their frequent ambiguity and openness to interpretation has not made them lastingly popular with American audiences. Beginning with *Blood Feud (Revenge)* in 1979 and *A Joke of Destiny, Lying in Wait Around the Corner Like a Robber* in 1983, she slipped out of favor with most filmgoers and critics in the United States, although she continued to create productions in Italy for various media. In 1992, she began to win back her audiences with *Ciao, Professore* (originally titled *Me, Let's Hope I Make It*), released in the U.S. in 1994 to favorable reviews. A departure from her political-sexual films of the past, *Ciao, Professore* concerns a teacher and his reluctant students. "Lina's uncanny savvy in picking the right faces and figures for each character builds instant audience rapport," wrote John Simon, who further observed that the film "returns Miss Wertmüller to the heights she achieved with her early movies." Wertmüller remains, meanwhile, one of the first women to build an international reputation as an artist in film, and the creator of a number of the medium's truly lasting works.

SOURCES:
Contemporary Authors. Vols. 97–100. Detroit, MI: Gale Research, 1981.
Contemporary Literary Criticism. Vol. 16. Detroit, MI: Gale Research, 1981.
Current Biography Yearbook, 1976. NY: H.W. Wilson, 1977.
Ferlita, Ernest, and John R. May. *The Parables of Lina Wertmüller.* NY: Paulist Press, 1977.
Film Index International. British Film Institute, 1994.
Gerard, Lillian. "The Ascendance of Lina Wertmüller," in *American Film.* Vol. 1, no. 7. May 1976, pp. 20–27.
Michalczyk, John J. *The Italian Political Filmmakers.* Rutherford, NJ: Fairleigh Dickinson University Press, 1986.

SUGGESTED READING:
Wakeman, John. *World Film Directors.* NY: H.W. Wilson, 1988.

Evelyn Bender, Ed.D.,
librarian, Philadelphia School District, Pennsylvania

Wesley, Cynthia (d. 1963).

See Davis, Angela for sidebar.

Wesley, Emilia (1692–1771)

Sister of John and Charles Wesley. Name variations: Emily. Born in South Ormsby, England, in 1692; died in London in 1771; third child of Samuel Wesley (a curate) and Susanna Wesley (1669–1742); married Robert Harper (a chemist).

Born in South Ormsby, England, in 1692, Emilia Wesley was the third child of Samuel Wesley, a curate, and *Susanna Wesley. As the eldest girl, she was a second mother to the younger Wesleys, including John and Charles, later the founders of Methodism. She was 17 when the fire burned down their house at Epworth. Because of family finances, she was sent to Lincoln to teach in a private boarding school; she later opened her own school in the Lincolnshire township of Gainsborough. At 43, at her brother John's urging, Emilia married an Epworth apothecary by the name of Robert Harper. Sadly, the marriage was a disaster. The spendthrift Harper quickly ran through Emilia's hard-earned savings, then deserted her and their baby for the United States. After her baby's death in 1740, Emilia moved to London to live with John Wesley in Moorfields. She died there at age 79.

SOURCES:
Appleyard, Simon. "The Family World of the Wesleys," in *This England*. Winter 1984.

Wesley, Martha (1706–1791)

Sister of John and Charles Wesley. Name variations: Patty. Born in Epworth, England, in 1706; died in City Road, London, in 1791; 17th child of Samuel Wesley (a curate) and Susanna Wesley (1669–1742); married Reverend Westley Hall, in 1735; children: out of ten confinements only one child survived, a boy who died of smallpox at age 14.

Born in Epworth, England, in 1706, Martha Wesley was the 17th child of Samuel and *Susanna Wesley. A solemn, level-headed girl known as Patty, Martha was exceptionally close to her brother John and listened carefully to her mother's teachings. When young, she lived in London with an uncle and while there married a curate, Westley Hall, in 1735. Though Martha was pregnant ten times, only one of her children survived infancy; the boy would eventually die of smallpox at age 14. As was the case with many of her sisters, hers was a dismal marriage. Her constantly straying husband would eventually desert her, fleeing with a mistress to the West Indies. Martha remained calm and turned her attention to the Methodism of her brothers, John and Charles, while enjoying the friendship of Dr. Samuel Johnson and other literary personages in 18th-century London. Martha outlived her beloved brother

John by four months and was buried in the same vault behind the City Road chapel.

SOURCES:
Appleyard, Simon. "The Family World of the Wesleys," in *This England*. Winter 1984.

Wesley, Mehetabel (1697–1750)

Sister of John and Charles Wesley. Name variations: Hetty. Born in Epworth, England, in 1697; died in London in 1750; eighth child of Samuel and Susanna Wesley; married William Wright (a plumber), in 1725.

Born in Epworth, England, in 1697, Mehetable Wesley was the eighth child of Samuel Wesley, a curate, and *Susanna Wesley. Since Hetty was the most intellectually gifted child, her father took a personal interest in her education. She had a number of suitors, but the authoritarian Samuel found them all wanting and sent her to be a governess in the home of a wealthy landowner in Kelstern village near Louth, Lincolnshire. While there, she fell in love with a lawyer named William Atkins, and once more begged her father for permission to marry. Declaring the man "unprincipled," Samuel again said no. In May 1725, the couple ran away to London to elope, "but the honeymoon began a day too soon," writes Simon Appleyard. After promising to marry Hetty following one night of bliss, Atkins backed out, leaving her a "ruined" woman. Hetty Wesley returned home to the scorn of the town and her father's undying fury. In October, he married her off to the next suitor, a traveling plumber named William Wright. A baby was born four months later, but died before the year was out. The once-promising Hetty, who was now tied to an illiterate and hard-drinking man, was determined to be a good wife. She had three more children, all of whom died young. According to Hetty, the deaths were caused by the lead fumes from her husband's workshop. For the rest of his life, her father forbade the entire family to have any contact with her. When Hetty died at age 53, only Charles Wesley attended the funeral.

SOURCES:
Appleyard, Simon. "The Family World of the Wesleys," in *This England*. Winter 1984.

Wesley, Susanna (1669–1742)

English mother of John and Charles Wesley whose "kitchen prayers" were thought to be the seed of the Methodist movement. Born Susanna Annesley in London, England, in 1669; died at Bunhill, London, in 1742; daughter of Dr. Annesley (a minister); married

Samuel Wesley (a London curate), in 1689 (died 1735); children: of 19 confinements only 10 survived, including daughters *Emilia Wesley (1692–1771); Susanna Wesley (1695–1764); Maria Wesley (1696–1734); *Mehetabel Wesley (1697–1750); Anne Wesley (b. 1702); *Martha Wesley (1706–1791); Kezziah Wesley (1709–1741); sons Samuel Wesley, Jr. (b. 1690); John Wesley (b. 1703, founder of Methodism); Charles Wesley (b. 1708, co-founder of Methodism and writer of 6,500 hymns, including "Hark! The Herald-Angels Sing").

Born in London in 1669, Susanna Wesley was the youngest child of Dr. Annesley, a prominent dissenting minister who gave every attention to her education. She learned Greek, Latin, French, logic and metaphysics and was deeply interested in the religious discussions of the day. At age 19, she met and married Samuel Wesley, a curate in London, who was earning a meager income of £30 a year. Though Samuel had also come from a strong Non-Conformist family, the couple would later decide to renounce dissent and abide by the Church of England.

In the summer of 1690, the Wesleys moved to the rural parish of South Ormsby in Lincolnshire; after seven years, they relocated to the larger parish of Epworth, where Samuel began to earn £200 per annum. During the first 20 years of this marriage which extended over a period of 46 years, Susanna Wesley had 19 children; the 15th was John Wesley (b. June 1703), destined to be the most famous preacher of his time; the 18th was Charles Wesley (b. 1705), his partner. Of the 19, only 10 survived infancy.

The Wesleys were "not the strait-laced martinets of high principle and narrow virtue that some chroniclers have tried to portray," wrote Simon Appleyard. The hot-tempered Samuel was a staunch Orangeman (a supporter of the usurping William III of Orange, champion of Protestant liberties); the stubborn but calm Susanna was a Jacobite, a supporter of the usurped James II. This led to numerous quarrels, as Susanna would refuse to say "Amen" at the end of any daily prayers that included a plea for the well-being of the king. In 1701, in a fit of pique, Samuel announced, "If we have two kings, we must have two beds," quit the Epworth rectory, and set out for London, leaving Susanna with their then six children. Differences were resolved by 1702 when the horse bearing William of Orange tripped over a molehole, killing the king. Enter Queen *Anne, the family pacifier. Though she was the daughter of James II, she also supported Protestants.

That same year, Samuel was arrested for non-payment of debt (£30) and incarcerated in Lincoln Prison for three months. Four years later, "within a month of what was to prove her last confinement," a fire broke out in the Epworth rectory, wrote Appleyard. Susanna "staggered to safety through the front door while several of her children clambered out of a window to the sanctuary of the garden. A maid brought out the baby." But John was missing; his cries could be heard from an upstairs bedroom. Seconds before the roof fell in, he was snatched out by two neighbors, convincing Susanna that God had spared John for a special purpose. The rectory was destroyed.

Because of the family's constant struggle with poverty, the task of educating the ten children had been left to Susanna, and for six hours a day for 20 years, she continued this work. She believed in forming children's minds by "conquering their will and bringing them to an obedient temper," though she also believed in overlooking small transgressions. "Self-will is the root of all sin and misery," she said. "Whatever checks it promotes their future happiness." Each night of the week was set aside for one child. (The math holds out, for Sunday was set aside for Emilia and Susanna,

Susanna Wesley

known as Sukey, Samuel, Jr., was away at school, and Kezzy was still a baby.)

Her noted son John followed her teachings, her will was his law, her letters through college were his oracles, her life was his example. "I do intend to be more particularly careful of the soul of this child, that Thou hast so mercifully provided for," she wrote in her private diary, "that I may do my endeavor to instil into his mind the principles of Thy true religion and virtue." Though they grew up under her strict and closely guided regimen, none of the Wesley children seem to have resented their mother; in fact, they matured into caring and loving adults.

In 1710, when Samuel journeyed to London to attend a lengthy convocation, he appointed a substitute curate. But Susanna found the young man's sermons so tedious that she began to hold service every Sunday evening in the rectory kitchen for the benefit of her children and servants. Word of mouth spread, others asked permission to come, until Susanna was preaching to around 200 people crammed into and out of the kitchen. Though Samuel protested on his return that it was unseemly for a woman to hold prayers, Susanna continued this practice for years in spite of hearty opposition. Many historians contend that the "kitchen prayers" were the seed of the Methodist movement.

After Samuel died in 1735, Susanna continued her ways until her own death in 1742. At her burial in Bunhill Fields, London, her son John preached one of his most eloquent and impressive sermons. She was the "mother of Methodism in a religious and moral sense," wrote Isaac Taylor, "for, her courage, her submissiveness to authority, the high tone of her mind, its independence and its self-control, the warmth of her devotional feelings, and the practical directions given to them, . . . were visibly repeated in the character and conduct of her son."

It is generally agreed that without the example set by Susanna Wesley, her sons would have not had the impenetrable hides needed for reforming. Wrote Appleyard: "There seems little doubt that without the strong personality and dogged persistence in the pursuit of goodness that so characterized their mother, Susanna, her sons would have been unfitted for the great reforming tasks that lay ahead of them, and the world would have been a poorer place for that alone."

SOURCES:
Appleyard, Simon. "The Family World of the Wesleys," in *This England*. Winter 1984.

SUGGESTED READING:
Stevens, Abel. *The Women of Methodism; Its Three Foundresses, Susanna Wesley, the Countess of Huntingdon, and *Barbara Heck; With Sketches of Their Female Associates and Successors in the Early History of the Denomination*. NY: Carlton & Porter, 1866.

Wessely, Paula (1907–2000)

Austrian actress and celebrated star of stage and film for over a half-century. Born in Fünfhaus, Vienna, Austria, on January 20, 1907; died on May 11, 2000, in Vienna; daughter of a butcher and a former ballerina of the Hofoper (Court Opera); attended Vienna's Theater-Akademie; studied with Max Reinhardt; married Attila Hörbiger (an actor), in 1935; children: Elisabeth, Christiane, and Maresa.

Became famous as a stage actress prior to her first film appearance in Maskerade *(1934); during World War II, made Nazi propaganda films; formed own movie production company (1949); reestablished successful stage career (late 1940s); became member of the ensemble of Burgtheater in Vienna (1953).*

One of the most celebrated actresses in Central Europe for over a half-century and one of the superstars of Vienna's Burgtheater, Paula Wessely achieved acclaim for her freshness and charm, her subtle sense of comedy and pathos, and her ability to convey a comfortable image of a familiar friend to her audience. She gained an interest in acting from her aunt, **Josephine Wessely**, an actress of reputation with the Vienna Burgtheater, and began studying the expressions, gestures, and gaits of the customers who came to her father's butcher shop. She started a more serious study of the acting craft with the Hungarian actress **Valerie Gray** before auditioning for Max Reinhardt's Theater-Akademie in Vienna, one of the most prestigious theater schools in Europe.

Wessely's first professional performance was at the Deutsches Volkstheater in Vienna in 1924, and thereafter she was continually engaged in theaters in Vienna, Prague, and Berlin until 1945. She played a wide variety of roles, in genres from French farce to serious drama, showing unusual vocal range and flexibility. Her close personal and artistic rapport with Reinhardt helped her to broaden her repertoire from flirtatious and superficial characters to a host of classical roles. Her most memorable artistic achievements are considered to be Gretchen in Reinhardt's production of Goethe's *Faust* in Salzburg in 1935 and the title role in George Bernard Shaw's *St. Joan*, translated into German, in Berlin in 1936.

Wessely's success on stage led to a flood of film offers. She rejected these opportunities until the script for *Maskerade* was submitted to her by Willi Forst and Walter Reisch. She found it too appealing to resist since the role so completely suited her Viennese temperament and used the dialect of her hometown. Released in 1934, *Maskerade* was a tremendous success and established her as a leading film actress. In 1935, she was directed by Reisch in *Episode*, another success, and later that year married Attila Hörbiger, an actor who became her frequent co-star.

Wessely's work in *Maskerade* brought her to the attention of Joseph Goebbels, the minister of propaganda under Adolf Hitler's Third Reich. Goebbels saw in the plain Wessely his ideal of the "wholesome" German woman, as opposed to the erotic *Marlene Dietrich (who was vehemently anti-Nazi anyway). Wessely reliably delivered the Aryan image required of her as she starred in a string of melodramatic propaganda films, the most blatant of which was *Heimkehr* (Homecoming) in 1941. This production gave Wessely dubious transatlantic fame when footage from it was included in a number of postwar documentaries on Nazi Germany.

After the war, Wessely was thought of in mythic terms as the grande dame of Austrian film culture. Although she made few films in the postwar period, she revitalized her interrupted stage career, becoming a member of the Burgtheater in Vienna, an honorary member of the Akademie für Musik und Darstellende Kunst of Vienna, and a special member of the Akademie der Künste of Berlin. Among her many awards were the Max-Reinhardt-Ring (1949), the Josef-Kainz-Medaille (1960), and the Goldmedaille der Stadt Wien (1967). Until her death in May 2000, Austro-German audiences continued to hold her in great affection for her down-to-earth persona and exceptional talent.

SOURCES:

Romani, Cinzia. *Tainted Goddesses: Female Film Stars of the Third Reich*. NY: Sarpedon, 1992.

Malinda Mayer,
writer and editor,
Falmouth, Massachusetts

Wessex, countess of.

See Thyra (d. 1018).
See Gytha (fl. 1022–1042).

Wessex, queen of.

See Sexburga (c. 627–673).
See Eadburgh (c. 773–after 802).
See Redburga (fl. 825).
See Osburga (?–c. 855).
See Martel, Judith (c. 844–?).

Paula Wessely

West, Claire (1893–1980)

One of the first costume designers in the American film industry. Born in 1893; died in 1980; graduated from college sometime in the 1910s; studied fashion in Paris.

Selected films: Intolerance *(1916);* The Affairs of Anatol *(1921);* Adam's Rib *(1923);* The Ten Commandments *(1924);* The Merry Widow *(1925).*

In the early days of film, there was no such thing as a studio designer, and stars were expected to dress themselves. In fact, an actress' personal wardrobe was considered to be one of her assets, and if she came into an audition properly dressed for the part, she stood a good chance of being cast. Claire West changed that when she began working for D.W. Griffith, and later Cecil B. De Mille, as the first studio costume designer.

While she was still in high school, West began selling her sketches of clothing designs to women's magazines. She went on to college, and graduated sometime in the 1910s. Traveling to Paris for the purpose of studying a variety of fashion lines, she became one of a group of successful fashion designers. She had the rare good fortune of starting at the top of her chosen profession when her first film project was D.W. Griffith's *Intolerance*, released in 1916. The two-year project required all of her talent and skill to dress the famous scenes of Babylon, and it provided the perfect showcase for West's abilities.

When West went to work for De Mille, he was making expensive, sophisticated films with stars like *Gloria Swanson who expected to have a different lavish outfit for every scene. Foregoing realism in favor of the extravagant costumes which were part of the De Mille formula for success, West worked closely with De Mille and scene designer *Jeanie Macpherson in dressing, on average, three pictures a year for De Mille Studios. She left in 1923 to enter into a contract with the actresses *Norma and *Constance Talmadge as their personal costumer.

SOURCES:

Acker, Ally. *Reel Women*. NY: Continuum, 1991.

Leese, Elizabeth. *Costume Design in the Movies*. NY: Dover, 1991.

Malinda Mayer,
writer and editor,
Falmouth, Massachusetts

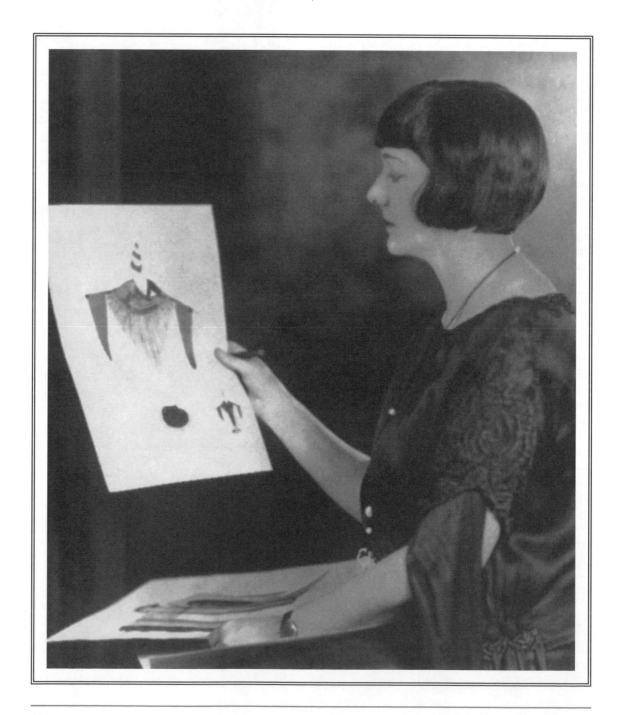

Claire West

West, Dorothy (1907–1998)

Youngest writer of the Harlem Renaissance of the 1920s who went on to develop a literary career spanning eight decades. Name variations: (pseudonyms) Mary Christopher; Jane Isaac. Born Dorothy West on June 2, 1907, in Boston, Massachusetts; died, age 91, on August 16, 1998, in Boston, Massachusetts; daughter of Isaac Christopher West (an entrepreneur) and Rachel Pease (Benson) West; attended public schools in Boston and graduated from Girls' Latin School in 1923; attended Columbia University; never married; no children.

Wrote her first short story at age seven; began publishing stories in the Boston Post *while still in her teens; shared second place award with Zora Neale Hurston in* Opportunity *writing contest (1926); moved to New York with cousin Helene Johnson during the height of the Harlem Renaissance; spent a year in Russia; founded* Challenge *magazine (1934) and* New Challenge *(1937); worked as a welfare investigator and as a writer for the Federal Writers' Project during the Great Depression; published more than two dozen short stories in the New York* Daily News *(1940s–1950s); moved to the island of Martha's Vineyard (mid-1940s), where she wrote a column for the local newspaper; published first novel,* The Living Is Easy *(1948); published a collection of stories and reminiscences,* The Richer, the Poorer, *and her second novel,* The Wedding *(1995).*

Selected works: "The Typewriter," in Opportunity *(Vol. 4, July 1926, pp. 220–222, 233–234); "An Unimportant Man," in* Saturday Evening Quill *(Vol. 1, June 1928, pp. 21–32); "Prologue to a Life," in* Saturday Evening Quill *(Vol. 2, April 1929, pp. 5–10);* The Living Is Easy *(Boston: Houghton, Mifflin, 1948); "Elephant's Dance: A Memoir of Wallace Thurman," in* Black World *(Vol. 20, November 1970, pp. 77–85); "My Mother, Rachel West," in* Invented Lives: Narratives of Black Women 1860–1960 *(ed. by Mary Helen Washington, Garden City, NY: Anchor Press, 1987, pp. 381–383);* The Richer, the Poorer: Stories, Sketches, and Reminiscences *(NY: Doubleday, 1995);* The Wedding *(NY: Doubleday, 1995). Contributed to the* Boston Post, *the New York* Daily News, *and the* Vineyard Gazette.

By the time Dorothy West moved from her family's home in Boston to a room at the YWCA in New York City's Harlem in 1926, the New Negro Movement, also later known as the Harlem Renaissance, was well under way. The 1920s ushered in a decade-long interest in African-American culture and an outpouring of art, music, and writing enjoyed by whites as well as blacks. The young poets Langston Hughes and Countee Cullen and fiction writers Wallace Thurman and Claude McKay were beginning to gain national reputations, and novelists *Zora Neale Hurston, ☙ Jessie Redmon Fauset and *Nella Larsen were hard at work, intent on doing the same. Still in her teens but already a published short-story writer, West became the youngest participant in the Harlem Renaissance. More than six decades later, she would become its oldest living survivor and experience a renaissance of her own.

Dorothy West was born in 1907, the only child of Isaac West, a former slave from Virginia who had moved to Boston and developed a thriving wholesale produce company, and **Rachel Benson West**, who was originally from South Carolina. Rachel apparently married the much older Isaac for the financial security he provided for her and her numerous brothers and sisters and their children.

When she was four, Dorothy was enrolled in the Boston public schools, where working-class students occasionally taunted her with racial epithets. At ten, she started attending the private, upper-class Girls' Latin School. She had begun crafting short stories at age seven and, by fifteen, was publishing fiction in the *Boston Post*, which frequently awarded her cash prizes in its weekly writing contests. When she was 17, she entered her story "The Typewriter" in a contest sponsored by *Opportunity*, the National Urban League's magazine, and won second place, which she shared with the older and more experienced writer Zora Neale Hurston. West traveled to New York City to accept the prize and decided to stay, sharing with her cousin, poet ☙ **Helene Johnson**, first a Harlem-area YWCA room and then Hurston's old apartment. In addition to being published in *Opportunity*, "The Typewriter" was reprinted in *The Best Short Stories of 1926*. That year another of West's stories, "Hannah Byde," appeared in the radical magazine the *Messenger*. While in New York City, she attended classes at Columbia University, studying philosophy and journalism.

Between 1928 and 1930, the *Saturday Evening Quill*, a little magazine produced by a black literary organization called the Boston Quill Club, published more of West's stories, including "An Unimportant Man" and "Prologue to a Life." Around the same time, the *Mary Roberts Rinehart Foundation awarded her a grant to support her creative writing.

In 1927, she landed a small part in the play *Porgy* by DuBose and *Dorothy Heyward

Jessie Redmon Fauset. See *Women of the Harlem Renaissance.*

Helene Johnson. See Women of the Harlem Renaissance.

(which was later adapted by George Gershwin into the opera *Porgy and Bess*) and traveled with the theater group in 1929 for a summer-long engagement in London. Three years later, at the suggestion of journalist Henry Moon, West joined an entourage of about two dozen African-American actors and intellectuals in Russia to shoot a movie exposing American racism, although the project was never completed. Despite this, West stayed a year to work with the film company and to do some writing and teaching. Even though she considered this period the most carefree time of her life, she ultimately rejected Communism, declaring herself too independent to claim a cause, and returned late in 1933 to Boston where her ill mother was coping with the death of West's father.

I remember turning to my father and saying, "I don't belong to you," and turning to my mother and saying, "I don't belong to you either. I belong to myself."

—Dorothy West

Feeling that, at age 25, she had not fulfilled her early promise as a writer and that the Harlem Renaissance had waned without giving young people like herself a chance to be heard, West launched a new little magazine, *Challenge*, in 1934. She published well-known writers, including Hurston, Johnson, Hughes, Cullen, McKay, and Arna Bontemps, as well as a few newcomers, such as Frank Yerby, but she also complained of a lack of good writing from younger authors. The last issue, which appeared in the spring of 1937, acknowledged that Richard Wright and other activists and Communists living in Chicago had criticized the magazine, and she offered them a section of the next issue. Instead, Wright, West, and **Marian Minus** collaborated in New York on a revamped magazine called *New Challenge*, with the first issue published that fall. However, financial hardship, philosophical differences over content, and a threat by radical University of Chicago students to take over the magazine led West to discontinue publication.

Although romantically linked to Langston Hughes, Claude McKay, Countee Cullen, Henry Moon and others, West never married or had children. (This latter caused her great sorrow.) After her father's death during the worst of the Great Depression, she had to support herself, but her experience with *Challenge* had shown her that publishing was not a profitable endeavor. To earn her living, West became a welfare worker in Harlem, a job she held for a year and a half before moving on to the Federal Writers

Project (FWP), a Depression-era program that hired writers for various assignments. "Mammy," a story based on her welfare work experience, appeared in *Opportunity* in October 1940; a memoir she wrote of Wallace Thurman for the FWP would appear as "Elephant's Dance" in *Black World* in 1970. In the 1940s, she launched a two-decade-long stint of regular short-story writing for the New York *Daily News*. Her stories typically are brief and simply plotted, often with universal themes that make race irrelevant. Perhaps because both her parents, although they were able to raise West as a proper Bostonian, had come from Southern poverty, the stories depict characters from all strata of society. Despite her publishing success, West also received numerous rejections from magazines that either printed only a small quota of stories about blacks or did not approve of her stories when they were not overtly about blacks. Still, they praised the author's storytelling and writing abilities. "I always said that my rejection letters read like acceptances until the end," West told interviewer **Deborah E. McDowell**.

West moved to the island of Martha's Vineyard, where her family had spent many happy summers, in the mid-1940s. In 1948, her semi-autobiographical novel, *The Living Is Easy*, was published. It is the story of a domineering woman, Cleo Judson, who ultimately destroys her marriage in an effort to protect and provide for her extended family. The inspiration for the Cleo character seems to have come from West's own mother Rachel, who brought several of her relatives from South Carolina to live with the Wests in their four-story house in Boston and who, as "chief mother," ran the household with an iron will tempered by a tendency to tell funny stories. Literary critic Robert Bone called the work "bitingly ironic" in his book *The Negro Novel in America* (1958), and **Florence Codman**, in her *Commonweal* review, considered the protagonist "a wholly plausible, tantalizing creature." Only years after the book's publication would West recognize Cleo as a feminist. The novel was not roundly welcomed, in part because it appeared at a time when readers were not interested in feminist women and middle-class blacks. *Ladies' Home Journal* considered serializing it, but decided not to risk losing Southern white subscribers who would object to its depiction of privileged African-American life.

West began a second novel based on the lives of upper-middle-class blacks on Martha's Vineyard, but as the civil-rights protest movement gained strength, she shelved the project, feeling that the timing was not right for this

book either. She feared that revolutionaries, particularly those in the Black Panther movement, would vilify her expression of the view that African-Americans needed elite blacks to serve as doctors, lawyers, and other professionals who would also help other less fortunate members of their race. Nevertheless, she continued writing, and many of her stories appeared in the *Vineyard Gazette*, the local newspaper where she had begun working as a billing clerk. Meanwhile, a summer resident on the island who worked as an editor with the Doubleday publishing firm,

*Jacqueline Kennedy, began encouraging West to complete her second novel. She eventually did so, and Doubleday published it as *The Wedding* in 1995. Doubleday also issued *The Richer, the Poorer: Stories, Sketches, and Reminiscences* that year. Critics praised both books. **Susan Kenney**, in *The New York Times Book Review*, wrote of the novel, "It's as though we've been invited not so much to a wedding as to a full-scale opera, only to find that one great artist is belting out all the parts." Literary historians, critics, and general admirers rediscovered West and her connection to the Harlem Renaissance, and, much to her genial enjoyment (and occasional bemusement), she became greatly sought after for interviews and lectures. A sign outside her home politely requesting "Please no unannounced visitors" was largely ignored by the legions of fans who trooped to her A-frame cottage in Oak Bluffs.

Although West's work features themes of racial mixing, the promises and pitfalls of middle-class values for black people, and love and admiration for African-American men in all their struggles, it also sounds the mother's voice and acknowledges women's strength and influence, notes **Mary Helen Washington**. In *The Living Is Easy*, West skewers her own mother's largely successful efforts to manipulate her father and his money for the benefit of her large and needy birth family. But in a brief sketch titled "My Mother, Rachel West," written after her mother's death, West paid tribute to Rachel's lasting legacy. In the essay, West recalled her relatives' relief that her mother, now dead, could no longer meddle in their lives, then considered how often she and her various aunts and cousins quoted her mother and heard the derisive response, "You sound just like Rachel." Eventually, West wrote, the family admitted that the ones "'who sound just like her are the ones who laugh a lot, love children a lot, don't have any hang-ups about race or color, and never give up without trying.' . . . I suppose that was the day and the hour of our acknowledgment that some part of her was forever embedded in our psyches."

West remained active and continued writing until the end of her long life. She enjoyed the attention garnered by the publication of her second novel, although she occasionally was wearied by the steady stream of admirers whom she was too gracious to turn away. At the time of her death in August 1998, she was working on a history of the African-American community in Martha's Vineyard, having scrupulously followed her own advice to "write, write, write."

SOURCES:

Bambara, Toni Cade. "Golden Age," in *The Boston Sunday Globe.* July 23, 1995, pp. B37, B40.

Dalsgard, Katrine. "Alive and Well and Living on the Island of Martha's Vineyard: An Interview with Dorothy West," in *Langston Hughes Review.* Vol. 12, Fall 1993, pp. 28–44.

Ferguson, Sally Ann H. "Dorothy West," in *Dictionary of Literary Biography.* Vol. 76: *Afro-American Writers, 1940–1955.* Detroit, MI: Gale Research, 1988.

Jacobs, Sally. "Dorothy West's Vineyard renaissance," in *The Boston Globe.* October 11, 1995, pp. 61, 66.

McDowell, Deborah E. "Conversations with Dorothy West," in *The Harlem Renaissance Re-examined.* Ed. by Victor A. Kramer. NY: AMS Press, 1987, pp. 265–282.

"Obituary," in *The Boston Globe.* August 19, 1998, p. C9.

Roses, Lorraine Elena. "Interviews with Black Women Writers: Dorothy West at Oak Bluffs, Massachusetts July, 1984," in *Sage.* Vol. 2. Spring 1985, pp. 47–49.

Skow, John. "The Second Time Around," in *Time.* July 24, 1995, p. 67.

Steinberg, Sybil. "Dorothy West: Her Own Renaissance," in *Publishers Weekly.* Vol. 242. July 3, 1995, p. 34.

Washington, Mary Helen, "I Sign My Mother's Name: Alice Walker, Dorothy West, Paule Marshall," in *Mothering the Mind.* Ed. by Ruth Perry and Martine Watson Brownley. NY: Holmes & Meier, 1984, pp. 142–163.

SUGGESTED READING:

West, Dorothy. *The Living Is Easy.* Boston, MA: Houghton, Mifflin, 1948 (republished by the Feminist Press, 1981, 1991).

———. *The Richer, the Poorer: Stories, Sketches, and Reminiscences.* NY: Doubleday, 1995.

———. *The Wedding.* NY: Doubleday, 1995.

COLLECTIONS:

Papers located in the Mugar Memorial Library, Boston University; the James Weldon Johnson Memorial Collection, Yale University, New Haven, Connecticut; and an interview in the Black Women's Oral History Project and papers in the Schlesinger Library, Radcliffe College, Boston.

RELATED MEDIA:

"As I Remember It: A Portrait of Dorothy West" (VHS, 56 mins.), written, produced, and directed by Saleem Merkuria, Merkuria Productions, in association with WGBH, 1991.

"The Wedding" (television miniseries), starring **Halle Berry**, Eric Thal, and Lynn Whitfield, produced by *Oprah Winfrey, first aired in 1998.

Cheryl Knott Malone,
University of Texas, Austin, Texas

West, Dottie (1932–1991)

American country-western singer and songwriter who was the first female vocalist to win a Grammy Award for country music. Born Dorothy Marie Marsh in McMinnville, Tennessee, on October 11, 1932; died of injuries sustained in a car accident in Nashville, Tennessee, on September 4, 1991; daughter of Hollis Marsh; Tennessee Technological University, B.A. in music; married Bill West (a guitarist, divorced 1969);

married Byron Metcalf (a drummer, divorced 1980); married Al Winters (a sound technician), in 1983 (divorced 1991); children: four, including country star **Shelly West.**

Recorded celebrated duets with Jim Reeves, Don Gibson, Jimmy Dean, and Kenny Rogers; became first female vocalist to win a Grammy Award for country music (1964).

Dottie West was born Dorothy Marie Marsh on October 11, 1932, in McMinnville, Tennessee, the first of ten children. Her position as the oldest sibling in a large, poverty-stricken family forced her to shoulder a significant amount of backbreaking work, including laboring in the cotton and sugar-cane fields and cooking Paul-Bunyan-sized meals. Worse, she suffered physical and sexual abuse at the hands of her father, an alcoholic.

West's extreme childhood circumstances could not derail her dreams. She began formal music lessons while still a teenager, financed by a series of part-time jobs which also paid for her college education at the Tennessee Technological University in Cookeville. There the music major met her future first husband, Bill West, who played a mean steel guitar in addition to his engineering studies. The pair began to perform together around campus and soon married. Although Bill held a job with a Cleveland electronics company after graduation, the Wests continued to make appearances together, including a regular slot on a local Cleveland television show, "Landmark Jamboree." The exposure was enough to win Dottie a contract with Starday Records in 1959, and she moved with Bill to the nation's country-western capital, Nashville, in expectation of making it big in the entertainment business.

Success was not so immediate, but West profited from her exposure to future country-western greats such as Willie Nelson, Hank Cochran, Roger Miller, and *Patsy Cline. Through informal jam sessions with these and other musicians, Dottie discovered a latent songwriting ability which she quickly put to good use. Her first hit "Is This Me?," recorded by Jim Reeves in 1961, gained her a BMI Writer's Award. She started a successful duet career with Reeves which included the top-ten "Love is No Excuse," but Reeves' premature death in a 1964 plane crash brought their partnership to an end. It was the first of several profitable duet-pairings for West which, at times, overshadowed her solo work.

Chet Atkins of RCA Records liked the combination of her voice and her compositions enough to give her a long-term contract in 1962, and within two years she wrote the first of her smash hits, "Here Comes My Baby." The song became a landmark in the music business, and earned her a Grammy Award in 1964, as the first female country star to win the coveted industry award. The song eventually made it into the repertoires of over 100 pop and country artists to cement its place in the pantheon of country classics.

West produced several other chart-topping songs in the 1960s, including "Would You Hold It Against Me?," "Paper Mansions," "Rings of Gold," "I was Born a Country Girl," "Gettin' Married Has Made Us Strangers," "What's Come Over My Baby?," and "Mommy, Can I Still Call Him Daddy?" Her songs about breakups proved prophetic as Dottie and Bill West divorced in 1969.

West's talent and beauty made her a good fit for television, and she became a regular cast member on the long-running "Grand Ole Opry" television show. Besides this permanent position, West did guest spots on several other country-themed programs throughout the 1960s, such as "The Jimmy Dean Show," "Country Music Hall," and "The Faron Young Show," and even branched briefly into movies with appearances in *Second Fiddle to a Steel Guitar* and *There's a Still on the Hill.* However, her greatest television success proved to be in commercial spots she wrote for the Coca-Cola company. In 1970, West contributed an ad for Coke, based on her "Country Girl" song, that proved so popular the company gave her a lifetime contract. In the first seven years, she provided music for 15 Coke commercials, including the "Country Sunshine" jingle that won her a Clio Award for best commercial of the year in 1973. Her success in advertising helped bolster her singing career, which had declined in the early 1970s, even though her European tours won her the honor of being named England's best American female country-music singer in 1972 and 1973.

In 1976, West made a pivotal career move when she switched to the United Artists record company and recorded the hit single "When It's Just You and Me." The change freed her up to record duets with her good friend Kenny Rogers, who was also on the label. His contribution to her song "Every Time Two Fools Collide" helped propel it to the top of the country charts and led to a full album of West-Rogers songs. Within three years, the album *Every Time Two Fools Collide* had gone gold with over 550,000 copies sold. Their follow-up album, *Classics,*

Dottie
West

was an even bigger success after its release in 1979, and several hit singles, such as "Anyone Who Isn't Me Tonight," "Til I Can Make It On My Own," and "All I Ever Need Is You," opened up new avenues for both country artists. West and Rogers commanded some of the largest concert halls in the United States for their performances, and West was a guest on "The Tonight Show" as well as several other talk shows. In both 1978 and 1979, the pair took home the Vocal Duo of the Year award from the Country Music Association.

West's whirlwind schedule of television work, concerts, and recording continued into the 1980s, with 320 appearances in 1980 alone. She also released solo albums such as *Special Delivery* in 1980 and *Wild West* the next year, both of which yielded significant hits, such as "Are You Happy Baby?" and "A Lesson in Leavin'." However, her career took a nosedive as the 1980s drew on, with only minor hits between 1981 and 1985. The beginning of the 1990s proved to be even more cruel, as disaster descended on the middle-aged star. Not only did she divorce her third husband, Al Winters, she also faced several lawsuits stemming from her declaration of bankruptcy in 1991. The IRS demanded almost $1 million in back taxes and fines and auctioned off virtually everything she owned, including the rights to some 400 songs she had written.

On August 30, 1991, West was running late for her appearance on the "Grand Ole Opry," and car trouble forced her to solicit the help of an elderly neighbor to drive her there. Barreling at high speeds to get West to her engagement on time, the neighbor drove off the ramp of the car park and crashed. Both West and the driver received critical injuries in the accident, with West in more serious condition with a ruptured liver. A series of operations failed to control the bleeding, and she died a few days later, on September 4, 1991.

SOURCES:
Read, Phyllis J., and Bernard L. Witlieb. *The Book of Women's Firsts.* NY: Random House, 1992.
Stambler, Irwin and Grelun Landon. *The Encyclopedia of Folk, Country & Western Music.* 2nd ed. NY: St. Martin's Press, 1983.

RELATED MEDIA:
"Big Dreams & Broken Hearts: The Dottie West Story" (2 hr. television movie), starring **Michele Lee**, first aired on CBS on January 22, 1995 (also includes reminiscences by Larry Gatlin, Kris Kristofferson, *Loretta Lynn, Willie Nelson, and **Dolly Parton**).

Malinda Mayer,
writer and editor,
Falmouth, Massachusetts

West, Harriet (1904–1999).

See Waddy, Harriet.

West, Jane (1758–1852)

British novelist and poet. Born Jane Iliffe in London, England, on April 30, 1758; died in Little Bowden, Northamptonshire, on March 25, 1852; only child of John Iliffe and Jane Iliffe; self-educated; married Thomas West (a farmer), around 1780 (died 1823); children: three sons.

Selected writings: Miscellaneous Poetry *(1786);* Miscellaneous Poems and a Tragedy *(1791);* The Advantages of Education *(1793);* The Gossip's Story *(1796);* Elegy on Edmund Burke *(1797);* A Tale of the Times *(1799);* Letters to a Young Man *(1801);* The Infidel Father *(1802);* Letters to a Young Lady *(1806);* The Loyalists: An Historical Novel *(1812);* Alicia de Lacey: An Historical Romance *(1814);* Ringrove; or Old Fashioned Notions *(1827).*

Jane West achieved a measure of celebrity for her writing of educational tracts and didactic novels for English audiences of the 18th and 19th centuries in a career that spanned over 50 years. Wholly self-taught, she began with poetry at the age of 13 and, by her own account: "The catalogue of my compositions previous to my attaining twenty would be formidable. Thousands of lines flowed in very easy measure. I scorned correction, and never blotted." Her husband's family was proud of their connection with the minor poet Gilbert West, an attitude that presumes her husband and his family's support of her literary efforts.

West was careful not to arouse criticism as a woman writer by maintaining the supremacy of her duties to her family above all else. Her novels, poetry, and plays reflect this domesticity as well as her conservative politics and devotion to the Anglican Church, all the while conveying the high moral tone expected of "acceptable" literature of the day. West aided her career by being a persistent self-promoter. Her initial volumes were books of poetry, *Miscellaneous Poetry* (1786) and *Miscellaneous Poems and a Tragedy* (1791). Her first novels, *The Advantages of Education; or The History of Maria Williams* (1793) and *The Gossip's Story* (1796), pre-date the anti-sentimentality of ***Jane Austen's** *Sense and Sensibility.* West next published *An Elegy on the Death of Edmund Burke* (1797) and *A Tale of the Times* (1799), the latter of which was declared by critics to be anti-Jacobin and an attack on William Godwin's *Political Justice.* She also assailed atheism in *The Infidel Father* (1802). Up until 1810, West used the character Prudentia Homespun as a narrator for her novels; the spinster's ironic and humorous observations flavored West's early works.

After the "death" of Prudentia in 1810, West embarked on the writing of historical novels. *The Loyalists* (1812) was set during the English Civil War and provided its author with the opportunity to further delve into her conservative politics. Her penultimate novel, *Alicia de Lacey* (1814), justified her use of historical characters in fiction, and her final novel, *Ringrove* (1827), was a story in the mold of instructional evangelical works. Her moral beliefs were reflected in two books she wrote for young adults to instruct them in good conduct, *Letters to a Young Man* (1801) and *Letters to a Young Lady* (1806). The second of these she dedicated to England's Queen *Caroline of Brunswick, including in the dedication an appeal for better education for young women to properly fit them for their moral and social responsibilities.

West lived for 25 years after she stopped publishing, outliving her husband and all three of her sons. She was plagued with fading eyesight as she got older, which aggravated the sense of loneliness she experienced without family or celebrity in her twilight years. She died at age 93 on March 25, 1852.

SOURCES:

Schlueter, Paul, and June Schlueter, eds. *An Encyclopedia of British Women Writers.* NY: Garland, 1988.

Shattock, Joanne. *The Oxford Guide to British Women Writers.* Oxford: Oxford University Press, 1993.

Malinda Mayer,
writer and editor,
Falmouth, Massachusetts

West, Jessamyn (1902–1984)

American writer who gained particular renown for novels and short stories set in Quaker communities in the American West. Born Mary Jessamyn West near North Vernon, Indiana, on July 2, 1902; died of a massive stroke in Napa, California, on February 23, 1984; daughter of Eldo Roy West (a teacher, citrus grower, and businessman) and Grace Anna (Milhous) West; graduated from Fullerton High School, 1918; graduated from Whittier College, 1923; graduate work at Oxford University, England, summer 1929; worked on Ph.D. at University of California, Berkeley, 1929–31; married Harry Maxwell (Max) McPherson, on August 16, 1923; became guardian for Ann McCarthy (Cash) from Limerick, Ireland (1955).

Moved to California (1909); contracted tuberculosis and entered a sanitorium (1931); published first story, "99.6" (1939); published The Friendly Persuasion *(1945); served as technical director for film* Friendly Persuasion *(1956); film won Gold Palm Award, Cannes Film Festival (1957) and was nominated for an Academy Award; received Indiana Authors' Day Award (1957); received Thormod Monson Award (1958); performance of operetta, "A Mirror for the Sky," Eugene, Oregon (May 1958); sister Carmen committed suicide (October 26, 1963); Ann McCarthy Cash adopted by Max McPherson (1990).*

Jessamyn West was a Quaker, a Westerner, and a woman, but she refused to be defined solely by these labels. She loved the western United States with its vast panoramas, and her attitudes and values reflected her gentle Quaker background. But she was more than an accumulation of places, family, or religious beliefs; "Who was I?" she asked, "I was all that was behind me. I had built myself. I was part of all I had loved. And hated?"

West lived a relatively quiet, uneventful life; she treasured solitude, enjoyed a long, stable marriage, and became a bestselling and wealthy writer. In one of her later novels, she used an epigram from Oscar Wilde: "One's real life is the life one does not lead." For Jessamyn West, her books "may be her 'real' life," the life of the mind and imagination. As a writer, West is still best known for her first collection of stories, *The Friendly Persuasion* (1945), based on her Quaker ancestors in Indiana. This, however, revealed only one facet of her writing, and she would admonish interviewers not to think of her as "a sweet little old Quaker lady."

Mary Jessamyn West was born near North Vernon, Indiana, in 1902, the oldest of four children. Her father Eldo Roy West came from a poor farm family, a man whom Jessamyn described as "easily discouraged, and given to melancholy." **Grace Milhous West** married Eldo over the objection of her parents; he was not a Quaker and was poor, which Grace never let him forget, even after the family prospered in California. West modeled several of her characters after Grace, the "practical, amusing, sex-fearing mother" who loved exotic names (hence Jessamyn, which was not "common"). Through the Milhous family, West was the second cousin of President Richard Milhous Nixon, whose grandfather moved to Whittier, California, and invested in real estate. In 1909, Eldo and Grace moved their family to the West Coast. Eldo bought a lemon grove in Yorba Linda, Orange County; he later engaged in several businesses and was active in local affairs. Jessamyn loved her new home in the time before railroads and irrigation made it a fruitful mecca for new migrants. The arid, windy, open spaces appealed to her, and California became her permanent home. Writes West's biographer, Alfred S. Shivers: "An artist cannot live by bread alone; she needs orchids for her soul," and California provided that for West.

Prosperity brought increasing materialism into the lives of West's California relatives. Despite this, she was subject to a rather strict up-

Jessamyn
West

bringing. Dancing, card-playing, drinking, and frivolous pleasures were not allowed to members of the Religious Society of Friends (the Quakers). But more important for the life and eventual writing career of Jessamyn West were the beliefs held by Quakers; God is love and abides in every human, the emphasis on human worth and responsibility, equality of men and women, and an optimistic, but realistic, view of life. These principles were embraced by Jessamyn and are embodied in her work. Consequently, West's female characters are complex and independent, never mere "shadows or reflections" of men.

By age 12, West was collecting story ideas in notebooks and keeping a journal; by 1975, she had filled nearly 50 journals. Unlike her brothers and sister, Jessamyn loved reading and each day made lists of new words to enhance her vocabulary. Her attitudes and views, and later her writings, were influenced by Henry David Thoreau, *Emily and *Charlotte Brontë, *Virginia Woolf, and *Eudora Welty. However, her desire to be a writer was undoubtedly inhibited by the Quaker notion that if one had a talent for language it should be employed to benefit the faith. Jessamyn's brother Myron, a college-educated engineer, typifies this opinion, declaring that writing was a "show-off business" and that he had never read one line of Jessamyn's stories. With no encouragement from her family, her ambition to be a writer remained unfulfilled until she was in her 30s.

Education was important to the West family, and three of the children graduated from college. Jessamyn attended Fullerton Union High School which shared a campus with Fullerton Junior College. A good student, she took the usual subjects, including Latin; her writing impressed her teachers, and her compositions were read to other English classes. She also served as editor of New Pleiades, a joint weekly publication of the high school and college. In 1919, West entered Whittier College (founded in 1901 by the Quakers) where she joined the debate team. A reserved, serious student, Jessamyn had an unfortunate experience that affected her for years. Her composition instructor, Miss Fisher, disliked a story she had written and told her "to curb her imagination." Later, West's essay "Live Life Deeply" elicited a more critical response. Fisher copied it on the blackboard for her class and "spent the rest of the period demonstrating the author's moral and intellectual shortcomings." "Shocked and humiliated," West contemplated suicide. Years later she published a story dealing with this crushing episode in her life.

With her confidence shaken, her grades dropped, and she transferred to the junior college. In 1921, Jessamyn returned to Whittier College. Despite prohibitions against "immoral" pleasures on the campus, she was happy there. She participated in many extracurricular activities, appeared in theater productions, and held office in the Palmer Literary Society. In the spring of 1923, West graduated from college with a B.A. in English. While an undergraduate, she became engaged to Harry Maxwell (Max) McPherson, son

of a Quaker family in Whittier. Intelligent and gregarious, Max had no interest in literature. He later earned a doctorate, served as principal in several schools, was a professor at the University of California, and became superintendent of the Napa Valley Unified School District. He was also the founder and first president of Napa Valley College. Max supported and encouraged Jessamyn to write and respected her need for privacy after they were married in the Yorba Linda Friends Church on August 16, 1923.

The following year they moved in with his parents in Hemet, California. Jessamyn worked as a school secretary for a year and then began teaching in a one-room schoolhouse near her in-laws' apricot orchard. She enjoyed teaching and her students (grades one through six). During her four-year teaching career, she gained insights into young people which she used in her writings. West now set her sights on graduate school; her goal was to earn a doctorate and teach English in a college, an ambitious, independent course for a young, married woman in 1929. More unusual was her decision to enroll in summer classes at Oxford University in England while Max attended the University of California at Berkeley. She traveled to Paris, and in mid-winter she rejoined her husband. Work toward her doctorate in American Studies was satisfying, but she still had an urge to write, a desire she had suppressed for years.

While in her 20s, West suspected she had a "medical problem." As she got out of bed one morning, a few days before her oral exams were to be taken (1931), she "tasted some warm-salty arterial blood in her mouth—a tubercular hemorrhage." Three days later, West was admitted to La Vina Sanitorium in the Sierra Madre foothills, near Pasadena. The diagnosis was "advanced bilateral tuberculosis," and doctors frankly informed her that 95% of patients with this form of the disease would not live more than five years. After nine months, she was able to return home to her husband in Yuba City. A few weeks later, she suffered a relapse. The doctors concluded that nothing could save her, and told her parents to take her home to die among her "loved ones." But Grace West, the "repressive backwoods Quaker," refused to accept her daughter's death penalty. (Richard Nixon's older brother, Harold, had died from the disease.) By November 1933, Jessamyn was able to join her husband.

While recuperating, she read a great deal, and she finally began to write. Her first effort was a short story, "99.6," about life in the sanitorium. When a female acquaintance suggested that Jessamyn make a quilt so her mother would have a remembrance, West decided, "Hell, if I've reached the end of the road, I am not going to leave a quilt. I'll put Grace's stories down on paper. And I began writing." Jessamyn West's experience with tuberculosis was not the end, but the beginning of her "real" life. The possibility that her hold on life was precarious made her more aware of the world and gave her a heightened appreciation of being alive, "that elation which is the chief fact of my life," as she expressed it.

West still had no intention of publishing her writing. But after reading a few of her stories, Max pressured her to submit them to magazines. She sent the stories to various "little magazines" that did not pay for entries, and they were accepted. Jessamyn West was a published author. She never wrote to earn money, for her needs were simple and few, and Max's salary had always sufficed. Despite her lack of interest in material things, West earned a great deal of money which Max invested well.

There was no longer a need for West "to curb her imagination." Her mother had provided the "germs" that developed into tales of Jessamyn's Indiana Quaker ancestors. In November 1945, Harcourt Brace published her collection of stories entitled *The Friendly Persuasion*; and in 1946, it came out in England. This "love poem to Indiana," as West called it, became an international bestseller and was translated into Dutch, French, German, Spanish, and Italian—all in 1945. The Quaker couple, Jess and Eliza Birdwell, are modeled on her Milhous ancestors, and Mattie and Gard Bent are based on West's own parents. In response to protests from family members, Jessamyn did change the name of her "fictitious" characters from Millhouse to Birdwell. Her cousin **Olive Marshburn** also objected to the frank language attributed to the Birdwells; words such as "pa, ain't, and duck dung" were offensive, and she insisted the language be "linguistically deodorized, scrubbed, and dressed in such proper attire as would befit a genteel family tradition." Jessamyn was furious—she changed the family's name, but the language remained "common." Ironically, when the book became a popular seller, this same cousin "donned Quaker costume and gave readings from it." Favorable reviews of the book soon appeared, but not from the Quaker press; West was criticized for using the "commonest of words," a practice the Quakers themselves had always advocated.

The Friendly Persuasion translated well into a motion picture. Jessamyn served as a technical advisor for the United Artists' film, directed by William Wyler and starring Gary Cooper, Tony

Perkins, and *Dorothy McGuire (1956). It was nominated for an Academy Award and won the Gold Palm Award at the Cannes Film Festival in France. West was paid well for the rights to her book, and she received an even greater sum from Metro-Goldwyn-Mayer for her novel *South of the Angels*. In 1960, future president Ronald Reagan produced and starred in "Learn to Say Goodbye," West's story about a boy who had raised a bull and cried when it was given over for auction; this televised version was on Reagan's "General Electric Hour."

> *W*riting is so difficult that I often feel that writers, having had their hell on earth, will escape all further punishment hereafter.
>
> —**Jessamyn West**

Except for Me and Thee, the sequel to *The Friendly Persuasion*, was published in 1969, and also became a bestseller. That West was a second cousin to then President Richard Nixon may have helped increase sales, and she was invited to appear on NBC's "Today" show which introduced her to a wide audience. Once again, Jess and Eliza Birdwell are portrayed as "sober, God-fearing, orderly, practical, and artistically starved" rural Quaker folk who are forced to deal with the Civil War, the question of slavery, and social change. The outside world infringes on their innocent, quiet, "even charming mode of existence," just as the modern world was making inroads into West's own rural surroundings. When Jess Birdwell relents and allows a Christmas tree in the house, he says to Eliza, "People are getting more worldly every day." And she responds, "Except for me and thee, Jess." Eliza had given expression to Jessamyn's own thoughts. In these two novels, West "quite gently reminds us that everything is an adventure . . . in order to return, turn back and find yourself."

West's most popular works are set in the past, in rural or small-town America. But she did not shy away from controversial subjects such as adultery, pederasty, rampant materialism, and declining religious faith which affected society in post-World War II America. In *Cress Delahanty* (1953), she describes the problems of growing up, a "thinly disguised story of her girlhood" in Yorba Linda, according to one critic. Her science-fiction novel *The Pismire Plan* (1948), also set in California, satirizes 20th-century American civilization; tastelessness and vulgarity, advertising that exploits sex, soap operas, "infantile motion pictures," and crass consumerism exemplify "a brave new world of the absurd," as West saw it, where humans were reduced to consumers.

In addition to fiction, West wrote memoirs, but not a complete autobiography. *To See the Dream* (1957) recounts the filming of *Friendly Persuasion*; *Hide and Seek* (1973) is an account of the time she lived alone in a trailer on the banks of the Colorado River, seeking the solitude she found so necessary for her well-being. She muses on her childhood, her mother's avoidance of sexual subjects, and her own thoughts on love and sex and "the joy of living." In *Double Discovery* (1980) West discusses her time in England and France in 1929, based on letters she had written to her mother. When Jessamyn read the letters, she told an interviewer she was "an older woman, a much older woman, discovering the young woman. That's why the book is called *Double Discovery*. It was a young woman's discovery of travel in Europe and the older woman's discovery of the younger woman."

The most biographical of all her works of fiction is *A Matter of Time* (1966), which deals with euthanasia. It was "sensational" and "agonizing to write," and it was controversial. The book is based on her sister **Carmen West**'s sui-

cide in 1963, during the terminal stages of intestinal cancer. In the novel Blix (Carmen) asks her sister Tasmania (Jessamyn) to help her end her life, which she did. The sisters save up pills and Tasmania (Tassy) agrees to be present so the suicide will be successful. Blix's decision is viewed by West as a "celebration of life"; to the end Blix controlled her own life and chose the time and how she would die. Interestingly, West did not question the morality of euthanasia, and "disavowed advocating any general practice" of mercy killing. To West, dying was a part of living: "It seems to me to be facing the whole of life." *A Matter of Time* did not sell well, and West received irate letters hoping she "would rot in hell." Her response was "I may, but not for those last days with Carmen."

In 1976, West "went public with the facts" of assisting in her sister's suicide when the statute of limitations for this illegal act had run out. In *The Woman Said Yes*, West pays tribute to her mother and sister, both victims of cancer. Jessamyn writes that she had no regret for helping Carmen whom she said "had the courage . . .

From the movie Friendly Persuasion, *starring* Dorothy McGuire and Gary Cooper.

[t]o depart like a courteous guest." Max McPherson confirmed to Shivers that West had indeed actively assisted in the suicide; it was not a fictional account. "Fiction reveals truths that reality obscures," West declared, and her writings dealt with lives of "real" people with whom she was familiar. None of her characters are truly wicked, she noted, for the simple reason that she had never met such a person.

West's poetry never gained much attention; only one collection was ever published, *The Secret Look* (1974). Her screenwriting for the films *Stolen Hours* and *The Big Country* brought her recognition and an offer from Raoul Péne duBois to write the script and lyrics for a musical based on the life of John James Audubon. The musical ran for only one performance at the University of Oregon in Eugene in May 1958. It was more spectacle than story, and the life of Audubon was eclipsed by the elaborate staging. But West's novels and stories made her reputation and earned her awards, including nine honorary doctorates from colleges and universities. Her books were selected by national book clubs, and a documentary film, *My Hand—My Pen*, was made on her philosophy of writing. West became a trustee at Whittier College and taught classes and workshops in creative writing. As a speaker she was much in demand, but she never read from her works in public. While writing, only her current project received her attention; as she admitted to an interviewer, "I never look inside a book once it's written, and I even forget them." West most often wrote about the past, but she did not live there.

Jessamyn and her husband had no children of their own, but at age 53 she "found" an 11-year old, red-headed girl during a trip to Ireland. Outside a Woolworth store in Limerick, West met a scantily clad child, **Ann McCarthy (Cash)**, shivering from the cold. After this chance encounter, Jessamyn stayed in Limerick to get to know Ann's family. Her aim was to take Ann to live with her in California. Ann's mother, a widowed scrubwoman, supported six children and a grandmother. Mrs. McCarthy finally agreed to the proposed arrangement, but West's husband hesitated; he was 57 years old and considered the idea "crazy." The Irish Catholic authorities gave permission for Ann and her sister **Jean** to live with the McPhersons, but the archbishop of San Francisco objected to Quakers becoming guardians of Catholic children. It finally took the intercession of then vice-president Richard Nixon to convince everyone that the McPhersons would be good parents. And they were. Ann remained with the family after her sister returned to Ireland; she graduated from California

State University and married Alan Cash. In 1990, Max adopted her and willed his and Jessamyn's estate to her and her husband.

During the last years of her life, West suffered a series of strokes which interfered with her writing and giving speeches. Memory loss, slurred speech, and occasional disorientation curtailed her activities for long periods. When able, however, she spoke before her appreciative audiences. On Wednesday, February 22, 1984, she had a massive stroke at home. Jessamyn West died at Queen of the Valley Hospital the next day at 5:00 AM without having regained consciousness. She was cremated, and no funeral service was held. Her ashes were buried in back of her house in Napa. The quiet, gentle Quaker lady who almost died before she was 30, lived to be 81 years old.

With the publication of her first book in 1945, West became "the most accomplished Quaker writer of the age," according to Shivers. An independent, private woman who loved solitude, her family, and the western United States, she spoke to her readers through her memorable Quaker ancestors. The words of Jess Birdwell in *Except for Me and Thee* echo the views of the author: "The world suits me to a T. . . . That's my trouble. Why, sometimes I think the Lord made it especially for me. I like its colors. I don't see how the flavor of spring water can be improved on. . . . Yellow lamplight on white snow. Thee ever seen anything prettier." These simple words reflect West's own sensitivity to, and appreciation of, a world that had vanished.

SOURCES:

Crider, Bill. "Jessamyn West," in *Dictionary of Literary Biography*. Vol. 6. Edited by James E. Kibler, Jr. Detroit, MI: Gale Research, 1980.

Farmer, Ann Dahlstrom. *Jessamyn West*. Western Writers Series, no. 53. Boise, ID: Boise State University, 1982.

———. "Jessamyn West," in *Dictionary of Literary Biography Yearbook: 1984*. Edited by Jean W. Ross. Detroit, MI: Gale Research, 1985.

Shivers, Alfred S. *Jessamyn West*. Rev. ed. NY: Twayne, 1992.

Yalom, Marilyn, ed. *Women Writers of the West Coast*. Santa Barbara, CA: Capra Press, 1983.

SUGGESTED READING:

Bakerman, Jane S. "Jessamyn West: A Wish to Put Something into Words," in *Writer's Digest*. No. 56. January 1976, pp. 28–29.

Dempsey, David. "Talk with Jessamyn West," in *The New York Times Book Review*. January 3, 1954, p. 12.

Graham, Lee. "An Interview with Jessamyn West," in *Writer's Digest*. No. 47. May 1967, pp. 24–27.

King, Brenda. "Jessamyn West," in *Saturday Review*. No. 40. September 21, 1957, p. 14.

Williams, Nick B. "Jessamyn West: Portrait of Author as Lives Really Lived," in *Los Angeles Times West Review*. January 13, 1980, p. 3.

Jessamyn West's manuscripts, journals, and letters are located in the Whittier College Library, Whittier, California.

Jeanne A. Ojala,
Professor Emerita, Department of History,
University of Utah, Salt Lake City, Utah

West, Mae (1893–1980)

American actress, singer and comedian, one of the great perennial figures of American popular culture in the 1920s and 1930s, who was a legend in her own lifetime. Name variations: known to her family as Mamie; early appeared on stage as May West; on occasion, used the pen name Jane Mast; known as the "Brooklyn Bernhardt" or "Vamp of High Camp." Born Mary Jane West on August 17, 1893 (the date is now certain), in the Bushwick section of Brooklyn, New York; died in her Hollywood home at age 87 on November 22, 1980; daughter of John West (a boxer of Irish background who died in 1935) and Matilda Dilker (or Doelger) West (a German-born corset model who died in 1930); second of four children, she had an older sister who died in infancy, a younger sister Mildred (a sometime actress, who appeared on the stage for a time as Beverly Osborn), and a ne'er-do-well brother John West, Jr.; briefly attended public school between the ages of 8 and 14; married Frank Wallace (né Szatkus), on April 11, 1911 (divorced 1942); no children.

First appeared on stage at an amateur night in Brooklyn singing "Movin' Day" (c. 1900); played children's roles with Hal Clarendon's Stock Company (1901–04); appeared as Maggie O'Hara in A La Broadway *and* Hello Paris *(September 22, 1911, NY), as a dancer, singer and chorus girl in* Vera Violetta *(November 11, 1911, NY), as La Petite Daffy in* A Winsome Widow *(April 11, 1912, in San Francisco), as Mame Dean in* Sometime *(October 4, 1918, NY), as Shifty Liz, Madelon and Cleopatra in* The Mimic World *(April 15, 1921, NY), as Margie LaMont in* Sex *(April 26, 1926, NY), as Evelyn "Babe" Carson in* This Wicked Age *(November 4, 1927, NY), in the title role in* Diamond Lil *(April 11, 1928, NY); toured in* Diamond Lil *(1929); toured in* Sex; *published first novel* Babe Gordon *(reissued as* The Constant Sinner, *1930); appeared as Babe Gordon in the play* The Constant Sinner *(October 14, 1931, NY); debuted on radio on the "Chase and Sanborn Hour" (1938); opened in play* Catherine Was Great *(August 2, 1944, toured 1945); toured as Carliss Dale in* Come on Up *(1946); appeared in London revival of* Diamond Lil *(1947–48), New York revival (February 5, 1949); toured night clubs in "The Mae West Show"*

(1954–59); published memoirs Goodness Had Nothing to Do With It *(1959); toured in* Sextette *(summer 1961); semi-retired (1961–69); appeared as Leticia Van Allen in* Myra Breckinridge *(20th Century-Fox, 1970); semi-retired (1971–76); published novelized version of her play* Pleasure Man *(1975); virtually retired (1976).*

Filmography: Night After Night *(Par., 1932);* She Done Him Wrong *(Par., 1932);* I'm No Angel *(Par., 1933);* Belle of the Nineties *(Par., 1934);* Goin' To Town *(Par., 1934);* Klondike Annie *(Par., 1936);* Go West Young Man *(Par., 1937);* Every Day's a Holiday *(Par., 1938);* My Little Chickadee *(Par., 1940);* The Heat's On *(Columbia, 1943);* Myra Breckinridge *(Fox, 1969);* Sextette *(Fox, 1976).*

Born in 1893 in Brooklyn, New York, Mae West grew up in a middle-class home in the Bushwick section. Her father, a prize fighter in his youth, operated a livery stable and later a private detective agency. Her mother, to whom she was devoted, sacrificed her own life to further her daughter's career. It is not known exactly when West first appeared on the stage—the story varied each time she told it—but an appearance at an amateur night in Brooklyn appears to have taken place when she was seven, either in 1900 or 1901. Thereafter, she joined Hal Clarendon's Stock Company doing little girl impersonations of such popular vaudevillians as *Eva Tanguay, Eddie Foy, and Bert Williams, and playing children's roles in such melodramas as* Little Nell, The Marchioness, Mrs. Wiggs of the Cabbage Patch, Ten Nights in a Barroom, For Their Child's Sake, *and* The Three Claudias; *she was also cast as Little Eva in* Uncle Tom's Cabin.

Except for a brief hiatus in her career during her awkward age, Mae West rarely attended school and on most subjects outside of her profession and her real-estate investments she appears to have been uninformed. She spoke with a broad Brooklyn accent that she never lost (punctuating her conversation with double negatives and referring to the bathroom as the "terlet"), and her creativity as a writer extended to her spelling and grammar.

By 1907, she was working again, singing and dancing in vaudeville. About 1910, she formed a song-and-dance team with Frank Wallace, and in April 1911 they were married. Since she was not yet 18, she had to lie about her age; this is why her birth year is often given as 1892. The account of her marriage in her autobiography is suspect, and it seems to have lasted for longer than the brief period she claimed. In any case, the two separated early and, after she became famous, she pretended that Wallace did not exist.

Little is known of Mae's life between her marriage and her sudden Broadway stardom in the mid-1920s. By her own account, she toured the country for years in vaudeville, learning her trade by carefully observing other performers and enjoying a number of romantic affairs. She performed as a ragtime singer, did a song-and-dance act with the Girard Brothers, did an act with her sister Mildred, who used the stage name **Beverly Osborn**, and appeared as a singer with Harry Richmond on piano. Gradually, West developed the self-mocking persona of the exaggerated siren, with a purring, insinuating voice and a slinky, undulating walk that came to be her trademarks and which she seems to have derived at least in part from watching female impersonators. Reviews of her various acts in the trade papers were rarely laudatory, but West nevertheless managed to secure an engagement at the Palace, the highest goal of all vaudeville artists after its opening in New York in 1913. From time to time, she appeared on the Broadway stage, usually in a musical revue such as *Vera Violetta* with Al Jolson and *Gaby Deslys (1911) and *Sometime* with Ed Wynn (1918), in which she introduced a dance called the "shimmy" that she had seen in Chicago cabarets, and which briefly became a craze.

The years between 1921 and 1926 are the most obscure. West seems to have continued touring in vaudeville, but there is some evidence that she may have had to support herself by working burlesque. In any case, she surfaced again in 1926, opening on Broadway in a play of her own devising called by the then scandalous title *Sex*. A dreadful piece of goods by all reports, it achieved notoriety by the refusal of the newspapers to carry ads for it and the necessity of opening at an obscure theater far uptown. Although West claimed repeatedly that *Sex* was her first venture as a playwright, the copyright-deposit collection at the Library of Congress has at least two earlier manuscripts by her pen, *The Hussy* (1922) and *Chick* (1924). *Sex* ran for months in New York until February 21, 1927, when it was raided, together with two other productions, during a periodic cleanup of the Broadway stage. Though the other producers agreed to pay the fine and close their shows, West—recognizing a million dollars worth of free publicity—allowed the case to go to court. She lost and was sentenced to ten days in jail, during which she kept busy, writing an article for *Liberty* magazine. Once released, she found herself a national celebrity and the darling of the tabloid press. While *Sex* was still running, West announced the production of a new play "by Jane Mast" entitled *The Drag* and billed as "A Homosexual Comedy in Three Acts." It opened in New Haven, Connecticut, on January 31, 1927, and, although West did not appear in it, the play did good business for two weeks despite dreadful reviews. The New York police, however, warned her against bringing it to Broadway, and she followed their advice. West's next vehicle was her own *This Wicked Age* (1927), which also received bad reviews. It ran for only 19 performances.

Mae West's next opus, however, was of a different order, the now legendary *Diamond Lil* (1928). Although one critic opined that as a melodrama, *Diamond Lil* was so bad that it had considerable merit as parody, it turned out to be the best vehicle that West ever concocted for herself. Set in the seamy and raffish world of the Bowery at the turn of the century, the play tapped a wellspring of nostalgia never before exploited, and enabled her to display her ample figure in the costumes and plumage of the era when women of her type had been fashionable. Speckled with clever dialogue, *Diamond Lil* presented West at her very best as a stage personality. Spicy, but in no way indecent, even by the standards of the day, *Diamond Lil* ran for nine months in New York.

During its successful run, West found time to stage another of her own plays, *Pleasure Man*, which she wrote and produced but did not appear in. As in *The Drag*, the theme was homosexuality, and the police raided the theater after its opening night performance. Once again, West opted to go to court, receiving even more free publicity, and this time being acquitted.

After the closing of the Broadway run of *Diamond Lil*, West took the play on tour. It was about this time that she began writing novels, *The Constant Sinner* (1930) and a novelized version of *Diamond Lil* (NY: McCauley, 1932). Neither of them qualify as literature, but both made a good "read," sold well and were occasionally being reissued as late as the 1950s. Back in New York, Mae opened in a stage version of *The Constant Sinner*, dealing with the then daring theme of a white woman and her black lover. Whatever redeeming social import the play might have had, however, was vitiated by the poor writing, for, while there is no question that West took her art as seriously as did Eugene O'Neill, she just wasn't very good at it. *The Constant Sinner* lasted only eight weeks.

In 1932, West accepted an invitation to make a film at Paramount Studios. Her first appearance was in a George Raft vehicle called *Night After*

Night in which, as Raft later stated, West stole everything but the scenery. Delighted with her impact, the studio immediately accepted her idea of filming *Diamond Lil*, which, for some reason not entirely clear, was retitled *She Done Him Wrong* (1932), and in which she played opposite Cary Grant. Though phenomenally successful, the film was falsely credited with saving Paramount from bankruptcy. Running for an entire year in Paris, it catapulted West to international fame. This picture was followed almost immediately by *I'm No Angel* (1933), a modern-dress story set in the circus world, again with Grant. Equally as successful as *She Done Him Wrong*, it left its star the most talked-about actress of the day, and by 1935 she would be the most highly paid woman in America ($485,000 per year). Mae West thus achieved the astonishing feat of becoming an international sex goddess at age 40. Her picture was on every magazine cover, and over the next few years, *Life* did a spread on her "many-mirrored apartment," Britain's Royal Air Force named its new two-chambered life jacket a "Mae West," and Salvador Dali used her face as the basis for a "still life." In an era that liked its women slim as reeds, West openly flaunted an hourglass figure; in a profession that prized youth, she triumphed in full-blown maturity; in an age that still gave lip-service to traditional morality, she treated sex openly and honestly, portraying women who knew what they wanted, saw nothing wrong in going after it, and suffered no pangs of remorse at the story's end.

Judge: "Are you trying to show contempt for this court?"

Mae West: "I'm doin' my best to hide it."

But Hollywood had gone too far in the early days of talking films, and Mae appears to have been the straw that broke the camel's back. Under threat of government intervention, the Hays Office had been formed to police the film industry from within, and West became its first major target. Her fourth film, originally called *It Ain't No Sin* (1934), was butchered to the point where its plot makes little sense, and it was forced to change its title to the innocuous *Belle of the Nineties*. Thereafter, although she continued to make films, she never made them with the frequency that film stars of the '30s usually did, and each seemed to be more innocuous, if not downright duller, than the last. Of these, it should be noted that, although she is usually associated with turn-of-the-century settings and costumes, only two of West's many plays and

only five of her twelve films were set in the past. She was assiduous in keeping her image and her material up to date.

In Hollywood, West settled down in a four-room apartment on the top floor of the Ravenswood Apartments, which had been rented for her by the studio before her arrival. Here, having decorated the place herself in a white-on-white Louis the Umpteenth style in the worst taste of 1932 (which she never redid), surrounded by her air-brushed photos, nude portrait, and a nude statue of herself by sculptor **Gladys Lewis Bush**, she lived for the rest of her life. Over the years, she invested heavily in real estate, including the Ravenswood (which she later sold for a handsome profit), a 22-room beach house in Santa Monica, and a ranch in San Fernando Valley near Van Nuys. When not making films, West attended prize fights and horse races, played with her increasing collection of diamonds, cut an occasional phonograph record, dabbled in the occult, awaited her muse, worked on her scripts, received her gentlemen callers, and let herself get fat. Once a film was scheduled, however, she became an athlete in training, working out, shedding pounds and, when necessary, having her face lifted.

Although she dropped broad hints that she was quite different in her private life from the characters she portrayed on stage and screen, the opposite was true. If anything, her taste in men was on a lower plane than that of the heroines in her vehicles. Boxers, wrestlers, body builders, weight lifters and miscellaneous gangsters, roughnecks, gigolos, and toughs were regulars at the Ravenswood, all grist for her mill when she was not bedding such actors as George Raft, Gary Cooper, and Cary Grant (the last of whom, with some exaggeration, she claimed to have discovered). Fond of mustachioed Latins, and an early supporter of giving roles to black actors and musicians, West freely practiced affirmative action in her libidinous adventures. Given the climate of the time, however, she worked hard to keep this a secret, even going so far as to deny it under oath. Whatever her relations with her men, however, West, ever preoccupied with her "dignity" and fancying herself "a lady," insisted on being treated with respect; no one was allowed to call her "Mae" in public.

Although West cavorted with many men, the only one with whom she was long associated in her heyday was Jim Timony, a heavy-set Irishman who had once been her mother's lawyer. Serving as her manager and gentleman-in-waiting for 25 years, and intensely jealous, Timony

supervised her increasing real-estate holdings and did everything he could to curb her amorous adventures. In Hollywood, it was even whispered that they were secretly married. Eventually, in 1935, West's real marriage was discovered, and, after first vigorously denying even knowing Wallace, she was finally forced to admit that he was her husband and made a settlement with him in order to obtain a divorce granted in 1942.

The late '30s brought another *succès d'scandale* when West made her radio debut on "The

Chase and Sanborn Hour," hosted weekly by the ventriloquist Edgar Bergen and his dummy, Charlie McCarthy. She so shocked radio audiences with her burlesque of the Adam and Eve story that she was not allowed to appear on radio again for a dozen years.

In the midst of all this, West appeared in her last important film, *My Little Chickadee* (1940), in which, sensing that she was slipping, the studio co-starred her with the famed comedian W.C. Fields. This picture, long popular on the cult-film circuit, is far less the hilarious comedy that it could have been, largely due to the jealousy of the two stars that led them to play most of their scenes without the other being involved. Detesting alcoholics, West took an immediate dislike to the hard-drinking Fields and even after his death did nothing to hide her bitterness over their squabbles on the set. Three years later, the first phase of her film career closed with *The Heat's On* (Columbia, 1944), which was not only her worst film until that time—*Myra Breckinridge* still lay ahead—but her first released as the "B" picture on a double feature.

The disaster of *The Heat's On* convinced West that there was no longer a future for her in Hollywood, and at 50 she returned to the New York stage with a script for which she had been unable to obtain support at Paramount. The play, *Catherine Was Great*, was originally intended to be a satire on the great Russian empress of the 18th century, famed for many things, including her sexual escapades. Unfortunately, the production, which opened in New York on August 2, 1945, with lavish costumes and no less than a dozen sumptuous sets, represented the high water mark of West's tendency to take herself too seriously. Though it was peppered with feeble one-liners and occasional smut to give the audience what it had come for, West tried to present a serious portrait of *Catherine II the Great*'s career and, in over her head, received appalling reviews. So hungry was the public for a glimpse of Mae West in the flesh, however, that the play managed five and a half months in New York (191 performances) and packed theaters on tour all through 1945. In 1946–47, she appeared in Oakland, California, in a play called *Ring Twice Tonight*, which she had adapted to her style and which she later toured in under the title *Come on Up*, without bringing it to New York.

In September 1948, West revived *Diamond Lil* in England, the only trip that she ever made abroad. The new production followed the film version, stressing the humor and featuring the star in song. *Diamond Lil* toured the British provinces for 12 weeks before opening in London on January 24, 1948, where West—if not her play—received good notices. The production ran for four months. Returning to America, she then staged the play on Broadway, where, relatively slimmed down, swathed in ostrich feathers, crowned with plumes, corseted within an inch of her life, and stuffed into tightly fitted turn-of-the-century gowns of lavender, beige, and vermilion, she was one of the sights of New York. The opening night of the revival was probably the high point of West's long career. A certified legend at 55 and still a handsome, voluptuous woman, she received a standing ovation, generally rave reviews, a layout in *Life*, and a portrait on the cover of *Theater Arts Monthly*. The play (temporarily closed when West broke her ankle) reopened in September to run for another six months after which she toured the country for the next three years, finally closing the play after a second Broadway run in November 1951 only to attend to Jim Timony who by now was clearly failing.

After his death and without his restraining influence, West opened a new phase in her career. In August 1954, turning 61, she launched a night-club act at the Sahara Hotel in Las Vegas, appearing with nine scantily clad, title-holding body builders. For five years, she took this act from coast to coast, breaking box-office records everywhere with what she called "the first bare-chest act for ladies." The show came to an end in 1959 in a swirl of bad publicity after West became involved in an altercation between two of her men, and it became common knowledge that she had been sleeping with most of her cast, some of whose members were less than half her age. The one durable result of this last major phase of her career was the acquisition of one of the body builders as her companion for the rest of her life.

Thereafter, West returned to Hollywood where she dictated a witty but largely ghosted autobiography *Goodness Had Nothing to Do With It* (1959). On the strength of this, she staged a revival of *Sextette* in Chicago in the summer of 1961. Though the show was well received by the local critics, as well as in Detroit and Miami, the death of her co-star cast a pall over the production, and West closed it without bringing it to New York.

The closing of *Sextette* was not meant to be the end of West's career but to a certain extent it was, for she never starred on stage again. Entering her 70s, she devoted her remaining years to a

WOMEN IN WORLD HISTORY

variety of activities, recording albums (*Way Out West, Wild Christmas* and *Great Balls of Fire*, 1966), appearing on television ("The Red Skelton Show," 1960, twice on "Mr. Ed," 1964, 1965), eating her health foods, riding her stationary bicycle, pursuing her interest in the supernatural, publishing a novelized version of *Pleasure Man* and an updated version of her "memoirs," coping with her sister's alcoholism, nursing her investments and her diabetes, and granting preposterous "interviews" (*Esquire, Playboy, The New York Times Magazine, Life, The Gay Advocate*, etc.), during which she claimed to have started whatever happened to be fashionable at the time, from the sexual revolution and women's liberation to civil rights for blacks and homosexuals. As the years passed, she became increasingly the object of a Mae West cult, receiving a steady volume of mail from fans who lived from one rare public appearance of their idol to another and who stood in line for hours to see revivals of her films. The University of Southern California football team chose her as its mascot, *After Dark* magazine honored her with a banquet and its "Ruby Award," and she was voted the "Sweetheart of Sigma Chi." She was adored by many homosexuals, whom she had early depicted in her plays and whom she had always defended, and "doing Mae West" became a standard feature of the female impersonator's art.

The collapse of film censorship in the '60s and the continued devotion of her fans prompted West to return to the screen in 1969 after an absence of 27 years. The vehicle chosen was Gore Vidal's bizarre but brilliant novel *Myra Breckinridge* with West given top billing in the much built-up role of "singer-agent" Leticia Van Allen. Unfortunately, the production, which might have been a comic masterpiece, was entrusted to an inexperienced English director, Michael Sarne, who made a fiasco of it. Released in 1970, it has often been cited as one of the worst films ever made. West's songs were poor; she was badly lit and badly photographed; most of her best lines and scenes were cut; and the reviews were savage. The premier in New York, however, was a personal triumph. A mob greeted her arrival at the theater, and afterwards she held a press conference, basking in the attention of New York reporters as in days of yore. Then, in 1976, after her successful appearance on "The Dick Cavett Show," she unwisely allowed herself to be induced into making yet another picture, a film version of *Sextette*, in which, at age 83, she played a glamorous movie star of 26, an incredible tour de

force of interest only to her die-hard fans. In many ways a better film than *Myra Breckinridge*, *Sextette* had a fine cast and good production values, but was vitiated by the fact that, except in a few startling scenes, West, stiff in movement, artlessly painted and blurred in soft focus, was no longer able to bring off what had once been her forte. After glittering openings in Los Angeles and San Francisco, followed by scathing reviews and empty seats, the film was unable to find a distributor and ended up being shown only at a few cult theaters. West lingered a few years longer, teetering on the edge of senility, and increasingly reclusive, attended by her companion of 30 years. Suffering a stroke on August 10, 1980, she died on November 22, three months after her 87th birthday; her last professional activity had been a radio advertisement for Poland Spring Mineral Water earlier the same year. She had thus been a performer for some 80 years.

Mae West was essentially a personality. Amazingly easy to impersonate, she nevertheless remained her own unique creation, and there was never anyone else like her on stage or screen. She was neither beautiful nor talented, and historians have gone to considerable lengths to explain her ability to capture the imagination of the public and to become a legend in her lifetime. Above all, one has to make an attempt today to explain the now almost incomprehensible public outcry over an actress who used no foul language, bared no flesh, and engaged in no sexual activity on screen beyond an occasional kiss or a momentary embrace. The best suggestion has been that at a time when women were still supposed to be sex objects, Mae West tossed hypocritical conventions out the window and conveyed, however implicitly, that she was as interested in having a physical relationship with her men as they were in having one with her. It would not be until the 1960s that the public was willing to accept the open sexuality of women and the fact that "decent" women could desire men as much as men desired them. Mae West disturbed many women, who feared or envied her frank sexuality, and many men resented her unwillingness to play the female role on their terms. In all her films and plays, however crude they may be, there is a continuing theme wherein we find a heroine ready to face the world and unwilling to pretend that life is anything other than what it really is.

To this extent, Mae West was well ahead of her time and this was something that she, though usually anything but introspective, appreciated herself. It must be left to psychology, however, to explain a female who flaunted her femininity but who comported herself more like a female impersonator than a real woman, and who, for all her sexual escapades, never seemed to be able to love any one man as an individual. Her colossal ego undoubtedly masked a very insecure person, who may have had grave doubts about her own worth as a woman to the point that she was driven over and over again to prove it to the world and in this way to herself.

Strong willed but good natured, Mae West was devoted to her family, helped many individuals quietly, and was able to earn the devotion of the few people whom she trusted enough to allow to get close to her, among them the designer *Edith Head, who created the costumes for *She Done Him Wrong, Myra Breckinridge*, and *Sextette*, and who stood by her on the set during the filming of her last two pictures. West looked after the people who had worked well with her and was always ready to cast one in her later productions. Shrewd, cunning and a good business woman, she nevertheless lacked sagacity and never seemed able to distinguish herself from her stage persona or to understand the demons that drove her. She took herself seriously as an actress, boldly sang in her small voice, and, having amassed an oeuvre consisting of several dreadful plays, clumsily written novels, and pedestrian film scripts, fancied herself a lady of letters. Though she had beautiful eyes and a dazzling smile, Mae West was otherwise a 5'4" bleached blonde, round-shouldered and somewhat dumpy. Famed for the size of her bosom, she was not, in fact, particularly endowed but simply big-boned and generally heavy set. The rest was padding. Only her legs were really beautiful, and these she rarely showed. Badly dressed off screen, she waged (and usually lost) a lifelong battle with obesity, yet she never ceased to consider herself irresistible to men, mindlessly accepting, as early as the 1920s, outrageous and often crude airbrushed publicity photographs as proof of her unfading charms.

A brilliant showwoman, however, West understood her craft to its very depths, and there was no one to whom the word "professional" was more fittingly applied. Sensuous by nature, she triumphed over her physical limitations by shrewd costuming and by allowing her natural sexuality to project itself through an uncanny use of voice, movement and gesture that bordered on genius. In comedy, she was the unparalleled mistress of the "one-liner" and, in her delivery, had a genius for timing. Her casual quip in *Diamond Lil*, "Come up and see me sometime," so innocuous on paper, when presented in her own particular inflection and tone of voice, became the most famed of salacious invitations. She knew, to the finest detail, what worked for her to the point where the limitations imposed upon her by the censors in the 1930s probably deprived us of some of her most brilliant work. Ironically, she remains best remembered for *My Little Chickadee*, still viewed today because of the popularity of W.C. Fields. Mae West would not have been pleased.

SOURCES:

Eels, George, and Stanley Musgrove. *Mae West*. NY: William Morrow, 1982.

Tusca, Jon. *The Films of Mae West*. Secaucus, NJ: Citadel, 1973.

West, Mae. *Goodness Had Nothing to Do With It*. NY: Prentice-Hall, 1959 (2nd ed. NY: Macfadden-Bartell, 1970).

SUGGESTED READING:

Hamilton, Marybeth. *"When I'm Bad, I'm Better."* CA: University of California Press, 1996.

*Lawrenson, Helen. "Mirror, Mirror, on the Ceiling: How'm I doin'?," in *Esquire*. July 1967.

Leider, Emily Wortis. *Becoming Mae West*. NY: Farrar, Straus, 1997.

"Mae West: America's Favorite Hussy Comes Back Again as 'Diamond Lil,'" in *Life*. May 23, 1949.

"Mae West; Goin' Strong at 75," in *Life*. April 18, 1969.

Meryman, Richard. "Mae West; a Cherished, Bemusing Masterpiece of Self-Preservation," in *Life*. April 18, 1969.

Parish, James Robert. *The Paramount Pretties*. Castle Books, 1972.

Roberts, Stephen B. "76 and Still Diamond Lil," in *The New York Times Magazine*. November 2, 1969.

Ward, Carol. *Mae West: A Bio-Bibliography*. Westport, CT: Greenwood Press, 1989.

Robert H. Hewsen,
Professor of History, Rowan University,
Glassboro, New Jersey

West, Rebecca (1892–1983)

English feminist, novelist, and critic, considered by many to be the leading woman journalist of her generation. Name variations: Cicely Isabel Fairfield; "Cissie"; Mrs. Henry Maxwell Andrews; Rachel East. Born Cicely Isabel Fairfield on December 21 (December 25 incorrectly claimed by some sources), 1892, in London, England; died at Kingston House, London, on March 15, 1983; daughter of Charles Fairfield and Isabella (Mackensie) Fairfield; attended day school; at age 11, given scholarship to George Watson Ladies' College, Edinburgh, Scotland; attended Academy of Dramatic Art, London; married Henry Maxwell Andrews, on November 1, 1930; children: (with H.G. Wells) Anthony Panther West (b. August 4, 1914).

Awards: Companion of the British Empire (1949); French Legion d'Honneur (1957); Dame of the British Empire (1959); Benson Medal of the Royal Society of Literature (1966); Hon. D.Litt. from New York University (1966); and others.

Was teen-aged participant in suffragist demonstrations; attended Academy of Dramatic Art in London for three terms; made an unsuccessful attempt at an acting career; joined staff of the feminist paper The Freewoman, *later* The New Freewoman; *adopted pseudonym Rebecca West (1912); joined staff of socialist paper* The Clarion; *wrote for* The New Republic, The New Yorker, *and numerous other publications; published her first book of nonfiction,* Henry James *(1916); published first novel,* The Return of the Soldier *(1918); published major work of nonfiction* Black Lamb and Grey Falcon *(1941); published* The Meaning of Treason *(1941); published major novel* The Fountain Overflows *(1956); went on British Council lecture tours in Finland and Yugoslavia (1935 and 1936); was a member of the first executive committee of PEN, the worldwide writers' organization; reported on Nuremberg trials (1946); was an eyewitness reporter at the siege of the Iranian Embassy in London (1980), at age 87.*

In 1912, a beautiful young would-be actress, fresh from three terms at the Academy of Dramatic Art in London, re-christened herself. Rebecca West, the name she chose, was that of the strong-willed heroine of Henrik Ibsen's *Rosmersholm,* a role which she herself had briefly played. The production in which she appeared failed to make theatrical history, but the resolute young woman, not yet 20 years old, was to make her chosen pseudonym famous.

In 1892, Rebecca West had been born Cicely, or to her family "Cissie," the youngest of three talented daughters of a gifted but impecunious couple, Charles and **Isabella Fairfield**. The parents were passionately devoted to music, art, literature and, in the case of Charles, the world of politics. Isabella was Scottish, daughter of Alexander Mackensie, a man of modest means but leader of the orchestra at the Theatre Royal in Edinburgh. Isabella was a fine pianist who might have had a career on the concert stage, so her daughters believed, if she had not been burdened with heavy family responsibilities. Charles Fairfield was of an Anglo-Saxon family, a learned but impractical anti-socialist thinker and journalist, whose shifting plans for supporting his wife and children regularly met with failure. When West was

13, he died alone and penniless in Liverpool after an improbable attempt to make his fortune in Sierra Leone in West Africa. "If he had been found dead in a hedgerow he could not have been more picked bare of possessions," his daughter would later write.

Isabella Fairfield took her young family home to her native Edinburgh. Their fortunes did not mend, nor were her daughters happy. Returning to London, the eldest, **Letitia Fairfield**, who had attended Edinburgh Medical College for Women on a Carnegie scholarship, took a position as a medical officer; the second, **Winifred Fairfield**, found a post as a teacher, while Cicely enrolled in the Academy of Dramatic Arts. Despite her good looks and abounding energy, West did not please her teachers. Losing a false mustache when she played Antonio in *The Merchant of Venice* seemed symbolic of her ill fortune. Acting jobs outside the Academy proved to be few.

It was at that point that West turned to journalism, the field in which her father had been most productive. Writing was natural to her, she said; she had always written. A sympathetic observer of her mother's long and largely unassisted struggle to survive, West was an ardent feminist, a suffragist, a socialist, an anti-imperialist, a New Woman. She had no abnormal "bump of reverence," and she gloried in her ability to enflame.

In November 1911, a feminist newspaper called *The Freewoman* began publication. For the second issue, West contributed a review of a book on women in India, a review which began with the then shockingly worded declaration, "There are two kinds of imperialists—Imperialists and Bloody Imperialists." She was paid two guineas and featured on billboards. The fledgling journalist was on her way.

West was offered and accepted a staff position on *The Freewoman*, an appointment which soon introduced her to some of the liveliest minds in the London literary world—Ezra Pound, George Bernard Shaw, and **Dora Marsden**, her editor, among others. West had already, with her sisters, attended meetings of the Fabian Society, which, under the leadership of Shaw and Sidney and *Beatrice Webb, was devoted to "reconstructing society in accordance with the highest moral responsibilities." Socialist but not Marxist, the Fabians sought to achieve their goal through education and political democracy.

London was rife with reformers whose varied causes were intoxicating to a young and idealistic journalist. In 1903, *Emmeline Pankhurst** had founded the Women's Social and Political

Union, dedicated to winning the vote for English women, a goal which was to be achieved fully in 1928, a month after Pankhurst's death. West, always independent minded, saw suffrage as only one of many reforms needed to improve the lives of women. She acknowledged that someone had to fight the suffragists' battle, and the WSPU with the Pankhursts in the lead had taken on that task. West championed them eagerly. Her greatest indignation was aroused by the death of *Emily Davison, the suffragist who had been imprisoned 8 times and force-fed 49 times until at last she threw her crippled body under a horse's hooves at the Epsom Derby in final protest at injustices committed against women by men. "Oh, men are miserably poor stuff!" cried West. They had proven themselves notoriously inefficient at governing an England which she saw "black with industrialism, foul with poverty, iridescent with the scum of luxury."

The arguments of her adversaries fell like corpses before the fury of her intelligence.

—Bernard Kalb

The chance to use her scathing tongue was wonderful to Rebecca, whose idol as a writer was Mark Twain in his satiric mode. Such an attitude was a matter of deep concern to her long-suffering but conservative mother. Isabella Fairfield banned *The Freewoman* from her house and forbade its being read. To preserve family unity and to save her mother pain, Cicely Fairfield overnight became Rebecca West. The pseudonym was immediately successful. From 1912 on, with the exception of brief essays signed Rachel East, she wrote under the name of Ibsen's heroine.

From *The Freewoman* and, briefly, the succeeding *The New Freewoman*, West moved to the socialist paper *The Clarion*. Soon she was contributing reviews to the *Daily News*. In 1914, she began to write for a newly founded American periodical, *The New Republic*. Her first *New Republic* contribution was an essay entitled "The Duty of Harsh Criticism." "A little grave reflection," she wrote, "shows us that our first duty is to establish a new and abusive school of criticism." In the meantime her own application of this "duty" had wrought important changes in her personal life. In 1911, she had reviewed H.G. Wells' latest novel *Marriage*, for *The Freewoman*. The review was acerbic, taunting the author with displaying the literary prudishness of an old maid. Wells, a noted womanizer and too famous to be intimidated, was nevertheless intrigued. He invited the youthful reviewer to lunch at his home. Soon they became lovers. Not long afterwards West found herself pregnant. On August 14,

1914, the day on which England entered World War I, Anthony, West's only child, was born. Despite West's high hopes, there was no question of marriage, since Wells was already married to ◄Catherine Wells, an infinitely patient wife whom he had no intention of divorcing.

Edwardian society still considered an unmarried mother a "fallen woman," and West herself proved not quite the New Woman she had fancied herself to be. For a number of years, she lived a lonely life, moving about from place to place in England and on the Continent. She kept her baby with her but taught him to call her "Auntie" and his father, who took considerable interest in the boy, "Mr. Wells." In time, West legally adopted the child, giving him her pseudonymous surname. Young Anthony adored his father, but, mixed with affection, held a keen and lifelong resentment toward his mother. It was at the time of the publication of Anthony West's own first novel that, against his mother's wishes, he publicly announced his true parentage.

Rebecca West's stormy relationship with H.G. Wells ended after ten years. In 1930, at age 38, she married Henry Maxwell Andrews, who was then an investment banker. A scholarly man, he seems to have given her a measure of happiness and peace. Together, they purchased Ibstone House in Buckinghamshire where the famous Rebecca West could be simply Mrs. Andrews. She enjoyed the countrywoman's life, and both she and Henry took an active part in the affairs of their village. They were generous hosts and patrons, helping many in the troubled Europe of that time. The marriage endured until Henry's death in 1968.

Neither joy nor grief, nor her own always somewhat fragile health, interrupted West's voracious reading or the flow of her own writing. It is estimated that during the course of her professional life she wrote nearly a thousand reviews, many of them still uncollected. "I doubt whether any such brilliant reviews of novels were ever seen before," wrote Frank Swinnerton. "[T]he difficulty of writing any form of criticism which is sensitive to the aims of authors and at the same time inexorable in appraisal of their performance is extreme. This difficulty . . . Rebecca West mastered." George Bernard Shaw judged that she could "handle a pen as brilliantly as ever I could, and much more savagely." (Of Shaw himself, West was to write, "I passionately resent the fact that God gave him a beautiful style and that he used it to preach tedious and reactionary ideas.") West's basic sympathy in her reviews was always with the poor and underprivileged. Although her

❧►

Wells, Catherine.
*See Richardson,
Dorothy for
sidebar.*

Opposite page
ℛebecca
𝒲est

socialist ardor abated with the years, she continued to believe that literature should have social significance and a moral purpose.

She was not content with criticism alone, however. In 1918, her first brief novel, *The Return of the Soldier*, was published. It was to be followed by ten other novels, of which *The Fountain Overflows*, a Literary Guild selection, has been the most popular. *The Fountain Overflows* is an autobiographical work, an account enriched by the novelistic imagination of West's own childhood with three sisters and a young brother thrown in for good measure, a valiant and long-suffering mother, a beloved but unreliable father and, pressing down upon them all, the desolations of poverty. Two posthumously published novels, *This Real Night* and *Cousin Rosamund*, continue the story of the semi-fictional Aubrey family.

Even voluminous literary criticism and her own fiction failed, however, to express everything that Rebecca West had to say. Her biographer **Victoria Glendinning** lists ten books of nonfiction. These deal with a wide range of topics, beginning with *Henry James* published in 1916 and ending with the autobiographical *1900* published in 1982.

The climax of West's writing in this genre—perhaps the climax of all her writing—came with the publication in 1941 of *Black Lamb and Grey Falcon* which would be followed some years later with *The Meaning of Treason* and still later by *The New Meaning of Treason*. The monumental—500,000 word—*Black Lamb and Grey Falcon* was the result of three trips which West took to Yugoslavia, a troubled, bewildering, and beautiful country with which she fell in love. The book condensed the three journeys into one undertaken with her husband Henry in 1937 when the approach of World War II already shadowed Europe and, with special poignancy, the Balkans. West used the literary form of the travelogue, vividly detailing people met and places visited, but her intention was much broader—to understand this tempestuous world of which she had been ignorant but whose history, art and politics seemed to her to have influenced all European lives.

In the course of her traveling and writing, West came to empathize strongly with the Serbs whom she saw as "poets and philosophers" who had persevered in a centuries-long struggle for freedom, while the Croats were "lawyers," though brave and freedom-loving, too. She was an ardent supporter of the Serb partisan General Draza Mihailovic whom the Yugoslavian Com-

munist leader Marshal Tito executed at the end of World War II. She refused to view Mihailovic as a pro-Nazi traitor.

Throughout her adult life, West traveled and lectured widely in Europe and the United States, a country which she much enjoyed. A list of her friends, male and female, reads like a Who's Who of the influential writers and thinkers of her time. A partial tally would include Shaw, John Gunther, Lord Beaverbrook, Sinclair Lewis, *Dorothy Thompson, *Fannie Hurst, *Anais Nin, Alexander Woollcott, *Emma Goldman, Noel Coward and Bertrand Russell. She looked on Wells, Shaw, Arnold Bennett and John Galsworthy as her literary "uncles." Among the modernists, she especially admired, although she was not personally close to, James Joyce, D.H. Lawrence, and *Virginia Woolf.

Prolific and immensely varied in her own work, West escapes literary classification. Perhaps as a result, she has not received wide critical attention. She herself was never an easy optimist. "All good biography, as all good fiction," she wrote, "comes down to the study of original sin, to our inherent disposition to choose death when we ought to choose life." Nor was she sanguine about the possibility of mutual understanding among people. "I wonder if we are all wrong about each other," she mused, "if we are just composing unwritten novels about the people we meet." And "there is something in the mind of humanity that turns again and again to anti-feminism. . . . Men are cruel to women . . . just as we are all cruel to our differences." She considered the 20th century "appalling."

West was never able to give herself completely to any organization. Even early in her career she had left the Women's Social and Political Union because she differed sharply with the Pankhursts, though she continued to support women's suffrage. In a challenging and often hostile world, she was determined to make the most of her own gifts. "She preferred to see herself," writes Motley Deakin, "as a free agent, a free thinker, and she championed the symbols of progress—individual freedom and social democracy." "The best artist, she said," writes Harold Orel, "starts an argument with his audience, and demonstrates through his art that the difficult problems of life can be endured (if not solved)."

SOURCES:
Deakin, Motley F. *Rebecca West*. Boston, MA: Twayne, 1980.

Glendinning, Victoria. *Rebecca West: A Life*. London, England: Weidenfeld and Nicolson, 1987.

Orel, Harold. *The Literary Achievement of Rebecca West*. London, England: Macmillan, 1986.

West, Rebecca. *Family Memories*. NY: Viking, 1988.

SUGGESTED READING:

Rollyson, Carl. *Rebecca West: A Life*. NY: Scribner, 1996.

Scott, Bonnie Kime, ed. *Selected Letters of Rebecca West*. New Haven, CT: Yale University Press, 2000.

West, Rebecca. *The Young Rebecca*. Bloomington, IN: Indiana University, 1982.

Wolfe, Peter. *Rebecca West Artist and Thinker*. Carbondale, IL: Southern Illinois University Press, 1971.

COLLECTIONS:

Principal archives located in the Special Collections Department, McFarlin Library, the University of Tulsa, and the Beinecke Rare Book and Manuscript Library, Yale University Library. Smaller collections located at the Humanities Research Center, University of Texas at Austin, the Berg Collection, New York Public Library, the George Arents Research Library, Syracuse University, and the Lilly Library, Indiana University.

RELATED MEDIA:

Rebecca West appeared as herself, a "witness" to the past, in the film *Reds*, co-written and directed by Warren Beatty, 1981.

Margery Evernden,
Professor Emerita, English Department,
University of Pittsburgh, and freelance writer

West, Vera (1900–1947)

American costume designer. Born in 1900; died in 1947; educated at the Philadelphia School of Design.

Born in 1900, Vera West served as head costume designer for Universal Studios from 1928 to 1947. Her many films include *Back Street* (1932), *Diamond Jim* (1935), *Magnificent Obsession* (1935), *That Certain Age* (1938), *The Sun Never Sets* (1939), *My Little Chickadee* (1939), *The Bank Dick* (1940), *Never Give a Sucker an Even Break* (1941), *Pardon My Sarong* (1942), *Frankenstein Meets the Wolfman* (1942), *Follow the Boys* (1943), *She Gets Her Man* (1944), *Terror By Night* (1945), *The Killers* (1946), and *Pirates of Monterey* (1947).

SOURCES:
Leese, Elizabeth. *Costume Design in the Movies*. NY: Dover, 1991.

Malinda Mayer,
writer and editor,
Falmouth, Massachusetts

West, Victoria Mary Sackville- (1892–1962).

See Sackville-West, Vita.

West, Winifred (1881–1971)

British-born Australian progressive school founder. Born in Frensham, Surrey, England, on December 21,

1881; died on September 26, 1971; eldest daughter and second child of Charles William West (a schoolmaster) and Fanny (Sturt) West; attended Queen Anne's School, Cavesham; studied medieval and modern languages at Newnham College, Cambridge, 1900–03; studied art at Julian Ashton Art School.

Traveled to Sydney, Australia (1907); was an illustrator for the Australian Museum; convened first meeting of the New South Wales Women's Hockey Association (1908); founded experimental and progressive Frensham boarding school (1913); opened Sturt school and arts center (1941); opened Gibgate primary school (1952); opened Holt physical education college for women (1953); named Officer of the British Empire (OBE, 1953); opened Hartfield boarding school (1968).

Winifred West realized her progressive ideas of education, especially education for women, by opening a succession of schools in Australia focused on encouraging independent thinking, freeing the creative spirit, and nurturing girls to become whole and physically healthy modern women. She was also a vocal critic of the state education system's emphasis on learning for the purpose of passing university entrance examinations, which she said resulted in "an overcrowded syllabus" that left "little room for original work and imaginative thinking." West disagreed with the promotion of science and technology at the expense of the humanist value of education, and sought to develop her students' interests in the arts and humanities with her unique curriculum.

West was born in England on December 21, 1881, to Charles William West and **Fanny West**. She engaged in studies at Queen Anne's School in Cavesham, followed by a study of medieval and modern languages at Newnham College in Cambridge from 1900 to 1903. Beyond her book work, West enjoyed both hockey and art, the latter passion taking her to Australia in 1907 to become an illustrator for the Australian Museum. She continued her education while there, adding to her knowledge of art at the Julian Ashton Art School. She also pursued her interest in hockey, convening the first meeting of the New South Wales Women's Hockey Association in 1908.

West's return to England in 1910 proved to be brief, as she traveled back to Australia in 1913. That year she established the Frensham boarding school for girls in Mittagong as the embodiment of her educational ideals for girls. The experimental curriculum highlighted the arts and physical education—an unusual combination, particularly for girls—and West had the grounds designed to reflect "the inward and spiritual grace of Fren-

sham," with open spaces, beautiful buildings and lush gardens. Her ideas had much less to do with contemporary progressive and feminist theories than with her own personal ideals regarding the training of girls to be strong and independent women. West adopted the symbol of the tree to represent the school as a growing, living, and regenerative entity, and encouraged her students to think of themselves as responsible, cooperative members of a community rather than competitive individuals. West remained at Frensham as headmistress until 1939, and maintained a connection with the school thereafter.

West founded four more schools between 1941 and 1968, all of which fell under the authority of Frensham as the parent school. Two years after giving up her post at Frensham, she opened the Sturt school, partly in response to what she felt were shortcomings in the state's secondary educational system. The arts and crafts school provided an alternative education to local teenage girls who engaged in a full-time curriculum related to the creation of textiles, woodwork, physical health, and the arts. Eventually Sturt dropped its age and gender requirements to include male and female students of all ages. It later became a community craft center with a professional staff. West also opened a co-educational primary school, Gibgate, in 1952, and the next year established a girls' college, Holt, to provide students with a complete physical education. Hartfield, opened in 1968, was West's last project. Founded at a time when there was renewed interest in progressive education, it was opened to girls who were more interested in arts and crafts than in attending a university. It closed in 1978. West was awarded the OBE in 1953 and died in 1971.

SOURCES:

Radi, Heather, ed. *200 Australian Women: A Redress Anthology.* NSW, Australia: Women's Redress Press, 1988.

Malinda Mayer,
writer and editor,
Falmouth, Massachusetts

Westbrook, Harriet (1795–1816).

See Shelley, Mary for sidebar.

Westerbotten, duchess of.

See Sybilla of Saxe-Coburg-Gotha (1908–1972).

Westley, Helen (1875–1942)

American actress who was one of the founders of the Theatre Guild. Name variations: Helen Ransom. Born Henrietta Remsen Meserole Manney in Brooklyn, New York, on March 28, 1875; died in Franklin

Township, New Jersey, on December 12, 1942; younger of two children and only daughter of Charles Palmer Manney and Henrietta (Meserole) Manney; educated at Brooklyn School of Oratory, Emerson College of Oratory in Boston, Massachusetts, 1894–95, and the American Academy of Dramatic Art in New York City; married Jack Westley (an actor), in New York on October 31, 1900 (separated 1912); children: one daughter, Ethel Westley.

Made stage debut in The Captain of the None-such *(September 13, 1897); acted in vaudeville and stock companies; member of the Liberal Club; with Lawrence Langner and others, formed the Washington Square Players; was one of the founders of the Theatre Guild and was on its board of directors for 15 years; had a successful career in Hollywood beginning in 1934, acting in nearly 30 films.*

Helen Westley had a long and successful career as an actress, both on stage and in the early decades of film. Born Henrietta Manney, she decided in childhood that she wanted to act. She prepared for this by studying first at the Brooklyn School of Oratory, then for a year in 1894–95 at Emerson College of Oratory in Boston, eventually ending at the American Academy of Dramatic Art in New York City. She started her career touring with the stock company headed by **Rose Stahl**, making her New York debut with Stahl at the Star Theater on September 13, 1897, in a production of *The Captain of the Nonesuch*, in which she acted under the stage name Helen Ransom. She then performed in vaudeville and with a number of stock companies for about three years. When she married actor Jack Westley, on October 31, 1900, she gave up the stage for the domestic life, and eventually gave birth to their only child, **Ethel Westley**. In 1912, Helen separated from her husband and returned to the stage.

As a settled New Yorker, she joined Greenwich Village's famous Liberal Club, which counted such notables as Sinclair Lewis, Theodore Dreiser, *Susan Glaspell, George Cram Cook, and Lawrence Langner among its membership. In 1915, Westley, Langner, and some of their friends organized the Washington Square Players, an off-Broadway resident theater company. In its first production of one-act plays, Westley appeared as the Oyster in *Another Interior*, a spoof of Maeterlinck's *Interior*. In 1916, she performed in Anton Chekhov's *The Seagull*. She subsequently performed in several Broadway plays as well.

Even in her youth, Westley was known as a character actress, portraying stern, unpleasant, eccentric, and even evil women, as well as more mature roles. In late 1918, she was among the players who formed the Theatre Guild, and served actively on its board for the next 15 years. She played Doña Sirena in *The Bonds of Interest*, the Guild's first production that opened on April 19, 1919, and afterwards appeared in at least one Guild production every season.

The next phase of her career took Westley to Hollywood where she played Mrs. Morris in *Moulin Rouge* (1934) and launched herself successfully into film work. Although she returned to Broadway once, to play Grandma in *The Primrose Path* at the Biltmore Theater in 1939, she spent the rest of her working life performing in films. In less than a decade, she made almost 30 films, including *The House of Rothschild* and *Death Takes a Holiday* (both 1934), *Roberta* (1935), *Showboat* (1936), *Heidi* (1937), *Rebecca of Sunnybrook Farm* and *Alexander's Ragtime Band* (both 1938), and *My Favorite Spy* (1942).

Cardiovascular disease forced Westley's resignation from the board of the Theatre Guild during the Guild's 1941–42 season, and she died shortly thereafter, in December 1942, of a coronary thrombosis, at age 67. Her friends eulogized her as a forthright person, honest, outspoken, and uninhibited, who maintained the highest standards and was unwilling to sacrifice art for money.

SOURCES:

James, Edward T., ed. *Notable American Women, 1607–1950*. Cambridge, MA: The Belknap Press of Harvard University, 1971.

Malinda Mayer,
writer and editor,
Falmouth, Massachusetts

Westmacott, Mary (1890–1976).

See Christie, Agatha.

Westmoreland, countess of.

See Stafford, Margaret (d. 1396).
See Beaufort, Joan (1379–1440).
See Percy, Elizabeth (d. 1437).
See Stafford, Catherine (fl. 1530).
See Howard, Jane (d. 1593).

Weston, Elizabeth Jane (1582–1612)

British scholar and writer who was ranked with the best Latin poets of her day. Born in London, England, on November 2, 1582; died in Prague, Czechoslovakia, on November 23, 1612; married Johann Leon (a lawyer), around 1602; children: three daughters and four sons.

A prodigy in languages, Elizabeth Jane Weston was greatly admired in her day as a scholar and Latin poet. Although born in England in 1582, she spent most of her life on the Continent, eventually settling in Prague. It is unclear why the Weston family moved from London to Brux in Bohemia, but it is likely to have been because the family property had been confiscated as a result of its Catholicism or politics. While in Brux, Weston began writing verse and corresponding with the leading scholars of her day. Although her primary spoken language was German, she did all of her writing, both poetry and prose, in Latin. She also spoke and wrote Greek, Italian, and Czech. English scholars thought so highly of her work that she was ranked with Sir Thomas More among the best Latin poets of her day, and her reputation on the Continent was even higher.

Weston's father enjoyed high living, and when he died suddenly in Prague in 1597, the debts he had accumulated left the family not only destitute but badly served by his creditors. Weston, then in her 15th year, traveled with her mother to Prague to sort out the situation, appealing to the emperor, Rudolph II, for his sympathy. The combination of her beauty and her scholarly accomplishments won Weston many powerful friends and supporters to advocate for her, among them England's James I who is thought to have assisted her in her suit. The lawsuit was successful, and Weston stayed in Prague, marrying about 1602. Her husband Johann Leon was a lawyer and agent at the imperial court for the duke of Brunswick and the prince of Anhalt.

A Silesian noble, Georg Martin van Baldhoven, so much admired her poems that he collected them and had them published in several volumes as *Parthenicon Elisabethae Joannae Westoniae, virginis nobilissimae, poetriae florentissimae, linguarum plurimarum peritissimae.* Many of these poems were addressed to princes, including her advocate, James I. The third volume contained a list of learned women, ending with Weston herself. The first edition was printed in Frankfurt an der Oder; succeeding editions were published in Prague (1605–06), Leipzig (1609), Amsterdam (1712), and Frankfurt (1723). Weston died in Prague in 1612 and was buried there.

SOURCES:
The Concise Dictionary of National Biography. Oxford: Oxford University Press, 1992.
Shattock, Joanne. *The Oxford Guide to British Women Writers.* Oxford: Oxford University Press, 1993.

Malinda Mayer,
writer and editor,
Falmouth, Massachusetts

Westphalen, Jenny von (1814–1881).

See Marx, Jenny von Westphalen.

Westphalia, princess of.

See Mathilde (1820–1904).

Westphalia, queen of.

See Catherine of Wurttemberg (1783–1835).

West Saxons, queen of.

See Sexburga (c. 627–673).
See Eadburgh (c. 773–after 802).
See Redburga (fl. 825).
See Osburga (?–c. 855).
See Martel, Judith (c. 844–?).

Wetamoo (c. 1650–1676)

Sunksquaw of the Pocassets. Name variations: Namumpam; Tatatanum; Tatapanum; Weetammo; Wetamou; Wetamoe; Weetamore; Queen Wetamoo; Squaw Sachem of the Pocasset. Born around 1650 on tribal lands of the Pocassets (now parts of Tiverton, Rhode Island, and Fall River, Massachusetts); daughter of a Wampanoag Federation sachem, Chief Corbitant of the Pocasset tribe; mother unknown; married Winnepurket, sachem of Saugus (died); married Wamsutta, also known as Alexander (died 1662), grand sachem of the Wampanoag Federation and brother to Metacom (King Philip); married Quequequamanchet (Ben); married Quinnapin (d. 1676); children: (with Wamsutta) one son (after he was taken hostage with Wamsutta, no record exists of his life).

Though the word *queen* is used incorrectly in reference to the Wampanoag Federation female head of state, it is clear why British colonists applied it to Wetamoo. She inherited her position, properly called *Sunksquaw*, from her father Corbitant, one of the most powerful *sachems* (chiefs) in the Wampanoag Federation.

Though Wetamoo probably only lived to be about 26, she experienced a life filled with adversity and contradictions. Of her several marriages (the first was to the *sachem* Winnepurket who died of disease), the most notable was that to Wamsutta (also known as Alexander) who was brother to Metacom. As the eldest son, Wamsutta succeeded his father as *sachem* of the Wampanoag tribe. He died in 1662 apparently from illness, but, at a time in early American history of great conflict between Indian tribes and the English, some Indians believed he had been poisoned. Succeeding Wamsutta as *sachem*, Metacom (also known as King Philip) intended to drive out the English settlers who were overwhelming his land. Siding with Metacom, Wetamoo was an Algonquin leader in the ensuing King Philip's War (1675–76), which, notes Douglas

Edward Leach, was "one of the most serious Indian wars in all of American history. . . . Although the Indian uprising had been unsuccessful, it had tremendous repercussions. Fifty-two of the 90 Puritan towns had been attacked, and 12 of these had been destroyed. Far worse damage was done to the Indian villages. As many as 1,000 colonists died from direct action; the Indian number is not known. Whole tribes practically ceased to exist."

After the death of Wamsutta, Wetamoo married Quequequamanchet but left her new husband when he sided with the colonists at the beginning of the war. Her next husband Quinnapin was a Narraganset, and during the war they captured *Mary Rowlandson, an Englishwoman held captive by the Narragansetts. Rowlandson seems to have worked for Wetamoo and provided the following description: "Wetamore, of whom I lived [with] and served all this while [was] a severe and proud dame . . . dressing herself near as much as any gentry in the land." Wetamoo's husband Quinnapin was a leading warrior in the infamous "Swamp Fight," where he was captured by the English and put to death. After he was killed, the Indian wars raged on.

Though we know little else about Wetamoo, we know that she was a valiant, proud warrior who continued to lead her people into battle. But by August 1676, the whites seemed to be gaining the upper hand. Supposedly, an Indian traitor revealed the location of Wetamoo's camp, leading to the capture of dozens of her warriors. Though Wetamoo escaped down river, her raft collapsed, and she drowned. When the soldiers found the body, she was beheaded. As was the English custom, Wetamoo's head was displayed on a pole.

Though ultimately unsuccessful, King Philip's War had far-reaching repercussions in New England. Notes Leach: "[E]ven though New Englanders had won and their land claims were now secure, the line of frontier settlements would not achieve their pre-1675 limits until 1720. Although the New Englanders survived the most severe test of English survival in colonial history, New England's development was set back by decades."

SOURCES:

Bataille, Gretchen, ed. *Native American Women*. NY: Garland, 1993.

Leach, Douglas Edward. "Metacom," in *Historic World Leaders*. Detroit, MI: Gale Research, 1994.

Travers, Milton A. *The Wampanoag Indian Federation of the Algonquin Nation: Indian Neighbors of the Pilgrims*. Boston, MA: Christopher, 1950.

Deborah Jones,
Studio City, California

Wethered, Joyce (1901–1997)

British golfer whose textbook swing won her five English Ladies' championships and four British Women's championships. Name variations: Lady Heathcote-Amory. Born in Maldon, Surrey, England, on November 17, 1901; died in London, England, in December 1997; married Lord Heathcote-Amory.

Won the English Ladies' championship five times (1920, 1921, 1922, 1923, 1924); was a four-time winner of the British Women's Amateur championships (1922, 1924, 1925, 1929); with various partners, including her amateur star brother Roger, won the Worplesdon mixed foursomes (1922, 1923, 1927, 1928, 1931, 1932, 1933, 1936); thought, by some, to be the greatest woman golfer of all time.

Bobby Jones, America's all-time golfing great, once played the Old Course at St. Andrews on the Lancashire coast of Scotland with Joyce Wethered. Soon after, he noted:

> She did not miss one shot; she did not even half miss a shot; and when we finished, I could not help saying that I had never played golf with anyone, man or woman, amateur or professional, who made me feel so utterly outclassed. . . . I have no hesitancy in saying that, accounting for the unavoidable handicap of a woman's lesser physical strength, she is the finest golfer I have ever seen.

Wethered was often compared to Bobby Jones. In the 1920s, she dominated the course and was considered to be the equal of all but a half-dozen male golfers in Britain. Wethered was only 19 when she began playing in tournaments, beating *Cecil Leitch at the English Ladies' championship. In that era, golf, like many sports, was dominated by wealthy amateurs, but there were some remarkable players. Many would later compare Jack Nicklaus, the American champion, to Wethered, as both had a great ability to concentrate. She never noticed the opposition on the course. It was as if she were the only player. "If I could only bring myself to forget the excitement and importance of the match I was playing in," she said, "then I gave myself an infinitely better chance of reproducing my best form." Her force of concentration, her timing, her fluid swing and long hitting ability, led to her winning five English Ladies' championships and four British Women's championships. Wethered's most memorable match may have been in 1929 in the British Women's final at St. Andrews. Her main opponent was American great *Glenna Collett Vare. One by one, the other 126 contestants were eliminated in the competition. Down by 5 at the end of the first 9 holes, Wethered played the next 18 in 73, and won on the 35th green.

Wethered married Lord Heathcote-Amory who also played golf, though he was never in his wife's class. She loved trout fishing and gardening at her country estate but continued to play some golf, competing in the Worplesdon Tournament 15 times and winning 8. Said Henry Cotton, the British Open champion in the 1930s, "I do not think a golf ball has ever been hit except perhaps by Harry Vardon, with such a straight flight by any other person." In 1975, Wethered and Vare were inducted into the PGA World Golf Hall of Fame.

SOURCES:

Condon, Robert J. *Great Women Athletes of the 20th Century*. Jefferson, NC: McFarland, 1991.

Karin Loewen Haag,
Athens, Georgia

Wetherell, Elizabeth (1819–1885).

See Warner, Susan Bogert.

Wetherell, Emma Abbott (1850–1891).

See Abbott, Emma.

Wetmore, Elizabeth Bisland
(1863–1929).

See Seaman, Elizabeth Cochrane for sidebar on Elizabeth Bisland.

Wharton, Anne (1659–1685)

English poet. Born in Ditchley, Oxfordshire, England, in 1659; died at age 26 (of a venereal disease caught from husband) in Adderbury, Oxfordshire, England, on October 29, 1685; second daughter of Sir Henry Lee (a wealthy landowner) and Anne (Danvers) Lee; married Thomas Wharton, marquis of Wharton and Whig leader, in 1673; no children.

Although none of her work was published during her lifetime, Anne Wharton was one of the best-known poets of the Restoration because her poems had such wide private circulation. She was a wealthy orphan from birth, as her father, Sir Henry Lee, had died of the plague before she was born and her mother **Anne Danvers Lee** died giving birth to her. Anne grew up under the care of her grandmother, **Anne Wilmot**, mother of John Wilmot, earl of Rochester, and married at age 14 to Thomas Wharton, later marquis of Wharton and prominent figure in the Whig faction of Parliament. The considerable wealth of her deceased father resulted in a substantial dowry for Anne, but the marriage was loveless and plagued by Thomas Wharton's ceaseless

Joyce Wethered

womanizing, for which he earned a reputation as the greatest rake in all of England. Anne Wharton was also bothered by poor health which kept her largely confined to her husband's country estate, where she occupied herself with reading and writing.

Through her uncle, John Wilmot, Wharton made the acquaintance of Gilbert Burnet, who later became the bishop of Salisbury. The two established a friendship and Anne began to send him copies of her poetry in her correspondence to him. Burnet, in turn, distributed them to all his female friends as well as Edmund Waller, a renowned lyric poet. Waller, highly impressed by Wharton's poetry, also began passing her work around his social circle, resulting in wide circulation and praise from other eminent poets of the day such as John Dryden and *Aphra Behn, the first English woman to earn her living by writing.

Wharton died at the age of 26 at her uncle's home of a venereal disease she had contracted from her husband. At the time of her death, her verse paraphrases of the Bible were considered her best work, although her lyric poems proved to be more enduring. Her tragedy *Love's Martyr, or Witt Above Crowns*, a political allegory of the Exclusion Crisis, was never produced or published. Perhaps reflecting her unhappy marriage, her poetry, which appeared in many anthologies after her death, often had a despairing tone.

SOURCES:

Buck, Claire, ed. *The Bloomsbury Guide to Women's Literature*. NY: Prentice Hall, 1992.

The Concise Dictionary of National Biography. Oxford: Oxford University Press, 1992.

Shattock, Joanne. *The Oxford Guide to British Women Writers*. Oxford: Oxford University Press, 1993.

Todd, Janet, ed. *A Dictionary of British and American Women Writers*. Roman & Allanheld, 1985.

Malinda Mayer,
writer and editor,
Falmouth, Massachusetts

Wharton, Anne Hollingsworth

(1845–1928)

American writer. Born in Pennsylvania in 1845; died in 1928.

A founder and first historian of the National Society of Colonial Dames of America, Anne Wharton wrote a number of entertaining and instructive books, her favorite subjects being those of Colonial and Revolutionary times. In 1893, she was appointed a judge at the Chicago World's Fair, and she was an honorary member of the Pennsylvania Historical Society. Her works include *St. Bartholomew's Eve, The Wharton Family* (1880), *Colonial Days and Dames* (1895), *Life of *Martha Washington, Social Life in the Early Republic, An English Honeymoon* (1908), *A Rose of Old Quebec* (1913), and *English Ancestral Homes of Noted Americans* (1915).

Wharton, Edith (1862–1937)

Acclaimed American writer whose novels, novellas and short stories meticulously document both high-society New York and Europe during the late 19th and early 20th centuries and the way in which lives are shaped and dominated by social strictures and community pressure. Name variations: Pussy; Lily. Born Edith Newbold Jones on January 24, 1862, baptized in Grace Church, Manhattan; died on August 11, 1937, at Pavillon Colombe, her house in Saint-Brice-sous-Foret, and buried at the Cimetiere des Gonards at Versailles, France; daughter of George Frederic Jones (a real-estate investor) and Lucretia (Rhinelander) Jones; had two older brothers, Frederic (b. 1848, the father of *Beatrix Jones Farrand) and Henry Edward (b. 1850); privately tutored in German; married Edward Robbins Wharton (divorced 1913), in 1885; no children.

Awards: Pulitzer Prize for The Age of Innocence and Legion of Honor for her war relief work during World War I in France.

Novels and novellas: The Touchstone (1900); The Valley of Decision (2 vols., 1902); Sanctuary (1903); The House of Mirth (1905); Madame de Treymes (1907); The Fruit of the Tree (1907); Ethan Frome (1911); The Reef (1912); The Custom of the Country (1913); Summer (1917) The Marne (1918); The Age of Innocence (1920); The Glimpses of the Moon (1922); A Son at the Front (1923); Old New York: False Dawn (The 'Forties); The Old Maid (The 'Fifties); The Spark (The 'Sixties); New Year's Day (The 'Seventies, 4 vols., 1924); The Mother's Recompense (1925); Twilight Sleep (1927); The Children (1928); Hudson River Bracketed (1929); The Gods Arrive (1932); The Buccaneers (1938).

Short stories: The Collected Short Stories of Edith Wharton (2 vols., ed. by R.W.B. Lewis, NY: Scribner, 1968).

Abraham Lincoln was president in 1862, the year Edith Newbold Jones was born into an old upper-class New York family. Her great-grandfather Ebenezer Stevens, an artillery officer at the Boston Tea Party, was immortalized in John Trumbull's canvases displayed in the Rotunda of the capitol in Washington, D.C. In 1900, the estate of Edith's grandfather, William Rhinelander, was estimated to be worth more than $50 million. Edith Wharton had an insider's view of *la belle époque*, a time of majestic splendor between the turn of the century and the outbreak of war in 1914; she would live to see the Victorian age give way to the Modern, and Germany fall under the sway of Adolf Hitler. Wharton would see the motor-car replace the horse-drawn carriage, try out the new typewriting machines, become dependent upon the telephone, and witness air flight. The force of such dramatic historical change would become one of the major themes of her fiction.

In Wharton's world a lady's name could be mentioned in public only three times: at her birth, her marriage, and her death. Under no circumstances did a well-bred woman publish fiction. The struggle to overcome this stricture and see herself as an artist was a part of Edith's young adulthood.

Storytelling and the "making up" of stories was an activity she engaged in from a very early age, during a childhood spent in Paris and Rome. After the Civil War, real-estate values declined and, since her father's income derived from property, George Frederic Jones decided to leave Newport and Manhattan and take his family to Europe where they could live on the same scale for less money; the Whartons did not return to America until Edith was ten. In Paris, a six-year-old Edith would walk up and down the living room suite making up stories about "real people" while pretending to read *The Alhambra*, written by her father's friend Washington Irving. Wharton's passion for pretending to read books prompted her father to teach her how to read. When a visitor from Newport dramatized tales of Olympian gods and goddesses so that they resembled the ladies and gentlemen Edith saw riding in carriages in the Bois de Boulogne, she became engaged by the notion of Greek myths redone in a contemporary setting. Later, she would play with this theme in her short stories "The Lamp of Psyche" (1894) and "Pomegranate Seed" (1929).

When Wharton returned to America, she could speak French, German, and Italian. The variety of European styles and manners she had observed would heighten her sense of contrast and comparison with those she encountered in her native New York. In Europe, she was tutored in German, and looked after by her Irish nurse, **Hannah Doyle**. In New York, her education was mainly gleaned from the books in her father's library. There she read Plutarch and the great poets from Homer to Dante, Milton, Pope, and the Romantics, Keats and Shelley. Edith's mother **Lucretia Rhinelander Jones** forbade her to read any new fiction. Girls of her class did not attend schools, though their brothers went on to Harvard, Columbia, or English universities.

Time spent reading in her father's library was "a secret ecstasy of communion." Most adults around Edith had "an awe-struck dread of . . . intellectual effort," though her father enjoyed poetry. George Jones had intense blue eyes and a romantic side Edith would write about in the novella *False Dawn*, describing his secret courtship of her mother, and the way he stole out at sunrise to sail down Long Island Sound by rigging up a sail on a rowboat.

The mother Edith knew, however, bore no resemblance to a romantic heroine, and was most passionate about acquiring a new wardrobe from Paris. Wharton thought that her mother's "matter-of-factness must have shrivelled up" something in her father's spirit that never bore fruit. According to biographer

R.W.B. Lewis, Lucretia Jones was the model for Mrs. Welland in *The Age of Innocence*, with her "firm placid features, to which a lifelong mastery over trifles had given an air of factitious authority." Wharton felt that her mother's pettiness overruled her father's larger spirit, and relationships like these, in which the smaller-minded individual gets the better of the larger-spirited one, would become a central theme in Wharton's fiction, as in *Ethan Frome*.

Edith had abundant red hair and large anxious brown eyes. Her brothers teased her about having big hands and feet, and she became shy and self-conscious. Lucretia Jones disapproved of the "long words" Wharton used and thought her daughter had "less heart" than her brothers because her nature was not openly affectionate. Still, Edith was experiencing herself as vital and sensual, feeling "vague tremors when I rode my pony, or swam through the short bright ripples of the bay, or raced and danced and tumbled" with the boys. Hesitantly, she asked her mother to explain these feelings, and was told: "it's not nice to ask about such things." When an older cousin told Edith that babies came from people, not flowers, Wharton again went to her mother and received a scolding about subjects that were "not nice."

Wharton told no one about a nameless fear that began to haunt her at this time. The fear had first visited her five years earlier, in Germany when she was recovering from typhoid fever; she read a tale of mystery and violence that frightened her to the point of causing a relapse. Now, she was revisited by "some dark undefinable menace forever dogging my steps, lurking and threatening." At night, she slept with the light on and a nursemaid in the room.

Edith had one good friend, **Emelyn Washburn**, who was six years Wharton's senior, and it was to Emelyn and no one else whom Edith, at 15, showed her first novella *Fast and Loose*. Its heroine, Georgie Rivers, was a lively girl with a yearning for material comfort who rejected her penniless fiancé for marriage to an aging and wealthy lord and later regretted it. Georgie is a precursor of Lily Bart, the heroine of Wharton's bestselling novel *The House of Mirth* (1905). Wharton was also writing a great deal of poetry which was competent but not original, and reflected her reading of such poets as Browning, Swinburne, Tennyson, and Rossetti. At 16, she managed to publish one of her poems in the *Atlantic Monthly*, and then nothing more was published for ten years.

At 18, Wharton had her social debut in the private ballroom of Mrs. Levi Morton (**Anna**

Morton), a well-known millionaire living on Fifth Avenue near 42nd Street. Lucretia Jones chose a private ballroom because she abhorred the kind of public display she associated with the newly wealthy *arrivistes* who made a great show in Delmonico's. For Edith, the elegant event was "a long cold agony of shyness." Dressed in white muslin with a low-necked bodice of green brocade, she carried a bouquet of lilies of the valley. Most of the evening she kept close to her mother and felt frozen, unable to respond to invitations to dance or to enjoy being the center of attention. Later, she was to refer to this time as an "age of innocence." Her mother arranged for her to attend the social activities where she would meet a suitable husband, but she left her daughter in the dark about what married people did when the party was over.

One can remain alive long past the usual date of disintegration if one is unafraid of change, insatiable in . . . curiosity, interested in big things, and happy in small ways.

—Edith Wharton

The social season began in December with dancing—the waltz, quadrilles, and "germans"—at Delmonico's; in Central Park there was ice skating, sleigh riding and tobogganing. In summer, there were boating parties, lawn tennis, or picnics in Newport or Bar Harbor. Edith and her older brother Harry were permitted to go around unchaperoned. Shortly after her coming-out party, she met Henry Leyden Stevens, son of Mrs. Paran Stevens [**Marietta Reed Stevens**] who belonged to the nouveau riche; Lucretia discouraged her children from mixing with this new element whose members she considered pushy and showy, without moral values, restraint, and integrity. Mrs. Stevens would engineer the marriage of her own daughter, **Mary Fisk Stevens**, to British royalty, a measure of social distinction Wharton would discuss in her last, unfinished novel, *The Buccaneers*. Despite her mother's reservations about socializing with *arrivistes*, in the summer of 1880 Edith spent a good deal of time with Henry Stevens and talk began to focus about the couple. That winter, Henry visited the Joneses in Venice where the family had gone for George's health. The following year Henry had become a devoted family friend, staying with the Joneses in Cannes throughout the last illness of Edith's father who was stricken by paralysis and then, shortly after, died. "I am still haunted by the look in his dear blue eyes," Wharton wrote about her father, remembering how his death-bed paralysis had left

him unable to deliver any parting message to her. In the summer of 1882, Lucretia publicly announced Edith's engagement to Henry Stevens. Henry, then 23, would receive his sizable inheritance when he married or when he became 25. In the meantime, his widowed mother Marietta, while controlling a few of the purse strings and able to use some of the income from her son's sizable fortune for her own ends, intervened and refused to approve the marriage. It was rumored that she broke up the relationship because she had been snubbed by members of Lucretia's old-monied set, but it is more likely that Marietta Stevens broke off her son's engagement out of greed. Edith provided no explanation in the note she wrote to her friend Emelyn, saying only that she had *had* to break the engagement.

In the summer of 1883, in Bar Harbor, Edith met Walter Van Rensselaer Berry, a cultivated young man with whom she could discuss art and literature and feel intensely involved. They went for long walks and canoed on the lake, and when Berry departed without a serious word about sharing a future together, Wharton was deeply disappointed. When, on the heels of the triple loss of her father, Harry Stevens, and Walter Berry, the 33-year-old Edward Wharton came into Edith's circle, she was ready to have a reliable suitor. Teddy Wharton, a friend of Edith's older brother Harry, was well born and lived in Brookline with his mother and sister. Though he had no money of his own, he was provided with an allowance of $2,000 a year. Teddy was handsome, extremely affable, and interested in the outdoors. At Harvard, he cut more classes than he attended, and he was without worldly ambition. Teddy was completely available to be of service to Edith and when, after a very brief engagement, they married, Wharton believed herself to be in love for the first time. The wedding at Trinity Chapel "was a quiet one," *The New York Times* reported. In 1885, the year of the wedding, Edith was close to 24, an age considered to be verging upon "spinsterhood."

According to R.W.B. Lewis, it was three weeks before the marriage was consummated, and the newlyweds' sexual life was nearly nonexistent, thereafter. Wharton blamed her mother for failing to provide a basic sexual education; to Edith's questions about marriage, Lucretia responded, "You've seen enough pictures and statues in your life. Haven't you noticed that men are . . . made differently than women? . . . You can't be as stupid as you pretend." Wharton felt that the sexual ignorance her mother perpetuated "did more than anything else to falsify and misdirect my whole life."

Edith
Wharton

The newlyweds settled into an amiable if passionless relationship. Teddy was good natured and admired Edith, and she began to act maternally towards him even though he was 13 years her senior. They never had children, and always kept numerous small lap dogs as pets. In the early years of their marriage, the Whartons lived in Newport from June to February and traveled in Europe, mostly Italy, the rest of the year. In the winter of 1888, in Athens, at the end of a four-month cruise through the Aegean that had cost the Whartons their annual income of $10,000,

Edith learned that she had come into a substantial legacy of $120,000, an amount equivalent to $500,000 at the end of the 20th century.

In 1889, the Whartons bought a home in New York, and Edith accumulated a group of friends from old New York families who shared her interest in books and painting. She tended to draw around her a group of unmarried men who fed her intellectual interests and might give her a measure of attention. Among an early group were Ogden Codman, an architect, John Cadwalader, a lawyer, and Egerton Winthrop, a cosmopolitan widower twice Edith's age who introduced her to the scientific theory of evolution and directed her reading to Darwin, Spencer, Huxley, and Haeckel. Her fiction would reflect this influence as she created characters who were at once shaped by their surroundings and defeated by the unbending forces in their social environments.

At 26, with an independent fortune, Wharton began asserting herself in new ways; she was separating herself from her mother by putting distance between them, living in houses in New York (884 Park Avenue) and Newport (Land's End) that were at opposite ends of town from Lucretia's houses, and she was beginning to write poetry again. Three years later, her first short story was published by Edward Burlingame in *Scribner's Magazine*, but it would be a year before she completed another, as she began to suffer from bouts of illness which took the form of nausea, fatigue, and depression. The stories she wrote at this time, "The Fullness of Life," "The Valley of Childish Things," and "The Lamp of Psyche," are concerned with a theme that held Wharton captive in these years: a woman's disenchantment with the man she has loved. Moreover, Edith was becoming frustrated with the social life at Newport; entertaining depressed her because she felt that unlike their European counterparts, members of American high society were isolated and completely out of touch with cultural movements. Eventually, she would abandon Newport for Lenox, Massachusetts, where she would build a house modeled on Christopher Wren's Belton House in Lincolnshire. Wharton began to make new friends, such as Paul Bourget, a French intellectual and novelist, who would introduce her to the scholarly Englishwoman *Violet Paget, who wrote under the pseudonym Vernon Lee and was the author of *Studies of the Eighteenth Century in Italy*, a book Edith knew and admired. Then, after a 14-year absence, Walter Berry re-entered her life to play a crucial role in supporting her ambition and her sense of identity as a creative artist. Berry helped her rewrite a book on *The Decoration of Houses* (1897) which she had been working on with Ogden Codman—an attack on the interior design of houses like the one in which she grew up for being unlivable, dreary places full of "exquisite discomfort." And it was Berry who was sympathetic during her periodic depressions, reminding her how, like herself, such writers as Flaubert and George Eliot (*Mary Anne Evans) were also prone to a loss of perspective after intense periods of concentration.

Wharton's steady, productive literary career did not begin until she was 37, in 1898. That year she made a list of "favorite books," which included the poetry of Walt Whitman, *Madame Bovary*, and Stendhal's *La Chartreuse de Parme* and *Le Rouge et le noir*. Her collection of short stories, *The Greater Inclination*, was published by Scribner's and the *Bookman* praised it for its "rare creative power called literary genius." Others spoke of her particular talent for conveying women's interior lives. Between 1900 and 1902, she would complete a novella, *The Touchstone*, another book of short stories, *Crucial Instances*, and a massive two-volume novel, *The Valley of Decision*. Moreover, she would make her mark in every literary genre, publishing poems, travel sketches, literary and dramatic criticism, and translations, as well as three plays of her own. As Wharton's creative energy grew, she added new friends to her inner circle, such as the art critic Bernard Berenson and the eminent novelist Henry James. Teddy's health worsened, and at 54, he suffered the first of a number of nervous breakdowns. His health always improved on a motor trip, and Edith took him to Italy where they drove through Tuscan cities for a magazine assignment that would become *Italian Villas and Their Gardens*. In 1904, in Paris, the couple purchased a Panhard-Levassor which Teddy drove happily through the French countryside, and in England they often picked up Henry James at his home in Rye, Sussex, and toured the area. James sometimes complained that Wharton could be a difficult and demanding, though never mean, companion. At times, he may very well have been envious of the enormous financial success of Wharton's fiction, especially in light of her already considerable independent wealth. *The House of Mirth* (1905), a satiric portrait of fashionable New York which maps the destruction of its beautiful and vital protagonist Lily Bart, sold more than 140,000 copies. Some said they recognized Walter Berry in the book's weak hero, Lawrence Selden, and Lily was the nickname Edith had been given by the Rutherford children in her youthful Newport days. The success of *The House of Mirth* inspired Paul Bourget to introduce Wharton to the intellectual and social circle of the Faubourg St. Germain in Paris where artists mixed with royalty. She was particularly taken with Comtesse ***Anna de Noailles**, a beautiful, intense artist who entertained such guests as Marcel Proust. The atmosphere in these worldly salons of *la belle époque* gave individuals a wide berth in which to experiment and express themselves, and it was in this milieu that, at 45, Edith ventured into a love affair with a Parisian-based American journalist, Morton Fullerton. Wharton confided her thoughts in a journal addressed to Fullerton in which she expresses her joy in feeling an uninhibited sensual pleasure she had never before experienced, and she wrote a fictional fragment, "Beatrice Palmato," which specifically reflects this erotic knowledge. And, at the height of her involvement during an unwanted separation from Fullerton, she wrote a story, "The Choice," about a married woman who wishes that her husband would die. In 1908, her collection of short stories, *The Hermit and the Wild Woman*, reflects the themes of imprisonment and the failed desire to escape. Fullerton did not respond to the kind of escalating commitment Wharton desired, and it was a sense of hopelessness concerning their future together, as well as a growing despair about her relationship with Teddy, which dominated her life at this time. The intensity of these private feelings seemed to go directly into the fiction she was then working on, *Ethan Frome*, a novella, and the novel *The Reef*.

Teddy began to experience dramatic mood swings, and during a manic period he embezzled $50,000 out of Edith's trusts and admitted to purchasing an apartment in Boston for his mistress as well as renting out apartments for several chorus girls. He became extremely remorseful and Edith forgave him, although his emotional instability caused her to insist that he no longer be in charge of her financial arrangements. Teddy had no profession of his own and once he gave up this one function in Edith's life which caused her to rely upon him, he felt forlorn and useless and became abusive, insisting that she reinstate him in his financial position. In 1913, after various fruitless attempts to reconcile, they divorced.

Wharton remained in Paris and did not return to the United States to live. She never remarried. Though Fullerton remained part of her life for some time after their affair ended in 1910, she stayed closest to Walter Berry. After her divorce, she traveled extensively, but she kept to a daily routine of writing each morning, and except for an interruption during the Great War, sustained her enormous creative energy, publishing a book each year until her death.

In 1913, her most powerful novel to exploit her knowledge of prewar American and European society, *The Custom of the Country*, was serialized in *Scribner's Magazine*, and its reception confirmed her major importance as an American writer. Wharton felt that World War I permanently altered the nature of life, and found it difficult to get her literary bearings afterwards. With André Gide, she discussed the possibility of translating her novella *Summer* and *The Custom of the Country* into French. In 1920, she published *The Age of Innocence*, the story of a New York lawyer who attempts without success to escape from the society that shaped him. The novel won the Pulitzer Prize, making Wharton the first woman to be so honored. As a writer approaching the final stages of life, Wharton explored inter-generational relationships in novels like *The Mother's Recompense* and *The Children*. She published stories, novellas and novels, yet by the late 1920s feared that her current work would be considered old-fashioned, or that she had been away from America too long and was no longer writing in a current idiom. Wharton continued to receive enormous advances for her work and relied upon making large amounts of money to support her two homes, Pavillon Colombe, 12 miles outside of Paris, and her château, Ste. Claire, in southern France. Her style of living had always been lavish, with servants, a cook, chauffeur, and gardeners, and she was personally responsible for the support of a number of individuals. Sinclair Lewis and F. Scott Fitzgerald paid her homage, and she was the first woman to whom Yale offered an honorary doctorate. Wharton was also recommended for the Nobel Prize in Literature. She published her autobiography, *A Backward Glance*, in 1934, and at the time of her death in 1937 left unfinished a novel that would be published the following year as *The Buccaneers*.

Although Edith Wharton lived in and wrote about a world vastly different than that of the early 21st century, her work remains not only respected but widely popular with readers. A number of her novels also have been made into movies or television series, proving that her later fears of her writing being out of touch were wholly unfounded. While many of the conventions and strictures of society that she detailed with such a keen eye have vanished, the human impulses both behind and against them remain universal.

SOURCES:

Lewis, R.W.B. *Edith Wharton: A Biography*. NY: Harper & Row, 1975.

Lubbock, Percy. *Portrait of Edith Wharton.* NY: D. Appleton-Century, 1947.

Wharton, Edith. *A Backward Glance: The Autobiography of Edith Wharton.* NY: Scribner, 1934.

Wolff, Cynthia Griffin. *A Feast Of Words: The Triumph of Edith Wharton.* NY: Oxford University Press, 1977.

SUGGESTED READING:

Howe, Irving, ed. *Edith Wharton: A Collection of Critical Essays.* Englewood Cliffs, NJ: Prentice-Hall, 1962.

COLLECTIONS:

Correspondence and papers located in the Yale University Library, New Haven, Connecticut.

RELATED MEDIA:

The Age of Innocence (81 min. film), starring *****Irene Dunne**, Lionel Atwill, and Helen Westley, released in 1934.

The Age of Innocence (133 min. film), starring **Michelle Pfeiffer**, Daniel Day-Lewis, and **Winona Ryder**, narrated by *****Joanne Woodward**, released in 1993.

The Children (115 min. film), starring Ben Kinglsey, *****Kim Novak**, and *****Helen Westley**, screenplay by **Timberlake Wertenbaker**, released in 1990.

Ethan Frome (107 min. film), starring Liam Neeson, **Joan Allen**, and **Patricia Arquette**, released in 1993 (an earlier televised adaptation of *Ethan Frome* starred *****Julie Harris** and Sterling Hayden).

The House of Mirth (film), starring **Gillian Anderson** and Eric Stoltz, released in 2000.

The Old Maid (95 min. film), starring *****Bette Davis**, **Miriam Hopkins**, and George Brent, screenplay by *****Zoe Akins** and Casey Robinson based on Akins' Pulitzer Prize-winning play, released in 1939.

Alice Goode-Elman,
author of various publications and Department Head, Humanities, Suffolk Community College, Selden, New York

Wheatley, Phillis (c. 1752–1784)

Leading American poet of the Revolutionary era and the first African-American of either gender to publish a book. Name variations: Phillis Peters. Pronunciation: WEET-lee. Born around 1752 in Gambia, West Africa; died of complications associated with childbirth in Boston, Massachusetts, on December 5, 1784; daughter of unknown parents; renamed Phillis by master John Wheatley after enslavement in 1761; tutored during childhood in the Wheatley household by family members; married John Peters, in April 1778; children: three (all died in infancy).

Captured by slavers in West Africa (1761), and transported to Boston; purchased by merchant tailor John Wheatley; published first poem in the Newport Mercury *(December 21, 1767); published first notable poem, "On the Death of the Rev. Mr. George Whitefield" (1770); only collection,* Poems on Various Subjects, Religious and Moral, *first printed in London (1773); traveled to England as a literary celebrity (summer 1773); wrote notable poem commemorating George Washington's appointment as commander of Continental Army (1775); John Wheatley died (1778),* leaving Phillis without a home; unable to publish second volume of poems during married years (1778–84).

In 1761, slave traders shattered the life of a seven or eight-year-old young girl. Uprooted from her home near the Gambia River in West Africa, she was placed aboard a slave ship bound for the Americas. This child, whose birth name has been lost to history, was one of 10 to 24 million Africans transported against their will to the "New World" between the early 1500s and the mid-1800s. Purchased by merchant tailor John Wheatley in Boston, the Fulani girl was taken into his household as a domestic servant. Renamed Phillis, she learned to communicate in English with amazing ease. Before she was 20 years old, this remarkable poet would become the first black American to author a published book.

At the time the Wheatleys purchased Phillis, Boston was the largest city in British North America with around 17,000 inhabitants. This included about 1,000 blacks, slightly more than half of whom were slaves. Most wealthy elites owned one or two house servants; the Wheatley household was one of very few that contained more than two. Compared to most slaves, Phillis experienced a privileged childhood in the Wheatley home. She had her own room, took meals with the family, and was held responsible for only light domestic chores. The other two or three family slaves, who were all adults, failed to receive similar treatment. **Susanna Wheatley**, her mistress, ultimately came to nurture Phillis as if she were a daughter. Nathaniel and **Mary**, twins who were about 18 years old when the young slave arrived in their parents' Boston home, served as her tutors. "Without any assistance from school education," John Wheatley reported, "and by only what she was taught in the family, she, in sixteen months time from her arrival, attained the English language . . . to such a degree as to read any of the most difficult parts of the sacred writings."

The education Phillis received under the direction of the Wheatley family was typical of that afforded male children of urban elites of the era. The daughters of even the most aristocratic families rarely enjoyed access to the knowledge and training that helped shape the attitudes, intellect, and art of Phillis Wheatley. An extensive education was considered unnecessary, if not dangerous, for women. The fact that she was also an African-American slave rendered this opportunity even more extraordinary. Very few Americans of the late colonial period questioned

*P*hillis
*W*heatley

the prevailing notions of African inferiority. They believed simply that blacks could not be educated. But the Wheatleys proved willing to challenge this view because of their evangelical religious beliefs and early recognition of the natural intellectual gifts of the young girl.

Susanna Wheatley, the family member most responsible for Phillis' training, was herself quite a remarkable individual who entertained unusual views about what was appropriate for women to think and do. Influenced by the ideas of the Great Awakening, she became active in humanitarian concerns inspired by religion. She was a young adult when the great itinerant revivalist George Whitefield toured New England in 1740 with his call for spiritual regeneration, or "New Birth," for all who would listen. In a 45-day period, he delivered 175 sermons—nearly every inhabitant of the region heard at least one. The surge in popular piety associated with the Great Awakening created a new interest in improving society through the conversion of people regardless of social status or race. Susanna not only embraced such notions, she developed friendships with a number of leading British evangelicals devoted to philanthropic causes who shared this view, including *Selina Hastings, countess of Huntingdon (1707–1791), and wealthy London merchant and philanthropist

John Thornton. She also aided the efforts of Native American evangelist Samson Occom and likeminded whites who promoted the idea of education for Native Americans at Eleazer Wheelock's Indian Charity School (later Dartmouth College). Susanna (and later Phillis) corresponded frequently with Occom, and he often visited the Wheatley home.

Susanna Wheatley was thus far more likely than most New Englanders to recognize the precociousness of her young servant and wish to prepare the girl for religious conversion. Phillis said that Susanna provided "unwearied diligence to instruct me in the principles of true religion." Little is known about the specific details of this training or other aspects of Phillis' childhood, but her extant poems and letters reveal an acceptance of Susanna's religious views. Not all of her poems have been discovered, and copies of some certainly will never be found, but based on the many that have survived it is clear that the Bible was the primary inspiration for her art.

Phillis began corresponding with Samson Occom, the Mohegan preacher, in 1765, only four years after her forced relocation to Massachusetts. She was probably writing to others at this time, including her friend from Newport, Rhode Island, **Obour Tanner**. Later letters to Tanner, herself a young female slave, have survived. Some biographers of Wheatley believe that Phillis and Obour came to America on the same slave vessel in 1761. In any event, letter writing no doubt helped to refine Phillis' literary skills. The *Newport Mercury*, a newspaper from the town where Tanner lived, carried what may have been Phillis' first published poem on December 21, 1767, "On Messrs. Hussey and Coffin." Like some of her later poems, this verse was concerned with a memorable incident that occurred in the life of people she knew personally. Hussey and Coffin, traveling from Nantucket to Boston, were nearly shipwrecked off Cape Cod. Afterward, they visited the Wheatleys in Boston, telling of their "narrow escape" at dinner. Phillis, "at the same Time 'tending Table, heard the Relation," and composed two dozen lines of verse.

"On Messrs. Hussey and Coffin" reveals a good deal about Phillis Wheatley's education and early influences. She asks:

> Did Fear and Danger so perplex your Mind,
> As made you fearful of the whistling wind?
> Was it not Boreas knit his angry Brow
> Against you? Or did Consideration bow?
> To lend you Aid, did not his winds combine?
> To stop your passage with a churlish Line,
> Did haughty Eolus with Contempt look down
> With Aspect Windy, and a study'd Frown?

Classical references, in this case to Greek gods of wind, appear throughout her poetry. Here, the pagan gods personify forces that evoke terror derived from man's fear of nature's uncontrollable power, a theme she addressed in other poems, including "Ode to Neptune" and "To a Lady on Her Remarkable Preservation in a Hurricane in North Carolina." She goes on to counsel her subjects to take comfort in the fact that the hand of "the Great Supreme" was in this harrowing adventure. Had they been "snatch'd away . . . to the raging Sea," they would go "with the supreme and independent God . . . To Heaven." As she closes, she praises God in a brief prose passage: "Had I the Tongue of a Seraphim, how would I exalt thy Praise; thy Name as Incense to the Heavens should fly, and the Remembrance of thy Goodness to the shoreless Ocean of Beatitude!—Then should the Earth glow with seraphick Ardour."

About 14 when she composed this poem, Phillis had not known a word of English a mere six years before. But what renders "On Messrs. Hussey and Coffin" even more fascinating is the instructive tone of the verse. Through her poetry, Wheatley adopts a posture, or a separate *persona*, that is hardly that of a 14-year-old slave girl. A "lowly" servant would barely make eye contact with visitors Hussey and Coffin, much less speak to them. But through her poetry, Phillis assumes the lofty position of one imparting the word of God. Through her poetry, Phillis Wheatley escaped from, and actually transcended, her role as a black slave.

Wheatley drew her inspiration for her poetry from a number of sources, including Scripture, the neoclassical verse of Alexander Pope and other English artists, and the work of American poets, primarily Samuel Cooper. It is also interesting that Phillis wrote about what she knew from firsthand experience. She certainly understood the terrors of the sea, for what could be more horrifying than being placed on a large vessel at the age of seven and transported across a vast ocean, only to wonder what awful, uncertain fate loomed at the end of the ordeal? She may have witnessed fellow captives thrown overboard because they were sick or a threat to order on the slave ship, common practices on the part of European crews. Children were generally allowed to roam the decks during daylight hours in good weather; Wheatley no doubt had memories that rivaled the darkest of nightmares. But she came to terms with her fears through her devotion to God, and in part through her poetry.

This printing of Wheatley's verse did not produce widespread recognition of her genius.

Certainly, visitors to the Wheatley home were continually amazed by her talent, but it was not until the publication of her "Elegiac Poem" memorializing George Whitefield that Phillis began to receive special notice. "On the Death of the Rev. Mr. George Whitefield, 1770," first advertised for sale in Boston newspapers on October 13 of that year, received wide publication throughout the American colonies and in England. Certainly, the revivalist's death was greeted with great sorrow in the Wheatley household. He had converted Susanna, who had then converted Phillis. In her verse, the young poet noted that Whitefield "pray'd that grace in ev'ry heart might dwell." His message was for all to "Take him, . . . Impartial Savior" and "You shall be sons and kings, and Priests to God," whether "wretched," "starving sinners," "preachers," "Americans," or "Africans." Phillis also consoled Susanna's English friend, Selina Hastings (Whitefield's principal benefactor), with the line:

Great Countess, we Americans revere
Thy name, and mingle in thy grief sincere

Little did Wheatley know when she penned these lines that Hastings would soon come to play a pivotal role in her life.

As any student of American history knows, George Whitefield's death in Newburyport, Massachusetts, hardly represented the most consequential demise of an inhabitant of the leading American colony in that year. On the night of March 5, five men were killed by British soldiers during the so-called Boston Massacre, and the very month that Phillis published her memorial to Whitefield, the trial of the soldiers began in the city. It was a time of great excitement for Boston's population. Phillis Wheatley was admitted to membership in the Old South Church that same year, thus joining a congregation dominated by patriot sentiment. She wrote a poem about the massacre, "On the Affray in King-Street, on the Evening of the 5th of March," and other verse sympathetic to the patriot cause. Unfortunately, this and many others addressing similar themes of the tumultuous period have been lost.

By early 1772, Wheatley was encouraged enough by her growing notoriety to propose the publication of a volume of her work. The original collection included, among poems on various subjects, "On the Death of Master Seider, who was killed by Ebenezer Richardson, 1770," "On the Arrival of the Ships of War, and the Landing of the Troops," and other patriotic verse. This project failed to receive enough backing in Boston, however, probably because of the color of the author's skin and the divisive state of local politics. It was at this point that the connection between Susanna Wheatley and Selina Hastings came into play. The countess, who knew that Phillis' poetry was genuine, agreed to help sponsor a London publication of a collection of her poems. Not all titles included were the same as the original proposal—ones devoted to controversial American themes were replaced by others—but the book would ultimately include 39 verses. *Poems on Various Subjects, Religious and Moral*, published by Archibald Bell, appeared in late 1773.

Wheatley visited England that year at the very height of her notoriety. She had become quite ill during the winter, and doctors advised sea air as a cure, so the Wheatleys sent her off with Nathaniel Wheatley to London. Her visit attracted a great deal of attention. While Selina Hastings and John Thornton looked after her, she met the colonial secretary, Lord William Dartmouth, about whom she had been asked to compose a poem, "To the Right Honourable William, Earl of Dartmouth" (1772). Impressed by the verse and a letter he had received previously from Phillis, he presented her with a copy of Cervantes' *Don Quixote* and gave her five guineas to purchase Alexander Pope's *Complete Works*. Brook Watson, later lord mayor of London, gave her a copy of Milton's *Paradise Lost*. American agent Benjamin Franklin "went to see the Black Poetess and offer'd her any Services I could do her." Many British notables, including literary figures, met the young celebrity. The time she spent abroad would be the highlight of her life.

> *I*, young in life, by seeming cruel fate
> Was snatch'd from Afric's fancy'd happy seat
> —**Phillis Wheatley**

Wheatley was to have an audience with King George III at court and remain in London until the publication of her book. But after only five weeks there, she received word that Susanna Wheatley had fallen gravely ill. She returned home immediately, arriving in September to find "my mistress was so bad as not to be expected to live above two or three days." She would survive, however, until March 3, 1774; her death was the first in a series of events that would bring sorrow and disappointment to Phillis. As she told John Thornton shortly after Susanna's death:

> By the great loss I have sustain'd of my best friend, I feel like One forsaken by her parents in a desolate wilderness, for such the world appears to me, wandering thus without my friendly guide. . . . She gave me many precepts and instructions; which I hope I

shall never forget, Hon'd Sir, pardon me if after the retrospect of such uncommon tenderness for thirteen years from my earliest youth—such unwearied diligence to instruct me in the principles of the true Religion, this in some degree Justifies me while I deplore my misery.

Not all was dark, however, when the young notable came back home. The *Boston Gazette* reported the return of "Phillis Wheatley, the extraordinary Poetical Genius," and in general her reputation soared. Shortly thereafter, "at the desire of [her] friends in England" and consistent with Susanna's wishes, John Wheatley granted Phillis her freedom. She remained in John's home for the next four years, until his death in early 1778. These were the most trying years of the Revolutionary period in Boston where public attention was diverted from all but the contest between patriots and their "oppressors." It was thus impossible for Wheatley to get a second volume of her poems published.

Her support for the revolutionary cause, however, did receive attention when she wrote a poem commemorating George Washington's appointment "by the Grand Continental Congress to be Generalissimo of the armies of North America." She sent a copy to Washington in October 1775. He liked it, as he told his friend Joseph Reed, but initially refrained from having it published. He wrote back to Wheatley in early 1776, thanking her for the "elegant lines" and explaining that he had not as yet asked to see it published because he feared he "might have incurred the imputation of vanity." He did, though, note that "the style and manner exhibit a striking proof of your poetical talents" and invited her to visit him at his headquarters in Cambridge. The poem would be published in a number of sources in 1776, including Thomas Paine's *Pennsylvania Magazine*. Moreover, Wheatley accepted the invitation and subsequently met in private with the general for about half an hour at his headquarters. She may have also composed a similar panegyric for John Paul Jones, who asked a friend to deliver this message: "pray be so good as to put the Inclosed into the hands of the Celebrated Phillis, the African Favorite of the Muse and of Apollo." Obviously, the naval hero was familiar with her reputation, and may have known her personally.

Two years after Wheatley's meeting with George Washington, her life began to change dramatically. John Wheatley's death in March 1778 marked the final dissolution of the Wheatley household where Phillis grew up. Mary Wheatley left the home in 1771 when she mar-

ried minister John Lathrop, and her brother Nathaniel remained in England. A month after her former master's passing, Phillis married John Peters, a charismatic free black shopkeeper of some means. Peters has often been blamed for bringing misery to Phillis' last years, for abandoning her and, through his reputed laziness, forcing her to work in a boardinghouse. But there is really no reliable historical evidence on this or the nature of any aspect of their marriage. In fact, the tax records of the period reveal that the Peterses had a home of above average value. All else that is known for certain is that the married couple had two children between 1779 and 1784, but they both died in infancy. Wheatley continually sought to have a second volume of poems published, which she dedicated to Benjamin Franklin, but could not get backing in the middle of the Revolution. This 300-page manuscript has been lost and thus many of her poems are still awaiting rediscovery. She did continue to publish verse under her married name, including "Liberty and Peace" (1784), written to celebrate the victory over the British. Late in that year, Wheatley gave birth to a third child. But complications associated with the ordeal took the lives of both mother and child. The death of the remarkable poet on December 5, 1784, received but a little attention, even in Boston.

Three years later, an American edition of *Poems on Various Subjects* finally appeared, and five reprints followed during the next three decades. Two more London editions were also brought out. During the first half of the 19th century, anti-slavery activists kept alive the poetry of Phillis Wheatley to help illustrate the natural abilities of African-Americans. Since then, historians and scholars of American literature often mentioned the poet as an interesting oddity, but serious analyses of her works were rare. In recent years, partly as the result of the discovery of some of her poems and letters, interest in Phillis Wheatley's life and poetry has increased dramatically. No longer dismissed as a mediocre artist who deserves but a footnote in studies of American history or literature, she is beginning to receive long-overdue acclaim as not just a "literary curio," but a woman of remarkable talent and accomplishments.

Modern critics may not rank her among the vanguard of the leading poets of all time, but as Arthur Schomburg argues, "There was no great American poetry in the eighteenth century, and Phillis Wheatley's poetry was as good as the best American poetry of her age." Sentimental neoclassical poems inspired by the Bible hardly seem the stuff of verse that transcends the ages. But many of her poems reveal a sophisticated mastery of poetic technique and some, particularly "On Imagination," "Niobe in Distress," and "To Deism," are powerful compositions that deserve a careful reading by serious students of American literature.

As Wheatley's reputation among literature scholars in general has risen, inclusion of her verse in anthologies of African-American writing has become more common. In the past, she was often ignored or even condemned for neglecting, as Vernon Loggins suggests, "her own state of slavery and the miserable oppression of thousands of her race." It is true that her references to Africa—"the land of errors" and "those dark abodes"—contrasted the continent of her birth to the "enlightened" Christian world in an unfavorable manner. But Phillis Wheatley's poetry did address subjects connected to slavery and race. Principal themes evident in her poems were freedom, escape, and equality before God. Her oft-quoted "On Being Brought from Africa to America" talks about her deliverance from a "Pagan land," but closes with the admonition:

> Remember, Christians, Negroes, black as Cain,
> May be refin'd, and join th' angelic train.

In her poem to the earl of Dartmouth, she explains "from whence my love of freedom sprung." After telling about the experience of being "snatch'd from Afric's fancy'd happy seat," she concludes:

> Such, such my case. And can I then but pray
> Others may never feel tyrannic sway?

Furthermore, it is important to note that Phillis Wheatley did directly and openly condemn the institution of slavery, if not in any extant poems. In a letter to Samson Occom in March 1774, which was reprinted in a number of newspapers throughout New England, she attacked the hypocrisy of so-called "patriots" who pleaded for liberty but would deny the same to slaves:

> [I]n every human Breast, God has planted a Principle, which we call Love of Freedom; it is impatient of Oppression, and pants for Deliverance; and by the Leave of our Modern Egyptians I will assert, that the same Principle lives in us. God grant Deliverance in his own way and Time, and get him honor upon all those whose Avarice impels them to countenance and help forward the Calamities of their Fellow Creatures. This I desire not for their Hurt, but to convince them of the strange Absurdity of their Conduct whose Words and Actions are so diametrically opposite. How well the Cry for Liberty, and the reverse Disposition for the Exercise of oppressive Power over others agree.

If she failed to use her poetry as a vehicle for overt political messages, or social commentary, this hardly means she did not care about the plight of other African-Americans, or that she was somehow "less" African. The themes she addressed, the literary *persona* she adopted, and the personal experiences that helped spark her creative genius cannot be understood without appreciating the role of her African roots. The girl stolen from her homeland at a young age became the most talented American poet of the Revolutionary era. Any discussion of America's rich African-American literary tradition must acknowledge the greatness of Phillis Wheatley.

SOURCES:

Mason, Julian D., ed. *The Poems of Phillis Wheatley.* Chapel Hill, NC: University of North Carolina Press, 1966.

Rawley, James R. "The World of Phillis Wheatley," in *New England Quarterly.* Vol. 50, 1977, pp. 667–677.

Robinson, William H. *Phillis Wheatley and Her Writings.* NY: Garland, 1984.

Wheatley, Phillis. *The Collected Works of Phillis Wheatley.* John C. Shields, ed. NY: Oxford University Press, 1988.

SUGGESTED READING:

Akers, Charles W. "'Our Modern Egyptians': Phillis Wheatley and the Whig Campaign Against Slavery in Revolutionary Boston," in *Journal of Negro History.* Vol. 60, 1975, pp. 397–410.

Kaplan, Sidney, and Emma Nogrady Kaplan. *The Black Presence in the Era of the American Revolution.* Rev. ed. Amherst, MA: University of Massachusetts Press, 1989.

COLLECTIONS:

Wheatley materials are contained in the Schomburg Center for Research in Black Culture, New York Public Library; the Countess of Huntingdon Papers, Cambridge University, Cambridge, England; and the Massachusetts Historical Society, Boston, Massachusetts.

John M. Craig,
Professor of History,
Slippery Rock University, Slippery Rock, Pennsylvania,
author of *Lucia Ames Mead and the American Peace Movement*
and numerous articles on activist American women

Wheaton, Anne (1892–1977)

First woman to serve as a spokesperson for the president of the United States. Born in Utica, New York, on September 11, 1892; died in March 1977; eldest of nine children of John Williams (a politician and labor commissioner) and Elizabeth Ann (Owen) Williams; graduated from Albany High School; attended Simmons College in Boston, Massachusetts, 1911–12; married Warren Wheaton (a journalist), on February 19, 1926 (divorced November 1946).

Worked for Knickerbocker Press (1912–21); was one of the first female political correspondents at New York state capitol; moved to Washington, D.C.

(1924); served as public relations consultant to the National League of Women Voters (1924–39); was director of women's publicity for the Republican National Committee (1939–57); was a public relations representative for wives of Republican presidential candidates; as associate press secretary, was first female presidential spokesperson during the Dwight D. Eisenhower administration (1957–61); was public relations representative for Nelson Rockefeller's presidential campaign (1964).

Anne Wheaton became the first woman to serve as a spokesperson for the president of the United States when she was appointed associate press secretary for the White House under press secretary James C. Hagerty. Raised in a family staunchly supportive of the Republican Party, she spent her childhood under the influence of a father who provided an excellent example of dedicated public service. John Williams served as a Republican member of the state assembly in New York beginning in 1906, then as state labor commissioner for 20 years under appointment by 5 governors. Wheaton spent one year in secretarial courses at Simmons College in Boston, Massachusetts, before entering into a career in journalism on the staff of the *Knickerbocker Press* in Albany, New York. From 1912 to 1921, she advanced from copying recipes for the women's section to being a full-fledged news reporter, and was one of the first women reporters to cover the New York state legislature and the governor's office.

In 1924, Wheaton moved to Washington, D.C., to advance her journalistic career as a political correspondent, and for the next 15 years served as a public relations consultant for several national organizations, focusing on projects of special interest to women. These included the Cause and Cure of War Conference, chaired by *Carrie Chapman Catt; the Women's Organization for Prohibition Reform; and the League of Women Voters.

In late 1939, Wheaton was asked to work for the Republican National Committee by GOP national chair John D.M. Hamilton. As assistant to the director of publicity, she was responsible for all public relations involving women's activities. These included serving as public relations manager and press representative to the wives of several presidential candidates: Mrs. Wendell Willkie (**Edith Wilk Willkie**) in 1940, Mrs. Thomas Dewey (**Frances Hutt Dewey**) in 1944, and *Mamie Eisenhower, wife of Dwight Eisenhower, in 1952. After Eisenhower's victory, she was assigned to his headquarters in New York

City to work as liaison for the Eisenhower family in planning the January 1953 inauguration.

On April 3, 1957, at the fifth annual Republican Women's Conference in Washington, D.C., President Eisenhower made a surprise announcement appointing Wheaton, who at the time was handling publicity for the conference, as associate White House press secretary under James Hagerty. Eisenhower had a policy of appointing women to high-level positions whenever he could, and Wheaton made a point of this to the press, noting that she was the 130th woman he had appointed. Hagerty later made it clear that her appointment was not merely to cover women's issues, but to be his assistant in all matters. This included being in charge of presidential press relations when Hagerty was away from Washington. Her duties included participating in the discussions preceding Eisenhower's weekly press conference, anticipating reporters' questions, and briefing the president on information he might need to answer them.

When asked how she had managed to survive her many years with the Republican National Committee, during which she worked with 11 different chairs and observed many party upheavals, Wheaton replied, "A newspaper person faces a job in politics on a different basis from a top Republican official. You're doing a professional job. Your personal opinions do not prevail. You pursue your job as someone might sell some product." Her presidential appointment was met with widespread approval. She was known to be the perfect publicity representative—efficient, competent, serene, and factual. To the press corps, she was "Our Annie." Wheaton, who was public relations consultant to Nelson Rockefeller when he ran for president on the Republican ticket in 1964, moved to Dallas in 1973. She died in 1977.

SOURCES:
Current Biography 1958. NY: H.W. Wilson, 1958.
Read, Phyllis J., and Bernard L. Witlieb. *The Book of Women's Firsts*. NY: Random House, 1992.

Malinda Mayer,
writer and editor,
Falmouth, Massachusetts

Wheeldon, Alice (fl. 1917)

British pacifist and socialist tried for a plot to assassinate David Lloyd George.

Alice Wheeldon, a socialist and pacifist who joined the No-Conscription Fellowship during World War I, was tried in 1917 (February 3–March 10) for having joined with Alfred and

Winnie Mason in a plot to assassinate British Prime Minister David Lloyd George, whom they held responsible for the carnage of war. The plan was said to have called for Wheeldon to stab the prime minister at a public rally with poison-dipped needles, but after Winnie Mason revealed their intentions to a friend prior to the event all three were arrested. At their trial, they were found guilty and sentenced to prison. Wheeldon was later found to be innocent; some maintain that the story of the assassination plot had been fabricated by the British government because Wheeldon was hiding Conscientious Objectors during World War I. She was released from prison to live out her days as a recluse in Derby where she died and was buried.

SUGGESTED READING:

Rowbotham, Sheila. *Friends of Alice Wheeldon.* NY: Monthly Review Press, 1986.

Malinda Mayer,
writer and editor,
Falmouth, Massachusetts

Wheeler, Anna Doyle (1785–c. 1850)

Irish feminist writer. Born Anna Doyle in Clonbeg, County Tipperary, Ireland, in 1785 (month and day unknown); year and date of death unknown, but approximately 1850; youngest daughter of Nicholas Doyle and Anna (Dunbar) Doyle; educated at home; married Francis Massey Wheeler, in 1800 (died 1820); children: Henrietta Wheeler (d. 1825); Lady Rosina Bulwer-Lytton (1802–1882).

Select publications: (with William Thompson) Appeal of One Half of the Human Race, Women, Against the Pretensions of the Other Half, Men, to Retain Them in Political, and Thence in Civil and Domestic Slavery (1825, new ed. Virago Press, 1983).

Born in Ireland in 1785, Anna Doyle was the youngest of three children of a Church of Ireland cleric who was a dean in the diocese of Fenner and Leighlen. Her father died when she was very young, and the family was looked after by her paternal uncle, General Sir John Doyle. The Doyle family had a long military tradition. Anna, who had a liberal education at home where she was taught fluent French, was 15 when she married Francis Massey Wheeler, son of a wealthy landowning family in County Limerick. Her mother had grave reservations about the marriage which were soon justified. Anna was abused and neglected by her husband and she also suffered a number of miscarriages. By the time their marriage broke up in 1812, they had two surviving daughters, **Henrietta** and *****Rosina (Bulwer-Lytton).**

Anna, her children and her sister **Bessie Doyle** then went to live in Guernsey in the Channel Islands where her uncle was governor. In 1816, she left Guernsey and went to Caen in France where she became part of a group of social reformers and thinkers. Anna had read widely since her childhood and one of her earliest influences was *****Mary Wollstonecraft**'s *A Vindication of the Rights of Woman* (1792). She was also familiar with the philosophical works of Denis Diderot and Paul von Holbach. In Caen, many of the people Wheeler associated with were followers of Claude-Henri Saint-Simon, one of the founders of French socialism. Although Saint-Simon was not particularly interested in the position of women, he believed, rather vaguely, that women could play "useful and productive" roles in his new socialist society.

Wheeler returned to Ireland when her husband died in 1820, and for the next few years she moved between Dublin and London. In London, she became acquainted with members of the co-operative movement who were strongly influenced by the ideas of Robert Owen. After her years in Caen, Wheeler was struck by the similarities between Owen's ideas and those of Saint-Simon. Writes her biographer **Dolores Dooley:** "She regularly introduced [Owen] to French and Irish reformers, and circulated his writings to enthusiasts in both countries. Wheeler excelled at facilitating meetings with potential disciples, expanding networks and smoothing differences between Owen and some of his antagonists."

Wheeler also got to know the English Utilitarian leader Jeremy Bentham. It was through these connections that she met the Irishman William Thompson, who was associated both with Owen and Bentham. Dooley describes this meeting as a turning point in Wheeler's personal and professional life. In 1825, Thompson was cited as the author of *Appeal of one Half of the Human Race . . . Against the pretensions of the Other Half* but in the introductory letter to the volume he emphasized her contribution to the volume: "I have endeavoured to arrange the expression of those feelings, sentiments and reasoning, which have emanated from your mind." The *Appeal* was written primarily to refute the argument of the Utilitarian philosopher James Mill that women were the responsibility of their fathers and husbands. But it developed into a sustained analysis of the social and economic causes of sexual inequality. Wheeler and Thompson did not argue that women would achieve equality when the laws changed; they recognized that culture and public opinion would also have to change. Without equality, not only would women not respect themselves, but men would not respect them either. A central theme of Wheeler's arguments was that improvements in the condition of women would benefit men just as much as women. The *Appeal* is now recognized as a key text in feminist history.

During a sojourn in Paris in the early 1820s, Wheeler met the utopian socialist François Fourier who became a regular visitor to her salon. Fourier envisaged a society organized into small communities called phalanxes. Wheeler was attracted to his ideas because for Fourier the position of women was a barometer of social progress. She popularized his beliefs, which were expressed in rather obscure and difficult terms, in lectures and articles. Wheeler's stay in Paris was marred by the death of her daughter Henrietta in 1825. After this she moved back to London where she lived a withdrawn existence and wrote little. In 1827 her surviving daughter Rosina married the writer Edward Bulwer-Lytton and by 1831 she had two children, a daughter **Emily Bulwer-Lytton** and a son Edward Robert Bulwer-Lytton. By 1833, Wheeler was once again writing in various cooperative journals. Family troubles intervened in 1836 when Rosina's marriage ended in a bitter and tempestuous divorce which had long-lasting consequences. Little is known about Wheeler's last years, although she seems to have remained in London. A friend of Fourier wrote to her in May 1848 urging her to come to Paris and experience at first hand the revolution which was sweeping the city. Circumstantial evidence, discussed by Dooley, suggests that she was dead by 1851. Her granddaughter Emily had died of typhoid in 1848.

After her divorce Rosina wrote a number of publications in which she charged her former husband with cruelty and adultery. In 1858, Bulwer-Lytton kidnapped her and put her in a mental home in order to stop her public accusations; ironically, her mother had once accused mental institutions of colluding with men who wanted to rid themselves of inconvenient relatives. In a memoir, Rosina's son, Edward Robert, attacked his grandmother Anna Wheeler as an unreasoning fanatic on the subject of women's rights. Unfortunately for Edward Robert, his third daughter, *Constance Lytton, became a prominent member of *Emmeline Pankhurst's Women's Social and Political Union and was imprisoned in 1909 for her suffragist activities.

SOURCES:

Dooley, Dolores. "Anna Doyle Wheeler (1785–1850)," in *Women, Power and Consciousness in 19th Century Ireland: Eight Biographical Studies.* Ed. by Mary Cullen and Maria Luddy. Dublin: Attic Press, 1995, pp. 19–53.

————. *Equality in Community: Sexual Equality in the Writings of William Thompson.* Cork: Cork University Press, 1996.

Deirdre McMahon, lecturer in history at Mary Immaculate College, University of Limerick, Limerick, Ireland

Wheeler, Anna Pell (1883–1966)

American analytical mathematician, educator, and administrator, longtime chair of the mathematics department at Bryn Mawr College, whose achievements helped to break down barriers for women. Born Anna Johnson in Hawarden, Iowa, on May 5, 1883; died on March 26, 1966; buried beside Alexander Pell in the Lower Merion Baptist Church Cemetery, Bryn Mawr; daughter of Amelia (Frieberg) Johnson and Andrew Gustav Johnson; University of South Dakota, A.B., 1903; University of Iowa, A.M., 1904; Radcliffe College, A.M., 1905; University of Chicago, Ph.D., 1910; married Alexander Pell, in Göttingen, Germany, on July 19, 1907 (died 1921); married Arthur Leslie Wheeler, on July 6, 1925 (died 1932).

Awards: was starred in American Men of Science *(1921); elected to Phi Beta Kappa (1926); was the first woman to deliver the Colloquium Lectures at the American Mathematical Society (1927); honorary degree from the New Jersey College for Women (1932) and Mt. Holyoke College (1937); honored by the Women's Centennial Congress (1940); seminar series created in her honor, Bryn Mawr College (1964).*

Moved to Akron, Iowa (1892); enrolled at the University of South Dakota (1899); granted scholarship at University of Iowa (1903); granted scholarship at Radcliffe College (1904); awarded Alice Freeman Palmer fellowship at Wellesley College (1906); studied at Göttingen University (1906); taught at the University of South Dakota (1907); returned to Göttingen University (1908); returned to U.S. (1908); enrolled at University of Chicago (January 4, 1909); her husband Alexander Pell suffered a stroke (1911); took over his classes at the Armour Institute of Technology (1911); accepted a position at Mt. Holyoke College (1911); promoted to associate professor (1914); accepted a position at Bryn Mawr College (1918); her father died (1920); succeeded Charlotte A. Scott as chair of the mathematics department, Bryn Mawr College (1924); appointed to the Board of Trustees of American Mathematical Society (1923); promoted to full professor (1925); delivered the Colloquium Lectures at the American Mathematical Society (1927); was editor of Annals of Mathematics *(1927); Emmy Noether moved to Bryn Mawr College (1933); death of Emmy Noether (1935); successfully petitioned for an American analog to the German journal Zentralblatt für*

Mathematik und ihre Grenzgebiete *(1939); retired from Bryn Mawr College (1948).*

Selected writings: *"The Extension of Galois Theory to linear differential equations" (master's thesis, Iowa City: University of Iowa, 1904); "On an integral equation with an adjoining condition,"* in Bulletin of the American Mathematical Society *(vol. 16, 1910); "Existence theorems from certain unsymmetric kernels,"* in Bulletin of the American Mathematical Society *(vol. 16, 1910); "Biorthogonal systems of functions" (Ph.D. thesis, Chicago: University of Chicago, 1910); "Non-homogeneous linear equations in infinitely many unknowns,"* in Annals of Mathematics *(1914); "A general system of linear equations,"* in Transactions of the American Mathematical Society *(vol. 20, 1919); "Linear ordinary self-adjoint differential equations of the second order,"* in American Journal of Mathematics *(vol. 49, 1927); "Spectral theory for a certain class of nonsymmetric completely continuous matrices,"* in American Journal of Mathematics *(vol. 57, 1935).*

Anna Pell Wheeler was born Anna Johnson in Hawarden, Iowa, on May 5, 1883, the daughter of immigrants from Lyrestad parish in Skaraborglän, Västergötland, Sweden. **Amelia Frieberg Johnson** and Andrew Gustav Johnson had arrived in the United States in 1872, and were married soon after. They subsequently moved to Hawarden in 1882, and then to Akron ten years later. It was in Akron that Wheeler first attended public school. A failed farmer, Andrew Johnson became a furniture retailer and undertaker in Akron.

In 1899, Anna enrolled at the University of South Dakota. After a qualifying year as a "subfreshman," she completed her degree in three years. Her grades in the arts and the social sciences were average, but she was an "A" student in chemistry, mathematics, and physics.

As an undergraduate, Anna had the good fortune to have Alexander Pell as one of her mathematics instructors. Alexander, a Russian revolutionary, had come to the United States in the 1880s. His real name was Sergei Degaev, and he was one of the assassins of Colonel George Sudeykin, an officer in the tsarist secret police. Once in America, Degaev changed his identity, and began a career as a mathematician. Alexander Pell was impressed by Wheeler's rare talent for mathematics, and took considerable pains to advise and assist her on her academic career.

Anna's sister **Ester Johnson** also attended the University of South Dakota; the two shared many classes, lived with Alexander and his wife **Emma Pell**, and participated in extra-curricular activities. Anna was secretary-treasurer of the French club, as well as the class historian. It was clear almost from the outset, however, that her principle ability lay in mathematics. In her yearbook, Wheeler wrote beneath her photograph, "I know mathematics better than my own name."

In 1903, she won a scholarship to the University of Iowa. There she took graduate courses and wrote her master's thesis, "The Extension of Galois Theory to Linear Differential Equations." The quality of Wheeler's research won her admission to the Iowa branch of Sigma Xi. While at the University of Iowa, she also taught undergraduate courses in mathematics. Following graduation, Wheeler won a scholarship to attend Radcliffe. There she completed a second master's degree in 1905. For the next year, she remained at Radcliffe on scholarship, taking courses from M. Bôcher, C.L. Bouton, and W.F. Osgood.

> [T]here is such an objection to women that they prefer a man even if he is inferior both in training and research.
> —Anna Pell Wheeler

Each year Wellesley College offered the *Alice Freeman Palmer fellowship to an outstanding female graduate from an American university. In 1906, Wheeler won the grant, beating out four other applicants. She used the money to travel to Germany, where she studied at Göttingen University. One of the stipulations of the Palmer fellowship was that Wheeler remain unmarried during the period of the award. Studying in Germany fulfilled a long-held ambition.

At Göttingen, Wheeler studied under the renowned mathematicians David Hilbert and Felix Klein. She was particularly intrigued by integral equations, a field of mathematics which was gaining increasing prominence at the time. Hilbert, as one the pioneers of integral equations, offered Anna his encouragement and assistance. Integral equations thus became the focus of most of her subsequent research.

Alexander Pell followed her career from a distance, and the two corresponded frequently. He wrote to her sister to express the pride he felt in Wheeler's accomplishments. "I consider her something like a demi-goddess now, for whatever she wants she gets and whatever she studies she makes a success of." When Alexander's wife died in 1904, Anna agreed to marry him over the objections of her family, even though he was 25 years her senior. After their wedding in Germany in July 1907 and the completion of her research at Göttingen, the couple returned to the U.S., where Alexander had recently been appointed the dean of engineering at the University of South Dakota. There Wheeler taught two courses, one on the theory of differential equations, the other on the theory of functions.

Having left her doctoral work unfinished, Wheeler returned to Göttingen University in the spring of 1908 to complete her dissertation. Alexander remained in South Dakota. He was quite at a loss without her, but work and finances prevented him from traveling to Germany. He wrote to his wife, "I am awfully sorry I cannot go this summer to Germany but we must pay our debts and then we can live a little bit better, i.e., we may go to Germany next summer together." In time, Wheeler's family came to accept Alexander, who spent considerable time with them during her absence.

By the fall of 1908, Wheeler was ready to take her doctoral examination. Alexander wrote to her sister in November:

> I send you the sample of Anna's dress goods—she has to appear before the examiner in a black dress. Oh, I wish this was all over and I could have her with me again. It is now 8 months since she is gone and I feel very, very lonesome.

During the summer, Alexander Pell had a disagreement with the president of the University of South Dakota which led to Pell's resignation. He accepted a position at the Armour Institute of Technology in Chicago.

On the eve of her Ph.D. examination, Wheeler had a falling out as well with David Hilbert. She never explained the circumstances surrounding the event, but she failed to complete her degree at Göttingen. She wrote to **Mary Coes**, then dean at Radcliffe, stating simply that "in Göttingen I had some trouble with Professor Hilbert and came back to America without a degree." Whatever the circumstances of her failure to complete her degree at Göttingen University, Wheeler remained undeterred. On January 4, 1909, she enrolled at the University of Chicago. She studied under Professors E.H. Moore, F.R. Moulton, and W.D. MacMillan. Wheeler completed her degree in record time, explaining to Coes:

> Since my thesis had been written independently of Hilbert, I had a right to use it at C.U. And so after a year of residence I took my degree under Professor E.H. Moore with magna cum laude. I was the second woman to receive a Ph.D. in mathematics at the University of Chicago and the first to receive it under Professor Moore.

After graduation, Wheeler taught a class at the University of Chicago, while searching for a full-time teaching position. "I had hoped for a position in one of the good universities like Wisconsin, Illinois, etc.," she wrote a friend, "but there is such an objection to women that they prefer a man even if he is inferior both in training and research." In 1911, when Alexander Pell suffered a stroke, she took over his classes at the Armour Institute of Technology. Wrote Wheeler:

> Mr. Pell was sick and they were practically forced to take me for they could not get a man. After a couple of weeks they told Mr. Pell he need not return this semester but take a good rest. I have fifteen hours of subjects in math and have shown them that a woman is capable of doing a man's work in a technical school. The math men at the Univ. of Chicago were very much pleased that at last a woman had the chance to show her ability in such a place as Armour Inst. But I know it will take a great number of years, to break down the prejudice.

Throughout her career, Wheeler was lauded for her teaching skills. A letter from a former president of the University of South Dakota is just one example of the high esteem in which she was held:

> She gives all her mind and energy to her teaching and is always willing to assist individual students out of hours. She is instinctively kind and interested thus winning her students to her cause—and her own enthusiasm soon communicates itself to her students.

In 1911, Wheeler accepted a position teaching at Mt. Holyoke College. Originally hired as an instructor, in 1914 she was promoted to the position of associate professor. The same year, she published a paper on linear equations of infinite unknowns. She also did joint research with **Ruth L. Gordon**, resulting in a work on the highest common factor of two polynomials. Alexander, despite his illness, taught at Northwestern University for one year beginning in 1915. He also remained actively engaged in research, and presented papers in 1915 and 1917 at the conferences of the American Society of Mathematics.

In 1918, a position became available at Bryn Mawr College. Wheeler happily accepted it. Bryn Mawr offered a distinguished graduate program under the direction of *Charlotte A. Scott. Wheeler hoped to assume the position of chair upon Scott's retirement and would indeed succeed Scott in 1924.

In 1920, Wheeler was promoted to full professor, but her early years at Bryn Mawr were dogged by tragedy. That year, her father died,

Anna
Pell
Wheeler

followed by the death of her husband three months later in 1921. Her professional accomplishments, however, did not go unrecognized. In 1921, she was starred in *American Men of Science*, which listed the most prominent American scientists of the day.

In 1925, Wheeler remarried. A widower since 1915, Arthur Leslie Wheeler was a well-known classicist who had taught at Bryn Mawr for several years. Just before their marriage, he accepted a position as professor of Latin at Princeton University. The couple moved to Princeton.

In 1923, Wheeler was appointed to the Board of Trustees of the American Mathematical Society. The next year, she was elected to the Council. She served on a three-person committee which selected the first recipient of the Chauvenet Prize in 1926. In 1927, Wheeler was invited to deliver the Colloquium Lectures at the American Mathematical Society, an annual series of three or four lectures delivered by a respected mathematician. She was the first and only woman to be so honored until 1980, when *Julia B. Robinson delivered the lectures. In 1927, Wheeler also became editor of *Annals of Mathematics*, a distinguished journal.

Wheeler continued to lecture at Bryn Mawr on a part-time basis. The reduced teaching load allowed her to pursue her research interest, and to became more involved with mathematics at Princeton University. In 1926, she had been elected to Phi Beta Kappa.

The Wheelers built a summer retreat in the Adirondacks, naming their hideaway Q.E.D. in reference to their mutual interests. There, Wheeler indulged her passion for wildflowers and bird watching. Unfortunately her husband died suddenly in 1932 of apoplexy. Thus, Wheeler returned to Bryn Mawr and resumed teaching full time. In 1939, she was one of a group of scholars who successfully petitioned for an American analog to the German journal *Zentralblatt für Mathematik und ihre Grenzgebiete*.

Wheeler's research centered on linear algebra of infinite variations. Her work was part of what has come to be known as functional analysis. Her interest sprang from the potential of various applications to differential and integral equations. Wheeler's mathematical training coincided with a period during which functional analysis was emerging as a field in its own right. Thus her research focused primarily on analysis, though she did investigate some purely algebraic problems. Of particular note was her work on biorthogonal systems of function, and their analytical uses in integral equations.

With the exception of brief absences, Wheeler remained chair of the Bryn Mawr mathematics department until her retirement in 1948. During those years, she supervised seven Ph.D. students and worked diligently to enhance the college's reputation. During the Great Depression, she tried to cultivate an atmosphere of intellectual inquiry and career opportunity despite the severe financial constraints placed upon the institution. Recognizing the important role which research played in the fostering of teaching excellence, she advocated reduced teaching loads during a period of fiscal restraint. Wheeler was aware of the difficulties faced by women in the profession, and urged her students to participate in the professional forums, and to do so on an equal basis with male colleagues. As one colleague subsequently wrote her:

> I shall always look back on those years with deep gratitude that the opportunity was given me to share them with you. You never wavered. The shrine of mathematics didn't need any apologies. There was no compromising. There was work to be done and you kept the path free from pitfalls and blind alleys. You know,—when it comes right down to it,—you have not only been a mathematician and mathematics teacher,—you have been a sort of Institute for Advanced Study.

During her tenure as chair of the mathematics department, Wheeler was instrumental in securing a position at Bryn Mawr for the prominent German mathematician *Emmy Noether who had been driven out of Germany because of her Jewish ancestry. Wheeler also sought to organize an exchange program between Bryn Mawr and the University of Pennsylvania, in which Noether was to be intimately involved. At the time of Noether's sudden death in 1935, Wheeler was attempting to fund a tenured position for Noether at Bryn Mawr. As a personal friend, Wheeler was deeply shocked by Noether's untimely death, as was the entire Bryn Mawr community.

Wheeler received an honorary degree from the New Jersey College for Women in 1932, and in 1937 she was also honored in the same fashion with a degree from Mt. Holyoke College. She was acclaimed by the Women's Centennial Congress in 1940, as one of 100 women who had flourished in careers traditionally closed to women. Wheeler was also praised for her devotion to her students. She was generous with her time, expertise, and finances. Poor students often received copies of books which Wheeler claimed she no longer used. Her home in the Adirondacks was open to graduate students seeking encouragement and a quiet place to work. She inspired her students with her passion for mathematics, and her willingness to discuss theoretical problems.

When Wheeler retired from Bryn Mawr in 1948, her former students and colleagues held a testimonial dinner for her. In retirement, Wheeler did not withdraw from mathematics. Despite severe arthritis, she continued to attend conferences and seminars. In 1964, a seminar series was created in her honor at Bryn Mawr.

Anna Pell Wheeler suffered a stroke and died on March 26, 1966, at age 82. She was buried alongside Alexander Pell in the Lower Merion Baptist Church Cemetery at Bryn Mawr. Wheeler's research was always well received, and respected. Her determination to pursue a career in the male-dominated field of mathematics speaks volumes of her force of character and courage. Her teaching, particularly at Bryn Mawr, inspired a generation of women to pursue careers in mathematics, and to do so with vigor and a pioneering spirit which attempted to negate the male prejudices of the mathematics profession in the United States.

SOURCES:

Green, Judy, and Jeanne LaDuke. "Contributors to American Mathematics: An Overview and Selection," in *Women of Science.* G. Kass-Simon and Patricia Farnes, eds. Bloomington, IN: Indiana University Press, 1990.

Grinstein, Louise S. "Wheeler, Anna Johnson Pell," in *Notable American Women: The Modern Period.* Barbara Sicherman and Carol Hurd Green, eds. Cambridge, MA: The Belknap Press of Harvard University, 1980.

———, and Paul J. Campbell. "Anna Johnson Pell Wheeler: Her Life and Work," in *Historia Mathematica.* NY: Academic Press, 1982, vol. 9, pp. 37–53.

Iyanga, S., and Y. Kawada, eds. *Encyclopedic Dictionary of Mathematics.* Cambridge, MA: MIT Press, 1977.

SUGGESTED READING:

Grinstein, Louise S., and Paul J. Campbell. "Anna Johnson Pell Wheeler," in *Women of Mathematics.* NY: Greenwood Press, 1987.

Hugh A. Stewart, M.A.,
Guelph, Ontario, Canada

Wheeler, Candace (1827–1923)

American designer who was the first woman to work professionally in the decorative arts in America. Born in Delhi, New York, on March 24, 1827; died in New York City on August 5, 1923; second daughter and third of eight children of Abner Gilman Thurber (a dairy farmer and fur dealer) and Lucy (Dunham) Thurber; educated at home in the arts; attended Delaware Academy in Delhi, New York; married Thomas M. Wheeler (a bookkeeper and businessman), on June 28, 1844 (died 1895); children: Candace (1845–1876); James Cooper (b. 1853); Dora Wheeler Keith (1856–1940); Dunham (b. 1861).

Encouraged by Eastman Johnson to take up painting (1854); studied painting in Dresden, Germany; eldest daughter died (1876); founded the Society of Decorative Art of New York City (1877); founded the Women's Exchange with Mrs. William Choate (1878); invited to join Louis Comfort Tiffany, Samuel Coleman, and Lockwood de Forest in Associated Artists to create textiles and embroideries; left Tiffany and founded own Associated Artists (1883); worked on advisory council of Woman's Art School of Cooper Union; directed exhibit of women's work for Chicago World's Columbian Exposition and was color director of Women's Building (1893); retired from Associated Artists (1900); published Principles of Home Decoration *(1903).*

Candace Wheeler opened up the world of decorative arts as a profession not only for herself but for many indigent women who provided for themselves through the institutions she founded. Her textile designs and skills in interior decoration were much admired as she became a key figure in the art nouveau movement in the United States. At a time when American textile designs were emerging into prominence, Wheeler was the first woman to work professionally in the decorative arts.

Wheeler was born Candace Thurber in Delhi, New York, in 1827 and grew up in a creative family headed by her father, an abolitionist and Presbyterian deacon. Both her parents encouraged her interests in artistic endeavors such as drawing, poetry, weaving, spinning, sewing, knitting, and embroidery, much of which she learned under the tutelage of her mother. At age 17, she married Thomas Wheeler who also appreciated art and literature, and together they became friends and patrons of the artists in their community on the outskirts of New York City. Their country home, Nestledown, in Jamaica, New York, was a gathering place for many of the artists of the day, a circle which included Eastman Johnson, who encouraged Wheeler to take up painting after noting her interest in drawing and her fine eye for color.

Wheeler did not seriously pursue artistic studies until the fall of 1865, when the entire Wheeler family went abroad to visit the artists and galleries in Italy, France, and Germany. They ended up in Dresden where Wheeler's husband left the family for the winter, and Wheeler was able to study for an entire season with a professor of painting. She described this period in her life as "the beginning of preparation for work in the world."

Tragedy struck Wheeler when her eldest daughter died in June 1876. To cope with her grief, she turned to charitable work that put to use all of her skills. While visiting the Centennial Exposition in Philadelphia shortly after her daughter's death, she found inspiration in an exhibit of art needlework from a London school set up specifically to teach "decayed gentlewomen" how to earn a living by means of this decorative art. Women who were educated yet destitute, with no respectable means of support, were often called "surplus women," living in the direst poverty or as poor working dependents in the homes of well-off relatives. Scorned and ridiculed by society, they often performed the drudgery of keeping house with none of the status of married women and no means to achieve independence. Wheeler felt compelled to organize a similar project at home to aid women in such circumstances in New York City. With the support of some of the wealthiest women in Manhattan, she founded the Society of Decorative Arts of New York City in 1877. The group exhibited and sold women's handicrafts and taught classes in embroidery and china painting. Wheeler left the organization the following year and, with the help of **Mrs. William Choate**, established the Women's Exchange to market a variety of products made by women.

In 1879, Wheeler was approached by Louis Comfort Tiffany with an offer to join him in his new interior design company, Associated Artists. Tiffany, a painter and glassmaker, was among those who introduced art nouveau to America. Two other artists, Samuel Coleman and Lockwood de Forest, managed woodworking and carving, and Wheeler was in charge of the soft arts, including textiles, embroidery, tapestry and needlework. As was the style of art nouveau, she made much use of floral motifs and showed the influence of Japanese art and design. Among Wheeler's commissions were Mark Twain's house in Hartford, Connecticut, the Union League Club in New York City, and the White House, redecorated at the beginning of the Chester A. Arthur administration.

In 1883, Wheeler decided that the textile department could survive on its own, and she founded her own company, also called Associated Artists, made up entirely of women. She was expressly concerned with showing that women could make a good living if properly trained. Her first assistant was her daughter **Dora Wheeler Keith**, who had studied painting in Paris. Candace experimented with color and texture, designing rich new fabrics of printed silk, velvets, damasks, and brocades. Fitting her designs to their settings, she created a Scottish thistle pattern for Andrew Carnegie and a pattern featuring bells, wheels, and drifting smoke for a railway parlor car. She invented new methods, techniques, and stitches, for which she held British and American patents. Her tapestries were based on American themes such as *Evangeline*, after Longfellow, and *Hester Prynne*, after Nathaniel Hawthorne's character from *The Scarlet Letter*.

At the same time, Wheeler was working on the advisory council of the Woman's Art School of Cooper Union and lecturing at the New York Institute for Artist-Artisans. In 1893, during the planning of the Chicago World's Columbian Exposition, she was named both director of the exhibit of women's work in the applied arts and color director of the Women's Building. She and her daughter Dora collaborated on decorations for the library of the Women's Building in vivid blues and greens to harmonize with the sky and water visible from the window. "Fifteen years ago, no American manufacturer thought of buying an American design for his carpet, or wallpaper, or textile," said Wheeler. "Today the manufacturers all agree that the most popular designs they can furnish are made by our native designers, who are, to a very large extent, women."

In 1900, Wheeler retired from Associated Artists, handing the reins over to her son, Dunham Wheeler, then took up her pen. She wrote innovative articles and essays on color and decoration; an autobiography, *Yesterdays in a Busy Life* (1918); and an important and influential book, *Principles of Home Decoration*, published in 1903. Candace Wheeler died at age 96, writing and painting to the end. Although tastes and styles have changed over time, Wheeler's legacy of opening the professions of textile design and interior decoration for women and giving higher status to American designers has lasted.

SOURCES:

James, Edward T., ed. *Notable American Women, 1607–1950.* Cambridge, MA: The Belknap Press of Harvard University, 1971.

Rubinstein, Charlotte Streifer. *American Women Artists.* NY: Avon, 1982.

Uglow, Jennifer S., comp. and ed. *The International Dictionary of Women's Biography.* 2nd ed. NY: Continuum, 1985.

Malinda Mayer,
writer and editor,
Falmouth, Massachusetts

Wheeler, Ella (1850–1919).

See Wilcox, Ella Wheeler.

Wheeler, Lucille (1935—)

Canadian skier. Name variations: Lucile Wheeler. Born in 1935 in St. Jovite, Quebec; daughter of Harry Wheeler; married Kaye Vaughan (an Ottawa Roughrider football player).

*Won an Olympic bronze in the downhill (1956), behind gold medalist **Madeleine Berthod** of Switzerland; won the World championship in skiing (1958).*

At Grey Rocks Inn, a large resort in the Laurentian Mountains north of Montreal founded by her grandmother in 1902, Lucille Wheeler grew up on skis, plunging down slopes at age three. The resident ski instructor, Herman Gadner of Austria, began her instruction at age 5; by age 10, Wheeler was competing against Canada's best of all ages. At 12, she won the Canadian Junior championship; at 14, she competed at the World championships in Aspen, Colorado. Wheeler moved to Kitzbuhel, Austria, in 1952, for rigorous winter training under the tough tutelage of Pepi Salvenmoser. In February 1958, at the World championships in Bad Gastein, Austria, she blitzed the downhill, finishing a full five seconds ahead of the second-place finisher. She then went out and won the giant slalom, becoming the first Canadian to win a skiing World championship. Following her victory, she promptly retired, married, and settled down to raise a family.

SOURCES:

Batten, Jack. *Champions: Great Figures in Canadian Sport.* Toronto: New Press, 1971.

Wheeler, Rosina (1802–1882).

See Bulwer-Lytton, Rosina, Lady.

Wheelock, Lucy (1857–1946)

American proponent of kindergartens who founded what became Wheelock College. Born in Cambridge, Vermont, on February 1, 1857; died in Boston, Massachusetts, on October 2, 1946; second daughter and second of six children of Edwin Wheelock (a Congregational minister) and Laura (Pierce) Wheelock; attended Underhill Academy in Vermont for one year; graduated from public high school in Reading, Massachusetts, in 1874; entered Chauncy Hall School in Boston, Massachusetts, in 1876; graduated from the Kindergarten Training School in 1879.

Directed inaugural one-year training course for kindergarten teachers at Chauncy Hall School; elected member of National Education Association (1892); served as second president of International Kindergarten Union (1895–99); organized free kindergarten for poor children in Hope Chapel, Boston (1895); established Wheelock Training School (1896); expanded curriculum to include teacher training for primary grades (1899); appointed to committee on education of the National Congress of Mothers (1899), and became chair (1908); served as chair of the Committee of Nineteen (1905–09); organized and led group of American kindergarten teachers to the home of Friedrich Froebel in Germany (1911); erected first permanent building for Wheelock School (1914); chaired committees to foster cooperation among educational and parent associations (1913–18); visited eight Southern states to promote the kindergarten movement (1916); included preparation for nursery school teachers in Wheelock Training School program (1926); served on the Educational Committee of the League of Nations (1929); incorporated Wheelock School as nonprofit institution (1939); Wheelock Training School became Wheelock College (1941).

Lucy Wheelock devoted her life to advocating for kindergartens, and training teachers of the very young. Her advocacy involved her in numerous committees concerned with children's education, and her teacher training programs resulted in her founding and directing the Wheelock School in Boston, Massachusetts, which later became Wheelock College.

Wheelock was born in Cambridge, Vermont, in 1857. Her first teaching assignment was in the village school in Cambridge, where she grew up. With the intention of enrolling in Wellesley College, she entered Chauncy Hall School in Boston, Massachusetts, in 1876. Her plans changed dramatically, however, when she was introduced to the school's kindergarten. She said she felt as if "the gates of heaven were opened and I had a glimpse of the kingdom where peace and love reign." On the advice of *Elizabeth Palmer Peabody (1804–1894), the founder of Boston's first kindergarten, Wheelock enrolled in the Kindergarten Training School in Boston conducted by **Ella Snelling Hatch**, where Peabody was one of the lecturers. Wheelock received her diploma in 1879 and taught for ten years in the kindergarten of the Chauncy Hall School. In 1888, kindergartens were made part of the public school system in Boston, and Chauncy Hall responded by inaugurating a one-year training course for teachers that Wheelock directed. The program was a tremendous success, the initial class of six students growing to accommodate students from all over the country. In 1893, the course was lengthened to two years, and in 1896 Wheelock established the Wheelock Kindergarten Training School, independent of Chauncy Hall. As Wheelock's school continued to grow, she added training for primary grade teachers in 1899, for nursery school teachers in 1926, and in 1929 extended the kindergarten training program to three years.

The kindergarten movement engendered strong feelings among educators in the late 19th and early 20th centuries. Based on the philosophy and methods originally developed by German educator Friedrich Froebel, kindergartens were first opened in Germany. Enthusiastic disciples spread Froebel's ideas throughout Europe and America, instituting a new phase in public education based on the premise that children are essentially dynamic and creative, rather than merely receptive. Froebel's belief in learning through activity and play gave rise to a series of specialized toys designed to stimulate learning by well-directed play accompanied by songs and music. Wheelock's students were trained in fundamental Froebelian methods as well as other progressive techniques, and were taught to consider the kindergarten classroom as only one of the important elements in the total process of socialization.

As the kindergarten movement took hold and public schools began adding kindergartens to their systems, educators started to divide into several camps of thought regarding the future development of the kindergarten. Wheelock was in the center of the movement and of the controversies that grew out of it. From 1892, when she became a committee member of the National Education Association to plan a national organization of kindergarten teachers, she served on many committees to foster the growth of kindergartens: the International Kindergarten Union (co-founder and president, 1893–99), the committee on education of the National Congress of Mothers (chair), and the Committee of Nineteen (chair, 1905–09).

Her function on the latter committee was as mediator among the factions that had grown up among educators who differed about the role of Froebel's system as applied to contemporary kindergartens. There was a conservative majority, represented by *Susan Elizabeth Blow, who felt that there should be no alteration of Froebel's original ideas; *Patty Smith Hill represented a smaller, more liberal group who believed in adopting flexible routines to allow the child more freedom in the choice of activities and play materials; a small minority, which included Wheelock and *Elizabeth Harrison, favored a gradual, intentional evolution of the Froebelian system. The Committee of Nineteen, appointed to study the areas of disagreement, issued a report in 1913, edited by Wheelock, entitled *The Kindergarten*.

Other committees she served on were intended to foster cooperation among teachers and parents. These included the committee on education of the National Congress of Mothers (later called the National Congress of Parents and Teachers) in 1899, a committee on coopera-

tion between the National Congress of Mothers and the International Kindergarten Union in 1916, and a similar committee of the Kindergarten Union and the National Education Association from 1913 to 1918. In 1929, she was appointed to the Educational Committee of the League of Nations.

Wheelock's activities included extending the benefits of kindergarten education to the children of the poor. To this end, she helped organize a free kindergarten at Hope Chapel, sponsored by Boston's Old South Church, served on the board of directors of the Ruggles Street Neighborhood House in Roxbury and of the House of Good Will in Boston, and helped to organize a kindergarten at the South End House, a Boston social settlement, at the request of founder Robert A. Woods. In 1916, she was one of a team of speakers who traveled through eight Southern states giving speeches to promote the kindergarten movement. She published many articles in educational journals, and in 1920 co-authored *Talks to Mothers* with **Elizabeth Colson**. She also translated stories for children from German and edited several books about the kindergarten movement.

Wheelock retired as director of Wheelock School in 1939, the year it became incorporated as a nonprofit institution. At that time, it had 325 students and 23 faculty members. It became Wheelock College in 1941, five years before Lucy Wheelock's death on October 2, 1946.

SOURCES:

James, Edward T., ed. *Notable American Women, 1607–1950.* Cambridge, MA: The Belknap Press of Harvard University, 1971.

McHenry, Robert, ed. *Famous American Women.* NY: Dover, 1980.

Malinda Mayer,
writer and editor,
Falmouth, Massachusetts

Whiffin, Blanche (1845–1936)

English-born actress. Name variations: Blanche Galton; Mrs. Thomas Whiffin. Born Blanche Galton in London, England, on March 12, 1845; died in Montvale, Virginia, of bronchial pneumonia at the home of her children on November 25, 1936; daughter of Joseph West Galton (a secretary in the London general post office) and Mary Ann (Pyne) Galton (an accomplished singer and piano teacher and sister of Louisa Pyne and Susan Pyne of the three well-known musical Pyne sisters); sister of Susan Galton; attended boarding schools in Gravesend, Kent, and in London; married Thomas Whiffin (a musician and actor), on July 11, 1868 (died 1897); children: Mary Blanche

Whiffin (died young); Thomas Whiffin (an actor turned farmer); Peggy Whiffin (an actress).

Blanche Whiffin, better known as Mrs. Thomas Whiffin, came to the United States in 1868 and was the original Buttercup in the American production of Gilbert and Sullivan's *H.M.S. Pinafore.* She joined the Lyceum Theater Company in New York in 1887, later played at the Empire, and became a great favorite with the public. She remained active into her 80s.

Whigham, Margaret.

See Margaret (d. 1993).

Whitby, abbess of.

See Hilda of Whitby (614–680).
See Elflaed (d. 714).

Whitcher, Frances Miriam Berry

(1811–1852)

American satirist and cartoonist who created the characters of the Widow Bedott and Aunt Magwire. Name variations: Miriam Berry; Miriam Whitcher; Widow Bedott; (pseudonym) Frank. Born in Whitesboro, New York, on November 1, 1811; died of tuberculosis in Whitesboro on January 4, 1852; 11th of 15 children of Lewis Berry (a tavern owner) and Elizabeth (Wells) Berry; educated at the village academy; married Benjamin W. Whitcher (an Episcopal cleric), on January 6, 1847; children: one daughter, Alice Miriam (b. 1849).

Showed early talent for drawing caricatures and writing satirical verse and parodies; published "Widow Spriggins" in weekly paper in Rome, New York; began publishing "The Widow Bedott" monologues in Neal's Saturday Gazette *(1846); submitted "Aunt Magwire's Experience" to* Godey's Lady's Book *(1847–49); posthumous collection* The Widow Bedott Papers *published (1856) and sold over 100,000 copies; her characters were dramatized by "Petroleum V. Nasby" (David Ross Locke) as* The Widow Bedott, or a Hunt for a Husband, *an acting vehicle for Neil Burgess (1879).*

Frances Miriam Berry Whitcher, known as Miriam, was the first American woman to publish a series of satirical sketches. Her work appeared regularly in popular periodicals and was itself extremely popular, outliving her in a posthumously published collection *The Widow Bedott Papers* (1856) that sold over 100,000 copies, and in a dramatization of her characters written in 1879, *The Widow Bedott, or a Hunt for a Husband,* that actor Neil Burgess used as a vehicle for his talents.

Whitcher's satiric ability, both in drawing and in writing, exhibited itself early in her life. She was born in 1811 in Whitesboro, New York, and used her fellow classmates and teacher at the local school as her early subjects; her caricature-artistic efforts were not much appreciated. The negative responses of her family and peers caused her to withdraw, growing up lonely and reserved, but they did not stop her from exercising her unique art into adulthood.

Her first public presentation of her parodies occurred before the Maionian Circle, a local social and literary association, to which she read a piece called "Widow Spriggins." The outlandish parody of *Regina Maria Roche's popular sentimental novel *The Children of the Abbey* was written as an extended monologue in colloquial dialect, and drew from the country humor of the satirists Seba Smith and Augustus Baldwin Longstreet. The malapropisms and incongruous situations that form the foundation of the humor of the piece also figured largely in her future satires. "Widow Spriggins" became her first published piece when part of it was printed in a weekly newspaper in Rome, New York, by a friend.

However, Whitcher did not truly achieve literary fame until her creation of another widow, the Widow Bedott. The horrid, aging woman served as the voice of a set of monologues which Miriam sent to Joseph C. Neal, editor of *Neal's Saturday Gazette*, in Philadelphia; they were published in 1846. The character's competition with other women for potential husbands and her pretensions to being a society lady revolve around Whitcher's larger satire on rural life and all its politics and customs. Neal, himself a well-known humorist, printed them immediately under the name "Frank" and encouraged her to contribute more on a regular basis. These stories, filled with send-ups of pretentious behavior and malapropisms, were so popular that Louis Godey of *Godey's Lady's Book* requested a series of monologues for his publication using the character of Aunt Magwire, sister of the Widow Bedott. The monologues from "Aunt Magwire's Experience" are told from the point of view of this slightly nicer character, but are no less biting in their humorous commentary on female hypocrisy, gossiping and social competitiveness. One example is the Sewing Society, intended as an outlet for charitable works, which turns into a battleground of personal pride and prejudice, and is ultimately undermined by the vulgar rich woman who dominates the village. Whitcher's satire included women's rights advocates—both male and female—as well as petty gossips and those with materialistic ambitions and false sophistication. She wrote in a broad dialect, and often illustrated the pieces herself. The "Aunt Magwire" series ran from 1847—the year of Miriam's marriage—to 1849.

Miriam's profession conflicted with that of her husband, Benjamin Whitcher, who was a minister of an Episcopal church in Elmira, New York. Several members of the church and community saw themselves in Miriam's foolish characters and considered such portrayals unforgivable in their minister's wife. A resulting lawsuit eventually forced her husband's resignation from his pastorate. The irony of the situation was that Whitcher herself was very devout. Brought up in Calvinism as a member of the Presbyterian Church, she took great solace in her Episcopal faith, and published several hymns and devotional poems. She also published the lesser-known "Letters from Timberville," of slightly less colloquial flavor.

After the birth of a daughter in 1849, Whitcher contracted tuberculosis, from which she never recovered, dying three years later at the age of 40.

SOURCES:

Buck, Claire, ed. *The Bloomsbury Guide to Women's Literature.* NY: Prentice Hall, 1992.

James, Edward T., ed. *Notable American Women, 1607–1950.* Cambridge, MA: The Belknap Press of Harvard University, 1971.

McHenry, Robert, ed. *Famous American Women.* NY: Dover, 1980.

Read, Phyllis J., and Bernard L. Witlieb. *The Book of Women's Firsts.* NY: Random House, 1992.

Weatherford, Doris. *American Women's History.* NY: Prentice Hall, 1994.

Malinda Mayer,
writer and editor,
Falmouth, Massachusetts

White, Alma Bridwell (1862–1946)

Founder of the Pillar of Fire Church and the first woman ordained a bishop in the United States. Born Mollie Alma Bridwell on June 16, 1862, near Vanceburg, Lewis County, Kentucky; died on June 26, 1946, in Zarephath, New Jersey; fifth daughter and seventh of eleven children of William Moncure Bridwell (a tanner and farmer) and Mary Ann (Harrison) Bridwell; attended Vanceburg Seminary and Millersburg Female College, both in Kentucky; married Kent White (a Methodist minister), on December 21, 1887; children: two sons, Arthur Kent White (b. March 14, 1889) and Ray Bridwell White (b. August 24, 1892).

Alma Bridwell White was born in 1862, near Vanceburg, Lewis County, Kentucky, the fifth daughter and seventh of eleven children of William Moncure Bridwell, a tanner and farmer, and **Mary Ann Bridwell**. In 1869, the family moved to Vanceburg so that her sisters might continue their schooling at the Vanceburg Female Seminary; in 1879, White began to study there as well. In 1880, the Bridwells moved to Millersburg where she and her sisters continued their education at the Millersburg Female College.

Receiving her teaching certificate in 1881, White taught first in the local school district and then in 1882 moved to Montana where she lived with an aunt, while teaching in the Dillon School District. She returned to Kentucky in 1884 and attended Millersburg College for another year. Unable to find a teaching position upon her return to Dillon, she moved to Salt Lake City and took a teaching position at the Methodist Seminary. In 1886, she became engaged to Kent White, whom she had met in Dillon; they were married on December 21, 1887, in Denver.

Living in Denver, where Kent was studying at the University of Denver for the ministry in the Methodist Church, the Whites became involved in the Colorado Holiness Association. In March 1893, White experienced the "second blessing" of sanctification of the Holy Spirit in Erie, Colorado, where her husband had been transferred by his conference of the Methodist Church. Following her sanctification, her religious vocation increased, and she began preaching, leading meetings, and organizing prayer sessions. In late 1895, Kent withdrew from regular ministerial duties within the Colorado conference of the Methodist Church to join his wife's endeavors. On July 7, 1896, White established an independent mission of the holiness movement within the Methodist Church. Believing that Methodism had departed from true Christianity and was confined by its refusal to ordain women or affirm their right to preach, White soon felt the need to sever ties with the Methodist Church. On December 29, 1901, she founded the Pentecostal Union Church, a religious, educational, and benevolent organization soon known as the Pillar of Fire, and on March 16 was ordained into the Pentecostal Union Church. Her husband relinquished his Methodist clergy credentials on March 14, 1902. In 1906, White began work to establish a central location for the church on land it had obtained in Zarephath, New Jersey, and on January 19, 1908, she officially moved the church headquarters there. That same year, the Zarephath Bible Training School (later known as the Zarephath Bible Institute) was established, quickly followed by the establishment in

1912 of the Zarephath Academy, later renamed the Alma Preparatory School. She would purchase Westminster College, renamed Belleview, from the Presbyterian Church in 1920 and found Alma White College in 1921.

The Whites' marriage, never perfect, had started to spiral downward in 1908 when Kent began advocating a more evangelical spiritualism and the speaking in tongues. On August 11, 1909, he renounced his church membership and left Zarephath. Despite sporadic reconciliations over the years, on March 13, 1918, Kent assumed the pastorate of Apostolic Faith's Stone Church in Chicago and then moved to a pentecostal pastorate in Bournemouth, England, in 1919. He would return to Denver in 1939, dying at the home of their son Ray White, on July 30, 1940. While serving as an ordained minister and as the spiritual and administrative leader of the Pillar of Fire following Kent's final renunciation of the church, White was consecrated a bishop on September 1, 1918, by William Godbey. She thereby became the first woman ordained as a bishop in the United States. That same year, the church accepted its first official church discipline, written by Ray White. Her second son Arthur White became a bishop in the Pillar of Fire in 1932 and its second president and general superintendent following his mother's death. White died from heart disease on June 26, 1946, in Zarephath and was buried at Fairmont Cemetery in Denver.

The Pillar of Fire Church has had questionable associations with the Ku Klux Klan. It was also known for its virulently anti-Catholic and anti-immigration rhetoric and often served as a divisive element in American social relations. But by rejecting the male dominance of the institutional church by forming a pentecostal union that opened the pulpit and its administration to women, White led the way for the ordination of women in more mainstream churches and denominations across America.

SOURCES:

Stanley, Susie Cunningham. *Feminist Pillar of Fire: The Life of Alma White*. Cleveland, OH: Pilgrim Press, 1993.

SUGGESTED READING:

White, Alma. *Alma White, The Story of My Life and the Pillar of Fire*. 5 Vols. Zarephath: Pillar of Fire Church, 1935–43.

———. *Looking back from Beulah*. Women in American Protestant Religion, 1800–1930 Series, no. 32. NY: Garland, 1987.

COLLECTIONS:

Personal papers are held by the family. Some personal papers and material pertaining to the church are held by the Pillar of Fire Church, Zarephath, New Jersey.

Amanda Carson Banks,
lecturer, Vanderbilt Divinity School,
Nashville, Tennessee

White, Anna (1831–1910)

American Shaker eldress and reformer. Born in Brooklyn, New York, on January 21, 1831; died in New Lebanon, New York, on December 16, 1910; third daughter of five children of Robert White (a hardware merchant) and Hannah (Gibbs) White; in early teens, sent to Mansion Square Seminary in Poughkeepsie, New York.

Raised as a Quaker; learned of Shakers through father's business; joined the Shaker community in New Lebanon, New York, as a member of the North Family (1849); appointed associate eldress (1865); became first eldress of the North Family (1887); worked for peace and women's rights outside the community.

Anna White was born in Brooklyn, New York, on January 21, 1831. She was the daughter of Quakers, her father having converted to the Society of Friends while Anna was still quite young. Both her faith and her parents encouraged her to do good works, particularly on behalf of the poor, so White's social conscience was already quite developed in childhood. She particularly remembered hearing anti-slavery lecturer *Lucretia Mott speak at a Friends meeting. After some schooling at a Friends school in Poughkeepsie, New York, White returned to her father in New York City and took up the tailoring trade.

White's father Robert underwent another religious conversion when he joined a Shaker community in New Lebanon, New York, having been exposed to the faith through business dealings with the Hancock, Massachusetts, Shaker community. Although this conservative, apocalyptic sect advocated both celibacy and communal living, Robert White retained his connection to his family. Anna White, who had occasionally joined her father on his trips to Hancock, likewise fell in love with the Shakers' rural community, songs, and lively meetings, and converted to Shakerism on September 16, 1849, contrary to the wishes of her family.

The New Lebanon Shaker community was to be White's home for the rest of her life, and she met several other prominent Shakers such as Mother **Ruth Landon**, successor to Mother **Lucy Wright**, Elder Fredrick Evans and Eldress **Antoinette Doolittle**. Within 15 years, White herself had ascended to a leadership position as associate eldress, responsible for the care of the girls. Upon the death of Eldress Antoinette in 1887, White took her position as first eldress of the North Family. In over 60 years of Shaker life, White created valuable documents on Shaker songs and history. She compiled two books of Shaker music, including some of her own compositions, and collaborated with Eldress **Leila S. Taylor** on the book *Shakerism: Its Meaning and Message*, published in 1904. At the time, it was the only published history of the movement written by one of its members. Her other interests included vegetarianism, spiritualism, and the tenets of Christian Science.

White's heavy involvement with the community did not preclude her activities in the "outside world." In the 1890s, she wrote a letter for a group of French women, "The Shaker Sisters Plea for Dreyfus," in support of Alfred Dreyfus, a Jewish officer in the French army falsely accused and convicted of selling military secrets to the Germans. She also participated in leadership capacities in such women's organizations as the Alliance of Women for Peace and the National Council of Women of the United States, both of which benefited from her efforts as vice-president. White was also a member of the National American Woman Suffrage Association. She spoke on behalf of all these interests before the Universal Peace Union in Mystic, Connecticut, in 1899, the Equal Rights Club of Hartford in 1903, and a conference in the New Lebanon meeting house in 1905, with the resulting resolutions presented by White to President Theodore Roosevelt. She died at the New Lebanon community in 1910 and was buried there in the cemetery of the North Family.

SOURCES:

James, Edward T., ed. *Notable American Women, 1607–1950*. Cambridge, MA: The Belknap Press of Harvard University, 1971.

Malinda Mayer,
writer and editor,
Falmouth, Massachusetts

White, Antonia (1899–1980)

British novelist and translator. Name variations: Eirene Adeline Botting. Born Eirene Adeline Botting in London, England, on March 31, 1899; died in London on April 10, 1980; only child of Cecil George Botting (a senior classics master at St. Paul's School in London) and Christine Julia (White) Botting; expelled from the Convent of the Sacred Heart in Roehampton, 1914; attended St. Paul's Girls' School in London, 1914–16; attended Royal Academy of Dramatic Art in London, 1919–20; married in 1921 (annulled 1924); married in 1924 (annulled 1929); married writer Tom (H.T.) Hopkinson, in 1930 (divorced 1938); children: two daughters, Susan Chitty and Lyndall.

At 14, expelled from convent school; left St. Paul's Girls' School against father's wishes; attended Royal Academy of Dramatic Art for one year (1919–20); actress in provincial repertory; first mar-riage annulled on grounds of non-consummation (1924); had mental breakdown followed by nine months in mental hospital; became fashion editor and drama critic; published Frost in May *(1933); mental instability recurred (1934); recovered using Freudian analysis; during World War II, wrote for BBC and worked in Foreign Office; became prolific translator (1949 on); published first volume of trilogy,* The Lost Traveller *(1950), followed by* The Sugar House *(1952) and* Beyond the Glass *(1954); received Clairouin Prize for translation (1950); became fellow of the Royal Society of Literature (1957).*

Antonia White was born on March 31, 1899, to Cecil George Botting and **Christine White Botting** in London, England. She converted with her parents to Catholicism at the age of seven and received an education at two different Catholic schools. White was a voracious reader but had a troubled academic career. Her first school, the Convent of the Sacred Heart in Roehampton, expelled her in 1914 after the nuns discovered a love story White had been writing. She had hoped that the manuscript's overt Catholicism would please her father, but the hints of illicit behavior in her writing overshadowed that element. Finding herself the target of the disapproval of the two most important authorities in her life—her father and the Catholic Church—White stopped writing until those influences in her life diminished. Even when she did resume writing at age 30 after her father's death and the lapse of her faith, she could never shake accompanying feelings of guilt and anxiety.

White's strained relationship with her father did not improve after she left her next school, St. Paul's Girls' School in London, where her father was a senior classics master. She studied at the Royal Academy of Dramatic Art in London from 1919 to 1920, and acted with a touring company the following year. She accepted a variety of teaching and clerical jobs after leaving the stage and landed more permanently in the field of journalism when she became an advertising copywriter for a magazine. Now writing again, she expanded her style to become a theater critic and fashion editor, in addition to copywriting for an advertising agency, teaching in an acting studio, and working for British intelligence during World War II.

At the same time White was making her mark in the professional world, she struggled with mental illness and failed marriages. Her first marriage in 1921 was disrupted by her breakdown and confinement to an insane asylum for nine months. It was annulled in 1924 on the grounds of non-consummation, and White married for a second time that same year. This marriage fared no better, and was likewise annulled in 1929. Although her third marriage, to journalist H. Tom Hopkinson, ended unhappily in divorce, White received encouragement from Hopkinson in her fiction writing after he discovered her long-neglected first novel. She gradually finished the work which she had begun at age 16, and published it as *Frost in May* in 1933.

As with the other three novels which made White's reputation, *Frost in May* was highly autobiographical, recounting her experiences at the convent school and including the details of her expulsion. In it, White attempted to reconcile her own conflicting feelings about faith and the Catholic Church, questioning why people become Catholic and how it is possible for people to subjugate their will to God's. The book was White's only commercial success, and a critic from *Commonweal* hailed it as a "minor classic" and its author "one of the best Catholic women writers of the generation." White, for her part, referred to the novel as "a kind of legend, the perfect thing I brought off once and never will again." It would be another 15 years before she produced her next book, possibly because of the loss of her "muse" after her divorce from Hopkinson in 1938. Another mental breakdown led her to try Freudian analysis, which she credited with ultimately curing her after four years of therapy. She also reconverted to the Catholic Church in 1940.

Starting in 1950, White wrote three novels in a five-year period, forming what was known as the Clara Batchelor trilogy. It was largely autobiographical, and despite the change of name of the heroine, from Wanda Grey in *Frost in May* to Clara Batchelor in the trilogy, the three novels are a sequel to her first work. The first of the three, *The Lost Traveller* (1950), re-explores the traumas of White's Catholic upbringing; the second novel, *Sugar House* (1952), examines the failure of her marriage; and the final novel, *Beyond the Glass* (1954), recreates the author's bouts with mental illness and institutionalization. Catholicism remains the underlying theme throughout her writing, yet there is a profound absence of hope. Critics suggested that White hoped to exorcise her own demons through the act of dramatizing her painful memories, but her inability to fully confront those memories resulted in a cold, distant narrative style. White acknowledged her struggle to express herself in writing, saying, "'Creative joy' is something I haven't felt since I was fourteen and don't expect to feel again." The four novels inspired a television series, "Frost in

Antonia White

May," in 1982. White also published an account of her return to the Catholic Church as *The Hound and the Falcon* in 1965.

In addition to her own writing, White began a career as a translator in 1949, taking the Clairouin Prize for translation the following year. Her English translations of such noted French authors as *Colette, Guy de Maupassant, and *Marguerite Duras, among others, numbered over 30, and in 1957 she became a fellow of the Royal Society of Literature. White died in 1980. One year later her unfinished autobiography, *As Once in May*, appeared, with an introduction by her daughter, **Susan Chitty**. Chitty also edited and published White's *Diaries 1926–1979*, in 1991.

SOURCES:

Buck, Claire, ed. *The Bloomsbury Guide to Women's Literature*. NY: Prentice Hall, 1992.

Contemporary Authors Online, 1999.

Schlueter, Paul, and June Schlueter, eds. *An Encyclopedia of British Women Writers*. NY: Garland, 1988.

Shattock, Joanne. *The Oxford Guide to British Women Writers*. Oxford: Oxford University Press, 1993.

Turner, Roland, ed. *The Annual Obituary 1980*. 1st ed. NY: St. Martin's Press, 1980.

Malinda Mayer,
writer and editor,
Falmouth, Massachusetts

White, Eartha M. (1876–1974)

African-American entrepreneur who was a major philanthropist in her hometown of Jacksonville, Florida. Name variations: Eartha White; Eartha Mary Magdalene White; Eartha M.M. White. Born in Jacksonville, Florida, on November 8, 1876; died in Jacksonville on January 18, 1974; daughter of Molly (or Mollie) Chapman (a former slave) and a white father, name unknown; adopted as an infant by Lafayette White and Clara (English) White; attended Stanton School in Jacksonville and Dr. Reason's School in New York City; studied hairdressing and manicuring at Madam Hall's School in New York City; attended Madam Thurber's National Conservatory of Music; attended Florida Baptist Academy, 1896–98; never married; no children.

Eartha M. White was born on November 8, 1876, in Jacksonville, Florida, to a mother who had been a slave and who never revealed the name of her baby's father, a young man from a "good" white family. She was soon adopted by Lafayette White, a former slave who had fought in the Civil War, and **Clara English White**. The devout and charitable daughter of freed slaves, Clara worked on steamships as a domestic and cook, and after Lafayette's death in 1881 raised young Eartha on her own. The two would remain close throughout the remainder of Clara's life, and her mother's example of consistent charity to the needy (she frequently gave meals to the poor) proved a lasting influence on Eartha.

White's education at Stanton School in Jacksonville was interrupted in 1888 by a yellow fever epidemic, which caused Clara to move with her daughter to New York City. There White attended Dr. Reason's School before transferring to Madam Hall's School to study hairdressing and manicuring. Later she attended Madam Thurber's National Conservatory of Music, where Harry T. Burleigh conducted her voice lessons. In 1895, she accepted an invitation to join the Oriental-American Company, one of the nation's first opera companies comprised entirely of African-Americans, and embarked on a world tour. During this time she became engaged to a young Southerner named James Lloyd Jordan, but he died a month before their planned wedding. Grief stricken, White gave up her singing career and returned to Jacksonville, where she spent the rest of her life unmarried.

After furthering her education at the Florida Baptist Academy from 1896 to 1898, White took a teaching post at her alma mater, Stanton School, while also working as a secretary for the Afro-American Life Insurance Company. Having saved $150 from her teacher's salary, in 1904 she opened a department store aimed at African-American consumers. The store was the first of numerous entrepreneurial successes, and over the next 25 years White bought a variety of small businesses in succession, including an employment agency, a dry-goods store, a steam laundry, a general store, a janitorial service, and a real-estate business. After working to make the business profitable, she typically would sell it and use the proceeds to buy another. In this way, she gradually built up an investment portfolio worth more than $1 million.

White never lived lavishly, however, and used her considerable business profits and skills to create a network of philanthropic organizations and institutions. The first black social worker and census taker in Jacksonville, she was also a tireless advocate of education and of social improvement, working for children, the elderly, the business community, the poor, and for African-Americans in general. In 1900, she became a charter member of Booker T. Washington's National Negro Business League (of which she long served as official historian), believing as did he that the best way to eradicate racism was to improve the education and business standing of the African-American community. That philosophy continually came to bear in White's numerous philanthropic interests. For years she operated the sole orphanage for black children in north Florida. In 1904, after the failure of an effort to recruit funding for a recreational center for at-risk boys, she began using her own money to staff and run such a center, on land donated by a friend; 12 years later, the city council finally took over responsibility for the center. White also volunteered at the county prison for over 50 years, conducting Sunday Bible classes and working for better conditions for inmates.

During World War I, White served as coordinator of recreational services for soldiers in Savannah, Georgia. She was also the only woman member of the Southeast War Camp Community Service, held in Jacksonville, in her position as director of the War Camp Community Services, and the only black woman to attend a White House meeting of the Council of National Defense. A moderate Republican, she worked in local Republican politics and in 1920 became the head of the Negro Republican Women Voters. During World War II she was active in the Red Cross and was named an honorary colonel in the Women's National Defense Program. A planned march on Washington, D.C., to protest racism and job discrimination in war employment that she organized with A. Philip Randolph in 1941 never materialized, but the idea itself had far-reaching consequences. The organization of the march led President Franklin D. Roosevelt to issue Executive Order 8802, which established the Fair Employment Practices Committee and banned discrimination in the federal government and in employment in defense industries.

However, White remains best known for her philanthropic work, including a rest home for tuberculosis patients, the *Harriet Beecher Stowe Community Center, a child placement center, and a home for unmarried pregnant women. In 1928, eight years after her mother died, she established the Clara White Mission in her honor. White lived for years on the second floor of the mission, which provided shelter and sustenance for the homeless and needy. Its services became even more important during the Depression; in 1932, she moved the mission to a larger building, and in February of the following year it fed over 2,500 people. The building also provided space for a Works Progress Administration office as well as various community services, and became a destination for a number of famous figures: among those who traveled there to meet with White were *Eleanor Roosevelt and *Mary McLeod Bethune. Rebuilt by White after a fire in 1944, the Clara White Mission is now a historic landmark, a homeless center and soup kitchen (the only non-profit soup kitchen in Jacksonville) as well as a museum of African-American history in the city. However, White was proudest of another project, the Eartha M. White Nursing Home, which she began with her own money. Completed in 1967 with federal funds, the home provided 120 beds for county and state welfare patients as well as occupational and physical therapy.

White lived to be 97, enjoying a busy and productive life almost to the end despite having to use a wheelchair after breaking her hip. She received numerous civic awards for her philanthropy, including the Good Citizenship Award from the local Jaycees (1969), the Lane Bryant Volunteer Award (1970), the American Nursing Home Association Better Life Award (1971), and an appointment to the President's National Center for Voluntary Action, for which she was honored at a White House reception (1971). Always believing that "service is the price we pay for the space we occupy on this planet," she died of heart failure on January 18, 1974, with her debt paid in full.

SOURCES:

Sicherman, Barbara, and Carol Hurd Green, eds. *Notable American Women: The Modern Period*. Cambridge, MA: The Belknap Press of Harvard University, 1980.

Smith, Jessie Carney, ed. *Notable Black American Women*. Detroit, MI: Gale Research, 1992.

COLLECTIONS:

White's papers are held in the Eartha M.M. White Collection in the library of the University of North Florida and at the Clara White Mission, both in Jacksonville, Florida.

Linda S. Walton,
freelance writer,
Grosse Pointe Shores, Michigan

White, Eliza Orne (1856–1947)

American novelist and children's author. Name variations: (pseudonym) Alex. Born on August 2, 1856, in Keene, New Hampshire; died on January 23, 1947, in Brookline, Massachusetts; daughter of William Orne White (a Unitarian minister) and Margaret Eliot (Harding) White; granddaughter of portrait artist Chester Harding; attended Miss Hall's School for Girls in Roxbury, Massachusetts; never married; no children.

Selected writings: As She Would Have It *(1873);* Miss Brooks *(1890);* When Molly was Six *(1894);* A Little Girl of Long Ago *(1896);* A Lover of Truth *(1898);* John Forsyth's Aunts *(1901);* Leslie Chilton *(1903);* A Borrowed Sister *(1906);* The Enchanted Mountain *(1911);* The First Step *(1914);* The Blue Aunt *(1918);* Peggy in Her Blue Frock *(1921);* Diana's Rosebush *(1927);* Sally in Her Fur Coat *(1929);* The Green Door *(1930);* Where Is Adelaide *(1933);* Anne Frances *(1935);* Helen's Gift House *(1938);* I: The Autobiography of a Cat *(1941);* Training of Sylvia *(1942);* When Esther Was a Little Girl *(1944).*

Eliza Orne White wrote over 40 books, the most popular of which were aimed at young girls, despite lacking the educational background that might be expected of a such prolific author. Born in 1856, she attended public schools in Keene, New Hampshire, and a boarding school in Massachusetts, but childhood illnesses interrupted her studies; eye trouble caused her to miss a year of school when she was 14, and an attack of typhoid two years later prevented her from graduating. Nevertheless, as a child of educated parents—her father William Orne White was a Unitarian minister who had graduated from Harvard, and her mother **Margaret Harding White**, the daughter of portrait painter Chester Harding, had attended *Elizabeth Palmer Peabody's school—she developed a strong interest in writing. Her father frequently read aloud to her from Homer, Spenser, and Dickens (whom they also heard lecture during one of his visits to the U.S.), and her mother encouraged her in and was delighted by all her creative efforts. Margaret White also had longtime connections to friends in literary circles. Young Eliza was especially fond of her mother's close friend *Lucretia Peabody Hale, whose serialized stories would later be published as the popular *Peterkin Papers*, and perhaps as a result of her influence Eliza wrote a series of romance stories around age 11. By age 18, she had begun writing short stories for publications including *The Christian Register* and *The Atlantic Monthly*, using the pseudonym "Alex." White traveled with her family for a year in Europe when she was 20, and upon her return moved with them to Brookline, Massachusetts, into a house that became her lifelong home.

White's first serious venture into writing books was a novel for adults, *Miss Brooks*, published in 1890. Although she continued to write literature for adults, her most popular works proved to be those aimed at children. Between 1894 and 1944, she wrote 29 children's books, chiefly for girls between the ages of six and ten, drawing on her own happy childhood memories for much of her vivid writing. *A Borrowed Sister* (1906), for example, grew out of her memory of the arrival of her beloved younger sister Rose, whom her parents had adopted when White was nine years old. "The good thing about imagination," she once wrote, "is that it defies time and bridges the gap between childhood and what to the uninitiated seems like age." Her work frequently explored middle-class family relationships in New England in various historical contexts, using what then seemed charming characters and a gentle sense of humor to tell her simply plotted stories. (Like those of many popular writers of her time, her books have not aged well.) Among the rare exceptions to her domestic stories focusing on well-behaved little girls was 1941's *I: The Autobiography of a Cat*, one of four books she wrote about cats.

White became totally blind in the late 1910s, and deaf not long thereafter, but continued to write. Her final book, *When Esther Was a Little Girl*, was published in 1944, just three years before her death from arteriosclerosis at age 90.

SOURCES:

Edgerly, Lois Stiles, ed. *Give Her This Day*. Gardiner, ME: Tilbury House, 1990.

James, Edward T., ed. *Notable American Women, 1607–1950*. Cambridge, MA: The Belknap Press of Harvard University, 1971.

Mainiero, Lina, ed. *American Women Writers*. NY: Frederick Ungar, 1972.

The National Cyclopaedia of American Biography. Ann Arbor, MI: University Microfilms, 1967.

Pendergast, Sara, and Tom Pendergast, eds. *St. James Guide to Children's Writers*. 5th ed. Detroit, MI: St. James Press, 1999.

Linda S. Walton,
freelance writer,
Grosse Pointe Shores, Michigan

White, Ellen Gould (1827–1915)

American religious leader who co-founded the Seventh-Day Adventist Church which she led for over 50 years, directing its expansion throughout North America, Europe, and Australia. Name variations: Ellen Gould Harmon. Born Ellen Gould Harmon on November 26, 1827, in Gorham, Maine; died on July 16, 1915, at her home in northern California; daughter of Robert Harmon (a hat maker) and Eunice Harmon; formal education ended at age nine; married James White, on August 30, 1846; children: Henry (1847–1863); James Edson (1849–1928); William (1854–1937); Herbert (September 1860–December 1860).

As a teenager, became involved in Adventist movement started by William Miller; at 17, began to have religious visions and began public career as religious leader; joined with husband to found the Seventh-Day Adventist Church (1863) and began to have visions regarding health reform; established the Western Health Reform Institute in Battle Creek, Michigan (1866); established churches in Europe (1885–87); established churches and a Bible school in Australia (1891–1900); established the College of Medical Evangelists, later Loma Linda University and Medical Center, in southern California (1909).

Publications: 26 books and over 5,000 periodical articles, including Spiritual Gifts (1858), Spirit of Prophecy (1870), Patriarchs and Prophets (1890), Ministry of Healing (1905), and her autobiography, Life Sketches of Ellen G. White (1915). All of White's writings are still in print and are available through the international headquarters of the Seventh-Day Adventist Church, located in Silver Spring, Maryland.

When the morning sun rose over New England on October 23, 1844, it was distressing proof to the "Millerites" (named after their leader William Miller) that the Second Coming of their Lord, Jesus Christ, was not at hand. Based on their reading of the Scriptures, they had believed that October 22nd would be the day of the apocalypse and had spent the preceding weeks preparing for the event. Some had given away their money and dispersed their earthly goods, while others had neglected their farms or left their jobs. They had looked toward October 22nd not with despair or fear, but with joy, believing that at the moment of the Last Judgment they would be among the ones chosen to spend eternity with Christ.

When the apocalypse failed to materialize as the Millerites had predicted, the men and women who had gathered together to witness the end of the age were dealt a crushing blow, from which many never fully recovered. The events of that October day, which became known as the "Great Disappointment," left them in a spiritual wilderness, stripped of the faith that had once helped them to make sense of their lives. A young girl, barely in her teens when she first heard William Miller speak, was among those who had prepared for that fall day. Ellen Gould Harmon had arrived at Miller's first lecture already full of anxiety about her personal salvation. Miller's words about Christ's imminent descent to earth touched at the heart of her concern and opened up to her a new way of understanding her religious faith. Ultimately, this belief in the imminent advent of Christ would become the focus of her life's work.

Ellen Gould Harmon was born in 1827 on a small farm near Gorham, Maine. She and her twin sister **Elizabeth Harmon** were the last of Robert and **Eunice Harmon**'s eight children. Within a few years of the twins' birth, their parents gave up their farm and moved the family to Portland, Maine, where they started a hat-making business. The business was based in the Harmon home, and Ellen and her siblings worked alongside their parents in producing the hats for sale. Religion was an important part of their family life, and all of the children were introduced to the Methodist faith at an early age.

As an adult, Ellen White would look back on her early childhood as a happy and generally uneventful period. An accident that occurred in her ninth year, however, marked the end of this childhood idyll. Crossing the street with her sister one afternoon, she was hit by a stone thrown by a schoolmate. The blow knocked her to the ground, and for three weeks she lay unconscious in her parents' home, hovering, she said later, between life and death. She eventually regained consciousness and began to resume some of her normal activities, but the effects of the accident continued to take their toll. Weak and having difficulty breathing, she was forced to withdraw permanently from school. Even more painful, perhaps, than this premature end to her schooling was the disfigurement that the accident caused and the rejection she suffered because of it. As she later wrote, the experience taught her the "bitter lesson that our personal appearance makes a difference in the treatment we receive from our companions."

In her autobiography, White described this childhood accident and its aftermath as the event that changed, and perhaps determined, the course of her life. The health problems she endured as a consequence of the accident isolated her from her peers and forced her to confront her own mortality. Even after the most serious stage of her illness had passed, she continued to be deeply interested in religious matters and intensely insecure about her personal salvation. Her parents encouraged her interest in religion, bringing her with them to revival meetings sponsored by their Methodist church. At one of these meetings, barely three years after the accident, White received what she believed was a sign from God that her salvation was assured. The experience made her feel as though she had been spiritually reborn, and soon after it she formalized her new relationship with God by becoming a member of the Methodist Church.

Ellen Gould White

Over the next few years, she maintained her membership in the Methodist Church while also studying William Miller's teachings about the Second Coming of Christ. As the Millerites (also known as the Adventists) became more specific in their teachings, eventually warning people of the exact date of Christ's appearance, White's confidence in her salvation began to weaken. The contradictions between the teachings of the Millerites and the Methodists were becoming more and more apparent to her, and she felt that she needed to choose between the two theological systems. She chose the Millerites, and, as October 1844 approached, found that by joining with them to prepare for Christ's return to earth she had regained confidence in her salvation.

An unspeakable awe filled me, that I, so young and feeble, should be chosen as the instrument by which God would give light to His people.

—Ellen Gould White

In the aftermath of the Great Disappointment, White, like other believers, sought a way to make sense of the events of that day. She still believed that there was truth to William Miller's message, but she did not know how to reconcile her faith in Adventist teachings with her disappointment over the Millerites' failed prophecy. Help came to her, as it would for the remainder of her life, in the form of detailed religious visions. Through these visions, it was said, God showed her that the Adventists had not been wrong to believe that October 22nd would be a critical day in world history; they simply had misunderstood its significance. October 22nd, she learned, was merely the beginning of a special time of preparation that eventually would culminate in the coming of Christ. In these early visions, God also revealed to White that she had been selected as the prophet through whom God would prepare the world for Christ's Second Coming.

Initially, she felt unworthy and incapable of living up to God's expectations of her. Only 17 years old and still physically frail, she did not think that people would believe that God had chosen her for this sacred duty. As a woman in a society that limited public leadership roles to men, she also found it difficult to envision herself as a religious leader. However, as public interest in her early visions grew, she began to gain courage and strength in her calling. Soon she was traveling throughout Maine and New Hampshire, sharing her visions with others who believed in the imminent Second Coming of Christ. Still fearful that she would be criticized for the unusual role she had assumed, White was careful to reiterate to people that she, a young, single woman, would never have embarked on so public a career if God had not demanded it of her.

During her travels, she met a young man, James White, who, although not a visionary, was engaged in similar work on behalf of the Adventist cause. The two were married in 1846, and from that time until the death of James in 1881 they worked together to spread the Adventist message. Her marriage in some ways made it easier for White to continue her work, since having James at her side bestowed on her an aura of respectability that she had lacked as a single woman. In other ways, however, it complicated her life, by adding the care of her husband and later of their four children to her religious responsibilities.

The early years of the Whites' marriage and joint ministry were difficult. They did not have a home of their own or a steady income but were forced to rely instead on the goodwill of other Adventists who provided them with temporary housing and money to feed and clothe their family. Because the Whites' ministry forced them to travel frequently, they also had to rely on other Adventists to help them care for their children. Asking other women to help raise her children always made White uneasy, however, because it violated her own beliefs about the role of women in society. Although her public career as a religious leader flew in the face of social convention, White never lent her voice to the call for women's rights. She remained, throughout her long life, an essentially conservative woman who viewed her own powerful and public position within her religious community as an exceptional situation that was uniquely sanctioned by God. Women, she said repeatedly, should remain home with their children and keep out of public debate, just as she would have done had not God called her to a special ministry.

Although she accepted that her religious calling required of her some personal sacrifice, White still found it difficult initially to make the necessary compromises regarding the care of her children. Her first child, Henry, was born in 1847, and after his birth White decided to restrict her travel and stay at home with him. When the baby became sick, however, and it looked like his life was in danger, she feared that God had sent the illness as a way of punishing her for neglecting her prophetic duties. "We had made the child an excuse for not traveling and laboring for the good of others," she wrote later, "and we feared that the Lord was about to remove him." White asked God to spare her son and promised that she would resume her travels as soon as he had recovered. She was true to her promise. When she was certain that the baby was well, she entrusted him to the care of friends and resumed her ministry.

Throughout the 1850s, White's religious visions increased in frequency and expanded in scope. The prominence of both Ellen White and her husband within the Adventist movement also grew, and in 1863 they solidified their place in the movement by founding the Seventh-Day Adventist Church. James White initially took charge of the administrative aspects of the church, leaving Ellen White, through her visions, to provide the inspiration and present the teachings of the church. By the 1870s, however, Ellen had become equally involved in the church's administration. During these years, she traveled more extensively than ever before, establishing Adventist communities in the Midwest and Western states. Membership in the church increased five-fold between 1863 and 1880, largely due to her effectiveness as an evangelist and her skill at mediating conflicts between church leaders.

The imminence of the Second Coming of Christ was White's central message, but after 1863 she added another dimension to her work. In that year, she had the first of what became known as her health-reform visions. Through these visions, she was made to understand that God sanctioned particular dietary habits and medical procedures and prohibited others. Health issues had been a part of her religious message since at least 1848, when she first began counseling people to abstain from tobacco, tea, and coffee, but White had never before made them a main focus of her ministry. After 1863, however, she made vegetarianism and hydropathy (the use of water as a treatment for disease) defining characteristics of Seventh-Day Adventism.

White's interest in health reform is not surprising given her own history of health problems. Sickness dictated the course of her late childhood and adolescence, and physical suffering became a recurring theme of her adult life. Indeed, whether it was a pain in her heart, a stomach ailment, an attack of debilitating weakness, or, as she called it, "nervous prostration," White was often sick as an adult. Even after she began to promote the new health regimens and therapies that appeared to her in her visions, she continued to have health problems of her own.

Perhaps because she knew sickness so well, she understood how effective a church institution devoted to healing could be as a way of introducing people to the Adventist message. When, in 1865, she received a vision directing her to build an institution "for the benefit of the diseased and suffering among us who wish to have health and strength," she immediately saw an opportunity to both serve the sick and promote the church. The Western Health Reform Institute that opened in Battle Creek, Michigan, in 1866 was operated by the church with both these goals in mind. Eventually known as the Battle Creek Sanitarium and operated under the direction of John Harvey Kellogg, who during his years there invented the cornflake breakfast cereal that still carries his name, the health institute attracted patients from all over the nation and was an overwhelming success.

As the Battle Creek Sanitarium increased awareness of the Seventh-Day Adventist Church within the United States, White began bringing her church's message overseas. Although she had some success in Europe in the mid-1880s, her most rewarding work was done in Australia. There, she founded the first Adventist college and for the first time recognized how valuable medical missionaries could be to the work of the church. Missionaries originally were trained at the Battle Creek Sanitarium, but after it left the church's control in 1906 following a dispute between White and Kellogg, she established a new medical center that is known today as Loma Linda University and Medical Center. Loma Linda is the crown jewel in a rich network of schools and hospitals founded by White, a network that has grown in the years since her death and continues to be a vital part of the mission of the Seventh-Day Adventist Church.

Ellen White died in 1915, five months after a fall that left her confined to a wheelchair. In the years since her death, she has continued, through the extensive writings she left behind, to guide the church she founded well over a century ago. The church has grown far beyond what even she could have anticipated, claiming by 1990 a membership of nearly 6 million people in over 190 different countries. Yet, despite the fact that she founded one of America's largest indigenous denominations, one that by 1990 had established the largest Protestant, nonprofit health-care system in the country, Ellen White is a little-known figure. This is unfortunate, since on the basis of her accomplishments as an American religious leader alone she merits more attention from historians.

Perhaps even more important, however, is the potential that the more private dimensions of her life have for helping us to understand the struggles of women of faith, past and present, who, like her, have found their religious vocation to be in conflict with their essentially conservative beliefs about the position of women in society. As a woman leader in a religious world managed by men, and as a wife and mother with a very public career, she defied convention without challenging its foundation. Although her life story tells little about the struggle for the emancipation of women in America, it offers a reminder that women's lives do not conform to a single pattern, and that women have not always spoken with one voice even on issues that bear intimately on their lives.

SOURCES:

Land, Gary., ed. *Adventism in America*. Grand Rapids, MI: William B. Eerdmans, 1986.

Numbers, Ronald L. *Prophetess of Health: Ellen G. White and the Origins of Seventh-day Adventist Health Reform*. Knoxville, TN: University of Tennessee Press, 1992.

White, Ellen Gould. *Life Sketches of Ellen G. White*. Boise, ID: Pacific Press, 1915.

SUGGESTED READING:

Butler, Jonathan. "Prophecy, Gender, and Culture: Ellen Gould Harmon [White] and the Roots of Seventh-day Adventism," in *Religion and American Culture*. Vol. 1, 1991, pp. 3–29.

———, and Rennie B. Schoepflin. "Charismatic Women and Health: *Mary Baker Eddy, Ellen G. White, and *Aimee Semple McPherson," in *Women, Health, and Medicine in America: A Historical Handbook*. Ed. by Rima Apple. NY: Garland, 1990, pp. 337–365.

COLLECTIONS:

Ellen White's personal papers are available, with some restrictions, at the international headquarters of the General Conference of Seventh-Day Adventists, located in Silver Spring, Maryland.

Kathleen M. Joyce,
Assistant Professor in the Department of Religion,
Duke University, Durham, North Carolina

White, Helen C. (1896–1967)

American educator and writer. Born Helen Constance White on November 26, 1896, in New Haven, Connecticut; died on June 7, 1967, in Norwood, Massachusetts; daughter of John White and Mary (King) White; attended Girls' High School in Boston, 1909–13; Radcliffe College, A.B., A.M., 1916; University of Wisconsin, Ph.D., 1924; never married; no children.

Selected works—nonfiction: The Mysticism of William Blake *(1927),* English Devotional Literature (Prose) 1600–1640 *(1931),* The Metaphysical Poets: A Study in Religious Experience *(1936),* Social Criticism in Popular Religious Literature of the Sixteenth Century *(1944),* The Tudor Books of Private Devotion *(1951),* Prayer and Poetry *(1960); (novels)* A Watch in the Night *(1933),* Not Built with Hands *(1935),* To

the End of the World *(1939),* Dust on the King's Highway *(1947),* The Four Rivers of Paradise *(1955),* Bird of Fire: A Tale of St. Francis of Assisi *(1958).*

Born in 1896, Helen C. White was raised until the age of five in New Haven, Connecticut, and then in Roslindale, Massachusetts, in a strong Irish Catholic tradition which remained an influence throughout her life. She attended Girls' High School in Boston where she received both an education in literature and, from sympathetic teachers, a greater understanding of the suffrage movement and Boston's immigrant population. After high school, she enrolled at Radcliffe College, graduating Phi Beta Kappa in 1916. The following year she accepted a teaching position at Smith College, where she remained until being hired as an English instructor at the University of Wisconsin in 1919.

White combined her teaching responsibilities with her own doctoral studies at the university, earning a Ph.D. in 1924 with her dissertation "The Mysticism of William Blake." Published as a book three years later, White's study on Blake demonstrated her interest in the exploration of literature in the context of the social and intellectual traditions in which authors worked, paying particular attention to the impact of religion. In her later scholarly studies, she focused on medieval and Renaissance literature in such works as *The Metaphysical Poets: A Study in Religious Experience* (1936), *Social Criticism in Popular Religious Literature of the Sixteenth Century* (1944), which one critic called a work of "impeccable scholarship," and *Prayer and Poetry* (1960). She was aided in her research by Guggenheim and Huntington Library fellowships. Aside from one year in the early 1940s spent as a visiting professor at Barnard College, White remained at Wisconsin for the rest of her working life, becoming a full professor in 1936—the first woman to achieve such status at the university—and ultimately chair of the English department.

In addition to her academic career, White published a number of novels which also reflected her triad interests in religion, literature, and ideas. Her first, *A Watch in the Night* (1933), the story of a 13th-century Franciscan monk, was a heavy favorite to win that year's Pulitzer Prize. In the opinion of many critics, she lost to **Caroline Miller**'s *Lamb in His Bosom!* only because the prize committee wanted to give the award to a novel with an American setting. *Not Built with Hands*, published two years later, also featured historical figures, this time Pope Gregory VII and

Countess *Matilda of Tuscany during the Investiture Conflict, a pivotal moment in Roman Catholic history. *Not Built with Hands* received generally more favorable reviews than had her first book, although Catholic authorities raised questions about its historical accuracy. Four more novels, including *To the End of the World* (1939), set during the French Revolution, and *Bird of Fire: A Tale of St. Francis of Assisi* (1958), adhered to the pattern of portraying characters in a time of pronounced ideological change.

As president of the American Association of University Women during the turbulent years from 1941 to 1947, White emphasized the importance of the role of educated women in achieving peaceful social change while also supporting the war effort. During this same period she served on the national commission of UNESCO and on the boards of the National Conference of Christians and Jews (1940–49) and several Catholic educational foundations. She also aided the careers of fellow scholars and students as an advisor to the Whitney Foundation and as president (in 1963) of the Modern Humanities Research Association. Among the tributes she received were three honorary degrees and the 1942 Laetare Medal from the University of Notre Dame. A self-admitted absentminded professor who was known on campus as "the lady in purple" (she considered it easier to dress all in one color), White retired from the University of Wisconsin in 1965. After suffering from heart disease, she died two years later of a stroke.

SOURCES:
Current Biography 1945. NY: H.W. Wilson, 1945.
Sicherman, Barbara, and Carol Hurd Green, eds. *Notable American Women: The Modern Period.* Cambridge, MA: The Belknap Press of Harvard University, 1980.

Linda S. Walton,
freelance writer,
Grosse Pointe Shores, Michigan

White, Helen Magill (1853–1944)

First American woman to earn a doctorate. Name variations: Helen Magill. Born on November 28, 1853, in Providence, Rhode Island; died on October 28, 1944, in Kittery Point, Maine; daughter of Edward Hicks Magill (an educator) and Sarah (Beans) Magill; attended Boston Public Latin School; graduated in the first class at Swarthmore College, 1873; Boston University, Ph.D. in Greek, 1877; graduate studies at Cambridge University, England, 1877–81; married Andrew D. White (a diplomat and former president of Cornell University), on September 10, 1890 (died 1918); children: Karin Andreevna; one who died in infancy.

Became the first American woman to receive a doctorate (1877); teaching career ended (mid-1880s); lived with husband in Russia (1892–94) and Germany (1897–1903); spoke out against women's suffrage (1913).

Born in 1853 in Providence, Rhode Island, Helen Magill White was one of five daughters of Quakers Edward Hicks Magill, a classicist, and **Sarah Beans Magill**. Her father's commitment to the education of women allowed for all the Magill girls to become sufficiently well educated to pursue careers as college teachers. Helen showed special promise as a student, and when her father assumed the position of sub-master at the prestigious Boston Public Latin School for boys, she became the only girl to study there. At age 15, she enrolled in the first class of the recently founded Swarthmore College in Pennsylvania, shortly before her father became the school's president. After graduating in 1873 as the second in her class, White spent two more years at Swarthmore in what would now be called postgraduate studies. She then began studying Greek at Boston University. In 1877, she became the first American woman to earn a doctorate, with a dissertation on Greek drama. The following four years she spent in England, pursuing classical studies at Newnham College of Cambridge University.

Upon her return to the United States, White embarked on a teaching career with an appointment as principal of a private school in Johnstown, Pennsylvania. She left this position in 1883, to accept the opportunity to organize the Howard Collegiate Institute, a newly established women's school in West Bridgewater, Massachusetts. With authority to select teachers, she appointed two of her sisters to the school, and her father contributed by investing in a laboratory and a gym. Although the student body grew under White's administration, a combination of family problems and a conflict with the trustees over her campaign for better sewage caused her to resign in 1887. She then briefly held teaching positions at Evelyn College, a women's annex to Princeton University that soon shut down, and at Brooklyn High School, but her career was effectively over by the time she turned 35. Plagued by illness and depression, White blamed herself for her failure to mold her phenomenal education into a successful career.

In 1890, she married Andrew Dickson White, a diplomat, contemporary of her father's, and former president of Cornell University whom she had met three years earlier, around the time his first wife died. Their initial introduction had come at a meeting of the American Social Science Association, at which he had been impressed with a paper she read. Now the wife of a diplomat, and soon a mother, she lived with her family in Russia while Andrew served as U.S. minister and ambassador there from 1892 to 1894. In 1897, he received a similar position in Germany, where they lived until 1903. As a diplomat's spouse White generally avoided involvement in political or social issues, preferring to indulge in her interest in music. She also earned a reputation as a brilliant conversationalist, well able to discuss such subjects as architecture, sculpture, music and literature with the kaiser himself. After witnessing the actions of militant suffragists in England in 1913, she became a public and vocal opponent of women's suffrage, which she believed (despite, or perhaps in part because of, her own educational experiences) would be detrimental to women's well being. Some years after her husband's death in 1918 White retired to Kittery Point, Maine, where she died in 1944.

SOURCES:

James, Edward T., ed. *Notable American Women, 1607–1950*. Cambridge, MA: The Belknap Press of Harvard University, 1971.

McHenry, Robert, ed. *Famous American Women*. NY: Dover, 1980.

Linda S. Walton,
freelance writer,
Grosse Pointe Shores, Michigan

White, Katharine S. (1892–1977)

Longtime editor at The New Yorker *whose skill, eye for talent, and uncompromising taste helped to elevate the magazine to the near-mythic status it enjoyed in the mid-20th century. Name variations: Katharine S. Angell; Kay White. Born Katharine Sergeant in Winchester, Massachusetts, on September 17, 1892; died of heart failure in North Brooklin, Maine, on July 20, 1977; daughter of Charles Spencer Sergeant (a vice president of West End Railway Co., Boston) and Elizabeth Blake (Shepley) Sergeant; attended the Winsor School, Boston, 1903–09; graduated from Bryn Mawr, 1914; married Ernest Angell (a lawyer), in Brookline, Massachusetts, on May 22, 1915 (divorced 1929); married E(lwyn) B(rooks) White (the writer), in Bedford Village, New York, on November 13, 1929; children: (first marriage) Nancy Angell and Roger Angell; (second marriage) Joel McCoun White.*

Joined the staff of The New Yorker *magazine (August 1925); retired from* The New Yorker *(1961); Ernest Angell died (1973); Onward and Upward in the Garden published (1979).*

Katharine S. White was of the opinion that "a writer is a special being, as fascinating as a bright beetle," according to her second husband, E.B. White. As an editor for *The New Yorker* magazine for over 36 years, she sought out and encouraged promising young writers such as John Updike, J.D. Salinger, **Jean Stafford*, John O'Hara, and Vladimir Nabokov. As a female editor in a masculine environment, White earned the respect of her colleagues and the often highly sensitive creative artists with whom she worked. Intelligent, refined, elegant, and opinionated, she was the epitome of the stylish New England upper-middle-class female. She was also reserved and self-controlled, confident of her ability to judge writing and writers. A loyal friend and a loving wife, White was a mediocre mother and a complete failure in anything domestic; she never learned to cook and disliked housekeeping. Work was the focus of her life, and *The New Yorker* was the center of her world.

Born in 1892 in Winchester, Massachusetts, the youngest of three daughters, Katharine Sergeant enjoyed a happy, comfortable childhood. Her parents were descended from old New England stock; her father's family came to New York "in a company of Puritans" around 1644, and produced an illustrious progeny who had early connections to Princeton University and married well. Charles Sergeant's name appeared in the Boston Blue Book, and he belonged to clubs whose members included men from the Cabot, Lodge, and Saltonstall families. Similarly, **Elizabeth Blake Shepley Sergeant**, Katharine's mother, was from a prominent family that arrived in Massachusetts in 1636, and became lawyers, governors, and generals in the 19th century. Katharine was six years old when her mother died and her father's sister **Caroline** (Aunt Crully) moved into their spacious Georgian house in Brookline. A graduate of Smith College, she provided an intellectually stimulating environment for Katharine and her two sisters, **Elizabeth** (Elsie) and **Rosamond Sergeant**. The family was rather "stiff and inhibited," but White acquired "a sense of security and a strong sense of her own self-worth" from her father and aunt.

White was tutored at home until she entered the seventh grade at the Winsor School in Boston, which had an excellent reputation. She did well in the college-preparatory courses that included mastery of French, Latin, and German. Called "Goody Sergeant" by her classmates, Katharine already revealed a maturity beyond her age; what emerged was "the picture of a girl who was in some ways a curiously old child of impossibly high standards, easily disappointed in people, and judgmental," according to **Linda H. Davis.**

In 1910, White entered Bryn Mawr College, known for its "high order of learning and the lofty aspirations of its students." A full two-thirds of applicants failed the entrance examinations. Three foreign languages were also required for admission. The formidable female president of Bryn Mawr, Dr. *****M. Carey Thomas,** believed that a girls' school was preferable to a co-educational institution. Interest in love and marriage would be postponed until the young women had made some contribution to science or the humanities, but it was also hoped that "even after graduation the Bryn Mawr woman would resist the temptation to marry." However, if they chose to marry, women should be financially independent of their husbands. White took this admonition as a firm rule and followed it all of her life. Typically, she pursued her own path, and during her freshman year became engaged to Ernest Angell, a senior at Harvard. When Katharine told a fellow student about this, her friend exclaimed, "Oh, Katharine, how perfectly awful." At college, White majored in English and philosophy, worked on school magazines, and wrote stories and poems. One of the brightest students, she graduated 4th out of 79 students in her class in 1914. After graduation, she worked as a volunteer at Massachusetts General Hospital, interviewing patients; women of White's social class were expected to be productive, but not to earn a living.

A year after graduation, Katharine married Ernest at her home in Brookline. She had first met him through his sister **Hildegard Angell** (Katharine was 12 and he was 15) when their families spent summer holidays at Lake Chocorua in New York State. The young couple had much in common. Both were intelligent, spoke foreign languages, and had an interest in culture and elegant living. Ernest graduated from Harvard Law School in 1913 and practiced law in Cleveland, his hometown. In Cleveland, the couple lived around the corner from Ernest's strong-willed mother, **Lily Curtis Angell.** Katharine and Ernest were socially active and helped found a theater company. In 1916, their daughter **Nancy Angell** was born and less than a year later, when America entered the First World War, Ernest enlisted in the army as a first lieutenant and was sent to France.

Ernest's army pay was inadequate to support his family, and Katharine found a job conducting a survey of disabled people in Cleveland. She went on to work for the Consumers' League,

lobbying for laws to protect workers. In late 1918, she took Nancy and moved back to her father's house in Brookline, continuing to do volunteer work and auditing writing classes at Boston University. By Bryn Mawr standards, White felt obliged to contribute something to society. Moreover, she was undeniably ambitious and admitted that she was unhappy "when I cannot do the work of the mind, not hands, for which I am best fitted."

After Ernest was discharged from the army in September 1919, he and Katharine moved to New York, and he joined a law firm. White worked for the Bryn Mawr Alumna Endowment Fund, which required her to travel around the country, until her son Roger was born in 1920. In France, Ernest had developed a taste for elegant living and for keeping a mistress. By 1922, White was aware that her husband was unfaithful, but his affairs were not serious enough to destroy the family. They lived a full and exciting life in New York where they had a three-story house and a quiet refuge at their summer house upstate in Sneden's Landing. White wanted to become a writer and contributed articles to *The New Republic* in addition to book reviews for the *Atlantic Monthly* and the *Saturday Review of Literature.* She also accompanied Ernest to Haiti and Santo Domingo. He was representing their interests in a U.S. Senate investigation of the American occupation of the areas. White's articles on conditions she personally observed in these states "are passionate indictments of the occupation and the racial prejudice and segregation," writes Davis.

> *M*y particular way of "saving the world" is rather indirect, I must admit, since it mostly involves trying to make *The New Yorker* a good magazine.
>
> —**Katharine S. White**

But White thought her life lacked focus and direction. She needed to be productive, to earn money, to be independent. Lavish living, which included several servants, strained the Angells' finances since neither she nor Ernest could handle money well and appeared unwilling, or unable, to alter their extravagant tastes.

In the summer of 1925, a neighbor in Sneden's Landing, Fillmore Hyde, who was a staff member on the newly founded *New Yorker*, suggested to White that she contact the editor, Harold Ross, about working for the magazine. In August, she was hired part-time to read manuscripts; two weeks later, she was working full-time, and in the fall she became an editor. Ross "recognized in her a person of taste, intelligence, and refinement, someone who could be of immense value to his fledgling magazine." In contrast to White, Ross was not well educated and was "rather uncouth" at times, but she appreciated his abilities, his humor, and his commitment to good writing. As Davis notes, White "was not a snob; like a true aristocrat, she did not need to be." Indeed, she had found a proven friend in Ross and a profession to which she could dedicate all her energy and loyalty.

In an article entitled "Home and Office" that she wrote for *The Survey* in 1926, White claimed that the job of editor provided her with "a way of life infinitely more satisfying than any I have yet known." And she defended her decision to be a working mother; work was a necessity, but not for financial reasons, and she admitted that she had made "honest attempts at the domestic life," but had not succeeded. Further, she wrote, her children preferred that she work. But Nancy later complained that "she never really knew" her mother whose interests were outside the family. Roger disagreed with this. Neither Katharine nor Ernest were openly affectionate with their children or, in fact, with each other. Ernest also made no attempt to be discreet in his philandering, which led to frequent quarrels.

Working at *The New Yorker*, White had found the career fulfillment she had sought. She was particularly adept at dealing with young writers and took a personal interest in their progress. She edited the early work of John O'Hara and James Thurber, the latter a writer for *The New Yorker* and office mate of Elwyn Brooks White. E.B. (called Andy by his friends) had contributed short pieces to the magazine in 1925. Harold Ross was impressed with his writing, and Katharine suggested to Ross that he hire Andy as a regular staff member. When Andy and Katharine developed an interest in one another is not certain—Katharine carefully guarded her private life and thoughts—but in a poem Andy published in early 1928, he wrote, "And if I love you truly/ Is anyone to blame?" Intelligent, sensitive, charming, and shy, Andy was seven years younger than Katharine.

In the summer of 1928, the Angells and their children went to Europe. Andy was in France, and after Ernest sailed for New York, Katharine met Andy in Paris. She always denied they had an affair; her New England upbringing and her personality make this appear plausible. The Angells' marriage was deteriorating, and in February 1929, Ernest struck her during a quar-

rel. Katharine moved to their house in northern New York, while the children remained with their father. White decided to divorce Ernest and went to Reno, Nevada, to establish residency and obtain the decree. Her family strongly objected to her decision. Divorce "was a bold action" to take at this time, but so was a demanding, full-time career for a woman. Moreover, Katharine agreed to joint custody of the children; they lived with their father during the week and with Katharine on weekends and holidays. In the settlement, she received $5,000 a year in alimony, even though she was making a better salary than Ernest, which he resented. After she obtained the divorce, she moved into an apartment in Greenwich Village, hired a housekeeper, and returned to work. In November 1929, Katharine married E.B. White. Their son Joel McCoun was born in December 1930.

Following the birth, White developed pyelitis (an inflammation of the renal pelvis) and was unable to work until the fall of 1931. In addition to her editorial duties, she began reviewing children's books, which previously had not been taken seriously by *The New Yorker*. She considered both text and illustrations as important, and criticized books that were condescending towards children or that engaged in "sentimentality, coyness, and moralizing." As fiction editor, White convinced Harold Ross to publish submissions he was prone to reject, such as stories by *Eudora Welty and John O'Hara. She also persuaded him to permit "possibly offensive language in the dialogue of stories in which the words were used to create character." During the 1930s, *The New Yorker* developed into "a more mature, sophisticated, urbane publication" due in large part to the cooperative efforts of Ross and of White who "became his literary counterpart, completing his education, supplying what he lacked in taste, tact, and literary judgment."

In 1937, White was associate editor of the magazine, earning a good salary plus stock options. Consequently, she and Andy lived well, employed servants, and bought a 36-acre farm in North Brooklin, Maine. Despite their successes, Andy found living in New York stressful and often complained of ill health. He decided to take a year off, travel, and relax. He would use his own money since Katharine had always kept her bank accounts separate from those of her husbands. Despite Katharine's opposition, Andy carried out his plan. On his return, he and Katharine decided to move to Maine, so Andy could write in a quieter, less demanding environment. But for Katharine the break with the magazine, her colleagues, her writers, and New York itself was a wrenching experience. Her leaving was "just too awful," said *Janet Flanner; to Flanner, who wrote for the magazine, White was "the best woman editor in the world."

In Maine, Katharine read manuscripts sent to her, reviewed children's books, and worked on an anthology of verse with Andy entitled *A Subtreasury of American Humor*. He wrote the introduction, and Katharine edited the 804-page book to which she had persuaded H.L. Mencken to contribute. In late 1943, Ross asked the Whites to return to New York and work on the magazine again. Both Katharine and Andy were already suffering from poor health; Katharine had a hysterectomy in 1943, and Andy experienced bouts of depression. However, Katharine was pleased to acquire new literary talent such as Vladimir Nabokov (author of the infamous novel *Lolita*) and Jean Stafford. As "the fighting female on the spot," White knew her influence would be greater with Ross than it had been when she lived in Maine.

Not everyone at *The New Yorker* got on well with Mrs. White (few people dared call her

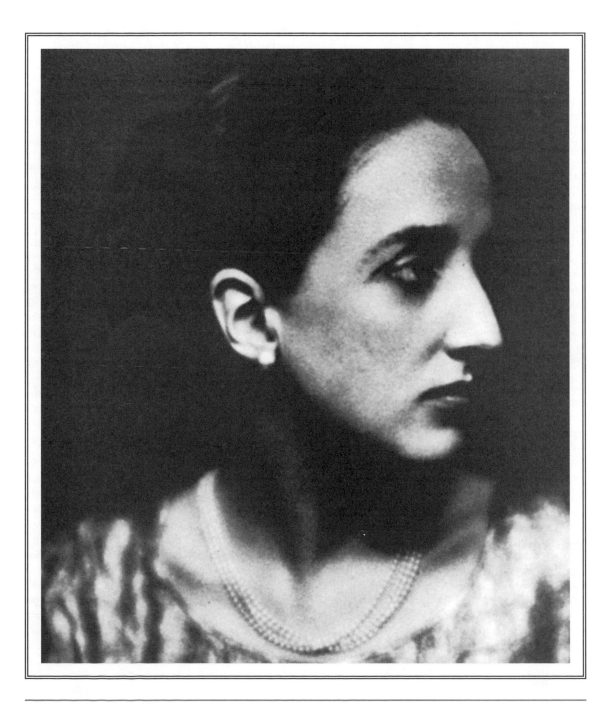

Katharine S. White

Katharine). Some staff members complained that she tended to intimidate less self-assured colleagues, but she and Ross dealt with one another as equals. A few, like humorist James Thurber, resented being edited by a demanding woman editor. In fact, White was "supremely self-confident, a woman of seemingly unshakable poise." She was able to remain friends with Thurber even though he was openly "hostile towards women," and with the often "pompous and arrogant" writer Edmund Wilson. Katharine was also editor and friend of Wilson's wife, the writer *Mary McCarthy (author of *The Group*); when her book was published, White told McCarthy she liked it, but "disliked the book's explicit sex scenes" and that it was "too much a social document and too little a novel about six or eight young women." White considered Vladimir Nabokov one of the magazine's "prized writers" and handled him "like an exotic hothouse flower." After rejecting his first submission to *The New Yorker*, she eventually edited about 30 of his published stories. Among her coterie of writers, Jean Stafford was an especially close friend. The subject of Stafford's excellent short story "Mountain Day" derived from a true-life experience of White's at Lake Chocorua in 1913.

When Harold Ross was diagnosed with cancer, White proposed that the editors take on his responsibilities to lighten his workload. The managing editor, St. Clair McKelway, claimed that she was planning to take over as Ross' successor, and he resented it. When Ross died in 1951, William Shawn became editor, and White approved the choice. She and Shawn shared common literary interests and worked well together.

Ill health began to plague Katharine's and Andy's lives during the 1950s. At various times she suffered from infectious hepatitis, mumps, and the flu. Absence from her office did not interfere, however, with reading manuscripts and encouraging new writers such as John Updike who began publishing in *The New Yorker* in 1954. As his editor, White "knew he was something special," and he never objected to her editorial suggestions; for example, the proper use of the colon and dash led to a long discussion on punctuation. Such meticulous attention to detail characterized White's editing and benefited "her" writers. She was an "uncommonly inspiring" editor, and her life revolved around her work which embodied her identity. However, family life was not as efficiently managed. Her sister Rosamond died in 1954, and Katharine took over caring for her elderly Aunt Caroline. She was unable to cope with housework or cooking, making domestic help a necessity, but Aunt

Caroline had been a loving surrogate mother to Katharine who would not consider sending her aunt to a nursing home. Relations between Katharine and her sister Elsie had been strained for several years; Katharine stopped supplementing Elsie's income in 1955, though the reason is not known. Elsie envied Katharine's success and claimed that her sister "had no feelings" (perhaps because Katharine did little to hide her negative appraisal of Elsie's writings).

After her aunt died, Katharine and Andy went to London, spent time with A.J. Liebling, a writer for *The New Yorker* later married to Jean Stafford, and visited John Updike in Oxford. On their return Katharine began thinking of moving out of New York and leaving her position at the magazine. Katharine wanted Andy to be happy, but the idea of a permanent move to Maine "oppressed her." The move was postponed, however, when the head of fiction at the magazine, Gus Lobrano, died in 1956, and for almost two years Katharine (now age 63) assumed his duties. Overwork and Andy's fragile health consumed her energies. She also worried that the written word was being replaced by oral communication, especially television, and noted the "decline in quality and quantity of manuscripts the magazine received, except in poetry."

By 1958, Katharine and Andy were living on their farm in Maine. She continued to read and comment on manuscripts and began writing her "charming and eloquent essays" on gardening. The first appeared in March 1958. The break with New York and the magazine was gradual; as White wrote to Updike, "I'll never stop being a New Yorker editor and will have strong opinions on everything." But after more than 35 years, her career came to an end on January 2, 1961, the day she normally would have returned to work after the holidays. Andy wrote that Katharine looked "as though she were entering Leavenworth" the day her retirement became official.

Without the challenge of work and living in a bustling urban center, Katharine's health rapidly deteriorated. She feared that dizzy spells might indicate the presence of a brain tumor or the symptoms of a stroke. She was also afraid that her illnesses might be psychosomatic, that her head, not her body, was diseased, and this bothered her. To White, "psychosomatic illness denoted a weak mind," and she was concerned that people might think she was a hypochondriac. Both Katharine and Andy were preoccupied with their health. Each was especially solicitous of the other which, Davis asserts, strengthened their marriage. But their marriage also became "too insulated, ultimately severing [White] from the work she needed and the friends she loved." Leaving *The New Yorker* undoubtedly affected Katharine's health. She developed an "uncomfortable new dependency on Andy" and felt "useless and restless." Nothing could fill the void that work had provided. And White did not write easily: an extremely private person, she had trouble expressing her personal feelings in her writings. Her garden essays did at times reflect her own experiences. The publisher Alfred Knopf wanted her to collect the essays into a book, but she did not feel up to the task at the time. In spite of her physical isolation, White kept in touch with *The New Yorker* and her former writer clients.

Winters spent in Florida failed to alleviate bouts of debilitating illnesses; in late 1963, "wild and hideous" skin eruptions covered her body which were finally diagnosed as "subcorneal pustular dermatosis." The assassination of President John F. Kennedy in November 1963, and her son Roger's divorce, further depressed her and, she claimed, affected her health. The death of her sister Elsie in 1965 was also deeply disturbing. However, White was still able to write a few garden pieces, correspond with friends, and read proofs for *The New Yorker*. She admitted to Stafford that "Like an old elephant, I don't forget and I can't stop being an editor." Work had kept her active and alive, but by the spring of 1969, White was becoming an invalid. Fractured vertebra, a case of shingles on top of her dermatosis, a kidney infection, and pneumonia, plus heart problems, now required expensive nursing care at home. In 1970, she resigned as garden writer at the magazine.

This official, final break with *The New Yorker* did not lessen her interest in the magazine's contents or in what people wrote about it. When Brendan Gill's book, *Here at The New Yorker*, was published in 1975, she accused Gill (a writer on the magazine) of having used "inaccurate, unsubstantiated gossip in various anecdotes." He had claimed White "was prepared to lead a palace revolution" to get rid of Harold Ross, which she vehemently denied. Gill also characterized Katharine as "loyally but not happily" moving to Maine at Andy's insistence in the late 1930s. Further, he implied that Katharine and Andy were hypochondriacs, who, in spite of their imaginary ills, were "the strongest and most productive couple that I have ever encountered." But Gill praised White's role as editor at *The New Yorker*: "Thanks in part to her . . . we would be a magazine as serious, and as ambitious, as she was, and we would be much the better for it." Ross

was depicted as "an aggressively ignorant man" in contrast to White who as a graduate of Bryn Mawr "had not only a superb confidence in herself and in her eye for quality" but also "must often have intimidated Ross . . . [and] gave him what amounted to an intellectual conscience." Katharine was furious, but her lawyer persuaded her not to sue Gill for libel. On the other hand, Dale Kramer's *Ross and The New Yorker* (1952) had provided a more balanced view of the roles of Ross and White, noting that "she possessed a cultivated taste. It was something [Ross] lacked and the magazine needed." White was quick to defend those whom she felt had been maligned or unfairly criticized—this included any review of Andy's writing that was not glowingly positive.

Her feisty defense of those for whom she cared was in contrast to her warm, open relations with her children and nine grandchildren. She was especially pleased that her children were happy and professionally successful. Curiously, she accepted the unconventional lifestyles of the younger generation. She wrote to her granddaughter, **Callie Angell**, that Ernest Angell had returned from France in 1919, "with the French idea that a wife and a mistress was the way to live." She admitted that she had never discussed this with her own children "because I wanted them to live and respect their father." White also stated that she was not against young people living together outside of marriage, but that "the new morals . . . may destroy 'the family'" in the future. She hoped that her grandchildren would not use marijuana, but she did not consider the drug "wicked." The formidable Mrs. White had become "a kind of grandmother par excellence."

By early 1977, Katharine's eyesight was failing, but she still smoked cigarettes, continued her correspondence with friends, and served traditional, formal dinners for her large family. In July 1977, her heart failed, and she died at 5:00 PM on July 20. Andy composed the eulogy, and she was buried in the small Brooklin cemetery about three miles from her house. As Brendan Gill noted, White was "militantly proud. . . of her fitness to take part in matters of importance in the world, she knew perfectly well who she was"; by the time she died the people who best knew Katharine S. White knew this, too.

SOURCES:

Davis, Linda H. *Onward and Upward: A Biography of Katharine S. White*. NY: Harper & Row, 1987.

Gill, Brendan. *Here at The New Yorker*. NY: Random House, 1975.

Kramer, Dale. *Ross and The New Yorker*. Garden City, NY: Doubleday, 1952.

SUGGESTED READING:

Angell, Katharine S. "Home and Office," in *The Survey*. December 1, 1926.

————. "Living on the Ragged Edge, Family Income vs. Family Expenses," in *Harper's Monthly*. Vol. 152. December 1925 (published anonymously).

Elledge, Scott. *E.B. White: A Biography*. NY: W.W. Norton, 1984.

Shawn, William. "Katharine S. White," in *The New Yorker*. August 1, 1977.

COLLECTIONS:

Katharine S. White's papers and books are located in the Bryn Mawr College Library, Bryn Mawr, Pennsylvania.

Jeanne A. Ojala,
Professor Emerita, Department of History,
University of Utah, Salt Lake City, Utah

White, Margaret Bourke (1904–1971).

See Bourke-White, Margaret.

White, Marilyn Elaine (1944—)

African-American Olympic track athlete. Born Marilyn Elaine White on October 17, 1944, in Los Angeles, California; daughter of Ela Nelson White and Mary Laurenza Susan (Johnson) White; attended University of California in Los Angeles; Pepperdine University, B.S., 1967; University of California, M.A., 1974; married Leon Leroy Milligan, on January 5, 1974; children: Leon Leroy, Jr.

Won a silver medal with the American relay team in the 4x100 event at the Olympics in Tokyo (1964).

Track star Marilyn Elaine White was born in Los Angeles, California, in 1944. She transferred from the University of California-Los Angeles to Pepperdine University on a track scholarship, and joined the elite group of sprinters who represented the United States in international track competitions during the 1960s. She medaled in the Pan Am Games in Sao Paulo, Brazil, in the 400-meter relay, the same event in which she won a silver medal at the Olympic Games in Tokyo in 1964. That year she narrowly missed medaling in the individual 100-meter race, coming in fourth. Following her track career, White earned a master's degree from the University of California in 1974 and in 1978 became a bilingual specialist for the Los Angeles Unified School District.

Linda S. Walton,
freelance writer,
Grosse Pointe Shores, Michigan

Opposite page
𝒫earl
𝒲hite

White, Maude Valerie (1855–1937)

English composer and writer who created some 200 songs over the course of her career. Name variations: Maude Valérie White. Born in Dieppe, France, on June 23, 1855; died in London, England, on November 2, 1937; studied at the Royal Academy of Music in London, 1876–79.

Maude Valerie White was a composer, translator and writer best known for some 200 songs she wrote, most of them in the style of the Victorian drawing-room ballad. She was born to English parents in Dieppe, France, in 1855, and studied with several eminent music teachers, including W.S. Rockstro and Oliver May. She also studied with G.A. Macfarren during her three years at the Royal Academy of Music in London. In 1879, her last year at the academy, she became the first woman to win the prestigious Mendelssohn Scholarship. Two years later, however, the ill health that plagued her throughout her life forced her to give up the scholarship, and she began traveling through Europe and South America in search of a curative climate.

White's travels gave her the opportunity to sharpen her linguistic skills, and she became an able translator. She translated several books into English, as well as poems by Hugo, Heine and others which she used as texts for her songs. Among the English poems which she set to music was Byron's "So we'll go no more a roving," which some critics consider her best work. She also produced several French songs noted for their spirited harmony. Lyricism is generally agreed to have been her greatest strength, although her work has been criticized for sentimentality. Besides her many songs, she also wrote instrumental works and music for the ballet *The Enchanted Heart* (1913).

A friend of American actress *Mary Anderson (1859–1940), White moved in artistic circles, and met both Shelley and Byron. She wrote two volumes of autobiography, *Friends and Memories* (1914) and *My Indian Summer* (1932), and died in London in 1937, at the age of 82.

SOURCES:

Sadie, Stanley, ed. *The New Grove Dictionary of Music and Musicians*. Vol. 20. London: Macmillan, 1980.

Uglow, Jennifer S., ed. *The International Dictionary of Women's Biography*. NY: Continuum, 1985.

Angela Woodward, M.A.,
Madison, Wisconsin

White, Pearl (1889–1938)

American actress best known for her starring role in the famous silent-film serial The Perils of Pauline. *Born Pearl Fay White on March 4, 1889, in Green Ridge, Missouri; died of liver disease on August 4, 1938, in Paris, France; daughter of Lizzie G. (House)*

White and Edward Gilman White; educated through the tenth grade in public schools in Springfield, Missouri; married Victor C. Sutherland (an actor), in 1907 (divorced 1914); married Wallace McCutcheon (an actor), around 1919 (divorced 1921); no children.

Selected filmography: The Girl from Arizona *(1910);* The New Magdalene *(1910);* The Woman Hater *(1910);* The Angel of the Slums *(1911);* Home Sweet Home *(1911);* Bella's Beau *(1912);* Oh Such a Night! *(1912);* The Chorus Girl *(1912);* Pearl as a Detective *(1913);* Girl Detective *(1913);* Heroic Harold *(1913);* Lizzie and the Iceman *(1914);* Shadowed *(1914);* The Perils of Pauline *(serial, 1914);* The Exploits of Elaine *(serial, 1915);* The New Exploits of Elaine *(serial, 1915);* The Romance of Elaine *(serial, 1915);* The King's Game *(1916);* The Iron Claw *(serial, 1916);* Pearl of the Army *(serial, 1916);* The Fatal Ring *(serial, 1917);* The Lightning Raider *(serial, 1918);* The House of Hate *(serial, 1918);* Black Secret *(serial, 1919–20);* The Dark Mirror *(1920);* The White Moll *(1920);* The Thief *(1920);* Beyond Price *(1921);* A Virgin Paradise *(1921);* The Mountain Woman *(1921);* Broadway Peacock *(1922);* Any Wife *(1922);* Plunder *(serial, 1923);* Terreur *(Fr. serial, released in U.S. as* The Perils of Paris, *1924).*

Pearl White was launched in a hot air balloon, hoisted up to the 20th story of a New York skyscraper, stalked by an evil secretary, left to sink off a dock, and tied to the railroad tracks in the path of an oncoming locomotive, surviving it all as the heroine of thrilling serial adventures that captivated silent-film audiences in the early years of the movie industry. She was one of the best-loved actresses of the 1910s, as her fans cheered her miraculous escapes and shouted at the screen to warn her of looming dangers in *The Perils of Pauline* and her other popular films. One of the best-paid actresses of the era as well, White performed many of her own stunts, and was renowned for her athletic skill and grace and her cheerful good looks.

She was born into a large farming family in rural Missouri in 1889. Her mother died when White was three, and the circumstances of her early life may have been difficult, although reliable information is scanty. She later encouraged the false story that she had joined the circus at age 15 and learned trapeze and stunt work there. Other sources contend that she left high school as a sophomore and took stage parts in a Springfield, Missouri, theater stock company. Her father was apparently so aghast at his daughter's line of work that he tried to find legal means to prevent her from acting. Nevertheless, White persisted.

She married an actor from the Springfield company, Victor Sutherland, in 1907, and continued to appear in live theater until around 1910.

At that point White was having difficulties with her voice, and she sought a career in films, where at the time emotive acting and title cards took the place of speech. She worked for several different silent-film companies in New York, New Jersey and Philadelphia, churning out footage at an exhausting rate. By 1912, she was starring in broad physical comedies, shooting on such a heavy schedule that she broke down and left the movies for a long European holiday. After her return, she was persuaded to star in a serial for the incredible salary of $250 a week. Run-of-the-mill actors earned about $30 a week at that time, so White was clearly a prize commodity when she began shooting *The Perils of Pauline*. A continuing story that left audiences with a classic cliff-hanger at the end of each episode (will she escape from that locomotive?), the serial was given huge publicity by the Hearst newspapers during its release in 1914, and an estimated 15 million Americans went to see it. Serials were an extremely popular genre in the late 1910s, with stars such as *Grace Cunard and Kathlyn Williams battling an astonishing array of dangers, but White topped them all with the 20-episode *Perils of Pauline*. After this success, her weekly salary was increased to $2,500. For a few years in the middle of the decade, she was more popular than *Mary Pickford. In 1915 alone she made three other serials, *The Exploits of Elaine*, which earned a profit of over $1 million, *The New Exploits of Elaine* and *The Romance of Elaine*. She went on to star in numerous other serials throughout the 1910s, including *The Iron Claw* and *Pearl of the Army* (both 1916), *The Fatal Ring* (1917), *The House of Hate* (1918), and *The Black Secret* (1919–20).

White initially did her own stunts, a fact that was amply advertised by Hearst and the film studios. During one hot-air balloon sequence in 1914, her balloon accidentally came untethered, and she floated through Manhattan in the rain before landing safely. Around that time she suffered an injury to her spine from a fall down a flight of stairs, the effects of which she would feel for the rest of her life. Eventually White persuaded her producers to use a double for the most dangerous stunts, although studio publicity continued to declare that she preferred to risk death and face danger in shooting her films. (Naturally a redhead, she wore a blond wig in her serials, and her stunt double was often an Irish boxer in a similar wig.) White's charm was in her pluck and daring, and she remained a screen darling

through World War I. In 1919, she published her autobiography, *Just Me*, from which a number of the romantic tales of her early life sprung. After 1919, she moved on to regular dramatic parts in more serious movies, none of which were nearly as successful as her serials. She made 13 serious films between 1919 and 1923, then made one more serial, *Plunder* (1923), before moving to France. Her last film was a French production entitled *Terreur* (1924), released in the United States as *The Perils of Paris*.

White saved an estimated $2 million in the years between 1914 and her retirement. She had been married and divorced twice, and had no children. (She had also never been to Hollywood: all her American films were shot in the East.) In France, she lived well, owning both a Parisian home and a villa in Rambouillet. She kept numerous racehorses, entertained on a sumptuous level and frequented fashionable European resorts. She was troubled, however, by failing eyesight as well as a scratchy voice that prevented her entry into talking films, and her health declined due to a liver ailment which apparently was exacerbated by the spinal injury she had suffered in 1914. She died in a Paris hospital on August 4, 1938, at age 49, and was buried in Passy Cemetery. *Betty Hutton played her onscreen in a popular, fictionalized 1947 musical comedy, as did Pamela Austin in a less successful film in 1967. Despite the fact that few living now have seen it, *The Perils of Pauline* remains, nearly 100 years after it was made, the best known of the silent serials, and Pearl White a surprisingly recognizable symbol of a long-gone era.

SOURCES:

Acker, Ally. *Reel Women: Pioneers of the Cinema 1896 to the Present.* NY: Continuum, 1991.

James, Edward T., ed. *Notable American Women, 1607–1950.* Cambridge, MA: The Belknap Press of Harvard University, 1971.

Katz, Ephraim. *The Film Encyclopedia.* 2nd ed. NY: HarperCollins, 1994.

McHenry, Robert, ed. *Famous American Women.* NY: Dover, 1980.

Quinlan, David, ed. *The Film Lover's Companion.* Secaucus, NJ: Citadel Press, 1997.

RELATED MEDIA:

The Perils of Pauline (96-min. film), starring Betty Hutton, John Lund, and *Constance Collier, released in 1947.

The Perils of Pauline (99-min. film), starring Pamela Austin, Pat Boone, and Terry-Thomas, released in 1967.

Angela Woodward, M.A.,
Madison, Wisconsin

White, Sue Shelton (1887–1943)

American lawyer, suffragist, and government official.

Born on May 25, 1887, in Henderson, Tennessee; died

of cancer on May 6, 1943, in Alexandria, Virginia; daughter of James Shelton White and Mary Calista (Swain) White; educated at Georgia Robertson Christian College and West Tennessee Business College; Washington College of Law, LL.B., 1923.

Sue Shelton White worked her way up from stenographer to lawyer to one of the architects of Democratic policies in the Roosevelt era. Born in the tiny town of Henderson, Tennessee, in 1887, White was one of three children in a family that, like so many others in the South, had been struggling financially since the Civil War. Her father, a lawyer as well as a Methodist minister, worked seven days a week, and died when White was nine years old. She was educated at home until age 13, when her mother died and she went to live with an aunt. White then attended Georgia Robertson Christian College in Henderson, with one year at another private school. When she was 16 she took a year-long teacher training course at Georgia Robertson, and then spent the next year in a secretarial course at West Tennessee Business College.

White started her working life as a stenographer in the town of Jackson, Tennessee. Because of her father's profession, she had always been interested in the law, and when her older sister **Lucy White** resigned her post as court reporter in 1907, Sue took the job and used it to get close to many area judges and politicians. As part of her duties as court reporter, a position she held until 1918, she served as private secretary to several members of the state supreme court. She also became interested in the fight for women's rights, and in 1913 served as the recording secretary for Tennessee's suffrage association. White had many political contacts and was an able organizer. She oversaw the formation of local suffrage groups, and during World War I held the position of chair of the Tennessee Division of the Woman's Committee of the U.S. Council of National Defense. Her work with the suffrage movement seems to have frustrated her, however, as she was stuck in the second tier of the Tennessee movement's hierarchy.

In 1917, White joined the radical National Woman's Party (NWP), the most militant branch of the suffrage movement. She also became chair of the Tennessee Woman's Party, though as its head she tried to maintain close ties to the more moderate wing of the movement. Her group was responsible for many theatrical and outrageous protests, and for this it was mostly reviled by the more mainstream National American Woman Suffrage Association (NAWSA). White tried to downplay her party's radicalism to allow both groups to work together, but some mutual bitterness persisted. In 1919, after the previous year's election of Woodrow Wilson, she was arrested for joining a NWP protest in Washington at which a cartoon of Wilson was burned. Jailed for five days, she then toured the country with a group of other women who had also been imprisoned, flaunting their prison uniforms to dramatize the struggle of the women's movement. While she was engaged in these militant actions, White also worked tirelessly to write and promote legislation that benefited women. She was responsible for drafting Tennessee's first married women's property act, a mother's pension act, and an old-age pension provision, all of which eventually became law.

In 1920, the year that saw ratification of the 19th Amendment granting women the right to vote, White began working in the nation's capital, first as a clerk and later as secretary to Tennessee Senator Kenneth D. McKellar, a supporter of women's suffrage. She also began attending night classes at Washington College of Law, and received her law degree in 1923. That same year, she helped to draft the Equal Rights Amendment. As a member of the NWP, White derided some of the moderate legislation advocated by the new federal Women's Bureau, and her uncompromising outlook seems to have been the reason she lost her job with McKellar in 1926. She returned to Jackson and began practicing law while continuing her work within the women's movement. Two years later, when the NWP decided to support Herbert Hoover's presidential campaign despite the fact that he had not endorsed the Equal Rights Amendment, White resigned her posts within the party and let her membership lapse.

After 1928, White became active in the Democratic Party, working to organize women voters. She closed her private practice in 1930 and returned to Washington, this time as executive assistant to the vice-chair of the Democratic National Committee in charge of women's issues. In this position White worked closely with *Eleanor Roosevelt, *Nellie Tayloe Ross and other prominent women, contributing to the campaign that swept Franklin Roosevelt to the presidency in 1932. Early in 1934 she became assistant chair of the Consumers' Advisory Board of the National Recovery Administration (NRA), and also served on the National Emergency Council, as assistant director of that group's Consumers' Division. After the Supreme Court dissolved the NRA, in 1936 she became attorney for the Social Security Board (later the

Federal Security Agency). In this position she helped to lay the foundations of Social Security as it exists today, although she died of cancer only seven years later, at age 56.

SOURCES:

James, Edward T., ed. *Notable American Women, 1607–1950*. Cambridge, MA: The Belknap Press of Harvard University, 1971.

Angela Woodward, M.A.,
Madison, Wisconsin

White, Willye B. (1939—)

African-American track-and-field champion, five-time Olympian, and the first American woman to win an Olympic medal in the long jump. Born in Money, Mississippi, on January 1, 1939; daughter of Willie and Johnnie White; married (divorced).

A Tennessee Tigerbelle and AAU indoor champion (1962); participated in five Olympics (1956, 1960, 1964, 1968, and 1972); won an Olympic silver medal in the long jump (1956) and a silver in the 4x100-meter relay (1964); traveled to 150 countries as a member of 35 international teams; served on the President's Commission on Olympic Sports; was the first American woman to jump over 21' in the broad jump.

During the Cold War in the 1950s and 1960s, athletic competition was fierce between the U.S. and the USSR. Competing against athletes of the Soviet subsidized system, African-American women did a great deal to maintain the honor of their country, and they did so often against a backdrop of difficult economic circumstances. Without the funds to finance an exclusively athletic existence, many had to work while they trained and attended school, seldom having the time or means to practice to the extent of their Soviet counterparts. Yet African-American women, including five-time Olympian Willye White, continued to set world records.

When White was born in Mississippi on January 1, 1939, her father left, and her mother abandoned her three days later. Raised by her maternal grandparents, White spent summers working in the cotton fields, as her illiterate grandfather tried to instill in her the knowledge that life offered choices: "Unless she made something of herself," writes Tom Callahan, "the cotton fields would be her future."

White, who changed the spelling of her name from "Willie" to "Willye" so that she would not be mistaken for a boy, tried out for track in elementary school, outrunning even the older, high-school girls. From 1953 to 1956, she led her high-school team to victory, participating in the 50-yard dash, the 50-yard hurdles, the 75-yard dash, and the running broad jump. Called by some a "one-girl track team," she was also on the relay team.

In 1956, Willye White was selected to attend Tennessee State University's summer track-and-field training program where she won a place on the Tennessee team. Coached by Ed Temple, the Tennessee Tigerbelles were a dominant force in American women's track and field for 40 years beginning in the mid-1950s. That summer, she traveled with the Tigerbelles to Philadelphia to compete in the national AAU meet where she set a new American record in the girls' broad jump at 18'6". She also began a rivalry with teammate *Margaret Matthews, a track-and-field champion from the Atlanta slums, which would spur both women to victories time and again. Matthews hated being beaten, particularly by White. The following week, the two met in Washington, D.C., for the Olympic trials. In the broad jump, White was 6' behind Matthews who jumped 19'19½" a new American record. The two would often exchange first and second place in the years to come.

In 1956, White began the first of her worldwide travels, going to Melbourne for the Olympics. She would later note:

> The Olympic Games introduced me to the real world. Before my first Olympics, I thought the whole world consisted of cross burnings and lynchings. After 1956 I found there were two worlds, Mississippi and the rest of the world. The Olympic Movement taught me not to judge a person by the color of their skin, but by the contents of their hearts. . . . I am who I am because of my participation in sports. I am what I am because of my Olympic experience.

In the long jump, White jumped 19'11½" to win the silver medal (**Elzbieta Krzesinska** of Poland took the gold with a world record 20'10"). In 1957, White won the broad jump in the girls' division at the national outdoor AAU meet, while placing 3rd in the women's division due to an injury. The following year (1958), her rival Matthews was the first American woman to break the 20' barrier with a jump of 20'1". Not long after, at a competition in Warsaw, White jumped 20'2½" to best Matthews. Two days later, Matthews took the competition an inch farther, jumping 20'3½".

After a disappointing 1960 Rome Olympics, where White's confidence was so high that she did not perform well, she left Tennessee for Chicago with the intention of studying nursing. She was kept out of nursing school, however, by a racial quota and took employment with the City of Chicago. In 1961, she was on the U.S. team which toured Europe coached by **Marian Armstrong-Perkins**, the famous African-American women's coach from Atlanta. In Moscow, with a jump of 20'11½", White placed second behind **Tatyana Schelkanova** who jumped 21'11" for a new world record. The superiority of the Soviet system was clearly demonstrated. In Karlsruhe, Germany, two days later, White became the first American woman to jump over 21' with a jump of 21'¼". And five days later, she bettered her own mark with in London with a 21'¾". White also continued as a sprinter, performing brilliantly. In Moscow, she ran the first leg of the 4x100-meter with **Ernestine Pollard**, **Vivian Brown**, and *****Wilma Rudolph**, and the team set a new world record with a time of 44.3.

In 1962 and 1963, though White did not better any of her records, she continued to win. She trained after work and on weekends and competed whenever she could. Despite the far from ideal training schedule, in 1964 White set a new American record with a broad jump of 21'6" in competition with the Soviets. She was also the member of the winning 4x100-meter relay team, and she won the 100-meters, 200-meters and the high jump. Later that year, she was a member of the U.S. Olympic team in Tokyo. Though she did not fare well in the long jump, she won a silver in the 4x100-meter relay. Also in attendance at the 1968 and 1972 Games, White became one of the few athletes to compete in five Olympiads.

After receiving an athletic scholarship at age 35, she graduated from Chicago State in 1976. That year, an injury made impossible her dream of winning gold at what would have been her sixth Olympics. During a 27-year career, White competed in 150 countries as a member of 35 international teams.

Believing in the power of sports to change young people's lives, she began to work with Chicago's youth. Her Willye White Foundation was established to honor women high-school athletes. As a result of an idea she developed for the foundation in 1994 came the Robert Taylor Girls Athletic Program, through which White offers free sports activities to the children of the Robert Taylor Homes, the U.S.'s largest public-housing project located on Chicago's South Side. Robert Taylor has more than 20,000 residents, and, notes Callahan, "The area is plagued by crime and related problems, with gangs controlling many of the 27 high-rise buildings. . . . Interviews in 1995 with 1,053 children on the South Side . . . found that, by age 11, 80% of these children had witnessed someone being assaulted, while 33% had seen a shooting or stabbing and 25% had witnessed a murder."

White's after-school program—with her motto: "If it is to be, it is up to me, for I believe in me"—provides a safe place for Robert Taylor's youth to engage in sports like track, bowling, swimming and basketball. "They have three personalities," notes White, "anger, fear and pain. I have to deprogram these children from violence and reprogram them for peace." Originally intended for girls, White's undertaking includes boys so that they too may play in safety. She told Callahan: "If you can turn the girls around, the girls will turn the boys around. . . . And together, they can turn the parents around." When asked by Callahan how her work with Chicago's youth compared to her Olympic career, she replied, "It took me 57 years to find the job of my life. This is my ministry. I am creating productive citizens for the year 2000 and beyond. When you jump in competition, it is measured by inches. I won the gold medal in life by a mile."

White received many honors during her long career. She was made a member of the Black Sports Hall of Fame, was the first individual to receive the Pierre de Coubertin International Fair Play Trophy from France, and received induction into the Women's Sports Foundation International Hall of Fame. The Willye White Award which bears her name is given to the top female athletes who attend Chicago high schools.

SOURCES:
Callahan, Tom. "She Gets Kids Back on Track," in *Parade Magazine*. September 14, 1997, p. 16.
Davis, Michael D. *Black American Women in Olympic Track and Field*. Jefferson, NC: McFarland, 1992.
Page, James A. *Black Olympian Medalists*. Englewood, CO: Libraries Unlimited, 1991.

Karin Loewen Haag,
Athens, Georgia

Whitehead, Nancy Dickerson

(1927–1997).

See Dickerson, Nancy.

White Lady of Chenonceau.

See Louise of Lorraine (1554–1601).

Whitelaw, Billie (1932—)

English actress who was the leading exponent of playwright Samuel Beckett. Born on June 6, 1932, in Coventry, England; youngest of two daughters of Percival Whitelaw (an electrician) and Frances Whitelaw; attended Thornton Grammar School, Bradford, Eng-

land; married Peter Vaughan (an actor), in 1952 (divorced 1964 or 1965); married Robert Muller (a writer), around 1983 (died 1998); children: (with Muller) son Matthew (b. 1967).

Selected theater: made London debut in Hotel Paradise *(1959); appeared in the Theater Workshop production of* Progress to the Park *(1960),* England, Our England *(1962),* The Dutch Courtesan *(National Theater, 1963–65); appeared as Desdemona in* Othello *(National Theater, 1963–65), in* Trelawney of the Wells *(National Theater, 1963–65), as Maggie in* Hobson's Choice *(National Theater, 1963–65); After Haggerty (1970), as the librarian in* Alphabetical Order *(1975); as Andromache and Athena in* The Greeks *(1980), in* Passion Play *(1981), in* Tales from Hollywood *(National Theater, 1981); appeared in the plays of Samuel Beckett:* Play *(1964),* Not I *(1973 and 1975),* Footfalls *(1976),* Happy Days *(1979),* Rockaby *(1982); appeared in New York (1984) and at London's Riverside Studios (1986) in a triple bill of* Rockaby, Enough, *and* Footfalls; *appeared as Martha in* Who's Afraid of Virginia Woolf? *(1987).*

Selected filmography: Bobbikins *(1959);* Hell Is a City *(1960);* Mr. Topaze *(I Love Money, 1960);* Make Mine Mink *(1960);* No Love for Johnnie *(1961);* Charlie Bubbles *(1968);* Twisted Nerve *(1968);* The Adding Machine *(1969);* Start the Revolution Without Me *(US, 1970);* Leo the Last *(1970);* Eagle in a Cage *(1971);* Gumshoe *(1972);* Frenzy *(1972);* Night Watch *(1973);* The Omen *(US, 1976);* The Water Babies *(1979);* The Dark Crystal *(US, voice only, 1982);* An Unsuitable Job for a Woman *(1982);* Slayground *(1984);* The Chain *(1986);* Shadey *(1986);* The Secret Garden *(US, 1987);* Maurice *(US, 1987);* The Dressmaker *(1988);* Joyriders *(1989);* The Krays *(1990);* Freddie as F.R.0.7 *(voice only, 1992);* Quills *(2000).*

Born in Coventry, England, in 1932, Billie Whitelaw stumbled into her acting career when her mother sent her to a local amateur theater (Bradford Civic Playhouse) for training to help cure a stutter. While still very young, she made her stage debut there in the Norman Ginsbury play *The Firstcomers,* about a group of people sailing to America on the *Mayflower.* Her performance led to an audition with the BBC and a role as a little boy on a series called "St. Jonathan's in the Country." A second role as Bunkle (another little boy), on the series by the same name, turned her into a "star" and made an important contribution to the family income for the next five years. Whitelaw's father had died of lung cancer when she was nine and, even with her mother working, money was always tight.

Before her 21st birthday, Whitelaw had acted with a number of small repertory companies and had appeared in enough television productions to be recognized on the street. She had also met actor Peter Vaughan, whom she married in 1952, after a whirlwind courtship. Whitelaw writes in her autobiography, *Billie Whitelaw . . . Who He?,* that Peter's jealousy grew as her career began to surpass his; as a result she became ambivalent about her own success. The marriage endured, however, until 1964, when Peter fell in love with someone else. Not long after her divorce was final, Whitelaw moved in with writer Robert Muller, with whom she had a son, Matthew, in 1967. They would remain together until Robert's death in 1998, although they did not marry until around 1983.

In the meantime, as a result of her performance in the musical revue *England, Our England* (1961), Whitelaw received an invitation from Laurence Olivier to join the National Theater. It was there that she first encountered Irish avant-garde writer Samuel Beckett, whose absurdist play *Waiting for Godot* (1953) had established his reputation as a playwright (he was also an essayist, poet, and novelist). Beckett visited the Old Vic during rehearsals of his one-act *Play,* in which Whitelaw was cast in one of the three roles. *Play* was performed by three actors standing in large urns, wearing makeup concocted from oatmeal, surgical glue, and jelly, covered over with another layer of white, brown, and slimy green pancake. The dialogue was spoken at breakneck speed, which Whitelaw described as "three people, all of them caught up in a loop of emotion, going over this emotion over and over again." *Play* opened in April 1964, and drew enough of the curious to remain in the repertory for several months. Whitelaw found performing Beckett a liberating experience. "Since then I've often said that it was never difficult for me to understand what Beckett wrote, because it always seemed to me about *me.* Doing *Play* made me feel more complete. Unconsciously I used the work as a therapy, not that I could have expressed any such thoughts at the time."

It would be 1972 before Whitelaw would work with Beckett again, performing the lead in *Not I* at the Royal Court Theater. In the interim, she had become a successful leading lady. With the National Theater, she had appeared as Maggie in *Hobson's Choice* and as Desdemona to Olivier's *Othello,* among other roles. She had played with the Royal Shakespeare Company and had won a British Film Academy Award for her role in *Charlie Bubbles* (1968), opposite Albert Finney. Whitelaw received the Beckett script for *Not I* while her son Matthew was still recovering from a bout of meningitis which almost killed him. The playwright wanted Whitelaw for the role of the play's single speaking character, Mouth. (All the audience sees of the character is a "mouth" on an invisible raised stage. The play's second character is a silent hooded man, the Auditor.) Three-quarters through her initial reading of the script, Whitelaw found that she couldn't stop crying. "Looking back, I think I understand my reaction," she explains. "What hit me was an inner scream, an endless nightmare that poured out of this old woman of seventy, who kept saying she was sixty. In her outpourings I recognized my own inner scream which I'd been sitting on ever since Matthew's illness began."

The play presented almost insurmountable problems for both the actress and the designers and technicians. It was, first of all, almost impossible to memorize. It also required extensive makeup and was performed with Whitelaw sitting perfectly still upon a chair placed on a high rostrum, wearing a mask and a great black cape, so that only her mouth remained visible. The play, which ran just over 15 minutes and was presented on a double bill with *Krapp's Last Tape*, opened on January 16, 1973, to great success. Whitelaw performed it again in 1975 and for a BBC filmed version for television.

Now fully established as Beckett's favorite actress, Whitelaw went on to perform in *Footfalls* (1976), *Happy Days* (1979), and *Rockaby* (1982 and 1984), as well as in several television productions written by the playwright. Beckett also directed *Footfalls*, in which Whitelaw played May, a woman of indeterminate middle age who spends the course of the action pacing up and down a single strip of carpet, having a conversation (possibly all in her head) with her invalid mother, who is never seen but is heard from an adjoining room. Whitelaw considers the play to be perhaps her most important work with Beckett as well as an entirely unique creative experience. "Sometimes I felt as if he were a sculptor and I a piece of clay. At other times I might be a piece of marble that he needed to chip away at," she writes of their rehearsals to-

Billie Whitelaw

gether. "He would endlessly move my arms and my head in a certain way, to get closer to the precise image in his mind. I didn't object to him doing this. As this went on, hour after hour, I could feel the 'shape' taking on a life of its own. Sometimes it felt as if I were modeling for a painter, or working with a musician. The movement started to feel like dance."

Beckett further described the character to Whitelaw as never being properly born, and in that spirit Jocelyn Herbert designed an extraordinary costume of pale grey tatters for the actress. "Like May, this costume was *never quite there*," Whitelaw explains. "It grew, it became organic, starting with bits of old lace and things Jocelyn had picked up in various markets. She dipped these bits in different shades of grey, then tore them to give the costume depth."

In 1980, Whitelaw made her American debut in the Beckett play *Rockaby*, performed along with his short story *Enough*, and presented first at the University of Buffalo and then at *Ellen Stewart's La Mama Theater in New York City. *Rockaby*, in which an old lady rocks herself to death as her last unspoken thoughts are played on a tape recorder, brought a flood of wonderful reviews, including one from Frank Rich of *The New York Times*: "It's possible that you haven't really lived until you've watched Billie Whitelaw die," he began. "Mr. Beckett and Miss Whitelaw make time stop, and it's a sensation that no theatergoer will soon forget."

As might be expected, Whitelaw's professional and personal relationship with Beckett grew over the years, developing into one of mutual admiration and profound respect. Apart from his intelligence and talent, Whitelaw describes him as having possessed a profound moral integrity. "He had no idea how to be untrue either to himself or to his friends; he never flattered; he showed no concern whatever with the promotion of Samuel Beckett, playwright. . . . The only thing that concerned him was to get his work *right*. . . . He didn't give a damn about becoming more famous or getting more prizes, nor did he care for money. When he got the Nobel Prize, rumour has it that he gave most of the money away. Beckett was the easiest touch of all time."

While Beckett was a major force in Whitelaw's career, she had equal success in more commercial ventures, of which Beckett often disapproved. She was notable as the young American revolutionary in David Mercer's *After Haggerty* (1970) and turned in a highly acclaimed performance as the inefficient librarian of a newspaper office in Michael Frayn's comedy *Alphabetical Order* (1975). During the 1980s, she appeared as an ex-Berlin barmaid in *Tales of Hollywood* (1984) and in 1987 played Martha in Edward Albee's *Who's Afraid of Virginia Woolf?* During the run of the production, she was hit by a crippling case of stage fright which caused her to temporarily give up the stage, although she continued to work in film and television.

When Samuel Beckett died in 1989, Whitelaw says it felt it like an amputation. She lost her desire to work and took to puttering around the country home in Suffolk that she and Robert had moved to in 1974. She participated in Beckett memorials in London, Paris, New York, and Dublin, and then served as a visiting lecturer at several United States colleges and universities, sharing her 25 years of experiences with Beckett with students. Eventually she put together a one-woman show comprised of selections from Beckett's works, linked with anecdotes about their preparation and rehearsals together. In June 1999, she performed the piece at Queen Elizabeth Hall, South Bank Centre, London. She also performed in a series of productions on the BBC, aired as a tribute to Beckett. In 2000, Whitelaw appeared in the movie *Quills*.

SOURCES:

Hartnoll, Phyllis, and Peter Found, eds. *The Concise Oxford Companion to the Theatre.* Oxford: Oxford University Press, 1992.

Katz, Ephraim. *The Film Encyclopedia.* NY: HarperCollins, 1994.

Whitelaw, Billie. *Billie Whitelaw . . . Who He?* NY: St. Martin's Press, 1995.

Barbara Morgan,
Melrose, Massachusetts

Whitfield, Beverly (1954–1996)

Australian swimmer. Name variations: Beverly Joy Whitfield. Born in Shellharbour, New South Wales, Australia, on June 15, 1954; died in 1996.

Beverly Whitfield became a powerful swimmer who reached her peak at the 1972 Olympic Games in Munich, where she won a gold medal in the 200-meter breaststroke and a bronze in the 100 meters. She was born in 1954 in the city of Shellharbour, New South Wales. Though her family was not well off, they supported her swimming, taking her to Sydney every weekend for coaching by esteemed Australian coach Terry Gathercole. When Gathercole took a coaching position in Texas in 1969, Whitfield went along. In 1970, she entered the British Commonwealth Games in Edinburgh and distinguished herself by winning two individual gold medals and another for her part in the 4x200-meter medley relay.

Two years later, she was in Munich. Over the course of her career, Whitfield won eight individual Australian championships, all in the 100- or 200-meter breaststroke, in addition to two Australian relay championships. She died in 1996.

Angela Woodward, M.A.,
Madison, Wisconsin

Whiting, Lilian (1847–1942)

American journalist and writer. Born Emily Lillian Whiting on October 3, 1847 (she often claimed 1859), in Olcott, New York; died on April 30, 1942, in Boston, Massachusetts; daughter of Lorenzo Dow Whiting and Lucretia Calistia (Clement) Whiting; educated at home.

Selected writings: The World Beautiful *(3 vols., 1894–96);* From Dreamland Sent *(poems, 1895);* After Her Death *(1897);* Kate Field *(1899);* A Study of Elizabeth Barrett Browning *(1899);* The Spiritual Significance *(1900);* Boston Days *(1902);* The Golden Road *(1918).*

Lilian Whiting was born in upstate New York in 1847, to parents who both were descended from clerics (on her father's side, she could claim relation to Cotton Mather). When she was still a baby, the family moved to rural northern Illinois, where her ex-schoolteacher father became a farmer and later a leading Republican member of the state legislature. Whiting was educated at home by her parents and by private tutors. The family was evidently well read and bookish, and Whiting showed her interest in writing from an early age. Her first job in this field was as editor of the Tiskilwa, Illinois, newspaper, Tiskilwa being the town closest to the Whiting family farm.

When she was 29, Whiting left Tiskilwa for a job at a newspaper in St. Louis, Missouri. In St. Louis, she met a group of mystic philosophers, including William T. Harris and Henry C. Brokmeyer, who fostered the religiosity and spiritualism that dominated her outlook and especially colored her later life. Whiting did well in Missouri, and in 1879 her writing on Transcendentalist *Margaret Fuller caught the attention of an editor in Cincinnati, who gave her a post on a paper there. After a year at the *Cincinnati Commercial*, she moved to Boston and worked as an art critic and then as literary editor for a local newspaper, the *Traveler*. Around 1880, on assignment for the *Traveler*, Whiting met the author and actress *Kate Field, with whom she formed an attachment that lasted the rest of Field's life. Whiting served as literary editor of the *Traveler* from 1885

to 1890, when she became editor of the weekly *Boston Budget*. After three years at the *Budget*, she began working as a freelance writer, contributing to many leading magazines and newspapers, including *Harper's* and the *New York Graphic*. The focus of many of her articles and columns was literary life in Boston, and she did much to publicize the culture of that city.

Besides her outpouring of journalism, Whiting also wrote and published essays and poetry. One of her most popular books was the three-volume *The World Beautiful* (1894–96), a detailing of her comfortingly optimistic spiritual philosophy which ran to 14 editions. Her poems, collected in *From Dreamland Sent* (1895), were of a similar nature, and were praised by such contemporaries and friends as *Julia Ward Howe, *Margaret Deland and *Mary A. Livermore. In 1895, Whiting had a vision which apparently instructed her to go to Italy, a trip that led her to write *A Study of *Elizabeth Barrett Browning* (1899), about the expatriate British poet. She traveled to Europe every year thereafter, and wrote many travel books based on her experiences in different cities abroad. Her companion Kate Field had died in 1896, and in tribute to her late friend she published *After Her Death* (1897) and *Kate Field* (1899). Whiting had psychic experiences after Field's death, leading her increasingly toward a mystical construction of the world. She published a book called *The Spiritual Significance* in 1900, and contributed regularly to the *National Spiritualist* magazine. After the turn of the 20th century she also advocated for women's suffrage and sought solace in numerous religious sects, becoming interested particularly in the Bahai faith and in Theosophy.

Among Whiting's last books were *Boston Days* (1902) and the semi-autobiographical *The Golden Road* (1918). During World War II, the government took over the Brunswick Hotel, where she had lived for over 40 years, and she moved to the Hotel Copley Plaza. After her death there in 1942, at the age of 94, her ashes were buried in Cambridge's Mount Autumn Cemetery, beside those of Kate Field.

SOURCES:

James, Edward T., ed. *Notable American Women, 1607–1950.* Cambridge, MA: The Belknap Press of Harvard University, 1971.

Angela Woodward, M.A.,
Madison, Wisconsin

Whiting, Margaret (1924—)

Popular American singer of the 1940s and 1950s. Born on July 22, 1924, in Detroit, Michigan; daughter of Richard Whiting (a songwriter); sister of Barbara Whiting (a singer and actress); attended high school in Hollywood; married Hubbell Robinson (an executive at CBS, divorced a year later); married Lou Busch (a pianist and conductor), in 1950 (divorced 1953); married John Richard Moore (a cinematographer, divorced); children: (second marriage) Debbie Whiting.

Biggest hits include: "Moonlight in Vermont," "That Old Black Magic," "My Ideal," "It Might As Well Be Spring," "Now is the Hour," "(I'm in Love with) A Wonderful Guy," "Come Rain or Come Shine," "What Are You Doing New Year's Eve," "Forever and Ever," "Baby, It's Cold Outside" (with Johnny Mercer), "A Tree in the Meadow," "Far Away Places," "Guilty," "Slippin' Around" (with Jimmy Wakely).

The daughter of popular songwriter Richard Whiting, whose oeuvre in the 1920s and 1930s included "Ain't We Got Fun," "Sleepytime Gal," "Hooray for Hollywood," and "Too Marvelous for Words," Margaret Whiting grew up in an environment saturated

Margaret Whiting

with music. (Her godmother was *Sophie Tucker.) Born in Detroit in 1924, she moved with her family a few years later to Beverly Hills, California. Her father often had her sing his new songs on demo records, and she studied piano and voice with him. At his frequent parties, she met other influential songwriters including Jerome Kern, Harry Warren, Harold Arlen, Jule Styne, and Frank Loesser. She was especially close to Richard's collaborator Johnny Mercer, who guided her career after her father's death when she was barely a teenager. In 1941, Mercer gave Whiting her first break when she sang on his radio show as part of an anniversary tribute to her father. Her rich alto voice was a hit with the audience, and by age 16 she was singing under contract with NBC on musical shows virtually every night.

Although Whiting was fired from her four-week test contract with the top popular-music program "Your Hit Parade" after she irritated the sponsor by not singing quickly enough, she found national success on the Capitol Records label (co-founded by Mercer) in 1943. Her first hit came serendipitously, after a pregnant *Ella Mae Morse canceled a session to record a new song by Mercer and Harold Arlen for the movie-star-studded, morale-boosting musical *Star-Spangled Rhythm*. Whiting already had a song waiting for release, but this new Mercer-Arlen one was guaranteed to open to a wider audience. Her recording of "That Old Black Magic" became a hit across the country (it was later sung memorably by *Marilyn Monroe in the movie *Bus Stop*). Columbia quickly followed up with the song she had recorded first, "My Ideal." It too became a hit, and with her first releases Whiting was a nationwide star.

In the turmoil of World War II, Whiting's warm, stable delivery embodied the sound of home to soldiers overseas and to their loved ones in the States. Along with *Peggy Lee and *Jo Stafford, Whiting was, as she noted in her autobiography, a "vocal pinup" whose "records were spun on beat-up phonographs all over the world." She credited her friend Art Tatum, the jazz pianist, as her greatest influence, remarking that his "happy approach" to music taught her to enjoy singing. In 1944, her recording of "Moonlight in Vermont" sold two million copies. Whiting also devoted much time and energy to the war effort, waiting tables and singing each week at the Hollywood Canteen and performing at air bases, Army camps, and Navy bases.

The innocence and optimism her voice conveyed were particularly well suited to the postwar era, as the Allied victory left the majority of Americans awash in patriotism and economic prosperity. Between 1946 and 1954, Whiting had 40 hit songs, including "It Might As Well Be Spring," "Faraway Places," "(I'm in Love with) A Wonderful Guy," "A Tree in the Meadow," and "Come Rain or Come Shine." Many of these are now regarded as standards, frequently heard on radio stations devoted to music of the era and covered by cabaret performers. Whiting was an unabashedly commercial singer with a smoothly polished style and—thanks to her songwriter father—great respect for songs as they had been written, and she rarely expressed any untoward emotion or experimented with the meanings or stylings of the songs she sang. She had 13 gold records, and was a staple on live radio broadcasts. In 1949, she teamed with country star Jimmy Wakely for a number of duets, including the #1 hit "Slippin' Around," which they performed to loud acclaim at the Grand Ole Opry. In the early 1950s, as more and more Americans began purchasing television sets and radio began to dim beside the new medium, Whiting made regular appearances on the live variety shows that were popular. She was the resident vocalist on "The Bob Hope Show," and in 1955 and 1956 had her own series, "Those Whiting Girls," a summer replacement for *Lucille Ball's "I Love Lucy." The story of two sisters in show business, the show costarred her sister **Barbara Whiting** and included Margaret singing a song in each episode.

When rock 'n' roll began to eat away at the popularity of the romantic ballad, Whiting's wide popularity also started to decline. After a brief attempt to fit her style to the new hard-edged music, she began singing in supper clubs and cabarets—often including new songs in her act—and appearing in charity benefits. Whiting also began starring off-Broadway and on tour in musicals, including *Call Me Madam, Anything Goes, Girl Crazy,* and *Gypsy*; *Gypsy Rose Lee called her the best Mama Rose (a part originated by *Ethel Merman) she had seen. In the later 1970s and 1980s, Whiting was a longtime member of the touring revue *4 Girls 4*, which also featured *Rosemary Clooney, *Helen O'Connell, and **Rose Marie**. And although she had always eschewed jazz in favor of the easy-listening pop that made her famous, she also began singing jazz standards and occasionally performing in jazz clubs.

Whiting, the mother of one daughter, **Debbie Whiting**, was married and divorced three times, and never lacked for male companionship. (She once had an affair with actor John

Garfield.) In 1976, she met Jack Wrangler, then a superstar in the world of gay pornography. Despite their disparate lives and the fact that she was 22 years his senior, they fell in love, and have been happily and unapologetically together since then. A resident of New York City since the mid-1960s, Whiting is the head of the Johnny Mercer Foundation and conducts a master class each summer at the Cabaret Symposium of the Eugene O'Neill Theater Center in Waterford, Connecticut. She published her autobiography, *It Might as Well Be Spring,* in 1987. After recovering from a knee injury caused by a fall on a city street in 1998, she returned to performing in concert and in cabarets in New York City and elsewhere. "I've never been a *Judy Garland or a Paul Newman," she once said, "but I've gone everywhere and seen everything. And I'm always learning new things. Charles Laughton once told *Bette Davis, 'Never be afraid to hang yourself.' I keep that in my wallet."

SOURCES:

Celebrity Register, 1990. Detroit, MI: Gale Research, 1990.

DeLong, Thomas A. *Radio Stars.* Jefferson, NC: McFarland, 1996.

Hemming, Roy, and David Hajdu. *Discovering Great Singers of Classic Pop.* NY: Newmarket, 1991.

Kinkle, Roger D. *The Complete Encyclopedia of Popular Music and Jazz, 1900–1950.* New Rochelle, NY: Arlington House, 1974.

The New York Times Biographical Service. August 1977, pp. 1168–1169.

People Weekly. May 4, 1987.

SUGGESTED READING:

Whiting, Margaret. *It Might as Well Be Spring.* NY: William Morrow, 1987.

Rebecca Parks, Detroit, Michigan

Whiting, Sarah F. (1847–1927).

See Cannon, Annie Jump for sidebar.

Whitlock, Mrs. Charles Edward (c. 1761–1836).

See Kemble, Eliza.

Whitlock, Mrs. Elizabeth (c. 1761–1836).

See Kemble, Eliza.

Whitman, Christine Todd (1946—)

American politician who was elected first woman governor of New Jersey in 1994. Name variations: Christie Whitman. Born Christine Todd on September 26, 1946, in New York; daughter of Webster B. Todd and Eleanor (Schley) Todd; studied at the American School in Paris, Foxcroft in Virginia, and the Chapin School, New York City; bachelor's degree in govern-

ment, Wheaton College, 1968; married John Whitman, in 1974; children: Kate Whitman (b. 1977); Taylor Whitman (b. 1979).

Born in New York in 1946, Christine Todd Whitman was the scion of one of New Jersey's wealthiest and best-connected political families. Both parents were active figures in Republican Party politics. Her father Webster B. Todd, a contractor whose projects included Rockefeller Center and Radio City Music Hall, served as chair of the Republican Party, while her mother **Eleanor Schley Todd** was active in both the Republican National Committee and the New Jersey Federation of Republican Women. Christine's husband John Whitman, a financial consultant, was also politically connected, the grandson of Charles S. Whitman, Sr., governor of New York from 1914 to 1916.

The youngest of four children, Whitman was raised on a farm in Oldwick, New Jersey, although some of her childhood was spent abroad. All the children were encouraged to pursue a life of public service, learning the mantra "good government was the best politics" from their parents, who were moderate "Rockefeller Republicans." Whitman's political indoctrination began early. She was chosen (along with a young Steve Forbes) to present dolls to six-year-old *Tricia and four-year-old *Julie Nixon during the 1952 presidential campaign, and she attended her first Republican National Convention at the age of nine.

Whitman studied at the American School in Paris, where her father served in the Eisenhower administration, as well as at private schools in the United States, including Foxcroft in Virginia and the Chapin School in New York City. She attended Wheaton College, in Norton, Massachusetts, graduating with a degree in government in 1968, the year she worked for Nelson A. Rockefeller during his presidential campaign. During the 1970s, Whitman worked in New York as a teacher and in Washington, D.C., with the Republican National Committee, also serving in the U.S. Office of Economic Opportunity, an anti-poverty program of the Nixon administration. After her marriage in 1974 to John Whitman, she lived for a time in England.

Whitman made her first bid for elective office in 1981, and served two terms on the Somerset County Board of Chosen Freeholders, a board of supervisors. In 1988, she was appointed president of the New Jersey Board of Public Utilities by Republican Governor Tom Kean, resigning in 1990 in order to run for the U.S. Sen-

ate against popular incumbent Bill Bradley. When she came within 2% of his votes, Whitman drew the attention of Republican Party leaders and began laying the groundwork for a campaign to oust Democratic Governor Jim Florio, building on opposition to his tax legislation and the anti-incumbent sentiments in the state. Despite damaging allegations during the Republican gubernatorial campaign (including charges that she had hired illegal aliens as household workers), Whitman entered the race as a favorite. Running on a platform of economic revival and tax cuts, she survived personal attacks, campaign disorganization, and numerous missteps to become the first woman governor in the history of the state. In her inaugural speech, Whitman declared: "Our principle problems are not the product of great global economic shifts or other vast, unseen forces. They are the creation of government." During her career as governor of New Jersey, she downsized government programs and provided a more conducive environment for private businesses.

A moderate Republican known for her steely character, firm beliefs, and intransigence, Whitman has made stands on many issues that oppose party orthodoxy, including her fervent advocacy of abortion rights. "It's when we get into government trying to manage morals and mores that we start to run into trouble. . . . But there's room in the party for people who believe differently on those issues." Her achievement in cutting taxes by the promised 30%, a feat she accomplished in two years instead of the promised three, inspired many politicians around the country, despite criticism of her reliance on a bullish stock market in order to balance the state budget and finance the state employees' pension plan. While the state income tax in New Jersey fell after she became governor, local property taxes increased. But through media exposure Whitman became one of the better-known politicians in the United States, spawning a growing number of "Christie Whitman Republicans" eager to emulate her success. In 1994 *People Weekly* dubbed her "a one-woman political slogan" and named her one of the most intriguing people of the year. She was also on the *Newsweek* list of the six most influential Republicans.

On the national scene, Whitman was chosen as the first governor to give the rebuttal to a Presidential State of the Union Address, counteracting President Bill Clinton in 1995. She made a promise on behalf of the Republican Party: "We will keep our word. We will do what you elected us to do." Her audience was impressed with her response and the buzz began about the possibilities of her candidacy for vice president in 1996.

Christine Todd Whitman

Bob Dole, the Republican candidate, ultimately chose Jack Kemp as his running mate.

Despite her national prominence, Whitman remained dedicated to her home state of New Jersey. She countered New York officials regarding their waste water mishaps that threaten her state's shores and also took them to court, claiming Ellis Island to be part of New Jersey. Annoyed by the typical New Jersey-bashing jokes, she worked to make sure that no one stepped on her state or on herself as governor.

Whitman raised local skepticism while keeping her promise to cut income taxes. Along the way, many people fell to her ruthless fiscal politics. For instance, Labor Commissioner Peter Calderone began to organize opposition to the privatization of the state's temporary disability insurance fund, a plan Whitman had proposed, and was asked to resign. Similarly, Robert Thompson, of the Whitman press office, was dismissed when he admitted that the privatization of the Department of Motor Vehicles was not going as well as Whitman herself had claimed. Countering an attack by minority leader John Lynch in 1997 regarding use of state money to settle a sexual harassment suit, Whitman made public a domestic violence dispute in the Lynch household that had required police intervention.

Despite her sometimes tough tactics, Whitman was known for getting the job done and keeping her promises. She was perceived as a dynamic force in Republican politics, and in 1999 surprised observers when she decided against running for the U.S. Senate. She lived on the family estate in New Jersey when not residing in the governor's mansion in Princeton. In 2000, her name was one of those suggested as a possible vice-presidential candidate for Republican presidential hopeful George W. Bush, although he eventually settled on Dick Cheney. Around that time she came under a firestorm of criticism when a 1996 photograph surfaced in the news media showing Whitman, with a wide grin, patting down a young African-American man who had been pulled over by state troopers she had been riding with. The timing of the photo's appearance was particularly bad, as it came on the heels of widespread allegations about racial profiling among New Jersey police, and brought the governor much negative publicity.

Whitman, who has also served on a variety of boards and commissions in New Jersey, left the governor's mansion in January 2001, when newly elected President Bush appointed her administrator of the Environmental Protection Agency. The first few months of her job there were made more difficult when the president undercut or disavowed statements she had made about EPA policy, although she steadfastly maintained her public loyalty to the administration.

SOURCES:

Collins, Louise Mooney, ed. *Newsmakers*. Detroit, MI: Gale Research, 1994.

Graham, Judith, ed. *Current Biography Yearbook*. NY: H.W. Wilson, 1995.

Mullaney, Marie Marmo. *Biographical Directory of Governors of the United States, 1988–1994*. Westport, CT: Greenwood Press, 1994.

Pulley, Brett. "Born With Politics in Her Veins," in *The New York Times Biographical Service*. October 1997.

Weissman, Art. *Christine Todd Whitman: The Making of a National Political Player*. Birch Lane, 1996.

Zworykin, Vitoria. *Encyclopedia of World Biography*. 2nd ed. Detroit, MI: Gale Research, 1998.

Paula Morris, D.Phil.,
Brooklyn, New York

Whitman, Narcissa (1808–1847)

First white woman to cross the Rocky Mountains by wagon train on the Oregon Trail, who established a Protestant mission in eastern Oregon Territory among the Cayuse Indians with her husband Dr. Marcus Whitman. Born Narcissa Prentiss on March 14, 1808, in Prattsburg, New York; killed on November 29, 1847, in Oregon Territory (now eastern Washington State); one of nine children of Stephen Prentiss (a landowner) and Clarissa (Ward) Prentiss (active in evangelical movement); attended Prattsburg common school through childhood; attended Auburn Academy for six months at age 15, and Franklin Academy in late teens and early 20s; married Dr. Marcus Whitman, in February 1836; children: Alice Clarissa (b. March 13, 1837, who died by drowning June 1839).

Had religious conversion at age 11; committed to missionary work with Presbyterian Church at age 15; in early 20s, taught in district schools but remained determined to become a missionary; active in local evangelical work; established infant school with her sister Jane in Bath, New York (1834); family moved to Angelica, New York (1835); encouraged through church connections to consider marriage to Dr. Marcus Whitman, newly commissioned missionary from neighboring village; applied independently to, and was accepted by, missionary board; married at age 27 and immediately began seven-month journey to Pacific Northwest (1836); Whitman mission, Waiilatpu, established among Cayuse Indians in eastern Oregon Territory (1836); daughter drowned in Walla Walla River (1839); took on care of seven orphaned Sager children (1844); rising unrest among Cayuse Indians, due to increasing waves of white settlers, and measles epidemic (1847); killed along with husband and 12 settlers in what came to be known as the Whitman Massacre (November 29, 1847).

On a gray morning in November 1847, 41 years after the Lewis and Clark expedition opened up the American West, Narcissa Whitman found the kitchen of her Protestant mission in a remote corner of Oregon Territory filled with angry Cayuse Indians. The small tribe she and her doctor husband had come to convert to

Narcissa Whitman

Christianity 11 years before had recently been decimated by a measles epidemic brought by white settlers. The Cayuse, noting that only one white child had died, believed the many deaths of their people to be the result of the "bad medicine" of Dr. Marcus Whitman, and their tribal customs demanded retribution. This most recent tragedy added fuel to other long-simmering conflicts between the missionaries and the Cayuse. A small group of chiefs and warriors, convinced that the very survival of their tribe was at stake, decided to take action. When Narcissa called her husband into the kitchen, he was struck down with tomahawks. Within hours, she too was dead, the only woman killed among 13 others over the course of several days in what came to be known as the Whitman Massacre.

Narcissa Whitman was born on March 14, 1808, in Prattsburg, New York, the third of nine children born to Stephen and **Clarissa Prentiss**. Whitman's parents had married in 1803 and settled in a newly formed township in western New York on what was then the frontier of the United States. The Prentisses quickly prospered with landholdings and mills and, by the time their first daughter was born, were becoming a well-established, middle-class family in a bustling community that was no longer on the western boundary of the United States.

Clarissa Prentiss was deeply influenced by a Christian evangelical movement of the early 19th century, the Second Great Awakening, that encouraged women to assume new roles of spiritual authority within their families and communities. Among the basic tenets of the movement was the belief that women were naturally pious and moral, and especially suited to religious work. Clarissa gave particular attention to the religious progress and salvation of her first daughter, Narcissa, born not long after her own religious conversion. Responding to her mother's influence, Narcissa believed from childhood that she was destined for a useful religious life. Within the large Prentiss family, she helped her mother maintain a religious routine of prayer meetings, revivals, and church activities. At age 11, Whitman was converted during a revival meeting, and, at age 15, pledged herself "without reserve" to missionary work.

Some [Cayuse Indians] feel almost to blame us for telling about eternal realities. One said it was good when they knew nothing but to hunt, eat, drink and sleep; now it was bad.

—Narcissa Whitman

In a period when few options were open to women other than marriage and domestic life, missionary field work represented a "heroic" and romantic alternative that appealed to independent, pious young women like Whitman. The Protestant Church saw its role as nothing less than converting the world to Christ, and during Narcissa's youth there was great excitement in church circles about the possibility of serving the Indians "beyond the Rocky Mountains." Although she had little notion of how to prepare in any practical sense for such a life, Narcissa throughout her youth read religious tracts and missionary biographies, assisted at revivals that came through Prattsburg, and followed her mother's example of doing "good works" in the community, such as visiting the poor and distributing Bibles.

Whitman was well educated by 19th-century standards. Her early schooling took place in the local Prattsburg common school. During her teens and early 20s, she studied intermittently at two private secondary schools, Auburn Academy in a neighboring village and Franklin Academy in Prattsburg. Both schools had strong ties to the evangelical community, and Whitman's resolve to become a missionary remained strong during these years.

By her early 20s, she had completed her formal education. She was healthy, skilled in household management, and felt spiritually prepared to begin her life's work as a missionary. She faced one serious obstacle, however: she had no husband. The American Board of Commissioners for Foreign Missions (ABCFM), the interdenominational organization that directed the vast network of 19th-century foreign missionary activities, would not at the time consider unmarried women. It was unwise, the board felt, to send a single woman into "heathendom" without a husband to protect her virtue. Married women, however, could accompany their husbands into the field as "assistant missionaries."

Narcissa could only await the "leadings of Providence" to provide a good missionary husband. In the meantime, she taught for several years in district schools, and in 1834 she and her sister **Jane Prentiss** established for a short while an infant school in Bath, New York. Whitman enjoyed her teaching, and was good with children, but she felt she was only biding her time until her real life's work began. According to her biographer **Julie Roy Jeffrey**, it was during this period that Narcissa began to demonstrate characteristics that would affect her future relations with the Cayuse:

> Revivalism and other evangelical activities reinforced what Narcissa had learned from her mother—that it was important to judge others, to draw distinctions between what was good and what was bad. While [her mother] had counseled charity and temperate speech at home, Narcissa developed a critical tongue.

An indicator of Whitman's strong, opinionated character was an event years earlier that was also to have future consequences in her life as a missionary. While a young woman attending Franklin Academy, Whitman had rejected the proposal of a fellow student, Henry Spalding. While he should have been an eminently suitable candidate for marriage—he was studying for the ministry and intended to enter the mission field—Narcissa viewed him as socially inferior because he was illegitimate and, she felt, lacked the middle-class manners and values she believed were so important to domestic life.

When Narcissa was 26, the "leadings of Providence," along with some behind-the-scenes matchmaking by church members, provided her with a husband. A doctor from a neighboring village, Marcus Whitman had been commissioned by the ABCFM the previous year to serve in the Indian mission field in Oregon Territory. He was seeking a missionary wife, and it is likely that a preacher traveling the revival circuit who had been instrumental in recruiting Dr. Whitman, suggested Narcissa Prentiss.

In February 1836, Marcus traveled to Narcissa's home, and in the course of a weekend visit they agreed to become engaged. There was no courtship nor pretense of romantic love between them; both saw marriage as a means of fulfilling their dreams to be missionaries. Marcus left immediately to make an exploratory trip west to the Oregon Territory, while Narcissa applied to, and was accepted by, the missionary board. One year later, having spent less than a week together, they were married. The next morning, Narcissa bid a sad farewell to her mother and the large family she would never see again, and the couple struck out on the initial leg of their missionary adventure. Their first destination was Cincinnati, where they were to join up with other missionaries heading West, among them Henry Spalding and his wife ✒▶ **Eliza Spalding**.

The seven-month journey through the Western plains and over the Rocky Mountains was the peak experience of Narcissa's life. From March to November 1836, her journal and letters reveal a woman thoroughly engaged in all that was happening around her, delighting in the novelty of new places, new people, and new experiences. In the early part of the journey, when the missionary party traveled leisurely by steamboat, Whitman had time to get to know her new husband, and she was pleased with what she found. "If you want to be happy," she wrote her sister, "get a good husband as I have got and be a missionary." It is also evident from her letters that she enjoyed her new status as a married woman, and basked in the attention she received as one of the first missionary women to cross the Rocky Mountains to save the "benighted heathen" of the West.

Curiously, in her letters home and in her journal, Narcissa rarely mentioned Eliza Spalding, the only other woman in the party headed for the Oregon Territory. Although their upbringings were similar, the two were very different, and there were no doubt some feelings of rivalry between them, at least on the part of Whitman. Narcissa was robust and proud of her good health and strength. "I think I shall endure the journey well, perhaps better than any of the rest of us," she wrote in a letter home. "[E]veryone who sees me compliments me as being the best able to endure the journey over the mountains from my looks." Of Eliza, she wrote: She "does not look nor feel quite healthy enough for our enterprise. . . . [R]iding affects her differently from what it does me."

Eliza was indeed frail and often sick—she had given birth to a stillborn child the year before—but in missionary circles she was considered the better qualified of the two for missionary life. Eliza was an intensely spiritual young woman who had actively prepared for her vocation in a way that Narcissa had not, studying Greek and Latin and immersing herself in missionary-related activities.

From St. Louis, then considered "the borders of civilization," the missionary party joined with other westward migrants to travel by wagon and horseback over the high prairies. Narcissa described their caravan as "a moving village—nearly four hundred animals with ours . . . and seventy men." Trail life agreed with her, and in letters home she enthusiastically described riding horseback, sleeping and eating out in the open, cooking over buffalo dung, and "wanting for nothing else" to eat but dried buffalo meat.

✒▶ **Spalding, Eliza** (1807–1851)

One of the first white women to cross the Rocky Mountains by wagon train who, with her husband, established a Protestant mission among the Nez Percé Indians in eastern Oregon Territory, now Washington State. Born Eliza Hart on August 11, 1807, near Berlin, Connecticut; died of tuberculosis on January 7, 1851, near Brownsville, Oregon; eldest of three daughters of Levi Hart (a farmer) and Martha (Hart) Hart; married Henry Harmon Spalding, on October 13, 1833 (died 1874); children: stillborn daughter (b. October 1835); Eliza Spalding (b. 1837, the first white child born in what is now Idaho); Henry Hart Spalding (b. 1839); Martha Jane Spalding (b. 1845); Amelia Lorene Spalding (b. 1846).

Born in 1807, Eliza Spalding spent her early life in New York State, where she was educated in academies and taught school. Converted at age 19 during a revival, she dreamed of becoming a missionary and corresponded with Henry Spalding, who also intended to enter missionary service as an ordained minister. Following their marriage, the couple moved to Cincinnati where Eliza prepared to enter missionary service while Henry attended Lane Theological Seminary. In 1836, they traveled West with Marcus and *Narcissa Whitman to establish Presbyterian missions in southeastern Oregon Territory. The Spalding mission, Lapwai, was established among the Nez Percé. During the Whitman Massacre in November 1847, the Nez Percé had such a high regard for Eliza that many of them protected her; Henry was absent at the time. The Spaldings later began to have serious trouble with the Nez Percé, however, and the family moved to the Willamette Valley, staking a claim on the Calapooya River, near present-day Brownsville, Oregon.

At a ten-day annual rendezvous of mountain men, traders, trappers, and native peoples in Green River, Wyoming, Whitman first met the Native Americans she had come to save. "I was met by a company of native women, one after the other, shaking hands and salluting [sic] me with a most hearty kiss," she wrote home. "This was unexpected and affected me very much." Nonetheless, she pitied "the poor Indian women" who were always on the move, and decided they were "complete slaves of their husbands." Biographer Jeffrey notes:

> Narcissa's journal and letters suggested much about her character and concerns. Her energy, resilience, and interest in what was going on around her come through clearly. So too do feelings that she only unconsciously revealed, misgivings about her vocation, an increasing ambivalence about the Indians she had come to save.

In November 1836, after a difficult trip over the mountains, the Whitmans' arrived in southeastern Oregon Territory (present-day Washington State) where they were to establish their mission, called Waiilatpu, among the Cayuse Indians. Whitman, several months pregnant, chose to remain with a family at a nearby military fort while her husband built an adobe and log house. The Spaldings traveled six days farther north to establish their mission, Lapwai, among the Nez Percé.

The Cayuse, who called themselves *te-aw'ken*, or "we the people," were a small, fierce tribe known by the fur companies as excellent horse breeders. Semi-nomadic, they followed an annual cycle of food-gathering activities, the men as hunters and fishers, the women as gatherers and processors. The Cayuse spent the winter months in small villages set up near water. Although they once had their own tribal language, by the time the Whitmans settled near their winter village on the banks of the Walla Walla River, they had adopted the language of the Nez Percé. (Whitman was never able to master Nez Percé, although Eliza Spalding did, and with her husband went on to write the first Nez Percé primer.)

In March 1837, Narcissa gave birth to a daughter, Alice Clarissa, and in her child she found the emotional sustenance she had missed in the year she had been separated from her family, and which her husband—increasingly preoccupied with the demands of the mission—was unable to provide. She reveled in her maternal role, and tried as best she could to keep up with the latest theories of child rearing. She worried about raising a Christian child in "heathen lands, among savages," and when Alice was a year old Narcissa made a commitment to "train her up for His glory," just as her mother had consecrated her to God.

The neighboring Cayuse, who were often at the mission house, were much taken with the missionary baby, and she with them as she grew older. Unlike her mother, Alice was quick to learn the language of the Cayuse, and she soon began to imitate them in other ways. Whitman was not pleased, and heeded other missionaries' warnings of "the evils of allowing a child to learn the native language" by trying to limit Alice's contact with the Cayuse.

In practical terms, the Whitman mission was a success. After five years, the small settlement on the banks of the river had grown to include two adobe houses, outbuildings, a sawmill and various gristmills. Narcissa and Marcus reported they had a thriving farm of 17 acres of wheat, corn, potatoes, and turnips, as well as a large vegetable garden. A herd of cattle provided meat, cheese, and milk.

The evangelical status of the mission was another matter. Despite an established routine of Christian education and worship, consisting of classes conducted in English by Narcissa in her kitchen, and evening and Sabbath worship led by Marcus, the Cayuse would not be converted. Communication remained a serious obstacle to Whitman's work with the Cayuse. She reported in 1839, three years into the mission, that she could not "converse satisfactorily with them hardly in the least degree."

Narcissa was also finding little satisfaction in the spiritual aspects of her work. Unable to suspend the middle-class, Christian values she held so dear, Whitman saw little to like in the people she had been sent to save. Her letters home are filled with negative descriptions of the Cayuse. They were "supremely selfish," she wrote, and "proud, haughty and insolent." The men invaded her house and made it dirty. She was repelled by their disregard for cleanliness and did not want them in her home. Applying her own standards to the women, she reported they were lazy workers, terrible housekeepers, and neglectful mothers. Her biographer writes:

> Despite her years of picturing herself as a missionary laboring among the heathen, despite her earnest desire to bring the Cayuse to Christ, Narcissa was making the terrible discovery, if not admitting it, that she was not really suited for missionary life.

Both Whitmans believed that the Indians, in order to be educated and converted, had to give up their semi-nomadic life and become sedentary, the same policy the U.S. government had applied in its dealings with Native Americans in the eastern states. Although a few Cayuse complied, the idea of plowing the land and building fences violated their traditional relationship with "mother earth." The Cayuse men were reluctant to give up their seasonal hunting expeditions. The missionaries preached that the Cayuse, before they could be saved, had to abandon their traditional religious beliefs and give up their "sinful practices" of dancing, gambling, and horse racing. But what the Whitmans held out to the Indians in exchange was hardly appealing. Though they preached of salvation, eternal life and heaven, they seemed to offer the Cayuse only hell and eternal damnation. Understandably, the native people showed little interest.

In June 1839, tragedy struck. On a quiet Sunday afternoon, while her parents were reading, Alice Clarissa, a little over two years old, wandered alone down to the river bank, fell in and drowned. In that instant, Whitman lost the emotional focal point of her life. She sat with her child's body for three days, and after the funeral, without family or close friends to share her grief and assuage her feelings of guilt that she was partly responsible for Alice's death, she took to her room with depression and ill health. Although she tried to find solace in the fact that her child was in heaven, her intense grief lasted into the fall and winter.

In 1840, the famous Oregon Trail over the mountains was completed, passing just to the north of Waiilaptu mission. The next year, annual wagon trains began to arrive, the settlers attracted by propaganda about Oregon's climate and agricultural possibilities. Among the settlers were more missionaries, and Waiilaptu became a popular "wintering over" stop where the travelers recovered after the rigors of the overland trip. Although Whitman and her husband had urged more missionaries to come to Oregon, she indicated in her letters that she now found her home uncomfortably crowded, the extra household work onerous, and the tensions and bickering between the missionary families disillusioning.

Both Narcissa and her husband were enthusiastic about the prospect of increased emigration, Dr. Whitman because he thought only the white men could settle and develop the country, and Narcissa because it held the promise of the community and social life she missed. Little consideration was given to what the Indians thought, watching in alarm as succeeding waves of white settlers invaded their territory.

"A tide of immigration appears to be moving this way rapidly," Whitman wrote her mother, "what a few years will bring forth we know not." The ABCFM mission board in Boston began to see new possibilities in Oregon, however. With so few Native Americans converted, perhaps the missionaries could better serve the settlers.

In the fall of 1844, the annual wagon arrived late at the mission, and the exhausted emigrants brought with them a family of seven orphaned children named Sager. Both parents had died on the trail, the mother soon after giving birth and the father of "camp fever." The father's last request was that the children be kept together and brought to the Whitman mission. Narcissa was touched by the plight of all the children—dirty, hungry and frightened—but it was the five-month old infant girl, barely alive and the size of a three-week-old, who captured her heart. Here was a child to replace the one she had lost. After some disagreement—Narcissa wanted to keep the Sager girls and send the boys on with the emigrants—the Whitmans agreed to take on the care of all seven.

With the demands of her new family, Whitman found an honorable means of retreat from the missionary work she found so unsatisfying. Undernourished, ill educated, lacking regular habits and good manners, the Sager children allowed Narcissa to use all her organizational skills and educational training. She established a rigid routine of daily activities, much like the one she had grown up with, alternating work and school, household chores, and religious training. Although she naively assumed the Cayuse would be pleased to see children growing up on the mission, she did not allow her adopted children to learn Nez Percé or to interact with the Cayuse children. She wrote to her father in 1846: "Bringing up a family of children in a heathen land, where every influence tends to degrade rather than elevate, requires no small measure of faith and patience, as well as great care and prayerful watchfulness."

Given new purpose in life, Narcissa grew robust and energetic. In a letter home, she reported having traveled 180 miles by horseback to the annual mission meeting, something she had not done since Alice's death. These were the happiest years of Narcissa's life, during which she felt useful and contented. She had successfully recreated a large family like the one she had left behind in New York eight years before, and with the increasing number of immigrants settling around the mission, she enjoyed a sense of community that she had never found with the Cayuse.

By 1846, three great emigrations totaling about 5,000 people had passed through Cayuse country, and the Indians knew no good could come of these waves of white settlers. Not only were the Cayuse forced to share their grazing lands with the emigrants, but other scarce resources as well, such as wild game and the fuel on which they depended. They had heard what happened to their counterparts in the Eastern states, and they could see their world changing and disappearing in the same way. Even more devastating to their culture were the infectious diseases that came with the white people: dysentery, malaria and measles. Marcus reported that one Cayuse chief accused the white men of preparing, "with poison and infection," to kill off the Native Americans in order to gain possession of their lands and horses.

In the winter of 1847, the Whitmans found themselves responsible for the welfare of 75 people living at Waiilatpu, and the number of hostile incidents and disputes with the Cayuse increased. In one confrontation, a chief told Marcus to leave the country, that he was not wanted there. The Cayuse knew that Narcissa and her husband had promoted emigration and settlement, and they understood that the Whitmans felt "the Americans" had the right to be there. Each year the Cayuse had observed the missionaries who had purportedly come to serve them ride out to help guide white settlers to safety, and watched as they were fed, sheltered and cared for through the winter. No such concern was extended to the Cayuse. The settlers were given supplies, while the mission charged the Cayuse for plowing their land or milling their grain. The Cayuse had demanded but never received payment for the mission land. The white children went to school, while there was no school for the Cayuse children.

In the same year, a virulent form of measles spread through the Oregon Territory with devastating effects. Although both settlers and Indians were affected, many more Native Americans than whites died, their high mortality rate caused both by their lack of immunity to the virus and their traditional practice of using sweat baths to treat illness, which only hastened the course of the disease.

Many tribal members, having seen Marcus Whitman kill predatory wolves with poison, believed he was killing the Cayuse with his medicines. Only one child at the mission had died of measles, while an estimated 30 Cayuse succumbed, despite Dr. Whitman's efforts to treat them. According to Cayuse custom, the relatives of a deceased person had the right to kill a medicine man if the treated person died of "bad medicine." The Whitmans were aware of this practice, and in the months leading up to the massacre they were repeatedly warned, both by Indians friendly to them and by settlers and traders who had heard rumors of unrest, that they were in danger. But either they did not take these warnings seriously, or they remained at the mission through their faith in God and a sense of duty. Although not a single Cayuse had been converted in the ten years they had been at Waiilatpu, the Whitmans felt they must stay to serve the settlement community as well as those emigrants traveling through each year. Neither appeared to believe they were in imminent danger.

They were wrong. On November 29, when a small group of Cayuse men appeared at the mission on the pretext of asking for medicine, they had already made the decision to kill Dr. Whitman in retribution for his "bad medicine." When Narcissa called her husband into the kitchen, he was immediately struck down with tomahawks. Narcissa gathered the other children into the house, while outside the Cayuse warriors, painted and dressed in ritual war regalia, attacked and killed the men and older boys who were working around the mission. The tribal women danced and sang nearby. At some point during the confusion of the next few hours, Narcissa looked out the door of the mission and was shot and wounded in the arm or breast. As dusk fell, the Cayuse began to break the windows of the mission, demanding that the women and children leave so they could burn the house. When Narcissa was carried outside lying on a sofa, several Indians gathered around, then shot and killed her. Her body was mutilated, indicating the great anger the Cayuse felt towards this woman who had lived in their midst for over ten years and had failed, as they saw it, to bring any good to their lives. The following morning, the survivors could hear the Indians chanting the "Death Song."

Not all the Cayuse were in favor of the killings, and survivors told of witnessing grief and distress among some Cayuse. Still, four more men would die in the following days, bringing the death toll to 14. Narcissa, just short of her 40th birthday, was the only woman to die in the Whitman Massacre. "If Narcissa had ever dreamed of martyrdom when, as a young girl, she had imagined herself as a missionary," writes Jeffrey, "her dream had come true. She had called her vocation a sacrifice, and a sacrifice it had been. . . . Martyrdom came at a time in Narcissa's life when she no longer desired to devote herself to the missionary cause."

SOURCES:

Drury, Clifford. *Marcus and Narcissa Whitman and the Opening of Old Oregon.* Vol. I and II. Seattle, WA: Pacific Northwest National Parks and Forest Association, 1986.

Jeffrey, Julie Roy. *Converting the West: A Biography of Narcissa Whitman.* OK: University of Oklahoma Press, 1991.

SUGGESTED READING:

Beaver, R. Pierce. *American Protestant Women in World Mission: A History of the First Feminist Movement in North America.* Grand Rapids, MI: William B. Eerdmans, 1968.

Ginzberg, Lori D. *Women and the Work of Benevolence: Morality, Politics and Class in the Nineteenth-Century United States.* New Haven, CT: Yale University Press, 1990.

Jessett, Thomas E. *The Indian Side of the Whitman Massacre.* Fairfield, WA: Ye Galleon Press, 1973.

Josephy, Alvin M., Jr. *The Nez Percé Indians and the Opening of the Northwest.* New Haven, CT: Yale University Press, 1965.

Miller, Christopher L. *Prophetic Worlds: Indians and Whites on the Columbia Plateau.* NJ: Rutgers University Press, 1985.

Sager, Matilda J. Delaney. *A Survivor's Recollections of the Whitman Massacre.* Seattle, WA: Shorey Bookstore, 1966.

The Whitman Massacre of 1847. Recollections of Catherine, Elizabeth and Matilda Sager. Fairfield, WA: Ye Galleon Press, 1981.

Judy Blankenship, author of *Scenes from Life: Views of Family, Marriage and Intimacy* (Boston: Little, Brown, 1976)

Whitman, Sarah Helen (1803–1878)

American transcendentalist, essayist, and journalist. Name variations: Sarah Power; Mrs. Whitman. Born Sarah Helen Power on January 19, 1803, in Providence, Rhode Island; died on June 27, 1878, in Providence; daughter of Nicholas Power and Anna (Marsh) Power; married John Winslow Whitman (a poet and editor), on July 10, 1828 (died 1833); no children.

Sarah Power Whitman enjoyed a long career as a journalist and poet, and for many years was an important figure in American literary circles. Born in 1803, the daughter of a merchant, Whitman was raised in comfortable surroundings in Rhode Island, until her father went bankrupt during the War of 1812. He was then captured by the British and after his release did not return to his family for nearly two decades. This left her mother in dire financial straits, and Sarah and her sister were sent to an aunt's home in Long Island. Sarah attended a Quaker school and became an avid reader of Gothic literature and poetry. She attended finishing school on her return to Providence and began writing poetry herself. At age 21, she became engaged to John Winslow Whitman, a poet and magazine editor of Boston. He published some of her verses in the *Boston Spectator* under the name "Helen." After their marriage in 1828, the couple lived in Boston, where they became part of the city's literary elite and Sarah made the personal friendships which would further her writing career in later years.

John Whitman died in 1833, and his widow returned to her family home in Providence. She continued to publish, always under a pseudonym. Through her essays in magazines, she took part in the literary debates over the works of authors such as Percy Shelley and Johann von Goethe. She also formed literary societies in the New England area. Whitman, who had by this time adopted Transcendentalist philosophy, became an outspoken advocate and practitioner of metaphysical science and spirituality, movements which were then growing in popularity across the United States. She read widely about mysticism, mesmerism, and the occult, and believed she developed the power to communicate with the dead. Whitman held séances and consulted with the leaders of the spiritualist movement. She also became actively involved in a range of progressive causes, including utopianism, women's rights, and new ideas in education. All the while her poetry, from humorous to romantic to spiritual, appeared regularly in literary and women's magazines.

It was in 1848 that Whitman published an anonymous valentine poem in *Home Journal* for the poet and novelist Edgar Allan Poe. He responded with a poem entitled "To Helen," and soon they met in person. In November, believing they were destined by a spiritual affinity to be together, they agreed to marry. However, a month later Whitman's mother and other friends convinced them to break off the engagement; Poe died the following year. Whitman composed a series of poems which found a wide readership on this strange and brief relationship.

In 1853, by now widely regarded as an important literary figure, Whitman published her first book, a collection of poems entitled *Hours of Life, and Other Poems.* Her work, both verse and prose, continued to appear in national newspapers and magazines until her last years. She concerned herself with social and political issues as well as literary ones, but now also wrote widely in defense of the life and work of Poe; her 1860 essay *Edgar Poe and His Critics* was a widely read, scholarly analysis praising Poe's literary style. Through this and other essays Whitman became one of the most important sources of information on the poet for his critics and biographers.

In 1868, Whitman became an officer in the Rhode Island woman suffrage organization, a cause she had championed for many years. She died ten years later, at age 75, in Providence after an illness. Showing her lifelong concern for social welfare, she left sizable bequests to organizations for African-American children in her will.

SOURCES:

James, Edward T., ed. *Notable American Women, 1607–1950*. Cambridge, MA: The Belknap Press of Harvard University, 1971.

Meyers, Jeffrey. *Edgar Allan Poe*. NY: Scribner, 1992.

Laura York, M.A. in History,
University of California,
Riverside, California

Whitney, Adeline Dutton

(1824–1906)

American writer. Born Adeline Dutton Train on September 15, 1824, in Boston, Massachusetts; died of pneumonia on March 21, 1906, in Milton, Massachusetts; daughter of Adeline (Dutton) Train and Enoch Train; educated at a private academy run by George Emerson; married Seth Dunbar Whitney, in 1843 (died 1890); children: Mary Adeline (b. 1844); Theodore Train (b. 1846); Marie Caroline (b. 1848, died in infancy); Caroline Leslie (b. 1853).

Selected writings: Mother Goose for Grown Folks *(poems, 1859);* Boys at Chequasset *(1862);* Faith Gartney's Girlhood *(1863);* The Gayworthys *(1865);* A Summer in Leslie Goldthwaite's Life *(1866);* Patience Strong's Outings *(1868);* We Girls *(1870);* Real Folks *(1871);* Pansies *(poems, 1872);* The Other Girls *(1873);* Bonnyborough *(1885);* Daffodils *(poems, 1887);* A Golden Gossip *(1890);* White Memories *(1893);* Friendly Letters to Girl Friends *(1897);* Square Pegs *(1899);* Biddy's Episodes *(1904).*

Adeline Dutton Whitney worked squarely in the tradition of Victorian women's writing, with prose, poems and essays overflowing with sentimentalized depictions of a good and happy life spent entirely within the sphere of the home. She was descended from early American settlers on both sides of her family, and her father Enoch Train was a prominent Boston merchant and trader. Adeline was educated at one of the best schools in Boston, a private academy run by George B. Emerson. She received a classical education, and later wrote approvingly that her study of Latin had helped her find the discipline she needed to accomplish her domestic chores.

When she was 19, she married Seth Dunbar Whitney, a wool and leather trader over twice her age. She had the first of her four children a year after the marriage, and with the exception of some European travel and one year spent in the West, Whitney lived the rest of her life with her family in the town of Milton, Massachusetts. Among her favorite authors was British writer *Elizabeth Gaskell, and in emulation of Gaskell's work she began submitting articles and poems to local newspapers in the 1850s. In 1859, she published her first book, a volume of poetry entitled *Mother Goose for Grown Folks*. This book was characteristic of her later work in its combination of humor, common sense, and didactic praise for domesticity. After *Mother Goose*, she published two novels for children, *Boys at Chequasset* (1862) and *Faith Gartney's Girlhood* (1863), the latter of which went through 20 editions.

While these publications were very popular, Whitney won even more widespread acclaim for a series of books she wrote over the ensuing years: *A Summer in Leslie Goldthwaite's Life* (1866), *We Girls* (1870), *Real Folks* (1871) and *The Other Girls* (1873). These were reissued as the "Real Folks" series, and sold over 10,000 copies in their first reprinting. The core of her work was always the hallowed home and the triumph of good young people. Despite her fame as an author, Whitney took no part in public life, though she did write one political tract, *The Law of Woman-Life*, excoriating the women's suffrage movement. Her depiction of woman's place as in the home won her much admiration from readers, and she was praised by prominent writers and critics, including the influential author of *Uncle Tom's Cabin*, *Harriet Beecher Stowe*.

Whitney published several more collections of poems, including *Pansies* (1872) and *White Memories* (1893), as well as a collection of advice and commentary on domestic issues entitled *Friendly Letters to Girl Friends* (1896). She also wrote many other stories for girls, as well as several more novels. Whitney continued to write and maintain her household in Milton after her husband's death in 1890. Her last book, *Biddy's Episodes*, was published in 1904, two years before she died at the age of 81. Though her work is markedly out of key with modern readers, she was fondly appreciated by her contemporaries.

SOURCES:

James, Edward T., ed. *Notable American Women, 1607–1950*. Cambridge, MA: The Belknap Press of Harvard University, 1971.

McHenry, Robert, ed. *Famous American Women*. NY: Dover, 1980.

Angela Woodward, M.A.,
Madison, Wisconsin

Whitney, Anne (1821–1915)

American sculptor, abolitionist and feminist—a major contributor to the 1893 Columbian Exposition in Chicago, with four busts sculpted for exhibition in its famed Woman's Building—whose work is displayed in the U.S. Capitol. Born on September 2, 1821, in Watertown, Massachusetts; died on January 23, 1915, in Boston, Massachusetts; daughter of Nathaniel R. Whitney II (a clerk in Middlesex courts and a gentleman farmer) and Sarah (Stone) Whitney; instructed at home except for her 13th year spent at Mrs. Samuel Little's Select School for Young Ladies in Bucksport, Maine; studied anatomy in a Brooklyn hospital, New York, and drawing at the Pennsylvania Academy of Fine Arts, 1859–60; received private instruction from sculptor William Rimmer, 1862–64; made several trips to Europe where she studied sculpture in France and learned bronze casting in Munich, Germany, between 1867 and 1871; never married; no children.

Taught school in Salem, Massachusetts (1847–49); lived in New York (1859–61); exhibited marble bust of Laura Brown at the National Academy of Design (1860); took a studio in Boston (1862); commissioned by the Commonwealth of Massachusetts to create a statue of Samuel Adams for the U.S. Capitol (1873); won (then lost) competition for monument of Senator Charles Sumner (1875); produced three sculptures for the Philadelphia Centennial Exhibition (1876); bought a house in Boston (1876); bought a farm in Shelburne, New Hampshire (1882); taught at Wellesley College (1885); moved into a penthouse duplex in Boston (1893), and exhibited busts of four prominent American women at the Woman's Building at the Columbian Exposition; included in Who's Who in America (1899).

Major works: Bust of Laura Brown (National Museum of American Art, Smithsonian Institution, 1859); Lady Godiva (private collection, Dallas, 1861); Samuel Adams (marble, United States Capitol, Statuary Hall); Le Modèle (bronze, Museum of Fine Arts, Boston, 1875); Senator Charles Sumner (plaster, Watertown Free Public Library, 1875); William Lloyd Garrison (plaster, Smith College, 1880); Leif Ericson (plaster, bronzed, National Museum of American Art, Smithsonian Institution, 1889); Roma (bronze, Wellesley College Museum, 1890); Frances E. Willard (Willard House, National Woman's Christian Temperance Union Museum, Evanston, Illinois, 1892); full-size bronze figure of Sumner erected in Harvard Square in Cambridge (1902).

The mid-19th century was a period of artistic awakening for American women, especially New Englanders. By the time of the Civil War in the 1860s, a colony of American women painters had settled in and around Paris, while the sculptors, following the lead of *Harriet Hosmer, had migrated to Rome. Anne Whitney was a latecomer to this group, as well as to her art. A small, intrepid woman who had shown a strong social conscience from an early age, she had dabbled in poetry and modeled in clay for many years before she became seriously committed to sculpture at age 38, just before the devastating years of the Civil War.

Anne Whitney was born in 1821 in Watertown, Massachusetts. Her father Nathaniel R. Whitney II was a clerk in the Middlesex courts and a gentleman farmer; her mother **Sarah Stone Whitney** raised their large brood of children in the liberal and supportive atmosphere of their Unitarian family. Anne was educated at home except for one year, at age 13, during which she attended Mrs. Samuel Little's Select School for Young Ladies in Bucksport, Maine. Unlike her brothers, she was not sent to college, but as a girl and the seventh child of the family, she was fortunate to get the education she did.

In 1847, when she was 26, Whitney opened a school in Salem, Massachusetts, where she taught for two years and made many friends. **Elizabeth Rogers Payne** writes that Whitney fell in love with a man she decided she could not marry because of hereditary insanity in his family. She never married, although she numbered Ralph Waldo Emerson and the Unitarian leader Theodore Parker among her men friends. Many of her women friends were feminists and activists like herself, including feminist leader *Lucy Stone, *Antoinette Brown, the first ordained woman minister in the United States, and pioneering physician *Elizabeth Blackwell. In 1850, Whitney was devastated by the passage of the Fugitive Slave Act, which required Northerners to return escaped slaves to the South. Abolitionism and the equality of women became two of the driving forces that guided her life and informed the body of her work.

The first of Whitney's poems to appear in print were published in *Harper's*, the *Atlantic Monthly*, and *Una*, a feminist journal. When Elizabeth Blackwell was working to raise money to establish a desperately needed women's hospital, Whitney helped by giving poetry readings and donating her earnings. In 1859, a collection of her poems was published in book form. In her hometown, Whitney had been a neighbor of Harriet Hosmer, a woman nine years her junior, who was already well established as a sculptor and had moved to Italy where she was selling her works for excellent prices. Now, in an unlikely move, Whitney shifted from poetry to a serious pursuit of sculpture. She found financial and emotional support of the change within her family; one brother transformed a shed on the family property into a studio, where her parents and her brother James posed as the subjects of some her earliest portraits.

That same year, when James and another brother, John, moved to Brooklyn, Whitney accompanied them in order to take anatomy lessons at a local hospital. There, she was reunited with close friends from her teaching days, the sisters **Eliza** and *****Fidelia Bridges** and the family of William Augustus Brown, a Quaker shipowner and merchant. Fidelia Bridges, the younger of the two sisters, was a talented artist who would become well known for her nature studies as well as her illustrations of *****Celia Thaxter**'s *Poems*. Orphaned at 15, Fidelia had been hired by the Brown family to care for their children. When the family moved to Brooklyn, Fidelia went with them. She also worked as a temporary governess for the children of Samuel Clemens, better known as Mark Twain. When Eliza Bridges joined her sister and opened a school in Brooklyn, her first students were the children of James and John Whitney.

> *It will take more than a Boston Arts Committee to quench me.*
>
> **—Anne Whitney**

The youngest of the Brown children, Laura (who did not live to adulthood), was immortalized on canvas by Bridges and in marble by Whitney. A marble bust of **Laura Brown**, at age three, became one of Anne Whitney's first commissions. To render in stone the ever-changing features of a three-year-old who refused to sit still might well have been one of the most difficult tasks the artist ever undertook. Nevertheless, the small marble statue is remarkably lively and free of affectations, showing the straightforward, simple, naturalistic style that was to characterize Whitney's work. In 1860, it was exhibited at the National Academy of Design.

During the two years Whitney remained in New York, she and Fidelia Bridges attended lectures by painter William Trost Richards and drawing classes at the Pennsylvania Academy of Fine Arts in Philadelphia. When Whitney began her first life-size sculpture, the subject she chose was Lady *****Godiva**, the legendary 11th-century English heroine who rode naked through the streets of Coventry after her husband told her that only on that condition would he lower the citizens' ruinously high taxes as she had requested. The piece of marble imported for the work cost Whitney $500, an enormous sum at the time. At Richards' suggestion, she represented her subject clothed. The result, unfortunately, was to weaken the impact of the work, since Whitney had chosen Godiva for her defiance of unjust authority, and the clothing became a major feature of the workmanship in stone. Nevertheless, *Lady Godiva* was well received in Boston and New York, and drew considerable attention as a work done by a woman.

Whitney's strong abolitionist views caused her to resist the magnetic pull of Europe until the war ended. In 1862, while the conflict was still under way, she acquired a studio in Boston, next to William Rimmer, a cobbler who had taught himself medicine before turning to sculpture and was considered one of the best anatomy instructors in the country. Rimmer's father had lived a tortured life, believing he was the son of *****Marie Antoinette** and Louis XVI, and the artist had inherited some of his father's somber intensity. His art anticipated modern concepts of sculpture, and many critics found his work controversial. Whitney studied for two years with this gifted and tormented man, and under his supervision she modeled what may well have been the first male nude done by an American woman. A later version of the work entitled *Lotus Eater* can still be seen at the Newark Museum in New Jersey.

During this period, Whitney's abolitionist concerns led her to produce a colossal figure called *Africa*, representing a black woman awakening from slavery, a work which the artist later destroyed. Another politically charged work she created was a statue of Toussaint L'Ouverture, the Haitian hero and liberator, often invoked by abolitionists, who opposed the forces of Napoleon Bonaparte and starved to death in a French prison. This work has also not survived.

In 1867, the war had been over for two years when Whitney sailed for Europe, at age 46, accompanied by Fidelia Bridges and another friend, **Adeline Manning**. Whitney remained for several years in Rome, joining the dynamic American women sculptors there (called "the White Marmorean Flock" by Henry James). Many Americans were both shocked and fascinated by these talented and emancipated women who seemed to prosper so well without men. Nathaniel Hawthorne, who was inspired by Hosmer when he wrote *The Marble Faun*, nevertheless described her patronizingly as "the bright little woman hopping about in her premises with a birdlike sort of fashion."

While in Rome, Whitney produced a remarkable work entitled *Roma*, a statue that depicts an old beggar woman, hunched and seated with two coins in her hand. The expression of resignation on her face gives the figure a disturbing hopelessness. It was a politically sensitive period in Italy, before the country's final unification, and Italian authorities were deeply antagonized by the realistic style of the work, as well as a title they took to be an insult to their national pride for representing Rome as a despairing old beggar. Whitney managed to smuggle the sculpture out of the country, and a ver-

sion of it in marble was exhibited in Philadelphia in 1876. Four years later, it was cast in bronze for Wellesley College. On the occasion of the 1893 Columbian Exposition in Chicago, she made a colossal version of *Roma*, which had to be lowered from the top floor of her Boston studio through a huge window.

While many American artists were still faithfully rendering the ideal forms of classical art, Whitney was seeking her own voice. In *Roma*, she had expressed her concern for a country torn by civil unrest; in *Le Modèle*, creat-

Anne
Whitney

ed during a stay in an artists' colony in France, she used irony to make her point. The concept of the artist's model had been so romanticized as to become trite. Using the same naturalistic style employed in *Roma*, Whitney went against the accepted classical-beauty standard of the period and showed an old peasant woman falling asleep as she poses for the artist.

Upon returning from Europe in 1871, Whitney moved into a new studio in Boston. Her reputation grew, and in 1873 the Commonwealth of Massachusetts offered her a commission to make a marble statue of Samuel Adams for Statuary Hall in Washington, D.C. Whitney made a larger-than-life model and took it to Florence to select the marble and advise the workers who would do the actual carving. When the large marble statue of Samuel Adams arrived in the United States, it was exhibited in Boston before being sent to its final destination. Bostonians liked the work so much that the city commissioned a bronze replica that was erected in Adams Square.

Charles Sumner, *sculpture by Anne Whitney, Harvard Square, Cambridge.*

With her work displayed in the U.S. Capitol, Whitney suddenly found the highest honor she had received thus far clouded by what was to be the greatest disappointment of her life. In a Boston Arts Committee competition to commemorate Charles Sumner, the abolitionist senator from Massachusetts, Whitney was one of 24 sculptors, along with Thomas Ball (whose studio she had used to apply the finishing touches to *Samuel Adams*), to submit models. Whitney felt a special affinity for the subject. Sumner had been a friend of her brother Alexander at Harvard, and the two men had remained close throughout their law school days. Whitney had not only known Sumner personally, but she had been an admirer and supporter of his views.

Submitted anonymously, Whitney's entry won first place—until it was discovered that the artist was a woman. To the outrage of Whitney and others, the Boston Arts Committee then decided to award the commission—and the $12,000 stipend—to Ball, on the grounds (and despite her acclaimed Samuel Adams) that it would be improper for a woman to sculpt a man. Along with Martin Milmore, a runner-up, Whitney instead received $500. Embittered by the unfairness, she swore never to enter another competition.

Nevertheless, Whitney did not allow the setback to destroy her. The following year, in 1876, she produced three sculptures for the Philadelphia Centennial Exhibition. At the age of 67, in 1888, Whitney had the opportunity to do a portrait bust of abolitionist leader William Lloyd Garrison, who was delighted by the work and wrote to his daughter, "It is admirably executed . . . and I am particularly pleased that it has been achieved by a woman." Meanwhile, her life remained guided by her social conscience and her feminist views. After her death, over 3,000 of her letters would be given to Wellesley College, where she had taught modeling in 1885, and the correspondence is a notable reflection of her activism and involvement in liberal causes. By the 1890s, she had embraced a modified form of socialism called nationalism which led her and her friend Adeline Manning, by then both elderly, to stand on street corners distributing pamphlets promoting the nationalization of basic industries.

By 1893, Whitney's renown had led to commissions for the four busts of leading American women for the World's Columbian Exposition held that year in Chicago. In her 70s at the time, she created portrait busts of *Frances Willard, president of the Woman's Christian Temperance Union; *Harriet Beecher Stowe, author of *Uncle

Tom's Cabin; *Mary A. Livermore, a tireless suffragist and writer who gave some 800 lectures across the country; and Lucy Stone, who had convened the first national Woman's Rights Convention in 1850 at Worcester, Massachusetts. The works were displayed in the Woman's Building, one of the most popular exhibits at the fair, which became pivotal in advancing the acceptance of women's causes in the United States.

Whitney's best work emerged in those subjects which permitted her to express her convictions. Her colossal statue of *Leif Ericson*, produced in 1889, was one of her less impassioned efforts. Recent scholarship and the discovery of a Scandinavian-type tower in nearby Cambridge had presented the view that Norsemen had landed in North America prior to Columbus, and money for the figure had been raised by the Scandinavian community for the city of Boston. The statue was modeled from a handsome, muscular young man who posed for Whitney, but he is encased in such a splendid chain-mail tunic that the eye is distracted by the detail. The statue was so appealing to popular tastes that the city of Milwaukee decided it wanted one also, to be placed with its back to Lake Michigan, as if Ericson had just stepped off his boat. The cost for casting the figure in bronze came to $11,000—with an additional charge of $33.65 to Whitney for train fare for the man who accompanied the statue to Milwaukee.

Today, the original plaster model of *Senator Charles Summer* can be seen at the Watertown Free Public Library, where the subject is shown seated on a solid and democratic chair. His nobility is in the thoughtful determination of his expression rather than in his clothes. Milmore had shown the figure draped in a Roman toga, while an earlier version of Thomas Ball's entry in the Boston Arts competition depicted the senator in bedroom slippers. In contrast, Whitney represents him in contemporary but unobtrusive attire. The manner in which she chose to have a single large button pull the two sides of the jacket together is particularly effective, indicating casual neglect and simplicity. Such details make Anne Whitney a remarkable portrait artist.

Twenty-five years after her statue of Sumner had been turned down by the Boston Arts Committee, Whitney still had not forgotten the affront. Even though she was approaching 80, she undertook the enormous task of making the monument from the model she had submitted in 1875. Several Harvard professors helped her raise money for the project. As her new penthouse studio was not large enough for what she

had in mind, she rented a studio outside of Boston. The finished statue was erected in Harvard Square in 1902. Anne Whitney, by then a diminutive white-haired woman, proved that indeed the Boston Arts Committee had not been able to quench her.

SOURCES:

Craven, Wayne. *Sculpture in America*. NY: Thomas Y. Crowell, 1968.

Rubinstein, Charlotte Streifer. *American Women Sculptors: A History of Women Working in Three Dimensions*. Boston, MA: G.K. Hall, 1990.

Tufts, Eleanor. *American Women Artists 1830–1930*. Exhibition catalogue for the National Museum of Women in the Arts, 1987.

SUGGESTED READING:

Payne, Elizabeth Rogers. "Anne Whitney, Sculptures: Art and Social Justice," in *Massachusetts Review*. Spring 1971.

COLLECTIONS:

Whitney Archives, Wellesley College Library, Wellesley, Massachusetts.

Claire Hsu Accomando,
writer on art and history and author of
Love and Rutabaga: A Remembrance of the War Years
(St. Martin's Press, 1993)

Whitney, Betsey Cushing Roosevelt

(1908–1998).

See Cushing Sisters.

Whitney, Charlotte Anita

(1867–1955)

American suffragist and political organizer who helped found what became the American Communist Party. Born on July 7, 1867, in San Francisco, California; died on February 4, 1955; educated at public and private schools in California; graduated from Wellesley College, 1889.

Later the defendant in the first major prosecution of California's "criminal syndicalism" law and a founder of the Communist Labor Party, which became the American Communist Party, Charlotte Anita Whitney was born into a wealthy family in San Francisco in 1867. Her father was a lawyer, and she was the niece of both Stephen J. Field, a justice on the Supreme Court from 1863 to 1897, and financier Cyrus W. Field. Whitney attended both public and private schools, and then went East to enroll at Wellesley College in Massachusetts, from which she graduated in 1889.

In 1893, Whitney visited the College Settlement House in New York City and was deeply impressed by the good works she saw there. Returning to her native California, she became a social worker in the Oakland slums, and served as secretary of the Council of Associated Charities of Alameda County from 1901 to 1906. By 1911, she had become active in the campaign for women's suffrage, and in that year she was elected president of the California College Equal Suffrage League as well as second vice-president of the National American Woman Suffrage Association (NAWSA). She organized California's drive to adopt a women's suffrage amendment to the state constitution and worked on similar campaigns in Oregon, Nevada and Connecticut.

Whitney's social work and suffrage politics put her in contact with leftist radicals in other movements. By 1914, she was a member of the Socialist Party, and was also active in the International Workers of the World (IWW), the radical labor union known as the Wobblies. Many states and towns in the West passed laws prohibiting street speaking to prevent Wobblies from spreading their message, and Whitney joined in the fight for freedom of speech. By 1919, when the post-World War I "Red Scare" was in full swing, spurred by fears of Communism, labor unions, and the first few of a string of bombings across the country, Whitney was part of the most radical wing of the Socialist Party. That year she helped orchestrate this wing's defection and the founding of a separate Communist Labor Party (CLP) which, after various tweakings, would become the American Communist Party. Late in 1919, Whitney was arrested after giving a speech at a CLP convention in Oakland. California had recently passed a criminal syndicalism law that, in short, 1) made illegal any doctrine advocating or aiding sabotage or violent acts aimed at changing industrial control or effecting political change and 2) made criminally liable anyone who organized or joined any group that advocated or aided criminal syndicalism. Whitney was indicted on five counts of criminal syndicalism. The law was aimed mainly at the Wobblies, some of whose objectives the CLP had endorsed; thus, because of that endorsement, and because Whitney did not deny that she was a member of the CLP, she was convicted on one count of criminal syndicalism (actually, guilt by association) and sentenced to one to fourteen years in jail. She served only 11 days of the sentence due to ill health, but her appeal of the conviction dragged through the courts for years before she was finally pardoned by California's governor in June 1927. It was during the Supreme Court's unanimous upholding of her conviction that justices Oliver Wendell Holmes and Louis Brandeis articulated the link between the due process clause of the 14th Amendment and the rights to freedom of speech and peaceful assembly of the 1st Amendment that eventually led to the enshrined concept of free and protected speech in America as we now know it.

Whitney's conviction and brief stint in jail did not end her involvement in political activities. In 1924, she ran on the Communist ticket for state treasurer, garnering more than 100,000 votes. She had another run-in with the law in 1935, when she was arrested for lecturing without a permit, falsely attesting Communist Party election petitions, and the distribution of radical literature. The following year she became national chair of the Communist Party, and in 1950, in her early 80s, she ran for the U.S. Senate. She died five years later in her hometown of San Francisco.

SOURCES:
McHenry, Robert, ed. *Famous American Women.* NY: Dover, 1980.

Angela Woodward, M.A.,
Madison, Wisconsin

Whitney, Dorothy Payne

(1887–1968)

American philanthropist. Name variations: Dorothy Straight; Dorothy Straight Elmhirst; Mrs. Willard Straight. Born in April 1887 in Washington, D.C.; died in 1968 in Devon, England; daughter of William Collins Whitney and Flora (Payne) Whitney (1843–1893); married Willard Dickerman Straight, on September 7, 1911 (died in 1919); married Leonard Knight Elmhirst, in 1925; children: (first marriage) Whitney Straight; Beatrice Straight (1918–2001, an actress); Michael Straight; (second marriage) two.

Born in 1887 in Washington, D.C., the youngest child of William Collins Whitney and *Flora Payne Whitney, Dorothy Payne Whitney was a mid-life baby; she was only six when her mother died of heart disease. William's subsequent marriage to **Edith Randolph Whitney** was regarded as treachery by the older Whitney children, Payne and **Pauline Whitney**, although Dorothy and her other brother Henry (Harry) Payne Whitney stood by their father and came to love their stepmother. Even after Edith succumbed to injuries sustained in a riding accident in 1898, the family remained divided in loyalties. William went on to amass quite a fortune and when he died in 1904, Dorothy became a wealthy young heiress. She was placed in the guardianship of her brother Harry and his wife *Gertrude Vanderbilt Whitney, who felt it their duty to protect her from the legions of young suitors they believed were out for her money.

Following a European tour and her introduction to society, Whitney enjoyed a busy social life (her diary for 1906 revealed dates with more than 40 men). Unlike her mother, however, whose life had been dominated by social activities, she was more attuned to the world. "Dorothy had a compassion that was ultimately to be translated into 'radicalism' displeasing to her set," writes W.A. Swanberg in *Whitney Father, Whitney Heiress*. "She was thrilled by such sonorous incitements to righteousness as Henley's *Invictus*. Although she took it for granted that she was of the elite, she shunned the more obtrusive snobberies of her circle and began her philanthropies—safely, through intermediary charities—by the distribution of her cast-off clothing to the poor."

In the summer of 1909, Dorothy embarked on a world tour. While in China, she met up with Willard Straight, who was negotiating banking transactions in Beijing (Peking) and serving as advisor to railroad magnate E.H. Harriman. Although Willard and Dorothy had met a few times previously at social gatherings, Willard had little money or family connections and appeared to be an unsuitable match for a Whitney. Over the course of two weeks in Beijing, however, the two fell in love, though family disapproval postponed their nuptials until September 7, 1911.

After 11 months of marriage, during which time they traveled extensively, the couple settled in New York. They eventually built a mansion on Fifth Avenue, where they entertained an endless stream of well-heeled and prominent personalities. Dorothy had three children, all of whom she cherished, but she entrusted them to English nannies to pursue her outside activities. She redoubled her charitable efforts, working with the Junior League, the drive for women's suffrage, the State Charities Aid, and the YWCA. She also supported her husband's frequent career changes, from banking to law, and subsidized *The New Republic*, a weekly newspaper devoted to "the improvement of the democracy" which he started with Herbert Croly in 1914.

During World War I, while her husband served overseas, Dorothy worked as a fund raiser for the Red Cross, and continued her service to the YMCA, although she came to abhor the pious, evangelical attitude of some of its members. "When I hear them say that their first duty is to put the soldier into proper relationship with God, I want to say, 'go to H——, the soldier is far closer to God than you are!'" At home, she cut her staff of some 26 servants almost in half, and cabled her husband for permission to sell off half of his polo ponies. In his absence, she also served as advisor to *The New Republic*, relaying messages from him to the editorial staff, attending weekly luncheon meetings, and working on particular projects. "You are wonderful, my dear Dorothy," editor Croly wrote to her. "There has never been a group of intellectual warriors, since the world began, who have had the kind assistance and support from a trustful friend that we have had from you." According to Swanberg, Whitney was also instrumental in starting the New School for Social Research in 1918, of which she also served as a director. The school provided "progressive" adult education and served as an independent social service institute.

Willard's unexpected death in November 1919 left Whitney bereft for months. The following summer, however, she undertook a request from General John Pershing to supervise the refurbishing of the cemetery at Suresnes, where Willard had been buried. The trip abroad revitalized her spirits, and by September her diary noted: "Most wonderful & happy day."

In 1925, Whitney married Leonard Knight Elmhirst, president of the Cosmopolitan Club at Cornell University. whom she had met while planning a union building at the university to honor her husband. The marriage surprised the social world as did the couple's subsequent move to England. There, they purchased Dartington Hall, a decaying mansion on 2,000 acres in Devon, and started a combined school and industrial-cultural center. Dorothy explained the enterprise to her friends back home in *The Junior League magazine*: "At Dartington, we regard the school as a part of the community in which adult education and rural enterprises of all kinds are being carried on," she wrote. "Fear of elders [on the part of the pupils, known as juniors] does not exist. . . . the juniors are exposed to the intellectual as well as the practical interests of the community."

At first, the school was judged a bit too progressive, especially in its informality and its lack of religious affiliation. The village cleric was censorious, and rumors about immorality and nudity ran rampant among the townsfolk. In time, however, Dartington became famous as an advanced school, particularly in the arts. Among its highly qualified teachers were Mark Tobey in painting, *Margaret Barr* in art history, and Michael Chekhov in drama. (Whitney's daughter **Beatrice Straight**, who became an acclaimed actress, received much of her training at Dartington.) The school also boasted occasional lecturers such as Bertrand Russell, Julian and Aldous Huxley, and Rabindranath Tagore. Whitney taught Shakespeare at the school and occasionally gave lectures to the convicts at nearby Dartmoor Prison.

Whitney continued to support *The New Republic* until it was sold in 1953, at which time her contributions totaled about $3 million. Not once in all those years did she seek to control the paper's opinions, even during World War II. Bruce Bliven, who succeeded Croly in 1930, noted that the "pacifist position of [*The New Republic*] must have grated on the Elmhirsts to a high degree, but never once did they make the slightest suggestion that we should alter our course."

Dorothy Payne Whitney died in 1968, at the age of 81, outliving all of her siblings. After a funeral ceremony at the Anglican church in the village, she was cremated and her ashes scattered in her own Dartington garden.

SOURCES:
Swanberg, W.A. *Whitney Father, Whitney Heiress.* NY: Scribner, 1980.

Barbara Morgan,
Melrose, Massachusetts

Whitney, Flora Payne (1897–1986)

American sculptor and art patron who was president of New York's Whitney Museum of American Art for 25 years. Name variations: Flora Whitney Miller. Born on July 29, 1897; died in Nassau, New York, on July 17, 1986; eldest of four children (two girls and two boys) of Harry Payne Whitney (1872–1930) and Gertrude Vanderbilt Whitney (1875–1942); attended the Brearley School, New York; graduated from Foxcroft School, Virginia; married Roderick Tower (1892–1961, a businessman), in 1920 (divorced); married George Macculloch Miller (1887–1972, an artist and businessman), on February 24, 1927; children: (first marriage) Pamela Tower; Whitney Tower; (second marriage) Flora Miller Biddle; Leverett Miller.

Upon the death of her mother *Gertrude Vanderbilt Whitney in 1942, Flora Payne Whitney took over the stewardship of the Whitney Museum of American Art, which Gertrude had established in 1931 and nurtured through its early years. For Flora Payne Whitney, the Museum "was her adored mother," says Flora's daughter **Flora Miller Biddle**. "Her longing and then her mourning poured into the Museum, enriching it for more than twenty-five years and holding Gertrude's passionate commitment fast."

Flora Payne Whitney was the eldest of four children born to Harry Payne Whitney and Gertrude Vanderbilt. She enjoyed a privileged but somewhat unpredictable childhood, her schooling frequently interrupted by family trips. At 14, she sojourned with Gertrude to Paris, where she had her own apartment near her mother's, with a maid and governess. "Had lunch with Mamma at her studio. It's awfully nice. I loved my first day in Paris," she wrote in her journal in 1912. In February, she recorded a shopping expedition. "Mamma got two coats and 16 evening dresses, suits, and afternoon dresses. . . . Then we went to get my clothes. I got 12 dresses, one suit (blue), three hats, and fours coats. I love them all." In her late teens, Flora went through a period of resenting her advantaged existence, feeling that it did not prepare her for a productive life. At the same time, she faulted her mother for not understanding her. "I really feel much worse about not being able to talk to Mamma than anyone thinks I do," she wrote in a letter at age 18. "Oh! It's awful. If only I could—I admire and respect and of course adore Mamma, but there is no companionship at all."

At 19, shortly after graduating from Foxcroft School in Virginia, Whitney fell in love with Quentin Roosevelt, Theodore's youngest son, to whom she became engaged shortly before he went overseas as a World War I pilot in the American Expeditionary Forces. On July 14, 1918, Quentin was shot down and killed in his plane inside the German lines. Flora was devastated by the loss, but found solace in the company of the Roosevelt family. She went to work as a transcriber for Theodore just weeks before his death in 1919. Reeling from a second loss, she stayed with *Alice Roosevelt Longworth in Washington, where she worked briefly for the Women's Republican Committee and attempted to keep up with Longworth's frantic social life.

In 1920, Whitney married Roderick Tower, a young oilman who had been a friend of Quentin's. The union produced two children but ended four year later. Following the divorce, Flora spent the summer with her mother in Paris. She began sculpting there and later in New York, exhibiting her work at the Society of Independent Artist and in the Whitney Studio Club's Tenth Anniversary Exhibition. In 1927, she married George Macculloch "Cully" Miller, a talented artist and businessman with whom she had much in common. Cully adored Whitney's children, and the couple added another two, Flora and Leverett. Hoping to raise their family in a "protected, healthy ambiance," they settled into a house in Aiken, South Carolina, given to them by Gertrude. Despite the idyllic setting, Biddle recalls that her parents were frequently absent. "Before World War II, when we were small, they actively sought pleasure, fun, the good life. They ate, drank, and made merry. We often felt left out, and were abandoned to the strict nanny who taught us discipline, restraint, and humility."

After the unexpected death of her mother, Whitney agonized over the museum, closing it briefly, then reopening it while she considered a merger with the Metropolitan Museum of Art. It was not until 1948 that she abandoned that idea and took over the institution herself. "My mother's decision to keep the Museum was a bold one," writes Biddle. "With fewer resources than her mother had, and mounting costs, she would have to count on her brother Sonny's and sister **Barbara [Whitney]**'s help. . . . And my mother would have to provide leadership."

Whitney did provide leadership, without the confidence of her mother but with warmth and enthusiasm. She oversaw moves in 1954 and 1966, the last to its present location on Madison Avenue, in a building designed by the famed architect Marcel Breuer. She also helped to expand the museum's collection and assisted fund-raising projects, often donating money from her own funds. In 1980, she sold a valuable Turner painting (*Juliet and Her Nurse*) from her own collection and donated a portion of the record proceeds ($6.4 million) to the museum. Like her mother, Whitney also took a great interest in nurturing new artists. "Her kindness tamed Philip Evergood's distrust of the rich and dispelled Charles Burchfield's social inarticulateness," recalled Jack Baur, who was director of the Whitney from 1968 to 1974. "After the latter's one-man show at the Whitney in nineteen fifty-six, Flora took his whole family back to Ten Gracie Square for a champagne dinner and bought his *Goldenrod in December*. Her spirit played a crucial part in establishing and nourishing the Whitney's policy of supporting living artists. We all loved her."

As age encroached, many of Whitney's duties were taken over by her daughter Flora Biddle. While Biddle had grieved over her mother's absences when she was a child, her work at the Whitney brought the two women closer. Following Whitney's death in the summer of 1986, the Biddles, together with the museum staff, put together a "Flora" memorial scrapbook, containing hundreds of photographs and tributes, and covered in yellow, her favorite color. The book

Flora Payne Whitney

was presented at a gala in Flora's honor held at her beloved museum. The party also marked a crucial juncture for the Whitney Museum, a time of moving forward and of change, not all of it easy. The museum is now a trustee-run business, no longer dominated by the Whitney family, although Whitney granddaughter **Fiona Biddle** sits on the board of trustees, representing the fourth generation of Whitney women to have a presence there.

SOURCES:

Biddle, Flora Miller. *The Whitney Women and the Museum They Made: A Family Memoir.* NY: Arcade, 1999.

Garraty, John A., and Mark C. Carnes, ed. *American National Biography.* Vol. 23. NY: Oxford University Press, 1999.

Barbara Morgan,
Melrose, Massachusetts

Whitney, Gertrude Vanderbilt

(1875–1942)

American sculptor, patron of the arts, and philanthropist who founded the Whitney Museum of American Art. Name variations: Mrs. Henry Payne Whitney; Mrs. Harry Payne Whitney; Mrs. H.P. Whitney. Born Gertrude Vanderbilt on January 9, 1875, in New York City; died in New York of heart complications on April 18, 1942; daughter of Alice Gwynne Vanderbilt (1845–1934, a socialite) and Cornelius Vanderbilt II (1843–1899, a banker, investor, and philanthropist); educated by private tutors and at the Brearley School for Girls; studied sculpture under Hendrik Andersen and James E. Fraser, and under Andrew O'Connor in Paris; married Henry (Harry) Payne Whitney, on August 25, 1896; children: Flora Payne Whitney (b. July 29, 1897); Cornelius Vanderbilt Whitney (b. February 20, 1899); **Barbara Whitney** (b. March 21, 1903).

Exhibited Aspiration at Pan American Exposition in Buffalo, New York, began studying with James Earle Fraser, and opened her first studio, on West 33rd Street, New York City (1901); joined the board of directors of the Greenwich House Social Settlement, moved her studio to 40th Street (1903); became student at Art Students League, finished American Athlete to exhibit at the St. Louis Exhibition, raised $7,000 for the Downtown Day Nursery (1904); organized Colony Club exhibition, opened 19 MacDougal Alley studio (1907); Paganisme Immortel accepted by the National Academy of Design and opened Paris studio (1910); Head of Spanish Peasant shown at the Paris Salon, Study of a Head exhibited at Independent Artists Show in New York City, began building studio at Westbury (1911); received commission for Titanic Memorial (1912); exhibited five works at all-women artists show at Gorham Art Gallery, New York City; opened Westbury Studio, bought Whitney Studio at 8 West 8th Street, New York City (1913); participated in Nassau Hospital benefit and Committee of Mercy for World War I benefit, held "50–50" exhibition at Whitney Studio, organized and funded American hospital in France, founded Friends of Young Artists (1914); started Whitney Studio prize competition to benefit Fraternité des Artistes, received Medal of Award at Panama-Pacific Exhibition for Fountain of El Dorado (1915); held single-woman show of her own works at Whitney Studio, exhibited personal art collection and her own works at the Newport (Rhode Island) Art Association, became member of Executive Committee of the Women's National Committee of the (Charles Evans) Hughes Alliance (1916); had retrospective show at San Francisco Art Association's Palace of Fine Arts, and Head of Titanic exhibited in Philadelphia Plastic Club all-woman sculptors show; made an associate member of National Sculpture Society (1916); created set design for Giovanitti's play As It Was in the Beginning, created decorations for the Hero Land Allied Bazaar, organized "Allies of Sculpture" benefit exhibition at Ritz-Carlton (1917); toured retrospective show of her sculptures in seven midwestern towns, and formed

Whitney Studio Club (1918); had own show entitled "Impressions of War" at Whitney Studio (1919); wrote five articles for Art and Decoration, organized traveling "Overseas Exhibition" (1920); had own shows at Luxembourg Museum and McLean's Gallery in London (1921); exhibited at National Association of Women Painters and Sculptors Show, awarded honorary degree from New York University (1922) and Tufts University (1924); Buffalo Bill won bronze medallion at Paris Salon (1924); awarded the French Legion of Honor medal, and opened Whitney Studio Club Shop (1926); disbanded Whitney Studio Club and Shop (1928); opened Whitney Museum of American Art (1932); published Walking the Dusk (1932); awarded honorary degree from Rutgers University (1934); court battle over custody of Gloria Vanderbilt (1934–38); had solo exhibition at Knoedler's Gallery (1936); elected associate of National Academy of Design, won Medal of Honor of the National Sculpture Society, awarded honorary degree from Russell Sage College (1940).

Sculptures: Aspiration (1901); American Athlete and Four Seasons (1904); Pan, Boy with Parrot, and pair of caryatids for Hotel Belmont (1905); Paganisme Immortel and Science (1907); Boy with Pipes, Study of a Head, Dancing Girl, and Wherefore (1910); Aztec Fountain, Head of Spanish Peasant, Despair, Portrait Head of an Athlete, Head of Young Man, and fountain for New Arlington Hotel in Washington, D.C. (1912); Caryatid, Bacchante, Chinoise, and Self-Sacrifice (1913); Titanic Memorial, El Dorado Fountain, and El Dorado Frieze (1914); Gassed, In the Trenches, Victory, At His Post, His Last Charge, His Bunkie, The Aviator, all undated but probably completed during the war years (1914–17); Spirit of the Daughters of the American Revolution (1917); Madison Square Victory Arch, Refugees, Honorably Discharged, Orders, Spirit of the Red Cross Nurse, Private in the 15th, The 102nd Engineers, Chateau-Thierry, and On the Top (1919); Washington Heights War Memorial (1921); Buffalo Bill and Damrosch medal (1922); St. Nazaire Monument and sculpture for Mt. Hope Community Mausoleum (1924); Samuel Untermyer's Woodlawn Cemetery shrine (1925); Columbus Monument (1928); Friendship Fountain (1931); Unemployed (1932); John, Leda and the Swan, Salome, Daphne, Woman With Child, and Pan with His Teacher (1933); Devotion, Nun, and Gwendolyn (1934); The Kiss (1935); Peter Stuyvesant Monument and Mercy (1936); Spirit of Flight (To the Morrow, 1939); other undated works include a fountain for the Colony Club and a frieze for the Daughters of the American Revolution.

Gertrude Vanderbilt Whitney, whose wealth shaped her every action and thought, was born into the richest family in the United States. Great-granddaughter of the famous, self-made millionaire "Commodore" Cornelius Vanderbilt and daughter of banker, investor, and philanthropist Cornelius Vanderbilt II and *Alice Gwynne Vanderbilt, Gertrude grew up in the pampered lap of luxury during America's Gilded Age. When Whitney was a young woman she hated the strictures that her money imposed. She disliked public scrutiny and feared that people cared for her only for her wealth. She wrestled with the expectations that came with being a Vanderbilt heiress: to marry a man from her class, to build show mansions, to be a consummate hostess, perhaps to give some of the money away, as her father had done. When she was older, however, Whitney learned how to use her money for personal happiness. She became a noted sculptor, was a patron of poverty-stricken artists, championed American art at a time when few believed it had any worth, and founded the Whitney Museum of American Art with her own art collection and left her fortune to the museum upon her death. In the end, it was her name and

Gertrude
Vanderbilt
Whitney

her money that allowed her to make an enormous and far-reaching contribution to the cultural life of the United States by her unflinching support for modern American art and artists.

Gertrude Vanderbilt was born on January 9, 1875, in New York City, one of two daughters in a family of six; her sister *Gladys Moore Vanderbilt, the seventh child, would not be born until Gertrude was eleven. Whitney confessed to her diary at age 18 that she wished she had been born a boy because boys could do things that girls could not. Even as a child, she longed for freedom of action, a freedom that would elude her throughout her life. Her childhood was not unpleasant, however. She had fine clothing made for her by Parisian couturiers, excellent schooling, countless toys, and beautiful surroundings. She also had a close and loving family. American aristocrats in the late 19th century were a world unto themselves, and Gertrude reaped the benefits of belonging to that tightly knit circle. The Vanderbilts socialized only with others of enormous means and married within their set.

I had to fight, fight all the time to break down the walls of half-sympathetic and half-scornful criticism based on no other concept than the one that [art] wasn't done by people in my position.

—Gertrude Vanderbilt Whitney

Whitney's girlhood consisted of daily lessons from tutors in her home (until 1889 when she attended the exclusive Brearley School in New York City), trips to Europe in the summers where she toured museums and historical sites and was fitted for her wardrobe, excursions to relatives' homes, formal social calls with her mother, dancing lessons, yachting, tennis, card games, swimming, and watching the men and boys race boats and horses. The Vanderbilts, like the rest of the very wealthy, followed the social season as it revolved among New York, Newport, and Europe. When she was a girl, most of Gertrude's activities took place in all-female groups, except dancing school. By the time of her social debut in 1895, when she was officially introduced to society in a series of balls, parties, and dinners, more of her doings involved men. Whitney, who was always chaperoned, as were all unmarried women of her class, was the object of much male attention. Intelligent but shy, tall and willowy, with dark hair and green eyes, she made a striking debutante. She turned down several marriage proposals, some because she thought the suitors were only fortune hunting.

On August 25, 1896, Gertrude Vanderbilt married Henry (Harry) Payne Whitney. Though the Whitneys had less money than the Vanderbilts, they boasted an older and more aristocratic lineage. Both families approved of the match. The newlyweds honeymooned in Japan and returned to begin the task of remodeling and furnishing their homes—a summer mansion in Newport, Rhode Island; the Whitney brownstone in New York City, at 2 West 57th Street, where Harry had grown up; and a huge, rambling country home on Long Island, called Westbury. The Whitneys entertained lavishly, but Gertrude found the social duties tedious and unenjoyable. She became pregnant with their first child, *Flora Payne Whitney, who was born less than a year after the wedding. In early 1899, Gertrude gave birth to their second child, Cornelius Vanderbilt Whitney.

By this time, Harry was spending more and more time with his father. They worked together on business projects and investments, and amused and enriched themselves by buying and racing thoroughbreds. In some years, Harry's stable won as much as a quarter of a million dollars. Harry was also a serious polo player. Both business and, more often, pleasure, took him away from Gertrude, and she suspected that he was involved in extramarital affairs. Since she considered Harry her one true love, the realization of his straying devastated her and made her circumscribed existence as a socialite even more hollow. In the absence of clear-cut and fulfilling roles, and with a small army of nursemaids, governesses, and tutors to tend to her children, she looked for something substantial to fill her time.

Whitney settled upon art. From her earliest years, art had held a special fascination. She had always sketched and painted, and while touring had lingered longest in the art museums. In 1900, she began taking classes with Hendrik Christian Andersen, a European sculptor who conceived mammoth works. The scale appealed to Whitney. Though she was a diligent student, it was not easy for her to carve out time away from the expectations of her husband, children, and society. In the summer of 1901, the Whitneys traveled to Europe without their children. Harry spent his hours playing polo and scouting for new horses while Gertrude haunted museums and dined with the local sculptors. Later that year, she exhibited her first work, *Aspiration*, at the Pan-American Exposition. The acceptance of *Aspiration* was the sort of encouragement that she needed to pursue what was, by then, clearly a calling.

Later that year, Whitney established two studios, as her determination to sculpt increased. One was in New York City, on West 33rd Street; the other was at Westbury. She also found another teacher, the noted American sculptor James Earle Fraser. In 1903, she combined art and philanthropy as she became a member of the board of directors of the Greenwich House Social Settlement in New York City, one of her lifelong charities. She subsidized and taught art classes there, and Greenwich House would continue to figure in her artistic endeavors. That year, Whitney was again pregnant. There are hints in her diary that the benevolent work at Greenwich and the pregnancy were attempts on her part to regain her husband's love. **Barbara Whitney** was born on March 21, 1903, but the marriage would never again be as it had in the early years. Initially disapproving, Harry would eventually become distantly supportive of his wife's work, but he did not cease having affairs. Ultimately, Whitney would also find solace outside the marriage.

During the early 1900s, she committed herself seriously to two main goals: becoming the finest sculptor possible and supporting artists in need. In pursuit of the first, she took classes at the Art Students League in New York City. In 1904, she exhibited *American Athlete* at the St. Louis Exhibition and the next year secured her first commission. By 1907, she had found ways to profitably combine her social standing and her art. That year, she put together an exhibit at the private, exclusive women's Colony Club—of which she was a founding member—that included antique lace, portraits of members, and contemporary American paintings by artists who were known to her, including Ernest Lawson, Blendon Campbell, Jerome Myers, Arthur B. Davies, and **Bridget Guinness**. She met these and other artists when she took a studio at 19 MacDougal Alley in Greenwich Village. There, in that mecca for artists, Whitney worked alongside *Malvina Hoffman, Lawson, and her old teacher, James Earle Fraser. To her continued disappointment, her family and society friends were only amusedly tolerant of her sculpting. Instead, it was the artists she met who responded to her seriousness and her dedication—as well as to her financial and emotional support of them.

Her second goal grew out of her understanding that the art being created around her was not greatly admired by most people. Whitney was especially fond of contemporary American realist painters, such as Robert Henri, John Sloan, William Glackens, and George Bellows, whose work would later be dubbed "the Ashcan

School." In the early 1900s, serious collectors, including museums and exhibitors, shunned these artists, because their style and subject matter did not conform to what was being defined and taught as *art* in the European academies. Without a showcase, these painters could not make a living. Whitney's wealth and profound esteem for the work of her colleagues put her in a position to become a strong supporter of American art. She bought their canvases or sculptures, gave or loaned them money, paid their rent or medical bills, sent them abroad to study, and paid for their art supplies. She did this for many artists—male and female, European and American—and almost always in secret. Sometimes her support was longterm; sometimes it was only to see an artist through a lean period. According to her biographer B.H. Friedman, patronage became "for her a co-equal means of expressing creative energy." There was "not a contemporary artist of note in America who has not been helped by Mrs. Whitney," wrote art critic Henry McBride. Ultimately, she turned her own studio into an exhibition space for their art.

In 1914, Gertrude opened the Whitney Studio next to her MacDougal space. Until 1927, she held regular exhibitions of the work of such then-struggling artists as Sloan, Hoffman, Guy Péne du Bois, **Florence Lucius, Grace Mott Johnson,** Charles Demuth, Henry Schnakenberg, and Walt Kuhn. Some of the exhibitions were centered on themes, such as "To Whom Shall I Go for My Portrait?," which garnered a steady stream of upper-class patrons seeking portraitists like Childe Hassam, Alfred Stieglitz, and Edward Steichen. One of the most famous exhibitions held at the Whitney Studio was the two-part "Indigenous Show" in 1918. She invited 20 painters to spend three days in the studio and supplied them with canvases (the size was randomly assigned—so a muralist had to contend with a tiny canvas), paints, brushes, food, whiskey, and cigars. Sculptors were allowed five days and varying amounts of clay. The public wandered through enthralled with the opportunity to watch creative geniuses at work. In 1923, Whitney held the "Negro Sculpture" show which combined the work of African and African-American sculptors as well as 20 paintings by Pablo Picasso, to highlight the connections between African art and modernism.

She held many other exhibitions for charity. The first was the 1914 "50–50 Art Sale," in which the profits were split evenly between the artists and the American Hospital in Paris which was tending to the wounded soldiers of World War I. Another, held in 1915 to benefit the Fraternité des Artistes in France, featured the works of Auguste Rodin, Edouard Manet, *Mary Cassatt, James McNeill Whistler, and Honoré Daumier. In 1918, the Whitney Studio held an exhibition of "Art by Children of the Greenwich House School." Whitney donated the proceeds to the settlement house and the child artists.

Her patronage extended beyond the art she collected, the artists she supported, and the exhibitions she held at the Whitney Studio. Whitney made up the deficit for John Sloan's Society of Independent Artists from 1917 through 1931. In 1923, she began to underwrite *The Arts*, a magazine devoted to the writings and work of contemporary, non-academic artists. She provided the funding for the defense of the Supreme Court case *Brancusi* v. *the U.S.*, in which the United States argued that Brancusi's sculpture *Bird in Space* was not a sculpture at all, but rather a heap of raw materials subject, as such, to an import tax. In 1928, the Court found in favor of Brancusi. In order to spread the word about American art—and, in some cases, because the Whitney Studio was too small—Whitney organized exhibitions in other galleries in New York City, Boston, Baltimore, and Newport, as well as abroad. The 1920 "Overseas Exhibition" toured four European cities, representing the work of 32 contemporary American artists. She also aided other art institutions, among them the National Sculpture Society, the Art Centre, the National Academy of Design, the Madison Gallery, the Art Alliance of America, and the Society of Beaux-Arts Architects. She donated $1,000 for decorations to the groundbreaking 1913 Armory Show. Whenever her exhibitions held competitions, she provided the purse.

Meanwhile, she sculpted. Whitney's own work was traditional, realistic, and often grand in scale. Many of her commissions memorialized events and people, such as the *Titanic Memorial* (Washington, D.C., 1914), *Spirit of the Daughters of the American Revolution* (Washington, D.C., 1917), *Madison Square Victory Arch* (New York City, 1919), *Washington Heights War Memorial* (New York City, 1921), *Buffalo Bill* (Cody, Wyoming, 1922), *St. Nazaire Monument* (St. Nazaire, France, 1924), *Columbus Monument* (Palos, Spain, 1928), and *Peter Stuyvesant* (New York City, 1936). If she accepted remuneration, she was criticized by members of memorial organizations who thought that she was wealthy enough to donate her art; if she worked for free, she was criticized by fellow artists who claimed she undercut the market. Though she did not always cash the checks, Whitney made certain that those who commis-

sioned her also paid her. Her smaller statues, such as *Paganisme Immortel* (1907), won a distinguished rating from the National Academy of Design in 1910 and caused her to begin exhibiting under her own name rather than anonymously; though *Chinoise* (1913) and *Salome* (1933) brought her satisfaction and occasionally money, she was best known for her monuments.

In 1910, Whitney began spending substantial time in Paris, where she found a studio space at 72 Rue de Flandrin and studied with Andrew O'Connor. She had always loved France, and in 1914, when World War I began, she set out to help the beleaguered country. Establishing an American Field Hospital just behind the battle lines in Juilly, she paid for the supplies, recruited and paid the salaries of its personnel, and administered it for the first year. In 1917, Whitney contributed more than $15,000 a month to the hospital. For her service, she was decorated with a gold medal by the French government. Tending to the wounded and dying soldiers, Whitney was touched and inspired. When the war ended, the subject matter and the timbre of her sculpture reflected her experiences. Many had martial subjects: *In the Trenches*, *Gassed*, *Victory*, *Honorably Discharged*, and *Refugees*, for example. In part because of her war work, the St. Nazaire Association commissioned her to create a monument to the first troops of the American Expeditionary Force to land in France, at St. Nazaire. It towered 60 feet above the rocky shoreline of the town's harbor. She continued to create war memorials into the 1920s.

In 1918, Gertrude organized the Whitney Studio Club. Begun with a core of 20 member artists and situated at 147 West 4th Street (it would move in 1923 to 8th Street), the Whitney Studio Club included two exhibition halls, an art library, a billiard room, and a squash court. It held annual member exhibitions and frequent classes, and served as a comfortable meeting place for artists of many stripes. Needy artists lived upstairs. Critical to the Club's success was ✥▶ Juliana Force, a secretary turned right-hand woman. Force had worked with Whitney on and off since the Colony Club exhibition in 1907. By 1918, Force had professionalized the exhibitions at the Whitney Studio, and operated nearly autonomously when Whitney spent months abroad. The Whitney Studio Club became famous for Force's dinners and teas, where artists discussed art, politics, and each other. By 1928, the Club had held 86 exhibitions but carried an unwieldy membership of 400 artists and a waiting list of 400 more. Whitney and Force decided to disband. Said Force, in a *New York Times* interview, "The pioneering work for which the club was organized had been done; its aim has been successfully attained. Opportunities for showing work by young American artists have increased tremendously. The liberal arts have won the battle." In fact, by the end of the 1920s, Whitney had helped make American art acceptable to the public and to its traditional arbiters.

During the last two years of the Club's existence, the Studio Club Shop sold the work of member artists, without charging a commission. This made the artwork less expensive, thus encouraging collectors, while the artists—sans dealers—retained a larger profit. The Whitney Studio Club and Shop gave way to the Whitney Studio Galleries, which was run as a commercial gallery, with single and group shows by contemporary artists. After two years, Whitney discontinued the Studio Galleries because she had opened what would become her most lasting monument to American art, the Whitney Museum of American Art.

By the end of the decade, she had acquired over 600 works in her personal art collection, and most of those languished in storage, unseen. Debating whether to add a wing to one of her houses or to give the collection away, Whitney and Force decided upon the latter course. To that end, Whitney sent Force to discuss the donation of her art collection, along with a $5 million endowment, to the director of the Metropolitan Museum of Art. The director cut Force off mid-proposal, saying, "What will we do with them, my dear lady? We have a cellar of those things already." Angrily, Force related the tale to Whitney who decided, on the spot, to create her own museum with her personal collection of "those things." Force was made director.

The Whitney Museum of American Art was born in the midst of the Great Depression, on November 18, 1931, with 4,000 in attendance. Harry Payne Whitney had died on October 26, 1930, while the planning was underway. He left an estate of $71 million. Most of this went to their children, but Gertrude had broad discretionary powers over the remainder. Some of his money and more of hers provided a solid financial base for the enterprise. Whitney's ongoing support of the museum included annual contributions of $160,000, a gift of $100,000 in 1935, and another gift of stocks valued at $790,000 in 1937. She would also donate $2.5 million to the museum in her will.

One unpublicized goal of Whitney's was to grant women artists the social and artistic sanction that generally eluded them. Born before the women's rights movement, she was acutely aware of the roles society prescribed for women and lamented the difficulties that women artists faced. In addition to the usual problems of finances, locating exhibition space, and securing commissions, women painters and sculptors suffered from public censure as they departed from their traditional roles of daughter, wife, and mother. In the early 20th century, it was not "nice" for middle- and upper-class women to have a career, to work in their own studios, to associate with the bohemians in Greenwich Village, to make money, to publicly display their work, or to compete with men. No other collector of her era bought or exhibited more work by women.

Whitney felt that she struggled against a double burden: being a woman and being wealthy. In an interview with *The New York Times* in 1919, she asserted: "[L]et a woman who does not have to work for her livelihood take a studio to do the work in which she is most intensely interested and she is greeted by a chorus of horror-stricken voices, a knowing lifting

---

❧➤ **Force, Juliana** (1876–1948)

American art museum administrator who was the first director of the Whitney Museum of American Art. Born Juliana Reiser (later changed name to Rieser) on December 25, 1876, in Doylestown, Pennsylvania; died in New York City on August 28, 1948; educated in local schools; married Dr. Willard B. Force.

After heading a secretarial school in New York City, Juliana Force signed on as secretary to *Helen Hay Whitney before she was asked to assist Helen's sister-in-law, *Gertrude Vanderbilt Whitney, with a novel Gertrude had written. Before long the book was forgotten, and Force was helping out at the Whitney Studio. When the Whitney Museum of American Art opened in 1930, Force was named director. She introduced a series of monographs on contemporary American artists, organized a series of morning and evening lectures, and energetically ran the Whitney until her death 18 years later. From 1933 to 1934, she also was regional director of the federal Public Works Art project. In her book *Off with Their Heads*, writer-artist *Peggy Bacon described Force: "Dependably indiscreet, brutally witty, she talks effectively, constantly, sparing no feelings, letting people know exactly where they stand. . . . Handsome auburn *chevelure*, cream-colored skin, and small menacing eyes that miss nothing. Nose of Cyrano de Bergerac, mouth like a circumflex accent. Figure erect, trim, magnetic, packed with audacity and challenge."

SOURCES:
Current Biography. NY: H.W. Wilson, 1941.

---

of the eyebrows, or a twist of the mouth that is equally expressive. And much more condemnatory." In the same article, she confessed her frustration upon receiving criticism from people who "could not understand how a woman [her] size could build up a statue of that height." While she was never clear about whether being rich or being a woman was more of a handicap, she ultimately capitalized on the first and ignored the second. Perhaps as a measure of how far she had come, upon her death in 1942, the *Times* obituary was headed: "Mrs. H.P. Whitney, Sculptor, Is Dead." "Sculptor" instead of "socialite" spoke volumes about the success of her battle. Writ large, that success was shared by the women artists whose work she hung in the Whitney Museum of American Art. (The fact that she was still called "Mrs. H.P. Whitney," however, spoke volumes about how far woman artists still had to go.)

Gertrude Vanderbilt Whitney devoted her later life to consolidating her financial empire, overseeing her large and increasingly troubled family (including the messy, tabloid custody case for her niece, *Gloria Vanderbilt), conserving her strength as her health failed, steering the Whitney Museum, and continuing to sculpt. Her last public sculptures were monuments of Peter Stuyvesant for Stuyvesant Square and *Spirit of Flight* for the 1939 World's Fair. In 1932, after a lifetime of writing diaries, travel journals, short stories, novellas, and plays, she published a novel under the pseudonym L.J. Webb, *Walking the Dusk* (Coward-McCann). In the depths of the Great Depression, it was not a great seller, but it did represent one success in the other main creative outlet in Whitney's life. From then on, she strove to professionalize her writing, taking a writing class and consulting with well-known authors. None of her other writings were ever published.

Although Whitney was a realist sculptor of merit who overcame familial animosity, public disbelief, and the limited expectations for her gender to create sculptures acclaimed around the globe, her greatest legacy was the Whitney Museum of American Art, the first museum anywhere to showcase artists from the United States. Behind that was the equally remarkable feat of making American art acceptable, even chic. As Whitney began sculpting, the members of the Ashcan School were unknowns. By the end of the 1920s, collectors were paying thousands of dollars for their paintings. The same could be said for most of the other artists whom she assisted, either directly—financially or through exhibitions at the Whitney Studio or Galleries—or indirectly, as a consequence of the rising status of American art. Whitney did not labor alone. Other artists and patrons assisted, such as Steichen and Stieglitz, but she was the true promoter of American realism. The fame of many of the 400 members of the Whitney Studio Club attests to her talent for discovering good art, promoting American art, and succoring the artist. Gertrude Vanderbilt Whitney put American art on the map.

SOURCES:

Berman, Avis. "The Force Behind the Whitney," in *American Heritage*. September–October 1989, pps. 102–113.

———. *Rebels on Eighth Street: Juliana Force and the Whitney Museum of American Art*. NY: Atheneum, 1990.

Friedman, B.H. *Gertrude Vanderbilt Whitney*. Garden City, NY: Doubleday, 1978.

"Hail and Farewell! Why the Whitney Studio Club Disbands," in *The New York Times*. September 23, 1928, p. 11.

Jewell, Edward Alden. "The Whitney Museum of American Art Opens This Week," in *The New York Times*. November 15, 1931, p. 14.

McCarthy, Kathleen D. *Women's Culture: American Philanthropy and Art, 1830–1930*. Chicago, IL: University of Chicago Press, 1992.

"Memorial Unveiled to First Americans Landing in France: Heroic Statue and St. Nazaire Celebration Revive Much of War's Idealism," in *The New York Times*. June 27, 1926, p. 1.

"Mrs. H.P. Whitney, Sculptor, Is Dead," in *The New York Times*. April 18, 1942, p. 16.

"Mrs. Whitney Left Fortune To Public," in *The New York Times*. May 5, 1942, p. 23.

"Mrs. Whitney on War Hospital," in *The New York Times*. March 28, 1915, section 5, p. 7.

"Poor Little Rich Girl and Her Art," in *The New York Times Magazine*. November 9, 1919, section 4, p. 7.

Tarbell, Roberta K. "Gertrude Vanderbilt Whitney as Patron," in *The Figurative Tradition and the Whitney Museum of American Art*. Patricia Hills and Roberta K. Tarbell, eds. Newark, NJ: University of Delaware Press, 1980.

SUGGESTED READING:

Biddle, Flora Miller. *The Whitney Women and the Museum They Made: A Family Chronicle*. NY: Arcade, 2000.

COLLECTIONS:

Gertrude Vanderbilt Whitney's personal papers are held at the Archives of American Art, Smithsonian Institution, Washington, D.C.

Stacy A. Cordery,
Associate Professor of History,
Monmouth College, Monmouth, Illinois

Whitney, Mrs. Harry Payne (1875–1942).

See *Whitney, Gertrude Vanderbilt*.

Whitney, Helen Hay (1876–1944)

American sportswoman and philanthropist who founded the Greentree Stable which produced numer-

*ous thoroughbreds including the 1931 Kentucky Derby winner Twenty Grand. Name variations: Mrs. Payne Whitney. Born Helen Hay on March 11, 1876, in New York; died in September 1944 in New York; daughter of John Hay (1838–1905, private secretary to Abraham Lincoln and U.S. secretary of state to presidents William McKinley and Theodore Roosevelt) and Clara Louise (Stone) Hay; sister of Alice Hay Wadsworth Boyd; attended Miss Masters' School, Dobbs Ferry, New York; married Payne Whitney (a financier), on February 6, 1902 (died 1927): children: *Joan Whitney Payson (1903–1975); Jock Whitney.*

Known as the "first Lady of the American Turf" because of her lifelong interest in horse racing, Helen Hay Whitney was the daughter of **Clara Stone Hay** and John Hay, private secretary to Abraham Lincoln and U.S. secretary of state to two presidents. After graduating from the exclusive Miss Masters' School, Whitney wrote several volumes of poetry, which so delighted her father that he had them published. Her writing career was cut short, however, by her marriage in 1902 to financier Payne Whitney. The wedding ceremony was a major social event in Washington; among the guests were President Theodore Roosevelt and his entire Cabinet. "The church was so crowded that one could not move without jostling a senator or dignitary of even higher rank," writes W.A. Swanberg. "Ambassadors from all nations were present, including the Wus from China and the Takahiras from Japan." Among the wedding gifts were a Fifth Avenue house, a yacht, and some impressive diamond jewelry.

Whitney purchased her first horse—a steeplechaser named Web Carter—in 1909 and by the mid-1920s had established Greentree Stable in Red Bank, New Jersey, a 150-acre facility recognized as one of the country's major stables and the largest run by a woman. It was also among the top money-winners in the country, particularly in 1931, when Whitney's horse Twenty Grand won the Kentucky Derby. Whitney sometimes found it necessary to use her wealth and power to protect her interests. She fought New York governor Charles Evans Hughes in his attempt to enact anti-gambling legislation in the state, and in 1939, she led the call for the legalization of parimutuel betting.

Whitney also supported a number of charitable organizations, including the New York Hospital and the Henry Street Settlement in New York City. Beginning in 1919, she hosted an annual Greentree Fair at her estate in Man-

hasset, New York, to benefit the Family Welfare Association of Nassau County and the New York Hospital. Following the death of her husband in 1927, she and her children donated money to Yale University for the construction of a new gymnasium in his memory. Whitney also served as honorary vice president of the Horticultural Society of New York. Helen Hay Whitney died in September 1944 in New York.

SOURCES:

Garraty, John A., and Mark C. Carnes, eds. *American National Biography.* Vol. 23. NY: Oxford University Press, 1999.

Swanberg, W.A. *Whitney Father, Whitney Heiress.* NY: Scribner, 1980.

Barbara Morgan,
Melrose, Massachusetts

Whitney, Mrs. Henry Payne

(1875–1942).

See Whitney, Gertrude Vanderbilt.

Whitney, Isabella (fl. 1567–1575)

English poet, considered one of the first women to publish secular literature.

Little is known of Isabella Whitney's life, yet she left her mark on English literature as one of the first women to publish non-religious writings. Her extant opus consists of two books of poetry. She is believed to have been the sister of another early English author, Geoffrey Whitney, who published a well-known book *A Choice of Emblemes* in 1586. Whitney belonged to a family of the minor gentry with a country home in Coole Pilate, near Nantwich, Cheshire. She had three sisters and two brothers. The sisters moved to London, and her brother Geoffrey attended Magdalene College in Cambridge. From her poems, it is clear that Whitney knew London well, and she also had something of an education, as she was evidently familiar with the classics, the Bible, and some contemporary literature.

Whitney's first book was *A Copy of a Letter lately written in Meeter by a Yonge Gentilwoman to Her Unconstant Lover* (1567). This consists of a long poem exhorting women to defend their chastity and virtue. It showed Whitney's knowledge of Greek and Roman literature in its many allusions to classical tragic heroines such as Dido, betrayed by Aeneas in Virgil's *Aeneid*, and Ariadne, left behind by Theseus after she helped him slay the minotaur in that Greek legend. Whitney drew parallels between these women's cruel fate and the perils attending modern women beset by men's lust-guided dishonesty.

Whitney's second book was a collection of poems entitled *A Sweet Nosegay, or Pleasant Posye: contayning a hundred and ten Philosophicall Flowers* (1573). These poems also contained a moral message, warning women of the temptations of worldliness, as particularly represented by the sinful city of London. Written in ballad meter, the poems were adaptations of maxims published in the 1572 book *The Floures of Philosophie* by Sir Hugh Platt. In her preface, Whitney acknowledged that she had borrowed her "flowers" from someone else's garden, yet the poems themselves were original. One poem included in the *Nosegay* was a "Wyll and Testament" addressed to the city of London, in which the author says farewell to the city, and describes in some detail its business district. Beyond her slim list of publications, Whitney remains a mystery. She may have married and had two children, and taken the name of Eldershae. Her importance remains in that she was essentially the first English woman to identify herself as a professional writer.

SOURCES:

Buck, Claire, ed. *The Bloomsbury Guide to Women's Literature.* NY: Prentice Hall, 1992.

Shattock, Joanne. *The Oxford Guide to British Women Writers.* Oxford: Oxford University Press, 1993.

Angela Woodward, M.A.,
Madison, Wisconsin

Whitney, Joan (1903–1975).

See Payson, Joan Whitney.

Whitney, Mrs. John Hay (1908–1998).

See Cushing Sisters for Betsey Cushing Whitney.

Whitney, Mary Watson

(1847–1921)

American astronomy teacher at Vassar College who was a protégé of Maria Mitchell. Born Mary Watson Whitney on September 11, 1847, in Waltham, Massachusetts; died on January 20, 1921, in Waltham; daughter of Samuel Buttrick Whitney and Mary Watson (Crehore) Whitney; attended Waltham public schools; Vassar College, B.A., 1868, A.M., 1872; attended lectures at Harvard and the University of Zurich; never married; no children.

Taught in Auburndale, Massachusetts (1868); was on staff at Dearborn Observatory, Chicago (1870); taught at Waltham High School (1876); was assistant at Vassar College Observatory (1881–88); was professor of astronomy and director of observatory at Vassar (1888–1910).

Selected writings: Observations of Variable Stars made During the Years 1901–12 *(1913);* "Scientific Study and Work for Women," *in* Education *(Vol. 3, 1882, pp. 58–69); numerous other observations of comets, asteroids and variable stars.*

Mary Watson Whitney, favorite student of *Maria Mitchell, dedicated most of her life to educating women at Vassar College. Whitney was born in 1847, in Waltham, Massachusetts, the eldest daughter of Samuel Buttrick Whitney, a successful real estate dealer, and **Mary Crehore Whitney**. Mary excelled as a student in the Waltham public schools and, after graduating from high school, attended the Swedenborgian Academy in Waltham for one year while Vassar College was being established. She entered Vassar as an advanced student in 1865, its inaugural year.

At Vassar, Whitney studied astronomy under Maria Mitchell, the noted woman astronomer, and became Mitchell's protégé. After graduating in 1868, Whitney taught and worked at the Dearborn Observatory in Chicago, both briefly. She kept up her own observing and joined Mitchell for a solar eclipse expedition in Iowa. Whitney also continued her education, first by attending classes at Harvard and then receiving her A.M. from Vassar in 1872.

Whitney and her family moved to Zurich in 1873, where her sister entered medical school and Whitney attended lectures at the University of Zurich. After returning to Waltham in 1876, she taught at the high school until she was summoned by her former teacher to return to Vassar as Mitchell's assistant, a position she would hold until Mitchell's retirement in 1888. When Mitchell recommended that Whitney be named her successor, Whitney became the second astronomy professor in Vassar's history and director of the Observatory.

Whereas Mitchell had stressed teaching, Whitney stressed research, directing observing programs in double stars, comet and asteroid measurements, and variable star observations. "Professor means more than teacher," said Whitney; "it means special application and experience, and a knowledge extending beyond books. A professor is not only leader in the classroom, [she] is a co-worker in the frontranks of thought." Her students would be hired by major American observatories upon graduation. Mary Watson Whitney was deeply committed to women's education, as reflected in her involvement with the Vassar Alumnae Association, the Association for the Advancement for Women and the Maria Mitchell Association of Nantucket. She was also a charter member of the American Astronomical Society.

Poor health forced Whitney's retirement from Vassar in 1910. She died of pneumonia in her hometown of Waltham on January 21, 1920. She is reported to have said on her deathbed: "I hope when I get to Heaven, I shall not find the women playing second fiddle."

SOURCES:

Furness, Caroline E. "Mary Watson Whitney," in Malone, Dumas, ed., *Dictionary of American Biography.* Vol. 20. NY: Scribner, 1936.

———. "Mary W. Whitney," in *Popular Astronomy.* Vols. XXX and XXXI, 1922 and 1923, pp. 597–608, pp. 25–35.

Wright, Helen. "Mary Watson Whitney," in James, Edward T., ed., *Notable American Women, 1607–1950.* Cambridge: The Belknap Press of Harvard University, 1971.

Kristine Larsen,
Associate Professor of Astronomy and Physics,
Central Connecticut State University,
New Britain, Connecticut

Whitney, Mrs. Payne (1876–1944).

See Whitney, Helen Hay.

Whitney, Phyllis A. (1903—)

Popular American author of romantic suspense novels. Born Phyllis Ayame Whitney on September 9, 1903, in Yokohama, Japan; daughter of Charles Whitney (a businessman) and Mary (Mandeville) Whitney; graduated from McKinley High School, Chicago, 1924; married George A. Garner, in 1925 (divorced 1945); married Lovell F. Jahnke, in 1950 (died 1973); children: one daughter, Georgia.

Selected writings: A Place for Ann (1941); Red Is for Murder (1943); The Silver Inkwell (1945); Writing Juvenile Fiction (1947); Ever After (1948); Mystery of the Black Diamonds (1954); The Quicksilver Pool (1955); The Moonflower (1958); Mystery of the Haunted Pool (1960); Mystery of the Hidden Hand (1963); Black Amber (1964); Sea Jade (1965); Columbella (1966); The Winter People (1969); Nobody Likes Trina (1972); The Golden Unicorn (1976); The Stone Bull (1977); Rainbow in the Mist (1989); Amethyst Dreams (1997).

Born in 1903 in Yokohama, Japan, to American parents, Phyllis A. Whitney spent portions of her childhood living with her family in the Philippines and China until her father's death when she was 15. Together with her widowed mother **Mary Mandeville Whitney**, Phyllis continued to lead a nomadic existence upon her return to the United States, spending time in both San Antonio, Texas, and California. After the death of her mother, Whitney—then in her late teens—was placed in the care of an aunt in Chicago, where she completed her high school education.

Financial circumstances forced her to begin working immediately after high school graduation. Whitney took a job in the children's book department of a Chicago department store, continuing to work there until her first short story was accepted by the *Chicago Daily News* in 1928. During World War II, Whitney began her reign as one of the best-known American writers of romantic suspense in the latter half of the 20th century, a field otherwise dominated by British authors such as **Mary Stewart**, Victoria Holt (**Eleanor Hibbert**), and **Dorothy Eden**.

Whitney's long career of writing for young people and adults produced more than 75 novels, a number of articles on the writing of fiction, and several textbooks for would-be writers of fiction. Although she wrote her first adult book, *Red is for Murder*, in 1943, it was not until the publica-

Phyllis A. Whitney

tion of *The Quicksilver Pool* in 1955 that she began writing regularly for adults. Over the years she evolved a particular form of romantic suspense novel, the family mystery, in which both the plot and the setting are thoroughly entwined in a complex history of sinister family feuds and secrets. Reflecting her international upbringing, Whitney made exotic or out-of-the-way settings a central part of her stories. Her novels alternate between foreign or American locales such as Turkey, Japan, Great Britain, Norway, the Caribbean, the Blue Ridge Mountains, or the Catskills. Although, or perhaps because, the books follow a fairly strict formula, usually involving a young woman who must solve an old family mystery before she can find safety, happiness, and love with a good man whom initially she distrusted, they were hugely popular with readers throughout Whitney's career.

After living in Chicago for several years, Whitney moved to New York in the late 1940s. A marriage in 1925 had finally ended in divorce, leaving her to care for her daughter, **Gloria**, with whom she would share her love of travel and the Massachusetts coast. Whitney also edited children's book review pages for both the *Chicago Sun* and the *Philadelphia Inquirer*, and taught writing courses at Northwestern University in 1945 and New York University from 1947 to 1958, despite never having had the opportunity to earn a degree herself. *Mystery of the Haunted Pool* (1960) and *Mystery of the Hidden Hand* (1963) each won her an Edgar Award from the Mystery Writers of America, while many of her other novels were propelled by their popularity into several printings. In 1997, at age 94, Whitney published her 76th book, *Amethyst Dreams*.

SOURCES:

McHenry, Robert, ed. *Famous American Women*. NY: Dover, 1980.

Mote, Dave, ed. *Contemporary Popular Writers*. Detroit, MI: St. James Press, 1997.

Pamela Shelton,
freelance writer,
Avon, Connecticut

Whittelsey, Abigail Goodrich

(1788–1858)

American editor of magazines for mothers. Born Abigail Goodrich on November 29, 1788, in Ridgefield, Connecticut; died on July 16, 1858, in Colchester, Connecticut; daughter of the Reverend Samuel Goodrich and Elizabeth (Ely) Goodrich; educated at home and at local schools; married the Reverend Samuel Whittelsey, on November 10, 1808 (died 1842); children: Samuel (b. 1809); Charles Chauncey *(b. 1812); Elizabeth (b. 1815); Henry (b. 1821); Charles Augustus (b. 1823); Emily (b. 1825); and one unnamed child who died at birth.*

Served as matron of a female seminary in upstate New York (1824–28); together with husband, founded a seminary for girls in Utica, New York (1828), and served as its matron; appointed editor of periodical Mother's Magazine *(1833); magazine moved to New York City, where circulation reached 10,000 by 1837; resigned (1848); was founder, editor, and publisher,* Mrs. Whittelsey's Magazine for Mothers *(1850–52).*

Abigail Goodrich Whittelsey was born in 1788 in Ridgefield, Connecticut, the third daughter of the Reverend Samuel Goodrich and **Elizabeth Ely Goodrich**, and sister of children's book author Samuel Griswold Goodrich (1793–1860), who wrote under the pseudonym Peter Parley. After receiving her education at local schools, she was married in 1808, at age 20, to Samuel Whittelsey, a minister. The couple made their home in Preston, Connecticut, where Reverend Whittelsey was pastor to the Congregational church, before moving to Hartford where for several years he headed what would become the American School for the Deaf. Six of Whittelsey's seven children were born during this period, although only two would live to adulthood. In 1824, the family moved to Canandaigua, New York, where Samuel headed the Ontario Female Seminary, and Abigail served as matron to the young students after the birth of her last child, **Emily Whittelsey (Curtis)**, in 1825. Three years later, the Whittelseys moved to nearby Utica to found their own seminary for young ladies.

While in Utica, Whittelsey joined the newly established Maternal Association. The organization espoused the same values as did Abigail—making it a priority to raise children in a pious, God-fearing home—and she volunteered to edit the association's new magazine, *Mother's Magazine*. Containing articles providing detailed, morally grounded instructions in the discipline, schooling, "proper government," and personal care of young children, the magazine was among the first of its kind in the United States. It gave special attention to children of the poor, as well as orphans.

After the family's move to New York City in 1834, Whittelsey continued to edit and publish *Mother's Magazine*, carrying on publication after Samuel's death in 1842 with the help of her late husband's brother. In 1848, Whittelsey resigned her editorial role at *Mother's Magazine* after the Maternal Association made the decision to merge its publication with *Mother's Journal and Family Visitant* and become more commercial in tone. Two years later, she renewed her journalistic efforts with *Mrs. Whittelsey's Magazine for Mothers*, which was very similar to her first endeavor. With the help of her son Henry, Whittlesey continued to promote a religious upbringing among America's youth until 1852. Returning to Connecticut late in life, she spent her final years with daughter Emily and Emily's husband, the Reverend Lucius Curtis, in Colchester, Connecticut. She died in 1858 at the age of 70 and was buried in the town of Berlin, Connecticut.

SOURCES:

James, Edward T., ed. *Notable American Women, 1607–1950*. Cambridge, MA: The Belknap Press of Harvard University, 1971.

McHenry, Robert, ed. *Famous American Women*. NY: Dover, 1980.

Read, Phyllis J., and Bernard L. Witlieb. *The Book of Women's Firsts*. NY: Random House, 1992.

Pamela Shelton,
freelance writer,
Avon, Connecticut

Whitton, Charlotte (1896–1975)

First female mayor of a major Canadian city. Born on March 8, 1896, in Renfrew, Ontario, Canada; died on January 25, 1975, in Ottawa, Ontario, Canada; daughter of John Edward Whitton (a civil servant) and Elizabeth (Langin) Whitton; Queen's University, M.A., 1917; lived with Margaret Grier, from 1918 to 1947.

Served in the social service sector, including as executive director of the Canadian Welfare Council (1926–41); was founder and editor of journal Canadian Welfare *and author of numerous social service pamphlets; appointed, elected, then served as mayor of Ottawa (1951–56 and 1960–64); was columnist and essayist, with work published in Canadian newspapers; wrote* A Hundred Years A-Fellin' *(1943) and* The Dawn of Ampler Life *(1943).*

Charlotte Whitton was born in Renfrew, Ontario, in 1896, the eldest of four children of **Elizabeth Langin Whitton** and John Edward Whitton, a forestry official for the province of Ontario. Entering Queen's University in Kingston, Ontario, with scholarships in six subjects, Whitton had a remarkable academic career. She was active in sports, debate, and student government (she was the first woman to participate in the school's elected office); she also won university medals in English and history and was the first female editor of the university newspaper. Graduating with honors in 1917, she remained active in alumnae affairs and was a member of the university's board of trustees until 1940.

Whitton began her career in public service as assistant secretary of Canada's Social Service Council in Toronto, where one of her tasks was editorship of the organizational periodical *Social Welfare*. She rose to the position of private secretary to Canada's minister in Trade and Commerce from 1922 to 1925, leaving at the age of 29 for a position as executive director of the Canadian Welfare Council, which she held until 1941. This position allowed her to pursue her interest in social welfare, particularly that of children, and she represented Canada in numerous international conferences, including as a delegate to the interwar League of Nations Social Questions section.

Resigning her government posts in 1941, Whitton turned to the private sector, working as a consultant, lecturer, publicist, and author. During the 1940s, she authored several studies of Canadian social conditions, among them the extensive survey *The Dawn of Ampler Life* (1943), as well as more than 50 pamphlets, among them *Canadian Women in the War Effort* (1942), *Security for Canadians* (1942), and *Welfare Must Be Planned and Paid For* (1945). A prolific writer, she also contributed articles on welfare-related topics to national periodicals, including *Maclean's* and *Saturday Night*, and wrote a syndicated column. Among her consultancy posts was a stint with the Province of Alberta, for which she undertook a study of the provincial welfare system. Whitton was also requested by Conservative Parliamentary leader John Bracken to develop a proposal for social insurance and health insurance that would serve as the basis for that country's socialized medicine system. Whitton herself felt such social welfare too costly and inflexible.

With her decidedly feminist beliefs, Whitton was not dissuaded from her political ambitions by the fact that no woman had yet served as mayor of the city of Ottawa, Canada's capital. When she was elected to the Board of Control in 1950 with backing from Ottawa's two main newspapers and the Ottawa Council of Women, her high percentage of votes qualified her as deputy mayor of the city. As such, Whitton was appointed to the mayoral seat by the Ottawa city council after the untimely death of Mayor Grenville Goodwin in October 1951. She ran another vigorous campaign the following year and won, becoming the first woman elected to that position. She served as mayor until 1956, when she left city politics to consider a federal

Charlotte
Whitton

position. In 1959, she ran for re-election as mayor of Ottawa, and after winning held that post until 1964.

The recipient of numerous tributes in appreciation for her lifelong career of public service, Whitton was honored as a Commander of the Order of the British Empire in 1934, and received the Jubilee Medal in 1935 and the Coronation Medal two years later. She collected honorary degrees from numerous Canadian colleges, and a poll of women's page editors at newspapers throughout the country voted her "Woman of the Year" twice during the early 1950s. Whitton lived with **Margaret Grier**, whom she had met in college, until Grier's death in 1947. She remained active in political and community affairs in Ottawa up until her own death in 1975. While public pursuits occupied much of her time, Whitton enjoyed swimming and spent summers renovating a cottage at Perkins Mills, Quebec. A keen student of history, particularly of the reign of England's Queen *Elizabeth I, she also inherited her father's interest in forestry. Her book *A Hundred Years A-Fellin'* (1943) is a history on lumbering in Ontario's Ottawa Valley.

SOURCES:

Current Biography 1953. NY: H.W. Wilson, 1953.

Locher, Frances C., ed. *Contemporary Authors.* Vols. 89–92. Detroit, MI: Gale Research, 1980.

Pamela Shelton,
freelance writer,
Avon, Connecticut

Whitty, Ellen (1819–1892).

See Vincent, Mother.

Whitty, May (1865–1948)

English actress who was celebrated for her skill both on stage and, later, on screen during a career that spanned over half a century. Name variations: Dame May Whitty. Born Mary Louise Whitty in Liverpool, England, on June 19, 1865; died in Hollywood, California, on May 29, 1948; youngest of three children (a boy and two girls) of Alfred Whitty (a newspaper editor) and Mary (Ashton) Whitty; privately educated; married Benjamin Webster (a lawyer turned actor), in August 1892; children: son (b. 1903 and died soon after); Margaret Webster (1905–1972, an actress and noted Shakespearean director).

Selected theater: made stage debut in the chorus of The Mountain Sylph *(Liverpool, 1881), and London debut as Fillippa in* Boccaccio *(Comedy Theater, 1882); appeared as Graham in* A Scrap of Paper *(St. James's, 1883), Suzanne in* The Ironmaster *(St. James's, 1884); toured as Lady Teazle, Kate Hardcastle, Lydia Languish, and Lady Gay Spanker (1885); toured as Dora Vane in* The Harbour Lights *and Ruth Herrick in* In the Ranks *(c. 1886 or 1887); appeared in* The Monk's Room, Prince Karl, She Stoops to Conquer, *and* The School for Scandal *(Globe Theater, 1888); appeared as Mary Melrose in* Our Boys *(Vaudeville, 1892), Mrs. Amhearst in* Flight *(Terry's, 1893); toured with Forbes-Robertson as the Comtesse Zicka in* Diplomacy *and Irene in* The Profligate *(1894); ap-*

peared as Kitty in A Loving Legacy *and Grace Dormer in* Fanny *(Strand, 1895); joined the Lyceum Company (June 1895) and played Marie in* Louis XI, *Julie in* The Lyons Mail, *Emilie in* The Corsican Brothers, *and the Gentlewoman in* Macbeth; *toured in America with Lyceum Company (1895–96); appeared as Edith Varney in* Secret Service *(Court, London, 1898), Mrs. Grace Tyrrell in* The Heather Field *(Terry's, 1899), Katherine Blake in* The Last Chapter *(Strand, 1899), Susan Throssell in* Quality Street *(Vaudeville, 1903), Carrie Hardinge in* Irene Wycherley *(in New York, 1907), Dame Dresden in* The Sentimentalists *and Mrs. Trafalgar Gower in* Trelawny of the Wells *(Duke of York's, London, 1910), Mrs. Daly in* The Home Coming *(Aldwych, 1910); *Peg Woffington in* The First Actress *(Kingsway, 1911), Mrs. John Tyler in* Ready Money *(New, 1912), Mrs. Channing in* A Matter of Money *(Little, 1913), Lay Cluffe in* Open Windows *(St. James's, 1913), Comtesse Malise in* The Grand Seigneur *(Savoy, 1913), Mrs. Talcot in* The Impossible Woman *(Haymarket, 1914), Mrs. Kesteven and Mrs. Luckman in* Forked Lightning *(Lyceum, Edinburgh, 1915), Mary Cumbers in* Iris Intervenes *(Kingsway, 1915), Madame Vagret in* The Arm of the Law *(His Majesty's, 1916), Mrs. Sharp in* The Passing of the Third Floor Back *(Playhouse, 1917); toured as Lady Marden in* Mr. Pim Passes By *(1920); appeared as Mrs. Corsellis in* The Enchanted Cottage *(Duke of York's, 1922), Lady Raunds in* Life's a Game *(Kingsway, 1922), Mrs. Henry Gilliam in* The Fool *(Apollo, 1924), Mrs. Janet Rodney in* March Hares *(Little, 1925), Mrs. Ebley in* The Last of Mrs. Cheyney *(St. James's, 1925), Mrs. Considine in* Sylvia *(Vaudeville, 1927), Lady Alethea Zaidner in* Come With Me *(New, 1928); toured in South Africa with *Zena Dare (1928–29); appeared as Lady Byfleet in* Sybarites *and Lady Blakeney in* Gentlemen of the Jury *(Arts, 1929), Mrs. Coade in* Dear Brutus *(Playhouse, 1929), Mrs. Mabley Jones in* A Business Marriage *(Court, 1930), Florence in* There's Always Juliet *(Apollo, 1931, and Empire, New York, 1932), Dame Frances Evers in* Behold We Live *(St. James's, London, 1932), Mildred Surrege in* The Lake *(Arts and Westminster, 1933), Mary Railton in* Man Proposes *(Wyndham's, 1933), Mrs. Voysey in* The Voysey Inheritance *(Sadler's Wells and Shaftesbury, 1934), Mrs. Crowborough in* Meeting at Night *(Globe, 1934), Mrs. May Maitland in* The Maitlands *(Wyndham's, 1934), Mrs. Sloane in* It Happened to Adam *(Duke of York's, 1934), Mrs. West in* Ringmaster *(Shaftesbury, 1935), Mrs. Bramson in* Night Must Fall *(Duchess, London, 1935, and Barrymore, New York, 1936), Mrs. Hesketh in* Grand Slam *("Q", London, 1939), the Nurse in* Romeo and Juliet

(51st Street, New York, 1940), Madame Raquin in Thérèse *(Biltmore, New York, 1945).*

Selected filmography: Enoch Arden *(1915);* Night Must Fall *(1937);* The 13th Chair *(1937);* Conquest *(1937);* I Met My Love Again *(1938);* The Lady Vanishes *(UK, 1938);* Raffles *(1940);* A Bill of Divorcement *(1940);* One Night in Lisbon *(1941);* Suspicion *(1941);* Mrs. Miniver *(1942);* Thunder Birds *(1942);* Forever and a Day *(1943);* Slightly Dangerous *(1943);* Crash Dive *(1943);* Stage Door Canteen *(1943);* The Constant Nymph *(1943);* Lassie Come Home *(1943);* Flesh and Fantasy *(1943);* *Madame Curie *(1943);* The White Cliffs of Dover *(1944);* Gaslight *(1944);* My Name is Julia Ross *(1945);* Devotion *(1946);* Green Dolphin Street *(1947);* This Time for Keeps *(1947);* If Winter Comes *(1948);* The Sign of the Ram *(1948);* The Return of October *(1948).*

"The first time [my mother] was ever taken to the theater she was so terrified that she screamed loudly till she was carried out," wrote *Margaret Webster, Dame May Whitty's daughter, in a memoir of her parents, *The Same Only Different*. "The piece was a pantomime called *The Three Bears*," she added. "Further visits to other pantomimes taught her that everything always came right in the end, and terror was replaced by enchantment." In good turn, May Whitty became the purveyor of the magic, delighting audiences in England and America with a wide range of stage and screen characterizations. In 1945, just three years before her death, the actress celebrated the 65th anniversary of her distinguished career on the stage. Whitty also had the distinction of being the first actress ever to be created a dame, receiving her DBE in 1918, both for her work in the theater and for her charity work during World War I.

May Whitty was born in Liverpool, England, on June 19, 1865, the youngest of three children of Alfred Whitty and **Mary Ashton Whitty**. Her paternal grandfather, Michael James Whitty, owned and edited the *Liverpool Journal* and later founded the *Liverpool Daily Post*, Great Britain's first penny daily. Whitty's father Alfred also worked for the *Post* until Michael sold it and brought in a new editor. Mary and her children were then deposited with her father, while Alfred went to seek his fortune in London. When May was ten, Alfred died of pneumonia, leaving Mary to support and educate the three Whitty children. She did so by opening a modest school for girls. It never prospered and eventually closed, but it was the only formal education May ever had.

At age 15, through her mother's friendship with *Madge Kendal, May received a note of introduction to the manager of the Court Theater in Liverpool, where in 1881 she made her first stage appearance, in *The Mountain Sylph*, an adaptation of the ballet *Les Sylphides*. A year later, she debuted in London as Fillippa in the comic opera *Boccaccio*, after which she moved to the St. James's Theater to work under the management of John Hare and William Kendal (husband of Madge). There, she served as understudy to **Annie Webster** ("Booey"), the actress sister of Ben Webster, a young law student who would give up the bar in 1887 and become an actor.

Whitty spent the time between meeting Ben and their marriage in August 1892 honing her craft and gaining experience. After leaving the St. James, she joined a touring stock company. "My mother played fourteen parts in two weeks, with one rehearsal for each—parts such as Lydia Languish and Kate Hardcastle, plus some meaty old melodramas and a farce or two," recalled daughter Margaret. "Between rehearsals and performances she made her own costumes." Whitty also toured briefly with Ben Greet's original Shakespearean company and with the Forbes-Robertson touring company. In addition to touring, she appeared in two or three plays a year, usually melodramas, which she later recalled had some extravagant scenic effects for the time. "In *Harbor Lights* the hero climbed down over the cliff to rescue the heroine. *Hoodman Blind* was about twin sisters, and I played both of them. One was good and the other bad, the bad one throwing herself over the Thames embankment."

During the first few years of their marriage, Whitty and her husband were frequently separated by their work. In June 1895, Whitty joined the Lyceum Company, then under the management of Sir Henry Irving and *Ellen Terry, whom she called "the kindest and grandest woman I have ever known." Her roles with the Lyceum Company included Marie in *Louis XI*, Julie in *The Lyons Mail*, Emilie in *The Corsican Brothers*, the daughter in *The Bells*, and the Gentlewoman in *Macbeth*. Together with her husband, she toured America with the company from 1895 to 1896.

Shortly after returning to England, Whitty left the Lyceum Company, unhappy with the quality of the roles she was assigned. She subsequently won some good notices for her portrayal of Susan Throssell in *Quality Street* (1902), then toured in the role. On Christmas Day, 1903, the couple's first child, a son, was born and died, at which time Whitty was warned that she should not have any more children. However, by the following summer, she was pregnant again, causing Ben great concern. During her confinement, she accompanied her husband to America, where daughter Margaret was born prematurely on March 15, 1905. May remained in New York for several years while Ben toured, and in 1907, she returned to the stage as Carrie Hardinge in *Irene Wycherly*, playing the role in Baltimore and New York.

In 1910, back in London, she played Amelia in *The Madras House*, the first of the character roles that would dominate the second half of her career. It was also her first experience with director H. Granville Barker, who was quite different in approach from the actor-managers with whom she had previously worked. Margaret Webster recalled that Granville-Barker gave her mother "a long dissertation on the history, habits, idiosyncrasies and antecedents of a character in *The Madras House*, all of which she was to convey to the audience by the significance with which she said her first line. The line was 'Good afternoon.'" Whitty also had a harrowing experience with Arthur Wing Pinero, who directed her in

Trelawny of the Wells, also in 1910. Pinero, wrote Webster, was a "martinet who drilled his actors in every detail of movement and inflection. Sometimes . . . imposed mannerisms supposed to indicate character. I remember my mother sedulously practicing a high screech demanded by Pinero, half giggle and half snort, till people on the streets turned round to stare, and the cook gave notice."

During World War I, Whitty juggled her performance schedule with charitable war work. As a member of the Actresses Franchise League, she helped organize the Women's Emergency Corps (WEC), which drafted women to replace men in jobs that had never been open to them before, in hospitals, offices, factories, and farms. In conjunction with the WEC, she also mounted several successful fund-raising campaigns for the Star and Garter Home for Disabled Sailors, Soldiers and Airman. Along with her war work, Whitty was also active in getting the British Actors' Equity Association established as a trade union.

In 1921, Whitty undertook the management of the Florence Etlinger Dramatic School, a post

From My Name is Julia Ross, *starring May Whitty.*

she held until 1926. During this period, she also appeared as Mrs. Corsellis in *The Enchanted Cottage* (1922), as Mrs. Henry Gilliam in *The Fool* (1924), and as Mrs. Ebley in *The Last of Mrs. Cheyney* (1925), among other varied roles. As she grew older, Whitty showed no signed of slowing down, and in fact gave some of her finest performances late in her career.

In 1935, the actress scored a major triumph as Mrs. Bramson in Emyln Williams' thriller *Night Must Fall*, which was brought to New York in 1936, after a year's run in London. "Her performance might give many a younger and more languid actress pause," wrote the critic for the *New York Herald Tribune*. "The scene in the last act where she finally rises from the wheel chair she has occupied all evening, strides vigorously around the stage and then bursts into wild hysterics, amazes those who know she is seventy-two years old." While admitting that the scene left her a bit "gaspy," Whitty said that the play was not otherwise stressful, even on her vocal chords. "I never even had a touch of laryngitis," she said.

A reprise of the role also launched Whitty's film career in 1937, although she had played in the silent film *Enoch Arden* as early as 1915. She was nominated for an Academy Award for her work in *Night Must Fall* and again for her portrayal of Lady Belden in *Mrs. Miniver* (1942). She was also memorable in the title role in Alfred Hitchcock's suspense film *The Lady Vanishes* (1938). "In a sense films are an unnatural medium, from the stage's point of view of logical development," Whitty said about acting in the new medium. "It surprised me that I could step in after a lifetime of stage training, and have so little difficulty in portraying a character."

In 1940, Whitty appeared with her husband in a New York production of *Romeo and Juliet*, and in 1945 she appeared with *Eva Le Gallienne and Victor Jory in *Thérèse*, an adaptation of Emile Zola's *Thérèse Raquin*, directed by her daughter. The critics, while not enthusiastic about the play, had nothing but praise for Whitty. "Her performance makes this contemporary version of a theatrical antique something more than a clever and entertaining stunt," wrote Howard Barnes in the *New York Herald Tribune*. "No matter what convolutions the plot takes in relating dark deeds, remorse and confession, she towers through the production with all the serenity she might have had in playing a great classic or modern tragedy. She quickens every scene of *Thérèse* with dramatic overtones which are not always discernible in the script."

"She is so wonderful," gushed critic Burton Roscoe, "that tears of gratitude came into my eyes that I was privileged to see such art."

For many years Whitty and her husband resided in a flat in Covent Garden which also served as a meeting place and refuge for both English and American actors. No one in need was ever turned away from the couple's doorstep. From 1939 on, they lived in Hollywood, where Whitty served as chair of the British Actors' Orphanage and as vice-president of the Los Angeles Branch of British War Relief. The couple's 55-year marriage ended with Ben's death in 1947, at age 82. Lewis Casson recalled that almost to the time of his death, Ben continued the nightly ritual of brushing his wife's hair. Dame May Whitty died a year later, on May 29, 1948, in Hollywood. A memorial plaque in St. Paul's Church, Covent Garden (the Actors' Church), pays homage to the couple. "They were lovely and pleasant in their lives," it reads, "and in their death they were not divided."

SOURCES:

Current Biography 1945. NY: H.W. Wilson, 1945.

Johns, Eric. *Dames of the Theatre*. New Rochelle, NY: Arlington House, 1974.

Katz, Ephraim. *The Film Encyclopedia*. NY: Harper-Collins, 1994.

Webster, Margaret. *The Same Only Different*. NY: Alfred A. Knopf, 1969.

Barbara Morgan,
Melrose, Massachusetts

Whitworth, Kathy (1939—)

American champion golfer. Name variations: Kathryne Whitworth. Born Kathryne Whitworth in Monahans, Texas, on September 27, 1939; youngest of three daughters of Dama Whitworth and Morris Whitworth (a hardware-store owner); grew up in Jal, New Mexico, just across the state line from El Paso, Texas.

Dominated the pro circuit (1960s); was the first recipient of the LPGA's Player of the Year Award (1966) which she would receive six more times; inducted into the LPGA Hall of Fame, the World Golf Hall of Fame, the Texas Sports Hall of Fame, and the International Women's Sports Hall of Fame; was the first female professional golfer to win over $1 million in purse money.

Kathy Whitworth entered her first professional golf tour at age 19, traveling for two days from Jal, New Mexico, to Augusta, Georgia, to participate in the LPGA Titleholders tournament. "I had a little Sunday bag," noted Whitworth, "and I didn't even have a full set of clubs." Her caddie was "almost too embarrassed" to carry them. For the next three years, Whitworth earned little money on the circuit, but she gained in skill and confidence. Finally her hard work paid off when she won the Baltimore Kelly Girl Open in 1962. For the rest of the 1960s, she dominated women's golf.

Sexism was responsible for Whitworth's choice of golf as a sport. She was born in Monahans, Texas, in 1939, the youngest of three daughters of Dama Whitworth and Morris Whitworth, a hardware-store owner. Her family moved from Texas to Jal when she was a small child. It was a happy time. Though an indifferent student, Whitworth was good at football, softball, and basketball. On reaching adolescence, however, she learned that these same sports were taboo for girls. The once active child became a withdrawn teenager. "I couldn't stay out of the refrigerator," she recalled. "My only sport was eating." Taller than most girls, she went from plump to plumper, then, feeling immense and ugly, she would comfort herself with more food. By the time she was 13, she weighed 200 pounds. "I didn't weigh myself after that, but they say I ballooned up to 250."

Exercise seemed to be the answer. Whitworth tried tennis, but had too much weight and too much self-hate to carry across the court. At 15, she decided to find a sport that was acceptable for women. She chose golf and took daily lessons from Hardy Loudermilk, the golf pro at the Jal Country Club; within a year, she lost 50 pounds. Loudermilk then suggested she travel to Austin for further lessons. For the next two years, Whitworth rode the bus every summer to take lessons from Harvey Penick, a well-known golf pro; she lost another 25 pounds. After she won the New Mexico State Amateur championship in 1957 and 1958, Whitworth decided to go to Augusta. Her weight was now down to 160 pounds.

Whitworth won eight tournaments in 1963, 1965, and 1967, nine in 1966, and ten in 1968. From 1965 to 1968 and 1970 to 1973, she was the leading money winner. She won the Vare Trophy seven times, from 1965 to 1967 and from 1969 to 1972. In 1984, at the Rochester International golf tournament, Whitworth claimed her 85th career title, surpassing Sam Snead's record for most professional golf tournament victories. She was the first golfer to be awarded the LPGA Player of the Year Award in 1966, receiving it a total of seven times. In 1965 and 1966, the Associated Press named her the Female Athlete of the Year. She now weighed 140 pounds.

Whitworth always championed women's golf. Serving as president of the LPGA, she worked tirelessly to raise the amount of the purses at women's professional events. By the 1970s, women's golf finally arrived as a major sport, due in part to Whitworth's efforts. At this point, she had earned over $1 million on the pro circuit, the first woman to do so. One of the 20th century's great golfers, Kathy Whitworth paved the way for younger golfers like *Nancy Lopez. "If it wasn't for golf," said Whitworth, "I'd probably be the fat lady in the circus now."

SOURCES:

Condon, Robert J. *Great Women Athletes of the 20th Century.* Jefferson, NC: McFarland, 1991.

Eldred, Patricia Mulrooney. *Kathy Whitworth.* Mankato, MN: Creative Education Society, 1975.

Sabin, Francene. *Women Who Win.* Random House, 1975.

Woolum, Janet. *Outstanding Women Athletes: Who They Are and How They Influenced Sports in America.* Phoenix, AZ: Oryx Press, 1992.

Karin L. Haag,
freelance writer,
Athens, Georgia

Whyte, Edna Gardner (1902–1992)

American pioneer aviator, flight instructor, and nurse who won over 120 racing trophies in the course of a nearly 60-year flying career. Name variations: Edna Marvel Gardner. Born Edna Marvel Gardner on November 3, 1902, in Garden City, Minnesota; died in Grapevine, Texas, on February 15, 1992; daughter of Walter Carl Gardner (a farmer and railroad laborer) and Myrtle (Marvel) Gardner (a schoolteacher); graduated from West Salem, Wisconsin, public school; married Ray L. Kidd, in 1935 (divorced 1940); married George Murphy Whyte, in 1946 (divorced 1967); children: one adopted daughter, Georgeann.

Awards: Woman of the Year, Women's National Aeronautical Association (1966); OX-5 Pioneer Pilots Association's Tiny Broadwick Award for promotion of women's aviation (1967); inducted in Curtiss-Wright Hall of Fame for Pioneer Pilots (1975); Jimmy Kolp Award Trophy for outstanding devotion to women pilots and 99ers (1977); inducted in Memory Lane Memorial Park, Amelia Earhart home, Atchison, Kansas; inducted into Texas Women's Hall of Fame (1984); inducted into Oklahoma Aviation and Space Hall of Fame (1985); inducted into Texas State Hall of Fame (1985); Charles Lindbergh Foundation, Life Time Achievement in Aviation Award (1986).

Father killed (1910); mother's illness led to family's dissolution (1912); began nurses' training, La

Crosse (Wisconsin) Hospital (1921); was certified as a registered nurse (1924); was a staff nurse, University of Wisconsin (1924), Parkland Hospital, Dallas (1925), and Virginia Mason Hospital, Seattle (1925); took first flying lesson (1927); was a staff nurse, University of Wisconsin (1927); received student pilot license (1929); joined U.S. Navy's Nursing Corps (1929); soloed and received pilot's license (1931); assigned to Newport Naval Hospital (1931); assigned to Naval Hospital Washington, D.C. (1934); resigned commission (1935); opened Southern Aviation School with husband at Shushan Airport, New Orleans; opened New Orleans Air College, Wedell-Williams Airport (1937); sold business, moved to Meacham Field, Fort Worth, as instrument instructor for U.S. Army (1941); joined Army Nursing Corps (1944); became instructor, Roy Taylor Flying School, Meacham Field (1946); was a saleswoman for Harry Pennington Channelcrome Co. (1955); built Aero Valley Airport, Roanoke, Texas, and created last flying school (1969); sold airport and retired (1988).

An aviator at a time when most women were excluded from the everyday life of airports and flying, Edna Gardner Whyte helped break down those barriers with her ambition, determination, skill, and intelligence. Her contribution was not as publicized as that of her friend *Amelia Earhart, but it was substantial enough that she was well known in aviation circles by the 1930s and remained prominent in them until her death in 1992. Said her friend, actor Cliff Robertson, "She flew with the heart of an eagle."

Whyte was born Edna Gardner in 1902 in Garden City, Minnesota, but moved frequently during the first half of her life. When she was ten, her father Walter Gardner was killed in a train wreck in Oregon; soon after, her mother Myrtle Gardner was stricken with tuberculosis. Placed in a sanitarium and unable to tend her children, Myrtle was forced to shift them from relative to relative. Whyte was reared by an aunt and uncle. Lacking money for college after her high school graduation, she did the practical thing, learning nursing on the job at the local hospital in La Crosse, Wisconsin.

Uncomfortable in the cold north, Whyte moved to Dallas, Texas, soon after completing her training in 1924, and then to Seattle, Washington, to practice nursing. While in Seattle, she met Bob Martin, an amateur pilot and Canadian bon vivant, and took her first flight with him in 1927, at age 25. Edna had been fascinated as a child with newspaper accounts of *Katherine

Stinson and her sister Marjorie, who trained military pilots at Dayton, Ohio, during World War I, and even though Martin was not an accomplished flier and announced after a rough ride that Edna owed him $7.50 for the 15 minutes aloft, she was hooked.

But wanting to fly and learning to fly were difficult matters for women in the 1920s. *Matilde Moisant, having been given the opportunity to learn, was told by her teacher to arrive at the airfield "at the crack of dawn dressed in men's clothing and have a hood over your hair so nobody can know you are a woman." Whyte was not subject to that demand, although her first instructors only reluctantly provided basic lessons in how to fly. They gladly tried to discourage her, convinced that aviation was for men only. (One of these teachers, Jim Peterson, flew in the movies *Wings* and *Hell's Angels*.) Edna started training in Seattle and then later in Madison, Wisconsin, but failed to progress as rapidly as she wished until she met Guerdon ("Guerd") Brockson at the Waukegan (Wisconsin) Flying Club. Having enlisted in the U.S. Navy Nursing Corps in 1929, she was stationed at the time at the Naval Hospital, Great Lakes Naval Training Station, near Chicago. Whyte had joined the flying club to practice at convenient times and to lower the price of instruction: flying time cost between $30 and $35 an hour, and her salary as a nurse was about $75 a month.

Guerd became both teacher and lover. In early 1931, Whyte flew solo; that May, she received her pilot's license. Though the government had begun certifying pilots in 1926, the official who tested Edna had never confirmed a female aviator. He showed his bias by sending two men up for tests before her, even though she had arrived first and had finished the written portions of the exams ahead of them. Fixing her with a stern gaze, the examiner asked, "Why do you want to fly? I've never given any woman a license and I'm not at all sure that I want to now." With tears and voice breaking, she begged for a chance. The examiner relented and found her skills such that he could not withhold license no. 20000 from her. Ultimately, this license would include the right to operate single and multi-engine land aircraft, seaplanes, rotor-crafts, and gliders. She would also hold certification as a flight instructor, instrument instructor, and ground instructor (Link Trainer).

Exuberant after receiving her pilot's license, Whyte entered a challenge race at Waukegan, piloting an OX-5 Robin monoplane 30 miles to victory. It was the first of many winning races.

Edna
Gardner
Whyte

Before her career ended, Edna Gardner Whyte would hold more than 100 trophies for closed course and cross-country racing, aerobatics, bomb dropping, spot landing, and the like. She entered the Powder Puff Derby, Angel Derby, Fair Lady Derby, the Sky Lady, Dallas Doll Derby, and a few that featured both men and women in head-to-head competition. Her most prestigious wins were The Men and Women Race (Curtiss-Wright Field, Baltimore, 1934); two Alcazar Trophy Races (1937 and 1941); two U.S.A. Rally, Men and Women Races (1964 and 1965); and four Women's International Air Races (1953, 1958, 1960, 1961). The latter were also among the most dangerous, in part because of the greater distances between countries and in part because of climatic variations.

Because it came early in her career and was followed by near tragedy, her most memorable victory was the *Kate Smith trophy race, National Charity Air Pageant, at New York's Roosevelt Field in 1933. She flew a borrowed Waco 10 and won $500. On her way home to Newport, Rhode Island, a heavy fog bank over Long Island convinced her to turn back to Roosevelt Field, but still she could not land. She had to circle the area until her fuel tanks were empty and then crashed on the lawn of the Woolworth estate on Oyster Bay. The Woolworths welcomed her, but the damage done to the aircraft cost her the $500 she had won in repairs.

At the time of the Kate Smith race, Whyte was working at the Naval Hospital in Newport, having transferred there from Great Lakes in 1931. The move had temporarily interrupted her love affair with Guerd, but he joined her in 1932, opening an airfield on land owned by the Vanderbilts at Coddington Cove. Before this, Edna had purchased her first airplane, a Travel Air that was powered by an OXX-6 engine, and kept it at an airport owned by Colonel Ned Green, the disabled playboy son of *Hettie Green. Green's Round Hill Airport was north of Newport, near New Bedford, Massachusetts, and although he did not fly, he knew a great deal about flying and shared his experience with Edna. She unwittingly became involved with bootleggers who paid $20 per trip to fly off Martha's Vineyard and report the color of flags flying from a designated ship there. The flags told when and where shipments of booze were to be landed. When Edna realized her complicity, she quit.

The publicity that she received as a racer, coupled with her profession, caused writers to begin calling her the "Flying Nurse." When in 1933 she heard that Dr. Leon M. Pisculli was organizing a "medical flight" across the Atlantic to Italy and that he intended to take a nurse as co-pilot, Whyte contacted Pisculli and arranged an interview. At journey's end, the nurse was to parachute into Italy to commemorate *Florence Nightingale's birth in Florence. A year earlier, Earhart had soloed across the Atlantic. Whyte was sure this trip could make her "as famous as Amelia." During the interview, Guerd, who accompanied her, repeatedly pointed out problems evident in the plan. Fearing that her companion's objections would hurt her chances, she became

angry and cut the meeting short. Later, when she was not chosen, blaming Guerd seemed natural, although she knew the Navy was the true reason; it had given her the option of resigning her commission or not taking part in the publicity stunt. Before she could decide, Pisculli chose another pilot-nurse, **Edna Newcomer**. Whyte was bitterly disappointed, but her attitude changed when the Bellanca carrying Pisculli, Newcomer, and others was lost at sea near the Azores. Nonetheless, ever confident, Whyte told Guerd, "I'll bet you anything, if I'd have been flying on that airplane it never would have crashed."

In March 1934, Whyte transferred to the naval hospital in Washington, D.C. By then, in addition to racing, she had begun to teach, scheduling students to fly at Congressional, Beacon, and Capital airports, and at College Park in Maryland. The move also required another separation from Guerd, which this time became permanent. In 1935, she met Ray Kidd, a writer for the U.S. Information Service, who promised to provide her the publicity she lacked in her quest for fame and recognition. They became close friends and eventually married. "Kidd held promise of being my G.P. Putnam," said Whyte. George Putnam, the head of a major publishing house and a first-rate publicist, had helped boost the careers of Charles Lindbergh, Admiral Richard Byrd, and Amelia Earhart, whom he married.

Whyte recognized Earhart as an aviation pioneer, "kind of a leader, helping to prove that women could do it," but she resented what she considered Earhart's lack of flying experience. In 1938, when *Look* magazine did a survey of the flying hours of female pilots, Whyte topped the list of Americans; Earhart would have been fourth had she not disappeared the previous July during her attempt to circle the globe. Earhart, who had been the first woman to cross the Atlantic in an aircraft as a passenger in 1928, had set a record in 1932 when she made the trip alone in 14 hours and 56 minutes. She also had broken several North American transcontinental crossing records in the 1930s. All her feats were promoted by Putnam. Whyte despised Putnam, "the heel," because of his alleged mistreatment of Earhart. Just before leaving on her ill-fated journey, Amelia and George had dined with Edna and Ray Kidd in New Orleans.

In 1935, Whyte resigned her commission in the Navy and took a job as an instructor at the Maynard Air Service in New Orleans. She soon quit and opened the Southern Aviation School at Shushan Airport with Ray. A mishap and trouble with governmental authorities caused them to move operations to an older facility, the Wedell-Williams Airport, where they renamed their flying school the New Orleans Air College. Whyte continued teaching and racing until 1941 when, following her divorce from Ray, she had the opportunity to sell most of her air service investment to the Army, which was acquiring such facilities to train military pilots.

With her newfound wealth and a friend, **Mary Dickey**, Whyte moved to Fort Worth, passed her certification for instrument flying, and served as an instruments instructor and examiner for the War Training Service until 1944 when the program at Meacham Field was terminated. Before this, she had trained men and women who flew for various branches of the military, including WASPs (Women's Airforce Service Pilots). In 1944, she joined the Army Nursing Corps and was posted to the Philippines where she served for two years. She then returned to Fort Worth to teach flying at a Veterans Administration-approved school owned by Roy Taylor.

In 1946, Edna met and married George Murphy Whyte, a former Army pilot and a fellow instructor. During the early 1950s, she and George were something of itinerant teachers, working in flight programs in Aberdeen, Mississippi, and Flint, Michigan, but always returning to Fort Worth. Whyte intensified her racing and won the bulk of her trophies in the next 20 years. In 1955, she became a sales representative for the Harry Pennington Channelcrome Company, the only such saleswoman in the United States. Assigned a territory extending from Central America into Canada, she sold various aircraft parts, especially chrome plated cylinders, logging thousands of flying hours and also representing Channelcrome in many air races.

While Edna flew for Channelcrome, George started his own Flying Base Operation, a school at Meacham Field called Aero Enterprises, in 1953. At times she worked with him, saying that he was a "terrific instructor and manager." But as had happened in her first marriage, her ambitions interfered with family life, and in the late 1960s she and George divorced. At the time he was suffering from cancer, having lost a leg to the disease. Earlier, she had helped rear George's daughter from his first marriage, and when **Georgeann Whyte** married and began having children, Edna, in addition to being known as the "Flying Nurse," and the "Flying Flapper," became the "Flying Grandmother." She and Georgeann piloted aircraft in races until the younger woman became more interested in a family than a career.

Edna left Channelcrome in 1969 and, at age 67, when most people would be planning retirement, founded an airport. Using her life savings and money borrowed from a local bank, she opened Aero Valley Airport on 85 acres of land near Roanoke, Texas, 20 miles northeast of Fort Worth. She started with 3 planes and a hangar but within 15 years had a facility that included 14 hangars and 126 aircraft. She owned six of the planes and leased two more for her flying school, which included several part-time instructors. In 1985, Whyte boasted of 240 pupils in various stages of training. Of her many achievements, the airport may have been the most unique. She began it without government aid and continued that way until she was forced to sell in 1989, following heart by-pass surgery.

Whyte knew she suffered from heart problems; she had tried to secure permission to fly in an Air Force jet but failed to pass the required physical. She regretted missing this chance almost as much as she rued never having been an airline pilot. In the late 1930s, she had tried to fly for Braniff Airlines, but the company president was incredulous. "Miss Gardner," he asked, "do you really think that passengers will get on the airplane if they saw a woman pilot up front there?" She did; he didn't.

Edna Gardner Whyte trained over 4,000 aviators to fly a variety of aircraft and logged more than 25,000 hours in the air over her lifetime. She had won many honors. In 1931, she joined the earliest women's flying sorority, the Ninety-Nines, an international organization of women pilots, serving as its president from 1956 to 1957. She was one of the original ten members of the Whirlygirls, an international organization of women helicopter pilots, and held additional memberships in Silver Wings, OX-5 Club of American, Women's National Aeronautical Association, Pioneer Pilots, and a variety of racing associations.

Whyte spent the last five years of her life lecturing in the Dallas-Fort Worth metroplex area. Her message was simple. Give women a chance, she said. A wall-hanging in her office at Aero Valley read: "A woman has to do twice as much as a man to be considered half as good. Fortunately, that's not too difficult."

SOURCES:

Baxter, Gordon. "Iron Edna," in *Flying*. Vol. III. May 1984, p. 108.
Dallas Morning News. April 29, 1970, sec. F, p. 1.
Dallas Times-Herald. October 31, 1974, sec. C, p. 4.
Fort Worth News-Tribune. December 6, 1985, sec. A, p. 12.
Fort Worth Star-Telegram. October 20, 1974, sec. I, p. 12.
Grit. December 15, 1974, p. 15.

"Interview with Edna Gardner Whyte by Floyd Jenkins, February 8, 1979," North Texas State University Oral History Collection (Business Archives Project) No. 28, Denton.

Obituary, in *Dallas Morning News.* February 18, 1992, sec. A, p. 13.

Obituary, in *Fort Worth Star-Telegram.* February 17, 1992, sec. A, p. 19.

O'Connor, D.C. "Flying High," in *Good Housekeeping.* Vol. CCI. September 1985, pp. 94, 96, 100.

The Washington Times. April 29, 1985, sec. B, p. 3.

Who's Who of American Women. 12th ed., 1981–1982.

Whyte, Edna Gardner with Ann L. Cooper. *Rising Above It: An Autobiography.* NY: Orion, 1991.

"Woman on Wings," in *Scene: The Dallas Morning News Sunday Magazine.* Vol. VIII. April 10, 1977, p. 17.

COLLECTIONS:

Edna Gardner Whyte Collection, Archives, Willis Library, University of North Texas, Denton.

SUGGESTED READING:

Ackermann-Blount, J. "She Flies Through the Air with the Greatest of Ease," in *Sports Illustrated.* Vol. LX. January 16, 1984, p. 94.

Lasher, Patricia. *Texas Women: Interviews and Images.* Austin, TX: Skoal Creek, 1980.

May, Charles Paul. *Women in Aeronautics.* NY: Thomas Nelson, 1962.

Robert LaForte,
Professor of History,
University of North Texas, Denton, Texas

Whyte, Kathleen (1909–1996)

Scottish embroiderer and teacher. Name variations: Helen Kathleen Ramsay Whyte. Born in August 1909 in Arbroath, Scotland; died in 1996; educated at Loreto Convent School in Darjeeling, India, and Arbroath High School in Scotland; studied at Gray's School of Art in Aberdeen, 1927–32; studied embroidery with Dorothy Angus, from 1920, and design with James Hamilton; graduated with Diploma of Design and Decorative Arts, 1932; attended Aberdeen Teacher Training College, 1932–33; studied weaving with Ethel Mairet at her Gospels studio in Ditchling, 1942–43.

Taught art at Frederick Street School, Central Secondary School, and Aberdeen High School for Girls; was a lecturer in embroidery and weaving in the Design and Craft section of Glasgow School of Art (1948–74); formed the Glasgow School of Art Embroidery Group (1957); awarded MBE for services to Scottish art education (1969).

Kathleen Whyte's early childhood was spent in Arbroath on the east coast of Scotland, where she was born in 1909. Her father was an engineer, the youngest of nine children of a master joiner. Her mother, an accomplished needlewoman, had been a lady's maid, employed by county families whom she accompanied on their fashionable seasonal visits to Italy. Both parents conveyed a sense of aesthetic appreciation to the young Kathleen, whose first efforts at embroidery began at age four.

From 1911 to 1913 and again from 1920 to 1923, Kathleen and her family joined her father in Jamshedpur, India, where he had been working. These years in India had a huge impact on her visual sense and appreciation of the variety of colors and textiles. Living in an isolated community, the family relied on visits by traveling "Box Wallahs" with their dazzling arrays of silks and white cottons. During her second visit to India, Whyte attended the Loreto Convent School in Darjeeling, in the foothills of the Himalayas, as a boarder. She enjoyed her time at Loreto, including the picnics in view of Mount Everest, and was encouraged by the nuns in drawing, crafts, and sewing.

On her family's return from India, Whyte attended Arbroath High School from 1923 to 1927, and then Gray's School of Art in Aberdeen, where she took the Diploma Course in General Design, an innovative four-year course introduced into the four Scottish art schools in 1920. Along with all art school subjects, embroidery enjoyed a revival in the late 1920s. **Dorothy Angus**, appointed teacher of embroidery in Aberdeen in 1920, was an important figure in the transformation of British embroidery into a dynamic modern art form and away from its nostalgic referencing of the arts and craft tradition established by William Morris. Angus introduced Whyte to "the vast potential of stitchery . . . an entirely new alphabet, the key to what I had been groping after all my life." Kathleen studied design with the eccentric James Hamilton, who stressed individuality and encouraged his students to produce large, decorative but highly disciplined charcoal drawings which were translated under Dorothy Angus' supervision into rich textile surfaces. This distinctive, expressive work done in Aberdeen in the early 1930s was to prove an influential force in the development of embroidery throughout Britain.

Whyte achieved much success at art school, winning prizes every year of her course, before her 1932 graduation with a Diploma of Design and Decorative Arts. After a year at Aberdeen Teacher Training College, Kathleen taught art at Frederick Street School in the East End of Aberdeen and at the Central Secondary School. She then moved to the Aberdeen High School for Girls, simultaneously teaching art school evening classes (instructing military personnel in

Kathleen
Whyte

leather work during the war) and occupational therapy. In the early 1940s, Whyte made several visits to the respected weaver **Ethel Mairet** at her Spartan workshop (known as "Gospels") in Ditchling, perfecting her weaving skills under Mairet's exacting tuition.

In 1948, supported by Angus, Whyte successfully applied for the post of embroidery and weaving lecturer in the Design and Craft section of Glasgow School of Art. She remained in this post until her retirement in 1974. Although the immediate postwar period was a boom time for art schools, Whyte faced numerous obstacles in Glasgow. Embroidery teaching had declined at the school since the early 1930s, and standards were low. She was helped by the re-emergence of the Needlework Development Scheme (NDS), which had been founded in 1934 to raise the standard of embroidery design and to encourage greater public interest. Responsible for numerous exhibitions and lectures, the NDS received new impetus after the war, in 1948 appointing as embroidery expert the Swedish **Ulla Kockum**, whom Kathleen befriended. Whyte was very impressed with Scandinavian design, having visited Stockholm, Gothenburg, and Boros, great centers of weaving and embroidery, after the war.

Kathleen Whyte revitalized embroidery teaching in Glasgow, with gradual introductions of new techniques, an emphasis on draftsmanship and experimentation, and a stimulating, demanding teaching style. To encourage students to develop their own ideas, she allowed no embroidery books in the department, apart from technical or history books. In 1951, the year of the Festival of Britain, the Design and Crafts Department was invited to exhibit at the Rayon Centre in Grosvenor Square, London, the first time representatives from any Scottish art school had exhibited in London. By the mid-1950s, the Design and Crafts Department was the largest in the school, although the status of weaving and embroidery there remained low, relegated to a separate building for much of the 1960s.

Whyte's teaching style was dynamic, incorporating exercises inspired by other art forms and trends, from ballet to pop art. Concerned that students needed a public outlet for their work and an incentive to continue producing work after graduating, she formed the Glasgow School of Art Embroidery Group, which held its first show in 1957. Without setting a rigid syllabus, she maintained exacting standards; three of her former students were to become heads of the Embroidery Departments at Dundee, Aberdeen, and Glasgow Schools of Art.

Kathleen Whyte's own work reflected her exceptional sense of color, wealth of inspirations and constant experimentation with the boundaries of the art form. She received a number of commissions from the Church of Scotland and worked on the Tay Road Bridge stole, commissioned on behalf of Queen *Elizabeth II in 1966. In 1969, Whyte was awarded the MBE for services to Scottish art education for her work on numerous boards and panels. After her retirement, she continued teaching small groups privately and pursuing her own work. She died in 1996.

SOURCES:
Arthur, Liz. *Kathleen Whyte, Embroiderer.* Batsford.

Paula Morris, D.Phil.,
Brooklyn, New York

Whyte, Sandra (b. 1970).

See Team USA: Women's Ice Hockey at Nagano.

Whyte, Violet (1856–1911).

See Winter, John Strange.

Whytock, Janet (1842–1894).

See Patey, Janet Monach.

Wiberg, Pernilla (1970—)

Swedish Alpine skier. Pronunciation: per-NEEL-ah VEE-berg. *Born in Norkoping, Sweden, on October 15, 1970.*

Won a gold medal in the giant slalom at the World championships in Saalbach, Austria (1991); won an Olympic gold medal in the giant slalom at Albertville (1992); finished 2nd overall in the World Cup standings and 2nd in the slalom (1993–94); won an Olympic gold medal in the combined at Lillehammer (1994); finished 10th in World Cup downhill standings (1995–96); won the gold in the slalom and combined in the World championships in Sierra Nevada, Spain (1996); registered eight World Cup victories (five in the slalom, two in the super G, and one in the downhill, 1996–97); won her first overall crown and set a single-season record for most World Cup points in the final World Cup standings—1,960 (1997–98).

Swedish Alpine skier Pernilla Wiberg won a gold medal in the giant slalom at Albertville in 1992 with a time of 2:12.74. **Diann Roffe** of the U.S.A. came in second; **Anita Wachter** of Austria came in third. Two years later, Wiberg won her second Olympic medal with a gold in the combined at Lillehammer, despite a great final run by second-place winner *Vreni Schneider. Third place **Alenka Dovzan**, who won the first medal for newly independent Slovenia, caused jubilation back home. Wiberg, who has won a World Cup victory in every discipline—downhill, super G, giant slalom, slalom, and combined—had a rough Olympics at Nagano in 1998. Coming in as the defending world cup overall and slalom champion, she fell in the slalom and the combined. She regrouped and took the silver in the downhill, finishing behind *Katja Seizinger.

Wickham, Anna (1883–1947)

English poet. Name variations: Edith Hepburn. *Born Edith Alice Mary Harper in Wimbledon, Surrey, Eng-*

land, in 1883 (some sources cite 1884); committed suicide in London in 1947; daughter of Geoffrey Harper and Alice (Whelan) Harper (both Australians); married Patrick Hepburn (a lawyer), in 1905 (died 1929); children: four, including sons James, John, and George.

Anna Wickham was the pseudonym of the prolific English poet Edith Harper Hepburn. Born in 1883 in Wimbledon, she grew up in Australia and then returned to England as a young adult. She was encouraged in the arts by her parents, a musician and a teacher, and at age ten she announced that she would become a poet. She earned a scholarship to the Tree's Academy of Acting, and studied opera in Paris. However, in 1905 she gave up music when she married an English lawyer, Patrick Hepburn, later secretary of the Astronomical Society. The marriage was unhappy and arguments were frequent; her husband disapproved of Wickham's liberal political views and creative writing.

Wickham, who gave birth to four sons between 1907 and 1919, found consolation in caring for her children and in writing poetry in her spare time. She also became interested in social welfare causes, especially with helping ease the burdens on working-class women. Her desire for freedom from the constraints of her married life intensified after Hepburn had her forcibly confined to an asylum for six weeks after an argument. A collection of her poems, *Songs for John Oland*, was privately printed in 1911, against her husband's wishes. Her poems also appeared in an anthology by the Poetry Bookshop in 1914. These were followed by three more volumes of poetry, *The Contemplative Quarry*, *The Man With a Hammer* (1916), and *The Little Old House* (1921). Her poetry followed rhyme conventions while expressing feminist views on oppression against women, especially against married women, and satirizing the bourgeois values held by her husband and his social class.

Wickham's poetry found a large audience among middle-class women in England and in the United States, and was frequently included in anthologies. In 1922, grief over the death of one of her sons led her to leave her husband and move to Paris. There she met the American writer *Natalie Clifford Barney, with whom Wickham would conduct a passionate correspondence for the next ten years, after her return to London. The wealthy Barney became a source of financial and emotional support for Wickham as she faced the disintegration of her marriage. In 1926, Wickham and Hepburn legally separated, though they briefly reconciled in 1928.

Wickham's letters to Barney, as well as much of her poetry from this period, has erotic undertones and testifies to her growing woman-centered consciousness.

After Patrick Hepburn drowned accidentally in 1929, Wickham continued to live in London with her three sons. The last of her works to appear in her lifetime were included in three anthologies edited by John Gawsworth in the 1930s, *Richards' Shilling Selections*, *Edwardian Poetry*, and *Neo-Georgian Poetry*. In 1943, Wickham's home in Parliament Hill in London was firebombed by the German army, destroying most of her correspondence and original manuscripts. She committed suicide by hanging in 1947. A book of *Selected Poems* was published in 1971 and several previously unpublished essays appeared in 1984 in *The Writings of Anna Wickham, Free Woman and Poet.*

SOURCES:

Shattock, Joanne, ed. *The Oxford Guide to British Women Writers*. NY: Oxford University Press, 1993.
Wickham, Anna. *The Writings of Anna Wickham, Free Woman and Poet*. Edited by R.D. Smith. Boston, MA: Salem House, 1984.

Laura York, M.A. in History,
University of California,
Riverside, California

Wieck, Clara (1819–1896).

See Schumann, Clara.

Wied, princess of.

See Marie of Nassau (1841–1910).
See Elizabeth of Wied (1843–1916).
See Pauline of Wurttemberg (1877–1965).

Wiedersheim, Grace Gebbie (1877–1936).

See Drayton, Grace Gebbie.

Wieland, Joyce (1931–1998)

Canadian director who built a reputation as an artist working with mixed media, conveying statements about women, the environment and Canada. Born on June 30, 1931, in Toronto, Ontario, Canada; died on June 27, 1998, in Toronto; educated at Central Technical Vocational High School in Toronto; married Michael Snow (an artist), in 1957 (divorced).

Joyce Wieland gained a reputation throughout Canada as a visionary artist who inspired women to pursue public recognition as professional artists in their own right. Born in Toronto in 1931, she was educated at that city's vocational high school, graduating in the mid-1950s to pursue a profession in the arts. Her first job was as an animator for Graphic Films, a position she held from 1955 to 1956. In 1957, Wieland married fellow artist Michael Snow, with whom she worked on numerous film projects throughout the remainder of the decade while also pursuing a variety of other creative projects.

When Toronto developed into a leading Canadian art center in the late 1950s and 1960s, Wieland became the only woman to achieve artistic prominence among the new group of Canadian painters influenced by Abstract Expressionism and Pop Art. Wieland funneled a good deal of her artistic vision into the medium of painting, producing a significant body of work in the process. Many of these works, presented in a distinctive abstract language on a large scale, conveyed sexual imagery from the viewpoint of women, a perspective most other artists would not pursue for several more years. In addition to her painting, Wieland produced a number of mixed-media assemblages and began making quilts in collaboration with her sister **Joan Stewart** and others.

Together with Snow, Wieland relocated to New York City in the early 1960s, and built a reputation as one of a group of experimental filmmakers who contributed to the creation of an avant-garde film style. She became friendly with many members of the underground film community, a group whose bohemian behavior and outrageously styled home movies were gaining increasing notoriety. The cinematic style that evolved out of several underground filmmakers' works became known by the late 1960s as "structural film," which paralleled painterly developments in minimal art and received international recognition as the new radical forefront of avant-garde film.

Influenced by underground filmmakers Harry Smith, Ken Jacobs, and George Kuchar, Wieland began making short, personal films, and her movies were soon included in the group's regular Greenwich Village screenings. Wieland's films formally investigate the limitations and shared properties of several media while they developed increasingly pointed themes regarding Canadian nationalism and feminism. Successful Wieland films of the 1960s included *Patriotism, Part II* (1964), in which she depicted hot dogs marching in unison to a John Philip Sousa song; *Rat Life and Diet in North America* (1968), which provides a sympathetic view of the flight of American draft dodgers into Canada, using gerbils as stand-ins for the draft protesters and menacing cats as their establishment jailers; and *Reason Over Passion/La Rai-*

son Avant la Passion (1969), a heartfelt declaration of her commitment to Canadian nationalism. This was the first of several cinematic efforts produced by the artist that would take Canadian political and social issues as their subjects. Wieland's films—often grouped and discussed along with those by such other structural filmmakers as Snow, Jacobs, Hollis Frampton, and Ernie Gehr—played at museums, film festivals, and colleges in Europe and North America.

Wieland reveled in the low-key atmosphere of New York's underground film community—a marked contrast to the fiercely competitive nature of the city's established art world—but by 1970 she found that even there she was discriminated against because of her gender. Her film *Reason Over Passion*, a longer and more ambitious effort than her earlier films, received a decidedly cold reception from her colleagues. "I was made to feel in no uncertain terms by a few male filmmakers that I had overstepped my place, that in New York my place was making little films," she later told **Kay Armatage** in an interview for *Take One*.

By 1971 Wieland had returned to Toronto, where she was honored as the first woman to be featured in a solo exhibit at the National Gallery of Art. That exhibit, "True Patriot Love/ Veritable Amour patriotique," included Wieland's paintings, sculpture, and a collection of quilts embroidered with the motto "Reason over Passion," made famous by Canada's then-president Pierre Trudeau. The publicity Wieland received in the wake of her groundbreaking solo exhibition served to inspire other Canadian women to take their artistic endeavors seriously, a movement that the artist herself actively encouraged in the many published interviews that followed the exhibit. During the 1970s and 1980s her varied works became increasingly associated with issues of Canadian identity, feminism, and the environment. Wieland worked primarily in paints and colored pencils, producing such memorable works as the mystical pencil drawing *The one above waits for those below* (1981) and the horrific and arresting *Experiment with Life* (1983).

Wieland did not abandon her filmmaking with her return to her homeland, however; she completed two additional short structural documentaries, *Pierre Vallières*, about a French-Canadian revolutionary and the problems between French and English Canada, and *Solidarity*, about a labor strike at an Ontario factory whose workers were mostly women. At the same time, Wieland co-wrote, co-produced, and directed a theatrical feature-length film, *The*

Far Shore, a romantic melodrama about a French-Canadian woman whose failing marriage to a stuffy Toronto bourgeois results in her liberating affair with a Canadian painter. While she continued to produce artworks in a variety of media throughout the 1970s, *The Far Shore* signaled the end of Wieland's filmmaking career. Wieland, considered one of Canada's most significant 20th-century artists, had her career cut short by Alzheimer's disease. After living under the care of her family for several years, she was finally removed to a Toronto nursing home and passed away in June 1998, three days before her 67th birthday.

SOURCES:

The Day [New London, CT]. June 30, 1998.

Hillstrom, Laurie Collier, and Kevin Hillstrom, eds. *Contemporary Women Artists*. Detroit, MI: St. James Press, 1999.

Unterburger, Amy L., ed. *Women Filmmakers & Their Films*. Detroit, MI: St. James Press, 1998.

Pamela Shelton, freelance writer, Avon, Connecticut, **Kevin Hillstrom** for *Contemporary Women Artists*, and **Lauren Ravinovitz** for *Women Filmmakers & Their Films*

Wienhausen, abbess of.

See Hoya, Katherina von (d. around 1470).

Wieniawska, Irene Regine

(1880–1932)

British composer, pianist and singer. Name variations: Lady Dean Paul; (pseudonym) Mme. Poldowski. Born Irene Regine Wieniawska in Brussels, Belgium, on May 16, 1880; died in London on January 28, 1932; daughter of the Polish violinist and composer Henryk (Henri) Wieniawski (1835–1880), who died six weeks before her birth; entered the Brussels Conservatory at age 12 to study piano and composition; went to London to complete her musical education, studying with Percy Pitt and Michael Hambourg; further studies took place in Paris; married Sir Aubrey Dean Paul, Bt. (who as a baritone gave concerts with his wife in England and the Continent), in 1901; children.

Irene Wieniawska was burdened throughout her life by being the daughter of Henryk Wieniawski, a world-famous violin virtuoso and composer whom she never knew, because he died six weeks before she was born in Brussels, Belgium, in 1880. Having received an excellent musical education in Brussels, London, and Paris, she was prepared for a significant career as a composer. Although she never penned a masterpiece, she composed finely crafted orchestral works, chamber music, piano pieces and

vocal works, as well as an operetta entitled *Laughter*. Wieniawska was primarily a composer of songs, and excelled in setting the French poets, from Victor Hugo to Paul Verlaine, to music. A number of noted singers of the day, particularly Gervase Elwes, gave excellent interpretations of her songs, but many felt that the best interpreter of these subtle works was Wieniawska herself, although she modestly noted that her readings of her own works were sung only "from the standpoint of the composer." Though her orchestral compositions did not enter the permanent repertoire, in their own day several of them were considered sufficiently excellent to be performed by major London orchestras. One of these, "Nocturne for Orchestra," which Wieniawska described as "an impression of night on an island off the West Coast of Scotland," was performed by Sir Henry Wood at one of his popular Promenade Concerts in 1912. Concerned that her music live on in future years, she urged her friends not to cancel an upcoming concert of her music as she lay on her deathbed in January 1932: "Do look after my music. Do let the concert go through."

SOURCES:

Cohen, Aaron I. *International Encyclopedia of Women Composers*. 2 vols. NY: Books & Music (USA), 1987.

John Haag,
Athens, Georgia

Wiesenthal, Grete (1885–1970)

Austrian dancer and choreographer who developed new dance forms based on the Viennese waltz and by 1914 had become an international star as the "ambassador of waltz." Born Margarete Wiesenthal in Vienna on December 9, 1885; died in Vienna on June 22, 1970; daughter of Franz Wiesenthal (a painter) and Rosa (Ratkovsky) Wiesenthal; had one brother and five sisters, including Elsa, Berta and Martha Wiesenthal; married Erwin Lang, in June 1910 (divorced 1923); married Nils Silfverskjöld (a Swedish physician), in 1923 (divorced 1927); children: son, Martin.

Born in Vienna in 1885 into an artistic family (her father was a successful academic painter), Grete Wiesenthal grew up at the center of the artistic and intellectual life of late imperial Austria. Avant-garde culture would be central to her career, but she began her life as a dancer within the traditions of ballet as it flourished in late 19th-century Vienna. Grete and her five sisters and brother grew up in an atmosphere saturated by music; thus, their transition from music to dance was a natural course of events. As a child, Grete was observant of the movements of the feet of peasants who came to Vienna on Sunday in order to perform dances in the open. To her, the dancers' feet seemed to be carrying on conversations with one another. Around the age of seven, when she was taken to see a ballet performance at Vienna's Hofoper (Court Opera), she was enthralled and wanted to leap from her seat in order to join the ballerinas on stage. The next day, she solemnly announced to her parents that she wanted to be a ballet dancer. In September 1895, she was enrolled at the Hofoper ballet school. A year later, her sister **Elsa Wiesenthal** also began to take instruction there.

In later years, Wiesenthal noted that when she began her ballet studies in Vienna the art was very much in a state of decline, routinely filled with kitsch and indifferent to any artistic expression, emphasizing instead a technique and drill that were boring, monotonous, and empty of meaning. Even so, Grete and Elsa continued their studies, and both sisters aspired to advance through the traditional ballet ranks of coryphée, corps leader, soloist, mimic and prima ballerina. Wiesenthal entered the corps in 1901 and one year later she and Elsa advanced to the level of coryphée. Grete's talents were recognized by Hofoper teacher and ballet master Joseph Hassreiter, but by this time she was finding it increasingly onerous to conform:

> It became difficult for me to dance in the line; too easily I leapt forward somewhat or stayed back out of fear that the ballet master, the next day in rehearsal, could say: 'And Wiesenthal had again danced out of line, yes; do you always want to be the star?' Oh, I so honestly endeavored to stay in the line correctly and had, for the time being, had enough of the effort to become a star. But I was obviously not created for the line.

In the early 1900s, innovation was rampant in Vienna. In February 1902, *Isadora Duncan danced there for the first time, introducing her influential new style to the Viennese, and artistic rebellion in general was in the air. Over the next few years, Wiesenthal's frustration with ballet only increased as it became clear to her that if she remained in a world dominated by individuals like Hassreiter her "desire for expression would stay unsatisfied and . . . I would have to experience everything lifeless." Feeling that the movements of ballet were severely limiting the expressive possibilities of the human body, the Wiesenthal sisters began to work on their own at home. While another sister accompanied them on the piano and their mother **Rosa** watched with sympathetic interest, Grete and Elsa chore-ographed new ways of moving and expressing themselves through dance. Their first completed dance routine was set to a Chopin waltz. Grete had found the path she would take for the remainder of her long, productive career. The second piece she worked on was the "Blue Danube Waltz" by Johann Strauss, Jr., a Viennese favorite she had seen performed many times at the Hofoper. In her autobiography, Wiesenthal tells how each time she saw the "Blue Danube Waltz" performed as part of the Strauss operetta *Die Fledermaus*, she would experience a shudder of ecstasy.

In 1907, Grete's opportunity presented itself when Hofoper scenic designer Alfred Roller and director Gustav Mahler decided to do away with the stuffy ballet conventions that had prevailed until then. Both men were aware of Wiesenthal's talent and ambitions, and Roller offered her the role of the mute woman Fenella in Daniel François Auber's opera *La Muette de Portici*, giving her considerable artistic freedom. The new production had its debut on February 27, 1907, and was a great success. Despite this, in late May, both Grete and Elsa left the Hofoper ballet, seeking artistic autonomy. Allied with the Secession circle of innovators, the sisters performed that June at an outdoor "Festival of Art, Nature, and Youth," the piece being a pantomime, *Die Tänzerinnen und die Marionette* (The Dancers and the Marionette).

That winter, on January 14, 1908, Grete and Elsa, joined by their sister **Berta Wiesenthal**, gave a performance of their new dance routines at Vienna's Cabaret Fledermaus. This fashionable cabaret had been opened some six months earlier by Fritz Wärndorfer, a founding member of the arts and crafts cooperative Wiener Werkstätte (Viennese Workshop). Reflecting the nascent international spirit in dance, that of New Dance (*Ausdruckstanz*), which reflected the passions found in Expressionist art, the performance of the Wiesenthal sisters that evening was both a triumph and a revelation for Vienna's artists and intellectuals. "One hardly finds artists in whom such an authentic and holy fire of enthusiasm is burning as is the case of the Wiesenthal sisters," wrote a reviewer for the *Fremdenblatt*.

Weeks after their appearance at the Cabaret Fledermaus, the Wiesenthal sisters were stars. With the support of the poet and playwright Hugo von Hofmannsthal, they performed in Berlin and most of Germany's other large cities. In Berlin, they danced at Max Reinhardt's innovative Deutsches Theater, ending a special performance of *Lysistrata* for which von Hofmannsthal had written a prologue. In 1909, the sisters performed again in Berlin and Vienna, with Grete dancing the role of the first elf in Reinhardt's production of Shakespeare's *A Midsummer Night's Dream* at Munich's Artist's Theater. For three months, from July through October 1909, the sisters performed at London's Hippodrome (between acrobatic acts, singers, and clown acts). That October, they followed their London success with an appearance at the Théâtre du Vaudeville in Paris.

The year 1910 brought significant changes in Grete's life. Professionally, in April she made her debut in Berlin in the pantomime *Sumurùn*, produced by Reinhardt. Wiesenthal regarded this as the first time that a truly modern pantomime had been seen on any stage. She made a distinction between traditional forms of pantomime using a sign language (*Zeichensprache*) to make the plot understandable, and the modern pantomime, which made its plot comprehensible to audiences through large movements of the characters, such as lying down, standing up, or walk-

ing. Personally, Wiesenthal married the painter Erwin Lang in June 1910. Lang, a son of Austrian feminist leader **Marie Lang** (1858–1934), had been inseparable from Wiesenthal for several years and had sketched costumes for her. That same year, Grete ended her dance partnership with her sisters. Elsa and Berta opened a dance school in Vienna, also giving performances of their own as a duo.

Grete made her United States debut at the Winter Garden in New York City on April 16, 1912, sharing a decidedly eclectic bill called "The Whirl of Society" with, among other performers, Al Jolson and the eight Texas Tommies. Her performance appears to have garnered more critical than popular acclaim, and a trade paper commented that she was "rather out of place in the noisy Texas Tommy and Bunny Hug affair." Upon her return to Europe, she created the role of the Kitchen Boy in Max Reinhardt's Stuttgart production of *Der Bürger als Edelmann*, with music by Richard Strauss. Soon after, Wiesenthal was pleased to discover that Hugo von Hofmannsthal had contracted with Sergei Diaghilev

Grete Wiesenthal (center).

for her to guest perform with the Ballets Russes during their upcoming 1913 Paris season. There were also plans to unite Reinhardt with Diaghilev for that production, but unfortunately Wiesenthal could not appear for health reasons. Instead, she discovered a new area for her art: the motion picture. In the spring of 1913, the German firm Deutsche Bioscop G.m.b.H. announced a "Grete Wiesenthal Series." Three films appeared before the summer of 1914: *Kadra Sâfa*, *Erlkönigs Tochter* (The Erl King's Daughter), and *Die goldne Fliege* (The Golden Fly). But the onset of World War I ended any further work by her in this medium.

The First World War left deep and lasting scars on Wiesenthal's life and art. The youthful innocence her dancing evoked was forever lost through that ghastly conflict. Her husband Erwin Lang became a prisoner of war in Russia, not returning to Vienna until 1920. Wiesenthal and Lang divorced three years later, but would remain friends until his death in 1962. By 1917, Vienna was a city of starving widows, orphans and beggars. Writing in the *Neue Freie Presse* in a forced spirit of optimism, Raoul Auernheimer insisted that "one could say of Wiesenthal that she danced Austria. And she dances it, one needs to note, in the midst of a war which threatens to devastate her art as well. . . . [I]t may not be so easy right now to come up with this exuberance of the limbs which constitutes her dance [but] nevertheless, being the determined Viennese that she is, . . . she dances toward a better future."

In 1919, soon after the end of a war that deprived the world, including Wiesenthal, of affluence and elegance, she opened her own dancing school in the "Hohe Warte," in Vienna's upscale suburb of Döbling. Despite postwar inflation and political chaos, she trained promising students, and soon went on tour with the best of them and her male partner Toni Birkmeyer. In 1923, she married a Swedish physician, Nils Silfverskjöld, but the union ended in divorce in 1927. That year, Wiesenthal triumphantly returned to the Vienna stage at the Staatsoper (State Opera House), in the lead role of her ballet *Der Taugenichts in Wien* (The Ne'er-Do-Well in Vienna). Despite Austria's desperate political and economic situation in the early 1930s, she remained active professionally, appearing in solo dance concerts and tours, including a return to New York in 1933, this time accompanied by her male dancing partner, Willy Fränzl, the ballet master of the Staatsoper, and her youngest sister **Martha Wiesenthal**, leader of a string quartet. Wrote dance critic John Martin in *The*

New York Times: "Grete Wiesenthal was one of a small number of pioneers who dedicated themselves to vitalizing the dance in a period when it was in dire need of their ministrations. . . . Hers was in its day exhilarating dancing, make no mistake. When it can be seen, at some future time, in relation to its period, it will again be exhilarating dancing. It has had the misfortune to be imported at exactly the wrong moment."

Although she was now seen by some as representative of the lost world of pre-1914 European culture, Wiesenthal remained popular in her home city of Vienna. In May 1934, she gave the opening performance at the International Dance Week held there. That September, she was appointed a professor of dance at Vienna's prestigious Academy for Music and the Performing Arts. But the world of Old Austria that she embodied was doomed, not only by the passage of time but by the rise of a Nazi Germany which despised the cosmopolitan and "decadent" style of prewar Austria. In January 1938, only a few weeks before the Anschluss that permitted Adolf Hitler to enter Vienna in triumph, Wiesenthal danced in public for the last time, partnered by Toni Birkmeyer, at a gala *Festabend* (evening of celebration). In August 1939, because of her close ties to Richard Strauss she was able to create the dances for the Salzburg Festival production of the Hofmannsthal-Strauss adaptation of *Der Bürger als Edelmann*. Within weeks, Europe was once again at war. For the next six years, Wiesenthal's career was in limbo. During the Nazi period, she presided over an informal salon that brought together artists of various shadings of anti-Nazi sentiments, allowing her to play a role, if only a modest one, in traditional Austria's cultural resistance to fascism.

After 1945, Wiesenthal's work enjoyed a renaissance in Austria, especially the dances she created for various Salzburg Festival productions. From 1945 until 1952, she held the post of director of the artistic dance section of the Academy for Music and the Performing Arts. A slightly revised edition of her autobiography, first published in 1919 as *Der Aufstieg* (The Way Upwards), appeared in 1947 under the title *Die ersten Schritte* (The First Steps). She even ventured into creative writing, publishing a novel, *Iffi: Roman einer Tänzerin* (Iffi: Novel of a Dancer), in 1951. Her last creative effort was her production of the dances for Mozart's *Don Giovanni* at the Salzburg Festival in July 1953. After Grete Wiesenthal died in Vienna on June 22, 1970, critics and audiences alike began to rediscover and reevaluate her remarkable legacy, a process that is still underway.

Above all else, Grete Wiesenthal will be remembered for having transformed the Viennese waltz from a monotonous one-two-three movement, performed by fixedly smiling dancers laced into corsets, into an ecstatic experience, performed by dancers with unbound hair and swinging dresses. For her, waltzing was bliss, but it could also represent suspicion and menace—something that George Balanchine would later embody in his choreography. Her legacy was a new method of dancing whose primary goal was to overcome the static quality of classical ballet, and, in an endless flow of movement, to dissolve all traces of posing. "Effortlessness, flying and swinging movement, rapture, and the capacity to be deeply moved by music were the characteristics of Grete Wiesenthal," writes **Maria Josefa Schaffgotsch**. "She specialized in translating into dance the flowing, wavelike quality of three-quarter time as embodied in Strauss waltzes."

SOURCES:

Arbeitsgemeinschaft "Biografisches Lexikon der österreichischen Frau," Dokumentationsstelle Frauenforschung im Institut für Wissenschaft und Kunst, Berggasse 17, Vienna, biographical file on Grete Wiesenthal.

Amort, Andrea. "Tänze der Verfemten," in *Tanzdrama Magazin*. No. 29. June 1995, pp. 24–26.

———. "Wiesenthal, Grete," in Taryn Benbow-Pfalzgraf and Glynis Benbow-Niemier, eds., *International Dictionary of Modern Dance*. Trans. by Zoran Minderovic. Detroit, MI: St. James Press, 1998, pp. 821–822.

Auernheimer, Raoul. "Eine Wiener Tänzerin im Kriege," in *Neue Freie Presse* [Vienna]. March 11, 1917.

Billinger, Richard. *Grete Wiesenthal und ihrer Schule. Lithographien von Erwin Lang*. Vienna: Haybach, 1923.

Caffin, Caroline, and Charles H. Caffin. *Dancing and Dancers of Today: The Modern Revival of Dancing as an Art*. Rep. ed. NY: Da Capo Press, 1978.

Craine, Debra, and Judith Mackrell. *The Oxford Dictionary of Dance*. Oxford, UK: Oxford University Press, 2000.

Ehler, P. "Grete Wiesenthal: Die Biene," in *Münchner Neueste Nachrichten*. November 21, 1916.

Fiedler, Leonhard M., and Martin Lang, eds. *Grete Wiesenthal: Die Schönheit der Sprache des Körpers im Tanz*. Salzburg: Residenz, 1985.

Grete Wiesenthal. Holzschnitte von Erwin Lang, mit einer Einleitung von Oscar Bie. Berlin: Erich Reiss, 1910.

Hofmannsthal, Hugo von. *Grete Wiesenthal in Amor und Psyche und Das fremde Mädchen*. Berlin: S. Fischer, 1911.

Howe, Dianne S. *Individuality and Expression: The Aesthetics of the New German Dance, 1908–1936*. NY: Peter Lang, 1996.

Huber-Wiesenthal, Rudolf. *Die Schwestern Wiesenthal: Ein Buch eigenen Erlebens*. Vienna: Saturn, 1934.

"Josef Hassreiter, Leben und Werk," in *Tanz Affiche* [Vienna]. Vol. 8, no. 60. December 1995–January 1996, pp. 18–37.

Koegler, Horst. "In the Shadow of the Swastika: Dance in Germany, 1927–1936," in *Dance Perspectives*. No. 57. Spring 1974, pp. 1–48.

———. "The Rediscovery of Grete Wiesenthal: Vienna International Ballet Festival Dance '86," in *Ballet International*. Vol. 9, no. 6. June 1986, p. 30.

Langer, Friedrich. "Grete Wiesenthal (1885–1969 [sic])," in *Neue Österreichische Biographie ab 1815: Grosse Österreicher*. Vol. 19. Vienna: Amalthea, 1977, pp. 140–145.

Oberzaucher-Schüller, Gunhild. "Wiesenthal, Grete," in Selma Jeanne Cohen *et al.*, eds., *International Encyclopedia of Dance*. Vol. 6. NY: Oxford University Press, 1998, pp. 386–388.

Prenner, Ingeborg. "Grete Wiesenthal, die Begründerin eines neuen Tanzstils." Ph.D. dissertation, University of Vienna, 1950.

Schaffgotsch, Maria Josefa. "Wiesenthal Technique," in Selma Jeanne Cohen, *et al.*, eds., *International Encyclopedia of Dance*. Vol. 6. NY: Oxford University Press, 1998, p. 388.

Wiesenthal, Grete. *Der Aufstieg: Aus dem Leben einer Tänzerin*. Berlin: Ernst Rowohlt, 1919.

———. *Die Biene: Eine Pantomime in zehn Bildern*. Berlin: Drei Masken, 1916.

———. *Iffi: Roman einer Tänzerin*. Vienna: Amandus, 1951.

Witzmann, Reingard. *Die Neue Körpersprache: Grete Wiesenthal und ihr Tanz. Historisches Museum der Stadt Wien, 94. Sonderausstellung, 18. Main 1985 bis 23. Februar 1986*. Vienna: Eigenverlag der Museen der Stadt Wien, 1985.

Zifferer, Paul. "Grete Wiesenthal," in *Neue Freie Presse* [Vienna]. January 5, 1912.

John Haag,
Associate Professor of History,
University of Georgia, Athens, Georgia

Wiggin, Kate Douglas (1856–1923)

American kindergarten pioneer and author of children's books who is best known for writing Rebecca of Sunnybrook Farm. *Born Kate Douglas Smith on September 28, 1856, in Philadelphia, Pennsylvania; died of bronchial pneumonia at a nursing home in Harrow, England, on August 24, 1923; daughter of Robert Noah Smith and Helen Elizabeth (Dyer) Smith; attended district school in Hollis, Maine, Gorham's (Maine) Female Seminary, Morison Academy in Baltimore, and Abbott Academy in Andover, Massachusetts; graduated from Emma J.C. Marwedel's Kindergarten Training School, Los Angeles, California, 1878; married Samuel Bradley Wiggin, on December 28, 1881 (died 1889); married George Christopher Riggs, on March 30, 1895.*

Organized Silver Street Kindergarten (1879) and California Kindergarten Training School (1880).

Selected writings: (children's stories) The Story of Patsy *(1883),* The Birds' Christmas Carol *(1887),* Timothy's Quest *(1890),* Rebecca of Sunnybrook Farm *(1903),* Mother Carey's Chickens *(1911); (other major works)* A Cathedral Courtship *(1893),* Penelope's English Experiences *(1900), (with Nora Smith)* Kindergarten Principles and Practice *(1896); (autobiography)* My Garden of Memory *(1923); also edited with Nora Smith, a five-volume collection of fairy tales and fables:* The Fairy Ring *(1906),* Magic Casements *(1907),* Tales of Laughter *(1908),* Tales of Wonder *(1909), and* The Talking Beasts *(1911).*

In 1878, Kate Douglas Wiggin and her family faced a desperate financial crisis. Her stepfather had died two years before, a tragedy which ultimately forced his widow to sell off substantial landholdings and other possessions to keep their home. Kate's younger sister, ◄❀ **Nora Archibald Smith**, having just graduated from Santa Barbara College, offered French and Spanish lessons to earn money. But Wiggin had little training that allowed her to do her part to keep the family afloat financially. She agreed to play the church organ for a local Episcopal Church for $15 a month, though she had never played this instrument before, only the piano. She also wrote a short story, "Half a Dozen Housekeepers," a work inspired by her own experiences as a student at a female seminary, and sent it to the *St. Nicholas Magazine.* Within a few months, a shocked Wiggin received a letter accepting the piece and a check for $150.

Four years later, she once again needed to raise some money, though this time not for her family. She hoped to add to the treasury of the Silver Street Kindergarten in San Francisco, California, which she had helped to organize two years before. So Wiggin turned to the "proven" approach of writing another story, this time a longer work entitled *The Story of Patsy,* a book

based in part on her personal experiences with poor children who attended the kindergarten. This piece, printed privately in 1883, was then followed by a second book in 1887, *The Birds' Christmas Carol.* Genuinely surprised by the popularity of the latter work, Wiggin decided to seek a regular publisher for it. When Houghton Mifflin reissued the story in 1889, the book became hugely successful, and its author quickly emerged as one of the most popular writers of children's books in the United States.

The career of this celebrated writer thus began virtually by accident, though her background and love for literature had certainly prepared Wiggin to write books for children. Born Kate Douglas Smith in Philadelphia on September 28, 1856, she was the eldest of two daughters of Robert Noah Smith and **Helen Dyer Smith**, both of New England ancestry. Each side of Kate's family included prominent individuals. Her maternal grandfather Jones Dyer, 3rd, was a wealthy businessman who devoted most of his time to intellectual pursuits and extensive travel, and to educating his 14 children. Her paternal grandfather Noah Smith, Jr., served in the Maine legislature, including as speaker of the house. He was later secretary of the U.S. Senate and legislative clerk. Robert Smith was born in Providence, Rhode Island, and educated at Brown University. He received a law degree from Harvard and moved to Philadelphia in the mid-1850s to begin his career. There, Kate and her sister Nora were born.

While traveling on business in 1859, Robert Smith died suddenly. Though only three years old when her father passed away, Wiggin maintained that this brilliant, charismatic man—and captivating storyteller—had a significant influence on her life. Upon his death, Helen Smith moved the family to Portland, Maine, and three years later married Albion Bradbury, a distant cousin. Kate would spend the rest of her childhood in Hollis, Maine, with sister Nora and half-brother Philip. Her stepfather, a physician and Bowdoin graduate, conducted lessons for his children at home.

The Bradbury home near the Saco River provided an idyllic setting for Kate's upbringing. She raised various pets (usually named after characters from the books of Charles Dickens), played with frogs, swam, went sledding, and generally lived in a protected and pleasant environment. With her sister, with whom she shared a very close relationship, she did chores, took piano lessons, and attended community functions. "These are the years that count most," Wiggin noted later. "The first years in the stock-

❀► **Smith, Nora Archibald** (1859?–1934)

American educator. Born around 1859 in Philadelphia, Pennsylvania; died in 1934; daughter of Robert Noah Smith and Helen Elizabeth (Dyer) Smith; sister of Kate Douglas Wiggin (1856–1923); graduated from Santa Barbara College.

With her sister *Kate Douglas Wiggin, Nora Archibald Smith helped run the California Kindergarten Training School and Silver Street Kindergarten, then took over Silver Street in 1881 and the training school in 1884, following Kate's marriage. With Wiggin Nora also co-authored *Kindergarten Principles and Practice* (1896); and co-edited a five-volume collection of fairy tales and fables. In 1925, Nora wrote her sister's biography, *Kate Douglas Wiggin as Her Sister Knew Her.*

ing of our memories and the development of our imaginations, in the growing of all those long roots out of which springs real life, these do far more for us than all the rest."

In her autobiography, *My Garden of Memory* (1923), Wiggin portrayed her childhood as full of happiness. But one of Kate's earliest memories was of tragedy, for she describes the reaction of her community and family to news of the death of Abraham Lincoln. "Families ate little, work in the fields stopped, men gathered in yards and by roadsides and talked in low voices. My mother sat with folded hands and my father paced to and fro in the grass in front of the house." It was Wiggin's first encounter with this sort of public sorrow, but also her "first conscious recognition of the greatness of individual character." She was glad her recollection of the event was so clear.

Within the Smith-Bradbury family, a love of reading prevailed. Wiggin believed that books represented "the most inspiring influence in human life." Her mother read aloud to her children from the time they were born. The family's most beloved author was Dickens, and Kate's mother would read his works, changing her voice to portray the various characters. No author would influence Wiggin's writing more than Dickens. But as a girl, she also read *Harper's Magazine* and *Littell's Living Age*, the Bible, and the most popular great novels of the era.

After studying at home as a young child, Kate attended the local district school for a few terms. When she was 13, she went to Gorham's Female Seminary as a boarding student. Here she formed a close relationship with Latin teacher **Mary Smith** and won prizes for elocution, French, and English. Two years later, Kate attended the Morison Academy in Baltimore, then spent a few months at the Abbott Academy in Andover, Massachusetts. Her formal education would end here, however, primarily because her stepfather moved the family to Santa Barbara, California, in 1873. Suffering from severe lung disease, he sought to recover his health on the West Coast.

Wiggin loved Maine but accepted the move to California as a great adventure and adjusted quickly to the new environment. But Albion Bradbury failed to regain his health. His death in 1876 plunged the family into difficult financial circumstances, a crisis they met with fortitude and even good humor. During these trying times, in the early summer of 1877, Kate met an activist woman who changed her life. *Caroline M. Severance*, a leader of the woman's club movement and proponent of the kindergarten method of education, visited Santa Barbara. Severance had embraced the views of the founder of the first kindergarten, Friedrich Froebel, who believed that childhood learning could be best promoted through games, music, exercise, art, and other active experiences. She convinced Kate to seek training as a kindergarten teacher.

After Severance left Santa Barbara, she helped found a kindergarten training school in Los Angeles, directed by **Emma Marwedel**. Severance asked Wiggin to come live with her and attend the training school. "You were born for this work," she told Kate, "and are particularly fitted to do pioneer service because you are musical, a good storyteller and fond of children." Though Helen Smith Bradbury had to mortgage their last property to scrape together the $100 for tuition, Kate went to Los Angeles to study. She completed the course in one year, then took charge of a small private kindergarten opened by Santa Barbara College. In 1878, the Public Kindergarten Society of San Francisco founded

Kate Douglas Wiggin

the first free kindergarten on the West Coast. Named to run the school, Wiggin turned the Silver Street Kindergarten into a model institution.

In 1880, she created the California Kindergarten Training School, which was attached to the Silver Street institution. Her sister Nora, a graduate of Santa Barbara College then serving as a girls' department principal in Tucson, entered the first class, then took over Silver Street in 1881 when Kate married Samuel Bradley Wiggin. Samuel was a childhood friend who had moved from Boston to San Francisco to practice law. Kate continued to help run the training school until her move in 1884 to New York City, and she continued to raise monies for it even after that point.

The book . . . is the most faithful of all allies and, after human friendship, the chief solace as well as the most inspiring influence in human life.

—Kate Douglas Wiggin

The year 1889 was both an exciting and terrible one for Kate Douglas Wiggin. Houghton Mifflin published *The Birds' Christmas Carol* and *The Story of Patsy*, launching the career of one of the nation's most successful authors of children's books. But while visiting the Silver Street school for commencement, Kate learned that Samuel Wiggin had died suddenly back East. Distraught and tired, Kate went back to Maine, to the family home in Hollis, where she mourned the loss of her husband, and tried to rest. She would retain the pen name "Kate Wiggin" for the rest of her life, though she did remarry.

While Kate rested, her fame as a writer spread quickly. *The Story of Patsy* and *The Birds' Christmas Carol* are highly sentimental tales where the protagonists—both young, fragile children—die. Patsy is the victim of an abusive father, who had thrown him down the stairs when he was a baby. This violence leaves Patsy badly deformed, a fate the young boy accepts without bitterness. In fact, his presence brightens the lives of those he touches, especially the narrator of the story, his kindergarten teacher. Like many of Wiggin's books, *Patsy* contains stereotyped characters, moral lessons, and healthy doses of both heart-rending sadness and humor. The *Birds' Christmas Carol* followed a similar formula. In her autobiography, *My Garden of Memory*, Wiggin herself describes the book that became her first big success:

> It was the simplest of all simple tales: the record of a lame child's life—a child born on Christmas day and named Carol. The [peri-od] in which I wrote [was] full of literary Herods who put to death all the young children in their vicinity. I was no exception with my fragile little heroine. What saved me was a rudimentary sense of humor.

Actually, it was this humor which "saved" most of Kate Wiggin's books; or to put it more accurately, it is what made them so popular.

Translated ultimately into French, German, Swedish, Japanese, and other languages, *The Birds' Christmas Carol* long remained a staple offering in the body of children's literature, selling over a million copies. Like many of Wiggin's stories, it remains in print. Its initial success allowed Kate Wiggin to become a full-time author and to travel extensively in Europe. Her first trips abroad in the 1890s led to the publication of three popular books for adults, *A Cathedral Courtship* (1893), *Penelope's Progress* (1898), and *Penelope's English Experiences* (1900). Also, on her way to England in 1894, she met an American linen importer, George Christopher Riggs. Before the ship had reached port, George had proposed. Kate Wiggin and George Riggs married in All Souls Church in New York City on March 30, 1895.

By this point, Wiggin had become one of the leading authors of children's books in the United States. *Timothy's Quest* (1890), the story of two orphans seeking a home, became almost as popular as *The Birds' Christmas Carol*, and represents the maturation of Wiggin as a writer. Like many of her works, it owes its theme and plot to Dickens, but the rural Maine setting renders this work special. It was the first time that Wiggin had set a story in the region she knew best and based her characters on Maine's unique culture. The characters were stern and stoic, but also compassionate and honorable despite their outward coldness. Kate Wiggin generally wrote about subjects with which she had firsthand experience, and she knew rural Maine and its people better than anything. Thus it is not surprising that her best works were located there. The success of *Timothy's Quest* set the stage for her later focus on Maine settings.

After marrying George Riggs, Kate settled into a life that changed little for the next 20 years. George and Kate would spend their summers at their Hollis home, Quillcote, winters in New York City, and springs in Europe (often in England). Kate did suffer from some bouts of ill health, and often spent short stints convalescing in hospitals and sanitariums. But she considered this more of a nuisance than a serious problem and continued to write prolifically before World War I. Much of this work was completed during the peaceful summer months she remained at Quillcote, the summer home in Hollis she purchased in the mid-1890s.

It is a bit ironic, however, that Kate Wiggin's most classic work, though set in Maine, was not written at Quillcote. Suffering from poor health in late 1903, she spent some time at a hospital in New York, and two sanitariums—in Pinehurst, North Carolina, and Dansville, New York. There, she penned *Rebecca of Sunnybrook Farm*, her most beloved creation. Set in Hollis ("Riverboro"), the book told the story of "the nicest child in American literature," as Thomas Bailey Aldrich described Rebecca. Though sometimes dismissed by modern critics as the epitome of the overly sentimental nature of the children's literature of the era, *Rebecca* is a book that deserves recognition as a genuine classic.

Rebecca of Sunnybrook Farm tells the tale of Rebecca Rowena Randall, a fatherless ten-year-old who goes to live with two maiden aunts in Riverboro. As the story opens, the young girl is the sole passenger on a stagecoach traveling country roads in Maine, recalling her past life at Sunnybrook Farm to driver Jeremiah Cobb. Her father, whose free-spirited ways Rebecca has inherited, had died, leaving wife Aurelia to look after seven small children. Rebecca had lightened the burden on her mother by going to live with aunts Miranda and Jane.

When she gets to Riverboro, there is immediate conflict between the domineering, materialistic, and stern Aunt Miranda and the carefree, creative, and optimistic child (Aunt Jane is more pleasant but dominated by her sister). Like Kate Wiggin, Rebecca loves the natural beauty of pastoral settings, romantic literature, and helping people. *Rebecca of Sunnybrook Farm* is the story of hard times, cruel fate, and duty—but it also glorifies fundamental decency and imagination. Rebecca ultimately wins over Aunt Miranda, acquires a useful education, helps her family financially and spiritually, and eventually inherits the house in Riverboro when Miranda dies. Her life is a triumph of goodness.

Rebecca of Sunnybrook Farm earned great praise when it appeared. Mark Twain called it "that beautiful book, beautiful and moving and satisfying," while other prominent literary figures also expressed their appreciation. To **Mary Mapes Dodge*, "*Rebecca* is delightful in every sense, a masterpiece of simple but vivid dramatization." The story lent itself to the stage, and Wiggin developed a play which opened in New York in 1910 and enjoyed a long run in the U.S. and Europe. As motion pictures were fast becoming the newest rage in American popular culture, *Rebecca* proved a natural choice for a film production. **Mary Pickford* portrayed Rebecca in the first screen version, while **Shirley Temple (Black)* played Rebecca in a 1937 movie.

In subsequent years, Wiggin adapted other stories to the stage, including the work that sold more copies than any other book other than *Rebecca of Sunnybrook Farm* and *The Birds' Christmas Carol, Mother Carey's Chickens*. Published in serial form beginning in 1909, and by Houghton Mifflin in 1911, the story depicts the struggles of a fatherless family who triumph over bad luck and poverty. Set in Maine, it was popular among children for many decades, though seldom read today. Between 1906 and 1911, Kate and her sister Nora Archibald Smith also compiled and edited *The Library of Fairy Literature*, a five-volume collection of fables and fairy tales.

World War I interrupted Kate's pattern of traveling abroad. She also wrote little during the period, no doubt because her moral tales seemed incongruous with the carnage in Europe. After the war, she wrote a number of short stories and her autobiography, *My Garden of Memory*. With her health failing, she put most of her energy into

From the movie Rebecca of Sunnybrook Farm, *starring Shirley Temple.*

the autobiography between 1919 and the spring of 1923. She was almost finished when she sailed for England with husband George in April of that year. Ill during the voyage, she feared she would not complete the book. But her health recovered enough to send the final chapters to her sister by early August. She had entered a nursing home at Harrow upon her arrival in Britain, and it was in this institution that Kate Wiggin died of bronchial pneumonia on August 24.

The beloved author and kindergarten pioneer had requested that her body be cremated, and the ashes taken home to Hollis, Maine. George Riggs followed her wishes by returning to Quillcote with Kate's remains. After a memorial service, he scattered her ashes on the Saco River. Following her death, her stories remained immensely popular for another two generations. When **Edna Boutwell** observed that "thousands of children found the world a better place because Kate Douglas Wiggin lived in it," she underestimated Wiggin's influence—the numbers of children were in the millions. If her stories are not read with the frequency of past years, many of her children's books are still in print, and still entertaining and instructing young people. If the name of Kate Wiggin is no longer known to most Americans, the author's legacy remains very tangible in the holdings of virtually every library in the country. Modern readers would do well to make their way to the area in the stacks where Wiggin's books still await new readers.

SOURCES:

Boutwell, Edna. "Kate Douglas Wiggin," in Siri Andrews, ed., *The Hewins Lecture, 1947–1962*. Boston, MA: Horn Book, 1963.

Moss, Anita. "Kate Douglas Wiggin," in Glenn E. Setes, ed. *Dictionary of Literary Biography*. Vol. 42. Detroit, MI: Gale Research, 1985.

Wiggin, Kate Douglas. *My Garden of Memory: An Autobiography*. Boston, MA: Houghton Mifflin, 1923.

SUGGESTED READING:

Smith, Nora Archibald. *Kate Douglas Wiggin as Her Sister Knew Her*. Boston, MA: Houghton Mifflin, 1925.

John M. Craig,
Professor of History,
Slippery Rock University, Slippery Rock, Pennsylvania,
author of *Lucia Ames Mead and the American Peace Movement*
and numerous articles on activist American women.

Wiggins, Myra Albert (1869–1956)

American artist, photographer, and writer. Born in 1869 in Salem, Oregon; died in 1956 in Seattle, Washington; educated at Art Students League in New York City, 1891–93; married Fred Wiggins, in 1894; children: one daughter.

Amateur photographer (1888–1929), with work exhibited internationally; began publishing photographs in periodicals (1903); admitted to Photo-Secession group; had retrospectives of paintings at Seattle Art Museum (1953) and M. H. De Young Memorial Museum in San Francisco (1954).

Myra Albert Wiggins was born in Salem, Oregon, in 1869. Artistic as a child and talented at both drawing and painting, she was quick to expand her interests to include the new medium of photography. Taking up a camera for the first time in 1888, Wiggins moved to New York City to attend the Art Students League three years later. There she studied under such artists as William Merritt Chase, John Twachtman, and Frank Vincent Dumond before leaving in 1893. Her photographs soon began appearing in such magazines as *American Amateur Photographer*, while her skills also extended to writing articles, including "Amateur Photography through Women's Eyes," which was published in *Photo-American* in 1894. That year, she married Fred Wiggins, with whom she would have one daughter.

A lover of the outdoors, Wiggins specialized in travel photography, and her work benefited from the many trips she took around the United States and abroad. An athletic woman, she won several awards for one photo series in particular, taken during an expedition over Oregon's Cascade Mountain range. Her book *Letters of a Pilgrim* detailed her journey to the Middle East through both text and photographs, while her poetry, which also reflected her love of travel, would be included in the anthology *Our Present-Day Poets: Their Lives and Works* (1926). After 1903, Wiggins' photographic work began appearing in journals both in the United States and internationally with increasing frequency, causing her to be one of three members from Oregon admitted to Photo-Secession, a national organization of women photographers. A move from Oregon to Toppenish, Washington, in 1907 presented the photographer with new vistas to shoot.

In addition to her outdoor photography, Wiggins developed something she called "Dutch genre" because of its roots in the paintings of the Old Masters. Using specially constructed sets, Wiggins would costume her subjects—often her daughter—in Dutch folk dress and other historic garb and pose them in a manner recalling the Dutch painters of earlier centuries. Many of these photographs were exhibited, interspersed with her travel photos, in the retrospectives of Wiggins' works staged at museums in Seattle and San Francisco in the early 1950s.

In 1929, at age 60, Wiggins ceased to pursue her photography, deciding instead to concentrate on painting, which she considered her primary form of artistic expression. Over the remainder of her career, she completed a number of landscapes and portraits. She and her family moved to Seattle in 1932, where she lived until her death in 1956. Her daughter donated 400 of Wiggins' photographs to the Portland, Oregon, art museum; a major exhibition of these works was held in the early 1990s.

SOURCES:

Rosenblum, Naomi. *A History of Women Photographers.* NY: Abbeville, 1994.

Pamela Shelton,
freelance writer,
Avon, Connecticut

Wightman, Hazel Hotchkiss

(1886–1974)

American tennis champion who revolutionized the way the women's game was played and won more national titles than any other player in the history of the game. Name variations: Hazel Hotchkiss; Mrs. George W. Wightman; Mrs. Wightie. Born Hazel Hotchkiss in Healdsburg, California, on December 20, 1886; died on December 5, 1974, in Chestnut Hill, Massachusetts; only daughter and fourth of five children of Emma Lucretia (Grove) Hotchkiss and William Joseph Hotchkiss; graduated from the University of California at Berkeley, 1911; married George William Wightman (a lawyer), in 1912 (divorced 1940); children: George, Jr. (b. 1913); Virginia; Hazel; Dorothy (b. 1922); William (b. 1925).

Won 44 national titles and 2 Olympic gold medals; played her last national tournament at age 73; the Hazel Hotchkiss Wightman Trophy or Wightman Cup (given to the winner of a match between British and Americans) was named in her honor.

Hazel Hotchkiss Wightman was born in 1886 and grew up on a 1,500-acre ranch in Healdsburg, in a remote area of California. Small and frail, she was encouraged to play outdoors with her brothers, indulging in a number of sports, football and baseball being particular favorites. When she was 16, the family moved to Berkeley where she was pressured to give up her roughneck ways. But after watching the 1902 Pacific Coast Tennis championship tournament, Wightman became an enthusiastic player. Fortunately, her parents thought tennis more genteel than other sports.

As a teenager, Wightman rose at first light to practice on the only asphalt tennis court in Berkeley, at the Faculty Club; girls were not allowed to play on the court after 8 AM. The remainder of the day she spent in the family's graveled backyard, hitting the ball against the side of the house or playing with her brothers. A rope had been strung across the yard to serve as a net.

After six months of practice, Wightman won the Bay Counties Women's Doubles in San Francisco with **Mary Radcliffe** as her partner. In many respects, Wightman had not given up her rugged approach to sports. At the turn of the century, women's tennis was played at the baseline with very little movement. But during her six-month apprenticeship, Hazel continued to recall that Pacific Coast championship: "It was a women's singles," noted Wightman, "and it was two of the Sutton girls, and they were the best in California—and *May Sutton was *the* best, she won the championship in England, too. She was the best all over the world—and she and her sister played singles. And it was boring to me because the points went on for so long. Just the ball over here and back." (Through the years, there would be no love lost between Wightman and Sutton.) Then Wightman had watched the men play, running to the net and volleying; she found that game far more interesting. Without instruction, her instincts prompted her to get the ball back in play quicker. A ball bouncing off backyard gravel may also have been an added influence. Wightman brought the volley and net play to the women's court, a much more aggressive style which was obviously successful.

This method made the restrictive nature of women's tennis togs immediately apparent, however. Hitting serves, volleys, and overhead smashes was a difficult task in a long-sleeved dress. Wightman had her mother run up a dainty white dimity dress, sans sleeves, on the Singer, giving her freedom in arm movement while retaining the proper ladylike look. It was the first fashion revolution on the court. "If it hadn't been for the fact that I had freedom of the arm, I never would have perfected the volley." "I think I wore corsets," said Wightman in an interview with **Barbara Klaw**. "I can't imagine. But I think I wore corsets, because how else would I have kept my stockings up? I wouldn't have known any better. And we wore high shoes, high sneakers. Hideous looking things!" The length of her dress still followed the rules, however, which demanded it be no shorter than four inches from the floor. Inadvertently, Wightman's playing style prompted the long and acrimonious battle which would eventually result in men and women wearing the same attire on the courts. Ironically, she did not much approve of modern-day tennis apparel, saying of the short tennis skirt, "It just isn't decent."

(In later life, Wightman had trouble accepting many of the changes in the world of women's tennis. Asked to comment before *Billie Jean King's match with Bobby Riggs, Wightman sadly predicted that King would lose. "Yet when she got to playing good tennis that night, outplaying Bobby, no one was happier than I," said Wightman. "I was so proud of her. I was *so* proud of her, and as a matter of fact, you know, I watched her lips, and I don't think she swore once.")

In 1909, Wightman won the national triple—the singles, doubles, and mixed doubles—repeating this feat again in 1910. In 1911, she did it again, only this time she played all three games on the same day. That year, she graduated from the University of California and met George Wightman while summering at tennis tournaments on the East Coast. They married in 1912 and eventually settled in Chestnut Hill, Massachusetts. Though George, Jr., arrived the following year, his birth did not keep Hazel Wightman off the court. She defeated the national champion at the Longwood Cricket Club

Hazel Hotchkiss Wightman

in Chestnut Hill months later. After two more children, **Hazel** and **Dorothy**, she recaptured the national singles title in 1919. Wightman had a total of five children, a fact which never interfered with her athletic career. She won on grass and clay, indoors and outdoors, and, in 1924, she took the trophy at Wimbledon in England and the gold medal at the Olympics in France.

Wightman worked hard to promote women's tennis and expand its opportunities; one of her major objectives was to bring France's *Suzanne Lenglen to compete in America. Pushing for an international competition for women to match the men's Davis Cup, she donated a silver vase, which became known as the Hazel Hotchkiss Wightman Trophy, to the U.S. Lawn Tennis Association (USLTA); it was first awarded in 1923. Teams of American women have been competing with their English counterparts for this prestigious cup every since. Wightman, who would play on the team for five years (1923, 1924, 1927, 1929, and 1931), was also a nonplaying coach-captain for 13 years. By the 1920s, she had begun to teach and write about tennis as well as play; *Helen Hull Jacobs was a student, as were **Sarah Palfrey**, *Helen Newington Wills, *Margaret Osborne, *Maureen Connolly and many others. Wightman often opened her enormous Chestnut Hill home to women tennis players so that they could socialize and form a support network. Wrote Billie Jean King:

> At Longwood, Hazel conducted clinics and numerous tournaments. During tournament weeks her three-story home became a kind of sorority house for aspiring young girls and women from all over the world. Guests slept everywhere, from the basement to the solarium, coexisting peacefully with Mrs. Wightie's cats, which came and went as they pleased through the open windows.

Hazel Wightman, who won more national tennis titles than any other player in history, did not retire from competitive tennis until 1960, when she was 73. She had been inducted into the International Tennis Hall of Fame three years earlier. In 1973, she was made an honorary Commander of the British Empire by Queen *Elizabeth II, in commemoration of the 50th anniversary of the Wightman Cup. Wightman died in 1974, two weeks before her 88th birthday.

In assessing her strategy, Wightman thought her strength was in the intelligence of her game; she felt her shots were limited, her backhand fair, her smash good, but "I'm a player that if any ball comes over the net and there isn't anybody to play it but me, I'll be there."

Women's tennis was profoundly shaped by Hazel Wightman. She revolutionized the style of play and tennis attire, and most important, widened professional opportunities. When she began playing, economic independence was unheard of for women, but thanks to her untiring efforts, women had the chance to support themselves while competing. Tennis became a gateway which fed women into other sports, such as track and field, gymnastics, basketball, and soccer. After Hazel Wightman rushed the net, the world of women's athletics was never quite the same.

SOURCES:

Clark, Alfred E. "Hazel Hotchkiss Wightman Dies; Holder of Tennis Titles Was 87," in *The New York Times Biographical Service*. December 1974, p. 1801.

King, Billie Jean, with Cynthia Starr. *We Have Come a Long Way, Baby: The Story of Women's Tennis*. NY: McGraw-Hill, 1988.

Klaw, Barbara. "Queen Mother of Tennis," in *American Heritage*. August 1975, pp. 17–24.

Wightman, Hazel Hotchkiss. *Better Tennis*. Boston, MA: Houghton Mifflin, 1933.

Woolum, Janet. *Outstanding Women Athletes*. Phoenix, AZ: Oryx Press, 1992.

Karin L. Haag,
freelance writer,
Athens, Georgia

Wigman, Mary (1886–1973)

German dancer who helped create the art form of modern dance with its emphasis on movement as an articulation of personal expression, emotions, and profound truths. Name variations: Wiegmann. Pronunciation: VEEG-mahn. Born Mary Wiegmann on November 13, 1886, in Hannover, Germany; died on September 18, 1973, in Berlin; daughter of a businessman and Amalie Wiegmann; attended secondary school at Hohene Töchterschule in Hannover, and boarding schools in England and Lausanne, Switzerland; never married; no children.

Enrolled for dance training in the school of Emile-Jacques Dalcroze in Dresden-Hellerau (1910); attended summer dance school taught by Rudolf Van Laban in Ascona, Switzerland (1913); made choreographic debut (1914); left Laban school to open own studio (1919); established dance group (1923); made first tour of U.S. under direction of Sol Hurok (1930–31); with Gret Palucca, Harald Kreutzberg and Dorothee Günther, choreographed "Olympic Youth" under Nazi supervision for the Berlin Olympics (1936); retired from performing (1942); served as teacher and choreographer until the closing of her school in West Berlin (1942–67); received Great Cross of the Order of Merit (Grosses Bundesverdienstkreuz) of the German Federal Republic (1957).

Works choreographed: Witch Dances Without Music (1914); Seven Dances of Life (1922–23); Ecstatic Dances (1919); Scenes from a Dance Drama (1924); Shifting Landscape (1929); Choric Movement (1929); Totenmal (1930); Dance of Silent Joy (1934); Farewell and Thanksgiving (1942).

At the start of the 20th century, Mary Wigman eschewed the principles of ballet to expose the unformulated, natural expression of the human body, and thereby became one of the preeminent founders of the German form of modern dance known as *Ausdruckstanz*. With her arresting face, framed by sharply tilted eyebrows and a square chin, she brought a seriousness to her performances that intrigued as often as it offended. Dancing with masks, and bringing movement to abstract idea, she aroused public adulation with her riveting solos and innovative choreography, but her greatest legacy was perhaps in the role of mentor. **Yvonne Georgi**, ***Gret Palucca** and Harald Kreutzberg, all crucial to the development of German modern dance, were students of hers, and yet another Wigman student, ***Hanya Holm**, conveyed her style and methods to America and became an influence on the careers of Alwin Nikolais, Murray Louis and Don Redlich. In the course of her career, while creating a new means of movement that embodied the emotional thrust of German expressionism, Wigman also maintained an ambiguous relationship to Nazism, enhancing the mystery of this woman who danced with masks and gave physical movement to abstract ideas.

She was born Mary Wiegmann on November 13, 1886, in Hannover, Germany, the eldest of three children in the family of a prosperous businessman. After the death of her father when she was nine, her mother soon married the twin brother of her late husband, who had also been his business partner, so the circumstances of the family were not greatly changed. Wigman's education included language study at boarding schools in England and Lausanne, Switzerland. She wrote poetry, read literature, and took lessons in comportment and social dance, but she was not encouraged toward the academic requirements of a gymnasium school, which would have prepared her for a university.

In 1908, at age 21, Wigman saw a performance in Hannover of ***Grete Wiesenthal** and her sister **Elsa**, dancers who represented a break then underway, in rebellion against the confined technique of classical ballet, toward freer forms of dance movement. But their performance lacked the more substantive originality Wigman saw later that same year in the works of another dancer, Emile-Jacques Dalcroze, which inspired her to take up dance training at a relatively late age. In 1910, she was 24 when she enrolled in the Dalcroze School in Hellerau, a town outside Dresden, and began to learn the system of eurythmics formulated by Dalcroze, which emphasized musical principles through movement.

*W*ithout ecstasy, no dance!

Without form, no dance!

—Mary Wigman

Dalcroze, essentially a music teacher, devised physical movements for particular sounds to help students gain an understanding of rhythm. While Wigman earned a lifelong attentiveness to music under his tutelage, she eventually rebelled against the idea of movement derived from music, as well as the more traditional forms of dance. In 1913, responding to advice from the German Expressionist painter Emil Nolde, Wigman enrolled in a summer dance course in Ascona, Switzerland, given by Rudolf van Laban, another founder of *Ausdruckstanz*. Laban's approach emphasized more structured movement but also encouraged expressiveness, freeing Wigman from the strictures she had felt in pantomiming music. Concentrating on space and form, Laban found ways to make these visible through dance as an aesthetic principle, particularly in the construction of large group works. He brought an underlying philosophy to Wigman's inchoate leanings

✤▶ Aakesson, Birgit (c. 1908–2001)

*Swedish dancer and choreographer. Name variations: Birgit Akesson; called "the Picasso of Dance." Born in Malmo, Sweden, around 1908; died in Stockholm in March 2001; studied with *Mary Wigman in Dresden, 1929–31; children: Mona Moeller-Nilesen.*

Birgit Aakesson, who made her debut in Paris at the Vieux Colombier in 1934, gave recitals in Sweden and in many European countries. She appeared in the Jacob's Pillow Dance Festival in the United States (1955); staged *Sisyphus* for the Royal Swedish Ballet, her first production with a professional troupe (1957); staged *The Minotaur* (1958), *Rites* (1960), and *Play for Eight* (1962); and choreographed *Icaros* (1963). Aakesson, while a member of the artistic council responsible for the policy of the Royal Swedish Ballet (1963 on), conceived many of her ballets in collaboration with Norwegian pianist **Kaare Gundersen**. Considered the founding mother of Swedish modern dance along with *Birgit Cullberg, Aakesson was awarded the gold medal of the Swedish Academy in 1998.

toward expressive movement, imparting a focus to her experimentation that would shape virtually all of her work thereafter.

On April 28, 1914, shortly before the outbreak of World War I, Wigman made her choreographic debut at the Laban school. She would remain there, at Monte Verita, an artists' colony in the Swiss Alps where she eventually became Laban's assistant, until the end of the war in 1918. By that time, Wigman was chafing under Laban's influence and wanted to open her own studio. But the recent death of her stepfather, the return of her brother from the war with an amputated limb, and the end of a love affair invoked stress that resulted in a nervous breakdown. In the winter of 1919, after a six-month stay in a sanatorium, 33-year-old Wigman returned to dance, making her first professional appearance at the Berlin Philarmonie.

But Wigman's performances were an assault on the expectations of audiences prepared for soothing visual splendors of movement, and reviewers decried her first concerts as too serious, abstract, and intense. *Ecstatic Dances* (1919), for example, was jarring in its lack of music. Both critics and audiences soon began to come around to the challenges she presented, however, and the thoughtfulness of her experiments was recognized, establishing her reputation as an innovator of an entirely new form of dance.

One distinction reviewers were quick to note was the dramatically different significance of women in Wigman's works. In the early 20th century, women outnumbered men in all performances of dance, but their appearances were determined by men offstage, producing, directing, and selecting who performed. Wigman played a large role in reversing this trend, establishing women as the directors, choreographers, and performers of modern dance. Replacing the romantic, piquant swans and sylphs of ballet with stark and forceful gestures of hands and bare feet, she also challenged the image of femininity on stage, highlighted by her remark that appeared in an interview in the German magazine *Die Weltwoche* in 1926: "My students must give such an impression that every man should enthusiastically call out: 'I would not like to be married to any one of them!'"

In 1920, Wigman opened a school in Dresden that served as her home base and provided the stability necessary for such creativity. Over the next decade, she would create 70 new solos and 10 major group works. By 1923, the dance group that had developed among her students gave her the opportunity to begin choreograph-

ing the larger works, and by 1926 the school boasted 360 students, including ◄⊰ **Birgit Aakesson.** Many, including Kreutzberg, Dore Hoyer, Palucca, Georgi, Kurt Jooss, and Holm, would go on to international fame. In the late 1920s, Wigman began touring, first to London and then in the United States, under the management of Sol Hurok. American tours from 1930 to 1933 solidified her reputation, preparing the way for her student Hanya Holm, who emigrated to New York and established the Mary Wigman School in 1931.

As Nazism burgeoned in Germany in the early 1930s, the aesthetic concepts Wigman had long propounded began to take on a fascistic tone. Her persistent interest in group works that combined principles of space and form now began to address the contingent realities of moving many people in patterned relation to one another. In *Deutsche Tanzkunst*, published in 1935, she wrote:

> We German artists today are more aware of the fate of the *Volk* than ever before. And for all of us this time is a trial of strength, a measuring of oneself against standards that are greater than the individual is able to fathom. The call of the blood, which has involved us all, goes deep and engages the essential.

In the early years of the Third Reich, *volk* (folk) was not only seen as a way of grouping all Germans together, but also bespoke the Nazi belief in an enduring, absolute German essence. The Nazi cultural ministry, seeking a dance form that utilized ballet and modern dance but would be more accessible to these *volk*, provided Wigman with support in the form of commissions, and touted her as the bearer of authentic German expression in dance that manifested the potent combination of artistic genius and the appeal and participation of the masses, the keystones of Nazi rhetoric.

In 1936, Wigman's collaboration reached its pinnacle when she joined Palucca, Kreutzberg and **Dorothee Günther** in choreographing "Olympic Youth" for the 1936 Berlin Olympics. Adolf Hitler wanted the Olympics and the accompanying International Dance Festival to be a spectacle of Aryan superiority and Germanic force. Olympic Youth realized his goals in orchestrating 10,000 young Germans through patterns eerily showcasing a unified mass. In New York, after dancers with leftist political leanings arranged a boycott of the Mary Wigman School because of Wigman's seeming acquiescence to Nazism, Hanya Holm renamed it the Hanya Holm School of Dance and even dropped "choric classes" in favor of focusing more on individual technique than the group work that was so instrumental to Wigman's ideas.

In Germany, meanwhile, Wigman's penchant for individual expression could not be contained by Nazism's predilection for art shaped to served its political goals. Soon after the Olympic spectacle, the cultural ministry stopped contributing to her support, although she continued to be recognized as the leader of modern dance in Germany. Between 1936 and 1942, Wigman supported her school through money raised from her solo tours, which reiterated the importance of individualism and the freedom of the artist.

In 1942, at age 56, Wigman ended her performing career with her appearance in *Farewell and Thanksgiving*, a dance expressing the inevitable loss a dancer faces in leaving the stage for good. But the "renunciation without resignation" that she hoped the number would also show already foreshadowed the inimitable energy and dedication she was to apply to choreography and to teaching for the next 30 years. That year, Wigman moved from Dresden to Leipzig, where she became a guest instructor at the Conservatory for Music and Dramatic Art. After Allied bombing of Leipzig destroyed the school in 1944, Wigman taught in her apartment, even as the bombing continued. In 1947, after the war had ended, she took on the role of stage director and choreographer for a production of *Orfeo ed Euridice*, the opera by Christoph Willibald Gluck. During the 1950s, she choreographed other operas as well as the ballet for Stravinsky's *Le Sacre du Printemps* in 1957, for the Berlin Municipal Opera. That same year, she received the Great Cross of the Order of Merit (*Grosses Bundesverdienstkreuz*) of the German Federal Republic.

But the end of World War II had left Leipzig under the control of Russian authorities, which Wigman found too restrictive. In 1949, she moved to West Germany, and opened a school in West Berlin. During the 1950s and 1960s, as ballet gained renewed interest in Germany, *Ausdruckstanz* became less popular, while Wigman's style of dance and its association with absolute Teutonic principles came back to haunt her. At a time when German artists in general deliberately moved away from the Expressionist styles formed earlier in the century, she was continually forced to refute claims that she had supported Nazism, and she struggled financially to keep her school alive. Insolvency forced its closure in 1967, and Wigman suffered in her last years from ill health. She died on September 18, 1973, at age 87.

SOURCES:

Manning, Susan A. *Ecstasy and the Demon: Feminism and Nationalism in the Dances of Mary Wigman.* Berkeley, CA: University of California Press, 1993.

Sorell, Walter. *The Mary Wigman Book.* Ed. and trans. by Walter Sorell. Middletown, CT: Wesleyan University Press, 1973.

Wigman, Mary. *The Language of Dance.* Ed. by Walter Sorell. Middletown, CT: Wesleyan University Press, 1966.

SUGGESTED READING:

Jowitt, Deborah. *Time and the Dancing Image.* NY: William Morrow, 1988.

COLLECTIONS:

Correspondence, articles, photographs, and videos located at the Dance Collection, Performing Arts Library, New York Public Library.

RELATED MEDIA:

"Mary Wigman 1886–1973: When the Fire Dances Between Two Poles" (50 min.), documentary by Allegra Fuller Synder and Annette MacDonald, 1991.

Julia L. Foulkes,
University of Massachusetts at Amherst

Wignolle, Yvonne (1894–1977).

See Printemps, Yvonne.

Wijsmuller-Meijer, Truus

(c. 1896–1978)

Dutch rescuer, who saved the lives of thousands of Jews, particularly children, both before and during the Holocaust. Name variations: Gertrude Wijsmuller; Geertruida or Gertruida Wijsmuller-Miejer; Gertruida Wijsmuller-Meijer; Truus Wijsmuller-Meijer; Truus Wysmuller. Born around 1896; died in Amsterdam in 1978.

In the still almost incomprehensible horror that was the Holocaust, 1.5 million Jewish children were killed by Nazi Germany. Hundreds of thousands survived, however, due in part to chance but also as a direct result of the efforts of individuals, both Jewish and non-Jewish, who chose to put their own lives at risk. Many of these women and men remain unknown to history, and only in recent years have their activities been subject to investigation by historians. In the Netherlands, one of the most remarkable of these rescuers was a Christian woman, Truus Wijsmuller-Meijer.

Wijsmuller-Meijer had a comfortable life (her husband was a banker), but after the Kristallnacht pogrom of November 1938 in Nazi Germany, she became a key participant in the Kindertransport system that helped German-Jewish children to safety by finding them temporary and, if at all possible, permanent places of refuge in the Netherlands and the United Kingdom. Within days of Kristallnacht, concerned individuals and organizations in the United Kingdom, both Jewish and non-Jewish, took immediate steps to save as many Jewish children as possible from a Nazi Reich that had recently grown in size and power through its annexation of Austria and the Sudetenland region of Czechoslovakia. On November 21, 1938, the British Parliament approved the entry into the country of 10,000 endangered children. By the time it was terminated with the outbreak of war in early September 1939, the Kindertransport was able to bring out 10,000 endangered children, 90% of them Jewish, from the recently expanded Reich. Ranging in age from infancy to 17, the children were sent alone by their desperate parents and placed with strangers in foster homes and hostels throughout the British Isles. Most of them would never see their parents again.

Convinced that what she was doing was right, from the outset of her involvement working with refugees from Nazism, Truus chose to ignore the powerful domestic currents of opinion on this issue. Many of her fellow countrymen were indifferent to the plight of Jewish refugees, and some sympathized with the goals of the Nazi German dictatorship. Significant numbers of the Dutch elite, including important officials within the government and some members of the royal family (though not Queen *Wilhelmina), believed they could appease Hitler and be "good neighbors" to the new Germany. Even after Kristallnacht, these influential elements of Dutch society condemned what they regarded as "a disorderly arrival of refugees." In a press release issued a week after the anti-Jewish violence, the Dutch government declared that on the question of Jewish refugees from Nazi Germany, its policy was one in which only "an orderly flow is permissible and that to a very limited extent."

Immediately following the creation of the Kindertransport, a situation developed at the German border town of Bentheim during one journey. The customs officers there were not the traditional officials but special SS guards who entered the train coaches. In the words of Norbert Wollheim, one of the German-Jewish leaders on the train, the SS men proceeded to behave "like animals," tearing into the children's luggage, presumably to discover contraband items such as jewels and foreign currency. Hearing about the incident, Truus came to Bentheim and lashed out at the SS crew. To their response of "We are doing our duty," she replied, "You're not doing your duty, you are behaving very badly." After her intervention, the SS vandalism ceased.

In early December 1938, authorized by British Jewish leader Norman Bentwich and Dutch Jewish leader David Cohen, Truus went to Nazi-occupied Vienna on behalf of the Council for German Jewry, a British organization that had gained laurels for its efforts to rescue Jews threatened by Nazi rule. She was to negotiate for the release of as many children as possible for emigration through the Kindertransport program. As she entered the Leopoldstadt, Vienna's traditional Jewish district, immediately after her Saturday arrival, Wijsmuller-Meijer found herself under arrest by the Gestapo. She was accused of being a foreign Jewess (*Jüdin*) with an unspecified agenda and was held for several hours before her release. On Monday, December 5, she found herself in the office of Adolf Eichmann, SS "Jewish expert" and the man in charge of all emigration matters pertaining to Vienna's large Jewish community. At first, Eichmann was skeptical of the validity of her mission, since she lacked authorization papers from the British government. Truus stubbornly held her ground with Eichmann, insisting on her mission's goal of rescuing as many Jewish children as possible. Eventually, Eichmann relented and gave permission for the release of 600 Viennese Jewish children. The children (now reduced to 470) left Vienna on December 10, which happened to be the Jewish Sabbath. Some on the scene regarded this as a final provocation on the part of the Nazis, since for Orthodox Jews travel was prohibited on the Sabbath. On December 11, the children departed safely from the Dutch port of Hoek van Holland on the steamer *Praag*, arriving safely in England some hours later.

Despite the continuing pro-German appeasement policies of the Dutch ruling elites, Nazi Germany launched a massive attack on the Netherlands on May 10, 1940. Within hours, the Blitzkrieg offensive began to break through Dutch defensive lines, and the population's morale plummeted. The Dutch-Jewish community particularly could now only stare at its immediate future with dread. At the time, the Netherlands' Jewish population totaled 140,000, of whom about 15,000 were refugees from the Greater German Reich (in 1939 and the first months of 1940, 34,000 refugees had entered the country, but by early May 1940, more than half of these had fortunately been able to find refuge in the United Kingdom, the United States and a number of other nations). These ex-Reich Jews, regarded by the invading Nazis as being legally stateless, were in even greater peril than the clearly threatened Jews of Dutch nationality.

As of May 10, with German Luftwaffe planes bombing Dutch cities indiscriminately, panic was the dominant mood among the Dutch, and rumors were rife. Among these was one claiming that Dutch Jews had little to worry about from the Nazis, since their government had provided a special ship to carry them to England and safety via the port of Ijmuiden. This baseless rumor was passed on, largely by word of mouth because telephone service had collapsed. In Amsterdam and other Dutch cities, the Special Committee for Jewish Affairs, an organization founded in 1933 to cope with emergencies facing the Jewish community, attempted as best it could to spread the word that the ship (or ships) would speed them to safety from several ports still under Dutch military control. While some Jews took matters into their own hands, making their way under chaotic conditions to coastal towns, including Scheveningen and Ijmuiden, where they hoped to board vessels bound for England, others found themselves overwhelmed by the enormity of events and resigned themselves to fate.

Determined to save as many lives as possible, Wijsmuller-Meijer managed to procure five buses. She then filled them with approximately 200 Jewish refugees from Germany and Austria who had recently been living in the Amsterdam Municipal Orphanage, among them about 80 children. With German troops approaching Amsterdam, and against great odds, she was able reach the port city of Ijmuiden with her precious cargo. Ijmuiden on May 14, 1940, was a scene of almost total confusion. One of the children, 14-year-old Harry Jacobi, would recall years later watching British troops land in the port as part of a desperate effort to bolster crumbling Dutch defenses. Wijsmuller-Meijer then persuaded the captain of the *Bodegraven*, a Dutch freighter set to sail for England, to accept 200 passengers. At 7:50 PM, just before the *Bodegraven* departed the port of Ijmuiden, Truus' Jewish refugees boarded the crowded vessel. Young Jacobi began to realize how truly fortunate he and the others in his group were as the *Bodegraven* steamed out of port: "Far away from the shore we looked back and saw a huge column of black smoke from the oil storage tanks that had been set on fire to prevent the Germans having them. At 9 PM, news came through, picked up by the ship's radio. The Dutch had capitulated." Soon, Jacobi and the other Jewish refugees reached Britain and safety. Their lives had been saved, but many near and dear to them would not be as fortunate. Neither Jacobi's parents, who had been unable to escape from Berlin, nor his grandparents who lived in the Netherlands but could not find space in those crowded motor coaches, would survive the Holocaust.

Some years after the war, Wijsmuller-Meijer would confide to the Dutch Jewish historian Jacob Presser, "If only I could have laid my hands on more cars, I could have saved a good many more people." In fact, she made a decision that gave her the opportunity to save many more lives during the harsh German occupation of her country. In May 1940, in the first days of Nazi

Germany's military victory over the Netherlands, she chose to remain behind to continue her participation in the struggle to save Jewish lives. By doing this, Wijsmuller-Meijer was able to take on a leadership role in the underground network that over the next five years would find ways to smuggle thousands of endangered Jews across Nazi-occupied Europe into neutral Spain and Switzerland. Cherished by the many whose lives she had saved, Truus Wijsmuller-Meijer died in Amsterdam in 1978. Some years before her death, she was honored in Jerusalem by Yad Vashem, the Martyrs' and Heroes' Remembrance Authority of Israel. As she later told Harry Jacobi, the finest hour of her life was the honor of planting a commemorative tree in Yad Vashem's Avenue of the Righteous Gentiles.

SOURCES:

Brinks, Jan Herman. "The Dutch, the Germans, & the Jews," in *History Today*. Vol. 49, no. 6. June 1999, pp. 17–23.

Cohen, David. *Zwervend en dolend: de Joodse vluchtelingen in Nederland in de jaren 1933–1940, met en inleiding over de jaren 1900–1933*. Haarlem: Erven F. Bohn, 1955.

Göpfert, Rebekka. *Ich kam allein: Die Rettung von zehntausend jüdischen Kindern nach England 1938–39*. Munich: Deutscher Taschenbuch, 1994.

———. *Der jüdische Kindertransport von Deutschland nach England 1938–39: Geschichte und Erinnerung*. Frankfurt am Main: Campus, 1999.

Harris, Mark Jonathan, and Deborah Oppenheimer. *Into the Arms of Strangers: Stories of the Kindertransport*. NY: Bloomsbury, 2000.

Jong, Louis de. *Koninkrijk der Nederlanden in de Tweede Wereldoorlog*. Vol. 3. The Hague: Staatsuitgeverij, 1969–1972, pp. 411–412.

Leverton, Bertha, and Shmuel Lowensohn. *I Came Alone: The Stories of the Kindertransports*. Sussex, England: Book Guild, 1990.

"The Little Refugees," in *American Heritage*. Vol. 51, no. 7. November 2000, p. 96.

Lynne, Edward. "Heroine from Holland: The Dutch Woman Who Rescued 10,000 Jewish Children. Condensed from 'Jewish Observer and the Middle East Review,'" in *Jewish Digest*. Vol. 13, no. 3. December 1967, pp. 39–40.

Michman, Dan. "The Committee for Jewish Refugees in Holland (1933–1940)," in Livia Rothkirchen, ed., *Yad Vashem Studies*. Jerusalem: Yad Vashem Martyrs' and Heroes' Remembrance Authority, 1981, Vol. XIV, pp. 205–232.

Moore, Bob. *Refugees from Nazi Germany in The Netherlands 1933–1940*. Dordrecht: Martinus Nijhoff, 1986.

———. *Victims and Survivors: The Nazi Persecution of the Jews in The Netherlands, 1940–1945*. NY: Arnold, 1997.

"Mrs. G. Wijsmuller-Meijer," in *Jewish Chronicle* [London]. No. 5710. September 29, 1978, p. 15.

Presser, Jacob. *Ashes in the Wind: The Destruction of Dutch Jewry*. Trans. by Arnold Ondergang. Detroit, MI: Wayne State University Press, 1988.

"600 Jewish Children Leave Vienna," in *The Times* [London]. December 6, 1938, p. 13.

Tulin, Anna. "She Saved 20,000 Children: An Interview with Truus Wysmuller," in *Hadassah Magazine*. July–August 1951, p. 5.

Wijsmuller-Meijer, Truus, and L.C. Vrooland. *Geen tijd voor tranen* (No Time for Tears). 2nd ed. Amsterdam: Em. Querido's Uitgeverij N.V., opgenomen in de Salamander, 1963.

RELATED MEDIA:

Harris, Mark Jonathan, and Deborah Oppenheimer. *Into the Arms of Strangers: Stories of the Kindertransport* (film), produced by Sabine Films in cooperation with the U.S. Holocaust Memorial Museum, Washington, D.C., released by Warner Bros., 2000.

John Haag,
Associate Professor of History,
University of Georgia, Athens, Georgia

Wilberforce, Octavia (1888–1963)

British physician. Born in 1888 in Lavington, Sussex, England; died in 1963 in Brighton; daughter of Reginald Wilberforce and Anna Wilberforce; great-granddaughter of William Wilberforce (leader of the antislavery movement in England); educated at the London School of Medicine.

A pioneer in the field of women's health, Octavia Wilberforce came from a distinguished family of social activists. Born in 1888 in Lavington, Sussex, England, she was the great-granddaughter of William Wilberforce, leader of Britain's campaign against the slave trade during the late 1700s, and the granddaughter of Samuel Wilberforce, a former bishop of Winchester. Both independent-minded and intelligent, Octavia refused to settle for the roles of wife and mother expected of upper-class British women of her generation. A 1910 meeting with **Louisa Martindale**, a doctor, inspired Wilberforce to consider a career in medicine for herself. Her parents were less than enthusiastic about their daughter's desire to have a career, however, and they refused to finance her education. When the willful Wilberforce again frustrated her parents' efforts to see her settled in the traditional role through an arranged marriage with Charles Buxton, the highly eligible eldest son of Lord Buxton, by voicing her intent to choose a career over marriage, her father grew so frustrated with his daughter that he rewrote his will and disinherited her.

Fueling Wilberforce's desire to break with tradition was another friendship, this one with suffragist *Elizabeth Robins. Robins agreed to help subsidize Wilberforce's education, while the rest of the money for her medical studies came from a surprising source: Lord Buxton, father of the spurned Charles. In 1913, Wilberforce enrolled at the London School of Medicine, and within a year was treating men who had been injured on the battlefields of World War I at St. Mary's Hospital. After the war Wilberforce moved to Dublin for a time before returning to Brighton to enter into private practice. Rekindling her friendships, she joined with Robins and Martindale in their successful efforts to gain public funding for a women's hospital; a short time after the 50-bed New Sussex Hospital for Women opened in the mid-1920s, Wilberforce was appointed head physician. Robins, Martindale, and Wilberforce continued their efforts to improve the region's medical care for women, founding a convalescent home for working women in the country town of Backsettown, near Brighton, that was designed to educate its patients in fitness, diet, coping with stress, and other health practices. Wilberforce retired from her position at New Sussex Hospital in 1954, although she remained an active proponent of women's health at Backsettown until her death in 1963.

Pamela Shelton,
freelance writer,
Avon, Connecticut

Wilcox, Ella Wheeler (1850–1919)

American poet and journalist. Born Ella Wheeler in Johnstown Center, Rock County, near Madison, Wisconsin, on November 5, 1850; died at her home in Short Beach, Connecticut, on October 30, 1919; attended the University of Wisconsin, 1867–68; married Robert Marius Wilcox, in 1884 (died 1916); children: one son, who died at birth.

Ella Wheeler Wilcox

Born in 1850 in Johnstown Center, Wisconsin, Ella Wheeler Wilcox grew up in Windsor and was weaned on the popular novels of *E.D.E.N. Southworth, *Mary Jane Holmes, and Ouida (*Louise de la Ramée). At age nine, she wrote an 11-chapter novel which was bound in kitchen wallpaper; at age 14, she was published. Following her marriage, Wilcox moved to Connecticut, then New York, where she became a successful contributor to magazines and wrote many short essays for the *New York Journal* and the

Chicago American. Though critics refused to take her work seriously, she found a large public for both her prose and poetry. Her populist career was ensured when one Chicago firm refused to publish a collection of her love poems, calling them immoral. The book *Poems of Passion*, by the now-dubbed "Poetess of Passion," sold 60,000 copies in 1883.

Wilcox produced over 20 volumes of verse and contributed a daily poem for newspaper syndication. Along with two autobiographies, *The Story of a Literary Career* (1905) and *The Worlds and I* (1918), her books included a collection of temperance verses entitled *Drops of Water* (1872), *Sweet Danger* (1902), *The Heart of New Thought* (about spiritualism, 1902), and *The Art of Being Alive* (1914). Following her husband's death, Wilcox became involved in the spiritualist movement, intent on contacting him. She had a nervous breakdown in 1919 and died three months later.

Wilcox, Elsie Hart (1879–1954)

First woman to serve in the Territory of Hawaii senate. Born on March 22, 1879, in Hanalei, Kauai, Hawaii; died on June 30, 1954, in Hawaii; daughter of Samuel Whitney Wilcox (a businessman) and Emma Washburn (Lyman) Wilcox; graduated from Wellesley College, 1902.

Active in community service, particularly in the area of public education; chair of International Institute of the YWCA (1919); served on Commission on Public Instruction (1920–32); helped organize first Pan-Pacific Women's Conference (1928); elected to Territorial Senate on Republican ticket (1932–40), served on the judiciary committee and as chair of the health and education committee (1937–39); active in Hawaiian Evangelical Association and other community organizations.

Born in 1879 on the island of Kauai, Hawaii, Elsie Hart Wilcox benefited from both inherited wealth and an inherited social consciousness. She was the granddaughter of Congregationalist missionaries to the Hawaiian islands, and part of a family who owned Grove Farm Plantation, a profitable concern that employed many family members. One of six children, Wilcox grew up in the shadow of her uncle, George N. Wilcox, a respected political figure in the Territory of Hawaii, and her own respect for the importance of education eventually motivated her to enter the political realm herself. After attending private schools because there were no English-language schools on Kauai, Wilcox was sent, like her sister **Mabel Wilcox**, to Wellesley College in New England for her advanced education. She returned to Grove Farm in 1902 after earning her college degree and remained there for the rest of her life.

Beginning in 1920, Wilcox served on Hawaii's Commission of Public Instruction, which set policy for public schools throughout the entire territory. Confronting problems relating both to inadequately trained teachers and to language difficulties resulting from the preponderance of Asian-born children within the territory's public school system, Wilcox was instrumental in increasing funding for "Americanization" programs and other educational activities, while also actively involving herself in public school activities. Her recognition of the political tensions of the early 20th century prompted Wilcox's involvement in several peace organizations. Through her affiliation with the Pan-Pacific Women's Union, she helped set up the first Pan-Pacific Women's Conference which in 1928 boasted *Jane Addams of Chicago's Hull House fame as chair and drew a gathering of over 300 delegates from around the world.

In addition to her public service, Wilcox was a lifelong volunteer at the Lihue Union Church, training novice Sunday school teachers and holding a number of church offices. She also extended her efforts to the Hawaiian Evangelical Association which coordinated the Territory's Congregational churches, and she actively supported ongoing missionary work in Asia. Wilcox's interest in the education of children spilled over from her professional life into her volunteer efforts with both the YMCA and YWCA programs on Kauai, where she taught summer-camp classes in astronomy and brought her expertise in areas of finance and public works to bear on budget matters and building expansions. Travel around the world also occupied much of her adult life; a tour to Europe shortly before World War I was augmented by several trips to Asia in the company of her uncle George and sister Mabel.

The high point of Wilcox's life of public service came with her election to the Territorial senate in 1932. In addition to serving on several important committees, she was elected vice-president of the senate in 1935 and continued to push for improved conditions in Hawaii's public schools. Among her goals was the reduction or elimination of the yearly ten dollar fee required to register a child for public school, a charge that made it impossible for many less affluent families to provide their children with a proper education. Serving in the senate for several terms, Wilcox was finally defeated in the 1940 election after several defections from the Republican Party eroded her base of political support. Despite her departure from public life, she remained active in the community around Grove Farm Plantation until her death in 1954.

SOURCES:
Peterson, Barbara Bennett, ed. *Notable Women of Hawaii.* Honolulu, HI: University of Hawaii Press, 1984.

Pamela Shelton,
freelance writer,
Avon, Connecticut

Wilde, Florence M. (1836–1914).

See Leslie, Miriam Folline Squier.

Wilde, Jane (1821–1896)

*Irish nationalist writer who was the mother of Oscar Wilde. Name variations: Jane Francesca Elgee; Lady Anna Francesca Wilde; Lady Jane Wilde; (pseudonyms) John Fanshawe Ellis, Albanus or A, and Speranza. Born Jane Francesca Elgee, probably on December 27, 1821 (place of birth unknown); died in London, England, on February 3, 1896; youngest child of Charles Elgee and Sarah (Kingsbury) Elgee; educated at home; married William Wilde (an ophthalmic surgeon), on November 12, 1851; children: William (Willie) Wilde (b. 1852, who was once married to *Miriam Leslie); Oscar Wilde (1854–1900, the writer); Isola Wilde (b. 1857).*

Selected writings: (translator) Sidonia the Sorceress (Reeves & Turner, 1849); Ancient Legends, Mystic Charms and Superstitions of Ireland (Ward & Downey, 1887); Notes on Men, Women and Books (Ward & Downey, 1891); Social Studies (Ward & Downey, 1893); Poems (M.H. Gill, 3rd ed., 1907).

In her later years Jane Wilde dismissed inquiries about her birth and birthplace as an impertinence. She sometimes admitted that she had been born in 1826, but when applying in 1888 for a grant from the Royal Literary Fund, she stated that her date of birth was December 27, 1821. This fits in with the information available about her family background. Her father Charles Elgee was a lawyer who died in 1824. Her mother **Sarah Kingsbury Elgee** came from a well-connected Dublin family prominent in business and politics. Sarah's sister **Henrietta Kingsbury** married the writer Charles Maturin. Jane was educated at home by tutors and governesses and was well read in the classics, a love she passed on to her younger son Oscar Wilde. She was also fluent in French and German and later translated books from Russian, Norwegian and Spanish.

Wilde's family was hostile to Irish nationalism, and she was initially uninterested in the social and political conditions existing in Ireland. This changed in the early 1840s when she read issues of the new journal *The Nation*, founded by a group of young nationalists who called themselves Young Ireland: "I read it eagerly and my patriotism was kindled." Her first poetry was published in *The Nation* in February 1846, and this and subsequent items were published under pseudonyms—John Fanshawe Ellis, Albanus or A—before she finally settled on the pen name which made her famous, Speranza. Most of her best-known poems were written between 1846 and 1848; these included "The Lament," "The Stricken Land," "The Exodus," and "The Brothers." As some of the titles indicate, they reflected the state of the country which was in the grip of the Great Famine. In 1848, the Young Irelanders were planning to stage a rebellion. In the July 29th issue of *The Nation*, Wilde wrote a famous headline "Alea Jacta Est" (The Die is Cast) which led to the government authorities seizing the issue, closing the paper, and arresting *The Nation*'s editor, Charles Gavan Duffy. When Duffy was brought to trial, Wilde stood up in court and announced that she was the author of "Alea Jacta Est," not Duffy, as was being alleged. After several trials and retrials, Duffy was finally released in 1849. These were the first of the dramatic trials which were to disrupt Jane Wilde's life.

In 1851, she married William Wilde, an eminent ophthalmic surgeon in Dublin who was also a distinguished antiquarian. At the time of the marriage, William had three illegitimate children but neither then nor in the future was Jane particularly troubled by her husband's infidelities. She regarded jealousy as vulgar and unworthy. Wilde admired and respected her husband although she found his sporadic depressions difficult to cope with. Her biographer **Joy Melville** has noted her ambivalent attitude to marriage: half feminist, half deferential. Her first son Willie was born in 1852, followed by Oscar in 1854 and her only daughter **Isola Wilde** in 1857. Jane adored her children and did not banish them to the nursery as was then the custom. Rather, she read poetry and stories to them, and when they were older they were present at her salons.

Although her family took up more of her time, she continued to write. In 1849, she had translated Meinhold's *Sidonia the Sorceress* which greatly influenced the pre-Raphaelites and was one of Oscar's favorite stories. The book features a double portrait, not unlike that in *The Picture of Dorian Gray*. She also wrote regularly for the *Dublin University Magazine*. Shortly after her marriage, she had become acquainted with **Lotten von Krämer** who was a leading campaigner for women's rights in Sweden where she had endowed a scholarship for women at Uppsala University. Through Krämer she met another leading Swedish feminist, **Rosalie Olivecrona**. These friends became extremely important to Jane, and her correspondence with them lasted for 25 years. She visited Sweden a number of times and also taught herself Swedish.

In December 1864, Jane was sued for libel by **Mary Travers** who alleged that she had been raped by William Wilde in 1862. Travers was mentally unstable, but it was clear that she had had a sexual relationship with William at some point. She began a campaign of public humiliation against William and his family, circulating leaflets around Dublin, and even pursuing Jane and the children when they went on holiday. The trial was a sensational event. It could possibly have been settled out of court but, as she was to urge Oscar to do in 1895, Jane was determined to fight the case. When she took the witness stand, she refused to play the role of the wronged wife although it might have helped her case more if she had. Travers won nominal damages of a farthing but the costs were awarded against the Wildes. William Wilde's health was never the same after the trial, and in 1867 Isola's sudden death devastated the family.

Towards the end of the 1860s, Jane began to hold soirées or *conversazioni* at her house in Merrion Square which soon became the most celebrated salon in Dublin. It attracted writers, journalists, lawyers, artists, dramatists and students, the latter being friends of Willie and Oscar who were studying at Trinity College, Dublin. But the family's fortunes changed after William Wilde's death in April 1876. Most of his estate was swallowed up in debts and the rest of the family property was heavily mortgaged. Financial problems dogged Jane for the rest of her life. In 1879, with Willie and Oscar both in London, she decided to move there and establish a new salon. She was to find, however, that she was much less well known in London and that her eccentricities, accepted in Dublin, were frowned upon.

Jane lived with her eldest son Willie who was pursuing a journalistic career. But he was feckless and sponged on his mother, to Oscar's great annoyance. Willie, like Oscar, was devoted to his mother, but his demands on her caused increasing friction between the brothers which Jane did her best to smooth over. As Oscar's writing prospered, he helped Jane financially and also secured writing commissions for her when he could.

When Oscar married **Constance Lloyd (Wilde)** in 1884, she and Jane developed a close relationship. It is uncertain whether Jane ever understood Oscar's sexuality, but in 1895, when he was charged with homosexual offenses, she urged him not to flee the country, as many of his friends were advising, but to stay and fight, as she had fought with Mary Travers. Oscar's conviction was a terrible blow, but even from prison he made sure that Jane had enough money from a fund set up by his friends. In 1896, however, Wilde came down with a debilitating attack of bronchitis, and, despite pleas to the prison authorities, Oscar was not allowed to see her. It was Constance who brought him the news of his mother's death that February. In *De Profundis*, which he wrote in prison, Oscar referred to the name "noble and honoured" which his parents had bequeathed to him but to which he had brought dishonor. Constance died in 1898, followed by Willie a year later, and then Oscar in 1900.

SOURCES:

Coakley, Davis. *Oscar Wilde: The Importance of Being Irish*. Dublin: Town House, 1994.

Melville, Joy. *Mother of Oscar: The Life of Jane Francesca Wilde*. London: John Murray, 1994.

Wyndham, Horace. *Speranza: A Biography of Lady Wilde*. London: T.V. Boardman, 1951.

Deirdre McMahon,
lecturer in history at Mary Immaculate College,
University of Limerick, Limerick, Ireland

Wilder, Laura Ingalls (1867–1957)

American author of the "Little House" books, a series of award-winning children's novels based on her own late 19th-century frontier childhood. Name variations: Bess or Bessie. Born Laura Elizabeth Ingalls on February 7, 1867, in Pepin, Wisconsin; died at Rocky Ridge Farm in Mansfield, Missouri, on February 10, 1957; daughter of Charles Philip Ingalls (a frontiersman, farmer, and carpenter) and Caroline Quiner Ingalls (a teacher); attended public schools until just short of high school graduation; married Almanzo James Wilder (a farmer), in 1885; children: Rose Wilder Lane (1886–1968, a writer); and one son who died shortly after birth.

Awards: six Newbery Honor Awards; first recipient (1954) of Laura Ingalls Wilder Award created by the American Library Association; many children's and public libraries named after her.

Traveled with her family from one place to another in search of a potentially profitable farm (1868–79); family ultimately settled in De Smet, (South) Dakota, where she met and married Almanzo Wilder with whom she moved (1894) to a farm outside Mansfield, Missouri, in the Ozarks where she lived until her death; wrote for The Missouri Ruralist (1911–24); served as secretary-treasurer of Mansfield Farm Loan Association (1919–27); from a 1930 autobiographical manuscript, "Pioneer Girl," elaborated the stories that would become the seven "Little House" books published in her lifetime; also wrote a book about the childhood of Almanzo Wilder.

Selected writings: Little House in the Big Woods *(1932);* Farmer Boy *(1933);* Little House on the Prairie *(1935);* On the Banks of Plum Creek *(1937);* By the Shores of Silver Lake *(1939);* The Long Winter *(1940);* Little Town on the Prairie *(1941);* These Happy Golden Years *(1943); (with Rose Wilder Lane)* On the Way Home: The Diary of a Trip from South Dakota to Mansfield, Missouri in 1894 *(1962);* The First Four Years *(1971);* West From Home: Letters of Laura Ingalls Wilder to Almanzo Wilder—San Francisco 1915 *(1974).*

Laura Ingalls Wilder's autobiographical children's novels, known as the "Little House" books, first began appearing in print in the early 1930s, but the series remains embedded in American life and is important to people all over the

Laura Ingalls Wilder

world. Tens of thousands of American school-children use the books in their classrooms to learn about pioneer life, or read and reread the books on their own. During the summer, countless tourists from the United States and other countries make pilgrimages to the sites of the homes where Laura Ingalls Wilder once lived. A manufacturer of collectible dolls, advertising in a national Sunday newspaper supplement, introduced the "Laura" doll as the first in a collection inspired by the books. Early in his presidency, Ronald Reagan indicated that the program based on the "Little House" books was his favorite television show. A well-known Japanese writer and director of television and film fled the materialism of Tokyo, taking with him five "Little House" books as his guides to a back-to-nature philosophy. A wire service report suggesting that Laura Ingalls Wilder's daughter, *Rose Wilder Lane, essentially was the ghostwriter of the books, provoked articles and columns in newspapers across the country and appeared as far away as the *South China Morning Post*.

I realized that I had seen and lived . . . all the successive phases of the frontier. . . . I wanted the children now to understand more about the beginnings of things . . . what it is that made America as they know it.

—Laura Ingalls Wilder

The life which formed the basis of these beloved books has come to be seen as especially expressive of the American pioneer experience. Yet that life was more complex than suggested by the widely known version of Wilder as a 65-year-old farm woman who sat down with a pencil and school tablet to tell with instinctive artistry the compelling story of her courageous 19th-century pioneer family. In fact, Wilder had been a columnist for a Missouri farm periodical for years, and in the chronicling of her childhood she had the active collaboration of her writer daughter, Rose Wilder Lane. Furthermore, the meaning of the pioneer life they related remains ambiguous: does one marvel at the Ingalls family's persistence or dwell on the reasons for their defeats?

Laura Ingalls was born in 1867 on a farm in Pepin, Wisconsin, not far from the Mississippi River. Both her mother's and father's families had migrated in stages from the East in search of fertile farmland. The goal of her parents, Charles and **Caroline Ingalls**, like that of most of the members of their families and of many other Americans at that time, was to establish themselves on affordable, fertile, easy-to-cultivate land so as to make a dependable living as farmers. During Laura's childhood, however, her parents ran afoul of virtually every setback experienced by those who sought to make their living from the land.

Their departure from Wisconsin in 1868 started the Ingalls family on an 11-year migration, zigzagging back and forth across the Midwest and the Great Plains in search of a piece of land that would grant them a living. It was from these efforts that the adult Laura would create the famous saga of her childhood. Their journeys took them to the treeless, open prairies of Montgomery County, Kansas, for almost three years (1868–71), then back to Pepin, Wisconsin, for about the same length of time (1871–74) before they headed across the Mississippi River once again for the prairies of western Minnesota. Their five-year stay (1874–79) in Walnut Grove, Minnesota, was broken in the middle by a year (1876–77) spent helping to run a hotel in Burr Grove, Iowa, and was further divided by an initial wheat farming venture (1874–76) and a later period (1877–79) of living and working in town.

Laura might have grown up in Walnut Grove were it not for the extension of the railroad into Dakota Territory and the availability of free land there under the terms of the 1862 Homestead Act. Through family contacts, Charles Ingalls obtained a white-collar job working for the railroad as it inched its way west. This job enabled him to pay off the debts accumulated during the difficult 1870s and to be in position to stake a homestead claim on Dakota land. At Caroline Ingalls' insistence, their homestead near De Smet, in what would become South Dakota in 1889, was as far west as the family, now including four daughters, ventured. It was in De Smet that Laura Ingalls grew to adulthood and married another homesteader, Almanzo ("Manly") Wilder.

Wilder's account of her childhood in the "Little House" books is wonderfully specific in its details of domestic and farm skills. It is a superb, if discreet, record of the socialization of a 19th-century roughneck into a young woman and capable partner for a farmer husband. Her depiction of the close, warm Ingalls family life is compelling, although sentimentalized. Her chronicle of the disasters faced by her family reflects the experiences of many other settlers as well: danger from panthers, bears, and wolves; frustration over government Indian policy and homesteading provisions; crop-destroying grasshoppers, blackbirds, and drought; prairie fires and endless blizzards.

There are other ways in which the books do not accurately reflect the Ingallses' experiences;

Wilder altered the chronology of events somewhat, accentuated the family's isolation, and deemphasized their dependence on wage work and their indebtedness for many of the years she chronicles. In her desire to portray the essential westward, pioneering movement of the family, she ignored the number of times they "backtrailed" (returned east), even to places they had once abandoned. Writing of her family's experiences 50 years after they occurred, Wilder stressed their hard work, persistence, ingenuity, and satisfaction in the face of all these challenges and downplayed the marginality of their existence on each farm, determinedly giving their lives as pioneers an optimistic tone. The original series of books, however, carries the family no further than Laura's marriage in 1885, two years before her parents abandoned for good their efforts to farm and moved to town.

Her husband Manly's prospects seemed better than her father's because he had more land and equipment and fewer people for whom he was responsible. Nonetheless, if Laura (whom Manly called Bessie) thought that in marriage she was escaping the chronic financial woes of her own family, she was wrong; Manly and Laura also failed at farming in De Smet, done in by personal tragedies and by hailstorms that destroyed their wheat, by drought that seemed to be the norm in South Dakota, and by the destruction of their farmhouse by fire.

These bleak happenings are all recounted in *The First Four Years*, a manuscript never published in Laura's lifetime. Even that book, however, ends on a note of optimism, although in reality the Wilders gave up on wheat farming on homestead land in South Dakota. In 1890, Laura, Manly, and their three-and-a-half-year-old daughter Rose began their own period of backtrailing, spending two years away, first in Minnesota and then in Florida. By August 1892, they had returned to De Smet to do wage work, saving money and pondering what to do next and where.

Eventually, the Wilders decided to go to the Ozark Mountains in southern Missouri, where the climate would be healthier and the land relatively cheap. They headed for the small town of

From the television series "Little House on the Prairie," starring Michael Landon and Melissa Gilbert as Laura.

Mansfield where they put a down payment on a farm—which they aptly named Rocky Ridge—that with years of hard labor would support orchards, livestock and poultry, and grain growing. In some respects, their experience was a reprise of Laura's childhood: starting from scratch with a farm that had to be cleared of stones and trees, enduring years of interminable physical labor, and moving into town for long periods to earn needed cash to develop the farm. The chronic anxiety about finances that had been a motif in her childhood and in her early married life followed her to Mansfield, where they arrived poor and without status and remained so for years.

Eventually, Wilder's accomplishments as a poultry raiser (a common task for farm wives) made her known throughout the Ozarks and attracted the attention of the editor of *The Missouri Ruralist* who asked her to submit articles for the farm weekly. Her first article, appearing in 1911, was soon followed by a wide range of writings for the periodical, and ultimately by her own column. She also sold occasional articles on farm life to regional newspapers. Such writing made only a small contribution to the finances of Rocky Ridge Farm which never provided the Wilders with the financial security that Laura especially craved. Even her paid job from 1919 to 1927 as secretary-treasurer of the Mansfield Farm Loan Association did not suffice to supplement inadequate income from their farm.

Fortunately for Wilder, her daughter Rose Wilder Lane, who had early left home to follow a variety of jobs all over the country, moved into journalism in 1915, becoming a very proficient and well-known writer who branched into fiction as well. Lane urged her mother to target broader markets for her writing so as to increase her earnings. From the 1910s, she helped Wilder with her writing and with ideas for articles. With Lane's editorial help and contacts, Wilder published three articles in national magazines by the mid-1920s. However, it was not until Lane had returned from several extended periods of living overseas and was ensconced for an eight-year interval at Rocky Ridge Farm, and the Wilders had retired from active farming, that Laura sat down in 1930 to write her autobiography.

Although Lane edited and typed "Pioneer Girl" for her mother, and sent it to her own literary agent, there were no takers for the first-person, adult-level narrative. However, a portion of the manuscript, dealing with the Wisconsin years, that Lane had separated out, conceiving of it as a children's book and titling it "When Grandma Was a Little Girl," did attract the interest of an editor who wished to see it expanded to 25,000 words. Wilder's task was to elaborate upon the original terse narrative, adding plenty of authentic detail about pioneer life. Lane's active role in conceptualizing and polishing the book that would be published in 1932 as *Little House in the Big Woods* exemplified her involvement with the series as a whole.

Wilder's special gifts were the creation of evocative word pictures and the telling of stories, skills probably enhanced by the five years when she served as her blind sister **Mary Ingalls**' eyes on the world and by an entire childhood spent listening to her father's storytelling. It took her a long time to realize that these talents did not result automatically in polished compositions. Lane's crucial role in seeing the overall theme of each book and making each chapter fit that theme caused considerable tension between mother and daughter as they worked on the books together throughout the 1930s and into the early 1940s when the eighth book was published.

Even before the first book was in print, Wilder began planning at least two more. The success, both popular and critical, of *Little House in the Big Woods* assured that she would carry on her project. Eventually readers' enthusiasm induced her to plan a whole series of novels covering her entire childhood.

As Lane worked with her on the stories, juggling her own writing with time spent on her mother's manuscripts, the two women began to believe that their family's experiences had political significance. As they recalled the struggles endured by the Ingallses and later by the Wilders, they became incensed by government farm-relief programs that implied that individuals could not cope with setbacks on their own. A lifelong Democrat, Wilder, like Lane, came to oppose Franklin Roosevelt adamantly and to see the "Little House" books as a rebuttal to the New Deal.

Whatever their underlying political convictions, the two women's collaboration produced compelling stories that created devoted fans who increased in numbers as each of the original eight novels appeared. The books about pioneering and farm life provided Wilder with the economic security that decades of actual farming had never accomplished; her fame assured her of a place of honor both in Mansfield and throughout the country. Her mailbox was constantly filled with letters from schoolchildren and librarians, and increasingly children's rooms or entire libraries were named in her honor. Although none of her books became Newbery Prize winners, only runners-up, she was the first recipient of the American Library Association's Laura Ingalls Wilder Award, given every five years to an author for a lifetime's contribution to children's literature. Even her death at 90 at home in Mansfield did not end her readers' fascination with the Laura of the "Little House" books. Given the tens of millions of her books that have been sold in numerous languages, Wilder's influence in perpetuating a specific version of American pioneer life cannot be underestimated.

SOURCES:

Anderson, William. *Laura Ingalls Wilder: A Biography.* NY: HarperCollins, 1992.

Fellman, Anita Clair. "'Don't Expect to Depend on Anybody Else': The Frontier as Portrayed in the Little House Books," in *Children's Literature.* Vol. 24, 1996.

Holtz, William. *The Ghost in the Little House: A Life of Rose Wilder Lane.* Columbia, MO: University of Missouri Press, 1993.

Miller, John E. *Laura Ingalls Wilder's Little Town: Where History and Literature Meet.* Lawrence, KN: University Press of Kansas, 1994.

SUGGESTED READING:

Anderson, William. *A Little House Sampler.* NY: Perennial Library, Harper & Row, 1989.

———. "The Literary Apprenticeship of Laura Ingalls Wilder," in *South Dakota History.* Vol. 13, no. 4. Winter 1983, pp. 285–331.

———. "Laura Ingalls Wilder and Rose Wilder Lane: The Continuing Collaboration," in *South Dakota History.* Vol. 16, no. 2. Summer 1986, pp. 89–143.

Fellman, Anita Clair. "Laura Ingalls Wilder and Rose Wilder Lane: The Politics of a Mother-Daughter Relationship," in *Signs: Journal of Women in Culture and Society.* Vol. 15, no. 3. Spring 1990, pp. 535–561.

Hackett, Christine Olivieri. *Little House in the Classroom: A Guide to Using the Laura Ingalls Wilder Books.* Carthage, IL: Good Apple, 1989.

COLLECTIONS:

Correspondence, papers, manuscripts, and memorabilia located in the Herbert Hoover Presidential Library in West Branch, Iowa; the Laura Ingalls Wilder Home Association in Mansfield, Missouri; and the Laura Ingalls Wilder Memorial Society in De Smet, South Dakota.

RELATED MEDIA:

"Little House on the Prairie," weekly television series based on the books, starring Michael Landon and **Melissa Gilbert**, NBC, 1974–82.

Anita Clair Fellman,
Director of Women's Studies and Associate Professor of History,
Old Dominion University, Norfolk, Virginia

Wilding, Dorothy (1893–1976)

British photographer. Born in 1893 in Longford, England; died in 1976 in England; self-educated; married Walter Portham, in 1920 (divorced 1932); married Thomas "Rufus" Leighton-Pearce (a designer and architect), in 1932 (died 1940).

Began to specialize in theatrical portrait photography in her London studio (1914); expanded her operation to seven studios within greater London; photographed members of the royal family (1937); was admitted to the Royal Photographic Society of Great Britain (1930); opened studio in New York City (1937); photographed coronation of Queen Elizabeth II (1953); retired (1957).

Dorothy Wilding was born in 1893 in Longford, England, the youngest of a long succession of Wilding children. She was uprooted at the age of four when she was sent by her harried parents to live with a childless aunt and uncle in Cheltenham, where, as Wilding would later note, she "was more or less taking the place of a pet dog." It was perhaps this early sense of being cut loose from security that made Wilding determined to be a success on her own terms, independent of her family, and in a way that would use her creativity. Fame of some sort became her goal, and the purchase of a camera in 1909 provided the then-16-year-old Wilding with the means of achieving that fame.

After three years teaching herself photographic methods, Wilding moved to London and found employment as a photo retoucher for Ernest Chandler. A term working alongside American portrait photographer Marion Neilson provided Wilding with the studio experience that would prove so invaluable when she embarked upon her own career as a portraitist, spending £60 in savings to open her first studio in London's West End, in 1914. Stashing her personal belongings behind a light green curtain at one end of the long room, Wilding set about building a clientele, fueled by her optimism and the sophisticated and innovative style that characterized both her personal and professional life.

Other studios soon followed, as Wilding quickly found herself in demand as a portraitist, particularly among young actresses expanding their portfolios. Many of her sitters were aggressive young women, self-made like Wilding herself, and against the white backdrop in Wilding's studio they were transformed into elegant, modern women of the world, their angular beauty emphasized by the stark setting and richly draped evening gowns they wore. Wilding's work also found its way into magazines such as *Sketch* and *Tatler*, and she was hired to do advertising photographs. Married in 1920 to Walter Portham, she moved her main studio to a set of rooms on Bond Street, long considered the

*L*ee
*W*iley

that decade being the coronation photographs of Queen *Elizabeth II.

SOURCES:

Rosenblum, Naomi. *A History of Women Photographers.* NY: Abbeville, 1994.

Williams, Val. *The Other Observers.* London, England: Virago, 1986.

Pamela Shelton,
freelance writer,
Avon, Connecticut

Wiley, Lee (1915–1975)

American vocalist. Born on October 9, 1915, in Fort Gibson, Oklahoma; died on December 11, 1975; married Jess Stacy (a pianist), in 1944 (divorced); married Nat Tischenkel (a businessman), in 1966.

Was featured vocalist on radio show "Kraft Music Hall" (1933–35); hired as dramatic actress on radio dramas; recorded a series of albums with noted jazz performers that showcased the works of modern composers (c. 1937–40); performed with Eddie Condon's orchestra for broadcast over the Armed Services Radio Network (c. 1939–45); toured with Jess Stacy Orchestra (1944–46).

Lee Wiley was born in 1915 in Fort Gibson, Oklahoma. Part Cherokee, she was an impulsive young woman, a talented singer with a disdain for the status quo and the ways of big business that would factor greatly in her career as a vocalist. At age 15, having been inspired by the recordings of *Ethel Waters, Wiley ran away from home and went to St. Louis, then to Chicago, in search of fame. A gig at a small Chicago nightclub found her sharing the stage with Victor Young, a young bandleader and composer who took Wiley under his wing and with whom Wiley, in turn, would fall in love. The pair eventually moved to New York City, where the demand for female vocalists was at a high point. Wiley found little difficulty in locating a job, even making several recordings with Leo Reisman's band. Her singing career was interrupted in 1931 when a fall from her horse temporarily blinded her. However, her sight was restored within a year, and she was soon appearing frequently on New York's nightclub stages.

In addition to her club work, Wiley was hired to sing on radio's "Pond's Cold Cream Hour" in 1933, and was soon approached by NBC radio to sign on as featured singer on the top-rated "Kraft Music Hall" radio show, which she accepted. By 1934, Wiley ranked just below *Kate Smith and Bing Crosby in national exposure to radio audiences, but the accompanying fame began to take a toll. Leading an active night

fashionable section of London, where she began to be visited by individuals who included screen actors Douglas Fairbanks, Jr., *Pola Negri, and *Tallulah Bankhead. A divorce from Portham in 1932 left her free to marry again, this time to interior decorator, architect, and painter Thomas "Rufus" Leighton-Pearce, who designed the modern interior of several of her studios. They would remain together until his death in 1940.

A talented visualist and an enterprising businesswoman, Wilding was soon grouped among England's most well-known photographers. Made a fellow of the Royal Photographic Society of Great Britain in 1930, she was honored with a solo exhibition at the society that same year. These accomplishments brought her to the attention of Great Britain's royal family, who commissioned Wilding to create portraits of King George VI and Queen *Elizabeth Bowes-Lyon in 1937. By the late 1930s, Wilding's renown had crossed the Atlantic, and she was encouraged to open a studio in New York City as well. She continued to work through 1957, with her major work of life, she began to drink heavily and gave up many of the local jobs that had fueled her success in New York City. Then, after two years on the "Music Hall" program, Wiley became frustrated that Young, who conducted the top-billed Paul Whiteman Orchestra during Wiley's performances, was not allowed on-air credit for his work. When she threatened not to renew her contract with NBC unless Young received public acknowledgment, the radio giant balked, and both she and Young were left without a job. Shortly thereafter, Wiley was diagnosed with tuberculosis and was forced to retire to Arizona to recover. Young moved on to California, where he built a successful career as a composer of film scores.

Upon Wiley's return to New York City in 1936, she performed regularly with Bunny Berigan on "Saturday Night Swing Club." Leaving that show in 1937, she spent the remainder of her career singing in nightclubs, guesting on local radio shows, and making recordings, expanding her predominantly swing-music repertoire to include jazz. Throughout the 1940s and 1950s, she was considered by many to be one of the most talented and underappreciated vocalists in the United States. Her singing style, which incorporated her naturally sultry alto voice with its Oklahoma accent, reflected her disdain for vocal gimmickry—flashy endings, excessive vibrato, and other flourishes—in favor of a simple rendition. A chic, attractive woman, she rubbed shoulders with everyone in the New York music world of her era, from the smartly decked-out club owners to the bohemians who frequented the city's lower-class bars. Working with such sidemen as Eddie Condon, Fats Waller, Pee Wee Russell, and Bud Freeman, she made a groundbreaking series of recordings that were the first to spotlight the works of individual composers like George Gershwin, Cole Porter, Rodgers and Hart, and Harold Arlen. Wiley's approach, which was orchestrated by a record buff named John DeVries as a way to promote her rich voice, would be mirrored by *Ella Fitzgerald and others in later years.

During World War II, Wiley performed with Eddie Condon and his band in weekly concerts that were aired for U.S. troops fighting overseas. At war's end, the 29-year-old vocalist married jazz pianist and bandleader Jess Stacy, and toured with his group around the country as lead singer. However, months on the road did not agree with Wiley, who enjoyed the fast-paced life of the city. She returned to her career in New York, finally remarrying a retired businessman in 1966, shortly before her retirement from the stage. Playing by her own rules, despite the repercussions of her refusal to bend to the wishes of others, Wiley remained true to her musical dictum "keep it simple." She died in December 1975, at the age of 60.

SOURCES:

Hemming, Roy, and David Hajdu. *Discovering Great Singers of Classic Pop.* NY: Newmarket, 1991.

Pamela Shelton, freelance writer, Avon, Connecticut

Wilhelmi, Jane Russell (1911–1967).

See Russell, Jane Anne.

Wilhelmina (1709–1758)

*Margravine of Bayreuth. Name variations: Friederike Sophie Wilhelmine. Born Frederica Sophia Wilhelmina in 1709; died in 1758; daughter of *Sophia Dorothea of Brunswick-Lüneburg-Hanover (1687–1757) and Frederick William I (1688–1740), king of Prussia (r. 1713–1740); sister of Frederick II the Great (1712–1786), king of Prussia; married Frederick, margrave of Bayreuth.*

Throughout both his childhood and adult life, Frederick II the Great maintained his closest relationship with his sister Wilhelmina. Corresponding regularly, they discussed literature, philosophy, affairs of state, and anything else of a public or private nature. It was she who provided solace during the darkest days of his relationship with their father.

Wilhelmina (1880–1962)

Queen of the Netherlands who, during her long reign, won the respect of her people for her intelligence and strength of character and became the living symbol of her country during its occupation in World War II. Pronunciation: Will-hell-MEE-nah. Born Wilhelmina Helen Pauline Mary in The Hague, the Netherlands, on August 31, 1880; died at Het Loo, in Apeldoorn, Gelderland, on November 28, 1962; daughter of William III (1817–1890), king of the Netherlands (r. 1849–1890) and grand duke of Luxemburg, and his second wife, Emma of Waldeck (1858–1934); married Henry (or Heinrich) Wladimir Albert Ernst, duke of Mecklenburg-Schwerin, on February 7, 1901; children: Juliana (b. April 30, 1909), queen of the Netherlands (r. 1948–1980).

Crowned at Amsterdam (September 6, 1898); fled to Britain (1940–41); encouraged Dutch resistance through radio broadcasts (1941–45); returned to the Netherlands (1945); abdicated in favor of her daughter, assuming the title Princess of the Netherlands (September 4, 1948).

Queen Wilhelmina of the Netherlands came to symbolize both her nation's hopes for peace and fierce love of freedom during the turbulent years of the first half of the 20th century. Throughout two world wars, a German occupation of her country, and the decline and fall of her nation's colonial empire, this deeply religious woman insisted that decency and morality should govern diplomacy between nations. One of the first world leaders to condemn Nazi treatment of European Jews, she argued that "this inhuman treatment is something being done to us personally."

Born in 1880, Wilhelmina spent a happy childhood at the castle of Het Loo near Apeldoorn in Gelderland. She received much parental attention, daily hours of play with her father William III, king of the Netherlands, and outings with her mother ◄❧ Emma of Waldeck, such as sleigh rides where they wore identical fur coats. Fond of horses, the young princess learned to drive Shetland ponies and later horses four-in-hand, activities she complemented with riding and skating lessons. The royal family divided their time between The Hague, where they spent the first four months of the year, Amsterdam, and Het Loo. Wilhelmina considered Het Loo her real home, and for the first seven years of her life she led an enchanted existence there.

Then her father fell ill shortly before his 70th birthday on February 9, 1887. At his death on November 23, 1890, Wilhelmina became queen of the Netherlands under the regency of her mother, who was sworn in by the Council of State. The ten-year-old Wilhelmina had been in training for her future task for the past five years. She had started English lessons at five, taught by a Miss Winter who aimed to train her character as well as her tongue. She wanted to make the little girl a "bold and noble woman, unflinching and strong," and Wilhelmina rewarded her by taking pride in her destiny. Her royal parents valued a good education, so French, arithmetic, and Dutch history lessons were started early on. After her father's death, Wilhelmina expanded her education further by trips abroad with her mother and tutor, while visits of state both at home and abroad informed her manners and trained her in the art of conversation. Vacations at home offered walks and the enjoyment of nature which she experienced keenly, especially the beauty of wildflowers. She took drawing lessons which centered on her rendition of those flowers and ultimately became skilled enough to venture an exhibition.

German, science, world history, geography and art history were gradually included in her regimen. Among those, she would find the teachings of science troublesome. Her spirit had taken a religious turn during her father's illness which did not square with the proposition that forces other than God had created the world. This devastating possibility was presented during a lesson in cosmography, and it left her mind in confusion and her soul in darkness. She struggled with what she perceived to be an irreconcilable dichotomy and resolved never to doubt God's authority again. "This never-again," she would later avow, "has been my life belt through trial and affliction and many difficult circumstances." Ever after, she would give precedence to the heart and soul and accord intelligence second place.

Following her confirmation in October 1892, she entered her adult life which, in addition to her studies, meant afternoon and evening receptions, state balls, dinners and concerts. She accompanied her mother to the openings of the States-General and attended conferences and audiences with her. Coming of age in August 1898, she was enthroned in Amsterdam's Nieuwe Kerk on September 6, well-enough prepared for her future task to write her own installation speech. A respectful daughter, she borrowed its key note from her father: "The House of Orange can never do enough for the Netherlands," and her first signatures were put to decrees honoring her mother's excellent work during her years as regent. She awarded Emma the Grand Cross of the Lion of the Netherlands and the Grand Cross of the Order of Orange-Nassau.

In the summer of 1900, Wilhelmina met Duke Henry of Mecklenburg on a visit to his grandmother's castle in Thuringia. A second

---

❧► **Emma of Waldeck** (1858–1934)

Queen and regent of the Netherlands. Name variations: Emma of the Netherlands; Emma of Waldeck-Pyrmont. Reigned as queen of the Netherlands from 1889 to 1898. Born in Arolsen, Hesse, Germany, on August 2, 1858; died at The Hague, the Netherlands, on March 20, 1934; daughter of George Victor, prince of Waldeck and Pyrmont, and *Helen of Nassau (1831–1888); sister of *Helen of Waldeck and Pyrmont (1861–1922); became second wife of William III (1817–1890), king of the Netherlands (r. 1849–1890) and grand duke of Luxemburg, on January 7, 1879; children: *Wilhelmina (1880–1962), queen of the Netherlands (r. 1898–1948). William III's first wife was *Sophia of Wurttemberg (1818–1877).

meeting was arranged at Wilhelmina's aunt's house at Konig in the Odenwald, Grand Duchy of Hesse, and on October 12, they announced their engagement. They were married on February 7, 1901, and spent their honeymoon at Het Loo. For 33 years, they enjoyed a harmonious marital relationship, which would end abruptly with Prince Henry's death of heart failure in 1934. They shared their joy in horses and rode about together in a carriage drawn by the prince's beautiful Lippizaners, or they drove four-in-hand next to one another, pulled by his gray and her bay horses. They shunned rather than sought popularity and conducted their daily lives without pomp; yet when meeting her people or giving speeches, the queen unfailingly conveyed her love of country and sincere desire and determination to see it prosper. Both she and her consort understood and accepted the cage of convention in which they were placed, but within it, they tried to live their lives as close to their own wishes and designs as possible. In 1909, Wilhelmina gave birth to Princess ◄❧ **Juliana**, their only child and the nation's only hope for a continued dynasty.

In her memoirs, Wilhelmina writes that the turning point in those years—1900 to 1914—was her discovery of God's image as present, no

❧▶ **Juliana** (1909—)

*Queen of the Netherlands. Name variations: Juliana of the Netherlands, Julia van Bueren. Reigned from 1948 to 1980. Born Juliana Louise Emma Marie Wilhelmina, princess of Orange-Nassau, duchess of Mecklenburg, in The Hague, the Netherlands, on April 30, 1909; only child of Wilhelmina (1880–1962), queen of the Netherlands (r. 1898–1948), and Duke Henry of Mecklenburg-Schwerin; studied at the University of Leyden, 1927–30; married Prince Bernard of Lippe-Biesterfeld, on January 7, 1937; children—four daughters: Beatrix (b. 1938), queen of the Netherlands (r. 1980—); *Irene Emma (b. 1939, who married Carlos Hugo of Bourbon-Parma); Margaret or *Margriet Francisca (b. 1943, who married Pieter von Vollenhoven), and *Maria Christina of Marijke (b. 1947).*

The day before the surrender of Holland to the Germans in 1940, Juliana and her family escaped to Canada. She left her children there for safety when she went to England in 1944, before her return to the Netherlands in 1945. On October 14, 1947, owing to the illness of her mother, Queen *Wilhelmina, Juliana temporarily assumed royal power in the Netherlands, ruling as princess regent until December 1, 1947, when Wilhelmina resumed her rule. Juliana became regent for the second time on May 14, 1948, and on September 4 of that year Queen Wilhelmina, after 50 years as ruler of the Netherlands, abdicated in her favor. On September 6, 1948, in the Nieuwe Kerk at Amsterdam, the unassuming and shy Juliana took her oath as queen of the Netherlands. She ruled until 1980, then abdicated in favor of her daughter *Beatrix.

A popular ruler, Juliana dealt with the postwar rehabilitation of the Netherlands, the plight of displaced persons, the granting of independence to Indonesia, and often devastating floods that threatened the economic structure of her country. Jettisoning formality, she discarded a great deal of the pomp and ceremony that went with monarchy, including the curtsy.

matter how faintly, in every human being. This belief opened the way for her to accept God as the guide who would lend significance to her work. She was aware of her relative solitude which the rigid attitudes of her entourage enforced, and she had been trained to perform the self-effacing task of a constitutional monarch, but she wanted to perform it with moral courage and apply her will-power to that purpose. She earnestly desired to better the lives of all her people and was a strong advocate of progressive social doctrines. Her spiritual revelation taught her that she could bring content to her ceremonial gestures and provide the tone and attitude which would serve the interest of her people.

It is a political fact that the Dutch Labor Party experienced an unprecedented growth during the early reign of Queen Wilhelmina. In 1897, the Socialist vote was 13,500. By 1913, it had jumped to 145,000, a leap indicative of a desire for electoral reform and social welfare legislation. A shift in temper had occurred in the process as well. With Dutch workers beginning to share in the general prosperity of the country, their party gradually became one of reform rather than revolution. On November 21, 1913, the queen addressed the nation, enumerating its blessings and rejoicing in its promising future. She mentioned the country's growing prosperity "under favor of an energetic spirit of enterprise and of improved labor conditions," its elevated "moral and spiritual plane" and its powers of competition in the fields of science and art. She concluded with the wish that the "concord of all Netherlanders, irrespective of social rank and religious conviction, . . . remain a strong foundation of the nation's independence."

The ensuing outbreak of World War I came as a surprise to the Dutch and a threat to the queen's vision of future progress. One generation after another had come to rely on the belief that Holland's policy of neutrality afforded the country sufficient protection. The Hague had been selected for the Peace Palace, a symbol of movement towards consensus and a civilization unthreatened by war, and yet, one year later, Holland's peace and freedom were in the balance. Wilhelmina stood firm in her declaration that the Netherlands would maintain its neutrality, fully realizing that sacrifices would be required from all to do so. She could rely on her Cabinet, which was formed of members independent of the parties represented in the Chamber but pledged to conform to the wishes of the electorate, to provide political stability. Leadership in psychological and spiritual matters, however, was imperative as well, and to that she pledged herself. The Dutch economy was hit hard by the war and many industries came to a complete standstill. The generosity of people and their government was tested as Belgian refugees streamed over the borders asking political asylum. Fleeing soldiers were interned to protect Dutch neutrality, which meant setting up internment camps. The queen's entourage was diminished, consisting only of her ladies and officers not fit for service. Wilhelmina stayed in contact with those employed in protecting Holland's neutrality by visiting different units of both the army and the navy. When 1916 brought staggering losses to the flooded areas of northern Holland, she paid visits there as well and offered to stand godmother to two babies born as the waves washed through their houses. Rumors circulated that her country would be drawn into the war. Wilhelmina made her presence known by taking up residence in The Hague, and taking a very public walk from her palace to her mother's home, some distance away. The public "correctly concluded from this that I had absolutely nothing to do and that the rumors were completely unfounded."

Neutrality involved the Dutch in constant bickering with both Germany, which on several occasions claimed the right to march its armies across Dutch land, and Britain, which claimed the right to search Dutch ships for any war materials bound for Germany. In 1918, Kaiser Wilhelm II and his empress *Augusta of Schleswig-Holstein asked for asylum in Holland. Wilhelmina was no admirer of Wilhelm, the emperor of Germany; she remembered the sight of Belgian refugees fleeing the German invasion of their country. Still, when he sought asylum, she believed that her country could not refuse. "I was called one November morning with the news that the Kaiser had crossed our frontier," she wrote. "I was astonished."

The flight and abdication of the kaiser induced the flight of other German princes which lit the sparks of revolution and caused dissension among the Dutch as well. It was a time for exercise of authority on a democratic basis. Both she and her government were put to the test when, after the war, the Supreme Council of the Allied Forces demanded the ex-kaiser's extradition. Wilhelmina refused, basing her argument on respect for "the laws of the Kingdom and love of that justice which is embodied in national tradition." For want of international laws by which the demand of the Council could be justified, those, she argued, were the only principles by which her government could be guided. Of the emperor, who spent much of his time gardening and growing tulips in the Netherlands until his death more than 20 years later, she noted, "Can any man have devised a punishment more humiliating than that which befell Wilhelm of Hohenzollern?"

Holland's subsequent membership in the League of Nations presented further challenges in foreign relationships, and the queen, by general consensus, contributed to the solutions of postwar problems to the extent the constitution permitted. She was given a distinguished compliment by Japan's crown prince Hirohito when he included Holland in his tour of Europe in 1921 to visit the countries with which Japan had been in contact during the war. In his toast to the queen he called himself fortunate "in addressing Your Majesty in person in the capital of her Kingdom whose name is ineffaceably written in the heart of every Japanese because Holland to them is the country which for more than two hundred years kept Japan in touch with Western civilization."

> *My* love for my fatherland was like a consuming fire, and not only in me; it reflected itself in fires around me. . . . Anyone who threatened to damage these interests was my personal enemy.
>
> —Wilhelmina

Wilhelmina adapted her household to the spirit of the times, defined by food and housing shortages as well as unemployment. Any ostentation was disallowed; her conduct, like that of her people, had to correspond with the feelings and attitudes towards life shaped by the war years. That meant increased contact with all classes of the population and the acknowledgment of rights as well as duties for her staff as for everyone else.

Wilhelmina watched the approach of World War II with undisguised impatience. She regarded Adolf Hitler as a brutal upstart, and she stood by uneasily as the Dutch Cabinet debated the possibility of reaching an understanding with him. Referring to *Mein Kampf*, she warned her subjects that neutrality might not last forever, since "Hitler has written a book, and the contents might be of some consequence."

At the outbreak of the hostilities, Holland declared her usual neutrality, but to little avail. When German troops crossed the Dutch frontier in May 1940, Wilhelmina, who was 60 years old, made her "flaming protest" at the German invasion of her country. In an attempt to capture her and the leaders of Holland's Cabinet, German paratroopers landed near The Hague. But

Wilhelmina evaded them by changing her residence, then boarding a British destroyer at Hook van Holland on May 13. She hoped that the British would be able to transport her to southwestern Belgium, where the Belgian royal family had hidden during World War I. Informed that the destroyer could not reach the desired area, she accepted advice to seek refuge in Great Britain (her daughter Juliana, along with her children, had preceded her there en route to Canada). And then she wept.

Wilhelmina was fully aware of the impression her departure would leave on her nation, but she thought herself obliged to go, not on her own but on their behalf. Perhaps the fact that King Leopold III of Belgium, who refused to leave his country even at the pleading of his foreign minister, was taken prisoner by the Germans may be seen as an argument for the rightness of her choice. Her Cabinet followed her to London, so the Dutch government was active in England throughout the war.

Queen
Beatrix

Juliana and her children, including ❧▶ **Beatrix**, had gone to Canada, to prevent both the queen and the heir to the throne from being exposed to the same danger during a time of war, but Juliana's husband Prince Bernhard, the prince consort, stayed in London. The queen spent the first part of her years in exile at a cottage with a garden at Roehampton, but when air raids became more frequent, she and the prince moved to Stubbings, one hour's journey from London. Pollution from neighboring factories ultimately made the air too oppressive, and so a small country place near South Mimms became her home. That move nearly proved fatal when a bomb was dropped within a yard and a half of the house, killing one sentry and wounding another. The queen remained unscathed but had to return to Stubbings.

Wilhelmina remained optimistic, relying on the lessons of Dutch history which showed that the Netherlands had always regained its freedom after a relatively short time. Her daughter and grandchildren were safe in Canada, so she could concentrate on keeping up the spirit of her people, both those who remained in Holland, some of whom became resistance fighters, and those who, like her, found their way to England.

Keeping in contact with these *England-vaarders* became an important task for her. It was facilitated by Mr. Van't Sand, the Dutchman in charge of the queen's security. A large house, Netherlands House, was put at the disposal of the Dutch for a meeting place, where British and Dutch women and men gathered for discussions and meals and where newly arrived *England-vaarders* brought news from home. They were people from all walks of life and could report the trials and tribulations of everyday life in Holland, such as shortages of food, fuel, clothing, blankets and soap. Due to the British blockade, bread had become so scarce in the Netherlands that large segments of the populations went hungry. At Wilhelmina's insistent, untiring urgings, supplies were sent from England, as well as from other European countries, as expeditiously as possible but never soon enough to ward off the suffering of the civilian population, especially the children.

For the resistance movement in the Netherlands, she became the symbol and rallying point. In broadcasts over Radio Orange, she imparted her own faith and conviction that holding out was only a matter of time. "A nation which has vitality and determination cannot be conquered simply by force of arms," she urged. "The device of my beloved mother, 'the palm flourishes under oppression,' is now being applied; our national pulse beats more strongly and resolutely than ever before. It is as a single and united people that we endure our trial." When liberation came in 1945, she returned home immediately, visiting the southern liberated areas in March 1945 and taking residence near Breda on April 27. Her return to Amsterdam on June 28 and to The Hague on July 7 was greeted by a jubilant people honoring their sovereign, whose voice in exile had been the strongest of all. They felt confident she would acquaint herself with their "wishes and desires" as she had pledged to do in her radio broadcasts and build a future in "consultation and co-operation with a free people."

The end of the war also terminated the separation from her daughter and granddaughters. She had been fortunate enough to have a reunion with them in 1942 when she paid a visit of state to President Franklin Roosevelt, during the course of which she had addressed the U.S. Con-

♔ Beatrix (b. 1938)

Queen of the Netherlands. Name variations: Beatrix Wilhelmina; Beatrix Wilhelmina Armgard van Orange-Nassau; Beatrice. Reigned 1980—. Born Beatrix Wilhelmina Armgard van Orange-Nassau on January 31, 1938, in Soestdijk, the Netherlands; daughter of Juliana (b. 1909), queen of the Netherlands (r. 1948–1980), and Prince Bernard of Lippe-Biesterfeld; received a doctorate in law, University of Leiden, 1961; married Claus Gerd von Amsberg (a German diplomat), on March 10, 1966; children: Willem or William Alexander, crown prince of the Netherlands (b. 1967); Johan Friso (b. 1968); and Constantijn or Constantine (b. 1969).

The granddaughter of Queen *Wilhelmina, Beatrix has reigned since the abdication of her mother Queen *Juliana in 1980. The first child born to Juliana, two-year-old Beatrix escaped from Holland to Ottawa, Canada, with the rest of her immediate family when the German army invaded the Netherlands in May 1940. Beatrix attended primary school in Ottawa until the family returned to Holland at the end of the war in 1945.

The Dutch constitution in effect in the 1940s provided that sons would inherit before daughters in the royal succession. Beatrix, being the first born of four girls, was recognized as heir to the throne in 1947 when it became clear that Juliana would not have any sons to succeed her. From then on Beatrix was treated as heir to the throne and prepared for her future role as queen.

In 1956, Beatrix turned 18 and officially joined the Dutch Reformed Church. As crown princess she also became a member of her mother's council of state. That same year, after graduating from secondary school, Beatrix entered the University of Leiden. She attended classes with other students and attempted to have as normal a college life as possible, studying sociology, law, and economics. These fields were intended to give her an understanding of the administration of the Netherlands and its place in the world economy. She also enjoyed painting, sculpture, and sailing. She made her first state visit to the United States in 1959.

In 1961, the princess graduated with a *doctorandus* degree, given to candidates who pass doctoral exams without completing a thesis, in political science. She then made other official visits to foreign countries, and helped launch a European version of the Peace Corps. In 1966, she announced her engagement to a 38-year-old German diplomat, Claus von Amsberg. When it was learned that von Amsberg had served in the Nazi army during World War II, the engagement caused a great scandal that cost the monarchy much of its popularity among the Dutch. Beatrix faced the scandal with her characteristic determination and candor, insisting that her fiancé regretted his past actions and was not a Nazi sympathizer. Von Amsberg adopted the Dutch spelling of his name, Van Amsberg, when he became prince of the Netherlands as well as quickly learning Dutch. These efforts combined with the birth of Beatrix's three sons between 1967 and 1969 improved the royal family's popularity.

Queen Juliana abdicated in favor of Beatrix on April 30, 1980, her 71st birthday. Although the constitution allows the Dutch monarch to play only an indirect role in government, Queen Beatrix, like her mother and grandmother, has the authority to sign all legislation passed by the States-General (the parliament), and acts as its adviser. She also has an important symbolic role as a moral leader of the Dutch nation and as representative of the Dutch in international affairs. In this capacity the queen has concerned herself with international problems such as underdevelopment in the Third World and other social welfare issues, especially involving the former Dutch colonies in Asia. She is currently one of the wealthiest women in the world, a result of her personal investments in the stock market and real estate.

SOURCES:

Encyclopedia of World Biography. Vol. 2. 2nd ed. Detroit, MI: Gale Research, 1998.

Moritz, Charles, ed. *Current Biography 1981.* NY: H.W. Wilson, 1981.

Laura York, M.A. in History, University of California, Riverside, California

gress, the first reigning queen to do so. She had landed at Ottawa airport where she was met by Juliana and her two granddaughters. Her stay with Franklin and *Eleanor Roosevelt at Hyde Park increased the respect and admiration she already felt for the president and awakened her deepest regard for the independence and uxorial loyalty of Eleanor. The following year, she had again crossed the ocean for an unofficial visit to her daughter and to welcome *Margriet Francisca, the granddaughter who had been born since her last stay. Juliana had subsequently joined Wilhelmina in London where she remained till the end of the war except for a trip in January 1945 to America to inform President Roosevelt of the suffering of the Dutch people.

During that same month, Wilhelmina's Cabinet had resigned. Well aware that the new government must be formed by people who were intimately familiar with Dutch conditions during the years of occupation, she had subsequently agreed with her advisors that the best solution for the time being would be a provisional government. Radio consultations had then been conducted between London and the Netherlands to ascertain the prevailing thinking regarding the nature and structure of the government which would take power following the liberation. Consensus had been reached that a college of "confidential counsellors" would be established, who would maintain law and order and get the country moving again as region after region was liberated.

Great demands were placed on the queen as she returned to her native land, and she found ample opportunity to demonstrate her leadership. The interim government had performed well given its limited resources, but the political structure had been disrupted, and a new government had to be formed in accordance with current needs. Leaders had to be chosen who were knowledgeable of the changes that had taken place in the past five years. Although Wilhelmina hoped that, in the postwar era, the monarchy would become the main institution leading the country, her hopes were not fulfilled. She had hoped that the resistance fighters would become her fervent supporters. As much as she was admired, however, the resistance had splintered into too many factions to be able to help her. The age of strong monarchies was over; hers was one of the last monarchies, of any kind, to remain in Europe. Careful deliberations on the part of the queen therefore resulted in her inviting Willem Drees to form a "national cabinet of recovery and reconstruction." Her goal was to establish a regime whose policy was democratic and whose program reflected the wishes of her people.

Another task was to compose an entourage of people who had lived in Holland during the occupation or who, in their capacity of *Englandvaarders*, had an understanding of the current situation and would promote regeneration. To further her own enlightenment, Wilhelmina visited different parts of her kingdom, and took in the undernourished looks and tense demeanors of a people whose country had been racked by war.

Only gradually did life return to a measure of normalcy. Juliana fetched her children from Canada, and she installed her family at the palace of Soestdijk. Awaiting her return to Het Loo, which was occupied by the staff of Holland's armed forces, Wilhelmina set herself up in two villas in Scheveningen, one for work, one for her personal use. Members of the States-General who had associated with the enemies were dismissed and their seats reappointed by the crown, which guaranteed the presence of a number of prominent representatives of the resistance. Yet the expected political and social changes did not immediately follow. The elections held in 1946 leading to the formation of a parliamentary Cabinet favored conservative leanings. The Dutch were too exhausted at this time to muster the energy for major reforms.

Continuing to live in a modest way and performing her official and unofficial duties with grace and sincerity, Wilhelmina strengthened the link between her people, her government and herself. She was dedicated to her wish to maintain the "fraternal" relationships between herself and the people which had grown and been nurtured in London during the difficult war years. Consequently, her subjects had ready access to the park surrounding the Huis ten Bosch, her winter residence, and she kept up her visits around the kingdom to get a firsthand impression of their living conditions.

Two years after the war, Wilhelmina approached her 68th birthday, which coincided with the 50th anniversary of her reign. The time had come, she decided, to consider abdicating in favor of Juliana. Great plans were being made for a state celebration, when she was gripped by increasing concerns about the physical and mental stamina needed for her participation in a round of celebrations countrywide while at the same time making considered decisions. She solved the problem by declaring Juliana a regent designate for a period ending immediately prior to her birthday and announcing her intention to abdicate immediately after.

The fourth of September became the day of abdication. The act itself was read to a table of dignitaries by the director of the queen's secretariat and signed by Wilhelmina and those present. She addressed everyone in general and spoke to Juliana in particular. She was pleased to hand over the reins to a woman as capable as her daughter, who loved her people as her mother did, and grateful to be alive to experience the beginning of her reign. At the stroke of noon, Wilhelmina and Juliana appeared on the balcony, hand in hand, followed by Bernhard. Wilhelmina told the crowd of her abdication, for which she had prepared them in a radio address the previous May. She introduced her daughter as the future queen of the Netherlands and invited the crowd to join her in a "long live the Queen," which they did with great feeling and elan.

Back at Het Loo, Wilhelmina allowed herself to give in to the fatigue which was the inevitable corollary to months of planning and tension. When she recovered, she devoted the greater part of her time to her painting and her grandchildren. She retired completely, maintaining only the honorary presidency of "Foundation 1940–45" and patronage of the Artists' Aid Society.

Yet Wilhelmina felt she still had work to do, although she was unsure of what it might be. She found the answer in the spring of 1949: she would do her part in bringing all people to Christ. It was a task for which she had begun preparing many years before, but at this point in her life she was able to declare her intention openly over the radio and in writing. While royal status gave her an audience, she spoke as an individual convinced that only with God's help could anyone carry out his assigned task on earth as she herself had demonstrated in her 50 years of rulership which earned her the title "Mother of the Netherlands."

SOURCES:

Barnouw, A.J. *Holland under Queen Wilhelmina*. NY: Scribner, 1923.

———. *The Pageant of Netherland's History*. NY: Longmans, Green, 1952.

H.R.H. Princess Wilhelmina of the Netherlands. *Lonely But Not Alone*. NY: McGraw-Hill, 1960.

Paneth, Philip. *Queen Wilhelmina: Mother of the Netherlands*. London: Alliance Press, 1943.

SUGGESTED READING:

de Jong, Louis. *The Netherlands and Nazi Germany*. Cambridge, MA: Harvard University Press, 1990.

Two Queens: Wilhelmina-Juliana, 1898–1948. NY: Netherlands Information Bureau, 1948.

Inga Wiehl,
a native of Denmark, teaches at
Yakima Valley Community College, Yakima, Washington

Wilhelmina Carolina (1683–1737).

See Caroline of Ansbach.

Wilhelmina of Brunswick
(1673–1742)

*Holy Roman empress of Austria. Name variations: Amalia Wilhelmine of Brunswick-Lüneburg. Born on April 21, 1673; died on April 10, 1742; daughter of John Frederick (b. 1625), duke of Brunswick-Luneburg, and **Benedicte Henriette Phileppine** (1652–1730); married Joseph I (1678–1705), Holy Roman emperor (r. 1705–1711); children: *Marie Josepha (1699–1757, who married Augustus III, king of Poland).*

Wilhelmina of Prussia (1751–1820)

Princess of Orange. *Born Frederica Sophia Wilhelmine on August 7, 1751, in Potsdam, Brandenburg, Germany; died on June 9, 1820; daughter of Augustus William (brother of Frederick II the Great) and *Louise of Brunswick-Wolfenbuttel (1722–1780); married William V (1748–1806), prince of Orange (r. 1751–1795, though he succeeded to the throne in 1751 did not actually begin ruling until 1766, deposed), on October 4, 1767; children: *Frederica Louise (1770–1819); William I (1772–1843), king of the Netherlands (r. 1813–1840); Frederick (1774–1799).*

Wilhelmina of Prussia (1774–1837).

See Frederica Wilhelmina of Prussia.

Wilhelmina Zahringen (1788–1836).

See Marie of Hesse-Darmstadt for sidebar on Wilhelmine of Baden.

Wilhelmine (1650–1706)

*Electress Palatine. Born Wilhelmine Ernestine on June 20, 1650; died on April 22, 1706; daughter of *Sophie Amalie of Brunswick-Lüneberg (1628–1685) and Frederick III (1609–1670), king of Denmark and Norway (r. 1648–1670); married Charles II, elector Palatine, on September 20, 1671.*

Wilhelmine (1747–1820)

*Electress of Hesse. Born Wilhelmina Caroline on July 10, 1747; died on January 14, 1820; daughter of *Louise of England (1724–1751) and Frederick V (1723–1766), king of Denmark and Norway (r. 1746–1766); married William IX, elector of Hesse-Cassel, on September 1, 1764; children: **Marie Frederica of Hesse-Cassel** (1768–1839, who married Alexis Frederick, prince of Anhalt-Bernburg); **Caroline Amelia of Hesse-Cassel** (1771–1848, who married Emile Leopold, duke of Saxe-Gotha); Frederick (b. 1772); William II, elector of Hesse (b. 1777).*

Wilhelmine (1808–1891)

*Princess of Schleswig-Holstein. Name variations: Wilhelmine Oldenburg. Born Wilhelmine Marie on June 18, 1808, in Kiel; died on May 30, 1891, in Glucksborg; daughter of *Marie Sophie of Hesse-Cassel (1767–1852) and Frederick VI, king of Denmark (r. 1808–1839); became first wife of Frederick VII (1808–1863), king of Denmark (r. 1848–1863), on November 1, 1828 (separated 1837); married Charles, prince of Schleswig-Holstein, on May 19, 1838. Frederick VII's second wife was *Caroline of Mecklenburg-Strelitz (1821–1876).*

Wilhelmine of Baden (1788–1836).

See Marie of Hesse-Darmstadt for sidebar.

Wilhelmine of Darmstadt (1765–1796)

*Bavarian royal. Name variations: Augusta Wilhelmine of Hesse-Darmstadt. Born on April 14, 1765, in Darmstadt; died on March 30, 1796, near Heidelberg, Germany; became first wife of Maximilian I Joseph (1756–1825), elector of Bavaria (r. 1799–1805), king of Bavaria (r. 1805–1825), on September 30, 1785; children: Ludwig I also known as Louis I Augustus (1786–1868), king of Bavaria (r. 1825–1848); *Amalie Auguste (1788–1851); *Caroline Augusta of Bavaria (1792–1873); Charles (1795–1875); Amelia (1790–1794).*

Wilkins, Mary Eleanor (1852–1930).

See Freeman, Mary E. Wilkins.

Wilkinson, Ellen (1891–1947)

English trade union organizer, feminist agitator, and politician. Name variations: Red Ellen. Born Ellen Cicely Wilkinson on October 8, 1891, in the Ardwick district of the city of Manchester, England; died in London at St. Mary's Hospital on February 6, 1947; daughter of Richard Wilkinson (an insurance agent) and Ellen (Wood) Wilkinson; attended elementary and secondary schools in Manchester; graduated from the University of Manchester, 1913; never married; no children.

Was involved in politics and women's movement in her teens; became Manchester organizer for National Union of Women Suffrage Societies (1913); was a full-time women's organizer for Amalgamated Union of Co-operative Employees (later National Union of Distributive and Allied Workers [NUDAW], 1915–24); served as a member of Parliament for Middlesbrough East (1924–31); was an official of NUDAW (1931–35); served as a member of Parliament for Jarrow (1935–47); was a leader of the Jarrow Crusade (1936); served as junior minister in the Coalition Government (1940–45); served as minister of education in the Labour Government (1945–47).

Selected writings: Clash *(Harrap, 1929);* Peeps at Politicians *(P.A. Allen & Co., 1930);* The Division Bell Mystery *(Harrap, 1932); (with Edward Conze)* Why Facism? *(Selwyn & Blount, 1934);* The Town that was Murdered *(Gollancz, 1939).*

On Monday, October 5, 1936, 200 men set out on a 300-mile march from Jarrow, a town in northeastern England, to London. All were unemployed, as were four out of five men in the area. They took with them a petition to be presented to the House of Commons. Carried in a box at the head of the march, beneath a banner bearing the words JARROW CRUSADE, the petition "humbly pray[ed] that the necessary active assistance be given by the Government for the provision of work in the town of Jarrow." By the time the marchers arrived in London, in pouring rain on Saturday, October 31, they had gained national attention. In Britain at that time many were unemployed and marches and demonstrations were commonplace; but the men of Jarrow, it has been said, "marched into History" and to the present day they are an abiding image of interwar unemployment. For parts of their journey, the men were led by the tiny figure—she was less than five feet tall—of Ellen Wilkinson, Jarrow's member of Parliament.

Born in Manchester in 1891, Wilkinson was the third of four children (two daughters and two sons) of working-class parents who struggled to improve their position. Her father Richard Wilkinson had worked in a cotton factory before obtaining a post as an insurance agent; he became well known in the district as he visited families to collect their small regular payments to the insurance company. He was also respected locally as a Methodist lay preacher, and the whole family was brought up under the influence of the chapel (one of Ellen's brothers became a Methodist minister). In keeping with the principles of their religious sect, the family consumed no alcohol and opposed the practice of gambling. The terraced house in which they lived provided respectable if rather austere accommodation. Recalling the time in a radio broadcast made when she was a public figure, Wilkinson spoke of "Manchester's acres of narrow streets and brick boxes with slate roofs" where "the weather was a mixture of soot and rain." Her mother's health was poor, but fortunately her father's income was sufficient to employ a woman to do heavy work such as the family's washing.

In politics, Richard Wilkinson was a Conservative, a man with a creed his daughter described as "a perfectly simple one. 'I have pulled myself out of the gutter, why can't they?' was his reply to every demand for sympathy or solidarity with his own class." Yet he did all he could to give his own children a start in life. Unlike many men at that time, he strongly believed that girls should have equal educational opportunities. Ellen was a bright child who stood out in the large classes at the local elementary school. She was regarded as someone who would become a teacher, an expectation that came nearer in 1906 when she won a £25 pupil teaching bursary. This led her, for two years, to spend half of each week at the Manchester Day Training College and the other half as a teacher in a local school, where she was only a little older than many of her pupils. Her next step up the educational ladder came when she successfully applied for a highly competitive scholarship to study history at the University of Manchester. Her course began in 1910.

In spite of long hours of hard work at her studies, she had found time for political activities. After reading the works of writers such as Robert Blatchford, perhaps the most popular socialist author of the period in England, she joined the Independent Labour Party at the age of 16. She was also active in the Manchester area in the campaign to win the parliamentary vote for women. In the city, *Emmeline Pankhurst was the leader of the suffragettes, who adopted militant tactics; but Wilkinson was a suffragist—a supporter of peaceful persuasion who employed constitutional methods to campaign for the vote. At university, she was a leading member of the Fabian Society, a socialist organization that advocated gradual reform. Though associated with these less militant groupings, she could take a vehement, and even angry, attitude to those questions on which she felt strongly, yet quarrels with colleagues were soon dissolved away by the warmth of her emotions.

In the summer of 1913, she took a degree in history and decided against a career in teaching. Instead, she accepted a post as the full-time Manchester organizer of the constitutionalist National Union of Women's Suffrage Societies. When, in August 1914, Britain entered what was to become World War I, the agitation to extend votes to women was suspended. Wilkinson was asked to concentrate instead on protecting the interests of those women who were affected by

the war. This led in 1915 to a post with the Amalgamated Union of Co-operative Employees as its national women's organizer.

The war allowed large numbers of women to find better-paid employment than had previously been available, and this in turn encouraged many to join trade unions. The work of the women's organizer therefore became increasingly important, and by the end of the war Wilkinson had become a prominent member of her union. An amalgamation with another trade union after the war created, in 1921, the National Union of Distributive and Allied Workers, a trade union that recruited many of its members from the ranks of shop assistants and warehouse workers.

As well as acting as women's organizer of the union, Wilkinson took part in the activities of other bodies. She became well known in the Women's Co-operative Guild, an organization made up of women supporters of the co-operative principle in retailing and manufacturing. Politically radicalized by the war, she was at this stage of her career well to the left and joined the Communist Party of Great Britain on its foundation in 1920. In 1921, she traveled to Moscow to attend a conference of the Red International

Ellen Wilkinson

of Labour Unions. At that time, it was possible to be a member of both the Communist Party and the Labour Party, but fairly soon relations between the two bodies became hostile. In September 1923, Wilkinson had been added to the list of candidates endorsed by the Labour Party—a step towards becoming a member of Parliament. At about this time, she decided her political future lay with Labour, and she resigned from the Communist Party.

> [S]he was as rock-like in her socialist idealism as in her feminism, abounding in mercurial anger yet overflowing with generosity of intent.
>
> —Betty Vernon

The decision was shrewd, as the Communists were never able to secure the election of more than the odd candidate to Parliament and small numbers to office in local government. In November 1923, she was elected as the representative of Gorton ward on Manchester City Council. At the general election of December 1923, she stood as the Labour Party's candidate at Ashton-under-Lyne, a constituency a few miles east of Manchester. She was defeated, but in April 1924 the local Labour Party in Middlesbrough East adopted her as its candidate for the next general election. That contest was not long delayed, as the minority Labour Government fell from office in October 1924.

At the time of the election Wilkinson was 33, but her slight build and youthful appearance led some opponents to claim she was not even old enough to vote (in 1918 the parliamentary franchise had been extended to women aged 30 and above; those over 21 had to wait until 1928 to obtain the vote on the same terms as male adults). The constituency was part of a town that depended on heavy industry, including shipbuilding, chemicals and steel; it had grown rapidly in the 19th century and looked, according to Wilkinson writing in her union's magazine, like "a book of illustrations to Karl Marx."

She won the contest and entered the House of Commons as one of only four women MPs, and the single woman Labour MP (her friend *Margaret Bondfield had been defeated). As such, she attracted much press attention, particularly as she dressed in an unusually colorful way—she had fine red hair and liked to set it off by wearing a green velvet dress. She became increasingly known by such terms as the "fiery particle," the "elfin fury," and, most often, "Red Ellen." Though she was a vigorous critic of the Conservative government, the most notable event of those years in which she was involved was the General Strike of May 1926. For nine days, the trade union movement attempted to put pressure on the government to protect the living standards of coalminers, and Wilkinson, as an MP sponsored by her union, was involved in the agitation. However, some labor leaders were reluctant to become embroiled in a lengthy dispute and brought the strike to an end. The coalminers continued the struggle—most were not to return to work until near the end of the year—and Wilkinson was among a group of trade unionists who visited the United States in August 1926, at the invitation of the American Federation of Labor, to raise funds in their support. Much of the passion and debate surrounding the General Strike was captured by Wilkinson in her novel *Clash*, which was published in 1929.

The general election of 1929 led to a second minority Labour Government. Wilkinson retained her Middlesbrough seat and was made the parliamentary private secretary to *Susan Lawrence, a junior minister in the new administration (which also included Margaret Bondfield, the first woman to occupy a post in the Cabinet). In the wake of the Wall Street crash, the British economy, already unsteady, suffered an increasing level of unemployment. Government policies were ineffective and in the summer of 1931 Labour fell from office. At the subsequent general election, the party lost a large proportion of its seats, including Middlesbrough East.

Supported by her union, which paid her a salary, Wilkinson was able to continue as a political activist. In 1932, she visited India where she met Mohandas Gandhi, who was then in prison. She went to Spain in 1934 to investigate the suppression of a workers' revolt (when the Civil War broke out in 1936 she was a passionate supporter of the Republic and worked hard on behalf of refugees from the conflict). Always a prolific writer for newspapers and magazines, she also wrote two books in the early 1930s: *Peeks at Politicians* (1931) and a detective novel, *The Division Bell Mystery* (1932). She returned to the House of Commons in the general election of 1935, as MP for Jarrow, a constituency some 30 miles north of Middlesbrough, near Newcastle upon Tyne in northeast of England.

She represented an area suffering heavy unemployment. To draw attention to its plight, members of all political parties on the town council decided to present a petition to the House of Commons. The petition was to be accompanied by 200 marchers; Wilkinson's part in the "Jarrow Crusade" is probably the single most important aspect of her public life. Whenever she could, she joined the march and, though her own small stride broke the men's rhythm, their spirits were always raised when she accompanied them.

In the short term, Jarrow's petition, presented in Parliament by her, made little difference to the town's economic well-being, as she made clear in her account *The Town that was Murdered: The Life-Story of Jarrow* (1939). Only with rearmament and then war in 1939 did full employment return. After the Labour Party joined the Coalition government of May 1940, Wilkinson was appointed to junior office, first at the Ministry of Pensions (May to October 1940) and then the Ministry of Home Security (October 1940 to May 1945).

Wilkinson was always a hard-working person, but the demands of wartime administration drained much of her energy. In 1940, her flat was destroyed in a bombing attack, and in 1943 she broke an ankle in an aircraft accident. One consequence of this was disturbed sleep which, with asthma attacks, led her to rely on regular medication. Nevertheless, her career received a boost in the summer of 1945 when, following the victory of the Labour Party at the general election, she was appointed to the Cabinet—becoming only the second woman to rise to this position—as minister of education. Like all ministers, she had to balance conflicting demands, in her case a commitment to raise to 15 the school-leaving age and to ensure that schools had sufficient space and qualified teachers to deal with larger numbers of children. In the autumn of 1946, she represented the government on a visit to Prague, to open a film festival, but became seriously ill after the ceremony. For the next few months, her health was always uncertain, though she continued in government. Early in February 1947, she was found ill in her flat suffering from pneumonia and admitted to hospital, where she died. Some speculated that she might have deliberately taken a drug overdose, though others insisted her fighting spirit would never allow such an action and that her frail body had simply become worn out.

SOURCES:

Pickard, Tom. *Jarrow March*. London: Allison & Busby, 1982.

Rubinstein, David. "Ellen Wilkinson Reconsidered," in *History Workshop Journal*. Vol. 7, 1979, pp. 161–169.

Vernon, Betty. *Ellen Wilkinson*. London: Croom Helm, 1982.

SUGGESTED READING:

Brookes, Patricia. *Women at Westminster*. London: Peter Davies, 1967.

D.E. Martin,
lecturer in the Department of History,
University of Sheffield, Sheffield, England

Wilkinson, Iris (1906–1939)

New Zealand writer. Name variations: Robin Hyde. Born Iris Guiver Wilkinson on January 19, 1906, in Cape Town, South Africa; died on August 23, 1939, in London, England; daughter of George Edward Wilkinson and Adelaide (Butler) Wilkinson; never married; children: Derek Challis (b. 1930).

One of the best-known journalists of New Zealand, Iris Wilkinson was also a celebrated poet and novelist. One of three children of an English-born civil servant and his Australian wife, Wilkinson was born in 1906 in South Africa. The family relocated to New Zealand soon after her birth, her father hoping to establish himself in the colonial bureaucracy. However, her family struggled with poverty and moved frequently throughout her childhood. An excellent student, Wilkinson entered a public secondary school in Wellington at age 13. She decided to become a writer when her stories and poetry were first published in the school newspaper in 1919. In writing she found a means of expressing herself and overcoming the stress of poverty and her parents' unhappy marriage. She won several literary competitions, and her poetry appeared in a number of monthly magazines. In 1922, she entered Victoria University College as a part-time student, and accepted a position writing for children in *The Farmer's Advocate* the following year. She was beginning to establish a name for herself as a fiction writer when she was stricken in 1924 with crippling arthritis of the knee joint. She underwent numerous surgeries but for the rest of her life suffered excruciating pain in her legs and could not walk without crutches. Her poetry again became an outlet for her emotional and psychological suffering at her sudden incapacitation.

Nonetheless Wilkinson returned to work, where she was promoted to write a women's column on Parliamentary proceedings for the *Dominion*, a pro-Conservative Party daily newspaper. To satisfy the editors, who believed women would not read serious articles, Wilkinson had to write in a breezy, gossipy style which she resented. However, her position brought her into contact with New Zealand's highest politicians, who courted her favor in order to influence her coverage of political issues.

She resigned from the *Dominion* in 1926 after discovering that she was pregnant from a brief love affair. She refused to marry the father but to avoid the scandal of an illegitimate child moved to Sydney, Australia, where she gave birth to a stillborn baby. Depressed, unemployed, and in ill health, she returned to her family in

Wellington. There she was hospitalized several times as a borderline psychotic. She became addicted to morphine and other painkillers, and in May 1927 committed herself to a mental institution. The regimen improved her health and spirit, but she would remain dependent on painkillers for the rest of her life. However, by the end of the year she was composing poems again. From this point on she would write under the pseudonym Robin Hyde, the name she had planned to give her stillborn son.

Wilkinson found work as a freelancer, writing for the Christchurch Publicity Bureau and contributing articles to the *Christchurch Press* and the *Sun*. She also wrote book reviews and a regular society column for the *Auckland Mirror*. Her vivid, colorful style subsequently brought her a position writing human interest stories aimed at women readers for the newspaper *The Truth* in 1928. She lost that position a few months later, after refusing to sign a contract stipulating that she would not sell her fiction or poetry to any other publisher.

In June 1929, Wilkinson moved to Wanganui, where she became the women's editor for *The Wanganui Chronicle*. There for the first time she was occasionally allowed to write articles on current events and issues, in addition to a society column and other articles for New Zealand's middle-class women. Her editorials addressed controversial topics, such as women's suffrage, education, the plight of the native Maori people, and immigration.

The publication in late 1929 of her first book of poetry, *The Desolate Star*, brought Wilkinson a national readership. In late 1930 another pregnancy following a love affair with a married journalist led to her dismissal by the editors of the *Chronicle*; she gave birth to a son, Derek, in October. Unemployed and destitute, Wilkinson placed the baby in a nursing home; he grew up with a foster family, although Wilkinson kept in contact with them, visiting her son occasionally and paying for his board.

She was soon offered another editorial position, at *The New Zealand Observer* in Auckland. Even with a regular salary, she felt obliged to remain separated from her child out of fear that she would lose her job if her employers learned of him. By 1933, overwork combined with emotional strain and morphine addiction led her to attempt suicide, after which she was hospitalized as a mental patient. Again she re-established her writing career, publishing more poetry and her first two novels in the mid-1930s. Residing in Auckland, she contributed articles to

The Observer on topics ranging from the Depression to feminism to the beauty of the New Zealand landscape, in addition to her prose and poetry. The works produced in her last few years include autobiographical and historical novels and travel pieces, all of which display Wilkinson's deep love for her native land's people and culture. They continue one of the overriding themes of her writings, the oppression of women and the need for economic and social equity for women. She also wrote passionately against the oppression of the Maori, and professed a strong sympathy with the Socialist movement.

In January 1938, Wilkinson left New Zealand to fulfill a childhood dream of seeing England. On an impulse she stopped for a long trip through China, sending back travel articles describing her journeys to *Woman Today* and *The Mirror*. As a journalist she was allowed to travel to the warfront, where she was moved to volunteer to nurse the Chinese soldiers and civilians wounded in the fight against the invading Japanese army. Witnessing firsthand the atrocities of war, Wilkinson wrote articles displaying a new-found and eloquent pacifism. Attacked by Japanese soldiers who thought she was a spy, she took refuge with the British ambassador in Tsingtao (Qingdao), who sent her to a Hong Kong hospital to recuperate. She finally left China in August, arriving in England in September. Through the help of old friends she was hospitalized for malnutrition, while at the same time she drove herself to write a book about her experiences in China. Depression and her continuing drug addiction kept her in and out of London hospitals.

In November 1938, her autobiographical *The Godwit's Fly* appeared to disappointing reviews. It was followed in early 1939 by her book on China, *Dragon Rampant*, which achieved considerable acclaim and high sales. Homesick and ill, Wilkinson had neither the mental or physical strength nor the money to go home. She also suffered, as her letters attest, from a debilitating lack of confidence in herself as a writer and a fear of the inevitability of the coming world war. While her friends were arranging government aid to send her home, Wilkinson took an overdose of pain medication and died in a hospital on August 23, 1939. She was 33 years old.

Iris Wilkinson was buried in a London cemetery. Her last book, a collection of poems, was published by her son and friends in 1952 as *Houses by the Sea*. It is considered her finest work.

SOURCES:

Boddy, Gillian, and Jacqueline Matthews, eds. *Disputed Ground: Robin Hyde, Journalist*. Wellington, New Zealand: Victoria University Press, 1991.

Roberts, Heather. *Where Did She Come From? New Zealand Women Novelists, 1862–1987*. London: Allen & Unwin, 1989.

Laura York, M.A. in History,
University of California,
Riverside, California

Wilkinson, Jemima (1752–1819)

Religious leader and self-proclaimed "Public Universal Friend." Born Jemima Wilkinson on November 29, 1752, in Cumberland, Rhode Island; died at Jerusalem, near Seneca Lake, New York, on July 1, 1819; eighth of twelve children of Jeremiah Wilkinson (a farmer and member of the Colony Council) and Elizabeth Amey (Whipple) Wilkinson; had some public school education; never married; no children.

Jemima Wilkinson was born in 1752 in Cumberland, Rhode Island, the eighth of twelve children of Jeremiah Wilkinson, a farmer and member of the Colony Council, and **Elizabeth Whipple Wilkinson**. She had some public education. As an adult, Wilkinson heard the preaching of George Whitefield and witnessed the meetings of the evangelizing "New Light Baptists." In 1775, while suffering a severe illness, she believed she died and was the recipient of a vision where she was "reanimated" by the spirit and power of Jesus. Given a charge by God to "warn a lost and guilty, gossiping, dying World to flee from the wrath . . . to come," she took the name "The Public Universal Friend" and began to speak at open-air meetings where the spirit of her personality rather than the content and message of her words held her audience captive. The basic content of her preaching involved the elevation of the state of celibacy over marriage, the importance of the church over family, and her assertion that she was indeed Jesus Christ come again. Although similarities exist between Wilkinson's thought and the Society of the Believers in Christ's Second Appearance (the Shakers), there is no evidence that she had any contact with this group. Furthermore, as the Shakers, having come to America only in 1774 and in 1775, were still a very small group located in New York City, influence by the teachings of Mother *Ann Lee is unlikely.

Beginning in 1776, Wilkinson gathered a group of about 20 of her most devoted followers and traveled a circuit through Rhode Island and Connecticut, preaching her message. In such processions, she rode wearing a flowing long robe, her followers riding two by two behind her. Unlike the Shakers, she was originally well received, in both the towns and countryside, founding churches in New Milford, Connecticut, and East Greenwich and South Kingston, Rhode Island, between 1777 and 1782. In conjunction with her church in South Kingston, Judge William Potter, a devoted follower, built a special addition to his mansion for Wilkinson, who gradually came to control his business and the management of his house and estate. Due to rising antagonism in Rhode Island and Connecticut against her and her followers, in 1783 Wilkinson transferred her headquarters to Philadelphia. It was here that her only published work appeared, *The Universal Friend's Advice, to Those of the Same Religious Society, Recommended to be read in their Public Meetings*. Philadelphia, however, was only slightly less intolerant and Wilkinson and her followers returned to New England in 1785. Three years later, she decided to try a different climate for her preaching and purchased a large parcel of land in Yates County near Seneca Lake in western New York state. A body of her follows began work to establish a colony, called Jerusalem, where "no intruding foot could enter." Wilkinson joined this group in 1790. Like the Shaker colonies nearby, the enterprise prospered in agriculture and lumbering, and by 1800 it had increased to about 260 members. Wilkinson was well liked by the neighboring Native Americans, who called her Squaw Shinnewanagistawge, or Great Woman Preacher, and she was often visited by European dignitaries and wealthy travelers. The prosperity of the colony, however, created difficulties among its members over land and profit divisions. Wilkinson, furthermore, developed a penchant for requesting gifts and personal effects from members by saying, "The Friend hath need of these things," and for assigning degrading forms of punishment for various infractions of the society rules. Over time a number of members began to leave, some after unsuccessful attempts at gaining some legal authority over the land, and others in anger over Wilkinson's domineering and greedy demands for precedence in person and in items. Having set aside 12,000 acres of the colony's property for her personal use, Wilkinson had an estate built on its farthest corner and remained there in luxury, although ailing with dropsy. She died on July 1, 1819, and the colony soon disintegrated.

SOURCES:

Adams, J.Q. "Jemima Wilkinson, the Universal Friend," in *Journal of American History*. April–May, 1915.

"Jemima Wilkinson," in *Quarterly Journal of New York State Historical Association*. April 1930.

SUGGESTED READING:

Wisbey, Herbert A. *Pioneer Prophetess: Jemima Wilkinson, the Publick Universal Friend*. Ithaca, NY: Cornell University Press, 1964.

Amanda Carson Banks,
lecturer, Vanderbilt Divinity School,
Nashville, Tennessee

Wilkinson, Marguerite Ogden

(1883–1928)

Canadian-born American poet. Born Marguerite Ogden Bigelow on November 15, 1883, in Halifax, Nova Scotia, Canada; died as the result of a swimming accident on January 12, 1928, in New York City; daughter of Nathan Kellogg Bigelow and Gertrude (Holmes) Bigelow; educated privately and at Northwestern University; married James G. Wilkinson (a school administrator), in 1909.

Published several volumes of poetry, beginning with In Vivid Gardens *(1911); became poetry reviewer for* The New York Times Book Review *(c. 1915); published* New Voices *(1919), an anthology of modern poetry, to critical acclaim; lectured on modern poetry at schools, library associations, and women's clubs.*

Selected writings: In Vivid Gardens *(1911); By a Western Wayside (1912); Golden Songs of the Golden State (1917);* New Voices *(1919); The Dingbat of Arcady (1922); Contemporary Poetry (1923); Yule Fire (1925); Citadels (1928).*

Marguerite Ogden Wilkinson was born in 1883 in Halifax, Nova Scotia, although she and her family left that area of Canada soon after for Evanston, Illinois. Wilkinson was raised with a love of the outdoors, despite her frail aspect, and her sensitive nature found an outlet in poetry, which she began to write during her student years at Northwestern University. In 1909, the 26-year-old Marguerite married James G. Wilkinson, a school principal in New Rochelle, New York, and moved there. In addition to taking on the domestic duties required of her married station, Wilkinson continued to write. Her first full collection of poetry, *In Vivid Gardens* (1911), was soon followed by several other collections which were characterized by her workmanlike approach to verse writing. Wilkinson also completed several prose works, including *The Dingbat of Arcady* (1922), a humorous volume that reflects her love of nature in its description of the events occurring during one of the many annual fishing excursions she took with her husband.

After publishing several volumes of her own poetry, Wilkinson began reviewing the poems of others in *The New York Times Book Review*,

becoming enough of an expert in 20th-century verse to lecture at colleges, library clubs, and other interested gatherings. Her *New Voices* (1919), an anthology and criticism of British and American contemporary verse, was hailed by many as a well-balanced presentation of the state of modern poetry. Among her own writings, *Citadels* (1928) reflects her interest in early Christianity, while *The Great Dream* (1923) is a long poem in which Wilkinson mused upon the changes that might be wrought in spirituality during the 20th century.

In her late 30s, Wilkinson began to grow increasingly drawn into spiritual concerns and fears for the future, and this obsession led to a nervous breakdown in 1928. In an attempt to cope with her increasing fears, she forced herself to learn how to fly a small plane and how to perform several flying stunts, paying for the course by writing a booklet advertising aviation training. In addition to flying every afternoon when the weather was good, Wilkinson arose each morning and took a bracing swim in the ocean off Coney Island, where she also tested her mettle by performing swimming stunts. It was on one of these morning swims, while practicing a new stunt, that she was drowned at the age of 44.

SOURCES:

Kunitz, Stanley J., and Howard Haycraft, eds. *Twentieth Century Authors*. NY: Wilson, 1942.

Pamela Shelton,
freelance writer,
Avon, Connecticut

Willard, Emma Hart (1787–1870)

*Founder of Troy Seminary, writer of textbooks, and partisan for the common-school movement who advocated female control of women's education with support from public funds and promoted change while urging stability during a boisterous historical era. Born Emma Hart on February 23, 1787, on a farm at Berlin, Connecticut; died on April 15, 1870, at Troy, New York; buried in Oakwood Cemetery overlooking Troy; ninth of ten children of Samuel Hart (a Revolutionary War hero) and Lydia (Hinsdale) Hart (Samuel Hart had seven other children from a previous marriage); older sister of *Almira Lincoln Phelps* (1793–1884), who also became a distinguished educator; attended the Berlin Academy, Connecticut; attended classes at schools in Hartford, Connecticut; married Dr. John Willard, in 1809 (died 1825); married Christopher Yates (a physician), in 1838 (divorced 1843); children: (first marriage) John Hart Willard (b. 1810).*

Attended a district school during "winter sessions"; studied at one of the first academies in Con-

necticut; began teaching at age 17; opened a boarding school for girls in her home (1814); presented plan for a female seminary to New York State Legislature (1819); opened Troy Seminary (1821); founded the Willard Association for the Mutual Improvement of Female Teachers (1837); wrote history textbooks; attempted, unsuccessfully, to establish seminaries for teachers in Greece; married Christopher Yates (1838); granted a divorce by the Connecticut Legislature (1843); elected superintendent of the common schools in Kensington, Connecticut (1840); toured extensively as a speaker for teachers' institutes (1845–46).

Selected writings: A Plan for Improving Female Education *(rep. of 2nd ed. of 1819 by VT: Middlebury College, 1918);* Advancement of Female Education: Or, a series of Addresses in Favor of Establishing at Athens, In Greece, A French Seminary, Especially Designed to Instruct Female Teachers *(Norman Tuttle, 1833);* History of the United States or Republic of America *(NY: White, Gallaher, and Whate, 1830);* Morals for the Young or, Good Principles Instilling Wisdom *(NY: A.S. Barnes, 1857);* "Political Position of Women-Letter to Dupont DeL'eure," *in* American Literary Magazine *(April 1848).*

Educators of the late 18th and early 19th centuries justified the need for "feminine schooling" on the basis of women's roles as wives, mothers, and teachers, and carefully constructed a separate, higher educational system aimed at training females. Sensing in this development opportunities for advancement, women of sensitivity, intelligence, and ambition, such as Emma Hart Willard (as well as *Mary Lyon and *Catharine Beecher), controlled the movement by successfully joining the needs of their society, their gender, and themselves to enhance female social authority and create public spaces wherein women educators could dominate. The ultimate consequences of their action were subversion of the status quo, promotion of feminism, and promotion of truly equal institutions of higher education for women. Women educators such as Willard, without openly rebelling against a culture determined to teach women to "know their place," developed significant political strategies for enlarging and expanding their dominion under the guise of defending society. Studying women such as Willard offers a way to understand how cultural change affected middle-class women in the early republican period because, by successfully founding the Troy Seminary, she arrived early in the seminary movement. Capable, sound, and respected, she advocated female control of women's education with

support from public funds. Emma Willard was not the first to propose that it was appropriate to educate women because they were women, but she was one of the most successful in using this idea to expand schooling for middle-class females, thus changing educational opportunities for women within the highly structured roles allocated to them.

In a letter to a friend in 1818, Emma Willard gave her reason for wanting to develop an educational institution for women: "My neighborhood to Middlebury College made me bitterly feel the disparity in educational *facilities* between the sexes." Willard's proximity to Middlebury and her interest in what went on there were the results of both marriage and an eager intellect. Born in Berlin, Connecticut, in 1787, she was the sixteenth child of Revolutionary War hero Stephen Hart and ninth child of his second wife **Lydia Hinsdale Hart**. Emma attended a district school and later studied at one of the first academies in Connecticut. The principal of this academy, Thomas Miner, was a Yale graduate, and Willard later claimed that there was no better instruction for young women at that time in the country.

In 1804, the summer she was 17, Willard began her teaching career. (Women were primarily allowed to attend and teach "public" school in the summertime when men were in the fields.) In the winters, she attended the schools of Misses Patten and Mrs. Royce of New Hartford. At age 20, Willard chose to teach at a private school run by two male graduates of Williams College in Westfield, Massachusetts. After only six months, she resigned and accepted another position at an academy in Middlebury, Vermont. The reasons for this change were never stated but, from this point on, Willard always maintained that women should be in charge of female education, an increasingly popular notion. From 1809 until 1821, Emma, while making her home at Middlebury, developed her concepts of female education and learned the political skills that later enabled her to work with opposing factions for the success of her seminary. In 1809, she married Dr. John Willard, an influential, wealthy man in the community much older than she. While he was away on frequent business trips, Willard read all his medical books plus studied the textbooks their nephew John brought home from his classes at Middlebury College. This was a most important educational experience for Willard since it demonstrated to her satisfaction that women could master the same curriculum as men and gave her what amounted to a college education.

In 1814, severe financial reverses, probably as a result of the disastrous War of 1812, caused the Willards to lose everything except their home. Emma opened a boarding school for girls that was an immediate success. This trauma was in fact fortuitous, since Emma, overeducated for the traditional roles she had been playing, quickly gained confidence in her own ability to initiate, develop, and direct institutions. She wrote to a Reverend Henry Fowler: "When I began my school in Middlebury my leading motive was to relieve my husband from financial difficulties [but] I had the further motive of keeping a better school than those around me."

[History] shows many [countries] whose legislatures have sought to improve their various vegetables . . . but none whose public councils have made it an object of their deliberations to improve the character of women.

—Emma Hart Willard

Her ambition thus somewhat providentially unleashed, Willard went on to tell Fowler that she had begun to secretly work on a plan to "effect an important change in education by a grade of schools for women higher than any heretofore known." For over a year, not even her husband knew of her idea. After receiving an encouraging letter from De Witt Clinton, governor of New York, in 1818, Willard determined that New York provided the most auspicious setting for her experiment since the state was anxious to surpass New England in progressive reform policies. The original copy of the plan, carefully handwritten by Willard and entitled *An Address to the Public: Particularly to the Members of the Legislature of New York, Proposing a Plan for Improving Female Education*, was read for her to the state legislature in the spring of 1819. Her willingness to go directly to a source of economic and political power demonstrates her understanding of the problems undermining opportunity for women.

Warning the legislators of the consequences of their neglect, Willard catalogued the evils perpetuated by women without "the preservatives of a good education" and advocated the use of seminary graduates as teachers for the republic so that they could perform a useful function and free the men for other important work. Anticipating some justifications and capitalizing on others all ready widely accepted, Willard listed other functions female schooling could perform for society. "Housewifery could be raised to a regular art. . . . [W]omen would acquire a taste for moral and intellectual pleasures [which would] extend the influence they possess over children." Ending the proposed plan with a perhaps unconscious personal statement, Willard noted that "there are *master spirits* among women who must have pre-eminence at whatever price." The solution, according to Willard, lay in allowing women to "govern and improve the seminaries for their sex."

Although the plan was formally approved by the New York Legislature, the request for funds was denied. Bitterly disappointed by what seemed to her a personal rejection, Willard made extensive efforts to publicize her attempt to gain public funding for female higher education and obtained financial support for a school in Troy, New York. The seminary opened in 1821 and proved to be a resounding success.

Proud of all she had accomplished but self-conscious in her role as innovator, Willard insisted on her own mode of schooling for women. Increasingly, she did not approve of attempts to widen women's public space, nor did she enjoy competition for her role as a leader in the field of female education. Rather, Emma Willard attempted to increase her own authority and that of her school by use of the strategies that had enabled her to prosper.

In 1833, she did risk her reputation, unknowingly, by becoming involved in a dubious scheme to enlist wealthy Americans in sponsoring female seminaries in Greece. One of the young men involved in the project was later tried by an ecclesiastical court in Chicago for misappropriation of church funds.

Willard sought to extend her authority among ex-students and "friends" of the school by founding the Willard Association for the Mutual Improvement of Female Teachers. Once more combining altruism with personal motives, her circulars nonetheless contain a remarkably thorough analyses of the qualities necessary for good teaching. Willard cautioned them to be alert; to trust their own judgment in curricular matters; and to govern their classrooms with a loving and patient heart. The Troy Seminary educated over 200 teachers before any teachers' normal schools were founded in the United States.

In 1838 an unfortunate second marriage hampered the widowed Emma Willard's ability to affect education broadly. In a letter to her good friend Amos Eaton, she admitted that she had made inquiries concerning the character of Christopher Yates, a physician from Albany, and that at one point she had broken off their engagement. Despite her doubts, she married Yates

Emma
Hart
Willard

on September 17, 1838, after carefully signing a prenuptial agreement that put Troy Seminary and the proceeds from the sale of her textbooks in the control of her son. After nine months of living with Yates in Boston (he was a gambler and a fortune hunter), Willard retired to Berlin, Connecticut, to live with a sister. In 1843, she petitioned for and was granted a divorce by the Connecticut Legislature with the legal right to use the name Emma Willard again.

Emma now eagerly accepted an offer from Henry Barnard, well-known Connecticut common-school reformer, to write an address on the pressing need for common schools in Kensing-

ton, Connecticut. Her speech so impressed the citizens that, in 1840, they elected her superintendent of their common schools. She energetically organized women's committees to supervise activities and raise funds for the common schools. She wrote, "I do not wish women to act out of their sphere; but it is time that modern improvements should reach their case and enlarge their sphere. . . . Why, in the name of common sense, should the school society hesitate to make a woman overseer of the schools?"

After completing her duties in the Connecticut common schools, Willard returned to New York where, her tarnished reputation restored, she became an active speaker for the new teachers' institutes springing up throughout the state. In the fall of 1845, she made a tour through southern New York and was heard by over 5,000 teachers. In 1846, she journeyed 8,000 miles through the South and the West, visiting seminaries and urging women to take an interest in the common schools.

Although there is no evidence that Willard was invited to or would have attended the women's rights convention held in Seneca Falls, New York, in July 1848, her published response on the issue of women's suffrage constituted a masterful display of her increasing comfort with halfway measures to achieve minimal change for women. In April 1848, she published an article in the *American Literary Magazine* addressed to a delegate to the French constitutional convention, entitled "The Political Position of Women." She carefully advocated a plan which partially enfranchised women and enlarged their political space to include care of the poor and of public morality as well as their role in education. Emma Willard's predilection for reform that guaranteed stability and promoted control of unruly elements was enhanced by increasing age and insecure social prominence.

Returning to Troy Seminary, she increasingly allowed her son and daughter-in-law **Sarah Lucretia Hudson** to govern the school while she remained an active and popular regional voice for women's education until her death in 1870.

Ambitious and hungry for recognition, Willard early perceived the personal rewards available in educational achievements for a bright, attractive young teacher. Encouraged by the significant men in her life, she eagerly sought the learning her intelligence demanded. Fortunate circumstances provided her with educational resources denied most women of the time; financial crisis gave her ample social justification for seizing control of her own and her family's destiny; power and prestige resulted from her efforts on behalf of women's higher education, and she achieved her ends without losing the admiration she sought and craved. Certainly the female seminary movement provided the vehicle for Willard's emergence on the American cultural scene during the exuberance of the Jacksonian period. Making controversial ideas palatable to people of influence by advocating the use of schooling and educated women as mediating forces, Willard pushed her sex toward a new definition of women and their role in American society.

SOURCES:

Goodsell, Willystine, ed. *Pioneers of Women's Education in the United States.* NY: AMS Press, 1931.

James, Edward T., ed. *Notable American Women, 1607–1950.* Cambridge, MA: The Belknap Press of Harvard University, 1971.

Lord, John. *Life of Emma Willard.* NY: D. Appleton, 1873.

Lutz, Alma. *Emma Willard: Daughter of Democracy.* Boston, MA: Houghton-Mifflin, 1929.

———. *Emma Willard, Pioneer Educator of American Women.* Boston, MA: Beacon Press, 1964.

Monroe, Paul, ed. *A Cyclopedia of Education.* Vol. 5. NY: Macmillan, 1913, pp. 795–811.

Scott, Ann. "A Widening Circle: The Diffusion of Feminist Values," in *The History of Education Quarterly.* Spring 1980.

Willard, Emma. *A Plan For Improving Female Education* (rep. of the 2nd ed. of 1819). VT: Middlebury College, 1918.

Woody, Thomas. *A History of Women's Education In The United States.* Vol. I. NY: Science Press, 1929.

SUGGESTED READING:

Cott, Nancy. *The Bonds of Womanhood.* New Haven, CT: Yale University Press, 1976.

Sklar, Kathryn Kish. *Catharine Beecher: A Study in American Domesticity.* New Haven, CT: Yale University Press, 1973.

COLLECTIONS:

Emma Willard's papers and letters are located in the Emma Willard Library Archives in Troy, New York.

Anne J. Russ,
Professor of Education and Sociology,
Wells College, Aurora, New York

Willard, Frances E. (1839–1898)

American president of the Woman's Christian Temperance Union, who actively advocated for the prohibition of alcohol and other reforms affecting women, including the "home protection ballot." Born Frances Elizabeth Caroline Willard on September 28, 1839, in Churchville, near Rochester, New York; died in New York City on February 17, 1898, of pernicious anemia; daughter of Josiah Willard (a farmer and businessman) and Mary (Hill) Willard (a teacher); educated at a district school near Janesville, Wisconsin; attended private school in Janesville (one winter), Milwaukee Normal Institute (one term), North Western Female College (three terms, Laureate of Science, 1860); never married; lived with Anna Adams Gordon (1853–1931); no children.

Moved with family to Oberlin, Ohio (1841–46); moved with family to a farm near Janesville on Wisconsin frontier (1846–58); moved to Evanston, Illinois, when she enrolled at North Western, where she lived for the rest of her life; taught school and published occasional articles (1862–66); traveled in Europe and Middle East (1868–70); served as president, Northwestern University's Ladies College (1871–74); served as president, Chicago Woman's Christian Temperance Union (1874–76); was secretary, National

WCTU *(1874–77); served as president, Illinois WCTU (1878); served as president, National WCTU (1879–98); served as president, World WCTU (1891–97); inducted into the Women's Hall of Fame at Seneca Falls, New York (autumn 2000).*

Selected writings: Nineteen Beautiful Years *(1863);* Woman and Temperance *(1883);* How to Win: A Book for Girls *(1886);* Woman in the Pulpit *(1888);* Glimpses of Fifty Years: The Autobiography of an American Woman *(1889);* Evanston: A Classic Town: The Story of Evanston by an Old-Timer *(1891);* A Great Mother *(1894);* A Wheel Within a Wheel: How I Learned to Ride the Bicycle *(1895); (ed. with Mary Livermore)* A Woman of the Century *(1893); (ed. with Helen Winslow and Sallie White)* Occupations for Women *(1897).*

"Do everything," said Frances Willard to her thousands of followers in the Woman's Christian Temperance Union (WCTU) and throughout America. And everything is what she herself tried to do, as leader of the first great organization of American women. When Willard initially used the phrase in an 1881 presidential address to the WCTU, she was referring to tactics rather than goals: lobbying, petition, moral suasion, gospel temperance, and publicity. Over the next decade, however, the term came to mean that the social issues of her day were all interrelated and must be attacked simultaneously. She expanded the WCTU, founded just five years before she became president, into a national and international political force. She tried to bring together various third party and reform groups into a strong coalition. She not only campaigned for a federal amendment for prohibition of alcohol but urged the adoption of a "home protection ballot" so that women could vote against the establishment of saloons in their neighborhoods, and eventually supported women's right to the full franchise. She argued for women to be ordained as ministers in churches and included in church government. She embraced diet and exercise fads as well as dress reform and schemes for easing the drudgery of housework. She worked with the WCTU to establish day nurseries for poor working women, and endorsed the free kindergarten movement, federal aid to education to compel Southern states to educate blacks, and a department of hygiene to study municipal sanitation. She lobbied for "social evil reform," to raise the age of consent, hold men equally guilty in prostitution offenses, and strengthen and enforce laws against rape. She personally supported the labor movement and Christian socialism. And at the end of her life, with her health in de-

cline, she still summoned energy to work for the relief of Armenian refugees. In addition, she wrote ten books, on everything from family biography to bicycle riding.

Frances Willard was a "welcome child," according to her own account. Her brother Oliver was four at the time of her birth in 1839, but her parents had lost their next two babies, including a 14-month-old daughter the year before Frances was born. Their mother remembered that child as having "a disposition without a flaw," and Willard's biographer **Ruth Bordin** suggests that Frances may have worked especially hard all her life trying to make up for the loss to her mother. **Mary Hill Willard** was a teacher for 11 years before her marriage and continued to teach her children and other pupils at home. In 1841, when the Willards moved to Oberlin where Josiah Willard intended to study for the ministry, Mary enrolled as well in the country's first co-educational college.

In 1846, Josiah gave up his ambition for the ministry, and moved to a farm on the Wisconsin frontier near Janesville, where he became a gentleman farmer. Oliver was sent to school, but Frances and her sister **Mary**, three years younger, were educated by their mother, who urged them to keep journals, and did not require them to do housework. "Frank" (a common nickname for Frances) enjoyed carpentry and outdoor activities shared with her brother; she also published occasional pieces in local farm journals. Josiah joined the Free Soil Party, was elected to the Wisconsin legislature in 1848, and was also active in the Washingtonians, a prewar organization that worked with recovering alcoholics. Although he could be authoritarian, he also cooked meals and tended babies. He made no secret of his preference for Frances' sister Mary, a docile and lovely girl, but he accompanied Frances to publish her first book and go to her first jobs.

Frances' formal education was limited to a short spell in 1857 at the Milwaukee Normal Institute (her father brought her and Mary back home after one term) and then at the North Western Female College in Evanston, where Frances quickly earned a reputation as "the wildest girl in the school" for pranks like climbing the college steeple during study hours. Perhaps for that reason, the Willards rented out their farm and moved to Evanston so Frances could live at home.

After leaving North Western, Willard tried a number of different career paths. During the next eight years, she taught for short periods of time at a Cook County one-room public school, an academy at Kankakee, as "preceptress" of natural sciences at North Western, at the Pittsburgh Female College, and a final two-year assignment at the Genesee Wesleyan Seminary in Lima, New York. She considered it a "hedged up life," however, and after the death from tuberculosis of her sister Mary in 1862, she spent the summer of 1863 writing a biography of her sister, *Nineteen Beautiful Years*. Her father sold the Evanston house which reminded him too powerfully of Mary and built a new one, "Rest Cottage," where Frances Willard would live for the rest of her life.

Do everything.

—Frances Willard

During her time at Genesee, Willard became corresponding secretary for the Methodist Ladies Centenary Association, to raise money for the Garrett Theological Seminary. Her signature on the acknowledgments which went out all over the country gave her great name recognition. At Genesee, Willard met **Katharine Jackson**, and traveled with her to Europe and the Middle East from 1868 to 1870, visiting European universities and studying foreign languages. Although Willard had become engaged in 1861 to Charles Fowler, later president of Northwestern University, she broke off the engagement because she was reluctant to give up her independence. Kate Jackson was the first of several close female friends who, along with her mother, provided Willard with emotional support throughout her life.

When Willard and Jackson returned to Evanston, they found that a new Ladies College had been chartered and Northwestern University had proposed a union. Willard, well educated after her stint in Europe and experienced in fund-raising through her work at Garrett, was named president of the new college. A number of problems, including the succession to the presidency of her former fiancé Fowler, harassment from male students, and financing problems with their building after the Chicago fire led to Willard's resignation in 1874.

Willard was at a crossroads. Her experiences in Europe had intensified her resolve to do something for women, but she was unsure of whether to continue as an educator or an administrator. An anti-saloon crusade, characterized as the "woman's war" in the press, began in December 1873 and lasted until the fall of 1874. Women marched by the hundreds, invaded bars with opened Bibles, or knelt in the streets outside. Temperance became the most important women's issue of the day, leading to the organization of the Woman's Christian Temperance Organization.

Willard was eager to work for the temperance movement. As a Methodist, she had been brought up to abstain from alcohol, although in Europe she had, on doctor's advice, taken wine instead of potentially contaminated water. She was, however, concerned that she could not earn a living through temperance work. On a visit to Maine to attend a temperance meeting, she opened a Bible in her hotel to the passage: "Trust in the Lord and do good. So shalt thou dwell in the land and verily thou shalt be fed." This technique was not unusual among her contemporaries, and throughout her life Frances Willard would be open to psychic investigations. She accepted a position as president of the Chicago Woman's Temperance organization and found she was good at preaching to men and boys whom she hoped to lure away from the temptation of drink. In the fall of 1874, she was elected secretary of the Illinois WCTU, and she represented Chicago at the first national convention of the WCTU, where she was elected corresponding secretary of the national organization, a position she held until 1877.

"Do everything" could have been her motto at this time in her life as well. In 1875, while she was president of the Chicago union and secretary of the Illinois WCTU, she took on the massive correspondence of the national group and yet still found time to work as before with derelicts in the Chicago Loop and to speak in the Chicago area. During 80 days over the summer, she wrote 2,000 letters and delivered 40 speeches.

Willard threw herself into the work she felt called to do, though not without sidelong glances at other possibilities over the next few years. In the spring of 1875, Willard met *Anna E. Dickinson, a celebrity on the lecture circuit. Willard tried to interest Dickinson in temperance work, but Dickinson preferred the podium. Willard had given many talks to temperance and church audiences and had even taken voice lessons; after she met Dickinson, she realized she could be a professional lecturer. In 1876, Willard spoke before ever larger forums, including the Centennial Exposition in Philadelphia and at Chautauqua. The following year, she was asked by evangelist Dwight Moody to join his lecture circuit, and although she was unable to work with him for long due to a number of differences, she earned a nationwide reputation from the association. On tour with him, she also met **Anna Adams Gordon**, a young woman who would be her companion and private secretary for the rest of her life.

Frances' brother Oliver died in the spring of 1878, and for a few months she took over his po-

❧▸ Gordon, Anna Adams (1853–1931)

American social reformer. Born in Boston, Massachusetts, on July 21, 1853; died in Castile, New York, on June 15, 1931; fourth daughter and fourth of seven children of James Monroe Gordon (a bank cashier and treasurer of the American Board of Commissioners for Foreign Missions) and Mary Elizabeth (Clarkson) Gordon; attended public schools in Newton, Massachusetts; attended Mt. Holyoke Seminary, 1871–72, and Lasell Seminary, Auburndale, Massachusetts; never married; no children; lived with Frances Willard.

Became secretary to Frances E. Willard (1877); joined Woman's Christian Temperance Union (1879), serving as vice president (1898–1925); appointed superintendent of juvenile work, World Woman's Christian Temperance Union (1891), and advanced to president (1922); author of several books, including The Beautiful Life of Frances E. Willard *(1898), and song collections, among them* Young People's Temperance Chorus Book *(1911),* Marching Songs for Young Crusaders *(1916), and* Jubilee Songs *(1923).*

Anna Adams Gordon was born in 1853 in Boston, Massachusetts, and attended college at both Mt. Holyoke Seminary (later to become Mt. Holyoke College) and Lasell Seminary. A studious young woman with a strong interest in music, Gordon found her life changed forever when she attended a revival program held by evangelist Dwight L. Moody that was held in Boston in 1877. There she met *Frances E. Willard, a young social idealist, and a lifelong friendship was formed. Gordon became Willard's secretary, moving from New England to Willard's native Midwest, where she resided with her friend and shared her interest in social change.

When Willard became active in the Woman's Christian Temperance Union (WCTU) in 1879, Gordon followed her lead, supporting Willard's term as president with her clerical and organizational skills. Both with Willard and on her own, Gordon traveled throughout

the United States on behalf of the WCTU, speaking out on the evils of strong drink and aiding in the organization of local branches and children's auxiliary units. Her work with young people particularly inspired Gordon, and she wrote several marching songs for use by the WCTU branch dealing directly with children. In 1891, at age 38, Gordon became supervisor of juvenile work for the World Woman's Christian Temperance Union (WWCTU), a new incarnation of the WCTU.

After Willard's death in 1898, Gordon became vice president of the U.S. branch of the WWCTU, and helped that organization expand its agenda to address the growing grassroots movement to urge the passage of legislation prohibiting the sale and distribution of alcoholic beverages within the United States. Lobbying efforts by Gordon convinced President Woodrow Wilson to curtail the commercial use of foods specifically used in the manufacture of alcoholic beverages, and after the 18th Amendment was passed, she pushed the WWCTU to aid in the enforcement of the government's new Prohibition legislation. President of the international organization by the early 1920s, Gordon resigned her vice-presidency with the national affiliate in 1925, devoting the remainder of her life to expanding the WWCTU's focus to include the Americanization of immigrants, child-welfare legislation, and improving the condition of working women throughout the industrialized world.

In addition to her dedication to social reform, Gordon remained dedicated to her friend even after Willard's death, publishing *The Beautiful Life of Frances E. Willard* (1898) and *What Frances E. Willard Said* (1905). Other books by Gordon include *Marching Songs for Young Crusaders* (1916) and *Everybody Sing* (1924), collections of many of the songs she wrote during her early years with the WCTU. Gordon died in Castile, New York, in 1931, age 78.

SOURCES:

McHenry, Robert, ed. *Famous American Women.* NY: Dover, 1980.

Pamela Shelton,
freelance writer, Avon, Connecticut

sition as editor of the *Chicago Post.* She could not save the financially troubled paper, and it was sold in the early summer. After that, Willard worked exclusively within the temperance movement.

In 1876, she began to call for woman suffrage, as a "home protection ballot." It was part of Willard's political genius to start with the non-controversial belief that a woman had a duty to her home, and then to extend the implications gradually from voting on local liquor licenses, to universal suffrage, to involvement in

other social issues which affect the family, such as education, economics and crime. In 1876, the WCTU convention voted against the suffrage resolution, as many women were horrified at the notion of "trail[ing] our skirts through the mire of politics." But by 1892, the WCTU's official publication would call for woman suffrage as a right, not merely as a means to an end.

In 1877, Willard resigned as secretary of the national WCTU, and challenged the leadership of president *Annie Wittenmyer, one of those opposed to suffrage. Willard's support meant much to suffrage leaders like *Susan B. Anthony, because the WCTU, which almost doubled its 1876 membership of 13,000 in one year, was much larger than the National Woman Suffrage Association. In 1878, Willard became president of the Illinois WCTU and led the first campaign for the home protection ballot. Although their petition to the state legislature failed, Willard received a great deal of publicity for her leadership. At the 1879 convention, Willard, 40, was elected president of the WCTU, a post she would hold for nearly 20 years. By 1881, the WCTU accepted the home protection ballot as part of its program.

During the 1880s, Willard became the most famous woman of her time. The WCTU expanded from 27,000 members to almost 200,000. During those ten years, she was away from home nearly continuously, averaging a meeting a day, and visiting 1,000 American cities and towns at least once. She supported her household, including herself, her mother and Anna Gordon, with lecture fees, even after she began to receive a salary from the WCTU in 1886.

Among Willard's most ambitious undertakings were her tours of the South, where women had little history of volunteer organizations or politics. There as elsewhere, her ability to reassure suspicious audiences by her gracious and womanly demeanor, and to lead them slowly toward her goal, were successful. The time was right, too, being after Reconstruction but before the repressive Jim Crow laws of the 1890s. She was invited to address not only white audiences but African-American ones as well.

During the 1880s, Willard published four more books. Due to her celebrity, they were all popular, even though they were hastily written and more propaganda than literature. Her autobiography, *Glimpses of Fifty Years*, published in 1889, was a bestseller. Her annual speech to the WCTU fall convention was the occasion for her principal message to the public at large, and she made a ritual of going into seclusion for some time beforehand to compose each one. The halls where she delivered the addresses were packed, and the press coverage she received was greater than that accorded to any other contemporary woman, according to Bordin.

Frances Willard customarily put in a long day, writing between 40 and 60 letters, often with the help of one or more secretaries. She liked domestic comforts but knew her surroundings would have to be made "wholesome and delightful by other hands than mine." Anna

Gordon functioned as Willard's capable chief of staff. After her brother's death, Frances Willard's two nephews had continuing problems with alcohol, which could have proved embarrassing to her as a temperance worker. She took much responsibility for their welfare.

As president of the first large women's organization, Willard was in a position to exert political force. This she was prepared to do, although she preferred to call it "influence." Her first move away from a narrow focus on prohibition and the home protection ballot was her support in 1883 of the free kindergarten movement. The WCTU also pledged to work for sexual purity laws, lobbying to raise the legal age of consent for females, which was ten years of age in twenty states and seven in one. By the middle of the decade, Willard became active in the American Social Science Association, joining those who believed that problems of alcohol abuse could not be solved solely by appeals to personal morality.

She broadened not only her agenda but her power base. Although she had Republican inclinations, bolstered by her admiration for *Lucy Webb Hayes, a temperance supporter, the Republican Party did not welcome women members. The Prohibition Party did. The largest third party from 1884 until 1892, it also supported the direct election of senators, an income tax, and votes for women. Willard served on the party's executive committee for ten years, from 1882 until 1891, and in 1888 campaigned for its presidential candidate. In 1886, WCTU delegates attended the national convention of the Knights of Labor, America's first mass labor organization, a union for skilled workers. They did not admit to membership anyone in the liquor trade; they were also women's rights advocates, demanding equal pay for equal work.

The publication in 1887 of Edward Bellamy's utopian novel *Looking Backward* provided a model for the national reform impulses of all these groups. Willard read the book soon after its release, and in her 1888 WCTU convention address, she urged all her listeners to read it. Bellamy, with whom she began corresponding, had a profound effect on the development of her idea that social reform must proceed on a wide front.

Frances Willard's political influence was at its peak in the early years of the 1890s. Even without the vote, WCTU members had successfully lobbied for local option and age of consent laws in numerous communities. Education on alcohol was part of the curriculum in nearly all

public schools. They had worked to establish institutions for disabled and "delinquent" women.

A second reform movement had grown up in the 1880s. Farmers' alliances grew steadily throughout the decade, while the Prohibition Party's appeal was waning. The alliances came together as the People's Party (also known as the Populists) in 1892, surpassing the Prohibition Party in size. The two groups had much in common: a Midwestern and Western constituency composed of alienated citizens—farmers and women—interested in basic reforms. It seemed logical for the two groups to unite in the cause of change. Willard invited a number of leading reformers to an informal meeting in Chicago in 1891, to position themselves for the 1892 election. It is a measure of her political stature that 28 of them accepted her invitation, including James B. Weaver, the first presidential candidate of the People's Party, and Samuel Dickie, Prohibition Party chair. The gap between the two parties was too wide, however. Even this small group was unable to reach agreement. Although Willard was made a member of the Populists' platform committee at their convention, the People's Party would not support either prohibition or woman suffrage, and the Prohibitionists could not support a group which ignored their two most basic tenets.

At the pivotal moment when her efforts at fusion were failing, two events shifted Willard's life in a new direction. In the fall of 1891, she met *Isabella Somerset, then known as Lady Henry Somerset, president of the British Woman's Temperance Association, and the two became friends and allies. And Willard's mother, long her mainstay, died. Shortly thereafter, in the summer of 1892, Willard and Gordon visited Lady Henry in England, where they spent much of the next four years. Willard came to terms with her loss by writing *A Great Mother*, Mary Hill Willard's biography.

The WCTU had, through missionary programs, already established an international presence. In 1884, they had begun to collect signatures on a "polyglot petition," a plea for world leaders to adopt prohibition. In 1891, Willard gathered 17 delegates from overseas to form the World WCTU and was elected president. As such, she had a reason for her protracted visits overseas, although her absence sometimes weakened her position at home. While in England, she met Sidney Webb, the socialist and husband of *Beatrice Webb, and in her 1893 address called for "Gospel Socialism" to bring about economic justice.

In the fall of 1892, Willard began to suffer from unaccustomed fatigue, and in the spring of 1893, she was diagnosed with pernicious anemia. She had always been interested in food fads and had given up tea and coffee in the late 1880s. By the 1890s, she was nearly a vegetarian, living on whole-wheat bread, vegetables and fruit, milk and a little fish. Her diet probably worsened her condition. Red meat, especially liver, was recommended at the time in the absence of iron supplements. Willard was too ill to

travel back to the United States and missed the opening of the Chicago World's Columbian Exposition, even though she was on its Board of Lady Managers. She tried to improve her health by exercise, and took up the new activity of bicycle riding, producing, characteristically, a book on the subject, *Wheel Within a Wheel: How I Learned to Ride the Bicycle*. She regretted her loss of energy. "I'm like a dog that has lost its bone," she lamented. "Work was my bone and a meaty one it has been."

Despite declining health, Willard was still the best-known woman in America and continued to influence WCTU policy. However, she was not unchallenged. In 1894, as the organization celebrated its 20th anniversary, she faced a number of difficult issues. At the annual convention, after a struggle, she was able to amend the constitution to appoint her successor. But back in England, she came under attack by *Ida Wells-Barnett, an African-American from Chicago who was critical of Willard's position on the controversial issue of the lynchings which were increasing throughout the South. Willard had made an ambiguous speech in 1893 condemning lynching, while seeming also to assume that accusations of black men raping white women were true.

In February 1895, Willard was on hand to present the Polyglot Petition to President Grover Cleveland, representing a demand by women for foreign policy influence. That same year, women in England and the United States took up another international cause, the plight of Armenian Christians in eastern Turkey who had become the victims of systematic mass murder. Willard and Lady Henry set up a refugee relief program in France in the summer of 1896, but the effort left Willard exhausted. A slight estrangement had begun between the two women—"Will we still be two cherries on a single stem?" Willard had worried before traveling to England that year—and the following year they disagreed over an English law proposing to license and regulate prostitution in order to control venereal disease. Lady Henry supported the law, while Willard held with those who saw it as governmental consent to the degradation of women.

After the WCTU national convention in 1896, Frances Willard retired to Dr. **Cordelia Green**'s sanatorium for women in Castile, New York, where she would spend most of the remainder of her life. She presided over one more meeting of the WCTU, where she promised to raise money for the WCTU's Temple office building, in financial difficulty ever since the depression of 1893. While in New York City for that purpose, her health worsened. She invited a New York *Tribune* reporter for a final interview, and gathered her family and friends for a sentimental Victorian deathbed scene. She died at midnight on February 17, 1898.

"No woman before or since was so clearly on the day of her death this country's most honored woman," Bordin wrote. Alcohol abuse was greater in the 19th century than in the 20th, and prohibition or severe regulation, Bordin said, was supported by most Protestant churchgoers, the business community, and the aspiring middle class. Willard, her biographer concludes, was more prominent than other 19th-century woman because her cause was more urgent. She attributes the fact that Frances Willard is little known today to the decline in popularity of prohibition, the cause with which she was most identified.

SOURCES:

Bordin, Ruth. *Frances Willard: A Biography.* Chapel Hill, NC: University of North Carolina Press, 1986.

COLLECTIONS:

Woman's Christian Temperance Union Papers, Willard Memorial Library, The National Headquarters of the WCTU, Evanston, Illinois; and Frances Willard papers, Schlesinger Library, Radcliffe College, Cambridge, Massachusetts.

SUGGESTED READING:

Leeman, Richard W. *Do Everything Reform.* Westport, CT: Greenwood, 1992.

Kristie Miller,
author of *Ruth Hanna McCormick: A Life in Politics 1880–1944*,
University of New Mexico Press, 1992

Willebrandt, Mabel Walker

(1889–1963)

American government official. Born Mabel Walker on May 23, 1889, in Woodsdale, Kansas; died of lung cancer on April 6, 1963, in Riverside, California; daughter of David William Walker (a newspaper editor) and Myrtle (Eaton) Walker (a teacher); expelled from Park College in Parksville, Missouri; graduated from the State Normal School in Tempe, Arizona, 1911; University of Southern California, LL.B., 1916, LL.M., 1917; married Arthur F. Willebrandt (a school administrator), in February 1910 (divorced 1924); children: one daughter, Dorothy Rae (adopted).

Career as educator included positions at public schools in Buckley, Michigan, and Phoenix, Arizona, and appointments as principal at both Buena Park School in Los Angeles, and Lincoln Park School in Pasadena, California; appointed head of Legal Advisory Board, District Eleven, Los Angeles (1914–19); admitted to the bar in California (1916); appointed assistant public defender of Los Angeles; appointed assistant attorney general of the U.S. (1921); argued over 40 cases before the U.S. Supreme Court; helped establish the first federal prison for women (c. 1925); became first woman to chair a committee on the Republican National Convention (1928); returned to private practice (1929); published monograph The Inside of Prohibition *(1929); obtained pilot's license (c. 1940).*

Mabel Walker Willebrandt was born in Woodsdale, Kansas, in 1889, into a family that valued education over financial gain. Her father, a newspaper editor, moved from town to town, working for small newspapers across the country while her mother found a suitable teaching job until the family's next relocation. Educated at home in her early years, Willebrandt did not receive formal schooling until the sixth grade, by which point she had developed an independent view of life. After graduating from high school, she enrolled at Park College in Parksville, Missouri, only to be expelled for openly expressing religious opinions that differed with those of the college administration. By age 17, Willebrandt had sufficient qualifications to pursue a career in

Mabel Walker Willebrandt

education; she got a job teaching high school classes in Buckley, Michigan, and then proceeded to marry the principal, Arthur F. Willebrandt.

Her husband's medical problems forced the family to move several times before they ultimately settled in the Los Angeles, California, area, where Willebrandt got a job as principal of Buena Park School, and then of Lincoln Park Grammar School. She next enrolled at the University of Southern California and graduated with an LL.B. in 1916. She passed the bar exam that year, and the following year received an LL.M. degree from the University of California. Adding her voice to those of other attorneys wishing to form a public defender's office in Los Angeles, Willebrandt saw this goal reach fruition. However, because of her married status, she was offered only a job as public defender for women charged with criminal offenses, a position that was unpaid, but which nonetheless offered her the opportunity to help over 2,000 poor individuals while starting her private practice as an attorney.

Willebrandt's volunteer efforts on behalf of justice, as well as her commitment to the Republican Party platform in California, continued through World War I, during which time she was appointed head of the Legal Advisory Board for draft cases for the largest draft board in Los Angeles. In 1921, at the age of 32, Willebrandt was appointed by President Warren G. Harding to the U.S. Justice Department, based on the recommendation of her Republican colleagues in California. The enforcement of Prohibition laws decreed by passage of the 18th Amendment to the U.S. Constitution would occupy much of Willebrandt's time in her new position as an assistant attorney general of the United States, despite the fact that she was not personally in favor of the constitutional revision. Earning the nickname "Prohibition Portia," Willebrandt successfully prosecuted the vast majority of cases charged to her, and successfully petitioned to have over 250 accepted for review by the U.S. Supreme Court in an effort to clarify the new law and regulate its enforcement. (One of her most widely publicized prosecutions involved popular singer *Helen Morgan, who had been duped into believing there was little danger in running a speakeasy.) Forty of those cases she argued before the Court herself. Willebrandt also wrote articles in support of Prohibition for magazines like *Ladies' Home Journal* and *Good Housekeeping*, and spoke out in an effort to gain public support for the new laws, encouraging law enforcement agencies to focus on the major lawbreakers rather than local speakeasies and still-owners.

In addition to her high-profile efforts on behalf of Prohibition, which she would later detail in *The Inside of Prohibition* (1929), Willebrandt accomplished much in other facets of government. In the area of prison reform, she was successful in establishing the first federal prison for women, Alderson Prison in West Virginia, and made other strides in modernizing the means by which the nation rehabilitated its criminals. In 1928, now the highest-ranking woman in a federally appointed position and actively involved in the campaign to elect Herbert Hoover to the office of president, Willebrandt was asked to chair a committee at that year's Republican National Convention. However, the public outcry over Prohibition and its factor as a central issue in the upcoming presidential campaign made her job as enforcer of laws banning the sale and distribution of alcohol a source of controversy. Resigning her post within the Republican National Convention, Willebrandt left the Justice Department in May 1929, and retired to private practice. Establishing offices in both Washington, D.C., and Los Angeles, she counted among her clients the California Grape Growers, the Aviation Corporation, and the Screen Director's Guild. Although she was divorced from her husband in 1924, Willebrandt remained determined to have a child, and in 1925 adopted two-year-old Dorothy Rae, whom she raised with the help of friends. In addition to teaching herself to fly at the age of 50, Willebrandt remained active in civic life and in the American Bar Association (ABA), where she became the first woman to chair an ABA committee—the committee on aeronautical law. Moving between homes in Washington, D.C., and California, and a farm she owned in Gettysburg, Pennsylvania, Willebrandt had a reputation as a generous woman, a skilled host, and an energetic debater. She died in 1963, at age 74.

SOURCES:

Sicherman, Barbara, and Carol Hurd Green, eds. *Notable American Women: The Modern Period*. Cambridge, MA: The Belknap Press of Harvard University, 1980.

Weatherford, Doris. *American Women's History*. NY: Prentice Hall, 1994.

Pamela Shelton,
freelance writer,
Avon, Connecticut

Williams, Abigail.

See Witchcraft Trials in Salem Village.

Williams, Anna (1706–1783)

English poet. Born in 1706 in Rosemarket, England; died on September 6, 1783, in London, England;

daughter of Zachariah Williams (a physician and inventor); educated at home.

Anna Williams was born in 1706 in Rosemarket, near Milford Haven, England, but moved with her widowed father to London when she was in her early teens. The daughter of a physician and inventor, Williams was unusually well educated for a young woman of her time, and through her father's efforts as an inventor—he worked, unsuccessfully, for many years on a method of determining precise longitude while at sea—she came into contact with several scientists. While supporting her now-impoverished father by taking on embroidery piecework, Williams also assisted Stephen Grey with his rudimentary experimentation with electricity. Fluent in several languages, she earned much-needed funds with her translation of *The Life of the Emperor Julian* (1746) from its original French. However, by middle age, Williams developed cataracts which caused her sight to diminish significantly. The family's troubles increased again when Williams' father lost the rooms he and his daughter had been living in; fortunately they were provided support by her father's friend, the eminent Dr. Johnson, and his wife **Elizabeth "Tetty" Porter Johnson**. Johnson also arranged for Williams to have an operation to restore her vision, but that operation—not surprisingly, given the times—was not a success, and instead rendered her totally blind.

In 1755, Zachariah Williams died, leaving his 49-year-old daughter blind and penniless, but fortunately not friendless. A benefit performance of the play *Merope* provided her with £200. In the meantime, Williams had developed a close relationship with Johnson, and resided with him, off and on, after his wife died in 1752. Several of her poems, which she had written throughout her life, were collected and published in *Miscellanies in Prose and Verse* (1766), a volume which also included contributions from both Johnson and the poet Hester Thrale (***Hester Lynch Piozzi**). Sales of her *Miscellanies*, received through subscriptions promoted by Johnson, earned Williams enough money to live in reasonable comfort for the rest of her life. Her health declined during her 70s, and she died at Johnson's house in 1783. She willed what few funds she had left to a home for deserted women, this reportedly at Johnson's suggestion.

SOURCES:

Shattock, Joanne. *The Oxford Guide to British Women Writers*. Oxford: Oxford University Press, 1993.

Pamela Shelton,
freelance writer,
Avon, Connecticut

Williams, Anna Wessels

(1863–1954)

American bacteriologist who made possible the widespread, cost-effective production of diphtheria antitoxin and also aided in the diagnosis of rabies. Born on March 17, 1863, in Hackensack, New Jersey; died of heart failure on November 20, 1954, in Westwood, New Jersey; daughter of William Williams (a teacher) and Jane (Van Saun) Williams; educated at home; graduated from the New Jersey State Normal School, 1883; New York Infirmary Woman's Medical College, M.D., 1891.

Joined staff of New York Infirmary upon receiving her M.D. (1891–1905); together with William Hallock Park, produced successful antitoxin for diphtheria (1894); produced method of determining presence of rabies in pathology (1896); served as assistant director of New York City Research Laboratories (1905–34); was the author of numerous medical papers, articles, and textbooks, including (as co-author) Pathogenic Microorganisms Including Bacteria and Protozoa *(1905) and* Who's Who among the Microbes *(1929).*

Anna Wessels Williams was born in 1863 into a large family in Hackensack, New Jersey. Her parents were very religious, and home schooled each of their children until grade six. Upon entering Hackensack's public school system at age 12, Williams was captivated by the books and other resources available for her use, particularly the microscope, which opened up a new world to her. After completing high school, she embarked upon a teaching career before switching to the study of medicine. The reason for this change of focus was a family tragedy: in 1887 her sister gave birth to a stillborn baby and almost died due to eclampsia, a toxemia incurred during pregnancy. With the support of both her parents, Williams enrolled at the New York Infirmary's Woman's Medical College, and received her M.D. in 1891. However, she decided against entering the medical profession, realizing that the number of diseases for which there was as yet no treatment would make that career path highly stressful to her. Instead, she determined to devote her life to finding those treatments, and remained at the infirmary through 1905, working as an assistant and as a consulting pathologist.

Meanwhile, Williams also volunteered at the city's Department of Health. Beginning in 1894, she assisted director William Hallock Park in his effort to find an easily produced antitoxin for diphtheria, then one of the major causes of death in children due to the scarcity of an antidote. Early in their joint research, Williams isolated a strain of the diphtheria bacillus—later referred to as Park-Williams #8—which generated substantially more toxin. This discovery made production of the corresponding antitoxin less costly and faster, allowing New York City health officials to fight the disease more rapidly, particularly among poorer residents who could now receive the antitoxin free of charge. Williams' discovery of Park-Williams #8 had resounding repercussions: New York's successful program was adopted by public health facilities nationwide, and an immunization program based on her work would take place in the mid-1940s, making diphtheria a rare occurrence.

In addition to diphtheria, Williams also did research in an effort to stop other diseases, such as chronic eye infections, measles, smallpox, and scarlet fever. A trip to France's Pasteur Institute in 1896 sparked her interest in combating the deadly rabies virus, and she obtained a quantity of the virus sufficient to allow large-scale vaccine production and distribution to begin by the end of the century. But it was not enough simply to produce a vaccine against rabies; Williams also recognized the need for quick diagnosis of potentially rabid animals, a process that at the time involved injecting cells from a suspected carrier into a healthy animal and awaiting the result. Identifying the presence of unusual cells within the brain tissue of infected animals through autopsies in a laboratory setting, she developed a means of staining brain tissue to reveal the presence of these cells almost immediately. For her work in this area, the American Public Health Association appointed Williams chair of its committee to standardize the diagnosis of rabies.

In 1905, Williams was named assistant director of the New York City Research Laboratories, a position she held until her retirement in 1934. During her tenure there, the presence of women on laboratory staffs greatly increased, team work was encouraged, and many processes were streamlined. During World War II, she put her talents to work developing a training program for war service laboratory workers both in the United States and abroad. In addition to her duties as director, she co-authored, with fellow bacteriologist Park, *Pathogenic Microorganisms Including Bacteria and Protozoa* (1905), a popular textbook considered the foundation in its field. A prolific writer, she also published several other books and articles, as well as numerous professional papers. Forced into mandatory retirement despite the objections of her co-workers, the 70-year-old Williams moved to New Jersey, where she lived with her sister until her death in 1954. Among the many honors she received over the course of her career was being elected to an office in the laboratory section of the American Public Health Association, the first woman to be given such office.

SOURCES:

Bailey, Brooke. *The Remarkable Lives of 100 Women Healers and Scientists.* Holbrook, MA: Bob Adams, 1994.

Sicherman, Barbara, and Carol Hurd Green, eds. *Notable American Women: The Modern Period.* Cambridge, MA: The Belknap Press of Harvard University, 1980.

Pamela Shelton,
freelance writer,
Avon, Connecticut

Williams, Augusta (1825–1876).

See Maywood, Augusta.

Williams, Betty and Mairead Corrigan

Co-founders of the Irish Peace People movement of the mid-1970s, the most successful of several early attempts to create a cross-community alliance against terrorism.

Williams, Betty (1943—). Name variations: Betty Williams Perkins. Born Betty Smyth in Belfast, Northern Ireland, on May 22, 1943; daughter of a butcher and a housewife; attended St. Teresa's Primary School and St. Dominic's Grammar School; married Ralph Williams (an engineer in the merchant marine), on June 14, 1961; emigrated to the U.S. where she later remarried; children: (first marriage) Paul; Deborah.

Awards: honorary doctorate from Yale University; Norwegian People Peace Prize (1976); Nobel Peace Prize (1976).

Corrigan, Mairead (1944—). Name variations: Máiread Corrigan; Mairead Corrigan Maguire. Born Mairead Corrigan in Belfast, Northern Ireland, on January 27, 1944; one of eight children of a window cleaning contractor and a housewife; married Jackie Maguire (her deceased sister's husband); children: Luke, Mark, Joanne, Marie Louise, and John.

Awards: honorary doctorate from Yale University; Norwegian People Peace Prize (1976); Nobel Peace Prize (1976).

Apart from a shared environment and a deep concern, shared also with many others, about the abysmal quality of life in troubled Northern Ireland, there was little to connect Betty Williams and Mairead Corrigan with each other, or either of them with the movement's third co-founder,

Ciaran McKeown (pronounced Key-rawn Ma-ki-own). Born within a few years of each other in Belfast, both came from Roman Catholic backgrounds (though Williams was of mixed parentage) and were educated locally and conventionally. By the mid-1970s, Williams was married to a seaman who was absent for most of each year. She lived in the Republican stronghold of Andersonstown, a suburb of Belfast, and much of the strain of bringing up two children in the war-torn terrorist enclave was borne by her. She found it best to live independently of political and religious or even women's groupings. Corrigan at that time also lived in West Belfast. But she was single and living with her parents and so perhaps was freer to respond to the intrusive and often outrageous behavior of both paramilitaries and soldiers in the surrounding streets. At one point in 1973, Corrigan had contemplated joining one such paramilitary organization. They had both spent several years, along with some two million inhabitants of Ulster, as unwilling participants/ victims in the province's "troubles," and but for one event it is likely that they would have remained anonymous. Their public existence, like that of the essayist Charles Lamb, "dated from the day of horrors."

On August 10, 1976, Corrigan's sister **Anne Maguire** was taking her three young children for a walk on a suburban street when a car smashed into them, seriously injuring Maguire and killing all three children—Joanne (8), John (3), and Andrew (6 weeks old). In a macabre characterization of the entire Ulster nightmare, it was discovered that the terrorist driver of the stolen car was already dead, shot moments before the crash by British soldiers during a running gun-battle. Betty Williams who lived nearby was a witness to the tragedy. It was Williams who organized, in the immediate aftermath, the petition calling for the IRA (Irish Republican Army) to cease its campaign, a petition signed by many thousands of Belfast people. Mairead Corrigan, the Maguire family's most vocal representative, helped to organize the massive public demonstration which took place on the day after the children's funeral. It was a show of public outrage unusual in that the Catholic women of West Belfast were joined by Protestant women from elsewhere in the city. It was unusual also in the depth and ferocity of its opposition to the terrorists' activities. As early as 1970, the Women Together movement, again a cross-community initiative in the divided society that is Ulster, had tried with some limited success to intercede between the embattled factions in a traditional men's world and to mediate with the political and military authorities. But the movement which followed the deaths of the Maguire children differed from previous efforts. It differed not only in the depth of its determination to endure and succeed, but also in its unambiguous and single-minded opposition to paramilitaries in a society ruled largely by them and in which terrorism had become a predominant way of life. The ruthless courage of those who led and made up the Peace People movement, together with their avowed rejection of the primacy of the paramilitaries' political aim, represented the first real threat to the popular support on which the moral position of the terrorists depended.

Mairead Corrigan's upbringing was in many ways closer to that of previous generations of Catholic families in Ulster than to the time into which she had been born. The family was large—two boys and five girls—though not uncommonly so by Ulster Catholic standards. Her father washed windows and her mother was kept fully occupied within the home. Her childhood, by her own account, was happy and her rather brief experience of Northern Ireland's segregated school system seemed to have left few real scars. But despite the fact that she was a contemporary of the first generation of Catholics to attend university, poverty determined that she would leave school at the age of 14. A short period at a business college equipped her for employment in one of Belfast's textile mills, a job she later abandoned for a more secure position in the legendary Guinness brewery.

Membership in a religious benevolent association, the Legion of Mary, eventually brought her into immediate contact with the "troubles" in 1969. Corrigan, a team leader in the Legion, worked with the children of Andersonstown, then a bleak featureless Catholic ghetto devoid of facilities, to prevent them from being drawn ever deeper into the surrounding unrest. She was responsible in part for the area's first nursery school and for a recreation center for Andersonstown's handicapped children. Her work with the Legion enabled her also to travel—to Russia, where she made a film on Catholic lifestyles, and as a delegate to the World Conference of Churches in Thailand. In the years before the events of 1976 made her into a household name, she was one of the Legionnaires who maintained close contact with the interned Catholics of Long Kesh prison camp, an old Ulster institution hastily brought back to life in 1971 to contain Catholics suspected of anti-establishment sentiments. Close friends were killed, and on more than one occasion, as she attempted to help those being harassed by soldiers, she was herself assaulted.

On these occasions, as on the evening when the British army teargassed a church in which she was holding a Legion meeting, Corrigan was presented with the choice open to all who endured in Ulster, of whether it might be better to meet violence with violence. Despite her Catholic upbringing, there was no history of overt Republicanism in Corrigan's family. As with many of her forebears it seemed to her simpler and less complicated to sublimate one's political urges, however strong, in religious passivism. Later her encounters with committed Republicans among the prisoners of Long Kesh convinced her of the aimlessness, futility, and eventual loss of direction of those who had resorted to violence. Her sense of personal identity cut across the divisions of life considered "normal" in Northern Ireland: Corrigan was uninterested in ending the partition arrangement whereby the island of Ireland had in 1921 been sundered into two political entities. Like many Ulster Catholics, she was very aware of cultural and attitudinal differences between herself and her co-religionists in the Irish Republic. Less like other Ulster Catholics however, she felt a keen bond with Northern Protestants. She regarded herself neither as British nor Irish: Northern Irishness was in itself a strong and self-contained identity.

Betty Williams' background was somewhat out of the ordinary for a woman who developed, with reservations, a largely conventional Catholic identity. Her mother was a Catholic from a large family, but one whose own father was Jewish. Betty's father, a butcher, was a Protestant. His marriage to Betty's mother led to his father being first assaulted and then shunned in the Belfast shipyard where he worked. Betty herself was born in 1943, attended a Catholic school and, like Mairead Corrigan, left to become a secretary. In 1961, she married Ralph Williams, who was English and Presbyterian, and who worked as an engineer in the merchant marine. The nature of his work meant long and frequent separation from his family. However, Betty appreciated the excellent salary (a rare thing in West Belfast) and being naturally fond of variety, she took evening jobs in addition to her regular daytime employment. Her two children, a boy and a girl, were five and twelve at the time of the Maguire family's ordeal in August 1976.

Unlike Mairead, who already had experience of cross-community work through her religious affiliations, Betty was uncertain as to whether any active role was open to her or what form that activity should take. She was, however, no less affected than Corrigan or anyone else in West Belfast by the surrounding conflict and the conditions created by it. In such an unstable environment, one acted and reacted according to the circumstances of each given situation: ideology and principles were luxuries. In the period before her involvement with the peace movement, Williams had successfully persuaded several local men to forsake Republicanism, transported a wounded paramilitary to safety in the Irish Republic, prayed with and comforted a dying British soldier, and gone through a period in which she ritually hurled abuse at even inoffensive soldiers on ground duty. Her sister's new home was burned by a Protestant mob during the summer disturbances of 1969, and she herself had been mistakenly arrested and detained as a terrorist (a not-uncommon experience in Northern Ireland). Two of her cousins had died in the "troubles"; one killed by Republicans, the other by loyalists.

Despite the never-ending pattern of terrorist atrocity followed by months of aggressive army activity in the locality, followed by a further atrocity and so forth, Williams gradually came to see the participants in the conflict—soldiers, paramilitaries, and their victims—simply as unfortunate human beings caught up in a tragedy that had largely been made before any of them had been born. Several years before the Maguire tragedy, Williams had become horrified at the gradual abandonment by her neighbors of any regard for the lives of fellow human beings. Paramilitaries, however personally unworthy and however questionable their motives, had become heroes; axiomatically all police and soldiers had become anonymous enemies to be destroyed on sight. Close to the localized heart of the struggle in Andersonstown, she was dismayed at the emptiness of the paramilitaries' tribal slogans and at the blind unthinking aggression of their tactics. Like Corrigan, Williams came of no strong Republican family tradition and so had the ability to see through the theoretical shibboleths of the gunmen and beyond their bland and facile justifications of even the most loathsome atrocities.

Unlike Corrigan, whose critical mind yet allowed her to work in close harmony with the Catholic Church, Betty Williams' deep faith in God was qualified by a slightly jaundiced view of the Church in the teachings of which she was reared. She was disturbed by the apparent failure of the Church to keep pace with modern human needs, and by its refusal to be more vocal in opposing the morally questionable behavior both of paramilitaries and the establishment. She was irritated by the prevalence of patriarchalism even in strife-ridden Belfast, by the ubiq-

Betty Williams and Mairead Corrigan.

uitous double standards, and by women's passive acceptance of this situation. The peace movement and its aims however, despite its mainly female leadership and predominantly female membership, transcended feminism. Survival made for a different kind of urgency.

No account of the roles of Corrigan and Williams would be complete (or even comprehensible) without considering that of Ciaran McKeown. Born in 1943 of the same generation as his two co-founders of the peace movement, McKeown shared with them also the ethos of a

Catholic upbringing, but in Londonderry. One of the bright pupils produced by the educational efforts of the Christian Brothers, he was one of the first generation of Catholics to attend Queen's University where he read philosophy. McKeown became concerned at the level of sectarianism which prevailed not only in Northern Ireland generally but even within the apparently liberal precincts of the region's only university. He became deeply involved in student politics, agitating for unity at least within student representative elections, and became president of an all-Ireland student council in 1966.

Every two or three hours we resurrect the past, dust it off and throw it in someone's face. Myself, I prefer tomorrow to yesterday.

—Betty Williams

In the later 1960s, while the Ulster civil-rights movement was being established, McKeown married and settled into professional journalism. Feeling his Catholic identity as much a responsibility as simply an accident of birth, he strove to report and write as impartially as possible, and to present the realities of the Northern Irish situation in a way in which they could be understood even by total strangers to that region and that situation. McKeown had already developed a deep respect for human life and an aversion to those who would destroy it. He was one of the relative few who regarded Michael Farrell and *Bernadette Devlin McAliskey, popular heroes of the civil-rights movement, as mere agitators who had subverted the movement's true purpose for political ends. As a journalist he preferred, when dealing with paramilitaries, to speak to rank-and-file members rather than to their commanders.

McKeown, sickened by the continuing daily diet of death and bloodshed which he was obliged to chronicle, had already decided to abandon news writing for some gentler or more scholarly form of journalism when he was detailed to cover the slaughter of the Maguire children in August 1976. His rapport with Corrigan and Williams was instantaneous and, between the three, the loosely structured Peace People movement emerged.

The movement began its work through a series of marches, designed partly to focus public attention on its objectives, but also with a view to gauging the level of popular response. A mere upsurge of emotion would not alone have carried it forward. Beginning with forays into each of the embattled areas of Belfast, the marches continued at Londonderry and throughout most of the

principal towns of Northern Ireland during the latter half of 1976. The character of the gatherings was that of intense emotion, expressed through impassioned speeches, interdenominational religious services, and singing which was intended to sustain and boost morale. The movement's central demands for peace were embodied in the short but pithy "Declaration of Peace" drawn up by McKeown and read at each march and gathering. Support continued to come from a wide range of organizations and individuals, including the trade union movement both within Ireland and internationally. Opposition came from the Republican elements who alleged that the movement's organizers and their followers, by adopting an explicitly apolitical stance in such a substantively political situation, were unwittingly offering support to the British-maintained establishment in Northern Ireland; that the peace sought by Corrigan, Williams and McKeown would, in fact, be "peace at any price."

Unsurprisingly, the ugliest manifestations of Republican opposition occurred at the Ulster-based marches. The publicity afforded these, however, was more than offset by the personal appearances of **Joan Baez** and veterans of the American civil-rights campaign who gave the Irish movement their unqualified support. All the marches, even with the vagaries of the Irish weather, were successful. Despite enormous attention from the world press, Corrigan and Williams refused to be drawn into conventional political debates on Ulster or on the British presence there; they wished, they said, to create a new type of politics and a new type of political response in Northern Ireland. The early marches in Belfast, especially in the Protestant stronghold of Shankill, were particularly crucial in that they convinced many waverers that the peace movement was not simply Catholic in character. Once the marches began to succeed outside of Belfast, the potential of the movement as a populist venture was made obvious not only to dismissive or hostile Republicans but also to the Northern Irish and British establishments. Journalists as well as Republican opponents began to query the source of the movement's funding, and the suspicion was created deliberately that the movement was a creature of the British establishment, set up with a view to drawing away local support from the terrorists. These insinuations continued as a march organized in London succeeded resoundingly and the leaders Corrigan, Williams and McKeown were awarded prizes by various international bodies, one being the coveted Nobel Peace Prize.

But spontaneity was the hallmark of the movement and structures came slowly; perhaps too slowly. At an early stage, the movement acquired somewhat inadequate office premises which soon became a clearing-house for members' details, phone numbers, and advice. A weekly newsletter was established. However, difficulties were soon created by the three leaders' relative lack of experience of such a large unwieldy organization, by continuing public speculation as to funding, and not least by the personalities and preoccupations of the leaders themselves. Once the early emotion had died down, exception (not always voiced aloud) began to be taken to the apparently casual assumption that Williams, Corrigan, and McKeown, elected by nobody, were to continue in the leadership role. Questions of accountability were raised in connection with the numerous and not infrequently large sums of money which were poured into the movement by individuals and institutions. Occasional cash-flow problems arose when tax exigencies caused a gap between acts of donation and actual receipt of money. At least one of the leaders was heavily in debt by the time the wave of marches came to an end in December 1976.

In the maelstrom of marches, meetings, and speeches some prospective members inevitably were offended by things they had heard the leaders say, or merely by one or another aspect of the movement when viewed at close quarters. Despite their unity on essential issues, the leaders had not thought to place any restraints on the utterance of their private views. McKeown (not unlike Williams in some respects) was critical of the supposed failure of the Catholic Church to speak out against the violence in other than a platitudinal fashion or to provide the sort of leadership which he, Williams, and Corrigan were being forced to assume. This was seen by some of the movement's more conservative Catholic supporters as an unjustified attack on their community's central icon. The divisions in Northern Irish society, after all, were as much religious as political. McKeown's fruitless attempt to force his Church to take up a moral stance, as he had done, was interpreted as an abuse of his position as leader. This led to the most serious challenge to the unity of the movement. Belfastman Tom Conaty expressed resentment that the leaders had endorsed such a view without consulting the rank-and-file members on whose behalf they claimed to speak. In a relatively short but wide-ranging statement, Conaty called for the active involvement of the Catholic Church and other churches in the peace movement, and also for the disbursement of funds to be placed in the hands of trustees. Further discussions led to further disagreement, and Conaty found himself in a sense expelled from the move-

ment, a decision he initially refused to accept. This drew attention to the Peace People's lack of proper representative structures—Conaty to all intents and purposes had been excluded by a set of non-elected leaders. An incalculable but possibly significant number of members left with him.

The movement recovered from the Conaty affair and tried to reorganize itself to prevent further similar rifts from occurring. In terms of media interest, however, the award of the Nobel Peace Prize to Corrigan and Williams in 1977 seems to have been the high watermark. Throughout Northern Ireland, the violence continued, escalating and decelerating by turns, but in response to sets of dynamics against which the Peace People movement clearly was working in vain. The early gibes that the movement was a "peace at any price" body stuck fast. Worse still, the disputes over funding continued to cause bitter wrangles within the movement. Betty Williams, exhausted and unable to find alternative employment in Northern Ireland, emigrated to the United States where she later remarried. Her once-stable relationship with Corrigan and McKeown foundered. Anne Maguire, whose tragedy had founded the movement, never recovered from that August day in 1976 and eventually committed suicide. A year later, Mairead married Anne's husband. She continued for many years to campaign internationally for the movement she had helped to establish, though Northern Irish audiences steadily diminished. McKeown eventually returned to journalism.

The development of peace studies and conflict management into a science of ever-increasing complexity will before too much longer place the Peace People of the 1970s and their founders in a historical context which at present can only dimly be ascertained. The probable end of the Northern Irish conflict will clarify also their role in that conflict and the position of Corrigan, Williams, and McKeown in Irish history and the role of women in the making of that history.

SOURCES:

Deutsch, Richard. *Mairead Corrigan; Betty Williams.* Woodbury, NY: Barron's, 1977.

SUGGESTED READING:

Dunne, Seamus, ed. *Facets of the Conflict in Northern Ireland.* NY: St. Martin's Press, 1995.

Gerard O'Brien, Senior Lecturer in History, University of Ulster, Northern Ireland

Williams, Camilla (1922—)

African-American soprano and teacher. Born in Danville, Virginia, on October 18, 1922; youngest of four children of Cornelius Booker Williams (a chauf-

feur) and Fannie (Carey) Williams; Virginia State College, B.S., 1941; married Charles Beavers (an attorney), on August 28, 1950.

Won the Marian Anderson Award twice; sang with the New York City Opera (1946–54).

Camilla Williams received a B.S. in 1941 from Virginia State College where she studied with **Marion Szekely-Freschl**, Hubert Giesen, and Sergius Kagen. In Philadelphia, she studied with Leo Taubman. In 1943 and again in 1944, Williams won the prestigious *Marian Anderson Award. In 1944, she also won the Philadelphia Orchestra Youth Award. Her operatic debut in 1946 took place at the New York City Opera, where she performed until 1954. Williams also toured widely as a concert artist. She taught at Brooklyn College and at the City College of New York from 1970 to 1973; from 1977, she taught at the Indiana University School of Music in Bloomington.

John Haag,
Athens, Georgia

Williams, Cicely (1893–1992)

British physician who discovered kwashiorkor (protein energy malnutrition). Born Cicely Delphine Williams in Kew Park, Jamaica, on December 2, 1893; died in Oxford, England, on July 13, 1992; daughter of Margaret (Farewell) Williams and James Rowland Williams; attended Bath High School for Girls, 1906–12; Oxford University, B.M., 1920; Oxford University, Ch.B., 1923; London University, diploma in tropical medicine and hygiene, 1929; never married; no children.

Awards: gold medal, British Paediatric Association (1965); Joseph Goldberger Award, American Medical Association (1967); Companion of the Order of St. Michael and St. George (1968); honorary Ph.D., University of the West Indies (1969); Martha May Elliot Award, American Public Health Association (1971); Dawson Williams Prize for Pediatrics, British Medical Association (1972); honorary member of the American Academy of Pediatrics (1973); honorary Ph.D., University of Maryland (1973), Tulane University (1973); fellow of the American Pediatric Association (1976).

Traveled to England (1906); passed the Oxford University entrance examination (1912); death of James Rowland Williams (1916); interned at King's College Hospital (1920); appointed house physician, South London Hospital for Women and Children (1923); worked for the American Farm School, Salonika, Greece (1927); was the first woman appointed

to the British Colonial Service, Gold Coast, Africa (1929); appointed head of the Princess Marie Louise Hospital for Children (1930); discovered kwashiorkor (1931); transferred to the General Hospital, Singapore, Malaya (1936); transferred to the Unfederated State of Trengganu (1941); interned by the Japanese, Changi Prison (1941); appointed commandant of the women's camp (February 1943); imprisoned by the Kempe Tai (October 1943); released by the Kempe Tai (March 25, 1944); served as head of the child health department, Oxford University (1948); was first head of the Section of Maternal and Child Health of the World Health Organization (1948); undertook research into vomiting sickness, Jamaica (1951); death of Margaret Williams (1953); was a senior lecturer in nutrition at London University (1953); studied toxaemia of pregnancy, University College (1955); joined the faculty of the American University of Beirut, Lebanon (1960); appointed advisor in Training Programs for the Family Planning Association of Great Britain (1964); joined the faculty of the University of Tulane (1971).

Selected writings: "Deficiency Diseases in Infants," *in* Gold Coast Medical Report *(Vol. 2, no. 93, 1931);* "A Nutritional Disease of Children Associated with a Maize Diet," *in* Archives of Disease of Childhood *(Vol. 8, no. 423, 1933);* "Clinical Malaria in Children," *in* Lancet *(Vol. 1, no. 441, 1940);* "Teaching Health in the Tropics," *in* Health Education Journal *(Vol. 8, no. 172, 1950);* "Maternal and Child Health Services in Developing Countries," *in* Journal of Tropical Paediatrics *(Vol. 1, no. 3, 1955);* "Factors in the ecology of Malnutrition," *in* Report of the Western Hemisphere Nutrition Congress *(1965);* "The needs of a Hungry World," *in* American Association for Advancement of Science *(1974).*

Cicely Williams made a discovery of stellar significance while working with the natives of West Africa. In 1931, she uncovered an illness known locally as kwashiorkor, or protein energy malnutrition. The earliest reference to kwashiorkor occurs in Psalm 131: "I will refrain my soul and keep it low like a child that is weaned from his mother; yea, my soul is even as a weaned child."

Stemming from a long line of plantations owners, Williams' family arrived in Jamaica during the 17th century from Glamorgan, Wales. It was at Kew Park, a plantation in Westmoreland, that she was born on December 2, 1893, the fourth of six children of James Rowland Williams and **Margaret Farewell Williams**, daughter of Major-General W.T. Freke Farewell, late of the

Cicely Williams

Indian Army. James met Margaret while studying in England. In 1888, the young couple married and moved to the family estate in Jamaica.

Cicely's childhood was one of privilege, surrounded by servants and the idyllic calm of sunshine and sea. The living conditions of the workers on the plantation, however, contrasted sharply with her own. Injuries were common, and from an early age Williams was taught the basics of first aid to help with emergencies. Margaret Williams founded a clinic for young mothers, and although she had no formal training she consulted frequently with local doctors. Thus, early in life Cicely Williams was confronted with the health-care concerns of an impoverished population.

In 1906, Williams was sent to school in England, where she attended the Bath High School for Girls. After graduating in 1912, she wrote the Oxford University entrance examination and passed. A devastating hurricane in the same year, however, did considerable damage to Kew Park. Due to financial constrains, Cicely returned to Jamaica, where she took a position teaching Montessori in Kingston. Though the financial situation at Kew Park gradually improved, in early 1916, James Rowland Williams died.

> *We* worry a great deal about the persons we want to liberate from political tyranny, and we ignore those we could and should liberate from the tyrannies of dirt, ignorance, and hunger.
>
> —Cicely Williams

Due to a shortage of doctors caused by the First World War, Williams was admitted to the school of medicine at Oxford University, arriving in England in October 1917. On October 14, 1920, she received a degree in medicine and found a position at King's College Hospital, where she was introduced to pediatrics by Sir George Frederick Still, a pioneer in the field of children's medicine. Traditionally, Oxford graduates were required to return and write final examinations for a medical degree. Williams did so in 1923.

That same year, she was appointed house physician at the South London Hospital for Women and Children, one of the few English hospitals which employed female doctors. There, her mentor became Dr. **Helen MacKay**, who was the first female fellow of the Royal College of Physicians and a pioneer in preventive and curative health services.

In 1927, after two years at South London and unable to find a permanent position, Williams moved to the American Farm School, near Salonika, Greece. There she instructed local farm boys in the rudiments of health and nutrition, and on the infectious diseases which could be transmitted from livestock to humans. In Greece, she met Dr. **Andrija Stampar**, who forever influenced her concept of community health care.

Returning to England in 1929, Williams earned a diploma in tropical medicine and hygiene from London University. The day after graduating, she was offered a position with the British Colonial Service. Williams was the first woman to be appointed to the British Colonial Service in the Gold Coast (now Ghana). In 1929, the population of the Gold Coast numbered some 3 million inhabitants. There were roughly 60 physicians, 30 nurses, and 10 technicians to serve the entire population. The Gold Coast was known as "The White Man's Grave," due to the epidemics of plague, smallpox, yellow fever, malaria, typhus, and sleeping sickness which swept the region.

Although disease control programs had been implemented, by the time of Williams' arrival new efforts were underway to initiate preventative health-care programs which targeted mothers and children. As Williams noted: "Hippocrates says that the physician 'must look after the patient's regimen while he is yet in health.'" After spending three months in Accra and Kumasi, she was transferred to the remote outpost of Koforidua. In 1930, she was appointed to head the Princess Marie Louise Hospital for Children. There she organized the out-patient services.

Williams identified a condition known as kwashiorkor in 1931. Her research was published in the *Gold Coast Colony Annual Medical Report* of 1932. The report included photographs, and charts measuring the weight of four children with the illness. The syndrome mainly affects infants and children, and if left untreated can result in death. As William J. Darby wrote, "the importance of her early descriptions of this syndrome and related concepts cannot be overestimated. . . . [Kwashiorkor] may well be the world's most appalling cause of early death and morbidity."

Her next publication in the *Archives of Diseases of Childhood*, published with the assistance of MacKay, hinted that an "amino acid or protein deficiency" might be responsible for the illness. Since kwashiorkor means "the disease of the deposed baby when the next one is born" it was a distinct possibility, as kwashiorkor is linked to the early weaning of children without adequate provision for protein.

Williams' hypothesis was not met by universal approval. She remembered the resistance of some of her colleagues. The controversy centered on whether or not kwashiorkor was a distinct disease or associated with pellagra, a syndrome which causes niacin deficiency. As late as 1954, Dr. Alvar Carrillo Gil wrote:

> The inconsistency and futility of Dr. Williams' arguments to establish a differential diagnosis between Kwashiorkor and Infantile Pellagra, are evident from the very first moment. . . . A greater carelessness and

deceit cannot be conceived in each and every one of the propositions presented by Dr. Williams. Taken as a whole they are the best argument to sustain the identity between Infantile Pellagra and Kwashiorkor.

Resistance to her diagnosis occurred largely because "many physicians have been dominated by ideas related to the study of infections," wrote Williams. "But nutritional disorders are an entirely different matter. . . . Disorders can exist as deficiencies, or as excesses or as imbalances. They can co-exist with any other form of disease."

After several years in Africa, Cicely Williams was transferred to the Far East in 1936. Thus, her research on kwashiorkor came to an abrupt end. As a pediatrician at the General Hospital in Singapore, she saw many cases of malnutrition, mainly related to beri beri and rickets. The prevalence of rickets came as a surprise, for Williams had been told that rickets was impossible only five degrees from the Equator.

While in Singapore, she fought the practice of feeding condensed milk to infants, and took on the Nestlé company in a highly controversial paper "Milk and Murder." She emphasized breast feeding and the education of mothers in family planning. As Herbert Ratner commented, "This defense of maltreated babies was probably the first salvo in the battle of breast versus bottle."

By early 1941, Williams was practicing in the Unfederated State of Trengganu when the Japanese invasion interrupted her work. She fled the territory ahead of the Japanese army, only to be trapped in Singapore when the city fell on February 15, 1942. She was interned in Changi Prison. Ironically, her cousin John Farewell had supervised the construction of the facility only a few years previous. The prison was designed to accommodate 700 prisoners. By the end of the war, it held 6,000.

During her two-year internment, Williams saw patients regularly, and was appointed commandant of the women's camp from February to June 1943. When a spy scare swept the prison, Williams was taken away for questioning on October 23, 1943, by the Kempe Tai, the Japanese secret police. She was not released until March 25, 1944, having endured terrible hardships at their hands. Of the treatment of fellow prisoners by the Kempe Tai, she wrote, "It is impossible to describe the courage of some of these men, who maintained their detachment and dignity in spite of hours of torture and threats and months of degradation." Mrs. Freddy Bloom, a fellow inmate, wrote of Williams: "She was tremendous fun. In the toughest situation, she could still see

the ridiculous. Even in the Kempe Tai 'cages' there were moments of uncontrolled hilarity. Later, in better times, the giggles were even worse when the pomposity and blatant vanity of 'authority' were evident."

Immediately following World War II, Williams spent several months in the United States as a postgraduate student at Johns Hopkins University. She had a lot of catching up to do. During the war, numerous medical advances had been made. But Williams eagerly plowed through the latest literature. She learned that serum analysis had been developed, and that her assumption about kwashiorkor, based on necropsy, was proven correct. As well, a treatment for pellagra had been developed which incorporated nicotinic acid. When tried on kwashiorkor patients, they all died. One of Williams' harshest critics, Dr. Hugh Trowell of the Colonial Service in the Gold Coast, wrote in 1975:

> Being a lady, and a very gracious lady at that, she arrived by instinct at the correct answer. . . . Experts nowadays tell me that I must call it Protein-Energy-Malnutrition (PEM), but never mind; probably they will change it again. Call it Energy-Protein-Malnutrition (EPM), but I will call it only and forever Kwashiorkor, in honor of Cicely, for she was right, and the experts had brought a needless dispute between us for more than a decade.

In 1945, the Colonial Office dispatched Williams to Malaya, where she reorganized health services. In 1948, she became the head of the child health department at the Institute of Social Medicine at Oxford University. After only five months at Oxford, the British Ministry of Health nominated her as the first head of Maternal and Child Health with the new World Health Organization. The preamble to the constitution of the World Health Organization states: "Healthy development of the child is of basic importance; the ability to live harmoniously in a changing total environment is essential to such development." The institutional bias of the organization towards large capital projects, rather than community-based health care, however, clashed with Williams' fundamental beliefs, which had been heavily influenced by Andrija Stampar. **Sally Craddock** summarizes these beliefs:

> The need for supervision of families on a regular basis; the need to involve mothers in caring for children in hospital; the need to listen to the local people if health education were to be effective—all of these and Cicely's constant cry for the proper training of nurses and health visitors.

In 1949, Williams was appointed to head the Maternal and Child Health department of the World Health Organization in South East Asia, a welcome reprieve from her administrative duties in Geneva. As well, South East Asia was a region of the world with which she was intimately familiar. From her headquarters in New Delhi, she set about implementing her theories, instituting a system of joint nursing to combat malaria, and encouraging doctors to visit people's homes. She also fought against the distribution of skim milk by UNICEF, because it is deficient in vitamin A and can cause xerophthalmia.

In October 1951, Williams resigned from the World Health Organization to care for her mother in Jamaica. Never one to remain idle for long, however, she soon applied for a position at the University of the West Indies, although she was turned down. When a serious outbreak of vomiting sickness swept the island, Williams set about investigating its causes, and discovered that a popular fruit, ackee, was responsible. She found that the fruit produced a toxic effect in malnourished children, which could be counteracted with a large dose of sugar.

In 1953, Margaret Williams died, and Cicely Williams returned to England as senior lecturer in nutrition at London University. After her contract expired, she moved to University College, where she studied toxaemia of pregnancy until 1957. In 1960, she traveled to Lebanon, where she joined the faculty of the American University in Beirut. She enjoyed teaching in Lebanon, and found the country "the most beautiful, exciting yet relaxed" that she had ever lived in.

Williams was appointed to the position of advisor in training programs for the Family Planning Association of Great Britain in 1964. She lectured and traveled extensively, visiting 70 countries on five continents. In 1968, she was made a companion of the Order of St. Michael and St. George, and introduced to Queen *Elizabeth II at a ceremony at Buckingham Palace. The queen reputedly remarked: "I can't remember where you've been." To which Williams replied, "Many places." "Doing what?" asked Her Majesty. With typical modesty, Williams replied, "Mostly looking after children."

In 1971, Cicely Williams joined the faculty at Tulane University. At the time, she was 78 and still going strong. She also lectured in Canada, Haiti, Mexico, and Colombia. While in America, Williams testified before the Committee on Public Welfare of the U.S. Senate, advising its members on development policy in the Third World.

Cicely Williams died in Oxford, England, on July 13, 1992. She was 98. A firm advocate of a more holistic approach to health care, Williams urged an integration of preventive and curative health services. She also sought to bridge the gap between health-care practitioners and their patients, particularly in the Third World. Today her model has been applied in many countries.

Williams was always an advocate of birth control and family planning. She argued that the surest way to curb overpopulation was to insure the survival of living children through the education of mothers, thus eliminating the need for large families. During her travels, she also witnessed many cases of female circumcision, a practice she abhorred. Her controversial ideas were often the target of criticism by her peers, but she took the criticism well, noting that "one of the most difficult things is to educate the educated."

Cicely Williams held honorary degrees from various universities, and was the recipient of numerous prizes and awards. Her accomplishments were many and varied. She is best remembered, however, for her identification of kwashiorkor as a primary cause of early mortality. Wrote William J. Darby, "It is through such rare practitioners of medicine as Cicely Williams . . . that the modern world repays its heritage from the early greats like Hippocrates and Galen."

SOURCES:

Craddock, Sally. *Retired Except on Demand: The Life of Dr. Cicely Williams*. Oxford: Green College, 1983.

Darby, William J. "Cicely D. Williams: Her Life and Influence," in *Nutrition Reviews*. Vol. 31, no. 11. Boston, MA: The Nutrition Foundation, 1973.

Farnes, Patricia. "Women in Medical Science," in *Women of Science*. G. Kass-Simon and Patricia Farnes, eds. Bloomington, IN: Indiana University Press, 1993.

O'Neill, Lois Decker. *The Women's Book of World Records and Achievements*. Garden City, NY: Anchor Press, 1979.

Uglow, Jennifer S., ed. *The International Dictionary of Women's Biography*. NY: Continuum, 1982.

SUGGESTED READING:

Dally, Ann. *Cicely: The Story of a Doctor*. London: Victor Gollancz, 1968.

Hugh A. Stewart, M.A.,
Guelph, Ontario, Canada

Williams, Elizabeth Sprague

(1869–1922)

American social worker. Born on August 31, 1869, in Buffalo, New York; died on August 19, 1922, in New York City; daughter of Frank Williams (a businessman) and Olive (French) Williams (a teacher); Smith College, B.S., 1891; Columbia University, A.M., 1896; children: (adopted) one.

Joined College Settlement as a resident (1896), and served as head worker (1898–1919); assisted in preparing Tenement House Exhibition by Charity Organization Society (1900); founded Mount Ivy (a summer camp for inner-city youth); founded the Lackawanna, New York, Social Center (1911); founded an orphanage in Serbia (1919).

Elizabeth Sprague Williams was born in 1869 in Buffalo, New York, the youngest of seven children of Frank Williams, a successful businessman, and **Olive French Williams**, a teacher. Elizabeth was a good student, and her academic achievements landed her at Smith College, from which she graduated in 1891. While at Smith, she had become interested in social settlement movements such as ***Jane Addams**' Hull House in Chicago, where individuals would take up residence in underprivileged communities and facilitate education, health-care awareness and, in the case of immigrant communities, "Americanization." Encouraged by her success in starting children's classes and organizing a small library within Buffalo, Williams moved to New York City, earning an A.M. from Columbia University in 1896. She also worked as a resident at the College Settlement near the Columbia campus, and became head worker there in 1898.

During its 21 years under Williams' guidance, the College Settlement grew in stature, becoming increasingly active through its participation in numerous programs designed to promote the welfare of the entire city. In an effort to improve the often dismal conditions in working-class neighborhoods like the city's Lower East Side, Williams promoted public participation in such programs as the Charity Organization Society, the Consumers' League, the Public Education Association, the Outdoor Recreation League, and the Manhattan Trade School for Girls. Taking an active role in individual programs, she also acted as the organization's representative, testifying on the College Settlement's successes before the state's Tenement House Commission in 1900. Among Williams' priorities was expanding educational opportunities among children, who, she reasoned, would be most receptive to the American values and habits presented, and she provided a link between the philosophies of the settlement movement and the theories underlying the push toward vocational and progressive education. She also encouraged group activities as a way to reduce the influence of dance halls, bars, and gangs among urban young people, and founded Mount Ivy, a summer camp located on a farm in

Rockland County, New York, that operated under the auspices of the College Settlement.

A compassionate and caring individual, Williams resigned her position as head of the College Settlement in 1919 to travel to war-torn Serbia, where she founded an orphanage near the Albanian border. With funding from various American sources, she was able to establish a train route to resupply the facility before turning control of its operation over to the Serbian government on her return to the United States two years later. Although Serbia was quick to acknowledge Williams' contribution in the form of a royal decoration, she was not alive to receive it, having succumbed to cancer in 1922, age 52, less than a year after coming home. She left behind an adopted child, a Serbian orphan she had brought with her from Eastern Europe.

SOURCES:
James, Edward T., ed. *Notable American Women, 1607–1950.* Cambridge, MA: The Belknap Press of Harvard University, 1971.

Pamela Shelton,
freelance writer,
Avon, Connecticut

Williams, Ella Gwendolen Rees
(1890–1979).

See Rhys, Jean (1890–1979).

Williams, Esther (1923—)

American actress and championship swimmer who became Hollywood's second "Million Dollar Mermaid." Born on August 8, 1923, in Inglewood, California; youngest of five children (three girls and two boys) of Lou Williams (a commercial artist) and Bula Williams (a schoolteacher); attended public schools in Los Angeles; graduated from Los Angeles City College; attended the University of Southern California; married Leonard Kovner (a physician, divorced); married Ben Gage (a radio announcer and singer), in 1945 (divorced); married Fernando Lamas (an actor), in 1967 (died 1982); married Edward Bell (a former professor and sometime actor); children: (second marriage) sons Benjamin and Kimball, and daughter Susan Gage.

Selected filmography: Andy Hardy's Double Life *(1942);* A Guy Named Joe *(1943);* Bathing Beauty *(1944);* Thrill of a Romance *(1945);* Ziegfeld Follies *(1946);* The Hoodlum Saint *(1946);* Easy to Wed *(1946);* Till the Clouds Roll By *(cameo, 1947);* Fiesta *(1947);* This Time for Keeps *(1947);* On an Island With You *(1948);* Take Me Out to the Ball Game *(1949);* Neptune's Daughter *(1948);* Duchess of Idaho

(1950); Pagan Love Song (1950); Callaway Went Thataway (unbilled cameo, 1951); Texas Carnival (1951); Skirts Ahoy! (1952); Million Dollar Mermaid (1952); Dangerous When Wet (1953); Easy to Love (1953); Jupiter's Darling (1955); The Unguarded Moment (1956); Raw Wind in Eden (1958); The Big Show (1961); The Magic Fountain (Sp., 1961).

A championship swimmer turned professional, Esther Williams emerged as "Hollywood's Mermaid" during the 1950s, starring in a string of lavishly mounted Technicolor aquamusicals. When big-budget musicals went out of fashion in the 1960s, however, her movie career came to a halt. Having already invested her earnings in a number of business ventures, Williams gracefully left Hollywood behind.

Esther Williams was born in 1923 and raised in the Los Angeles suburb of Inglewood, the youngest of five children. She learned to swim at the municipal pool across the street from the Williams' home, earning free swimming time by dispensing and collecting locker-room towels. In her early teens, Williams began entering and winning swim meets and became a member of the prestigious Los Angeles Athletic Club. At age 17, she rose to national prominence by winning every race she entered at the 1939 Women's Outdoor Swimming Nationals (100-meter freestyle, 300-meter and 800-yard relays, and 100-meter breaststroke). Recruited for the 1940 Olympic team, she was on her way to Tokyo when World War II intervened and the summer Games were canceled.

In 1940, after briefly attending the University of Southern California and modeling for a Los Angeles department story, Williams auditioned for and won a starring role in Billy Rose's Aquacade at the Golden Gate International Exposition in San Francisco. Paired with Olympian and screen star Johnny Weissmuller, she swam four shows a day (five on weekends) for eight months. When the show closed, she was offered a movie contract, but declined it believing that she couldn't act. However, a year later, when Louis B. Mayer offered her a contract which included six months of training, she accepted.

Williams' early film roles, in Andy Hardy's Double Life (1942) and A Guy Named Joe (1943), attracted some attention, but it was Hollywood's swimming movie Bathing Beauty (1944) that catapulted her to stardom. For the film, MGM constructed a special 90-foot square, 20-foot deep pool on the lot and outfitted it with hydraulic lifts, hidden air hoses, and special camera cranes for overhead shots. "No one had ever done a swimming movie before," Williams explained, "so we just made it up as we went along. I ad-libbed all my own underwater movements."

A series of aqua-musicals followed, among them *Ziegfeld Follies* (1944), *On an Island With You* (1948), *Neptune's Daughter* (1949), *Pagan Love Song* (1950), and *Million Dollar Mermaid* (1952), in which Williams portrayed ***Annette Kellerman**, the famed Australian swimmer who popularized swimming, pioneered the one-piece bathing suit, and appeared in early films. (Williams won the Golden Globe Award for *Million Dollar Mermaid*, putting her in the ranks of the most popular female stars in the world.) The films, though thin on plot, were big on musical numbers and had at least one beautifully photographed underwater sequence in which Williams—surrounded by hundreds of shapely, synchronized swimmers—executed a water ballet, amid flames, fountains, and rolling fog.

At the height of her Hollywood career, Williams was one of the top moneymakers for MGM, and was as popular abroad as she was in America, particularly in India and the Middle East. Although never cited for her acting ability ("I can't sing, I can't dance, I can't act," she once cheerfully confessed), Williams was one of the few female athletes to successfully cross over to movies, and her career played a major role in popularizing competitive and synchronized swimming. Her last swimming pictures were *Easy to Love* (1953) and *Jupiter's Darling* (1955), after which the genre fell out of favor.

Williams had invested her movie earnings wisely, however, and by the time of her retirement, she had a number of successful business enterprises, including a swimming pool company, a restaurant, and a bathing suit deal with Fred Cole of California. Ultimately she developed her own Esther Williams Collection, targeting older women. "I got into business because I knew those musicals couldn't go on forever," she said, also admitting that when she started in films she told her bosses to hold her modeling job. "This movie-making thing wouldn't last. I mean, how many swimming movies could they make?"

Williams was married briefly to a young medical intern, Leonard Kovner. After they divorced, she married actor-producer Ben Gage, a union which produced three children: Benjamin, Kimball, and Susan. That marriage ended in divorce in 1957, after which Williams married actor Fernando Lamas, who died of cancer in 1982. He was apparently the love of her life, although she says he was so jealous that he would not allow her three children to live with them. The actress is currently married to Edward Bell, a former French literature professor and sometime actor. In a tell-all autobiography, *Million Dollar Mermaid*, written with Digby Diehl and published in 1999, Williams writes candidly about her career, her love affairs, and her first three marriages.

SOURCES:
Current Biography 1955. NY: H.W. Wilson, 1955.
Johnson, Anne Janette. *Great Women in Sports.* Detroit, MI: Visible Ink, 1998.
Katz, Ephraim. *The Film Encyclopedia.* NY: Harper-Collins, 1994.
Lamparski, Richard. *Whatever Became Of . . . ?* 2nd Series. NY: Crown, 1968.
Purdum, Todd S. "Swimming Upstream," in *The New York Times.* September 2, 1999.
Shapiro, Laura. "Telling Tales Out of Pool," in *Newsweek.* September 13, 1999.

Barbara Morgan,
Melrose, Massachusetts

Williams, Fannie Barrier
(1855–1944)

African-American lecturer and civil-rights leader. Born on February 12, 1855, in Brockport, New York; died on March 4, 1944, in Brockport; daughter of Anthony J. Barrier (a businessman) and Harriet (Prince) Barrier; graduated from the New York State Normal School in Brockport, 1870; attended the New England Conservatory of Music and the School of Fine Arts in Washington, D.C.; married S. Laing Williams (an attorney), in 1887 (died 1921); no children.

Taught at freedmen's schools throughout the southern United States (c. 1880s); co-founded Provident Hospital and Training School for Nurses, Chicago (1891); spoke at World's Columbian Exposition (1893); co-founded National League of Colored Women (1893); inducted into Chicago Woman's Club as first black member (1895); co-founded National Association of Colored Women (1896); co-organized Colored Women's Conference of Chicago (1900); appointed director of Frederick Douglass Center (1905); elected to Chicago Library Board as first black and first female member (1924); published work included contributions to A New Negro for a New Century *(1900), co-authored with Booker T. Washington and others.*

Fannie Barrier Williams was born in 1855 in Brockport, New York, the youngest of three children born to Anthony J. Barrier and **Harriet Prince Barrier**, the only black couple in town. Accepted in the community throughout her childhood, she studied the classics and graduated from Brockport's State Normal School in

Opposite page
Esther
Williams

1870 with the intention of becoming a teacher. In contrast to her experiences in the northern United States were those Williams had as she moved throughout the South to teach at the freedmen's schools that had been established during Reconstruction. There she encountered the overt racial prejudice that proved disillusioning to such an idealistic young woman, but also shaped her later career.

Passionate about the arts, she left teaching in the South to attend classes at both the New England Conservatory and the Washington, D.C., School of Fine Arts before marrying attorney S. Laing Williams and moving to Chicago in 1887 to assist her husband in promoting his law practice. In Chicago, the couple was soon accepted as an integral part of the city's closely knit black community, and Williams became friends with well-known activist *Ida Wells-Barnett, who encouraged the transplanted young woman to become active in civil affairs, particularly in the club movement that would later result in the Colored Women's Conference of Chicago. Williams was up to the task, and helped organize the interracial Provident Hospital, as well as an affiliated training school for nurses, in 1891. A charismatic, attractive, articulate, and well-educated black woman, Williams was welcomed at many social organizations; in 1893, she addressed the World's Congress of Representative Women on "The Intellectual Progress of the Colored Women of the United States since the Emancipation Proclamation," and spoke as well before the World's Parliament of Religions. These engagements quickly put her in the national spotlight, and led to numerous speaking engagements across the nation. In 1893, she acted on her experiences of racial discrimination by co-founding the National League of Colored Women (NLCW), an organization that would later become the National Association of Colored Women and in which she was active throughout the remainder of her life. Her activities on behalf of the Colored Women's Conference of Chicago in 1900 resulted in support structures that benefited families throughout the city.

Ironically, a year after founding the NLCW, Williams again encountered racism, this time from a Northern source. When her name came up on the list of proposed members at the exclusive Chicago Woman's Club, it caused an extended debate among the members, all of whom were white. After a year of sometimes hostile discussion, but with the support of several influential friends, Williams broke the color barrier by becoming the club's first African-American member in 1895. This experience prompted Williams to take an even more active role in promoting the cause of blacks, most of whom lived in far less comfortable surroundings. Contributing essays on the subject of race to such newspapers as the *Chicago Record-Herald* and *New York Age*, she also enthusiastically spoke out in favor of Booker T. Washington's program of self-improvement and economic, rather than social, advancement. Perhaps because of her support, Washington supported Laing Williams in his successful bid to become assistant district attorney for Chicago in 1908. Sixteen years later, Williams became the first woman as well as the first African-American to be appointed a member of Chicago's Library Board. She held this position for two years, leaving Illinois in 1926 to return to her family in Brockport, where she died 18 years later, at the age of 89.

SOURCES:

James, Edward T., ed. *Notable American Women, 1607–1950.* Cambridge, MA: The Belknap Press of Harvard University, 1971.

McHenry, Robert, ed. *Famous American Women.* NY: Dover, 1980.

Smith, Jessie Carney, ed. *Notable Black American Women.* Detroit, MI: Gale Research, 1992.

Pamela Shelton,
freelance writer,
Avon, Connecticut

Williams, Grace (1906–1977)

Welsh composer. Born on February 19, 1906, in Barry, Wales; died on February 10, 1977, in Barry, Wales; educated at University of Cardiff, at the Royal College of Music, and in Vienna, Austria; studied with Ralph Vaughan Williams.

Grace Williams was born in 1906 in Barry, Wales, and attended the University of Cardiff before moving to London, England, early in her career to attend the Royal College of Music. While in London, she studied with composer Ralph Vaughan Williams, who was by this time approaching his transitional period wherein he would move from being a traditionalist whose music reflected the English rather than European musical past, to a modernist concerned with expressing contemporary moral dilemmas. Williams also traveled to Vienna to study with Egon Wellesz, an Austrian protégé of Schoenberg who would flee to England and a position at Oxford in the wake of Nazi occupation. Her compositions were heavily influenced by both of these men, as well as by the work of Benjamin Britten, for whom she had a particular admiration. Among Williams' most noted compositions are *Penillion*, an early work for full orchestra that is based on

Welsh barding songs and reflects the influence of Vaughan Williams; *Sea Sketches* (1944), a work for strings; and *The Parlour* (1961), a comedic opera that Williams composed 16 years before her death in 1977. Other works include a 1963 trumpet concerto, a symphony, and several works for both chorus and solo voice.

Pamela Shelton,
freelance writer,
Avon, Connecticut

Williams, Helen Maria (1762–1827)

English poet and correspondent. Born on June 17, 1762, in London, England; died on December 15, 1827, in Paris, France; daughter of Charles Williams (an army officer) and Helen (Hay) Williams; educated at home.

Helen Maria Williams was born in 1762 in London, England, and raised in Berwick-on-Tweed. She developed a talent for writing as a child, encouraged by her widowed mother, who supervised Williams' education. Moving to London in 1781, she began experimenting with verse and published her first work of poetry, the romance *Edwin and Eltruda: A Legendary Tale*, in 1782. Williams' writing proved popular enough with readers that book sales provided her with a respectable income, and she continued to publish both poetry and fiction during her 20s. Notable among her early works is "Poem on the Slave Trade" (1788), which describes her liberal reaction to the then-legal market in human flesh and firmly cemented her acceptance within London's more radical literary circles.

In 1790, at age 28, Williams moved to France at the invitation of an aristocratic friend, funding her first year there by translating and reworking Jean-Jacques Rousseau's novel *Julie* and submitting it to British readers that year. Living in Paris and quickly caught up in the political energy of the French Revolution, the impetuous Williams began a salon that drew such expatriates as Thomas Paine and *Mary Wollstonecraft. She also published several volumes of correspondence, among them *Letters Written in France in the Summer of 1790*, a series of radical pronouncements that appeared in England that year. Astute enough to realize that her writing might prove inflammatory, she also set to work on a translation of the popular novel *Paul et Virginie*, which she intended to use as a cover in case her workspace was ever raided. Despite her efforts at concealment, in 1793 Williams was arrested as a suspected member of the political faction known as Girondists and imprisoned by

Robespierre during his Reign of Terror—her arrest a result of her friendship with the late Girondist *Madame Roland, her irresponsible publishings, and her romantic, live-in relationship with divorced Englishman John Hurford Stone, a Unitarian radical.

Barely escaping the guillotine that brought the end to much of the French aristocracy, Williams managed to escape into Switzerland on a borrowed passport, a six-month journey recounted in her *A Tour in Switzerland* (1798). Her *Sketches of the State of Manners and Opinions in the French Republic* (1801) and *A Narrative of the Events Which Have Taken Place in France* (1815), while notorious for presenting a misinformed and naive portrait of the politics and events they purport to describe, have remained of interest to students of the Revolution. Despite her experiences during the Terror, Williams never wavered in her praise of Revolutionary principles, a position that lost her both friends and readers in her later years. Following Stone's death in 1818, she moved to Amsterdam to live with a nephew, returning eventually to Paris where she died in 1827.

SOURCES:

Buck, Claire, ed. *The Bloomsbury Guide to Women's Literature*. NY: Prentice Hall, 1992.

Kunitz, Stanley J., and Howard Haycraft, eds. *British Authors of the Nineteenth Century*. NY: H.W. Wilson, 1936.

Shattock, Joanne. *The Oxford Guide to British Women Writers*. Oxford: Oxford University Press, 1993.

Pamela Shelton,
freelance writer,
Avon, Connecticut

Williams, Ivy (1877–1966)

First woman to be called to the bar in England. Born in 1877 in England; died in 1966 in England; educated privately; graduated from the Society of Oxford Home-Students, B.C.L., 1902, LL.D., 1903; earned a D.C.L. from Oxford University.

Ivy Williams was born in 1877 into a well-to-do British family who deemed education to be of prime importance. Educated privately, she also enjoyed the learning experiences provided by a tour of Europe undertaken when she was a young woman. Returning to England, Williams joined the Society of Oxford Home-Students (which would later become St. Anne's College), where she studied under professors Edward Jenks and Sir William S. Holdsworth. She earned her baccalaureate degree in 1902, and her LL.D. the following year. She became the first woman to be called to the bar in England when she was accepted to the Inner Temple in 1922. Working as a tutor to aspiring lawyers beginning in 1920, Williams served as a lecturer in law at her alma mater until her retirement in 1945.

In addition to her teaching career, Williams contributed to the general study of law through several books, among them *The Sources of Law in the Swiss Civil Code* (1923) and the annotated *The Swiss Civil Code: English Version* (1925). A respected authority on international law, she was appointed a delegate to The Hague Conference for the Codification of International Law, held in the Netherlands in 1930. Among her other accomplishments, Williams earned a D.C.L. at Oxford University, making her the first woman to receive that degree, and at the age of 70 taught herself to read Braille and composed a booklet sharing her expertise for use by the National Institute for the Blind. Supportive of students striving for a career in the legal profession, Williams endowed two scholarships at Oxford, one to benefit only female students. She died in 1966 at the age of 89.

SOURCES:

The Concise Dictionary of National Biography. Oxford: Oxford University Press, 1992.

Pamela Shelton,
freelance writer,
Avon, Connecticut

Williams, Jody (1950—)

American who won the Nobel Peace Prize as coordinator of the International Campaign to Ban Landmines. Born Jo-Anne Williams on October 9, 1950, in Poultney, Vermont; daughter of John Williams and Ruth Williams; educated in public schools of Brattleboro, Vermont; University of Vermont at Burlington, B.A., 1972; School for International Training, Brattleboro, Vermont, M.A. in Spanish and teaching English as a second language, 1976; Johns Hopkins School of Advanced International Studies, M.A., 1984.

Served as co-coordinator for the Nicaragua-Honduras Education Project (1984–86); was deputy director of Medical Aid for El Salvador (1986–1992); drafted by the founder of the Vietnam Veterans of America Foundation to build a coalition to combat the widespread international use of antipersonnel land mines (1991); served as coordinator of the International Campaign to Ban Landmines (1992—), an effort for which she and her organization were awarded the Nobel Prize for Peace (1997); attended signing of Mine Ban Treaty (December 1997); treaty entered into force (March 1999).

The second child and first daughter of John and **Ruth Williams**, Jody Williams was born in 1950 in Poultney, Vermont, where her parents owned and operated a grocery store. Christened Jo-Anne as a child, Williams was called "Jody-kapody" by her father, and the first part of the nickname stuck; she later changed her name legally to Jody. An excellent student, she is recalled by her mother as an "achiever" who would become visibly upset if she had to miss school. Jody's older brother Stephen was born deaf, and her parents eventually sold the Poultney store and moved the family to Brattleboro where Stephen could receive specialized training at the Austin School for the Deaf. Jody, with younger siblings **Mary Beth**, Mark, and **Janet**, attended public schools in Brattleboro, while their parents ran a vending business.

Williams' underlying rebellious nature first surfaced while she was a student at the University of Vermont in Burlington. For Williams, the Vietnam War was "a defining experience." From that point on, she was no longer able to accept the pronouncements of those in authority without questioning their motivations. Her newfound militancy about the war made dinnertime discussions with the family far less amiable than they had been in the past, for her younger brother Mark and, initially, her father were strong supporters of the government's position on the conflict.

Although she was extremely focused on such issues as the Vietnam War, Williams was somewhat less decisive about her own future while studying at the University of Vermont. She changed majors five times, finally settling on psychology so that she could graduate. After graduation, she returned to Brattleboro and took a job as an assistant to an oral surgeon, a position that proved brief after she fainted a number of times during her first day at work. Instead, she decided to pursue studies at Brattleboro's School for International Training, where she earned a master's degree in Spanish and teaching English as a second language in 1976. She then spent some time in Mexico, putting her newly acquired teaching skills to work.

After working for three years in Washington, D.C., as a temporary secretary, Williams returned to school, earning a second master's degree from the Johns Hopkins School of Advanced International Studies in 1984. It was shortly after completing her studies that Williams by chance was handed a leaflet advertising a lecture about the cause of the El Salvador guerrilla movement, the FMLN. She attended the lecture and met Mario Velasquez, a leader of the FMLN, and before long was working for a change in U.S. policy toward Central America, frequently leading fact-finding tours in Nicaragua and Honduras as co-coordinator of the Nicaragua-Honduras Education Project. Two years later, she became deputy director of Medical Aid for El Salvador, an organization based in Los Angeles for which she initiated and supervised humanitarian relief projects. This involvement in the Central American cause was, for Williams, an epiphany. "The passion of doing what I considered to be the right thing captured me, and I've never looked back," she told graduates in a 1998 commencement address at the University of Vermont.

Williams' tireless work on behalf of the Central American cause brought her to the attention of Bobby Muller, founder of the Vietnam Veterans of America Foundation. A former marine left paralyzed by injuries received fighting in Vietnam, Muller hired Williams in 1991 to build a coalition of groups opposed to the use of antipersonnel mines. Land mines, potent weapons during wartime, are left behind after the fighting stops or moves away, and some 100 million live mines remain buried in various countries around the world. It is believed that Cambodia, where approximately a third of the population died during the bloody regime of Pol Pot, is seeded with over 10 million land mines, while Angola, after years of civil war, contains 9 million. The vast majority of those who stumble across the left-behind mines are civilians, often farmers or children, and those who do not die frequently require prosthetic limbs that are rarely available in their homelands.

In 1992, Williams left her job at Medical Aid for El Salvador to become the first coordinator of the International Campaign to Ban Landmines (ICBL), launched that October with a membership of six nongovernmental organizations (NGOs). Under Williams' leadership, the ICBL grew into a coalition of some 1,000 NGOs in more than 60 countries. In a matter of six years, she managed to rally support among governments, NGOs, the United Nations, and the International Red Cross for an international agreement that would outlaw land mines—which kill or injure 26,000 people annually—and also require countries to find and eliminate those land mines (usually unmapped) already buried. The cause attracted such high-profile figures as Nelson Mandela and Princess *Diana, who brought it much publicity. In October 1997, the Nobel Peace Prize was awarded jointly to the ICBL and its coordinator, Jody Williams. (She then came under attack from some quarters for choosing to keep her half of the million dollars in prize money for herself.)

In December 1997, at the 1997 Convention on the Prohibition of the Use, Stockpiling, Produc-

Jody Williams '72
Nobel Laureate

Jody Williams

tion and Transfer of Anti-Personnel Mines and on Their Destruction, held in Ottawa, Canada, the Mine Ban Treaty was signed by 125 governments. Ratification by at least 40 signatories was required for the treaty to go into effect. It did so in March 1999, and as of June 2001 it had been signed by 140 countries and ratified by 117. As coordinator of the ICBL, Williams continues to pressure both countries that signed the treaty to ratify it and countries that did not sign it to accede it. Among those non-signatories are China and Russia (both huge producers of land mines); much of the Middle East, including Israel and Saudi Arabia; Afghanistan, where land mines take a massive toll in human life each year; and the United States. Notable for its opposition to the treaty under both the Clinton and Bush administrations, the U.S. became one of Williams' primary targets. She frequently lectures and writes articles and studies for the ICBL, which has also expanded its mission to include assistance to those injured by land mines.

SOURCES:

Griffin, Lee. "Campaigning Against War's Legacy," in *Vermont Quarterly*. Summer 1998, pp. 21–25.
The New York Times Biographical Service. October 1997, pp. 1584–1585.

Don Amerman,
freelance writer,
Saylorsburg, Pennsylvania

Williams, Lucinda (1937—)

African-American track-and-field athlete. Name variations: Lucinda Williams Adams. Born on August 10, 1937, in Savannah, Georgia; daughter of Willie M. Williams and David Williams; graduated from Tennessee State University, B.S., 1959, M.S., 1961; married Floyd Adams, in 1959 (died); children: daughter Kimberly.

Became a world-class sprinter (1950s–1960s); earned a gold medal in the Rome Olympics in the 4x100-meter relay (1960).

Known as "Lady Dancer" for her graceful style of running, Lucinda Williams was born in Savannah, Georgia, in 1937. By the time she graduated from high school, she had perfected both her stride and her endurance, earning the twin titles of state track champion and outstanding senior athlete. She enrolled at Tennessee State University in 1954 and continued her outstanding performance with the famed Tennessee Tigerbelles track team, breaking records for the 100-meter relay and clocking times that qualified her for the U.S. Olympic trials. Her first appearance at the Olympics was at the summer Games in Melbourne, Australia, in 1956, but she failed to make the cut during the 100-meter heats.

Wins at the Amateur Athletic Union's track events for three straight years between 1957 and 1959 showed that Williams had the needed speed, and her top times won her a spot on the AAU women's All-American track-and-field team in both 1958 and 1959. She went on to put in a stellar performance in the sprint at the Pan Am Games in 1959, and her overall scores once again qualified her for the Olympic trials and a spot on the team, which headed to Rome, Italy, the following summer. Competition in the 1960 Olympic Games was stiff, and Williams missed the final cut for the individual 200-meter race. However, as part of the all-Tigerbelle relay team, she ultimately proved to be a winner as the second leg of the four-woman team that took home the gold medal in the 4x100-meter relay with a total time of 44.72 seconds.

After the Olympics, Williams returned to Tennessee State, graduating with a master's degree in physical education in 1961. Retiring from competition but wishing to remain involved with national track-and-field events, she served as a chaperon for the U.S. Olympic track-and-field team during their tour of Europe in 1963. In later years she put her college education to good use, taking a job as a physical education teacher at a high school in Dayton, Ohio, where she served as a role model and inspiration to aspiring young women—particularly African-Americans—interested in testing their skill and perseverance through competitive sports. She was elected to the Savannah, Georgia, Hall of Fame in 1968 and the Tennessee State University Hall of Fame in 1983.

SOURCES:

Hine, Darlene Clark, ed. *Facts on File Encyclopedia of Black Women in America: Dance, Sports, and Visual Arts.* NY: Facts on File, 1997.

Page, James A. *Black Olympian Medalists.* Englewood, CO: Libraries Unlimited, 1991.

Pamela Shelton,
freelance writer,
Avon, Connecticut

Williams, Margery (1881–1944).

See Bianco, Margery Williams.

Williams, Marietta (1911–1987).

See Sullivan, Maxine.

Williams, Marion (1927–1994)

African-American gospel singer. Born on August 29, 1927, in Miami, Florida; died of vascular complications arising from diabetes on July 2, 1994, in Philadelphia, Pennsylvania; dropped out of school at age 14; married; one son Robin.

Started singing career with the Clara Ward Singers (1947–58); sang with the Stars of Faith in the song-play Black Nativity; *her unique traditional gospel style influenced a host of secular artists, including Little Richard and Aretha Franklin, over the course of her career which lasted nearly half a century.*

Born in Miami, Florida, in 1927, Marion Williams was the youngest of eleven children, a group that included three sets of twins. Williams was one of only three children, however, who survived past their first year. Her father, who died when she was nine, was a West Indian who worked as a barber and also taught music. Her mother, originally from South Carolina, worked as a laundress and sang in a choir. Because of the family's poor financial circumstances, Williams dropped out of school at age 14 to work as a maid and child nurse. She later found work at a laundry and put in grueling hours to help support her family.

Williams started singing at age three and developed her natural ability with the encouragement of her father in her church's choir. Her roots were in sanctified singing in the Church of God and Christ, a denomination to which she remained faithful throughout her life. From her local Pentecostal church, she branched out to other churches in Miami, and to tent and street-corner revivals. Her life's ambition was to become a traveling gospel singer, like the many male quartets, the sanctified shouter *Rosetta Tharpe, and the Baptist mourner **Mary Johnson Davis**.

While visiting her sister in Philadelphia, Pennsylvania, in the mid-1940s, Williams encountered the Clara Ward Singers, the preeminent gospel group of the 1940s and 1950s, at the Ward African Methodist Episcopal (AME) Church. Upon invitation, Williams sang "What Could I Do (If It Wasn't for the Lord)" at the church. The teenager's stunning performance amazed and captivated the audience. *Clara Ward immediately asked Miami's premier gospel soloist to join her group. After about a year, she accepted the invitation. Between 1947 and 1958, Williams, as one of the now-famous Ward Singers, stood out as a backup member and excelled as a vocal leader.

Williams left the group in 1958, taking group members **Frances Steadman**, **Kitty Parham**, and **Henrietta Waddy** along with her to form another gospel group, the Stars of Faith. Williams made her theatrical debut in 1961 in the gospel song-play *Black Nativity*, the text of which was written by noted black author Langston Hughes. Hughes wrote the song-play especially for Williams, and it enjoyed a three-year run in the United States, followed by even greater success in Europe. During the Christmas season of 1963, *Black Nativity* was produced for national television.

Gospel diva Williams made her debut as a soloist in 1966 and continued in that capacity until her death. With her flamboyant, innovative style and her clear voicings, Williams incorporated such techniques as deep growls and octave-spanning whoops into the gospel repertoire she performed, influencing both gospel and pop singers, and bringing her brand of music to an international audience. Little Richard once credited Williams for inspiring the leap-frogging vocals and falsetto breaks in his hit "Tutti-Frutti," while vocalist **Aretha Franklin** paid her colleague the compliment of recording cover versions of Williams' two most popular gospel efforts: "Packin' Up" and "Surely God Is Able." During her career, Williams recorded ten albums of gospel and pop music, and experimented with a number of different musical genres, including blues, folk, and calypso.

During the late 1960s, Williams covered the college circuit, appeared at the Antibes Jazz Festival in France and the Dakar Festival of Negro Arts in Africa, did several television specials, and received from Princess Grace of Monaco (*Grace Kelly) one of Europe's top achievement honors, the International Television Award. Though the popularity of contemporary gospel rose in the 1970s, Williams, a gospel traditionalist, performed less frequently. Promoters and producers who envisioned Williams' ascension to the top of the pop charts made efforts to persuade her to sing more secular material and offered her lucrative contracts, but she stayed true to what she considered the purpose of her career: to spread her message of Christian love to her listeners. From the mid-1980s until her death, her concert career thrived, limited only by the physical disabilities she experienced from diabetes.

In addition to recording, Williams performed in churches and nightclubs around the nation, as well as in concert halls. She also contributed her talents as a singer to the motion pictures *Fried Green Tomatoes* and *Mississippi Masala* in the early 1990s. The year 1993 proved to be a high point in Williams' professional career: she was honored for her contributions to American culture by President Bill Clinton at New York's Kennedy Center, and also received a MacArthur Foundation "genius" grant for her contributions to American music, the first singer to be thus honored. Unfortunately, her televised appearance at the Kennedy Center was her last public performance; in 1994, at age 66, Williams died near her home in Philadelphia.

SOURCES:

Obituary, in *The Day* [New London, CT]. July 4, 1994.
Obituary, in *Time*. July 18, 1994.
Smith, Jessie Carney, ed. *Notable Black American Women, Book II*. Detroit, MI: Gale Research, 1996.

Pamela Shelton,
freelance writer,
Avon, Connecticut

Williams, Mary Lou (1910–1981)

African-American jazz pianist, arranger, and composer who absorbed and influenced the changing style of jazz—from boogie-woogie to Kansas City swing, bebop, symphonic and avant-garde—through six decades. Name variations: Mary Elfrieda Scruggs; Mary Elfrieda Winn; Mary Burleigh (or Burley). Born Mary Elfrieda Scruggs on May 8, 1910, in Atlanta, Georgia; died of cancer on May 28, 1981, in Durham, North Carolina; daughter of Joe Scruggs and Virginia Burley Winn; attended public grade school and Lincoln High School in Pittsburgh; married John Williams (a bandleader), in 1927 (divorced 1942); married Harold "Shorty" Baker (a trumpet player), in 1942 (marriage ended c. 1944); no children.

Began playing piano professionally at age six; toured, age 17, with John Williams' Synco Jazzers, and married the bandleader (1927); toured with John Williams when he joined Andy Kirk's Twelve Clouds of Joy (1928); made first solo recording, "Night Life" (1930); hired as pianist and arranger for Andy Kirk's group (1931); received commissions for arrangements from other bandleaders, including Benny Goodman, Jimmie Lunceford, Louis Armstrong, Earl Hines, and Tommy Dorsey (1930s); divorced John Williams and married trumpet player Harold "Shorty" Baker, with whom she led a six-piece band (1942); composed her first extended work, The Zodiac Suite, *performed at Town Hall in New York (1945); a portion of the suite performed at Carnegie Hall by New York Philharmonic (1946); appeared with an all-woman trio at Carnegie Hall (1947); had several long engagements at Cafe Society (1950s); after two years of living in England and France, quit music to devote herself to the study of religion and helping the poor (1954); joined the Catholic Church (1956); returned to music, appearing at the Newport Jazz Festival with Dizzy Gillespie (1957); founded her own record label, Mary Records (1963); commissioned by the Vatican, she wrote* Mary Lou's Mass, *premiered at Columbia University (1970); rewrote the mass for Alvin Ailey's City Center Dance Theater (1971); played at Jimmy Carter's White House Jazz Party (1978); became artist-in-residence at Duke University (1976); taught and arranged music up to a short time before her death (1981); was the first woman instrumentalist inducted into the* Down Beat *Hall of Fame (1990).*

Selected discography: Andy Kirk and His Clouds of Joy *(MCA 1343);* The Asch Recordings, 1944–47 *(Folkways 2966);* Zodiac Suite *(1946, Folkways 32844);* Mary Lou's Mass *(1970–72, Mary 102);* Zoning *(Mary 103); with Cecil Taylor:* Embraced *(1977, Pablo Live 2620–108);* My Mama Pinned a Rose on Me *(1977, Pablo 2310–819);* Solo Recital—Montreux Jazz Festival '78 *(Pablo Live 2308–218).*

When asked how she started her lifelong musical journey, Mary Lou Williams frequently related her earliest memory. She would be sitting on her mother's lap at the organ or piano, awed by the spirituals and ragtime her mother played. "One day," her mother would say (so often that it became a part of the daily ritual), "your hands are going to beat me to these keys." And one day, said Williams, they did. She was two and a half when her thrilled and astonished mother summoned the neighbors to witness her child actually playing the piano.

Williams also credited a deathly fear of lightning storms as the catalyst for her earliest musical expression. She described herself as a nervous child who needed a creative outlet to help her survive her fears. For an African-American growing up in rural Georgia in the early 1900s, there were plenty of dangers besides lightning to arouse fears. Lynchings, for instance, were still common. Williams witnessed lynchings at an early age and remembered them to her grave. Meanwhile, except for one relatively short period in which she relied on religion alone, music provided her with emotional and spiritual sustenance throughout her life. Eventually the inspiration of music and religion would be merged in the sacred jazz masses she composed.

Mary Elfrieda Scruggs was born on May 8, 1910, in Atlanta, Georgia. Her father's name was Joe Scruggs, but she never met him, and her early years were spent in a long wooden house in rural Georgia with her older sister **Mamie** and their mother **Virginia Burley Winn**, a church organist. By age three, Mary Lou had learned a ragtime piece her mother played; by the time she was four, word of her talent was out, and she began to perform for the local public. Her mother did not put much trust in formal training, believing that piano teachers had hampered her own ability to play by ear. Rather than arranging for lessons, Virginia began a routine of inviting professional musicians to the house, to play and to listen to Mary. Some of these frequent guests, particularly the great Atlanta boogie-woogie player Jack Howard, proved a tremendous influence.

By the time Williams was six, her mother had remarried twice, and the family had moved to Pittsburgh, Pennsylvania. There was an immediate affinity between the young pianist and her music-loving second stepfather Fletcher Burley (or Burleigh). For the exorbitant price of $1,000, Burley bought a player piano, which enabled Williams to learn from piano rolls made by groundbreaking musicians like Jelly Roll Morton and James P. Johnson, the father of stride piano. While other children were playing outside, Mary Lou was playing the piano up to ten hours a day. She was also learning by listening. In an oral history recorded for *Melody Maker* in 1954, Williams recalled a Saturday afternoon that influenced her later life, when she watched the pianist ◄❧ **Lovie Austin** leading the pit band in a local theater, "writing music with her right hand while accompanying the show with her swinging left." Williams often cited this image of the dynamic and multi-talented Austin as an inspiration for her own career as a musician-arranger-composer.

❧►
Austin, Lovie.
See Armstrong, Lil Hardin for sidebar.

Mary
Lou
Williams

Sometimes Burley took his stepdaughter with him to gambling houses, where she would play the piano for tips. By the age of seven, she was often the family's chief wage earner (she had many stepsiblings). By age 12, she had gone "pro" and was performing at dances, silent movie houses, and whorehouses throughout Pittsburgh. Wealthy families like the Mellons would send their chauffeurs to pick her up to play for their private parties. Everyone wanted to hear the "gigging piano gal from East Liberty."

In the early years of the century, African-American entertainers often got their music gigs through the Theater Owners' Booking Association or TOBA—commonly referred to by some performers as "Tough on Black Asses." Traveling on the TOBA route was often grueling, but as **Daphne Duval Harrison** points out, the circuit also provided "black entertainment professionals with the opportunity to appear on a regular basis." Many of the shows Williams saw as a young girl in Pittsburgh were put on by professionals on the TOBA circuit. When she was 12 years old, an act called *Hits and Bits* arrived in town, minus its piano player, and when the manager, "Buzzin'" Harris, began to ask around, he was told that someone called "the little piano girl" could learn the part quickly. Dubious but desperate, Harris hired Williams to play while the show was in town, and was so impressed that he persuaded her mother to allow Mary Lou to travel on the circuit, performing the show one summer. Touring in cities all over the Midwest, Williams got invaluable performing experience and exposure to top musicians, hearing Earl Hines (whom she had admired in Pittsburgh), Louis Armstrong in Chicago, and trumpet player Charlie Creath in St. Louis. On this tour she also met her future husband, baritone saxophone player and bandleader John Williams.

Jazz is whatever you are—playing yourself, being yourself, letting your thoughts come through.

—**Mary Lou Williams**

When *Hits and Bits* returned to Pittsburgh, Mary Lou went back to being a student. Then, just as she was nearing graduation, her stepfather fell ill, and young Williams needed to find work to help support her family. She contacted Harris, who placed her back on the TOBA circuit, playing with John Williams' Synco Jazzers. This tour proved harder than the last, and the young musicians were on the verge of destitution when they were saved by a last-minute offer to back a dance team, Jeanette and Seymour, on the Keith vaudeville circuit. Mary Lou, then calling herself Mary Burley, married John Williams that year, 1927.

The job with the dance team ended when Seymour died. The young marrieds were compelled to play in various bands, often in different towns. John Williams joined an Oklahoma-based group whose members had just voted to replace their leader with Andy Kirk, a talented and popular tuba player. The group moved to Kansas City, where Williams joined them in 1928, as driver, seamstress, water hauler, manicurist, and occasional substitute piano player. It

was three years later, after Williams had been discovered by Jack Knapp of the Brunswick label and had recorded two solos, "Night Life" and "Drag 'Em," when she was finally hired as pianist and arranger for Andy Kirk and His Twelve Clouds of Joy.

In the 1930s, Kansas City, Missouri, was a haven for everyone, including musicians, whose business had been hurt by Prohibition. The local political boss, Thomas Pendergast, created a "relaxed" atmosphere in the city by protecting gangster-owned night spots where unlawful drinking and gambling were allowed to flourish. Kansas City thus became a more profitable base for musicians than other U.S. cities during these years of the Great Depression, and out of this concentration of so many creative musicians in one spot a new style of music was born. A key figure in defining the blues-based, riff-oriented genre that would be called Kansas City Swing was Mary Lou Williams. In 1936, Andy Kirk's big band recorded an original piece of hers, "Froggy Bottom," which became a tremendous success, popular on juke boxes all over the country. Other compositions and arrangements of hers, often written by flashlight while the band was on the road, began to catch the ears of such eminent bandleaders as Benny Goodman, Jimmie Lunceford, and Earl Hines, and they began offering her commissions to write for them as well. In an interview for *Jazz Journal International*, Williams told Stan Britt that she once wrote 20 arrangements in one week for such well-known groups as Louis Armstrong's and Cab Calloway's bands and the Casa Loma Orchestra, and all became hits. Among her best-known pieces for other bandleaders were "What's Your Story Morning Glory" for Jimmie Lunceford, and the boogie-woogie-inspired "Roll 'Em," which became a hit for Benny Goodman.

On the heels of fame came new management and seemingly endless tours. After three years of zigzagging across the South, Williams grew tired of life on the road. Although the bands played to sellout crowds, there was often no place that served food to African-Americans in the towns they toured. There were times when the band members played five or six days of concerts without being able to eat properly; times when they were forced to steal from corn fields because there was no place they could buy food. And there was always the threat of lynchings. Also, audiences now expected the band to sound exactly as it had on record, which Williams found hampered her creativity. By this time she had met Thelonious Monk and Tadd Dameron, was interested by their new sounds, and wanted to try out her own harmonic experiments. Worn out by the combination of racism, physical hardship, and creative frustration, she quit Andy Kirk's band after 12 years and returned to Pittsburgh.

In 1942, she divorced John Williams and married trumpet player Harold "Shorty" Baker. Together they formed a combo which included drummer and bebop pioneer Art Blakey. When Baker went on tour with Duke Ellington, Williams continued leading the sextet for awhile, then quit to join Ellington. In six months on the road, she wrote 15 arrangements for Ellington, including the brilliant "Trumpets No End," which Ellington recorded in 1946, featuring his trumpet section. It became a classic.

By 1944, the marriage to Baker had ended. Mary Lou Williams was now based in New York, and surrounded, in a situation similar to Kansas City in the 1930s, by the exciting musical innovations being made by some of the best jazz musicians of the day. She became one of the few musicians to come out of the boogie-woogie, blues and even big-band traditions who were able to greet the dawn of bebop (also called bop) with enthusiasm, and to make the transition to this new beat. Bop was the rapid, densely noted, technically and harmonically challenging new music invented by young black musicians to counter the commercialization of swing which had been simplified and popularized by white orchestras by the 1940s. Bop utilized extended chords and emphasized the instantaneous composing skills of the soloist. Williams' apartment became the after-hours rehearsal spot and think-tank for such portentous bebop icons as Bud Powell, Thelonious Monk, Tadd Dameron, and *Sarah Vaughan. In an interview with The Village Voice, Williams once recalled how she, Monk and Powell worked on a piece for three pianos through many nights, the three of them sitting at a single piano—a piece which, unfortunately, was never finished. During this time, Williams herself composed the bebop tunes "Oo-Bla-Dee" and "Walking," and her first extended work, The Zodiac Suite, which was performed at New York's Town Hall in 1945, and part of which was performed the following year by the New York Philharmonic at Carnegie Hall. She made many appearances throughout the 1940s and early 1950s, including a 1947 Carnegie Hall performance with an all-woman trio consisting of **Marjorie Hyams** (who had played vibes with Woody Herman during World War II) and bassist **June Rotenberg**. The previous year, the three had recorded Girls in Jazz for RCA Victor with guitarist *Mary Osborne** and drummer **Rose Gottesman**. In 1948, Williams recorded some

bop experiments with trumpet player Idress Suleiman and bassist George Duvivier, and she had a number of engagements at Cafe Society Up Town and Downtown (1942–47).

From 1952 to 1954, Mary Lou Williams lived in England and France. At the end of this period, she gave up music to devote herself entirely to religious meditation and study. She returned to the U.S., having decided to dedicate her life to helping the poor, which included opening her apartment to homeless persons needing a place to sleep and clean up. She started the Bel Canto Foundation, a charitable organization aimed at rehabilitating ailing, alcoholic, and drug-addicted musicians. In 1956, she joined the Catholic Church. Her many musician friends, including Dizzy and **Lorraine Gillespie**, urged her to return to her art, but Williams continued to give all of herself to charitable works. Finally, in 1957, she agreed to appear with Dizzy Gillespie at the Newport Jazz Festival, playing for the first time in three years. After that, a Jesuit priest, Father Anthony Woods, is reported to have told her, "It's *my* business to help people through the church, and *your* business to help people through music."

In 1963, Williams founded her own record label, Mary Records, and began composing and recording pieces to express her religious devotion. Her modern jazz hymn entitled "Black Christ of the Andes" was recorded in 1964, and in 1969 she received a commission from the Vatican to write a sacred jazz mass. Mary Lou's Mass premiered in 1970 at Columbia University, and a year later she rewrote it as a ballet for Alvin Ailey's City Center Dance Theater. In 1978, another production of Mary Lou's Mass was the highlight of the First Women's Jazz Festival in Kansas City.

In her last years, Mary Lou Williams was honored many times for her distinguished career, including eight honorary university degrees and two Guggenheim Foundation grants. A street in Kansas City was named after her in 1973, and in 1978 she performed at Jimmy Carter's White House Jazz Party. Well into her 60s, she continued to experiment with new musical forms, joining avant-garde pianist Cecil Taylor for a duet concert and album in 1977. In 1976, she joined the music faculty as artist-in-residence at Duke University in Durham, North Carolina, where she wrote, gave concerts, and taught master classes and the history of jazz. Proud of her work at Duke, she continued to teach even while fighting the cancer that took her life, at age 71, on May 28, 1981. True to her calling to help people through music, she bequeathed her entire estate to the Mary Lou Williams Foundation, an organization she founded the year before her death for the purpose of providing individual jazz training for talented young musicians, ages six through twelve.

SOURCES:

Britt, Stan. "The First Lady of Jazz," in *Jazz Journal International*. Vol. 34, no. 9. September 1981, pp. 10–12.

Chilton, John. *Who's Who of Jazz: Storyville to Swing Street*. Time Life Records Special Edition, 1978.

Dahl, Linda. *Stormy Weather: The Music and Lives of a Century of Jazzwomen*. NY: Limelight Editions, 1989.

Handy, D. Antoinette. *Black Women in American Bands and Orchestras*. Metuchen, NJ: Scarecrow Press, 1981.

———. "Conversation with Mary Lou Williams: First Lady of the Jazz Keyboard," in *The Black Perspective in Music*, 1980, pp. 195–214.

Harrison, Daphne Duval. *Black Pearls: Blues Queens of the 1920s*. New Brunswick, NJ: Rutgers University Press, 1990.

Homzy, Andrew. *Mary Lou Williams: The Zodiac Suite Orchestra* (liner notes). Vintage Jazz Classics, VJC–1035, 1991.

Jones, Max. *Talking Jazz*. NY: W.W. Norton, 1987.

McDonough, John. "Mary Lou Williams," in *Down Beat*. September 1990, p. 21.

McPartland, Marian. "Into the Sun: an Affectionate Sketch of Mary Lou Williams," in *All in Good Time*. NY: Oxford University Press, 1987.

Mousouris, Melinda. "Mary Lou Williams: Musician as Healer," in *The Village Voice*. July 23, 1979, pp. 81–84.

Placksin, Sally. *Jazzwomen, 1900 to the Present*. London: Pluto Press, 1985.

SUGGESTED READING:

Dahl, Linda. *Morning Glory: A Biography of Mary Lou Williams*. NY: Pantheon, 2000.

Sherrie Tucker,
freelance writer and jazz disk jockey in
San Francisco Bay Area, California

Williams, Mary Wilhelmine

(1878–1944)

American historian. Born on May 14, 1878, in Stanislaus County, California; died following a stroke on March 10, 1944, in Palo Alto, California; daughter of Charles Williams and Caroline (Madsen) Williams; graduated from San Jose State Normal School, 1901; Stanford University, A.B., 1907, A.M., 1908, Ph.D., 1914; studied at the University of Chicago.

Appointed associate professor of history at Goucher College (1916); promoted to associate professor (1919), and professor (1920–40); organized first course in Canadian history to be offered in the United States (1916); was retained as a consultant by Honduran government (1918–19); co-founded Baltimore branch of Women's International League for Peace and Freedom (1923), serving as state chair (1934–36); toured 15 Latin American countries for the American Association of University Women (1926–27); wrote several texts and travel books, the most widely read being The People and Politics of Latin America *(1930).*

Mary Wilhemine Williams was born in 1878, one of six children of Scandinavian immigrants, and raised on a farm in rural California, with few luxuries due to her father's concern over the family's finances. Attending school only through grade eight, she eventually resumed her formal education at age 18, enrolling at the San Jose State Normal School and graduating in 1901. After teaching for three years, she enrolled at Stanford University and adopted an accelerated schedule that allowed her to graduate in only three years with a bachelor's degree, thus saving the fourth year to complete her master's. While money concerns forced Williams to return to teaching from 1908 to 1911, she resolved to pursue her love of history and spent her summers away from her own classroom studying at the University of Chicago. In 1911, she traveled to Europe, accumulating research toward her Ph.D. dissertation, "Anglo-American Isthmian Diplomacy, 1815–1915," which would win the American Historical Society's Justin Winsor Prize.

Upon her return home to the United States, Williams taught courses at Welleseley College during the 1914–15 school year, then moved to Goucher College in Baltimore, Maryland, where she began as an assistant professor and moved on to associate and then to full professor of history in 1920. During her long career at Goucher, she was instrumental in expanding the school's history program to include more Latin-American history classes and a history of the struggle for women's rights, and also organized and taught the first Canadian history course ever to appear at the college level in the United States. With her strong character, striking Scandinavian looks, and deeply held feminist beliefs, Williams served as an imposing role model for all her students. She was also respected within her field, working as a pioneer in developing new areas of Latin-American study as well as curricula, and served on several committees focusing in this region.

In 1918 Williams was asked to serve as a cartographer for the government of Honduras, which was attempting to resolve a border dispute with neighboring Guatemala and Nicaragua. Eight years later, under the auspices of the American Association of University

Women, she toured 15 Latin American nations as part of a survey of educational opportunities available to women internationally. Considered an authority on the region by the 1930s, Williams counseled aviator Charles Lindbergh on his proposed flight over South America, and was appointed by the U.S. State Department to a series of committees attempting to deal with problems related to U.S.-Latin American relations. In addition to her position on the board of editors of *Hispanic American Historical Review*, Williams also authored several books, among them *The People and Politics of Latin America* (1930), which remained a standard text on the subject for many years. A trip to the Scandinavian regions where her parents had been born and raised in 1916 resulted in *Cousin-Hunting in Scandinavia* (1916), a travel book.

For her dedication as both an educator and a promoter of an expanded world view, Williams was justly honored by her colleagues. The Dominican Republic also decorated Williams in 1940 for her efforts on behalf of increased international understanding. In addition to her career accomplishments, she also furthered the causes of both world peace and women's rights, publishing articles in magazines and actively lobbying her legislators. Active in the Women's International League for Peace and Freedom, she was also an energetic volunteer in activities of the National Woman's Party. Williams retired from her position at Goucher in 1940, and relocated to Palo Alto, California, where she died four years later at the age of 65. She left instructions that on her gravestone be carved the words "Teacher, Historian, Pacifist, Feminist."

SOURCES:
James, Edward T., ed. *Notable American Women, 1607–1950*. Cambridge, MA: The Belknap Press of Harvard University, 1971.

Pamela Shelton,
freelance writer,
Avon, Connecticut

Williams, Sarah (1841–1868)

British poet. Name variations: Sadie Williams. Born in 1841 in London, England; died on April 25, 1868, in London, England; daughter of a Welsh businessman; educated at Queen's College, London.

Sarah Williams was born in 1841 in London, England, and lived in that city throughout her brief life. The daughter of a transplanted Welsh businessman of some financial means, Williams often credited her father's ethnicity with her poetic nature. An only child, she was raised under the tutelage of a series of governesses, and eventually enrolled at Queen's College in London, from which she graduated in the early 1860s. She began writing poetry while at Queen's College, and received enough encouragement from Edward Hayes Plumptre, soon to be dean of Wells, to attempt publication. Her first work, *Rainbows in Springtide* (1866), earned a sum sufficient to encourage Williams to attempt a living from her poetry. She continued her writing and pursuit of various academic interests, even donating half the earnings from her poetry to London's poor. While Williams' works are little read today except for their historical value, they were reasonably popular at the time they were written, and consist mainly of children's verses and religious writings. In addition to *Rainbows in Springtide*, her other major published work is *Twilight Hours: A Legacy of Verse*, a commemorative anthology published shortly after her untimely death in 1868.

SOURCES:
Kunitz, Stanley J., and Howard Haycraft, eds. *British Authors of the Nineteenth Century*. NY: H.W. Wilson, 1936.

Pamela Shelton,
freelance writer,
Avon, Connecticut

Williams, Sherley Anne (1944–1999)

African-American poet, novelist, playwright, educator, and literary critic. Born in Bakersfield, California, on August 25, 1944; died of cancer in San Diego, California, on July 6, 1999; daughter of Jessee Winson Williams and Lelia Marie (Siler) Williams; attended junior and senior high school in Fresno, California; California State University at Fresno, B.A., 1966; spent one year in graduate studies at Howard University; Brown University, M.A., 1972; children: John Malcolm (b. 1968).

Selected writings: Give Birth to Brightness: A Thematic Study in Neo-Black Literature *(1972);* The Peacock Poems *(1975);* Some One Sweet Angel Chile *(1982);* Dessa Rose *(1986);* Letter from a New England Negro *(play, 1991);* Working Cotton *(1992);* Girls Together *(1997).*

Sherley Anne Williams was born in 1944 in Bakersfield, California, the daughter of Jessee Winson Williams and **Lelia Siler Williams**, migrant farm workers who struggled to make ends meet. The family lived in low-income housing projects throughout California's San Joaquin Valley, particularly in Fresno. To help earn enough to cover living expenses, young Sherley and her three sisters, **Ruby, Lois,** and **Jesmarie,** often picked cotton and fruit alongside their parents. When Sherley was just seven, her father died of tuberculosis, after which the family spent more time in Fresno, where she attended both junior and senior high school. Her mother died when she was 16, and the Williams sisters struggled even more desperately to survive and stay together as a family. Looking back on her childhood, Williams later described her upbringing as "the most deprived, provincial kind of existence you can think of."

Introduced to the delights of reading at an early age, Williams had been discouraged from this pursuit by her mother, who perhaps feared that reading might inspire her daughter towards goals that she could not possibly attain, given the family's impoverished state. Williams, however, was rescued by an eighth-grade science teacher who saw great promise and encouraged her to pursue college-prep courses. During high school, she rediscovered her love of language and determined that she would go to college. She later reflected: "To go from having no prospects at all to having seemingly limitless opportunity . . . well, in my case, I feel I just wasn't prepared for seemingly limitless opportunity."

After completing her high school studies, Williams attended California State University at Fresno, using earnings from farm work to help finance her tuition and earning a bachelor's degree in history in 1966. She then left California

for Washington, D.C., where she pursued graduate studies at Howard University for one year. In 1968, she began working at Federal City College in the capital, and became a single mother when she gave birth to her son John Malcolm. That same year she was published for the first time, in the *Massachusetts Review*, with the short story "Tell Martha Not to Moan." The first-person narrative of a young black woman pregnant with her second child and abandoned by her musician lover, it has since gone on to republication in several anthologies.

After a few years in Washington, Williams moved to Providence, Rhode Island, where she taught in the Black Studies department of Brown University and resumed her graduate studies. In 1972, she earned a master's degree from Brown and left shortly thereafter to assume an associate professorship at California State University in Fresno. Three years later, she traveled south to join the faculty of the University of California at San Diego, where she served as a professor of literature until her death.

Williams first attracted attention in literary circles with the 1972 publication of *Give Birth to Brightness: A Thematic Study in Neo-Black Literature*, a work of literary criticism in which she assessed the writings of such African-American notables as James Baldwin, Amiri Baraka, and Ernest Gaines and contended that most black heroes in contemporary fiction had their

Sherley Anne Williams

roots in black folklore. Three years later, she became known as a poet with the publication of *The Peacock Poems*, a nominee for both the Pulitzer Prize and the National Book Award in Poetry in 1976. The volume of autobiographical poems explored her early family life and her feelings as a single mother, as well as the precarious existence of low-income African-American women in general. The blues poetry so prevalent in *Peacock Poems* carried over into her next volume of poetry, 1982's *Some One Sweet Angel Chile*, which was also nominated for a National Book Award. Among the four sections in the book is one that focuses on *Bessie Smith, "Regular Reefer," and another, "Letters from a New England Negro," that details the life of a freeborn African-American woman teaching ex-slaves in the South after the Civil War. With these two collections, Williams was firmly established as an important new voice in African-American poetry. She later received an Emmy Award for a television performance of poems from *Some One Sweet Angel Chile*.

Williams made her debut as a novelist in 1986 with *Dessa Rose*, a work often compared to the writings of *Toni Morrison and **Alice Walker** because of its mystical qualities. Set in and around antebellum Charleston, South Carolina, the novel explores the unusual relationship between a wealthy young white plantation mistress and a slave named Dessa, who conspire to dupe white planters by selling them slaves who are later helped to escape. (Both were based on historical characters, a slave who led an insurrection while pregnant in 1829 and a white woman in North Carolina, although in real life their paths did not cross.) David Bradley, reviewing the novel in *The New York Times*, called it "artistically brilliant, emotionally affecting, and totally unforgettable," and went on to note that while Williams "shows that she can write a novel better than a lot of novelists, nowhere does she cut herself off from her poetic roots."

Williams' one-woman play, *Letter from a New England Negro*, was staged in 1991 at the National Black Theater Festival and a year later at the Chicago International Theater Festival. Her first children's book, *Working Cotton* (1992), won the Caldecott Award of the American Library Association as well as a *Coretta Scott King** Book Award. It was followed by a second children's book, *Girls Together*, in 1997. At the time of her death from cancer in 1999, at age 54, Williams was working on both a novel set in contemporary times and a sequel to *Dessa Rose*.

SOURCES:

The Day [New London, CT]. July 14, 1999, p. B5.

Green, Carol Hurd, and Mary Grimley Mason, eds. *American Women Writers*. NY: Continuum, 1994.

Hine, Darlene Clark, ed. *Black Women in America*. Brooklyn, NY: Carlson, 1993.

Magill, Frank N., ed. *Cyclopedia of World Authors*. Rev. 3rd ed. Pasadena, CA: Salem Press, 1997.

Don Amerman,
freelance writer,
Saylorsburg, Pennsylvania

Williams, Shirley (1930—)

*British politician who co-founded the Social Democratic Party. Name variations: Shirley Vivien Teresa Brittain Williams; Baroness Shirley Williams. Born Shirley Vivien Teresa Brittain on July 27, 1930, in Chelsea, England; daughter of Sir George Catlin (a professor of political science) and Vera Brittain (1893–1970); attended St. Paul's Girls' School in London; educated at Somerville College, Oxford; attended Columbia University; married Bernard Williams (a philosopher), in 1955 (annulled 1974); married Richard Neustadt (a professor of politics at Harvard), in 1987; children: (first marriage) one daughter, **Rebecca Clair Williams**.*

Began career as a journalist for Daily Mirror *and* Financial Times *(1954–59); ran for election to Parliament in Harwich (1954–55); served as general secretary of the Fabian Society (1960–64); elected as member of Parliament for Hitchin (1964–74), and Hertford-Stevenage (1974–79); served in numerous government posts in the Ministry of Health (1964–66), Ministry of Labor (1966–67), Ministry of Education and Science (1967–69), and Home Office (1969–70); appointed minister of Prices and Consumer Protection (1974–76), and minister for Education and Science and paymaster-general (1976–79); was a member of Labour Party National Executive (1970–81); appointed Professorial Fellow of London Policy Study Institute (1979); co-founded the Social Democratic Party (1981); served as president of the Social Democratic Party (1982–88); served as a member of Parliament for Crosby (1981–1984); published* Politics Is for People *(1981).*

Shirley Williams was born in 1930 in Chelsea, and the active civic lives of both her parents strongly influenced her choice of a career in politics. Her father Sir George Catlin was a professor of political science as well as a Labour Party candidate in the 1930s, and her mother, feminist *Vera Brittain, was widely known for advancing her socialist beliefs. Her parents entertained T.S. Eliot, Arthur Greenwood, and other celebrities; Jawaharal Nehru bounced Shirley on his knee when she was an infant. Her father taught at Cornell University in New York and at McGill University in Montreal in addition to acting as a special adviser to Wendell Willkie in 1940 when Willkie was Republican contender for the presidency of the United States. In British politics, he was adviser to the Labour Party from 1930 to 1979 and wrote extensively on U.S.-British cooperation.

Shirley Williams completed much of her education in London, although during the war years she went to St. Paul, Minnesota, to avoid the bombing. Returning to England in 1943, 13-year-old Williams attended St. Paul's Girls' School before enrolling in Somerville College, Oxford. At Somerville, she became active in politics, joining the Labour League of Youth during her freshman year. Following graduation, Williams chose to work alongside her Labour Party constituents, taking jobs in factories and waiting on tables before earning a year-long fellowship to Columbia University. While studying in New York in 1952, she met Bernard Williams, whom she married three years later.

Returning to London in 1954, Williams worked as a reporter for several London papers while beginning her political career. Nicknamed the "schoolgirl candidate," she ran for Parliament in 1954 and 1955 at Harwich, Essex, but lost. For three years she lived in Africa with her husband, teaching at the University of Ghana in Accra. She returned to England to run for a seat in Parliament from Southampton in 1959; she again failed. Williams became general secretary of the Fabian Society, the nucleus of socialism in England, from 1960 to 1964. Finally she was elected to Parliament at Hitchin, Hertfordshire, in October 1964. That year, after 13 years in opposition, the Labour Party returned to power, with Harold Wilson as prime minister.

Wilson gave Williams minor posts in the government. She served in the Ministry of Health (1964–66), the Ministry of Labor (1966–67), the Ministry of Education and Science (1967–69), and the Home Office (1969–70), where she concentrated on the Northern Ireland issue. The Protestants of Ulster never trusted her because she was a Catholic. During the 1960s, she voted against liberalizing divorce laws and against abortion rights. Williams was a self-confident, ebullient, popular, and decidedly unglamorous politician. With a rumpled appearance and unruly hair, she noted, "People like me because I look as crummy as they do."

When Wilson was defeated and the Labour Party became the opposition government in 1970, Williams became a member of the party's national executive board. She also became the voice of the party on Social Services, Home Affairs, and Prices and Consumer Protection. In May 1971, she was among 100 Labour members of Parliament who signed a declaration endorsing the Common Market despite criticism of the Common Market by many leftists in the party. Williams vehemently opposed isolationist policies and advocated joining the European Economic Community. She proclaimed that the Labour Party was opposed to the Common Market and threatened to resign from the opposition Cabinet unless Labour adopted a "more constructive" stance toward Europe. The Conservative government of Prime Minister Edward Heath brought Britain into the Common Market in July 1972, aided by Williams and other Labour Party members. "I am not as much a passionate European, as I am a passionate internationalist . . . with a deep sense of the special and unique nature of Britain," she said in an interview with the *Guardian* on April 15, 1975. "I see staying in Europe as being part of the price of living with reality."

In the election of February 1974, Williams won a new seat in Parliament, representing Hertford and Stevenage, and Wilson regained power. Williams was appointed minister of Prices and Consumer Protection, her first Cabinet office. As minister, she endorsed voluntary guidelines for combating inflation.

When Wilson, in a surprise move, resigned in March 1976, Williams removed herself from consideration for party leadership. The new leader was James Callaghan, who appointed her minister of Education and Science, where she led a campaign for comprehensive education but cut teacher-training positions. She also served as paymaster-general from 1976 to 1979.

In May 1979, the Conservatives under *Margaret Thatcher swept the elections, routing Labour. Williams lost her seat in Parliament and turned to a job as a senior research fellow at the Policy Studies Institute in London until 1985. Within the Labour Party, the leftists and the centrists battled. At a Labour Party conference in January 1981, the left, led by Anthony Wedgwood Benn, staged a showdown with the leaders of the center: Williams, Roy Jenkins, David Owen, and William Rogers, known as the "Gang of Four." Instead of letting the party's members of Parliament choose the party leader by themselves, Benn moved to give 40% of the vote to unions and 30% to local party organizations. Benn's faction won platform fights endorsing unilateral disarmament and withdrawal from the Common Market. Williams and others who opposed the platform resigned from the party. With Owen, Rogers, and Jenkins, she formed a new party, the Social Democratic Party (SDP), in March 1981.

Eight months later, she was elected to Parliament at Crosby, a suburb of Liverpool, as a candidate for the Social Democratic Party. By the end of 1981, the fledgling Social Democrats had 23 seats in the House of Commons and were gaining popularity. Williams became the party's president in 1982 and remained its leader until 1988. However, the Social Democrats quickly went into decline. By 1983, they had only six seats in the House of Commons, and Williams lost her seat at Crosby the following year. Popular support for the Falklands War against Argentina carried Margaret Thatcher's government and the Conservative Party to new heights of popularity, and the SDP never regained its initial momentum.

In 1985, Williams became director of the Turing Institute in Glasgow, Scotland. Having annulled her marriage to Bernard Williams in 1974, she married Richard Neustadt, a Harvard political economist, in 1987. That same year she ran again for Parliament at Cambridge and lost. In the 1990s, she became a member of the House of Lords, a Harvard University professor of electoral politics, and a director of Project Liberty, which assisted developing democracies in eastern and central Europe. She continued to play an active role in trying to bring peace to Northern Ireland.

SOURCES:

Encyclopedia of World Biography. 2nd ed. Detroit, MI: Gale Research, 1998.

Uglow, Jennifer S., comp. and ed. *The International Dictionary of Women's Biography.* 2nd ed. NY: Continuum, 1985.

Pamela Shelton,
freelance writer,
Avon, Connecticut

Williamsburg, countess of.

See Desmier, Eleanor (1639–1722).

Williams Perkins, Betty (b. 1943).

See joint entry under Williams, Betty and Mairead Corrigan.

Willing, Jennie Fowler (1834–1916)

Canadian-born American preacher and temperance reformer. Born on January 22, 1834, in Burford, Canada; died on October 6, 1916, in New York City; daughter of Horatio Fowler and Harriet (Ryan) Fowler; self-educated; married William C. Willing (an attorney), in 1853 (died 1894); no children.

Involved in the founding of the Woman's Christian Temperance Union (WCTU, 1874); served as editor of the WCTU's newspaper Our Union *(1875–76); founded the New York Evangelistic Training School to create settlement projects in New York City (1895).*

Jennie Fowler Willing was born in 1834 in Burford, Canada, and raised in farm country, first in western Canada and then in Newark, Illinois. Jennie had little exposure to formal schooling due to poor health. Her studies were instead fueled by her natural curiosity and the example of her mother, a devout reader and self-improvement advocate. By age 15, Jennie had been so successful in her own program of self-education that she was able to get a job at the local schoolhouse. Married to lawyer-turned-Methodist pastor William C. Willing by age 19, she moved with her husband to various pastorates in his home state of New York before returning to Illinois.

Encouraged by her husband, Willing obtained a preacher's license and presided over a number of services and revival meetings. More influential than her speaking, however, was Willing's writing—both fiction and nonfiction—which appeared in church pamphlets, books, and magazines. In her work she stressed the uplifting aspects of religion, calling upon her readers to live by Christian means and trust in their individual abilities. Well written and persuasive, if sometimes criticized for being "unladylike," her writing won Willing the respect of the Evanston College for Ladies, which awarded the 38-year-old author an honorary A.M. degree in 1872. Two years later both Willing and her husband were granted professorships at Illinois Wesleyan University, Willing to teach English language and literature and her husband to instruct students in the law.

While writing and literature occupied Willing's academic life, she pursued many other interests, most of which involved social causes. An early participant in the region's suffrage movement, Willing believed strongly in advancing the equality of women. One barrier to that equality was liquor, which Willing felt was at the root of many of the family-related problems then faced by women and children. In 1874, with the support of the national Women's Crusade, she helped the cause of temperance by lobbying for stricter liquor licensing laws in her adopted hometown of Bloomington, Illinois. That year, with the help of temperance reformer *Martha McClellan Brown and others, she organized a national women's temperance meeting that was held on November 18, 1874. The result of that meeting was the formation of the Woman's Christian Temperance Union (WCTU), which became one of the movement's most active organizations. Willing was elected to serve as the editor of the WCTU's newspaper, *Our Union*, a post she held from mid-1875 to early the following year.

Reform efforts stemming from her church involvement also competed for Willing's time, and after leaving *Our Union* she refocused her energies on the cause of home missions and settlements, particularly those to benefit immigrant girls. An active writer throughout her career, she now focused many of her articles on this area. After Willing and her husband relocated to New York City in 1889, she saw, firsthand, the hardships encountered by young working women in the inner city, where jobs were scarce and safe places to stay were even scarcer. A year after her husband's death in 1894, Willing founded the New York Evangelistic Training School, which, with the support of the Methodist Church, created settlement projects in the city. Upon her death in 1916, at age 82, half of Willing's estate was left to the Training School; the remainder was bequeathed to the WCTU.

SOURCES:

James, Edward T., ed. *Notable American Women, 1607–1950.* Cambridge, MA: The Belknap Press of Harvard University, 1971.

Pamela Shelton,
freelance writer,
Avon, Connecticut

Willis, Ann (b. 1933).

See Richards, Ann Willis.

Willis, Ann Bassett (1878–1956).

See Bassett, Ann.

Willis, Olympia Brown (1835–1926).

See Brown, Olympia.

Willis, Sara Payson (1811–1872).

See Fern, Fanny.

Willoughby, Catharine (1519–1580).

See Bertie, Catharine.

Wills, Helen Newington

(1905–1998)

Eight-time Wimbledon tennis champion who was the outstanding American woman player of her time. Name variations: Helen Wills Moody; Mrs. F.S. Moody. Born Helen Newington Wills on October 6, 1905, in Centerville, California; died in Carmel, California, on January 1, 1998; daughter of Clarence Wills (a doctor) and Catherine Wills; attended the University of California; married Frederick S. Moody, in 1929 (divorced 1937); married Aidan Roark, in 1939 (divorced around 1970).

*Won the U.S. Girls' championship (1921 and 1922); won the American Women's National Singles championship (1923, 1924, 1925, 1927, 1928, 1929), illness had prevented her from competing (1926); won the American Women's Doubles championship with Mrs. M.Z. Jessup (1922), with Hazel Hotchkiss Wightman (1924), with *Mary K. Browne (1925), and with Hazel Wightman (1928); won Olympic gold medals in singles and doubles at the Paris Olympics (1924); won the British Women's Singles championship at Wimbledon (1927, 1928, 1929, 1930, 1932, 1933, 1935, and 1938); won the French Women's Singles championship (1928, 1929, 1930, and 1932); retired from major competition (1938); devoted the rest of her life to painting and writing, producing an autobiography and a collection of mystery novels; admitted to the International Tennis Hall of Fame (1959).*

Journalist Paul Gallico once ventured the opinion, widely accepted in the early decades of the 20th century, that there were beautiful women, and then there were women athletes. Female sports figures, Gallico pronounced, were only using athletics to make up for a lack of beauty, a husband, a family, a home. Then Helen Wills won her first U.S. Open title in 1923. She was one of the most powerful and effective tennis players he had ever seen, male or female, and, he noted with surprise, she was strikingly attractive. Helen was, in fact, the first woman in America to become a tennis star, opening the door to later generations of her gender who attained international celebrity on and off the court, from *Billie Jean King to **Venus Williams**.

Born in Centerville, California, on October 6, 1905, she first picked up a tennis racket at the age of eight, when her father added the game to a variety of outdoor pursuits he had chosen to strengthen his daughter's delicate childhood health. Clarence Wills, a doctor, had introduced Helen to swimming, riding and hunting, among other sports, before he gave Helen her first tennis lesson in 1917 on a dirt court next to the hospital where he practiced medicine. "I was especially keen about nature and liked to hunt wild flowers as much as I liked to play any games at all," Wills later said, one of many statements proclaiming a rather nonchalant attitude toward the sport which would serve her so well. Tennis was at the time a relatively new public sport and a wildly

Helen
Newington
Wills

popular one, especially in California where, as one pundit of the game noted, "it's always June," and the game could be played all year round on the inexpensive, hard-paved courts to be found in any park or playground. Of all the sports that Clarence Wills had chosen for Helen, tennis seemed to have the most dramatic effect on her physical stamina, not the least because rackets of the time were made of solid wood, weighed a hefty 15 ounces and had handles that were five-and-a-half inches around. Helen herself was of the opinion that tennis "is more strenuous than swimming, more vigorous than horseback riding," and she quickly learned the volleying game that lent itself to the West Coast's hard court surfaces. Wills also came to the game at a time when the dominance of East Coast players was beginning to weaken. Maurice McLoughlin became the first California player to win the U.S. Open at Forest Hills in 1912, and Wills always remembered the thrill of watching him play an exhibition game—the first nationally ranked tennis player she had ever seen—and having him autograph one of her tennis balls.

When the Wills family moved to Berkeley after World War I and into a house conveniently located next to a park with tennis courts, Helen's interest in the game grew. She was now 13 and becoming a young woman. "Tennis was exchanged for the games of childhood," she wrote many years later, "and I am very happy that this happened." She still lacked formal training, depending on her father's suggestions and her observations of other players to improve her game; but when the tennis pro at the Berkeley Tennis Club, William "Pop" Fuller, heard about the Wills girl and ambled over to the park to watch her play, things became very formal indeed. Helen was given a junior membership in the Club and a series of lessons with Fuller, as a 14th birthday present from her parents. "When she steps on to a tennis court," Fuller later said of his most famous pupil, "all but the game ceases to exist." Fuller was especially impressed with the fact that Helen showed absolutely no emotion as she played, no matter what he asked her to do or how hard he lobbed balls to her. Helen later insisted her reputation as "Little Miss Poker-Face" grew from her father's suggestion that screwing up her face or grimacing during a game would put lines on her face, but Fuller thought it went deeper. "I never saw anyone more determined and cool about winning success nor more indifferent to failure," he reported. Fuller quickly built on the basics of the game instilled in Helen by her father, encouraging her to place her volleys with more subtlety and increasing the accuracy of her serves by having her aim at a white handkerchief he would move around the baseline across the net. Fuller did not interfere, however, with Helen's "open" stance, her manner of squarely facing the net for her strokes rather than with her shoulder forward; nor did he adjust her iron grip on the racket to a more relaxed and flexible hold. Although these deviations would today be considered highly unusual, one of Helen's frequent opponents reported that any shot drilled from Wills' racket made it seem as if the ball

"had been dipped in concrete" by the time it reached the other side of the court.

Within a few months, Fuller had moved her from matches with girls her own age to games with older boys at the Club, and eventually with adults. She loved speed, power volleys, rushing the net, and going after anything that was hit to her, no matter how much scrambling it entailed. But even though Fuller claimed her as his most famous pupil and was known until his death in 1956 as "Helen Wills' tennis coach," Helen herself held a different opinion. Outside of her father, she took pains to point out, "I have learned through observation of others and actual practice or contest. I practiced by playing games, not by drilling on strokes. I made up my mind to appear to be listening politely to what other people said, but not really to do what they suggested." Little wonder she became known as "Queen Helen."

By 1919, Wills had won a San Francisco Bay area tournament and had advanced to California State championship play, although she lost in straight sets to her opponent. In the gallery for the championship match, however, was *Hazel Hotchkiss Wightman, a top-ranked California player who was impressed enough with Helen's skill to spend three weeks after the state matches improving Wills' footwork and control of the ball. The two got on so well together that they would later team up in doubles tournaments, to great acclaim and admiration. By 1921, Wills had captured the California state singles title and Wightman had carried eastward the news about the stunning young West Coast player, laying the groundwork for Helen's first appearance on an East Coast grass court in a Providence, Rhode Island, tournament. She lost her chance at the singles title in the second round, but advanced all the way to the finals in doubles play; and quickly recovered by capturing the National Girls' championship at Forest Hills, returning to California in triumph. The following year, she won the California state title for a second time and once again traveled East to capture the National Junior Tournament in Philadelphia. She advanced all the way to the finals in the National Women's Singles at Forest Hills before losing to defending champion *Molla Mallory of Norway, and had become such a crowd pleaser that when the two women met again ten days later at the Longwood Cricket Club in Brookline, Massachusetts, the gallery actually booed court officials who made calls against Wills, reducing Mallory to tears even though Mallory once again defeated the newcomer. The Eastern tennis crowd had never seen anyone, man or woman, who looked or played like Helen Wills. She was wholesomely beautiful, combining great power and concentration with utter calm and composure, and the press came up with yet more sobriquets in dubbing her "the American girl" and "the Ice Queen." But it was Wills' game, not her fame, that mattered the most, and at the close of the 1922 season, she was ranked No. 3 in the country. The year 1923, the pundits said, would be Helen's.

Just before the 1923 season began, Wills graduated from a private girls' school and announced her intention to enter the fall term at the University of California at Berkeley as an art student. But the tennis world cared little for her educational plans, watching eagerly as Helen traveled East once more in the spring and played to victory in several small matches to accustom herself to playing on grass. When her association with Hazel Wightman led to a place on the American team of the U.S.-British competition named after Wightman, Wills and her American teammates swept the British team 7–0. Then, Helen advanced to the climax of her Eastern tour, the National Women's Singles championship. The title was still held by her old opponent, Molla Mallory, but a crowd of 5,000 at Forest Hills watched Wills polish Mallory off 6–1, 6–2 in little more than a half-hour to become the first American-born singles champion since 1919. Wills was, in the words of one of the journalists who crowded around her after the match, "a miracle in motion." She politely scoffed at the raised eyebrows over her aggressive playing style. "It's really much more fun to run to the net and try some smashing volleying shots," Wills told them. "They seem to call that a man's game. But I don't. I just call it fun."

As Wills returned to Berkeley to begin her college studies, tennis fans looked forward to the 1924 season and Helen's chance of capturing her first international title. Practicing every day after classes against some of California's best male players, Wills was in top form by the time she left for England in the late spring of 1924 for her first appearance at Wimbledon and at Olympic competition in Paris. The British press was just as helpless as their peers in America when faced with Wills' cool beauty and composure. "No lovelier or more striking girl has ever been seen on the historic courts here," the *Evening Standard* reported, even though Helen quickly lost in early rounds of the Wightman Cup competition, played that year near London. She made no excuses for her loss, although years later she admitted that she had played too hard in practice rounds and felt ill by the time the Wightman matches began. Hopes rose when Wills played triumphantly through her early matches for the Wimbledon singles title, but were dashed when she lost in finals play to Britain's **Kitty McKane**. It was the first and last time Helen was seen to burst into tears in public.

> *J*ust play the game.
> The thing is to have a good time.
> —**Helen Newington Wills**

She had recovered her composure by the time she arrived in Paris as a member of the American tennis team in that year's Olympics, held in a hastily constructed site in the industrial suburbs of the city. Wills handily arrived at finals play for the singles title to face France's top-ranked female player, **Didi Vlasto**, much remarked upon as one of the last women tennis players to use a genteel underhand serve that was no match for Wills' power drives. The competition was so unbalanced, in fact, that the gallery's French contingent loudly booed and hissed at what was seen as unfair tactics from the American, but Helen paid them no mind and defeated Vlasto 6–2, 6–2 in short order to win the gold medal for singles play, becoming the first American woman to win a major international singles title in 17 years. She won a second gold for doubles two days later. As Wills returned in triumph to New York and the long cross-country train journey home to California, she found that even people who knew nothing about tennis considered her a star. Crowds waited for her at every stop the train made, reporters swarmed toward her private car, all trying to get a glimpse of "the American girl."

America was, in fact, in love with her classic beauty at a time when flappers, bathtub gin and the excesses of the "Roaring Twenties" had been coarsening the national consciousness. Asked what he considered the most beautiful sight he had ever seen, Charlie Chaplin immediately replied, "The movement of Helen Wills playing tennis: it had grace and economy of action, as well as a healthy appeal to sex." Even Paul Gallico, so patronizing toward women in sports, waxed poetic when he recalled in later years "the gleam in the eyes of Helen Wills looking up at a tennis ball in the air during her service, and her lovely neck line." The fact that Wills neither drank alcohol, smoked, nor wore makeup was widely admired, as was the nearly constant presence of her mother **Catherine Wills**, and Helen's devotion to her art studies at Berkeley. It might all seem quaint today, but Helen came to personify these traditional values at a time when America was still reeling from the disillusionment of World War I and was being transformed from a mostly rural nation of farms and small businesses to a mechanized, urban-based economic giant. "She was," *The New Yorker* said simply, "what America needed."

For the next 14 years, Wills would not let America down. Between 1925 and 1931, she won the National Singles title at Forest Hills five more times. In 1927, she took home the first of eight Wimbledon Singles championships, defeating Spain's ◀❧ **Lili de Alvarez** 6–2, 6–4 in a furious, hard-hitting match that at one point left both players leaning on their rackets and gasping for breath. The following year, Wills won the first of her four French singles titles, the first American woman to do so, not to mention three doubles titles each at Forest Hills and at Wimbledon and two at the French nationals. By 1930, upwards of 20,000 fans were turning out to watch her play at Wimbledon for what one observer called the "ruthless execution" of her opponents. At one point, playing against her old nemesis Molla Mallory, Wills allowed only five points in a set that lasted all of five minutes; and in 1929, she nearly broke the world record for number of points scored in the shortest time by winning two sets at Forest Hills in 18 minutes. She lost only 8 games out of 80 played during the course of the tournament. Through all the pressure, "Miss Poker-Face" never lost her composure, never showed any sign of emotion on the court outside of a beatific smile at the end of a match, never objected to an umpire's call, never so much as stamped her foot. "I believe in taking things seriously, if one is trying hard for something," she told a friend in 1930. Even when she lost the doubles final at Forest Hills in 1933 because her exhausted partner, the newcomer *****Alice Marble**, had been playing for three consecutive days in other matches, Wills merely strode quietly off the court and declined to speak with reporters.

By the mid-1930s, in fact, the public and the press began to see Helen's impenetrable façade as cold and calculating, rather than as disciplined and focused, and her refusal to display normal emotions on the court as the behavior of a patronizing aristocrat. Top-seeded Bill Tilden, whom Wills had often beaten in mixed doubles, dared to say in print that he regarded her as "the coldest, most self-centered, most ruthless champion ever known to tennis. Her complete disregard for all other players and her fixed determination to play tennis only when she herself wished to and felt it was to her advantage, let her make little or no contribution to the ad-

vancement of the game." Alice Marble remembered when she was first introduced to Wills by Pop Fuller. "Wouldn't you like to help out a new player?" Fuller genially asked, to which Helen responded by saying "No, I wouldn't," before walking away. Even reporters who had been stunned by her earlier successes were now frankly bored, making bets on how long it would take Wills to finish off her opponents and commenting that she had become more of a businesswoman than a tennis player.

There was a brief buzz over Wills' 1929 marriage to Frederick Moody, a wealthy American stockbroker she had met while playing off-season matches on the Riviera, and reports about the new young couple made much of the fact that Helen was now wearing a hint of lipstick and might be loosening up a bit. But friends reported to one another by the mid-1930s that the marriage was in trouble, and at least some of them blamed the matrimonial strain for a series of humiliating losses to the new rising tennis star of the day, *****Helen Hull Jacobs**. Wills obtained her divorce in 1937 by temporarily moving to Nevada, where divorces were easily obtained if residency of even a few months could be proved, and cited mental cruelty as the reason for the end of her marriage. Fred Moody, on the other hand, blamed tennis and Wills' constant rounds of the tournament circuit. "I don't think we really got to know each other," Moody later said. Helen may have privately admitted the same thing, for she told reporters as she headed home from Nevada that she planned to "virtually desert the tennis court" and pursue other activities. But Wills had one more tennis drama to play out, at Wimbledon in 1938, in what became known as "the battle of the two Helens."

By June of that year, Wills was seeded first for Wimbledon singles play, Marble was seeded second, while Jacobs was unseeded as the early matches for the singles championship began. In a stunning performance that captured world attention, Helen Jacobs defeated all her opponents to arrive at finals play against Helen Wills. Even though the press referred to Wills as "Big Helen" and Jacobs as "Little Helen," it seemed for a time as if Jacobs would snatch the title from her illustrious opponent, until she incurred an ankle injury as she went for one of the famous Wills power lobs in the tenth set. Jacobs fought on painfully for the rest of the match as Wills mercilessly drove her deep to the baseline or made her scramble for the net. "In the way Helen Wills hit the ball with nearly mechanical perfection," said one reporter afterward, "there was a brutal thoroughness, almost sadistic in

❧▶
Alvarez, Lili de.
*See Aussem,
Cilli for sidebar.*

quality." It was widely noted that Wills never spoke to Jacobs, never looked at her as they passed each other changing courts, and only offered a perfunctory "Too bad, Helen" when it was all over. At the traditional courtside press conference, Wills made a few brief comments while Jacobs, with her throbbing ankle, sat on her racket behind her and had no chance to say anything. Then Helen Wills, without a handshake or a look at her opponent, walked off the court and disappeared. "The silence," said one onlooker, "was stifling."

On her return to the United States, Wills sent more ripples through the tennis world by announcing in a letter to the U.S. Lawn Tennis Association that she had decided to withdraw from national singles competition, citing a severe attack of "neuralgia." Even more of a shock, Helen publicized the letter in which she returned some $1,300 the USLTA had given her, ostensibly for Wimbledon expenses but actually, it was rumored, as an inducement for a reluctant Wills to appear at Forest Hills. It was the first time an amateur tennis player in the United States publicly acknowledged being paid. Then, in the spring of 1939, when she normally would have been heading East once again for national and European play, Wills announced from California that she was retiring from tournament competition. "I knew when it was over," she later wrote. "I was done. My time had passed. It was a beautiful spring. So I stayed at home." In the fall of that year, Helen married Aiden Roark, who listed his occupation as "film writer" but who was a well-known polo player. The couple settled near Los Angeles.

Wills never played serious tennis again and, true to her word after divorcing Fred Moody two years earlier, she turned to other pursuits. She published the first in a series of mystery novels late in 1939, inevitably revolving around the murders of several tennis players, and was undaunted by *The New York Times* review that opined: "In Mrs. Moody's hand, the racket is mightier than the pen." She began to paint, too, and exhibit her work in local art shows. She played tennis with friends and, just after World War II, with recovering soldiers at a military hospital near her home. She was inducted into the International Tennis Hall of Fame in 1959, for which occasion she made a rare public appearance, but she gave few subsequent interviews. In 1975, shortly after her divorce from Roark, she told a magazine reporter that she had turned most of her trophies into lamps. She was no more revealing in her last interview in 1984, when she was asked why she had retired so early

in her career. "I really don't know why," Wills said. "I just wanted to, I guess. It sure wasn't for the money. I played all those years, and you know why? Because I loved the game, I really did. I did all of that just because I loved the game." Helen Newington Wills died quietly at home in California on New Year's Day, 1998.

SOURCES:
Engelmann, Larry. *The Goddess and the American Girl: The Story of *Suzanne Lenglen* and Helen Wills*. NY: Oxford University Press, 1988.
Wills, Helen. *Fifteen-Thirty: The Story of a Tennis Player*. NY: Scribner, 1937.

Norman Powers,
writer-producer, Chelsea Lane Productions,
New York, New York

Willums, Sigbrit (fl. 1507–1523)

Powerful figure in Danish history as counsellor to King Christian II and mother of his royal mistress. Name variations: Sigbrit Villoms; Sigbrit Villems; Sibrecht Willumsdatter; Mother Sigbrit. Birth and death dates unknown; flourished in Danish history from 1507 to 1523, as counsellor to King Christian II and mother of Dyveke, his royal mistress.

Sigbrit Willums was a bright and enterprising Dutch woman who, with her young daughter, arrived in Norway in the early 1500s. There she obtained a license to sell bakery goods (or fish) from a booth at the harbor, or, as some historians maintain, run a tavern. She had been a tradeswoman in Holland as well, a seller of apples and nuts. Sources unanimously describe her as fat and ugly, sharp tongued and unafraid to speak the cause of poor and downtrodden farmers and traders. Although not born to nobility, she could read and write, and she taught her daughter both skills.

Neither talent for business nor intellectual prowess, however, accounts for her introduction into Danish history. That distinction she owes her daughter, a beautiful, gentle girl, called ❧▶ **Dyveke** (little dove). Dyveke attracted the attention of young King Christian II (1481–1559), who as viceroy of Norway made a trip to Bergen in 1507. He invited the girl and her mother to a ball at Bergen's town hall and negotiated with the latter an extended stay for the former. When Christian returned to Oslo, he tarried only long enough to build a stone house across from the royal palace before arranging for Dyveke and Sigbrit Willums to move in.

When Christian's father, King Hans, died in 1513, Christian was called to Copenhagen to assume the duties of king of Denmark-Norway.

❧▶
*See sidebar
on the
following page*

Dyveke and Sigbrit followed and moved into a royal manor north of Copenhagen. Contemporary historians note how Copenhagen citizens would gather at the city gates in the evening to see their king and master ride to the embrace of his beloved and, as they were to learn, seek the advice of her mother in matters of state.

For three years, the king kept up his nightly rides even after, in 1515, he had succumbed to increasing pressure from his Council of the Realm and the queen dowager to marry a foreign princess and secure an heir to the throne. No amount of pressure, however, could make him abandon his passion for Dyveke and his need for Sigbrit's counsel. Quite the contrary. He bought a house for them on the main street in Copenhagen, only a few blocks from the royal palace, and continued his visits. The subsequent scandal is easily imagined. Christian had married ◀❧ **Elisabeth of Habsburg**, granddaughter of Emperor Maximilian and sister of the future Charles V, and her mighty relatives were furious at Christian's obstinacy and breach of etiquette. To be tolerated, a king's mistress should be of noble blood, and the king himself was expected to carry out the duties of a husband even as he maintained his bachelor habits. Two years went by before Elisabeth showed visible signs of receiving Christian's sexual attentions. She was pregnant with her first child when Dyveke died very suddenly in the summer of 1517—allegedly from eating poisoned cherries, although modern historians have theorized that appendicitis caused her sudden demise.

By then Christian was tied with seemingly unbreakable bonds of loyalty and respect to Sigbrit, who between 1518 and 1523 became the king's most prominent and increasingly visible counsellor. Initially, their discussions took place in private, but by and by she would appear in the royal chancellery to dictate letters either on behalf of the king or herself. Extensive national and international correspondence kept her informed of happenings inside and outside of Denmark, and at times of the king's absence, she was his representative in negotiations with foreign secretaries of state. She was considered a clever negotiator, quick of wit, and well acquainted with the questions and problems at issue. She knew when to insist and when to yield and knew how and when to push the queen to the foreground to their reciprocal political advantage.

The question of how a foreign-born woman could gain such great influence over the monarch of a country other than her own may be answered in terms of shared interests and mutual ambitions. Both resented and distrusted the nobility and wanted their curtailment. Christian had inherited those sentiments from his father, King Hans, who had maintained that Denmark's welfare depended on industrious farmers and merchants rather than arrogant, power-hungry nobles. As a demonstration of this attitude, Hans had sent his son, the crown prince, to be reared in the home of a Copenhagen bookbinder where he might learn to value the life and work of common people. Christian had learned his lesson well and as viceroy of Norway shown himself a friend of the burghers. The Danish nobles, therefore, made him sign a coronation charter granting the Council of the Realm control of the country and granting men of nobility sole right to office under the crown. Sigbrit shared Christian's dislike of the nobles. A daughter of the people and a self-made woman, she loathed the arrogant ways of those whose inherited wealth had been amassed at the expense of working men and women like her. Against this common enemy, Christian and Sigbrit formulated and implemented their plans for Denmark's future based on government reforms and free trade, favoring the burghers and modelled on self-sufficient, flourishing Holland.

❧▶ **Dyveke** (c. 1491–1517)
*Paramour of Christian II. Name variations: (Dutch) Duiveke; Little Dove. Born around 1491; died suddenly, possibly poisoned, possibly of appendicitis, in the summer of 1517, age 26; daughter of *Sigbrit Willums (fl. 1507–1523); mistress of Christian II (1481–1559), king of Denmark and Norway (r. 1513–1523).*

❧▶ **Elisabeth of Habsburg** (1501–1526)
*Queen of Denmark and Norway. Name variations: Elisabeth of Hapsburg; Elizabeth of the Netherlands; Isabella or Isabel of Spain; Isabella Habsburg; Ysabeau. Born on July 18, 1501; died on January 19, 1526 (some sources cite 1525); daughter of *Juana la Loca (1479–1555) and Philip I the Fair (or Philip the Handsome), archduke of Austria, king of Castile and Leon (r. 1506, son of Maximilian I, Holy Roman emperor); sister of Charles V, Holy Roman emperor (r. 1519–1556), *Mary of Hungary (1505–1558), Ferdinand I, Holy Roman emperor (r. 1558–1564), and *Eleanor of Portugal (1498–1558); married Christian II (1481–1559), king of Denmark and Norway (r. 1513–1523), on August 12, 1515; children: John (b. 1518); twins Maximilian and Philipp (b. 1519); *Dorothea of Denmark (1520–1580, who married Frederick II, elector Palatine); *Christina of Denmark (1521–1590, who married Francesco Maria Sforza, duke of Milan, and Francis I, duke of Lorraine).*

At Sigbrit's instigation, Christian encouraged foreign businesses to invest in Danish trade and advertised for successful merchants to settle in Copenhagen which he envisioned as a center for trade in the Baltic. In 1520, after he had reclaimed Sweden for the Danish crown, Christian drew up plans for a Nordic trading association with offices in Copenhagen, Stockholm, Finland, and—characteristically—Holland. The association was to join forces with the south German merchant house of the Fuggers with the intent of crushing the Hanseatic league and ruling the Baltic. Nothing ultimately came of those grand plans, which suggest the vision of the king and his bourgeois counsellors, notably Sigbrit, but which also demonstrate the flaw in all their reforms: a lack of understanding of the difficulty with which people accept change.

While Christian was engaged in his war efforts to reunite Sweden with Denmark and Norway, Sigbrit took charge of the king's finances. In the spring of 1519, she became controller of the Sound tolls, the tariffs paid by all ships sailing between Denmark and Sweden for trading in the Baltic, and she moved the center for collecting those tariffs from Elsinore to Copenhagen. As an effort to centralize taxation, her strategy was sensible; the move, however, annoyed the captains who now had to maneuver their ships into the harbor of Copenhagen. She furthermore took charge of the generally despised taxes on wine and beer and aided Christian's efforts to grant Danish merchants special trading rights in disregard of privileges usually accorded only to the nobles.

To promote farming and farming methods, Sigbrit prevailed upon the king to import Dutch farmers to the flat land of Amager, south of Copenhagen. Their expertise in the making of butter and cheese and cultivation of gardens has been praised by Danish historians who have considered their efforts a positive trait among their mostly negative evaluations of Christian's innovations. Yet the farmers they replaced naturally resented their presence and only grudgingly yielded their land.

Sigbrit appears to have ignored whatever criticism reached her ears as she proceeded to put her stamp on city administration as well. She had Christian appoint a city administrator for the capital, as was the custom in Dutch cities, and draft ordinances to promote decency and cleanliness. Butchers were ordered to refrain from letting blood and other offal flow through the streets; to diminish air pollution, scavengers were told to bury their dead animals outside the city limits. Saturday nights were to be dedicated to sweeping of yards and scouring of floors and benches; garbage was to be stacked and carried into the street for collection by carriers on carts so tightly constructed that no refuse would fall out and litter the streets. Decent houses were to be built on empty lots and clay walls facing the streets of Copenhagen replaced with those of bricks and timber. Prostitutes were confined to plying their trade in a designated area of the city and to do so without benefit of wearing robes. The reason for the latter injunction is suggested by the 17th-century Danish historian Ludvig Holberg who credits Sigbrit with a specific ordinance pertaining to clearing the streets of beggars. She decreed, on the king's behalf, that only students who could pay for their own food would be matriculated into Copenhagen schools. Previously, school boys dressed in long robes leaving only their right arms free would be begging for food and money. Madame Sigbrit insisted, according to Holberg, that hands reaching out from those slits took more than alms and concealed the spoils in the folds of their robes, and he considers it likely that Sigbrit's experience with both boys and prostitutes had proven her point.

Danish historians unanimously report the animosity and hatred levelled against Sigbrit by members of the Council and the nobility in general, but they disagree on the extent to which she merited their detractions. One historian reports that when he as a child was on his way to school, he would pass by Madame Sigbrit's house and see the most prominent men in the kingdom beating their hands and stomping their feet against the cold as Sigbrit let them wait outside her door. They did not dare speak out against her openly, but they blackened her reputation by blaming her for the king's provocative administration and his thinly disguised desire to promote a hereditary monarchy. Holberg is less judgmental and less willing to ascribe to Sigbrit the title of evil counsellor. No one can be certain, he writes, whether the king in his dealings with the nobility followed his own nature or Sigbrit's advice. The coronation charter Christian had been forced to sign was so constraining that he was determined to curtail the power and authority of his nobles. Consequently, Holberg thinks, Christian would likely have taken the same measures without the presence of Sigbrit. Whichever the case may be, he concludes, Sigbrit was blamed for the king's actions. Holberg's concession is significant as a caveat against drawing overly hasty conclusions about distribution of fault and responsibility. No such prudence has tempered later historians' attributing to Sigbrit the engineering of Christian's brutal execution of 70 Swedish nobles on Stockholm's square in 1520, despite the fact that no evidence of her involvement exists.

The king she served was a gifted man, a visionary ruler with progressive plans for the future of his triple kingdom, a passionate and affectionate man, but, as his actions show, ruthless and brutal as well. He had been deeply devoted to his mistress, and when Dyveke died, Christian was inconsolable. He took revenge by executing Torben Oxe, administrator of the Castle of Copenhagen, who supposedly had brought Dyveke the cherries she ate before she died. By and by, however, the love and devotion of his young queen Elisabeth drew him to her, and gradually she moved into the place that had been Dyveke's in the affections of both Christian and Sigbrit. Sigbrit assisted at the birth of the queen's first child, three months after Dyveke's death. She was present also when the crown prince was born in early 1519 and again at the arrival of twins in December of the same year. Holberg reports that Sigbrit thought such fecundity reprehensible in a country as poor as Denmark; but despite that openly acknowledged opinion, she assumed the role of foster mother of Crown Prince Hans, and from then on was called Mother Sigbrit.

Sigbrit proved herself knowledgeable beyond mere midwifery and became a general physician for the royal house. Her fame spread after a visit by the renowned physician Paracelsus, who is known to have expressed his admiration for an herb brew she concocted and taught him to make. Yet because all she did was viewed with suspicion outside the royal household, Sigbrit's knowledge of medicine was by some perceived as knowledge of witchcraft. The same historian, Hans Svaning, who tells about the freezing nobles outside Sigbrit's door, reports that on one occasion her foster son, Crown Prince Hans, wandered into her bedroom which held a variety of bottles and glasses. He picked up a round bottle with a long neck because he saw something moving about inside it. Frightened, he dropped it, and the evil spirit escaped with a tremendous roar. Thunder rolled and a storm broke loose, and now the entire city knew for sure that Sigbrit was a witch.

Sigbrit and Christian ruled together from 1517 to 1523, when he was forced into exile. His queen and children accompanied him, as did Sigbrit. They separated on their arrival in Germany to the sorrow of all, because Sigbrit had by then become a loyal and trusted "mother" to the entire family. The headstone she had requested from Holland, she had to leave behind. On it was engraved her picture, her trademark, and an inscription: "here lies Sibrecht Willumsdatter, who died in the year of our Lord 15. . . Pray to God for my soul." A Danish noble, who had been charged with complicity in the "poisoning" of Dyveke and therefore been temporarily exiled, dragged it from its resting place in Sigbrit's courtyard and had it erected outside his own farmhouse. Word has it that he placed it in the gateway and ordered his farmhands to spit—or even urinate—on it as they passed through.

SOURCES:

Bech, Svend Cedergren. *Københavns Historie gennem 800 Aar.* Copenhagen: P. Haase og Søns, 1967.

Danmarks Historie. Eds. John Danstrup og Hal Koch. Copenhagen: Politikens, 1977.

Holberg, Johan Ludvig. *Danmarks Riges Historie.* Copenhagen: Thieles Bogtrykkeri, 1856.

Sources in English are scarce.

Inga Wiehl,
a native of Denmark, teaches at
Yakima Valley Community College, Yakima, Washington

Wilmot, Olivia (d. 1774)

*Duchess of Cumberland. Died on December 5, 1774; daughter of Reverend D. James Wilmot; allegedly married Henry Frederick (1745–1790), duke of Cumberland (brother of George III of England), on March 4, 1767; children: Olivia, princess of Cumberland (April 3, 1772–December 3, 1834, who married John Thomas Serres). Henry Frederick later married *Ann Horton (1743–1808).*

Wilson, Anne Glenny (1848–1930)

Australian romance writer and poet. Name variations: Lady Anne Glenny Wilson. Born in 1848 in Greenvale, Queensland, Australia; died in 1930; educated in Melbourne, Australia; married a sheep farmer, in 1874.

Selected writings: Themes and Variations *(1889);* Alice Lander, A Sketch *(1893);* Two Summers *(1900);* A Book of Verses *(1917).*

Anne Glenny Wilson, a poet and author of romance novels, was born in 1848 in Greenvale, a town in the state of Queensland in the northeastern corner of Australia, and educated in Melbourne, capital city of the state of Victoria. At age 26, she married a sheep farmer and moved to New Zealand. In the 1890s, Wilson began writing stories and poems which were published in literary journals throughout Australia and New Zealand. Her first long work, a collection of poetry, was followed by two novels, then a second volume of poems. Her novels were romantic tales with conventional situations and language, but they were distinctive in the incorporation of her arguments favoring women's independence. One volume of her verse was used as a textbook in New Zealand schools for a number of years.

Gillian S. Holmes,
freelance writer,
Hayward, California

Wilson, Augusta Evans (1835–1909)

Writer whose 1866 book St. Elmo *was one of the most popular American novels of the 19th century. Name variations: Augusta Evans. Born Augusta Jane Evans on May 8, 1835, in Wynnton, Georgia; died of a heart attack on May 9, 1909, in Mobile, Alabama; daughter of Matt Ryan Evans and Sarah Skrine (Howard) Evans; educated at home by her mother; married Lorenzo Madison Wilson (a financier and plantation owner), on December 2, 1868 (died 1891); children: four stepchildren.*

Selected writings: Inez: A Tale of the Alamo *(1855);* Beulah *(1859);* Macaria; or, Altars of Sacrifice *(1864);* St. Elmo *(1866);* Vashti *(1869);* Infelice *(1875);* At the Mercy of Tiberius *(1887);* A Speckled Bird *(1902);* Devota *(1907).*

Augusta Evans Wilson was a proud product of the South, and the region colored her attitudes and artistic output throughout her life. Her father Matt Ryan Evans owned a general store with his brother in Columbus, Georgia, when the town was newly founded on the Chattahoochee River. (As the land formerly had been inhabited by Native Americans, white settlers came under frequent attack from the tribes whom they had dispossessed.) The merchants prospered in the beginning, and in 1835, the year his first daughter Augusta was born, Evans began building a mansion named Sherwood Hall. The family, which eventually would grow to include eight children, moved into the home the following year. Prosperity deserted them when, in the early 1840s, the region was besieged by floods, Indian attacks, and financial panic. Evans, nearly bankrupt, mortgaged his 36 slaves and 143 acres of land and packed up his family in a covered wagon. They rode to Alabama and then west to Texas, where they settled first in Houston, then Galveston, and finally in prosperous San Antonio. Poverty followed them until Evans managed to reestablish his mercantile business. In 1849, the family returned to Alabama, settling in Mobile, which was to remain Wilson's home for the rest of her life.

Wilson's mother **Sarah Howard Evans** schooled her children at home, with particular emphasis on Methodist fundamentalism. Although she therefore had limited formal learning, Wilson broadened her education through extensive reading. Influenced by her time in Texas, she began writing a story about the Alamo. She was considered frail of health, and writing was not a proper occupation for women, so she stole time at night to work, with one of the family's slaves supplying her with lamp oil and helping to hide her manuscript. Wilson's parents had only praise for her work, however, when it was finally revealed to them, and it was published anonymously in 1855, when she was 20. Although (or because) its plot was laden with sentiment, moralizing, and anti-Catholic propaganda, *Inez: A Tale of the Alamo* was successful enough to earn Wilson the money to buy the home in which the Evans family lived.

*Augusta
Evans
Wilson*

A period spent doubting and scrutinizing her own Methodist faith and studying the works of authors like Emerson, Kant, and Carlyle led Wilson to a firm conviction in the importance of religion and high moral principles. Her second novel, *Beulah* (1859), centers on a character who similarly confronts her own doubts. Some 22,000 copies were printed in the book's first nine months of publication, and fellow novelist *Mary Virginia Terhune called it "the best work of fiction ever published by a Southern writer." The book also brought Wilson fame and a reprieve from the specter of poverty.

Wilson was an ardent secessionist, and her belief in the righteousness of the Confederate cause was only strengthened by the abolitionist and anti-Southern sentiment she saw on trips to New York to arrange the publication of her work. During these travels, she also met and became secretly engaged to James Reed Spalding, editor of the New York *World* and a strong supporter of Abraham Lincoln. In 1860, Wilson broke their engagement and dedicated herself to organizing a Confederate Army hospital (named Camp Beulah after her book) near Mobile. She worked at

Camp Beulah throughout the Civil War: "I have been constantly engaged in nursing sick soldiers, keeping sleepless vigil by day and night," she wrote to a friend. She also followed relatives who were soldiers to the battlefield and corresponded with Confederate leaders on matters including government appointments and military strategy. In her spare time, she wrote *Macaria; or, Altars of Sacrifice* (1864), published in Virginia with pages printed on wrapping paper and cardboard bindings covered with wallpaper. A piece of Confederate propaganda based on her own battlefield observations and first-person accounts of the Battle of Manassas, the book was intended to defend Confederate policy and lift the morale of her fellow Southerners. It won her a respect equal to that of male politicians and soldiers among many Southerners, and was so persuasive that a Northern general burned copies and banned its reading among his troops. A smuggled version printed in New York also sold well. When Wilson visited New York after the end of the war, her publisher gave her an unexpected cache of royalties not remitted during wartime, and the Northern currency (greatly valued in the South) helped her and her family survive comfortably during the privations of the Reconstruction.

The end of the Civil War did not stop Wilson's efforts for the Confederacy. She tried to have a monument to the Confederacy erected in Mobile and to insure the burial of the city's war victims in Magnolia Cemetery. Her family also sheltered General Robert Toombs, an old friend who was hunted as a fugitive in 1865. However, Wilson recognized that the cause was lost. She had hoped to write a history of the Confederacy, but abandoned that idea in favor of the novel *St. Elmo* (1866), which accomplished some of the same objectives. It sold beyond all expectation, for the nation's novel readers—mostly women— were fascinated by this tale of the virtuous Edna Earl, whose prayers, righteousness, and affection rescue a dashing hero from his sins. Behind *Harriet Beecher Stowe*'s *Uncle Tom's Cabin* and Lew Wallace's *Ben-Hur*, it was the third most popular novel of the 19th century, and made Wilson's name nationally known. Countless towns were renamed St. Elmo, and baby girls were christened Edna Earl. A dramatized version was written and staged many times from 1909 to about 1915, a silent film was made of *St. Elmo* in 1923, and William Webb's parody, *St. Twel'mo*, was also immensely popular.

Wilson continued to live at home, with a second occupation nursing her ill father and her brother Howard, who had been badly wounded during the war. She also visited sick neighbors, one of whom was the wife of Colonel Lorenzo Madison Wilson, a wealthy financier who owned a street railway company in Mobile. The father of four children, three of them adults, he was 68 years old when he proposed to Wilson after his wife's death. They delayed their wedding due to her father's objections, but married in December 1868 after Matt Evans' death and Sarah Evans' consent to their plans. Wilson proudly assumed the duties of caring for her husband and 13-year-old stepdaughter and running a large estate, with its extensive gardens, five greenhouses, and battery of servants. She also made daily visits to her mother on foot and wrote. (Her nursing experiences had forced Wilson into rigid time management, and she allotted four hours a day to writing.) Her next novel, *Vashti* (1869), was published only ten months after her wedding.

By 1870, Wilson's royalties from book sales amounted to $10,000 per year, an income that would remain steady for 30 years, although none of her subsequent novels were as popular as *St. Elmo*. Indeed, she was widely rebuked by critics for her use of difficult language and composition. Insomnia and severe hay fever forced her to travel widely with her husband seeking relief, and her writing slowed to accommodate these restrictions. In 1875, she published the melodramatic *Infelice*, followed in 1887 by *At the Mercy of Tiberius*. After her husband's death in 1891, Wilson, self-sufficient from her book sales, divided his estate between her stepchildren and went to live with a sister. A few years later, she moved into a large Victorian home in Mobile with her brother Howard, her closest companion until his death in 1908. Social conditions and causes preoccupied her, and, although she had long featured strong women characters triumphing over poverty, limitations, and insecurities, her 1902 novel *A Speckled Bird* opposed women's suffrage and labor unions. Her last work, *Devota*, a short story expressing her dislike of the Populist movement, was published in book form in 1907. She died of a heart attack two years later, on May 9, 1909, at the age of 74.

SOURCES:

Estes, Glenn, ed. *Dictionary of Literary Biography*, Vol. 42: *American Writers for Children Before 1900*. Detroit, MI: Gale Research, 1985.

James, Edward T., ed. *Notable American Women, 1607–1950*. Cambridge, MA: The Belknap Press of Harvard University, 1971.

McHenry, Robert, ed. *Famous American Women*. NY: Dover, 1980.

SUGGESTED READING:

Fidler, William Perry. *Augusta E. Wilson*. Birmingham, AL: University of Alabama Press, 1951.

Gillian S. Holmes,
freelance writer,
Hayward, California

Wilson, Cairine (1885–1962)

First woman appointed to the Canadian Senate. Pronunciation: Car-EEN WILL-son. Born Cairine Reay Mackay on February 4, 1885, at Montreal, Quebec, Canada; died on March 3, 1962, in Ottawa, Canada; seventh child of Robert Mackay (a businessman and politician) and Jane (Baptist) Mackay; attended private girls' school and the Trafalgar Institute, Montreal; married Norman Wilson, in 1909; children: Olive (b. 1910), Janet (b. 1911), Cairine (b. 1913), Ralph (b. 1915), Anna (b. 1918), Angus (b. 1920), Robert (b. 1922), Norma (b. 1925).

Elected joint president of the Eastern Ontario Liberal Association (1921); organized the National Federation of Liberal Women of Canada (1923); helped establish the Twentieth Century Liberal Association of Canada; appointed the first female member of the Canadian Senate (February 15, 1930); elected president of the League of Nations Society (1936); served as a member of the Canadian delegation to the General Assembly of the UN in New York (August 1949).

In October 1929, the Judicial Committee of the Imperial Privy Council in London (the supreme legal authority of the British Empire) brought down a landmark ruling based on Section 24 of the British North America Act. According to this ruling, women were henceforth to be considered "qualified persons" and thus entitled to sit in the second chamber of the Canadian Parliament, the Senate. This decision, the welcome outcome of a long struggle waged by Canadian feminists, was warmly endorsed by Prime Minister William Lyon MacKenzie King. MacKenzie King was particularly pleased because he was afforded the opportunity to appoint to the Senate one of his oldest friends, Cairine Wilson.

Wilson was born on February 4, 1885, into one of the richest and most influential Scots-Canadian families in Montreal, Quebec. Her father Robert Mackay, who had arrived in Canada 30 years earlier as a young and virtually penniless immigrant, had achieved rapid success in the city's burgeoning business environment. When he died in 1916, he held directorships in no fewer than 16 companies, including the highly prestigious Bank of Montreal and the Canadian Pacific Railroad. Robert's Presbyterian background imbued him with a deep and profound sense of religion. He believed in the virtues of hard work and thought that the principal duty of a good Christian was to employ his or her talents and wealth for the benefit of less fortunate members of society. It was this attitude of public service which was later to blossom so fruitfully in his daughter Cairine.

Cairine's mother **Jane Baptist Mackay** was the daughter of a prominent lumber baron in Quebec. Little is known of her apart from the fact that she suffered constant ill health, a condition probably aggravated by numerous pregnancies. Equally sparse are details concerning Cairine's younger years. Her strict, although not apparently unkindly, Presbyterian upbringing turned her into a shy child. It was perhaps for this reason that her father decided, rather unusually considering his wealth and social position, that Cairine was not to be educated by private tutors. Instead, she was sent to a small private girls' school, located near her home, which rejoiced in the name of "Misses Symmers and Smith's School for Young Ladies."

At age 14, Cairine was placed in the Trafalgar Institute which was, at that time, the most exclusive finishing school for women in Montreal. The three years she spent there (1899–1902) were, by all accounts, productive and happy. Wilson excelled in history and mathematics and, more important for her later career, became fluent in French. The headmistress of the Trafalgar Institute, **Grace Fairley**, actively encouraged her pupils to embrace the principles of patriotism and service to others. For the rest of her life, Wilson never forgot the lessons taught by Fairley. Indeed, shortly before her own death, Wilson established the Fairley Prize, an annual award presented to the graduating pupil who had made the most outstanding contribution to school life at the Institute.

Wilson did not continue her studies at a higher level. Though it was possible for women to be admitted to Montreal's McGill University, it was then considered unthinkable that anyone of Cairine's social background should do so. Rather, her time was filled with a continuous whirl of social functions and receptions. In 1904, however, her father encouraged Cairine and two school friends to undertake an extensive sightseeing trip of Britain and Europe (in the company of three chaperons). She repeated this excursion twice more in the next few years.

More significantly, it was during this period that Wilson began to take an active interest in politics. James Mackay had been appointed a Liberal member of the Canadian Senate in 1901 by his close friend, Sir Wilfrid Laurier, the prime minister. This position meant that James was required to spend a considerable amount of time in the nation's capital, Ottawa. Wilson began to accompany her father on these trips, and they frequently stayed at Laurier's private residence where she soon became a good friend of Lady **Zoe Laurier**, the prime minister's wife.

It was at one of the many social events organized in Ottawa that Cairine met her future husband, Norman Wilson. Like Cairine, Norman was descended from a prominent Scots-Canadian family that had achieved considerable business success in Quebec. When they first met, he was a member of Parliament for the Liberal Party. Although no intellectual, Norman had a gregarious and out-going character and was widely considered to be the most eligible bachelor in Ottawa.

Senator Wilson has made a contribution that is recognized throughout the world.

—**John Diefenbaker**

Shortly before their marriage in February 1909, Norman resigned his seat in Parliament. In April of that year, the couple moved to a new home in Rockland, a small town in Eastern Ontario, where Norman had become manager of the W.C. Edwards Company lumber mills. For the next ten years, Cairine devoted herself to running their large home and raising a rapidly growing family (her first child, **Olive**, was born in 1910). In 1912, Cairine's responsibilities were aggravated following the death of her mother. By this time, the family home in Montreal was inhabited only by her father and brother Edward, and Cairine had to frequently return from Rockland to help manage the house (as well as another family property in St. Andrews, New Brunswick).

These activities left Wilson very little time for other interests or concerns. When World War I broke out in 1914, however, she organized local women in Rockland into an auxiliary branch of the Red Cross to produce knitted woollen goods for Canadian military personnel overseas. Not long after, in 1916, her father died, leaving an estate valued at over $10 million (approximately $100 million at the close of the 20th century). The legacy which Wilson received made her family financially secure and allowed Norman to give up his job as manager of the lumber mill. He, Cairine and their children then returned to Ottawa.

In an interview given in 1931, Wilson explained how these early years of marriage had brought her "great happiness." She then went on to recount, however, how a family friend had remarked to her, on her return to Ottawa, that he had never "seen a person deteriorate mentally as I had" and that she had become "a most unin-

teresting individual." It was this frank, if rather brutal, assessment which prompted Wilson to seriously question the role she had adopted for herself in life. Deciding that she could do much more to be of service to others, she immediately plunged into an active involvement in political and social issues.

In 1921, Wilson was elected joint president of the Eastern Ontario Liberal Association and in this capacity traveled widely throughout Ontario speaking on behalf of the Liberal Party for the forthcoming federal election. This election, held in December of the same year, was the first occasion on which all Canadian women were allowed to vote. The then Liberal Party leader (and eventual victor in the election) was a close friend of her husband's named William Lyon MacKenzie King. MacKenzie King recognized the important contribution which Cairine had made to the party's success. Shortly after, he encouraged her to found the Ottawa Women's Liberal Club, an increasingly influential political association for which she served as president for three years.

Over the next few years, Wilson became more and more involved in various forms of political activity. In 1923, she began to organize the National Federation of Liberal Women of Canada, a country-wide coalition of women's Liberal Clubs. She then turned her attention to the party's youth and helped establish the Twentieth Century Liberal Association of Canada. This organization, which regularly convened young people in Ottawa for the purposes of dialogue and debate, was personally financed by Wilson. At the same time, her interests extended beyond the political realm. She became an executive member of the Victorian Order of Nurses and was an enthusiastic participant in the meetings of the Young Women's Christian Association.

On February 15, 1930, four months after the historic ruling by the Judicial Committee of the Privy Council in London, Prime Minister Mackenzie King appointed Cairine the first female member of the Canadian Senate. Although *Agnes Macphail had been the first woman elected to the House of Commons in 1921, Wilson's appointment had only been made possible thanks to the efforts of *Emily Gowan Murphy and other feminists from the province of Alberta. Indeed, it had been widely anticipated that it would be Murphy, and not Wilson, who would be given the Senate seat. The former, however, was a prominent supporter of the opposition Conservative Party and MacKenzie King pre-

Cairine
Wilson

ferred to select someone closely affiliated to his own party. Although Wilson was a personal friend of the prime minister, her appointment was due to the combination of her leading role in Liberal Party organizations, the fact that she was fluent in French (an important considera-

tion in Canadian politics) and, finally, because she was in a position to contribute financially to the party's funds.

Although Wilson's appointment met with general public approval, a number of critics (particularly from Alberta and Quebec) argued that some other, more qualified woman deserved this great honor. Wilson herself had her own doubts about her suitability and was only half-jesting when she wrote to MacKenzie King that "you are going to make me the most hated woman in Canada." Although her fears were unfounded, she was deeply concerned with the problem of reconciling her public duties with what she viewed was the proper role of a wife and mother. During her maiden speech before the Senate, delivered on February 25, 1930, she said, "I trust the future will show that while engaged in public affairs, the woman, the mother of a family, by reason of her maternal instinct and her sense of responsibility, will remain the faithful guardian of the home."

Over the next few years, Wilson used her influential position to advance many socially progressive causes. She spoke in favor of liberalizing the (highly restrictive) divorce laws and was in favor of legislation designed to limit the number of hours each individual was required to work each week. In 1936, she was elected president of the League of Nations Society in Canada which sought to oppose aggression and promote peace between nations through international arbitration and the creation of collective security agreements. The principal test of the League came in 1938. In September, the British and French prime ministers (Neville Chamberlain and Edouard Daladier) went to Munich, Germany, and signed an agreement with Nazi dictator Adolf Hitler which ceded the Sudetenland, the German-speaking portion of Czechoslovakia, to Germany. Chamberlain and Daladier called this policy, which effectively endorsed the dismemberment of a foreign sovereign state, "appeasement." Wilson, and her fellow members of the League, called it a "sell-out."

This courageous and principled stand put her in a difficult position. The Munich agreement was strongly supported by MacKenzie King and other important Liberal Party executives. Although no admirers of Hitler, they were extremely reluctant to be dragged into another European war on behalf of the British. Moreover, MacKenzie King remembered the divisive effect which the First World War had had on Canadian society when attempts, by another Liberal administration, to introduce national conscription had been fiercely resisted in the predominantly French-speaking province of Quebec. MacKenzie King correctly reasoned that a new war would require similar measures of conscription, and he was afraid that this would cause a split in his party which traditionally drew much of its support from Quebec. When Wilson publicly denounced the Munich agreement, along with the irresolute stance of the Liberal Party, she almost precipitated a complete break between herself and MacKenzie King. However, when Hitler attacked Poland in September of the following year, Wilson's position was fully vindicated.

Immediately prior to and during the war itself, Wilson served on the board of the Canadian National Committee on Refugees. This commission endeavored to raise public awareness of the plight of (particularly Jewish) refugees from Nazi tyranny. After the war, it continued to press the Liberal government to open the country's doors and admit any displaced person who wished to come to Canada. Unfortunately, the Canadian public, which had strong memories of the economic depression of the 1930s, was in no mood to countenance any program of large-scale immigration. Bowing to popular pressure, MacKenzie King refused to act. This narrow attitude came as a deep disappointment to Wilson, especially when the full enormity of Nazi crimes became evident. She continued to do what she could for individual refugees but was unable to effect any real alteration in government policy.

Another important issue during this period centered around policies for the reconstruction of postwar Canadian society and the reintegration of demobilized armed forces personnel back into the community. Some proposed a welfare state that would combine social security provisions with universal health insurance and a program of family allowances. Wilson took an active part in this debate, stressing, in particular, women's special needs for preventative health care and the extension of educational opportunities to the new generation of Canadian youth. Although proponents of these reforms initially met with stiff opposition from MacKenzie King (who was appalled at the potential cost of such measures), their proposals were eventually largely enacted. The progressive welfare legislation currently in effect in Canada is a direct result of their efforts.

In the years following the war, Wilson served on a wide variety of Senate committees, including banking and commerce, public health, and external relations. It was her prominence in the latter area which caused the new prime minister, Louis St. Laurent, to invite her to serve as a member of the Canadian delegation to the General Assembly of the United Nations in New York. Wilson, the first Canadian woman to be accorded this distinction, took up her appointment in August 1949. At the General Assembly, she was elected to what was known as the Third Committee, a standing commission of the United Nations which dealt with social, humanitarian, and cultural issues. Another member of this committee and subsequently a friend of Wilson's was the wife of a former president of the United States, *Eleanor Roosevelt.

Wilson served at the United Nations for two years before returning to Ottawa and her senatorial duties. In these last years, she continued to speak out on behalf of a variety of social issues, including the divorce laws and the injustices and abuses of the immigration system. Her husband Norman died in 1956 from Parkinson's disease and shortly afterwards Cairine was diagnosed with a heart condition. Three years later, she was found to be suffering from uterine cancer. Even then, Wilson refused to rest, and she continued to address various groups especially on immigration issues. In early 1962, her cancer entered a terminal stage, and she was admitted to the Civic Hospital in Ottawa where she died peacefully on March 3.

SOURCES:

Innis, Mary. *The Clear Spirit: Twenty Canadian Women and their Times.* Toronto: University of Toronto Press, 1967.

Iocavetta, Franca. "The Political Career of Senator Cairine Wilson, 1921–62," in *Atlantis.* Vol. 11, no. 1, Fall 1985.

Knowles, Valerie. *First Person.* Toronto: Dundurn, 1988.

Muir, Norma. "Senator Cairine Wilson—Woman," in *Canadian Home Journal.* Vol. 27, no. 2, June 1930.

Scott, S.L. "Our New Woman Senator," in *Macleans Magazine.* April 1, 1930.

SUGGESTED READING:

Cleverdon, Catherine. *The Woman Suffrage Movement in Canada.* Toronto: University of Toronto Press, 1974.

Dirks, Gerald. *Canada's Refugee Problem: Indifference or Opportunism?* Montreal: McGill-Queen's University Press, 1977.

COLLECTIONS:

Cairine Wilson's private papers are held in the National Archives of Canada.

Dave Baxter,
Department of Philosophy,
Wilfrid Laurier University, Waterloo, Ontario, Canada

Wilson, Catherine (1842–1862)

English nurse, poisoner, and executed murderer. Born in 1842; died by hanging on October 20, 1862, in London; parentage unknown; married a man named Dixon.

Not all women achieved their places in history through good works; Catherine Wilson made her mark as a notorious poisoner of innocent victims. Wilson's early life is unknown. From 1853 to 1862, she lived in London, England, and worked as a nurse and housekeeper to ailing persons who also happened to be wealthy. Wilson won the trust of her patients and persuaded them to make out new wills bequeathing their property and money to her. She then poisoned them.

Wilson first caught the attention of the authorities after she murdered her husband, a man called Dixon, in London. Doctors wanted to perform an autopsy on the dead man, but Wilson pleaded against the procedure, claiming her husband was terrified of being mutilated. The doctors relented, and Catherine's crime went undiscovered.

By 1862, Wilson was nursing and living with the ailing **Sarah Carnell** and her husband. Because of Catherine's tender ministrations, Sarah wrote a new will that left most of her property to Catherine. Soon after, Wilson brought the sick woman a "soothing drought." The drink burned Sarah's mouth, however, so she spat it on the carpet and called her husband who quickly entered the room. The Carnells stared in awe at the burned holes on the carpet where the fluid had landed. Wilson fled, and Mr. Carnell took the tainted glass to the police. The glass contained enough sulfuric acid to kill 50 people. Wilson was captured several days later and charged with attempted murder, but she was cleared of the charge thanks to her defense attorney who claimed a chemist (pharmacist) had given Wilson the wrong prescription. But time had run out. The bodies of seven other victims who had been attended by Wilson had been exhumed and were found to contain an assortment of poisons ranging from arsenic to colchicum. After her trial in London's Old Bailey, Wilson, who did not confess to a single murder, was condemned to die by hanging. On October 20, 1862, a crowd of 20,000 watched her swing from the gallows.

SOURCES:

Nash, Jay Robert. *Look For The Woman.* NY: M. Evans, 1981.

Gillian S. Holmes,
freelance writer,
Hayward, California

Wilson, Charlotte (1854–1944)

English anarchist and feminist who was the founder of the Freedom Press and the first female executive member of the Fabian Society. Born Charlotte Mary Martin on May 6, 1854, at Kemerton, near Tewkesbury, England; died at Irvington-on-Hudson, New York, on April 28, 1944; daughter of Robert Spencer

Martin (a physician) and Mary (Edgeworth) Martin; attended Merton Hall, Cambridge; married Arthur Wilson, in September 1876; no children.

Trial of Peter Kropotkin at Lyons, France (January 1883); founded Hampstead Marx Circle (October 1884); elected to executive committee of Fabian Society (December 1884); published first edition of Freedom (October 1886); founded Fabian women's group (March 1908).

Selected writings: series of articles (signed "An English Anarchist") entitled "Anarchism" in Justice *(November–December 1884); unsigned articles in* The Anarchist *(1885); "Social Democracy and Anarchism" in* Practical Socialist *(January 1886), "Anarchism" in* What Socialism Is, *(with George Bernard Shaw) Fabian Tract No.4 (June 1886), "The Principles and Aims of Anarchists" in* Present Day *(July 1886), all reprinted in* Three Essays on Anarchism *(Sanday, Orkney: Cienfuegos, 1979); "Anarchism and Outrage" in* Freedom *(December 1893).*

Anarchism is a political philosophy which is defined in terms of its overriding commitment to an ethical ideal of personal freedom. It views the legislative and administrative institutions of the state as exerting a coercive and constraining influence over the individual. Government compulsion, bureaucratic authoritarianism, economic exploitation, and sexual domination are the means through which state institutions combine to effectively crush the expression of a full and free human nature. It is for this reason, anarchists argue, that all such institutions must be completely abolished.

It is our aim to give conscious expression to the voiceless cry of the oppressed.

—**Charlotte Wilson**

The closing decades of the 19th century marked the high point of anarchist activity in Europe. Thanks to the revolutionary nature of these activities, many European governments did their best to suppress the anarchist movement. One result was that many prominent anarchists took refuge in Britain (where the government was more tolerant) and there resumed their activities in relative peace. The names of some of these refugees (such as Peter Kropotkin and Errico Malatesta) are well known in the lexicon of anarchist thought. Less well known is the name of an Englishwoman who played a significant part in facilitating the further work of these refugees and in laying the foundations of the British anarchist movement. That woman was named Charlotte Wilson.

She was born in 1854 into a prosperous middle-class family at Kemerton, a village near Tewkesbury, England. Atypically, for a family which enjoyed such a comfortable level of social and material well-being, she was an only child. There is some evidence to suggest that Charlotte's relationship with her mother **Mary Edgeworth Martin** (who was descended from the famous 18th-century theologian and philosopher, William Paley) was not altogether as it could have been. Later in life, she was to remark to a friend that her mother had always regarded her as "an infliction sent against her will from on high."

Nothing is known of Charlotte's association with her father who had a physician's practice in Kemerton, yet found time to combine his responsibilities as physician with several other positions. Robert Martin served as surgeon and referee to a number of leading insurance companies, as a certified factory surgeon, and as district medical officer of the Tewkesbury workhouse. It is possible to speculate that these duties had an important effect on his daughter's later development.

In the third quarter of the 19th century, conditions in most of the factories in England were appalling. Government legislation, regulating working practices and standards of health and safety, was not widely enforced. Moreover, because there was no state organized system of welfare, the old, the sick, and the unemployed were often forced to rely on charitable relief from the local workhouse.

The nature of his duties would have meant that Wilson's father often came in contact with factory workers and their families as well as the poor and unemployed. In these circumstances, there can be little question that Charlotte became aware, at a very early age, of the distressed circumstances in which many of these individuals found themselves. This disturbing lesson, in the practical social and economic effects of the factory system, seems to have played an important role in shaping her later political beliefs.

Charlotte's parents made a considerable effort to ensure that she received a good education. She spent three years at Cheltenham Ladies College, a finishing school widely regarded for its academic standards. According to Wilson's account, however, this was not a happy experience. Later in life, she recalled that her time at Cheltenham had been marked by much "mental and physical misery." In 1873, she entered Merton Hall, Cambridge, a recently opened educational institute for women (later to become part of Newnham College).

Over the next two years, Wilson took classes in English, logic, psychology, and political economy. The principal of Merton Hall was *Jemima Clough (the sister of the famous poet Arthur Hugh Clough), who sought to develop a syllabus that would provide the students with a thorough grounding in the work of contemporary thinkers (such as the famous social scientist Herbert Spencer and the philosopher John Stuart Mill). Charlotte's principal interest, however, was political economy (what we now call "economics"). In this regard, she had the good fortune to study under the guidance of Alfred Marshall, a man widely regarded then and now as one of the foremost economists of his generation.

Wilson successfully obtained passes in all these subjects but did not obtain a degree from Cambridge. Women were not then eligible to receive such awards (the university first granted degrees to women in 1923). More important than any formal degree was the effect that Cambridge had on Charlotte. The scholarly climate of the institution served to crystallize her intellectual capacities. Cambridge, she once wrote, was "the porch through which I entered the world."

Shortly after leaving Merton Hall, Charlotte married Arthur Wilson. A successful broker on the London Stock Exchange, Arthur was to take an active concern in his wife's political interests. From what little is known of their life together, it would appear that they were a devoted couple.

From 1876 to 1884, they led an outwardly unassuming life at Elm Lodge, Hampstead. Behind this quiet façade, however, Charlotte was beginning to immerse herself in the works of radical anarchist and socialist theoreticians (for instance, Michael Bakunin and Karl Marx). It is possible that this might have remained no more than an intellectual interest were it not for a particular incident that served to trigger a more active political involvement.

In the early 1880s, a series of bomb explosions had occurred in France. Although these explosions had been the work of a few fanatics with only a tenuous connection to the anarchist movement, the authorities seized the opportunity to initiate mass arrests of leading anarchists. Among those apprehended was the Russian Peter Kropotkin, one of the leading members of the anarchist movement and a theoretician of international renown.

Kropotkin's trial in January 1883 at Lyons, France, was widely reported in the British press. Public opinion was outraged; not at the crimes he and his compatriots were alleged to have committed, but, rather, at the palpable unfairness of the judicial proceedings and the severity of the sentences handed down. There is no doubt that this event made a strong impression on Wilson. Shortly after the trial ended, she wrote, "when the noble words of Kropotkin's defence ran through the length and breadth of France, they found an echo in the hearts of all honest seekers after truth."

Early in 1884, Wilson joined the recently founded Fabian Society and in December of that year became the first woman elected on its executive committee. Today, the Fabian Society is one of the key associations responsible for the formulation and guidance of policies in the British Labour Party. When it was originally founded, however, it comprised no more than a loose alliance of intellectuals (which included the famous playwright George Bernard Shaw) who ranged from being moderate socialists on the one hand to radical anarchists on the other. Although all the original Fabians were broadly committed to the need for some kind of fundamental social change there was no firm agreement as to precisely what this entailed or how it was to be achieved.

In October 1884, Wilson founded a study group which met regularly at Elm Lodge then, later, at her new home, the "Wyldes," an isolated cottage (once briefly occupied by Charles Dickens) at the edge of Hampstead Heath. Known variously as the Hampstead Marx Circle or the Hampstead Historical Club, this group of Fabians and anarchists met to discuss the ideas of various continental socialists as well as the history of the international labor movement. Sidney Webb, husband of *Beatrice Webb and a participant at one early meeting, was deeply impressed by the detailed and elaborate analysis Wilson gave of the first chapter of Karl Marx's *Capital* (a passage widely regarded as one of the most difficult in his entire corpus). More significant, perhaps, these meetings provided the intellectual impetus for many of the group to develop and publish their own views.

Wilson was no exception. In a series of articles published over the next two years, she provided what was the first native British contribution to anarchist theory. Her arguments consistently focused on how private property, state institutions, and the system of law all served to create a "spirit of domination" which is the "great cause of human misery and the present disorganization of social life." Wilson decried the divisive effects of economic competition and the struggle for individual aggrandizement at the expense of one's fellow human beings. In place of this, she argued for a new moral awareness in which the dignity and spontaneity of the individual comes to full fruition in the conditions of an associated humanity. Anarchism aims to bring about a revolution in every department of human existence because, in her words, "every man owes it to himself and to his fellows to be free."

Peter Kropotkin was released from prison in January 1886 and immediately took up the invitation issued by Charlotte Wilson and her anarchist friends to settle in England. His arrival inspired this small group to launch an anarchist newspaper which was modeled on Kropotkin's own highly influential paper *Le Révolté* (which had first appeared in Geneva, Switzerland, in 1879). The first issue of *Freedom* appeared in 1886. For the next eight years (with the exception of a break caused by illness in 1889), Charlotte Wilson was the chief editor, publisher, translator (of foreign contributions) and financial supporter of the newspaper. *Freedom* went on to publish articles by many leading anarchists and played a significant role in the dissemination of anarchist ideas among the British working class. It was the first publication of what eventually became the Freedom Press which remains to this day the most important publisher of anarchist literature in Britain.

Later in 1886, some leading Fabians proposed transforming the society into a socialist political party that would sponsor candidates for Parliament. Despite strong opposition, the motion to setup the Fabian Parliamentary League was successful. The anarchists found such participation unacceptable as they believed that state institutions like Parliament only served to crush and deny human freedom. Wilson thought that the majority of Fabians lacked an "earnest spirit of truth seeking" and shortly thereafter resigned from the executive committee and for many years remained a purely nominal member of the society. It says much for the high regard with which she was held that leading Fabians, such as Bernard Shaw, did everything in their power to persuade her to remain within the society.

Charlotte's frustration with the direction events were now taking was revealed in an editorial she wrote for *Freedom* in December of the same year. Subsequently republished in 1908 as a pamphlet entitled "Anarchism and Outrage," it was to become her most famous contribution to anarchist thought. Prior to this time, Wilson had argued that an anarchist society could only be achieved through peaceful means. She now suggested that, given the physical force and coer-

cion which the state authorities employed against anarchists, it might be necessary for these anarchists to respond in kind in order to defend their own rights. Although anarchists dislike violence, she said, situations will arise in which they are left with no choice but to resort to such methods. Wilson's contribution was important because it represented one of the earliest and clearest attempts by an anarchist to justify tactics of this kind.

Throughout the late 1880s, Wilson was constantly expanding the range of her political interests. She became involved with the Society of Friends of Russian Freedom and actively helped publicize the revolutionary cause in that country (for which there was much sympathy in Britain). More important, perhaps, she became interested in feminist issues through her friend Karl Pearson's Men and Women's Club. In correspondence with Pearson, Wilson suggested women were educated to believe that they should focus their whole attention on marriage and raising children. Once new political and economic arrangements are instituted then all the "horrible anomalies and shamefulness of our present sexual relations will naturally and inevitably disappear."

Unlike many other anarchist agitators of the period, Wilson was not well known as a public speaker. In 1887, however, the Freedom group organized a series of mass rallies to protest the sentences handed out at the Chicago Haymarket trial. Seven anarchists were condemned to death for a bomb explosion in which several police officers had been killed. There was considerable doubt as to whether the accused were in fact the perpetrators of this deed. Press reports of the case caused, if anything, even more protest in Britain than had the trial of Kropotkin several years earlier. It was at one of these meetings that Wilson spoke in defense of the rights of the accused and a contemporary account of her speech remains one of the few detailed portraits we have of her:

> Beside the table on the platform was standing a little woman dressed in black. Beneath the brow which was half hidden as by a wreath by her thick, short-cropped hair, shone a pair of black eyes beaming with enthusiasm. The white ruffle and the simple, almost monk-like, long, undulating garment seemed to belong to another century. A few only at the meeting seemed to know her; but whoever knew her, knew also that she was the most faithful, the most diligent, and the most impassioned champion [of anarchism] in England. . . . She was not a captivating speaker, but her voice had that iron ring of

unalterable conviction and honesty which often moves the listener more powerfully than the most brilliant eloquence.

In 1895, for reasons that are not entirely clear, Wilson severed all her connections with the anarchist movement. It is known that her father had recently died and that her mother (who had suffered a series of strokes) was an invalid who required constant attention. It may also be suggested, however, that by this time Charlotte had grown disillusioned with the prospects for the anarchist cause. By the last decade of the 19th century, the British working class had largely abandoned all thought of a radical, revolutionary overthrow of the capitalist system. Instead, it had chosen to concentrate its energies (largely through the auspices of the trades-union movement) in the day-to-day struggle to improve its conditions of existence within capitalist society. In such an atmosphere, anarchism in Britain had become little more than an irrelevant curiosity.

Charlotte Wilson eventually returned to political activity in 1908 and renewed her interest in feminist issues. In March, she formally rejoined the Fabian Society and founded their women's group. Over the next few years, she carried out important work on behalf of women in prisons and was responsible for preparing evidence for the royal commission on divorce. In 1911, she was again elected to the executive committee of the Fabian Society but in 1914 resigned for health reasons. She continued to work intermittently with the women's group until 1916 when she left to concentrate on her work as honorary secretary of the Prisoner of War Fund of the Oxford and Buckinghamshire Regiment.

Charlotte's husband Arthur died in 1932. Her own will, drawn up a year later, indicated that she remained an active supporter of women's issues. One of the chief benefactors of her will was the London School of Economics where she left money to be used in the support of studentships for research into the life of primitive people, especially women.

Shortly afterwards (the date is not certain), she left England with Gerald Hankin, a distant relation whom she and her husband appear to have adopted sometime before 1911. They moved to Washington, D.C., but practically nothing is known of her circumstances thereafter. Wilson eventually entered a home for the aged at Irvington-on-Hudson, New York, where she died on April 28, 1944, a few days short of her 90th birthday.

SOURCES:

Mackay, John H. *The Anarchists.* NY: Tucker, 1897.

Oliver, Hermia. *The International Anarchist Movement in Late-Victorian Britain.* London: Croom Helm, 1983.

Shaw, George Bernard. *The Fabian Society: Its Early History.* Fabian Tract No. 41, 1892.

Wilson, Charlotte. *Anarchism and Outrage.* London: Freedom Press, 1909.

———. *Three Essays on Anarchism.* Ed. by Nicolas Walter. Sanday, Orkney: Cienfuegos, 1979.

SUGGESTED READING:

Woodcock, George. *Anarchism.* Harmondsworth: Penguin, 1979.

Dave Baxter,
Department of Philosophy,
Wilfrid Laurier University, Waterloo, Canada

Wilson, Edith (1896–1981)

African-American blues singer and vaudeville performer. Born Edith Goodall on September 6, 1896, in Louisville, Kentucky; died of a brain tumor on March 30, 1981, in Chicago, Illinois; daughter of Susan (Jones) Goodall (a housekeeper) and Hundley Goodall (a teacher); educated in public schools in Louisville until about age 14, and received private tutoring in music beginning at age 13; married Danny Wilson (a pianist), in 1910s (died 1928); married Millard Wilson, in 1947.

Principal recordings include: "Nervous Blues" (1921); "Vampin' Liza Jane" (1921); "Frankie" (1921); "Old Time Blues" (1921); "(What Did I Do To Be So) Black and Blue" (c. 1928); "My Handy Man Ain't Handy No More" (c. 1929); "I'll Get Even With You" (c. 1929).

Edith Wilson was born on September 6, 1896, the third child of **Susan Jones Goodall**, a housekeeper, and Hundley Goodall, a schoolteacher. The family lived in a tidy, quiet neighborhood in Louisville, Kentucky, and social life centered around the church. It was at church that Wilson first sang and performed, as did her siblings. Louisville itself was also an early influence, with a lively music scene that over the years was home to numerous entertainers, including blues singers **Edmonia Henderson,** *Sara Martin,** and **Helen Humes,** tap dancers and comedians Buck and Bubbles, and musicians Dickie Wells, John Wickley, Elmo Dunn, and Jonah Jones. A show producer named Joe Clark spotted Wilson and put her onstage in "a little show down at White City Park," without her parents' knowledge, when she was only 13. Discovering her daughter's secret, Susan Goodall went to see the show for herself, and along with the rest of the audience was bowled over by Wilson's talent. The Goodalls hired a music tutor for their daughter, but made her promise to stay in school. Wilson kept the promise—briefly.

Singers were being paid $35 a week, and this amount of money was more than Wilson and her parents could resist. By 14, she was concentrating on her work as a singer and performer.

Shortly after her career began, she met pianist Danny Wilson, who expanded her repertoire of songs and began managing her career by booking her into shows in Chicago and Milwaukee. His professional interest expanded to include the personal, and the two married. Thanks to her husband's management, Wilson and his sister **Lena Wilson**, with Danny at the piano, sang in all the clubs in Chicago. Later, they traveled to Washington, D.C., Atlantic City, and New York. In New York City, record executive and composer Perry Bradford heard Wilson sing and negotiated a deal for her with Columbia Records. "Nervous Blues," which Bradford had written, was recorded on September 12, 1921, a version that was rejected by Columbia. On September 15, she rerecorded "Nervous Blues" and "Vampin' Liza Jane" in takes that pleased the record company. Several more unsuccessful recording sessions followed before October 6, when Wilson, backed by her husband on piano and her band Johnny Dunn's Original Jazz Hounds, recorded "Frankie" and "Old Time Blues." The songs were cheerful and danceable and began to sell well. As proof, she was signed to tour by the Theater Owners Booking Association (TOBA), the largest circuit for black entertainers.

Wilson's youth of church going and suburban gentility was never forgotten, and although blues singing of the day was frequently rough and graphically explicit, she refused to perform in raunchy skits or to sing songs with questionable lyrics. Instead, she chose sweeter songs with less suggestive lyrics (although some that she sang have double meanings), and songs that appealed to white audiences as well as black, leading her to become a crossover artist to the white market. Later, her repertoire grew to include show tunes, songs sung in foreign languages, and other material that classified her as more of a cabaret-style singer with some sophistication than a belter of "gutbucket" blues. (These qualities also have led some modern-day blues purists to question her authenticity.) At some of her club dates, Wilson sang double-entendre pieces like "He May Be Your Man (But He Comes to See Me Sometimes)" and "My Handy Man" as well as doing adult comedy skits and songs, but she was careful to remain within her own boundaries of propriety and good taste.

Vaudeville still demanded "plantation stereotypes" of African-American performers, and Wilson performed in many blackface numbers. She continued to develop her skills in acting and comedy and was acclaimed for her performances in a revue in the Dixieland Plantation Room of the Winter Garden in New York. Revamped as a musical comedy called *Dover Street to Dixie*, the show toured Europe starring ◄ **Florence Mills** and featuring Wilson in a number of set pieces. She returned to the United States in 1924 and played the Cotton Club and some other "name" theaters with the comic Doc Straine. She also continued to record with Columbia, which issued 26 out of the 32 single-record sides she made with them. As Wilson became known as the "Queen of the Blues," she also developed a reputation for tough-mindedness. She refused to be contracted to anyone and negotiated her own talent and terms; when committed to a project, she would not haggle over royalties and signed, particularly with Columbia, for recording deals with fixed and modest prices of as little as $125. She also made her own deals to sing as a solo act on the vaudeville circuit. In 1926, Wilson sang in Lew Leslie's *Blackbirds* and received her best reviews to date and the biggest boost to her career. This musical revue also toured Europe where she was hailed (particularly in Paris) as the "colored chanteuse with her naughty lyrics and impertinent humor."

Throughout the remainder of the 1920s, Wilson was a prominent performer in musical revues and vaudeville. She returned from Europe to work at the Cotton Club again and to sing on the Cotton Club's weekly radio programs broadcast by CBS (the club's house band was then led by Duke Ellington). Wilson's music appealed to white audiences, but blacks and whites did not perform together except for charity. Along with entertainers including Eddie Cantor, Ted Lewis, Buck and Bubbles, George Gershwin, the Hall Johnson Singers, James Weldon Johnson, Fletcher Henderson, Clifton Webb, **Ada Ward**, and J. Rosamond Johnson, she performed at many charity events for various African-American organizations.

In 1928, Wilson returned to Europe with *The Black Revue*. While she was overseas, Danny Wilson completed a day-long work session with composer Andy Razaf and died from exertion and complications from a long bout with tuberculosis. After a brief period of mourning, Wilson resumed her career. She performed with headliners like Louis Armstrong and Thomas "Fats" Waller, the latter of whom wrote the song "(What Did I Do To Be So) Black and Blue" for Wilson to record on the Brunswick label. He also arranged versions of "My Handy

Mills, Florence.
See Women of the Harlem Renaissance.

Man Ain't Handy No More" and "I'll Get Even With You" that she recorded for the Victor label. And then the Great Depression put an end to Wilson's recording career.

The Depression was tough on the careers of many performers, especially blues singers. Wilson's determination and extraordinary talent enabled her to survive by singing in revues and appearing with big bands. At the same time, whites regained control of parts of show business they had lost several decades ago; even the Apollo Theater in Harlem, which was "home" to many African-American performers, featured a growing number of white artists. Because she had always been so well received in Europe, Wilson returned there on tour often during the 1930s. Back home and performing at the Apollo, she captured the attention of Charlie Barnet, who led a racially mixed big band. She had often been upstaged by other performers in the upper echelon of talented entertainers, but Barnet convinced her to believe in herself as a superstar. His showcasing of her supreme talents essentially revived her career, and Wilson again became a well-known performer on the East Coast, singing with other renowned performers, including Eubie Blake in his *Shuffle Along* shows. For the first time, her reputation reached the West Coast, and she took engagements with both the Orpheum and Bert Levy circuits in Los Angeles, Seattle, Denver, Salt Lake City, and cities in Western Canada. The press described her "sparkling eyes" and "mischievous smile" and noted that she was "a blues singer of international reputation."

Opportunities in films and radio beckoned. After receiving offers for several small roles in movies, Wilson accepted a part in the 1944 Humphrey Bogart-**Lauren Bacall** classic *To Have and Have Not*. Her part required her to speak and sing in French; although most of her scenes ended up on the cutting-room floor, Wilson remained very proud of her work in the movie. In radio, she was stereotyped in roles such as a mother-in-law on "Amos 'n' Andy," bit parts in "The Great Gildersleeve," and Aunt Jemima on "The Breakfast Club." Based on the latter role, Quaker Oats hired Wilson for appearances as Aunt Jemima at fund-raising events for charity. Civil-rights groups protested the company's stereotyping and exploitation, but Wilson saw the character only as another role demanding skilled performances. She was hugely successful, despite the stereotyping, and raised almost $3 million for worthy causes before Quaker Oats was finally persuaded to retire the Aunt Jemima character in 1965.

Wilson's West Coast tours led to another change in her life in 1947, when she married Millard Wilson. They moved to Chicago in the 1950s and were active in black community organizations, civic events, and cultural activities. During the blues revival that gathered steam in the 1960s, Wilson often appeared at folk and blues festivals. In 1972, she returned to the recording studio for the first time in over 40 years, on an album that reunited her with Eubie Blake. On a 1976 album for Delmark Records, she sang classics from the blues and jazz repertoires with a jazz combo that included pianist "Little Brother" Montgomery. When her health began to fail in the mid-1970s, she refocused her energies on two objectives: singing as long as her weak heart permitted and establishing a home for indigent performers. Wilson had always been conservative with her money, but many of her show-business colleagues had not. (Sadly, this latter project never came to fruition.) She continued giving live performances, particularly in the clubs on the north side of Chicago, where, wearing "purple chiffon and a matching turban," she relished every minute of singing ballads and the blues.

Never having attended college in her youth, in 1978 Wilson became an artist-in-residence at the University of Maryland, where she and *Sippie Wallace regaled students with the experiences of their heyday to the delight of all. Wilson returned to the New York stage once more in 1980 in *Black Broadway*, an old-style revue that had Town Hall audiences cheering. That same year, the elegant if elderly Wilson guest-starred at the Newport Jazz Festival and stole the show with a mellow and mischievous rendition of "He May Be Your Man." She died of a brain tumor less than a year later, on March 30, 1981, after some 80 years on the stages of America and Europe.

SOURCES:

Harrison, Daphne Duval. *Black Pearls: Blues Queens of the 1920s*. New Brunswick, NJ: Rutgers University Press, 1988.

Smith, Jessie Carney, ed. *Notable Black American Women*. Detroit, MI: Gale Research, 1992.

Gillian S. Holmes,
freelance writer,
Hayward, California

Wilson, Edith Bolling (1872–1961)

First lady of the United States who may have run the country between 1915 and 1921. Name variations: Edith Bolling Galt; Edith Galt Wilson. Born on October 15, 1872, in Wytheville, Virginia; died on December 28, 1961, in Washington, D.C.; seventh child of William Holcombe Bolling (a lawyer and circuit judge) and Sallie (White) Bolling; married Norman

Galt, on April 30, 1896, in Wytheville, Virginia (died 1908); became second wife of Woodrow Wilson (president of the United States), on December 18, 1915, in Washington, D.C. (died 1924); children: (first marriage) one son who died in infancy.

It is ironic that Edith Bolling Wilson, who once referred to a parade of picketing suffragists as "detestable," was later accused of usurping her husband's power. However, in 1919, when President Woodrow Wilson suffered a life-threatening stroke, Edith Wilson embarked on what she termed her "stewardship," though it was characterized in the press as "Mrs. Wilson's Regency" and "petticoat government."

Edith Bolling, a ninth-generation descendant of *Pocahontas and John Rolfe, was born in 1872 and raised in the impoverished town of Wytheville, Virginia, the seventh of eleven children of William Holcombe Bolling and **Sallie White Bolling**. Her father, forced to surrender the family plantation after the Civil War, turned to law to support his large extended family, which included two grandmothers and two aunts. Money was scarce, and Edith's education consisted of home tutoring and two years at finishing schools.

When she was 18, Edith visited her sister in Washington, D.C., and there met and married Norman Galt, the cousin of her sister's husband and a partner in a family-held jewelry firm. The business flourished, and the couple lived comfortably for 12 years, traveling yearly to Europe and owning one of Washington's first electric cars. A son was born in 1903, but lived only three days. When her husband died suddenly in 1908, Edith inherited the business, which she managed for two years, then sold for a handsome profit. She took in **Altrude Gordon**, the orphaned, teenaged daughter of a friend. The two women traveled extensively, and even undertook a canoe trip in the wilderness of Maine. Through Gordon's fiancé, Admiral Gary Grayson, the White House physician, Edith met Woodrow Wilson's cousin, **Helen Woodrow Bones**, who had come to live in the White House after the death of Wilson's first wife *Ellen Axson Wilson.

It was through her friendship with Bones that Edith met Woodrow, literally colliding with him as she exited an elevator during a visit to the White House. The chance encounter led to tea in the Oval Room, at which time the president is said to have laughed for the first time since his wife's death, seven months earlier. From their first meeting, the president talked openly to Edith about state affairs, a practice he had begun with Ellen Wilson.

During their subsequent courtship, he installed a White House phone line to Edith's home, sending information on international and domestic issues by messenger, and calling her later to ask her opinions. This began what she called a "partnership of thought and comradeship," which served as her political internship. Two months after their chance meeting, the president proposed. With hopes of reelection in 1916, political advisors felt it might be too soon after the death of his wife for the president to remarry, and Edith had serious misgivings about the enormous responsibilities she would face as first lady. The wedding was postponed until nine months later, December 18, 1915. Soon after, the president barely squeaked out a reelection victory over his Republican challenger.

During the stressful years of World War I, Edith made sure the president took time to relax, often joining him for a morning golf game or an afternoon horseback ride. She ran a tight

Edith Bolling Wilson

wartime household in the White House, observing "wheatless and meatless days" and conserving heat and gas. The executive mansion became a hub of Red Cross work. Sheep grazed on the White House lawn, keeping it in trim, and providing wool to be sold for the war effort. Edith Wilson was even pressed into service naming battleships; she chose Native American names for many, in honor of her proud heritage.

After the Armistice in 1919, Edith accompanied the president to Europe, where he spent months pushing through an acceptable peace treaty, but Edith was alarmed by his recurring headaches and insomnia. Returning home, he waged a second battle to sell the League of Nations to the Senate. On an exhaustive cross-county train trip to take his case to the people, he suffered a collapse that was reported in the press as "a complete nervous breakdown." Back at the White House, on October 2, 1919, he suffered a massive stroke, which paralyzed his left side and threatened his life. The illness was shrouded in secrecy, and there were rumors that the president was dying or insane. No one but Edith and his doctors was allowed to see him.

Though Edith claimed that her "stewardship" lasted only six weeks, there are those who believe that she directed the executive branch of the government for the remaining 17 months of her husband's term. There is little doubt that she acted in what she believed to be her husband's best interest. When she proposed that the president resign, she was told by Dr. Grayson and other attending specialists that removing her husband's sense of purpose might kill him. "Have everything come to you," they advised. "Weigh the importance of each matter and see if it is possible to solve it by consultation with the head of the department involved without your husband's advice." Edith complied. To her many critics, she claimed, "I, myself, never made a single decision regarding the disposition of public affairs. The only decision that was mine was what was important and what was not." For four years, as the president's closest confidant, Edith had knowledge of his thoughts on many matters, but her detractors believe that she may have used the opportunity to distance the president from Cabinet level officials she did not like.

Woodrow Wilson never fully recovered. By November, he was seen in a wheelchair on the South Portico, but it was not until April that Cabinet meetings were resumed. Questions about his competency and Edith's influence persisted. When Wilson retired in 1921, after the Democrats and Warren Harding were elected by a landslide, Edith acted as nurse and companion until his death on February 3, 1924.

The remainder of her life was spent perpetuating her husband's memory and ideals. She was an active director of the Woodrow Wilson Foundation, traveled to Poland for the unveiling of a statue of him, and participated in the Woodrow Wilson Centennial Celebration in 1956. She had all of her husband's letters copyrighted and took personal pains to answer all her own mail. She remained a staunch Democrat, speaking on behalf of a number of candidates. One of her last public appearances was in a seat of honor at the inauguration of John F. Kennedy.

Edith Bolling Wilson died of heart failure on December 28, 1961, the anniversary of her husband's birth. It was not until 1967 that the 25th amendment to the Constitution, "Presidential Disability and Succession," became law, insuring that her particular situation would never be repeated.

SOURCES:
Healy, Diana Dixon. *America's First Ladies: Private Lives of the Presidential Wives.* NY: Atheneum, 1988.
Means, Marianne. *The Woman in the White House.* NY: Random House, 1963.
Melick, Arden David. *Wives of the Presidents.* Maplewood, NJ: Hammond, 1977.
Sicherman, Barbara, and Carol Hurd Green, eds. *Notable American Women: The Modern Period.* Cambridge, MA: The Belknap Press of Harvard University Press, 1980.

SUGGESTED READING:
*Ross, Ishbel. *Power with Grace: The Life Story of Mrs. Woodrow Wilson,* 1975.
Wilson, Edith Bolling, and Alden Hatch. *My Memoir,* 1961.

COLLECTIONS:
Edith Bolling Wilson Papers and Woodrow Wilson Papers, Library of Congress.

Barbara Morgan,
Melrose, Massachusetts

Wilson, Eleanora Mary Carus-
(1897–1977).

See Carus-Wilson, Eleanora Mary.

Wilson, Ellen Axson (1860–1914)

American first lady who was the first to use the position to advance worthwhile causes. Born Ellen Louise Axson on May 15, 1860, in Savannah, Georgia; died on August 6, 1914, in Washington, D.C.; daughter of Margaret (Hoyt) Axson and Samuel E. Axson (a third-generation minister); married (Thomas) Woodrow Wilson (future president of the United States), on June 24, 1885, in Savannah, Georgia; children: Margaret Wilson (1886–1944); Jessie Wilson (1887–1933);

Eleanor "Nell" Wilson McAdoo (1889–1967, who married William Gibbs McAdoo).

The first of four children of a third-generation Presbyterian minister, Ellen Louise Axson grew up in a deeply religious atmosphere. Little is know about her early education, but she graduated from the Rome (Georgia) Female College in 1876. "Tommy" Woodrow Wilson, whose father was also a minister, was the cousin of a childhood friend. The two first met as children and again soon after his graduation from Princeton. Completely enchanted the second time around by the girl "with hair like burnished copper," he proposed after only 11 meetings. However, marriage was postponed while he completed a doctorate and she pursued her dream of an art career at the Art Students League in New York City. Their separation prompted an exchange of daily letters that may represent some of the greatest love letters ever written in the English language. Ellen's are especially revealing of her philosophy, cultural interests and deep religious convictions.

Ellen Axson married Woodrow Wilson in June 1885, and shared academic life with him at Bryn Mawr, Wesleyan, and finally, Princeton, where he rose from professor to university president. Three daughters, Margaret, Jessie, and Eleanor, were born between 1886 and 1889. (**Margaret Wilson** [1886–1944], a singer who entertained troops in World War I, worked in advertising, then moved to India in 1940 because of her interest in Eastern religion, took the name Dista, and lived the last four years of her life as a virtual recluse. **Jessie Wilson** [1887–1933] was married in the White House in 1913. **Eleanor "Nell" Wilson McAdoo** [1889–1967] married widower William Gibbs McAdoo, her father's secretary of the treasury.) Ellen oversaw the children's early education and religious instruction at home. In the early 1890s, she worked in a volunteer women's employment society in Princeton and also found time to return to her painting.

Ellen's influence on Wilson's early career was profound.

*Ellen
Axson
Wilson*

Married to a man who has been characterized as "utterly dependent upon love and understanding for the realization of his own powers," she acted as his trusted advisor and confidante. Seeming to doubt her ability to fulfill all his needs, she saw to it that he was surrounded by interesting, lively people—often women—who would openly admire his intelligence and appreciate his humor. She proofread all his books, articles and speeches, and supported his political aspirations, becoming active in Democratic affairs. Wilson became governor of New Jersey in 1911 and president of the United States in 1913.

One of Ellen Wilson's first acts as first lady was to cancel the Inaugural Ball, which both she and her husband thought was frivolous and inappropriate with the world on the brink of war. A warm and charming Southern host, she preferred modest teas in the garden to lavish receptions. The most extravagant social events in the early Wilson years were the weddings of two of their daughters, Jessie in 1913 and Nell in 1914. Ellen's only personal indulgence in the White House was a skylight studio, which she had installed on the third floor.

Ellen Wilson's strong social conscience made her somewhat of an activist—a new role for a first lady. She personally toured the Washington slums and found the living conditions there deplorable for blacks and immigrants. As the "active" honorable chair of the advisory board for the housing committee of the Women's Department of the National Civic Federation, she worked to draft legislation to improve living conditions. The "alley bill" was introduced in Congress in February 1914. Ellen became aware of unsanitary conditions at government agencies, and worked to have rest rooms installed for hundreds of women employees. She used and promoted the hand-woven products made by women from the poor mountain states in the South, and was named honorary president of the Southern Industrial Association. Through her membership on the Board of Associated Charities, she supported a variety of other social causes and philanthropies, often donating her paintings anonymously to charitable auctions. They always brought a good price.

Ellen Wilson was diagnosed with tuberculosis and Bright's disease—a kidney disorder—after a serious fall in the spring of 1914. As her health worsened, one of her great disappointments was that Congress had still not moved on her housing legislation. Hearing that she was gravely ill, the Senate passed the "alley bill" one day before her death on August 6, 1914, at age

54. She is buried at Myrtle Hill Cemetery in Rome, Georgia.

SOURCES:

Healy, Diana Dixon. *America's First Ladies: Private Lives of the Presidential Wives*. NY: Atheneum, 1988.

James, Edward T., ed. *Notable American Women, 1607–1950*. Cambridge, MA: The Belknap Press of Harvard University, 1971, pp. 626–627.

Melick, Arden David. *Wives of the Presidents*. Maplewood, NJ: Hammond, 1977.

Paletta, LuAnn. *The World Almanac of First Ladies*. NY: World Almanac, 1990.

SUGGESTED READING:

McAdoo, Eleanor Wilson. *The Priceless Gift*, 1962.

———. *The Woodrow Wilsons*, 1932.

COLLECTIONS:

The Wilson Collection at Princeton University, New Jersey.

Barbara Morgan,
Melrose, Massachusetts

Wilson, Ethel (1888–1980)

South African-born Canadian novelist and short-story writer. Born Ethel Bryant in 1888 in Port Elizabeth, South Africa; died in 1980; educated in private school in Vancouver, Canada, and Trinity Hall in Southport, England; took the junior exams to enter Cambridge; received a teaching certificate in Vancouver; married a physician, in 1921.

Selected writings: Hetty Dorval *(1947);* The Innocent Traveller *(1949);* The Equation of Love *(1952);* The Swamp Angel *(1954);* Love and Saltwater *(1956);* Mrs. Golightly and Other Stories *(1961).*

Ethel Wilson was born Ethel Bryant in 1888 in Port Elizabeth, South Africa. When her mother died two years later, Ethel and her father returned to England, where they lived until his death in 1898. Wilson then traveled to Vancouver, British Columbia, Canada, to live with her maternal grandmother. She was educated in a Vancouver private school. Later, she resided at Trinity Hall, a boarding school in Southport, England, where she completed junior exams to enter Cambridge University. However, instead of attending Cambridge, she returned to Vancouver and earned a teaching certificate.

Wilson's teaching career lasted until she married her husband in 1921. This was the start of a long and happy period in her life. While her husband, a physician, made housecalls, Ethel waited in the car and wrote short stories. The couple traveled extensively, so Wilson's fiction features settings from around the world. Her first published writings appeared in *The New Statesman and Nation* in 1937. In 1947, *Hetty Dorval*, Wilson's premiere novel, was accepted for publication, and successfully established her reputation as a writer. Her next novel, *The Innocent Traveller* (1949), was a family saga. In 1952, two novellas were released under the title *The Equation of Love*.

Wilson's books feature the theme of deceptive appearances. Her characters, often ambivalent and unpredictable, are best represented in the novel *The Swamp Angel* (1954), which is considered her finest work. She also wrote *Love and Saltwater* (1956) and *Mrs. Golightly and Other Stories* (1961). Following Wilson's death in 1980, her life and work were commemorated in *Ethel Wilson: Stories, Essays, and Letters*.

SOURCES:

Buck, Claire, ed. *The Bloomsbury Guide to Women's Literature*. NY: Prentice Hall, 1992.

Gillian S. Holmes,
freelance writer,
Hayward, California

Wilson, Fiammetta Worthington (1864–1920)

English astronomer who observed over 10,000 meteors and discovered the 1913 return of Westphal's comet. Born in 1864 in Lowestoft, Suffolk, England; died in 1920; daughter of Helen Till Worthington and F.S. Worthington (a physician); educated by governesses; studied languages at schools in Lausanne, Switzerland (four years) and Germany (one year); studied music in Italy; no formal training in astronomy; married S.A. Wilson.

Selected writings: published several papers on astronomical subjects, the most notable being "The Meteoric Shower of January" in Monthly Notices of the Royal Astronomical Society *(January 1918, pp. 198–199).*

Fiammetta Worthington Wilson was born in Lowestoft in the Waveney district, Suffolk, England, in 1864. Her parents, **Helen Till Worthington** and Dr. F.S. Worthington, educated her at home under the care of governesses, but Fiammetta's father may have been her greatest educational influence. Dr. Worthington was an avid natural science enthusiast who spent his retirement performing microscopic studies. Although his daughter was tremendously gifted in languages and music, Dr. Worthington urged her to be aware of and to understand nature and her surroundings. Fiammetta attended private schools in Lausanne, Switzerland, and in Germany to study languages. She then went to Italy to study music and returned to London, England, to begin a career as a teacher at the Guildhall School of Music, where she also conducted the orchestra.

Wilson's interest in astronomy began when she attended astrophysicist Alfred Fowler's lecture series. She joined the British Astronomical Association and specialized in astronomical observations of meteors. World War I found Wilson serving as acting director (along with **A. Grace Cook**) of the British Astronomical Society's Meteor Section. From 1910 to 1920, Wilson observed over 10,000 meteors. She also became an expert in comets, zodiacal light, and the *aurora borealis*. In 1913, she discovered the return of Westphal's comet. After publishing several papers on meteors, Wilson was elected a fellow of the Royal Astronomical Society in 1916. In July 1920, the Harvard College Observatory awarded her a year-long research position, the E.C. Pickering Fellowship. However, she died that July, before being apprised of the honor.

SOURCES:

Ogilvie, Marilyn Bailey. *Women in Science*. Cambridge, MA: Cambridge Press, 1993.

Gillian S. Holmes,
freelance writer,
Hayward, California

Wilson, Harriet E. Adams

(c. 1827–c. 1870)

Writer whose 1859 novel was the first by an African-American published in the United States. Born around 1827 in Milford, New Hampshire; died around 1870; married Thomas Wilson, on October 6, 1851; children: George M. Wilson (died young).

Because very little documentation on her exists, the life story of Harriet E. Adams Wilson is virtually unknown. Census reports list her as a black woman. The death certificate of her son George M. Wilson shows that she was most likely born in Milford, New Hampshire, around 1827 or 1828, and a marriage record indicates that she married Thomas Wilson on October 6, 1851. This limited information is the fruit of research done by historian and critic Henry Louis Gates, Jr., who in the early 1980s discovered in a Manhattan bookstore a copy of Wilson's only known work, a novel published in 1859 titled *Our Nig: or Sketches from the Life of a Free Black, in a Two-Story White House, North, Showing That Slavery's Shadows Fall Even There*. The discovery of *Our Nig* restructured the chronology of black literature, for Gates also verified that Wilson's book was both the first novel by an African-American woman and the first novel by an African-American to be published in the United States. Prior to this, it was believed that the first novel written by an

African-American was *Clotel: or, The President's Daughter* (1853) by William Wells Brown, published only in London and written by a man. It was believed that the first novel (though not the first book) by an African-American woman was *Frances E.W. Harper*'s *Iola LeRoy, or the Shadows Uplifted*, which was not published until 1892. As well, critical studies of *Our Nig* establish it as a cornerstone of the African-American literary canon and a significant contribution to a number of genres, including the slave narrative, the sentimental novel, fictional autobiography, and women's fiction.

Although *Our Nig* is presented as a fictional autobiography, historians believe that many of the situations described in the novel reflect the author's own life. The story proves that racism in the period in which Wilson sets her tale—the early to middle 1800s—was just as strong in the North as it was in the South and was especially hard on free black women. The protagonist, Alfrado, is a child when she is taken in as a servant by a white family after her mother abandons her. Both the mother and sister in this "adoptive" family are cruel to her. As an adult, Alfrado suffers from illness and marries a man who is often absent and finally dies, leaving her poverty stricken with a sickly child.

Despite its veneer of fiction, *Our Nig* is historical in its depictions of gender, race, and class and how a harsh society dealt with these distinctions. Most of the works of black fiction and history in the pre-Civil War era addressed the evils of slavery; little attention was given to the "free" black living in the North. As a women's novel, *Our Nig* shows that African-American women were subjected to both severe economic restrictions and the idealization of femininity that became almost cult-like in the 19th century. *Our Nig* indicates that Wilson was aware of literary styles and conventions, and, more subtly, of what types of novels appealed to the largely white readership. Unlike *Clotel* and *Iola LeRoy*, the books it most resembles, Wilson's *Our Nig* has a believable story line and authentic dialogue, making it a landmark in the genre of the fictionalized autobiography. Wilson also leaned heavily on the tradition of the slave narrative, although hers is a story of a free woman. Alfrado's abuse at the hands of her white family is related in episodes throughout the book, and she yearns for freedom and sees education as the only means of escaping her difficult life. She does acquire an education and achieve freedom (the twin objectives of slave narrators), but she still fails to become self-sufficient. As a sentimental novel, Wilson's story was veiled from the public scrutiny that true autobiographies—particularly slave narratives—often received, thus preserving her feminine modesty as demanded by the times while still exposing the despicable care she received at white hands. The preface to *Our Nig* states that Wilson wrote the book "to aid me in maintaining myself and child." That, and the information Gates unearthed, is all that is known of her. She is thought to have died around 1870.

SOURCES:

Shockley, Ann Allen, ed. *Afro-American Women Writers, 1746–1933*. Boston, MA: G.K. Hall, 1988.

Smith, Jessie Carney, ed. *Notable Black American Women*. Detroit, MI: Gale Research, 1992.

Gillian S. Holmes,
freelance writer,
Hayward, California

Wilson, Harriette (1786–1855).

See Digby el Mesrab, Jane for sidebar.

Wilson, Helen Hopekirk (1856–1945).

See Hopekirk, Helen.

Wilson, Ida Lewis (1842–1911).

See Lewis, Ida.

Wilson, Kini (1872–1962)

Hawaiian dancer, singer and musician who was recognized as Hawaii's "Honorary First Lady." Name variations: Ana Kini Kuululani; Kini Kapahu; Jennie. Born Ana Kini Kuululani on March 4, 1872, in Honolulu, Hawaii; died after a stroke on July 23, 1962, in Honolulu; daughter of John N. McColgan (an Irish tailor) and a Hawaiian mother; hanai (adoptive) daughter of Kapahu Kula O Kamamalu; received three years of schooling, and was trained as a hula dancer, ballroom dancer, ukelele player, and singer; married John Wilson (an engineer who later served as mayor of Honolulu), on May 8, 1909.

Joined the royal troupe of hula dancers (c. 1888); began touring the U.S. and Europe (1893); returned to Hawaii (early 1900s) and became politically active in the Democratic Party (c. 1919); served as one of Hawaii's first presidential electors (1960).

Kini Wilson was born Ana Kini Kuululani in March 1872 in Honolulu, Hawaii, the 14th child of an Irish tailor and his "pure-blooded Hawaiian" wife. **Kapahu Kula O Kamamalu**, a stranger, was passing by the grass house by the sea near Honolulu Harbor when she heard the cries of the newborn. Entering the house, she bathed both infant and mother, who rewarded her in the Hawaiian tradition by giving her the child to raise as *hanai* (adoptive) mother. Kini

(Hawaiian for Jennie) thus became known by the name Kini Kapahu. Because Kapahu Kula O Kamamalu lived next door to the Hawaiian king's residence, the little girl grew up as a neighbor to King Kalakaua.

Wilson attended school for only three years. Her mother taught her how to dance the hula, and when she was 14, the king invited her to join the court's troupe of hula dancers. Kapahu, however, believed that the dance should be performed privately, and opposed the public nature of such display. When Wilson was 16, Queen *Kapiolani (1834–1899) approached Kapahu and persuaded her to allow her daughter to perform. By this time, Wilson had become a stunningly beautiful woman. She was nearly 6 feet tall and wore her long black hair like a splendid shawl on her shoulders. As one of the king's seven dancers (he called her "Lady Jane"), she was part of the royal court and was responsible for entertaining dignitaries, visitors to the Hawaiian court, and naval officers based on ships in Honolulu's Harbor. She danced the hula, played ukelele, and, as a member of the Kawaihau Glee Club, sang under the king's direction. She studied ballroom dancing in order to partner guests at court, and also continued her studies of Hawaiian dance. After the death of the king and the accession of his sister *Liliuokalani in 1891, Kini learned from teachers Nama-elua and Kapaona, who were from the island of Kauai.

White settlers were already scheming to gain control of Hawaii, and Queen Liliuokalani was deposed by rogue American troops in 1893. Wilson then decided to tour the United States and Europe, despite the objections of friends who considered this shameful. In the U.S., she performed in Portland, San Francisco, and at the Chicago World's Fair of 1893. She continued on to Europe the following year, dancing at the Folies-Bergère in Paris, for Tsar Nicholas II in Russia, and for Kaiser Wilhelm II in Germany. Refusing to believe Wilson's long hair was genuine, Wilhelm's wife *Augusta of Schleswig-Holstein gave it a yank; after the dancer cried out, the empress was so embarrassed she gave Wilson the necklace she was wearing. In 1895, Kini returned to Chicago, where the Royal Hawaiian Band had stopped while touring the United States. The band's manager, John Wilson, was a childhood friend, and they had a happy reunion. Of Irish, Scottish, Hawaiian, and Tahitian origins, he had been born and raised in Hawaii, where his father had served as chief engineer under Kalakaua and as marshal of Hawaii under Liliuokalani. John's mother had been a lady-in-waiting to Liliuokalani both before and after she ascended to the throne. Kini and John's renewed friendship soon blossomed into romance, although it would be 13 years before they married.

Meanwhile, Wilson continued touring with troupes of Hawaiian dancers to the Omaha Exposition of 1899 and the Buffalo Exposition of 1901, among others. It was during these tours that she claimed to have invented the ti-leaf skirt, now a staple of Hawaiian dancing along with the grass skirt. She also added zest (and, some have claimed, an unwonted sexuality) to the hula by rolling her eyes and wiggling as barkers introduced "the naughty girls from Honolulu [who] do the naughty hula dance." Early in the 1900s she returned to Hawaii, where she and Kapahu, her *hanai* mother, consulted (as unnamed sources) with Nathaniel B. Emerson regarding the hula legend, ritual, and dance forms. Emerson later published *Unwritten Literature of Hawaii: The Sacred Songs of the Hula* (1909). His book is still the definitive work on this native dance, although Wilson countered many of his statements and published corrections in academic journals.

During these years John Wilson had attended Stanford University, where he received an engineering degree. Kini and John married in 1909, and went to live in the Pelekunu Valley on the island of Molokai, where she served as postmistress and farmed small patches of taro while he worked as an engineer and contractor. In 1919, they moved back to Honolulu and became active in public life. John became the chief engineer for the city of Honolulu, and a year later, after the death of the incumbent, was appointed mayor. Hawaii was now a territory of the United States, and that same year, after the ratification of the 19th Amendment, Wilson organized the women of the territory in their first meeting to "discuss the new sphere of womanhood as created by the equal suffrage amendment."

Although her life on the stage had ended, and her remaining years were occupied with her husband's interests, Wilson's eye for detail, perfectionism, and strong opinions kept her in prominence beside her husband, not in his shadow. John headed Hawaii's Democratic Party for years, and was repeatedly elected mayor of Honolulu (in 1924, 1928, 1948, 1950, and 1952). Between mayoral stints, he was Honolulu's postmaster (1934–39) and administrator of Social Security and Public Welfare for the territory (1939–46). Wilson supported her husband's political endeavors and told reporters that she wanted him in office so she could "kick some shins."

Kini Wilson received many visitors over the years, including politicians seeking her endorsement, scholars researching Hawaiian lore, and dancers interested in learning traditional hula dancing styles. Her own importance to the community—she was known widely as "Auntie Jennie"—was commemorated after Hawaii was admitted to the union as the 50th state in 1959, when the legislature designated her as Hawaii's "Honorary First Lady." Her history with the Democratic Party, extending back to 1919, made her a figurehead for Democrats. In December 1960, after Hawaii participated in its first presidential election, Wilson was one of the four presidential electors who cast the new state's first electoral votes. At the time, she was 88 years old and was living in a cottage on the grounds of Maluhia Hospital, but she left her hospital bed to cast her electoral vote at Iolani Palace. Less than two years later, at age 90, she suffered a mild stroke and died on July 24, 1962.

SOURCES:
Peterson, Barbara Bennett, ed. *Notable Women of Hawaii.* Honolulu, HI: University of Hawaii Press, 1984.

Gillian S. Holmes, freelance writer, Hayward, California

Wilson, Margaret Bush (1919—)

African-American lawyer and civil-rights leader.
Born Margaret Berenice Bush on January 30, 1919, in St. Louis, Missouri; daughter of James Thomas Bush (a real-estate broker) and Margaret Berenice (Casey) Bush; educated in public schools in St. Louis; Talladega College, B.A. cum laude; Lincoln University School of Law, Jefferson City, Missouri, LL.B., 1943; married Robert Edmund Wilson, Jr., in 1944 (divorced 1968); children: Robert Wilson III.

Began practicing civil-rights and real-estate law (1943), and worked in private practice (1947–65, 1972—); served as assistant attorney general for Missouri (1961–62); worked for various state and federal agencies including the Missouri Department of Community Affairs, the St. Louis Model City Agency, and the St. Louis Lawyers for Housing; served as chair of the board of directors of the NAACP (1975–84).

Margaret Bush Wilson was born in 1919 in St. Louis, Missouri, one of three children of **Margaret Casey Bush** and James Thomas Bush. Although the family lived in a St. Louis ghetto, the children grew up in a beautiful home and a prominent, middle-class black family, for James Bush was the first successful African-American real-estate broker in St. Louis. Margaret's parents emphasized the importance of education and encouraged their children to look beyond their surroundings of the ghetto and the ubiquitous restrictions placed by American society on blacks in the decades before World War II.

Wilson attended local public schools, graduating from Sumner High School with honors in 1935. At Talledega College in Alabama, she studied economics and mathematics, won a *Juliette Derricotte Fellowship for her senior year, and received a B.A. degree *cum laude* in 1940. She then received a scholarship from Lincoln University School of Law in Jefferson City, Missouri, where she earned a law degree in 1943. That same year, Wilson was admitted to the Missouri bar and began working in St. Louis for the U.S. Department of Agriculture as an attorney in the Rural Electrification Administration. In 1944, she married Robert Edmund Wilson, Jr., whom she had met in law school. (Their only child would also become a lawyer.) Wilson helped her father and other members of the Real Estate Brokers Association, the first such organization for black brokers in St. Louis, in obtaining a charter. As the association's legal counsel, she led its legal battle against racially restrictive covenants in housing contracts, which culminated in 1948 with the Supreme Court's landmark decision in *Shelley* v. *Kraemer* that branded such covenants unconstitutional.

The previous year she had established a private practice, Wilson & Wilson, with her husband. Although the partnership would last nearly two decades, she often interrupted her practice to pursue other interests in the legal arena. In 1948, she followed her attraction to politics and ran for Congress on the Progressive ticket championed by Henry Wallace. Wilson was the first black woman from Missouri to run for Congress; after being defeated by the Democratic candidate, she joined the Democratic Party, in which she has remained active over the decades. From 1961 to 1962, she worked as assistant attorney general for the state of Missouri. She left Wilson & Wilson in 1965 (she and her husband would divorce in 1968), and for the next two years worked with the Missouri Office of Urban Affairs, attempting to improve housing conditions for poor blacks throughout the state. From 1967 to 1968, she served as an administrator for the Missouri Department of Community Affairs, responsible for continuing education programs and community services. She also helped to found and served as deputy director and then as acting director of the St. Louis Model City Agency, a corporation established to assist the poor in obtaining federal funds for better housing. Her focus on housing problems continued in her next

position, from 1969 through 1972, as director of St. Louis Lawyers for Housing. She then returned to private practice as a partner in the St. Louis firm of Wilson and Associates.

The respect Wilson earned in her many years of community service kept her in demand with boards and institutes, and she served on numerous local, state, and federal organizations. She was a member of the Council on Criminal Justice (1972–77), vice-chair (1973) and then chair (1975–77) of the Land Reutilization Authority of St. Louis, an instructor in civil procedure on the law school faculty of the St. Louis University Council on Legal Opportunities Institute, a member of the general advisory committee for the Arms Control and Disarmament Agency (1978–81), and a member of the President's Commission on White House Fellowships (1978–81). She also sat on the boards of directors of the American Red Cross (1975–81) and the United Way (1978–84) and was a trustee for several colleges.

A member since 1956 of the National Association for the Advancement of Colored People (NAACP), to which both her parents had belonged and to which she was elected a member of the board of directors, Wilson participated in

Margaret Bush Wilson

a number of councils within the organization. She also served as president of the St. Louis branch, president of the Missouri conference of state NAACP branches, and treasurer of the NAACP National Housing Corporation. She participated in the 1963 March on Washington, in task forces related to President Lyndon Johnson's antipoverty programs and the Civil Rights Act of 1964, and in the hearings that led to the desegregation of the school system in Atlanta, Georgia. Her crowning achievement came in 1975, when she was named chair of the board of directors of the 450,000-member NAACP. She was the first African-American woman elected chair of the venerable organization. (A founding white member, *Mary White Ovington, had served as chair from 1919 to 1932.) During her tenure, which lasted until 1984, Wilson emphasized not only housing, education, and job opportunities but also involving African-Americans in policy-making, government positions, and a wider range of fields that would extend their influence.

A sharp negotiator and tough administrator despite her small physical stature and soft voice, Wilson was once described as "Mary Poppins—with a razor blade." Among the many honors she has received are honorary degrees from Talladega College, Smith College, Alabama State University, Boston University, Kenyon College, Washington University, and St. Paul's College; the Bishop's Award of the Episcopal Diocese of Missouri (1963); the National Women's Division of the American Jewish Congress' *Louise Waterman Wise Laureate Award (1975); and the St. Louis Council of the American Jewish Congress' Democracy in Action Award (1978).

SOURCES:
Current Biography Yearbook 1975. NY: H.W. Wilson, 1975.
Smith, Jessie Carney, ed. *Notable Black American Women.* Detroit, MI: Gale Research, 1992.

Gillian S. Holmes,
freelance writer,
Hayward, California

Wilson, Margaret Oliphant (1828–1897).

See Oliphant, Margaret.

Wilson, Margaret W. (1882–1973)

Pulitzer Prize-winning American novelist. Name variations: Mrs. G.D. Turner; (pseudonym) An Elderly Spinster. Born Margaret Wilhelmina Wilson on January 16, 1882, in Traer, Iowa; died on October 6, 1973, in Droitwich, Worcester, England; daughter of West Wilson (a farmer and livestock trader) and

Agnes (McCornack) Wilson; educated in public schools including Englewood High School in Chicago, Illinois; University of Chicago, A.B., 1903, B.A. in philosophy, 1904; married George Douglas Turner (a British civil servant), in 1923 (died 1946); children: three stepdaughters.

Selected writings: The Able McLaughlins *(1923);* The Kenworthys *(1925);* The Painted Room *(1927);* Daughters of India *(1928);* Rural Populations and Agriculture in Mission Lands—Africa, Asia & Latin America *(nonfiction, 1928);* Trousers of Taffeta *(1929);* The Crime of Punishment *(nonfiction, 1931);* The Dark Duty *(1931, published in U.S. as* One Came Out, *1932);* Cardinal Points *(1933, published in U.S. as* The Valiant Wife, *1934);* The Law and the McLaughlins *(1936);* The Devon Treasure Mystery *(juvenile, 1939).*

Later describing herself as "the most Middle Western of all Middle Westerners," Margaret W. Wilson was born in 1882 in the small farming town of Traer, Iowa. She was the fourth child of **Agnes McCornack Wilson** and West Wilson, Scottish Presbyterian farmers and livestock traders who later abandoned farming and moved to Ames, Iowa, to concentrate on trading. The family next moved to Chicago, Illinois, where Wilson attended Englewood High School. She earned an associate degree from the University of Chicago in 1903, and the following year graduated with a bachelor's degree in philosophy. During her college years, Wilson had been moving toward a deep conviction in the Presbyterian faith of her parents. Largely unaware of her inward growth, her friends were astounded when, in 1904, she joined the United Presbyterian Church of North America as a missionary. A friend, **Katherine Scobey Putnam**, recalled her own reaction to the news as: "Margaret Wilson a missionary! Preposterous!"

Wilson spent six years working as a missionary in India. She later observed, "Being of a submerging disposition, I sank deeper into that country than the wise do, into Hindustan and Hindustani, into the Punjab and Punjabi, into Curmukha and Curmukhi, all of which are unsettling elements." She lived in the Punjab region of northern India, assisting Dr. **Maria White** at the Sailkot Hospital and teaching at and supervising the Gujranwala Girls' School. Wilson wrote regularly to Putnam that she was "happier than she had ever been in her life," but she was also witnessing aspects of existence she refused to write home about. In the end, missionary work proved too devastating to her emotional and mental health. She became ill with typhoid and in 1910 was forced to return to the United States, later writing, "I left India when I did because if I had not I should have died quite futilely of compassion."

After recovering her health, and still fueled with religious feeling, she reentered the University of Chicago in 1912 as a divinity student. Wilson completed the academic year and then began teaching at West Pullman High School, where she remained for five years. She officially resigned her missionary post in 1916, but her experiences in India still filled her imagination, and she began writing short stories. In 1917, she briefly resumed divinity school, but left after completing only two more quarters. Much of her time after that was spent nursing her father, whose health had been failing for years, but the free time she had was devoted to writing. She completed a set of short stories collectively called "Tales of a Polygamous City," some of which appeared in the *Atlantic Monthly* in 1917 under the pseudonym "An Elderly Spinster." (She was then 35.) "When I wrote of India . . . I signed myself 'An Elderly Spinster' because I was at that time the oldest woman in the United States," she later declared. Two more of the "Polygamous City" stories were published in *Asia* magazine in 1921.

In 1923, she published her first novel, *The Able McLaughlins*. A story of harsh life in the barely settled Midwest during the mid-19th century, examining especially the influence of religion in a sparse Scottish Presbyterian community, the book brought Wilson much critical and public attention, and won that year's Harper Prize. The following year, it won the Pulitzer Prize. It would go on to be republished four times, most recently in 1977. Meanwhile, Wilson's father had died in 1923 and she had sailed to Europe, where she became reacquainted with George Douglas Turner. An Englishman whom she had met in India, Turner had served the British government as a spy during World War I, and was the divorced father of three daughters. Wilson and Turner married in Paris on December 24, 1923, and settled in England, where Turner occupied positions of increasing responsibility within the penal administration system of the British Home Office, from warden to inspector of prisons to assistant commissioner of prisons for England and Wales.

Wilson published her second novel, *The Kenworthys*, in 1925. Considered a somewhat scattered book but nonetheless an important contribution to domestic novels of the period, it focuses on two brothers, one of whom previous-ly had been engaged to the woman the other marries. Wilson had written *The Kenworthys* prior to the publication of her first novel, and on the whole critics tended to think it a lesser work. None of her other novels would sell as well as had *The Able McLaughlins*, although they were read widely and critics remained interested in the controversies she raised. To Wilson, plot and character were secondary to the social themes she addressed, chief among them the influence of religion on both men and women. She once noted that she wrote "consciously and unconsciously for women," and her explorations of the various ways in which women were repressed in society have led to her reputation as one of the 20th century's early feminist writers.

The Painted Room (1927), a sequel to *The Kenworthys*, is an unflinching portrait of a young woman, duped and betrayed by a lover, who quickly comes to the belief that everyone is as vicious as her ex-lover and she should behave in a similar fashion, although the book's bitterness (and, indeed, point) is fairly well undermined by an inexplicable happy ending. Wilson's next two novels, *Daughters of India* (1928) and *Trousers of Taffeta* (1929), both set in India, focus on the low social status of Indian women. *Daughters of India* concerns the experiences of a young American woman serving as a missionary, while *Trousers of Taffeta* explores the impact of polygamy on women (with a whiff of the Biblical tale of *Rachel and Leah) through the story of two wives, one barren and beloved, the other fertile and unloved.

Her marriage allowed Wilson to observe prisons firsthand, and she was greatly influenced by her husband's opinions on crime and penology. In 1931, she wrote a nonfiction work on these subjects, *The Crime of Punishment*, in which she discussed the conflict she saw between the moral correctness of punishment and the innate goodness of human beings. She argued that laws create criminals and that prisons do not effectively stimulate rehabilitation. Although Turner was assaulted by inmates during riots at Dartmoor Prison the following year, Wilson remained resolute in her views on justice and the prison system. While her husband embarked on a crusade of prison reform, Wilson wrote three novels on these matters: *The Dark Duty* (1931, published in the U.S. as *One Came Out*), about a prison warden facing the impending execution of a man who may have been unjustly convicted; *Cardinal Points* (1933, published in the U.S. as *The Valiant Wife*), set in Dartmoor Prison during the War of 1812; and *The Law and the McLaughlins* (1936). This latter book, which returns to the characters from *The

Able McLaughlins, concerns an ultimately unsuccessful attempt to bring the perpetrators of a double lynching to justice.

With Turner's retirement in 1938, the couple moved to Droitwich in Worcester, England, but the onset of World War II interrupted their country idyll. The British government recruited Turner for wartime assignments, and filled their home with soldiers and refugees in need of temporary shelter with such frequency that the couple would spend weekends at a local hotel for some privacy and quiet. Aside from a children's book produced to earn money for home repairs in 1939, Wilson wrote nothing after the start of the war. Her husband suffered from illness throughout the fighting, and died in 1946. In poor health herself, Wilson was cared for by her stepdaughters until she outlived them. She died in a nursing home in Droitwich in 1973, at age 91.

SOURCES:

Contemporary Authors. Vol. 113. Detroit, MI: Gale Research, 1986.

Kunitz, Stanley J., and Howard Haycraft, eds. *Twentieth Century Authors*. NY: H.W. Wilson, 1942.

Wilkie, Everett C., Jr. "Margaret Wilson," in *Dictionary of Literary Biography*, Vol. 9: *American Novelists, 1910–1945*. Ed. by James J. Martine. Detroit, MI: Gale Research, 1981.

Gillian S. Holmes,
freelance writer,
Hayward, California

Wilson, Mary (1916—)

Wife of British Prime Minister Harold Wilson. Born Gladys Mary Baldwin in 1916 in Norfolk, England; father was a Congregational minister; educated at public and boarding schools including Wilton Mount, Sussex; trained as a stenographer and typist; married Harold Wilson (later prime minister of Britain, 1964–70, 1974–76), later Baron Wilson of Rievaulx, in 1940 (died 1995); children: sons Robin (b. December 1943) and Giles (b. May 1948).

Mary Wilson was born Gladys Mary Baldwin in Norfolk, England, in 1916. Her father was a Congregational minister who had begun life as a mill worker and nearly starved to death while studying theology at night, and her mother had also worked in a mill until shortly before her marriage. Among the Reverend Baldwin's many pastorates were Cambridge and Penrith at the edge of England's Lake District, where Mary, an only child, attended local schools. A good student who inherited a love of reading from her father (he quoted poetry as often as the Bible in his sermons), she also later attended Wilton Mount, a boarding school in Sussex. Travels

with her father to his pastorates exposed her to the rough working conditions at the mills and mines of Northern England, where she observed miners black with coal dust after a day in the pit mines. After studying shorthand and typing, Wilson began working in Cheshire in 1934.

That year she met and began seeing Harold Wilson, who was preparing to go to Oxford. He won a first-class degree in 1937 and became a don (professor) and lecturer in economics, and, with his future apparently secure at Oxford, they became engaged. With the beginning of World War II in September 1939, she moved to Oxford and worked for the Potato Marketing Board. Harold volunteered for Army service, but because of his reputation as an economist was channeled into civil service instead. They were married at Mansfield College in Oxford on January 1, 1940. Soon thereafter, Harold was appointed to the Ministry of Supply in London, and they moved to an apartment in Twickenham. His job took him to the unoccupied capitals of Europe, and the bombing raids on London forced Wilson to move back with friends in Oxford and then with family in Cornwall. She later returned to London and a flat in Richmond, where she served as an Air Raids Precaution Shelter Warden, guiding civilians to the shelters at night, and gave birth to their first son late in 1943. When German buzz-bombing raids began in the summer of 1944, she moved with her infant son to her parents' house in Cambridgeshire. Later that year the family was reunited in London, and in the spring of 1945 they returned to Oxford.

This resumption of university life was brief, however, for in July 1945 Harold was one of the victors in the Labour Party's postwar landslide victory. He also became one of three newly elected Labour members of Parliament (MPs) to obtain a position as a junior minister, thus entitling him to sit on the front bench. In 1947, he became a member of the Cabinet as president of the Board of Trade. Instead of the quiet university life of Wilson's dreams, the family, which by May 1948 included a second son, was being swept along on the political tide. On February 14, 1963, Harold was elected leader of the Labour Party. In 1964, he became prime minister with the Labour Party's minimal victory at the polls. That October, Mary rode with her husband to Buckingham Palace, where Queen *Elizabeth II* formally requested that he form a government. Wives usually did not attend such events, but Mary said, "It wouldn't occur to Harold to do anything else."

Four weeks later, the family took up residence at No. 10 Downing Street in London, the prime minister's official residence. Wilson sought as normal an existence as life in public permitted; she enjoyed being able to walk to the House of Commons to see her husband, and treasured her time to read and to write her own poetry. Although she objected to public speaking, she was quick to kill the "timid housewife image" associated with her and adapted well to the grander life and to public appearances, accompanying her husband on state visits to Washington, Paris, Rome, Ottawa, and Moscow. Harold Wilson served as prime minister until 1970, and was reelected in 1974. To some surprise, he then resigned in 1976. He was honored by the British government that year with a knighthood, and in 1983 received a life peerage, thus making Harold and Mary, Baron Wilson and Lady Wilson of Rievaulx.

SOURCES:

Frederick, Pauline. *Ten First Ladies of the World.* NY: Meredith Press, 1967.

Gillian S. Holmes,
freelance writer,
Hayward, California

Wilson, Mary (b. 1944).

See Supremes, The.

Wilson, Nancy (1937—)

African-American singer and actress. Born on February 20, 1937, in Chillicothe, Ohio; daughter of Olden Wilson and Lillian (Ryan) Wilson; educated at Burnside Heights Elementary School and West High School in Columbus, Ohio; spent one year at Central State College; married Kenny Dennis (a drummer), in 1960 (divorced); married Wiley Burton (a minister), in 1970; children: (first marriage) Kenneth, Jr. (b. 1963); (second marriage) Samantha (b. 1975) and Sheryl (b. 1976).

Nancy Wilson was born in Chillicothe, Ohio, in 1937, the first of Olden and **Lillian Ryan Wilson**'s six children. Both parents worked full time, Olden in an iron foundry and Lillian as a domestic, and during their workdays the children were cared for by a grandmother who lived near Columbus. Wilson, who first sang in a choir at church, knew by the time she was four years old that she wanted a career as a singer. She discovered a wide range of influences by listening to music with her father, including that of *Ruth Brown, Billy Eckstine, Nat King Cole, Louie Jordan, Jimmy Rushing and Little Jimmy Scott.

While attending West High School in Columbus, Ohio, Wilson won a talent contest and began singing professionally at local clubs at age 15. As

a teenager, she also began listening to other female singers, including *Sarah Vaughn and *Ella Fitzgerald. After graduating from high school, she enrolled at Central State College, intending to major in education and provide herself with some measure of financial security by obtaining teaching credentials. Nonetheless, she left school after one year, intent on pursuing a singing career. In 1956, Wilson joined the Rusty Bryant Band and met Julian "Cannonball" Adderly, a renowned alto saxophonist and skilled professional musician who became a mentor for her. From 1956 through 1959, Wilson toured the United States and Canada with the band.

She then moved to New York City with three definite objectives: to sign with manager John Levy (who also managed Adderly), to become known as an independent soloist, and to record for Capitol Records. She took a day job as a receptionist and decided to allow herself six months to meet her goals. In only one month, she was hired by a New York club to substitute for singer **Irene Reid**. Wilson's performances were so impressive that the club booked her to sing four nights a week indefinitely. John Levy heard her perform and set up a demo recording session during which she recorded "Guess Who I Saw Today" and "Sometimes I'm Happy," which were then sent to Capitol Records. Within six weeks of setting her goals, Wilson had signed a contract as a Capitol recording artist. Her debut single sold well, and between April 1960 and July 1962 she recorded five albums that were released by Capitol. One of these, *Nancy Wilson/Cannonball Adderly Quintet*, is now considered a classic. In 1963, Wilson had her first major hit with "Tell Me the Truth." In 1964, she won a Grammy Award for her song "How Glad I Am."

In the midst of all this activity, Wilson had married Kenny Dennis, a drummer, in 1960, and given birth to a son in January 1963. (The couple would later divorce.) She continued to release albums, and in the late 1960s began appearing regularly on television. During 1967–68, she had her own tv program, "The Nancy Wilson Show," which won an Emmy Award. Over the following years she also sang on "The Carol Burnett Show," "The Flip Wilson Show," "The Andy Williams Show" and "The Sammy Davis Jr. Show," among others, and acted in such popular shows as "Hawaii Five-O," "I Spy," "Police Story" and "Room 222." Wilson married again in 1970, to Wiley Burton, a minister with whom she would have two daughters. Following her second marriage, her career blossomed. She sang two shows per night every week of the year and was booked two years in advance.

Wilson remained with Capitol until 1980, when she switched to Japanese-based A.D.I. Records, a company that allowed her to record by singing each song completely, rather than in tracks that would then be spliced together. Of the American style of recording, Wilson noted, "The day the music died is the day . . . they stopped recording live, they started doing things you can't reproduce live." She preferred to start again from the top until she satisfied her producer, as opposed to singing select portions right in separate recordings. The switch to the Japanese label also gave her a new audience by making her one of the most popular recording artists in Japan. Of her preferences, Wilson noted, "I like a story in love songs. I don't want to sing something simplistic. Ballads ought to touch you," and she tended to avoid music that had been recorded frequently before. Her 1991 album *With My Lover Beside Me* featured Johnny Mercer's lyrics set to music by Barry Manilow; 1994's *Love, Nancy* showcased lush, romantic tunes; while 1997's *If I Had My Way* was a rhythm-and-blues set.

In addition to performing, acting and recording, Wilson has been active in community affairs and civic groups. A member of the NAACP and chair of Operation PUSH, she also has been a member of the Committee for the Kennedy Center for Performing Arts, the President's Council for Minority Business Enterprises, and the United Negro College Fund. She has worked for the Johnson & Johnson Prenatal Care Foundation, the Martin Luther King Jr. Center for Non-Violent Social Change, the National Urban Coalition, and her own Nancy Wilson Foundation, established with her family to help inner-city children experience life in the country. Her most visible charity work may be her frequent appearances on "The Lou Rawls Parade of Stars" and the "March of Dimes Telethon." Among the awards she has received are the Global Entertainer of the Year Award from the World Conference of Mayors (1986), the NAACP Image Award (1986), the Los Angeles Urban League's Whitney Young Award (1992), and the Paul Robeson Humanitarian Award.

Called "both cool and sweet, both singer and storyteller" by *Time* magazine, and now with some 60 albums to her credit, Wilson rejects critics' attempts to classify her as a jazz singer, pop singer, or rhythm-and-blues artist, preferring to consider herself "a song stylist." More specific labels, she believes, wrongly put people in boxes, and the only box she admits to is "I sing songs."

SOURCES:
"Nancy Wilson: a class act that defies classification," in *The Orange County Register.* April 17, 1997.
Smith, Jessie Carney, ed. *Notable Black American Women.* Detroit, MI: Gale Research, 1992.

Gillian S. Holmes,
freelance writer,
Hayward, California

Wilson, Romer (1891–1930)

English novelist. Name variations: Florence Roma Muir Wilson; (pseudonym) Alphonse Marichaud. Born Florence Roma Muir on December 16, 1891, in Sheffield, England; died of tuberculosis on January 11, 1930, in Lausanne, Switzerland; daughter of Arnold Muir (a solicitor) and Amy Letitia (Dearden) Wilson; educated at West Heath School, Kent, England; studied law at Girton College, Cambridge University, Cambridge, England, 1911–14; married Edward Joseph H. O'Brien (an anthologist), in 1923; children: one son.

Selected writings: Martin Schüler (1918); If All These Young Men (1919); The Death of Society: A Novel of Tomorrow (Hawthornden Prize winner, 1921); The Grand Tour of Alphonse Marichaud (1923); Dragon's Blood (1926); Greenlow (1927); Latterday Symphony (1927); The Social Climbers (play, 1927); All Alone: The Life and Private History of Emily Jane Brontë (1928); The Hill of Cloves: A Tract on True Love, with a Digression upon an Invention of the Devil (1929); Tender Advice (published posthumously, 1935).

As editor: Green Magic: A Collection of the World's Best Fairy Tales from All Countries (1928); Silver Magic: A Collection of the World's Best Fairy Tales from All Countries (1929); Red Magic: A Collection of the World's Best Fairy Tales from All Countries (1930).

Romer Wilson was born in England in 1891. Until the age of 16, she and her family lived in a manor house near the moors at Sheffield. The house and its heritage impressed Wilson's active imagination, as did summer holidays at chilly seasides and occasional trips to the Continent. Wilson attended boarding school at West Heath School in Kent, in the Thames Valley, and in the gentle landscape of the English Midlands. She stayed at West Heath (which, later in the century, schooled Lady *Diana, princess of Wales) for four years, then studied law at Girton College of Cambridge University in Cambridge. She completed college in three years, describing it as boring and leaving with mediocre marks; however, one of her professors suggested she consider writing as a career. On her graduation in 1914, she looked forward to a social life, but her expectations were frustrated by World War I. Again experiencing boredom, Wilson drafted her first novel *Martin Schüler* in 1915. She completed the first half of the book in three weeks but tore it up in disgust. A friend salvaged the manuscript, but Wilson did not continue work on it until 1917, when she finished it in another three-week period. It was accepted for publication that same year.

During the war, Wilson did a variety of war work, such as selling potatoes for the Board of Agriculture. She wrote the novel *If All These Young Men* followed shortly thereafter by the play *The Social Climbers*. Although both met with success, Wilson complained, according to *Twentieth Century Authors*, that *If All These Young Men* was understood by "no Americans and very few Englishmen." Wilson had also played at writing a private magazine produced on a typewriter and using the pen name of Alphonse Marichaud. Her own name had been shortened from Florence Roma Muir Wilson to Romer Wilson with the publication of *Martin Schüler*. In addition, she wrote *The Death of Society*, for which she was awarded the Hawthornden Prize of 1921.

Wilson then traveled to Paris for three weeks and wrote *The Grand Tour of Alphonse Marichaud*. She again visited the Continent with the manuscript proof in hand; in Portofino, Italy, she met Edward J. O'Brien, an anthologist from the United States. They were married in 1923, and returned to Portofino after their honeymoon. Although they both loved Portofino, a shortage of houses for rent led them to live in Rapallo, Italy. By 1928, Wilson had moved to Locarno, Switzerland. In the meantime, she had been commissioned to write a biography of *Emily Brontë, which forced her to call up memories of the wild English landscape and the country lifestyle that had vanished with World War I. Romer Wilson died of tuberculosis in Lausanne, Switzerland, at age 39. She had one son and was in the process of writing two novels at the time of her death. One of the novels, near completion, was published posthumously as *Tender Advice*.

Wilson had told *Twentieth Century Authors*, "I cannot, and never shall be able to write what I think people want. I cannot write for the public." A painstaking author, she apparently rewrote each of her books twice. In an assessment of her work, Maria Aline Seabra Ferreira writes: "Romer Wilson's novels, which possess a pronounced philosophical bent, address some of the most pressing concerns of the time in which she lived." Comparing her work to that produced during the same period by such writers as *Virginia Woolf, *Rebecca West, *Mary Agnes Hamilton, D.H. Lawrence, Richard Aldington, and Ford Madox Ford, Ferreira concludes that Wilson's works "mourn the passing of a civilization destroyed by World War I" and "dramatize the desirability of recovering the values embodied by the countryside."

SOURCES:

Ferreira, Maria Aline Seabra. "Romer Wilson," in *Dictionary of Literary Biography*, Vol. 191: *British Novelists Between the Wars*. Detroit, MI: The Gale Group, 1998, pp. 344–348.

Kunitz, Stanley J., and Howard Haycraft, eds. *Twentieth Century Authors*. NY: H.W. Wilson, 1942.

Gillian S. Holmes,
freelance writer,
Hayward, California

Wilson, Sarah (1750–?)

English thief, adventurer, and impostor. Name variations: (alias) Susanna (or Sophia) Carolina Matilda, Marchioness de Waldegrave. Born in 1750 in a village in Staffordshire, England; date and place of death unknown; married Captain William Talbot, after 1775.

Sarah Wilson was born in 1750 in a small village in Staffordshire, England. Little is known about her early years except that she apparently escaped country life while in her teens and journeyed to London. She found a job as a servant with **Caroline Vernon**, who was a maid of honor to Queen *Charlotte of Mecklenburg-Strelitz, wife of King George III (r. 1760–1782). In the spring of 1771, Wilson crept into the queen's boudoir and stole one of Charlotte's miniature portraits, a diamond necklace, and a gown. Attempting a second episode of thievery later that evening, Sarah was caught, tried, found guilty of burglary, and sentenced to death. Vernon and the queen intervened on her behalf, and her sentence was commuted to indentured servitude in the British colonies in North America.

The convict ship carrying Wilson arrived in Maryland in the autumn of 1771. William Devall of Bush Creek, Frederick County, Maryland, acquired Wilson's indenture, but she was hardly the ideal candidate for service, and she escaped soon after. Undetected, she had managed to keep the goods she had stolen in England, and she traveled throughout the Colonies styling herself as Susanna (or Sophia) Carolina Matilda, marchioness de Waldegrave, a sister of the queen of England. For approximately 18 months, from late 1771 through 1773, she cultivated friends among the upper ranks of society in Virginia, North Carolina, South Carolina, and Georgia by displaying the miniature portrait of "her sister" and exploiting her own wit, charm, and dramatic flair. Winning the confidence of the Colonies' finest citizens, and even gaining an introduction to the governor of North Carolina, Wilson duped several victims by claiming to be able to secure government posts and army commissions—for substantial fees.

Devall hired attorney Michael Dalton to find and return his servant, and posted a reward in the *Virginia Gazette* of June 3, 1773, describing her as possessing "a blemish in her right eye, black roll'd hair, stoops in her shoulders." Accounts differ from this point onward. One report indicates that she avoided capture and traveled to Boston—where she was spotted in January 1774—by way of Philadelphia, New York, and Newport. From Boston, she went to Portsmouth and Newcastle, New Hampshire, and then back to Newport, where the *Mercury* printed notices of her arrival and subsequent departure for New York in July 1775. According to this first account, she then vanished. Another report claims that she was apprehended and returned to Devall in 1773 but escaped again in 1775. Traveling north, she eventually met and married a British army officer, Captain William Talbot. After about 1775, no further traces of Sarah Wilson surfaced. Her epitaph seems to have been penned by a Boston printer who, in the *Providence Gazette* of January 22, 1774, characterized her as "the most surprizing [*sic*] genius of the female sex that was ever obliged to visit America."

SOURCES:

James, Edward T., ed. *Notable American Women, 1607–1950.* Cambridge, MA: The Belknap Press of Harvard University, 1971.

Read, Phyllis J., and Bernard L. Witlieb. *The Book of Women's Firsts.* NY: Random House, 1992.

Gillian S. Holmes,
freelance writer,
Hayward, California

Wilson, Mrs. Woodrow.

See Wilson, Ellen Axson (1860–1914).
See Wilson, Edith Bolling (1872–1961).

Wilson Carus, Eleanora (1897–1977).

See Carus-Wilson, Eleanora.

Wiltshire, countess of.

See Stafford, Catherine (d. 1474).
See Boleyn, Anne for sidebar on Elizabeth Howard (d. 1538).

Winchelsea, countess of.

See Finch, Ann (1661–1720).
See Seymour, Mary (d. 1673).

Winchester, countess of.

See Matilda (d. 1252).
See Beauchamp, Isabel (fl. 1285).

Winchester, Lady of.

See Emma of Normandy (c. 985–1052).

Windeyer, Mary (1836–1912)

Australian charity organizer and champion of orphans' welfare and women's suffrage. Name variations: Lady Mary Windeyer. Born Mary Elizabeth Bolton at Hove, England, in 1836; died in Raymond Terrace, New South Wales, Australia, in December 1912; daughter of Robert Thorley Bolton (a minister) and Jane (Ball) Bolton; married William Charles Windeyer (a barrister, judge, M.P., and government official), on December 31, 1857 (died 1897); children: nine, including Lucy Windeyer (namesake of Lucy Osburn) and Margaret Windeyer.

Mary Elizabeth Bolton was born in Hove, a town near Brighton on the south coast of England, in 1836, one of nine children of **Jane Ball Bolton** and the Reverend Robert Thorley Bolton. When Mary was a toddler, the family moved to Hexham in New South Wales, Australia, where her father ministered at Tarro Church.

On December 31, 1857, Mary married barrister William Charles Windeyer, who had been raised on "Tomago," a large estate in Raymond Terrace, about 100 miles north of Sydney on the southeast coast. Three years after their marriage, William was elected to Parliament. He later became solicitor-general and attorney-general. An ambitious and hard-working man, William was a protégé of Sir Henry Parkes, five-time prime minister of New South Wales and primary architect of the Australian Federation. Mary Windeyer busied herself with the public life that accompanied her husband's responsibilities and with raising their family. In 1864, her infant daughter died, a factor that likely influenced her future advocacy for the health and welfare of children; however, by 1872, the Windeyers had six young children. Critical of orphanages, Mary favored placing orphans in foster care with loving families in an attempt to replace the large orphanages that were virtually the only method of housing orphaned and abandoned children in Australia at that time. Her friend **Emily Clarke** had successfully initiated a "boarding out" program in

South Australia, and these views were shared by Mary's husband William. As royal commissioner, William Windeyer included this concept in his reports on public charities. In 1874, Mary helped to establish a foundling hospital that later became the Ashfield Infants' Home. As infanticide was a significant problem, Ashfield was reorganized to also admit mothers with illegitimate children.

Mary suffered from periodic bouts of serious illness, which handicapped her for several months during 1874 and again in 1876. She stayed with the children at "Tomago" during these incidents. Also in 1876, her ninth and last child was born. Mary enjoyed the friendship of *Lucy Osburn, a nursing pioneer, who encouraged Mary to channel her interests toward hospital training. (One of Mary's daughters was named Lucy Windeyer in her honor.) Mary continued her work with orphans by opening a cottage home for them and by appealing to Sir Henry Parkes regarding the "boarding out" issue. At his request, she drafted legislation for a State Children's Relief Board, which assumed responsibility for fostering children from the state-run orphanages; Mary Windeyer was appointed as an original member of this Board.

In 1879, William Windeyer became a judge and in 1881 began serving as a judge in divorce cases, promoting legal reforms related to desertion. Complementing her husband's work, Mary sought increased employment opportunities for women, holding that deserted wives could help themselves if varied employment and support were available. Women's work and self-sufficiency came to dominate Mary's charitable efforts and activism during this period. In 1887, the Windeyers traveled to Britain for the Jubilee celebrating Queen *Victoria's 50-year reign. Lucy Osburn was initiating an association to validate nursing as a profession and when the Windeyers returned from Britain, Mary helped organize an Exhibition of Women's Industries that concentrated on nursing and literature. The Exhibition raised sufficient funds for Windeyer to organize a Temporary Aid Society, which helped women make new starts in their lives by advancing them small amounts of money.

Another bout of illness slowed Mary in 1890, and her daughter Margaret Windeyer helped organize the first meeting of the Women's Literary Society, which had matured into the Womanhood Suffrage League by 1891. Mary Windeyer, now Lady Windeyer as a result of her husband's knighthood earlier in that year, became the first president of this new organization.

Also in 1891, she served as secretary for the second Australasian Conference on Charity, helped establish a Women's College at the University of New South Wales, and led the delegation on suffrage that met with Prime Minister Parkes.

The following year, she continued petitioning for suffrage and helped organize exhibits featuring women's work for inclusion in the 1893 Columbian Exhibition in Chicago. Windeyer was criticized for incorporating sculpture in the collection of exhibits; sewing, dressmaking, and other forms of needlework were considered the only suitable employment for women. She also supported new organizations to promote typewriting and silkgrowing as additional women's professions. A disagreement over rule changes led to her resignation in 1893 as president of the Womanhood Suffrage League. She had, however, begun a suffrage department within the Women's Christian Temperance Union, so the cause of suffrage remained a key focus of her attentions and influence.

Windeyer again organized a hospital in 1893 to care for poor women in their homes. Beginning as a district hospital, it opened its own facility in 1896, served as a training center, and later relocated to a larger premises as Crown Street Women's Hospital. In 1897, she further suggested that Queen Victoria's diamond jubilee fund should be dedicated to the extension of such provisions and accommodations. Sir William went to England in 1896, and Lady Mary followed him with the intention of attending the world conference of the Women's Christian Temperance Union. In September 1897, however, Sir William died suddenly. Lady Mary's larger charitable concerns ended; she returned to her children at "Tomago," the management of the family farms, and local charity work. Windeyer died in December 1912, having impacted public attitudes toward women and children; as she declared in many speeches, there is "no sex in religion, in intellect, in common sense."

SOURCES:
Radi, Heather, ed. *200 Australian Women: A Redress Anthology.* Australia: Women's Redress Press, 1988.

Gillian S. Holmes,
freelance writer,
Hayward, California

Windsor, Alice de (d. 1400).
See Perrers, Alice.

Windsor, Claire (1897–1972)
American silent film star. Born Clara Viola Cronk in Crawker City, Kansas, in 1897; died in 1972; educat-

ed at schools in Topeka and Seattle; married William Boyes (lasted one year); married Bert Lytell (an actor), in 1925 (divorced 1927); children: (first marriage) son Bill Boyes.

Claire Windsor starred in the silents during the 1920s, working for nearly every major Hollywood studio, but retired soon after the advent of sound. In addition to the movies she did for *Lois Weber—*To Please One Woman* (1920), *What's Worth While* (1921), *Too Wise Wives* (1921), *The Blot* (1921), *What Do Men Want?* (1921)—Windsor starred in *Little Church Around the Corner* (1923), *Rupert of Hentzau* (1923), *Dance Madness* (1926), *The Claw* (1927), *Captain Lash* (1929), and many others.

Windsor, duchess of.

See Windsor, Wallis Warfield, duchess of (1895–1986).

Windsor, Katherine (b. 1933).

See Worsley, Katherine.

Windsor, Wallis Warfield, duchess of (1895–1986)

American-born wife of Edward VIII, who abdicated the throne of England for the woman he loved. Name variations: Bessie Wallis Warfield (1895–1916); Wallis Spencer (1916–25); Wallis Simpson (1928–36); Duchess of Windsor (1936–86). Born out of wedlock as Bessie Wallis Warfield at the Monterey Inn, in Blue Ridge Summit, Pennsylvania, on June 19, 1895 (many sources incorrectly cite 1896); died in France on April 24, 1986; daughter of Teackle Wallis Warfield and Alice Montague Warfield (1869–1929); married Earl Winfield "Win" Spencer (a navy aviator), in 1916 (divorced 1925); married Ernest Simpson, in 1928 (divorced 1936); married Edward VIII (1894–1972), king of England (r. 1936–1936) and duke of Windsor, in 1937; no children.

King George V of England was a well-loved king, and greatly mourned at his death in 1936. His son Edward (VIII), prince of Wales, was almost universally admired by the British public who expected great things of their new monarch. But between his father's funeral and his own planned coronation, the news broke that Edward was involved in a love affair with an American woman, Wallis Simpson, who was not only a foreigner but also a double divorcée. He refused to give her up; the prime minister re-

fused to accept her, and so, in an unprecedented drama, the king abdicated his throne to marry Mrs. Simpson. Widely billed as "the romance of the century," the 1936 crisis led to a long, childless marriage in exile for the couple, ending with his death in 1972 and hers in 1986.

Wallis Warfield was born illegitimately in June 1895 and her parents, both from Southern families living in Baltimore, married only a year and a half later. Wallis later lied about the circumstances of her birth as about many other details. When her father Teackle Warfield died of tuberculosis six months after the marriage, her mother **Alice Montague Warfield** took her to live with her sister, who as "Aunt Bessie" would be a lifelong confidante. Poorer than many of her relatives—her uncle was one of America's wealthiest railroad entrepreneurs—Warfield early conceived the ambition to be socially successful and rich. She did not think of herself as a great beauty, but as historian Philip Ziegler notes she had "fine eyes, a radiant complexion, an excellent figure, and a sense of style which was refined with time but apparent from the moment she first took responsibility for her own appearance." Ziegler adds that she compensated for only modest intellectual and artistic accomplishments by deploying "wit, a blazing vitality . . . and a shrewd perception of masculine weaknesses. . . . In society she was ruthless and voracious." Her mother followed her ill-fated first marriage with an equally ill-fated second one in 1908, to a lazy alcoholic who died five years later: Wallis determined to do better.

She attended one of Maryland's most exclusive girls' boarding schools, Oldfields, and, thanks to the munificence of her uncle, had a successful debutante season in Baltimore in 1914. After a string of flirtations she married Earl Winfield Spencer, a Navy aviator, in 1916. He was stationed at Pensacola and during their engagement she witnessed several fatal air crashes, which gave her a persistent fear of flying. Spencer was popular, daring, and rich, but he too proved to be a flagrant alcoholic, so troublesome that, even in the early days of American involvement in World War I, the Navy declined to send him to active duty in France. The couple began spending longer periods apart after an unhappy stay in San Diego during which he also showed homosexual tendencies.

When, after the war, Spencer was stationed in China, Wallis moved to Washington, D.C., and undertook scandalous love affairs with an Argentinean diplomat and Prince Gelasio Caetani, ambassador from Mussolini's Italy, who taught her to admire fascism. In 1924, she was sent to the Far East, partly to be reunited with her husband but also, apparently, to carry confidential military information which the Navy did not want to broadcast by radio. During the later British abdication crisis, a variety of stories circulated to the effect that Wallis Spencer was really, at that point, a Russian spy, that she was selling opium, even that she was studying erotic arts in the Shanghai brothels. The stories emanated from an alleged 1935 "China dossier" which King George V was rumored to have ordered when he realized how serious his son's affair with Mrs. Simpson was becoming. Better documented is an affair she had there with another Italian fascist, Count Galeazzo Ciano. She became pregnant by him, underwent an abortion, and as a result was to suffer for the rest of her life with gynecological complications and infertility. Whatever the truth of the wilder "China" stories, we do know that her attempted reconciliation with Spencer failed and the couple was formally divorced in 1925.

Her second husband, in striking contrast to the first, was Ernest Simpson, an Anglo-American shipping entrepreneur who had served in an English Guards regiment. He was Jewish—the real family name was Solomons—but he kept the fact a secret even from his own daughter by a previous marriage and from Wallis herself. They began an affair in 1925 but his marriage and Wallis' lack of passion for him made it seem no more than another passing liaison at first. Then Ernest's first wife divorced him for adultery and Wallis, finding single life without much money too restrictive, accepted his long-standing offer of marriage. Ernest was a connoisseur of art and architecture, rich, complacent, and well read, and he tried to interest her in his many intellectual diversions. They married in 1928 and settled in London, where she soon became a popular hostess.

Among the Simpsons' circle of friends was **Thelma Furness**, an American heiress and one of the prince of Wales' many mistresses. Furness introduced Wallis to Edward in 1931, and they met periodically over the next few years, becoming steadily closer friends. The prince was already renowned in high society for his love affairs and his eccentric private behavior. He was obsessed with remaining thin and fit, liked to fly, play tennis, golf, and polo, did daily calisthenics and ate guardedly. His sartorial casualness stood in strong contrast to his father's formality, and his love of jazz transformed the mood of royal entertainments. His love affair with Wallis Simpson seems to have begun in early 1934 when

Thelma Furness was away, visiting New York. Ernest Simpson, fully aware of what was happening, connived in the affair, perhaps because he enjoyed the social distinction of being so regularly in royal company.

Most of the prince's household were appalled by Wallis Simpson, whom they found vulgar, ambitious, and hard-hearted. His equerry, John Aird, wrote in August 1934 that, when the royal party at Biarritz was out of the public eye, the prince "has lost all confidence in himself and follows W. around like a dog." Aiming to make her position permanent, Wallis persuaded the prince to cut off all contact with his former lovers, including Thelma Furness and even **Freda Dudley Ward**, the wife of a Liberal member of Parliament with whom he had been involved for more than a decade. Wallis herself was amazed at the way she had now become the cynosure of all eyes in high society. As one biographer records: "Wallis was immensely excited by these unfamiliar social attentions; there is something touchingly naive about her delight in them. . . . In her letters to her aunt that year she writes of her life with the Prince . . . as a fairy tale which is bound to come to an end sooner or later but which she is determined to enjoy while it lasts. . . . 'I never had so much fun before or things so easy and I might as well finish up what youth is left to me with a flourish.'" She was then 39.

Never, it was contended, had there been such a human-interest story since Mark Antony sacrificed an Empire for Cleopatra. . . . On this occasion, American journalists were determined that no leavings should remain to be used by some subsequent Shakespeare.

—**Malcolm Muggeridge**

Already familiar with Italian fascism, she now found herself being courted by the Nazi German diplomatic corps, which were cultivating the prince and understood the need to welcome his favorites too. These contacts, and the dogged support of the British Union of Fascists which she and the prince enjoyed during the abdication crisis, linked her name with fascism permanently and added to her unpopularity in later years. The Germans, knowing of the prince's horrified reaction to the First World War and his eagerness to avoid all future European conflicts, anticipated neutralizing Britain in the coming era of German expansion—he was the embodiment of "appeasement."

The old king's death and funeral in 1936 brought the prince of Wales to the throne. He now moved into Buckingham Palace, where Wallis was a frequent visitor, and together they made drastic changes in the economy of the royal palace and household. Her high-handedness was beginning to win Wallis enemies, however, and the situation escalated into a political crisis when Ernest Simpson declared that he and Wallis were getting a divorce, and the king told the Conservative prime minister, Stanley Baldwin, that he intended to marry her and make her queen. Her letters throughout the crisis show that, though she was determined to marry him if possible, she did not love him; that indeed she regarded his infantile sex play with her and his perpetual telephone calls as annoying. But even detractors had to admit that the king was far happier with her than he had been at any other stage of his life, that she had moderated his drinking and smoking, and that he was delighted by her brusque and domineering manner with him.

The British press of the 1930s was deferential to the royal family, and gave no hint of the mounting crisis or the prince's improprieties. Edward had to endure none of the glaring exposure of his descendants 50 years later. But the American press showed no such restraint, and began publishing lurid stories about the liaison, which fueled the rumors spreading rapidly through England. H.L. Mencken described the scandal as "the best news story since the Resurrection." For awhile, English distributors actually cut out the pages dealing with the affair from imported copies of *Time* magazine. Political opposition to her intensified when the government's Secret Intelligence Service began to suspect that official government business, conveyed to the palace in dispatch boxes, was being read by Mrs. Simpson and that she was passing on state secrets to her Nazi friends.

Esmond Harmsworth, one of the English press barons, met Wallis Simpson late in 1936 while the king was visiting south Wales, and suggested to her the possibility of a morganatic marriage, which would give her the title of duchess but exclude her from official functions and prevent any children she and the king had from succeeding to the throne. She listened favorably but, when this compromise was raised with the king, he indignantly refused and repeated that he planned to make her queen.

Baldwin also disliked the morganatic marriage compromise, and arranged in Cabinet that the government must either approve of Wallis as queen or else the king must abdicate. He knew that British public opinion, combined with the indignation of the British Empire (Australia, Canada, South Africa, and India), would not tolerate Mrs. Simpson as queen. Rumors of a plot against her life circulated in London, possibly started by one of the anti-marriage newspaper barons, and Wallis herself fled for the south of France, urging the king not to abdicate. She apparently hoped to be able to return to London some time after his coronation, when the furor had died down, and resume her position as the royal mistress. In letters, phone calls, and a statement to the gathering international press corps, she urged the king not to abdicate, insisting that rather than let that happen she would "withdraw forthwith from a situation which has been rendered both unhappy and untenable."

A speech by one of the Anglican bishops, hinting that the king was not taking his religious duties very seriously as defender of the faith, finally opened the floodgates of public sensation and details of the situation began to appear in the British newspapers. In London, demonstrations for and against the king gathered outside Buckingham Palace and the prime minister's house, 10 Downing Street. The Labour Party and younger Britons generally favored the marriage while the Conservatives, the Church of England, and older subjects generally opposed it. Winston Churchill, later to be prime minister during the Second World War, was particularly outspoken in his opposition to the marriage but also in his loyalty to the king, with whom he was on terms of close friendship and whom he wanted to preserve from folly. Edward would not be deterred, however, so Baldwin hammered out an abdication agreement by which Edward would get lifelong financial support in exchange for living abroad permanently and yielding the crown to his younger brother George (VI), the duke of York. Edward agreed and, far from being dismayed at the prospect of abdication, showed more signs of happiness, indeed euphoria, than he had in months.

In December 1936, he broadcast from Windsor Castle his decision to abdicate in favor of his brother, and then at once left the country, to stay with his wealthy Rothschild friends in their castle near Vienna, Austria. Ironically, in order for Wallis Simpson's divorce to be finalized without controversy, he was now prevented from seeing her for several months, but they wrote and telephoned daily until they could be reunited. The abdication was for her a bitter disappointment. She had come to believe that all her ambitions might be fulfilled. She had got her man and won from him the supreme sacrifice for her sake, but she had not got the office which had made this otherwise unpromising man supremely attractive in the first place.

The rest of her life was, in most respects, a protracted, 50-year anticlimax. Assured of lifelong wealth and international notoriety, the duke and duchess of Windsor were permanently excluded from Britain. They were married at the Château de Candé in June 1937, once her divorce decree had been finalized, and lived during the next few years in France. They remained on good terms with the Nazi regime in Germany, meeting Hitler at Berchtesgarden the following year. Despite his hopes, however, neither Edward nor his brother, the new King George VI, had any influence over the deteriorating diplomatic situation, and they could do nothing to stop the onset of the Second World War in 1939. Fleeing from France when it fell to Hitler's armies, the couple took refuge for a time in Franco's Spain, another fascist power, where the duke indiscreetly told the American ambassador that Britain ought to consider making a negotiated peace with Hitler. His old friend Winston Churchill, now prime minister, gave Edward a pointedly minor wartime post as governor of the Bahamas, so that he and Wallis spent most of the war years in the Caribbean, which she despised and where she fretted over constant snubs from Britain. They were frequent visitors to America in the postwar years, where they were greeted as social celebrities, members of what came in the 1950s to be called the "international jet-set," but rarely re-entered England.

Relations with the royal family remained chilly for decades. Edward's mother, the widowed Queen *Mary of Teck (1867–1953), had disliked Wallis from the beginning and found her son's behavior disgraceful. She wrote him in 1939: "I do not think you have ever realized the shock which the attitude you took up caused your family and the whole Nation. It seemed inconceivable to those who had made such sacrifices in the war [WWI] that you, as their King, refused a lesser sacrifice." She added that any attempt he might make to return to England "would only mean division and controversy." Queen Mary and the rest of the royal family remained implacably opposed to the duchess herself.

The duchess wrote a successful book of memoirs, *The Heart Has Its Reasons* (1956), which sold very widely and helped to support their lavish way of life. During a brief visit from France to London in 1965 for an eye operation, the duke met for the first time since her accession his niece, Queen *Elizabeth II, daughter and successor of George VI, who had been a young child at the time of his abdication. Two years later, the queen formally invited them both to a commemoration of the 100th anniversary of

Queen Mary's birth and so for the first time, after 31 years, Wallis Windsor appeared in public at a British royal function as duchess of Windsor alongside the queen. The duke died of cancer in 1972, and she lived on, still a famous hostess and international celebrity, until deteriorating health and senility made her reclusive. She died in 1986 at the age of 90 and was buried with full royal honors in Windsor, beside the body of her husband, with the queen in attendance. A subsequent auction of her possessions, chiefly jewelry, raised $50 million. One buyer for some of the more fabulous gems was *Elizabeth Taylor, who outbid Charles, prince of Wales, in the auction. The proceeds went to AIDS research.

SOURCES AND SUGGESTED READING:

Bloch, Michael, ed. *Wallis and Edward: Letters, 1931–1937*. London: Weidenfeld & Nicolson, 1986.

Higham, Charles. *The Duchess of Windsor: The Secret Life*. NY: McGraw-Hill, 1988.

Martin, Ralph G. *The Woman He Loved*. NY: Simon and Schuster, 1974.

Muggeridge, Malcolm. *The Sun Never Sets: The Story of England in the Nineteen Thirties*. NY: Random House, 1940.

Wilson, Edwina. *Her Name Was Wallis Warfield*. NY: E.P. Dutton, 1936.

Windsor, Wallis. *The Heart Has Its Reasons*. NY: McKay, 1956.

Ziegler, Philip. *King Edward VIII: The Official Biography*. London: Collins, 1990.

COLLECTIONS:

Public Records Office, London; British Museum, London; Captured German Materials Collections in the Library of Congress.

Patrick Allitt,
Professor of History, Emory University,
Atlanta, Georgia

Winfrey, Oprah (1954—)

Television talk-show host, actress, and producer, the first African-American woman to helm a national television program, who has become one of the most recognized and influential media personalities in America. Born out of wedlock on January 29, 1954, in Kosciusko, Mississippi; daughter of Vernon Winfrey and Vernita Lee; entered Tennessee State University, 1972.

Raised in poverty on her grandparents' farm before moving to Milwaukee to live with her mother; the following troubled years led to threats to place her in an institution before she moved to Nashville to live with her father, who introduced strict discipline and a respect for education into her life; entered Tennessee State University (1972); went to work as a reporter at a Nashville radio station (1973); moved to television, becoming the first African-American anchorwoman in Nashville (1974); had moved to Baltimore and was hosting a television talk show (1978), the ratings for which became impressive enough to bring an offer to host Chicago's "A.M. Chicago" (1984); show was renamed "The Oprah Winfrey Show" and syndicated nationally (1986); made her film debut in Steven Spielberg's The Color Purple *(1985), receiving an Oscar nomination for her performance (1986); now heads her own production company, which produces her television show along with television mini-series and feature films.*

Oprah Winfrey once recalled that during much of her lonely, poverty-stricken childhood in rural Mississippi, the only audience a talkative child like herself could find was pigs and chickens. She is no less talkative today, but her audience is numbered in the millions of Americans who watch television's most popular chat show or flock to see the feature films in which she performs and which are often produced by her own company. Beginning in the mid-1980s, in fact, Oprah Winfrey has remained America's most influential woman and one of its wealthiest, reported to have earned as much as $95 million in one year; but she is the first to admit that she got that way simply because of her childhood enthusiasm for talking. "I basically am no different from what I was when I was six," she says.

Although what few neighbors there were in tiny Kosciusko, Mississippi, knew all too well about the precocious Winfrey girl, little else about her early years indicated the reputation would spread. She had been born as the result of, as Oprah once put it, a "one day fling under an oak tree." Her father Vernon Winfrey never even knew that **Vernita Lee** was pregnant until the day he received a birth announcement mailed to him 250 miles away, where he had found work, telling him of the birth of a daughter on January 29, 1954, and carrying Vernita's hastily scribbled message, "Send clothes!" Vernon and Vernita never married and would not see each other again until many years later. Vernita had given birth to the child at home using the services of a midwife, who filled out the birth certificate by misspelling the Old Testament name chosen for the girl, *Orpah. With no husband and no chance of earning a living to support her daughter amid the farms of rural Mississippi, Vernita left the child in the care of her parents and moved to Milwaukee to find a job.

For the next seven years, Oprah grew up under the tutelage of her strict Baptist grandparents on an isolated farm in a rundown house with no plumbing. There were no other children within walking distance, the nearest neighbor being an old blind man who lived up the road. Although she came to love her grandmother **Hattie Mae Lee**, whom she called Mama, Oprah was terrified of her grandfather's temper tantrums and occasional beatings with a birch switch. She had become so talkative by the age of three that Hattie Mae was often obliged to tell her granddaughter to sit in a corner and keep her mouth shut when company came to call. When the two of them were alone, however, Hattie Mae took Oprah's education in hand by teaching her to read and write, and telling her not to be afraid of what lay beyond the confines of the farm. "God don't mess with His children," she would say, although Oprah had decided even at this early age that God's white children were the more favored ones. *Shirley Temple (Black) was her girlhood idle, and a clothespin clamped on the nose her favorite method of making it turn up, just like Shirley's did.

What little social life there was in Kosciusko—some 70 miles north of Jackson, the state capital—revolved around the Faith United Mississippi Baptist Church, of which her grandparents were proud members; and it was at a church event that Oprah gave her first public performance at the age of three by reciting her own essay about Jesus during the church's Easter observances. By the time she was ready for kindergarten, her recitations and readings had become so popular that other children at church were taunting her with the names "Preacher" and "Miss Jesus." No doubt it was equally irritating to them when 4-year-old Oprah, arriving in kindergarten and looking over the picture books around the room, wrote a letter to her teacher pointing out she did not belong in kindergarten, but in first grade. After a reading test, Oprah was promoted—not once, but twice, reaching third grade by the time she was six. The next year, Hattie Mae and her husband decided the child had become too much for them and sent their granddaughter north to live with Vernita, who was working in Milwaukee as a maid for $50 a week and who had given birth to a second daughter out of wedlock by the time Oprah arrived from Mississippi.

The temptations of a northern city after the rural isolation of Mississippi, coupled with Vernita's prolonged absences at work during the day and socializing at night, soon found Oprah stealing money from her mother's purse to buy candy and magazines. "I wanted to have money just like the other kids," Winfrey recalled of her first year in Milwaukee. It only took 12 months be-

fore Vernita arrived at the same conclusion as her parents in Mississippi had, sending Oprah off to live with Vernon in Nashville, Tennessee, where the environment was decidedly different. Vernon had married and settled down to a good job as a maintenance engineer at Vanderbilt University, where he saw firsthand the advantages that an education could give a child. His wife **Zelma Winfrey** was of the same mind and drilled Oprah at home in mathematics and the sciences while Vernon set strict rules about his daughter's after-school hours. "It was like military school there," Oprah once said of her father's household, although she admitted the discipline was precisely what she needed. Schools were better in Nashville, too, and Winfrey became particularly fond of a fourth-grade teacher who, she said, instilled the sense of self-confidence that would stand her in such good stead in coming years.

But her peripatetic childhood found her back in Milwaukee after another year, when Vernita married a man with his own son and had decided she wanted her own daughter with her. Oprah was to have spent only that summer of 1963 with her mother, but when September came and Vernon arrived to take her back to Nashville, Vernita refused to let her go. Away from the routine and discipline of the Winfrey household, often left alone with her half-sister and stepbrother while Vernita spent her evenings out, Oprah passed the time reading or watching television, where favorite sitcoms like "Leave It to Beaver" and "I Love Lucy" reinforced the notion of her Shirley Temple days that white skin was the passport to a better life. Then, too, there were the wealthy white families she began to visit when a junior high school teacher recommended her for a scholarship to an exclusive, all-white girls' school in the suburbs. There were earnest, if sometimes clumsy, attempts to treat her as an equal, but the differences between these families and her own were so sharp that Oprah often made up stories about her own home life to compensate. "I wanted a family like everyone else, because I was going to school where kids had mothers and fathers," she once said of this period.

It was only a matter of time before her frustrations began to burst out. There were the casual thefts of money from Vernita's purse, boyfriends of whom her mother had no knowledge, the clandestine entries through her bedroom window in the wee hours of the morning. There was the week Oprah spent living in a hotel room using money given to her by, of all people, **Aretha Franklin**, who stepped out of a limousine one night to give $100 to the teenaged girl who claimed she was penniless and trying to get home; and there was the night Oprah ransacked Vernita's apartment over some trifling dispute, then called the police to report a burglary and an assault. These were only symptoms of something Winfrey kept hidden, a secret so terrible she would be unable to reveal it for nearly 20 years, and then in the most dramatic way possible.

It was when Vernita finally threatened to put her daughter in a juvenile detention home that Vernon Winfrey came to the rescue, Vernita being only too glad to let Oprah return to her father in Nashville. "When my father took me in," Winfrey has often said, "it changed the course of my life. He saved me." An indication of Vernon's belief in strict discipline could be found in the sign which hung in the combination barbershop and grocery store he now owned. ATTENTION TEENAGERS, it said: IF YOU ARE TIRED OF BEING HASSLED BY UNREASONABLE PARENTS, NOW IS THE TIME FOR ACTION! LEAVE HOME AND PAY YOUR OWN WAY WHILE YOU STILL KNOW EVERYTHING.

To do less than your best is a sin.

—Oprah Winfrey

Vernon and Zelma saw to it that Oprah's merely average grades in school improved to the point where she became an honor student at Nashville's East High School, where she was one of the first black students enrolled after desegregation, and that her television viewing was restricted mostly to watching the news, Oprah being particularly impressed by the well-dressed, well-spoken newscasters. The *Today* show's *Barbara Walters became her early model. Zelma also set a reading list for Oprah that included the great authors of African-American literature—*Margaret Walker and *Zora Neale Hurston, among them. So effective were Vernon and Zelma's attentions that Oprah was elected student government president at East High and was chosen to represent her school at the Nixon administration's Conference on Youth in 1970. With natural poise and her gift for public speaking, Oprah was soon invited to enter the Nashville Fire Department's Miss Fire Prevention beauty pageant, sponsored by the city's most popular radio station, WVOL. She became the first African-American woman to win the event and, more important, entered the business that would bring her national fame when WVOL offered her a position as a part-time newscaster. "She was aggressive," an employee at the station recalled at the time, "not shy at all. She knew where she was going." Even Vernon had to approve when Oprah next won the Miss Black

Nashville beauty contest and its first prize of a four-year scholarship to Tennessee State University, where she enrolled in 1972 as a speech and drama major. That same year, she won the Miss Black Tennessee pageant, and had a good chance at the Miss Black America title had she not grown disillusioned with the whole process, deliberately presenting herself on the Miss Black America stage in a drab outfit with little makeup. Although she predictably lost the title, Winfrey later said she felt a sense of victory by taking control of her own life with her decision.

She arrived on the Tennessee State campus in the midst of the Black Pride movement of the 1970s, although she felt no need to demonstrate for something she had long taken for granted in light of Zelma's choice of reading. "I believe those women [authors] are part of my legacy, and the bridges that I crossed to get where I am today," Winfrey once said. Besides, Oprah had taken to heart Vernon's dictum that the best way to advance one's position in life was to be the best at one's chosen role. For Winfrey, that role increasingly seemed to be in broadcasting. In 1973, she was offered a job as a weekend television news anchor on Nashville's CBS affiliate, WTVF, becoming the city's first black news anchor. "I was a token," she said, "but I was a happy, paid token." After three years, a third job offer came along, this time at Baltimore's WJZ as a co-anchor on the station's evening newscast. Even though she was 22 by now, it was the first time Winfrey had been away from her family. Almost as bad as the loneliness and her apprehensions about moving to such a large market was the station's initial dissatisfaction with her personality on the air. She was not authoritative enough, the station complained, packing her off to New York for lessons with a voice coach to lend her delivery a more business-like air. The attempt failed to squelch Winfrey's natural friendliness and conversational tone, and her future in Baltimore was looking decidedly questionable when a change in management at the station brought a fresh and, as it would prove, momentous idea. Why not, the new station manager proposed, give Oprah Winfrey a talk show?

Winfrey was teamed as a co-host with one of the station's best-known reporters on "People Are Talking," WJZ's half-hour morning chat show meant to be a challenge to the top-rated "Phil Donahue Show." Within weeks, it was obvious that the very affability the station had complained about earlier was Winfrey's greatest asset. "People Are Talking" overtook the Donahue show and was syndicated to 12 other markets after its first year on the air. It should have

Oprah
Winfrey

been a triumphant vindication for Winfrey, but instead she found herself sinking into a deep depression, driven by several failed love affairs. The depression became so severe that Winfrey found herself one night writing out a suicide note before she forced herself to confront the fact that she had allowed herself to be emotionally abused by men. "You're not getting knocked around physically," she said, "but in terms of your ability to soar, your wings are clipped." Winfrey marks the beginning of her climb to the top of her career from this newfound commitment to determine the course of her own life.

While "People Are Talking" continued to gain in ratings, Oprah set as her goal a move to an even larger market; and when one of the producers of the show left to take on production duties for a morning chat show in Chicago, opportunity knocked. Like Baltimore's WJZ, Chicago's ABC-affiliate WLS needed to resuscitate its ailing "A.M. Chicago," also suffering at the hands of Phil Donahue. Winfrey was offered the show. She signed a four-year contract at $200,000 a year, even though friends warned her that Chicago, with its troubled racial history, would be a difficult challenge for a black woman thrust into such a public spotlight. The station's manager was more reassuring. "I don't care what color you are," he told Winfrey. "You can be green. All we want to do is win." Oprah made his wish come true, boosting the show's ratings after her first month on the air by abandoning the carefully scripted questions provided to her and using her instincts to interview her guests. Her first major interview on the show was with Paul McCartney, but Winfrey's obvious empathy with whomever she was talking to at the time and her ability to relate her personal experiences to the subject at hand convinced the show's producers that her guests and topics should be drawn from everyday life. "Talk show hosts didn't talk about themselves," fellow TV-host Maury Povitch said of television talk in those days. "Oprah opened up a lot of new windows." The show in which Winfrey interviewed three women from the Ku Klux Klan drew considerable attention, less for the crackpot theories the women espoused than for Winfrey's unruffled calm as her guests explained why blacks were inferior to whites and why their organization was committed to defending whites. Winfrey even managed to draw laughs from her audience when, after her invitation to lunch was refused by her guests, she innocently asked, "Not even if I pay?"

The decision to take the show national was hastened when Winfrey attracted major attention with her first film role in Steven Spielberg's *The Color Purple*, based on the **Alice Walker** novel and released in 1985. Winfrey had been recommended for the part of the abused wife Sofia by the film's co-producer, Quincy Jones, who was visiting Chicago when he saw her television show. The film starred two formidable Hollywood personalities, **Whoopi Goldberg** and Danny Glover, and Oprah found herself in the unusual position of being a subordinate. "I'm not accustomed to being intimidated by big stars or anybody," she said, "but this time I wasn't in control." Nevertheless, she held her own well enough to be nominated for Best Supporting Actress for her work in the film. The next year, she accepted a role in a film adaptation of Richard Wright's germinal novel *Native Son*, playing the mother of the film's central character, Bigger Thomas, and basing her role, she later said, on her own mother. With her growing fame came the decision to rename her television show "The Oprah Winfrey Show" and to syndicate it nationally, making Winfrey the first black woman to have her own national television program. Within six months, "The Oprah Winfrey Show" was America's highest-rated talk show.

The confessional nature of many of the programs fascinated Winfrey's daytime audience, no more so than the show in 1985 on childhood sexual abuse. As one of her guests told of being sexually molested as a girl, Winfrey suddenly burst into tears, threw her arms around her guest, and then revealed to her millions of viewers the secret she had hidden from the world for so long. She told of being raped at the age of nine by a 19-year-old cousin during her years in Milwaukee, and of being sexually molested over a period of five years by a boyfriend of her mother's and by an uncle. "You lose your childhood when you've been abused," Winfrey later told a Congressional committee which was considering a bill she had promoted to make an FBI database on known sexual molesters available to local police. Later still, Winfrey's half-sister sold a story to the tabloids claiming Oprah had become pregnant at the age of 14 and that her baby, born prematurely, had died. Winfrey never denied the truth of the story but has so far refused to discuss it publicly. These revelations of the mid-1980s underscored the lines Winfrey's character speaks in *The Color Purple*: "All my life I had to fight," Sofia says. "I had to fight my daddy, I had to fight my uncles, I had to fight my brothers. A child ain't safe in a family of mens."

Releasing the burden of her past history seemed to energize her career even further. "Doing good film is one of the best ways to raise consciousness," she told an interviewer in 1986 after announcing that she was forming her own production company, Harpo Films (Harpo is Oprah spelled backwards), housed in a block-long former warehouse in Chicago which she purchased for $20 million. Winfrey thus became the first black woman to own a studio, and only the third woman in American history, after *Mary Pickford** and *Lucille Ball**. Winfrey used her show to explore sometimes painful subjects, as when she broadcast live from Forsyth County,

Georgia, in 1987 with an all-white audience deliberately containing several outspoken white supremacists. (In one pre-taped segment, Winfrey ventured into a grocery store and offered her hand to the owner. "We don't shake hands with niggers here," the man proclaimed. "Good thing for the niggers," Winfrey shot back before turning and walking out.) That same year, after winning three daytime Emmy Awards, Winfrey announced an agreement to buy the rights to her show from Capitol Cities/ABC, with which she also negotiated a deal to broadcast her company's first major television film, "The Women of Brewster Place," based on the **Gloria Naylor** novel. Winfrey played the matronly Mattie Michael in Naylor's story of the African-American women who inhabit an inner-city brownstone. While the film received respectable ratings, the weekly series spun off from it failed to find a consistent audience and was soon canceled; but Oprah pressed on with a 1991 TV adaptation of Alex Kotlowitz's *There Are No Children Here*, examining the experiences of black children growing up in a Chicago housing project.

Meanwhile, the national addiction to confessional chat shows continued to grow. Although Winfrey's show held its own against newcomers, competition for viewers forced the nature of the shows' content to go beyond exploring real-life problems to sensational, even lurid, depictions of bizarre relationships and sexual abnormalities. "Trash Talk" became the byword of daytime television by the mid-1990s. Winfrey's show featured its share of such material, but when a former guest on a rival show was murdered by the man whom he had identified on the air as the object of his unspoken love, Oprah vowed to lift her own show's material to a higher plane. Among her innovations was "Oprah's Book Club," a regular discussion of notable books of the day, and examinations of legitimate social issues like welfare reform and women's rights. Viewers could also draw inspiration from Winfrey's descriptions of her battle with a long-time weight problem, and share her confession during a show on drug abuse of her own use of cocaine in the 1970s. Her pervasive influence on the national dialogue came to the fore in 1996 when she was sued for defamation by the Texas Cattlemen's Association after a militant vegetarian on one of her shows claimed that eating beef could lead to so-called "mad cow disease," prompting Winfrey to exclaim that the information "just stopped me cold from eating another burger!" A Texas court decided in Winfrey's favor two years later, although it gently expressed the opinion that she may have "melo-dramatized" the dangers of beef-eating. The incident only strengthened her show's ratings even further and allowed Oprah to negotiate a renewal contract in 1995 containing an unprecedented clause giving her the right to cancel the show without penalty at any point during the contract's five-year term.

By the time of the renewal, Winfrey had nearly completed another round of complex negotiations for a project she had first undertaken a decade earlier. In 1986, she had optioned the film rights to *Toni Morrison's Pulitzer Prize-winning novel *Beloved*, a spiritually tinged narrative of redemption set just after the Civil War. The book's story of Sethe, a former slave who must come to terms with a horrifying secret from her past, touched Oprah deeply. Ignoring warnings that the novel's complex structure, psychological texture and underlying theme of infanticide made it impossible to film, Winfrey guided the screenplay through several versions with three different writers and finally managed to bring the film to the screen after a tortuous process she described in her book *The Road to Beloved*. Winfrey not only produced the film as part of a multi-picture deal with Disney Entertainment, but took the emotionally difficult role of Sethe, playing opposite Danny Glover, as the ex-slave Paul D, and **Thandie Newton**, as the daughter known as Beloved. Winfrey described her own self-doubts as the film began production in North Carolina under Jonathan Demme's direction, but felt at the end of ten weeks of shooting that the film would be her crowning achievement. Unfortunately, critics and audiences alike did not agree. "Some audience members . . . will find it confusing or too convoluted," said Roger Ebert, although his review of the film was generally favorable. "It does not provide the kind of easy lift at the end that they might expect. Sethe's tragic story is the kind where the only happy ending is that it is over." **Janet Maslin**, writing in *The New York Times*, advised her readers that familiarity with the book would help them understand the film's structure. "In so ambitiously bringing this story to the screen, Ms. Winfrey underscores a favorite, invaluable credo: read the book," she wrote. But it was not only the structure of the picture that disturbed filmgoers. The picture's frank depiction of the brutalities of slavery and the horrifying murder at the center of the story proved too much for most audiences. Winfrey was devastated by the film's reception but discounted rumors that she was giving up the film business, preferring to look on the experience as a lesson in matching material to the market.

Meanwhile, "The Oprah Winfrey Show" continues as the nation's top-rated TV talk show and Oprah's remarkable influence on American thought and habit goes on unabated. But one thing is still missing—a long-awaited autobiography, which Winfrey completed and nearly published in 1993 but later withdrew. "I am in the heart of the learning curve," she says. "I feel there are important discoveries yet to be made."

SOURCES:

Mair, George. *Oprah Winfrey: The Real Story.* Secaucus, NJ: Carol Publishing, 1994.

Nicholson, Lois. *Oprah Winfrey.* NY: Chelsea House, 1994.

Norman Powers,
writer-producer, Chelsea Lane Productions,
New York, New York

Wingo, Effiegene Locke (1883–1962)

Effiegene Locke Wingo

American legislator and politician. Name variations: Effiegene Locke. Born on April 13, 1883, in Lockesburg, Arkansas; died on September 19, 1962, in Burlington, Ontario, Canada; descendant of Representative Matthew Locke of North Carolina; attended

public and private schools; studied music at the Union Female College in Mississippi; graduated from Maddox Seminary in Little Rock, Arkansas, 1901; married Otis Theodore Wingo (died 1930).

Completed her husband's term of office as a U.S. Representative following his death; aided her Arkansas district in the Depression years; served on the Committee on Foreign Affairs; created the Ouachita National Forest game refuge and Ouachita National Park; co-founded the National Institute of Public Affairs, offering Washington internships to students.

Effiegene Locke Wingo, the great-great-great-granddaughter of Representative Matthew Locke of North Carolina, rose to a seat in Congress upon the death of her husband Otis Wingo in 1930. Born in 1883, in Lockesburg, Arkansas, she received her early schooling at nearby public and private schools. She later studied music at the Union Female College in Oxford, Mississippi, and graduated from Little Rock's Maddox Seminary in 1901. She moved to Texarkana, Arkansas, in 1895 and two years later to De-Queen, Arkansas, where she made her home. She had met Otis Theodore Wingo at a Confederate veterans' reunion in DeQueen. Elected to the U.S. Congress as a Democrat representing Arkansas in 1912, Otis sustained serious injuries in an automobile accident in 1926, and Effiegene worked in his congressional office while he recuperated. When he died in 1930, Effiegene, who had support from both the Democratic and Republican central committees in the Fourth District, was nominated for election to finish her husband's unexpired term in the 71st Congress and to serve in the 72nd Congress to which Otis had been nominated prior to his death. On November 4, 1930, she won both the special election for the first term and the general election for the second.

Although Wingo had a broad base of support, her district faced formidable problems. The effects of the Great Depression had devastated the region, and agricultural woes beset the area as a result of the drought and other natural disasters that precipitated the Dust Bowl. After being sworn in on December 1, 1930, Wingo immediately sought a number of relief measures for the district. In the 71st Congress, she served on the committee on accounts and the committee on insular affairs. During the 72nd Congress, she held a seat on the committee on foreign affairs. Her sponsorships included a bill to complete the building of a railroad bridge near the Morris Ferry crossing of the Little River in Arkansas. She also developed legislation for a game refuge within the existing Ouachita National Forest and for the creation of the Ouachita National Park. These measures all aided the wounded economy of the area. In February 1932, Wingo declared that she would not stand for reelection. She ended her congressional career on March 3, 1933.

During her retirement years, Wingo co-founded the National Institute of Public Affairs to encourage interest in public service by sponsoring student internships in Washington, D.C. She also participated in research and educational work. Wingo lived the remainder of her life in DeQueen, Arkansas. She died on September 19, 1962, while visiting her son in Burlington, Ontario, Canada, and was interred in Rock Creek Cemetery in Washington, D.C.

SOURCES:

Office of the Historian. *Women in Congress, 1917–1990.* Commission on the Bicentenary of the U.S. House of Representatives, 1991.

Gillian S. Holmes,
freelance writer,
Hayward, California

Winkelmann, Maria (1670–1720).

See Kirch, Maria Winkelmann.

Winkworth, Catherine (1827–1878)

English poet and translator. Born on September 13, 1827, in London, England; died of heart failure on July 1, 1878; daughter of Henry Winkworth (a silk merchant) and Susanna (Dickenson) Winkworth; sister of Susanna Winkworth (1820–1884); educated by governesses and tutors; privately studied German language and literature.

Born in 1827, in the Holborn district of London, Catherine Winkworth was the fourth daughter of **Susanna Dickenson Winkworth**, a farmer's daughter from Kent, and Henry Winkworth, a silk merchant whose father was an evangelical cleric. The family moved to Manchester when she was young, and she and her sisters were privately educated by governesses and tutored by two celebrated Unitarian clerics: the Reverend William Gaskell (later husband of poet and novelist *Elizabeth Gaskell) and the Reverend James Martineau (brother of *Harriet Martineau, a fervent abolitionist and writer). The Gaskells shared friendships with many contemporary writers, including Charles Dickens, and Catherine later credited Reverend Gaskell for her appreciation and knowledge of English literature. In 1841, when Catherine was 14 years

old, her mother died; four years later, her father remarried. That year, Catherine traveled to Dresden, Germany, to live with an aunt and act as governess to her cousins.

Catherine developed a fluency in German and an intense interest in German literature; like her elder sister, *Susanna Winkworth, she was an extraordinarily gifted translator. Catherine studied and translated German hymns, including a first collection of translations of common hymns in *Lyra Germanica*, published in 1855. More than 20 editions of the book were published. In 1858, a second series was printed and a third set of hymns followed the next year. Scholars credit Catherine's translations with familiarizing English readers with German hymns. Baron Bunsen, a former German ambassador, suggested that the hymns be published with music, and Winkworth published *The Chorale Book for England* in 1862. Her subsequent writing extended to translations of German prose as well as hymns in *Veni Sancti Spiritus* (1865), and a set of biographical sketches, *Christian Singers of Germany* (1869).

In England, the Winkworths had endured financial losses and moved to Clifton on the outskirts of Bristol. Catherine, perceiving an opportunity to promote higher education for women, organized lectures and classes to prepare women to take the Cambridge examinations. She helped found Bristol University College, later Bristol University, and acted as a Cheltenham Ladies College council member. She also served as a governor for Red Maid's School in Bristol and promoted the creation of Clifton High School for Girls. In 1868, Winkworth joined the Committee on Higher Education for Women, becoming its secretary in 1870. With her older sister Susanna, she served as a delegate to the German Conference on Women's Work in 1872. In 1878, Winkworth traveled to Monnetier, France, to nurse her invalid nephew where she suffered a fatal heart attack and died on July 1, 1878. After her death, two scholarships for women were established in her memory at Bristol University.

SOURCES:

Kunitz, Stanley J., and Howard Haycraft, eds. *Twentieth Century Authors.* NY: H.W. Wilson, 1942.

Shattock, Joanne. *The Oxford Guide to British Women Writers.* Oxford: Oxford University Press, 1993.

Gillian S. Holmes,
freelance writer,
Hayward, California

Winkworth, Susanna (1820–1884)

English writer, translator, and social reformer. Born on August 13, 1820, in London, England; died on Novem-

ber 25, 1884, in Clifton, Bristol, England; daughter of Henry Winkworth (a silk merchant) and Susanna (Dickenson) Winkworth; sister of Catherine Winkworth (1827–1878); educated by governesses and tutors; privately studied German language and literature.

Selected writings: translation (with substantial addition of new material) of Niebuhr's Life *(1851–52); translation of* Theologica Germanica *(1854); translation and completion of Hare's* Life of Luther *(1855); translation of Bunsen's* Signs of the Times *(1856); translation of the life and sermons of John Tauler (1857); translation of Max Muller's* German Love from the Papers of an Alien *(1858); translation of Bunsen's* God in History *(1868–70).*

Born in London on August 13, 1820, Susanna Winkworth was one of four daughters of Henry Winkworth, a silk merchant and son of an evangelical cleric, and **Susanna Dickenson Winkworth**, daughter of a Kent farmer. In 1829, Henry moved his family to Manchester where the daughters were educated by governesses and tutors, including two distinguished Unitarian ministers, the Reverend William Gaskell and the Reverend James Martineau. Gaskell later married *Elizabeth Gaskell, a highly regarded novelist and friend of Charles Dickens and *Charlotte Brontë. Martineau was the brother of abolitionist and writer *Harriet Martineau.

Susanna became interested in German history during the course of her studies, and both she and her sister *Catherine Winkworth were extraordinarily gifted translators. Susanna confided to her friend Elizabeth Gaskell that she would like to translate the existing biography of the German historian and statesman Barthold Georg Niebuhr into English. Niebuhr, a professor of history in Berlin and Prussian ambassador to the Vatican, had altered the study of history by developing a critical approach. Following their conversation in 1850, Gaskell arranged for Winkworth to meet Baron Bunsen, the acting German ambassador to England in Rome. Susanna worked as Bunsen's secretary in Bonn, Germany, while completing translations and original research related to her interest in Niebuhr. She completed her translation of Niebuhr's *Life* in 1851, adding such extensive new material in the form of letters and essays that the biography essentially became an original work. Chapman & Hall published it in 1851–52.

Meanwhile, Bunsen had become Winkworth's mentor in German literature and suggested that she translate the *Theologica Germanica*, a text that had been discovered and published by Martin Luther in 1516. Her translation was completed and published in 1854, containing a preface by Charles Kingsley, the novelist and cleric probably best known for his children's book *The Water-Babies*. Historian Julius Charles Hare had begun a life of Martin Luther and Winkworth finished the biography in 1855. She also translated Bunsen's own works, *Signs of the Times* (1856) and *God in History* (1868–70). Winkworth further translated the biography and sermons of theologian John Tauler (1857) and the work *German Love from the Papers of an Alien* (1858), written by Max Muller.

After the Winkworth family suffered financial setbacks, Susanna moved with them to Clifton, a part of the city of Bristol in southwestern England. Both Susanna and Catherine became activists in local causes. Susanna's attention turned first to establishing higher standards of housing for the poor. She also shared Catherine's interest in promoting higher education for women. While Catherine accomplished more notable achievements with respect to women's education and betterment, both Winkworths were delegates to the 1872 German Conference on Women's Work. Susanna engaged in a number of other philanthropic efforts before she died in Clifton on November 25, 1884, having outlived her younger sister by six years.

SOURCES:
The Concise Dictionary of National Biography. Oxford: Oxford University Press, 1992.
Shattock, Joanne. *The Oxford Guide to British Women Writers.* Oxford: Oxford University Press, 1993.

Gillian S. Holmes,
freelance writer,
Hayward, California

Winlock, Anna (1857–1904)

American astronomer. Born in 1857 in Cambridge, Massachusetts; died in 1904 in Cambridge; daughter of Joseph Winlock (an astronomer) and Isabella (Lane) Winlock; received high school education; self-taught astronomer.

Anna Winlock was born in Cambridge, Massachusetts, in 1857, the elder daughter of Joseph and **Isabella Winlock**. Joseph, an astronomer, was the third director of the Harvard College Observatory. Anna took an avid interest in his work and exhibited remarkable abilities in mathematics from a young age. In 1869, when she was 12 years old, she and her father traveled to Kentucky to observe a solar eclipse. She completed grade school and high school just before her father died in June 1875. Winlock never received any further formal education, but taught herself astronomy and followed in her father's career, becoming one of the first women to hold a paid position as a staff member at the Harvard College Observatory.

Although Winlock did not contribute to the body of astronomical theory, she was a skilled observer, mathematician, calculator, and analyst of astronomical data. She could comprehend large amounts of raw information and assimilate it into a more accessible form. Performing a wide range of tasks, Winlock completed tedious calculations related to meridian circle observations, and made independent observations and computations. While still in school, she assisted staff at the Harvard College Observatory with work on a comprehensive star catalogue. The Cambridge observatory was one of many observatories worldwide that participated in the enormous project of producing the comprehensive *Astronomischer Gesellschaft*. The sky had been subdivided into zones or sections by circles that paralleled the celestial equator, and the Harvard Observatory worked on the "Cambridge zone." Winlock continued working on this project, which lasted nearly as long as her life, after formally joining the staff. Astronomer William Rogers, who was responsible for the project, observed a series of assistants who joined and left the tedious project while Winlock remained. Winlock earned Rogers' respect, not only as an assistant but as a true scientific colleague.

Winlock's other research at the Observatory included supervising the preparation of a table listing the relative positions of variable stars in clusters and their comparison stars; this work was published in Volume 38 of the Observatory's *Annals*. Winlock determined the path of the asteroid Eros, one of the largest inner asteroids. She also found the circular orbit for the asteroid Ocllo, and later assisted in determining its elliptical elements. Her most significant independent investigation, a catalogue of the stars near the North and South poles, was the most complete compilation assembled at that time. Documentation of her work was published in the *Annals*, volume 17, parts 9 through 10. Winlock's dedicated work contributed significantly to the growing field of astronomy. She died in Cambridge, Massachusetts, in 1904, still a member of the staff of the Harvard College Observatory.

SOURCES:

Ogilvie, Marilyn Bailey. *Women in Science*. Cambridge, MA: Cambridge Press, 1993.

Gillian S. Holmes,
freelance writer,
Hayward, California

Winn, Anona.

See Box, Muriel for sidebar.

Winnemucca, Sarah (1844–1891)

Native American who lectured and wrote about the ill-treatment of her people and campaigned for the rights of American Indians. Name variations: Sarah Winnemucca Hopkins; Paiute name was Thoc-me-tony, Thocmetony, or Toc-me-to-ne ("Shell-Flower"). Born in 1844 (some sources cite 1842) near Humboldt Lake, in present-day northern Nevada; died of tuberculosis at Henry's Lake, Nevada, on October 17 (some sources cite 16), 1891; daughter of Paiute Chief Winnemucca II and Tuboitonie (a Paiute woman and hunter-gatherer); attended St. Mary's Convent in San Jose, California, 1860; spoke English and Spanish as well as three Indian dialects; married an unidentified Paiute man, around 1861 (divorced); married Edward C. Bartlett (a first lieutenant), on January 29, 1871 (divorced 1876); married Joseph Satwaller, on November 13, 1878; married Lewis H. Hopkins, on December 5, 1881 (died 1887); children: none.

Lived with the family of Major William Ormsby, a stagecoach agent, in Mormon Station, Nevada, now known as Genoa, Nevada (1857); served as an official interpreter for the Army post at Camp McDermitt in northern Nevada (1868); interpreted for Sam B. Parrish, at the Malheur Agency in Oregon (1875); served the U.S. Army as an interpreter, scout, and peacemaker under General Oliver O. Howard, in the Bannock War (1878); following the war, lectured in major Western cities on behalf of justice for Indians and, accompanied by her father Chief Winnemucca II, went to Washington to plead for the Indians' cause (1880); went East to lecture on Indian rights and became the protege of Elizabeth Palmer Peabody and her sister Mary Peabody Mann (1883); wrote Life Among the Paiutes: Their Wrongs and Claims, *edited by Mary Peabody Mann; wrote a pamphlet, "Sarah Winnemucca's Practical Solution of the Indian Problem"; opened the Peabody Indian School for Paiute children; became an important lobbyist for Indian policy reform.*

Born in 1844 near Humboldt Lake, Nevada, Sarah Winnemucca was a member of the Northern Paiutes, an Indian tribe from the desert plateaus of western Nevada and southeastern Oregon. Her father Winnemucca II, whose name meant "the giver" or "one who looks after the Numa" people, was a shaman and, as his father before him, the recognized chief of the Northern Paiutes. Sarah's Paiute name was Thocmetony, meaning "Shellflower," although she was best known by her Christian name, Sarah, which she received from a white employer when she was 13 years old.

During Sarah Winnemucca's early childhood, her people's way of life was undergoing upheaval and change. The Paiutes' traditional hunting and gathering activities were increasingly curtailed by the advancement of white people onto their ancestral lands. In addition to appropriating Paiute land, the white settlers brought diphtheria and typhus to the Humboldt River. A peace-loving people, the Paiutes welcomed the white settlers, but Winnemucca developed an early fear of their noisy guns and pale skin. Her grandfather Chief Winnemucca I had accompanied Captain John Frémont on an expedition through the Sierra Nevada Mountains to California. Winnemucca grew up listening to his stories of white people traveling in "houses on water" (steamboats) and living in big brick buildings in cities.

In 1850, her grandfather took a group of 30 Paiutes to California, including six-year-old Sarah, her mother, and her four siblings. The journey did little to alleviate her fear of white people, and most of her time was spent huddled under a blanket, crying, or standing behind the protective shield of her brothers. When she returned home, her people were in mourning: Paiute families were dying of typhus as prospective gold miners continued to settle on Paiute lands. Winnemucca made additional trips to California with her grandfather and, by the time she was ten, she had learned to speak Spanish from some of her relatives who had married Spaniards.

When a more warlike tribe of Indians began to skirmish with the white settlers, the government moved all of the Indians in the region to the Pyramid Lake Reservation in northern Nevada. The Paiutes were told that life on the reservation would be advantageous. They would be given farms, food, and clothing.

In 1857, 13-year-old Winnemucca and her sister joined the household of Major William Ormsby, an agent of the Carson Valley Stage Company, in Genoa, where they worked as domestics and companions to Ormsby's daughter **Lizzie Ormsby**. During this time, Winnemucca learned to speak English and to read and write.

Two years later, the sisters returned home at their father's request; silver mines had been discovered in the Washoe district, and tension between the Paiutes and the whites was increasing. By spring of 1860, the situation was close to a state of war. When Major Ormsby led a group of

Opposite page

Sarah

Winnemucca

80 white settlers to attack the Paiutes at Pyramid Lake, he and his men were ambushed and slain before they could open fire. In spite of such violence, the Paiutes strongly desired peace, and by the end of the summer an armistice was settled.

Sarah's grandfather Chief Winnemucca, who had always advocated peaceful relations with the whites, fell ill shortly thereafter, in October 1860. According to his dying wishes, Sarah and her sister were sent to a convent school in San Jose, California. Their time there, however, would prove brief. After three weeks, the girls were sent home at the request of white parents who did not approve of Indians attending school with their children.

For the Paiutes, life on the reservation eroded their traditional nomadic existence. As white settlers destroyed the pine-nut trees needed for sustenance through the winter months, Paiute pleas to government officials fell on deaf ears. Consequently, Sarah and her father Chief Winnemucca sought to communicate their plight to the white populace. In 1864, they traveled to Virginia City, Nevada, where Chief Winnemucca addressed several crowds on the city streets. Acting as his interpreter, Sarah related how her people had befriended the whites, but that they were dying of starvation. She and her father were able to raise enough money to buy a few sacks of flour and some blankets, but their endeavor was not as successful as they had hoped.

When they returned home, conditions were the same. Food and supplies did not arrive as frequently as needed, and many of the 600 Paiutes living on the reservation were near starvation. Over the next few years, hostilities between whites and Paiutes broke out sporadically; in an attempt to stave off the destruction of his people, Chief Winnemucca eventually left the reservation with a group of Paiutes. Many whites continued to appropriate land on the reservation for their cattle and to make room for the new railroad.

In 1868, Sarah Winnemucca and her brother Natchez were invited by Captain Jerome of the Eighth Cavalry to come to Camp McDermit, where they were told to look for their father. Sarah was also hired as an interpreter and scout at $65 per month. In July, when her father and 490 Paiutes arrived at Camp McDermit and were given much-needed food and clothing, she was told about the ill-treatment of those Paiutes remaining on the Pyramid Lake Reservation. Indian agent Parker reported to his superiors that the "Indians were never so happy, or so well provided for," a great contradiction considering that many Paiutes were dying of measles, small-pox and starvation. With the hope that the new Indian superintendent to Nevada, Major Henry Douglass, would be more sympathetic, the Paiutes would agree to remain on the Pyramid Lake Reservation if they were given small farms and taught how to plant and harvest.

In April 1870, when Sarah Winnemucca wrote a letter to Major Douglass relating the situation, he was so impressed by her thoughtful and articulate communication that he had it circulated among his colleagues and sent on to Washington. She wrote of the existing reservation system:

> If this is the kind of civilization awaiting us on the Reserves, God grant that we may never be compelled to go on one, as it is much preferable to live in the mountains and drag out an existence in our native manner.

Nonetheless, she indicated that if they were given land to live on and taught the skills of farming, "the savage (as he is called today) will be a thrifty and law abiding member of the community fifteen or twenty years hence."

Winnemucca's fame as a spokesperson for her people spread, and several articles about her appeared in various magazines. After their meeting, Major Douglass described her as:

> A plain Indian woman, passably good looking, with some education and [she] possesses much natural shrewdness and intelligence. She converses well and seems select in the use of terms. She conforms readily to civilized customs, and will as readily join in an Indian dance.

In spite of his sympathy for the Paiutes, Douglass' plans for improving the reservation system were abated when he was replaced by the American Baptist Home Mission Society. For the next several years, the Pyramid Lake Reservation was run by agents from the Mission Society who were unable to meet the demands of the position.

During this time, Winnemucca was married briefly to Lieutenant Edward C. Bartlett, a soldier who had commanded Camp McDermit in 1870. Bartlett was a drunkard who not only spent any money that she made, but also began to pawn her jewelry. For the next several years, she worked at various jobs in an attempt to support herself; she also continued to write letters and travel to cities in an effort to present the problems that the Paiutes faced while living on the reservation.

In April 1875, the Paiutes were finally given an official home with good soil and a pleasant climate on a large tract of land in southeast Ore-

gon known as the Malheur Reservation. Winnemucca accepted an invitation by the Indian agent Samuel Parrish to be the reservation's interpreter. Unlike the previous agents, Parrish not only respected the Paiutes and taught them how to plant and harvest crops, but he also encouraged them to work hard and paid them for any job done. A year later, Winnemucca was happily working as a teacher's assistant at the reservation school run by Parrish's wife.

The Paiutes' happiness was short-lived, however, for Parrish was abruptly replaced by Major William V. Rinehart in June 1876. Violent and authoritarian, Rinehart, who had engineered his job through political influence, quickly alienated the Paiutes. Abolishing individual farms, he made the Indians work for him; instead of wages, they were paid with the food and clothing that had already been granted the Indians by treaty. When Winnemucca wrote a letter of protest, Rinehart dismissed her from her position as interpreter, and she was banished from the reservation. During this time, she married for a second time although no details of the marriage survive. Her second husband was Joseph Satwaller, a resident of Grant County, Oregon; unfortunately, this marriage, like her first, was disappointing and brief.

The woman who was called "The Princess" by Whites, and "Mother" by her tribe, was also surely the most famous Indian woman on the Pacific Coast.

—Frederick J. Dockstader

In April 1878, Winnemucca was asked to return to Malheur to obtain support from the soldiers at Camp Harney against Rinehart who was withholding supplies and food from the starving Paiutes. Many Bannock Indians, now living on the reservation, were becoming increasingly hostile towards Rinehart and other white settlers. Before she arrived at Malheur the hostilities had turned into open rebellion. Although the Paiutes did not wish to join the hostiles, Winnemucca's father and a small group of Paiutes were forced to travel with the Bannocks. Once apprised, Winnemucca took a daring trip over mountainous terrain to rescue her father and 75 men, women and children from the Bannock camp. The Bannock War, however, had just begun.

During the remainder of the war, Winnemucca worked as a scout for the military. The war finally ended in September 1878. Although the Paiutes wished to return to the Malheur Reservation, they were forced to travel with the Bannock Indians over 350 miles in December to the Yakima Reservation in Washington Territory. Several Paiutes died during the long winter trip. Upon their arrival, they were met by yet another unscrupulous and untrustworthy agent by the name of Wilbur.

Pressing again for public support, Winnemucca went to San Francisco to lecture on the history and hardships of the Paiutes. In 1880, she joined with her father and brother and traveled to Washington where they met the secretary of the interior, Carl Schurz. They also met briefly with President Rutherford B. Hayes and returned home with a letter and a promise from Schurz that the Paiutes would be allowed to return to the Malheur Reservation, where they would be given land and assistance with farming.

Her disappointment was acute when Agent Wilbur informed her that he had not received any such orders from Washington and would, therefore, not allow her people to leave Yakima. Undoubtedly frustrated, Winnemucca left Yakima and became a teacher and interpreter for the Bannock Indian prisoners at the Vancouver Barracks. She continued to write letters to Washington, and in 1881 she spoke with President Hayes for a second time. But again, her pleas for help were not acted upon. On December 5, 1881, she married her third husband, Lewis H. Hopkins, in San Francisco. Unlike her previous spouses, Hopkins appeared to support his wife who, as historian Gae Canfield notes, "walked a tightrope between two worlds."

On October 21, 1882, her father died. A year later, determined to fulfill his goal for the return of the Paiutes to their ancestral lands, Winnemucca and her husband traveled to Boston where they met two women who became her close friends and supporters. Seventy-nine-year-old *Elizabeth Palmer Peabody and her sister *Mary Peabody Mann (wife of eminent educator Horace Mann) arranged speaking engagements for Winnemucca: throughout the year, she lectured in New York, Connecticut, Rhode Island, Maryland, Massachusetts, and Pennsylvania on the ill-treatment of the Paiutes. She also wrote her autobiography, *Life Among the Paiutes: Their Wrongs and Claims*, which was one of the first published works of literature by a Native American.

But her lecture tour did nothing to endear her to the Indian agents and other governmental officials. Several articles and newspaper stories attempted to defame her by claiming that she had misused government money and that her character was morally suspect. Nonetheless, she defended herself ably and continued to speak in public.

In 1884, she presented a petition to Congress asking that the Paiutes be given lands and citizenship; she also spoke before the Senate subcommittee on Indian affairs. On July 6, 1884, the Senate passed a bill which gave permission for the Paiutes to return to Pyramid Lake Reservation. Although Winnemucca was disappointed that they had not been given land at Malheur, she returned to Pyramid Lake in August. She did not remain there long, however, since the agent was unable to remove white squatters from the reservation and did not hire Winnemucca as the interpreter.

As a result, in 1885 she went to live with her brother Natchez on his farm on the Humboldt River near the town of Lovelock, Nevada. She planned to open a school for Paiute children on Natchez's ranch and began more lecturing in a fairly successful attempt to raise money. With additional help from Elizabeth Peabody and revenue from the proceeds of her autobiography, the school was opened in 1887. That February, Congress passed the Dawes Act which granted citizenship and land to American Indians. Although the Act required Indian children to be educated in English-speaking institutions, Winnemucca continued to advocate for Indian schools.

On October 18, 1887, Lewis Hopkins died of tuberculosis. For the next four years, little information is known about Winnemucca's activities. After her Indian school closed in 1888, she went to live with her sister **Elma** at Henry's Lake, Nevada. Her health began to deteriorate, and Sarah Winnemucca died on October 17, 1891, of consumption at the age of 47.

SOURCES:

Canfield, Gae Whitney. *Sarah Winnemucca of the Northern Paiutes*. Norman, OK: University of Oklahoma Press, 1983.

Dockstader, Frederick J. *Great North American Indians, Profiles in Life and Leadership*. NY: Van Nostrand Reinhold.

Fowler, Catherine S. "Sarah Winnemucca, Northern Paiute, 1844–1891," in Liberty, Margot, ed., *American Indian Intellectuals*. St Paul, MN: West, 1978.

Gehm, Katherine. *Sarah Winnemucca: Most Extraordinary Woman of the Paiute Nation*. Phoenix, AZ: O'Sullivan Woodside, 1975.

Morrison, Dorothy Nafus. *Chief Sarah: Sarah Winnemucca's Fight for Indian Rights*. NY: Atheneum, 1980.

Richey, Elinor. "Sagebrush Princess with a Cause: Sarah Winnemucca," in *The American West*. Vol XIII. November 1975, pp. 30–33, 57–63.

Truman, Margaret. *Women of Courage*. NY: Bantam, 1976.

Waltrip, Lela and Rufus. "Sarah Winnemucca, Paiute Peace Maker," in *Indian Women*. NY: David McKay, 1964.

SUGGESTED READING:

Brimlow, George F. "The Life of Sarah Winnemucca: The Formative Years," in *Oregon Historical Quarterly*. Vol LIII, no. 2. June 1952, pp. 103–134.

Hopkins, Sarah Winnemucca. "Life Among the Paiutes: Their Wrongs and Claims," in *Old West*. Vol. 2. Fall 1965, pp. 49–96.

Peabody, Elizabeth. *Sarah Winnemucca's Practical Solution of the Indian Problem*. Cambridge, MA: John Wilson, 1886 (microfilm).

Winnemucca, Sarah. *Life Among the Paiutes: Their Wrongs and Claims*. Chalfant Press, 1969.

Margaret McIntyre,
Instructor of Women's History at Trent University,
Peterborough, Ontario, Canada

Winser, Beatrice (1869–1947)

American librarian and museum director. Born on March 11, 1869, in Newark, New Jersey; died of arteriosclerotic heart disease on September 14, 1947, in Newark, New Jersey; daughter of Henry Jacob Winser (a journalist) and Edith (Cox) Winser; educated in French and German languages at schools in Germany; studied at the Columbia University Library School.

Beatrice Winser was born in Newark, New Jersey, in 1869, the eldest of three children of Henry Jacob Winser and **Edith Cox Winser**. Her father, a journalist, was a native of Bermuda. Her maternal grandfather, Dr. Henry G. Cox, was a Bermudan whose career as a physician brought him prominence in New York City. When she was only two months old, her father took the position of U.S. consul general at the court of the duke of Saxe-Coburg in Germany. Previously an editor with *The New York Times*, Henry Winser became an assistant editor of the New York *Commercial Advertiser* and later the managing editor of the *Newark Advertiser* after he and his family returned to the United States.

During the 12 years she lived in Germany as a child, Beatrice learned to speak and read German and French and began what became a life-long captivation with books. In 1888, soon after Columbia University had opened its new Library School, Beatrice enrolled. A year later, she became the cataloguer of the French and German archives at the Newark Public Library. She was promoted to assistant librarian in 1894, working first under Frank P. Hill and then John Cotton Dana, an educational crusader. A dynamic man who had been appointed librarian in 1902, Dana believed education was the key to social reform. He considered the library system as a necessary resource for children and adults in pursuing education. Winser shared his enthusiasm for the library and became his assistant in advocating the open-shelf system, which made books more accessible to library patrons.

In 1909, Dana founded the Newark Museum, beginning with a collection of Japanese art that was held by the library. The museum also became a passion of Winser's; due to their mutual efforts, it grew rapidly to include not only art, but exhibits about science and industry. Believing that museums should complement the education system, Winser devoted attention to the Junior Museum Club and assumed many of the responsibilities for managing the new museum. She accepted an appointment to the Newark Board of Education in 1915, becoming the first woman to serve on any of the city's governing boards. Her tenure, however, was short lived. After a few months of participation, she submitted a proposal to reorganize the city's educational system by vesting broader responsibilities in the superintendent of schools and, consequently, diminishing the board's own powers. Her proposal was defeated, its primary opponent was elected president of the board, and Winser resigned on principle. Also in 1915, she became assistant director and assistant secretary of the museum, joining its board of trustees as a member the following year. When Dana died in 1929, Winser succeeded him as both head librarian of the Newark Public Library and director of the museum. She organized several landmark exhibitions while director, including "American Primitive Painting" (1930), "American Folk Sculpture" (1931), "Aviation" (1932), and "Three Southern Neighbors: Ecuador, Bolivia, Peru." During the Depression, Winser hosted Sunday concerts at the museum as well as an adult art workshop.

Winser's activities also extended to a number of organizations outside the library and museum. Beginning in 1890, she was a founding member of the New Jersey Library Association, serving as president from 1907 to 1908 and again from 1921 to 1922. She was active in the American Library Association (ALA) as a member of its Council of Fifty from 1909 to 1912 and again in 1930, and as the ALA's second vice-president in 1931. The New Jersey College for Women (later Douglass College) received Winser as a member of its women's committee beginning in 1918.

Winser resigned from the Newark Public Library in 1942, although she continued as director of the museum until a few months before her death in 1947. Her resignation as head librarian was done with the hope that the surprising action would stop the trustees' interference in administrative matters and protect the future of the library. Through her actions like the museum exhibit on aviation, which was one of Newark's key industries, she attempted to weave the library and museum into the fabric of the community. She generally avoided politics and national

issues, but remained opposed to the political control of libraries and other institutions, to the censorship of foreign books, and to prohibition. In 1937, Winser was awarded an honorary degree of Doctor of Laws from the University of Newark. The citation described her as "an ideal public servant and a luminous personality." She died of arteriosclerotic disease on September 14, 1947, in her home in Newark.

SOURCES:

James, Edward T., ed. *Notable American Women, 1607–1950*. Cambridge, MA: The Belknap Press of Harvard University, 1971.

Gillian S. Holmes, freelance writer, Hayward, California

Winsloe, Christa (1888–1944)

German playwright, screenwriter, novelist, and sculptor. Born in Germany in 1888; killed in 1944; married and divorced; had a relationship with *Dorothy Thompson (1893–1961).

"In pre-Hitler Germany there were a number of excellent anti-authoritarian films which were up front and direct with their messages," wrote Nash and Ross in their *Motion Picture Guide*. "This genre soon disappeared with the rise of the Nazis, because of the boldness of their stand for individual freedom." Perhaps the best of these was adapted by Christa Winsloe from her play *Gestern und Heute* (Yesterday and Today) which was first presented in Berlin in 1930. The following year, it was made into the classic German film *Mädchen in Uniform* (Girls in Uniform), starring **Dorothea Wieck** and **Hertha Thiele**, and directed by ***Leontine Sagan**. Written and directed by women with an-all woman cast, the film, says Nash, "has an assured quality. It knows what it wants to say and how to say it." The story concerns a young girl, Manuela von Meinhardis, struggling against the strict confines of a boarding school with its hardline Prussian principal who believes that, through discipline, hardship, stoicism, hunger, and "triumph of will," the Germans will rise again. But conformity is not in the girl's nature and she falls in love with her only listener, Fraulein von Bernburg, one of her teachers. Appalled, the principal forbids any further contact between the two until Manuela is found attempting suicide by jumping from a balcony. A novelization of the same story was published as *The Child Manuela* and released in Britain as *Life Begins* and in America as *Girl Alone*. A remake, starring ***Lilli Palmer** and ***Romy Schneider**, appeared in 1965, directed by **Geza Radvanyi**.

During World War II, Winsloe, who also wrote scripts for G.W. Pabst, lived in exile, helping fellow Germans escape to Switzerland. Just before the end of the war, she was shot and killed by a French criminal.

SOURCES:

Nash, Jay Robert, and Stanley Ralph Ross. *Motion Picture Guide, 1927–1983.* Evanston, IL: Cinebooks, 1986.

Winslow, Catherine Mary Reignolds

(1836–1911).

See Reignolds, Catherine Mary.

Winslow, Kate (1836–1911).

See Reignolds, Catherine Mary.

Winslow, Ola Elizabeth

(c. 1885–1977)

American writer and historian. Born around 1885 in Grant City, Missouri; died on September 27, 1977, in Damariscotta, Maine; daughter of William Delos Winslow and Hattie Elizabeth (Colby) Winslow; Stanford University, A.B., 1906, M.A., 1914; University of Chicago, Ph.D., 1922; pursued special studies at Johns Hopkins University.

Selected writings: Low Comedy as a Structural Element in English Drama from the Beginnings to 1642 *(1926);* (compiler) Harper's Literary Museum *(1927);* (compiler) American Broadside Verse *(1930);* Jonathan Edwards, 1703–1758 *(1940);* Meetinghouse Hill, 1630–1783 *(1952);* Master Roger Williams *(1957);* John Bunyan *(1961);* Samuel Sewall of Boston *(1964);* Portsmouth, the Life of a Town *(1966);* (editor) Jonathan Edwards: Basic Writings *(1966);* John Eliot: Apostle to the Indians *(1968);* "And Plead for the Rights of All": Old South Church in Boston, 1669–1969 *(1970);* A Destroying Angel: The Conquest of Smallpox in Colonial Boston *(1974).*

Highly regarded in the field of Colonial religious history, Ola Elizabeth Winslow was born around 1885 in Grant City, Missouri. After receiving a bachelor's degree at Stanford University in 1906, Winslow began her teaching career as an instructor at the College of the Pacific (now the University of the Pacific) in San Jose, California (1909–14). At the same time, she pursued advanced study at Stanford University, earning her master's degree in 1914. As a professor of English, Winslow headed the English department at Goucher College in Baltimore, Maryland, where she would remain until 1944. While also serving as assistant dean of the college from 1919 to 1921, she earned her doctorate at the University of Chicago in 1922. She also attended Johns Hopkins University for special studies.

In 1944, Winslow began a long affiliation with Wellesley College in Massachusetts, working as a professor of English there until 1950, when she retired and became professor emeritus until 1977. Beginning in 1950, she was also a professor of English at Radcliffe College in Cambridge, Massachusetts, where she stayed until 1962. Winslow specialized in early American cultural history and was particularly interested in religious subjects. Her biography of Jonathan Edwards won the Pulitzer Prize for biography in 1941. Winslow then spent four months at the British Museum in England reviewing original documents related to John Bunyan's life, after which she published his biography in 1961. She also contributed reviews and articles to various magazines. Goucher College granted her an honorary doctor of literature in 1951. Winslow died in Damariscotta, Maine, near her retirement home in Sheepscot, on September 27, 1977.

Christa Winsloe

Gillian S. Holmes,
freelance writer,
Hayward, California

Winsor, Kathleen (1919—)

Novelist whose bestseller Forever Amber *shocked 1940s America. Born on October 16, 1919, in Olivia, Minnesota; daughter of Myrtle Belle (Crowder) Winsor and Harold Lee Winsor; University of California, B.A., 1938; married Robert J. Herwig, in 1936 (divorced 1946); married Artie Shaw (the bandleader), in 1946 (divorced); married Arnold Robert Krakower (a lawyer), in 1949 (divorced 1953); married Paul A. Porter (a lawyer), in 1956 (died 1975).*

Selected writings; Forever Amber *(1944);* Star Money *(1950);* The Lovers *(1952);* America, with Love *(1957);* Wanderers Eastward, Wanderers West *(1965);* Calais *(1979);* Jacintha *(1985);* Robert and Arabella *(1986).*

Kathleen Winsor was born in Olivia, Minnesota, in 1919, the daughter of **Myrtle Crowder Winsor** and Harold Lee Winsor, who was in real estate. She graduated from the University of California in 1938 and began a career as a reporter and receptionist for the *Oakland Tribune* in Oakland, California. Winsor married four times, always retaining her maiden name. When her first husband Robert J. Herwig entered military service during World War II, she followed him to his various postings and occupied her time by reading over 350 books about English history before beginning her novel set in the period of the English Restoration, *Forever Amber*.

This book, her first, was published in 1944 and became a bestseller in 1945, selling millions of copies in the United States and abroad. Like *Margaret Mitchell*'s *Gone With the Wind* a decade earlier, *Forever Amber* enthralled a generation of readers. Its success has been attributed to its time of publication; it was released toward the end of World War II while many husbands and lovers remained overseas. Its heroine, Amber St. Claire, experiences an assortment of adventures—many of them sexual—at the court of Charles II until she eventually becomes the king's mistress. The book, considered shocking, was banned in Boston because it was "obscene and offensive," instigating several years of legal battles. "It wasn't such a daring book," said Winsor. "I wrote only two sexy passages, and my publishers took both of them out. They put in ellipses instead. In those days, you could solve everything with an ellipse." Despite the scandalous reviews and low recommendations from most critics, the book went through 11 printings and remained popular throughout the 20th century. In 1947, Hollywood added to the novel's mystique by filming *Forever Amber*. It was rumored that Winsor, herself a dark-haired beauty, would be its star. She instead served as a consultant on the film's production and *Linda Darnell portrayed the heroine. Box-office receipts totaled $20 million.

Winsor wrote other novels; though some gained more applause from the critics than her first, none were particularly successful with the general public. Most were similar in formula to *Forever Amber*, with robustly independent heroines living beyond society's restrictions. Her novel *Star Money*, however, was autobiographical in tone. It featured as its central figure a beautiful author who writes a bestseller set in the 18th century, gains power in publishing, and has affairs with high-profile men. *Calais* repeated this structure, exchanging the author for an actress. *America, with Love*, one of Winsor's more favorably reviewed works, offered a different story line, focusing on a year in the life of a young girl growing up in a Western town during the 1930s. For this novel, Winsor was applauded for her ability to enter into the young mind. Other novels included *Wanderers Eastward, Wanderers West* (1965), *Jacintha* (1985), and *Robert and Arabella* (1986). Winsor also served as a story consultant for the television series "Dreams in the Dust" in 1971.

SOURCES:

Contemporary Authors. Vols. 97–100. Detroit, MI: Gale Research, 1981.

Weatherford, Doris. *American Women's History*. NY: Prentice Hall, 1994.

Gillian S. Holmes,
freelance writer,
Hayward, California

Winter, Joanne (1924—)

Baseball player who pitched 63 consecutive shutout innings, a record which still stands. Born on November 24, 1924, in Illinois; never married; no children.

Born in 1924 and raised by her father from age ten, after her mother died, Joanne Winters spent part of her childhood living above a gym in Maywood, Illinois, where her brother John trained as a boxer. Describing herself as someone who "always liked to run, jump and holler," she not only learned how to handle a punching bag at an early age, but played baseball, earning 35 cents a game. When her father moved the family to Chicago, she was good enough to pitch warm-up games for the National Girls Baseball League teams. After her brother enlisted during World War II, Winter convinced her father to move to Arizona, where she hoped to try out for either the Phoenix Queens or the Ramblers, both nationally prominent women's softball teams at the time. Although she was accepted by the Ramblers, she was given so little opportunity to pitch that when she was offered a contract with the Racine Belles of the All-American Girls Baseball League, she headed back to Chicago without a second thought.

During her first year with the Racine Belles (1943), Winter started 29 games and ended the season with an 11–11 record. That first year, she also batted a respectable .253. She entered her second year totally committed to the team and to improving her record. However, she turned in a disappointing 15–23 in 40 starts, amassing the most losses in the league for the year. In 1945, her stats were not much better; in 34 starts, she posted a 7–22 record, again racking up the league high in losses. Winter blamed much of her problem on her slow pitch which she described as "feeble underhand like the figure eight."

Following her second disastrous season, Winter returned to Arizona, ready to quit the game. Her father suggested she contact Nolly Trujillo, a Phoenix softball pitcher who specialized in an underhand rise ball delivered in a slingshot manner, with minimal windup. Winter contacted Trujillo and ended up working with him several hours a day, attempting to master his technique.

When Winter returned to Chicago for spring training, she was armed with determination and her speedy new pitch. It changed everything for "the stately righthander," as she was referred to in the program. She ended the 1946 season with a 22–10 record, striking out 183 batters, more than three times above her past high, and setting a league record she shared with **Connie Wisniewski**. Unlike Wisniewski, however, Winter also pitched 63 consecutive shutout innings, a record that still stands. The Racine Belles also won the Shaughnessy Series championship that year, frosting on the cake for Winters.

Winters posted a 22–13 record in 1947, the year sidearm pitching was introduced into the league. "Many pitchers attempted it, but few succeeded," writes **Barbara Gregorich**. "The delivery was difficult to master, and umpires had a hard time determining if a pitch was legal (that is, if it truly came in sidearm, and not overhand)." Having just perfected her underhand pitch, Winters stuck with it during the season, figuring she could learn to pitch sidearm during the off-season.

She spent the off-season in the gym, working with Belles manager Leo Murphy to master the pitch. But during spring training, she began experiencing back pain during the eighth or ninth inning. She endured the pain for the entire season, ending with a 25–13 record. In 1949, she started 32 games, winning 11 and losing 13. As well, her batting suffered: she managed only 6 hits in 66 at-bats.

At the end of the 1950 season, plagued by poor attendance, the Belles folded, and Winters returned to softball, pitching for the Admiral Music Maids of the National Girls Baseball League in Chicago. She quit after a few years and moved back to Arizona, where she taught tennis at the Arizona Biltmore Hotel and took up the game of golf. Getting caught up in the new game, she eventually went professional, winning the Phoenix City Gold championship in 1959 and 1960, and the Arizona State championship in 1962. She later founded the Arizona Silver Belle Championship Gold Tournament and the Diamonds in the Rough Gold School in Payson and Scottsdale.

SOURCES:
Gregorich, Barbara. *Women at Play: The Story of Women in Baseball.* NY: Harcourt Brace, 1993.

Barbara Morgan,
Melrose, Massachusetts

Winter, John Strange (1856–1911)

British novelist. Name variations: Henrietta Stannard; Mrs. Arthur Stannard; Henrietta Palmer; (pseudonym) Violet Whyte. Born Henrietta Elizabeth Vaughan Palmer on January 13, 1856, in York, England; died from injuries suffered during an accident on December 13, 1911, in Putney, London, England; daughter of Henry Vaughan Palmer (a rector and former artillery officer) and Emily Catherine (Cowling) Palmer; educated at Bootham House School, York; married Arthur Stannard (a civil engineer), in 1884; children: one son, three daughters.

Wrote over 100 novels and various stories about military life, including Regimental Legends *(1883),* Bootles' Baby: A Story of the Scarlet Lancers *(1885),* Army Society *(1886),* Pluck *(1886),* Mignon's Husband *(1887),* Beautiful Jim of the Blankshire Regiment *(1888),* He Went for a Soldier *(1890),* A Soldier's Children *(1892),* That Mrs. Smith *(1893),* Grip *(1896),* A Summer Jaunt *(1899); began to contribute short fiction to periodicals (1875); founded magazine* Golden Gates *(1891), later renamed* Winter's Weekly, *suspended publication (1895); active in writers' societies; served as president of Society of Women Journalists (1901–03).*

A popular novelist and successful journalist, John Strange Winter was born Henrietta Eliza

Vaughan Palmer in York, England, in 1856, the daughter of an officer in the Royal Artillery who later became rector of St. Margaret's in York. She began her professional writing career at age 18, by contributing a number of short stories and serialized novels to the *Family Herald* under the pseudonym Violet Whyte in the mid-1870s. A decade later she published several novels, including *Cavalry Sketches* (1881) and *Regimental Legends* (1883). Many of her works deal with the life of a military family; Winter was descended from a long line of officers, including her father, and she had grown up hearing stories of life in the military. She published these works under the pseudonym John Strange Winter, considered more appropriate to their masculine subject matter, and kept this pen name for the rest of her life.

In 1884, the 28-year-old writer married Arthur Stannard, a civil engineer, with whom she would have three children. The year following her marriage saw Winter earn national prominence with *Bootles' Baby: A Story of the Scarlet Lancers*, which drew praise even from such critical luminaries as British philosopher John Ruskin due to what he deemed to be her accurate portrayal of the character of British soldiers. The novel, one of over 100 penned by Winter, was later adapted into a play. Other popular books include *Beautiful Jim of the Blankshire Regiment* (1888), *That Mrs. Smith* (1893), and *Grip* (1896).

In 1891, Winter founded her own magazine, *Golden Gates*, which was renamed *Winter's Weekly* in 1892, and served as that publication's editor for three years. Her election to the presidencies of the Writers' Club in 1892 and the Society of Women Journalists in 1901 attested to her sense of professionalism regarding her journalistic career, although she was equally devoted to her family. In 1896, both her husband and youngest daughter were ill, and the family moved to Dieppe, France, a port and resort city on the English Channel. Her residence there provided the settings for many of her works written during this time. Winter's diverse interests included passionate care for animals and a fascination with

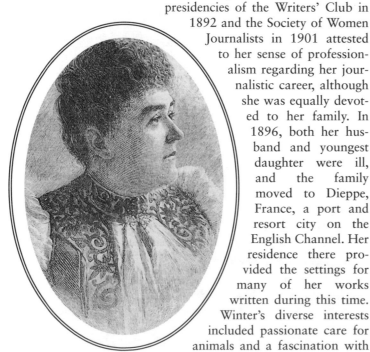

John Strange Winter

women's toiletries, grooming, and dress. Fifteen years later, she died while on a visit to London at the age of 55, the result of an accident. While she earned a good living through her writing, she invested money in a women's toiletries business late in her career, and left behind only £500 at her death.

SOURCES:

Buck, Claire, ed. *The Bloomsbury Guide to Women's Literature.* NY: Prentice Hall, 1992.

Kunitz, Stanley J., ed. *British Authors of the Nineteenth Century.* NY: H.W. Wilson, 1936.

Shattock, Joanne. *The Oxford Guide to British Women Writers.* Oxford: Oxford University Press, 1993.

Pamela Shelton,
freelance writer,
Avon, Connecticut

Winter Queen, the.
See Elizabeth of Bohemia (1596–1662).

Winters, Kay (1913–1971).
See Comingore, Dorothy.

Winters, Linda (1913–1971).
See Comingore, Dorothy.

Winters, Shelley (1922—)

American actress who won a pair of Oscars for her performances in **The Diary of Anne Frank** *and* **A Patch of Blue.** *Born Shirley Schrift on August 18, 1922 (also seen as 1923), in East St. Louis, Illinois; one of two daughters of Johan Schrift (a men's clothing designer and retailer) and Rose (Winter) Schrift (a singer); attended Birmingham Junior High School and Thomas Jefferson High School, in Brooklyn, New York; studied acting at the New Theater School and the Actors Studio; married Mack Mayer (a textile merchant), on January 1, 1943 (divorced 1948); married Vittorio Gassman (an actor), on April 28, 1952 (divorced 1954); married Anthony Franciosa (an actor), on May 4, 1957 (divorced 1960); children: (second marriage) daughter Vittoria Gassman.*

Selected theater: understudied **Julie Hayden** *as Kitty Duval in* The Time of Your Life *(Booth Theater, 1940); appeared as Miss Holvaag in the pre-Broadway tryout of* Conquest in April *(Locust Theater, Philadelphia, 1940), Flora in* The Night Before Christmas *(Morosco Theater, New York, 1941); toured in the revue* Meet the People *(1941); appeared as Fifi in* Rosalinda *(44th St. Theater, 1942); alternated with* ***Celeste Holm** *and Vivienne Allen as Ado Annie in* Oklahoma! *(St. James Theater, New York, 1947–48); appeared as Stella Kowalski in* A Streetcar Named Desire *(Circle Theater, Hollywood, 1952), Celia Pope in* A Hatful of Rain *(Lyceum, New York, 1955), Hilda Brookman in*

Girls of Summer *(Longacre Theater, 1956); succeeded *Bette Davis as Maxine Faulk in* The Night of the Iguana *(Royale Theater, NYC, 1961); portrayed the Prostitute in* Snowangel *and the Wife in* Epiphany *on the double bill* Cages *(York Playhouse, 1963); appeared as Flora Sharkey in* Part I, *Marcella Vankuchen in* Part II, *and Hilda in* Part III, *three one-act plays billed as* Under the Weather *(Cort Theater, 1966); appeared as Minnie Marx in* Minnie's Boys *(Imperial Theater, 1970); wrote three one-act plays presented as* One Night Stands of a Noisy Passenger *(Actors Playhouse, 1970); toured as Beatrice in* The Effect of Gamma Rays on Man-in-the-Moon Marigolds *(1973).*

Selected filmography: What a Woman! *(1943);* The Racket Man *(1944);* Nine Girls *(1944);* Two-Man Submarine *(1942);* Knickerbocker Holiday *(1944);* She's a Soldier Too *(1944);* Sailor's Holiday *(1944);* Cover Girl *(1944);* Tonight and Every Night *(1945);* A Thousand and One Nights *(1945);* Living in a Big Way *(1947);* The Gangster *(1947);* A Double Life *(1948);* Larceny *(1948);* Red River *(1948);* Cry of the City *(1948);* Take One False Step *(1949);* The Great Gatsby *(1949);* Johnny Stool Pigeon *(1949);* South Sea Sinner *(1950);* Winchester '73 *(1950);* Frenchie *(1951);* He Ran All the Way *(1951);* A Place in the Sun *(1951);* Behave Yourself *(1951);* The Raging Tide *(1951);* Phone Call From a Stranger *(1952);* Meet Danny Wilson *(1952);* Untamed Frontier *(1952);* My Man and I *(1952);* Saskatchewan *(1954);* Executive Suite *(1954);* Tennessee Champ *(1954);* Playgirl *(1954);* To Dorothy a Son *(Cash on Delivery, UK, 1954);* Mambo *(It.-US, 1955);* I Am a Camera *(UK, 1955);* The Night of the Hunter *(1955);* The Big Knife *(1955);* I Died a Thousand Times *(1955);* The Treasure of Pancho Villa *(1955);* The Diary of Anne Frank *(1959);* Odds Against Tomorrow *(1959);* Let No Man Write My Epitaph *(1960);* The Young Savages *(1961);* Lolita *(1962);* The Chapman Report *(1962);* The Balcony *(1963);* Wives and Lovers *(1963);* Gli Indifferenti *(Time of Indifference, It.-Fr., 1964);* A House Is Not a Home *(1964);* The Greatest Story Ever Told *(1965);* A Patch of Blue *(1965);* Alfie *(UK, 1966);* Harper *(1966);* Enter Laughing *(1967);* The Scalphunters *(1968);* Wild in the Streets *(1968);* Buona Sera Mrs. Campbell *(1969);* The Mad Room *(1969);* Bloody Mama *(1970);* How Do I Love Thee? *(1970);* Flap *(1970);* What's the Matter with Helen? *(1971);* Who Slew Auntie Roo? *(UK, 1971);* Something to Hide *(UK, 1972);* The Poseidon Adventure *(1972);* Blume in Love *(1973);* Cleopatra Jones *(1973);* Poor Pretty Eddie *(1975);* Diamonds *(Isr.-US-Switz., 1975);* That Lucky Touch *(UK-It.-Fr., 1975);* Journey Into Fear *(UK, 1975);* Next Stop Greenwich Village *(1976);* Le Locataire *(The Tenant, Fr., 1976);* La Dahlia Scarlatta *(It., 1976);* Mimi Bluette *(It., 1975);* Un Borghese Piccolo Piccolo *(It., 1977);* Tentacoli *(Tentacles, It., 1977);* Pete's Dragon *(1977);* Gran Bollito *(It., 1977);* The Three Sisters *(1977);* The Magician of Lublin *(Isr.-Ger., 1979);* City on Fire *(Can., 1979);* King of the Gypsies *(1979);* Redneck County Rape *(1979);* The Visitor *(1979);* Looping *(1981);* My Mother, My Daughter *(1981);* S.O.B. *(1981);* Fanny Hill *(UK, 1983);* Over the Brooklyn Bridge *(1983);* Very Close Quarters *(1984);* Ellie *(1984);* Deja Vu *(UK, 1984); (interview)* George Stevens: A Filmmaker's Journey *(1985);* Witchfire *(also assoc. prod., 1986);* The Delta Force *(1986); (interview)* Hello Actors Studio *(1987);* The Order of Things *(1988);* Rudolph and Frosty's Christmas in July *(voice, 1988);* Purple People Eater *(1988);* An Unremarkable Life *(1989); (interview)* Superstar: The Life and Times of Andy Warhol *(1990);* Touch of a Stranger *(1990);* Stepping Out *(1991);* The Pickle *(1992).*

Over the course of her career on stage and in films, Shelley Winters transformed herself from blonde bombshell to serious actress, winning a pair of Oscars for her work in *The Diary of Anne Frank* (1959) and *A Patch of Blue* (1965), and electrifying Broadway with her performance in *A Hatful of Rain* (1955). In the course of her metamorphosis, Winters kept the Hollywood gossip mills humming with reports of her colorful personal life. Outspoken and tempestuous, the actress had numerous affairs and was married and divorced three times, her second split, from Italian star Vittorio Gassman, making international headlines. From the 1960s, she was also a political activist.

Shelley Winters was born Shirley Schrift in 1922 in East St. Louis, Illinois, where her father Johan Schrift was a patternmaker and salesman for a large men's clothing manufacturer. Her mother **Rose Winter Schrift**, who once sang with the St. Louis Municipal Opera, made certain that Shelley and her sister **Blanche Schrift** had music lessons, despite the family's meager budget. In her first autobiography, *Shelley: Also Known as Shirley*, Winters recalls her mother as "the source of my strength, talent, chutzpa and ingenuity, and the lady I clung to no matter how many times I left home or got married." When Winters was 11, the family moved to Brooklyn, New York, where she attended the Birmingham Junior High School. Never a good student, she often cut classes to attend Wednesday afternoon theater matinees, a pattern which continued in high school. By that time, she was consumed with becoming an actress. During the nationwide search for a woman to play Scarlett O'Hara in the film version of *Margaret Mitchell's *Gone With the Wind*, she dressed herself up in her mother's straw hat and her sister's high heels and marched into the Grand Central Building on Park Avenue, where David Selznick, George Cukor and MGM's talent scout Bill Grady were interviewing women for the part. "With complete self-confidence I slithered in to see the film moguls," Winters recalled. "They stared at the sight before them—a tall, skinny teenager in a pastel violet dress, an off-the-shoulder bargain-basement special, with a black ribbon tied around my neck and three powder puffs stuffed in each bra cup. I managed to croak, 'Lawdy, folks, I'm the only goil to play Scarlett.'" While Selznick and Grady laughed out loud, George Cukor invited her to sit down, ordered her a Coke, and then seriously explained to her that she should take some acting lessons. "He was the first person to treat me as if I were really an actress," she remembered. Cukor, as it turned out, would later be instrumental in her becoming a star.

Winters quit high school six months short of graduation to take a modeling job in the garment district. She enrolled in night acting classes at the New Theater School, and worked odd jobs to pay her way, including a summer position on the staff at a Catskills resort, Aaron and Pinya Pasher's Lake Shore Chateau. In New York City, she haunted the offices of theatrical managers, sometimes riding up and down in the elevator when they would not see her. Her persistence eventually paid off with a string of small stage parts, including a singing role in the revue *Meet the People* (1941), in which she also toured.

It was Winters' performance as Fifi, the coquette, in *Rosalinda* (1942), that led to a contract with Columbia Pictures. Between 1942 and 1944, she played a series of bit parts in some ten films without gaining much attention. When her contract ended in 1944, she set out on a self-improvement campaign, taking dance lessons to improve her grace and studying speech and acting with Charles Laughton. It was her old mentor George Cukor, however, who rescued her from obscurity, hiring her to play the waitress and murder victim in *A Double Life* (1948), co-starring Ronald Colman. The role brought her an Academy Award nomination in the Supporting Actress category and a quick rise to stardom. She played leading roles in such films as *Cry of the City* (1948), *The Great Gatsby* (1949), *Take One False Step* (1949), and *South Sea Sinner* (1950), all of which exploited her earthy sexuality. Director George Stevens saw another side of

her, however, casting her as the pregnant factory worker who is drowned by her seducer (Montgomery Clift) in *A Place in the Sun* (1951), the second film version of Theodore Dreiser's *An American Tragedy*. At Stevens' request, Winters dyed her hair dark brown and abandoned all trappings of glamour for the part. She studied Dreiser's book and visited nearby factories to observe the young women workers. For her work on the film she won a second Academy Award nomination (as Best Actress) and established her reputation as a fine actress.

Winters' subsequent film roles were disappointing to her, however, as were the studio's demands about her behavior and the people she was to be seen with. In the mid-1950s, she returned to New York, convinced that her future lay in Broadway or London's West End. She enrolled in the newly formed Actors Studio, studying with Elia Kazan and Lee Strasberg. In 1955, she was cast as Celia Pope, the wife of a Korean war veteran and drug addict (Ben Gazzara), in the powerful ensemble drama *A Hatful of Rain* (1955). Although the original play was revised a number of times in tryouts, it opened on Broadway to glowing reviews. and played to standing ovations for a year.

It was a rounder, more mature Shelley Winters who returned to films in 1959, and during the 1960s, writes Ephraim Katz, "began displaying a unique talent for portraying suffering mothers, blowsy, promiscuous matrons, and veteran whores." She won Supporting Actress Oscars for her mother roles in *The Diary of *Anne Frank* (1959) and *A Patch of Blue* (1965) and, in the early 1970s, also won critical acclaim as the mother of the Marx Brothers in the Broadway production of *Minnie's Boys*. She later had a recurring role as the dotty mother on the television series "Roseanne."

Early in her second autobiography, Winters admits that for a long time she felt undesirable unless she was attached to an attractive man. Along with numerous affairs, she attempted marriage three times. She met her first husband Mack Mayer, a textile salesman and pilot, in 1941, while in Detroit on tour in the revue *Meet the People*. Following a whirlwind courtship, they were married on January 1, 1942, after which Mayer left for basic training with the Army Air Corps. The marriage did not survive the separations of war or Winters' career ambitions, and ended in divorce in 1948.

In 1951, on a European publicity junket for the movie *Behave Yourself*, Winters met Italian actor Vittorio Gassman, who was then involved in complicated divorce proceedings with his actress wife **Nora Ricci**. Winters, who at the time was "engaged to be engaged" to her co-star Farley Granger, fell in love with Gassman, although she could not converse with him in Italian and he knew little English. The two married in 1952, and had a daughter **Vittoria Gassman**. They divorced not long afterwards, in 1954, divided by cultural differences (neither one wanted to live and work in the other's country) as well as by Gassman's affair with a 16-year-old actress. The couple remained angry with one another for some time after the divorce, but eventually established a friendship for the sake of their daughter.

"Despite many years of self-examination, I have never been able to understand my affair with and subsequent marriage to Tony," writes Winters of her three-year relationship with actor Anthony Franciosa, with whom she acted in *A Hatful of Rain*. "It was a kind of obsessive compulsion. Perhaps for me, the rejection and failure of my marriage to Vittorio was so deep that I was unconsciously trying to find a substitute. But Tony was nobody's substitute. I don't know how he was in other relationships in his life, but for us it was fun and fights and grand passion and low comedy. We did some of the finest acting we ever did in our lives together."

Winters was involved in politics from the 1950s, when she supported Adlai Stevenson's first run for the presidency. The actress first met Dr. Martin Luther King, Jr., at a symposium at the home of Harry Belafonte. "My life suddenly seemed to have a different meaning after I listened to that remarkable man," she writes in *Shelley II*. "I pivoted back to being a woman who was conscious of her own humanity and responsibility to her brothers and sisters." Winters subsequently became friends with Martin Luther King and *Coretta Scott King, and began working in the civil-rights movement. Her involvement, she said, raised her self-esteem. With her new-found confidence, she wrote her first play, *Hansel and Gretel in the Oven*, about homosexuality and a young actor's struggle to hide it. It was performed at the Actors Studio quite successfully, after which she wrote several others. One, a series of three one-acters, *One Night Stands of a Noisy Passenger*, was produced off-Broadway, with fledgling actor Robert De Niro in one of the roles. It did not do well, however, and Winters gave up playwriting.

During the turbulent 1960s, Winters was also involved with the new Reform Democratic Committee of New York and was one of the first celebrities to take part in a sit-down demonstra-tion. (Along with Senator Hubert Humphrey and other civic leaders and Broadway stars, she sat in the middle of Times Square in a Ban the Bomb demonstration.) During the 1960 Democratic Convention, she supported Stevenson, then after he failed to win nomination, threw her support behind John F. Kennedy. During her political activities, she met *Life* photographer Paul Schutzer, with whom she had a long-distance affair and from whom she learned a great deal.

Winters continued to appear in plays and films throughout the 1980s and even into the 1990s, including interviews for several documentaries, *George Stevens: A Filmmaker's Journey* (1985), *Hello Actors Studio* (1987), and *The Life and Times of Andy Warhol* (1990). During the 1980s, she also published her two autobiographies. The second, published in 1989, ends with Winters' recollection of the assassination of John F. Kennedy, an event which devastated the actress along with the entire nation. One evening shortly after the tragedy, she was walking through Central Park and sat down on a bench at the Bethesda Fountain. "As usual, when I am in the depths of despair some survival mechanism deep within me activates and I summon up that tough survivor, Shirley Schrift," she wrote. "We held hands and she helped me home through Central Park that cold dawn."

SOURCES:
Current Biography 1952. NY: H.W. Wilson, 1952.
Katz, Ephraim. *The Film Encyclopedia*. NY: HarperCollins, 1994.
McGill, Raymond, ed. *Notable Names in the Theater*. Clifton, NJ: James T. White, 1976.
Winters, Shelley. *Shelley: Also Known as Shirley*. NY: William Morrow, 1980.
———. *Shelley II: The Middle of My Century*. NY: Simon and Schuster, 1989.

Barbara Morgan,
Melrose, Massachusetts.

Winthrop, F. (1888–1960).

See Jacob, Rosamund.

Winthrop, Margaret (c. 1591–1647)

English-born colonial, wife of the first governor of the Massachusetts Bay Colony, who was first lady for the colony's initial 16 years. Born Margaret Tyndal about 1591 in Great Maplestead, Essex County, England; died of uncertain causes in June 1647 in Boston, Massachusetts; daughter of Sir John Tyndal and Lady Anne Egerton Tyndal; married John Winthrop (Colonial governor), on April 24 or 29, 1618; children: eight, four of whom survived childhood, Stephen, Adam, Deane, and Samuel.

Information about Margaret Tyndal Winthrop's early life is not known. Her year of birth is estimated as 1591, which was based upon her husband's presumption that she was 56 at the time of her death. She was born in Chelmshey House, a country estate in Great Maplestead, Essex, England, the second daughter and fourth child of Sir John Tyndal and Lady **Anne Egerton Tyndal**. Lady Tyndal was the daughter of Suffolk's Thomas Egerton and the widow of William Deane of Deaneshall. Sir John was a master of chancery. Margaret was probably educated by tutors or governesses at home; her later letter writing suggests that she was a thoughtful and intelligent writer.

When she married attorney John Winthrop in 1618, her husband had already lost two previous wives to early death and had four sons. They moved into Groton Manor in Suffolk, his father's estate. Although John's father Adam was still master of the estate, **Lucy Winthrop** managed the household as the only unmarried daughter remaining at home. John's four sons ranged in age from three to twelve years old. Within three years, Margaret had the first two of her own children, Stephen and Adam. Life was complex at Groton Manor, with Margaret in charge of all the children and sharing household duties with Lucy. The manor was remote and had to be largely self-sufficient; journeys to markets, villages, and towns were rare. Although travel to and from the manor was only by horseback, the family entertained many visitors.

As an attorney with the Court of Wards and Liveries in London, John spent most of his time in chambers and seldom returned to Groton Manor. When plans to migrate to the New World became firm and the Massachusetts Bay Company, then still in England, elected him governor of their future colony in 1629, he was able to return less frequently. During these lengthy separations, Margaret wrote many letters to her husband which provide an important picture of her as an individual. Every letter begins and ends with commemoration of God's love; for both Margaret and John Winthrop, human love remained secondary to the love of God, and her letters provide dignified examples of this religious feeling. Edited by Joseph Hopkins Twichell and published in 1893 as *Some Old Puritan Love Letters: John and Margaret Winthrop, 1618–1638*, her letters imbue the Puritan way of life with personality and counteract many negative connotations.

John left Yarmouth, England, in March 1630, as part of the 700 original settlers of the Massachusetts Bay Colony, which matured into the city of Boston. Pregnant at the time, Margaret remained in England to give birth to her child and settle the family's estate. With correspondence impossible, the Winthrops relied on their spiritual strength to maintain a close bond during their two-year separation. In his last letter to Margaret before he sailed, John wrote, "Mondays and Fridays at five of the clock, we shall meet in spirit." John landed near Salem, Massachusetts, on June 12, 1630. Margaret, unable to join him in the New World until more than a year later, arrived on the ship *Lyon* in Boston Harbor on November 4, 1631. She was surprised by the welcome the ship received, but the *Lyon* carried a considerable cargo of supplies that the Colony needed for the winter. Anne, the child with whom Margaret had been pregnant when John sailed, had died at sea.

Margaret's responsibilities in England had prepared her well for her future duties in the Massachusetts Bay Colony. The Winthrops lived in a house on Beacon Hill in Boston which, although described as unpretentious, was large enough to accommodate their family as well as the governor's offices. John Winthrop was re-elected as the colony's governor 12 times. Among the Winthrops' neighbors were the Bradstreets and the Hutchinsons, with whom they shared well water. *Anne Bradstreet, a distinguished American colonial poet, was Margaret's friend. *Anne Hutchinson, a religious reformer whom the Puritans came to believe was subverting the moral laws, was tried, found guilty, and banished from the colony. Although Margaret was dedicated to her husband, her journals suggest that she was troubled by the actions taken against Hutchinson. However, she stayed out of the controversy, holding that God's will had been done despite her personal resistance.

Margaret became ill in June 1647, probably with influenza, and died the following day. Less than a year after her death, John married again, then died two years later. Margaret's place of burial is not commemorated, although she is thought to rest next to her husband in Boston's King's Chapel Churchyard.

SOURCES:

James, Edward T., ed. *Notable American Women, 1607–1950*. Cambridge, MA: The Belknap Press of Harvard University, 1971.

Weatherford, Doris. *American Women's History*. NY: Prentice Hall, 1994.

SUGGESTED READING:

Earle, Alice Morse. *Margaret Winthrop*. NY: Scribner, 1895.

Gillian S. Holmes,
freelance writer,
Hayward, California

Wischnewetzky, Florence Kelley

(1859–1932).

See Kelley, Florence.

Wisdom, Saint.

See Sophia (fl. early 2nd c.).

Wise, Brownie (1913–1992)

American entrepreneur who came up with the Tupperware party. Born in 1913 in the South and raised there; died in 1992; married at age 23 and moved to Detroit (divorced); children: one.

In 1947, when Earl Silas Tupper invented the flexible and indestructible plastic containers with the famous "Tupper seal" ("vermin and insect proof . . . unspillable"), there was little interest in the new product. While department store sales remained flat, Brownie Wise, a divorced single mother from Detroit, Michigan, was having great success selling the containers through Stanley Home Products. In 1948, Tupper met with Wise to discuss a new distribution plan. At that time she disclosed her merchandising strategy: the Tupperware party, a postwar version of the old quilting bee, but with the additional mission of selling a product and interesting the party-goers in becoming part of the sales force. "If we build the people, they'll build the business," Wise said. Tupperware parties became such a success that in 1951, Tupper made Wise vice president of the company, in charge of sales and distribution, and withdrew the product from stores. From that time on, sales were exclusively in-home.

The Tupperware party ultimately became a national institution, giving women in isolated suburbia an opportunity for adult companionship and a way to earn some extra money. The typical Tupperware hostess could make $25 to $30 for a two-hour party, have fun, and boost her self-esteem in the process. "When I had been with Tupperware for just two weeks," one woman said, "folks said I was no longer the shrinking violet they had once known." Wise, writes Alison Clarke, "offered women not just earning power but a measure of self-respect they weren't likely to find elsewhere."

In 1952, Tupper moved the company headquarters from Massachusetts to a 1,000-acre spread in Orlando, Florida, a site chosen by Wise. In 1958, Tupper sold the company for $9 million and retired. Wise, who once fretted over her meager wages as a secretary, was deemed a marketing genius and became the first woman ever featured on the cover of *Business Week*. Today, Tupperware is sold in 85 countries and has added such items as Kimono Keepers, Tortilla Keepers, and Kimchi Keepers to meet the needs of foreign markets. In the United States, the company has enhanced its existing products with Braille designations for the visually impaired. While much has changed, Brownie Wise's sales-force structure is still in place, as are her formats for sales incentives and conventions.

SOURCES:

Clarke, Alison. *Tupperware: The Promise of Plastic in 1950s America.* Washington, DC: Smithsonian, 1999.

Spake, Amanda. "Brownie Wise had one word for you: plastics," in *U.S. News & World Report*. October 18, 1999, p. 82.

Barbara Morgan,
Melrose, Massachusetts

Wise, Louise Waterman

(1874–1947)

American charitable leader and Zionist. Born Louise Waterman on July 17, 1874, in New York City; died of pneumonia on December 10, 1947; daughter of Julius Waterman (an artisan) and Justine (Mayer) Waterman; educated at a finishing school in Comstock, New York; married Stephen Samuel Wise (a rabbi), on November 14, 1900 (died 1949); children: James Waterman Wise (b. 1901) and Justine Wise (b. 1903).

Established the Free Nurses Association for medical assistance to poor mothers (1902); improved school buildings and started an adoption agency for Jewish orphans, previously placed in asylums (1909–16); began championing aid to children in Palestine (1923); completed paintings of social injustices; translated important French writings related to Judaism; created the Women's Division of the American Jewish Congress to heighten public awareness of the threats of Nazism and anti-Semitism; began establishing shelters for Eastern European refugees (1933); provided hostels for Allied military personnel; raised funds for wounded Russian and British civilians and for children evacuated during the Blitz in World War II; attempted to assist Holocaust survivors after the war.

Louise Waterman Wise was born in New York City in 1874, to German-Jewish immigrants Julius and **Justine Mayer Waterman**. Her father, a skilled artisan, had come to New Haven, Connecticut, from Bayreuth in Bavaria during the 1840s. His brother Sigmund was one of the first professors at Yale University to teach German. Julius started a factory to make hoop skirts and, after achieving some success, sent to Germany for his fiancée, Justine Mayer, who was well educated for a woman of her day. Before Louise's birth, the family moved to New York City where this second daughter and third child of the Watermans was born. Despite being members of Temple Emanu-El, the Watermans did not stress Jewish tradition, and Louise attended an Episcopal Sunday school. During her childhood, she earned the nickname "Quicksilver" due to her high spirits, and she attended a finishing school in Comstock, New York, studying fine arts as well as gaining fluency in French and German.

In 1890, after the unexpected death of her mother, Louise began to read the great literature of a variety of cultures, finding Ralph Waldo Emerson's writings particularly appealing because they advocated rebellion against tradition. She also met the moralist Felix Adler, founder of the Ethical Culture Society. Adler encouraged Louise to lead art classes for the underprivileged and to work in the settlement houses in the slums of New York, despite the protests of her family.

In January 1899, Louise met her future husband, Rabbi Stephen Samuel Wise. Although the family considered Wise an inappropriate suitor because of his poverty, Austro-Hungarian roots, and Zionist politics, he and Louise married in 1900 and would remain devoted companions for their 47 years together. Louise gave him constant support through his tumultuous career, and she found in him the Jewish background that had been neglected during her youth. The Wise family lived from 1900 to 1906 in Portland, Oregon, where he was the rabbi of Temple Beth Israel and she organized a social service agency, the Free Nurses Association. Founded in 1902, this agency pioneered free medical care for destitute young mothers. The Wises also had their own children while in Portland; James Waterman Wise, born in 1901, would become a writer, and **Justine Wise**, born in 1903, would become a lawyer and judge.

The family returned to New York in 1907 when Rabbi Wise established the Free Synagogue and began a lifelong crusade for social justice, honest local governments, the end of child labor, increased understanding between Jews and Christians, and the establishment of a Jewish homeland. Louise sympathized with her husband's ideals and practiced them in her own way by becoming a children's advocate. In 1909, she led efforts to improve classroom ventilation in badly designed New York public school buildings. In the process, she learned that Jewish orphans were routinely sent to asylums because there was no avenue for them to be adopted by Jewish families. Wise subsequently founded the Child Adoption Committee of the Free Synagogue in 1916. Physicians and nurses were asked to provide information on such children, and Wise herself gained legal custody to remove them from the asylums. She accepted applications for adoptions and tried to match each child and adoptive family.

In 1919, the Wises went to Europe where Rabbi Wise participated in the Paris Peace Conference as a delegate attempting to gain minority rights for Eastern European Jews and to foster an international agreement to form a Jewish homeland in Palestine. The Wises met Jews who represented all the countries of Europe and heard firsthand descriptions of all manner of suffering. In 1923, Louise traveled to Palestine, learning of *Henrietta Szold's attempts to improve conditions for children there; she supported this work with both words and money.

In the 1920s, with her children grown, Wise resumed her interest in art. She studied painting at the Art Students League in New York and captured on canvas images of injustice, with such titles as "Orphanage," "Sacrifice of Abraham," and "Flight from Belgium." Her paintings were critically acclaimed and exhibited, and a number of museums still house her work. Wise also completed important translations of French books about Judaism, such as *The Unknown Sanctuary* (1928) by Aimé Pallière, and *My Palestine* (1933) and *Why I am a Jew* (1934) by Edmond Fleg.

During the early 1930s, the Wises recognized the danger presented by the Nazis and Adolf Hitler. Wise normally avoided public speaking, but this issue drove her to the podium and to create the Women's Division of the American Jewish Congress. The division had wide-ranging aims, one of which was to publicize the horrors associated with fascism and anti-Semitism. Under the division's auspices, in 1933 Wise established the Congress House for Refugees to furnish refugees from Central and Eastern Europe with temporary housing. In 1935 and 1936, two more homes were added, and the three shelters housed 3,000 refugees before World War II. During the war, the houses were converted to Defense Houses at Wise's direction to shelter Allied military personnel of all religions. Wise also traveled across the United States to raise funds to provide medical care for wounded civilians in Russia and Britain and to care for children evacuated from London during the Blitz.

Despite poor health, at the war's end Wise went to Europe with her husband to identify ways and means of aiding Holocaust survivors. Most wanted to migrate to Palestine, but the British government blocked this option. When the British Foreign Office awarded the Order of the British Empire to Wise in July 1946 in acknowledgment of her war relief efforts, she refused the honor in protest of the Palestine immigration issue. She died of pneumonia at her home in New York City in December 1947. The United Nations had, by that time, called for the establishment of Israel; Rabbi Wise saw this come to pass in 1948 before dying himself the following year.

SOURCES:

James, Edward T., ed. *Notable American Women, 1607–1950.* Cambridge, MA: The Belknap Press of Harvard University, 1971.

Gillian S. Holmes,
freelance writer,
Hayward, California

Wiskemann, Elizabeth Meta

(1899–1971)

English historian, journalist, and educator. Born in Sidcup, Kent, England, on August 13, 1899; committed suicide on July 5, 1971, in London, England; daughter of Heinrich Odomar Hugo Wiskemann (a merchant) and Emily Myra (Burton) Wiskemann; educated at Notting Hill High School; awarded a first class degree in history from Newnham College, Cambridge University, Cambridge, England, 1921; Newnham College, M.Litt. in history, 1927; never married; no children.

Journalist and historian of international renown; forecasted the impending Nazi threat in articles for the New Statesman *in the years up to World War II; gathered intelligence against Germany during World War II; held Montague Burton chair as professor of history, Edinburgh University (1958–61); granted honorary doctorate from Cambridge University (1965).*

Selected writings: Czechs and Germans *(1938);* Undeclared War *(1939);* Italy *(1947);* The Rome-Berlin Axis *(1949);* Germany's Eastern Neighbours *(1956);* A Great Swiss Newspaper, the Story of the Neue Zürcher Zeitung *(1959);* Europe of the Dictators *(1966);* The Europe I Saw *(1968);* Fascism in Italy *(1969);* Italy since 1945 *(1971).*

Elizabeth Meta Wiskemann was born in Kent, England, in 1899, the youngest child of Heinrich Wiskemann, a German immigrant and merchant, and **Emily Burton Wiskemann**. Elizabeth attended Notting Hill High School in London and pursued both undergraduate and graduate degrees at Newnham College, Cambridge,

where she earned the honor of a first class degree in history in 1921 and later completed a master's degree in history in 1927. She had tried for a doctorate but felt that examiner bias caused her to receive only the master's degree; the experience left her distrustful of academia.

In 1930, Wiskemann left England for Berlin, occasionally returning to teach at Cambridge. While in Berlin, Wiskemann swiftly grasped the German political situation and discovered a strong fascination for European politics. As a correspondent for the *New Statesman*, she published magazine articles on German affairs and commentaries that warned of the growing menace of Hitler and Nazism. Her articles, informed by numerous German and British contacts, were so successful in their targeting of the Hitler regime that the Gestapo expelled her from the country in July 1936.

When she returned to Britain in 1937, Wiskemann earned a commission from the Royal Institute of International Affairs to explore the problem of Germans in Czechoslovakia. Her expertise in German affairs led to her first two books: *Czechs and Germans* (1938) and *Undeclared War* (1939). When the war began, her observations and predictions largely came to pass, and her standing as a journalist and scholar of the region was augmented as a result.

During World War II, Wiskemann lived in Berne, Switzerland, and worked as the assistant press attaché to the British legation from 1941 through 1945, responsible for collecting non-military intelligence from Germany and the countries it had conquered. Following the war, she moved to Rome, where she had previously developed strong ties, thanks to a network of friends from the Italian Resistance whom she met while in Berne. Serving as an occasional Rome correspondent to *The Economist*, she also published *Italy* (1947), *The Rome-Berlin Axis* (1949), and *Germany's Eastern Neighbors* (1956). *The Rome-Berlin Axis*, about the relationship between Hitler and Benito Mussolini, provided many scholars a point of departure for their own research. In homage to her time in Switzerland, she later wrote *A Great Swiss Newspaper, the Story of the Neue Zürcher Zeitung* (1959).

Wiskemann's growing reputation as an insightful and lucid scholar led to further opportunities for teaching. From 1958 to 1961, she held the Montague Burton chair as professor of international relations at Edinburgh University. She then tutored in modern European history at Sussex University from 1961 to 1964. Oxford University acknowledged her contributions to European historical study with an honorary doctorate in 1965. She continued to write books, including *Europe of the Dictators* (1966), *Fascism in Italy* (1969), and *Italy Since 1945* (1971). Wiskemann wrote her memoirs in 1968's *The Europe I Saw*, but the book reportedly disappointed friends, who felt that her personal manner, which often included acrid opinions on the personages she knew, did not translate well in the final product. When her eyesight began to fail in her final years, she felt that she could not live with the reduced freedoms and prohibition from reading that blindness would inflict and committed suicide on July 5, 1971.

SOURCES:

The Concise Dictionary of National Biography. Oxford: Oxford University Press, 1992.

Contemporary Authors. Vol. 111. Detroit, MI: The Gale Group, 1984.

The Dictionary of National Biography, 1971–1980. Ed. by Lord Blake and C.S. Nicholls. Oxford: Oxford University Press, 1986.

Gillian S. Holmes,
freelance writer,
Hayward, California

Wister, Sarah Butler (1835–1908).

See Kemble, Fanny for sidebar.

Witchcraft Trials in Salem Village (1692–1693)

The largest case of witchcraft mania in America, and one of the most famous incidents in colonial American history, in which uncorroborated accusations, mostly by children, sparked a mass delusion that resulted in the executions of 20 people and the imprisonment of several hundred more.

Those supposedly afflicted:

Ann Putnam (c. 1680–1716), daughter of Ann Putnam (also afflicted) and Thomas Putnam (parish clerk).

Elizabeth Parris (c. 1683–?). Name variations: Betsy. Daughter of Samuel Parris (a minister).

Rebecca Nurse (1621–1692). Name variations: Rebecca Nourse.

Abigail Williams (c. 1681–?). Lived in the Parris house.

As well as Mary Walcott (c. 1675–?), Elizabeth Hubbard (c. 1674–?), Elizabeth Booth (1675–?), Susannah Sheldon (c. 1675–?), Mary Warren, and Mercy Lewis.

Those condemned:

Sarah Osburn or Osborne; Giles and Martha Corey; Dorcas Goode.

Those executed:

Bridget Bishop, Sarah Goode, Sarah Wildes, Elizabeth How, Susanna Martin, Rebecca Nurse, George Burroughs, John Proctor, George Jacobs, Sr., Mary Parker, John Willard, Giles Corey, Martha Carrier, Martha Corey, Mary Easty, Alice Parker, Ann Pudeator, Margaret Scott, Wilmot Reed, Samuel Wardwell.

By the end of the 18th century, two million people in the Christian world had been executed for witchcraft. In the time of *Elizabeth I, those convicted were pilloried on first offense and executed for a second transgression. In the time of James I, those convicted on first offense were punished by death. The Puritans of Massachusetts, being English subjects of James I, lived under this law.

Puritanism was an important force in the religion and politics of England in the 17th century. Most Puritans were members of the Church of England who strenuously objected to its rituals and rites. Some Puritans felt it was their duty to "purify" (i.e. "de-Catholicize") the Anglican Church. Other Puritans were "separatists," who broke with the Church of England and created their own "Congregational" churches which were organized after what they believed was the pattern of the New Testament.

Puritans were to some extent Calvinists; that is, they believed in predestination. Predestination involved the conviction that God elected or chose certain individuals to be saved, while condemning the non-elect to damnation. It was the duty of all Puritans to live their lives in accordance with God's will, thereby demonstrating evidence of their election. The Puritans held the Bible to be the only infallible guide to God's will, and his ministers the only authoritative interpreters. The most adventurous of these Puritans crossed the Atlantic Ocean to Massachusetts in order to establish "a godly society" where Puritan ideals would govern every aspect of private and public life.

Ironically, the Puritans, who had left England because of religious persecution, persecuted anyone who did not agree with their beliefs. They felt "that since their religion was the truest, the devil was most anxious to destroy it," wrote *Shirley Jackson. They also believed that "most people outside the Puritan faith were helping the devil's cause because they were not strict enough." Like many others, *Anne Hutchinson was banished from the Massachusetts Bay Colony in 1638 following conviction of heresy.

After the Puritans of Massachusetts began to break away from England's governance by mint-ing their own money and settling legal disputes, the British sent Sir Edmund Andros to govern. When he declared that many land titles negotiated by colonists were worthless, they tossed him in prison for several months. Forthwith, England revoked their charter as a colony, casting more doubt on the legality of owner land rights. Increase Mather, president of Harvard College, was sent to Britain to negotiate a new charter. His son Cotton Mather, a passionate Boston Puritan who had developed a keen interest in studying cases of diabolical possession, had published some of his results in *Memorial Providences, Relating to Witchcrafts and Possessions*, as well as at least two other books on the subject. Although he would later strongly disapprove of the Salem judges' slaughter based on circumstantial evidence, his studies no doubt contributed to the panic over witchcraft in the first place. Cotton Mather, who entered into lively debates with Satan and then published them, was regarded by some as a hero for his valiant battles. Thus, his sermons helped set the climate for the events that took place in a small borough about a day's journey by horseback from Boston.

All this talk of demons had made the people of Salem Village uneasy. The winter of 1692 had been a hard one: villagers were jittery from Indian killings, rumors abounded about an imminent war with France, and pirates off the coast were interfering with trade. There had also been a great deal of spiritual infighting as well as family feuds. The townspeople had been so parsimonious and strict with their ministers that few would serve there. Though the new minister Samuel Parris was backed by half the town, the other half grumblingly took to attending church in nearby villages.

The life of the town was severe, revolving around work and religion. Pleasure and amusement were considered blasphemous. Wednesday evenings and most of Sunday were spent in church where Parris gave three-hour sermons on the work of the devil. Education consisted mostly of Bible study. Fifty years earlier, at a Salem town meeting, two attendees had been appointed to scout the town on Sunday and take note of those not attending church.

When a minister of a neighboring town was too lenient with a case of witchcraft (he told the accused to go home and behave), some conjectured that such a minister might be friendly with the dark forces. "This incident demonstrated an attitude toward witchcraft which contributed enormously to every witchcraft epidemic in history," wrote Jackson. "Anyone who defended or sympathized with or said a good word for a witch was automatically suspected."

The kindling for the eruption in Salem Village could be found in Parris' kitchen. Here the minister's cook **Tituba**, a slave who grew up in the West Indies and had been converted to Christianity from her voodoo faith, regaled Parris' nine-year-old daughter **Elizabeth Parris** and her friends with stories. Elizabeth's closest friend was **Abigail Williams**, her 11-year-old cousin who lived with them. Abigail's closest friend, 17-year-old **Mary Walcott**, was, like many of the others, heavily influenced by 12-year-old **Ann Putnam**. From most reports, Ann Putnam was filled with sweetness and light around adults but coldly cruel to peers. She wielded inordinate power over the others who gathered in that kitchen—**Mercy Lewis, Mary Warren, Elizabeth Hubbard, Elizabeth Booth**, and **Susannah Sheldon**—despite the fact that they were older. All were around 17 or 18 and worked as servants in village homes.

When Tituba began to tell them Biblical stories filtered through the lens of her childhood voodoo religion, several girls, including Elizabeth Parris, felt that they were doing something wrong, especially when Tituba told their fortunes by reading their palms. But Ann Putnam could not have been clearer. If Elizabeth Parris found it necessary to relieve her guilt by telling adults what was going on in that kitchen, Ann Putnam would personally see to it that Elizabeth Parris regretted it for the duration of her life.

Elizabeth held her tongue, and the girls learned about charms and how to make their hair curl and the meaning of dreams. Soon the adults of the village began to notice strange behavior in these girls: they seemed nervous, they cried easily, and they were prone to nightmares. Elizabeth Parris, especially, was prone to bad dreams and began to refuse the meals prepared by Tituba, saying they were poisoned. She would sit in a trance, then suddenly cringe and scream. Her father called in Dr. Griggs. After much inspection, Dr. Griggs diagnosed a bad case of witchcraft.

The other girls, now fearful that Elizabeth was about to expose them, took on the pallor of terror. By evening, news had spread that Ann Putnam had also been bewitched. The diagnosis of witchcraft had been a fortunate diversion for the kitchen ensemble. Those who had thought they were on the brink of severe punishment had been reprieved. By the next day, Mercy Lewis, Mary Warren, Abigail Williams, Mary Walcott, Elizabeth Hubbard, Elizabeth Booth, and Susannah Sheldon all seemed to be in a state of agitation. It was becoming increasingly certain that someone in the village had bewitched the entire pack.

Parris called a gathering of ministers from other towns. When the girls were brought before them, they shouted and were unintelligible. Parris begged them to confess who had done this. Finally, they all agreed: it was Tituba. Then Mercy Lewis, for good measure, threw out two more names, **Sarah Goode** and **Sarah Osburn**. The girls once more agreed.

Sarah Goode was an excellent candidate. Poor and half-crazed, she begged door-to-door with her children; she also cursed those who would not contribute. Sarah Osburn, however, lived on an outlying farm and was a respectable citizen—though, upon villager reflection, it was true she spent an inordinate amount of time sick in bed. And she could be cross. Come to think of it, she was also slovenly; she kept a messy house.

On February 29, 1692, warrants were issued for Goode, Osburn, and Tituba—signed by Joseph Hutchinson, Thomas Preston, and Thomas and Edward Putnam, father and uncle to Ann. Meanwhile, Minister Parris, who feared for his daughter, continued to fill his sermons with the evil and danger of witchcraft, while the girls wandered the village screaming, writhing, and throwing themselves on the ground and against walls.

There was a preliminary examination to determine whether or not there was enough evidence. In those days, in lieu of confession, "spectral evidence" was admissible. If a ghost, resembling the accused, appeared to another of the afflicted, it was regarded as undisputable proof that the accused was practicing witchcraft. If the accused protested, it was further proof. The harboring of witches' tools, like owning dolls, was further proof. Past comments could be brought up and analyzed in this new light. To give added heft to the investigation, Ann Putnam's mother (also named Ann Putnam) had joined the ranks of the afflicted.

On March 1, 1692, in front of presiding magistrate John Hathorne, an ancestor of author Nathaniel Hawthorne and a thinly disguised subject of his *House of Seven Gables*, and second magistrate Jonathan Corwin, the examinations were held in the Meeting House of Salem Village. The magistrates sat in front, most of the villagers in back, and the afflicted in the first row. When the prisoners Sarah Goode, Sarah Osburn and Tituba were brought in and placed before the magistrates, all pled not guilty.

Sarah Goode was the first to be examined. Since the records of the trials are still in existence, it is possible to quote responses verbatim. When asked if she were a witch, Goode replied that she was "falsely accused." But when the girls were asked if she was "the person who hurts you?" Ann Putnam jumped up, screamed, and then fell on the floor wailing for help. The other children followed suit. "She is pulling my arm," screamed Putnam, "pulling my arm and biting me because I told on her." They then began to fling themselves against walls. "She is going to bite Mary Warren," warned Mercy Lewis. Mary Warren let out a shriek. Finally, when the constables were ordered to turn Sarah Goode so that she would be unable to look at them, the girls became calm. Sarah Goode was dismayed and probably terrified. When asked again who was tormenting the children, she replied, "It was Osburn."

They brought in Sarah Osburn but had her keep her back to the children. Osburn admitted that she had once been frightened in her sleep "by a man all black, which did pinch me and pull my hair." When she turned to implore the spectators, "Will no one defend me?," the girls in the front row shrieked and wailed anew.

Tituba, with her earrings and colorful turban, was next. Upon hearing of Elizabeth Parris' affliction, Tituba cried and wanted to help all she could. She confessed that the devil had come to her and asked if she'd serve him. "There are four women who hurt the children," she said. "And a tall black man from Boston. They tell me if I will not hurt the children *they* will hurt *me*." She told the magistrates she'd been visited by apparitions—a black dog, a yellow bird, a black cat and a red cat—and the black man from Boston and four witches had pulled her to the Putnam house and made her pinch little Ann. At that point, Ann Putnam rose up and loudly corroborated the pinch. The other children said they'd seen the black man from Boston and, come to think of it, at least two of the witches. "No one stopped to wonder at the time," wrote Jackson, "how they all knew that the black man was from Boston, but they were all positive on that point."

Asked how they traveled, Tituba said that they "all rode upon sticks." Sarah Goode, she said, was given one of the yellow birds but Osburn's bird had a head like a woman and two legs and wings. Tituba continued to testify long into the day, agreeing with any suggestion. When the townsfolk left the meeting house, their purpose was clear; there were now two more witches unaccounted for.

Witchcraft trials in Salem Village.

For two weeks, the people of Salem observed their neighbors while the girls became more and more adept at possession. On March 7, the first three witches were carted to Boston and locked in prison. Those who had not attended the examinations were prime suspects. Those who did not believe in witchcraft had the most to fear. On March 19, 1692, a warrant was issued for the elderly **Martha Corey**. Martha Corey had not been in attendance; Martha Corey had boldly said that she "scorned to watch what she could not believe."

Goodwife Martha Corey was a departure from those previously named. She was educated, intelligent, highly regarded in the church, and could only laugh in amazement when the constables came to her house. Corey continued to believe that reason would prevail when she appeared in front of the magistrate and the town for her preliminary examination. Since it was common knowledge that witches could not pray, she told the judge she would answer all his questions, but first she would pray. But at that moment, Ann Putnam shouted: "Look, there is a black man whispering in her ear. Do you not see him?" When Magistrate Hathorne asked, "What did he say to you, when he whispered in your ear?" "Martha Corey smiled a little before she answered," wrote Jackson.

> At last she replied, "We must not believe all that these distracted children say." Her voice was patient, and she held out one hand to Judge Hathorne, as though she was sure he would understand. Immediately, in imitation of the gesture, Ann Putnam's arms were forced out in front of her and held stiff. Then the arms of the other girls stretched out. And as long as Martha Corey held out her hand, the arms of the afflicted children were held taut and rigid, while they begged Goody Corey to let them go.

Martha Corey had been allowed one brief prayer before entering the room for the examination. She had asked that the blindness of the judges be removed so they could see the truth. Apprised of this, Hathorne was indignant and asked her continually throughout what she meant by her statement that "the magistrate's eyes were blinded and I will open them?" Bound in chains, she was taken to prison. When her husband Giles Corey stood up for her, he too was escorted to Boston.

Religious old **Rebecca Nurse** was next. Rebecca Nurse, who had been regarded by most in the village as a saint, had quietly begun attending church in Topsfield, instead of the Salem Meeting House, after the first examinations were held. Rebecca Nurse was brought from her sickbed to stand before the magistrates. Over 70 and nearly deaf, she could not hear the questions; instead, she could only supply simple, pious answers to her accusers. Though some in the delegation were having trouble accepting Rebecca Nurse as a witch, Ann Putnam grew animated in her attack. Mary Walcott and Elizabeth Hubbard also swore that Goody Nurse had come into one of their rooms and sat on their chest to suffocate them. Rebecca Nurse stood in stunned silence. Wrote Jackson:

> During the first few trials, the afflicted children had confined their demonstrations to short periods of time, and between fits they were reasonably docile. However, with the trial of Rebecca Nurse, and urged on by the malice of Ann Putnam senior, their performances became largely uncontrollable. From that time on, the examinations were conducted through the unceasing howling and acrobatics of the children. Much of the court record shows gaps in the testimony, where the questions could not be heard because of the din in the room.

Rebecca Nurse went to prison, followed by **Dorcas Goode**, the daughter of Sarah Goode. Dorcas Goode had not met with a formal examination because it would have been futile to question her; Dorcas Goode was four years old. Another woman was arrested because in an earlier argument with her husband he had said she was bewitched. The next Sunday, **Sarah Cloyse** (also seen as Cloyce), sister of Rebecca Nurse, stood up in the middle of a typical Parris sermon about devils loose in the church and marched out. She was in prison within the week. They imprisoned **Abigail Hobbs** and her father and mother, as well as **Mary Easty**, sister of Rebecca Nurse and Sarah Cloyse. When Philip English and his wife were named by a man who had lost a lawsuit to him, the couple escaped to New York. Then **Elizabeth Proctor** was accused. Elizabeth Proctor was the wife of John Proctor who had once whipped Mary Warren. "The principal witness against Elizabeth Proctor was to be, strangely enough," wrote Jackson, "Mary Warren, who had waited a long time to get even."

Six weeks had passed. On April 11, court reconvened. But there had been a great deal of publicity over the doings in Salem Village, and the deputy-governor of the State of Massachusetts, Thomas Danforth, was now presiding, along with four new judges in addition to Hathorne and Corwin. Within five months, 200 to 300 more were imprisoned to await trial. The records of the examinations are still extant, replete with the disorder, the cries of the girls who could not be restrained, the constant interruptions and accusations.

It was Mary Warren who dropped the next bombshell. After the Proctors were remanded to prison to stand trial, Mary Warren had trouble living with the guilt. She confessed, admitting she "did but dissemble," that all the doings with the others were fake. Immediately, Mary was declared a witch and bound for trial. Clearly, she was not going to be believed. Her only recourse was to say that she had lied when she accused the others of perfidy. Mary Warren repented and recanted her confession.

The trials were about to begin. The new royal governor was Sir William Phips who appointed a Special Court. In June, the trial opened in Salem, with Cotton Mather attending. Rebecca Nurse, whose sickly condition had worsened while in prison, was the first to appear. She was now charged with murder by witchcraft. She stood accused of killing two Salem Villagers. When some testified that they were at the bedside of her supposed victims who had died a peaceful death, the jury found her not guilty. But, even though there was now order imposed in the court and the girls had been stifled, the judges ordered the jury to reconvene and reconsider their verdict. The jury then found Rebecca Nurse guilty. Sarah Goode, the Proctors, George Burroughs (a former minister in Salem who had not been liked by some), and Martha Corey were all tried and found guilty. Giles Corey was so outraged he refused to speak, even to answer how he pled.

By September 22, 1692, 19 had been executed publicly, hanged on Gallows Hill outside Salem. "Not one person who confessed to practicing witchcraft was executed," wrote Jackson. "The persons executed were those who insisted upon their innocence." Those hanged were Bridget Bishop, Sarah Goode, Sarah Wildes, Elizabeth How, Susanna Martin, Rebecca Nurse, George Burroughs, John Proctor, George Jacobs, Sr., Mary Parker, John Willard, Martha Carrier, Martha Corey, Mary Easty, Alice Parker, Ann Pudeator, Margaret Scott, Wilmot Reed, and Samuel Wardwell. Sarah Osburn had died in prison. Then a man in the town of Andover asked the girls to come there. His wife was sick and he wanted to see if witchcraft was involved. The plague went to Andover and 40 warrants were written.

Some think the turning point was the death of Giles Corey. He was pressed to death, crushed by rocks placed on his chest when he refused to plead guilty or not guilty. Then too, the girls began to cry out against the wrong people: Judge Corwin's mother-in-law; the wife of Sir William Phips; Mrs. Hale, the wife of Mr. Hale, an enthusiastic witch hunter. Some Andoverites filed for slander; the legality of "spectral evidence" came into question. A new court met in January 1693 and began to release prisoners; no one was found guilty in the new round of trials. In May, Sir William Phips issued a proclamation freeing 150, but they first had to pay jail and court fees and board for their time in prison. Some could not pay to get out; others were penniless by the time of their release and their property had been seized. Those with means fled the area, the care of the village declined, and farms were abandoned. Ann Putnam the elder died shortly after the hangings. Ann Putnam the younger lived the rest of her life in Salem Village, a semi-invalid. She publicly repented in 1706. Some of the jury had repudiated their participation years before, as had one of the magistrates.

"Although there were witchcraft trials and executions in England for a dozen years longer, and for as long as a hundred years more in some parts of Europe," wrote Jackson, "Massachusetts had taken the first step to end persecution. The state and its citizens had shown that although they had acted in panic, they were honestly prepared to confess their error, and make what restitution they could. Moreover, they had demonstrated that spectral evidence, guilt by association, and a belief that the prisoner was guilty before he was tried, are not means to be used in fighting any evil, no matter how frightening it may seem." On March 5, 1954, the lower house of the Massachusetts legislature cleared six of the women hanged as witches.

SOURCES:
Jackson, Shirley. *The Witchcraft of Salem Village.* NY: Random House, 1956.
Morison, Samuel Eliot. *Oxford History of the American People.* Oxford University Press, 1968.
Smithsonian. April 1992, p. 116.

SUGGESTED READING:
Carlson, Laurie Winn. *A Fever in Salem: A New Interpretation of the New England Witch Trials.* Ivan R. Dee, 1999.

RELATED MEDIA:
The Crucible (play) by Arthur Miller, opened at the Martin Beck Theater on January 22, 1953, starring **Beatrice Straight** as Elizabeth Proctor (replaced by *****Maureen Stapleton**), Arthur Kennedy as John Proctor, **Madeleine Sherwood** as Abigail Williams, and **Jacqueline Andre** as Tituba. (In the play, Miller was largely faithful to the court transcripts. He did, however, change Abigail Williams' age and create a relationship between her and John Proctor.)
Crucible (film), starring **Winona Ryder**, Daniel Day-Lewis, Paul Schofield, and Bruce Davison, produced by 20th Century-Fox, 1996.
Les Sorcières de Salem, French movie adaptation of Miller's play by Jean-Paul Sartre, starring *****Simone Signoret**, 1957.
"Three Sovereigns for Sarah" (3 hrs.), PBS drama, starring **Vanessa Redgrave** as Sarah Cloyce, with **Phyllis Thaxter** and *****Kim Hunter**.

Withburga
*Princess and nun. Daughter of *Saewara and Anna, king of East Anglia (r. 635–654); sister of *Elthelthrith and *Sexburga and half-sister of *Ethelburga (d. 665).*

Withers, Googie (1917—)
British stage and film actress. Born Georgette Lizette Withers on March 12, 1917, in Karachi, India (now

Pakistan); daughter of Edgar Clements Withers (a British captain) and Lizette Catarina Wilhelmina (van Wageningen) Withers; educated in convent schools in London; studied at Italia Conti Stage School; studied at Helena Lehmiski Academy, Birmingham, England; studied at Buddy Bradley School of Dancing; married John McCallum (an actor), in 1948; children: Joanna McCallum.

Selected theater: The Windmill Man *(1929);* Nice Goings On *(1933);* Happy Week-End *(1934);* This World of Ours *(1935);* Duet in Floodlight *(1935);* Ladies and Gentlemen *(1937);* Hand in Glove *(1937);* They Came to a City *(1943);* Private Lives *(1945);* Champagne for Delilah *(1949);* Winter Journey *(1952);* The Deep Blue Sea *(1952);* Waiting for Gillian *(1954);* Janus *(1957);* Hamlet *(1958);* Much Ado About Nothing *(1958);* The Constant Wife *(1960);* The Complaisant Lover *(1961);* Woman in a Dressing Gown *(1962);* Exit the King *(1963);* Desire of the Moth *(1966);* Getting Married *(1967);* The Cherry Orchard *(1971);* An Ideal Husband *(1971);* The Circle *(1976);* The Importance of Being Earnest *(1979);* Time and the Conways *(1983);* The Chalk Garden *(1986).*

Selected films: The Girl in the Crowd *(1934);* All at Sea *(1935);* Dark World *(1935);* Her Last Affaire *(1935);* The Love Test *(1935);* Windfall *(1935);* Accused *(1936);* Crime Over London *(1936);* Crown vs. Stevens *(1936);* King of Hearts *(Little Gel, 1936);* She Knew What She Wanted *(1936);* Action for Slander *(1937);* Pearls Bring Tears *(1937);* Convict 99 *(1938);* The Gaiety Girls *(Paradise for Two, 1938);* If I Were Boss *(1938);* Kate Plus Ten *(1938);* The Lady Vanishes *(1938);* Paid in Error *(1938);* Strange Borders *(1938);* You're the Doctor *(1938);* She Couldn't Say No *(1939);* Trouble Brewing *(1939);* Dead Men Are Dangerous *(1939);* Bulldog Sees It Through *(1940);* Busman's Honeymoon *(Haunted Honeymoon, 1940);* Murder in the Night *(Murder in Soho, 1940);* Girl in Distress *(Jennie, 1941);* Back Room Boy *(1942);* One of Our Aircraft Is Missing *(1942);* On Approval *(1944);* They Came to a City *(1944);* The Silver Fleet *(1945);* Four Against Fate *(Derby Day, 1952);* Dead of Night *(1946);* The Loves of Joanna Godden *(1947);* It Always Rains on Sunday *(1949);* Miranda *(1949);* Once Upon a Dream *(1949);* Night and the City *(1950);* Pink String and Sealing Wax *(1945);* Traveller's Joy *(1951);* The Magic Box *(1952);* White Corridors *(1952);* Devil on Horseback *(1954);* Port of Escape *(1955);* *Godiva Rides Again *(1955);* The Nickel Queen *(1970);* Time After Time *(1985);* *Jane Austen's "Northanger Abbey" (television, 1986);* "Hotel du Lac" (television, 1986);* Country Life *(1995);* Shine *(1996).*

Googie Withers was born Georgette Lizette Withers in the port city of Karachi, India (now Pakistan), in 1917, the daughter of Edgar Clements Withers and Lizette van Wageningen Withers, of British and Dutch nationality respectively. Educated in convent schools in London, she was only 12 when she made her stage debut in *The Windmill Man* in 1929.

Withers launched her film career in the 1930s and succeeded in creating a lasting image as a strong, passionate woman, classically dark and, when the occasion demanded, ruthless. Despite this marked screen persona, she also played dumb blonde roles in a string of lamentable British prewar comedies. Now and again, by way of a change, she portrayed bad girls, but the material was hardly an improvement.

Withers was rescued by the war and British director Michael Powell, who remembered her small roles in his early films and thought her possessed of a provocative beauty. He cast her as a Dutch resistance leader in *One of Our Aircraft Is Missing* (1942). It was perceptive casting. Withers was not only half-Dutch, but the role allowed her to play to her strengths as a resourceful, self-reliant woman who could perform well under pressure. She graduated to a female lead as another Dutch woman in *The Silver Fleet* (1943). In both films, she proved that drama was her forte.

As well, Withers was a gifted comedic actress, although the cinema seldom offered her much scope, with the exception of the stylish *On Approval* (1944). But the finest roles of her career were dramatic parts in three films she made with director Robert Hamer. For Hamer, Withers was invariably linked with dangerous passions that threatened to disrupt a tame world. Her best role, according to one critic, came in Hamer's *It Always Rains on Sunday* (1947), in which she played a woman trapped in a stultifying relationship, tempted by an alluring but destructive past.

For all her screen aptitude, Withers seemed unconcerned about building a conventional movie career, brushing aside studio requests that she change her name to something more euphonious than Googie (a childhood nickname that means "crazy" in Bengali). She often favored the theater over films, and eventually turned her back on Britain altogether. She married her costar from *It Always Rains on Sunday*, actor John McCallum, and settled with him in Australia in the late 1950s. She rarely appeared in movies thereafter, with one noted exception being 1996's acclaimed *Shine*, in which she portrayed an elderly writer. Her daughter **Joanna McCallum** is also an actress of stage and screen.

SOURCES:

Contemporary Theater, Film and Television. Vol. 9. Detroit, MI: Gale Research, 1991.

International Dictionary of Films and Filmmakers, Vol. 3: *Actors and Actresses.* Detroit, MI: St. James Press, 1996.

Katz, Ephraim, ed. *The Film Encyclopedia.* 3rd ed. NY: HarperPerennial, 1998.

Gillian S. Holmes,
freelance writer,
Hayward, California

Withers, Jane (1926—)

American vaudeville, radio, film, and television actress. Born on April 12, 1926, in Atlanta, Georgia; daughter of Walter Withers and Lavinia Ruth Withers; educated at Boston Academy, Atlanta, and Lawlor's Professional School; married William Moss, Jr., in 1947 (divorced 1954); married Kenneth Errair, in 1955 (died 1968); children: (first marriage) Wendy, William III, and Randy; (second marriage) Kenneth and Kendall.

Selected filmography: Handle with Care *(1932);* Bright Eyes *(1934);* Ginger *(1935);* The Farmer Takes a Wife *(1935);* This Is the Life *(1935);* Paddy O'Day *(1935);* Gentle Julia *(1936);* Little Miss Nobody *(1936);* Pepper *(1936);* Can This Be Dixie? *(1936);* The Holy Terror *(1937);* Angel's Holiday *(1937);* Wild and Woolly *(1937);* Forty-five Fathers *(1937);* Checkers *(1937);* Rascals *(1938);* Keep Smiling *(1938);* Always in Trouble *(1938);* The Arizona Wildcat *(1939);* Boy Friend *(1939);* Pack Up Your Troubles *(1939);* Chicken Wagon Family *(1939);* Shooting High *(1940);* High School *(1940);* Youth Will be Served *(1940);* The Girl from Avenue A *(1940);* Golden Hoofs *(1941);* A Very Young Lady *(1941);* Her First Beau *(1941);* Small Town Deb *(1941);* Young America *(1942);* Johnny Doughboy *(1942);* The Mad Martindales *(1942);* The North Star *(1943);* My Best Gal *(1944);* Faces in the Fog *(1944);* Affairs of Geraldine *(1946);* Danger Street *(1947);* Giant *(1956);* The Right Approach *(1961);* Captain Newman, M.D. *(1963);* Hunchback of Notre Dame *(1996). Also portrayed "Josephine the Plumber" in a series of television commercials (1963–75).*

Jane Withers was born in 1926, in Atlanta, Georgia. Her parents, who wanted her to have a career in the arts, placed her in Boston Academy of Atlanta at age three, where she studied dance. Following a move to the West Coast, she studied at Lawlor's Professional School and worked in vaudeville and radio when not in class. After a screen test at Twentieth Century-Fox, Withers made her screen debut with a small role in *Handle With Care* (1932) and went on to have an extensive career as one of Hollywood's leading child stars.

After *Shirley Temple (Black), Withers is considered one of the leading child actors of the 1930s, typically starring in two to four releases a year. Although she was chubby and not especially pretty, she had endless vitality and charm that communicated well on the silver screen. In her first major role, opposite Temple in *Bright Eyes* (1934), Withers won over audiences as a bratty child who, after Temple has requested a doll, tells Santa she wants a machine gun. From then on, her popularity grew, and she was one of 1937's top-ten box-office draws. As was the case with numerous popular child actors, when she matured into teen and ingenue roles, her box-office appeal dropped. She retired from films in 1947 when she married millionaire oil man William P. Moss, Jr., with whom she had three children. Following a severe bout of rheumatoid arthritis after divorcing Moss in 1954, she returned to act in character roles and married Kenneth Errair, a member of the Four Freshmen singing group, in 1955. They had two children, a son and a daughter, before Errair's death in a plane crash in 1968.

Surprisingly, Withers added to her fame in 1963, when she won the role of Comet Cleanser's "Josephine the Plumber," a character that became one of television's most popular advertising icons; the series of ads lasted until 1975. Her subsequent work was of a lower profile, although she did voice-over work for the Disney film *The Hunchback of Notre Dame* in 1996.

SOURCES:

Katz, Ephraim. *The Film Encyclopedia.* 3rd ed. NY: HarperPerennial, 1998.

Ragan, David. *Who's Who in Hollywood, 1900–1976.* New Rochelle, NY: Arlington House, 1976.

Gillian S. Holmes,
freelance writer,
Hayward, California

Witherspoon, Naomi (b. 1923).

See Madgett, Naomi Long.

Withington, Eliza (1825–1877)

American portrait and landscape photographer. Name variations: Elizabeth W. Kirby. Born in New York City in 1825 (some sources cite 1823); died in 1877 in Ione City (Amador City), California; educated in photographic technique in New York around 1857; married George V. Withington, in 1845 (separated around 1871); children: Sarah Augusta (b.

around 1847); Eleanor B. (b. around 1848); Everett (b. 1861, died five months later).

Elizabeth W. Kirby, called Eliza, was born in New York City in 1825. Nothing is known of her early years until 1845 when she married George V. Withington of Monroe, Michigan. The Withingtons' first two children, daughters **Sarah Augusta** and **Eleanor B.**, were born around 1847 and 1848, respectively. George, deciding to move to California, began his pioneer journey across the continent in 1849, while Eliza stayed home with their children. After he settled in Ione City, California, Eliza and Sarah Augusta (then about five) began their cross-country trek in 1852, from St. Joseph, Missouri, and ending in Ione City six months later. Eleanor would not be reunited with her parents until 1857.

Before 1857, Eliza journeyed back to the East Coast for the purpose of learning photography. She traveled throughout the Atlantic states after completing her studies and visited the galleries of the leading photographers of the day, including Matthew Brady's New York City gallery. Upon her return to California in January 1857, she opened her Excelsior Ambrotype Gallery in a rented house in Ione City, where she offered lessons in photography and oriental pearl painting, then a popular pastime for women. In 1861, the Withingtons had their only son, Everett, who died five months later. Some ten years later, Eliza separated from George.

Withington made stereographic photographs of people, landscapes, and other subjects. In stereographic photography, invented in 1838 by Sir Charles Wheatstone, two photographs of the same subject are taken from slightly different angles; when viewed through a stereoscope, they merge into one three-dimensional image. Stereoscopes were a popular form of entertainment found in many drawing rooms in the last half of the 19th century. Withington is best known for her stereographs of miners, mining operations, and the rugged landscapes of the Sierra Nevada Mountains that she took near Silver Lake, California, in 1873. She resolved the problem of cumbersome photographic equipment by devising her own traveling equipment, including special provisions for field developing, in which she used her own skirt as a tent.

Withington joined the San Francisco Photographic Art Society of the Pacific in 1875 and published an article detailing her techniques, entitled "How a Woman Makes Landscape Photographs," in *Philadelphia Photographer* in 1876; the magazine piece was reprinted in *Pho-*

tographic Mosaics in 1877. She died that year of cancer in Ione City.

SOURCES:

Rosenblum, Naomi. *A History of Women Photographers.* NY: Abbeville, 1994.

Gillian S. Holmes, freelance writer, Hayward, California

Witt, Katarina (1965—)

German figure skater, one of the last skating stars produced by the East German athletic training machine, who won six European championships, five world championships, and two Olympic gold medals. Born Katarina Witt in Karl-Marx-Stadt (now Chemnitz), in what was then the German Democratic Republic, in December 1965; daughter of Manfred Witt (a director of an agricultural cooperative) and Käthe "Katje" Witt (a physical therapist); trained at the Karl Marx Sports Club from a young age; never married; no children.

Won her first European championship (1982); won Olympic gold medal in figure skating (1984), and second Olympic gold medal (1988); in retirement from competitive skating, became television sports commentator for Olympics (1992); returned to Olympic skating at Lillehammer, Norway (1994); became a major staple of the professional figure-skating circuit; appeared in films, including Ronin, *and in television roles, including HBO's "Arli$$."*

In the late years of the Cold War that evolved between the East and the West after World War II, the career of the figure skater Katarina Witt came to epitomize how that international power struggle was played out through athletic contests. For several decades, when athletes from East German and Soviet countries vied against athletes from the West in international competitions—particularly the Olympics—wins and losses on the playing field of a number of sports were totted up as political. Regardless of how governments viewed the outcome, however, there were always some competitors who simply caught the fancy of sports fans. Thus it was that Katarina Witt, with all her Communist-backed training, was adored by millions in the West for the elegance of her performances on ice.

Witt was born in Karl-Marx-Stadt (now Chemnitz) in Saxony, German Democratic Republic, in December 1965. Her mother **Käthe Witt** was a physical therapist while her father Manfred Witt directed a cooperative that produced plants and seeds. Like her brother Axel, Katarina was athletic; he played soccer, while she was attracted to the ice rink. As a little girl, she would stop by Küchwald, a neighborhood ice arena, to watch the skaters. The first time she stepped onto the ice, she thought, "This is for me."

Witt had not been skating long when Bernd Egert, the head coach of the Karl-Marx-Stadt Club and school, spotted her and recognized her immediately as a natural. The club was one of the four major government-sponsored clubs, where some of East Germany's best athletes were trained, and Egert soon recruited Witt for the school's intensive training program. (Her selection had also involved inherited factors. According to Egert, "If the parents are too tall or have a tendency to be naturally heavy, these qualities mean the children are not suited for skating.") For Witt, life changed forever once she became a member of the East German "sports machine." "We never played at home," she said. "I left at six-thirty in the morning and I came back at six in the evening. There was only time to do your homework, then have dinner, and go to bed."

When Katarina was nine, her talent drew the attention of **Jutta Müller**, East Germany's most successful skating coach. Many of Müller's students were international and Olympic medal winners. "In many ways I am closer to Jutta than anyone," said Witt of the woman who became her surrogate mother. By the time Witt was 11, Müller's impact was apparent on the ice, when the girl made her first triple jump, called a "Salchow." As Witt entered into competition, Müller oversaw every detail of the young skater's life, choosing her costumes and choreographing her routines on the ice. Noting Witt's natural warmth, Müller encouraged her to let it shine through in performance, teaching her to pick one male face out of the audience crowd and perform solely for him. The coach spent countless hours fussing over Witt's makeup, coiffure, and every element of her personal style.

At age 14, Witt finished tenth in a World championship. Two years later, in 1982, she won her first European championship. From the beginning, her strength was as a performer, not simply an athlete. In competition, she hated skating compulsory figures, an endless series of figure eights, circles, and turns; she preferred doing the more elaborate double loop jumps and double Axels. Where she truly excelled, however, was in the four-minute freestyle or long program which let her artistic talent come to the fore. In many respects, she was as much a dancer as a skater. Witt loved skating to music of her own choosing, playing to the audience and creating a performance requiring countless hours of practice that raised her skills to the level of an art. Eleven months a year, she spent up to six hours a day on the ice, then worked on music, ballet, and choreography for as much as three more hours.

With the approach of the 1984 Olympics in Sarajevo, two Americans, **Rosalynn Sumners** and *****Elaine Zayak**, were expected to dominate the ice. Zayak had won the World title in 1982, Sumners in 1983; Katarina Witt was a relative unknown. Although compulsory figures had never been Witt's strength, she performed much better in them than did Zayak. Sumners remained in the lead until the short program, when Witt inched ahead. When the free-style skating program was all that stood between Witt and an Olympic gold medal, she was dazzling. According to Sumners, "Her Sarajevo performance was the first to hit the perfect blend of art and athleticism, pirouettes and panache." In the East German girl with the creamy complexion, dark hair, blue eyes, and perfect figure to complement her athletic abilities, the world discovered a new sports star.

The young East German received 35,000 pieces of fan mail, much of it from Americans. This product of the Eastern bloc sports machine in no way fit the stereotype of the impassive female athlete. She was graceful, elegant, flirtatious, and loved wearing jeans, going to discos, and driving sports cars. Although some tried to maintain that years of intense training damaged Eastern bloc athletes psychologically, there was no evidence in her of any ill effects. Questioned by the Western media, she always acknowledged her gratitude for the coaching and facilities made available to her, saying "few people could afford the training I have been given. Here, all you need is talent and desire." Parents of many American skaters could confirm this advantage, having gone nearly bankrupt trying to provide for their children what skaters like Witt received for free. But "Katarina the Great," as East Germans called her, now received much more than free training. She was rewarded with a penthouse apartment, a country retreat, a Porsche as well as a Lada sports car, clothes and cash. Because their salaries were tied directly to winning medal competitions, Jutta Müller and Bernd Egert benefited as well. From 1984 to 1988, Witt lost only one competition, the 1986 World championships held in Geneva, Switzerland, in which she was bested by American *****Debi Thomas**; the following year, Witt took the title back.

With the approach of the 1988 Olympics, however, Witt was feeling the political heat. As she won more and more competitions, the pressure mounted. Said Witt:

The 1988 Olympics were much more difficult for me. I had no clue in 1984; it was just another competition. But in Calgary, the moment I stepped onto the ice, I realized so many people were watching and my life depended on winning the gold medal. If I would be second, it would have been a major loss for the country. They never would have let me keep skating, and I knew it.

The pressures went deeper. The German Democratic Republic, still under Soviet control, was run by the secret police, known as the Stasi, who accumulated files on millions of East German citizens and encouraged neighbors to spy on neighbors. Star athletes were also expected to do their part for the Stasi. "They asked me to spy for them," said Witt, "and I would get all my endorsement contracts. They were worth a couple million dollars. I turned them down." Always quick to promote the East German system which had turned her into a superstar, Witt found herself forced to keep quiet about its dark side. "In East Germany nothing worked without the Stasi," she said. "They were everywhere." Under constant surveillance, Witt also was expected to light up the ice every time she stepped out onto the rink.

I do not want people to come up to me one day and say, "Aren't you that skater who used to be famous?" I am, and I will be, much more than that.

—**Katarina Witt**

At the 1988 Winter Olympics in Calgary, British Columbia, Witt found herself in the media spotlight, surrounded by scores of international reporters interested in every aspect of her career. The press had dubbed that year's women's figure-skating competition the "Battle of the Carmens," after both Witt and her American rival, Debi Thomas, had chosen to skate to the music of Bizet's opera. The two were very different skaters. The African-American Thomas was much more athletic than her East German counterpart, using choreography that stressed powerful leaps and turns; Witt had been trained for free by some of the world's best coaches while Thomas skated in tight secondhand boots, sewed her own costumes, repaired her skates with Elmer's glue, and choreographed her own routines. Planning to be a surgeon, Thomas struggled through school and through skating, without the rewards of penthouses or sports cars; and in the previous four years in international competition, Witt had lost only to Thomas.

On the ice or in a shopping mall, Witt had the media eating out of her hand. Debi Thomas, more abrupt and more direct, did not exude the natural star quality of her competitor. In addition, there was no love lost between the two skaters. And while the media was mesmerized by the "two Carmens," the judges' favorite was thought to be Canada's **Elizabeth Manley**, judged in some circles to be the best skater both technically and artistically. Thomas' artistic skills needed refining. In the compulsory figures, which counted for 20% of the score, Manley skated to first place, Thomas to second and Witt to third. During the short program, Witt's behavior was also faulted when she stayed on the edge of the rink watching Thomas execute the seven required moves. Some said Witt made Thomas nervous, though the American was perfect; going into the long program, which counts for 50% of the score, Thomas was first, Witt second, and Manley third. Thomas now aimed to demonstrate her superior athleticism, jumping higher and more often, but her program proved reckless.

Then Katarina Witt came on the ice, resplendent in red. Sensual in a way no other figure skater had ever been in competition, she quickly captivated both the audience and the judges. Technically her performance may have been weak, but artistically it was a triumph. Thomas, on the other hand, performed dismally, at least making the decision clear; poor landings and jumps cost her not only the gold but also the silver, which went to Manley. Katarina Witt joined the elite company of *Sonja Henie, winning her second gold medal for figure skating. On February 21, 1988, Phil Hershe rhapsodized in the *Chicago Tribune*, "Thomas skates brilliantly to Carmen. Witt is Carmen." Many felt Witt relied too heavily on flirting instead of technique. Pete Axthelm for *Newsweek* wrote: "She hardly seemed to skate. She flirted. In the slow segment of her *Carmen* program, she threw risk-taking to the wind. In lieu of daring jumps, the East German beauty seemed content to seek points with her coy shrugs, come-hither expressions and smiling eyes." Of her performance Witt said, "I want to be remembered as starting a new era in figure skating, where one tries to express the music, tell the whole story."

After the 1988 Olympics, Katarina Witt retired from competitive skating. In November 1989, the Berlin Wall came down, signifying the end of the Cold War, East Germany, and the state-financed athletic training cocoon which had nurtured her. Inevitably, there was some backbiting as Witt was criticized for her luxurious lifestyle in the former Communist country. She made no apologies, maintaining that stars in any country were given special privileges, and also pointed out the endorsements she had forfeited by refusing to cooperate with the Stasi. At the same time, she refused to repudiate completely the system which had trained her, a stance she has never abandoned.

Meanwhile, Witt and American skater Brian Boitano had become close friends, and the two began collaborating on an ice show. Joined by such world champions as Alexander Fadeev, Oleg Vasiliev, **Elena Valova**, Paul Martini, and **Barbara Underhill**, they built a show around acts that were both romantic and theatrical, with a far more athletic, demanding, and sophisticated style of skating than that of traditional ice shows. From childhood, both Witt and Boitano had skated solo, but now wanted to change their styles for this commercial endeavor. "We both like to express feelings and live within the characters and the story," said Witt. "I think more about a character when I'm with someone on the ice, so the acting is better." The tour was a triumph, and the possibilities for television specials, films, and other ice shows lay ahead. Witt also profited from endorsements such as Coca-Cola and was a television commentator for the 1992 Olympics. Everywhere she went, she was pursued by fans, and unlike some former Olympians, she flourished in the limelight.

By the time of the 1994 Winter Olympics in Lillehammer, Norway, women's skating had changed enormously. In the six years since Witt had won the gold, figure skating had become much more athletic. In the view of many, the sport that had once seemed very close to ballet now seemed to more closely resemble gymnastics. Realizing that she would not be able to compete at the same level as the new figure-skating stars, Witt had returned to her old rink in Karl-Marx-Stadt, now called Chemnitz, to train under Jutta Müller. For a year, she had subjected herself to the old discipline and worked hard to make the German team.

When she arrived in Lillehammer, the media was riveted by the **Nancy Kerrigan-Tonya Harding** scandal. During the final skating competition, Kerrigan, who had largely recovered from an attack instigated by Harding's former husband, skated exquisitely, dressed like a princess. **Oksana Baiul**, the young Russian skater, wooed audiences in pink. Witt wore a costume modeled on Robin Hood, because she noted, "I didn't want to be accused of seducing the judges this time." Dedicating her program to the people of wartorn Sarajevo, Witt skated to the antiwar anthem "Where Have All the Flowers Gone," reminding audiences worldwide of the Olympics which had taken place there in 1984, a time

Katarina Witt

when the peoples of the Balkans had lived in peace. The performance showed her typical grace, but she missed a triple loop when her hand touched the ice, and she had to turn a triple Salchow into a double. By the end, it was obvious that she was not nearly as athletic as her competitors that night, and she turned to the crowd with a sad smile, mouthing the words, "I'm sorry." To her surprise, the fans, tired of the tawdry antics which had dominated the championship, exploded into applause, showing their lasting affection for Witt. Although she placed seventh in the competition, far below what she once would have found acceptable, she knew the performance was still a triumph.

Dividing her time between Berlin and New York, Witt continued to perform with Boitano, and to do television commentary for international skating events. Now, she also has time to go to a ballet, a concert, or movies, or enjoy the simple pleasure of watching a sunset in the mountains or a sunrise at the beach. "I don't want to compete," she has said. "I want to skate for the joy."

SOURCES:

Axthelm, Pete. "Cool as Ice, Witt Hits Gold," in *Newsweek*. Vol. 111, no. 10. March 7, 1988, pp. 62–64.

Berkow, Ira. "Firepower Off the Ice," in *The New York Times Biographical Service*. April 1994, pp. 576–577.

Callahan, Tom. "The Word She Uses Is 'Invincible,'" in *Time*. Vol. 131, no. 7. February 15, 1988, pp. 44–46, 48, 57.

Condon, Robert J. *Great Women Athletes of the 20th Century*. Jefferson, NC: McFarland, 1991.

"For Medals and Television Glory," in *Newsweek*. Vol. 111, no. 7. February 15, 1988, pp. 78–81.

Janofsky, Michael. "East Germany's Tense Past Meets the Present," in *The New York Times Biographical Service*. February 1992, pp. 203–204.

Mansfield, Stephanie. "Katarina the Great," in *Vogue*. Vol. 181, April 1991, pp. 202–203, 210, 212.

Smolowe, Jill and Ellie McGrath. "Such Amazing Grace," in *Time*. Vol. 131, no. 10. March 7, 1988, pp. 64–66.

"A Spectacle for Thinking Adults," in *Time*. Vol. 136, no. 24. December 3, 1990, p. 98.

Starr, Mark. "Beauty is the Soul of Witt," in *Newsweek*. Vol. 122, no. 22. November 29, 1993, p. 83.

Wilson-Smith, Anthony. "Fire on the Ice," in *Maclean's*. Vol. 101, no. 4. February 1988, pp. 24–26, 28.

"Witt Switches Routine and Lands Smoothly," in *The New York Times Biographical Service*. February 1991, pp. 83–84.

Karin Loewen Haag,
freelance writer,
Athens, Georgia

Wittelsbach, Hedwig (fl. late 1600s).

See Hedwig Wittelsbach.

Wittenmyer, Annie Turner

(1827–1900)

American war relief worker, church leader, and charity organizer. Born on August 26, 1827, in Sandy Springs, Ohio; died of cardiac asthma on February 2, 1900, in Sanatoga, Pennsylvania; daughter of John G. Turner and Elizabeth (Smith) Turner; educated at a seminary in Ohio; married William Wittenmyer (a merchant), in 1847 (died around 1861); children: son Charles Albert, and four other children who died in infancy.

Annie Turner Wittenmyer was born in 1827 in Sandy Springs, Ohio, a small town on the Ohio River, one of several children of **Elizabeth Smith Turner**, a Kentuckian of Scots-Irish origins, and John G. Turner, born in Maryland of English descent. Annie spent some of her childhood years in Kentucky (where her father had also lived) and apparently attended a seminary in Ohio before marrying William Wittenmyer, a prosperous merchant, in 1847. Three years later, the couple moved to Keokuk, Iowa, with their children. They would eventually have five, but only one, Charles Albert, survived infancy.

With the move to Keokuk, Wittenmyer began a life dedicated to community service. She organized a Methodist church and a free school for destitute children. After losing her husband around 1861 and watching Civil War troops assemble at encampments along the Mississippi, Wittenmyer became secretary of Keokuk's Soldiers' Aid Society and spent much of her time comforting the sick. She sent Charles Albert to her mother and sister and began visiting Iowa soldiers. She also reported the conditions she observed back home to Keokuk, where they were published in the newspapers; other Iowa women began collecting the much-needed hospital supplies Wittenmyer requested and forming aid societies in their own communities. Wittenmyer's society in Keokuk became the central collection point for relief supplies dispatched throughout Iowa. Paying her own expenses at first, Wittenmyer also went to the front and nursed the wounded. Later, the Keokuk Soldiers' Aid Society helped fund her work, and in 1862 she was appointed a state sanitary agent under a new Iowa law.

Disputes plagued the various sanitary commissions, however. Wittenmyer's relief work was done in cooperation with the Western Sanitary Commission of St. Louis, but this organization conflicted with the men's organization, the Iowa Army Sanitary Commission, which was affiliated with the U.S. Sanitary Commission headquartered in New York. A convention was assembled in Muscatine, Iowa, in October 1863 to try to end the rivalry between these organizations and to merge both women's and men's work under the auspices of the U.S. Sanitary Commission. Wittenmyer resisted this action and headed an independent Iowa State Sanitary Commission. In November, however, another convention reorganized Iowa's relief work under the U.S. Sanitary Commission, Wittenmyer's opponent. Early in 1864, the Iowa legislature was presented with a bill penned by Wittenmyer's detractors requesting the repeal of her appointment and accusing her of profligate spending and of selling medical supply donations to hospitals. She successfully refuted the charges and her appointment was saved from repeal, but she nevertheless resigned in May 1864, having devised another plan to aid the wounded.

Realizing that army rations were not the best food for the injured, Wittenmyer planned to attach kitchens to hospitals to provide special diets for patients. In January 1864, she won support for the plan from another relief group, the U.S. Christian Commission, which both funded the project and provided special foods. A first kitchen was set up adjacent to the army hospital in

Nashville; after it proved highly successful, Wittenmyer directed the establishment of kitchens at other army hospitals. She also recruited women to serve as kitchen managers. These approximately 100 women supervised the soldiers assigned to furnish physical labor. The managers also made certain that patients actually received the food. In time, the kitchens were adopted as standards of the military hospital system.

Wittenmyer had also become concerned with the children of Iowa soldiers who had died in service. By 1865, she had organized a movement and called on Washington to convert barracks in Davenport for the use of the Iowa Orphans' Home Association and to provide medical supplies. In 1868, she was instrumental (through her affiliation with the Methodist Church) in creating the Ladies' and Pastors' Christian Union in which women visited the sick and needy with the guidance of their pastors. She became the corresponding secretary of this organization in 1871 and lectured frequently on its behalf.

Also in 1871, Wittenmyer moved to Philadelphia, where she established the *Christian Woman* magazine, which she published as a private enterprise and edited for 11 years. She also wrote hymns and books, including *Woman's Work for Jesus* (1871) and *Women of the Reformation* (1884). In 1872, Wittenmyer met Bishop Mathew Simpson who, on visits to Germany, had seen the work of deaconess orders there and thought their method could be adapted into American Methodism through the Ladies' and Pastors' Union. Although Wittenmyer went to Kaiserwerth, Germany, to observe the Lutheran deaconess centers, the Methodist deaconess project was assumed by *Lucy Meyer and *Jane Bancroft Robinson.

Wittenmyer's imagination had been captured by another, stronger cause. In 1873 and 1874, the Women's Crusade against alcohol had spread across western New York, Ohio, and throughout the Midwest. Wittenmyer lent her energies to this movement and represented Methodist women at a conference held in Cleveland in November 1874, which resulted in the birth of the National Woman's Christian Temperance Union (WCTU). Wittenmyer was elected the WCTU's first president. In 1875, she and *Frances E. Willard, the WCTU's corresponding secretary, toured extensively, lectured, and helped form local unions. That year, she also established the first official journal of the WCTU, *Our Union*. Wittenmyer again traveled to Washington, in both 1875 and 1878, bearing massive petitions to Congress that demanded the investigation of liquor traffic and the creation of a federal prohibition amendment. She documented these events in her *History of the Woman's Temperance Crusade* (1878), which expresses her strong belief that the WCTU was leading a divinely inspired movement to contest the liquor trade and its domination by a "low class of foreigners."

Wittenmyer was reelected president of the WCTU in 1877 and 1878, but she was opposed each year with increasing strength by Willard. The enterprising Willard represented women from the West who wanted the WCTU to advocate other causes, including women's suffrage. Finally, in 1879, Willard defeated Wittenmyer. During the five years of Wittenmyer's presidency, however, more than 1,000 local unions had been formed, and 26,000 members had joined the crusade. Wittenmyer remained active in both the Pennsylvania and national unions. When Willard had the WCTU endorse the Prohibition Party, Wittenmyer opposed this action by joining J. Ellen Foster and others in organizing the Non-Partisan Woman's Christian Temperance Union in 1890. Although Wittenmyer was simply a supporter at first, she eventually served as president from 1896 to 1898.

In 1889, she resumed her work on Civil War-related causes. She served as president from 1889 to 1890 of the Woman's Relief Corps (WRC), the women's branch of the Grand Army of the Republic. She also worked to found a national WRC rest home in Ohio for ex-nurses and for the female relations of veterans. As director of this home and another in Pennsylvania, she successfully lobbied Congress to pass an 1892 bill to pay pensions to former war nurses; Wittenmyer herself received a special pension in 1898. She lectured on behalf of the WRC and helped to edit publications by and about Civil War veterans. She also wrote about her war experiences in *Under the Guns*, published in 1895.

From the 1880s forward, Wittenmyer lived at her son's home in Sanatoga (now part of Pottstown), Pennsylvania. Upon celebrating her 70th birthday in 1897, she received gifts and congratulations from all over the United States. On February 2, 1900, she delivered a lecture in Pottstown, Pennsylvania, returned home, and died a few hours later from cardiac asthma.

SOURCES:

James, Edward T., ed. *Notable American Women, 1607–1950.* Cambridge, MA: The Belknap Press of Harvard University, 1971.

McHenry, Robert, ed. *Famous American Women.* NY: Dover, 1980.

Gillian S. Holmes,
freelance writer,
Hayward, California

Witty, Chris (1975—)

American speedskater. Born on June 23, 1975, in West Allis, Wisconsin.

Won U.S. Sprint championship (1995, 1996); won silver medal at World Sprint championship (1995); won World Sprint championship (1996); won nine medals in World Cup competition, including a sweep of the 1000 meters in Milwaukee (1996, 1997); won bronze medal at World Sprint championship (1997); won bronze and silver medals at Nagano Olympics (1998).

At the Nagano Olympics in 1998, Chris Witty surprised herself when she won the bronze medal in the 1500 meters, not her speciality, with a time of 1:58.97. *Marianne Timmer of the Netherlands took the gold medal. Witty was expected to medal in the 1000 meters, having come into the Olympics as the world-record holder with a time of 1:15.43, but Timmer, a good friend of Witty's, also took the gold in that event at 1:16.51. Witty finished second at 1:16.75 for the silver. *Catriona Le May-Doan won the bronze.

Wixom, Emma (1859–1940).

See Nevada, Emma.

Wöckel-Eckert, Bärbel (1955—)

East German track-and-field champion. Name variations: Barbel Eckert; Baerbel Woeckel; Bärbel Wockel. Born on March 21, 1955.

In 1976 in Montreal, Bärbel Wöckel-Eckert won Olympic gold medals in the 200 meters, with a time of 22.37, and in the 4x100 meters. She won two more gold medals in Moscow in 1980 in the same events; her time in the 200 meters was 22.03.

Woerishoffer, Carola (1885–1911)

American social activist and philanthropist who worked for the betterment of labor conditions. Born Emma Carola Woerishoffer in August 1885 in New York City; died in an automobile accident on September 11, 1911; daughter of Anna (Uhl) Woerishoffer and Charles Frederick Woerishoffer; granddaughter of Anna Uhl Ottendorfer (1815–1884); educated at the Brearley School, New York; graduated from Bryn Mawr College, Pennsylvania, 1907.

Carola Woerishoffer was born in New York City in 1885, the only child of **Anna Uhl Woer-**ishoffer and Charles Frederick Woerishoffer, a wealthy German-born Wall Street banker. Carola, who inherited her father's large fortune on his death in 1886, was raised by her mother Anna, a social reformer and advocate of the working class. (Anna's own mother ***Anna Uhl Ottendorfer** had managed a progressive German-language newspaper in New York.) Carola went to private schools, including the Brearley School, and then moved to Pennsylvania to attend Bryn Mawr College. There she excelled in both academics and athletics, studying economics, philosophy, languages, and political science. She graduated in 1907, and returned to New York City.

Although she did not need to work, Woerishoffer followed the example of her mother and became active as a social reformer. In 1908, she helped with the American Museum of Natural History to produce a Congestion Exhibit, which exposed New Yorkers to the crowded, unsanitary living conditions suffered by the city's poor. Her involvement with the exhibit led to associations with ***Florence Kelley**, founder of New York's National Consumers' League, and ***Mary Simkhovitch**, founder of the Greenwich House settlement home; she became a leader in both organizations.

Like many women activists at the turn of the 20th century, Woerishoffer was particularly concerned with the labor and living conditions of women, and in 1908 she was a founder of the New York Women's Trade Union League (WTUL). She served as its treasurer and worked in the union label shop as well. Her efforts on behalf of women expanded to include non-union work when she became a district leader for the New York Woman Suffrage Party.

The following year, Woerishoffer wanted to investigate the working conditions in the laundry industry herself, believing that social reform movements needed to be grounded in empirical evidence in order to effect change. As part of her desire to unite compassion with scientific research, for four months Woerishoffer took jobs under an assumed name in a dozen laundries. To be able to understand the lives of the workers better, she lived off her laundry pay and worked 15-hour days, six and seven days a week, in dangerous and unhealthy conditions. She then reported to the National Consumers' League on the terrible conditions laundresses endured.

She was hired by New York State's Wainwright Commission on employer liability to investigate employment agencies, again working under a false name as an immigrant service worker. Woerishoffer believed that the changing of public perceptions was important, and governmental regulation of labor conditions and wages was required. She saw her research and that of others, gathering evidence and statistical data, as vital to proving to the government the need for federal intervention. In 1910, she was appointed investigator to the Bureau of Industries and Immigration of the New York State Association for Labor Legislation. Her work involved traveling across the state investigating immigrant labor camps and reporting her findings to the bureau.

As a volunteer in her many organizations, Woerishoffer worked in menial tasks, refusing privileges for herself because of her wealth and status. Yet she enthusiastically devoted her personal wealth to her causes as well. In 1909, she supported striking garment workers by arguing for them in court and put up $75,000 in real estate as bond for jailed strikers. Although she was eager to discuss the strike and the workers' grievances with newspaper reporters, Woerishoffer refused to let herself become the center of the coverage, and maintained a low profile to keep attention on the workers themselves.

Carola Woerishoffer died in a car accident near Cannonsville, New York, in September 1911, while she was driving home from a labor camp investigation. She was 26 years old. Perhaps her most important legacy came from her will, which stipulated a bequest of $750,000 to her alma mater, Bryn Mawr. The college created an endowment fund and, in 1915, founded a new school in her honor. The Carola Woerishoffer Graduate Department of Social Economy and Social Research was the first professional school of social work in the world, and the first American school to offer a doctoral degree in social work.

SOURCES:

Garraty, John A., and Mark C. Carnes, eds. *American National Biography*. Vol. 23. NY: Oxford University Press, 1999.

Read, Phyllis J., and Bernard L. Witlieb. *The Book of Women's Firsts*. NY: Random House, 1992.

Laura York, M.A. in History,
University of California,
Riverside, California

Woffington, Peg (c. 1714–1760)

Irish actress who played leading roles in Dublin and London, achieving great success in comedy and in "breeches" parts. Name variations: Margaret Woffington. Born Margaret Woffington, possibly on October 18, 1714 (some sources cite 1717, 1718, or 1720), in Dublin, Ireland; died at Queen Square, Westminster, on March 26, 1760; daughter of John Woffington (a bricklayer) and Hannah Woffington (some sources give Murphy as the family name, Woffington being adopted later as a stage name); received a "genteel" education until her father's death c. 1720 left the family in poverty; never married; no children.

Taken on as a child performer by Madame Violante, who ran rope-dancing and theatrical entertainments in Dublin; appeared as Polly and in other parts in The Beggar's Opera *in Dublin and London; engaged (c. 1736) at Dublin's Aungier Street Theater; played Ophelia, her first major role (1737); first appeared as Sir Harry Wildair in Farquhar's* The Constant Couple *(1740); engaged by Rich for Covent Garden Theater, London (1740); opened (November 6, 1740) as Sylvia in* The Recruiting Officer *and subsequently in other parts, including that of Sir Harry Wildair; returned to Dublin and played opposite David Garrick at Smock Alley Theater (1742); played at Theater Royal, Drury Lane (1743–48); moved to Covent Garden, where she performed (1748–51); returned to Dublin (1751), receiving a record salary as a player at Smock Alley Theater; remained in Dublin until a riot closed Smock Alley (1754), when she returned to Covent Garden; collapsed on stage (1757); ill health prevented her return to the theater and she lived in retirement until her death three years later.*

On May 3, 1757, one of the most celebrated actresses of the century made her final stage appearance while doing Shakespeare's *As You Like It*. For almost two decades, Peg Woffington had, as one contemporary critic remarked, "carried the town captive," delighting audiences in Dublin and London by the charm of her personality no less than by the magic of her performances. Now, in an exit which, though unplanned, was as dramatic as any of her roles, she took leave of her public. The young actor Tate Wilkinson, who was present, described the scene:

> She went through Rosalind for four acts without my perceiving that she was in the least disordered; but in the fifth act she complained of great indisposition. . . . When she came off at the quick change of dress, she again complained of being ill, but got accoutred, and returned to finish the part, and pronounced the epilogue speech. . . . But, when arrived at, "If I were a woman I would kiss as many of you as had beards" etc., her voice broke and she faltered and endeavoured to go on, but could not proceed; then, in a voice of tremor exclaimed, "O God! O God!" and tottered to the stage-door speechless, where she was caught. The audience of course applauded till she was out of sight, and then sank into awful looks of astonishment, both young and old, before and behind the curtain, to see one of the most handsome women of the age, a favourite

principal actress . . . struck so suddenly by the hand of Death, in such a time and place, and in the prime of life.

Woffington's collapse and her subsequent retirement brought to an abrupt end a career which had taken her from the most obscure and unpromising beginnings to the pinnacle of her profession. Little is known of her family or early childhood, and even her date of birth is uncertain. The year 1720 cited on her memorial tablet is probably incorrect, and she may have been born as early as 1714. Some accounts describe her father John Woffington as a bricklayer, and Chetwood in his 1749 *General History of the Stage* reported that she was "born of reputable parents who gave her a genteel education." In about 1720, however, her father died, leaving his family in poverty. **Hannah Woffington**, with two small children to support, set up as a hawker, and, helped by Peg, her elder daughter, earned a precarious livelihood by selling watercress and salad stuffs on the street. Lee Lewes in his *Memoirs*, published in 1805, claimed to have talked to Dubliners, "who assured me that they remembered to have seen the lovely Peggy, with a little dish upon her head, and without shoes to cover her delicate feet, crying through College Green, Dame Street and other parts of that end of the town, 'All this fine young salad for a ha'penny, all for a ha'penny, all for a ha'penny here!'"

In about 1727, the young Peg attracted the attention of **Madame Violante**, a Frenchwoman, who was currently appearing in Dublin in a rope-dancing entertainment. Madame's performance entailed walking a tightrope with a basket containing a child suspended from each foot, and, according to some accounts, Peg made her first appearance on stage in this capacity. The show lasted for only one season, but some time later she was again engaged by Violante as a member of a "lilliputian" or children's company for which she played Polly Peachum and other parts in performances of John Gay's *The Beggar's Opera* in both Dublin and London. The young actress attracted the attention of Thomas Elrington, a noted Dublin actor manager, and was engaged by him to play at Aungier Street Theater, where she appeared in a number of minor parts as well as dancing and singing between the acts. In 1736 or 1737, she appeared in her first starring role, having reportedly persuaded the management to let her take over the part of Ophelia when the actress playing it was suddenly taken ill. She went on to take a number of other leading parts, including that of Sylvia in *The Recruiting Officer*, which required her to appear in disguise as a man and, in April 1740,

was first cast in the role for which she was to be most highly praised and with which her name was to become synonymous, that of Sir Harry Wildair in Farquhar's *The Constant Couple*.

The practice of actresses playing male or "breeches" parts was already well established, having been common since the introduction of women actors onto the English and subsequently the Irish stage in 1660. Prior to this date, female roles were played by boys; Elizabethan and Jacobean plays consequently included frequent scenes in which women characters assumed male disguise. When those characters began to be played by actresses such as *Nell Gwynn and *Elizabeth Barry, their appearance in men's dress had an erotic effect which made such roles extremely popular and prompted playwrights to include them in their new works. Thus, of the total of 375 plays publicly staged in London between 1660 and 1700, 89 contained one or more roles for an actress in male clothes, while at least 14 more had women playing roles originally written for men. The custom continued into the next century, with the Irish actress ❧➧ George Anne Bellamy enjoying a success in Dublin in *The Recruiting Officer*. However, Peg's performance as Wildair in 1740 surpassed all others in the popular and critical acclaim which it produced. She had an immediate success in the part, repeating it regularly throughout her career and making it her own to such an extent, wrote Murphy, that "the actors, even Garrick himself, made a voluntary resignation to her. She was the only Sir Harry Wildair during the remainder of her life."

Triumphant in Dublin, Woffington now took the traditional route of successful Irish actors to London. Traveling there in May 1740, she was engaged by John Rich, manager of the Covent Garden Theater, and on November 6, 1740, made her sensational London debut in *The Recruiting Officer*. Her success in the character of Wildair, in which she first appeared "by particular desire" on November 21, was even greater. She went on to play the part over 20 times during that particular season, and in January 1742, having moved to the Theater Royal at Drury Lane, assayed it once again in a royal command performance before Frederick Louis and *Augusta of Saxe-Gotha, the prince and princess of Wales. Not long afterwards, in May 1742, she made her first appearance with the newly arrived and already acclaimed young actor David Garrick, as Cordelia to his King Lear, and at about the same time began an affair with him which was to last for the next three years. In the following month, at the end of the London season, she and Garrick traveled to Dublin, where at the

Smock Alley Theater they played opposite one another in *Hamlet* and in *The Recruiting Officer*. Woffington was, of course, already a favorite with Dublin theatergoers, but Garrick, on his first visit to Ireland, was a sensation, attracting huge and enthusiastic audiences.

Back in London, the two set up house together, for a time in company with another actor, Charles Macklin, and later as a couple, agreeing to share household expenses. However, the relationship was increasingly strained by Garrick's carefulness with money and desire for respectability and by Woffington's relations with other men and her disregard of convention. Professional matters also may have come between them: in 1743, Garrick took on the part of Wildair, but, in contrast to Peg's many successes in this role, his attempt was an embarrassing failure. By May of that year, the couple were living apart. Woffington acquired a villa outside London, at Teddington, and when Garrick and other players became embroiled in a dispute with the management of Drury Lane, she took no part in it. Unlike Garrick, she appeared in the 1743–44 season, giving her first performance as Mistress Ford in Shakespeare's *The Merry Wives of Windsor* in November 1743. By the beginning of the following year, however, the two were once more appearing together on stage, and the affair itself was apparently continuing. There were rumors that they were to marry, and they did reportedly come close to doing so, but Garrick's earlier disquiet about the relationship resurfaced, resulting in a permanent split. Garrick was popularly regarded as having acted in an ungentlemanly manner in withdrawing his offer of marriage after such a long and public association. However, the breakdown of the relationship was probably inevitable: as Macklin, who knew both parties well, remarked, "dispositions so different as Garrick's and Woffington's, were not likely to produce a good matrimonial duet."

Woffington never married: the title "Mrs.," used in contemporary playbills and accounts, was a courtesy one, afforded to all actresses, and reports that she had secretly married her last lover, Colonel Caesar, were without foundation. The decision to remain single was, as **Elizabeth Howe** points out in her study of English actresses, not uncommon, and, at a time when a married woman surrendered control of her earnings to her husband, was probably motivated as much by economic as by emotional considerations. Unlike the great majority of her female colleagues, Woffington was in a position to command extremely high fees, and the estate which she would leave on her death suggests that she was an exceptionally capable manager of her own fi-

Bellamy, George Anne (1727–1788)

Irish actress. Name variations: Mrs. Bellamy. Born George Anne Bellamy at County Fingal, Dublin, Ireland, by her own account, on St. George's Day, April 23, 1733, but more probably in 1727; died in London, England, on February 16 (some sources cite February 10), 1788; illegitimate daughter of James O'Hara, 2nd Baron Tyrawley (British ambassador) and a Miss Seal; educated at a convent in Boulogne, France; married twice, once bigamously.

George Anne Bellamy was the illegitimate daughter of James O'Hara, 2nd Baron Tyrawley. Her mother, a Quaker named Miss Seal, married a Captain Bellamy, and the child received the name George Anne, a mishearing of the name Georgiana during her christening. Lord Tyrawley acknowledged the child and had her educated in a convent in Boulogne; through him she came to know a number of notable people in London. On his appointment as ambassador to Russia, she went to live with her mother in London, made the acquaintance of *Peg Woffington and David Garrick, and adopted the theatrical profession.

George Anne Bellamy was a celebrated actress, notes an 1888 theatrical reference book, "whose private history is of rather a sensational order." She first appeared at Covent Garden in *Love for Love* (1742) and went on to play Juliet to David Garrick's Romeo at Drury Lane at the time that Spranger Barry was giving rival performances as Romeo at Covent Garden. (Bellamy was considered the better of the Juliets.) Bellamy furnished the materials for her five-volume *Apology* to bookseller John Calcraft, who then asked Alexander Bicknell to whip them into shape; the memoirs containing her "amours, adventures, and vicissitudes" were published in 1785, the year of her retirement, and achieved great popularity. An early "as told to," the last volume was published with the following title page: "An apology for the life of George Anne Bellamy, late of Covent Garden Theater. Written by herself. To the fifth volume of which is annexed, her original letter to John Calcraft, Esq. advertised to be published in October 1767, but which was then violently suppressed." Her last years were unhappy, and passed in poverty and ill health.

nances. In such circumstances, marriage might well be regarded as an undesirable surrender of the autonomy which she had enjoyed throughout her career. However, she paid a price for this independence in the scurrilous rumors about her private life which circulated throughout her lifetime. The general perception of actresses as promiscuous, together with Peg's openness about her affairs, fuelled such gossip and greatly exaggerated the number of her lovers.

When Garrick returned to Dublin in autumn 1745, Peg remained at Drury Lane. Her

Peg
Woffington

professional relationship with Garrick was resumed when he became joint manager of the theater, where she stayed until 1748 when she moved back to Covent Garden. According to her rival, George Anne Bellamy, her departure from Drury Lane was prompted by her jealousy of other actresses: "Mrs Woffington," Bellamy reported, was "highly offended at her quondam admirer Mr Garrick, choosing rather to appear with Mrs Pritchard than with her." Peg's relations with other leading ladies were never good. Jealous of her status and professional integrity, she reacted strongly to any real or imagined slight, and her feuds with actresses such as *Hannah Pritchard, *Kitty Clive and the younger George Anne Bellamy were acrimonious and public. The quarrel with Bellamy culminated in an incident in 1755 when, during a performance of *The Rival Queens*, Woffington drove the other actress off the stage and stabbed her almost in view of the audience.

During the summer of 1748, Woffington visited Paris, where she reportedly met Voltaire and visited the playhouses frequently, regarding the French actors as superior to the English in tragedy. She had already appeared in London in her first major tragic role, though to a mixed public and critical response, as Cleopatra in Dryden's *All for Love*. She was never to reach the same heights in tragedy as in comedy, but in the following season at Covent Garden, while continuing to appear in the comedy parts in which she had made her reputation, she also won new praise for roles such as Portia in *Julius Caesar*, Andromache in *The Distress'd Mother*, Calista in Rowe's *The Fair Penitent* and the Lady in *Comus*. During the following two seasons at Covent Garden, Peg added more tragic parts to her repertoire. These included the Shakespearean heroines Desdemona and Lady Macbeth, as well as Arpasia in *Tamerlane* and Cleopatra again, this time with greater success than when she had played it previously.

In 1751, as a result of a quarrel with Rich and of dissatisfaction with the regime at Covent Garden, Peg revisited Dublin. Engaged by Thomas Sheridan at Smock Alley, she demanded, and received, the then astronomical salary of £400 for the season. The 1751–52 season was one of the most brilliant mounted by Sheridan's company, and Woffington's presence played a large part in this success. Soon after her opening as Lady Townley in *The Provoked Husband*, the *Dublin Journal* was reporting that her performances were attracting "the most crowded audiences hitherto known"; her two benefit performances were gala occasions, attended by the viceroy and the duke of Dorset, and the local critics and public were united in her praise. Her performance as Sir Harry Wildair was particularly popular and was repeated several times during the season. So successful was she, and so profitable for the company, that she was engaged for the next season at double the salary, earning in addition over £200 more from two benefits on her behalf. She remained the company's star attraction, staying on for two more seasons, one of her greatest successes being in another "breeches" part

which she acted here for the first time, that of Lothario in *The Fair Penitent*. She was honored by the viceroy, an enthusiastic patron of the theater, and by the fashionable Beefsteak Club, founded by Sheridan, which made her its president and its only woman member. However, eyebrows were raised when at Christmas 1752 she left Dublin, accompanied by Sheridan, for an unknown destination. In fact, their journey was to the latter's native county of Cavan, where Woffington, born a Catholic, was to be received discreetly into the Church of Ireland. The conversion was a purely pragmatic one, intended to allow Peg to inherit a legacy which was conditional on her becoming a Protestant, although one contemporary journal, noting the current prohibition on Catholics bearing arms, pretended to believe that "some eminent lawyers advised her to take this step, in order to qualify herself to wear a sword in the character of Sir Harry Wildair."

She had Beauty, Shape, Wit and Vivacity, equal to any theatrical Female in any Time, and capable of Undertaking in the Province of Comedy, nay of deceiving, and Warming into Passion, any of her own Sex, if she had been unknown and introduced as a young Baronet just returned from his Travels.

—Benjamin Victor

The 1753–54 season began as well as its predecessors, but was to end in disaster. Though not a political society, the Beefsteak Club had become associated in the public mind with the viceroy and his circle. The growing unpopularity of the government as a result of the perennially vexed question of crown control over Irish finances was reflected in public animosity towards Sheridan and Woffington herself, and by January 1754 she was reportedly playing to empty houses. On March 2, a performance of *Mahomet*, which included lines interpreted as having a bearing on the dispute, provoked violent protests in the theater. Woffington herself was a member of the cast on this occasion, and was no stranger to disturbances in the theater: a few years earlier at Covent Garden she had faced and quelled an angry audience. On this occasion, however, her appearance failed to quiet the mob, and a full-scale riot erupted, which wrecked the theater, bringing the season to a premature end and driving her, with other members of the company, back to London.

On October 22, 1754, Peg reappeared at Covent Garden as Maria in *The Nonjuror*, and followed this, among other roles, with Phaedra in *Phaedra and Hippolitus*, Lady Pliant in *The Double Dealer* and Jocasta in *Oedipus*. Over the next three seasons, and in spite of worsening health, she successfully repeated old parts, like Wildair, Sylvia, Millamant and Lady Townley, and appeared in a number of new parts, both in comedy and tragedy. Unlike many of her colleagues, she insisted on performing whenever possible, and Hitchcock, in his *Historical View of the Irish Stage*, praised her professionalism. "She had," he noted, "none of those occasional illnesses which I have sometimes seen assumed by capital performers, to the great vexation and loss of the manager and disappointment of the public." On May 3, 1757, she took the stage as Rosalind. Having broken down during the play, she returned to finish it, but within a few lines of the end, collapsed and had to be carried off. It was her final performance. Believed by both audience and colleagues to be dying, she did in fact survive for a further three years, but never recovered sufficiently to return to the stage. Her final years were spent as an invalid, in the company of her last lover, Colonel Caesar. She may have visited Dublin in the winter of 1757, before returning to London, where she received visitors, took an interest in various charities and had her portrait painted, probably by Arthur Pond, while lying on her sickbed. Peg Woffington died on March 26, 1760, in Colonel Caesar's house in Queen Square, Westminster, and was buried in Teddington churchyard. A memorial tablet, erected to her in the church there, described her as "Spinster. Born Oct. 18th 1720."

Throughout her career, Peg had supported both her mother and her sister **Mary Woffington**, who, after an unsuccessful stage career, had married into the aristocracy. According to Macklin, Peg, some years before her death, made a verbal agreement with Colonel Caesar "that the longest liver should have all." However, "Mrs Woffington having neglected to make a clause in favour of her sister until her last illness . . . the sister took advantage . . . of the Colonel's leaving the house one evening rather early, and had the will altered to her own mind." In the event, the estate, which amounted to £8,000 and some property, was left either to Mary or at her direction, except for an annuity of £42 to their mother.

Woffington was remembered with admiration and affection by most of her colleagues and contemporaries, although her reputed promiscuity dismayed those who wished to raise the status of professional actors at a time when the theater was still condemned by some moralists as "the house of the devil." Even her friend Thomas Sheridan reportedly refused to introduce her to his wife *Frances Sheridan, declaring that her "moral character was such as to exclude her from the society of her own sex." Garrick's biographer, Murphy, too, felt obliged to excuse that "one female error," apart from which, however:

> It might fairly be said of her that she was adorned with every virtue; honour, truth, benevolence and charity were her distinguishing qualities. Her understanding was superior to that of the generality of her sex. Her conversation was in a style of elegance, always pleasing and often instructive. She abounded in wit. . . . She possessed a fine figure, great beauty, and every elegant accomplishment.

Peg's beauty, recorded in several portraits, was matched by the charm of her personality. Witty and intelligent, her conversation, it was said, "was not less sought by men of wit and genius than by men of pleasure." Essentially unchanged by success, she remained, according to Hitchcock, "the same gay, affable, obliging, good-natured Woffington to everyone around her." A consummate professional, she had a keen sense of loyalty towards her fellow players, appearing frequently in benefit performances which supplemented their earnings. During the 1751–52 Dublin season, for instance, she took part in 22 benefits out of a total of 26 held.

As an actress, Woffington was generally agreed to excel in comedy parts. Together with Macklin and Garrick, she helped to popularize a new, more naturalistic and easy style of acting, which was admirably suited to this genre. "Genteel comedy," wrote Murphy, "was her province," and Davies, in his *Life of Garrick*, agreed, mentioning particularly her Millamant and Lady Townley. "Her chief merit in acting, I think, consisted in the representation of females in high rank and of dignified elegance, whose grace in deportment, as well as foibles, she understood and displayed in a very lively and pleasing manner." However, she "did not confine herself to parts of superior elegance; she loved to wanton [to play loosely] with ignorance combined with absurdity, and to play with petulance and folly, with peevishness and vulgarity" in parts such as that of Lady Pliant.

Woffington was less successful in tragic roles, to which her voice was reportedly unsuited: one critic described it as "croaking," and another complained that "she barked out her sentences with dissonant notes of voice as ever offended a critical ear." Her technique was also criticized, Victor suggesting that she had adopted the French tragic style, "which appeared too affected and extravagant for an English audience." However, there were differences of opinion on this topic. Victor himself commended her Andromache as displaying "the true spirit of the noble Grecian matron," and Thomas Wilkes, in his *General View of the Stage*, declared that throughout her career she had "stood in a capital light, both in tragedy and comedy, with a dignity in the former and a polite deportment in the latter that we despair of ever seeing equalled."

Above all, however, Woffington was admired for her appearances in male roles, most famously Sir Harry Wildair. A biography of her fellow actor James Quin noted, "there was no woman that ever yet had appeared on the stage, who could represent with such ease and elegance the character of a man," and she herself is said to have remarked, "I have played the part so often, that half the house believes me to be a real man." Yet, as Pat Rogers points out, the charm of such a performance lay not in the accurate impersonation by a woman of a man but rather in its "imperfect masculinity," in the titillation provided by the bending of gender stereotypes and in constant reminders of the actress' essential femininity, as conveyed in this contemporary verse in praise of her Wildair.

> That excellent Peg
> Who showed such a leg
> When lately she dressed in men's clothes—
> A creature uncommon
> Who's both man and woman
> And chief of the belles and the beaux!

Woffington's experience, as an actress and as a woman, was equivocal. As an actress, her talent and popularity brought critical acclaim and material reward. But the 18th-century theater, like society itself, was a male-dominated environment, and the occupational opportunities which it offered to women were offset by the inferior status of even its leading female players and by the exploitation of their sexuality both on and off the stage. Not the least of Woffington's achievements was the degree to which she overcame these disadvantages, to enjoy in her career and private life an independence which was, in contemporary terms, remarkable.

SOURCES:

Dunbar, Janet. *Peg Woffington and Her World*. London: Heinemann, 1968.

Gerard, Frances. *Some Celebrated Irish Beauties of the Last Century*. London: Ward and Downey, 1895.

Howe, Elizabeth. *The First English Actresses*. Cambridge University Press, 1992.

Lucey, Janet Camden. *Lovely Peggy: The Life and Times of Margaret Woffington*. London: Hurst and Blackett, 1952.

Rogers, Pat. "The breeches part," in *Sexuality in Eighteenth-century Britain*. Ed. by Paul-Gabriel Bouce. Manchester, England: Manchester University Press, 1982.

SUGGESTED READING:

Ferris, Lesley. *Acting Women: Images of Women in Theater*. London: Macmillan, 1990.

Reade, Charles. *Peg Woffington* (novel based on her life).

Rosemary Raughter,
freelance writer in women's history,
Dublin, Ireland

Wohmann, Gabriele (1932—)

German writer. Born Gabriele Guyot on May 21, 1932, in Darmstadt, Germany; daughter of Paul Daniel Guyot and Luise (Lettermann) Guyot; educated at the University of Frankfurt; married Reiner Wohmann, in 1953.

Received the Literary Prize of the City of Bremen (1971); elected to Berlin Academy of Art (1975); elected to Academy of Language and Literature (1980); awarded West German Order of Merit (1980).

Selected writings: Abschied für länger (*A Farewell for a Long Time, 1965*); Die grosse Liebe (*True Love, 1966*); Landliches Fest und andere Erzählungen (*Country Party and Other Stories, 1968*); Paulinchen war allein zu Haus (*Paulinchen Was Home Alone, 1974*); Schönes Gehege (*Beautiful Enclosure, 1975*); Frühherbst in Badenweiler (*Early Fall in Badenweiler, 1978*); Der Flötenton (*Sound of a Flute, 1987*); Aber das war noch nicht das Schlimmste (*But That Was Not Yet the Worst, 1998*); Frauen machens am späten Nachmittag: Sommergeschichten (*Summer Stories, 2000*).

Novelist Gabriele Wohmann was born in 1932 in Darmstadt, Germany, the daughter of **Luise Lettermann Guyot** and Paul Guyot, a parson. As she grew up during the Third Reich, her anti-fascist parents tried to shield her from Nazi propaganda and encouraged her education. After finishing high school in Norden, she studied German and foreign literatures and philosophy for three years at the University of Frankfurt. She left college in 1953 to marry another Frankfurt student, Reiner Wohmann. The Wohmanns taught for a year at a private school on the North Sea island of Langeroog, then took new teaching positions in Gabriele's native Darmstadt.

In 1956, Wohmann successfully submitted her first short story, "Ein unwiderstehlicher Mann" (An Irresistible Man), for publication. The critical acclaim which followed led her to quit teaching in order to write full-time in 1957. Three volumes of short stories appeared in 1958, 1960, and 1963, securely establishing

Wohmann as a leading figure in modern German literature. Since 1957 she has been a prolific writer, publishing short stories, novels, plays, and poetry as well as essays. Typical of postwar German literature, most of Wohmann's works are realistic in setting and pessimistic in theme, centering on the domestic conflicts of ordinary people. Deeply influenced by Irish novelist James Joyce, Wohmann has produced many works using Joyce's stream-of-consciousness narrative style. More recent works have addressed social issues such as drug abuse. Critics have consistently praised the depth of her characters and the universality of her themes, such as love, the fear of death, and loneliness. In 1974, her first television screenplay, "Entziehung" (Withdrawal), was produced, with Wohmann herself playing a drug addict in the film.

Her work has brought her numerous awards. In 1971 she won the Literature Prize of the City of Bremen, and she was elected to the Berlin Academy of Art in 1975. In 1980, she was elected to the Academy for Language and Litera-

Gabriele Wohmann

ture and was awarded the West German Order of Merit. Although they frequently travel to the United States and across Europe, the Wohmanns still make their home in Darmstadt.

SOURCES:

Bédé, Jean-Albert, and William B. Edgerton, eds. *Columbia Dictionary of Modern European Literature.* 2nd ed. NY: Columbia University Press, 1980.

Elfe, Wolfgang D., and James Hardin, eds. *Contemporary German Fiction Writers.* 2nd series. Detroit, MI: Gale Research.

Laura York, M.A. in History,
University of California,
Riverside, California

Wolcott, Marion Post (1910–1990)

American photographer of rural America in the 1930s and 1940s. Born Marion Post in Montclair, New Jersey, on June 7, 1910; died in Santa Barbara, California, on November 24, 1990; youngest of two daughters of Walter Post (a physician) and Helen (Hoyt) Post (a trained nurse); attended Bloomfield High School, Bloomfield, New Jersey; graduated from the Edgewood School, Greenwich, Connecticut; attended the New School for Social Research and New York University; attended the University of Vienna; married Leon Oliver Wolcott (a government official), on June 6, 1941; children: Linda Wolcott Moore; Michael Wolcott; (stepchildren) Gail Wolcott; John Wolcott.

During the brief period between 1938 and 1942, when she was a photographer for the Farm Security Administration (FSA), Marion Post Wolcott produced a vast body of compelling black and white photographs documenting life in rural America during the Depression. Through the years, Wolcott's photographs, along with those of Walker Evans, *Dorothea Lange, and others, found their way into numerous exhibits, publications, and major collections, including those of the Metropolitan Museum of Art, the Chicago Art Institute, and the Smithsonian Institution. Unlike many of her fellow FSA photographers, however, Wolcott slipped into obscurity. Her professional life ended abruptly in 1942, when, following her marriage to a widower with two small children, she resigned from her job to devote herself to her family. "You see, I guess I believed back then, or was supposed to believe, that my place was in the home," she told biographer Paul Hendrickson, who questioned the brevity of her career, "that I couldn't do both, you know, be a photographer, a would-be artist, and try to raise children. It just wasn't as easy in those days."

Wolcott was herself the product of a broken home, which may explain in part the choice she made. The youngest of two daughters of a physician, she spent her early years in Montclair, New Jersey, where her father had a homeopathic practice. The Posts underwent a bitter divorce when Wolcott was 14, after which she and her sister were sent to a boarding school in Pennsylvania. After an unhappy year there, she transferred to the Edgewood School in Greenwich, Connecticut, where she flourished in the more progressive environment. She spent weekends and summers with her mother Helen "Nan" Post, who had taken an apartment in Greenwich Village and was working with *Margaret Sanger to help establish health and birth control clinics around the country. After graduation, Wolcott lived with her mother while teaching at a progressive elementary school in New Jersey and attending classes at New York's New School for Social Research and later at New York University. Interested in such diverse subjects as modern dance, anthropology, and educational psychology, she finally decided that her talents lay in teaching young children. She had several different teaching positions during the early 1930s, one in a small western Massachusetts mill town where she watched with growing disillusionment as the school and the town struggled against encroaching poverty, then shut down.

In 1932, with money inherited from her father, Wolcott went to Europe, traveling in Paris and Berlin, and winding up in Vienna, where she studied child psychology at the University of Vienna. At the time, her sister Helen Post Modley was studying photography with Viennese photographer *Trude Fleischmann, who gave Wolcott her first little camera. "Sis, you've got a good eye," Fleischmann told Wolcott after developing some of her early pictures. Wolcott was encouraged, but dubious about entering the same field as her sister. Helen had always been the "artistic one."

With the frightening rise of Nazism and fascism in Europe, Wolcott returned to the United States, taking yet another teaching position and pursuing freelance photo assignments on the side. At age 25, she left teaching to devote herself to photography full time. After landing a photo on the cover of *The New York Times Magazine*, she joined the New York Photo League, where she was mentored by Ralph Steiner and Paul Strand. She also assisted on a film about labor organizing in the Cumberland Mountains of Tennessee, and worked briefly as a full-time staff photographer on the Philadelphia *Evening Bulletin*. In 1938, Paul Strand gave her a letter of introduction to Roy Stryker, head of the New Deal's Farm Security Administration Historical Section. Stryker offered her a trial position and she was off to Washington, D.C.

The FDA had been mandated by Franklin D. Roosevelt to assist farmers devastated by the Depression. In heading the Historical Section, Stryker's mission was both to document scenes of the country's economic plight and to sell the New Deal's agricultural programs. With these goals in mind, Wolcott traversed the South—the Carolinas, West Virginia, Florida, Georgia, Louisiana, and Texas. She also traveled less extensively in New England and the West. "Her views of migrant workers housing, coal mining families, and plantation farming demonstrate her flair for capturing subtle shifts in class and race hierarchies," writes Deborah L. Owen. "Her studies of New England architecture are clean and simple, yet reveal a bitterness in climate and attitude that lay beneath village surfaces."

Wolcott traveled alone, and according to her daughter, Linda Wolcott Moore, got lonely, tired, and eventually burned out. "She had to wrap her camera in hot water bottles to keep the shutters from freezing; write captions at night in flimsy motel rooms while fending off the men trying to enter through the transoms; deal with southern social workers, suspicious cops, chiggers and mosquitoes; mud, heat and humidity."

In order to achieve her revealing images, Wolcott first befriended her subjects, sometimes joining them to work in the fields, or tending the children left behind. Her daughter notes that Wolcott cared deeply about the people she photographed, and they in turn trusted her. "They liked her; they knew she cared; they thought that maybe she would, could, help. That the images would get back to others who would, and could, help. She gave them hope; and, she did what she had to do, with a passion and commitment that kept her on the backroad alone for up to a month at a time."

Despite loneliness and fatigue, Wolcott never lost her sense of humor, as evidenced in a letter from the road dated July 18, 1940:

> Chief Stryker! Calling all cars. Caution all photogs! Never take picture of pregnant woman sitting in rocking chair on sloping lawn while visiting family on Sunday afternoon! Consequences are—lady doesn't want photograph taken in present state, starts hurriedly to get up & run in house, but chair tips over backwards dumping (& embarrassing, not seriously damaging) her. Photog is surprised, sorry, tries to apologize, inquire after victim's health, etc., etc., & succeeds

only in almost being mobbed & beaten & driven off by irate & resentful & peace loving member of family—DOZENS of them. (P.S.—Camera was saved.)

In 1941, Wolcott met and fell in love with Leon "Lee" Oliver Wolcott, the handsome assistant to Henry Wallace, secretary of agriculture under President Roosevelt, and a widower with two small children. They married following a whirlwind courtship. Though she continued with her photography a while longer, she missed her husband and was conflicted about working, especially because she had two stepchildren, Gail and John, to care for. Lee offered no encouragement for her to stay on the job. She resigned in February 1942 and entered what Hendrickson termed "almost fifty years of photographic hiding."

The Wolcotts settled outside Washington, D.C. Over the next ten years, they owned three different farms and had two more children, Linda and Mike. They were not easy times for Wolcott, who was sometimes overwhelmed with the chaotic household and her responsibilities as

Marion Post Wolcott

a farm wife. "At the moment we are under a lot of strain and pressure, having bought a small dairy farm (1135 acres & 45 head) about 6 miles from this place, in January," she wrote her old boss Roy Stryker in April 1948, displaying none of the humor that had infused her earlier notes from the road. "We are still hoping to sell this, & move over there eventually but I'm afraid that this house is not to be sold very easily. Labor, both household & farm help, is still very scarce & poor & unreliable, making life difficult & keeping us tied down."

On several occasions Wolcott attempted to leave her husband, but she never followed through. Her neighbors from that time could attest to the tensions in the marriage. "I don't think I ever really heard Lee and Marion in an argument of their own," said **Betty Campbell**, Wolcotts' closest neighbor for a half-dozen years. "But I remember his stern voice with her now and then. He'd say something like, 'Now you listen to me!'" Wolcott took some pictures of Betty's children, but Betty noticed that she wasn't at all enthusiastic about photography at the time. "It seems such a shame, this business about Marion and the stopping. Why didn't she go on? . . . I don't think she truly wanted it after she had kids. On the other hand, I guess I've always secretly wondered if there wasn't a little part of him that wanted to put her down. Maybe he didn't want her to come up to him."

In 1953, Lee was involved in an accident with a gasoline-powered brush burner that badly burned his legs and ended his farming career. He was in the hospital for five months, during which time Wolcott contacted Stryker, telling him she wanted to work again, not for the money, but for something to do. Stryker was evasive, spending much of their luncheon meeting telling her that her place, especially now, was beside her husband. "A good man needs a good woman when he's recovering, Marion," he said. Wolcott came away filled with doubt about her talent.

After recuperating, Lee became a professor of government at the University of New Mexico, then took a position with the State Department. For the next 30 years, Wolcott accompanied her husband to various foreign posts in Iran, Pakistan, Egypt, Afghanistan, and India. She photographed children and captured some of her travels on film, but none of her images ever reached the public. After returning to the United States in 1968, the couple moved again several times before finally settling in Santa Barbara, California.

Wolcott's work came to the attention of the art world in 1976, through an influential FSA group exhibition at New York's Witkin Gallery. At that time, she briefly entered the public arena, granting some interviews and accepting speaking engagements. (Her daughter said she agonized over her speeches, spending weeks researching, note-taking, and doggedly rewriting.) In 1978, the first solo exhibition of her work occurred in California, and in 1983, the first monograph of her photographs was published, a project headed up by **Sally Stein**, a teacher, historian and feminist. There were subsequent retrospectives of her work at the Art Institute of Chicago and at the International Center of Photography in New York City.

Wolcott died on November 24, 1999, after a long battle with lung cancer. A few years before her death, she was the keynote speaker at a Women in Photography Conference at Syracuse University. "Women are tough, supportive, sensitive, intelligent, and creative," she told her audience. "They're survivors. Women have come a long way, but not far enough. Ahead still are formidable hurdles. Speak with your images from your heart and soul. Give of yourself. Trust your gut reactions. Suck out the juices—the essence of your life experiences. Get on with it; it may not be too late." Perhaps Wolcott was attempting to gear up a new generation of women to persevere in the battle that she had given up on years before.

SOURCES:

Hendrickson, Paul. *Looking for the Light: The Hidden Life and Art of Marion Post Wolcott.* NY: Alfred A. Knopf, 1992.

Owen, Deborah L. *American National Biography.* Vol. 23. Ed. by John A. Garraty and Mark C. Carnes. NY: Oxford University Press, 1999.

Rosenblum, Naomi. *A History of Women Photographers.* NY: Abbeville, 1994.

SUGGESTED READING:

McEuen, Melissa A. *Seeing America: Women Photographers Between the Wars.* KY: University Press of Kentucky, 1999.

Barbara Morgan,
Melrose, Massachusetts

Wolf, Christa (1929—)

German writer from the former German Democratic Republic whose internationally acclaimed novels and essays advocate the humanistic goals of Marxism while promoting a confrontation with Germany's past and present. Pronunciation: VOllff (O as in old). Born Christa Margarete Ihlenfeld on March 18, 1929, in Landsberg-Wartha (today Gorzów Wielkopolski, Poland); daughter of Otto Ihlenfeld (a merchant); attended Oberschule in Landsberg, 1939–45, Oberschule in Schwerin, 1946–47, Abitur in Bad Frankenhausen, 1949; studied Germanic languages and literature in Jena and Leibzig, 1949–53; married Gerhard Wolf (the Germanist and essayist), in 1951; children: Annette (b. 1952); Katrin (b. 1956).

Family fled to Mecklenburg (1945); took various jobs, including position as clerk typist for the mayor of Gammelin (1945–46); stayed at a sanitarium for pulmonary diseases (1946); was a member of the SED (Socialist Unity Party, 1949–89); moved to Berlin (1953); was a research assistant for the German Writers' Union (1953–55); was on staff of Neue deutsche Literatur (1954–59); served as chief editor for publishing company Neues Leben (1956–59); made first trip to the Soviet Union (1955); was a member and executive committee member of the Writers' Union, German Democratic Republic (GDR, 1955–77); moved to Halle, worked in a factory, became involved in the Association of Writing Workers, was a freelance editor of Mitteldeutscher Verlag (Halle), and editor of several anthologies of contemporary German literature (1959–62); awarded Artists' Prize of the City of Halle (1962); freelanced in Kleinmachnow near Berlin (1962—); given Heinrich Mann Prize of the Academy of Arts of the GDR (1963); was a candidate of the Central Committee of the Socialist Unity Party (1963–67); awarded National Prize Third Class of the Academy of Arts of the GDR (1964); awarded Wilhelm-Raabe Prize of the City of Braunschweig (1972); Theodor Fontane Prize for Art and Literature (1973); dismissed from the executive committee of the Berlin Section of the Writers' Union of the GDR (1976); granted Literature Prize of the City of Bremen (1977); traveled in Athens and Crete (1981); was a guest professor in Poetics at the University of Frankfurt am Main (1982); granted Schiller Prize, was a guest professor and given honorary doctorate at Ohio State University, and gave readings in New York, Los Angeles, San Francisco (1983); went on a reading tour through Italy and Austria (1984); awarded Austrian National Prize for Literature and an honorary doctorate, University of Hamburg (1985); traveled to Greece and Spain (1986); granted Geschwister-Scholl Prize of Munich and was a guest professor at the Technische Hochschule in Zürich (1987); after the fall of the Berlin Wall, withdrew Socialist Union Party membership (1989); gave various speeches and essays concerning German unification (1989); awarded honorary doctorates, University of Hildesheim and the Free University of Brussels; granted the Ordre des Artes et Lettres, France; given Literature Prize of the 16th Internationale, Mondello, Italy; received intense attention from the media and faced charges of cowardice after the publication of "What Remains?" (1990); discovery of a file of the Stasi, the secret security service of the

GDR, that listed Wolf (1959–62) as secret informer and informal collaborator of the Stasi (1993); given stipend at Getty Center, Santa Monica (1994).

Selected writings: Moskauer Novelle *(1961);* Divided Heaven *(1963, trans. 1965);* The Quest of Christa T. *(1968, trans. 1970);* The Reader and the Writer: Essays, Sketches, Memories *(1971, trans. 1977);* Till Eulenspiegel *(film script with Gerhard Wolf, 1972);* A Model Childhood *(1976, trans. 1980);* No Place on Earth *(1979, trans. 1982);* Cassandra *(1983, trans. 1984);* Accident/A Day's News *(1987);* The Fourth Dimension: Interviews with Christa Wolf *(1988, trans. 1989);* What Remains? *(1990, trans. 1993); numerous short stories, some published in* What Remains and Other Stories *(1993);* Auf dem Weg nach Tabou *(1994, trans. and released in U.S. as* Parting from Phantoms: Selected Writings, 1990–1994, *University of Chicago, 1997).*

When it became known in 1993, after the opening of the files of the former German Democratic Republic's Secret Security Service (Stasi), that Christa Wolf was listed from 1959 to 1962 by the Stasi, first as a secret informer and then as an informal collaborator, a lively debate ensued following earlier accusations of complicity with the former socialist regime. The most prominent East German writer, simultaneously idealized and sharply criticized in both Germanies, was known and respected as a tireless advocate of humanitarian and feminist ideals, personal truthfulness, and collective remembrance, and to many Wolf represented the very ideal of personal integrity and human decency. Her reputation at stake, Wolf wrote in her own defense, addressing some issues and raising only more questions concerning others. She was unable to exonerate herself in the eyes of some critics and readers, confirming the distrust of those critics who had always been suspicious of Wolf's support of socialism and disappointing others who until now had firmly believed in her honesty and integrity.

The discovery that she acted as an informant for the Stasi and had written a report about a fellow writer was the second controversy after the disintegration of East Germany concerning Wolf's ethical and political convictions, and in the eyes of many, Wolf became one of the idols fallen along with socialism and the border between East and West Germany. Wolf had received unfavorable attention shortly after the collapse of the East German State when she published *What Remains?*, a story chronicling her experience of being spied upon by the Stasi in

June and July 1979. Critics wondered why Wolf, who wrote about her ordeal in 1979, waited to publish the story until the East German State no longer existed. Some criticized the delayed publication as a sign of her lack of courage and her complicity with the regime. Was the most celebrated writer of the former German Democratic Republic (GDR) claiming to have secretly resisted the repressive regime? Why did she hold back until the party was no longer in power and when it was safe, and even politically correct, to come forward with a story criticizing the methods of the old regime? Did the fact that she was complaining about having been watched by the Stasi for a few weeks not make a mockery of the true suffering of the hundreds of writers and artists who were harassed, blackmailed, jailed, forbidden to publish, or expelled? Why, critics asked, was Wolf now portraying herself as a victim of the system she had supported intellectually for so many years?

Many of Wolf's earlier novels and stories are critical of certain aspects of the repressive East German State, and her subjective and individualistic style of writing defied the official call for an uncritical, non-experimental socialist-realist literature idealizing the life under socialism as the only way to truly achieve justice and equality. Despite her critical stance, Wolf always defended the ideals of socialism and consciously chose to remain in East Germany despite numerous opportunities for defection during her travels in Europe and the United States. Because of the skillful restraint in her explorations of the advantages and limitations of socialism, she managed—despite some sharp criticism from the political establishment—to have her works published and honored in the GDR. Through her work, Wolf promoted a confrontation with Nazism and the German past, thus countering the official East German point of view, which denied any responsibility for the past. Because the GDR was a socialist country, it was built—so went the official party line—upon an anti-fascist foundation and therefore must not share the guilt for the crimes of the Nazis.

Born in 1929, Christa Wolf grew up in Nazi Germany and witnessed the rise and fall of the Hitler regime. The advance of the Red Army toward the West forced her family to flee to the city of Mecklenburg. Within the next few years, Wolf held various jobs, including a clerk-typist position for the mayor of the small town of Gammelin. After a stay in a sanatorium for pulmonary diseases, Wolf completed her diploma in Bad Frankenhausen in 1949. Reading the works of Karl Marx and Friedrich Engels, she became

convinced that socialism was the bearer of hope for a new, anti-fascist beginning and a more humane and just society. In 1949, she became a member of the Socialist Unity Party, which was to rule the GDR until its collapse in 1989. Wolf remained a member until 1989.

Her desire to write developed in childhood. During her youth, Wolf wrote letters to friends and jotted down stories, daydreams, and poems. In retrospect, Wolf perceived her early ambitions as grounded in the longing to change and multiply her inner self and observes that her writings represented reality in a naive and carefree manner. Possibly meant to be an act of liberation and a sign of the hope for a new beginning, Wolf burned her diaries after the war. She planned to become a teacher and studied Germanic languages and literature at the universities of Jena and Leibzig. She finished her studies with a thesis on the problems of realism in the works of the German writer Hans Fallada, which she wrote under the direction of the well-known writer and Germanist Hans Mayer. In 1951, she married the essayist Gerhard Wolf, with whom she collaborated in several projects, including a film script entitled *Till Eulenspiegel*. Their first daughter, **Annette**, was born in 1952. Having given up her plans to become a teacher, Wolf worked as an assistant for the East German Writers' Union, a reader for the publishing house Neues Leben, and an editor of the periodical *Neue Deutsche Literatur*.

If we cease to hope, then that which we fear will surely come.
—Christa Wolf

In 1959, three years after her daughter **Katrin** was born, Wolf moved to Halle, and under the influence of the socialist writers' movement whose goal was to bridge the gap between physical, intellectual, and artistic labor, worked in a factory. The idea of having writers share the everyday lives of factory workers on the one hand and encouraging workers to write about their experiences on the other, was the result of the 1959 Bitterfeld writers' conference, which affirmed the tradition of the programmatic concepts of writing, socialist realism, and considered writing an instrument for the advancement of socialist consciousness. The realization of these attempts to overcome the division of art and life and to involve writers in material production and workers in creating literature failed, because few writers were willing to commit themselves to working in the factories for an extended period of time and few workers were interested in participating in the Circles of Writing Workers.

In 1961, Wolf published her first novel, *Moskauer Novelle*, for which she received the Artists' Prize of the City of Halle. It is the story of Vera, an East Berlin doctor, who travels to Moscow in 1959 and finds that Pavel, the Russian interpreter for her delegation, is the former lieutenant of the Red Army whom she had met 15 years earlier during the Soviet occupation of East Germany. Pavel's and Vera's love story is a parable of the relations between the Soviet Union and East Germany: Vera feels guilty about the German past and an accident which caused Pavel's eye injury, and Pavel is a model socialist who educates Vera to become a socially responsible member of the new system. Wolf's story, which did not receive much attention, already contained some of the themes important for her later work, including the search for truth, the longing for a new society and new values, and the connection between love and suffering.

Wolf's first success came with the 1963 publication of *Divided Heaven*. The factory worker Rita falls in love with the chemist Manfred, who is portrayed as an emotionally immature cynic unwilling to integrate himself into the socialist system. Manfred moves to the West and Rita follows him to West Berlin, but returns to the East just before the borders are closed and the Berlin Wall is built in 1961 in order to stop the mass exodus of skilled workers and professionals. In the GDR, the novel was hailed for its commitment to socialism, demonstrated by Rita's conscious decision to return to the East. In the West, the novel was interpreted as a critique of the Wall, and many critics pointed out that Rita's accident at the end of the novel could indeed be interpreted as a suicide attempt.

Wolf's novel *The Quest for Christa T.* focuses on the narrator's struggle to write about and come to terms with the life of Christa T., who dies of leukemia. The East German teacher Christa T. fails as a writer and ends up leading an ordinary existence as a housewife and mother, and the narrator asks: "How, if at all, and under what circumstances, can one realize oneself in a work of art?" Christa T. does not fit the mold of the socialist individual and does not conform to the pressures of the collective. Instead, she values imagination, spontaneity, and self-actualization and searches for a harmonious coexistence between her emotional and intellectual self. In opposition to the demands of the new system, Christa T. longs for personal fulfillment, and struggles, like the narrator, to find and say the truth. Because of its implied criticism of the socialist state, *The Quest for Christa T.* was largely ignored in East Germany, and Wolf was criticized for her departure from the socialist-realist model of literature. In the West, the novel enjoyed great success.

Wolf's next novel, *A Model Childhood*, is partly an autobiographical account of life under fascism and the difficulty of dealing with the fascist past in the present. With her husband and daughter, Nelly returns to her native Landsberg, now part of Poland, and recalls her childhood during the Third Reich. Nelly attempts to come to terms with the past, and the novel suggests that due to their failure to oppose Nazism, both East and West Germans must share the responsibility for the atrocities of fascism. This novel was received well in both Germanies.

In 1976, Wolf and her husband signed an open letter protesting the expulsion of the writer and singer Wolf Biermann from the GDR. She was one of the first 12 writers to sign and more than 70 artists and intellectuals followed within the next few days. The party reacted to this demonstration of solidarity with various sanctions and expelled some writers from the party and/or prohibited them from publishing their works. Wolf's husband was among those expelled, and Wolf herself was dismissed from the executive committee of the Berlin Section of the Writers' Union of the GDR.

In the 1970s, Wolf began to explore 19th-century German Romanticism, an enterprise allowing her to turn from contemporary events to an exploration of historical figures of German literature. In an interview, she described the period following the Biermann incident as a time when she felt obliged to examine the preconditions for failure and "the connection between social desperation and failure in literature. At the time, I was living with the intense feeling of standing with my back to the wall, unable to take a proper step." In 1979, Wolf published the story of a fictional encounter between the writer Heinrich von Kleist and the poet ✥➤ **Karoline von Günderrode**, both of whom eventually committed suicide. *No Place on Earth* is a novel critical of modern life and the consequences of technological advances and rationalized forms of human interaction. Kleist and Günderrode long for a life of passion, truth, and friendship, but despite their momentary closeness, their dialogue ultimately fails, both finding no place on earth for the fulfillment of their desires. Because of its thematization of issues of gender and its inherent critique of patriarchal society, *No Place on Earth* has been well received among feminists and was instrumental in a renewed interest in the role of women during the Romantic period.

The critique of patriarchy is the focus of *Cassandra* (1983), which develops a utopian vision of a female existence freed from male violence. Awaiting her death at the hands of her Greeks captors, the mythological figure of the Trojan Cassandra—who was able to foresee the future, but whose predictions were not believed—recalls the path of war and destruction and reflects upon the possibilities and impossibilities of a humane life under male domination, for which Greek culture stands as a paradigm.

For the Greeks there is no alternative but either truth or lies, right and wrong, victory or defeat, friend and enemy, life or death. They think differently than we do. What cannot be seen, smelled, heard, touched, does not exist. It is the other alternative that they crush between their clear-cut distinctions, the third alternative, which in their view does not exist, the smiling vital force that is able to generate itself from itself over and over: the undivided, spirit in life, life in spirit.

During the many years of war, however, the Trojans adopt the attitudes of their enemy, and the decline of its culture turns Troy into a repressive, corrupt society willing to sacrifice its own standards of liberty, justice, and morality for a chance to defeat the Greeks. As a woman, Cassandra becomes subject to the will and cruelty of both the Greek enemy and the men ruling Troy. After the fall of Troy, Cassandra chooses to die rather than to escape: "I had to reject at the cost of my life: submission to a role contrary to my nature." In both East and West Germany, *Cassandra* became a bestseller and instant classic; it is still Wolf's most successful novel.

One year after the nuclear accident at Chernobyl in the Soviet Union, Wolf published *Accident/A Day's News*, which explores the advantages and dangers of modern technology. The news of the nuclear accident confronts the narrator with the terrible consequences of technology, while she realizes simultaneously that her brother, who suffers from a brain tumor, depends upon medical technology to save his life.

After the opening of the Berlin Wall in 1989 and the publication of *What Remains?* in 1990, Wolf was at the center of a controversy involving East and West German intellectuals. In many ways, this controversy is an exemplar of the German dispute over morality and aesthetics, the role of the intellectual within society, the relationship between the German past and East German socialism, the loss of a utopian vision, and the reception of East German literature by West German critics. The intense debate over Wolf also testifies to the continued distance, the mistrust, and the failed efforts to come to an understanding between East and West. Although the border between the two countries has fallen, the border in the minds of the German people still exists and continues to divide.

Wolf's *Auf dem Weg nach Tabou* (1994) documents the doubts and uncertainty following the collapse of the GDR and the unification of Germany. It is a collection of Wolf's essays, speeches, diary entries, and correspondences with renowned intellectuals in East and West.

◀✥
*Günderrode,
Karoline von.*
See Arnim,
Bettine von for
sidebar.

Auf dem Weg nach Tabou testifies to Wolf's continued concern about the future of humanity and raises uncomfortable questions concerning the future of a unified Germany. It fails, however, to explain the author's personal involvement in the socialist regime.

Many critics insist that Wolf's claim to have forgotten and repressed her collaboration with the Stasi contradicts her efforts to counter the collective repression of the Nazi past by the German people. Her relationship to her own past brings to mind her critical analysis of the repression of history and memory in *A Model Childhood*: "What is past is not dead. It is not even past. We separate ourselves from it and pretend to be strangers."

SOURCES:

Anz, Thomas. *Es geht nicht um Christa Wolf.* Frankfurt: Fischer, 1995.

"Culture Is What You Experience—An Interview with Christa Wolf," in *New German Critique.* Trans. by Jeanette Clausen. Vol. 27, Fall 1982.

Emmerich, Wolfgang. *Kleine Literaturgeschichte der DDR.* Frankfurt: Luchterhand, 1989.

Fries, Marilyn Sibley, ed. *Responses to Christa Wolf.* Detroit, MI: Wayne State University Press, 1989.

Hilzinger, Sonja. *Christa Wolf.* Stuttgart: Metzler, 1986.

SUGGESTED READING:

Kuhn, Anna K. *Christa Wolf's Utopian Vision: From Marxism to Feminism.* Cambridge: Cambridge University Press, 1988.

Wilke, Sabine. *Ausgraben und Erinnern.* Würzburg: Königshausen & Neumann, 1993.

Karin Bauer,
Assistant Professor of German Studies, McGill University,
Montreal, Canada

Wolfe, Catherine L. (1828–1887)

American philanthropist. Born Catharine Lorillard Wolfe in New York City on May 8, 1828; died at her home in New York City on April 4, 1887; second and only surviving child of John David Wolfe (a hardware mogul) and Dorothea Ann (Lorillard) Wolfe (heir to the Lorillard family, manufacturers of tobacco); first cousin of **Catherine Wolfe Bruce** (patron of astronomy); educated at home by private tutors and abroad; never married; no children.

Following the death of her parents, Catherine Lorillard Wolfe was left with a large fortune, and devoted her life to works of charity. Besides giving generous sums to Grace Church, Union College, the American School at Athens, and St. Luke's Hospital in New York City, she founded a newsboys' lodging and a home for incurables. Wolfe also supplied the funds for Dr. Ward's archaeological expedition to Asia Minor, and gave a valuable collection of paintings to the Metropolitan Museum of Art, with an endowment of $200,000, for its preservation and enlargement.

Wolfe, Elsie de (1865–1950).

See de Wolfe, Elsie.

Wolff, Elizabeth Betjen (1738–1804).

See Deken, Aagje for sidebar on Elizabeth Bekker.

Wolff, Helen (1906–1994)

U.S.-German publisher and partner with Kurt Wolff—responsible for publishing many of the best-known books of this century such as Doctor Zhivago, The Tin Drum, *and* The Leopard—*whose influence on publishing was incalculable. Born Helen Mosel in Üsküb (Skopje), Macedonia, in 1906; died of heart failure on March 29, 1994, in Hanover, New Hampshire; father was an engineer with Siemens; mother was a cultivated Viennese of Austro-Hungarian descent; had one brother and two sisters; educated at Schondorf School as the only female pupil; married Kurt Wolff (the publisher), in 1933 (killed in an accident on October 21, 1963); children: son Christian Wolff (b. 1934).*

After the Balkan War, family left for Berlin (1915) where they remained until 1916; went to work for Wolff Verlag (1927); sent to Paris when Pegasus, part of Wolff Verlag, was sold (1929); lived in exile in Italy (1935–37) and in France (1937–39); interned with husband as enemy aliens (1939); left for U.S. (1941); founded Pantheon Books (1942); published Gift from the Sea *(1955),* Doctor Zhivago *(1958),* Born Free *(1960); established "A Helen and Kurt Wolff Book" imprint (1960s); after Kurt's death, continued as publisher for Konrad Lorenz, Amos Oz, Stanislaw Lem, as well as many other distinguished European writers.*

In 1941, as they headed for a boat out of Lisbon, Helen and Kurt Wolff were only one step ahead of the Nazi juggernaut. "I deliberately packed the kind of clothes that one would need in a concentration camp," said Helen, "including overalls and sturdy boots for my husband, our son, and myself." The Wolffs knew their fate was sealed should they be caught. They had already been interned in France as enemy aliens. Although she was Catholic and he was Protestant, both were viewed as enemies of the Third Reich and destined to be eliminated in Nazi-occupied France. Fortunately, the Wolff family was able to board the *Serpa Pinto* bound for New York. As they sailed westward, the

American shipping lines closed down this last remaining passenger service for the duration of the war. They were among the last to escape the Holocaust which would consume many of their friends and relatives.

Helen Mosel was born in 1906 in Macedonia and grew up in the town of Üsküb (formerly Skopje), where the inhabitants were a mixture of Turks, Greeks, Albanians, and Serbs. The town boasted a fortress, the Vardar River, and a predilection for earthquakes (a severe quake partially destroyed the city in 1963). Young Helen recalled a piece of nursery ceiling falling on her bed during one quake. Fortunately, it was unoccupied at the time. Helen's father, who was from Bonn and an employee of Siemens, was in Macedonia as part of a program to electrify Turkey. Her mother was Austrian and Hungarian. The family lived in Üsküb ten years, and her brother and two sisters were also born there.

Wolff's colorful childhood prepared her for an adventurous adult life. Living conditions were primitive. Although her father had come to electrify the area, their home was lit by kerosene lamps. Automobile traffic was unheard of. The children's favorite time of year was known as a "cholera vacation." During the annual epidemic, all lessons stopped, which they viewed as a great treat. Daily walks were another event she and her siblings anticipated. Before they left the house, however, her mother took out her binoculars to check if any bodies were hanging from the town gallows. If this were the case, the walk had to be terminated at the railroad tracks, as their mother felt this sight would be too traumatic for her children. Despite such gruesome sights, the inhabitants were friendly and kind to children, and invitations into homes for sweets were common. The young children had a sense of safety and moved about with a great deal of freedom. Even in remote Üsküb, Helen, who began reading at age four, was surrounded by books, as her parents had a decent library. She spoke German at home, but learned Turkish and Serbian as well. Her parents were regular contributors to German newspapers, and her mother wrote especially notable reports on events in Turkey.

When the Balkan Wars broke out (1912–13), shortly before World War I, and the Serbs took over the town, the Mosel family had to flee. Mother and children went to Vienna where they stayed with family while Helen's father went to Samsun, on the Black Sea in Turkey, as a member of the German consular service. The family was separated throughout the war. Food shortages in Vienna forced them to move to Berlin in 1916.

Here conditions were only slightly better, and at the end of the war they moved to Oberammergau in rural Bavaria where more food was available.

Despite much moving about, Helen was well educated, largely because her parents emphasized learning. She was taught by a series of tutors and when the family left Berlin, her mother brought along Fräulein Albrecht to school the two girls. "When you get private tutoring," said Wolff, "you learn nothing or a great deal. I owe a lot to Fräulein Albrecht." Among other subjects, she learned English, French, and piano. Later, the family moved again to be near the Schondorf School where her brother was enrolled as a day student. Enrolled in the all-boys' school as well, the 15-year-old Helen discovered her private tutoring in French and English had stood her in good stead, though this was not the case in geometry and mathematics. Being the only girl was harrowing at times, but she enjoyed Schondorf where she excelled in German composition.

Wolff was gifted with languages and an avid reader. Even as a teenager, she wanted to enter the world of publishing. She was offered a trainee position without pay, thanks to the intervention of **Leila von Meister**, a classmate's mother. Having heard of Helen's aspirations, von Meister spoke to the one publisher she knew, Kurt Wolff. Thus it was in 1927 that Helen Mosel went to Munich armed with von Meister's advice, "You have three months to make yourself indispensable." Helen's language skills were immediately required, and she plunged into work on an international art series which involved translating French, German, Italian, and English.

Helen had unknowingly joined one of the most innovative publishing firms of that or any era. In 1913, Kurt Wolff decided to publish the best work of his generation. Born into a highly cultured family in Bonn in 1887, Kurt had systematically collected German books from different styles and periods. His father, a Protestant, was a professor of music, while his mother, who loved books, was from an old, assimilated Jewish family. Uninterested in the financial aspects of the book trade, Kurt wanted to distribute the works of new authors in editions of high quality for relatively little cost. He published unknown authors such as Franz Kafka, Oskar Kokoschka, Franz Werfel, and Joseph Roth and produced prize-winning German translations of Emile Zola, Maxim Gorky, and Sinclair Lewis. Kurt Wolff Verlag books had bold and colorful jackets. Striking design also characterized the firm's advertising, rendered by such contemporary artists as Paul Klee, Alfred Kubin, and George Grosz. New thematic series with open-ended lists such as the "new novel," the "European novel," and "modern poetry in translation" were introduced. Kurt combined old and new in an interesting manner; for example, he reissued Voltaire's *Candide* with drawings by Klee.

Helen threw herself into this unique publishing venture with great enthusiasm and by the end of the trial period had, indeed, become indispensable. In 1929, currency problems forced Kurt to sell the Pantheon series on which Helen was working to a Parisian firm. "I was part of the deal," she said, "because I had been with the series almost from its inception. So I can only say that I was sold with it." In Paris, however, the venture continued to struggle so she soon found work in a branch of the League of Nations on the strength of her fluent French. Though he was married to his first wife at the time, she and Kurt remained in touch. It wasn't until 1933 that they were married, after he had been divorced for two years.

I never felt that I was in my husband's shadow; I always felt that I was in his light.

—Helen Wolff

Kurt had been brought up a Protestant, but he failed the "racial purity" test. According to Nazi guidelines, because his mother's maiden name was Marx, he was "half-Jewish." A Roman Catholic, Helen's mother was extremely cosmopolitan. She had leanings toward Islam and read the Koran to her children. The racial intolerance sweeping Europe was difficult for Helen Wolff to comprehend. Though France was accepting foreigners in the early 1930s, the Wolffs moved to Italy in 1935 to be in a safer, cheaper environment. They soon realized they would never go back to Germany. For two years, they remained in Italy until they felt impelled to return to Paris, as Florence by then was full of Gestapo agents. When war broke out in 1939, France no longer seemed a safe haven: concentration camps were already well known and Paris was full of Jewish refugees. One of their friends, Paul Ludwig Landsberg, went underground but was picked up, tortured, and died in a concentration camp in the south of France. The outlook was grim. Two professors who were friends offered to shoot the Wolffs if the Nazis occupied Paris.

The Wolffs' first thought was to save their small son, Christian. In May 1940, the six-year-old was sent to a convent school at La Rochelle. Shortly thereafter, Kurt was rounded up by the French and sent to an enemy alien camp at Le Cheylard in southeastern France. Then, the French began to round up alien women, and Helen was shipped south to Gurs, near the Pyrenees. When an armistice was declared between Germany and France in June 1940, Helen Wolff walked out of the camp (no one stopped her) and hitchhiked toward southeastern France where her husband and son were located. She ended up at Saint-Lary-près-Lach where she stayed with **Berthe Colloredo-Mansfeld**, an Austrian countess who hated the Nazis. While there, Wolff learned that Kurt had managed to leave the internment camp, and she joined him in Nice. They knew they must get Christian out of the convent school and leave Europe. But how? La Rochelle was under German occupation.

Tina Vinès, a friend who worked at the Louvre, retrieved their son from the convent and smuggled him out of town in a peasant's cart. As a French-born citizen, Christian was an enormous asset to his parents. The Wolffs were convinced that the reason they were allowed to leave France was because French authorities reasoned that a French child needed his parents. Once reunited with Christian, Kurt began to assemble documents to travel to America. These included an exit visa from France, a transit visa through Spain, and an American entry visa. It was almost impossible to get one document without the others. Thanks to the efforts of Varian M. Fry, an American scholar and editor who set up an American Aid Center in Marseilles, the documents were procured. *Eleanor Roosevelt** aided Fry by expediting paperwork through the State Department. Dr. **Thea Dispeker** obtained a sponsor in the States, asking Robert C. Weinberg, an architect and regional planner, to vouch for the Wolffs. The family's assets were traded in for two bars of gold.

Thus, the Wolffs—at great risk because of the U-boats patrolling the Atlantic—finally became passengers on the *Sera Pinto*, a ship overloaded with 600-plus passengers and makeshift bunks to accommodate everyone. The ship had to stop first in Bermuda where, for three days, the passengers were questioned before going on to New York. Despite all this, Helen termed the voyage "uneventful," and the family finally docked on March 30, 1941, at Staten Island. The Wolffs arrived penniless. Having paid $2,600 for the trip, they had exhausted most of their cash reserves. Dr. Dispeker met them at the dock and set them up in two rooms in a hotel on Columbus Avenue. Though they were free, they were now refugees from an enemy country in a new land with a new language. English was more a barrier for Kurt than for Helen. But the Wolffs were determined to rebuild their lives.

Kurt set out immediately to raise money to begin a new publishing firm. Though their assets in Europe were frozen, Barclays Bank in London lent them money based on those accounts. Then Kurt persuaded three investors—Weinberg, Gerald Neisser, and George Merke—to fund this new publishing enterprise. Thus, Pantheon Books was founded in February 1942 and run out of their apartment at 41 Washington Square. The venture required an enormous effort from both Wolffs. In the beginning, they decided to publish books already in the public domain, so many hours of research in libraries were required. They brought out Jakob Burckhardt's *Force and Freedom: Reflections on History*, Erich Kahler's *Man the Measure*, and Hermann Broch's *The Death of Virgil* among others. Many of the books chosen had not yet been translated into English. After a year, they were doing modestly well. Their first success was *The Complete Grimm's Fairy Tales* translated by **Margaret Hunt** with illustrations by Josef Scharl, which was issued in 1944. When word got out that the Wolff firm was publishing again, Paul and **Mary Mellon** asked the Wolffs to publish the Bollingen Series—handsome volumes on the arts, humanities, and psychology. Because of the beauty of the volumes and the prestige of its backers, this series marked a turning point and provided a steady income.

In 1949, Pantheon moved to offices at 333 Sixth Avenue. Helen's job was editing, copy editing, proofreading, advertising, and publicity; she also typed her own letters and ran the juvenile department. In the 1950s, only 12 people worked for the firm. Expanding into new areas, historical novels were added to their list. ***Mary Renault**'s *The Last of the Wine*, *The King Must Die*, and *The Bull from the Sea* were all bestsellers. The firm branched out into Zen Buddhism, publishing Allan Watts' *Behold the Spirit* and *The Way of Zen* due largely to Helen's influence as she was interested in Oriental philosophy. The Wolffs also brought out two phenomenal bestsellers, *****Anne Morrow Lindbergh**'s *Gift from the Sea* in 1955 and Boris Pasternak's *Doctor Zhivago* in 1958, as well as Günter Grass' *The Tin Drum*, and Giorgio Bassani's *The Garden of the Finzi-Continis*. Their authors included Max Frisch and Georges Simenon. At this point, Pantheon was "awash with money." (The Wolffs had struck up an epistolary friendship with Pasternak, thus they felt genuine anguish when the Soviet government forced the author to refuse the Nobel Prize for literature. Helen was responsible for the phrase which summed up the Russian author's situation: "Boris Pasternak rejects the prize, retains the honor.")

Helen Wolff's gifts as a linguist brought the firm another bestseller in 1960, *The Leopard* by Giuseppe Tomasi di Lampedusa. After reading the book in Italian, she had been determined to have it translated and published. The couple were living in Switzerland at the time, and success was beginning to take its toll. Because of Kurt's heart trouble, they sold their shares in Pantheon, though they kept their affiliation with the firm. While in Switzerland, they also acquired the rights to *****Joy Adamson**'s *Born Free*. The Wolffs had published a great deal of Carl Gustav Jung's work in the Bollingen Series and wanted another volume, though Jung was now in his 80s. He dictated large portions of *Memories, Dreams, and Reflections* to Aniela Jaffé before his death in 1961. Helen helped bring the book to final form, and it was published in 1963. In 1961, the Wolffs resigned from Pantheon altogether, considering this more or less the end of their publishing career.

This was changed by William Jovanovich, president of Harcourt, Brace, who offered them the opportunity to be co-publishers under the imprint "A Helen and Kurt Wolff Book." The Wolffs' many contacts proved useful to the venture. The special relationship with Harcourt, Brace continued for three years with productive results. Anne Morrow Lindbergh brought the Wolffs *Dearly Beloved*, while Günter Grass delivered *Dog Years*. Their close friend *****Hannah Arendt** delivered Karl Jaspers' *The Great Philosophers*. Then on October 21, 1963, while attending the Frankfurt Book Fair, Kurt was struck and killed by a truck, and a productive partnership was abruptly ended.

Two months later, Jovanovich asked Helen to continue the Wolff imprint, and she agreed. Noting that Konrad Lorenz's book *On Aggression* had not been published in the United States, she began publishing his works. Joy Adamson's *The Peoples of Kenya*, a follow-up to her bestselling *Born Free*, appeared under the Wolff imprint. Increasingly the best writers, agents, and editors decided that their books should be published only as "A Helen and Kurt Wolff Book" because of the excellent editing, literary translations, and artistic typography. Helen Wolff became a historic figure in publishing in her own right. Throughout a long and adventuresome life, she maintained high standards, and countless books published since 1963 were the result of her work alone, including Umberto Eco's *The Name of the Rose*. She maintained a presence at the Wolff imprint even after her retirement in 1986, and at the time of her death at her home in Hanover, New Hampshire, in 1994 was the undisputed grande dame of literary publishing in the United States.

SOURCES:

Bruckner, D.J.R. "The Prince of Publishers," in *The New York Times Book Review.* January 5, 1992, p. 12.

Ermarth, Michael. *Kurt Wolff: A Portrait in Essays & Letters.* Chicago, IL: The University of Chicago Press, 1991.

Mitgang, Herbert. "Profiles. Imprint," in *The New Yorker.* Vol. 58, no. 24. August 2, 1982, pp. 41–73.

"Obituary," in *Publishers Weekly.* October 28, 1963, p. 34.

"Obituary," in *Publishers Weekly.* April 4, 1994, p. 16.

John Haag,
Associate Professor of History,
University of Georgia, Athens, Georgia

Wolff, Sister Madeleva (1887–1964).

See Madeleva, Sister Mary.

Wolff, Mary Evaline (1887–1964).

See Madeleva, Sister Mary.

Wolfida of Saxony (c. 1075–1126)

Duchess of Bavaria. Born around 1075; died on December 29, 1126; daughter of Magnus, duke of Saxony, and Sophie of Hungary; married Henry the Black (c. 1074–1126), duke of Bavaria (r. 1120–1126), around 1095; children: Henry IV the Proud (c. 1100–1139), duke of Bavaria; *Judith of Bavaria (fl. 1120s); Guelph also known as Welf VI (d. 1191); and possibly *Sophia of Zahringen.

Wolfson, Theresa (1897–1972)

American labor economist and educator. Born on July 19, 1897, in Brooklyn, New York; died on May 14, 1972, in Brooklyn; daughter of Adolph Wolfson and Rebecca (Hochstein) Wolfson, Russian-Jewish radicals; Adelphi College, A.B., 1917; Columbia University, M.A., 1923; Brookings Institute, Ph.D., 1926; married Iago Galdston (a psychiatrist), in 1920 (divorced 1935); married Austin Bigelow Wood (a psychology professor), in 1938; children: (first marriage) Richard (b. 1926); Margaret Beatrice (b. 1930).

Selected writings: The Woman Worker and the Trade Unions; *(co-author)* Labor and the N.R.A. *(1934); (co-author)* Frances Wright, Free Enquirer: The Study of a Temperament *(1939).*

Theresa Wolfson was born in 1897 in Brooklyn, New York, where her Russian-Jewish immigrant parents, who were radical socialists, ran a boardinghouse. After graduating from high school, she entered Adelphi College. There she became politically active in progressive causes, founding an Adelphi chapter of the Intercol-

legiate Socialist Society, later known as the League for Industrial Democracy, and working for a time as an investigator of the women's clothing industry. Wolfson finished her A.B. degree in 1917 and took a job with the Meinhardt Settlement House in New York City. She then worked for two years (1918–20) as an investigator for the National Child Labor Committee, a position which involved heavy travel around the eastern United States. She published several magazine articles about her experiences with the problem of child labor.

In 1920, Wolfson married Iago Galdston, a medical student and later a psychiatrist. She returned to school, studying for a master's degree in economics at Columbia University. From 1920 to 1923, she worked for the New York Comsumers' League and the Joint Board of Factory Control in the women's clothing industry, gathering data for her master's thesis on women and labor economics. Graduating from Columbia in 1923, Wolfson continued to combine professional experience, trade-union activism, and academic work as a doctoral student at the Brookings Institute. She was convinced that progress for workers required education, so she became active as an educator, working with trade unions to arrange classes in economics and labor. Wolfson was motivated to educate workers, she later explained, because workers "cannot hope to solve the problems of their industry or of their economic world without specific information concerning both."

In 1925, she went to work for the International Ladies' Garment Workers' Union (ILGWU) as education director of the Union Health Center. Her study on discrimination against women in trade unions formed the topic of her doctoral dissertation, later published as *The Woman Worker and the Trade Unions*, and, she received her Ph.D. in 1926, the same year that she gave birth to her first child, Richard. In 1928, Wolfson accepted teaching positions in economics at the Bryn Mawr Summer School for Women Workers and at Brooklyn College; she would remain with Brooklyn College for the rest of her career.

Wolfson gave birth to her second child, **Margaret Beatrice Galdston**, in 1930 but divorced Galdston in 1935. In 1938, she married Austin Bigelow Wood, a Brooklyn College colleague and psychology professor. In addition to raising her family, teaching at Brooklyn College, and her union work, Wolfson published numerous articles on labor issues between 1919 and 1946. She co-authored two books, *Labor and the N.R.A.*

(1934) and a biography of the American labor leader *Frances Wright, *Frances Wright, Free Enquirer: The Study of a Temperament* (1939).

During World War II, Wolfson was appointed to the War Labor Board's public panel. In that capacity, she advised the federal government for the good of the economy not to force wartime female workers to leave their jobs after the war. Although the government largely ignored this advice in the late 1940s, Wolfson would continue to advocate expanded wage-earning roles for American women throughout the 1940s and 1950s. She also joined the American Arbitration Association, which provided conflict resolution services in union-management labor disputes. The League for Industrial Democracy, whose socialist labor organizing she had been involved with since college, honored her with the John Dewey Award in 1957. Wolfson retired from Brooklyn College in 1967, but taught part-time at Sarah Lawrence College's continuing education program for women. She died in Brooklyn in 1972, age 74.

SOURCES:

Sicherman, Barbara, and Carol Hurd Green, eds. *Notable American Women: The Modern Period.* Cambridge, MA: The Belknap Press of Harvard University, 1980.

Laura York, M.A. in History,
University of California,
Riverside, California

Wollerin, Cecilie (d. 1341)

Wool merchant of Germany. Died in 1341 in Regensburg, Germany; never married; no children.

Cecilie Wollerin, a German wool merchant, was born into a family of urban artisans of Regensburg. It is unclear why she never married; perhaps there was not enough money for a dowry sufficient to make her a desirable bride, or perhaps Wollerin herself rejected the idea of marriage and was permitted to act as she wished. Her single status was eventually part of her enormous financial success. She inherited her parents' wool-weaving company on her father's death (which would not have been likely had she been married) and managed the operation herself for many years. Wollerin's business acumen and independent status led her company to flourish, and she amassed enormous personal wealth; she was one of the richest citizens of Regensburg when she died.

SOURCES:

Klapisch-Zuber, Christiane, ed. *A History of Women in the West, vol. II: Silences of the Middle Ages.* Cambridge, MA: Belknap-Harvard, 1992.

Laura York, M.A. in History,
University of California,
Riverside, California

Wollstein, Martha (1868–1939)

American pathologist and researcher. Born on November 21, 1868, in New York City; died on September 30, 1939, in New York City; daughter of Lewis Wollstein and Minna (Cohn) Wollstein; received medical degree from the Woman's Medical College of the New York Infirmary, 1889; never married; no children.

Born in New York City in 1868 to German-Jewish immigrants, Martha Wollstein began medical school at age 18 at the Woman's Medical College of the New York Infirmary. She finished the program in 1889, specializing in pathology. After serving a two-year internship at Babies Hospital in New York, Wollstein was hired as a pathologist there in 1892. Her early years were spent researching malaria, tuberculosis, and typhoid fever. In 1903, a pathological laboratory was opened at Babies Hospital, and Wollstein began experimental work on the bacteriology of infant diarrhea. Her published studies proved important in the diagnosis and treatment of the disease. In recognition of her work, Simon Flexner, director of the Rockefeller Institute of New York, in 1906 offered her an assistant research position at the institute, where she would remain as a respected researcher, though without ever being granted membership status, for 15 years. In 1907, she began experimental research on polio.

Wollstein was keenly aware of the discrimination against women in medicine and their struggle for educational and professional opportunities. In 1908, she published one of the first histories in this area, with her article "The History of Women in Medicine" for the *Woman's Medical Journal.*

In 1910 Wollstein turned to researching pneumonia with the pathologist Samuel Meltzer, and by 1918 she was working on an anti-meningitis serum and researching the virus that causes mumps. In 1921, Wollstein returned full-time to Babies Hospital as a pediatric pathologist. Her research efforts there over the following 14 years included work on the pathology of influenzal meningitis, tuberculosis, jaundice, congenital defects, and leukemia. In 1928, the New York Academy of Medicine named Wollstein to be head of its pediatric section. Two years later, she became the first woman elected to the American Pediatric Society. Over the course of her career, Wollstein published 80 scientific papers.

The details of Wollstein's personal life are not well known. She never married, and few traces of close personal relationships have survived. After her retirement in 1935, she moved to Grand Rapids, Michigan, but returned to New York when she became terminally ill. She died there, at age 60, in 1939 and was buried in Beth-El Cemetery in Brooklyn.

SOURCES:

James, Edward T., ed. *Notable American Women, 1607–1950.* Cambridge, MA: The Belknap Press of Harvard University, 1971.

Read, Phyllis J., and Bernard L. Witlieb. *The Book of Women's Firsts.* NY: Random House, 1992.

Laura York, M.A. in History,
University of California,
Riverside, California

Wollstonecraft, Mary (1759–1797)

Writer for reformist, radical, and feminist causes, and first British feminist, who is best known for A Vindication of the Rights of Woman, *an analysis of the injustices and disadvantages women suffered as a result of social, economic, political, and educational inequality. Name variations: Mary Imlay; Mary Godwin; Mary Wollstonecraft Godwin. Pronunciation: WALL-stun-craft. Born Mary Wollstonecraft on April 21, 1759, probably at Spitalfields, a district at the eastern edge of London, England; died on September 10, 1797, in London, following complications of childbirth; second of seven children of Edward John Wollstonecraft (a weaver and unsuccessful farmer) and Elizabeth (Dickson) Wollstonecraft; attended village day schools, largely self-educated; had liaison with Gilbert Imlay, 1793; married William Godwin, in 1797; children: (with Imlay) Fanny Imlay (b. 1794); Mary Wollstonecraft Godwin Shelley (1797–1851).*

Father lost most of a substantial inheritance through incompetence; family moved frequently and became virtually dysfunctional; met Fanny Blood (1775), with whom she established a fervent longterm friendship; left home to go to Bath as a paid companion (1778); returned home to nurse her dying mother (1781); after mother's death, lived with the Blood family; "rescued" her sister Eliza from her husband's home following her postpartum breakdown (1784); established schools at Islington, then Newington Green with Fanny Blood and sisters Eliza and Everina; visited Fanny, who married (1785) in Lisbon, and found her dying in childbirth; returned to England to find the school had foundered (1786); wrote Thoughts on the Education of Daughters; took a position as governess with Kingsborough family; dismissed by Lady Kingsborough (1787); her novel, Mary, A Fiction, published by Joseph Johnson, printer of works by radical writers; hired by Johnson to write for the Analytical Review; earned an independent living as a reviewer, translator, and writer of fiction and children's stories (1788–90);

wrote A Vindication of the Rights of Men *(1790), a response to Burke's* Reflections on the Revolution in France; *published* A Vindication of the Rights of Woman *and went to Paris to observe the French Revolution (1792); met and established relationship with Gilbert Imlay; daughter Fanny Imlay born in LeHavre (1793); made first suicide attempt (May 1795); visited Scandinavian countries with infant daughter; made second suicide attempt (October 1795); renewed acquaintance with William Godwin, radical social and political philosopher (1796); married Godwin (March 1797); died ten days after the birth of their daughter, Mary (September 1797).*

Major writings: (a book on the education and conduct of women) Thoughts on the Education of Daughters *(1787); (a novel)* Mary, A Fiction *(1788); (a collection of tales for children)* Original Stories *(1788); (an anthology for women)* The Female Reader *(1789); (a defense of freedom and liberalism written in response to Burke's* Reflections*)* A Vindication of the Rights of Men *(1790); (treatise on the disabilities and injustices suffered by women)* A Vindication of the Rights of Woman *(1792); (an account based on her residence in France)* An Historical and Moral View of the Origin and Progress of the French Revolution *(1794); (travelogue and social commentary)* Letters Written During a Short Residence in Sweden, Norway, and Denmark *(1796); (an unfinished novel published posthumously)* The Wrongs of Woman: or, Maria *(1798).*

Mary Wollstonecraft, the first important English feminist, was the second of seven children and the oldest daughter of Edward John Wollstonecraft and **Elizabeth Dickson Wollstonecraft**. The family included Mary's older brother Ned; two sisters, **Eliza** and **Everina Wollstonecraft**; Henry, who died in infancy; and brothers James and Charles. Edward Wollstonecraft inherited a substantial fortune from his father, a member of the new manufacturing class, who amassed considerable capital by organizing the weaving industry in London and investing his earnings well. But Mary's father and mother, a young woman whose family came from County Donegal in Ireland, did not like London or the weaving trade. Hoping to rise in social status as a gentleman farmer, Edward moved his young family to a series of farms, settling first in the Epping Forest on the outskirts of London in 1763, then at Barking in Essex in 1765. Neither venture proved successful.

From 1768 to 1774, the family lived on a farm at Beverley in Yorkshire, where Wollstonecraft seems to have experienced the most stability of her early years. She enjoyed the freedom of exploring the surrounding countryside, and proved an eager and quick student at the day schools of the town, where she was to receive practically all of her formal education. One can trace Wollstonecraft's later views on social and sexual relationships and her often somber temperament to these formative years from age nine to fifteen when she witnessed the deterioration of her family. She saw her father fritter away his fortune, as well as any portion of it that might have come to his children, through incompetence and extravagance as he indulged a country squire's fondness for horses and alcohol. As his family grew and his prospects declined, his temper became increasingly uncontrolled and abusive. Wollstonecraft later described memories of a childhood in which she often protected her submissive mother from the drunken rages of her father, sometimes sleeping on the landing outside their bedroom in the event that she should have to intervene to shield her mother from physical violence.

Her mother favored and spoiled her oldest son, Ned, who was heir to one-third of his grand-

Mary Woll-stonecraft

father's fortune; she seemed to give her attention and affection to each new baby that came along while subjecting Mary, as the oldest daughter, to severe discipline. In time, her mother's resignation to her unhappy marital life gave way to passivity and indifference, and she showed little interest in or affection for her family. Feeling neglected on the grounds of both her sex and age, Mary became a solitary child, roaming the countryside and preferring the company of animals to people. During these years, she developed an abiding hatred of tyranny, cruelty, and the exercise of irrational authority. Her family situation also created in her the seemingly contradictory emotional tendencies that influenced her unconventional adult behavior: a yearning for freedom and independence on the one hand and, on the other, an intense need for loyal, accepting love and secure family relationships.

> [W]e hear her voice and trace her influence even now among the living.
>
> —*Virginia Woolf

Despite her eagerness to learn, the education Wollstonecraft received at the village day schools taught her little more than to read and write. Although her brother Ned was sent to a good grammar school and marked early for a career in law, the family's declining fortunes ruled out the possibility of a governess for the Wollstonecraft daughters or boarding school for Mary. She grew to adolescence nurturing a sense of grievance as her family's passive acceptance of failure and increasing poverty seemed to narrow her chances for independence and a satisfying life. She yearned for affection, and found an outlet for her emotional intensity in jealous and demanding friendships, first with **Jane Arden** when she was 14, and then, at 16, with **Fanny Blood**, a young woman two years her senior who had a strong and lasting influence on Wollstonecraft's life.

Mary met Fanny Blood after the Wollstonecrafts abandoned farming and moved back to Hoxton, on the outskirts of London, in 1774. A neighboring cleric and his wife, who took an interest in Mary and encouraged her self-education through reading, introduced her to Fanny, whose family situation seemed to mirror her own. Unlike Wollstonecraft, however, Blood had managed to develop her talents and assume some responsibility for her improvident family's wellbeing with competence and good spirits. She helped to support her family by selling her drawings. Wollstonecraft was attracted to Blood as a role model who inspired her to develop her abilities and assert her autonomy in a family drifting toward moral and financial ruin. When her father

made one last attempt at farming by relocating to Wales in 1776, Mary maintained her attachment to Fanny through letters, and dreamed of a day when she and Fanny could live together and earn their own living. Then when her family's latest venture failed, Mary persuaded her father to move back to Walworth, south of London, where she was within easy visiting distance of Fanny.

As her family life continued to deteriorate, Mary asserted her independence by accepting—against her parents' wishes—a position as a paid companion to a widowed Mrs. Dawson at Bath. In one of the few paid occupations open to women of her class and education, Wollstonecraft, at 19, observed for the first time what she judged as the frivolous and unproductive life led by the fashionable, wealthy, leisured class of her day. Although her new position was far from the ideal of independence she had hoped for, it seemed a decided improvement on her situation at home.

She remained with Mrs. Dawson for two years, until she was called home to nurse her dying mother in the autumn of 1781. Elizabeth Wollstonecraft's death in April 1872 dissolved any ties that might have kept the family together; shortly thereafter, Mary went to live at Walham Green with the Bloods. Her father remarried and returned to Wales. Her sister Eliza married Meredith Bishop in October, and her sister Everina went to live with their older brother Ned, who was married and practicing law in London. Her brother James went to sea, and Charles, her youngest brother, was eventually indentured to Ned. Throughout her life, Mary felt a responsibility for the welfare of her younger sisters and brothers, who did not share Ned's good fortune in receiving an inheritance from his grandfather as the oldest son.

Mary lived with the Bloods for two years, contributing to the support of the household by helping with the eye-straining needlework Mrs. Blood did for meager compensation. Over time, the relationship between Mary and Fanny changed. Mary had previously idealized Fanny as a model of competence and strength, but now her friend showed signs of unhappiness and dependence. Fanny had been engaged for some time to Hugh Skeys, who had moved to Lisbon without setting a marriage date; Mary blamed Skeys for Fanny's declining spirits and health, and became a source of support and strength for Fanny, who was, in fact, in the early stages of consumption.

Soon another unhappy relationship was to trouble Wollstonecraft. Her sister Eliza suffered a breakdown following the birth of her daughter in August 1783. When her condition did not improve by November, her husband sent for Mary to help. Wollstonecraft wrote Everina that she found Eliza with "her mind in a most unsettled state." According to Ralph Wardle, Mary concluded that "the root of Eliza's trouble . . . [was] a profound aversion which she had taken to her husband." In January, with some help from Fanny and Everina, Mary stole Eliza away from her home, husband, and baby, convinced that only separation from Bishop could heal her sister's ravaged mind. Mary wrote Everina that as they fled across London, Eliza, in her terror of being caught in this flagrant act of rebellion against sacred law and honored social convention, "bit her wedding ring to pieces."

After living in hiding with Eliza for about a month, Mary announced that she, Eliza, and Fanny would open a school together. Their first attempt, at Islington, failed, but a second attempt at Newington Green proved successful. Everina joined them, and for awhile it appeared that Wollstonecraft had managed to establish a community of independent, self-supporting women.

Newington Green had a century-long tradition of attracting religious Dissenters, political reformers, and dissident intellectuals. Here Wollstonecraft first came into contact with thinkers whose radical social and political views influenced her later writings. Through the famous Dissenting minister Dr. Richard Price and his friends, Wollstonecraft discovered a rational intellectual tradition that substantiated views regarding social and personal relationships she had developed through her own experience. Having acquired both a circle of sympathetic friends and a degree of financial independence, Wollstonecraft felt for the first time that a happy and useful life might be within her reach.

This new-found optimism about the future was tempered by concern for Fanny's health, which grew steadily worse. Hugh Skeys finally sent for Fanny to join him in Lisbon in 1784; they were married in February, and Fanny immediately became pregnant. In November, Wollstonecraft went to Lisbon to be with her friend during childbirth. On her arrival, she found Fanny already in labor and so weakened by rapidly advancing tuberculosis that there was no hope she would survive. Within days of the birth, both Fanny and her child were dead. As she relived in memory her earlier passionate and idealized love of Fanny, Wollstonecraft mourned her friend with bitter grief.

Wollstonecraft returned to England emotionally exhausted to find the school disintegrat-ing and the Blood family devastated by Fanny's death and once more in desperate financial straits. Almost overwhelmed by failure, debt, and depression, Mary wrote that she wished to die. Then with a characteristic recovery of energy and determination, she turned to a new direction by writing *Thoughts on the Education of Daughters*, for which she received an advance from Joseph Johnson, a publisher with Dissenting and radical tendencies, through whose friendship and help she later established her career as a writer. The book, rapidly written and fairly conventional in its pedagogical views, did not attract a great deal of attention; its importance lies in the way it sketches, in rudimentary form and somewhat random order, Wollstonecraft's emerging ideas regarding the role of education in shaping the social destiny of women. She spent the earnings of this first literary effort to send the Blood family to Ireland to make a fresh start.

Still faced with mounting debts, Wollstonecraft hastily learned French in order to take a position, obtained through friends of Dr. Price, as governess to the daughters of Lord and **Lady Kingsborough** in County Cork, Ireland. It was a position ill-suited for a woman of her pride and experience. As she waited patiently but fruitlessly for her charges to join her at Eton for the trip to Ireland, she once again experienced the disdain she had felt at Bath for the idle life, inconsiderate behavior, and shallow values of the privileged class. Once in Ireland, Wollstonecraft gained the affection and respect of her wards, but the awkward social position of a governess, privileged among servants but subject to the whims and desires of her employers, proved difficult for Wollstonecraft to maintain. She was discharged by Lady Kingsborough after ten months of service.

Upon her return to London in 1787 at age 28, Wollstonecraft was, as **Claire Tomalin** writes, "homeless again, without a job or a reference; she had nothing to live on, and she was in debt to several people." While in Ireland, however, she had prepared herself for a career as a writer by reading extensively in contemporary British and continental literature. She had also completed her first novel, *Mary, A Fiction*, based in part on her relationship with Fanny Blood, in part on her experiences with the Kingsboroughs, and held together by the conventions of popular fiction of sentiment and sensibility. Immediately upon her return to London, she went to Joseph Johnson's print shop in St. Paul's Churchyard with her manuscript. Johnson, the major English publisher of radical and reformist books, invited her to make his house her home for the time being and proposed to set her up in a house of her own while she undertook work for him, particularly in the expanding market of books aimed at women and children. She was to become, as she announced to Everina in a letter, the "first of a new genus" of women who could earn their livings as professional writers, reviewers, and editorial assistants.

In 1788, Johnson published two books by Mary Wollstonecraft: her novel *Mary, A Fiction*, and *Original Stories from Real Life*, a book for children, which was illustrated with engravings by William Blake in its second edition. Between 1788 and 1792, she wrote reviews, did translations, and assisted in the production of the *Analytical Review*, a new monthly periodical with a liberal and radical perspective founded by Johnson and his colleagues. She also compiled an anthology of prose and verse entitled *The Female Reader*.

Johnson's shop served as a center for radical and unconventional thinkers. Joseph Priestly, Thomas Paine, William Godwin, William Blake, *Anna Letitia Barbauld*, William Wordsworth, and Samuel Coleridge all at one time or another had associations with Johnson. Wollstonecraft thrived in this heady atmosphere, where she met, probably in 1788, Henry Fuseli, the flamboyant artist and scholar who excited her admiration, respect, and eventually love. Even though Fuseli had recently married, Wollstonecraft, convinced of the purity of her love, made no attempt to conceal her feelings from either Fuseli or their friends; nor did Fuseli seem to discourage her apparently hopeless pursuit of his attention and affection.

The outbreak of the French Revolution in July 1789 and the excitement it created among Johnson's circle provided a saving distraction from this unhappy infatuation for Wollstonecraft. She sublimated her passion for Fuseli by becoming a fervent supporter of the principles of the Revolution. When Edmund Burke, alarmed by the implications of radical British sympathy for the revolutionaries, responded with his *Reflections on the Revolution in France*, Wollstonecraft was inspired to refute his reactionary stance. She quickly wrote *A Vindication of the Rights of Men*, which made up in passionate conviction for what it lacked in reasoned argument. This first published reply to Burke (the most famous would be Thomas Paine's *Rights of Man*), printed anonymously in the first edition, became immediately popular, and when it was published in its second edition under her name, Wollstonecraft found herself famous and controversial.

Encouraged by the reception of the *Rights of Men*, Wollstonecraft soon began the work on which her reputation as a feminist of first importance and lasting influence rests, *A Vindication of the Rights of Woman*, the first sustained argument for female emancipation. According to William Godwin, she spent only six weeks on the composition of the work for which her whole life was in effect a preparation. Published in 1792, *A Vindication* affirms that the "rights of man" championed by the philosophical radicals imply also the rights of women. As **Miriam Brody** points out, before Wollstonecraft, "there were works suggesting the reform of female manners or proposals for improving female education, but there was no single-minded criticism of the social and economic system which created a double standard of excellence for male and female and relegated women to an inferior status." Wollstonecraft asserts that women are human beings before they are sexual beings, that they have the same rational capacity to effect their moral perfectibility as men, and that the social, economic, and political inequities and disadvantages under which they live result from social conditions and customary assumptions about the natures of women and men, not from inherent "inferiority."

Following the publication of the *Vindication*, Wollstonecraft planned a trip to Paris with Johnson and Henry and **Sophia Fuseli**, but news of trouble and danger in France caused them to stop at Dover. In fact, recent reports of revolutionary excesses such as massacres and executions were dampening the ardor of many English supporters of the Revolution. The party returned to London, and Wollstonecraft then proposed to Sophia that she be admitted to the Fuseli household on a permanent basis as Fuseli's "spiritual partner." Sophia, outraged, ordered Wollstonecraft never to return to their house. Wollstonecraft seems to have finally recognized the futility of her ardor, and rather than indulge her personal unhappiness in London, she determined to go to France alone to view the political situation at firsthand. There she was welcomed as the author of the *Vindication of the Rights of Woman* by a group of international literary and political writers.

By the end of 1792, she found herself in the midst of a frightening political crisis. Although she was still committed to the ideals of the Revolution, Wollstonecraft's lifelong revulsion against cruelty made her sympathize, despite her contempt for the claims of divine right and aristocracy, with the imprisoned King Louis XIV. In February 1793, France declared war on England, and by spring the situation in Paris had deteriorated to rioting, vandalism, and destruction of unpopular presses. Foreigners in France fell under suspicion, and Wollstonecraft considered leaving for Switzerland, but could not get an appropriate passport.

Then in April 1793 she met Gilbert Imlay, an American entrepreneur, author, and adventurer; soon she became involved in an affair that would bring her brief periods of happiness in a stormy relationship that lasted for three years. Although both claimed indifference to the bonds of formal marriage, Imlay registered Mary as his wife at the American Embassy to protect her when the Terror put English citizens in France in danger, and Wollstonecraft sometimes assumed his name for the sake of convenience. The two lived together in France briefly, and Imlay was with Wollstonecraft when their daughter ❧▶ **Fanny Imlay**—named for Fanny Blood—was born in Le Havre in May 1794. It seems unlikely, however, that he ever anticipated the kind of permanent union Wollstonecraft seemed to wish for. As their incompatibility grew more apparent, Imlay spent most of his time separated from Wollstonecraft, pursuing affairs of business and pleasure. She occupied herself in Paris during his extended absence in the winter of 1794 by finishing her *Historical and Moral View of the French Revolution*, in which she reaffirmed her faith in the principles that inspired the Revolution at the same time that she deplored violence as means of achieving a reformed social order.

When Imlay remained evasive regarding plans for a future together, Wollstonecraft returned to London in April 1795 in the hopes of making the relationship work. She found Imlay unwilling to set up house with her—he was involved in a new affair—and in her loneliness and depression made her first suicide attempt, probably with laudanum. She was revived by friends, and an alarmed Imlay asked her to undertake a journey to the Scandinavian countries as his business emissary. Wollstonecraft agreed and spent three months traveling on his behalf under difficult conditions with her infant daughter and a nurse.

Upon her return to London, Wollstonecraft was humiliated to learn that Imlay was preparing to set up house with an actress. She wrote a suicide letter to Imlay, walked to Battersea Bridge on the Thames, and decided the dismal spot she had chosen was too public for her plan. She hired a boat and rowed alone upstream to Putney Bridge, where she climbed to the railings and jumped into the darkness. Although she had first stood in the cold October rain to soak her clothes so that she would sink quickly, some boatmen who saw her fall fished her unconscious floating body from the river and took her to a public house where a doctor revived her.

Upon her physical and mental recovery, Wollstonecraft set about once again to mend the pieces of her shattered life. She moved to new lodgings, began reviewing again for Johnson, and prepared a new edition of *Original Stories*. She asked Imlay to return the letters she had written during her Scandinavian journey and published them in 1796 as *Letters Written During a Short Residence in Sweden, Norway, and Denmark*. The book contains some of Wollstonecraft's best and most lyrical writing in a travelogue that combines fine descriptions of the countries she visited and acute observations of the people and social conditions she encountered with a melancholy record of her need for love, her tortured relationship with Imlay, and her tender affection for Fanny.

In April 1796, Wollstonecraft renewed her earlier acquaintance with William Godwin, whose *Enquiry Concerning Political Justice* (1793) had established his reputation as the leading radical philosopher in England, and whose latest book, *Caleb Williams*, a novel, illustrated the flaws of the social system he attacked in *Political Justice*. Their friendship, based on their compatible political and social views and their situations as isolated and unregenerate radicals in an era that had become increasingly conservative, soon developed into passionate love. By December, Mary had reason to believe she was pregnant.

Both Wollstonecraft and Godwin opposed marriage as an artificial bond that could corrupt a freely chosen relationship between individuals. Godwin was so famous for his opposition to cohabitation that it was difficult for him and Wollstonecraft to announce their marriage at St. Pancras Church in March 1797 to their friends. The

---

❧▶ **Imlay, Fanny** (1794–1816)
*Daughter of Mary Wollstonecraft. Name variations: Fanny Imlay Godwin. Born in Le Havre, France, in May 1794; committed suicide in September 1816; illegitimate daughter of Mary Wollstonecraft (1759–1797) and Gilbert Imlay; half-sister of *Mary Shelley (1797–1851).*

Seven of Fanny Imlay's letters, written the year of her death, are included in *The Clairmont Correspondence*, published by Johns Hopkins in 1996. (*See also Shelley, Mary.*)

marriage was in some respects unconventional: both partners kept up their established friendships and visited independently of one another, and Godwin maintained a separate residence where he did his work. Perhaps because of this recognition of one another's individual needs, the marriage was a happy one.

Wollstonecraft had only a few months, however, in which to enjoy her long-sought and hard-won happiness. During her pregnancy, she worked on a second novel, *The Wrongs of Women, or Maria*, and an essay on childrearing, *Letters on the Management of Infants*. Having little patience with the tradition of a month-long confinement following childbirth, and anticipating an easy delivery with an experienced midwife's assistance, Wollstonecraft planned to join Godwin at dinner the day after their child's birth. Instead, she suffered a long and painful labor. She delivered a daughter, Mary Wollstonecraft Godwin (*Mary Shelley), on August 30, but failed to deliver the placenta. On the advice of the midwife, Godwin called in an obstetrician, who found the placenta broken, attempted to remove the pieces, and undoubtedly introduced infection in the process. Wollstonecraft appeared to recover, but within a few days, she showed symptoms of the onset of septicemia. She died of the infection on September 10. The daughter she gave birth to would become the wife of Percy Bysshe Shelley and the author of *Frankenstein*.

Most of the biographical information we have regarding Wollstonecraft is derived from the book Godwin began to write as a tribute to his wife within two weeks of her death, *Memoirs of the Author of A Vindication of the Rights of Woman*, which described her life with the honesty characteristic of both Wollstonecraft and Godwin. Its candor in describing her personal beliefs and behavior, her love affairs, pregnancies, and suicide attempts did little to rehabilitate her reputation with a public that had regarded her as a threat to social and domestic order. The book, in fact, seemed to strike a blow at both liberal and feminist causes; Wollstonecraft's life and death became, for the Tory press, a cautionary tale of the dangers of feminist and radical thought and principles. The pioneer of feminism was thus subject for nearly a century to the neglect resulting from a conservative atmosphere in which reference to her life and works would bring discredit to feminist causes. Even John Stuart Mill did not acknowledge her ideas or example in his essay *On the Subjection of Women* in 1869. It remained for the 20th century to rediscover, reevaluate, and reach a just appreciation of Mary Wollstonecraft's courageous life and influential body of work.

SOURCES:
Brody, Miriam. Introduction, in *A Vindication of the Rights of Woman by Mary Wollstonecraft*. NY: Penguin, 1992.

Ferguson, Moira, and Janet Todd. *Mary Wollstonecraft*. Boston, MA: Twayne, 1984.

Flexner, Eleanor. *Mary Wollstonecraft: A Biography*. NY: Coward, McCann & Geoghegan, 1972.

George, Margaret. *One Woman's "Situation": A Study of Mary Wollstonecraft*. Urbana, IL: University of Illinois Press, 1970.

Godwin, William. *Memoirs of Mary Wollstonecraft*. Ed. by W. Clark Durant. London: Constable, 1927.

Lorch, Jennifer. *Mary Wollstonecraft: The Making of a Radical Feminist*. NY: St. Martin's, 1990.

Sunstein, Emily W. *A Different Face: The Life of Mary Wollstonecraft*. NY: Harper & Row, 1975.

Tomalin, Claire. *The Life and Death of Mary Wollstonecraft*. London: Weidenfeld & Nicholson, 1974.

Wardle, Ralph M. *Mary Wollstonecraft: A Critical Biography*. Lawrence, KS: University of Kansas Press, 1951.

Wollstonecraft, Mary. *A Vindication of the Rights of Woman*. Edited with an Introduction by Miriam Brody. NY: Penguin Classics, 1992.

Woolf, Virginia. "Mary Wollstonecraft," in *The Second Common Reader*. NY: Harcourt, Brace & World, 1932.

SUGGESTED READING:
Jacobs, Diane. *Her Own Woman: The Life of Mary Wollstonecraft*. NY: Simon & Schuster, 2001.

Todd, Janet. *Mary Wollstonecraft: A Revolutionary Life*. NY: Columbia University Press, 2000.

Patricia B. Heaman, Ph.D.,
Professor of English, Wilkes University,
Wilkes-Barre, Pennsylvania

Wolstenholme-Elmy, Elizabeth
(1834–1913)

British feminist and suffragist who pioneered in women's education and the training of teachers. Name variations: Elizabeth Wolstenholme. Born in 1834 in England; died in 1913; only daughter and one of two children of a Methodist minister; had two years of formal education; married Benjamin Elmy (a poet), in 1874; children: one son.

Elizabeth Wolstenholme-Elmy was born in England in 1834, one of two children of a Methodist minister who held traditional views on the education of women. While her brother Joseph received advanced schooling, Wolstenholme-Elmy was limited to two years of formal education and, even after the death of her parents, was forbidden by her guardians to enter the newly opened Bedford College for Women. At age 19, upon receiving her inheritance, she purchased her own boarding school in Manchester.

Concerned with the quality of teacher training, in 1865 Wolstenholme-Elmy helped form the Manchester Schoolmistresses' Association. With *Josephine Butler, she later established the North of England Council for the Higher Education of Woman, which provided special lectures and examinations for women schoolteachers. Addressing the broader issue of women's education, Wolstenholme-Elmy later wrote an article on education for Butler's book *Women's Work and Women's Culture*, in which she set out a plan of high schools to educate girls in every town across Britain.

Wolstenholme-Elmy was also an avid suffragist, joining with *Lydia Becker as early as 1865 to form the Manchester Society for Women's Suffrage. She assisted Richard and *Emmeline Pankhurst on several endeavors, serving as a member of the Married Women's Property Committee, which led to the Married Women's Property Act (1882), and working for the Custody of Infants Act (1886). In 1889, she joined the Pankhursts to form the Women's Franchise League and the three also became members of the Manchester branch of the Independent Labour Party.

From 1874, Elizabeth was supported in her endeavors by her husband, poet Benjamin Elmy, whom she married in a civil ceremony in 1874. True to her principles, she rejected the promise of obedience to her husband and also refused to change her surname or wear a wedding ring. Three months after the ceremony, Wolstenholme-Elmy gave birth to the couple's only child, a son.

Late in life, Wolstenholme-Elmy became critical of what she termed the "fiddle-faddling" of the National Union of Women's Suffrage Societies, and jumped ship to join the Women's Social and Political Union. Now in her 70s, however, she was severely limited in her activities and could not participate in any actions that might have landed her in prison. Elizabeth Wolstenholme-Elmy died in 1913.

SUGGESTED READING:

Holton, Sandra. *Suffrage Days*. Routledge, 1996.

Wolter, Charlotte (1834–1897)

Austrian actress. Born in Cologne, Germany, in 1834; died in 1897.

Charlotte Wolter began her artistic career in Budapest in 1857. Four years later, she appeared at the Victoria Theater in Berlin where her performance of Hermione in *The Winter's Tale* took the playgoing world by storm. In 1862, she joined the Vienna Hofburg Theater, where she stayed until her death in 1897. According to her wish, she was buried in the costume of Iphigenia, in which role she had achieved her most brilliant success. Considered one of the great tragic actresses of her time, Charlotte Wolter excelled in a rich repertory of classic and historical characters.

Women of the Harlem Renaissance

Writers, artists, actresses, and social figures who were instrumental, though now less recognized than their male counterparts, in creating the hugely influential African-American cultural movement known as the Harlem Renaissance.

Bennett, Gwendolyn B. (1902–1981). American artist, poet, writer, and educator whose work as a columnist for Opportunity *encouraged the growth of cultural life in Harlem and whose poetry, incorporating themes of her African heritage and her training as a painter, placed her among the finest of the writers of the Harlem Renaissance. Born on July 8, 1902, in Giddings, Texas; died in Reading, Pennsylvania, on May 30, 1981; only child of Joshua Robin Bennett and Mayme F. (Abernathy) Bennett; graduated from Brooklyn Girls High School, 1921; studied fine arts at Teachers College, Columbia University for two years; transferred to the Pratt Institute in Brooklyn, where she finished her education; married Alfred Joseph Jackson (a physician), in 1927 (died); married Richard Crosscup (died January 9, 1980).*

Shortly after her birth, family relocated first to Nevada, where her parents taught on an Indian reservation, and later to Washington, D.C., where her father studied law and her mother became a beautician. While she was still young, her parents divorced, leaving her in her mother's custody; at age seven, her father kidnapped her, and she would not see her mother again until she was an adult; graduated from Brooklyn Girls High School (1921), where she became the first black student elected to the literary and dramatic societies; became an instructor of watercolor and design at Howard University; received Delta Sigma Theta's foreign scholarship (1924), which allowed her to travel to Paris to study at the Julian and Colarossi academies as well as at the École de Pantheon; in Paris, became acquainted with the modern French painter Frans Masereel; resumed teaching at Howard (1926) and became assistant editor of the magazine Opportunity, *where she wrote the column "The Ebony Flute" (1926–28); was one of two African-American artists selected to study the modern and primitive art collections of the Barnes Foundation (1927); writing appeared in numerous magazines, including* Fire!, Crisis, and the American Mercury *(1922–34); continued teaching at Howard University and also served as director of the Harlem Community Arts Center (1937–40); little is known of her life after the 1940s.*

Selected fiction: "Wedding Day," *in* Fire! *(1926);* "Tokens" *(1927).*

Selected nonfiction: "The Future of the Negro in Art" *(1924) and* "Negroes: Inherent Craftsmen" *(1925) in* Howard University Record; "Review of Plum Bun, *by Jessie Redmon Fauset," in* Opportunity *(1929);* "The Ebony Flute" *column, in* Opportunity *(1926–28);* "The American Negro Paints," *in* Southern Workman *(1928).*

Selected poetry: "Heritage," *in* Opportunity *(1923);* "To Usward," *in* Crisis *(1924);* "Wind" *in* Opportunity *(1924);* "Purgation" *in* Opportunity *(1925);* "Lines Written on the Grave of Alexander Dumas," *in* Opportunity *(1926);* "Dear Things" *and* "Dirge," *in* Palms *(1926);* "Hatred," *in* Opportunity *(1926).*

Fauset, Jessie Redmon *(1882–1961).* **American novelist, journalist, poet, and editor whose wide-ranging literary skills both influenced other writers of the Harlem Renaissance and vividly captured the struggles and successes of black Americans in the early part of the 20th century.** *Born Jessie Redmon Fauset on April 27, 1882, in Camden, New Jersey; died on April 30, 1961, in Philadelphia, Pennsylvania; seventh child of Redmon Fauset (a minister of the African Methodist Episcopal Church) and Annie (Seamon) Fauset; attended Philadelphia High School for Girls, graduating in 1900; graduated from Cornell University, 1905, with Phi Beta Kappa; attended summer classes at the Sorbonne in Paris; University of Pennsylvania, M.A., 1919; married Herbert E. Harris (a businessman), in 1929 (died 1958).*

Was the first black woman to graduate from Cornell University (1905); taught Latin and French in Washington, D.C., at the M Street High School (later Dunbar High School, 1906–19); served as the literary editor of Crisis *(1919–26); edited, with W.E.B. Du Bois, a children's magazine,* The Brownies' Book *(1920–21); wrote four novels (1924–33); taught French at DeWitt Clinton High School in New York City (1927–44); moved to Montclair, New Jersey, with husband (early 1950s); after his death, moved to Philadelphia (1958), where she died of heart disease (1961).*

Selected writings (all published in Crisis*): (poetry)* "Rondeau" *(1912),* "Again It Is September" *(1917),* "Oriflamme" *(1920),* "La vie c'est la vie" *(1922),* "To a Foreign Maid" *(1923),* "Courage! He Said" *(1929); (short stories)* "There Was a Time; A Story of Spring" *(1917),* "The Sleeper Wakes" *(1920),* "Double Trouble" *(1923); (nonfiction):* "The New Literature of the New Negro" *(1920),* "Impressions on the Second Pan-African Congress" *(1921),* "The 13th Biennial of the N.C.A.C." *(1923); (novels)* There Is Confusion *(1924),* Plum Bun *(1929),* The Chinaberry Tree: A Novel of American Life *(1931),* Comedy: American Style *(1933).*

Fuller, Meta Warrick *(1877–1968).* **Prolific American sculptor and illustrator known for sculptures symbolizing the aspirations of African-Americans as well as works depicting human suffering.** *Born Meta Vaux Warrick on June 9, 1877, in Philadelphia, Pennsylvania; died on March 13, 1968, in Framingham, Massachusetts; daughter of William Warrick and Emma Warrick, middle-class parents who encouraged her artistic talents; attended Pennsylvania School of Industrial Arts, 1899; studied for three years at Academie Colarossi, Paris, and École des Beaux-Arts, Paris, beginning in 1899; received instruction from Charles Grafly, Rodin, Gauqui, Rollard, and Raphael Collin in Paris; exhibited several works at L'Art Nouveau, a Paris gallery; attended Pennsylvania Academy of Fine Arts, 1907; married Liberian-born Solomon Fuller (a neurologist and psychologist), in 1909; children: three sons.*

Commissioned to sculpt 150 black figures (called The Progress of the Negro in America*) for the Jamestown Tercentennial Exposition (1907); most of her early sculpture destroyed in a fire in a Philadelphia warehouse (1910); exhibited life-size work* Awakening Ethiopia *at the New York Making of America Exposition (1922); invited by W.E.B. Du Bois to sculpt a piece for the 50th anniversary celebration of the Emancipation Proclamation, held in New York (1931); remained active in Boston art circles (1930s); lived and worked at her home in Framingham, Massachusetts, where she also taught students (1929–68).*

Selected sculpture: Crucifixion of Christ in Agony *(c. 1894);* Secret Sorrow *(also known as* Man Eating His Heart*),* The Thief on the Cross, The Wretched, Man Carrying a Dead Comrade *(most likely during years in Paris, 1899–1902);* John the Baptist *(1899);* Head of Medusa *(1903);* Oedipus, The Silent Appeal, Exodus, The Impenitent Thief, Warrick Tableau *(all n.d.);* Emancipation Group *(1913);* Awakening Ethiopia *(1914);* Water Boy *(1914);* Peace Halting the Ruthlessness of War *(1917);* The Talking Skull *(1937);* The Madonna of Consolation *(1961);* The Statue of Jesus on the Cross *(1962);* The Refugee *(1964);* Bust of Charlotte Hawkins Brown *(1965).*

Exhibits: Paris Salon (1898, 1899, 1903); Jamestown Tercentennial Exposition (1907); New York Public Library (1921); Making of America Ex-

hibit, New York (1922); Boston Public Library (1922); Art Institute of Chicago (1927); Emancipation Exhibit, New York (1931); Harmon Foundation (1931–33); Boston Art Club (1930s); Augusta Savage Studios (1939); American Negro Exposition (1940); Howard University (1961); Framingham Center Library (1964); City College of New York (1967).

Collections: Cleveland Art Museum; Schomburg Collection, New York City; Atlanta YMCA; Garfield School, Detroit; New York Public Library, 135th Street Branch; Framingham Center Library, Massachusetts; Framingham Union Hospital; St. Andrew's Episcopal Church, Framingham; San Francisco Museum of Fine Arts; Howard University; Livingston College Library, Salisbury, North Carolina; Business and Professional Women's Club, Washington, D.C. Awards: elected fellow, Academy of Fine Arts; silver medal in New Vistas in American Art Exhibition, Howard University (1961); honorary Doctor of Letters, Livingston College (1962).

Johnson, Georgia Douglas (1877–1966). American poet, playwright, educator, and political activist whose work, incorporating many threads of the artistic tapestry of the Harlem Renaissance, explored the duality women of color endure in American society. Born Georgia Blanche Douglas Camp on September 10, 1877, in Atlanta, Georgia; died in Washington, D.C., on May 14, 1966; daughter of George Camp and Laura (Jackson) Camp; received primary education in Atlanta public schools; completed Normal Program at Atlanta University, 1896; studied music at Oberlin Conservatory in Oberlin, Ohio, where she trained in violin, piano, voice, and harmony; also studied at Cleveland College of Music and Howard University; married Henry Lincoln Johnson (a lawyer and politician), in 1903 (died 1925); children: Henry Lincoln, Jr., and Peter Douglas.

Returned to Atlanta after studies to teach school and serve as an assistant principal; moved to Washington, D.C. (1910), where Henry Johnson established a law firm; their home became a literary salon known as the "Round Table," which met on Saturday nights and drew many of the major figures of the Harlem Renaissance; published her first poems in Crisis (1916); published first volume of poetry, The Heart of a Woman and Other Poems (1918); published more than 200 poems (1918–30), and became active in civil-rights activities and in politics, participating in the Pan-African movement, Congregational Church meetings, and the Republican Party; after the death of husband (1925), took various government jobs to support herself and her children; became the commissioner of conciliation

at the Department of Labor (1927) and began writing plays; won first prize in the Opportunity magazine play contest (1927); became involved with the Federal Theater Project, which was part of the New Deal; continued to write until her death (1966).

Selected writing: (poetry) The Heart of a Woman and Other Poems (1918), Bronze (1922), An Autumn Love Cycle (1928), Share My World (1962), also published in various anthologies, including "The Dreams of the Dream," "Hope," and others in Countee Cullen's Caroling Dusk (1927); (plays) A Sunday Morning in the South: A One-Act Play (1924), Plumes: Folk Tragedy (1927), Blue Blood (1928).

Johnson, Helene (1907—). American poet, part of the younger generation of writers of the Harlem Renaissance, whose literary career, though brief, had an important impact on American poetry. Name variations: Helen Johnson Hubbell. Born Helen Johnson on July 7, 1907 (some sources cite 1906), in Boston, Massachusetts; only child of Ella (Benson) Johnson and William Johnson; cousin of Dorothy West (1907–1998); attended Boston public schools and Boston University; attended Columbia University Extension School in 1926; married William Warner Hubbell (a motorman), early 1930s; children: Abigail Calachaly Hubbell (b. September 18, 1940).

While still living in Boston, was a member of the literary group, the Saturday Evening Quill Club; also won first prize for a short-story contest in the Boston Chronicle; moved to New York City with her cousin Dorothy West (1920s); published poems in numerous periodicals, including Opportunity, Vanity Fair, and Fire!; became active in A'Lelia Walker's literary salon, the Dark Tower, and in the Fellowship for Reconciliation, an international organization; won literary awards for her poems "My Race" and "Metamorphism" (1926); probably returned to Boston (c. 1929); disappeared from the Harlem literary scene (1929); published a few poems in Opportunity (early 1930s).

Poetry: "My Race," in Opportunity (1925); "Fulfillment," "Futility," "Metamorphism," "Night," "Mother," "The Road," in Opportunity (1926); "Love in Midsummer," in Messenger (1926); "Summer Matures," in Opportunity (1927); "Cui Bono?" in Harlem Magazine (1928); "A Missionary Brings Native," in Palms (1928); "Fiat Lux," in Opportunity (1928); "I Am Not Proud," "Invocation," "Regalia," "Remember Not," "Why Do They Prate," "Worship," in Saturday Evening Quill (1929); "Vers de Société," in Opportunity (1930); "Sonnet," in Opportunity (1931); "Sonnet," "Monotone," in Opportunity (1932); "Plea of a Plebian," in Opportunity (1934).

McClendon, Rosalie "Rose" (1884–1936). American stage actress who combined wide-ranging theatrical talents with a desire to promote and advance black theater during the Harlem Renaissance. Name variations: Rose McClendon. Born Rosalie Virginia Scott on August 27, 1884, in Greenville, North Carolina; died of pneumonia in 1936; daughter of Sandy Scott and Tena (Jenkins) Scott; grew up in New York City, where she was active in her church theater group; received a scholarship to study at the American Academy of Dramatic Art, 1916; married Dr. Henry Pruden McClendon (a chiropractor and Pullman porter), in 1904.

Following her marriage, spent the next ten years engaged in church work (1904–14); cast in first serious role in play Justice (1919); achieved critical acclaim for her role in Deep River (1926); had roles in nearly every important African-American play staged in New York City (1926–mid-1930s); began directing plays at the Negro Experimental Theater in New York (early 1930s); with Dick Campbell, organized the Negro People's Theater (1935); fell ill with pleurisy (1935).

Selected stage performances: Justice (1919); Roseanne (1924); Deep River (1926); In Abraham's Bosom (1926); Porgy (1927); The House of Connelly (1931); Never No More (1932); Black Souls (1932); Brainsweat (1934); Roll Sweet Chariot (1934); Mulatto (1935).

Collections: Rose McClendon Memorial Collection at Howard University includes hundreds of photographs of black artists and writers, gift of Carl Van Vechten, 1946.

Mills, Florence (1895–1927). American actress, singer, and dancer whose performances in musical theater productions like Shuffle Along and Blackbirds made her an international star and a popular figure of the Harlem Renaissance. Born Florence Winfree on January 25, 1895 (some sources cite 1896), in Washington, D.C.; died of appendicitis in New York on November 1, 1927; daughter of John Winfree and Nellie (Simons) Winfree; married Ulysses Thompson (a dancer and comedian).

By age five, was winning dance contests; made her first stage appearance at age eight in a Washington, D.C., production of Sons of Ham; toured with the Bonita Stage Company as a "pickaninny" with the singing and dancing chorus; performed in the Mills Trio with sisters **Olivia** and **Maude**; later formed the Panama Trio with Ada Smith and Cora Green; toured with the Tennessee Ten Company in a trio with her husband and Fredi Johnson; received important professional break with Shuffle Along (1921); performed in numerous other Broadway and Harlem produc-

tions, including Dixie to Broadway (1924) and Blackbirds (1926).

Selected stage performances: Shuffle Along (1921); Plantation Review (1922); From Dover to Dixie (London, 1923); Dixie to Broadway (1924); Blackbirds (1926).

Walker, A'Lelia (1885–1931). American heiress, hostess and literary patron whose social gatherings brought together some of the most colorful figures of the Harlem Renaissance. Name variations: Lelia Walker (changed her name to A'Lelia as an adult). Born Lelia McWilliams in Vicksburg, Mississippi, on June 6, 1885; collapsed at a dinner party and died in Long Branch, New Jersey, in August 1931; daughter of Sarah (Breedlove) McWilliams (the future Madame C.J Walker) and Moses (Jeff) McWilliams (a laborer); graduated from Knoxville College in Tennessee; married a man named Robinson, around 1905 (divorced 1914); married Wiley Wilson (a physician), in 1919 (divorced 1923); married James Arthur Kennedy (a physician, divorced); children: (adopted during first marriage) Mae Walker Robinson.

Raised in Indianapolis, Indiana; arrived in New York City to manage the Walker Corporation's Harlem headquarters (1914); her mother died (1919); wedding of Mae Walker Robinson, adopted daughter from first marriage (1923); opened the Dark Tower, a literary and artistic salon in her New York townhouse (1928).

The term "renaissance" means "rebirth," and in Harlem, the neighborhood in New York City above 125th Street, a rebirth is what took place in the 1920s. The Harlem Renaissance was a cultural explosion in African-American literature, art, theater, and dance which began around 1917 and lasted until the early 1930s. It was also, as historian Nathan Huggins has described, "a channeling of energy from political and social criticism into poetry, fiction, music and art." Participants in the Harlem Renaissance viewed art and literature not merely as expressions of creativity, but as agents of change. This was an age of freedom in art and literature, dance and theater, but it was also an age marked by racial segregation, the disenfranchisement of blacks, and heightened prejudice. An understanding of this contradiction informed the artists of the Harlem Renaissance.

Part of the impetus for the Harlem Renaissance was a demographic shift known as the Great Migration. Between 1910 and 1930, almost one million blacks left the South and migrated North to cities like Chicago, Detroit, Pittsburgh, and New York in search of better opportunities. Migration North reached its peak during 1915 and 1916, when factories producing war materials needed Southern workers to combat serious labor shortages. The Great Migration represented a significant change in the structure of the American population, and it meant that a new generation of African-Americans would become urban, rather than rural, dwellers.

New York City had a special appeal to those headed North, and for the African-Americans who would sustain the Harlem Renaissance, it was a promising destination. For aspiring writers, it was the center of the publishing industry; the many theaters of Broadway lured hopeful stage performers; art galleries and museums were plentiful. As a whole, the city had an unrivaled "metropolitan charisma" in the 1910s and 1920s which lured many talented writers and artists to its environs. New York became the headquarters for the two most influential publications of the Harlem Renaissance, *Crisis* and *Opportunity*. *Crisis* was the official organ of the National Association for the Advancement of Colored People (NAACP), and W.E.B. Du Bois, the founder, served as the magazine's editor. *Opportunity* served a similar function for the Urban League, and Charles S. Johnson was its editor. Both magazines published the latest work of African-American poets, writers, and critics.

Among these were a number of talented African-American women. Yet, as one historian of the era has noted, "although women were central within the Harlem Renaissance, the names which define the movement are usually male." Countee Cullen, Jean Toomer, and Langston Hughes appear frequently in discussions of the Renaissance, but the names of many of the hundreds of black women who wrote poetry, plays, fiction, essays, and children's books in the 1920s and 1930s have been lost to history. This was due in part to the vagaries of the patronage system, which for a number of reasons tended to exclude women. Without the assistance of a benefactor, many women artists of the Harlem Renaissance had to find alternative employment in order to support themselves.

Women not only contributed to the literature and art of the period, but also served as editors. The writer Jessie Redmon Fauset, for example, served for several years as literary editor of *Crisis*. In addition, women played an important role in fostering cultural discussions through "salons" like **Georgia Douglas Johnson**'s Saturday evening "Round Table," and **A'Lelia Walker**'s "Dark Tower" club. In all of these capacities, women contributed a great deal to the cultural vitality of the Harlem Renaissance.

Some of the most notable women of the Harlem Renaissance were writers, and of these, a large number expressed themselves through poetry. As critic **Gloria T. Hull** has noted, poetry during the Harlem Renaissance was "the preeminent form" of expression, "based on its universality, accessibility for would-be writers, suitability for magazine publication, and classical heritage as the highest expression of cultured, lyric sensibility." Yet the women writers of the Harlem Renaissance rarely limited themselves to one genre. They wrote plays, essays, and magazine columns; they painted; they became educators and civic leaders. Taken together, their contributions represent an important chapter not only in the history of 20th-century American literature, but in the history of American culture as a whole.

Jessie Redmon Fauset

Perhaps the best known of the women writers of the Harlem Renaissance was Jessie Redmon Fauset, a woman of letters who was admired for

her editorial skills as much as for her fiction and poetry. Fauset was a trailblazer from a young age: she was one of the first black students at the Philadelphia Girls' High School, and after Bryn Mawr rejected her college application because of race, she went on to become the first black woman graduate of Cornell University. These experiences influenced Fauset's later fiction, which had as its recurring theme women's struggle for autonomy in a world bedeviled by racial prejudice.

While she was a young teacher in Washington, D.C., Fauset began to submit articles on a wide range of topics to the magazine *Crisis*. Editor W.E.B. Du Bois was so impressed with her work that he persuaded her to move to New York City to serve as the publication's literary editor. In this capacity Fauset became, according to Langston Hughes, "one of those who midwifed the so-called New Negro literature into being." She used *Crisis* as a forum for new talent, giving much-needed exposure to young novelists and poets like *Nella Larsen and Gwendolyn Bennett.

To be a Negro in America posits a dramatic situation.
—Jessie Redmon Fauset

Fauset herself contributed to the literature of the Renaissance through her poetry and fiction. Her first novel, *There Is Confusion*, published in 1924, told the story of a young woman who fights racial prejudice and achieves success through self-sacrifice and perseverance. In many ways, the story mirrored Fauset's own experience as a young black woman in America. Her second novel, *Plum Bun*, published in 1929, had as its central character a light-skinned black woman who attempts to pass as white in New York society. Through this character, Fauset, with keen insight, deconstructed American ideas about skin color and showed, as one critic noted, how "the white disguise proves to be a heavier burden than dark skin."

Fauset's contemporaries and later critics characterized her novels as fully within the genre of "genteel black fiction" because they took as their setting the internal dynamics of the black middle class. One Harlem writer, Claude McKay, described Fauset as "prim, pretty, and well-dressed," and noted that she "talked fluently and intelligently." He went on to say, "Miss Fauset is . . . dainty as a primrose, and her novels are quite as fastidious and precious." Some of Fauset's contemporaries and many later critics dismissed her work as "novels of manners," unpersuasive in their descriptions of black life. Yet this overlooks the deeper dilemmas Fauset explored in her work. In her writing, she captured the predicament that all blacks faced in America: social and racial barriers which barred them from achieving their full potential. This theme found its way into a great deal of the literature of the Harlem Renaissance.

Fauset's contact with other artists of the Harlem Renaissance was not limited to her editing responsibilities at *Crisis*. During the late 1910s and 1920s, she was a frequent guest of another writer and literary host of the era, Georgia Douglas Johnson. In Johnson's Washington, D.C., living room, Fauset met writers like *Angelina Weld Grimké, Langston Hughes, Countee Cullen and *Alice Dunbar-Nelson. Fauset and Johnson formed a comfortable working relationship as well. Fauset helped Johnson assemble her first volume of poetry for publication. It is not surprising that Fauset and Johnson became friends, for in their work they both wrestled with the question of their place in society as women, as writers, and as African-Americans.

Georgia Douglas Johnson

Though she lived in Washington, D.C., rather than New York City, historians consider Georgia Douglas Johnson an important contributor to the literature of the Harlem Renaissance. First as a poet, and later as a playwright, Johnson tackled a wide range of contemporary social themes in her work, including the oppressiveness of sexual and racial stereotypes and the atrocity of lynching in the South.

An accomplished lyricist whose earlier musical training influenced her use of language and rhythm in her writing, Johnson, in her earliest poems, tells the stories of women who try to overcome the restrictive sexual stereotypes of the age. "Heart of a Woman," the title poem of her first collected anthology, described this struggle and the frustration it sometimes brought. The heart of a woman, Johnson wrote, is like a bird that flies "forth with the dawn," then "falls back with the night."

> And enters some alien cage in its plight.
> And tries to forget it has dreamed of the stars
> While it breaks, breaks, breaks on the sheltering bars.

Johnson experienced the restrictiveness of those "sheltering bars," for it was well known that her husband, a public official, did not approve of her career as a writer.

In her second volume of poetry, *Bronze*, Johnson went beyond sexual stereotypes to explore racial ones as well. As one biographer has noted, she tried to explain why women like herself "were expected to identify themselves as either black or female, but never both." This duality is revealed in poems like "Bondage" and "Alien." In "Octoroon," Johnson discussed the "sorrowful circumstances" of mixed heritage, and some scholars have speculated that her use of miscegenation as a theme in her poetry, combined with her reticence about her own family's history, suggest that her ancestry contained white blood. Her later writing, particularly the poems in *An Autumn Love Cycle*, explored universal literary themes such as love and aging.

As the Harlem Renaissance reached its high point in the late 1920s, Johnson turned her attention from poetry to playwriting and found a forum for her political concerns. Employing a mix of standard English and traditional black dialect, she used theater to convey powerful stories about African-American life in the early 20th century. *A Sunday Morning in the South*, for example, revealed the horrors of lynching and the nefarious activities of the Ku Klux Klan in the Southern states. Another play, *Plumes*, won the first prize in *Opportunity* magazine's playwriting contest in 1927.

Johnson's literary activities during these years were even more remarkable when one considers that she was not able to devote herself to them full-time. Starting with the death of her husband in 1925, she was employed in various government agencies in order to support herself and her children. Her work offered a unique description of African-American history from a woman's perspective, at the same time that it celebrated black efforts to achieve equality and freedom in American society. Like Jessie Fauset's novels, Georgia Douglas Johnson's plays and poetry were informed by her sense of history and by her personal experiences as a black woman in America.

Gwendolyn B. Bennett

In 1924, a dinner was held at New York City's Civic Club to honor the publication of Jessie Fauset's first novel, *There Is Confusion*. Celebrating with Fauset and other literary luminaries that evening was Gwendolyn Bennett, a 22-year-old artist, poet, and writer who represented a new, younger generation of the Harlem Renaissance. Bennett traveled in the most exciting artistic circles in Harlem. She knew Georgia Douglas Johnson through the lively and engaging Saturday-night meetings held at the Johnsons' Washington, D.C., home, and she corresponded with other women writers like *Zora Neale Hurston and *Regina Anderson.

Georgia Douglas Johnson

Gwendolyn Bennett's interest in literature began at an early age, and she became the first black girl to be elected to the Felter Literary Society at Brooklyn Girls High School. She also engaged in literary pursuits while she completed her higher education, penning two plays while a student at the Pratt Institute in Brooklyn. But it was as a columnist for the magazine *Opportunity* that Bennett first made her mark on Harlem's literary scene. Lifting a line from William Rose Benet's poem "Harlem"—"I want to sing Harlem on an ebony flute"—Bennett dubbed her column "The Ebony Flute," and from 1926 to 1928 she tracked the "literary chit-chat and artistic what-not" of Harlem. In addition, she used her column as a medium for discussing the African-American literary and artistic movements flourishing in other cities, like the Saturday Evening Quill Club in Boston.

Though her column had many devoted readers, Gwendolyn Bennett's most significant impact on the Harlem Renaissance came through her poetry. She never published her own volume of collected works, but she was a frequent contributor to publications like *Crisis*, where Jessie Redmon Fauset published her work, *Fire!* and *Palms*. Bennett's poetic themes ranged from love and death to nature, romance, and the dilemmas of race. She employed a variety of forms in her work, from traditional ballads and sonnets to more modern styles like free verse, and the length of her poems ranged from a few lines to four dozen.

Bennett's poetry was informed by her training as a visual artist, and she appears to have been particularly influenced by her encounter with modern art during her years of foreign study in Paris. There she met the well-regarded modern painter Frans Masereel, who encouraged her painting. One literary critic has called her poems, literally, "word paintings." In one verse, she linked the world of the painter to the world of the poet, saying "Brushes and paints are all I have/ To speak the music in my soul. . . . / A copper jar beside a pale green bowl." Bennett also used poems to explore her African heritage, capturing both the tumult and the joy of the African-American experience. In "To a Dark

Gwendolyn
B. Bennett

Girl," for example, Bennett praised black beauty, and in "Song" she described the "cry of the soul" of African-Americans.

Helene Johnson

Bennett was not the only young poet of her generation to make a lasting impression on the Harlem literary scene. A woman from Boston whose literary heroes included Alfred, Lord Tennyson, Percy Shelley, and Walt Whitman, she left her home city for New York in the early 1920s. Though her literary career would prove fleeting, Helene Johnson was, as Hull has noted, one of "the stellar poets of the younger generation" of the Harlem Renaissance. This generation included people like Gwendolyn Bennett and Arna Bontemps, who wanted to change the direction of Harlem culture away from the "polite" interests of the older generation and towards newer forms of literary and artistic expression. They wanted to stir things up. They launched a new magazine aptly named *Fire!* which had as its stated purpose: "to burn up a lot of old, dead, conventional Negro-white ideas of the past." Through this medium and others, as historian Jervis Anderson has noted, they "hoped to define the position of the black literary avant-garde and, in so doing, state their aesthetic and philosophical differences with the older literary leadership."

Though little is known of her early life, Johnson came to Harlem with a wealth of literary talent; established Harlem writers like Wallace Thurman expected much of her, calling her a "Negro prodigy." She immersed herself in the Harlem literary scene, attending meetings of A'Lelia Walker's Dark Tower group and publishing several prize-winning poems in *Opportunity* magazine. In her work, Johnson wrote about race in a way that the older generation of Harlem poets had not. She demonstrated, as one biographer has noted, a "fierce identification" with her racial heritage and a fascination with "ghetto life." As her contemporary James Weldon Johnson put it, "she took the 'racial bull' by the horns," often combining militant themes with the new colloquial-folk-slang style that was becoming popular at the time. According to some critics, her best poem was "Bottled," published in *Vanity Fair* in 1927, which compared a bottle of sand from the Sahara desert with a black man from Seventh Avenue in New York. Johnson concluded that although both the sand and the man had been "bottled" for the gaze of Western society, they retained the integrity of their own cultures and heritages.

Like many of the other women writers of the Harlem Renaissance, Helene Johnson found time amidst her literary activities to pursue political activities as well. She became a member of an international organization called the Fellowship of Reconciliation, which advocated pacifism and interracial cooperation. Johnson remained active in the organization until the late 1920s, when she suddenly retired from the Harlem scene. After marrying William Warner Hubbell, a motorman (Johnson's married name was not made public until the 1970s), she devoted herself full-time to raising their daughter **Abigail Calachaly Hubbell**. Critics generally agree that Johnson's early promise as a poet remained unfulfilled since her career spanned such a short period of time, preventing her work from growing in new directions and maturing.

Helene Johnson's departure from the Harlem literary scene, though driven by personal concerns, was emblematic of the shift in fortunes experienced by other writers of the era. When the full force of the nationwide economic depression hit Harlem in the 1930s, writers and poets like Fauset, Georgia Douglas Johnson, and Bennett suffered. Since the literary magazines that published their work were struggling to stay afloat financially, many of these women had to turn to other professions in order to support themselves. Jessie Fauset devoted herself almost entirely to teaching; Georgia Johnson turned her attention to New Deal-sponsored theater projects; and Gwendolyn Bennett returned to her earlier career as an educator, teaching watercolor and design at Howard University.

Unlike the women writers of the Harlem Renaissance, much of whose work is immortalized in anthologies and literary magazines, the female stage performers of the era live on only in black-and-white still photographs and in the accounts of their contemporaries. Nonetheless, these descriptions tell the story of women like Florence Mills and Rose McClendon, whose electrifying personalities lit up the stages of New York and Europe. Their skills found fertile soil in Harlem. According to Jervis Anderson, by the mid-1920s Harlem had become the "night-club capital of the city," and even of the nation. The Lenox Club at Lenox Avenue and 143rd Street, the Bamboo Inn on Seventh Avenue, and "Jungle Alley," the stretch of night clubs along West 133rd Street, all drew hordes of black and white New Yorkers in to experience the sounds and sights of Harlem. In addition to these cabarets and night clubs, Harlem has never had so many active theater groups as it did in the decade of the '20s. This flourishing theater culture provided a number of venues for young performers.

Florence Mills

One of the most beloved stage performers of the Harlem Renaissance was the actress, singer, and dancer Florence Mills. A theater veteran from a very young age, Mills was, according to the poet Countee Cullen, "all too slender and slight for the bright and vivacious flame of her being." James Weldon Johnson echoed this praise, calling Mills "exotic . . . pixie radiant . . . [with] a naivete that was alchemic." Mills was also a Harlemite, known for her down-to-earth demeanor and friendliness, even after achieving celebrity.

Though she had traveled with a number of theater companies, Mills' career gained momentum after her turn in the 1921 production *Shuffle Along*. A musical comedy written by collaborators Noble Sissle and Eubie Blake, *Shuffle Along*, according to one historian, "ushered in a vogue of Negro singing and dancing that lasted until the Great Depression." Though Mills was only in the chorus line of the production, she stole the show, and quickly became one of Harlem's biggest celebrities. She followed this breakthrough performance with appearances in Lew Leslie's *Plantation Review* the next year. *Plantation Review* toured in London and then returned to New York in 1924, enlarged and retitled *Dixie to Broadway*. There was no doubt that Mills was its star, and she became the first female performer around whom an entire musical was structured.

Mills was the maven of a new style of Harlem musical, which introduced novel forms of music and dance to the American stage and to the public. The plaintive tones of jazz and blues, and the swing-like beat of ragtime music, became as popular as new dances like the Charleston, the Cakewalk, and the Lindy Hop. But it was Mills' star turn in Lew Leslie's *Blackbirds* in 1926 that brought her international recognition. An American critic, assessing her performance, compared her to the male stage performer Al Jolson, and declared, "Florence Mills is, within the limits of her field of theatrical enterprise, America's foremost female player." Foreign audiences agreed. *Blackbirds* toured London and Paris for more than a year, and it was said that England's prince of Wales saw the show 20 times.

Mills returned from Europe to a parade in her honor that wound through the streets of Harlem. Tragically, just a few weeks later, she died after an operation for appendicitis. She was 32 and at the peak of her career. New Yorkers expressed their admiration for her talents by giving Mills one of the most elaborate funerals Harlem had ever seen, with floral tributes pouring in from all across the country and the world—$100,000 worth in one day, according to a reporter for the *Boston Evening Transcript*. Mills' body lay in state for a week at a Harlem funeral home, where thousands came to pay their respects.

Rose McClendon

If Florence Mills was the star of Harlem musicals, then Rose McClendon was the leading lady of the Harlem theater. McClendon embarked on a professional acting career late in life; she was 35 when she landed her first major role in the 1919 production *Justice*. Yet, like Florence Mills, she quickly gained critical acclaim for her acting skills. *Ethel Barrymore called McClendon's performance in the 1926 play *Deep River* "one of the memorable, immortal moments in the theater," and a critic commented on the "sensitive personality, bell-like voice," and "fineness of perception" she brought to her roles. By 1927, McClendon was a seasoned performer, appearing in such works as Paul Green's Pulitzer Prize-winning *In Abraham's Bosom*. Of the play, which also featured the actors Jules Bledsoe and Abbie Mitchell, one observer wrote:

> It is difficult to remember scenes in any play that were more compelling than the tragic scenes in which these three players appeared together—all artists, all with long theater training, all understanding that unity among players which the Russians call "communion."

Yet McClendon was not satisfied to remain merely a performer. She was also an important force behind the black community-theater movement in the late 1920s and 1930s. In a letter to *The New York Times*, McClendon outlined the need for the establishment of a permanent black theater in America. "Such a theater could," she said, "create a tradition that would equal the tradition of any national group" and develop "a long line of first-rate actors." In 1935, with this goal in mind, McClendon and actor Dick Campbell organized the Negro People's Theater in Harlem. Unfortunately, McClendon would not live to see her dreams realized. She died of pneumonia in 1936, having remained an active stage and community presence until her final days. Her Negro People's

Theater became part of the Works Progress Administration's Federal Theater Project during the New Deal, and in 1937, her friend Dick Campbell formed the Rose McClendon Players, which one historian has described as "dedicated to carrying out her vision of a community group for training in all aspects of the theater." Through her moving performances on the stage and her strenuous efforts on behalf of the Harlem theatrical community, McClendon left an enduring legacy.

Meta Warwick Fuller

In addition to the many talented writers and actresses of this period, the Harlem Renaissance spawned a number of gifted visual artists. One of the most well known of this group was the sculptor and illustrator Meta Warrick Fuller. Fuller's career would span nearly nine decades. Although she was born and raised in Philadelphia and did not live in New York, the themes she explored through her sculpture were those of the Harlem Renaissance. As a young woman, Fuller received a scholarship to study in Paris, where she arrived in 1899. Under the tutelage and encouragement of Auguste Rodin, Fuller's talents flourished. Despite her successes in Paris (including an exhibit at the Paris Salon gallery), upon returning to Philadelphia, Fuller faced prejudiced art dealers who refused to buy her sculptures. It was not until 1907, when she was commissioned to craft a piece for the Jamestown Tercentennial, that the American art world took notice of her work.

Human suffering fascinated Meta Fuller, and through sculpture she explored its various elements. In *The Wretched*, completed in 1903, she fashioned seven figures, each of which depicted a different form of human suffering. This interest reflected the very great influence of Rodin, and historian Nathan Huggins has argued that "her art was derivative of Rodin's rather than part of the new wave of impressionism and post-impressionism that was swelling around her." Fuller's contemporaries often found her focus on suffering extreme to the point of morbidity, and they labeled her a "sculptor of horrors." But Fuller's work was also about human aspirations, especially the aspirations of African-Americans. In *Water Boy*, she used the image of a small black child's struggle to carry a heavy water jar to symbolize this process. In this way, Fuller's work mirrored that of other Harlem Renaissance figures who used literature and the theater to explore contemporary social themes.

Meta Warrick Fuller

A'Lelia Walker

Many facilitated the exchange of ideas, art, and literature that took place during the Harlem Renaissance, but few did so with the flair of A'Lelia Walker. The daughter of *Madame C.J. Walker, the beautician who built an empire around the "Walker System" of hair-care products, A'Lelia Walker first came to New York in 1914 to manage the Harlem headquarters of her mother's beauty corporation. After her mother's death in 1919, Walker became the wealthiest woman in Harlem; she would use that wealth to create a social circle that included some of the most important figures of the Harlem Renaissance.

As one of her contemporaries noted, A'Lelia Walker's guest lists "read like a blue book of the seven arts." Poets, writers, artists, actors and actresses, musicians and journalists mingled at Walker's sumptuous parties, usually held at her mother's Westchester County mansion, Villa Lewaro, or at either of her two city residences.

Her wealth gave her access to a wide circle of acquaintances, including a well-known white patron of the Harlem Renaissance, Carl Van Vechten. Hull has suggested that Walker and Carl Van Vechten "were the fete-givers supreme of this party-mad era," and Anderson has said that she typified the social side of the Harlem Renaissance. While some of the older, established Harlem families grumbled about Walker's nouveau-riche style of entertaining, there is no doubt that the social activities she organized did a great deal to encourage the blossoming of culture in Harlem in the 1920s.

Walker was not college-educated, nor did she consider herself an intellectual or an artist. Instead, she was that most important of figures, the generous social organizer and artistic sponsor. Yet Walker was not a philanthropist on a large scale, as her mother had been (two-thirds of the Walker Corporation's profits went to charity); her generosity was considerable, but it was directed towards her immediate circle of friends. Indeed, Walker was infamous throughout her life for her conspicuous consumption of expensive jewelry, cars, and clothing. For years, Harlemites recalled the 1923 wedding she hosted for her adopted daughter, **Mae Walker Robinson.** It was one of the most elaborate and expensive celebrations Harlem had ever seen.

Walker's generosity flowed directly to the artists and writers she knew through her social circle. In 1928, she turned the bottom floor of her townhouse into a meeting-place for younger members of the Harlem Renaissance. According to Anderson, they named the place the Dark Tower Tea Club after a monthly column called "Dark Tower" that poet Countee Cullen wrote for the magazine *Opportunity*. It became a regular gathering-place for Walker's talented circle of friends.

Perhaps the best evidence of her impact on the Harlem Renaissance was the recognition given to her by her friends. Carl Van Vechten commented frequently on her charms, and after her death in 1931, a number of prominent figures paid their respects to Walker. At her funeral, Langston Hughes read a poem he had written, "To A'Lelia"; *Mary McLeod Bethune spoke, and Reverend Adam Clayton Powell delivered the eulogy. Though she left behind no published works, A'Lelia Walker had a significant influence on the Harlem Renaissance. Through her wealth, her social powers, and her generosity, she aided the community of writers and artists who produced the best work of the period.

For many observers, Walker's death in 1931 marked the end of an era. As Langston Hughes wrote, that spring "was really the end of the gay times of the New Negro in Harlem." The Depression brought hardship to artists and writers throughout the country, and by that time many prominent figures of the Harlem Renaissance had either died or moved away from New York. Yet the legacy—both artistic and political—of this vibrant period in American history lives on. One historian has described it as an important point "in the evolution of Afro-American literature." The works of Jessie Fauset, Georgia Douglas Johnson, Gwendolyn Bennett, Zora Neale Hurston, Alice Dunbar-Nelson, *Dorothy West, Nella Larsen, and Helene Johnson attest to this. Harlem in the 1920s also generated new and exciting forms of acting and musical theater, as seen through the careers of Florence Mills and Rose McClendon. Finally, the Harlem Renaissance created a sense of community among writers and artists and led to a new sense of racial identity among African-Americans. This new identity was both cultural and political, and it would have an important and lasting influence on American life.

SOURCES:

Anderson, Jervis. *This Was Harlem; A Cultural Portrait, 1900–1950.* NY: Farrar, Straus and Giroux, 1981.

Huggins, Nathan Irvin. *Harlem Renaissance.* NY: Oxford University Press, 1971.

Hull, Gloria T. *Color, Sex, and Poetry: Three Women Writers of the Harlem Renaissance.* Bloomington, IN: Indiana University Press, 1987.

Kellner, Bruce, ed. *The Harlem Renaissance: A Historical Dictionary for the Era.* NY: Methuen, 1984.

Roses, Lorraine Elena, and Ruth Elizabeth Randolph. *Harlem Renaissance and Beyond: Literary Biographies of 100 Black Women Writers, 1900–1945.* Boston, MA: G.K. Hall, 1990.

Sylvander, Carolyn Wedin. *Jessie Redmon Fauset: Black American Writer.* Troy, NY: Whitston, 1981.

SUGGESTED READING:

Bontemps, Arna, ed. *The Harlem Renaissance Remembered.* NY: Dodd, Mead, 1972.

Douglas, Ann. *Terrible Honesty: Mongrel Manhattan in the 1920s.* NY: Farrar, Straus and Giroux, 1995.

Christine Stolba, Ph.D. candidate in American History, Emory University, Atlanta, Georgia

Women of the Regional Theater Movement in America

American producers and directors whose regional theaters, renowned for their high level of quality and commitment, spawned the nationwide movement that revolutionized theater and cultural life in America.

Fichandler, Zelda (1924—). American theatrical producer and director who co-founded the Arena Stage

in Washington, D.C. Pronunciation: ZEL-da FICH-and-ler. Born Zelda Diamond on September 18, 1924, in Boston, Massachusetts; daughter of Harry Diamond (a scientist and inventor) and Ida (Epstein) Diamond; Cornell University, B.A. (Phi Beta Kappa) in Russian language and literature, 1945; George Washington University, M.A. in dramatic arts, 1950; married Thomas C. Fichandler (an executive director of Arena Stage until his retirement in 1986), on February 17, 1946; children: two sons.

Awards: honorary doctorates from Hood College (1962), Georgetown University (1974), George Washington University (1975), and Smith College (1977); Margo Jones Award (1971); Washingtonian of the Year Award (1972); Commonwealth Award for Distinguished Service in Dramatic Arts (1985); *Helen Hayes Award for best direction of The Crucible *(1988).*

Spent her early years in Washington, D.C., until moving to Ithaca, New York, for college; co-founded the Arena Stage in Washington, D.C. (1950); served as producing director of Arena Stage (1952–94); received a Ford Foundation director's grant (1959); received grant from the Rockefeller Foundation to create a training program for her acting company (1965); involved with the founding of the Theater Communications Group (1961); served as delegate to the International Theater Institute Conference in Moscow (1974); served as visiting professor at the University of Texas in Austin and Boston University (1970s); assumed position of artistic director of the Graduate Acting Program at New York University's Tisch School of the Arts (1984—); was artistic director of the Acting Company (1991–94).

Selected writings: "Theaters or Institutions?" in Theater 3: The American Theater 1969–1970 *(NY: Scribner, 1970, pp. 104–116);* "A Humanist View of the Theater," in Performing Arts Journal *(Vol. 7, no. 2, 1983, pp. 88–99);* "Our Town in Our Times," in American Theater *(October 1991, pp. 52–53, 143).*

Plays directed: over 50 during her tenure at Arena Stage, including the American premiere of *Agatha Christie's The Mousetrap *(1955); Jerome Lawrence and Robert E. Lee's* Inherit the Wind, *which toured to Moscow and Leningrad (1973); American premiere of Chingiz Aitmatov and Kaltai Mukhamedzhanov's Soviet play* The Ascent of Mount Fuji *(1975); Arthur Miller's* After the Fall *toured to the Hong Kong Arts Festival (1980); Arthur Miller's* The Crucible *performed at the Israel Festival in Jerusalem (1987).*

Jones, Margo (1911–1955). American theater director and producer who founded one of the nation's earli- est professional regional theaters, Theater '47, in Dallas, Texas. *Born Margaret Virginia Jones on December 12, 1911, in Livingston, Texas; died in Dallas, Texas, on July 24, 1955; daughter of Richard Harper (a lawyer) and Martha Pearl (Collins) Jones; Texas State College for Women in Denton, B.A. in speech, 1932, and M.S. in philosophy and education, 1933; postgraduate studies at Southwestern School of Theater, 1933–34, and Pasadena Playhouse, 1934; never married; no children.*

Awards: achievement award from the Dallas City Council (1954); the Margo Jones Award, established in her honor (1961) by playwrights Jerome Lawrence and Robert E. Lee to recognize those who, like Jones, demonstrate exemplary commitment to the production of new plays.

Spent most of her youth in Livingston until moving to Denton to enter college; worked as assistant director of the Houston Federal Theater Project (1935); founded the Houston Community Players (1936); served as faculty member in the drama department of the University of Texas at Austin (1942–43); was recipient of a Rockefeller fellowship (1944); founded Theater '47 in Dallas (1947).

Publications: Theater-in-the-Round *(Rinehart and Company, 1951).*

Plays directed: over 50, including several of Tennessee Williams' early plays, You Touched Me *(1943),* The Purification *(1944), and the Broadway premieres of* The Glass Menagerie *(1945, co-director) and* Summer and Smoke *(1948); and dozens of world premieres, such as William Inge's* Farther off from Heaven *(1947), *Dorothy Parker and Ross Evans'* The Coast of Illyria *(1949), and Jerome Lawrence and Robert E. Lee's* Inherit the Wind *(1955).*

Vance, Nina (1914–1980). American theater director and producer who founded the Alley Theater in Houston, Texas. *Born Nina Eloise Whittington on October 22, 1914, in Yoakum, Texas; died in Houston, Texas, on February 18, 1980; only daughter of Calvin Perry Whittington (a cotton broker) and Minerva (DeWitt) Whittington; Texas Christian University in Fort Worth, B.A. (cum laude) in public speaking, 1935; postgraduate work at the University of Southern California in Los Angeles, 1935, and the American Academy of Dramatic Art and Columbia University, 1936; married Milton Vance (a lawyer), on August 30, 1941 (divorced 1960); no children.*

Awards: honorary doctorates from Southern College of Fine Arts (1960) and the University of St. Thomas (1969); Distinguished Alumna Award from Texas Christian University (1964); Houston YMCA's

Woman of the Year (1965); inducted into Phi Beta, the national professional fraternity for women in music and speech (1966); recognized by the American Theater Association as a pioneer in the field of resident professional theater (1975).

Spent her youth in Yoakum, Texas, before moving to Fort Worth to enter college; was founder and artistic director of the Houston Jewish Community Center's Players Guild (1945–47); was founder and artistic director of the Alley Theater (1947–80); received a director's grant from the Ford Foundation (1959); was active in the Theater Communications Group (TCG), first as a member of its advisory board and later on its executive committee (1961–71); was invited by President John F. Kennedy to serve on the advisory committee for the proposed National Center for the Performing Arts (1961); was appointed to the U.S. Advisory Commission on International Education and Cultural Affairs (1963); received a director's grant from the Andrew W. Mellon Foundation (1974); hosted the second Conference of Volunteers of Professional Resident Theaters (1975); invited by the U.S. Department of State, the Soviet Ministry of Culture, and the Russian Copyright Agency to join a delegation of American theater directors to tour Leningrad and Moscow (1977); produced the American premiere of Mikhail Roschin's Echelon, *directed by **Galina Volchek** of Moscow's Sovremenik Theater, the first instance of such collaboration between a U.S. and Soviet theater (1978).*

Plays directed: over 125 during the course of her career, including the highly acclaimed Eugene O'Neill's Desire under the Elms *(1949) and* The Iceman Cometh *(1959), and Edward Albee's* Tiny Alice *(1976); world premieres included Ronald Alexander's* Season with Ginger *(1950), James Lee's* Career *(1956), Paul Zindel's* The Effect of Gamma Rays on Man-in-the-Moon Marigolds *(1965), and **Shirley Lauro**'s* The Contest *(1975).*

Margo Jones

While the young Margo Jones—with help from her sister and brothers—created plays in the family barn during the 1920s, virtually no professional theater existed in the United States outside New York City. Most road companies from the 19th century had long since folded, and movie screens had replaced the stages where live actors had once performed in cities across America. Professional theater meant "Broadway," named after the street that runs through the theater district in New York, and Broadway meant a certain kind of theater: commercial ventures created to make a profit,

not necessarily created with the goal of making great art.

Margo Jones envisioned a different kind of professional theater: one that was truly regional, where the people of every city in America with a population of more than 100,000 could enjoy quality live performances; one that was composed of a company of theater artists who worked together for at least an entire season rather than the one-time-only structure relied on in New York; one that was devoted to producing a combination of classic plays and new scripts; and one that embraced an avant-garde style of production Jones dubbed "theater-in-the-round." Known to many as "the dynamo," Margo Jones was just the person to lead the way; along with Nina Vance and Zelda Fichandler, she stood at the vanguard of a new idea for theater in America.

Born in 1911 in the sleepy little East Texas town of Livingston (population 2,000), Jones did not see a professional theatrical production until she was 19—a performance of *Cyrano de Bergerac* in Fort Worth. But after watching her lawyer-father at work creating real-life drama in the courtroom, Jones was smitten with the theater, and knew by age 11 that she desired to direct plays. She called the experiments created out in the barn her first directing ventures. When she enrolled at Texas State College for Women in 1927, Jones claimed that she was the only drama major interested in directing; everyone else seemed bent on acting careers.

During her undergraduate years, Jones ravenously devoured plays, claiming that she read a play a day, minimum, then and for the rest of her life. After receiving a B.A. in 1932, Jones entered Texas State College's one-year graduate program. Because the college did not offer a graduate degree in drama, Jones focused her studies on educational psychology, but the topic of her thesis proves that her interest in theater never waned. Its title was "The Abnormal Ways out of Emotional Conflict as Reflected in the Dramas of Henrik Ibsen," a study of three strong female characters including Ibsen's most famous heroine, Hedda Gabler.

The very day Jones received her M.S. in August 1933, she visited the Southwestern School of Theater in Dallas where she spent almost a year taking all kinds of classes. She then enrolled in the 1934 Pasadena Playhouse Summer School in southern California. As the highlight of her experience there, Jones co-directed the final play of the summer, *Enid Bagnold's *The Chalk Garden. Through a friend, she then landed the opportunity to direct several plays at California's Ojai Community Theater, including *Hedda Gabler*. In 1935, she spent several months traveling around the world as the assistant to a wealthy woman, and saw plays in such exotic places as Beijing, Hong Kong, and Singapore. After such an abundance of experience, Jones felt ready to return to Texas and build her theater dream at home.

In the fall of 1935, Jones joined the Houston Federal Theater as assistant director. The Federal Theater Project (FTP), founded in 1935 and funded by the Works Progress Administration (WPA), had been created to provide jobs for thousands of unemployed theater artists as a part of Franklin Roosevelt's New Deal. Although the Houston arm of the FTP lasted only six months, Jones met many theater people and found herself at home in Houston—at least temporarily. In 1936, she set sail again, this time to Europe and the Moscow Art Theater Festival, which she wrote about in articles for the *Houston Chronicle*.

When she returned to Houston this time, Jones took a job with the Houston Recreation Department teaching playground directors around the city how to create plays with children. She quickly took advantage of her connection with the recreation department, asking if she might use—free of charge—a small park building with a stage to produce plays for adults. With permission granted, Jones announced the formation of the Houston Community Players, and in December 1936, its first production, Oscar Wilde's *The Importance of Being Earnest*, premiered. By the fall of 1937, having directed three more successful shows for the troupe, Jones convinced the Houston Recreation Department to use the proceeds to pay her salary and production costs. Thus, she was finally paid to produce and direct plays full time. In the two years that followed, Jones produced and directed both contemporary and classical plays, including Shakespeare's *Macbeth*, Noel Coward's *Design for Living*, Molière's *The Learned Ladies*, and Maxwell Anderson's *High Tor*.

In the spring of 1939, she attended a community-theater conference in Washington, D.C., and saw a production performed in a hotel ballroom in which the stage was placed in the center of the room with seats for the audience surrounding it on all sides. Theater-in-the-round, also known as arena staging, soon became one of Jones' signatures as a director. She realized that theater-in-the-round had several advantages: it was relatively inexpensive because it did not require a lot of scenery; it created an intimate environment because the audience was in close proximity to the stage; and it allowed Jones to convert nontraditional spaces into theaters without much fuss. Her Community Players had taken a hiatus each summer because the Houston heat prevented them from using their traditional, proscenium theater. Jones simply persuaded Houston hotels to rent her their air-conditioned meeting rooms, and by the summer of 1939, she was directing plays year round.

The outbreak of World War II meant a shift in focus for all Americans, and such leisure activities as community theater were sacrificed for the war effort. Jones lost over 100 volunteers to the armed services, and in the fall of 1942, she decided the Houston Community Players must close. She taught in the drama department of the University of Texas at Austin from 1942 to 1943, continuing to direct productions in the round.

About this time, Jones conceived her idea for a new theater: a professional company dedicated to producing both new plays and classics in repertory, which meant that several different plays would be produced on a rotating basis. She also began to articulate her belief in decentral-

Margo Jones

ization: establishing professional theaters all across the country's hinterlands to counterbalance their current predominance in New York City. Thus, the idea of a "regional" theater was born—a professional theater for every region of the United States, not confined just to Broadway.

Jones met the influential drama editor and critic of the Dallas *Morning News*, John Rosenfield, and proposed her plan. He suggested Dallas as the site and introduced Jones to many Dallas citizens who also supported the idea. While she continued to develop her Dallas theater plan and garner support, Jones also accepted directing jobs.

> *N*either the building, nor the organization, nor the finest plays and actors in the whole world will help you create a fine theater if you have no consistent approach of your own, a true philosophy of the theater.
>
> —Margo Jones

In 1943, she had directed Tennessee Williams' *You Touched Me* at the Pasadena Playhouse; she returned there in 1944 to direct his work again. Jones had developed a zealous respect and deep affection for the young playwright, and this time she directed his one-act play, *The Purification*. She received notification that she had received a prestigious Rockefeller Foundation fellowship to study the American theater scene and seek potential artists to join her company. But another golden opportunity created a dilemma for Jones. Tennessee Williams was about to have his big break on Broadway with a play that was to become a modern classic: *The Glass Menagerie*. He invited Jones to co-direct the play with Eddie Dowling, who also played the lead character, Tom, in the production. She requested a leave of absence from her fellowship for the experience of working on Broadway.

When the play opened in 1945 to the accolades of critics and audiences, Jones returned to Dallas more determined than ever to forge ahead with her plan. She approached **Mrs. Eugene McDermott**, a local philanthropist and former member of the defunct Dallas Little Theater. When Jones described her concept of a "permanent, professional, repertory, native theater in Dallas," McDermott responded by donating $10,000 to the cause. Jones articulated a well-conceived operating plan that included a board of directors, season subscriptions, status as a nonprofit organization, and the preparation of a budget designed by a business manager. Her outline for success would become the prototype for

dozens of professional theaters that followed hers in the years to come—including those of Nina Vance and Zelda Fichandler.

After a long search for a suitable building, Jones found what she wanted on the grounds of Fair Park, a short drive from downtown Dallas. In just two months, she supervised its conversion into a theater-in-the-round, and on June 3, 1947, her Theater '47 was inaugurated with William Inge's drama *Farther off from Heaven* (which later received critical and commercial success under the new title *Dark at the Top of the Stairs*).

For the next eight years, Jones championed the work of unknown playwrights who were struggling for recognition. Her Theater '47, which changed its name to correspond with the current year, reflecting Jones' philosophy "to remain contemporary at all times," became the spawning ground for six plays that were later produced on Broadway. The most memorable of these, Jerome Lawrence and Robert E. Lee's *Inherit the Wind*, which was based on the (in)famous Scopes monkey trial, also succeeded as a major motion picture.

In a mere ten years, between 1945 and 1955, Jones produced and/or directed about 100 plays, many of which also reflected her commitment to the classics. She expanded her season from an initial 10 weeks to 30 and steadily increased the number of plays offered. At national theater conferences, Jones continued to preach her belief in a regional professional theater as well as her partiality to arena staging. She was, indeed, a "Texas Tornado," as Tennessee Williams claimed.

In July 1955, a freak set of circumstances claimed Margo Jones' life. One evening, as she often did, Jones settled down on her living-room carpet to read from the stacks of new scripts that sat piled around her. That same day her carpet had been professionally cleaned using carbon tetrachloride. Jones fell asleep on the carpet, inhaling the toxic chemical fumes, and 11 days later, on July 24, 1955, she died from their fatal effects on her liver and kidney. Jones' unexpected death at the age of 43 sent a tremor through the theater community around the country, for her dynamic personality and fervent belief in the theater as a cultural institution had influenced hundreds of people. Jones was the visionary who led what historian Joseph Wesley Zeigler aptly called a "theater revolution."

Nina Vance

Nina Vance was also a revolutionary. She shared Margo Jones' vision for a national network of professional theaters as well as her Texas roots. Born in 1914 in another small Texas town called Yoakum, located on its southeastern plains, Vance, too, felt her calling to the theater at a young age. At six, she was enraptured by elocution lessons and made her formal theatrical debut as a buttercup in elementary school. Vance also recalled playing a "dope fiend" in her first Yoakum High School production, which was followed by many other parts. When she arrived in Fort Worth to attend Texas Christian University (TCU) in 1931, Vance knew she wanted to study theater.

She graduated cum laude from TCU in 1935, and spent the following summer taking classes at the University of Southern California in Los Angeles—with the pipe dream of being in the movies. After landing only one part as a crowd-scene extra, Vance returned to Yoakum at the end of the summer to her first teaching job. But teaching speech at the local grade school did not hold her interest for long; she was off again, this time to New York City. She enrolled for the 1936 spring term at the American Academy of Dramatic Art. Although she took acting classes, Vance claimed that she learned more observing people on the streets of New York than through any of her formal training. After extending her stay through the summer, taking continuing-education classes for teachers at Columbia University, Vance returned once again to Yoakum. She taught speech and drama classes at Yoakum High School and there began her career as a director. After three years of teaching to her credit and the directing experience of approximately 25 high-school plays behind her, Vance turned her aspirations eastward—toward Houston.

When Vance arrived in Houston in the fall of 1939, its "cow-town" image was fading. That summer Margo Jones and her Community Players had first used arena staging in a rented meeting room of the Rice Hotel. Vance embarked on several new ventures: teaching in the Houston public-school system, as well as her associations with both the Houston Little Theater and Jones' Community Players. Margo Jones was undoubtedly the most influential person in Vance's early theatrical career. For Margo, Vance ran box office, worked backstage, sewed costumes, swept floors, acted in 14 productions—and most important—observed Jones' professionalism and the merits of arena staging.

Three years after Jones left Houston in 1942, Vance found herself following the example of her mentor. In 1945, she agreed to direct plays for the Jewish Community Center, christening her group the Players Guild, and converted rented rooms into arena theaters. For two seasons, Vance directed a series of crowd-pleasing comedies before the Players Guild folded, its operating funds exhausted. Then, in the summer of 1947, she and her theater friends began talking. They wanted a theater of their own, a nonprofessional (i.e., nonpaying) theater with standards of professionalism—a theater devoted to plays that were serious and socially relevant, in addition to the occasional comedy. But where would they find this theater and how could they make it a reality?

Bob Altfeld, a former member of the Players Guild, had an idea. His wife **Vivien Altfeld** ran a dance studio by day; perhaps they could convert it into an arena theater by night if Vance would direct. Over 100 people attended the organizational meeting on October 3, 1947, that gave birth to the Alley Theater and declared Nina Vance its artistic director. Only a month later, Vance and her group of theater enthusiasts made their Houston debut with *A Sound of Hunting*

Nina Vance

by Harry Brown, a drama about World War II. The theater had a hit, both critically and financially, and from the onset, the name Nina Vance became synonymous with the Alley Theater.

Vance directed six productions in a row before the Houston fire marshal condemned the tiny theater for lack of sufficient emergency exits. In February 1949, the Alley Theater opened its first permanent home, a converted fan factory just a few blocks away from the original dance studio, with *Lillian Hellman's *The Children's Hour*. For the next 19 years, Vance directed a total of 91 productions in-the-round on the Alley's famous "postage-stamp stage."

In many ways, Vance continued Jones' legacy in Houston. From its inception, the Alley Theater was established as a nonprofit organization. Vance's insistence on arena staging created an intimate theater experience for Houston audiences and kept production costs down because it required relatively little scenery. Vance also championed new plays; in the Alley's first decade alone, she produced six world premieres. Certainly her most famous discovery was the debut of Paul Zindel's script *The Effect of Gamma Rays on Man-in-the-Moon Marigolds* in 1965, which later premiered on Broadway and won the Pulitzer Prize for drama in 1971. And although her personal style was not nearly as flamboyant as that of Margo Jones, people also gravitated to Nina Vance. Many accounts confirm that she was a charismatic leader, an excellent director, and a wise producer who brought locally acclaimed productions of previous "Broadway flops," as she put it, to Houston's theatergoers. Vance believed in producing plays of literary merit, and she succeeded in persuading her Houston audiences to believe in them, too.

Even during the Alley's fledgling years, Vance's vision of professionalism informed all her choices for the theater's future. As early as 1951, she insisted on paying some of her actors, and in 1954 the Alley officially became a fully professional theater by adhering to the regulations of Actors' Equity Association, the professional actors' union. This also meant maintaining a core group of actors—as Vance had done from the beginning—that became the foundation for a permanent company in residence. Thus, alongside Jones' Theater '54, the Alley became one of the country's first professional resident theaters.

But Vance was interested in more than a play factory—she wanted to establish an institution in the fabric of Houston's cultural life; she wanted to impart an appreciation and understanding of the theater as an art form. To that end, she created the Alley Academy, a training school for children. She initiated an apprentice program for young people desiring to pursue careers in the theater. She developed a speakers bureau to talk to clubs around the city. This steady expansion of the theater as a multifaceted educational institution became one of the distinguishing hallmarks of the professional nonprofit resident theater movement that was to emerge nationwide in the 1960s.

Nina Vance and her Alley Theater were at the forefront of the resident theater movement in the late 1950s. Her work came to the attention of W. McNeil Lowry, director of the Ford Foundation's Division of Humanities and the Arts. Lowry led a plan he called "organized philanthropy," which was the first private funding of the arts on a national scale in American history. The Alley, in particular, benefited from several programs Lowry established. In 1959, in addition to Arena Stage in Washington, D.C., it was one of four theaters to receive monies to support a company of actors for three consecutive seasons. In the same year, Nina Vance received a director's grant. After the success of these and other programs, the Ford Foundation's commitment to theater took a dramatic turn. On October 10, 1962, newspaper headlines around the country announced the largest sum ever awarded to theaters by any philanthropic institution: a total of $6.1 million to nine nonprofit theaters. The Alley received the largest sum of all: $2.1 million specified for the construction of a new building.

For the next six years, Vance continued to direct on her postage-stamp stage while she consulted with engineers and architects from around the country, planning the most state-of-the-art theater imaginable. During this time, she also lent her expertise to Lowry as an advisor and was instrumental in the early development of the Theater Communications Group (TCG), a nationwide networking organization founded by the Ford Foundation in 1961. Vance's was one of the earliest voices to articulate the philosophy and goals of a national theater community, and when the new Alley Theater opened on November 26, 1968, the news made headlines around the world.

In the decade that followed, Vance continued her work at the helm of the Alley Theater, although her primary role evolved from director to producer. The Alley became known as one of the first-generation theaters of the revolution, a model for others to follow. When Vance died of cancer in February 1980, her death was mourned by America's most respected theater professionals. Her Alley Theater lives on, a constant tribute to her search for excellence.

Zelda Fichandler

One of those theater artists who spoke at Vance's memorial service was Zelda Fichandler. Along with Margo Jones and Nina Vance, Fichandler has been dubbed by historian **Dorothy B. Magnus** a "matriarch of the regional theater." Indeed, Fichandler reigned for decades as a leading artist and advocate representing the professional nonprofit theater. Although her career parallels those of Jones and Vance, Fichandler's early history was quite different. A city girl born in Boston in 1924, Fichandler grew up in Washington, D.C. She studied Russian language and literature at Cornell University, from which she graduated with a B.A. in 1945. She then studied dramatic arts at George Washington University, receiving an M.A. in 1950.

Just a year before, Fichandler's mentor at George Washington University, Edward Mangum, conceived of the idea to start a professional theater in Washington. Fichandler found herself—a graduate student—on the ground floor of a plan to create the city's first theater-in-the-round. Crediting Margo Jones for her early interest in arena staging, Fichandler says it was Jones "who took the time to talk to a frightened young girl, to encourage her objectives and stiffen her right arm." In 1950, the converted Hippodrome movie house opened its doors as Arena Stage.

When Mangum accepted a position with another theater in 1952, Fichandler was left in charge. From 1952 until 1991, Zelda Fichandler held the position of producing director at Arena Stage. During her tenure, the theater steadily expanded. By 1955, it had outgrown its original 247-seat space, and a new 500-seat arena theater was built inside an old brewery, home to Arena Stage for the next six years. The year 1961 was a momentous one for Arena Stage. The company moved into a new building, designed by architect Harry Weese, on the shores of the Potomac River. This landmark structure was one of the very first modern regional theaters built specifically for that purpose, rather than converted from a preexisting building. Then in 1962, Arena Stage was named the recipient of $863,000 from the Ford Foundation to be used for the new theater's operating costs. Like the Alley Theater, Fichandler and her Arena Stage received many Ford Foundation grants over the years. Culminating a decade of expansion, the Kreeger Theater, housing a proscenium stage, was constructed adjacent to the existing arena building 1971. This complex is now home to Arena Stage.

Under Fichandler's leadership, Arena Stage achieved a reputation as one of America's foremost resident theaters. She shared Jones' and Vance's dedication to producing a combination of classics and new plays. Throughout her tenure, Fichandler produced many original works that went on to Broadway and national acclaim, including *Moonchildren* by Michael Weller, *Indians* by Arthur Kopit, and *K2* by Patrick Meyers. She also introduced American audiences to foreign plays, such as Bertolt Brecht's *The Caucasian Chalk Circle* and Peter Barnes' *The Ruling Class*. But it was Fichandler's world premiere of Howard Sackler's *The Great White Hope* in 1967 that created a turning point for the resident theater in America. Starring James Earl Jones and **Jane Alexander**, the production received enormous critical acclaim, and Fichandler decided to move it to Broadway. The play then gained national recognition, including the Pulitzer Prize for drama. Since the commercial success of *The Great White Hope*, resident theaters have been established as the nation's most important spawning ground for new scripts.

Fichandler also pioneered international relations between the Arena Stage and foreign countries. In 1973, it was the first resident American company to tour the Soviet Union, with productions of Thornton Wilder's *Our Town* and Lawrence and Lee's *Inherit the Wind*. She directed the American premiere of the Soviet play *The Ascent of Mount Fuji*, by Chingiz Aitmatov and Kaltai Mukhamedzhanov, in 1975. In 1980, the company took Arthur Miller's *After the Fall* to the Hong Kong Arts Festival, and in 1987 Miller's *The Crucible* to the Israel Festival. This paralleled Fichandler's work at home: since the late 1960s, she sought to build a multicultural company of actors, bent on reflecting the diversity of her audiences in the composition of her productions. For these and many other strides made by the theater under Fichandler's aegis, in 1976 Arena Stage received the first *Antoinette Perry (Tony) Award designated to a regional theater for outstanding achievement.

In addition to her impact on the American resident theater through her work at the Arena Stage, Fichandler has been a prominent figure in other parts of the American theatrical landscape, as well. Since 1984, she has held the position of artistic director of the Graduate Acting Program at New York University's Tisch School of the

Arts. She has been actively involved with the Theater Communications Group since its inception in 1961 and also served on its executive committee. From 1991 to 1994, Fichandler acted as artistic director of the Acting Company, a touring ensemble composed of young actors and devoted to productions of the classics. Although she stepped down as producing director of Arena Stage in 1994, she continued her connection with the theater as an artistic associate, directing occasionally. During her remarkable career with Arena Stage, Fichandler produced more than 400 plays and directed more than 50 of them.

Spanning almost five decades, Fichandler's life in the theater is a testament to the work of her former colleagues Margo Jones and Nina Vance. They shared a philosophy that defined theater across America: an insistence on standards of professionalism; a desire to produce plays of literary merit; a belief in the importance of a resident ensemble company of actors; and a concept of the theater as a multifaceted, educational institution. Through their theaters and their work, these women made an indelible mark on contemporary theater practices and audiences in America.

Zelda Fichandler

SOURCES:

Robinson, Alice M., Vera Mowry Roberts, and Milly S. Barranger, eds. *Notable Women in the American Theatre: A Biographical Dictionary.* NY: Greenwood, 1989.

Sheehy, Helen. *Margo: The Life and Theatre of Margo Jones.* Dallas, TX: Southern Methodist University Press, 1989.

Stanley, N.J. "Nina Vance: Founder and Artistic Director of Houston's Alley Theatre, 1947–1980." Ph.D. diss., Indiana University, 1990.

SUGGESTED READING:

Dauphin, Sue. *Houston by Stages: A History of Theatre in Houston.* Burnet, TX: Eakin, 1981.

McAnuff, Des. "The Times of Zelda Fichandler," in *American Theatre.* March 1991, pp. 18–25, 58–61.

Zeigler, Joseph Wesley. *Regional Theatre: The Revolutionary Stage.* Minneapolis, MN: University of Minnesota Press, 1973.

COLLECTIONS:

The Margo Jones Collection, Dallas Public Library, Dallas, Texas.

N.J. Stanley,
Visiting Assistant Professor of Theater,
Bucknell University, Lewisburg, Pennsylvania

Women POWs of Sumatra

(1942–1945)

Several hundred women, mostly European, Dutch, and Australian, interned with some 40 children in Malaya by the Japanese during World War II, who organized their camp against conditions of brutality, deprivation, and disease, sustaining themselves with a vocal orchestra, newsletter, and dispensary.

Japan attacked Pearl Harbor, Hong Kong, Malaya, and Singapore (December 7, 1941); Singapore surrendered; women POWs began internment in Palembang (February 15, 1942); Philippines fell to Japan (May 1943); Allies landed in New Georgia, New Guinea, New Britain, and the bombing of Japan began (1943); Gilbert and Marshall Islands, Marianas, Saipan, and Guam recaptured and Tokyo bombed (1944); women POWs moved from Palembang to Muntok on Banka Island (October 20, 1944); 210 women died of Banka fever (October–December 1944); British, American, and Chinese forces retook Burma, now Myanmar (1945); Philippines reoccupied (February 4, 1945); Americans landed on Iwo Jima (February 19); survivors of Banka Island moved to Loebok Linggau, in Malayan interior (April 9); Margaret Dryburgh, camp spiritual leader, died (April 21); Victory in Europe Day (May 8); atomic bomb dropped on Hiroshima (August 6); atomic bomb dropped on Nagasaki (August 9); women discovered in Loebok Linggau camp by the British (August 26); Japan formally surrendered (September 2, 1945).

While debates have raged about whether or not women should take part in combat, they served in many capacities during World War II—flying aircraft, driving trucks, nursing the wounded—and they also became prisoners of war. In the Pacific theater, the death rate in Japanese camps was staggering: 20–50% of the POWs died in internment. Because of their status as "noncombatants," women like those held captive in Sumatra have generally been overlooked. When the war ended, they returned to their nations without parades, pensions, or recognition. In recent years, however, as many survivors write books to tell their stories and work to publicize the fate of their fellow captives, a good deal of interest has been awakened in the epic of survival of the women POWs of Sumatra.

Many came from Singapore, an island which was the site of what came to be regarded as the greatest military disaster ever inflicted on the British Empire. The East Indies were home to tens of thousands of British and Dutch colonists, and by 1940 Singapore had been a favorite posting for colonials for well over 100 years, with its wide streets, bustling shops, parks, manicured lawns, and attractive homes. Administrators, planters, and members of the armed forces and their wives were frequent visitors at the Raffles Hotel, which served the finest food and drink available to the region's white rulers.

On December 7, 1941, when the Japanese bombed Pearl Harbor, they also attacked Malaya, Singapore, and Hong Kong. Two assumptions were to prove the Europeans' undoing: they regarded the Japanese as inferior warriors, and they believed that the British navy and heavy artillery guarding Singapore made the island impregnable. When Japanese forces began making their way from Burma (now Myanmar) down the Malay peninsula, they were at first ignored. It was commonly believed that the island and its port were further protected by impenetrable jungle. Over the weeks, however, the Japanese hacked their way closer and closer to the British stronghold, and when they captured an entire airfield, British forces fled in panic. The Japanese army was suddenly pouring into Singapore's unguarded back door while its air force rained bombs down from on high, rendering the huge guns pointing out to sea useless. The Japanese navy made short work of the British ships guarding the harbor, and on February 15, 1941, they took Singapore.

The colonists' belief in the impenetrability of their stronghold up to the last moment accounted for the large numbers of women and children still in the city when Singapore fell. In the last days, when defeat was clearly imminent, hordes of people rushed to the harbor to board any available craft, and the Japanese sank many shiploads of refugees. On these vessels were many of the women who would become POWs in Sumatra, among them ◀❧ **Norah Chambers**, ❧▶ **Vivian Bullwinkel**, and **Betty Jeffrey**, on the *Vyner Brooke*; ◀❧ **Margaret Dryburgh** on the *Mata Hari*; and the adolescents **Helen, Antoinette** and **Alette Colijn** on the *Poelau Bras*. Built for 12 passengers, the *Vyner Brooke* held more than 300, including 65 nurses of the Australian Army Nursing Service (AANS), of which Bullwinkel was one. After a night passed hiding behind islands to avoid being spotted by the Japanese, the *Vyner Brooke* finally made its way toward escape, reaching the Banka Strait. After taking machine-gun fire which put holes in the starboard lifeboats, at 2 PM on February 14th the vessel suffered direct hits from three bombs. The order was made to abandon ship. Bullwinkel would later remember: "Those that weren't too

❧▶
*Chambers,
Norah* and *Dryburgh, Margaret.*
See sidebars on
pages 734–735.

*Norah
Chambers*

keen to leave, we gave a helping hand to." The *Vyner Brooke* was sunk in about 15 minutes, and the Japanese fired on the hundreds in the water. Throughout the night, despite persistent strafing by Japanese pilots, the survivors headed for a fire on Banka Island, lit as a beacon by the first among them to reach land. By morning, nearly 100 shipwrecked survivors were assembled there on Radji beach.

The decision was made to turn themselves in to the Japanese. One of the senior nurses, Matron Drummond, suggested that the mothers and children head for the village along with the other civilian women. That group departed but the nurses, including Drummond, remained with the men, whose injuries they attended, and were joined by one elderly woman who chose to stay with her husband. What followed would be long remembered. The Japanese arrived on the beach and marched half of the able-bodied men out of sight. They returned moments later to claim the remaining half, who also disappeared. The nurses and one civilian woman were left on the beach. Bullwinkel heard one nurse remark: "There are two things I hate the most, the sea and the Japs, now I've got them both." The ensuing laughter was broken by the sound of rifle fire. The Japanese returned, sat down in front of the women, cleaned their bloody bayonets, and saw to their rifles. They then lined the women up and ordered them to walk into the sea; when the women were waist high in the water, the soldiers opened fire. Bullwinkel was the only survivor. She would later recall:

> They just swept up and down the line and the girls fell one after the other. I was towards the end of the line and a bullet got me in the left loin and went straight through and came out toward the front. The force of it knocked me over into the water and there I lay. I did not lose consciousness. . . . The waves brought me back to the edge of the water. I lay there 10 minutes and everything seemed quiet. I sat up and looked around and there was no sign of anybody. Then I got up and went up in the jungle and lay down and either slept or was unconscious for a couple of days.

Bullwinkel was startled by the voice of a man, Private Kingsley, who had been bayoneted when the Japanese killed the men but was still alive. Injured herself, she nursed him until, about 12 days later, they began the walk to Muntok. There, notes Hank Nelson, Bullwinkel found 31 nurses who had landed in a different location on the island. "From the 65 nurses on the *Vyner Brooke*," he writes, "twelve were presumed drowned, 21 had been shot, and 32 had been

taken prisoner. Over 80 people had been killed on the beach; a quarter of them women." At war's end, Nelson notes, even with evidence of "other and greater horrors," "it was probably the shooting of the nurses and the miraculous escape of Sister Bullwinkel that became the best known of all the POW stories of death and defiance." Bullwinkel would later admit: "At the time I'd say, 'Why me? Why me?' And then as time went on I—you know, I still say, 'Why me?'"

Aware she was in particular danger as a witness to the massacre, Bullwinkel had intended not to speak of the killings to anyone so as not to endanger them as well. But in the emotion of the reunion, as she was pressed for details of what had become of the others, she told her fellow nurses of the murders. "And all agreed," writes Nelson, "that Bullwinkel's escape would have to be secret among the nurses: it was not to be talked about, even when they thought they were alone. Bullwinkel, the lone survivor and the one link with so many dead colleagues, was both precious and dangerous to the other nurses." Though the women would remain silent, the effect of her story would have far-reaching ramifications during their upcoming days of internment. The women POWs were now well aware that the Japanese were willing to kill them.

Unprepared for coping with so many captured European prisoners, the Japanese held those who surrendered to them in contempt, especially the women. The men at least could be put to work as common laborers, but women and children were "useless mouths." This attitude would dictate Japanese policy until the end of the war.

In all, Bullwinkel and the other women and children who were rounded up and sent to Irenelaan camp near Palembang, on the island of Sumatra, represented 27 nationalities and numerous walks of life, including nurses, nuns, doctors, teachers, and wives of administrators and planters. Until their capture, many had been members of the European elite. Thrust into the primitive conditions of the internment camp, they slept, often without blankets, on concrete floors, with only a well and one or two faucets to provide water. Their food was mostly contaminated rice; bathroom facilities were outside and public. The Japanese, unequipped for such numbers, did as little as possible, in the hope that the problem would simply take care of itself. The women were to move to four different camps during their three-and-a-half years of captivity.

Following the shock of their internment, they had to adjust to their inferior status if

Bullwinkel, Vivian (1915–2000)

Australian nurse and prisoner of war who was the sole surviving woman of a massacre on Banka Island. Name variations: *Vivian Stathem. Born in Kapunda, South Australia, in December 1915; died in Perth from cardiac arrest following leg surgery on July 3, 2000; daughter of George Bullwinkel (a mining company employee); educated in Broken Hill and District Hospital, 1938; married Colonel Frank W. Statham, in 1977 (died 1999); children: one stepson; one stepdaughter.*

Completed midwifery training (1939); served as staff nurse at Kiaora Private Hospital, Hamilton, Victoria (1939–40); served as staff nurse at Jessie McPherson Hospital, Melbourne (1940–41); volunteered with the 13th Australian General Hospital (September 1941); interned at Japanese prisoner-of-war camp (1941–44); named president of the College of Nursing (later the Royal College of Nursing), Australia (1970s).

After working as a staff nurse during the early years of World War II, Vivian Bullwinkel wanted to volunteer her services to the war effort. Initially rejected by the Royal Australian Army Nursing Service (RAAF) because of flat feet, she joined the Australian Army Nursing Service (AANS) in September 1941, as part of the fledgling 13th Australian General Hospital (AGH), and sailed to Singapore on a hospital ship. When Singapore was attacked by the Japanese and evacuated, Bullwinkel boarded the *Vyner Brooke*, which was bombed and sunk by the Japanese in the Banka Strait. She and other survivors reached Banka Island, where the Japanese soon arrived to push the women nurses and one civilian woman into the water and open fire on them. Bullwinkel, the only woman survivor of the massacre on the beach, reached Muntok some days later, where she joined other shipwrecked nurses who had landed in different locations on the island. With them, she was interned in the women's POW camp for three-and-a-half years. She reached Singapore at war's end, on September 16, 1945. Bullwinkel resumed her career as a nurse in Australia and, with fellow survivor **Betty Jeffrey**, toured Victoria to raise funds for a Nurses' Memorial Centre in Melbourne. Established to honor all nurses who had lost their lives during the war, the Centre was also created for the "welfare and advancement" of the profession of nursing.

they were to survive. They learned to bow repeatedly to the Japanese or suffer punishment. When food was delivered, dumped in front of them on the ground, they learned that it could be retrieved only after permission was given. The Japanese government had never agreed to the Geneva convention which mandated the treatment of prisoners, and requests for medical care were usually ignored. Red Cross shipments were confiscated and few of these supplies ever reached the 500 women and about 100 children interned in the Palembang camp.

❧ Chambers, Norah (1905–1989)

Scottish musician whose role in conducting a vocal orchestra of women POWs in Sumatra during World War II brought her retrospective recognition and inspired the movie Paradise Road. *Born Margaret Constance Norah Hope on April 26, 1905, in Singapore; died on June 18, 1989, on Jersey, Channel Islands, England; eldest of four children of James Laidlaw Hope (a mechanical engineer) and Margaret Annie Ogilvie (Mitchell) Hope; sister of Barbara Laidlaw, Ena Jessie, and James Affleck; attended boarding school in Aylesbury, England; graduated from the Royal Academy of Music, London, where she studied the violin, piano and chamber music, and played in the Royal Academy of Music orchestra under Sir Henry Wood; married John Lawrence Chambers (a civil engineer), on March 1, 1930, in Ipoh, Perak, Malaya; children: Sally Hope (b. October 28, 1933, in Ipoh, Perak, Malaya). Lived on and off in Malaya, first with parents, and later with husband; when the Japanese invaded Malaya, trekked through the jungle and arrived in Singapore as evacuation was in progress; evacuated daughter to Perth, Western Australia, but her own rescue vessel, the* Vyner Brooke, *was bombed and sunk; separated from husband and interned in Japanese prison camp; after 18 months, formed a vocal orchestra (1943); with Margaret Dryburgh, worked from memory to arrange scores of 30 classics for four-part women's voices; with husband after the war, returned to Malaya; retired to Jersey in the Channel Islands (1952); composed for and directed the choir of St. Mark's Church in St. Helier.*

During 1943, in an attempt to inspire her fellow prison-camp internees with the will to survive the south Sumatran camps, Norah Chambers conceived the idea of forming a vocal orchestra to perform orchestral works for the entertainment of the 600 women and children in the camp. She took the idea to *Margaret Dryburgh, a gifted Presbyterian missionary, and they worked from memory to transcribe and arrange over 30 miniature classics for four-part vocal harmonies.

Chambers was born to Scottish parents in Singapore in 1905, the eldest of three girls and one boy. From Malaya, where their father was an engineer, the children were sent to boarding school in Aylesbury, England. For three years during the 1920s, Chambers was a student at the prestigious Royal Academy of Music in London where she studied the violin under James Lockyer. According to correspondence exchanged in the 1980s between Chambers and New Zealand musician *Cara Hall, Chambers' greatest influence in those years came from

playing in the Academy orchestra under Sir Henry Wood. He was, wrote Chambers, "a brilliant man, very eccentric and he hammered anyone who made a mistake. . . . I can still see Sir Henry lifting his left hand and yelling 'VEE-BRATO!' What a man. I loved playing in the orchestra where I learned a lot. Unfortunately, I didn't have a hope of getting into one after I left—very few females allowed—they were mostly harpists. Fiddlers were two a penny. It took a prison camp to realise what I could do. Funny, isn't it?" Years later, when she came to conduct her own vocal orchestra in the prison camp, Chambers simply knew how to conduct. Sir Henry had made a lasting impression.

After graduating from the Royal Academy, Chambers, with her mother and two sisters, rejoined her father in Malaya. In March 1930, she married John Chambers, a civil engineer in the government service working in a small, up-country white community in the northeastern town of Kuala Trengannu. There, she began teaching violin to local children. Their daughter Sally was born in 1933 in Ipoh, Perak, Malaya.

When the Japanese invaded Malaya in 1941, the Chambers family made a harrowing five-day trek through the jungle, eventually finding a railway line and arriving in Singapore where a full-scale evacuation was in progress. The young Sally was safely evacuated to Perth, Western Australia, but her parents were not so lucky—their ship, the *Vyner Brooke*, was sunk, and after several days at sea they came ashore on Sumatra. There, they were captured and interned in separate camps—one for women and children, the other for men.

In the brutal conditions of the camp, Chambers came up with the idea of performing orchestral music, using voices as instruments. Even the guards in the camp fell completely under the spell of the music she made with her vocal orchestra and later came to all the concerts. When Chambers refused to add a Japanese song to the repertoire, she was made to stand for hours in the sun without water.

Unlike her musical partner Dryburgh, Chambers survived the years of internment and lived to see the music of the vocal orchestra widely performed in the postwar years. Three years before her death, she met a musician whom she felt precisely understood her music and interpretations, Dirk Jan Warnaar, music editor and director of the Dutch Vocal Orchestra from Bodegraven. He conducted a concert of the music the women had performed in the camps. Wrote Chambers to Cara Hall: "He seemed to know my mind. His girls sang exactly as mine did." In 1987, aware of the wide interest in the story and music of her vocal orchestra, Chambers wrote Hall: "I believe now that our music will not die."

Dryburgh, Margaret (1890–1945)

English Presbyterian missionary in China and Singapore who acquired the status of a kind of saint among the women POWs in Sumatra and gained posthumous recognition for her role in creating a repertoire for the vocal orchestra of women. Name variations: Daisy. Born in February 1890 in Sunderland, northern England; died on April 23, 1945, in a Japanese prisoner-of-war camp in Belalau, Sumatra (then the Dutch West Indies); first of three daughters of William Dryburgh (a Presbyterian minister) and Agnes Dryburgh; studied education and music at Newcastle College, a division of Durham University, B.A., 1911; never married. Taught at Ryhope Grammar Girls' School, where she led the school choir; worked for the Presbyterian Women's Missionary Association in Swatow, South China (1919–25); went to Singapore to work among the Teochow Chinese, whose language she spoke fluently; became the first principal of the Kuo Chuan Girls' School on Bishan Street, as well as organist in the Presbyterian Church in Orchard Road; was aboard the Mata Hari (February 1942) when it was seized by the Japanese in the Banka Strait off Sumatra; was a prisoner of war in a series of camps for women and children in southern Sumatra (1942–45); in the camps, quickly emerged as a religious and social leader whose regular church services as well as her verse, plays, songs and drawings of prison scenes served to inspire those around her; many of her creative works, including poems, drawings and a hymn, have been published in accounts of life in the prison camps.

Born into a devout Presbyterian family in 1890 in Sunderland, northern England, Margaret Dryburgh was the eldest of three daughters, all of whom were accomplished in music and the arts. She studied education and music at Newcastle College, a division of the University of Durham, and graduated with a B.A in 1911. Her first teaching post was at Ryhope Grammar Girls' School, where she led the school choir. Dryburgh subsequently spent more than 20 years as a Presbyterian missionary in China and Singapore, where she was much admired for the expression of her faith through music. She was 52 years old when she was taken prisoner by the Japanese in 1942. **Helen Colijn**, one of three adolescent sisters interned in the camp with her, recalls: "When I first met Miss Dryburgh, she had struck me as a rather dull bird: eyes peeping through thick round lenses, brownish hair in a tight bun at the back of her head, a short stocky figure wearing the sensible loose-fitting cotton dress and Mary Jane-type shoes. . . . But I soon discovered that Miss Dryburgh was not at all a dull woman."

Dryburgh was among 320 women and children who had been evacuated from Singapore in the last days before its fall. She was aboard the *Mata Hari* when it surrendered to the Japanese in the Banka Strait off Sumatra. Together with survivors from other fleeing ships sunk at sea, those from the *Mata Hari* were rounded up on Sumatra and interned in two separate camps—one for women and children, the other for men."

Survivors stress that one of the most dislocating aspects of their internment was their complete isolation from the outside world. Dryburgh understood the significance of being able to draw upon the culture which the internees had left behind to provide an alternative context for their present circumstances. Her composition of *The Captives' Hymn*, an early example of this, was first sung on July 5, 1942, and drew upon conventional and well-known patterns of hymnal music and verse to create a piece which also acknowledged the particular anguish of the internees. As if in testimony to its particular and universal relevance, when repatriation came it was carried by a Eurasian girl to Singapore to be sung by the prisoners there.

When fellow POW *Norah Chambers* decided to create a vocal orchestra for women in the camp, she collaborated with Dryburgh on the scores which would one day be used to recreate the women's performances around the world. Their music helped sustain the prisoners through three-and-a-half years of internment. Dryburgh, however, was among the many who died before seeing freedom.

Lavinia Warner and John Sandilands note that "the loss of Miss Dryburgh was sorely felt. . . . She was the vigorous and inventive spirit who made a large and disparate body of women coalesce to find strength against a common peril. . . . The church services she initiated, amid the doubts and impatience and even embarrassment of those around her at the start of the imprisonment, endured as a vital rallying point to the very end. But in fact she did more, fostering the tribal strength that became the foundation of survival when the desperate fight at Belalau forced each person there to call upon their last individual resources."

While performances of the vocal orchestra music have been held in many countries, perhaps the most specific tribute to Dryburgh's creativity has come from Dutch musician Dirk Jan Warnaar, whose oratorio *Margaret* was based on her prison-camp poems and first performed in Holland on May 4, 1990. It is dedicated to Norah Chambers, to honor the collaboration of the two women. So great was Dryburgh's impact on her fellow prisoners that although she died before peace was declared in 1945 her reputation as an inspiring figure, a musical genius, even a kind of saint lives on among the survivors today.

Prisoners suspected of treachery were taken to the Palembang Jail, which was run by the Kempei Tai, the Japanese version of the Gestapo. Women who survived the confinement and torture were often returned to camp without knowing the crime with which they had been charged.

Nevertheless, the women began to create a community. Two early leaders were Sister **Catherina**, a member of the Dutch Order of St. Borromeus, who had come to Sumatra in 1936, and Reverend Mother **Laurentia**, the order's mother superior, who organized the prisoners into groups, each headed by a captain. These representatives assessed their group's day-to-day needs, distributed their few precious resources when available, and carried out orders dictated by the Japanese. Mother Laurentia also marshaled the captive nuns to minister to prisoners, both physically and spiritually. Dr. **Jean McDowall**, a Scot who always carried her black medical bag with her, and **Margot Turner**, a British nurse, set up a crude dispensary staffed by nurses who were mostly Australian; **Zaida Short**, born in Baghdad and married to a British soldier, negotiated with the guards to procure many badly needed goods like cloth, medicine, and additional food.

The crowded and dismal conditions made organization and cooperation essential to survival. The rice supply had to be picked through, grain by grain, to remove glass shards, bits of straw, and rodent excrement. The meat and vegetables, dumped on the ground, had to be thoroughly cleaned. When the women learned to add ferns, bamboo, and other jungle plants to their diet, groups were sent out to forage. Firewood had to be gathered and chopped for the preparation of meals, laundry had to be done, and latrines had to be cleaned to prevent disease. Tasks were assigned on a daily and weekly basis, and cultural differences sometimes created tension, but the framework of a daily routine helped somewhat to soften the harsh conditions.

Three quarters of the 600 internees were Dutch. Apart from the 32 Australian army nurses, a group of Dutch nuns from Java and Sumatra, and a handful of Eurasian internees, most of the women in the camp were expatriate Dutch or British women accustomed to leading a life of leisure in the colonies. From the beginning, these women organized entertainments for each other and for the children in their national groups: in the squalid, crowded conditions of the camp there were concerts, theatrical performances, and lending libraries of the few books available. In the British group, the English missionary Miss Dryburgh (as she was always known to her fellow internees) quickly emerged as a leader.

Noted **Lavinia Warner** and John Sandilands: "On the very first morning in the barracks, equipped with her Bible and a prayerbook borrowed from young **Phyllis Liddelow**, she announced that each morning and night she would say prayers and read from the Bible, and invited anyone who wished to do so to join her. This was the first indication of some form of leadership emerging amongst the women." With musician Norah Chambers, the Scottish wife of a government official, Dryburgh prepared music for choral singing in a glee club and a choir which sang on Sundays at regular church services. Amidst the filth and suffering which characterized the life of the prison camps, Dryburgh urged the women to "Look up!"—a literal redirection of the attention from the sordidness below to the sky above. To help main-

Margaret Dryburgh

tain their spirits, she began a newsletter. When the children, left with little to do, began to form gangs and become increasingly disruptive, **Dorothy Moreton, Mamie Colley,** and Dryburgh restored some structure to their lives by founding a school. Holidays, birthdays, and anniversaries were observed in the camp. In December 1942, the women applied their ingenuity to the observance of the first Christmas as prisoners. The camp was decorated, a Christmas feast was improvised, and there were homemade games and toys for each child. On Christmas Eve, the men in another camp nearby, separated from their wives and children, were dumbstruck to hear the strains of "Oh Come, All Ye Faithful" ring out, followed by other carols.

Like Dryburgh, Chambers emerged as a central figure. **Helen Colijn** would recall in *Song of Survival*: "In charge of the kitchen were two women who worked every day—and most of the day unless they were ill—for the duration of our captivity. These were the British Norah Chambers and the Dutch **Saartje Tops**. At four or five every morning they rose to start the fires, wheedling the flames out of embers they kept alive from the previous evening. A match was a rarity in the camp. Another of Chambers' jobs was to carry water for the baths of the Japanese, whilst the women's own water—a cup a day for everything during the dry season—came from a dirty well and had to be boiled."

Warner and Sandilands argue that the difficult, dirty and dangerous jobs in the camps acted as a yardstick for character, drawing respect and admiration in more or less reverse proportion to the view taken of such tasks in normal life. Two of the first volunteers to empty the overflowing cesspools in the second camp were Chambers and her best friend there, the New Zealander **Audrey Owen**. Every day before breakfast, they each used a halved coconut shell to scoop the contents into kerosene tins and, using a yoke, carried the vile contents outside the camp. They returned to repeat the process until the job was done. Chambers would later note: "Audrey taught me a great deal. . . . She knew a lot about the stars and on clear nights we would sit outside and she would point out the constellations to me, a wonderful escape from everything around us. She was a very intelligent, gentle person and sometimes, to take our minds off our sanitary forays, she would recite poetry to me as we worked. And even in that ghastly mess we found flowers, beautiful passion flowers which we would pick and take back and give one bloom to anyone

who had a birthday." Chambers' ability to find hope in the midst of squalor would help sustain the other women as the effects of starvation worsened.

> *So* close your eyes, and try to imagine you are in a concert hall hearing Toscanini or Sir Thomas Beecham conduct his world-famous orchestra.
> —**Margaret Dryburgh at the first performance of the vocal orchestra in the women's POW camp**

After 18 months of captivity, when the 600 women and children were moved to a compound no larger than a football field, their creative energy began to evaporate, and entertainments slowed almost to a stop. Here starvation rations had to be eked out, the sick and dying nursed without medication, and latrines emptied. Margaret Dryburgh became ill with dengue fever, and the choir languished without her dynamism. Chambers, a graduate of the Royal College of Music, hit upon the notion of using voices instead of instruments to present orchestral pieces. She took her idea to Dryburgh, and together the two women, working entirely from memory, created exquisitely crafted miniature instrumental works arranged for four-part women's voices. Chambers would later recall of Dryburgh: "She had an infallible memory for both music and words, perfect pitch and an instant command of harmony. You could go to her, hum a tune and straight away she could write it down and harmonize it." The vocal parts were copied out in the smallest manuscript on precious scraps of paper. Rehearsals for the first concert were held in secret. It was to be a festive occasion and a surprise for the audience.

The first concert took place on December 27, 1943, introduced by Dryburgh:

> This evening we are asking you to listen to something quite new, we are sure: a choir of women's voices trying to reproduce some of the well-known music usually given by an orchestra or a pianist. The idea of making ourselves into a vocal orchestra came to us when songs were difficult to remember, and we longed to hear again some of the wonderful melodies and harmonies that uplifted our souls in days gone by.

Large gatherings were forbidden by the Japanese, and the guard rushed into the audience waving his bayonet. Chambers ignored him, raised her hands and the vocal orchestra began the hushed opening of the Largo from the *New World Symphony*. The guard, entranced, listened quietly. The Dvorak ended "with a great crescendo to give the impression of victory over all," recalls Colijn. "What the guard's private thoughts were we'll never know, but the impact on the internees was enormous. Many wept. They had not expected such beauty amid the hunger, the bed-bugs, the rats and the filth that had come to characterise their lives. The concert helped to renew the women's sense of human dignity, of being stronger than the enemy."

Recalled Bullwinkel:

There were 30 women in the choir. They were so weak from malnutrition that they had to sit on wooden stools as they sang, and it was difficult for them, at times, to sustain notes for their full strength. It was a spiritual moment; it transported us right away from our surroundings. Until then we were close to despair. Remember, it was our second Christmas in captivity, and we had no idea how long we would be there until liberation. But after that performance I don't think we ever despaired again. It stood out as the most joyful experience in three and a half years of captivity.

Because the songs sung by the vocal orchestra were without words, the music transcended the language barriers that had stood between the Dutch and the English-speaking women and helped create a cultural harmony the camps had not previously known. Musician ✤▶ **Cara Hall** notes that the remarkable thing about the Dryburgh-Chambers achievement was the way they condensed complex works (even movements from symphonies) entirely from memory, taking main themes with the right modulations and harmonic changes, then weaving them into miniature works complete in themselves. The process was a total collaboration between the two women. Chambers chose the works they could try, then Dryburgh worked them out. If Dryburgh ran into difficulties, Chambers lent a hand, completing such works as Ravel's *Bolero* and Rutland Boughton's *Faery Song*. Dryburgh "was a genius," wrote Chambers, "and we got on so well in every way. Though she was my senior by 20 years, age doesn't matter a hoot where music is concerned. It has a language all its own."

Though the first concert and those which followed lifted the women's spirits, it could not change their malnourishment. Most had the swollen bellies brought on by starvation and poor nutrition, and most had ceased to menstruate. Because of this, one woman did not realize she was pregnant until her seventh month. Mosquitoes were inescapable, causing malaria and septic sores, and dysentery, beriberi, and skin infections were common. Few medications were available and all medical treatment was crude; only the desperately ill were sent to the hospital. Despite these conditions, there were relatively few deaths from 1942 to 1944.

As the Allies drew closer to Malaya, and the Japanese troops became increasingly cut off from supply lines, the circumstances of the POWs deteriorated. On October 20, 1944, the women learned they would be moved to Muntok Camp, on Banka Island, just off the coast of Sumatra, which at first appeared to be an improvement. The new site had nine wells and large airy sleeping huts; chopped wood was even provided. But the island hosted the virulent Banka fever. The location of the latrines and the addition of 200 prisoners enhanced its spread, and malnourishment made the prisoners easy prey. The women sang for over a year, but when more than half of their number had died, the vocal orchestra was silenced. The deaths began in earnest in the last month of 1944. In late November there were 210 victims of Banka fever lying in the huts. In December, six Englishwomen and three Dutch nuns died; by Christmas Eve there were fifteen dead. By the end of January 1945, there were two or three funerals every day, as the women dug graves for their companions.

On April 9, 1945, the survivors were forced to move again. Packed first into the hold of a ship, and then into a train, they were transported without food or water to Loebok Linggau, an old rubber plantation. Several women died on the way, and conditions at the new camp proved even worse. Roofs full of holes provided little shelter from torrential downpours, and the prisoners were ordered to grow their own food supplemented by what they could gather from the jungle. In an act of particular cruelty, their captors did not allow the women to eat the many tropical fruits growing on the plantation, which were left to rot. After the harrowing journey, Dryburgh was desperately ill. Norah Chambers recalls her last moments: "She was semi-conscious and it was obvious that she was dying. She should have recovered but she was so weak from starvation that she just couldn't." On April 21, 1945, Margaret Dryburgh died at Loebok Linggau, a loss that symbolized all that the women had endured.

When Victory in Europe was declared less than three weeks later, on May 8, 1945, the women, still isolated from the outside world, were unaware. In early August, after the dropping of atomic bombs on Hiroshima and Nagasaki resulted in the surrender of Japan, word had still not reached the inmates. But the victori-

✥▸ Hall, Cara Vincent (1922—)

New Zealand concert pianist who has played a central role in providing creative artists with background information on the establishment of the vocal orchestra of women POWs in Sumatra. Name variations: Cara Kelson. Born Cara Vincent Hall on October, 16, 1922, in Christchurch, New Zealand; daughter of George Francis Hall (an accountant) and Gladys Amelia (Vincent) Hall; sister of Charles Stanley Vincent; educated at Fendalton and Elmwood schools, Christchurch, and Wellington East Girls' College; graduate of the Royal Academy of Music, London, where she studied the piano with Vivian Langrish; studied in Paris with Lazare-Levy and Olivier Messiaen (early 1950s); married Robert Natahaniel Kelson (a political scientist, academic, and author), on May 7, 1955, in Wellington, New Zealand; children: Stanley Crispin Kelson (b. February 11, 1957).

Performed on first radio broadcasts (1935); gained the LRSM and awarded a scholarship to study at the Royal Academy of Music in London (1937); performed extensively around the world (1940s–50s), and became especially known in New Zealand, where she performed solo in concert halls and schools, in recitals and concertos with the New Zealand Symphony Orchestra, and on radio and in film; known for her articles on musical subjects and for her collaboration with creative artists in providing background information on the vocal orchestra of women POWs in Sumatra.

Cara Hall grew up in Christchurch, New Zealand, during the Depression years of the late 1920s and 1930s. She learned piano from age 7, began to broadcast on New Zealand radio at 13, and at 15 gained her LRSM and a scholarship to study at the prestigious Royal Academy of Music in London (1937). Her studies at the Royal Academy, interrupted by her return to New Zealand during World War II, were resumed in 1945. After a short and successful career in England, she returned to New Zealand in 1948 to pioneer an innovative music-education program for the New Zealand Education Department, performing 100 live piano lecture-recitals for children in rural schools and colleges throughout the country. She returned to Europe in the early 1950s to study with Lazare-Levy and Olivier Messiaen in Paris. A further period of performances in England was followed by a return to New Zealand in late 1954 to take up engagements with the New Zealand Symphony Orchestra.

Within months of her return, she met and married Robert Kelson, an American Fulbright scholar from Boston, Massachusetts, who was lecturing at Victoria University, Wellington. They traveled extensively throughout South East Asia, the Middle East and Europe en route to Duke University, North Carolina, in the United States. Her performance career ended soon after the birth of their son in 1957.

During the 1980s, Hall lived in retirement with her husband in Perth, Western Australia, and turned to music journalism. She became particularly fascinated by the story of the formation of a vocal orchestra in a women's prisoner-of-war camp in Sumatra during World War II, and began a five-year correspondence with *Norah Chambers, conductor of that orchestra. After Chambers' death in 1989, Cara Hall was music adviser to the Red Cross organizers of a concert held in Perth, Western Australia, in 1990 to commemorate the 45th anniversary of the release of the Australian army nurses from the prison camp. Subsequently, she has provided information and inspiration to a number of creative artists who have adapted the story into various art forms, including the feature film *Paradise Road* and the play *Voices* by **Mary Morris** which premiered in Western Australia in May 1997.

---

ous Allies had heard rumors of large numbers of POWs in Japanese hands. Up to that time, their "island hopping" strategy had kept the Allied forces out of combat in Malaya, with the result that there were 80,000 well-armed Japanese troops still in the area. If these forces declined to surrender, there was a risk that their prisoners might be slaughtered. The British decided to parachute in a few men to negotiate the military settlement and locate any POWs, still without any notion that the women's camp even existed. On August 26, 1945, Major Gideon Jacobs was in charge of the first men to reach the shocking campsite, where the internees were now hardly more than skeletons. Jacobs radiocd immediately for an airdrop of food and medical supplies, and a huge four-engined Liberator bomber was soon raining provisions down on the camp. British soldiers took up the work of cooking, cleaning, and caring for the sick; by this time, the number of the original captives who had died had risen to 237.

In the first days of their postwar experience, even generous helpings of food, too much for frail bodies, could be dangerous. The visible reactions of outsiders were a reminder of the terrible physical toll the ordeal had exacted. The news of the past three-and-a-half years, both personal and public, had to be absorbed. One of the greatest problems for the women turned out to be the adjustment to solitude. After years of living without privacy, many were uneasy without constant companionship, a situation poignantly anticipated by Dryburgh's 1943 poem "Alone: A meditation on community life."

> I never can be quite alone,
> My soul I scarce can call my own,
> Five hundred voices fill the air,
> Five hundred figures cross the square. . . .
> I dress before a hundred eyes,
> A public bath the camp supplies
> I read, embroidered is my tale
> By stories of how others ail,
> I write, the cook says "Time to eat."
> "Remove your paper!" I retreat . . .
> Shrill blast of whistles, clang of bells.
> Alone! Alone! When shall I be
> All by myself in privacy?
> When that day comes, mayhap I'll own
> I rather fear to be alone.

Having grown close during their ordeal, the women found themselves abruptly, and often permanently, separated from the support network which had sustained them. The colonial lifestyle they had known was now vanished forever, and many could not return to their former existences. Most went back to Europe, where their homecomings were low-key, and resumed their lives as best they could, without public recognition of what they had endured. Governments offered them no financial aid.

The camp administrator, Captain Siki, was sentenced to 15 years' imprisonment for his brutal treatment of the inmates. But former captives showed surprisingly little bitterness toward the Japanese, demonstrating the same largeness of spirit, perhaps, which had sustained them in captivity. According to Major Jacobs, the morale of the women at the time of their liberation was much higher than that of the men in their camps. "Perhaps the women were more adaptable or had greater inner resources than the men," he said, "but they seemed to withstand the rigours of imprisonment more stoically."

On January 28, 1978, the story of the women POWs gained its first widespread attention after the broadcast of the British version of the television program "This Is Your Life," featuring one of the captives, Dame Margot Turner. More than 30 years after their liberation, some of the former prisoners were reassembled for the show. Since then, the story of the women's vocal orchestra has been retold many times. In Australia, Betty Jeffrey's autobiography *White Coolies* was published in 1952. Since Antoinette Colijn Mayer donated her original scores to Stanford University in 1980, performances of the vocal orchestra's music have been held throughout the world. In Britain, Lavinia Warner and John Sandilands' book *Women Beyond the Wire* was the basis for the BBC-TV series "Tenko" in the 1980s. In California during 1983, a documentary film was made of the performance of the music by the Peninsula Women's Chorus conducted by Dr. **Patricia Hennings**. In Pittsburgh, Pennsylvania, Bruce Wells, resident choreographer of the Pittsburgh Ballet Theater, prepared a dance work called *A Capella*, premiered by the **Mary Miller** Dance Company on November 1, 1990. In Holland, Dutch musician Dirk Jan Warnaar's oratorio *Margaret*, based on Dryburgh's prison-camp poems and first performed in Holland on May 4, 1990, was dedicated to Norah Chambers to honor her crucial role in helping so many women survive the horrors of prison-camp life. And in Australia, Martin Meader and David Giles wrote a film script which was subsequently used by Bruce Beresford as the basis for his film *Paradise Road*, released internationally in 1997.

By writing books, promoting the music of the vocal orchestra, and publicizing the events that they had survived, the women of Sumatra's POW camps made sure that those who perished there would be remembered. In December 1946, Bullwinkel gave evidence at the Tokyo war crimes trials. For her heroism, she was awarded many honors, including the Order of Australia, the MBE, and the Red Cross' *Florence Nightingale** Medal. After returning to Australia and working at the Heidelberg Military Hospital there, she retired from the AANS and returned to civilian nursing until her marriage to Colonel Frank W. Statham in 1977. Throughout her retirement, she participated in numerous philanthropic projects that benefited veterans and nurses. Fifty years after her imprisonment, she returned to Banka Island with other nurses to honor her fallen colleagues; near the place where she believed the massacre had occurred, they unveiled a memorial.

Although the 237 graves hacked out of the Malayan jungle by the women have long since disappeared, tributes to the fallen will continue. In the town of St. Helier on the island of Jersey in England's Channel Isles, near which Norah Chambers lived from 1952 until her death on June 18, 1989, a handmade wooden cross resides on the altar of the Lady Chapel in St. Mark's Church, bearing the inscription, "In the memory of those women who died in prison camps in Sumatra whose graves will never be found." This simple message, handcrafted in ancient oak by the husband of one of the camp survivors, belies the intensity of the events which occurred half a world away, half a century ago.

SOURCES:

Ager, Mary, ed. *Song of Survival*. CA: Song of Survival Productions, 1985.

Barber, Noel. *A Sinister Twilight: The Fall of Singapore 1942*. Boston, MA: Houghton Mifflin, 1968.

Caffrey, Kate. *Out in the Midday Sun: Singapore 1941–45*. London: André Deutsch, 1974.

Callahan, Raymond. *The Worst Disaster: The Fall of Singapore*. London: Associated University Press, 1977.

Colijn, Helen. *Song of Survival: Women Interned*. Sydney: Millennium, 1996.

Hall, Cara. "The Dolmetsch Tradition," in *Early Music Journal*. Vol 13, no 2. June–July 1990.

———. "Filming underway of wartime drama," in *Artswest*. May–June 1996, p. 23.

———. "Gift of Love," in *Artswest*. March–April 1992, pp. 22–24.

———. "Music gave them the will to survive," in *Destinations, Skywest*. November–December 1989, pp. 24–27.

———. "Parry's plea for national concert circuit," in *Music Maker*. September–October 1988, p. 31.

———. "Song of Survival—now an oratorio and a dance," in *Artswest*. March–April, 1991, p. 30.

———. "Vocal orchestra music to be heard in Perth," in *Music Maker*. March–April 1990, p. 9.

Ienaga, Saburo. *The Pacific War, 1931–1945: A Critical Perspective on Japan's Role in World War II*. NY: Pantheon, 1978.

Nelson, Hank. "A Map to Paradise Road: A Guide for Historians," in *Journal of the Australian War Memorial*. Issue 32. March 1999.

———. "The Nips are Going for the Parker. The Prisoners Face Freedom," in *War and Society*. Vol. 3, no. 2. September 1985, pp. 127–143.

Personal correspondence between Cara Kelson (Hall) and Norah Chambers, 1984–89.

Roland, Charles G. "Allied POWs, Japanese Captors and the Geneva Convention," in *War and Society*. Vol. 9, no. 2. October 1991, pp. 83–102.

———. "Stripping Away the Veneer: P.O.W. Survival in the Far East as an Index of Cultural Atavism," in *Journal of Military History*. Vol. 53, no. 1. January 1989, pp. 79–94.

———, and Harry S. Shannon. "Patterns of Disease Among World War II Prisoners of the Japanese: Hunger, Weight Loss, and Deficiency Diseases in Two Camps," in *Journal of the History of Medicine and Allied Sciences*. Vol. 46, no. 1. January 1991, pp. 65–85.

Warner, Lavinia, and John Sandilands. *Women Beyond the Wire: The True Wartime Story of Women Imprisoned by the Japanese*. London: Michael Joseph, 1982.

Wigmore, Lionel. *The Japanese Thrust*. Canberra: Australian War Memorial, 1968 (*Australia in the War of 1939–1945*, Series I [Army], IV).

SUGGESTED READING:

Crouter, Natalie. *Forbidden Diary: A Record of Wartime Internment, 1942–1945*. NY: B. Franklin, 1980.

Jackson, Daphne. *Java Nightmare: An Autobiography*. Padstow, Cornwall: Tabb House, 1979.

Jeffrey, Betty. *White Coolies*. Sydney: Angus & Robertson, 1954.

Keith, Agnes Newton. *Three Came Home*. Boston, MA: Little, Brown, 1947.

Leffelaar, H.L. *Through a Harsh Dawn: A Boy Grows Up in a Japanese Prison Camp*. Barre, MA: Barre, 1963.

Manners, N.G. *Bullwinkel*. Carlisle, WA: Hesperian Press, 1999.

Norman, E., and D. Angell. "Vivian Bullwinkel: Sole Survivor of the 1942 Massacre of Australian Nurses," in *Nursing History Review*. No. 7, 1999, pp. 97–112.

Simons, Jessie Elizabeth. *While History Passed: The Story of the Australian Nurses Who Were Prisoners of the Japanese for Three and a Half Years*. Melbourne: William Heinemann, 1954.

RELATED MEDIA:

Paradise Road (115 min. film), starring **Glenn Close, Pauline Collins, Frances McDormand, Julianna Margulies**, and **Cate Blanchett**, directed by Bruce Beresford, Fox Searchlight, 1997.

Song of Survival (video), produced by Helen Colijn and Brighton Video, New York, 1985.

Three Came Home (106 min. film), starring *Claudette Colbert*, covers the ordeal of *Agnes Newton Keith* in North Borneo internment camp, 1950.

A Town Like Alice (303 min.), internationally acclaimed Australian television miniseries, starring **Helen Morse, Dorothy Alison**, and Bryan Brown, teleplay based on the novel by Nevil Shute, adapted by **Rosemary Anne Sisson** and Tom Hegarty, produced by The Seven Network Australia, 1981.

COLLECTIONS:

Cara Hall's memorabilia are lodged in the Music Archives of the National Library of New Zealand in Wellington.

Cara Hall, former New Zealand concert pianist, now retired and living in Perth, WA, Australia;
Lekkie Hopkins, Co-ordinator of Women's Studies, Edith Cowan University, Perth, WA, Australia;
and **Karin Loewen Haag**, writer, Athens, Georgia

Women Prophets and Visionaries in France at the End of the Middle Ages

An overview of women, similar to but less heralded than Joan of Arc, whose mystic religion frequently brought them into conflict with authorities.

In Avignon, where the French pope resided in the South of France, the peasant **Marie Robine** (d. 1399) had visions of a great number of weapons and of a virgin bearing arms. A voice reassured her, however, that the weapons were not destined for her, but for a virgin who would come later to deliver the kingdom. It was the end of the 14th century, and the worst period of the Hundred Years' War between England and France. King Charles VI, stricken with madness since 1391, could not control the conflicting factions in France. The Burgundians, who fought in support of the duke of Burgundy, and the English and Armagnacs, who were loyal to the king and his allies, were involved in a fierce civil war.

The virgin savior who would accomplish Marie Robine's prophecy was none other than *Joan of Arc, the "Maid from Lorraine," herself viewed as a prophet by her contemporaries. The mythic stature of the young war leader, associated with Biblical heroines in chronicles of the time, generally outshines the interventions of many other self-proclaimed prophets then making predictions about the political and religious situation. The chaos and disruption of the period, in fact, proved an opportunity for women to voice their moral guidance and expressions of public will. Their visions and revelations, aimed at the king and his entourage, sought a resolution of the political troubles, and their challenge to leaders of the Church was to put an end to the Great Schism which had divided Christianity since 1378, with an Italian pope trying to rule from Rome and a French pope established at Avignon.

[Pieronne of Brittany] affirmed and swore that God often appeared to her in human form and talked to her as one friend does to another; that the last time she had seen him he was wearing a long white robe and a red tunic underneath, which is blasphemous. She would not take back her assertion that she frequently saw God dressed like this and so was this day condemned to be burned.

—*Journal d'un Bourgeois de Paris*

Marie Robine, known also as Marie of Gascony, or of Avignon, had arrived at Avignon in 1387, on a pilgrimage in the hope of being cured of an illness. Miraculously healed at the tomb of the cardinal Pierre of Luxembourg, she settled at the cemetery of St. Michael, where she lived as a recluse. Visions compelled her to advise her king, Charles VI, and particularly his queen, *Isabeau of Bavaria, whom the peasant woman reproached for her misconduct. On June 2, 1398, Marie was in Paris, where the French prelates were holding a council, when she tried in vain to speak before them in favor of the pope of Avignon. The following year, she warned the monarchy in apocalyptic tones that if the instructions coming from her voices were not followed, France and Paris would be destroyed by the Antichrist.

In the crisis of the two opposing popes, neither party was above capitalizing on the revelations of prophets. While Marie Robine advocated in favor of Avignon, **Constance of Rabastens**

was taking the side of the Roman pope, Urban VI. Constance first received revelations in 1384, transcribed by her confessor in 1386. What the prophecies had in common, and shared with the messages of two other famous prophets, *Bridget of Sweden and *Catherine of Sienna in Italy, was a disappointment with the institutions of the Church. The problem for these women was that their view of themselves as elected by God could reach an almost heretical dimension when they put their obedience to Him above their obedience to the Church.

It was Constance's wish to restore peace in France, reestablish the legitimacy of the pope, and reconquer the Holy Land. Her designated champion to accomplish these tasks was Gaston Fébus, count of Foix, a partisan of Charles VI and hostile to the English. For these views, she was forbidden to publish her visions and imprisoned by the Inquisitor of Toulouse, in 1385.

With these two prophets in mind, it is easier to understand both the destiny of Joan of Arc and her place in a broader context in which exceptional women felt compelled to play the role of spiritual and political leaders. Neither view weakens the extraordinary accomplishments of the Maid of Lorraine, which gave her a mythical dimension even in her own time. But it is interesting to see that in her campaign for the recognition of the legitimacy of the dauphin who was to be Charles VII, and to drive the enemies of France off her soil, she met—and sometimes even competed with—other women visionaries and warriors.

What is peculiar to Joan of Arc is the legend surrounding her, which helped to give substance to the belief that she was the savior virgin, coming from the eastern borderlands of the kingdom. Before 1429, the year she left her village of Domremy, there were already several prophecies circulating about a miraculous restorer of France. Two that are attributed to Merlin, the famous enchanter of Arthurian legend, played a decisive role in both her success and her fall: the first involved an armed warrior virgin destined to campaign against the English; the second announced that a miraculous maid would come from an oak wood. This wood later came to be identified with the large tree in Joan's village where she sometimes heard voices of St. *Margaret of Antioch, St. Michael, and St. *Catherine of Alexandria advising her. These prophecies were accepted not only by the populace and her followers, but by the clerics during her trial, who found in them the grounds for indicting Joan as a heretic.

It is fair to say that Joan identified with just such prophecies, and that she began to see herself as a thaumaturge and a prophet. She never questioned the sanctity of her visions or the powers she received from them. Among these powers were her ability to inspire terror in the English troops, and the conviction that she was invulnerable, shared among the French soldiers. Miraculous-seeming also was the perplexing sexual impotence that arose among her companions in arms when they came into close contact with her. Credited with such miracles as bringing a baby back to life after it had been dead for three days, she could not avoid the development of a cult around her.

To express her admiration for Joan's accomplishments in a masculine world, *Christine de Pizan wrote the *Ditié de Jeanne d'Arc*, a poem glorifying the image of the female warrior. The experience of the author, recognized as the first French woman of letters and one of the most important authors of the 15th century, was in some respects similar to Joan's, in that both took on masculine roles. Widowed at age 25, Christine succeeded in earning a living for herself and her three children as a professional writer and an intellectual in the modern sense of these terms, taking on a role usually restricted to men while sharing the prophets' sense of mission. Writing mostly essays, in which she gives firm expression to her political and social views, she discusses the condition of women, the responsibilities of the various components of society, war and peace and the obligations of those in power.

In the fall of 1429, the year before her trial and condemnation, Joan of Arc met another female lay prophet, **Catherine de La Rochelle**. Catherine was a follower of a Franciscan preacher, Brother Richard, who gathered a group of women visionaries around him to announce the imminent coming of a liberator of the French kingdom. When Catherine claimed to have seen an apparition in which a lady in white instructed her to raise money to hire soldiers to follow Joan, the Maid of Lorraine replied with a terse injunction for her to return home and look after her husband and children. To test Catherine's legitimacy, Joan decided to share her bed, stayed awake all night and then declared that she had witnessed nothing; one reason, probably, was that Catherine promoted peace negotiations with the Burgundians, while Joan was convinced that the solution lay in taking up arms. Catherine's revenge was to give testimony suggesting the devilish nature of Joan's visions.

Another disciple of Brother Richard, *Pieronne of Brittany**, along with another woman, had also taken up arms but on the side of the Armagnacs. The two were caught and tried in 1430. Once in jail, Pieronne declared her support of the Maid and insisted that God had appeared several times to her. She was burned at the stake in Paris.

The most intriguing woman linked to the story of Joan of Arc was another warrior, **Claude des Armoises**, the so-called Maid. Like Joan, she claimed to have been instructed by God to wear male attire, and to undertake the life of a soldier. According to a chronicler, she got into trouble in Germany with the inquisitor of Cologne, then fled to Italy where she fought in the pope's army, killing two men. From there she came to France, where she married a knight, Robert des Armoises, and also became mistress of the bishop of Metz. In 1436, six years after the Maid of Lorraine had died at the stake, Claude appeared as Joan, and many people, convinced that their heroine had not been burned at Rouen, were persuaded that a woman soldier clad like a man could only be Joan of Arc. Joan's two brothers even recognized Claude as their sister, gave her a horse and sword, and exhibited her on a tour. In 1439, she was received by the town of Orleans, although she was later arrested and tried, only to resume her life as a soldier. The "Bourgeois de Paris" who chronicles her story does not relate how her life ended.

In spite—or perhaps because—of her ambiguity, a figure like Claude des Armoises reveals a great deal about the role played by women who intervened in public events, particularly in times of crisis, at the end of the Middle Ages. On the one hand, they fulfilled collective expectations at every level of the social spectrum; in their personalities and their messages, believers found both hope and guidance. On the other hand, their behavior, projecting images of role reversal, was a potential threat to the norms of social order. It is not surprising, then, to find them greeted by clerics with hostility. Among the most prominent of their antagonists was Jean Gerson, a cleric and chancellor of the University of Paris. In several treatises, he expresses his skepticism toward the authenticity of visions and revelations claimed by women. His suspicion comes from his discomfort with both their femininity and the paranormal aspect of their mysticism. Surprisingly, he wrote a treatise in support of Joan of Arc, and against the majority of the theologians of the University of Paris, who played a crucial role in her condemnation. Years later, he manifested no such understanding for another visionary, arrested in 1424 for claiming to be one of five women sent by God for the redemption of souls. Tortured and tried in Lyons, she confessed her so-called imposture.

The phenomenon of female visionaries finds only part of its explanation in the war and religious crisis brought by the Great Schism. It must also be situated in the larger context of lay mysticism at the end of the Middle Ages, and its female subculture. During this time, both men and women found ways of leading religious lives without belonging to institutionalized religious orders. Groups of lay men, called beghards, and lay women, known as beguines, living in half-secular, half-religious convents, were often attacked and persecuted as heretics. Their worst enemies were the mendicant orders, Dominicans and Franciscans, who saw them as competitors and outside their control.

Women, particularly, seem to have been attracted to these less authoritarian, less hierarchical forms of community. A less formal environment offered them a suitable context for the expression of a religious urge characterized by the pursuit of mystic experience. Through the mystic experience, a woman could free herself from male authority as represented within the structure of the Church. By her direct communication with God or the saints, she was invested with a superior authority that allowed her to advise and instruct those in power like the pope or the king.

Delphine of Puimichel (1284–1360, also known as Delphine de Sabran) was one such influential mystic. In 1299, she married Elzéar of Sabran, scion of a powerful aristocratic family in Provence. Both were considered at the time to be saints, and at her request, the marriage was never consummated. After her husband's death in 1323, Delphine gave away all her patrimonial possessions, and in 1333 she made a vow of total poverty. Living as a recluse, she conversed several times with the pope in Avignon, very likely on the state of the Church.

The case of **Jeanne-Marie de Maillé** (1331–1414) was similar. Born in 1331 into an aristocratic family in the Touraine region, she grew up under the guidance of an erudite Franciscan monk who served the family as confessor and children's tutor. Taught to read and comment on the Scriptures, and influenced by the lives of the saints, she obtained an agreement from her husband at the time of their marriage, in 1347 or 1348, that the union would not be consummated. After her husband's death in 1362, she lived as a recluse, first settling in Tours and then moving near a Franciscan monastery in 1386. In a life divided between prayer and care of the poor and sick, she had visions and apparitions of *Mary the Virgin and St. Francis. In 1396, she prophe-

sied that the Great Schism would be brought to an end by a Franciscan, a prophecy that came true in 1409, with the election of Pope Alexander V. Despite her hermit's life, Jeanne-Marie de Maillé kept close links with the aristocratic families of Touraine and Vendée, exerting her spiritual influence on the members of the same aristocratic circle who were later supporters of Joan of Arc. She met King Charles VI privately and also reproached Queen Isabeau, who was mistress of the king's brother, Louis of Orleans. When she died after a long life, in 1414, Jeanne-Marie Maillé was considered to be a saint.

The Hundred Years' War and the Great Schism provided the context within which these women could play the role of spiritual leaders. However, conditions in the early 14th century had also been favorable for the emergence of a feminine spirituality characterized by its mysticism and by its prophetic dimension. One factor was the crisis which occurred when troubles in Rome first forced the popes to take refuge in Avignon.

One of these popes, John XXII, became the target of a visionary's curse, when a beguine of southern France, **Prous Boneta**, began receiving visions of Jesus. Believing that God had chosen her to be the incarnation of the Holy Ghost, she attacked John XXII, accusing him of being the Antichrist; it is no wonder that she was tried and burned at the stake at Carcassonne in 1325. But it is also probably significant in her case that she was linked with a branch of radical Franciscans who were denounced as heretics by the Inquisition. As a follower of Peter-John Olieu, or Olivi, a leading figure of the movement, who preached poverty and chastity even within marriage, Prous Boneta typified the Franciscan influence on lay piety, particularly among women. The women following Brother Richard—Joan of Arc, Delphine of Puimichel, and Jeanne-Marie de Maillé—can all be considered examples of the impact of the Franciscan movement on feminine mysticism.

Chastity and poverty were fundamental to the ideal of perfection espoused by groups of beghards and beguines. When they engaged in their preaching, hostility against them could turn at times into persecution. One victim was **Jeanne Daubenton** (also seen as Péronne Daubenton), burned in Paris in 1372 for belonging to an association of the poor called "Turlupins." Although associations of lay devout women had been granted permission by the pope to live together in 1216, they were not allowed to preach, translate or comment on the Scripture, and their autonomy from ecclesiastical supervision was not well accepted.

Another victim of this attitude of suspicion and hostility was the beguine **Marguerite Porete** (d. 1310, also seen as Poiret or Porret, or Marguerite of Hainault) who wrote a book at the very end of the 13th century that was burned in 1306 on the public square in the northern town of Valenciennes. The bishop of Cambrai prohibited its reading and forbade Marguerite to spread her ideas. In her book, the *Mirror of Simple Souls*, Marguerite taught the doctrine of the pure love of God. The soul contemplates God, and in that mirror she sees herself and unites with the object of her contemplation. It is an attitude of passivity to God, of liberation from will and desire, as indicated in the full title of one of the extant manuscripts: *The Mirror of Simple Annihilated Souls who only Dwell in the Will and Desire of Love.* Porete never questioned the essentials of the faith. However, her detachment and indifference to religious practices suggested heresy to the Inquisition. Some of her statements can easily be misunderstood, for example when she says that in its state of liberation, the soul "gives to nature, without remorse, all that it asks," or when she makes a distinction between the "Holy Church the Little," governed by reason, and the "Holy Church the Great," governed by divine love.

Despite the bishop's warnings, Marguerite disseminated both her ideas and her book. In 1308, she was brought before the new bishop of Cambrai and the Inquisitor of Haute Lorraine for having sent it to the bishop of Châlons-sur-Marne. Refusing to answer to questions or to take the necessary oath, she remained in prison for many months. Almost two years later, she was again interrogated in Paris where articles from her book had been examined by 21 theologians of the University of Paris and declared heretical. Refusing to retract, she was burned in the Place de Grève. The cleric who had supported her, Guiart de Cressonesart, had been arrested in Paris in 1308, but escaped death by retracting and was condemned to life imprisonment.

Marguerite's condemnation has been explained politically: supposedly, she had been the object of an exchange between the Inquisition and King Philip the Fair who wanted to have free hand for trying the Templars. However, the success of Marguerite's book—15 manuscripts remain, among them versions in Old French, Old Italian, Middle English and Latin—seems to justify the Church's concern. It clearly suggests that her ideas were in tune with a conception of personal spirituality shared by many others.

The French visionaries and prophets of the 14th and 15th centuries must be considered in the larger context of feminine mysticism, such women as *Julian of Norwich, *Margery Kempe, Bridget of Sweden and Catherine of Sienna. What is special with figures like Joan of Arc or Marie Robine, however, is their involvement in the political and religious conflicts of their time, along with their conviction that they had a mission to accomplish.

SOURCES AND SUGGESTED READING:

Fraioli, Deborah. "The Literary Image of Joan of Arc: Prior Influences," in *Speculum*. Vol. 56, 1981, pp. 811–830.

Porete, Marguerite. *The Mirror of Simple Souls*. Introd. by Elen L. Babinski. NY: Paulist, 1993.

Shirley, Janet. *A Parisian Journal 1405–1449*. Oxford: Clarendon, 1968.

Vauchez, André. *The Laity in the Middle Ages. Religious Beliefs and Devotional Practices*. Notre Dame, IN: University of Notre-Dame Press, 1993.

Zum Brunn, Emilie and Georgette Epiney-Burgard. *Women Mystics in Medieval Europe*. NY: Paragon House, 1989.

Dr. Madeleine Jeay,
Professor of Medieval Literature, Department of French,
McMaster University, Hamilton, Canada

Wong, Anna May (1907–1961)

Actress who was the first Chinese-American to succeed in the movie industry. Name variations: Wong Liu Tsong. Born Wong Liu Tsong on January 3, 1907 (some sources cite 1905), in Los Angeles, California; died of a heart attack on February 3, 1961, in Santa Monica, California; daughter of Sam Wong and Lee Gon Toy; educated in Los Angeles public schools.

Appeared in more than 80 films, including The Thief of Bagdad *(1924), with Douglas Fairbanks, and* Shanghai Express *(1932), with Marlene Dietrich.*

Born Wong Liu Tsong in 1907 in the Chinatown section of Los Angeles, Anna May Wong was the first successful Chinese-American film actor, popular in both the United States and Europe. Still, the prejudices of her times prevented Wong from ever reaching true stardom, and she struggled throughout her career against racial stereotyping in American movies.

One of eight children of second-generation Chinese laundry owners, she went to public schools but, inspired by American movies, decided at age 12 that she wanted to be an actress. Her parents saw acting as dishonorable and strongly disapproved of her untraditional career goal, but Wong defied them and made her first film appearance, as an extra, in *The Red Lantern* in 1919. Still a high school student, she appeared as an extra in two more films, then had her first screen credit playing the wife of Lon Chaney, Sr., in *Bits of Life* (1921). After her graduation later that year, Wong's dramatic talent and striking beauty—she was 5'7", with black hair and pale skin—led to the leading role of Lotus Flower in one of the first Technicolor films, *The Toll of the Sea* (1922).

Two years later, Wong became a Hollywood celebrity when she was cast in Douglas Fairbanks' lavish production of *The Thief of Bagdad* (1924). She played a supporting role as a Mongol slave, but her exotic performance captured the attention of critics and audiences. Until 1928, Wong appeared regularly in new movies, almost always cast as an "oriental villainess" as movie studios made many films set in China and Chinatown.

By 1928, she was frustrated with the lack of significant roles offered to her and with the stereotyping of Asian characters in movies as evil or mysterious. Hoping to find more substantial film roles in Europe, she went to Germany, where her performance in the silent film *Song* brought her praise from German critics. Over the next two years, Wong appeared in several movies made in Germany, France, and England, and enjoyed a considerably expanded range of roles and appreciation by European audiences. She appeared frequently on stage, including a long run in a Vienna musical. As talking pictures became popular, Wong learned fluent German and French in order to remain competitive for new roles; she was so successful that some critics accused the studio of dubbing her voice. In England her most notable work was in E.A. Dupont's *Piccadilly*, released in 1929. While in London, Wong's European successes made her a celebrity, an icon of style and sophistication who moved within high society.

However, her London stage debut in March 1929 was less successful. Appearing opposite Laurence Olivier, Wong opened in *A Circle of Chalk*, based on a Chinese legend and adapted specifically for her by the English director Basil Dean. Neither the actors nor the play received good reviews, and critics were especially harsh about Wong's American accent. When *Circle* closed in 1930, she returned to the United States. Her success in Europe brought her to the attention of casting directors again, and throughout the 1930s she accepted many leading roles in melodramas, although she was still often playing Chinese stereotypes. She performed in her first Broadway play in late 1930 as a "half-Chinese gangster's moll" in *On the Spot*. The following year she accepted a multi-film contract with Paramount Studios, and was given the lead in *Daughter of the Dragon*, released in 1932. Wong remained in the spotlight through 1932 when she was critically acclaimed for her supporting role

as a prostitute in the *Marlene Dietrich film *Shanghai Express*. She then made two movies in England in 1934, returned to the U.S. to make Paramount's *Limehouse Blues*, then once again sailed for Europe. There she toured extensively across Western Europe in a one-woman show.

Despite positive reviews of her work, in 1935 Wong was bitterly disappointed when she was passed over for the leading role of O-lan in *Pearl S. Buck's *The Good Earth*. (The part went to the Austrian *Luise Rainer, who won an Oscar for her performance.) Instead, Wong was offered a minor role in the movie, which she turned down. In January 1936, she and her sister traveled to China for a ten-month stay. Wong was surprised and saddened when Chinese officials publicly denounced her for playing stereotypical evil Chinese roles, even though she herself had been an outspoken critic of racism in Hollywood in her interviews and had mourned the lack of serious roles for Asian actors.

Wong returned to the United States in 1937 to star as a detective in Paramount's *Daughter of Shanghai*, her first positive portrayal of a Chinese woman in an American film. However, this success was followed by a string of low-budget mysteries. When her Paramount contract expired, Wong traveled to Australia and toured again in her one-woman show. During World War II, she performed in two American war films, *Bombs Over Burma* and *The Lady from Chungking*. She also worked as a scene coach—ironically teaching Caucasian actors how to be more believable as Asians—and entertained American troops. Offered little in the way of good film roles in the late 1940s and 1950s, Wong lived quietly with her brother Richard in her Santa Monica home.

She made her television debut in 1951, playing an art gallery owner and amateur detective in a series created for her, *The Gallery of Madame Liu Tsong*. The series was soon canceled, and she appeared only in bit roles on television and in live theater after that. In 1960, she made her final film, *Portrait in Black*, with *Lana Turner. Wong had to quit production on another film, *Flower Drum Song*, in late 1960 because of failing health due to cirrhosis of the liver caused by heavy drinking. After being bedridden for several months, she died of a heart attack in February 1961, at age 54. Anna May Wong was buried at Rosedale Cemetery in Los Angeles. Although she had supported her widowed father, despite their estrangement, and most of her siblings throughout her career, Wong left her small fortune entirely to her brother Richard Wong.

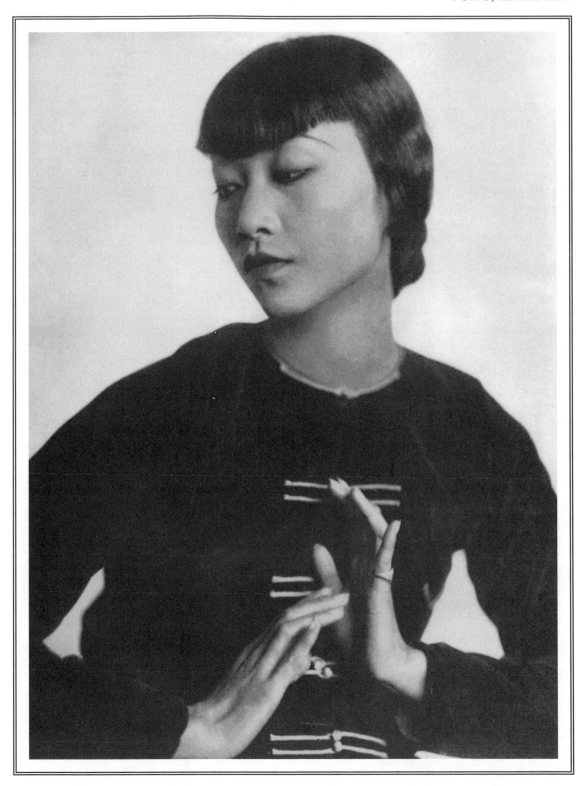

SOURCES:

Katz, Ephraim. *The Film Encyclopedia*. NY: Harper-Collins, 1998.

Roberts, Barrie. "Anna May Wong: Daughter of the Orient," in *Classic Images*. No. 270. December 1997, pp. 20–24.

Sicherman, Barbara, and Carol Hurd Green, eds. *Notable American Women: The Modern Period*. Cambridge, MA: The Belknap Press of Harvard University, 1980.

Laura York, M.A. in History,
University of California,
Riverside, California

Anna May Wong

Wong, Betty Ann (1938—)

American composer, pianist, instrumentalist and lecturer. Name variations: Siu Junn. Born in San Francisco, California, on September 6, 1938.

Co-managed the Flowing Stream Ensemble, a Chinese silk and bamboo orchestra whose repertoire covered 25 centuries; composed Chinese and Western music.

As a composer, who also played the piano, banjo, gong, Chinese recorder and zither, Betty Ann Wong combined her Chinese heritage with her love of American music. Her father, a scholar and poet, and her mother, a schoolteacher, taught their daughter Chinese studies. She studied music at Mills College under Morton Subotnick, Nathan Rubin, and Colin Hampton. In addition, Wong studied Chinese music under David Liang, Lawrence Lui, and Leo Lew. She became a piano teacher at the San Francisco Music Conservatory and the University of California at San Diego. She also set up the Community Center Chinese Music Workshops through a Rockefeller grant. Through her music, Wong was able to combine the culture from which she came with the culture in which she lives.

John Haag,
Athens, Georgia

Wong, Jade Snow (1919—)

Chinese-American writer. Born on January 21, 1919, in San Francisco, California; daughter of Hong Wong (a manufacturer) and Hing Kwai (Tong) Wong; San Francisco Junior College, A.A., 1940; Mills College, B.A., 1942; married Woodrow Ong (a travel agent), on August 29, 1950; children: Mark Stuart; Tyli Elizabeth; Ellora Louise; Lance Orion.

Wrote the autobiographical Fifth Chinese Daughter *(1945) and* No Chinese Stranger *(1975), considered landmarks in Chinese-American literature.*

Born in 1919, Jade Snow Wong was raised in a poor section of Chinatown, in San Francisco, where she attended public schools. As a teenager, she worked as a servant to help her family, a position she found degrading. She excelled in school, but her parents disapproved of education for girls, and refused to support her financially after she graduated at the head of her high school class. Wong then worked to pay her own way through college, graduating with honors from San Francisco Junior College in 1940. She entered the private Mills College in Oakland on a scholarship where she completed her undergraduate work in 1942.

After college, she worked for two years as a secretary for the War Production Board. Always drawn to writing, Wong won a National Congressional Award in 1944 for an essay on employee absenteeism. The next year, she chronicled her experiences growing up in America with a traditional Chinese family in her first book, *Fifth Chinese Daughter*. An insightful personal commentary on the struggles of Chinese-Americans to reconcile their two cultures, it was published in 1945 to critical acclaim and strong sales, and remains a classic of Asian-American literature.

Wong returned to Chinatown, where she became a professional potter and sculptor, opening her own ceramics gallery in 1946. Four years later, she married Woodrow Ong. The couple opened a travel agency, and, between the business and caring for their four children, Wong did not publish again until 1975. This second work, *No Chinese Stranger*, was a continuation of her memoirs. In 1976 she received an honorary doctorate from Mills College. Since the 1970s, Wong has occasionally contributed to magazines, such as *Holiday*, and written a column for the *San Francisco Examiner*.

SOURCES:

Bloom, Harold, ed. *Asian-American Women Writers*. Philadelphia, PA: Chelsea House, 1997.

Buck, Claire, ed. *The Bloomsbury Guide to Women's Literature*. NY: Prentice Hall, 1992.

Laura York, M.A. in History,
University of California,
Riverside, California

Wood, Beatrice (1893–1998)

American painter, sculptor, and ceramist who was known as the "Mama of Dada" because of her association with several early 20th-century artists and writers. Born on March 3, 1893, in San Francisco, California; died on March 13, 1998, in Ojai, California; attended several private schools in the United States and spent a year at a French convent school; studied drawing at the Académie Julien; studied with Viennese master ceramists Otto and Gertrude Natzler; married twice; no children.

Beatrice Wood, best known for her ceramic pieces known as lustreware, characterized by their opalescent glazes, was born in 1893 in San Francisco, but grew up in New York, where her family moved shortly after her birth. Her privileged upbringing included private schools and sojourns to Europe with her mother each summer. In her early teens, Wood rebelled against the confines of her Edwardian upbringing and ran off to Paris (accompanied by a chaperon). On a visit to

Giverny, during which she caught a glimpse through a hedge of Monet at work in his garden, she was inspired to take a garret room at a nearby inn and immerse herself in painting. She eventually returned to Paris, where she took drawing courses at the Académie Julien and later studied acting and dance at the Comédie Française.

Wood was in Paris in 1914 when the onset of World War I forced her to return to New York, also the destination of a number of renegade young French artists who would become part of the Dada movement. (Dada had no fixed theory and was more a "state of mind" than a movement, a revolt against bourgeois values in art and society.) It was at this juncture that she made the acquaintance of Marcel Duchamp (1876–1968), whose painting *Nude Descending a Staircase* had scandalized the art world in 1913. For several years, she became the companion of Duchamp and his friend Henri-Pierre Roché, a French diplomat turned novelist, sharing with them important avant-garde events, including an art exhibition in which she displayed a provocative drawing of a nude alongside Duchamp's sculpture called *Fountain* (a urinal turned upside down). They attended salons for the literati at the apartment of art patrons Walter and **Louise Arensberg**, and published a short-lived journal called *The Blind Man*. Roché became Wood's mentor and her lover, and when he betrayed her with another woman, she replaced him with Duchamp. (Roché later immortalized the trio in his novel *Jules and Jim*, which also became a celebrated François Truffaut film, starring *Jeanne Moreau.)

In 1917, Wood returned to the theater, moving to Montreal and marrying a theater manager whom she later divorced. She also married and divorced a second time, although little is known about the details. "I never made love to the men I married, and I did not marry the men I loved," she later proclaimed. "I do not know if that makes me a good girl gone bad, or a bad girl gone good."

Wood came into ceramics as the result of an adult education class she enrolled in at Hollywood High School, with the intention of creating a teapot to match six lustreware plates she had bought on a trip to the Netherlands in 1930. Instead of the teapot, she produced some much-admired small clay figures, the sale of which provided income while she went on to learn more about the new medium. She studied with Glen Lukens and Otto and **Gertrude Natzler**, then in 1941 established her own studio in Hollywood. In 1948, Wood moved her home and studio to Ojai, California, where her spiritual

guru, the Indian philosopher Jiddu Krishnamurti, had founded the Happy Valley School a year earlier. (Wood originally studied with Krishnamurti in the Netherlands, and first visited Ojai when he held a camp meeting there.) "Ojai was the pot of gold at the end of a long obstacle-strewn rainbow," wrote Wood in her 1985 autobiography *I Shock Myself*. "From the moment I arrived on March 3, 1948, time ceased." Fifty-five at the time, Wood continued to live and work in Ojai until her death in 1998.

Wood produced her clay vessels and modeled figures mainly to serve as a vehicle for her opalescent glazes. The pieces, many of which look as though they might have been dug up from long-ago civilizations, often emerged from the potter's wheel or the kiln with imperfections. The glazes were Wood's true passion and a source of constant experimentation. "The element of luster in her pieces, not used as an overglaze but as part of the formula for the body of the glaze, coalesced in surfaces shot through with many-colored light," writes **Barbara Cortland** in describing the characteristics which set Wood's lustreware apart. "They varied, say, from peach to apple green like the inside of an abalone shell, or the rainbow changes on a soap bubble, or a silver sheen over copper, or turquoise to pink to robin's egg blue."

Many of Wood's clay forms are small comical replicas of humans she liked to call her "naughty figures." Single images or groups, sometimes incised in tile, they are indicative of the artist's sense of humor and gift for biting commentary. One representative piece called *Career Women*, described by **Helen Dudar** in *Smithsonian*, consists of three naked ladies "stonily perched on the prone form of a clothed, bewildered-looking man." In another piece, a female figure is dressed in ankle-high boots, long gloves, and a large flowered hat, while the rest of her body is naked. The work is titled *Is My Hat on Straight?*

Wood was a prolific artist, at her wheel early each morning before breakfast, even before her sacrosanct period of silent meditation. Her passion for her work may have contributed to her longevity, although she was also a strict vegetarian and neither drank nor smoked. From 1961, when she toured India, she dressed exclusively in colorful saris, accessorized with quantities of oversized silver bangles and rings. Over the years, Wood received hundreds of visitors a month to her studio, which was listed in the visitors' guide for Ojai as a "Point of Interest." Since the artist once confessed to a lifelong addiction to "chocolate and young men," many of her male visitors came bearing boxes of candy.

On the occasion of her 104th birthday in 1998, Wood was honored by an exhibition at the American Crafts Museum in New York City. The bulk of the show was devoted to her lustreware although it also included some of her prints, painting, and drawings, as well as some of her early diary notes. Beatrice Wood died on March 13, 1998, shortly after her 105th birthday.

SOURCES:
"An Artist Seeking Her Own Way," in *U.S. News & World Report.* August 28–September 4, 1995.
Dudar, Helen. "Beatrice Wood in her second century: still going strong," in *Smithsonian.* March 1994.
Hill, Ann, ed. *A Visual Dictionary of Art.* Greenwich, CT: New York Graphic Society, 1974.
Hillstrom, Laurie Collier, and Kevin Hillstrom, eds. *Contemporary Women Artists.* Detroit, MI: St. James Press, 1999.
Morgan, Susan. "The Brimming Bowl of Beatrice Wood," in *Los Angeles Times Calendar.* February 28, 1993.

RELATED MEDIA:
Beatrice Wood: Mama of Dada (60 min. documentary), a portrait of the centenarian ceramicist, 1991.

Barbara Morgan,
Melrose, Massachusetts

Wood, Carolyn (1922–1982).

See Sherif, Carolyn Wood.

Wood, Edith Elmer (1871–1945)

American housing reformer. Born on September 24, 1871 (some sources cite 1872), in Portsmouth, New Hampshire; died on April 29, 1945, of a cerebral hemorrhage in Greystone Park, New Jersey; daughter of Horace Elmer (a Civil War veteran and naval officer) and Adele (Wiley) Elmer; educated privately; Smith College, B.L., 1890; Columbia University, in a joint program with the New York School of Philanthropy, M.A., 1917, Ph.D., 1919; married Albert Norton Wood (a naval officer), in 1893; children: Horace Elmer (b. 1895); Thurston Elmer (b. 1897); Horace Elmer II (b. 1900); and Albert Elmer (b. 1910).

Selected writings: Her Provincial Cousin *(1893);* Shoulder Straps and Sunbonnets *(1901);* Spirit of the Service *(1903);* An Oberland Chalet *(1910);* The Housing of the Unskilled Wage Earner *(1919);* Housing Progress in Western Europe *(1923);* Recent Trends in American Housing *(1931);* Introduction to Housing Facts and Principles *(1939).*

The daughter of a naval officer, Edith Elmer Wood traveled across the United States and abroad frequently as a child. She received her early education from private tutors before entering Smith College in Northampton, Massachusetts. She graduated in 1890 with a B.L. degree. Drawn to writing as a child, she became a novelist, publishing several books of romantic fiction and travelogues. In 1893, she married a naval officer, Albert Norton Wood, with whom she would have four sons, and again traveled frequently as his assignments changed. During the early years of her marriage, Wood divided her time between her family duties and fiction writing.

Her literary works were abandoned in 1906, when the family was living in Puerto Rico. Wood's servant became ill with tuberculosis; discovering that no treatment was available on the island, Wood started a crusade to improve public-health facilities especially for the poor. She founded the Anti-Tuberculosis League of Puerto Rico, and when the family moved to Washington, D.C., tried to improve housing conditions in the slums, though with limited success. Convinced that she needed more education to better understand the connections between public health and housing conditions, Wood entered Columbia University's graduate school in 1915, at age 44. She completed her M.A. in 1917 with a thesis on European housing policy, and also finished a diploma at the New York School of Philanthropy. In 1919, she earned a doctorate for her thesis, a detailed statistical analysis of low-income housing later published as *The Housing of the Unskilled Wage Earner.*

Wood would dedicate the rest of her life to housing-reform advocacy. A member of the Regional Planning Association of America, she wrote many articles for scholarly journals and published three more books on housing policy. In her writings Wood developed her argument that the free market system was incapable of providing affordable and sanitary housing for middle- and low-income families. Wood believed that the federal government needed to intervene in the housing market to ensure the availability of affordable, decent housing because housing conditions affected health, moral behavior, and happiness. Her constructive proposals for housing legislation included federal loans and tax abatement for the middle class, and direct government ownership of housing for the poor. After graduating from Columbia, Wood and her family settled in Cape May Court House, New Jersey.

A recognized expert on housing policy by 1920, Wood was appointed to numerous housing advisory boards, including the Women's Municipal League of Boston (1917–19) and the American Association of University Women's committee on housing, of which she was chair from 1917 to 1929. In addition, she lectured widely and from 1926 to 1930 taught courses on housing economics and public policy at Columbia University. She was also a member and later director of the National Public Housing Conference from 1932 to 1945, and of the Executive Committee of the New Jersey State Housing Authority from 1934 to 1935.

Overall, progress for low-income housing was slow before the implementation of Franklin Roosevelt's New Deal housing policies in the 1930s, many of which followed constructive practices such as Wood had proposed. During Roosevelt's tenure, Wood served as a consultant to the Public Works Administration from 1933 to 1937, and to the U.S. Housing Authority from 1933 to 1945, researching and shaping New Deal housing legislation. Her efforts made her one of the most respected analysts of American housing needs. She was awarded an honorary LL.D. from Smith College in 1940.

Wood suffered a heart attack in 1943 but continued her writing and advising activities even while bedridden. She was finally forced to retire from her campaign to improve the lives of the poorer classes in 1944, at age 73. She died in April 1945 in Greystone Park, New Jersey, and was buried in the Naval Academy Cemetery at Annapolis, Maryland.

SOURCES:

James, Edward T., ed. *Notable American Women, 1607–1950.* Cambridge, MA: The Belknap Press of Harvard University, 1971.

Trattiner, Walter I., ed. *Biographical Dictionary of Social Welfare in America.* NY: Greenwood Press, 1986.

Whitman, Alden, ed. *American Reformers.* NY: H.W. Wilson, 1985.

Laura York, M.A. in History,
University of California,
Riverside, California

Wood, Ellen Price (1814–1887)

Prolific English novelist who wrote the hugely popular East Lynne. *Name variations: Mrs. Henry Wood; Johnny Ludlow. Born Ellen Price on January 17, 1814, in Worcester, England; died on February 10, 1887, in London; daughter of Thomas Price and Elizabeth (Evans) Price; married Henry Wood (a banker), in 1836; children: Charles Wood (b. 1850).*

The popular Victorian novelist Ellen Price Wood was born in 1814 in Worcester, England, to a prosperous manufacturing family. After developing scoliosis as a child, she had to be educated at home. She would remain a semi-invalid throughout her life, able to write only while lying on a couch. At age 22, she married Henry Wood, son of a wealthy banking and shipping family. The couple lived in the Dauphiné, France, for most of the first two decades of their marriage.

While in France, Wood wrote stories which were published in *Bentley's Miscellany* and the *New Monthly Magazine.* In 1860, a setback in Henry Wood's financial fortunes led the family to return to England and settle in Norwood. There Ellen wrote her first novel, completed in one month, for a contest sponsored by the Scottish Temperance League. *Danesbury House* won first prize and was later published. Her second novel *East Lynne* appeared first serially in the *New Monthly Magazine* in 1861 and then in book form. It was highly praised by *The Times*, and by 1900 had sold over half a million copies. The most widely read of her novels, it was translated into many languages and frequently dramatized. Wood followed the success of *East Lynne* with the family sagas *Mrs. Halliburton's Troubles* and *The Channings.* All of her novels were published under the name "Mrs. Henry Wood." Though written in a variety of genres, her books share a melodramatic style and a similar theme, a stern Christian morality with severe punishment for those characters who transgress middle-class Victorian values. A politically conservative, pious Anglican, Wood also used her novels to argue against progressive social movements, such as trade unionism. *The Channings* was followed by the Gothic *The Shadow of Ashlydyat* (1863), *Lord Oakburn's Daughters* (1864), and *Roland Yorke* (1869) among others.

Henry Wood died in 1866. The following year Ellen and her son Charles bought a literary magazine, *The Argosy*, which they then co-edited. Wood also contributed to the magazine; her colorful stories based on her Worcestershire childhood and published under the name "Johnny Ludlow" are thought to be her best works from these years. Wood completed an additional 20 novels, most notably *Edina* (1876). In all, she published over 30 novels and 300 short stories. Wood died in 1887, at age 73.

SOURCES:

Shattock, Joanne, ed. *The Oxford Guide to British Women Writers.* NY: Oxford University Press, 1993.

Wood, Charles. *Memorials of Mrs. Henry Wood.* London: R. Bentley, 1894.

Laura York, M.A. in History,
University of California,
Riverside, California

Wood, Evelyn (1909–1995)

American developer of the speed-reading technique. Born Evelyn Nielsen on January 8, 1909, in Logan,

Utah; died on August 26, 1995, in Tucson, Arizona; daughter of Elias Nielsen and Rose (Stirland) Nielsen; University of Utah, B.A., 1929, M.S. in speech, 1947; postgraduate work at Columbia University, 1957; married Myron Douglas Wood, on June 12, 1929 (died 1987); children: one daughter **Carol Wood Evans**.

Born in 1909 in Logan, Utah, Evelyn Wood attended public schools there as a child. She entered the University of Utah, finishing her bachelor's degree in English in 1929. In June of that year, she married Myron Wood, with whom she had one daughter. Wood worked for one year as a professor of biology and English at Weber College in Ogden, Utah, but left the college in 1932. Later she returned to the University of Utah, completing her M.S. degree in speech in 1947. That year, she also developed and presented numerous radio programs on reading skills which were broadcast around the state.

Wood remained at the University of Utah as a researcher from 1947 to 1950, working with C. Lowell Lees on speech and reading studies. In 1948, she also accepted a position as girls' counselor at Jordan High School in Sandy, Utah, where she would remain until 1957. Especially interested in developing her students' reading skills, Wood began a remedial reading program. She discovered that the girls who read the fastest retained the most information. Using this insight, Wood planned a large-scale study of naturally fast readers. As part of her research, she traveled across the United States contacting 1,500 people who could read over 1,500 words per minute. She then studied their reading techniques and tested their comprehension.

From this work Wood developed a speed-reading technique which she further refined by teaching it in elementary, high school, and adult education classes between 1948 and 1959. Between 1957 and 1959, she taught reading skills courses at the University of Utah. The key to her technique was to train the eyes to skim a page top to bottom, seeking key words and phrases, rather than reading each line one word at a time.

In 1959, she named her program Evelyn Wood Reading Dynamics, and opened an institute to teach speed-reading in Washington, D.C. That same year, she outlined her program in her book *Reading Skills*, which promised to increase the student's reading speed from the average 250 words per minute to 1,500 words per minute. The book's simple techniques brought her considerable popularity and led to the establishment of other Reading Dynamics Institutes in major

U.S. cities. It was also translated into numerous European languages.

Three more books followed: *A Breakthrough in Reading* (1961), *A New Approach to Speed-Reading* (1962), and *Speed Reading for Comprehension* (1962). In 1961, Wood was appointed assistant professor at the University of Delaware. Two years later, the popularity of Wood's program was assured when John F. Kennedy, himself a speed-reader, asked her to teach Reading Dynamics to the joint chiefs of staff. Wood lectured across the United States, Canada, and in Europe, and was featured on many television and radio programs throughout the 1960s. She herself benefited from her program, and reportedly could read up to 15,000 words per minute.

The Woods sold the Institutes in 1966, but Evelyn Wood continued to teach courses until a stroke forced her to retire in 1977. At the peak of the program's popularity in the late 1970s, there were over 150 Reading Dynamics Institutes in the U.S. teaching thousands of Americans each year. In addition to her research and teaching on reading, Wood, a Mormon, was active in her church and in various civic organizations in Salt Lake City, where she made her home until the death of her husband in 1987. Wood then went to live with her daughter in Tucson, Arizona. She died there in 1995, at age 86.

SOURCES:
The National Cyclopedia of American Biography. Vol. 63. Clifton, NJ: James T. White, 1984.
Obituary, in *The Day* [New London, CT]. August 30, 1995, p. B4.
Obituary, in *Time*. September 11, 1995, p. 35.

Laura York, M.A. in History,
University of California,
Riverside, California

Wood, Mrs. Henry (1814–1887).

See Wood, Ellen Price.

Wood, Mrs. John (1831–1915).

See Wood, Matilda.

Wood, Mary Elizabeth (1861–1931)

American missionary and librarian who helped found the National Library of Peking (Beijing) with funds raised in the United States. Born on August 22, 1861, in Elba, New York; died on May 1, 1931, in Wuchang, China; daughter of Edward Farmer Wood and Mary Jane (Humphrey) Wood; educated at the Pratt Institute, New York, and Simmons College, Boston; never married.

Born in Elba, New York, Mary Elizabeth Wood was an Episcopal missionary and librarian in China for 30 years. Shortly after Wood's birth in 1861, her family moved to Batavia, New York, where she attended private and public schools. After graduating from Batavia High School, she worked for ten years as the librarian of the newly founded Richmond Library in Batavia.

A visit to China in 1899 to see her brother Robert Wood, an Episcopal missionary in Wuchang, turned into a lifelong educational and religious mission for Mary Wood. She learned to speak Chinese (although she did not learn to read it) and decided to stay to teach at her brother's Boone School. In 1904, Wood was made a lay missionary by the Episcopal Church. That year, the reigning Manchu government of China abolished the traditional Chinese education system in favor of Western-style learning. Chinese schools and colleges needed libraries to support the new learning, and Wood saw an opportunity to combine library science with her missionary work. She returned to the United States in 1906 to solicit private funding for a library building for the Boone School; her benefactors included philanthropist *Olivia Phelps Stokes and a former Columbia University president, Seth Low.

Wood made other trips back to the States in succeeding years, studying library science at the Pratt Institute and Simmons College while seeking additional patrons for her Chinese library campaigns. These campaigns included establishing a series of branch libraries at state and private colleges in Wuchang and Hankow, and arranging for "traveling libraries" to tour schools and factories so that workers could benefit from the Chinese and English books as well.

A tireless fund raiser, Wood also funded scholarships for two Chinese students to study library science in the United States; they returned to China to assist her in founding a school for library science at Boone College in 1920. The school had trained nearly 500 Chinese librarians before its closure after the Communist revolution of 1949; it was subsequently reopened as an affiliate of National Wuhan University.

As part of her ongoing effort to secure funding for a true national library system, in 1923 Wood had a petition signed by Chinese leaders asking the U.S. Congress to allot a part of the $6 million paid by China to the U.S. after the Boxer Rebellion of 1899 for public library development. She took the signed petition to Washington, D.C., where she made her case in personal interviews with hundreds of members of Congress, including Senator William Cabell Bruce,

who wrote of Wood's "unselfish zeal . . . tact and good sense." Her appeal was successful, and Congress passed a bill establishing a fund for educational activities in China, which later totaled $12 million.

The fund allowed Wood to return to China and establish the National Library of Peking (Beijing), as well as scholarships at the Boone Library School; she was also influential in the establishment of the Library Association of China in 1926. After she withdrew the Boone Library School from its affiliation with the missionary Huachung University, Wood devoted her last few years to raising funds to endow the Boone Library School under an American-controlled board (later called the Mary Elizabeth Wood Foundation). Mary Wood died of a heart attack in Wuchang in 1931, at age 69, mourned by many Chinese friends and colleagues for her devotion to her cause. Her body was cremated and her ashes buried in Batavia Cemetery.

SOURCES:

James, Edward T., ed. *Notable American Women, 1607–1950.* Cambridge, MA: The Belknap Press of Harvard University, 1971.

McHenry, Robert, ed. *Famous American Women.* NY: Dover, 1980.

Laura York, M.A. in History, University of California, Riverside, California

Wood, Matilda (1831–1915)

British actress and theater manager. Name variations: Mrs. John Wood. Born Matilda Charlotte Vining on November 6, 1831, in Liverpool, England; died on January 11, 1915, on the Isle of Thanet, Kent, England; daughter of Henry Vining (an actor) and an actress mother; married John Wood (an actor), in 1854 (separated 1858); children: Florence Wood.

The daughter of actors, Matilda Wood was born in 1831 and grew up in Liverpool, England. She made her stage debut in 1841 at age ten, and until 1854 appeared regularly in small theaters outside London. At age 22, she married John Wood, an actor, with whom she would have one daughter, **Florence Wood**, later an actress. Soon after their marriage, the couple signed a contract to appear on stage in vaudeville and burlesque productions at the new Boston Theater in Massachusetts. Wood's American debut was as a singing chambermaid in the vaudeville play *The Loan of a Lover* in September 1854; her husband performed in comedic roles as well. They remained at the Boston Theater for three seasons.

In 1856, the couple debuted in New York at the Academy of Music; Wood also appeared at Wallack's Theater for a month. From New York, the couple went on to theaters in St. Louis and New Orleans. By 1858, they reached San Francisco, where they performed at Maguire's Opera House, and then toured the Pacific coast. While in San Francisco, the couple separated; John Wood moved to British Columbia, where he died in 1863.

Matilda Wood remained in San Francisco for a season, then in 1859 took a job in Sacramento managing the Forrest Theater, followed by a managing position at San Francisco's American Theater. Later that year, she returned to New York, where she performed at the Winter Garden in September. Between 1860 and 1863, Wood appeared frequently on stage in Boston, Philadelphia, New Orleans, and New York. In October 1863, she opened a theater in New York, the Olympic, with her own company; she was both manager and performer. The Olympic's comedic productions made the company a success, and Wood, petite and charming, enjoyed popular and critical acclaim.

However, she decided to return to England in 1866, at age 34, and settled in London. After

Matilda Wood

appearing in numerous stage roles at London's best theaters, Wood accepted a management position at the St. James's Theater in 1869, where she remained for a decade. She next co-managed the New Royal Court Theater from 1888 to 1891, where she also performed in several productions. Wood retired to the Isle of Thanet, off Kent, after her final stage appearance in *The Prodigal Son* at the Drury Lane Theater in 1905. She died in 1915, at age 83.

SOURCES:

James, Edward T., ed. *Notable American Women, 1607–1950.* Cambridge, MA: The Belknap Press of Harvard University, 1971.

Laura York, M.A. in History,
University of California,
Riverside, California

Wood, Matilda Alice Victoria
(1870–1922).

See Lloyd, Marie.

Wood, Natalie (1938–1981)

American actress best known for her roles in the classics **Miracle on 34th Street** *and* **Rebel Without a Cause.** *Born Natasha Gurdin (also seen as Natasha Zakharenko) on July 20, 1938, in Santa Rosa, California; died on November 29, 1981, in a boating accident off the California coast; daughter of Maria Nikolaevna Gurdin (later Maria Wood) and Nicholas Gurdin; married Robert Wagner (an actor), in 1957 (divorced 1962); married Richard Gregson (an actor), in 1969 (divorced 1971); remarried Robert Wagner, in 1972; children: (with Gregson) Natasha Gregson (b. 1970, later Natasha Wagner, an actress); (with Wagner) Courtney Wagner (b. 1974); (stepdaughter)* **Katie Wagner.**

Cast as an extra in a film shooting in her hometown when she was four years old (1942); as Natalie Wood, became a popular child star in Hollywood (1940s); became famous with her appearance in Miracle on 34th Street *(1947); nominated for her first Academy Award for her work in* Rebel Without a Cause, *playing opposite James Dean (1955), followed by two more nominations for* Splendor in the Grass *and* Love with the Proper Stranger; *during later career, turned more toward television films.*

Filmography: Tomorrow Is Forever *(1945);* Driftwood *(1947);* The Ghost and Mrs. Muir *(1947);* Miracle on 34th Street *(1947);* Father Was a Fullback *(1949);* Green Promise *(1949);* Never a Dull Moment *(1950);* Our Very Own *(1950);* Just for You *(1953);* The Rose Bowl Story *(1953);* Star *(1953);* I'm a Fool *(1953);* The Silver Chalice *(1954);* Rebel Without a Cause *(1955);* The Burning Hills *(1956);* The

Searchers *(1956)*; Bombers B-52 *(1957)*; Kings Go Forth *(1958)*; Marjorie Morningstar *(1958)*; Cash McCall *(1959)*; Splendor in the Grass *(1961)*; West Side Story *(1961)*; Gypsy *(1962)*; Love with the Proper Stranger *(1963)*; Sex and the Single Girl *(1964)*; The Great Race *(1965)*; Inside Daisy Clover *(1965)*; This Property Is Condemned *(1966)*; Bob & Carol & Ted & Alice *(1969)*; The Affair *(1973)*; From Here to Eternity *(1979)*; Meteor *(1979)*; The Last Married Couple in America *(1980)*; Willie and Phil *(1980)*; Brainstorm *(released 1983)*.

It seemed to film director Irving Pichel that most of Santa Rosa, California, had turned out for his casting call one spring day in 1943, even though he was looking for only one particular extra—a little girl who would burst into tears when she dropped the ice cream cone she was eating. He and his cast and crew had come to the neat, all-American town near San Francisco for outdoor scenes for the romantic comedy *Happy Days*; and thus it was that Pichel was confronted with **Maria Gurdin** and her four-year-old daughter, Natasha. Pichel, struck by the child's lustrous dark eyes, bent down to ask if she could cry on cue, but Maria quickly answered for her daughter. "Of course she can!," she said as emphatically as a thick Russian accent would allow, launching the career she would assiduously tend from the wings for the next 20 years; for under her guidance, little Natasha would metamorphose into Natalie Wood.

Wood was the second of Maria Nikolaevna's two daughters, born from two different marriages—the first in her native Tomsk, Siberia, to a man who later abandoned her and her daughter **Olga Wood** after suggesting that they emigrate to America. Maria followed through on the advice, eventually arriving in California to marry another Russian immigrant, Nicholas Gurdin, variously described as a prop man or an architect, but whose talents as a carpenter constructing movie sets first brought Maria into contact with the film industry. The couple had settled in Santa Rosa by the time Natasha was born on July 20, 1938. A third daughter, **Lana Wood**, would follow eight years later. Three years after Natalie's brief movie debut, Pichel remembered the pretty little dark-haired girl from Santa Rosa and offered to cast her as Orson Welles' daughter in *Tomorrow Is Forever*. "She was a born professional, so good, she was terrifying," Welles said years later about acting with Pichel's discovery. Natalie was more modest about her first major role. "I could hardly read, so my part had to be told to me, and

then I would memorize it," she remembered. It was Pichel who guided Wood's early career, getting her signed with Twentieth Century-Fox and suggesting the name change, anglicizing Natasha to Natalie and borrowing the last name of his friend and fellow director, Sam Wood. Maria took Pichel's suggestion a step further and adopted the name Wood for herself and the rest of the family as well. Natalie was so young when she entered the film business that it never occurred to her at the time that anything was remarkable about her life. "It was only when I met people outside the studios . . . that it began to dawn on me that life was different for other people," she said.

It soon became evident that Maria's confidence in her daughter's abilities was well founded, for Natalie could hold her own on screen against such major Hollywood figures as *Gene Tierney (in *The Ghost and Mrs. Muir*) and *Bette Davis (in *The Star*), despite her youth and lack of formal training. In fact, the famously temperamental Bette Davis became so enamored of the ten-year-old playing her daughter that she rushed to her defense when the film's director insisted that Natalie dive from a boat, as required by the script, despite Wood's tearful protests that she was afraid of the water. "If you want a swimmer, go find Johnny Weissmuller!" Davis said, threatening to leave the picture if the director persisted. A double was quickly found. By the time Natalie appeared in the classic *Miracle on 34th Street* in 1947 as the little girl who discovers there really is a Santa Claus, she was well on her way to replacing a maturing *Shirley Temple (Black)** and an adolescent *Elizabeth Taylor** as Hollywood's favorite child actress. Under Maria's careful eye, Wood was friendly and compliant on the set, got along with cast and crew, and was well prepared for a scene by the time it was rehearsed. Even more important, she projected an innocent, transparent intensity on screen that made her performance entirely believable and her character an integral part of the picture, rather than a cloying adornment.

By 1954, Wood had appeared in over 20 films, although few of them are memorable and some were outright flops. One critic thought that 1954's *The Silver Chalice* would have been better left undeveloped in the can; and even Paul Newman, who co-starred in the picture, published a letter of apology when it aired for the first time on television. Most of Wood's films from this period, however, were modest family comedies, with titles like *Father Was a Fullback* and *Never a Dull Moment*, that performed reliably at the box office and provided Natalie and her family with an equally reliable income. Maria was content to bank her daughter's salary and keep her working, arranging for tutoring on the set and keeping Wood away from the normal activities of others her age; but she miscalculated the passions that frequently assail a young girl entering womanhood, particularly Natalie's desire to be more than just a wage-earner for her family. "I was a bit like a puppet," Wood once said of these years. "Acting was something I did automatically, obeying the director, who pulled the strings, and my mother, who ran my life." Now, in 1955, two pieces of the puzzle came together that would free her from Maria's control. One of them was the volcanic James Dean, and the other was the picture in which they co-starred, *Rebel Without a Cause.*

Nicholas Ray's explosive examination of teenage angst found a huge audience among young moviegoers who were just discovering their collective voice as the country's new protest generation. Wood's portrayal of the high-school sweetheart Judy who defies her parents and falls for Dean's misfit Jimmy Stark electrified audiences and brought Natalie her first Academy Award nomination; but it was the off-screen relationship between Dean and Wood that was of more significance for her career. The two had first met two years earlier, when both had been cast in a television play. "I couldn't take my eyes off him," she said of their first encounter at a rehearsal for the play. "His words were slow and laborious and sometimes you couldn't hear him at all. I never ever worked with anyone quite like him." Her fascination was probably helped by the fact that Dean arrived at the rehearsal on his revered motorcycle and used a window to enter the room, rather than the door. Dean, who would complete only one more picture before dying in a motorcycle crash in 1955, the year *Rebel* was released, encouraged Natalie to trust her own emotions and take control of her life away from her mother; and it was Dean's fascination with psychoanalysis that marked the beginning of Wood's own search for self-knowledge under professional guidance, which in turn brought a new emotional intensity to her acting under Ray's direction. For the rest of her life, Wood's most prized possession would be a bust of Dean that accompanied her whenever she was working on a picture.

Just 17 when *Rebel* was released, Natalie was soon appearing in Hollywood gossip sheets as she moved further away from her mother's influence and toward a life of parties, celebrity dates and scandalous rumors, all of which added to her box-office appeal. Warner Bros. took ad-

vantage of the publicity and cast Wood against type in John Ford's classic Western *The Searchers.* Her role as John Wayne's long-lost niece, abducted by Native Americans only to become one of them in the post-Civil War West, was her first mature character and an indication of the range of which she was capable.

During 1956, Wood met a young actor who had moved to Hollywood six years earlier from Detroit and who quickly became her most ardent suitor. "When I saw them together, I sensed romance in the air," reported Natalie's younger sister, Lana, of Robert Wagner's first visit to the Woods' home. Wagner had made a promising start in the film business as a dark-haired, strikingly handsome supporting actor and, like Natalie, had been quickly signed by Twentieth Century-Fox. (Natalie had moved to Warner's before they met.) By the time he proposed to Natalie (by famously placing a wedding ring in the bottom of a champagne-filled glass), he was attracting attention for his work as a cold-blooded killer in *A Kiss Before Dying* and seemed destined for leading-man status. When Wood went to work shooting *Marjorie Morningstar* in early 1957, a posse of photographers and gossip columnists followed her and Wagner all the way to the shoot's location in the Adirondacks; and in December of that year, Natalie and "R.J.," as he was nicknamed, were married in Scottsdale, Arizona, later moving into a plush Beverly Hills mansion where, as the press would have it, they enjoyed "the most glittering union of the 20th century." Wagner was 26, Natalie just 19.

But the union suffered from professional pressures, as the careers of each seemed to stall. Wood had entered the dangerous territory between child stardom and more adult roles, while Wagner's prospects dimmed in the face of competition from more dynamic newcomers like Newman and Marlon Brando, even after he and his new wife co-starred in 1960's *All the Fine Young Cannibals.* Natalie, for her part, almost didn't get the job that would bring her another Academy Award nomination and restart her career, as Elia Kazan told friends he didn't want to cast "some washed-up child star" as the lead in his upcoming *Splendor in the Grass.* But Kazan reconsidered when Wood came to audition for him. "I detected a twinkle in her eyes," he said. "I knew there was an unsatisfied hunger there. I could see that the crisis in her career was preparing her for a crisis in her personal life. She told me she was being psychoanalyzed. That did it." Kazan cast Wood opposite Warren Beatty in his story of ill-starred love in a small town, based on a narrative by playwright William Inge. Natalie's

Opposite page
𝒩atalie
𝒲ood

radiant performance (and her affair with Beatty during the shoot) proved his instincts right. With her marriage to Wagner in trouble, Wood invited a 14-month suspension by Warner's for refusing to leave Wagner to shoot a film in England. Finally, in April 1962, Hollywood's perfect young couple divorced, a decision that would haunt both of them for the next ten years.

Ironically, those years would mark the most prolific period of Wood's career, with her most varied collection of roles, including two musicals—as Maria in Robert Wise's 1961 screen adaptation of *West Side Story* (with Natalie's singing voice dubbed by **Marnie Nixon**) and as *Gypsy Rose Lee in Mervyn LeRoy's 1962 film version of *Gypsy* (this time Natalie insisting on doing her own singing). Astute Hollywood observers remarked how closely the musical's story of **Rose Hovick**, the overbearing show-business mother whose daughter eventually strikes out on her own, described the relationship between Maria Gurdin and Natalie Wood. Having by now played a Puerto Rican street girl from New York and a blossoming stripper on the 1930s vaudeville circuit, Natalie won her third Academy Award nomination for her work as the Italian Catholic working girl Angie Rossini in Robert Mulligan's 1963 film *Love with the Proper Stranger*. A gritty, quirky love story shot on location in New York, the film tackled the subject of abortion as Natalie's character discovers she's pregnant from a passing affair with Steve McQueen's itinerant trumpet player. Wood's performance, one critic wrote, "is the linchpin of the film, played with pluck and humor."

Despite the ebullient spirit with which she infused the character of Angie, Wood's off-screen life was unraveling. A series of short-lived, painful affairs following her divorce from Wagner, some of them with whoever her leading man was in whatever film she happened to be shooting, drove her even further into therapy, anti-depressant medications and increased alcohol consumption. None of her pictures fared well at the box office and, without Wagner, she was lonely and depressed enough to take an overdose of sleeping pills late in 1966. Recovering in a hospital under an assumed name, she told sister Lana, "I just didn't want to live any more."

Things seemed to take a turn for the better when Wood met Richard Gregson, a British entrepreneur who dabbled in the film business as a producer and writer. "When she was with Richard, Natalie was settled, calm, and happy," Lana Wood remembered some years later. The two married in 1969 at a lavish Russian Ortho-

dox wedding planned by Maria, after which the happily married Natalie began work on Paul Mazursky's spoof of married life, *Bob & Carol & Ted & Alice*—her first film in three years and another reach for her, since she had never taken on a purely comic role. The film was one of the biggest hits of the year and seemed to put her career back on track, not to mention her life, for Wood announced during shooting that she had just discovered she was pregnant. In September 1970, Natalie gave birth to a girl that she and Gregson named Natasha, later **Natasha Wagner**.

But before little Natasha was barely a year old, the marriage that had begun so hopefully was over, Wood accusing Gregson of having an affair with her secretary and ordering him out of her life. Gregson complied, plaintively telling a Hollywood gossip sheet, "I was totally unprepared for living with an actress." The two were divorced in 1971. "She was . . . deeply and seriously unhappy, her safe, secure world destroyed," Lana wrote in her memoir of the months after the marriage ended. "Some women accommodate themselves to husbands like Richard. Not Natalie."

All my life I've been looking for someone to love me.
—Natalie Wood as Judy in *Rebel Without a Cause*

Wood did not appear in another film after *Bob & Carol & Ted & Alice* for three years; so it was with some surprise that she arrived at the 1972 Academy Awards in the company of none other than Robert Wagner. "There are happy endings after all," she told a gaggle of reporters who were astonished as much by the fact they had been unaware of the reconciliation as by the story itself. It had begun, Wood explained, a year earlier at a dinner party arranged by thoughtful mutual friends. At the time, Wagner was recently divorced after a brief European marriage and Wood was about to bring an end to her marriage to Gregson. The two lovers had managed to keep their renewed relationship a secret even from Natalie's family, who only learned of it when Wagner attended a family dinner at Wood's home. Wagner and Wood married for the second time in July of that year. As if to reinforce the rematch, Natalie returned to the screen with Wagner as her co-star in 1973's *The Affair*, in which she played a wheelchair-bound songwriter who falls in love with her lawyer, played by Wagner. It was the first of many collaborations for the couple.

In 1974, Natalie gave birth to a second daughter, **Courtney Wagner**, and announced that she would accept no further film roles that required her to be away from home and her children for extended periods. It was one reason why she turned increasingly to making television films, with their shorter shooting schedules on local stages and locations. In 1979, she and Wagner appeared in a television version of *Cat on a Hot Tin Roof*, in which Laurence Olivier played Big Daddy; that same year, Wagner debuted in "Hart to Hart," a mystery series which cast him and **Stefanie Powers** as married sleuths, a contemporary Nick and Nora Charles. The Wagner-Wood marriage was marked by a mature view of the quixotic business in which both spouses had staked their careers, Wagner accepting his failure as a major box-office star and Wood content to look back on a stunning 20 years at the top of the business.

There were occasional returns to the world she had once known only too well, but the last few films of her life were unremarkable and pale comparisons to the triumphs of her earlier years. She completed work on what would be her last film, *Brainstorm*, in the summer of 1981. That fall, she, Wagner, and actor-friend Christopher Walken, who had co-starred with Natalie in *Brainstorm*, departed on Wagner's beloved yacht for a weekend vacation on Catalina Island, off the California coast near Los Angeles. Wagner had named the boat *Splendor* in honor of what he considered her best film role in Kazan's picture. Despite Wood's terror of water that had first come to the surface so many years before, and that had brought Bette Davis to her defense, she enjoyed sailing on the *Splendor*. On the night of November 29, 1981, the three friends moored in the island's harbor and went ashore in a dinghy to have dinner. The *Splendor*'s captain later reported that, upon returning to the yacht, an argument had broken out below decks as the three friends sat drinking and Wood began flirting with Walken, much to Wagner's irritation. The three then retired, each to a separate bedroom. Wagner, Walken, and the ship's captain all claimed they heard no splash or cry for help when Natalie went overboard that night. A medical examiner later suggested that the heavy down coat she wore had quickly dragged her under when she apparently slipped while trying to secure the dinghy's loose rope, its banging against the hull perhaps keeping her awake. The official report also indicated that Natalie's blood-alcohol level had been well above legal limits, confirmed by her husband and Walken, who admitted that they had all drunk rather heavily during and after dinner. Natalie's body washed ashore the next morning, the empty dinghy bobbing nearby. She was 43 years old.

"I had lived a charmed life, and then I lost a beautiful woman I loved with all my heart," Wagner said in 1988. It was virtually the only public comment he ever made about his loss, despite the usual Hollywood rumors of the circumstances surrounding the incident. Relations with Natalie's family soured when Lana Wood's memoir appeared in 1984, suggesting that Wagner was ultimately responsible for his wife's death; and when *Vanity Fair* attempted to arrange a photo shoot in the spring of 2000 with every actress who had ever played in a James Bond film, Wagner's present wife **Jill St. John** and Lana, both of whom had been "Bond girls," engaged in such a furious verbal assault on each other that the shoot had to be cancelled. Close friends claim that Wagner will remain in mourning for Natalie Wood for the rest of his life.

Despite her early death, Wood's career in films spanned nearly 40 years, from the little girl who cried at the loss of her ice cream in 1943 to a tremulous young lover in *Splendor in the Grass*, an alluring stripper in *Gypsy*, and a working-class girl in *Love with the Proper Stranger*. Off screen, she had confronted the upheavals of her private life, ultimately producing a happy ending as an actress, wife, and mother. She seemed to take to heart the lines from Wordsworth that she recites in a scene in *Splendor in the Grass*:

We will grieve not, rather find
Strength in what remains behind.

SOURCES:
Parker, John. *Five For Hollywood*. NY: Carol, 1991.
Wood, Lana. *Natalie*. NY: Putnam, 1984.

SUGGESTED READING:
Finstad, Suzanne. *Natasha*. Harmony, 2001.
Kashner, Sam. "Natalie Wood's Final, Fatal Hours," in *Vanity Fair*. February 2000.

Norman Powers,
writer-producer, Chelsea Lane Productions,
New York, New York

Wood, Peggy (1892–1978)

American actress and singer. Born Margaret Wood on February 9, 1892, in Brooklyn, New York; died of a cerebral hemorrhage on March 18, 1978, in Stamford, Connecticut; daughter of journalist Eugene Wood and Mary (Gardner) Wood; educated at Manual Training High School in New York City; married John van Alstyne Weaver (a poet, novelist, and playwright), on February 14, 1924 (died from tuberculosis, 1938); married William H. Walling (an executive in the printing business), on October 1, 1946 (died 1973); children: (first marriage) David (b. 1927).

Began a long theater career at age 18; made film debut (1919); one of the founders of Actors' Equity; was president of American National Theater and Academy; nominated for Academy Award for her performance in The Sound of Music *(1965); campaigned for many theater causes during her life.*

Selected filmography: Almost a Husband *(1919);* Women of Wonder *(1929);* Handy Andy *(1934);* The Right to Live *(1935);* Jalna *(1935);* A Star is Born *(1937);* Call It a Day *(1937);* The Housekeeper's Daughter *(1939);* The Bride Wore Boots *(1946);* Dream Girl *(1948);* The Sound of Music *(1965). Also starred on television series "Mama" (1949–57).*

Born in 1892 in Brooklyn, New York, actress Peggy Wood was the daughter of **Mary Gardner Wood** and Eugene Wood, a feature writer for the *New York World*. She began studying voice as a child because her father wanted to ensure that she had a marketable skill; her instructors included Arthur Van der Linde and *Emma Calvé. Wood attended Manual Training High School and, after graduating in 1910, made her professional singing debut in the chorus of the Broadway production of *Naughty Marietta*. She appeared on stage in New York regularly through the 1910s, including starring roles in the drama *Young America* in 1915, and as Marietta in *Naughty Marietta* in 1916. The next year she began a two-year run as Ottilie in *Maytime*, for which she drew praise from New York theater critics.

In 1919, Wood appeared in her first film, Will Rogers' *Almost a Husband*. That year she also became involved with the formation of the Actors' Equity Association, a union for stage and screen performers. In 1924, she married John van Alstyne Weaver, a poet. Her family had frowned on the match, but the marriage proved to be happy. The next year Wood starred in *Candida* on stage in New York and abroad. After her son David was born in 1927, she took time off from acting and wrote several plays, including *The Flying Prince*. She returned to the stage in Noel Coward's *Bitter Sweet* in London, and would appear in plays continually through the 1930s and 1940s, primarily in London and New York.

Wood found time to write as well. In the 1920s and 1930s, she contributed many articles on her experiences and on theater personalities to such periodicals as the *Saturday Evening Post*, *Ladies' Home Journal*, *Theater Arts Monthly*, and *Collier's*. In 1930, she published *Actors and People*, describing her conversations with playwright George Bernard Shaw and opera diva Calvé. Six years later, her novel *Star Wagon* was published, to mixed reviews.

Wood appeared in only a few films throughout her long career. In 1935, she was seen as Meg in *Jalna*, followed by *A Star Is Born* in 1937. Also in 1937 she starred in *Miss Quis*, a play she cowrote with Ward Morehouse. A year later, Wood had to take time off from performing after the death of her husband from tuberculosis. In 1941, she published a book of memoirs, *How Young You Look*, to popular acclaim. She remained an active member of Actors' Equity, having served on its council from 1919 to 1940, and was elected vice-president of the Episcopal Actors Guild in 1942. In that year Wood opened in London in what became one of her most popular roles, as Ruth in Noel Coward's *Blithe Spirit*, earning critical praise during the one-year run. During World War II, she was a member of the American Theater Wing, performing for Allied troops at army bases in Britain. In 1946, she married William H. Walling, an executive in the printing business.

Despite decades on stage, Wood is best remembered for a pioneering television role. In 1949, she was cast in the title role as the matriarch of a Norwegian-American family in "Mama," adapted from John Van Druten's Broadway play *I Remember Mama*, which was itself based on ◄❧ Kathryn Forbes' book *Mama's Bank Account*. The show was an immediate success and ran for eight seasons, ending in 1957. (*Ms.* editor **Robin Morgan** played her daughter Dagmar.) Wood was honored by the Swedish King Haakon VII with the Order of St. Olaf medal for her portrayal, which was seen as fostering international understanding. During the 1950s, Wood's political conservatism led her to oppose much of the union activity she had earlier supported. Active politically, she also worked to pass a federal bill to require theater producers to verify the financial viability of their productions.

In 1959, Wood became president of the American National Theater and Academy, serving until 1966. She published her second memoir, *Arts and Flowers*, in 1963. Her final film was *The Sound of Music* (1965), which brought Wood an Academy Award nomination for Best Supporting Actress for her portrayal of the Mother Abbess. She retired from the stage in 1967, at age 75, due to failing health, but remained active in various theater organizations. Widowed again in 1973, Peggy Wood died in March 1978, at age 86.

SOURCES:

Herbert, Ian, ed. *Who's Who in the Theatre*. Detroit, MI: Gale Research, 1977.

Jackson, Kenneth T., ed. *Dictionary of American Biography, 1976–1980*. NY: Scribner, 1980.

Robinson, Alice M., *et al.*, eds. *Notable Women in the American Theater*. NY: Greenwood Press, 1989.

Laura York, M.A. in History,
University of California,
Riverside, California

Wood, Sara Bard Field (b. 1882).

See Bryant, Louise for sidebar on Field, Sara Bard.

Wood, Yvonne (1914—)

American costume designer. Born in 1914; educated at Chouinard Art School.

Selected filmography: A Bell for Adano *(1945);* L'il Abner *(1959);* One-Eyed Jacks *(1959);* The Cheyenne Social Club *(1969);* The Life and Times of Judge Roy Bean *(1972);* "Quincy" *(TV, 1976);* Zoot Suit *(1981).*

After attending Chouniard Art School, Yvonne Wood worked for Fox and Universal studios as a sketch artist. Her first film credit as a costume designer came in 1943 in *The Gang's All Here* with *Carmen Miranda. Ultimately, her career spanned some 75 films through 1981.

Mary McNulty,
freelance writer,
St. Charles, Illinois

Woodard, Lynette (1959—)

African-American athlete, the first woman signed with the Harlem Globetrotters, who captained the 1984 American basketball team to an Olympic gold medal. Born in Wichita, Kansas, on August 12, 1959; daughter of Dorothy Woodard and Lugene Woodard; graduated from University of Kansas, 1981.

Was a star national player at the University of Kansas; won a gold medal as a member of the World University Games team (1979); played in the Pan American games (1981 and 1983); was on the World championship team (1983 and 1990); was the first woman signed with the Harlem Globetrotters (1985); captained the first American women's basketball team in the Olympics (1984) and won a gold medal; had nine years of professional play; became a stockbroker for Magna Securities in New York City; signed to the Cleveland Rockers in the WNBA (February 27, 1997).

Lynette Woodard, who captained the American women's basketball team to an Olympic gold-medal victory and became the first woman to play day-to-day professional basketball on a men's team, once told *The New York Times*: "I don't know how long it will

❧▶
Forbes, Kathryn.
See Dunne, Irene for sidebar on Kathryn McLean.

Lynette Woodard

take, but a woman will play in the NBA. I want people to see me play with the Globetrotters and say a woman could also have the ability to play in the NBA." Woodard's ambition was realized when the first American women's professional basketball league, the WNBA, began its inaugural season on June 21, 1997. Her participation in the sport—which began in Wichita, Kansas, where she played pick-up games with her older brother Darrell—helped light the path to this major achievement in the history of women's sports.

Born in 1959, Woodard received early inspiration from her cousin Hubie "Geese" Ausbie, who was a member of the Harlem Globetrotters. In addition to playing "sockball" with her brother and father ("We'd roll up socks for a ball and shoot off the bedroom door," she told *People*), Woodard practiced the moves taught to her by Ausbie: "Geese showed us how to spin a basketball on our fingers and do all those Globetrotter tricks. . . . It was a joy to my heart." She played her first organized basketball as a sophomore in high school and went on to become a collegiate star for the University of Kansas Jayhawks. The 5'11" Woodard led the nation in rebounds with a 14.8 average, and her 25.2 points per game were second in the country. She was named freshman player of the year by *Street and Smith's* and *Basketball Weekly*. During her sophomore year, Woodard led the nation in scoring, averaging 31 points per game and setting a single-season scoring record with 1,177 points. With 33 rebounds, she also set a single-game record. Woodard's college scoring points totaled 3,649. A four-time collegiate All American from 1978 to 1981, she was a serious student, maintaining a 3.04 gradepoint average in her last two years of college, and *Great Women in Sports* notes that she "eventually broke 24 of the 32 records the NCAA kept, regarding women's basketball. . . . She was the first UK student ever to have a jersey number retired at the end of her college career." She received her bachelor's degree in speech communications and human relations in 1981 and would go on to study for her master's.

In the 1979 World University Games, Woodard played on the gold-medal winning American team. Chosen as a member of the U.S. Olympic Team in 1980, she was disappointed at being unable to attend when the U.S. protested the Soviet invasion of Afghanistan by boycotting the Games. With professional opportunities for women in basketball almost nonexistent, Woodard played for a year in Italy where she was the only English-speaking member of her team. Although her time there proved to be isolating and she was homesick, Woodard would later note that she was grateful for the experience. On her return to America in 1982, she took a position at her alma mater as an academic advisor and volunteer assistant basketball coach. Meanwhile, she trained for the 1984 Olympic team tryouts and also became recognized for her community service. Woodard's efforts included her assistance in initiating a Big Brother-Big Sister program in Kansas and serving as a volunteer at the American Cancer Society. The Wichita branch of the NAACP conferred upon her the title of Woman of the Year in 1982.

That year, she was captain of the U.S. national team which defeated the Soviet Union (Woodard scored 21 points). In 1983, as a member of the U.S. team, she won a gold medal at the Pan American Games and a silver medal at the World University Games. In Los Angeles during 1984, she captained the first American women's basketball team to capture an Olympic gold medal.

In 1985, Woodard became the first woman to be signed by the Harlem Globetrotters. During tryouts, she had been one of ten finalists, and Earl Duryea, team manager, called her "a 10 in a group of 9¾." *Great Women in Sports* notes that she started out on the team as a "'hopper,' or straight ball player who helped the comic players set up their routines. Gradually she was given her own chance to play the comic." The experience was rewarding. Woodard told the *Los Angeles Times*, "It's entertainment. . . . I see laughter and smiles on people's faces. . . . There are so many terrible things happening in the world. You can make people forget about their problems just for a couple hours. That's good. . . . You see those little kids. Those eyes sparkle. And I know their hearts, because that used to be me." It was Woodard's hope that her visibility as a woman player on a men's team would help "a women's professional basketball league become viable and stable." Her dream, and that of many other women players in the country, would become a reality about a decade later.

Contractual disputes prompted her to leave the Globetrotters after two seasons, and she returned to the University of Kansas as a coach. The Women's Sports Foundation named her Professional Sportswoman of the Year in 1986. Once noting that there were a lot of women who had the same dream she had, "but they don't have any place to go after their college days," Woodard went on to see the creation of the WNBA and was signed to the league's Cleveland Rockers in February 1997. Having developed an interest in the financial world from her play for Daiwa Securities in Japan, she also became a registered stockbroker for Magna Securities in New York.

SOURCES:

Johnson, Anne Janette. *Great Women in Sports*. Detroit, MI: Visible Ink, 1998.

Newman, Matthew. *Lynette Woodard*. Mankato, MN: Crestwood House, 1986.

Rosenthal, Bert. *Lynette Woodard: The First Female Globetrotter*. Chicago, IL: Children's Press, 1986.

Woolum, Janet. *Outstanding Women Athletes*. Phoenix, AZ: Oryx, 1992.

Karin L. Haag,
freelance writer,
Athens, Georgia

Woodbridge, Louise Deshong

(1848–1925)

American photographer. Born in 1848 in Chester, Pennsylvania; died in 1925, possibly in Chester; married Jonathon Edwards Woodbridge, in 1877.

Although she devoted much of her energy to society affairs, Louise Deshong Woodbridge undertook photography in 1884. Nine years later, her photographs, primarily landscapes, were featured in the Sixth Joint Annual Exhibition of Photography in Philadelphia and the World's Columbian Exhibition in Chicago. Woodbridge left a collection of her work to the Delaware County Historical Society.

SOURCES:

Rosenblum, Naomi. *A History of Women Photographers.* NY: Abbeville, 1994.

> **Mary McNulty,**
> freelance writer,
> St. Charles, Illinois

Woodbridge, Margaret (b. 1902).

See Bleibtrey, Ethelda for sidebar.

Woodbury, Helen Sumner

(1876–1933)

American historian and public official. Born Helen Laura Sumner on March 12, 1876, in Sheboygan, Wisconsin; died on March 10, 1933, in New York City; daughter of George True Sumner (a Colorado judge) and Katherine Eudora (Marsh) Sumner; Wellesley College, A.B., 1898; University of Wisconsin, Ph.D., 1908; married Robert M. Woodbury (an economist), in November 1918.

Helen Sumner Woodbury was born in 1876 in Sheboygan, Wisconsin, the daughter of George True Sumner, a district attorney, and **Katherine March Sumner**. When she was five, the family moved to Durango, Colorado, where her father became a judge; they moved again in 1889 to Denver. Woodbury attended public schools and then entered Wellesley College, a private women's school in Massachusetts. Wellesley's faculty was particularly active in liberal political and social reform movements in the 1890s, and Woodbury was deeply influenced by her professors, including *Vida Scudder, *Katherine Lee Bates (literature), **Katharine Coman** (economics and history), *Emily Greene Balch (economics), and *Mary Whiton Calkins (philosophy and psychology). Drawn to social and political causes, she majored in economics, and in 1896 tried to aid the populist presidential campaign of William Jennings Bryan by publishing a short story, "The White Slave, or, 'The Cross of Gold,'" which supported Bryan's "free silver" platform.

In 1898, she graduated with a bachelor of arts degree. Sympathetic to the growing American labor movement, in 1902 Woodbury went on to study labor economics with Richard T. Ely and John Commons at the University of Wisconsin. In 1904, she was named an honorary fellow in political economy at the university. Perhaps the major economist of the early 20th century, Commons would have a marked impact on Woodbury's career; she contributed to his *Trade Unionism and Labor Problems* in 1905 and for the next several years was an important figure in his American Bureau of Industrial Research. With Thomas S. Adams, Woodbury also co-authored a college textbook, *Labor Problems* (1905).

In 1906, she conducted a long investigation of women's suffrage in Colorado for the New York State Collegiate Equal Suffrage League. Two years later, she graduated with a doctorate for her thesis, "The Labor Movement in America, 1827–1837"; her report on women's suffrage was published as *Equal Suffrage* in 1909. Her thesis would appear revised in Commons' two-volume *The History of Labor in the United States* (1918), the first serious study on the topic. Another part of her research, on women in the American labor force, formed the basis of the U.S. Bureau of Labor Statistics' "History of Women in Industry in the United States," in its *Report on Condition of Woman and Child Wage-Earners in the United States* (1910). Woodbury also served as associate editor on Commons' *A Documentary History of American Industrial Society* (1910–11).

A member of the Socialist Party, Woodbury rejected Marxist theory as inapplicable to American capitalism. She belonged to the Intercollegiate Socialist Society and was a longtime member of the national council of its successor, the League for Industrial Democracy. She traveled to Western Europe in 1910 to study labor law and the special labor courts European democracies had established; the U.S. Bureau of Labor Statistics published the results of her study as *Industrial Courts in France, Germany, and Switzerland* that year. She would later publish several articles arguing that the United States would benefit from a similar labor justice system.

Although she did not initially secure a full-time government position, Woodbury published regularly between 1910 and 1913 and produced labor studies for many federal labor agencies while living with her widowed mother in Washington, D.C. In 1913, Woodbury joined *Julia Clifford Lathrop and the staff of the newly formed U.S. Children's Bureau. Over the next five years, she would head numerous studies on child-labor issues, most of which were published; her most important publications with the Bureau include *Child Labor Legislation in the United States* (1915) and *The Working Children of Boston: A Study of Child Labor under a Modern System of Legal Regulation* (1922). Well respected among her colleagues, Woodbury was eventually promoted to director of investigations for the Bureau in June 1918. She resigned in November when, at age 42, she married an economist, Robert Morse Woodbury. However, she would remain affiliated with the Bureau until 1924.

The Woodburys accepted positions at the Institute of Economics in 1924, where Helen worked to establish standards for gathering labor statistics. She also served as a contributor to the *Encyclopedia of the Social Sciences* between 1926 and 1928, as well as to the *Dictionary of American Biography*. She remained ac-

Cecil Woodham-Smith

tive as a researcher and writer until her death in 1933, age 56, at her home in New York City.

SOURCES:

James, Edward T., ed. *Notable American Women, 1607–1950*. Cambridge, MA: The Belknap Press of Harvard University, 1971.

McHenry, Robert, ed. *Famous American Women*. NY: Dover, 1980.

Laura York, M.A. in History, University of California, Riverside, California

Woodby-McKane, Alice (1865–1948).

See McKane, Alice Woodby.

Woodham-Smith, Cecil (1896–1977)

British biographer and historian. Name variations: (pseudonym) Janet Gordon. Born Cecil Blanche FitzGerald on April 29, 1896, in Tenby, Wales; died on March 16, 1977, in London, England; daughter of James FitzGerald (an army colonel) and Blanche Elizabeth Philipps FitzGerald; educated at the Royal School for Officers' Daughters in Bath, a French convent school, and at St. Hilda's College, Oxford; married George Ivon Woodham-Smith (an attorney), in 1928 (died 1968); children: Elizabeth Sarah Woodham-Smith; Charles James Woodham-Smith.

Selected writings: (under pseudonym Janet Gordon) April Sky (1938); Tennis Star (1939), Just Off Bond Street (1940); (as Cecil Woodham-Smith) Florence Nightingale, 1820–1910 (1950), The Reason Why (1953), The Great Hunger: Ireland 1845–1849 (1962), Queen Victoria: Her Life and Times (1972).

Born in 1896 in Tenby, Wales, Cecil Woodham-Smith was the daughter of James FitzGerald, a British army officer of Irish descent, and **Blanche Philipps FitzGerald**, from Wales. Expelled from the Royal School for Officers' Daughters in Bath, England, for traveling to France without permission, Woodham-Smith then enrolled at a French convent before entering St. Hilda's College at Oxford University. She graduated in 1917, and supported herself for the next decade as a typist and copywriter for a London advertising firm. In 1928, she quit working when she married George Ivon Woodham-Smith, a prosperous attorney. She then devoted herself to caring for her two children, but when they were old enough to enter boarding school, Woodham-Smith used her new leisure time to begin writing seriously. She published three novels under the pseudonym "Janet Gordon," beginning with *April Sky* in 1938.

Drawn to the challenges of biography, in 1941 Woodham-Smith began research for her first nonfiction work, a life of the pioneering nurse *Florence Nightingale. Published under her own name in 1950 as *Florence Nightingale: 1820–1910*, it was hailed as a scholarly, witty, and sympathetic work, brought Woodham-Smith considerable acclaim among critics, and won the James Tait Black Memorial Prize.

Woodham-Smith continued her work on the 19th century with her next book about the British Light Brigade. *The Reason Why*, examining the intrigues and poor planning which sent 600 British soldiers charging into a death trap of Russian artillery forces during the Crimean War, appeared in 1953. Again Woodham-Smith earned critical and popular acclaim for her lively detail and thorough research; such was its success with scholarly readers that a television program planned as a discussion of the book, "Author Meets the Critics," had to be canceled when the producers could find no historian willing to attack the work.

Cecil Woodham-Smith, who always considered herself Irish, then turned to an investigation of the tragedy of the Irish potato famine. The result, *The Great Hunger: Ireland 1845–1849* (1962), remained in print for decades and is still considered the classic work on the forces that led to the death or emigration of millions of Irish men and women.

Woodham-Smith was honored in 1960 when she was named a Commander of the Order of the British Empire; she also received honorary doctorates from the National University of Ireland in 1964 and St. Andrews in 1965. In 1967, St. Hilda's College named her an honorary fellow; two years later, she received the A.C. Benson Medal for her contributions to British literature.

When she was widowed in 1968, Woodham-Smith lost much of her impetus and inspiration as a writer. Nevertheless, she continued researching her biography of Queen *Victoria. She gained access to the archives of the Windsors, which allowed her to draw complex portraits of the queen and her family. The first volume of the planned multivolume biography was published as *Queen Victoria: Her Life and Times*, in 1972. Woodham-Smith did not live to complete the work, however, dying at age 80 in March 1977.

SOURCES:

Blake, Lord, and C.S. Nicholls, eds. *The Dictionary of National Biography 1971–1980*. Oxford: Oxford University Press, 1986.

Current Biography 1955. NY: H.W. Wilson, 1955.

Locher, Frances Carol, ed. *Contemporary Authors*. Vols. 77–80. Detroit, MI: Gale Research, 1979.

Laura York, M.A. in History, University of California, Riverside, California

Woodhouse, Chase Going (1890–1984).

See Woodhouse, Margaret Chase Going.

Woodhouse, Margaret Chase Going (1890–1984)

American educator and politician. Name variations: Mrs. Chase Going Woodhouse; Margaret Woodhouse. Born Margaret Chase Going in Victoria, British Columbia, Canada, on March 3, 1890; died on December 12, 1984, in Sprague, Connecticut; daughter of Seymour Going (a mining and railroad executive) and Harriet (Jackson) Going; educated at public schools in California, South Dakota, and Kentucky; McGill University in Montreal, Canada, B.A., 1912, M.A., 1913; married Edward Woodhouse (a professor of government), in 1917; children: Noel Robert (b. 1921) and Margaret (b. 1925).

Worked as an economics professor at a number of American universities throughout her career; served as senior economist with the Bureau of Home Economics of the U.S. Department of Agriculture (1926–28); acted as founder and managing director of the Institute of Women's Professional Relations (1929–46); elected secretary of state for Connecticut (1941); elected to the U.S. Congress (1944); failed in reelection bid (1946); became executive director of the women's division of the Democratic National Committee (1947); won a second term in Congress (1948); lost reelection bid (1950); became the special assistant to the director of Price Stabilization (1951); served as the director of the Service Bureau for Women's Organizations in Hartford, Connecticut (1952–80).

Margaret Chase Going Woodhouse, known as Chase, was born in 1890 in Victoria, British Columbia, Canada, the only child of **Harriet Jackson Going** and Seymour Going, a prominent railroad and mining businessman. The family moved frequently between Canada and the United States, so she attended public schools in California, South Dakota, and Kentucky. In 1908, she graduated from Science Hill School in Shelbyville, Kentucky. She then entered McGill University in Montreal, Canada, completing a bachelor's degree in economics in 1912 and a master's degree a year later. After a few months as a social worker, Woodhouse decided she needed to continue her education abroad. She studied economics in Germany and England before returning to the U.S. at the outbreak of World War I in 1914 to begin graduate studies at the University of Chicago. She was named a fellow in political economy in 1917; later that year she married Edward Woodhouse, a professor of government at the university.

When Edward joined the armed forces with the United States' entrance on the European battlefield, Woodhouse accepted a professorship in economics at Smith College in Northampton, Massachusetts, where her first child, Noel, was born in 1921. She also taught during the summer at Smith's School for Social Work. After the birth of her second child, **Margaret**, in 1925, Woodhouse left Smith to join the home economics bureau of the Department of Agriculture as a senior economist; she remained there until 1928. That year, she took on a new position, as director of personnel at the Woman's College at the University of North Carolina at Greensboro. While in North Carolina, Woodhouse combined scholarship with political and civic activism. On behalf of professional women, she chaired the research division of the North Carolina Federation of Business and Professional Women's Clubs. She was also co-founder of the Institute of Women's

Professional Relations, of which she served as director from 1929 to 1946. The Institute was established to study the economic and educational needs of working women, and to work with colleges to create curricula to meet the needs of that growing population. Woodhouse served as editor of the Institute's numerous publications, including *Women's Work and Education*. In addition to her teaching, family, and Institute duties, she was a leader in many civic and women's organizations in the 1930s, including the League of Women Voters, the Altrusa Clubs, the American Home Economics Association, and the American Sociological Society. She also found time to contribute articles on labor policy to various scholarly journals, and published several books aimed at women, including *After College—What?* (1932), *Dentistry, Its Professional Opportunities* (1934), and *Business Opportunities for the Home Economist* (1934).

Also in 1934, Woodhouse began a 12-year tenure as professor of economics at the Connecticut College for Women. A committed liberal Democrat, she was active politically in Connecticut state politics, serving as president of the Connecticut Federation of Democratic Women's Clubs. In 1940, Woodhouse decided to enter electoral politics, campaigning for Connecticut secretary of state. She won the election by a record-breaking majority for a Connecticut state election.

When her term ended in 1942, Woodhouse returned to teaching at Connecticut College, and published *The Big Store* the following year. In 1944, she entered politics again, running for election to the U.S. House of Representatives from Connecticut's second district. She built her campaign around solutions to the economic and labor issues America would face when World War II ended and military personnel returned home; she supported a revised tax system to keep inflation down, and advocated the creation of an international body to maintain peace in Europe. Woodhouse won the 1944 election, becoming the second Connecticut woman to serve in Congress.

Sworn into office in January 1945, Woodhouse faced controversy on her first roll-call vote when she opposed a bill to make the House Committee on Un-American Activities a standing committee. Assigned to the important Committee on Banking and Currency, Woodhouse traveled in Western Europe to observe the state of postwar European economies. She returned keenly aware of the global dimensions of the postwar American economy and became a strong voice in favor of the establishment of an international monetary fund and world bank to

Margaret
Chase
Going
Woodhouse

aid in the reconstruction of postwar Europe and promote political stability. However, she also favored continued federal price controls as a member of the Congressional Committee for the Protection of the Consumer. Woodhouse also defended liberal positions on issues such as child welfare, federally funded women's health clinics, and public education.

Although she was defeated in her bid for re-election in 1946, Woodhouse regained her seat in 1948 but was defeated again in 1950. After leaving Congress, she worked in the public sector. She was assistant to the director of Price Stabilization from 1951 to 1953, and, from 1952 to 1980, was director of the Service Bureau for Women's Organizations in Hartford, Connecticut. Woodhouse died at the age of 94 in Sprague, Connecticut.

SOURCES:
Current Biography 1945. NY: H.W. Wilson, 1945.
Office of the Historian. *Women in Congress, 1917–1990.* Commission on the Bicentenary of the U.S. House of Representatives, 1991.

Laura York, M.A. in History,
University of California,
Riverside, California

Woodhull, Victoria (1838–1927)

American advocate of free love, women's suffrage and workers' rights, one of the most notorious women of her era, who lectured, operated a stock brokerage, ran for the U.S. presidency, precipitated a scandalous adultery trial, and flaunted Victorian social and sexual mores throughout most of her life. Name variations: Victoria Woodhull-Martin; Victoria Claflin; "The Woodhull" and "The Wicked Woodhull." Born Victoria Claflin on September 23, 1838, in Homer, Ohio; died on June 9, 1927, at her estate in Worcestershire, England; daughter of Reuben Buckman Claflin (a gristmill operator) and Roxanna (Hummel) Claflin; sister of Tennessee Claflin (1846–1923) and Utica Claflin Brooker (d. 1873); mostly self-taught; married Canning Woodhull, c. 1853; married Colonel James Harvey Blood, in 1866; married John Martin, in 1882; children: (first marriage) Byron; Woodhull; Zulu Maude Woodhull.

Promoted by their father, toured as a clairvoyant with her sister Tennessee; moved with husband Canning Woodhull and children to New York City; while touring as a spiritualist, met Colonel Blood, an advocate of free love, whom she married (1866); with her sister Tennie, opened the first women-owned brokerage firm on Wall Street (1870); announced her candidacy for the presidency (April 1870); founded Woodhull & Claflin's Weekly (May 1870); addressed the House Judiciary Committee regarding women's right to vote (January 1871); publicly declared herself a practitioner of free love (November 1871); nominated by the Equal Rights Party as candidate for the U.S. presidency, with Frederick Douglass as vice-president (1872): in a direct challenge to the Victorian standards of morality of the day, revealed the extramarital affair of the Reverend Henry Ward Beecher and Elizabeth Tilton, leading to charges of criminal libel and mailing obscene literature (November 1872); moved with family to England, with probable financial support of the heir of Commodore Cornelius Vanderbilt (1877); married millionaire John Martin (1882); became a philanthropist on behalf of agriculture and education.

On the evening of November 20, 1871, Victoria Woodhull waited to walk on stage at New York City's Steinway Hall and speak on the subject of free love, wondering whether the Reverend Henry Ward Beecher would accept her challenge for him to appear as the introductory speaker. By all accounts, the scene a few days earlier, when she had extended the invitation, had been dramatic. A fiery evangelical minister, Beecher was the brother of the author of *Uncle Tom's Cabin*, *Harriet Beecher Stowe, and pastor of Plymouth Church in Brooklyn. Privately, Beecher was widely rumored to have had many affairs with women of his parish, but from the pulpit he had publicly denounced sexual activity outside the institution of matrimony as immoral. In the meeting, which had included Theodore Tilton, a current lover of Woodhull's and formerly Beecher's best friend, Woodhull had threatened to expose Beecher unless he agreed to validate her views by introducing her. Years later Tilton described how Beecher, with tears streaming down his face, begged Woodhull to "let him off," on the grounds that associating himself with a leader of the free-love movement would cause him to lose his reputation, if not his entire parish. "Mr. Beecher," Woodhull replied, "if I am compelled to go onto that platform alone, I shall begin by telling the audience why I am alone and why you are not with me."

Beecher did not appear, but at the last moment Tilton did, offering his arm to lead Woodhull on stage. As a member of Beecher's Plymouth Church, editor of religious and liberal newspapers, author, and titular head of the National Women's Suffrage Association, Tilton had the credentials to enhance Woodhull's stature as a speaker, and he gave her a grand introduction.

Her speech had not gone far when Woodhull declared, "Yes! I am a free lover!," and was met with hisses and howls. "I have an inalienable, constitutional, and natural right to love whom I may," she continued, "to love as long or as short a period as I can, to change that love every day if I please! And with that right neither you nor any law you can frame have any right to interfere." Tilton, like the audience, was astounded by this admission, which had not been planned. That night she would refrain from exposing Beecher (who had recently ended an affair with Tilton's wife), but the speech was to be a singular milestone in a highly controversial public life.

Victoria Woodhull . . . has faced and dared men to call her names that make women shudder.

—Elizabeth Cady Stanton

The childhood of Victoria Claflin Woodhull had prepared her for a life of publicity and drama. Born on September 23, 1838, to Reuben Buckman Claflin and **Roxanna Claflin**, in Homer, Ohio, she was the fifth of seven children. Her father ran a gristmill and had a penchant for gambling, scheming, lawsuits, and any other opportunity to get rich quick. Her mother, quick-witted with a fiery temper, and inclined toward clairvoyance, instilled in her children a sense of familial loyalty that would lead Victoria to provide financial support for many of her family members in later years. An ardent follower of evangelical religion, Roxanna brought her children to camp meetings in the woods led by traveling preachers, including the respectable and invigorating revivals made famous by the Reverend Lyman Beecher (the father of Victoria's later adversary). Drawn into a state of religious ecstasy, Roxanna would join others at the meetings in whirling and speaking in tongues.

Victoria grew up imitating preachers, gathering other children around her to captivate them with her fiery preaching. If she failed to hold their attention with shouts of "Sinners repent! Repent or know the burning flames of hell!," she sometimes shifted to gory tales of Indian scalpings. She also showed signs of what was considered clairvoyance, playing childhood games with the spirits of her deceased baby sisters, and asserting that she saw the devil. From an early age, she was especially close to her sister *Tennessee Claflin, who shared her gift for "second sight," which their father saw as a golden opportunity. In an era when séances, replete with raps on walls and moving furniture, were immensely popular, Buck Claflin became "Dr. R.B. Claflin, American King of Cancers," and took his two daughters on a road show where they drew audiences as healers with psychic powers.

Because of these entertaining and profitable activities, Victoria reached the age of 15 with only a few years of education. She was blossoming into a beauty, however, with large blue eyes, delicate features, and rose-petal skin. Before turning 16, she married Dr. Canning Woodhull, a well-born and well-educated man who soon proved to be an alcoholic and a womanizer. As a physician, he had difficulty maintaining a practice, and, after the birth of their son Byron, Woodhull convinced Canning to move the family to San Francisco, where she became the breadwinner as a cigar girl and actress.

Her sister Tennie had meanwhile moved to New York City with their father, and from San Francisco Woodhull felt she heard Tennie's voice "call out" to her. In 1860, the Woodhulls packed up and moved to New York, where Tennie proved to be untroubled. Perhaps Woodhull's impulse came out of her own need for her family. In New York, the sisters set up a new practice as "magnetic healers" and spiritualists, with the Woodhulls and the Claflins all living in a single hectic household. That year, Victoria's young son Byron fell from a second-story window. Though he recovered after lying near death for several days, he was left severely and permanently brain damaged. Nursing her son, and caring for Canning through his bouts with alcohol, Woodhull continued to see clients, and in 1861 her life was brightened by the birth of a daughter, **Zulu Maude Woodhull**.

In 1864, the need for new clientele prompted the clan to move to Cincinnati. Tennie and another sister, **Utica Claflin Brooker**, were by now as attractive as Victoria, and all were vibrant like their mother, with passions that extended beyond religious zeal. After charges of illicit sexual activities and scandals forced the group from their home, they resettled in Chicago, where the pattern was repeated. By this time, Woodhull had been all but deserted by Canning, who came home only when he needed money. Given the mores of the times, the relations of the sisters with men may have been sexual or merely flirtatious, but they were shocking enough to their neighbors to give the appearance of prostitution, and, combined with the family's generally raucous behavior, caused them to be chased out of their homes more than once.

The two sisters were on the road again as clairvoyants when Woodhull met Colonel James Harvey Blood in St. Louis. He was a courteous, educated, and respected man, and a believer in the doctrine of free love. Victoria now had a name and a theory for the lifestyle that she and her sisters had been leading.

Victoria
Woodhull

In an era when divorce was extremely rare and difficult for women to obtain in most states, advocates of free love viewed marriage as an institution that could trap people in unhappy lives. In their view, marriage should be recognized as a social partnership, and if some element—such as sexual gratification or companionship—were missing in the relationship, then spouses should be allowed to find that element through loving more than one individual. As Woodhull would later write, "Copulation without love is prostitution."

Through her acquaintance with Blood, Woodhull became highly articulate about her views of free love; her own life had taught her to despise the hypocrisy of a sexual double standard that allowed men to engage in extramarital sex without social repercussions (and without fear of, or responsibility for, pregnancy). Almost everywhere, a man could divorce a wife who had committed adultery much more easily than a woman could obtain a divorce from an adulterous husband. Respectable women could not admit publicly to having sexual desire. Respectable men supported the same lie, even while having mistresses, frequenting houses of prostitution, or profiting from the ownership of buildings that housed prostitutes. Yet prostitutes were shunned by society for their profession (then legal in many communities and not widely outlawed until the end of the century).

Among a number of radical beliefs that gained hold during the 19th century, the doctrine of free love was seen by many as the most dangerous, presenting a serious threat to the social order by desanctifying the family unit. If people were allowed to have sex with anyone they pleased, who would take responsibility for the children? Furthermore, venereal disease—often spread through prostitution—was commonplace, and had no cure; and there were no reliable methods of birth control. For advocates of the movement, these social ills were precisely the reasons for needing a change in sexual standards. According to their argument, if human sexuality were more openly discussed, and people were not forced to deny their desires, prostitution would be unnecessary, women would be exploited less, and lives could be saved, because sexually transmitted disease would be recognized and treated more quickly.

Advocacy of free love was not advocacy of sexual licentiousness. Instead, men and women were encouraged to choose sexual partners based on mutual feelings rather than according to the dictates of church and state; to the extent that individuals acted responsibly and openly, marriage laws would not be needed.

As a spiritualist, Woodhull found the movement compatible with her belief that the soul transcended the boundaries of the material world represented by marriage laws. Such a view also resembled anarchy in many ways, and many followers of free love were anarchists, at a time when anarchy was considered a threat to the nation. Politically, Woodhull's outlook was actually closer to early communism, and she became a member of the Marxist International Working-

men's Association (from which she was later expelled). Clearly, the free-love doctrine carried some fiercely political undertones.

By 1866, Victoria Woodhull had divorced her first husband and married James Blood. They settled with Tennie and others of her family in New York City, where Woodhull established a salon attended by the brightest and most articulate radicals of the day, who met to socialize and spar intellectually. The prosperity of the family was greatly increased after Tennie met the New York millionaire Commodore Cornelius Vanderbilt, then a 76-year-old widower whose wife *Sophia Johnson Vanderbilt had just died in 1868. Sought after for her powers of spiritual healing, Tennie, in this case, turned her "magnetic powers" to arousal, and she became Vanderbilt's lover. When the two sisters approached Vanderbilt for financial advice, he became indispensable, advising them at first on business strategy, and later backing them in the opening of a brokerage office, Woodhull, Claflin & Co., the first run by women on Wall Street. The firm was an immense success, and the sisters were referred to by the *New York Herald* as the "Bewitching Brokers."

With this prosperity, the sisters were able to support their parents, a sister and her husband, and even Canning Woodhull all in one large home. Although many were scandalized, Woodhull found the presence of her first husband, as the father of her children, entirely appropriate and made her reasoning clear: "Dr. Woodhull, being sick, ailing and incapable of self-support, I felt it my duty to myself and to human nature that he should be cared for. . . . My present husband, Colonel Blood, not only approves of this charge, but cooperates in it. I esteem it one of the most virtuous acts of my life."

Woodhull gained fame as a stunning conversationalist among the intellectuals and politicians who frequented her salon. Two who were charmed by her attractiveness, intellect, and flair for making ideas dramatic were the brilliant Stephen Pearl Andrews and Congressman Benjamin F. Butler of Massachusetts. Both were sympathizers with the free-love doctrine, as well as supporters of women's right to vote, and schooled Woodhull in the limitations of women's legal and political rights.

Salon discussions frequently centered on the hypocrisies of American social and political life, as freethinkers argued for nothing less than a social revolution. Intent on exposing injustices between genders, classes, and races, Woodhull, Tennie, and Blood took every opportunity to call attention to cases of individual rights being denied. On one occasion, the sisters arrived to dine at Delmonico's, the famous restaurant near Wall Street, and were denied service because the establishment followed a rule common to many restaurants, holding that ladies were not welcome without male escorts after 6 PM. Tennie went to the door and waved to the cab driver waiting with a carriage for them outside. The man was seated with them, and the women ordered soup for three, breaking the conventional codes of both gender and rank, as Delmonico's was forced into serving two independent women and an embarrassed working-class man.

In May 1870, the sisters began the publication of *Woodhull & Claflin's Weekly*, with a masthead that read "Don't Fail to Read the Lady Broker's Paper! The Organ of the Most Advanced Thought and Purpose in the World!" The paper lasted until June 1876, advertising their business and spreading the ideas that flourished in their salon, with its opinions and exposés about free love, workers' rights, political scandals, and social injustice. It also became a platform for Woodhull's presidential candidacy, announced that April. Her plan was to run as an independent, giving her two years to publicize her ideas before the national presidential campaign.

Of all the ideas she brought to the public, Woodhull was most dedicated to free love. But once she grasped how few legal and political rights women actually had, she also made "Votes for Women" her personal mission and inspired many gatherings about women's rights. On January 11, 1871, she appeared before the House Judiciary Committee to deliver a memorial on the topic of woman suffrage. A "memorial" was a speech that was printed, circulated, and personally presented by a citizen before Congress in order to persuade it to enact a law. Since no woman had ever before been recognized by a congressional committee, Woodhull's appearance caused a huge stir. That same morning, the liberal suffragists of the National Woman's Suffrage Association (NWSA) had planned the opening of their annual convention in Washington, but Woodhull's appearance threatened to upstage them; many in the movement also feared that Woodhull's radical advocacy of free love would give suffragists a bad name if the public associated her position with votes for women. After much arguing, the NWSA postponed its morning session and sent a delegation, including *Susan B. Anthony, to hear Woodhull.

Woodhull was by this time a brilliant orator. When she spoke her face brightened, her whole body seemed to communicate her words to the crowd, and her speeches always built up momentum. That day, her argument was sharp and clear, invoking the 14th and 15th amendments as proof of women's right to the vote. Not surprisingly, the congressional majority report written in response to the speech was not favorable, but the minority report—signed by Benjamin Butler—issued the strongest official argument to date in favor of women's rights under the Constitution.

The suffragists, meanwhile, were so impressed that they invited Woodhull to repeat her memorial before their convention as the keynote speaker. Leaders of NWSA, including Susan B. Anthony, ✥ **Isabella Beecher Hooker** (sister of Henry Ward Beecher and Harriet Beecher Stowe), and *Elizabeth Cady Stanton, would continue to defend Woodhull's beliefs, and to welcome the publicity she brought to the issue of women's suffrage.

But the number of Woodhull's enemies also grew. Harriet Beecher Stowe attacked her through a comic novel then being serialized, parodying Woodhull as a brainless free lover who spoke about women's rights without knowing what they were. *Catharine Beecher, Harriet's older sister, wrote prolifically on the subject of women's role within family and education and was famous for her efforts to gain respect for women's work; she lectured Woodhull about morality and threatened to pull her down personally if she continued her mission of promoting free love.

Family conflicts also created bad publicity. When Woodhull's mother took James Blood to court, claiming that he was spending money improperly, the press published stories revealed on the witness stand about life in the Claflin home, including lovers who visited Victoria and Tennie, and Tennie's relationship with Vanderbilt. The public was scandalized, Vanderbilt's advice ceased, and the sisters began to lose money on Wall Street.

What galled Woodhull was to have to defend her own character publicly, while others who lived similarly were held up as pillars of morality. Her outrage grew when she learned that the minister Henry Ward Beecher was exercising free love privately while his sisters condemned her publicly. Woodhull learned of the affair through *Pauline Wright Davis, a fellow suffragist and friend of *Elizabeth Tilton, who had told Davis of her anguish over the recently ended romance. Lib Tilton had felt compelled to confess her affair to her husband, Theodore Tilton, who had been the Reverend Beecher's

◄ **Hooker, Isabella Beecher.** See Stowe, Harriet Beecher for sidebar.

closest friend until that day, and Theodore had since become obsessed with thoughts of revenge. On the afternoon during which Davis heard Lib Tilton's grief-stricken story, Davis met with Woodhull, pledging "not to leave Brooklyn until I had stripped the mask from that infamous, hypocritical scoundrel, Beecher."

Woodhull debated whether to reveal the Beecher-Tilton affair, aware of the harm that the scandal could cause to the spouses and children involved. Testing the waters, she sent vague letters to the editors of New York newspapers, alluding to a love scandal involving "teachers of eminence," which led to her first meeting with Theodore Tilton. In the ensuing months, Tilton edited and published a biography of Woodhull, and a romance developed, fueling the desires of them both to see Beecher "unmasked."

But in 1871, after her speech at Steinway Hall, the forces of contemporary social propriety rallied strongly against her. Woodhull and her family were evicted from their mansion, ending her salon; the brokerage firm was closed, and all financial advice had ceased. Yet she received more speaking invitations than ever.

In 1872, members of the NWSA organized the Equal Rights Party. Woodhull was nominated at its convention to run for president of the United States and Frederick Douglass (who was not present) as vice-president. Suffragists were soon divided over whether to throw support behind this new party or work for the established ones. Susan B. Anthony believed Woodhull was too involved with her own agenda, and that her many causes were too radical to be useful to the suffrage movement, but Elizabeth Cady Stanton remained a Woodhull supporter for the rest of her life.

As more suffragists distanced themselves from her and the free-love doctrine, Woodhull lost speaking engagements and began to despair. Finally, at a speech before the National Association of Spiritualists she revealed the Beecher-Tilton affair, and published an account of it in her *Weekly*, leading to indictments against Woodhull and Tennie for criminal libel and charges of sending obscene literature through the mail. Despite the several weeks the sisters spent in jail, a judge biased against them, and hours of testimony about their private life, they were found not guilty. Following a mock investigation held at Plymouth Church, led by the closest friends of the Reverend Beecher to "prove" that he was innocent of immoral acts, Theodore Tilton filed a lawsuit against the minister for willfully alienating him from the affections of his wife, resulting in one of the most sensational tri-

als of the century. Tickets for a courtroom seat were scalped to the highest bidders, and refreshment booths and souvenir stands appeared outside of the courthouse. Although the jury ruled against Tilton, the ultimate result, according to Stanton, was a strong pull "toward making the standard of tolerated behavior of men and women equal." Finally, people were speaking more openly about sexuality.

Woodhull was not asked to testify at the trial, and in fact was retreating by then from the sexuality spotlight. As she and her mother began turning to the Bible, then toward Catholicism, for new mystic explanations, Colonel Blood had no place in her life. They divorced in 1876, the same year that publication of the *Weekly* ceased. In 1877, she was barely supporting herself through lectures and spiritual healing, when Commodore Vanderbilt died, leaving the bulk of his millions to his eldest son. Woodhull apparently received a stroke of good fortune when the remainder of the Vanderbilt family planned to contest the will and to call Woodhull and Tennie into court as proof of the Commodore's incompetency. Shortly afterward, Woodhull, her children, Tennie, and their mother departed to England, where they lived in comfort for some years; it was assumed that the eldest Vanderbilt had safeguarded his inheritance by providing for their new life.

In England, Woodhull continued to lecture about the Bible, spiritualism, and sexuality, but with a significant difference evident in her point of view. Now when she spoke about "The Human Body, the Temple of God," the emphasis was shifted from sexual activity to consideration of the body within the context of marriage and responsibility. At one such lecture, she met the conservative banker and millionaire, John Biddulph Martin, who fell in love with her. After an extensive courtship, they were married in 1882.

In England, Woodhull embraced humanitarian causes. She took frequent trips back to the United States, and during her courtship with Martin became involved with the small Humanitarian Party, which nominated her as its presidential candidate in 1892. Settled with her new husband on their country estate in Worcestershire, Woodhull took up new interests with her usual missionary zeal, including new methods of agriculture. After the death of her husband, she divided up one of the estate farms and rented small shares to women where they could learn farming techniques. The estate included a school for experimenting with the latest educational methods. Still living each day to the fullest, she established an annual agricultural show, entertained the prince of Wales, and worked fervently during World War I for the war effort. She owned one of the first automobiles in England and always had her chauffeur drive as fast as possible through the countryside. Hoping to cheat death, she slept upright in the last years of her life. In 1927, at age 88, she died in her night chair.

Victoria Woodhull perhaps summed up her own life best to a reporter after losing the 1892 election, when she explained why she had not expected to win: "The truth is that I am too many years ahead of this age and the exalted views and objects of humanitarianism can scarcely be grasped as yet by the unenlightened mind of the average man." It is a statement hard to dispute.

SOURCES:

D'Emilio, John, and Estelle B. Freedman. *Intimate Matters: A History of Sexuality in America.* NY: Harper & Row, 1988.

Johnston, Johanna. *Mrs. Satan: The Incredible Saga of Victoria C. Woodhull.* NY: Putnam, 1967.

Sears, Hal D. *The Sex Radicals: Free Love in High Victorian America.* Lawrence, KS: The Regents Press of Kansas, 1977.

SUGGESTED READING:

Gabriel, Mary. *Notorious Victoria: The Life of Victoria Woodhull, Uncensored.* Algonquin, 1997.

Sachs, Emanie. *The Terrible Siren.* NY: Harper & Bros., 1928.

Tilton, Theodore. *The Life of Victoria Claflin Woodhull.* NY: Golden Age, 1871.

COLLECTIONS:

Books and papers at the Sterling Memorial Library and the Beinecke Rare Book Library, Yale University; files, papers, and newspapers at the New York Historical Society Library; books and newspapers, New York Public Library.

Susan Gonda,
Instructor of History at Grossmont College,
San Diego, California

Woodsmall, Ruth F. (1883–1963)

American YWCA official whose studies of the condition of women around the world aided in international relief and development efforts. Born Ruth Frances Woodsmall on September 20, 1883, in Atlanta, Georgia; died on May 25, 1963, in New York City; daughter of Hubert Harrison Woodsmall (a Union soldier and lawyer) and Mary Elizabeth (Howes) Woodsmall (an art teacher); educated at Franklin College, Indiana University, Columbia University, and the University of Heidelberg; University of Nebraska, B.A., 1905; Wellesley College, M.A., 1906.

Started her career with the Young Women's Christian Association (YWCA), as a director of hostess houses (1917); worked as a liaison to the American military during the occupation of Germany following World War I, specifically reporting on conditions in Germany, Poland, and the Baltic and Balkan regions; became executive secretary of the YWCA in the Near East and secretary of the YWCA Eastern Mediterranean Federations (1920); published germinal study on the changing status of Muslim women (1930); published further research into the status of women in the Far East (1933); served as a specialist on international affairs to the national board of the YWCA (1932–35); became general secretary of the World's YWCA (1935); conducted studies of women in Nazi Germany (1930s) and Latin America during World War II; became chief of Women's Affairs in Germany following World War II; received the Commander's Cross of the Order of Merit of West Germany (1962).

Born in 1883 in Atlanta, Georgia, Ruth Frances Woodsmall was one of four children of Hubert Harrison Woodsmall, a lawyer and former Union soldier, and **Mary Howes Woodsmall**, a Southerner. Mary supported the family after her husband's death in 1889 by teaching painting and decorative arts in Indianapolis, Indiana. There Ruth attended public schools, followed by studies at Franklin College (1901–03) and Indiana University (1903–05). She then went to the University of Nebraska, where she finished her bachelor's degree Phi Beta Kappa in 1905. She studied briefly at the University of Heidelberg in Germany, as well as at Columbia University before completing her master's degree in German at Wellesley College in Massachusetts in 1906.

She accepted a position as principal of a high school in Ouray, Colorado, and then worked as a German and English teacher in schools in Colorado and Nevada. In 1916, she left teaching to pursue a year abroad, traveling through India and East Asia. On her return in 1917, Woodsmall, a Baptist, joined the Young Women's Christian Association (YWCA), the organization she would remain with the rest of her career. Serving first as director of hostess houses near U.S. army bases in America and France, she worked as a liaison to the U.S. military after World War I as part of the American occupation forces in Germany and Poland. To help establish YWCA services in Eastern Europe, Woodsmall investigated social conditions in those countries and in the Baltic and Balkan regions between 1918 and 1920.

Woodsmall's field reports proved one of her greatest contributions to the YWCA. In 1920, she was made executive secretary of the organization in the Near East and secretary of the its

Eastern Mediterranean Federations. In this capacity, she conducted research on topics such as the changing status of women and American financial involvement in Muslim-dominated states, including Turkey, Lebanon, Iraq, Iran, India, and Palestine. Her findings were later published as *Moslem Women Enter a New World* in 1936. As part of the Laymen's Foreign Mission Inquiry, Woodsmall then turned her attention to the status of women in Burma (now Myanmar), Japan, China, and India. Her findings were published in 1933 as *Eastern Women Today and Tomorrow*.

In 1932, Woodsmall returned to the United States to serve as international affairs staff specialist on the YWCA National Board. By 1935, she was traveling abroad again, moving to Geneva, Switzerland, to become the general secretary of the World's YWCA. She would spend time in Britain, North Africa, Sweden, and Latin America over the course of her term as secretary, organizing conferences and helping establish YWCA efforts. Woodsmall's research on the status of women in Nazi Germany and Latin America in the 1930s and during World War II was important in guiding the YWCA's efforts to improve the legal and social status of women in those areas.

She stepped down as secretary in 1947 after 12 years of service. However, she continued to devote her time to the YWCA on the staff of the Special Service in China, Japan, and Korea. Returning to government work in 1949, Woodsmall went back to Allied-occupied Germany for a five-year tenure as chief of the Women's Affairs Section, where she worked to improve German women's access to public health facilities, education, welfare, and religious organizations. She also sought to re-establish communication between German women's groups and other European women's organizations. For this work, Woodsmall would receive the Commander's Cross of the Order of Merit of West Germany in 1962. Awarded honorary doctorates by the University of Nebraska and the University of Indiana in the 1940s, Woodsmall also served as adviser to the UN's Commission on the Status of Women in 1949 and 1951 and was a key participant in the 1951 UNESCO Working Party on the Equality of Access of Women to Education in Paris.

Woodsmall returned from Germany in 1954 and settled in New York City. Until her death in 1963, she devoted herself to new research on the status of women in East Asia, updating her previous two books to include the new data. They were republished as *Study of the Role of Women, Their Activities and Organizations in* *Lebanon, Egypt, Iraq, Jordan and Syria* (1955) and *Women and the New East* (1960). Ruth Woodsmall died in New York in May 1963. Her ashes were scattered in a wooded area near Geneva, Switzerland.

SOURCES:

Current Biography 1949. NY: H.W. Wilson, 1949.

Sherrow, Victoria. *Women and the Military: An Encyclopedia*. Denver, CO: ABC-CLIO, 1996.

Sicherman, Barbara, and Carol Hurd Green, eds. *Notable American Women: The Modern Period*. Cambridge, MA: The Belknap Press of Harvard University, 1980.

Laura York, M.A. in History,
University of California,
Riverside, California

Woodville, Anne (b. around 1458)

Countess of Kent. Born around 1458; daughter of Richard Woodville, 1st earl Rivers, and *Jacquetta of Luxemburg; sister of *Elizabeth Woodville (1437–1492), queen of England; married William Bourchier, Viscount Bourchier; married George Grey, 2nd earl of Kent; children: (first marriage) Henry Bourchier, 2nd earl of Essex, and Cecily Bourchier; (second marriage) Richard Grey, 3rd earl of Kent.

Woodville, Catherine (c. 1442–1512).

See Woodville, Katherine.

Woodville, Elizabeth (1437–1492)

Queen of England and wife of Edward IV. Name variations: Dame Elizabeth Grey; Elizabeth Wideville. Born Elizabeth Woodville around 1437 in Grafton Regis, Northamptonshire, England; died on June 7 or 8, 1492, in Bermondsey Abbey, London; eldest and one of six daughters and seven sons of Sir Richard Woodville, 1st earl Rivers, and Jacquetta of Luxemburg; married Sir John Grey, 2nd baron Ferrers of Groby (died); married Edward IV, king of England, on May 1, 1464 (died 1483); children: (first marriage) Thomas Grey, 1st marquess of Dorset (d. 1501) and Richard Grey (c. 1453–1483); (second marriage) Elizabeth of York (1466–1503, who married Henry VII); *Mary Plantagenet (1467–1482); *Cecilia (1469–1507); King Edward V (1470–1483, who was murdered in the Tower of London); Margaret (1472–1472); Richard (1473–1483, who was murdered in the Tower); *Anne Howard (1475–1511); George (1477–1479, who died of the plague); ❧➤ Katherine Plantagenet (1479–1527); Bridget (1480–1517, who became a nun at Dartford).

Elizabeth Woodville, queen of Edward IV, was the product of the blissful union between ❧➤ **Jacquetta of Luxemburg**, a Luxemburg princess, and Sir Richard Woodville, an English squire who married despite family disapproval. As the eldest of the couple's 13 children, Elizabeth became a second mother to her younger siblings, whom she continued to nurture and protect throughout her life. She was described as a beautiful young woman, with "silver-gilt hair" down to her knees.

Elizabeth's first husband was John Grey, with whom she had two sons. Because John was a staunch supporter of the Lancastrians, Elizabeth became a lady of the bedchamber to Henry VI's queen, *Margaret of Anjou (1429–1482). John, however, was killed in battle, and when Yorkist Edward IV had himself proclaimed king, Elizabeth lost all her husband's estates and was left penniless. She then set out to petition the new king to provide support for her children. Rather than seeking an audience, Elizabeth purportedly waylaid Edward while he was on a hunting expedition near her mother's home in Northamptonshire. Under an oak tree (which was known as the Queen's Oak until the 19th century), flanked by her small sons, she approached the king, who, known for his weakness for beautiful women, lost no time in propositioning the young widow. Indignant at his suggested impropriety, Elizabeth was said to have replied: "My Liege, I know I am not good enough to be your Queen, but I am far too good to be your mistress." Edward apparently found Elizabeth irresistible, and they were married a short time later, although the ceremony was kept secret so that the king could avoid the anger of his family and court over his marriage to a commoner. Edward did not make the marriage public until negotiations with Louis XI of France for him to marry a French princess took a serious turn.

Elizabeth was finally crowned in a splendid ceremony at Westminster, after which she busied herself with having more babies and situating her many siblings within wealthy marriages, a task made simpler by her ability to favorably influence her husband. (One of the most notorious results of her matchmaking was the marriage of her eldest brother, just 20, to the dowager duchess of Norfolk, who was 80.) Elizabeth's leverage over Edward remained in the realm of what **Norah Lofts** terms "gossipy bedroom influence" and did not extend to sensitive affairs of state. Nonetheless, Elizabeth was not popular among many Yorkist supporters, who were incensed over the favors granted to her upstart relatives, many of whom had Lancastrian connections.

While Edward was out of the country during the Wars of the Roses, Elizabeth was forced by the dangers of war to take refuge in the sanctuary at Westminster for the birth of her fourth child, Edward V, heir to the throne. Hard times eventually gave way to victory for the Yorkists, and the royal court was restored to a place of luxury and lavish entertainment. While Elizabeth produced five more children, Edward began to ignore his royal duties in favor of the high life, which included liaisons with a number of other women, including *Elizabeth Lucy and *Jane Shore. After Edward's death in 1483, at age 40 (attributed by some to sheer overindulgence), Elizabeth was immediately caught up in the attempt of her power-hungry brother-in-law, Richard (III) of Gloucester, to keep Edward V, then 12, from succeeding to the throne. Villainous in his approach, Richard accused Elizabeth of witchcraft and, declaring that her children were illegitimate because her marriage had been irregular, had himself declared king. Most devastating to Elizabeth was the sudden disappearance of both Edward V and his brother Richard, who had been confined to the Tower of London, supposedly to await the coronation. Thought to have been murdered by agents of Richard III, their bodies went undiscovered for 200 years. (After two centuries of speculation, workmen repairing a staircase in the Tower found the bones of two youths, believed to be the brothers.)

❧ **Katherine Plantagenet** (1479–1527)
*English princess and duchess of Devon. Born around August 14, 1479, in Eltham, Kent, England; died on November 15, 1527, in Tiverton, Devon, England; daughter of Edward IV, king of England, and *Elizabeth Woodville (1437–1492); married William Courtenay, earl of Devon, in October 1495; children: three, including Henry Courtenay (c. 1498–1539), marquess of Exeter.*

❧ **Jacquetta of Luxemburg** (c. 1416–1472)
*Luxemburg princess. Name variations: Duchess of Bedford. Born in Luxemburg around 1416; died on May 30, 1472; daughter of Peter of Luxemburg, count of St. Pol, and Margaret del Balzo; married John of Lancaster, duke of Bedford (son of Henry IV and *Mary de Bohun), on April 20, 1433; married Richard Woodville, 1st earl Rivers, in 1436; children: (second marriage) *Elizabeth Woodville (1437–1492); Anthony Woodville, 2nd earl Rivers (c. 1442–1483); John Woodville (c. 1445–1469); Lionel Woodville, bishop of Salisbury (c. 1453–1484); Richard, 3rd earl Rivers (d. 1491); Edward Woodville (d. 1488); *Margaret Woodville (who married Thomas Fitzalan, 14th earl of Arundel); *Anne Woodville (who married William Bourchier, viscount Bourchier, and George Grey, 2nd earl of Kent); *Jacquetta Woodville; *Katherine Woodville (c. 1442–1512); *Mary Woodville (c. 1443–c. 1480); Eleanor Woodville (who married Anthony Grey).*

During the two-year reign of Richard III (r. 1483–1485), Elizabeth, once dowager queen, became simply Dame Elizabeth Grey, and lived under the king's control in Bermondsey Abbey. When Henry VII finally defeated the Yorkists and took Elizabeth's daughter (***Elizabeth of York**) as his bride in 1486, he restored the dowager queen's lands. One of the last pleasures of Elizabeth Woodville's life was attending the christening of Henry's and Elizabeth's first son Arthur, to whom she was godmother as well as grandmother. After her death in 1492, at age 55, Elizabeth was buried without ceremony beside Edward IV at Windsor. A likeness of her adorns a stained-glass window in Canterbury Cathedral.

SOURCES:

Hall, Walter Phelps, and Robert Greenhalgh Albion. *A History of England and the British Empire.* Boston, MA: Ginn, 1953.

Lofts, Norah. *Queens of England.* NY: Doubleday, 1977.

SUGGESTED READING:

MacGibbon, David. *Elizabeth Woodville, 1437–1492,* 1938.

Barbara Morgan,
Melrose, Massachusetts

Elizabeth Woodville

Woodville, Jacquetta

Sister of the queen of England. Name variations: Lady Strange of Knockin. Daughter of Richard Woodville, 1st earl Rivers, and *Jacquetta of Luxemburg; sister of *Elizabeth Woodville, queen of England (1437–1492); married John, Lord Strange of Knockin.

Woodville, Katherine (c. 1442–1512)

English royal. Name variations: Duchess of Buckingham, Duchess of Bedford; Catherine Woodville; Catherine Wydeville. Born around 1442; died in 1512; daughter of Richard Woodville, 1st earl Rivers, and *Jacquetta of Luxemburg; sister of *Elizabeth Woodville, queen of England (1437–1492); married Henry Stafford (1455–1483), 2nd duke of Buckingham (r. 1460–1483), in 1466 (executed on November 2, 1483); married Jasper Tudor, duke of Bedford, in 1485; married Richard Wingfield; children: (first marriage) Edward Stafford, 3rd duke of Buckingham (1478–1521); Henry Stafford, earl of Wiltshire (c. 1479–1523); *Elizabeth Stafford (d. 1532, mistress of Henry VIII).

Woodville, Margaret (fl. 1450s)

Countess of Arundel. Flourished in the 1450s; daughter of Richard Woodville, 1st earl Rivers, and *Jacquetta of Luxemburg; sister of *Elizabeth Woodville, queen of England (1437–1492); married Thomas Fitzalan, 14th earl of Arundel.

Woodville, Mary (c. 1443–c. 1480)

Countess of Pembroke. Born around 1443; died before 1481; daughter of Richard Woodville (b. 1405), 1st earl Rivers, and *Jacquetta of Luxemburg; sister of *Elizabeth Woodville, queen of England (1437–1492); married William Herbert (1455–1491), 2nd earl of Pembroke; children: possibly Elizabeth Herbert (c. 1476–c. 1511). William Herbert's second wife was Katherine Herbert (c. 1471–?).

Woodward, Ellen Sullivan (1887–1971)

American government official. Born on July 11, 1887, in Oxford, Mississippi; died of arteriosclerosis on September 23, 1971, in Washington, D.C.; daughter of William Van Amberg Sullivan (a state congressional representative and U.S. senator) and Belle (Murray) Sullivan; educated at Sans Souci and Washington (D.C.) College; married Albert Young Woodward (a judge and state legislator), in 1906; child: Albert Young, Jr.

Ellen Sullivan Woodward was born in 1887 into a prominent Southern family. Her father William Van Amberg Sullivan, the first law graduate of Vanderbilt University, served as both a Mississippi congressional representative and as a U.S. senator. Her mother **Belle Murray Sullivan** died when Ellen was seven, a circumstance which led to a particularly close relationship between William Sullivan and his children. Ellen spent many hours with her father as he argued court cases.

Her informal education in government was traded for a more formal education at Oxford High School. In 1906, one year after graduating from Sans Souci College in South Carolina, Ellen married Albert Young Woodward, a man with a background similar to her father's. Albert was an attorney, state district judge, and member of the state legislature. Their only child, Albert, Jr., was born in 1909.

The couple resided in Louisville, Mississippi, where Woodward became deeply involved in the community and organized her husband's legislative campaign. When Albert, Sr., died unexpectedly in 1925, Ellen Woodward took his place in the next election, winning a decisive victory and thus becoming the second woman to serve in the Mississippi House of Representatives. As a widow and single mother, however, she did not seek reelection. Instead, Woodward took a position as the director of civic development for the Mississippi State Board of Development in 1926. She served as executive director from 1929 to 1933. During this time, she remained involved with community organizations, serving as trustee of various charities and as an executive with the Mississippi State Board of Public Welfare.

Woodward also served as a delegate to the 1928 Democratic National Convention and as a campaign worker for Franklin Delano Roosevelt's 1932 presidential bid. Her dedication to public service was recognized when Harry L. Hopkins, director of the Works Progress Administration (WPA), appointed her to direct women's work programs. Woodward focused on women's traditional work roles and introduced programs to provide household training, establish sewing rooms, and develop rural libraries. She also believed in equal pay for equal work and advocated the inclusion of work training in all emergency aid programs. Most of the state directors in liaison with her program were women.

In July 1936, Woodward became director of WPA projects for writers, musicians, actors and artists. This position made her the second-highest ranked woman in the federal government, second only to *Frances Perkins. She also began a lifelong friendship and professional relationship with *Eleanor Roosevelt. After Hopkins' resignation, Woodward was appointed to the Social Security board, a position she held until the board was abolished in 1946. In this federal position, Woodward vigorously managed a politically sensitive agency while still supporting the needs of artists and writers. In 1938 she defended, though unsuccessfully, her cultural projects before a congressional investigating committee.

Upon her resignation from this position, Harry Truman appointed Woodward director of the Office of Inter-Agency and International Relations of the Federal Security Administration. She organized the expansion of social security benefits to women and children and was encouraged by jobs available to women during World War II, a situation which allowed her to extend unemployment insurance as well. After her retirement in January 1954, Woodward remained active in a number of women's organizations, including the National Federation of Business and Professional Women's Clubs. She died of arteriosclerosis at home in Washington, D.C., in 1971.

SOURCES:

Sicherman, Barbara, and Carol Hurd Green, eds. *Notable American Women: The Modern Period*. Cambridge, MA: The Belknap Press of Harvard University, 1980.

Mary McNulty,
freelance writer,
St. Charles, Illinois

Woodward, Joanne (1930—)

American actress of stage and screen, one of the most respected of her generation, who won an Academy Award for her performance in The Three Faces of Eve. *Born Joan Woodward on February 27, 1930, in Thomasville, Georgia; attended Louisiana State University; daughter of Wade Woodward and Elinor Woodward; married Paul Newman (the actor), on January 29, 1958; children: Elinor "Nell" Teresa Newman (b. April 1959); Melissa "Lissy" Newman (b. September 1961); Claire "Clea" Newman (b. April 1963); and three stepchildren.*

Enrolled in the Neighborhood Playhouse in New York to study under Sanford Meisner; while performing on the New York stage and on television, was given her first feature film role (1955); won an Academy Award for Best Actress for her career-making performance in The Three Faces of Eve *(1957); has since been nominated twice more for Best Actress and has won two Emmy Awards for her work in distinguished television films; has worked frequently with husband Paul Newman, who has not only acted with her but also directed some of her most well-received roles;*

with husband, awarded the Kennedy Center honors for lifetime achievement (1992).

Selected filmography: Count Three and Pray (Calico Pony, *1955); A Kiss Before Dying (1956); The Three Faces of Eve (1957); No Down Payment (1957); The Long, Hot Summer (1958); Rally 'Round the Flag, Boys! (1958); The Sound and the Fury (1959); The Fugitive Kind (1959); From the Terrace (1960); Paris Blues (1961); The Stripper (1963); A New Kind of Love (1963); Signpost to Murder (1964); A Big Hand for the Little Lady (1966); A Fine Madness (1966); Rachel, Rachel (1968); Winning (1969); WUSA (1970); They Might Be Giants (1971); The Effect of Gamma Rays on Man-in-the-Moon Marigolds (1972); Summer Wishes, Winter Dreams (1973); The Drowning Pool (1975); The End (1978); Harry and Son (1984); The Glass Menagerie (1987); Mr. and Mrs. Bridge (1990); Philadelphia (1993); (narrator) The Age of Innocence (1993).*

Laurence Olivier never forgot the night Joanne Woodward jumped into his lap. No matter that she was only nine years old at the time, or that Olivier happened to be passing by in an open limousine in Atlanta, Georgia, as part of a motorcade escorting *Vivien Leigh to the world premiere of *Gone With the Wind*. The ear-splitting shriek and the mad leap into his car by the little girl from rural Georgia remained with him all his life.

Joanne had seen Olivier in *Wuthering Heights*, but he was just one of the stars she had come to admire during countless afternoons at the movies with her mother **Elinor Woodward** in Thomasville, Georgia, where she had been born on February 27, 1930. Her father Wade Woodward, an administrator in the local school system, remained skeptical of his daughter's enthusiasm for "movie people," but Joanne's mother was an indefatigable film fan. She had, in fact, named her daughter Joan, after one of her favorite Hollywood stars, *Joan Crawford; but a thick Georgia drawl would soon lengthen the name to Joanne. Elinor needed little convincing when Joanne suggested they drive to Atlanta for the *Gone With the Wind* premiere in December 1939. By the time the Woodwards moved to Greenville, South Carolina, six years later, Joanne had already been entering beauty contests and had adopted *Bette Davis as her favorite actress. At 15, she was tall, slim, and strikingly attractive, with blonde hair and light blue eyes; and it was the opinion of her high school drama teacher that she was accomplished enough as an actress to go directly to New York. Instead,

Woodward was accepted at Louisiana State University, where she majored, of course, in drama.

Her parents had separated by the time Joanne returned to Greenville after only two years at LSU; but when Wade attended Joanne's performance in *The Glass Menagerie* at the Greenville Little Theater, even he had to acknowledge his daughter's talent. In 1949, after a season of summer stock in Massachusetts, Woodward arrived in New York and Sanford Meisner's Neighborhood Playhouse to begin seriously studying her craft. "I hated him at first," she said of the man she would later credit with much of her success. "For two years, I was slapped down, torn apart, and taught to act by Sandy Meisner." In addition to the rigors of Meisner's intensely psychological approach to acting, there was her Southern accent to contend with, slowly eradicated by speech lessons; and there was Joanne's conviction that all that 1950s show business in New York wanted was "dark neurotic girls from the wrong side of the tracks" rather than attractive Southern blondes. "I tried to turn myself into that type," she said, "but it didn't work." Fortunately, the advertising business still had need of clean-cut young women and provided Woodward with a small income from modeling.

Her fortunes improved when an agent from MCA, then the most powerful talent agency in both New York and Hollywood, saw her perform in a Neighborhood Playhouse production and signed her to a one-year contract. Also in Joanne's favor was the dawning of television's "Golden Age," distinguished by a number of live weekly drama series needing unknown young actors. One such series was NBC's "Robert Montgomery Presents." Thus it was that on June 9, 1952, millions of Americans got their first look at Joanne Woodward in a drama called "Penny." But her contract with MCA would mean more to her future than commercial success, for it introduced her to the man who would become her partner in one of Hollywood's longest-lived marriages.

Joanne had first seen Paul Newman in the hallways and waiting rooms of MCA. "I had been making the rounds and I was hot, sweaty, and my hair was all stringy around my neck," she said of the summer afternoon she first met Newman, who was four years her senior and whom she later described as "funny and pretty and neat." They seemed, at first glance, an unlikely pair. While Joanne had grown up in straitened circumstances in a small Southern town, Newman came from an upper-middle-class

Cleveland family and had been educated at Ivy League schools; and while Joanne had arrived in New York as a single woman and had remained unattached, Newman had been married for some years to a fellow Midwesterner, **Jacqueline Witte,** and had three children. But when Woodward and Newman were cast as understudies in Josh Logan's landmark 1953 Broadway production of William Inge's *Picnic*, the relationship deepened. "I think Paul and Joanne had a certain discipline about their lives," Logan later said. "I'm talking about outside of talent; I'm talking about intelligence." The couple grew even closer when both began studying with Lee Strasberg at the Actors Studio as part of a now legendary class that included Marlon Brando, *Eva Marie Saint, *Julie Harris and Eli Wallach.

In 1954, Woodward was flown to Los Angeles to appear in a filmed television play for "Four Star Playhouse." She played a teenager who falls in love with an older man, performed by veteran film actor Dick Powell. Powell was so impressed by his 24-year-old co-star's ability to metamorphose for the camera into a starry-eyed adolescent that he sent a print of the show to his agent at Twentieth Century-Fox, which promptly signed her to a seven-year feature film contract that allowed her to continue working in television in New York while the studio looked for a suitable role for her. It took a year before Fox finally loaned Woodward out to Columbia to star with Van Heflin in a Civil War drama, *Count Three and Pray*. "It was a helluva good part," Woodward said years later of her first feature film role as the roughneck teenager Lissy. (She would give the nickname to her second-born daughter.) Even at this early stage in her career, Joanne's work drew attention for its integrity and depth, a tribute to her years studying with Meisner and Strasberg. "All she delivers is talent," one director said of her at the time. "No particular glamour, not publicity—just talent." But her next role for Hollywood proved more trying. *A Kiss Before Dying* (1955), in which she played the remarkably unperceptive girlfriend of Robert Wagner's homicidal killer ("No wonder he wants to kill her!" one critic wrote), would become, for her, "the worst picture ever made in Hollywood." The picture drew audiences, however, for the controversy which arose over the use of the word "pregnant" in one scene. Conservative elements became so incensed that the word was actually edited out of the soundtrack in Chicago theaters.

Hollywood, in fact, was not proving to her taste at all. Woodward found herself frustrated by the slow pace of making a feature film, spending on one picture weeks that might have provided

work in three or four television dramas; and the studio's suggestion that she accept more glamorous roles rather than challenging ones was, she thought, insulting to her craft. Her future, she became certain, lay in television and on Broadway, both of which she tackled after the release of *A Kiss Before Dying* with a string of TV dramas and her official Broadway debut in a play called *The Lovers*. The stage play didn't attract much favorable attention, but her television work led one critic to call her "another Bette Davis." She didn't warm to the compliment, even though Davis had, indeed, been one of her childhood idols. "I'd rather be the *first* Joanne Woodward than a second Bette Davis," she said, adding that she preferred "a small role that I felt would be good for me than a star part unsuited to me."

Acting is like sex.

You should do it, not talk about it.

—Joanne Woodward

Her personal life was proving frustrating, too. By 1956, her relationship with Newman was well known, especially when she and Newman stayed together at a house in Malibu owned by mutual friend Gore Vidal. Newman was, of course, still married; and both lovers were warned by friends that their professional lives could be ruined by the affair, even if their respective careers were the talk of Hollywood. (Newman had just been praised for his performance as boxer Rocky Graziano in *Somebody Up There Likes Me*.) The tension was especially difficult for Newman to handle, his arrest in New York on drunk-driving charges being just a slight indication of a serious drinking problem that developed at this point in his life.

Woodward, meanwhile, was presented with the role that made her career as a respected film actress. She later claimed she had been given the role of Eve in *The Three Faces of Eve* only because the part had been turned down by stars like *Judy Garland and *Susan Hayward. Even Joanne later admitted that she had serious reservations about the picture that would make her a star in her own right. "If I hadn't needed something really big right then," she said, "I wouldn't have played it. I was afraid I couldn't make the part believable." But the film's veteran producer-writer Nunnally Johnson, a fellow Georgian, claimed he had wanted a newcomer all along and had based his choice on her television work. The two spent hours discussing the part and watching films of actual patients suffering from schizophrenia. Woodward spent more hours alone learning what was in essence the three separate characters she would be

required to alternately assume, sometimes switching from one to another in just a few seconds of screen time. "It was frightening," she said, "but it was a great opportunity for any actress." The daily rushes caused such excitement at the studio that Joanne immediately started production on another picture, *No Down Payment*, as soon as *Eve* wrapped; and when *Eve* previewed in August 1957 before its national release Woodward, it was said, was destined for an Oscar.

The attention was agonizing for her, since Hollywood gossips were already wondering when Newman would divorce his wife to marry Woodward. The talk escalated when the two stars worked together on screen for the first time in *The Long, Hot Summer*, a steamy romance set in a small Southern town in which Joanne's Clara Varner falls for Paul's knockabout vagabond Ben Quick; and it reached such intense speculation that gossip columnist **Sheila Graham** finally asked Woodward point blank when she and Newman would marry. Joanne evaded the question by pointing out that because of her own parents' divorce, she was being especially cautious about marrying. But just after shooting wrapped on *The Long, Hot Summer*, Newman left Hollywood for Mexico and obtained a divorce from Witte. On January 29, 1958, Joanne Woodward and Paul Newman were married in Las Vegas.

Meanwhile, *The Three Faces of Eve* had opened nationally in the late fall of 1957. It was a tremendous hit, Joanne's name appearing at the top of lists of "most important new actresses" of that year; and true to predictions, she received her first Academy Award nomination for her work in the film. But by now, Woodward had acquired a reputation for speaking her mind and began to make Fox executives uneasy with her nonchalant attitude toward her chance for the industry's top award. "If I had an infinite amount of respect for the people who think I gave the greatest performance, then it would matter to me," she said, adding that she herself thought *Deborah Kerr, who had been nominated for *Heaven Knows, Mr. Allison*, deserved the Best Actress Oscar. "It's *not* telling the truth that would destroy me as a person and destroy my integrity as an actress," she claimed. But on Oscar night, 1957, Woodward leaped to her feet, jubilant, when John Wayne opened the envelope and announced she had won the award. Even Hollywood insiders hadn't expected the award to go to a relative newcomer, and one who didn't fit the mold of a glamorous movie star. "She did it on acting ability," one of her classmates from the Neighborhood Playhouse later said, "because that part was incredibly challenging. It just never occurred to anybody that you could win an Academy Award just by being good."

For awhile, it seemed she might be too good, for the studio was unsure how to follow up Woodward's stunning work in *Eve* and Joanne herself rejected several parts offered to her. It was Newman who managed to sell the studio on the idea of following up their work together in *The Long, Hot Summer* with another pairing, but this time in a spoof of American suburbia called *Rally 'Round The Flag Boys*. Joanne soon discovered, however, that her considerable talents did not lie in light comedy and complained that all she was doing in the picture was "making faces." The film was moderately successful at the box office, but it would be some years before Woodward would tackle another purely comic role. The experience, in fact, soured both of them on traditional studio films, and Newman, exercising a clause in his contract that allowed stage work in New York, agreed to take the lead in the Broadway premiere of Tennessee Williams' *Sweet Bird of Youth*. By early 1959, the couple had moved back to New York's Greenwich Village with great relief; and in April of that year, Joanne gave birth to the couple's first child—a daughter they formally named Elinor Teresa but nicknamed Nell (**Nell Newman**).

Woodward returned to work soon after in *The Fugitive Kind*, a film adaptation of Williams' *Orpheus Descending* shot by Sidney Lumet in a small town in upstate New York, and then went back to Los Angeles to co-star with Newman in Fox's adaptation of the John O'Hara novel *From the Terrace*. She caused further discomfort for the studio's publicity department when she said in one interview that she had taken the part of O'Hara's lonely heiress only because of the glamorous wardrobe. Both films were only moderate successes. An international phase of her career ensued during late 1959 and early 1960 as Newman shot *Exodus* in Israel and both Joanne and her husband appeared in *Paris Blues*, filmed in that city during a time Joanne would later remember as one of the happiest of their marriage. The film, directed by Martin Ritt, featured Newman and Sidney Poitier as itinerant jazz musicians in Paris who fall in love with two American tourists, played by Joanne and **Diahann Carroll**.

After nearly a year of travel and work, Woodward and Newman returned to Los Angeles, where Paul began work on *The Hustler* and Joanne turned to family matters. To begin with, she was pregnant again while little Nell was going

through "the terrible twos"; and there were the difficulties to be expected between Joanne and her three stepchildren from Newman's previous marriage, all of whom were considerably older than Nell. But by the time Joanne gave birth to a second daughter, **Melissa Newman** (the daughter who was nicknamed after Joanne's favorite character, Lissy) in September 1961, domestic harmony seemed restored. Both parents were intent on giving the children as normal a life as possible. "As a child, my parents hid me from the theater, the press, and all those other chaotic elements," Scott Newman, Paul's eldest son, later said. To prove their point, the Newmans returned to the East Coast and bought a house in Westport, Connecticut, where Paul's older children attended local schools, and the family lived as quietly as possible in between pictures.

After playing the real-life part of mother and homemaker for nearly a year, it must have been with some degree of irony that Woodward chose as her next film role a fading showgirl who can only keep working by turning to stripping. Her work in *The Stripper* (for which Joanne was coached by *Gypsy Rose Lee, who has a small part in the picture) was followed by the kind of film with Newman she had sworn she would never do again—a sex comedy called *A New Kind of Love*, in which Newman played a sports journalist who mistakes Woodward's fashion-model character for a high-priced call girl. Both pictures performed poorly at the box office. Friends concerned about Joanne's career urged her to be more careful about her roles and her image . . . *any* image, since it was apparent the public preferred stars, not actors. "It isn't important for me to have an image," Woodward insisted. "If you have an identifiable personality, you end up playing the same role all the time." (Newman, on the other hand, was solidifying his image as the rugged, brooding leading man with the successful release of *Hud* and *The Prize*.) Once again abandoning Hollywood, the couple returned East to star in an Actors Studio production of a new play by James Costigan called *Baby Want a Kiss?* that played to sold-out houses for four months.

After the show closed, Woodward retired to Connecticut to give birth, in April 1963, to her third daughter, **Claire Newman**, nicknamed Clea. But she returned to work in two films she hoped would help restore her career after several mediocre and, sometimes, disastrous films. (*Signpost to Murder*, shot before her pregnancy but not released until after it, had been so poorly received that some critics predicted her career was over.) The first new project was a comedy set in the Old West, *A Big Hand for the Little*

Lady, in which she played Henry Fonda's poker-playing wife; in the second, she was Sean Connery's wife in *A Fine Madness*. Although both pictures played well, neither was the major vehicle Woodward was looking for. She realized she would have to try something more daring to regain her professional footing. She candidly admitted that raising a family and pursuing an acting career were not compatible activities, and that she now wanted to focus on her work. "I've done my bit for the population explosion," she said in 1966, "and raised the children to where I feel I'm not depriving them if I'm working." Newman, too, was looking for a new challenge after a successful string of what he called his "H" pictures—*The Hustler, Hud,* and *Harper,* in all of which he had played the tough. The result was another joint venture between husband and wife, but this time Newman would direct Woodward. "Why merely be a first violinist," he said, "when you feel you can conduct?"

Rachel, Rachel did for Woodward's later career what *Three Faces* had done for her early working years. Newman himself had developed the adaptation of *Margaret Laurence's *A Jest of God,* about a prim New England schoolteacher forced to face her inhibitions; but Warner Bros. was the only studio that would take the picture on, despite the value of his name on any film, and only if Newman and Woodward would accept a percentage of the box office rather than a salary. Further, Newman would have to agree to star in two future pictures of Warner's choosing. "So much for loyalty," Newman groused, although the project was important enough to both of them that the terms were accepted. Shooting began in the summer of 1967, not far from the couple's Westport home, and all went smoothly despite dire predictions that an actor-husband could never direct his actor-wife. (The couple's eldest daughter Nell also had a part in the film, playing Rachel as a child.) "Who could direct better than the person you live with?" Joanne later said. "He knows all there is to know about you." After six weeks of shooting and eight months of meticulous editing, *Rachel, Rachel* premiered in New York and Los Angeles in the fall of 1968 to great acclaim. "Beautifully sensitive," one critic wrote of Woodward's performance, while another thought the picture was "visually impressive and compelling." The picture garnered an armful of Academy Award nominations—for Best Picture, for Joanne as Best Actress, and for screenwriter Stewart Stern for his work in adapting Laurence's novel to the screen. Woodward won the Hollywood Foreign Press Association's Golden Globe for Best Actress while Newman won the same for Best Director for

his work; and the National Board of Review named the picture one of the best English-language films of 1968. "I guess *Rachel* has revived my career," Woodward finally admitted. "Some people thought I'd gone underground."

But the increased public scrutiny after their success proved difficult. There were reports of Newman's problems with alcohol and of strains within the marriage. Gossip columns claimed the pair intended to divorce, forcing them to take an ad in *The Los Angeles Times* denying the reports and leading Paul to famously declare that "for two people with almost nothing in common, we have an uncommonly good marriage." Paul's infatuation with race-car driving, born from his research in preparation for the racing film *Winning,* and Woodward's mounting anxiety for his physical safety, added further tension, as did the worsening alcoholism of Newman's eldest son Scott, now 19 and said to be psychologically troubled. Within the film business, traditionally conservative Hollywood worried about the couple's political liberalism, Woodward being a vocal supporter of Planned Parenthood and several environmental and feminist causes, while Newman was said to be contemplating a run for one of Connecticut's Senate seats at the urging of Gore Vidal. (Newman ultimately chose not to run.) Both of them were openly critical of the Nixon administration. "I am in despair about this country," Woodward said, "and working very hard to do something about it in as many ways as I can."

Propelled by the success of *Rachel, Rachel,* she returned to film work nearly fulltime; but while Newman's career went from strength to strength with such films as *Butch Cassidy and the Sundance Kid* and *The Sting,* Woodward's failed to reach similar heights. "He's the big movie star, and I'm the character actress," she said after the lukewarm reception for her next film, *They Might Be Giants,* a dark comedy in which she played a psychiatrist who becomes involved in the fantasy of one of her patients, played by George C. Scott. Hopes rose when Newman directed her a second time in the film version of the Broadway play *The Effect of Gamma Rays on Man-in-the-Moon Marigolds,* but a slow-paced adaptation and Joanne's painful portrayal of a monstrous mother who dominates and bullies her daughters again left audiences cold. Drawing on her Actors Studio training, she was so submersed in the character's self-loathing that it took a toll, and the entire family avoided her even at home. It wasn't until 1973's *Summer Wishes, Winter Dreams* that critics and audiences alike were again drawn to Woodward's meticulous character work as she portrayed a middle-aged woman's efforts to conquer sexual frigidity. The role brought her a second Academy Award nomination.

Tragedy struck the Newmans in 1978 when Scott Newman died of a drug and alcohol overdose. Although Scott's interest in acting and his budding career in small film roles had been a bond with his father (he had had a small part in *Towering Inferno*, in which Newman starred), relations between the two had been distant. Scott was said to resent his father's abandonment of his mother Jacqueline Witte and to have never felt comfortable in the new family Newman built with Joanne. The family did not attend the public memorial service for Scott, Newman remaining at Kenyon College in Ohio, his alma mater, where he had agreed to direct a student production. Later, however, he and Joanne created and endowed the Scott Newman Foundation for troubled young people.

Woodward herself didn't return to feature film work until the mid-1980s. She decided, instead, to return to the medium that had given her a start in the business, appearing in a string of quality television movies. "See How She Runs," about a bored housewife who wins the Boston Marathon, won her an Emmy Award, as did her portrayal of a woman suffering the first stages of Alzheimer's disease in "Do You Remember Love?" It wasn't until 1990 that she turned in another of her signature feature film performances, and once again with her husband, in *Mr. and Mrs. Bridge*, a touching domestic drama set during the 1930s and 1940s based on the three "Bridge" novels by Evan S. Connell. The role brought her a third Academy Award nomination. It was quickly followed by a third Emmy nomination for her performance as the hapless Maggie Moran in the television adaptation of Anne Tyler's *Breathing Lessons*.

With her marriage to Paul Newman intact and thriving and unqualified recognition as one of America's finest actresses of the second half of the 20th century, Joanne Woodward can look back on a satisfying, if occasionally tumultuous, personal and professional life. But looking back isn't Woodward's style. "You never really make it once and for all," she has said. "Every new part, every picture, you have to make it all over again."

SOURCES:

Katz, Ephraim. *The Film Encyclopedia.* 2nd ed. NY: HarperCollins, 1994.

Morella, Joe, and Edward Epstein. *Paul and Joanne.* NY: Delacorte, 1988.

Norman Powers,
writer-producer, Chelsea Lane Productions,
New York, New York

Woolf, Virginia (1882–1941)

Major 20th-century British novelist who, besides being one of the chief architects of the modern novel, was a pioneer in the use of the literary technique of stream-of-consciousness. Name variations: Virginia Stephen. Born Adeline Virginia Stephen on January 25, 1882, at 22 Hyde Park Gate, in Kensington, London; drowned herself in the River Ouse near Monk's House in Rodmell on March 28, 1941, at age 59; daughter of Sir Leslie Stephen (an editor, critic, historian) and Julia (Jackson Duckworth) Stephen; educated mostly by home tutoring; later took Greek and history classes at King's College, London, prior to studying with Janet Case, graduate of Girton College; married Leonard Woolf (a writer, publisher, and editor), on August 10, 1912; no children.

Grew up in and around London, in low end of upper-middle-class Victorian household, where she remained throughout her life, in addition to regular stays at a country retreat; mother died when she was 13; oldest half-sister and mother-substitute, Stella Duckworth, died two years later; experienced the first serious signs of mental illness that shadowed and, ultimately, claimed her life; in adolescence, authored the Hyde Park Gate News; *began to keep a diary, which she sustained during various periods throughout her life (1897); had second breakdown and made first suicide attempt (1904), following her father's death by cancer; became a part of the Bloomsbury group of Cambridge intellectuals and published her first article in* The Guardian *(1904); after establishing a career in writing through reviews and criticism, embarked on a remarkable literary career that would see her become a novelist of the first order; published her first novel,* The Voyage Out *(1915); suffered two more breakdowns (1910, 1913), resulting in extended "rest cures" and a second suicide attempt (1913); besides activity in the women's suffrage movement, enrolled in Women's Co-operative Guild (1915); established Hogarth House with Leonard Woolf, publishing the work of renowned writers like James Joyce and T.S. Eliot in addition to their own writing (1917); active in the "1917 Club," a resurgence of Bloomsbury intellectuals and antiwar socialists; saw the publication of Hogarth Press' first full-length novel, Woolf's* Jacob's Room *(1922); published* Orlando—*based on love affair with Vita Sackville-West—which marked an upward turn in her commercial and critical success (1928); gave famous lectures on "Women and Fiction" at Girton and Newnham Colleges (1928) which became the basis for that most original of feminist tracts,* A Room of One's Own; *continued writing and publishing throughout middle age, her literary accomplishments alternating with mental breakdowns.*

Selected works: The Voyage Out *(Duckworth, 1915);* The Mark on the Wall *(Hogarth, 1917);* Kew Gardens *(Hogarth, 1919);* Night and Day *(Duckworth, 1919);* Monday or Tuesday *(Hogarth, 1921);* Jacob's Room *(Hogarth, 1922);* Mr. Bennett and Mrs. Brown *(Hogarth, 1924);* The Common Reader *(Hogarth, 1925);* Mrs. Dalloway *(Hogarth, 1925);* To the Lighthouse *(Hogarth, 1927);* Orlando: A Biography *(Hogarth, 1928);* A Room of One's Own *(Hogarth, 1929);* The Waves *(Hogarth, 1931);* Letter to a Young Poet *(Hogarth, 1932);* The Common Reader: Second Series *(Hogarth, 1932);* Flush: A Biography *(Hogarth, 1933);* Walter Sickert: A Conversation *(Hogarth, 1934);* The Years *(Hogarth, 1937);* Three Guineas *(Hogarth, 1938);* Roger Fry: A Biography *(Hogarth, 1940);* Between the Acts *(Hogarth, 1941);* A Writer's Diary *(ed. by Leonard Woolf, Hogarth, 1953).*

Posthumous publications: (ed. by Leonard Woolf) A Writer's Diary *(Hogarth, 1953);* The Death of the Moth and other Essays *(Hogarth, 1942);* A Haunted House and other Short Stories *(Hogarth, 1943);* The Moment and Other Essays *(Hogarth, 1947);* The Captain's Death Bed and Other Essays *(Hogarth, 1950);* Granite and Rainbow *(Hogarth, 1958);* Contemporary Writers *(Hogarth, 1965);* Collected Essays *(Hogarth, 4 vols., 1966–67); (ed. by Leonard Woolf and James Strachey)* Virginia Woolf & Lytton Strachey: Letters *(Hogarth & Chatto & Windus, 1956).*

Unquestionably, Adeline Virginia Stephen Woolf was born and bred to be a writer. No angel in her middle-class household, she resisted the Victorian ideal of womanhood that sent her mother and older sister prematurely to their graves. As with all artists, separating the life from the work, the personal demons from the creative genius, requires delicate critical surgery. One of the most important novelists of her century, man or woman, Virginia Woolf has also been one of the most intriguing, particularly to biographers intent on explaining the origins of her lifelong "madness." Even more beguiling was the stable conventional life that gave rise to her singular literary genius, combined with the intermittent yet relentless bouts of mental illness.

She was born in 1882 at 22 Hyde Park Gate, London, to **Julia Jackson Duckworth Stephen** and Leslie Stephen. Both were widowers before coming to this second marriage with four children already between them: George, Gerald and **Stella Duckworth** from Julia's first marriage to Herbert Duckworth, and **Laura Stephen** from Leslie's marriage to **Harriet Thackeray**, daughter

of the novelist. Julia and Leslie added four more children to the brood: *****Vanessa Bell** (1879), Adeline Virginia (1882), Thoby (1880) and Adrian (1883). Well bred and literate, both parents had a hand in the children's schooling, particularly with that of the girls who were educated at home. Julia was more renowned for her compassion and charitable acts, although she is also credited with having published a manual on "how to manage sick rooms" in 1883, according to biographer-critic Lyndall Gordon. Leslie fancied himself a philosopher and man of the pen. Together, the parents apparently fashioned a strict but intellectually stimulating and nurturing atmosphere in a household that consisted of eight children, seven servants and a dog or two. This image of the stable Victorian home, as projected by biographer and nephew Quentin Bell, has been challenged by other biographers like **Louise DeSalvo**. Not only was Laura Stephen viewed as incorrigible, she was also confined to a separate part of the house from childhood onward, much like *****Charlotte Brontë**'s "mad woman of the attic." Moreover, both Vanessa and Virginia suffered sexual abuse at the hands of their half-brother George Duckworth. Whether or not these aspects of her home life caused her lifelong instability can never be proved with certainty. But her childhood experience with sexual abuse and her sister's perceived insanity certainly had to figure into Virginia's compromised mental health.

Nevertheless, Woolf's giftedness became evident early on in the *Hyde Park Gate News*, which she "published" weekly from the age of nine until thirteen or so. She used such journalistic writing as a kind of apprenticeship throughout her youth and early adulthood, eventually developing into an adept and able professional writer of reviews and criticism. These efforts, besides providing her with a livelihood most uncommon for a Victorian woman, also formed a solid base for her most mature and original fictional writing. In addition to the juvenilia, her precocity was also evident in her insatiable appetite for books, particularly the English classics. Her father maintained an extensive library and took pride in his daughter's voracious literary appetite. According to Quentin Bell, Leslie also encouraged his daughter to be an independent thinker and to "learn to read with discrimination, to make unaffected judgments, never admiring because the world admires or blaming at the order of a critic." While she took his admonishment to heart with respect to her judgment of others, she suffered from severe hypersensitivity to any criticism of her own work.

Her mother's death when Virginia was 13 not only put an end to the *Hyde Park Gate News*, it also cast a pall over Leslie and the entire household and made the way for Virginia's first serious breakdown. It was at this time that her half-brother's unwanted sexual advances were occur-

ring and, as expressed in her diary and paraphrased in the Bell biography, "spoilt her life before it had fairly begun." Stella Duckworth was compelled to replace her mother in the caregiving role, most particularly as it related to the demanding and inconsolable widower. Stella's untimely death within just two years of her mother's left the females of the house, Vanessa and Virginia, prey to Leslie's gloom and extravagant demand for sympathy, especially female sympathy.

In the absence of their mother's and older sister's protection, both Virginia and Vanessa became prey to half-brother George Duckworth's conventional notions regarding females and their "proper" introduction to society. He escorted them in public, saw to their wardrobe and manners, and in all ways acted the part of the ingratiating patron. Though uncomfortable, they had little choice in the matter. Their father's prolonged death by cancer in 1904 initially rendered them even more vulnerable to George's unwanted advances and involvement in their lives. After her father's death, Virginia experienced a second breakdown that saw her first suicide attempt during a stay at the home of a close friend, **Violet Dickinson**. Her mental illness ultimately extricated her from her London home, however, as well as from her half-brother's strangle-hold. Moreover, Virginia's intimacy with Violet Dickinson established a kind of template for the powerful female friendships and love affairs yet to come in Virginia's life, the most famous one being the love affair with *Vita Sackville-West.

A woman must have money and a room of her own if she is to write fiction.

—Virginia Woolf

But her mental illness did not prevent her from publishing her very first article—a book review—in *The Guardian* (December 1904). By 1905, Virginia Woolf was a published writer with an established career. She had also moved, along with her sister and two brothers, from the Kensington home of their childhood to Bloomsbury, where the Bloomsbury group of Cambridge intellectuals was born. Younger brother Thoby enjoyed all the privileges of an upper-middle-class male, which, of course, meant that a Cambridge education was emphatically denied to Virginia and her sister. This prejudice aggrieved Woolf greatly, but she did manage to enjoy the benefits of the regular gathering of Thoby's fellow students at 46 Gordon Square, including such prominent people (to be) as John Maynard Keynes, Lytton Strachey, Clive Bell and her future husband Leonard Woolf. Even more than the heady intellectual air of the Bloomsbury group, Virginia enjoyed being freed from the marriage market and social designs of George Duckworth and the narrow strictures of Victorian society.

By 1905, at age 23, Woolf was writing for *The Times Literary Supplement*, participating in her sister Vanessa's fine arts group, the "Friday Club," and instructing young working adults in the evening at Morley College. Besides taking classes in Greek and Latin at King's College, she was also tutored by **Janet Case**, one of the first graduates of Girton College, the institution for women that figures so prominently in Woolf's later work, the influential feminist tract *A Room of One's Own* (1929). Later, under Case's influence, she also took up the cause of women's suffrage, although Woolf always leaned more toward the aesthetic than to the political both in her life and in her work.

Tragedy once again struck the Stephen family when young Thoby contracted typhoid fever and died in November 1906. Shortly afterwards, Vanessa married Clive Bell and Virginia was compelled to move to a flat in Fitzroy Square with a younger, duller, and less companionable brother Adrian Stephen. But the Bloomsbury group was recycled and Virginia continued to sharpen her intellect as well as her writing techniques in the company of, among others, Lytton Strachey, critic, literary rival, and lifelong friend.

The year 1909 sounded the death knell of the Bloomsbury group, as Vanessa, an aspiring painter, and her husband Clive Bell grew more interested in the fine arts. A year later, Virginia succumbed to yet another breakdown and, under the care of a Dr. Savage, was advised to remove herself entirely from the hustle and bustle of London life and to undergo a rest "cure" at a home in Twickenham. Woolf was forced to submit to such treatments periodically, although the lack of intellectual and social stimulation they required seemed at times to engender rather than to relieve her anxiety. Famed feminist writer *Charlotte Perkins Gilman provides a scathing but telling fictional account of such cures in *The Yellow Wallpaper*, which is based on her own experience with the male medical model for the treatment of mental illness in women at that time. While it is unlikely that Woolf knew of Gilman's account, she certainly shared her experience of helplessness and victimization, resulting not only from the illness but also from patriarchal society's lack of understanding and questionable methods in dealing with it.

With age, the Stephen sisters grew more unconventional, no doubt to the dismay of Mr. "Victorian" Duckworth. By 1911, Vanessa's marriage to Clive Bell had disintegrated and she took up with an artist, Roger Fry, while Virginia shared a home at Brunswick Square with Adrian and several friends, including Maynard Keynes and Leonard Woolf. This form of communal living in the early 1900s had to be viewed as no less than outrageous. But, characteristically, Virginia balked at social prescriptions for women and revelled in the relaxed egalitarian atmosphere of her primarily male circle. She apparently agonized over whether or not she might find a suitable marriage partner, and experienced some jealousy of Vanessa's more successful love life. By 1912, after some initial misgivings, she agreed to marry Leonard Woolf, but not before experiencing another relapse that once again found her installed at the Twickenham home. The signs were always the same—depression, headaches, sleeplessness, inability to eat—and, worst of all, during her most severe bouts, she heard voices. After their marriage, Leonard kept a strict accounting of these periods of "illness," and in many ways he functioned as her caretaker—looking after her, consulting with specialists, removing her from town life and the activity which apparently promoted the anxiety that precipitated her periodic breakdowns. In consultation with her doctors, they agreed it would not be advisable for Virginia to have children, a choice which dismayed her.

They were married on August 10, 1912, at the St. Pancras Registry Office before honeymooning abroad, and thus began a reasonably successful social and intellectual, if not sexual, union: "Their love and admiration for each other," wrote Quentin Bell, "based as it was upon a real understanding of the good qualities in each, was strong enough to withstand the major and minor punishments of fortune, the common vexations of matrimony and, presently, the horrors of madness." Virginia had found her long-sought intellectual equal and worthy companion in Leonard. He was a well-educated man of the world, having lived and worked for the British government in Ceylon (now Sri Lanka), and was a writer himself. Ironically, however, he was the man behind the famous woman, as his writing never achieved the quality or stature of his wife's. But he was intelligent enough to recognize superior work, and demonstrated this with the co-founding (with Virginia) of Hogarth Press in 1915. In March of that same year, Virginia published her first novel, *The Voyage Out*, to enthusiastic reviews, including one by the well-respected writer E.M. Forster. But prior to both these achievements, she had already experienced her first post-marriage breakdown, during which she made another unsuccessful suicide attempt with an overdose of prescription medication. Another Dr. Savage rest-cure, followed by a period of recuperation at the home of George Duckworth, with the support of Leonard, close

friend **Ka Cox**, and a team of nurses, finally resulted in her recovery. But as Quentin Bell notes, "It was one of the horrors of Virginia's madness that she was sane enough to recognise her own insanity." The madness persisted in shadowing her life. Woolf, the writer, captured this experience in one of her most mature novels, *Mrs. Dalloway*. Through the character of Septimus Smith, whose eerie descent into madness and suicide we witness, Woolf captures the machinations of her own demons which she could not kill off, either in or through her fiction.

Throughout most of their married life, Virginia and Leonard maintained a home in the city (Richmond, Bloomsbury) along with a country retreat (Asham, Monk's House). Virginia nurtured fond memories of the Talland House of her childhood, the beach home in St. Ives that is thought to be the basis for the Ramsey resort in one of her most well-known novels, *To the Lighthouse*. Although she could not recapture the carefreeness associated with those early summers, retaining a country home relieved her from the stresses of her social and professional life. It also allowed her to enjoy the arduous rambling walks she so enjoyed, as did her father and grandfather before her; Lyndall Gordon points up the uncanny parallel between her physical and mental exertions: "As though she were tracking a metaphor for her future work, she followed natural paths which ignored artificial boundaries." Indeed, her novels' success depended "on their conclusions where she would justify the mind's keen ramble by some astonishing find." In her fiction, too, not inclined to stay on the well-trod conventional path, Virginia Woolf insisted on exploring the intricate streams of the mind and on investigating the different levels of reality. Content and form merge harmoniously as her best work—*Mrs. Dalloway, To the Lighthouse, The Waves*—succeeds in capturing these streams and levels simultaneously and brilliantly. In this mature work, Quentin Bell points out, we also see her conscious efforts to make literature "radial" rather than "linear." In a 1919 essay entitled "Modern Fiction," Woolf, the self-conscious critic as well as the creative writer, contended that "true knowledge resides in the interior of the narrator and her subject, not in the external details of life." In line with the shift to a modern consciousness that occurred in the early 20th century, Virginia Woolf's writing reflects this emphasis on the inner truth and self. According to Quentin Bell, Woolf saw herself and others like her as making major aesthetic breakthroughs. Hers is a startling achievement, as she helped to refashion the novel, thus reflecting the significant epistemological developments of her era.

From 1915 until 1931, Woolf wrote prolifically and produced some of the major work of her career. Quentin Bell tells us that she fell into a pattern, in which an intense and serious-minded effort was invariably followed by a lighter, less taxing one. For example, *To the Lighthouse* was succeeded by *Orlando*, which was written as a lark and a kind of love letter to Vita Sackville-West. In the book *Orlando*, the protagonist who is inexplicably transformed into a woman, also mysteriously traverses several centuries. During the course of his/her astonishing journey, Orlando learns that, essentially, a woman is no different from a man save as society views and treats her. The ambiguity of his/her sexual identity also casts the issue of same-sex love in an unconventional but more accepting light, that is, it is not one's sex that we love but one's inner person and gender is an accidental rather than a defining aspect of one's self. In her 1994 film adaptation of *Orlando*, **Sally Potter** renders Woolf's poignant playfulness in strikingly visual terms. The film's self-consciousness—reflected in Orlando's relationship with the camera—parallels the meta-narrative at work in Woolf's frisky yet earnest novel.

But despite her literary achievement and the recognition it engendered, Virginia Woolf could not escape the monster of madness that persisted in haunting her. In a diary entry of 1926, she likened its relentless attacks to a "fin rising on a wide blank sea." *Orlando* (1928) marked a turning point in her career, one that saw her reputation cinched and her bank account assured. Moreover, loath to accept awards or honorary degrees, she nevertheless agreed that same year to accept a French prize, the Femina Vie Heureuse, and the small sum it brought. But her formidable accomplishments failed to subdue the "fin" rising out of the darkness. Having lived through one war, during the 1930s she watched as the world took on Hitler and the fascist threat, dismayed that violence and military might were necessary to subdue them. She disapproved of her husband's aggressive stance and disagreed with her nephew Julian Bell's decision in 1937 to join the crusade against Francisco Franco in Spain. His death seemed unnecessary and no less acceptable for his idealism. The decade of the 1930s saw the death of other good friends as well, like Lytton Strachey, Janet Case, and her sister's lover, Roger Fry. In addition to these inestimable losses, Woolf's predisposition to gloom was also exacerbated by the movement toward leftist politics in literature, which had to be anathema to Woolf and her band of aesthetes. But the overriding factor in her despondency during this period emanated from the onslaught of increasingly hostile criticism of her work, particularly that of Wyndham Lewis.

Virginia and Leonard made a suicide pact, according to Quentin Bell, in the event that Hitler was successful. After all, Leonard was a Jew and the prospects of a Nazi takeover were frightening. That agreement obviously proved unnecessary, and the two went on as usual, Virginia with her writing (*Three Guineas*, an anti-war novel, and *The Years*), and Leonard with his editorship as well as with the ever-expanding Hogarth Press. But Virginia's "madness" again resurfaced and this time she felt totally hopeless and incapable of wrestling with it. She wrote her last words, a touching farewell to her best friend and husband, placed some stones in her pockets and walked into the River Ouse.

Known for her acute sensitivity to criticism and occasional professional jealousies, Virginia Woolf is better remembered, indeed, revered, for her daring in art and for her long battle against the inexplicable illness that claimed the woman and stole one of the century's finest and most extraordinary writers. It remains ironic that Virginia Woolf's most memorable words are contained in a feminist tract that has influenced generations of feminists, despite having been penned by a writer whose work was characteristically apolitical.

SOURCES:

Bell, Quentin. *Virginia Woolf: A Biography*. NY: Harcourt, Brace, Jovanovich, 1972.

DeSalvo, Louise. *Virginia Woolf: The Impact of Childhood Sexual Abuse on Her Life and Work*. Boston, MA: Beacon, 1989.

Gordon, Lyndall. *Virginia Woolf; A Writer's Life*. NY: W.W. Norton, 1984.

Mepham, John. *Criticism in Focus: Virginia Woolf*. NY: St. Martin's, 1992.

Woolf, Virginia. *A Room of One's Own*. NY: Harcourt, Brace, Jovanovich, 1957.

SUGGESTED READING:

King, James. *Virginia Woolf*. NY: Norton, 1995.

Leaska, Mitchell. *Granite and Rainbow: The Life of Virginia Woolf*. NY: Farrar, Straus & Giroux, 1998.

Lee, Hermione. *Virginia Woolf*. NY: Alfred A. Knopf, 1997.

Nicholson, Nigel. *Virginia Woolf: A Penguin Life*. NY: Viking, 2000.

COLLECTIONS:

The Berg Collection; the New York Public Library; The Monk's House papers at the University of Sussex; and the Charleston papers at King's College, Cambridge.

RELATED MEDIA:

Orlando (93 min. film), starring **Tilda Swinton**, Billy Zane, and Lothaire Bluteau, with Quentin Crisp as Queen *Elizabeth I, directed by Sally Potter, 1994.

A Room of One's Own (play), adapted by Patrick Garland, starred **Eileen Atkins**, and opened off-Broadway in New York in March 1991 (also first aired on PBS "Masterpiece Theater," in 1992).

Virginia Woolf's Mrs. Dalloway (film), starring **Vanessa Redgrave, Natascha McElhone**, and Rupert Graves, 1998.

Vita & Virginia (play based on the letters of Woolf and Sackville-West), written by Eileen Atkins, starred **Vanessa Redgrave** and Atkins, directed by **Zoe Caldwell**, opened off-Broadway at Union Square Theater in December 1994.

Kathleen A. Waites Lamm,
Professor of English and Women's Studies,
Nova Southeastern University, Fort Lauderdale, Florida

Woolgar, Sarah Jane (1824–1909).

See Mellon, Sarah Jane.

Woolley, Helen (1874–1947)

American psychologist who was one of the first to study child development. Born Helen Bradford Thompson on November 6, 1874, in Chicago, Illinois; died of an aortic aneurysm on December 24, 1947, in Havertown, Pennsylvania; daughter of David Wallace Thompson and Isabella Perkins (Faxon) Thompson; graduated from Englewood High School; University of Chicago, Ph.B., 1897, Ph.D., 1900; studied in Paris and Berlin; married Paul Gerhardt Woolley (a physician), in 1905 (separated 1924); children: Eleanor Faxon Woolley; Charlotte Gerhardt Woolley.

Born in 1874 in Chicago, Illinois, Helen Woolley was the daughter of David Wallace Thompson, a shoe manufacturer, and **Isabella Faxon Thompson**. She attended public schools before entering the University of Chicago, where she majored in psychology and philosophy. She earned a bachelor of philosophy degree in 1897, and in 1900 completed her doctorate in psychology. This was followed by a year of study in Paris and Berlin through a fellowship from the Association of Collegiate Alumnae (later the American Association of University Women), after which she became an instructor at Mt. Holyoke College in South Hadley, Massachusetts. In 1902, she became director of the psychological lab and professor of psychology there. Her dissertation appeared in print in 1903 under two titles, *Psychological Norms in Men and Women* and *Mental Traits of Sex*.

In 1905 she resigned from Mt. Holyoke and traveled to Yokohama, Japan, where she married Paul Gerhardt Woolley, a physician whom she had known at the University of Chicago. Settling in Manila in the Philippines, they would

have two daughters, **Eleanor Faxon Woolley** (b. 1907) and **Charlotte Gerhardt Woolley** (b. 1914). In Manila, Woolley worked as an experimental psychologist in the Philippines Bureau of Education, while her husband served as director of the Serum Laboratory.

In April 1906, the family moved to Bangkok, Thailand, where Paul Woolley had been appointed director of a new laboratory; in 1907 he was promoted to chief inspector of health. The family eventually returned to the U.S. to settle in Cincinnati, Ohio, where Paul and Helen both taught at the University of Cincinnati. In 1911 Helen was named director of the new Bureau for the Investigation of Working Children. In that capacity, she developed the Cincinnati Vocation Bureau in 1914 as a part of the public school system, and conducted studies of the impaired physical and mental development of working children compared to non-working children. Her findings were published in parts between 1914 and 1923, and in 1926 as the comprehensive work *An Experimental Study of Children at Work and in School between the Ages of Fourteen and Eighteen Years*. Throughout the years of her research at the Bureau, Woolley used her studies to advocate compulsory school attendance and a new child labor law in Ohio. The result, the Bing Law of 1921, would become a model bill for other states.

In addition, during World War I Woolley served on the Council of National Defense and worked to set up a scholarship fund, which became part of the Cincinnati War Chest. She was elected president of the National Vocational Guidance Association in 1921, and participated on the boards of the Cincinnati Community Chest and the Woman's City Club. A longtime activist on behalf of women's suffrage, she was chair of the Ohio Women's Suffrage Committee of Greater Cincinnati until the 19th Amendment securing women's suffrage was ratified. Woolley also showed courage in fighting for the progressive causes she believed in, for example when in 1921 she led a walkout from a professional meeting when a black colleague was mistreated by the staff of the hotel hosting the event.

In 1921, the Woolley family moved to Detroit, where Helen was appointed the staff psychologist at the Merrill-Palmer School, established by *Lizzie Merrill Palmer; the next year, she was named associate director of the school. In this capacity Woolley organized one of the first nursery schools in the nation and researched children's personality and mental development patterns. Her findings led to several publications in professional journals, as well as to a teaching position at the University of Michigan. She worked with **Elizabeth Cleveland**, a graduate student at the University of Michigan, to investigate the effectiveness of *Maria Montessori's pedagogical work.

A frequent public speaker, Woolley was active in women's groups, educational organizations, and scientific societies. Other articles appeared in popular journals, such as *Mother and Child*, *Child Study*, and *New Republic*, and did much to spread the scientific understanding of child psychology to parents. As vice-president of the American Association of University Women (1923–25) and chair of its committee on educational policy, Woolley began a program for studying preschool children, designed to promote interest in education and child welfare studies among women college graduates. The program was funded by a grant from the *Laura Spelman Rockefeller Memorial Fund.

By 1924, Woolley's marriage had failed, and she separated from her husband, who moved to California. In 1925, at age 50, she became professor of education and director of the new Institute of Child Welfare Research at the Teachers College of Columbia University in New York. In 1926, depression over the end of her marriage, loneliness, and ill health led her to take a two-year leave from Columbia, during which she traveled in Europe to visit psychological research institutes. She returned in 1928, but the decline in her effectiveness as a teacher and interest in research caused the college to request her resignation in 1930.

She moved in with her daughter Eleanor in Havertown, Pennsylvania. Despite her long career of scientific achievement in the field of child psychology and her social activism, Woolley's final years passed in obscurity. Her last publication was a chapter in *A Handbook of Child Psychology* (1931) titled "Eating, Sleeping, and Elimination." Helen Thompson Woolley died in December 1947 of heart disease, age 73.

SOURCES:

James, Edward T., ed. *Notable American Women, 1607–1950*. Cambridge, MA: The Belknap Press of Harvard University, 1971.

Laura York, M.A. in History,
University of California,
Riverside, California

Woolley, Mary E. (1863–1947)

American educator, college president, and activist.
Born Mary Emma Woolley on July 13, 1863, in South Norwalk, Connecticut; died on September 5, 1947, in Westport, New York; daughter of Joseph Judah Woolley (a Congregational cleric) and Mary Augusta (Ferris) Woolley (a schoolteacher); educated at Mrs. Fannie Augur's school in Meriden, Connecticut; attended schools of Miss Bliss, Mrs. Lord, and Mrs. Davis in Pawtucket, Rhode Island; Providence High School, Rhode Island; graduated from Wheaton Seminary (now College), 1884; one of the first seven women admitted to Brown University, A.B., 1894, M.A. in history, 1895, Ph.D., 1900; became first woman senator in Phi Beta Kappa, 1907; studied educational problems in Great Britain, 1900.

The first child of cleric Joseph Judah Woolley and schoolteacher **Mary Ferris Woolley**, Mary E. Woolley was born on July 13, 1863, in South Norwalk, Connecticut. When she was eight, the family moved to Pawtucket, Rhode Island, where Woolley was educated at home and at small private girls' schools. Growing up, she was deeply influenced by her parents' religious devotion, pacifist beliefs, and dedication to serving God through social reform and improving the lives of the working class. She attended high school in Providence but finished her secondary education in 1884 at Wheaton Seminary in Norton, Massachusetts. After teaching there for five years, Woolley traveled to Europe, where she observed the educational opportunities available to European women and decided to pursue a higher education. She was one of the first group of seven women admitted to Brown University in 1891. After spending the first few months as a "guest" in men's classes, Woolley joined the separate classes opened for women. An exceptional student and a natural leader, she earned her bachelor's degree in three years, graduating with one other woman student in 1894. After a further year of study, she earned a master's degree in history. She would publish three historical articles in the 1890s.

In 1895, Woolley accepted a position as instructor of Biblical history and literature at Wellesley College; by 1899 she was a full professor. A popular teacher, at Wellesley she introduced new elective courses in church history and headed her department, as well as serving as head of a large dormitory. In 1899, Woolley was offered two considerable appointments, as dean of the women's college at Brown University, and as president of Mt. Holyoke College in South Hadley, Massachusetts, replacing *Elizabeth Storrs Mead. She accepted Mt. Holyoke's offer, but delayed beginning work there until 1901, after studying a year in England. She would remain president of Mt. Holyoke for over three decades.

Woolley's long tenure is seen as crucial in the development of Mt. Holyoke, one of the most respected of American women's colleges. She continued the tradition of Mt. Holyoke's founder *Mary Lyon, who emphasized scholarship as well as community and religious service. She doubled the size of the faculty and improved it by raising salaries and establishing sabbaticals for research, increasing academic freedom in teaching, and publicly recognizing her faculty's achievements. She also set up fellowships for needy students, and made Mt. Holyoke a member of the Carnegie Foundation's pension program.

The college's students benefited from Woolley's curriculum reforms. She extended the proportion of free electives in the program, and introduced honors courses and comprehensive exams in major fields of study. In addition, she loosened regulations which required students to belong to the Congregationalist Church, allowing students of any denomination to attend. She consistently refused efforts by the college's board to implement a home economics program, believing that would be detrimental to the college's mission. Woolley also replaced the YWCA with a "Fellowship of Faiths."

To inspire her students, Woolley frequently brought guest speakers to campus. To maintain an open collegiate environment, she decided to end secret societies and implemented an honor system for both social and academic responsibility. Woolley was also a tireless fund raiser, despite her personal distaste for it, and saw the college's endowment grow from less than $1 million to almost $5 million during her presidency.

A dedicated instructor and administrator, Woolley served on many educational boards and conducted research on ways to improve higher education throughout her career. She was the first woman senator of Phi Beta Kappa, served as chair of the College Entrance Examination Board (1924–27), and led the movement to improve funding and academic standards at American women's colleges. She was also active in federal conferences on education and child-care issues, and from 1921 to 1922 traveled across China for the Foreign Missions Conference, observing educational institutions. A member of the advisory board of the American Association of Labor Legislation, Woolley opposed sweatshops and urged consumers to boycott the products of sweatshop labor.

Always active in spiritual causes as well, Woolley was made chair of the Federal Council of Churches in 1936, served as honorary moderator for the General Council of the Congrega-

tional-Christian Churches, and was vice-president of the American Peace Society from 1907 to 1913. A leader in the women's peace movement which preceded World War I, Woolley remained dedicated to fostering international understanding all of her life. She was appointed by President Herbert Hoover to represent the United States at the Geneva Conference on Reduction and Limitation of Armaments in 1932, the first woman to represent the nation at a major diplomatic event. As chair of the Peoples' Mandate to End War in 1936, she recommended economic sanctions as an alternative to military action. Besides the peace movement, Woolley was also closely associated with the woman suffrage movement, and among other achievements cofounded the College Women's Equal Suffrage League in 1908. Other offices Woolley held include vice-chair of the American Civil Liberties Union, member of the Daughters of the American Revolution (DAR) in Pawtucket, and president of the American Association of University Women (AAUW), from 1927 to 1933.

Mary E. Woolley

In 1937 Woolley resigned as president of Mt. Holyoke after facing increasing opposition from the board of directors, who disapproved of her extended absences from the school and accused her of mismanagement of college funds. Woolley was disappointed by the board's actions against her, and angered by their decision to replace her with a male candidate. She saw a male president of a women's college as an implication that no woman was qualified for the position, and as running counter to the institution's mission to prepare women for leadership. She never returned to the campus after the new president was installed.

Woolley moved to Westport, New York, where she continued to work on international issues. An organizer of the Committee on the Participation of Women in Post-War Policy during World War II, she was also a member of the feminist National Women's Party. She frequently published articles in the late 1930s and 1940s on education and international peace, as well as one book, *Internationalism and Disarmament* (1935).

In 1941, Woolley was honored for a lifetime of achievement for outstanding educational service by the American Federation of Women's Clubs. Recipient of 20 honorary doctorates, she also held honorary memberships in many organizations, including the New England Press Women's Association, the American Women's Club in Vienna, the Business and Professional Women's Club, the Cosmopolitan, and the Women's University Club of New York City. In 1944, Mary Woolley suffered a cerebral hemorrhage which left her partially paralyzed. She died in Westport in 1947, age 84, and was buried in Wilton, Connecticut.

SOURCES:

Current Biography 1942. NY: H.W. Wilson, 1942.

James, Edward T., ed. *Notable American Women, 1607–1950*. Cambridge, MA: The Belknap Press of Harvard University, 1971.

McHenry, Robert, ed. *Famous American Women*. NY: Dover, 1980.

Read, Phyllis J., and Bernard L. Witlieb. *The Book of Women's Firsts*. NY: Random House, 1992.

Laura York, M.A. in History, University of California, Riverside, California

Woolsey, Sarah Chauncey

(1835–1905)

*American author and poet. Name variations: Sarah Chauncy Woolsey; (pseudonym) Susan Coolidge. Born on January 29, 1835, in Cleveland, Ohio; died of a heart condition on April 9, 1905, in Newport, Rhode Island; daughter of John Mumford Woolsey (a land agent and businessman) and Jane (Andrews) Woolsey; cousin of **Abby Howland Woolsey** (1828–1893), **Jane Stuart Woolsey** (1830–1891), and **Georgeanna Muirson Woolsey** (1833–1906), all Civil War relief and hospital workers; niece of Theodore Dwight Woolsey (1801–1889), an educator; studied at private schools in Cleveland; educated at the Select Family School for Young Ladies in Hanover, New Hampshire; never married.*

Selected writings: The New-Year's Bargain *(1872);* What Katy Did *(1873);* What Katy Did at School *(1874);* Mischief's Thanksgiving, and Other Stories *(1874);* Nine Little Goslings *(1875);* For Summer Afternoons *(1876);* Eyebright *(1879);* Verses *(1880);* The Diary and Letters of ***Frances Burney**, Madame d'Arblay *(ed., 1880);* Crosspatch, and Other Stories, Adapted from the Myths of Mother Goose *(1881);* A Guernsey Lily; or, How the Feud Was Healed *(1881);* My Household of Pets by Théophile Gautier *(trans., 1882);* A Round Dozen *(1883);* A Little Country Girl *(1885);* What Katy Did Next *(1886);* A Short History of the City of Philadelphia from its Foundation to the Present Time *(1887);* Clover *(1888);* Just Sixteen *(1889);* A Few More Verses *(1889);* In the High Valley: Being the Fifth and Last Volume of the Katy Did Series *(1890);* Rhymes and Ballads for Girls and Boys *(1892);* The Letters of ***Jane Austen**, Selected from the Compilation of Her Great Nephew Edward, Lord Bradbourne *(ed., 1892);* The Barberry Bush, and Eight Other Stories about Girls for Girls *(1893);* Not Quite Eighteen *(1894);* An Old Convent School in Paris, and Other Papers *(1895);* Curly Locks *(1899);* A Rule of Three *(1904);* A Sheaf of Stories *(1906);* Last Verses *(1906).*

The eldest of five children, Sarah Chauncey Woolsey was born in 1835 in Cleveland, Ohio, the daughter of John Mumford Woolsey and **Jane Andrews Woolsey**. Her father, a descendant of Jonathan Edwards, had graduated from Yale University and moved to Cleveland five years earlier to start his own business. The Woolsey children, consisting of four girls and one boy, were encouraged to pursue active lives in the outdoors and grew up in an attractive home on Euclid Avenue. From an early age, Woolsey enjoyed telling and writing stories. An independent student, she enthusiastically pursued literature and history while neglecting less-favored subjects. After attending private schools in Cleveland, Sarah and her sisters were sent to a private school for girls in New Hampshire, the setting of which later inspired Woolsey's successful children's stories.

At age 20, Sarah moved with her family to New Haven, Connecticut, where her uncle, Theodore Dwight Woolsey, was president of Yale University. During the Civil War, Woolsey worked in different hospitals for the wounded. She met and began a close lifelong friendship with the author *Helen Hunt Jackson, known by the pseudonym "H.H." A story published in *Scribner's Monthly Magazine* by H.H., "Joe Hale's Red Stockings," features a character closely modeled after Woolsey. Following the death of her father in 1870, Woolsey traveled abroad for two years and, upon returning to the United States, followed her family to Newport, Rhode Island, where Jackson was living. The Woolseys built a charming house where Sarah would live for the remainder of her life, except for summer excursions to Maine and occasional visits to Europe.

Woolsey had previously published articles in magazines, and she submitted a collection of her children's stories to Roberts Brothers, which published them in 1872 under the pseudonym of Susan Coolidge. (Woolsey chose the name because her sister **Jane Woolsey** had previously published stories under the name "Margaret Coolidge.") The most popular of her children's books was the "Katy Did" series, published between 1873 and 1890. Basing the central character, Katy, upon herself, Woolsey depicted the lives of children in ways that were heavily influenced by her own family's experiences. These stories broke with the more traditional popular forms of moralizing tales to depict heroic, bold schoolgirls.

In addition to her children's books, Woolsey wrote poetry for adults, edited scholarly works, and continued to submit stories, verse, and travel articles to such prominent publications as *Outlook*, *Woman's Home Companion*, and *Scribner's*. She also worked as a manuscript reader for Roberts Brothers and then Little, Brown.

Woolsey built a summer home with her unmarried sister **Dora Woolsey** in Oneonta, New York, during the late 1880s. The two also visited their sister Jane on Mount Desert Island in Maine during the summers. In Boston, she stayed with **Sarah Wymann Whitman** and visited with *Sarah Orne Jewett and William James. In her later years, Woolsey enjoyed a modest amount of wealth and leisure. She died of a heart condition in her home in Newport on April 9, 1905. She was buried on Dorset Island at Glen Cove, Long Island, where the first Woolsey had settled in 1623.

SOURCES:

Jackson, Kenneth T., ed. *Dictionary of American Biography*. NY: Scribner.

James, Edward T., ed. *Notable American Women, 1607–1950*. Cambridge, MA: The Belknap Press of Harvard University, 1971.

MacDonald, Ruth K. "Sarah Chauncy Woolsey," in *Dictionary of Literary Biography*, Vol. 42: *American Writers for Children Before 1900*. Detroit, MI: Gale Research, 1985, pp. 397–400.

Drew Walker,
freelance writer,
New York, New York

Woolson, Abba Goold (1838–1921)

American teacher, author, and advocate of dress reform. Born Abba Louisa Goold on April 30, 1838, in Windham, Maine; died of arteriosclerosis on February 6, 1921, in Portland, Maine; daughter of William Goold (a politician and local historian) and Nabby Tukey (Clark) Goold; educated in Portland public schools; graduated from Portland High School for Girls, 1856; married Moses Woolson, in 1856; no children.

Selected writings: Woman in American Society *(1873); (ed.)* Dress-Reform *(1874);* Browsing Among Books *(1881);* George Eliot and Her Heroines *(1886).*

One of seven children, Abba Goold Woolson was born in 1838 in Windham, Maine, near Portland, and graduated from Portland High School for Girls as valedictorian of her class. Proficient in French and Latin, she later learned to speak German, Greek, Italian, and Spanish. At age 18, she married her former principal, Moses Woolson, a man 17 years her senior. Soon after, Woolson began teaching at Portland High School and writing for various publications. In 1862, she moved with her husband to Cincinnati, Ohio, where she taught literature at the Mount Auburn Young Ladies' Institute. Returning to the East after three years in Ohio, Abba spent her time assisting her husband in his duties as a school administrator and writing her own essays for publication in such popular magazines as the *Home Journal*, the *Portland Transcript*, and *Boston Journal*.

In 1873, Woolson published her first collection of essays, *Woman in American Society*, to favorable reviews. While supporting the women's rights movement, Woolson critiqued the many difficult and disadvantageous cultural situations encountered by both married and self-supporting women in America. Most prominent among the demands made of women, according to Woolson, were those involving standards of fashionable dress. Arguing that the constraints of women's clothing were not only unnecessary but unhealthy, she maintained that a reform in dress standards was a key issue in the emancipation of women. The Bloomer costume, she contended, had been resisted not because it was unfashionable, but because it had originated in America and not Paris.

In 1873, Woolson also chaired the dress-reform committee of the New England Women's Club, which endorsed what was commonly referred to as a "union suit" because it combined a flannel shirt with attached pantlets (**Susan Taylor Converse** later improved the design in 1875 by making it a two-piece garment and calling it the Emancipation Suit). One of the first organizations to promote reforms in dress design, the New England Women's Club sponsored a series of lectures by four important women physicians on the potentially harmful effects of such constrictive undergarments as corsets. Contributing an essay of her own, Woolson edited these lectures as *Dress-Reform* in 1874, and provided examples of alternative forms of dress, including designs and directions.

Throughout the 1870s and later decades, Woolson continued to publish on various topics, from smoking to popular forms of amusement. She also maintained her lifelong literary interests by presenting lectures on English literature and by publishing *George Eliot and Her Heroines* in 1886. She also lectured on the topic of Spain, an interest that she furthered by visits there in 1883–84 and 1891–92. Her enthusiasm for Spain inspired her in 1887 to help found the Castilian Club in Boston, of which she served as president. Among her many other activities during this time was her work as president and co-founder of the Massachusetts Moral Education Association, which addressed the social problems leading women into prostitution. She was also president of the Massachusetts Society for the Education of Women.

Surviving her husband by 25 years, Abba Woolson died of arteriosclerosis in 1921, age 83. She was buried in Windham, Maine, in the Goold family tomb. In memory of her paternal grandfather, Woolson had provided an endowment to Bowdoin College, establishing the Nathan Goold Prize to be awarded annually to the senior who achieved the highest standing in Greek and Latin studies.

SOURCES:

James, Edward T., ed. *Notable American Women, 1607–1950*. Cambridge, MA: The Belknap Press of Harvard University, 1971.

Drew Walker,
freelance writer,
New York, New York

Woolson, Constance Fenimore

(1840–1894)

American author and friend of Henry James. Name variations: (pseudonym) Anne March. Born on March 5, 1840, in Claremont, New Hampshire; died from injuries resulting from a fall after a protracted period of illness on January 24, 1894, in Venice, Italy; daughter of Charles Jarvis Woolson (a stove manufacturer) and Hannah Cooper (Pomeroy) Woolson; grandniece of author James Fenimore Cooper; during 1840s, attended Miss Hayden's School, Cleveland, Ohio; graduated from Cleveland Female Seminary, 1858; attended Mme. Chegaray's School in New York City; never married; no children.

Selected writings: (as Anne March) The Old Stone House (1872); Castle Nowhere: Lake-Country Sketches (1875); Two Women, 1862: A Poem (1877); Rodman the Keeper: Southern Sketches (1880); Anne: A Novel (1882); For the Major: A Novelette (1883); East Angels (1886); Jupiter Lights: A Novel (1889); Horace Chase: A Novel (1894); The Front Yard, and Other Italian Stories (1895); Dorothy, and Other Italian Stories (1896); Mentone, Cairo, and Corfu (1896).

Constance Fenimore Woolson was born in New Hampshire in 1840, the sixth and youngest daughter among Charles and **Hannah Woolson**'s nine children. Three of her sisters died of scarlet fever within weeks of her birth, and while she was still an infant, the family relocated to Cleveland, Ohio. The grandniece of novelist James Fenimore Cooper, Constance received a cultured upbringing. She attended Miss Hayden's school in Cleveland before entering the Cleveland Female Seminary, graduating in 1858 at the top of her class. She then attended Mme Chegaray's finishing school in New York City. The family spent summers on Mackinac Island in Michigan and in Wisconsin, where long walks in the woods and voluminous reading became lifelong customs. During the Civil War, she volunteered as a nurse.

After the death of her father in 1869, Woolson began to write seriously. She and her mother traveled extensively throughout the eastern and southern United States, which informed the distinctly American settings in Woolson's writings. She began publishing in 1870, and for the next few years contributed travel and descriptive sketches to such magazines as *Harper's* and *Putnam's*. She also wrote local color stories situated in the Great Lakes region, the Ohio Valley, and Cooperstown, New York. Her first novel, which had been serialized previously in *Harper's*, proved to be one of her biggest successes; *Anne*, a mystery thriller set on Mackinac Island, had sales topping 57,000 copies following its publication in 1882.

As Woolson became ever more familiar with the South during her travels, she wrote a series of short works that were collected as *Rodman the Keeper: Southern Sketches* (1886). Many of her stories concern the themes of responsibility and sacrifice. According to *Notable American Women*, she was probably "the first Northern writer to treat the postwar South honestly and sympathetically, without sentimentality." Although Woolson considered herself a realist because she based her stories on strong characters and carefully detailed settings, critics regard her use of remote and unusual locations and exhilarating plots more representative of romanticism.

When her mother died in 1879, Woolson traveled to Europe, where she remained the rest of her life. In Florence, Italy, during the spring of 1880, Woolson developed a notable friendship with American author Henry James, who apparently referred to her affectionately as "Fenimore." Biographer Lyndall Gordon, in *Henry James: Two Women and His Art*, presents Woolson as having had "a muselike influence" on James and suggests that James may have used plots originally devised by Woolson. However, James was no less an important influence on her, as she adopted his introspective, psychological style in her later works of fiction, particularly in *For the Major*, which is considered one of her best efforts.

Living in different parts of Europe throughout the 1880s and 1890s, and traveling to Greece and Egypt during the winter of 1889–90, Woolson wrote prolifically. During these years, she published four novels which, like her earlier works, first appeared in serial form in *Harper's* and were then published as books. Woolson's final short stories revolve around American expatriates living abroad, and are commonly regarded as inferior to her works with American settings.

In 1890, Woolson returned to England, residing in Cheltenham and Oxford until the summer of 1893, when she found an apartment on the Grand Canal in Venice. Her physical health had deteriorated, and that winter she battled the flu, which eventually turned into typhoid fever. On January 24, 1894, she either fell or jumped to her death from an upper-floor window. Woolson had suffered from depression her entire life, a condition she believed to be inherent to a creative temperament. Although Henry James speculated that she had committed suicide, the absence of a witness precludes a definite opinion. She was interred in the Protestant Cemetery in Rome.

SOURCES:

Boren, Lynda S. "Constance Fenimore Woolson," in *Dictionary of Literary Biography*, Vol. 12: *American Realists and Naturalists*. Detroit, MI: The Gale Group, 1982, pp. 456–463.

Constance Fenimore Woolson

Dean, Sharon L. "Constance Fenimore Woolson," in *Dictionary of Literary Biography*, Vol. 221: *American Women Prose Writers, 1870–1920*. Detroit, MI: The Gale Group, 2000, pp. 370–380.

Edwards, Mary P. "Constance Fenimore Woolson," in *Dictionary of Literary Biography*, Vol. 74: *American Short-Story Writers Before 1880*. Detroit, MI: The Gale Group, 1988, pp. 365–370.

James, Edward T., ed. *Notable American Women, 1607–1950*. Cambridge, MA: The Belknap Press of Harvard University, 1971.

McHenry, Robert, ed. *Famous American Women*. NY: Dover, 1980.

Publishers Weekly. March 1, 1999, p. 51.

Wadsworth, Sarah. "Constance Fenimore Woolson," in *Dictionary of Literary Biography*, Vol. 189: *American Travel Writers, 1850–1915*. Detroit, MI: The Gale Group, 1998, pp. 353–359.

SUGGESTED READING:

Gordon, Lyndall. *A Private Life of Henry James: Two Women and His Art*. NY: W.W. Norton, 1999.

Drew Walker,
freelance writer,
New York, New York

Wootten, Bayard (1875–1959)

American landscape photographer. Born Mary Bayard Morgan in 1875 in New Bern, North Carolina: died in 1959 in New Bern; educated at North Caroli-

na State Normal and Industrial School (later the University of North Carolina at Greensboro); married Charles Thomas Wootten, in 1897 (separated 1901); children: two sons.

Became the first woman to take aerial photographs in North Carolina; photographed the landscapes of the southeastern U.S., and also produced a series portraying Appalachian life.

Bayard Wootten was born Mary Bayard Morgan in 1875 in New Bern, North Carolina. She received her education, although not a degree, at the North Carolina State Normal and Industrial School from 1892 to 1894, and accepted a teaching position at a Georgia state school for the deaf. During her time in Georgia, she entered a short-lived marriage with Charles Thomas Wootten and had two sons in the four years they were together. Separating from her husband in 1901, she returned to New Bern.

Wootten began her photography career around 1904, opening a studio in New Bern and joining the Women's Federation of the Photographers' Association of America in 1909 or 1910. In 1914, flying over New Bern in an airplane built and owned by the Wright Brothers, Wootten made what were probably the first aerial photographs of North Carolina—and possibly anywhere—by a woman to that date. In 1917, she decided to try her luck in New York City, but the studio she opened there closed after only a few months, and she returned to New Bern.

Wootten pursued work in photography with renewed interest and finally settled in Chapel Hill in 1928, in the hopes of capitalizing on the presence of the University of North Carolina in that city. Throughout the 1930s, she continued to photograph landscapes of the southeastern United States, and also produced a series portraying the impoverished inhabitants of that area. In 1954, her photographs illustrated books depicting Appalachian life and crafts. She retired that year and died in 1959.

SOURCES:

Rosenblum, Naomi. *A History of Women Photographers.* NY: Abbeville, 1994.

Drew Walker,
freelance writer,
New York, New York

Wootton, Barbara (1897–1988)

English educationalist, social scientist and public servant who advocated liberal and progressive causes. Name variations: Baroness Wootton of Abinger. Born Barbara Frances Adam on April 14, 1897, in Cam- bridge, England; died in Surrey on July 11, 1988; daughter of James Adam (a university teacher) and Adela Marion (Kensington) Adam; educated at home; Perse High School for Girls, Cambridge, 1910–15; Girton College, Cambridge, 1915–19; married John Wesley Wootton, in 1917 (died 1917); married George Percival Wright, in 1935 (died 1964); no children.

Made research student, London School of Economics (1919–20); named director of studies in economics, Girton College, Cambridge (1920–22); hired as researcher, Trades Union Congress and Labour Party Joint Research Department (1922–26); named principal of Morley College for Working Men and Women (1926–27); named director of studies for tutorial classes, University of London (1927–44); named reader in social studies, University of London (1944–52), professor from 1948; named Nuffield research fellow, Bedford College, University of London (1952–57).

Selected writings: Twos and Threes (Howe, 1933); Plan or No Plan (Gollancz, 1934); London's Burning (Allen & Unwin, 1938); Lament for Economics (1938); Freedom under Planning (Allen & Unwin, 1945); Testament for Social Science: An Essay in the Application of Scientific Method to Human Problems (Allen & Unwin, 1950); The Social Foundations of Wage Policy: A Study of Comparative British Wage and Salary Structure (Allen & Unwin, 1955); Social Science and Social Pathology (Allen & Unwin, 1959); Crime and Criminal Law (1963); In a World I Never Made: Autobiographical Reflections (Allen & Unwin, 1967); Crime and Penal Policy: Reflections on Fifty Years' Experience (Allen & Unwin, 1978).

While studying classics at the University of Cambridge, the 20-year old Barbara Adam married, on September 5, 1917, John Wootton, an army officer who was serving in the war. On the eve of their wedding, a telegram had arrived ordering him to be in London on September 7 to return to active service in France. Their honeymoon was canceled. Instead, they spent two nights together, one near Cambridge, the other in a London hotel close to the railway station from which John Wootton had to leave. Five weeks later, he was shot in the eye. He survived for two days, dying of his wounds on October 11, 1917. The tragedy, not unusual at a time of massive casualties, was to alter the course of Barbara Wootton's life. She moved from classics to social inquiry, from Christian faith to agnosticism, and from conservatism to socialism. But she always retained the intellectual discipline and sense of purpose with which she was brought up.

Barbara Wootton was born in 1897 into a moderately prosperous and intellectually distinguished household in Cambridge. Her father's social origins were humble: James Adam was the only son of an Aberdeenshire farm worker, but by means of scholarships he rose to become a classics don and senior tutor of Emmanuel College in the University of Cambridge. In contrast, her mother **Adela Kensington Adam**, was the daughter of a banker; she went to Cambridge as a student of classics and married her tutor, James Adam. They had two sons before the birth of their third and last child, Barbara.

The regime under which the Adams children were brought up insisted on academic achievement, although in keeping with the attitudes of the time Barbara was educated at home, while her brothers went to preparatory and public schools (by a peculiarity of the British system, public schools are in reality both private and exclusive). At age three, she was a fluent reader, and by ten she could read from the New Testament in Greek to her father as part of the family's Sunday routine.

The death of her father, at age 47 in August 1907, clouded Barbara's early years, especially

Barbara Wootton

as her mother had a somewhat austere personality. It was to a family servant (known for obscure reasons as "The Pie") that Barbara turned for reassurance. There was some respite from an emotionally arid home life when, at the age of thirteen and a half, she was sent to school, where she made friends with girls her own age.

In 1915, Barbara entered the University of Cambridge to study Greek and Latin and moved to student accommodation in Girton College; she did so partly in obedience to her mother's wish that she too should become a classicist. In September 1916, her younger brother, who was serving in the war, died in action. A few months later, she became engaged to John ("Jack") Wootton, a friend of her elder brother. Many years later, she wrote in her autobiography that similar tragedies had affected many others, but the premature deaths of a father, a brother, and a husband had inevitably left permanent marks.

Again and again I have had the satisfaction of seeing the laughable idealism of one generation evolve into the accepted commonplace of the next.

—Barbara Wootton

In some respects, her studies kept her mind occupied, while her upbringing had ingrained in her perseverance and self-discipline—characteristics she showed throughout her life. However, in the summer of 1918 an attack of tonsillitis prevented her from sitting some of her examinations; she later wondered if the illness had been psychosomatic, a reaction to family pressure to study classics. But in the following year, after she switched to economics, the examiners awarded her scripts a distinction, for the best-ever performance in the subject. At that time, women could not formally be conferred with the full degree of the University of Cambridge, and Barbara Wootton was not permitted to add the letters "B.A." after her name. She was always resentful of the slights to which women were subject because of gender prejudice. Among the forms of this discrimination, she included the tendency to draw attention to a woman's achievements when no comment would be made were a man to have a similar record. She was exasperated when women were "elaborately treated as equals" and disliked intended compliments such as those attributing to her a "masculine brain."

Typical of the way she kept to personal principles, Barbara Wootton refused to accept a war widow's pension: she believed she was able to make a living by her efforts and abilities. In 1919, she was awarded a research scholarship at the London School of Economics, and then, after a year, she returned to Cambridge as director of studies in economics at Girton College. Social attitudes, while less rigid than some of those encountered by *Emily Davies and earlier generations of women at Cambridge, could still be annoying, especially to someone of Wootton's sensibilities. On one occasion, because she was not formally a member of the university, the name of a male colleague was printed instead of hers as the lecturer, although it was known that she had been given responsibility for the course. Such slights were to some extent compensated for by the lively intellectual atmosphere of the time, and she came into contact with several younger scholars who shared, and helped to develop further, her left-wing views. As well as refining her political ideas, she thought deeply about ethical and religious questions. The Christian beliefs of her parents were abandoned in favor of agnosticism. This aspect of her moral code was as deeply seated as her feminism, and on one occasion she was far from flattered when a well-meaning Christian friend wrote that she was not truly an agnostic: to her that was equivalent to suggesting that a devout believer was not genuine in their Christian faith.

A sense that academic life was too restrictive—a feeling that, as she put it in her autobiography, "a wider world was calling"—led her to resign her Cambridge post in 1922. She moved to London to work as a researcher for the Trades Union Congress and the Labour Party. She was, in her own words, "absolutely whole-hearted" in her devotion to the labor movement and content therefore to work for a lower salary. Her abilities were widely recognized. She was offered the chance to become a candidate for the House of Commons, but declined it (and never stood for election to a public office). Her appointment in 1924 to a government inquiry into taxation aroused much press comment, on the grounds of her age and sex; such comments would no doubt have been heightened had it become known that she wrote the entire report that appeared under the names of those who formed a minority on the inquiry. She noted wryly that much of what she wrote as a researcher was credited to others.

On several further occasions, she sat on official inquiries, developing a reputation as a shrewd and constructive committee member. On that first occasion, she was acutely aware that while entrusted by the state to be a member of a public inquiry—and, from 1925, to be a justice of the peace—she was denied a parliamentary vote. Only in 1918 had women received the franchise, and then only if they had reached the age 30; it was not until 1928 that a common age, 21, applied to both sexes. To Barbara Wootton it showed the piecemeal, inconsistent, and often grudging process by which women's civil and other rights were conceded.

Even as a busy researcher, she had retained an interest in teaching, particularly adult education, and in 1926 Wootton decided to accept the post of principal of Morley College for Working Men and Women. In 1927, she moved to the University of London, to hold the directorship of studies—an appointment dealing with part-time students, and one free of the "marriage bar" (the requirement, then common in some of the professions open to women, that obliged marriage to be accompanied by resignation). She held the director's post until 1944.

A highly efficient administrator, Wootton was always capable of undertaking several tasks at apparently the same time. Her reputation ensured that she was regularly invited to speak at conferences throughout the world. In 1927, for example, she attended a League of Nations economic conference in Geneva; in 1930, she made her first visit to the United States (and was shocked in Chicago by the squalid slums "separated by one block only from the magnificent lakeside frontage"); and, in 1932, she traveled to the Soviet Union. As well as academic work, she experimented with expressing her social ideas in fictional form: in this she was influenced by H.G. Wells, but a collection of short stories, *Twos and Threes* (1933), and a novel about a fascist uprising, *London's Burning* (1938), were regarded as too stilted and enjoyed little success.

Her scholarly work, however, was widely noticed. Almost everything she wrote grew out of interests that were practical as well as academic. Her *Plan or No Plan* (1934) reflected the debate over the extent to which the state should enter into the field of economic organization. She believed state intervention was preferable to the unfettered competition of the market. She also maintained that economists should make their writings relevant to the issues of the period. Her *Lament for Economics* (1938) was a statement of what she believed was wrong with the approach taken by many of her contemporaries who were writing on the subject, although, some two decades after her brilliant degree in economics, she saw the book as marking the point at which she began to regard herself as no longer an economist.

Subsequently, writings in the field of social administration formed the basis of her scholarly reputation. The outbreak of world war in 1939

ended for several years opportunities to travel abroad. One of her last overseas journeys was to the United States to hold a lectureship founded in tribute to the American feminist *Anna Howard Shaw. However, Wootton's interest in the wider world took the form of activity in organizations dedicated to promoting a system of international government. As she ruefully observed in her autobiography, "hard-headed practical men" regarded people such as herself as "a hopeless lot of woolly idealists, if not actually near-traitors"; but, she added, practical men "can always demonstrate the impracticability of idealistic proposals by the simple device of making sure that these are never tried."

Having moved in 1944 to Bedford College, which was part of the University of London, she was promoted to a professorship in 1948. There were renewed opportunities to travel abroad, including a visiting professorship at Columbia University, which in 1954 conferred on her an honorary degree. This was the first of several such awards: in subsequent years, no fewer than 13 British universities recognized her scholarship in the form of honorary degrees. What she regarded as her most substantial book, *Social Science and Social Pathology*, appeared in 1959 and attempted to explore the concept of "the criminal personality." Her many years as a magistrate specializing in cases of juvenile delinquency gave her practical insights into the problems of deviancy which were also evident in her *Crime and the Criminal Law* (1963). Similarly, an earlier book, *The Social Foundations of Wage Policy* (1955), drew upon another of her activities—membership of a civil service arbitration board—in discussing those influences which determined wages and salaries.

At the age of 60, in 1957, Barbara Wootton decided to retire from her university post, though she accepted visiting appointments in Ghana in 1958 and Australia in 1961. In 1961, she was invited by Japan Airlines to join the inaugural flights over the North Pole on the London to Tokyo route. When her hosts inquired what she would like to see during her visit, she characteristically asked to be taken to inspect a prison. Invitations such as this came because of her position as a member of the House of Lords. In 1958, she had been raised to the peerage with the title of Baroness Wootton of Abinger. Her elevation had been made at the request of the Labour Party, which had relatively few representatives in the upper chamber of Parliament. She took her duties, as always, very seriously and was prominent in the debates and other functions of the House of Lords.

She took the Surrey village of Abinger as part of her title to acknowledge having settled there, in a converted barn, two years earlier. The move had marked also a change in her personal circumstances—separation from her second husband, George Wright. Their marriage was somewhat unconventional. When they met in the 1930s, her husband was the driver of a taxi, though he was about to begin a scholarship at the London School of Economics. To Wootton's great annoyance, the circumstances were picked up by the newspapers which ran "cabby marries don" stories. The wedding took place in July 1935, and subsequently George Wright became a Labour Party official and was elected as a member of the London County Council. Nevertheless, the original story remained on file, and when she entered the House of Lords the press pestered her for a photograph of the couple "standing beside his taxi." Reflecting on their life together a few years after his death, which occurred in 1964, she acknowledged that she had been "too much occupied with my own affairs, and too reluctant to modify my way of life, to make an easy marriage partner," while her husband had been "a natural polygamist." Even after they had separated, there was no divorce; they continued to spend time in each other's company, and she helped to support him financially.

For most of her adult life, Barbara Wootton was called upon to serve on many voluntary or nominally paid bodies. These included four Royal Commissions (on Workmen's Compensation, 1938, the Press, 1947, the Civil Service, 1954, and the Penal System, 1964–66), membership of the University Grants Committee, 1948–50, and the board of governors of the British Broadcasting Corporation, 1950–56; and the chair of the University Grants Committee, 1968–70. A frequent broadcaster, she also put forward her views in articles in newspapers and periodicals. The House of Lords provided another platform, although she usually limited her speeches to the topics about which she had an expert knowledge. Her standing among her fellow peers was recognized when she was made a deputy-speaker, the first woman to occupy that post. In 1977, she was made a Companion of Honor, and so joined an order limited to 65 distinguished persons; she was one of only two women members.

When Barbara Wootton wrote *In a World I Never Made: Autobiographical Reflections* in 1967, she assumed it would be her final book. She was, however, to continue to write until her mid-80s, when fading powers brought an end at last to a career of over 60 years of public and academic work. In advanced old age, some time before her death on July 11, 1988, she moved to a nursing home. She had taken the title of her autobiography from a poem by A.E. Housman which includes the lines: "I, a stranger and afraid/ In a world I never made." Yet if she could not make the world, she did see social changes of the sort that she approved. While she preferred not to label herself as a feminist—she was always wary of the forms of discrimination that could be tied into the apparently enlightened treatment of women—the principles by which she lived were those that advanced the woman's status. Her formidable intellect, with both its constructive and iconoclastic characteristics, was combined with immense self-discipline and a sturdy conviction that she could help to change society for the better. When asked as a child what she would grow up to be, she replied "an organizing female with a briefcase," and she was content to believe that she had been.

SOURCES:

Bean, Philip, and David Whynes, eds. *Barbara Wootton, Social Science and Public Policy: Essays in her Honour.* London: Tavistock, 1986.

Clywd, Ann. "Women of Our Century. IV: Barbara Wootton," in *Listener.* July 26, 1984.

Seal, Vera G., and Philip Bean, eds. *Selected Writings: Barbara Wootton.* 4 vols. Basingstoke: Macmillan, 1992.

Wootton, Barbara. *In a World I Never Made: Autobiographical Reflections.* London: Allen & Unwin, 1967.

SUGGESTED READING:

Caldecott, Leonie. *Women of our Century.* London: BBC, 1984.

D.E. Martin,
Lecturer in History, University of Sheffield,
Sheffield, England

Wordsworth, Dorothy (1771–1855)

English diarist and natural historian who was companion to—and caretaker of—her brother William, and friends with other influential British Romantics. Born on December 25, 1771, in Cockermouth, England; died on January 25, 1855, at Rydal Mount after 20 years of mental and physical illness; daughter of John Wordsworth and Anne (Cookson) Wordsworth; sister of William Wordsworth (the poet); never married; no children.

Caretaker and companion of her brother William, even after his marriage to Mary Hutchinson, a childhood friend (1802); published nothing during her lifetime, with the exception of a few poems included by her brother in a collection Poems by William Wordsworth, Including Lyrical Ballads, and the Miscellaneous Pieces of the Author *(1815); died (1855), five years after William.*

Selected writings: her work is in various collections and editions of her journals, correspondence, poetry and short fiction; these include Recollections of a

Dorothy Wordsworth

Tour Made in Scotland, A.D. 1803 (1874); Journals of Dorothy Wordsworth (first complete edition 1941, ed. by Ernest de Selincourt); George & Sarah Green: A Narrative by Dorothy Wordsworth (1936, ed. by de Selincourt); The Letters of William and Dorothy Wordsworth (1967–82, 6 vols., ed. by Alan G. Hill, Mary Moorman, and Chester L. Shaver); "The Collected Poems of Dorothy Wordsworth," in Susan M. Levin's Dorothy Wordsworth & Romanticism (Rutgers University Press, 1987, pp. 175–237).

Like so many women of the 18th and 19th centuries, Dorothy Wordsworth focused her at-tention and energies on local concerns: her family and the home she shared with them. Until comparatively recently, most women who wrote did so in private, and their lit-erary production revolved around correspon-dence, diaries, poetry and fiction never intended for eyes other than those of family and friends. Thus the diary-journal forms an especially fertile area in which to recapture not only women's his-tory but also women's writing as literary produc-tion. For this reason, many scholars now turn their attention to women's diaries, letters, and other forms of autobiography as a source of women's literature, no longer brushing aside such forms as somehow lesser because they were private and sometimes, as in the case of much of what Dorothy Wordsworth wrote, intended for an audience of one, herself, or two, herself and her brother William Wordsworth. That Wordsworth did not seek public acclaim through the validation that publication affords should not be taken to mean that she had nothing of value to say: her writings, like those of so many women working in these modes, tell us differently. And, her reticence aside, Wordsworth's ideas, perceptions, and very language were appreciated by at least two monuments of the British Romantic period: her brother William and their friend, Samuel Taylor Coleridge. In fact, Dorothy Wordsworth noted on several occasions that she kept her records in large part as an aid to her prestigious brother's memory; he, in turn, delved into them, borrowing events, descriptions, and even close turns of phrase in such poems as "I Wandered Lonely as a Cloud," "Beggars," and "Resolution and Independence."

Dorothy and her four brothers (of whom William was one year her senior) led a happy early childhood in Cockermouth, Westmoreland, with their parents John and **Ann Wordsworth**. John was steward and agent (lawyer) for wealthy landowner Sir James Lowther. But in 1778, when Dorothy was six, her mother died and the children were separated. Until 1795, she lived with a succession of relatives and was never brought back to her father's home, even though her brothers frequently visited there from boarding school. Her experiences were not the happiest ones for a child suffering the loss of a parent; after her mother's death, in 1778 she stayed with her mother's cousin, **Elizabeth Threlkeld**, in Halifax, along with five other orphan cousins; from her accounts, this was a pleasant home. She attended boarding school beginning in 1781, but was forced to switch to a Halifax day school owing to the sudden death of her father in December 1783 and the resulting lack of funds for private schooling. At 15, Dorothy was sent to live with her maternal grandparents, the William Cooksons, in Penrith, where her mother's cleric brother, William, tutored her in geography, math, and French. Her schooling in Halifax was the only truly formal education that Wordsworth would receive.

Her stay in Penrith was unhappy: her grandparents were cold to her and would not allow her brothers to visit. By October 1788, however, her uncle William married **Dorothy Cowper** and brought Dorothy Wordsworth to live with them at his new parish in Forncett, Norfolk, a happier situation. While at Forncett, Dorothy helped start and run a small school for local country girls. She remained there until 1794; for the next year, she moved from relative to relative. But, in 1795, she achieved her fondest wish and moved into a house at Racedown, Dorsetshire, with her brother William, something made possible by a small legacy from one of his friends. Until her death in 1855, five years after William's own demise, Dorothy remained a welcomed part of her brother's household. At Racedown, she undertook the business of managing their domestic affairs, cooking, cleaning, helping William with his work, and corresponding with friends. Throughout her life, Dorothy Wordsworth devoted herself to the well being of William, tending to the mundane so that he could write; accompanying him on walking trips; keeping journals of these trips and of her local observations, to which both he and Coleridge would refer for information; and, later, minding the children of William and his wife, **Mary Hutchinson Wordsworth**, whom he married on October 4, 1802.

It was at their first home at Racedown in 1797 that Dorothy and William made the acquaintance of Samuel Taylor Coleridge, with whom William had previously corresponded. Subsequently that year, they moved closer to Coleridge, living in Alfoxden House in Nether Stowey. From this initial friendship came the intense intellectual engagement that produced some of British Romanticism's most powerful poetry: the *Lyrical Ballads*. Additionally, from their stay at Alfoxden House came Dorothy's own *Alfoxden Journal*, a record of the natural world and the people of the area—work to which both men allude and for which they praise her for her artistic ability. While Coleridge and William wrote and talked, not only was Dorothy writing in her journal, but she was also tending to the multitude of household responsibilities so that the men could have the luxury of time to think, talk, and write. It is no surprise that her brother remarks in Book IX of his autobiographical poem, *The Prelude*, that Dorothy, "in the midst of all, preserved me still/ A Poet."

In 1798, Dorothy, William, Coleridge and his student John Chester traveled to Germany; an account recorded in her journal, *Journal of Visit to Hamburgh and of Journey from Hamburgh to Goslar*, was not published in full until 1941. After this at times unpleasant trip, owing in part to the weather, the unfriendliness of the locals, and the isolation, Dorothy and William settled in Dove Cottage in Grasmere in December 1799. It was this home that provided Dorothy with the source of some of her most critically acclaimed observations, now referred to as the *Grasmere Journals*, covering May 1800 through January 1803. Like the *Alfoxden Jour-*

nal, the *Grasmere Journal* was not published in its entirety until 1941, although excerpts had been printed in 1897. It is clear from Dorothy's recorded material and William's poetry that he owed her more than a debt of gratitude for her painstaking record of local detail and natural events; Dorothy herself remarks that, at times in his poetry, her words had become William's, yet she seems not to begrudge him the borrowing.

Dorothy Wordsworth never separated herself from her beloved brother, and as she records in the *Grasmere Journals*, on the night prior to William and Mary's wedding, she slept with the wedding ring on her forefinger and that, when she gave it to him privately the day of the wedding, he slipped it again on her hand before taking it with him to the church. Understandably, particularly considering the bleak prospects open to an unmarried woman in the 18th—or 19th—century, Dorothy was distressed at this shift in circumstances. In fact, she did not attend the wedding. After this initially difficult adjustment, however, she continued as a faithful and devoted member of William's household until her death, and, by all accounts, deeply loved and was loved by Mary and the children.

Throughout much of her adult life, until illness made it no longer possible, Dorothy continued to travel with her brother and with friends, while he often left his wife and children at home. Dorothy and William were keen walkers, as were the other Romantics, and her journals record her observations of nature, local custom, and the day-to-day business that contributes significantly—as do other women's diaries—to our understanding of domestic and personal life during these times. In 1803, she began a recounting of a six-week trip that she, William, and Samuel Coleridge made to Scotland; totaling over 300 pages and existing in at least five manuscripts, *Recollections of a Tour Made in Scotland, A.D. 1803* is a brilliantly rendered example of the travel writing of her day. Although friends urged her to publish it, it did not see print until 1874 as a posthumous edition. Of particular interest to scholars of women's history are Wordsworth's accounts of the domestic scenes she observed on her travels. Throughout her adult life, she continued to record her travel experiences and observations of domestic life and natural history. "Excursion on the Banks of Ullswater" was an account of a November 1805 trip with William (not published until 1941). In her *Journal of a Tour on the Continent 1820*, she recounts finally seeing Mont Blanc, but as a woman well past youth, her narrative reflects the disappointment of time and choices past and passed by (not pub-

lished in its entirety until 1941). Her *Journal of my Second Tour in Scotland* (also not published in its entirety until 1941) is an account of her 1822 trip with **Joanna Hutchinson** in which she looks at herself now as an older, less sturdy woman than the one who accompanied William on the same journey in 1803—needless to say, she expresses regrets. Lastly, her *Journal of a Tour in the Isle of Man*, an account of an 1828 trip, is filled with negative images (published for the first time in 1941).

I should detest setting myself up as an Author.
—Dorothy Wordsworth

Although Dorothy Wordsworth did write several dozen poems and a few short stories, only a handful were available to the public while she was alive—those being the ones William included in the 1815 edition of his *Poetical Works*. As in her journals, her poems and stories have much to do with children and mothering; some critics suppose that her focus on these issues stems from the early loss of her own mother. Loss affects much of Dorothy Wordsworth's life on many levels: not only was she orphaned early in life, but her beloved brother John drowned in 1805, and two of Mary and William's children also died. This same concern reflects itself in *A Narrative Concerning George & Sarah Green of the Parish of Grasmere*, an account she wrote in part to raise money for the support of the eight children orphaned by the 1808 death by drowning of a local couple. Yet, when friends urged her to publish it, she declined.

In April 1829, while keeping house for her nephew John Wordsworth in Whitlock, Dorothy grew seriously ill—perhaps with dysentery—and for a time there was concern that she might not recover. For the rest of her life, her physical health deteriorated, confining her to a wheelchair. More tragically, her mental capacity diminished, perhaps from arteriosclerosis, and she entered a private world from which she was less and less able to emerge. In 1850, however, she did respond when told of her brother William's death; it was not until five years later that Dorothy Wordsworth died, a month after her 83rd birthday.

SOURCES:
de Selincourt, Ernest. *Dorothy Wordsworth: A Biography*. Oxford: Clarendon, 1933.
Gittings, Robert, and Jo Manton. *Dorothy Wordsworth*. Oxford: Clarendon, 1985.
Levin, Susan M. *Dorothy Wordsworth and Romanticism*. New Brunswick, NJ: Rutgers University Press, 1987.
Maclean, Catherine Macdonald. *Dorothy Wordsworth: The Early Years*. Freeport, NY: Books for Libraries, 1932, rep. 1970.

Mullane, Janet, and Robert Thomas Wilson, eds. "Dorothy Wordsworth," in *Nineteenth-Century Literature Criticisms*. Vol. 25. Detroit, MI: Gale Research, 1990.

Taylor, Elisabeth Russell. "Dorothy Wordsworth: Primary and Secondary Sources," in *Bulletin of Bibliography*. Vol. 40, no. 4, 1983, pp. 252–255.

SUGGESTED READING:

Bond, Alec. "Reconsidering Dorothy Wordsworth," in *Charles Lamb Society Bulletin*. July–October 1984, pp. 194–207.

de Selincourt, Ernest, ed. *Journals of Dorothy Wordsworth*. 2 vols. NY: Macmillan, 1941.

Ellis, Amanda M. *Rebels and Conservatives: Dorothy and William Wordsworth and Their Circle*. Bloomington, IN: Indiana University Press, 1967.

Greenfield, John R., ed. *Dictionary of Literary Biography*, Vol. 107: *British Romantic Prose Writers, 1789–1832*. 1st series. Detroit, MI: Gale Research, 1991.

Jones, Kathleen. *A Passionate Sisterhood: Women of the Wordsworth Circle*. St. Martin's, 2000.

Levin, Susan. "Subtle Fire: Dorothy Wordsworth's Prose and Poetry," in *Massachusetts Review*. Vol. 21, 1980, pp. 345–363.

McGavran, James Holt, Jr. "Dorothy Wordsworth's Journals: Putting Herself Down," in *The Private Self: Theory and Practice of Women's Autobiographical Writings*. Ed. by Shari Benstock. Chapel Hill, NC: University of North Carolina Press, 1988, pp. 230–253.

Moorman, Mary, ed. *Journals of Dorothy Wordsworth*. London: Oxford University Press, 1971.

Wolfson, Susan J. "Individual in Community: Dorothy Wordsworth in Conversation with William," in *Romanticism and Feminism*. Ed. by Anne K. Mellor. Bloomington, IN: Indiana University Press, 1988, pp. 139–166.

Woof, Pamela, ed. *The Grasmere Journal*. London: Joseph, 1989.

COLLECTIONS:

Dove Cottage Library, Grasmere, England, houses most of Wordsworth's manuscripts; Cornell University Library holds photocopies of this material and other original manuscripts. The following libraries hold holographs: Bristol Central Library, Bristol, England; Ashley Collection, British Museum; Brown University Library; Lilly Library, Indiana University; Pierpont Morgan Library; Swarthmore College Library; Coleridge Collection, Victoria University Library, Toronto.

Melissa E. Barth, Coordinator of the Office of Women's Concerns and Women's Studies and Professor of English, Appalachian State University, Boone, North Carolina

Wordsworth, Elizabeth

(1840–1932)

British leader in women's education at Oxford University. Name variations: (pseudonym) Grant Lloyd. Born on June 22, 1840, at Harrow-on-the-Hill, England; died on November 30, 1932, in Oxford; daughter of Christopher Wordsworth (the bishop of Lincoln) and Susanna (Hatley) Wordsworth; sister of John Wordsworth (the bishop of Salisbury); great-niece of poet William Wordsworth and diarist Dorothy Wordsworth (1771–1855).

Was first principal of Lady Margaret Hall at Oxford University; opened St. Hugh's Hall (later St. Hugh's College) at Oxford, and encouraged the opening of Lady Margaret Hall Settlement in Lambeth; made a Dame of the British Empire (1928).

Elizabeth Wordsworth was born in 1840 into a prosperous family of great renown in English society. Her father Christopher Wordsworth was later bishop of Lincoln; her brother John Wordsworth was later bishop of Salisbury, and she was the great-niece of poet William Wordsworth and his sister, diarist *Dorothy Wordsworth. Although Elizabeth spent a year at a boarding school in Brighton, she received most of her education under the guidance of her father and several governesses who instructed her in classics, history, English, languages, music, and painting. Her family connections and impressive intellect gave her entrance to social circles particularly devoted to scholarship, art, and church and social improvement.

In 1878, Wordsworth accepted an appointment as the first principal of Oxford University's Lady Margaret Hall. During her distinguished 30-year career as an administrator, she expanded the student body, hired tutors, added new buildings, and began plans for the construction of both a hall and a library. More important, she was an advocate of women's entrance to Oxford University, and to this end opened St. Hugh's Hall (later St. Hugh's College) in 1886 and encouraged the establishment of the Lady Margaret Hall Settlement in Lambeth in 1897.

Wordsworth retired from administrative work in 1909, but was no less active in retirement. She had previously published two novels under the pseudonym Grant Lloyd and returned to writing in her retirement. She published *Glimpses of the Past* (1912), *Essays Old and New* (1919), and *Poems and Plays* (1931). Her most notable literary work was the biography of her father, published in 1888. For her efforts on behalf of education, she received several honorary degrees and was named a Dame of the British Empire in 1928. She died on November 30, 1932, in Oxford, where she had made her home since 1899.

SOURCES:

The Concise Dictionary of National Biography. Oxford: Oxford University Press, 1992.

The Dictionary of National Biography, 1931–1940. Ed. by L.G. Wickham Legg. Oxford: Oxford University Press, 1949.

Drew Walker, freelance writer, New York, New York

Workman, Fanny (1859–1925)

American explorer and mountain climber who won acclaim in both the U.S. and Europe for the extensive travels she undertook with her husband. Born on January 8, 1859, in Worcester, Massachusetts: died in Cannes, France, on January 22, 1925; daughter of Alexander Hamilton Bullock (1866–1868, Massachusetts governor) and Elvira (Hazard) Bullock; granddaughter of wealthy Connecticut gunpowder manufacturer Augustus George Hazard; educated by tutors, at Miss Graham's finishing school in New York City, and subsequently at schools in Paris and Dresden; married William Hunter Workman, in 1881; children: one daughter, Rachel Workman (b. 1884).

Traveled extensively throughout the world for nearly three decades, exploring mountainous areas, traveling by bicycle, and publishing accounts of travels and exploration which she co-authored with her husband, including Algerian Memories *(1895),* In the Ice World of the Himalaya *(1900), and* Two Summers in the Ice Wilds of Eastern Karakorum *(1917); set world records for mountain climbing.*

On January 8, 1859, Fanny Workman was born in Worcester, Massachusetts, the youngest of three children of Alexander Hamilton Bullock and **Elvira Hazard Bullock**. As the granddaughter of wealthy Connecticut merchant Augustus George Hazard, the premiere manufacturer of gunpowder in the mid-19th century, Fanny laid claim to a distinguished New England heritage, which was enhanced by her father's election to the governor's post in Massachusetts in 1866. Money and political connections provided Workman with a cosmopolitan education at Miss Graham's finishing school in New York City and in Europe.

Returning to Worcester after completing her studies in Paris and Dresden, Fanny met a successful physician named William Hunter Workman, and the two married in June 1881. The Workmans had one child, **Rachel**, born in 1884, who spent much of her childhood in boarding schools while her parents traveled the world. Fanny and William began their travels together in 1886, visiting Germany, Sweden, and Norway. William's illness-induced retirement from medicine in 1889 hardly meant economic hardship given their independent wealth, so the pair spent the following nine years in Europe, keeping a residence in Germany. Enjoying the high culture of Europe, Fanny loved the German operas of Richard Wagner, often attending performances of them in Bayreuth. However, her interest in mountaineering—sparked by her husband while the

two still lived in the United States—became her primary passion as she embarked on a series of mountain climbs of such Alpine peaks as Mont Blanc, Zinal Rothorn, and the Matterhorn.

By the mid-1890s, the Workmans had begun traveling throughout the Mediterranean region, visiting several North African countries (including Egypt), Greece, and Palestine. In Algeria and Spain, they made a great many long trips on bicycle about which they co-authored two books. The Workmans' adventures in bicycle travel remains a remarkable undertaking even by modern standards. Between bicycling in Ceylon (modern-day Sri Lanka), Java, Sumatra, India, and what is today Vietnam, they logged over 17,000 miles.

In 1899, Fanny and William, aged 40 and 52 respectively, began their long travels through the Himalayas, first visiting the Karakorum range in the northwest, at that time mostly unmapped and unexplored by those from the West. They thus began the first of seven expeditions to this region, mapping, photographing and recording scientific data as they went along. The Workmans worked together as a great team, equally sharing in the dull and more exciting parts of these expeditions and equally proficient in all tasks which needed to be performed. The pair devoted themselves to scientific studies, mapmaking, and photography during their climbs and published their findings in five volumes between 1900 and 1917. They studied the weather, glaciers, and the effects of altitude on the body, in addition to charting their courses in the harshest conditions. As a result of their work, scientists learned of previously unmapped areas and glaciers, including the watersheds of many rivers. Undertaking many arduous and treacherous climbs, Fanny set an altitude climbing record for women in 1903 by climbing Mt. Koser Gunga to 21,000 feet. She broke her own record three years later by ascending to 23,300 feet on Pinnacle Peak.

Fanny's hobby was unconventional for a woman to say the least, but she was not one to conform to society's expectations of a woman. Workman was a lifelong suffragist, and was photographed reading a paper with the headline "Votes For Women" on her record-setting trek up Pinnacle Peak. William shared his wife's belief regarding the equality of men and women. Despite her convictions, Fanny did dress "appropriately" in a long dress even during the most difficult climbs, although she shortened the length to her boot tops as she aged.

In 1908, another woman climber, ***Annie Smith Peck**, claimed to have broken Fanny's record with a 24,000-foot ascent of the Huascarán peak in the Andes mountains of Peru. However, Workman had Peck's assertion discredited by hiring a team of French engineers to measure the true height of that peak, which came to 21,812 feet. Workman's own record climb was later found to have reached only 22,815 feet, but even that lower number continued to stand as a record until 1934.

This inaccuracy was not the only one to be linked to the Workmans' research in the course of their expeditions. Lacking the training of skilled surveyors and unwilling to take the time needed to painstakingly prepare charts, the Workmans often included inaccurate maps and

data in their publications. Criticism of the Workmans extended to their treatment of their Asian guides and porters; the couple's rushed approach to mountain climbing and general disdain for those helping them resulted in strained relationships with their often-enormous crews of 100 or more people. In one instance, 150 members of a climbing party in Karakorum deserted the Workmans, taking much of the food with them.

In spite of these indiscretions, few historians dispute the fact that Fanny Workman's achievements were remarkable for the time in which she lived. She lectured extensively in Eu-

Fanny Workman with her husband William.

rope and America, earning the distinction of being the first American woman to lecture at the Sorbonne. She was also a member of prominent geographic societies, including the Royal Geographical Society (of which she was a fellow) and the Royal Asiatic Society. She earned the highest medals of ten different geographic societies in Europe.

Following World War I, the Workmans retired to France. Although 12 years the junior of her husband, Fanny preceded him in death, passing away at the age of 66 after enduring a long illness. Ever-mindful of women's issues, she bequeathed some $125,000 to four women's colleges—Bryn Mawr, Radcliffe, Smith, and Wellesley—continuing to support the causes of feminism and women's rights after her death.

The principle works of Fanny Workman, in collaboration with William Workman, include: *Algerian Memories* (1895), *Sketches Awheel in Modern Iberia* (1897), *Through Town and Jungle: 14,000 Miles Awheel among the Temples and People of the Indian Plain* (1904), *In the Ice World of the Himalaya* (1900), *Ice-bound Heights of Mustagh* (1908), *Peaks and Glaciers of Nun Kun* (1909), *The Call of the Snowy Hispar* (1910), and *Two Summers in the Ice Wilds of Eastern Karakorum* (1917). In addition, Workman also contributed articles to such prominent publications as *Putnam's* and *Harper's*.

SOURCES:

Garraty, John A., and Mark C. Carnes, eds. *American National Biography*. NY: Oxford University Press, 1999.

James, Edward T., ed. *Notable American Women, 1607–1950*. Cambridge, MA: The Belknap Press of Harvard University, 1971.

Magill, Frank N., ed. *Great Lives From History*. Vol. 5. Pasadena, CA: Salem Press, 1995.

McHenry, Robert, ed. *Famous American Women*. NY: Dover, 1980.

Drew Walker,
freelance writer,
New York, New York

Wormeley, Katharine Prescott

(1830–1908)

English-born American translator, author and philanthropist. Born on January 14, 1830, in Ipswich, Suffolk, England; died of pneumonia on August 4, 1908, in Jackson, New Hampshire; daughter of Ralph Randolph Wormeley (a rear admiral) and Caroline (Preble) Wormeley.

Selected writings: The Other Side of War *(1889);* The United States Sanitary Commission: A Sketch of Its Purpose and Work *(1864);* A Memoir of Honoré de Balzac *(1892).*

Selected translations: Honoré de Balzac's La Comédie Humaine *(40 vols., 1885–96);* The Works of Balzac *(1899); Paul Bourget's* Pastels Man *(1891, 1892), various works by Alexander Dumas (1894–1902), plays by Molière (1894–97),* The Works of Alphonse Daudet *(1898–1900),* Memoirs of the Duc de Saint-Simon *(1899),* Letters of **Mlle. de Lespinasse (1901),* Diary and Correspondence of Count Axel Fersen *(1902), Sainte-Beuve's* Portraits of the Eighteenth Century *(1905).*

Katharine Prescott Wormeley was born in Ipswich, England, in 1830. Her mother **Caroline Wormeley** was a daughter of an East India merchant from Boston and was also the niece of Commodore Edward Preble of the U.S. Navy. Her father Ralph Wormeley, a sixth-generation Virginian and a great-nephew of Edmund Randolph, who had served as George Washington's attorney general, spent his childhood in England. He eventually became a British subject and retired from the Royal Navy as a rear admiral. Politically liberal in his views, Ralph bequeathed a sense of social responsibility to his children. Katharine spent most of her childhood in various genteel environments in Europe; she lived in London from 1836 to 1839, followed by three years in Switzerland and France, and lived again in London from 1842 to 1847. Spending the following year again in France, her family returned to the United States in 1848, planning an extended visit. When her father died in 1852, Katharine and her family remained in the United States.

At the onset of the Civil War, Wormeley was one of the first to initiate and participate in relief work in Newport, Rhode Island, where her family was then living. In July 1861, she helped form and direct the local Women's Aid Society. Assisting the families of soldiers who were experiencing rough economic times, Wormeley secured a government contract to make clothing, which furnished work for the wives and daughters of soldiers. Under her direction, the women made more than 50,000 shirts during the winter of 1861–62. After leaving her position in the Women's Aid Society, Wormeley became a member of the hospital transport service of the U.S. Sanitary Commission, caring for the sick and wounded on hospital ships on the York and Pamunkey rivers. Much later, in 1889, she published the letters she had written during this period under the title *The Other Side of the War.*

Wormeley returned home in August 1862 and, the following month, accepted the position of lady superintendent of Lowell General Hospital, at nearby Portsmouth Grove, Rhode Island. Her duties at the hospital included directing the female nurses and the dietary kitchen, as well as the laundry and linen departments. During this time she was aided by assistant superintendents, including *Sarah Chauncey Woolsey and Sarah's cousins Jane Stuart Woolsey and Georgeanna Woolsey. After a year of difficult and stressful work, however, Wormeley became ill, resigned her position, and returned home to Newport to recover.

In the postwar years, Wormeley concentrated on charity work. One of her prominent achievements during this time was the founding of the Newport Charity Organization Society in 1879. She also administered classes in sewing and domestic work for impoverished women. In 1887, Wormeley founded an industrial school for girls where they could learn cooking, dressmaking, household work, and sewing. Wormeley was the school's director and financial supporter until it became a part of Newport's public school system in 1890.

Although she gave much of her time to charitable efforts, Wormeley is best known for her translations of noted French writers, particularly Honoré de Balzac, to which she devoted herself from the early 1880s to the end of her life. She also wrote *A Memoir of Honoré de Balzac* (1892). According to *Dictionary of American Biography*, Wormeley had made the translation of his voluminous (40 volumes) *La Comédie Humaine* such an obsession that "she apparently came to look upon its author as a personal charge" and suffered no criticism of him or his work. An accomplished French scholar with a profound understanding of French culture, Wormeley translated Balzac's work without losing its spirit or sense.

She spent the last years of her life in Jackson, New Hampshire, and died there on August 4, 1908, from pneumonia after breaking her hip from falling on the steps of her house. Her cremated remains were buried near Newport, Rhode Island, beside the grave of her father.

SOURCES:

Jackson, Kenneth T., ed. *Dictionary of American Biography*. NY: Scribner.

James, Edward T., ed. *Notable American Women, 1607–1950*. Cambridge, MA: The Belknap Press of Harvard University, 1971.

Drew Walker,
freelance writer,
New York, New York

Elsie Fogerty.
See Ashcroft, Peggy for sidebar.

Worns, Eila (1862–1934).

See Almeida, Julia Lopes de.

Worontsova, Ekaterina (1744–1810).

See Dashkova, Ekaterina.

Worsley, Katherine (1933—)

Duchess of Kent. Name variations: Katherine Windsor. Born Katherine Lucy Mary Worsley on February 22, 1933, in Hovingham Hall, York, Yorkshire, England; daughter of William Worsley and Joyce Brunner; married Edward Windsor (b. 1935), 2nd duke of Kent, on June 8, 1961; children: George, Lord St. Andrews (b. 1962); Lady Helen Windsor (b. 1964, who married Timothy Taylor); Nicholas (b. 1970).

Worth, Irene (1916—)

American actress and creative director. Born in Nebraska on June 23, 1916; University of California at Los Angeles, B.Edn., 1937; studied for the stage in London under Elsie Fogarty, 1944–45.

Born on June 23, 1916, in Nebraska, Irene Worth took to music as a child, studying piano and cello. After graduating from the University of California at Los Angeles in 1937, she worked as a schoolteacher until 1942, when at age 26 she made her first appearance on stage, touring with *Elizabeth Bergner in the play *Escape Me Never*. Later that year, Worth made her first appearance on Broadway in *The Two Mrs. Carrolls* at the Booth Theater. She then traveled to London where she studied acting with ◄ Elsie Fogerty. In February 1946, Worth made her London debut playing Elsie in *The Time of Your Life* at the Lyric Theater in Hammersmith. Remaining in Britain for over three years, she played a variety of parts in different productions, including that of Cella Copplestone in T.S. Eliot's *The Cocktail Party*, a role which she created. After six months back in New York in 1950, she returned to London.

Touring with various productions in the following years, Worth visited many countries including Germany and South Africa. She joined the Old Vic Company in October 1951, appearing at the Berlin Festival as Desdemona in *Othello*. She repeated her performance upon her return to London and earned praise from **Audrey Williamson**: "The girl who could flout convention and choose love not colour, who 'saw Othello's visage in his mind,' and concentrated all the spiritual and physical warmth and intensity of her nature on this one figure who held her tenderness, respect and imagination, became at last fully alive on the stage." Worth continued her Shakespearean performances as Helena in *A Midsummer Night's Dream* with the Old Vic that season. She also played Catherine de Vausselles in *The Other Heart*. With the same company in South Africa, she continued in these two roles and added Lady Macbeth to her Shakespearean repertoire. Back in London, she played Portia in *The Merchant of Venice*, a performance for which she received mixed reviews from the critics.

In 1953, after two highly successful years with the Old Vic, she collaborated with Tyrone Guthrie and Alec Guinness in founding the Stratford Festival in Ontario, Canada. This marked the starting point for one of the most interesting experiments in the North American theater, influencing production techniques everywhere by its abandonment of the proscenium arch and consistent use of an open, uncurtained stage. In addition to her role in Stratford as an organizer, Worth acted as well, performing Helena in *All's Well that Ends Well* and Queen Margaret in *Henry VI*.

The next years brought travel between London and New York and a 1958 appearance in the Edinburgh Festival. She returned to Stratford again in 1959, performing Rosalind in *As You Like It*. While in England in 1962, she joined the Royal Shakespeare Company to play the Marquise de Merteuil in *The Art of Seduction* (*Les liaisons dangereuses*). In 1964, playing the role of Alice in Edward Albee's *Tiny Alice*, Worth received the *Antoinette Perry (Tony) Award. The next year she received the *Evening Standard* Award for Best Actress for her work in Noel Coward's *Suite in Three Keys*.

A British Council tour in 1966 brought her to South America and various universities in the United States. In 1967, Worth performed at Yale University in *Prometheus Unbound*. Three years later, she returned again to Stratford, where she was critically acclaimed for her work in the starring role in *Hedda Gabler*. In 1974, she played Mrs. Alving in Greenwich Theater's *Ghosts*. She had already perfected her interpretation of this possessive, anguished mother at Stratford, an interpretation regarded as one of her greatest triumphs. Worth effectively conveyed the double guilt felt by Ibsen's heroine at her failure to live her own life satisfactorily and her terror at having transmitted the unmentionable disease of syphilis to her adored son Oswald. Her ability to dominate the stage had earlier been evident when she played Queen Margaret in Shakespeare's *Henry VI*.

Although she worked less in the cinema that many other actresses of her generation, Worth won the British Film Academy Award for her performance as Leonie in 1958's *Orders to Kill*, a drama set in occupied France in 1944. She has also had a distinguished career as a television actress and received awards for her performance in "The Lady from the Lake" and "The Lady from the Sea" in 1954. She has played all the great classic roles, and her fame in her native United States was recognized by the Obie Award for Sustained Achievement in the Theater in 1989. She received the Order of the British Empire as well.

SOURCES:

Herbert, Ian. *Who's Who in the Theatre*. Detroit, MI: Gale Research, 1977.
Morley, Sheridan. *The Great Stage Stars*. Australia: Angus & Robertson, 1986.

Drew Walker,
freelance writer,
New York, New York

Wortley, Emmeline Stuart- (1806–1855).

See Stuart-Wortley, Emmeline.

Wortley-Montagu, Lady Mary (1689–1762).

See Montagu, Lady Mary Wortley.

Wotton, Margaret

*Marquise of Dorset. Daughter of Robert Wotton; married Thomas Grey (1477–1530), 2nd marquess of Dorset; children: Henry Grey, duke of Suffolk; *Katherine Fitzalan (b. around 1520, who married Henry Fitzalan, 16th earl of Arundel); Elizabeth Grey (who married Thomas Audley). Thomas Grey was first married to Eleanor St. John.*

Wrather, Bonita Granville (1923–1988).

See Granville, Bonita.

Wray, Fay (1907—)

Canadian-born American actress best known for her performance as the giant ape's love interest in King Kong. *Born Vina Fay Wray on September 15, 1907, in Alberta, Canada; daughter of Joseph Wray; educated at Hollywood High School, Hollywood, California; married John Monk Saunders (a playwright and screenwriter), in 1928 (divorced 1939); married Robert Riskin (a screenwriter), in 1942 (died 1955); children: (second marriage) Susan, Robert, Victoria.*

Selected filmography: Blind Husbands *(1919)*; Gasoline Love *(1923)*; The Coast Patrol *(1925)*; Lazy Lightning *(1926)*; The Man in the Saddle *(1926)*; The Saddle Tramp *(1926)*; The Wild Horse Stampede *(1926)*; Loco Luck *(1927)*; A One Man Game *(1927)*; Spurs and Saddles *(1927)*; The First Kiss *(1928)*; The Honeymoon *(1928)*; Legion of the Condemned *(1928)*; The Street of Sin *(1928)*; The Wedding March *(1928)*;

The Four Feathers *(1929)*; Pointed Heels *(1929)*; Thunderbolt *(1929)*; Behind the Makeup *(1930)*; Border Legion *(1930)*; Captain Thunder *(1930)*; Paramount on Parade *(1930)*; The Sea God *(1930)*; The Texan *(1930)*; The Conquering Horde *(1931)*; Dirigible *(1931)*; The Finger Points *(1931)*; The Lawyer's Secret *(1931)*; Three Rogues *(Not Exactly Gentlemen, 1931)*; The Unholy Garden *(1931)*; Doctor X *(1932)*; The Most Dangerous Game *(The Hounds of Zaroff, 1932)*; Stowaway *(1932)*; Ann Carver's Profession *(1933)*; Below the Sea *(1933)*; The Big Brain *(Enemies of Society, 1933)*; The Bowery *(1933)*; King Kong *(1933)*; Master of Men *(1933)*; Mystery of the Wax Museum *(1933)*; One Sunday Afternoon *(1933)*; Shanghai Madness *(1933)*; The Vampire Bat *(1933)*; The Woman I Stole *(1933)*; The Affairs of Cellini *(1934)*; Black Moon *(1934)*; The Captain Hates the Sea *(1934)*; Cheating Cheaters *(1934)*; The Countess of Monte Cristo *(1934)*; Madame Spy *(1934)*; Once to Every Woman *(1934)*; The Richest Girl in the World *(1934)*; Viva Villa *(1934)*; White Lies *(1934)*; Woman in the Dark *(1934)*; Alias Bull Dog Drummond *(Bull Dog Jack, 1935)*; The Clairvoyant *(Evil Mind, 1935)*; Come Out of the Pantry *(1935)*; Mills of the Gods *(1935)*; Roaming Lady *(1936)*; They Met in a Taxi *(1936)*; When Knights Were Bold *(1936)*; It Happened in Hollywood *(1937)*; Murder in Greenwich Village *(1937)*; Once a Hero *(1937)*; The Jury's Secret *(1938)*; Navy Secrets *(1939)*; Smashing the Spy Ring *(1939)*; Wildcat Bus *(1940)*; Adam Had Four Sons *(1941)*; Melody for Three *(1941)*; Not a Ladies' Man *(1942)*; Small Town Girl *(1953)*; Treasure of the Golden Condor *(1953)*; The Cobweb *(1955)*; Queen Bee *(1955)*; Hell on Frisco Bay *(The Darkest Hour, 1956)*; Crime of Passion *(1957)*; Rock Pretty Baby *(1957)*; Tammy and the Bachelor *(Tammy, 1957)*; Dragstrip Riot *(1958)*; Summer Love *(1958)*; *"Gideon's Trumpet"* (television, 1980).

Selected writings: (with Sinclair Lewis) Angela Is 21 *(1939)*; (film, with Sinclair Lewis and Wanda Tuchock) This Is the Life *(1944)*; (autobiography) On the Other Hand: A Life Story *(1989)*.

One of six children, Fay Wray was born in 1907 near Cardston on her father's ranch in Alberta, Canada. She was a young child when her family moved first to Arizona and then Salt Lake City, Utah, so that her father could find better employment. After they relocated in California, her parents divorced, which created financial difficulties for the family. Wray was raised in Los Angeles and attended Hollywood High School, where she became interested in acting.

Wray and her mother began visiting casting offices, and at age 13, after many unsuccessful attempts to get into the movies, she finally received her first role in a comedy called *Blind Husbands* in 1919. She took small parts and worked as an extra in films for the next several years, in addition to participating in her high school's annual Hollywood Pilgrimage Play. Wray's break came in 1926 when director Erich von Stroheim selected her to star in his film *The Wedding March*. Described by Richard Lamparski as "a choppy but memorable silent film with some splendid photography," it was released in 1928 and transformed Wray into a star. That same year, she married playwright and screenwriter John Monk Saunders.

Although Wray had doubted she would have a career in the "talkies," throughout the 1930s she starred in film after film with such leading men as Gary Cooper, William Powell, Richard Arlen, Jack Holt, Ronald Colman, and Fredric March. However, it would be the 1933 film *King Kong*, with a gargantuan ape as her co-star, which secured her cinematic immortality. Wildly popular and financially successful when it was released, the film has since attained the status of a pop-cultural phenomenon. Although Wray later claimed that she had no idea

Fay Wray

about the plot of the film before signing the contract, she reportedly has quipped, "They told me I was going to have the tallest, darkest, leading man in Hollywood."

From the mid-1930s, Wray began starring in a series of low-budget action pictures, while continuing her own work as a playwright and Broadway actress, though without great success. In 1939, she and Saunders divorced. Wray retired in 1942 when she married her second husband, screenwriter Robert Riskin (who wrote *It Happened One Night*). She remained in retirement until the death of her husband in 1953, when she made a comeback as *Jane Powell's mother in *Small Town Girl*. The sale of *King Kong* to television in the 1950s introduced Wray, and her screams, to a new generation of fans. It also provided her the opportunity to make several films and episodic appearances on television programs such as "Alfred Hitchcock Presents" and "Perry Mason" in the mid-to-late 1950s, after which she again retired. She spent her time traveling and enjoying her cliff-side home in the Brentwood district of Los Angeles until 1980, when she came out of retirement to appear in the television movie "Gideon's Trumpet." Although Wray wrote several plays and stories that were largely unsuccessful, she also published her autobiography, *On the Other Hand*, in 1989. She continues to receive fan mail—mostly from adolescent boys—generated by repeated showings of *King Kong*.

SOURCES:

Contemporary Theatre, Film, and Television. Vol. 8. Detroit, MI: Gale Research, 1990.

Katz, Ephraim. *The Film Encyclopedia*. 3rd ed. NY: HarperPerennial, 1998.

Lamparski, Richard. *What Ever Became Of . . . ?* 2nd series. NY: Crown, 1968.

Drew Walker,
freelance writer,
New York, New York

Wrede, Mathilda (1864–1928)

Finnish prison reformer. Born on March 8, 1864, in Vaasa, Finland; died on December 25, 1928, in Finland; daughter of Baron Carl Gustav Wrede (governor of Finland's Vaasa district) and Baroness Eleonora Glansenstjerna; educated by tutors; attended a boarding school in Fredrikshamn (Hamina); spent one year in a Finnish folk school.

Born in 1864 in Vaasa, Finland, prison reformer and peace activist Mathilda Wrede was the daughter of the governor of Vaasa. One of nine children, she was raised by her father and her older sister **Helena Wrede** after her mother's death

in 1875. As a child, she developed the extraordinary sympathy for others which would drive her career. At a young age she developed a strong affection for animals, horses in particular, which lasted throughout her life. While still a girl she began to feel a great sympathy with and pity for prisoners whom she would encounter working on her father's estate—such prison labor being customary at that time. Despite the discouragement of her father and tutors, she began to interact with the prisoners, talking to them and showing them kindness. While some worried about what they felt to be her naive approach to hardened convicts, Mathilda showed a great deal of strength and respect for these men that was very unusual in her day. One of the first such instances occurred in her father's home where a prisoner had been sent to fix a door knob. Mathilda talked to this man, eventually sharing with him a deep religious experience she had recently had. The man showed interest in her conversation and had a friendly disposition, securing her lifelong belief that every person had some good in them, but that bad circumstances led them to crime.

She re-echoed this sentiment at the International Penal Conference in Petrograd, Russia, in 1890. A distinguished scholar had spoken regarding the incorrigibility of certain criminals and the uselessness of spending public money on reform efforts. Not a native speaker of the language nor an established scholar in the area, Mathilda courageously rose to speak of her personal experiences and deny the statement. She was applauded enthusiastically for contending that reform efforts should first concentrate on the spiritual being of the individuals involved, looking to God rather than specific laws and systems to transform the incorrigible. She was invited to a dinner with the tsar, an invitation she refused believing that the participation in luxury would threaten the trust she had earned from the prisoners that she was so dedicated to helping.

The Penal Conference was the beginning of Wrede's long career dedicated to improving Finnish prisons and reforming criminals through religious instruction. At first concentrating her efforts only on her father's estate, she worked closely with individual prisoners, earning their respect by respecting them. When they were released, Wrede helped them re-establish themselves as free men; each man who returned to an honest life reaffirmed her beliefs and inspired her to continue her efforts with other convicts. Wrede's family wealth and her social status allowed her to travel across Finland, meeting alone with thousands of incarcerated men. In 1886, her father gave her a farm for her own use, which she immediately put to use as a shelter and church for freed convicts.

Gradually Wrede gave up the luxuries she had been accustomed to, spending her considerable wealth not for her own comfort but on caring for her charges and their families; she is said to have owned only two dresses. In 1912 she gave an interview to a newspaper criticizing the state prison system for neglecting the physical well-being of its convicts. This sort of direct public criticism brought her the ire of prison officials, who began to deny Wrede private interviews with prisoners, and refused to let her visit them alone. She persisted in contacting freed prisoners, and as she became well respected in Finland for her charitable efforts, prison officials eventually relented.

During World War I, Wrede turned her efforts to helping Finnish soldiers, volunteering as a relief worker for their families. She refused to take sides in the Finnish War of Liberation of 1917, in which the Finnish tried to overthrow Russian rule, instead aiding the soldiers of both sides of the conflict. Her experiences of war led Wrede to dedicate herself to peace activism in Finland and abroad. During the Russian Civil War of 1917–18, she opened her home to the many refugees fleeing Russia who came to Finland. In 1919, she met with other peace activists in the Netherlands, where they formed the Fellowship of Reconciliation, dedicated to promoting international peace. Wrede's work for the Fellowship was largely concentrated on negotiating between Russia and Finland, trying to find an acceptable settlement to the issue of control of Finland. She was also active in protecting freedom of conscience and the rights of religious minorities in Finland. She was particularly successful in helping a group of Greek Orthodox priests living in Finland who were being forced to neglect the Orthodox calendar of holy days. Wrede appealed their case to the Finnish government and even to the League of Nations, eventually winning for them the right to worship by their own calendar.

In addition to peace, minority rights, and prison reform, Wrede was dedicated to helping animals as a member of the Society for the Prevention of Cruelty to Animals. Through all these efforts Mathilda Wrede became celebrated as a national heroine; on her 60th birthday she was given a house by a group representing the women of Finland, called the House of Honor. Wrede died there after a long illness at age 64, in 1928.

SOURCES:

Kenworthy, Leonard S. *Twelve Citizens of the World.* Garden City, NY: Doubleday, 1953.

Laura York, M.A. in History, University of California, Riverside, California

Wright, Frances (1795–1852)

British-born freethinker, writer, and public speaker who advocated radical social reform, abolition of slavery, and women's rights in the U.S., based on her criticism of the superstitions and immorality of Christianity. Name variations: Fanny Wright; Frances Wright d'Arusmont; Frances Darusmont. Born Frances Wright on September 6, 1795, in Dundee, Scotland; died in Cincinnati, Ohio, on December 13, 1852, from complications from a broken hip; daughter of James Wright (a linen merchant) and Camilla (Campbell) Wright; married William Phiquepal d'Arusmont, on July 22, 1831 (divorced); children: daughter (name not known, b. 1831 and died at age six months); Frances Sylva d'Arusmont (b. April 14, 1832).

Orphaned at age two, grew up in London and Dawlish, England; age 18, moved to Dundee, Scotland (1813); traveled to U.S. (1818–19); settled in U.S. (1824); established and lived with emancipation community at Nashoba, Tennessee (1825–29); moved to New Harmony, Indiana (1828); assumed editorship of New Harmony paper, changed its name to Free Enquirer, and moved with it to New York City (1828–29); purchased Hall of Science for weekly lectures and meetings on freethought subjects (1829); became frequent lecturer and writer on freethought and reform (1828–52).

Selected writings: Altorf: A Tragedy (1819); Views of Society and Manners in America (1821); A Few Days in Athens (1822); Course of Popular Lectures, with Three Addresses on Various Public Occasions, and a Reply to the Charges against the French Reformers of 1789 (1829); Biography, Notes, and Political Letters (1844); England the Civilizer (1848); and numerous articles and lectures published in the Free Enquirer.

At a time when few women assumed a public role, Frances Wright became the first woman in America to ascend to fame as a public speaker and social reformer. By 1830, her notoriety had reached such a level that the New York City press labeled her "The Red Harlot of Infidelity." Never afraid to air her views or scoff at the conventions of proper society, Frances Wright bore the double stigma in the early 19th century of being a religious skeptic and an educated, independent woman. As a result of her lectures and writings, she became the most well-known leader of the freethought movement in the 1820s and 1830s.

The goal which shaped the career of Frances Wright was simple: to rekindle in America an understanding of the principles upon which it was founded and to call on its people and its government to live up to the promise which the Revolution had begun—in short, to recreate American society into a nation truly dedicated to liberty of conscience and to legal, economic, and social equality for all its citizens—male and female, black, red, and white. To accomplish this, she believed, radical change in society and in education was needed. Not until the superstitions of Christianity were replaced by the principles of reason, she argued vehemently, would society be freed from its bonds to the inequities and oppression of the past.

Wright was born in Dundee, Scotland, in 1795, to a family of means, but was orphaned at age two. Raised by their mother's aristocratic relatives, Frances and her younger sister **Camilla Wright** spent their childhood in London and in Dawlish, Devonshire, England. Though she chafed at the rigidness of her maiden aunt and the conservative views of an unsympathetic grandfather, Wright was fortunate to receive a solid education and opportunities for learning well beyond those provided for most females in her society. In addition, to fill the lonely hours of her youth, Wright took advantage of the libraries and learned people around her. Indeed, according to biographers Alice Perkins and Theresa Wolfson, she began to think of herself as possessing extraordinary "gifts of genius" and worried that she would die before she could put her talents to use. Her pursuit of knowledge, it seemed, was unquenchable, and she began at a very young age to question what she perceived to be the injustices and inconsistencies of the world around her. The death of her older brother Richard (raised by another uncle), as a young soldier in the Napoleonic Wars, confirmed Fanny's suspicion that she was marked for special suffering and strengthened the lifelong bond between the two sisters.

In her quest for understanding, Wright did not limit herself to reading. During her youth, she was struck by the misery of many, both workers in London and the peasantry in Devonshire, who had not been fortunate enough to have been born into the higher classes. As she recalled in her biography, her sympathies "were powerfully drawn towards the sufferings of humanity, and thus her curiosity was vividly excited to discover their causes." On a trip through the countryside with her aunt, the young Fanny observed peasants living at subsistence level, and she began to think about the lives of the poor, burdened with taxes, tithes, poor-rates, game laws, unemployment, and other economic hardships. Do these people also have no rights? she

wondered. Are they entitled to nothing? Soon after, she claimed, she took a solemn oath "to wear ever in her heart the cause of the poor and helpless; and to aid in all that she could in redressing the grievous wrongs which seemed to prevail in society." It is that oath which guided the course of her adult life.

During this period, Wright also developed a fascination with the United States. It was while engrossed, perplexed, and often depressed with silent and unsuccessful efforts to arrive at a satisfactory view of truth in anything, she explained, that she first came across a history of America by the Italian writer Bocca which filled her with excitement. "Life was full of promise," she reported. Finally she knew that "there existed a country consecrated to freedom, and in which man might awake to the full knowledge and full exercise of his powers." She determined there and then, at age 16, to direct her sights and her life toward America.

At age 18, Wright moved with her sister to Glasgow, Scotland, to escape the restrictions of her mother's family. There they were welcomed into the family of their great-uncle, James Milne, respected professor of moral philosophy at the University of Glasgow and leader in the rationalist empiricism of the Scottish Enlightenment. She had finally found a lively and progressive intellectual environment which suited her tastes and talents. The Milne family and their friends stimulated and encouraged Wright in her pursuit of truth and engaged her in parlor discussions on literature, philosophy, and current issues ranging from republican principles to legislation against the slave trade.

Wright also indulged her continuing fascination for the United State by reading everything available on its history. She even tried her hand at playwriting, composing a short drama, entitled *Altorf: A Tragedy*, which extolled republican principles in the guise of a fictitious event in the aftermath of the Swiss war for independence from the Habsburgs. She found no stage or publisher for such a play in Britain, but it would eventually be performed in Philadelphia in 1819, to limited success, and then published in America. In the preface, Wright criticized the lack of freedom in the press of Great Britain and revealed her affinity for the United States, explaining to American readers that she "sought their country uninvited, from a sincere admiration of the government, a heart-felt love of its freedom, a generous pride and sympathy in its rising greatness."

In September 1818, after three years in Glasgow, Frances and her sister Camilla sailed to

New York, and, for the next 19 months, they traveled from New York City through the western frontier of New York State, from Niagara through Canada, down through the battle sites at Lake Champlain, through Vermont, to Philadelphia and Washington, and briefly to Virginia. Fanny kept account of her experiences in a series of letters to an older friend in Scotland, subsequently published in 1821 as *Views of Society and Manners in America*. Filled with observations on America's tolerance and freedom, and on the limits to those ideals in areas such as slavery and female education, this book launched her career as a public figure. *Views and Manners* was read widely in both countries, bringing criticism of Wright from conservatives in New York for identifying America's faults, and praise from liberals in Europe for identifying its virtues. Yet perhaps its most important effect on Wright's career was that it brought her two new and important acquaintances upon her return to Europe: the utilitarian philosopher Jeremy Bentham in England, and the Marquis de Lafayette in France, both of whom were impressed with her defense of republicanism.

Has treason gone so far in this land, for EQUALITY to be denounced as a dream of enthusiasts, an innovation of foreigners?

—Frances Wright

Over the course of the next several years, Bentham, whom she affectionately referred to as "her Socrates," introduced her to many leading intellectuals of the day. Wright's later writings and addresses reveal strong affinities with the basic tenets of utilitarianism she absorbed during these years. Testifying to the extent of Bentham's influence, in 1822 Wright published a second play (actually written in 1818), *A Few Days in Athens*, and dedicated it to Bentham, "as a testimony of her admiration of his enlightened sentiments, useful labors, and active philanthropy, and of gratitude for his friendship." In this play, two ideas surfaced which would remain characteristic of her thought: an abhorrence of intolerance; and the inklings of a materialist epistemology which would lead her to reject all dogma and superstition as the enemies of reason, freedom, and equality. The play centered around a figure in ancient Athens who investigated various schools of philosophy, concluding that all have their prejudices and that rather than choosing one school to which to belong, the best advice is "think for yourself." At play's end, its only female character sums up Wright's message: "Trust me, there are as many ways of living as there are men, and one is no

more fit to lead another, than a bird to lead a fish, or a fish a quadruped."

Wright's friendship with Lafayette proved even more influential. For the next three years, she became his almost constant companion, and through him, met many of the most influential liberals in Europe. When Lafayette accepted the invitation of President James Monroe to tour America as its honored guest in 1824, Wright accompanied him (raising more than a few American eyebrows) and met many of America's leaders as well. She then remained in the United States with a specific mission in mind.

Wright's first visit to America had made her keenly aware of the disparity between the country's theory and practice of equality on one vital issue: slavery. Her comments on it ran through her letters home, both published and private. Appalled by the moral inconsistency of slavery continuing in her ideal country, she determined to undertake a social experiment which, she hoped, would lead to the emancipation of all African-American slaves.

On her travels westward with Lafayette in the spring of 1825, Wright passed through New Harmony, Indiana, the site of the new communitarian experiment of Robert Owen, the British socialist. Owen's social and economic theories strongly influenced Wright's ideas and specifically her budding plan for an experimental emancipation community. She also met Owen's son, Robert Dale Owen, who would become her friend and associate in the active days ahead. After a second trip westward that summer, she published *A Plan for the Gradual Abolition of Slavery in the United States Without Danger of Loss to the Citizens of the South*, in the Baltimore newspaper *Genius of Universal Emancipation*.

The plan entailed convincing the U.S. Congress to establish model plantations in the southwest cotton belt on which slaves would be educated to be economically self-sufficient, trained in the principles of freedom and equality, and then colonized elsewhere, outside the United States. It was a fairly conservative plan, compared to calls by other abolitionists for the immediate general emancipation of slaves. But she defended her scheme as good for both the slaves and the Southern economy: the slaves would be properly educated for freedom, and the economy of the South would be strengthened at the same time. In her view, the necessary moral reform could be accomplished only by choice and not by coercion. Wright was convinced that if she could demonstrate that the moral imperative was economically advantageous, slaveowners would gradually see

Frances Wright

the light and participate voluntarily. To provide a model, she purchased some land in western Tennessee in December 1825 and began an emancipation community at Nashoba with about a dozen manumitted slaves and a handful of co-workers.

The experiment was a miserable failure. Wright suffered in the climate of western Tennessee and the community suffered from inexperience with farming and from scandal. Based on reports that one of the white leaders, James Richardson, had begun living with one of the mulatto women residents, Nashoba was derided as a community which fostered free love and miscegenation. This put Wright in a bind. On

the one hand, she did reject the sanctity of the marriage bond and did not see any moral barrier to interracial relationships. Part of the purpose of the Nashoba experiment had been to remove the obstacles created by all forms of slavery, including the tyranny of marriage laws which subjugated women to men and bound people together long after affection between them had died. On the other hand, such reports damaged the community's image in the public mind, and she would have preferred to keep the details quiet. The hoped-for public support never materialized.

In the fall of 1829, Wright announced the end of the Nashoba experiment. Accompanied by William Phiquepal d'Arusmont (her future husband), she traveled with the emancipated slaves to their new home in Haiti in January 1830. By then, however, she already had embarked upon a new, and broader, mission.

Because of Nashoba, Wright concluded that small experiments were not the best means to accomplish real social reform. She had "begun at the wrong end." Instead, the place to start must be with the public mind. "Reform, to be effective," she insisted in her biography, "must be rightly understood *in its principles* by a collective body politic, and carried forward wisely, consistently, with due regard to the interests of all concerned, by that body politic." The task now was to convince others of the rightness of reform. It was to the process of educating the American public in the basic principles of liberty—in effect, retraining society—that she dedicated the remainder of her life.

The years 1828–30 were Wright's most active and public. She undertook lecture tours through the western frontier and the cities of the eastern seaboard, focusing on the principles of reason and the problems of inequality and injustice in areas of class, sex, and race. To disseminate her views more widely, with Robert Dale Owen she edited a weekly paper called the *Free Enquirer* (1828–35) in New York City, whose motto explained their purpose: "Just opinions are the result of just knowledge,—just practice of just opinions." By encouraging free enquiry on all subjects, she hoped to instruct society in "truth" and in "reason," in order to lay the foundation for the rational reform of society in all its laws and institutions. The problem, as she saw it, was that the U.S. was a land of great hope and promise, but it was not living up to its promise. "The great principles stamped in America's declaration of independence," she declared in one lecture, "are true, are great, are sublime, and are *all her own.* But her usages, her law, her religion, her education, are false, narrow, prejudiced, ignorant, and are the relic of dark ages." The reason for its shortcomings, she argued, was at base the negative influence of Christianity and its clergy.

Faced with what seemed to her to be an increase in revivalism on the frontier and in the cities and a rise in evangelical religion, Wright sought to replace what she considered emotionalism and superstition with an appeal to reason. Religion, she argued in her lectures, preys on "human credulity and nervous weakness," especially in women and youth, and interferes with a rational understanding of the principles of morality and truth. Worse, she feared that Christian clergy were attempting to form a "Christian party in politics" which would undermine the American principle of religious freedom.

Attacked as an infidel, Wright welcomed the label, for she firmly believed in the need to reject all religious dogma, just as she rejected all forms of tyranny over the mind and heart of society. Instead, she emphasized the need to doubt, to inquire, and to break away from the unwarranted dominance of the clergy. When an opponent asked on one occasion whether or not there is a God, she responded, as she reported in the *Free Enquirer*: "I am unable to inform him" one way or the other. She insisted that one should concentrate on what one *can* know, rather than hypothesize about what one cannot know with any certainty. Christianity claimed knowledge where it had none, which led it to assert as true doctrines which were inconsistent, contradictory, and absurd. What Wright advocated was a morality based on the principles of reason rather than on some fictitious God. People then would need no outside influence to explain what is morally right, and certainly not the influence of "priests" who have a vested interest in perpetuating the authority of the Church and its "outdated" beliefs. Then, as a result of rational investigation, people would come to support the causes of equality and justice for slaves, women, laborers, and other disenfranchised members of society.

Thus criticism of Christianity was a product of her philosophy and a means to an end. The consequences of Wright's insistence on reason and the principles of freedom and equality were a passionate commitment to reform on a number of issues: free and universal public education for citizens of all classes and both sexes; opposition to state and federal laws based on Christian belief and practice (such as Sunday "blue laws," prohibition of Sunday mail service, and blasphemy laws); involvement in the nascent labor movement of New York City to secure political rights for the working classes; and reform of laws and attitudes on a variety of social issues ranging from marriage, divorce, and contraception to civil rights, improved status for women, and criminal justice. She also became perhaps the most notorious woman in America, derided not only as that "bold blasphemer and voluptuous preacher of licentiousness," but also as a "female monster" who, against all propriety, took the public-lecture platform, stepping far over the line of acceptable female behavior.

Wright was not alone in her work. By the late 1820s and early 1830s, there were a number of writers and lecturers on the freethought circuit—most notably Robert Dale Owen, Abner Kneeland, Benjamin Offen, George Houston, and Gilbert Vale—and freethinking citizens in numerous cities had organized into societies to support the cause. But Fanny Wright remained the most infamous leader. The movement achieved little in real reform; but its legacy continued in the writings of leaders like Wright and in the power of its vision as inspiration for future reformers. Through the pages of her newspapers, lectures and debates, and tireless devotion to the activities of the freethought movement, Wright helped define the vision of a more rational and just society in America.

Frustrated by lack of widespread popular support, Wright virtually disappeared from the American scene between the years 1831 and 1836. For most of that time she was in France, preoccupied with marriage and family. In 1831, soon after the death of her sister, Wright married William d'Arusmont after learning she was pregnant with his child. The marriage was mostly one of convenience; Wright had sharply criticized contemporary marriage laws which reduced wives to little more than the property of men, but she feared the effects of society's condemnation upon a bastard child. Sadly, their daughter died at six months, but a second daughter, **Frances Sylva d'Arusmont**, born in April 1832, survived.

Marriage and family could not consume Wright's energies for long. She returned to the U.S. in late 1835 and began a new series of lectures in the spring of 1836 in Cincinnati, and then in New York, Philadelphia, and Boston. The winter of 1836–37 found Wright in Philadelphia engaged in publishing her own monthly paper, *A Manual of American Principles*. The motto recalled the earlier days of the *Free Enquirer*: "Independence, Liberty, Justice; from the three, shall proceed happiness." Yet the paper soon folded.

By 1838, Wright broadened her interest in political philosophy and practical reform to encompass the history of civilization. The result was her magnum opus, *England the Civilizer*, which, though never well received, was the capstone on a lifetime search for the causes of injustice in society. Her concern still centered on republican principles, the rights of women, and the needs of the laboring classes, but now she ranged back through the history of Western civilization to explore both the origins and pervasiveness of injustice and the history of innovation and efforts for justice. What she discovered, she believed, was that the problems endemic in American society were products of millennia of

subjection and degradation of those not in power. Progress would occur only when society turned its attention from the individual to the public good. It was up to women, she argued, to "give the tone in this" and place themselves "everywhere on the side of humanity, union, order, right reason, and right feeling."

In the 1840s and early 1850s, Wright continued her moral and educational crusade. One might expect that she would have joined the lead of the rising abolitionist movement; she did not. Her strong antipathy to the churches, whose members formed much of the abolitionist movement, kept her away. Moreover, her belief that immediate abolition would be detrimental to both slaves and society at large remained intact. It also may be, as Perkins and Wolfson suggest, that she did not want to "play second fiddle in a field where she had already made the supreme sacrifices of fortune, health, and personal reputation." In any case, her conviction that progress could only be achieved through a slow process of education ran counter to the calls of William Lloyd Garrison and other advocates of abolition and immediate emancipation.

On women's rights, too, Wright remained aloof from the blossoming suffrage movement. This is not to say, however, that Wright had no connection at all to the movement. Since 1828, Wright had forcefully and repeatedly argued for women's rights and for the value of women, and many women and men heard and read her views, including reformers like *Lucretia Mott and Orestes Brownson. *Susan B. Anthony displayed a picture of Frances Wright on a wall in her study, along with portraits of other past reformers she admired; and both Anthony and *Elizabeth Cady Stanton recognized Wright's contribution as a lecturer on behalf of women.

Much of Wright's energy in the decade before her death was consumed by personal concerns. Her husband's long illness, his legal and financial difficulties, estrangement and child custody problems, and finally divorce took their toll. Following a year of suffering after falling and badly breaking a hip, Wright died on December 13, 1852. The press, which 20 years earlier had excoriated her so often, barely noticed.

Frances Wright was a precursor of progress, a prophet of an idea whose time had not yet come. As with most prophets, her legacy lies not in reforms she accomplished, but in the inspiration she gave to others of more practical bent. As a vocal, confident, articulate woman who refused to be limited in her role because of her sex, Wright stands out as a model for women who followed. Her public career on behalf of equality and freedom has earned her an honored place in the pages of American and Western history as one of the outspoken voices of dissent from complacency, credulity, injustice, and intolerance.

SOURCES:

d'Arusmont, Frances Wright. *Life, Letters, and Lectures, 1834–1844.* NY: Arno, 1972.

Eckhardt, Celia Morris. *Fanny Wright: Rebel in America.* Cambridge, MA: Harvard University Press, 1984.

Perkins, Alice, and Theresa Wolfson. *Frances Wright, Free Enquirer: The Study of a Temperament.* NY: Harper Bros., 1939.

Post, Albert. *Popular Freethought in America, 1825–1850,* 1943 (rep. ed., NY: Octagon Books, 1974).

Wright, Frances. *Altorf: A Tragedy.* Philadelphia, PA: Mathew Carey & Son, 1819.

——. *England the Civilizer: Her History Developed in its Principles; With Reference to the Civilizational History of Modern Europe (America Inclusive) and with a View to the Denouement of the Difficulties of the Hour.* London: Simpkin, Marshall, 1848.

——. *A Few Days in Athens, being the translation of a Greek manuscript discovered in Herculaneum.* London: Longman, Hurst, Rees, Orme, and Brown, 1822.

——. *Views of Society and Manners in America,* 1821 (rep. ed., Cambridge, MA: Harvard University Press, 1963).

——, and Robert Dale Owen, eds. *Free Enquirer.* New York, 1828–32.

SUGGESTED READING:

Kolmerton, Carol A. *Women in Utopia: The Ideology of Gender in the American Owenite Communities.* Bloomington, IN: Indiana University Press, 1990.

Lockwood, George B. *The New Harmony Movement,* 1905 (rep. ed. NY: Augustus M. Kelley, 1970).

Taylor, Anne. *Visions of Harmony: A Study in Nineteenth-Century Millenarianism.* Oxford: Clarendon, 1987.

COLLECTIONS:

Correspondence and papers located in the Houghton Library, Harvard University; the National Library of Scotland, Edinburgh; the British Library, London; the Bloomsbury Science Library, University College, London University; the Theresa Wolfson Papers, Labor-Management Documentation Center, Martin P. Catherwood Library, Cornell University; and the Cincinnati Historical Society.

Terry E. Sparkes,
Assistant Professor of Religion,
Luther College, Decorah, Iowa

Wright, Haidée (1868–1943)

*English actress. Name variations: Haidee Wright. Born in London, England, on January 13, 1868; died on January 29, 1943; daughter of Fred Wright (an actor-manager) and Jesse (Frances) Wright (an actress); sister of Fred, Huntley, Bertie, and **Marie** Wright (all actors).*

Like her sisters and brothers, Haidée Wright was trained for the stage in her father's touring company. She first appeared in April 1878 as Diamond Wetherwick in *The Hoop of Gold.* In 1887, Wright made her London debut at the Pavilion Theater as Esther Forester in *False Lights.* Her initial West End appearance was at the Lyric in 1896, as Stephanus in *The Sign of the Cross,* opposite Wilson Barrett. In 1908, Wright portrayed Miss Kite in *The Passing of the Third Floor Back* at the St. James and toured the United States in the same role from 1909 to 1911. In 1911, she played Anna in Maxim Gorky's *The Lower Depths* at the Kingsway Theater. The year 1913 found her back in New York playing Miss Scrotton in *Tante* at the Empire. Returning to London in 1917, she appeared as Mrs. Hilperty in *The Melody of Youth,* as Mother Marguerite in *Cyrano de Bergerac* (1919), as Madame de Musset in *Madame Sand* (1920), as Queen *Elizabeth I in *Will Shakespeare* (1921), as Mrs. David Garrick (***Eva-Maria Veigel**) in *Ned Kean of Old Drury* (1923), and once again as Queen Elizabeth in *Dark Lady of the Sonnets* (1923). Crisscrossing the Atlantic, Wright appeared in New York as Fanny Cavendish in the *Royal Family* in 1927. In 1932, in London, she took on the part of Napoleon's mother ***Letizia Bonaparte** in *Napoleon;* her last stage appearance was as Martha Blackett in *Gentle Rain* in 1936. Wright's films include *The Blarney Stone, Jew Süss,* and *Tomorrow We Live.*

Wright, Helen (1914–1997)

American astronomer and author. Name variations: Helen Wright Greuter. Born Helen Wright in Washington, D.C., on December 20, 1914; died of heart failure at the Thomas House Retirement Home in Washington, D.C., on October 23, 1997; only daughter of four children of Frederick Eugene Wright (a well-known petrologist and consultant for the National Parks) and Kathleen Ethel (Finley) Wright (who graduated from McGill University in Montreal with the governor-general's medal for highest honors in history and languages); attended Madeira School in Washington, the Mont Choisi in Lausanne, Switzerland, and Bennett School in Millbrook, New York; graduated from Bennett Junior College, 1934; Vassar College, B.A., 1937, M.A., 1939; married John Franklin Hawkins (an artist), in 1946 (divorced); married Rene Greuter (died early 1970s); no children.

Helen Wright was a pioneering American astronomer who founded and directed the great California observatories: Mount Wilson, in Pasadena, and Mount Palomar. She also founded

The Astrophysical Journal, one of the preeminent journals of astronomy and physics, before turning to freelance writing and editing in the 1940s; her subjects included mathematics, physics, anthropology, and archaeology. Wright's career began at Vassar College, where she worked as a student assistant in the astronomy department and won the Lucy Kellogg English Prize in astronomy and physics. While doing graduate work at Vassar, she wrote her M.A. thesis on "A Preliminary Investigation of the Topography of the Moon."

During World War II, Wright was a junior astronomer at the U.S. Naval Observatory. She is best known for her books *Sweeper of the Sky: The Life of *Maria Mitchell* (Macmillan, 1949) and *Explorer of the Universe: A Biography of George Ellery Hale* (Dutton, 1966). Wright also chronicled the creation of Palomar, then the world's largest telescope (1952).

Wright, Helena (1887–1982)

English medical practitioner, early advocate of family planning in England, China, and India, and author. Name variations: Helena Rosa Lowenfeld. Born Helena Rosa Lowenfeld on September 17, 1887, in Brixton, London, England; died on March 21, 1982; daughter of Heinz Lowenfeld; educated at the Cheltenham Ladies' College and the London School of Medicine for Women; married Henry Wardel Snarey Wright (a surgeon).

Worked as a medical missionary, medical officer of a woman's health-care clinic, and as a gynecologist in private practice; published seven books, including The Sex Factor in Marriage *(1930) and* Sex and Society *(1968); advocated improvement and reform of women's health care.*

Helena Wright was born Helena Rosa Lowenfeld in London, England, in 1887, where she studied at Cheltenham Ladies' College and the London School of Medicine for Women. She became a member of the Royal College of Surgeons, England, and a Licentiate of the Royal College of Surgeons, London, in 1914, going on to earn an M.B. and B.S. in 1915. Afterwards she married surgeon Henry Wardel Wright of the Royal Army Medical College. The two traveled to Shantung Christian University, in Tsinan, China, where they worked as medical missionaries from 1919 to 1927. Helena Wright was an associate gynecologist at the university.

Returning to England thereafter, Wright became involved in the movement for birth control. She worked as a medical officer for the North Kensington Women's Welfare Centre and then in private practice as a gynecologist until 1975; she also helped set up the International Committee on Planned Parenthood (later known as the International Planned Parenthood Federation). Wright upheld women's rights to free choice and was prepared to recommend abortion for unplanned pregnancies. As well, she actively worked as an advocate for prisoners and had a great deal of success as a writer, authoring seven books, including *The Sex Factor in Marriage* (1930), which sold over one million copies. *Sex and Society* (1968) initiated public awareness regarding the effects of voluntary fertility on society. Serving as a family planning consultant to several underdeveloped countries, Wright traveled to India at age 88 to continue this work. She died on March 21, 1982, at age 94.

Drew Walker,
freelance writer,
New York, New York

Wright, Judith (1915–2000)

Australian writer, conservationist, and campaigner for Aboriginal rights, who is considered the doyenne of Australia's women poets. Born Judith Arundell Wright on May 31, 1915, in Armidale, New South Wales (NSW), Australia; died of a heart attack on June 26 (some sources cite June 25), 2000, in Canberra; daughter of Phillip Arundell Wright (a pastoralist and businessman) and Ethel (Bigg) Wright; had two brothers Bruce (b. 1917) and Peter (b. 1919); educated at the New England Girls School, 1929–33, and University of Sydney, 1934–36, as a non-matriculating student in English honors; married Jack McKinney, 1944 (died 1966 or 1967); children: one daughter, Meredith McKinney (b. April 21, 1950).

Moved to Tambourine Mountain in Queensland (1948); awarded a Commonwealth Literary Fund Scholarship to write a novel and the Grace Leven Poetry prize (1949); edited a book of Australian verse and gave Commonwealth Literary Fund Lectures at the University of Queensland (1956); co-founded the Wildlife Preservation Society of Queensland (WPSQ, 1962) and held the post of president (1962–76); awarded honorary doctorates from the University of New England and the University of Queensland (1963); given the Encyclopaedia Britannica award (1964); appointed a fellow of the Australian Academy of Humanities (1970); granted an Australian National University creative fellowship (1973); appointed a member of the Commonwealth Government Committee of Enquiry into the National Estate (1973); awarded a Creative Arts fellowship from the Australian Na-

tional University and appointed to the University Council (1974); awarded the Robert Frost Medallion of the Fellowship of Australian Writers (1975); awarded an honorary doctorate of letters from the University of Sydney and an ANZAC fellowship to visit New Zealand (1976); awarded an honorary doctorate of letters from Monash University and a Senior Writer's fellowship from the Literature Board of the Australia Council (1977); awarded the Order of Golden Ark: Degree of Ridder (1980); became an honorary life member of the Australian Conservation Foundation (1981); awarded the ASAN World Prize for Poetry (1984); lived in Braidwood, NSW.

Selected works: The Moving Image (1946); Woman to Man (1949); The Gateway (1953); The Two Fires (1955); The Generations of Men (history, 1959); Australian Bird Poems (1961); Birds (1962); Judith Wright (1963); Five Senses (1963); City Sunrise (1964); The Nature of Love (short stories, 1966); The Other Half (1966); Collected Poems, 1942–1970 (1971); Alive (1973); Because I Was Invited (1975); Fourth Quarter and Other Poems (1976); The Coral Battleground (1977); The Double Tree: Selected Poems, 1942–1976 (1978); Reef, Rainforest, Mangroves, Man (1980); Phantom Dwelling (1985); We Call for a Treaty (1985); A Human Pattern (1990); as well as various children's books and literary criticism.

Both the work and activism of Judith Wright, who is considered one of Australia's greatest poets, were marked by her relationship with her country's landscapes, from the bush and farming land to the rainforests of Queensland. While these settings were perhaps intrinsically linked to her poetic development, it was also via the land, which she sought to protect as a conservationist, that she came to her support for Aboriginal rights, penning lines like: "Did we not know their blood channelled our rivers/ and the black dust our crops ate was their dust?" On her death in 2000, fellow poet Robert Gray spoke the thoughts of many when he called Wright "the conscience of this country."

She was born Judith Arundell Wright during 1915 in Armidale, New South Wales (NSW), into a family which still maintains a strong presence in the district. From the time of their move to Australia in 1828, her ancestors were pastoralists and landowners in this fertile area; she would later say of them: "They were those who chose to adapt themselves to the new environment rather than superimpose their class values of Englishness upon it." Wright lived with her family on a remote sheep and cattle station,

"Wollomombi," and her enduring connection with the Australian landscape was encouraged early. In the introduction to *The Double Tree* (1978), she would write that it was her father, a wealthy pastoralist, who "taught me to look at the country with seeing eyes."

Her mother encouraged the children to work outside, establishing in Wright a love and respect for the work of her family, and encouraged her daughter's poetic tastes by reading to her children from classic English and Australian poets—Tennyson, Burns, Shelley, Henry Lawson, and A.B. Patterson. Wright's grandmother, **May**, recited nursery rhymes to the children, and Wright would later acknowledge that she was never able to write successfully without such rhythm.

Although she had two younger brothers, Wright led a solitary youth. The station, now the home of the University of New England, is still sparsely, though diversely populated. While Wright's biographer Bill Scott has noted that she started composing poems as soon as she could put pen to paper, the young Wright was not confined to study. Her father believed in the freedom of youth and let his children range over the property, doing as they wished, an experience Wright found "confidence producing."

Her mother died when Judith was 12 as a result of the 1919 influenza pandemic. Wright was educated by governesses, not an uncommon practice for families living on the land, especially due to the availability of correspondence courses by the New South Wales department of education. Writer Alec Derwent Hope maintains that this was a fortunate arrangement for Wright. As a member of a literate family, she was encouraged to read and—without the time constraints of school attendance—was able to follow her own interests. The children were taught in the morning, leaving the rest of the day for reading, then roaming on foot or horseback (Wright was riding by age two). Particularly lonely after her mother's death, Wright visited with the nearest girl of her own age, a cousin who lived about 20 miles away. Often they rode and met halfway, sharing lunch and talk before their rides back home.

Following her father's remarriage, at age 14 Wright was sent to boarding school at the New England Girls School in Armidale (the area around Armidale is known as New England). She was by this time already a published writer, having had six letters and six poems published in the *Sydney Mail* sometime between 1927 and 1929. In Armidale, her work was published in the school's *Chronicle*. Wright, however, was "miserable" by her own account, later noting that the "only thing I had to treasure was poetry and the knowledge that I was going to be a poet." If this desire deviated from the path her family might have laid out for her, Wright was not to be deterred. Her biographer **Veronica Brady** would later note: "She was born into a pastoral family who expected her to become a grazier's wife and just bear children, but she was determined to become a writer. She was a woman who simply went her own way. Nobody was going to stop her and she did what she wanted to." Away from her own family of strong personalities and ideas, she could not have been accustomed to the regimentation imposed by school life. One positive influence at the time was an English teacher who fostered her interest in, and talent for, poetic composition.

From 1934 to 1936, Wright followed an unconventional course of study at the University of Sydney, where she did not enroll in classes for any particular degree, despite the university's disapproval of such a choice. Rather, she studied in a wide range of areas. She read widely in Eng-

lish, participating in the Honors stream under Professor Waldock, and sources indicate that she learned French and Italian independently and read poetry in these languages. Her further studies included anthropology, in order to gain greater understanding of the native Aboriginals of Australia; philosophy and psychology, because of an interest in people's motives, thoughts and emotions; and history with particular emphasis on Oriental history (under Professor Salder who entertained a number of students at his home). Wright's reading was directed by the *Guide to Kulchur* by Ezra Pound who along with modernist poet T.S. Eliot impacted her work (although A.D. Hope would note them to be ambiguous influences). Wright would take her dislike of academics ("ackers")—for their inclination to anatomize poetry—into later life. Jim McIlroy would note: "Wright was critical of the way poetry was taught in schools, but like so many others I recall Judith's poems as the soul of Australian poetry from my school days."

Scott maintains that a more formal university training would not have been much use to Wright,

Judith Wright

who by this age not only was determined to be a writer but also possessed a clear sense of the sort of writer she would be. Wright would later remark that she had hoped her diverse studies "might offer a useful insight into society and its mysterious failures and achievements." While at the university, she was involved with the student newspaper *Honi Soit*, a publication which still serves as an early stomping ground for Australian writers.

> *W*hat the hell are people doing, and why are they doing it?
>
> —Judith Wright

Following her time at the University of Sydney, Wright embarked on a year's travel in Europe with a cousin, a not uncommon choice for young people of families able to fund such expeditions. Nonetheless, she had little money with which to manage day to day. With her cousin, she took walking tours in Austria, Germany, Hungary, and Scotland, feeling a personal connection to the latter, as Rob Roy (immortalized in the novel by Sir Walter Scott) was related through family tradition (the Wright family was part of the Macgregor clan). Whereas many young Australian writers undertook such journeys as apprenticeship to English literary culture, creating almost a literary genre in Australia of the expatriate, Wright was not subject to the same influences, and her admiration for the European landscape seems to have only intensified the poet's connection with her own native land. Likely reminded of home, she was much taken with Hungary's wide plains, brown summer grass and grazing herds of horses. The country also provided a safe haven after the nervousness of events in Germany and Austria; Wright had witnessed one of Hitler's Nuremberg rallies and had her first experience with what she termed "the military-industrial complex." Additional travels included Switzerland and France, and she also stayed with a relative for a few months on a tea plantation in Ceylon (now Sri Lanka).

After her return from Europe, knowing that she had to support herself, Wright enrolled in a secretarial course for six months. She took positions in commercial firms at various office jobs, invariably choosing employment that would allow her to put in overtime, though she deplored the work. She would work in a position until she could fund a period of writing; when the money ran out, she would take up a new position. Wright also worked as an assistant to the professor of geography at the University of Sydney who undertook some field work on the Wright property with respect to soil erosion.

With the outbreak of World War II, Wright returned to help run the family station in her brothers' absence. The return was a defining moment in her life:

> As the train panted up the foothills of the Moonbis and the haze of dust and eucalypt vapour dimmed the drought-stricken landscape, I found myself suddenly and sharply aware of it as "my country." These hills and valleys were—not mine, but me; the threat of Japanese invasion hung over them as over me; I felt it under my own ribs. Whatever other blood I held, this was the country I loved and knew.

Here, she heard from the older workers on her family's property of the part the pioneers had played in violently dispossessing the Aboriginal people. Wright took the crimes of her fathers onto her own back, and would bear what she likely regarded as her own responsibility through her writings and activism. She would write in the *Tasmanian Wilderness Calendar* in 1981: "The love of the land we have invaded and the guilt of the invasion have become part of me."

In 1943, she took up a newly created post at the University of Queensland, in the Universities Commission as a statistician. At this time, she established contact with C.B. Christensen, editor of *Meanjin*. Wright spent much time helping Christensen with various aspects of the magazine, and it was to become one of the most influential and respected literary periodicals in Australia, a status it has held to the present. In 1943 or early 1944, at Christensen's home, Wright met Jack McKinney, a philosopher who was 23 years her senior. They married in 1944 and would have a daughter **Meredith McKinney** five years later. Wright told Glover that it was Jack who gave her hope and enabled her to become a poet.

Christensen was not only influential in Wright's personal life. He was responsible for the publication in 1946 of her first volume of poetry *The Moving Image*. Writes A.D. Hope, this book "marked a dividing line and an important change in Australian poetry and in Australian life." The work included "South of My Day's Circle," which would count among Wright's well-known poems. The year *The Moving Image* was published brought the beginnings of her next project when she read the 25 diaries of her grandfather Albert Wright. The resulting work, the three-part *The Generations of Men*, was a history of her family on the land in New South Wales and would be published in 1959.

In 1948, Wright moved to Mount Tambourine in Queensland, a remarkably beautiful area covered in rainforests. Her second published book, *Woman to Man*, appeared the following year. Later in her career, she would grow tired of comparisons between her new works and her acclaimed early efforts: "I had turned away from the simple nationalistic poems of the 1940s and was entering fields where no one wanted to follow."

In addition to poetry, Wright authored fiction and literary essays. Over the years, her work was to address the issues of the day, including subjects like the Vietnam War, as well as ecological causes and the fight for Aboriginal rights. Notes Brady: "Her poems were not descriptive eulogies of nature or heritage buildings, but took sides and put the blame for neglect, ignorance or destruction where it belonged." She was a conservationist before the word was even in common parlance in Australia. Co-founder of the Wildlife Preservation Society of Queensland in 1962, Wright served as president until she moved to Mongarlowe Near Braidwood in NSW during 1976. Her 1977 work *The Coral Battleground* addressed the issues regarding the Great Barrier Reef. "If the Great Barrier Reef could think, it would fear us," she wrote to a friend. "Slowly but surely we are destroying those great water-gardens, lovely indeed as cherry boughs and flowers under the once clear sea."

Wright's husband died in 1966 (some sources cite 1967). Her energies turned from writing poetry to promoting poetry in the schools, and to protest for the causes she believed passionately in, including the land rights of Aboriginals. She was good friends with Australian poet Oodgeroo Noonuccal (*Kath Walker), to whom Wright wrote: "I am born of the conquerors,/ you of the persecuted." After Wright's death, **Joan Williams** would write in *The Guardian*: "To the end she refused to give up and continued her public commitment to reconciliation with the indigenous people by leading the historic walk across the Sydney Harbour Bridge, which could be seen as endorsement of her efforts over three decades for Aboriginal land rights, a Makarrata (treaty), preservation of our indigenous heritage and reconciliation."

In the month before her death, Wright, by now a deaf woman in her mid-80s, made another public appearance when her friend, poet **Barbara Blackman**, presented a portrait of Wright's family to the National Portrait Gallery. She had stopped writing poetry at age 70, going on to tell Richard Glover that poetry requires emotional energy, that it is a compulsion that springs from physical passions which she no longer felt. "I've also stopped," she continued, "because . . . [t]he fact of the matter is that the world is in such a bloody awful state that I cannot find words for it."

She died of a heart attack in June 2000, having been twice nominated for a Nobel Prize. Australia's Judith Wright Prize, valued at $10,000, was created with funds from private benefactors to honor the poet's life, poetry, and convictions.

SOURCES:

Glover, Richard. "World Without Words," in *Sydney Morning Herald*, Good Weekend supplement, June 26, 1993, pp. 34–39.

Hope, Alec Derwent. *Judith Wright*. Melbourne: Oxford University Press, 1975.

Scott, Bill. *Focus on Judith Wright*. St. Lucia: University of Queensland Press, 1967.

Strauss, Jennifer. *Judith Wright*. "Oxford Australian Writers series." Melbourne: Oxford University Press, 1995.

Walker, Shirley. *Flame and Shadow: A Study of Judith Wright's Poetry*. St. Lucia: University of Queensland Press, 1991.

Williams, Joan. "Judith Wright," in *The Guardian*. July 5, 2000.

"Wright, Judith," in *The Australian Encyclopedia*. Vol 11. 4th ed. Sydney: Grolier Society of Australia, 1983.

SUGGESTED READING:

Rowbotham, David. *The Poetry of Judith Wright*. Galmahra, 1947.

Smith, Graeme Kinross. "Judith Wright," in *Australia's Writers*. Melbourne: Thomas Nelson, 1980.

Walker, Shirley. *Judith Wright*. Melbourne: Oxford University Press, 1981.

Wright, Judith. "Statements: Judith Wright," in *Poetry and Gender: Statements and Essays in Australian Women's Poetry and Poetics*. Ed. by David Brooks and Brenda Walker. St. Lucia: University of Queensland Press, 1989.

COLLECTIONS:

Extensive archival material including book reviews, biographical clippings, personal papers, letters and photographs held at the National Library of Australia.

RELATED MEDIA:

Oral History recordings and taped and video interviews held at the National Library of Australia.

Annabelle Mooney,
freelance writer,
Canberra, Australia

Wright, Laura Maria (1809–1886)

American missionary to the Seneca Indians who, with her husband, developed a written Seneca language. Name variations: Auntie Wright. Born Laura Maria Sheldon on July 10, 1809, in St. Johnsbury, Vermont; died on January 21, 1886, near Iroquois, New York; daughter of Solomon Sheldon and Dorothy (Stevens) Sheldon; granddaughter of pioneer Willard Stevens; educated in local schools and at the Young Ladies' School of St. Johnsbury; married Asher Wright (a cleric), on January 21, 1833 (died 1875).

Laura Maria Wright was born in 1809 in St. Johnsbury, Vermont, the 10th of 12 children. From age seven, she was raised by a married sister in the nearby town of Barnet, which her grandfather, Willard Stevens, had pioneered. As a youngster, she sought contact with the Native American children living nearby and later held prayer meetings for them. At age 17, she spent a year at the nearby Young Ladies' School, improving her education, after which she taught school in the Vermont towns of Barnet and Newbury for several years. In 1833, she married missionary Reverend Asher Wright of Hanover, New Hampshire. The day after their wedding, they began their journey by stagecoach to the Buffalo Creek Reservation in western New York State. During the cold, 15-day trip, Asher taught Laura the Seneca language, and within their first few months in their new home, she became a proficient speaker. This skill enabled her to work closely with the Seneca women and children, an accomplishment denied to her husband due to the strict separation of the sexes in that community.

Living in a two-story log building called the Seneca Mission House at Buffalo Creek, the Wrights traveled on horseback to local Native American settlements, carrying medicine, food, and their Bibles and notebooks. Working to render the Seneca language into written form, the Wrights became fluent speakers of the difficult language and began teaching the Seneca to read. The Wrights also translated hymns, prayers, and scripture into Seneca. An enlarged version of Asher's hymnal, first printed in 1843, was still in use in the 20th century. As part of their literacy work, Laura wrote a bilingual schoolbook that was published in 1836 in Boston. She wrote a speller in 1842 and a bilingual journal between 1841 and 1850, both of which were printed at the mission by means of a printer her husband designed especially to accommodate Seneca phonetics.

Between the years of 1837 and 1845, the Wrights entered into a series of conflicts with local white land developers. Their efforts proved mainly unsuccessful, and the Buffalo Creek Reservation on which many of the Seneca lived was lost. After a treaty was signed in 1842, the Seneca retained only two reservations in that area of New York. Soon, the chiefs were overthrown by a group dominated by the Wrights' students, and the republican Seneca Nation was formed in 1848. Both the move and the rebellion brought hunger, disease, and dependence to the Seneca people. After years of hardship amongst the Seneca, the Wrights, with the aid of a wealthy Boston merchant named Philip E. Thomas, were able to take a great many orphaned Seneca children into their newly founded Thomas Asylum for Orphan and Destitute Indian Children. Now known as "Auntie Wright," Laura was revered for honoring an ancient Seneca virtue; before the official founding of the orphanage, she had taken several parentless Seneca children into her home. She also founded the Iroquois Temperance League as the abuse of alcohol had further burdened the Seneca. When Asher Wright died in 1875, Laura moved into the house of Nicholson H. Parker, a long-time Seneca friend. She died there 11 years later, in 1886, of pneumonia. As late as the 1930s, "Auntie Wright" was still remembered with great respect by the elder members of the Seneca community.

SOURCES:

James, Edward T., ed. *Notable American Women, 1607–1950.* Cambridge, MA: The Belknap Press of Harvard University, 1971.

McHenry, Robert, ed. *Famous American Women.* NY: Dover, 1980.

Drew Walker,
freelance writer,
New York, New York

Wright, Mabel Osgood
(1859–1934)

American nature writer, conservationist, and novelist. Name variations: (pseudonym) Barbara. Born on January 26, 1859, in New York City; died from hypertensive myocardial disease on July 16, 1934, in Fairfield, Connecticut; daughter of Samuel Osgood (a cleric) and Ellen Haswell (Murdock) Osgood; educated at home and at a private school in New York City; married John Osborne Wright, on September 25, 1884 (died 1920).

Selected writings: The Friendship of Nature (1894); Birdcraft: A Field Book of Two Hundred Song, Game, and Water Birds (1895); (with naturalist Elliot Coues) Citizen Bird (1897); Gray Lady and the Birds (1907); The Garden of a Commuter's Wife (1901); The Open Window; Poppea of the Post Office; The Woman Errant (1904); The Stranger at the Gate (1913); My New York (1926).

The youngest of three children, Mabel Osgood Wright was born in 1859 in New York City. Her father Reverend Samuel Osgood was a graduate of Harvard and Harvard Divinity School. Originally a Unitarian, he served as pastor for the Church of the Messiah in New York for two decades before taking orders in the Episcopal Church. Mabel's paternal grandfather, John Osgood, was one of the founders of Andover, Massachusetts, while her mother **Ellen Haswell Osgood** was related to *Susanna Haswell Rowson, author of *Charlotte Temple.*

Mabel grew up in an atmosphere of learning and culture. Her father was well known for his translations of religious works, especially German theology. Moreover, her parents shared close associations with literary figures and other members of the New York cultural scene. It was supposedly during trips to the country that Mabel developed her lifelong interest in nature and the study of birds in particular. In 1884, at age 25, she married James Osborne Wright, an English rare-book dealer. After a long trip to England, they returned to the United States, settling in Fairfield, Connecticut.

Wright's first noted publication, "A New England May Day," appeared in the New York *Evening Post* in 1893. This and subsequent published pieces were collected and republished in book form in 1894 under the title *The Friendship of Nature*. In the several years that followed, Wright produced books that varied between impressionistic nature writing to actual field manuals for the study of birds. In the late 1890s, she began to advocate conservation. She also wrote books on plants and mammals, nature stories, and fables for children. When the magazine *Bird-Lore* began publication, Wright worked on projects for its executive and school departments from 1899 to 1910, thereafter serving as a contributing editor for the remainder of her life.

As her writing on conservation continued throughout the late 1890s, so did her work as an activist for the cause. In 1898, she helped to found the Connecticut Audubon Society, an organization of which she served as president for many years. She was also appointed director of the National Association of Audubon Societies, a post she held from 1905 to 1928. In 1901, she was made a full member of the American Ornithologists Union, an organization with which she had been affiliated since 1895. In addition to this work she also planned and constructed a Birdcraft Sanctuary on a tract of land near her home in Connecticut.

While highly regarded as an accomplished nature writer and prominent conservationist, Wright was also the author of several romance novels, which she published under her own name or under the pseudonym Barbara. Between 1901 and 1913, she wrote a total of ten such works, half being conventional in form and the others containing letters, social criticism, diary entries, natural history, and gardening advice. These largely unsuccessful works were often reviewed and reprinted, but lacked engaging settings, plots, characters, and dialogue. In 1926, she published a largely autobiographical book

entitled *My New York*. Mabel Wright died of a heart ailment on July 16, 1934, in Fairfield, Connecticut, at the age of 75.

SOURCES:

James, Edward T., ed. *Notable American Women, 1607–1950.* Cambridge, MA: The Belknap Press of Harvard University, 1971.

Drew Walker,
freelance writer,
New York, New York

Mabel Osgood Wright

Wright, Maginel (1881–1966)

American artist known primarily for her illustrations of children's classics, including Hans Brinker *and* Heidi. *Name variations: Maginel Wright Barney; Maginel Wright Enright. Born Maginel Wright on June 19, 1881, in Weymouth, Massachusetts; died on April 18, 1966, in East Hampton, New York; daughter of William Cary Wright (a minister) and Anna (Lloyd-Jones) Wright; sister of architect Frank Lloyd Wright; studied drawing under her brother; attended the Chicago Art Institute; married Walter J. Enright (divorced); married Hiram Barney (died 1925); children: (first marriage) Elizabeth Enright (1909–1968, an author).*

Selected writings: (self-illus.) The Baby's Record through the First Year in Song and Story *(1928); (compiler and illus.)* Weather Signs and Rhymes *(1931); (autobiography)* The Valley of the God-Almighty Joneses *(1965).*

Selected illustrations: (under name Maginel Wright Enright) Clara Whitehill Hunt, About Harriet *(1916); (under name M.W. Enright) *Mary Mapes Dodge,* Hans Brinker; or, The Silver Skates *(1918); (under name M.W. Enright)* Songs from Mother Goose, for Voice and Piano *(1920); (under name M.W. Enright) *Johanna Spyri,* Heidi: A Story for Children and Those Who Love Children *(1921); Ruth Sawyer,* This Way to Christmas *(1924); Caroline D. Snedeker,* Downright Dencey *(1927, selected as Newbery honor book, 1928); Sophie de Ségur,* Sophie: The Story of a Bad Little Girl *(1929); Philip Broughton,* Pandy *(1930); Ethel Calvert Phillips,* Calico *(1937).*

Under name Maginel Wright Enright; all written by Laura Bancroft (the pseudonym of L. Frank Baum): Bandit Jim Crow *(1906);* Mr. Woodchuck *(1906);* Prairie-Dog Town *(1906);* Sugar-Loaf Mountain *(1906);* Prince Mad-Turtle *(1906);* Twinkle's Enchantment *(1906);* Policeman Bluejay *(1907, also published as* Babes in Birdland, *1911);* Twinkle and Chubbins: Their Astonishing Adventures in Nature Fairyland *(1911).*

Born in 1881, Maginel Wright spent her early childhood with her mother's family in the idyllic Wisconsin valley, near Madison. Although she was born in Massachusetts, where her father was the pastor of a church near Boston, her parents had separated when she was still very young, and her mother **Anna Lloyd-Jones Wright**, homesick for the Wisconsin air, had returned to the large, protective circle of the Lloyd-Jones clan.

Wright was tutored at home by her mother and learned to draw under the guidance of her brother, the future renowned architect Frank Lloyd Wright, who was 12 years her senior. She later spent a year at her aunt's school, the Hillside Home School (one of Wright's first architectural designs), which provided her with a nurturing educational environment. "I learned more than in all the other years of my schooling put together," she said. At 12, she moved with her mother to Chicago, where Frank was beginning his career as an architect. After some difficulty deciding where they should live, her mother fi-

nally settled on Oak Park, a village suburb half an hour by train from the city. Wright found her new school, unlike Hillside, to be a cold, terrifying place. But the most popular girl at school took the frightened Maginel under her wing. "She gave me courage and confidence in myself and I began to know how to deal with boys."

After graduation, Wright attended the Chicago Art Institute, leaving after a year to take a job as a commercial artist at a Chicago engraving house. Although she wanted desperately to be an illustrator, earning a living took precedence. The job, working on page layouts for catalogues, paid $50 a week, a good income for a young woman at the time. In three years, she had saved enough for a European trip with her mother.

Returning to the States, Wright married illustrator and cartoonist Walter Enright, known as Pat. After their daughter *Elizabeth Enright was born, they moved to New York to pursue careers as artists. Finding a large apartment on the top floor of a building that overlooked the Hudson River, Wright set up a home studio, found someone to look after the baby, and went to work. As her nostalgic pictures gained popularity, she soon had as much work as she could manage. Along with her illustrations for children's books, she painted covers for a number of leading magazines, including *Woman's Home Companion* and *Ladies' Home Journal*. Although Wright described her life as "happy and busy," her marriage to Enright ended in divorce. She subsequently married a lawyer named Hiram Barney, who died in 1925.

Elizabeth Enright, who also became a popular author and illustrator, remembered standing with her nose pressed to the glass door of her mother's studio, to which she was forbidden entrance unless invited. While the young Elizabeth was often resentful and resorted to whining for attention, for the most part she took her mother's work for granted. Later, she would realize the impact of her mother's art on her own life, remarking: "For she took the responsibility of my upbringing nearly single handed; and in her case the phrase is particularly apt, because she did this by means of her skillful right hand guided by her imaginations."

In addition to creating illustrations for some classic children's stories like *Heidi* and *Hans Brinker; or, The Silver Skates*, Maginel Wright also revolutionized textbook illustrations, which up to that time, in her daughter's words, were "nearly as deadly as the text: 'Ned has gone to the shed. Tom has a red sled. . . .' What my mother did was to bring grace, liveliness, and, above all, imagination to the pages of these books."

During the Depression, Wright created tapestries with colored wools, which she called "long point" because of the lengthy stitches that distinguished them from other tapestry. Several exhibitions of her work were held in New York. In the 1940s, she distinguished herself as a shoe designer, creating high-fashion jeweled and sequined shoes manufactured by Capezio.

In 1965, just before her death, Wright published her autobiography *The Valley of the God-Almighty Joneses*, which focused on her mother's family, the Lloyd-Joneses, and detailed her relationship with her famous brother. She died on April 18, 1966, at the Hunting Lane Rest Home in East Hampton, Long Island.

SUGGESTED READING:

Barney, Maginel Wright. *The Valley of the God-Almighty Joneses*. NY: Appleton-Century, 1965.

Barbara Morgan,
Melrose, Massachusetts

Wright, Martha Coffin (1806–1875)

American women's rights leader. Born on December 25, 1806, in Boston, Massachusetts; died from pneumonia on January 4, 1875, in Boston; daughter of Thomas Coffin, Jr. (a merchant and ship's captain) and Anna (Folger) Coffin; sister of suffragist Lucretia Mott (1793–1880); educated at Kimberton Boarding School near Philadelphia, Pennsylvania; married Peter Pelham, on November 18, 1824 (died 1826); married David Wright (a lawyer), in 1829; children: (first marriage) Marianna Pelham (b. 1825); (second marriage) Eliza Wright Osborne (b. 1830, a suffragist), Matthew Tallman Wright (b. 1832), Ellen Wright (b. 1840, a suffragist), William Pelham Wright (b. 1842), Frank Wright (b. 1844), Charles Wright (b. 1848).

Martha Coffin Wright, the youngest of eight children, was born in Boston, Massachusetts, in 1806. Her father and mother were descendants of Tristram Coffyn and Peter Folger, respectively, two of the original settlers of Nantucket Island in 1662. Both of her parents were devout Quakers and raised the family within the church community known as the Society of Friends. Wright's family had moved from Nantucket to Boston in 1804, two years before her birth. When she was three, however, the family moved once again, this time to Philadelphia where her father Thomas Coffin, Jr., thought they might find a cultural environment better suited to the practice of their religion. When Martha's father died a few years later, her mother **Anna Folger Coffin** operated a boardinghouse and small shop to support her large family.

After three years in boarding school, Martha fell in love with Peter Pelham, an army captain and one of her mother's boarders. Although Captain Pelham was not a Quaker, which elicited objections from Martha's family, the couple married on November 18, 1824, and soon thereafter moved to Florida. Two years later, however, Peter died and Martha returned to her family in Philadelphia with her baby daughter, **Marianna Pelham**, who had been born in August 1825. Ousted from the Quaker faith because of her marriage, Wright maintained many of the Quaker characteristics and grew to have little affinity for organized religion.

During the following year, Wright entered into an engagement with Julius Catlin, the brother of the famous painter George Catlin. This was short-lived as neither had the financial means for marriage. In 1827, she moved with her mother to Aurora, New York, where she taught in a school that her mother had opened there. It was in Aurora that Martha met and married a lawyer from Philadelphia, David Wright. The two lived in Aurora until 1839, and then moved to Auburn, New York, where they remained for many years. During this time they had six children together, two of whom, **Eliza Wright Osborne** and **Ellen Wright**, became active in the women's suffrage movement in their adult years.

Martha Wright's long career in the women's movement began in 1848 when she worked with her sister *Lucretia Mott and *Elizabeth Cady Stanton in organizing the first convention for women's rights in the United States. The conference took place in Seneca Falls, New York, in July of that year. Wright continued to organize and lead women's rights conventions over the following years, serving as secretary of a convention in Syracuse in 1852, vice-president of a convention in Philadelphia in 1854, and then president of three different conventions in 1855. She also presided over the New York State Woman's Rights Committee's tenth annual women's rights convention held in New York City in 1860. Over the years she played an important role as an advisor to Stanton and *Susan B. Anthony, both of whom were her good friends. When the movement split after the Civil War, Wright remained loyal to both Anthony and Stanton during those turbulent years, and helped them organize the American Equal Rights Association in 1866 and the National Women's Suffrage Association in 1869.

Although Wright published only a few magazine articles on women's rights, she was known to have written poetry, sketches, and short stories. In 1874, she was elected president of the National Women's Suffrage Association; however, she died the following year of pneumonia while on a visit to a daughter in Boston.

SOURCES:

James, Edward T., ed. *Notable American Women, 1607–1950*. Cambridge, MA: The Belknap Press of Harvard University, 1971.

Drew Walker,
freelance writer,
New York, New York

Wright, Mary Clabaugh

(1917–1970)

American scholar of Chinese history who was the first woman to be named a full professor at Yale University. Born Mary Oliver Clabaugh on September 25, 1917, in Tuscaloosa, Alabama; died from lung cancer on June 18, 1970, in Guilford, Connecticut; second of five children of Samuel Francis Clabaugh (a newspaper publisher) and Mary Bacon (Duncan) Clabaugh; attended Ramsay High School in Birmingham, Alabama; graduated from Vassar College, 1937; Radcliffe College, Ph.D., 1951; married Arthur Frederick Wright (1913–1976, a scholar of Chinese history), on July 6, 1940; children: two sons, Charles Duncan (b. 1950) and Jonathan Arthur (b. 1952).

Published several academic works, including The Last Stand of Chinese Conservatism: The T'ung-chih Restoration 1862–1874 *(1957), and* China and Revolution: The First Phase, 1900–1913 *(1968); founded the Society for Ch'ing Studies; created journal for this society,* Ch'ing-shih wen-t'i; *established prominent collection of Chinese resources for the Hoover Library; became associate professor of history, Yale University (1959), later became a full professor, the first woman in such a position at Yale; worked on the Joint Committee on Contemporary China.*

Mary Clabaugh Wright was born in Tuscaloosa, Alabama, in 1917, the second of five children of Samuel Francis Clabaugh and **Mary Duncan Clabaugh**. Both parents had graduated from the University of Alabama and both had deep Alabama roots. Her father, a prosperous businessman, published the *Tuscaloosa News*, and was later involved with the insurance industry in Birmingham.

Wright enjoyed an active childhood and particularly liked swimming, tennis, and horseback riding. In high school she served as president of the student body and was a member of the National Honor Society. Earning a scholarship, she attended Vassar College where she became president of the student political union. She graduated Phi Beta Kappa from Vassar and entered graduate school at Radcliffe College to study European history. Her scholarly interests soon turned to China, a country she had visited in 1934.

At age 21, she met Arthur Frederick Wright, an advanced graduate student at Harvard who was studying China and Japan. Arthur had already earned a degree from Stanford University in 1935 and had studied Chinese Buddhism at Oxford. The couple married in 1940, in Washington, D.C., and soon left for Kyoto, Japan, where both had been granted fellowships to pursue studies toward their doctorates.

After a year in Kyoto, the couple planned to spend an additional year in Beijing (Peking), China. Although both China and Japan were precarious locations for American citizens during the early 1940s, the Wrights continued to pursue their resident studies. With the Japanese occupying or indirectly controlling many portions of China, including Beijing, deteriorating relations between the United States and Japan intensified, finally dissolving into war with the Japanese attack on Pearl Harbor on December 7, 1941. Nevertheless, the couple chose to remain in Beijing studying Chinese history and culture. They lived in relative academic freedom until March 24, 1943, when all citizens of nations at war with Japan were gathered and sent to a detention camp at Wei-hsien, in the Shantung province of China. They remained in the camp in oppressive conditions for more than two years until the war ended and they were released.

Returning to Beijing, the Wrights found themselves in the middle in a revolution in which Communist forces under Mao Zedong seemed to be gaining control of China. It was during this time that the Hoover Library hired the couple to amass contemporary materials for a collection pertaining to the Chinese revolution. Traveling around China in American military planes, the Wrights gained access to a great many records and historical resources, including an audience with Mao in October 1946.

Upon returning to the United States in April 1947, Arthur completed his dissertation and received his doctorate from Harvard. Soon thereafter, he was hired as an assistant professor of history at Stanford University. Moving with him to Palo Alto, California, Mary became the China curator at the Hoover Library. She also received her doctorate from Radcliffe in 1951, between the birth of their two sons. Her dissertation was finally published in 1957 as *The Last Stand of*

Chinese Conservatism: The T'ung-chih Restoration 1862–1874.

In the years preceding the publication of her book, Mary had lectured at Stanford and was promoted to assistant and then to associate professor at the Hoover Library. She built a unique and extensive collection of Chinese materials and also sponsored several bibliographic studies on such topics as the overseas Chinese, the Chinese Red Army, and the student movement. In 1959, the Wrights took positions in the history department at Yale University, he as a professor and she as an associate professor. She later became the first woman to be named a full professor at Yale. Their presence at the university, in addition to its established strength in Chinese language and literature, instantly made Yale a highly respected center of Chinese studies.

The Wrights returned to Asia on their first sabbatical in 1953 and 1954 and again with their two sons in 1962 and 1963. During her career at Yale, Mary published influential collections and studies on modern Chinese history, including *China and Revolution: The First Phase, 1900–1913,* in 1968. She also founded the Society for Ch'ing Studies, created a journal of the society, *Ch'ing-shih wen-t'i,* and worked with a development agency, the Joint Committee on Contemporary China. In addition to receiving several honorary degrees, she became the first woman trustee of Wesleyan University. The rigorous combination of academic and family life led to nervous exhaustion in 1965. Although she returned to the bustle of academics, she developed incurable lung cancer in 1969. After ordering her affairs and visiting friends and family, Mary Clabaugh Wright died on June 18, 1970, at age 52. She was buried in Grove Street Cemetery in New Haven, Connecticut.

SOURCES:

Contemporary Authors. Vol. 109. Detroit, MI: Gale Research, 1983.

Sicherman, Barbara, and Carol Hurd Green, eds. *Notable American Women: The Modern Period.* Cambridge, MA: The Belknap Press of Harvard University, 1980.

Drew Walker,
freelance writer,
New York, New York

Wright, Mickey (1935—)

*American golfer, considered one of the all-time greats.
Name variations: Jay Wright; Mary Kathryn Wright.
Born Mary Kathryn Wright in San Diego, California,
on February 14, 1935; attended Stanford University,
1953–54.*

Turned pro (1954); won LPGA championship (1958, 1960, 1961, 1963); won U.S. Women's Open (1958, 1959, 1961, 1964); won Titleholders (1961 and 1962); won the Western Women's Open (1962, 1963, 1966); only woman to hold all four major titles simultaneously; achieved a record 14 wins (1963); was LPGA all-time leading money winner (1964–68); inducted into the LPGA Hall of Fame (1964), the World Golf Hall of Fame (1976), and the International Women's Sports Hall of Fame (1981).

Teased for her unusual height, the 5'8", 11-year-old Mickey Wright was called "Moose" by classmates. She looked to a sport to boost her self-confidence and became one of the greatest women golfers in history.

Wright was born in San Diego, California, in 1935, into an industrious family. Her grandmother was the first woman pharmacist in Illinois and her grandfather was an inventor. Wright's father, a lawyer who had once crossed from the Midwest to the West Coast on horseback, likely provided an example of competitiveness. He bought her a set of golf clubs, and Wright began practicing when she was 9 at the La Jolla Country Club. By the time she was 13, she was shooting in the low 80s. A year later, Wright took the Southern California Girls' championship, a victory followed at age 15 by a win at the Invitational Tournament at La Jolla, where she made her first hole-in-one. Early on, such notable pros as Johnny Bellante, Harry Pressler, and Les Bolstad helped to develop the swing that would make her famous.

In 1952, Wright was 17 when she won the national U.S. Golfing Association Junior Girls' championship. As a freshman at Stanford University, she was the low amateur at the U.S. Women's Open and runner-up in the U.S. Amateur championship. Since her low scores were comparable to those of the top female professionals, Wright decided to leave college to dedicate herself to golf. Joining the Ladies' Professional Golf Association (LPGA) in 1954, she intended to become a leader in the sport. Such surety of her abilities would pave the way. "Winning really never crossed my mind that much," she later noted. "It's trite, but I knew if I did it as well as I could, I would win. If I did as well as I could, it would have been better than anybody else did it, and therefore it would win."

The year she turned pro, Wright was paired with her idol *Babe Didrikson Zaharias at the U.S. Women's Open (1954). Zaharias, watching the young golfer on the practice tee, commented, "I didn't think anyone but the Babe could hit 'em like that." Zaharias won the tournament, and

Wright was the low amateur. On the professional circuit a year later, Wright began the first of her 82 professional victories. In 1958, she won the U.S. Women's Open with a four-round total of 290, breaking Zaharias' standing record. She beat her own record by three strokes the following year. By 1963, she earned $32,000 in winnings, the highest of any woman golfer, and she was proof positive that women's golf had come of age. Wright outdrove most male players; her fairway shots were often 225 to 270 yards long. (Once, with the help of strong winds in Dallas, she overdrove on a 385-yard hole.) She finished play during 1964 holding first place for lifetime earnings ($176,994), a distinction she would maintain for the next several years (until her 1969 all-time earnings of more than $268,000 were surpassed by *Kathy Whitworth).

During her long career, Wright would win each of the four major tournaments—the U.S. Women's Open, the LPGA championship, the Western Women's Open, and the Titleholder's Tournament—at least twice. She took both the LPGA and U.S. Open titles four times and during one period between 1960 and 1962 became the only woman to hold all four majors titles simultaneously. While performing at such a consistently high level of play, Wright confronted both her own perfectionism and the public pressure that accompanied success. She would later recall in *The Illustrated History of Women's Golf*: "The main emotion going into any new season was fear. Every season, just every season. It was the fear that no matter how good the previous year had been, this year would not be as good, and the pressure to win that first tournament was unbelievable."

Each year between 1960 and 1964, Wright received the Vare Trophy, indicating that she had the best year-long average on the LPGA tour. She won 13 tournaments in 1963, averaging 72.81 strokes per 18 holes and earning the Female Athlete of the Year award from the Associated Press both that and the following year (1963 and 1964). Wright was inducted into the LPGA Hall of Fame (1964) and into the World Golf Hall of Fame (1976), before being named to the International Women's Sports Hall of Fame in 1981.

Popular with the spectators, the once-gangly teenager had turned her height into an asset, becoming arguably the best golfer in the world. By virtue of her excellence, as well as her acceptance of speaking engagements, she brought great attention to her sport. In 1965, a combination of publicity activities, stressful competitions, and a wrist injury brought her to a short-lived retirement. She returned to the tour a year later. By the time wrist and foot injuries prompted her second retirement from full-time touring in 1970, the 35-year-old Wright had changed the face of women's golf with her enormous drives and what some still describe as her perfect swing. Noted one colleague: "Mickey got the outside world to take a second hard look at women golfers, and when they looked, they saw the rest of us."

Wright continued to enter tournaments after her retirement. She took the Colgate-*Dinah Shore championship in 1973 and participated in the 1979 Coca-Cola Classic. Looking back, she called her extraordinary career "a dream, another life." That dream changed the face of her sport by emphasizing a remarkable standard of excellence. It also made her in the minds of many perhaps the greatest player ever in women's golf.

SOURCES

Johnson, Anne Janette. *Great Women in Sports*. Detroit, MI: Visible Ink, 1998.

McHenry, Robert, ed. *Famous American Women*. NY: Dover, 1980.

Woolum, Janet. *Outstanding Women Athletes*. Phoenix, AZ: Oryx, 1992.

Karin L. Haag and **Richard Wasowski**, freelance writer, Mansfield, Ohio

Wright, Muriel Hazel (1889–1975)

Native American writer and historian. Born near Lehigh, Choctaw Nation (later Coal County, Oklahoma), on March 31, 1889; died of a stroke in Oklahoma City on February 27, 1975; daughter of Eliphalet Nott Wright and Ida Belle (Richard) Wright; attended Presbyterian and Baptist elementary schools; tutored by her mother, 1902–06; attended Wheaton Seminary, 1906–08; studied French, piano, and voice lessons privately in Washington, D.C., 1908–11; attended East Central State Normal School, 1911–12; pursued master's in English and history, 1916–17.

Selected writings: (with Joseph Thoburn) Oklahoma: A History of the State and Its People (1929); A Guide to the Indian Tribes of Oklahoma (1951); contributed to The Chronicles of Oklahoma (1922–73), was associate editor (1943–55), and editor (1955–73).

The Native American historian Muriel Hazel Wright was born in 1889 near Lehigh, Choctaw Nation, in Oklahoma Territory. Her father Eliphalet Nott Wright, a physician for the Missouri-Pacific Coal Mines, was half Choctaw and the son of the chief of the Choctaw Nation; her mother **Ida Richard Wright** was an Anglo-

Scotch Presbyterian missionary. When Wright was five years old, the family moved to Atoka, Oklahoma, where she attended Presbyterian and Baptist schools. In 1902, the family returned to Lehigh, and Wright continued her studies with her mother.

Wright entered Wheaton Seminary (now Wheaton College) in Norton, Massachusetts, in 1906. After two years of study, she went with her family to Washington, D.C., where her father had been named delegate of the Choctaw Nation to the federal government. She studied French, piano, and voice with private tutors. In 1911, Wright enrolled in East Central State Normal School in Ada, Oklahoma, graduating in 1912 and beginning a teaching career in the Coal County, Oklahoma, school system. In 1914, she became high school principal in Wapanucka, also teaching Latin, English, and history. She decided to further her education in 1916 in New York, where she studied history and English. American involvement in World War I led Wright to return to Oklahoma in 1917, where she served again as a principal and teacher in Coal County until 1924. In 1922, she became secretary of the Choctaw Committee, leaders of the Choctaw people. In that position, which she held until 1928, she assisted in the complicated legal process and business affairs which resulted from the change in tribal land status when Oklahoma had become a state in 1906. Wright also began contributing articles to *The Chronicles of Oklahoma*, the journal of the Oklahoma Historical Society, and other periodicals. Drawn to researching her Native American heritage, in 1924 Wright left school administration to investigate the history of the Choctaw and other Oklahoma tribes, hoping to learn how the tribes had shaped American history and culture.

In the late 1920s, she collaborated in her research with Joseph B. Thoburn; their four-volume scholarly work, *Oklahoma: A History of the State and Its People*, was published in 1929. She then published three textbooks of Oklahoma history. In 1934, Wright helped organize the Choctaw Advisory Council, serving as secretary until 1944. She was a leader in the fight to make the federal and state governments pay compensation to the Native American tribes for the loss of their former lands. She also initiated a statewide historical marker program, including sites of importance to its native inhabitants.

By 1943, Wright was a respected scholar whose reputation extended well beyond Oklahoma. She was named associate editor of *The Chronicles of Oklahoma*, becoming editor in

Opposite page
Mickey
Wright

1955, where she remained until her retirement in 1973. In 1951, Wright published her nationally known reference work, *A Guide to the Indian Tribes of Oklahoma.*

Muriel Wright's dedication to helping Oklahoma Indians and to preserving state heritage led to her induction into the Oklahoma Hall of Fame in 1940. In 1949, the University of Oklahoma awarded her a Distinguished Service Citation. She was also honored by the North American Indian Women's Association as the outstanding Indian woman of the century in 1971. She remained active as a writer in the Oklahoma Historical Society after retirement. Muriel Wright died in Oklahoma City, at age 85, in 1975.

SOURCES:

Sicherman, Barbara, and Carol Hurd Green, eds. *Notable American Women: The Modern Period.* Cambridge, MA: The Belknap Press of Harvard University, 1980.

Laura York, M.A. in History, University of California, Riverside, California

Patience Lovell Wright

Wright, Patience Lovell

(1725–1786)

American wax sculptor who was particularly popular in England. Born in Bordentown, New Jersey, in 1725;

died in London, England, on March 23, 1786; daughter of John Lovell and Patience (Townsend) Lovell; married Joseph Wright, in 1748 (died 1769); children: Mary Wright (who married Benjamin Van Cleef); *Elizabeth Wright* (who married Ebenezer Platt); Joseph Wright (1756–1793, studied with Benjamin West and was the first engraver and diesinker of the U.S. mint); *Phoebe Wright* (b. 1761, modeled for Benjamin West and married the renowned English portrait painter John Hoppner); Sarah Wright (b. 1769, died young).

One of the first American sculptors; opened one of the world's first successful wax museums; was commissioned to create wax works of many famous figures in America and England.

One of the first American professional sculptors, Patience Lovell Wright was born in Bordentown in colonial New Jersey in 1725, the daughter of prosperous Quaker farmers. She was raised a vegetarian by her devout father, who saw meat-eating as a sin, and who dressed all of his children in white. In 1748, when she was 22, she married a cooper, Joseph Wright of Philadelphia. Little is known about her years of marriage, except that she gave birth to five surviving children before her husband's death in 1769. As he left her little money, Patience was desperate for a way to support her children. Though she had always been artistically inclined, she had not pursued art seriously. Now she decided to launch a career as a sculptor, modeling well-known public figures in wax. Wright created a remarkably successful series of portraits, and made them into a traveling exhibit which was the first of its kind, charging the public to see them in Charleston, New York, and Philadelphia.

Wright's strikingly realistic wax sculptures were an instant success, but a fire destroyed most of them while on exhibit in New York in 1771. Nonetheless, she was encouraged to travel to England in 1772, where her works and her eccentric personality captivated spectators. She created popular exhibits representing contemporary English politicians, nobles, and actors, many of them introduced to her by her friend Benjamin Franklin. Wright seems to have deliberately cultivated a bohemian artist persona, and was known as the "American Sibyl"; when granted an audience with the British monarchs, she reportedly addressed King George III and Queen *Charlotte of Mecklenburg-Strelitz as George and Charlotte. *Abigail Adams once said of Wright, "her appearance is quite the slattern." Wax sculptures of contemporary figures were novelties in England, and she faced little competition (*Madame Tussaud would not open the first wax museum for another 30 years). Among Wright's most important sitters was Prime Minister William Pitt, whose life-size sculpture was installed in Westminster Abbey after his death.

During the American Revolution, Wright corresponded with Franklin and sheltered American prisoners of war. She clearly enjoyed political gossip, which she shared with her British friends despite her patriotism. Her 1780 trip to Paris, where she hoped to open a wax museum, also found her meeting with Franklin to discuss her odd plans for fostering a rebellion in England and Ireland. Still, there is little evidence for the many legends of Wright's other exploits, such as that she acted as a spy for Franklin or that she sent military information to the Continental Congress by hiding letters in wax figures sent to her sister **Rachel Wright Wells**, who ran a wax museum in Philadelphia. Her plans for commercial success in Paris came to nothing; Philippe Curtius, uncle of the celebrated wax sculptor Madame Tussaud, had already captured the Parisian market for wax spectacles, and Wright returned to London in 1781.

One of her final works was an ambitious reproduction in wax figures of the meeting of peace commissioners following the war. Although Wright wanted to return to Pennsylvania before her death because she did not want "to have her native bones laid in London," she was in fact buried in London after her sudden death in March 1786. Her son Joseph Wright, elected to the British Royal Academy, became a well-known painter and wax sculptor.

SOURCES:

James, Edward T., ed. *Notable American Women, 1607–1950*. Cambridge, MA: The Belknap Press of Harvard University, 1971.

McClelland, Elizabeth. "Patience Lovell Wright: Sculptor," in *Early American Life*. April 1976.

McHenry, Robert, ed. *Famous American Women*. NY: Dover, 1980.

Read, Phyllis J., and Bernard L. Witlieb. *The Book of Women's Firsts*. NY: Random House, 1992.

Laura York, M.A. in History,
University of California,
Riverside, California

Wright, Susanna (1697–1784)

American colonial writer and poet. Born in Manchester, England, on August 4, 1697; died in Columbia, Pennsylvania, on December 1, 1784; daughter of John Wright and Patience (Gibson) Wright; educated in England.

The Quaker writer Susanna Wright was born in Manchester, England, in 1697, one of six children of **Patience Gibson Wright** and John Wright, a Quaker minister and bodice-maker. Hoping to find prosperity in the English colonies in the New World, in 1714 John took his family to Chester, Pennsylvania, and set himself up as a shopkeeper. After her mother's death in 1722, Susanna managed her father's household; five years later, the Wrights moved to Hempfield on the banks of the Susquehanna River, where John became a successful ferryman. Because his ferry (two canoes tied together) forded the most important river crossing into what was then the midwest, the Wrights' home became a retreat for officials, travelers, traders, and pioneers. Over the course of her 20 years heading the family at Wright's Ferry (later the town of Columbia), Susanna Wright became known as a genteel and gracious host.

In 1745, Susanna Wright was bequeathed land and a house by the settler Samuel Blunston. The exact nature of Wright's relationship to Blunston is not clear, nor is why she never married, but it seems probable that she and Blunston had had a love affair. She moved to the house and took in her brother James and his family.

Settled in her own homestead, Wright became an intellectual and artist while at the same time managing a frontier home and establishing a successful silk farm. She served her community as a scribe, writing wills, indentures, and deeds for her illiterate neighbors. Highly respected, Wright became an informal arbitrator and notary as she settled disputes between local settlers. She also acted as a doctor and pharmacist for her neighbors on the colonial frontier, where professional doctors were scarce.

Well educated, fluent in French and Italian, and interested in philosophy, poetry, and science, Wright established friendships with other colonial intellectuals. These included James Logan, Benjamin Franklin, and Charles and Isaac Morris, who supplied her with the latest books and journals for what she termed her "large and well-chosen library." She was celebrated as a witty conversationalist who could discuss poetry and natural philosophy with ease and grace. She also drew and wrote verse, though few examples of her work survive. Wright's intelligence and vivacity earned her numerous friends and supporters, and in her final years many visited the "celebrated Susanna Wright." She died in 1784, at age 88, in Columbia.

SOURCES:

James, Edward T., ed. *Notable American Women, 1607–1950*. Cambridge, MA: The Belknap Press of Harvard University, 1971.

Laura York, M.A. in History,
University of California,
Riverside, California

Wright, Teresa (1918—)

Academy Award-winning American actress best known for her performances in such classics as Shadow of a Doubt *and* The Little Foxes. *Born Muriel Teresa Wright in Harlem, New York, on October 27, 1918; daughter of Arthur Wright and Martha (Espy) Wright; attended Rosehaven, a private school in Tenafly, New Jersey, 1925–28, and public schools in Maplewood, New Jersey, 1929–36; studied acting at the Wharf Theater, Provincetown, Massachusetts, 1937–38; married Niven Busch, in 1942 (divorced 1952); married Robert Woodruff Anderson (the playwright), in 1959 (divorced); married Carlos Pierre (marriage ended); remarried Robert Anderson.*

Selected filmography: The Little Foxes *(1941);* Mrs. Miniver *(1942);* The Pride of the Yankees *(1942);* Shadow of a Doubt *(1943);* Casanova Brown *(1944);* The Best Years of Our Lives *(1946);* Pursued *(1947);* Enchantment *(1948);* The Capture *(1950);* The Men *(1950);* Something to Live For *(1952);* California Conquest *(1952);* The Steel Trap *(1952);* The Actress *(1953);* Track of the Cat *(1954);* The Search *for Bridey Murphy (1956);* Escapade in Japan *(1957);* The Restless Years *(1958);* Hail Hero! *(1969);* The Happy Ending *(1969);* Roseland *(1977);* Somewhere in Time *(1979);* The Good Mother *(1988).*

The American actress Teresa Wright enjoyed a film and stage career which spanned six decades. Born Muriel Teresa Wright in New York City in 1918, Wright spent her first years with relatives after her parents separated. When she was eight, her father sent her to Rosehaven, a private girls' school in New Jersey. After three years there, she attended public school in Maplewood, New Jersey.

It was during her high school years that Wright decided on an acting career. She was inspired by *Helen Hayes'* performance in *Victoria Regina* and by her uncle and father, both amateur actors. She studied drama at Columbia High School as well as at summer programs in 1937 and 1938 at the Wharf Theater in Provincetown, Massachusetts. After graduating from high school in 1938, she moved back to New York City.

From the movie Mrs. Miniver, *starring Greer Garson and Teresa Wright (right).*

There, she successfully auditioned for the lead's understudy in *Our Town*. In the spring of 1939, after both the lead actress *Martha Scott and her understudy *Dorothy McGuire left the production, Wright played the lead through that summer. She had the opportunity to perform in the hometown of the playwright Thornton Wilder where he coached the actors. After a season in summer stock, in 1939 Wright landed a role in the Broadway production of *Life with Father*, which ran for two years. Although she always went by Muriel in her private life, Wright was forced to use her middle name of Theresa as a performer, since there was already a Muriel Wright registered with Actors' Equity.

While playing in *Life with Father*, she was hired by Samuel Goldwyn to appear with *Bette Davis in the film version of *Lillian Hellman's *The Little Foxes*. Her contract for this production is thought to be unique in movie history; clause 39 spelled out the many poses and shots that the actress could not be required to perform, such as appearing in a bathing suit, "running on the beach with her hair flying in the wind," or "wearing a bunny cap with long ears for Easter." Although this was part of Wright's efforts to protect her reputation as a serious actress by avoiding "cheesecake" publicity photos, the stipulations aroused an array of comments from the press. However, once *The Little Foxes* was released in 1941, her performance earned high praise from critics, and she was nominated for an Academy Award for Best Supporting Actress.

The following year Wright enjoyed two more critical and popular successes. In 1942, she portrayed **Eleanor Gehrig** opposite Gary Cooper in *The Pride of the Yankees*, which earned her an Oscar nomination for Best Actress; as well, she appeared with *Greer Garson in *Mrs. Miniver*, the wartime family drama that won six Academy Awards. One of those went to Wright, for Best Supporting Actress. Also in 1942, she married screenwriter and novelist Niven Busch; they would divorce in 1952.

Although Wright earned critical praise for her roles in two classics, Alfred Hitchcock's *Shadow of a Doubt* and William Wyler's *The Best Years of Our Lives*, later roles in Hollywood pictures did not enhance her career. Part of this may be related to Wright's consistent refusal to do publicity work for her films; her intense desire for privacy may have prevented her from becoming a true Hollywood star by keeping her out of the public's eye.

Wright appeared in several television movies, most notably "The Miracle Worker" (1957) and "The *Margaret Bourke-White Story" (1960), for which she was nominated for Emmy Awards. Then, in 1959, she married playwright Robert Anderson, and retired from the screen to further pursue her love of Broadway. They divorced and she later married Carlos Pierre. This marriage also ended and Wright subsequently remarried her second husband. She returned to Broadway, most notably in *Mary, Mary* in 1962 and *Death of a Salesman* in 1975. She also made several television appearances in the 1970s and 1980s, earning a third Emmy nomination for Outstanding Guest Actress in a Drama Series for her performance in a 1989 episode of "Dolphin Cove."

SOURCES:

Contemporary Theatre, Film, and Television. Vol. 17. Detroit, MI: Gale Research, 1997.
Current Biography, 1943. NY: H.W. Wilson, 1943.
Katz, Ephraim. *The Film Encyclopedia*. 3rd ed. NY: HarperPerennial, 1988.
Quinlan, David, ed. *The Film Lover's Companion*. Secaucus, NJ: Citadel, 1997.

Laura York, M.A. in History, University of California, Riverside, California

Wrightson, Patricia (1921—)

Australian children's novelist. Born Alice Patricia Furlonger in Lismore, New South Wales, Australia, in June 1921; daughter of Charles Radcliff Furlonger (a solicitor) and Alice (Dyer) Furlonger; attended St. Catherine's College, Stanthrope, Queensland, 1932; State Correspondence School, 1933–34; married, in 1943 (divorced 1953); children: Jennifer Mary Wrightson Ireland; Peter Radcliff.

Selected writings: The Crooked Snake (1955); The Bunyip (1958); The Rocks of Honey (1960); The Feather Star (1962); Down to Earth (1965); I Own the Racecourse! (1968); An Older Kind of Magic (1972); (ed.) Beneath the Sun: An Australian Collection for Children (1972); The Nargun and the Stars (1973); The Ice is Coming (1977); (ed.) Emu Stew (1977); The Dark Bright Water (1979); Behind the Wind (1981); A Little Fear (1983); Night Outside (1985); Moon-Dark (1987); Baylet (1989); The Sugar-Gum Tree (1992); Shadows of Time (1994); Rattler's Place (1997); four-time Children's Book of the Year Award winner.

Patricia Wrightson was born Alice Patricia Furlonger in Linsmore, New South Wales, Australia, in June 1921, the third daughter of Charles Radcliff Furlonger, a solicitor, and **Alice Dyer Furlonger**. She spent the first four years of her life on a farm before her parents relocated to Sydney. After selling most of their furniture and making the week-long journey to the city, the family remained for only a year, their experiment with city life being unsuccessful. In this short time, however, Wrightson had a new brother, and their father began reading Charles Dickens to them in the evening. This nighttime tradition persisted through her teens. The next three years brought a series of transfers as the Furlongers prepared to move into a newly built house in a larger Australian town of the river-country.

Wrightson entered grammar school as a dutiful student and developed a love for composition. Before she was 12, her family again moved from the river planes to the hills, a place absent of such conveniences as electricity. Although she was originally jealous of her sisters' continued residence in the city, she eventually learned to love this Australian land and began to develop an Aboriginal consciousness. "I'm glad it happened like that," she wrote: "that I came abruptly from city and town into this country and learnt to love it." After a year spent homesick in boarding school, she returned home to complete her high school diploma in 1939 by correspondence from the New South Wales Correspondence School. At the outbreak of World War II, she moved to Sydney and worked in a munitions factory. She married in 1943 and had two children, but divorced her husband in 1953.

It was while living with her children and parents and managing the Bonalbo District Hospital that Wrightson began to write seriously. None of the stories she had read as a child had been set in Australia, and only as an adult was Wrightson able to appreciate and value her own experiences as an Australian native; she hoped to teach her children to value their heritage and homeland through her stories. Set in the Australian landscapes of her childhood, Wrightson's stories show her young readers that Australia is a beautiful, exciting country, and try to help them develop a sense of pride in being Australian. Her first attempt at a full-length novel was published in 1955 as *The Crooked Snake*, to immediate popular and critical acclaim. It was named Australia's Book of the Year by the Children's Book Council; Wrightson would later win this award in 1974, 1978, and 1984 as well.

When her children were old enough to enter high school, Wrightson moved with them to Sydney in 1960. There she joined the staff of the Sydney District Nursing Association. Four years later she accepted a position as assistant editor of Sydney's *School Magazine*, a publication for elementary school students, moving up to serve as editor from 1970 to 1975. Despite holding full-time jobs, Wrightson published a new book every year or two between 1955 and 1997. She has been consistently popular with young readers, who respond to her imaginative settings and characters and the lack of condescension in her stories.

Although she is best known for her realistic children's books, Wrightson has also published science fiction and fantasy novels for children, including several series, most notably the "Wirrun" trilogy: *The Ice is Coming* (1977), *The Dark Bright Water* (1979), and *Behind the Wind* (1981). She has written numerous fantasy novels for adults as well, and edited two collections of juvenile stories, *Beneath the Sun* (1972) and *Emu Stew* (1976).

Wrightson's fantasy works are in large part the result of her involvement with Australian Aboriginal culture and traditions. She has researched the folklore of native Australians and uses elements of their stories to structure her books and add depth to her Australian settings. She sees native folk magic as integral to Australian culture, and as a part of the Australian landscape: as she

Patricia Wrightson

has written, "Magic belongs to simple people, and is shaped by the things that simple people know: the places where they live and the lives they lead. It fits the scene where it was made."

Wrightson has received many awards for her work. In 1978, she was awarded the Order of the British Empire for her contributions to children's literature. The following year, she received the New South Wales Premier's Award for ethnic literature. Other prizes include the Boston Globe-Horn Book award (1984) and the *Young Observer* Prize (1984). She was honored with the Hans Christian Andersen Medal in 1986, and with the New South Wales Premier's Special Occasion Award in 1988.

SOURCES:

St. James Guide to Fantasy Writers. NY: St. James Press, 1996.

Something About the Author Autobiography Series. Vol. 4. Detroit, MI: Gale Research, 1987.

Wilde, William H., *et al.,* eds. *The Oxford Companion to Australian Literature.* Melbourne: Oxford University Press, 1985.

Laura York, M.A. in History,
University of California,
Riverside, California

Wrinch, Dorothy (1894–1976)

English physicist and philosopher. Name variations: Dorothy Wrinch Nicholson; Dot Wrinch; (pseudonym) Jean Ayling. Born Dorothy Wrinch to English parents in Rosario, Argentina, in 1894; died in February 1976; educated in England; Girton College, Cambridge, B.A. and M.A, 1918; University of London, M.Sc. and D.Sc.; Oxford University, M.A., and was the first woman to receive a D.Sc. from Oxford, 1929; married John Nicholson (an Oxford physicist known for his work on atomic structure), in 1922 (divorced 1938); married O.C. Glaser, in 1941; children: (first marriage) Pamela Wrinch Schenkman (1928–1975).

Appointed lecturer in pure mathematics, University College, London (1918); was a member of the Executive Committee of the Aristotelian Society (1925–26); moved to U.S. (1939); was a member of the chemistry department, Johns Hopkins University (1940–41); taught at Amherst, Smith, and Mt. Holyoke (1941–44); taught physics at Smith College (1944–71).

Selected works: "On the Nature of Judgement" in Mind *(Vol. 28, 1919); "On the Nature of Memory" in* Mind *(Vol. 29, 1920); "On the Structure of Scientific Inquiry" in* Proceedings of the Aristotelian Society *(New Series 21, 1920–21); "On Certain Methodological Aspects of the Theory of Relativity" in* Mind *(Vol. 31, 1922); "The Idealist Interpretation of Einstein's Theory"; "On Certain Aspects of Scientific Thought" in* Proceedings of the Aristotelian Society *(New Series 24, 1923–24); Chemical Aspects of Polypeptide Chain Structures and the Cyclal Theory (1965).*

Scientist Dorothy Wrinch has been labeled variously as a mathematician, biochemist, physicist, and philosopher. Indeed, her work bridged the disciplines of several fields, and helped to reconcile divergences between the biological and physical sciences. Considered brilliant and hard-driven, Wrinch was also known to be zealous and competitive, often so impatient with the politics of science that she was viewed by colleagues as abrasive. Although these charges must be viewed in light of Wrinch's status in a male-dominated profession, she was hardly afraid of controversy. In a 1948 letter, Michael Polanyi told her, "You and I have much in common in the manner we managed to make our scientific careers less dull than usual."

Born in 1894, Wrinch, whose father was an engineer, spent her childhood in Rosario, Argentina, entering Girton College of Cambridge University in 1913, where she specialized in philosophy and epistemology. While there, she excelled in mathematics and was elected a member of the prestigious Aristotelian Society, established to encourage philosophical dialogue. (Her circle of friends during this period is said to have included Bertrand Russell, with whom she studied philosophy.) After receiving her B.A. and M.A. degrees in 1918, she was appointed lecturer in pure mathematics at the University College of the University of London (1918–20), then went on to become a member of the university's research staff (1920–24). In 1922, she also became a member of the faculty of physical science at Oxford University, retaining her association with that university for 17 years. That same year, she married John Nicholson, an Oxford physicist known for his work on atomic structure. Their only child, **Pamela Wrinch Schenkman,** was born in 1928.

In addition to teaching, Wrinch was a prolific writer. By 1930, she had published 16 papers on philosophy and another 20 on mathematics. Her academic achievements also included advanced degrees from the University of London and Oxford. (In 1929, she was the first woman awarded a D.Sc. from that institution.) In spite of her credentials and seven years' experience teaching mathematics, Wrinch failed in her application for a Rhodes traveling fellowship because, according to her sponsors, she was a woman. She was more successful, however, in subsequent requests, receiving research fellowships from Girton College and Oxford University that allowed her to study at the University of Vienna, the University of Paris, and in Prague and Leyden.

Most of Wrinch's early research focused on mathematics, and the allied studies of mathematical physics, methodology, and the theory of probability, although in 1930, under the pseudonym Jean Ayling, she published *The Retreat from Parenthood*, a sociological study proposing a broad plan for restructuring social services to make them more compatible with the professional lives of both men and women. Around 1934, she took up the study of structural problems in physiology and chemistry (molecular biology). By means of a Rockefeller Foundation fellowship (1935–41), Wrinch furthered her studies in this direction, concentrating on chromosomes and proteins, and evolving models of protein molecules based on mathematical computations of constructional possibilities. Her findings were presented in 1937, at the meeting of the British Association for the Advancement of Science.

Wrinch's "cyclol" theory of the structure of the protein molecules startled the emerging world of molecular biology and caused division within the scientific community between those believing Wrinch had proven her hypothesis and those rallying around her leading and most vocal critic, Linus Pauling. The controversy, which went on for a decade, grew quite heated and led to harsh words between Wrinch and her colleagues, and to her eventual blacklisting by most of the scientific community. The argument completely unnerved Wrinch's 12-year-old daughter, who wrote a letter to Pauling requesting that the two scientists stop attacking one another. "There are many quarrels in the world alas," she wrote. "Don't please let yours be one; it is these things that help to make the world a kingdom of misery!!" (It was some 13 years before the work of Swiss chemist Arthur Stoll verified Wrinch's cyclol hypothesis, but by that time the scientific community had moved on to other things, and paid little attention to the new findings.)

Wrinch was divorced from John Nicholson in 1938, and subsequently moved with Pamela to the United States, where she took a position with the chemistry department of Johns Hopkins University (1940–41). In 1941, amid some local opposition, she was appointed a visiting professor at Amherst, Smith, and Mt. Holyoke colleges, where she introduced a series of lectures on the structural problems of biology, chemistry, and the medical sciences, and also offered seminars in molecular biology. That same year, she married Otto Charles Glaser, a biology professor at Amherst, and settled permanently in Massachusetts.

From 1944 until her retirement in 1971, Wrinch was associated exclusively with the physics department at Smith College, where she lectured, conducted seminars and continued her research. In the summers, she taught courses in crystallography at the Marine Biology Laboratory at Woods Hole, Massachusetts. The body of her work was impressive, and included techniques for the interpretation and application of 7X-ray data of crystal structures, as well as studies in mineralogy. Before the end of her career, she had produced some 192 publications, covering many branches of science.

Wrinch spent her later years in Woods Hole, where she lost her daughter Pamela in a tragic house fire in November 1975. She died three months later, at age 82. After her death in 1976, a three-day commemorative symposium was held at Smith College.

SOURCES:

Kass-Simon, G., and Patricia Farnes. *Women of Science: Righting the Record*. Bloomington, IN: Indiana University Press, 1993.

Ogilvie, Marilyn Bailey. *Women in Science*. Cambridge, MA: Cambridge Press, 1993.

Rothe, Anna, ed. *Current Biography 1947*. NY: H.W. Wilson, 1947.

Waithe, Mary Ellen, ed. *A History of Women Philosophers*. Boston, MA: Martinus Nijhoff, 1987–1995.

Catherine Hundleby, M.A. Philosophy, University of Guelph, Guelph, Ontario, Canada

Wriothesley, Rachel (1636–1723).

See Russell, Rachel.

Wriothesly, Elizabeth (d. 1690)

*Countess of Northumberland. Died in September 1690; daughter of Thomas Wriothesly (b. 1607), 5th earl of Southampton, and **Elizabeth Leigh**; married Josceline also known as Jocelyn Percy (d. 1670), 11th and last earl of Northumberland, on December 23, 1662; married Ralph Montagu, 1st duke of Montagu; children: (first marriage) *Elizabeth Percy (1667–1722).*

Wroth, Mary (c. 1587–c. 1651)

*English poet, prose writer, and literary patron. Born Mary Sydney in Penshurst Place, Kent, England, around 1587; died around 1651; daughter of Robert Sidney, 1st earl of Leicester, and Barbara Gamage; niece of **Mary Herbert** (1561–1621); married Sir Robert Wroth, in 1604 (died 1614); children: (first marriage) son James (died 1616); (with William Herbert, 3rd earl of Pembroke) two illegitimate children.*

Selected writings: The Countesse of Montgomerie's Urania *(1621);* Pamphilia to Amphilanthus; Love's Victorie.

Born in Penshurst Place in Kent, England, Lady Mary Wroth was the eldest daughter of **Barbara Gamage** and Sir Robert Sidney, 1st earl of Leicester. Her paternal uncle was Sir Philip Sidney, the Elizabethan poet best known for his *Arcadia.* Her own work would be deeply influenced by Philip, although he died about the time of her birth. In 1604, Mary married the wealthy Sir Robert Wroth, eldest son of a member of Parliament. As with many upper-class marriages in the 17th century, the couple did not freely choose one another; instead, the marriage was arranged as a union between the two families. Lady Mary and her husband had one son, but spent most of their years of marriage apart. Mary was prominent at the English court, where she circulated her verses and was a generous supporter of other writers; those who dedicated works to her in the hope of a reward included Ben Jonson, George Chapman, and George Wither. Jonson dedicated *The Alchemist* to her in 1610, after she had performed in one of his masques.

Despite his large landholdings, Sir Robert Wroth lived well beyond his means; when he died in 1614, Mary was left in considerable debt. Her son James died two years later. Sometime in the late 1610s, Wroth began a relationship with her cousin, William Herbert, 3rd earl of Pembroke, with whom she had two children.

In 1621, Wroth sought patrons of her own when she issued a prose romance, *The Countesse of Montgomerie's Urania,* which imitated her uncle's popular *Arcadia* and is considered the first English novel published by a woman. It included verses and a set of sonnets entitled *Pamphilia to Amphilanthus,* written in the form of letters between two lovers, thought to have been drawn from her affair with Herbert. Both romantic and satirical, the *Urania* provides a female perspective on the joys and sorrows of courtly love, as do her few other known works. However, the *Urania* did not bring Wroth the financial success she needed; the work's satirical depiction of court figures caused a great scandal at court and forced her to withdraw it six months later.

In addition to these works, she authored a play, a tragicomedy titled *Love's Victorie* which was not published until 1853. Wroth retired from court and spent her final years at her country estates. The year of her death is not known. In the late 20th century, literary scholars rediscovered her works and began using them as sources to understand women's experiences in 17th-century England. Lady Mary Wroth's collected verses were published in 1983; in 1995, the first part of *Urania* was newly made available again to readers, drawn from surviving manuscripts.

SOURCES:

Buck, Claire, ed. *The Bloomsbury Guide to Women's Literature.* NY: Prentice Hall, 1992.

The Concise Dictionary of National Biography. Vol. III. Oxford: Oxford University Press, 1992.

Shattock, Joanne. *The Oxford Guide to British Women Writers.* Oxford: Oxford University Press, 1993.

Laura York, M.A. in History,
University of California,
Riverside, California

Wu, Chien-Shiung (1912–1997)

Chinese-American experimental physicist who supplied the proof for the hypothesis that the principle of the conservation of parity was invalid, overthrowing what had been a fundamental concept of physics. Name variations: *Wu Chien-Shiung.* Pronunciation: *CHEN-shoong WOO. Born Chien-Shiung Wu on May 29, 1912, in Shanghai, China; died in New York City after suffering a stroke on February 16, 1997; daughter of Wu Zhongyi (a school principal) and Fuhua H. Fan Wu; National Central University, Nanjing, B.S., 1934; University of California, Berkeley, Ph.D., 1940; married Luke Cha-Liou Yuan (a physicist), on May 30, 1942, in Pasadena, California; children: son, Vincent Weichen Yuan (b. 1947).*

Hired as physics instructor, Smith College (1942); became physics instructor, Princeton University (1943); joined scientific staff, Division of War Research, Manhattan Project, Columbia University (1944–45); was research physicist, Columbia University (1945–81); received tenure as associate professor at Columbia (1952); became naturalized citizen (1954); determined invalidity of principle of parity (1957); received Research Corporation Award (1958); was seventh woman elected to the National Academy of Sciences (1958); promoted to full professor at Columbia (1959); named "Woman of the Year" by the American Association of University Women (1962); was first woman to receive the National Academy of Sciences Comstock Award (1964); won the National Medal of Science (1975).

Selected writings: "I. The Internal and External Continuous X-Rays Excited by the Beta Particles of 32/15P. II. Some Fission Products of Uranium" *(Ph.D. dissertation, University of California, Berkeley, 1940);* "Recent Investigations of the Shapes of Beta-Ray Spectra," *in* Reviews of Modern Physics *(Vol. 22, October 1950, pp. 386–398); with I. Shaknov, "The Angular Correlation of Scattered Annihilation Radia-*

tion," in Physical Review (Vol. 77, 1950, p. 136); with Ernest Ambler, Raymond W. Hayward, Dale D. Hoppes, and R.P. Hudson, "Experimental Test of Parity Conservation in Beta Decay," in Physical Review (Vol. 105, 1957, p. 1413); with Luke C.L. Yuan, Nuclear Physics (2 vols., NY: Academic, 1961–63); "The Universal Fermi Interaction and the Conserved Vector Current in Beta Decay," in Reviews of Modern Physics (Vol. 36, 1964, p. 618); with Steven A. Moszkowski, Beta Decay (NY: Interscience, 1966); with Lawrence Wilets, "Muonic Atoms and Nuclear Structure," in Annual Reviews of Nuclear Science (Vol. 19, 1969, p. 527); "One Researcher's Personal Account," in Adventures in Experimental Physics (1973); edited with Vernon W. Hughes, Muon Physics (3 vols., NY: Academic, 1975–77); "Subtleties and Surprises: The Contribution of Beta Decay to an Understanding of the Weak Interaction," in Annals of the New York Academy of Sciences (Vol. 294, November 8, 1977, pp. 37–51).

On January 16, 1957, at a press conference held at Columbia University in New York City, a petite Chinese-American woman, her hair twisted into a bun, declared the results of an experiment in nuclear physics she had recently completed. Nuclear particles, said Chien-Shiung Wu, did not always behave symmetrically. The scientific principle of conservation of parity was therefore proved invalid. If the nature of her pronouncement were arcane, the scientific implications of it were huge. For the first time in the relatively short history of the science of physics, one of its universally accepted laws regarding the structure and behavior of the universe was being struck down.

For the 45-year-old research physicist, the experimental results were the culmination of her life's work. Explaining the reward she found in physics research, Wu later told **Gloria Lubkin**, senior editor of *Physics Today*, "I've always felt that in physics you must have total commitment. It's not just a job. It's my whole life."

The name Chien-Shiung Wu means "Courageous Hero," a fitting designation for the daughter of a fighter in the Chinese Revolution of 1911. Wu Zhongyi was a former engineering student, and his only daughter was born the year after he helped in the overthrow of the Manchu Dynasty. Enlightened about gender issues by his reading of Western books, he established a girls' school and became one of the foremost feminists in China. "I want every girl to have a school to go to," he declared. "I want everyone who has suffered to have a place to go to air his [or her] sufferings."

Chien-Shiung Wu was on born May 29 (other sources cite the 31st), 1912, in the Chinese port city of Shanghai. She grew up some 30 miles away in the small town of Liuho, in Chiangsu Province, where her father's school was located. Wu's mother **Fuhua H. Fan Wu** visited local families to persuade parents to send their daughters to her husband's school, and to end the ancient and brutal Chinese practice of binding young girls' feet. School principal Wu Zhongyi, committed to preparing both young men and women for life in a modernized China, filled the family's home with scholarly books and encouraged questioning and the exploration of new ideas in his daughter and two sons; at night, the family read together. Wu Zhongyi held the culture and traditions of China in high regard, and believed music, arts and literature enriched the lives of his children and helped to prepare them for the future.

"It was a wonderfully happy life. I had a fortunate and happy childhood," Wu told biographer **Edna Yost**. Curious about the world around her, she enjoyed playing with other children, but was particularly delighted by the solving of problems her father would pose for her. In Liuho, where few people recognized the scope of political change then abroad in China and the Far East, Wu Zhongyi advised his daughter, "Ignore the obstacles. Just put your head down and keep walking forward." Father and daughter grew especially close.

Chien-Shiung Wu knew from an early age that she wanted to be a scientist. When she was nine, she completed the training available at her father's school and asked to be allowed to go to boarding school. Her great-great-grandmother, the family matriarch, insisted that she be sent to the best school available. A teacher at the Soochow Girls School who was a family friend agreed to be her guardian, and the school's Western curriculum opened many new subjects to her, including English. Lecturers came from such prominent American schools as Columbia University, where she was to spend most of her career.

At Soochow, girls entered either an academic program or a training course to become a teacher. Wu elected at first to pursue the teaching curriculum because it was free and prepared students for jobs. Soon, however, she became fascinated by what friends in the academic program were learning in their science classes. She would get students in her dormitory to loan her their science textbooks during the evening so that she could learn the principles of physics, mathematics and chemistry for herself. The puz-

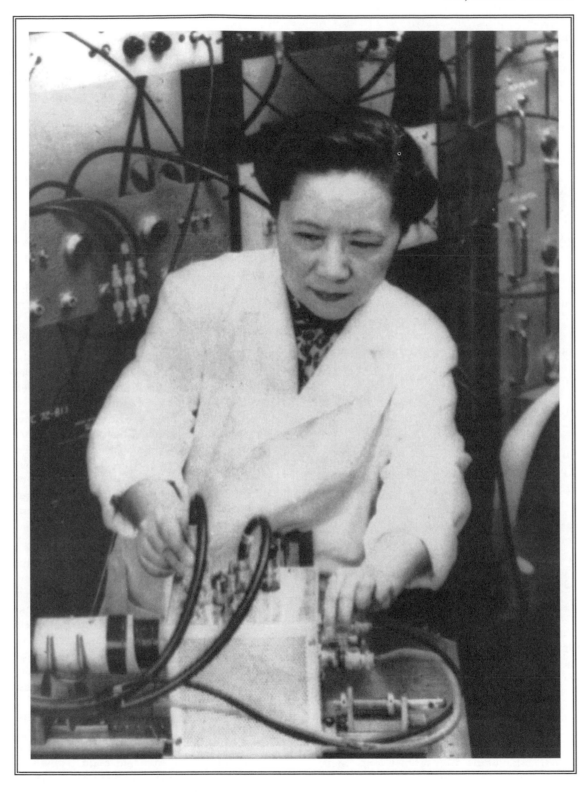

zles posed by physics intrigued her most. "Some-how I soon knew," she later said, "it was what I wanted to go on with."

In the seven years she spent at Soochow, Wu also led the local chapter of China's under-ground student movement, protected from ex-pulsion by her father's revolutionary record and her excellent grades as she represented the stu-dents at meetings and strikes. Graduated in 1930 at the top of her class, she received notice that summer of her selection as a student at the

National Central University, the elite government-supported school located at Nanjing, the capital of the nationalist government. Eager to study physics, she confessed her doubts about her background in mathematics and science to her father. "There's ample time to prepare yourself," responded Wu Zhongyi, who bought her three advanced textbooks—in mathematics, chemistry, and physics—which she studied until the school year began.

It is the courage to doubt what has long been established, the incessant search for its verification and proof that pushed the wheel of science forward.

—Chien-Shiung Wu

Enrolled initially in mathematics, Wu had enough confidence by her sophomore year to transfer to physics. Thriving in this intellectual setting, she completed every physics and mathematics course she could and led every class. In the tumultuous atmosphere of pre-World War II China, she also participated in the students' nationalist movement, boycotting Japanese products and protesting at the presidential mansion of General Chiang Kai-shek. With other student leaders, she appeared before the general to urge his resistance against Japanese aggression. In 1934, despite her political activism, she completed her thesis on X-rays and was awarded a degree in physics.

"If it hadn't been for my father's encouragement," Wu later said, "I wouldn't have had the courage to select physics as a major field and I would be teaching grade school somewhere in China now." As it was, graduation was followed by a teaching position at a provincial university, then research work, in X-ray crystallography, at Shanghai's National Academy of Sciences. At the academy, a female physicist with a Ph.D. from the University of Michigan became an influential mentor, encouraging Wu to attend her alma mater for graduate physics courses unavailable in China.

Wu's parents supported her desire to go to the U.S.; at that time she saw the degree she could get in America as a way to help in the modernization of her country. An uncle who had made a fortune establishing China's first long-distance bus company financed the trip, and at age 24, in the fall of 1936, she set sail across the Pacific.

In San Francisco, friends of her family introduced her to Luke Cha-Liou Yuan, a graduate student in physics at the University of California at Berkeley. The grandson of a famous Chinese general, Luke Yuan warned her against the University of Michigan, with its large Chinese student population and rules that did not even allow women to use the student union. Berkeley, on the other hand, had one of the best physics programs in the world. Eager to meet Americans and put off by thoughts of discrimination, Wu followed his advice and enrolled at Berkeley.

In the fascinating and demanding program she entered, some of the world's best nuclear physicists were teaching and carrying out their research. Dr. Ernest O. Lawrence, director of the radiation laboratory, was then devising an atom-smashing cyclotron, and won the Nobel Prize in physics for research in atomic structure and transmutations while Wu was his student. In the classes of Robert Oppenheimer, she heard lectures about new quantum theories, concerning the behavior of atoms and subatomic particles. She was unintimidated among these brilliant figures, later explaining, "I didn't see a man there who could compare with my father."

At ease in the classroom, Wu had some difficult cultural adjustments. In the cafeteria of the International House, where Asian, European and American graduate students lived together, she was bewildered by the confusing buffet faced at breakfast time instead of the expected rice. Going off campus to find Chinese food, she met a German student, **Ursula Schaefer**, in a bakery, and they became friends. The two learned about the cooking and customs and civilization of America while sharing opera, theater, books and their native foods. Wu grew fond of Western folk songs and classical music.

In her slit-skirt, high-collared dresses, Wu was exquisitely exotic to Berkeley's male students. One described her as "a smasher—a gorgeous, willowy girl with a smile that would melt anybody's heart." Wu, in turn, was dignified and reserved, addressing everybody formally by their titles. Her students called her "Miss Wu," and only Oppenheimer and close friends dared to address her affectionately as "Jiejie," meaning "elder sister" in Chinese. Charming, modest and polite, she also insisted on rationality and truth, even when her opinions forced her to be disapproving of friends. Schaefer described Wu as "the only one who gave me real hell," and also "an absolutely, totally reliable friend. If anything happened she would be right there. She's very reserved, but very, very human and warm."

At Berkeley, Wu focused on the study of atomic particles, including protons, electrons, neutrons and other invisible components such as mesons, that were central to research in nuclear physics at the time. Emilio Segré, who assisted Lawrence and was known for his rudeness to many students, including Wu (when she forgot to secure a mercury bottle, he left her a note, "The vapor is poisonous. Do you want to see your grandchildren?"), admired her. "Wu's will power and devotion to work are reminiscent of *Marie Curie," he once commented, "but she is more worldly, elegant and witty." Urging her to read more physics and spend less time in the laboratory, Segré advised, "You have to stand back from things and see the whole picture."

In the classroom and laboratory, Wu performed admirably; her professors considered her work to be brilliant, original and insightful. Because they were Asian, however, both she and Yuan were denied fellowships; $200 each to grade papers was the best they could get. Yuan left for the California Institute of Technology in southern California to accept a $600 fellowship.

In July 1937, learning that Japan had invaded China, Wu realized she was cut off from all contact with her family. "We are all very, very sorry," she was told by the chair of the physics department. "But you don't have to worry about yourself. We will take care of you now." In International House, two Japanese students sent her flowers. Worried about her family and friends, she endured months of reading about Japanese atrocities against Chinese civilians.

Meanwhile, she immersed herself in her work. "I have always felt that in physics, and probably in other endeavors too, you must have total commitment," she once said. "It is not just a job. It is a way of life." Patterning her career after that of Marie Curie, who also emigrated to a new home and labored to succeed in physics, Wu worked late into the night. Caring professors would request that a graduate student drive her home so she would not walk alone in the dark. Wu panicked at each test, afraid that a failure in schoolwork would leave her with nowhere to go, and celebrated in Chinese restaurants when she passed. Insecure about her pronunciation of English, she carefully wrote out each lecture. But she was happy in her work. "It is hard to push the door open and to get inside a subject," she explained. "But once you understand it, it is very interesting."

In 1940, Wu completed her Ph.D. in nuclear physics and was elected to Phi Beta Kappa. For her doctoral dissertation, she performed two investigations. The first involved ingeniously devised methods of separating two types of rays emitted during beta decay, a type of radioactivity (known as a weak interaction) in which a nucleus ejects high-speed electrons and becomes another element. Wu studied the electromagnetic energy emitted when a particle traveling through matter decelerated, validating her theoretical predictions with her experimental results.

In her second investigation, she studied radioactive noble gases derived from uranium fission (the atomic nucleus was first split by German scientists in 1939). Working with Dr. Segré, she demonstrated that "two complete chains of radioactive decay" resulted "with the half lives, radiations and isotope numbers completely identified." The wartime climate of secrecy prevented the work from being published at that time, but the results were requested by and delivered to the U.S. government's Los Alamos Laboratories.

No major research university employed a woman as a professor of physics at the time; and in the discriminatory atmosphere against Asians, especially on the West Coast (although the Chinese were U.S. military allies), Berkeley's administrators refused to hire Wu for such a position. Berkeley's physics department, hoping to retain their outstanding young physicist, created a position for Wu in the radiation laboratory as a research assistant to Dr. Lawrence. Gaining expertise in fission, she lectured throughout the country in 1941.

On May 30, 1942, in the midst of World War II, Wu married Luke Yuan in the garden of Nobel Prize-winner Robert Millikan. The couple moved to New Jersey, where Yuan was employed to design radar devices for RCA and Wu was hired to teach physics at Smith College. Within that same year, she was invited to become a lecturer on nuclear physics at Princeton University. While she was reluctant to leave a position in which she could influence female students, Wu finally elected to teach at the all-male Princeton, where she became the first woman instructor, in order to have access to physics research equipment that was unavailable at Smith. She had been at Princeton only a few months when she was interviewed to work for the wartime Manhattan Project at Columbia University.

Pleased to be able to contribute to the Allied war effort, Wu joined the scientific staff of the Division of War Research at Columbia, in New York City, in March 1944. In a converted automobile warehouse, she worked on designing radiation detectors for the atomic bomb project and perfecting Geiger counters, as well as neutron and uranium enrichment research.

In 1945, with World War II ended, Wu finally received news that her family in China was alive. At Columbia, she became a senior investigator for a large federal research grant. In 1947, her son Vincent Weichen Yuan was born, and the family moved into an apartment at 15 Claremont Avenue, only two blocks from her laboratory. Filled with Chinese art, furniture and cooking utensils, the apartment was Wu's place to relax and enjoy her family. Luke commuted to Brookhaven National Laboratory on Long Island, where he designed accelerators, and Vincent went to local private academies and European boarding schools. Wu considered "a nice husband," a home near work, and reliable child care as essential for married female scientists.

In her research, Wu now renewed her studies of beta decay. Because of discrepancies between theories and experimental results due to the primitive state of beta spectroscopy (the optical examination of a particle's spectrum), she attempted to discover new ways to study the shapes of beta spectra and their interaction during beta decay. She developed a technique for spectra study, using a scintillation counter and beta detector inside a magnetic spectrometer, and after several years of research with thin copper sheets, she offered proof in support of Enrico Fermi's theory of beta decay about the travel of electrons at specific speeds.

Because she was a full-time researcher at Columbia, Wu was not promoted to associate professor of physics with tenure until 1952, when she began to teach part-time. This was an academic rank few women had achieved in universities or research laboratories. Two years later, in 1954, Wu became a naturalized American citizen. She and her husband had been invited to join the faculty of the National Central University in China, but they elected to become Americans due to China's civil war with the communists. Wu never saw her family again, and received only infrequent letters.

Dr. Wu advised graduate students focused on problems regarding beta decay, seeking new methods and materials with them for conducting their research. In the 13th-floor laboratory of the Pupin physics building, she had a reputation among some as a slave driver who expected her students to work as hard as she did, day and night, and on weekends. But according to Schaefer, "if she felt that a student was performing below par, she gave him hell, because she was anxious that he wasn't going to make it." A demanding teacher, known for the high-necked Chinese dresses she wore under her laboratory coat, she monitored experiments, adjusting equipment and criticizing her students' methods, while also warning them to guard their data until it was published to prevent intellectual

theft. Most who worked under her admired her for her intense devotion to her research, and for her competitiveness, while she in turn was motivated by their youthful enthusiasm.

Some students showed their Asian bias by dubbing Wu the "Dragon Lady," after a comic-strip character defaming Madame Chiang Kai-shek (*Song Meiling). Others regarded her as one of the nicest professors at Columbia, comparing her to male professors, in particular, with reputations for self-centeredness and disdain toward their students. Wu, in contrast, ate lunch with her students every Friday in Chinese restaurants, and hosted parties to celebrate the degrees and honors they earned; she was particularly caring toward her Asian students, warning them that they would have to work harder than others to overcome discrimination in their chosen field. With these loyal and dedicated students, Wu established Columbia as a center for some of the most outstanding experimentation being done in physics, and the work was monitored by other leading physicists, who sought her out for consultations.

In the spring of 1956, Wu was approached by two fellow physicists, both of Chinese-American background, with an intriguing proposition. Tsung Dao Lee was a colleague of Wu's at Columbia and Chen Ning Yang worked at the Princeton Institute for Advanced Study, and what they were seeking was help in testing the validity of one of the underlying principles of physics.

The so-called principle of conservation of parity belonged to the body of laws, including those of gravity, which are understood by physicists to govern the nature of the universe at the subatomic level. The principle of conservation of parity applied to the behavior of particles at the subatomic level, where an object and its mirror image were believed to be symmetrical. Albeit unproven, it had been accepted for three decades as one of the fundamental underpinnings of physics.

As early as 1946, however, the validity of the parity principle was brought into question by the work of some theoretical physicists. In the early 1950s, doubts were increased after the discovery of the subatomic particles known as K-mesons, which did not follow the pattern of disintegration that the principle of parity should have made predictable. Then when Lee and Yang, working together, began to investigate the principle, they found behavioral anomalies at the subatomic level and incomplete information. Suspecting by then that the principle was invalid, they sought out Wu to help in the proof of their hypothesis because of her lengthy experience with another type of subatomic particle, the electrons in the nucleus of radioactive substances known as beta rays. They proposed that Wu design an experiment using beta rays, to determine if particles were sloughed from the nucleus during beta decay, regardless of the direction in which the nucleus spun. If this were true in the case of beta rays, the conservation of parity would be proven invalid as a universal law.

The experiment would be extremely complex and difficult to set up; the odds against arriving at a conclusive proof were about one in a million. Wu's initial reaction was to loan the men her copy of the study *Beta- and Gamma-Ray Spectroscopy*. But in June 1956, when they submitted their article "Question of Parity Conservation in Weak Interactions" to *Physical Review*, she began preparing her approach to the problem, fearing some other scientist might get ahead of her. She even decided not take the ocean cruise to the Far East she and her husband had planned to celebrate the anniversary of their immigration.

Since Columbia's facilities were not adequate for the job, Wu contacted the National Bureau of Standards in Washington, D.C., where she could have the help of Ernest Ambler, who had pioneered research with radioactive nuclei at extremely cold temperatures. Working with the bureau's Low Temperature Physics Group and scientists from the Atomic Energy Commission, she was engaged in the project for the next six months, commuting between Washington and her students in New York every two weeks, and sleeping no more than fours hours a night.

Her design for the test involved a radioactive nucleus of cobalt 60, put into a complex cooling and vacuum system capable of being cooled with gases and crystals to the temperature of 0.01° above absolute zero (-459° Fahrenheit). The extremely low temperature reduced thermal motion during beta decay so that the spinning cobalt nuclei could be aligned with a magnetic field, and thus be more easily manipulated and observed. A scintillation counter recorded the results by enumerating the electrons discharged by the disintegrating cobalt nuclei. As Wu explained, "The essence of the experiment was to line up the spins of the Cobalt 60 nuclei along the same axis, then to determine whether the beta particles were emitted preferentially in one direction or the other along the axis." Scientists in Washington, intensely monitored by Wu, stayed with the equipment day and night, readjusting it as needed. Those hectic sessions, she said later, were "like a nightmare. I wouldn't want to go through them again."

As her careful measurements began to yield repeated verifications, Wu remained doubtful of her findings. Researchers at Columbia and the University of Chicago began to duplicate her results with experiments in meson decay, and her sleepless nights continued while she sought other means of confirming her results. Finally, after weeks of deliberation, she agreed to announce her findings, at the press conference hosted by Columbia.

Declaring her results, Wu asserted that nuclear particles did not always behave symmetrically. In fact, statistics proved that electrons preferred going in the opposite direction of the nuclei's spin in an almost predetermined pattern. Scientists began to suggest that Wu and her colleagues had revealed a "preference" in electrons for "handedness." Nuclear particles, like humans, could be designated as being right-handed or left-handed as they moved along the axis of rotation and were discharged according to the direction of their spin.

While physicists adjusted to the idea of discarding one of the fundamental concepts of their science, Wu enjoyed the "moments of exaltation and ecstasy" in what she described as the "sudden liberation of our thinking on the very structure of the physical world." According to the *New York Post*, "This small modest woman was powerful enough to do what armies can never accomplish," and she was featured on the front page of *The New York Times* as well as in *Time* and *Newsweek*. For Wu, however, the thrill was in the "new level of understanding" for physicists, and the meanings that still lay ahead. "When we arrive at this understanding," she said, "we shall marvel how neatly all the elementary particles fit into the Great Scheme. Indeed, how deeply privileged our generation is to have been challenged with this fascinating task."

Reaping the professional accolades due her for the research, Wu also ensured international acclaim for Lee and Yang, whose names appeared along with hers on her findings, published in the *Physical Review* (signed "C.S. Wu," as were all her articles). In 1957, the Nobel Prize in physics went to the two theoretical physicists, but not to Wu. According to the strict rules of eligibility, the award was given for discovery or invention, and did not cover the work of supplying the proof. Many physicists felt it an unjust oversight, however, that the work of Wu and her experimental group was ignored.

At Columbia, Wu was promoted to full professor, and the following year she became the first woman to receive the Research Corporation

Award, and only the seventh woman to be elected to the National Academy of Sciences. She also won the Franklin Institute's Wetherill Medal and $10,000 from Taiwan's Chi-Tsin Culture Foundation, and was elected to the Academy of Sciences of China. When she was awarded the first honorary doctorate in science ever given to a woman by Princeton University, its president declared that Wu had "richly earned the right to be called the world's foremost female experimental physicist," and congratulated her for revealing "the unwisdom of underestimating the powers of a woman."

In 1960, Wu was named Woman of the Year by the American Association of University Women; two years later, she was the first woman to receive the National Academy of Sciences Comstock Award. In 1975, while Gerald Ford was president, she would receive the National Medal of Science, America's highest science award.

Continuing her research in beta decay, Wu experimented on other weak interactions in nuclei. In 1963, with two Columbia colleagues, she confirmed a theory, proposed in 1958 by Murray Gell-Mann and Richard P. Feynman, concerning the conservation of vector current in beta decay, considered an important contribution to physicists' ongoing efforts to establish a unified theory of fundamental forces. Her review article, "The Universal Fermi Interaction and the Conserved Vector Current in Beta Decay," appeared in *Reviews of Modern Physics* and is often cited by physicists. Wu also measured X-rays and gamma rays emitted by muonic atoms (in which a muon, a particle 200 times heavier, replaces an external electron) to describe nuclear properties. With Lawrence Wilets, she published a watershed review article, "Muonic Atoms and Nuclear Structure," in *Annual Reviews of Nuclear Science*. The treatise *Beta Decay*, which she wrote with Steven A. Moszkowski in 1966, now considered a classic in the field; she also published *Nuclear Physics* with her husband and edited *Muon Physics* with Vernon W. Hughes.

Believing that "even the most sophisticated and seemingly remote basic nuclear physics research has implications beneficial to human welfare," Wu turned to research in biophysics in quest of a cure for sickle-cell anemia. Her proximity at Columbia to Harlem led to her interest in the genetic predisposition among African-Americans to produce the irregularly shaped blood cells that underlie this devastating disease, and Wu's work concentrated on molecular changes in hemoglobin.

In 1972, Columbia awarded Wu an endowed professorship. She also became the first living scientist to have an asteroid named in her honor. In 1973, she returned to China, but her parents were by then dead, and her brothers had been killed during the Cultural Revolution. Two years later, she became the first woman to serve as president of the American Physical Society, and she was made an honorary fellow of the Royal Society of Edinburgh.

In 1981, Chien-Shiung Wu, known as Madame Wu to colleagues and students, retired from Columbia University after a 36-year career. She continued to lecture in Asia and America, and her love for her homeland and for physics was passed on to her son, Vincent, also a physicist. Believing that more time and money had to be devoted to education and research if her adopted country were to remain politically and economically powerful, Wu also denounced attitudes that discouraged American women from pursuing physics. "I doubt that the tiny atoms and nuclei or the mathematical symbols or the DNA molecules have any preference for either masculine or feminine treatment," she asserted, and her financial prizes often went to fund scholarships. Wu died in Manhattan, after suffering a stroke, on February 16, 1997.

Shortly after disproving the parity principle, Chien-Shiung Wu spoke to student winners of the National Science Award, explaining the willingness and daring to doubt that lay behind her work in a way that could be taken as her personal philosophy. "The overthrow of the parity law drives home again the idea that science is not static, but ever-growing and dynamic," she said. "It is the courage to doubt what has long been established, the incessant search for its verification and proof that pushed the wheel of science forward."

SOURCES:

Gilbert, Lynn, and Gaylen Moore. *Particular Passions: Talks with Women Who Have Shaped Our Times.* NY: Crown, 1981.

Lubkin, Gloria. "Chien-Shiung Wu, the First Lady of Physics Research," in *Smithsonian.* January 1971, pp. 52–57.

McGrayne, Sharon Bertsch. *Nobel Prize Women in Science.* Secaucus, NJ: Carol, 1993.

Noble, Iris. *Contemporary Women Scientists of America.* NY: Messner, 1979.

"Wu, Chien-Shiung," in *Current Biography.* NY: H.W. Wilson, 1959, pp. 491–492.

Yost, Edna. *Women of Modern Science.* NY: Dodd, Mead, 1959.

SUGGESTED READING:

Crease, Robert P., and Charles C. Mann. *The Second Creation: Makers of the Revolution in Twentieth-Century Physics.* NY: Macmillan, 1986.

Mattfeld, Jacquelyn A., and Carol G. Van Aken, ed. *Women and the Scientific Professions: The MIT Symposium on American Women in Science and Engineering.* Cambridge: MIT, 1965.

Segré, Emilio. *From X Rays to Quarks: Modern Physicists and Their Discoveries.* San Francisco, CA: W.H. Freeman, 1980.

Weisskopf, Viktor F. *Privilege of Being a Physicist.* NY: W.H. Freeman, 1989.

COLLECTIONS:

Photographs of Wu and material about American physicists are available at the American Institute of Physics, Center for History of Physics, Niels Bohr Library, New York City.

Elizabeth D. Schafer, Ph.D.,
freelance writer in history of technology and science,
Loachapoka, Alabama

Wu, Empress (624–705).

See Wu Zetian.

Wu Chao (624–705).

See Wu Zetian.

Wu Chien-Shiung (1912–1997).

See Wu, Chien-Shiung.

Wu Hou (624–705).

See Wu Zetian.

Wei Hsing Chün fu-jen (1262–1319).

See Guan Daosheng.

Wu Lanying (d. 1929).

See Kang Keqing for sidebar.

Wuldetrada of the Lombards

Duchess of Bavaria. Daughter of Wacho, king of the Lombards; married Garibald I, duke of Bavaria, in 555; children: Theudeline of Bavaria; Gundoald, duke of Asti.

Wulfetrud of Nivelles

Abbess of Nivelles. Daughter of Grimoald, mayor of Austrasia (d. 656); sister of Childebert, king of Austrasia and the Franks (r. 656).

Wulfhild

West Saxon princess. Name variations: Wulfhilda. Daughter of *Elfgifu (c. 963–1002) and Aethelred or Ethelred II the Unready (c. 968–1016), king of the English (r. 979–1013, deposed, 1014–1016); married Ulfcytel Snylling, ealdorman of East Anglia; married Thurchil, earl of East Anglia.

Wulfrid (c. 945–1000).

See Wulfthryth.

Wulfthryth (fl. 860s)

Queen of the English. Flourished in the 860s; married Ethelred I (c. 843–871), king of the English (r. 865–871), around 868; children: Ethelhelm, archbishop of Canterbury (d. 923); Ethelwald, king of York (c. 868–902).

Wulfthryth (c. 945–1000)

Mistress of a king. Name variations: Wulfrida; Saint Wulfrid. Born around 945; died in 1000; mistress of Edgar the Peaceful (944–975), king of the English (r. 959–975); children: *Edith (c. 961–984).

Wulz, Wanda (1903–1984)

Italian photographer. Born in 1903 in Trieste, Italy; died in Italy in 1984; daughter of Carlo Wulz.

Wanda Wulz was born in 1903 in Trieste, Italy, into a family of portrait photographers and likewise made a name for herself by taking portraits and experimental photographs. Family photographers included her grandfather Guiseppe Wulz and her father Carlo Wulz, who created portraits of local intellectuals and fellow artists and photographed various social events. Like her father, Wanda often photographed artists in the field of theater, dance, and music. Her work of the late 1930s is usually associated with late Futurists because her experimental photography often incorporated motion and superimposed images. Wulz's initial success was limited to Trieste, but in 1930 she earned recognition in Rome for her exhibition of six photographs. During the Tenth Anniversary of the Fascist Revolution in 1932, Wulz established her greatest success, exhibiting experimental work with the "Futurist Collection." Here, her work was displayed in proximity to that of Arthur Bragaglia and other noted artists. Wulz died in Italy, in 1984, at age 80.

SOURCES:

Rosenblum, Naomi. *A History of Women Photographers.* NY: Abbeville, 1994.

Richard Wasowski,
freelance writer,
Mansfield, Ohio

Wunderlich, Frieda (1884–1965)

German-born American sociologist, feminist and social-political activist. Born in 1884; died in 1965.

Frieda Wunderlich served as a judge in Berlin from 1926 to 1933, during which time she was also a member of both the Berlin City Council (1926–33) and the Prussian Diet

(1930–33). She fled Nazi Germany in 1933 and made it to New York, where she was the first woman to be a faculty member of the "University in Exile," the precursor of the New School for Social Research. In 1939, she became its first female dean. Wunderlich wrote a handbook on labor in Nazi Germany for the Office of Strategic Services during World War II.

SOURCES:

Wobbe, Theresa. "Karrieren im nationalen Kontext: Soziologinnen in Deutschland," in *Jahrbuch für Soziologiegeschichte*, 1993, pp. 93–114.

John Haag,
Athens, Georgia

Wu Mei (624–705).

See Wu Zetian.

Wu Meiliang (624–705).

See Wu Zetian.

Wu of Huang He or Hwang Ho (624–705).

See Wu Zetian.

Wuolijoki, Hella (1886–1954)

Estonian-born Finnish writer, social critic, and unofficial diplomat. Name variations: (pseudonyms) Juhani Tervapää or Juhani Tervapaa; Felix Tuli. Born Ella Maria Murrik on July 22, 1886, in Helme, Estonia; died on February 20, 1954, in Helsinki, Finland.

Born Ella Maria Murrik in Estonia in July 1886, Hella Wuolijoki witnessed the cultural repression of the Estonian nation by tsarist Russia while she was growing up. By the early 1900s, she was moving in radical circles and had befriended, among other writers, the noted novelist Maxim Gorky. Wuolijoki moved to Finland at age 18 in order to continue her education, enrolling at the University of Helsinki. Here she mastered the Finnish language and became intrigued with Finland's rich traditions of epic poetry.

A wealthy Communist, she was arrested by the Finns on charges of treason during the bloody Finnish-Soviet conflict and sentenced to death. Bertolt Brecht's statements on her behalf, made to the Swedish consul in Los Angeles, were relayed to Finland and played a major role in saving her life. (Her play *The Sawdust Princess* had served as model for Bertolt Brecht's *Herr Puntila und sein Knecht Matti*, but Brecht had declined to pay her a share of the royalties even though Wuolijoki was then impoverished.) Released in 1944, Wuolijoki soon became involved in international diplomacy, using her friendship with *Alexandra Kollontai to initiate contacts between Helsinki and Moscow that led to an armistice between Finland and the USSR. Her radical social commentaries and sharp critiques of patriarchal society made her a controversial writer who was often ahead of her time.

SOURCES:

Kitching, Laurence P.A. "Brecht's *Der kaukasische Kreidekreis* and Wuolikoji's *Das estnische Kriegslied*," in *Journal of Baltic Studies*. Vol. 13, no. 4, 1982, pp. 314–326.

Kummituksia ja kajavia. Helsinki, 1947.

Laitinen, K. *Suomen kirjallisuus 1917–1967.* Helsinki, 1967.

Lasilla, Pertti, and Risto Hannula. "Hella Wuolijoki: A Versatile Talent," in *Books from Finland*. Vol. 20, no. 2, 1986, pp. 90–95.

Lounela, Pekka, and David Barrett. "Hella Wuolijoki (1886–1954): A Woman of Contrasts," in *Books from Finland*. Vol. 13, 1979, pp. 120–129.

Wuolijoki, Hella. *Und ich war nicht Gefangene: Memoiren und Skizzen.* Ed. by Richard Semrau. Trans. by Regine Pirschel. Rostock: Hinstorff, 1987.

"Wuolijoki, Hella," in Olli Alho, Hildi Hawkins and Päivi Vallisaari, eds., *Finland: A Cultural Encyclopedia.* Trans. by Hildi Hawkins and David McDuff. Helsinki: Finnish Literature Society, 1997.

John Haag,
Associate Professor of History,
University of Georgia, Athens, Georgia

Wurm, Mathilde (1874–1935).

See Fabian, Dora.

Wurttemberg, duchess of.

See Gonzaga, Barbara (1455–1505).

See Sabine of Bavaria (1492–1564).

See Maria Augusta of Thurn and Taxis (1706–1756).

See Sophia Dorothea of Brandenburg (1736–1798).

See Elizabeth Frederike of Bayreuth (fl. 1750).

See Antoinette Saxe-Coburg (1779–1824).

See Henrietta of Nassau-Weilburg (1780–1857).

See Catherine Charlotte of Hildburghausen (1787–1847).

See Marie d'Orleans (1813–1839).

See Theodelinde (1814–1857).

See Vera Constantinovna (1854–1912).

See Margaret Sophie (1870–1902).

See Maria Immaculata (1878–1968).

See Nadejda of Bulgaria (b. 1899).

See Helene (1903–1924).

See Rosa (1906–1983).

Wurttemberg, queen of.

See Augusta of Brunswick-Wolfenbuttel (1764–1788).

See Catherine of Russia (1788–1819).

See Pauline of Wurttemberg (1800–1873).

See Olga of Russia (1822–1892).

Wu Tse-t'ien (624–705).
See Wu Zetian.

Wu Tso Tien (624–705).
See Wu Zetian.

Wu Zetian (624–705)

Controversial ruler of Tang China who dominated Chinese politics for half a century, first as empress, then as empress-dowager, and finally as emperor of the Zhou Dynasty (690–705) that she founded. Name variations: Wu Ze-tian; Wu Chao, Wu Hou, or Wu Zhao; Wu Mei or Wu Meiliang; Wu Tse-t'ien, Wo Tse-tien, or Wu Tso Tien; Wu of Hwang Ho or Huang He; Empress Wu, Lady Wu. Pronunciation: Woo-jeh-ten. Born née Wu (first name at birth not known) in 624 in Taiyuan, Shanxi province; died in 705 in Luoyang, Henan province; daughter of a high-ranking official, Wu Shihuo, and his aristocratic wife; married Emperor Taizong (r. 626–649), in 640 (died 649); married Emperor Gaozong (r. 650–683), in 654; children: (second marriage) Crown Prince Li Hong; Crown Prince Li Xian; Emperor Zhongzong; Emperor Ruizong; Princess Taiping; another daughter (died in infancy).

Became concubine to Emperor Taizong (640); entered Buddhist nunnery (649); returned to the palace as concubine (654), then as empress (657) to Taizong's son Emperor Gaozong; became empress dowager and regent to her two sons (684–89); founded a dynasty (Zhou, 690–705) and ruled as emperor for 15 years.

The China that Wu Zetian was born in was the Tang Dynasty (618–906), a strong and unified empire after four centuries of political discord and foreign interaction. Tang China during the 7th century was a period of military strength and cultural attainments, its empire stretching into Central Asia and Southwest Asia and ruled by the Li-Tang imperial family from the capital city of Xi'an (Xian), Shanxi province. Missions from Japan, Korea, and Vietnam arrived at Xi'an bearing tribute and seeking education in Buddhism and Confucianism. Traders from the Mediterranean and Persia also came from both the overland and maritime trade routes, where Buddhism and Central Asian culture, dress, and music reached China. The Tang Dynasty also witnessed significant military, political, and social changes, as reflected in the transformation of an aristocracy into a meritocracy from the 7th to the 10th centuries. The Confucian dynastic system of government, based on the mandate of heaven, or the claim of heaven-sanctioned military conquest and benevolent rule, was first pro-

pounded by the Zhou Dynasty in 1045 BCE and perpetuated by subsequent dynasties until 1911.

The founding emperor of a dynasty and his descendants constituted the imperial family, which through male succession produced emperors who were normally the eldest son born to the empress. A brother or a clan grandson at times ascended the throne during usurpation or when the emperor died without issue, but female succession through descent from a daughter was never permitted. To ensure imperial male progeny, the Chinese emperor's harem was an elaborate organization of eunuchs who attended to hundreds of concubines, of whom one was appointed empress, the principal wife of the emperor.

The primary and secondary sources on Wu Zetian are abundant and problematic, reflecting an almost exclusively male authorship that has portrayed her as a beautiful, calculating, brutal woman who ruled China as the only woman emperor in name and in fact. Recent revisionist reappraisals have focused on the feminist slant of her rule and her record as an emperor rather than a woman, but no new primary sources have appeared to resolve conflicting information and gaps in her biography.

Wu Zetian's father was a successful merchant and military official who reached ministerial ranks. Her mother née Yang was of aristocratic birth with mixed Chinese and Turkic blood, the result of generations of intermarriage when five nomadic tribes overran north China and founded dynasties in the 4th to 6th centuries. When she was an infant dressed in boy's clothes, Wu Zetian's potential for emperorship was predicted by an official. She first entered the imperial harem at the age of 13 as a lowly ranked concubine to Emperor Taizong (r. 626–649), who has been praised as the most capable ruler of the Tang period and hailed as the "heavenly khan" by Central Asian states. Wu Zetian's tough character and good equestrian skills were perceived by observers even when she was a teenager. When her mother was distressed about losing her to an uncertain life fraught with intrigues in the emperor's harem, she firmly reassured her: "Isn't it a fortune to attend the emperor! Why should you weep for me?" She later volunteered to tame Taizong's wild horse with an iron whip, hammer, and knife. While serving as his concubine, she risked a death penalty in engaging in an incestuous affair with the crown prince and her stepson, the later Emperor Gaozong (r. 649–683).

When Taizong died, Gaozong became emperor, and Wu Zetian joined a Buddhist nunnery, as required of concubines of deceased emperors. But several years later, she returned to the palace as Gaozong's concubine and gave birth to sons. We are told that through cruel manipulations, including strangulating her own infant daughter to falsely implicate Gaozong's then current barren empress, Wu Zetian replaced her as empress in 657 and dominated the rest of Gaozong's reign. When Gaozong died in 683, she became empress dowager and ruled on behalf of two adult sons, emperors Zhongzong (r. 684, 705–710) and Ruizong (r. 685–689, 710–712). In 690, she declared herself emperor after deposing her sons and founding her own dynasty—Zhou.

For Wu Zetian, the rise to power and consolidation involved manipulations, murders, and support of the intellectual and religious establishments. Traditional historians grudgingly acknowledged that she surpassed her sons, the legitimate heirs, in both vision and statecraft. Her daunting task was convincing the Confucian establishment about the legitimate succession of a woman who was the widow of the deceased emperor and the mother of the currently legitimate ruler. Wu Zetian was in effect taking the unprecedented step of transforming her position from empress dowager to emperor. She could not become an emperor under the Tang Dynasty because of the long tradition of male succession and the fact that she was not a member of the imperial family by birth. The answer was to proclaim another dynasty, not by military conquest, but by interpreting omens that favored her to carry out a change of dynasties and become enthroned as a woman emperor.

Give me three tools to tame that wild horse.
First, I'll beat it with the iron whip. If it does not yield,
I'll hit it with the iron hammer. If it still won't be tamed,
I'll cut its throat with the knife.

—Wu Zetian

Changing the dynasty was the easier task and was accomplished by securing the approval of the Confucian establishment. Historians have documented Wu Zetian's resort to slander, torture, and murders to reinforce the propaganda of omens. Princes and ministers loyal to the Tang Dynasty and princes suspected of rebellious motives against her were executed. Setting up a new dynasty meant installing a new imperial family to replace the Li-Tang imperial house, from which she had married two emperors who were father and son, Taizong and Gaozong. To entrench her biological family as the imperial house, she bestowed imperial honors to her ancestors through posthumous enthronement and

constructed seven temples for imperial sacrifices. Traditionally, only the emperor, as the son-of-heaven, could communicate with heaven and carry out sacrifices to heaven and earth. But already in 666 when Wu Zetian was empress to the reigning Gaozong, she had prepared for her imperial ambitions by defying tradition and mockery as she led the unprecedented procession of imperial ladies to sacrifice to earth, believed to be a female deity. To enhance her position as a woman, in 688 she constructed a "hall of light" in the eastern capital of Luoyang to serve as a cosmic magnet to symbolize the harmony of heaven and earth and the balance of male (*yang*) and female (*yin*) forces.

In preparing for the legitimacy of her emperorship, she claimed the Zhou Dynasty (1045–256 BCE) and its founders among her own ancestors. She herself would thus be seen as a restorationist of the Zhou Dynasty, with the Wu family replacing the Li-Tang family. She gave titles of royalty to her own Wu family: her brothers and nephews became princes while her sisters, aunts, and nieces became princesses. The remaining Li-Tang family who survived the murders, including Wu Zetian's own son on whose behalf she was serving as empress dowager, begged to take the surname of Wu to replace their birth surnames of Li. Thus the Wu family was now elevated to the imperial house. Anticipating Wu Zetian's political ambitions, 60,000 flatterers—including Confucian officials, imperial relatives, Buddhist clergy, tribal chieftains, and commoners—supported the petition to proclaim the Zhou Dynasty with herself as the founding emperor.

On the question of succession after her death, Wu Zetian entertained notions of an heir from a Wu and Li marriage. She thus arranged marriages between her children and grandchildren with her brothers' sons and their grandchildren. Her upright Confucian minister, Di Renjie (d. 700, the protagonist of Robert van Gulik's popular Judge Dee detective novels), convinced her to bring back her son, the deposed emperor Zhongzong, to be appointed as her successor.

Wu Zetian's politics can be considered as feminist initiatives to reinforce the legitimacy of women in the political arena. She shocked the Chinese officialdom by arranging to send male grooms to the daughters and aunts of the tribal chieftains at the empire's borders, although it was customary to send female brides. When the Turkic ruler asked for a marriage arrangement, she sent her nephew's son to become the groom to the chieftain's daughter. The Turkic chieftain was insulted by the fact that the groom did not come from the Li-Tang imperial family but descended from what he perceived to be the inferior Wu clan, so he promptly imprisoned the unlucky groom and in 698 returned him to China.

Replacing the dynasty and imperial house through Confucian ideology still could not legitimize a woman on the throne. Wu Zetian turned to the Buddhist establishment to rationalize her position. Long a supporter of Buddhism through her mother's devotion and her own refuge in the nunnery after her first husband Taizong's death, Wu Zetian counted on Buddhist ideology to legitimize her reign and her dynasty. Her Buddhist supporters interpreted the *Madamegha* (Great Cloud) sutra to predict a *maitreya Buddha* (Buddha-to-come) in female form, presumably Wu Zetian herself, who would embody the concept of the *cakravartin* (wheel-turner, universal emperor, or the ideal man who is king). To reinforce her legitimacy, Wu Zetian also invented about a dozen characters with a new script. One of these served as her new personal name, Zhao, which articulates the fundamental Buddhist notion of universal emptiness.

Nevertheless, the legitimation was not without problems, and there was continued resistance from among the high officials who collaborated with the Li-Tang crown princes, princes, and princesses to get her dismissed as empress in 674 and dethroned as de facto ruler in 684, but both events failed. The insurrections had received little popular support and in the years that she dominated politics as empress, empress dowager, and finally as emperor, there were no widespread military unrests. But in 705, when she was 81 years old, the combined forces of the Li-Tang family took advantage of her weakening grip on the state and removed her from power. Wu Zetian died within a year.

Her overall rule, in spite of the change of dynasty, did not result in a radical break from Tang domestic prosperity and foreign prestige. But she changed the composition of the ruling class by removing the entrenched aristocrats from the court and gradually expanding the civil service examination to recruit men of merit to serve in the government. The development of the examination system during her reign was a critical step in the eventual transformation of the aristocracy to a meritocracy in the government. Although she gave political clout to some women, such as her capable secretary, she did not go as far as challenging the Confucian tradition of excluding women from participating in the civil service examinations. Already in 674 she had drafted 12 policy directives ranging from encouraging agriculture to formulating social rules of conduct. She maintained a stable economy and a moderate taxation for the peasantry. Her reign witnessed a healthy growth in the population; when she died in 705 her centralized bureaucracy regulated the social life and economic well-being of the 60 million people in the empire.

Wu Zetian's collected writings include official edicts, essays, and poetry, in addition to a treatise to instruct her subjects on moral statecraft. She changed the compulsory mourning period for mothers who predeceased fathers from the traditional one year to three years—the same length as the mourning for fathers who predeceased mothers. Wu Zetian argued that since mothers were indispensable to the birth and nourishment of infants, the three years when the infant totally depended on the mother as caregiver should be requited with three years of mourning her death. On a similar tone, she ordered that the mother of the Daoist sage Laozi (Lao Tzu, c. 600 BCE) be honored.

Overall Wu Zetian was a decisive, capable ruler in the roles of empress, empress dowager, and emperor. According to almost all her biographers, she was extremely cruel in her personal life, murdering two sons, a daughter, sister, niece, grandchildren, and many Li and Wu princes and princesses who opposed her. Such killings were not uncommon among emperors before and after her. Her significance as an emperor and founder of a new dynasty lies in her redefining of the gender-specific concepts of the emperorship and the Confucian state.

As an effective woman ruler, she challenged the traditional patriarchical dominance of power, state, sovereignty, monarchy, and political ideology. Her experience reflected a reversal of the gender roles and restrictions her society and government constructed for her as appropriate to women. While functioning and surviving in the male-ruled and power-focused domain, she exhibited strengths traditionally attributed to men, including political ambition, long-range vision, skillful diplomacy, power drive, decisive resolve, shrewd observation, talented organization, hard work, and firm dispensal of cruelty. The political success of Wu Zetian indicates that the attributes needed in diplomacy and rulership were not restricted to men. Functioning in a male-oriented patriarchy, Wu Zetian was painstakingly aware of the gender taboos she had to break in political ideology and social norm. She worked against the Confucian dictum that women must restrict their activities to the home and in the wildest imagination could not become emperors. She contended with petitions against female dominance which argued that her unnatural position as emperor had caused several earthquakes to occur and reports being filed of hens turning into roosters.

The reversal of gender roles was nowhere more objectionable than Wu Zetian's sexuality, in the eyes of the traditional historians. Wu Zetian's first two sexual partners were emperors and related to each other as father and son. After the latter died in 684, she took on four or five lovers, including a monk whom she ordered executed when weary of his greed and abuse of power. Her last two lovers were the young and handsome Zhang brothers who put on makeup and exploited the relationship by obtaining offices, honors, and gifts for themselves and their family. In 705, Wu Zetian's grandson, the later Emperor Xuanzong (r. 712–756), slaughtered the Zhang brothers in spite of Wu Zetian's protest and forced her to return the Li-Tang imperial family to power.

The earliest sources on Wu Zetian already contained rumors of sex scandals in her court. An active imagination produced pornographic novels in the 16th century focusing on her alleged sexual practices. Modern popular novels and plays, in Chinese, Japanese, and English, also exaggerate the sexual aspect of her rule. If Wu Zetian is judged by the traditional female virtues of chastity and modesty, then she falls short of expectations. But if she is observed in the context of the sexuality of male rulers, then the number of her favorites is insignificant. In the last three decades, Marxist historiography on Wu Zetian in Mainland China has yielded a positive but unreliable and ideologically charged reappraisal. She appears in influential plays as a feminist and champion of the lower classes while her male rivals are shown to be aristocrats, landlords, and conservatives against the tide of history.

In sum, within the social and political context of her time, Wu Zetian was a leader who went beyond the traditional roles of submissive wife and home-bound mother to emerge as ruler, lawmaker, and head of state and society while her second husband, lovers, and sons were relegated to less powerful positions than traditionally expected. Some historians have viewed her as blazing the trail for the women who came after her, and indeed her daughter, daughter-in-law, and granddaughter aspired to emulate her success, but they failed and even died violently in the process. Thus Wu Zetian's experience might have caused some redefinition of gender in her time, but this direction has not translated into enduring gains in the society and political organization that she left behind.

SOURCES:

Chen, Jo-shui. "Empress Wu and Proto-Feminist Sentiments in T'ang China," in Frederick P. Brandauer and Chün-chieh Huang, eds., *Imperial Rulership and Cultural Change in Traditional China.* Seattle, WA: University of Washington Press, 1994, pp. 77–116.

Guisso, Richard W.L. "The Reigns of the Empress Wu, Chung-tsung and Jui-tsung," in Denis Twitchett, ed., *Cambridge History of China.* Cambridge: Cambridge University Press, 1979. Vol. 3, no. 1, *Sui and T'ang,* pp. 290–332.

Jay, Jennifer W. "Vignettes of Chinese Women in Tang Xi'an (618–906): Individualism in Wu Zetian, Yang Guifei, Yu Xuanji and Li Wa," in *Chinese Culture.* Vol. 31, no. 1, 1990, pp. 77–89.

Liu, Xu. *Jiu Tangshu* [Old history of the Tang]. Beijing: Zhonghua shuju, 1975.

Ouyang, Xiu. *Xin Tangshu* [New history of the Tang]. Beijing: Zhonghua shuju, 1975.

Sima, Guang. *Zizhi tongjian* [Comprehensive mirror as guide to history]. Shanghai: Sibu congkan ed., 1929.

Twitchett, Denis, and Howard J. Wechsler. "Kao-tsung and the Empress Wu," in Denis Twitchett, ed. *Cambridge History of China.* Cambridge: Cambridge University Press, 1979. Vol. 3, no. 1, *Sui and T'ang,* pp. 242–289.

SUGGESTED READING:

Forte, Antonino. *Political Propaganda and Ideology in China at the End of the Seventh Century.* Naples: Institute Universitario Orientale, 1976.

Guisso, Richard W. *Empress Wu Tse-t'ien and the Politics of Legitimation in T'ang China.* Bellingham, WA: Center for Asian Studies, Western Washington University, 1978.

Guo, Moruo. *Five Historical Plays.* Beijing: Foreign Languages Press, 1984.

Lin, Yutang. *Lady Wu.* NY: Putnam, 1965.

McMullen, David. "The Real Judge Dee: Ti Jen-chieh and the T'ang Restoration of 705," in *Asia Major.* 3rd Series. Vol. 6, no. 1, 1993, pp. 1–81.

Paul, Diana Y. "Empress Wu and the Historians: A Tyrant and Saint of Classical China," in Nancy Auer Falk and Rita M. Gross, eds., *Unspoken Worlds: Religious Lives of Women.* Belmont: Wadsworth, 1989, pp. 145–154.

Su, Tong. *Wu Zetian.* Hong Kong: Cosmos, 1994.

Van Gulik, Robert. *The Chinese Bell Murders.* Chicago, IL: University of Chicago Press, 1977.

Wills, John E., Jr. "Empress Wu," in *Mountain of Fame: Portraits in Chinese History.* Princeton, NJ: Princeton University Press, 1994, pp. 127–148.

Jennifer W. Jay,
Professor of History and Classics,
University of Alberta, Edmonton, Canada

Wu Zhao (624–705).

See Wu Zetian.

Wyatt, Jane (1912—)

American actress best known for her role as the quintessential 1950s housewife in the television series "Father Knows Best." Born on August 10, 1912 (some sources cite 1910), in Campgaw, New Jersey; daughter of Christopher Billop Wyatt (a lawyer) and Eupemia Van Rensselaer (Waddington) Wyatt (a writer); graduated from the Chapin School, New York, 1928; Barnard College, 1928–30; Apprentice School of Berkshire Playhouse; married Edgar Bethune Ward, on November 9, 1935; children: Christopher, Michael.

Selected theater: The Tadpole; Trade Winds *(1930);* Give Me Yesterday *(1931);* The Mad Hopes *(1932);* Evensong *(1933);* Conquest; Dinner at Eight *(1933);* The Love Story *(1934);* The Joyous Season *(1934);* The Bishop Misbehaves *(1935);* Save Me the Waltz *(1938);* Night Music *(1940);* Quiet Please *(1940);* Hope for the Best *(1945);* The Skin of Our Teeth *(1946);* The Winslow Boy *(c. 1950);* The Autumn Garden *(1961).*

Selected filmography: One More River *(1934);* Great Expectations *(1934);* We're Only Human *(1936);* Luckiest Girl in the World *(1936);* Lost Horizon *(1937);* Girl from God's Country *(1940);* Hurricane Smith *(1941);* Weekend for Three *(1941);* Kisses for Breakfast *(1941);* The Navy Comes Through *(1942);* Army Surgeon *(1942);* Buckskin Frontier *(1943);* The Kansan *(1943);* None but the Lonely Heart *(1944);* The Bachelor's Daughters *(1946);* Boomerang *(1947);* Gentlemen's Agreement *(1947);* Pitfall *(1948);* No Minor Vices *(1948);* Bad Boy *(1949);* Canadian Pacific *(1949);* Task Force *(1949);* Our Very Own *(1950);* House by the River *(1950);* My Blue Heaven *(1950);* The Man Who Cheated Himself *(1951);* Criminal Lawyer *(1951);* Interlude *(1957);* Never Too Late *(1965);* "Tom Sawyer" *(for television, 1973);* Treasure of Matacumbe *(1976);* "Amelia Earhart" *(television, 1976);* "A Love Affair: The Eleanor and Lou Gehrig Story" *(television, 1978);* "Superdome" *(television, 1978);* "The Nativity" *(television, 1978);* "The Millionaire" *(television, 1978);* Star Trek IV: The Voyage Home *(1986);* Amityville IV: The Evil Escapes *(1990).*

Selected television: starred as Margaret Anderson in "Father Knows Best" (series, 1954–60); was host and moderator for "Confidential for Women"; episodic appearances include: "Bob Hope Presents the Chrysler Theater," "The Virginian," "Wagon Train," "U.S. Steel Hour," "Bell Telephone Hour," "Kraft Music Hall," "Hollywood TV Theater," "Star Trek," "Love American Style," "The Ghost and Mrs. Muir," "Here Come the Brides," "Alias Smith and Jones," "Fantasy Island," and "St. Elsewhere."

Jane Wyatt was born in 1912, in Campgaw, New Jersey. Her father Christopher Billop Wyatt was a lawyer and her mother **Eupemia Waddington Wyatt**, once president of the Catholic Big Sisters, wrote for *Commonweal* and *Catholic World*. The family moved to New York when Jane was young. Before graduating from the Chapin School in 1928, Wyatt had begun acting in school performances as well as in plays written by her sister, **Elizabeth Wyatt**, and directed by their mother. Both sisters frequently attended the theater, and it was after a performance by *Maude Adams that Jane decided she wanted to become an actress.

Following her graduation from Chapin, Wyatt, who chose Barnard College because of the drama classes available, majored in history. In 1930, she enrolled in the Apprentice School of the Berkshire Playhouse in Stockbridge, Massachusetts. In that same year, she acquired a professional role as a walk-on in *Trade Winds* in Philadelphia, and understudied for a production of *The Vinegar Tree* on Broadway. She first appeared on stage in New York City a year later, in 1931, as Freda Mannock in A.A. Milne's *Give Me Yesterday* at the Charles Hopkins Theater. She remained with the Berkshire Stock Company for three summers and continued appearing in minor Broadway roles. In May 1933, Wyatt replaced *Margaret Sullivan in *Dinner at Eight*, a production that subsequently began a lengthy tour.

In the midst of this long run, Wyatt married Edgar Bethune Ward on November 9, 1935. Together they had two sons, Christopher and Michael. The tour with *Dinner at Eight* brought an offer from Hollywood, and Wyatt appeared in *Lost Horizon* in 1937. Still maintaining her love for Broadway, she had roles in *Save Me the Waltz* in 1938, and *Night Music* and *Quiet Please* in 1940. She accepted a number of film roles, only to reappear on Broadway in *Hope for the Best* opposite Franchot Tone for 117 performances beginning February 1945. In 1945, she was also nominated as one of the best-dressed women of the nation by the Fashion Academy.

Jane Wyatt

Wyatt continued acting in film throughout the early 1950s and appeared in what she considered her favorite role, that of Mary Morgan in *Task Force*, in 1950. In several of these later films, Wyatt was cast as a housewife.

She had her greatest success, however, playing opposite Robert Young on the television series "Father Knows Best," which aired from 1954 to 1956 on CBS before switching to NBC, where it stayed until 1960. For three successive years, 1958 to 1960, Wyatt won an Emmy Award for her role as the all-American wife and mother. She made numerous episodic appearances on television series before filming the 1973 television movie "Tom Sawyer" and a feature film entitled *Treasure of Matacumbe* in 1976. Although Wyatt suffered a mild stroke in 1995, she made a fine recovery and was able to continue her television and film work until she was well into her 80s. She has also been active in the March of Dimes from its inception.

SOURCES:

Contemporary Theatre, Film, and Television. Vol. 3. Detroit, MI: Gale Research, 1986.

Current Biography, 1957. NY: H.W. Wilson, 1957.

Katz, Ephraim. *The Film Encyclopedia.* 3rd ed. NY: HarperPerennial, 1998.

Richard Wasowski,
freelance writer,
Mansfield, Ohio

Wychingham, Elizabeth

*Lady Hoo. Married Thomas Hoo, Lord Hoo and Hastings; mother of *Anne Hoo (c. 1425–1484); great-great-grandmother of *Anne Boleyn.*

Wydeville.

Variant of Woodville.

Wyeth, Henriette (1907–1997)

American artist. Name variations: Henriette Wyeth Hurd. Born Ann Henriette Wyeth on October 22, 1907, in Wilmington, Delaware; died on April 3, 1997, in Roswell, New Mexico; daughter of Newell Convers Wyeth (the artist) and Carolyn Brenneman (Bockius) Wyeth; home schooled by father; attended an academy at the Museum of Art, Boston, 1921–23; Pennsylvania Academy of Fine Arts, Philadelphia, beginning in 1923; married Peter Hurd (the artist), in 1929 (died 1984); children: Peter, Jr., Michael, and Carol Rogers Hurd.

Works featured in several exhibits: Roswell Museum and Art Center; Gerald Peters Gallery, Sante Fe; Brandywine River Museum, Chadds Ford, Pennsylva-nia; works displayed in several collections: Art Institute of Chicago; Carnegie Institute, Pittsburgh; Columbus Museum of Art, Ohio; Delaware Art Museum; Foundation of New York State University; Museum of Texas Tech University; New Britain Museum of American Art, Connecticut; National Portrait Gallery, Washington, D.C.

Daughter of **Carolyn Bockius Wyeth** and celebrated American illustrator and painter N.C. Wyeth, artist Henriette Wyeth was born in 1907 in Wilmington, Delaware. At age three, she contracted life-threatening polio, but recovered fully, suffering only a deformation of her right hand. She and her four siblings were trained as artists by their father at their home in Chadds Ford, Pennsylvania, near Wilmington, North Carolina. N.C. also chose to home-school his children because he distrusted public education. Along with her brother Andrew Wyeth, Henriette was the most artistically promising of the Wyeth children. She began formal art lessons with her father at age 11, doing charcoal studies and geometric shapes. She learned to paint with her left hand but was able to draw with her injured right hand.

In 1921, Wyeth entered the Boston Museum of Art academy, and two years later began to study painting at the Pennsylvania Academy of Fine Arts in Philadelphia. Specializing in portraiture, she received commissions for paintings of Wilmington residents. Despite her personal success, Wyeth would remain heavily influenced by her father's unique realistic style, and reject painting genres, such as Impressionism and Cubism, which he disliked. She would also follow his political and social conservatism, rejecting as destructive to society the progressive movements of the 1960s and 1970s, including the women's movement, and criticizing television and modern culture for harming children.

At age 21, Wyeth married artist Peter Hurd, her father's apprentice and a fellow student at the Pennsylvania Academy. Two years later, the couple settled in Santa Fe, New Mexico. They were part of the first wave of visual artists to make the Santa Fe-Roswell area into a thriving arts community in the 1930s.

Wyeth had three children, and divided her time between her art and caring for her family. During World War II, she remained at home while Hurd worked as a war artist and correspondent for *Life* magazine. In the 1940s and 1950s, she received many commissions from wealthy patrons, including *Helen Hayes,

*Paulette Goddard, and Mrs. John D. Rockefeller III (*Blanchette Hooker Rockefeller), for which she earned a lasting celebrity. She also explored painting still-lifes and the New Mexico landscape and rendered a portrait of *Pat Nixon for the White House.

In 1963, Wyeth created a portrait of her brother Andrew Wyeth for the cover of *Time* magazine. The following year both Hurd and Wyeth were commissioned to produce a cover portrait of Lyndon B. Johnson for *Time*'s "Man of the Year" issue. Solo exhibitions of Wyeth's work were held at the Roswell Museum and Art Center, and at the Gerald Peeters Gallery in Santa Fe. Individual works were purchased by many museums and private collectors, including the Art Institute of Chicago, the National Portrait Gallery in Washington, D.C., the Carnegie Institute in Pittsburgh, and the Delaware Art Museum in Wilmington. In 1981, Wyeth received the New Mexico Governor's Award in recognition of her contributions to New Mexican culture.

After Peter Hurd's death in 1984, Wyeth continued to paint on their ranch in San Patricio until ill health caused her to retire in the mid-1990s. Henriette Wyeth died in 1997 in Roswell, New Mexico, at age 89. She was survived by her son Michael Hurd and daughter **Carol Rogers Hurd**, both artists, and son Peter Hurd, a musician.

SOURCES:

Magill, Frank N., ed. *Great Lives From History*. Vol. 5. Pasadena, CA: Salem Press, 1995.

Obituary, in *The Day* [New London, CT]. April 4, 1997.

Laura York, M.A. in History,
University of California,
Riverside, California

Wylie, Elinor (1885–1928)

American poet and novelist who became a social celebrity as well as a leading literary figure of the post-World War I years. Born Elinor Hoyt on September 7, 1885, in Somerville, New Jersey; died on December 16, 1928; first born of Henry Hoyt and Anne (McMichael) Hoyt; married Philip Hichborn (a Washington lawyer), in 1906 (committed suicide 1916); married Horace Wiley, in 1916 (divorced 1923); married William Rose Benét (the poet).

Although her mother privately printed some of her early poetry, she came to public attention with the appearance of her collection of poems Nets to Catch the Wind *(1921); with impressive social connections, her widely admired beauty, and a well-publicized extramarital affair during her first marriage, became a social celebrity as well as a leading literary figure of*

the post-World War I years; published three more volumes of poetry, as well as four novels, before her early death at the age of 43 (1928); her poetry is known for the contrast between its meticulous structure and its sensuality, while her novels correspondingly display a classic formality combined with a sense of fantasy. Benét later edited and published her Collected Poetry *(1932) and* Collected Prose *(1933).*

Most everybody remembered the first time they set eyes on Elinor Wylie. Thomas Wolfe was so impressed after meeting her in New York's Greenwich Village in the mid-1920s that the memory was still fresh when he set about creating the heroine for his 1939 novel *The Web and the Rock*. "Anyone who ever saw her would retain the memory of her lovely, slender girlishness, her proud carriage, the level straightness of her glance," he wrote of his Rosalind Bailey, "and a quality of combined childishness and maturity, of passion and ice." He could just as well have been describing Wylie's literary personality, too, for her poetry and fiction were much admired for a combination of formality and fantasy that had made her the shimmering centerpiece of Greenwich Village's rich artistic milieu. To millions of other, less broad-minded Americans, however, it was her scandalous love life that had made her a household name during the early 20th century.

Her life had begun comfortably and conventionally enough in Somerville, New Jersey, as the first child, born on September 7, 1885, of Henry and **Anne McMichael Hoyt**. Both parents were from socially prominent Philadelphia families, although Henry Hoyt was obliged to support his young family by working in a bank in nearby New York City. Four more Hoyt children followed—two brothers, Henry Jr., and Morton; and two sisters, **Constance** and **Anne Hoyt**. The children were tutored at home during their early years before being sent off to private schools. Wylie's fondest memories of her childhood were of the family's Irish maid who would entertain her with folk tales and Irish folk songs, providing strong images that would later surface in Wylie's poetry; and her earliest memory of a poem was Coleridge's *Christabel*, the strange imagery of which she later said "scared me into seven fits." Nevertheless, she wrote her first poem (about the moon) at the age of eight, and her first short story (about four mischievous mice) when she was nine. Even at this early stage, Wylie's flights of fancy were making her famous among her friends. She "could lie like a trooper," one of them said. "Nothing was too strange in connection with Elinor."

When her father took a job as an assistant attorney general in the McKinley administration in 1897, the family moved to Washington and Elinor moved to a new private school, where a favorite English teacher instilled in her a deep love for the classics and for the Metaphysical poets—Donne, Blake and especially Shelley, for whom Wylie would form a lifelong infatuation. By 1903, as she turned 18 and faced the social rituals of her "coming out" as a young debutante in Washington society, Elinor met a young lawyer named Philip Hichborn, three years her senior. Her mother mistrustfully called Hichborn "a Rudolph Valentino" and strove for the next three years to discourage the romance, but on December 1, 1906, Wylie and Hichborn were married. "I never had such a lovely time in my life, and Philip's absolutely perfect," Elinor burbled in a letter to her mother written during her honeymoon in New York City. She did not mention Hichborn's moodiness and fits of jealousy, but by the time a son was born to the couple in September 1907, Wylie's marital raptures had cooled and Hichborn had been diagnosed as suffering from "dementia praecox," the era's catchall phrase for a host of mental illnesses not yet fully understood. (Today, Hichborn would probably have been diagnosed with bipolar disorder.)

I cannot help making fables and bitter fairy tales out of life.

—Elinor Wylie

Shortly after the birth of her son, Elinor met another Washington lawyer, Horace Wylie, at one of the numerous functions that occupied the calendar of Washington society's season. Horace was also married, but he, too, recalled vividly his first sight of Elinor. "I thought at once she was the most beautiful person I had ever seen," he wrote years later. "I really almost gasped." By 1909, the two had embarked on the dangerous business of a full-blown affair, and Elinor was capturing her love for Horace in such lines as:

> I think the holy angels might
> Look down on me from Heaven's height,
> And envy my pure heart,
> My pure and happy heart.

The clandestine lovers seemed to entice gossip by lunching together in public and to court disaster as each of them encouraged the friendship that had grown between the Hichborns and the Wylies, allowing them to see each other more often than they otherwise would have. Finally, in 1910, Elinor and Horace decided to run away together. Even the death of Elinor's father in November of that year failed to discourage their plans, especially when it came out that Henry Hoyt had maintained a mistress in a nearby house for years. The revelation only seemed to strengthen Wylie's resolve to disappear with her own lover. "When you found out that your father had been in love with someone not your mother," wrote novelist *Rebecca West, a friend of Wylie's in those tumultuous days, "why *of course* you left your own husband. It was something she could no more help than her blood pressure."

Finally, in December 1910, Anne Hoyt woke up one morning to find a letter from her daughter. "Don't let this kill you," Elinor had written. "I have run away." The following years provided gossip for the newspapers and a good deal of work for the army of investigators that Wylie's mother and husband hired. Even President Taft tried to help when Anne Hoyt called on her husband's years of loyal service in Washington for a favor. As the story unfolded, it became evident that Elinor and Horace had simply driven out of Washington to a remote train station, boarded a train for Canada, and then taken ship from Montreal for Europe. For the next six years, the two lovers traveled all over Europe as virtual exiles, identifying themselves on hotel registers and documents as "Mr. and Mrs. Waring" and moving on as soon as there was the least sign they had been recognized. Horace's attempts to see his children by offering his wife $10,000 a year for the right to annual visits only made things worse, while Elinor was portrayed in the press as the mother who abandoned her little son for a life of sin. Hichborn filed for divorce and custody of little Philip in 1912, but the high drama turned to tragedy when he committed suicide by shooting himself in the head in his sister's library, leaving a note behind that read, "I am not to blame for this." He was just 29 years old. Now labeled not only as an adulterer but as a murderer for causing Hichborn's death, Wylie began to suffer from severe headaches, high blood pressure, and temporary blindness. Still, she refused to accept responsibility for her husband's suicide, writing more than ten years after the event, "If Philip had killed himself over me, he could not have waited over two years to do it." The statement only confirmed the image of a cold-hearted, dangerous femme fatale. Further strains ensued when Elinor's pregnancy by Horace ended in a stillbirth, and again when the onset of World War I forced the couple to return to the United States from England, unable to produce the legal identity papers required of all foreigners by the British government.

The affair of the notorious Mrs. Hichborn seemed to resolve itself when Horace's wife finally granted the divorce he had been seeking in

1916, allowing him to marry Elinor on August 7 of that year. Life was still difficult, to be sure, with Horace ruined financially by the years of living abroad and forced to ask for a loan from Elinor's mother, while Elinor suffered two more unsuccessful pregnancies between 1917 and 1919. It was during these years that Wylie produced what would become some of her most famous poetry, matured by the sufferings and upheavals of the previous ten years. Not a few of them were apologetically addressed to Horace, as in these lines written in 1919:

I would for you that I were decked
In honor and the world's respect.
Before God's mercy we must all
Stand naked, and so stand or fall.

"It was Horace who made a poet and scholar of me," Elinor said six years later.

But it was fellow poet and editor William Rose Benét who publicly took up Elinor's cause. Benét, from a literary-minded family that included his poet-brother Stephen Vincent Benét and his novelist-sister **Laura Benét**, had, like Horace, first seen Elinor on the Washington social circuit. Relations between the two families were cordial, and it was to Benét that Elinor's mother sent the poems her daughter had passed on to her during the tumults of the late 1910s; and it was Benét who in turn showed Wylie's work to Louis Untermeyer of *The Saturday Review*, for whom Benét worked as an associate editor. The poems, Untermeyer said, were "a little *too* brilliant," but he joined Benét in seeing Wylie's first collection of poetry into print; *Nets to Catch the Wind* appeared in 1921. Benét further attached himself to Wylie by informally representing her to major publishing houses (jokingly calling himself "The Bennay Literary Agency"), encouraging her to try her hand at short stories and essays, and even rooming with Elinor's brother Henry, who had survived World War I to become an artist of some repute. Benét's interest in Wylie quickly became more than a literary one, evidenced by the lines he wrote describing her as having

. . . the bronze mane of a little lion.
She was tall, with wrists and ankles
Reminding him of the fragile China deer.

Nets to Catch the Wind quickly attracted the attention of New York's literati, although few knew of the grief that Wylie had poured into some of the poems after her brother Henry, who had returned from the war despondent and troubled, killed himself in 1920, the second suicide among those close to Elinor. Her "Heroics" and "Lonesome Rose," which was the centerpiece of *Nets*, were written in response to the tragedy. The collection was awarded the Poetry Society's prize for best first volume of poetry, cited for its innovative use of imagery and its precise meter. "Its accuracy never misses," Edmund Wilson told his readers in *Vanity Fair*, "its colors are always right. Mrs. Wylie's tone is always certain and pure." Elinor's work, said *Edna St. Vincent Millay, was "austere and immaculate," comparable to the best of *Emily Dickinson, John Donne, even William Blake. Louis Untermeyer's pithy observation that Wylie "burned, but gave

no warmth," neatly combined his assessment both of her personality and her poetry.

By 1921, when Elinor had left Horace and Washington to settle near Washington Square in Greenwich Village, Benét was writing to her: "You want the truth. Have it. I fell in love with you. As for you having anything to do with it, except being yourself, that is nonsense." Benét helped Wylie arrange her second collection of poems, *Black Armour*, before proposing marriage. In September 1922, Elinor initiated divorce proceedings against Horace, who chose not to contest the suit. "You're better off without me, Elinor," he wrote to her. "You are a fantastic creature and I understand you." The divorce was granted in January 1923, and in October of that same year, Wylie and Benét were married.

Wylie's first novel, *Jennifer Lorn*, appeared a month after her third marriage. It was a Gothic melodrama set in 18th-century Britain and in India, but close friends recognized much of Elinor and Horace in the book's two lovers, and it became the talk of New York society. Two years later, with the publication of a second work of fiction, *The Venetian Glass Nephew*, Wylie was the toast of literary society. Her lace-embroidered wardrobe and cascading hair were widely copied, and no gathering of literary lights was complete unless she made an appearance. *The Venetian Glass Nephew*, another historical drama, set this time in 18th-century Venice, was as meticulously researched as the previous book but is today considered Wylie's best production, with the intricate balance between the virtuous and the profane, between light and darkness, that marks her poetry. In 1926, yet another novel appeared, this one inventively based on the premise that Wylie's poetic idol, Shelley, had not drowned in Italy in 1822 but had, in fact, been rescued by the crew of an American clipper ship and brought to the United States. *Orphan Angel* caused an uproar among other Shelley admirers, who accused Elinor of vulgar commercialism at the expense of their hero. But Wylie perversely produced a sequel in 1928, *Mr. Hodge and Mr. Hazard*, which brought Shelley back to England after his American sojourn. This time, she inserted thinly veiled fictional versions of some of her critics into the story. "I say it is meringue," she wrote to a perceptive friend, "but you will see it is really meringue flavoured with strychnine rather than vanilla bean." She had, in fact, already warned her readers that her patience was growing thin in a poem called *Portrait* published anonymously in *The New Yorker* the previous year:

Sometimes she gives her heart, sometimes instead
Her tongue's sharp side.

By the time *Mr. Hodge and Mr. Hazard* appeared in bookstores, Wylie was already planning her next book, despite increasingly troublesome health. Persistent headaches, high blood pressure and fainting spells were all exacerbated by a third suicide when her sister Constance killed herself, although Constance had been living in Germany since before World War I and the two sisters had seen little of each other. Another collection of poetry, *Trivial Breath*, appeared early in 1928 as Wylie embarked for Europe to research her planned novel about witchcraft, to be set in Italy, France and England. In November of that year, during a stay in London, she fell and injured her spine, while a temporary facial paralysis diagnosed as Bell's palsy forced her to return to New York in early December. On December 16, while working in her study on the proofs for her last published poetry collection, she suddenly called out to Benét for a glass of water. He reported that she tried to walk toward him as he entered the room, then collapsed from a stroke and died. Her last words, he said, had been: "Is that all there is?" She was 43 years old.

Angels and Earthly Creatures appeared posthumously, in February 1929. Benét never spoke publicly about the fact that Elinor had been on the verge of leaving him to return to Horace, to whom she had written a letter suggesting they resume their relationship. In the years following her death, Benét diligently prepared her *Collected Poetry* and *Collected Prose*, which appeared in 1932 and 1933, respectively, and wrote a study of her work which appeared in 1934. The harsh realities of World War II and the second half of the century eventually overpowered the delicately textured style that Wylie had perfected in a public career that spanned less than ten years, while what fame remained to her was due more to the wake of the personal tragedies and ruinous love affairs she left behind. "How like a comet through the darkening sky you raced!" wrote Edna St. Vincent Millay ten years after Elinor Wylie's death. "The soaring mind outstripped the tethered heart."

SOURCES:
Olson, Stanley. *Elinor Wylie: A Life Apart.* NY: Dial, 1979.

Norman Powers,
writer-producer, Chelsea Lane Productions,
New York, New York

Wylie, Ida A.R. (1885–1959)

Australian-born English novelist. Name variations: I.A.R. Wylie. Born Ida Alexa Ross Wylie in Melbourne, Australia, in 1885; died on November 4, 1959; attended finishing school in Brussels, Belgium; attended Cheltenham Ladies' College; educated at a private school in Karlsruhe, Germany; lived with Louise Pearce (1885–1959).

Selected writings: The Germans *(1909, published as* My German Year, *1910);* The Rajah's People *(1910);* Rambles in the Black Forest *(1911);* In Different Keys *(1911);* Dividing Hands *(1911);* The Daughter of Brahma *(1912);* The Red Mirage *(1913);* The Paupers of Portman Square *(1913);* Eight Years in Germany *(1914);* Happy Endings *(short stories, 1915);* The Temple of Dawn *(1915);* Armchair Stories *(short stories, 1915);* Tristram Sahib *(1916);* The Shining Heights *(1917);* The Duchess in Pursuit *(1918);* All Sorts *(short stories, 1919);* Towards Morning *(1920);* Brodie and the Deep Sea *(1920);* The Dark House *(1922);* Ancient Fires *(1924);* Black Harvest *(1925);* The Silver Virgin *(1929);* Some Other Beauty *(short stories, 1930);* The Things We Do *(1932);* To the Vanquished *(1934);* Furious Young Man *(1935);* Prelude to Richard *(1935);* A Feather in Her Hat *(1937);* The Young in Heart *(1939);* My Life with George *(autobiography, 1940);* Strangers Are Coming *(1941);* Keeper of the Flame *(1942);* Storm in April *(short stories, 1946).*

Ida A.R. Wylie was born in 1885 in Melbourne, Australia, the daughter of a Scottish barrister. The family returned to England soon after her birth, and her mother died when Wylie was still a young child. Wylie had an unusual early education; her father financed her independent travels throughout England and the Continent when she was ten. This experience prepared her for handling all sorts of situations even before she reached her teens. She also read the entirety of her father's extensive library and assumed, even before her formal schooling had begun, that she would be an author.

When she was 14, she began attending finishing school in Brussels, becoming fluent in French during her three years there. She spent the subsequent two years at Cheltenham Ladies' College and then attended a school in Karlsruhe, Germany, where she perfected her German and developed a deep understanding of German culture and consciousness. Here Wylie officially began her writing career and several of her stories were published in English magazines. She wrote several novels about her experiences in Germany, including *My German Year* (1910) and *Eight Years in Germany* (1914). She considered her first successful novel, however, to be 1920's *Towards Morning*.

Wylie returned to England prior to World War I and participated in the women's suffrage movement there. She traveled to the United States in 1917, purchasing a farm near Princeton, New Jersey, where she lived with American physician *Louise Pearce beginning in 1951. She died in November 1959.

SOURCES:

Companion to Twentieth Century Literature. Longman, 1970.

Dictionary of Literary Biography. D.C. Browning, comp. London: J.M. Dent, 1960.

Kunitz, Stanley J., and Howard Haycraft, eds. *Twentieth Century Authors.* NY: H.W. Wilson, 1942.

Richard Wasowski,
freelance writer,
Mansfield, Ohio

Wylie, Wilhelmina (b. 1892).

See Durack, Fanny for sidebar.

Wyman, Jane (1914—)

American actress who won an Academy Award for her wordless performance in Johnny Belinda *and was married to Ronald Reagan, long before he became president. Name variations: sang on radio as Jane Durrell. Born Sarah Jane Fulks on January 4 or 5, 1914, in St. Joseph, Missouri; youngest of three children (a boy and two girls) of Richard Fulks (a city official) and Emma (Reise) Fulks; graduated from Los Angeles High School; married Myron Futterman (a dress manufacturer), in 1937 (divorced); married Ronald Reagan (the actor and future president of the U.S., 1981–89), on January 26, 1940 (divorced 1948); married Fred Karger (a bandleader), on November 1, 1952 (divorced 1955, remarried March 1961, divorced 1965); children: (second marriage) Maureen Reagan (1941–2001, singer-actress turned political activist); (adopted) Michael Edward Reagan.*

Selected filmography: Gold Diggers of 1937 *(1936);* My Man Godfrey *(1936);* King of Burlesque *(1936);* Smart Blonde *(1937);* Stage Struck *(1937);* The King and the Chorus Girl *(1937);* Ready, Willing, and Able *(1937);* Slim *(1937);* The Singing Marine *(1937);* Public Wedding *(1937);* Mr. Dodd Takes the Air *(1937);* The Spy Ring *(1938);* He Couldn't Say No *(1938);* Wide Open Faces *(1938);* Fools for Scandal *(1938);* The Crowd Roars *(1938);* Brother Rat *(1938);* Tail Spin *(1939);* Private Detective *(1939);* The Kid From Kokomo *(1939);* Torchy Plays With Dynamite *(1939);* Kid Nightingale *(1939);* Brother Rat and a Baby *(1940);* An Angel From Texas *(1940);* Flight Angels *(1940);* My Love Came Back *(1940);* Tugboat Annie Sails Again *(1940);* Gambling on the High Seas *(1940);* Honeymoon for Three *(1941);* Bad Men of Missouri *(1941);* You're in the Army Now *(1941);* The Body Disappears *(1941);* Larceny Inc. *(1942);* My Favorite Spy *(1942);* Footlight Serenade *(1942);* Princess O'Rourke *(1943);* Make Your Own Bed *(1944);* Crime by Night *(1944);* The Doughgirls *(1944);* Hollywood Canteen *(1944);* The Lost Weekend *(1945);* One More Tomorrow *(1946);* Night and Day *(1946);* The Yearling *(1947);* Cheyenne *(1947);* Magic Town *(1947);* Johnny Belinda *(1948);* A Kiss in the Dark *(1949);* It's a Great Feeling *(cameo, 1949);* The Lady Takes a Sailor *(1949);* Stage Fright *(1950);* The Glass Menagerie *(1950);* Three Guys Named Mike *(1951);* Here Comes the Groom *(1951);* The Blue Veil *(1951);* Starlift *(1951);* The Story of Will Rogers *(1952);* Just for You *(1952);* Let's Do It Again *(1953);* So Big *(1953);* Magnificent Obsession *(1954);* Lucy Gallant *(1955);* All That Heaven Allows *(1956);* Miracle in the Rain *(1956);* Holiday for Lovers *(1959);* Pollyanna *(1960);* Bon Voyage! *(1962);* How to Commit Marriage *(1969).*

Born Sarah Jane Fulks in 1914 in St. Joseph, Missouri, Jane Wyman would later sum up her childhood as strictly disciplined. Her parents Richard and **Emma Fulks** already had a teenage son and daughter at the time of Wyman's birth. When Jane was eight, Emma took her to Hollywood, ostensibly to visit relatives, but actually to try and get her into the movies. When she was unsuccessful, they returned home, where Wyman continued to study dancing and singing.

Following her father's death in 1929, Wyman and her mother returned to Los Angeles, where Wyman attended high school and attempted once again to obtain a studio contract. The best she could do was an occasional part in the dancing chorus of a musical. In 1935, she enrolled at the University of Missouri, but soon after was discovered by a radio executive who heard her sing at a party. She quit college and toured the country as a radio vocalist under the name Jane Durrell.

After her success on the radio, Wyman tried again to break into pictures, at which time she was advised to improve her speaking voice. She underwent another stint at the University of Missouri, for diction and elocution training, then returned to Hollywood. In 1936, following a featured role in *My Man Godfrey*, she signed a contract with Warner Bros.

Wyman faced still another uphill struggle to find a breakthrough role. For eight years, she played leads and second leads in a string of light comedies, receiving encouragement from critics who noted her "brightness and charm," and winning polls as the starlet most likely to suc-

ceed. As a beautiful young Hollywood contract player, Wyman also enjoyed a lively social life. After a brief marriage in 1937 to dress manufacturer Myron Futterman, a divorced man almost twice her age, Wyman set her sights on fellow contract player Ronald Reagan, although they did not begin dating seriously until 1939 while they were working together in *Brother Rat* (1940). The couple had little in common aside from acting. Reagan, an outdoor fellow, was very politically minded; Wyman, at the time, preferred night-clubbing. By most accounts, it was Wyman who most aggressively pursued the relationship, even taking up golf so she could accompany Reagan when he played.

The year-long courtship ended in marriage on January 26, 1940, and after a brief honeymoon they returned to the studio to co-star in *An Angel From Texas*, which Warner Bros. hoped to release while the two were still newlyweds. A year later, on January 4, 1941, they had their first child, ❧▶ **Maureen Reagan**, and built a house to accommodate a nursery. The Reagans expanded the family again in 1944, adopting an infant son, Michael Reagan. By that time, the nation was at war, and the Reagans went from "storybook" couple to "Mr. and Mrs. America Fighting the War." In truth, the war did not disrupt their lives to any great extent; Reagan spent eight weeks in San Francisco then returned to Hollywood, where he served with a special services unit of the Army Air Corps at the Hal Roach Studios in Culver City. Wyman entertained at the Hollywood Canteen and toured with the Victory Committee, selling war bonds.

Wyman's career finally took off with her role as the long-suffering sweetheart of alcoholic writer Ray Milland in *The Lost Weekend* (1945), although the picture, finished in 1944, was not released immediately, because the studio feared that the subject of alcoholism might not play well with audiences. The liquor industry lobby also did its best to delay release of the film, offering the studio a hefty sum to keep it shelved. When it did finally reach movie houses, it was an overwhelming success and opened the door to better roles for Wyman. The following year, she won an Oscar nomination (and a ten-year contract with Warner's) for her portrayal of Ma Baxter in an adaptation of *Marjorie Kinnan Rawlings' The Yearling*, a turn-of-the-century story about a backwoods Florida family. "While she does not have the physical characteristics of the original 'Ma,'" wrote critic Bosley Crowther, referring to the character in the Rawlings novel, "she compels credulity and sympathy for a woman of stern and Spartan stripe." With her role in *The Yearling*, Wyman began thinking of herself as a serious actress and selected roles more thoughtfully. "For the first time in my life, I was no longer shy, or afraid of being ridiculed about my ambition," she said.

In 1948, Wyman won an Academy Award for her superb portrayal of a deaf-mute rape victim in *Johnny Belinda*. The actress spent six months at a school for the deaf to prepare for the part, which she played with her ears sealed with wax. "Miss Wyman brings superior insight

and tenderness to the role," observed Crowther in *The New York Times*. "Not once does she speak throughout the picture. Her face is the mirror of her thoughts. Yet she makes this pathetic young woman glow with emotional warmth. . . . Miss Wyman, all the way through, plays her role in a manner which commands compassion and respect." Archer Winsten in the *New York Post* was equally impressed. "Jane Wyman gives a performance surpassingly beautiful in its slow, luminous awakening of joy and understanding. It is all the more beautiful in its accomplishment without words, perhaps *because* it is so wordlessly expressive."

Before shooting began on *Johnny Belinda*, Wyman had prematurely delivered an infant daughter who had died within several hours of birth. By the time the film was nearing completion, there were rumors of difficulties in the Reagan marriage. Wyman's career was beginning to eclipse Reagan's, and he was becoming increasingly involved in union work for the Screen Actor's Guild (SAG), which required frequent travel. In December 1947, Wyman announced that she was separating from her husband. After an attempt at reconciliation, the couple separated and eventually divorced. "Finally, there was nothing in common between us," Wyman said, "nothing to sustain our marriage." The couple continued to see each other frequently because of the children, who remained with Wyman, although she had little time to be a hands-on mom. Michael later said: "I didn't get to know my mother and father personally until I was twenty-five. Mom was working double time. I was more or less raised by Carrie, who was Mom's cook. I would go to her with my problems and inner feelings."

Both Wyman and Reagan remarried in 1952, Ronald to Nancy Davis (*Nancy Reagan), whom he had dated off and on for two years, and Jane to Fred Karger, a musician who worked for Columbia Pictures, and the father of a young daughter by a previous marriage. Wyman would subsequently divorce, remarry, and divorce again. After her second divorce from Karger in 1965, she remained single.

Meanwhile, her career hummed along. The actress moved with ease from melodrama to comedy and received two additional Oscar nominations, for *The Blue Veil* (1951), in which her character aged 40 years during the course of the film, and *Magnificent Obsession* (1954), the quintessential tearjerker about a reckless playboy (Rock Hudson) who accidentally blinds a woman, then falls in love with her, and finally becomes a doctor and cures her blindness. During the 1950s,

Reagan, Maureen (1941–2001)

American activist and first daughter. Born on January 4, 1941, in Los Angeles, California; died on August 8, 2001, in Sacramento, California; first child and one of two children of Ronald Reagan (president of the U.S.) and Jane Wyman (b. 1914, an actress); stepdaughter of Nancy Reagan (b. 1921); attended boarding school in Palos Verdes, California; briefly attended Marymount Junior College, Arlington, Virginia; married and divorced twice; married third husband Dennis Revell (a lobbyist and public relations firm owner), in 1991; children: (adopted) Rita Revell.

The eldest child of actors Ronald Reagan and *Jane Wyman, Maureen Reagan (nicknamed "Mermie" by her father) had a difficult childhood from the age of seven, when her parents divorced. Packed off to boarding school by her working mother, she grew up lonely. "To this day I am very sad at goodbyes," she said later. "When someone goes to the market, I get sick to my stomach."

At 17, Reagan briefly attended Marymount Junior College but left after a few months and took a secretarial job in Washington, where she also became interested in politics. She changed her party affiliation at the time from Democrat to Republican, later teasing her father that she became a Republican before he did. During the 1960s, she married and divorced twice. "I didn't like being married," she recalled years later. "I don't like being a nonperson. I've been someone's daughter all my life, and I'm not going to spend the rest of my life being someone's wife."

Reagan found her identity in the political arena, where she flourished. An outspoken feminist who disagreed with her father on abortion rights and the Equal Rights Amendment, Reagan chaired the United States delegation to the 1985 World Conference of the UN Decade for Women, and served as U.S. representative to the UN Commission on the Status of Women. From 1987 to 1989, she served as co-chair of the Republican National Committee and created a political action committee that supported over 100 women candidates.

During her father's 1980 bid for the presidency, Reagan left her job to join his campaign. "Maureen was very active," said Frank Donatelli, a regional campaign director. "She was good to put with groups of women, especially younger women. She's an excellent campaigner, well informed. She understands politics. She had a reputation for being brash, but she was an asset really." Reagan later mounted her own campaigns for public office,

the first in 1982, running unsuccessfully against Pete Wilson for a U.S. Senate seat. In 1992, she finished second among 11 candidates for the Republican nomination for a new House seat.

Over the years, Reagan was also a political analyst, a radio and television talk-show host, and author of *First Father, First Daughter: A Memoir* (1989). The third of the Reagan children to write a book about their famous father, Maureen presented an honest but loving portrait, free of the anger that seemed to permeate the accounts of her siblings. *Nancy Reagan, who at first shuddered at the idea of another Reagan child exposé, was pleasantly surprised. "Maureen's book is frank and interesting, and in it she provides details and insights about Ronnie that even I hadn't known," she wrote in her own memoir, *My Turn*.

In 1991, Reagan married Dennis Revell, a lobbyist and owner of a public-relations firm. On one of several trips she made to Africa for her father, they met a Ugandan child, Rita, whom they adopted in 1994. Most of Maureen's later years were spent raising public awareness of Alzheimer's disease, the memory-robbing and fatal affliction that her father was diagnosed with in 1994. As a board member and representative for the Chicago-based Alzheimer's Association, she lobbied for more funding for Alzheimer's research and caregiver support. In October 2000, she received the association's Distinguished Service Award for her efforts.

In 1996, Reagan was diagnosed with malignant melanoma, a deadly skin cancer, which she battled privately for two years. While in remission in 1998, she broke her silence, becoming a speaker for the American Academy of Dermatology and helping to raise awareness and promote the importance of skin examinations. In 2000, however, it was discovered that the cancer had spread to her spine, and she underwent renewed treatment. She lost her battle when the disease invaded her brain, and died on August 8, 2001. At her funeral on August 18, attended by both her mother Jane Wyman and Nancy Reagan, Maureen was eulogized as "a valiant, passionate fighter against Alzheimer's disease and melanoma, as well as an advocate for women inside and outside the Republican Party."

SOURCES:

Allen, Jane E. "Maureen Reagan dies of cancer at 60," in *Los Angeles Times*. August 8, 2001.

Leamer, Laurence. *Make-Believe: The Story of Nancy and Ronald Reagan*. NY: Harper & Row, 1983.

Reagan, Nancy, with William Novak. *My Turn*. NY: Random House, 1989.

Wilson, Jeff. "Obituary," in *Boston Globe*. August 9, 2001.

Wyman also tentatively entered television, filming an episode of the "General Electric Theater" (hosted by her ex-husband Ronald Reagan).

In 1955, sensing that television might hold more of a future for her than movies, Wyman took over the already established anthology series "Fireside Theater" (which became "Jane Wyman Presents the Fireside Theater," and then "The Jane Wyman Theater"), serving as actress and later as executive producer of the popular program. "She is a very astute businesswoman and a devoted and hard worker," said William Asher, who produced the show during its first season. "She can—and does—jump into any kind of business negotiation in competition with men. She has a tremendous understanding of the value of a dollar." After three grueling years of nonstop acting and producing, Wyman left the series but continued to make guest appearances on other popular television shows. Her film career was pretty much over by 1962, although in 1969 she appeared in *How to Commit Marriage* with Jackie Gleason, the first "class" production she had been offered in years.

The intense media interest that had surrounded Wyman's marriage to Ronald Reagan was rekindled at various intervals during Reagan's political career. Wyman consistently refused to comment. "It's not because I'm bitter or because I disagree with him politically," she once said. "I've always been a registered Republican. But it's bad taste to talk about ex-husbands and ex-wives, that's all." While her children Maureen and Michael, who figured prominently in their father's presidential campaigns, were attending his inauguration in January 1981, Wyman was telling reporters that she had "no regrets" about not being first lady. "Oh no, the White House is not for me. . . . Mark you, I have perfectly wonderful memories of him. We are good friends and we will always remain good friends."

Wyman's status as Reagan's first wife, however, did not hurt her show-business marketability, and may have indeed led to her successful run as the mean-spirited matriarch Angela Channing on the evening soap opera *Falcon Crest*. Nominated for a Golden Globe Award in 1984, for Best Performance by an Actress in a Dramatic Series, Wyman was stunned to win. In her acceptance remarks, the actress shocked the audience by acknowledging her character as a "bitch," then went on to express her delight. "I'm having the best time of my life," she said. "I'm a little too old to be happy, but just old enough to be grateful."

SOURCES:

Katz, Ephraim. *The Film Encyclopedia*. NY: HarperCollins, 1994.

Morella, Joe, and Edward Z. Epstein. *Jane Wyman: A Biography*. NY: Delacorte, 1985.

Rothe, Anna, ed. *Current Biography 1949*. NY: H.W. Wilson, 1949.

Barbara Morgan,
Melrose, Massachusetts

Wyndham, Mary (1861–1931)

English actress and co-founder of Wyndham's Theaters. Born Mary Moore in London, England, on July 3, 1861; died on April 6, 1931; daughter of Charles Moore; attended Warwick Hall, Maida Vale; married James Albery (a playwright), in 1878 (died 1889); married Sir Charles Wyndham, in 1916 (died 1919); children: (first marriage) son Bronson.

Mary Wyndham was born in London, England, in 1861. Her first stage appearance was at the Gaiety Theater, under the direction of John Hollingshead. She retired from acting in 1878 upon marrying playwright James Albery, with whom she would have one son Bronson before Albery's death in 1889. In 1885, Mary joined Sir Charles Wyndham's company, appearing as Lady Dorothy in *The Candidate* in the Theater Royal, Bradford. Charles also managed the Criterion, and Mary acted there in 1885 as well. Wyndham, whose claim to fame was playing silly yet attractive women, appeared in command performances at Windsor Castle for King Edward VII in both 1903 and 1907. At one time, she was president of the Actors' Benevolent Fund.

Mary partnered with Sir Charles in the Criterion, beginning in 1897, and together they built Wyndham's Theater in 1899, on Charing Cross Road in London. They opened with *David Garrick*, a proven success for the two performers, and later partnered to build the New Theater. Although they had an established professional relationship, they were not married until 1916. When Charles died in 1919, Mary maintained her positions as co-proprietor of Wyndham's Theater and the New Theater and co-lessee of the Criterion in conjunction with Sir Charles' executors. When Lady Mary Wyndham died in 1931, the theater continued under the management of her son Bronson Albery and Howard Wyndham, the son of Sir Charles by a previous marriage.

Richard Wasowski,
freelance writer,
Mansfield, Ohio

Wynette, Tammy (1942–1998)

Enduringly popular country music singer, the first woman in the genre to record a million-selling song, who was beloved by fans for both her talent and the resilience she showed throughout a hard life. Born Virginia Wynette Pugh on May 5, 1942, in Itawamba County, Mississippi; died of a blood clot in Nashville, Tennessee, on April 6, 1998; daughter of Hollice Pugh and Mildred Lee Pugh; married Euple Byrd, around 1959 (divorced c. 1965); married Don Chapel (a musician), in 1965 (divorced 1968); married George Jones (the singer), in 1969 (divorced 1975); married Michael Tomlin (a real-estate agent), in 1978 (divorced six weeks later); married George Richey (a songwriter and producer), in 1978; children: six, including (first marriage) Gwendolyn Byrd; Jacqueline "Jackie" Byrd Daly; Tina Byrd; (third marriage) Georgette Jones.

Taught herself to play the guitar and, after separation from first husband and a move to Birmingham, Alabama, began singing on local television programs; signed first recording contract in Nashville (1966), and over the next 30 years had 20 #1 hits; released "Stand By Your Man" (1968) which became the first country music recording by a female artist to sell more than a million records; later career marred by illness and financial difficulties, but won two Grammy Awards and was three times named the Country Music Association's Female Vocalist of the Year; was inducted into the Country Music Hall of Fame (1998).

She was known as the "Heroine of Heartbreak," a description that could be applied to Tammy Wynette's life as well as to her music. She was trapped in a loveless marriage at 17, when she had the first of six children in a ramshackle cabin in the middle of Mississippi cotton fields; came to Nashville with little else than a guitar and stars in her eyes; overcame two abusive marriages, financial problems, and ill health to become one of the most famous country music stars of all time, famous enough to demand and receive a personal apology from **Hillary Rodham Clinton**; and died young amid controversy so vituperative over the cause of her passing that a second autopsy had to be performed. "Her story is really the story of country music," said one official of the Country Music Foundation at her death, "from humble beginnings . . . to superstardom."

She was born in such rural isolation that there was no village or town that could lend its name to her birthplace. Virginia Wynette Pugh was born on May 5, 1942, to Hollice and **Mildred Lee Pugh** in Itawamba County, Mississippi, not far from the Alabama border. Everyone called her Wynette, except for her beloved grandfather, who called her Nettiebelle. Tammy remembered little of her father, who died of a brain

tumor when she was just nine months old without realizing his ambition to become a professional musician. "The only legacy my father left me was his love of music," she wrote almost 40 years later, claiming that one of Hollice Pugh's last wishes was that the same passion would be instilled in his daughter. While Mildred left Mississippi to find high-paying war work at an aircraft factory in Memphis, little Virginia was raised by her grandparents, who became "Mama" and "Daddy" to her. "My grandfather was the rock of my childhood," Wynette wrote, filling the early chapters of her autobiography with stories of him. "From him I formed the images of what a father and a husband should be." But true to Hollice Pugh's wishes, she learned to pick guitar and sing from an uncle and could play songs on the piano after hearing them only once by the time she was six. Her favorite time was Sunday morning, when the nearby Baptist church attended by her grandparents was filled with hearty voices floating on strong chords from piano and organ. Everything else revolved around the cotton season, from the spring planting to the late summer's picking, and Wynette worked the fields like every other child, daydreaming about one day meeting her favorite country music star, George Jones.

By the time Tammy's mother had moved back from Memphis at war's end and Tammy had entered Tremont High School, an hour's drive from her grandparents' home, her dreams of escaping from the tedium of farm life had grown even stronger. As it had been for her father, music was one path to freedom, if only a temporary one. She and a high school friend were invited to sing once or twice on a local radio station and, later, formed a band that sang at school events, peppering their shows with country music, current best sellers from those early days of rock 'n' roll, and even some of the gospel songs they had all been singing in church for so many years. But for most young women of the 1950s in the rural South, marriage beckoned as the only sure way to a new life. "Marriage meant escape," Wynette once remembered, "and I began daydreaming about meeting someone, falling in love, getting married and, of course, living happily ever after." The someone that Tammy settled on was Euple Byrd, the attractive son of a family she had known since childhood. Just back from the service and with stories of what lay beyond the Mississippi cotton fields, Euple proposed to Tammy one Sunday morning during a church service. Over her mother's furious objections, Tammy accepted and drove with Euple to the nearest town where a preacher could be found to conduct the service. Tammy was just 17. The next day, after the young couple had moved into the Byrd family homestead, Tammy went back to high school but was later barred from graduating because she had neglected to tell the school of her marriage.

Six months later, with Euple finding only sporadic work in construction and Tammy pregnant, the couple moved into an old cabin on her grandparents' farm, lacking indoor plumbing or electricity, where Tammy had a daughter, **Gwendolyn Byrd**, followed little more than a year later by a second girl, Jacqueline (**Jackie Daly**). "By the time Jackie was born, I put music out of my head altogether," Wynette once recalled. "I resigned myself to the fact that I had a family to raise . . . and music wouldn't bring in any money." She settled on hairdressing as a useful trade, driving 40 miles each way every day of the week to Tupelo, Mississippi, to attend the classes paid for by her mother, but Wynette actually ended up working nights as a waitress in a Memphis bar when Euple took his family north to find work. Mary's Place, on the Memphis waterfront, was more of an education for Tammy than any amount of hairdressing classes. "It was like throwing a lamb to the wolves," Wynette said. "I was married and the mother of two children, but I was still a country girl who had never been anywhere." What made the job bearable was the music that filled the place all night, a mix of Memphis blues, rock 'n' roll, and country. Before long, Wynette was singing a few tunes for the customers every night and was listening half-seriously to the piano player's suggestion that her voice was good enough to make it in Nashville.

But it was her failing marriage that finally set Wynette on the road to independence. After four years of nearly constant moving as her husband quit one job after another, she found herself back in Tupelo, ill from a persistent kidney infection, and carrying her third child. A severe depression followed—cured, Wynette later revealed, by a series of 12 electroshock treatments—after which she tried to leave Euple for good. Euple attempted to have her children taken from her because of what he claimed was her "mental instability," followed her constantly, and claimed the child she was carrying was not his. But not long after the birth of Tammy's third daughter, named **Tina Byrd**, Euple finally agreed to a divorce and Tammy moved with her children to Birmingham, Alabama, where she found work as a beautician and where, as it happened, an uncle worked as an engineer at a local television station that broadcast a morning country music show. Noticing that the group that performed each morning had no girl singer, Wynette asked her uncle to put in a good word and soon found herself singing two songs each morning on the station for $35 a week. Frequent visits to Nashville to make the rounds of record companies followed, but it was not until the great Porter Wagoner brought his traveling country music show to Birmingham that Wynette got her first real taste of show business.

Almost all country stars of the time were male; and Wagoner's road show, like others of the day, always opened with a female singer to warm up the crowd before Wagoner himself stepped on stage. But the show arrived in Birmingham with no warm-up act after Wagoner's longtime girl singer quit. Recommended by her friends at the television station, Wynette auditioned for the job, ended up opening the show for Wagoner and was invited to join the road company for the next ten days for $50 a night. Thus began Wynette's long love affair with life on the road. It was, she said, "like I was playing hooky from real life." But Wagoner hardly spoke to her during her time with the show and her hopes of an offer to find her a recording contract vanished when the Wagoner show left Alabama without her. Angry at the way she had been treated, Wynette headed back to Nashville with her daughters vowing not to leave until she had been signed. "I bet I'm the only one [Wagoner] has helped by not helping," Wynette later said.

She had begun to doubt her rash decision after more fruitless rounds of recording company front offices, leaving her two older daughters in the car to look after little Tina for the few minutes it took to be told there was no opening for a female country singer, and certainly not for one called Wynette Byrd. But that was before she arrived in the office of Billy Sherrill, a producer for Epic Records who listened to her sing two numbers and offered her a song he had just heard called "Apartment #9"; and it was Sherrill who suggested that with her blonde hair and ponytail, she adopt the name Tammy Wynette. "Apartment #9," released in October 1966, was hardly the big hit Wynette had been hoping for; but it was enough to finally get her in the door at one of Nashville's most prominent agencies, which she chose to approach because George Jones was the agency's major client; and it was enough to prepare the ground for her second single, "Your Good Girl's Gonna Go Bad," which became the first of four consecutive #1 hits and the beginning of a string of 20 chart-toppers she would record under Sherrill's guidance over the next 15 years.

By 1968, only three years after leaving Alabama, Wynette was well on her way to becoming a genuine country music star, earning several thousand dollars a week in bookings. It was Tammy's unique ability to combine a robust country voice with an underlying vulnerability that attracted attention and sold her records. "She was as soulful a singer as I've ever heard," the prominent music producer Don Was once said of her. "In her own way, she was every bit as soulful as someone like **Aretha Franklin**." But with her success came hard lessons in surviving in a business run by men. "The same men who treated wives and girlfriends with respect and consideration treated girl singers like merchandise," she complained. "Everyone joked about what 'the boys' did, but if a woman stepped out of line her career was ruined." Years after receiving minor injuries in a plane crash on her way to a concert and arriving an hour-and-a-half late, she would still write bitterly of the reprimand she got from the show's cigar-chomping promoter. "Every career woman knows the fine line you walk to succeed, and there are times when you can't help but resent it," she said. At the same time, it was with men that Wynette sought security and safety, although a short marriage to musician Don Chapel, who played in the band backing up Wynette on the road, ended in divorce after Chapel became jealous of her relationship with the country star she had dreamed of meeting as a little girl, George Jones.

Wynette had been booked on the same bill with Jones for several concerts during 1968, the same year she was presented with the first of three awards as the Country Music Association's Female Vocalist of the Year. Even though they never actually shared the stage for a duet, Wynette always made sure to watch from backstage when Jones, more than ten years her senior, began his set. "He could hold an audience in the palm of his hand from the first note," she said. "He made it so easy, you would have thought he was singing in his own living room." Then, during a show in Winnipeg, Canada, Jones surprised Wynette by inviting her on stage for a duet as a suspicious Don Chapel looked on. Some weeks later, after Jones had announced his divorce from his wife of 17 years, he showed up unexpectedly at a benefit concert Wynette was doing in Alabama, just over the state line from her childhood home in Mississippi; still later, Jones began intervening in the vituperative arguments that broke out backstage between Wynette and Chapel over everything from arrangements to the men Tammy was seeing. Events reached a climax in Wynette's kitchen one night when the two men nearly came to blows; Jones dramatically announced that he loved her and then swept Tammy and her three daughters out of the house. Overnight, Wynette became known as the singer who'd left her husband to hitch her star to Jones', an ironic turn of events for the woman whose two biggest hits would be "Stand By Your Man" and "D-I-V-O-R-C-E." But Wynette insisted she had acted out of love. "My heart was so full of love for this man I had worshiped since childhood that I felt as if it would burst in my chest," she proclaimed.

The messy issue of a divorce was neatly solved by a judge in Alabama, who pointed out that Wynette's marriage to Chapel had never been legal under Alabama law because she had been divorced from Euple Byrd for less than two months at the time. Still, Jones and Wynette waited until February 1969—a month after they had both been inducted into the Grand Ole Opry—to become legally married in a civil ceremony in Georgia. Such was her affection for Jones that Wynette felt sure she could deal with her new husband's alcoholism and erratic, sometimes violent, behavior. The incidents were infrequent enough at first for the couple to buy a huge estate in Florida, on which Jones planned to create a "country music park," and for Tammy to give birth in 1970 to another girl, named **Georgette Jones**. The marriage seemed to settle down after Georgette's birth. Jones' "Old Plantation Park" in Lakeland, Florida, became a major tourist attraction; Wynette released "Stand By Your Man," the crossover hit that sparked a considerable backlash from the women's movement of the 1970s and an equal amount of comment over the fact that Wynette was on her third husband in ten years at the time; and the couple made a series of wildly popular joint appearances, even though Jones frequently had to be fetched from local watering holes while Wynette paced backstage. But even Tammy had to finally admit that the marriage was doomed. "There's no love in the world that can't be killed if you beat it to death long enough," she later said.

Jones' drinking, held in abeyance after Georgette's birth, returned even more violently than before. Wynette's bruises and injuries grew more alarming, interfering with her performance schedule; on one occasion when she threatened to leave him, Jones pointed a 30/30 rifle at her and swore he'd kill her first. Wynette finally left Jones in December 1974, pouring out her grief in songs like "Till I Can Make It on My Own" and "These Days I Barely Get By" which never failed to draw a sympathetic response from her audiences. "The audience responded to me with equal intimacy," she said, "and I would come off the stage feeling that I had actually known or experienced these people in such a close way it's difficult to put into words."

It was during these first years after her separation and divorce from Jones that Wynette's health became increasingly troublesome. In the three years after her divorce from Jones in 1975, she underwent four operations—one a hysterectomy and two for intestinal disorders; and it was also during these years that mysterious phone calls, some threatening her life, began to plague her. These were followed by 15 break-ins at her Nashville home in 9 months. Obscenities were scrawled over her windows and doors, and a fire was started in her basement while Wynette was in an upstairs room, causing major damage but fortunately resulting in no injuries. None of it was ever satisfactorily explained, least of all by Wynette, although she later linked the incidents to the months in which she had been dating Rudy Gatlin, one of country music's Gatlin Brothers, pointing out that the incidents ceased when she and Gatlin broke off their relationship.

The personal crises that marred her life only seemed to bind her more firmly to her audience and make her an object of interest outside of traditional country markets. One of the first country music stars to break out of the traditional mold, Wynette was a frequent guest on network television variety shows and daytime chat shows and performed at the White House during a state dinner arranged by President Gerald Ford. Her brief relationship with Burt Reynolds was much reported in the mainstream press, as was a fourth, brief marriage in 1976 to real-estate agent Michael Tomlin. ("An expensive lesson in my life," Wynette later said, claiming that Tomlin's taste for luxury had cost her more than $30,000 in their six weeks together.) A grueling tour schedule did little for her increasingly fragile health, resulting in another operation for a gallbladder disorder. Two years later, Wynette married the man who would finally give her the support she had been seeking. He was George Richey, a songwriter and producer whom she had known since her days with George Jones, for whom Richey had written two hits. Their time together after their marriage in July 1978, she wrote, was "the most contented I've known since I was a little girl, when Daddy was always there to take care of me."

But the upheavals that had marked her earlier years could not be kept at bay. There was a bizarre incident late in 1978 in which Wynette claimed she had been abducted at gunpoint from a shopping mall in Nashville. She was later seen flagging down cars on a busy highway, her clothes soiled and torn. Mysteriously, no one was ever charged with the crime when Wynette herself refused to press charges against her assailant by saying he had already been sent to jail for another crime. In 1988, Wynette was forced to file for personal bankruptcy after investing in two failed Florida shopping malls. But there was always her music to keep her going. By the early 1990s, she was universally acknowledged as "the first lady of country music"; and her career

seemed to attain a certain dignified maturity when she recorded a duet, "Two Story House," with George Jones and produced a joint album with him in 1995, called *One*. She made national headlines when she angrily challenged soon-to-be-First Lady Hillary Rodham Clinton's 1992 remark while campaigning for her husband, "I'm not sitting here like some little woman standing by my man, like Tammy Wynette." Wynette's response included the barbed observation that the comment had offended everyone who had made it on their own "with no one to take them to the White House. I can assure you, in spite of your education," Tammy continued, referring to Hillary Clinton's Yale degree, "you will find me to be just as bright as yourself." Clinton later telephoned to apologize for the remark, to such effect that Wynette agreed to perform at a fundraiser organized by the Clintons. That same year she explored new musical territory by joining the British pop group KLF for the song "Justified and Ancient," which became an international dance-pop hit; while in 1993, she teamed with two other country music divas, **Dolly Parton** and *Loretta Lynn, for the landmark album *Honky Tonk Angels*.

> *W*hen Tammy opened her mouth,
> it was the soul of country music.
> —Patty Loveless

But everyone in the country music business knew that Wynette's health was growing steadily worse through the 1990s. She underwent several operations between 1990 and 1997 for recurring infections and inflammations of the bile duct, and by 1998 it was widely believed that she was terminally ill. On the afternoon of April 6, 1998, Wynette laid down on a couch in the living room of her Nashville home for a nap. She died in her sleep, a medical examiner ruling after an autopsy that she had died of blood clots in her lungs.

Even in death, the world would not let Tammy Wynette alone. Nearly a year after her passing, her daughters with Euple Byrd filed a $50-million wrongful death suit against her doctor and George Richey. The doctor, they charged, had given their mother powerful narcotics while Richey had "improperly and inappropriately maintained her narcotic addiction." Richey retaliated by winning a court order to have Tammy's body exhumed and another autopsy performed by Tennessee's chief medical examiner, who ruled in May 1999 that Tammy Wynette had died of natural causes, specifically heart failure. "I am saddened that part of Tammy's legacy is this fiasco," Richey told the press, charging that Wynette's daughters had wanted a larger share of her estate than was left to them in her will.

But in the end, even this final controversy failed to overpower that legacy, one Wynette herself admitted was not without its flaws. "Sometimes the notes were flat and the words didn't rhyme," she once said of the life and the career that were so inseparable. "All the people I love . . . have contributed the notes. But the melody is mine. I sing it for them."

SOURCES:

Wynette, Tammy, with Joan Dew. *Stand By Your Man.* NY: Simon & Schuster, 1979.

SUGGESTED READING:

Daly, Jackie, with Tom Carter. *Tammy Wynette: A Daughter Recalls Her Mother's Tragic Life and Death.* NY: Putnam, 2000.

Norman Powers,
writer-producer, Chelsea Lane Productions,
New York, New York

Wynyard, Diana (1906–1964)

English actress. Born Dorothy Isobel Cox on January 16, 1906, in London, England; died of a kidney ailment on May 13, 1964, in London; daughter of Edward Cox and Margaret Cox; attended Woodford

Diana
Wynyard

School, Croydon; married Sir Charles Reed, in 1943 (divorced 1947); married Tibor Csato (divorced).

Selected theater: The Grand Duchess *(1925);* Sorry You've Been Troubled *(1929);* The Old Bachelor *(1930);* The Devil Passes *(1932);* Wild Decembers *(1933);* Sweet Aloes *(1934);* Pygmalian *(1937);* Design for Living *(1939);* No Time for Comedy *(1941);* Watch on the Rhine *(1942);* Marching Song *(1954);* The Bad Seed *(1955);* Toys in the Attic *(1960);* Camino Real *(1957).*

Selected filmography: Rasputin and the Empress *(*Rasputin the Mad Monk, *1933);* Cavalcade *(1933);* Men Must Fight *(1933);* Reunion in Vienna *(1933);* Where Sinners Meet *(*The Dover Road, *1934);* Hollywood on Parade No. 13 *(1934):* One More River *(*Over the River, *1934):* Let's Try Again *(*Marriage Symphony, *1934);* On the Night of the Fire *(*The Fugitive, *1939);* Angel Street *(1941);* Freedom Radio *(*A Voice in the Night, *1941);* The Prime Minister, Kipps *(*The Remarkable Mr. Kipps, *1941);* An Ideal Husband *(1947);* Tom Brown's Schooldays *(1951);* The Feminine Touch *(*The Gentle Touch, *1956);* Island in the Sun *(1957);* "The Second Man" *(television, 1959).*

Born Dorothy Isobel Cox in London in 1906, Diana Wynyard attended Woodford School in Croydon, where she and *Peggy Ashcroft acted in Shakespearean plays and studied the art of public speaking. Making her London debut in 1925, she worked with William Armstrong's Liverpool Repertory Company from 1927 to 1930, laying the foundations of her career. Wynyard then appeared at the St. Martin's Theater in London in *Sorry You've Been Troubled.* After a successful Broadway appearance opposite Basil Rathbone in *The Devil Passes* in 1932, Wynyard was signed to a supporting role with John, Lionel, and *Ethel Barrymore in *Rasputin and the Empress*—the only film in which the three Barrymores performed together. Although she made only seven films in America, Wynyard garnered an Academy Award nomination for Best Actress for her performance in Noel Coward's Oscar-winning *Cavalcade* in 1933. Hollywood honored her in a ceremony on January 26, 1933, by adding her imprint in cement outside Grauman's Chinese Theater.

Wynyard resumed her career on the British stage when no other substantial roles were presented in Hollywood. She continued to appear in British films that generally lacked box-office appeal but were hallmarked by quality, especially *Reunion in Vienna* in 1933 in which she teamed once more with John Barrymore, and the role of the wife being driven mad by a psychotic husband in *Angel Street* in 1940, which some critics believe to be superior to the 1944 Hollywood remake titled *Gaslight*, starring *Ingrid Bergman. Wynyard wed film director Charles Reed in 1942, but that marriage ended as did her later marriage to Tibor Csato. Although she continued to appear in films, she devoted most of her career to the stage. After World War II, Wynyard spent two years with the Stratford Memorial Theater at Stratford upon Avon, where she successfully performed numerous leading roles, including Desdemona, Beatrice, and Queen Catherine. She then toured Australia with the Memorial Theater Company in 1949 and 1950.

Throughout her career she was known for her bold choices of plays, especially those by dramatists Dennis Cannan, John Whiting, André Roussin, Tennessee Williams, and *Lillian Hellman. According to an obituary in the London *Times*, "She was a restraining influence in the theater, an enemy of emotional self-indulgence whether on stage or in the auditorium." Wynyard was honored for her service to the British stage by being named a Companion of the Order of the British Empire in 1953. She died of a kidney ailment in London on May 13, 1964.

SOURCES:

The Concise Dictionary of National Biography. Oxford: Oxford University Press, 1992.

The Film Lover's Companion. Ed. by David Quinlan. Secaucus, NJ: Citadel, 1997.

Katz, Ephraim. *The Film Encyclopedia.* 3rd ed. NY: HarperPerennial, 1998.

Obituaries from the Times, 1961–1970. Frank C. Roberts, comp. Reading, UK: Newspaper Archive Developments, 1970.

The Oxford Companion to Theatre. 3rd ed. London: Oxford University Press.

Richard Wasowski,
freelance writer,
Mansfield, Ohio

Wyse Power, Jennie (1858–1941)

Irish suffragist and nationalist. Name variations: Jennie Wyse-Power. Born Jane O'Toole in Baltinglass, County Wicklow, Ireland, in May 1858 (exact day unknown but was baptized May 23, 1858); died in Dublin, Ireland, on January 5, 1941; seventh child of Edward O'Toole and Mary (Norton) O'Toole; married John Wyse Power (a journalist), on July 5, 1883; children: Kathleen (died in infancy); Maire Wyse Power; Nancy Wyse Power; Charles Stewart Wyse Power.

Jennie Wyse Power was born in 1858, the last child and third daughter of Edward O'Toole and **Mary Norton O'Toole**; although christened Jane she was always called Jennie. The O'Tooles came from farming families in the Baltinglass area of west Wicklow, but two years after Jennie's birth the family moved to Dublin. Her education is unknown, but as she was well educated and knew several languages she may possibly have gone to one of the good convent schools near the family home. Wicklow was a county with a strong rebel tradition, and Edward O'Toole, when he moved to Dublin, allowed his house to be used as a refuge and shelter for members of the Fenian Brotherhood, a radical republican group which wanted complete separation from Britain.

Jennie's parents died within 18 months of each other in 1876–77. After this, she lived with her brother, but she enjoyed a degree of freedom and independence remarkable for the time. Her farming background kindled her interest in the land issue which was agitating Irish politics at the time. Tenant farmers were campaigning for fair rents, security of tenure, and the right of free sale. They also wanted the opportunity to buy their farms from their landlords. The campaign intensified between 1879 and 1881 and led to increasing violence. *Anna Parnell, sister of the Irish nationalist leader Charles Stewart Parnell, set up the Ladies' Land League (LLL) in January 1881. An auxiliary organization of the Land League which had been founded in 1879, it soon had hundreds of branches in Ireland, Britain, the U.S., Canada, and Australia. By August of that year, Jennie, who was a great admirer of Anna Parnell, was a member of the LLL executive. The League kept records of landlords and evictions and also gave relief to evicted tenants who were destitute and homeless.

There was some ecclesiastical criticism of the LLL from the archbishop of Dublin who objected to women taking "their stand in the noisy arena of public life. They are asked to forget the modesty of their sex and the high dignity of their womanhood by leaders who seem utterly reckless of the consequences." However, other Catholic churchmen approved of the LLL. When Charles Parnell and additional Land League leaders were arrested in October 1881, the LLL carried on its work despite police harassment. Members reported on evictions, and a newspaper reported on "an altercation" at one meeting held near Baltinglass between Jennie and the authorities. When Parnell was released in May 1882, he paid tribute to the work of the LLL. Privately, however, he felt it was becoming too radical, and the LLL was dissolved shortly thereafter. This created a serious rift between Charles and his sister Anna.

In July 1883, Jennie married John Wyse Power, a journalist of Fenian sympathies who had been imprisoned during the land agitation. He remained closely involved in various radical nationalist movements and was under regular police surveillance. By 1889, they had three daughters, Kathleen (who died in infancy), Maire and Nancy. In 1890, the country was convulsed by the divorce scandal involving Charles Parnell and *Katherine O'Shea which split the Irish nationalist party. Jennie and her husband supported Parnell, although she reportedly said to him: "[T]hings would have been different if you had given us votes for women; you'd have swept the country." Parnell supposedly replied: "I daresay you are quite right." Jennie was expecting another baby when Charles died suddenly in October 1891, and when her only son was born the following year he was christened Charles Stewart Wyse Power. She also compiled and edited a book of Parnell's speeches, *Words of the Dead Chief* (1892), which had an introduction by Anna.

Jennie Wyse Power

After Parnell's death, the Wyse Powers were no longer active in politics, although Jennie remained interested in women's suffrage. In 1899, she set up her own shop in Dublin. The Irish Farm Produce Company, which also had its own restaurant, prospered and soon became a mecca for various nationalist groups. In 1900, she joined *Maud Gonne's Inghinidhe na hEireann and became one of its four vice-presidents. In 1903, Jennie was elected a poor-law guardian for North Dublin and as such had responsibility for social welfare issues affecting the poor. She retained this post until 1911. Her business continued to expand and her three children were also gifted academically. **Nancy Wyse Power** was studying for a doctorate in Bonn when war broke out. On her return, she became involved in the Irish Neutrality League which was opposed to the war. Son Charles had become a barrister and defended nationalists arrested under war regulations.

The family was aware of the plans being hatched for a rebellion against British rule. The proclamation declaring an Irish Republic on Easter Monday 1916 was actually signed at the Wyse Power house which was soon in the thick of the fighting. The house and Jennie's shop were destroyed, but this mattered little compared to the sudden death in July 1916 of her daughter **Maire Wyse Power** who had established herself as a brilliant philological scholar. As radical nationalism regrouped after the rebellion, Jennie was active in most of the key organizations, including Cumann na mBan (the Women's League) and Sinn Fein. In December 1918, she and her daughter Nancy canvassed for Countess *Constance Markievicz's successful election to a Dublin constituency.

During the Irish War of Independence, the Wyse Powers sheltered people who were on the run from the British authorities. Fortunately, none of Jennie's family were arrested. In 1920, she won a seat in the municipal elections; she was also on the executives of Sinn Fein and Cumann na mBan and was a member of the industrial commission set up by the revolutionary parliament, the Dail. Nancy was engaged in Irish propaganda work in Germany. When the terms for Irish independence were finally agreed between Irish and British representatives in December 1921, they caused a split in Ireland which deeply affected Jennie and her family. She decided reluctantly to accept the terms, although some were unpalatable to her. Events spiraled towards civil war in 1922 but Jennie maintained friendships across the political divide, with Markievicz, *Kathleen Lynn and others.

In December 1922, Wyse Power was nominated to the senate by the new Irish prime minister, W.T. Cosgrave, one of only four women senators. She told an American paper in 1923: "I do not hold that women should be everywhere just because they are women but because they are able to be there." She was elected vice-president of the government party, Cumann na nGaedheal, but she was increasingly disenchanted with the government's policies and became an independent senator in 1926. She fought particularly against legislation which tried to restrict women's employment in the civil service and to prevent them from serving on juries.

After her husband's death in May 1926 and the sale of her business in 1929, Jennie lived with Nancy who was a senior civil servant. Charles was a judge in Galway. She remained active in the senate until 1934 when her term ended. In her last years, Wyse Power was contemplating writing her memoirs but regrettably never got around to writing them before her death in January 1941.

SOURCES:

O'Neill, Marie. *From Parnell to de Valera: A Biography of Jennie Wyse Power 1858–1941.* Dublin: Blackwater Press, 1991.

Deirdre McMahon, lecturer in history at Mary Immaculate College, University of Limerick, Limerick, Ireland

Wysmuller, Truus (c. 1896–1978).

See Wijsmuller-Meijer, Truus.

X

Xanthippe (c. 435 BCE–?)

Athenian wife of Socrates whose name, thanks to the philosopher's disciples, has for centuries been a byword for a sharp-tongued shrew. Name variations: Xantippe. Born around 435 BCE; death date unknown; married Socrates (the Greek philosopher); children—only sons are known: Lamprocles, Sophroniscus, and Menexenus.

Xanthippe was the much maligned—if not silent—wife of the famous Socrates. (It is possible that Socrates was married once before Xanthippe, for a suspect ancient tradition also associates him with a **Myrto**, reportedly the daughter of the prominent Athenian politician Aristides the Just.) With Xanthippe, Socrates had three known sons: Lamprocles, Sophroniscus, and Menexenus (none of whom, according to Aristotle, ever amounted to much).

Xanthippe is harshly treated by most of the extant sources which characterize Socrates' life and its impact: these (all of which sanctify Socrates and everything he stood for, although they are not entirely consistent as to what he did actually stand for) portray Xanthippe as a vicious nag. The reason for this characterization is obvious. Whereas Socrates was charismatic and a man who inspired many to revere his memory, when his disciples sought to reminisce about their days in his presence, they also remembered that Xanthippe had the audacity to scold Socrates in public for his failure to shoulder his familial responsibilities. Such boldness was thought to be out of place in any "respectable" Athenian woman of the period, and to verge on the criminal when the one thus embarrassed by his wife's brazen behavior was the saintly Socrates. It is undoubtedly true that Xanthippe occasionally overstepped the bounds of propriety, as when she did such things as douse Socrates with water when she caught him philosophizing with his (mostly wealthy) friends when he should have been earning a living, but even Socrates understood that when she thus flew off the handle, she did so because the interests of her family were being hurt. This appears to have been the case, anyway, from a report that once, when Lamprocles was bitterly objecting to his mother's habit of censuring him in public, Socrates berated his oldest son as an ingrate for not understanding that Xanthippe's bite was unleashed only to improve those whom she loved: that is, her husband and sons. At another time and with somewhat more acid, when friends asked him how he tolerated Xanthippe, Socrates replied that he lived with a shrew for the same reason good equestrians love to ride spirited horses. That is, just as the spirited mount forces the rider to hone his skill, coping with Xanthippe gave Socrates the wherewithal to tolerate anybody. However "useful" as a spur to improvement Socrates may have deemed Xanthippe, he did little to accommodate her criticisms, for philosophy was his passion and his life. What did it matter if his family did not eat as well as they could, if the Athenian people could be won over to his search for truth?

However acrimonious Xanthippe appears in the sources, she had every reason to be upset at how she was treated by her husband and his (at times) ungrateful sons. Although trained from birth to accept her second-rate status (as a woman) in democratic Athens, Xanthippe nevertheless expected her husband to do what was expected of every Athenian husband: that is, that he should actually make an effort to support his family. This Socrates did not do, regardless of what he has come to mean for philosophy. In fact, in the *Apology*, Plato portrays Socrates as admitting that he had neglected his family's interests as he sought truth. Thus, Xanthippe not only had to virtually raise her sons by herself, she also had to attempt to run a household without her husband actually attempting to earn enough income to sustain it. (Socrates was a stonecutter by profession, and apparently once possessed enough wealth to be enrolled in Athens' hoplite class [that which provided its own arms and armor to fight in the infantry]. However, when he died, he did so a poor man.) Socrates seems not to have personally suffered much from his lack of concern with money, for he was of simple wants and was frequently wined and dined at his friends' expense. How much food and drink he brought back to his own household after a night at a symposium, however, is simply not recorded.

Regardless, perhaps the most callous experience Xanthippe had to suffer at Socrates' hands occurred on the eve of his death. An emotional woman by nature, Xanthippe was banished by Socrates from his presence when she could not refrain from bewailing the injustice of his death sentence at the hands of the Athenian people. Socrates (never one to have much sympathy for any expression of emotion) could not tolerate Xanthippe's diatribes as his hours grew few. Thus, Xanthippe was expelled on account of pathos, so that Socrates could quietly engage in reasoned debate with his masculine friends. Of course, thereafter Socrates became a cultural icon . . . while Xanthippe has been consigned to the rubbish-heap of the overly emotional and the overly concerned with the futures of their families.

William S. Greenwalt,
Associate Professor of Classical History,
Santa Clara University, Santa Clara, California

Xene (fl. 1300s).

See Maria of Armenia.

Xenia (1582–1622).

See Godunova, Xenia.

Xenia Alexandrovna (1876–1960)

Grand duchess. Name variations: Xenia Romanov or Romanof. Born on April 6, 1876 (some sources cite April 18, 1875); died on April 20, 1960, in London, England; daughter of *Marie Feodorovna (1847–1928) and Alexander III (1845–1894), tsar of Russia (r. 1881–1894); sister of Nicholas II, tsar of Russia (r. 1894–1917); married Alexander Michaelovitch (1866–1933, grandson of Nicholas I of Russia), grand duke, on July 25, 1894; children: *Irina (1895–1970, who married Felix Yussoupov, count Soumarokov-Elston); Andrew (b. 1897); Theodore (b. 1898); Nikita (b. 1900); Dmitri (b. 1901); Rostislav (b. 1902); Basil (b. 1907).

Xenia Chestov or Shestov (1560–1631).

See Martha the Nun.

Xiang Jingyu (1895–1928)

Most prominent of the earliest leaders of the women's movement of the Chinese Communist Party who was executed in 1928 and became a revolutionary model for the first generation of Chinese communist female activists. Name variations: Xiang Jingyu; Hsiang Ching-yu or Hsiang Chin-yu; incorrectly Hsiang Ching Yu and Xiang Chingyu. Pronunciation: SEE-ahng JING-yew. Born in Hunan, China, in 1895; captured by the Chinese Nationalist Party and executed on May 1, 1928; her father was a well-to-do merchant in the town of Xupu; received a traditional Confucian education and then attended a modern academy, the Zhou-nan Girls' School in Changsha; married fellow provincial Cai Hesen (1890–1931), in 1921; children: daughter Yi-yi (b. 1921); son Bo-bo (b. around 1924).

Started a modern co-educational primary school in Xupu; went to France (1919); attended a French women's school and worked part-time in a rubber plant and a textile mill; returned to China (around 1921) and joined the Chinese Communist Party, becoming the first female member of the Central Committee and head of its women's movement; organized and led strikes in foreign factories in Shanghai (1924) and worked at the Shanghai University; went to Moscow for further education and training (1926–27); returned to China and engaged in radical labor activity; captured and executed (May 1, 1928).

Selected writings: Only surviving writings are a collection of love poems, "Toward a Brighter Day" (Xiang-shang Tong-meng), which she exchanged with husband Cai Hesen during their trip to France (November 1919); there are excerpts from other pieces of her work in Lieh-shih Hsiang Ching-yu (*The Martyr Xiang Chingyu*), *published in Beijing (1958).*

Xiang Jingyu was a leader in the first generation of radical women who saw in the Communist Party the vehicle for the liberation of Chinese women. She is remembered with great reverence as "the grandmother of the Chinese revolution." While she dedicated her life to building the Communist Party, particularly among women, she also had a strong interest in education and a love of poetry and literature. She was not only a tireless agitator and organizer who gave her life for her beliefs, but also a lively, generous, and thoughtful person who was both respected and loved by her comrades.

Xiang Jingyu was born in 1895 into a comfortable Chinese merchant's home in Hunan, the province of China which produced far more revolutionary leaders than any other. At the time she was born, China was in critical transition. The Chinese were the heirs of an incredibly continuous culture, usually characterized as "Confucian," because the scholar Confucius (551–

479 BCE) had become the central intellectual of the society. Confucian China was an extremely hierarchical and well-ordered society characterized by a reverence for the past and an emphasis upon authority, particularly that of the government and the males who dominated that society. Women had a distinctly secondary place.

While Confucianism had provided for a stable and satisfactory life for many Chinese for more than a millennium, by the time Xiang Jingyu was born, it had failed to keep pace with the challenges of the modern world. By 1895, China was threatened by its own weaknesses, particularly by an extremely large population which put incredible pressure upon resources, and by predatory foreign powers attracted to the legendary wealth of the "Center Kingdom." The central government, rather than responding effectively to these challenges, simply became ultra-conservative and hostile to any reforms which threatened the monarchical institution.

People's Republic of China postage stamp issued in 1978 in honor of Xiang Jingyu.

Seeing that Confucianism was becoming more of a burden than an advantage, Chinese intellectuals began casting about for alternatives. As a child, Xiang Jingyu received a Confucian education, but one of her brothers, like many children of wealthy and progressive families,

studied in Japan. There Jingyu's brother observed a dynamic society which prized modern education, including co-educational institutions, above all. Many Chinese students returned from Japan determined to see China follow a similar path. Japanese expansionists, however, began to view the weaker China as their natural prey.

In Hunan, there were many Chinese women who saw the liberation of Chinese women from the Confucian tradition as the key to Chinese modernization. These women supported modern schools, including those for women. Xiang Jingyu's family sent her to one of these, the Zhou Nan Girls' Normal School in Changsha, the provincial capital. The scholar and journalist Nym Wales (*Helen Foster Snow), who studied the lives of many radical Chinese women, dubbed it "the cradle of the Chinese communist women's movement."

One of the women who had attended Zhou Nan was **Yu Manzhen**, mother of the noted Chinese feminist and writer *Ding Ling (1904–1985). Ding Ling, who would later attend the school, would be encouraged by her mother to model herself upon Xiang Jingyu, who had become known as an exceptionally serious and mature student. Ding Ling and Xiang Jingyu became good friends and revolutionary comrades. Many young female radicals saw the education of women in modern schools as a *sine qua non* for reform or revolution. Xiang Jingyu, like the female rebel before her, *Qiu Jin (c. 1875–1907), started a school, opening a primary co-educational school in her hometown.

Xiang, Yu Manzhen, and Ding Ling were all active in the series of student protests which occurred in the region. Students, like many of the Chinese, were alarmed at the steady pace of foreign encroachments. They increasingly criticized the inability of the series of Chinese military governments (the "warlords"), which had replaced the monarchy in 1912, to stem the tide of failures. One of Xiang's first public radical acts was to organize students to protest the failure of the Chinese government to resist extortionate demands from Japan for special economic privileges.

Within this inflammatory environment, student-organized protests became more frequent and more violent. Mao Zedong, who eventually brought the Chinese Communist Party to power in 1949, was also a student in Hunan. Mao and several radical comrades, the female leader *Cai Chang and her brother, Cai Hesen, together organized the New People's Study Society, a group which would produce many of the leaders of the Communist movement. Xiang Jingyu was

among its first members and soon distinguished herself for her fiery essays of protest. Because of their Confucian literary heritage, Chinese intellectuals were extremely respectful of those like Xiang Jingyu who could write well and on a variety of subjects. The writings of modern European and American authors were particularly important in exposing them to new ideas coming from the modern West.

Excited by Western ideas, many young radicals wished to travel abroad to better learn how to reform China. Xiang Jingyu and Cai Chang organized a group of Hunanese to go to France on a work-study program. In 1919, the two, as well as Cai's brother Cai Hesen and many other students, set out for France. On the long ocean voyage, Xiang Jingyu fell in love with Cai Hesen. But the fiery radicals felt that the political revolution in China was more important than their own happiness and agreed to postpone their marriage. In France, the two became noted for their leadership of the Hunanese students' movement. Xiang Jingyu attended a French school and worked in factories. She soon learned of the hard life of the industrial laborer, particularly the women often employed in textile mills such as the one in which she worked.

France was a hotbed of revolutionary Marxism. Not only were such international radicals as the Vietnamese leader Ho Chi Minh active there, but many French intellectuals were Marxists as well. Xiang Jingyu came to see a Marxist revolution as an answer to the many problems of China. In particular, she believed that in an egalitarian Marxist society, the difficulties of Chinese women would at last be solved. For her, then, Marxism was a vehicle which both embraced and was broader than the contemporary feminism of the United States and Europe.

Xiang and Cai Hesen married about 1921, and she soon gave birth to their daughter, Yi-yi. At about this same time, Mao Zedong and others were founding the Chinese Communist Party (CCP) in Shanghai. When Xiang and her husband were expelled from France for engaging in a demonstration, the two went to Shanghai and quickly became members of the party. Xiang Jingyu, as a noted female radical, was made a member of the governing body of the CCP, the Central Committee, and given the important responsibility of heading the Women's Department, charged with organizing Chinese women to support the revolutionary cause.

Xiang Jingyu's enthusiasm, energy, and prolific pen served her well. A photograph taken of her at about this time shows an attractive woman with the short hair characteristic of the modern Chinese girl and broad features believed by many Chinese to be a trait of the fiery Hunanese. Although she was said to be soft-spoken and slow to put herself forward, it is evident that Chinese female workers in particular found her a sympathetic figure. She is credited with being the guiding intelligence behind the extremely successful work of the CCP among the working women of Shanghai. In 1924, Xiang gave birth to a son, Bo-bo.

> [Xiang Jingyu], the famous Communist and leader of the woman's movement in China, is known as the "Grandmother of the Chinese revolution."
>
> —Nym Wales

The following year Xiang Jingyu and her husband Cai Hesen, frequently said to have been more important than Mao in shaping the ideology and activities of the early Chinese Communist Party, went to Moscow for additional study. The Russians believed that their own revolution was threatened by such world powers as Great Britain. Therefore, they decided to support the young Chinese Communist Party, both as a means of distracting the British, who had important interests in China, and as a way of bringing about a worldwide revolution.

The almost two years that Xiang Jingyu spent in Russia were probably a happy time. She could study and was with her beloved husband in a supportive atmosphere which did not require arduous work or dangerous political activities. Xiang and Cai were said to be at their most contented when they were reading together in their apartment. However, no matter where they lived, in France, the Soviet Union, or China, their living quarters inevitably became the scene of lively salons where radicals met and talked.

In China, the course of revolution was proving tortuous. The Russians had chosen to sponsor not only the young Chinese Communist Party, but also the Chinese Nationalist Party (Guomindang). The Guomindang, founded by the noted Chinese nationalist leader Sun Yat-sen (1866–1925), had been taken over by Chiang Kai-shek, a young military leader, at the time of Sun's death. The Russians then forced the CCP and the Guomindang into an alliance, though each regarded the other with suspicion. The division of labor between the two saw the Guomindang concentrating upon building a military force, and the CCP organizing among peasants, workers, and women, looking forward to the day when their alliance was strong enough to unite China under a modern-reform regime.

But the two parties disagreed on a critical issue: the importance of social revolution. The Guomindang felt that a strong government alone could solve China's problems; the CCP felt that only a complete revolution which overturned the rigid social structure of China would finally modernize China. The CCP-Guomindang alliance was initially successful, marching north from Canton defeating warlord armies. But with victory in sight, the inevitable final split between the two occurred in Shanghai in the spring of 1927. Chiang Kai-shek, with his superior army, massacred many of the young Communists in Shanghai, and drove the party into a retreat which lasted for decades.

During this period, the life of a Communist was a dangerous and arduous one of constant flight and omnipresent fear of the "White Terror" of the Guomindang. Those thought to be Communists were often shot without trial. Xiang Jingyu courageously continued her work, but in 1928 she was captured by the Guomindang in Hangzhou, where she was working in the Communist underground. She was executed on May 1. It is said that she was defiant to the last, and died bravely. Cai Hesen survived her for three more years before he, too, was captured and executed.

Although Xiang Jingyu was now one of the multitude of the early martyrs to the Communist cause, the revolution itself did not die. Due to a combination of its own bad policy and Japanese aggression which prevented it from ever consolidating power, the Guomindang failed to establish a successful government. Mao Zedong, Xiang Jingyu's fellow Hunanese, eventually led the CCP to victory, establishing the People's Republic of China in 1949. Xiang Jingyu was said to be the grandmother of that revolution and was spoken of with great reverence by all the first generation of Chinese leaders, but especially by Chinese female leaders who idealized her.

The Chinese Communists themselves were to prove to be less than perfect rulers of China, but under their leadership China made great progress. Today it is one of the great powers of the globe, quite different from the backward country into which Xiang Jingyu had been born in 1895. And despite the many charges of Communist failure or excess, virtually no one has argued that the women of China were not far better off than they had been. It is sometimes difficult for those educated in contemporary Western feminist ideals to understand the circumstances which persuaded Chinese women that the Communist revolution was the single key to their own progress. But the history of China's 20th century suggests that women like Xiang Jingyu had good cause for their optimism, even if the revolution did not ultimately solve all of China's problems.

SOURCES:

Boorman, Howard L., ed. "Hsiang Ching-yu," in *Biographical Dictionary of Republican China*. Volume II. NY: Columbia University Press, 1970, pp. 86–87.

Brandt, Conrad. *The French-Returned Elite of the Chinese Communist Party*. Reprint no. 13. Institute of International Studies, Berkeley, CA: University of California, 1961.

Klein, Donald W., and Anne B. Clark, eds. "Hsiang Ching-yu," in *Biographic Dictionary of Chinese Communism 1921–1965*. Vol I. Cambridge, MA: Harvard University Press, 1971, pp. 317–318.

SUGGESTED READING:

China Reconstructs. No. 14. March 1965, pp. 24–26.

Chow Tse-tsung. *The May Fourth Movement: Intellectual Revolution in Modern China*. Stanford, CA: Stanford University Press, 1960.

Wales, Nym. *Inside Red China*. NY: Doubleday, 1939.

Women of China. Vol. 33, no. 233, 1963, pp. 22–25.

Jeffrey G. Barlow,
Professor in the Department of Social Studies,
Pacific University, Forest Grove, Oregon

Xiao Hong (1911–1942)

Chinese author. Name variations: Hsiao Hung; Chang Nai Ying; Zhang Naiying; Chiao Yin. Born near Harbin, China, in 1911; died on January 22, 1942, in Hong Kong; attended a girls' school in Harbin, beginning 1926; fled from an arranged marriage, in 1928; became common-law wife of Duanmu Hongliang, in 1938.

Selected novels: The Field of Life and Death (1935); Ma Bole (1941); Tales of the Hulan River; also wrote short stories and collaborated on the journal Qu-yne.

The Chinese novelist Xiao Hong was born Zhang Naiying in a wealthy landholding family in northeast China's Heilongjiang Province. When she was nine, her mother died, and Xiao Hong was raised by her cold and strict father, nurtured only by a loving grandfather who read classical poetry to her. She attended a girls' school in nearby Harbin for about five years, starting at age 15. Exposed to Chinese, American, and Russian literature, she became politically liberal, espousing democratic views, but was expelled for her activities. Her father quickly arranged a marriage for her to ensure that she would not dishonor their family.

To avoid the forced marriage, Xiao Hong fled first to Harbin, where she lived with a married teacher, then followed him to Beijing. The details of her months in Beijing are unknown—she may have spent time with her intended husband after separating from her lover—but two years later she was back in Harbin, pregnant and homeless. She began a relationship with a newspaper writer, Xiao Jun, who helped launch her literary career in Harbin. They published a collection of short stories, *Bashe* (*The Long Journey*) in 1933. The following year they went to Shandong, where Xiao Hong wrote *Shengsi Chang* (*The Field of Life and Death*), published in Shanghai in 1935. Although she would publish under several names, she is best known as Xiao Hong. The work, which describes life in northeast China during the Japanese occupation, reflects both Xiao Hong's rural upbringing and her Chinese patriotism in the face of Japanese aggression. Critically acclaimed, the novel made Xiao Hong a celebrity in Shanghai. She followed up in 1936 with a second novel, *Shangshi Jie* (*Market Street*). However, as the Chinese struggle against invading Japanese forces continued, Xiao Hong and Xiao Jun had to leave Shanghai and settle in Chonquig. There Xiao Hong collaborated with writer Hu Feng and published a leftist journal, *Qu-yne.*

Her relationship with Xiao Jun ended in 1936, and she moved to Hong Kong with writer Duanmu Hongliang, who became her common-law husband. Despite ill health, Xiao Hong continued writing. *Minzu Hun* (*Soul of a Nation*) was written in 1940 to commemorate the life of her friend and mentor Lu Xun. *Hulan He Chuan* (*Tales of Hulan River*), published in 1941, was largely an autobiographical work which described her unhappy childhood. She sent a copy of *Tales* to Upton Sinclair, initiating a warm literary friendship. Many of Xiao Hong's best-known short stories, including the poetic "Hands" and "The Bridge," as well as her longer works, reveal a feminist consciousness and criticize the oppression of women in Chinese law and culture. However, as these themes are integrated into others, few of her works can be labeled as specifically feminist fiction. Other themes developed in her work examine the harsh life of peasants in rural China and the need for Chinese to unite and protect Chinese civilization against Japan.

During the Japanese attack on Hong Kong in December 1940, Xiao Hong became ill, spending her final days in Queen Mary's Hospital. She died of a throat infection in January 1942. Xiao Hong is now considered one of the most important modern Chinese writers. Her poetry and prose works have been often reprinted and have been translated into several languages, including English.

SOURCES:

Colby, Vineta, ed. *World Authors, 1975–1980.* NY: H.W. Wilson, 1985.

Magill, Frank N., ed. *Cyclopedia of World Authors.* 3rd ed. Englewood Cliffs, NJ: Salem Press, 1997.

Robinson, Lillian S., ed. *Modern Women Authors.* NY: Continuum, 1996.

Laura York, M.A. in History,
University of California,
Riverside, California

Xiaoqin Xian Huanghou (1835–1908).

See Cixi.

Ximena.

Variant of Jimena.

Xi Taihou (1835–1908).

See Cixi.

Xoc, Lady (c. 660–c. 720)

Ritual partner of Shield Jaguar, Mayan king. Born about 660; died about 720.

Although actual biographical information regarding Lady Xoc is limited, what survives illustrates the essential role that royal women played in the Mayan religion. The Maya placed a great emphasis on personal sacrifice and blood-letting. Not only did blood provide nourishment for the gods, but it also allowed the divine to enter into the performer's being. Lady Xoc was the ritual partner of King Shield Jaguar, of Yaxchilan, a ceremonial city of Mayan culture. The specific actions of Lady Xoc are recorded on two carved lintels, currently housed in the British Museum.

In one lintel, Lady Xoc kneels next to a standing Shield Jaguar who is dressed in ceremonial costume. Lady Xoc is shown drawing a thorn-lined rope through her mutilated tongue. The rope falls into a basket, and her blood is caught by a sting-ray spine. The basket would have been burned later to send the blood to the gods. The second lintel, set in 681, depicts a hallucination of Lady Xoc that was induced by a ritual experience. In it, she holds a plate of bloody paper and lancets—examples of ritual paraphernalia—as she gazes up at a large serpent that springs from another plate. On the floor of the apparition's plate lie bloody paper lancets and a rope. An armed warrior emerges from the serpent's mouth.

These artifacts demonstrate the role of women during the reigns and changes of rulers. For the Maya, auto-sacrifice, or the act of letting one's own blood, and the visionary experiences of the king's ritual partner, connected the present ruler to his ancestors and divinities, helping him see and understand the mythic past, present, and future. Other royal women, such as **Lady Balam-Ix** and **Lady 6-Tun**, performed such rituals as part of their role as the partner of a king.

SOURCES:

Who's Who of World Religions. Ed. by John R. Hinnells. NY: Simon & Schuster, 1992.

Richard Wasowski,
freelance writer,
Mansfield, Ohio

Xostaria, Anastasia Eristavi (1868–1951).

See Eristavi-Xostaria, Anastasia.

Xuan, Bui Thi (d. 1771).

See Ba Trieu for sidebar.

ACKNOWLEDGMENTS

Photographs and illustrations appearing in *Women in World History, Volume 16,* were received from the following sources:

Courtesy of ABC News "20/20", **p. 177;** Courtesy of Allied Artists, **p. 394;** Painting by Heinrich von Angeli, **p. 7;** Photo by Virgil Apger, **p. 582;** Courtesy of Arena Stage, **p. 730;** Painting by Bonifazio Bembo, **p. 48;** Photo by Walter Bird, **p. 797;** Courtesy of Bryn Mawr College Archives, **p. 429;** Courtesy of National Archives of Canada, **pp. 498, 613;** © CBS Records, Inc., 1989, **p. 867;** Courtesy of Columbia Pictures, **p. 501;** Courtesy of Columbia University, **p. 841;** From a painting by John Singleton Copley, **p. 217;** Courtesy of *Crafts* Magazine, **p. 509;** From the collection of the Texas/Dallas History and Archives Division, Dallas Public Library, **p. 725;** Photo by Trude Fleischmann, **p. 692;** © HARPO Productions, Inc., 1998, All Rights Reserved, photo by Timothy White, **p. 645;** Painting by Sir George Hayter, **p. 6;** Courtesy of Moorland-Springarn Research Center, Howard University, Washington, D.C., **p. 721;** From a painting by James Latham, **p. 686;** Painting by Sir Peter Lely, **p. 37;** Photo by Herman Leonard, **p. 233;** Photo by Joan Levine, **p. 596;** Courtesy of the Library of Congress, **pp. 153, 289, 355, 385, 405, 419, 479, 565, 591, 715, 747, 766, 832;** Photo by Peter M. Lockner, **p. 391;** © MGM, 1942, **p. 834;** Courtesy of Mississippi Department of Archives and History, **p. 363;** Courtesy of The National Gallery, London, **p. 23;** Courtesy of the National Park Service, **p. 143;** Courtesy of National Portrait Gallery, London, **pp. 11, 195, 639, 705, 785;** Courtesy of The Navajo Tribal Museum, photo by James Bosch, **p. 267;** © NBC, **p. 537;** Courtesy of the Royal Netherlands Embassy, **pp. 543, 546;** Courtesy of the Nevada Historical Society, **p. 653;** Photo by Fiorenzo Niccoli, **p. 375;** Courtesy of the Oregon Historical Society, **p. 469;** © Helga Paris, 1982, Courtesy of University of Chicago Press, **p. 695;** Painting by Charles Willson Peale, **p. 241;** Engraving by Howard Pyle, **p. 671;** Painting by Schumatoff, **p. 278;** Painting by William Shevill, **p. 119;** © Twentieth Century-Fox, **p. 81,** 1965, **p. 521,** 1938; Courtesy of the U.S. House of Representatives. **pp. 92, 317, 648;** © United Artists, **p. 259;** Courtesy of the United Nations, **p. 352;** Courtesy of United Reformed Church, London, **p. 736;** Courtesy of *Vermont Quarterly,* **p. 587;** Courtesy of Virago Press, **p. 205;** © WNBA Enterprises, LLC, photo by Bill Baptist, **pp. 269, 761;** Courtesy of the Wyoming State Museum, **p. 257;** Courtesy of Collection of American Literature, Beinecke Rare Book and Manuscript Library, Yale University, **p. 857.**

ISBN 0-7876-4075-1

9 780787 640750

90000